RHS PLANT FINDER 2009-2010

Devised by Chris Philip
and Realised by Tony Lord

Consultant Editor
Tony Lord

RHS Editors
James Armitage Janet Cubey
Dawn Edwards Neil Lancaster

Compiler
Judith Merrick

A Dorling Kindersley Book

LONDON, NEW YORK, MUNICH, MELBOURNE, DELHI

Published by
Dorling Kindersley Ltd
80 Strand, London WC2R 0RL
A Penguin company

First edition April 1987
Twenty-third edition April 2009

British Library Cataloguing Publication Data.
A Catalogue record for this book is available from the British Library.

ISBN 978-1-4053-4176-9

Compiled by
The Royal Horticultural Society
80 Vincent Square,
London SW1P 2PE
Registered charity no: 222879/SCO38262

www.rhs.org.uk

Illustrations by Sarah Young
Maps by Alan Cooper

Produced for Dorling Kindersley Ltd by
COOLING BROWN

Printed and bound in England by Clays Ltd, St Ives Plc

The Compiler and the Editors of the *RHS Plant Finder* have taken every care, in the time available, to check all the information supplied to them by the nurseries concerned. Nevertheless, in a work of this kind, containing as it does hundreds of thousands of separate computer encodings, errors and omissions will, inevitably, occur. Neither the RHS, the Publisher nor the Editors can accept responsibility for any consequences that may arise from such errors.

If you find mistakes we hope that you will let us know so that the matter can be corrected in the next edition.

Back cover photographs from top to bottom: *Gentiana sino-ornata, Helleborus × sternii* 'Boughton Beauty', *Heuchera* 'Plum Pudding', *Inula magnifica, Salvia officinalis* 'Tricolor'
Front cover and spine: *Meconopsis betonicifolia* by Mark Bolton/GAP Photos

Contents

Introduction

The *RHS Plant Finder* exists to put enthusiastic gardeners in touch with suppliers of plants. The book is divided into two related sections – **Plants** and **Nurseries. Plants** includes an A–Z Plant Directory of more than 70,000 plant names, against which are listed a series of nursery codes. These codes point the reader to the full nursery details contained in the **Nurseries** section towards the back of the book.

The *RHS Plant Finder* is comprehensively updated every year and provides the plant lover with the richest source of suppliers known to us, whether you are looking for plants locally, shopping from your armchair or touring the country in search of the rare and unusual.

As you will see from the entries in the **Nursery Details by Code** many nurseries do not now publish a printed catalogue but produce an online version only. This is a growing trend, fuelled by the cost of printing a full catalogue.

It is important to remember when ordering that many of the nurseries listed in the book are small, family-run, businesses that propagate their own material. They cannot therefore guarantee to hold large stocks of the plants they list. Some will, however, propagate to order.

New in this edition

For the topical essay this year, Dr Paul Alexander, RHS Soil Scientist, in collaboration with others, has produced an informative review of the debate on container growing media in the UK.

This year, the decisions of the RHS Advisory Committee on Nomenclature and Taxonomy (ACONAT) are perhaps more noticeable than usual in the Plant Directory. *Michelia* and *Manglietia* have been included within *Magnolia* following widely accepted practice and × *Solidaster* is no longer distinct from *Solidago* following the move of *Aster ptarmicoides* to *Solidago ptarmicoides*.

A long-deliberated decision was that of transferring *Chamaecyparis nootkatensis* into the relatively new genus *Xanthocyparis*, as *X. nootkatensis*. As one of the parents of the well-known Leyland cypress, this has the knock on effect of changing the botanical name from × *Cupressocyparis leylandii* to × *Cuprocyparis leylandii*.

Not all the decisions of ACONAT result in name changes; each year it is agreed on numerous occasions that the status quo will be retained. For example, *Androcymbium*, *Bulbocodium* and *Merendera* have been retained as distinct from *Colchicum*, though situations such as this will continue to be monitored in the future.

If there is a botanical issue that you would like to bring to the attention of the editors, then please don't hesitate to contact us.

Available from the Compiler

Application for Entry

Nurseries appearing in the *RHS Plant Finder* for the first time this year are printed in bold type in the *Nursery Index by Name* starting on p.931.

If you wish your nursery to be considered for inclusion in the next edition of the *RHS Plant Finder* (2010-2011), contact the Compiler at the address below.

Plants Last Listed in Earlier Editions

Plants cease to be listed for a variety of reasons. For more information turn to *How to Use the Plant Directory* on p.18. A listing of the 45,000 plus plants listed in earlier editions, but for which we currently have no known supplier, is available online at www.rhs.org.uk/RHSPlantFinder/documents/PF_Lastlisted_2009.pdf.

Lists of Nurseries for Plants with more than 30 Suppliers

To prevent the book from becoming too big, we do not print the nursery codes where more than 30 nurseries offer the same plant. The plant is then listed as being "Widely available". This is detailed more fully in *How to Use the Plant Directory* on p.18.

If any readers have difficulty in finding such a

plant, we will be pleased to send a full list of all the nurseries that we have on file as stockists. All such enquiries must include the full name of the plant being sought, as shown in the *RHS Plant Finder*, together with an A5 size SAE. For more than one plant, please send an A4 1st class SAE.

The above may be obtained from:
The Compiler, *RHS Plant Finder*, RHS Garden Wisley, Woking, Surrey GU23 6QB

Email: plantfinder@rhs.org.uk

This information is also available online.

THE RHS PLANT FINDER ONLINE

The *RHS Plant Finder* is available on the Internet. Visit the Royal Horticultural Society's website **www.rhs.org.uk** and search the *RHS Plant Finder* database online.

ACKNOWLEDGMENTS

Judith Merrick, supported by Karin Wilson, and with the help of June Skinner and Patty Boardman, compiled this edition. Richard Sanford managed the editing of the plant names on the database. Rupert Wilson and Julia Barclay administered the Horticultural Database, using the BG-BASE™ Collection Management Software, from which the book is produced.

We should like to acknowledge the help of Simon Maughan, RHS Publications, John David, RHS Head of Botany, Christopher Whitehouse, RHS Keeper of the Herbarium, Sharon McDonald, RHS Botany, Angela Lee, RHS Science & Learning, Kerry Walter of BG-BASE (UK) Ltd., Max Phillips of Strange Software Ltd. and Alan Cooper, who produces the nursery maps.

As always, we are greatly indebted to Peter Cooling of Cooling Brown Ltd., for his skill in enabling us to turn our mass of raw data into a published format.

RHS Botanists James Armitage, Dawn Edwards and Neil Lancaster, have undertaken the task of editing the new plant names in this edition of the book.

Our colleagues on the RHS Advisory Committee on Nomenclature and Taxonomy, along with the RHS International Cultivar Registrars, have all provided valuable guidance and information. Many nurseries have supplied helpful information on plants, which has proved useful in verifying some of the more obscure names, and have suggested corrections to existing entries. Some of these remain to be checked and will be entered in the next edition, although those that contravene the Codes of Nomenclature may have to be rejected. We appreciate your patience while these checks are made. We are also grateful to all our regular correspondents and to the many readers who have made comments and suggestions; we look forward to receive your letters and emails in the coming year.

Clematis	V. Matthews ('00-'06) & D. Donald ('07-'08), International Cultivar Registrar, RHS
Chrysanthemum	J. Barker ('07-'08)
Conifers	L. Springate, Int'l Cultivar Registrar, RHS
Dahlia	R. Hedge, RHS Wisley
Dianthus	Dr A.C. Leslie, Int'l Cultivar Registrar, RHS
Geranium	D.X. Victor ('03), Int'l Cultivar Registrar
Heathers	Dr E.C. Nelson, Int'l Cultivar Registrar
Ilex	S. Andrews ('06)
Iris	J. Hewitt ('05, '07-'08)
Lavandula	S. Andrews ('03 & '05)
Lilium	K. Donald, Int'l Cultivar Registrar, RHS
Meconopsis	Dr E. Stevens ('03, '05 & '07)
Narcissus	S. McDonald, Int'l Cultivar Registrar, RHS
Rhododendron	Dr A.C. Leslie, Int'l Cultivar Registrar, RHS
Sorbus	Dr H. McAllister
Thymus	M. Easter ('03-'08)
Viburnum	C. Sanders

Janet Cubey, RHS Principal Botanist and **Tony Lord**, Consultant Editor,
February 2009

CONSERVATION AND THE ENVIRONMENT

As the ***RHS Plant Finder*** demonstrates, gardens in Britain have been greatly enriched by the diversity of plants introduced to cultivation from abroad. Whilst the vast majority of those introduced have enhanced our gardens, a few have proved to be highly invasive and to threaten native habitats. Once such plants are established it is very difficult, costly and potentially damaging to native ecosystems to eradicate or control the invasive "alien" species. Gardeners can help by choosing not to buy or distribute non-native invasive plants and by taking steps to prevent them escaping into the wild and by disposing of them in a responsible way.

The top eight invasive non-native species are no longer listed in the *RHS Plant Finder*. Any cultivars or varieties of them that are listed are believed to be less invasive than the species themselves. These eight plants are:

Azolla filiculoides – fairy fern
Crassula helmsii – New Zealand pygmy weed
Fallopia japonica – Japanese knotweed
Heracleum mantegazzianum – giant hogweed
Hydrocotyle ranunculoides – floating pennywort
Impatiens glandulifera – Himalayan balsam
Ludwigia grandiflora – water primrose
Myriophyllum aquaticum – parrot's feather

Bringing plants back from abroad

Travelling can be a great source of inspiration for gardeners and often provides an introduction to new and interesting plants. Anyone thinking of bringing plants back into Britain from overseas must realise, however, that this is a complex matter. Various regulations are in force which apply to amateur gardeners as well as to commercial nurseries. The penalties for breaking these can be serious.

Some of the most important regulatory bodies are listed below.

Plant Health regulations are in place to control the spread of pests and diseases. Plants are divided into the categories of prohibited, controlled and unrestricted, but there are also limits that vary according to the part of the world you are travelling from. For full details contact the Plant Health division of DEFRA, or visit www.defra.gov.uk/planth/ph.htm

DEFRA has produced a leaflet that summarises the Horticultural Code of Practice. This is available online at www.defra.gov.uk or by phoning the helpline on 08459 335577.

The Convention on International Trade in Endangered Species (CITES) affects the transport of animal and plant material across international boundaries. Its aim is to prevent exploitative trade and thereby to prevent harm and the ultimate extinction of wild populations. Export and import licences are required for any plants listed on the CITES Appendices. A broad range of plants is covered in these Appendices, including *Cactaceae* and *Orchidaceae* and, although species are mentioned in the convention title, the restrictions cover all cultivars and hybrids too. Details of the plants listed in the Appendices can be found on the CITES website, www.ukcites.gov.uk/intro/cites_species.htm, or in the leaflets detailed below.

The Convention on Biological Diversity (CBD or the "Rio Convention") recognises the property rights of individual countries in relation to their own biodiversity. It exists to enable access to that biodiversity, but equally to ensure the sharing of any benefit derived from it. Export permits are required for plant material taken from the country of origin, with prior informed consent being gained for any uses that the material will be used for in the future. Further information on the Convention can be found on the CBD website, www.cbd.int.

If you would like to read more about these subjects, *Conservation and Environment Guidelines* leaflets are available on request from the RHS. Please write to the Compiler at the address given on page 4 enclosing an A4 SAE, or find them online at www.rhs.org.uk/publications. Leaflets are also available on a wider range of subjects, with topics including:

Peat and the gardener
Potentially harmful garden plants
The use of limestone in horticulture
Trees and timber products
Wild and endangered plants in cultivation
Wildlife in gardens

Container Growing Media in the UK: Balancing the Needs of Horticulture and Conservation

Peat has been the main material used in growing media, or "compost", for over 30 years. However environmental concerns surrounding its extraction have recently led to a change in attitudes about its continued use.

Although there are around 1.65 million hectares of peat soils in Great Britain, mostly greater than 1m deep, only 70,000ha are lowland raised bogs, the type having potential commercial interest for horticultural peat. Yet of this, little remains recognisable as lowland raised bog, with only 3,836ha in a near natural condition and 5,032ha degraded or drained but capable of regeneration. Accordingly, the UK Government has established targets to limit the use of peat in horticulture. The 2005 target of 40% peat replacement has been met but, as 2010 approaches, the target of 90% peat-free across growing media and soil conditioners appears increasingly out of reach. One recent industry-wide initiative has seen UK horticulture look forward and take positive steps towards meeting this challenging target.

Early Developments in Growing Media

The terms growing media, compost and potting mix are all used interchangeably to describe the material that growers use to fill pots and trays in order to raise and grow plants. The primary requirements of the material are to provide anchorage for the plant while balancing air and water provision in the rooting zone. Commercially, the material also needs to be available in large volumes and to be of consistent quality.

In the 1930s Lawrence and Newel developed what are known as the "John Innes" mixes, which were the first commercially available standardised growing media in the UK. Made from blends of "loam" (composted grass turves), peat and sand, these mixes were slowly accepted by the industry over a 10-15 year period. Loam is not an ideal constituent of growing media, however, as it is heavy, making transport and handling more expensive; and sourcing large volumes of good-quality loam is difficult. Replacing the loam with peat in the 1970s solved both of these problems. As with the "John Innes" mixes, the peat-based mixes took a number of years to be accepted as growers had to alter their systems to accommodate the "new" material.

Peat has many properties that make it an ideal constituent of growing media, being generally low in nutrients and having low pH, low bulk density and a good air-filled porosity value. Many growers have become conditioned to using peat and there is a myth that there is nothing like peat and that it is one consistent material. However, peat is a very variable material. Each peat type has a unique set of properties and these affect how it will perform in growing media. The suggestion of a "generic" peat being a panacea is ill-founded, as is the suggestion that peat can be replaced with one material.

Increasing Environmental Awareness

In the late 1980s concerns over the use of peat in horticulture in the UK arose from the damage it caused to natural habitats and the archaeological artefacts preserved within the peat body, as well as the detrimental effects it had on the hydrological cycle. For the environmental lobby, the debate grew into a broader one of wider environmental responsibility. They believed it to be both illogical and immoral to export the UK's environmental footprint to other countries by importing their peat.

The sustainability of peat use is of particular concern. Peat bogs can take up to six years to prepare for commercial extraction. Vegetation is cleared and the site drained (which also affects the surrounding landscape) prior to milling. Commercial operations can remove depths of up to 22.5cm per annum but peat only forms at approximately 1mm per annum. Within any biogeographical area, this is widely regarded as unsustainable. Some industry interests have, however, widely promoted UK peat use in terms of overall global peat formation, ignoring the specific biodiversity and archaeological interests of biogeographic regions, let alone the issue of whether extraction from all bogs is economically viable. There is now a much better understanding and an acceptance of the need for sustainability to be assessed with more sophistication than at the global level.

Restoration to raised bog cannot be taken for granted as this after-use in some cases is not a requirement of the original planning permission. Some "restored" bogs have been turned into amenity wetland sites (e.g. in Somerset and Ireland) and these do not substitute for the original fully functioning peat bog in terms of its nature conservation resource and biodiversity and, of course, its archaeological and palaeo-ecological archive will have been destroyed.

The Peat Debate in Horticulture

In 1990 a UK peat-free campaign began with calls to ban the use of peat and stop all peat extraction. Public awareness was raised with a bold and clear message but the uncompromising call to "ban peat" increased anger and defensiveness within the horticultural industry. The prospect of peat replacement was seen by some as unrealistic, a view exacerbated by the scarcity of good-quality peat-free alternatives at that time. The opposing positions became entrenched. The "peat debate" flared and raged for much of the 1990s with feelings running high on both sides.

In response to the debate the UK Government set up a Peat Working Group. In 1994, this made a variety of recommendations which attempted to balance the needs and interests of conservation and the horticultural industry. Through its Biodiversity Action Plan (BAP) the UK Government introduced a target for 40% of growing media and soil improvers to be of non-peat materials by 2005. This Habitat Action Plan (HAP) target reflected the issues of conservation, sustainability and peat extraction in the UK and has informally recognised the desire not to export the UK's environmental footprint by curtailing domestic peat extraction. The HAP built on the initial target, by including a second target for the use of alternatives to be 90% non-peat by 2010.

Growing media manufacturers began to recognise the problems and investigate peat replacement. Up until now, research into alternative materials had focussed on using the advantageous properties of these materials in small quantities to improve the quality of the peat-based growing media. However, investment in new technology and a greater knowledge and understanding of the materials, improved the results of plant-growing trials. By the late 1990s, although many of the peat-free and peat-reduced growing media trials were proving very successful, commercial uptake was limited.

Industry-Wide Agreement

Despite the Government targets, factors such as conflicts of interest, technical problems, increasing costs, reluctance and apathy saw slower progress towards achieving the 90% target by 2010.

In 2004, a small group was formed to discuss the potential for encouraging a greater take-up of peat alternatives. This group has subsequently grown to include key Non-Government Organisations (NGOs), retailers (big and small), growing media manufacturers, growers and the Department of Environment, Food and Rural Affairs (Defra). In spring 2008, the group launched the Growing Media Initiative (GMI), managed by the Horticultural Trades Association, to raise awareness of peat-use replacement particularly among retailers and encouraged them to join and achieve the peat reduction targets of the scheme.

Participants in the scheme agree to set themselves targets to reduce peat year on year and to have policies that illustrate how they will do this. Companies' peat-use figures and policies are independently audited and those that meet certain targets, agreed by all members of the scheme, are then allowed to promote themselves as members of the GMI and display a logo on products that meet set criteria. As more manufacturers join the scheme, it is hoped to widen its membership to include growers and to begin promotion of the logo to help the public make a more informed choice.

Current Peat Use and Progress with Alternative Materials

Defra's 2008 research shows current total market use (growing media and soil conditioners) as 47% peat, with 99% of the peat being used in growing media. UK horticulture currently sources its peat from three areas, 38% from UK bogs, 60% from Ireland and 2% from Northern Europe.

Much of the UK's peat extraction was, until recently, on designated nature conservation sites. This has changed markedly over the last 10 years as the conservation value of the bogs has become more widely recognised. The government has spent several millions of pounds in compensating companies to end peat extraction and embark on the lengthy process of restoration.

The main peat-replacement products used are either bark, wood fibre, coir or specifically selected composted green wastes. There is also continued interest by some to use by-products or waste stream materials. The ultimate goal of peat-replacement is to use sustainable components, preferably sourced as close to market as possible, which actually add value to the final "compost" mix (including factors such as potential disease suppressive properties and enhanced shelf life both in terms of water holding and nutrient release). Although many by-products and waste stream materials carry greater environmental benefits, they often require greater effort (technically and logistically) and can therefore be more expensive.

Consumer Awareness

Despite public awareness campaigns by different organisations, the issue of peat and the destruction of peatlands has failed to capture the imagination of the general public in the same way as those on tropical hardwoods and deforestation.

Those who tried the early peat-free products often judged that they performed badly and reverted to peat-based products. Since then, formulations have been improved and customer confidence has increased.

The part played by major retailers in encouraging peat replacement in horticulture in the UK should not be underestimated. They were the first to encourage peat-reduced mixes, marking a significant step forward in reducing peat use since partial dilution is becoming the norm for products that were previously all-peat. Three major national gardening retail companies (B&Q, Homebase and Focus) have policies that are driving the replacement of peat in the direction of meeting government targets. B&Q believes there is a demand from their customers as just over 50% of its current growing media sales are peat-free.

Professional growers are also beginning to use peat-reduced and peat-free mixes as demand, and their confidence in using these media, increases. These growers have been prepared to take the risk and make the investment, familiarising themselves with new mixes and placing themselves at the forefront of the modern market. The reluctance of other professional growers stems from a variety of factors, probably associated with the financial implications of increased nursery costs and of familiarity with established practices.

The Carbon Economy

The importance of peat soils as a carbon store, and hence its role in both adapting to and mitigating climate change, is focusing more attention on conserving peatlands. Although the carbon dynamics of peatlands are complicated and often site-specific, the large quantity of carbon stored in peatlands is incontrovertible, as is the need to keep this carbon safely stored away and out of the active, greenhouse-impacting carbon pool. Peatlands in the UK are believed to store more carbon than the forests of the UK and France combined.

Conserving peatland carbon stores is increasingly recognised by the UK Government as a significant contribution towards climate change mitigation, analogous, in the post-Kyoto talks, to avoiding deforestation.

Peat formation takes carbon out of the active carbon cycle, whereas peat extraction brings this carbon, stored slowly at the rate of a metre depth per millennium, back into the cycle. Many peat alternatives also cause the release of carbon but this is much more recently sequestered and most materials are considered as being much more carbon-neutral.

Conclusion

The development and initiation of the GMI scheme has enabled environmental and business interests to share issues and concerns and build a common understanding to develop a practical way forward to achieve peat-replacement in the UK. The Government's peat replacement target for 2010 has been a key stimulus for encouraging the group to come together and find a common purpose.

The development of growing media based on non-peat materials will attract increasing attention as the need for a coherent EC policy on peat use becomes ever more relevant. With peat bogs and mires becoming increasingly recognised as important carbon stores, together with the wider benefits of having peatland habitats in good condition, the need to establish peat replacement will become more important in Europe, and Europe will need a more coordinated approach linking carbon management with habitat protection.

We hope that the UK experience of working towards peat replacement will help to develop sustainable growing media throughout Europe, as an important contribution by the horticulture industry to resolving some of today's key environmental issues.

Paul Alexander, Soil Scientist, RHS
Neil Bragg, Bulrush Horticulture Ltd.
George Padelopoulos, B&Q plc
Olly Watts, Royal Society for the Protection of Birds
Roger Meade, Roger Meade Associates

EXTENDED GLOSSARY

This glossary combines some of the helpful introductory sections from older editions in an alphabetical listing. A fuller, more discursive account of plant names, *Guide to Plant Names*, and a detailed guide to the typography of plant names, *Recommended Style for Printing Plant Names*, are both available as RHS Advisory Leaflets. To request a copy of either please send an A4 SAE to The Compiler at the contact address given on page 5.

ADVISORY COMMITTEE ON NOMENCLATURE AND TAXONOMY

This Panel advises the RHS on individual problems of nomenclature regarding plants in cultivation and, in particular, use of names in the *RHS Horticultural Database*, reflected in the annual publication of the *RHS Plant Finder*.

The aim is always to make the plant names in the *RHS Plant Finder* as consistent, reliable and stable as possible and acceptable to gardeners and botanists alike, not only in the British Isles but around the world. Recent proposals to change or correct names are examined with the aim of creating a balance between the stability of well-known names and botanical and taxonomic correctness. In some cases the Panel feels that the conflicting views on the names of some groups of plants will not easily be resolved. The Panel's policy is then to wait and review the situation once a more obvious consensus is reached, rather than rush to rename plants only to have to change them again when opinions have shifted.

The Panel is chaired by Dr Alan Leslie (RHS) with Dr Janet Cubey (RHS) (Vice-Chair) and includes: Dr Crinan Alexander (RBGE), Susyn Andrews, Chris Brickell, Dr James Compton, Dr John David (RHS), Mike Grant (RHS Publications), John Grimshaw, Dr Stephen Jury (University of Reading), Dr Tony Lord, Dr Charles Nelson, Julian Shaw (RHS) & Adrian Whiteley, with Dr Christopher Whitehouse (RHS) as Secretary.

AUTHORITIES

In order that plant names can be used with precision throughout the scientific world, the name of the person who coined the name of a plant species (its author, or authority) is added to the plant name. Usually this information is irrelevant to gardeners, except in cases where the same name has been given to two different plants or a name is commonly misapplied. Although only one usage is correct, both may be encountered in books, so indicating the author is the only way to be certain about which plant is being referred to. This can happen equally with cultivars. Authors' names, where it is appropriate to cite them, appear in a smaller typeface after the species or cultivar name to which they refer and are abbreviated following Brummitt and Powell's *Authors of Plant Names*.

🏆 AWARD OF GARDEN MERIT

The Award of Garden Merit (AGM) is intended to be of practical value to the ordinary gardener and is therefore awarded only after a period of assessment by the Society's Standing and Joint Committees. An AGM plant:

- must be available
- must be of outstanding excellence for garden decoration or use
- must be of good constitution
- must not require highly specialist growing conditions or care
- must not be particularly susceptible to any pest or disease
- must not be subject to an unreasonable degree of reversion

The AGM symbol is cited in conjunction with the **hardiness** rating. A full list of AGM plants may be found on the RHS website at www.rhs.org.uk/plants/award_plants.asp.

BOTANICAL NAMES

The aim of the botanical naming system is to provide each different plant with a single, unique, universal name. The basic unit of plant classification is the species. Species that share a number of significant characteristics are grouped together to form a genus (plural **genera**). The name of a species is made up of two elements; the name of the genus followed by the specific epithet, for example, *Narcissus romieuxii*.

Variation within a species can be recognised by division into subspecies (usually abbreviated to subsp.), varietas (or variety abbreviated to var.) and forma (or form abbreviated to f.). Whilst it is unusual for a plant to have all of these, it is possible, as in this example, *Narcissus romieuxii* subsp. *albidus* var. *zaianicus* f. *lutescens.*

The botanical elements are always given in italics, with only the genus taking an initial capital letter. The rank indications are never in italics. In instances where the rank is not known it is necessary to form an invalid construction by quoting a second epithet without a rank. This is an unsatisfactory situation, but requires considerable research to resolve.

In some genera, such as *Hosta*, we list the cultivar names alphabetically with the species or **hybrid** to which they are attributed afterwards in parentheses. For example, *Hosta* 'Reversed' (*sieboldiana*). In other situations where the aim is not to create a list alphabetically by cultivar name we would recommend styling this as *Hosta sieboldiana* 'Reversed'.

Classification of Genera

Genera that include a large number of species or with many cultivars are often subdivided into informal horticultural classifications or more formal Cultivar Groups, each based on a particular characteristic or combination of characteristics. Colour of flower or fruit and shape of flower are common examples and, with fruit, whether a cultivar is grown for culinary or dessert purposes. How such groups are named differs from genus to genus.

To help users of the *RHS Plant Finder* find the plants they want, the classifications used within cultivated genera are listed using codes and plants are marked with the appropriate code in brackets after its name in the Plant Directory. To find the explanation of each code, simply look it up under the genus concerned in the **Classification of Genera** starting on p.28. The codes relating to edible fruits are also listed here, but these apply across several genera.

Collectors' References

Abbreviations (usually with numbers) following a plant name refer to the collector(s) of the plant. These abbreviations are expanded, with a collector's name or expedition title, in the section **Collectors' References** starting on p.20.

A collector's reference may indicate a new, as yet unnamed range of variation within a species. The inclusion of collectors' references in the *RHS Plant Finder* supports the book's role in sourcing unusual plants.

The Convention on Biological Diversity calls for conservation of biodiversity, its sustainable use and the fair and equitable sharing of any derived benefits. Since its adoption in 1993, collectors are required to have prior informed consent from the country of origin for the acquisition and commercialisation of collected material.

Common Names

In a work such as this, it is necessary to refer to plants by their botanical names for the sake of universal comprehension and clarity. However, at the same time we recognise that with fruit and vegetables most people are more familiar with their common names than their botanical ones. Cross-references are therefore given from common to botanical names for fruit, vegetables and the commoner culinary herbs throughout the Plant Directory.

Cultivar

Literally meaning cultivated variety, cultivar names are given to denote variation within species and that generated by hybridisation, in cultivation. To make them easily distinguishable from botanical names, they are not printed in italics and are enclosed in single quotation marks. Cultivar names coined since 1959 should follow the rules of the International Code of Nomenclature for Cultivated Plants (**ICNCP**).

Descriptive Terms

Terms that appear after the main part of the plant name are shown in a smaller font to distinguish them. These descriptive elements give extra information about the plant and may include the **collector's reference**, **authority**, or what colour it is. For example, *Fritillaria thessala* SBEL 443, *Penstemon* 'Sour Grapes' M. Fish, *Lobelia tupa* dark orange.

Families

Genera are grouped into larger groups of related plants called families. Most family names, with the exception of eight familiar names, end with the same group of letters, *-aceae*. While it is still acceptable to use these eight exceptions, the modern trend adopted in the *RHS Plant Finder* is to use alternative names with *–aceae* endings. The families concerned are *Compositae* (*Asteraceae*), *Cruciferae* (*Brassicaceae*), *Gramineae* (*Poaceae*), *Guttiferae* (*Clusiaceae*), *Labiatae* (*Lamiaceae*), *Leguminosae* (split here into *Caesalpiniaceae*, *Mimosaceae* and *Papilionaceae*), *Palmae* (*Arecaceae*) and *Umbelliferae* (*Apiceae*). Also the traditionally large family *Liliaceae* is split into a number of smaller, more natural, families that as yet may be unfamiliar to readers.

Apart from these exceptions we currently follow Brumitt's *Vascular Plant Families and Genera* for our family names.

GENUS (plural – GENERA)

Genera used in the *RHS Plant Finder* are almost always those given in Brummitt's *Vascular Plant Families and Genera.* For spellings and genders of generic names, Greuter's *Names in Current Use for Extant Plant Genera* has also been consulted. See **Botanical Names.**

GREX

Within orchids, hybrids of the same parentage, regardless of how alike they are, are given a grex name. Individuals can be selected, given cultivar names and propagated vegetatively. For example, *Pleione* Versailles gx 'Bucklebury', where Versailles is the grex name and 'Bucklebury' is a selected **cultivar**.

GROUP

This is a collective name for a group of cultivars within a genus with similar characteristics. The word Group is always included and, where cited with a cultivar name, it is enclosed in brackets, for example, *Actaea simplex* (Atropurpurea Group) 'Brunette', where 'Brunette' is a distinct cultivar in a group of purple-leaved cultivars.

Another example of a Group is *Rhododendron polycladum* Scintillans Group. In this case *Rhododendron scintillans* was a species that is now botanically 'sunk' within *R. polycladum*, but it is still recognised horticulturally as a Group.

Group names are also used for swarms of hybrids with the same parentage, for example, *Rhododendron* Polar Bear Group. These were formerly treated as **grex** names, a term now used only for orchids. A single clone from the Group may be given the same cultivar name, for example, *Rhododendron* 'Polar Bear'.

HARDINESS

Hardiness ratings are shown for **Award of Garden Merit** plants. The categories used are as follows:

H1 = plants requiring heated glass in the British Isles

H2 = plants requiring unheated glass in the British Isles

H3 = plants hardy outside in some regions of the British Isles or in particular situations, or which, while usually grown outside in summer, need frost-free protection in winter (eg. dahlias)

H4 = plants hardy throughout the British Isles

H1-2, H2-3, H3-4 = plants intermediate between the two ratings given

H1+3 = requiring heated glass; may be grown outside in summer

HYBRIDS

Some species, when grown together, in the wild or in cultivation, are found to interbreed and form hybrids. In some instances a hybrid name is coined, for example hybrids between *Primula hirsuta* and *P. minima* are given the name *Primula* × *forsteri*, the multiplication sign indicating hybrid origin. Hybrid formulae that quote the parentage of the hybrid are used where a unique name has not been coined, for example *Rhododendron calophytum* × *R. praevernum*. In hybrid formulae you will find parents in alphabetical order, with the male (m) and female (f) parent indicated where known. Hybrids between different genera are also possible, for example × *Mahoberberis* is the name given to hybrids between *Mahonia* and *Berberis*.

There are also a few special-case hybrids called graft hybrids, where the tissues of two plants are physically rather than genetically mixed. These are indicated by an addition rather than a multiplication sign, so *Laburnum* + *Cytisus* becomes +*Laburnocytisus*.

ICNCP

The ICNCP is the International Code of Nomenclature for Cultivated Plants. First published in 1959, the most recent edition was published in 2004, although a new edition is due to be published in 2009.

Cultivar names that do not conform to this Code, and for which there is no valid alternative, are flagged I (for invalid). This code states that the minimum requirement is for a cultivar name to be given in conjunction with the name of the genus. However, in the ***RHS Plant Finder*** we choose to give as full a name as possible to give the gardener and botanist more information about the plant.

NOTES ON NOMENCLATURE AND IDENTIFICATION

The **Notes on Nomenclature and Identification**, starting on p.23, give further information for names that are complex or may be confusing. See also **Advisory Committee on Nomenclature and Taxonomy**.

PLANT BREEDERS' RIGHTS

Plants covered by an *active* grant of Plant Breeders' Rights (PBR) are indicated throughout the Plant Directory. Grants indicated are those awarded by both UK and EU Plant Variety Rights offices. Because grants can both come into force and lapse at any time, this book can only aim to represent the situation at one point in time, but it is hoped that this will act as a useful guide to growers and gardeners. UK grants represent the position as of the end of December 2008 and EU grants as of the end of October 2008. We do not give any indication where PBR grants may be pending.

To obtain PBR protection, a new plant must be registered and pass tests for distinctness, uniformity and stability under an approved name. This approved name, under the rules of the **ICNCP**, established by a legal process, has to be regarded as the cultivar name. Increasingly however, these approved names are a code or "nonsense" name and are therefore often unpronounceable and meaningless, so the plants are given other names designed to attract sales when they are released. These secondary names are often referred to as selling names but are officially termed **trade designations**.

For further information on UK PBR contact:

Plant Variety Rights Office, White House Lane, Huntingdon Road, Cambridge CB3 0LF
Tel: (01223) 342396
Fax: (01223) 342386.
Website: www.defra.gov.uk/planth/pvs/default.htm

For details of plants covered by EU Community Rights contact:

Community Plant Variety Office (CPVO), 3 Boulevard Maréchal Foch, BP 10121 FR-49101 Angers, Cedex 02, France
Tel: 00 33 (02) 41 25 64 00
Fax: 00 33 (02) 41 25 64 10
Website: www.cpvo.europa.eu

The *RHS Plant Finder* takes no responsibility for ensuring that nurseries selling plants with PBR are licensed to do so.

REVERSE SYNONYMS

It is likely that users of this book will come across names in certain genera that they did not expect to find. This may be because species have been transferred from another genus (or **genera**). In the list of **Reverse Synonyms** on p.33, the name on the left-hand side is that of an accepted genus to which species have been transferred from the genus on the right. Sometimes all species will have been transferred, but in many cases only a few will be affected. Consulting **Reverse Synonyms** enables users to find the genera from which species have been transferred. Where the right-hand genus is found in the Plant Directory, the movement of species becomes clear through the cross-references in the nursery code column.

SELLING NAMES

See **Trade Designations**

SERIES

With seed-raised plants and some popular vegetatively-propagated plants, especially bedding plants and pot plants such as *Petunia* or *Impatiens*, Series have become increasingly popular. A Series contains a number of similar cultivars, but differs from a **Group** in that it is a marketing device, with cultivars added to create a range of flower colours in plants of similar habit. Individual colour elements within a series may be represented by slightly different cultivars over the years.

The word Series is always included and, where cited with a cultivar name it is enclosed in brackets, for example *Aquilegia* 'Robin' (Songbird Series). The Series name usually follows the rest of the plant name, but sometimes in this book we list it before the cultivar name in order to group members of a series together when they occur next to one another on the page.

SPECIES

See under **Botanical Names**

SUBSPECIES

See under **Botanical Names**

SYNONYMS

Although the ideal is for each species or cultivar to have only one name, anyone dealing with plants soon comes across a situation where one plant has received two or more names, or two plants have received the same name. In each case, only one name and application, for reasons of precision and stability, can be regarded as correct. Additional names are known as synonyms. Further information on synonyms and why plants change names is available in *Guide to Plant Names*. See the introduction to this glossary for details of how to request a copy.

See also **Reverse Synonyms**.

TRADE DESIGNATIONS

A **trade designation** is the name used to market a plant when the cultivar name is considered unsuitable for selling purposes. It is styled in a different typeface and without single quotation marks.

In the case of **Plant Breeders' Rights** it is a legal requirement for the cultivar name to appear with the trade designation on a label at the point of sale. Most plants are sold under only one trade designation, but some, especially roses, are sold under a number of names, particularly when cultivars are introduced from other countries.

Usually, the correct cultivar name is the only way to ensure that the same plant is not bought unwittingly under two or more different trade designations. The *RHS Plant Finder* follows the recommendations of the **ICNCP** when dealing with trade designations and PBR. These are always to quote the cultivar name and trade designation together and to style the trade designation in a different typeface, without single quotation marks.

TRANSLATIONS

When a cultivar name is translated from the language of first publication, the translation is regarded as a **trade designation** and styled accordingly. We endeavour to recognise the original cultivar name in every case and to give an English translation where it is in general use.

VARIEGATED PLANTS

Following a suggestion from the Variegated Plant Group of the Hardy Plant Society, a (v) is cited after those plants which are "variegated". The dividing line between variegation and less distinct colour marking is necessarily arbitrary and plants with light veins, pale, silver or dark zones, or leaves flushed in paler colours, are not shown as being variegated unless there is an absolutely sharp distinction between paler and darker zones.

For further details of the Variegated Plant Group, please write to:

Jerry Webb, Esq.,
17 Heron Way, Minster Heights,
Ilminster TA19 0BX

VARIETY

See under **Botanical Names** and **Cultivar**

'The question of nomenclature is always a vexed one. The only thing certain is, that it is impossible to please everyone.'

W.J. BEAN – PREFACE TO FIRST EDITION OF *Trees & Shrubs Hardy in the British Isles*

Symbols and Abbreviations

Symbols Appearing to the Left of the Name

*	Name not validated. Not listed in the appropriate International Registration Authority checklist nor in works cited in the Bibliography. For fuller discussion see p.10
I	Invalid name. See *International Code of Botanical Nomenclature 2000* and *International Code of Nomenclature for Cultivated Plants 2004*. For fuller discussion see p.10
N	Refer to Notes on Nomenclature and Identification on p.23
§	Plant listed elsewhere in the Plant Directory under a synonym
×	Hybrid genus
+	Graft hybrid genus

Symbols Appearing to the Right of the Name

✿	Plant Heritage (NCCPG) National Plant Collection® exists for all or part of this genus. Provisional Collections appear in brackets. Full details of the NCCPG Plant Collections are found in the *National Plant Collections® Directory 2008* available from: www.nccpg.com or NCCPG, 12 Home Farm, Loseley Park, Guildford, Surrey GU3 1HS
♀H4	The Royal Horticultural Society's Award of Garden Merit, see p.10
(d)	double-flowered
(F)	Fruit
(f)	female
(m)	male
(v)	variegated plant, see p.14
PBR	Plant Breeders Rights see p.12
new	New plant entry in this edition

For abbreviations relating to individual genera see **Classification of Genera** p.28
For **Collectors' References** see p.20
For symbols used in the **Nurseries** section see p.823

Symbols and Abbreviations used as Part of the Name

×	hybrid species
aff.	affinis (akin to)
agg.	aggregate, a single name used to cover a group of very similar plants, regarded by some as separate species
ambig.	ambiguous, a name used by two authors for different plants and where it is unclear which is being offered
cf.	compare to
cl.	clone
f.	forma (botanical form)
gx	grex
sensu lato	in the broadest sense
sp.	species
subsp.	subspecies
subvar.	subvarietas (botanical subvariety)
var.	varietas (botanical variety)

It is not within the remit of this book to check that nurseries are applying the right names to the right plants or to ensure nurseries selling plants with Plant Breeders' Rights are licensed to do so.

Please, never use an old edition

RHS PLANT TRIALS BULLETINS

In January 2009 the 23rd Trials Bulletin, entitled *Hydrangea paniculata*, was published. These publications give the results and findings of RHS Trials. The detailed descriptions and images of the plants that have been given the Award of Garden Merit are included, as well as updates on nomenclature, cultivation details and a table comparing the different characteristics of the entries in the trial.

Begonia Rex Cultorum Group
Canna
Clematis alpina and *C. macropetala*
Daisies (yellow perennial)
Delphinium
Fuchsia, hardy
Geranium, hardy (Stage 1)
Geranium, hardy (Stage 2)
Geranium, hardy (Stage 3)
Hyacinthaceae (little blue bulbs)
Hydrangea paniculata
Iris, bearded
Lavandula, hardy
Miscanthus
Peppers, chilli
Peppers, sweet
Potatoes, salad
Potentilla, shrubby
Rhododendron yakushimanum and hybrids
Runner Beans
Saxifraga, silver
Sedum, herbaceous
Spiraea japonica

If you would like a copy of any of these, please contact:
The Trials Office, RHS Garden Wisley, Woking, Surrey GU23 6QB. Please enclose an A4 SAE and a cheque for £2.00 per copy (as a donation towards costs) made out to the Royal Horticultural Society.

In addition to the above there are three bulletins that are only available on the RHS Website: *Caryopteris*, *Perovskia* and *Pittosporum*.
To view and download any of these RHS Plant Trials Bulletins online, please visit:
www.rhs.org.uk/plants/trials_bulletins.asp

PLANTS

Whatever plant you are looking for, maybe an old favourite or a more unusual cultivar, search here for a list of the suppliers that are closest to you.

How to Use the Plant Directory

Nursery Codes

Look up the plant you require in the alphabetical Plant Directory. Against each plant you will find one or more four-letter codes, for example WCru, each code represents one nursery offering that plant. The first letter of each code indicates the main area of the country in which the nursery is situated. For this geographical key, refer to the **Nursery Codes and Symbols** on p.822.

Turn to the **Nursery Details by Code** starting on p.826 where, in alphabetical order of codes, you will find details of each nursery which offers the plant in question. If you wish to visit any nursery, you may find its location on one of the maps (following p.939). Please note, however, that not all nurseries, especially mail order only nurseries, choose to be shown on the maps. For a fuller explanation of how to use the nursery listings please turn to p.823. **Always check that the nursery you select has the plant in stock before you set out.**

Plants with more than 30 Suppliers

In some cases, against the plant name you will see the term 'Widely available' instead of a nursery code. If we were to include every plant listed by all nurseries, the *RHS Plant Finder* would become unmanageably bulky. We therefore ask nurseries to restrict their entries to those plants that are not already well represented. As a result, if more than 30 nurseries offer any plant the Directory gives no nursery codes and the plant is listed instead as having 'Widely available'.

You should have little difficulty in locating these in local nurseries or garden centres. However, if you are unable to find such plants, we will be pleased to send a full list of all the nurseries that we have on file as stockists. To obtain a list, please see the Introduction on p.4.

Finding Fruit, Vegetables and Herbs

You will need to search for these by their botanical names. Common names are cross-referenced to their botanical names in the Plant Directory.

If you have Difficulty Finding your Plant

If you cannot immediately find the plant you seek, look through the various species of the genus. You may be using an incomplete name. The problem is most likely to arise in very large genera such as *Phlox* where there are a number of possible species, each with a large number of cultivars. A search through the whole genus may well bring success. Please note that, for space reasons, the following are not listed in the Plant Directory: annuals, orchids, except hardy terrestrial orchids; cacti, except hardy cacti.

Cross-references

It may be that the plant name you seek is a synonym. Our intention is to list nursery codes only against the correct botanical name. Where you find a synonym you will be cross-referred to the correct name. Occasionally you may find that the correct botanical name to which you have been referred is not listed. This is because it was last listed in an earlier edition as explained below.

Plants Last Listed in Earlier Editions

It may be that the plant you are seeking has no known suppliers and is thus not listed.

The loss of a plant name from the Directory may arise for a number of reasons – the supplier may have gone out of business, or may not have responded to our latest questionnaire and has therefore been removed from the book. Such plants may well be still available but we have no current knowledge of their whereabouts. Alternatively, some plants may have been misnamed by nurseries in previous editions, but are now appearing under their correct name.

To obtain a listing of plants last listed in earlier editions please see the Introduction on p.4.

Please, never use an old edition

USING THE PLANT DIRECTORY

The main purpose of the Plant Directory is to help the reader correctly identify the plant they seek and find its stockist. Each nursery has a unique identification code which appears to the right of the plant name. Turn to **Nursery Details by Code** (p.826) for the address, opening times and other details of the nursery. The first letter of each nursery code denotes its geographical region. Turn to the map on p.822 to find your region code and then identify the nurseries in your area.

Another purpose of the Directory is to provide more information about the plant through the symbols and other information. For example, if it has an alternative names, is new to this edition or has received the RHS Award of Garden Merit.

Euonymus (*Celastraceae*)

	B&L 12543	EPla EWes
	B&SWJ 4457	WPGP
	CC 4522	CPLG
	alatus ♀H4	Widely available
	- B&SWJ 8794	WCru
	- var. ***apterus***	EPfP
	- Chicago Fire	see *E. alatus* 'Timber Creek'
	- 'Ciliodentatus'	see *E. alatus* 'Compactus'
§	- 'Compactus' ♀H4	Widely available
§	- 'Fire Ball'	EPfP
	- Little Moses = 'Odom'	MBlu
*	- 'Macrophyllus'	EPfP
	- 'Rudy Haag'	CPMA EPfP
	- 'Select'	see *E. alatus* 'Fire Ball'
	- 'Silver Cloud' **new**	EPfP
§	- 'Timber Creek'	CPMA EPfP MBlu MBri NLar
	americanus	EPfP GIBF MBlu NLar
	- 'Evergreen' **new**	EPfP
	- narrow-leaved	EPfP NLar
	atropurpureus	EPfP
	'Benkomoki' **new**	MGos
	bungeanus	CMCN EPfP EPla NLar
	- 'Dart's Pride'	CPMA EPfP NLar
	- 'Fireflame'	EPfP NLar
*	- var. ***mongolicus***	EPfP
	- 'Pendulus'	EPfP MBlu SIFN
	- var. ***semipersistens***	CPMA EPla
	carnosus	EPfP NLar
	'Copper Wire'	EMil SPoG
	cornutus var. ***quinquecornutus***	CPMA EPfP LPan MBlu NBhm NLar SIFN SPoG WPGP WPat
	'Den Haag'	EPfP MBri
	echinatus	EPfP EPla
	- BL&M 306	SLon
	europaeus	Widely available
	- f. ***albus***	CPMA CTho EPfP LTwo NLar
	- 'Atropurpureus'	CMCN CTho EPfP MBlu MBri NLar SIFN
	- 'Atrorubens'	CPMA
	- 'Aucubifolius' (v)	EPfP
*	- 'Aureus'	CNat
	- 'Brilliant' **new**	EPfP
*	- f. ***bulgaricus***	EPfP
	- 'Chrysophyllus'	EPfP MBlu NLar
	- 'Howard'	EPfP
	- var. ***intermedius***	ENot EPfP MAsh MBlu NLar
	- 'Miss Pinkie'	CEnd CMCN
	- 'Pumilis' **new**	EPfP
	- 'Red Cascade' ♀H4	Widely available
	- 'Scarlet Wonder'	CPMA EPfP MBri NLar
	- 'Thornhayes'	CTho EPfP
I	- 'Variegatus' **new**	EPfP
	farreri	see *E. nanus*
	fimbriatus	EPfP
	fortunei Blondy = 'Interbolwi'PBR (v)	Widely available

ABBREVIATIONS
To save space a dash indicates that the previous heading is repeated. If written out in full the name would be Euonymus alatus *'Fire Ball'.*

NEW
Plant new to this edition.

DESCRIPTIVE TERM
See p.11.

SYMBOLS TO THE LEFT OF THE NAME
Provides information about the name of the plant. See p.15 for the key.

SYMBOLS TO THE RIGHT OF THE NAME
Tells you more about the plant itself, e.g. (v) *indicates that the plant is variegated,* (F) *= fruit. See p.15 for the key.*

SELLING NAMES
See p.13.

♀H4
This plant has received the RHS Award of Garden Merit. See p.10.

CROSS-REFERENCES
Directs you to the correct name of the plant and the nursery codes. See p.18.

NURSERY CODE
A unique code identifying each nursery. Turn to p.826 for details of the nurseries.

Widely available
Indicates that more than 30 Plant Finder nurseries supply the plant, and it may be available locally. See p.18.

PBR
Plant Breeders' Rights. See p.12.

SUPPLEMENTARY KEYS TO THE DIRECTORY

COLLECTORS' REFERENCES

Abbreviations following a plant name, refer to the collector(s) of the plant. These abbreviations are expanded below, with a collector's name or expedition title. For a fuller explanation, see p.11.

A&JW A. & J. Watson
A&L Ala, A.; Lancaster, Roy
AB&S Archibald, James; Blanchard, John W; Salmon, M.
AC Clark, Alan J.
AC&H Apold, J.; Cox, Peter; Hutchison, Peter
AC&W Albury; Cheese, M.; Watson, J.M.
ACE AGS Expedition to China (1994)
ACL Leslie, Alan C.
AER Robinson, Allan
AGS/ES AGS Expedition to Sikkim (1983)
AGSJ AGS Expedition to Japan (1988)
AH Hoog, A.
AIM Avent, Tony Mexico 1994
Airth Airth, Murray
Akagi Akagi Botanical Garden
AL&JS Sharman, Joseph L.; Leslie, Alan C.
ARG Argent, G.C.G.
ARJA Ruksans, J. & Siesums, A.
B Blanchard, John
B&F MA Brown, Robert & Fisher, Rif & Middle Atlas 2007
B L. Beer, Len
B&L Brickell, Christopher D.; Leslie, Alan C.
B&M & BM Brickell, Christopher D.; Mathew, Brian
B&S Bird P. & Salmon M.
B&SWJ Wynn-Jones, Bleddyn; Wynn-Jones, Susan
B&V Burras, K. & Vosa, C.G.
BB Bartholomew, B.
BC Chudziak, W.
BC&W Beckett; Cheese, M.; Watson, J.M.
Beavis Beavis, Derek S.
Berry Berry, P.
Berry & Brako Berry, P. & Brako, Lois
BKBlount Blount, B.K.
BL&M University of Bangor Expedition to NE Nepal
BM Mathew, Brian F.
BM&W Binns, David L.; Mason, M.; Wright, A.
BOA Boardman, P.
Breedlove Breedlove, D.
BR Rushbrooke, Ben
BS Smith, Basil
BSBE Bowles Scholarship Botanical Expedition (1963)
BSSS Crûg Expedition, Jordan (1991)
Bu Bubert, S.
Burtt Burtt, Brian L.
C Cole, Desmond T.
C&C Cox, P.A. & Cox, K.N.E.
C&Cu Cox, K.N.E. & Cubey, J.
C&H Cox, Peter; Hutchison, Peter
C&K Chamberlain & Knott
C&R Christian & Roderick
C&S Clark, Alan; Sinclair, Ian W.J.
C&V K.N.E. Cox & S. Vergera
C&W Cheese, M.; Watson, J.M.
CC Chadwell, Christopher
CC&H Chamberlain, David F.; Cox, Peter; Hutchison, P.
CC&McK Chadwell, Christopher; McKelvie, A.
CC&MR Chadwell, Christopher; Ramsay
CCH&H Chamberlain, D.F.; Cox, P.; Hutchison, P.; Hootman, S.
CCH&H Chamberlain, Cox, Hootman & Hutchison
CD&R Compton, J.; D'Arcy, J.; Rix, E.M.
CDB Brickell, Christopher D.
CDC Coode, Mark J.E.; Dockrill, Alexander
CDC&C Compton, D'Arcy, Christopher & Coke
CDPR Compton, D'Arcy, Pope & Rix
CE&H Christian, P.J.; Elliott; Hoog
CEE Chengdu Edinburgh Expedition China 1991
CGV Vosa, Canio
CGW Grey-Wilson, Christopher
CH Christian, P. & Hoog, A.
CH&M Cox, P.; Hutchison, P.; Maxwell-MacDonald, D.
CHP&W Kashmir Botanical Expedition
CL Lovell, Chris
CLD Chungtien, Lijiang & Dali Exped. China (1990)
CM&W Cheese M., Mitchel J. & Watson, J.
CN&W Clark; Neilson; Wilson

CNDS	Nelson, C. & Sayers D.
Cooper	Cooper, R.E.
Cox	Cox, Peter A.
CPC	Cobblewood Plant Collection
CPN	Compton, James
CS	Stapleton, Christopher
CSE	Cyclamen Society Expedition (1990)
CT	Teune, Carla
CWJ	Colley, Finlay; Wynn-Jones, Bleddyn, Taiwan 2007
Dahl	Dahl, Sally
DBG	Denver Botanic Garden, Colorado
DC	Cheshire, David
DF	Fox, D.
DG	Green, D.
DHTU	Hinkley, D., Turkey 2000
DJH	Hinkley, Dan
DJHC	Hinkley China
DJHV	Hinkley, Dan, Vietnam
DM	Millais, David
Doleshy	Doleshy, F.L.
DS&T	Drake, Sharman J.; Thompson
DWD	Rose, D.
DZ	Zummell, D.
ECN	Nelson, E. Charles
EDHCH	Hammond, Eric D.
EGM	Millais, T.
EKB	Balls, Edward K.
EM	East Malling Research Station
EMAK	Edinburgh Makalu Expedition (1991)
EMR	Rix, E.Martyn
EN	Needham, Edward F.
ENF	Fuller, E. Nigel
ETE	Edinburgh Taiwan Expedition (1993)
ETOT	Kirkham, T.S.; Flanagan, Mark
F	Forrest, G.
F&M	Fernandez & Mendoza, Mexico
F&W	Watson, J.; Flores, A.
Farrer	Farrer, Reginald
FK	Kinmonth, Fergus W.
FMB	Bailey, F.M.
G	Gardner, Martin F.
G&K	Gardner, Martin F.; Knees, Sabina G.
G&P	Gardner, Martin F.; Page, Christopher N.
GDJ	Dumont, Gerard
GG	Gusman, G.
GS	Sherriff, George
Green	Green, D.
Guitt	Guittoneau, G.G.
Guiz	Guizhou Expedition (1985)
GWJ	Goddard, Sally; Wynne-Jones, Bleddyn & Susan
G-W&P	Grey-Wilson, Christopher; Phillips
H	Huggins, Paul
H&B	Hilliard, Olive M.; Burtt, Brian L.
H&D	Howick, C.; Darby
H&M	Howick, Charles; McNamara, William A.
H&W	Hedge, Ian C.; Wendelbo, Per W.
Harry Smith	Smith, K.A.Harry

Hartside	Hartside Nursery
HCM	Heronswood Expedition to Chile (1998)
HECC	Hutchison, Evans, Cox, P., Cox, K.
Hird	Hird
HH&K	Hannay, S&S & Kingsbury, N
HLMS	Springate, L.S.
HM&S	Halliwell, B., Mason, D. & Smallcombe
HOA	Hoog, Anton
Hummel	Hummel, D.
HW&E	Wendelbo, Per; Hedge, I.; Ekberg, L.
HWEL	Hirst, J.Michael; Webster, D.
HWJ	Crûg Heronswood Joint Expedition
HWJCM	Crûg Heronswood Expedition
HWJK	Crûg Heronswood Expedition, East Nepal (2002)
HZ	Zetterlund, Henrik
ICE	Instituto de Investigaciónes Ecológicas Chiloé & RBGE
IDS	International Dendrological Society
ISI	Int. Succulent Introductions
J&JA	Archibald, James; Archibald, Jennifer
J. Jurasek	Jurasek, J.
JCA	Archibald, James
JE	Jack Elliott
JJ	Jackson, J.
JJ&JH	Halda, J.; Halda, J.
JJH	Halda, Joseph J.
JLS	Sharman, J.L.
JM-MK	Mahr, J.; Kammerlander, M.
JMT	Mann Taylor, J.
JN	Nielson, Jens
JR	Russell, J.
JRM	Marr, John
JW	Watson, J.M.
K	Kirkpatrick, George
K&LG	Gillanders, Kenneth; Gillanders, L.
K&Mc	Kirkpatrick, George; McBeath, Ronald J.D.
K&P	Josef Kopec, Milan Prasil
K&T	Kurashige, Y.; Tsukie, S.
KC	Cox, Kenneth
KEKE	Kew/Edinburgh Kanchenjunga Expedition (1989)
KGB	Kunming/Gothenburg Botanical Expedition (1993)
KM	Marsh, K.
KR	Rushforth, K.D.
KRW	Wooster, K.R. (distributed after his death by Kath Dryden)
KW	Kingdon-Ward, F.
KWJ	Crûg-World of Ferns Joint Expedition, Vietnam 2007
L	Lancaster, C. Roy
L&S	Ludlow, Francis; Sherriff, George
LA	Long Ashton Research Station clonal selection scheme
LB	Bird P., Salmon, M.
LEG	Lesotho Edinburgh/Gothenburg Expedition (1997)
Lismore	Lismore Nursery, Breeder's Number

LM&S	Leslie, Mattern & Sharman
LP	Palmer, W.J.L.
LS&E	Ludlow, Frank; Sherriff, George; Elliott, E. E.
LS&H	Ludlow, Frank; Sherriff, George; Hicks, J. H.
LS&T	Ludlow, Frank; Sherriff, George; Taylor, George
M&PS	Mike & Polly Stone
M&T	Mathew; Tomlinson
Mac&W	McPhail & Watson
McB	McBeath, R.J.D.
McLaren	McLaren, H.D.
MDM	Myers, Michael D.
MECC	Scottish Rock Garden Club, Nepal (1997)
MESE	Alpine Garden Society Expedition, Greece 1999
MF	Foster, Maurice
MH	Heasman, Matthew T.
MK	Kammerlander, Michael
MP	Pavelka, Mojmir
MPF	Frankis, M.P.
MS	Salmon, M.
MS&CL	Salmon, M.; Lovell, C.
MSF	Fillan, M.S.
NICE	North India Expedition 1997
NJM	Macer, N.J.
NNS	Ratko, Ron
NS	Turland, Nick
NVFDE	Northern Vietnam First Darwin Expedition
Og	Ogisu, Mikinori
OS	Sonderhousen, O.
P. Bon	Bonavia, P.
P&C	Paterson, David S.; Clarke, Sidney
P&W	Polastri; Watson, J. M.
PB	Bird, Peter
PC&H	Pattison, G.; Catt, P.; Hickson, M.
PD	Davis, Peter H.
PF	Furse, Paul
PJC	Christian, Paul J.
PJC&AH	P.J. Christian & A. Hogg
PNMK	Nicholls, P.; Kammerlander, M.
Polunin	Polunin, Oleg
Pras	Prasil, M.
PS&W	Polunin, Oleg; Sykes, William; Williams, John
PW	Wharton, Peter
R	Rock, J.F.C.
RB	Brown, R.
RBS	Brown, Ray, Sakharin Island
RCB AM	Brown, Robert, Expedition to Armenia
RCB/Arg	Brown, Robert, Argentina, (2002)
RCB E	Brown, Robert, Expedition to Spain (Andalucia)
RCB/Eq	Brown, Robert, Ecuador, (1988)
RCB RA	Brown, Robert
RCB RL	Brown, Robert, Expedition to Lebanon
RCB/TQ	Brown, Robert, Turkey (2001)
RH	Hancock, R.
RKMP	Ruksans, J., Krumins, A., Kitts, M., Paivel, A.
RM	Ruksans, J. & Kitts, M.
RMRP	Rocky Mountain Rare Plants, Denver, Colorado
RS	Suckow, Reinhart
RSC	Richard Somer Cocks
RV	Richard Valder
RWJ	Crûg Farm-Rickards Ferns Expedition to Taiwan (2003)
S&B	Blanchard, J.W.; Salmon, M.
S&F	Salmon, M. & Fillan, M.
S&L	Sinclair, Ian W.J.; Long, David G.
S&SH	Sheilah and Spencer Hannay
Sandham	Sandham, John
SB&L	Salmon, Bird and Lovell
SBEC	Sino-British Expedition to Cangshan
SBEL	Sino-British Lijiang Expedition
SBQE	Sino-British Expedition to Quinghai
Sch	Schilling, Anthony D.
SD	Sashal Dayal
SDR	Rankin, Stella; Rankin, David
SEH	Hootman, Steve
SEP	Swedish Expedition to Pakistan
SF	Forde, P.
SG	Salmon, M. & Guy, P.
SH	Hannay, Spencer
Sich	Simmons, Erskine, Howick & Mcnamara
SJ	Johansson, Stellan
SLIZE	Swedish-Latvian-Iranian Zagros Expedition to Iran (May 1988)
SOJA	Kew / Quarryhill Expedition to Southern Japan
SS&W	Stainton, J.D.Adam; Sykes, William; Williams, John
SSNY	Sino-Scottish Expedition to NW Yunnan (1992)
T	Taylor, Nigel P.
T&K	Taylor, Nigel P.; Knees, Sabina
TH	Hudson, T.
TS&BC	Smythe, T and Cherry, B
TSS	Spring Smyth, T.L.M.
TW	Tony Weston
USDAPI	US Department of Agriculture Plant Index Number
USDAPQ	US Dept. of Agriculture Plant Quarantine Number
USNA	United States National Arboretum
VHH	Vernon H. Heywood
W	Wilson, Ernest H.
WM	McLewin, William
Woods	Woods, Patrick J.B.
Wr	Wraight, David & Anke
WWJ	Wharton, Peter; Wynn-Jones, Bleddyn & Susan
Yu	Yu, Tse-tsun

Notes on Nomenclature and Identification

These notes refer to plants in the Plant Directory that are marked with a 'N' to the left of the name. 'Bean Supplement' refers to W.J. Bean *Trees & Shrubs Hardy in the British Isles* (Supplement to the 8th edition) edited by D L Clarke 1988.

***Acer davidii* 'Ernest Wilson' and *A. davidii* 'George Forrest'**
These cultivars should be grafted in order to retain the characteristics of the original clones. However, many plants offered under these names are seed-raised.

***Acer palmatum* 'Sango-kaku' / 'Senkaki'**
Two or more clones are offered under these names. *A. palmatum* 'Eddisbury' is similar with brighter coral stems.

***Achillea ptarmica* The Pearl Group / *A. ptarmica* (The Pearl Group) 'Boule de Neige' / *A. ptarmica* (The Pearl Group) 'The Pearl'**
In the recent trial of achilleas at Wisley, only one of the several stocks submitted as 'The Pearl' matched the original appearance of this plant according to Graham Stuart Thomas, this being from Wisley's own stock. At rather less than 60cm (2ft), this needed little support, being the shortest of the plants bearing this name, with slightly grey, not glossy dark green, leaves and a non-invasive habit. This has been designated as the type for this cultivar and only this clone should bear the cultivar name 'The Pearl'. The Pearl Group covers all other double-flowered clones of this species, including seed-raised plants which are markedly inferior, sometimes scarcely double, often invasive and usually needing careful staking. It has been claimed that 'The Pearl' was a re-naming of Lemoine's 'Boule de Neige' but not all authorities agree: all plants submitted to the Wisley trial as 'Boule de Neige' were different from each other, not the same clone as Wisley's 'The Pearl' and referrable to The Pearl Group.

***Anemone nemorosa* 'Alba Plena'**
This name is used for several double white forms including *A. nemorosa* 'Flore Pleno' and *A. nemorosa* 'Vestal'.

***Artemisia ludoviciana* subsp. *ludoviciana* var. *latiloba* / *A. ludoviciana* 'Valerie Finnis'**
Leaves of the former are glabrous at maturity, those of the latter are not.

***Artemisia stelleriana* 'Boughton Silver'**
This was thought to be the first validly published name for this plant, 'Silver Brocade' having been published earlier but invalidly in an undated publication. However, an earlier valid publication for the cultivar name 'Mori' has subsequently been found for the same plant. A proposal to conserve 'Boughton Silver' has been tabled because of its more widespread use.

***Aster amellus* Violet Queen**
It is probable that more than one cultivar is sold under this name.

Aster dumosus
Many of the asters listed under *A. novi-belgii* contain varying amounts of *A. dumosus* blood in their parentage. It is not possible to allocate these to one species or the other and they are therefore listed under *A. novi-belgii.*

***Aster* × *frikartii* 'Mönch'**
The true plant is very rare in British gardens. Most plants are another form of *A.* × *frikartii*, usually 'Wunder von Stäfa'.

Aster novi-belgii
See note under *A. dumosus*. *A. laevis* is also involved in the parentage of most cultivars.

***Berberis buxifolia* 'Nana' misapplied / 'Pygmaea'**
See explanation in Bean Supplement.

Betula utilis* var. *jacquemontii
Plants are often the clones *B. utilis* var. *jacquemontii* 'Inverleith' or *B. utilis* var. *jacquemontii* 'Doorenbos'

Brachyscome
Originally published as *Brachyscome* by Cassini who later revised his spelling to *Brachycome*. The original spelling has been internationally adopted.

***Calamagrostis* × *acutiflora* 'Karl Foerster'**
C. × *acutiflora* 'Stricta' differs in being 15cm taller, 10–15 days earlier flowering with a less fluffy inflorescence.

Calceolaria integrifolia sensu lato
Christine Ehrhart (*Systematic Botany*. (2005. 30(2):383–411) has demonstrated that this is a complex involving nine distinct species (*C. andina, C. angustifolia, C. auriculata, C. georgiana, C. integrifolia sensu stricto, C. rubiginosa, C. talcana, C. verbascifolia* and *C. viscosissima*). However, it is not yet clear to which species plants in cultivation belong or whether they are hybrids.

Caltha polypetala
This name is often applied to a large-flowered variant of *C. palustris*. The true species has more (7–10) petals.

***Camassia leichtlinii* 'Alba'**
The true cultivar has blueish-white, not cream flowers.

***Camassia leichtlinii* 'Plena'**
This has starry, transparent green-white flowers; creamy-white 'Semiplena' is sometimes offered under this name.

***Campanula lactiflora* 'Alba'**
This refers to the pure white-flowered clone, not to blueish- or greyish-white flowered plants, nor to seed-raised plants.

***Carex morrowii* 'Variegata'**
C. oshimensis 'Evergold' is sometimes sold under this name.

Carya illinoinensis
The correct spelling of this name is discussed in *Baileya*, **10(1)** (1962).

Cassinia retorta
Now included within *C. leptophylla*. A valid infraspecific epithet has yet to be published.

***Ceanothus* 'Italian Skies'**
Many plants under this name are not true to name.

***Chamaecyparis lawsoniana* 'Columnaris Glauca'**
Plants under this name might be *C. lawsoniana* 'Columnaris' or a new invalidly named cultivar.

***Chrysanthemum* 'Anastasia Variegated'**
Despite its name, this seems to be derived from 'Mei-kyo', not 'Anastasia'.

Clematis chrysocoma
The true *C. chrysocoma* is a non-climbing erect plant with dense yellow down on the young growth, still uncommon in cultivation.

Clematis montana
This name should be used for the typical white-flowered variety only. Pink-flowered variants are referable to *C. montana* var. *rubens*.

***Clematis* 'Victoria'**
Raised by Cripps (1867). There is also a Latvian cultivar of this name with petals with a central white bar in the collection of Janis Ruplēns which is probably, though not certainly, of his own raising.

***Colchicum* 'Autumn Queen'**
Entries here might refer to the slightly different *C.* 'Prinses Astrid'.

***Cornus* 'Norman Hadden'**
See note in Bean Supplement, p.184.

Cotoneaster dammeri
Plants sold under this name are usually *C. dammeri* 'Major'.

***Cotoneaster frigidus* 'Cornubia'**
According to Hylmø this cultivar, like all other variants of this species, is fully deciduous. Several evergreen cotoneasters are also grown under this name; most are clones of *C.* × *watereri* or *C. salicifolius*.

Crataegus coccinea
C. intricata, *C. pedicellata* and *C. biltmoreana* are occasionally supplied under this name.

***Crocus cartwrightianus* 'Albus'**
The plant offered is the true cultivar and not *C. hadriaticus*.

***Dianthus* fringed pink**
D. 'Old Fringed Pink' and *D.* 'Old Fringed White' are also sometimes sold under this name.

***Dianthus* 'Musgrave's Pink' (p)**
This is the registered name of this white-flowered cultivar.

***Epilobium glabellum* misapplied**
Plants under this name are not *E. glabellum* but are close to *E. wilsonii* Petrie or perhaps a hybrid of it.

Erodium glandulosum
Plants under this name are often hybrids.

Erodium guttatum
Doubtfully in commerce; plants under this name are usually *E. heteradenum*, *E. cheilanthifolium* or hybrids.

***Fagus sylvatica* Atropurpurea Group / Cuprea Group**
It is desirable to provide a name, Cuprea Group, for less richly coloured forms, used in historic landscapes before the purple clones appeared.

***Fagus sylvatica* 'Pendula'**
This name refers to the Knap Hill clone, the most common weeping form in English gardens. Other clones occur, particularly in Cornwall and Ireland.

Fuchsia loxensis
For a comparison of the true species with the hybrids 'Speciosa' and 'Loxensis' commonly grown under this name, see Boullemier's Check List (2nd ed.) p.268.

***Geum* 'Borisii'**
This name refers to cultivars of *G. coccineum* Sibthorp & Smith, especially *G.* 'Werner Arends' and not to *G.* × *borisii* Kelleper.

Halimium halimifolium
Plants under this name are sometimes *H.* × *pauanum* or *H.* × *santae*.

***Hebe* 'Carl Teschner'**
See note in Bean Supplement, p.264.

***Hedera helix* 'Caenwoodiana' / 'Pedata'**
Some authorities consider these to be distinct cultivars while others think them different morphological forms of the same unstable clone.

***Hedera helix* 'Oro di Bogliasco'**
Priority between this name and 'Jubiläum Goldherz' and 'Goldheart' has yet to be finally resolved.

***Helleborus* × *hybridus* / *H. orientalis* misapplied**
The name *H.* × *hybridus* for acaulescent hellebore hybrids does not seem to follow the *International Code of Botanical Nomenclature* Article H.3.2 requiring one of the parent species to be designated and does not seem to have been typified, contrary to Article 7 of the Code. However, the illustration accompanying the original description in Vilmorin's *Blumengärtnerei* 3(1): 27 (1894) shows that one parent of the cross must have been *H. guttatus*, now treated as part of *H. orientalis*. Taking this illustration as the type for this hybrid species makes it possible to

retain *H.* × *hybridus* formally as a hybrid binomial (rather than *H. hybridus* as in a previous edition), as the Code's requirement to distinguish one parent is now met.

Hemerocallis fulva **'Kwanso', 'Kwanso Variegata', 'Flore Pleno' and 'Green Kwanso'**
For a discussion of these plants see *The Plantsman*, 7(2).

Heuchera villosa **'Palace Purple'**
This cultivar name refers only to plants with deep purple-red foliage. Seed-raised plants of inferior colouring should not be offered under this name.

Hosta montana
This name refers only to plants long grown in Europe, which differ from *H. elata.*

Hydrangea macrophylla **Teller Series**
This is used both as a descriptive common name for Lacecap hydrangeas (German *teller* = plate, referring to the more or less flat inflorescence) and for the series of hybrids raised by Wädenswil in Switzerland bearing German names of birds. It is not generally possible to link a hydrangea described by the series name plus a colour description (e.g. Teller Blau, Teller Rosa, Teller Rot) to a single cultivar.

Hypericum fragile
The true *H. fragile* is probably not available from British nurseries.

Hypericum **'Gemo'**
Either a selection of *H. prolificum* or *H. prolificum* × *H. densiflorum.*

Ilex* × *altaclerensis
The argument for this spelling is given by Susyn Andrews, *The Plantsman*, 5(2) and is not superseded by the more recent comments in the Supplement to Bean's Trees and Shrubs.

Iris
Apart from those noted below, cultivar names marked 'N' are not registered. The majority of those marked 'I' have been previously used for a different cultivar.

Iris histrioides **'Major'**
Two clones are offered under this name, the true one pale blue with darker spotting on the falls, the incorrect one violet-blue with almost horizontal falls.

Juniperus* × *media
This name is illegitimate if applied to hybrids of *J. chinensis* × *J. sabina*, having been previously used for a different hybrid (P.A. Schmidt, *IDS Yearbook 1993*, 47–48). Because of its importance to gardeners, a proposal to conserve its present use was tabled but subsequently rejected.

Lavandula spica
This name is classed as a name to be rejected (*nomen rejiciendum*) by the *International Code of Botanical Nomenclature.*

Lavatera olbia **and** ***L. thuringiaca***
Although *L. olbia* is usually shrubby and *L. thuringiaca* usually herbaceous, both species are very variable. Cultivars formerly ascribed to one species or the other have been shown to be hybrids and are referable to the recently-named hybrid species *L.* × *clementii.*

Lobelia **'Russian Princess'**
This name, originally for a pink-flowered, green-leaved cultivar, is now generally applied to a purple-flowered, dark-leaved cultivar that seems to lack a valid name.

Lonicera periclymenum **'Serotina'**
See note in Bean Supplement, p.315.

Lonicera sempervirens **f.** ***sulphurea***
Plants in the British Isles usually a yellow-flowered form of *L. periclymenum.*

Malus domestica **'Dummellor's Seedling'**
The phonetic spelling 'Dumelow's Seedling' contravenes the ICBN ruling on orthography, i.e. that, except for intentional latinisations, commemorative names should be based on the original spelling of the person's name (Article 60.11). The spelling adopted here is that used on the gravestone of the raiser in Leicestershire.

Meconopsis **Fertile Blue Group**
This Group comprises seed-raised and intrinsically perennial tall blue poppies of as yet indeterminate origin. The only cultivars so far established are 'Lingholm' (synonyms 'Blue Ice' and 'Correnie') and 'Kingsbarns'.

Meconopsis napaulensis **misapplied**
In his revision of the evergreen monocarpic species, Dr C. Grey-Wilson has established that *M. napaulensis* DC., a dwarfish yellow-flowered species not usually more than 1.1m tall and endemic to C Nepal, is not currently in cultivation. The well-known plants of gardens which pass for *M. napaulensis* are hybrids, for the present to be known as *M. napaulensis* misapplied. The parents of the hybrids are *M. staintonii* (from W Nepal) and *M. paniculata* (a yellow-flowered species with a purple stigma) or *M. staintonii* and *M. regia* or a complex mixture of all three species. *M. staintonii*, newly described by C. Grey-Wilson (*Bot. Mag.* (2006) 23(2):176–209), is a tall (to 2.5m), robust species with red or pink flowers and a dark green stigma, near in appearance to *M. napaulensis* of gardens, but less so to true *M. napaulensis.* As *M. staintonii*, like its near relatives, readily hybridises in cultivation, it is rarely seen in an unadulterated form.

Melissa officinalis **'Variegata'**
The true cultivar of this name has leaves striped with white.

***Nemesia caerulea* 'Joan Wilder'**
The lavender-blue clone 'Joan Wilder', described and illustrated in *The Hardy Plant,* 14(1), 11–14, does not come true from seed; it may only be propagated from cuttings.

***Osmanthus heterophyllus* 'Gulftide'**
Probably correctly *O.* × *fortunei* 'Gulftide'.

***Pelargonium* 'Lass o' Gowrie'**
The American plant of this name has pointed, not rounded leaf lobes.

Pelargonium quercifolium
Plants under this name are mainly hybrids. The true species has pointed, not rounded leaf lobes.

***Penstemon* 'Taoensis'**
This name for a small-flowered cultivar or hybrid of *P. isophyllus* originally appeared as 'Taoense' but must be corrected to agree in gender with *Penstemon* (masculine). Presumably an invalid name (published in Latin form since 1958), it is not synonymous with *P. crandallii* subsp. *glabrescens* var. *taosensis.*

Pernettya
Botanists now consider that *Pernettya* (fruit a berry) is not separable from *Gaultheria* (fruit a capsule) because in some species the fruit is intermediate between a berry and a capsule. For a fuller explanation see D. Middleton, *The Plantsman,* 12(3).

Pinus ayacahuite
P. ayacahuite var. *veitchii* (syn. *P. veitchii)* is occasionally sold under this name.

***Pinus nigra* 'Cebennensis Nana'**
A doubtful name, possibly a synonym for *P. nigra* 'Nana'.

Polemonium archibaldiae
Usually sterile with lavender-blue flowers. A self-fertile white-flowered plant is sometimes sold under this name.

***Prunus laurocerasus* 'Castlewellan'**
We are grateful to Dr Charles Nelson for informing us that the name 'Marbled White' is not valid because although it has priority of publication it does not have the approval of the originator who asked for it to be called 'Castlewellan'.

Prunus serrulata* var. *pubescens
See note in Bean Supplement, p.398.

***Prunus* × *subhirtella* 'Rosea'**
Might be *P. pendula* var. *ascendens* 'Rosea', *P. pendula* 'Pendula Rosea', or *P.* × *subhirtella* 'Autumnalis Rosea'.

Rheum* × *cultorum
The name *R.* × *cultorum* was published without adequate description and must be abandoned in favour of the validly published *R.* × *hybridum.*

***Rhododendron* (azaleas)**
All names marked 'N', except for the following, refer to more than one cultivar.

***Rhododendron* 'Hinomayo'**
This name is based on a faulty transliteration (should be 'Hinamoyo') but the spelling 'Hinomayo' is retained in the interests of stability.

Rhus hirta and R. typhina
Linnaeus published both *R. typhina* and *R. hirta* as names for the same species. Though *R. hirta* has priority, it has been proposed that the name *R. typhina* should be conserved.

Rosa gentiliana
Plants under this name are usually the cultivar 'Polyantha Grandiflora' but might otherwise be *R. multiflora* 'Wilsonii', *R. multiflora* var. *cathayensis, R. henryi* or another hybrid.

***Rosa* 'Gros Chou de Hollande' (Bb)**
It is doubtful if this name is correctly applied.

***Rosa* 'Jacques Cartier' misapplied**
For a discussion on the correct identity of this rose see *Heritage Rose Foundation News,* Oct. 1989 & Jan. 1990.

***Rosa* 'Kazanlik'**
For a discussion on the correct identity of this rose see *Heritage Roses,* Nov. 1991.

***Rosa* Sweetheart**
This is not the same as the Sweetheart Rose, a common name for *R.* 'Cécile Brünner'.

Rosa wichurana
This is the correct spelling according to the ICBN 1994 Article 60.11 (which enforces Recommendation 60C.1c) and not *wichuraiana* for this rose commemorating Max Wichura.

***Rubus fruticosus* L. agg.**
Though some cultivated blackberries do belong to *Rubus fruticosus* L. *sensu stricto,* others are more correctly ascribed to other species of *Rubus* section *Glandulosus* (including *R. armeniacus, R. laciniatus* or *R. ulmifolius)* or are hybrids of species within this section. Because it is almost impossible to ascribe every cultivar to a single species or hybrid, they are listed under *R. fruticosus* L. agg. (i.e. aggregate) for convenience.

Salvia microphylla* var. *neurepia
The type of this variety is referable to the typical variety, *S. microphylla* var. *microphylla.*

***Salvia officinalis* 'Aurea'**
S. officinalis var. *aurea* is a rare variant of the common sage with leaves entirely of gold. It is represented in cultivation by the cultivar 'Kew Gold'. The plant usually offered as *S. officinalis* 'Aurea' is the gold variegated sage *S. officinalis* 'Icterina'.

***Sambucus nigra* 'Aurea'**
Plants under this name are usually not *S. nigra.*

***Skimmia japonica* 'Foremanii'**
The true cultivar, which belongs to *S. japonica* Rogersii Group, is believed to be lost to cultivation. Plants offered under this name are usually *S. japonica* 'Veitchii'.

***Spiraea japonica* 'Shirobana'**
Shirobana-shimotsuke is the common name for *S. japonica* var. *albiflora*. Shirobana means white-flowered and does not apply to the two-coloured form.

Staphylea holocarpa* var. *rosea
This botanical variety has woolly leaves. The cultivar 'Rosea', with which it is often confused, does not.

***Stewartia ovata* var. *grandiflora*.**
Most, possibly all, plants available from British nurseries under this name are not true to name but are derived from the improved Nymans form.

***Thymus* Coccineus Group**
Thymes under this name have dark crimson (RHS 78A) flowers whereas those of 'Alan Bloom' are purplish-pink (RHS 78C).

***Thymus serpyllum* cultivars**
Most cultivars are probably correctly cultivars of *T. polytrichus* or hybrids though they will remain listed under *T. serpyllum* pending further research.

***Thymus* 'Silver Posie'**
The cultivar name 'Silver Posie' is applied to several different plants, not all of them *T. vulgaris*.

***Tricyrtis* Hototogisu**
This is the common name applied generally to all Japanese *Tricyrtis* and specifically to *T. hirta*.

Tricyrtis macropoda
This name has been used for at least five different species.

Uncinia rubra
This name is also misapplied to *U. egmontiana* and *U. uncinata*.

***Viburnum opulus* 'Fructu Luteo'**
See note below.

***Viburnum opulus* 'Xanthocarpum'**
Some entries under this name might be the less compact *V. opulus* 'Fructu Luteo'.

Viburnum plicatum
Entries may include the 'snowball' form, *V. plicatum* f. *plicatum* (syn. *V. plicatum* 'Sterile'), as well as the 'lacecap' form, *V. plicatum* f. *tomentosum*.

Viola labradorica
See Note in *The Garden*, **110(2)**: 96.

***Wisteria floribunda* 'Violacea Plena' and *W. floribunda* 'Yae-kokuryū'**
We are grateful to Yoko Otsuki, who has established through Engei Kyokai (the Horticultural Society of Japan) that there are two different double selections of *Wisteria floribunda*. 'Violacea Plena' has double lavender/lilac flowers, while 'Yae-kokuryū' has more ragged and tightly double flowers with purple/indigo centres. Each is distinctive but it is probable that both are confused in the British nursery trade. 'Yae-fuji' might be an earlier name for 'Violacea Plena' or a Group name covering a range of doubles but, as *fuji* is the Japanese common name for the species, it would not be a valid name under the ICNCP.

CLASSIFICATION OF GENERA

Genera including a large number of species, or with many cultivars, are often subdivided into informal horticultural classifications, or formal cultivar groups in the case of *Clematis* and *Tulipa*. The breeding of new cultivars is sometimes limited to hybrids between closely-related species, thus for *Saxifraga* and *Primula*, the cultivars are allocated to the sections given in the infrageneric treatments cited. Please turn to p.11 for a fuller explanation.

ACTINIDIA

(s-p)	Self-pollinating

BEGONIA

(C)	Cane-like
(R)	Rex Cultorum
(S)	Semperflorens Cultorum
(T)	× *tuberhybrida* (Tuberous)

CHRYSANTHEMUM

(By the National Chrysanthemum Society)

(1)	Indoor Large (Exhibition)
(2)	Indoor Medium (Exhibition)
(3a)	Indoor Incurved: Large-flowered
(3b)	Indoor Incurved: Medium-flowered
(3c)	Indoor Incurved: Small-flowered
(4a)	Indoor Reflexed: Large-flowered
(4b)	Indoor Reflexed: Medium-flowered
(4c)	Indoor Reflexed: Small-flowered
(5a)	Indoor Intermediate: Large-flowered
(5b)	Indoor Intermediate: Medium-flowered
(5c)	Indoor Intermediate: Small-flowered
(6a)	Indoor Anemone: Large-flowered
(6b)	Indoor Anemone: Medium-flowered
(6c)	Indoor Anemone: Small-flowered
(7a)	Indoor Single: Large-flowered
(7b)	Indoor Single: Medium-flowered
(7c)	Indoor Single: Small-flowered
(8a)	Indoor True Pompon
(8b)	Indoor Semi-pompon
(9a)	Indoor Spray: Anemone
(9b)	Indoor Spray: Pompon
(9c)	Indoor Spray: Reflexed
(9d)	Indoor Spray: Single
(9e)	Indoor Spray: Intermediate
(9f)	Indoor Spray: Spider, Quill, Spoon or Any Other Type
(10a)	Indoor, Spider
(10b)	Indoor, Quill
(10c)	Indoor, Spoon
(11)	Any Other Indoor Type
(12a)	Indoor, Charm
(12b)	Indoor, Cascade
(13a)	October-flowering Incurved: Large-flowered
(13b)	October-flowering Incurved: Medium-flowered
(13c)	October-flowering Incurved: Small-flowered
(14a)	October-flowering Reflexed: Large-flowered
(14b)	October-flowering Reflexed: Medium-flowered
(14c)	October-flowering Reflexed: Small-flowered
(15a)	October-flowering Intermediate: Large-flowered
(15b)	October-flowering Intermediate: Medium-flowered
(15c)	October-flowered Intermediate: Small-flowered
(16)	October-flowering Large
(17a)	October-flowering Single: Large-flowered
(17b)	October-flowering Single: Medium-flowered
(17c)	October-flowering Single: Small-flowered
(18a)	October-flowering Pompon: True Pompon
(18b)	October-flowering Pompon: Semi-pompon
(19a)	October-flowering Spray: Anemone
(19b)	October-flowering Spray: Pompon
(19c)	October-flowering Spray: Reflexed
(19d)	October-flowering Spray: Single
(19e)	October-flowering Spray: Intermediate
(19f)	October-flowering Spray: Spider, Quill, Spoon or Any Other Type
(20)	Any Other October-flowering Type
(21a)	Korean: Anemone
(21b)	Korean: Pompon
(21c)	Korean: Reflexed
(21d)	Korean: Single
(21e)	Korean: Intermediate
(21f)	Korean: Spider, Quill, Spoon, or any other type
(22a)	Charm: Anemone
(22b)	Charm: Pompon
(22c)	Charm: Reflexed
(22d)	Charm: Single
(22e)	Charm: Intermediate
(22f)	Charm: Spider, Quill, Spoon or Any Other Type
(23a)	Early-flowering Outdoor Incurved: Large-flowered

(23b)	Early-flowering Outdoor Incurved: Medium-flowered
(23c)	Early-flowering Outdoor Incurved: Small-flowered
(24a)	Early-flowering Outdoor Reflexed: Large-flowered
(24b)	Early-flowering Outdoor Reflexed: Medium-flowered
(24c)	Early-flowering Outdoor Reflexed: Small-flowered
(25a)	Early-flowering Outdoor Intermediate: Large-flowered
(25b)	Early-flowering Outdoor Intermediate: Medium-flowered
(25c)	Early-flowering Outdoor Intermediate: Small-flowered
(26a)	Early-flowering Outdoor Anemone: Large-flowered
(26b)	Early-flowering Outdoor Anemone: Medium-flowered
(27a)	Early-flowering Outdoor Single: Large-flowered
(27b)	Early-flowering Outdoor Single:Medium-flowered
(28a)	Early-flowering Outdoor Pompon: True Pompon
(28b)	Early-flowering Outdoor Pompon: Semi-pompon
(29a)	Early-flowering Outdoor Spray: Anemone
(29b)	Early-flowering Outdoor Spray: Pompon
(29c)	Early-flowering Outdoor Spray: Reflexed
(29d)	Early-flowering Outdoor Spray: Single
(29e)	Early-flowering Outdoor Spray: Intermediate
(29f)	Early-flowering Outdoor Spray: Spider, Quill, Spoon or Any Other Type
(30)	Any Other Early-flowering Outdoor Type

CLEMATIS

(Cultivar Groups as per Matthews, V. (2002) *The International Clematis Register & Checklist 2002*, RHS, London.)

(A)	Atragene Group
(Ar)	Armandii Group
(C)	Cirrhosa Group
(EL)	Early Large-flowered Group
(F)	Flammula Group
(Fo)	Forsteri Group
(H)	Heracleifolia Group
(I)	Integrifolia Group
(LL)	Late Large-flowered Group
(M)	Montana Group
(T)	Texensis Group
(Ta)	Tangutica Group
(V)	Viorna Group
(Vb)	Vitalba Group
(Vt)	Viticella Group

DAHLIA

(By the National Dahlia Society with corresponding numerical classification according to the RHS's International Register)

(Sin)	1 Single
(Anem)	2 Anemone-flowered
(Col)	3 Collerette
(WL)	4 Waterlily (unassigned)
(LWL)	4B Waterlily, Large
(MWL)	4C Waterlily, Medium
(SWL)	4D Waterlily, Small
(MinWL)	4E Waterlily, Miniature
(D)	5 Decorative (unassigned)
(GD)	5A Decorative, Giant
(LD)	5B Decorative, Large
(MD)	5C Decorative, Medium
(SD)	5D Decorative, Small
(MinD)	5E Decorative, Miniature
(SBa)	6A Small Ball
(MinBa)	6B Miniature Ball
(Pom)	7 Pompon
(C)	8 Cactus (unassigned)
(GC)	8A Cactus, Giant
(LC)	8B Cactus, Large
(MC)	8C Cactus, Medium
(SC)	8D Cactus, Small
(MinC)	8E Cactus, Miniature
(S-c)	9 Semi-cactus (unassigned)
(GS-c)	9A Semi-cactus, Giant
(LS-c)	9B Semi-cactus, Large
(MS-c)	9C Semi-cactus, Medium
(SS-c)	9D Semi-cactus, Small
(MinS-c)	9E Semi-cactus, Miniature
(Misc)	10 Miscellaneous
(Fim)	11 Fimbriated
(SinO)	12 Single Orchid (Star)
(DblO)	13 Double Orchid
(B)	Botanical
(DwB)	Dwarf Bedding
(Lil)	Lilliput (in combination)

DIANTHUS

(By the RHS)

(b)	Carnation, border
(M)	Carnation, Malmaison
(pf)	Carnation, perpetual-flowering
(p)	Pink
(p,a)	Pink, annual

FRUIT

(B)	Black (*Vitis*), Blackcurrant (*Ribes*)
(Ball)	Ballerina (*Malus*)
(C)	Culinary (*Malus, Prunus, Pyrus, Ribes*)
(Cider)	Cider (*Malus*)

(D) Dessert (*Malus, Prunus, Pyrus, Ribes*)
(F) Fruit
(G) Glasshouse (*Vitis*)
(O) Outdoor (*Vitis*)
(P) Pinkcurrant (*Ribes*)
(Perry) Perry (*Pyrus*)
(R) Red (*Vitis*), Redcurrant (*Ribes*)
(S) Seedless (*Citrus, Vitis*)
(W) White (*Vitis*), Whitecurrant (*Ribes*)

FUCHSIA

(E) Encliandra
(T) Variants and hybrids of F. triphylla

GLADIOLUS

(B) Butterfly
(E) Exotic
(G) Giant
(L) Large
(M) Medium
(Min) Miniature
(N) Nanus
(P) Primulinus
(S) Small
(Tub) Tubergenii

HEPATICA NOBILIS

(Adapted from the International Hepatica Society classification for *Hepatica nobilis*)
(1) Hyoujun (normal)
(2) (degenerated anther)
(3) Otome (degenerated stamen)
(4) Henka (petal deformity)
(5/d) Herashibe (semi-double, primitive)
(5A/d) Choji (semi-double, primitive)
(6/d) Nidan (semi-double, advanced)
(7/d) Sandan (double, primitive)
(8/d) Karako (double, advanced)
(9/d) Sene-e (double, completed)

HYDRANGEA MACROPHYLLA

(H) Hortensia
(L) Lacecap

IRIS

(By the American Iris Society)
(AB) Arilbred
(BB) Border Bearded
(Cal-Sib) Series *Californicae* × Series *Sibiricae*
(CH) Californian Hybrid
(DB) Dwarf Bearded (not assigned)
(Dut) Dutch
(IB) Intermediate Bearded
(J) Juno (subgenus) *Scorpiris*
(La) Louisiana Hybrid
(MDB) Miniature Dwarf Bearded
(MTB) Miniature Tall Bearded
(Rc) Regeliocyclus (Section *Regelia* × Section *Oncocyclus*)
(SDB) Standard Dwarf Bearded
(Sino-Sib) Series *Sibiricae*, chromosome number 2n=40
(SpH) Species Hybrid
(Spuria) Spuria
(TB) Tall Bearded

LILIUM

(Classification according to *The International Lily Register* (ed. 4, 2007))
(I) Asiatic hybrids derived from *L. amabile, L. bulbiferum, L. callosum, L. cernuum, L. concolor, L. dauricum, L. davidii, L.* × *hollandicum, L. lancifolium, L. lankongense, L. leichtlinii, L.* × *maculatum* and *L. pumilum, L.* × *scottiae, L. wardii* and *L. wilsonii.*
(II) Martagon hybrids derived from *L. dalhansonii, L. hansonii, L. martagon, L. medeoloides and L. tsingtauense*
(III) Euro-Caucasian hybrids derived from *L. candidum, L. chalcedonicum, L. kesselringianum, L. monadelphum, L. pomponium, L. pyrenaicum* and *L.* × *testaceum.*
(IV) American hybrids derived from *L. bolanderi*, L. × *burbankii, L. canadense, L. columbianum, L. grayi, L. humboldtii, L. kelleyanum, L. kelloggii, L. maritimum, L. michauxii, L. michiganense, L. occidentale, L.* × *pardaboldtii, L. pardalinum, L. parryi, L. parvum, L. philadelphicum, L. pitkinense, L. superbum, L. vollmeri, L. washingtonianum* and *L. wigginsii.*
(V) Longiflorum lilies derived from *L. formosanum, L. longiflorum, L. philippinense and L. wallichianum.*
(VI) Trumpet and Aurelian hybrids derived from *L.* × *aurelianense, L. brownii, L.* × *centigale, L. henryi, L* × *imperiale, L.* × *kewense, L. leucantheum, L. regale, L. rosthornii, L. sargentiae, L. sulphureum* and *L. sulphurgale* (but excluding hybrids of *L. henryi* with all species listed in Division VII).
(VII) Oriental hybrids derived from *L. auratum, L. japonicum, L. nobilissimum, L.* × *parkmanii, L rubellum* and *L. speciosum* (but excl. all hybrids of these with *L. henryi*).
(VIII) Other hybrids not covered by any of the previous divisions (I-VII)
(IX) Species and cultivars of species

a/	upward-facing flowers
b/	outward-facing flowers
c/	downward-facing flowers
/a	trumpet-shaped flowers
/b	bowl-shaped flowers
/c	flat flowers (or with only tepal tips recurved)
/d	recurved flowers

MALUS *SEE* FRUIT

NARCISSUS

(By the RHS, revised 1998)

(1)	Trumpet
(2)	Large-cupped
(3)	Small-cupped
(4)	Double
(5)	Triandrus
(6)	Cyclamineus
(7)	Jonquilla and Apodanthus
(8)	Tazetta
(9)	Poeticus
(10)	Bulbocodium
(11a)	Split-corona: Collar
(11b)	Split-corona: Papillon
(12)	Miscellaneous
(13)	Species

NYMPHAEA

(H)	Hardy
(D)	Day-blooming
(N)	Night-blooming
(T)	Tropical

PAPAVER

(SPS)	Super Poppy Series

PAEONIA

(S)	Shrubby

PELARGONIUM

(A)	Angel
(C)	Coloured Foliage (in combination)
(Ca)	Cactus (in combination)
(d)	Double (in combination)
(Dec)	Decorative
(Dw)	Dwarf
(DwI)	Dwarf Ivy-leaved
(Fr)	Frutetorum
(I)	Ivy-leaved
(Min)	Miniature
(MinI)	Miniature Ivy-leaved
(R)	Regal
(Sc)	Scented-leaved
(St)	Stellar (in combination)
(T)	Tulip (in combination)
(U)	Unique
(Z)	Zonal

PRIMULA

(Classification by Section as per Richards. J. (2002) *Primula* (2nd edition). Batsford, London)

(Ag)	*Auganthus*
(Al)	*Aleuritia*
(Am)	*Amethystinae*
(Ar)	*Armerina*
(Au)	*Auricula*
(A)	Alpine Auricula
(B)	Border Auricula
(S)	Show Auricula
(St)	Striped Auricula
(Bu)	*Bullatae*
(Ca)	*Capitatae*
(Cf)	*Cordifoliae*
(Ch)	*Chartaceae*
(Co)	*Cortusoides*
(Cr)	*Carolinella*
(Cu)	*Cuneifoliae*
(Cy)	*Crystallophlomis*
(Da)	*Davidii*
(De)	*Denticulatae*
(Dr)	*Dryadifoliae*
(F)	*Fedtschenkoanae*
(G)	*Glabrae*
(Ma)	*Malvaceae*
(Mi)	*Minutissimae*
(Mo)	*Monocarpicae*
(Mu)	*Muscarioides*
(Ob)	*Obconicolisteri*
(Or)	*Oreophlomis*
(Pa)	*Parryi*
(Pe)	*Petiolares*
(Pf)	*Proliferae*
(Pi)	*Pinnatae*
(Pr)	*Primula*
(Poly)	Polyanthus
(Prim)	Primrose
(Pu)	*Pulchellae*
(Py)	*Pycnoloba*
(R)	*Reinii*
(Si)	*Sikkimenses*
(So)	*Soldanelloides*
(Sp)	*Sphondylia*
(Sr)	*Sredinskya*
(Su)	*Suffrutescentes*
(Y)	*Yunnannenses*

PRUNUS *SEE* FRUIT

PYRUS *SEE* FRUIT

RHODODENDRON

(A)	Azalea (deciduous, species or unclassified hybrid)
(Ad)	Azaleodendron
(EA)	Evergreen azalea
(G)	Ghent azalea (deciduous)

(K)	Knap Hill or Exbury azalea (deciduous)
(M)	Mollis azalea (deciduous)
(O)	Occidentalis azalea (deciduous)
(R)	Rustica azalea (deciduous)
(V)	Vireya rhododendron
(Vs)	Viscosa azalea (deciduous)

RIBES *SEE* FRUIT

ROSA

(A)	Alba
(Bb)	Bourbon
(Bs)	Boursault
(Ce)	Centifolia
(Ch)	China
(Cl)	Climbing (in combination)
(D)	Damask
(DPo)	Damask Portland
(F)	Floribunda or Cluster-flowered
(G)	Gallica
(Ga)	Garnette
(GC)	Ground Cover
(HM)	Hybrid Musk
(HP)	Hybrid Perpetual
(HT)	Hybrid Tea or Large-flowered
(Min)	Miniature
(Mo)	Moss (in combination)
(N)	Noisette
(Patio)	Patio, Miniature Floribunda or Dwarf Cluster-flowered
(Poly)	Polyantha
(Ra)	Rambler
(RH)	Rubiginosa hybrid (Hybrid Sweet Briar)
(Ru)	Rugosa
(S)	Shrub
(SpH)	Spinosissima Hybrid
(T)	Tea

SAXIFRAGA

(Classification by Section from Gornall, R.J. (1987). *Botanical Journal of the Linnean Society,* 95(4): 273-292)

(1)	*Ciliatae*
(2)	*Cymbalaria*
(3)	*Merkianae*
(4)	*Micranthes*
(5)	*Irregulares*
(6)	*Heterisia*
(7)	*Porphyrion*
(8)	*Ligulatae*
(9)	*Xanthizoon*
(10)	*Trachyphyllum*
(11)	*Gymnopera*
(12)	*Cotylea*
(13)	*Odontophyllae*
(14)	*Mesogyne*
(15)	*Saxifraga*

TULIPA

(Classification by Cultivar Group from *Classified List and International Register of Tulip Names* by Koninklijke Algemeene Vereening voor Bloembollenculture 1996)

(1)	Single Early Group
(2)	Double Early Group
(3)	Triumph Group
(4)	Darwin Hybrid Group
(5)	Single Late Group (including Darwin Group and Cottage Group)
(6)	Lily-flowered Group
(7)	Fringed Group
(8)	Viridiflora Group
(9)	Rembrandt Group
(10)	Parrot Group
(11)	Double Late Group
(12)	Kaufmanniana Group
(13)	Fosteriana Group
(14)	Greigii Group
(15)	Miscellaneous

VERBENA

(G)	Species and hybrids considered by some botanists to belong to the separate genus *Glandularia.*

VIOLA

(C)	Cornuta Hybrid
(dVt)	Double Violet
(ExVa)	Exhibition Viola
(FP)	Fancy Pansy
(PVt)	Parma Violet
(SP)	Show Pansy
(T)	Tricolor
(Va)	Viola
(Vt)	Violet
(Vtta)	Violetta

VITIS *SEE* FRUIT

REVERSE SYNONYMS

The following list of reverse synonyms is intended to help users find from which genus an unfamiliar plant name has been cross-referred. For a fuller explanation see p.13.

Abelmoschus – Hibiscus
Abronia – Verbena
Abutilon – Corynabutilon
Acacia – Racosperma
Acca – Feijoa
× *Achicodonia – Eucodonia*
Achillea – Anthemis
Achillea – Tanacetum
Acinos – Calamintha
Acinos – Clinopodium
Acinos – Micromeria
Acis – Leucojum
Acmella – Spilanthes
Actaea – Cimicifuga
Actaea – Souliea
Aethionema – Eunomia
Agapetes – Pentapterygium
Agarista – Leucothoe
Agastache – Cedronella
Agathosma – Barosma
Agave – Manfreda
Agave – × *Mangave*
Ageratina – Eupatorium
Agrostis – Eragrostis
Aichryson – Aeonium
Ajania – Chrysanthemum
Ajania – Dendranthema
Ajania – Eupatorium
Albizia – Acacia
Alcea – Althaea
Allardia – Waldheimia
Allocasuarina – Casuarina
Aloysia – Lippia
Althaea – Malva
Alyogyne – Anisodontea
Alyogyne – Hibiscus
Alyssum – Ptilotrichum
Amana – Tulipa
× *Amarygia – Amaryllis*
Amaryllis – Brunsvigia
Amberboa – Centaurea
Amomyrtus – Myrtus
Amsonia – Rhazya
Anacamptis – Orchis
Anaphalis – Gnaphalium
Anchusa – Lycopsis
Androsace – Douglasia
Androstoma – Cyathodes
Anemanthele – Oryzopsis
Anemanthele – Stipa
Anemone – Eriocapitella
Anisodontea – Malvastrum
Anisodus – Scopolia
Anomatheca – Freesia
Anomatheca – Lapeirousia
Anredera – Boussingaultia
Antirrhinum – Asarina
Aphanes – Alchemilla
Arctanthemum – Chrysanthemum
Arctostaphylos – Arbutus
Arctotis – Venidium
Arctotis – × *Venidioarctotis*
Arenga – Didymosperma
Argyranthemum – Anthemis
Argyranthemum – Chrysanthemum
Armoracia – Cochlearia
Arnoglossum – Cacalia
Arundinaria – Pseudosasa
Asarina – Antirrhinum
Asarum – Hexastylis
Asparagus – Myrsiphyllum
Asparagus – Smilax
Asperula – Galium
Asphodeline – Asphodelus
Asplenium – Camptosorus
Asplenium – Ceterach
Asplenium – Phyllitis
Asplenium – Scolopendrium
Aster – Crinitaria
Aster – Doellingeria
Aster – Erigeron
Aster – Microglossa
Aster – Symphyotrichum
Astilboides – Rodgersia
Asyneuma – Campanula
Athanasia – Hymenolepis
Atropanthe – Scopolia
Aurinia – Alyssum
Austrocedrus – Libocedrus
Austromyrtus – Myrtus
Azorella – Bolax
Azorina – Campanula

Bambusa – Arundinaria
Barnadesia- Mutisia
Bashania – Arundinaria
Bassia – Kochia
Beaucarnea – Nolina
Bellevalia – Muscari
Bellis – Erigeron
Bignonia – Campsis
Blechnum – Lomaria
Blechnum – Struthiopteris
Blepharocalyx – Temu
Bolax – Azorella
Bolboschoenus – Scirpus
Bonia – Indocalamus
Borago – Anchusa
Bothriochloa – Andropogon
Bouteloua – Chondrosum
Boykinia – Telesonix
Brachychiton – Sterculia
Brachyglottis – Senecio
Brimeura – Hyacinthus
Brodiaea – Triteleia
Brugmansia – Datura
Brunnera – Anchusa
Buglossoides – Lithospermum
Bulbine – Bulbinopsis

Cacalia – Adenostyles
Caladium – Xanthosoma
Calamagrostis – Stipa
Calamintha – Clinopodium
Calamintha – Thymus
Calibrachoa – Petunia
Callisia – Phyodina
Callisia – Tradescantia
Calocedrus – Libocedrus
Calomeria – Humea
Caloscordum – Nothoscordum
Calylophus – Oenothera
Calytrix – Lhotzkya
Camellia – Thea
Campanula – Symphyandra
Cardamine – Dentaria
Carmichaelia – × *Carmispartium*
Carmichaelia – Chordospartium
Carmichaelia – Corallospartium
Carpobrotus – Lampranthus
Cedronella – Agastache
Centaurium – Erythraea
Centella – Hydrocotyle
Centranthus – Kentranthus
Centranthus – Valeriana
Cephalaria – Scabiosa
Ceratostigma – Plumbago
Chaenomeles – Cydonia
Chaenorhinum – Linaria
Chamaecytisus – Cytisus
Chamaedaphne – Cassandra
Chamaemelum – Anthemis
Chamerion – Chamaenerion
Chamerion – Epilobium
Chasmanthium – Uniola
Cheilanthes – Notholaena
Chiastophyllum – Cotyledon
Chimonobambusa – Arundinaria
Chimonobambusa – Qiongzhuea
Chionohebe – Parahebe
Chionohebe – Pygmea

× Chionoscilla – Scilla
Chlorophytum – Diuranthera
Chromolaena – Eupatorium
Chrysanthemum – Dendranthema
Chrysopsis – Heterotheca
Cicerbita – Lactuca
Cionura – Marsdenia
Cissus – Ampelopsis
Cissus – Parthenocissus
× Citrofortunella – Citrus
Clarkia – Eucharidium
Clarkia – Godetia
Clavinodum – Arundinaria
Claytonia – Calandrinia
Claytonia – Montia
Clematis – Atragene
Clematis – Clematopsis
Cleyera – Eurya
Clinopodium – Calamintha
Clytostoma – Bignonia
Clytostoma – Pandorea
Cnicus – Carduus
Conoclinium – Eupatorium
Codariocalyx – Desmodium
Codonopsis – Campanumoea
Collospermum – Astelia
Colobanthus – Arenaria
Consolida – Delphinium
Cordyline – Dracaena
Cornus – Chamaepericlymenum
Cornus – Dendrobenthamia
Coronilla – Securigera
Cortaderia – Gynerium
Corydalis – Capnoides
Corydalis – Fumaria
Corydalis – Pseudofumaria
Cosmos – Bidens
Cotinus – Rhus
Cotula – Leptinella
Crassula – Rochea
Crassula – Sedum
Crassula – Tillaea
× Crataegosorbus – Sorbus
Cremanthodium – Ligularia
Crinodendron – Tricuspidaria
Crocosmia – Antholyza
Crocosmia – Curtonus
Crocosmia – Montbretia
Cruciata – Galium
Ctenanthe – Calathea
Ctenanthe – Stromanthe
Cupressus – Chamaecyparis
× Cuprocyparis – Chamaecyparis
× Cuprocyparis – Cupressocyparis
Cyclosorus – Pneumatopteris
Cymbalaria – Linaria
Cymophyllus – Carex
Cyperus – Mariscus
Cypripedium – Criogenes
Cyrtanthus – Anoiganthus
Cyrtanthus – Vallota
Cyrtomium – Phanerophlebia
Cyrtomium – Polystichum
Cytisophyllum – Cytisus
Cytisus – Argyrocytisus
Cytisus – Genista
Cytisus – Lembotropis
Cytisus – Spartocytisus
Daboecia – Menziesia
Dacrycarpus – Podocarpus
Dactylorhiza – Orchis
Dalea – Petalostemon
Danae – Ruscus
Darmera – Peltiphyllum
Datura – Brugmansia
Davallia – Humata
Delairea – Senecio
Delosperma – Lampranthus
Delosperma – Mesembryanthemum
Dendrocalamus – Bambusa
Desmodium – Lespedeza
Deuterocohnia – Abromeitiella
Dicentra – Corydalis
Dichelostemma – Brodiaea
Dicliptera – Barleria
Dicliptera – Justicia
Diervilla – Weigela
Dietes – Moraea
Diplazium – Athyrium
Dipogon – Dolichos
Disporopsis – Polygonatum
Dolichothrix – Helichrysum
Dracaena – Pleomele
Dracunculus – Arum
Dregea – Wattakaka
Drepanostachyum – Bambusa
Drepanostachyum – Chimonobambusa
Drepanostachyum – Gelidocalamus
Drepanostachyum – Thamnocalamus
Drimys – Tasmannia
Duchesnea – Fragaria
Dypsis – Chrysalidocarpus
Dypsis – Neodypsis

Echeveria – Cotyledon
Echinacea – Rudbeckia
Echinospartum – Genista
Edraianthus – Wahlenbergia
Egeria – Elodea
Elatostema – Pellionia
Eleutherococcus – Acanthopanax
Elliottia – Botryostege
Elliottia – Cladothamnus
Elymus – Agropyron
Elymus – Leymus
Ensete – Musa
Epipremnum – Philodendron
Epipremnum – Scindapsus
Episcia – Alsobia
Eranthis – Aconitum
Eremophila – Myoporum
Erepsia – Semnanthe
Erigeron – Haplopappus
Erysimum – Cheiranthus
Eucalyptus – Corymbia
Eupatorium – Ageratina
Eupatorium – Ayapana
Eupatorium – Bartlettina
Euphorbia – Poinsettia
Euryops – Senecio
Eustachys – Chloris
Eustoma – Lisianthus
Euthamia – Solidago

Fallopia – Bilderdykia
Fallopia – Polygonum
Fallopia – Reynoutria
Farfugium – Ligularia
Fargesia – Arundinaria
Fargesia – Borinda
Fargesia – Semiarundinaria
Fargesia – Sinarundinaria
Fargesia – Thamnocalamus
Fatsia – Aralia
Felicia – Agathaea
Felicia – Aster
Fibigia – Farsetia
Filipendula – Spiraea
Ficinia – Isolepis
Foeniculum – Ferula
Fortunella – Citrus
Frangula – Rhamnus

Galium – Asperula
Gaultheria – Chiogenes
Gaultheria – Pernettya
Gaultheria – × Gaulnettya
Gelasine – Sisyrinchium
Genista – Chamaespartium
Genista – Cytisus
Genista – Echinospartum
Genista – Teline
Gethyum – Ancrumia
Geum – Sieversia
Gladiolus – Acidanthera
Gladiolus – Anomalesia
Gladiolus – Homoglossum
Gladiolus – Petamenes
Glebionis – Chrysanthemum
Glebionis – Xanthophthalmum
Glechoma – Nepeta
Gloxinia – Seemannia
Gloxinia – Sinningia
Gomphocarpus – Asclepias
Gomphocarpus – Asclepias
Goniolimon – Limonium
Goniophlebium – Polypodium
Graptopetalum – Sedum

Graptopetalum – Tacitus
Greenovia – Sempervivum
Gymnadenia – Nigritella
Gymnospermium – Leontice

Habranthus – Zephyranthes
Hacquetia – Dondia
× *Halimiocistus – Cistus*
× *Halimiocistus – Halimium*
Halimione – Atriplex
Halimium – Cistus
Halimium – Helianthemum
Halimium – × *Halimiocistus*
Halocarpus – Dacrydium
Hanabusaya – Symphyandra
Harrimanella – Cassiope
Hedychium – Brachychilum
Helianthella – Helianthus
Helianthemum – Cistus
Helianthus – Coreopsis
Helianthus – Heliopsis
Helichrysum – Gnaphalium
Helicodiceros – Dracunculus
Helictotrichon – Avena
Helictotrichon – Avenula
Hepatica – Anemone
Herbertia – Alophia
Hermodactylus – Iris
Heterocentron – Schizocentron
Heteromeles – Photinia
Heterotheca – Chrysopsis
× *Heucherella – Heuchera*
× *Heucherella – Tiarella*
Hibbertia – Candollea
Hieracium – Andryala
Himalayacalamus – Arundinaria
Himalayacalamus – Chimonobambusa
Himalayacalamus – Drepanostachyum
Himalayacalamus – Drepanostachyum
Himalayacalamus – Thamnocalamus
Hippocrepis – Coronilla
Hippolytia – Achillea
Hippolytia – Tanacetum
Hoheria – Plagianthus
Homalocladium – Muehlenbeckia
Howea – Kentia
Hyacinthoides – Endymion
Hyacinthoides – Scilla
Hydrangea – Schizophragma
Hylomecon – Chelidonium
Hymenocallis – Elisena
Hymenocallis – Ismene
Hymenoxys – Dugaldia
Hymenoxys – Helenium
Hyophorbe – Mascarena
Hypoxis – Rhodohypoxis

Incarvillea – Amphicome
Indocalamus – Sasa
Iochroma – Acnistus
Iochroma – Cestrum
Iochroma – Dunalia
Iostephane – Coreopsis
Ipheion – Tristagma
Ipheion – Triteleia
Ipomoea – Calonyction
Ipomoea – Mina
Ipomoea – Pharbitis
Ipomopsis – Gilia
Ischyrolepis – Restio
Isolepis – Scirpus
Isotoma – Laurentia
Isotoma – Solenopsis

Jamesbrittenia – Sutera
Jeffersonia – Plagiorhegma
Jovibarba – Sempervivum
Juncus – Scirpus
Junellia – Verbena
Jurinea – Jurinella
Justicia – Beloperone
Justicia – Duvernoia
Justicia – Jacobinia
Justicia – Libonia

Kadsura – Schisandra
Kalanchoe – Bryophyllum
Kalanchoe – Kitchingia
Kalimeris – Aster
Kalimeris – Asteromoea
Kalimeris – Boltonia
Kalopanax – Acanthopanax
Kalopanax – Eleutherococcus
Keckiella – Penstemon
Keckiella – Penstemon
Kitagawia – Peucedanum
Knautia – Scabiosa
Kniphofia – Tritoma
Kohleria – Isoloma
Krascheninnikovia – Ceratoides
Kunzea – Leptospermum

Lablab – Dolichos
Lagarosiphon – Elodea
Lagarostrobos – Dacrydium
Lamium – Galeobdolon
Lamium – Lamiastrum
Lampranthus – Mesembryanthemum
Laserpitium – Siler
Lavatera – Malva
Ledebouria – Scilla
× *Ledodendron – Rhododendron*
Ledum – Rhododendron
Leontodon – Microseris
Lepechinia – Sphacele
Lepidothamnus – Dacrydium
Leptecophylla – Cyathodes
Leptinella – Cotula
Leptodactylon – Gilia
Leucanthemella – Chrysanthemum
Leucanthemella – Leucanthemum
Leucanthemopsis – Chrysanthemum
Leucanthemum – Chrysanthemum
Leucochrysum – Helipterum
Leucocoryne – Beauverdia
Leucophyta – Calocephalus
Leucopogon – Cyathodes
Leucopogon – Styphelia
× *Leucoraoulia – Raoulia*
× *Leucoraoulia – Raoulia* x *Leucogenes*
Leymus – Elymus
Ligularia – Senecio
Ligustrum – Parasyringa
Lilium – Nomocharis
Limonium – Statice
Linanthus – Linanthastrum
Lindelofia – Adelocaryum
Ligularia – Cacalia
Lindera – Parabenzoin
Lindernia – Ilysanthes
Liriope – Ophiopogon
Lithodora – Lithospermum
Lobelia – Monopsis
Lophomyrtus – Myrtus
Lophospermum – Asarina
Lophospermum – Maurandya
Lophostemon – Tristania
Lotus – Dorycnium
Lotus – Tetragonolobus
Ludwigia – Jussiaea
Luma – Myrtus
× *Lycene – Lychnis*
Lychnis – Agrostemma
Lychnis – Silene
Lychnis – Viscaria
Lycianthes – Solanum
Lytocaryum – Cocos
Lytocaryum – Microcoelum

Macfadyena – Bignonia
Macfadyena – Doxantha
Machaeranthera – Xylorhiza
Machaerina – Baumea
Mackaya – Asystasia
Macleaya – Bocconia
Maclura – Cudrania
Macropiper – Piper
Magnolia – Manglietia
Magnolia – Michelia
Magnolia – Parakmeria
Mahonia – Berberis
Maianthemum – Smilacina
Mandevilla – Dipladenia
Mandragora – Atropa
Marrubium – Ballota

Matricaria – Tripleurospermum
Maurandella – Asarina
Maurandya – Asarina
Melanoselinum – Thapsia
Melicytus – Hymenanthera
Melinis – Rhynchelytrum
Mentha – Preslia
Merremia – Ipomoea
Merwilla – Scilla
Mimulus – Diplacus
Minuartia – Arabis
Minuartia – Arenaria
Moltkia – Lithodora
Moltkia – Lithospermum
Monochoria – Pontederia
Monopsis – Lobelia
Morina – Acanthocalyx
Morina – Acanthocalyx
Mukdenia – Aceriphyllum
Muscari – Hyacinthus
Muscari – Leopoldia
Muscari – Muscarimia
Muscari – Pseudomuscari
Myrteola – Myrtus

Naiocrene – Claytonia
Naiocrene – Montia
Nectaroscordum – Allium
Nematanthus – Hypocyrta
Nemesia – Diascia × Linaria
Neolitsea – Litsea
Neopanax – Pseudopanax
Neopaxia – Claytonia
Neopaxia – Montia
Neoregelia – Nidularium
Nepeta – Dracocephalum
× Niduregelia – Guzmania
Nipponanthemum – Chrysanthemum
Nipponanthemum – Leucanthemum
Nolina – Beaucarnea
Notospartium – Carmichaelia
Nymphoides – Villarsia

Ochagavia – Fascicularia
Oemleria – Osmaronia
Oenothera – Chamissonia
Olsynium – Sisyrinchium
Onixotis – Dipidax
Onoclea – Matteuccia
Ophiopogon – Convallaria
Orbea – Stapelia
Orchis – Anacamptis
Orchis – Dactylorhiza
Oreopteris – Thelypteris
Orostachys – Sedum
Oscularia – Lampranthus
Osmanthus – Phillyrea
Osmanthus – × Osmarea
Othonna – Hertia
Othonna – Othonnopsis
Oxygraphis – Ranunculus
Oziroë – Fortunatia
Ozothamhus – Helichrysum

Pachyphragma – Cardamine
Pachyphragma – Thlaspi
Pachystegia – Olearia
Packera – Senecio
Paederota – Veronica
Pallenis – Asteriscus
Papaver – Meconopsis
Parahebe – Derwentia
Parahebe – Hebe
Parahebe – Veronica
Parasenecio – Cacalia
Paraserianthes – Albizia
Paris – Daiswa
Parthenocissus – Ampelopsis
Parthenocissus – Vitis
Passiflora – Tetrapathaea
Paxistima – Pachystema
Pecteilis – Habenaria
Pelargonium – Geranium
Peltoboykinia – Boykinia
Penstemon – Chelone
Penstemon – Nothochelone
Penstemon – Pennellianthus
Pentaglottis – Anchusa
Pericallis – Cineraria
Pericallis – Senecio
Persea – Machilus
Persicaria – Aconogonon
Persicaria – Antenoron
Persicaria – Bistorta
Persicaria – Polygonum
Persicaria – Tovara
Petrocoptis – Lychnis
Petrophytum – Spiraea
Petrorhagia – Tunica
Petroselinum – Carum
Phalocallis – Cypella
Phegopteris – Thelypteris
Phlebodium – Polypodium
Phoenicaulis – Parrya
Photinia – Stransvaesia
Photinia – × Stravinia
Phuopsis – Crucianella
Phyla – Lippia
Phymatosorus – Microsorum
Phymosia – Sphaeralcea
Physoplexis – Phyteuma
Physostegia – Dracocephalum
Pieris – Arcterica
Pilosella – Hieracium
Platycladus – Thuja
Plecostachys – Helichrysum
Plectranthus – Coleus
Plectranthus – Solenostemon
Pleioblastus – Arundinaria
Pleioblastus – Sasa
Podophyllum – Dysosma
Podranea – Tecoma
Polianthes – Bravoa
Polygonum – Persicaria
Polypodium – Phlebodium
Polyscias – Nothopanax
Polyspora – Gordonia
Poncirus – Aegle
Potentilla – Comarum
Pratia – Lobelia
Prenanthes – Nabalus
Pritzelago – Hutchinsia
Prumnopitys – Podocarpus
Prunus – Amygdalus
Pseudocydonia – Chaenomeles
Pseudogynoxys – Senecio
Pseudopanax – Metapanax
Pseudopanax – Neopanax
Pseudosasa – Arundinaria
Pseudotsuga – Tsuga
Pseudowintera – Drimys
Pterocephalus – Scabiosa
Pteryxia – Cymopterus
Ptilostemon – Cirsium
Pulicaria – Inula
Pulsatilla – Anemone
Purshia – Cowania
Puschkinia – Scilla
Pycreus – Cyperus
Pyrrocoma – Aster
Pyrrocoma – Haplopappus

Reineckea – Liriope
Retama – Genista
Retama – Lygos
Rhapis – Chamaerops
Rhodanthe – Helipterum
Rhodanthemum – Argyranthemum
Rhodanthemum – Chrysanthemopsis
Rhodanthemum – Chrysanthemum
Rhodanthemum – Leucanthemopsis
Rhodanthemum – Leucanthemum
Rhodanthemum – Pyrethropsis
Rhodiola – Clementsia
Rhodiola – Rosularia
Rhodiola – Sedum
Rhododendron – Azalea
Rhododendron – Azaleodendron
Rhododendron – Rhodora
Rhododendron – Therorhodion
Rhododendron – Tsusiophyllum
Rhodophiala – Hippeastrum
× Rhodoxis – Hypoxis × Rhodohypoxis
× Rhodoxis – Rhodohypoxis
Rhus – Toxicodendron
Rhyncospora – Dichromena

Rosularia – Cotyledon
Rosularia – Sempervivella
Rothmannia – Gardenia
Ruellia – Dipteracanthus

Saccharum – Erianthus
Sagina – Minuartia
Sanguisorba – Dendriopoterium
Sanguisorba – Poterium
Sasa – Arundinaria
Sasaella – Arundinaria
Sasaella – Pleioblastus
Sasaella – Sasa
Sauromatum – Arum
Saussurea – Jurinea
Scadoxus – Haemanthus
Schefflera – Brassaia
Schefflera – Dizygotheca
Schefflera – Heptapleurum
Schizachyrium – Andropogon
Schizostachyum – Arundinaria
Schizostachyum – Thamnocalamus
Schizostylis – Hesperantha
Schoenoplectus – Scirpus
Scilla – Oncostema
Scirpoides – Scirpus
Securigera – Coronilla
Sedum – Cotyledon
Sedum – Hylotelephium
Sedum – Sedastrum
Semiaquilegia – Aquilegia
Semiaquilegia – Paraquilegia
Semiarundinaria – Arundinaria
Semiarundinaria – Oligostachyum
Senecio – Cineraria
Senecio – Kleinia
Senecio – Ligularia
Senna – Cassia
Seriphidium – Artemisia
Shortia – Schizocodon
Sibbaldiopsis – Potentilla
Sieversia – Geum
Silene – Lychnis
Silene – Melandrium
Silene – Saponaria
Sinacalia – Ligularia
Sinacalia – Senecio
Sinningia – Gesneria
Sinningia – Rechsteineria
Sinobambusa – Pleioblastus
Sinobambusa – Pseudosasa
Siphocranion – Chamaesphacos
Sisymbrium – Hesperis
Sisyrinchium – Phaiophleps
Smallanthus – Polymnia
Solanum – Lycianthes
Soleirolia – Helxine
Solenostemon – Coleus
Solidago – Aster
Solidago – × Solidaster
× Solidaster – Aster
× Solidaster – Solidago
Sophora – Styphnolobium
Sorbaria – Spiraea
Sparaxis – Synnotia
Sphaeralcea – Iliamna
Sphaeromeria – Tanacetum
Spirodela – Lemna
Spraguea – Calyptridium
Stachys – Betonica
Stemmacantha – Centaurea
Stemmacantha – Leuzea
Stenomesson – Urceolina
Stenotus – Haplopappus
Stewartia – Stuartia
Stipa – Achnatherum
Stipa – Agrostis
Stipa – Calamagrostis
Stipa – Lasiagrostis
Stipa – Nassella
Strobilanthes – Parachampionella
Strobilanthes – Pteracanthus
Styphnolobium – Sophora
Succisa – Scabiosa
Sutera – Bacopa
Syagrus – Arecastrum
Syagrus – Cocos
Syncarpha – Helipterum
Syzygium – Caryophyllus

Talbotia – Vellozia
Tanacetum – Achillea
Tanacetum – Balsamita
Tanacetum – Chrysanthemum
Tanacetum – Matricaria
Tanacetum – Pyrethrum
Tanacetum – Spathipappus
Tecoma – Tecomaria
Telanthophora – Senecio
Telekia – Buphthalmum
Tetradium – Euodia
Tetraneuris – Actinella
Tetraneuris – Actinella
Tetraneuris – Hymenoxys
Tetrapanax – Fatsia
Thamnocalamus – Arundinaria
Thlaspi – Hutchinsia
Thlaspi – Noccaea
Thlaspi – Vania
Thuja – Thujopsis
Thymus – Origanum
Tiarella – × Heucherella
Tonestus – Haplopappus
Toona – Cedrela
Trachelium – Diosphaera
Trachycarpus – Chamaerops
Tradescantia – Rhoeo
Tradescantia – Setcreasea
Tradescantia – Zebrina
Trichopetalum – Anthericum
Trichophorum – Scirpus
Tripetaleia – Elliottia
Tripleurospermum – Gentiana
Tripleurospermum – Matricaria
Tripogandra – Tradescantia
Tristaniopsis – Tristania
Triteleia – Brodiaea
Tritonia – Crocosmia
Tritonia – Montbretia
Trochiscanthes – Angelica
Tropaeolum – Nasturtium hort.
Tupistra – Campylandra
Tutcheria – Pyrenaria
Tweedia – Oxypetalum

Ugni – Myrtus
Utricularia – Polypompholyx
Uvularia – Oakesiella

Vaccaria – Melandrium
Vaccinium – Oxycoccus
Verbascum – Celsia
Verbascum – × Celsioverbascum
Verbena – Glandularia
Verbena – Lippia
Veronicastrum – Veronica
Vigna – Phaseolus
Viola – Erpetion
Vitaliana – Androsace
Vitaliana – Douglasia

Wedelia – Zexmenia
Weigela – Diervilla
Weigela – Macrodiervilla

Xanthocyparis – Cupressus
Xanthorhiza – Zanthorhiza
Xerochrysum – Bracteantha
Xerochrysum – Helichrysum

Yushania – Arundinaria
Yushania – Sinarundinaria
Yushania – Thamnocalamus

Zantedeschia – Calla
Zauschneria – Epilobium
Zephyranthes – × Cooperanthes
Zephyranthes – Cooperia

THE PLANT DIRECTORY

A

Abelia ✿ (*Caprifoliaceae*)

chinensis misapplied	see *A.* × *grandiflora*
§ ***chinensis*** R.Br.	CBcs CPLG EBee EPfP GKir MAsh MMuc SBfd SDnm SEND SKHP SPer SRms WFar WGrn
'Edward Goucher'	Widely available
engleriana	CPLG CWan EBee EPfP LRHS MAsh MMuc NLar SEND SLon WFar
floribunda ♀H3	CBcs CBgR CDul CMac CPLG CSBt CSam CWib EBee ECre ELan EPfP LRHS MAsh NLar SDnm SEND SKHP SPer SPoG SSpi WAbe WFar WGob WPat WSHC
§ × ***grandiflora*** ♀H4	Widely available
- 'Aurea'	see *A.* × *grandiflora* 'Gold Spot'
- 'Compacta'	CBar WFar
- Confetti = 'Conti'PBR (v)	Widely available
- dwarf	CDoC
§ - 'Francis Mason' (v)	Widely available
§ - 'Gold Spot' (v)	CWSG EBee EPfP LRHS MGos MWat MWhi NMun SPoG WGob
- 'Gold Strike'	see *A.* × *grandiflora* 'Gold Spot'
- 'Goldsport'	see *A.* × *grandiflora* 'Gold Spot'
- 'Hopleys'PBR (v)	CBcs CDoC CDul CMac CSBt CWib EBee EBtc ELan EPfP LHop LRHS MAsh MGos NHol SEND SLim SLon SPoG SWvt WCot WFar WGob WGrn WHar
- 'Kaleidoscope' (v)	CAbP CDoC CMac CSBt EShb EWTr LRHS LSRN MAsh MGos NCGa SBfd SLim SPoG SWvt WGob WGrn
- 'Panache' (v)	CAlb CDoC LLHF LTen MGos MRav WCot WPat
- 'Prostrate White'	MAsh NLar SBfd
- 'Semperflorens'	EMil LRHS SBfd
- 'Sherwoodii'	EMil EPfP LRHS SLim WPat
- 'Sunrise' (v)	EBee ELan EPfP MGos NLar SLim
- 'Tanya'	EBee
- 'Variegata'	see *A.* × *grandiflora* 'Francis Mason'
mosanensis	EBee EPfP IVic LRHS MAsh MBlu MBri NLar SLon SPoG SSpi
parvifolia 'Bumblebee' **new**	SPoG
rupestris misapplied	see *A.* × *grandiflora*
rupestris Lindl.	see *A. chinensis* R.Br.
schumannii ♀H4	Widely available
- 'Saxon Gold'PBR	EBee
spathulata	WFar
triflora	CAbP CBot CPLG CWib EBee ECre EPfP LAst LHop MMuc NLar SEND SKHP WFar WGob WSHC

Abeliophyllum (*Oleaceae*)

distichum	Widely available
- Roseum Group	CBcs CDoC CPLG CPMA EBee ELan ELon EPfP LAst LHop LRHS MAsh MGos MMuc MRav NSti SKHP SLon SPer SPoG WCot WFar

Abies (*Pinaceae*)

alba	CDul IFFs NWea
- 'Bystricka'	MAsh
- 'Compacta'	CKen
- 'King's Dwarf'	CKen
- 'Microphylla'	CKen
- 'Münsterland'	CKen
- 'Nana' misapplied	see *Picea glauca* 'Nana'
- 'Nana' ambig.	CKen
- 'Pendula'	CKen
amabilis	GLin WEve
- 'Spreading Star'	GKir
× ***arnoldiana***	MGos
balsamea	CDul GKir NWea
- 'Cook's Blue' **new**	CKen
- Hudsonia Group ♀H4	CDoC CKen ECho EHul EMil GKir LRHS NHol NLar NMen SLim SPoG WEve
- 'Jamie'	CKen MAsh NLar
- 'Le Feber'	CKen
- 'Nana'	CKen ECho EHul EPla MAsh NPCo WDin WFar
- var. ***phanerolepis*** 'Bear Swamp'	CKen NHol NLar
- 'Piccolo'	CDoC CKen ECho EHul LRHS NHol NLar WEve WFar WGor
- 'Prostrata'	ECho EHul WEve
- 'Renswoude'	CKen
- 'Tyler Blue'	CKen
- 'Verkade's Prostrate'	CKen
* ***borisii-regis*** 'Pendula'	CKen
brachyphylla dwarf	see *A. homolepis* 'Prostrata'
cephalonica	CDul CKen CMCN NWea
- 'Greg's Broom'	CKen ECho
§ - 'Meyer's Dwarf'	ECho EHul GKir LRHS MBri NLar NPCo SCoo SLim SPoG WEve
- 'Nana'	see *A. cephalonica* 'Meyer's Dwarf'
chensiensis subsp. ***salouensis***	GKir
cilicica 'Spring Grove' **new**	CKen
concolor ♀H4	CBcs CDul CTho EMac EWTr GKir IFFs LMaj LTen MMuc NWea SEND WDin WEve
- 'Archer's Dwarf'	CKen ECho MGos NLar SLim
- 'Argentea' Niemetz, 1903	CKen
- 'Aurea'	MGos NLar WEve
- 'Birthday Broom'	CKen
- 'Blue Sapphire'	CKen
- 'Blue Spreader'	CKen ECho MGos
§ - 'Compacta' ♀H4	CDoC CKen ECho GKir LRHS MAsh MGos NHol NLar SCoo SLim SPoG WEve WFar
- 'Fagerhult'	CKen
- 'Gable's Weeping'	CKen
- 'Glauca'	see *A. concolor* Violacea Group
- 'Glauca Compacta'	see *A. concolor* 'Compacta'
- 'Hillier Broom'	see *A. concolor* 'Hillier's Dwarf'
§ - 'Hillier's Dwarf'	CKen

	- 'Husky Pup'	CKen
	- (Lowiana Group) 'Creamy'	CKen
	- 'Masonic Broom'	CKen
	- 'Mike Stearn'	CKen
	- 'Mora'	CKen
	- 'Ostrov nad Ohri'	CKen
	- 'Piggelmee'	CKen ECho MAsh NLar
	- 'Pygmy'	CKen
	- 'Scooter'	CKen
	- 'Sherwood's Blue'	ECho
*	- 'Swift's Silver'	LRHS WBVN WEve
§	- Violacea Group	CKen ECho MGos SLim WEve WFar
	- 'Wattez Prostrate'	LRHS NLar SCoo SLim SPoG WFar
	- 'Wattezii'	CKen ECho GKir
	- 'Wintergold'	CKen ECho GKir MGos NLar NPCo SLim WEve
	delavayi	CDul GKir MGos NWea
	- SDR 3269	GKev
	- var. ***delavayi*** Fabri Group	see *A. fabri*
I	- 'Nana'	CKen
	- 'Nana Headfort'	see *A. fargesii* 'Headfort'
§	***fabri***	CDul CKen GKir
	fargesii	CKen NLar
§	- 'Headfort'	NLar
	firma	GKir NWea
	forrestii	CKen GKir
	- var. ***georgei***	GKir NWea
	fraseri	IFFs MMuc NWea WEve
	- 'Blue Bonnet'	CKen
	- 'Piglet's' witches' broom	NLar
	- 'Raul's Dwarf'	CKen ECho
	grandis	CBcs CDul EMac IFFs NWea WDin
	- 'Compacta'	CKen
	- 'Van Dedem's Dwarf'	CKen MAsh NLar SLim WEve
	holophylla	GKir NLar
	homolepis	CDul CKen GKir NLar
§	- 'Prostrata'	CKen
	kawakamii	CKen
	koreana	Widely available
	- 'Alpin Star'	CKen MAsh
	- 'Aurea'	see *A. koreana* 'Flava'
	- 'Blaue Zwo'	CKen NLar
	- 'Blauer Eskimo'	CKen MAsh NLar SLim
	- 'Blauer Pfiff'	CKen ECho NLar
	- 'Blinsham Gold'	CKen
	- 'Blue Emperor'	CKen NLar
	- 'Blue Magic'	CKen MAsh NLar
	- 'Blue 'n' Silver'	ECho NLar WEve
	- 'Bonsai Blue'	NLar
	- 'Cis'	CDoC CKen NHol NLar SCoo SLim SPoG
	- 'Compact Dwarf'	ECho MGos NLar WEve
	- 'Crystal Globe'	CKen NLar
	- 'Dark Hill'	NLar
	- 'Doni Tajuso'	CKen
	- 'Eisregen'	CKen
	- 'Festival'	NLar
§	- 'Flava'	CKen MGos NPCo WEve
	- 'Frosty'	SPoG
	- 'Gait'	CKen ECho MAsh NLar
	- 'Golden Dream'	CKen
	- 'Golden Glow'	NLar SLim WFar
	- 'Green Carpet'	CKen GKir NLar SLim
	- 'Grübele' witches' broom	CKen
	- 'Horstmann' **new**	CKen
	- 'Inverleith'	CKen
	- 'Kleiner Prinz'	NLar
	- 'Kohout'	CKen
	- 'Kristallkugel'	MAsh
	- 'Lippetal'	CKen
	- 'Luminetta'	CKen MBri MGos NLar SLim
	- 'Nadelkissen'	CKen NHol
	- 'Nisbet'	ECho NPCo SCoo SLim SPoG WEve WGor
	- 'Oberon'	CDoC CKen MAsh NHol NLar SLim
	- 'Piccolo'	CKen
	- 'Pinocchio'	CDoC CKen MGos
	- 'Prostrata'	see *A. koreana* 'Prostrate Beauty'
§	- 'Prostrate Beauty'	ECho NPCo WEve WFar WGor
	- 'Scherenbach'	NLar
	- 'Schweden König'	NLar
	- 'Sherwood Compact'	CKen
	- 'Silberkugel'	CKen CMen ECho NLar SLim
	- 'Silberlocke' ♀H4	CDoC CDul CKen ECho EPla GKir LRHS MBlu MBri MGos NBea NEgg NLar SCoo SLim SPer SPoG SSpi WEve WFar
	- 'Silbermavers'	CKen
	- 'Silberperl'	CKen CMen LRHS MAsh NLar SPoG
	- 'Silberschmelze'	ECho MGos NLar
	- 'Silberzwerg' **new**	CDoC
	- 'Silver Show'	CDoC CKen NWea
	- 'Taiga'	NLar
	- 'Threave'	CKen
	- 'Vengels'	NLar
	- 'Verdener Dom'	NLar
	- 'Winter Goldtip'	ECho WEve
	lasiocarpa	CDul NWea
	- 'Alpine Beauty'	CKen MAsh NLar
	- var. ***arizonica*** 'Argentea'	WEve
	- - 'Compacta' Hornibr. ♀H4	CDoC CKen CMac ECho EHul ELan EPla GKir LRHS MBri MGos SCoo SLim SPoG WFar WGor
	- - 'Kenwith Blue'	CKen ECho MGos SLim WFar
	- 'Compacta' Beissn.	NHol WEve WFar
	- 'Day Creek'	CKen
	- 'Duflon'	CKen
	- 'Elaine' **new**	CKen
	- 'Glauca'	see *A. lasiocarpa* var. *arizonica* 'Argentea'
	- 'Green Globe'	CKen ECho LRHS NLar WEve
	- 'Joe's Alpine'	CKen
*	- 'King's Blue'	CKen
	- 'Logan Pass'	CKen NLar
	- 'Mulligan's Dwarf'	CKen ECho
	- 'Prickly Pete'	CKen NLar
I	- 'Prostrata' **new**	CMac
	- 'Toenisvorst'	CKen
	- 'Utah' **new**	CKen
	magnifica	GKir
I	- 'Nana'	CKen
	- witches' broom	CKen
	marocana	see *A. pinsapo* var. *marocana*
	nebrodensis	CKen
	nephrolepis	GKir
	nobilis	see *A. procera*
	nordmanniana ♀H4	CAlb CDul CMac CTri EHul EMac EPfP GKir IFFs LBuc LMaj LTen MGos MMuc NEgg NWea SEND SPer SPoG WDin WEve WMou
	- 'Arne's Dwarf'	CKen
	- 'Barabits' Compact'	ECho EPla MBri MGos NLar
	- 'Barabits' Gold'	ECho
	- 'Barabits' Spreader'	CKen ECho
	- subsp. ***equi-trojani***	NWea
	- - 'Archer'	CKen NPCo
	- 'Golden Spreader' ♀H4	CDoC CKen CMac ECho EPla GKir LRHS MAsh MBri MGos NLar NPCo SCoo SLim SPoG WEve WFar
	- 'Hasselt'	CKen
	- 'Jakobsen'	CKen

	- 'Pendula'	MBri
	- 'Silberspitze'	CKen
	numidica	CKen
	- 'Glauca'	CKen
	- 'Lawrenceville'	ECho NPCo WFar
	pindrow	ECho GKir
	pinsapo	CDul EWTr GKir IFFs SEND
	- 'Atlas'	MAsh NLar
	- 'Aurea'	CKen ECho GKir MGos MPkF NLar SLim WEve WFar
I	- 'Aurea Nana'	CKen
	- 'Fastigiata'	MGos MPkF
	- 'Glauca' ♀H4	CDoC CDul CKen CTho ECho EHul ELan GKir LMaj LRHS MBlu NLar SCoo SLim SPoG WDin WEve
	- 'Hamondii'	CKen
I	- 'Horstmann'	CKen ECho GKir NLar NPCo SLim WEve
	- 'Kelleriis'	NLar
§	- var. ***marocana***	GKir
	- 'Pendula'	CKen ECho MGos MPkF NLar WEve
	- 'Quicksilver'	CKen
§	***procera*** ♀H4	CAlb CBcs CDul EMac GKir IFFs NWea WBVN WDin WEve
	- 'Bizarro'	ECho NLar
	- 'Blaue Hexe'	CKen ECho NLar SLim SPoG WFar
	- Glauca Group	CDoC CDul CTho LTen MAsh MBlu MBri MGos SLim WEve WFar
	- - 'Glauca Prostrata'	ECho EPla GKir MGos SCoo SLim WEve WFar
	- 'La Graciosa'	NLar
	- 'Noble's Dwarf'	ECho GKir SLim
	- 'Obrighofen'	NLar
	- 'Prostrata'	MAsh
	- 'Seattle Mount'	NLar
	- 'Sherwoodii'	CKen ECho SLim
	recurvata	NLar
	- var. ***ernesti***	GKir
	Rosemoor hybrid	CKen
	sachalinensis	CKen
	sibirica	NWea
	veitchii	CTho GKir
	- 'Heddergott'	CKen ECho MGos NLar SLim
	- 'Heine'	CKen
	- 'Kramer' **new**	CKen
I	- 'Pendula'	CKen
	- 'Rumburg'	CKen NLar
	- 'Syców' **new**	CKen

Abromeitiella see *Deuterocohnia*

Abrotanella (*Asteraceae*)

sp.	ECho

Abutilon ✿ (*Malvaceae*)

	sp.	CArn
	'Amiti'	ELar
	'Apricot Belle'	SMDP
	'Ashford Red'	CBcs CCCN CWGN ELan IVic LRHS MAsh SAga SBfd SKHP SMDP SOWG WKif
*	'Benary's Giant'	CPLG
	'Boule de Neige'	CBot SMrm SOWG
	'Canary Bird' ♀H2	CBcs CBot CCCN CHEx ELon ERea SAga SMDP SUsu
	'Cannington Carol' (v) ♀H2	CCCN ELan ERea IVic LSRN SEND SMDP WCot
	'Cannington Peter' (v) ♀H2	CCCN ERea LSRN SMDP
	'Cannington Sonia' (v)	SMDP
	'Cloth of Gold'	CMac ERea
	'Cynthia Pike' (v)	LRHS
	'Flamenco'	CWGN LRHS NEgg
	'Frances Elizabeth'	SMDP
	'Heather Bennington'	SMDP
	'Henry Makepeace'	ELar SMDP
	'Hinton Seedling'	CCCN CRHN
	× ***hybridum***	CHEx
	apricot-flowered	
	- red-flowered	CHEx
	indicum	CCCN
	'Isles of Scilly'	CCCN
	'Jacqueline Morris'	LRHS MAsh SMrm
	'John Thompson'	CCCN CWGN LSRN
	'Kentish Belle' ♀H2-3	CBcs CCCN CDoC CHEx CMHG CMac CRHN CSBt EBee ELan ELon EPfP GGar LRHS LSRN NEgg NPal SBfd SCoo SEND SKHP SLim SPer SPlb WClo WFar
I	'Kentish Belle Variegatum' (v)	ELan
	'Kreutzberger'	ELar
	'Lemon Queen'	ELar
	'Linda Vista Peach' ♀H2	ELar SMDP
	'Louis Marignac'	ELar
	'Marion' ♀H2	CRHN ELar LRHS LSRN SMDP SMrm SPoG WCot
	'Master Michael'	CMac SMDP
	megapotamicum ♀H3	CBcs CBot CCCN CHEx CMHG CMac CRHN CSBt CTri EBee ELan EPfP EShb IVic LOck LRHS MAsh MGos MRav MSCN SEND SKHP SLim SOWG SPer SPoG SRms WClo WSHC
	- 'Variegatum' (v)	CBcs CCCN CMac CSBt EBee ELan ELar EPfP LRHS MAsh MGos NEgg SBfd SKHP SLim SLon SOWG SPer SPoG SWvt WFar
	- 'Wisley Red'	CRHN CSBt SMDP
	× ***milleri*** hort. ♀H2	CMac CRHN WCot WWlt
	- 'Variegatum' (v)	CCCN CHEx CMac EBee LRHS NEgg SEND WCot
	- 'Ventnor Gold'	SBfd
	'Nabob' ♀H2	CCCN CDoC CHGN CRHN ERea EShb EUJe LRHS SBfd SMDP SMrm SOWG SPoG
	'Old Rose Belle'	SMDP
	'Orange Glow' (v) ♀H2	ERea
	'Orange Vein'	EShb SMDP WPrP
	'Patrick Synge'	CCCN CHGN CMHG CWit EBtc EShb SBfd SOWG SPhx SUsu
	pictum	ERea
	- 'Thompsonii' (v)	CHEx EShb IDee SBfd SMDP WDyG
	'Pink Lady'	EShb SMDP
	'Red Bells'	ELar
	'Red Queen'	ELar
	'Rotterdam'	ERea
	'Russels Dwarf'	CCCN
	'Satin Pink Belle'	SMDP
	'Savitzii' (v) ♀H2	MCot MSCN SBfd SMDP SOWG
	'Silver Belle'	SMDP
	'Simcox White'	CCCN
	'Snow Boy'	ELar
	'Snowfall'	SMDP
	'Souvenir de Bonn' (v) ♀H2	ELar ERea EShb LSou SBfd SMDP SMrm
	× ***suntense***	CBcs CCCN CMHG CPLG CSBt EBee ELan EPfP ESwi GGar LHyd LRHS NPer SChF SEND SOWG
	- 'Jermyns' ♀H3	CAbP EBee EPfP EWTr GCra LRHS LSRN MAsh MBri SCoo SEND SKHP SPoG SSpi SWvt WFar
	- Ralph Gould seedling	ECGP
	- 'Violetta'	CEnd WKif
	'Tango'	CWGN LRHS SEND SLim

variegated, salmon-flowered (v)	LAst SEND
'Victory'	CCCN CWGN SKHP
vitifolium	CBcs CBot CCCN CDTJ CWib EPfP EQua EWTr GGar NBid NEgg NLar SPad SPer SPoG WBor WKif
- 'Album'	CBcs CDul CHll EBee EPfP EQua GCal GQui LHyd MAsh SEND SPer SSpi WFar WSpi
- 'Buckland'	CGHE
- 'Ice Blue'	CBot
- 'Tennant's White' ♀H3	CAbP CBot CCCN EBee EPfP GGal LRHS MBri SKHP
- 'Veronica Tennant' ♀H3	CPLG GQui WKif
'Wakehurst'	WCom
'Waltz'	CWGN LRHS SLim
'Westfield Bronze'	CRHN SMDP

Acacia (*Mimosaceae*)

sp. **new**	NLar
acinacea	IDee SPlb
adunca	EBee SPad SPlb
armata	see *A. paradoxa*
axillaris **new**	SPlb
baileyana ♀H2	Widely available
- var. ***aurea***	SPlb
- 'Purpurea' ♀H2	Widely available
brachybotrya	CDTJ
caven	EBee
- NJM 08.0021	WPGP
cultriformis	CCCN CTrC CTsd ESwi SBfd SEND
dealbata ♀H2	Widely available
- 'Gaulois Astier'	CAbb CDoC CSBt EBee ELon LRHS LSRN MBri MGos MREP SBfd SSpi SWvt WBrE WPGP
- subsp. ***subalpina***	WPGP
erioloba	CPLG
'Exeter Hybrid'	CDoy CSBt
fimbriata	CRHN
floribunda 'Lisette'	EPfP
julibrissin	see *Albizia julibrissin*
juniperina	see *A. ulicifolia*
karroo	CArn CCCN CDTJ CPLG
kybeanensis	EBee WPGP
longifolia	CBcs CCCN CDTJ CTsd EBee EPfP LRHS SEND SPer SRms
- subsp. ***sophorae***	CCCN
macradenia	SPlb
mearnsii	CCCN SEND
melanoxylon	CBcs CDTJ CDul CTsd CWit EBee ELan GGar SLim
mucronata	CTrC EShb
obliquinervia	MWya
§ ***paradoxa*** ♀H2	CCCN ECou ELon ESwi IDee LRHS SEND WPat
pataczekii	CSBt EBee EPfP EWes
pendula	IDee
podalyriifolia	CAbb CCCN CWit EBee ETod SPlb
pravissima ♀H2-3	Widely available
- 'Bushwalk Baby'	SOWG
retinodes ♀H2	CBcs CCCN CDTJ CDoC CRHN CTsd CWit EAmu EBee EPfP ESwi ETod IFFs LRHS LSRN SBfd SEND SLim SPad SWvt WCFE
- blue-leaved	ESwi SEND
- 'Palme d'Or' **new**	LRHS
riceana	CCCN CTsd
rubida	IDee MGos MREP SPlb
senegal	CArn
sentis	see *A. victoriae*
spectabilis	CCCN SPlb
suaveolens	SPlb
§ ***ulicifolia***	CPLG CSBt
verticillata	CBcs CCCN CDTJ CHGN CHll CTsd CWit EBee SOWG
- riverine	CPLG CTrC EPfP LRHS SPoG
§ ***victoriae***	ECre

Acaena (*Rosaceae*)

adscendens misapplied	see *A. affinis*, *A. saccaticupula* 'Blue Haze'
adscendens Vahl	see *A. magellanica* subsp. *laevigata*
adscendens ambig. 'Glauca'	EHoe NBir
§ ***affinis***	ECha SDix
anserinifolia misapplied	see *A. novae-zelandiae*
§ ***anserinifolia*** (Forst. & Forst. f.) Druce	MRav
buchananii	CTri EBee ECho EHoe GAbr GGar MMuc NLar SRms STre WCom WFar WPer
caerulea hort.	see *A. caesiiglauca*
§ ***caesiiglauca***	CTri GAbr GGar GQue MLHP NBid SGar WCom
- 'Frikart'	EBee
eupatoria **new**	EBee
inermis	MMuc SPlb WCom
- 'Purpurea'	CAby EBee ECha EHoe GAbr GBin GGar GQue LRHS NDov NLar SPlb WHoo WMoo WPtf
macrocephala	EBee
magellanica	EBee GCal GGar GKev MSCN
§ - subsp. ***laevigata***	GGar
microphylla ♀H4	CSam CTri EBee ECho LBee LRHS MBrN MLLN NLar NMen SPlb SRms WCon WFar WMoo
- 'Braune Feder' **new**	EBee
- Copper Carpet	see *A. microphylla* 'Kupferteppich'
- 'Dichte Matte' **new**	EBee
- 'Glauca'	see *A. caesiiglauca*
- 'Grüner Zwerg'	EBee
§ - 'Kupferteppich'	EBee ECho ECtt EHoe ETod GAbr GCal GGar GKir GQue LHop LRHS MBri MMuc MRav NBir NDov NLar SBch WCom WMoo WPat WPer WWEG
myriophylla	EBee ECho EDAr
§ ***novae-zelandiae***	CTri EBee GGar SDix WCom WMoo
ovalifolia	EBee
'Pewter'	see *A. saccaticupula* 'Blue Haze'
profundeincisa	see *A. anserinifolia* (Forst. & Forst. f.) Druce
'Purple Carpet'	see *A. microphylla* 'Kupferteppich'
'Purple Haze'	CSpe
saccaticupula	WFar
§ - 'Blue Haze'	CMoH EBee ECha ECho EDAr EHoe EShb GGar GKir LHop LRHS MRav SPer SPlb SRms WFar WHoo WMoo WPtf
sanguisorbae	see *A. anserinifolia* (Forst. & Forst. f.) Druce
splendens	SPlb
viridior	see *A. anserinifolia* (Forst. & Forst. f.) Druce

Acalypha (*Euphorbiaceae*)

hispida ♀H1	ERea MBri
pendula	see *A. reptans*
§ ***reptans***	CCCN EShb

Acanthocalyx see *Morina*

Acantholimon (*Plumbaginaceae*)

glumaceum	GKev

Acanthopanax see *Eleutherococcus*

ricinifolius	see *Kalopanax septemlobus*

Acanthus ✿ (*Acanthaceae*)

balcanicus misapplied	see *A. hungaricus*
dioscoridis	EBee GCal MAvo SMHy WHil
- var. ***perringii***	CDes ECha GBin LHop MAvo MNrw WCot WFar WHil WPGP WSHC
- smooth-leaved	WCot WHil
eminens	WHil
hirsutus	IFoB LPio NBre SBig SPav WCot
- f. ***roseus***	WFar
- subsp. ***syriacus***	EHrv EWTr GCal NBre NLar WCot WFar
'Hollande du Nort'	EBee GBin
§ ***hungaricus***	CArn CHid CMac EBee EBla EBrs ECtt ELan EShb EWTr GAbr GBBs GKir LBMP LRHS MLLN MMuc MSCN NLar SDix SEND SPav SPer SPhx SWat WCot WFar WHil WMnd WWEG
- MESE 561	EPPr
longifolius Host	see *A. hungaricus*
mollis	Widely available
- from Turkey	GCal
- 'Fielding Gold'	see *A. mollis* 'Hollard's Gold'
- free-flowering	GCal MAvo
§ - 'Hollard's Gold'	Widely available
- 'Jefalba'	see *A. mollis* (Latifolius Group) 'Rue Ledan'
- Latifolius Group	EBee EPfP MCot MRav NHol SPer SRms WHil WHoo WTin
§ - - 'Rue Ledan'	EBee EShb GBin IPot LHop LPio MAvo MDKP NBPC NGdn NLar SMHy SPhx SUsu WCot WFar WHil WTin
- 'Long Spike'	EBee GCal
- 'Tasmanian Angel' (v)	CBow WCot
montanus **new**	WHil
'Morning Candle'	EBee ECtt MAvo
sennii	CMdw EBee LPio SMad SPhx WHil WSHC
spinosus misapplied	see *A. spinosus* Spinosissimus Group
spinosus L. ♀H4	Widely available
- Ferguson's form	WCot WHil
- 'Lady Moore' (v)	IBlr IPot MCCP NLar WCot WHil
- 'Royal Haughty'	EWes GBin GCal WFar
§ - Spinosissimus Group	CBct CFir CMHG CTca EBee ECha EHrv ELan ELon GBin GCal GCra LEdu LPio MCCP MRav SAga SBfd SPhx SWat WCot WFar WHil WMnd WTin
'Summer Beauty'	EBee EWes GBin GCal GKir LHop LPio LRHS MAvo MBri NBre NLar WCon WCot WFar WHil

Acca (*Myrtaceae*)

sp.	SWvt
sellowiana (F)	CBcs CDul CMHG CMac CPLG CSBt EBee ECrN ELan EPfP ERom GQui IVic LAst LHop LRHS MGos MREP SBfd SLim SOWG SPer SPlb SPoG SVic WBrE WFar WSHC
- 'Apollo' (F)	EBee ERea
- 'Coolidge' (F)	CAgr ERea
- 'Gemini' (F) **new**	LRHS
- 'Mammoth' (F)	CAgr CBcs CCCN ERea
- 'Marian' (F)	EBee
- 'Triumph' (F)	CAgr CBcs CCCN ERea
- 'Unique' (F)	CAgr ERea
- 'Variegata' (F/v)	CCCN EBee ELan LAst SPoG

Acer ✿ (*Aceraceae*)

amoenum B&SWJ 10916	WCru
barbinerve	EPfP
buergerianum	CDul CLnd CMCN CMen CPMA LMaj MMuc MPkF NEgg NLar SCoo SEND
- var. ***formosanum*** B&SWJ 7032	WCru
- - CWJ 12477	WCru
- 'Himcode'	NLar
- 'Mino-yatsubusa'	MPkF
- 'Miyasama-yatsubusa'	MPkF
- 'Naruto'	CMCN MPkF
calcaratum	CDul CMCN
campbellii B&SWJ 7685	WCru
- subsp. ***campbellii*** var. ***serratifolium*** GWJ 9360 **new**	WCru
* - var. ***fansipanense*** B&SWJ 8270	WCru
- - HWJ 569	WCru
- - HWJ 944	WCru
campestre ♀H4	Widely available
- 'Carnival' (v)	CCVT CDul CEnd CPMA CWib EBee ECrN ELon EMil MAsh MBlu MBri MPkF NLar NPCo SBfd SMad SPer SPoG SPur SWvt
- 'Elsrijk'	CCVT CLnd EBee LMaj SCoo
- 'Evelyn'	see *A. campestre* 'Queen Elizabeth'
- 'Pendulum'	CEnd ECrN
- 'Postelense'	CMCN CPMA EBee MBlu MGos MPkF
- 'Pulverulentum' (v)	CEnd CMCN CPMA MGos NPCo SMad SSta
§ - 'Queen Elizabeth'	LMaj MGos
- 'Red Shine'	EBee GKir MGos
- 'Royal Ruby'	CPMA CWSG MGos WFar
* - 'Ruby Glow'	CEnd ECrN
- 'Schwerinii'	CDul
I - 'Silver Celebration' (v)	CPMA
- 'William Caldwell'	CEnd CTho ECrN
capillipes ♀H4	CAlb CBcs CCVT CDul CLnd CMCN CTho CWib EBee ECrN GKir IFFs LAst LMaj LRHS MGos MMuc NBea NWea SPer WDin WFar WHCr WHar WPGP WPat
- B&SWJ 11473	WCru
- 'Candy Stripe'	see *A.* × *conspicuum* 'Candy Stripe'
- 'Gimborn'	WPGP
- 'Honey Dew'	NLar
cappadocicum	CCVT CDul CEnd CMCN ECrN GKir IFFs LMaj MMuc MSnd NWea SEND WDin
- 'Aureum' ♀H4	CBcs CDoC CDul CEnd CLnd CMCN CTho EBee ECrN ELan EPfP GBin GKir IArd MBlu MBri MGos MRav NBea NLar SLim SPer SSpi SWvt WDin WFar
§ - subsp. ***divergens***	CMCN MPkF
§ - subsp. ***lobelii***	CLnd
- var. ***mono***	see *A. pictum*
- 'Rubrum' ♀H4	CBcs CDul CLnd CMCN EBee ECrN EPfP GKir LAst LMaj MBlu MBri MGos MRav SLim SPer WDin WFar WHer
- var. ***sinicum***	EPfP GBin WFar WPGP

	- var. ***tricaudatum***	CPLG
	carpinifolium	CMCN IArd MBlu MPkF NLar SBir
	- B&SWJ 10955	WCru
	- B&SWJ 11124	WCru
	catalpifolium	see *A. longipes* subsp. *catalpifolium*
§	***caudatifolium***	CMCN
	- B&SWJ 6734	WCru
	- RWJ 9843	WCru
§	***caudatum*** CWJ 12403	WCru
	- GWJ 9279	WCru
	- GWJ 9317	WCru
	- HWJK 2240	WCru
	- HWJK 2338	WCru
	- subsp. ***ukurunduense***	MPkF
	- - B&SWJ 8658	WCru
	circinatum	CBcs CDoC CDul CLnd CMCN CPMA EBee ECrN EPfP GBin IFFs IVic MBlu MMuc MPkF MSnd NBea NLar NWea SPlb SSta WDin WFar
	- B&SWJ 9565	WCru
	- 'Little Gem'	CPMA
	- 'Little Joe'	CPMA
	- 'Monroe'	CPMA
	- 'Pacific Fire'	CPMA
	- 'Sunglow'	CPMA NLar
	circinatum* × *palmatum	GKir SBig
	cissifolium	CMCN EPfP EPla IArd NLar
	- B&SWJ 10801	WCru
§	× ***conspicuum*** 'Candy Stripe'	CBcs CLnd CPMA GKir NLar SLim SSpi SSta
	- 'Elephant's Ear'	CPMA EPfP NLar
	- 'Mozart'	CPMA MBlu MPkF
	- 'Phoenix'	CBcs CEnd CMCN CPMA EBee EPfP GKir IArd IVic MAsh MBlu MBri NLar SSpi WDin WPGP WPat
	- 'Red Flamingo'	CPMA GKir LRHS MBri MGos MPkF SOkt WClo
	- 'Silver Ghost'	MPkF
§	- 'Silver Vein'	CDoC CEnd CMCN CPMA EBee EPfP MWea NLar SSta WPGP
	crataegifolium B&SWJ 11036	WCru
	- B&SWJ 11355	WCru
	- 'Meuri-keade-no-fuiri' (v)	MPkF
	- 'Meuri-no-ōfu' (v)	MPkF
	- 'Veitchii' (v)	CMCN CPMA EBee EPfP MBri MPkF SBig SSpi
	creticum L., non F. Schmidt.	see *A. sempervirens*
	dasycarpum	see *A. saccharinum*
	davidii	CBcs CCVT CDoC CDul CLnd CMCN CSam ECrN GAuc GKir IFFs LMaj LTen MBlu MGos MRav NBea NHol SLim SPer WDin WFar WPat
	- B&SWJ 8183	WCru
§	- 'Canton'	CPMA MPkF
	- 'Cantonspark'	see *A. davidii* 'Canton'
	- 'Cascade' **new**	CPMA
	- 'Chinese Temple'	SBir
N	- 'Ernest Wilson'	CBcs EBee MBlu NLar
N	- 'George Forrest' ♀H4	CCVT CDoC CDul CMCN CMac CTho EBee ECrN ELan EPfP GBin IFFs LAst LRHS MAsh MBlu MMuc NBea NWea SBfd SEND SLim SPer SPoG WDin WFar WPat
	- 'Hagelunie'	MPkF SBir
	- 'Karmen'	CBcs CDul CGHE CPMA EBee LRHS MPkF WPGP
	- 'Madeline Spitta'	CMCN CPMA MBri MPkF
	- 'Purple Bark'	NLar SBir
	- 'Rosalie'	CBcs CPMA EPfP MBlu MBri SBir

	- 'Serpentine' ♀H4	CBcs CDoC CMCN CPMA EBee EPfP GBin IDee MBlu MBri NEgg NLar SBir SSpi SSta WFar WPGP
	- 'Silver Vein'	see *A.* × *conspicuum* 'Silver Vein'
	***discolor* new**	CMCN
	distylum	CMCN
	divergens	see *A. cappadocicum* subsp. *divergens*
	elegantulum	CDoC CPLG CPMA GBin WPGP
	erianthum	MSnd
	erythranthum B&SWJ 11733	WCru
	- DJHV 06147	WCru
	fabri	CDul CPLG
	flabellatum B&SWJ 8057	WCru
	- var. ***yunnanense***	EBee IFFs MSnd
	forrestii	CMCN CPLG EPfP NBea NHol
	- BWJ 7515	WCru
	- 'Alice'	CBcs CEnd CPMA
	- 'Sirene'	CPMA
	- 'Sparkling'	CPMA
	× ***freemanii***	CMCN
	- 'Armstrong'	WFar
	- Autumn Blaze = 'Jeffersred'	CBcs CCVT CDoC CDul CMCN EBee EPfP GKir LMaj LRHS MBlu MGos SCoo SMad WDin WFar WPat
	- Autumn Fantasy = 'Dtr 102'	LRHS
	- Celebration = 'Celzam'	CCVT MGos WFar
	- 'Indian Summer'	see *A.* × *freemanii* 'Morgan'
§	- 'Morgan'	CEnd CPMA SBir
	fulvescens	see *A. longipes*
	ginnala	see *A. tataricum* subsp. *ginnala*
	globosum	see *A. platanoides* 'Globosum'
	grandidentatum	see *A. saccharum* subsp. *grandidentatum*
	griseum ♀H4	Widely available
	grosseri	CDul CMCN CTri
	- var. ***hersii*** ♀H4	CBcs CCVT CDoC CDul CLnd CMac CWib EBee ECrN EPfP GKir MRav NBea NLar NWea SPer SPoG SWvt WDin WFar WHCr WPGP
	- 'Leiden'	EPfP
	heldreichii	EGFP EPfP
	henryi	CDul CLnd EPfP LMaj NEgg NLar
	heptaphlebium B&SWJ 11713	WCru
	- DJHV 06063	WCru
	hyrcanum	CMCN
	japonicum	CMCN MMuc SEND SSta WHCr
	- B&SWJ 5950	WCru
§	- 'Aconitifolium' ♀H4	Widely available
	- 'Ao-jutan'	CPMA
	- 'Attaryi'	MPkF
	- 'Aureum'	see *A. shirasawanum* 'Aureum'
	- 'Ezo-no-momiji'	see *A. shirasawanum* 'Ezo-no-momiji'
	- 'Filicifolium'	see *A. japonicum* 'Aconitifolium'
	- 'Green Cascade'	CEnd CMCN CMac CMen CPMA ECho IVic LRHS MPkF NEas NLar NPCo SBig WPGP WPat
	- 'Kalmthout'	NLar
	- 'King's Copse'	LRHS MAsh
	- 'Laciniatum'	see *A. japonicum* 'Aconitifolium'
	- f. ***microphyllum***	see *A. shirasawanum* 'Microphyllum'
	- 'Ogurayama'	see *A. shirasawanum* 'Ogurayama'
	- 'Ō-isami'	EPfP MPkF SBig
	- 'Ō-taki'	CPMA
	- 'Vitifolium' ♀H4	CDoC CDul CEnd CMCN CMac CPMA CSBt ECho ELan EPfP GBin LRHS LTen MBlu MBri MGos MPkF

		NBea NEgg NLar NPCo SBig SPer SSpi SSta WCFE WDin WGPG WPat
	kawakamii	see *A. caudatifolium*
	laevigatum	CMCN
§	- var. ***reticulatum*** B&SWJ 11698	WCru
	laxiflorum HWJK 2240	WCru
	lobelii Bunge	see *A. turkestanicum*
	lobelii Ten.	see *A. cappadocicum* subsp. *lobelii*
§	***longipes***	CMCN
§	- subsp. ***catalpifolium***	CMCN
	macrophyllum	CDul CMCN CTho EPfP LHyd MBlu
	mandschuricum	CDul EPfP MPkF WDin
§	***maximowiczianum***	CBcs CDul CMCN CTho ELan MPkF WFar
	maximowiczii	ECrN MPkF NWea WHCr
	metcalfii GWJ 9360	WCru
	micranthum	CDoC CDul CGHE CMCN EBee EPfP LRHS MPkF NLar SSpi WPGP
	miyabei	MPkF
	mono	see *A. pictum*
*	- f. ***ambiguum*** B&SWJ 8806	WCru
	monspessulanum	CLnd CMCN SEND
	morifolium	EBee MPkF
	morrisonense	see *A. caudatifolium*
	negundo	CDul CMCN CWib ECrN IFFs LMaj NWea
	- 'Auratum'	CMCN WDin
	- 'Aureomarginatum' (v)	ECrN LAst LMaj
	- 'Aureovariegatum' (v)	CBcs
§	- 'Elegans' (v)	CDul CEnd CMCN ECrN EPfP SCoo SPer WFar
	- 'Elegantissimum'	see *A. negundo* 'Elegans'
	- 'Flamingo' (v)	Widely available
	- 'Kelly's Gold'	CBcs CCVT CWSG MGos NLar NMun NWea SBfd SLim SPoG WDin WFar WHar
	- subsp. ***mexicanum*** F&M 48	WPGP
	- 'Variegatum' (v)	ECrN LAst SPer WDin WFar
	- var. ***violaceum***	CEnd CMCN EPla
	- 'Winter Lightning'	CPMA
	nikoense	see *A. maximowiczianum*
	oblongum	CMCN
	- var. ***concolor*** HWJ 869	WCru
	- - WWJ 11851	WCru
	oliverianum	CPLG EBee EPfP
	- subsp. ***formosanum*** B&SWJ 6773	WCru
	- - RWJ 9912	WCru
	opalus	CMCN SEND
	orientale	see *A. sempervirens*
	orizabense	EBee
	Pacific Sunset = 'Warrenred'	EBee
	palmatum	CBar CBcs CCVT CDoy CDul CMCN CMHG CMen CSBt CTho CTri CWib EPfP GKir IFFs LRHS MBlu MGos NEgg NWea SPlb SSpi SSta STre SWvt WBVN WDin WFar WHar WPat
	- 'Akane'	CMen MPkF
§	- 'Aka-shigitatsu-sawa'	CBcs CMCN CMac CMen CPMA ECho LRHS MGos MPkF NLar WFar
	- 'Akegarasu'	NLar
	- 'Akita-yatsubusa'	MPkF
	- 'Alpenweiss'	CPMA
	- 'Alpine Sunrise'	MPkF
	- 'Amagi-shigure'	CPMA
	- 'Aoba-jo'	CMen CPMA ECho MPkF NLar NPCo
	- 'Ao-kanzashi' (v)	MPkF
	- 'Aoshime-no-uchi'	see *A. palmatum* 'Shinobuga-oka'
	- 'Aoyagi'	CEnd CMCN CMen CPMA ECho EPfP LRHS MGos MPkF NEas NHol NLar NPCo WFoF WPat
§	- 'Arakawa'	CEnd CMCN CMac CMen ECho MPkF NPCo
	- 'Arakawa-ukon'	CPMA
	- 'Aratama'	CBty CPMA LRHS MGos MPkF NEas NLar SCoo
	- 'Ariake-nomura'	CMen MPkF
	- 'Asahi-zuru' (v)	CBcs CDoC CMCN CMen CPMA EBee ECho LRHS MBri MGos MPkF NEas NHol NLar NPCo SPer WDin WFar WFoF WPat
	- 'Ashurst Wood'	SBig
	- 'Atrolineare'	CMen MPkF NBea NLar WPat
	- 'Atropurpureum'	Widely available
	- 'Atropurpureum Novum'	MPkF
	- 'Attraction'	CMCN CMen NPCo
	- 'Aureum'	CMCN CMac CMen CWib ECho EPfP LAst LMil LRHS MAsh MBlu MGos MPkF NEas NHol NLar NPCo SPoG SSpi WCFE WFar
	- Autumn Glory Group	CEnd CMac CPMA ECho
	- 'Autumn Red'	ECho NPCo
*	- 'Autumn Showers'	CEnd CPMA
	- 'Azuma-murasaki'	CMen CPMA MPkF
	- 'Beni-chidori'	CMen
	- 'Beni-gasa'	CPMA MPkF
	- 'Beni-hime'	MBri MPkF NLar
	- 'Beni-hoshi'	MPkF WPat
	- 'Beni-kagami'	CEnd CMCN CPMA EPfP MPkF NBea NLar
	- 'Beni-kawa'	CMen CPMA MPkF NPCo SBig WPat
	- 'Beni-komachi'	CBty CEnd CMCN CMen CPMA ECho EGxp ELon EPfP LRHS MBri MGos MPkF NEas NLar WPat
	- 'Beni-maiko'	CEnd CMCN CMen CPMA CWib EPfP GKir LRHS LSou MBri MGos MPkF MWea NLar NPCo SBig SCoo SWvt WDin WPGP WPat
	- 'Beni-musume'	MPkF NLar
	- 'Beni-otake'	CBcs CBty CLnd CMen CPMA ECho EPfP LRHS MBri MGos MPkF NEas NLar NPCo SBig SPer WClo WPat
	- 'Beni-otome'	MPkF
	- 'Beni-schichihenge' (v)	CBcs CBty CEnd CMCN CMen CPMA CWCL CWGN ECho EPfP LRHS MAsh MBri MGos MPkF NEas NHol NPCo SBig SCoo WClo WPGP WPat
	- 'Beni-shi-en'	CPMA MPkF NLar
	- 'Beni-shigitatsu-sawa'	see *A. palmatum* 'Aka-shigitatsu-sawa'
	- 'Beni-tsukasa' (v)	CEnd CMen CPMA ECho LMil LRHS MAsh MPkF NPCo SSpi WPGP
	- 'Beni-ubi-gohon'	CPMA LRHS MPkF NEas NLar
	- 'Berry Broom'	MPkF
	- 'Berry Dwarf'	MPkF
	- 'Bloodgood' ♀H4	Widely available
	- 'Bonfire' misapplied	see *A. palmatum* 'Seigai'
	- 'Bonfire' ambig.	CPMA
	- 'Bonnie Bergman'	CPMA
	- 'Boskoop Glory'	ECho
	- 'Brandt's Dwarf'	MPkF WPat
	- 'Burgundy Lace' ♀H4	Widely available
	- 'Butterfly' (v)	Widely available
	- 'Calico'	CPMA
	- 'Caperci Dwarf'	MPkF
	- 'Carlis Corner'	CPMA MPkF

	– 'Carminium'	see *A. palmatum* 'Corallinum'
	– 'Chikuma-no'	MPkF
	– 'Chirimen-nishiki' (v)	MPkF
	– 'Chitose-yama' ♀H4	CBty CEnd CMCN CMac CMen CPMA CWCL EBee EPfP LMil LRHS MAsh MBri MGos MPkF MRav NHol NLar NPCo SCoo SLim SPoG SSpi SSta WFar WPat
§	– 'Chiyo-hime'	ELan EPfP MGos NPCo WClo
	– 'Coonara Pygmy'	CBty CCVT CMCN CMac CMen CPMA ECho LRHS MGos MPkF NLar NPCo SCoo WFar WPat
	– 'Coral Pink'	CMen CPMA MPkF
§	– 'Corallinum'	CDul CEnd CMCN CMen CPMA MPkF NLar NPCo NPal WDin WPat
	– var. ***coreanum***	CMCN
	– – B&SWJ 8606	WCru
	– – 'Korean Gem'	CPMA MPkF NPCo
	– 'Crimson Prince'	CBcs EMac LRHS LTen MPkF NEas SCoo
	– 'Crippsii'	CBcs CBty CMac CMen ECho GBin LRHS MGos MPkF SCoo WFar WPat
	– 'Curtis Strapleaf'	MPkF
	– 'Demi-sec'	ECho
	– 'Deshōjō'	CBty CMCN CMen CWSG CWib EGxp LRHS MBlu MGos MPkF NHol NLar SCoo
	– 'Diana'	CMen MPkF
	– 'Diane Verkade'	MPkF
	– var. ***dissectum*** ♀H4	Widely available
	– – 'Ao-shidare'	CPMA LRHS
	– – 'Ariadne' (v)	CBty CEnd CPMA CWib LRHS MBri MGos MPkF NLar SBig SCoo SPoG WPat
	– – 'Autumn Fire'	CPMA
	– – 'Baby Lace'	CPMA CWGN MPkF NLar
	– – 'Balcombe Green'	SBig
	– – 'Baldsmith'	CPMA LRHS MGos MPkF NEas NLar WPat
	– – 'Barrie Bergman'	CPMA
	– – 'Beni-fushigi'	MPkF WPat
	– – 'Beni-shidare Tricolor' (v)	CMen MPkF NLar
	– – 'Beni-shidare Variegated' (v)	CMCN CPMA
	– – 'Berrima Bridge'	CPMA
	– – 'Bewley's Red'	CPMA
	– – 'Brocade'	IVic MPkF WPat
	– – 'Bronzewing'	CPMA
	– – 'Chantilly Lace'	CPMA
	– – 'Crimson Princess' **new**	MPkF
	– – 'Crimson Queen' ♀H4	Widely available
	– – Dissectum Atropurpureum Group	CBcs CCVT CMac CPMA CTri ELan EPfP LHyd LRHS MGan MGos NBea NEas NHol NLar NWea SBig SCoo SLim SReu SSpi SSta WBVN WDin WFar
	– – 'Dissectum Flavescens'	CEnd CMac CMen CPMA ECho MBlu MPkF NPCo
§	– – 'Dissectum Nigrum'	CMac CMen CPMA CTri ECho MAsh MPkF NBea NHol NLar NPCo SSpi WPat
	– – 'Dissectum Palmatifidum'	CDoC CLnd CMen EQua MPkF NPCo SCoo SPer WFar
	– – 'Dissectum Rubrifolium'	MGos MPkF
§	– – 'Dissectum Variegatum' (v)	CBcs CPMA EPfP MPkF NPCo
	– – Dissectum Viride Group	CBcs CMCN CMac CMen CPMA CSBt CWSG ECho ELan ELon EPfP GKir LMil LRHS MAsh MBlu MGos MSwo NBea NEas NEgg NPCo NWea SBfd SLim SPer SSta WFar

	– – 'Ellen'	CPMA WPat
	– – 'Emerald Lace'	CPMA LRHS MBri MPkF NLar WCFE WClo
	– – 'Felice'	CPMA MPkF WPat
	– – 'Filigree' (v)	CMCN CMen CPMA ECho EPfP MGos MPkF NLar NPCo SBig SSpi WDin WPGP WPat
	– – 'Garnet' ♀H4	Widely available
	– – 'Goshiki-shidare' (v)	CEnd CMen CPMA MPkF
	– – 'Green Globe'	LRHS NLar
	– – 'Green Hornet'	CPMA WPat
	– – 'Green Lace'	CMen MPkF
	– – 'Green Mist'	CPMA WPat
	– – 'Hanzel'	WPat
	– – 'Inaba-shidare' ♀H4	Widely available
	– – 'Jeddeloh Orange'	MPkF
I	– – 'Kawaii'	CPMA
	– – 'Kiri-nishiki'	CMen CPMA MPkF NLar NPCo
*	– – 'Lionheart'	CMen CPMA CWGN ECho EMac LRHS MGos MPkF NEas NLar SCoo WFar
	– – 'Nomura-nishiki' (v)	CMen
	– – 'Octopus'	CPMA
	– – 'Orangeola'	CBcs CBty CMen CPMA CSBt IVic LRHS MAsh MBri MGos MPkF NEas NHol NLar NPCo SBfd SBig SCoo SPer WPat
	– – 'Ornatum'	CMCN CMen CWCL CWib ECho ELon EPfP GBin LSRN LTen MGos MPkF MRav NEas NEgg NPCo SBfd SCoo WCFE WDin WFar
	– – 'Otto's Dissectum'	CPMA
	– – 'Pendulum Julian'	CMCN LRHS MPkF NEas NLar
	– – 'Pink Ballerina' (v)	CPMA
	– – 'Pink Filigree'	CMen MPkF
	– – 'Raraflora'	CPMA
	– – 'Red Autumn Lace'	CPMA WPat
	– – 'Red Dragon'	CDoC CMen CPMA CWGN ECho EQua LMil LRHS MPkF NEas NLar NPCo SBig WPat
	– – 'Red Feather'	CPMA
	– – 'Red Filigree Lace'	CEnd CMCN CMen CPMA CWGN ECho EPfP MGos MPkF NHol NPCo SBig WPat
	– – 'Red Select'	CBty LRHS MPkF
	– – 'Seiryū' ♀H4	Widely available
§	– – 'Shōjō-shidare'	CDul CEnd CMen CPMA MPkF NLar
	– – 'Spring Delight'	CPMA MPkF NLar
	– – 'Suisei' (v)	MPkF
	– – 'Sunset'	CPMA MPkF WPat
	– – 'Tamukeyama'	CBcs CBty CLnd CMCN CMen CPMA EBee ECho ELan EMac LMil LRHS MBri MGos MPkF NEas NLar NPCo SCoo SLau WFar WPat
	– – 'Toyama-nishiki' (v)	CMCN CMen CWGN ECho LRHS MPkF NEas NPCo
	– – 'Waterfall'	CMCN CPMA
	– – 'Watnong'	CPMA
	– – 'Zaaling'	CMen ECho NPCo
	– 'Doctor Tilt'	MPkF
	– 'Dormansland'	SBig
	– 'Earthfire'	MPkF NEas WPat
I	– 'Ebbingii' **new**	CMac
	– 'Eddisbury'	CEnd CMen CPMA MPkF NBea NLar SSta WPGP WPat
	– 'Edna Bergman'	CPMA
	– 'Effegi'	see *A. palmatum* 'Fireglow'
	– 'Eimini'	MPkF
	– 'Elegans'	CMen EPfP MPkF NPCo WDin
	– 'Elizabeth'	MPkF
	– Emperor 1	see *A. palmatum* 'Wolff'

	- 'Enkan'	CBty CEnd CMen CPMA CWGN LRHS MBri MGos MPkF NEas NLar WPat
	- 'Eono-momiji'	CMen
	- 'Ever Red'	see *A. palmatum* var. *dissectum* 'Dissectum Nigrum'
	- 'Fall's Fire'	CPMA
	- 'Fascination'	CPMA
	- 'Fior d'Arancio'	CPMA IVic MPkF NBea NLar NPCo WClo
§	- 'Fireglow'	CBcs CBty CDoC CEnd CLnd CMCN CMen CPMA CSBt CWCL CWib ECho LMaj LRHS MBlu MBri MGos MPkF NBea NEas NEgg NLar NPCo SCoo SPer WClo WFar WPGP WPat
	- 'First Ghost'	CPMA
	- 'Fjellheim'	CPMA MPkF
	- 'Frederici Guglielmi'	see *A. palmatum* var. *dissectum* 'Dissectum Variegatum'
	- 'Garyū'	MPkF
	- 'Geisha'	CPMA MGos MPkF
	- 'Germaine's Gyration'	CPMA
	- 'Gibbsii'	ECho NPCo
I	- 'Globosum'	MPkF
	- 'Glowing Embers'	CPMA MPkF WPat
	- 'Golden Pond'	CPMA
	- 'Goshiki-kotohime' (v)	CBty CMCN CPMA LRHS MPkF
	- 'Green Trompenburg'	CMen CPMA MGos MPkF NEgg NLar NPCo
	- 'Groundcover'	MPkF
§	- 'Hagoromo'	CMac CMen ECho MPkF NPCo SCoo WFar
	- 'Hanami-nishiki'	CMen MPkF NEgg WPat
	- 'Haru-iro'	CPMA
	- 'Harusame' (v)	MPkF
	- 'Hazeroino' (v)	CMen MPkF
	- 'Heartbeat'	CPMA MPkF
	- 'Helena'	see *A. shirasawanum* 'Helena'
	- var. ***heptalobum***	CMCN
§	- 'Heptalobum Elegans'	CMCN LRHS MBlu SSpi
	- 'Heptalobum Elegans Purpureum'	see *A. palmatum* 'Hessei'
	- 'Herbstfeuer'	CPMA MPkF
§	- 'Hessei'	CEnd CMCN MBlu MPkF NBea NLar
	- 'Higasayama' (v)	CBcs CEnd CMCN CMen CPMA ECho GKir IVic LRHS MGos MPkF NEas NHol NLar NPCo WPGP WPat
	- 'Hino-tori-nishiki'	CMen
	- 'Hōgyoku'	CMCN CMen CPMA MPkF WPat
	- 'Hōno-o' **new**	MPkF NLar
	- 'Hoshi-kuzu'	MPkF
	- 'Hupp's Dwarf'	MPkF
	- 'Ibo-nishiki'	CMen MPkF
	- 'Ichigyōji'	CEnd CMen CPMA ECho IVic NPCo SBig SChF WPGP WPat
	- 'Iijima-sunago'	CMen MPkF
	- 'Inazuma'	CBcs CDoC CMCN CMen CPMA EPfP LRHS MGos MPkF NEas NLar SCoo SLau WFar WPat
	- 'Irish Lace'	CPMA MPkF
	- 'Iso-chidori'	MPkF
	- 'Issai-nishiki'	ECho MPkF NPCo
*	- 'Issai-nishiki-kawazu'	MPkF
	- 'Jane'	MPkF
	- 'Japanese Sunrise'	CPMA MPkF NEas WPat
	- 'Jerre Schwartz'	MGos MPkF NLar WPat
	- 'Jirō-shidare'	CPMA EPfP MPkF NLar SBig
	- 'JJ'	CPMA
	- 'Julia D.'	CPMA NLar
	- 'Kaba'	CMen IVic MPkF
	- 'Kagero' (v)	MPkF WFar
§	- 'Kagiri-nishiki' (v)	CBcs CDul CMCN CMac CMen CPMA ECho IVic LRHS LTen MPkF NEgg NHol NLar WFar
	- 'Kamagata'	CBty CEnd CMCN CMen CPMA ECho EPfP IVic LMil LRHS MGos MPkF NEas NHol NLar NPCo SCoo SPer WPGP WPat
	- 'Kandy Kitchen'	CPMA MBri MGos MPkF
	- 'Karaori-nishiki' (v)	CMen ECho MPkF NLar
	- 'Karasugawa' (v)	CMen CPMA MGos MPkF NLar NPCo
	- 'Kasagiyama'	CEnd CMCN CMen CPMA MGos MPkF NBea WPGP
	- 'Kasen-nishiki'	CMen ECho MPkF
	- 'Kashima'	CEnd CMCN CMen CPMA ECho MPkF NPCo WFar
	- 'Kashima-yatsubusa'	LRHS MPkF
	- 'Katja'	CMen MPkF
	- 'Katsura' ♀^{H4}	Widely available
	- 'Ki-hachijō'	CMCN CMen CPMA EPfP MPkF NLar WPat
	- 'Kingsville Variegated' (v)	MPkF
	- 'Kinran'	CMen CWit MPkF NPCo WPat
	- 'Kinshii'	CBty CEnd CMCN CMen CPMA EPfP IVic LRHS MPkF NBea NHol NPCo SPoG WPat
	- 'Kiyohime'	CDoC CMCN CMen ECho MPkF NBea WFar WPat
	- 'Kogane-sakae'	CPMA MPkF
	- 'Kokobunji-nishiki' (v)	MPkF
	- 'Komache-hime'	CMen CPMA ECho WPat
*	- 'Komaru'	NLar
	- 'Komon-nishiki' (v)	CMen CPMA ECho MPkF
	- 'Koriba'	CPMA MPkF NLar
	- 'Koshibori-nishiki'	MPkF
§	- 'Koshimino'	CPMA
	- 'Kotohime'	CAbP CMCN CMen CPMA IVic MBri MGos MPkF NLar SBig SCoo SPoG
	- 'Koto-ito-komachi'	CMen CPMA ECho ELon LRHS MPkF NLar NPCo WPat
	- 'Koto-maru'	MPkF
	- 'Koto-no-ito'	CMCN CWGN LRHS MGos MPkF NEas NLar WPat
	- 'Koya-san'	CMen MPkF
	- 'Krazy Krinkle'	CPMA
	- 'Kurabu-yama'	CMen MPkF
	- 'Kurui-jishi'	MGos MPkF
	- 'Kyōryū'	MPkF
	- 'Kyra'	CMen MPkF
	- 'Leather Leaf' **new**	MPkF
	- 'Linearilobum'	ECho EPfP IVic LHyd LMil MBlu MGos MPkF NBea NLar NPCo SCoo WFar
	- 'Linearilobum Atropurpureum'	NBea
	- 'Little Princess'	see *A. palmatum* 'Chiyo-hime'
	- 'Lozita'	WPat
	- 'Lutescens'	MPkF NPCo
	- 'Lydia'	MPkF
	- 'Maiko'	CMen MPkF
	- 'Mama'	CMen NPCo
	- 'Mapi-no-machihime'	CEnd CMCN CMen CPMA ELan LRHS MAsh MBri MGos MPkF NHol WPGP WPat
	- 'Marakumo'	MPkF
	- 'Marasaki-yama' **new**	MPkF
	- 'Mardi Gras'	CPMA
	- 'Margaret'	MPkF
	- 'Margaret Bee'	MPkF
	- 'Marjan'	MPkF NLar

	– 'Masamurasaki'	CMen MPkF WPat
	– 'Masukagami' (v)	CEnd CPMA MPkF NLar
	– 'Matsuga-e' (v)	CMen MPkF NPCo
	– 'Matsukaze'	CMCN CMen CPMA
	– var. ***matsumurae*** B&SWJ 11100	WCru
	– 'Matsuyoi'	CPMA
	– 'Meihō-nishiki'	CPMA
	– 'Melanie'	CPMA SBig
	– 'Midori-no-teiboku'	MPkF
	– 'Mikawa-yatsubusa'	CMCN CMac CMen EPfP IVic LRHS MGos MPkF NLar NPCo SOkt WPat
	– 'Mimaye'	CPMA
	– 'Mini Mondo'	MPkF
	– 'Mirte'	CMen CPMA MPkF SBig WFar WPat
	– 'Mizuho-beni'	CPMA NPCo
	– 'Mizu-kuguri'	MPkF NLar
	– 'Momoiro-koya-san'	CPMA MPkF WPat
	– 'Mon Papa'	CMen CPMA NLar
	– 'Monzukushi'	CPMA MPkF
	– 'Moonfire'	CMCN CPMA EPfP LRHS MGos MPkF NEas NLar WClo WPat
	– 'Mr Sun'	CPMA
*	– 'Muncaster'	SBig
	– 'Murasaki-hime'	MPkF
	– 'Murasaki-kiyohime'	CBty CEnd CMCN CMen CPMA ECho GBin LRHS MPkF NPCo WPat
	– 'Mure-hibari'	CPMA MPkF
	– 'Murogawa'	CMen CPMA NPCo
	– 'Nanase-gawa'	MPkF
	– 'Nicholsonii'	CMCN CMen CTri EPfP IVic MPkF NLar NPCo WFar WPat
	– 'Nigrum' ♀H4	CMCN NLar WPat
	– 'Nishiki-gasane' (v)	MPkF
§	– 'Nishiki-gawa'	CEnd CMCN CMen CPMA CWit ECho MPkF NPCo WPGP
	– 'Nishiki-momiji'	CMen
	– 'Nomura'	CMen CPMA
	– 'Nomurishidare' misapplied	see *A. palmatum* var. *dissectum* 'Shojo-shidare'
	– 'Nomurishidare' Wada	SSpi
	– 'Nuresagi'	CEnd CPMA MPkF WPat
	– 'Ōgi-nagashi' (v)	MPkF NLar
	– 'Ōgi-no-sen'	MPkF
	– 'Ōgon-sarasa'	CPMA MPkF
	– 'Ojishi'	CMen MPkF
	– 'Ō-kagami'	CBcs CBty CDoC CEnd CMac CMen CPMA CSBt ECho ELon GKir LMil LRHS MAsh MGos MPkF NLar NPCo SCoo WPGP
	– 'Okukuji-nishiki'	CPMA
	– 'Okushimo'	CEnd CMCN CMen CPMA CWit IVic LRHS MPkF NHol NLar NPCo WPGP
	– 'Omato'	CPMA MPkF SBig WFar
	– 'Omurayama'	CBcs CBty CDoC CEnd CMCN CMen CPMA ECho EPfP LMil LRHS MGos MPkF NEas NLar NPCo SCoo SPer SSta WFar
	– 'Orange Dream'	Widely available
	– 'Oregon Sunset'	MGos MPkF WPat
	– 'Oridono-nishiki' (v)	Widely available
	– 'Ōsakazuki' ♀H4	Widely available
	– 'Ōsakazukidy Lace' **new**	CWit
	– 'Ōshio-beni'	CMen CPMA NPCo
	– 'Ōshū-shidare'	CMen CPMA ECho EPfP MPkF WFar
	– 'Oto-hime'	CMen CPMA ECho MPkF NPCo
	– 'Otome-zakura'	CMen CPMA ECho LRHS MPkF WPat
	– 'Peaches and Cream' (v)	CBcs CMen CPMA MPkF NLar NPCo SPer WPat
	– 'Peve Chameleon'	MPkF NLar
	– 'Peve Dave'	MPkF NLar
	– 'Peve Multicolor'	CPMA MGos MPkF NLar
	– 'Peve Ollie'	MPkF NLar
	– 'Peve Stanley' **new**	MPkF NLar
	– 'Phoenix'	MBri MPkF
	– 'Pine Bark Maple'	see *A. palmatum* 'Nishiki-gawa'
	– 'Pixie'	CBty CMen CPMA IVic MGos MPkF NLar WPat
	– 'Pung-kil'	IVic MPkF
	– 'Purple Ghost'	NLar SLim
	– 'Red Baron'	CPMA
	– 'Red Cloud'	MPkF NLar
	– 'Red Crusader'	NLar
	– 'Red Elf'	MPkF
	– 'Red Embers'	CWib
	– 'Red Emperor'	CWGN GBin MBri NEas NLar SPer WPat
	– 'Red Flame'	NLar
	– 'Red Flash'	CMen MPkF
	– 'Red Jonas'	MPkF NLar
	– 'Red Pygmy' ♀H4	Widely available
	– 'Red Spider'	CPMA
	– 'Red Wood'	CDoC CPMA GBin MPkF SCoo SLau SPer WPat
	– 'Renjaku-maru'	MPkF
	– 'Reticulatum'	see *A. palmatum* 'Shigitatsu-sawa'
	– 'Ribesifolium'	see *A. palmatum* 'Shishigashira'
*	– 'Rigassii'	LMaj
	– 'Rising Sun'	CPMA
	– 'Rokugatsu-en-nishiki'	WPat
	– 'Roseomarginatum'	see *A. palmatum* 'Kagiri-nishiki'
	– 'Rough Bark Maple'	see *A. palmatum* 'Arakawa'
	– 'Royle'	CPMA
	– 'Rubrum'	CMen
I	– 'Rubrum Kaiser'	CPMA
	– 'Ruby Ridge'	CPMA
	– 'Ruby Star'	CPMA MPkF NLar
	– 'Rufescens'	MPkF
	– 'Ryokū-ryū'	CMen MPkF
	– 'Ryuzu'	CPMA MPkF WPat
	– 'Sagara-nishiki' (v)	CEnd CMen CPMA ECho MPkF NPCo
	– 'Sai-ho'	MPkF
	– 'Saint Jean'	MPkF
	– 'Samidare'	CPMA EPfP MPkF NLar
	– 'Sandra'	CMen MPkF
N	– 'Sango-kaku' ♀H4	Widely available
	– 'Saoshika'	CMen CPMA MPkF
	– 'Sa-otome'	CMen MPkF
	– 'Satsuki-beni'	CMen ECho NPCo
	– 'Sazanami'	CDoC CEnd CMen CPMA CWCL MPkF NBea NLar WPGP WPat
	– 'Scolopendriifolium'	CBcs CBty CDoC GBin LMil LRHS MPkF NEas SCoo SLau WFar
§	– 'Seigai'	CPMA MPkF
	– 'Seigen'	CEnd CMCN CMen CPMA ECho MPkF NPCo WPGP
I	– 'Seigen Aureum'	CPMA
	– 'Seiun-kaku'	CMen CPMA ECho MPkF WPat
	– 'Sekimori'	CPMA SBig
	– 'Sekka-yatsubusa'	CMCN CMen ECho MPkF
N	– 'Senkaki'	see *A. palmatum* 'Sango-kaku'
	– 'Septemlobum Elegans'	see *A. palmatum* 'Heptalobum Elegans'
	– 'Septemlobum Purpureum'	see *A. palmatum* 'Hessei'
	– 'Sessilifolium' dwarf	see *A. palmatum* 'Hagoromo'
	– 'Sessilifolium' tall	see *A. palmatum* 'Koshimino'
	– 'Shaina'	CBcs CDoC CEnd CMen CPMA CSBt CWCL CWGN CWib EPfP IVic LRHS LTen MBri MGos MPkF NEas

NLar NPCo NPal SCoo SLim WFar WPat
- 'Sharp's Pygmy' CBty CMen CPMA ECho GBin LRHS MPkF NPCo WPat
- 'Sherwood Flame' CDoC CMCN CMen CPMA CWib ECho LRHS MAsh MGos MPkF NLar NPCo SCoo WClo WFar WPat
- 'Shichigosan' CMen LRHS
- 'Shidava Gold' CPMA MPkF
- 'Shi-en' MPkF
- 'Shigarami' CPMA MPkF
§ - 'Shigitatsu-sawa' (v) CBcs CBty CEnd CMCN CMac CMen CPMA ECho LRHS MGos MPkF NLar NPCo SBig
- 'Shigure-bato' CPMA MPkF
- 'Shigurezome' MPkF
- 'Shikageori-nishiki' CMen CPMA MPkF
- 'Shime-no-uchi' CPMA MPkF SBig
- 'Shindeshōjō' Widely available
§ - 'Shinobuga-oka' CBcs CMCN CMen CPMA MPkF NEas SLau
- 'Shinonome' CPMA MPkF
- 'Shirazz' (v) CBty CDoC CWGN LRHS MBri MGos MPkF
§ - 'Shishigashira' CDoC CMCN CMac CMen CPMA CWGN EBee ECho EPfP IArd IVic LMil LRHS MBlu MBri MGos MPkF NBea NEas NLar NPCo SBfd SCoo SPoG WDin WFar WPat
- 'Shishio' CBcs CBty CMCN CMen LAst LHyd LRHS MPkF NPCo SBig SSpi WPat
- 'Shishio Improved' CEnd CMCN CMac CPMA CTho CWSG ELon EPfP LRHS MAsh MGos MPkF NHol NLar NPCo SBig SWvt
- 'Shishio-hime' MPkF
- 'Shishi-yatsubusa' CPMA MPkF
- 'Shōjō' CMCN CPMA WFar
- 'Shōjō-no-mai' CPMA
- 'Shōjō-nomura' CAbP CEnd CMen MGos MPkF NLar WPGP WPat
- 'Sister Ghost' CPMA
- 'Skeeter's Broom' CBcs CBty CMen CPMA ELon LBuc LRHS MBri MGos MPkF NEas NPCo SBig SCoo WPat
* - 'Sode-nishiki' CPMA MPkF NLar
- 'Stella Rossa' CEnd CPMA MPkF NBea NLar WPat
- 'Suminagashi' CBcs CBty CDoC CMen CWCL CWit GBin LMil LRHS MGos MPkF NEas NLar NPCo SChF SCoo SLau WPat
I - 'Summer Gold' MBri SWvt
* - 'Sunago' NLar
- 'Susan' MPkF
- 'Taiyō-nishiki' CPMA MPkF NEas
- 'Takao' CMen
- 'Tama-hime' CMen CPMA MPkF NPCo
- 'Tana' CMCN CMen CPMA EPfP MPkF WFar WPat
- 'Tarō-yama' CPMA WPat
- 'Tatsuta' CMen MPkF WHar
- 'Taylor'[PBR] (v) CEnd CWGN EGxp GKir IVic LRHS LSou MBri MGos MPkF NLar SCoo WPat
- 'Tennyo-no-hoshi' CMen CWit MPkF NLar NPCo
- 'Tiger Rose' CPMA NLar
- 'Tiny Tim' CPMA
- 'Trompenburg' ♡H4 Widely available
- 'Tsuchigumo' CMen CPMA MPkF NLar
- 'Tsukubane' WPat
- 'Tsukuma-no' MPkF
- 'Tsukushigata' MPkF NEas WPat
- 'Tsuma-beni' CMCN CMen EPfP MPkF NPCo
- 'Tsuma-gaki' CDoC CMen CPMA ECho EGxp EPfP MBri MGos MPkF NLar NPCo WPat
- 'Tsuri-nishiki' CMen CPMA MPkF NLar
- 'Twombly's Red Sentinel' **new** MPkF
- 'Ueno-homare' LRHS MPkF SCoo WPat
- 'Ueno-yama' CBcs CPMA GBin MGos MPkF NEas WPat
- 'Ukigumo' (v) CBcs CEnd CLnd CMCN CMac CMen CPMA CSBt CWib ELan LMil LRHS MBlu MBri MGos MPkF NEas NHol NLar NPCo SBfd SBig SCoo SPer SPoG SSta WDin WFar WPat
- 'Ukon' CCVT CMen CPMA ECho GBin LMil MPkF NEas NPCo SCoo
- 'Umegae' CPMA
- 'Uncle Ghost' CPMA
- 'Usu-midori' CPMA
- 'Utsu-semi' CPMA MPkF
- 'Van der Akker' CPMA
- 'Versicolor' (v) CEnd CMCN CPMA MPkF
- 'Vic Pink' CPMA
- 'Victoria' MPkF
- 'Villa Taranto' CBty CDoC CEnd CMCN CMen CPMA ECho ELon EPfP IVic LMil LRHS MBri MGos MPkF NEas NHol NLar NPCo SCoo SSpi SSta WPGP WPat
- 'Volubile' CMCN CMen EPfP MPkF NPCo
- 'Wabito' CMCN CMen CPMA LRHS MPkF
- 'Waka-midori' CMen
- 'Waka-momiji' (v) CPMA
- 'Wakehurst Pink' (v) CMCN MPkF WPat
- 'Wendy' CMen CPMA IVic MPkF NLar WPat
- 'Wetumpka Red' CPMA
- 'Whitney Red' CMen
- 'Wildgoose' MPkF
- 'Will D' CPMA
- 'Wilson's Pink Dwarf' CBty CEnd CMen CPMA CWib CWit ECho ELon IVic LRHS MBri MGos MPkF NLar NPCo SCoo SLim SPoG
- 'Winter Flame' CPMA GBin LRHS MPkF NEas NHol NLar WPat
§ - 'Wolff' MPkF NEas WPat
- 'Wolff's Broom' MPkF
- 'Wou-nishiki' CMCN CMen ECho MPkF NPCo
- 'Yana-gawa' CMen
- 'Yasemin' CMen CPMA IVic MPkF NLar NPCo SBig
- 'Yatsubusa' MPkF NLar
- 'Yezo-nishiki' CMen MPkF WFar
- 'Yūba e' MPkF WFar WPat
- 'Yūgure' IVic MPkF NLar WFar
- 'Yuri-hime' **new** MPkF

papilio see *A. caudatum*

pensylvanicum ♡H4 CBcs CCVT CDul CMCN CTho EBee ECrN ELan EPfP IFFs LMaj MGos MMuc MRav NHol NWea SEND SLim SPer SSpi WDin WFar WHCr
- 'Erythrocladum' CEnd CMCN CPMA EPfP GKir MAsh MBri NEgg NHol NLar SBig SLim SPur SSta WFar WPGP

pentaphyllum CDul SBig SBir SSpi

* ***phlebanthum*** B&SWJ 9751 WCru

§ ***pictum*** CMCN
- subsp. ***okamotoanum*** CMCN
- - B&SWJ 8516 WCru
- 'Shufu-nishiki' CMCN

	- 'Usugomo'	WPat
	platanoides ♀^{H4}	CBcs CCVT CDoC CDul CLnd CMCN CSBt CTri CWib EBee ECrN EMac EPfP IFFs MGos MMuc MSwo NWea SBfd SEND SPer STre WDin WFar WHar WMou
	- 'Charles Joly'	LMaj
	- 'Cleveland'	CBcs
	- 'Columnare'	CCVT CDul CLnd CMCN CWib SCoo
	- 'Crimson King' ♀^{H4}	Widely available
	- 'Crimson Sentry'	CCVT CDoC CDul CEnd CLnd CMCN CWib EBee ECrN ELan EPfP IArd IVic LAst LTen MAsh MGos MRav SBfd SCoo SLim WDin WFar WHar
	- 'Deborah'	CBcs CTho LMaj MWya SCoo
	- 'Drummondii' (v)	Widely available
	- 'Emerald Queen'	CCVT CLnd CWib ECrN LMaj WDin
	- 'Faassen's Black'	CPMA
§	- 'Globosum'	CLnd CMCN EBee ECrN LMaj NLar SWvt
	- 'Goldsworth Purple'	CLnd NEgg
	- 'Laciniatum'	CEnd CMCN
	- 'Lorbergii'	see *A. platanoides* 'Palmatifidum'
	- 'Marit'	WPat
§	- 'Palmatifidum'	CLnd
	- Princeton Gold = 'Prigo'^{PBR}	CBcs CDoC CDul EBee ELan EMil LRHS MAsh MBri MGos SBfd SCoo SLim SPoG WHar
	- 'Reitenbachii'	CDul LMaj
	- 'Royal Red'	CBcs CDul CWib EBee ECrN EWTr LMaj MRav NLar SCoo
	- 'Schwedleri' ♀^{H4}	CDul CMCN EPfP MGos WDin
	- 'Walderseei'	CLnd
	pseudoplatanus	CBcs CCVT CDul CLnd CMCN CSBt CTri ECrN ELan EMac IFFs LBuc MGos NWea SBfd SPer WDin WFar WHar WMou
§	- 'Atropurpureum'	CDoC CDul CLnd ECrN EWTr NWea WDin WHar
	- 'Brilliantissimum' ♀^{H4}	Widely available
	- 'Erectum'	WFar
	- 'Erythrocarpum'	CMac
	- 'Gadsby'	EBee
	- 'Leopoldii' misapplied	see *A. pseudoplatanus* f. *variegatum*
	- 'Prinz Handjéry'	CBcs CDul CEnd CLnd CMCN CTri CWib EBee MAsh MGos NHol NLar NWea SPer SPoG WHar
	- f. ***purpureum***	SEND
	- 'Spaethii' misapplied	see *A. pseudoplatanus* 'Atropurpureum'
§	- f. ***variegatum*** (v)	NEgg
	- - 'Esk Sunset' (v)	CBcs EBee ECho MGos MPkF NLar
	- - 'Leopoldii' ambig. (v)	CBcs CDul CLnd CMCN ECrN ELan LAst SCoo SEND SPer SWvt WDin WFar
	- - 'Leopoldii' Vervaene (v)	SCrf
	- - 'Simon-Louis Frères' (v)	CCVT CDul CEnd CLnd CMCN CWSG CWib CWit EBee ECrN LAst MAsh MGos NEgg NLar SBfd SCrf SPer SPoG SWvt WFar WFoF WHar
	- 'Worley'	CBcs CCVT CDul CLnd CMCN CMac EBee ECrN MRav NWea SBfd SEND SLim SPer WDin
	pseudosieboldianum	CMCN CPMA IArd MBlu MPkF
	- B&SWJ 8746	WCru
	- B&SWJ 8769	WCru
	- var. ***microsieboldianum*** B&SWJ 8766	WCru
	pycnanthum	EPfP
	reticulatum	see *A. laevigatum* var. *reticulatum*
	rubescens	CPMA WPGP
	- B&SWJ 6735	WCru
	- RWJ 9840	WCru
	- variegated seedlings (v)	CPMA WPGP
	rubrum	Widely available
	- 'Autumn Flame'	EBee
	- 'Autumn Spire'	CPMA
	- 'Bowhall'	SBir
	- 'Brandywine'	CPMA EBee GKir LRHS MAsh MBlu MBri SCoo SPoG
	- 'Candy Ice' (v)	CPMA
	- 'Columnare'	CMCN EPfP
	- 'Embers'	CPMA
	- Fireball = 'Firzam'	CPMA
	- 'Firedance'	CPMA
	- 'New World'	GKir NLar SCoo
	- 'Northwind'	CPMA
	- 'Northwood'	CPMA
	- 'October Glory' ♀^{H4}	Widely available
	- 'Red King'	CPMA
	- 'Red Rocket'	SPoG
	- Red Sunset = 'Franksred'	CDul CEnd CMCN CPMA CTho EBee EPfP GKir LMaj LRHS LTen MBlu NLar SBir SCoo SLim SMad SPoG SSta
	- 'Scanlon'	CBcs CDul CEnd CMCN CPMA CTho EBee ECho EPfP LAst LMaj MBlu SPer
	- 'Schlesingeri'	CEnd CMCN CMac CPMA EPfP
	- 'Somerset'	CPMA CTri EBee LRHS MBri SCoo
	- Summer Red = 'Hosr'	CPMA EBee GKir LRHS SCoo SPoG
	- 'Sun Valley'	CPMA EBee GKir MAsh SCoo
	- 'Tilford'	CPMA SCoo SSta
§	***rufinerve*** ♀^{H4}	CAlb CBcs CCVT CDoC CDul CLnd CMCN CTho CTri EBee ECrN EPfP EPla IFFs LMaj LRHS MBri MMuc NBea NEgg NLar NWea SCoo SPer WBVN WDin WPGP
	- B&SWJ 10845	WCru
	- B&SWJ 10959	WCru
	- B&SWJ 11571	WCru
	- 'Albolimbatum'	see *A. rufinerve* 'Hatsuyuki'
	- 'Erythrocladum'	CBcs CPMA EBee
§	- 'Hatsuyuki' (v)	CEnd CMCN CPMA SBig
	- 'Winter Gold'	CPMA EPfP NLar SPur
§	***saccharinum***	CBcs CCVT CDoC CDul CLnd CMCN CMac CTri CWib EBee ECrN ELan EMac EPfP EWTr IFFs LRHS MGos MMuc MSnd NWea SCoo SPer WDin WFar WHar
	- 'Born's Gracious'	CPMA IFFs
	- 'Fastigiatum'	see *A. saccharinum* f. *pyramidale*
	- f. ***laciniatum***	EBee LAst MBlu MGos MMuc SPer WDin
	- 'Laciniatum Wieri'	CDul CMCN ECrN LAst WDin
	- f. ***lutescens***	CDul CMCN
§	- f. ***pyramidale***	CDoC CLnd EBee ECrN IFFs LMaj SPer WDin
	saccharum	CAgr CBcs CDoC CDul CLnd CMCN CTho ECrN EPfP MBlu MPkF NWea SPer
	- 'Brocade'	CPMA MPkF
	- 'Fiddlers Creek'	CPMA
§	- subsp. ***grandidentatum***	EPfP MBlu NLar
§	***sempervirens***	CGHE CPMA EBee LEdu MBlu WPGP
	'Sensu'	CPMA
	serrulatum B&SWJ 6760	WCru
	- CWJ 12437	WCru
	- RWJ 9912	WCru
	shirasawanum	CMCN

§	- 'Aureum' ♀H4	Widely available
	- 'Autumn Moon'	CBcs CBty CEnd CMCN CMen CPMA CWGN EPfP IArd LRHS MBri MPkF NEas NLar NPCo SBfd SCoo SLim WPat
§	- 'Ezo-no-momiji'	CMen CPMA MPkF NLar NPCo
	- 'Gloria'	CBty MPkF
§	- 'Helena'	MPkF
	- 'Johin'	CPMA
	- 'Jordan' PBR	CEnd CWGN EBee MBri MGos NLar
	- 'Lovett'	CPMA
§	- 'Microphyllum'	MPkF
§	- 'Ogurayama'	CPMA NPCo
	- 'Palmatifolium'	CPMA
	- 'Susanne'	CPMA MPkF
	- var. ***tenuifolium*** B&SWJ 11073	WCru
	sieboldianum	CDul CMen CTho CTri ECho IFFs MMuc WHCr WHar WPat
	- B&SWJ 10962	WCru
	- B&SWJ 11049	WCru
	- 'Sode-no-uchi'	CMen MPkF NPCo
	- var. ***tsushimense*** B&SWJ 10962 new	WCru
	sikkimense B&SWJ 11613 new	WCru
	- WWJ 11853	WCru
	aff. ***sikkimense*** HWJK 2040	WCru
	'Silver Cardinal' (v)	CBcs CDul CEnd CMCN CPMA EBee EPfP MBlu MGos MPkF NLar WHar
	'Silver Vein'	see *A.* × *conspicuum* 'Silver Vein'
	spicatum	EPfP LLHF NLar
§	***stachyophyllum***	EBee GAuc GQui
	- BWJ 8101	WCru
§	***sterculiaceum***	CMCN WPGP
	- subsp. ***franchetii***	NLar
	- subsp. ***sterculiaceum*** GWJ 9317	WCru
	takesimense B&SWJ 8500	WCru
	tataricum	CMCN GKir
	- subsp. ***aidzuense*** B&SWJ 10958	WCru
§	- subsp. ***ginnala***	CBcs CDul CLnd CMCN CTri CWSG ECrN EMac EPfP IFFs LMaj MBlu MGos NBea NLar NPal NWea SEND SPer WDin
	- - 'Flame'	CPMA CWSG EBee ECrN ELan EPfP IFFs LRHS MGos MMuc MSnd NLar NWea SPoG
	- - 'Red Wing'	CPMA EBee
	tegmentosum	CBcs CMCN CPMA EPfP MBlu
	- B&SWJ 8421	WCru
	- subsp. ***glaucorufinerve***	see *A. rufinerve*
	tetramerum	see *A. stachyophyllum*
	tonkinense DJHV 06173	WCru
	trautvetteri	CMCN EPfP
	triflorum ♀H4	CBcs CCVT CDul CMCN CPMA EPfP LMaj MBlu NBea NLar SSpi WDin WFar
	truncatum	CMCN MPkF
	- 'Akikaze-nishiki' (v)	CPMA MPkF
	tschonoskii	GQui
	- subsp. ***koreanum***	MPkF
§	***turkestanicum***	WFar
	velutinum	CMCN
	villosum	see *A. sterculiaceum*
	'White Tigress'	CDoC CDul CPMA CTho NLar WPGP
	wilsonii	CSam
	× ***zoeschense***	CMCN
	- 'Annae'	NHol

Aceriphyllum see *Mukdenia*

× *Achicodonia* (*Gesneriaceae*)

	'Dark Velvet'	WDib

Achillea (*Asteraceae*)

	ageratifolia ♀H4	EBla ECho ECtt EDAr LBee LRHS MTho NBre SMad SRms WClo WFar
	- subsp. ***serbica***	ECho
§	***ageratum***	CArn CHby CPrp ECho ELau EOHP GBar GPoy MHer MNHC NGHP SIde SRms WGwG WHer WJek WPer
	'Alabaster'	EBee NDov SAga SPhx
	aleppica subsp. ***zederbaueri***	GKev
	Anthea = 'Anblo' PBR	CKno CPrp CWCL EBee EBla ECtt GBBs LBMP LPio LRHS LSRN MCot MRav NChi NCob NLar SRGP SRms WFar
§	'Apfelblüte' (Galaxy Series)	CWCL EBee EBla ECha ECtt ELan EPfP EWTr GMac LRHS LSRN MLLN MMuc MRav NDov NGdn NHol NSti SEND SPer SPoG WCAu WFar WMnd WPer WPtf WWEG
	Appleblossom	see *A.* 'Apfelblüte' (Galaxy Series)
	'Apricot Beauty'	EBee ECtt GBBs GMaP GQue LSRN WCon
	argentea misapplied	see *A. clavennae*, *A. umbellata*
	argentea Lamarck	see *Tanacetum argenteum*
	argentea ambig.	NMen
	aurea	see *A. chrysocoma*
	'Bahama'	GBin GQue NBre NBro
	'Belle Epoque' ♀H4	WWEG
	brachyphylla	EHoe
	'Breckland Bouquet'	ECtt EWes
	'Breckland Ruby'	ECtt EWes
	'Carmina Burana'	CMea
	cartilaginea	see *A. salicifolia*
	'Christine's Pink' ♀H4	EShb MSpe MTis SUsu
§	***chrysocoma***	ECho EDAr MMuc MWat WMoo
	- 'Grandiflora'	EBee ECha ELan LPla NGdn
§	***clavennae***	CMea ECho EDAr LPio MWat SMrm SRms WAbe WFar WPat
	clypeolata Sibth. & Sm.	EBee EPPr LPio LRHS NBre NLar SPlb SRms
	coarctata	NBir WPer
	Colorado Group	CWCL GAbr LRHS NChi SPav WFar
	'Coronation Gold' ♀H4	CDoC CPrp CWCL EBee EBla ECtt ELan EPfP LAst MNFA MRav MWat NDov SAga SWvt WCAu WCot WEas WFar WWEG
	'Credo' ♀H4	Widely available
	decolorans	see *A. ageratum*
	erba-rotta	WPer
	- subsp. ***moschata***	NBro
§	'Fanal'	Widely available
	'Faust'	CHar EBla ELon MNrw SMrm STes SUsu WCon WPGP
	'Federsee' new	MArl
	'Feuerland'	CMac CSam CWit EBee EBla ECha ECtt ELon EPPr EPfP LRHS MLLN MRav MTis NBir NDov NGdn NSti SMad SMrm SPer SPoG SWat WCAu WCot WFar WPer WWEG
	filipendulina	GKir MLLN SWal WHrl
	- 'Cloth of Gold' ♀H4	Widely available
	- 'Gold Plate' ♀H4	Widely available
	- 'Parker's Variety' ♀H4	EBee GQue NBre WFar WMoo

	'Fleur van Zonneveld' **new**	NDov
	Flowers of Sulphur	see *A.* 'Schwefelblüte'
	(Forncett Series) 'Forncett Beauty'	WPtf
	- 'Forncett Bride'	NBre WHil
	- 'Forncett Candy'	NDov WWEG
	- 'Forncett Citrus'	MAvo NBre WPGP
	- 'Forncett Fletton'	CFir CWCL EBee ECtt ELon EPPr EPfP EShb GBin LHop LRHS MAsh MNFA MNrw MRav MSpe MTis NCGa NCob NGdn NHol WFar WPtf WWEG WWlt
	- 'Forncett Ivory'	EPPr NBre WPtf
	fraasii	MDKP
	Galaxy Series red-flowered	WSpi
	glaberrima hybrid	WPtf
	'Gloria Jean'	SHar SPhx
	'Gold and Grey'	SMrm WWEG
	'Goldstar'	EBee NBPC NDov WFar
	grandifolia misapplied	see *Tanacetum macrophyllum* (Waldst. & Kit.) Sch.Bip.
§	***grandifolia*** Friv.	CElw COlW CPrp CSam EBee LPla MRav NBro SMad SSvw WAul WBor WFar WHer WMnd WMoo
	'Gravat' **new**	MArl
	'Great Expectations'	see *A.* 'Hoffnung'
	'Hannelore Pahl'	NDov
	'Heidi' ♀H4	CCVN WPtf WWEG
	'Heinrich Vogeler'	EBee
	'Hella Glashoff' ♀H4	CMea CWCL CWan EBee ECho ECtt ELon GBin LRHS MWea SAga WCot WFar
§	'Hoffnung'	CPrp CWCL EBee EBla ECtt MRav MSpe SPer WMnd WPer WWEG
	× ***huteri***	EBla ECho ECtt EDAr EPfP LBee LRHS MMuc MRav SPoG WCom WFar WNew
	'Inca Gold'	CWCL EBee EBla ECha ECtt EHrv EPPr EShb GQue LRHS MRav MTis NCob NGdn NHol NSti SAga SPhx WWEG
	'Jacqueline'	EWll MSpe
	'King Alfred'	LAst WClo
	× ***kolbiana***	MWat NMen SRms WPat
§	- 'Weston'	ECho NBre
§	'Lachsschönheit' (Galaxy Series) ♀H4	Widely available
	× ***lewisii***	NMen
	- 'King Edward' ♀H4	ECho EDAr EPfP GMaP LPio NBir SPoG WClo WCom WFar
	ligustica	WCot
	'Lucky Break' ♀H4	EBla SDix SUsu
	macrophylla	MBNS NBre
	'Marie Ann'	CWCL EBee ECtt EKen GQue LPio LSRN MNrw NBPC NLar NSti SPhx SRGP
	'Marmalade'	MSpe NDov SMrm WMnd WPGP WWEG
	'Martina' ♀H4	CDoC CMMP CPrp EBee ECtt EPPr EPfP GAbr IPot LAst LBMP LHop MAsh MBNS MBri MCot MLLN MRav MSCN NCGa NDov NGdn NHol SRGP WWEG
	'McVities'	CWCL ECtt EPPr LEdu MLLN MSpe MTis SDnm STes WMnd WPtf WWEG
	millefolium	CArn COld CWan EBWF ELau GBar GPoy MNHC NLan NMir NSco SPlb WHer WJek WSFF
	- 'Bloodstone'	EBee ECtt EWes GBar MRav
	- 'Bright Cerise'	WFar
	- 'Carla Hussey'	WFar
	- 'Cassis'	CCVN CSpe GQue LRHS MNHC NGBl NLar SDnm SPav WFar
§	- 'Cerise Queen'	Widely available
	- 'Christel'	CCVN EWes GBin SUsu
	- 'Christine'	GBin
	- 'Dark Lilac Beauty'	EWTr
	- 'Excel'	EBee
	- 'Harlekin'	EBee
	- 'Kelwayi' ♀H4	WPtf
	- Kirschkönigin	see *A. millefolium* 'Cerise Queen'
	- 'Lansdorferglut' ♀H4	EBee EBrs SPhx
	- 'Lavender Beauty'	see *A. millefolium* 'Lilac Beauty'
§	- 'Lilac Beauty'	CAby CBar CHar COlW EBee EBrs ECha EHrv ELon EPfP GBin GKir IPot LBMP LRHS LSRN MAsh MMuc MRav NBir NEgg NGHP NHol NPri NSti SBfd WFar WHoo WPer WWEG
*	- 'Lilac Queen'	MArl
	- 'Oertels Rose'	WFar
	- 'Old Brocade'	EShb NDov WPGP WPtf WWEG
	- Pastel Shades	GKir IFoB WMoo
	- 'Prospero'	WCot WCra WWEG
	- 'Raspberry Ripple'	GBin
	- 'Red Beauty'	CWCL EBee EPfP MAsh MBNS MSpe MWea SMad SMrm SRms SWat WCFE WWEG
	- 'Red Salmon' **new**	EWes
	- 'Red Velvet'	Widely available
	- 'Rose Madder'	CAby CPrp CWCL EBee EBla ECtt EHoe EPPr GMaP LPla LRHS MBri MLHP MLLN MNrw MSCN MSpe NBir NCGa NGHP NGdn NHol NLar NSti SPav SWvt WCot WGwG WPrP
	- 'Rosie'	GBar
	- 'Ruby Port'	WFar
	- 'Salmon Pink'	WFar
	- 'Salmon Queen'	NGHP NHol
	- 'Sammetriese'	CWan EBee LRHS MNrw NCGa SMad SPhx WFar WWEG
	- 'Schneetaler'	EBee GBin
	- 'Serenade'	EBee EBla ECtt WFar
	- 'Sue's Pink'	CSam
	- 'Summertime'	LAst
	- 'Tickled Pink'	WPer
	- 'White Queen'	EBee
	'Mondpagode' ♀H4	CHar CPrp CWit EBee EPPr EWTr LPla LRHS LSRN MAvo MBNS MNFA MRav MWea NGdn SBfd SMHy SPhx WFar WKif
*	'Moonbeam'	SEND
	'Moonshine' ♀H3	Widely available
	'Moonwalker'	CAbP EBee NBre NGBl SIde SPav WCot WFar WPer
	nana	GEdr
	nobilis	MMuc SEND
	- subsp. ***neilreichii***	EBee EBla ECGP EHoe EHrv EWTr IKil LRHS MNrw NSti WHal WPrP WPtf WTin WWEG
	'Nostalgia'	EBee
*	***odilis*** **new**	MAsh
	'Paprika' (Galaxy Series)	Widely available
	'Peardrop'	NBre
	'Petra'	EBee WCAu
	pindicola subsp. ***integrifolia***	EWes
	'Pink Lady'	EBee EBla GBBs WCon
	pink-flowered from Santa Cruz Island	CKno CWCL
	'Pretty Belinda'	EBee ECtt EPfP GMac IPot LSou MAsh MBNS MSpe NBPC NCGa NLar NPri NSti SPoG WWlt

	ptarmica	CArn CBre EBWF ELau GBar LLWG MHer NMir NPri SIde
*	- 'Ballerina'	LRHS MBNS MWhi NBre NDov NLar
	- Innocence	see *A. ptarmica* 'Unschuld'
	- 'Major'	NBre
	- 'Nana Compacta'	CSpe EBee EBla ECha EPPr GBin IGor NBir NCGa SPlb SUsu WCFE WFar WWEG
	- 'Perry's White'	CBcs CBre EBee ECha MNrw NGdn NHol SRGP WCot
	- 'Stephanie Cohen'	see *A. sibirica* 'Stephanie Cohen'
N	- The Pearl Group seed-raised (d)	CTri ELan MMuc NVic SPlb SPoG SWat WFar WMoo WPer WTin
N	- (The Pearl Group) 'Boule de Neige' (clonal) (d)	EPfP GKir MRav MSpe NBre NCob NPer NSti SPer SPet WFar
N	- (The Pearl Group) 'The Pearl' (clonal) (d) 𝕐^{H4}	Widely available
§	- 'Unschuld'	NBir
	- 'Weihenstephan'	EBee
	'Rougham Salmon'	WPtf
§	***salicifolia***	WFar
	- 'Silver Spray'	EBee GQue NBre NLar SDnm SPav WOut
	'Sally'	EBee EPPr
	Salmon Beauty	see *A.* 'Lachsschönheit'
	'Sandstone'	see *A.* 'Wesersandstein'
§	'Schwefelblüte'	MRav NBir SBch SMrm
	'Schwellenburg'	CDes CHar NBre WPGP
	sibirica	SRGP
	- subsp. ***camschatica***	WPtf
	- - 'Love Parade'	EAEE EBee EPfP IPot ITim LBMP LRHS MBNS MMuc MNFA MNrw MRav NBPC NGdn NLar SAga SGSe SPer SRGP SSvw WFar WMoo WWEG
§	- 'Stephanie Cohen'	CPrp EBee ECtt GBee GBin LLWG MLLN NGdn WFar WWEG
	'Stephanie'	ECtt EPPr EWes LSRN NBre
	Summer Berries Group	WOut
	Summer Pastels Group	GKir IFro LLWG LRHS NBir NHol NLar SBfd SPav SPoG SRms SWal WClo WFar WHil
	'Summerwine' 𝕐^{H4}	Widely available
	'Sunbeam'	SHar
I	'Taygetea'	CSam EBee EBla ECtt ELan EPPr EPfP EShb LRHS MBNS NPnk SDix SPer SPet WCAu WCot WFar WKif WPer WSHC WWEG
	'Terracotta'	Widely available
	'The Beacon'	see *A.* 'Fanal'
	'Tissington Old Rose'	MAvo MSpe MTis
	tomentosa 𝕐^{H4}	CTri ECha ECho ECtt EPfP
§	- 'Aurea'	EBla ECho MSCN NBre NBro
	- 'Maynard's Gold'	see *A. tomentosa* 'Aurea'
	'Tri-colour'	NGdn
§	***umbellata***	EBee WBox WBrk
	- 'Weston'	see *A.* × *kolbiana* 'Weston'
	'W.B. Childs'	ECha ELan MCot MNrw NDov SHar
	'Walther Funcke'	Widely available
§	'Wesersandstein'	CHar CWCL EBee ECtt EPPr EShb GBin GMaP LPla LRHS MAvo MLLN MNrw NBir STes WCot WFar WPer WWEG
	'Wilczekii'	NBre SRms
	'Yellowstone'	EBee EWes

× *Achimenantha* (*Gesneriaceae*)

'Aries'	WDib
'Himalayan Sunrise' **new**	LAma
'Inferno' 𝕐^{H1}	EABi WDib
'Tyche'	EABi

Achimenes (*Gesneriaceae*)

	'Addano' **new**	WDib
	'Ambroise Verschaffelt' 𝕐^{H1}	EABi LAma WDib
	'Ami Van Houtte'	WDib
	'Ballerina' **new**	WDib
	'Blue David'	EABi
	'Boy David'	EABi
	'Cascade Violet Night'	WDib
	'Cattleya'	LAma
	'Charity'	WDib
	'Clouded Yellow'	EABi
	'Coral Cameo Mix'	EABi
	'Cornell Favourite'	EABi
	'Crummock Water'	WDib
	'Derwentwater'	EABi
	'Donna'	EABi
	'Dot'	EABi
	'English Waltz'	EABi
	erecta	WDib
	'Erlkönig' **new**	WDib
	'Extravaganza'	WDib
	'Glory'	WDib
	grandiflora 'Robert Dressler'	EABi
	'Harry Williams'	LAma WDib
	'Hilda Michelssen' 𝕐^{H1}	WDib
	'Jay Dee Pink' **new**	WDib
	'Jennifer Goode'	EABi
	'Jubilee Gem'	EABi
	'Just Divine'	EABi
	'Kim Blue'	WDib
	'Light Lilac' **new**	WDib
	'Little Beauty'	WDib
	longiflora	EABi
	'Luneberg'	EABi
	'Maxima'	LAma
	'Menuett' **new**	WDib
	'Mozelle'	EABi
	'Orange Delight'	WDib
	(Palette Series) 'Palette Mix Lilac'	EABi
	- 'Palette Mix Red Dwarf'	EABi
	- 'Palette Mix Salmon'	EABi
	- 'Palette Mix White'	EABi
	- 'Palette Red Mix'	EABi
	'Pally'	WDib
	'Patens Major'	WDib
	'Peach Blossom'	LAma WDib
	'Pearly Queen'	EABi
	'Pink Beauty'	EABi
	'Pink Rose' (d)	EABi
	'Platinum'	EABi
I	'Purple Hybrid'	EABi
	'Purple Queen' **new**	WDib
	'Rainbow'	WDib
	'Red Giant'	EABi
	'Rose Dream'	EABi
	'Stan's Delight' (d) 𝕐^{H1}	EABi WDib
	'Summer Sunset'	EABi
	'Tarantella'	EABi WDib
	'Teresa'	EABi
	(Tetra Series) 'Tetra Verschaffelt'	EABi
	- 'Tetra Wine Red Charm'	EABi
	'Tiger Eye' **new**	WDib
	'Trailing Yellow'	EABi
	'Vivid'	EABi WDib
	'Weinrot Elfe'	WDib

'Wetterflow's Triumph'	EABi WDib
'Yellow Beauty'	WDib

Achlys (*Berberidaceae*)

japonica	GEdr WCru
triphylla	GGar WCon WCru

Achnatherum see *Stipa*

Achyranthes (*Amaranthaceae*)

bidentata	CArn

Acidanthera see *Gladiolus*

Acinos (*Lamiaceae*)

§ ***alpinus***	CArn CPBP EBee EDAr GJos GPWP LLHF LRHS MHer MMuc SEND SPhx WJek
§ ***corsicus***	NMen NWCA WHoo

Aciphylla (*Apiaceae*)

aurea	EBee GBin GCal GKev NWCA SMad SPlb
dieffenbachii	CTrC EUJe GBin ITim
ferox	GBin
glaucescens	ECou GAbr GBin GCrs
kirkii	GBin
'Lomond'	GBin
monroi	LLHF
montana	GLin
pinnatifida	GGar SMad
scott-thomsonii	GBin
squarrosa	CTrC EUJe GBin
subflabellata	ECou

Acis ✿ (*Amaryllidaceae*)

§ ***autumnalis*** ♀H4	Widely available
- 'Cobb's Variety'	EBee ECho WCot
- var. ***oporantha***	CWCL
- - from Morocco	ECho
- var. ***pulchella***	ECho
§ ***longifolia***	ECho
nicaeensis ♀H2-3	CPBP EBur ECho EPot GCrs ITim LRHS MAsh MTho SCnR WAbe WCom WCot
§ ***rosea***	CStu EBur ECho NMen SCnR WAbe WThu
§ ***tingitana***	ECho WCot
- SB&L 203	WCot
§ ***trichophylla***	ECho LLHF SCnR WCot
- f. ***purpurascens***	ECho WCot
* - var. ***rosea***	ECho
§ ***valentina***	CPBP ECho EPot SCnR SRot WCot

Acmella (*Asteraceae*)

§ ***oleracea***	CArn EOHP SCoo

Acmena (*Myrtaceae*)

smithii	EShb

Acnistus (*Solanaceae*)

australis	see *Iochroma australe*

Acoelorrhaphe (*Arecaceae*)

wrightii	EAmu

Aconitum (*Ranunculaceae*)

B&SWJ 2954 from Nepal	WCru
CNDS 036 from Burma	WCru
GWJ 9393 from northern India	WCru
GWJ 9417 from northern India	WCru
SDR 4842	EBee
SDR 4912	EBee
alboviolaceum	WCot
- var. ***alboviolaceum*** f. ***albiflorum*** B&SWJ 4105	WCru
- - B&SWJ 8444	WCru
altissimum	see *A. lycoctonum* subsp. *vulparia*
anglicum	see *A. napellus* subsp. *napellus* Anglicum Group
§ ***anthora***	EBee EDif EPfP IKil
arcuatum	see *A. fischeri* var. *arcuatum*
austroyunnanense	EBee WSHC
- BWJ 7902	WCru
autumnale misapplied	see *A. carmichaelii* Wilsonii Group
autumnale Rchb.	see *A. fischeri* Rchb.
× ***bicolor***	see *A.* × *cammarum* 'Bicolor'
'Blue Opal'	CDes EBee ECtt EWes WPGP
'Blue Sceptre'	NMoo
'Bressingham Spire' ♀H4	EBee EBrs ECtt EDif EHrv ELan EPfP GCra GKir GMaP IKil LAst LRHS MAvo MBri MCot MRav NBPC NCGa NDov NPer SPer SRms WHil WMoo WWEG
§ × ***cammarum*** 'Bicolor' ♀H4	Widely available
- 'Eleanora'	CFir EBee ECtt EPPr EWes GCra LHop LSou MBri MSCN NBPC NGHP NGdn NLar NMoo SPer WCot WHil WWEG
- 'Grandiflorum Album'	CAby EWld LPla
- 'Pink Sensation'PBR	CAby CFir EBee ECtt EKen EPfP GQue LLHF MBNS MLLN NBPC NBre NDov NGHP NLar NPnk NSti SSvw WSpi WWEG
§ ***carmichaelii***	CArn CBot CMea CSam CWit EBee EBrs ELan EPfP GKir IFoB IFro LAst LRHS LSou MBri MMuc MNrw NBro NChi NEgg SMrm SPoG SRms WCot WFar WHoo WHrl WTin
- Arendsii Group	ECtt LAst LRHS SPhx SRot
- - 'Arendsii' ♀H4	Widely available
- 'Blue Bishop'	LSou
- 'Redleaf'PBR	see *A. carmichaelii* 'Royal Flush'
- 'River Arrow'	WCot
- 'River Avon' **new**	WCot
- 'River Lune'	WCot
- 'River Nene'	WCot
- 'River Ouse'	WCot
- 'River Tees'	WCot
- 'River Teifi' **new**	WCot
- 'River Trent'	WCot
- 'River Usk' **new**	WCot
- 'River Welland' **new**	WCot
§ - 'Royal Flush'PBR	CWGN EBee MNrw NCob NGdn NLar WCot
- var. ***truppelianum***	EBee
- - HWJ 732	WCru
§ - Wilsonii Group	CPrp EBee GGar GKir GMaP LEdu LRHS MCot MRav MWat NDov NEgg SPhx WFar WPGP WPer
- - 'Barker's Variety'	CFir CKno EBee ECtt ELon EPfP GBee GCal GQue LPio NHol NLar NSti SMrm SSvw WCot
- - 'Kelmscott' ♀H4	EBee ECtt EWes MCot MRav SDix SMHy SMrm SSvw WFar WRHF WSpi
- - 'Spätlese'	CAbP CWGN EBee ECtt ELon EPfP GCal LEdu MCot MNFA NBir NDov

	NGdn SAga SMHy SMrm SPer STes SUsu WCot WWEG
chasmanthum	LRHS
chiisanense B&SWJ 4446	WCru
cilicicum	see *Eranthis hyemalis* Cilicica Group
'Cloudy'	CPrp EBee ECtt NBPC NGdn SPer
§ ***columbianum***	WCru
subsp. ***viviparum*** HWJK 2120 **new**	
compactum	see *A. napellus* subsp. *vulgare*
confertiflorum	see *A. anthora*
elwesii	EBee EBrs LRHS NBre
episcopale	NDov WCru WFar
aff. ***episcopale***	WSHC
- CLD 1426	WFar
excelsum	see *A. lycoctonum* subsp. *lycoctonum*
ferox	EBee ELon EWes
- HWJK 2217	WCru
fischeri misapplied	see *A. carmichaelii*
§ ***fischeri*** Rchb.	CWib EBee MMuc NCGa NMoo WHil
- B&SWJ 8809	WCru
§ - var. ***arcuatum*** B&SWJ 774	WCru
formosanum	LEdu
- B&SWJ 3057	WCru
fukutomei	MRav NBre
- B&SWJ 337	WCru
gammiei GWJ 9418	WCru
gmelinii	see *A. lycoctonum* subsp. *lycoctonum*
§ ***hemsleyanum***	CAby CBot CPLG CPrp CRHN CStu CWGN EBee ECtt EPfP GCra GGar GKev GQue MMuc NBid NHol SGSe SPhx WBrE WCru WFar
howellii	see *A. columbianum* subsp. *viviparum*
hyemale	see *Eranthis hyemalis*
'Ivorine'	CBot CMac CRow CTri EBee ECha ELan EPfP GCra GGar GMaP LAst LRHS LSRN MAvo MCot NCGa SPer WFar WPnP WSpi WTin WWEG
jaluense B&SWJ 8741	WCru
japonicum	EBee GCal LRHS WCon WFar
- var. ***montanum*** B&SWJ 5507	WCru
§ - subsp. ***napiforme***	EBee EWes SAga WPGP
- - B&SWJ 943	ELon WCru
§ - subsp. ***subcuneatum*** B&SWJ 6228	WCru
laciniatum GWJ 9254	WCru
lamarckii	see *A. lycoctonum* subsp. *neapolitanum*
lasianthum	see *A. lycoctonum* subsp. *vulparia*
longecassidatum B&SWJ 4277	WCru
- B&SWJ 8486	WCru
- B&SWJ 8488	WCru
lycoctonum	GKir LRHS NLar SRms
- 'Darkeyes'	CAbP CFir LOck LRHS LSou NCob NGdn WCot
§ - subsp. ***lycoctonum***	SRms WCot
§ - subsp. ***moldavicum***	WCot
§ - subsp. ***neapolitanum***	ECtt ELan EPfP GCal GKir GMaP MLLN MMuc NBPC NGdn NLar WFar WSpi WWEG
- 'Russian Yellow'	EWld GCal

§ - subsp. ***vulparia***	CArn CMac CPrp EBee GMac GPoy LPio MNFA MRav NEgg WAul WCot WPer
mairei	see *A. vilmorinianum*
moldavicum	see *A. lycoctonum* subsp. *moldavicum*
napellus	Widely available
- 'Bergfürst'	CAby CMea EBrs LPla LRHS MBri MNFA SPhx
- 'Blue Valley'	EBee EPfP EWes MSCN NCGa WFar
- subsp. ***napellus***	LEdu
§ - - Anglicum Group	CRow CSev CWan MCot NLar WCot WPen WSpi
- 'Rubellum'	EBee ECtt ELan EPfP MMuc NBir NBro NEgg NPri SMrm SPur WMnd WSpi
- 'Schneewittchen'	EBee EWes SSvw
§ - subsp. ***vulgare***	WFar
- - 'Albidum'	CPrp EBee EHrv ELan ELon EPfP GAbr GMaP LEdu LRHS NBid NGHP NHol NLar NPri SPer SPet WAul WBrE WFar
- - 'Carneum'	EBrs GCra LRHS WFar WHer WKif
napiforme	see *A. japonicum* subsp. *napiforme*
neapolitanum	see *A. lycoctonum* subsp. *neapolitanum*
'Newry Blue'	EBee EBrs ELan NBir NHol NLar SPoG SRms WFar WPer WWEG
orientale misapplied	see *A. lycoctonum* subsp. *vulparia*
paniculatum	see *A. variegatum* subsp. *paniculatum*
pendulum	EBee
piepunense	EBee GKev
proliferum B&SWJ 4107	WCru
pseudohuiliense	CPLG
pseudolaeve	EWld
- B&SWJ 8663	WCru
- var. ***erectum*** B&SWJ 8466	WCru
pubiceps	GCal
white-flowered **new**	
pyramidale	see *A. napellus* subsp. *vulgare*
pyrenaicum	see *A. lycoctonum* subsp. *neapolitanum*
ranunculifolius	see *A. lycoctonum* subsp. *neapolitanum*
sachalinense	LLHF
seoulense B&SWJ 694	WCru
- B&SWJ 864	WCru
septentrionale	see *A. lycoctonum* subsp. *lycoctonum*
'Spark's Variety' ♀H4	Widely available
spicatum	GKir
- GWJ 9418	WCru
'Stainless Steel'	Widely available
subcuneatum	see *A. japonicum* subsp. *subcuneatum*
× ***tubergenii***	see *Eranthis hyemalis* Tubergenii Group
uchiyamae	EPPr NLar
- B&SWJ 1005	WCru
- B&SWJ 1216	ELon WCru
variegatum	EBee
§ - subsp. ***paniculatum***	MBri NBre
- - 'Roseum'	EBee WFar
§ ***vilmorinianum*** BWJ 8055	WCru
volubile misapplied	see *A. hemsleyanum*
volubile Pall.	CFir EBee GCal
vulparia	see *A. lycoctonum* subsp. *vulparia*
yamazakii	WCru
yezoense	GCal

Aconogonon see *Persicaria*

Acorus ✿ (*Acoraceae*)

	calamus	CArn CBen CKno CWat EHon ELau GKir GPoy LPBA MCCP MSKA NPer SWat WHer
	- subsp. ***angustatus***	GPoy
	- 'Argenteostriatus' (v)	CBen CRow CWat EBee ECha ECtt EHon LPBA MMuc MWts SEND SGSe SWat WMAq
*	***christophii***	EBee ELon EPPr EWes SApp WMoo
	gramineus	ELau LPBA MSKA NPer SWat WHer WMoo WTin
	- 'Golden Delight'	SGSe
	- 'Golden Edge' (v)	EBee NHol WMoo WRHF
	- 'Hakuro-nishiki' (v)	EBee ECtt EHoe EHul EPPr EShb GKev GKir IFFs LPBA MCCP MGos MMoz NBid NHol SBfd SGSe SRms SWvt WMoo
	- 'Kinchinjunga' (v)	IFro
	- 'Licorice'	EBee EPPr GCal MBNS MDKP NHol SPoG WGrn WMoo WPnP
	- 'Masamune' (v)	EBee EPla EWes GBin GCal IFro NHol SApp WMoo WPat WTin
	- 'Minimus Aureus'	CBre GCal
	- 'Oborozuki' misapplied	see *A. gramineus* 'Ogon'
	- 'Oborozuki' (v)	EBee EHoe SMrm
§	- 'Ogon' (v)	Widely available
	- 'Omogo'	EBee
	- var. ***pusillus***	EBee EPla NBro WWEG
	- 'Variegatus' (v)	Widely available
	- 'Yodo-no-yuki' (v)	EBee EPla IFro
	'Intermedius'	NPer

Acradenia (*Rutaceae*)

	frankliniae	CBcs CCCN CMHG CMac CPne CTrC CTsd EBee GGar GKir SEND SKHP WFar WPGP WSHC

Actaea (*Ranunculaceae*)

	alba misapplied	see *A. pachypoda*, *A. rubra* f. *neglecta*
	arizonica	CLAP EBee GCal WCru
	asiatica	CLAP WPGP
	- B&SWJ 616	WCru
	- B&SWJ 6351 from Japan	WCru
	- B&SWJ 8694 from Korea	WCru
	- BWJ 8174 from China	WCru
	biternata	CLAP
	- B&SWJ 5591	WCru
	- B&SWJ 11190	WCon WCru
§	***cimicifuga***	CLAP EBee GCal GPoy
	- B&SWJ 2657	WCru
§	***cordifolia***	EBee EBrs GBin GMaP LPBA LRHS MLLN NBPC WBor
	- 'Blickfang'	CLAP
	dahurica	EBee GKir LRHS NLar SWat
	- B&SWJ 8426	WCru
	- B&SWJ 8573	WCru
	- tall	GCal
	erythrocarpa	see *A. rubra*
	europaea	SPoG
	frigida B&SWJ 2966	WCru
	heracleifolia B&SWJ 8843	WCru
	- DJHC 970139	CDes
§	***japonica***	CLAP GAbr GCal LRHS WFar
	- B&SWJ 5828	WCru
	- B&SWJ 11136	WCru
	- var. ***acutiloba*** B&SWJ 6257	WCru
	- compact	GBin
	- - B&SWJ 8758A	WCru
I	- 'Minima'	LRHS
	mairei	LRHS
	- BWJ 7635	WCru
	- BWJ 7939	WCru
§	***matsumurae***	CPLG
	- B&SWJ 11528	WCru
	- 'Elstead Variety' ♀H4	CPLG GCal MBri MRav NBre
	- 'Frau Herms'	CLAP LRHS
	- 'White Pearl'	CBcs CRow EBee ECha EHrv ELan EPfP GAbr GGar GMaP LHop LLWG LRHS MLLN MMuc MRav NBPC NBid NCGa NGdn NSti SMad SPer SPoG WCAu WFar WMnd WPGP WWEG WWlt
§	***pachypoda*** ♀H4	COld EBee ECGP ECha EPfP GCal GGar GKev GKir GPoy IGor MCot NBid NLar SMad SPoG WCru
	- f. ***rubrocarpa***	GCal
§	***podocarpa***	SPlb SRms WCru
	racemosa ♀H4	CArn CMac COld CRow EBee ELan EPfP GCal GPoy LRHS MHer MLLN MRav NBid NGdn NSti SPer SWvt WFar WMnd
	- 'Washfield' **new**	WCot
§	***rubra*** ♀H4	CHid CMHG EBee ECha ELan GCal GGar GKir MCot MMHG MRav NBid SMad SPoG WCru WFar WPGP
	- B&SWJ 9555	WCru
	- ***alba***	see *A. pachypoda*, *A. rubra* f. *neglecta*
§	- f. ***neglecta***	GAbr GCal GGar GQue WCot WCru
	simplex	CBot EBee ECha GCra GKir LRHS NEgg NPri SWat
	- B&SWJ 8664	WCru
§	- Atropurpurea Group	Widely available
	- - 'Bernard Mitchell'	CFir
	- - 'Black Negligee'	CLAP CWGN EBee EBrs ECtt LLHF LRHS LSou MTis SBfd SPad SPoG WCot WWEG
	- - 'Brunette' ♀H4	Widely available
	- - 'Hillside Black Beauty'	CCVN CLAP EBee ECtt GMaP IPot MNrw NBir NCob NPnk WBor WCAu WCot
	- - 'James Compton'	Widely available
	- - 'Mountain Wave'	CLAP EBee ECtt EWll IPot WFar
	- 'Pink Spike'	Widely available
§	- 'Prichard's Giant'	CLAP EBee EBrs ECha GBin GKir LRHS MRav MSpe NDov WFar
	- ***ramosa***	see *A. simplex* 'Prichard's Giant'
	- 'Silver Axe'	GCal LRHS NBre
	- variegated (v)	CDes WCot
	spicata	COld EBee EWTr GBin GCra GKir GPoy NLar WCot WCru
	- from England	GCal WCru
	taiwanensis	CLAP
	- B&SWJ 343	CLAP
	- B&SWJ 3413	WCru
	- RWJ 9996	WCru
	yesoensis B&SWJ 6355	WCru
	yunnanensis	EBee GCal

Actinella see *Tetraneuris*

Actinidia (*Actinidiaceae*)

	BWJ 8161 from China	WCru
	arguta (f/F)	CAgr NLar WPGP
	- B&SWJ 569	WCru
	- 74-32 (m)	CAgr
	- 'Ananasnaya' (f/F)	CAgr
	- var. ***cordifolia*** (f/F)	CAgr
	- 'Geneva 2' (f/F)	CAgr

- 'Issai' (s-p/F) CAgr CBcs CCCN CDul EPfP ERea LBuc LSRN MGos NLar
- 'Ken's Red' (F) CAgr
- 'Kiwai Vert' (f/F) CAgr
- LL#1 (m) CAgr
- LL#2 (f/F) CAgr
- LL#3 (m) CAgr
- 'Meader' (m) CAgr
- 'MSU' (F) CAgr
- 'Shoko' (F) WCru
- 'Unchae' (m) WCru
- 'Weiki' MGos

chinensis misapplied see *A. deliciosa*
chinensis ambig. CDoy
§ ***deliciosa*** EBee ERom EUJe MGos SBfd WFar WSHC
- 'Atlas' (m) CAgr ERea IArd NLar WBVN
* - 'Boskoop' ELan EUJe MCoo MGos MWat
- 'Buitenpost' new IArd
- 'Hayward' (f/F) CAgr CBcs CCCN CDoC CHEx CMac EBee EPfP ERea LHop LRHS LSRN MCoo MREP NLar NPal SDea SPer SWvt WBVN WFar
- hermaphrodite (F) SBfd
- 'Jenny' (s-p/F) CAgr CMac CSut CTri ERea LAst LBuc LRHS MAsh MBri MGos SBfd SDea SLim SPoG SVic
- 'Solo' CCCN CDoC CMac CSBt CWit EPfP LBuc LRHS LSRN MCoo NLar SBfd SEND SPer SPoG SWvt WPGP
- 'Tomuri' (m) CBcs CCCN CDoC CHEx CMac EBee EPfP ERea LRHS LSRN MCoo NLar NPal SPer SWvt

hypoleuca B&SWJ 5942 WCru
kolomikta ♀H4 Widely available
- (m) MBlu NPla
- B&SWJ 4243 WCru
- 'Red Beauty' (F) CAgr
- 'Tomoko' (f/F) WCru
- 'Yazuaki' (m) WCru

latifolia B&SWJ 3563 WCru
petelotii HWJ 628 WCru
pilosula CBcs CCCN CPLG CSPN CWGN EBee EPfP EWTr GCal GGal GKir LEdu LHop LRHS LSRN LTen MBri MGos SBfd SCoo SPoG WCru WPGP WSHC
polygama (F) GCal IDee
- B&SWJ 5444 WCru
- B&SWJ 8525 from Korea WCru
- B&SWJ 8923 from Japan WCru

rufa B&SWJ 3525 WCru
aff. ***strigosa*** HWJK 2367 WCru
tetramera B&SWJ 3564 WCru

Adansonia (*Bombacaceae*)

grandidieri new SPlb
gregorii SPlb

Adelocaryum see *Lindelofia*

Adenanthos (*Proteaceae*)

sericeus new EUJe

Adenia (*Passifloraceae*)

glauca LToo

Adenium (*Apocynaceae*)

obesum ♀H1 LToo
- subsp. ***boehmianum*** LToo
- subsp. ***oleifolium*** new LToo
- 'Scooby' LRHS
- subsp. ***swazicum*** new LToo

Adenocarpus (*Papilionaceae*)

complicatus SEND
decorticans SPlb

Adenophora (*Campanulaceae*)

BWJ 7696 from China WCru
'Afterglow' see *Campanula rapunculoides* 'Afterglow'
asiatica see *Hanabusaya asiatica*
aurita CFir EWTr WCot
bulleyana CFir EBee ELan GCra GJos IKil NBid SDnm SGSe SPav SPlb WCot WFar
capillaris subsp. ***leptosepala*** BWJ 7986 WCru
coelestis GKev NBid NBre
- B&SWJ 7998 WCru

confusa LHop MDKP NBre SAga WFar WHer WSHC
* ***cymerae*** LEdu MAvo
divaricata WFoF
forrestii NBre WFar
grandiflora B&SWJ 8555 WCru
jasionifolia EBee GKev
- BWJ 7946 WCru

khasiana LLHF MDKP NLar WPrP
koreana NBre
lamarkii B&SWJ 8738 WCru
latifolia misapplied see *A. pereskiifolia*
latifolia ambig. white-flowered MMuc
latifolia Fischer WFar
liliifolia CMoH EBee ECtt ELan EPfP GCal GGar GJos MMuc NPer SMrm WFar WHal WPtf
morrisonensis RWJ 10008 WCru
§ ***nikoensis*** GAuc NBid
§ - var. ***stenophylla*** NBre
nipponica see *A. nikoensis* var. *stenophylla*
§ ***pereskiifolia*** EWes NBre SGSe SHar SPlb WCot
polyantha EHrv NLar SRms WFar
polymorpha see *A. nikoensis*
potaninii CFir EBee EHrv ELan MMuc SEND SPav WFar WHal WWEG
- pale-flowered EHrv MMuc WHal

remotiflora B&SWJ 8562 WCru
- B&SWJ 11016 WCru

stricta subsp. ***sessilifolia*** NBre
takedae var. ***howozana*** MLHP
taquetii EBee
tashiroi CPrp ECtt EPfP
triphylla NBir SGSe SPav
- B&SWJ 8608 WCru
- B&SWJ 10916 WCru
- var. ***hakusanensis*** LLHF NBre
- var. ***japonica*** B&SWJ 8835 WCru

uehatae GEdr
- B&SWJ 126 WCru

Adiantum ✿ (*Adiantaceae*)

aethiopicum CHVG WRic
§ ***aleuticum*** ♀H4 CLAP EBee ELan NBid NBro NLar WAbe WFib WPGP WRic
- 'Imbricatum' CBty CElw CLAP EBee EDif ELon GBin IKil LRHS MAsh MGos NLar NMyG SBfd SDix SRms WCot WFar WFib WRic

§	- 'Japonicum'	CDes CLAP CMil EBee ELan NBir SRms WAbe WFar WHal WPGP
	- 'Laciniatum'	SRms
	- 'Miss Sharples'	CDTJ CLAP CMil EBee ELan LRHS MAsh MGos NLar SRms WFar WRic
§	- 'Subpumilum' 🏆^{H4}	CLAP MRav NBid NMyG SRms WAbe WFib WRic
	bonatianum	CPLG
	capillus-veneris	ISha SChr SGSe WCot WFib WRic
	- 'Mairisii'	see *A.* × *mairisii*
	chilense	EFtx GBin WCot WRic
	cuneatum	see *A. raddianum*
	fulvum	WRic
	hispidulum	CBty CCCN CMil EBee ISha LRHS SRms WRic
	- 'Bronze Venus'	CCCN CDes EBee LRHS
§	× ***mairisii*** 🏆^{H3}	EFtx ISha WRic
	pedatum misapplied	see *A. aleuticum*
	pedatum ambig.	CBty EBee GKir ISha
	pedatum L. 🏆^{H4}	CBcs CHEx CLAP ECha EFer ELan EPfP GEdr GMaP LAst LPBA LRHS MAsh MBri MMoz NMoo NVic SApp SPer SSpi SWat WFar WPGP
	- Asiatic form	see *A. aleuticum* 'Japonicum'
	- 'Japonicum'	see *A. aleuticum* 'Japonicum'
	- 'Roseum'	see *A. aleuticum* 'Japonicum'
	- var. ***subpumilum***	see *A. aleuticum* 'Subpumilum'
	pubescens	WRic
§	***raddianum*** 🏆^{H2}	EFtx
	- 'Fragrans'	see *A. raddianum* 'Fragrantissimum'
§	- 'Fragrantissimum'	EShb WRic
	- 'Micropinnulum'	EFtx WRic
	- 'Monocolor'	WRic
	sulphureum new	WRic
	venustum 🏆^{H4}	CGHE CHEx CLAP EFer EFtx EPot EWTr MCot MWat SChr SDix SKHP SRms SSpi SWat WAbe WCom WCot WEas WFar WFib WHal WIvy WPGP WRic

Adina (*Rubiaceae*)

rubella	NLar

Adlumia (*Papaveraceae*)

fungosa	CSpe LBMP

Adonis (*Ranunculaceae*)

	amurensis misapplied	see *A.* 'Fukujukai', *A. multiflora*
	- 'Pleniflora'	see *A. multiflora* 'Sandanzaki'
	amurensis ambig.	CMea EBee EPot GEdr LAma LEdu LLHF SCnR WCon WCru WFar
	annua	MNHC
	brevistyla	GKir
§	'Fukujukai'	ECha GEdr WFar WWst
§	***multiflora***	CAby SRot
§	- 'Sandanzaki' (d)	EBee EPot EWes GEdr MMHG SMrm WCot
	vernalis	GKir GPoy NLar

Adoxa (*Adoxaceae*)

moschatellina	CRWN EBWF NMen NRya WAbe WHer WSFF WShi

Adromischus (*Crassulaceae*)

cooperi	STre WEas

Aechmea (*Bromeliaceae*)

sp.	XBlo
caudata var. ***variegata***	CHEx
fasciata 🏆^{H1}	MBri XBlo
ramosa	XBlo
victoriana	XBlo

Aegle (*Rutaceae*)

sepiaria	see *Poncirus trifoliata*

Aegopodium (*Apiaceae*)

podagraria	CHid
'Dangerous' (v)	
- gold-margined (v)	EBee EPPr
- 'Variegatum' (v)	CDoC COIW CRow CWit ECha ECrN EHoe EHrv EPPr EPla GMaP LHop LRHS MLLN MMuc MRav MSCN NBid NSti SEND SPer SPoG WCFE WCot WHil WMoo WWEG

Aeonium (*Crassulaceae*)

	sp.	CArn
	arboreum 🏆^{H1}	CAbb CDTJ CHEx CTsd ERea EShb GCal LPio NPal SBfd SEND SMrm
	- 'Albovariegatum' (v)	LPio MSCN
	- 'Atropurpureum' 🏆^{H1}	CAbb CHEx COIW EAmu EPfP ERea EShb IDee MAsh MRav NEgg NPer SBfd SEND SPer SPoG
	- green-leaved	SEND
I	- 'Magnificum'	EPfP ETod GBin SAPC SArc
	- 'Variegatum' (v)	CBow NPer
	balsamiferum	CCCN CDTJ CHEx COIW EPfP IDee SBfd SChr WCom
	'Black Cap'	CCCN
	'Blush'	MRav
	'Blushing Beauty'	CAbb SBst SPoG
	canariense	CCCN CDTJ CHEx ETod LPio
	castello-paivae	EShb
	ciliatum	SPlb
	'Cristata Sunburst'	WCot
	cuneatum	SEND
	decorum	SEND
*	- 'Variegatum' (v)	CBow LPio WCot
	'Dinner Plate'	CHEx CTsd
	'Dinner Plate' × ***haworthii***	CHEx
	gomerense	STre
	goochiae	CBow
	haworthii 🏆^{H1}	CHEx EOHP LPio MSCN SBHP SEND
	- 'Variegatum' (v)	EOHP EShb LPio SChr
	holochrysum Webb & Berth.	CAbb
	lindleyi	SChr
	nobile	CBrP IDee
	percarneum	EShb SChr
	simsii variegated (v)	EShb
	tabuliforme 🏆^{H1}	CCCN CDTJ CSpe ERea WCot
	- 'Cristatum'	WCot
	urbicum	CHEx
	'Zwartkop' 🏆^{H1}	Widely available

Aeschynanthus (*Gesneriaceae*)

	'Big Apple'	WDib
	Black Pagoda Group	WDib
	buxifolius KR 7798 new	WAbe
	'Fire Wheel'	WDib
	hildebrandii	WDib
	'Hot Flash'	WDib
	longicalyx	WDib
§	***longicaulis*** 🏆^{H1}	WDib
	marmoratus	see *A. longicaulis*
	radicans 🏆^{H1}	WDib
	'Scooby Doo'	WDib
	speciosus 🏆^{H1}	WDib

Aesculus ✿ (*Hippocastanaceae*)

arguta	see *A. glabra* var. *arguta*

× ***arnoldiana***	CDul CMCN
- 'Autumn Splendor'	EPfP
assamica WWJ 11886	WCru
§ × ***bushii***	CDul CMCN MGos NLar
californica	CDul CMCN CMac EPfP SKHP WPGP
× ***carnea***	CDul CTri ELan IFFs
- 'Aureomarginata' (v)	LLHF SMad WHar WPat
- 'Briotii' ♀^{H4}	Widely available
- 'Marginata' (v)	MBlu
- 'Plantierensis'	CDul ECrN MBlu
* - 'Variegata' (v)	CDul CMCN MGos
chinensis	CMCN MBri
'Dallimorei' (graft-chimaera)	WPat
flava ♀^{H4}	CCVT CDul CMCN CTho EBee ECrN EPfP EWTr GKir LMaj MBri MMuc NWea SEND SLim SPer SSpi WFar
- f. ***vestita***	CDul MBlu
georgiana	see *A. sylvatica*
glabra	CDul CMCN CTho EGFP GKir
- 'April Fire' **new**	MBlu
§ - var. ***arguta***	CMCN GKir
- 'Autumn Blaze'	EPfP MBlu SMad
- 'October Red'	EPfP MBlu MBri
glaucescens	see *A.* × *neglecta*
hippocastanum ♀^{H4}	Widely available
- 'Aureomarginata' (v)	CMac
§ - 'Baumannii' (d) ♀^{H4}	CDoC CDul CLnd CMCN EBee ECrN ELan EPfP GKir IFFs LMaj MGos MSwo NWea SPer WDin WFar
- 'Digitata'	CDul CMCN WPat
- 'Flore Pleno'	see *A. hippocastanum* 'Baumannii'
- 'Hampton Court Gold'	CBcs CMCN CMac
- f. ***laciniata***	CDul CMCN IArd IFFs MAsh MBlu NLar SMad WPat
- 'Monstrosa'	MBri SMad
- 'Wisselink'	CDul CMCN ECrN MBlu SMad
indica	CDul CHEx CLnd CMCN CTho EBee ECrN ELan EPfP GKir IArd IDee IFFs LMaj SEND SPer SSpi WDin
- 'Sydney Pearce' ♀^{H4}	CDul CEnd CMCN EBee EPfP EWTr GKir MBlu MBri MGos NLar SSpi WClo WDin WPat
× ***marylandica***	CDul
× ***mississippiensis***	see *A.* × *bushii*
× ***mutabilis*** 'Harbisonii'	NLar WPat
- 'Induta'	CDul CLnd CMCN EBee EPfP MBri NLar NSti SKHP SMad SSpi WFar
§ - 'Penduliflora'	CDul CEnd MBlu
§ × ***neglecta***	CLnd CMCN
- 'Autumn Fire'	MBlu
- 'Erythroblastos' ♀^{H4}	CBcs CDul CEnd CMCN CPMA EBee EPfP GKir LRHS MAsh MBlu MBri MRav NLar SCoo SMad SPoG SSpi SSta WCot WDin WPat
parviflora ♀^{H4}	CBcs CDul CLnd CMCN CMac CTri EBee ELan EPfP EWTr GKir IDee IFFs LMaj MBlu MGos MMuc MPkF MRav NBea NEgg SEND SLPl SLim SMad SPer SSpi SWvt WDin WFar
§ ***pavia*** ♀^{H4}	CBcs CDul CLnd CMCN CTho EPfP SSpi WDin
- 'Atrosanguinea'	CEnd CLnd CMCN EPfP MBlu MBri SDix SKHP SMad
I - 'Biltmore Buckeye'	MPkF
- var. ***discolor*** 'Koehnei'	CDul CMCN EBee EPfP LRHS MBlu MBri NLar SPoG
- 'Penduliflora'	see *A.* × *mutabilis* 'Penduliflora'
- 'Purple Spring'	MBlu
- 'Rosea Nana'	CMCN LLHF WPat
splendens	see *A. pavia*
§ ***sylvatica***	CMCN
turbinata	CDul GKir SSpi
wilsonii	CDul CPLG CTho

Aethionema (*Brassicaceae*)

armenum	EDAr
- 'Mavis Holmes' **new**	EDAr
capitatum	EDAr
§ ***grandiflorum*** ♀^{H4}	EDAr LRHS NBro SRms WFar
- Pulchellum Group ♀^{H4}	CSpe
iberideum	MDKP MWat SRms
* ***kotschyi*** hort.	ECho WAbe
membranaceum	CPBP ECho EDAr WFar
oppositifolium	MWat
pulchellum	see *A. grandiflorum*
schistosum	EDAr LLHF
spicatum	WFar
'Warley Rose' ♀^{H4}	ECho ELan GKev GKir GMaP LHop LRHS MWat MWea NBir NMen SBch SRms WFar
'Warley Ruber'	CMea CPBP NBir NMen WAbe WFar

Aextoxicon (*Aextoxicaceae*)

punctatum	EBee

Afrocarpus (*Podocarpaceae*)

falcatus	CTrC ECou

Agapanthus ✿ (*Alliaceae*)

sp.	XPde
from Johannesburg	ECha
'Aberdeen'	CPne XPde
'Adonis'	IBlr
'African Moon'	CPen CPne CPrp MAvo
africanus misapplied	CElw COlW CWib EBee ECho EHrv ELan EPfP EUJe GAbr LEdu MNHC SAPC SArc SPav SPer SRot SSwd SWat WBor WBrE WFar WPer WWEG
- 'Albus' misapplied	CBcs CDoC EBee ECho ELan EPfP IFoB ITim LAst LSRN LTen MGos SEND SPav SPer WFar WGwG WHil WPer WWEG
'Albatross'	CPne ECha GCra
'Albus' ambig.	CPLG GKev GMaP LRHS MGos MHer MWat SAga SHom
'Amsterdam'	CPen EBee NHoy XPde
'Angela'	CBgR CPen CPne CYeo ELon IBal NHoy XPde
'Anthea'	XPde
'Aphrodite'	IBlr
'Apple Court'	XPde
'Aquamarine'	CAvo CFFs NHoy SBch
'Arctic Star'	CKno CPLG CPar CPen CPne CPou CTca EBee IBal LRHS LSou NHoy STes XPde
Ardernei hybrid	CAby CDes CPrp EBee ECha ECtt EWes GAbr GCal GQue IBal IBlr LPio LSou MAvo NEgg SAga SMrm WClo WCot WGwG WPGP XPde
§ 'Argenteus Vittatus' (v) ♀^{H1}	CPen CPne CPrp ELan EPfP EUJe NHoy WPGP
'Atlas'	IBlr
'Aureovittatus' (v)	CYeo IBal NHoy
'Baby Blue'	see *A.* 'Blue Baby' Rom.
Back in Black = 'B in B'^{PBR}	CPne CSpe CWCL CWGN CYeo ELan EPfP EWTr EWes IPot LPio LRHS MAsh MBNS NBPC NBid NCob NHoy
'Ballyrogan'	IBlr

	'Balmoral'	CPne
	'Bangor Blue'	IBal IBlr
	'Barnsley'	NHoy
	'Basutoland'	EBla EBrs LRHS
	'Beatrice'	CPne XPde
	'Beeches Dwarf'	CPne ELan NHoy
	'Beloved'	NHoy
	'Ben Hope'	CPrp IBal IBlr NHoy SDnm WCot XPde
	'Beth Chatto'	see *A. campanulatus* 'Albovittatus'
	'Bethlehem Star'	CBgR CPne
	'Bianco'	XPde
	'Bicton Bell'	CPne IBal IBlr
*	'Bicton Hybrid'	CPrp
	'Big Blue'	EBee EPfP GKev LSRN LSou SBfd SEND SRkn
	Birr hybrids **new**	WCot
	'Black Buddhist'	CPMA CPrp EBee ECtt EWTr EWll MCot MGos MSCN NGdn NHoy SPer
	'Black Magic'	CPne
	'Black Pantha' PBR	Widely available
§	'Blue Baby' Rom.	CCCN CChe CPen CPrp CYeo EBee ELan ELon EPfP IBlr LRHS NHoy SMrm WCom WFar XPde
	'Blue Bird'	LRHS XPde
	'Blue Boy'	XPde
	'Blue Brush'	CMac CPrp CSBt EBee IBal LRHS LSou NHoy SCoo SEND SPoG
	'Blue Cascade'	IBlr
	'Blue Companion'	CPne CPrp IBal IBlr NHoy WMnd
	'Blue Crane'	EBla
	'Blue Diamond' ambig.	CMac EHrv NHoy
	'Blue Dot'	CPrp EAEE EBee LBMP LRHS
	'Blue Dragon'	NHoy
	'Blue Formality'	IBal IBlr
	'Blue Fortune'	WWEG
	'Blue Giant'	CBcs CCVN CKno CPrp EBee EBrs EPfP IBal IBlr LRHS MBri MGos MNFA MNHC NHoy SAga SWat WCFE WCot WFar WPGP WSpi WWEG
	'Blue Globe'	CHid CMMP EBee GMaP LAst MSCN WWEG
	'Blue Gown'	CPne CSam IBal
	'Blue Haze'	XPde
	'Blue Heaven' PBR	CPne EBee EWTr NHoy NPnk WCot
	'Blue Ice'	CAvo CPne
	'Blue Imp'	EBee GBin IBlr NHol SApp
	'Blue Jay' **new**	CPen
	'Blue Lakes'	XPde
	'Blue Méoni'	XPde
	'Blue Moon'	CAbP CPen CSev CYeo EBee ECha IBal IBlr LRHS LSou MCot NHoy SAga SMrm WCot
	'Blue Nile'	CPen CPne XPde
	'Blue Peter' **new**	CSpr
	'Blue Prince'	CPen CPrp EBee LBuc LRHS NHoy
	'Blue Ribbon'	XPde
	'Blue Skies' ambig.	NCGa NHoy XPde
I	'Blue Skies' Dunlop	IBlr
	'Blue Sparkler' **new**	CPne
	'Blue Spear'	CPen
	'Blue Triumphator'	CTca EBee EPfP EWTr EWll GMaP IBlr LRHS MHer NHoy NPla SMrm SPhx WWEG XPde
	'Blue Umbrella'	EBee NHoy
	'Blue Velvet'	CPne XPde
	Bluestorm = 'Atiblu' PBR	CPrp LBuc NHoy
	'Bluety' PBR	CPen NHoy
	'Bressingham Blue'	CPne CPrp CTri CWit EBrs ECtt EWes GCal GKir IBal IBlr IFoB LRHS MRav NHoy NVic SMHy SWat WCot XPde
	'Bressingham Bounty'	EBrs LRHS XPde
	'Bressingham White'	CPne EBee EBrs ECGP ECtt EHrv LEdu MBri MRav NHoy SWat XPde
	'Bristol'	CPne XPde
	'Brody' **new**	CPne
	'Buckingham Palace'	CDes CPrp EBee EWes GAbr IBal IBlr NHoy WCot WPGP XPde
	'Cally Blue'	GAbr GCal IBal NHoy
	'Cally Longstem'	GCal
	'Cally Pale Blue'	GCal IBal
	'Cambridge'	CPne XPde
	campanulatus	CMac CPLG CPMA CPrp CWCL EBee EBla ECho ELan EPfP IBal IBlr IGor ITim LPio LRHS MCot MMuc MRav NCob NEgg NHoy NSti SEND SWat WCot WFar WPGP
	- var. ***albidus***	CDes CPMA CWCL CYeo EBee EBrs ECha ECho ELan EPfP EShb GKev IBlr LHop LPio LRHS MCot MMuc NBid NGdn NHol NHoy NSti NVic SEND SPer WFar WHoo WPGP XPde
§	- 'Albovittatus'	CPrp CSam ECho EWTr IBal LPio MCot NHoy
	- 'Beth Chatto' (v)	CPrp EBla IBal
	- bright blue-flowered	CWCL GCal
	- 'Buckland'	IBlr
	- 'Cobalt Blue'	CPrp EBee LRHS NGdn NHoy
	- dark blue-flowered	XPde
	- 'Oxford Blue'	CPen CPrp EBrs IBal IBlr LRHS NHoy WPGP XPde
	- subsp. ***patens*** ♀H3	CPrp EBla EPfP GKev IBal LPio SWat WPGP
	- - deep blue-flowered	CFir CPrp EBrs IBlr LRHS NHoy XPde
	- 'Profusion'	CPne EBrs ECha IBal IBlr LRHS NHoy WFar XPde
	- variegated (v)	EBla ECha NPer
	- 'Wedgwood Blue'	CPrp EBee EBrs IBal IBlr LRHS NHoy XPde
	- 'Wendy'	CPne CPrp EBrs IBal IBlr LRHS NHoy XPde
	- 'White Hope'	IBal IBlr
	'Carefree'	CPrp IBal
	'Castle of Mey'	CPen CPne CPrp GAbr IBal IBlr LPla NHoy SMrm WPGP XPde
	'Catharina'	CPne XPde
§	***caulescens*** ♀H1	EBrs IBal IBlr IGor SMHy WCot WPGP XPde
	- subsp. ***angustifolius***	EBee IBlr SPer WCot WPGP
	- subsp. ***caulescens***	CPne IBlr SWat
	- 'Nigel Marshall'	GCal
	'Cedric Morris'	IBlr LPio NHoy SMHy XPde
	'Celebration' **new**	CPne
	'Chandra'	IBlr
	'Charlotte' PBR	CMac EBee LRHS NHoy SPoG XPde
	'Cherry Holley'	CPne ELon XPde
	'Chika's Blue' **new**	MAvo
	'Clarence House'	XPde
	coddii	CPLG EWes IBlr WCot WHil XPde
	'Colin Edward' **new**	NHoy
	'Columba'	CPen CPne CTca CYeo EBee ELon IBal LAma NBid NHoy XPde
	comptonii	see *A. praecox* subsp. *minimus*
	'Congratulations'	NHoy
	'Cool Blue'	CPne XPde
	'Corina'	EBee
	'Cornish Sky'	CPne

	'Crystal Drop'	CBgR CPne CPou SWat
	'Dainty Lady'	NHoy
	Danube	see *A.* 'Donau'
	'Dark Star'	WFar
	'Dartmoor'	CPne
	'Davos'	IPot
	'Dawn Star'	CPne XPde
	'Debbie'	XPde
	'Delft'	CPrp IBal IBlr
	Dell Garden hybrids	LRHS
	'Density'	IBlr
	'Devon Dawn'	CPne
	'Diana'	XPde
	'Dnjepr'	XPde
	'Dokter Brouwer'	CCVN CPen CPne CYeo EBee IBal IKil LRHS LSRN MCot MDKP NBid NHoy WGwG XPde
§	'Donau'	CDoC CPen CYeo EBee EShb IBal LAst LSou NBid NBir NHoy SMrm SWat WFar WHil XPde
	'Dorothy Kate'	CPne
	'Double Diamond'	CPen CPne CWGN IBal LSRN LSou NBid NHoy SPoG SUsu WClo
	'Dream'	NHoy
	'Dublin'	CPne
	'Duivenbrugge Blue'	CPne XPde
	'Duivenbrugge White'	CPne XPde
	dyeri	see *A. inapertus* subsp. *intermedius*
	'Ed Carman' (v)	EBee LSou SPoG WCot
	'Eggesford Sky' **new**	CPne
	'Elisabeth'	CPne XPde
	'Elizabeth Salisbury' **new**	CPne
	'Enigma'	CAbb CCCN CPar CPen CPne CWGN CYeo EBee ECha EKen EShb GBin IBal IPot LRHS LSRN LSou MWea NHoy SBfd SRkn SUsu SWat
	'Essence of Summer'	WCot
	'Ethel's Joy'	CPen
	'Eve'	IBlr XPde
	'Evening Star'	CPne ECha XPde
	'Exmoor'	CPne
	'Farncombe'	NCot
	'Fast Track'	WCot
	'Findlay's Blue'	SMHy WHil WPGP
	'Finnline' (v)	CPne CPrp
	'Flanders Giant'	XPde
	'Flore Pleno' (d)	Widely available
	'Forget-me-not'	NHoy
	'Gayle's Lilac'	CBcs CElw CPne CPrp CSam CWGN CYeo EBee ECtt ELan ELon IBal LPio LRHS LSRN LSou MRav NBPC NCob NHoy NSti SApp SBfd SDnm SEND SMrm WCAu WCot WWEG
	'Gem'	CPne MAvo
	'Getty White'	GBin
I	'Giganteus Albus'	CPne XPde
	'Glacier Stream'	CPen EBee ECtt EHrv IKil NHoy WSpi
	'Glen Avon'	CAbb CFir CPne CPrp CYeo EBee IBal LRHS LSRN NBPC NHoy NLar SApp SCoo SEND WSpi XPde
	'Golden Rule' (v)	CBow CPne CPrp EBee EHoe IBal IBlr WPGP XPde
	'Goliath'	CPne
	'Grey Ruler'	LSou WCot
	'Hanneke' **new**	CPen
	'Happy Birthday'	NHoy
	'Harvest Blue'	XPde
§	Headbourne hybrids	Widely available
	Headbourne hybrids dark blue-flowered	EBrs LRHS
	Headbourne hybrids dwarf	LRHS
	'Heather Gail' **new**	NHoy
	'Heavenly Blue'	CCCN CPne
	'Helen'	IBlr
	'Holbeach'	CPen CPne XPde
	'Holbrook'	CSam XPde
	'Holly Ann'	NHoy
	'Hoyland'	NHoy
	'Hyacinth'	NHoy
	'Hydon Mist'	XPde
	'Ice Blue Star'	XPde
	'Ice Lolly'	CPen EBee EWTr IKil XPde
	inapertus	CAvo CPLG CPrp CSpe EWes GGal IGor LPio MHer SAga SMHy SMrm SWat WCot WPGP XPde
	- dwarf	IBlr
	- subsp. ***hollandii***	CPne CPom EBee GCal IBal IBlr MAvo NHoy SWat WCot XPde
	- - 'Zealot'	IBlr
	- 'Icicle' **new**	GCal
	- subsp. ***inapertus***	IBlr SWat WCot
I	- - 'Albus'	IBlr LRHS SMHy
	- - 'Cyan'	IBlr
	- - 'White'	CPMA CPne
§	- subsp. ***intermedius***	CBgR CBro CPne CPrp EBee IBal IBlr NHoy SWat
	- - white-flowered	CPen CPou
	- large **new**	IBal
	- 'Midnight Cascade'	CPar CPne NBid NHoy SUsu SWat
I	- 'Nigrescens'	WCot
	- subsp. ***parviflorus***	IBlr
	- subsp. ***pendulus***	CDes CFir CPne EBrs GCal IBlr IPot WPGP
	- - 'Graskop'	CAbb CBgR CCCN CHVG CPne CWGN EBee ELon GBin IBal IBlr LRHS LSou NHoy NSti SGSe SKHP SPoG
	- - 'Violet Dusk'	IBlr
	- 'Sapphire Cascade'	NHoy SWat
	'Inkspots' **new**	EBee IBal SPoG
	'Innocence'	IBlr
	'Intermedius' Leichtlin	IBal XPde
I	'Intermedius' van Tubergen	EBee NBid
	'Isis'	CAvo CFir CPne CPrp CSam CTri EBla EBrs ECha IBal IBlr LRHS NHoy XPde
	'Jack's Blue'	Widely available
	'Jersey Giant'	IBal NHoy XPde
	'Jodie'	CPne MAvo XPde
	'Johanna'	CPne EBee XPde
	'Jolanda'	CPne ELon
	'K. Wiley'	SUsu
	'Kew White'	SDix
	'Kingston Blue'	CYeo EBee ECha EHrv IBal IBlr NBid NHoy WFar WPrP WSHC WWEG XPde
	'Kirsty'	CPne
	'Kobaltglocke' **new**	EBee
	'Kobold'	EBee NHoy WFar
	'Lady Edith'	IBlr
§	'Lady Grey'	IBlr
	'Lady Moore'	IBlr IGor SMHy SMrm XPde
	'Lady Wimborne'	CPne
	'Latent Blue'	CPrp IBlr
	'Lavender Haze'	CPen CPne CPrp EPfP IBal LRHS LSou NHoy SBfd
	'Leicester'	CPne XPde
	'Liam's Lilac'	CPar CPen CPne CPou ELon IBal
	'Lilac Bells'	CPne
	'Lilac Flash'	CPen CPne

'Lilac Time'	CPen CPne IBlr SAga XPde
'Lilliput'	Widely available
'Limoges'	XPde
'Little Beauty'	NHoy
'Little Diamond'	LRHS
'Littlecourt' **new**	CBro
'Loch Hope' ♀H3	CDoC CPMA CPne CPrp CSam EBee EBrs GAbr GGar IGor LAst LRHS LSou MRav NCob NHoy SApp SPer SUsu WCot WHoo WSpi XPde
'Lowland Nursery'	XPde
'Luly'	CPne CPrp IBal LRHS NHoy SWat XPde
'Lydenburg'	CPen IBal IBlr NHoy
'Lyn Valley'	CPne
'Mabel Grey'	see *A.* 'Lady Grey'
'Magnifico'	IBal IBlr
'Malaga'	XPde
'Malvern Hills'	XPde
'Marchants Cobalt Cracker' **new**	SMHy
'Margaret'	NHoy
'Marianne'	XPde
'Mariètte'	CPen CPne EBee XPde
'Marjorie'	CPne SApp XPde
'Martine'	CPne EBee MAvo
'May Snow' (v)	WCot
'Megan's Mauve' **new**	CPne
'Meibont' (v)	CPne IBal WCot XPde
'Mercury'	CPne IBlr
'Metalica'	NHoy
Midknight Blue = 'Monmid'	MWte NHoy
'Midnight'	EWes SAga WSHC
'Midnight Blue' ambig.	CAby CMea EBrs ECha ELan IBal IGor LRHS MGos SMHy SPav WFar
'Midnight Blue' P. Wood	GCal IBlr
§ 'Midnight Star'	Widely available
'Miniature Blue'	SWat
minor **new**	CKno
mixed seedlings	CPne EPfP IBal MGos NHoy SEND WHil XPde
mixed whites	WBVN WCFE
'Montreal'	XPde
'Mood Indigo'	CPne
'Moonshine' **new**	CPen
I 'Mooreanus' misapplied	EBee EPfP IBal IBlr NBid SMrm WPGP XPde
'Morning Star'	CPne
'Mount Stewart'	IBal IBlr
'My Love'	NHoy
'Navy Blue'	see *A.* 'Midnight Star'
'New Love'	EBee
'New Orleans'	XPde
'Newa'	XPde
'Night Sky' **new**	CPne
'Nikki'	CPne
'Norman Hadden'	IBlr
'Northern Light' **new**	CPen
'Northern Star' **new**	CPen CPne ELon LRHS
nutans	see *A. caulescens*
'Nyx'	IBlr
'NZ Blue'	XPde
'NZ White'	XPde
'Oslo'	CPne NHoy XPde
'Oxbridge'	IBlr
Palmer's hybrids	see *A.* Headbourne hybrids
'Paris'	CPen XPde
'Patent Blue'	IBlr
'Patriot'	CYeo LRHS
'Pauline' **new**	NHoy
'Penelope Palmer'	CPrp IBal IBlr
'Penny Slade'	SAga XPde
'Peter Pan' ambig.	Widely available
'Phantom'	CDes CPne CPrp GCal IBal IBlr XPde
'Pinchbeck'	CPne XPde
'Pinky'	XPde
'Pinocchio'	CPen CWib EBee ECho NHol NHoy XPde
'Plas Merdyn Blue'	CPrp IBal IBlr
'Plas Merdyn White'	CFir CPne CPrp IBal IBlr NHoy XPde
'Podge Mill'	CPne IBlr XPde
'Polar Ice'	CFir CPen CYeo EBee ECtt ELon GBin IBal IBlr LRHS SPad WFar XPde
'Polar White'	NHoy
'Porcelain'	IBal IBlr
praecox	CPrp EBrs EShb GAbr IBal IBlr LRHS NHoy
- 'Albiflorus'	CPne CPou IBal LAst LBMP LRHS NEgg NHoy SEND XPde
- 'Floribundus'	SWat
- 'Maximus Albus'	CPou IBal IBlr WBrE
§ - subsp. ***minimus***	CElw CPne CPou IBal IBlr LPio NHoy SWat XPde
- - 'Adelaide'	CPrp EBee
- - blue-flowered	SWat
- - white-flowered	CPne SWat
- 'Neptune'	IBlr
§ - subsp. ***orientalis***	CCCN CPne CSut EHrv GGar IBlr SAga SBfd SWat
- - 'Cape Blue' **new**	CPrp
- subsp. ***praecox***	IBlr IGor
- - azure-flowered	CPrp SWat
- - 'Variegatus'	see *A.* 'Argenteus Vittatus'
- 'Saturn'	IBlr
- Slieve Donard form	IBlr
- 'Uranus'	IBlr
- 'Venus'	IBlr
- 'Vittatus' (v)	CStu NHoy WCot WFar
'Premier'	CPrp EBee EBrs IBal IBlr LRHS NHoy WPGP
'Pride of Bicton'	CPne
'Princess Margaret'	CPne XPde
'Proteus'	XPde
§ 'Purple Cloud'	Widely available
'Purple Star'	CCCN CKno
'Queen Anne'	NHoy SEND
'Queen Elizabeth The Queen Mother'	CPrp XPde
'Quink Drops'	SMHy
'Raveningham Hall'	XPde
'Regal Beauty'	CPar CPne CPrp CSBt CWGN EBee EShb IBal IPot LRHS LSRN LSou MBri NBid NHoy SBfd SRkn
'Remembrance'	NHoy
'Rhone'	IBlr XPde
rich blue-flowered	XPde
'Rosemary'	CPne XPde
'Rosewarne'	CCCN CChe CKno CMac CPrp EBee EPfP GBin IBal IBlr LRHS NHoy SBfd SEND XPde
'Rotterdam'	CPen CPne EBee NHoy XPde
'Royal Blue'	CHar GBin GMaP NHol NHoy SBfd WSpi
'Royal Lodge'	XPde
'Royal Purple'	XPde
'Sally Anne'	CPne
'San Gabriel' (v)	CPne XPde
'Sandringham'	CDes CPne CPrp EBee EWes IBlr WPGP XPde
'Sapphire'	CPrp IBlr XPde
'Sarah' PBR	LSou NCGa NHoy

'Sea Coral'	CCCN CFir CPne CPrp EAEE EBee GAbr GGar LRHS MAvo NHoy NSti SHom
'Sea Foam'	CPen CPne CPrp EBee IBal NLar SBfd WSpi XPde
'Sea Mist'	CCCN CPne EBee IBal WSpi
'Sea Spray'	CCCN CKno CPne EBee GGar IBal LRHS LSRN NHoy XPde
'Selma Bock'	CPen CPne
'Senna' **new**	CWGN EBee IBal LRHS LSou NHoy
'Septemberhemel'	CPen XPde
'Sevilla'	XPde
'Silver Baby'	CPMA CPen CPne CPrp CWGN CYeo ELon LRHS MAvo MNrw NHoy
'Silver Jubilee'	XPde
'Silver Mist'	CBgR CPMA CPne EBee IBlr SWat XPde
Silver Moon = 'Notfred'[PBR] (v)	CBow EBee EHrv ELan EPfP IBal LRHS MGos NCob NHoy SPoG XPde
'Silver Sceptre'	IBlr
'Silver Stream' **new**	NHoy
'Sky'	CAbb CPar CSBt CWGN CYeo EBee GBin IBal IBlr LBuc LRHS LSRN LSou NBid SBfd SHar SKHP SPoG SRkn SWat
'Sky Rocket'	CPne CPrp IBal IBlr
'Sky Star'	IBal XPde
'Slieve Donard'	IBlr WFar
'Sneeuwwitje'	XPde
'Snow Cloud'	CAbb CPMA CPne CSBt EBee ELon IBal LRHS NEgg NHoy SBfd SLon WSpi XPde
'Snow Pixie'	CPne CSpe CWGN EBee IBal LSRN LSou NHoy SPoG WSpi
'Snow Princess'	CPen IBal LRHS MGos
'Snow White' **new**	CSpr
'Snowball'	CDoC COlW CPne CPrp EBee EWTr GAbr GKev LSou NBPC NHoy NPnk SBfd SGSe WClo WSpi WWEG XPde
'Snowdrops'	CCCN CPrp EBee EHrv GAbr IBal LHop LSRN MLLN MNrw NCob SApp SDnm SGSe SKHP SMrm SPav WCFE WFar
'Snowstorm'[PBR]	IPot
'Southern Star'	CPne
'Spokes'	IBlr
'Starburst'	IBlr
'Stéphanie'	XPde
'Stéphanie Charm'	CPen XPde
'Storm Cloud' Reads	see *A.* 'Purple Cloud'
'Storm Cloud' (d)	CFir
'Streamline'	Widely available
'Summer Clouds'	CPne ELan NHoy
'Summer Skies'	CPne IBal NHoy
'Summer Snow'	CPne
'Sunfield'	CKno CPen CPrp EBee GBin IBal LAma LRHS LSRN MCot NHoy NLar NPer SPad XPde
'Super Star'	CPne XPde
I 'Supreme'	IBal IBlr
'Suzan'	XPde
'Sylvia'[PBR]	NHoy
'Sylvine'	CPen CPne XPde
'Tall Boy'	CPrp IBal IBlr
'Tarka'	CPne EBee IBal
'Taw Valley'	CHVG CPne
'Thumbelina'	CPne CSpe EBee IBal LSou NHoy
'Timaru'	Widely available
'Tinkerbell' (v)	Widely available

'Tiny Tim'	EBee XPde
'Titan'	IBlr
'Tom Thumb'	CAvo ECtt IBal LRHS LSou NHoy SRot WGor
'Torbay'	CBgR CPne CPrp CYeo EAEE EBee ECtt EShb IBlr LLWG LRHS MWte NCGa NEgg SUsu WWEG XPde
'Tornado'	EBee NHoy
'Tranquil'	NHoy
Tresco hybrid	CHEx
'Tresco Select'	NHoy
'Triangle'	CPne
'Trudy'	XPde
'Twilight'	IBlr
umbellatus Redouté	see *A. praecox* subsp. *orientalis*
'Underway'	EWes GCal IBal IBlr SMrm XPde
'Vague Bleue'	XPde
'Velvet Night'	CPen
'Violetta' **new**	CPne
'Virginia'	XPde
'Wedding Day' **new**	CPne
'Wembworthy'	CPne
'White Dragon'	NHoy
'White Dwarf'	see *A.* white dwarf hybrids
§ white dwarf hybrids	CPen EBee ECha ECtt EPfP EShb GGar IBal LRHS NBir SMrm WFar
'White Heaven'[PBR]	CKno CPen CPne EBee IBal LRHS LSou MAvo NHoy NPnk SMrm SPoG SUsu SWat WAul WCot WFut WWEG
'White Ice'	CBcs CPne EBee LRHS SApp WSpi
'White Orb'	IBal MBri NHoy
'White Star'	XPde
'White Starlet'	NHoy XPde
'White Superior'	CMMP CSpe GMaP LAst MSCN SPet WCAu WHil XPde
'White Triumphator'	WCot
'White Umbrella'	NHoy
white-flowered	CHEx GGar NCob
'Whitestorm'	NHoy
'Whitney'[PBR]	IBlr
'Wholesome'	IBal
'Windlebrooke'	CCCN CPne ECha XPde
'Windsor Castle'	CPen CPrp IBal IBlr XPde
'Windsor Grey'	Widely available
'Winsome'	IBlr
'Winter Sky'	XPde
'Wolga'	CPMA EWll
'Wolkberg' Kirstenbosch	CPne IBlr
'Woodcote Paleface'	SRms
'Yellow Tips'	CPne XPde
'Yolande'	LAma
'Yves Klein'	CPrp IBlr
'Zachary'	CPen CPne CPou EBee ELon IBal STes
'Zebra'	NHoy
'Zella Thomas'	CPne EBee LHyd XPde
'Zomba'	CPne

Agapetes (*Ericaceae*)

'Ludgvan Cross' 🏆H1-2	CCCN EBee SSpi
serpens 🏆H1	CCCN CHEx CWib EShb SLon
– 'Scarlet Elf'	CCCN EBee WCot
smithiana var. ***major***	GGGa

Agarista (*Ericaceae*)

§ ***populifolia***	WFar

Agastache (*Lamiaceae*)

(Acapulco Series)	LRHS
Acapulco Orange = 'Kiegador'[PBR] 🏆H3-4	

	- Acapulco Purple = 'Kiegapur'PBR (Acapulco Series)	LRHS
	'After Eight'	EBee NDov
	anethiodora	see *A. foeniculum* (Pursh) Kuntze
	anisata	see *A. foeniculum* (Pursh) Kuntze
	aurantiaca	CMea GCal NLar SPhx SUsu WFar
	- 'Apricot Sprite'	EBee EPfP LRHS MHav MHer MNHC NEgg SBch SDnm SPoG SRkn WFar
	- 'Navajo Sunset'	GJos
	'Black Adder'	Widely available
	'Blue Delight'	SBch
	'Blue Fortune' ♀H3-4	CBcs EBee EPfP LPio LRHS MBri MCot MSCN NBro NDov NMoo SMrm SPhx WFar WHlf WWEG
§	***cana***	WFar
	- 'Cinnabar Rose'	NBir WFar
	- 'Purple Pygmy'	CCVN CSpe EBee EPfP EWll LRHS LSou MWea SMrm SPer SRot
	'Firebird'	CBot EAEE EBee EBla ECtt EHrv ELan LHop LRHS MBri MCot MLLN MNrw NBir NDov SMrm SPer SUsu SWat SWvt WAul WFar WWEG
	'Fleur' **new**	EBee
	foeniculum misapplied	see *A. rugosa*
§	***foeniculum*** (Pursh) Kuntze	CArn CChe CMea EBee ECha ELan GMaP GPoy MHer MNHC NGHP SPav SPhx SRms WFar WJek WPer WWEG
	- 'Alabaster'	CBcs EBee NLar SPhx
	- 'Alba'	NBre NGHP SBfd SHDw SPav WFar
	'Glowing Embers'	ECtt EPfP
	'Hazy Days'	LSou
	'Kolibri' **new**	EBee
	'Linda'	NDov
§	***mexicana***	LPio SDnm SPav
	- 'Marchants Pink'	SMrm
	- 'Red Fortune'PBR	CWGN EAEE EBee EBla ECtt EPPr LHop MBri MWea NDov NEgg SMrm
	- 'Rosea'	see *A. cana*
	- 'Sangria'	EBee EDif EWTr LBMP NDov SBch SBfd
	nepetoides	EPPr SDnm SPav
	'Painted Lady'	CSpe ECtt LPio MNrw MWea SMrm
	pallidiflora var. ***neomexicana*** 'Lavender Haze'	EBee EPfP EWTr GAbr
	'Pink Beauty'	ECtt
	'Pink Pop'	EBee EPfP LRHS
	pringlei	WMoo
	'Purple Candle'	EWes
	'Purple Haze'	NDov
	'Raspberry Summer' **new**	NDov
§	***rugosa***	CArn ELau GKev GKir GPoy LHop MNHC NDov NEgg SDnm SGar SPav SPhx SWat WHfH WJek WMoo WPer
	- B&SWJ 4187 from Korea	WCru
	- f. ***albiflora***	NBre NEgg SDnm
	- - 'Liquorice White'	EBee EPfP GQue LRHS NBre NLar SPer WHrl
	- 'Golden Jubilee'PBR	CSam CSpe EAEE EBee EBla ECha ECtt ELan EPfP LBMP LHop LPio MCCP MHer MNHC NHol NLar SBfd SPoG WFar WJek WMoo WWEG
	- Heronswood strain **new**	NDov
	- 'Honey Bee Blue'	NHol
	- 'Korean Zest'	WCru
	- 'Liquorice Blue'	EBla LBMP LRHS MLLN NEgg NGBl NGdn NLar SBfd SDnm SPer SPoG WBox WFar WMoo WPer
	- pink-flowered	CEnt
	rupestris	CSpe EDif NLar SBch SPhx
	- 'Apache Sunset'	CBow MBri SBch SDnm SGar SPlb WHal WWEG
	scrophulariifolia	WBox
	'Serpentine'	EBee EWTr NDov SPhx
	'Spicy'	ECha
	'Summer Love' **new**	EBee
	'Tangerine Dreams' ♀H3	CDoC EBee EBla ECtt EDif LHop LRHS MWea NEgg NGdn SCoo SMrm SPoG SUsu
	'Tutti-frutti'	CWGN ECtt EHrv MBri SDnm SPhx
	urticifolia	CSpe NBre
	- 'Alba'	CSpe NBre WPer
	- 'Liquorice'	EBee WFar

Agathaea see *Felicia*

Agathis (*Araucariaceae*)

	australis	CDoC

Agathosma (*Rutaceae*)

	ovata	CCCN

Agave ✿ (*Agavaceae*)

	acicularis	MAga
	aktites	MAga
	albescens	MAga
	albomarginata	CDTJ MAga
	amaniensis	MAga
	americana ♀H1	Widely available
	- var. ***expansa***	MAga
I	- - 'Mediopicta Pallida' **new**	MAga
	- 'Marginata' (v) ♀H3-4	CBrP CDTJ CHll IBlr MAga MREP SDnm SEND SSwd STre WCot
	- 'Mediopicta' misapplied	see *A. americana* 'Mediopicta Alba'
	- 'Mediopicta' (v) ♀H1	CDTJ CHEx ETod SAPC SArc SBig WEas
§	- 'Mediopicta Alba' (v) ♀H1	CBrP CDTJ EAmu ESwi MAga SChr SEND WCot
	- 'Mediopicta Aurea' (v)	MAga WCot
	- var. ***oaxacensis***	MAga
	- subsp. ***protamericana***	MAga WPGP
	- subsp. ***protamericana*** × ***scabra*** F&M 310	WPGP
	- - NJM 05.057	WPGP
	- 'Striata' (v)	EShb MAga MCot WCot
	- 'Variegata' (v) ♀H1	Widely available
	angustiarum	MAga
	angustifolia	see *A. vivipara* var. *vivipara*
	- var. ***marginata*** hort.	NExo SBig WCot
	applanata	MAga WPGP
	asperrima	CDTJ MREP
§	- subsp. ***maderensis***	MAga SPlb
	- subsp. ***potosiensis***	MAga
§	- subsp. ***zarcensis***	MAga
	attenuata	CAbb CBrP CHEx EAmu ETod EUJe MAga SAPC SArc SBig SPlb WPGP
	attenuata × ***shawii***	MAga
	aurea	MAga
	avellanidens	MAga
	beauleriana	EAmu MAga SBig
	'Blue Glow'	NExo
	boldinghiana	MAga WCot
	bovicornuta	MAga WCot
	bracteosa	CCCN MAga SChr
	brittoniana	MAga
	cantala	MAga
	capensis	MAga

	celsii	see *A. mitis* var. *mitis*
	cerulata subsp. ***nelsonii***	MAga
	chazaroi new	MAga
	chiapensis	MAga
	chrysantha	CCCN CTrC EAmu EBee ETod MAga WCot WGrn WPGP
	- 'Black Canyon'	WCot
	chrysoglossa	MAga WPGP
	cocui from Venezuela new	MAga
	colimana	see *A. ortgiesiana*
	colorata	CCCN CDTJ NExo WCot
	- dwarf	MAga
	congesta	MAga
	'Cornelius' new	WCot
	cundinmarcensis from Columbia	MAga
	cupreata	ETod MAga
	dasylirioides	MAga
	datylio	MAga
	decipiens	MAga
	- dwarf	MAga
	delamateri	MAga
	de-meesteriana	EAmu ETod MAga
	- var. ***marginata***	MAga
	- variegated (v)	EAmu
	deserti	CBrP LRHS WCot
	- var. ***simplex*** variegated (v)	MAga
	difformis	ETod MAga
	- NJM 05.034	WPGP
	durangensis	MAga
	eggersiana	MAga
	ellemeetiana	MAga
	elongata	see *A. vivipara* var. *vivipara*
	ensifera	MAga
	- var. ***marginata***	MAga
	- variegated (v)	MAga
	evadens	MAga
	felgeri	CDTJ MAga
	ferdinandi-regis	see *A. victoriae-reginae*
	ferox	see *A. salmiana* var. *ferox*
	filifera ♀H1	CCCN CDTJ CHEx EAmu ETod MAga SBst SChr SEND SPlb WCot
	- 'Compacta'	MAga
	- subsp. ***microceps*** ISI 1184	MAga
I	- 'Variegata' (v) new	MAga
	flexispina	ETod MAga SPlb
	fortiflora	MAga
	fourcroydes	MAga MREP
	funkiana	MAga
	- blue-leaved	MAga
	garciae-mendozae	CDTJ
	- NJM 05.073	WPGP
	geminiflora	CCCN CDTJ EAmu EShb MAga WCot
	gentryi	CDTJ ETod MAga
	- F&M 213A	WPGP
	ghiesbreghtii	MAga MREP
	gigantea	see *Furcraea foetida*
	gigantensis	MAga
	× ***glomeruliflora***	MAga
	goldmaniana	see *A. shawii* subsp. *goldmaniana*
	× ***gracilipes***	MAga WPGP
	guadalajarana	CDTJ MAga NExo WCot WPGP
	- dwarf	MAga
	guiengola	MAga
	gypsophila	MAga
	havardiana	CTrC EAmu EUJe MAga WCot WPGP
	- dwarf	MAga
	hiemiflora	MAga
	hookeri	MAga
	horrida	ETod EUJe MAga SBig
	- subsp. ***horrida*** new	SPlb
	- 'Perotensis'	EShb
	hurteri	CDTJ MAga
	impressa	WCot
	inaequidens	MAga
	isthmensis	NExo
	'Joe Hoak' (v)	NExo
	karwinskii	MAga
	kerchovei	MAga WCot
	lechuguilla	CDTJ MAga SChr WPGP
	lechuguilla × ***univittata***	MAga
	lechuguilla × ***victoriae-reginae***	MAga
	lophantha	see *A. univittata*
	- var. ***caerulescens***	see *A. univittata*
	lurida Aiton	see *A. vera-cruz*
§	'Macha Mocha' new	WCot
	macroacantha	CDTJ MAga
	maculosa	WCot WPGP
	maculosa × ***obscura*** new	MAga
	mapisaga	MAga
	- NJM 05.036	WPGP
	- var. ***lisa***	MAga
	marmorata	MAga WCot
	maximilliana	MAga SPlb
	- 'Katharinae'	MAga
	missionum from The Virgin Islands	MAga
	mitis var. ***albidior***	MAga WPGP
§	- var. ***mitis***	CDoC MAga SAPC SArc SChr
	- var. ***mitis*** × ***variegata***	WCot
	montana	CDTJ CGHE EAmu ETod MAga SBst SPlb
	- F&M 221	WPGP
	moranii	MAga
	multifilifera	MAga
	nayaritensis	MAga
	neglecta	MAga
	neomexicana	CCCN EAmu ETod IDee MAga WPGP
	- S&B 948	WCot
	× ***nigra*** hort.	EAmu
	nizandensis	CHEx MAga
§	***obscura***	CDTJ ETod MAga
	ocahui	ETod MAga
	- var. ***longifolia***	MAga
	ornithobroma	MAga
	oroensis	MAga
§	***ortgiesiana***	MAga
	ovatifolia	MAga SKHP SPlb
	pachycentra	MAga
	palmeri	CCCN CTrC MAga WPGP
	panamana	see *A. vivipara* var. *vivipara*
	parrasana	EAmu MAga WCot WPGP
	- dwarf	MAga
	parryi	CBcs CDTJ CDoC CSpe EAmu ETod GKev MAga SBst SChr SPlb WGrn WPGP
	- var. ***couesii***	SKHP
	- 'Cream Spike' (v)	WCot
	- var. ***huachucensis***	CDTJ CTsd WCot
	- 'Ohi Kissho ten Nishiki' (v)	WCot
	- subsp. ***parryi***	CBrP CDTJ MAga MREP WPGP
	- - JCA 1.035.000	WPGP
	- var. ***truncata***	EAmu NExo
I	- 'Variegata' (v) new	MAga
	parvidentata	MAga
	- blue-leaved	MAga
	parviflora ♀H1	MAga

	- subsp. ***flexiflora***	MAga
	- - dwarf	MAga
	× ***peacockii***	MAga
	pedunculifera	MAga NExo
	pelona	MAga
	pendula	MAga
	petiolata	MAga
	polianthiflora	MAga
	polyacantha	MAga
	- F&M 120	WPGP
	- var. ***xalapensis***	see *A. obscura*
	potatorum ♀H1	ETod NExo
	- var. ***potatorum***	MAga
	- var. ***verschaffeltii***	EAmu MREP
	- - dwarf	MAga
	promontorii	MAga
	pumila	MAga NExo
	pygmaea	see *A. seemanniana*
	rhodacantha	MAga
	× ***romani*** new	MAga
	salmiana	CDTJ EAmu MAga SBig SPlb
	- F&M 290	WPGP
	- var. ***angustifolia***	MAga
	- subsp. ***crassispina***	MAga SPlb
§	- var. ***ferox***	CDTJ CDoC CTrC EAmu ETod EWll MAga MREP SAPC SArc SBig SChr WCot
	- - 'Marginata' (v)	MAga
	- subsp. ***salmiana***	MAga
	variegated (v)	
	scabra	CCCN CDoC EBee MAga
	- subsp. ***maderensis***	see *A. asperrima* subsp. *maderensis*
	- subsp. ***zarcensis***	see *A. asperrima* subsp. *zarcensis*
	scabra × ***univittata***	MAga
	scaposa	MAga
	schidigera	CBrP ETod MAga WCot
	- 'Shira-ito-no-ohi' (v) new	WCot
	schottii	CDTJ MAga
	- var. ***treleasei***	MAga
§	***seemanniana***	MAga
	'Sharkskin' new	WCot
	shawii	MAga
§	- subsp. ***goldmaniana***	MAga
	shrevei	ETod
	- subsp. ***magna*** new	SPlb
	- subsp. ***matapensis***	MAga
	sileri	WCot
	sisalana	ETod MAga
I	- f. ***armata***	MAga
	- 'Mediopicta'	MAga
	sobria	MAga
	- subsp. ***frailensis***	MAga
	- subsp. ***sobria***	MAga
§	***spicata***	MAga
	striata	EAmu ETod
	- subsp. ***falcata***	MAga WCot
*	- ***rubra***	CDTJ SPlb
	stricta ♀H1	CCCN CDTJ EAmu ETod MAga MREP
	- dwarf	CBrP MAga
	- 'Nana'	CDTJ
	- 'Nana' blue-leaved	MAga
	stringens	MAga
	subsimplex	MAga
	tecta	MAga
	tenuifolia	MAga
	tequilana blue-leaved	MAga
	- green-leaved	MAga
	- variegated (v)	MAga WCot
	thomasiae	MAga
	titanota	ETod MAga
	toumeyana	MAga SChr WCot
	- var. ***bella***	CDTJ MAga
	triangularis	ETod MAga
	underwoodii	MAga
§	***univittata***	CDTJ EUJe MAga WCot
	- 'Quadricolor' (v)	NExo
	utahensis ♀H1	ETod MAga SEND
	- var. ***discreta***	MAga
	- dwarf	MAga
	- var. ***eborispina***	MAga
	- var. ***nevadensis***	MAga
	valenciana new	MAga
	variegata new	WCot
§	***vera-cruz***	MAga
§	***victoriae-reginae*** ♀H1	CBrP CCCN CDTJ EAmu EShb EWll MAga SChr SWal WCot
	- dwarf	MAga
I	- 'Marginata Pallida' new	MAga
	- f. ***ornata***	MAga
	vilmoriniana	MAga
	virginica new	WCot
	vivipara	MAga
	- var. ***letonae***	MAga
	- 'Marginata'	MAga
	- var. ***nivea***	MAga
	- var. ***sargentii***	MAga
§	- var. ***vivipara***	MAga SBig
	vizcainoensis	MAga
	warelliana	MAga
	weberi	EAmu MAga
	wendtii	MAga
	wercklei	MAga
	× ***winteriana***	MAga
	wocomahi	MAga
	xylonacantha	ETod MAga SChr SPlb
	yuccifolia	see *A. spicata*
	zebra	MAga

Ageratina (*Asteraceae*)

§	***altissima***	CHid CMac EBee ELan EPfP GBar LRHS MAvo MCot WFar WHfH WSpi WTin
	- 'Braunlaub'	CPrp EBee ECtt EHrv GKir LPla NBir NBre NGdn SWat WCAu WHrl WMnd WPtf
	- 'Chocolate' ♀H4	Widely available
§	***aromatica***	EBee EDAr MAvo MRav NBre NBro SWat WSFF
§	***glechonophylla***	MAvo WHil
§	***ligustrina*** ♀H3	Widely available
§	***occidentalis*** NNS 94-53	WCot

Ageratum (*Asteraceae*)

	corymbosum	CHll CSpe MWea SUsu

Aglaomorpha (*Polypodiaceae*)

	coronans	WRic

Aglaonema (*Araceae*)

	'Maria Christina'	LRHS

Agonis (*Myrtaceae*)

	flexuosa	CCCN CTrC

Agrimonia (*Rosaceae*)

	eupatoria	CArn COld CRWN EBWF EBee GPoy MHer MNHC NMir SIde SWat WHer WHfH
*	- var. ***alba***	NBre NLar
	grandiflora	EBee NBre
	odorata misapplied	see *A. procera*
	odorata (L.) Mill.	see *A. repens*

pilosa	CArn EBee
§ ***procera***	EBWF EBee
§ ***repens***	GBar WMoo

Agropyron (*Poaceae*)

glaucum	see *Elymus hispidus*
magellanicum	see *Elymus magellanicus*
pubiflorum	see *Elymus magellanicus*

Agrostemma (*Caryophyllaceae*)

coronaria	see *Lychnis coronaria*
githago	CArn MNHC MPet SBch
- 'Ocean Pearl'	CSpe

Agrostis (*Poaceae*)

calamagrostis	see *Stipa calamagrostis*
§ ***canina*** 'Silver Needles' (v)	CBre EWes GKir NBir WFar WWEG
karsensis	see *A. stolonifera*
'Lago Lago'	EBee
§ ***montevidensis***	CBod NWsh SMad
nebulosa	CKno
- 'Fibre Optics'	CSpe MCot
§ ***stolonifera***	EBWF
- 'Julia Ann' (v)	WCot

Aichryson (*Crassulaceae*)

× ***aizoides***	EBak EBee WCot
var. ***domesticum*** 'Variegatum' (v) 🏆H1	
tortuosum	CFee
villosum new	ESem

Ailanthus (*Simaroubaceae*)

§ ***altissima***	CBcs CCVT CDul CHEx CLnd CMac CPLG CTho EBee ECrN EPfP EWTr IFFs LAst MBlu NMun NWea SAPC SDnm SEND SPer SPlb SWvt WBVN WDin
- var. ***tanakae*** B&SWJ 6777	WCru
- - RWJ 9906	WCru
glandulosa	see *A. altissima*

Ainsliaea (*Asteraceae*)

acerifolia B&SWJ 4795	WCru
- B&SWJ 6059	WCru
apiculata B&SWJ 11397	WCru
cordifolia	EBee
aff. ***elegans*** WWJ 11720	WCru
petelotii B&SWJ 11732	WCru
tonkinensis B&SWJ 11819	WCru
uniflora B&SWJ 11336 new	WCru

Ajania (*Asteraceae*)

§ ***pacifica***	CSpr
- 'Silver Edge'	EBee

Ajuga (*Lamiaceae*)

ciliata var. ***villosior***	CFir GBin WHil
genevensis	CArn NMun WOut
- 'Tottenham'	EBee
incisa	EBee GCal
- 'Bikun' (v)	CLAP CMoH EBee EPPr LOck LRHS NCGa SRGP
- 'Blue Enigma'	CLAP EBee EWes NCGa NHol
'Little Court Pink'	see *A. reptans* 'Purple Torch'
lupulina new	GKev
metallica hort.	see *A. pyramidalis*
'Pink Spires'	NCot
§ ***pyramidalis***	CFee GKir WHer
- 'Metallica Crispa'	CBct CBow EBee ECho ECtt EPfP EWes GCrs LBMP MBNS NBPC NHol NLar SPoG SRms SWvt WCot WFar
reptans	CArn CRWN CTri CWan EBWF EBee ECtt EWTr GKev GKir GPoy LPBA LRHS MCot MHer MNHC NMir NSco SGar WFar WJek
- f. ***albiflora*** new	WHfH
- - 'Alba'	CArn EBee ECtt EPfP GGar MRav MSCN NBro SBfd SRms WAlt WFar WMoo
- - 'Sanne'	EBee
- - 'Silver Shadow'	NChi WHil
- 'Arctic Fox' (v)	EBee ECho EHrv MNrw MRav MSCN NRya SWvt WCot WFar WHer
- 'Argentea'	see *A. reptans* 'Variegata'
§ - 'Atropurpurea'	CBar CWan EBee ECha ECho ELan EPfP GAbr GGar LPBA LRHS MAvo MGos MLHP MSCN NHol NVic SPer SPlb SRms SWvt WBrk WFar WJek WWEG
- Black Scallop = 'Binblasca'PBR	Widely available
- 'Braunherz'	CTri EBee ECho ECtt EHoe ELan EPfP EShb GAbr GGar GKir GMaP IFoB LHop LRHS LTen MBri MHer MWat NMir NPri SBfd SPer SWvt WFar WHoo WMoo WTin
- 'Burgundy Glow' (v)	CArn CBcs CWCL EBee ECha ECho EPfP GKir GMaP LAst LBuc LHop LRHS MGos MHer MSCN NPri SBfd SEND SPer SPet SPlb SPoG SRms SWvt WBrE WFar WGwG WMoo WWEG
§ - 'Catlin's Giant' 🏆H4	Widely available
- 'Chocolate Chip'	see *A. reptans* 'Valfredda'
- 'Delight' (v)	EBee ECho
- 'Dixie Chip' new	MLLN
- 'Ebony'	LSRN
- 'Evening Glow'	GGar WMoo
- 'Flisteridge'	CNat WAlt
- 'Golden Beauty'	CBow EBee ECho ECtt LAst WNew
- 'Harlequin' (v)	SWvt WBrE
- 'Jumbo'	see *A. reptans* 'Jungle Beauty'
§ - 'Jungle Beauty'	EAEE EBee EPfP LRHS MRav WFar
- 'Lush Blue'	WAlt
- 'Macrophylla'	see *A. reptans* 'Catlin's Giant'
§ - 'Multicolor' (v)	CBcs EBee ECho ELan GKir LRHS MAvo MCot MRav NHol SPer SPlb SPoG SRms SWvt WFar WMoo WNew WWEG
- 'Palisander'	EAEE EBee LRHS NEgg NLar
- 'Party Colours'	CLAP SBfd
- 'Pink Elf'	CMHG ECho MRav NBro SWat WBrk WFar
- 'Pink Splendour'	NBre NChi
- 'Pink Surprise'	EBee ECtt EHoe GBar MHer MLHP NRya WFar WGwG WMoo WWEG
- 'Purple Brocade'	EHoe
§ - 'Purple Torch'	EBee GKir LRHS NLar WOut WWFP
- 'Purpurea'	see *A. reptans* 'Atropurpurea'
- 'Rainbow'	see *A. reptans* 'Multicolor'
- 'Rosea'	EAEE EBee NPnk WAlt WCAu WFar WMoo
- 'Rowden Amethyst'	CRow
- 'Rowden Royal Purple'	CRow
- 'Silver Carpet'	EBee
- 'Silver Queen'	EBee ECtt
- 'Stölzle' new	EBee
- 'Sugar Plum'	SBfd
- 'Toffee Chip' (v)	CBow
- 'Tricolor'	see *A. reptans* 'Multicolor'

§ - 'Valfredda'	CEnt EBee ECho ECtt EPfP EShb GBar GGar LAst LRHS MAvo NEgg NLar SHar WCot WFar WGwG WMoo WOut WPtf WWEG
- 'Vanilla Chip' (v)	EBee
§ - 'Variegata' (v)	EBee ECho ECtt EPfP NPri SPer SPoG SRms SWat WFar
- 'Wild Purple'	WAlt

Akebia ✿ (*Lardizabalaceae*)

longeracemosa	LEdu NLar WCot
- B&SWJ 3606	WCru
× ***pentaphylla***	EBee ELan EPfP LRHS MAsh NLar SPer
- B&SWJ 2829	WCru
quinata	Widely available
- B&SWJ 4425	WCru
- 'Alba'	CBcs CSPN CWGN NLar WPat
- 'Amethyst'	SKHP
- 'Amethyst Glow'	EPfP LRHS MAsh MBri SPer SPoG
- cream-flowered	EBee EPfP EWTr LRHS LSRN MAsh MRav MWea SBfd SKHP SPer SPoG SSta SWvt WCru WPGP
- variegated (v)	CBcs CBow LLHF SMad WCot WCru WPat
- 'White Chocolate'	ESwi NLar WCru WSHC
trifoliata	CBcs EBee EPfP GKir LRHS SLim SLon WOld
- B&SWJ 2829	WCru
- B&SWJ 5063	WCru

Alangium (*Alangiaceae*)

chinense	EPla WBVN
platanifolium	CAbP CBcs CPLG MBlu MBri NLar WPGP
- var. ***macrophyllum***	EPfP SPoG
- var. ***platanifolium***	NLar

Albizia (*Mimosaceae*)

chinensis	LRHS
distachya	see *Paraserianthes lophantha*
§ ***julibrissin***	CArn CChe CDTJ CTrC CWib EAmu EPfP EUJe LAst LMaj NEgg NMun SMad WDin
- Ombrella = 'Boubri'PBR	EBee ELan EMil LRHS MBri SBfd SCoo SPoG
- f. ***rosea*** ♀H2-3	Widely available
- 'Rouge d'Été'	EBee
I - 'Rouge Selection'	LRHS SLim WPGP
- 'Summer Chocolate'	CAbP CBcs CWGN EPfP LRHS MAsh SCoo SMad SPoG
lophantha	see *Paraserianthes lophantha*

Albuca (*Hyacinthaceae*)

sp.	WCot WHil
JCA 15856	NWCA
from Lesotho	GCal
§ ***abyssinica*** new	EBee
angolensis	CPou
aurea	CTca EBee WCot WHil WPrP
bainesii	see *A. abyssinica*
* ***batliana***	ECho
batteniana	CFir CPrp EBee ECho WCot
canadensis	MAvo WHil
clanwilliamigloria	WHil WPrP
cooperi	ECho
'Dirk Wallace'	CPLG
fastigiata	ECho
flaccida	WHil
fragrans	CDes EBee WHil
glauca new	CPrp EBee ECho
humilis	CDes CPLG CPrp CStu EBee ECho LLHF NMen NRya WAbe WCot WPat WPrP
longifolia new	ECho
maxima	CPou CTca EBee ECho WCot
nelsonii	CAvo CPne CPrp CTca EBee ECho ERea WPGP
rupestris	WCot
setosa	CTca EBee ECho
shawii	CBgR CDes CPne CPou CPrp CStu CTca EAEE EBee EBla ECho LAst LRHS NWCA SAga SGar SPad SPet SPoG WAbe WCot WHil WPGP WPrP
tortuosa	ECho
trichophylla	ECho MHer

× *Alcalthaea* (*Malvaceae*)

suffrutescens 'Parkallee' (d)	CAbP CDes EBee ECtt ELon EPPr GMac LHop LOck LPla LRHS LSou MAvo MCCP MCot MNrw NDov NGdn NLar NSti SMad SPhx SUsu WClo WCot WCra WHil WHoo
- 'Parkfrieden' (d)	CSpe EBee ECtt EPPr MAvo SPhx WCot
- 'Parkrondell' (d)	EBee ECha ECtt EPPr GMac LHop LPla LRHS MAvo MNrw NDov WCot WFut WHil
- white-flowered	IFro

Alcea (*Malvaceae*)

'Apple Blossom' (d)	GMac NCGa
'Arabian Nights'	SPav
'Blackcurrant Whirl'	SPav
ficifolia	MCCP NChi SDnm SPav SWal WCon WFar WMoo
'Happy Lights'	CWib
kurdica	WCot
pallida	GMac NPri
'Peaches 'n' Dreams'	CWib EBee NCGa NGBl
§ ***rosea***	GKir SVic WFar
- Chater's Double Group (d)	CWib ECtt EPfP MBri MWat SPoG SRms WRHF
- - chamois (d)	EPfP GKir
- - chestnut brown-flowered (d)	EPfP
- - pink-flowered (d)	EPfP NPri SPer
- - purple-flowered (d)	EGxp EPfP LAst SPer SPoG
- - red-flowered (d)	EPfP NPri SPoG
- - salmon pink-flowered (d)	EPfP
- - scarlet-flowered (d)	EPfP SPoG
- - violet-flowered (d)	EPfP SPer
- - white-flowered (d)	EPfP MWat NPri SPer SPoG
- - yellow-flowered (d)	EPfP NPri SPer SPoG
- Cottage Mixed new	GKev
- 'Crème de Cassis'	EPfP MWat NBPC NCGa NGBl SPav WHil
- double pink-flowered (d)	MHer
- double red-flowered (d)	MHer
- double rose-flowered (d)	EBee SPer
- double scarlet-flowered (d)	SPer
- double white-flowered (d)	MHer
- double yellow-flowered (d)	EBee MHer
- Fruity Mix new	WRHF
- 'Nigra'	CMea CSpe EBee ECtt EHrv ELan EPfP GAbr LHop LSRN MCot MHer MNHC MWat NGBl NGdn NPri SPer WCAu WFar WWEG
- single-flowered	MWat
- Summer Carnival Group	CWib LAst SRms
- 'Victoria Ann' (v)	CPla
§ ***rugosa***	CMea GAbr MCot NPri SPav WPGP

Alchemilla ✿ (*Rosaceae*)

	abyssinica	EBee WHrl WWEG
	alpina misapplied	see *A. conjuncta*
	alpina ambig.	EOHP MCot
	alpina L.	CEnt CFee CMea EBla ECho EHoe EPfP GKir LEdu LHop LRHS MMuc MRav MWat NChi SBch SPet SRms SWat WFar WKif WMoo WNew WPer
	aroanica	EBee EBla
§	***conjuncta***	Widely available
	ellenbeckii	CDes CMoH EBee ECho EDAr EPfP GBar GGar LAst MTho NChi WFar WMoo WPGP WWEG WWFP
	epipsila	EBee EShb NBPC NLar SPhx WPer WPtf
	erythropoda ♀H4	Widely available
	faeroensis	WMoo WPer WPtf WWEG
	- var. ***pumila***	EBla GEdr NMen WAbe
	filicaulis	EBWF
	- 'Minima'	CNat
§	***fulgens***	EWTr LEdu
	glaucescens	CNat EBla
	hoppeana (Reichenb.) Dalla Torre	EBee
	iniquiformis	EBee WPGP
	lapeyrousei	EBee NChi
	mollis ♀H4	Widely available
*	- 'Robusta'	MMuc SEND SPlb SWat WFar WMoo WPnP
*	- 'Senior'	LHop
	- 'Thriller'	EBee LRHS WSpi
	monticola	WPer
	'Mr Poland's Variety'	see *A. venosa*
	pedata	NChi
	pentaphylla	EBee
	peristerica new	EBee
	pumila	NBre
	saxatilis	IFoB
*	***sericophylla***	EBee
	splendens misapplied	see *A. fulgens*
	straminea	MRav NBre
§	***venosa***	CMoH
	vetteri	EBee GMac WHrl
	vulgaris misapplied	see *A. xanthochlora*
§	***xanthochlora***	CArn EBee GBar GPoy NBre NLar NSco SRms WCon WFar WHer

Aldrovanda (*Droseraceae*)

vesiculosa	EFEx

alecost see *Tanacetum balsamita*

Alectorurus (*Liliaceae*)

yedoensis var. ***platypetalus***	EBee

Alectryon (*Sapindaceae*)

excelsus	CBcs ECou

Alisma (*Alismataceae*)

plantago-aquatica	CBen CRow CSpe EHon LPBA MSKA NPer NSco SWat WMAq WPnP XBlo
- var. ***parviflorum***	CBen LPBA MSKA MWts SPlb SWat WMAq

Alkanna (*Boraginaceae*)

tinctoria	CArn
- HH&K 345	CMdw

Allamanda (*Apocynaceae*)

§	***blanchetii***	SOWG
	cathartica	CCCN ERea MBri
	- 'Birthe'	MBri
	'Cherries Jubilee'	SOWG
	'Jamaican Sunset'	SOWG
	neriifolia	see *A. schottii*
§	***schottii*** ♀H1	CCCN SOWG
	violacea	see *A. blanchetii*

Alliaria (*Brassicaceae*)

petiolata	CArn EBWF GPoy NLan WHer WSFF

Allium (*Alliaceae*)

	SSSE 250	GEdr
§	***acuminatum***	CPom EBee ECho GBin NBir NMen WWst
I	- 'Album'	ECho
	acutiflorum	LAma
	aflatunense misapplied	see *A. hollandicum*
	aflatunense ambig.	EBrs ECho IBal LRHS LSRN SDeJ SEND WCot WFar WWEG
	aflatunense B. Fedtsch.	ECho SApp
I	- 'Alba'	EBee ECho
	'Akbulak'	EBee ECho ERCP LAma
	albopilosum	see *A. cristophii*
	altaicum	ECho
	altissimum	LAma
	- 'Goliath'	CTca EBee ECho WCot
	amabile	see *A. mairei* var. *amabile*
	'Ambassador'	CMea CTca EBee EBrs ERCP LAma LRHS MNrw SPhx WClo
	ampeloprasum	CPrp EBWF EBee ECha ECho LAma NGHP WHer WShi
	- var. ***babingtonii***	CAgr CArn CPrp CTca ECho GPWP GPoy ILis LEdu WHer WHil WShi
§	- 'Elephant'	CArn ECho
	amphibolum	EBee ECho EHrv EPot LAma
	amplectens	EBee ECho LAma
§	***angulosum***	CAvo CMea EBee ECho LAma WCot
	angustitepalum	see *A. jesdianum* subsp. *angustitepalum*
	atropurpureum	CBgR EBee EBrs ECha EHrv ELan EPfP ERCP LAma LEdu LRHS MWat SDeJ SEND SPer
	atropurpureum × ***schubertii***	LSRN
	atroviolaceum	EBee ECho
	azureum	see *A. caeruleum*
	backhousianum	LAma
	balansae	ECho
	barszczewskii	ECho
	'Beau Regard' ♀H4	CTca CWCL EBee EBrs ECho ERCP LAma NLar
	beesianum misapplied	see *A. cyaneum*
	beesianum W.W. Smith	CDes CPom GEdr NBir NRya
	- from Sichuan, China	ECho GCrs
	- 'Album'	EBrs ECho
	blandum	see *A. carolinianum*
	bolanderi	ECho
	brevicaule	ECho
	bucharicum	ECho
	bulgaricum	see *Nectaroscordum siculum* subsp. *bulgaricum*
§	***caeruleum*** ♀H4	Widely available
	- ***azureum***	see *A. caeruleum*
	caesium ♀H4	EBrs ECho SMad
	- RS 188/84	WWst
	- tall	WWst
	- 'Tashkent'	ECho

	caespitosum	ECho
	callimischon	ECho SPhx WWst
	subsp. ***callimischon***	
	- subsp. ***haemostictum***	CBgR CDes CPom EBrs ECho NMen WAbe
	canadense	CArn EBee ECho GPWP SHar
§	***carinatum***	ECho
§	- subsp. ***pulchellum*** ♀H4	CArn CAvo CBgR CMea EBee ECha ECho ELon EPot LAma LHop LLWP LRHS MHer MNrw MTho MWat NMen SMrm SPhx WCom WPer
	- - f. ***album*** ♀H4	CArn CAvo CBgR CMea CSWP EBee ECha ECho ELon ERCP LEdu LLWP LRHS MNrw NMen SBch SMrm SPhx WCom WCot
	- - 'Tubergen'	ECho
	'Carlito' **new**	LAma
§	***carolinianum***	EBee ECho LAma
	cepa	SVic
	- Aggregatum Group	ELau GPoy
	- 'Kew White'	WCot
	- 'Perutile'	CArn CHby GPoy ILis LEdu MHer SBfd SHDw
	- Proliferum Group	CArn CHby CPrp CSev CWan ECho EOHP GBar GPoy ILis LEdu MHer MNHC NGHP SBfd SIde WGwG WHer WJek
	- var. ***viviparum***	EBrs ECho LAma
	- 'White Lisbon' ♀H4	SVic
	cernuum	Widely available
§	- 'Hidcote' ♀H4	CSam ECho WBVN WKif
	- 'Major'	see *A. cernuum* 'Hidcote'
	- var. ***neomexicanum***	ECho
	- var. ***obtusum***	ECho
	- pink-flowered	NBir
	- 'White Dwarf' **new**	CBgR EBee ECho
	chinense **new**	GPoy
	cirrhosum	see *A. carinatum* subsp. *pulchellum*
	colchicifolium **new**	CPom
	commutatum	ECho
	cowanii	see *A. neapolitanum* Cowanii Group
	crenulatum	EBrs ECho LAma
	crispum **new**	WWst
§	***cristophii*** ♀H4	Widely available
	cupanii	EBee ECho
	- subsp. ***hirtovaginatum***	ECho
	cupuliferum	CPom ECho WWst
	curtum RCB RL 13 **new**	WCot
	cuthbertii	WWst
§	***cyaneum*** ♀H4	CBgR CPBP CPom EBee ECho GCrs GEdr LAma LBee LRHS NMen NRya WAbe WCot
*	- ***album***	ECho
	- 'Cobalt Blue'	ECho
	cyathophorum	ECho EWld NWCA
§	- var. ***farreri***	CArn CAvo CBgR CBre EBee EBrs ECho EPot GAuc GCrs GEdr GKir LBee LEdu LLWP LRHS MLHP MRav NChi NRya SBch WAbe WBVN WCot WPrP
	darwasicum	ECho
	decipiens	ECho LAma
	dichlamydeum	ECho WWst
§	***drummondii***	CPom ECho LRHS
	'Early Emperor'	EBee ERCP LAma LRHS WClo
	elatum	see *A. macleanii*
	'Emir'	EBee ECho
	ericetorum	EBee ECho WCot WWst
	falcifolium	EBee ECho EPot LAma NMen NMin
	farreri	see *A. cyathophorum* var. *farreri*
	fasciculatum	LAma
	fimbriatum	ECho
	- var. ***abramsii***	ECho
	- var. ***purdyi***	ECho
	'Firmament'	CAvo EBee ECGP ECha ECho ERCP LAma LRHS NLar SDeJ
	fistulosum	CArn CHby CWan EBee ECho ELau GBar GPoy ILis LAma LEdu MHer MMuc MNHC NGHP NHol NPri SIde SVic WGwG WJek WPer
	- 'Red Welsh'	CPrp ILis WJek
	- red-flowered	CHby
	flavum ♀H4	CAby CArn CTca ECha ECho EDAr EPot ERCP IFoB LAma MRav SBch SDeJ SMad SMrm WGwG WWEG
§	- 'Blue Leaf'	ECho NBir SMrm
	- subsp. ***flavum***	EBee EBrs ECho MMHG MNrw
	- - var. ***minus***	EBee ECho IFro MTho NWCA WAbe
	- 'Glaucum'	see *A. flavum* 'Blue Leaf'
	- var. ***nanum***	EPot GCrs GEdr GKir
	- subsp. ***tauricum***	CSpe EBee ECho SPhx
	'Forelock'	CHid CMea CPom CTca EBee EBrs ERCP LAma MNrw WCot
	forrestii	EBee ECho GBin MDKP WCot
	geyeri	EBee ECho GCrs WCot
	giganteum ♀H4	Widely available
	'Gladiator' ♀H4	CFir CFox CTca CWCL EBee EBrs ECho ECtt ERCP LAma LRHS LSRN MNrw MRav SBfd SDeJ SPad WClo WWEG
	glaucum	see *A. senescens* subsp. *glaucum*
	'Globemaster' ♀H4	Widely available
	globosum	ECho
	'Globus'	CTca EBee ECho IBal LAma
	goodingii	CPom EBee EBrs ECho GCrs
	guttatum	EBee ECho
	subsp. ***dalmaticum***	
	- - HOA 9114	WWst
	- subsp. ***sardoum***	EBee ECho
	- - CH 859	WWst
	haematochiton	ECho WCot
	- NNS 95-23	EBee WWst
	'Hair'	see *A. vineale* 'Hair'
	heldreichii	EBee EBrs ECho WWst
*	***hirtifolium*** var. ***album***	EBee ECho LAma LRHS
	'His Excellency'	CBgR CFir EBee EBrs ERCP IBal LAma LRHS WClo
§	***hollandicum*** ♀H4	CAvo CFFs CTca CWCL EBee EBrs ECha ECho ECtt EHrv EPfP GKev GKir LAma MWat NEgg SPer SPlb WFar
	- 'Purple Sensation' ♀H4	Widely available
	- 'Purple Surprise' ♀H4	GKir
	hookeri ACE 2430	EBee EPot WCot
	- var. ***muliense***	GEdr
	howellii var. ***clokeyi***	WWst
	huber-morathii	WWst
	humile	ECho GEdr WCot
	- CC 1818	WCot
	hyalinum	EBrs
	- pink-flowered	EBee WCon WCot WPrP
	hymenorrhizum	ECho
	inconspicuum **new**	LAma
§	***insubricum*** ♀H4	EBrs ECho GCrs GEdr NBir NHol
	jajlae	see *A. rotundum* subsp. *jajlae*
	jesdianum	ECho
§	- subsp. ***angustitepalum***	EBrs
	- 'Michael Hoog'	see *A. rosenorum* 'Michael H. Hoog'
	- 'Purple King'	CPom EBee ECho LAma LRHS MNrw
	- white-flowered	EBrs

	kansuense	see *A. sikkimense*
	karataviense ♀H3	Widely available
	- subsp. ***henrikii***	WWst
	- 'Ivory Queen'	CAby CAvo CFFs CFox CMea CTca EBee EBrs ECha ECho ECtt EPfP ERCP GKev IBal IFro LAma LRHS LSRN NHol NLar SBfd SDeJ SPad SPlb WAul WFar
	- 'Kara Tau'	ECho
	kazemunii	WWst
	komarovianum	see *A. thunbergii*
	komarovii new	CPom
	lacunosum var. ***lacunosum***	ECho
	ledebourianum	EBee ECho LAma
	lenkoranicum	CAvo EBee ECho LAma WCot WWst
	libani	WPer
§	***lineare***	ECho
	litvinovii new	ECho LAma
	longicuspis	ECho
	loratum	LAma WWst
	'Lucy Ball'	EBee EBrs ECho ERCP LAma LRHS NBir NLar SDeJ
	lusitanicum	CTca EBla ECha ECho EPot ERCP GAuc LAma LEdu LPio NBre NMen SDix SMHy WAbe WClo
§	***macleanii***	CArn EBee ECho LAma LRHS
	macranthum	CBgR CPom EBee EBrs ECho GEdr LAma LRHS WCot
	- S&L 5369	WWst
	macrochaetum	ECho
	macropetalum	ECho
	mairei	EBrs ECho EPot LHop LLWP LRHS NMen NRya WTin
§	- var. ***amabile***	ECho GEdr LRHS NChi NRya NSla WThu
	- - pink-flowered	ECho
	- - red-flowered	ECho
	maximowiczii	EBee ECho
	- white-flowered new	LAma
	'Mercurius' PBR	EBee ERCP LAma LRHS MNrw SPhx WCot
	meteoricum	EBee
	moly	CArn CWCL EBee EBrs ECho EDAr GKir IFoB LAma LRHS MBri MMuc MRav NBPC NRya SBfd SDeJ SEND SMrm SRms SWal WCot WTin
	- 'Jeannine' ♀H4	CTca EBee ECho EPot LAma LRHS MMHG WShi
	'Mont Blanc'	CMea EBee ECho ELan ERCP GBin LAma LRHS MNrw NLar
	multibulbosum	see *A. nigrum*
	murrayanum misapplied	see *A. unifolium*
	murrayanum Reg.	see *A. acuminatum*
	myrianthum	ECho LAma
	narcissiflorum misapplied	see *A. insubricum*
§	***narcissiflorum*** Villars	ECho GCrs
	neapolitanum	CArn CMea EBee ECho EPot LAma LRHS MBri MCot SEND SPer SRms WGwG
§	- Cowanii Group	EBee ECho EHrv LHop LRHS MWat SDeJ WCot
	- 'Grandiflorum'	CSam EBee ECho WBrE WRHF
	nevii	WWst
	nevskianum	EBee ECho LAma LRHS
§	***nigrum***	CArn CAvo CFFs EBee EBrs ECho EHrv EPot ERCP LAma LRHS MCot MWat NBir SDeJ SPhx WCot
	nutans	CBod CPrp EBee ECho LAma LEdu MHer NGHP SHDw WHal WJek
	nuttallii	see *A. drummondii*
§	***obliquum***	CArn CAvo EBee EBrs ECha ECho ERCP LRHS SPhx WCot WPrP WTin WWst
	ochotense new	WCot
	odorum L.	see *A. ramosum* L.
	oleraceum	EBee ECho WHer
	olympicum	ECho WWst
§	***oreophilum***	CArn CSam CYeo EBee ECha ECho ECtt EHrv EPfP LAma LRHS MWat NRya NWCA SMrm SPer SRms WHoo WTin WWEG
	- 'Agalik'	ECho
	- 'Agalik Giant'	ECho
	- 'Zwanenburg' ♀H4	ECho EPot WCot
	oreoprasum	ECho
	oschaninii new	LAma
	ostrowskianum	see *A. oreophilum*
	ovalifolium var. ***leuconeurum***	WCot
	palentinum new	LAma
	pallasii	ECho WWst
	pallens	CBre ECho NBir
§	***paniculatum***	CAvo EBee ECho GKir SCnR WWst
*	- var. ***minor*** new	LAma
	paradoxum	ECho LEdu NBir
	- var. ***normale***	CBgR CDes CPom EBee EBrs ECho EPot ERCP MMHG NBir NMen WCot
	pedemontanum	see *A. narcissiflorum* Villars
	pendulinum	ECho WWst
	peninsulare	WWst
	'Pinball Wizard'	CTca EBee EBrs ECho ERCP LAma LRHS
	platycaule	ECho LAma WCot
	platyspathum	ECho
	plummerae	EBee EBrs ECho GCrs SKHP
	plurifoliatum	ECho LAma
	polyastrum	CPom
	polyphyllum	see *A. carolinianum*
	polyrrhizum	ECho
	przewalskianum	ECho LAma
	pskemense	EBee ECho LAma WCot
	pulchellum	see *A. carinatum* subsp. *pulchellum*
	'Purple Giant'	ECho
	'Purple Rain' new	LAma
	pyrenaicum misapplied	see *A. angulosum*
	pyrenaicum Costa & Vayreda	ELan
	ramosum Jacquin	see *A. obliquum*
§	***pyrenaicum*** L.	EBee ECho LAma LEdu NCob NGHP WPer
	'Renaissance'	ECho ERCP
	'Rien Poortvliet'	ECho LAma
	robustum	EBrs ECho
	rosenbachianum misapplied	see *A. stipitatum*
	rosenbachianum Regel	EBee EPot
	- 'Akbulak'	ECho LRHS
	- 'Album'	EBee ECha ECho EPot ERCP LAma LRHS WCot
	- 'Michael Hoog'	see *A. rosenorum* 'Michael H. Hoog'
	- 'Purple King'	ECho
	- 'Shing'	EBee IBal LAma LRHS MNrw
§	***rosenorum*** 'Michael H. Hoog'	CPom EBee ECho EPot LAma LRHS
	roseum	CArn CMea CPBP CStu EBee ECho ECtt EPfP EPot LAma LLWP MDKP SMrm
	- ***album***	ECho
§	- var. ***bulbiferum***	ECho
	- 'Grandiflorum'	see *A. roseum* var. *bulbiferum*

	rotundum	ECho
§	– subsp. ***jajlae***	EBee ECho LLWP
	– subsp. ***rotundum***	ECho
	'Round and Purple'	CPom EBee EBrs ERCP LAma LRHS
	sanbornii var. ***sanbornii***	ECho
	sarawschanicum	ECho WWst
	– 'Bright Boy'	EBee ECho WWst
	– 'Chinoro'	ECho
	sativum	CArn ECho MHer NPri SIde SPoG SVic
	– 'Albigensian Wight'	NGHP
	– 'Chengdou'	ECho
	– 'Elephant'	see *A. ampeloprasum* 'Elephant'
	– golden	GPoy
	– 'Iberian Wight'	NGHP
	– 'Lautrec'	NGHP
	– 'Mediterranean Wight'	NGHP
	– var. ***ophioscorodon***	EBee ECho GPoy ILis LAma
	– – 'Early Wight' ♀H4	NGHP
	– – 'Purple Wight'	NGHP
	– 'Purple Heritage Moldovan'	NGHP
	– 'Solent White' ♀H4	NGHP
	– 'Thermidrôme'	ECho
	saxatile	EBee ECho
	schmitzii	ECho
	schoenoprasum	Widely available
	– f. ***albiflorum***	CArn CPbn CPrp CSWP EBrs ECha ECho GPWP LEdu MHer NBir NCGa NHol SIde WHer
	– 'Black Isle Blush'	CPbn CTca GPoy LEdu LPla MHer SMHy
	– 'Corsican White'	LEdu
	– fine-leaved	ELau
	– 'Forescate'	CPrp CTca EBee EBla EBrs ECha ECho EWes GBar LAma LAst LHop LRHS MRav NBir NGdn SBch SIde SPet SSvw
	– medium-leaved	ELau
	– 'Netherbyres Dwarf'	CArn ECho
	– 'Pink Pérfection'	GPoy LPla MHer SMHy
	– 'Polyphant'	CBre
	– var. ***sibiricum***	ECho GBar GGar SDix WShi
	– 'Silver Chimes'	CDes CWan EBee MRav SBfd SHDw
	– thick-leaved	ELau NPri
	– 'Wallington White'	GBar
	– 'Wilau' new	ELau
	schubertii	Widely available
	scorodoprasum	EBWF EBee ECho SIde
	– subsp. ***jajlae***	see *A. rotundum* subsp. *jajlae*
	– subsp. ***scorodoprasum***	ECho LAma LEdu
	semenowii	ECho
	senescens	CArn CTca CTri EBee ECGP LAma LRHS MRav NChi NWsh SApp SBch SEND SRms SSvw WTin
§	– subsp. ***glaucum***	CArn CBgR CMea CPBP CPom CPrp CSpe EAEE EBee EBla EBrs ECha ECho EPla GEdr LEdu LPio LRHS NGdn NRya SAga SPet SWat WBox WCot WPer WTin
	– subsp. ***senescens***	CAvo EBee ECho LEdu LPio WPrP
	serra	WCot
	sessiliflorum	ECho
	setifolium	ECho
	sewerzowii	ECho WWst
	sibthorpianum	see *A. paniculatum*
	siculum	see *Nectaroscordum siculum*
	sieheanum	EBee
§	***sikkimense***	CFir CWCL EBee EBla EBrs ECho GCrs LRHS MDKP NSla SMHy SPet SSvw WCon WCot WPer WPrP
	– SBQE B	EDAr
	'Silver Spring'	CAvo CTca EBee EBrs ECho ERCP LAma LRHS MNrw SPer SPhx WCot
	siskiyouense	ECho
	– NNS 02-43	WWst
	sordidiflorum new	CPom
	sphaerocephalon	Widely available
	splendens	ECho
I	– var. ***kurilense*** new	WWst
	stellatum	LRHS WGwG WWst
	stellerianum	WPer
	– var. ***kurilense***	CPBP ECho WThu
§	***stipitatum***	EBrs ECho ERCP IFro LAma LRHS WCot
	– 'Album'	CArn EBee EBrs ECho EPot LRHS
	– 'Glory of Pamir'	ECho
	– 'Mars'	CFir EBee EBrs ECho EPfP ERCP LAma LRHS MCot MWat NLar
	– 'Mount Everest'	CAvo CFFs CFir CHid CTca EBee EBrs ECho EPfP EPot ERCP GKev GMaP LAma LRHS MNrw MWat NBPC NLar SDeJ SMrm SPer SPhx WClo WCot WShi
	– 'Violet Beauty'	CMdw CWCL EBee ECho LAma WCot
	– 'White Giant'	CTca EBee EBrs ECho ERCP LAma LRHS MNrw
	stracheyi	WCot
	'Stratos'	EBee ERCP LAma
	strictum Ledeb.	see *A. szovitsii*
	strictum Schrad.	see *A. lineare*
	suaveolens	ECho
	subhirsutum	CPom EBee ECho
	subvillosum	WCot
	'Summer Beauty'	see *A. lusitanicum*
	'Summer Drummer'	EBee ERCP
	'Sweet Discovery'	EBee ECho LAma LRHS
§	***szovitsii***	ECho
	tanguticum	LRHS
	tauricola	WWst
	texanum new	LAma
§	***thunbergii*** ♀H4	CAvo EBee EBrs ECho GCrs LAma NBir NRya SCnR WAbe WWEG
	– 'Album'	WAbe
	– 'Ozawa'	EBee ECho NMen WAbe WCot
	tibeticum	see *A. sikkimense*
	togashii	ECho
*	***tournefortii***	EBee ECho
	triquetrum	CTca EBee EBrs ECho ELan ELau EPfP EPot GGar GPWP IBlr LAma LEdu NBir NLar NSti SEND WCot WHer WMoo
	tschimganicum new	LAma
	tuberosum	Widely available
	– B&SWJ 8881	WCru
	– purple/mauve-flowered	CHby ECho ELau
	tubiflorum	ECho
	turkestanicum	ECho
	umbilicatum	WWst
§	***unifolium*** ♀H4	CArn CAvo CBgR CFFs CPom CSam EBee EBrs ECho EPfP EPot ERCP GKev LAma MNrw MRav NBir NLBP SDeJ SGar WAbe WBrE WCot WFar WPer
	ursinum	CArn CBgR CHby CWan EBWF EBee EBrs ECho EOHP GGar GPWP GPoy LAma MWat NMir SVic WAul WFar WJek WSFF WShi
	'Valerie Finnis'	CPBP
	victorialis	ECho
	– 'Cantabria'	EBee WWst
	– 'Kemerovo'	EBee
	vineale	CArn EBWF NMir WHer

§ - 'Hair'	CTca EBee EBrs ECho EPfP ERCP ITim LAma LRHS MCot NBir SGar WCon WHoo
violaceum	see *A. carinatum*
virgunculae	CMea CPBP CStu ECho WAbe
wallichii	EBee ECho GAuc GMaP MBNS NBir NChi SKHP WCot WTin
- ACE 2458	WCot
- dark-flowered	ECho WCot
- purple-flowered	GEdr
woronowii	WWst
zaprjagajevii	ECho WCot
zebdanense	EBee ECho LAma LRHS

Allocasuarina (*Casuarinaceae*)

monilifera	ECou

almond see *Prunus dulcis*

Alnus ✿ (*Betulaceae*)

cordata ♀H4	Widely available
cremastogyne	EGFP NLar
crispa	see *A. viridis* subsp. *crispa*
fauriei from Niigata, Japan	CSto
firma	CDul CMCN CSto
glutinosa	CBcs CCVT CDoC CDul CLnd CMac CRWN CSBt CTri EBee ECrN EMac EPfP EWTr GKir IFFs LBuc LMaj MGos NWea SPer WDin WMou WSFF
- from Corsica	CSto
- 'Aurea'	CDul CEnd CLnd CTho CWib ECrN GKir MBlu MGos SPer
- var. ***barbata***	CSto
- 'Imperialis' ♀H4	CCVT CDoC CDul CEnd CPMA CTho EBee ECrN ELan EPfP EWTr GKir IFFs LBuc LHop MAsh MBlu MBri MDun MMuc NBro NLar NWea SBfd SEND SPer SPoG WDin
- 'Laciniata'	CDoC CDul CMac CTho ECrN GKir MBlu MGos WFar
hirsuta	CMCN CSto NWea
incana	CCVT CDoC CDul CLnd CMCN CWib EBee ECrN EMac GKir IFFs LBuc MGos MSnd NLar NWea SPer WDin WMou
- 'Aurea'	CBcs CDul CEnd CLnd CMac CTho EBee ECrN ELan EPfP GAuc GKir IArd LMaj LRHS MBlu MBri MGos NBea NBro NEgg NLar NPal SBfd SPer SPoG WDin WFar WMou WPat
- 'Laciniata'	CTho MGos NLar SCoo WDin WFar
- 'Pendula'	CTho
§ - subsp. ***rugosa***	CMCN
japonica	CSto NLar
maximowiczii	CSto NLar
nitida	CMCN CSto
oregana	see *A. rubra*
pendula	CSto
- B&SWJ 10895	WCru
§ ***rubra***	CCVT CDoC CDul CLnd CMCN ECrN ELan EMac GKir NWea WDin
- f. ***pinnatisecta***	CMCN CTho MBlu
serrulata	see *A. incana* subsp. *rugosa*
sieboldiana	CSto
× ***spaethii***	GKir MBlu MMuc
subcordata	CSto
viridis	CAgr CSto ECrN NWea
§ - subsp. ***crispa***	CSto GKir
- subsp. ***sinuata***	CAgr CSto GAuc

Alocasia ✿ (*Araceae*)

sp. **new**	SArc
× ***amazonica*** ♀H1	ERea XBlo
'Aurora' **new**	EAmu
'Calidora'	CDTJ EUJe SBst
cucullata	XBlo
gageana	CDTJ
lauterbachiana **new**	EAmu
macrorrhiza	CDTJ CFir EAmu SAPC SBig SBst
- 'Variegata' (v) ♀H1	EUJe
odora	CDTJ EAmu EUJe XBlo
plumbea	XBlo
'Portodora'	EAmu EUJe WCot
wentii	CDTJ EAmu WCot
- 'Aline'PBR (v) **new**	EAmu

Aloe ✿ (*Aloaceae*)

aculeata	CAbb EShb WCot
africana	CAbb
arborescens	CAbb CBrP CDTJ CHEx EAmu EShb EUJe IDee LRHS MAga SBst SChr SEND
aristata ♀H1	CAbb CHEx ERea ETod EUJe MAga SAPC SArc SBfd SChr SEND SWvt WPGP
bakeri × ***descoingsii*** × ***parvula***	MAga
barbadensis	see *A. vera*
barberae	CAbb CCCN
'Bedford's Beau'	MAga
bellatula	MAga
'Black Frost'	MAga
bowiea	MAga
branddraaiensis	WCot
'Brazen'	MAga
brevifolia ♀H1	CAbb CBrP EAmu EShb EUJe MAga SAPC SBst
broomii	CAbb CCCN EPfP MAga SChr
camperi	MAga
- 'Maculata'	SChr SEND
castanea	CAbb
chabaudii	MAga
ciliaris	ERea EShb SChr
comptonii	CAbb EShb MAga
cooperi	CCCN CDTJ EShb
* ***delaetii***	MAga
deltoideodonta ISI 898	MAga
descoingsii ♀H1 ISI 948	MAga
descoingsii × ***haworthioides***	MAga
descoingsii × ***rauhii***	MAga
dewetii	CAbb
dichotoma	CAbb
distans	SEND
'Doran Black'	MAga
dyeri	MAga
ecklonis	CCCN CTrC SPlb
ferox	CAbb CBod CBrP CCCN CDTJ CTrC EAmu EShb GPoy MAga SBfd SBig SChr SEND
'Firebird'	MAga
'Flurry'	MAga
fosteri	CDTJ
gariepensis	MAga
globuligemma ISI 1248	MAga
'Gold Rush'	MAga
'Grande'	MAga
greatheadii	CTrC
- var. ***davyana***	SChr
harlana ISI 334	MAga
haworthioides ♀H1	MAga

hereroensis ISI 89-34	MAga
'Hey Babe'	MAga
humilis	CBrP CTrC MAga SChr SEND
imalotensis	MAga
immaculata	WCot
jucunda ISI 533	MAga
juvenna	MAga
karasbergensis	MAga
kedongensis	SEND
krapohliana	CAbb
littoralis	CAbb
maculata	CDTJ CTrC SEND SWal
- ISI 537	MAga
marlothii	CAbb CCCN EShb
- ISI 92-37	MAga
melanacantha ♀H1	STre
microstigma	CCCN
- ISI 1249	MAga
'Midnight'	MAga
'Midnight Child'	MAga
'Midnight Exchange'	MAga
'Midnight Feast'	MAga
millotii	MAga
mitriformis	CBrP EPfP MAga SChr SEND
mutabilis	CHEx CTrC SChr SEND
parvula ISI 23	MAga
peglerae	CAbb MAga
'Pepe'	MAga
petricola	CAbb
'Pink Lace'	MAga
plicatilis	CAbb CCCN CDTJ EShb MAga
polyphylla	CAbb EAmu WPGP
pratensis	CCCN CDTJ SChr
'Quicksilver'	MAga
rauhii ♀H1	MAga
rauhii* × *sinkatana ISI 97-54	MAga
rauhii* × *somaliensis	MAga
reitzii	CAbb CTrC
sinkatana	MAga
'Snowflake'	MAga
somaliensis ♀H1 ISI 133	MAga
speciosa	CAbb EShb
spicata	CAbb
× ***spinosissima***	SChr STre
striata	CAbb CCCN EShb SChr
- ISI 627	MAga
striatula	CAbb CBrP CDTJ CGHE CHEx CSam CTca CTrC EAmu EBee EShb EUJe IBlr LPJP LTen SAPC SArc SBHP SBig SChr SEND SKHP WCot WPGP
- var. ***caesia***	IBlr
succotrina	CAbb
suprafoliata	MAga
swynnertonii	MAga
'Teigelberg Triumph'	MAga
thraskii	CAbb
vaombe ISI 95-21	MAga
variegata (v) ♀H1	EShb STre SWal SWvt
§ ***vera*** ♀H1	CArn CCCN CDoC CHby COld EOHP ERea EShb EUJe GPoy ILis LRHS MNHC NPer NPla NPri SBch SBfd SEND SIde SVic SWal WCot WJek
'White Diamond'	MAga
wickensii	CAbb

Aloe × *Gasteria* see × *Gasteraloe*

Alonsoa (*Scrophulariaceae*)

'Bright Spark'	CSpe
incisifolia	CCCN CSpe
meridionalis	CCCN
- 'Rebel'	LAst LSou SBfd SRkn
- 'Shell Pink'	SPhx
'Pink Beauty'	CSpe
warscewiczii	CCCN ELan
- 'Peachy-keen'	CSpe

Alopecurus (*Poaceae*)

alpinus	see *A. borealis*
§ ***borealis***	MMoz
- subsp. ***glaucus***	EBee EHoe ELan EPPr GBin SPer WWEG
geniculatus	CRWN
lanatus	NBea
pratensis	EBWF
- 'Aureovariegatus' (v)	CWan EBee EHoe EPPr EPla GKir GMaP LBMP MMoz NBid NHol SApp SLim SPer WFar WMoo
- 'Aureus'	ECha GBin LRHS MRav NBro SPlb WWEG
- 'No Overtaking' (v)	EPPr

Alophia (*Iridaceae*)

lahue	see *Herbertia lahue*

Aloysia (*Verbenaceae*)

citriodora	see *A. citrodora*
§ ***citrodora*** ♀H2	Widely available
gratissima	EOHP WJek

Alpinia (*Zingiberaceae*)

B&SWJ 3775	WPGP
formosana	LEdu
galanga	CArn
japonica	CPLG LEdu
- B&SWJ 8889	WCru
officinarum	CArn
zerumbet 'Variegata' (v)	XBlo

Alsobia see *Episcia*

Alstroemeria (*Alstroemeriaceae*)

'Adonis' PBR	LRHS WViv
'Aimi'	CFir LRHS SPer SWvt WFar
'Alexis' PBR	LRHS WViv
'Angelina'	LRHS SWvt
'Apollo' ♀H4	CBcs CTsd MBNS MNrw NBre SPer SWvt WViv
'Athena'	LRHS WViv
aurantiaca	see *A. aurea*
§ ***aurea***	GGar MRav NBPC NLar SRms
- 'Apricot'	GCal
- 'Dover Orange'	IGor SCoo SEND
- 'Lutea'	EWll NBre SPlb
- 'Orange King'	CTsd EBee EGxp ELan EPfP NLar SMrm WCot
'Avanti'	LRHS
'Blushing Bride'	CFir ELon LRHS MBNS SWvt
'Bolero'	WViv
'Bonanza'	SLon SPer
brasiliensis	CTsd EBee EShb GCal MNrw NChi WCot WSHC WViv
'Cahors'	GKir LRHS
'Candy Floss'	EBee EPfP
'Ceres'	GKir LRHS
'Charm'	WFar WSpi WViv
§ 'Christina' PBR	LRHS MBNS NPri SLon SWvt WHlf WViv
'Coronet' ♀H4	MBNS
'Dandy Candy'	CAbP CWGN ELon EWll ITim MNrw NBPC NLar SPad SPoG WBrk WClo WCot

'Devotion'	MGos
Diana, Princess of Wales = 'Stablaco'	LRHS NLar
diluta subsp. ***chrysantha*** F&W 8700	WCot
Doctor Salter's hybrids	ECGP LLHF SRms
'Douceur d'Automne'	GKir LRHS
'Dutch Pink'	SEND
'Dwarf Lemon'	SEND
'Dwarf Pink'	SEND
'Elvira'	LRHS SPer WViv
'Evening Song'	CFir EKen LRHS MBNS SLon SPer SWal SWvt WViv
'Flaming Star'	CBcs LRHS WViv
'Freedom'	CAbP CWGN EBee ELon GBin LAst MBNS NBPC NEgg NGdn NLar SPad SPoG SUsu WClo WCot WSpi
'Friendship' ♀^{H4}	CBcs CTsd LRHS NBre SWvt WViv
'Gloria'	MBNS SWvt WViv
'Glory of the Andes' (v)	CWGN NGdn NLar WWEG
'Golden Delight'	LRHS SPer WViv
'Golden Queen'	WFar
H.R.H. Princess Alexandra = 'Zelblanca' ♀^{H2}	GKir
§ H.R.H. Princess Alice = 'Staverpi' ♀^{H2}	GKir
haemantha	MDKP
I 'Hatch Hybrid'	GCal
'Hawera'	GCal SMrm
hookeri	EBee ECho GBin GCal GGar NLar SCnR
- subsp. ***cummingiana***	LLHF WCot
Inca Adore = 'Koadore'^{PBR}	LHop MBri NBPC
Inca Azure = 'Konazur' **new**	WViv
Inca Birdy = 'Konirdy' **new**	WViv
Inca Classic = 'Konclassic'	WViv
Inca Desert = 'Konesert'	WViv
Inca Devotion = 'Konevotio'	MBri
Inca Exotica = 'Koexotica'^{PBR}	LRHS MBri MGos NBPC WViv
Inca Glow = 'Koglow'^{PBR}	LRHS MGos WViv
Inca Ice = 'Koice'	CWGN LHop LRHS MBri MGos NLar WViv
Inca Moonlight = 'Komolight'	WViv
Inca Obsession = 'Koobsion'	LRHS WViv
Inca Pride = 'Kopride'	WViv
Inca Pulse = 'Konpulse'^{PBR}	LRHS MBri WViv
Inca Rocky = 'Konyrock' **new**	WViv
Inca Serin = 'Koserin'^{PBR}	CWGN LRHS MBri WViv
Inca Tropic = 'Kotrop'	CWGN LRHS MBri MGos WViv
Inticancha Purple = 'Tespurplin' **new**	WViv
Intichana Red = 'Tesrobiri'	EGxp WViv
Jazze Series **new**	WGor
kingii	see *A. versicolor*
'Laguna'	WViv
ligtu hybrids	CAvo CBcs CFFs ECha ELan EPfP IFoB LAst LHop MNrw NLar NPer NVic SRms SRot SWvt WBrE WFar WHoo WWEG
- var. ***ligtu***	SMHy WCot
'Little Eleanor'	GBin WFar WViv
'Little Miss Charlotte'	WFar WViv
'Little Miss Christina'^{PBR}	see *A.* 'Christina'
'Little Miss Davina'	NPri WViv
'Little Miss Isabel'	LRHS WViv
'Little Miss Lucy'	WViv
'Little Miss Matilda'	WViv
'Little Miss Natalie'^{PBR}	see *A.* 'Natalie'
'Little Miss Roselind'	see *A.* 'Roselind'
'Little Miss Sophie'^{PBR}	see *A.* 'Sophie'
'Little Miss Tara'^{PBR}	see *A.* 'Tara'
'Little Miss Veronica'	MBNS WViv
'Lucinda'	CBcs SWvt
magnifica	WCot
- subsp. ***magnifica***	WCot
'Marina'	MBNS
'Marissa'	GMaP
'Mars'	GKir SWal
'Mauve Majesty' **new**	LSou SPoG WCot
'Moulin Rouge'	LRHS MBNS SLon WViv
§ 'Natalie'^{PBR}	LRHS NPri WViv
'Neptune'	LRHS
'Orange Gem' ♀^{H4}	MBNS WFar
'Orange Glory' ♀^{H4}	ELon GKir GMaP LRHS MBNS SWvt WFar WViv WWlt
'Orange Supreme'	LRHS WViv
'Oriana'	LRHS SWvt WViv
patagonica	WAbe
pelegrina	ECho
'Perfect Blue'	LRHS WViv
'Perfect Love'	MNrw
philippii	WCot
'Phoenix' (v)	CFir LRHS SLon SWal SWvt WViv
'Pink Perfection'	NLar
Pink Triumph = 'Stapink' **new**	GKir
'Polka'	MBNS SWal WViv
presliana RB 94103	WCot
- subsp. ***australis***	SMrm
Princess Aiko = 'Zapriko'	LRHS
Princess Alice	see *A.* H.R.H. Princess Alice
Princess Angela = 'Staprilan'^{PBR}	CBcs LRHS MBNS NLar SCoo
Princess Anouska = 'Zaprinous'^{PBR}	LRHS MNrw NLar SLon WViv
Princess Ariane = 'Zapriari' **new**	WViv
Princess Beatrix = 'Stadoran'	GKir
Princess Camilla = 'Stapricamil'^{PBR}	CBcs LRHS SLon SPer SPoG
§ Princess Charlotte = 'Staprizsa'^{PBR}	GKir LRHS
Princess Daniela = 'Stapridani'^{PBR}	SCoo SPoG
Princess Diana = 'Zapridapal'^{PBR} **new**	WViv
Princess Elizabeth	see *A.* Queen Elizabeth The Queen Mother
Princess Ella = 'Staprirange'	LRHS NLar
Princess Emma = 'Zaprimma' **new**	WViv
Princess Fabiana = 'Zaprifabi'^{PBR}	LRHS SPoG WViv
Princess Felicia = 'Zapricia' **new**	LRHS
Princess Frederika = 'Stabronza'	GKir
Princess Grace = 'Starodo'	GKir
Princess Isabella = 'Zapribel'^{PBR}	LRHS NLar WViv
Princess Ivana = 'Staprivane'^{PBR}	LRHS NLar SPoG
Princess Juliana = 'Staterpa'	GKir SPoG
Princess Julieta = 'Zaprijul'^{PBR}	LRHS NLar SPoG WViv
Princess Letizia = 'Zaprilet'	LRHS MNrw

	Princess Leyla = 'Stapriley'PBR	CBcs LRHS MBNS MNrw SLon SPer SPoG
	Princess Louise = 'Zaprilou' new	WViv
	Princess Margaret	GKir NLar
	Princess Marilene = 'Staprilene'PBR	LRHS MBNS
	Princess Mary = 'Zaprimary'PBR	LRHS MNrw NLar
	Princess Mathilde = 'Zaprimat' new	WViv
	Princess Monica = 'Staprimon'PBR	GKir MBNS SPoG
	Princess Oxana = 'Staprioxa'PBR	MNrw NLar SCoo
	Princess Paola = 'Stapripal'PBR	MBNS MNrw SCoo WViv
	Princess Ragna	see *A.* Princess Stephanie
	Princess Sara = 'Staprisara'PBR	LRHS MNrw SPoG
	Princess Sarah = 'Stalicamp'	MBNS
	Princess Sissi = 'Staprisis'PBR	MNrw SPoG
§	Princess Sophia = 'Stajello'	SPoG
§	Princess Stephanie = 'Stapirag'	GKir NLar
	Princess Susana = 'Staprisusa'PBR	LRHS NLar SCoo SPoG
	Princess Theresa = 'Zapriteres'PBR	LRHS NLar
	Princess VictoriaPBR	see *A.* 'Victoria'
	Princess Zavina = 'Staprivina'PBR	CBcs CFir LRHS MBNS MNrw NLar SPer
	Princess Zsa ZsaPBR	see *A.* Princess Charlotte
§	***psittacina***	CAvo CGHE CHll CMea CSam CStu EBee EBla ECha ECho EHrv ELan EPfP EPla EWoo GBin GCal GCra GGar GKir IFoB LHop MHer NChi SGSe WFar WPGP WPtf WSHC WViv
	- 'Mona Lisa'	EShb EWll LLHF NLar WCot
	- 'Royal Star' (v)	CPLG CWCL EBee EBla ELan ELon EPPr EPfP EPla GCal GGar MAvo MRav NLar SHar WCom WCot WFar WHil WHoo WPrP WSHC WWEG
	pulchella Sims	see *A. psittacina*
	pulchra	LLHF
	'Purple Rain'	LRHS MNrw SLon SWvt WViv
	pygmaea	WAbe
§	Queen Elizabeth The Queen Mother = 'Stamoli'	GKir
	'Red Beauty' (v)	see *A.* 'Spitfire'
	'Red Beauty'	GKir GMaP LRHS MBNS NBir SPer SPlb SWvt WCot
	'Red Elf'	MBNS SUsu SWvt WFar WViv
	'Regina'PBR	see *A.* 'Victoria'
	'Rhubarb and Custard'	EBee EPfP
§	'Roselind'	CFir LRHS MBNS NPri SWvt WHlf WViv
	'Rosy Wonder'	NMoo
	'Saturne'	GKir LRHS
	'Selina'	MBNS NBre SWal WFar WViv
	'Serenade'	CBcs CFir LRHS
	'Short Purple'	LSou WCot WFut
	'Solent Wings'	WFar
	'Sonata'	WViv
§	'Sophie'PBR	LRHS MBNS NPri SLon SWvt WViv
§	'Spitfire' (v)	GKir LRHS SLon SWvt WCom WViv
	'Spring Delight' (v)	WCot
	'Strawberry Lace'	EBee EPfP
	'Sunrise'	WWlt
	'Sunstar'	GMaP
	'Sweet Laura'PBR	CAbP CSam ECtt ELon GGar LLHF LSRN MBNS NBPC NEgg NLar SPoG WClo WCot
	'Tanya'	WViv
§	'Tara'PBR	MBNS NPri SWvt WViv
	'Tessa'	LRHS MBNS NBre SLon WViv
	'Turkish Delight'	EBee EPfP
	'Uranus'	GKir LRHS
	'Ventura'	LRHS WViv
§	***versicolor***	WCot
§	'Victoria'PBR	GKir
	'Yellow Friendship' 🏆H4	MBNS NLar SPlb SWvt WFar
	Yellow King	see *A.* Princess Sophia

Alternanthera (*Amaranthaceae*)

	dentata 'Purple Knight'	EShb SBst

Althaea (*Malvaceae*)

	armeniaca	EBee LPla NLar WCot
	cannabina	CAby CFir CSpe EBee ELan GCal GQui MHer MWea NGBl SGSe SUsu WBor WHal WHoo WOld WSHC
	officinalis	CArn CPrp CSev CWan EBWF EBee ELan GBar GPoy ILis MHer MNHC SIde WGwG WHfH WJek WSpi
	- ***alba***	LSou NLar WCom WHer
§	- 'Romney Marsh'	EBee EWll GCal MRav WFar WKif WSHC
	rosea	see *Alcea rosea*
	rugosostellulata	see *Alcea rugosa*

Altingia (*Hamamelidaceae*)

	gracilipes	WPGP
	poilanei B&SWJ 11756	WCru

× *Alworthia* (*Aloaceae*)

	'Black Gem'	EBee EPfP EShb LSou

Alyogyne (*Malvaceae*)

	'Attraction'	ECou
	hakeifolia	CSpe ECou
	- 'Elle Maree'	ECou SOWG
	- 'Melissa Anne'	ECou SOWG
§	***huegelii***	CBcs CBod EBee ECou EShb SRkn WDyG
	- 'Lavender Lass'	ECou
	- 'Santa Cruz'	CCCN CHll CMdw CSpe EBee ECou ERea LHop SEND SOWG SUsu WPGP

Alyssoides (*Brassicaceae*)

	utriculata	NBre

Alyssum (*Brassicaceae*)

	argenteum new	NBre
	cuneifolium	WAbe
	montanum	ECha ECho SPlb SRms WMoo
§	- 'Berggold'	ECho EPfP LRHS MMuc
	- Mountain Gold	see *A. montanum* 'Berggold'
	repens	NBre
	saxatile	see *Aurinia saxatilis*
	scardicum	LLHF
§	***spinosum*** 'Roseum' 🏆H4	CMea CTri ECha ELan EPot GMaP LBee MLHP MWat NMen NWCA SBch WAbe WFar
*	- 'Roseum Variegatum'	EPot
	- 'Strawberries and Cream'	WAbe WFar
	tortuosum	SEND WMoo
	wulfenianum	EDAr IFoB LLHF NBre SEND WAbe

Amana (*Liliaceae*)

edulis	ECho

Amaranthus (*Amaranthaceae*)

caudatus	WTou
hypochondriacus	CSpe
'Pygmy Torch' ♀H3	

× *Amarcrinum* (*Amaryllidaceae*)

'Dorothy Hannibal'	GCal WCot
memoria-corsii	CPrp ECho
- 'Howardii'	CFir EBee ECho EShb LEdu WCot WHlf

× *Amarine* (*Amaryllidaceae*)

tubergenii	CAvo
- 'Zwanenburg'	CStu EBee WCot

× *Amarygia* (*Amaryllidaceae*)

parkeri	ECho
§ - 'Alba'	EBee ECho WCot

Amaryllis (*Amaryllidaceae*)

§ ***belladonna*** ♀H2-3	CAby CBcs CHEx CPne CPrp CTca EBee EBrs ECho EPfP ERCP EShb EWTr GBin LAma LEdu MBri NBPC NCGa SChr SDeJ SDnm SEND SMrm SPav WClo WCot WHil
- 'Bloemfontein'	CAvo
- 'Johannesburg'	CAvo WCot
- 'Kimberley'	CPne
- 'Major'	CAvo
- 'Parkeri Alba'	see × *Amarygia parkeri* 'Alba'
- 'Purpurea'	WCot
- white-flowered	EBee ECho SDeJ WCot

Amberboa (*Asteraceae*)

§ ***moschata***	WCot

Ambrosina (*Araceae*)

bassii from Tunisia	ECho

Amelanchier ✿ (*Rosaceae*)

alnifolia	EPla MWya
- 'Forestburg'	MBri
- 'Obelisk'PBR	CDoC CDul EBee GKir LBuc LHop LLHF LRHS MAsh MBri MGos NCGa SCoo SSta
§ - var. ***pumila***	CPMA LHop WTin
- var. ***semi-integrifolia*** new	NLar
- 'Smokey'	CDul
§ ***arborea***	SRms
asiatica var. ***sinica*** new	NLar
bartramiana	CTho SSta
- 'Eskimo'	NLar
canadensis K. Koch	see *A. lamarckii*
canadensis Sieb. & Zucc.	see *A. arborea*
canadensis ambig.	GAuc GKir IFFs NPri
canadensis (L.) Medik.	Widely available
- 'Prince William' new	SSta
- Rainbow Pillar = 'Glenn Form'	MBlu SSta
denticulata F&M 176	WPGP
× ***grandiflora*** 'Autumn Brilliance'	CEnd CPMA MBri NHol NLar
- 'Ballerina' ♀H4	Widely available
- 'Cole's Select'	EBee LRHS
- 'Princess Diana'	EBee MBlu NLar SCoo
- 'Robin Hill'	CBcs CMac EBee ECrN ELon GKir LAst LBuc LRHS MBlu MGos MRav NEgg NLar SCoo SLim SMad WFar WPat
- 'Rubescens'	CDul CEnd CPMA EBee EPfP
humilis	GAuc
'La Paloma'	CWSG EBee GKir LRHS MBri NLar SCoo
laevis	CBcs CDul CTri EPfP MGos NLar SPer STre
- 'Cumulus'	NLar
- 'Prince Charles'	NLar
- 'R.J. Hilton'	EBee GKir MBri SCoo
- 'Snow Cloud'	CDoC
- 'Snowflakes'	CEnd CPMA CWSG EBee GKir LRHS MGos NHol NLar SLim SPer SPoG SPur
§ ***lamarckii*** ♀H4	Widely available
ovalis misapplied	see *A. spicata* (Lam.) K. Koch.
ovalis Medik.	SPlb
- 'Edelweiss'	CEnd CPMA MBlu MGos NEgg NLar SCoo
- 'Helvetia'	NLar WEas
pumila	see *A. alnifolia* var. *pumila*
rotundifolia ambig.	MCoo
spicata (Lam.) K. Koch.	ECrN IFFs MCoo SSta

Amianthium (*Melanthiaceae*)

muscitoxicum	LRHS

Amicia (*Papilionaceae*)

zygomeris	CBot CHEx CHGN CHll CMdw CPom CSpe EBee ELon EWes EWld GBin GCal MCot SAga SDix SMad SMrm SPoG SUsu WCot WSHC

Amitostigma (*Orchidaceae*)

Enomotoe	NLAp WWst
gx 'Kou Itten' new	

Ammi (*Apiaceae*)

majus	CArn CSpe SDix SMrm
visnaga	CArn CBre CHby CSpe ELau WHal

Ammocharis (*Amaryllidaceae*)

coranica	ECho WCot

Ammophila (*Poaceae*)

arenaria	CBod CKno CRWN EBWF EBee GFor SMea
breviligulata	SPhx

Amomyrtus (*Myrtaceae*)

§ ***luma***	CAgr CDoC CDul CHEx CTri EBee ELan GQui IDee IFFs SAPC SArc WCot WJek

Amorpha (*Papilionaceae*)

canescens	CBcs EBee GKir LRHS MBri SEND SPlb WBVN WSHC
fruticosa	CBcs EBee EShb EWTr LEdu MBlu MBri NLar SPlb
herbacea	NLar
ouachitensis	NLar
paniculata	NLar

Amorphophallus ✿ (*Araceae*)

Chen Yi A-102 new	WCot
albispathus	WCot
albus	CDTJ LEdu WCot
bulbifer	CDTJ EAmu EBee EUJe LAma SBig WPGP
dunnii	CDTJ
kerrii	CPLG WCot

kiusianus	WCot
- B&SWJ 4845	WCru
konjac	CDTJ CDes CFir CGHE CHEx CPLG EAmu EUJe LEdu SHaC WCot WPGP WWst
nepalensis	CDTJ EBee EUJe
rivieri	EBee GCal WCot
stipitatus	CAby WCot

Ampelocalamus (*Poaceae*)

scandens	CGHE EPla WPGP

Ampelocissus (*Vitaceae*)

sikkimensis HWJK 2066	WCru

Ampelodesmos (*Poaceae*)

mauritanica	CHar CHid CKno COlW CSam CSpe EBee ECha EHoe EPPr EShb EWes GFor LEdu LOck LRHS MNrw MWhi SEND SMHy SPlb WBox WCot WHrl WPGP WRHF WWEG

Ampelopsis (*Vitaceae*)

aconitifolia	CWit MGos NLar
- 'Chinese Lace'	EBee LRHS MRav NLar WPGP
brevipedunculata	ELan MMHG SCoo SGar SKHP SLim SPer SPoG WDin WFar
- var. ***maximowiczii*** 'Elegans' (v)	CBcs CHEx CMac CWib EBee ELan EPfP EShb LAst LHop LRHS MGos MRav MSwo NBro SAga SPad SPer SPoG SWvt WCot WDin WPat WSHC
delavayana	EBee
henryana	see *Parthenocissus henryana*
megalophylla	CBot CHEx EBee ELan EPfP EShb GCal IArd IDee MBri NCGa NLar SPer WBVN WCru WFar
sempervirens hort. ex Veitch	see *Cissus striata*
tricuspidata 'Veitchii'	see *Parthenocissus tricuspidata* 'Veitchii'

Amphicome see *Incarvillea*

Amsonia (*Apocynaceae*)

ciliata	CHid CPom EBee EDif ELan IKil
elliptica	EBee
'Ernst Pagels' new	NDov
hubrichtii	CAby CEnt CFir CMdw CPom CSpe EBee EBrs ECha ELon EPPr LEdu LHop NLar SMad SPad WHoo WPer WPnP WPtf WSHC
- from Hans Kramer	SMHy
illustris	CAbP CEnt CPom EBee EBrs EPPr GCal GKir LRHS NLar SHar SMHy SUsu WHoo WHrl WPer WSHC WTin
jonesii	SMHy
§ ***orientalis***	CFir CHar CHll CMea CTri EBee ECha EHrv GBBs GCal LEdu LHop MLHP MRav NDov NLar SAga SGar SMHy SMrm SPoG SUsu WAul WBor WFar WPnP WPtf WTin
tabernaemontana	Widely available
- var. ***salicifolia***	CEnt CSpe EBee GKir NBPC NDov WCAu WTin
tomentosa	EBee

Amygdalus see *Prunus*

Anacamptis (*Orchidaceae*)

× ***callithea***	NLAp
champagneuxii	NLAp
coriophora new	NLAp
fragrans	NLAp
§ ***laxiflora***	NLAp
§ ***morio***	NLAp
- ***alba*** × ***sancta***	NLAp
morio × ***papilionacea***	NLAp
palustris	NLAp
pyramidalis	EFEx NLAp WHer
sancta	NLAp

Anacyclus (*Asteraceae*)

pyrethrum	GPoy
- var. ***depressus***	CTri EBee ECho ELan EPfP GGar GKir GMaP LRHS NVic NWCA SPlb SRot WCFE WFar WHoo WPer WRHF
- - 'Garden Gnome'	CTri ECho MSCN SRms WFar
- - 'Silberkissen'	EDAr NBre SBch

Anagallis (*Primulaceae*)

arvensis	MNHC
- var. ***caerulea***	EDif
monellii ♀H4	MNrw
- Blue Compact = 'Wesanacomp'	LSou SVil
- subsp. ***linifolia*** 'Blue Light'	CSpe
- 'Skylover'	CCCN CFox LAst NPri SAga
- 'Sunrise'	CPBP LAst SUsu
tenella	LLWG
- 'Studland'	CEnt GAbr NWCA WAbe

Ananas (*Bromeliaceae*)

comosus (F)	CCCN
- 'Champaca' (F) new	CCCN

Anaphalioides (*Asteraceae*)

§ ***bellidioides***	CTri ECha ECou GAbr GGar

Anaphalis (*Asteraceae*)

alpicola	EBee EPot NBre NMen
margaritacea	CBcs CSBt EBee ECha ECtt GMaP MLLN NBid SRms WFar WMoo WPtf
§ - 'Neuschnee'	CTri CWan EBee EPfP NBPC NBre NGdn NPri WFar WPer WWEG
- New Snow	see *A. margaritacea* 'Neuschnee'
- var. ***yedoensis*** ♀H4	CTri EBee MCot MLHP NBre SDix SGar SPer WBrE
§ ***nepalensis*** var. ***monocephala***	ELan MCot NBre NSti
nubigena	see *A. nepalensis* var. *monocephala*
transnokoensis	EBee EWes
§ ***trinervis***	CPLG
triplinervis ♀H4	EBee ECrN EHoe ELan EPPr EPfP GGar GKev GKir GMaP IFoB LRHS MCot MRav NBid NBir NLar NVic SMrm SPer SRms WCot WFar WHoo WMoo WWEG
- 'Silberregen'	EBee
§ - 'Sommerschnee' ♀H4	CMac EBee ECha ECtt EHoe EPfP GKir LBMP LRHS MCot MRav NEgg NLar SPer WMnd WPer
- Summer Snow	see *A. triplinervis* 'Sommerschnee'

Anchusa (*Boraginaceae*)

angustissima	see *A. leptophylla* subsp. *incana*
§ ***azurea***	CArn EBee EGxp MLLN NLar
- 'Dropmore'	CTri EBee ELan EPfP GJos LAst LRHS MNHC NBPC NEgg NLar SMrm SPav SRms WPer WWEG
- 'Feltham Pink' new	CHid

- 'Feltham Pride'	CSBt EBee GJos GKir LRHS SPav SRms SWvt WFar WHoo WPGP WPer
- 'Little John'	EBee SRms
- 'Loddon Royalist' ♀H4	Widely available
- 'Opal'	EBee ECtt EPfP EWTr GCal LRHS MMHG
- 'Royal Blue'	GKir
caespitosa misapplied	see *A. leptophylla* subsp. *incana*
capensis 'Blue Angel'	MNHC SWvt WFar
cespitosa Lam.	ECho ELan EWes LLHF WAbe
italica	see *A. azurea*
laxiflora	see *Borago pygmaea*
§ ***leptophylla*** subsp. ***incana***	SBch
- - F&W 9550	MDKP
myosotidiflora	see *Brunnera macrophylla*
officinalis	CArn MNHC SPav
sempervirens	see *Pentaglottis sempervirens*

Ancylostemon (*Gesneriaceae*)

convexus B&SWJ 6624	WCru

Andrachne (*Euphorbiaceae*)

colchica	EBee WCot

Androcymbium (*Colchicaceae*)

cuspidatum 'Karoopoort' new	ECho
dregei 'Loeriesfontein' new	ECho
eucomoides 'Varsputs' new	ECho
gramineum	ECho
- from Morocco	ECho
melanthioides new	ECho
volutare 'Tanqua' new	ECho

Andrographis (*Acanthaceae*)

paniculata	CArn

Andromeda (*Ericaceae*)

glaucophylla f. ***latifolia*** new	IVic
polifolia	ECho GAuc GKev MAsh NWCA WDin WFar
- 'Alba'	ECho EPot GKev LRHS MAsh NRya SPer SPlb SWvt WFar
- 'Blue Ice'	ELan EPfP GKir LRHS MAsh MBri MNHC NHar NLar NMen SLim SPer SPoG SSpi WAbe WFar WPat
- 'Compacta' ♀H4	CDoC CMac EBee ECho EPfP EPot GEdr GGar GKir LSRN LTen MAsh MBri MMuc NHol NMen SBfd SPer SPoG SRms SWvt WGwG WSHC
- 'Compacta Alba' ♀H4	ECho
- 'Grandiflora'	ECho GEdr GKev
- 'Kirigamine'	GKir LRHS MAsh NHar NHol
- 'Macrophylla' ♀H4	ECho EPot GEdr NHar WAbe WPat WThu
- 'Nana'	CSBt ELan EPfP LRHS MAsh NMen
- 'Nikko'	CMac NHol
- 'Shibutsu'	NMen

Andropogon (*Poaceae*)

gerardii	CKno CRWN EBee EHoe EHul EPPr GFor LEdu MWhi NWsh SApp SGSe SPhx WWEG
scoparius	see *Schizachyrium scoparium*
virginicus	EBee

Androsace (*Primulaceae*)

albana	ECho GKev
alpina	WAbe
armeniaca var. ***macrantha***	EDAr GAbr
bulleyana	WAbe WWEG
caduca	WAbe
cantabrica	EPot
carnea	CPBP ECho
- ***alba***	ITim
- subsp. ***brigantiaca***	ECho GAbr GKev NLAp NRya NSla WAbe WHoo
- var. ***halleri***	see *A. carnea* subsp. *rosea*
- subsp. ***laggeri*** ♀H4	ECho LLHF NLAp NSla WAbe WFar
§ - subsp. ***rosea*** ♀H4	ECho
carnea × ***pyrenaica***	ECho NMen
chamaejasme	ECho
ciliata	WAbe
cylindrica	ECho GKev ITim LRHS NMen WFar
cylindrica × ***hirtella***	ECho ITim LRHS WAbe
delavayi	WAbe
- ACE 1786	WAbe
foliosa	GKev
geraniifolia	EBee ECha SRms
globifera	EPot WAbe
gracilis PB 99/20	EPot
halleri	see *A. carnea* subsp. *rosea*
hedraeantha	ECho GKev NRya NSla WAbe
helvetica	ECho
himalaica	CPBP EPot GEdr NMen WAbe
hirtella	WAbe
idahoensis	WAbe
idahoensis × ***laevigata*** new	WAbe
incana	GKev WAbe
jacquemontii	see *A. villosa* var. *jacquemontii*
kosopoljanskii	WAbe
lactea	GAbr WAbe
laevigata	ITim NMen WAbe
- from Columbia River Gorge, USA	WAbe
- var. ***ciliolata***	NWCA
- 'Gothenburg'	WAbe WPat
- 'Saddle Mount'	WAbe
lanuginosa ♀H4	CMea CPBP CSpe ECho ECtt EHoe EPot GEdr MWat NHar NMen NPri NWCA SRms SRot WAbe WFar WNew
- compact	EPot
- 'Leichtlinii'	GKev
lehmanniana	WAbe
yellow-flowered new	
limprichtii	see *A. sarmentosa* var. *watkinsii*
mariae	WAbe
× ***marpensis***	EPot NMen WAbe
mathildae	EPot
microphylla	see *A. mucronifolia* G. Watt
minor	WAbe
§ ***mollis***	CPBP
montana	WAbe
mucronifolia misapplied	see *A. sempervivoides*
§ ***mucronifolia*** G. Watt	WAbe
mucronifolia × ***sempervivoides***	EPot
muscoidea	WAbe
- SEP 132	CPBP
- 'Breviscapa'	EPot
- f. ***longiscapa***	WAbe
- Schacht's form	WAbe
nivalis 'Chumstick Form'	LLHF
ochotensis	WAbe
primuloides	see *A. studiosorum*
pubescens	ECho LLHF LRHS NMen
pyrenaica	ECho LRHS NMen

	rigida	EPot WAbe
	robusta subsp. ***purpurea***	WAbe
	rotundifolia	GEdr GKev
	- stoloniferous new	GEdr
	sarmentosa misapplied	see *A. studiosorum*
	sarmentosa ambig.	EDAr GAbr GJos MWat
	sarmentosa Wall.	SRms WHoo
	- from Namche, Nepal	EPot EWld WAbe
	- Galmont's form	see *A. studiosorum* 'Salmon's Variety'
	- 'Sherriffii'	ECho EPot GEdr SRms WHoo
§	- var. ***watkinsii***	EPot GKev NMen
	- var. ***yunnanensis*** misapplied	see *A. studiosorum*
	- var. ***yunnanensis*** Knuth	see *A. mollis*
	selago	WAbe
	- 'Red Eye' new	WAbe
§	***sempervivoides*** ♀H4	CYeo ECho EDAr EPot GEdr GJos GKev GMaP LHop LRHS NHol NLAp NMen NWCA SPlb SRms WAbe WPat
	- CC 4622	GKev
	- CC 4631	GKev
	- 'Greystone'	NMen
	- 'Susan Joan' (v)	CPBP EPot GEdr GKev WAbe
	septentrionalis	GKev
	- 'Stardust'	ECho NBre
	spinulifera SDR 4808	GKev
	- SDR 5948	GKev
	strigillosa	GKev WAbe
§	***studiosorum*** ♀H4	ECho EPot GEdr GKev WAbe WPat
	- 'Chumbyi'	GEdr LLHF NLAp NWCA SRms WPat
	- 'Doksa'	CPBP EPot GEdr NLAp NMen WAbe WPat
§	- 'Salmon's Variety'	CMea CTri ECho WAbe
	tangulashanensis new	WAbe
	tapete	EPot
	- ACE 1725	WAbe
	vandellii	GKev ITim
§	***villosa*** var. ***jacquemontii***	CPBP EDAr GEdr NHar NWCA
	- - lilac-flowered	EPot
	- - pink-flowered	EPot NLAp WAbe
	- subsp. ***taurica***	ECho
	vitaliana	see *Vitaliana primuliflora*
	wardii new	WAbe
	watkinsii	see *A. sarmentosa* var. *watkinsii*
	yargongensis	GKev WAbe
	zambalensis	WAbe
	zayulensis new	WAbe

Andryala (*Asteraceae*)

	agardhii	WPat
	lanata	see *Hieracium lanatum*

Anemanthele (*Poaceae*)

§	***lessoniana*** ♀H4	Widely available
	- 'Gold Hue'	CKno

Anemarrhena (*Anthericaceae*)

	asphodeloides	CArn WCot

Anemone ✿ (*Ranunculaceae*)

	Chen Yi T49	WCot
	aconitifolia Michx.	see *A. narcissiflora*
	aconitifolia ambig.	GKir
	afghanica	LRHS
	altaica	ECho NLar SRms
	amurensis	CPLG EBla ECho
	apennina ♀H4	CAvo CLAP EBla ECGP ECho WShi WTin
	- var. ***albiflora***	CDes CLAP EBee ECho EPPr EPot LRHS MAvo WPnP
	- double-flowered (d)	CDes CPBP EBla ECho EPPr MAvo SMHy WCru
	- 'Petrovac'	CBgR CLAP EBee EPot LLHF WCot
	baldensis	EBee ECho EDAr GKev ITim SRms
	barbulata	CPLG ECho EWes GAuc GEdr GMac NLar SMad WSHC
	blanda ♀H4	EBrs ECho GKir LAma LRHS MAvo MBri MLHP MNHC NChi NLar SEND SGar SWal WBor WFar WShi
I	- 'Alba'	LRHS
	- 'Blue Star'	ECho
	- blue-flowered	Widely available
	- 'Charmer'	ECho EPot ERCP NMen
	- 'Ingramii'	EPot WCot
	- pink-flowered	GKir SMrm
	- var. ***rosea*** ♀H4	ECho ELan EPfP GKev LAma LRHS SPer SPoG WFar
	- - 'Pink Charmer'	ECho NLar
	- - 'Pink Star'	ECho ERCP LAma MCot NBir
	- - 'Radar' ♀H4	CMea ECho EPot ERCP LAma MNrw NBir SDeJ WAbe
	- 'Violet Star'	ECho EPot ERCP NLar SDeJ SPhx
	- 'White Charmer'	ECho
	- 'White Splendour' ♀H4	CAvo CFFs CFox CMea CSam CTri EBrs ECho ELan EPfP EPot ERCP GAbr GKev LAma LRHS MCot NBir NChi NLar NMen SDeJ SPer SPhx SPoG SRms WCot WFar
	- white-flowered	SMrm
	blue-flowered from China	CDes
	canadensis	CSpe CWCL EBee ECho ELon EPPr GGar ITim WBVN WCot
	caroliniana	EBee ECho GKev GKir
	caucasica	ECho SCnR WWst
	chapaensis HWJ 631	WCru
	coronaria De Caen Group	EBrs EPfP GKir LAma LRHS SPoG WFar
§	- - 'Die Braut'	CFox CMea ERCP GKev LRHS NBir SDeJ WFar
	- - 'His Excellency'	see *A. coronaria* (De Caen Group) 'Hollandia'
§	- - 'Hollandia'	CFox
	- - 'Mister Fokker'	CFox CTca EBrs ERCP GKev LAma WFar
	- - The Bride	see *A. coronaria* (De Caen Group) 'Die Braut'
	- - 'The Governor'	CFox CTca SDeJ WFar
	- Jerusalem hybrids	WFar
	- Saint Bridgid Group (d)	EBrs EPfP LAma WFar
	- - 'Lord Lieutenant' (d)	CFox CMea EPfP ERCP EWTr NBir WFar
	- - 'Mount Everest' (d)	CFox ERCP NBir SDeJ
	- - 'Saint Bridgid' (d)	EBrs LRHS
	- - 'The Admiral' (d)	CFox EPfP NBir SDeJ WFar
	- Saint Piran Group	CBgR
	- 'Sylphide' (Mona Lisa Series)	CFox ERCP NBir SDeJ WFar
	crinita	LLHF WBVN
	cylindrica	CSam EBee MDKP NBre NLar
	decapetala	MHer
	demissa	WCot
	- SDR 3307	EBee GKev
	- SDR 4306	GKev
	dichotoma	SSvw
	drummondii	EBee GAbr GKev NChi WBVN
	eranthoides	EBee ECho WWst
	fanninii	GCal
	fasciculata	see *A. narcissiflora*
	flaccida	CAby CDes CLAP EBee ECho EHrv EPPr GEdr GMac LRHS MAvo

		MNrw SBch WCot WCru WFar WHal WSHC
	× ***fulgens***	ECha ECho
	- 'Annulata Grandiflora'	ECGP
	- 'Multipetala'	ECho
	globosa	see *A. multifida* Poir.
	gortschakowii* × *petiolulosa	WWst
	'Guernica'	EBee ECho EWes
	'Hatakeyama Double' (d)	CMdw GCal LPla
	'Hatakeyama Single'	CDes CMdw LPla
	hepatica L.	see *Hepatica nobilis*
§	***hortensis***	CMea ECho NBre
	- subsp. ***heldreichii***	ECho
§	***hupehensis***	CBot CPLG EBee GBBs GMaP IGor WFar WPer
	- BWJ 8190	WCru
	- f. ***alba***	CLAP CSpe EBla IFro WPGP
§	- 'Bowles's Pink' ♀H4	CElw CPLG EBee ECho IGor MWat SPet WCru WPGP WTin
	- 'Crispa'	see *A.* × *hybrida* 'Lady Gilmour' Wolley-Dod
	- 'Eugenie'	EBee ECtt MWea NBir NGdn NHol
	- 'Hadspen Abundance' ♀H4	Widely available
	- 'Hadspen Red'	WFar
§	- var. ***japonica***	CPou EWTr MLLN NBPC NCob
	- - B&SWJ 4886	WCru
	- - 'Bodnant Burgundy'	CDes EBee ECtt WPGP
§	- - 'Bressingham Glow'	CMHG CMac CPLG CSam EAEE EBee ECtt ELan EPfP EPot GKir LRHS MBri MRav NBir NGdn NHol NVic SPer SPet WAbb WBrk WCAu WFar
§	- - 'Pamina' ♀H4	Widely available
	- - 'Pink Saucer' **new**	LBuc
	- - Prince Henry	see *A. hupehensis* var. *japonica* 'Prinz Heinrich'
§	- - 'Prinz Heinrich' ♀H4	Widely available
§	- - 'Rotkäppchen'	EBee EBla EBrs ECtt GAbr GBin GGar GQue IVic LRHS LSou MAvo NGdn NHol NLar SMrm SWvt WBrk WCot WHoo WSHC
	- - 'Splendens'	CMHG COIW EBee EBrs GBBs LAst LHop MAsh MCot MMuc MRav NEgg NGdn SPur SWal SWvt WAbb WFar WHal WWEG
	- 'Ouvertüre'	EBee ECtt MAvo WCot WPGP
	- 'Praecox'	CKno CMea EAEE EBee EBla EHrv EPfP GBBs LRHS MBNS NBPC NBir NGdn NHol NPri SBfd SWvt WAbb WFar WHal WMnd WWEG
	- 'September Charm'	see *A.* × *hybrida* 'September Charm'
	- 'Superba'	EPfP WKif
§	× ***hybrida***	ECho LRHS MWat NChi NCob NEgg SGar WFar WMoo
	- 'Alba' misapplied (UK)	see *A.* × *hybrida* 'Honorine Jobert'
	- 'Alba Dura'	see *A. tomentosa* 'Albadura'
	- 'Albert Schweitzer'	see *A.* × *hybrida* 'Elegans'
	- 'Andrea Atkinson'	Widely available
	- 'Bowles's Pink'	see *A. hupehensis* 'Bowles's Pink'
	- 'Bressingham Glow'	see *A. hupehensis* var. *japonica* 'Bressingham Glow'
	- 'Coupe d'Argent'	EBee IKil NBre WCot
§	- 'Elegans' ♀H4	CSam CWCL EBee ECtt GMaP LHop MLLN MMuc MRav NBPC NBir NGdn SMrm SWat SWvt WFar WHil WSpi
§	- 'Géante des Blanches'	EBee IGor LPla LRHS MAvo
§	- 'Honorine Jobert' ♀H4	Widely available
§	- 'Königin Charlotte' ♀H4	Widely available
	- 'Kriemhilde'	EBee GBin
	- 'Lady Gilmour' misapplied	see *A.* × *hybrida* 'Montrose'
	- 'Lady Gilmour' ambig.	GMaP MCot MLLN MSCN NBPC SPad
§	- 'Lady Gilmour' Wolley-Dod	CSam CSpe EBee ECtt EHrv EPfP GAbr GCra GKir GMac LEdu LRHS MBri MRav NBPC NBir NEgg NGdn SAga WCot WCru WFar WWEG
	- 'Little Princess'	CHid EBee ECtt
	- 'Loreley'	CMea CPrp EBee EPfP MWat NLar SBfd SWvt WWEG
	- 'Luise Uhink'	CPou IGor LRHS NBir
	- 'Märchenfee' **new**	EBee
	- 'Margarete' Kayser & Seibert	CPLG CPar EBee EBrs ECtt ELan EPPr EPfP LAst LHop MBri MGos MWat NGdn SBfd WCot WCru
	- 'Max Vogel'	see *A.* × *hybrida* 'Elegans'
	- 'Monterosa'	see *A.* × *hybrida* 'Montrose'
§	- 'Montrose'	CPou EBee ECha EHrv EWes GCal GKir GMaP LSou MLLN NBir NLar SRms SWat WCAu
	- 'Pamina'	see *A. hupehensis* var. *japonica* 'Pamina'
	- Prince Henry	see *A. hupehensis* var. *japonica* 'Prinz Heinrich'
	- 'Profusion'	CTri LBuc WHal
	- Queen Charlotte	see *A.* × *hybrida* 'Königin Charlotte'
	- 'Richard Ahrens'	EBee ECtt EShb GCal GKir GMaP GMac LAst LHop LRHS MGos MLHP MSCN NBPC NEgg NGdn NHol NLar SBfd SWat WCru WFar WMnd WWEG
§	- 'Robustissima'	EBee ECtt EPfP GBBs GMaP GMac LLWP LRHS LSRN MCot MGos MRav NBir NCob NDov NGdn NSti SPer SWat SWvt WAbb WFar WMnd WMoo WWEG
	- 'Rosenschale'	EBee GMac WCru
	- 'Rotkäppchen'	see *A. hupehensis* var. *japonica* 'Rotkäppchen'
§	- 'September Charm' ♀H4	Widely available
	- 'Serenade'	CChe CPar CSam EBee ECtt EPfP GBBs GMac IVic LSRN MAsh MRav NBir NLar SMrm SPad SPoG SRkn WCAu WCot WFar WHoo WMoo WWEG
	- Tourbillon	see *A.* × *hybrida* 'Whirlwind'
§	- 'Whirlwind'	Widely available
	- 'White Queen'	see *A.* × *hybrida* 'Géante des Blanches'
	- Wirbelwind	see *A.* × *hybrida* 'Whirlwind'
	japonica	see *A.* × *hybrida*, *A. hupehensis*, *A. hupehensis* var. *japonica*
	keiskeana	EBee GEdr WCru WWst
§	× ***lesseri***	CFir CSpe EBee ECha ECho ECtt EDAr EHrv ELan GKev LHop MHer SPhx SRms WFar
	leveillei	Widely available
	- BWJ 7919	WCru
§	× ***lipsiensis***	CAby CAvo CDes CPBP EBee EBla ECho EPfP EPot EShb GBBs GEdr GMaP IFro LRHS MAsh MAvo MNrw MTho NDov NLar NMen NRya NWCA WCot WCru WFar WHal WPGP WSHC
	- 'Pallida' ♀H4	CPMA EBee EBla ECho ELon GCrs GEdr GKev IGor LLWP LRHS MAvo NLar NWCA SKHP SMrm SSvw WCot
	- 'Vindobonensis' **new**	WCot
	lyallii	WBrE
N	***magellanica*** hort. ex Wehrh.	see *A. multifida* Poir.

	matsudae B&SWJ 1452	WCru
	multifida misapplied red-flowered	see *A.* × *lesseri*
§	***multifida*** Poir.	CStu EBee ECha ECho EPfP GGar GKev IFoB LHop LRHS MAvo NBir NChi NSti NSum SPoG SRms WFar WHoo WPtf WTin
	- NNS 06-49	EPPr
	- Annabella Series	GAbr
	- 'Major'	CFir CHar CMea CPrp CSpe EPfP NCob NGdn NWCA WBVN WFar
	- f. ***polysepala***	NEgg
	- 'Rubra'	CMea CPrp EAEE EBee EDAr EHrv EPfP EWll GAbr GEdr GGar GKev LBMP LRHS MAvo MBNS MNrw NBPC NBir NEgg NLar NWCA SMrm SPoG STes WHoo WPtf
	- yellow-flowered	GBBs GGar NSum
§	***narcissiflora***	CSpe ECho EHrv GKev IGor NBir NBre NChi NPnk WCom WFar
	nemorosa 🏆H4	Widely available
N	- 'Alba Plena' (d)	CPMA CSWP CSam CStu EBee EBla ECha ECho EPPr GEdr GGar GMac MTho NMen NPnk SMad WAbb WCru WFar WPnP WSHC
	- 'Allenii' 🏆H4	CAby EBee EBla EBrs ECha ECho ELon EPot GEdr GMaP ITim LRHS MAvo MNFA MRav NMen NRya WCom WCot WCru WFar WShi
	- 'Amy Doncaster'	CLAP ECho
	- 'Atley' **new**	EBee
	- 'Atrocaerulea'	CLAP IBlr NLar WCru WFar
	- 'Atrorosea'	EBee
	- 'Ballyrogan Blue' **new**	MNrw
	- 'Bill Baker's Pink'	CDes CLAP MAvo
	- 'Blue Beauty'	CLAP CPMA EBee ELon GMaP IBlr MAvo NMen SBch WCru
	- 'Blue Bonnet'	CElw CPMA ECho IGor ITim MAvo MNrw SMrm
	- 'Blue Eyes' (d)	CAby CDes CElw CLAP CStu EBee EBla GCrs GEdr GMaP IBlr IGor ITim MAvo NBir NDov NMen WCot WCru WFar
	- 'Blue Queen'	GAbr
	- 'Bowles's Purple'	CAby CPMA CPom EBee ECho GBBs GMaP IBlr LRHS MAvo MNrw NBid NHar NMyG NRya SKHP SPoG WCot WCru WFar WPnP WTin
	- 'Bracteata'	ECho EHrv GEdr LRHS NMen
	- 'Bracteata Pleniflora' (d)	CBow CLAP CPMA CStu EBee EBla EBrs ECho GMaP IBlr IGor LHop MAvo MNrw NBir NMen WCot WCru WFar WHal
	- 'Buckland'	CDes CFwr CLAP EBee EHrv EPfP IBlr SKHP SMad WCru WFar
	- 'Caerulea'	ITim
	- 'Cedric's Pink'	CLAP CPMA EBla ECho EPPr IBlr IGor LLHF MNrw WCru WFar
	- 'Celestial'	EBee EBla ECho EPPr
	- 'Dee Day'	CLAP EBee EHrv MNrw SCnR SMrm WFar
	- 'Dell Garden' **new**	EPPr
	- 'Evelyn Meadows' 🏆H4	CLAP
	- 'Flore Pleno' (d)	CDes EBla ECho GAbr GKir MMoz NBir NMen
	- 'Frühlingsfee'	CPMA EBee ECho NLar
	- 'Gerda Ramusen'	CLAP EBla ECho LLHF
	- 'Green Fingers'	CLAP CPMA EBla ECho EHrv EPPr EPot GEdr GMaP IGor IPot ITim MAvo MNrw SCnR WCot WCru
	- 'Hannah Gubbay'	CLAP IBlr IGor MAvo MNrw
	- 'Hilda'	ECho EPot GCrs GEdr MAvo MNrw NBir NDov NMen NRya
	- 'Ice and Fire'	MAvo SSvw
	- 'Jack Brownless'	CLAP ITim
	- 'Kentish Pink'	GBBs GCrs GMaP
	- 'Knightshayes Vestal' (d)	CLAP EBee ECho MRav NHol WCot
	- 'Lady Doneraile'	CDes CLAP EPot ITim MDKP NBir NLar SSvw WCru WFar
	- 'Latvian Pink'	EBee ECho EPot
	- 'Leeds' Variety'	CLAP CSam EPot GCrs GMaP IGor ITim MAvo MNrw MTho NMen
	- 'Lionel Bacon'	WWst
	- 'Lismore Blue'	EBee ECho EPPr EPot
	- 'Lismore Pink'	EHrv GEdr
	- 'Lucia'	EPot
	- 'Lychette'	CHid CPMA EBee ECho EHrv EPPr EPot GAbr IBlr IPot ITim LPio MAvo MNrw NWCA SHar WCru WFar
	- 'Marie Rose'	EPot
	- 'Martin'	CStu
	- 'Mart's Blue'	GCrs IPot
	- 'Miss Eunice'	CLAP
	- 'Monstrosa'	EBee EBla EBrs ECho SSvw
	- 'New Pink'	CLAP CPom IBlr
	- 'Parlez Vous'	EBee ECho EHrv EPPr GEdr LPio MAvo MNrw NCGa NMen SCnR SSvw WFar
	- 'Pat's Pink'	WShi
	- 'Pentre Pink'	EPot IBlr MAvo MCot MNrw MSSP MTho WBVN WCru WFar
	- 'Picos Pink'	EHrv SCnR WWst
	- 'Pink Carpet'	GEdr
	- pink-flowered	CLAP ECho WCru
	- 'Polar Star'	CLAP
	- 'Robinsoniana' 🏆H4	Widely available
	- 'Rosea'	CLAP EBrs ECho GEdr MNrw SMrm WCru
	- 'Royal Blue'	CAby CDes CLAP CPMA EBee ECho EHrv EPPr GAbr GEdr GMaP LAma MAvo NHol NMen NPnk WCot WCru WFar WPnP WTin
	- 'Rubra'	EPot GKev MNrw
	- 'Salt and Pepper'	MAvo
	- 'Stammheim' (d)	CLAP
	- 'Super Allenii'	EBee
	- 'Tinney's Blush'	CLAP
	- 'Tomas'	CLAP EBee ECho ELon EPot GBin GEdr ITim NHar NWCA SPoG
	- 'Vestal' (d) 🏆H4	Widely available
	- 'Virescens' 🏆H4	CAby CAvo CFFs CLAP CWCL EBee ECho EHrv EPPr EPot GAbr GCrs GEdr GKir GMaP MAvo NBir NHar NWCA WCom WPtf WShi
	- 'Viridiflora'	CFwr CLAP ECho EPfP GAbr LHop MNrw MTho NBir NSti SSvw WCon WCot WCru WFar WSHC
	- 'Westwell Pink'	CAby CLAP CPMA CSWP EBee ECho EPPr LLHF MAvo MNrw MSSP WCot
	- white-flowered	GKir
	- 'Wilks' Giant'	ITim MAvo WCru WFar
	- 'Wilks' White'	EBla ELon EPPr GEdr WCru WFar
	- 'Wisley Pink'	EPot
	- 'Wyatt's Pink'	CLAP CPMA ELon MAvo NCGa WCru WFar WPnP WTin
	- 'Yerda Ramusem'	EBee ECho EPPr MAvo
	nemorosa* × *ranunculoides	see *A.* × *lipsiensis*
	nikoensis	ECho WWst
	obtusiloba	CLAP GEdr GKir MTho SRms WAbe
	- CLD 1549	GEdr

	- 'Alba'	GMac WAbe
I	- 'Sulphurea'	CDes GEdr NMen
	- yellow-flowered	WAbe
	palmata	EDAr GKir MDKP MWea NBre NPnk SGSe SMad WCru WFar
	parviflora	EBee ECho
	patens	see *Pulsatilla patens*
	pavonina	CAby CMea CPMA CSpe ECha GMac LRHS MAsh MBri MSSP MTho NBir SMHy SPoG SUsu WAbe WCom WCot WCru
	- 'Chapeau de Cardinal'	MAsh
	- 'Grecian Sunset'	MAsh
	- lilac-flowered	MAsh NBir
	- pink-flowered	MAsh NBir SUsu
	polyanthes	CSpe WCot
	prattii	CLAP CPLG EPPr GEdr WCot WHal
	pseudoaltaica	EBee GEdr WCru WWst
	- pale blue-flowered	CLAP
	- 'Yuki-no-sei' (d)	GEdr WWst
	pulsatilla	see *Pulsatilla vulgaris*
	quinquefolia	CLAP WCot
	raddeana	EBee EBrs ECho WWst
*	- f. ***rosea*** new	WWst
	ranunculoides ♀H4	Widely available
	- 'Frank Waley'	WCot
*	- ***laciniata***	CLAP NMen WCot
	- 'Pleniflora' (d)	CFwr CLAP EBla EBrs ECha ECho EHrv GBBs NLar NMen WCom WCot WFar
	- subsp. ***ranunculoides***	ECho GKev WHil
	- 'Semi Plena'	EBee EBrs ECho
	- subsp. ***wockeana***	CDes CSam EBee ECho MAvo
	reflexa	EBee GKev LLHF
	richardsonii	CPla
	riparia	see *A. virginiana* var. *alba*
	rivularis	Widely available
	- BWJ 7611	WCru
	- CC 4587	GKev
	- GWJ 9391	WCru
	- SDR 5943	GKev
	- 'Blue Back' new	GCal
	- 'Glacier'	NEgg WPer
	aff. ***rivularis*** new	WPtf
	rupicola	CAby EBee GMac NBir
	× ***seemannii***	see *A.* × *lipsiensis*
	stellata Lam., non Risso.	see *A. hortensis*
	stolonifera double-flowered (d)	CAby CElw ECho MAvo WCot
	sulphurea	see *Pulsatilla alpina* subsp. *apiifolia*
	sylvestris	Widely available
	- 'Elise Fellmann' (d)	EBee EPfP GMac IGor MAvo WCot WHal
	- 'Flore Pleno' (d)	CDes WCot
	- 'Macrantha'	CDes EBee EPfP GAbr NGdn SMrm WBrE WPrP
	tetrasepala	WCot
§	***tomentosa***	EBee ECha GGar IGor LBMP LRHS NBre SDix SRms SWat WBVN WFar WPtf
§	- 'Albadura'	EBee NBre
	- 'Robustissima'	see *A.* × *hybrida* 'Robustissima'
	trifolia L.	CAby EBee EPPr NBid SCnR SRms WPGP WPat
	- pink-flowered	CLAP WFar
	trullifolia	EBee EPfP GAbr GBin GCra GCrs GEdr GGar GKev GKir GMac ITim MRav NSla WAbe
	- ***alba***	GCrs GMac
	- var. ***coelestina***	NBir
	vernalis	see *Pulsatilla vernalis*
	virginiana	EBee GAbr MDKP NBid NPnk SPhx WBVN WFar WWEG
§	- var. ***alba***	EKen NSti WBVN WPrP WPtf
	vitifolia misapplied	see *A. tomentosa*
	vitifolia DC.	EBee
	- B&SWJ 8202 from Vietnam	WCru
	- GWJ 9434	WCru
	- HWJK 2044	WCru

Anemonella (*Ranunculaceae*)

	thalictroides	Widely available
	- 'Alba Plena' (d)	ECho
	- 'Amelia'	CLAP EPPr GEdr NHar SCnR WAbe
	- 'Babe'	WWst
	- 'Betty Blake' (d)	ECho GEdr WCot
	- 'Big'	WWst
	- 'Cameo'	CLAP EBee EFEx EPPr GEdr MAvo NHar SCnR WAbe WCot WCru WFar WWst
	- 'Charlotte'	WWst
	- 'Diamante'	WWst
	- 'Double Green' (d)	CLAP EBee EFEx GEdr IMou WWst
	- 'Full Double White' (d)	EFEx GEdr WWst
	- 'Green Hurricane' (d)	EBee EFEx GEdr ITim WWst
	- 'Jade Feather'	CElw
	- f. ***rosea***	CAby CElw CLAP WAbe WCru WFar
	- - 'Oscar Schoaf' (d)	CLAP EBee GEdr WAbe WWst
	- - semi-double (d)	CElw CLAP EHrv GKir MAvo NLar WWst
	- semi-double white-flowered (d)	CElw CLAP EBee EHrv EPPr NMen WAbe WCot
	- 'Tairin'	EBee GEdr WWst
	- white-flowered	WSpi

Anemonopsis (*Ranunculaceae*)

	macrophylla	CDes CElw CLAP CMoH CPBP ECha ECho GCal GEdr GKev GKir GMac IGor MNrw MTho SMad SPhx WCru WFar WSHC
	- 'White Swan'	ECho WCru

Anemopsis (*Saururaceae*)

	californica	CDes EBee IFoB LLWG MSKA MWts NLar WCot WPGP

Anethum (*Apiaceae*)

	graveolens	CArn GKir GPoy MHer MNHC SBfd SIde SWal
	- 'Dukat'	CSev ELau NGHP

angelica see *Angelica archangelica*

Angelica (*Apiaceae*)

	acutiloba	CSpe MMHG NLar WFar
	- var. ***iwatensis*** B&SWJ 11197	WCru
	anomala B&SWJ 10886	WCru
	archangelica	Widely available
	- subsp. ***archangelica***	GAuc
	- 'Corinne Tremaine' (v)	CBow ITim MDKP NExo
	atropurpurea	CArn EBee ECtt EPfP EWll GKev LRHS MHer MNHC MNrw MRav NCGa SWat WFar WJek WMnd WWEG
	dahurica B&SWJ 8603	WCru
	decursiva	CArn WCot
	- B&SWJ 5746	WCru
	'Ebony'	CAby CBod CMea GKev LEdu MDKP MHer NExo SBfd WCot
	edulis	LEdu
	- B&SWJ 10968	WCru
	florentii	WPGP

gigas	Widely available
- B&SWJ 4170	WCru
hispanica	see *A. pachycarpa*
japonica B&SWJ 8816a	WCru
- B&SWJ 11480	WCru
montana	see *A. sylvestris*
morii RWJ 9802	WCru
§ ***pachycarpa***	CArn CSam CSpe EBee EBrs ELan EOHP EPyc GMaP LHop LRHS MCCP MCot MHer NBir NGHP NPnk SBfd SGar SIde SMrm SPad SPav WFar WJek WPGP WWEG
pubescens	IMou SPhx
- B&SWJ 5593	WCru
- var. ***matsumurae*** B&SWJ 6387	WCru
sinensis	CArn GPoy
'Summer Delight'	see *Ligusticum scoticum*
§ ***sylvestris***	CArn CRWN EBWF GBar NGHP NSco
* - 'Purpurea'	CAby CKno CSpe EWes MCot SDnm WPGP
- 'Vicar's Mead'	CDes EBee IPot LEdu LHop LPla LSRN MDKP MLLN NBPC NCGa NChi NLar NPnk NSti SPhx SRkn WCot WJek
taiwaniana	CArn CDTJ CWan EBee ELan LRHS MDKP MLLN SGar
ursina	GAuc
- B&SWJ 10829	WCru

Angelonia (*Scrophulariaceae*)

(Angelface Series) Angelface Blue = 'Anzwei'^{PBR}	CSpe
- Angelface Blue Bicolour = 'Anstern'	LAst
- Angelface Wedgewood Blue = 'Anwedg'	LAst NPri
AngelMist Lavender Pink = 'Balanglapi'^{PBR}	LAst

Anigozanthos (*Haemodoraceae*)

sp. **new**	WHil
'Big Red'	SOWG
(Bush Gems Series) 'Bush Eclipse'	SOWG
- 'Bush Haze'	SOWG
- 'Bush Ranger'	CCCN CWit
flavidus	CHEx CTrC EAmu ECre EOHP SOWG SPlb
- 'Ember'	CCCN CWit SPoG
- 'Illusion'	CCCN
- 'Opal'	CCCN
- 'Orange Cross'	SOWG
- 'Pearl'	CCCN CWit SPoG
- red-flowered	CTrC
- 'Splendour'	CCCN
- yellow	WBrE
- 'Yellow Gem' **new**	CCCN CWit
humilis Lindl. ♀H1	SOWG
manglesii ♀H1	CTrC SOWG SPlb
- 'Bush Dawn' (Bush Gems Series)	SOWG
'Regal Claw'	SOWG
'Royal Cheer'	SOWG

Anisacanthus (*Acanthaceae*)

quadrifidus var. ***wrightii***	WCot

anise see *Pimpinella anisum*

Anisodontea (*Malvaceae*)

§ ***capensis***	CCCN CHGN EBee ELan ERea EShb GBee GKir IDee LAst MCot NBir SBfd SChF SLim SMrm SOWG SPlb SRkn SRms SWvt WDyG
- 'Tara's Pink'	CSpe EBee EWes IFoB MAsh SAga SMrm SPhx
'El Royo' **new**	WCot
elegans	SAga
'Elegant Lady'	CSpe GFai SUsu
huegelii	see *Alyogyne huegelii*
× ***hypomadara*** misapplied	see *A. capensis*
julii	SPlb
'Lady in Pink' **new**	LSou SVil
malvastroides	WWlt
scabrosa	CChe

Anisodus (*Solanaceae*)

§ ***luridus***	EWld GCal

Anisotome (*Apiaceae*)

lyallii	EBee GBin GKev ITim

Annona (*Annonaceae*)

cherimola (F)	CCCN XBlo

Anoiganthus see *Cyrtanthus*

Anomalesia see *Gladiolus*

Anomatheca (*Iridaceae*)

cruenta	see *A. laxa*
grandiflora	CHll CPLG ECho WCot
§ ***laxa*** ♀H2-3	CArn CAvo CFFs CPLG CRHN CSev CSpe CStu CTri EBee ECha ECho EHrv ELan EPfP EPot IFoB LRHS MAvo MCot MTho NMen NWCA SHom SRms WAbe WBrk WCom WPat WPer
- var. ***alba*** ♀H2-3	CPLG CPom CRHN CSev CSpe CStu EBee ECho EDif EHrv ELan ITim MCot MTho MWea NMen WAbe WBrk WCom
- ***albomaculata***	GCrs
- blue-flowered	CRHN ECho WAbe WBrk
- 'Joan Evans'	CRHN EBee ECho ELan LLHF NMen NWCA SBch SHom SRms WAbe WBrk WHrl
- red-spotted	CPLG ECho EDif ITim SGar
- ***viridiflora***	ECho
viridis	CDes CPLG CPou EBee ECho LRHS WBrk WPGP

Anopterus (*Escalloniaceae*)

glandulosus	IBlr WPGP WSHC

Anredera (*Basellaceae*)

§ ***cordifolia***	CRHN ECho EShb LEdu

Antennaria (*Asteraceae*)

aprica	see *A. parvifolia*
aromatica **new**	EDAr
dioica	CArn CTri ECtt EDAr GAbr GJos GKir GPoy SPlb SRms WFar
- 'Alba'	EHoe
- 'Alex Duguid'	GEdr GMaP LBee LRHS NLAp WCom
- 'Aprica'	see *A. parvifolia*
- 'Minima'	ECho EPot MWat NBro NMen WAbe
- 'Nyewoods Variety'	EPot NLAp
- red-flowered	ECho

- var. ***rosea***	see *A. rosea*
- 'Rotes Wunder'	EPot
* - 'Rubra'	CTri ECha ECho ECtt EDAr GBin LBMP LRHS MHer NMen NWCA WAbe
'Joy'	WAbe
macrophylla hort.	see *A. microphylla*
§ ***microphylla***	ECho SRms WEas
§ ***parvifolia***	CTri ECho NPri SRms SRot
- var. ***rosea***	see *A. microphylla*
plantaginifolia	EBee
'Red Wonder'	CMea
§ ***rosea*** Υ^{H4}	ECho GKir LRHS NHol NLAp NMen SPlb SRms WFar

Antenoron see *Persicaria*

Anthemis ✿ (*Asteraceae*)

from Turkey	ECtt EWes LLWP
arvensis	MNHC
§ 'Beauty of Grallagh'	GMac IGor MDKP SDix WSpi
'Cally Cream'	GCal SMrm
'Cally White'	GCal
carpatica	NBro
- 'Karpatenschnee'	EBee EBrs GGar LBMP LRHS NBre
'Catforth White'	NCob
§ ***cretica*** subsp. ***cretica***	CMac NWCA
'Daisy Bee'	EBee MAvo
frutescens Hort. & Siebert & Voss.	see *Argyranthemum frutescens*
'Grallagh Gold' misapplied, orange-yellow	see *A.* 'Beauty of Grallagh'
'Grallagh Gold'	CMoH EBla ECha ECtt EWes MWat NPer WFar WSpi
§ ***marschalliana***	CMea CPBP EBee ECha ECho ECtt EDAr EPot LBee LRHS SMrm SPlb SUsu WAbe WCot
montana	see *A. cretica* subsp. *cretica*
nobilis	see *Chamaemelum nobile*
punctata	WNew
- subsp. ***cupaniana*** Υ^{H3-4}	Widely available
- - 'Nana'	NPer
rudolphiana	see *A. marschalliana*
sancti-johannis	CWib EAEE EBee EBla EPfP GKir IGor LRHS LSou NDov NPer SBfd SMrm SPer SRms WMoo
'Sauce Béarnaise'	GCra WMnd
Susanna Mitchell = 'Blomit'	Widely available
'Tetworth'	EBee EBla ECha ECtt EHrv ELan EPfP LSRN MBNS MRav SMad SUsu WFar WWEG
tinctoria	CArn CHby CMac EBee GPoy LRHS MHer NPer SWvt WHfH WJek WSFF WTou
- 'Alba'	EBee GGar GKir NBre NLar WClo WFar WWEG
- 'Charme'^{PBR}	EBee ECtt LAst LSou MWea NDov SBfd SPoG
- 'Compacta'	EWes GCal NBre NCob NGdn
- dwarf	EBee EBla SBri WFar
- 'E.C. Buxton'	Widely available
- 'Eva'	LRHS NBre NLar WEas WWEG
I - 'Golden Rays'	MDKP SBfd SDix SSvw WWEG
- 'Kelwayi'	CPrp CSBt CTri EBee EPfP GKir LRHS NBPC NBro NLar NPer SBfd SPer SPoG SRms SWat WFar WMoo WWEG
- 'Lemon Ice' **new**	MAvo
- 'Lemon Maid'	CFir ELon EPfP GBin LRHS NBre NCob SMrm
- 'Sauce Hollandaise'	Widely available
- subsp. ***tinctoria***	SMrm
- 'Wargrave Variety'	Widely available
'Tinpenny Sparkle'	CSam EBee ECtt EWll LSou MAvo NLar NSti WBrk WCot WHoo WTin
triumfettii	EBee NPer NPnk
tuberculata	SAga SBch
'White Water'	WAbe WFar

Anthericum (*Anthericaceae*)

algeriense	see *A. liliago*
baeticum	EBee
§ ***liliago***	EBee ECho ELan EWTr GCal GKev GMaP IFoB LHop LRHS MAvo MCot MLLN MRav NCGa NLar WAul WHrl WPer WWEG
- 'Major' Υ^{H4}	ECGP ECha ECho EHrv IGor MLHP NBre SUsu WPGP
ramosum	CAby CDes CSpe EBee ECha ECho ELan EPot EWes GCal GMac MBrN MLLN NBid NBir NCGa NLar NWCA SMrm SPhx SUsu WPGP WPer
- ***plumosum***	see *Trichopetalum plumosum*

Antholyza (*Iridaceae*)

coccinea	see *Crocosmia paniculata*
× ***crocosmioides***	see *Crocosmia* × *crocosmioides*
paniculata	see *Crocosmia paniculata*

Anthoxanthum (*Poaceae*)

odoratum	CArn CRWN EBWF ELau GBar GPoy

Anthriscus (*Apiaceae*)

cerefolium	CArn CHby CSev ELau EPfP GPoy ILis MHer MNHC SBfd WJek
sylvestris	CArn EBWF NMir NSco WSFF
- 'Broadleas Blush'	CNat
- 'Clair' **new**	CNat
- 'Kabir'	CNat
- 'Moonlit Night'	EHoe
- 'Ravenswing'	Widely available

Anthurium (*Araceae*)

amazonicum	MBri
andraeanum Υ^{H1}	MBri
- 'Glowing Pink'	XBlo
- 'Red Heart'	XBlo
- 'Tivolo'	XBlo
'Aztec'	XBlo
Baleno = 'Anthauf4'^{PBR}	LRHS XBlo
'Caribo'	XBlo
crenatum	XBlo
'Crimson'	XBlo
'Magenta'	XBlo
'Mikra'	XBlo
'Octavia'	XBlo
'Pico Bello'	XBlo
'Pink Champion'	XBlo
'Porcelaine White'	XBlo
Red Champion = 'Anthbnena'^{PBR}	LRHS XBlo
scherzerianum Υ^{H1}	MBri
'Vitara'	XBlo
White Champion = 'Anthefaqyr'^{PBR}	LRHS XBlo

Anthyllis (*Papilionaceae*)

barba-jovis	CSpe EBrs LRHS
hermanniae	WPat
- 'Compacta'	see *A. hermanniae* 'Minor'
§ - 'Minor'	NLar NMen

montana	LRHS
subsp. ***atropurpurea***	
- 'Rubra' ♀H4	ECho EDAr EPot EWes LHop LLHF NLar NMen
vulneraria	CFee EBWF ECho EDAr NMir NRya NSco WSFF
- var. ***coccinea***	CMea CSpe EBee EDAr ELan GAbr GBin GGar GKev MCCP MLLN MSCN MTho MWea NLar NSla NWCA SGSe WCFE WCom WFar WHal WHil

Antigonon (*Polygonaceae*)

leptopus	SOWG

Antirrhinum (*Scrophulariaceae*)

asarina	see *Asarina procumbens*
barrelieri	SEND
braun-blanquetii	CSpr SEND WCot WMoo WPtf
'Carambola Yellow' (Fruit Salad Series)	LSou
glutinosum	see *A. hispanicum* subsp. *hispanicum*
§ ***hispanicum***	CPBP
- 'Avalanche'	ECtt
§ - subsp. ***hispanicum***	SRot
- - 'Roseum'	CMea CSpe
(Luminaire Series) Luminaire Deep Purple = 'Balumdepur'	LAst
- Luminaire Yellow = 'Balumyell'	LAst
majus	WCot
- 'Black Prince'	CSpe ECtt LHop SPhx
- 'Night and Day'	CSpe
molle	CPom CSpe ECtt GKev MCot NBir NPer NWCA SChF SRot SUsu WAbe
- pink-flowered	WAbe
pulverulentum	SAga WAbe WSHC
sempervirens	SAga WAbe
siculum	EWTr

añu see *Tropaeolum tuberosum*

Aphelandra (*Acanthaceae*)

squarrosa	MBri
- 'Citrina'	XBlo

Aphyllanthes (*Aphyllanthaceae*)

monspeliensis	CFee ECho

Apios (*Papilionaceae*)

§ ***americana***	CAgr CMdw CPom EBee ECho GBin LEdu NBir NLar NSti WBVN WCot WCru WSHC
tuberosa	see *A. americana*

Apium (*Apiaceae*)

graveolens	CArn CBgR CPrp EBWF ELau GPoy MHer MNHC SBfd SIde WJek
- (Secalinum Group) 'Par-cel'	MHer NGHP
nodiflorum	EBWF

Apium × *Petroselinum* (*Apiaceae*)

hybrid, misapplied	see *A. graveolens* Secalinum Group

Apocynum (*Apocynaceae*)

cannabinum	CArn COld GPoy

Apodolirion (*Amaryllidaceae*)

macowanii	ECho

Aponogeton (*Aponogetonaceae*)

distachyos	CBen CRow CWat EHon LPBA MSKA MWts NPer SCoo SVic SWat WFar WMAq WPnP

apple see *Malus domestica*

apricot see *Prunus armeniaca*

Aptenia (*Aizoaceae*)

cordifolia ♀H1-2	CCCN NPer SChr SDnm SEND SPet
- 'Variegata' (v)	CCCN MRav

Aquilegia ✿ (*Ranunculaceae*)

sp.	SVic
akitensis misapplied	see *A. flabellata* var. *pumila*
* ***alba variegata*** (v)	ECho WEas
alpina	CBot CMea CPrp EBee ECho ECtt EPfP GGar MNHC MRav SBfd SPer SRms WCAu WFar WMoo WPer
amaliae	see *A. ottonis* subsp. *amaliae*
amurensis	CLAP
'Apple Blossom'	WTou
aragonensis	see *A. pyrenaica*
§ ***atrata***	CLAP CPou EBee ECho MDKP MWea NBre SMrm WHil WTou
atrovinosa	MWea
aurea misapplied	see *A. vulgaris* golden-leaved
aurea Janka	GKev
barnebyi	CMea EBee
bernardii	NMun
bertolonii ♀H4	CMea ECho GKev LHop LRHS NMen NRya SRms WHoo WTou
- ***alba***	NWCA
Biedermeier Group	EBee ECho GAbr GKir LRHS NNor SBfd SPoG SRot WFar WPer WTou
'Blue Jay' (Songbird Series)	GKir LRHS MHer NPri SMrm STes SWvt
'Blue Star' (Star Series)	CSam EAEE EBee ELan EPfP LRHS NEgg WPer WTou
'Bluebird' (Songbird Series) ♀H2	NPer
brevistyla	WCot
buergeriana	GEdr MDKP WTou
- 'Calimero'	LBMP LRHS MDKP NLar WFar WHil
- var. ***oxysepala***	see *A. oxysepala*
'Bunting' (Songbird Series) ♀H2	NLar SCoo SWal WFar
canadensis ♀H4	CLAP CMHG CSpe EBee ELan GKev MNFA NBir NBro NWCA SBfd SGar SRms WTou
- 'Corbett'	GEdr MDKP WHil WTou
- 'Little Lanterns'	CTsd ECtt EPPr GGar GKev LBMP LHop MDKP NLar NSum SGSe SPad SVil WFar WHil
- 'Nana'	CStu GEdr GKev WThu
- 'Pink Lanterns'	NPri SMrm WHil
'Cardinal' (Songbird Series)	GKir LRHS MBri MHer NLar NPri WFar
chaplinei	CBot NBir SBch
chrysantha	CSam GKev MNFA NBre SGSe SRms WBrE WEas WKif WTou
- 'Yellow Queen'	CPLG CPrp CWCL EBee EBrs EPPr EPfP GMaP LBMP LHop LRHS MBri MDKP MWat NBre NLar NMoo SPad SPur SSvw STes WCFE WHil WTou
clematiflora	see *A. vulgaris* var. *stellata*
Clementine Series	EPfP LRHS
coerulea ♀H4	EBee GKev MDKP NNor SRms
- var. ***coerulea***	GKev

	- 'Himmelblau'	NBre
	- 'Mrs Nicholls'	WSpi
	- var. ***ochroleuca***	WCot
	'Colorado' (State Series)	MBri
	'Crimson Star'	EBee EPfP GKir LRHS MDKP SPer SPoG SPur WMoo WTou WWEG
	'Debutante'	EBee LLWP MDKP MWea
	desertorum	MDKP
	discolor	EPot GKev LLHF WThu WTou
	'Double Rubies' (d)	LSRN WMoo
	'Dove' (Songbird Series) ♀H2	EWll LRHS MHer NLar NPri SMrm WFar
I	'Dragonfly'	CBcs CTsd CWib EPfP LRHS MAvo MNHC NBre SBfd SPer SPet SPoG WFar WTou WWEG
	ecalcarata	see *Semiaquilegia ecalcarata*
	einseleana	EBee LLHF
	'Elegance' **new**	WTou
	elegantula	MWea
	flabellata ♀H4	GCra GGar GKir WAbe WKif
	- f. ***alba***	CTri ECho ELan NWCA WEas
	- Cameo Series	GKev GMaP LRHS WFar WGor
	- - 'Cameo Blue and White'	CWib ECho NCGa SRot WFar
	- - 'Cameo Blue'	ECho
	- - 'Cameo Blush'	WFar
	- - 'Cameo Pink and White'	ECho MHer NCGa SRot WFar
	- - 'Cameo White'	SRot
	- 'Georgia' (State Series) ♀H3-4	MBri SMrm
	- Jewel Series	ECho
	- - 'Amethyst'	GKir
	- - 'Blue Jewel'	ECho
	- 'Ministar'	ECho EPfP GKir NVic WBrE WFar
	- 'Nana Alba'	see *A. flabellata* var. *pumila* f. *alba*
I	- ***nana yezoense***	ECho
§	- var. ***pumila*** ♀H4	CFir CSam CWCL ECha ECho EPfP GGar GKir LHop LRHS MDKP NPri WFar WTou
§	- - f. ***alba*** ♀H4	CBot ECha ECho GKev LHop LRHS NChi SMrm SRms WTou
	- - 'Atlantis'	LRHS NPri SVil
	- - 'Flore Pleno'	ECho
I	- - f. ***kurilensis*** 'Rosea' **new**	CFir GKev NWCA
	- - 'Silver Edge' (v)	CPla
	'Flamboyant'	WTou
	flavescens	WCot
	formosa	CBot CMea EBee ECho GKev LBMP MDKP NChi NPri NWCA SMHy WCot WGwG WKif WTou
	- var. ***truncata***	EBee
	formosa* × *pubescens NNS 05-76	WCot
§	***fragrans***	CLAP CPrp CTsd EBee EPfP GEdr GKev LBMP LRHS NWCA SPad STes WGwG WHoo WTou
	glandulosa	LLHF NLar WEas
	glauca	see *A. fragrans*
	'Golden Guiness'	WPnP WTou
	'Goldfinch' (Songbird Series)	LRHS MHer NBir NPri SCoo SWal
	grata	MDKP
	'Heavenly Blue'	CChe NGdn SMrm WTou
	'Hensol Harebell' ♀H4	SRms WPtf WSpi
	japonica	see *A. flabellata* var. *pumila*
	jonesii* × *saximontana	GKev
	'Kansas' (State Series)	MBri
	kitaibelii	GKev
	'Koralle'	MDKP NBre WFar WHil
	'Kristall'	EBee EShb LSRN MDKP NBre STes
	laramiensis	CPBP
	'Leprechaun Gold' (v)	NGdn SMrm WTou
	longissima ♀H4	CMea MDKP MHer MLLN MWea NPnk SGSe SHar STes WEas WGwG WHoo WPen
	'Louisiana' (State Series) ♀H2	MBri SMrm
	'Magpie'	see *A. vulgaris* 'William Guiness'
	'Maxi'	LRHS MDKP NBre WTou
	McKana Group	Widely available
	micrantha	GKev
	'Milk and Honey'	CBre
	'Montana' (State Series)	MBri
	Mrs Scott-Elliot hybrids	CSBt EPfP GAbr SGar SPer SPet WFar
	Music Series ♀H4	SRms
	'Nightingale' (Songbird Series)	LRHS NPri
	nigricans	see *A. atrata*
	nivalis	LLHF
	olympica	EBee EWes
	'Oranges and Lemons'	LSou SGSe WRHF
	Origami Series	WFar
§	***ottonis*** subsp. ***amaliae***	CPBP GEdr WAbe
§	***oxysepala***	CPLG EBee GCal WPrP WTou
	- B&SWJ 4775	WCru
	'Perfumed Garden'	CPla
	pleated burgundy-flowered	EBrs LRHS
	'Purple Emperor' PBR	LRHS
§	***pyrenaica***	EPot GKev
	'Red Hobbit'	CBct CChe CSBt CSpe EAEE EBee EPfP GGar GKev GKir LHop LRHS LSou MBri MDKP MHer NBre NEgg SUsu WFar WHil WHoo WTou
	'Red Star' (Star Series)	CPrp EAEE EBee EPfP NEgg WFar WHil WPer WRHF
	'Robin' (Songbird Series)	MHer NPri SCoo SMrm SWal WFar
	rockii	CFir CLAP EBee EWes GCal GKev GKir MDKP SSvw WTou
	- B&SWJ 7965	WCru
	'Roman Bronze'	see *Aquilegia* × *Semiaquilegia* 'Roman Bronze'
	'Rose Queen'	CSam EBee EPfP MAvo MDKP NBre NNor SSvw WHoo WTou
	saximontana	EPot GEdr GKev NLar WPer
§	'Schneekönigin'	CWCL GMaP LRHS WCFE
	scopulorum	EBee GKev LLHF WAbe
	shockleyi	CDes NWCA
	sibirica	CFir LLHF WTou
	'Silver Queen'	EBee ELan MDKP
	skinneri	CPLG CSpe EBee EShb IFro WMnd WMoo WSpi WTou
	- 'Tequila Sunrise'	CWib EBee ECtt LSRN LSou NHol NNor NPri NWsh
	Snow Queen	see *A.* 'Schneekönigin'
	Songbird Series	NPri WFar
	(Spring Magic Series) 'Spring Magic Blue and White'	LBuc LRHS WTou
	- 'Spring Magic Pink and White'	LRHS WTou
	- 'Spring Magic Rose and Ivory' **new**	WTou
	stellata	see *A. vulgaris* var. *stellata*
	'Stoulton Blue'	WSpi
	'Sunburst Ruby'	CPla MDKP WMoo WTou
	'Sweet Rainbows' (d)	CPla
	triternata	NNor
	'Virginia' (State Series)	MBri
	viridiflora	CBot CLAP EBee ELan EPfP GCal LBMP MCot SGar SUsu WCot WEas WFar WHil WMnd WPGP WTou
	- 'Chocolate Soldier'	CSpe CWCL LEdu MWea
	vulgaris	CArn CMHG CRWN EPfP GPoy LLWP LRHS MHer MNHC NBro

		NMir NSco SGar SPlb WCAu WMoo WShi WTin WWEG
	- SDR 5436	GKev
	- 'Adelaide Addison'	ECGP ECha WEas WFar WHoo WTou
	- var. ***alba***	CMea EBee EPPr LBMP LLWP LRHS MNFA SMrm WCAu WTou
	- 'Altrosa'	NBre
*	- 'Anemoniflora'	WSpi
	- 'Aureovariegata'	see *A. vulgaris* Vervaeneana Group
	- 'Burnished Rose'	CPla ECtt WHil WTou
	- ***clematiflora***	see *A. vulgaris* var. *stellata*
	- (Clementine Series) 'Clementine Dark Purple' (d)	EPfP
	- - 'Clementine Red' (d)	EPfP
	- - 'Clementine Salmon Rose' (d)	EPfP
	- - 'Clementine White' (d)	EPfP
	- 'Crystal Star'	LRHS
	- var. ***flore-pleno*** (d)	LLWP
	- - bicolour **new**	WTou
	- - black-flowered (d)	LRHS LSou WCot WTou
	- - 'Blue Bonnet' (d)	WTou
	- - blue-flowered (d)	WTou
	- - 'Dorothy Rose' (Dorothy Series) (d)	LSRN MPnt
	- - 'Double Pleat' (d)	GGar
	- - 'Double Pleat' blue/white-flowered (d)	CPrp WHil WPer
	- - 'Double Pleat' pink/white-flowered (d)	CPrp NGdn
*	- - 'Frilly Dilly Rose' (d)	WTou
	- - 'Jane Hollow' (d)	CPou
	- - pale blue-flowered (d)	LLWP WCot WTou
	- - 'Pink Bonnet' (d)	WFar
	- - pink-flowered (d)	GGar WTou
	- - purple-flowered (d)	LLWP WTou
	- - red-flowered (d)	WTou
	- - 'Strawberry Ice Cream' (d)	NBro NNor WTou
	- - 'Tower Light Blue' (Tower Series) (d)	CSpr WRHF
*	- - 'White Bonnet' (d)	SMrm SRos
	- - white-flowered (d)	LLWP WTou
	- 'Foggy Bottom Blues'	GKir LRHS
§	- golden-leaved	ECho WOut WTou
	- Grandmother's Garden Group	WTou WWEG
	- 'Granny's Gold'	LRHS
	- 'Heidi'	CBot NBre
	- 'Mellow Yellow'	CPla CTsd ELon GKev MDKP SDix SGSe WMoo
	- 'Miss Coventry'	SMHy
	- Munstead White	see *A. vulgaris* 'Nivea'
	- subsp. ***nevadensis***	EBee
§	- 'Nivea' ♀H4	CBot CPou CSpe EBee ECha LAst MBri NChi SPoG
	- 'Pink Spurless'	see *A. vulgaris* var. *stellata* pink-flowered
	- (Pom Pom Series) 'Pom Pom Crimson'	MTis NBro WCot
	- - 'Pom Pom Violet'	WSpi
	- scented	WTou
§	- var. ***stellata***	ELan GKev LEdu LSou NBro NNor WMoo WTou
	- - Barlow Series (d)	WFar WTou WWEG
	- - - 'Black Barlow' (d)	Widely available
	- - - 'Blue Barlow' (d)	CElw CSpe EBee ECtt EPfP GKir GMaP IBal LRHS LSRN NBre SPer WMnd WPer WTou WWEG
	- - 'Blue Fountain'	WTou
	- - blue-flowered	LRHS WTou
	- - 'Bordeaux Barlow' (Barlow Series) **new**	WTou
	- - 'Christa Barlow' (Barlow Series) (d)	EBee EPfP NBre NGdn SMrm SPer WTou
	- - double-flowered (d)	WTou
	- - 'Firewheel'	WMoo
	- - 'Gisela Powell'	EBee
	- - 'Greenapples' (d)	CBre CWCL EBee MNFA MTis NGdn NPri SMrm SPad WCot WTou WWEG
*	- - 'Iceberg'	WSpi
	- - 'Nora Barlow' (Barlow Series) (d) ♀H4	Widely available
§	- - pink-flowered	LLWP WTou
	- - purple-flowered	LLWP MGos WTou
	- - red-flowered	ELan LLWP MGos WTou
	- - 'Rose Barlow' (Barlow Series) (d)	EBrs EPfP IBal LRHS LSRN WMnd WTou
	- - 'Royal Purple' (d)	NBro NNor WMoo
	- - 'Ruby Port' (d)	CBcs CWCL EAEE EBee EPfP EShb GCal GGar GMaP IBal LHop LRHS LSRN MLHP MNrw NBPC NDov NPri SPad SPer SSvw STes WFar WPrP
	- - 'Ruby Port' crimped (d)	WPnP
	- - (Vervaeneana Group) 'Sweet Dreams' (v/d) **new**	WTou
	- - 'White Barlow' (Barlow Series) (d)	GKir LRHS SPer WTou
	- - white-flowered	CSpe GCra LRHS NBro WFar WTou
	- variegated foliage	see *A. vulgaris* Vervaeneana Group
§	- Vervaeneana Group (v)	CMHG CWCL ECtt EPfP LRHS MCot MNrw NBir NBre NPer SBfd SGSe SPer SPlb SRms SWat WFar WHoo WMoo WTou
	- - 'Woodside Blue' (v)	GKir LRHS NHol WTou WWEG
	- - 'Woodside Pink' (v)	MGos
	- - 'Woodside White' (v)	NBir WBrk WWEG
§	- 'William Guiness'	Widely available
	- 'William Guiness Doubles' (d)	WMoo WTou
	'White Star' (Star Series)	CPrp EBee ELan EPfP LAst LRHS MRav NDov NEgg WPer WTou WWEG
	white-flowered	WTou
	Winky Series	NNor
	- 'Winky Blue-White'	LRHS MHer NLar NPri SMrm WCFE WFar WHil
	- 'Winky Dark Blue-White' **new**	WHil
	- 'Winky Double White-White' (d)	NPri WHil
	- 'Winky Purple-White'	NLar NPri WFar WHil
	- 'Winky Red-White'	NLar NPri SRot SWvt WFar WHil
	- 'Winky Rose-Rose'	LRHS SMrm
	yabeana	EBee EWld GAbr GGar GKev MWhi SPad WCot WMoo

Aquilegia × *Semiaquilegia* (*Ranunculaceae*)

	hybrid, blue-flowered	WCru
§	'Roman Bronze'	CPla WMoo WTou

Arabis (*Brassicaceae*)

	albida	see *A. alpina* subsp. *caucasica*
	alpina	SPlb
§	- subsp. ***caucasica***	ECho GKev WFar
	- - 'Corfe Castle'	ECho ECtt
	- - 'Douler Angevine' (v)	ECtt NPri SPoG WFar
	- - 'Flore Pleno' (d) ♀H4	CElw CSpe CTri CWCL ECho ECtt ELan EWld GAbr GMaP MTho SBch

	SRms WCom WEas WFar WHoo WNew
- - 'Pink Pearl'	ECho
- - 'Pinkie'	ECho ELon SGar
- - 'Pixie Cream'	EWTr LBMP
- - 'Rosea'	GJos LRHS NBir NPri SRms WFar WMoo
§ - - 'Schneehaube' ♀H4	CTri CWib ECho ECtt EPfP GKir GMaP LRHS NBir NPri SPoG SRms SWal WMoo
- - Snowcap	see *A. alpina* subsp. *caucasica* 'Schneehaube'
- - 'Snowdrop'	WFar
- - 'Variegata' (v)	ECho ECtt ELan GMaP LAst LBee LRHS NPri SAga SPoG SRms WEas WFar
androsacea	SRms WCom WFar
× ***arendsii*** 'Compinkie'	GJos LBMP SPlb SRms
- 'Rosabella' (v)	LRHS
blepharophylla	EPfP WCot WFar
§ - 'Frühlingszauber' ♀H4	CTri EPfP GJos GKir NBir SPoG SRms WFar
- 'Rose Delight'	LRHS
- 'Rote Sensation'	ELon GKev NPri WRHF
- Spring Charm	see *A. blepharophylla* 'Frühlingszauber'
bryoides	NMen
caucasica	see *A. alpina* subsp. *caucasica*
cypria	LSou
double white-flowered (d)	CFee
ferdinandi-coburgi	ECho MWat WNew
- 'Aureovariegata' (v)	CMea CTri ECho ECtt EDAr SPet SWvt
- 'Old Gold'	ECho EDAr EHoe EPfP GKir LBee LRHS MHer NHol NPri SPoG SRms SRot SWvt WCFE WFar WHoo WRHF
- 'Variegata'	see *A. procurrens* 'Variegata'
glabra	EBWF
§ ***procurrens*** 'Variegata' (v) ♀H4	CMoH CTri ECha ECho ECtt EHoe ELan EPfP EWes GEdr GKev LBee LEdu LRHS MBrN MHer NHol NPri SPlb SRms SRot WFar WNew
purpurea	EDAr
§ ***scabra***	CNat
Snow Cap	see *A. alpina* subsp. *caucasica* 'Schneehaube'
stelleri **new**	NBre
stricta	see *A. scabra*
'Tu Tu'	LRHS
× ***wilczekii***	EPot

Arachniodes (*Dryopteridaceae*)

davalliaeformis **new**	EBee ISha WRic
simplicior (v)	CBty CCCN CKel EBee ISha LRHS WCot WRic
standishii	WRic

Araiostegia (*Davalliaceae*)

faberiana	CPLG
hymenophylloides	SKHP WCot
perdurans	WCot WRic

Aralia ✿ (*Araliaceae*)

CD&R 2289 from China	WCru
apioides EDHCH 9720	WCru
armata B&SWJ 6719	WCru
- RWJ 10060	WCru
cachemirica	CDTJ CLAP EWes GAbr GCal NBid NLar SDix SMad SPlb WCru WHal
- CC 4578	GKev
californica	COld EBee GCal GPoy LEdu NLar SDix SKHP WCru
chapaensis B&SWJ 11812	WCru
- HWJ 723	WCru
chinensis misapplied	see *A. elata*, *A. stipulata*
chinensis L.	WBVN
- BWJ 8102	WCru
continentalis	CLAP IMou NLar
- B&SWJ 4152	WCru
- B&SWJ 8524	WCru
cordata	EBee EWes GCal GKev LEdu NLar
- B&SWJ 5511	WCru
decaisneana RWJ 9910	WCru
§ ***elata*** ♀H4	Widely available
- B&SWJ 5480	WCru
- 'Albomarginata'	see *A. elata* 'Variegata'
- 'Aureo-marginata' (v)	CMac EBee
- 'Aureovariegata' (v)	CBcs CDoC ELan EWes MBlu NLar NMoo NPal SCoo WDin
- 'Golden Umbrella' (v)	LSRN NLar WDin
- 'Silver Umbrella'	CDoC MGos NLar
§ - 'Variegata' (v) ♀H4	CBcs CBot CDoC CDul EBee ELan EPfP MBlu MGos NLar NMoo NPal SCoo WDin
foliolosa B&SWJ 8360	WCru
kansuensis BWJ 7650	WCru
leschenaultii B&SWJ 11789	WCru
- HWJK 2385	WCru
montana RWJ 10101	WCru
papyrifera	see *Tetrapanax papyrifer*
racemosa	CArn EBee GPoy GQue LPla MLLN MNrw NLar SRms WFar
- B&SWJ 9570	WCru
searelliana B&SWJ 11736 **new**	WCru
sieboldii de Vriese	see *Fatsia japonica*
spinifolia B&SWJ 11745	WCru
spinosa L.	GKev MBlu NLar SPlb
§ ***stipulata***	NLar
subcordata HWJK 2385	WCru
verticillata B&SWJ 11797	WCru
vietnamensis B&SWJ 12349E	WCru

Araucaria (*Araucariaceae*)

angustifolia	WPGP
§ ***araucana***	Widely available
bidwillii	CTrC
cunninghamii	ECou
excelsa misapplied	see *A. heterophylla*
§ ***heterophylla*** ♀H1	CCCN CDoC CTsd ECho EShb MBri SAPC SArc SEND
imbricata	see *A. araucana*

Araujia (*Asclepiadaceae*)

sericifera	CHII CMac CPne CRHN CSam CSpe EBee GEdr GQui SDnm SGar SPav WCot WFoF WSHC

Arbutus ✿ (*Ericaceae*)

sp. **new**	MWya
andrachne	EPfP
- from Cyprus **new**	SKHP
× ***andrachnoides*** ♀H4	CAbP CBcs CHGN CPMA CTri EBee ELan EPfP GGal LRHS LSRN MAsh MRav SAPC SArc SDnm SPer SPoG SReu SSta WPGP WPat WSpi
glandulosa	see *Arctostaphylos glandulosa*
'Marina'	CAbP CDoC CEnd CPMA CTrC EBee ELan EPfP IVic LHop LRHS MAsh MBlu NLar SBfd SEND SMad

	SPer SPoG SSpi SWvt WFar WPGP WPat
menziesii ♀H3	CBcs CDoC CEnd CMCN CTho EBee ECrN EPfP LRHS LSRN MGos MMuc MSnd NLar SMad SPer WDin WFar
unedo ♀H4	Widely available
- 'Atlantic'	CAlb CCCN CPMA ECrN GGar GKir IVic LRHS LSRN MAsh MGos SBfd SBig SWvt WPat
- 'Compacta'	CAlb CBcs CCCN CDoC GKir LRHS MAsh MGos NLar SLon SWvt WCFE WDin
- 'Elfin King'	ELan EPfP LRHS MAsh NLar SDnm SLon SPoG SSta SWvt
- 'Quercifolia'	CPMA EBee ELan MMHG NLar SDnm WFar WPat
- Roselily = 'Minlily'	SBig
- f. ***rubra*** ♀H4	Widely available

Archontophoenix (*Arecaceae*)

alexandrae	EAmu LPal
cunninghamiana ♀H1	CBrP EAmu LPal XBlo

Arctanthemum (*Asteraceae*)

§ ***arcticum***	CKno EBrs ECha LBMP NBre NLar WPer
- 'Roseum'	EBee GBin
- 'Schwefelglanz'	NCGa

Arcterica see *Pieris*

Arctium (*Asteraceae*)

lappa	CArn GBar GPoy MHer NMir SIde SVic
- 'Takinogawa Long'	MNHC
minus	CArn EBWF NSco
- 'Plus'	WAlt

Arctostaphylos (*Ericaceae*)

§ ***glandulosa***	SAPC SArc
uva-ursi	GPoy NLar NMen SLon SPlb SSta WDin
- 'Massachusetts'	GKir NLar
- 'Snowcap'	NHol
- 'Vancouver Jade'	CDoC EBee GKir LRHS LSRN MAsh MBri SBfd SCoo SLon SPer SPoG SReu SRms SSta SWvt

Arctotis (*Asteraceae*)

Hannah = 'Archnah'PBR	CSpe CWit LAst MBNS SUsu SVil WHil
Hayley = 'Archley'PBR	CCCN CWit LAst MBNS SUsu SVil
× ***hybrida*** hort. cream-flowered	CHEx SAga
- 'Apricot'	CCCN CHEx LAst SAga SMrm WHil
- 'China Rose'	SMrm
- 'Flame' ♀H1+3	CAby CCCN LAst MBNS SAga SCoo SMrm WHil WHlf
- 'Red Devil'	CCCN LAst LSou MBNS SAga SCoo SMrm SUsu
- 'Wine'	CCCN CHEx LAst LSou MBNS SCoo SMrm SRkn SUsu SVil WHil
'Prostrate Raspberry'	SAga

Ardisia (*Myrsinaceae*)

japonica var. ***angusta***	WCot
- var. ***minor*** B&SWJ 1841	WCru
- - B&SWJ 3809	WCru
- 'Miyo-nishiki' (v)	WCot
pusilla	GBin

Areca (*Arecaceae*)

triandra	XBlo

Arecastrum see *Syagrus*

Arenaria (*Caryophyllaceae*)

SDR 6134	GKev
alfacarensis	see *A. lithops*
balearica	CWCL CYeo ECho EWes GKir LLWG LRHS NSla SPlb SRms
capillaris	CTri
grandiflora	GKev
ledebouriana	EDAr MWat NLar
§ ***lithops***	EPot
magellanica	see *Colobanthus quitensis*
montana ♀H4	CMea ECha ECho ECtt EDAr EPfP EWTr GGar GMaP LHop LRHS MDun MGos MLHP NMen NPri NVic NWCA SPet SPlb SRms WAbe WBVN WCot WFar WWFP
- 'Avalanche'	ECtt
- 'Blizzard'	EPfP
pinifolia	see *Minuartia circassica*
pseudacantholimon	WAbe
pulvinata	see *A. lithops*
purpurascens	ECho EDAr EPot EWes LLHF NLar NMen NWCA SRms SRot WFar
- 'Elliott's Variety'	NMen WPat
serpyllifolia	EDAr
tetraquetra subsp. ***amabilis***	EPot NMen NSla WAbe
tmolea	NMen
verna	see *Minuartia verna*

Arenga (*Arecaceae*)

engleri	EAmu LPal
micrantha	WCot

Argania (*Sapotaceae*)

spinosa	WPGP

Argemone (*Papaveraceae*)

grandiflora	CSpe SBch SPav
mexicana	ELan
pleiacantha	EBee

Argyranthemum ✿ (*Asteraceae*)

'Anastasia'	MAJR
'Beth'	GBee MAJR
'Blanche' (Courtyard Series)	MAJR
Blazer Rose = 'Supaglow' (Daisy Crazy Series)	MAJR
§ 'Blizzard' (d)	MAJR
Blushing Rose = 'Supaellie' (Daisy Crazy Series)	MAJR
'Bofinger'	MAJR
'Bon Bon'	MAJR
'Bridesmaid'	CCCN MAJR
Bright Carmine = 'Supalight'PBR (Daisy Crazy Series)	LSou MAJR
broussonetii	MAJR
Butterfly = 'Ulyssis' ♀H1+3	MAJR WGor
'Camilla Ponticelli'	MAJR
canariense hort.	see *A. frutescens* subsp. *canariae*
'Champagne'	MAJR
Cherry Love = 'Suparcher' (Daisy Crazy Series)	CCCN EPfP MAJR
'Christy Bell'	MAJR
* ***compactum***	MAJR
'Comtesse de Chambord'	MAJR SPet

'Cornish Gold' ♀H1+3	CBcs CCCN CFox LSou MAJR SBfd
coronopifolium	MAJR
'Dana' **new**	LAst
'Donington Hero' ♀H1+3	MAJR MHom
double white-flowered (d)	MAJR
'Edelweiss' (d)	MAJR
'Ella'	MAJR
'Flamingo'	see *Rhodanthemum gayanum*
§ ***foeniculaceum*** misapplied	CTri ELan GKir WKif
- pink-flowered	see *A.* 'Petite Pink'
§ ***foeniculaceum*** (Willd.) Webb & Sch.Bip.	MAJR MCot
- 'Royal Haze' ♀H1+3	CCCN CHll MAJR NPer
'Frosty'	MAJR
§ ***frutescens***	CHEx MAJR
§ - subsp. ***canariae*** ♀H1+3	CCCN MAJR
- Cherry Harmony (Daisy Crazy Series)	MAJR
- subsp. ***succulentum***	MAJR
- - 'Margaret Lynch'	MAJR
'Fuji Sundance'	MAJR
'George'	MAJR
'Gill's Pink'	CCCN MAJR MHom WPnn
'Golden Treasure'	GBee MAJR
gracile	CHll
- 'Chelsea Girl' ♀H1+3	CCCN CHEx COIW MAJR MCot MHom WKif
'Gretel'	GBee MAJR
'Guernsey Pink'	MAJR MHom
Gypsy Rose = 'M9/18d'	CCCN MAJR
'Harvest Snow'	LAst
'Henriette'	MAJR
'Icknield Jubilee'	MAJR
'Icknield Lemon Ice'	MAJR
'Icknield Pink'	MAJR
'Icknield Surprise'	MAJR
'Icknield Sylvia'	MAJR
'Icknield Yellow'	MAJR
'Jamaica Primrose' ♀H1+3	CBot CHEx CSpe CTri ECtt MAJR MAsh MCot SAga SDix
'Jamaica Snowstorm'	see *A.* 'Snow Storm'
'Julie Anna' (d)	SAga
'Julieanne'	CBcs COIW LAst MAJR MBNS SMrm
'Lemon Delight'	LAst MAJR
lemsii	MAJR
'Levada Cream' ♀H1+3	MAJR MHom
'Libby Brett'	MAJR
'Lilliput'	MAJR
Machio Double Pink = 'Ohar01245' (Madeira Series)	MAJR
Madelana = 'Ohmadmade'PBR (Madeira Series)	SVil
§ ***maderense*** ♀H1+3	CHll GBee GCal MAJR
- pale-flowered	MAJR
'Mary Cheek' (d) ♀H1+3	CCCN MAJR SPet SRGP
'Mary Wootton' (d)	ECtt MAJR MHom
mawii	see *Rhodanthemum gayanum*
'Mike's Pink'	MAJR
'Millennium Star'	MAJR
'Mini-snowflake'	see *A.* 'Blizzard'
Molimba Duplo Pearl = 'Argydupea'PBR	MAJR
Monte = 'Ohar01241'PBR (Madeira Series)	MAJR
§ 'Mrs F. Sander' (d)	MAJR MCot MHom
ochroleucum	see *A. maderense*
'Pacific Gold'	CBcs MAJR
§ 'Petite Pink' ♀H1+3	CCCN ECtt LAst MAJR MHom
Ping-Pong = 'Innping'PBR (d)	CCCN MAJR SVil
'Pink Australian' (d)	CCCN GBee MAJR MHom
'Pink Delight'	see *A.* 'Petite Pink'
'Pink Pixie'	MAJR
Pink Wonder = 'Supalily' (Daisy Crazy Series)	MAJR
pinnatifidium subsp. ***succulentum***	MAJR
Polly = 'Innpolly'PBR	CFox MAJR SBfd SMrm SVil
'Pomponette Pink'	CBcs
'Porto Moritz'	MAJR
'Powder Puff' (d)	ECtt MAJR
'Primrose Petite'PBR (Courtyard Series)	MAJR SVil
prostrate double pink-flowered (d)	MAJR
'Rising Sun'	MAJR
'Saimi'	MAJR
Santana = 'Ohmadsant' (Madeira Series)	MAJR SVil
'São Catarina'	MAJR
São Martinho = 'Ohmadsaom' (Madeira Series)	MAJR SVil
São Vicente = 'Ohmadsavi'PBR (Madeira Series)	MAJR
'Silver Leaf'	MAJR
'Silver Queen'	see *A. foeniculaceum* misapplied
§ 'Snow Storm' ♀H1+3	LAst MAJR MHom WClo WPnn
'Snowball'	MAJR
'Snowflake' misapplied	see *A.* 'Mrs F. Sander'
'Sole Mio'	CWCL MAJR
'Starlight'	LAst MAJR
Strawberry Pink = 'Suparosa' (Daisy Crazy Series)	EPfP LRHS
'Sugar and Ice'	CCCN MAJR
'Sugar Baby'PBR	CCCN
Sugar Cheer = 'Cobeer'	MAJR
'Sugar Lace'	MAJR
Sultan's Dream = 'Supadream' (Daisy Crazy Series)	EPfP
Sultan's Lemon = 'Supalem'PBR (Daisy Crazy Series)	EPfP MAJR
Sultan's Pride = 'Cosupri' (Daisy Crazy Series)	MAJR
'Summer Angel' (d)	MAJR
'Summer Cloud'	MCot
'Summer Eyes'	GBee
'Summer Melody'PBR (d)	CBcs CCCN CFox CSpe MAJR
'Summer Pink'	CCCN LAst MAJR
'Summer Stars' (Daisy Crazy Series) (d)	MAJR
Summersong Lemon = 'Supa601' (Daisy Crazy Series)	LSou MAJR
Summersong White = 'Supa594' (Daisy Crazy Series)	LSou MAJR
'Summertime'	MAJR
Summit Pink = 'Cobsing'PBR (Daisy Crazy Series)	EPfP MAJR
'Sweety'	MAJR
'Tony Holmes'	MAJR
'Tweeny'	MAJR
'Tweety'	MAJR

'Vancouver' (d) ♀$^{H1+3}$	CBot CCCN CHll CWCL ECtt EShb LAst MAJR SBHP SPet
Vanilla Ripple = 'Supabright' (Daisy Crazy Series)	MAJR
* 'Vera'	CCCN MAJR
'Wellwood Park'	CCCN
'Weymouth Pink'	MAJR
'Weymouth Surprise'	MAJR
White Blush = 'Supamorni' (Daisy Crazy Series)	MAJR
White Crystal = 'Supagem' (Daisy Crazy Series)	MAJR
'White Spider'	CCCN ELan GBee MAJR MHom
'White Star' (d)	MAJR
'Whiteknights' ♀$^{H1+3}$	GBee MAJR
'Yellow Australian' (d)	CCCN MAJR

Argyrocytisus see *Cytisus*

Arisaema ✿ (*Araceae*)

sp.	NWCA
C&H 7026	NMen WWst
CC 4904	CPLG
CC 5511	CPLG
Chen Yi 14	WCot
Chen Yi 38	WCot
Chen Yi 41	WCot
Chen Yi 97	WCot
album	EBee
amurense	CElw CLAP EBee ECho EWld GAuc GCal GGar LAma MMoz WCot WFar WPnP
§ - subsp. ***robustum***	ECho NMen WCot WWst
* ***angustatum*** var. ***amurense***	GEdr LAma
asperatum	LAma WCot
auriculatum	EBee
biauriculatum	see *A. wattii*
brachyspathum	see *A. heterophyllum*
brevipes	CPLG GEdr
candidissimum ♀^{H4}	Widely available
- pink-flowered	NWCA
- white-flowered	GEdr LAma LEdu WCot
ciliatum	CDes CPom EBee EBla ELon GEdr LAma LEdu MMoz MNrw NHar NLar SRot WBVN WCot WSHC
- var. ***liubaense***	CAby CFwr CGHE CLAP CMea CPLG CWCL EBee EPfP EPot EUJe EWld GEdr MMoz WFut WIvy WPGP
- - CT 369	CSpr SCnR SDys SKHP WCot WWst
- variegated (v) <u>new</u>	WCot
concinnum	CFir EAmu EBee EPot EWld GAuc GBin GEdr LAma NHol NLar WPnP
consanguineum	CAby CDes CFwr CGHE CHEx CLAP CPLG CRow EBee ECho EPfP EUJe EWld GBin GCal GCrs GEdr GGar LAma MLLN MMoz MTho NHar NHol NLar NMen WCot WFar WHil WPGP
- B&SWJ 071	WCru
- PJ 277	WCot
- dark-flowered	WCot
- 'J. Balis'	WCot
- subsp. ***kelung-insulare*** B&SWJ 256	WCru
- marble-leaf red	WCot
- 'Qinling'	WCot
cf. ***consanguineum***	CArn
- ACE 2031	WCot
costatum	CCCN CHEx CLAP CPom CStu EAmu EBee ECho EPfP EPot EUJe GBin GEdr GGar LAma LEdu LRHS MMoz NHol NMen WClo WPGP
- CC 3237	WCot
dilatatum	EBee LAma
dracontium	CLAP EBee ECho LAma NLar NMen
du-bois-reymondiae	EBee
ehimense	WWst
elephas	EBee ECho LAma WCot WWst
erubescens	CPom NLar WBVN
- marbled-leaved	GEdr
aff. ***erubescens***	WCot
exappendiculatum	CDes EBee MMoz WPGP
fargesii	CLAP CPLG EBee ECho GEdr LAma MMoz SChF SKHP WCot WWst
flavum	CDes CGHE CLAP CStu EBee ECho ELon EPfP EPot EWld GCal ITim LAma MMoz MTho NHar NHol NLar NMen SGSe SPlb WAbe WBVN WCot WFut WPGP WPrP
- subsp. ***abbreviatum***	EUJe
* - ***minus***	NWCA
- tall	ECho
- subsp. ***tibeticum***	EBee
formosanum B&SWJ 280	WCru
- var. ***bicolorifolium*** B&SWJ 3528	WCru
- f. ***stenophyllum*** B&SWJ 1477	WCru
§ ***franchetianum***	CPLG EBee GEdr LAma WCot
fraternum	WWst
galeatum	EBee ECho EPot LAma NHol
grapsospadix B&SWJ 7000	WCru
§ ***griffithii***	EBee ECho GAuc GEdr GGar LAma LRHS NHol WPnP
- 'Numbuq'	GCra
- var. ***pradhanii***	EBee GAuc WWst
handelii	CPom
helleborifolium	see *A. tortuosum*
§ ***heterophyllum***	EBee GEdr WWst
intermedium	EBee ECho GEdr LAma MNrw NHol NMen
iyoanum subsp. ***nakaianum***	GEdr WWst
jacquemontii	CAby CLAP EBee EBla ECho EWld GCra GEdr GKir NLar NMen WCot WPGP
- CC 5184	ITim
aff. ***jacquemontii***	GCrs
- MECC 29	NMen
- MECC 76	NMen
japonicum Blume	see *A. serratum* var. *mayebarae*
japonicum Komarov	see *A. serratum*
jinshajiangense	CPLG
kishidae	EBee GEdr WWst
kiushianum	EBee EFEx GEdr LAma MMoz WCot WWst
leschenaultii	LAma WWst
lichiangense	LAma WCot
lingyunense	WCot
§ ***lobatum***	CPLG EBee LAma
maximowiczii	EBee GEdr WWst
meleagris	LAma
negishii	WWst
§ ***nepenthoides***	CBcs EAmu EBee ECho EHrv EPot GBin GEdr ITim LAma LRHS MNrw NHol NLar WPnP
ochraceum	see *A. nepenthoides*
omeiense	EBee WCot
onoticum	see *A. lobatum*

	petelotii B&SWJ 9706	WCru
	polyphyllum B&SWJ 3904	WCru
	propinquum	CLAP CPom EBee ECho EWld GBin LAma NMen
	purpureogaleatum	see *A. franchetianum*
	rhizomatum	LAma
	rhombiforme	EBee LAma WCot WWst
	ringens misapplied	see *A. amurense* subsp. *robustum*
	ringens ambig.	SKHP
	ringens (Thunberg) Schott	CDes EBee EFEx EUJe GEdr LAma LEdu WWst
	- f. ***praecox*** B&SWJ 1515	WCru
	- f. ***sieboldii*** B&SWJ 551	WCru
	robustum	see *A. amurense* subsp. *robustum*
	saxatile	EBee LAma WCot WWst
	sazensoo	EBee GEdr LAma LRHS WWst
§	***serratum***	EBee ECho LAma LRHS MMoz MNrw WPGP
§	- var. ***mayebarae***	WWst
	sikokianum	CBcs EBee ECho EFEx EHrv EPPr EPot EUJe GCrs GEdr LAma LRHS SKHP SPoG
	- green-flowered **new**	LRHS
	- var. ***serratum***	CFir
	- variegated (v)	GEdr LRHS WWst
	speciosum	CHEx CPLG EAmu EBee ECho EPot EUJe EWld GAbr GEdr GGar LAma LRHS NHol NLar NMen SPlb WCot WFar WPnP
	- CC 3100	WCot
*	- var. ***magnificum***	EBee EHrv EWld GEdr NHol WCot
	- var. ***mirabile***	EBee GEdr
*	- var. ***sikkimense***	LAma
	taiwanense	CFwr CLAP CPom SKHP WCot
	- B&SWJ 269	WCru
	- var. ***brevipedunculatum*** B&SWJ 1859	WCru
	- f. ***cinereum*** B&SWJ 19121	WCru
	- silver-leaved	WCot
	tashiroi	GEdr WWst
	ternatipartitum	EBee GEdr WWst
	thunbergii	CPom EFEx EPPr LRHS SPoG WCot
	- subsp. ***autumnale*** B&SWJ 1425	WCru
	- subsp. ***urashima***	CLAP EBee EFEx GEdr LAma LRHS WCot WWst
§	***tortuosum***	CArn CLAP CPLG EAmu EBee ECha ECho EPot EUJe EWld GBin GEdr GGar LAma LEdu MNrw MTho NEgg NHol NLar NWCA SChF WAbe WCot WPGP WPnP
	- CC 1452	CPou
	- CC 1760	WCot
	- CC 4596	WCot
	- from high altitude	NMen
	tosaense	EBee WWst
	triphyllum	CElw CLAP CPLG CStu EBee ECho EPot GGar ITim LAma LEdu LRHS MTho NHol NLar NWCA SPlb WCot WFar WPGP WPnP
	- subsp. ***stewardsonii***	EBee GGar NMen WWst
	- subsp. ***triphyllum*** var. ***atrorubens***	CLAP
§	***utile***	EAmu EBee ECho EPot GAuc GBin GEdr LAma WPnP
	- CC 3101	WCot
	verrucosum	see *A. griffithii*
	- var. ***utile***	see *A. utile*
§	***wattii***	LAma
	yamatense	WWst
	- subsp. ***sugimotoi***	LAma
	yunnanense	CLAP EBee LAma

Arisarum (*Araceae*)

	proboscideum	Widely available
	vulgare	CStu ECho WCot
	- from Crete	ECho
*	- f. ***maculatum***	ECho
	- subsp. ***simorrhinum***	EBee ECho WCot
	- subsp. ***vulgare***	ECho WCot WHal

Aristea (*Iridaceae*)

	sp.	GGal
	africana 'Worcester' **new**	ECho
	angolensis **new**	EBee
	ecklonii	CDes CHEx CPLG CPou CPrp CTca CTrC CTsd EBee EShb IGor MCot SGar SHom WBor WCot WDyG WHil
	ensifolia	CMdw ELan MWea SAga WSHC
	grandis	CFir WCot
	inaequalis	CDes
§	***major***	CHll CSpe CTrC
	- pink-flowered	CDes CTrC WPGP
	spiralis 'Paarl' **new**	ECho
	thyrsiflora	see *A. major*
	woodii 'Clarens' **new**	ECho

Aristolochia (*Aristolochiaceae*)

	baetica	CArn CPLG SKHP WPGP
	californica	LEdu SKHP
	chilensis	CCCN
	clematitis	CArn EBee ECho GPoy LEdu
	cucurbitifolia B&SWJ 7043	WCru
	delavayi	CHEx
	durior	see *A. macrophylla*
	elegans	see *A. littoralis*
	gigantea	CCCN CHll
	grandiflora	CCCN CHll
	griffithii B&SWJ 2118	WCru
	heterophylla	see *A. kaempferi* f. *heterophylla*
	kaempferi	CCCN WSHC
	- B&SWJ 293	WCru
§	- f. ***heterophylla*** B&SWJ 3109	WCru
	× ***kewensis***	CCCN
§	***littoralis*** ♀H1	SOWG
	liukiuensis B&SWJ 4960 **new**	WCru
	longa	WThu
§	***macrophylla***	CBcs CBot CCCN CHEx CMac EBee EPfP GKir MRav NEgg NPal SLim WDin WSpi
	manshuriensis B&SWJ 962	WCru
	moupinensis BWJ 8181	WCru
	onoei B&SWJ 4960	WCru
	pearcei	CCCN CPla
	rotunda	SKHP
	sempervirens	SKHP WDin WSHC
	sipho	see *A. macrophylla*
	tomentosa	SKHP

Aristotelia (*Elaeocarpaceae*)

§	***chilensis***	LEdu
	- 'Variegata' (v)	CCCN CMac CWib CWit EBee GQui MAsh SPlb WCom
	fruticosa (f)	ECou
	- (m)	ECou
	- black-fruited (f)	ECou
	- white-fruited (f)	ECou
	macqui	see *A. chilensis*
	peduncularis	CPLG

	serrata	ECou
	- (f)	ECou
	- (m)	ECou

Armeria (*Plumbaginaceae*)

§	***alliacea*** (Cav.) Hoffsgg. & Link.	CSpe ECha
	- f. ***leucantha***	SRms WMoo
	alpina	GAuc MWat
	arenaria	EBWF
	Bees' hybrids	WMoo
	'Bloodgood'	ECho ECtt
	'Brutus'	MAvo SUsu
	caespitosa	see *A. juniperifolia*
	- 'Bevan's Variety'	see *A. juniperifolia* 'Bevan's Variety'
	euscadiensis	CSpe
§	***girardii***	EPot
	Joystick Series	ECho GJos NVic SPoG
	- 'Joystick Lilac Shades'	EBee EPfP EShb NLar SPoG
	- 'Joystick Pink'	SPoG SWal
	- 'Joystick Red'	EBee EPPr EPfP EShb GKir SPoG
	- 'Joystick White'	EPfP GKir LRHS NLar SPoG
§	***juniperifolia*** ♀H4	CMea ECho ELan EPfP GMaP LBee LRHS MAsh MHer MWat NHol NMen NWCA SPoG SRms
	- 'Alba'	CMea ECho ELan EPfP EPot GBin GMaP LRHS MAsh MHer MMuc NMen NPri NWCA SPoG SRms WAbe WFar WHoo WThu
§	- 'Bevan's Variety' ♀H4	ECha ECho ECtt ELan EPfP EPot GGar GKir GMaP LEdu LRHS MMuc MWat NLAp NLar NMen NPri NRya SPoG SRms SRot WAbe WFar WHoo WNew WPat
	- 'Brookside'	EPot
	- dark-flowered	WAbe
	- rose-flowered	ITim
§	***maritima***	CArn EBWF ECho EPfP GJos GKir LAst LRHS MNHC MSCN NEgg SPet WCFE WFar WHfH WJek WMoo WNew
	- 'Alba'	CArn CBcs COlW CTri ECha ECho ELan EPfP GJos GKev GMaP LEdu LRHS MCot MLHP MMuc NChi NPri NRya SBfd SPet SPlb SPoG SWal WCFE WFar WMoo WNew
	- 'Armada Rose' **new**	LRHS
	- 'Bloodstone'	CTri ECho ECtt ELan MWat
	- 'Corsica'	CMea CTri ECha NBir SBch WFar
	- Düsseldorf Pride	see *A. maritima* 'Düsseldorfer Stolz'
§	- 'Düsseldorfer Stolz'	CElw CPBP ECha ECho ECtt EDAr ELan EPfP GGar GKev GKir GMaP LHop LRHS MCot MLHP NDov NMen NPri SPoG
	- 'Laucheana'	SBch WHoo WMoo
*	- 'Pink Lusitanica'	ECho LBMP
	- 'Rosa Stolz' **new**	NDov
I	- 'Rubrifolia'	Widely available
	- 'Ruby Glow'	CTri
	- 'Splendens'	CBcs CTri ECho EDAr EPfP GGar GMaP LAst MGos MMuc NMir NRya NVic SBch SBfd SPoG WFar WMoo WPer
	- 'Vindictive' ♀H4	CMea CTri EPfP
	morisii	SBch
	'Nifty Thrifty' (v)	CBod CMea CTri EBee ECho ECtt EHoe EWes LRHS MAsh MHer MSCN NLAp SCoo SIde SPoG SRot WCom WFar WPat WWFP
	'Ornament'	SBfd
	plantaginea	see *A. alliacea* (Cav.) Hoffsgg. & Link.
	pseudarmeria	EBee ECho ELan EPfP GCal GKir MWhi
	- 'Drumstick Red'	ECho
	- 'Drumstick White'	WPer
	- hybrids	CTri ELan GGar
	pungens SDR 5622	GKev
	setacea	see *A. girardii*
	'Vesuvius'	NDov
	vulgaris	see *A. maritima*
	welwitschii	IFoB SRms
	'Westacre Beauty'	EWes

Armoracia (*Brassicaceae*)

§	***rusticana***	CArn CBod CHby COld CPrp CSev CTri ELau EPfP GAbr GPoy ILis MHer MMuc MNHC NPer NPri SBfd SIde SVic WHer WJek WSpi
	- 'Variegata' (v)	CPrp ELau GCal IFoB LHop MAvo NSti SMad WHer WJek WMoo

Arnica (*Asteraceae*)

	angustifolia subsp. ***alpina***	SRms
	- subsp. ***iljinii***	NBir
	chamissonis Schmidt	see *A. sachalinensis*
	chamissonis Less.	CHby EBee MNHC NBre NLar WJek
	longifolia	NBre
	montana	CArn EBee GBar GPoy MHer MNHC NMun SRms SWat
§	***sachalinensis***	NBre
	- RBS 0206	EPPr

Aronia (*Rosaceae*)

	arbutifolia	CBcs CDul CTri EPfP LSRN MBlu MGan SLon SPlb WDin WEas
	- 'Erecta'	CBgR CDul EBee ELan EPfP GBin LHop LRHS MBlu MBri MMuc NLar SBfd SLPl SPoG SRms SSpi
	melanocarpa	CDul CMCN CSpe CTsd CWib EBee ELan EPfP EWTr GKir LEdu LRHS MAsh SSpi WDin WFar
	- 'Autumn Magic'	CBcs CDoC CPMA EBee EPfP EWTr GBin IVic LAst LHop LRHS MAsh MMuc NMyG SCoo SLPl SLon SPer
	- var. ***grandifolia***	CPMA
	- 'Hugin'	CAgr CPMA NLar
*	- 'Red Viking'	GGar
	× ***prunifolia***	CDoC CDul GAbr GKir LEdu
	- 'Aron' (F)	CPMA
	- 'Brilliant'	CDoC CTri EBee EMil EPfP IFFs MAsh NEgg NLar SCoo SPer SPur
	- 'Nero' (F)	CAgr GBin NLar
	- 'Serina' (F)	CPMA NLar
	- 'Viking' (F)	CAgr CAlb CMCN CPMA EBee ECrN EMil EPfP GKir LBuc LHop LRHS MAsh MBlu MMuc NBro NLar SLim WDin

Aronia × *Sorbus* (*Rosaceae*)

§	'Burka'	WPat

Arracacia (*Apiaceae*)

	B&SWJ 9023 from Guatemala	WCru

Arrhenatherum (*Poaceae*)

	elatius var. ***bulbosum***	WFar
	- - 'Variegatum' (v)	EBee EHoe ELan EPPr GBin GMaP LBMP LEdu MMoz MMuc MWhi NBid NHol NOak WFar WMoo WPtf WWEG

Artemisia ✿ (*Asteraceae*)

RBS 0207	CPLG
from Taiwan	WHer
§ ***abrotanum*** ♀H4	Widely available
absinthium	CArn CEls CPbn CSev CWan GPWP GPoy MHer MNHC NSti SIde SVic SWat WJek
- 'Corinne Tremaine' (v)	WHer
- 'Lambrook Giant'	CEls
- 'Lambrook Mist' ♀H3-4	CEls CMac CPrp CSev EBee EBla ECtt ELan EPfP GBar GCal GKir GMaP GMac LRHS MRav SWat WMnd WWEG
- 'Lambrook Silver' ♀H4	CArn CEls CPLG CSam EBee ECha EHrv EPfP GBar GKir GMaP LHop LRHS LSRN MHer MMuc MRav NBro SLim SPer SWat SWvt WDin WFar WMnd WPer
- 'Silver Ghost'	CEls
afra	CArn CEls EBee IFro
§ ***alba***	CEls EOHP GBar GPoy MHer SIde WJek WPer
§ - 'Canescens' ♀H4	CArn CEls CSam CTri EBee ECha ECtt EHrv ELan EPfP GBar GMaP LAst LBMP LRHS MCot MHer MRav SDix SMrm SPer WAul WCFE WCot WFar WMnd WPer
annua	CEls SIde
anomala	CArn CEls
arborescens ♀H3	CArn CEls CMHG EBrs LRHS NEgg SDix SPer WDin WKif
- 'Brass Band'	see *A.* 'Powis Castle'
- 'Faith Raven'	CEls EBee EPfP GBin GMac MBNS WFar
- 'Little Mice'	CEls EBee SSvw WGwG WWEG
- 'Porquerolles'	CEls
argyi	CEls
§ ***armeniaca***	CEls ECho
assoana	see *A. caucasica*
atrata	CEls
barrelieri	CEls
caerulescens	see *Seriphidium caerulescens*
californica	CEls
- 'Canyon Gray'	CEls
campestris subsp. ***borealis***	CEls
- subsp. ***campestris***	CEls
- subsp. ***maritima***	CEls
- - from Wales	CEls
camphorata	see *A. alba*
cana	see *Seriphidium canum*
canariensis	see *A. thuscula*
canescens misapplied	see *A. alba* 'Canescens'
canescens Willd.	see *A. armeniaca*
capillaris	CArn CEls
§ ***caucasica*** ♀H3-4	CEls ECho EPot EWes MBrN MHer SChF SPhx SRms SRot WEas WPer
- ***caucasica***	CEls WFar
chamaemelifolia	CEls EBee GPWP IGor MHer NBre WJek
cretacea	see *Seriphidium nutans*
discolor Dougl. ex Besser	see *A. michauxiana*
douglasiana	CEls
- 'Valerie Finnis'	see *A. ludoviciana* 'Valerie Finnis'
dracunculus	ECha MCot MNHC MRav NVic SBfd SPlb SWal WBrk WFar WHfH WPer
- French	CArn CBod CEls CHby CSev CWan ELau GBar GPoy LEdu MHer NGHP NPri SBfd SIde WGwG WHil WJek
- Russian	CArn CEls GBar SVic
ferganensis	see *Seriphidium ferganense*
filifolia	CEls
fragrans Willd.	see *Seriphidium fragrans*
frigida ♀H3-4	CEls WCot
genipi	CEls
glacialis	CEls
gmelinii	CEls
gnaphalodes	see *A. ludoviciana*
gorgonum	CEls EBee EWes
herba-alba	CEls
'Huntington'	CEls WFar
japonica **new**	CEls
kawakamii B&SWJ 088	CEls WCru
kitadakensis	CEls
- 'Guizhou'	see *A. lactiflora* Guizhou Group
laciniata	CEls
lactiflora ♀H4	CArn CDoy CEls EBee ECha ECtt ELan GAbr GBar GBee GMaP MRav NGdn SDix SMrm SPer SRms WFar WHfH WMoo WTin
- 'Elfenbein'	EBee GBin GCal LHop LPla SMHy
§ - Guizhou Group	Widely available
- - 'Dark Delight'	CSpe CWit EBee ECtt EWes GBin NBPC NSti
- 'Jim Russell'	CBow CDes CElw EBee ECtt EWes NBre NDov
- ***purpurea***	see *A. lactiflora* Guizhou Group
- 'Stonyford'	MSCN
- 'Weisses Wunder'	EBee
lagocephala	CEls
lanata Willd. non Lam.	see *A. caucasica*
laxa	see *A. umbelliformis*
§ ***ludoviciana***	CEls ELan GBee IFoB MRav NLar NPer SBch SRms WCFE
- var. ***latifolia***	see *A. ludoviciana* subsp. *ludoviciana* var. *latiloba*
- subsp. ***ludoviciana*** var. ***incompta***	CEls LAst
§ - - var. ***latiloba***	CEls EBee EHoe GBar LHop NBro NPnk SBch SWvt WCot WHoo WPer
- subsp. ***mexicana*** var. ***albula***	CEls SMrm WFar
- 'Silver Queen' ♀H4	Widely available
N - 'Valerie Finnis' ♀H4	Widely available
maritima	see *Seriphidium maritimum*
mauiensis **new**	CEls
§ ***michauxiana***	CEls EBee NSti
molinieri	CEls
mutellina	see *A. umbelliformis*
niitakayamensis	CEls GBar
nitida	CEls
nutans	see *Seriphidium nutans*
palmeri hort.	see *A. ludoviciana*
pamirica	CEls
aff. ***parviflora*** CLD 1531	CEls
pedemontana	see *A. caucasica*
pontica	CArn CEls CWan EBee ECha ECrN EHoe ELan GBar GMaP GPWP GPoy MBNS MHer MRav NBro NSti SPer SSvw WFar WHfH WHil WHoo WJek WPer WWEG
§ 'Powis Castle' ♀H3	Widely available
princeps	CArn CEls ELau GPWP SIde WTou
procera Willd.	see *A. abrotanum*
purshiana	see *A. ludoviciana*
pycnocephala	CEls
- 'David's Choice'	CEls SMad
ramosa	CEls
'Rosenschleier'	CAby EWes LPla NBre WFar WPGP WTin WWEG
schmidtiana ♀H4	CEls ECha MWat SRms
- 'Nana' ♀H4	Widely available
- 'Nana Attraction' **new**	LRHS

	selengensis	CEls
	splendens misapplied	see *A. alba* 'Canescens'
	splendens Willd.	ELan SPhx
	- var. ***brachyphylla***	MAsh
	stelleriana	CArn CEls CTri EBee ECha EWTr GBee GKev IFoB LBMP LHop MAvo MCot MHer NBro NPri SRms WCAu
	- RBS 0207	CEls NLar
N	- 'Boughton Silver'	CEls EBee ECtt EHoe ELan EPfP EWTr GBBs GGar GMaP GMac IKil LRHS MAsh MCot MRav MWat NSti SMrm SPer SRms SWvt WCom WFar WMnd WWEG
N	- 'Mori'	see *A. stelleriana* 'Boughton Silver'
	- 'Nana'	CEls SWvt
	- 'Prostrata'	see *A. stelleriana* 'Boughton Silver'
	- 'Silver Brocade'	see *A. stelleriana* 'Boughton Silver'
	taurica	CEls
§	***thuscula***	CEls
	tridentata	see *Seriphidium tridentatum*
§	***umbelliformis***	CEls
	vallesiaca	see *Seriphidium vallesiacum*
	verlotiorum	CEls GBar
	vulgaris L.	CArn CEls EBWF ELau GBar GPoy MHer MNHC WHer
	- 'Cragg-Barber Eye' (v)	CEls EBee NBid WCom
	- Oriental Limelight = 'Janlim' (v)	CEls CFox COlW EBee ECtt EHoe EPfP EWTr GAbr LBMP LEdu LHop LRHS MCCP MWhi NBir NEgg NPri SBfd SWvt WFar WHer WJek
	- 'Variegata' (v)	CEls CEnt EBee EPfP NBir WAlt WFar WHer WMoo
	- 'Woolaston' (v)	WAlt
	× ***wurzellii***	CEls

Arthropodium (*Anthericaceae*)

	candidum	CBot CStu ECGP ECho ECou EHoe MSCN NWCA WPtf
	- 'Cappucino'	CBcs CBod
	- ***maculatum***	ECho GEdr LEdu SGSe SPlb WWEG
	- ***purpureum***	CWit EBee ECho GGar IKil NWCA WPGP
	cirratum	CHEx CSpe ECho ECou GAbr IKil LEdu MHer SBch SGar SWal
	- 'Matapouri Bay'	CAbb CBcs CDes CHEx EBee ECre MAvo WPGP
	minus	CPLG

Arthrostylidium (*Poaceae*)

	naibuense	CDTJ CGHE WPGP

artichoke, globe see *Cynara cardunculus* Scolymus Group

artichoke, Jerusalem see *Helianthus tuberosus*

Arum (*Araceae*)

	alpinum	see *A. cylindraceum*
	besserianum	ECho
	byzantinum	ECho
	'Chameleon'	CDes EBee ELon EPPr MAvo MNrw MTho NBir NLar SKHP SMad SPer WCot WCru WFar WHil WHoo WPGP WPrP WTin WWEG
§	***concinnatum***	EBee ECho NLar SChr SKHP WPrP
	- black-spotted	ECho
	- 'Mount Ida'	ECho SKHP
	- purple	ECho
	- variegated (v)	MAvo WCot
	concinnatum × ***cyrenaicum***	ECho GKev
	concinnatum × ***cyrenaicum*** from Crete	WWst
	cornutum	see *Sauromatum venosum*
	creticum	CArn CBgR CFir CMea CSpe CStu EBee ECha ECho EPot GCal LRHS MNrw MRav MTho NLar SCnR SRot SUsu WBVN WBor WCom WFar
	- MS 696	MNrw
	- FCC form	CPLG ECho LAma MMoz SKHP WAbe WPGP WWst
	- 'Karpathos' FCC form	WCot
	- 'Marmaris White'	SCnR WCot
	- white-spotted	MNrw MTho
	- yellow-spotted	NBir WFar WIvy
	creticum × ***italicum***	MAvo WFar
§	***cylindraceum***	ECho
	- CE&H 741	WWst
	cyrenaicum	CStu EBee ECho EWld LEdu MTho WCot WPGP WWst
	- from Crete	ECho WCot
	dioscoridis	CEnt CPom CStu ECho EWes GKev MMoz MTho NLar SKHP WCot
	- JCA 195.197	WCot
	- var. ***cyprium***	EBee ECho GKev WPrP WWst
§	- var. ***dioscoridis***	WCot
	- - JCA	WWst
	- - JCA 195200	WPrP
	- var. ***liepoldtii***	see *A. dioscoridis* var. *dioscoridis*
	- var. ***philistaeum***	WWst
	- var. ***smithii***	see *A. dioscoridis* var. *dioscoridis*
	dracunculus	see *Dracunculus vulgaris*
	elongatum	CPom WWst
	- RS 274/87	EBee
	euxinum	ECho
	hygrophilum	WWst
	italicum	CArn CEnt CLAP CTri ECho LAma LBMP MTho NBPC NLar SDeJ SEND SWat WCot WFar WPnP WSHC WShi
	- subsp. ***albispathum***	CHid CPom EBee ECho EDAr MMoz WCot WFar WPGP
	- 'Black Spot' **new**	EPPr
	- black-spotted	ECho SCnR WFar
	- giant	ECho WHil
	- 'Green Marble'	CBct WFar WWEG
	- subsp. ***italicum***	CBct EBee EBrs ECho EPla EShb EWTr NDov NWCA WBrk
	- - 'Bill Baker'	WFar
	- - 'Cyclops'	CHid WWEG
§	- - 'Marmoratum' ♀H4	Widely available
	- - 'Sparkler'	WCot
	- - 'Spotted Jack'	EBee MNrw WCot WCru WWEG
	- - 'Tiny'	CFir CPLG GCal SCnR SMHy WFar WWEG
§	- - 'White Winter'	CElw EBee ECGP NCGa WBrk WCot
	- 'Nancy Lindsay'	MAvo
	- subsp. ***neglectum***	SChr WFar
	- - 'Castle Brissac'	MAvo
	- - 'Miss Janay Hall' (v)	EBee EWes LLHF MDKP WCot
	- 'Pictum'	see *A. italicum* subsp. *italicum* 'Marmoratum'
	- 'Splish Splash'	CAvo CBow
	- 'Tresahor Beauty'	MAvo
	jacquemontii	ECho
	korolkowii	WCot
	maculatum	CArn CRWN EBee ECho EPot GPoy LAma MCot MHer MRav NLar NMir WHer WPrP WShi
	- 'Painted Lady' (v)	MAvo WCot
	- 'Pleddel'	MAvo MRav

nickelii	see *A. concinnatum*
§ ***nigrum***	CPom ECho EWes LLHF WGwG
- CE&H 524	EBee WWst
orientale	EPot
palaestinum	EBee WWst
petteri misapplied	see *A. nigrum*
pictum	CBgR CLAP CMac CPLG CStu EBee ECho EWes LEdu LLHF WCot WWst
- from Majorca	WCot
- 'Taff's Form'	see *A. italicum* subsp. *italicum* 'White Winter'
purpureospathum	CPom EBee ECho EPPr WCot WPGP
rupicola var. ***rupicola***	ECho
- var. ***virescens***	ECho WWst
sintenisii	WCot

Aruncus ✿ (*Rosaceae*)

AGSJ 214	NHol
aethusifolius 🏆H4	Widely available
- 'Little Gem'	ECho WCru
asiaticus B&SWJ 8624	WCru
dioicus	Widely available
§ - (m) 🏆H4	CDoC CRow ECha ELan EPla MBNS MRav MWts NBro NHol NSti SBfd SGar SMad SPer SRms SWat WMoo WPer
- var. ***acuminatus***	EBee
- Child of Two Worlds	see *A. dioicus* 'Zweiweltenkind'
- 'Glasnevin'	CSev EBrs ECtt GBee LRHS MRav WFar
- var. ***kamtschaticus***	EBee EWes MCCP MGos NBre NHol NLar WPGP WPnP
- - AGSJ 238	NHol
- - RBS 0208	NGdn WBVN
- 'Kneiffii'	Widely available
§ - 'Zweiweltenkind'	CEnt EBee EHrv LRHS NBre NLar SMad
'Guinea Fowl' new	EBee
'Horatio'	EBee GBin IPot LPla NDov SAga SPhx WCot
'Johannifest'	CDes EBee ECtt GBin IPot NDov WPGP
'Misty Lace'	EBee NGdn NLar SMrm
'Noble Spirit'	CEnt EBee NGdn NLar SGSe SWat
plumosus	see *A. dioicus*
sinensis	EBee NBre WFar
sylvestris	see *A. dioicus*
'Woldemar Meier'	EBee GBin NDov

Arundinaria (*Poaceae*)

amabilis	see *Pseudosasa amabilis* (McClure) Keng f.
anceps	see *Yushania anceps*
angustifolia	see *Pleioblastus chino* 'Murakamianus'
auricoma	see *Pleioblastus viridistriatus*
chino	see *Pleioblastus chino*
disticha	see *Pleioblastus pygmaeus* 'Distichus'
falconeri	see *Himalayacalamus falconeri*
fargesii	see *Bashania fargesii*
fastuosa	see *Semiarundinaria fastuosa*
fortunei	see *Pleioblastus variegatus*
funghomii	see *Schizostachyum funghomii*
§ ***gigantea***	CDTJ MWht WJun
- subsp. ***tecta***	CBcs MGos
hindsii	see *Pleioblastus hindsii*
hookeriana misapplied	see *Himalayacalamus falconeri* 'Damarapa'
hookeriana Munro	see *Himalayacalamus hookerianus*
humilis	see *Pleioblastus humilis*
japonica	see *Pseudosasa japonica*
jaunsarensis	see *Yushania anceps*
maling	see *Yushania maling*
marmorea	see *Chimonobambusa marmorea*
murielae	see *Fargesia murielae*
nitida	see *Fargesia nitida*
oedogonata	see *Clavinodum oedogonatum*
palmata	see *Sasa palmata*
pumila	see *Pleioblastus argenteostriatus* f. *pumilus*
pygmaea	see *Pleioblastus pygmaeus*
quadrangularis	see *Chimonobambusa quadrangularis*
simonii	see *Pleioblastus simonii*
spathiflora	see *Thamnocalamus spathiflorus*
tessellata	see *Thamnocalamus tessellatus*
vagans	see *Sasaella ramosa*
variegata	see *Pleioblastus variegatus*
veitchii	see *Sasa veitchii*
viridistriata	see *Pleioblastus viridistriatus*
'Wang Tsai'	see *Bambusa multiplex* 'Floribunda'

Arundo (*Poaceae*)

donax	Widely available
- 'Golden Chain' (v)	CChe CEnt CKno EBee ELan EPPr EShb EWes LHop SBfd SEND SMad SPoG
- 'Macrophylla'	CGHE CHGN CKno ETod LEdu LPJP SApp WPGP
- 'Variegata'	see *A. donax* var. *versicolor*
§ - var. ***versicolor*** (v)	Widely available
I - - 'Aureovariegata'	CDTJ EUJe MDKP
formosana	CKno EBee EPPr
- 'Golden Showers'	EBee SBfd
plinii	WPGP

Asarina (*Scrophulariaceae*)

antirrhiniflora	see *Maurandella antirrhiniflora*
barclayana	see *Maurandya barclayana*
erubescens	see *Lophospermum erubescens*
hispanica	see *Antirrhinum hispanicum*
lophantha	see *Lophospermum scandens*
lophospermum	see *Lophospermum scandens*
§ ***procumbens***	CEnt CMea CTri ECho EPfP EWTr LBMP MTho NRya SGar SRms WBrk WFar WKif
- 'Alba'	IFro
'Victoria Falls'	see *Maurandya* 'Victoria Falls'

Asarum (*Aristolochiaceae*)

Chen Yi 5	WCot
albomaculatum	ECho
- B&SWJ 1726	WCru
arifolium	EHrv EPPr GBBs NLar
asaroides	WWst
campaniflorum	EBee ECho EHrv LAma WCot WCru WWst
canadense	CArn EBee ECho EHrv EPfP EWld GBBs GEdr GPoy MMoz NLar WCru WWEG
caudatum	CDes CHEx CLAP CRow EBee ECha ECho EPfP GEdr LEdu NBro NHol NLar NWCA SRms WCot WCru WFar WPGP WSpi
- white-flowered	CLAP EBee EHrv SKHP WCru
caudigerum	WCot
- B&SWJ 1517	WCru
caulescens	EBee ECho EHrv EPPr LAma LEdu WCru WWst
- B&SWJ 5886	WCru

delavayi	EBee ECho EHrv LAma WCot WCru WWst
epigynum B&SWJ 3443	WCru
- 'Kikko'	GEdr
- 'Silver Web'	WCru
europaeum 𝕐H4	Widely available
fauriei	WCru
forbesii	EBee ECho EHrv MMoz NLar WWst
geophilum	MMoz
hartwegii	CLAP EHrv GKev NLar WCot WCru WPGP WPtf WWst
- NNS 00-78	WCot
- NNS 05-85	WCot
hatsushimae	EBee GEdr
himalaicum GWJ 9341 **new**	WCru
hypogynum B&SWJ 3628	WCru
infrapurpureum B&SWJ 1994	WCru
kumageanum	WCot
leptophyllum B&SWJ 1983	WCru
longirhizomatosum	WCru
macranthum	WCot
- B&SWJ 1691	WCru
maculatum B&SWJ 1114	WCru
magnificum	EHrv LAma MMoz WCru WWst
maximum	CFir CLAP EBee ECho EHrv LAma MMoz NMen WCot WCru
- 'Silver Panda'	CBct CDes CMil CSev CWGN CWit EBee ECtt EHrv EUJe GEdr LOck LRHS LSou MLLN NPnk SKHP SMad SPoG WCot WRHF
megacalyx	GEdr
minamitanianum	EBee
naniflorum 'Eco Decor'	CLAP EBla EHrv GEdr LAst LOck LRHS LSou MBNS MCot NPnk WClo WCot
nipponicum	GEdr WCot
petelotii HWJ 1043	WCru
pulchellum	CAby EHrv WCot WCru WWst
rigescens	EHrv
satsumense	GEdr
sieboldii	EBee GEdr WCru WFar
simile	GEdr
splendens	Widely available
taipingshanianum B&SWJ 1688	WCot WCru
- 'Elfin Yellow'	WCru
taitonense	WWst
takaoi	EBee
unzen	GEdr
viridiflorum	GEdr WWst
wulingense	WCru

Asclepias (*Asclepiadaceae*)

'Cinderella'	EBee LSou NBPC NGdn
curassavica	CCCN CSev EShb EWld NBre SRkn
incarnata	CEnt CMoH ELan EPau IFoB LRHS MRav NBre SMrm SPlb SUsu WPer
- 'Alba'	CPom ELan MMuc
- 'Ice Ballet'	CPrp EBee ELan IFoB LHop LLWG LSou NBPC NBre NGdn NLar SAga SGSe SPer SPoG WPer
- 'Soulmate'	EBee ELan EPfP MMHG MMuc MSCN NBPC NBre NGdn SGSe
- 'White Superior'	EBee LLWG
physocarpa	see *Gomphocarpus physocarpus*
purpurascens	CArn CPom
speciosa	EBee NBre NLar
sullivantii	EBee NBre
syriaca	CArn CPom EBee LRHS MLLN NBre SGSe
tuberosa	CArn CBcs CEnt CPom CWib EBee EShb GKir GPoy GQue LLWG LSou MHer NEgg SGSe SMad SPet SPoG
- Gay Butterflies Group	NBre NGdn
- 'Hello Yellow'	EBee SGSe
verticillata	NBre

Asimina (*Annonaceae*)

triloba (F)	CBcs CDTJ MBlu MBri NLar SPlb
- 'Davis' (F)	CAgr
- 'Sunflowers'	CCCN

Askidiosperma (*Restionaceae*)

chartaceum	CTrC

Asparagus (*Asparagaceae*)

B&SWJ 8309 from northern Vietnam	WCru
RCB AM 23	WCot
from Malawi, hardy **new**	SKHP
asparagoides 𝕐H1	EShb
cochinchinensis	WPGP
crassicladus	EShb
densiflorus 'Mazeppa'	EShb
- 'Myersii' 𝕐H1	ERea EShb SEND
- Sprengeri Group 𝕐H1	SEND
- - 'Variegatus'	EShb
denudatus	EShb
falcatus	EShb SEND
officinalis	SEND WFar
- 'Ariane'	MAsh
- 'Backlim' 𝕐H4	ECrN EMil ERea
- 'Butler'	SDea
- 'Cito' (m)	LRHS NPri SDea
- 'Connover's Colossal' 𝕐H4	CSBt CWan ECrN ERea LSRN MAsh MNHC SEND
- 'Dariana'	EMil ERea SDea
- 'Franklim'	SEND WFar
- 'Gijnlim' 𝕐H4	EMil ERea SDea WFar
- 'Jersey Knight'	SVic
- 'Mary Washington'	SVic
- 'Pacific 2000'	LSRN
- var. ***prostratus*** from Britain	GCal
- 'Purple Jumbo'	EBee ECrN
- 'Stewart's Purple' **new**	MAsh
plumosus	see *A. setaceus*
pseudoscaber 'Spitzenschleier'	EBee EShb MAvo SDix SMad
racemosus	CArn EShb
retrofractus	EShb WPGP
scandens	EShb
schoberioides	LEdu
§ ***setaceus*** 𝕐H1	EShb
suaveolens	EShb
verticillatus	SGSe
virgatus	EShb WCot WPGP

Asperula (*Rubiaceae*)

§ ***arcadiensis*** 𝕐H3	ECho WAbe WPat WThu
aristata subsp. ***scabra***	CSpe EBee ECha ELan WCot
- subsp. ***thessala***	see *A. sintenisii*
boissieri	ECho
daphneola	ECho EWes WAbe
gussonei	CMea ECho GCrs MWat NLAp NMen WAbe
lilaciflora	ECho
- var. ***caespitosa***	see *A. lilaciflora* subsp. *lilaciflora*
§ - subsp. ***lilaciflora***	ECho NMen
nitida	CPBP ECho
- subsp. ***puberula***	see *A. sintenisii*

odorata	see *Galium odoratum*
orientalis	WPGP
§ ***sintenisii*** Υ^{H2-3}	CMea ECho NMen WAbe WHoo WPat WThu
suberosa misapplied	see *A. arcadiensis*
suberosa Sibth. & Sm.	ECho
taurina subsp. ***caucasica***	CMoH NLar WBor
tinctoria	CArn GBar GPoy MHer SRms

Asphodeline (*Asphodelaceae*)

§ ***brevicaulis***	GAuc WCot
Cally hybrids	EDAr
liburnica	CAvo CMoH CSam EBee ECha ELan GAbr MRav SEND WCAu WCot WFar WHoo WPer
§ ***lutea***	Widely available
§ - 'Gelbkerze'	EPfP GKir LRHS NBre
- Yellow Candle	see *A. lutea* 'Gelbkerze'
taurica	EBee ECho GAuc LBMP MBNS NBre WPer

Asphodelus (*Asphodelaceae*)

acaulis	ECho LLHF SCnR WAbe WCot
- SF 37	WCot
§ ***aestivus***	EWes GCal MLLN SMrm SPhx SSvw WPer
- Cally Spear strain	GCal NCGa
albus	CArn CAvo CBot CSpe EBrs ECha EPPr GAuc GBin IFoB LBMP LRHS MCot NBid NCGa SPer SPlb SRms WAul WPer WWEG
asiaticus	EBee
brevicaulis	see *Asphodeline brevicaulis*
cerasiferus	see *A. ramosus*
fistulosus	LEdu NBir SAga SPhx WPrP
lusitanicus	see *A. ramosus*
luteus	see *Asphodeline lutea*
microcarpus	see *A. aestivus*
§ ***ramosus***	CPar EBee ECho GAuc GCal MCot MNrw MTho NCGa WBVN WPer

Aspidistra (*Convallariaceae*)

Chen Yi 135 **new**	WCot
from China	WCot
attenuata	IBlr
- B&SWJ 377	WCru
caespitosa 'Jade Ribbons'	IBlr WCot
'China Star'	IBlr WCot
daibuensis	IBlr
- B&SWJ 312b	WCru
elatior Υ^{H1}	CBct CHEx CTsd EBak EBee EShb IBlr NLar NPal NPla SAPC SArc SEND SMad STre WCot
- 'Akebono' (v)	WCot
- 'Asahi' (v)	IBlr WCot WFut
- 'Goldfeather'	IBlr
- 'Hoshi-zora' (v)	IBlr WCot
- 'Lennon's Song' (v)	WFut
- 'Milky Way' (v)	CBct CBow CHid EShb EWld IBlr MTho SEND SMad WCot WFut
- 'Morning Frost'	IBlr WFut
- 'Okame' (v)	IBlr WCot
- 'Variegata' (v) Υ^{H1}	CBct CHEx EShb IBlr IFoB MTho NBir SEND WCom WCot
- 'Variegata Exotica'	XBlo
leshanensis (v)	IBlr
linearifolia 'Leopard'	IBlr WCot
lurida	CBct EBee IBlr
- 'Ginga Giant' (v)	WFut
- 'Irish Mist' (v)	IBlr
marbled-leaved (v) **new**	WCot
minutiflora	WCot
mushaensis B&SWJ 1953 **new**	WCru
aff. ***mushaensis*** 'Spotty Dotty' (v)	WCru
omeiensis	WCot
patentiloba **new**	WCot
punctata	IBlr
saxicola 'Uan Fat Lady'	see *A. zongbayi* 'Uan Fat Lady'
'Singapore Sling' (v)	WCot WFut
sutepensis B&SWJ 5216	WCru
typica	IBlr
- 'China Sun'	IBlr WCot
- 'Old Glory' **new**	WCot
urceolata	IBlr
zongbayi	WCot
§ - 'Uan Fat Lady'	WCot WCru

Asplenium ✿ (*Aspleniaceae*)

adiantum-nigrum	GKir SRms WAbe
australasicum	EShb
boltonii **new**	WRic
bulbiferum misapplied	see *A.* × *lucrosum*
bulbiferum ambig. 'Suze'	SMad
bulbiferum ambig. × ***oblongifolium***	EUJe WRic
bulbiferum Forst.f.	ESwi
§ ***ceterach***	EFer WAbe WHer WRic
daucifolium	EOHP
× ***ebenoides***	WRic
flaccidum	WRic
incisum **new**	WRic
§ × ***lucrosum*** Υ^{H1-2}	CBty CDTJ CKel EFtx
lyallii	WRic
'Maori Princess'	GBin WFib
nidus Υ^{H1}	WRic XBlo
oblongifolium	GBin WRic
obovatum subsp. ***lanceolatum***	WRic
oligosorum **new**	WRic
onopteris **new**	WRic
polyodon	WRic
ruprechtii	WRic
ruta-muraria	EFer
§ ***scolopendrium*** Υ^{H4}	Widely available
- 'Angustatum'	Widely available
* - 'Circinatum'	WPGP
- 'Conglomeratum'	SRms
- Crispum Group	CBgR CLAP EFer ELan GBin MRav NBid NHol SApp SRms SRot WAbe WFib WPGP WPtf
- - 'Crispum Bolton's Nobile' Υ^{H4}	WCot WFib WPGP
- - 'Golden Queen'	CLAP
- Crispum Cristatum Group	CLAP LTen MMuc NVic SEND
- Crispum Fimbriatum Group	CLAP GQui
- Cristatum Group	Widely available
- Fimbriatum Group	CLAP WRic
- 'Furcatum'	CBty CDTJ CLAP EBee GEdr MAsh NHol NLar WRic
- 'Kaye's Lacerated' Υ^{H4}	CLAP EFer WFib WRic
- Laceratum Group	CLAP SRms
- Marginatum Group	EFer SWat WPGP
- - 'Irregulare'	SRms
- 'Muricatum'	CLAP ELan GBin MRav NBid NHol SRms WFib WTin
- 'Ramocristatum'	CLAP
- Ramomarginatum Group	CLAP ELan SRms WFar WRic
- 'Sagittatocristatum'	SRms WPGP
- 'Sagittatoprojectum Sclater'	WFib

*	- 'Sagittatum'	SRms
	- 'Stagshorn'	SRms
	- Undulatum Group	CBgR CBty CDTJ CLAP EAEE EBee ECha EFtx EPfP GBin LRHS MAsh MMoz MMuc NBir NEgg NHol NLar NMyG SBfd SEND SRms SWat WIvy WPnP WRic
	- Undulatum Cristatum Group	CLAP
	trichomanes 𝕐H4	Widely available
	- Cristatum Group	SRms WFar
	- Incisum Group	CLAP EBee EFer SRms WAbe WRic

Astelia (*Asteliaceae*)

	alpina	IBlr
	banksii	CBcs CDoC CHEx CHll CSWP CTrC EBee ECou EUJe GCal GGar IBal LRHS LSRN LTen MGos SBfd SPoG WCot WPGP
§	***chathamica*** 𝕐H3	Widely available
	- 'Silver Spear'	see *A. chathamica*
	chathamica × ***fragrans***	ECou
	cunninghamii	see *A. solandri*
	fragrans	CSpe ECou GGar IBlr LEdu WCot
	graminea	GCal IBlr
	grandis	IBlr LEdu
	nervosa	CTrC CTsd ECou GKir IBlr LEdu LSRN SAPC SArc WPat
	- 'Alpine Ruby' PBR	IBlr
	- 'Bronze Giant'	IBlr
	- 'Silver Sabre'	IBlr
	- 'Westland'	CBcs CBod CDoC CKno CPen CSBt CTrC CWit EBee EUJe GBin GCal GKir IBlr LEdu LRHS LSRN MBri MDun MGos MRav SBfd SEND SMrm SPad SPlb SPoG WCon WCot WGrn
	nivicola 'Golden Gem'	IBlr
	- 'Red Gem'	GCal LEdu
	petriei	IBlr
	'Red Devil'	WHer
	'Silver Mound'	EPfP
§	***solandri***	ECou IBlr
	trinervia	IBlr

Aster ✿ (*Asteraceae*)

	SDR 5969	GKev
	acris	see *A. sedifolius*
	ageratoides 'Starshine' PBR **new**	NSti WCot
	alpigenus var. ***alpigenus*** NNS 07-48	GKev
	alpinus 𝕐H4	ECho EPfP GJos GKir MWat SRms WClo WFar
	- var. ***albus***	EBee EDAr EPfP NBre NBro SPoG SRGP
	- Dark Beauty	see *A. alpinus* 'Dunkle Schöne'
	- var. ***dolomiticus***	GKev
§	- 'Dunkle Schöne'	EBee ECho ELon NBre NVic SPoG SRGP SRms WRHF
	- 'Goliath'	EBee ECho EPfP NBre NBro SPlb WFar
	- 'Happy End'	CMMP ECho NBre NBro NLar SPoG SRGP SRms WFar
	- 'Märchenland' (d)	NBre
	- 'Pinkie'	CSam EBee EDAr EPfP NBre NLar
	- 'Trimix'	ECho NBir SRms WFar
	- 'White Beauty'	SRms
*	- 'Wolfii'	SRms
	amelloides	see *Felicia amelloides*
	amellus	CArn ITim LRHS LSou WMoo
	- 'Blue King'	EBee NWsh SMrm SWvt
	- 'Breslau'	EBee
	- 'Brilliant'	CPrp EBee EBla ECtt EPPr LAst LSou MAvo MBNS MNFA MRav MWat SMrs SPer SRGP WHoo WOld
	- 'Butzemann'	EBee
	- 'Forncett Flourish'	WOld
	- 'Framfieldii' 𝕐H4	NDov SMHy WCot WOld
	- 'Gründer'	ECtt WOld
	- 'Jacqueline Genebrier' 𝕐H4	CHar ELon WSHC
	- 'King George' 𝕐H4	Widely available
	- 'Kobold'	LRHS
	- 'Lac de Genève'	EBee LRHS WCot WOld
	- 'Lady Hindlip'	CSam EBee ECtt WFar
	- 'Louise'	LRHS MBrN SUsu
	- 'Moerheim Gem'	LRHS
	- 'Nocturne'	WCot WOld
	- 'Peach Blossom'	EBee NBPC
	- Pink Zenith	see *A. amellus* 'Rosa Erfüllung'
§	- 'Rosa Erfüllung'	CMac EBee EBla ECtt EPPr EPfP GBin GMaP GMac LAst LHop LRHS MCot MRav NDov NWsh SAga SRGP SWvt WCot WMnd WOld
	- 'Rotfeuer'	ELon GQue WCot
	- 'Rudolph Goethe'	EBee EBrs ECtt EMil EPPr EPfP GKir LAst LRHS MRav SBHP SRGP WFar WMoo WOld WWEG
	- 'September Glow'	SHar
	- 'Silbersee'	CSam LRHS NDov
	- 'Sonia'	EBrs LRHS MRav
	- 'Sonora'	CPrp ECGP LHop LPla NBre SAga SMrm SRGP WCom WOld
	- 'Sternkugel'	WOld
	- 'Vanity'	LRHS WOld
§	- 'Veilchenkönigin' 𝕐H4	Widely available
N	- Violet Queen	see *A. amellus* 'Veilchenkönigin'
	- 'Weltfriede'	WOld
	'Anita Pfeiffer'	LRHS
	'Anja's Choice'	EBee LHop NBre NWsh WOld
	asper	see *A. bakerianus*
	asperulus misapplied	see *A. peduncularis*
§	***bakerianus***	WFar
	capensis 'Variegatus'	see *Felicia amelloides* variegated
§	***carolinianus***	EShb WFar
	'Cassandra'	WOld
	'Cheavers'	LRHS
	'Climax' misapplied	see *A. laevis* 'Arcturus', *A. laevis* 'Calliope'
	'Climax' ambig.	CAby CElw GCal MMuc MRav NBid NSti SAga SMrm
	'Climax' Vicary Gibbs	WOld
	coelestis	see *Felicia amelloides*
	coloradoensis	CPBP LLHF NSla
	'Connecticut Snow Flurry'	see *A. ericoides* f. *prostratus* 'Snow Flurry'
	conspicuus **new**	GCal
	'Coombe Fishacre' 𝕐H4	CAby COIW CPrp CSam EBee ELan GCal LPla MCot MNFA MRav NBre NCGa NLar SBfd SMrm SSvw SUsu WCAu WCot WFar WHoo WOld WTin
	cordifolius	WFar
	- 'Blutenregen'	EBee
	- 'Chieftain' 𝕐H4	CAby IGor MNFA MNrw SAga SPhx WOld
	- 'Elegans'	CAby CSam EBee IGor MWea WCot WMnd WMoo WOld
	- 'Ideal'	EBee NLar WOld
	- 'Silver Queen'	WOld
	- 'Silver Spray'	CPrp EBee ECtt GMaP GMac GQue MHom MWat NBre SRGP WOld WPer

	- 'Sweet Lavender' ♀H4	WOld
	- 'White Chief' **new**	WOld
	corymbosus	see *A. divaricatus*
	'Cotswold Gem'	WCot WOld
	'Dark Pink Star'	WOld
	delavayi	SUsu
	diffusus	see *A. lateriflorus*
	diplostephioides	CAby EBee EDAr EPPr EPfP GBin GCal GGar GQue IKil LBMP LRHS MBNS MMHG NBPC NBre NLar SGSe SGar SPlb WAul WPer WPtf
§	***divaricatus***	Widely available
§	- 'Eastern Star'	NCGa WBVN WCot WFar WOld
	- Raiche form	see *A. divaricatus* 'Eastern Star'
	- 'Tradescant'	IMou
N	***dumosus***	CPLG WFar WPer
	- 'Biteliness'	NBre NLar
	- Sapphire = 'Kiesapphire'PBR	CBow CPrp LHop LRHS LSRN NEgg NPri SPoG
	'Dwarf Barbados' **new**	LRHS
	ericoides	CKno MCot NBre WWEG
	- 'Blue Star' ♀H4	CPrp CSam EBee EBrs IGor LRHS NBPC NBid NLar SPer WMnd WOld
	- 'Brimstone' ♀H4	IGor MRav NBre WOld
	- 'Cinderella'	COIW CPrp GBee GMac LRHS NSti WOld WWEG
	- 'Cirylle'	NBre
	- 'Constance'	WOld
	- 'Erlkönig'	EBee ECGP GCal GQue LAst MRav MWea NDov NGdn NLar NPnk SWat WCot WMnd WOld WPer
	- 'Esther'	CPrp EBee ECha ELan NCGa SMrm WOld
	- 'Golden Spray' ♀H4	EBee EPfP GMaP GQue NLar SPer WFar WMnd WOld
	- 'Herbstmyrte'	CSam
	- 'Hon. Edith Gibbs'	WOld
	- 'Monte Cassino'	see *A. pilosus* var. *pringlei* 'Monte Cassino'
	- 'Pink Cloud' ♀H4	CHVG COIW CPrp EBee ECtt EPfP EWTr GCal GGar GMac LAst LRHS MNFA MRav NCGa NCob NLar SPer SRGP SWat WCAu WFar WMnd WOld WPer WTin WWEG
	- f. ***prostratus***	EPot WFar
§	- - 'Snow Flurry' ♀H4	CAby CMea CSam EBee ECha ECtt GMac IGor IMou LEdu MAvo MNFA MNrw NLar SAga SMrm WCom WCot WMnd WOld WOut
	- 'Rosy Veil'	CKno GMac IGor MHom NBir NGdn
	- 'Schneegitter'	EBee WCot WFar WOld
	- 'Schneetanne'	NBre
	- 'Sulphurea'	MWat
	- 'Vimmer's Delight'	WCot
	- 'White Heather'	CPrp IGor NLar WMnd WOld WPer WRHF
	- 'Yvette Richardson'	MHom SMHy WOld WWEG
	falcatus	WCot
	- var. ***commutatus***	WCot
	'Fanny's Fall'	see *A. oblongifolius* 'Fanny's'
	foliaceus	WHil
	- from Montana	EPPr
	- var. ***parryi***	EBee
	× ***frikartii***	CMac EBee ELan EPfP EShb LOck LRHS MRav SAga SRms SWvt WEas WOld WSHC
	- 'Eiger'	WOld
	- 'Flora's Delight'	EBrs GCal LRHS NDov WOld WWEG
	- 'Jungfrau'	CWGN EBee EPPr GMaP GQue LPio LRHS MRav NLar SPhx WOld WWEG
N	- 'Mönch' ♀H4	Widely available
	- Wonder of Stafa	see *A.* × *frikartii* 'Wunder von Stäfa'
§	- 'Wunder von Stäfa' ♀H4	CEnd CKno CPLG EBee ECtt ELan ELon EPfP GKir GMaP LHop LPio LRHS LSRN MBNS MCot MRav NBir NLar NVic WCot WMnd WOld WPGP WWEG WWlt
	glehnii 'Aglenii' **new**	EBee
	greatae	EBee
	hayatae B&SWJ 8790	WCru
	'Herfstweelde'	CPrp EBee MAvo SMad SUsu WFar WOld
	× ***herveyi***	CAby CFir CMoH CSam EBee EBla EBrs ECtt ELan EPfP GCal LLWP LRHS MMuc NDov NSti NWsh SAga SDix SPer SPhx SPoG SRGP WCAu WCot WFar WMnd WOld
	himalaicus	SRms
	'Hittlemaar'	WHil
	'Hon. Vicary Gibbs' (*ericoides* hybrid)	MNFA WOld WOut
	hybridus luteus	see *Solidago* × *luteus*
	'Ivy House'	ECtt
	'Kylie' ♀H4	CAby CHVG CPrp ECtt GMac IGor LRHS LSRN MHom NCGa NDov SRGP WBor WBrk WFar WOld WTin
	laevis	NBre NLar WPer WTin
	- 'Anneke Van der Jeugd'	EBee
§	- 'Arcturus'	CBgR CFir LRHS MHom MNrw NBir NBre NCGa NSti SSvw WCot WFar WWlt
	- 'Blauhügel'	LPla
	- 'Blue Bird'	LRHS SUsu
§	- 'Calliope'	Widely available
	- 'Cally Compact' **new**	GQue
	- var. ***geyeri***	MNrw
	- 'Nightshade'	MNrw WOld
	- white-flowered **new**	WOld
	lanceolatus Willd.	CSam EPPr NCGa
	- 'Edwin Beckett'	CBre MHom WOld
§	***lateriflorus***	EBee WOld WPer
	- 'Bleke Bet'	WCot WOld
	- 'Buck's Fizz'	ELan NDov NLar SBfd WOld
	- 'Chloe'	EBee NCGa SPhx
	- 'Datschi'	NDov WFar
	- var. ***horizontalis*** ♀H4	Widely available
	- 'Jan'	WOld
	- 'Lady in Black'	Widely available
	- 'Lovely'	EBee EBrs LRHS NBre NNor SRGP WCot
	- 'Prince'	Widely available
	laterifolius 'Snow Flurry'	see *A. ericoides* f. *prostratus* 'Snow Flurry'
§	***linosyris***	EBee EPfP EWes GBin GQue NBre NLar SMrm WHer WOld
	- 'Goldilocks'	see *A. linosyris*
	'Little Carlow' (*cordifolius* hybrid) ♀H4	Widely available
	'Little Dorrit' (*cordifolius* hybrid)	NWsh WOld
	maackii	SMrm
	macrophyllus	ELan LRHS NLar WOld
	- 'Albus'	EBee EPPr GBin WFar WOld
	mongolicus	see *Kalimeris mongolica*
	'Mrs Dean'	ECtt
	natalensis	see *Felicia rosulata*
	'Natasha'	LSRN
	'Noreen'	MAvo
	novae-angliae	CArn NBPC NBre WOld

	– 'Alex Deamon'	WOld
	– 'Andenken an Alma Pötschke'	Widely available
	– 'Andenken an Paul Gerber'	EBee ECtt MAvo MHom MNrw NDov WBrk WOld
	– 'Annabelle de Chazal'	ECtt MAvo WOld
	– 'Augusta' **new**	WOld
	– Autumn Snow	see *A. novae-angliae* 'Herbstschnee'
	– 'Barr's Blue'	CAby CMac EBee EPfP GCra LRHS MAvo MHom MMuc MWat NLar NWsh SPer SRms WBrk WMoo WOld
	– 'Barr's Pink'	CBre CMac EBee ECtt EPfP LRHS MCot MHer MHom MLHP MMuc MRav MWat NLar SEND WBrk WFar WOld WPer WSFF WWEG
*	– 'Barr's Purple'	ECtt WCFE WOld
	– 'Barr's Violet'	CAby ECtt EPPr MAvo MHom SRms WBrk WCot WHal WHoo WHrl WMoo WOld WPer WTin WWEG
	– 'Bishop Colenso'	NBre
	– 'Brockamin' **new**	WBrk
	– 'Brockamin Margaret' **new**	WBrk
	– 'Christopher Harbutt'	SRGP WOld
	– 'Colwall Constellation'	WOld
	– 'Colwall Galaxy'	MAvo WHrl WOld
	– 'Colwall Orbit'	WOld
	– 'Crimson Beauty'	EPPr GMac MAvo MHom MWat WBrk WCom WOld WWEG
	– 'Evensong'	ECtt WOld
	– 'Foxy Emily' **new**	MAvo
	– 'Harrington's Pink' 🏆[H4]	Widely available
	– 'Helen Picton'	CSam ECtt MAvo MBrN MHom MWat WBrk WCom WOld
§	– 'Herbstschnee'	Widely available
	– 'Indian Summer'	GJos
	– 'James Ritchie'	LLHF WHoo WOld
	– 'John Davies'	MAvo WOld
	– 'Lachsglut'	CAby GMac MAvo SMrm WCot
	– 'Lou Williams'	ECtt MAvo MWat WOld
I	– 'Lucida'	WHal WOld
	– 'Lye End Beauty'	CAby CKno ECtt EPyc LLWP LRHS MAvo MHom MNFA MRav MWat MWte WCot WHoo WMoo WOld WTin
	– 'Marina Wolkonsky'	CAby CBgR EBee ECtt EWes LHop MAvo MNrw SPhx SUsu WBrk WCot WOld
	– 'Millennium Star'	MAvo WOld
	– 'Miss K.E. Mash'	MHom SRGP WBrk WOld WWEG
	– 'Mrs S.T. Wright'	CAby CPrp CTri ECtt EWes MBrN MHom MWea SMrs SRGP WFar WOld WWEG
	– 'Mrs S.W. Stern'	WOld
	– 'Pink Parfait'	CAby CSam ECtt GMac LRHS NBre NGdn SRms WCot WOld
	– 'Pink Victor'	CTri EPPr SEND SRms WMoo
	– 'Primrose Upward'	CAby MNrw NWsh WCom WCot WOld
	– 'Purple Cloud'	CAby GMac LHop MHer MHom MWat NBre NGdn WBrk WCom WHal WOld WWEG
I	– 'Purple Dome'	Widely available
	– 'Quinton Menzies'	CSam WCom WOld WWEG
	– 'Red Cloud'	NBre WOld
	– 'Rosa Sieger' 🏆[H4]	CAby CBre CElw CPrp EBee ECtt MAvo MHom NGdn SMrs SUsu WBor WBrk WOld WWEG
	– 'Rose Williams'	MAvo WOld
	– 'Roter Stern'	ECtt LRHS
	– 'Rubinschatz'	CAby EBee LRHS MAvo MHom NBre SRms WOld
	– 'Rudelsburg'	MAvo NDov
	– 'Saint Michael's' **new**	WOld
	– 'Sayer's Croft'	CAby LRHS MHom MWat NBre WCot WHil WHoo WOld WTin
	– September Ruby	see *A. novae-angliae* 'Septemberrubin'
§	– 'Septemberrubin'	CAby CBgR CMea EBee ECtt ELon EPfP EWTr GMac IFoB LEdu LHop LRHS MNFA MRav NWsh SPhx SRGP SUsu WFar WOld WPrP
	– 'Treasure'	CBre EBrs ECtt EWes LRHS NBre SMrm SMrs WMoo WOld
	– 'Violet Haze'	CMea
	– 'Violetta'	CAby EBee ECtt LRHS LSou MAvo MHom MNFA MWea NMRc WBrk WFar WHoo WOld WTin
	– 'W. Bowman'	WOld
	– 'Wow'	NBre SMrm
N	***novi-belgii***	NSco WHer
	– 'Ada Ballard'	CMac CWit EBee EBrs LRHS LSRN NBre NEgg NGdn SBfd SMrm SMrs SPer SPoG SRGP WOld WWEG
	– 'Albanian'	WOld
	– 'Alderman Vokes'	WOld
	– 'Alex Norman'	WOld
	– 'Algar's Pride'	ECtt WOld WWEG
	– 'Alice Haslam'	CMac EBee ECtt GKir LRHS MCCP NEgg NPri SBfd SPoG SRGP SRms WOld WPer WWEG
	– 'Alpenglow'	WOld
	– 'Angela Peel'	EBrs
	– 'Anita Ballard'	WOld
	– 'Anita Webb'	NBir WOld
	– 'Anneke'	EBee LRHS MBri NLar SRGP SRkn WOld
	– 'Apollo'	EBrs NEgg NLar WFar WOld
	– 'Apple Blossom'	WOld
	– 'Arctic'	WOld
	– 'Audrey'	CEnt CMac EBee ECtt GKir GMaP LRHS LSRN MBNS NEgg NGdn SRGP STes WFar WOld
	– 'Autumn Beauty'	WOld
	– 'Autumn Days'	WOld
	– 'Autumn Glory'	WOld
	– 'Autumn Rose'	SMrs WOld
	– 'Baby Climax'	WOld
	– 'Bahamas' (Island Series)	EWll GKir LRHS LSou NWsh SGar SOkt
	– 'Barbados' (Island Series)	EPfP GKir LRHS LSou MBri
	– 'Beauty of Colwall'	WOld
	– 'Beechwood Challenger'	WOld
	– 'Beechwood Charm'	WOld
	– 'Beechwood Rival'	CTri EBee MBri
	– 'Beechwood Supreme'	WOld
	– 'Bewunderung'	WOld
	– 'Blandie'	CTri EBee EPfP MBNS SRGP WOld
	– 'Blauglut'	WOld
	– 'Blue Baby'	CMac WPer
	– 'Blue Bouquet'	CTri SRms WOld
	– 'Blue Boy'	WOld WWEG
	– 'Blue Danube'	SMrs WCom WOld
	– 'Blue Eyes'	CAby CElw EWTr SMrs SUsu WOld
	– 'Blue Gown'	CMdw GCal GQue SMrs WOld WOut
	– 'Blue Lagoon'	CMea ELan SMrs SRGP WBrk WOld
	– 'Blue Patrol'	WOld
	– 'Blue Radiance'	WOld
	– 'Blue Spire'	WOld
	– 'Bonanza'	WOld

- 'Boningale Blue'	WOld
- 'Boningale White'	NDov WOld
- 'Bridesmaid'	WOld
- 'Bridgette'	NBPC NPnk
- 'Bright Eyes'	SRGP
I - 'Brightest and Best'	WOld
- 'Cameo'	WOld
- 'Cantab'	WOld
- 'Cantonese Queen' (v)	EPPr
- 'Carlingcott'	WOld
- 'Carnival'	CMMP EBee ECtt MMHG MWea NEgg SMrs SPer SRGP WOld
- 'Cecily'	WOld WWEG
- 'Charles Wilson'	WOld
- 'Chatterbox'	CPrp EPfP MRav MWat NEgg NLar SRms WOld
- 'Chelwood'	WOld
- 'Chequers'	CAby CMMP CWit EBee MBNS MWea NEgg SMrs SRGP WOld
- 'Christina'	see *A. novi-belgii* 'Kristina'
- 'Christine Soanes'	WOld
- 'Cliff Lewis'	WOld
- 'Climax Albus'	see *A.* 'White Climax'
- 'Cloudy Blue'	WOld
- 'Coombe Gladys'	WOld
- 'Coombe Joy'	WOld
- 'Coombe Margaret'	WOld
- 'Coombe Queen'	WOld
- 'Coombe Radiance'	WOld
- 'Coombe Ronald'	MWat WOld
- 'Coombe Rosemary'	EBrs ECtt LRHS NLar WBor WOld
- 'Coombe Violet'	CAby MWat WOld
- 'Countess of Dudley'	WOld WPer
- 'Court Herald'	WOld
- 'Crimson Brocade'	CFir EBee ECtt ELan MRav MWea NLar SBfd SPoG SRGP WOld
- 'Dandy'	CMac EBee ELan LRHS NBir NEgg NGdn SRGP WFar WOld
- 'Daniela'	SRms WBrk WOld
- 'Daphne Anne'	WOld
- 'Dauerblau'	GBin WOld
- 'Davey's True Blue'	CTri SMrs WOld
- 'David Murray'	WOld
- 'Dazzler'	WOld WWEG
- 'Destiny'	WOld
- 'Diana'	NWsh WOld
- 'Diana Watts'	WOld
- 'Dietgard'	WOld WWEG
- 'Dolly'	NBir SRms WOld WWEG
- 'Dora Chiswell'	WOld
- 'Dusky Maid'	WOld
- 'Dwarf Ibiza' **new**	LRHS
- 'Elizabeth'	CAby CElw WOld
- 'Elizabeth Bright'	WOld
- 'Elizabeth Hutton'	WOld
- 'Elsie Dale'	WOld
- 'Elta'	WOld
- 'Erica'	CElw MWat WOld
- 'Ernest Ballard'	WOld
- 'Eva'	SRms WOld
- 'Eventide'	CAby CElw CTri EBee LSRN WOld WRHF
- 'Fair Lady'	EBrs LRHS MWat WOld
- 'Faith'	WOld
- 'Farncombe Lilac'	EBrs
- 'Farrington'	WOld
- 'Fellowship' ♀H4	CBgR CDes CFir CMoH COlW EBee ECtt LEdu MAvo MBri MMuc MWat NCGa NDov SHar SRGP SRms WBrk WCot WOld WWEG
- 'Flamingo'	LRHS WOld
- 'Fontaine'	WOld
- 'Freda Ballard'	ECtt EWll GMaP LSRN MWat NGdn SMrs SRGP WCAu WNew WOld WWEG
- 'Freya'	LSRN WOld WSHC
- 'Fuldatal'	WOld
- 'Gayborder Blue'	WOld
- 'Gayborder Royal'	CFir WOld
- 'Glory of Colwall'	WOld
- 'Goliath'	WOld
- 'Grey Lady'	WOld
- 'Guardsman'	WOld
- 'Gulliver'	WOld WWEG
- 'Gurney Slade'	WOld
- 'Harrison's Blue'	SMrs WBrk WOld WPer
- 'Heinz Richard'	CMMP COlW EBee ECha EWTr MHer NBir NBre NGdn SBch SMrs SRGP SRms WOld WWEG
- 'Helen'	WOld
- 'Helen Ballard'	CMoH SRms WBrk WOld
- 'Herbstgruss vom Bresserhof'	EWTr LRHS NBre NLar WOld
- 'Herbstpurzel'	WOld
- 'Hilda Ballard'	WOld
- 'Ibiza' **new**	LRHS
- 'Ilse Brensell'	WOld WWEG
- 'Irene'	WOld
- 'Isabel Allen'	WOld
- 'Janet Watts'	WOld
- 'Jean'	MWat SBfd SRms WOld
- 'Jean Gyte'	WOld
- 'Jeanette'	SRms WOld
- 'Jenny'	Widely available
- 'Jollity'	WOld
- 'Julia'	WOld
- 'Karminkuppel'	NBre WOld
- 'Kassel'	SRms WOld
- 'King of the Belgians'	WOld
- 'King's College'	WOld
§ - 'Kristina'	CBgR COlW CWan EBee EBrs ECha EPPr LRHS MBri MRav WCot WOld WWEG
- 'Lady Evelyn Drummond'	WOld
- 'Lady Frances'	EBee SRms WOld
- 'Lady in Blue'	Widely available
- 'Lady Paget'	WOld
- 'Lassie'	CElw MWat WOld
- 'Lavender Dream'	WOld
- 'Lawrence Chiswell'	WOld
- 'Lederstrumpf'	NDov
- 'Lilac Time'	WOld
- 'Lisa Dawn'	CSpr ECtt SMrs WOld
- 'Little Boy Blue'	NBre SRms WOld
- 'Little Man in Blue'	WOld WWEG
- 'Little Pink Beauty'	CEnt COlW EBee ECtt ELan EPfP EWTr LAst LHop LRHS MAsh MBNS NBid NEgg NGdn NVic SPer SRGP SRms WFar WOld WWEG
- 'Little Pink Lady'	EBrs SRms WOld
- 'Little Pink Pyramid'	SRms WWEG
- 'Little Red Boy'	WOld
- 'Little Treasure'	WOld
- 'Lucy'	WOld
- 'Madge Cato'	MAvo WOld
- 'Mammoth'	WOld
- 'Margaret Rose'	WOld
- 'Margery Bennett'	WOld
- 'Marie Ballard'	CAby CMac COlW CSBt EBee GKir GMaP LRHS MBri MHer MRav MWat MWhi NBre NCGa NGdn NPer SBfd SMrm SPer SPoG SRGP SRms SWat WBrk WCAu WNew WOld WPer WWEG

- 'Marie's Pretty Please'	WOld
- 'Marjorie'	SBfd SPoG WOld
- 'Marjory Ballard'	WOld
- 'Martonie'	WOld WPer
- 'Mary Ann Neil'	SMrs WOld
- 'Mary Deane'	WOld WPer
- 'Mauve Magic'	SRms WOld WWEG
- 'Melbourne Belle'	WOld
- 'Melbourne Magnet'	WOld
- 'Michael Watts'	WOld
- 'Midget'	WOld
- 'Mistress Quickly'	MCot SMrs WOld WWEG
- 'Mount Everest'	LHop NCGa SPhx WOld WPer WWEG
- 'Mrs J. Sangster'	WOld
- 'Mrs Leo Hunter'	WOld
- 'Neron'	NDov
- 'Nesthäkchen'	WOld
- 'Niobe'	CMac WOld
- 'Nobilis'	WOld
- 'Norman's Jubilee'	EBee EPfP NBir NEgg WOld WWEG
- 'Nursteed Charm'	WOld
- 'Oktoberschneekuppel'	WOld
- 'Orlando'	WOld
- 'Pamela'	WOld
- 'Patricia Ballard'	CBcs CFir CMac CPrp CSBt GCra GMaP LRHS MBri MWat MWhi NLar NPer SBfd SMrs SPer SPoG SRGP WCAu WFar WNew WOld WPer WWEG
- 'Peace'	WOld
- 'Percy Thrower'	ECtt SMrs WOld
- 'Peter Chiswell'	SRms WOld
- 'Peter Harrison'	GMaP GMac NBir WMnd WOld WPer
- 'Peter Pan'	GBee LRHS WOld
- 'Picture'	NBre WOld
- 'Pink Gown'	WOld
- 'Pink Lace'	MBNS WOld WPer
- 'Pink Pyramid'	WOld
- 'Plenty'	MBri WOld
- 'Porzellan'	CAby CElw CMMP COlW EBee ECGP ECtt MAvo MBNS NDov NGdn SMrs SRGP WCot
- 'Priory Blush'	CAby WOld
- 'Professor Anton Kippenberg'	CEnt CWan EBee EBrs EPfP GKir GMaP LLWP LRHS MRav NBre NLar SPer SRGP WMnd WOld
- 'Prosperity'	NBre WOld
* - 'Prunella'	CBgR GAbr WOld
- 'Purple Dome'	ECha LEdu LSRN MCCP MHer MWat NMoo SHar SRkn WOld WOut
- 'Queen Mary'	WOld
- 'Queen of Colwall'	WOld
- 'Ralph Picton'	WOld
- 'Raspberry Ripple'	WOld
- 'Rector'	see *A. novi-belgii* 'The Rector'
- 'Red Robin'	MWat
- 'Red Sunset'	SRms WOld
* - 'Reitlinstal'	EBee
- 'Rembrandt'	ECtt EWll NEgg NGdn SMrs SRGP
- 'Remembrance'	CAby SRms WBrk WOld WWEG
- 'Reverend Vincent Dale'	WOld
- 'Richness'	MAvo SAga WOld
- 'Robin Adair'	WOld
- 'Roland Smith'	WOld
- 'Rose Bonnet'	CSBt SPlb
- 'Rose Bouquet'	WOld
- 'Roseanne'	WOld
- 'Rosebud' ambig.	WOld WWEG
- 'Rosebud' Ballard	ECtt
- 'Rosenschein' **new**	NDov
- 'Rosenwichtel'	MMuc NLar WBrk WOld WWEG
- 'Royal Ruby'	EBee EBrs ECtt LRHS WOld WWEG
- 'Royal Velvet'	WOld
- 'Rozika'	WOld
- 'Rufus'	WOld
- 'Sailor Boy'	NCGa WOld
- 'Saint Egwyn'	WOld
- 'Sam Banham'	WOld
- 'Samoa' (Island Series)	EPfP EWll GKir LRHS LSou NBPC SOkt
- 'Sandford White Swan'	MHom WBrk WEas WWEG
- 'Sapphire'	LSRN SRGP SVil WOld
- 'Sarah Ballard'	SRGP WOld
§ - 'Schneekissen'	CPrp EBee ECtt EPfP EWTr GMaP LRHS MBNS MHer MMuc NPri SBfd SPer SRGP SWvt WFar WOld WWEG
- 'Schöne von Dietlikon'	CAby MAvo WBox WOld
- 'Schoolgirl'	WOld WWEG
- 'Sheena'	SRGP WOld
- 'Silberblaukissen'	GBin WOld
- Snow Cushion	see *A. novi-belgii* 'Schneekissen'
- 'Snowdrift'	NWsh WOld
- 'Snowsprite'	CBcs CSBt ELan LRHS MWat NEgg NLar SMrs SRGP SRms SWat WBrk WOld
- 'Sonata'	GMaP WOld
- 'Sophia'	SMrs WOld
- 'Starlight'	EBee NLar NMoo WFar WOld WRHF
- 'Steinebrück'	WOld
- 'Sterling Silver'	WOld
- 'Sunset'	WOld
- 'Susan'	WOld
- 'Sweet Briar'	CElw WOld
- 'Tapestry'	WOld
- 'Terry's Pride'	EBee SRGP WOld WWEG
- 'The Archbishop'	ECtt WOld
- 'The Bishop'	WOld
- 'The Cardinal'	WOld
- 'The Choristers'	WOld
- 'The Dean'	WOld
§ - 'The Rector'	WOld
- 'The Sexton'	WOld
- 'Thundercloud'	CAby WBrk WOld
- 'Timsbury'	SRms WBrk WOld WWEG
- 'Tony'	WOld
- 'Tovarich'	WOld
- 'Trudi Ann'	NBir WOld
- 'Twinkle'	WOld
- 'Victor'	WOld
- 'Vignem'	NSti
- 'Violet Lady'	WOld
- 'Waterperry'	MWat WOld
- 'Weisses Wunder'	WOld
- 'White Ladies'	CBcs EBrs ECtt GCra GMaP MMuc MWat NLar SBfd SPer SPoG SRGP
- 'White Swan'	CAby ECtt WOld
- 'White Wings'	WOld
- 'Winston S. Churchill'	CMMP CMoH COlW CTri EBee ELan EPfP GMaP LRHS MBri MWat SBfd SPer SPlb SPoG SRGP WBrk WOld WSpi
oblongifolius	GCal SAga WOld WPer
§ - 'Fanny's'	CPrp EBee EBla ECtt GCal GQue MMuc MNFA SMrm SPoG SRGP WCot WFar WOld
'Ochtendgloren' (*pringlei* hybrid) ♀H4	CDes CPrp CSam EBee ECtt EPPr EWes MAvo MNrw NCGa SMrm WCot WFar WHal WOld WOut
Octoberlight	see *A.* 'Oktoberlicht'

§ 'Oktoberlicht'	EBrs NCGa SMrm WOld
oolentangiensis	LRHS
'Orchidee'	ECtt EWTr EWes
'Orpheus'	MNrw
pappei	see *Felicia amoena*
'Pearl Star'	WOld
§ ***peduncularis***	EBee EBrs EPPr LPla LRHS SPhx SUsu
petiolatus	see *Felicia petiolata*
'Photograph' ♀H4	EBee EBrs GMac LRHS MAvo MHom SMrm WFar WMnd WOld
§ ***pilosus*** var. ***demotus*** ♀H4	ECha EWes MRav WFar WOld WTin
§ - var. ***pringlei***	CHid CSBt EBee EBla ECtt EPfP
'Monte Cassino' ♀H4	GQue LHop LRHS MBNS MRav MWat NBPC SMrm SPav SPer SPhx SRGP WFar WMoo WOld WWEG
- - 'October Glory'	CMdw WFar
- - 'Phoebe'	WOld
- - 'Pink Cushion'	CMHG WCot
'Pink Star'	CAby CMea CMoH EBee ECtt GMac MNFA MRav MWat NDov NSti SBch SBfd WBrk WFar WHoo WOld WTin
'Pixie Dark Eye' (*ericoides* hybrid)	CDes EBee WCot
'Pixie Red Eye' (*ericoides* hybrid)	WCot
'Plowden's Pink'	WOld
'Prairie Lavender'	WOld
'Prairie Pink'	WOld
'Prairie Violet'	WOld
'Primrose Path'	EBee WCot
puniceus	EBee NBre
pyrenaeus 'Lutetia'	CPrp CSam EBee ECha GAbr GCal GMaP MAvo MHom MMuc MNFA MWat NCGa NDov NLar SPoG SRGP WCAu WCot WFar WOld WWEG
radula	EBee EPPr EWes IMou LPla MAvo MNrw NBre NLar WOld WSHC
'Ringdove' (*ericoides* hybrid) ♀H4	CAby CKno CPrp EBee EBla ECGP ECtt GMac MCot MHom MNFA NCGa NSti SRGP WCot WOld
'Rosa Star'	WOld
'Rose Queen' **new**	MAvo
rotundifolius 'Variegatus'	see *Felicia amelloides* variegated
rugulosus 'Asrugo'	EBee
× ***salignus***	WOld
- Scottish form	WOld
§ ***scaber***	EBee NWsh WCon WCot WPGP
scandens	see *A. carolinianus*
schreberi	CFir EBee EPPr EWes MAvo NBre NWsh WCot WOld
§ ***sedifolius***	EBee ECtt ELan GQue LEdu LPio MDKP MWat MWea NBid SDix SEND WCot WFar WHil WMnd WOld WPer
- RCBAM -5	WCot
- 'Nanus'	CPLG ELan GCal MNFA MRav MWea NBir NLar SPer WAbe WCot WFar WMnd WOld WOut WSpi WTin
§ ***sibiricus***	NBre NLar
'Snow Flurry'	see *A. ericoides* f. *prostratus* 'Snow Flurry'
'Snow Star'	LRHS WOld
spectabilis	IMou LRHS WOld
stracheyi	EDAr
subcaeruleus	see *A. tongolensis*
'Sunhelene'	CBgR CDes EBee WCot
'Sunqueen'	EBee WCot
tataricus	LPla
- 'Jindai'	EBee WFar
thomsonii	WFar WOld
- 'Nanus'	CAby CMdw CMoH GMaP GQue LRHS MCot MWea NDov SAga SBch SPoG WCot WOld WSHC WSpi
Tonga = 'Dasfour'	CWGN EWTr GKir LRHS LSou NWsh SWvt WCot
§ ***tongolensis***	GKev SBHP SRms
- 'Berggarten'	CHar EBee LRHS NMoo WAbe
- 'Dunkleviolette'	NBro SRms
- 'Napsbury'	EBee WPGP
- 'Wartburgstern'	CFir CPrp EBee EPfP NGdn STes WWEG
tradescantii misapplied	see *A. pilosus* var. *demotus*
tradescantii L.	EBee ELan MBNS MRav NBre NHol NSti SMad WBrk WCot WOld WTin
'Treffpunkt'	IMou
trinervius	CPou WOld
subsp. ***ageratoides***	
- - 'Ashvi' **new**	WCot
- - 'Asran'	CWan EBee ECtt EWes LSou MMuc SSvw WCot WOld
- - 'Harry Smith'	EBee NDov
- var. ***harae***	SSvw WOld
tripolium	EBWF WHer
'Triumph'	WCot
turbinellus misapplied ♀H4	CAby CKno EBee EPfP GCal IKil LPla SMHy SPhx SRkn SUsu WBox WBrk WCot WHoo WOld WPtf WTin
turbinellus Lindl.	CSam EPfP EWTr GBee LRHS MWat NCGa
- hybrid	SMrm SSvw WFar
umbellatus	CBre CKno EBee GBin GQue NBir NBre NCGa NLar NSti SMrm SRms WCot WOld WPrP WTin
'Vasterival'	EBee NCGa NDov SMHy SSvw WBrk
vimineus Lam.	see *A. lateriflorus*
- 'Ptarmicoides'	see *Solidago ptarmicoides*
§ 'White Climax'	CAby EBee MHom WBox WBrk WCot
'Wood's Pink'	EBee WSpi
'Yvonne'	CBre

Asteranthera (*Gesneriaceae*)

ovata	CGHE GGGa GGar LRHS LSou MAsh SLon SPoG WAbe WPGP WSHC

Asteriscus (*Asteraceae*)

'Gold Coin'	see *Pallenis maritima*
maritimus	see *Pallenis maritima*

Asteromoea (*Asteraceae*)

mongolica	see *Kalimeris mongolica*
pinnatifida	see *Kalimeris pinnatifida*

Asteropyrum (*Ranunculaceae*)

cavaleriei	GEdr WCot WCru

Asterotrichion (*Malvaceae*)

discolor	ECou GGar

Astilbe ✿ (*Saxifragaceae*)

CC 5201	CPLG
'Alive and Kicking'	MBri
'Amerika' (× *arendsii*)	CMHG CSBt ECtt
'Amethyst' (× *arendsii*)	CMHG CMac EPfP GBin LLWG LRHS MRav NBir NBre SApp SPer SPoG WCAu WFar WHoo WMoo WWEG

	'Anita Pfeifer' (× *arendsii*)	CMHG EBrs ELon GBin GKir LPBA NLar WFar WPnP
	'Aphrodite' (*simplicifolia* hybrid)	CBcs CWCL GCal GKir MDKP MLHP MSCN NBre NGdn NHol WBrE WGor WWEG
	× ***arendsii***	IFoB NBre WMoo WPer
	astilboides	CMHG NHol SWvt
	'Atrorosea' (*simplicifolia* hybrid)	NCot SRms
	'Avalanche'	GAbr GBin GKir NHol WMnd WWEG
§	'Beauty of Ernst' (× *arendsii*)	LPBA LRHS SPoG
§	'Beauty of Lisse' (× *arendsii*)	LRHS
	Bella Group (× *arendsii*)	NBre SPet WMnd
	'Bergkristall' (× *arendsii*)	CMHG
	'Betsy Cuperus' (*thunbergii* hybrid)	CMHG EBee GBin MRav NBre SApp WCAu
	'Bonn' (*japonica* hybrid)	CWCL CWat LRHS SCoo SRms
§	'Brautschleier' (× *arendsii*) 🏆H4	CBgR CMHG CMMP CMac CTri EBrs ECtt EPfP GBin GCra GKev LSRN MDun MSCN NGdn NLar NPri WPnP WPtf
	'Bremen' (*japonica* hybrid)	CMHG EBrs GBin LPBA LRHS NHol
	'Bressingham Beauty' (× *arendsii*)	Widely available
	Bridal Veil (× *arendsii*)	see *A.* 'Brautschleier'
§	'Bronce Elegans' (*simplicifolia* hybrid) 🏆H4	CFir CMHG CPrp EBee ECha EPfP GBin GKir GMaP MRav NHol WFar WMoo WOut WWEG
	'Bronzelaub' (× *arendsii*)	GBin GKir
*	***bumalda*** 'Bronze Pygmy'	MMoz NHol STes
	'Bumalda' (× *arendsii*)	CFir CSBt CWCL GBin GMaP LLWG MWts NChi NGdn NMyG SBfd SPlb WFar WMoo
	'Burgunderrot' (× *arendsii*)	CWCL GAbr MAsh MBri MLLN MNrw NCGa NLar SMrm
*	'Carmine King'	WHil
	'Carnea' (*simplicifolia* hybrid)	CMHG
	'Catherine Deneuve'	see *A.* 'Federsee'
	'Cattleya Dunkel' (× *arendsii*)	CMHG WFar
	'Cattleya' (× *arendsii*)	CMHG CSam EBrs NBPC NLar NMoo WFar WMoo
	'Ceres' (× *arendsii*)	CMHG NHol
	'Cherry Ripe'	see *A.* 'Feuer'
	chinensis	CMHG ECho LRHS NBre WFar WSHC
	- B&SWJ 8178	WCru
	- from Russia	GCal
	- 'Brokat'	GBin
	- 'Christian'	GBin
	- var. ***davidii***	CMHG
	- - B&SWJ 8583	WCru
	- - B&SWJ 8645	WCru
	- 'Diamonds and Pearls' PBR	CWGN MBri MWea
	- 'Finale'	CHar COlW EWTr NHol SPer WFar
	- 'Frankentroll'	CMHG
	- 'Intermezzo'	GCal GMaP NLar
	- 'Love and Pride'	MBri
	- 'Milk and Honey' PBR	ECtt
§	- var. ***pumila*** 🏆H4	Widely available
	- - 'Serenade'	CMac NGdn WFar
	- 'Purple Glory'	CMHG EWll GKir IKil MDun
	- 'Spätsommer'	CMHG
	- var. ***taquetii***	CMac EBee NBre NSti SRms
	- - Purple Lance	see *A. chinensis* var. *taquetii* 'Purpurlanze'
§	- - 'Purpurlanze'	Widely available
§	- - 'Superba' 🏆H4	CMHG CMac CRow CTri ECha EPfP GBin GGar LRHS MCCP MCot MLHP NBro NGdn NHol SDix SPer SRms STes WFar WMoo WPGP
	- 'Troll'	GBin
	- 'Veronika Klose'	CMHG EBee GBin GKir NLar WCAu WWEG
	- 'Vision in Pink' PBR	CMil CWCL LSou MBNS SBfd WHil
	- 'Vision in Red' PBR	CMil CWCL CWat ECtt EKen EWll GBin GGar LRHS LSou MBNS MBri MNrw NLar NMyG SBfd SPoG WCAu WFar WHil
	- 'Visions'	CMHG CMac CMil CWCL EBee EBrs GBin GQue LRHS LSou MBNS MBri NBro NGdn NMyG SBfd STes WFar
	Cologne	see *A.* 'Köln'
	Color Flash	see *A.* 'Beauty of Ernst'
	Color Flash Lime	see *A.* 'Beauty of Lisse'
	'Crimson Feather'	see *A.* 'Gloria Purpurea'
	× ***crispa***	ECho WCFE WFar
	- 'Gnom'	NHar
	- 'Lilliput'	ECtt GBee GBin GGar GKir NBir NHar NLar NRya SMad WWEG
§	- 'Perkeo' 🏆H4	CBcs CFir ECha ECho ECtt ELan EPfP GBin GGar GKir GMaP MLLN NBir NHar NLar NMen NPri NSla SRms WAul WBVN WFar WMoo WWEG
	- 'Peter Pan'	see *A.* × *crispa* 'Perkeo'
	- 'Snow Queen'	NBir NHar NMen WFar
	'Darwin's Dream'	NLar NPri WFar
	'Darwin's Favourite' (× *arendsii*)	CWCL
	'Deutschland' (*japonica* hybrid)	Widely available
§	'Diamant' (× *arendsii*)	CMHG EBrs EShb LRHS MMuc NGdn NHol WFar
	Diamond	see *A.* 'Diamant'
	'Drayton Glory' (× *arendsii*)	see *A.* × *rosea* 'Peach Blossom'
	'Drum and Bass' PBR	LSou NLar
	'Dunkelachs' (*simplicifolia* hybrid)	CBgR LRHS LTen MSCN NBPC NMyG WFar
	'Dusseldorf' (*japonica* hybrid)	CMHG CSam CWCL EBrs GKir NHol
	'Eden's Odysseus'	GBin NHol
	'Elegans' (*simplicifolia* hybrid)	CMHG CMac GKir WFar
	Elizabeth Bloom = 'Eliblo' PBR (× *arendsii*)	CHVG EBee EBrs EPla GKir LLWG LRHS MRav NDov NEgg NHol WFar
	'Elizabeth' (*japonica* hybrid)	CMHG EBee
	'Ellie' (× *arendsii*)	CMHG CMac CWCL GBin GQue LSRN LSou MAsh MBNS MBri NBPC NGdn NHol NLar SAga SMrm WPtf
	'Else Schluck' (× *arendsii*)	ECha
	'Erica' (× *arendsii*)	CMHG CTri EWll GKir MRav NLar NPnk WFar WMnd WMoo WWEG
	'Etna' (*japonica* hybrid)	CBcs CMHG CSam EBee IFFs LRHS MMuc NEgg NGdn NHol NLar SMrm SRms WPnP
	'Europa' (*japonica* hybrid)	CMHG CMac EBrs ECtt GBin GKir LRHS MGos MRav SBfd SPoG WFar WMoo
	'Fanal' (× *arendsii*) 🏆H4	Widely available
	'Fata Morgana' (× *arendsii* hybrid)	CMHG
§	'Federsee' (× *arendsii*)	CBcs CMHG EBrs ECha ECtt ELan EPyc GKir LRHS MBNS NBPC NBre NBro NDov NGdn SMrm SPer WFar
§	'Feuer' (× *arendsii*)	CMHG CMMP CMac CPrp ECtt ELan EPfP GKir LBMP NEgg NGdn NHol NLar NVic WBor WMoo
	Fire	see *A.* 'Feuer'
	'Flamingo' PBR (× *arendsii*)	GAbr GBin MAvo MBNS SMrm

	'Gertrud Brix' (× *arendsii*)	CBcs CWat GKir MMuc NBir NGdn
§	***glaberrima***	NBid NHol NMen
§	- var. ***saxatilis*** 🏆H4	CRow EBee EPfP GBin GGar IFro NHar NSla WAbe WHal WThu
	- ***saxosa***	see *A. glaberrima* var. *saxatilis*
	'Gladstone' (× *arendsii*)	see *A.* 'W.E. Gladstone'
	'Gloria' (× *arendsii*)	CMHG CMac CTri EBrs ECtt LPBA LRHS MRav WFar
§	'Gloria Purpurea' (× *arendsii*)	CMHG GKir NHol NMoo NMyG WMoo
	Glow	see *A.* 'Glut'
§	'Glut' (× *arendsii*)	CFir CMHG CWCL EBrs ECtt EPPr GBin GKir LLWG NGdn NHol NMyG SRms WFar
	'Granat' (× *arendsii*)	CMHG CMMP CMac NBir NBre NEgg NHol WFar WMoo
*	Grande Group (× *arendsii*)	NBre
	grandis	CMHG GBee WHer
	'Grete Püngel' (× *arendsii*)	ECha GBin GKir WFar WWEG
	'Harmony' (× *arendsii*)	CMHG
	'Heart and Soul'PBR	EPfP MBri MWea
	'Hennie Graafland' (*simplicifolia* hybrid)	CBcs CMHG CWCL GAbr GBin GKir GQue LRHS LSou MLLN NCGa NLar SHar
	'Henry Noblett' new	GBin
	'Holden Clough' (*japonica* hybrid)	NHol
	Hyacinth	see *A.* 'Hyazinth'
§	'Hyazinth' (× *arendsii*)	CMHG CPLG CPrp EBrs GBin GMaP LBMP LLWG LSou NGdn NHol WFar
	'Inshriach Pink' (*simplicifolia* hybrid)	CBcs CCVN CMHG CPrp EBrs EHoe ELan GBin GKir LRHS MBri NBir NHar NHol SAga SBch WFar WHal
	'Irrlicht' (× *arendsii*)	CMHG CMac EBrs ELan EPfP EPla EShb GGar GKir LHop LPBA MCot MGos NHol SMrm SPer SWat WAul WPnP WWEG
	japonica	CPLG
*	- 'Pumila'	NBir NGdn
	- var. ***terrestris***	see *A. glaberrima*
	'Jo Ophorst' (*davidii* hybrid)	CMHG ECtt GBin LRHS MRav NEgg NGdn NHol NLar WFar
	'Jump and Jive'PBR	LSou MAsh
	'Koblenz' (*japonica* hybrid)	CMHG CWCL MDKP NMyG
§	'Köln' (*japonica* hybrid)	CMHG CWat EBrs GBin LPBA LRHS NMyG WFar
	koreana	GGar WCot WPGP
	- B&SWJ 8611	WCru
	- B&SWJ 8680	WCru
	'Kriemhilde'	CMHG MSCN
	'Kvële' (× *arendsii*)	CMHG GKir WFar WMoo
§	'Lachskönigin' (× *arendsii*)	CMHG GKir
	'Lilli Goos' (× *arendsii*)	CMHG GBin GCal
	'Lollipop'	GBin MBNS MBri SRms
	longicarpa B&SWJ 6711	WCru
	macroflora	GCal
	'Maggie Daley'	CMMP EBee NBro WMoo
	'Mainz' (*japonica* hybrid)	CHVG CMHG ECtt ELan LPBA
	'Mars' (× *arendsii*)	CMHG
	microphylla	CMHG NHol
	- B&SWJ 11085	WCru
	- pink-flowered	CMHG NHol
	'Moerheim Glory' (× *arendsii*)	CMMP GBin MSCN NBre NGdn NLar
	'Moerheimii' (*thunbergii* hybrid)	CMHG GKir
	'Mont Blanc' (× *arendsii*)	CMHG
	'Montgomery' (*japonica* hybrid)	Widely available
	'Nikki'	NCGa NLar
	'Obergärtner Jürgens' (× *arendsii*)	CMMP GBin
	Ostrich Plume	see *A.* 'Straussenfeder'
	'Paul Gaärder' (× *arendsii*)	CMHG
	'Peaches and Cream'	EBee GKir MMHG NBro NLar NPnk
	'Peter Barrow' (*glaberrima* hybrid)	GBin SRms
	'Pink Fanal'	EBrs LRHS
	'Pink Lightening'PBR (*simplicifolia* hybrid)	CBow CWCL EBee EShb MAvo MBNS MBri NBPC NLar SMrm WBor
	Pink Pearl (× *arendsii*)	see *A.* 'Rosa Perle'
	'Poschka'	CFir
I	'Poschka Alba'	CFir
	'Professor van der Wielen' (*thunbergii* hybrid)	CFir CMHG EBee EBrs GGar GKir MDun MWte NHol NLar SDix SPer SRms WCAu WFar WSpi WWEG
	pumila	see *A. chinensis* var. *pumila*
*	'Queen'	LPBA
	'Queen of Holland' (*japonica* hybrid)	MGos
	'Radius'	CBgR CMMP EBee GBin LPBA MSCN NGdn NLar WPnP
	Red Light	see *A.* 'Rotlicht'
	'Red Sentinel' (*japonica* hybrid)	CBcs CMMP CWCL CWat EPfP GBin GMaP MAsh MBri MSCN NBro NGdn NHol SBfd SPoG WFar WHrl
	'Rheinland' (*japonica* hybrid) 🏆H4	CBcs CMHG CMMP CWCL EPfP GBin LPBA MLLN MMuc NPri SRot STes WFar WHoo WPnP
	'Rhythm and Blues'PBR	ECtt NLar
	rivularis	CMHG EBee GBin WCot
	- CC 5201	GKev
	- GWJ 9366	WCru
§	- var. ***myriantha***	NBre
	- - BWJ 8076a	WCru
	- - SICH 757	CPLG
	'Rock and Roll'PBR	CMil LPBA NBPC WHil
§	'Rosa Perle' (× *arendsii*)	CHVG CMHG CSam NHol
§	× ***rosea*** 'Peach Blossom'	CBcs CBgR CHVG CMHG CMMP CMoH EBrs ELon GCra GKir LPBA LRHS NBir NCGa NHol SBfd SPoG WFar WHoo WMoo
	- 'Queen Alexandra'	WFar
	'Rosea' (*simplicifolia* hybrid)	EBrs GBin LRHS NHol WFar
	'Rot Straussenfeder' (× *arendsii*)	GBin MNrw MSCN
§	'Rotlicht' (× *arendsii*)	CMHG CMac EBrs GKir LRHS NHol NMyG SBfd WFar WGor
	'Salland' new	GCal
	Salmon Queen	see *A.* 'Lachskönigin'
	'Salmonea' (*simplicifolia* hybrid)	CMHG
	'Saxosa'	see *A. glaberrima* var. *saxatilis*
	'Sheila Haxton' (*chinensis* hybrid)	EBee EBrs NHar NHol
	Showstar Group (× *arendsii*)	LRHS MMuc MSnd NBre
	simplicifolia 🏆H4	CAby CRow SKHP WFar
	- 'Alba'	CMHG
	- Bronze Elegance	see *A.* 'Bronce Elegans'
	- 'Darwin's Snow Sprite'	CMac GBin MBri NHol NLar NMyG NPri WFar
	- 'Jacqueline'	EBee LSou NHol WFar
	- 'Praecox Alba'	EBee GBin NEgg WWEG
	- 'White Sensation'PBR	NBPC NLar
	'Snowdrift' (× *arendsii*)	CHid CMHG CWat EBrs EPla EWTr GKir GMaP IKil LBMP LLWG LRHS MBNS MDKP MLLN MMuc MWat NBir NEgg SPer SWat WFar WWEG
	'Solferino' (× *arendsii*)	CMHG
	'Spartan' (× *arendsii*)	see *A.* 'Rotlicht'

'Spinell' (× *arendsii*) CWCL LRHS MDun NBre NMRc WFar WPnP WWEG
'Sprite' (*simplicifolia* hybrid) ♀H4 Widely available
'Stand and Deliver'PBR ECtt MBri
§ 'Straussenfeder' (*thunbergii* hybrid) ♀H4 CMHG CMac CTri EBrs ECtt EPfP EPla GBin GKir GMaP LBMP LHop LRHS NBid NBir NBro NHol NLar SPer WAul WCAu WClo WFar WMoo WPnP WPtf WWEG
'Sugar Plum' (*simplicifolia* hybrid) EBee NGdn
'Superba' see *A. chinensis* var. *taquetii* 'Superba'
thunbergii CEnt CPLG EBrs
- var. ***congesta*** B&SWJ 10961 **new** WCru
- var. ***hachijoensis*** EBee
- - B&SWJ 5622 WCru
- var. ***sikokumontanum*** B&SWJ 11164 WCru
- var. ***terrestris*** B&SWJ 6125 WCru
'To Have and To Hold' **new** LSou
'Venus' (× *arendsii*) CSam EBrs ECha ECtt GBin GGar GMaP LPBA MBNS MCot NDov NHol NVic SPer SWat WCAu WFar WMoo
'Vesuvius' (*japonica* hybrid) CBcs EBrs MDKP NBro
virescens see *A. rivularis* var. *myriantha*
§ 'W.E. Gladstone' (*japonica* hybrid) CWat NHol WGor
'Walküre' (× *arendsii*) CMHG
'Walter Bitner' GBin LLWG MBNS NHol SRGP
'Washington' (*japonica* hybrid) EBee IFFs LAst MDKP NBre NGdn SHar
§ 'Weisse Gloria' (× *arendsii*) CMHG CMac CPrp EBrs ECha GBin GKir LLWG LPBA LRHS NBPC NBro NDov NEgg NHol NMyG SBfd SCoo SMrm SPad WBor WClo WMoo WTin
'Weisse Perle' (× *arendsii*) GKir
White Gloria see *A.* 'Weisse Gloria'
'White Queen' (× *arendsii*) NHol
'White Wings'PBR (*simplicifolia* hybrid) NLar
'William Reeves' (× *arendsii*) CMHG NHol
'Willie Buchanan' (*simplicifolia* hybrid) CBcs CHid CMHG CPrp EHoe GAbr GBin GGar GKev GKir GMaP LBMP NEgg NGdn NHar NHol NMen SApp SPer SRms WAbe WFar WMoo WNew WWEG
Younique Carmine = 'Verscarmine' **new** WHil
Younique Silvery Pink = 'Versilverypink' **new** WHil
'Zuster Theresa' (× *arendsii*) CBgR CMHG EBee EBrs GKir LPBA MBNS MNrw MSCN NBPC NBro WFar

Astilboides (*Saxifragaceae*)

§ ***tabularis*** Widely available

Astragalus (*Papilionaceae*)

canadensis GKir SPhx
glycyphyllos CArn SPhx
membranaceus CArn MNHC
purshii ECho

Astrantia ✿ (*Apiaceae*)

'Atomic Sunburst' **new** GQue
bavarica GCal MDKP MFie WFar
'Berendien Stam' EBee MAvo MFie
'Bloody Mary' CBct EBee ELan LSRN MAvo MFie NBPC NGdn NLar SPer
'Buckland' Widely available
carniolica EPyc NEgg WCAu
- ***major*** see *A. major*
- 'Rubra' CBcs EBee GMaP MFie NBre WHal
- 'Variegata' see *A. major* 'Sunningdale Variegated'
'Dark Shiny Eyes' CBct CLAP EBee ECtt MFie NCGa NGdn NLar NSti
'Hadspen Blood' Widely available
Harptree hybrid CHar
'Helen' NLar
helleborifolia misapplied see *A. maxima*
'Larch Cottage Magic' **new** NLar
'Madeleine' see *A. major* 'Madeleine van Benekom'
§ ***major*** Widely available
- 'Abbey Road'PBR CBct CKno CLAP EBee EBla LAst LHop LLWG LSou MBNS MFie MGos NBPC NEgg NLar SHar SMrm STes WAul
I - 'Alba' CBcs CMHG CPrp CWCL EBee EBla ECha EHrv IBal IKil MCot MFie MRav NBir NGdn NPer SPer STes WMnd WMoo
- 'Ann Cann' CBct MFie
- subsp. ***biebersteinii*** EBla LRHS MFie NBir NBre
- 'Bo-Ann' EBla LPio MFie NCob NLar WAul WFar
- 'Celtic Star' EBee EBla MFie NCob NGdn SWvt
- 'Claret' Widely available
- Cliff's form MFie
- 'Côte d'Azur' MFie
- 'Cyril James' MFie
- dwarf WFar
- 'Elmblut' MFie
- 'Enduring Love' MFie
- 'Florence' **new** LRHS NDov STes
- 'Gill Richardson' Widely available
- 'Gracilis' EBee
- 'Greenfingers' EWes
- 'Gwaun Valley' WFar
- Gwen's form MFie
- 'Hillview Red' CElw EBee MFie
- subsp. ***involucrata*** EBee EBla EHrv LRHS MFie SWat WFar
- - 'Barrister' CSam LRHS MFie NLar WFar
- - 'Canneman' EBee EBla EWes LPla MFie NLar WCot WFar
- - 'Jumble Hole' MFie NDov
- - 'Margery Fish' see *A. major* subsp. *involucrata* 'Shaggy'
- - 'Moira Reid' Widely available
- - 'Orlando' CLAP EBee MAvo MFie
§ - - 'Shaggy' ♀H4 Widely available
- - 'Wattisfield White' **new** MAvo
- 'Jade Lady' WFar
- 'Jitse' EBee MAvo
- 'Lars' Widely available
- 'Little Snowstar' EHrv IBal MBNS
- 'Lola' EBee LLWG NCGa
§ - 'Madeleine van Bennekom' CLAP GMac MAvo WCra
- 'Magnum Blush' EBee LRHS
- 'Paper Moon' WFar
- 'Penny's Pink' **new** MFie
- 'Percy Picton' **new** MAvo
- 'Pink Pride' EBee LSou NCGa WHil
- 'Primadonna' EBee EBla EHrv GMaP MFie NHol NLar NWsh SPlb WFar WPer WSpi WWEG

- 'Princesse Sturdza' EBee
- 'Reverse Sunningdale Variegated' MAvo MFie
- 'Rosa Lee' EBee IBal MFie NCGa NCob NLar NPnk WAul
- var. ***rosea*** CBre CWCL EBee EBla EHrv EPfP EWTr IBal LHop LRHS LSRN MFie MRav MWat MWhi NGdn SAga SMrm SPer WCAu WFar WMoo WWEG
- - George's form CBct CKno CLAP CMac CSam EAEE EBee EBla ECtt LAst LHop LRHS LSRN MBNS MFie NCGa NCob NEgg NHol NPnk SMrs SPur
- 'Rosensinfonie' EBee EBla GMaP MFie NBro NGdn NPnk WFar WMnd
§ - 'Rubra' Widely available
- 'Ruby Cloud' CHid EBee EBla EHrv IBal LLWG MCot MFie MNrw NBro NGdn NLar NSti SGSe WFar WFoF WMnd WPnP WSpi WWEG
- 'Ruby Glow' LRHS MFie
- 'Ruby Star' CLAP ECGP ECtt MFie MTis NDov NLar SUsu WCra WFut
- 'Ruby Wedding' Widely available
- 'Silver Glow' CSpr EBee ECtt IBal MFie NBPC NGdn NMyG WFar
- 'Star of Summer' EBee EKen MFie MWea
- 'Starburst' MFie WFar
- 'Sue Barnes' (v) EBee GCal MAvo MFie
§ - 'Sunningdale Variegated' (v) ♀H4 Widely available
- 'Titoki Point' MFie WCot
- 'Venice'PBR CWCL CWGN IPot LRHS LSou MBri MLLN MNrw NDov NLar NSti STes
- 'White Giant' LRHS NLar WCot
§ ***maxima*** ♀H4 Widely available
- 'Mark Fenwick' MFie NBir
* - ***rosea*** EBla ECtt MDKP MNrw MWhi NBir NGdn WWEG
minor EBee WCru WFar
'Moulin Rouge'PBR Widely available
'Queen's Children' EBee MFie
'Rainbow' MFie NLar
'Roma'PBR Widely available
rubra see *A. major* 'Rubra'
'Sheila's Red' **new** LRHS NDov
'Snow Star'PBR CWCL CWib EBee EHrv GBin IPot MBri MFie NLar NPnk WHlf
'Star of Beauty'PBR CWCL ECtt LSou MBri MFie NLar NSti SMrm WWlt
'Star of Heaven' **new** NLar
'Star of Royals'PBR **new** ECtt
'Stonehouse Perpetual' ECha
'Warren Hills' CCVN CLAP EBee EBla GMaP MFie NLar NPnk
'Washfield' **new** NDov

Astrodaucus (*Apiaceae*)

orientalis SPhx

Asyneuma (*Campanulaceae*)

canescens CEnt LSou NBre SGar
§ ***prenanthoides*** SMrm
pulvinatum CPBP WAbe

Asystasia (*Acanthaceae*)

bella see *Mackaya bella*
§ ***gangetica*** CSev EShb
violacea see *A. gangetica*

Athamanta (*Apiaceae*)

turbith CSpe
- subsp. ***haynaldii*** EBee

Athanasia (*Asteraceae*)

§ ***parviflora*** SPlb

Atherosperma (*Monimiaceae*)

moschatum CBcs CHII IRar SKHP WSHC

Athrotaxis (*Cupressaceae*)

cupressoides CDoC CDul CKen GKir WThu
laxifolia CDoC CKen GKir MGos WThu
selaginoides CDoC

Athyrium ✿ (*Woodsiaceae*)

'Branford Beauty' CBty CCCN CDes CLAP EBee EFtx ISha LRHS NLar WPGP WRic
'Branford Rambler' CLAP ISha WRic
filix-femina ♀H4 Widely available
§ - subsp. ***angustum*** CBty CLAP EBee ELan GBin MMoz NHol SPer SRms WMoo WRic
- - f. ***rubellum*** 'Lady in Red' CCCN CDes CElw CKel CLAP EBee EFtx ELon ISha LBMP LLHF LRHS LSRN MAsh MAvo MBri MGos NBid NLar SPoG WMoo WRic WWEG
- 'Corymbiferum' SRms
- 'Crispum Grandiceps Kaye' SRms
- Cristatum Group CLAP EBee EFer EFtx ELan LSRN MMoz SWat WFib
- 'Dre's Dagger' EFtx MAsh SPoG WFar WWEG
- 'Encourage' SPoG WFar
- 'Fieldii' CLAP SRms
- 'Frizelliae' ♀H4 Widely available
- 'Frizelliae Capitatum' CLAP WFib WPGP
- 'Frizelliae Cristatum' EFtx SRms
- 'Grandiceps' CLAP EBee SRms
- 'Minutissimum' CDes CGHE CLAP EBee ECha ELan ISha MMoz WPGP
* - 'Nudicaule' SRms
- Plumosum Group CLAP WAbe WFib
- 'Plumosum Axminster' CBty CLAP EFer MAsh NMyG NWsh WFar
- 'Plumosum Divaricatum' SRms
- 'Plumosum Druery' CLAP
- Red Stem see *A. filix-femina* 'Rotstiel'
§ - 'Rotstiel' CDTJ CFwr CLAP EBee MMoz MMuc SBfd WFar WMoo WPnP WRic WWEG
- 'Vernoniae' ♀H4 CBty CDTJ CLAP CWCL ELan LPBA MMoz NHol NLar NWsh SGSe WRic
- 'Vernoniae Cristatum' CLAP NHol WFib
- 'Victoriae' CBty CCCN CDTJ CDes CFwr CPrp CWCL EBee EFer EKen GEdr GMaP ISha LPBA LRHS MAsh MMuc NBPC NBid NGdn NHol NLar NMyG SGSe STes WMoo WPat WWEG
- Victoriae Group see *A. filix-femina* subsp. *angustum*
- 'Victoriae' seedling MBri WPtf
'Ghost' CBty CCCN CDes CKel CLAP EBee EFtx ISha LRHS LSou LTen MGos NLar NSti WPat WRic WWEG
goeringianum 'Pictum' see *A. niponicum* var. *pictum*
niponicum LRHS MLLN WHal
- f. ***metallicum*** see *A. niponicum* var. *pictum*
§ - var. ***pictum*** ♀H3 Widely available
- - 'Apple Court' CBty CCCN EBee EFtx ISha LRHS NLar WPat WRic
- - 'Burgundy Glow' CBow

- - 'Burgundy Lace'PBR	CBcs CBty CLAP EBrs EFtx LRHS MAsh MNrw NMyG NPri SHeu SMrm WFut WPat WPtf
* - - 'Cristatoflabellatum'	CLAP EBrs ELan LRHS
- - 'Pewter Lace'PBR	CBty EFtx MAsh
- - 'Red Beauty'	CBcs CBty CDTJ CEnt CLAP CWit EBee ECha EPfP GAbr GBin GCal LRHS LSRN MAsh MAvo NHol NLar SBfd SPad SPoG WClo WCot WPat WPnP WWEG
- - 'Regal Red' new	ISha
- - 'Silver Falls'	CBcs CBty CLAP CMil EAmu EBee EBrs EShb GBin GKev NCob NMyG SPoG WCot WHal WPGP
- - 'Soul Mate'	CLAP
- - 'Ursula's Red'	Widely available
- - 'Wildwood Twist'	CBty CLAP EFtx
'Ocean's Fury' new	EFtx
oppositipinnum new	WRic
otophorum ♀H4	ISha NBid NHol SRms WIvy WPGP WRic
- var. ***okanum***	Widely available
reflexipinnum new	WRic
vidalii	CBow CDTJ CFwr CLAP EBee ISha LSou MMoz NEgg NLar NMyG WFib WRic WWEG
wardii new	WRic

Atractylodes (*Asteraceae*)

japonica	EFEx
macrocephala	CArn EFEx

Atragene see *Clematis*

Atriplex (*Chenopodiaceae*)

canescens	NLar WDin
cinerea	ECou
halimus	CArn CBcs CBot EBee ECha EHoe ELau EPPr LTen MBlu MBri MRav NLar SDix SLon SPer SPlb WCom WCot WDin WKif
hortensis var. ***rubra***	CArn CEnt CSpe ELan LSou MHer MNHC MWte NGHP SIde SMrm WCot WEas WJek WTou

Atropa (*Solanaceae*)

acuminata	CArn
bella-donna	CArn GBar GPoy SEND WTin
mandragora	see *Mandragora officinarum*

Aubrieta (*Brassicaceae*)

'Alba'	see *A.* 'Fiona'
albomarginata	see *A.* 'Argenteovariegata'
'Alix Brett'	CMea ECho LRHS
'Ann Kendall'	ECtt
§ 'Argenteovariegata' (v) ♀H4	ECho ELan GKir LRHS WAbe WFar
'Astolat' (v)	ECho SRms
§ 'Aureovariegata' (v) ♀H4	ECho ELan GKir NPer WAbe WFar
(Axcent Series) 'Axcent Antique Magenta' new	WGor
- 'Axcent Antique Rose' new	WGor
Blaue Schönheit	see *A.* 'Blue Beauty'
'Blaumeise'	GKir LRHS WSpi
§ 'Blue Beauty'	ECtt EPfP NWCA WClo WNew WSpi
'Blue Chip'	ECtt
'Blue Emperor'	NCGa WSpi
'Blue Gown'	GKir
'Blue Whale'	ECtt GAbr LHop SRot
§ 'Bob Saunders' (d)	CMea ECho LLHF LRHS NCGa
'Bressingham Pink' (d) ♀H4	CMea ECtt ELan EPfP SPoG WFar
'Bressingham Red'	ECho ECtt EPfP GKir NCGa SPoG
'Bubble Purple'	EPfP
Cascade Series	GJos GKir SPoG
- 'Blue Cascade'	EPfP GKir MBNS MWat SPlb SPoG WGor WRHF
- 'Lilac Cascade'	SPoG
- 'Purple Cascade'	CTri CWib EPfP LSRN MBNS MWat SPlb SPoG SRms WFar WGor
- 'Red Cascade' ♀H4	CTri CWib ECtt EPfP LSRN MBNS SPlb SPoG SWal
deltoidea	SVic WClo
* - 'Gloria'	SRot
- 'Nana Variegata' (v)	CPBP EPot WGor
- Variegata Group (v)	ECtt EPot NPri NSla WFar WRHF
- - 'Shaw's Red'	GKir
'Doctor Mules' ♀H4	ECtt GKir LRHS SRms WAbe
'Doctor Mules Variegata' (v)	CTri ECho ECtt EPfP LAst MHer NWCA SPoG SWvt WFar WHoo
Double Stock-flowered Group pink-flowered	LAst
'Downers Variegata' (v)	LRHS
'Eila' (d)	STre
'Elsa Lancaster'	NMen WAbe WPat
§ 'Fiona'	ECtt
§ 'Frühlingszauber'	SRms
glabrescens	WAbe
'Gloriosa'	GAbr
'Golden King'	see *A.* 'Aureovariegata'
gracilis	EPot WAbe
- 'Kitte Rose'	ECtt
* 'Graeca'	LRHS
'Greencourt Purple' ♀H4	CMea ECho ELan MHer MWat
'Gurgedyke'	SRms
'Hamburger Stadtpark'	CWCL ECho ECtt EPfP SRot
'Harknoll Red'	ECtt
'Hemswell Purity'PBR	see *A.* 'Snow Maiden'
'Hendersonii'	SRms
'J.S. Baker'	SRms
'Jeeves'	LRHS
'Joy' (d)	ECtt LLHF
'Kati' new	NCGa
'Kitte'	ECho ECtt EPfP NLar NPri SPoG
'Leichtlinii'	LRHS
macedonica	WAbe
'Moerheim' new	GQue
'Mrs Rodewald' ♀H4	SRms
'Novalis Blue'	SRms
'Oakington Lavender'	GKir
pinardii	WAbe
'Pink Beauty'	ECtt
'Purple Charm'	SRms
'Red Carpet'	ECho ECtt ELan EPot MHer SPoG SRms
'Red Carpet Variegated' (v)	CMea
'Rose Queen'	CMea CPBP
Royal Series ♀H4	COIW
- 'Royal Blue'	EPfP LRHS NEgg WFar WMoo
- 'Royal Lavender'	LRHS WFar
- 'Royal Lilac'	WFar
- 'Royal Red'	EPfP LRHS NPri SBch SRms WClo WFar WGor WMoo
- 'Royal Rose'	LRHS NBre WFar
- 'Royal Violet'	CTri EPfP LRHS NHol SBch WFar WMoo
'Schloss Eckberg'	GQue
'Schofield's Double'	see *A.* 'Bob Saunders'
'Silberrand'	ECha
§ 'Snow Maiden'PBR	ECtt NPri WFar
'Somerfield Silver'	EPfP NPri
'Somerford Lime' (v)	ECtt EPfP NPri
Spring Charm	see *A.* 'Frühlingszauber'

'Swan Red' (v)	ECtt EPot GKev LAst LIMB MHer NEgg NSla SPoG WClo WFar WHoo
thessala	CPBP
'Triumphante'	ECtt LLHF LRHS
'Whitewell Gem'	LRHS NHol SRms WMoo

Aucuba ✿ (*Aucubaceae*)

japonica	CAlb
- (f)	CDul WDin
- (m)	SReu
- 'Crassifolia' (m)	CMac EQua SAPC SArc
- 'Crotonifolia' (f/v) ♀H4	Widely available
- 'Crotonifolia' (m/v)	CMac LBMP MAsh SRms WRHF
- 'Dentata'	CHEx
- 'February Star' (f/v) **new**	SDix
- 'Gold Splash' (v)	GKir
- 'Golden King' (m/v) ♀H4	CAlb CDoC CMac CWib EBee ELan ELon EPfP GKir LRHS LSRN MAsh MGos MWat NLar SLim SPer WBrE
- 'Golden Spangles' (f/v)	CAlb CBcs CDoC EBee IVic LRHS NLar NMun SLim SWvt
- 'Goldstrike' (v)	EBee LRHS LSRN MAsh NEgg SMad
- 'Hillieri' (f)	EQua
- f. ***longifolia*** ♀H4	CMac NHol NLar SAPC SArc SDix WCru
- - 'Lance Leaf' (m)	EPla EQua
- - 'Salicifolia' (f)	CHEx LAst MRav NLar WCru WDin WFar WPGP
- 'Maculata' hort.	see *A. japonica* 'Variegata'
- 'Marmorata'	LRHS
- 'Mr Goldstrike' (m/v)	EPfP SBfd SLim
- 'Nana Rotundifolia' (f)	EPla
- Pepper Pot = 'Shilpot' (m/v)	CHEx EPfP LRHS MAsh SLon SPoG SSta
- 'Picturata' (m/v)	CBow CDul CHEx CMac CSBt EBee ELan GKir LRHS MAsh MGan MGos MRav NHol NLar SLim SPer SPoG WFar
- 'Rozannie' (f/m) ♀H4	Widely available
- 'Sulphurea Marginata' (f/v)	CBcs CBow CMac CTri EBee ECrN ESwi LRHS NLar SPer
§ - 'Variegata' (f/v)	Widely available
- Windsor form (f)	EQua MBri
omeiensis	WPGP
- BWJ 8048	WCru

Aurinia (*Brassicaceae*)

§ ***saxatilis*** ♀H4	ECho EPfP LAst MMuc SPlb WFar WNew
- 'Argentea'	ECho
- 'Citrina' ♀H4	ECha ECho ECtt MWat SRms
- 'Compacta'	CTri ECho ECtt GJos LRHS
- 'Dudley Nevill'	ECho
- 'Dudley Nevill Variegated' (v)	ECha ECho ECtt ELon EWes GMaP LIMB MHer NBir WFar
- 'Flore Pleno' (d)	ECho
- Gold Ball	see *A. saxatilis* 'Goldkugel'
- 'Gold Dust'	ECho ECtt SRms
- 'Golden Queen'	ECtt MHer
§ - 'Goldkugel'	ECho EPfP GKir IFoB SPoG WFar
- 'Silver Queen'	WEas
- 'Variegata' (v)	NPri SPoG

Austrocedrus (*Cupressaceae*)

§ ***chilensis***	CBcs CKen CTho GBin SBig
- 'Thornhayes Ghost'	CTho

Austromyrtus (*Myrtaceae*)

§ ***dulcis***	ECou

Avena (*Poaceae*)

candida	see *Helictotrichon sempervirens*
sativa 'French Black'	CSpe

Avenula see *Helictotrichon*

avocado see *Persea americana*

Azalea see *Rhododendron*

Azara ✿ (*Flacourtiaceae*)

sp.	NEgg
celastrina **new**	IArd
dentata	CBcs CHll CMac EBee GGal GKir LAst WDin WFar
- 'Variegata'	see *A. integrifolia* 'Variegata'
* ***integerrima***	GQui
integrifolia	CBcs CCCN
- 'Uarie'	CCCN
§ - 'Variegata' (v)	CWib EBee IRar LRHS NEgg SDnm
lanceolata	CDul CMCN CPLG CTri EBee GGal IDee LEdu NSti SPer WFar
microphylla ♀H3	CBcs CChe CDoy CDul CLnd CMCN CMac CPLG CTri EBee EPfP GGal GKir IVic LAst LBMP LRHS MAsh NSti SAPC SArc SDnm SLim SPer SPlb SSpi WFar WPGP WSHC WSpi
- 'Gold Edge' (v)	WFar
- 'Variegata' (v)	CBcs CDoC CMac CPLG CPMA CWGN CWib EBee EBtc EHoe EPfP GQui LAst LBMP LRHS MAsh MRav MSCN NHol NLar NSti SDnm SLon SPoG SSpi SSta WFar WPat WSHC
* ***paraguayensis***	CDoC GGar SDnm SPlb WFar
petiolaris	EPfP
serrata ♀H3	CBcs CDul CEnd CMCN CSBt CWib CWit EBee EPfP GBin GGar GKir LRHS MSCN NCGa NMun SDix SGar SPer SPoG SRms WBor WDin WFar WHar WSHC WSpi
uruguayensis	CCCN CPLG EBee EBtc GBin

Azorella (*Apiaceae*)

filamentosa	ECou
glebaria misapplied	see *A. trifurcata*
glebaria A. Gray	see *Bolax gummifer*
gummifer	see *Bolax gummifer*
lycopodioides	GEdr WAbe
* ***speciosa***	EPot
§ ***trifurcata***	CPar CSpe CTri ECho ECtt GAbr GEdr GKir MMuc NLAp NWCA SAga SPlb WPer
- 'Nana'	ECho GGar MWat WPat WThu

Azorina (*Campanulaceae*)

§ ***vidalii***	CBot CSpe EShb IDee SGar

B

Babiana (*Iridaceae*)

sp.	SAga
ambigua	CStu
angustifolia	CDes CGrW CPLG ECho GGar
'Blue Gem'	ECho
disticha	see *B. fragrans*
ecklonii	WCot
§ ***fragrans***	CGrW
- 'Porterville' **new**	ECho
- 'Rawsonville' **new**	ECho
framesii	CStu

- var. ***kamiesbergensis***	CPLG
nana	CGrW CPBP
odorata	CGrW
plicata	see *B. fragrans*
pygmaea	WCot
ringens	CGrW CPLG
rubrocyanea	CGrW
sinuata	CGrW
stricta ♀H1-2	CCCN CPLG ECho
- var. ***erectifolia***	WPrP
- 'Purple Star'	CPLG ECho EPot
- 'Tubergen's Blue'	ECho
- white-flowered	CGrW
tubulosa	CGrW
vanzyliae	WCot
villosa	ECho WCot
- 'Tulbagh' **new**	ECho
'Zwanenburg's Glory'	ECho SAga

Baccharis (*Asteraceae*)

glomeruliflora	MBri
halimifolia	CBcs CTrC GLin GQui IFFs LRHS SEND
magellanica	EBee
patagonica	EBee GGar LRHS MMuc SAPC SArc SEND WPat
salicifolia	WCot
sphaerocephala **new**	IDee

Backhousia (*Myrtaceae*)

citriodora **new**	CArn

Bacopa (*Scrophulariaceae*)

'Snowflake'	see *Sutera cordata* 'Snowflake'

Baeckea (*Myrtaceae*)

densifolia	ECou
gunniana	CPLG
linifolia	SPlb
virgata	CBcs CTrC ECou SPlb

Baeometra (*Colchicaceae*)

uniflora 'Malmesbury' **new**	ECho

Baillonia (*Verbenaceae*)

juncea	WSHC

Balbisia (*Geraniaceae*)

peduncularis	CCCN

Baldellia (*Alismataceae*)

ranunculoides	CRow WMAq
- f. ***repens***	LLWG

Ballota ✿ (*Lamiaceae*)

acetabulosa ♀H3-4	ECha EWes WCot
'All Hallow's Green'	see *Marrubium bourgaei* var. *bourgaei* 'All Hallow's Green'
nigra	CArn EBWF GPoy MHer MNHC NMir WMoo
§ - 'Archer's Variegated' (v)	CBow MAvo
- 'Variegata'	see *B. nigra* 'Archer's Variegated'
pseudodictamnus ♀H3-4	Widely available
- from Crete	ECha SEND
rupestris 'Frogswell Carolyn' (v)	IFro

Balsamita see *Tanacetum*

Balsamorhiza (*Asteraceae*)

deltoidea	GEdr
sagittata	ECho

Bambusa (*Poaceae*)

glaucescens	see *B. multiplex*
gracilis	see *Drepanostachyum falcatum*
§ ***multiplex***	XBlo
- 'Alphonso-Karrii'	CEnt CGHE EBee EPla SBig
- 'Elegans'	see *B. multiplex* 'Floribunda'
- 'Fernleaf'	see *B. multiplex* 'Floribunda'
§ - 'Floribunda'	CHEx EShb XBlo
- 'Golden Goddess'	XBlo
- 'Silverstripe'	see *B. multiplex* 'Variegata'
§ - 'Variegata' (v)	XBlo
- 'Wang Tsai'	see *B. multiplex* 'Floribunda'
pubescens	see *Dendrocalamus strictus*
textilis	WJun
ventricosa	SBig XBlo
vulgaris	XBlo
- 'Vittata'	XBlo

banana see *Ensete, Musa*

Banksia (*Proteaceae*)

aemula	SOWG
burdettii	SOWG
canei	SPlb
coccinea	SOWG
ericifolia var. ***ericifolia***	CCCN CTrC SOWG
- var. ***macrantha***	SPlb
grandis	CBcs CCCN LTen SOWG
integrifolia	CBcs CCCN CTrC EAmu SOWG SPlb WCot
marginata	CTrC CTsd EBee ECou SOWG SPlb
- mauve-flowered	SOWG
media	SPlb
oblongifolia	SPlb WCot
occidentalis	SOWG
paludosa	CTrC SPlb
robur	CBcs CCCN SPlb
serrata	LEdu SOWG SPlb
serratifolia	CPla
speciosa	SPlb
spinulosa	CTrC
- var. ***collina***	CTrC SOWG SPlb
- pink-flowered	SOWG
- var. ***spinulosa***	CBcs CCCN
violacea	SPlb

Baptisia (*Papilionaceae*)

§ ***alba***	EBee NLar WCot
§ - var. ***macrophylla***	CMdw EWes LPla LRHS NBir NLar SDix WCot
australis ♀H4	Widely available
- 'Caspian Blue'	CWCL EWll LEdu MWat WFar WSHC
- 'Exaltata'	ELan LHop
- var. ***minor***	EBee NLar SPhx WPGP
- 'Nelson's Navy'	LRHS MMHG
bracteata var. ***leucophaea***	EBee EBrs LRHS LSou WCot WFar
'Carolina Moonlight'	EPPr
lactea	see *B. alba* var. *macrophylla*
leucantha	see *B. alba* var. *macrophylla*
megacarpa	SKHP
pendula	see *B. alba*
'Purple Smoke'	CSpe EBee EWll MMuc MNrw NBre SMHy SPhx WCot WCra
tinctoria	CArn

Barbarea (*Brassicaceae*)

praecox	see *B. verna*
rupicola 'Sunnyola'	EDAr

§ ***verna***	GPoy MHer NGHP SVic
vulgaris 'Variegata' (v)	CArn CMoH EBee LBMP NBro NCob WCom WMoo
- 'Variegated Winter Cream' (v)	CSpr WFar

Barleria (*Acanthaceae*)

lupulina	EShb
micans	CCCN
suberecta	see *Dicliptera sericea*

Barosma see *Agathosma*

Bartlettina (*Asteraceae*)

§ ***sordida***	CCCN EBee EUJe IRar SPoG

Basella (*Basellaceae*)

rubra	SVic

Bashania (*Poaceae*)

faberi Og 94053	EPla
§ ***fargesii***	CDoC ENBC EPla MRav MWht SEND WJun
I ***qingchengshanensis***	CGHE EBee EPla MWht WJun WPGP

basil see *Ocimum basilicum*

Basutica (*Thymelaeaceae*)

aff. ***aberrans***	WAbe

Bauera (*Cunoniaceae*)

rubioides new	WAbe
- var. ***alba***	ECou
- pink-flowered	ECou

Bauhinia (*Caesalpiniaceae*)

corymbosa	SOWG
galpinii	EShb SOWG SPlb WSHC
* ***lutea***	CCCN
monandra	SOWG
natalensis	EShb SPlb
purpurea L.	CCCN
tomentosa	CCCN EShb
'White Lady'	CCCN
yunnanensis	EDif SOWG

Baumea see *Machaerina*

bay see *Laurus nobilis*

Beaucarnea (*Dracaenaceae*)

recurvata ♀H1	CTrC EShb LPal MBri WFar
stricta	SPlb

Beaufortia (*Myrtaceae*)

sparsa	SOWG
squarrosa	SPlb

Beaumontia (*Apocynaceae*)

grandiflora	EShb SOWG

Beauverdia see *Leucocoryne*

Bedfordia (*Asteraceae*)

linearis	GGar

Beesia (*Ranunculaceae*)

calthifolia	CFir CLAP CPLG EBee EHrv EWld IMou LLHF WCon WCru WPGP
- DJHC 98447	CDes
deltophylla	WCot

Begonia ✿ (*Begoniaceae*)

B&SWJ 6881 from Taiwan	WCru
B&SWJ 10279 from Mexico	WCru
B&SWJ 10442 from Guatemala	WCru
B&SWJ 10479 from Costa Rica	WCru
BWJ 7840 from China	WCru
Chen Yi 5	WCot
Chen Yi 7	WCot
DJHC 580	WCot
from Argentina new	CSpe
- hardy new	SKHP
from China	NShi
from Ruwenzori, Uganda	NShi
from Sikkim, India	WCot
from Vietnam	ERhR NShi
'Abel Carrière' (R)	ERhR NShi WDib
acetosa	NShi
acida	ERhR NShi
aconitifolia (C)	ERhR EShb NShi
acutifolia Jacq.	ERhR
'Aladdin'	ERhR NShi
'Alamo III'	ERhR NShi
albopicta (C)	EBak ERhR
- 'Rosea' (C)	EShb WDib
'Albuquerque Midnight Sky' (R)	NShi
alice-clarkiae	ERhR
'Alleryi'	ERhR
alnifolia	ERhR
'Alto Scharff' ♀H1	ERhR NShi
'Alzasco' (C)	ERhR
'Amigo Pink' (C)	ERhR
ampla	NShi
'Andre' (R)	NShi
'Anita Roseanna' (C)	ERhR
'Ann Anderson' (C)	ERhR
'Anna Christine' (C)	ERhR
§ ***annulata***	ERhR NShi
'Aquarius'	ERhR NShi
'Arabian Sunset' (C)	ERhR
arborescens var. ***arborescens***	ERhR
'Argentea' (R)	EBak MBri NShi
'Argenteo-guttata'	ERhR EShb
'Aries'	ERhR NShi
'Arthur Mallet' (Mallet Series) (C)	ERhR
'Aruba'	ERhR
'Atlanta Jazz' (R)	NShi
'Autumn Glow' (T)	ERhR NShi
'Avalanche' (T)	ERhR
'Axel Lange' (R)	NShi
'Aya' (C)	WDib
'Baby Perfection'	NShi
'Bahamas'	ERhR
'Bantam Delight'	ERhR NShi
'Barbara Ann' (C)	ERhR
'Barbara Hamilton' (C)	ERhR
'Barbara Parker' (C)	ERhR
'Barclay Griffiths'	ERhR NShi
'Baronessa'	NShi
'Beatrice Haddrell'	ERhR NShi WDib
'Benitochiba' (R)	ERhR LOck LSou NShi WCot WDib
'Bess'	ERhR
'Bessie Buxton'	ERhR
'Bethlehem Star'	ERhR NShi WDib
§ 'Bettina Rothschild' (R)	ERhR NShi WDib
'Beverly Jean'	ERhR NShi

	'Big Mac'	ERhR NShi
	'Bill's Beauty'	ERhR NShi
	'Black Jack' (C)	ERhR
	'Black Knight' (R)	NShi
	'Black Raspberry'	ERhR
	'Black Velvet'	NShi
	'Blackberry Swirl' (R)	WDib
	'Blanc de Neige'	ERhR
	'Blue Sky Appleblossom' **new**	LAst
	'Blue Vein'	ERhR
	'Bokit'	ERhR WDib
	'Bokit' × ***imperialis***	NShi WDib
	boliviensis (T)	CAbb CDes CDoC CSpe GCal WCot WCru
	- 'Firecracker' **new**	WDib
	Bonfire = 'Nzcone'	LBuc
	'Boomer' (C)	ERhR NShi
	bowerae	ERhR NShi
§	- var. ***nigramarga***	ERhR NShi
	'Boy Friend'	ERhR NShi
	bracteosa	ERhR
	bradei	ERhR
	brevirimosa	ERhR
	- subsp. ***exotica***	ERhR
	'Bronze King' (R)	NShi
	'Brown Lace'	NShi
	'Brown Twist'	NShi WDib
	'Bunchii'	ERhR NShi
	'Burgundy Velvet'	ERhR NShi WDib
	'Burle Marx' ♀^{H1}	ERhR EShb NShi SDix WDib
	'Calico Kew'	ERhR
	'Calla Queen' (S)	ERhR
	'Can-can'	see *B.* 'Herzog von Sagan'
	'Candy Floss'	NShi WCru
	'Captain Nemo' (R)	ERhR NShi
	cardiocarpa	ERhR NShi
	'Carol Mac'	ERhR NShi
	'Carolina Moon' (R) ♀^{H1}	ERhR NShi
	carolineifolia	NShi WDib
	carrieae	ERhR
	× ***carrierei***	see *B.* Semperflorens Cultorum Group
	'Casey Corwin' (R)	WDib
	'Cathedral'	ERhR NShi WDib
	'Champagne'	SPer
	'Chantilly Lace'	ERhR NShi
*	***chapaensis***	NShi
	- HWJ 642	WCru
	'Charles Chevalier'	ERhR
	'Charles Jaros'	ERhR
	'Charm' (S)	ERhR
	'Cherry Sundae' (S)	ERhR
	'Chesson'	ERhR NShi
	'China Curl' (R) ♀^{H1}	ERhR NShi
	'China Doll'	NShi
	chitoensis B&SWJ 1954	WCru
	chloroneura	ERhR WDib
	'Chocolate Box'	ERhR
	'Chocolate Chip'	ERhR NShi
	'Christmas Candy'	ERhR
	'Chumash'	ERhR NShi
	'Cistine'	ERhR NShi
	'Clara' (R)	MBri NShi
	'Cleopatra' ♀^{H1}	ERhR NShi WDib
	'Clifton'	ERhR NShi
	coccinea (C)	ERhR WDib
	'Coconut Ice'	EShb
	conchifolia f. ***rubrimacula***	ERhR NShi
	'Concord'	ERhR NShi
	'Connee Boswell'	ERhR NShi WDib
	convolvulacea	ERhR NShi
	cooperi	ERhR
	'Cora Anne'	ERhR
	'Cora Miller' (R)	ERhR NShi
§	***corallina*** (C)	EBak
	- 'Lucerna Amazon' (C)	ERhR
	'Corbeille de Feu'	ERhR
	'Cowardly Lion' (R)	ERhR NShi
	'Cracklin' Rosie' (C)	ERhR
	crassicaulis	ERhR
	'Crestabruchii'	ERhR NShi
	'Crystal Brook'	ERhR
§	***cubensis***	ERhR NShi
	cucullata (S)	ERhR NShi
	'Curly Fireflush' (R)	ERhR MSCN NShi WDib
	'Dales' Delight' (C)	ERhR
	'Dancin' Fred'	ERhR
	'Dancing Girl'	ERhR
	'Dannebo'	MBri
	'Dark Mambo'	NShi
	'D'Artagnon'	ERhR NShi
	'David Blais' (R) ♀^{H1}	NShi WDib
	'Dawnal Meyer' (C)	ERhR WDib
I	'de Elegans'	ERhR NShi WDib
	'Decker's Select'	ERhR NShi
	'Deco Diamond Dust'	ERhR
	decora	ERhR
	deliciosa	ERhR NShi
	'Delray Silver'	NShi
	(Devil Series) 'Devil Red' (S)	LAst
	- 'Devil Rose' (S)	LAst
	- 'Devil White' (S)	LAst
	Devotion (Million Kisses Series) **new**	SVil
	'Dewdrop' (R) ♀^{H1}	ERhR NShi WDib
	diadema	ERhR NShi
	'Di-anna' (C)	ERhR
	'Dibleys Pink Showers'^{PBR} **new**	WDib
	dichotoma	ERhR NShi
	dichroa (C)	ERhR
	'Dielytra'	ERhR
	'Di-erna' (C)	ERhR
	dietrichiana	ERhR NShi
	'Digswelliana'	ERhR NShi
	dipetala	ERhR
	discolor	see *B. grandis* subsp. *evansiana*
	domingensis misapplied	see *B. obliqua* L.
	domingensis ambig.	ERhR
	'Don Miller' (C)	ERhR WDib
	'Doublet Pink'	ERhR SVil
	'Doublet Red'	ERhR SVil
	'Doublet White'	ERhR SVil
	'Doublonia Rose'	SVil
	'Douglas Nisbet' (C)	ERhR
§	***dregei*** (T) ♀^{H1}	ERhR GCal NShi
	- 'Bonsai' (T)	STre
	- var. ***dregei*** (T)	ERhR
	- 'Glasgow' (T)	ERhR NShi
	- var. ***macbethii*** (T)	NShi
	'Druryi'	ERhR
	'Dwarf Houghtonii'	ERhR
	'Earl of Pearl'	ERhR NShi
	'Ebony' (C)	ERhR
	echinosepala	ERhR NShi
	echinosepala × ***sanguinea***	NShi
	edmundoi (C)	ERhR
	egregia	ERhR
	'Elaine'	ERhR
	'Elaine Ayres' (C)	ERhR
§	'Elaine Wilkerson'	ERhR NShi

'Elaine's Baby'	see *B.* 'Elaine Wilkerson'
'Elda'	ERhR NShi
'Elda Haring' (R)	ERhR NShi
Elegance (Million Kisses Series) **new**	LAst SVil
'Elizabeth Hayden'	ERhR NShi
'Elsie M. Frey'	ERhR NShi
emeiensis	CSpe SKHP
'Emerald Beauty' (R) ♀H1	ERhR NShi
'Emerald Giant' (R)	ERhR NShi WDib
'Emerald Isle'	NShi
'Emerald Princess'	NShi
'Emma Watson'	ERhR NShi
'Enchantment'	ERhR
'Enech'	ERhR NShi
'English Knight'	ERhR NShi
'English Lace'	ERhR NShi
epipsila	ERhR
'Erythrophylla'	EShb NShi
'Erythrophylla Bunchii'	ERhR NShi
§ 'Erythrophylla Helix'	ERhR NShi
'Escargot' (R) ♀H1	NShi WDib
'Essie Hunt'	ERhR
'Esther Albertine' (C) ♀H1	ERhR
'Etna' (R)	NShi
'Evening Star'	ERhR
'Fairy'	ERhR NShi
feastii 'Helix'	see *B.* 'Erythrophylla Helix'
fernando-costae	ERhR
§ 'Feuerkönigin' (S)	ERhR
'Fever' (R)	NShi
'Fiji Islands'	WJun
'Filigree' (R)	ERhR
'Fire Flush'	see *B.* 'Bettina Rothschild'
'Fireworks' (R) ♀H1	ERhR NShi WDib
'Five and Dime'	ERhR NShi
'Flamboyant' (T)	ERhR LSou MBri SVil WGor
Flaming Queen	see *B.* 'Feuerkönigin'
'Flamingo' (C)	ERhR
'Flamingo Queen' (C)	ERhR
'Flo 'Belle Moseley' (C)	ERhR WDib
'Florence Carrell'	ERhR
'Florence Rita' (C)	ERhR
'Flutterbye Salmon' **new**	LAst LSou
'Flying High'	ERhR
foliosa	ERhR NShi
- var. ***amplifolia***	see *B. holtonis* var. *holtonis*
§ - var. ***miniata*** ♀H1	CDoC CTsd EBak ERhR EShb LPio MArl NShi SDix WDib
- - pink-flowered	CCCN CDTJ GGar LAst NShi
- - red-flowered	CCCN CDTJ
- - 'Rosea'	CDoC NShi
formosana	NShi
- B&SWJ 7041	WCru
'Frances Lyons' (C)	ERhR
'Freckles' (R)	ERhR
'Fred Bedson'	ERhR NShi
'Fred Martin'	NShi
friburgensis	ERhR
'Friendship'	ERhR NShi
'Frosty Fairyland'	ERhR
'Frosty Knight'	ERhR NShi
'Fuchsifoliosa'	ERhR NShi
fuchsioides	see *B. foliosa* var. *miniata*
fusca	ERhR
'Fuscomaculata'	ERhR NShi
'Gaystar'	NShi
gehrtii	ERhR NShi
geranioides (T)	ERhR
glabra	ERhR
glandulosa misapplied	see *B. multinervia*
glandulosa ambig.	ERhR
glaucophylla	see *B. radicans* Vell.
'Gloire de Sceaux'	ERhR
goegoensis	ERhR
'Good 'n' Plenty'	ERhR
'Granada'	ERhR
grandis	NShi
§ - subsp. ***evansiana*** ♀H3-4	CHEx CSam CSpe CStu EBee ERhR EShb ETod EUJe GCal LEdu LPio LPla MTho NMRc NShi SBch SDix SGSe SKHP SMad SPlb SUsu WCot WCru WFar WMoo
- - var. ***alba*** hort.	CAby ERhR EShb ESwi EWld EWll GCal LOck LPla MTho SGSe SKHP SMad SSpi SUsu WCot WPGP
- - 'Claret Jug'	EBee ELon EShb ESwi LPio NShi WCot WGrn WPGP WWEG
- - hybrid	NShi
- - 'Pink Parasol'	EBee ESwi NShi WCru
- - 'Simsii'	WFar
- 'Maria'	EBee
- 'Sapporo'	EBee EPPr GCal LPio NShi WCru
§ - subsp. ***sinensis***	EBee NShi WCot
- - BWJ 8011	WCru
aff. ***grandis*** subsp. ***sinensis***	NShi SKHP
- - BWJ 8133	WCru
* 'Great Beverly'	ERhR NShi
'Green Acres'	ERhR
'Green Gold' (R)	NShi WDib
'Green Lace'	ERhR NShi
'Grey Feather'	ERhR
griffithii	see *B. annulata*
'Gustav Lind' (S)	ERhR
'Gypsy Maiden' (T)	NShi
haageana hort. ex W. Watson	see *B. scharffii*
handelii	ERhR
* 'Happy Heart'	ERhR
'Harbison Canyon'	NShi
* 'Harry's Beard'	ERhR NShi
'Hastor'	ERhR NShi
hatacoa	ERhR NShi
- silver-leaved	ERhR EShb NShi WDib
- spotted-leaved	ERhR NShi
'Hazel's Front Porch' (C)	ERhR
'Helen Lewis' ♀H1	ERhR NShi
'Helen Teupel' (R)	ERhR WDib
'Helene Jaros'	ERhR NShi
hemsleyana	NShi
'Her Majesty' (R)	ERhR
§ ***heracleifolia***	ERhR NShi
- var. ***longipila***	see *B. heracleifolia*
- var. ***nigricans***	see *B. heracleifolia*
§ 'Herzog von Sagan' (R)	ERhR NShi
'Hilo Holiday' (R) ♀H1	NShi WDib
hispida var. ***cucullifera***	ERhR NShi
'Holmes Chapel'	ERhR NShi
§ ***holtonis*** var. ***holtonis***	ERhR
homonyma	see *B. dregei*
'Honeysuckle' (C)	ERhR
'Hot Tamale'	ERhR
'Houston Fiesta' (R)	NShi
hydrocotylifolia	ERhR NShi
hypolipara	see *B. sericoneura*
(Illumination Series) 'Illumination Apricot'	SCoo WGor
- 'Illumination Orange' ♀H2-3 **new**	WGor
- 'Illumination Rose'	SCoo WGor
- 'Illumination Salmon Pink' ♀H2-3	SCoo

	- 'Illumination Scarlet' **new**	WGor
	- 'Illumination White'	SCoo
	imperialis	ERhR NShi
	incarnata	ERhR NShi
	- 'Metallica'	see *B. metallica*
	'Ingramii'	ERhR
	'Interlaken' (C)	ERhR
	'Ironstone' (R) ♀H1	NShi
	'Ivy Ever'	ERhR
	'Jade'	NShi
	'Jelly Roll Morton'	ERhR
	'Joe Hayden'	ERhR
	'John Tonkin' (C)	ERhR
	johnstonii	ERhR
	'Jolly Silver'	NShi
	'Jubilee Mine'	ERhR
	juliana	ERhR
	'Jumbo Jeans'	ERhR NShi
	'Jumbo Jet' (C)	ERhR
	'Kagaribi' (C)	ERhR
	kellermanii	ERhR NShi
	keniensis	GCal
	'Kentwood' (C)	ERhR
	kenworthyae	ERhR
	kingiana	NShi
	'Kit Jeans'	ERhR NShi
	'Kit Jeans Mounger'	ERhR NShi
	'Knutsford'	NShi
	'Kyoto'	NShi
	'La Paloma' (C)	WDib
	'Lacewing'	ERhR
	'Lady Clare'	ERhR
*	'Lady France'	ERhR MBri
	'Langeana'	NShi
	'Laurie's Love' (C)	ERhR
	'Lawrence H. Fewkes'	ERhR
	'Lazy River' (R)	NShi
	leathermaniae (C)	ERhR
	'Legia'	ERhR
	'Lenore Olivier' (C)	ERhR
	'Leopard'	ERhR MBri NShi
	'Lexington'	ERhR
	'Libor' (C)	ERhR
	'Lillian' (R)	NShi
	'Lime Swirl'	ERhR NShi WDib
	'Limeade'	WDib
	limmingheana	see *B. radicans* Vell.
	'Linda Dawn' (C)	ERhR
	'Linda Harley'	ERhR
	'Linda Myatt'	ERhR
	lindeniana	ERhR NShi
	listada ♀H1	ERhR MBri NShi WDib
	'Lithuania'	ERhR
	'Little Brother Montgomery' ♀H1	ERhR EShb GGar NShi SDix WDib
	'Little Darling'	ERhR NShi
	'Little Iodine'	NShi
	'Lois Burks' (C)	ERhR WDib
	'Loma Alta'	ERhR
	'Looking Glass' (C)	ERhR MNrw WDib
	'Lospe-tu'	ERhR NShi
	'Lubbergei' (C)	ERhR
	'Lucerna' (C)	EBak ERhR
	'Lucky Colours' (R)	NShi
	'Lucy Closson' (R)	NShi
	'Lulu Bower' (C)	ERhR NShi
	luxurians ♀H1	CHII CSpe ERhR NShi WCot
	- 'Ziesenhenne'	ERhR
	lyman-smithii	ERhR
	'Mabel Corwin'	ERhR NShi
	'Mac MacIntyre'	NShi
	macduffieana	see *B. corallina*
	'Mac's Gold'	ERhR NShi
	maculata (C) ♀H1	ERhR
	- 'Wightii' (C)	CSpe ERhR WDib
	'Mad Hatter'	ERhR NShi
	'Madame Butterfly' (C)	ERhR
	'Magic Carpet'	ERhR NShi
	'Magic Lace'	ERhR NShi
	'Magma' (R)	NShi
	'Manacris'	ERhR NShi
	manicata	ERhR NShi
	'Maphil'	MBri NShi
	'Mardi Gras' (R)	NShi
	'Margaritae'	ERhR NShi
*	'Marginata Crispa White'	SPer
	'Marmaduke' ♀H1	CTsd NShi WDib
	'Martha Floro' (C)	ERhR
	'Martin Johnson' (R) ♀H1	ERhR NShi WDib
	'Martin's Mystery'	ERhR
	masoniana ♀H1	CTsd ERea ERhR NShi WDib WSFF
	- light-leaved	NShi
	- var. ***maculata***	NShi
	'Maui Mist' (R)	NShi
	'Maurice Amey'	ERhR
	'Maverick'	ERhR
	mazae	ERhR NShi
	'Medora' (C)	ERhR
	'Melissa' (T)	NShi
	'Merry Christmas' (R) ♀H1	ERhR NShi WDib
	metachroa	ERhR NShi
	'Metallic Mist' **new**	EUJe
§	***metallica*** ♀H1	ERhR EShb NShi
	'Meteor' (R)	NShi
	meyeri-johannis	CFir
	'Miami Storm' (R)	NShi
	'Michaele'	ERhR
	'Midnight Magic' (R) ♀H1	NShi
	'Midnight Sun'	ERhR NShi
	'Midnight Twister'	ERhR NShi
	'Mikado' (R) ♀H1	ERhR NShi
	minor	ERhR
	'Mirage' ♀H1	ERhR NShi
	mollicaulis	ERhR
	'Moon Maid'	ERhR
	'Mr Kartuz' (T)	NShi
	'Mrs Hashimoto' (C)	ERhR NShi
	'Mrs Hatcher' (R)	ERhR NShi
§	***multinervia***	ERhR
	'Munchkin' ♀H1	ERhR NShi WDib
	'My Best Friend'	NShi
*	'Mystic'	ERhR
	'Mystique'	ERhR
	'Namur' (R) ♀H1	NShi WDib
	'Nancy Cummings'	ERhR
	natalensis	see *B. dregei*
	'Nelly Bly'	ERhR
	nelumbiifolia	ERhR NShi
	'Niagra Scarlet Picotee' **new**	LAst
	nigramarga	see *B. bowerae* var. *nigramarga*
	nigritarum	ERhR NShi
	nitida alba	see *B. obliqua* L.
	'Nokomis' (C)	ERhR
	'Norah Bedson'	ERhR NShi
	'Northern Lights' (S)	ERhR
§	***obliqua*** L.	ERhR
	obscura	ERhR NShi
	'Obsession' (C)	ERhR
	odorata	see *B. obliqua* L.
	'Odorata Alba'	ERhR
	olbia	ERhR
	'Old Gold' (T)	ERhR
	'Oliver Twist'	ERhR

	'Orange Dainty'	ERhR
	'Orange Pinafore (C)'	ERhR
	'Orange Rubra' (C) ♀H1	ERhR
	'Orient' (R)	ERhR NShi
	'Orococo'	NShi
	'Orpha C. Fox' (C)	ERhR
	'Orrell' (C)	ERhR
	'Othello'	ERhR NShi
	'Pachea' (R)	NShi
	paleata	ERhR NShi
	palmata	CDes CHEx EBee EBla EShb GCal NShi SKHP WCot WPGP
	- from China	EBla NShi
	- from Sikkim	WCot
	- B&SWJ 2692 from Sikkim	WCru
	- var. ***palmata***	NShi
	'Palomar Prince'	ERhR NShi
	'Panasoffkee'	ERhR
	'Panther'	ERhR NShi
	'Papillon' (T)	ERhR
	paranaënsis	ERhR
	parilis	ERhR
	partita	see *B. dregei*
	'Passing Storm'	ERhR NShi
§	Passion (Million Kisses Series)	LAst LBuc LSou WBor
	'Patricia Ogdon'	ERhR NShi
	'Paul Bee'	ERhR NShi
	'Paul Harley'	ERhR NShi
	'Paul Henry'	NShi
	paulensis	ERhR
	'Peace' (R)	NShi
	'Peach Parfait' (C)	ERhR
	pearcei (T)	ERhR
	'Peardrop' new	SVil
	'Pearl Ripple'	ERhR NShi
	'Pearls' (C)	ERhR
	pedatifida	EBee SKHP
	- DJHC 98473	WCru
	'Peggy Stevens' (C)	ERhR
	peltata	ERhR NShi
*	'Penelope Jane'	ERhR
	'Persian Brocade'	ERhR NShi
	'Petite Marie' (C)	ERhR
	'Phil Corwin' (R)	NShi
	'Piccolo'	ERhR NShi
	'Pickobeth' (C)	ERhR
	'Picotee' (T)	CSut
	'Pinafore' (C) ♀H1	ERhR
	'Pink Champagne' (R) ♀H1	NShi WDib
	'Pink Frosted' (R)	NShi
I	'Pink Lady'	WCru
	'Pink Nacre'	ERhR
	'Pink Parade' (C)	ERhR
	'Pink Spot Lucerne' (C)	ERhR
	'Pink Taffeta'	ERhR
	'Pinkpop'	NShi
	plagioneura	see *B. cubensis*
	'Plum Rose'	ERhR NShi
	plumieri	ERhR
	'Pollux' new	WDib
	polyantha	ERhR
	polygonoides	ERhR
	popenoei	ERhR
	'Potpourri'	ERhR
	'Président Carnot' (C)	ERhR
	'Pretty Rose'	ERhR
	'Preussen'	ERhR
	'Princess of Hanover' (R) ♀H1	ERhR NShi WDib
	'Princessa Rio de Plata'	ERhR NShi
	prismatocarpa	ERhR
	procumbens	see *B. radicans* Vell.
	'Purple Snow' (R)	NShi
	pustulata 'Argentea'	ERhR
	putii B&SWJ 7245	WCru
	'Queen Mother' (R)	ERhR
	'Queen Olympus'	ERhR GGar NShi WDib
	'Quinebaug'	ERhR NShi
§	***radicans*** Vell. ♀H1	ERhR MBri
	'Raquel Wood'	ERhR NShi
	'Raspberry Swirl' (R) ♀H1	ERhR NShi WDib
	ravenii (T)	CHEx EBee GCal NShi SKHP WCot
	'Raymond George Nelson' ♀H1	ERhR NShi
	'Razzmatazz' (R)	NShi WDib
	'Red Berry' (R)	ERhR NShi
	'Red Bull'	NShi
	'Red Dragon' (R)	WDib
	'Red Flame' (R)	NShi
	'Red Kiss' (R)	NShi
	'Red Planet'	ERhR NShi
	'Red Reign'	ERhR NShi
	'Red Robin' (R)	NShi WDib
	'Red Spider'	ERhR NShi
	'Red Undies' (C)	WCru
	'Red Wing' (R)	NShi
	'Regal Minuet' (R)	NShi WDib
	'Reine des Neiges' (R)	NShi
	reniformis	ERhR
	rex (R)	MBri NShi
	'Richard Galle'	LAst
	'Richmondensis' (S)	ERhR EShb NShi
	'Ricinifolia'	ERhR GCal NShi
	'Ricky Minter' ♀H1	ERhR NShi
	'Rip van Winkle'	ERhR NShi
	'Robin' (R)	ERhR NShi
	'Robin's Red' (C)	ERhR NShi
	'Rocheart' (R) ♀H1	NShi WDib
	'Roi de Roses' (R) ♀H1	ERhR NShi
	Romance (Million Kisses Series) new	LAst SVil
	roxburghii	ERhR NShi
	'Royal Lustre'	ERhR NShi
	'Rubacon'	ERhR NShi
	rubro-setulosa	ERhR
	'Sabre Dance' (R)	ERhR
	'Sachsen'	ERhR
	'Sal's Comet' (R) ♀H1	NShi WDib
	'Sal's Moondust'	NShi WDib
	'San Diego Sunset' (R)	NShi
	sanguinea	ERhR NShi
	'Savannah Pink Parfait' (R)	NShi
	'Scarlett O'Hara' (R)	ERhR
§	***scharffii***	EBak ERhR SDix
	'Scherzo'	ERhR NShi WDib
	'Scottish Star'	NShi
	'Sea Captain'	NShi
	'Sea Serpent' ♀H1	NShi
	'Secpuoc'	ERhR
	semperflorens hort.	see *B.* Semperflorens Cultorum Group
§	Semperflorens Cultorum Group (S)	MBri
§	***sericoneura***	ERhR
	'Serlis'	ERhR NShi
	serratipetala	EBak ERhR MBri WDib
	'Shamus'	ERhR NShi
*	***sheperdii***	NShi WDib
	'Shiloh' (R)	ERhR NShi
*	'Shinihart'	ERhR
	'Sierra Mist' (C)	ERhR NShi
	sikkimensis	EBee GCal

'Silbreen'	NShi
silletensis	EBee GCal
subsp. ***mengyangensis***	
'Silver Cloud' (R) 𝕐H1	ERhR NShi WDib
'Silver Dawn' (R)	ERhR
'Silver Dots'	NShi
'Silver Giant' (R)	ERhR NShi
'Silver Jewell'	NShi WDib
'Silver Lace'	NShi WDib
'Silver Mist' (C)	ERhR
'Silver Points'	ERhR
'Silver Queen' (R) 𝕐H1	NShi
'Silver Sweet' (R)	ERhR NShi
'Silver Wings'	ERhR
'Sinbad' (C)	ERhR
sinensis	see *B. grandis* subsp. *sinensis*
* 'Sir Charles'	ERhR
'Sir John Falstaff'	ERhR
sizemoreae	NShi WDib
Skeezar Group	ERhR
- 'Brown Lake'	ERhR NShi
'Snow Storm'	NShi WDib
* 'Snowcap' (C) 𝕐H1	ERhR EShb WDib
socotrana (T)	ERhR
solananthera A. DC. 𝕐H1	ERhR EShb GGar NShi WDib
soli-mutata	NShi WDib
sonderiana (T)	GCal WBor
'Speckled Roundabout' (T)	NShi
'Speculata' (R)	ERhR NShi
'Spellbound'	ERhR NShi
'Spindrift'	ERhR NShi
'Spitfire' PBR	NShi
'Splotches'	ERhR
'Stained Glass'	NShi WDib
'Stichael Maeae'	ERhR
stipulacea ambig.	ERhR
subvillosa	ERhR
'Sugar Plum'	ERhR
'Summer Maid'	NShi
'Sun God'	NShi
(Super Olympia Series) 'Super Olympia Red' (S)	LAst
- 'Super Olympia Rose' (S)	LAst
- 'Super Olympia White' (S)	LAst
(Superba Group) 'Irene Nuss' (C) 𝕐H1	ERhR
- 'Lana' (C)	ERhR
- Sophie Cecile' (C) 𝕐H1	ERhR
sutherlandii (T) 𝕐H1	CAvo CCCN CFFs EABi EBak EOHP ERhR EWld GGar LOck LPio NBir NPer SBch SDix WCot WDib WEas WFar WHer
- 'Papaya' (T)	CSpe
'Swan Song'	ERhR
'Sweet Magic'	ERhR NShi
'Swirly Top' (C)	ERhR
'Sylvan Triumph' (C)	ERhR
taiwaniana	NShi
taliensis	SKHP
- EDHCH 042	WCru
- 'White Boned Demon' **new**	SKHP
'Tapestry'	ERhR NShi
'Tar Baby' (T)	ERhR
'Tea Rose'	ERhR
teuscheri	ERhR
'Texastar'	ERhR NShi WDib
'The Wiz'	ERhR
thelmae	ERhR
'Think Pink'	NShi
'Thrush' (R)	NShi
'Thumotec'	ERhR
'Thunderclap'	ERhR NShi
'Thurstonii' 𝕐H1	ERhR EShb NShi
'Tiger Paws' 𝕐H1	CTsd ERhR MBri NShi
'Tim Anderson' (R)	NShi
'Tingley Mallet' (Mallet Series) (C)	ERhR
'Tiny Bright' (R)	ERhR NShi
'Tiny Gem'	ERhR
'Tom Ment' (C)	ERhR
'Tom Ment II' (C)	ERhR
'Tomoshiba'	ERhR
'Tondelayo'	ERhR NShi
'Tornado' (R)	NShi
'Tribute'	ERhR
'Trinidad'	ERhR NShi
* ***tripartita*** (T)	ERhR NShi WDib
'Tucson Bonfire' (R)	NShi
'Twilight'	ERhR
'Two Face'	ERhR NShi WDib
ulmifolia	ERhR NShi
undulata (C)	ERhR
'Universe'	ERhR NShi
'Valentine' (R)	NShi
'Venetian Red' (R)	ERhR NShi
venosa	ERhR NShi
'Venus'	ERhR NShi
'Verschaffeltii'	ERhR
versicolor	ERhR
'Vesuvius' (R)	NShi WDib
'Viaudii'	ERhR
'Viau-Scharff'	ERhR
'Vista' (R)	NShi
'Wally's World'	NShi
'Wanda'	NShi
'Weltonensis'	ERhR NShi
'Weltoniensis Alba' (T)	ERhR
'Westland Beauty'	NShi
'White Cascade'	ERhR
'Wild Swan'	NShi WCru
williamsii Rusby & Nash	see *B. wollnyi*
'Witchcraft' (R)	ERhR NShi
'Withlacoochee'	ERhR NShi
§ ***wollnyi***	ERhR
'Wood Nymph' (R)	ERhR NShi
'Zuensis'	ERhR

Beilschmiedia (*Lauraceae*)

berteroana	IDee

Belamcanda (*Iridaceae*)

chinensis	CArn CBro CHll EBee ELan EPfP GKev GPoy MAvo MHer SDnm SGar SMrm SPav SPlb SRms WGwG WOut WPer WPtf WSHC
- B&SWJ 8692B	WCru
- 'Crûg Colossal' **new**	WCru
- 'Freckle Face'	EBee EKen LSou MSpe NBPC SGSe SPad WHil
- 'Hello Yellow'	EShb MAvo

Bellevalia (*Hyacinthaceae*)

atroviolacea	ECho
brevipedicellata	ECho
ciliata	ECho
'Cream Pearl'	ECho WCot
desertorum JCA 0.227.690	WCot
dubia	EBee ECho WCot
- subsp. ***hackelii***	ECho
forniculata	ECho
hyacinthoides	CStu ECho WCot
longipes	ECho
* ***maura***	ECho

§	***paradoxa***	CAby CBgR CHid CMea CTca EBee EBrs ECho EHrv ERCP LLHF LRHS MNrw WCot
	- white-flowered	ECho
	pycnantha misapplied	see *B. paradoxa*
	romana	CPom CTca EBee ECho ERCP MTho WCot WHil
	sarmatica	ECho
	sessiliflora	ECho
	tabriziana	ECho WCot
	trifoliata	ECho
	webbiana	ECho

Bellis (*Asteraceae*)

§	***caerulescens***	GAbr NBro
	perennis	CArn EBWF GKir NSco
	- 'Alice'	GAbr WCot
	- 'Changeling'	WAlt
	- 'Dresden China'	ECho EWes GAbr MTho WCom
	- 'Galaxy White' (Galaxy Series)	EPfP
	- Hen and Chickens	see *B. perennis* 'Prolifera' single-flowered
	- 'Hula'	CNat
	- 'Parkinson's Great White'	GAbr
§	- 'Prolifera' single-flowered	WAlt WCom WHer
	- 'Robert'	GAbr
	- 'Rusher Rose'	EPfP
	- 'Single Blue'	see *B. caerulescens*
	- 'The Pearl'	GAbr WCot
	- 'Upper Seagry'	WAlt
	rotundifolia 'Caerulescens'	see *B. caerulescens*
	sylvestris	CArn

Bellium (*Asteraceae*)

*	***crassifolium canescens***	WPer

Beloperone see *Justicia*

	guttata	see *Justicia brandegeeana*

Bensoniella (*Saxifragaceae*)

	oregona	CPLG

Benthamiella (*Solanaceae*)

	nordenskjoldii	WAbe
	patagonica	WAbe
	- F&W 9345	WAbe

Berberidopsis (*Flacourtiaceae*)

	sp.	GGal
	beckleri	SSpi WPGP
	corallina	Widely available

Berberis ✿ (*Berberidaceae*)

	CC 4730	CPLG
	SDR 4219	GKev
	aetnensis	GAuc
	aggregata	EMac GKir NBir SPer SRms
	amurensis var. ***latifolia*** B&SWJ 4353	WCru
	- - B&SWJ 8539	WCru
	angulosa	GCal
	aquifolium	see *Mahonia aquifolium*
	- 'Fascicularis'	see *Mahonia* × *wagneri* 'Pinnacle'
	aristata misapplied	see *B. glaucocarpa*
	asiatica	CPLG GPoy
	'Baby Bear' new	CPMA
	bealei	see *Mahonia japonica* Bealei Group
	'Blenheim'	WFar
	brevipaniculata Schneider	GAuc
	brevipedunculata Bean	see *B. prattii*
	× ***bristolensis***	SRms
N	***buxifolia*** 'Nana' misapplied	see *B. microphylla* 'Pygmaea'
	calliantha	WFar
	candidula C.K. Schneid.	CDul EPfP GKir LRHS MGan MMuc MSwo NHol NLar SLon SPer WDin
	- 'Jytte'	see *B.* 'Jytte'
	× ***carminea*** 'Barbarossa'	WDin
	- 'Buccaneer'	EPfP
	- 'Pirate King'	CSBt LRHS SPoG SWvt WFar WPat
	centiflora new	GKir
	chrysosphaera	WFar
	coxii	GBin GGar
	darwinii 🏆H4	Widely available
I	- 'Compacta'	CChe CDoC CMac EBee EPfP GKir LBuc LHop LRHS LTen MAsh NEgg NLar SBfd SLim SPoG
	dictyophylla 🏆H4	CPMA EBee EPfP GKir LHop LRHS MGos MMuc NLar SEND SKHP SPer SPoG SSpi WDin WKif WPat WSHC WSpi
	dulcis 'Nana'	see *B. microphylla* 'Pygmaea'
	dumicola new	MSnd
	empetrifolia	WSpi
	× ***frikartii*** 'Amstelveen' 🏆H4	CDoC EBee ECrN ELan EPfP GKir LAst LRHS MBNS MRav NHol NLar NPri SBfd SEND WDin WFar
	- 'Telstar'	EBee LAst LBuc MGos MRav NLar SLim WMoo
	gagnepainii misapplied	see *B. gagnepainii* var. *lanceifolia*
	gagnepainii C.K. Schneid.	CMac EBee EMac GKir NHol SLPl
§	- var. ***lanceifolia***	CTri EBee ECrN EPla GKir MGos MMuc NHol NWea SEND SLim WDin WFar
	- - 'Fernspray'	EPfP EPla MRav SRms
	- 'Purpurea'	see *B.* × *interposita* 'Wallich's Purple'
	'Georgei' 🏆H4	CMHG CWib EPfP GQui LRHS SSpi
§	***glaucocarpa***	EPfP EPla NHol
	'Goldilocks'	CPMA EPfP GKir LAst LSRN MBlu SEND SSpi
	goudotii B&SWJ 10769	WCru
	× ***hybridogagnepainii*** 'Chenaultii'	ELan NHol
	- 'Robin Hood'	WPat
	hypokerina	CMac
	insignis	GCal IDee WFar
	- subsp. ***insignis*** var. ***insignis***	WFar WPat
	- - B&SWJ 2432	WCru
§	× ***interposita*** 'Wallich's Purple'	CCVT EBee ECrN EPfP MRav MSwo SPer WDin WMoo
	jamesiana	WPat
	julianae 🏆H4	Widely available
§	'Jytte'	EBee EMil WDin
	kawakamii	SLPl
	koreana	EBee EPfP NLar WFar
	- 'Rubin'	CAgr
	linearifolia 'Orange King'	CBcs CMac CTri EBee ELan EPfP GKir LRHS MAsh MBlu MGos NEgg NLar SCoo SPer SPoG WClo WDin WFar WHar WPat
	'Little Favourite'	see *B. thunbergii* f. *atropurpurea* 'Atropurpurea Nana'
	× ***lologensis***	MGos WDin
	- 'Apricot Queen' 🏆H4	CBcs CMac EBee EPfP GKir LRHS MAsh MGos MHav MRav NLar SCoo SPer SPoG WDin WPat
	- 'Mystery Fire'	EBee GKir MAsh MBri MGos NHol NLar SPoG SWvt WDin WFar WHar WMoo

- 'Stapehill'	CMac CSam ELan EPfP GKir LRHS MAsh NHol SPoG WClo
× ***media*** Park Jewel	see *B.* × *media* 'Parkjuweel'
§ - 'Parkjuweel'	CBcs CMac EBee ECrN IArd MRav NLar SCoo WDin WFar WMoo
- 'Red Jewel' $\mathbb{Y}^{H4}$	CDoC CMac EBee ECrN EPfP EPla LRHS MGos MMuc MRav SCoo SEND SPer SPoG WCFE WDin WFar WMoo
microphylla	CAlb EPfP GKir LEdu WCFE WClo
§ - 'Pygmaea'	CAbP CAlb CBcs CSBt EBee EPfP EWTr GKir LRHS MAsh MGos MRav NHol NLar SLim SPer SPoG WDin WFar
mitifolia	NLar
montana	WCFE WPGP WPat
morrisonensis	GBin
morrisonicola	GAuc
× ***ottawensis*** 'Auricoma'	LTen MMuc SEND SWvt
- f. ***purpurea***	CCVT CMac CWib LRHS MGos WDin WFar WHar
§ - - 'Superba' $\mathbb{Y}^{H4}$	Widely available
§ - 'Silver Miles' (v)	EHoe MRav NLar WFar WPat
panlanensis	GCal
'Cally Rose' **new**	
poiretii	CPLG NLar
polyantha misapplied	see *B. prattii*
§ ***prattii***	GAuc
- var. ***laxipendula***	SMad
'Red Tears'	CPMA CSam EBee MGos MRav NLar SPer WMoo
'Rubrostilla'	EBee
× ***rubrostilla*** 'Cherry Ripe'	CMac
sargentiana	SLPl
sieboldii	LLHF MRav WCFE WPat WSpi
soulieana	EPfP LRHS MGan
stenophylla Hance	see *B. soulienana*
× ***stenophylla*** Lindl. $\mathbb{Y}^{H4}$	CBcs CCVT CDoC CDul CSBt CTri EBee ECrN EPfP GKir LBuc LTen MAsh MBri MRav NWea SBfd SEND SPer SPoG WBVN WDin WFar WHar WMoo
- 'Claret Cascade'	EBee MGos MMuc MRav NHol NLar SEND SPer WFar
- 'Corallina Compacta' $\mathbb{Y}^{H4}$	CMac CMea ECho ELan EPfP EPot GKir LHop LRHS MAsh NRya SPer SPoG SRms WAbe WPat
- 'Crawley Gem'	GBin MGos NHol NLar WFar
- 'Etna'	ELan LRHS MAsh SPoG
- 'Irwinii'	CMac EBee LAst LRHS MGos SPer WFar
- 'Nana'	LRHS SRms
- 'Pink Pearl' (v)	CMHG MGos
taliensis	CPLG
temolaica $\mathbb{Y}^{H4}$	CGHE CPMA CSam EBtc EPfP MDun MGos MRav MSnd NEgg NLar NSti NWea SDnm SMad SPer SSpi SSta WCot WDin WPGP WPat WSpi
thunbergii $\mathbb{Y}^{H4}$	CBar CBcs CDoC CDul CMac EMac EPfP GBin GKir LBuc MRav NLar NWea SCoo SPer SPlb SPoG SWvt WDin WFar
- f. ***atropurpurea***	CBar CBcs CCVT CDul CMac CSBt CTri EBee EMac EPfP EWTr GGar LAst LBuc LTen MAsh MGan MGos MSwo NEgg NLar NWea SCoo SPer WBVN WDin WFar WMoo
- - 'Admiration'[PBR]	CAbP CBcs CDoC CEnd CSBt CWit ELan EPfP LBuc LLHF LRHS LSRN LSqu MAsh MBri MGos MMHG NEgg NLar NPri SBfd SCoo SLim SLon SPer SPoG SWvt WClo WPat
§ - - 'Atropurpurea Nana' $\mathbb{Y}^{H4}$	Widely available
- - 'Bagatelle' $\mathbb{Y}^{H4}$	Widely available
- - 'Carmen'	MGos
- - 'Dart's Purple'	WFar
- - 'Dart's Red Lady'	CPLG CPMA CSBt CWib EBee ECrN EHoe ELan EPfP GGar LRHS LSRN MAsh MRav NLar SCoo SLim SPer SPoG SWvt WDin WFar WPat
- - 'Golden Ring' $\mathbb{Y}^{H4}$	Widely available
- - 'Harlequin' (v)	CBcs CChe CDoC EBee ELan EPfP GKir LRHS LSRN MAsh MBri MGos MRav NEgg SBfd SLim SPer SPoG SWvt WClo WDin WFar WHar WPat
- - 'Helmond Pillar'	Widely available
- - 'Red Chief' $\mathbb{Y}^{H4}$	CBcs CMHG CMac EBee ECrN EHoe ELan EPfP GKir LRHS LSRN MAsh MGos MMuc MRav MSwo NEgg NPri SBfd SLim SLon SPer SPoG SWvt WDin WFar WHar WMoo WPat
- - 'Red King'	MRav WDin
- - 'Red Pillar'	CAlb CChe CDoC CMac CWit EBee EHoe ELan EPfP IVic LAst LRHS MAsh MGos MWat NEgg NHol SLim SWvt WDin WFar WPat WRHF
- - 'Red Rocket'	LBuc MCCP MGos NLar
- - 'Rose Glow' (v) $\mathbb{Y}^{H4}$	Widely available
- - 'Rosy Rocket' (v)	CWit LBuc LRHS MGos SPoG
- 'Atropurpurea Superba'	see *B.* × *ottawensis* f. *purpurea* 'Superba'
- 'Aurea'	Widely available
- Bonanza Gold = 'Bogozam'[PBR]	CBcs CDoC EBee ELan EPfP GKir LBMP LRHS MAsh MRav NLar SLim SPer SPoG WDin WFar WPat
- 'Boum'	EMil MAsh
- 'Carpetbagger'	WHar
- 'Crimson Pygmy'	see *B. thunbergii* f. *atropurpurea* 'Atropurpurea Nana'
- 'Diabolic'	GKir LRHS SPer WClo
- 'Erecta'	CMac EPfP MGos MRav SPer WCFE WDin
- 'Golden Rocket'	EPfP LBuc LLHF LRHS MAsh MGos SBfd SPer
- 'Golden Torch'	CAlb CSBt EBee ELan EMil EPfP GKir LRHS LSRN MBri MRav NEgg SBfd SLim SWvt WPat
- 'Green Carpet'	CMac EBee GKir LHop LRHS MBlu NLar SPoG WFar
- 'Green Mantle'	see *B. thunbergii* 'Kelleriis'
- 'Green Marble'	see *B. thunbergii* 'Kelleriis'
- 'Green Ornament'	NHol
- 'Green Ring'	EQua
§ - 'Kelleriis' (v)	LHop LRHS MGos MMuc MRav NHol NLar SLon WClo WDin WFar
- 'Kobold'	CMac EBee EPfP LHop LRHS MAsh MGos NEgg NHol NLar SLim SPer SPoG WFar
- 'Maria'[PBR]	LLHF LRHS LSou MGos NCGa NEgg NHol NLar SPoG WHar
- 'Moia'	EKen
- 'Orange Rocket'	CWit EPfP LRHS MAsh MGos
- 'Pink Queen' (v)	CDul EBee ELan EPfP EWTr LHop LRHS MAsh NLar SMad SPur WDin WFar WPat
- 'Pow-wow'	CBcs CDoC EBee IVic LRHS MBri MGos NEgg NLar SCoo SLim SPoG SWvt WDin WPat
- 'Silver Beauty' (v)	CBcs CMHG EBee ELan MGos MSwo WDin

- 'Silver Mile'	see *B.* × *ottawensis* 'Silver Miles'
- 'Somerset'	CMac
- 'Starburst'^{PBR} (v)	CBcs CDoC CDul CSBt EPfP GKir LRHS LSRN MAsh MBri MGos NEgg NLar NPri SBfd SCoo SLim SLon SWvt
- Sunsation = 'Monry' **new**	IVic
- 'Tiny Gold'^{PBR}	CEnd GBin LBuc LRHS LSRN LSqu MAsh MGos SLim SLon SPoG SWvt
* - 'Tricolor' (v)	CMac MRav WFar WPat
valdiviana	CBcs CDul CGHE CMHG CPLG CPMA EBee EPfP EPla SKHP SMad SSpi WPGP WPat
verruculosa ♀^{H4}	CBcs CDoy EBee EPfP GKir LAst LHop LRHS MGan MGos NHol NLar NWea SCoo SEND SPer SRms SWvt WCFE WDin WFar
- 'Hard's Rob'	NLar
aff. ***verticillata*** B&SWJ 10672	WCru
virescens B&SWJ 2646D	WCru
vulgaris	CArn CNat EMac EPfP GPoy IFFs MCoo
- 'Wiltshire Wonder' (v)	CNat
wilsoniae	CBcs CDoy CDul CMac CTri EBee ELan EMac EPfP GKir LHop MMuc MSnd NHol NLar NWea SCoo SPer WCFE WClo WDin WFar
- L 650	CGHE WPGP
- blue-leaved	WFar WPat
- var. ***guhtzunica***	EWes

Berchemia (*Rhamnaceae*)

racemosa	CMen NLar WSHC

bergamot see *Citrus bergamia*

Bergenia ✿ (*Saxifragaceae*)

'Abendglocken'	CMac EBee ECGP ECha ECtt EPfP GKir LRHS MNFA NGdn NSti WCom WCot WEas WFar
§ 'Abendglut'	Widely available
'Admiral'	CBct CMoH ECha MLHP WCot
* ***agavifolia***	CBct
'Andrea'	WCot
'Autumn Magic'	CBct COIW CWit GAbr GQue LAst LHop LSou NEgg NPri SPoG WFar WSpi
'Baby Doll'	Widely available
'Bach'	WCot
§ 'Ballawley' clonal ♀^{H4}	CMoH EBrs ECha GCal IBlr IGor LRHS MLHP MRav NEgg WCot WFar WMnd WWEG
'Ballawley Guardsman'	EBee EHrv
§ Ballawley hybrids	GBin SDix WSpi
'Ballawley Red'	GBin NEgg
'Ballawley' seed-raised	see *B.* Ballawley hybrids
'Bartók'	WCot
beesiana	see *B. purpurascens*
'Beethoven'	CBct CDes CMoH EBee ECha EWTr GCra IGor MRav NBir NBre SUsu WCot WPGP
Bell Tower	see *B.* 'Glockenturm'
'Biedermeir'	ECha
'Bizet'	CBct
'Borodin'	CBct
'Brahms'	CBct WCot
'Bressingham Beauty'	GKir
'Bressingham Bountiful'	CBct
'Bressingham Ruby'^{PBR}	CBcs CBct CLAP EBee EBrs ECha ECtt GKir LAst LBMP LRHS LSRN MGos MRav NBir NEgg WCot WPGP WSpi
'Bressingham Salmon'	CMoH EBee ELan ELon GMaP LRHS LSRN MBri MRav NLar WCot WMnd
'Bressingham White' ♀^{H4}	Widely available
'Britten'	WCot
ciliata	CBct CDes CHEx CLAP CMac CTca EBee EBla EShb IFro LEdu LRHS MCot MLHP MRav NBir NHol NLar SDix SUsu WCom WPGP WSHC WTin
- f. ***ligulata***	see *B. pacumbis*
- 'Patricia Furness'	CLAP
- 'Wilton'	CBct CDes CLAP WCot
ciliata × ***crassifolia***	see *B.* × *schmidtii*
'Claire Maxine'	GCal
cordifolia	Widely available
- 'Jelle'	GBin
- 'Purpurea' ♀^{H4}	CBcs CDoC EAEE EBee ECha ELan EPfP GKir LBuc LRHS MLHP MNFA MRav NBir NEgg SMrm SPer SRms WFar WPnP
- 'Rosa Schwester'	ECha
- 'Rosa Zeiten'	GBin
- 'Tubby Andrews' (v)	CBct CBow EBla ECtt GEdr LEdu LLHF LRHS MAvo MBrN MBri MCCP MDKP MLLN NEgg NLar SBfd WCom WWEG
- 'Vinterglöd'	EBee ELan ELon GMaP IFoB LRHS MWat NBre NGdn NLar SWvt WFar WHil WPnP
crassifolia	EBee EPfP GKev NBre SRms WWEG
- 'Autumn Red'	CBct CMoH ECha
- 'Orbicularis'	see *B.* × *schmidtii*
- var. ***pacifica*** 'Cally Gem' **new**	GCal
* ***cyanea***	CLAP WCot
'David'	ECha EWes GBin WWEG
'Delbees'	see *B.* 'Ballawley' clonal
'Doppelgänger'	EBee SUsu
'Eden's Dark Margin'	CBct EBee WCot
'Eden's Magic Giant'	CBct CFir EBee EWll GBin MBNS
emeiensis	CDes CLAP CPom IMou SMrs WCot WPGP
- hybrid	CBct
'Eric Smith'	CBct EBee ECha GBin GCal GCra IGor MBri WCot WMnd
'Eroica'	CBct COIW CSpe EBee EBrs ECha ECtt ELan EPfP GBin LAst LHop LRHS LSou MBri MMuc MRav NBre NSti SPoG WCAu WHoo WMnd WPtf WSpi
'Evening Glow'	see *B.* 'Abendglut'
'Frau Holle'	EBee MBri
§ 'Glockenturm'	CBct NEgg
'Harzkristall'	GQue LHop LRHS
'Hellen Dillon'	see *B. purpurascens* 'Irish Crimson'
'Herbstblute'	EBee
'Jo Watanabe'	CBct MRav
'Lambrook'	see *B.* 'Margery Fish'
§ 'Margery Fish'	CBct ECha SPer
milesii	see *B. stracheyi*
§ 'Morgenröte' ♀^{H4}	CBcs CBct EBee EBrs ECha ELon EPfP GEdr GKir GMaP LAst LRHS LSRN MGos MRav NHol NLar NSti SBfd SPer SRms SWvt WCAu WCFE WCot WWEG
'Morning Light'	ECtt
Morning Red	see *B.* 'Morgenröte'
'Mrs Crawford'	CBct ECha
'Oeschberg'	CBct GBin GCal
'Opal'	CBct EBee
'Overture'	CAby CBct CSpe EBee EBrs ECtt EHrv ELan ELon EUJe GBin GEdr

	LAst LHop LRHS LSRN MAvo MBri MGos MNFA NCob NGdn NLar SUsu WCot WFar WWEG WWFP
§ ***pacumbis***	CDes CHEx CLAP EBtc GBin GCal GEdr NBid NBre NSti WCot WPGP WSpi
- CC 1793	SBch
- CC 3616	CBct WCot
'Perfect'	EBee WMnd
'Pink Dragonfly'	CMac CMil CWGN EBee ECtt GBin SPoG WCot WFut
'Pinneberg'	GBin
'Profusion'	SPer
'Pugsley's Pink'	CBct
'Purple Queen'	LRHS
§ ***purpurascens*** ♀H4	CMac CMoH EBee EPfP GMaP IFoB IGor MBrN SBfd SDix SPer WCot WTin WWEG
- SDR 4548	GKev
- var. ***delavayi*** ♀H4	EBrs LRHS MBri NBre SRms
§ - 'Irish Crimson'	CGHE WCot
aff. ***purpurascens*** ACE 2175	WCot
'Purpurglocken'	EBee ECtt WAul
'Red Beauty'	CMoH LRHS MGos MSnd SBfd WPnP
'Reitheim'	EBee
'Rosi Klose'	CDes CFee CLAP EBee EBrs ECha ECtt EHoe EHrv EWes GBin GCra GEdr GQue LAst LHop LRHS MBri MNFA MRav MWat NBre NCob NGdn SUsu WCot WFar WGwG WHoo WWEG
'Rosi Ruffles'	EBee MBNS
'Rotblum'	CBct EBee ECGP ECtt EHoe ELon EPfP GKir GMaP LAst MSCN NBir NCob NGdn NVic WClo WFar
§ × ***schmidtii*** ♀H4	CBct CMac IGor LRHS MRav NBir NBre NLar WCot
'Schneekissen'	CBct CMac CPrp EBee ECGP ECtt LRHS MRav WCAu
§ 'Schneekoenigin'	CBct ECha GBin GCal MRav
§ 'Silberlicht' ♀H4	Widely available
Silverlight	see *B.* 'Silberlicht'
'Simply Sweet'	WCot
Snow Queen	see *B.* 'Schneekoenigin'
'Solar Flare' (v)	CBow
§ ***stracheyi***	CBct CFir CMoH CPLG EBee ECha GCal IGor MLHP MRav NBid NLar SApp SDix WCot WEas
- CC 4609	GKev
- CC 5225	GKev
- Alba Group	CMoH EBee ECha GCal SMHy SUsu WPGP
- 'Ice Queen' **new**	WCot
'Sunningdale'	CBcs CMac EBee ECha ECrN ELan EPfP GCra GKir GMaP LHop LRHS MLLN MRav NBir NGdn SWvt WClo WMnd WWEG
tianquanensis	CDes EBee WPGP
'Walter Kienli'	EBee GBin
Winter Fairy Tales	see *B.* 'Wintermärchen'
§ 'Wintermärchen'	CBct CChe EBee ECha ECtt ELan ELon EPfP GBin GCra LAst LRHS MGos MMuc MRav NHol SBfd SPoG WCot WMnd WWEG
'Winterzauber'	EBee

Bergeranthus (*Aizoaceae*)

multiceps	SChr
scapiger	WCot

Berkheya (*Asteraceae*)

multijuga	GMac NBre SBHP WSHC
- 'Golden Spike' **new**	EBee
purpurea	CBcs CCVN CPom CSpe EBee EBrs ELon EPfP GCal GKev GMac IGor LLWG LOck LRHS MCCP MDKP MLLN MWea NEgg SBch SMad SMrm SPet SPlb WClo WCot WHil WKif WSHC
- 'Silver Spike'	EAEE EPfP GKir LBMP LHop LRHS LSRN MBri WCon
- 'Zulu Warrior'	EDif EKen GBin IPot LSou MWea NGBl SBHP SRkn

Berlandiera (*Asteraceae*)

lyrata	CArn EBee

Berneuxia (*Diapensiaceae*)

thibetica	IBlr

Berula (*Apiaceae*)

erecta	EBee NPer

Berzelia (*Bruniaceae*)

galpinii	SPlb
lanuginosa	GGar

Beschorneria (*Agavaceae*)

albiflora	WPGP
rigida	WPGP
septentrionalis	CAbP CChe CDTJ CFir CGHE CSpe CTrC EBee ESwi LOck LRHS LSou MAvo MBNS MSCN SBfd SPad WClo WCot WGrn WPGP
tubiflora	CDTJ CHEx
yuccoides ♀H3	CAbb CBcs CHEx CPne CTrC CWit EAmu EBee EShb ESwi GAbr IBlr IDee LEdu NVic SAPC SArc SDnm SEND SLim
- subsp. ***dekosteriana*** F&M 102	WPGP
- 'Quicksilver'	CBcs CCCN CDoC CEnd CKno CSBt CTrC EBee EPfP EUJe IVic LRHS MBri MGos MPkF SBfd SDix SDnm SLim SSpi WCot WGrn WPGP

Bessera (*Alliaceae*)

elegans	CAvo CFFs CFir EBee ECho EPot LAma WCot

Beta (*Chenopodiaceae*)

trigyna	WCom WCot
vulgaris	SVic WHer
- 'Bull's Blood'	CArn CSpe WJek
- subsp. ***cicla***	CArn SVic
var. ***flavescens*** 'Bright Lights' ♀H3	
- - - 'Rhubarb Chard' ♀H3	WJek
- subsp. ***maritima***	CAgr EBWF

Betonica see *Stachys*

Betula ✿ (*Betulaceae*)

alba L.	see *B. pendula*, *B. pubescens*
albosinensis misapplied	see *B. utilis*
albosinensis Burkill ♀H4	CDul CLnd CMCN CTri EBee EPfP NWea WDin WFar WMou
- W 4106	CSto
- from Gansu, China	CSto
- 'Bowling Green'	CPMA WPGP

	- 'China Ruby'	CPMA GKir MBri MWya SMad SSpi WPGP
	- 'Chinese Garden'	CPMA MBlu
	- clone F	see *B. albosinensis* 'Ness'
	- 'Fascination'	CMCN EBee GKir IFFs LMaj LTen MGos
	- 'K.Ashburner'	CPMA CTho
	- 'Kansu'	CEnd CPMA EBee GKir SBig SCoo SMad SSpi WHCr
§	- 'Ness'	CPMA CTho
	- 'Pink Champagne'	CPMA CSto
	- 'Rhinegold'	MBlu
	- 'Sable'	SLim SPer
	- var. ***septentrionalis*** ♀H4	Widely available
	- - 'Purdom'	CPMA GKir SBig SMad
§	***alleghaniensis***	CBcs CCVT CDul CMCN CSto EBee EPfP GKir IFFs MMuc NLar NWea WDin
	alnoides B&SWJ 11751	WCru
	apoiensis 'Mount Apoi'	CPMA GKir SBig
§	× ***caerulea***	WSpi
	caerulea-grandis	see *B.* × *caerulea*
	chichibuensis	CSto EPla WHer
	'Conyngham'	CPMA CTho MBlu SLau
	cordifolia	see *B. papyrifera* var. *cordifolia*
	costata misapplied	see *B. ermanii* 'Grayswood Hill'
	costata ambig.	CMCN ECrN MMuc
	costata Trautv.	CLnd EBee ELan GKir MSwo WDin
*	- 'Fincham Cream'	CPMA GKir SBig WHCr
I	× ***cruithnei***	GAuc
	cylindrostachya	EBee
	dahurica Pall.	CDul CMCN CSto GAuc
	- B&SWJ 8462	WCru
	- 'Maurice Foster'	CPMA CTho SBir
	- 'Stone Farm'	CPMA
	delavayi	EBee GKir
	ermanii	Widely available
	- B&SWJ 8801 from South Korea	WCru
	- from Hokkaido, Japan	CSto
	- 'Blush'	CLnd CPMA GKir MBlu SBig SCoo WHCr
	- var. ***ermanii***	LSRN
	- - MSF 825	EBee
	- - MSF 865	WPGP
§	- 'Grayswood Hill' ♀H4	CDul CEnd CLnd CMCN CPMA CSBt CTho CTri EBee EPfP GKir GQui LRHS MBlu MBri MGos NLar SCoo SLim SMad SPer WHCr WPGP
	- 'Hakkoda Orange'	CPMA CTho GKir MBri SCoo WPGP
	- 'Holland'	LMaj NLar
	- 'Moonbeam'	GKir
	- 'Mount Zao'	CPMA CSto WPGP
*	- 'Pendula'	CPMA EBee MBlu NPal SBig SBir SCoo
	- 'Polar Bear'	CPMA CWSG EBee GKir MBlu MBri NLar NPal SCoo SMad WHCr WHar
*	- ***ussuriensis***	GKir
	- 'Zao Purple'	CDul
	'Fetisowii'	CDul CEnd CPMA CTho ECrN GKir LRHS MBlu SBig SCoo SSta
	fruticosa	see *B. humilis*
	globispica	CPMA
	'Hergest'	EBee EPfP GKir LRHS MAsh MBri MGos NPal SCoo SLau SLim SMad SPoG WHCr WPGP
§	***humilis***	GKir GQui WDin
	insignis	CSto
	'Inverleith'	see *B. utilis* var. *jacquemontii* 'Inverleith'
	jacquemontii	see *B. utilis* var. *jacquemontii*
	kamtschatica	see *B. humilis*
	lenta	CDul CMCN CSto EPfP IArd IFFs MBlu MMuc NLar NWea WDin
	luminifera	CPMA EBee EBtc GKir LRHS NLar SBir
	lutea	see *B. alleghaniensis*
§	***mandshurica***	CSto GQui NEgg WHCr
§	- var. ***japonica***	ECrN GKir MMuc MSnd NLar NWea
	- - 'Whitespire Senior'	CDul
	maximowicziana	CDoC CDul CMCN CTho CWib EGFP EPfP LHop NMun WDin
	medwedewii	CDul CMCN CSto EBee EPfP SCoo
	- 'Gold Bark'	CMCN MBlu
	michauxii	NLar
	nana	CDul EWTr GAuc GKir MGos MRav NHar NHol NWea SRms SSta STre WDin
	- 'Glengarry'	EPot GEdr NLar
	nigra	CBcs CCVT CDoC CDul CEnd CLnd CMCN CSBt CTho CTri EBee ECrN IFFs LMaj MAsh MBri NWea SSta WDin WFar WMou
	- Dura-Heat = 'Bnmtf'	MGos NLar
	- Heritage = 'Cully' ♀H4	CDul CLnd CPMA EBee LHop LRHS LTen MGos NWea SBig SBir SCoo SSta WDin WFar WHCr WMoo
	- 'Little King'	CPMA MGos NLar SKHP SPoG
	- 'Summer Cascade'	SKHP
	- Tecumseh Compact = 'Studetec'	MBlu MPkF
	- Wakehurst form	EPfP GKir SPer
	papyrifera	Widely available
	- var. ***commutata***	WDin
§	- var. ***cordifolia***	CSto
	- - 'Clarenville'	WPGP
	- 'Saint George'	CPMA CTho
	- 'Vancouver'	CPMA CTho MBlu
§	***pendula*** ♀H4	Widely available
	- 'Bangor'	CLnd CPMA
	- f. ***crispa***	see *B. pendula* 'Laciniata'
	- 'Dalecarlica' misapplied	see *B. pendula* 'Laciniata'
	- 'Dalecarlica' ambig.	CBcs CCVT CSBt ECrN LRHS MRav SCrf SLim WFar
	- 'Dark Prince'	CPMA
	- 'Fastigiata'	CDul CEnd CLnd CSBt CTho EBee ECrN ELan GKir LMaj MGos NEgg NWea SCoo SLim SPer WDin WFar WMoo
*	- 'Golden Beauty'	CCVT CDoC CMac EBee ECrN ELon GKir IFFs MAsh MGos NLar NPal SBfd SCoo SLim SPer SSpi WDin WFar
	- 'Golden Cloud'	CMac LAst
§	- 'Laciniata' ♀H4	CDoC CDul CMCN CMac CTho CWib EBee ECrN ELan EPfP GKir IFFs LAst LMaj MBlu MGos MRav MSwo NBea NWea SBfd SCoo SPer WCFE WDin WHar WPat
	- 'Long Trunk'	CDul EBee ECrN LSRN MBlu MWya SLim
	- 'Purpurea'	CCVT CDul CLnd CMCN CMac CSBt CWib EBee ECrN ELan ELon EPfP LAst LSRN MGos MSwo NBea SBfd SCoo SPer WDin WFar
	- 'Silver Grace'	CPMA EBee ECrN LSRN SSpi
	- 'Swiss Glory'	CLnd LMaj
	- 'Tristis' ♀H4	Widely available
	- 'Youngii'	Widely available
	platyphylla misapplied	see *B. mandshurica*
	platyphylla (Regel) V.N.Voroschilov subsp. ***kamtschatica***	see *B. mandshurica* var. *japonica*

	platyphylla Sukaczev	CMCN NWea
	- Dakota Pinnacle = 'Fargo'	EBee GKir LRHS SCoo SPoG
	populifolia	CSto
	pseudomiddendorffii new	GKev
§	***pubescens***	CCVT CDul CLnd CSto CTri ECrN GQue IFFs NWea SLPl WDin WFar WMou
I	***refugia***	GAuc
	'Royal Frost'	CDul CPMA EBee GKir IArd IFFs LRHS MAsh MWya NLar NPal SLim SPoG WHar
	saposhnikovii	GKir
	schmidtii	EWTr
	szechuanica	GQui NEgg NPCo WDin WPGP
	- 'Liuba White'	CPMA CTho
	- 'Moonlight'	SLau
	'Trost's Dwarf'	CBcs WDin WFoF
§	***utilis***	CDul CMCN CSBt CSto EBee ECrN EMil LMaj MMuc NWea SSta WDin WFar WPGP
	- BL&M 100 from central Nepal	CSto
	- F 19505 from Sichuan, China	CSto
	- H&M 1480 from Sichuan, China	CSto
	- RSC 1 from Langtang, Nepal	CSto
	- SICH 667 from Sichuan, China	CSto
	- S&L from Nepal	CDul
	- Yu 10163 from Yunnan, China	CSto
	- from eastern Nepal	CSto
	- from Uttar Pradesh, India	GAuc
	- 'Buckland'	ECrN
	- 'Darkness'	SLon
	- 'Fascination'	CCVT CDul CEnd CPMA EPfP GKir IArd LRHS MBri MGos NWea SBir SCoo SLim SSpi WHCr
*	- 'Fastigiata'	CLnd CPMA SBig
	- 'Forrest's Blush'	CDul CEnd CPMA EBee GKir LSRN MBri SBig SBir
	- 'Himalayan Pink'	WSpi
N	- var. ***jacquemontii***	Widely available
	- - Polunin	WPGP
	- - 'Doorenbos' ♀H4	Widely available
	- - 'Grayswood Ghost' ♀H4	CDul CEnd CMCN CPMA CTho CTri EBee ECrN EPfP GKir LRHS MBlu MBri MDun NWea SBig SBir SLau SLim SPer SSpi WPGP
§	- - 'Inverleith'	CEnd CLnd CPMA EBee GKir MAsh SBig SBir SCoo SLim WFar WPGP
	- - 'Jermyns' ♀H4	CDul CEnd CLnd CMac CPMA CTri EBee EPfP GKir LMaj LRHS LSRN MBlu MBri SCoo SLau SMad SPer SSpi WHCr
	- - 'McBeath'	SLau
	- - 'Silver Shadow' ♀H4	CDul CEnd CPMA CTho EBee EPfP GKir LRHS LSRN MAsh MBlu MWya NLar NWea SBig SBir SCoo SKHP SLau SLim SMad SPer SPoG SSpi SSta WSpi
	- - 'Trinity College'	CPMA CTri EBee GKir MBri SBig SBir SSpi WHCr
	- 'Knightshayes'	CTho
	- 'Moonbeam'	CDul CLnd CPMA EBee GKir LRHS MAsh MBri MWya SBig SBir SCoo SPoG SPur WClo WHar
	- var. ***occidentalis*** 'Kyelang'	CPMA CTho
	- 'Polar Bear'	GKir
	- var. ***prattii***	CEnd
	- - Parkwood 1123	CSto EBee
	- 'Ramdana River'	CLnd
	- 'Wakehurst Place Chocolate'	CDul CPMA CSBt CWSG GKir LRHS MAsh MBlu MBri NPal SBig SCoo SLim SMad SSpi WHCr
	cf. ***utilis***	CTri
	- GWJ 9259	WCru
	- HWJK 2345	WCru
	verrucosa	see *B. pendula*

Biarum (Araceae)

	S&L 604	WCot
	SB&L 597	WCot
	arundanum	WCot
	bovei	ECho WCot
	- LB 351	WCot
	carratracense	WCot
	- from Spain	WCot
	davisii	ECho EPot WCot
	dispar	WCot
	- S&L 290/2	WCot
	- SB&L 294	WCot
	- SB&L 564	WCot
	ditschianum	WCot
	- from Turkey	WCot
	marmarisense	EBee ECho WCot WWst
*	***ochridense***	WCot
	tenuifolium	EBee ECho WCot
	- LB 223	WCot
	- LB 295	WCot
	- PB 357	WCot
	- SL 174	WCot
	- subsp. ***abbreviatum***	WWst
	- - MS 974	WCot
	- - from Greece	ECho
	- subsp. ***galianii*** PB 435	WCot
	- subsp. ***idomenaeum*** MS 738	WCot
	- subsp. ***zelebori***	ECho WCot
	- - CRL 502	WCot
	- - LB 300	WCot
	- - PB 224	WCot
	- - PB 334	WCot

Bidens (Asteraceae)

	B&SWJ 10276 from Mexico	WCru
	atrosanguinea	see *Cosmos atrosanguineus*
§	***aurea***	CEnt EBee EBla ECtt EPPr EWes GCal GGar LAst LEdu MDKP MNrw NCGa NPer SAga SGar SMrm SPet SPhx STes WBor WFar WOld
	- B&SWJ 9049 from Guatemala	WCru
	- 'Blacksmith's Flame'	EBla
	- 'Cream Streaked Yellow'	GCal GQue WPrP
	- cream-flowered	MNrw
	- 'Golden Drop'	EBee EWes
	- 'Hannay's Lemon Drop'	CAby CCVN CEnt CKno CSev EBee EBla ECtt ELon EPPr EPfP GCal LHop LPla MDKP MNrw NCGa SAga SPoG SSvw STes SUsu WBor WHrl WMoo WPGP
	- 'Julia's Gold'	STes
	- 'Rising Sun'	EBee EWes
	- white-flowered	GCal
	'Eldorado' new	LAst
	ferulifolia ♀H1+3	ECtt MLLN NPer
	- Peter's Gold Rush = 'Topteppich'PBR	LSou
	- Peter's Surprise = 'Petersurpr'PBR	SVil
	- Solaire = 'Bidtis 1'PBR	WGor

'Golden Star' LAst LSou
heterophylla misapplied CAby CEnt CKno CPrp ECtt MCot MRav MWat SMrm WFar WHal WHrl WMoo WPrP
- CD&R 1515 LPla
heterophylla Ortega see *B. aurea*
humilis see *B. triplinervia* var. *macrantha*
integrifolia SMad
pilosa EBee
'Southon Star' new LSou
triplinervia B&SWJ 10413 WCru
- B&SWJ 10696 WCru
§ - var. ***macrantha*** EBee ELon LHop

Bignonia (*Bignoniaceae*)

capreolata CCCN EBee WCot WSHC
- 'Dragon Lady' SKHP WCot
lindleyana see *Clytostoma calystegioides*
tweedieana see *Macfadyena unguis-cati*
unguis-cati see *Macfadyena unguis-cati*

Bilderdykia see *Fallopia*

Billardiera (*Pittosporaceae*)

cymosa SOWG
longiflora 🏆H3 Widely available
- 'Cherry Berry' CBcs CMac CWan EBee ELan GAbr LPio LRHS LSRN MAsh MCCP NLar SLim SPer SPoG SRms SWvt WSHC
- ***fructu-albo*** CBcs EBee ELan EWes GKev LRHS SLim SLon SPer SPoG SWvt WBVN
- red-berried GGar

Billbergia (*Bromeliaceae*)

nutans CBen CHEx CHll CPen EBak EOHP EShb ESwi EUJe IBlr IMou LEdu MBri MRav NPal SChr SEND SRms WGwG WSFF
- var. ***schimperiana*** EShb
* - 'Variegata' (v) CFir CHll EShb NPal SChr WCom WCot
pyramidalis 🏆H1 XBlo
I - 'Variegata' (v) IBlr
× ***windii*** 🏆H1 CFir CHEx EBak SRms

Bismarckia (*Arecaceae*)

nobilis CCCN EAmu EUJe LPal WCot

Bistorta see *Persicaria*

Bituminaria (*Papilionaceae*)

bituminosa WSHC

blackberry see *Rubus fruticosus*

blackcurrant see *Ribes nigrum*

Blechnum (*Blechnaceae*)

alpinum see *B. penna-marina* subsp. *alpinum*
arcuatum new WRic
auriculatum WRic
brasiliense 🏆H1 WRic
chambersii WRic
§ ***chilense*** 🏆H3 CBty CDTJ CDes CGHE CHEx CLAP EBee EFtx EPfP GCal GCra GGar IBlr LEdu MMoz NVic SAPC SArc SBig SDix SGSe SKHP WCru WMoo WPGP WRic
colensoi CKel WRic
discolor CBcs CKel CLAP CTrC EFtx EUJe GBin IDee LPal WRic
fluviatile CBcs CDTJ CKel CLAP CTrC EFtx EUJe GBin IDee MMoz SGSe WRic
fraseri WRic
gibbum EFtx EShb MBri
- 'Silver Lady' CTrC WRic
magellanicum misapplied see *B. chilense*
magellanicum (Desv.) Mett. CKel EBee EFtx SBig SKHP WPGP WRic
minus CBty MGos WRic
§ ***niponicum*** EBee GBin
novae-zelandiae CBcs CDTJ CKel CTrC EFtx EUJe GBin WRic
nudum CBty CDTJ CKel EAmu EFtx EPfP EQua LTen NMoo WRic
penna-marina 🏆H4 CBty CCCN CElw CKel CLAP CPLG EFer EFtx GAbr GCal GGar GMaP LEdu MAvo MBri NBir NRya NVic NWCA SRms WAbe WFib WMoo WOut WRic WWEG
§ - subsp. ***alpinum*** CLAP EBee ECha GGar SGSe SKHP WAbe WMoo
- 'Cristatum' CLAP GAbr GGar SRms WPGP
punctulatum WRic
spicant 🏆H4 Widely available
tabulare misapplied see *B. chilense*
tabulare (Thunb.) Kuhn 🏆H1 CBcs CDTJ CKel EFtx EPfP GGal NMun WPGP WRic
vulcanicum WRic
wattsii CDes

Blepharocalyx (*Myrtaceae*)

cruckshanksii CPLG
- 'Heaven Scent' CCCN EBee GGar LAst MCCP NLar WBor

Blephilia (*Lamiaceae*)

ciliata SPhx

Bletilla ✿ (*Orchidaceae*)

sp. new NDav
Brigantes gx CDes EBee
hyacinthina see *B. striata*
ochracea CPLG EBee NLAp WCot WWst
Penway Bouquet gx NLAp
Penway Classic gx NLAp
Penway Coral gx NLAp
Penway Fancy gx NLAp
Penway Fantasy gx NLAp
Penway Harlequin gx NLAp
Penway Majestic gx NLAp
Penway Paris gx NLAp
Penway Pixie gx NLAp
Penway Prelude gx NLAp
Penway Pride gx NLAp
Penway Rainbow gx NLAp
Penway Rose gx NLAp
Penway Sunset gx NLAp WCot
sinensis CPLG
§ ***striata*** CAby CBct CBgR CDes CPLG CPom CSWP CTri EBee ECho GBBs LAma LEdu LRHS MNrw MREP NCGa NHol NLAp NMen NWCA SPer WCot WFar WPGP
- ***alba*** see *B. striata* f. *gebina*
- 'Albostriata' CBct CDes EBee ECho ELan LAma NCGa NLAp NWCA WCot
§ - f. ***gebina*** CBgR CDes CMdw CTri EBee ECho LAma LEdu LRHS NLar WCot WFar WPGP
- - variegated (v) LEdu NMen WCot WHal
- var. ***japonica*** EPot
- 'Lips' new WWst

- 'Soryu' new — WWst
- variegated (v) — CBow
- yellow-flowered — ECho

szetschuanica — EBee WWst

Bloomeria (*Alliaceae*)

crocea — ECho
- var. **aurea** — EBee ECho
- var. **montana** — ECho

blueberry see *Vaccinium corymbosum*

Bocconia (*Papaveraceae*)

cordata — see *Macleaya cordata* (Willd.) R. Br.
frutescens F&M 358 new — WPGP
microcarpa — see *Macleaya microcarpa*

Boehmeria (*Urticaceae*)

nipononivea 'Kogane-mushi' (v) — WCot
platanifolia — IMou
sylvatica — NLar
tricuspis — IMou

Boenninghausenia (*Rutaceae*)

albiflora — CSpe
- B&SWJ 1479 — WCru
- BWJ 8141 from China — WCru
- pink-flowered B&SWJ 3112 — WCru

japonica — EBee GKev
- B&SWJ 4876 — WCru

Boesenbergia ✿ (*Zingiberaceae*)

rotunda — CArn

Bolax (*Apiaceae*)

glebaria — see *B. gummifer*
§ **gummifer** — ECho WAbe

Bolboschoenus (*Cyperaceae*)

§ **maritimus** — CRWN EBWF GFor LPBA WFar

Boltonia (*Asteraceae*)

asteroides — CFee CSam CSpe ECtt EHrv GCra LEdu NGdn SMrm SPer STes SWat WBVN WCom WRHF
- var. **latisquama** — EBee GMaP GQue LSou MAvo MRav MWat NCGa NLar SHar SSvw WBor WFar WHal
- - 'Nana' — EWTr LEdu MRav NBre SGSe WFar
- - 'Snowbank' — EBee EBla ELan GCal LHop NDov NWsh
- 'Pink Beauty' — EBla LEdu LHop

decurrens — EBee MAvo NBre
incisa — see *Kalimeris incisa*

Bomarea (*Alstroemeriaceae*)

F&M 130 — WPGP
acuminata — see *B. andreana*
acutifolia — SKHP
- B&SWJ 10388 — WCru
- B&SWJ 9094 — WCru WPrP

aff. **andreana** B&SWJ 10617 — WCru
boliviensis — EBee WCru
caldasii — see *B. multiflora*
costaricensis — ERea
- B&SWJ 10467 — WCru

distichifolia new — WCot
§ **edulis** — CBgR CDes CGHE CRHN CWGN EBee EWld LEdu WCot WPGP WThu
- B&SWJ 9017 — WCru
- F&M 104 — WPGP

frondea — see *B. multiflora*
hirtella — see *B. edulis*
§ **multiflora** ♀H1 — CBcs CCCN CFir CHEx CRHN EBee ERea EWld GCal IKil SMad SKHP SOWG WBor WFoF WPGP WSHC
aff. **multiflora** B&SWJ 10681 — WCru
salsilla — CCCN CRHN CStu EBee SKHP WCot WPGP WSHC

Bongardia (*Berberidaceae*)

chrysogonum — CAvo CFFs ECho LRHS WCot WHal

Bonia (*Poaceae*)

§ **solida** — CHEx MMoz MMuc MWht SEND WDyG WJun

Borago (*Boraginaceae*)

alba — MNHC
laxiflora — see *B. pygmaea*
officinalis — CArn CFox CHby CSev CWan ELau EPfP GKir GPoy MHer MNHC NBir NGHP NVic SBch SBfd SVic WJek
- 'Alba' — CBre CSev ELau ILis NGHP SBch SBfd SDnm SIde WJek
- 'Bill Archer' (v) — CBow CNat

§ **pygmaea** — CArn CHid CPLG CSev CSpe ELan GBar MHer MNrw MTho NGHP NSti STes SWat WGwG WHer WJek WMoo WPrP

Borinda (*Poaceae*)

albocerea — EPla MWht WDyG WJun
- Yunnan 1 — EPla WJun WPGP
- Yunnan 2 — CDTJ CEnt EPla MMoz WJun WPGP
- Yunnan 3a — CDTJ CEnt EPla WJun WPGP
- Yunnan 3b — WJun
- Yunnan 4 — CDTJ CEnt EPla WPGP

boliana — EPla SBig WJun
edulis — EPla WJun
frigida — CDTJ CEnt EPla WJun WPGP
- KR 4059 — MWht

grossa — EPla
- KR 5931 — MWht

lushuiensis — EPla WJun
macclureana — EPla
- KR 5050 — WJun
- KR 5177 from Gyala, Nepal — ESwi MWht WJun WPGP
- KR 6236 — ESwi
- KR 6243 — WJun
- KR 6438 from Pasm Tso new — ESwi
- KR 6400 from Show La new — ESwi

* **muliensis** — WJun
papyrifera — CEnt EPla WJun WPGP
- CS 1046 — WJun
- KR 3968 — WJun
- KR 7613 — MWht WJun

scabrida — CDTJ CEnt CGHE EPla ETod MMoz MWht WJun WPGP
- 'Asian Wonder' — EBee ENBC EPla LRHS MBlu MGos NLar SPoG

Boronia (*Rutaceae*)

citriodora — SOWG
denticulata — ECou
heterophylla — CBcs CCCN CTsd ECou SOWG WAbe
- 'Ice Charlotte' — CBcs IDee

- white-flowered	ECou
mollis	SOWG
pinnata	ECou SOWG
serrulata	ECou

Bossiaea (*Papilionaceae*)

riparia new	SPlb

Bothriochloa (*Poaceae*)

§ ***bladhii***	CKno EPPr
caucasica	see *B. bladhii*

Botryostege see *Tripetaleia*

Bougainvillea (*Nyctaginaceae*)

'Ailsa Lambe'	see *B.* (Spectoperuviana Group) 'Mary Palmer'
'Alexandra'	LRHS MBri
'Apple Blossom'	see *B.* 'Elizabeth Doxey'
'Audrey Grey'	see *B.* 'Elizabeth Doxey'
'Aussie Gold'	see *B.* 'Carson's Gold'
'Begum Sikander'	ERea
'Brilliant' misapplied	see *B.* × *buttiana* 'Raspberry Ice'
× ***buttiana*** 'Ametyst'	MBri
- 'Asia'	ERea
- 'Audrey Grey'	see *B.* 'Elizabeth Doxey'
- 'Barbara Karst'	SOWG
- 'Coconut Ice' (v)	SOWG
- 'Killie Campbell' 𝕐H1	ERea
- 'Lady Mary Baring'	ERea SOWG
§ - 'Mahara' (d)	ERea SOWG
§ - 'Miss Manila' 𝕐H1	SOWG
§ - 'Mrs Butt' 𝕐H1	ERea
§ - 'Poultonii'	ERea
§ - 'Poulton's Special' 𝕐H1	ERea
§ - 'Raspberry Ice' (v)	ERea EShb SOWG
- 'Ratana Red' (v)	ERea
§ - 'Roseville's Delight' (d)	SOWG
- 'Tiggy'	ERea
§ Camarillo Fiesta = 'Monle' (*spectabilis* hybrid)	ERea SOWG
§ 'Carson's Gold' (d)	ERea
§ 'Chiang Mai Beauty'	ERea
§ 'Closeburn'	SOWG
'Crimson Lake' misapplied	see *B.* × *buttiana* 'Mrs Butt'
'Donya'	ERea
'Double Yellow'	see *B.* 'Carson's Gold'
§ 'Elizabeth Doxey'	SOWG
'Flamingo Pink'	see *B.* 'Chiang Mai Beauty'
'Floribunda'	ERea
glabra 𝕐H1	CMen ERea LRHS MBri
§ - 'Harrissii' (v)	ERea
§ - 'Magnifica'	SOWG
§ - 'Sanderiana'	ERea EUJe
'Gloucester Royal'	SOWG
'Glowing Flame' (v)	ERea
'Golden Doubloon'	see *B.* × *buttiana* 'Roseville's Delight'
'Golden Tango'	ERea
'Harrissii'	see *B. glabra* 'Harrissii'
'Hawaiian Scarlet'	see *B.* 'San Diego Red'
'James Walker'	ERea
'Jennifer Fernie'	ERea
'Juanita Hatten'	ERea
'Klong Fire'	see *B.* × *buttiana* 'Mahara'
'Little Caroline'	SOWG
'Lord Willingdon' misapplied	see *B.* 'Torch Glow'
§ 'Louis Wathen'	ERea
'Magnifica'	see *B. glabra* 'Magnifica'
'Mahara Double Red'	see *B.* × *buttiana* 'Mahara'
'Mahara Orange'	see *B.* × *buttiana* 'Roseville's Delight'
'Manila Magic Red'	see *B.* × *buttiana* 'Mahara'
'Mini-Thai'	see *B.* 'Torch Glow'
'Mrs Butt'	see *B.* × *buttiana* 'Mrs Butt'
* 'Orange Flame'	SOWG
'Orange Glow'	see *B.* Camarillo Fiesta
'Orange King'	see *B.* 'Louis Wathen'
'Orange Stripe' (v)	ERea
'Pixie'	see *B.* 'Torch Glow'
'Poultonii'	see *B.* × *buttiana* 'Poultonii'
'Poultonii Special'	see *B.* × *buttiana* 'Poulton's Special'
'Princess Mahara'	see *B.* × *buttiana* 'Mahara'
'Purple Robe'	ERea MREP
'Ratana Orange' (v)	ERea
'Red Fantasy' (v)	ERea
'Reggae Gold' (v)	ERea
'Rubyana'	ERea SOWG
§ 'San Diego Red' 𝕐H1	ERea SOWG
'Sanderiana'	see *B. glabra* 'Sanderiana'
Scarlett O'Hara	see *B.* 'San Diego Red'
'Smartipants'	see *B.* 'Torch Glow'
'Snow Cap'	see *B.* (Spectoperuviana Group) 'Mary Palmer'
§ (Spectoperuviana Group) 'Mary Palmer'	ERea
- 'Mrs H.C. Buck'	ERea
Surprise	see *B.* (Spectoperuviana Group) 'Mary Palmer'
'Tango'	see *B.* × *buttiana* 'Miss Manila'
'Temple Fire'	see *B.* 'Closeburn'
'Thai Gold'	see *B.* × *buttiana* 'Roseville's Delight'
§ 'Torch Glow'	EAmu
'Tropical Rainbow'	see *B.* × *buttiana* 'Raspberry Ice'
'Variegata'	see *B. glabra* 'Harrissii'
'Vera Blakeman'	SOWG
'Wac Campbell' (d)	SOWG

Boussingaultia (*Basellaceae*)

baselloides Hook.	see *Anredera cordifolia*

Bouteloua (*Poaceae*)

curtipendula	CRWN EBee GFor SGSe
§ ***gracilis***	EBee EBrs EHoe GFor LRHS MWhi NWsh SGSe SMea SMrm SUsu SWal WPGP WWEG

Bouvardia (*Rubiaceae*)

× ***domestica***	EShb
longiflora	ERea SOWG
ternifolia	WCot

Bowiea (*Hyacinthaceae*)

volubilis	EBee EShb

Bowkeria (*Scrophulariaceae*)

cymosa	SPlb
gerrardiana	CHII
verticillata	WBor

Boykinia (*Saxifragaceae*)

aconitifolia	CAbP EBla EBrs EWld GGar MRav NLar NRya SMad WCru WMoo WSHC
elata	see *B. occidentalis*
heucheriformis	see *B. jamesii*
§ ***jamesii***	GEdr GKev NWCA
lycoctonifolia	EBee NLar
major	EBee GAuc
§ ***occidentalis***	EBee EPot GGar MMHG WCru WMoo WPtf

rotundifolia EBee EWld GKev NBir WCru WMoo
tellimoides see *Peltoboykinia tellimoides*

Brachychilum see *Hedychium*

Brachychiton (*Sterculiaceae*)

acerifolius CHEx EShb
discolor EShb
§ ***rupestris*** EShb

Brachyelytrum (*Poaceae*)

japonicum GFor NLar

Brachyglottis ✿ (*Asteraceae*)

§ ***bidwillii*** CBcs IDee IRar
- 'Basil Fox' WAbe
§ ***buchananii*** GKir WSHC
- 'Silver Shadow' GGar
§ ***compacta*** ECou ELan EPfP LRHS MAsh SLon SPer SPoG
compacta × ***monroi*** ECou LRHS
'County Park' ECou
'Drysdale' ELan EPfP GGar LRHS MAsh MBri SBfd SLon SRGP SWvt
§ (Dunedin Group) 'Moira Reid' (v) CPLG GGar
§ - 'Sunshine' ♀H4 Widely available
'Frosty' ECou
greyi misapplied see *B.* (Dunedin Group) 'Sunshine'
§ ***greyi*** (Hook. f.) B. Nord. CMac EBee EPfP MWhi
greyi × ***repanda*** CDoC GGar SAPC
huntii × ***stewartii*** GGar
laxifolia misapplied see *B.* (Dunedin Group) 'Sunshine'
'Leith's Gold' CBcs CTrC
§ ***monroi*** ♀H4 CBcs CMac CSBt CWib EBee ECou EHoe ELan EPfP GGar IVic LRHS MMuc MRav SEND SLon SPoG WDin
- 'Clarence' ECou
repanda WCot
§ ***rotundifolia*** CBcs CCCN CDoC GGal GGar NLar
'Silver Waves' ECou
§ ***spedenii*** GGar
I 'Sunshine Improved' CBcs EHoe NBir SWvt
'Sunshine Variegated' see *B.* (Dunedin Group) 'Moira Reid'
Walberton's Silver Dormouse = 'Walbrach'PBR LBuc LRHS MAsh SPoG

Brachypodium (*Poaceae*)

pinnatum EHoe
sylvaticum EBWF EHul GCal GFor MMuc SEND

Brachyscome (*Asteraceae*)

'Blue Mist' MMuc
formosa ECou
melanocarpa WCom
'Metallic Blue' NPri
multifida MBri
nivalis var. ***alpina*** see *B. tadgellii*
'Pink Mist' SPet
rigidula ECou GKev
'Strawberry Mousse' LAst SPet
§ ***tadgellii*** ECou
tenuiscapa new GGar

Brachysema (*Papilionaceae*)

celsianum SOWG

Brachystachyum (*Poaceae*)

densiflorum EPla NLar

Brachystelma (*Asclepiadaceae*)

angustum LToo
bracteolatum LToo
caffrum LToo
circinatum LToo
filifolium LToo
foetidum LToo
gracile new LToo
longifolium new LToo
meyerianum new LToo
nanum LToo
tuberosum new LToo
vahrmeijeri new LToo

Bracteantha see *Xerochrysum*

Brahea (*Arecaceae*)

armata CAbb CBrP CDTJ CPHo EAmu EPfP EShb ESwi ETod EUJe IDee LPal MGos MREP SAPC SBst SChr STrG WCot
edulis CBrP EAmu LPal SChr
'Super Silver' WCot

Brainea (*Blechnaceae*)

insignis WRic

Brassaia see *Schefflera*

Brassica (*Brassicaceae*)

japonica see *B. juncea* var. *crispifolia*
§ ***juncea*** var. ***crispifolia*** CArn MNHC
nigra CArn
oleracea EBWF SVic WHer
- 'Nine Star Perennial' new CAgr
* ***rapa*** var. ***japonica*** CArn

Bravoa (*Agavaceae*)

geminiflora see *Polianthes geminiflora*

Brillantaisia (*Acanthaceae*)

kirungae CCCN ECre EShb WHil

Brimeura (*Hyacinthaceae*)

§ ***amethystina*** ♀H4 CAvo CBgR CPLG CPom ECho GBin GKev GMac NWCA SDeJ SPhx WCot
- 'Alba' CAvo CBgR EBrs ECho GKev LRHS SDeJ SMrm SPhx WCot

Briza (*Poaceae*)

maxima CEnt CKno CTri EHoe EPla LEdu LHop NGdn NSti SBch WHal WHer WTou
media Widely available
- 'Golden Bee' CKno EPPr
- 'Limouzi' CBod CElw CFir CKno EBee EBrs EHoe EHrv ELon EPPr GCal GKir LEdu LRHS MAvo MBri NSti SDys SMad SMea SPoG WPrP
- 'Russells'PBR CHid CKno EBee EHoe EPPr GBin GKir LHop LRHS NBPC NCGa SBfd SMea SPer SPhx SPoG SWvt WPtf
subaristata EBee EPPr GCal MWhi WHrl
triloba EWes MMHG NWsh

Brodiaea (*Alliaceae*)

§ ***californica*** CPou EBee ECho NMen WCot
- NNS 00-108 WCot
capitata see *Dichelostemma capitatum*
coronaria CPBP GAuc WCot

'Corrina'	see *Triteleia* 'Corrina'
elegans	EBee ECho GAuc WCot
ida-maia	see *Dichelostemma ida-maia*
laxa	see *Triteleia laxa*
pallida	WCot
peduncularis	see *Triteleia peduncularis*
stellaris	ECho

Bromus (*Poaceae*)

inermis	EBee EHoe EHul EPPr EWes NLar
'Skinner's Gold' (v)	SMea SMrm WCot WWEG
sterilis	CSpe
'Chinese Brushstrokes'	

Broussonetia (*Moraceae*)

kazinoki	CArn EBee IFFs NLar WDin
papyrifera	CAbP CBcs CDul EGFP ELan GBin IVic LMaj MBri SPer WDin WPGP
- 'Laciniata'	MBri NLar SMad

Browallia (*Solanaceae*)

from Sikkim	CSpe

Bruckenthalia see *Erica*

Brugmansia ✿ (*Solanaceae*)

§ ***arborea***	CArn CDTJ SEND SRms
§ - 'Knightii' (d) ♀H1	CDTJ ELan ERea
aurea	CCCN CHEx
× ***candida***	CCCN CHEx
§ - 'Grand Marnier' ♀H1	CBot CDTJ CHEx CHll ELan ERea SOWG
- 'Plena'	see *B. arborea* 'Knightii'
- ***plena*** 'Mon Amoure M' (d)	ERea
§ - 'Variegata' (v)	CCCN CDTJ CSam ERea
§ ***chlorantha***	CBcs
× ***cubensis*** 'Charles Grimaldi'	CSam
'Flowerdream' (d)	ERea
'Herzenbrucke'	ERea
'Igea Pink'	CSam
§ × ***insignis***	CHll
- 'Pink'	SEND
§ - pink-flowered	CHEx SEND
'Mobishu'	EShb
rosei	see *B. sanguinea* subsp. *sanguinea* var. *flava*
§ ***sanguinea***	CBcs CCCN CHEx CHll EGxp EShb IDee IRar SEND SOWG
- red-flowered	CHEx
- 'Rosea'	see *B.* × *insignis* pink-flowered
§ - subsp. ***sanguinea*** var. ***flava***	CHEx
§ ***suaveolens*** ♀H1	CHEx CHll EGxp ELan SPlb
- 'Flore Pleno' (d)	EGxp
- pink-flowered	EShb
- ***rosea***	see *B.* × *insignis* pink-flowered
- 'Variegata' (v)	EShb
- yellow-flowered	EShb
suaveolens × ***versicolor***	see *B.* × *insignis*
'Variegata Sunset'	see *B.* × *candida* 'Variegata'
versicolor misapplied	see *B. arborea*
§ ***versicolor*** Lagerh.	CCCN SOWG

Brunfelsia (*Solanaceae*)

americana	CCCN ERea SOWG
calycina	see *B. pauciflora*
eximia	see *B. pauciflora* 'Eximia'
jamaicensis	SOWG
lactea	CCCN ERea EShb
nitida	ERea
§ ***pauciflora*** ♀H1	CCCN ELan ERea EUJe MBri
§ - 'Eximia'	ERea
- 'Floribunda'	ERea SOWG
- 'Macrantha'	ERea

Brunia (*Bruniaceae*)

albiflora	SPlb

Brunnera ✿ (*Boraginaceae*)

§ ***macrophylla*** ♀H4	Widely available
- 'Agnes Amez'	CLAP
- 'Alba'	see *B. macrophylla* 'Betty Bowring'
§ - 'Betty Bowring'	Widely available
- 'Blaukuppel'	CLAP EAEE EBee EBla EWes GBin LRHS NBir NCob WFar
- 'Dawson's White' (v)	Widely available
- 'Gordano Gold' (v)	CBow EHoe EPPr MAvo NBir WCot
- 'Hadspen Cream' (v) ♀H4	Widely available
- 'Jack Frost'PBR ♀H4	Widely available
- 'Langford Hewitt' (v)	MNrw
- 'Langtrees'	Widely available
- 'Looking Glass'PBR	Widely available
- 'Marley's White'	CAbP CLAP EBee EHrv GAbr LLHF MCot NCob NEgg SUsu WCot WPtf
- 'Mr Morse' (v)	CHid CWGN ECGP ECtt ELon EPPr EPfP GEdr GQue LLHF MAsh MAvo MCot MTis NBPC NBir NDov NEgg NLBP NLar NPnk NSti SMrm SPoG WBrk WCot WCra WFut WHoo WWEG
- 'Silver Wings'	CElw EBee ECtt EPfP EWll GEdr LRHS NBir SWat
- 'Spring Yellow'	EBee NLar SHeu
'Mrs Morse'	MMuc NGdn
sibirica	CDes CLAP EBee EPPr EWes NBid

Brunsvigia (*Amaryllidaceae*)

bosmaniae	ECho
marginata	ECho
pulchra	ECho WCot
radula 'Vanrhynsdorp' **new**	ECho
radulosa	ECho
rosea 'Minor'	see *Amaryllis belladonna*
striata	ECho

Bryonia (*Cucurbitaceae*)

dioica	CArn GPoy NMir

Bryophyllum see *Kalanchoe*

Buchloe (*Poaceae*)

dactyloides	CRWN EBee

Buddleja ✿ (*Buddlejaceae*)

HCM 98.017 from Chile	WPGP
agathosma	CBot CPLG SLon SOWG WCom WKif WLav WPGP WSHC
albiflora	SLon WLav
alternifolia ♀H4	Widely available
- 'Argentea'	CBcs CBot CDoC EBee ELan EPfP GBin GKir LRHS MBNS MRav NLar NSti SKHP SPer SPoG SRGP SSpi WCot WLav WPat WSHC
asiatica ♀H2	CBot EShb IDee SLon SOWG WLav
- B&SWJ 7214	WCru
- B&SWJ 11278	WCru
auriculata	CBcs CBgR CBot CDul CMCN CPLG CTca CWib EBee ECre ELan EPfP EShb LRHS MRav NSti SDix SKHP SLon SOWG SPlb SPoG WBor WCru WLav WPGP WPat
* 'Blue Trerice'	CPLG
caryopteridifolia	EBee GQui SEND SLon

colvilei	CBcs CDoC CDul ELan EPfP GCal GGal GKir IDee LAst MBri SDnm SLon WBor WPat WSpi
- B&SWJ 2121	WCru
- GWJ 9399	WCru
- 'Kewensis'	CBot CHGN CPLG CRHN CSam EBee EWes GCal GGal GKir NLar NSti SLon WCFE WCom WCru WLav WPat WSHC WSpi
cordata	SLon SOWG
- B&SWJ 10433	WCru
- F&M 220	WPGP
coriacea	SLon
§ ***crispa***	CBcs CBot CDul CPLG CSpe CTca ECha ELan EPfP LRHS SDnm SLon SOWG SPer SRkn WClo WEas WFar WKif WPGP WSHC WSpi
- var. ***farreri***	CHGN CWit SLon
crotonoides subsp. ***amplexicaulis***	SLon
curviflora f. ***venenifera***	SLon
- - B&SWJ 6036	WCru
davidii	CArn NWea SGar STre WDin
- B&SWJ 8083	WCru
- Adonis Blue = 'Adokeep'PBR	CBcs MGos
- 'African Queen'	CAni SLon SRGP
- var. ***alba***	CWib
§ - 'Autumn Beauty'	CAni ECrN SLon
- 'Bath Beauty'	CAni
- 'Beijing'	see *B. davidii* 'Autumn Beauty'
- 'Bishop's Velvet'	CAni
- 'Black Knight' Y^{H4}	Widely available
- 'Blue Horizon'	CAni CSam MMuc NLar SEND SLon SRGP WCot WLav WMoo WRHF
- 'Border Beauty'	CAni SLon
- 'Boskoop Beauty'	CAni
- 'Brown's Beauty'	CAni
- Camberwell Beauty = 'Camkeep' (English Butterfly Series)	CSBt MGos NHol SLon WClo
- 'Car Wash'	CAni
- 'Castle Blue' **new**	SLon
- 'Castle School'	CAni CSam
§ - 'Charming'	CDul WMoo WSHC WWlt
- 'Clive Farrell'	see *B. davidii* 'Autumn Beauty'
- 'Croyde'	CSam
- 'Dartmoor' Y^{H4}	CAni CDul CFee CMHG CMac CPLG CTri EBee ECtt ELan EPfP GCal GKir LRHS MAsh MCot MGos MRav NLar NPer SDix SIde SPer SPlb SPoG SSta WCom WFar WSHC WSpi
- 'Dart's Ornamental White'	MRav SLon
- 'Dart's Papillon Blue'	CAni SLon
- 'Dart's Purple Rain'	CAni SLon
- 'Dubonnet'	CAni SLon WLav
- 'Dudley's Compact Lavender'	CAni
- 'Ecolonia'	CAni SLon
- 'Empire Blue' Y^{H4}	Widely available
- 'Fascinating'	CAni GCal MGan MRav NBir SLon WLav
- 'Flaming Violet'	CAni SLon WLav
- 'Florence'	CWit EBee LLHF LSRN LSou NEgg NHol NLar SLon SPoG SRGP WFar WHar WMoo
- 'Fortune'	CAni
- 'Glasnevin Hybrid'	CAni NSti SDix SLon WLav
- 'Gonglepod'	CAni SLon
- 'Greenway's River Dart'	CAni SLon
- 'Harlequin' (v)	Widely available

- 'Ile de France'	CAni CBcs CWib EBee MGos NWea SLon SRms WLav
- 'Leela Kapila'	LBuc MGos SLon
- 'Les Kneale'	CAni SLon
- 'Lyme Bay'	CAni
- Marbled White = 'Markeep'	CSBt NHol SLon
- Masquerade = 'Notbud'PBR (v)	MBri MGos MRav SLon WGor
§ - 'Nanho Blue' Y^{H4}	Widely available
- 'Nanho Petite Indigo'	see *B. davidii* 'Nanho Blue'
- 'Nanho Petite Plum'	see *B. davidii* 'Nanho Purple'
- 'Nanho Petite Purple'	see *B. davidii* 'Nanho Purple'
§ - 'Nanho Purple' Y^{H4}	CAlb CAni CDoC CMHG CTri CWib EBee ELan EPPr EPfP LRHS LSRN MAsh MGos MRav NLar SLim SLon SPer SPlb SPoG SRGP WHar
- Nanho White = 'Monite'	ELan EPfP GKir LRHS SLon SPer SPoG SRms WFar
- var. ***nanhoensis***	CAni CDul EBee SEND SIde WLav
- - blue-flowered	NHol SLon SPer
- 'Orchid Beauty'	CAni SLon WLav
- 'Orpheus'	CAni SLon WLav
- 'Panache' **new**	SLon
- 'Peace'	CMac CTri EBee EPfP LSRN MBri MRav NLar SLon SPoG WLav
- Peacock = 'Peakeep'PBR (English Butterfly Series)	CBcs
- 'Persephone'	SLon WLav
- 'Petite Indigo'	see *B. davidii* 'Nanho Blue'
- 'Pink Beauty'	GKir IFFs LAst LSRN SRGP
- 'Pink Charming'	see *B. davidii* 'Charming'
- 'Pink Pearl'	CAni MMuc SEND SLon WLav
- 'Pink Spreader'	CAni SLon
- 'Pixie Blue'	CAni LAst LBMP LBuc LRHS MAsh NMyG NPri SRGP
- 'Pixie Red'	CAni LBMP LBuc LRHS MAsh MMuc NEgg NLar NMyG NPri SEND
- 'Pixie White'	LBuc LRHS MAsh MMuc NLar NPri SEND SRGP WLav
- Purple Emperor = 'Pyrkeep' (English Butterfly Series)	CBcs NBir SLon
- 'Purple Friend'	CAni SLon WLav
- 'Purple Prince'	CAni
- 'Red Admiral'	CAni LLHF LRHS MAsh SLon SPoG SRGP
- Rêve de Papillon = 'Minpap'	EMil
- 'Royal Purple'	CAni SLim
- 'Royal Red' Y^{H4}	Widely available
- 'Saith Ffynnon Early' **new**	WSFF
- 'Santana' (v)	CAni CDul CMac CWit EBee EHoe ELon EPfP EWes LRHS LSou MGos MRav MWea NEgg NHol NLar SAga SBfd SWvt WCot WHar WMoo WPat WRHF WSpi
- 'Shapcott Blue'	CAni
- 'Shire Blue'	WLav
- 'Southcombe Splendour'	CAni
- 'Summer Beauty'	CAni CWib EBee LRHS MGos MRav SLon WLav
- 'Summer House Blue'	SLon
- 'Twotones'	WLav
- 'Variegata' (v)	CAni LRHS MAsh SLon WLav
- 'White Ball'	EBee ELan EPfP NLar SLon
- 'White Bouquet'	CAlb CAni CCVT CDul CSBt CWit EBee EPfP GKir IFFs LAst LRHS MAsh MHer MMuc MSwo MWat NPri NWea SEND SPer SRGP SReu WLav

	- 'White Cloud'	CAni ECrN GKir GQui MGos SRms WGwG
	- 'White Harlequin' (v)	SLon WCFE
	- 'White Profusion' ♀H4	CAlb CAni CBar CBcs CDul CSam EBee ECtt ELan EPfP GKir LRHS MGan MGos MRav NBir NEgg NLar NWea SBfd SLim SPad SWat SWvt WCFE WDin WFar WHar
	- 'White Wings'	SLon WLav
	- 'Widecombe'	CAni
§	***delavayi***	CPLG EBee GKir SEND WCru
	fallowiana misapplied	see *B.* 'West Hill'
	fallowiana Balf. f.	ELan GQui LRHS WCom WLav
	- ACE 2481	LRHS
	- BWJ 7803	WCru
	- var. ***alba*** ♀H3	CBot CDoC CHGN CMac EBee ECrN ELan EPfP GBin LRHS MAsh MRav NLar NSti SLon SPer SPoG WFar WPGP WSHC
	'Flower Power'	see *B.* × *weyeriana* 'Bicolor'
	forrestii	CBot CRHN WCru
	globosa ♀H4	Widely available
	- RCB/Arg C-11	WCot
	- 'Cally Orange'	GCal GGar
	- 'Lemon Ball'	MBlu NPer SLon WLav
	glomerata	EBee EShb SLon WCom WPGP
	- 'Silver Service' **new**	CMHG ELan EWTr LRHS SKHP
	'Gulliver'	NLar SLon
	heliophila	see *B. delavayi*
	indica	SLon WBor
	japonica	SLon
	- B&SWJ 8912	WCru
	× ***lewisiana*** 'Margaret Pike'	CBot SLon SOWG
	limitanea	SLon
	lindleyana	Widely available
	aff. ***lindleyana*** B&SWJ 11478	WCru
	'Lochinch' ♀H3-4	Widely available
	longifolia	SLon
	loricata	CBgR CBot CFee CHGN CPLG CTca CWib EBee GBin GQui IDee LRHS MMuc SEND SGar SLon SOWG SPlb WCFE WLav WPGP
	macrostachya	GBin GLin
	- HWJ 602	WCru
§	***madagascariensis*** ♀H1	CRHN NLar SGar SLon SOWG SPlb WHar
*	'Malvern Blue' (English Butterfly Series)	CAni
	megalocephala B&SWJ 9106	WCru
§	'Morning Mist' PBR	CDoC CMHG CPLG CWGN EBee EGxp ELan EPfP GBin LLHF LSRN LSou MGos NBir NEgg NHol NLar SBfd SLim SLon SOWG SPoG WClo WCot WHar WPGP
	myriantha	CPLG SLon
*	- f. ***fragrans***	WCot
	nappii	NMun SLon
	nicodemia	see *B. madagascariensis*
	nivea	CBot CPLG SLon SOWG WCom WLav
	- B&SWJ 2679	WCru
	- pink-flowered	SLon
	officinalis ♀H2	CBot CPLG CTca SLon SOWG
	paniculata	MAsh SLon
	parvifolia	SLon
	- MPF 148	WLav
	× ***pikei*** 'Hever'	GCal
	'Pink Delight' ♀H4	Widely available
	'Pink Perfection'	CAni WFar
	'Pride of Hever'	SOWG
	'Pride of Longstock'	LRHS SLon
	'Purple Splendour'	GGal
	'Rosebud' **new**	EWTr
	saligna	SLon
	'Salmon Spheres'	SLon
	salviifolia	CBcs CBgR CBot CDul CPLG CRHN CSWP CSam CTca CTsd EBee ELan GGal GGar GQui IDee LAst LRHS MBlu NSti SDnm SPlb SWal WAbe WCom WGwG WHer WLav
	- white-flowered	CRHN SLon
	Silver Anniversary PBR	see *B.* 'Morning Mist'
	stachyoides	SOWG
	stenostachya	CPLG SLon
	sterniana	see *B. crispa*
	tibetica	see *B. crispa*
	tubiflora	CBot SLon SOWG WLav
	venenifera B&SWJ 895	WCru
§	'West Hill'	SLon SRGP WLav
	× ***weyeriana***	CBgR CDul CRHN CSam EBee ECtt EPfP GQui IFFs MMuc MNrw MSwo NBir SBfd SGar SPlb SWvt WBVN WBor WDin WFar WLav
§	- 'Bicolor' **new**	MNrw
	- 'Golden Glow' (v)	CBow CTri ECrN EPfP GBin LSRN SLon WLav WSFF
	- 'Lady de Ramsey'	MMuc SEND
	- 'Moonlight'	CBcs CPLG ELan GKir IFro SBfd SLon WCot WLav WSpi
	- 'Sungold' ♀H4	CBcs CMac CWib EBee ELan EPPr EPfP GBin GGar GKir GQui IVic LSRN MBlu MCCP MGan MLLN MRav NBir SLon SPer SRGP WBVN WCot WFar WHar WLav WSpi
	'Winter Sun'	SLon
	yunnanensis	GCal GGar SLon WCFE
	- B&SWJ 8146	WCru

Buglossoides (*Boraginaceae*)

§	***purpurocaerulea***	CEnt CHll CMHG CPom CSpe CWGN EBee ECha ELan LHop MLHP MWhi NBid NBir WCot WSHC

Bukiniczia (*Plumbaginaceae*)

cabulica	WAbe

Bulbine (*Asphodelaceae*)

	SH 74	CMdw
	abyssinica	ECho
	alooides	ECho
	annua misapplied	see *B. semibarbata*
	bulbosa misapplied	see *B. semibarbata*
	capitata	ECho
	'Bloemfontein' **new**	
	caulescens	see *B. frutescens*
§	***frutescens***	CDoC CHll CTca GGar MBNS WBrk WJek WPrP
	- 'Hallmark'	CCCN
	latifolia	CCCN EShb
	narcissifolia	ECho
	'Ladybrand' **new**	
§	***semibarbata***	CCCN

Bulbinella (*Asphodelaceae*)

angustifolia	ECho WCot
cauda-felis	WCot
- 'Tulbagh' **new**	ECho
eburnifolia	ECho
elata	WCot

floribunda	IBlr
gibbsii var. ***balanifera***	ECho
graminifolia	ECho
'Clanwilliam' new	
hookeri	CPom EBee ECho ECou EWld GBee GEdr GGar GKev GKir ITim LRHS NChi NLAp NWCA SRms WHal
latifolia	ECho
- subsp. ***doleritica*** new	ECho
nutans	CDes ECho WPGP
punctulata	ECho
'Piketberg' new	

Bulbinopsis see *Bulbine*

Bulbocodium (*Colchicaceae*)

vernum	EBrs ECho EPot GKev GKir LAma LLHF MBri NHol NMin SDeJ
- white-flowered	ECho

bullace see *Prunus insititia*

Bunias (*Brassicaceae*)

orientalis	CAgr ELau

Bunium (*Apiaceae*)

bulbocastanum	IMou LEdu SBfd SHDw

Buphthalmum (*Asteraceae*)

salicifolium	CSam EBee ELan EPfP GKir MMuc MNFA NBro NGdn SEND SPer SRms SWat WCAu WCot WFar WPer WWEG
- 'Alpengold'	ECha GMaP NBre NLar
- 'Dora'	ECtt WCot
§ - 'Golden Wonder'	GKir
- 'Sunwheel'	EWll GKir LRHS NBre SRms
speciosum	see *Telekia speciosa*

Bupleurum (*Apiaceae*)

angulosum	CSpe LRHS NBir SMrm WFar
- copper-leaved	see *B. longifolium*
candollei GWJ 9405	WCru
falcatum	CArn CSpe ECGP ECha LRHS NDov SPur WCot WFar
fruticosum	CBcs CBot CSpe EBee ECGP ECtt EPfP LRHS MAsh SDix SDnm SEND SKHP SPer SPoG SSpi SSta WCot WDin WEas WPGP WPat WSpi
gibraltaricum	EBee
§ ***longifolium***	CAby CElw CFee CPom CSpe EBee EWes GBBs GBin GKir LEdu LRHS MDKP MNrw NCGa NChi SKHP WHoo
- subsp. ***aureum***	MAvo NLar SPhx WFar
- bronze-leaved	LSou MAvo
spinosum	SMad
tenue	CArn

Bursaria (*Pittosporaceae*)

spinosa	CCCN EBee ECou EShb NLar

Butia (*Arecaceae*)

capitata	CAbb CBcs CBrP CCCN CDTJ CHEx CPHo CTrC EAmu EPla ESwi ETod EUJe IDee LMaj LPJP LPal LTen MGos MREP NPal SAPC SArc SBst SChr
§ - var. ***odorata***	EAmu LPal
eriospatha	CDTJ EAmu EUJe LPal
odorata	see *B. capitata* var. *odorata*
yatay	CDTJ EAmu LPal SBig

Butomus (*Butomaceae*)

umbellatus ♀H4	CBen CRow CWat ECha EHon EPfP LPBA MCCP MNrw MRav MSKA MWts NPer NSco SWat WMAq WPnP WTin
- f. ***albiflorus*** new	MSKA
- 'Rosenrot'	CRow LLWG
- 'Schneeweisschen'	CRow LLWG MNrw MWts NLar

butternut see *Juglans cinerea*

× *Butyagrus* (*Arecaceae*)

nabonnandii	EAmu

Buxus ✿ (*Buxaceae*)

aurea 'Marginata'	see *B. sempervirens* 'Marginata'
balearica ♀H4	CSWP EPla EQua IDee SLan SLon WPGP
bodinieri	EPla EQua SLan
- 'David's Gold'	WPen
colchica	SLan
'Glencoe'	SLan
'Green Gem'	NHol SLan
'Green Mound'	SLan
'Green Mountain'	SLan
'Green Velvet'	EPfP NHol SLan
harlandii hort.	CMen EPla SLan SRiv
- 'Richard'	SLan STre
henryi	MBri
japonica 'Nana'	see *B. microphylla*
macowanii	SLan
§ ***microphylla***	CSWP MHer NHol SLan STre WBVN WSpi
- 'Asiatic Winter'	see *B. microphylla* var. *japonica* 'Winter Gem'
§ - 'Compacta'	CMen LLHF MHer NMen SLan SRiv WCot WPat WThu
- 'Curly Locks'	EPla MHer SLan
- 'Faulkner'	CCVT EBee ELan EPfP EQua IFFs LBuc LHop LRHS MAsh MBNS MGos MREP NHol SLan SPer SPoG SRiv WDin WMoo WSpi
- Golden Dream = 'Peergold'PBR	NLar
- 'Golden Triumph'PBR	EPfP MWat SLan
- 'Grace Hendrick Phillips'	SLan
- 'Green Pillow'	EPfP MHer SLan SRiv WSpi
- 'Helen Whiting'	SLan
- 'Henry Hohman'	SLan
- 'Herrenhausen'	SLan
- var. ***insularis***	see *B. sinica* var. *insularis*
- var. ***japonica*** 'Belvédère'	SLan
- - 'Gold Dust'	SLan
- - 'Green Beauty'	SLan
- - 'Green Jade'	SLan
- - 'Jim Stauffer'	SLan
- - 'Morris Dwarf'	SLan
- - 'Morris Midget'	IArd NHol SLan
- - 'National'	SLan WPGP
- - 'Sunnyside'	SLan
- - 'Trompenburg'	SLan
- - 'Variegata' (v)	CStu
§ - - 'Winter Gem'	MHer MRav NHol NLar SLPl SLan
- - f. ***yakushima***	SLan
- 'John Baldwin'	SLan SRiv
- 'Kagushima'	SLan
- var. ***koreana***	see *B. sinica* var. *insularis*
- 'Quiet End'	SLan
'Newport Blue'	see *B. sempervirens* 'Newport Blue'
riparia	EPla SLan
rugulosa	SLan

	sempervirens ♀H4	Widely available
	- 'Abilene'	SLan
	- 'Agram'	SLan
	- 'Anderson'	SLan
§	- 'Angustifolia'	EPla MGos MHer MRav NHol SLan
	- 'Arabeske'	SLan
	- 'Arborescens'	EQua
	- 'Argentea'	see *B. sempervirens* 'Argenteo-variegata'
§	- 'Argenteo-variegata' (v)	EPfP IFoB NEgg SLan WFar
	- 'Aristocrat'	SLan
	- 'Aurea'	see *B. sempervirens* 'Aureovariegata'
	- 'Aurea Maculata'	see *B. sempervirens* 'Aureovariegata'
	- 'Aurea Marginata'	see *B. sempervirens* 'Marginata'
	- 'Aurea Pendula' (v)	CPMA EPla SLan WDin
§	- 'Aureovariegata' (v)	EBee EPfP GBar LRHS MAsh MGan MGos MHer MNHC MRav NHol NSti SLan SPer SRiv WDin WFar WMoo
	- 'Belleville'	SLan
	- 'Bentley Blue'	NHol NWea
	- 'Berlin'	SLan
	- 'Blauer Heinz'	ELan IVic MHer MRav NHol SLan SRiv WSpi
	- 'Blue Belle'	SLan
§	- 'Blue Cone'	NHol
	- 'Blue Spire'	see *B. sempervirens* 'Blue Cone'
	- 'Bowles's Blue'	EQua SLan
I	- 'Brilliantissima'	NHol
	- 'Bullata'	SLan
	- 'Claverton'	SLan
	- clipped ball	CWib EPfP LSRN MGos NLar SLan SLim SRiv WFar
	- clipped bird	SRiv
	- clipped cone	LSRN SRiv
	- clipped pyramid	CWib EPfP LSRN MGos NLar SLan SLim SRiv
	- clipped spiral	LSRN SLan SLim SRiv
	- 'Crossley'	SLan
	- 'Dark Sky'	SLan
	- 'Dee Runk'	SLan
	- 'Denmark'	SLan
	- 'Egremont'	SLan
	- 'Elegans'	IFoB LRHS
§	- 'Elegantissima' (v) ♀H4	Widely available
	- 'Emir'	SLan
	- 'Fiesta'	SLan
	- 'Fleur de Lys'	SLan
	- 'Giant'	SLan
	- 'Glauca'	SLan
	- 'Gold Tip'	see *B. sempervirens* 'Notata'
	- 'Golden Frimley' (v)	LHop
§	- 'Graham Blandy'	MHer NHol SLan SRiv WSpi
	- 'Grand Rapids'	SLan
	- 'Green Balloon'	EPfP LBuc SLan
	- 'Greenpeace'	see *B. sempervirens* 'Graham Blandy'
	- 'Haller'	SLan
	- 'Handsworthiensis'	CLnd EBee NHol NLar SEND SLan SPer WMoo
	- 'Handsworthiensis' blue-leaved	SLan
	- 'Handsworthii'	CTri NWea SRms
	- 'Hardwickensis'	SLan
	- 'Henry Shaw'	SLan
	- 'Hermann von Schrenk'	SLan
	- 'Herman's Low'	SLan
	- 'Holland'	SLan
	- subsp. ***hyrcana***	SLan
	- 'Ickworth Giant'	SLan

	- 'Inglis'	SLan
	- 'Ingrid'	SLan
	- 'Inverewe'	SLan
	- 'Ipek'	SLan
	- 'Jack'	SLan
	- 'Japonica Aurea'	see *B. sempervirens* 'Latifolia Maculata'
	- 'Kensington Gardens'	SLan WSpi
	- 'King Midas'	IVic SLan
	- 'Kingsville'	see *B. microphylla* 'Compacta'
	- 'Kingsville Dwarf'	see *B. microphylla* 'Compacta'
	- 'Krakow'	NLar SLan
	- 'Lace'	NSti SLan
§	- 'Langley Beauty'	SLan
	- 'Langley Pendula'	see *B. sempervirens* 'Langley Beauty'
	- 'Latifolia Macrophylla'	SLan SLon
§	- 'Latifolia Maculata' (v) ♀H4	CAbP CDoC CWib EBee EPfP EPla MNHC NHol NPer SEND SLan SPoG SRiv STre WJek WSpi
*	- 'Latifolia Pendula'	NHol SLan
	- 'Lemmens'	SLan
	- 'Linda'	SLan
	- 'Longifolia'	see *B. sempervirens* 'Angustifolia'
§	- 'Marginata' (v)	CTca EPla GBar IFoB LHop LRHS LTen SLan SLon WHar WSpi
	- 'Mary Gamble'	SLan
	- 'Memorial'	MHer NHol SLan SMHy SRiv WSpi
	- 'Molesworth'	SLan
	- 'Myosotidifolia'	CMHG SLan SRiv WPGP WSpi
	- 'Myrtifolia'	CBot EPla MHer NHol SLan SLon WSpi
	- 'Natchez'	SLan
§	- 'Newport Blue'	SLan
	- 'Northern'	SLan
§	- 'Notata' (v)	IFoB MAsh SBfd WDin WRHF WSpi
	- 'Obelisk'	SLan
	- 'Ornament'	SLan
	- 'Parasol'	MHer SLan
	- 'Pendula'	GKir SLan SLon
	- 'Pinnacle'	SLan
I	- 'Planifolia'	SLan
	- 'Prostrata'	NHol NWea SLan WSpi
	- 'Pylewell'	WSpi
	- 'Pyramidalis'	SEND SLan WFar
	- 'Raket'	SLan
	- 'Rosalia'	SLan
	- 'Rosmarinifolia'	MHer MRav SLan
	- 'Rotundifolia'	ELan MGos SEND SIde SLan WDin WSpi
	- 'Roy Lancaster'	SLan
	- 'Saint Genevieve'	SLan
	- 'Salicifolia Elata'	SLan
	- 'Sentinelle'	SLan
	- 'Silver Beauty' (v)	MAsh MGos NEgg
	- 'Silver Variegated'	see *B. sempervirens* 'Elegantissima'
	- 'Suffruticosa' ♀H4	Widely available
I	- 'Suffruticosa Blue'	NHol
	- 'Suffruticosa Variegata' (v)	EOHP SRms SWvt
	- 'Sultan'	SLan
	- 'Sunningdale Silver'	EQua
	- 'Twisty'	SLan WFar
	- 'Undulifolia'	SLan
	- 'Vardar Valley'	NHol SLan SLon SRiv WSpi
*	- 'Variegata' (v)	ELan SLan
	- 'Varifolia'	SLan
	- 'Waterfall'	MHer SLan
	- 'Welleri'	SLan
	- 'William Borek'	SLan
	- 'Wisley Blue'	SLan WSpi
	sinica	SLan
§	- var. ***insularis***	MAsh NHol SLan

- - 'Chegu' SLan
- - 'Filigree' NHol SLan WSpi
- - 'Justin Brouwers' MHer SLan SRiv WSpi
- - 'Pincushion' SLan
- - 'Tall Boy' SLan
- - 'Tide Hill' MHer SLan SRiv WFar WSpi
- - 'Winter Beauty' SLan
- - 'Wintergreen' SLan
- var. ***intermedia*** SLan
wallichiana CGHE EPla SLan WPGP

C

Cacalia see *Parasenecio*

Caesalpinia (*Caesalpiniaceae*)

gilliesii CBcs CDTJ EBee EUJe LSRN SOWG SPlb
- RCB/Arg N-1 WCot
mexicana EGFP WPGP
pulcherrima CCCN SOWG SPlb
spinosa new WSHC

Calamagrostis (*Poaceae*)

from Korea IPot NDov
× ***acutiflora*** 'Avalanche' CKno EBee EHoe EPPr
- 'Eldorado' (v) new WCot
N - 'Karl Foerster' Widely available
- 'Overdam' (v) Widely available
- 'Stricta' EBee EPPr GKir NWsh
- 'Waldenbuch' EBee GBin
argentea see *Stipa calamagrostis*
arundinacea CElw COIW CPLG CSpe ECou EPla LEdu NBid NHol NVic SDix SGar SPlb WFar WMoo WPGP WPrP
'Avalanche' CKno GBin
§ ***brachytricha*** ♀H4 Widely available
emodensis CEnt CKno CWCL EBee ECha EHoe EPla IMou LEdu LRHS MAvo MMoz NOak NWsh SMad WGrn WMoo WPGP
epigejos EBee GFor NBre NHol WHrl WPrP
nutkaensis EPPr
splendens misapplied see *Stipa calamagrostis*
splendens Trin. new NDov
varia CKno EHoe EPPr NDov SMrm WHrl

Calamintha (*Lamiaceae*)

alpina see *Acinos alpinus*
§ ***ascendens*** CArn EBee SPhx WMoo
clinopodium see *Clinopodium vulgare*
cretica EBee WPer
* 'Fritz Kuhn' WWEG
§ ***grandiflora*** CArn EBee ECha EDAr ELan GGar GJos GPoy LEdu MHer MMuc MNHC MRav MWhi NBir NPer SEND SMad SMrm SPer SPlb SSvw SWat WCAu WFar WJek WMoo WTin
- 'Elfin Purple' EBee EPfP SBfd
- 'Variegata' (v) CPrp EBee ECtt ELan EPPr EPfP LAst LSou NPri WCom WFar
§ ***menthifolia*** NBre NLar WJek
mimuloides 'Supernova' WCot
§ ***nepeta*** CArn CWan CWit EBWF EBee ECha ECtt GMaP LAst LBMP LRHS MNHC NBir NBro NWCA SMrm SPhx SPlb SPoG SWat WFar WJek WMoo WPer
- subsp. ***glandulosa*** CEnt EBee ECGP WMoo
- - ACL 1050/90 WHoo
- - 'White Cloud' CSpe EBee EHrv ELan GBar LLWP MBri MRav NBir WCAu WMoo
- 'Gottfried Kuehn' EBee LPla MRav
§ - subsp. ***nepeta*** CPrp ELan ELon EPfP GBar GKir MHer MLHP MRav MWat NSti SPer SUsu WClo WEas WFar WHal WTin
- - 'Blue Cloud' CSam CSpe EBee ECha EHrv EPfP MBri MMuc NBir NDov SPhx SWat WCAu WFar WMoo
- 'Weisse Riese' SPhx
nepetoides see *C. nepeta* subsp. *nepeta*
officinalis misapplied see *C. ascendens*
sylvatica see *C. menthifolia*
I - 'Menthe' EBee
vulgaris see *Clinopodium vulgare*

calamondin see × *Citrofortunella microcarpa*

Calandrinia (*Portulacaceae*)

grandiflora GKev LLHF
* ***ranunculina*** CPBP
sericea CPBP
sibirica see *Claytonia sibirica*
umbellata EDAr GKev LBMP LRHS WPer
- 'Ruby Tuesday' NPri

Calanthe (*Orchidaceae*)

alismifolia EFEx
arcuata EFEx
arisanenesis EFEx
aristulifera EFEx GEdr WWst
bicolor see *C. striata*
discolor EBee EFEx GEdr LAma NLAp WCot WWst
- subsp. ***amamiana*** EFEx
- var. ***flava*** see *C. striata*
- subsp. ***tokunoshimensis*** EFEx
fargesii WCot WWst
graciliflora EFEx
Hizen gx GEdr WWst
Kozu gx GEdr LEdu WWst
- red-flowered GEdr WWst
mannii EFEx
nipponica CBct EBee EFEx GEdr LAma WWst
reflexa EBee EFEx GEdr LAma NLAp WCot WWst
sieboldii see *C. striata*
§ ***striata*** CBct EBee EFEx GEdr LAma WCot WWst
Takane gx GEdr WWst
tricarinata CBct EFEx GEdr LAma NLAp WWst

Calathea (*Marantaceae*)

argyrophylla 'Exotica' XBlo
louisae 'Maui Queen' XBlo
§ ***majestica*** ♀H1 XBlo
makoyana ♀H1 XBlo
oppenheimiana see *Ctenanthe oppenheimiana*
ornata see *C. majestica*
picturata 'Argentea' ♀H1 XBlo
roseopicta ♀H1 XBlo
rufibarba XBlo
* ***stromata*** XBlo
zebrina ♀H1 XBlo
'Zoizia' XBlo

Calceolaria (*Scrophulariaceae*)

acutifolia see *C. polyrhiza* Cav.
alba NLar
arachnoidea SKHP WCom
× ***banksii*** WCom
bicolor EBee

§ ***biflora***	ECho EPfP GGar GKev NLar
- 'Goldcap'	ECho SMrm
- 'Goldcrest Amber'	ECho SPlb
'Briga Elite'	EBee LSou
'Camden Hero'	GCal MAJR
chelidonioides	GGar MTho
corymbosa	GKev
falklandica	ECho GKev GKir NLAp SRms
fothergillii	GKev NLAp SMrm WAbe
'Goldcrest'	ECho LRHS SRms
'Hall's Spotted'	NWCA
N ***integrifolia*** ♀H3	CAbb CDTJ CPLG CSpe EBee ECtt ELan EPfP GKir MSCN SEND SGar SPer SPoG SRms WAbe WCom WHer WWlt
- bronze	MSCN
- 'Gaines' Yellow'	EBee GCal
'John Innes'	ECho
'Kentish Hero'	CSpe GCal MAJR WAbe WCom
aff. ***pavonii***	CRHN
perfoliata B&SWJ 10638	WCru
plantaginea	see *C. biflora*
§ ***polyrhiza*** Cav.	ECho NRya
rugosa	see *C. integrifolia*
'Stamford Park'	WCom
Sunset Series	EPfP SRot SWal
tenella	NSla WAbe
teucrioides F&W 11440 new	GKey
uniflora var. ***darwinii***	ECho NLAp WAbe
'Walter Shrimpton'	ECho EPot EWes WAbe WCom

Calendula (*Asteraceae*)

arvensis	CCCN
meuselii	CFee
officinalis	CArn ELau GPoy MHer MNHC SBfd SIde SPav SWvt WJek
- Fiesta Gitana Group ♀H4	CPrp WJek
- 'Touch of Red' (Touch of Red Series)	CSpe

Calibanus (*Dracaenaceae*)

hookeri	EShb

Calibrachoa (*Solanaceae*)

(Cabaret Series) Cabaret Apricot = 'Balcabapt'	LAst SVil
- Cabaret Cherry Rose = 'Balcabcher' PBR	SVil
- Cabaret Hot Pink = 'Balcabhopi' PBR	NPri
- Cabaret Light Pink = 'Balcablitpi' PBR new	LAst
- Cabaret Peach = 'Balcabpea'	LAst NPri
- Cabaret Purple = 'Balcabpurp'	LAst NPri SVil
- Cabaret Scarlet = 'Balcabscar' PBR	LAst NPri
- Cabaret White Improved = 'Balcabwitim'	NPri SVil
- Cabaret Yellow ' = 'Balcabyel	NPri SVil
- Cabaret Yellow Improved new	LAst
(Dream Kisses Series) Dream Kisses Deep Red new	SVil
- Dream Kisses Orange Sunset = 'Wescaosu' PBR new	SVil
(Million Bells Series) Million Bells Cherry = 'Sunbelchipi' PBR	LSou WGor
- Million Bells Crackling Fire = 'Sunbelfire' PBR	LAst LSou
- Million Bells Lemon = 'Sunbelkic'	WGor
- Million Bells Orange Glow = 'Sunbelore'	LSou
- Million Bells Trailing Blue = 'Sunbelkubu' PBR	LAst WGor
- Million Bells Trailing Fuchsia = 'Sunbelrkup' ♀H3	WGor
- Million Bells Trailing Ice = 'Sunbelkuriho' PBR	LAst LSou
- Million Bells Trailing Lavender Vein = 'Sunbelbura' PBR	LAst WGor
- Million Bells Trailing Pink = 'Sunbelkupi' PBR ♀H3	LSou
- Million Bells Trailing Pink Morn = 'Sunbelkupapi' PBR	LAst
(Noa Series) Noa Magenta new	WGor
- Noa Mega Pink new	WGor
- Noa Orange Eye	LSou WGor
- Noa Ultra Purple	LSou
(Superbells Series) Superbells Amarena	LAst
- Superbells Candy White = 'Uscali48' PBR	LSou
- Superbells Indigo = 'Uscali51' PBR	LAst LSou
- Superbells Magenta = 'Uscali17' PBR	LAst LSou
- Superbells Orange	LAst
- Superbells Pink = 'Uscali11' PBR ♀H3	LAst
- Superbells Royal Blue = 'Uscali4' PBR	LAst
- Superbells Strawberry Pink = 'Uscali47' PBR	LAst
- Superbells White = 'Uscali6'	LAst
- Superbells Yellow	LAst

Calibrachoa × *Petunia* see × *Petchoa*

Calicotome (*Papilionaceae*)

spinosa	CArn

Calla (*Araceae*)

aethiopica	see *Zantedeschia aethiopica*
palustris	CRow CWat EHon EPfP LPBA MCCP MSKA MWts NPer SWat WFar WMAq WPnP

Calliandra (*Mimosaceae*)

'Dixie Pink'	CCCN
haematocephala	SOWG
portoricensis	CCCN
surinamensis	CCCN
tweediei	CCCN SOWG

Callianthemum (*Ranunculaceae*)

coriandrifolium	GEdr
kernerianum	WAbe
miyabeanum new	WWst

Callicarpa (*Verbenaceae*)

americana	CPLG NLar
- var. ***lactea***	CMCN
bodinieri	GKir NBir WFar
- var. ***giraldii***	GBin GKev MGan MRav NLar WDin
- - 'Profusion' ♀H4	Widely available
cathayana	CMCN NLar
dichotoma	CBcs CPLG EBee ELan NLar WFar
- 'Issai'	IVic MBri MGos NLar SBfd SPur WPat
- 'Shirobana'	NLar
japonica	CMen CPLG NLar
- B&SWJ 8587	WCru
- f. ***albibacca***	NLar
- 'Koshima-no-homate'	MBri NLar
- 'Leucocarpa'	CBcs CMac CPLG EBee ELan EPfP MRav NLar SPer SPur WFar
- var. ***luxurians*** B&SWJ 8521	WCru
kwangtungensis	CBcs CMCN EPfP MBri NLar
mollis	CPLG NLar
shikokiana	NLar
× ***shirasawana***	NLar
yunnanensis	NLar

Callirhoe (*Malvaceae*)

bushii new	SMad
involucrata	CSpr EBee GGar MWea NWCA WHrl

Callisia (*Commelinaceae*)

repens	MBri

Callistemon ✿ (*Myrtaceae*)

acuminatus	CCCN
'Awanga Dam'	ECou
'Burgundy'	SOWG
* 'Burning Bush'	SOWG
'Candy Pink'	SOWG
chisholmii	SOWG
citrinus	CHll CTri EBee ECou EPfP ERom EShb GGar MCot MMuc MREP MSCN NHol SOWG SPlb WBrE WDin WHar
- 'Albus'	see *C. citrinus* 'White Anzac'
- 'Angela'	SOWG
- 'Canberra'	SOWG
- 'Firebrand'	CDoC LRHS SOWG
- 'Splendens' ♀H3	Widely available
§ - 'White Anzac'	CDoC CMac ELan EPfP EUJe SEND SOWG SPoG SSta
comboynensis	CCCN GBin SOWG
'Coochy Coochy Station'	SOWG
'Dawson River Weeper'	SOWG
'Eureka'	SOWG
flavescens	SOWG
flavovirens	SOWG
formosus	SOWG
glaucus	see *C. speciosus*
'Hannah's Child'	SOWG
'Happy Valley'	SOWG
'Harkness'	SOWG
'Horse Paddock'	SOWG
'Injune'	SOWG
'Kings Park Special'	SOWG
laevis hort.	see *C. rugulosus*
linearifolius	LSRN
linearis ♀H3	CBcs CMac CTrC CTri CWit ECou ECrN ELan EPfP LRHS LSRN MHer MMuc SCoo SEND SLim SLon SOWG SPlb SRms SSpi SWal SWvt WSHC
macropunctatus	SOWG SPlb
'Mauve Mist'	CCCN CDoC EBee ELan ELon EPfP GBin LRHS MAsh SOWG SPoG
pachyphyllus	ECou SOWG
- var. ***viridis***	SOWG
pallidus	CCCN CHEx CMHG CMac CWib EBee ECou ELan EPfP LRHS MAsh MHer MRav SEND SOWG SPer SPlb SPoG SSta WKif
- 'Candle Glow'	SOWG
- 'Father Christmas'	SOWG
paludosus	see *C. sieberi* DC.
pearsonii	SOWG
- prostrate	SOWG
- 'Rocky Rambler'	SOWG
'Perth Pink'	CBcs CCCN CDoC ELan EPfP IVic LRHS SLim SOWG
'Phil May'	SOWG
phoeniceus	ECou SOWG
- 'Pink Ice'	SOWG
pinifolius	CTsd SOWG SPlb
- green-flowered	SOWG
- red-flowered	SOWG
- 'Sockeye'	SOWG
'Pink Champagne'	SOWG
§ ***pityoides***	CPLG ECou SOWG
- from Brown's Swamp, Australia	ECou
polandii	SOWG
- dwarf	SOWG
'Purple Splendour'	SOWG
recurvus	SOWG
'Red Clusters'	CDoC CMac CTsd CWit EBee ELan EPfP EUJe IArd LRHS MAsh NEgg NLar NPri SBfd SChF SLim SOWG SWvt
'Reeve's Pink'	SOWG
rigidus	CBcs CChe CDoC CEnt CHEx CMHG CTri CWib EBee ELan EPfP GGar IArd IFFs LRHS LTen MBlu MGos MMuc MRav NLar SBfd SOWG SPer SWvt WDin
'Rose Opal' new	CTrC
§ ***rugulosus***	CCCN EBee EQua IDee IFFs SOWG SWvt
'Running River'	SOWG
salignus ♀H3	CBcs CCCN CDoC CDul CEnt CHEx CMac CTrC CTri EBee EPfP GLin MHer MMuc MRav NEgg NLar SEND SLim SOWG SPer WDin
- Flaming Fire = 'Flaipp'	NLar
sieberi misapplied	see *C. pityoides*
§ ***sieberi*** DC.	CDoC CMHG CTrC EBee ECou ELan EPfP GGar IVic LRHS MMuc NBir NLar NPal SLim SOWG SPlb SPoG WFar
- purple-flowered	SOWG
§ ***speciosus***	CDul CTrC EBee NLar SEND SOWG SPlb
subulatus	CDoC CHEx CTrC EBee ECou GGal MCCP NLar SAPC SArc SOWG SPlb WMoo
- 'Crimson Tail'	EBee GBin MMuc NHol NLar SBfd SEND
- 'Packer's Selection'	ECou SOWG
'Taree Pink'	SOWG
teretifolius	SOWG
viminalis	CBcs CCCN SGar SOWG SPlb
- 'Captain Cook'	CAlb CMac ECou IDee LBuc LRHS LSRN MDun MGos NLar SOWG SRms SWvt WBrE
- 'Endeavor'	CCCN

	- 'Hannah Ray'	EBee SOWG
	- 'Little John'	CAlb CSBt CTrC CWSG EBee LRHS LSRN NLar SBfd SOWG SPad SWvt WBrE
	- 'Malawi Giant'	SOWG
	- 'Wilderness White'	SOWG
	'Violaceus'	IRar
	viridiflorus	CTrC ECou GGal GQui LRHS MCCP SEND SOWG SPlb SWal WGwG
	- 'County Park Dwarf'	ECou
	- 'Sunshine'	ECou
	'White Anzac'	see *C. citrinus* 'White Anzac'
	'Wildfire'	CTrC

Callitriche (*Callitrichaceae*)

§	***palustris***	EHon MSKA MWts
	stagnalis	NSco
	verna	see *C. palustris*

Callitris (*Cupressaceae*)

	oblonga dwarf **new**	CStu
	rhomboidea	CTrC

Calluna ✿ (*Ericaceae*)

	vulgaris	EBWF
	- 'Aberdeen'	SHeS
	- 'Adrie'	SHeS
	- 'Alba Argentea'	SHeS
	- 'Alba Aurea'	SHeS
	- 'Alba Carlton'	SHeS
	- 'Alba Dumosa'	SHeS
	- 'Alba Elata'	SHeS
	- 'Alba Elegans'	SHeS
	- 'Alba Elongata'	see *C. vulgaris* 'Mair's Variety'
	- 'Alba Erecta'	SHeS
	- 'Alba Jae'	SHeS
	- 'Alba Minor'	SHeS
	- 'Alba Multiflora'	SHeS
	- 'Alba Pilosa'	SHeS
§	- 'Alba Plena' (d)	SHeS
	- 'Alba Praecox'	SHeS
	- 'Alba Pumila'	SHeS
§	- 'Alba Rigida'	SHeS SRms
	- 'Alec Martin' (d)	SHeS
	- 'Alex Warwick'	SHeS
	- 'Alexandra'^{PBR} (Garden Girls Series) 🏆^{H4}	NHol SHeS SPoG SRms
	- 'Alice Knight'	SHeS
	- 'Alicia'^{PBR} (Garden Girls Series) 🏆^{H4}	CBcs NHol SHeS SPoG SWhi
	- 'Alieke'	SHeS
	- 'Alina'	SHeS
	- 'Alison Yates'	SHeS
	- 'Allegretto'	SHeS
	- 'Allegro' 🏆^{H4}	EPfP MMuc SHeS SPer SRms SWhi
	- 'Alportii'	GKir SHeS
	- 'Alportii Praecox'	SHeS
	- 'Alys Sutcliffe'	SHeS
	- 'Amanda Wain'	SHeS
	- 'Amethyst'^{PBR} (Garden Girls Series)	IVic MMuc NHol SHeS SPoG SWhi
	- 'Amilto'	CBcs SHeS SRms
	- 'Andrew Proudley'	SHeS
	- 'Anette'^{PBR} (Garden Girls Series) 🏆^{H4}	SHeS SWhi
	- 'Angela Wain'	SHeS
	- 'Anna'	SHeS
	- 'Annabel' (d)	SHeS
	- 'Anne Dobbin'	SHeS
	- 'Annegret'	see *C. vulgaris* 'Marlies'
	- 'Anneke'	SHeS
	- 'Annemarie' (d) 🏆^{H4}	CSBt EPfP NHol SCoo SHeS SPer SPlb SRms SWhi
	- 'Anne's Zwerg'	SHeS SRms
	- 'Anthony Davis' 🏆^{H4}	NHol SHeS
	- 'Anthony Wain'	SHeS
	- 'Anton'	SHeS
	- 'Antrujo Gold'	SHeS
	- 'Aphrodite'^{PBR} (Garden Girls Series)	CBcs SHeS SWhi
	- 'Apollo'	SHeS
	- 'Applecross' (d)	SHeS
	- 'Arabella'^{PBR}	SHeS SRms
	- 'Argentea'	SHeS
	- 'Ariadne'	SHeS
	- 'Arina'	SHeS
	- 'Arran Gold'	SHeS
	- 'Ashgarth Amber'	SHeS
	- 'Ashgarth Amethyst'	SHeS
	- 'Ashgarth Shell Pink'	SHeS
	- 'Asterix'	SHeS
	- 'Atalanta'	SHeS
	- 'Atholl Gold'	SHeS
	- 'August Beauty'	SHeS
	- 'Aurea'	SHeS
	- 'Aurora'	SHeS
I	- 'Autumn Glow'	SHeS
	- 'Babette'	SHeS
	- 'Baby Ben'	SHeS
	- 'Baby Wicklow'	SHeS
	- 'Barbara'	SHeS
	- 'Barbara Fleur'	SHeS
	- 'Barja'	SHeS
	- 'Barnett Anley'	SHeS
	- 'Battle of Arnhem'	SHeS
	- 'Bayport'	SHeS
	- 'Beechwood Crimson'	SHeS
I	- 'Bella Rosa'	SHeS
	- 'Ben Nevis'	SHeS
	- 'Bennachie Bronze'	SHeS
	- 'Bennachie Prostrate'	SHeS
	- 'Beoley Crimson'	SHeS
	- 'Beoley Crimson Variegated' (v)	SHeS
	- 'Beoley Gold' 🏆^{H4}	CSBt CTri EPfP GKir MGos NHol SHeS SRms SWhi
	- 'Beoley Silver'	SHeS SWhi
	- 'Bernadette'	SHeS
	- 'Betty Baum'	SHeS
	- 'Bispingen'	SHeS
	- 'Blazeaway'	CTri EPfP GKir NHol SHeS SPer SRms SWhi
	- 'Blueness'	SHeS
	- 'Bognie'	SHeS
	- 'Bonfire Brilliance'	CSBt IVic NHol SHeS
	- 'Bonita'^{PBR} (Garden Girls Series)	IVic SHeS SWhi
	- 'Bonne's Darkness'	SHeS
	- 'Bonsaï'	SHeS
	- 'Boreray'	SHeS
	- 'Boskoop'	NHol SHeS SWhi
	- 'Bradford'	SHeS
	- 'Braemar'	SHeS
	- 'Braeriach'	SHeS
	- 'Branchy Anne'	SHeS
	- 'Bray Head'	SHeS
	- 'Brita Elisabeth' (d)	SHeS
	- 'Bronze Beauty'	SHeS
	- 'Bud Lyle'	SHeS
	- 'Bunsall'	SHeS
	- 'Buxton Snowdrift'	SHeS
	- 'C.W. Nix'	CSBt SHeS
	- 'Caerketton White'	SHeS

	- 'Caleb Threlkeld'	SHeS
	- 'Calf of Man'	SHeS
	- 'Californian Midge'	NHol SHeS
	- 'Camla Variety'	SHeS
	- 'Carl Röders' (d)	SHeS
	- 'Carmen'	SHeS
	- 'Carngold'	SHeS
	- 'Carole Chapman'	SHeS
	- 'Carolyn'	SHeS
	- 'Cassa'	SHeS
	- 'Catherine'	SHeS
	- 'Catherine Anne'	SHeS
	- 'Celtic Gold'	SHeS
	- 'Charles Chapman'	SHeS
§	- 'Chernobyl' (d)	NHol SHeS
	- 'Chindit'	SHeS
I	- 'Christin'	SHeS
	- 'Christina'	SHeS
	- 'Cilcennin Common'	SHeS
	- 'Clare Carpet'	SHeS
	- 'Coby'	SHeS
	- 'Coccinea'	SHeS
	- 'Colette'	SHeS
	- 'Con Brio'	MMuc SHeS SRms SWhi
	- 'Copper Glow'	SHeS
	- 'Coral Island'	SHeS
	- 'Corbett's Red'	SHeS
	- 'Corrie's White'	SHeS
	- 'Cottswood Gold'	NHol SHeS SRms
	- 'County Wicklow' (d) ♀H4	CBcs CTri EPfP GGar GKir MMuc NHol SHeS SPer SRms SWhi
	- 'Craig Rossie'	SHeS
	- 'Crail Orange'	SHeS
	- 'Cramond' (d)	SHeS
	- 'Cream Steving'	SHeS
	- 'Crimson Glory'	SHeS
	- 'Crimson Sunset'	SHeS
	- 'Crinkly Tuft'	SHeS
	- 'Crowborough Beacon'	SHeS
	- 'Cuprea'	EPfP NHol SHeS SWhi
	- 'Dainty Bess'	MSwo SHeS
	- 'Dapiali'	SHeS
	- 'Dark Alicia'	SHeS
	- 'Dark Beauty' PBR (d) ♀H4	CBcs EPfP IVic MMuc NHol SHeS SWhi
	- 'Dark Star' (d) ♀H4	CBcs EPfP MGos MMuc NHol SCoo SHeS SRms SWhi
	- 'Darkness' ♀H4	CTri EPfP NHol SCoo SHeS SRms SWhi
	- 'Darleyensis'	SHeS
	- 'Dart's Amethyst'	SHeS
	- 'Dart's Beauty'	SHeS
	- 'Dart's Brilliant'	SHeS
	- 'Dart's Flamboyant'	SHeS
	- 'Dart's Gold'	NHol SHeS
	- 'Dart's Hedgehog'	SHeS
	- 'Dart's Parakeet'	SHeS
	- 'Dart's Parrot'	SHeS
	- 'Dart's Silver Rocket'	SHeS
	- 'Dart's Squirrel'	SHeS
	- 'David Eason'	SHeS
	- 'David Hagenaars'	SHeS
	- 'David Hutton'	SHeS
	- 'David Platt' (d)	SHeS
	- 'Denkewitz'	SHeS
	- 'Denny Pratt'	SHeS
	- 'Desiree'	SHeS
	- 'Devon' (d)	SHeS
	- 'Diana'	SHeS
	- 'Dickson's Blazes'	SHeS
	- 'Dirry'	NHol SHeS
	- 'Doctor Murray's White'	see *C. vulgaris* 'Mullardoch'

	- 'Doris Rushworth'	SHeS
	- 'Drum-ra'	SHeS SRms
	- 'Dunnet Lime'	SHeS SPlb
	- 'Dunnydeer'	SHeS
	- 'Dunwood'	SHeS
§	- 'Durford Wood'	SHeS
	- 'Dwingeloo Delight'	SHeS
	- 'E.F. Brown'	SHeS
	- 'E. Hoare'	SHeS
	- 'Easter-bonfire'	NHol SHeS SWhi
	- 'Eckart Miessner'	SHeS
	- 'Edith Godbolt'	SHeS
	- 'Elaine'	SHeS
	- 'Elegant Pearl'	SHeS
	- 'Elegantissima'	MMuc SHeS
	- 'Eleonore' (d)	SHeS
	- 'Elkstone White'	SHeS
	- 'Ellen'	SHeS
	- 'Ellie Barbour'	SHeS
	- 'Elly'	SHeS
	- 'Else Frye' (d)	SHeS
	- 'Elsie Purnell' (d) ♀H4	EPfP MGos NHol SHeS SPlb SRms
	- 'Emerald Jock'	SHeS
	- 'Emma Louise Tuke'	SHeS
	- 'Eric Easton'	SHeS
	- 'Eskdale Gold'	SHeS
	- 'Eurosa'	SHeS
	- 'Fairy'	SHeS
	- 'Falling Star'	SHeS
	- 'Feuerwerk'	SHeS
§	- 'Finale'	SHeS
	- 'Findling'	SHeS
	- 'Fire King'	SHeS
	- 'Fire Star'	SHeS
	- 'Firebreak'	NHol SHeS
	- 'Firefly' ♀H4	CBcs CSBt EPfP MMuc NHol SHeS SRms SWhi
	- 'Flamingo'	CSBt MMuc MSwo NHol SHeS SPer SRms SWhi
	- 'Flatling'	SHeS
	- 'Flore Pleno' (d)	SHeS
	- 'Floriferous'	SHeS
	- 'Florrie Spicer'	SHeS
	- 'Fokko' (d)	SHeS
	- 'Fort Bragg'	SHeS
	- 'Fortyniner Gold'	SHeS
	- 'Foxhollow Wanderer'	SHeS
	- 'Foxii'	SHeS
	- 'Foxii Floribunda'	SHeS
	- 'Foxii Lett's Form'	see *C. vulgaris* 'Velvet Dome', 'Mousehole'
	- 'Foxii Nana'	NHol SHeS SRms SWhi
	- 'Foya'	SHeS
	- 'Fraser's Old Gold'	SHeS
	- 'Fred J. Chapple'	SHeS SWhi
	- 'Fréjus'	SHeS
	- 'French Grey'	SHeS
	- 'Fritz Kircher' PBR	SHeS
	- 'Gaia'	SHeS
	- Garden Girls Series	MMuc
	- 'Gerda'	SHeS
	- 'Ginkel's Glorie'	SHeS
	- 'Glasa'	SHeS
	- 'Glen Mashie'	SHeS
	- 'Glencoe' (d)	SHeS
	- 'Glendoick Silver'	SHeS
	- 'Glenfiddich'	CSBt NHol SHeS
	- 'Glenlivet'	SHeS
	- 'Glenmorangie'	SHeS
	- 'Gloucester Boy'	SHeS
	- 'Gnome'	SHeS
	- 'Gold Charm'	SHeS

	- 'Gold Finch'	SHeS
	- 'Gold Flame'	SHeS
	- Gold Hamilton	see *C. vulgaris* 'Chernobyl'
	- 'Gold Haze' $\mathbb{Y}^{H4}$	CTri GKir NHol SCoo SHeS SPer SRms SWhi
	- 'Gold Knight'	EPfP SHeS
	- 'Gold Kup'	SHeS
	- 'Gold Mist'	SHeS
	- 'Gold Spronk'	SHeS
	- 'Goldcarmen'	SHeS
	- 'Golden Blazeaway'	SHeS
	- 'Golden Carpet'	CSBt MGos NHol SHeS SPer SRms
	- 'Golden Dew'	SHeS
	- 'Golden Dream' (d)	SHeS
	- 'Golden Feather'	SHeS
	- 'Golden Fleece'	SHeS SRms
	- 'Golden Max'	SHeS
	- 'Golden Rivulet'	MSwo SHeS
	- 'Golden Turret'	NHol SHeS
	- 'Golden Wonder' (d)	SHeS
	- 'Goldsworth Crimson'	CSBt SHeS
	- 'Goldsworth Crimson Variegated' (v)	SHeS
	- 'Goscote Wine'	SHeS
	- 'Grasmeriensis'	SHeS
	- 'Green Cardinal'	SHeS
	- 'Grey Carpet'	SHeS SRms
	- 'Grijsje'	SHeS
	- 'Grizabella'	SHeS
	- 'Grizzly'	SHeS
	- 'Grönsinka'	SHeS
	- 'Guinea Gold'	SHeS
§	- 'H.E. Beale' (d)	CTri EPfP MGos NHol SHeS
	- 'Hamlet Green'	SHeS
	- 'Hammondii'	SHeS
	- 'Hammondii Aureifolia'	SHeS SPlb SWhi
	- 'Hammondii Rubrifolia'	SHeS SRms SWhi
	- 'Harlekin'	SHeS
	- 'Harry Gibbon' (d)	SHeS
	- 'Harten's Findling'	SHeS
	- 'Hatje's Herbstfeuer' (d)	SHeS
	- 'Hayesensis'	SHeS
	- 'Heidberg'	SHeS
	- 'Heidepracht'	SHeS
	- 'Heidesinfonie'	SHeS
	- 'Heideteppich'	SHeS
	- 'Heidezwerg'	SHeS
	- 'Heike' (d)	SHeS
	- 'Herbert Mitchell'	SHeS
	- 'Hester'	SHeS
	- 'Hetty'	SHeS
	- 'Hibernica'	SHeS
	- 'Hiemalis'	SHeS
	- 'Hiemalis Southcote'	see *C. vulgaris* 'Durford Wood'
	- Highland Cream	see *C. vulgaris* 'Punch's Dessert'
	- 'Highland Rose'	SHeS SPlb SRms
	- 'Highland Spring'	SHeS
	- 'Hilda Turberfield'	SHeS
	- 'Hillbrook Limelight'	SHeS
	- 'Hillbrook Orange'	SHeS
	- 'Hillbrook Sparkler'	SHeS
	- 'Hinton White'	SHeS
	- 'Hirsuta Albiflora'	SHeS
	- 'Hirsuta Typica'	SHeS
	- 'Hollandia'	SHeS
	- 'Holstein'	SHeS
	- 'Hookstone'	SHeS
	- 'Hoyerhagen'	SHeS
§	- 'Hugh Nicholson'	SHeS
	- 'Humpty Dumpty'	NHol SHeS
	- 'Hypnoides'	SHeS
	- 'Ide's Double' (d)	SHeS
	- 'Inchcolm'	SHeS
	- 'Inchkeith'	SHeS
	- 'Ineke'	SHeS
	- 'Inge'	SHeS
	- 'Ingrid Bouter' (d)	SHeS
	- 'Inshriach Bronze'	SHeS
	- 'Iris van Leyen'	SHeS
	- 'Islay Mist'	SHeS
	- 'Isle of Hirta'	SHeS
	- 'Isobel Frye'	SHeS
	- 'Isobel Hughes' (d)	SHeS
	- 'J.H. Hamilton' (d) $\mathbb{Y}^{H4}$	CTri GKir NHol SHeS SRms SWhi
	- 'Jan'	SHeS
	- 'Jan Dekker'	NHol SHeS SWhi
	- 'Janice Chapman'	SHeS
	- 'Japanese White'	SHeS
	- 'Jenny'	SHeS
	- 'Jill'	SHeS
	- 'Jimmy Dyce' (d)	SHeS
	- 'Joan Sparkes' (d)	SHeS
	- 'Jochen'	SHeS
	- 'Johan Slegers'	SHeS
	- John Denver	see *C. vulgaris* 'Marleen Select'
	- 'John F. Letts'	NHol SHeS SRms
	- 'Johnson's Variety'	SHeS
	- 'Jos' Lemon'	SHeS
	- 'Jos' Whitie'	SHeS
	- 'Josefine'	SHeS
	- 'Joseph's Coat'	SHeS
	- 'Joy Vanstone' $\mathbb{Y}^{H4}$	EPfP GKir MGos NHol SHeS SRms
	- 'Julia'	SHeS
	- 'Julie Ann Platt'	SHeS
	- 'Juno'	SHeS
	- 'Kaiser'	SHeS
	- 'Karin Blum'	SHeS
	- 'Kermit'	SHeS
	- 'Kerstin' $\mathbb{Y}^{H4}$	MMuc MSwo NHol SHeS SPlb SRms SWhi
	- 'Kerstin Jacke'	NHol
	- 'Kinlochruel' (d) $\mathbb{Y}^{H4}$	CBcs CSBt CTri EPfP GGar GKir IVic MGos MMuc NHol SHeS SPlb SRms SWhi
	- 'Kir Royal'	SHeS
	- 'Kirby White'	NHol SHeS SPlb SWhi
	- 'Kirsty Anderson'	SHeS
	- 'Kit Hill'	SHeS
	- 'Klaudine' PBR **new**	IVic
	- 'Knaphill'	SHeS
I	- 'Kontrast'	SHeS
	- 'Kuphaldtii'	SHeS
	- 'Kuppendorf'	SHeS
	- 'Kynance'	SHeS
	- 'Lady Maithe'	SHeS
	- 'Lambstails'	SHeS
	- 'L'Ancresse'	SHeS
	- 'Larissa' PBR (Garden Girls Series)	SHeS
	- 'Lemon Gem'	SHeS
	- 'Lemon Queen'	SHeS
	- 'Leprechaun'	NHol SWhi
	- 'Leslie Slinger'	NHol SHeS SWhi
	- 'Lewis Lilac'	SHeS
	- 'Liebestraum'	SHeS
	- 'Lilac Elegance'	SHeS
	- 'Lime Glade'	SHeS
	- 'Lime Gold'	SHeS
	- 'Little John'	LSRN SHeS
	- 'Llanbedrog Pride' (d)	SHeS
	- 'Loch Turret'	SHeS
	- 'Loch-na-Seil'	SHeS
	- 'Long White'	SHeS SWhi
	- 'Loni'	SHeS

	- 'Lüneberg Heath'	SHeS
	- 'Lyle's Late White'	SHeS
	- 'Lyle's Surprise'	SHeS
	- 'Lyndon Proudley'	SHeS
	- 'Macdonald of Glencoe'	SHeS
§	- 'Mair's Variety' ♀H4	SHeS
	- 'Mallard'	SHeS
	- 'Manitoba'	SHeS
	- 'Manuel'	SHeS
	- 'Marianne'	SHeS
	- 'Marie'	SHeS
	- 'Marion Blum'	SHeS
	- 'Marleen'	NHol SHeS
§	- 'Marleen Select'	SHeS
§	- 'Marlies'	SHeS
	- 'Martha Hermann'	SHeS
	- 'Martine Langenberg'	SHeS
	- 'Masquerade'	SHeS
	- 'Matita'	SHeS
	- 'Mauvelyn'	SHeS
	- 'Mazurka'	SHeS
	- 'Melanie' (Garden Girls Series)	MSwo NHol SHeS
	- 'Mick Jamieson' (d)	SHeS
	- 'Mies'	SHeS
	- 'Minima'	SHeS
	- 'Minima Smith's Variety'	SHeS
	- 'Miniöxabäck'	SHeS
	- 'Minty'	SHeS
	- 'Mirato'	IVic SHeS
	- 'Mirelle'	SHeS
	- 'Miss Muffet'	NHol SHeS
	- 'Molecule'	SHeS
	- 'Monika' (d)	SHeS
	- 'Moon Glow'	SHeS
	- 'Mountain Snow'	SHeS
§	- 'Mousehole'	NHol SHeS
	- 'Mrs Alf'	SHeS
	- 'Mrs E. Wilson' (d)	SHeS
	- 'Mrs Pat'	NHol SHeS
	- 'Mrs Pinxteren'	SHeS
	- 'Mrs Ronald Gray'	SHeS
	- 'Mullach Mor'	SHeS
§	- 'Mullardoch'	SHeS
	- 'Mullion' ♀H4	SHeS
	- 'Multicolor'	NHol SHeS SRms
	- 'Murielle Dobson'	SHeS
§	- 'My Dream' (d) ♀H4	CSBt EPfP NHol SCoo SHeS
	- 'Nana'	SHeS
	- 'Nana Compacta'	SHeS
	- 'Natasja'	SHeS
	- 'Naturpark'	SHeS
	- 'Nele' (d)	SHeS
	- 'Nico'	SHeS
	- 'Nofretete'	SHeS
	- Nordlicht	see *C. vulgaris* 'Skone'
	- 'October White'	SHeS
	- 'Odette'	SHeS
	- 'Oiseval'	SHeS
	- 'Old Rose'	SHeS
	- 'Olive Turner'	SHeS
	- 'Olympic Gold'	SHeS
	- 'Orange and Gold'	SHeS
	- 'Orange Carpet'	SHeS
	- 'Orange Max'	NHol SHeS
	- 'Orange Queen'	CSBt SHeS
	- 'Öxabäck'	SHeS
	- 'Oxshott Common'	SHeS
	- 'Pallida'	SHeS
	- 'Parsons' Gold'	SHeS
	- 'Parsons' Grey Selected'	SHeS
	- 'Pastell' (d)	SHeS
	- 'Pat's Gold'	SHeS
	- 'Peace'	SHeS
	- 'Pearl Drop'	SHeS
	- 'Peggy'	SHeS
	- 'Penhale'	SHeS
	- 'Penny Bun'	SHeS
	- 'Pennyacre Gold'	SHeS
	- 'Pennyacre Lemon'	SHeS
	- 'Pepper and Salt'	see *C. vulgaris* 'Hugh Nicholson'
	- 'Perestrojka'	SHeS
	- 'Peter Sparkes' (d) ♀H4	CBcs CSBt EPfP MGos MMuc NHol SHeS SRms SWhi
	- 'Petra'	SHeS
	- 'Pewter Plate'	SHeS
	- 'Pink Alicia' PBR (Garden Girls Series)	SHeS
	- 'Pink Beale'	see *C. vulgaris* 'H.E. Beale'
	- 'Pink Dream' (d)	SHeS
	- 'Pink Gown'	SHeS
	- 'Pink Spreader'	SHeS
	- 'Pink Tips'	SHeS
	- 'Plantarium'	SHeS
	- 'Platt's Surprise' (d)	SHeS
	- 'Polly'	SHeS
	- 'Poolster'	SHeS
	- 'Porth Wen White'	SHeS
	- 'Prizewinner'	SHeS
*	- 'Procumbens'	SHeS
	- 'Prostrata Flagelliformis'	SHeS
	- 'Prostrate Orange'	SHeS
§	- 'Punch's Dessert'	SHeS
	- 'Purple Passion'	EPfP
	- 'Pygmaea'	SHeS
	- 'Pyramidalis'	SHeS
	- 'Pyrenaica'	SHeS
	- 'R.A. McEwan'	SHeS
	- 'Radnor' (d) ♀H4	CSBt SHeS
	- 'Radnor Gold' (d)	SHeS
	- 'Raket'	SHeS
	- 'Ralph Purnell'	SHeS
	- 'Ralph Purnell Select'	SHeS
	- 'Ralph's Pearl'	SHeS
	- 'Ralph's Red'	SHeS
	- 'Randall's Crimson'	SHeS
	- 'Rannoch'	SHeS
	- 'Rebecca's Red'	SHeS SRms
	- 'Red Carpet'	SHeS
	- 'Red Favorit' (d)	CBcs IVic SHeS SRms
	- 'Red Fred'	NHol SHeS
	- 'Red Haze'	EPfP NHol SHeS
	- 'Red Max'	SHeS
	- 'Red Pimpernel'	EPfP NHol SHeS SWhi
	- 'Red Rug'	SHeS
	- 'Red Star' (d)	NHol SHeS
	- 'Red Wings'	SHeS
	- 'Redbud'	SHeS
	- 'Redgauntlet'	SHeS
	- 'Reini'	SHeS SWhi
	- 'Rica'	SHeS
	- 'Richard Cooper'	SHeS
	- 'Rieanne'	SHeS
	- 'Rigida Prostrata'	see *C. vulgaris* 'Alba Rigida'
	- 'Rivington'	SHeS
	- 'Robber Knight'	SHeS
	- 'Robert Chapman' ♀H4	CSBt CTri GKir NHol SHeS SRms SWhi
I	- 'Rock Spray'	SHeS
	- 'Röding'	SHeS
	- 'Rokoko'	SHeS
	- 'Roland Haagen' ♀H4	SHeS
	- 'Roma'	SHeS
	- 'Romina'	MSwo NHol SHeS

- 'Ronas Hill' SHeS
- 'Roodkapje' SHeS
- 'Rosalind' ambig. EPfP
- 'Rosalind, Crastock Heath' SHeS
- 'Rosalind, Underwood's' EPfP NHol SHeS
- 'Rosita' **new** IVic
- 'Ross Hutton' SHeS
- 'Roswitha' SHeS
- 'Roter Oktober' IVic SHeS
- 'Rotfuchs' SHeS
- 'Ruby Slinger' NHol SHeS SWhi
- 'Rusty Triumph' SHeS
- 'Ruth Sparkes' (d) NHol SHeS
- 'Sabrina' (d) SHeS
- 'Saima' SHeS
- 'Saint Nick' SHeS
- 'Salland' SHeS
- 'Sally Anne Proudley' SHeS
- 'Salmon Leap' NHol SHeS
- 'Sam Hewitt' SHeS
- 'Sampford Sunset' SHeS
- 'Sandhammaren' SHeS
- 'Sandwood Bay' SHeS
- 'Sandy'^{PBR} (Garden Girls Series) NHol SHeS SPoG SWhi
- 'Sarah Platt' (d) SHeS
- 'Saskia' SHeS
- 'Schneewolke' SHeS
- 'Scholje's Jimmy' SHeS
- 'Scholje's Rubin' (d) SHeS
- 'Scholje's Super Star' (d) SHeS
- 'Schurig's Sensation' (d) IVic SHeS
- 'Schurig's Wonder' (d) SHeS
- 'Scotch Mist' SHeS
- 'Sedloňov' SHeS
- 'Sellingsloh' SHeS
- 'September Pink' SHeS
- 'Serlei' SHeS
- 'Serlei Aurea' ♀^{H4} CSBt EPfP NHol SHeS SRms
- 'Serlei Grandiflora' SHeS
- 'Serlei Purpurea' SHeS
- 'Serlei Rubra' SHeS
- 'Sesam' SHeS
- 'Sesse' SHeS
- 'Shirley' SHeS
- 'Silberspargel' SHeS
- 'Silver Cloud' SHeS
- 'Silver Fox' SHeS
- 'Silver King' SHeS
- 'Silver Knight' CSBt EPfP GGar MGos NHol SHeS SPer SPlb SRms SWhi
- 'Silver Pearl' SHeS
- 'Silver Queen' ♀^{H4} NHol SHeS SRms SWhi
- 'Silver Rose' ♀^{H4} SHeS
- 'Silver Sandra' SHeS
- 'Silver Spire' SHeS
- 'Silver Stream' SHeS
- 'Silvie' SHeS
- 'Simone' SHeS
- 'Sir Anthony Hopkins' SHeS
- 'Sir John Charrington' ♀^{H4} CSBt EPfP MGos NHol SHeS SWhi
- 'Sirsson' SHeS
- 'Sister Anne' ♀^{H4} CSBt EPfP MMuc NHol SHeS SRms SWhi
- 'Skipper' NHol SHeS

§ - 'Skone' (v) SHeS
- 'Snowball' see *C. vulgaris* 'My Dream'
- 'Snowflake' SHeS
- 'Soay' SHeS
- 'Sonja' (d) SHeS
- 'Sonning' (d) SHeS
- 'Sonny Boy' SHeS
- 'Sophia' (d) SHeS
- 'Sparkling Stars' NHol SHeS
- 'Sphinx' SHeS
- 'Spicata' SHeS
- 'Spicata Aurea' SHeS
- 'Spicata Nana' SHeS
- 'Spider' SHeS
- 'Spitfire' NHol SHeS
- 'Spook' SHeS
- 'Spring Cream' ♀^{H4} GKir MMuc NHol SHeS SPoG SWhi
- 'Spring Glow' SHeS
- 'Spring Torch' CSBt GKir NHol SCoo SHeS SPer SPoG SRms SWhi
- 'Springbank' SHeS
- 'Stag's Horn' SHeS

I - 'Startler' SHeS
- 'Stefanie' NHol SHeS SRms
- 'Stranger' SHeS
- 'Strawberry Delight' (d) EPfP SHeS
- 'Summer Elegance' SHeS
- 'Summer Gold' SRms
- 'Summer Orange' NHol SHeS
- 'Summer White' (d) SHeS
- 'Sunningdale' see *C. vulgaris* 'Finale'
- 'Sunrise' CSBt EPfP SHeS
- 'Sunset' ♀^{H4} CSBt SHeS SRms SWhi
- 'Sunset Glow' SHeS
- 'Talisker' SHeS
- 'Tenella' SHeS
- 'Tenuis' SHeS
- 'Terrick's Orange' SHeS
- 'The Pygmy' SHeS
- 'Theresa' (Garden Girls Series) SHeS
- 'Tib' (d) ♀^{H4} CSBt NHol SHeS SRms SWhi
- 'Tijdens Copper' SHeS
- 'Tino' SHeS
- 'Tom Thumb' SHeS
- 'Tomentosa Alba' SHeS
- 'Torogay' SHeS
- 'Torulosa' SHeS
- 'Tremans' SHeS
- 'Tricolorifolia' EPfP NHol SHeS SPer SWhi
- 'Underwoodii' SHeS
- 'Unity' SHeS
- 'Valorian' SHeS
- 'Van Beek' SHeS

§ - 'Velvet Dome' SHeS
- 'Velvet Fascination' ♀^{H4} EPfP NHol SHeS SWhi
- 'Violet Bamford' SHeS
- 'Visser's Fancy' SHeS
- 'Walter Ingwersen' SHeS
- 'Waquoit Brightness' SHeS
- 'Westerlee Gold' SHeS
- 'Westerlee Green' SHeS
- 'Westphalia' SHeS
- 'White Bouquet' see *C. vulgaris* 'Alba Plena'
- 'White Carpet' SHeS
- 'White Coral' (d) EPfP SHeS
- 'White Gold' SHeS
- 'White Gown' SHeS
- 'White Lawn' ♀^{H4} MMuc MSwo NHol SHeS SRms SWhi
- 'White Mite' SHeS
- 'White Pearl' (d) SHeS
- 'White Princess' see *C. vulgaris* 'White Queen'

§ - 'White Queen' SHeS
- 'White Star' (d) SHeS
- 'Whiteness' SHeS
- 'Wickwar Flame' ♀^{H4} CBcs CSBt EPfP MGos MMuc NHol SHeS SPer SPlb SRms SWhi
- 'Wilma' SHeS

	- 'Wingates Gem'	SHeS
	- 'Wingates Gold'	SHeS
	- 'Winter Chocolate'	CSBt EPfP MSwo NHol SHeS SPer SWhi
	- 'Winter Fire'	SHeS
	- 'Winter Red'	SHeS
	- 'Wollmer's Weisse' (d)	SHeS
	- 'Wood Close'	SHeS
	- 'Yellow Basket'	SHeS
	- 'Yellow Beauty' PBR	SHeS
	- 'Yellow Globe'	SHeS
	- 'Yellow One'	SHeS
	- 'Yvette's Gold'	SHeS
	- 'Yvette's Silver'	SHeS
	- 'Yvonne Clare'	SHeS

Calocedrus (*Cupressaceae*)

§	***decurrens*** ♀H4	CBcs CDoC CDul CLnd CMac CTho CTri EHul EPfP EWTr GKir IFFs LRHS MBlu MGos MMuc NPCo NWea SBfd SLim SPer SPoG WEve WFar
	- 'Aureovariegata' (v)	CBcs CWib EHul EPla LRHS MBlu MBri MWya NLar SCoo SLim SPoG WEve WFar
	- 'Berrima Gold'	CDoC CKen EPfP GKir LRHS MGos NLar SLim SPoG WEve
	- 'Columnaris'	LMaj
§	- 'Depressa'	CKen
	- 'Intricata'	CKen NLar SLim
	- 'Maupin Glow' (v)	NLar SLim
	- 'Nana'	see *C. decurrens* 'Depressa'
	- 'Pillar'	CKen MBri NLar
	formosana	WFar
	macrolepis	NMun

Calocephalus (*Asteraceae*)

	brownii	see *Leucophyta brownii*
	'Silver Sand'	EPPr LSou

Calochortus (*Liliaceae*)

	'Cupido' PBR	ECho ITim LAma
	invenustus	ECho
	luteus Douglas ex Lindl.	EPot
	- 'Golden Orb' PBR	CGrW ECho LAma SDeJ
	splendens	LAma
	- 'Violet Queen'	CGrW EBrs ECho LAma
	superbus	EBrs ECho EPot SDeJ
	'Symphony' PBR	ECho EPot LAma
	venustus	CGrW ECho EPot LAma SDeJ

Calomeria (*Asteraceae*)

§	***amaranthoides***	WJek

Calonyction see *Ipomoea*

Calopogon (*Orchidaceae*)

	tuberosus	NLAp

Calopsis (*Restionaceae*)

	paniculata	CCCN CDTJ CHEx CTrC CTsd IArd WPGP

Caloscordum (*Alliaceae*)

§	***neriniflorum***	EBur WAbe

Calothamnus (*Myrtaceae*)

	blepharospermus	SOWG
	gilesii	SOWG
	homolophyllus	SOWG
	quadrifidus	ECou EUJe SOWG
	- yellow-flowered	SOWG
	rupestris	SOWG
	sanguineus	SOWG
	validus	SOWG SPlb

Caltha ✿ (*Ranunculaceae*)

	appendiculata	EPot WAbe
	howellii	see *C. leptosepala* subsp. *howellii*
	introloba	SWat
	laeta	see *C. palustris* var. *palustris*
	leptosepala	CLAP CRow EBee EPot EWTr GKev LLHF NLar
§	- subsp. ***howellii***	EBee GKev
	- - NNS 02-92	GKev
	palustris ♀H4	Widely available
	- var. ***alba***	Widely available
	- 'Auenwald'	CLAP CRow
	- var. ***barthei***	CFir GEdr
	- - f. ***atrorubra***	GEdr
	- 'Flore Pleno' (d) ♀H4	Widely available
	- 'Honeydew'	CDes CLAP CRow LRHS WPGP WSHC
	- 'Marilyn'	CLAP
	- 'Multiplex' (d)	EBee SRot
	- Newlake hybrid	LLWG
§	- var. ***palustris***	CBen CBre CRow ECha EHon ELan GGar LPBA SWat WCra WFar
	- - 'Plena' (d)	CRow CWat EPfP EUJe GGar LRHS MCot MSKA NBPC WFar
	- var. ***radicans***	CRow
	- - 'Flore Pleno' (d)	CRow
	- 'Stagnalis'	CRow MSKA MWts
	- 'Tyermannii'	CRow
N	***polypetala*** misapplied	see *C. palustris* var. *palustris*
N	***polypetala*** Hochst. ex Lorent	CFir CWat EBee EWll GCal GKir MSCN MSKA NPer SMad SWat WBor WMAq
	- from Turkey	SGSe
	sagittata	WSHC
	scaposa	GKev

Calycanthus (*Calycanthaceae*)

	fertilis	see *C. floridus* var. *glaucus*
	floridus	CAgr CArn CBcs CDul CMCN CPMA CTri CWib EBee ELan EPfP EWTr IDee LAst LEdu LRHS MAsh MBNS MBlu MBri MMuc NBea SDnm SPer SPlb SPoG SSpi WCFE WDin
	- 'Athens'	CBcs CPMA NLar
§	- var. ***glaucus***	EPfP LRHS MGos NLar WSHC
	- - 'Purpureus'	CBcs CPMA MBlu MBri NLar
	- var. ***laevigatus***	see *C. floridus* var. *glaucus*
	- 'Michael Lindsay'	CPMA MBri NLar
	occidentalis	CAgr CArn CBcs CDul CMCN CWib CWit EPPr MBlu MMuc SGar SSpi WBVN WCFE

Calystegia (*Convolvulaceae*)

	'Angel's Trumpets' **new**	SKHP
§	***hederacea*** 'Flore Pleno' (d)	ELan SMad
	japonica 'Flore Pleno'	see *C. hederacea* 'Flore Pleno'
	silvatica 'Incarnata'	EBee
	soldanella NNS 99-85	WCot

Calytrix (*Myrtaceae*)

	tetragona	SPlb
	- compact, pink-flowered	SOWG

Camassia ✿ (*Hyacinthaceae*)

	biflora	EBee
	cusickii	Widely available

	- white-flowered	IFoB
	- 'Zwanenburg'	CTca EBee ERCP GKev LRHS WCot
	esculenta Lindl.	see *C. quamash*
	howellii	EBee
	leichtlinii misapplied	see *C. leichtlinii* subsp. *suksdorfii*
	leichtlinii (Baker) S.Watson	ECho
N	- 'Alba' hort.	see *C. leichtlinii* subsp. *leichtlinii*
*	- 'Alba Plena'	MNrw MWat NBPC NBir
	- Blue Danube	see *C. leichtlinii* subsp. *suksdorfii* 'Blauwe Donau'
	- 'Blue Wave'	NHol
§	- subsp. ***leichtlinii*** Υ^{H4}	Widely available
	- 'Magdalen'	CAvo
N	- 'Plena' (d)	ECha
	- 'Sacajawea'	CMea CTca ERCP GGar
	- 'Semiplena' (d)	CAvo CFFs CMea CMil CTca EBee ERCP GGar LRHS MLLN MNrw NSti SPhx WAul WCot WHoo
	- 'Sky Blue' **new**	CMea
§	- subsp. ***suksdorfii***	CSam ECho GCra
§	- - 'Blauwe Donau'	GKev
	- - Caerulea Group	Widely available
	- - 'Electra'	CAvo ECha SMHy SUsu
	- - 'Lady Eve Price' **new**	SMHy
§	***quamash***	Widely available
	- 'Blue Melody' (v)	CBow CTca EBee EBrs EPot ERCP GKev GMaP GMac LEdu LRHS MCCP NMRc NMen SDeJ SPhx WRHF
	- var. ***breviflora***	EBee
	- 'Orion'	EBee GMac NSti SPhx WAul WCot
*	***scolymus*** 'Argenteuil' **new**	SMHy

Camellia ✿ (*Theaceae*)

	'Adorable' (*pitardii* hybrid)	LRHS LSRN
	'Annette Carol'	CDoC
	'Ariel's Song'	CDoC
	'Auburn White'	see *C. japonica* 'Mrs Bertha A. Harms'
	'Baby Bear'	CDoC
	'Barbara Clark' (*saluenensis* × *reticulata*)	CDoC LRHS LSRN MGos SCog SCoo
	'Bertha Harms Blush'	see *C. japonica* 'Mrs Bertha A. Harms'
	'Bett's Supreme'	CDoC
	'Black Lace' Υ^{H4}	CAlb CBcs CTrh CTri EPfP GGGa LBuc LRHS LSRN MAsh MBri NPri SAPC SCam SCog SCoo SEND WBVN WGob
	'Blissful Dawn'	CBcs CTrh
	'Bonnie Marie'	CBcs CDoC MGos SCog
	'Canterbury'	CDoC
*	'Chatsworth Belle'	CTrh
	'China Lady' (*granthamiana* × *reticulata*)	MBri
	'Christmas Daffodil' (*japonica* hybrid)	LRHS
	'Cinnamon Cindy'	CDoC LRHS SCam SCog
	'Cinnamon Sensation'	SCog
	Classique = 'Kerguelen' PBR **new**	MPkF
	'Congratulations'	CSBt LSRN
	'Contessa Lavinia Maggi'	see *C. japonica* 'Lavinia Maggi'
	'Cornish Snow' (*cuspidata* × *saluenensis*) Υ^{H4}	CBcs CDoC CSBt CSam CTri EPfP GGal LHyd MGos SCam SCog SPer SSpi WFar
	'Cornish Spring' (*cuspidata* × *japonica*) Υ^{H4}	CAlb CCCN CDoC CSBt CTrh EPfP LHyd LRHS MGos SCam SCog SPer
	'Crimson Candles' **new**	LRHS
	cuspidata	LHyd
	'Czar'	see *C. japonica* 'The Czar'
	'Dainty Dale'	CDoC LRHS SCam
	'Debut' (*japonica* × *reticulata*)	LRHS
	'Delia Williams'	see *C.* × *williamsii* 'Citation'
	'Diamond Head' (*japonica* × *reticulata*)	CBcs LHyd
	'Diana's Charm'	CDoC LSRN
	'Doctor Clifford Parks' (*japonica* × *reticulata*) Υ^{H2}	CDoC LHyd LRHS SCam SCog
	'Donckelaeri'	see *C. japonica* 'Masayoshi'
	edithae **new**	LRHS
	'El Dorado' (*pitardii* × *japonica*)	CDoC
	'Elizabeth Bolitho'	SCam
	'Extravaganza' (*japonica* hybrid)	CBcs CTrh IArd MBri SCam SCog
	'Fairy Blush'	CDoC LRHS MPkF
	'Fairy Wand'	CDoC LRHS MPkF
	'Faustina Lechi'	see *C. japonica* 'Faustina'
	'Felice Harris' (*reticulata* × *sasanqua*)	CDoC MBri SCam SCog
	'Fiesta Grande' **new**	LRHS
	'Fire 'n' Ice'	CDoC SCam SCog
	forrestii	NLar
	'Forty-niner' (*reticulata* × *japonica*)	CBcs
	'Fox's Fancy'	CDoC
	'Fragrant Joy'	LRHS
	'Fragrant Pink' (*japonica* subsp. *rusticana* × *lutchuensis*)	CTrh SCam
	'Francie L' (*reticulata* × *saluenensis*) Υ^{H3-4}	CDoC CDul EPfP LHyd LRHS SCam SCog SSta
	'Freedom Bell' Υ^{H4}	CDoC CMHG CTrh ELon GGGa GGal GGar LRHS MAsh MMuc MPkF SCam SCog SCoo
	'Gay Baby'	CDoC
	'Golden Anniversary'	see *C. japonica* 'Dahlohnega'
	grijsii	CPLG CTrh LHyd SCam
	handelii	CPLG
	'Happy Anniversary'	CSBt LSRN
§	***hiemalis*** 'Bonanza'	CTrh
	- 'Chansonette'	CDoC ELon SCam SCog
§	- 'Dazzler'	CBcs CSBt SCam SCog
	- 'Interlude'	LRHS
	- 'Kanjirō'	CDoC LHyd SCam
	- 'Shishigashira' **new**	CTrh
	- 'Showa Supreme'	SCam
	- 'Shōwa-no-sakae'	LRHS SCog
§	- 'Sparkling Burgundy' Υ^{H3}	CBcs CDoC ELon EPfP LHyd LRHS MGos SCam SCog
	'Hierathlyn'	GGal
	'High Fragrance'	LRHS MPkF
	'Hooker'	CDoC
	'Ice Follies'	SCog
	'Imbricata Rubra'	see *C. japonica* 'Imbricata'
	'Innovation'	SCoo
	'Inspiration' (*reticulata* × *saluenensis*) Υ^{H4}	CDoC CMHG CMac CSBt CTrh CWSG EPfP GGGa GGar LHyd LRHS LSRN MBri MGos NLar SCam SCog SPer SSpi SVic WGob
	japonica	SArc
	- 'Aaron's Ruby'	CBcs CDoC ELon LRHS SCog
	- 'Ace of Hearts'	MBri
	- 'Ada Pieper'	CTrh
	- 'Adelina Patti' Υ^{H4}	CBcs CDoC CMHG CSBt CTrh LHyd SCog SCoo
	- 'Adolphe Audusson' Υ^{H4}	Widely available
	- 'Adolphe Audusson Special'	LSRN

§	- 'Akashigata' ♀H4	CBcs CDoC CMac EPfP LRHS LSRN MGos SCog SLim SPer SPoG SSta
	- 'Alba Plena' ♀H4	CTrh CWSG LHyd MGos SCog SPer WFar
	- 'Alba Simplex'	CAlb CDoC CMac CTrh CWit ELan EPfP LRHS MGos SCam SCog SPer SSta
	- 'Alexander Hunter' ♀H4	CDoC LHyd LRHS SCog
	- 'Alison Leigh Woodroof'	CDoC
§	- 'Althaeiflora'	CBcs CDoC ELon MGos SCam SCog
	- 'Ama-no-gawa'	LHyd
	- 'Amazing Graces'	CDoC
	- 'Anemoniflora'	CDoC ELan LRHS SCam SCog WFar
	- 'Angel'	CBcs LSRN SCam SCog WBor
	- 'Angello'	CWit LSou WGob
	- 'Ann Sothern'	CBcs
	- 'Annie Wylam' ♀H4	CTrh LHyd SCog
	- 'Apollo' ambig.	CBcs CDoC CTsd LRHS MGos WGob
	- 'Apollo' Paul, 1911	CSam EPfP MGos MSwo SCam SCog
§	- 'Apple Blossom' ♀H4	CBcs ELan
	- 'Arajishi' misapplied	see *C. japonica* subsp. *rusticana*
*	- 'Augustine Supreme'	CMac
	- 'Australis' ♀H4	MAsh SCam
	- 'Ave Maria' ♀H4	CDoC CTrh
	- 'Baby Pearl'	LSRN
	- 'Baby Sis'	LRHS
	- 'Ballet Dancer' ♀H4	CDoC ELon LSRN MGos SCam SCog SVic
	- 'Bambino'	CDoC
	- 'Barbara Woodroof'	CBcs
	- 'Baron Gomer'	see *C. japonica* 'Comte de Gomer'
	- 'Baronne Leguay'	SCam
	- 'Beau Harp'	LRHS SCam
	- 'Bella Lambertii'	NMun
	- 'Bella Romana'	SCam
	- 'Benten' (v)	SCam SMad
	- 'Berenice Boddy' ♀H4	CTrh
	- 'Berenice Perfection'	CDoC WFar
	- 'Betty Foy Sanders'	CTrh
	- 'Betty Robinson'	CDoC LRHS
	- 'Betty Sheffield'	MAsh MGos SCog SCoo WFar
	- 'Betty Sheffield Pink'	LRHS SCam
	- 'Betty Sheffield Supreme'	CBcs
	- 'Billie McCaskill'	SCam
	- 'Black Tie'	CDoC ELon LRHS MAsh MGos SCam SCog SPur SVic WGob
	- 'Blackburnia'	see *C. japonica* 'Althaeiflora'
	- 'Blaze of Glory'	NLar SCog
§	- 'Blood of China'	CBcs CDoC CSBt LBuc LRHS LSRN LSou MAsh MGos MMuc SCam SCog SCoo SPer WFar WGob WMoo
	- 'Bob Hope' ♀H4	CBcs CDoC CTrh LHyd MAsh MGos
	- 'Bob's Tinsie' ♀H4	CBcs CDoC CMHG CSBt CTrh EPfP GBin LRHS LSRN NLar SCog SPoG WGob
§	- 'Bokuhan' ♀H4	CDoC EPfP MPkF
	- 'Bonomiana'	SAPC
	- 'Bright Buoy'	CDoC
	- 'Brushfield's Yellow' ♀H4	CBcs CDoC CMHG CSBt ELan EPfP IArd LHyd LMil LRHS LSRN LSou MAsh MBri MDun MGos NEgg NLar SBfd SCam SCog SCoo SPer SSta SVic WFar WGob
	- 'Bush Hill Beauty'	see *C. japonica* 'Lady de Saumarez'
§	- 'C.M. Hovey' ♀H4	CMHG CMac LRHS MAsh
	- 'C.M. Wilson'	CDoC CMac SCog
N	- 'Campbellii'	LHyd
	- 'Campsii Alba'	CDoC
	- 'Can Can'	CBcs CDoC SCog
	- 'Candy Apple' **new**	CTrh

	- 'Candy Stripe'	CDoC SCam
	- 'Cara Mia'	CDoC SCam
	- 'Carolina Beauty'	LRHS
	- 'Carter's Sunburst' ♀H4	CBcs CDoC CTrh ELan EPfP SCog WGob
	- 'Cassandra' **new**	LRHS
	- 'Chandleri Elegans'	see *C. japonica* 'Elegans'
	- 'Charlotte de Rothschild'	CTrh CTri EPfP SCam
	- 'Cheryll Lynn'	CDoC CTrh
	- 'Christmas Beauty'	SCam
	- 'Cinderella'	CDoC SCog
	- 'Clarise Carleton'	GGGa LHyd MBri
	- 'Colonel Firey'	see *C. japonica* 'C.M. Hovey'
	- 'Commander Mulroy' ♀H4	CDoC CTrh MBri
§	- 'Comte de Gomer'	CDoC ELan ELon EPfP LRHS NPri SCog
	- 'Conspicua'	CBcs
	- 'Contessa Samailoff'	CDoC
§	- 'Coquettii' ♀H4	CBcs CDul LRHS MAsh SCog
	- 'Coral Beauty'	WFar
	- 'Coral Pink Lotus'	CDoC
	- 'Coral Queen'	CDoC
	- 'Cornish Excellence'	SCam
	- 'Curly Lady' PBR	MPkF NPri
§	- 'Dahlohnega'	CDoC CSBt CTrh LSRN MPkF
	- 'Daikagura'	CBcs
	- 'Daitairin'	see *C. japonica* 'Dewatairin'
	- 'Dark of the Moon'	CDoC
	- 'Dear Jenny'	CBcs
	- 'Debutante'	CBcs CDoC CMac ELon LHyd SCam SCog
	- 'Deep Secret' ♀H4	SCog
	- 'Desire' ♀H4	CBcs CDoC CMHG CSBt CTrh EPfP LRHS LSRN MAsh MDun MPkF NMun SBfd SCam SCog SCoo SPoG WGob
	- 'Devonia'	CBcs EPfP LHyd SCog
§	- 'Dewatairin' (Higo)	CBcs CDoC MGos SCam SCog
	- 'Dixie Knight'	CBcs CDoC MGos SCam SCog
	- 'Dobreei'	CMac
	- 'Doctor Burnside'	CBcs CDoC CTrh LRHS SCam SCog
	- 'Doctor King'	LRHS
	- 'Doctor Tinsley' ♀H4	CDoC LRHS MAsh NPri SCoo
	- 'Dolly Dyer'	CDoC
	- 'Dona Herzilia de Freitas Magalhaes'	CDoC SCam
	- 'Dona Jane Andresson'	SCam
	- 'Donckelaeri'	see *C. japonica* 'Masayoshi'
	- 'Donnan's Dream'	CTrh
	- 'Drama Girl' ♀H2	CBcs CDoC EPfP MGos SCam SCog SVic
	- 'Dream Time'	CBcs
	- 'Duc de Bretagne'	SCog
	- 'Duchesse Decazes'	CBcs MBri
	- 'Ed Combatalade' **new**	CDoC
	- 'Edelweiss'	CDoC MGos SCam SCog
	- 'Effendee'	see *C. sasanqua* 'Rosea Plena'
	- 'Eleanor Hagood'	CBcs
§	- 'Elegans' ♀H4	CBcs CDoC EPfP LRHS NEgg SBfd SCam SCog SCoo SLim SPer SPoG SSta WFar
	- 'Elegans Champagne'	EPfP NPri
	- 'Elegans Splendor'	CDoC
	- 'Elisabeth'	CDoC WFar
	- 'Elizabeth Dowd'	CBcs SCog
	- 'Elizabeth Hawkins'	CTrh CWit LHyd LRHS MAsh MMuc NCGa SCam
	- 'Emily Wilson'	CDoC
	- 'Emmett Barnes'	SCam
	- 'Emmett Pfingstl'	SCam
	- 'Emperor of Russia'	CBcs
	- 'Eric Baker'	SCam

- 'Erin Farmer' CBcs
- 'Eugène Lizé' SCam
- 'Evelyn' SCam
- 'Eximia' EPfP LRHS SCam SCog
- 'Faith' CBcs
- 'Fashionata' CDoC SCam
§ - 'Faustina' MAsh
- 'Feast Perfection' CDoC
- 'Finlandia Variegated' CDoC SCam SCog SVic
- 'Fire Dance' CDoC
- 'Fire Falls' ♀H4 CMHG
- 'Firebird' CBcs
- 'Flame' CBcs
- 'Flamingo' LHyd
- 'Flashlight' CDoC EPfP SCam
§ - 'Fleur Dipater' LRHS LSou SCam WGob
- 'Flowerwood' SCog WFar
- 'Forest Green' CDoC ELan MAsh
- 'Fortune Teller' CBcs
- 'Frans van Damme' CBcs
- 'Fred Sander' CDoC ELon MGos NMun SCam SCog
- 'Frizzle White' SApp
- 'Frosty Morn' CBcs CDoC ELan
- 'Furo-an' CBcs MAsh
- 'Geisha Girl' SCam SCog
- 'Général Lamoricière' LRHS
§ - 'Gigantea' SCam
§ - 'Gigantea Red' LRHS
- 'Giuditta Rosani' CDoC
- 'Giuseppina Pieri' LHyd
- 'Gladys Wannamaker' SCog
- 'Glen 40' see *C. japonica* 'Coquettii'
- 'Gloire de Nantes' ♀H4 CTrh NMun SCam SCog
- 'Gold Tone' CDoC MGos SCam
- 'Goshozakura' **new** CDoC
- 'Grace Bunton' CBcs CDoC ELon MGos SCam SCog
- 'Granada' SCog
- 'Grand Prix' ♀H4 CDoC CTrh ELon LSRN MGos SCam SCog SVic
- 'Grand Slam' ♀H2 CDoC CDul CTrh MAsh SCam
- 'Guest of Honor' CBcs CDoC LSou
- 'Guilio Nuccio' ♀H4 CBcs CDoC CTri EPfP IArd LRHS LSRN MGos NEgg NPri SBfd SCam SCog SCoo SLim SPer SVic
- 'Gus Menard' SCam
- 'Gwenneth Morey' CBcs CDoC ELan EPfP SCam
- 'H.A. Downing' CDoC SCam
§ - 'Hagoromo' ♀H4 CBcs CDoC CTrh ELan EPfP SBfd SCam SCog SPer WFar
- 'Hakugan' EMil EPfP NLar
§ - 'Hakurakuten' ♀H4 CDoC CMHG CTri IArd SCog
- 'Hanafûki' CDoC MGos SCam SCog
- 'Happy Birthday' LSRN
- 'Hatsuzakura' see *C. japonica* 'Dewatairin'
- 'Hawaii' CBcs CDoC CMac CTrh LHyd MGos SCog
- 'Her Majesty Queen Elizabeth II' CDoC
- Herme see *C. japonica* 'Hikarugenji'
- 'High Hat' CBcs SCog
- 'High, Wide 'n' Handsome' CDoC
§ - 'Hikarugenji' CDoC MGos SCog
- 'Hinomaru' CDoC CMac
- 'Holly Bright' CTrh SCam
- 'Honeyglow' CDoC
- 'Ichisetsu' SCog
§ - 'Imbricata' CAlb LBuc LRHS MAsh SCog
- 'Italiana Vera' LBuc LRHS MAsh
- 'J.J. Whitfield' CMac SCam
- 'Jack Jones Scented' CMHG
- 'Janet Waterhouse' CBcs SCam WFar
- 'Jean Clere' CDoC MGos MWea SCog
- 'Jennifer Turnbull' CDoC
- 'Jessie Katz' CDoC
- 'Jingle Bells' CBcs
- 'Jitsugetsusei' CDoC
- 'Joseph Pfingstl' ♀H4 CDoC CTri EPfP LRHS MMuc NPri SCam SCog WBVN
- 'Joshua E. Youtz' LHyd SCog
- 'Jovey Carlyon' CBcs LRHS MAsh
- 'Joy Sander' see *C. japonica* 'Apple Blossom'
- 'Julia France' SCog
- 'June McCaskill' CDoC
- 'Juno' CBcs LRHS SCam SCoo
- 'Jupiter' Paul, 1904 ♀H4 CBcs CDoC CMac CTri EPfP GKev LHyd LRHS LSRN MGos SCog SCoo SPer
§ - 'K. Sawada' SCam
- 'Kellingtoniana' see *C. japonica* 'Gigantea'
- 'Kentucky' LRHS
- 'Kick-off' CBcs CTrh SCog
- 'Kimberley' CBcs CDoC EPfP NMun SCog WBVN
- 'King Size' CDoC MGos SCam
- 'King's Ransom' CDoC CMac LRHS MAsh
- 'Kingyoba-shiro-wabisuke' CDoC
- 'Kingyo-tsubaki' SCam
- 'Kitty Berry' CTrh
- 'Kokinran' CDoC SCam
§ - 'Konronkoku' ♀H4 CBcs CDoC LRHS MAsh SCog
- 'Kouron-jura' see *C. japonica* 'Konronkoku'
- 'Kramer's Beauty' LRHS SCoo
- 'Kramer's Supreme' CBcs CCCN CDoC LBuc LRHS LSRN MGos NLar SCam SCog SCoo WCot WFar
- 'Lady Campbell' CTri GAbr GGar GKev LRHS LSou NLar NMun NPri SPad
- 'Lady Clare' see *C. japonica* 'Akashigata'
§ - 'Lady de Saumarez' CDoC CMac
- 'Lady Erma' CBcs
- 'Lady Loch' CTrh MAsh MBri MGos SCam
- 'Lady Mackinnon' MAsh
- 'Lady McCulloch' LRHS SCam
- 'Lady Saint Clair' CDoC
- 'Lady Vansittart' CAlb CChe CDoC CTrh ELan EPfP LHyd LRHS LSRN MAsh MGos MPkF SBfd SCam SCog SCoo SLim SPer SPoG WGob
§ - 'Lady Vansittart Pink' CMac SBfd
- 'Lady Vansittart Red' see *C. japonica* 'Lady Vansittart Pink'
- 'Lady Vansittart Shell' see *C. japonica* 'Yours Truly'
- 'Lady Vere de Vere' (d) CDoC
- 'Latifolia' SCam
- 'Laurie Bray' SCog WFar
§ - 'Lavinia Maggi' ♀H4 CAlb CBcs CDoC CTrh CTri ELan ELon EPfP LBuc LHyd LRHS LSRN MAsh MGos NPri SCam SCog SCoo SPer SPoG SReu SRms SSta WBVN WGob
- 'L'Avvenire' SCog
§ - 'Le Lys' SCam
- 'Lemon Drop' CTrh
- 'Leonora Novick' CDoC SCog
- 'Lillian Rickets' CDoC
- 'Lily Pons' ♀H4 CDoC CTrh LHyd
- 'Little Bit' CBcs CDoC CMHG CTrh ELon MGos SCam SCog SPer
- 'Little Slam' CDoC
- 'Lovelight' ♀H4 CTrh
- 'Ludgvan Red' LRHS SCam
- 'Lulu Belle' SCog
- 'Mabel Blackwell' SCam

- 'Madame de Strekaloff'	CMac CSBt SCam
- 'Madame Hahn'	CDoC
- 'Madame Lebois'	CBcs CDoC SCam
- 'Madame Martin Cachet'	SCog
- 'Magic Moments'	SCog
- 'Magnoliiflora'	see *C. japonica* 'Hagoromo'
- 'Magnoliiflora Alba'	see *C. japonica* 'Miyakodori'
- 'Maiden's Blush'	CMac
- 'Man Size'	CDoC
- 'Margaret Davis'	CCCN CDoC CSBt ELan ELon EPfP LBuc LHyd LRHS LSRN MAsh MDun MGos MPkF MWea NEgg NPri SBfd SCam SCoo SLim SPoG SVic WGob
- 'Margaret Davis Picotee' ♀H4	CBcs CMHG CTrh SCog SPer SSta
- 'Margaret Rose'	SCam
- 'Margaret Short'	CDoC
- 'Margherita Coleoni'	LHyd
- 'Marguérite Gouillon'	CBcs CDoC LHyd
- 'Marian Mitchell'	SCam
- 'Mariana'	CDoC SCog
- 'Marie Bracey'	CBcs SCam
- 'Marjorie Magnificent'	LBuc LRHS MAsh SCoo
- 'Mark Alan'	CDoC LSRN
- 'Maroon and Gold'	CDoC LSRN SCog
- 'Marquis of Exeter'	NMun
- 'Mars' ♀H4	CBcs MGos SCam SCog SPer WFar
- 'Mary Alice Cox'	CDoC
- 'Mary Costa'	CBcs CDoC CTrh WFar
- 'Mary J. Wheeler'	LSRN
§ - 'Masayoshi' ♀H4	CBcs CSBt LHyd LRHS MAsh SCam SCog
- 'Mathotiana Alba' ♀H4	CDoC CMac CSBt CTri ELan EPfP LSRN MGos SCam SCog SPer
§ - 'Mathotiana Rosea' ♀H4	CMac SCam
- 'Mathotiana Supreme'	CDoC SCam SCog
- 'Matterhorn'	CTrh MAsh
- 'Mattie Cole'	CDoC LHyd SCam
- 'Maui'	CDoC
- 'Mercury' ♀H4	CMac CWSG GGGa SCog
- 'Mercury Variegated'	CMHG
- 'Mermaid'	CDoC
- 'Midnight'	CBcs CDoC CMHG LBuc LRHS MAsh SCoo WFar
- 'Midnight Magic'	CTrh CTri
- 'Midnight Serenade'	CDoC
- 'Midsummer's Day'	CBcs
§ - 'Mikenjaku'	CBcs EPfP LBuc LRHS MAsh NMun SCog WGob
- 'Minnie Maddern Fiske'	SCam
- 'Miriam Stevenson'	SCam
- 'Miss Charleston'	CBcs LHyd SCog
- 'Miss Lyla'	NLar
- 'Miss Universe'	CTrh
- 'Mississippi Beauty'	CTrh
§ - 'Miyakodori'	EPfP
- 'Modern Art' **new**	MPkF
- 'Monsieur Faucillon'	CBcs
- 'Monstruosa Rubra'	see *C. japonica* 'Gigantea Red'
- 'Monte Carlo'	CDoC SCam SCog SVic
- 'Moonlight'	CDoC
- 'Moonlight Bay'	CTrh SCog
- 'Moshe Dayan'	CAlb CDoC LBuc LRHS LSou MAsh NPri SCog SCoo WGob
- 'Moshio'	CDoC
§ - 'Mrs Bertha A. Harms'	CDoC MGos SCam SCog SVic
- 'Mrs Charles Cobb'	LRHS
- 'Mrs D.W. Davis'	CBcs CDoC EPfP SCam
- 'Mrs Lyman Clarke'	CDoC
- 'Mrs William Thompson'	SCam
- 'Nagasaki'	see *C. japonica* 'Mikenjaku'
- 'Nigra'	see *C. japonica* 'Konronkoku'
- 'Nina Avery'	CDoC
- 'Nioi-fubuki' (Higo) **new**	CDoC
- 'Nobilissima'	CBcs CDoC CMac CTrh CTri EPfP GAbr GKev LHyd LRHS MBlu MMuc NLar NPri SCam SCog SCoo SPer SPoG WFar
- 'Nuccio's Amigo'	MAsh
- 'Nuccio's Cameo'	CDoC CTrh LRHS MAsh SCoo
- 'Nuccio's Carousel' **new**	MPkF
- 'Nuccio's Gem' ♀H4	CDoC CMHG ELan EPfP LHyd LRHS MGos SCam SCog SCoo SSta
- 'Nuccio's Jewel' ♀H4	CDoC CSBt CTrh CWSG EPfP LBuc LHyd LRHS LSRN MAsh SCam SCog SCoo SPer WBVN WGob WMoo
- 'Nuccio's Pearl'	CBcs CDoC CWit EPfP LRHS LSRN LSou MMuc NEgg NPri SCam SCog SCoo WBVN WGob
- 'Nuccio's Pink Lace'	CDoC CTri
- 'Olga Anderson'	CDoC MGos
- 'Onetia Holland'	CBcs CDoC EPfP LSRN MGos SBfd SCam SCog SLim
- 'Oo-La-La' **new**	MPkF
- 'Optima'	CBcs CDoC LRHS SCam SCog SCoo
- 'Optima Rosea'	SPoG
- 'Ōrandako' **new**	LRHS
- 'Paeoniiflora Alba'	SCam
- 'Patricia Ann'	LSRN
- 'Paul Jones Supreme' **new**	CDoC
- 'Paulette Goddard'	SCam
- 'Paul's Apollo'	see *C. japonica* 'Apollo' Paul, 1911
- 'Peachblossom'	see *C. japonica* 'Fleur Dipater'
- 'Pearl Harbor'	SCam
- 'Pensacola Red'	CDoC SCam
- 'Pink Champagne'	NPri
- 'Pink Clouds'	CBcs
- 'Pope Pius IX'	see *C. japonica* 'Prince Eugène Napoléon'
- 'Preston Rose'	CBcs CDoC NMun
- 'Primavera'	CTrh LHyd SCog
§ - 'Prince Eugène Napoléon'	SCam
- 'Prince Murat'	CDoC
- 'Princess Baciocchi'	CBcs SCam
- 'Princess du Mahe'	CMac
- 'R.L. Wheeler' ♀H4	CBcs CDoC CSBt CTri EPfP LHyd LRHS LSRN MWea SBfd SCog SCoo SLim
- 'Red Dandy'	CDoC MGos SCam SCog
- 'Red Elephant'	SCam
- 'Red Red Rose'	CDoC
- 'Reg Ragland'	CDoC CMHG MGos SCam SCog
- 'Robert Strauss'	SCam
- 'Roger Hall'	CBcs CDoC CTrh LRHS LSRN MAsh MPkF SCog SCoo SPoG WGob
- 'Roman Soldier'	CBcs
- 'Rosa Mundi' **new**	LRHS
- 'Rosularis'	CDoC SCam SCog
- 'Royal Velvet'	CDoC
- 'Rubescens Major' ♀H4	CBcs LHyd
- 'Ruddigore'	CTrh SCam
§ - subsp. ***rusticana***	CBcs CDoC SCog SCoo SLim WFar
- - 'Arajishi' misapplied	see *C. japonica* subsp. ***rusticana***
- - 'Arajishi'	SCam
- - 'Reigyoku' (v)	CBcs CDoC
- 'Sabiniana'	LRHS MAsh
- 'Saint André'	CMac LRHS MAsh SCoo
- 'Sally Harrell'	SCam
- 'San Dimas' ♀H4	CDoC CTrh SCam SCog SVic
- 'Saturnia'	CDoC ELon LBuc LRHS MAsh WBor
- 'Sawada's Dream'	CDoC SCog
- 'Scented Red'	CDoC SCam SCog
- 'Scentsation' ♀H4	CDoC CMHG CTri NPri SCog

	- 'Sea Foam'	LHyd LRHS SSta
	- 'Sea Gull'	CTrh
	- 'Senator Duncan U. Fletcher'	CDoC
	- 'Shikibu'	CTrh
	- 'Shiragiku'	CBcs CDoC SCog SPer
	- 'Shiro Chan'	CDoC MGos SCam SCog
	- 'Shirobotan'	CDoC ELon LRHS MAsh MGos SCam SCog SCoo SPur SVic
	- 'Silver Anniversary'	CAlb CBcs CDoC CMHG CSBt CTrh CTri ELan ELon EPfP LHyd LMil LRHS LSRN MAsh MGos NEgg NPri SBfd SCam SCog SCoo SLim SPer SPoG SReu SSta SVic WGob
	- 'Silver Moon'	see *C. japonica* 'K. Sawada'
	- 'Silver Ruffles'	CDoC
	- 'Silver Triumph'	SCam
	- 'Snow Chan'	CMHG
	- 'Something Beautiful'	CDoC
	- 'Souvenir de Bahuaud-Litou' ♀H4	SCam SCog
	- 'Spencer's Pink'	CBcs CDoC
	- 'Splendens Carlyon'	LRHS MAsh SCoo
	- 'Spring Fever'	SCam
	- 'Spring Fling'	CTrh
	- 'Spring Formal'	CTrh
	- 'Spring Frill'	SCam SCog
	- 'Stardust'	SCam
	- 'Strawberry Blonde'	SCog
	- 'Strawberry Parfait'	CDoC CTrh LRHS SCog
	- 'Strawberry Swirl'	CBcs SCog
	- 'Sugar Babe'	CDoC CSBt CTrh LRHS SCam SCog SCoo WGob
	- 'Sunset Glory'	CMHG SCam
	- 'Sweetheart'	SCog
	- 'Sylva' ♀H4	GGGa GGal SSpi
	- 'Sylvia'	CMac
	- 'Takanini'	CDoC CTrh
	- 'Tama-no-ura' **new**	CDoC
	- 'Tammia'	EPfP
	- 'Tarō'an'	GGal
	- 'Teresa Ragland'	CDoC SCam
	- 'Teringa'	CDoC
§	- 'The Czar'	CBcs
	- 'The Mikado'	CDoC SCog
	- 'Tickled Pink'	CDoC
	- 'Tiffany'	CBcs CDoC LHyd LRHS MGos SCam SCog SCoo SVic
	- 'Tiki'	MBri WFar
	- 'Tinker Bell'	CDoC MAsh MBri SCog
	- 'Tom Thumb' ♀H4	CDoC CTrh LRHS SRms SSta WGob
	- 'Tomorrow'	CDoC LRHS MAsh NEgg SCam SCog
	- 'Tomorrow Park Hill'	CBcs SCog
§	- 'Tomorrow Variegated'	MGos SCam
	- 'Touchdown'	SCam
	- 'Trewithen White'	CDoC CSam
§	- 'Tricolor' ♀H4	CBcs CDoC CMHG CMac CSBt CTrh LHyd LRHS MAsh MGos SBfd SCam SCog SCoo SPer WFar
	- 'Tricolor Red'	see *C. japonica* 'Lady de Saumarez'
	- 'Trinkett'	CDoC
	- variegated (v)	SCog
	- 'Victor de Bisschop'	see *C. japonica* 'Le Lys'
	- 'Victor Emmanuel'	see *C. japonica* 'Blood of China'
	- 'Ville de Nantes'	MGos
	- 'Ville de Nantes Red'	SCog
	- 'Virginia Carlyon'	CBcs CDoC
	- 'Virginia Robinson'	SCam
	- 'Virgin's Blush'	SCam
	- 'Vittorio Emanuele II'	CDoC CTrh LBuc LRHS MAsh MGos SCoo
	- 'Volcano' **new**	MPkF
	- 'Vosper's Rose'	CDoC
	- 'Warrior'	SCog
	- 'White Giant'	CBcs
	- 'White Nun'	CBcs SCog
	- 'White Perfection' **new**	SAPC
	- 'White Swan'	CSBt LRHS MAsh SCoo
	- 'Wilamina' ♀H4	CDoC CMHG LRHS
	- 'Wildfire'	LRHS SCam
	- 'William Bartlett'	CTrh LRHS
	- 'William Honey'	CTrh
	- 'Wisley White'	see *C. japonica* 'Hakurakuten'
§	- 'Yours Truly'	CBcs CDoC CMac CTrh LHyd LRHS LSRN MAsh MDun SCog
	- 'Yukimi-guruma'	CDoC
	'John Tooby'	CDoC
	'Jury's Yellow'	see *C.* × ***williamsii*** 'Jury's Yellow'
	'Lasca Beauty' (*japonica* × *reticulata*)	CBcs LHyd
	'Lavender Queen'	see *C. sasanqua* 'Lavender Queen'
	'Leonard Messel' (*reticulata* × *williamsii*) ♀H4	CBcs CDoC CDul CMHG CMac CTrh CTri EPfP GGGa GGal LHyd LRHS MAsh MDun MGos MPkF NPri SCam SCog SCoo SPer SPoG SReu SVic
	'Liz Henslowe'	CDoC
	'Madame Victor de Bisschop'	see *C. japonica* 'Le Lys'
§	***maliflora*** (d)	CBcs
	'Milo Rowell'	CDoC
	'Mimosa Jury'	CDoC LRHS
	'Monticello'	CDoC
	'Mystique'	see *C. reticulata* 'Mystique'
	'Nicky Crisp' (*japonica* × *pitardii*)	CDoC LHyd
	'Night Rider'	CDoC
	'Nijinski' (*reticulata* hybrid)	CDoC
	'Nonie Haydon' (*pitardii* hybrid)	CDoC
	oleifera	CPLG NLar SCog WFar
	'Phyl Doak' (*reticulata* × *saluenensis*)	CDoC
	'Pink Spangles'	see *C. japonica* 'Mathotiana Rosea'
	pitardii	SCog
	- 'Snippet'	CDoC
	'Polar Ice' (*oleifera* hybrid)	CDoC SCog
	'Polyanna'	CDoC SCog
	'Quintessence' (*japonica* × *lutchuensis*)	CDoC CTrh LRHS SCog
	reticulata 'Captain Rawes'	SCam
	- 'Les Jury'	LHyd LMil
	- 'Mary Williams'	GKev LMil NLar SCoo
	- 'Miss Tulare'	CDoC LHyd
	- 'Mouchang' **new**	CBcs
§	- 'Mystique'	CDoC
	- 'Satsuma-kurenai'	CTrh
	- 'William Hertrich'	CBcs
	rosiflora 'Roseaflora Cascade'	CDoC
	'Royalty' (*japonica* × *reticulata*) ♀H3	CBcs
	rusticana	see *C. japonica* subsp. ***rusticana***
	saluenensis 'Bartley Pink'	LHyd
	sasanqua Thunb.	CDul
I	- 'Apple Blossom'	MAsh
	- 'Baronesa de Soutelinho'	SCam SCog
	- 'Bettie Patricia'	SCog
	- 'Bonanza'	see *C. hiemalis* 'Bonanza'
	- Borde Hill form	SCam
	- 'Cleopatra'	EPfP MAsh
	- 'Cotton Candy'	CDoC
	- 'Crimson King' ♀H3	CDoC CHVG CTrh NMun SCam

	- 'Dazzler'	see *C. hiemalis* 'Dazzler'
	- 'Early Pearly'	CDoC LRHS
	- 'Evangelica'	LRHS
I	- 'Exquisite'	CDoC
	- 'Flamingo'	see *C. sasanqua* 'Fukuzutsumi'
	- 'Flore Pleno'	see *C. maliflora*
	- 'Fragrans'	SCog
	- 'Fuji-no-mine'	ELon SCog
§	- 'Fukuzutsumi'	CSBt LRHS SCam
	- 'Gay Sue'	CDoC CTrh SCam
	- 'Hiryū'	LRHS SCam
	- 'Hugh Evans' ♀H3	CAbP CBcs CDoC CTrh ELon LRHS SCam SCog SCoo SRkn SSta
	- 'Jean May' ♀H3	CDoC ELon EPfP LHyd LRHS SCam SCog SCoo SPer SSta WGob
	- 'Kenkyō'	SCam SCog SSta
§	- 'Lavender Queen'	SCam
	- 'Lucinda'	LHyd SCog
	- 'Maiden's Blush'	LRHS SCam SCog WFar WSpi
	- 'Mignonne'	SCam
	- 'Narumigata'	CAbP CBcs CDoC CMac CSBt CTrh EPfP LRHS MBlu SCam SCog SCoo SPoG SSta WGob
	- 'New Dawn'	SCam SCog
	- 'Nyewoods'	CMac
	- 'Papaver'	SCam SCog
	- 'Paradise Belinda'PBR	CDoC SCam
	- 'Paradise Blush'	CBcs CDoC SCog
	- 'Paradise Glow'	CBcs CDoC SCam SCog
	- 'Paradise Helen' **new**	SCam
	- 'Paradise Hilda'	CBcs CDoC SCam SCog
	- 'Paradise Joan'	CDoC
	- 'Paradise Little Liane'PBR	CBcs CDoC SCam SCog
	- 'Paradise Pearl'	CBcs CDoC SCam SCog
	- 'Paradise Petite'PBR	SCog
	- 'Paradise Sayaka'	CDoC
	- 'Paradise Venessa'PBR	CDoC EPfP SCam SCog
	- 'Peach Blossom'	CBcs LHyd
	- 'Plantation Pink'	CSBt CTrh EPfP LHyd LRHS SCam SCog SLim SPer SPoG SRkn WCot
	- 'Rainbow'	CAbP CDoC CHVG CTrh ELon EPfP GGal LRHS NMun SCam SCog SCoo SRkn SSta WFar WGob
	- 'Rosea'	SCam SCog
§	- 'Rosea Plena'	CBcs CHVG CMac SCam
	- 'Sasanqua Rubra'	CMac SCam SCog
	- 'Sasanqua Variegata' (v)	MPkF SCam SCog SSta
	- 'Setsugekka'	CDoC SCam SCog
I	- 'Shishigashira' Nihon Engei Kai Zasshi, 1894	LHyd
	- 'Silver Dollar'	CDoC
	- 'Snowflake'	SCam SCog SSta
	- 'Sparkling Burgundy'	see *C. hiemalis* 'Sparkling Burgundy'
	- 'Tanya'	CDoC
	- 'Versicolor'	LRHS MPkF
	- 'Winter's Snowman'	CDoC LRHS SCam SCog
	'Satan's Robe' (*reticulata* hybrid)	CDoC MGos SCam SCog WFar
	'Scented Gem' **new**	MPkF
	'Scented Sun'	CTrh
	'Scentuous' (*japonica* × *lutchuensis*)	CDoC CTrh SCam
	'Show Girl' (*reticulata* × *sasanqua*)	LHyd SCam SCog
	'Shōwa-wabisuke' (wabisuke)	CTrh
§	***sinensis***	CCCN CTrh GPoy LRHS SCam
	'Sir Victor Davis'	CDoC
	'Snow Flurry' (*oleifera* hybrid)	LRHS SCam SCog
	'Spring Festival' (*cuspidata* hybrid) ♀H4	CDoC CMHG CTrh LHyd LRHS MPkF NLar SCog SPoG WMoo
	'Spring Mist' (*japonica* × *lutchuensis*)	CDoC CMHG CTrh LHyd
	'Sugar Dream'	CDoC CTrh
	'Superscent'	CTrh
	'Survivor' **new**	LRHS MPkF
	'Swan Lake'	SCog
	'Sweet Emily Kate' (*japonica* × *lutchuensis*)	CDoC
	'Sweet Jane' **new**	MPkF SBfd
	'Tarōkaja' (wabisuke)	SCam
	thea	see *C. sinensis*
	'Tinsie'	see *C. japonica* 'Bokuhan'
	'Tiny Princess' (*fraterna* × *japonica*)	CMac
	'Tom Knudsen' (*japonica* × *reticulata*) ♀H3	CDoC CTrh
	'Tomorrow Supreme'	see *C. japonica* 'Tomorrow Variegated'
	transnokoensis	CMac CPLG
	'Tricolor Sieboldii'	see *C. japonica* 'Tricolor'
	'Tristrem Carlyon' (*reticulata* hybrid) ♀H4	CBcs CDoC CTri CWit EPfP LSou NPri SCam WGob
	tsaii	CDoC
	'Valley Knudsen' (*reticulata* × *saluenensis*)	SCog
	× ***vernalis*** 'Ginryû'	SCam
	- 'Star Above Star'	CMHG
	- 'Yuletide'	CDoC CTrh LHyd LRHS MPkF SCam
	'Volcano'	CDoC
	× ***williamsii*** 'Angel Wings'	LRHS
	- 'Anticipation' ♀H4	CBcs CDoC CDul CMHG CMac CSBt CSam CTrh CWSG EPfP GGGa LHyd LMil LRHS MAsh MBri MDun MGos MSwo NEgg NPri SBfd SCam SCog SLim SPer SPoG SSpi WFar WGob
	- 'Ballet Queen'	CBcs CDoC CSBt MGos SVic WFar
	- 'Ballet Queen Variegated'	CDoC MGos SCog
	- 'Bartley Number Five'	CMac
	- 'Beatrice Michael'	CMac
	- 'Bow Bells'	CDoC CDul CTri GKir LHyd SCam SSta
	- 'Bowen Bryant' ♀H4	CTsd GGGa SCog
	- 'Bridal Gown'	GGGa LHyd
	- 'Brigadoon' ♀H4	CBcs CDoC CMHG CTrh CTri EPfP GGGa GGal GGar GKir LHyd MBri MGos SCam SCog
	- 'Burncoose'	CBcs
	- 'Burncoose Apple Blossom'	CBcs CDoC
	- 'Buttons 'n' Bows'	CDoC SCog
	- 'C.F. Coates'	CDoC SCog SSta
	- 'Caerhays'	CBcs SCam
	- 'Carnation'	MAsh
	- 'Carolyn Williams'	CBcs SCam
	- 'Celebration'	CBcs CSBt LSRN
	- 'Charlean'	CDoC SCam
	- 'Charles Colbert'	CDoC LRHS
	- 'China Clay' ♀H4	CBcs CDoC EPfP LHyd
§	- 'Citation'	CBcs CMac LHyd SCog
	- 'Clarrie Fawcett' ♀H4	CDoC
	- 'Contribution'	CTrh
	- 'Crinkles'	CDoC CDul SCam SSta
	- 'Daintiness' ♀H4	CDoC LHyd SCog
	- 'Dark Nite'	CMHG
	- 'Debbie' ♀H4	Widely available
	- 'Debbie's Carnation'	CDoC CMHG
	- 'Donation' ♀H4	Widely available
	- 'Dream Boat'	CDoC LHyd LRHS

- 'E.G.Waterhouse'	CBcs CDoC CMHG CTrh CTri ELon EPfP LHyd LRHS MAsh MGos MMuc SCam SCog SCoo SPoG SSta SVic WGob
- 'E.T.R. Carlyon' 🏆H4	CBcs CDoC CTrh CTri CTsd ELon EPfP LBuc LHyd LRHS MAsh MPkF NLar SCog SCoo SLim SPoG
- 'Elegant Beauty' 🏆H4	CBcs CDoC CSBt SCam SCog SPer SVic
- 'Elizabeth Anderson' 🏆H4	CTrh SCam
- 'Ellamine'	CBcs
- 'Elsie Jury' 🏆H3	CBcs CDoC CMac CTri CWSG GQui LHyd MGos SCam SCog SPer SVic
- 'Exaltation'	CDoC SCog
- 'Fiona Colville'	CDoC
- 'Francis Hanger'	CDoC CTrh LHyd SCam SCog SPer
- 'Galaxie' 🏆H4	CBcs CDoC SCog
- 'Garden Glory'	LHyd
- 'Gay Time'	CBcs
- 'George Blandford' 🏆H4	CBcs CMac GGal
- 'Glenn's Orbit' 🏆H4	CBcs CDoC SCam SCog SLim
- 'Golden Spangles' (v)	CBcs CDoC CMac CTrh CTsd CWit ELan EPfP LHyd LRHS MDun MGos MMuc NLar SBfd SCam SCog SLim SPer WGob
- 'Grand Jury'	LRHS
- 'Gwavas'	CBcs CCCN CDoC LHyd LRHS MAsh SCam SCog SCoo
- 'Hilo'	CDoC SCam
- 'Hiraethlyn'	LHyd
- 'Holland Orchid'	SCog
- 'J.C.Williams' 🏆H4	CBcs CMac CSam CTri EPfP MMuc SCog
- 'Jamie'	CDoC
- 'Jean Claris'	CDoC SCog
- 'Jenefer Carlyon'	CBcs CDoC SCog
- 'Jill Totty'	CTrh SCog
- 'Joan Trehane' 🏆H4	CTsd SCam
- 'Julia Hamiter' 🏆H4	CBcs CDoC
§ - 'Jury's Yellow' 🏆H4	Widely available
- 'Lady's Maid'	CBcs
- 'Laura Boscawen'	CDoC LHyd SCam
- 'Les Jury' 🏆H4	CDoC CGHE CMHG CSBt CTrh LMil LSRN MWea NEgg NPri SBfd SCog SLim SPoG
- 'Little Lavender'	CDoC
- 'Margaret Waterhouse'	CBcs CDoC SCam SCog
- 'Marjorie Waldegrave'	LRHS
- 'Mary Christian' 🏆H4	CBcs GGal LHyd SCam SSta
- 'Mary Jobson'	CBcs
- 'Mary Larcom'	CBcs
- 'Mary Phoebe Taylor' 🏆H4	CBcs CDoC CWSG GGal MPkF NLar SCam SCog SCoo SLim
- 'Mildred Veitch'	CDoy CSBt
- 'Mirage'	CDoC SCam
- 'Moira Reid'	CDoC
- 'Monica Dance'	CBcs CDoC SCam
- 'New Venture'	CBcs
- 'November Pink'	CBcs
- 'Palaxie'	SCam
- 'Phillippa Forward'	CBcs CMac
- 'Red Dahlia'	CBcs
- 'Rendezvous'	CDoC MGos SCam SCog SVic
- 'Rose Bouquet'	CDoC
- 'Rose Parade'	LHyd SCoo
- 'Rosemary Williams'	CBcs
- 'Ruby Bells'	CMHG
- 'Ruby Wedding' (d)	CDoC CMHG CSBt CTrh CWSG EPfP GQui LHyd LMil LRHS LSRN MAsh MWea NEgg NPri SBfd SCog SCoo SLim SPoG

- 'Saint Ewe' 🏆H4	CBcs CDoC CSBt CTrh CTri EPfP GGal GKev LBuc LHyd LRHS MBri MGos MMuc NLar NPri SCam SCog SCoo SPer WGob
- 'Saint Michael'	CBcs CDoC
- 'Sayonara'	CBcs SCam SCog
- 'Senorita' 🏆H4	CDoC CTrh ELon LHyd SCam SCog SVic
- 'Simon Bolitho'	LHyd SCog
- 'Sun Song'	SCog
- 'Taylor's Perfection'	SCam
- 'The Duchess of Cornwall'	CDoC SCam
- 'Tiptoe'	CDoC MBri
- 'Waltz Time'	CDoC SCam
- 'Water Lily' 🏆H4	CBcs CDoC CTri ELon EPfP MGos SCam SPur SVic
- 'Wilber Foss' 🏆H4	CDoC CMHG LHyd MGos MMuc SCog
- 'Wynne Rayner'	CDoC SCam
- 'Yesterday'	MMuc
'Winter's Charm' (*oleifera* × *sasanqua*)	SCog
'Winter's Dream' (*hiemalis* × *oleifera*)	SCog
'Winter's Interlude' (*oleifera* × *sinensis*)	CDoC SCam SCog
'Winter's Joy'	SCog
'Winter's Toughie' (*sasanqua* hybrid)	CDoC SCam SCog
'Winton' (*cuspidata* × *saluenensis*)	CBcs CDoC SCam WFar
'Wirlinga Belle'	SCog
'Yoimachi' (*fraterna* × *sasanqua*)	CDoC CTrh LRHS

Campanula ✿ (*Campanulaceae*)

RCB AM 13	WCot
from Morocco	ECtt
abietina	see *C. patula* subsp. *abietina*
§ ***alliariifolia***	Widely available
- DHTU 0126	WCru
- 'Ivory Bells'	see *C. alliariifolia*
- 'Minor'	GKev
allionii	see *C. alpestris*
§ ***alpestris***	ECho
alpina	MDKP
argaea	GKev
armena	ELan
arvatica	EACa ECho EDAr EPot GMaP LRHS MDKP NHar NMen
- 'Alba'	EACa ECho GMaP
aucheri	see *C. saxifraga* subsp. *aucheri*
autraniana	EACa GKev
'Azure Beauty'	CSpe EBee ECtt ELan NCGa WCot
§ 'Balchiniana' (v)	CBow
barbata	CFir EACa EBee ECho EDAr GMaP MWat NWCA WAbe WMoo
'Belinda' <u>**new**</u>	CPBP
bellidifolia	NBir NBre
- subsp. ***saxifraga***	EBur GKev ITim NMen
besenginica	GKev WAbe
§ ***betulifolia*** 🏆H4	CSam WFar
'Birch Hybrid' 🏆H4	EACa EBee ECho ECtt EDAr ELan EPfP GKir LRHS MMuc WFar
bononiensis	LLHF NBre SRms STes
'Bumblebee'	WAbe
'Burghaltii' 🏆H4	CHar CPom EBee EHrv ELan GCal GMac SMrm WCot WFar WMnd WOut WPer
calaminthifolia	EBur
'Cantata'	EPot WAbe

§	***carnica***	ECho
	carpatica ♀^{H4}	ECho EPfP GKir ITim MLHP MLLN NBre NBro NGdn SPlb SRms SWat
	- f. ***alba***	GKev LRHS MLLN NBre NGdn SPlb SWat
	- - 'Snowdrift'	GKir
§	- - 'Weisse Clips'	CBar EAEE EBee ECho ECtt ELan EPfP EPot GGar GKir GMaP LAst LHop LRHS NDov NEgg NGdn NPri SBfd SPer SPoG SRms STes SWvt WFar
§	- 'Blaue Clips'	CBar CBcs EBee ECho ECtt ELan EPfP EPot GGar GKev GKir GMaP IFoB LAst LHop LRHS MGos NDov NEgg NGdn NPri SBfd SPer SPoG SRms STes SWvt WFar WRHF
	- Blue Clips	see *C. carpatica* 'Blaue Clips'
	- 'Blue Moonlight'	EACa EBur ECho LHop LRHS
	- 'Chewton Joy'	CTri EACa ECho GKir LLHF LRHS
	- 'Ditton Blue'	GMaP
	- dwarf	EACa
	- 'Karpatenkrone'	EBee
	- 'Kathy'	CMoH
*	- var. ***pelviformis***	SMHy
	- 'Silberschale'	NBre
	- 'Suzie'	IPot
	- var. ***turbinata***	ECho GKev SRms WAbe
	- - 'Foerster'	EACa ECho IPot LRHS
	- - 'Georg Arends'	ECtt
	- - 'Isabel'	EACa ECho LLHF LRHS
	- - 'Jewel'	EACa ECho LHop LRHS
	- White Clips	see *C. carpatica* f. *alba* 'Weisse Clips'
§	***cashmeriana***	EBur
	- 'Blue Cloud'	CWib
	cenisia	WFar
	cephallenica	see *C. garganica* subsp. *cephallenica*
	cespitosa	CPBP WAbe
§	***chamissonis***	ECho GEdr LLHF WPat
	- 'Alba'	GEdr
	- 'Major'	EWes LBee
	- 'Oyobeni'	NLAp
§	- 'Superba' ♀^{H4}	EBur ECho ELan NMen WAbe
§	***cochlearifolia*** ♀^{H4}	CEnt CSpe CTri EBee ECho EDAr EPfP GJos GKir GMaP LRHS MMuc SBch SBfd STre WClo WFar WHoo
	- var. ***alba***	CSpe CTri EDAr GMaP MHer MMuc NRya NWCA SBch SRms WAbe WHoo WPer
	- - 'Bavaria White'	ECho WFar
	- - double white-flowered (d)	WPat
	- - 'White Baby' (Baby Series)	ECho ECtt EPfP EPot GAbr GGar GJos GKir IVic LRHS NHol SPet SPoG
	- 'Annie Hall'	ECho
	- 'Bavaria Blue'	ECho ITim IVic NHol NWCA SMrm SPet
	- 'Blue Baby' (Baby Series)	CSpr ECho EPfP GGar GJos GKir IVic MHer SPoG SRms SRot
	- 'Blue Wonder'	ITim
	- 'Cambridge Blue'	EACa WFar
	- 'Elizabeth Oliver' (d)	CFir CTri ECho ECtt EDAr EPot GCal GKev GKir GMaP LHop LRHS MAvo MHer NLAp NWCA SMrm SPlb SRms WAbe WCom WFar WHoo WPat
	- 'Miss Willmott'	NBir
	- 'Oakington Blue'	GKir LLHF WAbe WCom
	- var. ***pallida*** 'Silver Chimes'	ECho ITim
	- 'R.B. Loder' (d)	LRHS
	- 'Tubby'	ECho EPot GKev LLHF MHer SRms
	- 'Warleyensis'	see *C.* × *haylodgensis* W. Brockbank 'Warley White'
	collina	CTri EACa LLHF NBre
	'Covadonga'	CMea EACa EBee ECho LHop LLHF LRHS
	crenulata new	GKev
	cretica	ELan NBPC NBre
	'Crystal'	ECtt MAvo MNrw SUsu
	dasyantha	see *C. chamissonis*
	dolomitica	EBee GKev LLHF NMen
	'E.K. Toogood'	CElw CFir CPBP ECho ECtt NVic NWCA SRms
	elatines	EBee
	ephesia	GKev
	- SDR 1111	GKev
	'Faichem Lilac'	EBee GCra GKev LLHF NChi STes
	fenestrellata	ITim NMen SRms WAbe WFar
	finitima	see *C. betulifolia*
	foliosa	EACa WPer
	formanekiana ♀$^{H2-3}$	EBur
	fragilis	EBur ECho IFoB WPat
	- 'Hirsuta'	ECho
	garganica ♀^{H4}	EACa ECho EPfP GGar GKev GMaP LAst LRHS MDKP MMuc MRav NEgg SBfd SEND SWvt WFar WMoo
	- 'Aurea'	see *C. garganica* 'Dickson's Gold'
	- 'Blue Diamond'	ECho IVic LHop WAbe WFar
§	- subsp. ***cephallenica***	CElw EACa NBro
§	- 'Dickson's Gold'	Widely available
	- 'Erinus Major'	IVic
	- 'Hirsuta'	ECho
	- 'Major'	ECho GKir LAst SPoG WFar
	- 'Mrs Resholt'	ECtt ESwi EWll GKir LAst SDix SMrm SWvt WFar
	- 'W.H. Paine' ♀^{H4}	ECho ECtt IFoB MDKP NMen WAbe WFar WHoo
	glomerata	CBot CElw CEnt CPLG CRWN EBWF GCra GJos LSRN MNHC NBro NLan NMir SPet WBrk WEas WFar
	- var. ***acaulis***	EACa EBee EPfP GAbr GKev GKir NLar NWCA SBfd SPoG WFar WPer
	- var. ***alba***	CBcs CFir EAEE EBee ECtt ELan EPfP EShb GJos GKir GMaP LBMP LRHS MLHP MNFA MRav NBPC NHol SBfd SPer SPlb SPoG STes SWat WCAu WClo WFar WMnd WPer WWEG
§	- - 'Schneekrone'	ECha EPfP GKir NBre SMrm WFar
	- 'Caroline'	Widely available
	- Crown of Snow	see *C. glomerata* var. *alba* 'Schneekrone'
	- var. ***dahurica***	CFir ELon NBre NLar SMrm SPet WPer
	- 'Emerald'	EBee ECtt LLHF MHer WCot WHlf
	- 'Joan Elliott'	CMac EBee ECha ECtt LEdu LSRN MNFA MRav MWat WAul WCra
	- 'Purple Pixie'	LRHS MGos
	- 'Superba' ♀^{H4}	Widely available
	grossekii	CFir EHrv LLHF NBre WHrl
	hakkiarica	WCot
	'Hannah'	EACa ECho LHop LRHS
	× ***haylodgensis*** misapplied	see *C.* × *haylodgensis* 'Plena'
§	- 'Marion Fisher' (d)	CPBP ECtt EDAr EPot WAbe WCot WHoo
§	- 'Plena' (d)	ECho ECtt ELan EPot LBee LHop LRHS NMen NPri SRms WAbe WCot WFar WHoo WKif
§	- 'Warley White' (d)	EBur ECho ELan

	- 'Yvonne'	ECtt EPot GMaP LHop LRHS SMrm SPoG WFar WNew
	'Hemswell Starlight'	WAbe
	hercegovina 'Nana'	EACa LLHF WAbe
	'Hilltop Snow'	CPBP NMen WAbe WCom
	hofmannii	EBee EBur EDAr ELan GKev MBNS NLar WFar
§	***incurva***	CSpe EBee EBur ELan EWTr GJos GKev WMoo
	isophylla ♀H2	ECho EPot
	- 'Alba' ♀H2	ECho
	- 'Flore Pleno' (d)	EBur
	- 'Mayi' misapplied	see *C.* 'Balchiniana'
	- 'Variegata'	see *C.* 'Balchiniana'
	'Jenny' **new**	CWGN EPPr SHar
	'Joe Elliott' ♀H2-3	ECho WAbe
	kemulariae	LLHF WCom
	- ***alba***	ITim
	'Kent Belle' ♀H4	Widely available
	khasiana	EBee GKev
	'Kifu' (v)	CBow
	komarovii **new**	WCot
	lactiflora	CAby CElw CMac CSev EBee ECha EPfP GAbr GCra GKev GKir GMaP IFoB MCot MLHP MSCN MWhi NEgg NVic SPer WBrE WFar WHoo WMoo WPer WTin WWEG
	- ***alba***	see *C. lactiflora* white-flowered
N	- 'Alba' ♀H4	EBee EBla EPfP GAbr GKir GMaP IVic MAvo MDKP MLHP STes WFar WMnd
	- 'Avalanche'	LRHS WCot
	- 'Blue Cross'	CMoH EBee GKir GMac LEdu LRHS NBre NLar WSpi
	- 'Blue Lady'	NBre WFar
	- 'Dixter Presence'	IPot NDov SMHy SUsu
	- dwarf pink-flowered	EBee EPfP MBNS NBre NCGa
	- 'Favourite'	CFir CSpe EBee MNrw NBPC NCGa NGdn NLar STes WFar
	- 'Loddon Anna' ♀H4	Widely available
	- 'Marchants Nimbus' **new**	SMHy
	- 'Moorland Rose'	WMoo
	- new hybrids	GJos
	- 'Pink Star'	EBee
	- 'Pouffe'	CHid CPrp EAEE EBee EBla ECtt ELan ELon EPfP GKir GMaP IVic LRHS MBri MDKP MRav NBro NGdn SMrm SPer SWat SWvt WFar
	- 'Prichard's Variety' ♀H4	Widely available
	- 'Superba' ♀H4	EBee ECtt IVic MCot SMad WClo
	- 'Violet'	GKir SWat WPer
	- 'White Pouffe'	CPrp EAEE EBee ECtt ELan ELon EPfP GKir GMaP IVic LRHS MBri MDKP NBPC NLar SPer SPoG STes SWat WFar
§	- white-flowered	CBot ECha GKir MBNS NBir SMrm SPer SWat WFar WPer
	lasiocarpa	CPBP GKev
	latifolia	EBWF ECha GAbr GJos LRHS MCot NBid NMir NVic SPer SRms WFar WMoo WTou
	- var. ***alba***	EBee ELan EPfP GAbr GCra GJos MWea NGdn SEND SPav SPer SRms SUsu WFar WHal WPer WSpi WTou WWEG
*	- 'Amethyst'	CPrp SDnm
	- blue-flowered	WSpi
	- 'Brantwood'	EBee GAbr GKir MRav MWhi SDnm SPav SRms SWat WCot WMnd WSpi
	- 'Gloaming'	ECtt MCot NPnk
	- var. ***macrantha***	EBee ELan EPfP GMaP LHop MBri MCot MWat NGdn NHol NSti SBfd SPav SPer SWat SWvt WMoo WPer WWEG
	- - 'Alba'	CMMP EBee ECha ECtt EShb EWTr GMaP LHop MCot MRav SBfd WCot WMoo WPer WWEG
	- 'Misty Dawn'	WCot WFar
§	***latiloba***	CElw CMHG GKir MWhi SBch SGar WBrk WCot WFar
§	- 'Alba' ♀H4	CElw EBee ELan EPPr EPfP GCal GCra MCot MDKP NEgg NGdn SBch SGar WBrk
	- 'Hidcote Amethyst' ♀H4	Widely available
	- 'Highcliffe Variety' ♀H4	CPrp EBee ECtt ELan EPfP GCra MDKP MRav NDov SGSe SMrm WCot WKif WMnd WWEG
*	- 'Highdown'	WFar
	- 'Percy Piper' ♀H4	EACa EBrs ELan GKir MRav NBre NBro NLar WFar WSpi
	- 'Splash'	CElw EBee MAvo
	linifolia	see *C. carnica*
	longestyla 'Isabella Blue'	EBee
	'Lynchmere'	CPBP WAbe WCom
	makaschvilii	CEnt CPla CSpe EACa EBee ECtt GKev GMac IGor MHer MWhi NLar SGSe SMad STes WCot WHrl WPer WSHC
	'Marion Fisher'	see *C.* × *haylodgensis* W. Brockbank 'Marion Fisher'
	massalskyi	GKev
	medium	LAst WTou
§	- var. ***calycanthema*** hort.	EPfP
	- 'Cup and Saucer'	see *C. medium* var. *calycanthema* hort.
	mirabilis 'Mist Maiden'	WFar
	moesiaca	GKev
	'Molly Pinsent'	EBee
	'Monic'	EPfP
	muralis	see *C. portenschlagiana*
	nitida	see *C. persicifolia* var. *planiflora*
	'Norman Grove'	ECtt EPot
	ochroleuca	CMea CPom CSpe EBee MCot SGSe STes SWat WCFE WCot WHrl WMoo
	- 'White Beauty'	CWib
	- 'White Bells'	MWhi
	odontosepala	EBee EWTr
	- from Iran	EPPr NBre
	'Oliver's Choice'	WHrl
	olympica misapplied	see *C. rotundifolia* 'Olympica'
	ossetica	EBee ECtt ELan MLHP
	pallida subsp. ***tibetica***	see *C. cashmeriana*
	parviflora Lam.	see *C. sibirica*
	patula	GJos NLar
§	- subsp. ***abietina***	NBre NLar
	'Paul Furse'	EBee ECtt MAvo MDKP MLLN NBre NCGa NSti WTin WWEG
	pelviformis	MNrw
	pendula	CSpe EPfP EWes MBNS NLar
	persicifolia	Widely available
	- var. ***alba***	Widely available
§	- 'Alba Coronata' (d)	GAbr GKir NBir WEas WFar
	- 'Alba Plena'	see *C. persicifolia* 'Alba Coronata'
	- Ashfield double ice blue (d)	NBre
	- 'Beau Belle'	EBee EPfP LSou NBPC NLar NMoo
§	- 'Bennett's Blue' (d)	EBla EHrv ELan EPfP MRav NHol NSti SPer SRms SWat WFar
	- 'Blue Bloomers' (d)	CElw CHar CLAP EBee ECtt EWes GGar IKil LLWP LRHS MAvo MLLN MNFA MRav NHol SGSe SMrm WBrk WCot WHal WPer
	- blue cup-in-cup (d)	EBla ELon MDKP MTis WFar WPtf
	- 'Blue-eyed Blonde' (v) **new**	NCGa
	- blue-flowered	GKir IFoB LAst MRav SGSe SPlb WFar

	- 'Boule de Neige' (d)	CMMP CMoH EBla ECtt WCFE WEas WSpi WWEG
	- 'Caerulea Coronata'	see *C. persicifolia* 'Coronata'
§	- 'Chettle Charm'PBR ♀H4	Widely available
	- 'Cornish Mist'	CBgR CFir CPLG EBee ECtt EHrv ELan EPfP LSou MAvo MTis NSti WCot WFut WSpi
§	- 'Coronata' (d)	ECtt GCra
	- cup and saucer blue (d)	GCra
§	- cup and saucer white (d)	EBla ELan WClo WFar
	- double blue-flowered (d)	NBro WEas
	- double white-flowered (d)	ELan WMoo
	- 'Fleur de Neige' (d) ♀H4	ECtt NBre WCot WHoo WWEG
	- 'Frances' (d)	CLAP WCom
	- 'Gawen'	EBee ECtt GBee GMaP GMac MAvo MTis NBre NHol SMrm WCot
	- 'George Chiswell'PBR	see *C. persicifolia* 'Chettle Charm'
	- 'Grandiflora'	NBre SMrm
	- 'Grandiflora Alba'	NBre NHol SMrm
	- 'Grandiflora Caerulea'	NLar
§	- 'Hampstead White' (d)	ECtt EHrv GCal NBro WEas WHil WMnd WSpi WWEG
	- 'Hetty'	see *C. persicifolia* 'Hampstead White'
	- Irish double white-flowered (d)	MAvo
	- 'Kelly's Gold'	CFir EBee EBla EPfP LAst MCCP MTis NBir NLar NPri WWEG
	- 'La Belle'	EBee ECtt EPyc NLar STes
	- 'La Bello'PBR	EBee ECtt
	- 'La Bonne Amie'	CDes EBee ECtt IKil IPot NLar
	- 'Moerheimii' (d)	EBee EPfP EShb NBir STes
	- 'Monita White'	CMoH
	- 'Perry's Boy Blue'	NPer
§	- var. ***planiflora***	CPBP WCom WThu
	- - f. ***alba***	MWat
	- 'Powder Puff' (d)	CBgR EBee GBin GMac ITim LSou MLLN MWea NEgg SMrm WCot
	- 'Pride of Exmouth' (d)	CHar CMMP ECtt EHrv ELan EShb MCCP MHer MSpe MWea WCFE WClo WMnd WPer WSpi WWEG
	- subsp. ***sessiliflora***	see *C. latiloba*
	- - 'Alba'	see *C. latiloba* 'Alba'
	- 'Snowdrift'	ELan SRms
	- Takion Series	CSpe
	- - 'Takion Blue'	MSCN
	- - 'Takion White'	WHil
	- 'Telham Beauty' misapplied	CSBt CWCL EBee ECtt ELan EPfP EShb GAbr GKir LRHS MRav NHol SMrm SPer SRms SWvt WFar WMnd WPer
	- 'Telham Beauty' ambig.	EAEE LAst MCot MSCN NEgg NGBl SBfd SWvt WSpi WWEG
	- 'Tinpenny Blue'	WTin
	- 'White Cup and Saucer'	see *C. persicifolia* cup and saucer white
	- 'White Queen' (d)	WMnd
	- 'Wortham Belle' misapplied	see *C. persicifolia* 'Bennett's Blue'
	- 'Wortham Belle' ambig.	CWGN EShb WSpi
	- 'Wortham Belle'	ECtt MAvo MBNS NDov NEgg NHol WCAu WFar
	petrophila	WAbe
	pilosa	see *C. chamissonis*
	- 'Superba'	see *C. chamissonis* 'Superba'
	'Pink Octopus'	CSev CWGN EBee ECtt LLHF LOck LRHS MBNS MCot MTis NBPC NCGa NGdn NPnk SMrm WCot WCra WFut WSpi
	'Pinkie' **new**	SBch
	pinnatifida var. ***robusta*** **new**	GKev
	planiflora	see *C. persicifolia* var. *planiflora*
	'Polly Henderson'	CPBP WAbe
§	***portenschlagiana*** ♀H4	Widely available
	- 'Catharina'	ECtt
	- 'Lieselotte'	CElw LIMB LLHF
	- 'Major'	LAst WCom WFar WMoo
	- 'Resholdt's Variety'	CBar CMea CSam EBee ECho ECtt EDAr EPfP GMaP LBee LHop LRHS MRav NPri SAga WMoo WPer
	poscharskyana	Widely available
	- 'Blauranke'	EBee EWes
	- 'Blue Gown'	GMaP IPot MNFA
	- 'Blue Waterfall'	CWGN EBrs LRHS MBNS NCGa NDov SPoG WFar
	- 'E.H. Frost'	CBre CElw EACa EBee ECho ECtt EDAr EPPr EPfP EWTr GKev GMaP LHop MBri MCot MLLN MMuc MWat NBro NRya SAga SEND SPer SRGP SRms SWvt WBrk WFar WMoo WPer
	- 'Lilacina'	EPPr
	- 'Lisduggan Variety'	CElw EBee EBur ECtt EDAr ELon EPPr EWes GKir GMaP LHop LIMB MBri MHer MNFA NBro SBch WBrk WCom WCot WFar WMoo WPer
	- 'Nana Alba' **new**	EPPr
	- 'Stella' ♀H4	EBee ECha ECho ECtt EPfP LSRN MAvo MRav NBro SDix SPer SRGP SWvt WCom WFar WMoo WRHF
	- 'Trollkind' **new**	EPPr
	- variegated (v)	EHoe
	- white-flowered	CTri ECho ELan LAst MDKP WFar
	prenanthoides	see *Asyneuma prenanthoides*
	primulifolia	EACa ELan GAbr GKir LRHS MNrw SRms SWat WMoo
	- 'Blue Oasis'	LSRN
	× ***pseudoraineri***	EACa EBur EWes LRHS NMen WCom
	ptarmicifolia **new**	GKev
	pulla	CPBP CSpe CWCL EBur ECho ECtt EDAr GGar GMaP IFro LAst LRHS NWCA SPoG SRot WAbe WFar WHoo
	- ***alba***	EBur ECho ECtt EDAr EPot LRHS WAbe
	× ***pulloides*** hort. 'G.F. Wilson' ♀H4	EACa EBee EBur ECho ECtt EPot SRkn WFar
	punctata	CBot CMHG CSpe EBee EHrv GJos GKev GKir LEdu MCot NBPC NBro NSti SBfd SPer SWat WFar WGwG WMoo WPer
	- f. ***albiflora***	GKev MNrw SHar WFar WMnd
	- - 'Alba'	CCVN
	- - 'Nana Alba'	SBch
	- 'Alina's Double' (d)	GBee GMac MNrw MSpe WWEG
	- 'Cherry Pie' **new**	EPfP
	- dwarf **new**	CPBP
	- 'Einhorn JP' **new**	IVic
	- 'Golddrache JP' **new**	IVic
	- 'Hexe JP' **new**	IVic
	- var. ***hondoensis***	GKev IGor MLHP SAga
	- - 'Bossy Boots'	SMrm
	- hose-in-hose (d)	EBla MMHG NLar WFar WGwG
	- 'Hot Lips'	CChe CMMP EBee EBla ECtt ELan EPPr EPfP EShb LRHS LSRN MBri NBPC NPnk NSti SAga SBfd SPet SPoG SRGP WClo WCot WPrP WWEG
*	- var. ***howozana***	GKev
	- var. ***microdonta*** B&SWJ 5553	WCru
	- 'Milky Way'	EPPr

	- 'Millennium'	WFar
	- 'Milly'	IVic LLHF WPGP
	- 'Moorgeist JP' **new**	IVic
	- 'Mottled' (v)	NBre
*	- 'Nana'	CCVN
	- 'Nasachtal' **new**	IVic
	- 'Pantaloons' (d)	CMac EBee EBla ECtt EWTr LRHS LSRN MBri MDKP MSpe NLar SMrm WCra
	- 'Pink Chimes' PBR	EBee GKev IVic LSou MBNS MBri MTis NCGa
	- 'Plum Wine'	MSpe
	- 'Pumpernickel JP' **new**	IVic
	- 'Reifrock'	IVic SMrm
	- 'Rosea'	SRms WFar
	- f. ***rubriflora***	CCVN ECtt ELan EPfP EPla GAbr GCra GJos LBMP LHop LRHS MCot MNrw MWat MWhi NEgg NHol SBfd SGar SMad SMrm SPer WFar WMnd WPat WPer WWEG
	- - 'Beetroot'	EBee EBla ECtt GKir IKil ITim IVic LAst MHer MTis NLar WHrl WPGP WPer
	- - 'Bowl of Cherries' PBR	EBee EBla ECtt EShb ESwi GKir IVic LLHF LSRN LSou MBri MMHG MTis NLar NMoo NPnk NSti SRkn SRot
	- - 'Cherry Bells'	EAEE EBla ECtt EPfP GMac IVic LRHS LSRN MBri MCCP MNrw NLar SPoG
	- - 'Vienna Festival'	CSBt EBee ECtt GKev GMac LEdu LSou NLar NSti WCot
	- - 'Wine 'n' Rubies'	ECtt EHrv GMac LSRN LSou MDKP MNrw MSCN SHar WCot
	- 'Seejungfrau JP' **new**	IVic
	- 'Troll JP' **new**	IVic
	- 'Twilight Bells'	NBre
	- 'Wedding Bells'	CMMP EBee EBla ECtt EHrv ELan GKev IVic LAst LRHS LSRN MBri MHer MSCN NBPC NCGa NLar NMoo NSti SPet SRkn WCAu WFar WHil WWEG
	- 'Weisser Schwan JP' **new**	IVic
	- 'Weisser Turm JP' **new**	IVic
I	- 'White Bells'	ELan EPPr MDKP
	- white hose-in-hose (d)	MNFA MNrw WBrk
	'Purple Sensation' PBR	CSpe EBee ECtt EPfP GMac LSou MBNS MNrw NCGa NPnk NSti WCot
	pusilla	see *C. cochlearifolia*
	pyramidalis	CBot CMea CMoH CSpe EBee ELan EPfP GJos GKir MCCP MLLN MMuc NGBl SBfd SDnm SPav SPlb WKif WTou WWEG
	- 'Alba'	CSpe CWib EBee ELan EPfP GJos MMuc NBre NLar SBfd SDnm SPav SPlb WWEG
	- lavender blue-flowered	CWib LAst
	raddeana	ITim MDKP WBrk
	raineri ♀H4	ECho EPot NMen NSla WAbe
*	- ***alba***	CPBP ECho EPot WAbe
	- 'Nettleton Gold'	ECho EPot
§	***rapunculoides***	EBee GJos GKev NBre SWat WFar
§	- 'Afterglow'	EBee MAvo WCot WDyG
	- 'Alba'	MAvo
	rapunculus	CArn ILis
	recurva	see *C. incurva*
	rhomboidalis Gorter	see *C. rapunculoides*
	rotundifolia	CArn CRWN EBWF ECho EPfP GJos GKir LAst LRHS MCot MHer MMuc MNHC NBre NGBl NLan SGSe SIde SPlb SWat WAbe WBrk WPer
	- var. ***alba***	EWes WAbe
§	- 'Olympica'	EBee EBur IGor MBNS MMuc NLar NPri WFar WHoo
	- 'Superba'	ECho
	- 'White Gem'	EBee EPfP GJos LBMP MBNS NBre WPtf
	'Royal Wave'	ECtt IPot NCGa
	rupestris	EBur LLHF WPat
	rupicola	WAbe
	'Samantha'	CBow CSpe EBee EBla ECtt GMac LHop LRHS LSRN MWea NPri SHar SMrm SPoG SRGP
	'Saragamine'	EBee
	'Sarastro'	Widely available
	sarmatica	ECGP EPfP GAbr GKev MNFA MWhi NBid SMrm SRms WKif
	- 'Hemelstraling'	EBee
	sartorii	EBur
§	***saxifraga***	EBur EDAr EWTr GKev ITim NWCA
	subsp. ***aucheri***	WFar
	scabrella	GKev
	scheuchzeri	CSpr
	'Senior'	EBee EPPr IVic
	'Serafinental' **new**	IVic
	seraglio	GKir
§	***sibirica***	NBre
	speciosa	EBee MWhi NBre
	'Stansfieldii'	CPBP EBur ECho LLHF LRHS NMen WPat
	'Summer Pearl'	ECtt EWll GKev SBfd SMrm
§	'Swannables'	CPou EBee ECtt LLHF MNFA MRav NCGa NChi WOut
	takesimana	Widely available
	- B&SWJ 8499	WCru
I	- 'Alba'	CSpr EBee EBla GKir LBMP MDKP NBre SHar WMoo
	- 'Beautiful Trust'	CCVN CFir CLAP EBee EBla ECtt GBee GMac LHop LRHS MCot NBPC NPnk NSti SGSe SHar SRkn SUsu WCru WPGP
	- 'Elizabeth'	Widely available
	- 'Elizabeth II' (d)	ECtt MDKP WCot
	teucrioides	NWCA
	thyrsoides	EBee ELan GKev MCot NBre SDnm SPav
	'Timsbury Perfection'	CPBP NHar WAbe
	'Tiny Bells'	LLHF
	tommasiniana ♀H4	EACa WAbe
	trachelium	CEnt CMHG EBWF EBee ELon EPfP GAbr GKir MNrw MRav NBPC NLan SAga SGar STes SWat WCot WFar WHer WMoo WPer WWEG
	- var. ***alba***	CEnt CLAP EBee GKev GKir MNrw MWhi NLar STes SWat WBrE WCot WFar WMoo WPer
	- - 'Alba Flore Pleno' (d)	CHar CLAP MAvo STes WFar
	- 'Bernice' (d)	Widely available
	- lilac-blue-flowered	SWat
	- 'Snowball'	EShb LAst LSRN LSou
	tridentata	GKev
	troegerae	GKev
	'Tymonsii'	CPBP EBur ECho LLHF NBir NMen WAbe WFar
	'Van-Houttei'	CElw CHar EBee EWes GMac SAga WCot WFar WPer
	versicolor	EACa NBre
	vidalii	see *Azorina vidalii*
	waldsteiniana	CPBP WAbe
	wanneri	EBee EBur EPfP NLar
	'Warley Gem'	GKir
	'Warley White'	see *C.* × *haylodgensis* W. Brockbank 'Warley White'

	'Warleyensis'	see *C.* × *haylodgensis* W. Brockbank 'Warley White'
	× ***wockei*** 'Puck'	EACa EBur ECho ECtt EPot LHop LLHF LRHS WAbe
	zangezura	EBee EBur EDAr EPfP GKev IKil NGdn SBfd SGar STes
	zoysii	GKev

Campanula × *Symphyandra* see *Campanula*

Campanumoea see *Codonopsis*

Campsis (*Bignoniaceae*)

	grandiflora	CArn CBcs CSBt CSPN CWGN EBee ELan EPfP LRHS LSRN MAsh SPer SRms SWvt WCFE
	radicans	CArn CBcs CDul CMac CRHN CWib EBee ECrN ELan EPfP IFFs LRHS LSRN MCot MPet MSwo SBfd SLon SPer SPlb WBVN WDin
	- 'Atrosanguinea'	EPfP
	- 'Flamenco'	CDoC CMac EBee ELan LAst LRHS LSRN MAsh NLar SBfd SCoo SLim SWvt WFar WGwG
§	- f. ***flava*** ♀H4	CBcs CDoC CHEx CMac CTri EBee ELan ELon EPfP LHop LRHS MAsh MBlu MCCP MGos NLar NPal NPla NSti SBfd SLim SPer SPoG SWvt
	- 'Indian Summer'	CBcs CSBt CWGN EBee EPfP LRHS LSRN LSou MBlu MBri MGos MREP NLar SBfd SCoo SLim SPoG
	- 'Stromboli'	EPfP
	- 'Yellow Trumpet'	see *C. radicans* f. *flava*
	× ***tagliabuana*** Dancing Flame = 'Huidan' PBR	CWGN CWit EBee LRHS MAsh NLar
	- 'Madame Galen' ♀H4	Widely available

Camptosema (*Papilionaceae*)

	praeandinum	WPGP

Camptosorus see *Asplenium*

Camptotheca (*Cornaceae*)

	acuminata	WPGP

Campylandra see *Tupistra*

Campylotropis (*Papilionaceae*)

	macrocarpa	EPfP NLar

Canarina (*Campanulaceae*)

	canariensis ♀H1	CCCN ECho ERea SOWG WPGP

Candollea see *Hibbertia*

Canna ✿ (*Cannaceae*)

	'Adam's Orange'	CDTJ CHEx XBlo
	'Alberich'	CSam SBfd
	altensteinii	CDTJ SHaC SPlb XBlo
	'Ambassador'	LAma
	'Ambassadour'	SBfd
	'Angie Summers'	SBfd
	'Annaeei' ♀H3	EAmu
	'Argentina'	SBfd SHaC
	'Assaut'	SBfd SHaC
	'Atlantis'	XBlo
	'Australia'	CDTJ EPfP EUJe SBfd SHaC XBlo
	'Black Knight'	CFir ECGP LAma LSRN SBfd SEND SHaC SPad WWlt XBlo
	'Bonfire'	CDTJ CHEx
	brasiliensis	CFee CFir CHII CRHN SBfd SHaC XBlo
	'Brillant'	LAma SBfd SBst SHaC WDyG
	'Caballero'	SBfd
	'Caliméro'	SBfd
	'Canary'	XBlo
	'Carnaval'	SBfd SHaC
	'Centenaire de Rozain-Boucharlat'	SBfd
	'Centurion'	LAma
	'Champigny'	SBfd
	'Champion'	SBfd SHaC
	'Cherry Red' misapplied	see *C.* 'Pfitzer's Cherry Red'
	'Chinese Coral' Schmid	CHEx LAma
I	'Citrina'	SHaC XBlo
§	'City of Portland'	LAma SBfd SChr SHaC
§	'Cleopatra'	CCCN EAmu EPfP LAma SBfd WGwG XBlo
	coccinea	SAPC
§	'Colibri'	LAma SBfd
	'Conestoga'	SBfd
	'Confetti'	see *C.* 'Colibri'
	'Corail'	SBfd SHaC
	'Corrida'	SBfd
	'Corsica' (Island Series)	SBfd
	'Creamy White'	CHEx XBlo
	'Crimson Beauty'	LAma
	'Délibáb'	CSam LAma SBfd SHaC WDyG
	'Di Bartolo'	XBlo
	'Dondo'	SBfd SHaC
	'Durban' ambig.	CChe CWGN CWit EBee ECtt EPfP EUJe LAma LAst LSRN MAvo SAga SPad WClo WCom WGwG
	'Durban' Hiley, orange-flowered	see *C.* 'Phasion'
	edulis	CDTJ CHEx EUJe SBfd SHaC
	- green-leaved	SHaC
§	× ***ehemanii*** ♀H3	CAvo CDTJ CRHN CSev ETod EUJe LPJP SBfd SChr SDix SHaC WCom WPGP
	'Emblème'	SBfd SHaC
	'En Avant'	CDTJ CHEx LAma SBfd SHaC SPlb
	'Endeavour'	CHEx EUJe LPJP MSKA SHaC
	'Erebus' ♀H3	CHVG MSKA SBfd SDix SHaC
	'Ermine'	SHaC WCot
	'Espresso Festival'	NGdn
	'Étoile du Feu'	XBlo
	'Eureka'	SBfd
	'Evening Star'	LAma
	'Extase'	SBfd
	'Fatamorgana'	LAma SBfd SHaC
	'Felix Ragout'	LAma
	Firebird	see *C.* 'Oiseau de Feu'
	flaccida	SHaC
	'Flame'	SHaC XBlo
§	'Florence Vaughan'	SBfd
	'General Eisenhower' ♀H3	SHaC
	× ***generalis***	SHaC
	× ***generalis*** × ***indica***	SHaC
	glauca	EUJe SDix SHaC
	'Gnom'	SBfd
*	'Gold Ader'	LAma
	'Gold Dream'	LAma
	'Golden Girl'	SBfd
	'Golden Lucifer'	ELan LAma
	'Golden Orb' **new**	SBfd
	'Gran Canaria'	SBfd SHaC
	'Grand Duc'	SHaC
	'Grande'	CFir MAJR SBfd SHaC
	'Heinrich Seidel'	CHEx SBfd
	heliconiifolia **new**	SBfd
	Henlade	CDTJ
	'Hercule'	CHEx SBfd
	'Ibis'	EAmu EPfP SHaC

	indica	CAbb CDTJ CSpe EShb LTen SAPC SArc SBfd SHaC SPlb
	- 'Kreta' (Island Series)	SBfd
	- 'Purpurea'	CDTJ CHEx EAmu EUJe MCot SBfd SChr SDix SHaC SMrm SPlb WDyG WPGP
	- 'Red King Rupert'	CCCN
	- 'Russian Red' ♀H3	SBfd SHaC
	- Tropicanna Gold = 'Mactro' **new**	EPfP
	'Ingeborg' ♀H3	LAma
	'Intrigue'	SHaC
	iridiflora misapplied	see *C.* × *ehemanii*
	iridiflora Ruiz & Pav.	CDTJ CHEx CSpe SAPC SArc
	'Italia'	WHil
	'Jivago'	SHaC
	'Kalimpong'	CDTJ
I	'King Humbert' (blood-red)	CBcs CDTJ CHEx EPfP LAma LAst LRHS SBfd XBlo
	King Humbert (orange-red)	see *C.* 'Roi Humbert'
	'King Midas'	see *C.* 'Richard Wallace'
	'Königin Charlotte'	SBfd SHaC
	'La Bohème' (Grand Opera Series)	LAma
	latifolia **new**	SHaC
	'Lenape' ♀H3	SBfd
	'Lesotho Lil'	CHll SBfd SHaC
	'Liberté'	see *C.* 'Wyoming'
	'Louis Cayeux' ♀H3	SDix
	'Louis Cottin'	CBcs CCCN CDTJ CHEx EPfP LAma LRHS SBfd SHaC WHil
	'Lucifer'	CCCN CHEx LAma LRHS NEgg NPer SEND SPlb WBrE
	lutea	CHEx XBlo
	'Madame Angèle Martin'	SBfd XBlo
	'Madame Paul Casaneuve'	SBfd
	'Madeira' (Island Series)	SBfd
	'Malawiensis Variegata'	see *C.* 'Striata'
	'Marabout'	SBfd SBst SHaC
	'Margaret Strange'	SBfd SHaC
	'Marvel'	LAma
	'Maudie Malcolm'	EPfP
	'Montaigne'	SHaC
	'Mrs Oklahoma'	LAma SBfd
	'Mrs Tim Taylor'	SHaC
	'Musifolia' ♀H3	CDTJ CHEx EAmu ETod EUJe EWes LPJP SBfd SDix SEND SHaC WDyG XBlo
	'Mystique' ♀H3	EUJe EWes SBfd SDix SHaC
	'Ointment Pink'	XBlo
§	'Oiseau de Feu'	LAma
	'Oiseau d'Or'	WHil
	'Orange Perfection'	CFir CSam LAma LAst SBfd SMrm
	'Orange Punch'	SBfd WCot
	'Orchid'	see *C.* 'City of Portland'
	'Osric'	CSpe
	'Pacific Beauty'	CSpe CWit EAmu ECtt EUJe NGdn SBfd WCot
	'Panache'	CDTJ CHEx EUJe SBfd SHaC WCot WDyG
	paniculata	SHaC
	'Peach Pink'	XBlo
	'Pearlescent Pink'	XBlo
	'Perkeo'	LAma SBfd
§	'Pfitzer's Cherry Red' **new**	WHil
§	'Phasion' (v) ♀H3	CHEx CHll CSpe ELan EPfP EUJe EWes LSRN MSCN NGdn NPer NPla NVic SBfd SBst SDix SHaC SPoG WCot XBlo
	'Picadore'	SBfd SHaC
	'Picasso' ♀H3	CBcs CCCN CDTJ CHEx CPLG LAma LRHS SBfd SEND XBlo

	'Pink Champagne'	XBlo
	'Pink Futurity' (Futurity Series)	SBfd
	'Pink Perfection'	SHaC
	'Pink Sunburst' (v)	CDTJ EUJe NGdn SBfd SHaC SPlb
	'Plaster Pink'	XBlo
	'President'	LAma LRHS SBfd SHaC WBrE XBlo
	'Pretoria'	see *C.* 'Striata'
	'Primrose Yellow'	WHil
	'Prince Charmant'	SBfd
	'Pringle Bay' (v)	SBfd SHaC
	'Professor Lorentz'	see *C.* 'Wyoming'
	'Ra' ♀H3	MSKA SHaC
	'Red Futurity' (Futurity Series)	SBfd
	'Red Wine'	LRHS
§	'Richard Wallace'	CPLG CSam LAma SBfd SHaC SPlb XBlo
	'Robert Kemp'	SBfd
§	'Roi Humbert'	CSam LAst SBfd SChr SHaC
	'Roi Soleil' ♀H3	LAma
	'Roitelet'	CHEx
	'Rose Futurity' (Futurity Series)	SBfd
	'Rosemond Coles'	CHEx CSam LAma SBfd SHaC XBlo
	'Russian Red'	SBfd
	'Saladin'	SHaC
	'Sémaphore'	SBfd XBlo
	'Shenandoah' ♀H3	SBfd
	'Singapore Girl'	SBfd
	'Snow-white'	XBlo
	'Soudan'	CDTJ SBfd
	speciosa	CDTJ XBlo
	'Strasbourg'	CSam LAma NPer
	'Strawberry Pink'	XBlo
	'Striata' misapplied	see *C.* 'Stuttgart'
§	'Striata' (v) ♀H3	CCCN CDTJ CHEx CSpe CWGN EBee ECtt EPfP EUJe LPJP LRHS LSRN MAvo MREP NGdn NMoo NPla SAga SBfd SEND SHaC SMad WCom WCot WDyG XBlo
	'Striped Beauty' (v)	CCCN CDTJ CHVG EUJe SBfd
§	'Stuttgart' (v)	CDTJ CSpe EAmu EPfP EWes LRHS NMoo SBfd SHaC WCom WCot
	'Südfunk'	SBfd
	'Summer Gold'	XBlo
	'Summer Joy'	SHaC
	'Sunset'	CWGN NGdn SBfd WCot
	'Talisman'	LAma XBlo
	'Taney'	EUJe MSKA
	'Tchad'	SHaC
	'Tricarinata'	CHEx
	'Triomphe'	SBfd SHaC
	(Tropical Series) 'Tropical Red'	SBfd SGar SHaC
	- 'Tropical Rose'	SBfd SHaC SRms WCot
	- 'Tropical Salmon'	SHaC
	- 'Tropical White'	SBfd SGar SHaC WHil
	- 'Tropical Yellow'	SBfd SGar SHaC
	Tropicanna	see *C.* 'Phasion'
	tuerckheimii **new**	SBfd SHaC
	'Valentine'	WCot
	'Vanilla Pink'	XBlo
*	'Variegata' (v)	LAma
	'Velvet Red' **new**	WHil
	'Verdi' ♀H3	CSpe LAma SBfd SHaC
	warscewiczii	CDTJ CPLG CSpe SBfd SBst SHaC
	'Weymouth'	CDTJ
	'Wine 'n' Roses'	SHaC
	'Woodbridge Pink'	XBlo
§	'Wyoming' ♀H3	CBcs CCCN CDTJ CHEx CHVG CSam ECGP ETod EUJe LAma LRHS

	MCCP NVic SBfd SBst SEND SHaC XBlo
'Yellow Humbert' misapplied	see *C.* 'Richard Wallace', *C.* 'Cleopatra', *C.* 'Florence Vaughan'
'Yellow Humbert'	LAma WHil

Cantua (*Polemoniaceae*)

buxifolia 🏆H2-3	CAbb CBcs CCCN CFee CPLG EBee ECre EShb LRHS SOWG SSpi WPGP
- 'Alba'	CCCN
- 'Dancing Oaks'	WCot

Cape gooseberry see *Physalis peruviana*

Capnoides see *Corydalis*

Capparis (*Capparaceae*)

spinosa	CCCN

Capsicum (*Solanaceae*)

annuum	CCCN CSim MBri
- var. ***annuum*** (Grossum Group) 'Corno di Toro Rosso' 🏆H2	ELau
- - (Longum Group) cayenne	CCCN
- - - 'Bolivian Rainbow'	ELau
- - - jalapeno	SVic
- - 'Prairie Fire' 🏆H2	CCCN
- 'Apache' 🏆H2	CCCN SEND
baccatum	CSim
- 'Lemon Drop'	NExo
chinense	CSim
- Habanero Group 🏆H2	SVic
frutescens	CSim
pubescens	CSim

Caragana (*Papilionaceae*)

CC 3945	CPLG
arborescens	CAgr CArn CDul CMCN EBee EPfP GKir NWea SEND SPer SPlb WDin
- 'Lorbergii'	CEnd GKir MBlu SPer WFoF
- 'Pendula'	CLnd CMac CWib ELan GKir LAst MAsh NEgg NHol NLar SCoo SLim SPer WDin
- 'Walker'	CDul CEnd CMac CWib EBee ELan EPfP GKir MAsh MBlu MBri MGos NHol NLar NWea SCoo SLim SMad SPer SPoG WSpi
jubata	NLar
pygmaea	NLar

caraway see *Carum carvi*

carambola see *Averrhoa carambola*

Cardamine ✿ (*Brassicaceae*)

angustata new	WCru
asarifolia misapplied	see *Pachyphragma macrophyllum*
bulbifera	CLAP EBee ELon EPPr GBin GEdr LEdu NRya WCom WCru WSHC
californica	EBee EPPr NRya WCru WMoo
concatenata	WCru
digitata	EBee GCrs MTho
diphylla	CDes CLAP EBee LEdu NLar SKHP WCot WCru WFar
- 'American Sweetheart'	WCot
- 'Eco Cut Leaf'	CDes EBee WCot WCru WPGP
- 'Eco Moonlight'	IMou WCru
enneaphylla	CLAP GMaP LEdu NDov NLar
glanduligera	EBee ELon EPPr GEdr LEdu MMoz MNrw SMrm WCot WCru WPGP
§ ***heptaphylla***	CAby CLAP ECha ELon EWTr GKir
- 'Big White'	GCal NCGa SPoG
- Guincho form	CLAP EPPr GBin WCot WPGP
- white-flowered	CLAP GBBs GMaP
§ ***kitaibelii***	CLAP ECha GBin LEdu WCot WCru
latifolia Vahl	see *C. raphanifolia*
macrophylla	CLAP EBee EWld GCrs LEdu SWat WCot
- CD&R 561	NCGa
- 'Bright and Bronzy'	GEdr WCru
maxima	LEdu WCru
microphylla	EBee
pentaphylla 🏆H4	CSpe EBee EBrs ECho ELan ELon EPPr EWTr GBBs GEdr GGar GKir IFro LPla MCot MNFA NBir NLar SUsu WBor WCot
- bright pink-flowered	CLAP WCot
pratensis	CArn CRWN CWat EBWF EBee EHon MCot MHer MNHC MSKA MWts NLan NMir NPri SIde SWat WFar WHer WMoo WSFF WShi
- 'Diane's Petticoat'	MHer MNrw WHoo
- 'Edith' (d)	CLAP GBin MMoz MNrw
- 'Flore Pleno' (d)	CAby CBre CFee CHVG CSpe CWan EBee ECha ELan IFro MHer MNrw MTho NBid NBir NBro NLar NPnk NPri SBch SUsu SWat WAlt WCom WFar WSFF WSHC
- white-flowered	WAlt
- 'William' (d)	EPPr MNrw WMoo
quinquefolia	CAby CDes CElw CLAP CMea CPom EBee ECha EHrv ELon LEdu MMoz NDov NLar NMyG SDys SMrm SSvw WBrk WCot WCru WOut WPGP
§ ***raphanifolia***	CBre CDes CRow EBee ECha EPPr GAbr GBin GCal GGar IFro LEdu LLWG NBid NBro NChi NSti SKHP SWat WMoo WOut WPGP WTin
trifolia	CMac CSpe EBee ECha EHrv ELon EPPr EWTr GBin GCal GCrs GEdr GGar GKir GMaP IFro MRav NBir NBro NHol NLar NRya NVic SWat WCot WCru WFar WMoo
waldsteinii	CAby CDes CLAP CSpe EBee ECho EHrv GEdr IMou LEdu NCGa SBch SCnR SUsu WCru WHoo WSHC
yezoensis B&SWJ 4659	WCru

cardamon see *Elettaria cardamomum*

Cardiandra (*Hydrangeaceae*)

alternifolia	CLAP
- B&SWJ 5719	WCru
- B&SWJ 5845	WCru
- B&SWJ 6354	WCru
- 'Pink Geisha'	WCru
amamiohshimensis	EWld WCru
formosana	CGHE CLAP CPLG WPGP
- B&SWJ 2005	WCru
- 'Crûg's Abundant'	WCru
- 'Hsitou'	WCru
- 'Hsitou Splendour'	WCru

Cardiocrinum (*Liliaceae*)

cathayanum	CBct GAuc GEdr WCot WPGP WWst
cordatum	ECho GAuc WAul WBVN
- B&SWJ 4841	WCru
- var. ***glehnii***	CCCN ECho GAuc GEdr
- - B&SWJ 4758	WCru
- red-veined	GEdr
giganteum	Widely available

- B&SWJ 2419	WCru
- HWJK 2158 from Nepal	WCru
- var. ***yunnanense***	CBcs CMil CPom EBrs ECho EPfP GAbr GAuc GEdr GGGa GKir GLin GMaP ITim LRHS NBid WCot WCru WPGP

cardoon see *Cynara cardunculus*

Carduus (*Asteraceae*)

benedictus	see *Cnicus benedictus*

Carex (*Cyperaceae*)

from Uganda	MMoz SApp
acuta	GFor GKir MSKA
- 'Variegata' (v)	CBen CRow EHoe EHon EPla EShb GMaP LLWG LPBA MMoz MMuc MWts NBro NOak SApp SBfd WCot WFar WHal WMoo WPnP WWEG
acutiformis	CRWN EBWF GFor NMir NSco
alba	EPPr GFor WCot
albida	EHul LRHS
albula	MMoz
'Amazon Mist'	EPPr GFor LRHS WNew
appalachica	EPPr
appressa	SApp
arenaria	EBWF GBin GFor
atrata	EBee EHoe EPla WHrl
§ - subsp. ***pullata***	GCal
- - KEKE 494	EBee WPGP
aurea	EPPr GFor IFoB NHol
baccans	CPLG EBee GCal NOak SGSe
bebbii	EPPr
berggrenii	EBee ECou EHoe ELan EPPr GKir LEdu LPBA NCob NLar NWCA SPlb SWat WTin WWEG
binervis	CRWN EBWF
boottiana	EWes
brizoides	IMou
brunnea	EWes SBfd SHDw
- 'Jenneke' (v)	CChe CKno EBee EPPr EPfP EPla LBMP LRHS MBri SBfd SGSe SHDw SLim SMrm SWvt WCot
- 'Variegata' (v)	CChe CEnt EHoe MMoz SApp SBfd SHDw WWEG WWFP
buchananii ♀^{H4}	Widely available
- 'Viridis'	ELan EPPr GBin
bushii	NCob
buxbaumii	SRms
§ ***canescens*** subsp. ***canescens***	CRWN EBWF
chathamica	CAby EBee LRHS MMuc SApp
'China Blue'	EPPr MMoz SApp SGSe
ciliatomarginata 'Treasure Island' (v)	EPPr
comans	EPPr EPfP EShb GKir NBro NHol NWsh
- from Dunedin, New Zealand **new**	EPPr
- 'Bronze Perfection'	SMea SWal WFar
- bronze-leaved	Widely available
- 'Bronzita'	EPPr LRHS
- 'Copper Green'	SMea
- 'Dancing Flame'	CPrp CWCL EBee ELon MBri NWsh
- 'Feebers Dwarf'	WWEG
- 'Frosted Curls'	Widely available
- green-leaved	GFor
- 'Kupferflamme'	EBee EPPr
- red-leaved	CWCL LAst MGos NLar SRms
- 'Small Red'	see *C. comans* 'Taranaki'
§ - 'Taranaki'	EBee EPPr EPfP GKir MBNS MMoz SCoo SWal
conica	MWat
- 'Hime-kan-suge'	see *C. conica* 'Snowline'
- 'Kiku-sakura' (v)	EPPr NHol
§ - 'Snowline' (v)	EBee ECha EHoe ELan EPfP EPla GKev GKir GMaP LEdu LLWP LPBA LRHS LTen MMoz NBro NHol NLar NWsh SBfd SGSe SPer SWal SWvt WMoo WPer WTin
crinita	EPPr
cristatella	EPPr
§ ***cuprina***	CRWN EBWF
'Curly Whirly'	SPad
curta	see *C. canescens* subsp. *canescens*
* ***cyperus***	GKir
dallii	EKen EWes MMoz MMuc SGSe WHrl
davisii	EPPr
demissa	see *C. viridula* subsp. *oedocarpa*
depauperata	CRWN EBWF EHoe
digitata	CRWN
dioica	CRWN EBWF
dipsacea	CKno CWCL EBee EBrs ECou EHoe EHul EPPr EShb GFor GGar GMaP LRHS MMoz MNrw NGdn NHol NWsh SBfd WDin WHal WMoo WPer WPnP WTin WWEG
- 'Dark Horse'	CKno EBee EHoe EPPr ETod GCal LLHF LRHS SBfd SMea WClo WPtf
divulsa subsp. ***divulsa***	CRWN EBWF
§ ***dolichostachya*** 'Kaga-nishiki' (v)	CSBt EBee EPPr LEdu LHop MMoz SLim WPnP WPrP WWEG
duthiei	see *C. atrata* subsp. *pullata*
echinata	CRWN EBWF
elata	GKir
§ - 'Aurea' (v) ♀^{H4}	Widely available
- 'Bowles's Golden'	see *C. elata* 'Aurea'
- 'Knightshayes' ♀^{H4}	CKno EBee EWes GBin MMoz NLar SGSe WCot
'Evergold'	see *C. oshimensis* 'Evergold'
firma 'Variegata' (v)	GEdr MWat NMen NWCA WAbe WThu
flacca	CKno CRWN EBWF EHoe EPPr GBin GFor GKir
- 'Bias' (v)	EPla MMoz
- 'Blue Zinger' **new**	CKno WWEG
§ - subsp. ***flacca***	EBee EWes MMoz NSti SMea WPGP
flagellifera	Widely available
- 'Auburn Cascade'	EBee EPfP LRHS NBPC NHol SApp SBfd
- 'Coca-Cola'	NOak SGSe
- 'Rapunzel'	EBee EPPr MMoz WPGP
flava	CKno EHoe EPPr GFor
fortunei	see *C. morrowii* Boott
fraseri	see *Cymophyllus fraserianus*
fraserianus	see *Cymophyllus fraserianus*
glauca Bosc. ex Boott	see *C. glaucescens*
glauca Scop.	see *C. flacca* subsp. *flacca*
§ ***glaucescens***	CWCL EPPr EPla SBfd WPGP
'Gold Fountains'	see *C. dolichostachya* 'Kaga-nishiki'
granularis	EPPr
I 'Grayassina'	CKno EPPr
grayi	CDes EBee EBrs EHoe GFor LEdu LLWG LRHS MAvo MBlu MSCN MSKA NCGa NLar NOak NPnk SGSe WPtf
§ ***hachijoensis***	WFar
'Happy Wanderer'	SLPl
hirta	CRWN EBWF NSco
hispida	MCCP
hostiana	CRWN EBWF
'Ice Dance' (v)	CKno CWGN EBee EHon EPPr EPla GGar GKev GQue LEdu LRHS

		MMoz NHol NOak SBch SBfd STes SWvt WPGP WPrP WPtf WWEG
	kaloides	EBee EHoe EPPr
	'Kan-suge'	see *C. morrowii* Boott
§	***leporina***	CRWN EBWF
	limosa	EBWF
	lupulina	NOak
	lurida	CKno EPfP GFor MAvo MBNS
	- 'Silver'	EPPr MBNS
	macrocephala	GFor
	'Majken'	GFor
	maorica	EPPr
	maritima Gunnerus	CRWN EBWF
	mertensii NNS 07-98	EPPr
	Milk Chocolate = 'Milchoc'PBR (v)	CWGN EBee EPfP LRHS NMun SApp
	montana	EBee LRHS
	morrowii misapplied	see *C. oshimensis*, *C. hachijoensis*
§	***morrowii*** Boott	CWCL EPPr
I	- 'Fisher's Form' (v)	CKno CTri EBee EPPr EPla LEdu LHop MMoz MMuc MRav NGdn NHol NLar NWsh SApp SBfd SEND SGSe SWvt WFar WPGP WPer WWEG
	- 'Gilt' (v)	EAEE EBee EHoe EPPr EPla LBMP LRHS MBNS NHol
	- 'Nana Variegata' (v)	CTri NBir WPGP
	- var. ***temnolepis***	IMou
	- - 'Silk Tassel' (v)	EPPr SGSe WWEG
N	- 'Variegata' (v)	EHoe EHrv EHul ELan EPPr EPfP EPla GCal GKev GMaP LAst LPBA MMoz MRav NBir NHol NSti SLPl SRms WCot WEas WFar WPnP
	muehlenbergii	EPPr
	muricata	EPPr
	muskingumensis	Widely available
	- 'Ice Fountains' (v)	EPPr WWEG
	- 'Little Midge'	CKno EBee EBrs EPPr GCal GKir LRHS WCot WWEG
	- 'Oehme' (v)	CKno CWCL EBee EBrs EPPr EPla EShb GBin GCal LEdu LLWG LRHS MSCN NBid NHol SGSe WPtf WTin WWEG
	- 'Silberstreif' (v)	CKno EBee EPPr GBin GGar LEdu MMuc NLar SApp
	nigra (L.) Reichard	CRWN EBWF EHon EPPr
§	- 'On-line' (v)	CKno EHrv EPPr MBNS MMoz NHol NWsh SApp
	- 'Variegata'	see *C. nigra* 'On-line'
	No 1, Nanking (Greg's broad leaf)	MMoz
	No 4, Nanking (Greg's thin leaf)	EPPr MMoz SApp
	normalis	EPPr
	obnupta	CKno EPPr WWEG
	ornithopoda 'Aurea'	see *C. ornithopoda* 'Variegata'
§	- 'Variegata' (v)	EBee ECtt EHul EPPr GFor MBrN MMoz NBro NGdn NHol NOak NWsh SBch WMoo WWEG
§	***oshimensis***	EPPr MMoz
§	- 'Evergold' (v) ♀H4	Widely available
	- 'Variegata' (v)	NBir
	otrubae	see *C. cuprina*
	ovalis	see *C. leporina*
	pallescens 'Breckland Frost' (v)	EPPr
	panicea	CKno CRWN CSBt CWCL EBWF EBee EHoe EPPr EPla LLWG MMoz MSKA SApp SBch SGSe WGrn WMoo

	paniculata	CRWN GFor NSco
	parviflora new	SMea
	pendula	Widely available
	- 'Cool Jazz' (v)	EPPr MAvo WAlt
	- 'Moonraker' (v)	CBot CWCL EBee EHoe EPPr EPla MAvo MBNS MLLN MSKA NOak SApp WCot WSpi WWEG
	petriei	CWCL ECha ETod EWes LLWP MBNS MMoz NVic WCot WFar WTin
	phyllocephala	EShb
	- 'Sparkler' (v)	CBod CKno EBee ECtt EHoe ELon EPla EShb GGar LAst LEdu LHop LRHS MCCP MMuc NCGa NSti SBfd SGSe SPad SPoG SRms SWvt WClo WCot WFar WGrn WPGP
	plantaginea	EBee EBrs EHoe EPPr EPla GBin LEdu SApp WCot WMoo WPGP WWEG
	praegracilis	CKno EPPr
	Pritchard's selection (v)	IFro
	projecta	EPPr
	pseudocyperus	CPom CRWN EBWF EHoe EHon GBin GFor GKir LPBA MMoz MMuc MSKA NPer NWsh SEND SWat WMoo WPnP
	pulicaris	CRWN
	'Red Rooster'	WNew
	remota	CRWN EBWF EHoe EPPr
	riparia	CRWN EBWF LPBA MMoz MMuc MSKA NHol NPer NSco SWat WFar WShi
	- 'Bowles's Golden'	see *C. elata* 'Aurea'
	rostrata	CRWN EBWF
	sabynensis	see *C. umbrosa* subsp. *sabynensis*
	secta	CKno ECou EPPr GFor GGar GMaP MNrw SGSe SHDw WDyG WMoo
	- from Dunedin, New Zealand	EPPr
	siderosticha	EPla SLPl WPGP
	- 'Banana Boat'	see *C. siderosticha* 'Golden Falls'
	- 'Echigo-nishiki' (v)	EPPr
§	- 'Golden Falls' (v)	LEdu LRHS SGSe SMad
	- 'Golden Fountains'	WCot
	- 'Kisokaido' (v)	EPPr LEdu LRHS WCot
	- 'Old Barn'	EBee
	- 'Shima-nishiki' (v)	CPMA CPrp EBee ECtt EPPr EPfP LAst LBMP LEdu LRHS MBNS NOak SAga SMad WFar WWEG
	- 'Variegata' (v)	Widely available
	'Silver Sceptre' (v)	Widely available
	'Silver Sparkler'	NBir
	'Silver Streams'	WWEG
	solandri	CSam LEdu NWsh SApp SBfd SGSe SHDw WMoo WPtf
	spissa	CKno MNrw
	stricta Gooden. 'Bowles's Golden'	see *C. elata* 'Aurea'
	sylvatica	CRWN EBWF EHoe GFor
	tenuiculmis	CKno CWCL EBee EBrs EPPr EShb LBMP LHop MAvo NBPC NHol NOak NSti NWsh SBfd SGSe SRms SWal WCot WTin WWEG
	- 'Cappucino'	CKno
	testacea	Widely available
	- dark new	EPfP
	- 'Old Gold'	EBee ELan EPPr EWes LRHS MMuc NOak SBfd SMad SPlb WFar WGrn WMoo
	- 'Prairie Fire'	EPPr LRHS
	texensis	EPPr
	'The Beatles'	EBee EHoe EPPr MMoz NBir NHol

trifida	CHEx CKno EHoe EKen GFor GGar MNrw NWsh SMad WFar WMoo WPnP
- 'Chatham Blue'	CHid EPPr GBin LRHS MAvo MMoz MMuc NBir SEND
- 'Rekohu Sunrise' (v) **new**	CKno EBee EPPr SGSe
umbrosa	CKno EBee EPPr EShb
subsp. ***sabynensis*** 'Thinny Thin' (v)	
uncifolia	ECou
viridula	EBWF
§ - subsp. ***oedocarpa***	CRWN EBWF
- subsp. ***viridula***	CRWN EBWF
vulpina	EPPr
vulpinoidea	EPPr

Carica (*Caricaceae*)

papaya 'Babaco'	CCCN

Carissa (*Apocynaceae*)

grandiflora	see *C. macrocarpa*
§ ***macrocarpa*** (F)	CCCN EShb MWya

Carlina (*Asteraceae*)

acanthifolia	ECho
- subsp. ***cyanara*** JJA 274.101	NWCA
acaulis	CArn ECho ELan EPfP GEdr GKev GKir GPWP MNHC NWCA SDnm SPav SPlb WFar
- SDR 3566	GKev
- subsp. ***acaulis***	GPoy
- bronze-leaved	MCCP NBPC
- var. ***caulescens***	see *C. acaulis* subsp. *simplex*
§ - subsp. ***simplex***	EBee ECha GGar GKir GMaP NPri WFar
- - bronze-leaved	CBow SMad SPhx
vulgaris	EBWF
- 'Silver Star'	GEdr SPhx

Carmichaelia (*Papilionaceae*)

'Abundance'	ECou
'Angie'	ECou
angustata 'Buller'	ECou
appressa	ECou GGar
- 'Ellesmere'	ECou
astonii	ECou
- 'Ben More'	ECou
- 'Chalk Ridge'	ECou
australis	EBee WSHC
'Charm'	ECou
'Clifford Bay'	ECou
corrugata	ECou
curta	ECou
enysii	CCCN EBee
fieldii 'Westhaven'	ECou
flagelliformis 'Roro'	ECou
glabrata	WCot
'Hay and Honey'	ECou
× ***hutchinsii*** 'County Park'	GGar
kirkii	ECou
'Lilac Haze'	ECou
monroi	ECou
- 'Rangitata'	ECou
- 'Tekapo'	ECou
odorata	CPLG ECou
- 'Lakeside'	ECou
- 'Riverside'	ECou
ovata 'Calf Creek'	ECou
'Parson's Tiny'	ECou
petriei	ECou SMad
- 'Aviemore'	ECou
- 'Lindis'	ECou
- 'Pukaki'	ECou
- Virgata Group	ECou
'Porter's Pass'	ECou
'Spangle'	ECou
stevensonii	EPfP WBVN WSHC
'Tangle'	ECou
uniflora	ECou
- 'Bealey'	ECou
'Weka'	ECou
williamsii	ECou

× *Carmispartium* see *Carmichaelia*

Carpenteria (*Hydrangeaceae*)

californica ♀H3	CBot CPMA CSBt CTri EBee ELan EPfP EPla EWTr GKev GKir LAst LRHS MBri MGos MWat NLar NPal NPri SEND SPer SReu SSpi SWvt WCot WDin WPat WSpi
- 'Bodnant'	CDul EBee ELan LRHS MBri MGos MWea SWvt WPGP WSpi
- 'Elizabeth'	CAbP CBcs CPMA CSBt CWGN ELan EPfP GKir LRHS LSRN MAsh SPer SPoG SSpi SSta WCot WDin WPGP WPat
- 'Ladhams' Variety'	CBcs CPMA EBee EPfP LRHS MGos MRav NLar SRkn SWvt WCFE WSpi

Carpinus ✿ (*Corylaceae*)

sp.	CMen LSRN
betulus ♀H4	Widely available
- 'Columnaris'	CDul CLnd CTho EBee GKir
* - 'Columnaris Nana'	CMCN
§ - 'Fastigiata' ♀H4	CCVT CDoC CDul CEnd CLnd CMCN CMac CSBt CTho CWib EBee ECrN ELan EPfP GKir LAst LBuc LHop LMaj LRHS MGos NEgg NPri NWea SBfd SCoo WDin WFar WHar WMou
- 'Frans Fontaine'	CCVT CDoC CDul CEnd CMCN CTho EBee EPfP GKir IArd LMaj MBlu MBri MGos NLar NWea SCoo SLim SPer SPoG
- 'Globus'	MBlu
- 'Incisa'	WMou
I - 'Monumentalis'	LMaj
- 'Pendula'	CDul CEnd CLnd CTho EBee GKir MBlu SPoG WDin
- 'Purpurea'	CEnd LMaj MBlu MGos NLar
- 'Pyramidalis'	see *C. betulus* 'Fastigiata'
- 'Quercifolia'	CDul EBee
caroliniana	CLnd CMCN SBir SMad
- 'Sentinel Dries'	MBlu
cordata	MBlu SBir WDin
coreana	SBir
fangiana	CEnd CGHE CPLG CTho EBee SKHP WPGP
fargesiana	EGFP
fargesii	see *C. viminea*
henryana	CMen CPLG SBir
japonica ♀H4	CDul CEnd CMCN CMen CTho EGFP EPfP GKir LLHF MBlu SBir SCoo WDin
- B&SWJ 10803	WCru
- B&SWJ 11072	WCru
kawakamii	WCru
CWJ 12412 **new**	
laxiflora	CMen CPLG MPkF WFar WPGP
- B&SWJ 10809	WCru
- B&SWJ 11035	WCru

- var. ***longispica*** B&SWJ 8772	WCru
- var. ***macrostachya***	see *C. viminea*
macrocarpa	EGFP
orientalis	CMCN SBir
polyneura	SBir
pubescens	GKir WPGP
rankanensis RWJ 9839	WCru
× ***schuschaensis***	EBtc GKir SBir
shensiensis	CDul
tschonoskii B&SWJ 10800	WCru
turczaninowii ♀H4	CBcs CDul CMHG CMen GKir IDee NLar NPal SBir STre WDin WPGP
§ ***viminea***	CEnd CPLG MBri SBir

Carpobrotus (*Aizoaceae*)

§ ***edulis***	CCCN CDTJ CDoC EShb SAPC SArc SChr SEND WHer
- var. ***edulis***	CHEx
- var. ***rubescens***	CCCN CHEx
muirii	CCCN EShb
rossii	GGar
sauerae	CCCN

Carpodetus (*Escalloniaceae*)

serratus	CBcs CTrC

Carrierea (*Flacourtiaceae*)

calycina	WPGP

Carthamus (*Asteraceae*)

tinctorius	CArn MNHC SPav

carrot see *Daucus carota*

Carum (*Apiaceae*)

carvi	CArn CWan ELau GPoy MHer MNHC NPri SIde SVic WJek
petroselinum	see *Petroselinum crispum*

Carya ✿ (*Juglandaceae*)

aquatica	CMCN
cordiformis	CTho EPfP MBlu
glabra	CBcs
N ***illinoinensis*** (F)	CAgr CBcs MBri
- 'Carlson No 3' seedling (F)	CAgr
- 'Colby' seedling (F)	CAgr
- 'Cornfield' (F)	CAgr
- 'Lucas' (F)	CAgr
laciniosa (F)	CBcs CTho EPfP
- 'Henry' (F)	CAgr
- 'Keystone' seedling (F)	CAgr
ovata (F)	CAgr CMCN CTho EPfP MBlu MBri SSpi WDin
- 'Grainger' seedling (F)	CAgr
- 'Neilson' seedling (F)	CAgr
- 'Weschcke' (F)	EGFP
- 'Weschcke' seedling (F)	CAgr
- 'Yoder no 1' seedling (F)	CAgr
pallida	EGFP
texana	EGFP
tomentosa	EGFP EPfP

Caryophyllus see *Syzygium*

Caryopteris ✿ (*Verbenaceae*)

× ***clandonensis***	CMac ECtt MGan MLHP MWat NBir WCFE WDin WFar
- 'Arthur Simmonds' ♀H4	CSam CTri EBee ECha EPfP GKir LHop LSRN SPer WGor
- 'Dark Knight'	EBee EPfP LAst LBuc LRHS MBri MWat NPnk SBfd SPur SWvt WClo WRHF
- 'Ferndown'	CDoC CWib EBee ELon EPfP EWTr GKir MMuc NLar SEND SPer SPoG SReu SRms
- 'First Choice' ♀H3-4	CAbP CDul CMac CSpe EBee ELan EPfP EShb LAst LHop LRHS LSRN LSqu MAsh MGos SLim SPer SPoG SRkn SWvt WSpi
- 'Gold Giant' **new**	LRHS MAsh SPer
- Grand Bleu = 'Inoveris'PBR	CMac CSBt EBee ELan EPfP EQua EShb LRHS LSRN MGos MSwo NLar SMad SWvt WCot WPat WRHF WSpi
- 'Heavenly Baby' ♀H3-4	LRHS MAsh SLon SPoG
- 'Heavenly Blue'	Widely available
- Hint of Gold = 'Lisaura' ♀H3-4	LRHS MAsh SBfd
- 'Kew Blue'	Widely available
- 'Longwood Blue'	CMdw ELan EPfP LRHS MAsh
- 'Moody Blue' (v)	EPfP
- Sterling Silver = 'Lissilv' **new**	LRHS MAsh
- 'Summer Gold'	GKir MRav
- 'Summer Sorbet'PBR (v) ♀H3-4	CBcs CBow CDoC CWit EBee EHoe ELan EPfP EWes LBuc LHop LRHS MAsh MGos MMuc NEgg NHol NLar NPnk SBfd SCoo SEND SLim SPer SPoG SWvt WGrn WHar WPat WSpi
- 'Worcester Gold' ♀H3-4	Widely available
divaricata	EBee MBri
- 'Electrum'	ECtt LSou
- 'Jade Shades'	EBee ECtt LSou
- variegated (v)	CBow
§ ***incana***	EBee EPfP GKir SPer WPat WSHC
- 'Autumn Pink'PBR	EBee ECrN ELan EPfP LSRN NLar SEND
- 'Blue Cascade'	EBee EBtc ELan GQue MRav NLar WGrn WPat
§ - 'Jason'PBR	EPfP MGos NEgg SPoG WPat
- Sunshine BluePBR	see *C. incana* 'Jason'
mastacanthus	see *C. incana*

Caryota (*Arecaceae*)

mitis ♀H1	CCCN EAmu LPal
- 'Himalaya'	EAmu LPal
urens	LPal

Cassandra see *Chamaedaphne*

Cassia (*Caesalpiniaceae*)

corymbosa Lam.	see *Senna corymbosa*
marilandica	see *Senna marilandica*

Cassinia (*Asteraceae*)

aculeata	GGar
leptophylla	CBcs GGar SPer
- 'Avalanche Creek'	ECou
- subsp. ***fulvida***	CBcs ECou EHoe GGar
- subsp. ***vauvilliersii***	GGar SEND SPer
- - BR 55	GGar
- - var. ***albida***	SPer
- - 'Silberschmelze'	SOWG
N ***retorta***	ECou
'Ward Silver'	CBot ECou EHoe EWes SEND

Cassiope ✿ (*Ericaceae*)

'Askival Snowbird'	GCrs ITim
'Badenoch'	ECho EPot GEdr GGar GKev
'Edinburgh' ♀H4	ECho EPot GBin GCrs GEdr IVic NHar NHol

fastigiata Askival strain	GCrs
× ***wardii***	
lycopodioides 'Beatrice Lilley'	ECho GGar GKev LLHF NHar SRms WThu
- 'Jim Lever'	GCrs WAbe
- 'Rokujō'	ITim
mertensiana	ECho EPot GEdr SRms
- 'California Pink'	NHar
- var. ***gracilis***	IVic WThu
'Muirhead' ♀H4	ECho GCrs NHar SRms WThu
'Randle Cooke' ♀H4	ECho EPot GEdr NHar SRms WThu
selaginoides	GKev
- LS&E 13284	GCrs WAbe
- McBeath's **new**	GCrs
tetragona	GCrs ITim SRms

Castanea ✿ (*Fagaceae*)

'Bouche de Bétizac' (F)	CAgr
crenata	CAgr
dentata	EGFP
'Ferosacre' (F)	MCoo
henryi	CMCN EGFP
'Maraval' (F)	CAgr CTho MBlu MBri MCoo
'Maridonne' (F)	CAgr
'Marigoule' (F)	CAgr MCoo
'Marlhac' (F)	CAgr
'Marsol' (F)	CAgr MCoo
mollissima	EGFP
'Précoce Migoule' (F)	CAgr ECrN
pumila var. ***pumila*** NNS 05-190 **new**	GKev
sativa ♀H4	Widely available
§ - 'Albomarginata' (v) ♀H4	CDoC CDul CEnd CTho EBee EPfP LHop LMaj MBlu MBri MGos NBea SPoG WDin WFar WPat
- 'Anny's Red'	MBlu
- 'Anny's Summer Red'	CDul
- 'Argenteovariegata'	see *C. sativa* 'Albomarginata'
- 'Aspleniifolia'	CDul
- 'Aureomarginata'	see *C. sativa* 'Variegata'
- 'Belle Epine' (F)	CAgr
- 'Bournette' (F)	CAgr
* - 'Doré de Lyon'	CAgr
- 'Marron Comballe' (F)	CAgr
- 'Marron de Goujounac' (F)	CAgr
- 'Marron de Lyon' (F)	CAgr CDul CEnd EPfP MBri SVic
- 'Pyramidalis'	WDin
§ - 'Variegata' (v)	CBcs CLnd CMCN ELan LMaj MGos

Castanopsis (*Fagaceae*)

eyrei	CMCN
sclerophylla	CBcs WPGP

Castanospermum (*Papilionaceae*)

australe	CArn

Castilleja (*Scrophulariaceae*)

applegatei subsp. ***pinetorum***	GKev
elegans	WAbe
hispida	WAbe
miniata	WAbe

Casuarina (*Casuarinaceae*)

cunninghamiana	ECou

Catalpa (*Bignoniaceae*)

bignonioides ♀H4	Widely available
- 'Aurea' ♀H4	Widely available
* - 'Aurea Nana'	CEnd EBee MBri
- 'Nana'	CWit EBee LMaj LRHS MBri WDin WPat
- 'Purpurea'	see *C.* × *erubescens* 'Purpurea'
- 'Variegata' (v)	EPfP EWTr LRHS MGos NWea SPer WPat
bungei	EGFP MBlu MGos MREP SAPC SArc
- 'Purpurea'	ELan LAst
§ × ***erubescens*** 'Purpurea' ♀H4	CBcs CBot CDoC CDul CEnd CMac CTho CWit EAmu EBee EPfP EWTr LRHS LTen MAsh MBlu MBri MGos MRav NLar SBfd SPer SSta WDin WFar WPGP WPat
fargesii f. ***duclouxii***	CDul CEnd EPfP MBlu MBri NLar WPGP
ovata	CMCN EGFP
- 'Slender Silhouette'	NLar
speciosa	CDul EWTr MMuc SEND WBVN
- 'Frederik'	MBri
- 'Pulverulenta' (v)	CDoC CDul CEnd CMCN LRHS MGos NLar SBig

Catananche (*Asteraceae*)

caerulea	Widely available
- 'Alba'	CMea EBee EBla ECha EPfP GKir IFoB LRHS NBir NPri SBfd SGar SMrm SPer SPoG SWvt WMoo WPer
- 'Amor Blue'	LRHS
- 'Amor White'	WOut
- 'Bicolor'	CMMP MHer STes WHoo WMoo
- 'Major' ♀H4	LRHS SRms

Catha (*Celastraceae*)

edulis	CArn GPoy WHfH WJek

Catharanthus (*Apocynaceae*)

roseus ♀H1	GPoy

Caulophyllum (*Berberidaceae*)

thalictroides	CArn EBee GBBs GEdr GKir IMou LEdu SRot WCru WFar WMoo WPnP WSHC
- subsp. ***robustum***	WCru

Cautleya ✿ (*Zingiberaceae*)

cathcartii	CPLG LEdu WHil
- 'Tenzing's Gold'	CLAP WCru WWst
§ ***gracilis***	CDTJ CPLG CPrp EBee EPfP ETod EUJe GCal IBlr LEdu MNrw NMyG SBig WHal
- B&SWJ 7186	WCru WDyG
- 'Edinburgh Lemon'	IBlr
lutea	see *C. gracilis*
spicata	CBct CCCN CDTJ CDoC CHEx CPLG CSpe CTsd CWit EBee ECho EPPr EUJe GGar IBlr NPal SBHP SBig
- SDR 3844	GKev
- 'Arun Flame'	LEdu WCru
- 'Crûg Canary'	LEdu WCru
* - var. ***lutea***	CBct CHEx CPne ETod
- 'Robusta'	CAvo CGHE CHEx CPLG CPne CPrp EAmu EBee EBrs EShb GCal GCra IBlr LEdu MNrw NPal SChF SGSe SMad WBor WCru WPGP WSHC

Cayratia (*Vitaceae*)

japonica B&SWJ 6636	WCru
§ ***thomsonii*** BWJ 8123	WCru

Ceanothus ✿ (*Rhamnaceae*)

'A.T. Johnson'	ECrN SLim SPer SRms
americanus	CArn

	arboreus	SAPC SArc
	- 'Trewithen Blue' 🏆H3	Widely available
	'Autumnal Blue' 🏆H3	Widely available
	'Blue Cushion'	CAlb CBcs CDoC CPMA CWSG EBee LRHS MAsh MGos MRav NHol NLar SEND SLim SLon SWvt WBVN WBrE WFar
	'Blue Diamond'PBR	LSRN
	'Blue Dreams'	WFar
	'Blue Jeans'	EBee ELan IArd LRHS MMuc SPoG WPat
	'Blue Mound' 🏆H3	Widely available
	'Blue Sapphire'PBR	CAlb CBcs CDoC CMac CWGN CWSG EBee ELan EPfP GBin LAst LRHS LSRN MAsh MGos MRav NEgg NLar NPri SPer SPoG SWvt WClo
	'Burkwoodii' 🏆H3	CAlb CBcs CDoC CDoy CDul CSBt CWSG EPfP GKir LAst LRHS LSRN MAsh MGan MGos MRav NEgg NHol SBfd SLim SPer SPoG SWvt WClo WFar
	'Cascade' 🏆H3	CBcs CWSG EBee GKir LRHS LSRN MGos MWat NSti SLim SLon SPer SPlb
	'Centennial'	LBuc LRHS MRav
	'Comtesse de Paris'	see *C.* × *delileanus* 'Comtesse de Paris'
	'Concha' 🏆H3	Widely available
§	***cuneatus*** var. ***rigidus***	SRms WSHC
	- - 'Snowball'	ELan EPfP
	'Cynthia Postan'	EBee EPfP IArd LRHS MBlu MWat NLar SCoo WAbe
	'Dark Star' 🏆H3	CAlb CBcs CChe CDoC CMHG CSPN CTri CWSG EBee EPfP LAst LBMP LRHS LSRN MAsh MGos NHol NSti SBfd SCoo SEND SOWG SPoG SSta SWvt
	'Delight'	CBcs EBee ELan EPfP MGos WDin WFar
§	× ***delileanus***	EBee
	'Comtesse de Paris'	
	- 'Gloire de Versailles' 🏆H4	CBcs CBot CDoC CDul CWib EBee ECrN ELan ELon EPfP GKir LAst LHop LRHS MAsh MCot MGos MRav MSwo MWhi SPer SWvt WDin WFar
	- 'Henri Desfossé'	ELan EPfP LRHS LSRN MRav NLar SOWG SPer SPoG WDin
	- 'Indigo'	EBee EPfP
	- 'Topaze' 🏆H4	EBee ELan EMil EPfP LRHS NLar SLon SOWG WDin WHar WKif
	dentatus misapplied	see *C.* × *lobbianus*
	dentatus Torr. & A.Gray	MAsh SPlb
	- var. ***floribundus***	CSBt ELan SDix
*	- 'Superbus'	EBee
	'Diamond Heights'	see *C. griseus* var. *horizontalis* 'Diamond Heights'
	'Edinburgh' 🏆H3	EPfP WFar
	El Dorado = 'Perado' (v)	LRHS MAsh MGos
	'Eleanor Taylor'	EBee
	gloriosus	EBee EWes
	- 'Anchor Bay'	EBee ELan EPfP LRHS SOWG
	- 'Emily Brown'	CAlb CBcs CDoC CSPN CTrC CWit EBee ELan LAst LRHS LSRN LSou MRav NLar SBfd
	griseus **new**	SGar
§	- var. ***horizontalis*** 'Diamond Heights' (v)	CMac EPfP LSRN MAsh MBri SPer WFar
	- - 'Silver Surprise'PBR (v)	CBcs CSPN EBee ELan EPfP LBuc LRHS LSRN MAsh MGos NEgg NLar SLim SPoG
	- - 'Yankee Point'	CAlb CBcs CDoC CMac CSBt CWib EBee ECrN EPfP GGar GKir LRHS LSRN LTen MGos MRav MSwo NHol NLar SBfd SCoo SLim SPlb SPoG SWvt WDin
	- 'Kurt Zadnik'	SPoG
	impressus	CMHG CSBt CTri EBee EPfP MAsh MBlu SEND SPer SWvt WCFE WFar
	- 'Victoria'	EBee LSRN LSou MAsh MGos MHav NLar SBfd SRGP
N	'Italian Skies' 🏆H3	CAlb CBcs CDoC CSBt CWSG CWib EBee ELan EPfP GKir LAst LRHS LSRN MAsh MGos MSwo NEgg SCoo SLim SLon SPer SPlb SPoG SWvt WDin WFar
	'Julia Phelps'	CMHG EBee WEas
§	× ***lobbianus***	CTri WDin
	- 'Russellianus'	EBee
	'Madagascar'	LRHS SPoG
	Marie Bleue = 'Minmari'	LRHS
	Marie-Rose = 'Minmarose'	LRHS
	× ***pallidus*** 'Georges Simon'	EPfP
	- 'Marie Simon'	CBcs CBot CWib EBee ELan EPfP LAst LBMP LRHS LSRN MAsh MGos SPer SPoG SRms SWvt WCFE WDin WHar WKif
	- 'Perle Rose'	CBcs EBee EPfP LAst LLHF LRHS MGos NLar SOWG SPer SPoG WKif WSHC
§	'Pershore Zanzibar'PBR (v)	CBcs CChe CMac CSBt CSPN CWSG CWit EBee EHoe ELan EPfP LAst LBuc LRHS LSRN MGos MNHC MRav MSwo MWat NEgg NLar SCoo SLim SPer SPoG SWvt WBrE
	'Pin Cushion'	CWSG CWib EBee EPfP LRHS MAsh NHol
	'Point Millerton'	see *C. thyrsiflorus* 'Millerton Point'
	'Popcorn'	EBee LRHS MGos
	prostratus	MAsh SMad WAbe
	'Puget Blue' 🏆H4	Widely available
	'Ray Hartman'	NLar
	repens	see *C. thyrsiflorus* var. *repens*
	rigidus	see *C. cuneatus* var. *rigidus*
	'Sierra Blue'	EBee
	'Snow Flurries'	see *C. thyrsiflorus* 'Snow Flurry'
	'Southmead' 🏆H3	CDoC CTri EBee ELan EPfP LRHS MAsh MGos MSwo MWat NHol WDin WMoo
	thyrsiflorus	CTri CWSG CWib MAsh NHol SPer SRms SWvt WDin WHar
§	- 'Millerton Point'	EBee EPfP LAst LRHS MGos NLar SBfd SCoo SLim SPoG WGwG
§	- var. ***repens*** 🏆H3	Widely available
	- 'Skylark' 🏆H3	CAlb CBar CChe CDoC CMac CSam CWSG EBee ELan EPau EPfP GGar GKir LHop LRHS LSRN LTen MAsh MBri MGos MLHP NLar NPri SDix SGar SLim SSpi WDin WFar WPat
§	- 'Snow Flurry'	CBcs CWib EGxp EPfP MSwo WAbe WFar
	'Tilden Park'	LRHS
	'Tuxedo' **new**	GKir LRHS MAsh
	× ***veitchianus***	CDoy CSBt EBee ELan LRHS MAsh NHol SCoo SEND SPer
	'White Cascade'	EBee
	'Zanzibar'PBR	see *C.* 'Pershore Zanzibar'

Cedrela (*Meliaceae*)

	sinensis	see *Toona sinensis*

Cedronella (*Lamiaceae*)

§	***canariensis***	CArn CBod CHby CPrp EShb GBar GPoy ILis MHer MNHC NGHP SIde SOWG SWat WJek

mexicana	see *Agastache mexicana*
triphylla	see *C. canariensis*

Cedrus (*Pinaceae*)

atlantica	CDul CLnd CMac CMen CPMA ECrN EHul IFFs NWea SEND WBVN WEve WMou
- 'Aurea'	CDul MBri MGos NLar NPCo NWea SSta WDin WHar
- 'Fastigiata'	EHul MGos NLar SCoo SLim WEve
- Glauca Group ♀H4	Widely available
- - 'Glauca Fastigiata'	CKen CMen GKir NLar WEve
- - 'Glauca Pendula'	CDoC CDul CMen ECrN EHul EPfP GKir LMaj LRHS MBlu MBri MGos NEgg NPCo NWea SCoo SLim SPoG SSta WBVN WDin WEve WFar
- - 'Silberspitz'	CKen
- 'Pendula'	ECho MAsh WBVN
- 'Sahara Frost' **new**	NLar
- 'Saphir Nymph'	MAsh NLar SLim
brevifolia	CAlb ECho GKir LTen MGos NLar SBfd STre WEve
- 'Epstein'	MGos NLar
- 'Hillier Compact'	CKen MGos NLar
- 'Kenwith'	CKen ECho MAsh NLar
deodara ♀H4	Widely available
- 'Albospica' (v)	SWvt
- 'Argentea'	MGos
- 'Aurea' ♀H4	CDoC CDul CKen CSBt CTho ECho EHul EPfP GBin GKir LMaj LRHS MBri MGos MWya NEgg NLar NWea SLim WDin WEve WFar
I - 'Aurea Pendula'	ECho
- 'Blue Dwarf'	CKen ECho NLar WEve
* - 'Blue Mountain Broom'	CKen
- 'Blue Snake'	CKen NLar
- 'Blue Surprise'	SLim
- 'Bush's Electra'	CPMA NLar
- 'Cream Puff'	ECho MGos
- 'Devinely Blue'	CKen SLim SPoG
- 'Feelin' Blue'	CDoC CDul CKen ECho EHul EPla GKir LBee LRHS MAsh MBri MGos NEgg NHol NLar NPCo SCoo SLim SWvt WEve WFar
- 'Gold Cascade'	SLim
- 'Gold Cone'	ECho MGos
- 'Gold Gowa'	MGos
- 'Gold Mound'	CKen WEve
- 'Golden Horizon'	CDoC CKen CMac CMen CSBt ECho ECrN EHul EPla LBee LRHS MAsh MBri MGos NEgg NPCo SCoo SLim SPoG WDin WEve WFar
- 'Green Prince'	NLar
- 'Hedgehog'	NLar
- 'Karl Fuchs'	EWTr GKir LTen MAsh MBri NLar WGor
- 'Kelly Gold'	WEve
- 'Lime Glow'	SLim
- 'Miles High'	CPMA
- 'Mountain Beauty'	CKen
- 'Nana'	CKen
- 'Nivea'	CKen
- 'Pendula'	CKen ECho EHul LMaj MGos SLim WEve WGor
- 'Pygmy'	CKen
- 'Raywood's Prostrate'	CKen
- 'Robusta'	WEve
- 'Roman Candle'	CSBt ECho NPCo WEve WFar
- 'Scott'	CKen
- 'Silver Mist'	CKen MGos
- 'Silver Spring'	EPla MGos NLar
libani ♀H4	Widely available
- 'Blue Angel'	NLar SLim
- 'Comte de Dijon'	ECho EHul NLar
- 'Fontaine'	NLar
- 'Gold Tip'	NLar
- 'Home Park'	CKen NLar
- 'May'	NLar
- Nana Group	CKen ECho NPCo
- 'Pampisford'	NLar
- 'Sargentii'	CKen ECho EHul MGos NLar NPCo WEve
- 'Taurus'	NLar

Celastrus (*Celastraceae*)

flagellaris B&SWJ 8572	WCru
hookeri B&SWJ 11667 **new**	WCru
orbiculatus	CBcs CDoC CMac ELan LHop LRHS MRav MWya NSti SLon SPer WBor
- 'Diana' (f)	CMac EBee NBea
- 'Hercules' (m)	CMac EBee NBea
- Hermaphrodite Group ♀H4	EBee MREP SDix SEND SKHP WSHC
- var. ***punctatus*** CWJ 12439	WCru
scandens	CMac EBee SPhx SPlb WDin
stephanotiifolius B&SWJ 4727	WCru

Celmisia (*Asteraceae*)

allanii	IBlr WAbe
angustifolia	IBlr
argentea	ECho GCrs WAbe
armstrongii	ECho
Ballyrogan hybrids	IBlr
bellidioides	ECho EPot EWes GCrs MDKP NSla WAbe
bonplandii	GCrs IBlr
brevifolia	IBlr
coriacea misapplied	see *C. semicordata*
coriacea Raoul	see *C. mackaui*
costiniana	IBlr
'David Shackleton'	IBlr
densiflora	GKev IBlr
- silver-leaved	IBlr
discolor	IBlr
glandulosa	IBlr
gracilenta	GCrs NSla
- CC 563	NWCA
graminifolia	ECho
haastii	IBlr
'Harry Bryce'	IBlr
hectorii	IBlr WAbe
hectorii × ***ramulosa***	WAbe
hookeri	IBlr
Inshriach hybrids	IBlr
insignis	IBlr
latifolia	IBlr
- large-leaved	IBlr
longifolia large-leaved	IBlr
- small-leaved	IBlr
§ ***mackaui***	GGar IBlr
monroi	IBlr
prorepens	IBlr
pugioniformis	IBlr
ramulosa var. ***tuberculata***	GCrs IBlr NSla
§ ***semicordata***	EPot GAbr GCra IBlr NSla WAbe
- subsp. ***aurigans***	GKev IBlr
- subsp. ***stricta***	IBlr
sessiliflora	GKev
spectabilis	ECho GGar GKir

- 'Eggleston Silver'	GKev NEgg
- subsp. ***magnifica***	GKev
tomentella	IBlr
verbascifolia	IBlr
§ ***walkeri***	EPot IBlr
webbiana	see *C. walkeri*

Celsia see *Verbascum*

× *Celsioverbascum* see *Verbascum*

Celtica see *Stipa*

Celtis (*Ulmaceae*)

australis	CBcs EBtc MGos MMuc NMun SEND
biondii	EGFP
bungeana	NLar
caucasica	GAuc NLar
julianae	IArd NLar
koraiensis	EGFP
occidentalis	CDul ELan IArd WBVN
reticulata	EGFP
sinensis	CMen
tenuifolia new	EGFP

Cenolophium (*Apiaceae*)

denudatum	CDes EBee ECha EPPr NChi WPGP

Centaurea ✿ (*Asteraceae*)

sp.	ECtt
HH&K 271	NBid
RCB AM -6	WCot
RCB EA-1	WCot
from Turkey	MAvo MSpe WPGP
achtarovii	GKev
alpestris	EBee NBre NLar WPGP WPer
argentea	CBot
athoa	EBee GKev
§ ***atropurpurea***	CDes CSpe EBee EWes GMac GQue MAvo MRav MSpe NBPC NLar SHar SMrm SPhx SUsu WClo WHil WHrl WPGP
bagadensis	GKev
bella	Widely available
benoistii misapplied	see *C. atropurpurea*
benoistii × ***orientalis*** ambig. new	SPhx
cana	see *C. triumfettii* subsp. *cana*
candidissima misapplied	see *C. cineraria*
'Caramia'	SAga
carniolica SDR 5443	GKev
cheiranthifolia	EPPr MAvo MSpe NBir WFar WPGP
- var. ***purpurascens***	MAvo
§ ***cineraria***	ECre SRms WEas
- subsp. ***cineraria*** ♀H3	EBee WCot
clementei	CSpe
cyanus	CArn MHer MNHC NPri WJek
- 'Black Ball'	CSpe MNHC
cynaroides	see *Stemmacantha centaureoides*
dealbata	CBot CMac COIW CPrp CWib EBee EPfP GJos GKir IFoB LBMP LTen MLHP MMuc MSpe NBPC NBro NLar NMir NPri SBfd SEND SMrm STes WBor WCot WFar WMoo WPer WWEG
- 'Steenbergii'	CMac EBee EBla ELan GCal GGar GKir MNFA MSpe NBid NBir NGdn NPer NSti SGSe SPer SPoG WAbb WCAu WCot WFar WHoo WMnd
debeauxii subsp. ***nemoralis***	NLar
fischeri Willd.	CDes EBee MSpe WPGP
glastifolia	EBee GCal MSpe NBre WPGP
gymnocarpa	see *C. cineraria*
hypoleuca	NBid
jacea	CSam EBee EShb GAbr GKev GQue IMou MSpe NBid NLar WCot WPer
'Jody'	WCAu
'John Coutts'	Widely available
'Jordy'	EBee ECtt IPot MAvo SPhx SSvw
karabaghensis new	WPGP
kotschyana	CDes EBee NBre WPGP
macrocephala	Widely available
mollis	NBid
montana	Widely available
- 'Alba'	Widely available
- 'Amethyst in Snow' new	CSpr GBin IPot NLar
§ - 'Carnea'	CCVN CElw CPom CSam CTca EBee EBla GCra GMaP GMac LLWP MAvo MSpe NBir NChi NLar SAga SPhx STes WCAu WMoo WSHC WWEG
- 'Gold Bullion'	CDes CPrp CSpe CTca CWGN EBla EBrs ECtt ELan ELon EPfP EWes EWll GKir GMaP LRHS MBri MCCP MRav MSpe NBid NBir NLar NSti SAga SMad WWEG
- 'Gold Strike'	EBee
- 'Grandiflora'	EBee MBri
- 'Joyce'	CDes CElw CPom EBee EBla MAvo MSpe NBid NLar
- 'Lady Flora Hastings'	CBre CDes CElw CKno CMdw CPom CSam CSpe CTca EBee EBla LEdu MAvo MSpe NBid WPGP WWEG
- lilac-flowered	NBid
- 'Ochroleuca'	CDes EBee NBid NBre WPGP
- pale pink-flowered	NChi
- 'Parham'	CElw CPrp CSev EBee EBla ECtt ELan EPPr GCal LBMP LLWP LSRN MCot MLLN MNrw MRav MWat NEgg NSti SPer SPlb SPoG WFar WMnd WWEG
- 'Purple Heart'	EBee EBla EKen ELon IPot LSou MAvo MBri MLLN MNrw MSpe NBPC NLar NPri
- 'Purple Prose'	MAvo WWEG
- 'Purpurea'	CAby CDes CPom EBee MSpe SUsu
- 'Rosea'	see *C. montana* 'Carnea'
* - ***violacea***	NBid
- 'Violetta'	EBee MAvo NBir WCAu WFar WMoo
montana × ***triumfettii***	CDes EBee
moschata	see *Amberboa moschata*
nervosa	see *C. uniflora* subsp. *nervosa*
nigra	CArn COld CRWN EBWF EBla GJos MNHC NBre NLan NMir NSco SMrm WMoo WSFF
- var. ***alba***	CArn CBre NBid
- subsp. ***rivularis***	ECha MMuc NBid NBre SEND
nogmovii	CDes EBee
orientalis	CMea CSpe EBee EWes GCal LBMP LLWG MNFA MSpe NBre NDov NLar SPhx SPoG WHoo
pannonica subsp. ***pannonica***	NBid WSHC
phrygia	COIW EBee MSpe NBre WPer
pulcherrima	EBee GMac LRHS NBre WCom
'Pulchra Major'	see *Stemmacantha centaureoides*
pumilio new	GKev
rupestris	EBee EPfP MAvo MSpe NBre NDov SGar SPhx WPer

ruthenica	EBee GMac MAvo NBre NDov NGdn NLar SMad SPer SPhx SPlb WCot WHil
salonitana RCB AM 1	WCot
scabiosa	CArn CRWN CWib EBWF GPWP MHer MNHC NBid NBre NLan NLar NMir NSco WPer
- f. ***albiflora***	EBee ECtt
simplicicaulis	CDes CSam CWan EBee GAbr MSpe MTho SBch SMrm SRms WCom WEas WHoo WSHC
thracica	SAga WCot
'Totnes Fat Lemon'	CDes
triumfettii	CPBP
- 'Blue Dreams'	MSpe
I - subsp. ***cana*** 'Rosea'	WBrk
- 'Hoar Frost'	CDes EBee MSpe NDov WCot WPGP
- subsp. ***stricta***	CPrp CSpr EBee MSpe WFar
uniflora	CDes EBee
§ - subsp. ***nervosa***	NBid NBre NBro NLar WPer
woronowii	MSpe

Centaurium (*Gentianaceae*)

erythraea	CArn EBWF GPoy MHer
scilloides	CPBP MTho NLAp NMen NSla NWCA WAbe

Centella (*Apiaceae*)

§ ***asiatica***	CArn EOHP GPoy WJek

Centradenia (*Melastomataceae*)

floribunda	LAst
inaequilateralis	CCCN
- 'Cascade'	MBri SPet

Centranthus (*Valerianaceae*)

§ ***lecoqii***	EBee ECtt EWes LPla SPhx WCot
§ ***ruber***	Widely available
* - 'Alba Pura'	NBPC
§ - 'Albus'	Widely available
- 'Atrococcineus'	ECha MMuc SEND SPoG WPer
- 'Clair'	CNat
- var. ***coccineus***	CBcs CKno EBee ELan EPfP GAbr GBin GMaP LAst LBMP LRHS MCot MNHC MRav MWat NPri NVic SBfd SEND SMrm SPer SPhx SRot SWat WCAu WCot WFar WWEG
- mauve-flowered misapplied	see *C. lecoqii*
- mauve-flowered	NBir
- 'Roseus'	WMoo
- 'Snowcloud'	CSev ECtt EPfP MNHC WClo WHil
'White Cloud'	WJek

Centropogon (*Campanulaceae*)

§ ***ayavacensis*** subsp. ***ayavacensis*** B&SWJ 10663	WCru
cordifolius B&SWJ 10282	WCru
costaricae B&SWJ 10455	WCru
ferrugineus B&SWJ 10665 **new**	WCru
hirsutus B&SWJ 10657	WCru
aff. ***valerii*** B&SWJ 10341 **new**	WCru
willdenowianus	see *C. ayavacensis* subsp. *ayavacensis*

Cephalanthera (*Orchidaceae*)

falcata	EFEx GEdr NLAp WWSt
longibracteata	EFEx GEdr NLAp WWSt

Cephalanthus (*Rubiaceae*)

occidentalis	CBcs CWib EBee ELon GBin LRHS LSou MAsh MBNS MBlu MBri MGos MWya NLar SLim SPer SPoG SRms WBVN WFar WGob

Cephalaria (*Dipsacaceae*)

§ ***alpina***	COIW EBee EBla EHrv EPfP LBMP LRHS MHer MNrw MRav NLar SPhx SRms SWat WCot WFar WPer
- RCB/TQ E-1	WCot
- 'Nana'	NWCA
ambrosioides	MLLN
- MESE 503	EBee
anatolica KM T-04-72	EBee
caucasica	see *C. gigantea*
dipsacoides	CEnt CFee CSam EBee EBla ECha LPio MSpe NBre NLar SKHP SMHy SPhx SPoG STes WHal WMoo
§ ***flava***	EBee NBre
galpiniana	SPlb
- subsp. ***simplicior***	EBee
§ ***gigantea***	Widely available
graeca	see *C. flava*
leucantha	CArn EBee EWTr MLLN NBid NBre SMrm SPhx STes WFar WMoo
litvinovii	CElw
radiata	CSam EBee GBin LPio
tatarica hort.	see *C. gigantea*
tchihatchewii	EBee MLLN

Cephalotaxus (*Cephalotaxaceae*)

fortunei	CDul SPer
- 'Prostrate Spreader'	SLim
harringtonii	ECho ERom GKir LEdu WPGP
- var. ***drupacea***	CDoC NWea
- 'Fastigiata'	CBcs CDoC CDul ECho EHul GKir IArd IDee LRHS MAsh MBri MGos NPal SCoo SLim SPoG WDin WFar
- 'Korean Gold'	CKen GKir LRHS MBri NLar SLim SPoG
- 'Prostrata'	LRHS SPoG
sinensis	CMCN

Cephalotus (*Cephalotaceae*)

follicularis	SHmp

Cerastium (*Caryophyllaceae*)

alpinum	ECho IFoB SRms
- var. ***lanatum***	CMea ECho EDAr EWes LRHS
candidissimum	EWes LBMP
tomentosum	CBar ECho EPfP GKir LAst LRHS MMuc NPri SEND SPer SPet SPlb SPoG WFar
- var. ***columnae***	ECha ECho EHoe EPfP EWes
- 'Silberteppich'	LBMP
- 'Yo Yo'	WFar

Ceratonia (*Caesalpiniaceae*)

siliqua	CBcs NMun SEND

Ceratophyllum (*Ceratophyllaceae*)

demersum	CBen CRow CWat EHon MSKA MWts NSco SWat WMAq

Ceratostigma ✿ (*Plumbaginaceae*)

abyssinicum	ELan
asperrimum B&SWJ 7260	WCru
'Autumn Blue'	EPfP
capensis **new**	CMac
- 'Alba' **new**	CMac

griffithii	CBcs CBot CChe CDoC CDul CHll CMac CWSG EBee ECtt EHoe ELan EPfP LAst LBMP LEdu LRHS MCCP MRav MSwo SBfd SLim SPer SPoG SWal WDin WFar WHoo WKif WSHC
- wild-collected **new**	GCal
§ ***plumbaginoides*** ♀H3-4	Widely available
willmottianum ♀H3-4	Widely available
- BWJ 8140	WCru
- Desert Skies = 'Palmgold' PBR	CBcs EBee ELan EPfP LAst LRHS MBlu MGos NLar SBfd SCoo SLim SMad SPer SSta SWvt
- Forest Blue = 'Lice' PBR	CAbP CDoC CMac CSBt CSpe CWSG EBee ELan EPPr EPfP LAst LRHS LSRN LSqu MAsh MBri MGos NLar NPri SBfd SCoo SLim SPer SPoG SReu SWvt WDin WPat

Cercidiphyllum ✿ (*Cercidiphyllaceae*)

japonicum ♀H4	Widely available
- 'Boyd's Dwarf'	CPMA LRHS MAsh NLar SSpi WAbe WCot
- 'Herkenrode Dwarf'	NLar
- 'Heronswood Globe'	CPMA EPfP MBlu NLar SSta WSpi
- 'Kreukenberg Dwarf'	CPMA
- 'Morioka Weeping'	CPMA CTho SMad SSta WPGP
- 'Peach'	CPMA NLar
§ - f. ***pendulum*** ♀H4	CBcs CDul CEnd CLnd CMCN CMac CPLG CPMA CTri CWSG EBee EPfP GBin GKir LRHS MAsh MBlu MGos NEgg NLar SCoo SLim SPoG SSpi WDin
- - 'Amazing Grace'	CTho LLHF MBlu SSta
- 'Raspberry'	CPMA MBri NLar
- Red Fox	see *C. japonicum* 'Rotfuchs'
§ - 'Rotfuchs'	CBcs CEnd CMCN CMac CPMA EBee EPfP EWTr GBin GKir IVic LRHS MAsh MBlu MBri MGos MPkF NCGa NLar NPCo SCoo SLim SMad SPoG SSpi SSta WPGP
- 'Ruby'	CPMA MBlu MBri NLar
- 'Strawberry'	CBcs CPMA EBee MBlu NLar
- 'Tidal Wave'	CPMA NLar
magnificum	CBcs CDoC CDul CEnd CMCN CPLG EPfP IDee NEgg NLar WCru WPGP
- f. ***pendulum***	see *C. japonicum* f. *pendulum*

Cercis (*Caesalpiniaceae*)

sp.	WFoF
canadensis	CBcs CDul CMCN CWGN EPfP IFFs MGos NEgg NLar NWea SCoo SLim SPer WPat
- f. ***alba***	CBcs ESwi LSRN
- - 'Royal White'	CPMA EPfP IArd MBlu SSta
- 'Appalachian Red'	CBcs CPMA LSRN MBlu NLar SKHP
- 'Cascading Hearts'	CBcs ESwi MBri NLar
- 'Flame'	CPMA SSta WPat
- 'Floating Clouds' (v)	MGos
- 'Forest Pansy' ♀H4	Widely available
- 'Hearts of Gold'	CWGN EBee LRHS MAsh MBlu MBri MGos MPkF NLar SBfd SKHP SLim SPoG WClo
- Lavender Twist = 'Covey'	CBcs EBee ESwi LAst LRHS LSRN MBlu MBri MGos NLar SBfd SLim SPoG
§ - var. ***occidentalis***	LEdu NLar NMun SOWG SSta
- 'Pauline Lily'	NLar
- 'Rubye Atkinson'	CPMA NLar SSpi
- 'Tennessee Pink'	CPMA NLar
- 'Texan White'	LRHS
- var. ***texensis*** 'Traveller'	NLar SSta
- 'Wither's Pink Charm' **new**	SSta
chinensis	CBcs NLar SPer WDin
- 'Avondale'	Widely available
- 'Don Egolf'	CPMA LRHS LSRN MGos MPkF NLar SKHP SSta
chingii	CPLG
gigantea	NLar
griffithii	EGFP LLHF NLar NMun SSta
occidentalis	see *C. canadensis* var. *occidentalis*
racemosa	CPLG IDee NLar WPGP
reniformis 'Oklahoma'	CPMA EBee ESwi LRHS LSRN MGos MPkF NLar NPCo SKHP
- 'Texas White'	CBcs CPMA EBee MBri MPkF NLar SKHP SLim WPat WSpi
siliquastrum ♀H4	Widely available
- f. ***albida***	CBcs CBgR CBot CTho ECrN EPfP LRHS SKHP SSpi WCFE WSpi
- 'Bodnant'	EBee EPfP EWes LAst LLHF LRHS LSRN MBlu MBri MGos NLar
- 'White Swan'	CPMA EWes
yunnanensis	EBee LRHS NLar

Cerinthe (*Boraginaceae*)

glabra	LBMP NBre SPlb
major	MLLN SWvt WEas
- 'Kiwi Blue'	CHll MDKP
- 'Purpurascens'	CMea CSpe EHrv ELan EPfP EWTr IFoB LBMP MCot MNHC MSCN NLar SEND SGar SMad SMrm SPer SPoG WWEG
- 'Yellow Candy'	SEND
- 'Yellow Gem'	CPla NLar
retorta	CSpe

Ceropegia (*Asclepiadaceae*)

barklyi	LToo
conrathii	LToo
floribunda **new**	LToo
fusca	EShb
§ ***linearis*** subsp. ***woodii*** ♀H1	EShb LRHS MBri SRms STre
§ - - 'Lady Heart' (v)	EShb
- - 'Variegata'	see *C. linearis* subsp. *woodii* 'Lady Heart'
multiflora	LToo
oculata **new**	LToo
pubescens GWJ 9441	WCru
rendallii **new**	LToo
woodii	see *C. linearis* subsp. *woodii*

Ceroxylon (*Arecaceae*)

alpinum	LPal
ventricosum	LPal

Cestrum (*Solanaceae*)

aurantiacum	ERea EShb
auriculatum	SOWG
× ***cultum***	CHll EShb
- 'Cretan Pink' **new**	SOWG
- 'Cretan Purple'	CBcs CHGN CHid CHll EBee ELan ELon EPfP ERea EShb EWTr LHop SEND SMad SOWG SPoG WCFE WSHC
diurnum × ***nocturnum***	EShb
§ ***elegans***	CDoC CHEx CHll CPLG CSev CTsd EBee ELon EPfP EWTr LRHS NEgg SEND SLon SOWG WCFE WDin WGob
fasciculatum	EShb SOWG
'Newellii' ♀H2	CBcs CMHG CPLG CSev CWCL CWGN CWib EBak EBee ELan ELon

	EPfP ERea EShb LRHS SDnm SEND SGar SOWG WBor WKif WSHC
nocturnum	CCCN CDoC CHll EBak EOHP ERea EShb IDee NExo SOWG WCFE
parqui ♀H3	CAbb CBcs CHll CMHG CWib EBee ELan EPfP ERea EShb LRHS SDix SDnm SEND SGar SLon SMad SMrm SOWG SUsu WJek WKif WSHC WWlt
psittacinum	CPLG
purpureum (Lindl.) Standl.	see *C. elegans*
roseum	CPLG
- 'Ilnacullin'	ERea
* ***splendens***	SOWG

Ceterach (*Aspleniaceae*)

officinarum	see *Asplenium ceterach*

Chaenomeles (*Rosaceae*)

cathayensis	CAgr CTho LEdu NLar
§ ***japonica***	MMuc WDin WFar
- 'Chojubai'	CMen
- 'Cido'	CAgr LBuc MCoo
- 'Orange Beauty'	LRHS SPer WFar WRHF
- 'Sargentii'	CMac EPfP MGos NBro
'John Pilger'	NHol
lagenaria	see *C. speciosa*
Madame Butterfly = 'Whitice'	CDoC EBee GKir LAst LRHS LSRN MAsh MBri MMuc MRav NEgg SBfd SEND SLim SPer SPoG WClo WGrn
maulei	see *C. japonica*
'Orange Star'	CEnd EBee MNHC NLar
sinensis	see *Pseudocydonia sinensis*
§ ***speciosa***	CSam MGan NWea SMrm
- 'Apple Blossom'	see *C. speciosa* 'Moerloosei'
- 'Brilliant'	EPfP
- 'Contorta'	LRHS MAsh
- 'Eximia'	CAlb LRHS LTen NLar
- 'Falconnet Charlet' (d)	LRHS MRav
- 'Friesdorfer'	LRHS
- 'Geisha Girl' (d) ♀H4	Widely available
- 'Grayshott Salmon'	NHol WFar
- 'Kinshiden'	EPfP LRHS
- 'Knap Hill Radiance'	SLim
§ - 'Moerloosei' ♀H4	CDoC CDul CPMA CSBt CSam EBee ELan EPfP EWTr GBin LAst LRHS MAsh MBlu MBri MGos MMuc MRav MSwo MWat NLar SAga SEND SLim SPer SSta WDin WMoo WPat WTin
- 'Nivalis'	Widely available
- 'Rosea Plena' (d)	LAst
- 'Rubra Grandiflora'	LRHS WBVN
- 'Simonii' (d)	CBcs EBee EPfP MGos MRav NHol NWea SPer WFar
- 'Snow'	MAsh MSwo NHol
- 'Umbilicata'	EBee NLar SPer SRms
- 'Yukigoten'	CDoC EBee GKir LRHS MMuc NLar SBfd WClo
× ***superba***	STre
- 'Boule de Feu'	CTri CWib EBee ECtt MCoo
- 'Cameo' (d)	CBot CChe CEnd CSBt EBee ELon EPfP LHop MBNS MBri MHav MRav NCGa NLar SLPl WClo
- 'Clementine'	CWib EBee
- 'Crimson and Gold' ♀H4	Widely available
- 'Elly Mossel'	CMac CWib NLar WFar
- 'Ernst Finken'	EBee
- 'Etna'	CAlb
- 'Fascination'	NLar
- 'Fire Dance'	CDul CWib CWit EBee ECtt MSwo NHol NLar SPer
- 'Fusion' **new**	CAgr
- 'Hever Castle'	CPMA
- 'Hollandia'	MGos
- 'Issai White'	MRav
- 'Jet Trail'	CAlb CBar CBcs CSBt EBee ELan EPfP GKir LAst LRHS LSRN MAsh MGos MRav MSwo NLar SLPl SLim SPoG SSta WFar
- 'Knap Hill Scarlet' ♀H4	CDoC CDul EBee EPfP GGal GKir LRHS MAsh MGos MMuc NHol SLim SPer SPoG SRms WDin WFar
- 'Lemon and Lime'	ELan EPfP MGos MRav NSti SLon SPer
- 'Nicoline' ♀H4	CBcs CDoC CDul EBee EPfP GKir MBri NEgg NPri SLim WDin WFar
- 'Pink Lady' ♀H4	Widely available
- 'Red Joy'	NLar WGrn
- 'Red Trail'	MRav
- 'Rowallane' ♀H4	CWit EBee ELan EPfP LOck MRav SPer
- 'Salmon Horizon'	EBee EPfP MGos NLar
- 'Tortuosa'	EBee LHop
'Toyo-nishiki'	MBlu NLar

Chaenorhinum (*Scrophulariaceae*)

§ ***origanifolium***	ECho EShb NRya SBch SPlb
- 'Blue Dream'	CSpe EBee ECho ECtt EPfP GGar GKev LRHS NVic SPoG SWvt WFar WMoo WPer WRHF
- 'Dreamcatcher'	EPfP
- 'Summer Skies'	NPri SPet WFar
villosum 'Little Dragons' **new**	NBre

Chaerophyllum (*Apiaceae*)

hirsutum	CRow IMou
- 'Roseum'	Widely available

Chamaecyparis ✿ (*Cupressaceae*)

'Erecta Viridis'	CSBt MGos MHav
formosensis	CKen
lawsoniana	CDul EHul EMac NWea WBVN WDin WMou
- SIN 1820	GLin
- 'Albospica' (v)	GKir WFar
- 'Allumii Aurea'	see *C. lawsoniana* 'Alumigold'
- 'Allumii Magnificent'	CDul NLar
§ - 'Alumigold'	CSBt CWib GKir MAsh MGos SCoo WDin
- 'Alumii'	EHul GKir IFFs MAsh MGos NWea
- 'Argentea'	see *C. lawsoniana* 'Argenteovariegata'
§ - 'Argenteovariegata' (v)	GKir
- 'Aurea'	CDul
- 'Aurea Densa' ♀H4	CKen CMac CSBt CTri ECho EHul EPfP GKir MAsh MGos NEgg SCoo WEve WGor
- 'Aureovariegata' (v)	GKir
§ - 'Barabits' Globe'	GKir
- 'Bleu Nantais'	CKen CMac ECho EHul GKir LBee LRHS MGos SCoo SLim SPoG WCFE WEve WFar
- 'Blom'	CKen EHul
§ - 'Blue Gown'	EHul MGos SRms
§ - 'Blue Jacket'	NWea
- 'Blue Surprise'	CKen EHul WFar
- 'Brégéon'	CKen NLar
- 'Broomhill Gold'	CDoC CSBt EHul GKir LRHS MAsh MGos NHol NPri SCoo SLim SPer SPoG WDin WEve
- 'Caudata'	CKen NLar
- 'Chantry Gold'	EHul SCoo WEve

§	- 'Chilworth Silver' $\mathbb{Y}^{H4}$	CSBt EHul GKir IFFs LBee LRHS MAsh SCoo SLim SPer SPoG SRms WBVN WDin WFar
	- 'Columnaris'	CBcs CDoC ECho EPfP EWTr GKir IFFs LAst LBee LMaj LRHS MBri MGos NEgg NWea SCoo SPoG WFar
	- 'Columnaris Aurea'	see *C. lawsoniana* 'Golden Spire'
N	- 'Columnaris Glauca'	CMac CSBt CWib EHul GKir MAsh MGos NEgg NWea SCoo SPer WDin WFar
	- 'Crawford's Compact'	CMac
	- 'Cream Crackers'	EHul
	- 'Cream Glow'	CKen CSBt GKir LRHS MGos NLar SCoo SLim SPoG WFar WGor
	- 'Croftway'	EHul
	- 'Dik's Weeping'	CDoC GKir NLar NWea SLim WEve
	- 'Duncanii'	ECho EHul
	- 'Dutch Gold'	EHul
	- 'Dwarf Blue'	see *C. lawsoniana* 'Pick's Dwarf Blue'
	- 'Eclipse'	CKen
	- 'Elegantissima' ambig.	CKen GKir MGos
	- 'Ellwoodii' $\mathbb{Y}^{H4}$	CChe CDul CMac CSBt CTri CWib ECho EHul EPfP GKir IFFs LAst MAsh MGos NPri NWea SCoo SLim SPer SPoG WDin WFar WMoo
I	- 'Ellwoodii Glauca'	SPlb
	- 'Ellwood's Empire'	EHul GKir
	- 'Ellwood's Gold' $\mathbb{Y}^{H4}$	CBcs CChe CDoC CSBt CWib ECho EHul ELan EPfP GKir IFFs LBee LRHS MAsh MBri MGos NHol NPri NWea SPer SPlb SPoG STre WDin WEve WFar WMoo
	- 'Ellwood's Gold Pillar'	ECho EHul GKir LBee LRHS MAsh MGos NHol SCoo SLim SPoG WFar
§	- 'Ellwood's Nymph'	CKen ECho GKir LRHS MAsh SCoo SLim WFar WGor
	- Ellwood's Pillar = 'Flolar'	CChe CDoC CMac EHul GKir LAst LBee LRHS MAsh MBri MGos NHol NLar SCoo SLim WCFE WDin WFar
	- 'Ellwood's Pygmy'	CMac GKir
	- 'Ellwood's Silver'	ECho MAsh WFar
	- 'Ellwood's Silver Threads'	CMac GKir
	- 'Ellwood's Variegata'	see *C. lawsoniana* 'Ellwood's White'
§	- 'Ellwood's White' (v)	CKen CSBt ECho EHul EPfP WFar
I	- 'Emerald'	CKen
	- 'Emerald Spire'	MAsh NHol
	- 'Empire'	WFar
	- 'Erecta Aurea'	ECho EHul MGos SCoo
	- 'Erecta Viridis'	CBcs GKir NEgg NWea WDin WFar
	- 'Ericoides'	EHul
	- 'Filiformis Compacta'	EHul
	- 'Filip's Golden Tears' **new**	SLim
	- 'Fleckellwood'	CWib EHul MAsh
	- 'Fletcheri' $\mathbb{Y}^{H4}$	CMac EHul GKir NWea WDin WFar
	- 'Fletcheri Aurea'	see *C. lawsoniana* 'Yellow Transparent'
	- 'Fletcher's White'	EHul
	- 'Forsteckensis'	CKen ECho EHul GKir NLar NWea SCoo SRms WFar WGor
I	- 'Forsteckensis Aurea'	NLar
	- 'Fraseri'	NWea
	- 'Gimbornii' $\mathbb{Y}^{H4}$	ECho EHul GKir LBee SCoo SLim SRms WFar
	- 'Glauca'	CDul
	- 'Glauca Spek'	see *C. lawsoniana* 'Spek'
	- 'Globosa'	MGos
	- 'Globus'	see *C. lawsoniana* 'Barabits' Globe'
	- 'Gnome'	CDoC CMac ECho EHul GEdr LAst LRHS MGos SCoo SLim SPoG WEve WGor

	- 'Gold Flake'	MGos
§	- 'Golden Pot'	CDoC CMac CSBt CWib EHul GKir LBee LRHS MGos NHol SCoo WDin WFar
§	- 'Golden Queen'	EHul
	- 'Golden Showers'	EHul
§	- 'Golden Spire'	NLar WFar
	- 'Golden Triumph'	EHul
	- 'Golden Wonder'	EHul MGos NEgg NLar NWea SCoo SRms WDin WEve WFar
	- 'Goldfinger'	NLar
	- 'Grayswood Feather'	CDoC CSBt EHul GKir LBee LRHS MAsh MGos SCoo SPlb WEve
	- 'Grayswood Gold'	EHul GKir LRHS WEve
	- 'Grayswood Pillar' $\mathbb{Y}^{H4}$	CDul EHul GKir MGos
	- 'Green Globe'	CDoC CKen CMen CSBt EHul LBee MAsh MGos NLar SCoo SLim WAbe WDin WEve
§	- 'Green Hedger' $\mathbb{Y}^{H4}$	CSBt MHav NWea SCoo SRms WFar
§	- 'Green Pillar'	CWib IFFs LAst LBee LRHS NEgg SCoo
	- 'Green Spire'	see *C. lawsoniana* 'Green Pillar'
	- 'Hillieri'	GKir
	- 'Hogger's Blue Gown'	see *C. lawsoniana* 'Blue Gown'
	- 'Imbricata Pendula'	CDoC CKen GKir IDee LRHS NLar SLim SMad
	- 'Intertexta' $\mathbb{Y}^{H4}$	GKir WEve
	- 'Ivonne'	EHul GKir MGos WEve
	- 'Jackman's Green Hedger'	see *C. lawsoniana* 'Green Hedger'
	- 'Jackman's Variety'	see *C. lawsoniana* 'Green Pillar'
	- 'Jeanette'	MGos
	- 'Kelleriis Gold'	EHul
	- 'Killarny Salmon' **new**	CMac
	- 'Kilmacurragh' $\mathbb{Y}^{H4}$	CDul CMac GKir MGos NWea
	- 'Kilworth Column'	CDoC MGos NLar NWea
	- 'Knowefieldensis'	CMac ECho EHul GKir
	- 'Lane' misapplied	see *C. lawsoniana* 'Lanei Aurea'
	- 'Lane' den Ouden	CSBt CWib MGos MRav NEgg SCoo WDin WFar
§	- 'Lanei Aurea' $\mathbb{Y}^{H4}$	EHul MGos NWea WFar
	- 'Lemon Pillar'	WDin WEve
	- 'Lemon Queen'	CSBt EHul LBee
	- 'Limelight'	MGos
	- 'Little Spire' $\mathbb{Y}^{H4}$	CDoC ECho EPla GKir LRHS MBri MGos NHol NLar SBfd SCoo SLim SPoG WEve WGor
	- 'Lombartsii'	WFar
	- 'Lutea' $\mathbb{Y}^{H4}$	CMac EHul GKir MGos NWea
§	- 'Lutea Nana' $\mathbb{Y}^{H4}$	CMac EHul EPla MAsh MGos NLar SCoo
§	- 'Lutea Smithii'	NWea
	- 'Luteocompacta'	LBee
*	- 'MacPenny's Gold'	CMac
	- 'Milford Blue Jacket'	see *C. lawsoniana* 'Blue Jacket'
§	- 'Minima'	SRms
	- 'Minima Argentea'	see *C. lawsoniana* 'Nana Argentea'
	- 'Minima Aurea' $\mathbb{Y}^{H4}$	CDoC CDul CKen CMac CSBt CWib ECho EHul EPfP EPla EPot GKir IFFs LAst LBee LRHS MAsh MBri MGos NEgg NHol NWea SLim SPer SPoG WCFE WDin WEve WFar WMoo
	- 'Minima Densa'	see *C. lawsoniana* 'Minima'
	- 'Minima Glauca' $\mathbb{Y}^{H4}$	CDul CMac CSBt ECho EHul EPfP GEdr GKir IFFs LAst MAsh MGos NEgg NHol NWea SCoo SLim SPer WDin WEve WFar
	- 'Moonlight'	MGos
*	- 'Moonsprite'	ECho EHul NLar SCoo SLim SPoG
	- 'Naberi'	GKir
	- 'Nana'	CMac

	- 'Nana Albospica' (v)	ECho EHul LBee LRHS NPri SCoo WFar WGor
§	- 'Nana Argentea'	CKen CMac EHul EPfP SCoo WFar WGor
	- 'Nana Lutea'	see *C. lawsoniana* 'Lutea Nana'
	- 'New Silver'	MGos
	- 'Nicole'	ECho EHul MAsh SCoo WGor
	- 'Nidiformis'	EHul NWea SCoo SRms
	- 'Nyewoods'	see *C. lawsoniana* 'Chilworth Silver'
	- 'Nymph'	see *C. lawsoniana* 'Ellwood's Nymph'
§	- 'Pelt's Blue' ♀^{H4}	CBcs CDoC CDul CKen CSBt EHul GKir IFFs LBee LRHS MGos NLar SBfd SCoo SLim SPoG WDin WFar
	- 'Pembury Blue' ♀^{H4}	CDoC CDul CSBt CWib ECho EHul EPfP GKir LBee LRHS MAsh MGos NEgg NLar NWea SCoo SLim SPer SPoG WDin WFar
§	- 'Pick's Dwarf Blue'	LRHS MGos NHol SCoo WEve WGor
	- Pot of Gold	see *C. lawsoniana* 'Golden Pot'
	- 'Pottenii'	CMac CSBt ECho EHul GKir LBee MAsh MGos NWea SCoo WDin WFar
	- 'Pygmaea Argentea' (v) ♀^{H4}	CKen CMac CSBt CWib ECho EHul ELan EPfP EPla GKir LBee LRHS MAsh MBri MGos NEgg NHol SLim SPer SPoG SRms WBor WCFE WDin WFar
	- 'Pygmy'	EHul GKir NHol NLar NWea SCoo SLim WEve
	- 'Rijnhof'	EHul LBee
	- 'Rimpelaar'	CDoC MGos
	- 'Rock Gold' **new**	WEve
	- 'Rogersii'	SRms WFar
	- 'Romana'	MBri
	- 'Royal Gold'	EHul
	- 'Silver Queen' (v)	CKen
	- 'Silver Threads' (v)	ECho EHul EPla GKir LBee LRHS MAsh NHol WFar
	- 'Silver Tip' (v)	EHul LRHS SCoo SLim
	- 'Smithii'	see *C. lawsoniana* 'Lutea Smithii'
	- 'Snow Flurry' (v)	CKen ECho EHul WFar
	- 'Snow White'^{PBR} (v)	ECho EHul GKir LBee LRHS MAsh MBri MGos NHol SCoo SLim SPoG WFar WGor
	- 'Somerset'	MGos
§	- 'Spek'	GKir
	- 'Springtime'^{PBR}	CSBt EHul LBee LRHS SCoo SLim SPoG WGor
	- 'Stardust' ♀^{H4}	CBcs CDoC CDul CSBt CTri CWib EHul ELan GKir IFFs LRHS MAsh MBri NEgg NPri SCoo SLim SPer SPoG WDin
	- 'Stewartii'	CDul CTri NEgg NWea SCoo
	- 'Stilton Cheese'	NHol
*	- 'Summer Cream'	EHul
	- 'Summer Snow' (v)	CDoC ECho EHul EPfP GKir LBee LRHS MGos NHol NPri SCoo SLim SRms WFar
	- 'Sunkist'	CSBt LRHS SCoo SLim WFar
	- 'Tamariscifolia'	CDoC EHul GKir WCFE WDin WFar
	- 'Tharandtensis Caesia'	WFar
	- 'Tilford'	EHul
	- 'Treasure' (v)	CSBt ECho EHul EPfP EPla LRHS MAsh NHol SCoo SLim SPoG WFar
	- 'Triomf van Boskoop'	GKir
	- 'Van Pelt'	see *C. lawsoniana* 'Pelt's Blue'
	- 'Waterfall'	SMad
	- 'Westermannii' (v)	CMac LRHS SCoo

	- 'White Edge'	WFar
	- 'White Spot' (v)	ECho EHul GKir LBee MBri NPri SCoo WFar
	- 'White Wonder'	MGos
	- 'Winston Churchill'	CSBt GKir MGos NWea
	- 'Wisselii' ♀^{H4}	CDoC CKen CMac ECho EHul GKir IFFs NLar NWea SCoo SRms WDin WFar WMoo
	- 'Wisselii Nana'	CKen EHul
	- 'Wissel's Saguaro'	CDoC CKen MGos NLar SLim
	- 'Witzeliana'	CDul CSBt ECho MGos NLar
	- 'Yellow Queen'	see *C. lawsoniana* 'Golden Queen'
	- 'Yellow Success'	see *C. lawsoniana* 'Golden Queen'
§	- 'Yellow Transparent'	CMac
	- 'Yvonne'	CDoC CDul GKir LRHS MAsh MGos NEgg NHol NLar SCoo SLim SPoG WEve
	leylandii	see × *Cuprocyparis leylandii*
	nootkatensis	see *Xanthocyparis nootkatensis*
	- 'Aurea'	GKir IFFs WDin
	- 'Aureovariegata' (v)	EHul
	- 'Compacta'	CTri
	- 'Glauca'	CTho IFFs
	- 'Gracilis'	EHul
	- 'Green Arrow'	CKen ECho LRHS NLar SCoo SLim
	- 'Jubilee'	NPCo SCoo SLim WMou
	- 'Kanada'	NLar
	- 'Lutea'	CTri LRHS NWea
	- 'Nordkroken'	NLar
	- 'Strict Weeper'	CKen GKir NLar SLim
	obtusa 'Albovariegata' (v)	CKen
	- 'Arneson's Compact'	CKen
	- 'Aurea'	CDoC SCoo WEve
	- 'Aurora'	CKen ECho ELan MBri MGos SLim WEve
	- 'Bambi'	CDoC CKen MGos NLar WAbe WEve WThu
	- 'Barkenny'	CKen
	- 'Bartley'	CKen
	- 'Bassett'	CKen
	- 'Bess'	CKen
	- 'Brigitt'	CKen
	- 'Buttonball'	CKen MGos
	- 'Caespitosa'	WAbe
	- 'Chabo-yadori'	CDoC ECho EHul GKir LRHS MGos SCoo SLim WFar
	- 'Chilworth'	CDoC CKen MGos NLar
	- 'Chima-anihiba'	CKen
	- 'Chirimen'	CDoC CKen MGos NHol NLar SLim
	- 'Clarke's Seedling'	CDoC NLar
	- 'Confucius'	CDoC EHul MGos NHol
	- 'Corley Gold'	MGos
§	- 'Crippsii' ♀^{H4}	CBcs CDoC CDul CMac GKir MGos SCoo SLim
	- 'Crippsii Aurea'	see *C. obtusa* 'Crippsii'
	- 'Dainty Doll'	CDoC CKen MGos NLar
	- 'Densa'	see *C. obtusa* 'Nana Densa'
	- 'Draht'	CDoC MGos NLar SCoo
	- 'Draht Hexe'	CKen
	- 'Elf'	CKen
	- 'Ellie B'	CKen
	- 'Ericoides'	CKen ECho
	- 'Erika'	ECho
	- 'Fernspray Gold'	CDoC CDul CKen CTri ECho EHul GKir IFFs LRHS MAsh NEgg SBfd SCoo SLim SPer SPoG WFar
	- 'Flabelliformis'	CKen
	- 'Gnome'	CKen CMen GKir
	- 'Gold Fern'	CKen MGos WFar
	- 'Golden Fairy'	CDoC CKen MGos WAbe WEve
	- 'Golden Filament' (v)	CKen
	- 'Golden Nymph'	CDoC CKen MGos NLar

	- 'Golden Sprite'	CDoC CKen MGos NLar WAbe WEve WThu
	- 'Goldilocks'	EHul
	- 'Gracilis Aurea'	CKen CMac
	- 'Green Diamond'	CKen
	- 'Hage'	CKen
	- 'Hypnoides Nana'	CKen
	- 'Intermedia'	CDoC CKen MGos WAbe
	- 'Ivan's Column'	CKen
	- 'Junior'	CKen
	- 'Juniperoides'	CKen WThu
	- 'Juniperoides Compacta'	WAbe
	- 'Kamarachiba'	CDoC CKen CSBt ECho EHul EPla LBee LRHS NLar SCoo SLim SPoG WEve WFar
	- 'Kerdalo'	LRHS NLar SLim SPoG
	- 'Konijn'	ECho EHul
	- 'Kosteri'	CDoC CKen CMac ECho EHul ELan EPot LBee MAsh NEgg NHol SCoo WEve
	- 'Kyoto Creeper'	CKen
	- 'Laxa'	MGos
	- 'Leprechaun'	MGos NLar
	- 'Limerick'	CKen
	- 'Little Markey'	CKen
	- 'Lucas' **new**	SLim
	- 'Lycopodioides'	ECho MGos
	- 'Marian'	CKen MGos NLar
§	- 'Mariesii' (v)	CKen SCoo
	- 'Melody'	CKen NLar
	- 'Meroke'	NLar
	- 'Minima'	CKen MGos
	- 'Nana' 🏆H4	CDoC CKen CMac CMen LBee MGos NHol WEve
	- 'Nana Albospica'	GKir
	- 'Nana Aurea' 🏆H4	CDoC CMac CMea CSBt ECho EHul EPfP GKir MAsh MGos NHol WBrE WEve WFar
I	- 'Nana Confucius'	MGos
§	- 'Nana Densa'	CDoC CKen CMac NLar
	- 'Nana Gracilis' 🏆H4	CDoC CDul CKen CMen CSBt ECho EHul ELan EPfP EPla EPot GEdr GKir IVic LAst MAsh MBri MGos NEgg NHol NWea SCoo SLim SPoG WBor WDin WEve WFar
I	- 'Nana Gracilis Aurea'	CMen EHul WEve
I	- 'Nana Lutea'	CDoC CKen CSBt ECho EHul EPfP EPot GKir LBee LRHS MAsh MGos NHol NWea SCoo SLim SPoG WBor
	- 'Nana Pyramidalis'	LBee
	- 'Nana Rigida'	see *C. obtusa* 'Rigid Dwarf'
	- 'Nana Variegata'	see *C. obtusa* 'Mariesii'
	- 'Pygmaea'	CSBt EHul MGos SCoo SLim WEve
	- 'Rashahiba' **new**	SLim
§	- 'Rigid Dwarf'	CDoC CKen EHul LBee NLar SCoo SPoG WEve
	- 'Saffron Spray'	LRHS MBri SLim
	- 'Snowflake' (v)	CDoC CKen ECho SBfd WEve WFar
	- 'Snowkist' (v)	CKen
	- 'Spiralis'	CKen
	- 'Stoneham'	CKen
	- 'Suirova-hiba'	SLim
	- 'Tempelhof'	CKen CSBt ECho EHul LRHS MAsh MGos MHav NEgg NLar SCoo SLim WEve
	- 'Tetragona Aurea'	CBcs CMac ECho EHul MGos NLar SCoo SLim WEve
	- 'Timothy' **new**	CMac
	- 'Tonia' (v)	CKen EHul EPla GKir NHol NLar SLim WEve WGor
	- 'Topsie'	CKen NLar
	- 'Tsatsumi'	CDoC EMil SCoo
	- 'Tsatsumi Gold'	CDoC CKen ECho EHul LRHS NLar SCoo SLim SPoG
	- 'Verdon'	CKen
	- 'Winter Gold'	WEve
	- 'Wissel'	CKen MGos
	- 'Wyckoff'	CKen
	- 'Yellowtip' (v)	CKen MGos NLar WEve
	pisifera 'Aurea Nana' misapplied	see *C. pisifera* 'Strathmore'
	- 'Avenue'	EHul
	- 'Baby Blue'	ECho EHul ELan EPfP LRHS MGos SCoo SLim
	- 'Blue Globe'	CKen
	- 'Boulevard' 🏆H4	CBcs CDoC CDul CMac CSBt CWib ECho EHul ELan EPfP GKir IFFs LAst LBee LRHS MAsh MGos MHav NEgg NWea SBfd SLim SPer SRms WBVN WDin WEve WFar WMoo
	- 'Compacta Variegata' (v)	NEgg
	- 'Curly Tops'	CSBt ECho EHul GKir LRHS MGos SCoo SLim WBor WEve
	- 'Devon Cream'	ECho MAsh MGos NEgg SCoo WFar
	- 'Filifera'	CMac CSBt GKir SCoo WFar
	- 'Filifera Aurea' 🏆H4	CKen CMac CWib ECho EHul EPla GKir LBee MAsh MGos NEgg NHol NWea SCoo SRms WCFE WDin WEve WFar
	- 'Filifera Aureovariegata' (v)	EHul SCoo
	- 'Filifera Nana'	ECho EHul ELan SLim SPoG STre WDin WFar
	- 'Filifera Nana Aurea'	see *C. pisifera* 'Golden Mop'
	- 'Filifera Sungold'	see *C. pisifera* 'Sungold'
	- 'Fuiri-tsukomo'	CKen
*	- 'Gold Cascade'	MGos
	- 'Gold Cushion'	CKen
	- 'Gold Dust'	see *C. pisifera* 'Plumosa Aurea'
	- 'Gold Spangle'	CKen ECho EHul WFar
§	- 'Golden Mop' 🏆H4	CKen EHul GKir MAsh NLar
	- 'Green Pincushion'	CKen CMen
	- 'Hime-himuro'	CKen
	- 'Hime-sawara'	CKen CMen
	- 'Margaret'	CKen
	- 'Nana'	CKen CMen ECho EHul EPfP MAsh MGos NHol WFar
I	- 'Nana Albovariegata' (v)	CDoC ECho MAsh SPoG WFar WThu
	- 'Nana Aureovariegata' (v)	CDoC CSBt ECho EHul LBee LRHS MAsh SCoo SLim SPer WEve WFar
I	- 'Nana Compacta'	CMac SRms
	- 'Nana Variegata' (v)	CMac LBee SCoo SLim WFar
I	- 'Parslorii'	CKen
	- 'Pici'	CKen
§	- 'Plumosa Aurea'	CKen EHul GKir WDin WFar
	- 'Plumosa Aurea Compacta'	CKen
	- 'Plumosa Aurea Nana'	ECho GKir MGos NHol WFar
I	- 'Plumosa Aurea Nana Compacta'	CMac
	- 'Plumosa Aurescens'	CDoC CMac
§	- 'Plumosa Compressa'	CDoC CKen ECho EHul MAsh SCoo SLim WFar WGor
	- 'Plumosa Densa'	see *C. pisifera* 'Plumosa Compressa'
	- 'Plumosa Flavescens'	EHul SCoo
I	- 'Plumosa Juniperoides'	CKen ECho EHul SCoo SLim WFar WGor
I	- 'Plumosa Pygmaea'	MGos WGor
§	- 'Plumosa Rogersii'	EHul NHol WGor
I	- 'Pygmaea Tsukumo'	MGos NLar
	- 'Rogersii'	see *C. pisifera* 'Plumosa Rogersii'
	- 'Silver and Gold' (v)	EHul
	- 'Silver Lode' (v)	CKen

	- 'Snow' (v)	CKen
	- 'Snowflake'	CKen ECho EHul MGos NHol
	- 'Spaan's Cannon Ball'	CKen ECho
§	- 'Squarrosa'	WDin WFar
	- 'Squarrosa Dumosa'	CKen EHul
I	- 'Squarrosa Lombarts'	CSBt ECho EHul GKir IFFs SCoo
	- 'Squarrosa Lutea'	CKen
	- 'Squarrosa Sulphurea'	CSBt ECho EHul EPfP LRHS SLim WBVN WDin WFar
	- 'Squarrosa Veitchii'	see *C. pisifera* 'Squarrosa'
§	- 'Strathmore'	CKen EHul NHol WDin
§	- 'Sungold'	CDoC CKen CSBt ECho EHul EPla GKir LRHS MAsh SCoo SLim SPer SPoG WEve
	- 'Tama-himuro'	CKen
	- 'Teddy Bear'	MBri NLar
	- 'True Blue'	EHul MBri MGos NLar
	- 'Winter Beauty'	LRHS
	thyoides 'Andelyensis'	CMac CSBt ECho EHul GKir LAst NEgg SCoo WFar
	- 'Andelyensis Nana'	CKen
	- 'Aurea'	EHul
	- 'Conica'	CKen
	- 'Ericoides' ♀H4	CKen CTri ECho EHul GKir LBee SPlb WDin WFar
	- 'Little Jamie'	CKen
	- 'Red Star'	see *C. thyoides* 'Rubicon'
§	- 'Rubicon'	CMac CSBt ECho EHul EPfP EPla GKir IFFs LBee LRHS MAsh MGos NEgg SBfd SLim SPoG WBor WFar
	- 'Top Point'	ECho LBee LRHS MAsh MGos SCoo SLim SPoG
	- 'Variegata' (v)	EHul

Chamaecytisus (*Papilionaceae*)

§	***albus*** (Hacq.) Rothm.	GQui WDin
§	***hirsutus***	WPGP
	prolifer	CPLG NLar
§	***purpureus***	CBgR CSBt EBee ELan EPfP GKir LHop MRav NPri NWea SPer WBVN WDin WFar WPat
	- f. ***albus***	EPfP SPer
§	- 'Atropurpureus' ♀H4	MMuc SPer
	- 'Incarnatus'	see *C. purpureus* 'Atropurpureus'
	- 'Lilac Lady'	LRHS
§	***supinus***	CPLG IRar SRms

Chamaedaphne (*Ericaceae*)

calyculata	CBcs EBee IVic WSHC
- 'Nana'	NHar

Chamaedorea (*Arecaceae*)

	elegans ♀H1	CTsd LPal
	erumpens	see *C. seifrizii*
	metallica misapplied	see *C. microspadix*
	metallica O.F. Cook ex H.E. Moore ♀H1	LPal
§	***microspadix***	CPHo EAmu LPal SChr
	radicalis	CBrP CPHo EAmu LPJP LPal SChr
§	***seifrizii*** ♀H1	LPal

Chamaemelum (*Asteraceae*)

§	***nobile***	CArn CHby CPrp CSev CTri CWan ECho ELau EPfP GBar GKir GMac GPoy MBri MHer MMuc MNHC NGHP NGdn NPri SBfd SEND SPlb SRms SVic WJek WPer
	- dwarf	GBar LMor SVic
	- dwarf, double-flowered (d)	GBar
	- 'Flore Pleno' (d)	Widely available
	- 'Treneague'	Widely available

Chamaenerion see *Chamerion*

Chamaepericlymenum see *Cornus*

Chamaerops (*Arecaceae*)

	excelsa misapplied	see *Trachycarpus fortunei*
	excelsa Thunb.	see *Rhapis excelsa*
	humilis ♀H3	Widely available
§	- var. ***argentea***	CBrP CDTJ CPHo CTrC EAmu EGxp ETod EUJe LPJP MGos NPal SBfd WCot
	- var. ***cerifera***	see *C. humilis* var. *argentea*
	- 'Vulcano'	CDTJ EAmu LRHS MBri MGos SChr

Chamaespartium see *Genista*

Chamaesphacos (*Lamiaceae*)

ilicifolius misapplied	see *Siphocranion macranthum*

Chambeyronia (*Arecaceae*)

macrocarpa	EAmu LPal

Chamelaucium (*Myrtaceae*)

axillare	SOWG
floriferum new	CFee
uncinatum	SOWG

Chamerion (*Onagraceae*)

§	***angustifolium***	EBWF GBar NSco SWat WSFF
§	- 'Album'	Widely available
	- 'Isobel'	CSpe MRav WCot
	- 'Stahl Rose'	CBot CElw CHid CMea EBee EWes LPla NSti SMrm SPhx SSvw STes SWat WCot WPGP WSHC
§	***dodonaei***	ELan EWes EWld IMou MMuc MTho SPhx WFar

Chasmanthe (*Iridaceae*)

aethiopica	CPou GGar
bicolor	CDes CPLG CPou CTca EBee IDee
floribunda	CAbb CHEx CPrp CTca EBee
- var. ***duckittii***	CFir CPrp EBee ECho EPfP WPGP
- 'Saturnes'	CDes EBee
- 'Venus'	EBee

Chasmanthium (*Poaceae*)

§	***latifolium***	Widely available

Cheilanthes (*Adiantaceae*)

albomarginata new	WAbe
argentea	WAbe WRic
cucullans	WAbe
distans	SRms WAbe WRic
eatonii	WAbe
eckloniana	WAbe
grisea	WAbe
lanosa	CBty CCCN CHid CLAP EBee EFer EPPr EWes LRHS SGSe SRms WCot
lindheimeri	WAbe
microphylla	WAbe
myriophylla	WAbe
nivea	WAbe
pulchella	WAbe
sieberi	WAbe
sinuata	ISha
tomentosa	CBty CCCN CLAP EBee ISha LRHS SRms WAbe WRic
wootonii	WAbe

Cheiranthus see *Erysimum*

Cheirolophus (*Asteraceae*)

benoistii misapplied	see *Centaurea atropurpurea*
benoistii (Humb.) Holub new	CSpe EBee
teydis new	SPlb

Chelidonium (*Papaveraceae*)

hylomeconoides new	EBee
japonicum	see *Hylomecon japonica*
majus	CArn CRWN EBWF GPoy GQui MHer MNHC NMir WHer WSFF
- 'Flore Pleno' (d)	CBre MMHG NBid NBro WCFE WHer
- var. ***laciniatum***	NBir WCot

Chelone (*Scrophulariaceae*)

barbata	see *Penstemon barbatus*
§ ***glabra***	Widely available
lyonii	EBee ELan GGar LEdu MBri MDKP NBre NGdn NLar SPad SPet WMoo WPer WPnP WShi
- 'Pink Temptation'	EBee EWTr GJos SPet
obliqua	Widely available
- var. ***alba***	see *C. glabra*
- 'Forncett Foremost'	GQui
- 'Forncett Poppet'	NBre
- 'Pink Sensation'	EBee NBre WFar
* - ***rosea***	EBee MLLN MMHG NBPC WGwG

Chelonopsis (*Lamiaceae*)

moschata	CLAP CPom LEdu MMoz SMad WMoo WPGP WPrP
yagiharana	EBee MBri MCCP MDKP MWea NBPC NBid NPnk WMoo

Chengiopanax (*Araliaceae*)

sciadophylloides B&SWJ 4728	WCru

Chenopodium (*Chenopodiaceae*)

bonus-henricus	CAgr CArn CHby CWan GBar GPWP GPoy ILis MCoo MHer MNHC SBfd SIde WHer WJek
giganteum	GPWP ILis MNHC WJek

cherimoya see *Annona cherimola*

cherry, Duke see *Prunus* × *gondouinii*

cherry, sour or morello see *Prunus cerasus*

cherry, sweet see *Prunus avium*

chervil see *Anthriscus cerefolium*

chestnut, sweet see *Castanea sativa*

Chiastophyllum (*Crassulaceae*)

§ ***oppositifolium*** ♀H4	CBcs CSam CStu CTri EBee ECha ECho EDAr ELan EPfP GAbr GEdr GGar GJos GKev LAst LRHS MLHP MRav NBid NMen NWCA SPlb SRms WCot WKif WMoo WSHC
- 'Frosted Jade'	see *C. oppositifolium* 'Jim's Pride'
- 'Jane's Reverse'	EBee WCot
§ - 'Jim's Pride' (v)	Widely available
simplicifolium	see *C. oppositifolium*

Chiliotrichum (*Asteraceae*)

diffusum (G. Forst.) Kuntze	CWib GGar
- dark-leaved	GGar
- 'Siska'	CBcs GBin IFFs SMad

Chilopsis (*Bignoniaceae*)

linearis (Cav.) Sweet	CArn EGFP

Chimonanthus ✿ (*Calycanthaceae*)

fragrans	see *C. praecox*
nitens	CBcs CMCN NLar
§ ***praecox***	Widely available
- 'Grandiflorus' ♀H4	CEnd CPMA EPfP LRHS MAsh MBri SPoG SSpi SSta WPGP WPat
- 'Luteus' ♀H4	CEnd CPMA ECrN ELan EPfP LRHS LSRN MAsh MBri MGos MRav SPer SPoG SSpi SSta WPGP WPat
- 'Sunburst'	CPMA
- 'Trenython'	CEnd CPMA WPat
yunnanensis	CPne NLar

Chimonobambusa (*Poaceae*)

KR 7592 new	MWht
falcata	see *Drepanostachyum falcatum*
hejiangensis	EPla
hookeriana misapplied	see *Himalayacalamus falconeri* 'Damarapa'
macrophylla f. ***intermedia***	EPla
§ ***marmorea***	CDTJ CEnt EAmu EBee EPla LPal MMoz MMuc MWht NPal SBig WDyG WJun WPGP
- 'Variegata' (v)	CDTJ EPla MMoz SLPl WDyG WJun WPGP
§ ***quadrangularis***	CBcs CDTJ CDoC CEnt CGHE CHEx EBee EPfP EPla ESwi IMou LEdu MAvo MMoz MWht NPal SBig WDyG WJun WPGP
- 'Nagaminei' (v)	EPla WJun
- 'Suow' (v)	CDTJ CGHE EPla WPGP
- 'Tatejima'	EPla WJun
tumidissinoda	CDTJ CEnt CGHE EBee EPfP EPla ESwi IMou MMoz MWhi MWht NPal SBig WDyG WJun WPGP

Chinese chives see *Allium tuberosum*

Chiogenes see *Gaultheria*

Chionanthus (*Oleaceae*)

retusus	CBcs CDul CMCN EBee EPfP LRHS MBri MPkF NLar SKHP SSpi WDin
virginicus	Widely available

Chionochloa (*Poaceae*)

beddiei	GBin
conspicua	CAby CBod CGHE CKno EBee EKen GBin GCal GKev GQue MAvo MMuc NBir NLar SGSe SMad WPGP WWEG
- subsp. ***conspicua***	GGar
- 'Rubra'	see *C. rubra*
flavescens	EHoe GBin LRHS MAvo
flavicans	CKno GBin IMou MMuc SGar SMad
rigida	EBee
§ ***rubra***	CElw CGHE CKno CSpe EBee EBrs EHoe ELan EPla EWes GCal GMaP IMou LEdu LHop MAvo MMoz MRav NChi SApp SGSe SMrm WCot WMoo WPGP WTin WWEG
- subsp. ***cuprea***	CAby EBee GBin GGar NDov SMad

Chionodoxa ✿ (*Hyacinthaceae*)

cretica	see *C. nana*

§ ***forbesii***	CWCL EBrs ECGP ECho EPfP EPot LRHS NBir SDeJ SMrm SPer SRms WFar WShi
- 'Alba'	ECho LAma
- 'Blue Giant'	ECho EPot ERCP LRHS
- 'Rosea'	ECho LAma
- 'Tmoli'	ECho
- 'Violet Beauty'	ECho
- 'Zwanenburg'	ECho
gigantea	see *C. luciliae* Gigantea Group
lochiae	EBrs
luciliae misapplied	see *C. forbesii*
luciliae ambig.	ECho SEND
luciliae Boiss. 🏆H4	CAvo EPfP EPot LAma MBri MMuc SPer
- 'Alba'	EBrs ECho GGar LRHS MCot SDeJ SMrm SPer
§ - Gigantea Group	ECho ELan EPot GKev LAma
- - 'Alba'	EPot GKev
§ ***nana***	ECho
'Pink Giant'	CAvo CFox CStu EBrs ECho ELan EPfP EPot ERCP EWTr GGar GKev LAma LRHS MCot SDeJ SMrm WCot
sardensis 🏆H4	CBgR ECho EPot ERCP LAma LRHS MCot SDeJ SPhx WCot WShi

Chionographis (*Melanthiaceae*)

japonica	EFEx WCru

Chionohebe (*Scrophulariaceae*)

§ ***densifolia***	GCrs
pulvinaris	GCrs NSla

× *Chionoscilla* (*Hyacinthaceae*)

§ ***allenii***	CAvo CBgR ECho SPhx WCot

Chirita (*Gesneriaceae*)

'Aiko'	WDib
'Candy' **new**	WDib
'Chastity'	WDib
'Diane Marie'	WDib
'Erika' **new**	WDib
flavimaculata	WDib
heterotricha	WDib
'Keiko'	WDib
* ***latifolia*** × ***linearifolia***	WDib
linearifolia	WDib
linearifolia × ***sinensis***	WDib
longgangensis	WDib
'New York'	CSpe WDib
sinensis 🏆H1	WDib
- 'Hisako'	CSpe WDib
speciosa 'Crûg Cornetto'	WCru
'Stardust'	WDib
tamiana	CSpe WDib

Chironia (*Gentianaceae*)

baccifera	SPlb

× *Chitalpa* (*Bignoniaceae*)

sp. **new**	MWya
tashkentensis	CBcs CEnd CMCN EBee EPfP IDee MBri NLar WPGP WPat
- 'Morning Cloud'	MBlu
- 'Pink Dawn'	IFFs MBri NLar
- Summer Bells = 'Minsum'	CDoC EBee LHop LRHS MAsh MGos MMuc MREP SBig SCoo WCot

chives see *Allium schoenoprasum*

Chlidanthus (*Amaryllidaceae*)

fragrans	CCCN CStu ECho EShb GGar SEND

Chloranthus (*Chloranthaceae*)

fortunei	CDes CLAP EBee WPGP
japonicus	CLAP WCru
oldhamii	CLAP EWld GEdr LEdu
- B&SWJ 2019	WCru
serratus	EBee WCru

Chloris (*Poaceae*)

distichophylla	see *Eustachys distichophylla*

Chlorophytum (*Anthericaceae*)

comosum	EShb SEND SVic
- 'Aureomarginata'	SEND
- 'Variegatum' (v) 🏆H1+3	CDTJ MBri SEND SRms
- 'Vittatum' (v) 🏆H1+3	EShb SRms
krookianum	CFir EBee WCot
macrophyllum	EShb
majus	WCot
nepalense	WCot
- B&SWJ 2393	WCru
- B&SWJ 2528	WCru
orchidastrum	EShb
saundersiae	CPLG SHom

Choisya (*Rutaceae*)

× ***dewitteana*** 'Aztec Pearl' 🏆H4	Widely available
- White Dazzler = 'Londaz' **new**	LBuc MAsh SLon WGrn
dumosa	LHop
- var. ***arizonica***	WCot
'Golden Gift' **new**	LRHS LSqu MAsh SSpi
Goldfingers = 'Limo' PBR	CBcs CDul CWGN EBee ELan ELon EPfP IVic LAst LHop LRHS LSRN MAsh MBri MGos MRav MSwo NEgg NHol NLar SBfd SCoo SLim SLon SPad SPer SPoG SSta SWvt WCot
ternata 🏆H4	Widely available
- Moonshine = 'Walcho' PBR	EBee GBin NHol NLar WCot
- Moonsleeper PBR	see *C. ternata* Sundance
- Snow Flurries = 'Lisflurry' **new**	LRHS LSqu MAsh SPoG
§ - Sundance = 'Lich' PBR 🏆H3	Widely available

Chondropetalum (*Restionaceae*)

* ***elephantinum***	CFir LTen
hookerianum	NEgg
mucronatum	CTrC WPGP
tectorum	Widely available
- dwarf	CDes CTrC WPGP

Chondrosum (*Poaceae*)

gracile	see *Bouteloua gracilis*

Chordospartium see *Carmichaelia*

Chorisia (*Bombacaceae*)

speciosa	CCCN EAmu

Chorizema (*Papilionaceae*)

cordatum 🏆H1	ECou
ilicifolium	CBcs CCCN CSPN ERea

Chromolaena (*Asteraceae*)

arnottiana RCB/Arg L2	CDes

- 'Salsipuede'	MAvo WCot

Chronanthus see *Cytisus*

Chrysalidocarpus see *Dypsis*

Chrysanthemopsis see *Rhodanthemum*

Chrysanthemum ✿ (*Asteraceae*)

'Action Bronze' **new**	MCms
'Action Yellow'PBR (22) ♀H3 **new**	MCms
'Agnes Ann' (21d)	MNrw
'Alec Bedser' (25a)	NHal
'Alehmer Rote' (21)	MNrw WWEG
'Alexandra'	NHal
'Aline' (21)	MNrw SPhx
'Alison' (29c)	MNrw
'Alison's Dad' **new**	MNrw
'Allouise' (25b) ♀H3	NHal
'Allyson Peace' (14a) **new**	NHal
alpinum	see *Leucanthemopsis alpina*
'American Beauty Lemon' **new**	MCms
'American Beauty White' **new**	MCms
'Anastasia' (21c)	CHid EBee ECtt MNrw MRav NSti SPhx WFar WHoo WWEG
'Anastasia White' (28)	WWEG
'Angela Blundell'	WCot
'Anja's Bouquet'	see C. 'Mei-kyō'
'Anne Ratsey' (21)	CSam MNrw
'Anne, Lady Brocket' (21d)	ECtt MNrw NWsh SSvw
'Antigua'PBR **new**	MCms
'Apollo' **new**	LLHF WCom
'Apollo' (21)	EBee EWll NCGa SPhx SSvw WHoo
'Apricot'	see *C.* 'Cottage Apricot'
'Apricot Chessington' (25a)	NHal
'Apricot Courtier' (24a)	NHal
'Apricot Enbee Wedding'	see *C.* 'Bronze Enbee Wedding'
'Arctic Queen'PBR (23a) **new**	MCms
arcticum L.	see *Arctanthemum arcticum*
argenteum	see *Tanacetum argenteum*
'Astro'	NHal
'Aunt Millicent' (21d)	LLHF MNrw NHal SPhx
'Balcombe Perfection' (5a)	NHal
balsamita	see *Tanacetum balsamita*
Barbara = 'Yobarbara' (22)	EPfP NHal
'Beacon' (5a) ♀H2	NHal
'Belle' (21d)	MNrw
'Beppie Bronze' (29)	MCms
'Beppie Purple' (29)	MCms NHal
'Beppie Red' (29)	MCms
'Beppie Rose' **new**	MCms
'Beppie Yellow' (29)	MCms
'Bernadette Wade' (23a)	NHal
'Bill Wade' (25a)	NHal
'Billy Bell' (25a)	NHal
'Blanche Poitevene' (5b)	EMal
'Blaze Away' **new**	MCms
'Blenda'	ECtt
'Blenda Pink'	MCms
'Blenda Purple'	MCms
'Bobby Swinburn' (13b) **new**	NHal
Bravo = 'Yobra' (22c) ♀H3	EPfP NHal
* 'Breitner's Supreme'	MNrw WWEG
'Brennpunkt'	SMrs
'Brierton Violet' (17b) **new**	NHal
'Brietner' (24b) ♀H3	NHal
'Bright Eye' (21b)	MNrw WMnd
'Brightness' (21)	SSvw SUsu
'Bronze Beauty' (25b)	WFar
'Bronze Cassandra' (5b) ♀H2	NHal
'Bronze Dee Gem' (29c)	NHal
§ 'Bronze Elegance' (28b)	EBrs LRHS MLLN MNrw NBir NGdn NSti SMrs SRms SSvw WEas WMnd WPer
§ 'Bronze Enbee Wedding' (29d) ♀H3	NHal
'Bronze Matlock' (24b)	NHal
'Bronze Max Riley' (23b) ♀H3	NHal
'Bronze Mayford Perfection' (5a) ♀H2	NHal
'Bronze Mei-kyo'	see *C.* 'Bronze Elegance'
'Bronze Pamela'	see *C.* 'Pamela'
burnt orange-flowered	CPrp MNrw
'Burnwood Belle' (3b) **new**	NHal
'Candy Floss' (7a) **new**	NHal
'Capel Manor'	EBee WCot
'Carmine Blush' (21)	EBee MNrw SPhx SSvw WBrk WCot
'Cassandra' (5b) ♀H2	NHal
'Caukeel Cadet' (29c) **new**	NHal
'Caukeel Copper' (29c) **new**	NHal
'Chelsea Physic Garden'	EBee MNrw SPhx SSvw SUsu WCot
'Cherry Chessington' (25a)	NHal
Chesapeake = 'Yochesapeake'PBR	NHal
'Chorus'PBR (22) **new**	MCms
'Christopher Lawson' (24b)	NHal
'Cinderella'	WMnd
cinerariifolium	see *Tanacetum cinerariifolium*
'Clapham Delight' (23a)	NHal
'Clara Curtis' (21d))	Widely available
'Clive Skinner' (25b)	NHal
coccineum	see *Tanacetum coccineum*
'Conjuror'PBR **new**	MCms
'Coral Reef'	NHal
'Cornetto' (25b)	NHal
corymbosum	see *Tanacetum corymbosum*
§ 'Cottage Apricot'	CPrp EBee EBrs ECGP EWoo LHop MBNS MLHP MNrw MRav SSvw WEas
'Cottage Bronze'	MNrw
'Cottage Lemon'	MNrw
'Cottage Pink'	see *C.* 'Emperor of China'
'Cottage Yellow'	SSvw WHoo
'Courtier' (24a)	NHal
'Cousin Joan'	EBee MNrw NCGa WCot
'Cream Elegance' (9c)	NHal
'Cream Patricia Millar' (14b)	NHal
Dana = 'Yodana' (25b) ♀H3	NHal
Dance = 'Fidance'PBR **new**	MCms
Dance Salmon = 'Fidance Salmon' **new**	MCms
'Daniel Cooper' (21)	MNrw
'Darren Pugh' (3b)	NHal
Debonair = 'Yodebo'PBR (22c) ♀H3	EPfP
'Dee Gem' (29c) ♀H3	NHal
'Delta' (5b) **new**	NHal
'Delta Copper Bronze' **new**	NHal
'Delta Crimson' (29d) **new**	NHal
'Delta Yellow' (29)	NHal
'Dezianne' **new**	MCms
'Dezianne Yellow' **new**	MCms
§ 'Doctor Tom Parr' (21c)	CPLG EBee ELan GCal IGor LAst LHop MNrw WPtf
'Doreen Statham' (4b)	NHal

'Doris Ozols' (25a) **new**	NHal
'Dorothy Stone' (25b)	NHal
'Dorridge Crystal' (24a)	NHal
'Duchess of Edinburgh' (21d)	CPrp EBee ECtt ELan EPfP EShb GBin MNrw SBfd SPhx SSvw WMnd
'Duke of Kent' (1)	NHal
'Dutchy'PBR **new**	MCms
'Egret' (23b)	NHal
'Elaine Johnson' (3b)	NHal
'Elegance' (9c)	NHal
'Elizabeth Lawson' (5b)	NHal
'Elizabeth Shoesmith' (1)	NHal
'Ellen' (29c)	MCms NHal
* 'Emma Jane' (25a)	NHal
'Emperor' **new**	MCms
§ 'Emperor of China' (21)	CElw CSam EBee ECha ECtt GCal IGor MNrw MRav NHal SMad SPhx SSvw WBor WCot WFar WMnd WWEG
'Enbee Gift' (29d) **new**	NHal
'Enbee Wedding' (29d) ♀H3	NHal
'Energy'PBR **new**	MCms
'Esther' (21d)	MNrw NCGa
'Feeling Green Dark' **new**	MCms
'Feeling Sunny' **new**	MCms
'Feeling White'PBR **new**	MCms
foeniculaceum misapplied	see *Argyranthemum foeniculaceum* misapplied
foeniculaceum (Willd.) Desf.	see *Argyranthemum foeniculaceum* (Willd.) Webb & Sch.Bip.
'Fondant' **new**	NHal
'Foxtrot'PBR ♀H3	MCms
'Froggy'PBR **new**	MCms
frutescens	see *Argyranthemum frutescens*
'Gala Burgundy' **new**	MCms
'Gala Crimson' **new**	MCms
'Gambit' (24a)	NHal
'Geof Brady' (5a)	NHal
'Geoff Amos' (3b) **new**	NHal
'Geoff Sylvester' (25a)	NHal
'George Griffiths' (24b) ♀H3	NHal
'Gerrie Hoek Pink' **new**	MCms
'Gigantic' (1)	NHal
'Gladys' (24b)	ELan EWoo
'Gladys Emerson' (3b)	NHal
'Golden Cassandra' (5b) ♀H2	NHal
'Golden Chalice' (12a)	NHal
'Golden Courtier' (24a)	NHal
'Golden Gigantic' (1)	NHal
'Golden Mayford Perfection' (5a) ♀H2	NHal
'Golden Plover' (22)	NHal
'Golden Rain' (10a) ♀H2	NHal
'Golden Wedding' (21)	MNrw
'Golden William Florentine' (15a)	NHal
'Golden Woolman's Glory' (7a) **new**	NHal
'Goldengreenheart' (21)	LLHF MNrw WHoo
'Goldmarianne' (21)	GBin
'Gompie Bronze'	MCms
'Gompie Purple' **new**	MCms
I 'Gompie Rose'	MCms
'Gompie White' **new**	MCms
'Gompie Yellow'	MCms
'Grace Wade' (25b)	NHal
'Grandchild' (21c)	LLHF MNrw NHal SPhx
§ × ***grandiflorum***	SRms
- 'Corinna'	GBin
'Handsome'PBR **new**	MCms
'Hanenburg'	NHal
haradjanii	see *Tanacetum haradjanii*
'Harold Lawson' (5a)	NHal
'Harry Gee' (1)	NHal
'Heather James' (3b)	NHal
'Hebe' (21d)	EBee
'Heide' (29c) ♀H3	NHal
'Herbstbrokat' **new**	GBin
'Herby'PBR **new**	MCms
'Herby Sunny' **new**	MCms
'Hesketh Knight' (5b) ♀H2	NHal
Holly = 'Yoholly' (22b) ♀H3	NHal
'Honey Enbee Wedding' (29d)	NHal
'Horningsea Pink' (19d)	ECGP WBor
hosmariense	see *Rhodanthemum hosmariense*
'Husky' **new**	MCms
Ibis Lime = 'Fibis Lime' **new**	MCms
'Innocence' (21)	CSam EBee ECtt ELan IGor MNrw MRav NGdn NSti SAga SSvw WHoo
'Jacky' **new**	MCms
'Janet South' **new**	MNrw
'Jante Wells' (21b)	MNrw WEas WWEG
'Jenny Wren' (12a) **new**	NHal
'John Harrison' (25b)	NHal
'John Hughes' (3b)	NHal
'John Riley' (14a)	NHal
'John Wingfield' (14b)	NHal
'Joyce Fountain' (24a)	NHal
'Joyce Frieda' (23b)	NHal
'Julia' (28)	EPfP SRGP
Julia = 'Yojulia'	EBee
'Julia Peterson'	WCot
'Julie Lagravère' (28)	MNrw WPtf
'Juweeltja'	NHal
'Karen Taylor' (29c) ♀H3 **new**	NHal
'Kath Stephenson' (7b) **new**	NHal
'Kath Stephenson Primrose' (7b) **new**	NHal
'Kath Stephenson Rose' (7b) **new**	NHal
'Katie Jane' (7b) **new**	NHal
'Katinka'PBR **new**	MCms
'Katinka Salmon'PBR **new**	MCms
'Kay Woolman' (13b)	NHal
'Kimberley Marie' (15b)	NHal
'Kingfisher' (12a)	MCms
'Kiyominomeisui'	NHal
'Kleiner Bernstein' **new**	WCot
× ***koreanum***	see *C.* × *grandiflorum*
'La Muns' **new**	MCms
'Lady in Pink' (21)	MNrw
'Lakelanders' (3b)	NHal
'Le Bonheur Red'	NHal
leucanthemum	see *Leucanthemum vulgare*
'Lexy Red'PBR **new**	MCms
'Lilac Chessington' (25a)	NHal
Linda = 'Lindayo'PBR (22c) ♀H3	NHal
'Lollipop'PBR **new**	MCms
Lollipop Purple = 'Filollipop Purple'PBR **new**	MCms
'Lorna Wood' (13b)	NHal
'Louise' (25b)	MNrw
'Lucy' (29a) ♀H3	NHal
'Lundy' (2)	NHal

'Luv Purple'	NHal
'Lynn Johnson' (15a)	NHal
Lynn = 'Yolynn' (22c) ♀H3	NHal
macrophyllum	see *Tanacetum macrophyllum* (Waldst. & Kit.) Sch.Bip.
'Malcolm Perkins' (25a)	NHal
'Mancetta Comet' (29a)	NHal
maresii	see *Rhodanthemum hosmariense*
'Margaret' (29c) ♀H3	WCot
'Marion' (25a)	SPhx WCot
'Mark Woolman' (1)	NHal
'Mary' (21f)	MNrw NHal
'Mary Stoker' (21d)	CPrp CSam EBee EBrs ECtt ELan EPfP MLHP MNrw MRav NCGa NHal NLar NSti SRGP SSvw SUsu WAul WCAu WFar WMnd WWEG
'Matador' (14a)	NHal
'Matlock' (24b)	NHal
'Mauve Gem' (21f)	MNrw
mawii	see *Rhodanthemum gayanum*
'Max Riley' (23b) ♀H3	NHal
maximum misapplied	see *Leucanthemum* × *superbum*
maximum Ramond	see *Leucanthemum maximum* (Ramond) DC.
'Maxine Johnson' (25b)	NHal
'May Shoesmith' (5a) ♀H2	NHal
'Mayford Perfection' (5a) ♀H2	NHal
§ 'Mei-kyō' (28b)	CMea EBee ECtt IGor MNrw SPhx SRms WBor WCot WFar WHil WPer WWEG
'Membury' (24b)	NHal
'Mermaid White' **new**	MCms
'Mermaid Yellow' ♀H3	MCms
'Michelle Preston' (13b)	NHal
'Millennium' (25b) ♀H3	NHal
'Misty Cream' **new**	MCms
'Misty Golden' **new**	MCms
'Misty Lemon' **new**	MCms
'Moonlight' (29d/K)	MRav
'Morning Star' (12a)	NHal
'Moulin Rouge' PBR (22b) ♀H3 **new**	MCms
§ 'Mrs Jessie Cooper' (21)	CHGN ELan GQue MNrw NBir NLar NWsh SSvw WCom WCot WHil WHoo WPtf WTin
'Mrs Jessie Cooper No 1'	NCGa WBrk
'Mrs Jessie Cooper No 2'	MNrw
'Muriel Odell' (7b) **new**	NHal
'Music' (23b)	NHal
'Muxton Sable' (10a) **new**	NHal
'Myss Carol' (29c) **new**	NHal
'Myss Debbie' (29e) **new**	NHal
'Myss Jem' (29e) **new**	NHal
'Myss Jem Red' (29e) **new**	NHal
'Myss Marion' (29c) **new**	NHal
'Myss Saffron' (29c) **new**	NHal
'Nancy Perry' (21d)	CSam ELan MNrw MRav SSvw
nankingense	WFar
'Nantyderry Sunshine' (28b) ♀H4	CPrp CSam EBee EBrs LLHF MNrw SPhx SSvw WCot WEas WMnd WPer WWEG
'Naru' (9c)	NHal
'Naru Crimson' (9c) **new**	NHal
'Nell Gwynn' (21d)	MNrw
'Netherhall Moonlight'	MNrw SSvw
Nicole = 'Yonicole' (22c) ♀H3	NHal
nipponicum	see *Nipponanthemum nipponicum*
'Norton Vic' (5b) **new**	NHal
'Olwyn' (4b) **new**	NHal

'Orange Allouise' (25b)	MCms NHal
'Orange Enbee Wedding' (29d)	NHal
'Oxana' PBR **new**	MCms
pacificum	see *Ajania pacifica*
§ 'Pamela' (29c)	MCms
'Pamela Gold' **new**	MCms
parthenium	see *Tanacetum parthenium*
'Patricia Millar' (14b)	NHal
'Paul Boissier' (30Rub)	ECtt MNrw NSti SPhx SSvw WCot WMnd
'Peach Courtier' (24a)	NHal
'Peach Enbee Wedding' (29d) ♀H3	NHal
'Peach John Wingfield' (14b)	NHal
'Pennine Bullion'	NHal
'Pennine Gift' (29c)	NHal
'Pennine Marie' (29a) ♀H3	NHal
'Pennine Oriel' (29a) ♀H3	NHal
'Pennine Point' (19c)	NHal
'Pennine Polo' (29d) ♀H3	NHal
'Pennine Ranger' (29d)	NHal
'Pennine Swan' (29c)	NHal
'Pennine Toy' (19d)	NHal
'Penny's Yellow'	LLHF
'Perry's Peach' (21a)	LLHF MNrw NCGa NHal NPer SPhx SSvw
'Peter Rowe' (23b)	NHal
'Peter Sare' (21d)	EBrs LRHS
'Peterkin'	CMac CPrp EBrs ECGP ECtt WWEG
'Pink Allouise' **new**	MCms
'Pink Fantasy' **new**	MCms
'Pink John Wingfield' (14b)	NHal
'Pink Progression'	MNrw NBir WWEG
'Polar Gem' (3a)	NHal
'Primrose Allouise' (24b) ♀H3	NHal
'Primrose Courtier'	see *C.* 'Yellow Courtier'
'Primrose Dorothy Stone' (25b)	NHal
'Primrose Enbee Wedding' (29d) ♀H3	NHal
'Primrose John Hughes' (3b)	NHal
'Primrose Mayford Perfection' (5a) ♀H2	NHal
'Primrose West Bromwich' (14a)	NHal
'Princess' (21d)	LLHF
'Promise' (25a)	NHal
ptarmiciflorum	see *Tanacetum ptarmiciflorum*
'Puma' PBR **new**	MCms
'Puma Sunny' **new**	MCms
'Purleigh White' (28b)	CPrp ECtt MNrw NSti SSvw WCot
'Purple Chempak Rose' (14b)	NHal
'Purple Gem' (29c) **new**	NHal
'Ralph Lambert' (1)	NHal
'Raquel' (21)	EPfP MNrw
'Red Balcombe Perfection' (5a)	NHal
'Red Mayford Perfection' (5a)	NHal
'Red Pennine Gift' (29c)	NHal
'Red Regal Mist' (25b)	MCms
'Red Shirley Model' (3a)	NHal
'Red Wendy' (29c) ♀H3	MCms
'Redbreast'	NHal
'Regal Mist Purple' **new**	MCms NHal
'Richmond' (3b)	NHal
'Ringdove' (12a)	NHal

'Rita McMahon' (29d) 🏆H3	NHal
'Robeam' (9c) 🏆H2	NHal
Robin = 'Yorobi' (22c)	NHal
'Roen Sarah' (29c)	NHal
'Romany' (2)	CElw WEas
'Rose Enbee Wedding' (29d)	NHal
'Rose Madder'	MNrw WCot
'Rose Mayford Perfection' (5a) 🏆H2	NHal
'Rose Patricia Millar' (14b)	NHal
'Rosetta' **new**	WCot
roseum	see *Tanacetum coccineum*
'Royal Command' (21)	MNrw WCot
rubellum	see *C. zawadskii*
'Ruby Enbee Wedding' (29d) 🏆H3	NHal WPtf
'Ruby Mound' (21c) 🏆H3	LLHF MNrw NHal SDys SPhx SSvw SUsu WEas
'Ruby Raynor' (21) 🏆H4	MNrw SPhx SSvw
'Rumpelstilzchen' (21d)	CElw CMea ECtt MNrw WPer
'Salhouse Joy' (10a)	NHal
'Salmon Allouise' (25b)	NHal
'Salmon Enbee Wedding' (29d) 🏆H3	NHal
'Sam Vinter' (5a)	NHal
'Sarah Louise' (25b)	NHal
'Sea Urchin' (21f) 🏆H3	MNrw NHal SPhx SSvw
'Sheena' (9f/10) **new**	NHal
'Sheila Coles' (7b) **new**	NHal
'Shining Light' (21f)	LLHF MNrw
'Shirley Primrose' (1)	NHal
sinense	see *C.* × *grandiflorum*
'Skylark' (22a)	NPri
'Sonnenschein'	LHop
'Sophie Elizabeth' (24a)	NHal
'Southway Sheba' (29d) **new**	NHal
'Southway Shimmer' (29d) **new**	NHal
'Southway Shiraz' (29d)	NHal
'Southway Snoopy' (29d)	NHal
'Southway Snowcap' (29d) **new**	NHal
'Southway Spice' (29d) **new**	NHal
'Southway Strontium' (29d)	NHal
'Southway Sunkissed' (29d) **new**	NHal
'Spartan Canary'	SWal
'Spartan Display'	SWal
'Spartan Fire'	SWal
'Spartan Glory' (25b)	SWal
'Spartan Linnet'	SWal
'Spartan Raspberry' (21d)	SWal
'Spartan Seagull' (21d)	MNrw SSvw SWal
'Spartan Star' (29d)	SWal
'Starlet' (21f)	LLHF
'Starling' **new**	MCms
'Stockton' (3b) 🏆H2	NHal
'Sunbeam' (28)	EBee
'Sundae' PBR (22c) **new**	EPfP MCms
Sundoro = 'Yosun' (22d)	NHal
Swan = 'Fiswan' PBR **new**	MCms
'Syllabub' 🏆H3	ECtt
'Symphony' (10a) **new**	NHal
'Taiga White'	NHal
'Tapestry Rose' (21d)	CMea IGor MCot MNrw NCGa SPhx SSvw WBor
'Thoroughbred' (24a)	NHal
'Tom Parr'	see *C.* 'Doctor Tom Parr'
'Tom Snowball' (3b)	NHal
'Tracy Waller' (24b)	NHal
Triumph = 'Yotri' (22)	NHal
'Tuvalu' PBR **new**	MCms
'Tuvalu Sunny' **new**	MCms
'Tweety' **new**	MCms
uliginosum	see *Leucanthemella serotina*
'Universe' PBR **new**	MCms
'Uri'	SAga SPhx
'Vagabond Prince'	MNrw NCGa SPhx WCot WHoo
'Venice' (24b)	NHal
'Venus' (21)	NCGa WCot
'Venus One'	SPhx
'Vibrant' (9c) 🏆H2 **new**	NHal
'Virginia' (21)	NHal
'Vivid' **new**	MCms
'Wedding Day' (29k)	EBee MNrw WTin
'Wedding Sunshine' (21)	MNrw
welwitschii	see *Glebionis segetum*
'Wembley' (24b)	NHal
'Wendy Bronze'	MCms
'Wendy Tench' (21d)	ECtt
'West Bromwich' (14a)	NHal
weyrichii	EBee ECho ECtt LEdu MTho MWea NRya NWCA SRms WWEG
'White Allouise' (25b) 🏆H3	MCms NHal
'White Beppie' (29e)	MCms
'White Cassandra' (5b)	NHal
'White Enbee Wedding' (29d)	NHal
'White Gem' (21f)	NHal
'White Gerrie Hoek' (29c)	MCms
'White Gloss' (21e)	LLHF MNrw SSvw
'White Skylark' (22)	NHal
'White Tower'	MNrw
'William Florentine' (15a)	NHal
'Win' (9c)	NHal
'Winning's Red' (21)	LHop NCGa SMad SSvw
'Wizard' PBR	MCms
'Woolman's Glory' (7a) **new**	NHal
'Woolman's Star' (3a)	NHal
'Woolman's Venture' (4b)	NHal
'Yellow Allouise' (25b)	MCms
'Yellow American Beauty' (5b) 🏆H2 **new**	MCms
'Yellow Billy Bell' (15a)	NHal
'Yellow Clapham Delight' (23a) **new**	NHal
§ 'Yellow Courtier' (24a)	NHal
'Yellow Egret' (23b)	NHal
'Yellow Ellen' (29c)	MCms NHal
'Yellow Enbee Wedding' (29d)	NHal
'Yellow Harold Lawson' (5a)	NHal
'Yellow Heide' (29c) 🏆H3	NHal
'Yellow John Hughes' (3b) 🏆H2	NHal
'Yellow John Wingfield' (14b)	NHal
'Yellow May Shoesmith' (5a)	NHal
'Yellow Mayford Perfection' (5a) 🏆H2	NHal
'Yellow Pennine Oriel' (29a) 🏆H3	NHal
'Yellow Starlet' (21f)	LLHF MNrw
yezoense 🏆H4	CSam ELan LRHS MNrw WPer
- B&SWJ 10872	WCru
- 'Roseum'	CSam ECtt NSti WBor
§ ***zawadskii***	CMac WFar

Chrysocephalum (*Asteraceae*)

'Desert Flame'	LSou

Chrysocoma (*Asteraceae*)

ciliata JJH 9401633	NWCA

Chrysogonum (*Asteraceae*)

australe	EBee
virginianum	CMea CPrp ECha EShb EWes LRHS MRav SBch SPer WFar WWEG
- 'Allen Bush'	EBee
- var. ***australe***	EBee
'Andre Viette' **new**	

Chrysopogon (*Poaceae*)

gryllus	EBee SApp WPGP

Chrysopsis (*Asteraceae*)

§ ***mariana***	WOld
villosa (Pursh) Nutt. ex DC.	see *Heterotheca villosa*

Chrysosplenium (*Saxifragaceae*)

davidianum	CBre CSam EBee ECha EPot EWld GEdr GGar GJos GKev IMou NBir NLar NSla WBor WCon WCot WCru WFar WMoo WPrP WPtf
- SBEC 233	CPLG
flagelliferum B&SWJ 8902	WCru
forrestii	WPtf
lanuginosum	WCru
var. ***formosanum*** B&SWJ 6979	
macrophyllum	CDes CPLG EWld GMaP IMou MAvo WBor WCot WCru
macrostemon	WCru
var. ***shiobarense*** B&SWJ 6173	
oppositifolium	EBWF EBee GPWP WSFF WShi

Chusquea (*Poaceae*)

breviglumis misapplied	see *C. culeou* 'Tenuis'
breviglumis Phil.	NMoo
culeou ♀H4	CAbb CBcs CDoC CEnd CEnt CGHE CHEx CHid EBee ENBC EPfP EPla GBin LAst LEdu LPal MAvo MGos MMoz MWht NBea NMoo SBig SDix SSta WDyG WJun WPGP
- 'Breviglumis'	see *C. culeou* 'Tenuis'
- 'Purple Splendour'	EPla WJun WPGP
§ - 'Tenuis'	EPla WJun
- weeping	CDTJ WPGP
cumingii	CBcs EBee GBin WJun WPGP
delicatula	WPGP
from Machu Picchu, Peru	
gigantea	CDTJ CEnt CPLG EPfP EPla ESwi MMoz MWht SBig WDyG WJun WPGP
- 'Bracken Hill'	MMoz
macrostachya	EBee WPGP
montana	CBcs CDTJ EBee EPla GBin
mulleri from Mexico F&M 104A	WPGP
quila	EPla MMoz WPGP
valdiviensis	EPla WJun WPGP

Cibotium (*Dicksoniaceae*)

glaucum	WRic
schiedei **new**	WRic

Cicerbita (*Asteraceae*)

sp.	ECtt
BWJ 7891 from China	WCru
§ ***alpina***	EBee NBid NLar SGar SPlb
plumieri	CSpr EWes IFro SPhx WCot WFar WHrl WMoo WPtf
- 'Blott' (v)	WCot

Cichorium (*Asteraceae*)

intybus	CArn CHby CPom CPrp EBWF EBee EBla ELan ELau GMac GPoy LHop MAvo MLLN MNHC NBir NCGa NGHP NMir NPri SBfd SIde SPer SPlb SPoG SVic WFar WHrl WJek WMoo
- f. ***album***	CPrp EBee EBla ECha ECtt EPfP LHop MAvo MLLN MRav NBir NCGa NCob NGdn SBch SWat WCAu
- var. ***foliosum***	EBee
- 'Roseum'	CPrp EBee EBla ECha ECtt ELan EPfP EWTr GMac LHop MAvo MCot MLLN MRav NBir NCGa NCob NGdn SBch SPer SWat WHrl

Cicuta (*Apiaceae*)

virosa **new**	MMuc

Cimicifuga see *Actaea*

acerina	see *Actaea japonica*
americana	see *Actaea podocarpa*
cordifolia (DC.) Torrey & A.Gray	see *Actaea cordifolia*
cordifolia Pursh	see *Actaea podocarpa*
foetida	see *Actaea cimicifuga*
racemosa var. ***cordifolia***	see *Actaea cordifolia*
- 'Purpurea'	see *Actaea simplex* Atropurpurea Group
ramosa	see *Actaea simplex* 'Prichard's Giant'
rubifolia	see *Actaea cordifolia*
simplex var. ***matsumurae***	see *Actaea matsumurae*

Cineraria (*Asteraceae*)

saxifraga	EShb

Cinnamomum (*Lauraceae*)

camphora	CBcs CHEx CPLG
micranthum	WPGP

Cionura (*Asclepiadaceae*)

oreophila	EBee WSHC

Circaea (*Onagraceae*)

alpina	EBee MMuc
lutetiana	EBWF NSco WHer
- 'Caveat Emptor' (v)	CBow CHid EBee NBid WCot WHer

Cirsium (*Asteraceae*)

acaule	NLar
anartiolepis F&M 252	WPGP
arvense	WSFF
* ***atroroseum***	SWat
diacantha	see *Ptilostemon diacantha*
helenioides	see *C. heterophyllum*
§ ***heterophyllum***	CPom EWld LEdu NBre NChi NLar SHar SPhx WCot WHil WPGP
japonicum	GKir
- 'Early Pink Beauty'	NBre
- 'Early Rose Beauty'	NBre
- 'Pink Beauty'	WWEG
- 'Rose Beauty'	EBee
'Mount Etna'	CDes CPrp CSam EBee EBla LRHS MBNS MMuc MSpe NCob NDov NGdn SPoG WPGP

	oleraceum	LEdu NBid NBre NLar
	purpuratum	MNrw WCot WPGP
	rivulare	CSam GKir
	- 'Atropurpureum'	Widely available
	tuberosum	NDov SKHP SPhx
	vulgare	WSFF

Cissus (*Vitaceae*)

	antarctica ♀H1	CCCN CTrC EShb MMuc SEND
	pedata B&SWJ 2371	WCru
	quadrangularis	SBfd
	rhombifolia ♀H1	EOHP MMuc SEND
§	***striata***	CBcs CDoC CHEx CMac CRHN CTrC EBee ELon EShb IFFs LRHS MRav SBfd SEND SLim SWvt WSHC

Cistus ✿ (*Cistaceae*)

	acutifolius misapplied	see *C. inflatus*, *C.* × *pulverulentus*
	× ***aguilarii***	CBcs CHEx CSBt CTri EPfP LAst MRav WSHC
	- 'Maculatus' ♀H3	CBot CDoC CDul CPLG CSam EBee ELan EPfP GBin GGar GKir LRHS LSRN MMuc NCGa NLar NPri SBfd SCoo SLPl SPer SPoG SWvt WAbe WCFE WKif
	albidus	CArn WKif
	algarvensis	see *Halimium ocymoides*
	'Ann Baker'	MBrN SLPl
	'Anne Palmer'	see *C.* × *fernandesiae* 'Anne Palmer'
	× ***argenteus*** 'Blushing Peggy Sammons'	CDoC
	- Golden Treasure = 'Nepond' (v)	CBow EPfP SWvt
	- 'Paper Moon'	LSRN
§	- 'Peggy Sammons' ♀H3	CBgR CBot CDoC EBee ECha ECrN ELan EPfP GGar GKir LAst LBMP LRHS LSRN MAsh MGos MMuc MWte NLar SCoo SEND SLim SPer SWvt WBrE WFar WHar WSHC
	- 'Silver Pink' ambig.	Widely available
	'Blanche'	see *C. ladanifer* 'Blanche'
	× ***bornetianus*** 'Jester'	CSBt EBee LRHS MAsh
	× ***canescens***	EBee
	- f. ***albus***	CWib EQua WEas WKif
§	***clusii***	NLar
	× ***corbariensis***	see *C.* × *hybridus*
	creticus	CDoC CPLG CSam CWit ELau EQua LAst MAsh MBri MGos MLHP NMun SBfd SLon SPoG WKif WPGP
§	- subsp. ***creticus***	EBee ELan ELon EPfP MRav SCoo SPer WAbe
§	- subsp. ***incanus***	LRHS
§	× ***crispatus*** 'Warley Rose'	GMaP
	crispus misapplied	see *C.* × *pulverulentus*, *C.* × *purpureus*
§	***crispus*** L.	EBee MMuc SEND WEas
	- 'Prostratus'	see *C. crispus* L.
	- 'Sunset'	see *C.* × *pulverulentus* 'Sunset'
§	× ***cyprius*** ♀H4	CArn CDul EBee ECtt ELan EPfP GBin MGos MNHC MRav MWat SDix SEND SPer SRms WDin WFar
§	- var. ***ellipticus*** 'Elma' ♀H3	ELan EPfP LRHS MAsh SPer WEas WPGP
§	× ***dansereaui***	CMHG CSBt CWib EBee LRHS MGos MRav SWvt WFar WSpi
	- 'Albiflorus'	see *C.* × *dansereaui* 'Portmeirion'
	- 'Decumbens' ♀H4	CBcs CChe CDul CMHG CTri EBee ELan EPfP LAst LHop LRHS MAsh MBNS MNHC MRav MSwo NCGa SAPC SArc SBfd SCoo SPer SPoG SWvt WAbe WClo WDin WPGP
	- 'Jenkyn Place'	CDoC EBee GMaP IVic LSRN MBNS MBri MGos SLPl SPer SPoG SUsu WKif
§	- 'Portmeirion'	WAbe WFar
	'Elma'	see *C.* × *cyprius* var. *ellipticus* 'Elma'
	'Enigma'	CDoC EBee
§	× ***fernandesiae*** 'Anne Palmer'	CBgR EBee EPfP GBin LHop LLHF LRHS LSRN MAsh SEND SPoG SRGP WFar
	× ***florentinus*** misapplied	see × *Halimiocistus* 'Ingwersenii'
§	× ***florentinus*** Lam.	CAbP EBee GMaP
	formosus	see *Halimium lasianthum* subsp. *formosum*
	'Gordon Cooper'	CWan EBee LSRN MMuc SCoo SPoG
	× ***heterocalyx*** 'Chelsea Bonnet'	EBee EPfP GMaP MBNS SCoo SLim SPoG WPGP WPen
	hirsutus Lam. 1786	see *C. inflatus*
	- var. ***psilosepalus***	see *C. inflatus*
§	× ***hybridus***	Widely available
	- 'Gold Prize' (v)	CMHG CWGN CWit EBee ELan MBri MGos NEgg NLar SBfd SWvt WFar WGrn WHar WPat
	- Rospico = 'Rencis' (v)	EMil LBuc LRHS
	incanus	see *C. creticus* subsp. *incanus*
§	***inflatus***	MMuc
	ingwerseniana	see × *Halimiocistus* 'Ingwersenii'
	'Jessamy Beauty'	EBee SLPl
	'Jessamy Bride'	SLPl
	ladanifer misapplied	see *C.* × *cyprius*
	ladanifer ambig.	CMac SAPC SArc WKif
	ladanifer L. ♀H3	CDoC CSBt CTri ECha ELan EPfP EWTr GCra GPoy MRav MSwo SBfd SPer SWvt WEas WFar WHar WSHC
	- var. ***albiflorus***	EQua
§	- 'Blanche'	CBgR EBee LLHF LSRN SEND SSpi WKif
	- 'Minstrel'	LRHS
§	- 'Paladin'	CBgR EBee SBfd WAbe
	- Palhinhae Group	see *C. ladanifer* var. *sulcatus*
	- 'Pat'	EBee ELan EPfP LRHS LSRN MAsh NBir SPoG SSpi
§	- var. ***sulcatus***	CDoC EBee ELan EPfP LRHS WFar
	- - f. ***bicolor***	EBee
	lasianthus	see *Halimium lasianthum*
	laurifolius ♀H4	CDoC EBee EPfP EWTr MGos NBir NEgg NLar SKHP SLPl SPer SPoG WCom
	× ***laxus***	WAbe
	- 'Snow White'	CAbP CDoC EBee EPfP LAst LRHS MGos NPer SLPl SLim SLon SRms SUsu WGrn
	× ***ledon***	SLPl
§	× ***lenis*** 'Grayswood Pink' ♀H4	Widely available
	libanotis	MSpe
	× ***longifolius***	see *C.* × *nigricans*
	× ***loretii*** misapplied	see *C.* × *dansereaui*
	× ***loretii*** Rouy & Foucaud	see *C.* × *stenophyllus*
	× ***lusitanicus*** Maund	see *C.* × *dansereaui*
	'Merrist Wood Cream'	see × *Halimiocistus wintonensis* 'Merrist Wood Cream'
	monspeliensis	CAbP CMac EBee EPfP EQua LRHS MBNS MMuc SEND SLon SPer WFar WPGP
	- CMBS 62	WPGP
	- 'Vicar's Mead'	CCCN CDoC EBee ELan EPfP LRHS MBNS MMuc SEND SRms
§	× ***nigricans***	WCot
	× ***obtusifolius*** misapplied	see *C.* × *nigricans*
	× ***obtusifolius*** ambig.	LRHS SKHP WNew
	× ***obtusifolius*** Sweet	EPfP EWes SLPl WEas
§	- 'Thrive'	LRHS MBri SCoo

	ochreatus	see *C. symphytifolius* subsp. *leucophyllus*
	ocymoides	see *Halimium ocymoides*
	'Paladin'	see *C. ladanifer* 'Paladin'
	palhinhae	see *C. ladanifer* var. *sulcatus*
	parviflorus misapplied	see *C.* × *lenis* 'Grayswood Pink'
	parviflorus Lam.	CBot WSHC
	'Peggy Sammons'	see *C.* × *argenteus* 'Peggy Sammons'
	× ***platysepalus***	SLPl
	populifolius	CMHG CMac ECha LLHF LRHS SPer WPGP
	- var. ***lasiocalyx***	see *C. populifolius* subsp. *major*
§	- subsp. ***major*** 🏆^{H3}	CBgR EBee EPfP LRHS LSRN SKHP WPGP
	psilosepalus	see *C. inflatus*
§	× ***pulverulentus***	CPLG CTri EBee ECha EPfP MMHG SWal WDin WSHC
§	- 'Sunset' 🏆^{H3}	Widely available
	- 'Warley Rose'	see *C.* × *crispatus* 'Warley Rose'
§	× ***purpureus*** 🏆^{H3}	Widely available
	- 'Alan Fradd'	CBcs CMac EBee ECrN EPfP GBin GGar LAst LBMP LHop LRHS LSRN MAsh MDun MGos MMuc MSpe MSwo NLar SBfd SCoo SEND SLim SMrm SPoG SRGP SWvt WBor WFar
	- var. ***argenteus*** f. ***stictus***	EBee LRHS LSRN WAbe
	- 'Betty Taudevin'	see *C.* × *purpureus*
	× ***rodiaei*** 'Jessabel'	CBgR EBee LRHS MAsh MMuc SCoo SEND SPoG
	- 'Jessica'	EBee NLar WAbe
	rosmarinifolius	see *C. clusii*
	'Ruby Cluster'	CCCN EBee LRHS LSRN MMuc SRms WClo
	sahucii	see × *Halimiocistus sahucii*
	salviifolius	CAbP CArn CCCN WFar
	- 'Avalanche'	EBee MRav WAbe
	- 'Gold Star'	EBee
	- 'May Snow'	LRHS
	- 'Prostratus'	ELan EPfP IRar MMuc WPGP
	salviifolius × ***monspeliensis***	see *C.* × *florentinus* Lam.
	'Silver Pink' misapplied	see *C.* × *lenis* 'Grayswood Pink'
	× ***skanbergii*** 🏆^{H3}	CBcs CBgR CHEx CMac CSBt CTri CWib EBee ELan EPfP LHop LIMB LRHS MGos MLHP MMuc MRav MWat NBir SCoo SDix SEND SMrm SPer SPoG WEas WFar
	'Snow Fire' 🏆^{H4}	CAbP CBgR CCCN CDoC EBee EPfP LRHS LSRN MAsh MGos MMuc SBfd SCoo SLPl SPoG SSpi WClo WGrn
§	× ***stenophyllus***	CWib MMuc SPer
	'Summer Snow' **new**	LRHS
	symphytifolius	WPGP
§	- subsp. ***leucophyllus*** MSF 98.019	WPGP
	'Thornfield White'	EBee
	'Thrive'	see *C.* × *obtusifolius* 'Thrive'
	tomentosus	see *Helianthemum nummularium* subsp. *tomentosum*
	× ***verguinii***	LHop SDix
	- var. ***albiflorus*** misapplied	see *C.* × *dansereaui* 'Portmeirion'
	villosus	see *C. creticus* subsp. *creticus*
	wintonensis	see × *Halimiocistus wintonensis*

Citharexylum (*Verbenaceae*)

spicatum	CPLG EUJe WBor WPGP

× *Citrofortunella* (*Rutaceae*)

	sp.	CCCN
§	***microcarpa*** (F) 🏆^{H1}	CBcs CCCN CDoC EPfP ERea LRHS MBri NLar
	mitis	see × *C. microcarpa*

citron see *Citrus medica*

Citrullus (*Cucurbitaceae*)

colocynthis	CArn

Citrus ✿ (*Rutaceae*)

	amblycarpa djeruk lime (F)	ERea
I	***aurantiata*** 'Chinese Citron' (F)	ERea
	aurantiifolia (F)	CCCN EPfP ERea SVic
	- key lime (F)	ERea
	- 'Paduk' (F)	ERea
	aurantium	ERea SPlb
	- 'Bouquet de Fleurs' (F)	CCCN ERea
	- var. ***myrtifolia*** 'Chinotto' (F)	ERea
	- 'Seville' (F)	ERea LSRN
	bergamia bergamot	ERea
	calamondin	see × *Citrofortunella microcarpa*
	'Fukushu' (F)	CCCN ERea
	hystrix	CCCN CDoC ERea LSRN NPla
	jambhiri 'Otaheite' (F) **new**	CCCN
	japonica	see *Fortunella japonica*
	'Kulci' (F)	CCCN
	kumquat	see *Fortunella margarita*
	'La Valette' (F)	CCCN ERea LSRN SEND
	× ***latifolia*** (F/S)	CCCN CDoC EPfP LRHS MREP
	limetta	CCCN
	- 'Romnya' (F)	ERea
	limettoides (F)	CArn ERea
	limon (F)	CHEx CTsd EPfP EUJe LRHS MREP STrG SVic
	- 'Amalfitanum' (F)	ERea
	- 'Eureka' (F) **new**	CCCN
	- 'Fino' (F)	CCCN
	- 'Four Seasons' (F)	CCCN ERea LSRN NLar
§	- 'Garey's Eureka' (F)	CDoC EPfP ERea
	- 'Genova' (F)	ERea
	- 'Imperial' (F)	ERea
	- 'Lemonade' (F)	ERea
	- 'Mosquito' (v)	CHll ERea
	- 'Quatre Saisons'	see *C. limon* 'Garey's Eureka'
	- 'Toscana' (F)	ERea
	- 'Variegata' (F/v) 🏆^{H1}	CCCN ERea
	- 'Verna' (F)	CCCN
	- 'Villa Franca' (F)	ERea SVic
	- 'Yen Ben' (F)	ERea
	× ***limonia*** 'Rangpur' (F)	ERea
	'Lipo'	CCCN NLar
	macrophylla	ERea
	madurensis	see *Fortunella japonica*
	maxima (F)	ERea
	medica (F)	CHll ERea
	- 'Cidro Digitado'	see *C. medica* var. *digitata*
§	- var. ***digitata*** (F)	ERea
	- 'Ethrog' (F)	ERea
	- var. ***sarcodactylis***	see *C. medica* var. *digitata*
	× ***meyeri***	CHEx
	- 'Improved Meyer' (F)	ERea
	- 'Meyer' (F) 🏆^{H1}	CBcs CCCN CHll CTri CTsd EPfP ERea LRHS LSRN NLar SPer
	microcarpa Philippine lime	see × *Citrofortunella microcarpa*
	mitis	see × *Citrofortunella microcarpa*
	× ***nobilis*** Ortanique Group (F)	CCCN
	- 'Silver Hill Owari' (F)	ERea

- Tangor Group (F)	ERea
× ***paradisi*** (F)	CCCN MREP SVic
- 'Foster' (F)	ERea
- 'Golden Special' (F)	ERea SVic
- 'Marsh' (F)	ERea
- 'Red Blush' (F/S)	ERea
- 'Star Ruby' (F/S)	CCCN ERea
'Ponderosa' (F)	ERea
'Pursta' (F)	CCCN ERea
reticulata (F)	CCCN MREP
- 'Hernandina' (F)	CCCN
- Mandarin Group (F)	CDoC EPfP
- - 'Clementine' (F)	CDoC ERea LRHS
- - 'Esbal' (F) **new**	CCCN
- - 'Nules' (F/S)	CCCN ERea
- 'Nova'	see *C.* × *tangelo* 'Nova'
- 'Orogrande'	ERea
- 'Suntina'	see *C.* × *tangelo* 'Nova'
sinensis (F)	CCCN LRHS SVic
- 'Egg' (F)	ERea
- 'Fukumoto' (F) **new**	CCCN
- 'Harwood Late' (F)	ERea
- 'Jaffa'	see *C. sinensis* 'Shamouti'
- 'Lane Late' (F)	CCCN ERea
- 'Malta Blood' (F)	ERea
- 'Moro Blood' (F)	ERea
- 'Navelate' (F)	ERea
- 'Navelina' (F/S)	CCCN CDoC
- 'Newhall' (F)	ERea
- 'Saint Michael' (F)	ERea
- 'Sanguinelli' (F)	CCCN ERea
§ - 'Shamouti' (F)	ERea
- 'Tarocco' (F)	ERea
- 'Trovita' (F)	ERea
- 'Valencia' (F)	CCCN
- 'Valencia Late' (F)	ERea
- 'Washington' (F/S)	EPfP ERea
× ***tangelo*** 'Minneola' (F)	ERea
§ - 'Nova' (F/S)	CCCN
- 'Seminole' (F)	ERea
- 'Ugli' (F)	ERea
unshiu 'Miyagawa'	CCCN ERea
- 'Okitsu' (F/S)	CCCN

Cladanthus (*Asteraceae*)

B&F MA 20	WCot

Cladothamnus see *Elliottia*

Cladrastis (*Papilionaceae*)

§ ***kentukea***	CArn CBcs CDul CLnd CMCN EBee ELan EPfP EWTr LRHS MBlu MBri MMuc MRav NLar SSpi WDin
§ - 'Perkins Pink'	MBlu MBri SSpi
- 'Rosea'	see *C. kentukea* 'Perkins Pink'
lutea	see *C. kentukea*
sinensis	CBcs CGHE CPLG EBee EPfP EPla IDee IFFs MBlu SKHP SSpi WPGP

Clarkia (*Onagraceae*)

* ***repens***	CSpe

Clavinodum (*Poaceae*)

§ ***oedogonatum***	EPla MWht

Claytonia (*Portulacaceae*)

alsinoides	see *C. sibirica*
caroliniana	NLar
§ ***perfoliata***	CArn GPoy ILis WHer
§ ***sibirica***	CAgr CArn CElw IMou LSou WPtf
- f. ***albiflora***	CElw WCot WMoo
virginica	EHrv LAma WFar WMoo

Clematis ✿ (*Ranunculaceae*)

BWJ 7630 from China	WCru
BWJ 8169 from China	WCru
CC 711	CPLG
CC 4710	CPLG
CC 5904	GKev
SDR 6109	GKev
SDR 6151	GKev
'Abundance' (Vt) ♀H4	CDoC CRHN CSPN CWCL EBee EPfP ETho LOck LRHS LSRN MBri MRav NBea NHol SBfd SDix SPer SPet
acuminata var. ***sikkimensis*** B&SWJ 7202	WCru
addisonii	CBcs CSPN CWGN EBee MWhi NHaw
aethusifolia	CSPN
afoliata	CSPN ECou WThu
afoliata × ***forsteri***	ECou
'Ai-Nor' (EL)	ETho
'Akaishi' (EL)	CWGN EBee ETho
akebioides SDR 5966	GKev
- SDR 6110	GKev
Alabast = 'Poulala'PBR (EL) ♀H4	CSPN EBee ETho LRHS MAsh NHaw SCoo SPoG SWCr
'Alba Luxurians' (Vt) ♀H4	Widely available
'Albatross'	LSRN
'Albiflora' (A)	CSPN ECtt NSti
'Albina Plena' (A/d)	ETho MGos
'Aleksandrit' (EL)	NHaw
'Alice Fisk' (EL)	CSPN EBee EPfP ETho LSRN MSwo NBea NHaw SLim WGor
'Alionushka' (I) ♀H4	CRHN CSam EBee ELan ELon EPfP ETho LOck LPio LRHS LSRN MAsh MBri MGos NBea NPri SLim SPer SPet SPoG SWCr WCot
'Allanah' (LL)	EBee ELon ETho LOck LRHS LSRN MGos NHaw SCoo SLim SPet SPoG WFar
alpina ♀H4	CBot ECtt EPfP GGal GKev GKir LSRN MRav MWhi NHaw NPer SPlb WBVN WFar
- SDR 3611	GKev
- 'Albiflora'	see *C. sibirica*
- 'Columbine White'	see *C.* 'White Columbine'
I - 'Odorata'	CSPN LPio MGos NHaw
§ - 'Pamela Jackman' ♀H4	CChe CDoC CMac CSPN CWSG EBee ELan GKir IBal LOck LRHS LSRN MAsh MGos NBea NEgg NHol NSti SCoo SDix SLim SPer SPet SPoG SWvt WFar
- pink-flowered	GKir
- 'Stolwijk Gold'	EBee ETho LPio MBlu MGos NHaw
alternata	CWGN EBee ETho
'Amelia Joan' (Ta)	MWat
'Ameshisuto' (EL)	ETho
'Andromeda' (EL)	CSPN EBee ETho LRHS NBea NHaw NPri SGar WFar
Angelique = 'Evipo017' (EL)	EPfP ETho LBuc LRHS LSqu MAsh SCoo SLon SPer SPoG SWCr
'Anita' (Ta)	EPfP ETho LSRN NHaw SLim SMDP
'Anna' (EL)	LPio
'Anna Carolina'	LPio
Anna Louise = 'Evithree'PBR (EL) ♀H4	CLng CSPN CWCL EBee EPfP ETho IBal LBuc LRHS LSRN LSqu MAsh MBri SCoo SLim SPer SPoG SWCr
'Annabel' (EL)	CSPN LSRN
'Annemieke' (Ta)	MGos
Anniversary = 'Pynot' (EL)	LSRN SCoo
'Anti' (LL)	LPio NBea

'Aotearoa' (LL)	EBee LPio NHaw
Aphrodite = 'Aphrodite Elegafumina'	CFir CRHN CWGN LPio LRHS MAsh NBea NHaw SWCr
apiifolia	MWhi
- B&SWJ 4838	WCru
'Apple Blossom' (Ar) ϒH4	Widely available
'Arabella' (I) ϒH4	CChe CRHN CSPN CSam CWCL EBee ELan ELon EPfP EShb ETho LAst LBMP LOck LPio LRHS LSRN MAsh MBri NBea NPri SLim SPer SPet SPoG SWCr SWvt WFar
§ Arctic Queen = 'Evitwo'^{PBR} (EL) ϒH4	CLng CSPN CWCL EBee EPfP ETho LBuc LRHS LSRN LSqu MAsh NPri SCoo SPer SPoG SWCr WFar
armandii	Widely available
- 'Enham Star'	LRHS MBri MGos
§ - 'Little White Charm'	CBcs CSPN LRHS SBfd SKHP SPoG
- 'Meyeniana'	see *C. armandii* 'Little White Charm'
§ - 'Snowdrift'	CAlb CBcs CSBt CSPN CSam CWSG ELan ELon EPfP ETho LPio LRHS LTen MAsh MGos MSwo NEgg NLar NSti SBfd SKHP SPer SPoG SRms SWCr WSpi
× ***aromatica***	CBcs CFir CSPN CWGN EAEE EBee ELan EPfP ETho LOck LPio LRHS MCot MRav NBea NSti SCoo SPoG WSpi
§ 'Asagasumi' (EL)	EBee ETho LPio
'Asao' (EL)	CElw CRHN EBee ELan EPfP ETho LOck LRHS MAsh MGos MRav SCoo SPer SPet SPoG SWCr
'Ascotiensis' (LL)	CBcs CLng CRHN CSPN EBee EPfP ETho LRHS MAsh NHaw SCoo SPoG SWCr WFar
'Ashva'	CWGN LPio MGos
'Aureolin' (Ta)	CSPN CWSG EBee EPfP ETho NHol WPGP
Avant-garde = 'Evipo033'^{PBR} (Vt)	CWGN EPfP ETho LPio LRHS LSqu MAsh SLon SPoG SWCr
§ 'Bagatelle' (LL)	CLng CSPN LRHS LSRN NHaw NPri SMDP WFar
'Bal Maiden' (Vt)	CRHN NHaw
§ 'Ballerina in Blue' (A/d)	NHaw
'Ballet Skirt' (A/d) ϒH4	MGos NHaw
'Bałtyk' (EL)	CSPN LPio
'Barbara' (LL)	ETho MRav NHaw
'Barbara Dibley' (EL)	CLng CTri CWSG LOck LPio LRHS NBea NHaw SCoo SDix SLim SPet
'Barbara Harrington'^{PBR} (LL)	CLng LRHS LSRN MAsh NHaw SWCr
'Barbara Jackman' (EL)	CMac EBee ECtt ETho GKir LOck LPio LRHS LSRN MAsh MGos MRav MSwo NBea SCoo SLim SPer SPoG SWCr WFoF
cf. ***barbellata*** CC 5144 **new**	GKev
'Basil Bartlett' (Fo)	ECou
'Beata' (LL)	LPio MGos NBea NHaw
'Beauty of Richmond' (EL)	CWSG LPio
'Beauty of Worcester' (EL)	CFir CMac CSPN CWSG ELan ELon EPfP ETho GKir LOck LPio LRHS LSRN MSwo NBea NHaw SCoo SDix SLim SPer SPet SPoG WFar
'Bees' Jubilee' (EL)	CBcs CChe CMac CRHN CWSG EBee ECtt ELan ETho GKir LPio LRHS LSRN MAsh MGan MGos MRav MSwo NBir SDix SLim SPer SPet SPoG SWCr SWvt WFar
'Bella' (EL)	NHaw
'Belle Nantaise' (EL)	EBee LPio SCoo SPet SRms
'Belle of Woking' (EL)	CRHN CSPN CWSG EBee ECtt ELan ELon ETho LOck LPio LRHS LSRN MAsh MRav NBea NPri SCoo SDix SLim SPet SPoG SWCr
'Bells of Emei Shan'	ETho SMDP WCru
'Benedictus' (EL)	LPio
'Berry Red' (A)	CWGN
§ 'Beth Currie' (EL)	CLng CSPN EBee EPfP LPio LRHS MAsh NPri SWCr
'Betina'	see *C.* 'Red Beetroot Beauty'
'Betty Corning' (Vt) ϒH4	CRHN CSPN CWGN EBee ELan ELon EPfP ETho LPio LRHS LSRN MAsh MBri MGos NBea SCoo SLim SLon SWCr WFar WGwG
'Betty Risdon' (EL)	EBee ETho LPio
'Bill MacKenzie' (Ta) ϒH4	Widely available
'Black Prince' (Vt)	CRHN CWGN EBee ELan ETho LOck LPio LRHS LSRN MGos NBea NHaw NHol NLar SLim SLon SMDP SRms
'Black Tea' (LL)	LPio LRHS LSRN NHaw SLim
§ 'Błękitny Anioł' (LL) ϒH4	CElw CLng CMac CRHN CSPN ETho LOck LRHS MAsh MGos NBea NLar SCoo SLim SPer SPet SPoG SWCr WFar
Blue Angel	see *C.* 'Błękitny Anioł'
'Blue Belle' (Vt)	CRHN ELan NSti SLon SMDP SPoG WFar
'Blue Bird' (A/d)	CBcs CWCL CWSG EBee ECtt GKir LRHS MBlu NHol SMDP SPoG SRms
Blue Blood	see *C.* 'Königskind'
'Blue Boy' (I)	see *C.* × *diversifolia* 'Blue Boy' (I)
'Blue Boy' (EL)	see *C.* 'Elsa Späth'
'Blue Dancer' (A)	CLng EBee EPfP EShb ETho IBal LPio LRHS MAsh MGos NBea NLar SWCr
'Blue Eclipse' (A)	CSPN CTri CWGN LPio MBri MGos NHaw
'Blue Eyes' (EL)	CSPN EBee ELon ETho LPio LSRN NBea NHaw SLim
'Blue Fizz'	LPio
§ 'Blue Light'^{PBR} (EL/d)	CSPN ELan ETho LRHS MGos NLar WFar
Blue Moon = 'Evirin'^{PBR} (EL)	CLng EPfP ETho LAst LPio LRHS LSRN MAsh NLar SCoo SLim SWCr WFar
Blue Pirouette = 'Zobluepi'^{PBR} (I)	CWGN LPio LRHS MAsh NLar SMDP
Blue Rain	see *C.* 'Sinii Dozhd'
'Blue Ravine' (EL)	EBee EPfP LRHS MGos NLar SCoo
Blue River = 'Zoblueriver' **new**	CWGN
'Blue Sensation' (I)	LPio
'Blue Tapers' (A)	NHaw
§ 'Blushing Ballerina' (A/d)	LPio
Bonanza = 'Evipo031'^{PBR}	CLng EPfP ETho LPio LRHS LSqu MAsh SCoo SPer SPoG SWCr
§ × ***bonstedtii*** 'Campanile' (H)	LPio NBir
- 'Crépuscule' (H)	EBrs LPio MCot SMDP SRms
'Boskoop Beauty' (EL)	NHaw
Bourbon = 'Evipo018'^{PBR}	EPfP ETho LBuc LMor LRHS LSqu MAsh NPri SCoo SPer SPoG SWCr
'Bowl of Beauty' (Ar)	MGos
'Bracebridge Star' (EL)	ECtt NBea
brachiata	CPne
'Brocade' (Vt)	CRHN CSPN ETho LPio NHaw
'Broughton Bride'	CSPN CTri CWGN LPio MBri NHol
'Broughton Star' (M/d) ϒH4	CElw CMac CRHN CSBt CSPN CWib CWit EBee ELan EPfP ETho GKir LPio LRHS LSRN LTen MBlu

		MBri MGos MRav MSwo NBea NBir NHol NSti SLim SPet SPoG WFar
	'Brunette' (A)	CSPN EBee ELan EPfP ETho LPio LRHS MAsh MGos NHaw NLar SPoG SWCr
	buchananiana Finet & Gagnep.	see *C. rehderiana*
	buchananiana DC. B&SWJ 8333a	WCru
	'Buckland Beauty' (V)	CWGN GMac NBea
	'Buckland Cascade' **new**	SMDP
	'Buckland Longshanks' (H)	SMDP
	'Burford Princess' (Vt)	CRHN NHaw
	'Burford White' (A)	CSPN EBee EPfP NLar
	'Burma Star' (EL)	CWGN EPfP ETho LOck LPio LRHS NBea NHaw
	Caddick's Cascade = 'Semu'	CSPN CWGN ETho LPio NHaw
	'Caerulea Luxurians' (Vt)	CRHN CWGN LPio NHaw WSHC
	calycina	see *C. cirrhosa* var. *balearica*
	campaniflora	see *C. viticella* subsp. *campaniflora*
	'Campanile'	see *C.* × *bonstedtii* 'Campanile'
	'Candida' (EL)	EBee LPio
	'Candleglow' (A)	CSPN MBri
	'Candy Stripe'	CLng EBee LPio LRHS MAsh SCoo SLim SPoG SWCr
	'Capitaine Thuilleaux'	see *C.* 'Souvenir du Capitaine Thuilleaux'
	'Cardinał Wyszyński'	see *C.* 'Kardynal Wyszynski'
	'Carmencita' (Vt)	CRHN CSPN EBee LPio LRHS NBea NHaw SCoo SLon SPet WFar
	'Carnaby' (EL)	CSPN CWCL CWSG EBee ELan ELon EPfP ETho LOck LPio LRHS LSRN MAsh MBri MGos NBea SCoo SLim SPoG SWCr WPGP
	'Carnival Queen'	CSPN CWSG LPio
	'Carol Leeds' (Vt) **new**	NHaw
	'Caroline' (LL)	CSPN CWGN EBee ETho LPio LSRN NHaw SMDP
*	× ***cartmanii*** hort. (Fo)	SAga
	- 'Avalanche' PBR (Fo/m) ♀H3	CSPN ELan ETho GBin LBuc LPio LRHS MGos NLar NPri SBfd SCoo SLim SPoG
	- 'Joe' (Fo/m)	CBcs EBee ELan EPfP EPot ETho EWes ITim LRHS LSRN MAsh MGos NHol SBfd SCoo SPoG SWCr WHil
	- 'Joe' × ***marmoraria*** (Fo)	ECho MGos
	- 'Joe' × 'Sharon'	LSRN
	- 'White Abundance' PBR (Fo/f)	ETho LPio LRHS NLar SPoG
	× ***cartmanii*** hort. × ***petriei*** (Fo)	ECho
	Cassis = 'Evipo020' PBR	CWGN EPfP ETho LBuc LRHS LSRN LSqu MAsh SCoo SLon SPer SPoG SWCr
	Cezanne = 'Evipo023' PBR (EL)	EPfP ETho LBuc LRHS LSqu MAsh SCoo SLon SPer SPoG SWCr
	'Chacewater' (Vt)	CRHN
	'Chalcedony' (EL)	CSPN CWGN ETho LPio MGos
	Chantilly = 'Evipo021' PBR	EPfP ETho LBuc LRHS LSqu MAsh SCoo SPer SWCr
	'Charissima' (EL)	CSPN CWGN EPfP LRHS MAsh MGos NLar SCoo SPet SWCr WFar
	'Chatsworth' (Vt)	CRHN EPfP LRHS MAsh
	Chevalier = 'Evipo040' **new**	ETho LRHS MAsh SLon SPer SPoG
	chiisanensis	CSPN
	- B&SWJ 4560	WCru
	- B&SWJ 8706	WCru
	- 'Korean Beauty'	GKev
	- 'Lemon Bells' (A)	ELan EPfP ETho LOck LRHS MAsh SCoo SPoG SWCr
	- 'Love Child' (A)	CSPN ELan SLim
	chinensis misapplied	see *C. terniflora*
	chinensis Osbeck RWJ 10042	WCru
	Chinook = 'Evipo013' PBR	CLng LRHS MAsh SLim
	'Christian Steven' (LL)	CSPN LPio
	chrysantha	see *C. tangutica*
	chrysocoma misapplied	see *C. spooneri*, *C.* × *vedrariensis*
N	***chrysocoma*** Franch.	EPfP NHol SMDP WSpi
	- ACE 1093	CPou
	'Cicciolina' (Vt)	CRHN ETho NHaw
	cirrhosa	CBot CTri ELan GKir LOck LRHS MAsh MGos MWhi NHol SWCr
§	- var. ***balearica***	Widely available
	- 'Ourika Valley'	EBee EPfP ETho LPio LRHS MAsh NBea NLar SWCr WFar
	- var. ***purpurascens*** 'Freckles' ♀H3	Widely available
	- - 'Jingle Bells'	CLng CMac CRHN EBee EGxp EPfP ETho LOck LPio LRHS LSRN MAsh NBea NHol NPri SCoo SLim SPoG SWCr WFar WSpi
	- - 'Lansdowne Gem'	CMac CSPN CWGN CWib NBea NHol SKHP SMDP SPoG WSpi
	- 'Wisley Cream' ♀H3	Widely available
	clarkeana misapplied	see *C. urophylla* 'Winter Beauty'
	columbiana var. ***tenuiloba*** 'Ylva' (A)	WAbe
	'Columbine' (A)	CWSG EBee ETho LPio LRHS MSwo NBea NHol SDix SPer SPoG
	'Columella' (A)	ETho MGos NHaw NLar
	'Comtesse de Bouchaud' (LL) ♀H4	Widely available
	Confetti = 'Evipo036' PBR	CLng ETho LRHS LSRN SLim
	confusa HWJK 2200	WCru
	'Congratulations'	ELon LOck LSRN SLim
	connata	GQui
	- GWJ 9386	WCru
	- HWJCM 132	WCru
	aff. ***connata*** GWJ 9431 from West Bengal	WCru
	- HWJK 2176 from Nepal	WCru
	'Constance' (A) ♀H4	CElw CMac CSPN CWCL EBee EPfP ETho IBal LRHS LSRN MAsh NBea NHaw NSti SAga SCoo SPer SRms SWCr WPGP
	'Continuity' (M)	CWGN EBee
	'Cornish Spirit' (Vt) **new**	CRHN
	'Corona' (EL)	CLng CSPN ELan EPfP NHaw SCoo WFar
	'Corry' (Ta)	NLar
	'Côte d'Azur' (H)	CMdw CPLG ECtt GCal LPio MCCP
	'Countess of Lovelace' (EL)	CBcs CSPN CWSG EBee ELan EPfP ETho LRHS LSRN MAsh MBri MGos MRav NBea SCoo SLim SPet WFar
	County Park hybrids (Fo)	ECou
	'Cragside' (A)	EBee ETho NBea
§	'Crimson King' (LL)	ETho LPio NHaw WGor
	'Crinkle' PBR (M)	CCCN CLng SLim
§	***crispa***	CElw CSPN GAuc MWhi NBea NHaw
§	Crystal Fountain = 'Evipo038' PBR (EL)	CLng CWCL CWGN EPfP ETho LPio LRHS LSqu MAsh SCoo SPer SPoG SWCr
	× ***cylindrica***	CSPN
	'Danae' (Vt)	CRHN NHaw
	Dancing Queen = 'Zodaque' (EL) **new**	ETho
	'Daniel Deronda' (EL) ♀H4	CDoC CDul CSPN CWSG ECtt ELan ELon ETho GKir LOck LPio LRHS LSRN MAsh MGos MRav NBea NBir SCoo SDix SLim SPoG SWCr WFar

	'Darius' (EL)	LPio
	'Dark Eyes' (Vt)	CWGN LPio
	'Dark Secret' (A)	CSPN EPfP MBri
	'Dawn' (EL)	CCCN CLng CSPN ELon ETho LOck LPio LRHS LSRN MAsh NBea SCoo SLim SPoG SWCr
	'Débutante' (EL)	LPio NHaw
	'Denny's Double' (EL/d)	CSPN CWGN CWSG ETho LPio
	'Diana' (LL)	ETho LPio LSRN
	Diana's Delight = 'Evipo026' **new**	ETho LRHS LSqu MAsh SLon SPer SPoG
	dioica F&M 100	WPGP
	dioscoreifolia	see *C. terniflora*
§	× ***diversifolia***	CRHN EBee MGos NHaw NHol SDix SGar WSpi
§	- 'Blue Boy' (I)	CElw CMoH CRHN CSPN EBee LPio MGos NHaw
	- 'Heather Herschell' (I)	CRHN CSPN EBee ELon LPio NBea NHaw SMDP
§	- 'Hendersonii' (I)	EAEE EBee ELan ELon EPfP ETho GGar GKir LHop LOck LPio LSRN MRav MSwo NBea NBir NHol NSti SDix SWat WKif WSpi
§	- 'Olgae' (I)	CMoH CPLG CSPN LPio NBea NHaw SMDP WGwG
	'Doctor Ruppel' (EL)	CMac CSPN CWCL CWSG ECtt ELon EPfP ETho GKir LOck LPio LRHS LSRN MAsh MBri MGos MRav MSwo NBea NBir NPri SDix SLim SPer SPet SPoG SWCr WFar
	'Dominika' (LL)	CSPN CWGN LPio NHaw
	'Dorath'	ELon LPio NBea
	'Dorothy Tolver' (EL)	ETho LPio
	'Dorothy Walton'	see *C.* 'Bagatelle'
	'Double Cross'	ECou
	'Dubysa'	LPio
	'Duchess of Albany' (T)	CSPN CTri CWSG CWib EBee ELan EPfP ETho IBal LAst LOck LRHS LSRN MAsh MGos NBea NEgg NHol NSti SLim SPer SWCr WFar WSHC
	'Duchess of Edinburgh' (EL)	CBcs CMac CRHN CWSG EBee ECtt ELan EPfP ETho GKir GMac LAst LPio LRHS LSRN MAsh MGos MSwo NBea NEgg SDix SLim SPet SPoG SWCr WFar
	'Duchess of Sutherland' (EL)	MGos NHaw SDix SPet
	'Dulcie'	NHaw
	× ***durandii*** 🏆H4	CBcs CBot CRHN CSPN CWCL EBee ELan EPfP ETho LPio LRHS LSRN MAsh MBri MRav NBea NHol NPri NSti SCoo SLim SPer SPoG SWCr WCot WFar WSpi
	'Dusky Star' (M)	CWGN EBee
	'Dutch Sky'	MBri
	'Early Sensation' (Fo/f)	Widely available
	'East Malling' (M)	NHaw
	'Eclipse' (H) **new**	SMDP
	'Edith' (EL) 🏆H4	ECtt ETho LPio LSRN NBea NHaw WGor
	'Edomurasaki' (EL)	LPio
	'Edouard Desfossé' (EL)	CLng
	'Edward Prichard'	CMoH CSPN EBee ELon EPfP LPio MGos MWea NBea NHaw SDix SMDP
	'Eetika' (LL)	CRHN ETho LPio NBea
	'Ekstra' (LL)	EBee ETho LPio
	'Eleanor' (Fo/f)	ECou GEdr
	'Elfin' (Fo/v)	ECou
	'Elizabeth' (M) 🏆H4	Widely available
§	'Elsa Späth' (EL)	CElw CMac CPLG CSPN CTri EBee ELan EPfP ETho GKir LPio LRHS LSRN MAsh MBri MGan MGos MRav NBea SDix SLim SPer SPoG SWCr WFar
	'Elten' (M)	CSPN CWGN SMDP
	'Elvan' (Vt)	CRHN EBee NHaw NLar SPet
	'Emilia Plater' (Vt)	CRHN CSPN ETho LOck LPio MGos NBea NHaw SLon
	Empress = 'Evipo011'PBR (EL)	EPfP ETho LBuc LRHS LSqu MAsh SLon SWCr
	'Entel' (Vt)	CRHN CWGN ETho LPio NHaw
	'Erik' (A)	LPio NBea
	× ***eriostemon***	see *C. × diversifolia*
	'Ernest Markham' (LL) 🏆H4	Widely available
	'Esperanto' (LL)	EBee LPio MGos NBea SMDP
	'Essex Star' (Fo)	ECou
	'Étoile de Malicorne' (EL)	LPio WGor
	Etoile Nacrée	see *C.* 'Sakurahime'
	'Étoile Rose' (Vt)	CMac CRHN CSPN CTri CWCL ELan EPfP ETho GKir LAst LOck LPio LRHS LSRN MAsh MGos MRav NBea NHol SCoo SDix SLim SPer SWCr WBor WFar WPGP
	'Étoile Violette' (Vt) 🏆H4	Widely available
	'Eva' (LL)	LPio
	Evening Star = 'Evista'	EPfP WFar
	'Evipo039'PBR	ETho
	'Eximia'	see *C.* 'Ballerina in Blue'
	'Fair Rosamond' (EL)	EBee EPfP MGos NBea NHaw SPet
	'Fairy' (Fo/f)	ECou
	Fairy BluePBR	see *C.* Crystal Fountain
	× ***fargesioides***	see *C.* 'Paul Farges'
	fasciculiflora	CBot CMHG CRHN CSPN
	- L 657	WCru WPGP
	'Fascination'PBR (I)	CWGN EBee EPfP LPio NHaw SMDP
	fauriei	WSHC
	Filigree = 'Evipo029'PBR	LRHS MAsh SWCr
	finetiana misapplied	see *C. paniculata* J.G. Gmel.
	'Firefly' (EL)	MGos
	'Fireworks' (EL)	CAlb CChe CSPN CWGN EBee ECtt ELon EPfP ETho LOck LPio LRHS LSRN MAsh MBri MGos MRav NBea NEgg SLim SPer SPoG SWCr WFar WFoF WGor
	'Flamingo' (EL)	CWCL CWSG
	flammula	CMac CRHN CSPN CTri CWib EBee ELan EPfP LOck LRHS LSRN MAsh MBlu MRav MWhi NBea NSti SDix SLim SPer SPoG SWCr SWvt WBVN WFar WGwG WSHC WSpi
	- 'Rubra Marginata'	see *C. × triternata* 'Rubromarginata'
	Fleuri = 'Evipo042'	EPfP ETho LBuc LRHS MAsh SCoo SPoG SWCr
§	'Floral Feast' (A/d)	CSPN NBea
	'Floralia'	see *C.* 'Floral Feast'
	florida	CSPN CWGN LPio
	- 'Bicolor'	see *C. florida* var. *sieboldiana*
	- var. ***flore-pleno*** (d)	CCCN CSPN CWCL EBee ELan EPfP ETho GMac LAst LOck LPio LRHS LSRN MAsh NBea NEgg SPer SPoG SWCr WFar WGwG
	- Pistachio = 'Evirida'PBR (LL)	CCCN CLng CSPN CWCL CWGN EBee EPfP ETho IBal LBuc LPio LRHS LSRN LSqu MAsh NLar SLim SPer SWCr WFar
§	- var. ***sieboldiana*** (d)	CBcs CSPN CWCL CWSG EBee ELan EPfP ETho GMac IBal LAst LBMP LPio LRHS LSRN MAsh MBri MGos NBea NLar SLim SPer SPoG SRkn SWCr WFar WGwG WPGP
	- 'Thorncroft' (LL)	ETho
	'Floris V'	IPot LPio NHaw NLar

	'Flutter' (M)	LRHS
	foetida	CSPN
	foetida × 'Lunar Lass' (Fo)	ECho ECou
	foetida × ***petriei***	ECho ECou
	'Fond Memories' (EL)	ETho LPio LSRN
	'Forever'	ETho
I	'Forget-me-not'	LPio LSRN
	forrestii	see *C. napaulensis*
§	***forsteri***	CBcs CSPN ETho WPGP WSHC
	'Foxtrot' (Vt)	CRHN NBea NHaw
	'Foxy' (A) 🏆^{H4}	CLng EBee LPio LRHS NHaw SLon WGob
	'Fragrant Joy' (Fo/m)	ECou
	'Fragrant Oberon'	ECou
	'Fragrant Spring' (M)	CSPN CWGN ECtt ELon ETho LOck LRHS MGos NHaw NLar SLim SMDP WFar WGwG
	'Frances Rivis' (A) 🏆^{H4}	Widely available
	'Francesca' (A)	LSRN MGos NBea
	'Frankie' (A) 🏆^{H4}	CLng CSPN EBee ELan EPfP ETho LRHS LSRN MAsh SCoo SWCr
	Franziska Maria = 'Evipo008' (EL)	CLng EBee EPfP ETho LBuc LRHS LSqu MAsh SCoo SLon SWCr
	'Frau Mikiko' (EL)	ETho LPio MGos
	'Frau Susanne' (EL)	ETho
	'Freda' (M) 🏆^{H4}	CRHN CTri CWSG EBee ECtt ELan EPfP ETho LRHS LSRN MAsh MBlu MBri MGos MRav NBea NHol NSti SDix SLim SPer SPoG SWCr WCru
	fruticosa 'Mongolian Gold'	CWGN
	'Fryderyk Chopin' (EL)	CSPN EBee LPio NHaw NLar
	'Fuji-musume' (EL) 🏆^{H4}	CSPN CWGN EBee ETho LOck LPio LRHS NBea NHaw NLar SLim SPet SPoG SWCr WFar
	'Fujinami' (EL)	LPio MAsh
	'Fukuzono'	EBee ETho LOck LRHS LSRN MAsh NBea NHaw SWCr
	fusca misapplied	see *C. japonica*
	fusca Turcz.	WIvy WSHC
	- dwarf	CWGN NHaw
§	- var. ***fusca***	ETho WSHC
	- var. ***kamtschatica***	see *C. fusca* Turcz. var. *fusca*
	'Fuyu-no-tabi' (EL)	ETho LPio
	'G. Steffner' (A)	MGos
	'Gabrielle' (EL)	CSPN LPio LSRN NHaw
	Galore^{PBR}	see *C.* Vesuvius
	Gazelle = 'Evipo014'^{PBR}	CLng LRHS MAsh SKHP SPoG
	'Gemini' (EL)	LPio MGos
	'Generał Sikorski' (EL)	CBcs CMac CRHN CSPN CWSG ECtt ELan EPfP ETho LOck LPio LRHS LSRN MAsh MBri MGos NBea SCoo SLim SPer SPoG SWCr
	gentianoides	ETho LSRN WAbe WCot
	'Geoffrey Tolver' (LL)	ETho
	'Georg' (A/d)	MGos NHaw
	'Georg Ots' (LL)	LPio
	Giant Star = 'Gistar'^{PBR} (M)	CLng CWGN LRHS MGos NEgg NLar NPer SLim SPoG
	'Gillian Blades' (EL) 🏆^{H4}	CLng CRHN CSPN EBee ELan EPfP ETho LOck LPio LRHS LSRN MAsh NBea NHaw SCoo SPer SPet SPoG SWCr
§	'Gipsy Queen' (LL) 🏆^{H4}	CBcs CMac CSPN CWCL CWSG EBee ECtt ELan EPfP ETho GKir LPio LRHS LSRN LTen MAsh MRav NBea SDix SLim SPoG SVic SWCr WFar
	'Girenas'	LPio
	'Gladys Picard' (EL)	LPio NHaw WFar
	glauca Turcz.	see *C. intricata*
	glauca ambig.	GAuc
	glaucophylla	WCru
	'Glynderek' (EL)	LPio
	'Gojōgawa' (EL) **new**	ETho
	'Golden Harvest' (Ta)	NHol NLar WFar
	Golden Tiara = 'Kugotia'^{PBR} (Ta) 🏆^{H4}	CSPN CWGN ETho LSRN MGos NBea NLar SRms
	'Gothenburg' (M)	NBea NHaw WFar
I	'Gothenburg Superba'	SMDP
	'Grace' (Ta)	CRHN CSPN EBee NBea NHaw NLar SMDP
I	'Grandiflora' (F)	SLim WFar
	'Grandiflora Sanguinea' Johnson	see *C.* 'Södertälje'
	grata misapplied	see *C.* × *jouiniana*
	grata Wall. B&SWJ 6774	WCru
	'Gravetye Beauty' (T)	CMac CRHN CSPN EBee ELan EPfP ETho GMac LAst LOck LRHS LSRN MAsh MBri MGos MRav NBea NHol NSti SDix SLim SPer SRkn SRms SWCr WCot WGwG WSpi
§	'Grażyna'	LPio
	'Green Velvet' (Fo/m)	ECou
	grewiiflora B&SWJ 2956	WCru
	'Guernsey Cream' (EL)	CFir CSPN CWCL CWSG EBee ETho LOck LPio LRHS LSRN MAsh MBri MGos NBea SCoo SDix SLim SPet SPoG SWCr WFar
	'Guiding Star' (EL)	NHaw
	'H.F. Young' (EL)	CSPN CWSG EBee ELan EPfP ETho GKir GMac LOck LPio LRHS LSRN MAsh MBri MGos NBea SCoo SDix SLim SPer SPet SPoG SWCr
	haenkeana **new**	NHaw
	'Hagley Hybrid' (LL)	Widely available
	'Haku-ōkan' (EL)	CSPN EBee EPfP ETho LOck LPio LRHS LSRN NBea NLar SCoo SLim
	'Hakuree' (I)	ETho LOck LPio LRHS SMDP
	'Hanaguruma' (EL)	CSPN EBee ETho LPio LRHS LSRN NBea NHaw SLim WFar
	'Hanajima' (I)	ETho LPio SMDP WAbe
	'Hania'	CWGN ETho LPio
	'Happy Anniversary' (EL)	ETho LBuc LSRN
	Harlow Carr = 'Evipo004'^{PBR}	CLng CMac CWGN EBee EPfP LRHS MAsh SCoo SLim SWCr
	'Harmony' (EL/d)	LPio
	'Haru Ichiban' (EL)	ETho
	'Haruyama' (EL)	LPio
	Havering hybrids (Fo)	ECou
	'Helen Cropper' (EL)	ETho
	'Helios' (Ta)	CSPN EPfP ETho LRHS MGos NBea NSti SCoo SPer SPoG
	'Helsingborg' (A) 🏆^{H4}	CLng CSPN EBee ECtt ELan EPfP ETho LPio LRHS MAsh NBea NHol NPri NSti SCoo SLim SPoG SRms SWCr
	hendersonii Koch	see *C.* × *diversifolia* 'Hendersonii'
	hendersonii Stand.	see *C.* × *diversifolia*
I	'Hendersonii' (I)	LSRN MAvo MNFA NHol SRkn
	'Hendersonii Rubra' (Ar)	CSPN NLar SPoG
	'Hendryetta'^{PBR} (I)	CWGN EPfP ETho LBMP LPio LRHS MAsh SMDP SPoG SRkn
	henryi	EShb LPio LSRN MAsh
	- B&SWJ 3402	WCru
	- var. ***morii*** B&SWJ 1668	WCru
	- 'Snow Bells' **new**	LRHS
	'Henryi' (EL) 🏆^{H4}	CDul CMac CRHN CSPN CTri CWCL CWSG EBee ELan EPfP ETho LRHS LSRN MBri MGos MRav MSwo NBea NEgg SDix SPer SPet SPoG SWCr WFar WGwG

	Name	Suppliers
	heracleifolia	CAby CBcs CBot CFir CPou ECtt GAuc MWhi NHol NLar SBfd SGSe WAbe WClo WCom WWEG
	- Alan Bloom PBR	see *C. tubulosa* Alan Bloom
I	- 'Alba' (H)	LPio
	- 'Blue Dwarf'	ETho LPio MGos SMDP WAbe
	- 'Campanile'	see *C.* × *bonstedtii* 'Campanile'
	- 'Cassandra'	CSam CWGN EAEE EBrs ECGP ECtt EPfP EShb ETho GCal LHop LPio LRHS MAvo MCot MGos NCGa NHol NLar SAga SChF SMDP WWlt
	- 'China Purple'	CPLG GKev LPio LSou MNrw MSCN NLar SMDP WHil WHoo
	- var. ***davidiana***	see *C. tubulosa*
	- 'Pink Dwarf'	CWGN ETho NLar SMDP WAbe
	- 'Roundway Blue Bird'	CBot LHop NHaw SMDP
	hexapetala misapplied	see *C. recta* subsp. *recta* var. *lasiosepala*
	hexapetala Forster	see *C. forsteri*
	hexasepala	see *C. forsteri*
	'Hikarugenji' (EL)	CSPN LPio NHaw
	'Honora' (LL)	CSPN CWGN EGxp LOck LPio LRHS NBea SCoo SPoG
	'Horn of Plenty' (EL)	LOck NHaw SPet
	'Huldine' (LL) 🏆H4	CBcs CRHN CSPN EBee ELan EPfP ETho LPio LRHS LSRN MAsh MRav NBea NSti SDix SPer SPet SPoG SWCr
	'Huvi' (LL)	CWGN ETho LPio NBea NHaw
	'Hybrida Sieboldii' (EL)	CRHN EBee SCoo
	Hyde Hall = 'Evipo009' PBR	CLng CMac CWGN EBee EPfP ETho IBal LRHS LSqu MAsh SCoo SLim SLon SWCr
	'Hythe Egret' (Fo)	ECho ITim LLHF
	I Am a Little Beauty = 'Zolibe' (Vt)	CRHN CWGN LPio NHaw
	I Am Lady Q = 'Zoiamladyq' (Vt)	CWGN LPio
	'Ialtinskii Etiud' (LL)	LPio
	ianthina	WPGP
	- var. ***ianthina***	CRHN
	- var. ***kuripoensis*** B&SWJ 700	WCru
	'Ibi' (EL)	CWGN LPio
	Ice Blue = 'Evipo003' PBR (Prairie Series) (EL)	CLng EPfP ETho LBuc LPio LRHS LSqu MAsh SCoo SLim SLon SWCr
	'Ideal' (EL)	LPio
	'Ilka' (EL)	LPio
	'Imperial' (EL)	LPio NHaw
	indivisa Willd.	see *C. paniculata* J.G. Gmel.
	Inspiration = 'Zoin' PBR (I)	CSPN ELan EPfP ETho LPio LRHS MGos NLar SCoo
	integrifolia	CElw CPLG CPou EBee EHrv EPfP GKir GMac IFoB LHop LRHS MBri MGos MHer MLLN MTho MWat MWhi NBPC NLar NPer SBfd SGar SMrm SPer SPoG SRms WHoo WPer WWEG
I	- 'Alba'	CBcs CBot CElw CSPN EBee ECtt ELon LHop LPio LSRN MBNS MCot MDKP NBea NBir NHaw NSti SCoo SPer SPoG
	- blue-flowered	ITim
	- 'Budapest'	LPio NHaw
	- 'Cora' (I)	CWGN
	- 'Hendersonii' Koch	see *C.* × *diversifolia* 'Hendersonii'
	- var. ***latifolia***	CElw
	- mid-blue-flowered	MGos
	- 'Olgae'	see *C.* × *diversifolia* 'Olgae'
	- 'Ozawa's Blue'	CWGN EAEE ETho LPio LRHS MCot
	- white-flowered	see *C. integrifolia* 'Alba'
§	***intricata***	CBcs CPLG CSPN MGos SGar SLim
	'Iola Fair' (EL)	CSPN NHaw
	ispahanica	SGar
	'Iubileinyi-70' (LL)	LPio
	'Ivan Olsson' (EL)	CSPN EBee ETho LPio MGos NBea
	'Izumi' (LL)	LPio
	'Jackmanii' (LL) 🏆H4	CBcs CMac CTri EBee EPfP ETho GKir LOck LPio LRHS LSRN MAsh MGos NBea NWea SCoo SLim SPer SPet SPoG SWCr WFar
	'Jackmanii Alba' (EL)	ELan ELon EPfP ETho LRHS LSRN MAsh NBea SCoo SLim SPet SPoG SWCr
	Jackmanii Purpurea = 'Zojapur'	LPio
	'Jackmanii Rubra' (EL)	ETho NBea
	'Jackmanii Superba' misapplied	see *C.* 'Gipsy Queen'
	'Jackmanii Superba' ambig. (LL)	CChe CDul CMac CSPN CWCL CWSG ECtt ELan EPfP ETho LAst LRHS MAsh MBri MGan MGos MRav MSwo NBea NEgg NPer NPri SDix SLim SPer SPoG WFar
	'Jacqueline du Pré' (A) 🏆H4	CAlb CBcs CMac CSPN CWCL EBee ELan EPfP ETho LOck MGos NBea NHaw SLim SMDP
	'Jacqui' (M/d)	ETho MGos NHaw NLar
	'James Mason' (EL)	CSPN ETho NBea NHaw
	'Jan Fopma' PBR (I)	CWGN ETho LPio SMDP
	'Jan Lindmark' (A/d)	CLng EPfP ETho LPio LRHS MAsh MGos NBea NHol NLar NSti SCoo WFar
§	'Jan Paweł II' (EL)	CWSG EBee ECtt EGxp ELan ETho GKir LOck LRHS NBea SCoo SPer
	'Janina'	CWGN
§	***japonica***	CSPN NHaw SMDP
	- B&SWJ 11204	WCru
§	- var. ***obvallata*** B&SWJ 8900	WCru
	'Jenny' (M/d)	CWGN ETho LPio LRHS MAsh MGos NHaw NLar SMDP SWCr
	'Jenny Caddick' (Vt)	CSPN ETho LPio NHaw SMDP
	'Jerzy Popiełuszko' (EL)	ETho LRHS
	'Joan Picton' (EL)	CWSG LRHS
	John Howells = 'Zojohnhowells' (Vt) **new**	ETho SLon
	'John Huxtable' (LL) 🏆H4	CLng CRHN EPfP ETho LPio LRHS MAsh NBea NHaw NPri WGor
	John Paul II	see *C.* 'Jan Paweł II'
	'John Treasure' (Vt)	CRHN EBee LOck LRHS NHaw NLar SLim
	'John Warren' (EL)	CWSG EBee ETho LRHS MAsh NHaw SCoo SLim SPer SPoG SWCr WFar
	Jolly Good = 'Zojogo' (LL)	CWGN ETho
	'Jorma' (LL)	LPio
	Josephine = 'Evijohill' PBR (EL) 🏆H4	CLng CSPN CWCL EBee EPfP ETho LAst LOck LPio LRHS LSRN LSqu MAsh NLar NPri SCoo SPer SPoG SWCr WFar
§	× ***jouiniana***	EBee LPio MRav NHol SWCr WSHC
	- 'Chance' (H)	NHaw
	'Julka' (EL)	ETho LPio NHaw
	'June Pyne'	ETho
	'Justa' (Vt)	CWGN LPio NHaw
	'Juuli' (I)	LSRN
	'Kaaru' (LL)	CRHN CSPN ETho LPio
	'Kacper' (EL)	CSPN EBee ETho LPio MGos NHaw
	'Kaen'	CWGN ETho LPio
	'Kaiu' (V)	CWGN LOck LRHS NBea NHaw SLim SMDP

	Name	Suppliers
§	'Kakio' (EL)	CLng EBee ETho LOck LRHS LSRN MAsh MGos NBea SDix SLim SWCr WFar
	'Kalina' (EL)	ETho LPio NHaw
	'Kamilla' (EL)	CWGN LPio
§	'Kardynał Wyszyński' (EL)	EBee ETho GKir MGos NBea SMDP
§	'Kasmu' (Vt)	LPio NHaw
	'Katharina' (EL)	LPio
	'Kathleen Dunford' (EL)	LSRN NBea NHaw SCoo SMDP SPoG
	'Kathryn Chapman' (Vt)	CRHN LPio NHaw
	'Keith Richardson' (EL)	LPio
	'Ken Donson' (EL) 🏆^{H4}	EBee LPio MGos SCoo
	'Ken Pyne'	LPio
	'Kermesina' (Vt) 🏆^{H4}	CElw CFir CRHN CWCL EBee ELan EPfP ETho GKir LOck LPio LRHS MAsh MBri MGos MHer MRav NBea NHol NSti SCoo SDix SLim SPer SPet SPoG SRms SWCr
	'Kiev' (Vt)	NHaw
	'Killifreth' (Vt)	CRHN NHaw
	'King Edward VII' (EL)	EBee EPfP NBea WGor
	Kingfisher = 'Evipo037'^{PBR}	EPfP ETho LBuc LRHS LSqu MAsh NPri SCoo SLon SPoG SWCr
	'Kiri Te Kanawa' (EL)	CSPN EBee ELon ETho LOck LRHS LSRN MGos NBea NHaw SMDP
	'Kommerei' (LL)	ETho NHaw
§	'Königskind' (EL)	CSPN ETho LPio MGos NBea
	koreana	NHol WCru
	- var. ***lutea***	WCru
	'Kosmicheskaia Melodiia' (LL)	CSPN EBee
	'Kuba' (LL)	LPio
	'Küllus' (LL)	CWGN ETho LPio
	'Kunpū'	LPio
	ladakhiana	CElw CSPN GQui MWhi NHaw SMDP WPGP
	'Lady Betty Balfour' (LL)	CElw CLng CMac CSPN CWSG ETho LRHS LTen SCoo SDix SPet SPoG WFar
	'Lady Bird Johnson' (T)	EBee ELon EPfP LOck LRHS LSRN MAsh SCoo SLim SWCr
	'Lady Caroline Nevill' (EL)	CRHN LPio
	'Lady Londesborough' (EL)	EBee EPfP LPio NBea NHaw SCoo SDix
	'Lady Northcliffe' (EL)	CLng CSPN CTri CWSG EPfP ETho LPio LRHS MAsh NPri SDix SPet
	'Lambton Park' (Ta) 🏆^{H4}	CFir CRHN EBee EPfP ETho LOck LRHS LSRN NBea NHaw NLar SMDP
	'Lantern Light' (A)	LRHS
	lasiandra	EBee NHaw
	- B&SWJ 6252	WCru
	- B&SWJ 6775	WCru
	'Last Dance' (Ta)	CRHN
	Lasting Love	see *C.* 'Grażyna'
	'Lasurstern' (EL) 🏆^{H4}	CBcs CMac CPLG CRHN CSPN CTri EBee ECtt ELan EPfP ETho GKir GMac LAst LPio LRHS LSRN MAsh MBri MRav SDix SPoG SWCr WFar
	'Laura' (LL)	NHaw
	'Laura Denny' (EL)	ETho
	'Lavender Lace'	LPio
	'Lawsoniana' (EL)	CMac CRHN CWSG LAst
	'Lech Wałęsa'	CWGN
	'Lemon Chiffon' (EL)	CLng CSPN EBee ETho LPio LRHS MAsh NHaw SWCr
	Liberation = 'Evifive'^{PBR} (EL)	CLng EBee LRHS MAsh SCoo SPoG SWCr
§	***ligusticifolia***	NHaw
	'Liisu' (LL)	LPio
	'Lilacina Floribunda' (EL)	EBee NHaw
	'Lilactime' (EL)	NHaw
	'Lincoln Star' (EL)	CLng CMac ELon GKir LOck LPio LRHS MGos NBea SDix SLim SPer SPet SPoG
	'Little Bas' (Vt)	CRHN CSPN LPio MBri NHaw NLar SLon
	'Little Butterfly' (Vt)	CRHN LPio MGos NBea NHaw
	'Little Mermaid' (EL)	CWGN
	'Little Nell' (Vt)	CCCN CElw CRHN CSPN ELan EPfP ETho GKir LOck LPio LRHS MRav NBea NHol SCoo SDix SPer SPet WFar WSpi
	'Lord Herschell'	CWGN ETho LOck LRHS SMDP
	'Lord Nevill' (EL)	CRHN CWSG EPfP ETho LOck LPio LRHS NBea WFar
	'Louise Pummell'	ECou
	'Louise Rowe' (EL)	CElw CLng EBee ELan ETho LOck LRHS LSRN MAsh MGos NBea NHaw SWCr
	loureiroana HWJ 663	WCru
	'Love Jewelry'	CWGN ETho LPio NHaw
	'Loving Memory' **new**	ETho
	'Lunar Lass' (Fo/f)	ECho EPfP ETho ITim LRHS NBea SBfd WPGP
I	'Lunar Lass Variegata' (Fo/v)	ECho LLHF
	'M. Koster' (Vt)	CDoC CRHN CSam EBee EPfP ETho LOck LRHS NBea NHaw SRms
	macropetala (d)	CBcs CDoy CSBt EBee ELan EPfP ETho LAst LRHS MAsh MGan MGos MRav MWhi NBea SDix SPer SPet SWCr WBrE WFar
	- 'Alborosea'	see *C.* 'Blushing Ballerina'
	- 'Blue Lagoon'	see *C. macropetala* 'Lagoon' Jackman 1959
	- 'Lagoon' Jackman 1956	see *C. macropetala* 'Maidwell Hall' Jackman
	- 'Lagoon' ambig.	LSRN MAsh SLim SPet SWCr
§	- 'Lagoon' Jackman 1959 (A/d) 🏆^{H4}	CSPN EBee ETho LRHS LSRN MSwo NBea NHol NSti SCoo SLim SPoG
§	- 'Maidwell Hall' Jackman (A/d)	CSPN CTri CWSG EBee ECtt EPfP ETho LPio LSRN MGos NBea NHol WPGP
	- 'Maidwell Hall' O.E.P. Wyatt (A)	MRav SCoo
	- 'Wesselton' (A/d) 🏆^{H4}	CSPN CTri EPfP ETho LRHS MAsh MBri MGos NBea NHaw NHol SWCr WFar
	- 'White Moth'	see *C.* 'White Moth'
	'Madame Baron-Veillard' (LL)	CLng ECtt LAst LRHS NEgg SCoo SDix WFar
	'Madame Edouard André' (LL)	CLng CRHN CSPN EPfP LPio LRHS MAsh NBea SCoo SLim SPet SPoG SWCr WFar
	'Madame Grangé' (LL) 🏆^{H4}	CSPN EPfP LPio LRHS MAsh NBea NHaw SCoo SPoG SWCr
	'Madame Julia Correvon' (Vt) 🏆^{H4}	Widely available
	'Madame le Coultre'	see *C.* 'Mevrouw Le Coultre'
	'Majojo' (Fo)	EPot GEdr LLHF SMrm
	mandschurica	ETho GCal LPio NHaw
	- B&SWJ 1060	WCru
	marata	WThu
	'Marcelina' (EL)	LPio
	'Margaret Hunt' (LL)	CSPN EGxp ELan ETho LSRN NBea NHaw
	'Margaret Jones' (M/d)	NHaw
	'Maria Cornelia' (Vt)	CWGN
	'Maria Louise Jensen' (EL)	LPio
	'Marie Boisselot' (EL) 🏆^{H4}	CBcs CMac CRHN CSPN CTri CWCL CWSG EBee ECtt ELan EPfP ETho GKir LOck LPio LRHS LSRN

		MAsh MBri MGos MRav MSwo NBea NSti SDix SLim SPer SPet SPoG SWCr
	'Marinka' (H)	SMDP
	'Märjamaa' (LL)	LPio
	'Marjorie' (M/d)	CBcs CDoC CSPN CTri CWSG EBee ECtt ELan EPfP ETho LOck LRHS MAsh MGos MRav NBea NEgg NHol SLim SPer SPet SPoG SRms SWCr WCru WFar
	'Markham's Pink' (A/d) ♀H4	Widely available
	marmoraria ♀H2-3	CMoH ECho LHop LRHS WFar
	- hybrid (Fo)	ITim
	marmoraria × ***petriei***	ECho
	'Marmori' (LL)	CWGN EBee ETho MAsh NBea NHaw SLim SWCr
	'Mary Rose'	see *C. viticella* 'Flore Pleno'
	'Mary Whistler' (A)	LPio MGos
§	'Maskarad' (Vt)	CSPN
	Masquerade (Vt)	see *C.* 'Maskarad'
I	'Masquerade' (EL)	LPio MBri
	'Matilda' (EL)	LPio
	'Matka Siedliska' (EL)	CSPN LPio
	'Maureen' (LL)	CSPN CWGN CWSG
	maximowicziana	see *C. terniflora*
	'Mayleen' (M) ♀H4	CPou CSBt CTri CWSG EBee ECtt EPfP ETho EWTr LOck LRHS MAsh MBri MGos MRav NBea NEgg SAga SBfd SCoo SLim SPer SPet SPoG SRms SWCr WFar
	Medley = 'Evipo012'PBR	CLng LPio LRHS MAsh
	'Meeli' (LL)	EBee LPio
	'Meloodia' (LL)	NBea
	'Mercurius' (LL) new	LPio
§	'Mevrouw Le Coultre' (EL)	MBlu MGan MGos
	meyeniana var. ***insularis*** B&SWJ 6700 new	WCru
	microphylla	ECou
	Mienie Belle = 'Zomibel' (T)	CWGN ETho
	'Mikelite' (Vt)	EBee LPio NHaw
	'Mikla' (LL)	LPio
	'Miniseelik' (LL)	SMDP
	'Minister' (EL)	EBee LPio
	'Minuet' (Vt) ♀H4	CRHN CSPN EBee ELon EPfP ETho GKir LOck LPio LRHS MSwo NBea SCoo SDix SPer WSpi
	'Miriam Markham' (EL)	LPio NBea NHaw
	'Miss Bateman' (EL) ♀H4	CDoC CMac CRHN CSPN CTri CWCL CWSG EBee ECtt ELan EPfP ETho GKir LBMP LPio LRHS LSRN MAsh MBri NBea SDix SLim SPer SPet SPoG SWCr WBor
	'Miss Christine' (M)	ETho LSRN SMDP WFar
	'Miss Crawshay' (EL)	NHaw
	'Moniuszko' (EL)	CWGN LPio
N	***montana***	CBcs CPLG CSBt EBee ECtt GGal MGos NBea NHol SBfd SDix SPet SSta WFar
	- B&SWJ 6724 from Taiwan	WCru
	- B&SWJ 6930	WCru
	- BWJ 8189b from China	WCru
	- HWJK 2156 from Nepal	WCru
	- var. ***alba***	see *C. montana* var. *montana*
	- 'Alexander'	CPou CWSG EPfP LRHS MAsh MGos
	- var. ***grandiflora*** (M) ♀H4	Widely available
I	- 'Lilacina'	LRHS
§	- var. ***montana*** new	CBar CDoy
	- 'Peveril'	CSPN
	- 'Prosperity'	LPio
	- var. ***rubens*** misapplied	see *C. montana* var. *montana*
	- var. ***rubens*** E.H.Wilson	CDoC CSBt CTri ELan EPfP ETho GGal GGar LOck LRHS LTen MBri MSwo NBea NHol NWea SDix SPet SPlb SReu SWCr WFar
I	- - 'Odorata'	EBee ETho LPio MGos MRav SCoo SLim SPoG WGor WGwG
	- - 'Pink Perfection'	CDoC CMac CWSG EBee ECtt ELan EPfP EWTr LAst LPio LRHS LSRN MAsh NBea NEgg NHol SCoo SPer SPoG SWCr WFar
	- - 'Tetrarose' ♀H4	Widely available
	- - 'Veitch'	CBot
I	- 'Rubens Superba'	CMHG CTri CWSG ECtt LBuc MAsh MGan NPri SRms WFar
	- var. ***sericea***	see *C. spooneri*
	- 'Snow' (M)	LPio
§	- var. ***wilsonii***	CSPN CSam EBee ECtt ELan EPfP ETho GGar LOck LPio LRHS LSRN MAsh MGos MNHC MRav MSwo NBea SDix SMDP SPet SRms SWCr WFar
	'Monte Cassino' (EL)	CRHN CSPN CWGN EBee ETho LPio LRHS NBea SMDP
	'Moonbeam' (Fo)	CMHG EAEE EBee ECou ELan EPot GEdr ITim LRHS MGos MRav NBea WCot
§	'Moonlight' (EL)	CElw CSPN LPio
	'Moonman' (Fo)	LLHF
	Morning Cloud	see *C.* 'Yukikomachi'
	Morning Star = 'Zoklako'PBR	CWGN ETho LPio
	Morning Yellow = 'Cadmy'PBR (M)	CCCN CLng EWTr LRHS NEgg
	'Mrs Cholmondeley' (EL) ♀H4	CMac CRHN CSPN CWSG EBee ELan ELon EPfP ETho GKir LOck LPio LRHS LSRN MAsh MBri MGan MGos MSwo NBea NPri SDix SLim SPoG SRms SWCr WFar
	'Mrs George Jackman' (EL) ♀H4	CLng CSPN ETho LPio LRHS LTen MGos NBea NLar SCoo
	'Mrs Hope' (EL)	LPio
	'Mrs James Mason' (EL)	LPio NBea NHaw SMDP
	'Mrs N.Thompson' (EL)	CMac CSPN CTri CWCL EBee ELan ETho LOck LPio LRHS LSRN MAsh MBri MGos NBea NBir NEgg NPer SDix SLim SPer SPet SPoG SWCr WFar
	'Mrs P.B.Truax' (EL)	EBee LPio LRHS NBea SMDP
	'Mrs P.T.James' (EL)	LPio
	'Mrs Robert Brydon' (H)	ECtt IPot MBNS NBPC NCGa NHol NLar NSti SRms STes WCot WFar
	'Mrs Spencer Castle' (EL)	CSPN ETho LPio NBea
	'Mrs T. Lundell' (Vt)	CRHN CSPN EBee LPio MGos NHaw
	'Multi Blue' (EL)	CBcs CRHN CWSG EBee ECtt ELan ELon EPfP ETho LAst LOck LPio LRHS LSRN MAsh MBri MGos MRav NBea SLim SPer SPoG SRms SWCr WBrE WFar WGwG
	'My Angel'PBR (Ta)	CSPN ELan MGos NHaw NLar WSpi
	'Myōjō' (EL)	CSPN EBee LPio
	'Nadezhda' (LL)	LPio NBea SMDP
§	***napaulensis***	CSPN CTri ETho LPio MNrw WCru WFar WSHC WSpi
I	'Natacha' (EL)	EBee LOck LPio MAsh NBea NHaw SCoo SWCr
	'Natascha' (EL)	CLng LRHS LSRN NPri
	'Neapolitan'	LPio

'Negritianka' (LL)	CSPN EBee EPfP LPio LRHS LSRN NBea NHaw SPoG
'Negus' (LL)	LPio MGos
'Nelly Moser' (EL) ♀H4	Widely available
'New Dawn' (M)	CSPN NHaw
'New Love'PBR (H)	CSPN ETho LSRN MGos NHaw NLar
New Zealand hybrids (Fo)	ECou
'Night Veil' (Vt)	ETho
'Nikolai Rubtsov' (LL)	CSPN LPio SMDP
'Niobe' (EL) ♀H4	CMac CSPN CWCL CWSG EBee ELan EPfP EShb ETho GMac LOck LPio LRHS LSRN MAsh MBri MGos MSwo NBea NPri NSti SDix SLim SPer SPet SPoG SRms SWCr WFar WSpi
North Star (LL)	see *C.* 'Põhjanael'
'North Star' (EL)	LPio LRHS
'Nuit de Chine' (EL)	LPio
'Nunn's Gift' (Fo)	ETho
nutans var. ***thyrsoidea***	see *C. rehderiana, C. veitchiana*
obvallata	see *C. japonica* var. *obvallata*
'Ocean Pearl' (A)	ETho NLar
ochotensis	CSPN SDys
'Odoriba' (V)	CWGN ETho NHaw NLar SMDP
'Ola Howells' (A/d)	LPio NBea
'Omoshiro' (EL)	CWGN EBee ETho LPio MGos NBea NHaw
Ooh La La = 'Evipo041'	EPfP ETho LBuc LRHS MAsh SCoo SWCr
'Oonagare Ichigoo' (Vt)	LPio MGos
Opaline	see *C.* 'Asagasumi'
orientalis misapplied	see *C. tibetana* subsp. *vernayi*
orientalis L.	CElw EBee GCra NHol SCoo WFar
- 'Orange Peel'	see *C. tibetana* subsp. *vernayi* var. *vernayi* 'Orange Peel'
'Otto Fröbel' (EL)	CSPN LPio
'Paddington' (EL)	ETho
'Pagoda' (Vt) ♀H4	CDoC CRHN EBee EPfP LPio MBri MRav NBea NHol NSti SCoo SRms
Palette = 'Evipo034'PBR	CLng LPio LRHS MAsh
'Pamela' (F)	CSPN ETho LPio NHaw
'Pamela Jackman'	see *C. alpina* 'Pamela Jackman'
'Pamiat Serdtsa' (I)	EBee ETho LPio NHaw
'Pamina' (EL)	CWGN ETho LPio
'Pangbourne Pink' (I) ♀H4	CSPN CWCL EBee EPfP ETho LPio LRHS MAsh NBea NHaw SCoo SWCr
paniculata Thunb.	see *C. terniflora*
§ ***paniculata*** J.G. Gmel.	CSPN
- (f)	ETho LPio
- var. ***lobata***	LPio
'Paola' (EL/d)	CWGN LPio
'Paradise Queen' (EL)	LBuc LPio NLar WFar
'Parasol' (EL)	CSPN LPio
Parisienne = 'Evipo019'PBR	EPfP ETho LBuc LRHS LSqu MAsh SCoo SLon SPer SWCr
parviflora DC.	see *C. viticella* subsp. *campaniflora*
parviloba var. ***bartlettii*** B&SWJ 6788	WCru
'Pastel Blue' (I)	ETho LPio NBea SMDP
'Pastel Pink' (I)	ETho LPio SMDP
'Pastel Princess' (EL)	NHaw
'Pat Coleman' (EL)	ETho
patens	CElw
- 'Korean Moon' (EL)	WCru
§ - 'Manshuu Ki' (EL)	CRHN CSPN CWSG EBee ECtt ELon EPfP ETho GKir LPio LRHS NBea SLim SPer SRms
- 'Yukiokoshi' (EL)	ETho LPio
Patricia Ann Fretwell = 'Pafar' (EL)	CSPN
§ 'Paul Farges' (Vb) ♀H4	CSPN CWGN EBee ETho NHaw NHol NSti SMDP
'Pauline' (A/d) ♀H4	CBcs CLng CWSG EBee ETho LRHS LSRN MAsh MGos NBea SCoo SLim SWCr
'Pearl Rose' (A/d)	CWSG
'Pendragon' (Vt)	CRHN CWGN NHaw
'Pennell's Purity' (LL)	NBea NHaw
Peppermint = 'Evipo005'PBR	EPfP ETho LBuc LRHS LSqu MAsh SCoo SPer SPoG SWCr
'Perle d'Azur' (LL)	Widely available
'Perrin's Pride' (Vt)	CLng LPio LRHS MAsh MGos NBea NLar SCoo
Petit Faucon = 'Evisix'PBR (I) ♀H4	CLng EBee ECtt EPfP ETho LAst LOck LPio LRHS LSRN LSqu MAsh MBri NBea NPri NSti SCoo SLim SPer SPoG SWCr WCot
petriei	ECou GBBs NHar WThu
- 'Princess' (Fo/f)	ECou
- 'Steepdown' (Fo/f)	ECou
'Peveril Pearl' (EL)	EBee ETho
Picardy = 'Evipo024'PBR (EL)	EPfP ETho LBuc LRHS LSqu MAsh SCoo SPer SWCr
I 'Picton's Variety' (M)	CTri EBee NHaw NHol SMDP WFar
pierotii B&SWJ 6281	WCru
'Piilu' (EL)	CSPN CWGN EBee ELan ETho LBuc LOck LPio LRHS LSRN MAsh MBNS MBri MGos MWea NBea NHaw SCoo SLim SMDP SPoG SVic SWCr
'Pink Celebration'	CWGN ETho LPio
Pink Champagne	see *C.* 'Kakio'
'Pink Delight'PBR	CWGN
'Pink Fantasy' (LL)	CLng CRHN CSPN CTri CWSG ETho LPio LRHS MAsh MGos NBea SCoo SLim SRkn SWCr
'Pink Flamingo' (A) ♀H4	CLng CSPN CWCL EBee ECtt EGxp ELan EPfP ETho LRHS MAsh NSti SCoo SLim SPet SPoG SRkn SWCr WBrE
'Pink Ice' (I)	LOck LPio LRHS
'Pink Pearl' (EL)	LPio
'Pirko' (Vt)	LPio NHaw
§ ***pitcheri***	NHaw WSHC
'Pixie' (Fo/m)	CSPN ECou ELan EPfP ETho GGar ITim LRHS MGos NHaw NHol NLar SCoo SLim SPoG SRms
I 'Pleniflora' (M/d)	MGos NHaw
§ 'Plum Beauty' (A)	CSPN MGos NHaw
§ 'Põhjanael' (LL)	CSPN CWSG LPio MGos NBea
'Pointy' (A)	LPio
Polar BearPBR	see *C.* Arctic Queen
'Poldice' (Vt)	CRHN
'Polish Spirit' (LL) ♀H4	Widely available
'Polonez' (Vt)	ETho
potaninii	CFir CSPN ECtt GCra MWhi WPtf WSHC
- 'Summer Snow'	see *C.* 'Paul Farges'
'Praecox' (H) ♀H4	CRHN CSam CWCL EAEE EBee ECtt ELan EPfP ETho LHop LRHS MBri MWhi NBea NBir NHol SDix SPoG WCot
'Prairie River' (A)	ETho
Pretty in Blue = 'Zopre'PBR (F)	EBee
'Pribaltika' (LL)	LPio
'Primrose Star'PBR	see *C.* 'Star'
'Prince Charles' (LL) ♀H4	CPou CRHN CSPN CTri EBee ELan EPfP ETho GMac LOck LPio LRHS LSRN MGos NBea

		SCoo SDix SLim SPer SPet SPoG WFar WGwG
	'Prince Philip' (EL)	LPio WFar
§	'Princess Diana' (T) Υ^{H4}	CBcs CRHN CSPN CWCL CWGN CWSG EBee ELan ETho GMac LBuc LOck LRHS LSRN MAsh MBlu MGos MLLN MRav MSwo NBea NHol SCoo SLim SPer SPoG SRkn SWCr WGwG
§	'Princess of Wales' (EL)	LSRN NLar NSti WFar
	'Prins Hendrik' (EL)	WGor
	'Prinsesse Alexandra'^{PBR}	EBee ETho LPio
	'Propertius' (A)	CWGN EBee ETho LRHS MGos NHaw SMDP
	'Proteus' (EL)	CLng CSPN ELan ELon EPfP ETho LPio LRHS MAsh MGos NBea SCoo SDix SLim SWCr
	'Pruinina'	see *C.* 'Plum Beauty'
	psilandra CWJ 12377	WCru
	'Purple Haze' (Vt)	CRHN NHaw
	'Purple Princess' (H)	CMac MAvo
	'Purple Rain' (A)	CTri LPio LRHS NHol
	'Purple Spider' (A/d)	CMac CSPN EBee ETho MBlu NHaw NHol NLar SCoo SPoG
	'Purpurea Plena Elegans' (Vt/d) Υ^{H4}	Widely available
	'Queen of Holland'^{PBR}	CWGN
	'Radar Love' (Ta)	LLHF NLar
	'Radost' (EL)	LPio
	'Ragamuffin' (EL/d)	MGos
	'Rahvarinne' (LL)	ETho LPio
	'Ramona' (LL)	CLng LRHS LSRN MAsh NHaw
	Rebecca = 'Evipo016'	EPfP LBuc LRHS LSqu MAsh SCoo SLon SPer SPoG SWCr
	recta	CSPN ECtt GKir LPio MNrw MWhi NBea NLar WTin
§	- 'Lime Close' (F)	LPio
	- 'Lime Close' seedlings **new**	CAby
I	- 'Peveril' (F)	NBea
	- 'Purpurea' (F)	CBcs CBot CSpe EBee EHoe ELan EPfP EWTr LHop LOck LPio LRHS MAsh MAvo MWhi NBPC NBea NBir NSti SDix SPer SWCr WCom WCot WHil WHoo WTin
§	- subsp. ***recta*** var. ***lasiosepala***	CSPN
	- Serious Black	see *C. recta* 'Lime Close'
	- 'Velvet Night' (F)	CMHG CSpe CWGN ECtt ETho MGos MLLN NBea NEgg NLar SMDP WCot
	'Red Ballon' (Ta)	SMDP
§	'Red Beetroot Beauty' (A)	CSPN
	'Red Cooler'	see *C.* 'Crimson King'
	'Red Pearl' (EL)	ETho LPio MGos SLim
§	***rehderiana*** Υ^{H4}	CBot CDul CFir CRHN CSPN CSam CTri EBee ELan EPfP ETho GAuc LRHS MBlu MRav MWhi NBea NBir NHol NSti SDix SPer WBVN WGwG WPGP WSHC
	- BWJ 7700	WCru
	'Remembrance' (LL)	ETho LPio LSRN
	repens Finet & Gagn.	see *C. montana* var. *wilsonii*
	'Rhapsody' ambig.	CLng EPfP ETho LRHS MAsh MGos SCoo SLim SPoG SWCr WFar
I	'Rhapsody' B. Fretwell (EL)	CSPN LPio LSRN NHaw
	'Richard Pennell' (EL) Υ^{H4}	EBee ETho LOck LPio LRHS MAsh NBea SDix SLim SWCr
	'Rising Star' **new**	LRHS NHaw
	'Roko-Kolla' (LL)	CSPN ETho LPio
	'Romantika' (LL)	CSPN EBee ELan ELon ETho LPio LRHS NBea NHaw SCoo SLim SPoG
	'Roogoja' (LL)	LPio
	'Rooguchi' (I)	CWGN EBee ETho GMac LPio LRHS MAsh NBea SMDP SPoG SWCr
	'Rosa Königskind' (EL)	ETho LPio
	'Rose Supreme' (EL)	ETho LPio
I	'Rosea' (I) Υ^{H4}	CSPN EAEE EBee EPfP ETho LHop LOck LRHS LSRN MCot MTho NBea NSti SPoG
	'Rosea' (Vt)	LPio
	Rosebud = 'Robud'^{PBR} (M/d)	CLng NLar NPer SMDP
	Rosemoor = 'Evipo002'^{PBR}	CLng CWCL CWGN EPfP ETho IBal LPio LRHS LSqu MAsh MBri SCoo SLim SWCr
	'Rosy O'Grady' (A) Υ^{H4}	CWCL EBee ELan ETho MBri MGos NHol NLar NSti
	'Rosy Pagoda' (A)	EBee ELan EPfP LOck MBri NBea NBir NHaw NLar SLim
	'Rouge Cardinal' (LL)	CChe CMac CRHN CSPN CWSG EBee ECtt ELan EPfP ETho IBal LOck LPio LRHS LSRN MAsh MBri MCot MGos NBea NEgg SDix SLim SPer SPet SPoG SRms SWCr WBVN WFar
	'Royal Velours' (Vt) Υ^{H4}	CDoC CElw CRHN CSPN CTri EBee ELan EPfP ETho GKir LOck LPio LRHS LSRN MAsh MGos NBea NHol NSti SCoo SDix SLim SPer SWCr
	Royal Velvet = 'Evifour'^{PBR} (EL)	CLng CSPN CWCL EPfP ETho IBal LPio LRHS LSRN MAsh MBri SCoo SLim SWCr
	'Royalty' (EL) Υ^{H4}	CLng CSPN ELan EPfP IBal LOck LPio LRHS LSRN MAsh NBir SCoo SLim SPer SPoG SWCr
	'Rubens Superba'	see *C. montana* 'Rubens Superba'
	'Rubra' (Vt)	MBlu
	'Ruby' (A)	CMHG CSPN CWSG EBee EPfP ETho LOck LRHS LSRN MGos NBea NHol NSti SCoo SLim SPer SPoG SRms
	'Ruby Glow' (EL)	CLng EPfP LPio LRHS LSRN MAsh SCoo SWCr
	'Rüütel' (EL)	ETho LOck LPio LRHS MGos NBea NHaw SCoo SLim SMDP SPoG
	'Saalomon' (LL)	LPio
	'Sakala' (EL)	LPio
§	'Sakurahime' (EL)	LPio
	'Sally Cadge' (EL)	LPio NHaw
	'Samantha Denny' (EL)	CSPN LPio NBea NHaw
	'Sander' (H)	CSPN ETho SMDP
	'Sandra Denny' (EL)	ETho
	'Sano-no-murasaki' (EL)	LPio
	Saphyra Indigo = 'Cleminov 51'^{PBR}	CLng
	'Satsukibare' (EL)	LPio MGos
	'Saturn' (EL)	LPio
	Savannah = 'Evipo015'^{PBR} (Vt)	CLng LRHS MAsh SLim SWCr
	'Scartho Gem' (EL)	CLng LPio LRHS MAsh SCoo
	'Sealand Gem' (EL)	LPio NBea NHaw
	'Serenata' (EL)	LPio
	serratifolia	ETho GLog MDKP MWhi SDix SWal WBVN WFar
	- B&SWJ 8458 from Korea	WCru
	'Sheila Thacker' (EL)	ETho
	'Shin-shigyoku' (EL)	CWGN LPio MGos
	'Shirayukihime' (LL)	CSPN LPio
§	'Shiva' (A)	MBri
	'Sho-un' (EL)	EBee LPio
	'Sialia' (A/d)	MGos
§	***sibirica***	EPfP LPio NBea

	'Signe' (EL)	LPio
	'Signe' (Vt)	see *C.* 'Kasmu'
	'Silmakivi' (EL)	LPio
	'Silver Moon' (EL)	CLng CSPN ETho LOck LPio LRHS NBea NLar SCoo
	'Simplicity' (A)	CSPN MBri
	simsii Small	see *C. pitcheri*
	simsii Sweet	see *C. crispa*
	'Sinee Plamia' (LL)	LPio NHaw
§	'Sinii Dozhd' (I)	CSPN LPio
	'Sir Garnet Wolseley' (EL)	LRHS SDix
	'Sir Trevor Lawrence' (T)	CSPN EBee ETho LRHS MAsh NBea NHaw NHol NSti SPer WFar
	'Sizaia Ptitsa' (I)	ETho LPio
	'Snow Queen' (EL)	CFir CLng CSPN EBee ELon EPfP ETho LOck LPio LRHS MAsh MBri MGos NBea SLim SPet SRms SWCr
	'Snowbells'	CBcs EGxp NPri
	'Snowbird' (A/d)	CSPN EPfP LPio LRHS MAsh NHaw NHol SPoG SWCr
	'Snowdrift'	see *C. armandii* 'Snowdrift'
§	'Södertälje' (Vt)	CRHN ETho LRHS NBea SCoo SPoG WFar
	'Solidarność' (EL)	ETho LRHS
	songarica	NHol
	'Sonnette'	CWGN
	'Souvenir de J.L. Delbard' (EL)	LPio
§	'Souvenir du Capitaine Thuilleaux' (EL)	GKir LPio MGos NBea
	'Special Occasion' (EL)	CLng CSPN CWGN EBee ETho LPio LRHS LSRN MAsh NBea NHaw NLar NPri SCoo SPoG SWCr WFar
§	***spooneri***	CTri CWSG ECtt EPfP GQui MGan NHol SCoo SLim SRms WFoF
	'Sputnik' (I)	CSPN CWGN NHaw
	'Stanislaus' (H)	LPio SMDP
	stans	CElw CPLG CPou EPfP IFro LPio LRHS MAsh NBea NLar NWCA SMDP SWCr
	- B&SWJ 5073	WCru
	- B&SWJ 6345	WCru
§	'Star'[PBR] (M/d)	CSPN CWGN EBee EPfP ETho LOck LRHS MAsh MGos MRav MSwo NHol NLar SLim SRms SWCr WFar
	'Star of India' (LL)	CElw CLng CRHN EBee EPfP ETho LPio LRHS MAsh MGos MRav NBea SCoo SPer SPoG SWCr WFar
	Star River = 'Zostarri' **new**	CWGN
	'Starfish' (EL)	LPio MGos NHaw
	'Starlight' (M)	ELon LRHS NBea SLim
	'Stasik' (LL)	LPio NHaw
	'Stephanie' (A)	LPio
	Still Waters = 'Zostiwa'	CWGN ETho
	Sugar Candy = 'Evione'[PBR] (EL)	CLng IBal LRHS MAsh MBri SCoo SLim SPoG
	Summer Dream = 'Zosumdre' **new**	CWGN
	Summer Snow	see *C.* 'Paul Farges'
	'Sundance'	CSPN SMDP
	'Sunrise'[PBR] (M/d)	CSPN CWGN EBee ELon ETho LOck LRHS MSwo NHaw NLar SLim WFar
	'Sunset' (EL) ♀H4	CLng ELon LPio LRHS LSRN MAsh MBri NBea NLar SCoo SLim SPoG SWCr WFar
	'Suruga' (EL)	LPio
	'Susan Allsop' (EL)	LPio
	'Swedish Bells' (I)	ETho
	'Sylvia Denny' (EL)	CWSG EBee ELan EPfP ETho GKir MRav NBea SPet
	'Sympatia' (LL)	NHaw
	'Syrena' (LL)	NBea NHaw
	szuyuanensis B&SWJ 6791	WCru
	- CWJ 12455	WCru
	'Tae' (EL) **new**	ETho
	'Tage Lundell' (A)	CLng CSPN EBee EPfP LRHS MGos NBea SMDP
	'Tamula'	LPio
	'Tango' (Vt)	CRHN EBee LPio NBea NHaw
§	***tangutica***	Widely available
	- subsp. ***obtusiuscula*** 'Gravetye Variety' (Ta)	LPio
	'Tapestry' (I)	NHaw SMDP
	'Tartu' (EL)	CSPN ETho
	tashiroi purple-flowered B&SWJ 7005	WCru
	- 'Yellow Peril'	WCru
	'Teksa' (LL)	LPio
	'Tentel' (LL)	LPio
§	***terniflora***	CBcs EBee EPfP ETho NHaw NSti SKHP
	- B&SWJ 5751	WCru
	'Teshio' (EL)	CSPN EBee NHaw SPoG
	texensis	CBcs CElw WSHC
	- 'The Princess of Wales'	see *C.* 'Princess Diana'
	'The Bride' (EL)	CSPN CWGN ETho LPio LRHS LSRN MGos NBea NHaw
	'The First Lady' (EL)	CSPN ETho LPio
	'The President' (EL) ♀H4	Widely available
	'The Princess of Wales' (EL)	see *C.* 'Princess of Wales' (EL)
	'The Princess of Wales' (T)	see *C.* 'Princess Diana' (T)
	'The Vagabond' (EL)	CSPN CWSG ELan ELon ETho LOck LRHS LSRN MGos NBea NHaw NLar SCoo SLim SPet
	Thumbelina = 'Evipo030'[PBR]	LRHS
	thunbergii misapplied	see *C. terniflora*
	'Thyrislund' (EL)	CSPN LPio
	'Tibetan Mix' (Ta)	CSPN SMDP
	tibetana	NHaw
	- 'Black Tibet'	SMDP
§	- subsp. ***vernayi***	CMHG GKir
	- - var. ***laciniifolia***	NHol
§	- - var. ***vernayi*** 'Orange Peel' LS&E 13342	CBcs CDoC ETho GKir MRav NHol SEND SGar SLim WFar WSpi
	Timpany NZ hybrids (Fo)	ITim
	'Tinkerbell'	see *C.* 'Shiva'
	'Toki' (EL)	CWGN EBee
	tongluensis GWJ 9358	WCru
	- HWJK 2368	WCru
	'Treasure Trove' (Ta)	CSPN NHol SMDP
	'Triibu' (LL)	LPio
§	× ***triternata*** 'Rubromarginata' ♀H4	CDoC CFir CMac CRHN CSPN CSam CWGN EBee ELan ELon EPfP ETho GMac LOck LRHS LSRN MAsh MBri MGos MRav NBea NHol NSti SDix SLim SPer SPoG SRkn SWCr
	'Tsuzuki' (EL)	CSPN EBee LPio
§	***tubulosa***	CSPN EBee ETho MGos NHol SMDP
§	- Alan Bloom = 'Alblo'[PBR] (H)	GKir LRHS
	- 'Wyevale' (H) ♀H4	CMac CSPN EAEE ELan EPfP ETho GGar LHop LRHS MAvo MCot MRav NHol SAga SCoo SDix SMDP WCot WEas
	'Tuchka' (EL)	LPio
	'Twilight' (EL)	CLng CSPN EPfP LPio LRHS MAsh WFar

	uncinata B&SWJ 1893	WCru
	– B&SWJ 11368	WCru
§	***urophylla*** 'Winter Beauty'	CDoC CSam ETho MGos MRav SPoG
	urticifolia	GMac
	– B&SWJ 8651	WCru
	– B&SWJ 8852	WCru
	'Valge Daam' (LL)	CWGN ETho LPio NHaw
	'Vanessa' (LL)	CRHN LPio
	'Vanilla Cream' (Fo)	ECou
	'Vanso'^{PBR}	see *C.* 'Blue Light'
	× ***vedrariensis*** 'Hidcote' (M)	NHaw SMDP
§	***veitchiana***	NHaw
	'Venosa Violacea' (Vt) $\mathbb{Y}^{H4}$	CElw CMac CRHN CSPN CSam EBee ELan ELon EPfP EShb ETho LOck LPio LRHS LSRN MAsh MRav NBea NHol NSti SCoo SDix SPer SPoG SRms SWCr WFar
	'Vera' (M)	CSPN EBee ECtt ETho LRHS LSRN SCoo SLim WFar
	vernayi	see *C. tibetana* subsp. *vernayi*
	'Veronica's Choice' (EL)	CRHN CSPN ELan EPfP LOck LPio MGos MRav NBea NHaw SPet
	Versailles = 'Evipo025'^{PBR} (EL)	LRHS MAsh
§	Vesuvius = 'Evipo032'^{PBR}	CLng EPfP LRHS LSqu MAsh SCoo SLon SWCr
	Victor Hugo = 'Evipo007'^{PBR}	CLng EPfP ETho IBal LBuc LPio LRHS MAsh NLar NPri SCoo SWCr
N	'Victoria' (LL) $\mathbb{Y}^{H4}$	CRHN CSPN ETho LPio LRHS LSRN MAsh MGos MRav NBea NHaw SCoo SDix SPoG SWCr
	Viennetta = 'Evipo006'^{PBR}	EPfP ETho LBuc LRHS LSqu MAsh SCoo SLon SPer SPoG SWCr
	'Vilhelmīne'	CWGN LPio
	'Ville de Lyon' (LL)	CBcs CMac CRHN CSPN CWCL EBee ELan EPfP GKir LPio LRHS LSRN MAsh MBri MGan MGos NBea NEgg SDix SLim SPer SPet SPoG SVic SWCr WFar
	'Vince Denny' (Ta)	NHaw SMDP
	Vino = 'Poulvo'^{PBR} (EL)	CLng IBal LRHS MAsh NHaw SCoo SLim SPoG
I	'Viola' (LL)	CSPN CWGN EBee ELon ETho LPio LRHS MBri MGos NBea NHaw SLim WFar
	'Violet Charm' (EL)	CWSG
	'Violet Elizabeth' (EL)	LPio MRav
	'Violet Purple' (A)	MGos NHaw
	'Violetta' (EL)	LPio
	viorna	NHaw WSHC
	virginiana misapplied	see *C. vitalba*
	virginiana Hook.	see *C. ligusticifolia*
	virginiana L.	CElw
§	***vitalba***	CArn CRWN EBWF ECrN ETho NHaw WHer WSFF
	viticella $\mathbb{Y}^{H4}$	CElw CRHN CWib ETho MBri NBea NHaw SDix WSHC
§	– subsp. ***campaniflora***	CBot CMea CSPN EPla EShb ETho GCal NBea NHaw NWCA WCru
§	– 'Flore Pleno'	CRHN ELon EPfP ETho LOck LRHS LSRN MAsh NHaw SWCr WCot
	– 'Hågelby Pink'	CRHN CWGN LPio
	– 'Hågelby White'	CWGN ETho NHaw
	– 'Hanna' (Vt)	LPio LSRN NHaw
	– 'Mary Rose'	see *C. viticella* 'Flore Pleno'
	'Vivienne'	see *C.* 'Beth Currie'
	'Vivienne Lawson' (LL)	LPio
	'Voluceau' (Vt)	CLng CPou CRHN ELan GKir LRHS LSRN MAsh MGos MRav NBea SPer SRms SWCr
	'Vostok' (LL)	LPio MGos
	'Vyvyan Pennell' (EL)	CBcs CMac CSPN CTri EBee ECtt ELan EPfP ETho GKir LPio LRHS LSRN MAsh MBri MGan MGos MSwo NBea NEgg SLim SPer SPet SPoG SWCr WFar
	'W.E. Gladstone' (EL)	CRHN ETho GKir LRHS NBea SDix
	Wada's Primrose	see *C. patens* 'Manshuu Ki'
	'Walenburg' (Vt)	CRHN CWGN ETho NBea NHaw SLon
	'Walter Pennell' (EL)	CBcs CLng CWSG EBee ETho IBal LPio LRHS MAsh NBea SCoo SLim SWCr WGor
	'Warsaw' (Ta)	SWCr
	'Warszawska Nike' (EL) $\mathbb{Y}^{H4}$	CLng CMac CRHN EBee ELan EPfP ETho LOck LPio LRHS MAsh MBri MGos NBea SCoo SPer SPet SPoG
	'Warwickshire Rose' (M)	CLng CRHN CSPN CTri CWGN CWSG ECtt ETho EWTr GKir LOck LRHS LSRN MAsh MGos MWat NBea NHaw NHol SLim SPoG SWCr WFar
	'Waterperry Star' (Ta)	MWat
	'Wedding Day' (EL)	ETho LSRN NLar
	'Wee Willie Winkie' (M)	CWGN LRHS SCoo
	'Westerplatte' (EL)	CLng CRHN CSPN CWGN EPfP ETho LOck LPio LRHS MAsh MGos NBea NHaw SMDP SPoG SWCr WFar
	'Whirligig' (A)	CSPN
§	'White Columbine' (A) $\mathbb{Y}^{H4}$	EBee EPfP ETho LOck LPio LRHS MGos NBea NSti SDix SLim SPet
	'White Lady' (A/d)	NHaw
	'White Magic' (Vt)	CRHN CWGN ETho MGos
§	'White Moth' (A/d)	CSPN CWSG EBee ELan ETho LRHS LSRN MGos MRav NHaw NHol SPer SPoG SRms
	'White Satin' **new**	LRHS MAsh
	'White Swan' (A/d)	CSPN EPfP MBri MGos NHol NPri NSti SCoo WFoF
	'White Tokyo' (A/d)	MGos
	'White Wings' (A/d)	EBee SPet
	'Wilhelmina Tull' (EL)	CSPN LPio
	'Will Goodwin' (EL) $\mathbb{Y}^{H4}$	CBcs CLng CMac CWCL EBee ELan EPfP ETho LPio LRHS MAsh MBri NBea SLim SRms SWCr
	'William Kennett' (EL)	CWSG EBee ELan EPfP ETho LPio LTen MBri MGan MGos SDix SVic
	'Willy' (A)	CBcs CSPN EBee ECtt ELan EPfP ETho GKir GQui LOck LRHS MAsh MBri MGos MSwo NBea NHol NSti SDix SLim SPer SPet SPoG SWCr
	Wisley = 'Evipo001'^{PBR}	CBcs CLng EPfP IBal LPio LRHS MAsh MBri NLar SLim SLon SPer SWCr
	'Xerxes' misapplied	see *C.* 'Elsa Späth'
	'Yatsuhashi'	CFir LRHS NBea
	'Yellow Queen' Holland	see *C. patens* 'Manshuu Ki'
	'Yellow Queen' Lundell/Treasures	see *C.* 'Moonlight'
§	'Yukikomachi' (EL)	CSPN ETho NBea NHaw
	'Yvette Houry' (EL)	NHaw NLar
	'Yvonne Hay' **new**	SMDP

Clematopsis see *Clematis*

Clementsia see *Rhodiola*

Cleome (*Capparaceae*)

hassleriana 'Helen Campbell' $\mathbb{Y}^{H3}$ **new**	CFox CSpe
'Senorita Rosalita'	GBin SVil

Clerodendrum (*Verbenaceae*)

bungei	Widely available
- 'Herfstleu'	MGos
- 'Pink Diamond' (v)	CCCN CDoC CDul CWGN EBee ELon EPfP EWes LAst LBuc LHop LRHS LSRN MGos MPkF NLar NPri NSti SBfd SEND SPer SPoG WCot WFar
§ ***chinense*** var. ***chinense*** (d) ♀H1	CCCN ERea
- 'Pleniflorum'	see *C. chinense* var. *chinense*
fragrans var. ***pleniflorum***	see *C. chinense* var. *chinense*
* ***mutabile*** B&SWJ 6651	WCru
myricoides 'Ugandense' ♀H1	CCCN CHll CRHN CSpe CTsd ELan ERea LPio SAga SMrm SOWG WSFF
philippinum	see *C. chinense* var. *chinense*
quadriloculare	CCCN
aff. ***serratum*** DJHV 06074	WCru
× ***speciosum***	ERea SOWG
splendens ♀H1	SOWG
aff. ***subscaposum*** WWJ 11735	WCru
thomsoniae ♀H1	ELan ERea MBri SOWG WSFF
trichotomum	Widely available
- 'Carnival' (v)	CAbP CBcs CCCN CDul CMac CPLG CPMA EBee ELan ELon EPfP EWes IArd LRHS MAsh MBri MCCP NLar SBfd SKHP SLim SPer SPoG WBrE WPat
- var. ***fargesii*** ♀H4	Widely available
- 'Purple Blaze' **new**	EPfP
- 'Purple Haze'	CPMA MBri NLar
- 'Shiro' **new**	WCru
wallichii	CSpe EShb SOWG

Clethra ✿ (*Clethraceae*)

acuminata	EPfP
alnifolia	CBcs CDul CEnd CMCN CMHG CPLG CTrC EBee EPfP MMuc MPkF SRms WCFE WDin WFar
- 'Anne Bidwell'	MBri NLar
- 'Creel's Calico' (v)	NLar
- 'Fern Valley Pink'	CCCN CMac CSBt ELon LLHF LRHS MDun NLar
- 'Hokie Pink'	MBri NLar
- 'Hummingbird'	CCCN CDoC CEnd CMac CPLG CWib CWit EBee ELan EPfP GGGa GKir IVic LRHS MAsh MBlu MBri MGos MWat NLar NPCo SLim SPoG SSpi SWvt WBVN WFar WSHC
- 'Paniculata' ♀H4	CDoC EBee EPfP LRHS MMuc SPoG SPur WBor WFar
- 'Pink Spire'	CBcs CDoC CDul CPLG EBee ECrN EPfP GGGa MMHG MMuc MRav NEgg NLar NPal SCoo WDin WFar
- 'Rosea'	CBot CTri GQui MGos MMHG MPkF SPer WFar
- 'Ruby Spice'	Widely available
- 'September Beauty'	MBri NLar
- 'Sixteen Candles'	GGGa NLar
arborea	CBcs CHEx CMHG CTrC SSpi
barbinervis ♀H4	CBcs CDoC CMCN CPLG EBee EPfP GAuc IVic LRHS MBlu MBri NLar SPer SSpi WFar WSHC
- B&SWJ 11562	WCru
delavayi Franch.	CBcs CCCN CDoC EBee EPfP EWes GGGa GQui NLar SKHP SSpi
- SBEC 1513	CPLG
- Stone's hardy strain **new**	SKHP
fargesii	CPLG EBee EPfP MBri MGos NLar WBVN
monostachya	CPLG
pringlei	WSHC
tomentosa 'Cottondale'	NLar

Cleyera (*Theaceae*)

fortunei	see *C. japonica* 'Fortunei'
- 'Variegata'	see *C. japonica* 'Fortunei'
§ ***japonica*** 'Fortunei' (v)	CCCN CMac CWib GKir IArd IDee LRHS SSta WFar
- var. ***japonica***	CGHE WPGP
- 'Tricolor' (v)	CBcs IDee
- var. ***wallichii***	EBee WPGP

Clianthus (*Papilionaceae*)

maximus	ECou
§ ***puniceus*** ♀H2	CAbb CDoy CHEx CHll CMHG CPLG CPne CPom CSBt CSpe CStu CTsd CWCL CWib CWit EBee ECou EPfP GGar IVic LRHS SChF SEND SOWG SPer SPlb SPoG WCru WPGP WSHC
§ - 'Albus' ♀H2	CBcs CBot CHEx CHGN CHll CPLG CSpe CTsd CWib CWit EBee EPfP IDee LRHS SOWG SPer SPoG WPGP
- 'Flamingo'	see *C. puniceus* 'Roseus'
- 'Kaka King'	CBcs EWes
- 'Red Admiral'	see *C. puniceus*
- 'Red Cardinal'	see *C. puniceus*
- 'Red Kakatoo'	EGxp
§ - 'Roseus'	CBcs CPLG CSpe SPer SPoG WCot WPGP
- 'White Heron'	see *C. puniceus* 'Albus'

Clinopodium (*Lamiaceae*)

ascendens	see *Calamintha ascendens*
calamintha	see *Calamintha nepeta*
grandiflorum	see *Calamintha grandiflora*
§ ***vulgare***	CArn CRWN EBWF EBee GBar MHer MNHC NGHP NMir NSco SGar SIde WDyG WFoF WMoo WOut WPtf

Clintonia (*Convallariaceae*)

andrewsiana	CLAP EBee ECho EHrv EWes GGGa GGar WCot WCru
udensis	WCru
- HWJK 2339 from Nepal	WCru
umbellulata	CLAP GCal WCru
uniflora	CLAP ECho EHrv EWes GGar WCru

Clivia ✿ (*Amaryllidaceae*)

caulescens	ERea WCot
× ***cyrtanthiflora***	ERea
gardenii	ERea WCot
gardenii × ***miniata***	WCot
miniata ♀H1	CBcs CBgR CTca CTsd ECho ERea MMuc SMrm SRms WCot
- 'Aurea' ♀H1	CSpe
- var. ***citrina*** ♀H1	CFwr CTca ECho LAma WCot
- - 'Butterball'	ERea
- - 'New Dawn'	ERea
- 'Citrina Spider'	CFwr
- 'Daruma'	WCot
- hybrids	NPal SEND
- 'Orange Spider'	CFwr
- pastel shades	CFwr
- 'Striata' (v)	CFwr ERea
- 'Vico Yellow'	ERea
- 'Viscy Yellow'	CTsd

- 'Wide Leaf Monk'	WCot
nobilis 𝒀^{H1}	ERea WCot
'San Marcus Yellow' ×'Solomone Yellow'	WCot
'Solomone Yellow'	ERea

Clusia (*Clusiaceae*)

rosea	CCCN

Clypeola (*Brassicaceae*)

jonthlaspi	WCot

Clytostoma (*Bignoniaceae*)

§ ***calystegioides***	CHll CRHN ERea EShb

Cneorum (*Cneoraceae*)

tricoccon	SKHP WSHC

Cnicus (*Asteraceae*)

§ ***benedictus***	CArn SIde

Cnidium (*Apiaceae*)

officinale	GPoy

Coaxana (*Apiaceae*)

purpurea B&SWJ 9028	WCru

Cobaea (*Cobaeaceae*)

lutea B&SWJ 9142A	WCru
pringlei	WPGP WSHC
- CD&R 1323	WCot
scandens 𝒀^{H3}	CCCN CDTJ CFox CSpe EBee ELan EShb EWld IFoB SBfd SGar SPer
- f. ***alba*** 𝒀^{H3}	CFox CSpe SPer

cobnut see *Corylus avellana*

Cocculus (*Menispermaceae*)

laurifolius new	EUJe
§ ***orbiculatus***	CPLG
- B&SWJ 535	WCru
trilobus	see *C. orbiculatus*

Cochlearia (*Brassicaceae*)

armoracia	see *Armoracia rusticana*
officinalis	CArn EBWF ELau MHer WHer

Cocos (*Arecaceae*)

plumosa	see *Syagrus romanzoffiana*
weddelliana	see *Lytocaryum weddellianum*

Codonanthe (*Gesneriaceae*)

gracilis	WDib
'Paula'	WDib

× *Codonatanthus* (*Gesneriaceae*)

'Golden Tambourine'	WDib
'Sunset'	WDib
'Tambourine'	WDib

Codonopsis ✿ (*Campanulaceae*)

HWJK 2105 from Nepal	WCru
SDR 4718	GKev
SDR 5965	GKev
from Chollipo, Korea	EWld
affinis HWJCM 70	WCru
- HWJK 2151	WCru
benthamii GWJ 9352	WCru
bhutanica	NEgg SPhx
bulleyana	GKir IGor
cardiophylla	EWld GCal
celebica HWJ 665	WCru
clematidea	CSpe EBee ECha ECho ECtt EPfP EWld GCal GKev LRHS MCCP MTho MWhi NChi NEgg NSum SAga SBfd SGSe SPhx SPlb SRms SWvt WKif WSpi WWEG
- 'Lilac Eyes'	MCCP SGSe
convolvulacea misapplied	see *C. grey-wilsonii*
convolvulacea Kurz J&JA 4.220.705	NWCA
- 'Alba'	see *C. grey-wilsonii* 'Himal Snow'
- Forrest's form	see *C. forrestii* Diels
- var. ***hirsuta*** Kurz	CStu IGor ITim MTho NSla
- - B&SWJ 7812	WCru
'Dangshen'	see *C. pilosula*
dicentrifolia HWJCM 267	WCru
forrestii misapplied	see *C. grey-wilsonii*
§ ***forrestii*** Diels	ECho GKev GKir NHar
- BWJ 7776	WCru
- BWJ 7847	WCru
§ ***grey-wilsonii*** 𝒀^{H4}	CAby EBee ECho EWld GEdr IGor ITim WFar WIvy
- B&SWJ 7532	WCru
§ - 'Himal Snow'	CAby ECho EWld GEdr MDKP NCGa
inflata GWJ 9442 new	WCru
javanica B&SWJ 8145	WCru
kawakamii B&SWJ 1592	WCru
- RWJ 10007	WCru
§ ***lanceolata***	CAby EWld IGor SGSe
- B&SWJ 562	WCru
lancifolia B&SWJ 3835	WCru
meleagris Diels	IGor
mollis	ECho NLar NSum WFar WWEG
nepalensis Grey-Wilson	see *C. grey-wilsonii*
obtusa	GKir
ovata	CBot IGor MTho NBro SPhx SRms
§ ***pilosula***	EBee EWld GKev GPoy IGor MTho SGSe SPhx
- BWJ 7910	WCru
§ ***rotundifolia*** var. ***angustifolia***	EBee EWld GKev IGor MDKP WCru
- var. ***grandiflora***	EBee EWld GKev
silvestris	see *C. pilosula*
subsimplex BWJ 7502	WCru
tangshen misapplied	see *C. rotundifolia* var. *angustifolia*
tangshen Oliv.	CArn EBee GKev GKir MTho
thalictrifolia CC 5491	ITim
- MECC 93	WCru
ussuriensis	see *C. lanceolata*
vinciflora	CPBP CPne ECho GEdr GKev IGor WIvy
viridiflora	WCru
viridis HWJK 2435	WCru

Coffea (*Rubiaceae*)

arabica	CCCN

coffee see *Coffea*

Colchicum ✿ (*Colchicaceae*)

agrippinum 𝒀^{H4}	CAvo CFee CTca EBla ECha ECho EPot GGar GKev MRav NBir NMen NRya NSla WHoo WTin WWst
'Antares'	ECha MBri NBir
atropurpureum	ECho EPot LAma
- Drake's form	ECho
'Attlee'	LAma
'Autumn Herald'	ECho GKev LAma LRHS
N 'Autumn Queen'	CTca ECho EPot GKev LAma LRHS
§ ***autumnale***	CArn CAvo CFee EBrs ECho EPot GAuc GKir GPoy ITim LAma LRHS NMen NRya SDeJ WFar WShi

*	- 'Albopilosum'	NBir
	- 'Alboplenum'	CTca EBrs ECho EPot ERCP LAma LRHS WTin WWst
	- 'Album'	CAvo CTca ECho EPot ERCP GAbr GGar LAma LRHS NBir SPer WGwG WHoo WShi WTin
	- 'Atropurpureum'	ECho
	- 'Drama Bunch'	WWst
	- var. ***major*** hort.	see *C. byzantinum* Ker Gawl.
	- var. ***minor*** hort.	see *C. autumnale*
§	- 'Nancy Lindsay' $\mathbb{Y}^{H4}$	EBla ECho EPot LRHS MBri SCnR WCot WShi
	- 'Pannonicum'	see *C. autumnale* 'Nancy Lindsay'
§	- 'Pleniflorum' (d)	ECho EPot LAma MMHG
*	- ***roseum***	ECho
	- 'Roseum Plenum'	see *C. autumnale* 'Pleniflorum'
	baytopiorum	ECho GAuc
	- from Turkey	ECho
§	***bivonae***	ECho EPot
	- HOA 9139	WWst
	- 'Apollo'	ECho GKev
	Blom's hybrid	WTin
§	***boissieri***	ECho EPot WWst
	bornmuelleri misapplied	see *C. speciosum* var. *bornmuelleri* hort.
	bornmuelleri Freyn	ECho EPot GAuc GKev LAma
	bowlesianum	see *C. bivonae*
§	***byzantinum*** Ker Gawl. $\mathbb{Y}^{H4}$	EPot GKev LAma LRHS NBir SDeJ WTin
	- ***album***	see *C. byzantinum* 'Innocence'
§	- 'Innocence'	EBla ECho EPot
	cilicicum	ECho EPot LAma WHoo
	- Bowles's form	ECho
	- 'Purpureum'	CTca ECho GKev LAma LRHS WWst
	'Conquest'	see *C.* 'Glory of Heemstede'
	corsicum	ECho NMen WThu
	cupanii	CPBP ECho GKev WWst
	- var. ***pulverulentum***	ECho
	davisii	ECho WWst
	'Dick Trotter'	ECho EPot
	'Disraeli'	CTca ECho GKev
	falcifolium	ECho WWst
§	***giganteum***	ECho EPot LAma LRHS
§	'Glory of Heemstede'	ECho GKev
	graecum	ECho WWst
	'Harlekijn'	CTca ECho ERCP
	hierosolymitanum	WWst
	hungaricum	CFee ECho WWst
	- f. ***albiflorum***	ECho EPot WWst
	- 'Valentine' new	WWst
	- 'Velebit Star' new	ECho WWst
	illyricum	see *C. giganteum*
	'Jochem Hof'	ECho GKev LRHS
	'Jolanthe'	WWst
	kesselringii	ECho WWst
	kotschyi	EPot WWst
	laetum misapplied	see *C. parnassicum*
	laetum Stev.	EPot
	'Lilac Bedder'	ECho EPot GKev
	'Lilac Wonder'	ECho EPfP GKev LAma MRav SDeJ SEND SPer WCot WFar
	lusitanum	LAma
	luteum	ECho WWst
	macrophyllum	ECho LAma WWst
	micranthum	ECho
	minutum	ECho
	munzurense	WWst
	'Oktoberfest'	EPot
	parlatoris	ECho WWst
§	***parnassicum***	CPBP ECha ECho WWst
	- CH 835	WWst
	- HOA 8942	WWst
	peloponnesiacum	WWst
	'Pink Goblet' $\mathbb{Y}^{H4}$	LAma
	'Poseidon'	ECho
	procurrens	see *C. boissieri*
	pusillum	WWst
	'Rosy Dawn' $\mathbb{Y}^{H4}$	CTca EBrs ECha ECho GGar LRHS NRya
	sfikasianum	ECho WWst
	sibthorpii	see *C. bivonae*
	speciosum $\mathbb{Y}^{H4}$	CAvo EBrs ECho EPot GKir LAma LRHS NBir
	- 'Album' $\mathbb{Y}^{H4}$	CAvo CFee EBla EBrs ECha ECho EPfP EPot GKev LAma LRHS MBri NBir SDeJ
	- 'Atrorubens'	ECha ECho MBri
I	- var. ***bornmuelleri*** hort.	ECho WWst
	- var. ***illyricum*** hort.	see *C. giganteum*
	- 'Maximum'	MBri
	- 'Ordu'	ECho
	- 'Rubrum'	ECho
	szovitsii Fisch. & B. Mey.	ECho
	- 'Snow White' new	WWst
	- 'Tivi'	ECho WWst
	- white-flowered	ECho
	tenorei $\mathbb{Y}^{H4}$	ECho EPot GKev LAma LLHF NBir
	'The Giant'	CTca EBrs ECho EPot GKev LAma LRHS SDeJ
	triphyllum	ECho WWst
	troodi ambig.	ECho WWst
	variegatum	ECho LAma WWst
	'Violet Queen'	ECho EPot GAbr LAma
	'Waterlily' (d) $\mathbb{Y}^{H4}$	CAvo CTca EBla EBrs ECho ELan EPfP EPot ERCP GGar GKev ITim LAma LRHS NBir SDeJ SPhx WGwG WHoo
	'William Dykes'	EBla ECho
	'Zephyr'	ECho LAma

Coleonema (*Rutaceae*)

	album	CSpe
§	***pulchellum***	CCCN CHEx CSpe NSti
	pulchrum misapplied	see *C. pulchellum*
	'Sunset Gold'	CSpe CTrC CWit SPlb

Coleus see *Solenostemon*

Colignonia (*Nyctaginaceae*)

	ovalifolia B&SWJ 10644	WCru

Colletia (*Rhamnaceae*)

	armata	see *C. hystrix*
	cruciata	see *C. paradoxa*
§	***hystrix***	CBcs CMac CTri CTsd EBee GGar SAPC SArc SMad SOWG WBor WSHC
	- RCB RA S-3	WCot
	- 'Rosea'	CMac CTrC GCal SKHP
§	***paradoxa***	CBcs CCCN CWib ELan EPfP GCal LAst LPJP NLar SAPC SKHP SMad SPoG WHil
	paradoxa × ***spinosissima***	SMad

Collinsonia (*Lamiaceae*)

	canadensis	CArn ELan

Collomia (*Polemoniaceae*)

	grandiflora	WCot

Colobanthus (*Caryophyllaceae*)

§	***quitensis***	ECho

Colocasia (Araceae)

	affinis var. ***jeningsii***	CDTJ CFir EAmu
	antiquorum	see *C. esculenta*
§	***esculenta*** ♀H1	CBct CDTJ CFir CHEx EAmu EGxp EShb EUJe LPio MSKA SDix SPlb XBlo
	- 'Black Beauty'	EAmu
	- 'Black Magic'	Widely available
	- 'Black Marble'	EUJe
	- 'Black Ruffles'	CDTJ EUJe
	- burgundy-stemmed	CDTJ EUJe SBig
	- 'Chicago Harlequin'	CDTJ EAmu EUJe
	- 'Fontanesii'	CDTJ CHEx EAmu EUJe WCot
	- 'Hilo Beauty'	EAmu XBlo
	- 'Illustris'	CDTJ EUJe SBst SGar SUsu WClo WCot
	- 'Nancy's Revenge'	EAmu
	- 'Nigrescens'	EAmu
	- 'Pink China' **new**	EAmu
	- 'Ruffles'	EUJe
	- 'Tea Cup' **new**	EAmu EUJe
	fallax	CFir CHEx EAmu EUJe WPrP
	formosana B&SWJ 6909	WCru
	gaoligongensis **new**	CFir
	gigantea	CDTJ EAmu EUJe MSKA SBst
	'Himalayan Dragon' **new**	SKHP

Colquhounia (Lamiaceae)

	coccinea	CArn CHll CSam CTrC EShb MBlu MRav NLar SGar SLon SSpi WCom WSHC
	- Sch 2458	WPGP
§	- var. ***mollis*** B&SWJ 7222	WCru
	- var. ***vestita*** misapplied	see *C. coccinea* var. *mollis*
	- var. ***vestita*** ambig.	CBcs CTsd EBee EPfP GGar LRHS MMuc MWea SEND WBor

Columnea (Gesneriaceae)

	'Aladdin's Lamp'	WDib
	'Apollo'	WDib
	× ***banksii*** ♀H1	EOHP WDib
	'Bold Venture'	WDib
§	'Broget Stavanger' (v)	WDib
	'Chanticleer' ♀H1	WDib
I	'Firedragon'	WDib
	'Gavin Brown'	EOHP WDib
	gloriosa	EBak
	hirta ♀H1	WDib
	- 'Variegata'	see *C.* 'Light Prince'
	'Inferno'	WDib
	'Katsura'	WDib
§	'Light Prince' (v)	WDib
	'Merkur'	WDib
I	'Midnight Lantern'	WDib
	'Rising Sun'	WDib
	'Robin'	WDib
	schiedeana	EOHP WDib
	'Stavanger' ♀H1	WDib
	'Stavanger Variegated'	see *C.* 'Broget Stavanger'

Colutea (Papilionaceae)

	arborescens	CArn CBcs CMac CPLG CWib EBee ELan GKir MBlu MGos MMuc NMun NWea SEND SPer SPlb SPoG WDin
§	***buhsei***	SOWG
	× ***media***	CPom GKir MBlu SGar
	- 'Copper Beauty'	CBcs EBee EPPr GKir LRHS MBri MGos NLar SPer
	orientalis	CCCN
	persica misapplied	see *C. buhsei*

Comarum see *Potentilla*

Combretum (Combretaceae)

	fruticosum	CCCN

Commelina (Commelinaceae)

	coelestis	see *C. tuberosa* Coelestis Group
	dianthifolia	GCal LPio MTho NWCA SRms WPer
	- 'Electric Blue'	LRHS
	robusta	EBee LPio WCot
	tuberosa	ELan EPfP LPio WBrE
	- B&SWJ 10353	WCru
	- 'Alba'	ELan GCal LPio
	- 'Axminster Lilac'	WPer
§	- Coelestis Group	CPom CSpe EBee ECha ELon EPfP IGor LHop LRHS MCot SGar SRkn SRms WKif WSHC
	- - 'Hopleys Variegated' (v)	CBow
	- - 'Sleeping Beauty'	MSpe

Comptonia (Myricaceae)

	peregrina	WCru

Conandron (Gesneriaceae)

	ramondoides B&SWJ 8929	WCru
	- 'Akabana' **new**	GEdr

Conanthera (Tecophilaeaceae)

	bifolia	ECho
	campanulata	ECho

Conicosia (Aizoaceae)

	pugioniformis	EBee

Coniogramme (Adiantaceae)

	emeiensis	WCot
	intermedia	WRic

Conium (Apiaceae)

	maculatum	CArn

Conoclinium (Asteraceae)

§	***coelestinum***	EBee EWes GKir LHop MDKP NBre SMad WSFF
	dissectum	WSFF

Conopodium (Apiaceae)

	majus	CRWN EBWF WShi

Conostylis (Haemodoraceae)

	candicans	ECou

Conradina (Lamiaceae)

	verticillata	WPat

Consolida (Ranunculaceae)

§	***ajacis***	MNHC
	ambigua	see *C. ajacis*

Convallaria ✿ (Convallariaceae)

	japonica	see *Ophiopogon jaburan*
	keiskei	EBla EPPr GAuc WWEG
	majalis ♀H4	Widely available
	- 'Albostriata' (v)	Widely available
	- 'Berlin Giant'	EBla NBre NRya
	- 'Bordeaux'	CHid CPLG EBee ELon
	- 'Bridal Choice' **new**	EBee NLar
	- 'Dorien'	CBct CBre EBee EPPr WCom
	- 'Flore Pleno' (d)	EBee EHrv MTho SGSe WPnP WWEG

- 'Géant de Fortin'	CBct CFir CLAP CPLG CRow EBla ECho EPot GCal GEdr MMoz MRav NBir NBre NLar SBch SMad WCAu WCom WCot WFar
- 'Gerard Debureaux'	see *C. majalis* 'Green Tapestry'
§ - 'Green Tapestry' (v)	CBct CBow CLAP CRow MAvo
- 'Haldon Grange' (v)	CLAP EPPr SMad
- 'Hardwick Hall' (v)	CAvo CBct CBow CLAP CMdw CPLG CRow EBee EBla ECha ECho EHoe EHrv EPla EPot MAvo NBre SMHy WAul WCot WFar WTin WWEG
- 'Hofheim' (v)	CLAP CRow MAvo WWEG
- 'Marcel' (v)	CLAP WCom
- 'Prolificans'	CAvo CBct CBgR CFir CLAP CMdw EBee ECho EPPr GAbr LSou MAvo MRav NBir NLar NMyG NPnk NSti SSvw WCAu WCom WCot WFar WHil
- var. ***rosea***	Widely available
- 'Variegata' (v)	CAvo CBgR CHar EBee EBla EPla EPot LHop NMen NMyG SBch SMad SSvw SWal WCom WHil WWEG
- 'Vic Pawlowski's Gold' (v)	CAby CBct CDes CLAP CMac CPLG CRow EBee ELon EPPr MAvo
transcaucasica	ECho EPot

Convolvulus (*Convolvulaceae*)

althaeoides	CBot CMea ECGP ECho ELan MCot NBir SEND SPhx WAbb WEas WPat
§ - subsp. ***tenuissimus***	CSpe EBee ECtt EWes WCFE WCom WSHC
- - 'Pink Fanfare'	WSpi
§ ***boissieri***	WAbe
cantabricus	CHll MDKP SGSe WHil WSHC
chilensis	CCCN WHil
cneorum ♀H3	Widely available
- 'Snow Angel'	EBee GBin GGar LBuc LRHS LSou MAsh MNHC SWvt WCot
elegantissimus	see *C. althaeoides* subsp. *tenuissimus*
humilis	ECho
lineatus	EBee ECho EWes MTho NMen NWCA
mauritanicus	see *C. sabatius*
nitidus	see *C. boissieri*
remotus	WBox
§ ***sabatius*** ♀H3	CCCN CFox CHEx CSam CTri EBee ECho ECtt ELan EPfP LAst LHop MCot MMuc MSCN NMen NWCA SBfd SEND SGar SPer SPlb SPoG WCFE WEas WFar WPtf
- 'Compton Lane'	WCom
- dark-flowered	CCCN CSpe ECho ELan GCal SMrm SUsu

× *Cooperanthes* see *Zephyranthes*

Cooperia see *Zephyranthes*

Copernicia (*Arecaceae*)

alba	EAmu EUJe LPal

Coprosma (*Rubiaceae*)

acerosa	CTrC
- 'Hawera'	CBcs
- 'Live Wire' (f)	ECou
- 'Red Rocks'	CBcs CTrC
atropurpurea (f)	ECou NWCA
- (m)	ECou
'Autumn Orange' (f)	ECou
'Autumn Prince' (m)	ECou
baueri misapplied	see *C. repens*
'Beatson's Gold' (f/v)	CBcs CBot CDTJ CFee CHGN CHll CPLG CTsd EBee ELan EPfP GGar IVic LRHS MSCN SEND SLim STre SWvt WDin WGrn WSHC
'Black Cloud'	CTrC
'Blue Pearls' (f)	ECou
'Blue Skies' **new**	NHar WThu
brunnea	ECou
- 'Blue Beauty' (f)	ECou
- 'Violet Fleck' (f)	ECou
'Bruno' (m)	ECou
'Cappuccino'	CBcs EBee GBin IFFs LSou
cheesemanii (f)	ECou
- (m)	ECou
- 'Hanmer Red' (f)	ECou
- 'Mack' (m)	ECou
- 'Red Mack' (f)	ECou
'Clearwater Gold'	CTrC
'Coppershine'	CPLG CTrC
crassifolia × ***repens*** (m)	ECou
× ***cunninghamii*** (f)	ECou
- ***macrocarpa*** (m)	ECou
'Cutie' (f)	CTrC ECou
'Dark Spire' **new**	CTrC
depressa	ECou
- 'Orange Spread' (f)	ECou
'Evening Glow' PBR (f/v)	CBgR CCCN CDTJ CDoC CSBt CWit EBee ELan EPfP EShb GGar IFFs IVic LSou MGos SLim
'Fire Burst' PBR	CBcs CCCN CDoC CWit ELan EPfP EShb GGar IFFs LSou MRav SLim WCFE
grandifolia	ECou
'Green Girl' (f)	ECou
'Green Globe'	CHll
'Hinerua' (f)	ECou
'Indigo Lustre' (f)	ECou
'Jewel' (f)	ECou
'Karo Red' PBR (v)	CDoC CTrC CWit EBee ELan ELon EPfP IFFs MGos SLim
× ***kirkii*** 'Gold Edge'	ECou
I - 'Kirkii' (f)	CHll ECou STre
I - 'Kirkii Variegata' (f/v)	CBcs CBot CDoC CTrC CTsd EBee ECou EPfP GGar LRHS SEND SOWG STre WSHC
'Kiwi' (m)	ECou
'Kiwi Red'	GGar
'Kiwi-gold' (m/v)	ECou
'Lemon and Lime' (v) **new**	EPfP
'Lemon Drops' (f)	ECou
linariifolia (m)	ECou
lucida (f)	ECou
- 'Mount White' (m)	ECou
- 'Wanaka' (f)	ECou
macrocarpa (f)	ECou
- (m)	CTrC ECou
nitida (f)	ECou
parviflora (m)	ECou
- red-fruited (f)	ECou
- white-fruited (f)	ECou
'Pearl Drops' (f)	ECou
'Pearl's Sister' (f)	ECou
'Pearly Queen' (f)	ECou
petriei	ECou WThu
- 'Don' (m)	ECou
- 'Lyn' (f)	ECou
'Pride'	CDoC
propinqua (f)	ECou
- (m)	ECou
- var. ***latiuscula*** (f)	ECou

- - (m)	ECou
'Prostrata' (m)	ECou
pseudocuneata (m)	ECou
quadrifida	ECou
'Rainbow Surprise'PBR (v)	CCCN CDoC CPLG CSBt CWit EBee ELan GGar IFFs LSou MGos MRav SLim SPoG
§ ***repens***	CPLG EShb SPlb
- (f)	ECou
- (m)	ECou
- 'County Park Plum' (v)	ECou ELon
- 'County Park Purple' (f)	ECou ELon
- 'County Park Red'	ECou ELon
- 'Exotica' (f/v)	ECou
- 'Marble King' (m/v)	ECou
- 'Marble Queen' (m/v) 🏆H1-2	CBcs ECou MGos SLim
- 'Orangeade' (f)	ECou
- Pacific Night = 'Hutpac'	CDoC CSBt ECou ELan EPfP IVic LBuc LRHS MDKP MGos MWea SPoG
- 'Painter's Palette' (m)	CBcs EBee ECou GGar SLim WDin
- 'Picturata' (m/v) 🏆H1-2	EBee ECou EShb
- 'Pink Splendour' (m/v)	CBcs CDoC ECou GGar MGos
- 'Rangatiri' (f)	ECou
- 'Silver Queen' (m/v)	ECou
- 'Variegata' (m/v)	ECou MSCN
rigida	ECou
- 'Ann' (f)	ECou
- 'Tan' (m)	ECou
robusta	ECou
- 'Cullen's Point' (f)	ECou
- 'Sally Blunt' (f)	ECou
- 'Steepdown' (f)	ECou
- 'Tim Blunt' (m)	ECou
- 'Variegata' (m/v)	ECou
- 'William' (m)	ECou
- 'Woodside' (f)	ECou
rotundifolia	ECou
'Roy's Red' (m)	CBgR CDoC EBee ECou GGar LSRN SPoG
rugosa	CPLG
- (f)	ECou
'Snowberry' (f)	ECou
'Taiko'	CTrC
tenuifolia (m)	ECou
'Translucent Gold' (f)	ECou
'Violet Drops' (f)	ECou
virescens (f)	ECou
'Walter Brockie'	CHGN CHll CTrC SEND
'White Lady' (f)	ECou
'Winter Bronze' (f)	ECou
'Yvonne'	MGos

Coptis (*Ranunculaceae*)

japonica	WCru
- var. ***dissecta***	WCru
- var. ***major***	CDes WCru WSHC
omeiensis	WCru
quinquefolia B&SWJ 1677	WCru
ramosa B&SWJ 6000	WCru
- B&SWJ 6030	WCru
trifolia	WCru

Corallospartium see *Carmichaelia*

Cordyline ✿ (*Agavaceae*)

australis 🏆H3	Widely available
- 'Albertii' (v) 🏆H3	CBcs CCCN CTrC MBri MMuc NMoo SAPC SArc SEND
- 'Atropurpurea'	CCCN CDoC EUJe IFoB SEND WDin WFar
- 'Black Night'	CCCN CTrC ESwi
- 'Black Tower'	CDoC MGos
- 'Claret'	CBcs CTrC
- 'Coffee Cream'	CBcs CCCN ELan EPfP SBfd SPer WDin WFar
- 'Olive Fountain'	CCCN
- 'Peko'PBR	CCCN MGos
- 'Pink Champagne'	CBcs CCCN LBuc LRHS LSRN MAsh MGos NEgg SLim SPoG
- Pink Passion = 'Seipin' **new**	LRHS NPri SBfd
- 'Pink Stripe' (v)	CBcs CCCN CDoC EBee ELan EPfP ESwi LRHS LSRN MBri MCCP NPla SEND SLim SWvt
- 'Purple Heart'	CCCN CTrC MSwo
- Purpurea Group	CBcs CBot CChe CDTJ CMHG CTrC CWSG EBee ELan ELon EPfP GKir LAst LRHS MGos MMuc SEND SPer SPlb SWal WClo WFar
- 'Red Sensation'	CCCN CHEx CTrC CTsd SWvt
- 'Red Star'	CAbb CBar CBcs CCCN CChe CDoC CSBt CTrC CWSG CWib EBee ELan EPfP GKir IVic LAst LRHS LTen MCCP MSwo NPer SPoG SWvt WBrE WFar WGwG
- 'Sparkler'	CBcs CCCN CChe ESwi LRHS MGos
- 'Sundance' 🏆H3	CBcs CDoC CEnd CMac CSBt CTrC CWSG CWib EBee EPfP IFFs LAst LRHS MBri MCCP MGos MMuc MSwo NPer SEND SLim SPad SPoG SRms SWvt WFar
- 'Torbay Dazzler' (v) 🏆H3	Widely available
- 'Torbay Red' 🏆H3	CBcs CCCN CDoC CDul CMHG CMac CWSG EBee ELan ELon EPfP LRHS LSRN MAsh MBri MMuc NPri SBfd SPer SWvt WFar
- 'Torbay Sunset'	CCCN CDoC CTrC ELan
- 'Variegata' (v)	CBot
'Autumn'	CCCN IFFs
banksii	CPne CTsd GCal GGar
'Candy Cane' **new**	EAmu ESwi
'Cardinal'PBR	CBcs CWit EUJe
'Dark Star'	CBcs CCCN CDTJ CDoC CMac SLim
'Eurostar' **new**	CWit
'Firecracker' **new**	LRHS
fruticosa 'Atom'	MBri
- 'Baby Ti' (v)	MBri
- 'Calypso Queen'	MBri
- 'Kiwi'	MBri
- 'Orange Prince'	MBri
- 'Red Edge' 🏆H1	MBri XBlo
- 'Yellow King'	MBri
'Green Goddess'	SBfd SLim
§ ***indivisa***	CBcs CDTJ CTsd CWit EAmu EBak GCal GGar LMaj MBri SAPC SArc SPlb WPGP
'Jurassic Jade'	CBcs CTrC
'Jurassic Jasper'	CTrC
kaspar	CCCN CHEx CTsd SAPC SArc
obtecta	CCCN CTsd
- bronze-leaved	CTsd
'Pacific Coral'	MGos
'Pacific Dawn' (v)	EGxp
pumilio	LRHS
'Purple Sensation'	CBcs CCCN CMHG CTrC EUJe LRHS NPri
'Purple Tower' 🏆H3	CDoC CHEx EPfP EUJe MGos SLim SPad
'Red Bush'	XBlo
'Red Fountain'PBR	ESwi

	'Red Heart' **new**	LRHS
	'Southern Splendour' **new**	CBod CCCN ELon ESwi LRHS
§	***stricta***	CHEx MBri
	'Sunrise' (v) **new**	EAmu LRHS
	terminalis	see *C. fruticosa*

Coreopsis (*Asteraceae*)

	'Astolat'	EAEE EBee MNFA MWea SPer
	auriculata Cutting Gold	see *C.* 'Schnittgold'
	- 'Elfin Gold'	EBee EDAr LBMP WFar
	- 'Nana'	EBee MNrw NBre WFar WWEG
	- 'Zamphir'	EBee ECtt EPfP MNrw NBre NCGa
	'Autumn Blush'	EBee MWea NBre NCGa NDov SBfd
	'Baby Gold'	see *C. lanceolata* 'Sonnenkind' (unblotched)
	Baby Sun	see *C.* 'Sonnenkind' (red-blotched)
	'Butterfly Flame'	LRHS
	'Caluroso'	LRHS
	'Calypso' (v)	ECtt EWes LBuc LRHS MAsh SCoo SMad
	'Cutting Edge'	CEnt
	'Full Moon' (Big Bang Series) **new**	EBee STes
	'Gold Nugget' **new**	SBfd
	'Golden Ballerina'	LRHS
	'Golden Pom Pom' (d) **new**	EBee LSou NDov
	grandiflora	MPet NEgg
	- 'Badengold'	EBee
	- 'Bernwode' (v)	CMac EBee LSou NLar SPoG SWvt
	- 'Domino'	EBee NBre SMrm
	- 'Early Sunrise' ♀H4	CSBt EBee ECtt EPfP GKir LBMP LRHS MAsh MBri MHer NBir NGBl NPer SAga SGar SPet SPoG STes SWal SWvt WFar WWEG
	- Flying Saucers = 'Walcoreop' PBR	EBee GKir LBuc LRHS MAsh SCoo SPoG
	- 'Heliot'	SAga
	- 'Mayfield Giant'	CSBt EBee EShb LHop MNrw MWea NPri SPer SRms SWvt WHrl WWEG
	- 'Presto' (d)	LBuc SBfd WHil
	- 'Rising Sun'	EBee MAsh MBri NPri SPet SPhx WPer
	- 'Sunburst'	EBee EPfP LTen NBre WPer
	- 'Sunfire'	MHer SPhx STes
	- 'Sunray'	CBcs CDoC CSBt CWib EBee ECtt ELon EPfP EShb GKir LRHS LSRN MAvo MBri MGos NGdn NPri SBfd SMrm SPlb SPoG SRms SWvt WMoo WWEG
	- 'Tetra Riesen'	EBee NBre
	heterophylla	see *Iostephane heterophylla*
	'Jethro Tull'	EBee MBri
	lanceolata	NBre NSti
	- 'Goldfink'	GKir MRav SRms
	- 'Goldteppich'	LRHS
	- 'Little Sundial'	EBee LSou
§	- 'Sonnenkind' (unblotched)	EBee EPfP MAsh WWEG
	- 'Walter'	EAEE EBee ECtt LRHS MBri MWea NDov NEgg SPoG
	'Limerock Dream'	ECtt LRHS NDov SBfd SMrm WHlf
	'Limerock Passion' PBR	LRHS LSou MWea NDov NLar NPri SBfd SRkn SUsu WSpi
	'Limerock Ruby' PBR	Widely available
	major	CSam EBee
	maximiliani	see *Helianthus maximiliani*
	palmata	EBee MDKP
	'Pinwheel'	EBee NDov SBfd
	pubescens	EBee LSou
	- 'Sunshine Superman'	EBee LSou WWEG
	rosea	WFar WPer
	- 'American Dream'	CSBt EBee ELan EPfP GKir LAst LBMP LRHS LSRN NBir NGdn NPri SBfd SGSe SGar SPer SPlb SPoG SRms SWal SWvt WBrE WFar
	- 'Heaven's Gate' PBR	EBee ELan EPfP EWll MAvo MBri NBPC NBre
	- 'Sweet Dreams' PBR	EBee LHop LSRN MWea NCGa SPer SRkn SUsu WFar
	'Rum Punch' **new**	GKir MWea SUsu WHil
	'Sangria'	LAst LHop MWea SPoG SUsu WHil
§	'Schnittgold'	CWan EBee NBre WPer
	'Snowberry'	CCVN CWGN EBee ECtt IPot MWea SBfd
I	'Sonnenkind' (red-blotched)	EBee ECtt LBMP LRHS NBre WPer
	'Sterntaler'	CFir CMea CPrp EBee EPPr EPau EPfP EShb GKir LRHS MAsh MBri MWat NCGa NPri SBfd SMrm SPet SWvt WPer
	Sun Child	see *C.* 'Sonnenkind' (red-blotched)
	'Tequila Sunrise' (v)	EBee ELan MBNS NMoo SPad
	tripteris	CAby CSam LPla LRHS MDKP MMuc NBre SAga SGSe SMad SPhx WMoo
	- 'Mostenveld'	EBee
	'Turkish Delight'	LRHS
	verticillata	CMac EBee ECha EHrv EPfP GCal MBrN MDun MGos MHer MWat NPer SBfd SDix SRms WFar WHal
	- Crème Brûlée = 'Crembru' PBR	CSam EBee EBrs ECtt EWes LRHS LSou MAvo MWea NBPC NDov NEgg NLar NPnk SCoo SMrm SPer SPoG SRkn SUsu WCot WCra WSpi WWEG
I	- 'Golden Gain'	EBee ECtt LHop LRHS MArl NGdn SBfd WFar WMnd WWEG
	- 'Golden Shower'	see *C. verticillata* 'Grandiflora'
§	- 'Grandiflora' ♀H4	CBcs COlW CPrp CTca EAEE EBee EBrs ELan EPfP GMaP LRHS MRav NCGa NGdn NHol NVic SMad SPer WCAu WFar WMnd
	- 'Moonbeam' ♀H4	Widely available
	- 'Old Timer' ♀H4	SDix SUsu
	- 'Ruby Red'	CAbP CMac EBee SMad SUsu
	- 'Zagreb' ♀H4	Widely available

Corethrogyne (*Asteraceae*)

	californica	EBee

coriander see *Coriandrum sativum*

Coriandrum (*Apiaceae*)

*	***citratus*** **new**	ELau
	sativum	CArn CSev GPoy ILis MHer MNHC NVic SBfd SIde SPoG
	- 'Confetti'	MNHC
	- 'Leisure'	NPri SVic
	- 'Santo'	ELau NGHP
	- 'Slobolt'	ELau NGHP

Coriaria ✿ (*Coriariaceae*)

	arborea	WCru
	intermedia B&SWJ 019	WCru
	japonica	IFFs NLar WCru
	- B&SWJ 2833	WCru
	- subsp. ***intermedia*** B&SWJ 3877	WCru
	kingiana	EBee WCru WPGP
§	***microphylla***	WCru
	- B&SWJ 8999	WCru
	myrtifolia	EWld NLar WCru WFar
	nepalensis	NLar WCru
	- BWJ 7755	WCru
	pteridoides	WCru
	ruscifolia	WCru

	- HCM 98178	WCru
	sarmentosa	WCru
	terminalis	GCal
	f. ***fructu-rubro***	
	- var. ***xanthocarpa***	CBcs EBee EPfP GCal GGar LSou WCot WCru
	- - GWJ 9204	WCru
	- - HWJK 2112c	WCru
	thymifolia	see *C. microphylla*

Cornus ✿ (*Cornaceae*)

	KWJ 12225 from northern Vietnam **new**	WCru
	alba L.	CBar CCVT CDoC CDul CLnd ECrN EMac EWTr MHer MRav NWea SRms WDin WMou
	- 'Alleman's Compact'	CPMA
	- 'Argenteovariegata'	see *C. alba* 'Variegata'
	- 'Aurea' 🏆H4	Widely available
	- Baton Rouge = 'Minbat'	LRHS SBfd
	- Chief Bloodgood = 'Chblzam'	CPMA
	- 'Cream Cracker'PBR (v)	EBee
	- 'Elegantissima' (v) 🏆H4	Widely available
	- 'Gouchaultii' (v)	CAlb CBcs CPMA EBee ECrN EMac GKir IFFs LBMP LRHS LTen MAsh MRav MWat NLar SBfd SLim SPer SRms WDin WFar
	- 'Hessei' misapplied	see *C. sanguinea* 'Compressa'
	- 'Hessei'	CPMA WPat
	- Ivory Halo = 'Bailhalo'PBR	EBee EMil EPfP LSRN MBri MGos MRav NLar NWea SLim SPer SPoG SRms
	- 'Kesselringii'	Widely available
	- Red Gnome = 'Regnzam'	CPMA LLHF WPat
	- 'Ruby'	CPMA
	- 'Siberian Pearls'	CBcs CPMA ELan MBlu MGos NLar SSta
§	- 'Sibirica' 🏆H4	Widely available
	- 'Sibirica Variegata' (v)	CBow CDoC CMac CPMA EBee EPfP EPla GCra LRHS LSRN MAsh MBlu MGos NCGa NEgg SBfd SLim SPer SPoG SSpi SSta SWvt WCFE WFar
	- 'Snow Pearls'	CPMA
	- 'Spaethii' (v) 🏆H4	Widely available
§	- 'Variegata' (v)	CBcs ECho EQua LAst MGos
	- 'Westonbirt'	see *C. alba* 'Sibirica'
	alternifolia	CBcs CCVT CMCN ELan WPat
§	- 'Argentea' (v) 🏆H4	Widely available
	- 'Brunette'	NLar
	- 'Golden Surprise' **new**	CPMA
	- 'Silver Giant' (v)	CPMA MBri WSpi
	- 'Variegata'	see *C. alternifolia* 'Argentea'
	- 'Yellow Spring'	NLar
	amomum	CAbP EBee EBtc NLar WFar
	- 'Blue Cloud'	CPMA
	- 'Lady Jane'	NLar
	angustata	SKHP SSpi
	'Ascona'	CBcs CEnd CPMA ELan EPfP NLar SSpi SSta WPat
	Aurora = 'Rutban' (Stellar Series)	CPMA IArd MBlu NLar SSpi
	australis	GAuc
	canadensis 🏆H4	Widely available
	candidissima Marshall	see *C. racemosa*
	capitata	CBcs CBgR CChe CDoC CDul CEnd CMac CPne CTsd EBee EPfP GGar GKev IFFs ITim LHop MMuc MWya SEND SGar SKHP SPoG SSpi WBVN WCru WFar WPGP WPat WSHC WSpi
	capitata × ***florida***	CSam
§	Celestial = 'Rutdan' (Stellar Series)	CPMA IArd LRHS NLar SKHP
	'Celestial Shadow' **new**	MPkF
	'Centennial'	LRHS SSpi
	chinensis	LMil SWvt
	'Constellation' (Stellar Series)	CPMA MAsh SSpi
	controversa	CBcs CCVT CDul CLnd CMCN CTri ECho ECrN ELan EPfP EWTr GKir IFFs MBlu MMuc NLar NWea SEND SLPl SLim SReu SSpi SSta SWvt WDin WFar WHar
	- 'Candlelight'	MBlu MBri NLar
§	- 'Frans Type' (v)	CBcs CBot CEnd CPMA ECho ELan ERom LSRN SReu SSta WDin
I	- 'Marginata Nord'	NLar NPal
	- 'Pagoda'	EPfP MBlu MBri NLar
	- 'Troya Dwarf'	CPMA NLar
	- 'Variegata' (v) 🏆H4	Widely available
	- 'Variegata' Frans type	see *C. controversa* 'Frans Type'
	- 'Winter Orange'	CPMA EPla NLar
	'Dorothy' **new**	NLar
	'Eddie's White Wonder' 🏆H4	Widely available
	florida	CCVT CDul CLnd CMCN CTho EBee IFFs LAst LRHS MMuc MSnd SPer WBVN WDin WHCr
	- 'Alba Plena' (d)	CPMA NLar
	- 'Andrea Hart'	CPMA
	- 'Appalachian Spring'	LRHS MGos
	- 'Apple Blossom'	CMac CPMA CSBt ECho NPCo WGob
	- 'Aurea' × ***kousa***	MPkF
	- 'Autumn Gold'	CPMA
	- Cherokee Brave = 'Comco No 1'	CBcs CPMA ECho ESwi LMil LRHS MAsh MGos MPkF NPCo SBfd SPoG SSpi
	- 'Cherokee Chief' 🏆H4	CBcs CEnd CPMA CTri CWit ECho IVic LAst LSRN MGos MPkF NPCo SBfd SLim SPer WDin WFar WGob WHar WSpi
	- 'Cherokee Daybreak'	see *C. florida* 'Daybreak'
	- 'Cherokee Princess'	CPMA ECho LRHS MAsh SPoG
	- 'Cherokee Sunset'	see *C. florida* 'Sunset'
	- 'Cloud Nine'	CBcs CDoC CPMA CWGN ECho MGos MPkF NLar NPCo WSpi
	- 'Daniela' (v)	NLar
§	- 'Daybreak' (v)	CBcs CEnd CPMA ECho ESwi LRHS LSRN MAsh MBri MGos MPkF SBfd SPer
	- 'Eternal Dogwood' (d)	CBcs ESwi LRHS LSRN MGos
	- 'Firebird'	LRHS MGos
	- 'First Lady' (v)	CBcs CMac CPMA CWit ECho NPCo
	- 'Fragrant Cloud'	ECho
	- 'G.H. Ford' (v)	CPMA NLar
	- 'Golden Nugget' (v)	CPMA ECho
	- 'Junior Miss'	CEnd
	- 'Moonglow'	CPMA LMaj
	- 'Pendula'	CBcs CPMA MPkF
	- 'Pink Flame' (v)	NLar
	- f. ***pluribracteata*** (d)	NLar
	- var. ***pringlei***	CPMA
	- 'Purple Glory'	CBcs CPMA ECho MPkF NLar
	- 'Pygmaea'	NLar
	- 'Rainbow' (v)	CAbP CBcs CPMA CWib EBee GKir LAst LRHS MBri MGos MPkF SBfd SLim SPer SPoG SSpi WDin
	- 'Red Giant'	CAbP CBcs CPMA ELan LMil NLar
	- f. ***rubra***	CAlb CBcs CSBt CTri CWib ECho ELan EWTr GKir LAst

	LMaj LRHS MGos MMuc MWea NPCo SPer WDin WFar WSpi
- 'Spring Day'	CSBt ECho NPCo
- 'Spring Song'	CMac CPMA CSBt ECho NPCo
- 'Springtime'	CPMA ECho NLar
- 'Stoke's Pink'	CEnd CPMA CSBt CWit ECho NPCo WSpi
§ - 'Sunset' (v)	CBcs CEnd CPMA CWib ECho ELon LRHS MAsh MBri MGos NLar NPCo SBfd SPer SWvt
- 'Sweetwater'	CBcs CEnd CPMA
- 'Tricolor'	see *C. florida* 'Welchii'
- 'Weaver's White'	CBcs ECho MPkF
§ - 'Welchii' (v)	CEnd CPMA
- 'White Cloud'	CPMA ELan MBri
- 'Xanthocarpa'	MPkF
aff. ***gigantea*** HWJ 834	WCru
'Gloria Birkett'	CAbP ECho ELon LMil LRHS MAsh NPCo SSpi WGob
hemsleyi	EPla
hessei misapplied	see *C. sanguinea* 'Compressa'
hongkongensis WWJ 11700	WCru
- subsp. ***tonkinensis*** B&SWJ 11791	WCru
- - HWJ 1022	WCru
'Kelsey Dwarf'	see *C. sericea* 'Kelseyi'
'Kenwyn Clapp'	CPMA SSpi
kousa	CDoC CDul CMCN CMac CPne CSam CTho ECho ELan EMac EPfP ERom GKir IFFs LMaj LRHS MSnd NEgg NLar SBfd SLim SPer SPlb WDin WFar WHar
- B&SWJ 5494	WCru
- 'Aget'	CPMA
- 'Akabana'	CPMA
- 'All Summer'	CPMA
- 'Angyo Issai'	NLar
- 'Autumn Rose'	CPMA EPfP NLar
- 'Beni-fuji'	CPMA IVic MWya NLar
- 'Big Apple'	CPMA LRHS MAsh NLar SSpi
- 'Blue Shadow'	CPMA IArd IDee MBri NLar
- 'Boldre Beauty'	SSpi
- 'Bonfire' (v)	CPMA
- 'Bultinck's Beauty'	MWya NLar
- 'Bush's Pink'	CPMA
- 'Cherokee'	CPMA SLim
- 'China Dawn' (v)	CPMA
- var. ***chinensis*** 🏆H4	Widely available
- - 'Bodnant Form'	CEnd CPMA ECho ELon GKir NPCo
- - 'China Girl'	CAbP CDul CEnd CPMA EBee ELan EPfP GKir LBuc LMil LRHS LSRN MAsh MBlu MBri MGos MSwo MWya NLar SLim SPer SPoG SSpi SSta WDin WPat
- - 'Claudia'	IVic NLar
- - 'Great Star'	MAsh
- - 'Greta's Gold' (v)	CPMA
- - 'Ikone' **new**	IVic
- - 'Milky Way'	CMCN CPMA EBee ECho LBuc LSRN MBlu MGos MPkF NLar NPCo SSpi WPat WSpi
- - 'Snowflake'	CPMA
- - 'Spinners'	CPMA
- - 'Summer Stars'	CPMA NLar WPat
- - 'White Dusted' (v)	CPMA EPfP NLar
- - 'White Fountain'	LRHS MBri MPkF MPnt MWya NLar
- - 'Wieting's Select'	CPMA IVic MPkF
- - 'Wisley Queen'	CAbP CPMA LMil LRHS MAsh SSpi
- 'Claudine'	CPMA
- 'Doctor Bump'	CPMA
- 'Doubloon'	CPMA ECho WPat
- 'Dwarf Pink'	CPMA
- 'Ed Mezitt'	CPMA NLar SSpi
- 'Elizabeth Lustgarten'	CPMA MPkF
- 'Eurostar' **new**	IVic
- 'Fanfare'	CPMA NLar
- 'Fernie's Favourite'	CPMA
- Galilean = 'Galzam'	CPMA
- 'Gay Head'	CPMA
I - 'Girard's Nana'	CPMA
- 'Gold Cup' (v)	CPMA MPkF
- 'Gold Star' (v)	CAbP CBcs CEnd CMac CPMA CWGN EBee ECho ELan EPfP LMil LRHS MAsh MBlu MBri MGos MPkF NLar NPCo SPoG SSpi
- 'Greensleeves'	CPMA
- 'Heart Throb'	CBcs CPMA LRHS MGos NLar
- 'Highland'	CPMA
- 'John Slocock'	NLar
- 'Kim'	NLar
- 'Kreutzdame'	CPMA IArd MBri
- 'Laura'PBR	MBri
- 'Little Beauty'	CPMA
- 'Lustgarten Weeping'	CPMA NLar
- 'Madame Butterfly'	CEnd CPMA MBlu NLar NPCo
- 'Milky Way'	ESwi GBin
- 'Milky Way Select'	CBcs CPMA ECho LMaj MGos
- 'Minuma'	NLar
- 'Miss Petty'	CPMA MPkF NLar
- 'Miss Satomi' 🏆H4	Widely available
- 'Moonbeam'	CPMA MBri NLar WPat
- 'Mount Fuji'	CPMA MBri NLar
- 'National'	CPMA ECho EPfP LMil MAsh MGos MPkF NLar SSpi WPat
- 'Nicole'	CDoC LRHS NLar WDin WGob WPat
- 'Pevé Limbo' (v)	CPMA NLar
- 'Pevé Satomi Compact'	NLar
- 'Polywood'	CPMA NLar
- 'Radiant Rose'	CPMA LRHS MBri MPkF NLar SSpi
- 'Rasen'	CPMA MBri NLar
- 'Rel Whirlwind'	CPMA
- 'Rosea'	CPMA
- Samaratin = 'Samzam' (v)	CBcs CEnd CPMA ESwi LRHS LSRN MBri MGos MPkF SKHP
- 'Schmetterling'	CPMA IArd NLar WPat
- 'Silver Pheasant' (v)	NLar
- 'Snowbird'	CPMA
- 'Snowboy' (v)	CBcs CEnd CPMA NPCo SMad
- 'Snowflurries'	CPMA
- 'Southern Cross'	CPMA GBin
- 'Square Dance'	CPMA
- 'Steeple'	CPMA
- 'Summer Fun'	CPMA LRHS SSpi
- 'Summer Majesty'	CPMA
- 'Sunsplash' (v)	CPMA NLar
- 'Temple Jewel' (v)	CPMA
- 'Teutonia'	CPMA IVic LRHS MBri MPkF NLar
- 'Tinknor's Choice'	CPMA
- 'Trinity Star'	CPMA SSpi
- 'Triple Crown'	CPMA
- 'Tsukubanomine'	CPMA NLar
- 'U.S.A.'	MPkF
- 'Vale Milky Way' (v)	NLar
- 'Weaver's Weeping'	CPMA MPkF
- 'Weisse Fontäne'	CPMA NLar
- 'White Dream'	CPMA NLar
- 'White Giant'	CPMA
- 'Wolf Eyes' (v)	CPMA LRHS MAsh MBlu MPkF NLar SPoG SSpi SSta WPat
macrophylla Wall.	CMCN EPfP NLar WPGP
mas	Widely available

- 'Aurea' (v)	CAbP CBcs CDul CPMA EBee ELan EPfP EPla LRHS MAsh MBri MGos MRav NEgg NLar NPCo SLim SPer SPoG SSpi SSta WDin WPat
§ - 'Aureoelegantissima' (v)	CEnd CGHE CMac CPMA EPla LRHS MBri NEgg NLar SPer SSpi WFar WPat WSHC
- 'Devin'	NLar
- 'Elegantissima'	see *C. mas* 'Aureoelegantissima'
- 'Golden Glory' ♀^{H4}	CPMA EPfP MBri NLar
- 'Gourmet' **new**	CAgr
- 'Happy Face'	NLar
- 'Hillier's Upright'	CPMA
- 'Jolico'	CPMA MBlu NLar
- 'Kasanlaker'	MBri NLar
- 'Pioneer'	CPMA
- 'Redstone'	CPMA
- 'Spring Glow'	CPMA NLar
- 'Titus'	NLar
- 'Variegata' (v) ♀^{H4}	CAbP CBcs CBot CMCN CPMA EBee EPfP LRHS MAsh MBlu MBri MGos NLar NPCo NPal SKHP SPer SPoG SSpi WDin WFar
- 'Xanthocarpa'	CPMA NLar
N 'Norman Hadden' ♀^{H4}	Widely available
nuttallii	CDul CTho CTri CWib ECho ELan EPfP GAuc GLin IFFs MGos MMuc SPer SWvt WDin WFar
- 'Colrigo Giant'	CPMA MPkF
- 'Gold Spot' (v)	CMac CPMA ECho MGos NPCo NWea
- 'Monarch'	CPMA CTho NLar SSpi
- 'North Star'	CPMA ECho MWya NLar
- 'Osmunda'	ECho
- 'Pink Blush'	MPkF NLar
- 'Portlemouth'	CEnd CPMA WGob WSpi
- 'Zurico'	CPMA MPkF NLar
officinalis	CAgr CAlb CMCN CMac EBee EMil EPfP LRHS MAsh MBri MMuc MWea NLar SKHP SPur WDin
- 'Ellen' **new**	NLar
- 'Kintoki' **new**	SKHP
'Ormonde'	CPMA CWGN CWit ECho NLar NPCo SSpi WGob
'Pink Blush'	CPMA
'Porlock' ♀^{H4}	CDul CMCN CPMA EPfP GKir ITim LRHS LSRN MBri NLar SSpi WDin WPat
pumila	CPMA NLar
§ ***racemosa***	MBri NLar WFar
rugosa	EBtc NLar
× ***rutgersiensis*** Galaxy	see *C.* Celestial
Ruth Ellen = 'Rutlan' (Stellar Series)	CPMA NLar
sanguinea	CBcs CCVT CDul CLnd CRWN CTri ECrN EMac EPfP IFFs LBuc LMaj MMuc MRav MSwo NWea SPer SVic WBVN WDin WHar WMou
- 'Anny'	CPMA MAsh MBlu WPat
- 'Anny's Winter Orange'	CPMA
§ - 'Compressa'	EBee EPfP MRav NLar WFar
- 'Magic Flame'	CPMA MBri
- 'Midwinter Fire'	Widely available
- 'Winter Beauty'	CAlb CPMA CSBt CWib CWit EBee EPfP LSou MAsh MBlu NEgg NLar NWea SLon SWvt WCFE WFar WHar WPat
§ ***sericea***	CArn EMac EPla GKir SRms WMoo
- 'Budd's Yellow'	GKir LRHS MBlu MBri
- 'Cardinal'	CHGN EPfP LRHS MAsh MBri NLar
- 'Coral Red'	CPMA
- 'Flaviramea' ♀^{H4}	Widely available
- 'Hedgerows Gold' (v)	CPMA CSBt EBee ELan EMil LHop LRHS MAsh SBfd SPoG SPur WPat
- 'Isanti'	CPMA
§ - 'Kelseyi'	CAlb CMac CPMA EBee EPla LTen MNHC MRav NLar SLPl SPer WDin WMoo
- Kelsey's Gold = 'Rosco'	MAsh WPat
- subsp. ***occidentalis*** 'Sunshine'	CPMA NLar
§ - 'White Gold' (v) ♀^{H4}	CBow CDoC CPMA EBee EHoe MAsh MBri MRav MSwo SLon SPer SPoG WDin WFar WMoo
- 'White Spot'	see *C. sericea* 'White Gold'
Stardust = 'Rutfan' (Stellar Series)	CPMA
Stellar Pink = 'Rutgan' (Stellar Series)	CBcs CPMA CWib IVic LRHS MBri MGos NLar SKHP SSpi
stolonifera	see *C. sericea*
suecica	NHar
× ***unalaschkensis***	LLHF
Venus = 'Kn30-8'	CPMA LRHS MBlu MBri SPoG
walteri	CBcs CMCN WFar
- B&SWJ 876	WCru

Corokia (*Escalloniaceae*)

buddlejoides	CBcs CDoC CHGN CMHG CTrC CTsd EBee ECou GGar SEND SOWG SPoG WFar
'Coppershine'	CMHG
cotoneaster	CAbP CMac CTri EBee ECho ECou ELan EPfP EPot LRHS MAsh MGos MPkF NLar SBfd SMad SPer SPoG SWvt WBrE WCot WFar WPat WSHC
- 'Boundary Hill'	ECou
- 'Brown's Stream'	ECou
- 'Geenty's Ghost' **new**	CTrC
- 'Hodder River'	ECou
- 'Little Prince'	GGar
- 'Ohau Scarlet'	ECou
- 'Ohau Yellow'	ECou
- 'Swale Stream'	ECou
- 'Wanaka'	ECou
macrocarpa	CDoC ECou SDix
* ***parviflora***	CTrC
× ***virgata***	CAbP CBcs CDoC CMHG CMac CTrC CTri ECou ELan EPfP GBin GGal GKir MCCP NLar SAPC SArc SPer SWvt WBVN WHar WSHC
- 'Bronze King'	CDoC CSam CWit EBee EPfP LRHS MPkF SOWG SPer
- 'Bronze Lady'	ECou
- 'Cheesemanii'	ECou GGar
- 'County Park Lemon'	ECou SOWG
- 'County Park Orange'	ECou
- 'County Park Purple'	ECou
- 'County Park Red'	ECou
- 'Envy'	ECou
- 'Everglades'	ECou
- 'Frosted Chocolate'	CAlb CBcs CDoC CSam CTrC CTsd EBee ECou ELan EPfP ETod IVic LBMP LHop LLHF LRHS MAsh MGos MPkF SKHP SLim SOWG SPoG SSta SWvt WCot WDin WFar WGrn
- 'Geenty's Green'	CTrC ECou LRHS
- 'Havering'	ECou
- 'Mangatangi'	CTrC MGos
- 'Pink Delight'	CDoC EBee ECou EPfP ESwi MAsh MRav SSta
- 'Red Wonder'	CAlb CDoC CMHG CMac CPen CTrC EBee ELan EPfP GGar IVic

		LRHS MMHG MPkF SEND SLim SOWG SPoG WDin WFar WGrn
	- 'Sandrine'	ECou
	- 'Silver Ghost'	CDoC ECou
	- 'Sunsplash' (v)	CAlb CBcs CDoC CMac CTrC CTsd EBee ECou EPfP ESwi LBMP LHop LLHF LRHS MAsh MGos MPkF NLar SEND SPoG SWvt WFar WGrn WHar
I	- 'Virgata'	CChe ECou MGos
	- 'Wingletye'	ECou
	- 'Yellow Wonder'	CBcs CDoC CMHG CPen CTrC EBee ECou ESwi GGar LRHS MGos NLar SEND SLim SPoG SWvt WDin

Coronilla (*Papilionaceae*)

	comosa	see *Hippocrepis comosa*
	emerus	see *Hippocrepis emerus*
	glauca	see *C. valentina* subsp. *glauca*
	minima	WAbe
	valentina	CDoC CRHN CSPN EBee LHop SDix WSHC
	- 'Creamed Corn'	WCot WFut
§	- subsp. ***glauca*** ♀H3	CAlb CBot CDul CFee CMac CSBt CTri CWib EBee ELan ELon EPfP LAst LEdu LRHS LSRN MMuc MREP MSCN SEND SGar SLim SPer SRms SWvt WAbe WFar WPat
	- - 'Brockhill Blue'	CWGN EBee IVic LRHS WCot
	- - 'Citrina' ♀H3	Widely available
*	- - 'Pygmaea'	LRHS WCot WWFP
	- - 'Variegata' (v)	CBcs CBot CDoC CMac CSPN CTri CWib EBee EHoe ELan ELon EPfP LRHS MAsh MCot SBfd SEND SLim SLon SMrm SPer SPoG WCot WFar
	varia	see *Securigera varia*

Correa (*Rutaceae*)

	alba	CCCN CDoC CPLG CTrC EBee ECou EPfP LBMP MAsh WGwG WHar
	- 'Pinkie' ♀H2	CBcs CPLG ECou LBMP MAsh SAga SOWG WCot
	alba × ***backhouseana*** new	SOWG
	backhouseana ♀H2	CAbb CBcs CBgR CDoC CMac CPLG CTrC CTri CWit EBee ECou ELan EPfP EWld GGar IDee IVic LHop LRHS MAsh MMuc NLar SAga SEND SGar SMrm SOWG WGwG WHar WSHC
	- 'Peaches and Cream'	CSBt IVic SRkn
	baeuerlenii	ECou SOWG
	decumbens	CAbb CTrC ECou IDee MAsh SEND SOWG
	'Dusky Bells' ♀H2	CBcs CCCN CDoC CHll CSWP CTri EBee ECou EPfP GGar IVic LBMP LHop LRHS MAsh MMuc SAga SEND SLim SMrm SOWG SPlb SPoG SRkn
	'Dusky Maid'	CCCN CPLG WAbe
	'Federation Belle'	CDoC ECou SOWG
	glabra	SOWG
	- red-flowered	ECou
	'Gwen'	CDoC ECou SOWG
	'Harrisii'	see *C.* 'Mannii'
	'Inglewood Gold'	ECou
	'Ivory Bells'	ECou EPfP
	lawrenceana	CDoC CTrC ECou SEND WAbe
§	'Mannii' ♀H2	CBcs CDoC CPLG CPom CTsd EBee ECou ELan EPfP IVic LRHS SEND SOWG SPoG WSHC
	'Marian's Marvel' ♀H2	CBgR CCCN CDoC CMHG CPLG CTrC ECou EWld IDee LBMP MAsh MMuc SEND SGar SOWG SPoG SRkn WAbe
	'Peachy Cream'	CDoC EPfP LRHS
	'Pink Mist'	CDoC ECou
	'Poorinda Mary'	ECou SOWG
	pulchella ♀H2	CDoC CPLG CTri IRar LBMP MAsh SOWG
	- orange-flowered	ECou SOWG
	- 'Pink Mist' new	SOWG
	reflexa ♀H2	CDoC CPLG ECou IDee SOWG WAbe
	- var. ***nummulariifolia***	ECou LBMP MAsh WAbe WCot
	- var. ***reflexa***	CPLG
	- - 'Mary's Choice'	CDoC
	- var. ***scabridula*** 'Yanakie'	ECou SOWG
*	- ***virens***	CPLG WEas
	schlechtendalii	ECou

Cortaderia ✿ (*Poaceae*)

	argentea	see *C. selloana*
	fulvida misapplied	see *C. richardii* (Endl.) Zotov
§	***fulvida*** (Buchanan) Zotov	CBcs CKno EBee EWes GBin IDee MNrw WDin
	jubata 'Candy Floss'	CKno
	'Point du Raz'	CKno
	richardii misapplied	see *C. fulvida* (Buchanan) Zotov
	richardii ambig.	CFir CPLG EHoe EPau GBin IMou MMuc NLar WWEG
§	***richardii*** (Endl.) Zotov ♀H3-4	CBcs CKno EPPr ESwi EWes GGar GMaP IBlr IMou MAvo NVic SAPC SArc WCot WCru WMnd WPGP
	- BR 26	GGar
§	***selloana***	CBcs CDul CHEx CSBt CTri CWib CWit EHul EPfP GKir MAvo MGos MRav NBir NGBl SAPC SBfd SPlb WFar WMoo
§	- 'Albolineata' (v)	CBcs CBct EBee EHoe ELon EWes MMuc MSCN MWht NOak SBfd SEND SLim SPer SPoG SWvt WFar WGrn WPat
§	- 'Aureolineata' (v) ♀H3	CBcs CBct CDoC CMac EHoe ELan EPfP GKir IVic MAsh MGos MMoz MMuc MWhi NBid NLar NOak NWsh SBfd SEND SLim SPer SPoG SWvt WFar WGrn WPat
	- 'Cool Ice'	CPen
	- 'Evita'PBR	CKno EPPr LHop SMad SPer WCot
	- 'Gold Band'	see *C. selloana* 'Aureolineata'
	- 'Icalma'	CPen
	- 'Monstrosa'	MMuc SEND SMad
	- 'Patagonia'	EHoe EPPr
	- 'Pink Feather'	EBee EPfP GKir IFFs LTen MMuc SApp SEND SPer
	- 'Pumila' ♀H4	Widely available
	- 'Rendatleri'	CBcs CDoC ELan EPfP GKir LSRN SCoo SLim SPer SPoG WDin
	- 'Rosea'	CWit EBee EGxp EPfP MGos NBPC NGdn NLar WBrE WFar WWEG
	- 'Silver Comet'	EWes
	- Silver Feather = 'Notcort' (v)	MGos SLim
	- 'Silver Fountain' (v)	ELan EPfP LRHS MAsh
	- 'Silver Stripe'	see *C. selloana* 'Albolineata'
	- 'Splendid Star'PBR (v)	CBcs CDoC CKno EBee EGxp EHoe GBin LBuc LHop LRHS LTen MAsh MBri MGos MREP NLar NOak SBfd SLim SMad SPoG SRms SWvt WCot
	- 'Sunningdale Silver' ♀H3	CDoC CDul CMac CWit EBee ECha ECtt EHoe EHul ELan ELon EPfP GKir LRHS LSRN MAsh MBri MGos MMuc SBfd SEND SLim SMad SPer SPoG SWvt WDin WFar WSpi

*	- 'White Feather'	CChe IFFs MWhi NGdn NPri SApp SLim WFar WMoo WWEG
	Toe Toe	see *C. richardii* (Endl.) Zotov

Cortia (*Apiaceae*)

	SDR 3922	EBee

Cortiella (*Apiaceae*)

	aff. ***hookeri*** HWJK 2291	WCru

Cortusa (*Primulaceae*)

	brotheri	ECho
	- CC 2987	EBee
*	***caucasica*** **new**	GKev
	matthioli	CElw EBee ECho EPfP GBBs GKev GKir NMen SRms WBVN WFar
	- 'Alba'	CElw EBee ECho GEdr GKev GKir NMen NWCA SRms
	- subsp. ***pekinensis***	CFir ECho EDAr GEdr GGar GKir NLar NMen NWCA SGSe SPet SRms WCot WFar WSHC
	turkestanica	ECho GAuc LLHF

Corydalis ✿ (*Papaveraceae*)

	from Sichuan, China	CPom MDKP
	ambigua misapplied	see *C. fumariifolia*
	ambigua Cham. & Schldlt.	EBee WWst
	angustifolia	WWst
	- white-flowered	GCrs WWst
	anthriscifolia	CLAP MDKP WCot
	'Berry Exciting'	CBow EBee
	'Blackberry Wine'	CPLG EBee ECtt EWTr IPot MDKP MPnt NPri WFar
	'Blue Panda'	see *C. flexuosa* 'Blue Panda'
	'Bronze Beauty'	CBow WMoo
	bulbosa misapplied	see *C. cava*
	bulbosa (L.) DC.	see *C. solida*
	buschii	CAby CLAP EBee ECho GBin GCrs GEdr GKev NCot NHar NRya SCnR WPGP
	'Canary Feathers'	EBee LSou MPnt NPri SBfd SRot
	cashmeriana	GEdr GKir LRHS NBid NHar NMen WAbe WHal
	cashmeriana × ***flexuosa***	CLAP ECho WAbe
	caucasica	ECho NMen
	- var. ***alba*** misapplied	see *C. malkensis*
§	***cava***	CLAP CPom EBee ECho EPot GCrs LAma SPhx WShi
	- 'Albiflora'	CLAP ECho SPhx
	- subsp. ***cava***	ECho
	chaerophylla	IBlr
	cheilanthifolia	CPLG CRow CSpe EBee ECha EDAr EHrv EPfP LBMP LEdu LRHS MDun MSCN SBfd SGar SPhx SRms WEas WFar WPGP WTin
	chionophila	WWst
	'Craigton Blue'	GCrs NHar
	curviflora	CPLG EWes SSvw WCot
	subsp. ***rosthornii***	
	- - 'Blue Heron'	IPot
	darwasica	WWst
	davidii	CPLG
	decipiens misapplied Υ^{H4}	CPom ECho EPot
I	- purple-flowered	EBee ECho WWst
I	***decipiens*** Schott, Nyman & Kotschy	see *C. solida* subsp. *incisa*
	decumbens B&SWJ 11142	WCru
	densiflora	ECho WWst
	'Early Bird'	EWes
	elata	Widely available
	- 'Blue Summit'	CLAP EBrs EPPr IMou LRHS
	elata × ***flexuosa***	IMou
	elata × ***flexuosa*** clone 1	CLAP CMdw CPLG GEdr WPrP
	erdelii	ECho WWst
	flexuosa Υ^{H4}	CFee CSpe EBee ECho EPfP IFro MArl MLHP MNrw MTho NCob SGar WAbe WBor WFar WSHC
	- CD&R 528	NRya
	- 'Balang Mist'	CLAP CPLG GCrs
	- 'Blue Dragon'	see *C. flexuosa* 'Purple Leaf'
§	- 'Blue Panda'	CPLG EBee EPPr EWes GMaP LRHS NHar NSla WFar
	- 'China Blue'	Widely available
	- 'Copperhead'	ECho
	- 'Golden Panda'^{PBR} (v)	CBct CBow CHid CYeo EBee ECho ECtt MCCP MPnt WCot WFut
	- 'Hale Cat'	EBee ECtt EPPr
	- 'Hidden Purple'	CHid
	- 'Nightshade'	CPLG CYeo ECtt EWTr NBid NCob WCot WFar WHoo WPrP
I	- 'Norman's Seedling'	ECtt EPPr IVic WPGP
	- 'Père David'	Widely available
§	- 'Purple Leaf'	Widely available
§	***fumariifolia***	ECho MTho
	glauca	see *C. sempervirens*
	glaucescens	ECho WWst
	- 'Early Beauty'	ECho WWst
	'Golden Spinners' **new**	IVic
	gracilis	WWst
	haussknechtii	WWst
	henrikii	NMen WWst
	heterocarpa	IMou
	incisa	ECho ERCP LAma NMen
	- B&SWJ 4417	WCru
	integra	WWst
	'Kingfisher'	CDes CLAP EWes GCrs IPot NHar NLar NSla SBch WAbe WFar
	kusnetzovii	WWst
	ledebouriana	ECho EPot WWst
	leucanthema	CLAP CPLG EBee
	- DJHC 752	CDes WPrP
	- 'Silver Spectre' (v)	CBow CPLG EBee ECtt LLHF MNrw NLar NSti WFar
	linstowiana	CPLG
	- CD&R 605	CLAP
§	***lutea***	CBcs CRWN EBee EPfP IBlr IFoB IFro MMuc MSCN NBir NCob NPer NVic SEND SRms WCot WMoo
	magadanica	LLHF MMoz WHil
§	***malkensis*** Υ^{H4}	CAvo EBee ECho EPot GBin GCrs LLHF MAsh NBir NRya SCnR WFar WThu
	maracandica	WWst
	moorcroftiana	CPLG
	nariniana	WWst
	'New Contender' **new**	WWst
	nobilis	CPom CSpe ECho IFoB IFro SPhx WFar WWst
	nudicaulis	ECho WWst
	ochotensis	IMou
	- B&SWJ 917	WCru
§	***ochroleuca***	CElw CMac CPom CRow CSpe EBee EPot GCal GKir LPla MSCN MTho WFar WMoo
	ophiocarpa	CSpe EHoe ELan GCal IBlr SBfd WHil WMoo
	oppositifolia	WWst
	- subsp. ***kurdica***	WWst
	ornata	WWst
	pachycentra	CPLG
	paczoskii	ECho GGar GKev GKir LRHS MNrw NMen
	- RS 12180	EBee
	paschei	WWst

popovii	MTho SCnR WWst
pseudofumaria alba	see *C. ochroleuca*
pumila	EBee ECho
quantmeyeriana	CBow CWGN EBee ECtt EPPr LLHF
'Chocolate Stars'	LSou MBNS SBfd SMrm SPhx SPoG WCot WFar
'Rainier Blue'	IVic
repens	WWst
rosea 'American Dream'	CWCL
scandens	see *Dicentra scandens*
schanginii	ECho WWst
subsp. ***ainii*** ♀H2	
- subsp. ***schanginii***	ECho WWst
scouleri	NBir
seisumsiana	WWst
§ ***sempervirens***	CBod WWEG
- 'Alba'	CBow ECho WFoF
sewerzowii	WWst
siamensis	IFoB IMou
- B&SWJ 7200	WCru
smithiana	WFar WHil
§ ***solida***	CAby CAvo CPom EBee EBrs ECho ECtt ELan EPfP EPot GAbr IBlr ITim LAma LEdu LRHS MRav NLar NMen NPnk NRya SDeJ SMrm SPhx WBVN WCot WFar WPnP WShi WTin
- 'Firecracker'	ECho LLHF LRHS
- 'First Kiss'	WWst
- 'Frodo'	IPot LAma
- 'Harkov'	WFar WWst
- 'Highland Sunset'	GCrs
- 'Ice Pink'	NMen
§ - subsp. ***incisa*** ♀H4	EBee ECho GKev LAma MNrw MTho SPhx WCot WShi
- - CH 850	WWst
- - HOA 8943	WWst
- - white-flowered **new**	WWst
- lilac-flowered	IFoB
- 'Margaret'	WWst
- 'Maxima'	NMen
- 'Merlin'	WWst
- 'Moonlight Shade'	ECho
- Nettleton seedlings	EPot
- pink and red shades	GCrs MAsh
- 'Pink Discovery'	WWst
- 'Purple Beauty'	EBee ECho EPot GKev MNrw SPhx WWst
- 'Quiet Elegance' **new**	LAma
- 'Snowlark'	WWst
§ - subsp. ***solida***	CLAP CMil EBrs ECho EPot GGar GKev NBir NRya SPhx
- - from Penza, Russia	LAma NCot WWst
- - 'Alba'	NSla
- - 'Beth Evans'	CAvo CWCL EBee ECha ECho ECtt ELon EPPr EPot ERCP GBin GEdr GKev IPot LAma LEdu LLHF MCot NCGa NHar NHol NLar NMen SCnR SDeJ SPhx WCot WFar WWEG
- - 'Blushing Girl'	ECho IPot LAma
- - dark pink-flowered **new**	NDov
- - 'Dieter Schacht' ♀H4	EBee ECho EPot GBin GCrs ITim LAma LLHF NMen WCot
- - 'Evening Shade'	ECho LAma
- - 'George Baker' ♀H4	Widely available
- - 'Lahovice'	NMen WCot WFar
- - pale pink-flowered **new**	NDov
- - Prasil Group	CBgR EPot GKev SPhx
- - 'White Knight'	GCrs LAma WCot
- f. ***transsylvanica***	see *C. solida* subsp. *solida*
- 'White King'	WWst
- 'White Swallow'	ECho GKev WWst
- 'Zwanenberg'	WWst
'Spinners'	CDes CElw CLAP CMea EBee ECha ECtt EPPr GCal GKev IPot IVic MDKP SBch SSvw SUsu WPGP WPrP WSHC
stipulata B&SWJ 2951	WCru
taliensis	CPLG GLog SBfd WHil
tauricola	GEdr NMen WWst
tomentella	GEdr
'Tory MP'	CDes CEnt CHid CLAP CPLG CPne CPom CSam CSpe EPPr GAbr GEdr MDKP MNrw NBid NChi NHar WCom WHoo WMnd WPGP WPrP
transsylvanica	see *C. solida* subsp. *solida*
turtschaninovii	SKHP
vittae	ECho IFoB WWst
vivipara	ECho EPot
wendelboi	ECho IFoB
- subsp. ***congesta***	WWst
- - 'Abant Wine'	EPot
- Jonus form	NMen
- subsp. ***wendelboi*** **new**	WWst
'Wildside Blue'	CLAP
wilsonii	CPLG GEdr IFoB IGor WEas
zetterlundii	WWst

Corylopsis ✿ (*Hamamelidaceae*)

glabrescens	CHGN CPMA
- var. ***gotoana***	EPfP MAsh NLar SSpi SSta
- - 'Chollipo'	CAbP CBcs LRHS SSta
glandulifera	NLar SSpi
himalayana	NLar
multiflora	SSpi
pauciflora ♀H4	Widely available
platypetala	see *C. sinensis* var. *calvescens*
- var. ***laevis***	see *C. sinensis* var. *calvescens*
sinensis	WPGP
§ - var. ***calvescens***	CBcs CPMA MBri NLar SSpi WPGP
§ - - f. ***veitchiana*** ♀H4	CDoy CPMA CSam ELan EPfP NLar SSpi WDin
- - - purple-leaved	CPMA
§ - var. ***sinensis*** ♀H4	CDoC CPMA CWit EBee ELon EPfP IVic LAst LRHS MAsh MBlu NLar SLon SPoG SReu WDin WFar WSpi
- - 'Spring Purple'	CAbP CBcs CEnd CGHE CMac CPMA EBee EPfP IDee IVic LRHS NCGa NLar SKHP SSpi SSta WDin WFar WPGP
spicata	CBcs CDoy CDul CPMA EBee IDee LRHS LTen MBlu MGos MRav NEgg NLar SLim SSpi WBVN
- 'Golden Spring'	EPfP MBlu NCGa NLar
- 'Red Eye'	IVic NLar
veitchiana	see *C. sinensis* var. *calvescens* f. *veitchiana*
willmottiae	see *C. sinensis* var. *sinensis*

Corylus ✿ (*Corylaceae*)

avellana (F)	Widely available
- 'Anny's Red Dwarf'	WPat
- 'Aurea'	CBcs CDul CEnd CLnd CSBt CTho CTri EBee ECrN ELan EPfP EWTr GBin GKir LBuc LRHS MAsh MBlu MBri MGos MRav NHol NLar NWea SLim SPer SSta SWvt WDin WFar
- 'Bollwylle'	see *C. maxima* 'Halle'sche Riesennuss'
- 'Casina' (F)	CAgr CTho
- 'Contorta'	Widely available
- 'Corabel' (F)	CAgr MCoo

	- 'Cosford Cob' (F)	CAgr CCVT CDul CMac CSBt CTho CTri ECrN ERea GKir GTwe LBuc MBlu MBri MGos SDea SKee SPer
	- Emoa Series	MCoo
	- 'Fortin' (F)	ECrN
§	- 'Fuscorubra' (F)	CPMA GKir MRav MWat
	- 'Gustav's Zeller' (F)	CAgr LRHS MBri MCoo
§	- 'Heterophylla'	CDul CEnd EBee EPfP GKir IFFs MBri NLar
	- 'Laciniata'	see *C. avellana* 'Heterophylla'
§	- 'Lang Tidlig Zeller' (F)	CAgr MCoo
	- 'Merveille de Bollwyller'	see *C. maxima* 'Halle'sche Riesennuss'
	- 'Nottingham Prolific'	see *C. avellana* 'Pearson's Prolific'
	- 'Pauetet' (F)	CAgr
§	- 'Pearson's Prolific' (F)	CAgr CSBt GTwe LBuc MMuc SDea SKee
	- 'Pendula'	EBee GKir MBlu SCoo SLim WPat
	- 'Purpurea'	see *C. avellana* 'Fuscorubra'
	- 'Red Majestic'^{PBR}	Widely available
	- 'Tonda di Giffoni' (F)	CAgr MCoo
	- 'Webb's Prize Cob' (F)	CAgr CDul ECrN ERea GTwe MBlu MMuc NLar SDea SEND SKee SVic WMou
	avellana* × *colurna 'Freeoka'	MCoo
	colurna ♀^{H4}	CCVT CDul CLnd CMCN CMac CTho EBee ECrN EPfP EWTr GKir IFFs MGos MWat NLar NWea SCoo SPer WBVN WDin WMou
	- 'Te-Terra Red'	CMCN CPMA EBee GKir MAsh MBlu MBri NLar SMad SSpi WMou
	× ***colurnoides*** 'Chinoka' (F)	MCoo
	- 'Laroka' (F)	ECrN
	Early Long Zeller	see *C. avellana* 'Lang Tidlig Zeller'
	ferox GWJ 9293	WCru
	maxima (F)	CLnd CMac CTri EMac ERea GTwe MSwo NWea SDea WDin
	- 'Butler' (F)	CAgr CMac CTho ECrN ERea GTwe MBri SKee
	- 'Ennis' (F)	CAgr ECrN ERea GTwe SDea SKee
	- 'Fertile de Coutard'	see *C. maxima* 'White Filbert'
	- 'Frizzled Filbert' (F)	ECrN
	- 'Frühe van Frauendorf'	see *C. maxima* 'Red Filbert'
	- 'Garibaldi' (F)	NLar
	- 'Grote Lambertsnoot'	see *C. maxima* 'Kentish Cob'
	- 'Gunslebert' (F)	CAgr CCVT CMac CSBt CTho ECrN ERea GTwe MBri SDea SKee
	- Halle Giant	see *C. maxima* 'Halle'sche Riesennuss'
§	- 'Halle'sche Riesennuss' (F)	CAgr ECrN EPfP GTwe MMuc NLar SEND SKee
§	- 'Kentish Cob' (F)	CAgr CBcs CDul CMac CSBt CTho CWSG ECrN ELan EPfP ERea GTwe LBuc MAsh MBlu MBri MGan MGos SBfd SDea SKee SLim SPer SRms WHar
	- 'Lambert's Filbert'	see *C. maxima* 'Kentish Cob'
	- 'Longue d'Espagne'	see *C. maxima* 'Kentish Cob'
	- 'Monsieur de Bouweller'	see *C. maxima* 'Halle'sche Riesennuss'
	- 'Purple Filbert'	see *C. maxima* 'Purpurea'
§	- 'Purpurea' (F) ♀^{H4}	Widely available
§	- 'Red Filbert' (F)	CEnd CTho CWSG ERea GTwe IFFs LRHS MAsh MBlu MBri NLar SCoo SKee SLim WPat
	- 'Red Zellernut'	see *C. maxima* 'Red Filbert'
	- 'Spanish White'	see *C. maxima* 'White Filbert'
§	- 'White Filbert' (F)	ERea GTwe MAsh SKee WHar
	- 'White Spanish Filbert'	see *C. maxima* 'White Filbert'
	- 'Witpit Lambertsnoot'	see *C. maxima* 'White Filbert'
	'Nottingham Early' (F)	NLar

Corymbia see *Eucalyptus*

Corynabutilon see *Abutilon*

Corynephorus (*Poaceae*)

canescens	EBee GFor GQue NBir WWEG

Corynocarpus (*Corynocarpaceae*)

laevigatus	CHEx ECou MBri

Cosmos (*Asteraceae*)

§	***atrosanguineus***	Widely available
	- 'Chocamocha'	CAvo CBcs CCCN CChe CHar CMea CSpe CWCL CWit EBee ECtt EPfP GBin LAst LHop LSRN LSou MTis NPri SBfd SMrm SPoG SRot STes SUsu
	bipinnatus	CSpe
	Bright Lights mixed (d)	
	- 'Purity'	CFox CSpe
	- 'Sonata Carmine'	LSou NPri
	- 'Sonata Pink'	LSou NPri SPoG
	- 'Sonata White'	CSpe LAst LSou NPri SPoG
	peucedanifolius	CSpe MCot
	- 'Flamingo'	EBee EPfP LSou SPoG

Cosmos × *Dahlia* (*Asteraceae*)

'Mexican Black'	EBee ERCP GMac MCot WCot WFut

costmary see *Tanacetum balsamita*

Cotinus ✿ (*Anacardiaceae*)

	americanus	see *C. obovatus*
§	***coggygria*** ♀^{H4}	CArn CBcs CDoC CMCN CMac CSBt CTri CWSG EBee ECrN ELan EPfP GAbr GKir LHop MBri MMuc MRav MSwo MWat NBea NWea SBfd SEND SPer SWvt WDin WFar WHar
	- Golden Spirit = 'Ancot'^{PBR}	Widely available
	- Green Fountain = 'Kolcot'^{PBR}	LRHS
	- 'Kanari'	CPMA EBee NLar WPat
	- 'Nordine'	NLar
	- 'Notcutt's Variety'	ELan EPfP GKir MGos MRav NSti
	- 'Old Fashioned' **new**	MBri MPkF
	- 'Pink Champagne'	CBcs CPMA EPfP MBri NLar SSpi WPat
	- Purpureus Group	GKir LRHS
	- 'Red Beauty'	CPMA NLar
	- Red Spirit = 'Firstpur'	NLar
	- 'Royal Purple' ♀^{H4}	Widely available
	- Rubrifolius Group	CBcs EBee EPfP LRHS NHol SPer SWvt WDin WFar
	- Smokey Joe = 'Lisjo'^{PBR}	CWit EPfP LRHS MAsh NCGa SBfd SLon SPoG SSta
	- 'Smokey Joe Purple'	LSou
	- 'Velvet Cloak'	CAbP CPMA EBee ELan EPfP EWTr GKir LBuc LRHS MBri MGos MRav NLar SLon SWvt
	- 'Young Lady'^{PBR}	Widely available
	Dusky Maiden = 'Londus'	EPfP GKir LRHS MAsh SLon WPat
	'Flame' ♀^{H4}	CAbP CBcs CDul CPMA EBee ELan EPfP EWTr GKir LRHS MBri MGos MRav NLar SKHP SLim SPer SSpi WPat
	'Grace'	Widely available
§	***obovatus*** ♀^{H4}	CPMA EBtc EPfP IArd LRHS MBlu MPkF MRav NLar SSpi WPat

Cotoneaster ✿ (*Rosaceae*)

	acuminatus	EMac SRms
	adpressus ♀H4	MGos MSwo
§	- 'Little Gem'	EBee ECho MGos NHar NLar
	- var. ***praecox***	see *C. nanshan*
	- 'Tom Thumb'	see *C. adpressus* 'Little Gem'
	affinis	SRms SSpi
	albokermesinus	SRms
	amoenus	SLPl SRms
§	***apiculatus***	EBee SRms
§	***ascendens***	SRms
	assamensis	SRms
§	***astrophoros***	CMac GKir MBlu NHar
	atropurpureus	SRms
§	- 'Variegatus' (v) ♀H4	CBcs CBot CDul CMac CSBt CWSG CWib EBee EHoe ELan EPfP GKir LBMP LRHS MAsh MGos MMuc NEgg NPer SBfd SCoo SEND SLim SPer SPoG SRms SWvt WDin WFar WMoo
	boisianus	SRms
	bradyi	SRms
§	***bullatus*** ♀H4	CDul CLnd CTri ECrN EMac EPfP GKir IFFs MGos MMuc NLar SPer SRms
	- 'Firebird'	see *C. ignescens*
	- f. ***floribundus***	see *C. bullatus*
	- var. ***macrophyllus***	see *C. rehderi*
	- 'McLaren'	SRms
	bumthangensis	SRms
	buxifolius blue-leaved	see *C. lidjiangensis*
	- 'Brno'	see *C. marginatus* 'Brno'
	- f. ***vellaeus***	see *C. astrophoros*
	camilli-schneideri	SRms
	canescens	SRms
§	***cashmiriensis*** ♀H4	MGos
	cavei	MBlu SRms
	cinnabarinus	SRms
§	***cochleatus***	CDul EBee LAst MGos NMen SRms
§	***congestus***	CSBt CWib EBee GKir MGos MSwo NHol SPlb SRms WDin WHar
	- 'Nanus'	CMea ELan GEdr MGos NHol WPat
	conspicuus	CBcs EWTr LAst SRms
	- 'Decorus' ♀H4	CAlb CCVT CDoC CDul CSBt CWSG EBee EPfP GKir IFFs LHop LRHS MGan MGos MMuc MSwo NEgg NHol NLar NWea SBfd SLim SPer SPlb SPoG SWvt WDin WMoo
	- 'Leicester Gem'	SRms
	- 'Red Glory'	CMac
	cooperi	SRms
*	'Coral'	LAst
	cornifolius	SRms
	cuspidatus	MBlu
N	***dammeri*** ♀H4	Widely available
§	- 'Major'	CBar LBuc
§	- 'Mooncreeper'	MBri
	- 'Oakwood'	see *C. radicans* 'Eichholz'
	- var. ***radicans*** misapplied	see *C. dammeri* 'Major'
	- var. ***radicans*** C.K.Schneid.	see *C. radicans*
	dielsianus	EMac IFFs NLar NWea SRms
	distichus var. ***tongolensis***	see *C. splendens*
	divaricatus	EMac EPfP NLar NWea SPer SRms WFar
	duthieanus 'Boer'	see *C. apiculatus*
	elatus	SRms
	elegans	SRms
	emeiensis	SRms
	'Erlinda'	see *C.* × *suecicus* 'Erlinda'
	'Exburiensis'	CBcs CDoC CDul EPfP GKir LAst MAsh MBri MGos MMuc MRav NLar WDin WFar
	falconeri	EBee SRms
	fangianus	EMac
	fastigiatus	SRms
	flinckii	SRms
	floccosus	IVic NWea
	floridus	SRms
	forrestii	SRms
	franchetii	Widely available
	- var. ***cinerascens***	SRms
	frigidus	SRms WDin
N	- 'Cornubia' ♀H4	Widely available
	- 'Notcutt's Variety'	EPfP
	- 'Saint Monica'	MBlu
	gamblei	SRms
	ganghobaensis	SRms
	glabratus	SLPl SRms
	glacialis	SRms
	glaucophyllus	IArd SEND SRms
§	***glomerulatus***	SRms
	gracilis	SRms
	granatensis	SRms
	harrovianus	SLPl SRms
	harrysmithii	GAuc GKir
I	***hedegaardii*** 'Fructu Luteo'	SRms
	henryanus	SRms
	'Herbstfeuer'	see *C. salicifolius* 'Herbstfeuer'
	'Highlight'	see *C. pluriflorus*
§	***hjelmqvistii***	EBee LBuc SRms
	- 'Robustus'	see *C. hjelmqvistii*
	- 'Rotundifolius'	see *C. hjelmqvistii*
	hodjingensis	SRms
	horizontalis ♀H4	Widely available
	- 'Variegatus'	see *C. atropurpureus* 'Variegatus'
	- var. ***wilsonii***	see *C. ascendens*
	hualiensis	SRms
	humifusus	see *C. dammeri*
	hummelii	SRms
§	'Hybridus Pendulus'	Widely available
§	***hylmoei***	SLPl SRms
	hypocarpus	SRms
	ignavus	SLPl SRms
§	***ignescens***	MMuc NWea SRms
	ignotus	SRms
	induratus	SLPl SRms
	insculptus	SRms
	integerrimus	SRms
§	***integrifolius*** ♀H4	EBee EPfP EPla NMen SCoo SPoG SRms WMoo
	- 'Silver Shadow'	NLar
	kangdingensis	SRms
	lacteus ♀H4	Widely available
	lancasteri	SRms
	langei	SRms
	laxiflorus	SRms
§	***lidjiangensis***	SRms
§	***linearifolius***	GCra GKir
	lucidus	NLar SRms
	ludlowii	SRms
	magnificus	SRms
§	***mairei***	SRms
	marginatus	SRms
§	- 'Blazovice'	SRms
§	- 'Brno'	SRms
	marquandii	GKir SRms
§	***meiophyllus***	MBlu
	meuselii	SRms
	microphyllus misapplied	see *C. purpurascens*

	microphyllus Wall. ex Lindl.	CDul CTri EBee LRHS MGos NPla NWea SDix SPer SPoG STre WDin WMoo
	- NICE 004	WCFE
	- var. ***cochleatus*** misapplied	see *C. cashmiriensis*
	- var. ***cochleatus*** (Franch.) Rehd. & Wils.	see *C. cochleatus*
	- var. ***cochleatus*** ambig.	NSla
	- 'Donard Gem'	see *C. astrophoros*
	- 'Ruby'	SRms
	- 'Teulon Porter'	see *C. astrophoros*
	- var. ***thymifolius*** misapplied	see *C. linearifolius*
	- var. ***thymifolius*** (Lindl.) Koehne	see *C. integrifolius*
	milkedandai	SRms
	miniatus	SRms
	mirabilis	SRms
	monopyrenus	SRms
	'Mooncreeper'	see *C. dammeri* 'Mooncreeper'
	morrisonensis	SRms
	moupinensis	SRms
	mucronatus	SRms
	multiflorus Bunge	NLar SRms
§	***nanshan***	CAbP NLar NWea SRms
	- 'Boer'	see *C. apiculatus*
	'Naoujanensis' **new**	GKir
	newryensis	SRms
	nitens	SRms
	nitidifolius	see *C. glomerulatus*
	nohelii	SRms
	notabilis	SRms
	nummularioides	SRms
	nummularius	SRms
	obscurus	SRms
	obtusus	SRms
	pangiensis	SRms
	pannosus	SLPl SRms WFar
	- 'Speckles'	SRms
	paradoxus	SRms
	parkeri	SRms
	pekinensis	SRms
	permutatus	see *C. pluriflorus*
	perpusillus	SRms WFar
§	***pluriflorus***	SRms
	poluninii	SRms
	polycarpus	SRms
	praecox 'Boer'	see *C. apiculatus*
	procumbens	SLon SRms WDin
	- 'Queen of Carpets'	CDoC CDul EBee EPfP EQua GKir LRHS LSRN MAsh MGos MRav MWhi NLar SBfd SCoo SLim SPoG SRms SWvt WMoo
	- 'Streib's Findling'	see *C.* 'Streib's Findling'
	prostratus	SRms
	przewalskii	SRms
	pseudo-obscurus	SRms
§	***purpurascens***	CSBt GKir MGos WFar
	pyrenaicus	see *C. congestus*
	qungbixiensis	SRms
	racemiflorus	SRms
§	***radicans***	IFFs MWat SPoG
§	- 'Eichholz'	EBee MGos NHol SBfd SPoG WDin
§	***rehderi***	CMHG NLar SRms
	roseus	SRms
	'Rothschildianus' ♀H4	Widely available
	rotundifolius	SLon
	rubens	GKir
	rugosus	SRms
	salicifolius	EBee GKir MSwo SRms WDin WFar
	- Autumn Fire	see *C. salicifolius* 'Herbstfeuer'
§	- 'Avonbank'	CDoC CEnd LTen NLar
	- 'Bruno Orangeade'	SRms
	- 'Gnom'	CChe CDul CMac EBee ELan EPfP EQua LRHS MAsh MBlu MGos MRav NBir NEgg SPer SPoG SRms WDin WFar WHar WMoo
§	- 'Herbstfeuer'	MGos MRav MSwo SRms WFar
	- 'Pendulus'	see *C.* 'Hybridus Pendulus'
	- 'Repens'	CDoC CWib EPfP MGan MWhi NHol NPla NWea SLim SPer SPoG SRms WDin WFar
	- var. ***rugosus*** hort.	see *C. hylmoei*
	- 'Scarlet Leader'	CMac
	salwinensis	SLPl SRms
	sandakphuensis	SRms
	scandinavicus	SRms
	schantungensis	SRms
	schlechtendalii 'Blazovice'	see *C. marginatus* 'Blazovice'
	- 'Brno'	see *C. marginatus* 'Brno'
	schubertii	SRms
	serotinus misapplied	see *C. meiophyllus*
	serotinus Hutchinson	NLar SLPl SRms
	shannanensis	SRms
	shansiensis	SRms
	sherriffii	SRms
	aff. ***sichuanensis***	GAuc
	sikangensis	SLon SRms
	simonsii ♀H4	CCVT CDoC CDul CLnd CMac CTri EBee ECrN ELan EMac EPfP GKir IFFs LBuc MGos NHol NLar NPla NWea SCoo SPer SPoG SRms WDin WFar WHar
§	***splendens***	GKir SRms WFar
	- 'Sabrina'	see *C. splendens*
	spongbergii	SRms
	staintonii	SRms
	sternianus ♀H4	EBee EPfP SLPl SRms
§	'Streib's Findling'	MAsh NLar
	suavis	SRms
	subacutus	SRms
	subadpressus	SRms
	× ***suecicus*** 'Coral Beauty'	Widely available
§	- 'Erlinda' (v)	NLar SCoo SRms
	- 'Ifor'	SLPl SRms
	- 'Juliette' (v)	EHoe GGar LAst LRHS LSRN MAsh NLar SCoo SLim SPoG WFar WRHF
	- 'Skogholm'	CBcs CDul CWib EBee GKir IFFs LRHS MAsh MGos SCoo SPer SRms WDin WFar WHar
	taoensis	SRms
	tardiflorus	SRms
	tauricus	SRms
	teijiashanensis	SRms
	tengyuehensis	SRms
	thimphuensis	SRms
	tomentellus	WCFE
	tomentosus	SRms
	turbinatus	SLPl SRms
	'Valkenburg'	SRms
	vandelaarii	GKir SLPl SRms
	veitchii	MBri NLar SRms
	verruculosus	SRms
	villosulus	SRms
	vilmorinianus	SRms
	wardii misapplied	see *C. mairei*
	wardii W.W. Sm.	GGal SRms
	× ***watereri***	CCVT CWib LAst MMuc MSwo NWea SBfd SEND WDin WJas
	- 'Avonbank'	see *C. salicifolius* 'Avonbank'
	- 'Corina'	SRms
	- 'Cornubia'	see *C. frigidus* 'Cornubia'
	- 'John Waterer' ♀H4	EPfP MGos SPoG WFar
	- 'Pendulus'	see *C.* 'Hybridus Pendulus'

- 'Pink Champagne'	CMac EQua MRav
wilsonii	SRms
yallungensis	SRms
yinchangensis	SRms
zabelii	SRms

Cotula (*Asteraceae*)

C&H 452	NWCA
atrata	see *Leptinella atrata*
coronopifolia	CBen CWat EHon LPBA NPer SWat
§ ***hispida*** (DC.) Harv.	CMea CTri EBee ECho EDAr EHoe EPot GKev GMaP LRHS MHer MSCN MTho MWat NPer NRya NWCA SPoG SRms WCom WEas WFar WJek WPat
leariloba (DC.) Hilliard	ECha ECho EWes LBee LRHS
minor	see *Leptinella minor*
'Platt's Black'	see *Leptinella squalida* 'Platt's Black'
potentilloides	see *Leptinella potentillina*
pyrethrifolia	see *Leptinella pyrethrifolia*
rotundata	see *Leptinella rotundata*
serrulata	see *Leptinella serrulata*
squalida	see *Leptinella squalida*

Cotyledon (*Crassulaceae*)

chrysantha	see *Rosularia chrysantha*
gibbiflora var. ***metallica***	see *Echeveria gibbiflora* var. *metallica*
oppositifolia	see *Chiastophyllum oppositifolium*
orbiculata	CHEx CStu ETod SDix
- var. ***oblonga***	EBee WEas
- var. ***orbiculata***	EShb
- 'Silver Waves'	MCot
simplicifolia	see *Chiastophyllum oppositifolium*
tomentosa subsp. ***ladismithensis***	EShb

Cowania see *Purshia*

Crambe (*Brassicaceae*)

cordifolia 🏆H4	Widely available
maritima 🏆H4	CArn CSev CSpe EBWF EBee EBrs ECha EPfP GMaP GPoy LRHS MCoo MCot MMuc MRav NEgg NPnk NSti SEND SMad SPer SWat WCot WFar WJek WMnd WPer WSpi WWEG
- 'Lilywhite'	CAgr EBee ILis SVic WCom WCot
tatarica	WPer

cranberry see *Vaccinium macrocarpon*, *V. oxycoccos*

Crassula (*Crassulaceae*)

anomala	see *C. atropurpurea* var. *anomala*
arborescens	EShb SRms STre
argentea	see *C. ovata*
§ ***atropurpurea*** var. ***anomala***	SChr
- subsp. ***arborescens*** 'Blue Mist'	SEND
coccinea	EShb
dejecta	EShb
§ ***exilis*** subsp. ***cooperi***	STre
lactea	STre
lycopodioides variegata	see *C. muscosa* 'Variegata'
multicava	CHEx
muscosa	EShb NWCA SChr SRot STre
§ - 'Variegata' (v)	EShb
obtusa	SRot
orbicularis	WCot
§ ***ovata*** 🏆H1	CDoC CHEx CTsd EBak EOHP EPfP EUJe MMuc NPer NPla SEND SWal WThu
- 'Gollum'	STre SWal
- 'Hummel's Sunset' (v) 🏆H1	STre SWal
* - ***nana***	SEND STre
- 'Obliqua'	STre
- 'Variegata' (v)	EBak STre
perfoliata var. ***falcata*** 🏆H1	CTsd EShb NWCA SRot WCot
perforata	NWCA SPlb
- 'Variegata' (v)	CBow LSou SRot
picturata	see *C. exilis* subsp. *cooperi*
portulacea	see *C. ovata*
rupestris 🏆H1	STre
§ ***sarcocaulis***	CBcs CHEx CTri ECho ELan ELon EPot GEdr GMaP MMuc MTho NMen NVic NWCA SEND SGar SPlb SPoG SRms SRot STre WAbe WEas WFar WPat WSHC
I - ***alba***	GEdr STre
- 'Ken Aslet'	STre
sedifolia	see *C. setulosa* 'Milfordiae'
sediformis	see *C. setulosa* 'Milfordiae'
§ ***setulosa*** 'Milfordiae'	CTri ECho GKir NBir
socialis	STre WAbe
- 'Major'	SChr
tetragona	MMuc SEND
* ***tomentosa*** 'Variegata' (v)	EShb
'Très Bon'	STre

+ *Crataegomespilus* (*Rosaceae*)

'Jules d'Asnières'	NLar

× *Crataegosorbus* (*Rosaceae*)

miczurinii 'Ivan's Belle'	CAgr

Crataegus (*Rosaceae*)

F&M 196	WPGP
altaica	GKir
arnoldiana	CAgr CDul CEnd CLnd CTri EBee ECrN EPfP GKir LRHS MCoo MMuc NWea SCoo SEND SLPl SPer
'Autumn Glory'	CEnd CLnd EBee ECrN GKir WFar
azarolus	CTho EPfP
champlainensis	CLnd
chrysocarpa	EPfP
chungtienensis	SSpi WSpi
- SDR 5104	GKev
N ***coccinea*** misapplied	see *C. intricata*
N ***coccinea*** ambig.	NWea
§ ***coccinea*** L.	CAgr CLnd CTho EBee EPfP GKir MCoo SCoo
coccinioides	EPfP
cordata	see *C. phaenopyrum*
crus-galli misapplied	see *C. persimilis* 'Prunifolia'
crus-galli L.	CCVT CDoC CDul CLnd CTho EBee ECrN EPfP LAst NWea SPer WDin WFar WJas
dahurica	EPfP
× ***dippeliana***	EPfP
douglasii	EPfP GAuc
dsungarica	EPfP
× ***durobrivensis***	CAgr CDul CLnd EPfP GKir MBri MCoo NLar
ellwangeriana	CAgr ECrN EPfP
- 'Fire Ball' new	MBlu
eriocarpa	CLnd
flabellata	GKir
gemmosa	CEnd GKir MCoo NLar NWea SSpi

greggiana	EPfP
× ***grignonensis***	CBcs CDul CLnd CTho ECrN LMaj MAsh SEND SPer WJas
§ ***intricata***	EPfP NWea
irrasa	EPfP
jonesiae	ECrN EPfP
laciniata Ucria	see *C. orientalis*
§ ***laevigata***	CDul GKir NWea
- 'Coccinea Plena'	see *C. laevigata* 'Paul's Scarlet'
- 'Crimson Cloud'	Widely available
- 'Gireoudii'	CBcs CDul CEnd CPMA CWib EBee LAst MGos NLar WPat
- 'Mutabilis'	CLnd CTri
§ - 'Paul's Scarlet' (d) ♀H4	Widely available
- 'Pink Corkscrew'	EPfP LLHF MBlu MGos NHol SMad WPat
- 'Plena' (d)	CBcs CDoC CDul CLnd CMac CSBt CTho CTri CWib EBee ECrN EPfP GKir LAst MGos MSwo MWat NWea SBfd SCrf SLim SPer WDin WFar WHar
- 'Punicea'	GKir
- 'Rosea'	SEND
- 'Rosea Flore Pleno' (d) ♀H4	Widely available
× ***lavalleei***	CCVT CDul CLnd CTri EBee ECrN ELan EPfP GKir LAst LMaj MAsh MMuc MSwo NWea SCoo SPer SPur WDin
- 'Carrierei' ♀H4	CDoC CMac CTho EBee EPfP EWTr GKir IVic LHop LMaj LRHS MBri NWea SCoo WCot WMou
lobulata	EPfP
mexicana	see *C. pubescens* f. *stipulacea*
mollis	CAgr CTho ECrN EPfP MBri WSpi
monogyna	CArn CBcs CCVT CDoC CDul CLnd CMac CRWN CTri ECrN ELan EMac EPfP GKir LAst LBuc LRHS MAsh MBri MGos NPri NWea SBfd SPer SPoG WDin WFar WHar WMou WSFF
§ - 'Biflora'	CDul CEnd CLnd CTho CTri CWit EBee ECrN GKir LRHS MCoo MGos NPal NWea SLim
- 'Compacta'	MBlu WPat
- 'Flexuosa'	MGos WCot
- 'Praecox'	see *C. monogyna* 'Biflora'
- 'Stricta'	CCVT CDul CLnd CSBt EBee ECrN EPfP GKir LMaj MMuc SEND
- 'Variegata' (v)	ECrN
× ***mordenensis*** 'Toba' (d)	CDul CLnd EPfP
nigra	EPfP
§ ***orientalis***	CCVT CDul CEnd CLnd CMCN CTho CTri EBee ECrN EPfP GKir IArd MAsh MBlu MBri MCoo MGos NWea SCoo SLPl SLim SMad SSpi WJas WMou WSpi
oxyacantha	see *C. laevigata*
pedicellata	see *C. coccinea* L.
pentagyna	EPfP
§ ***persimilis*** 'Prunifolia' ♀H4	Widely available
- 'Prunifolia Splendens'	CCVT EBee EWTr GBin GKir LBuc MBri MCoo SCoo WPat
§ ***phaenopyrum***	CDul CLnd CTho EBee EPfP MGos SLPl SMad
pinnatifida	EPfP GKir
- var. ***major***	CDul CEnd EPfP MBri MCoo NWea SCoo SMad
- - 'Big Golden Star'	CAgr CLnd CTho CWit ECrN GKir MBlu MCoo NLar SCoo
'Praecox'	see *C. monogyna* 'Biflora'
prunifolia	see *C. persimilis* 'Prunifolia'
pseudoheterophylla	EPfP
§ ***pubescens*** f. ***stipulacea***	CDul CTho ECrN EPfP
punctata	CTho SLPl
- f. ***aurea***	EPfP
sanguinea	EPfP
schraderiana	CAgr CDul CLnd CTho EBee EBtc EPfP GKir LRHS MBri NWea SCoo SPoG
songarica	GAuc
sorbifolia	EPfP
succulenta	EPfP GKir
- var. ***macracantha***	EPfP GKir
suksdorfii	EPfP
tanacetifolia	CAgr CDul CPMA CTho EPfP GKir LLHF MBlu MBri SPer
* - 'Fructu Albo'	GKir
turkestanica	EPfP
viridis 'Winter King'	CPMA EPfP GKir MBlu MCoo SLim
wattiana	ELan EPfP

× *Crataemespilus* (*Rosaceae*)

grandiflora	CBcs CDul CEnd CLnd CTho WSpi

Crawfurdia (*Gentianaceae*)

pasquieri B&SWJ 11725 new	WCru
speciosa B&SWJ 2138	WCru

Cremanthodium (*Asteraceae*)

SDR 5953	GKev
arnicoides	EBee

Cremastra (*Orchidaceae*)

variabilis	NLAp WWst

× *Cremnosedum* (*Crassulaceae*)

§ 'Little Gem'	CStu EPot NMen WAbe

Crenularia see *Aethionema*

Crepis (*Asteraceae*)

aurea	CSpr ECho WCom
incana ♀H4	CMea CMoH CPla EBee ECho ECtt MAvo MTho NChi NMen NSla NWCA SPhx SRms WPat
- 'Pink Mist'	GBin MBri NLar SDix

Crinitaria see *Aster*

Crinodendron (*Elaeocarpaceae*)

hookerianum ♀H3	Widely available
- 'Ada Hoffmann'	CBcs CDoC CMac CSam EBee ELan ELon GAbr GCal GGGa GGar GKir IVic LRHS LSRN MBlu MBri MGos MPkF MREP NLar NMun SBfd SChF SKHP SLim SPoG WAbe WBrE
patagua	CBcs CCCN CSam CWib EBee EQua ESwi GGar IArd IDee IVic MBri MMuc NEgg NLar SLon SPoG WAbe WFar WSHC

Crinum (*Amaryllidaceae*)

amoenum	CCCN EBee ECho WCot
asiaticum	WCot
- DJHC 970606	WCot
- var. ***sinicum***	WCot
§ ***bulbispermum***	CFir CPrp EBee ELan GCal LRHS WCot
campanulatum	CDes
capense	see *C. bulbispermum*
'Carolina Beauty'	WCot

'Elizabeth Traub'	WCot
'Ellen Bosanquet'	CCCN CDes CFir CTca EBee WCot
'Emma Jones'	WCot
erubescens	WCot
'Hanibal's Dwarf'	CDes EBee WCot WPGP
moorei	CAvo CDes CFir CRHN CTca EBee ECho IVic LEdu LPio SChr WCot WPGP
- f. ***album***	CCCN CTca EBee LPio WCot
'Ollene'	WCot
§ × ***powellii*** Ψ^{H3}	Widely available
- 'Album' Ψ^{H3}	Widely available
- 'Longifolium'	see *C. bulbispermum*
- 'Roseum'	see *C.* × *powellii*
'Regina's Disco Lounge'	WCot
'Sangria' **new**	WCot
'Summer Nocturne' **new**	WCot
variabile	EBee WCot
'White Queen'	WCot
yemense misapplied	IMou WCot

Criogenes see *Cypripedium*

Crithmum (*Apiaceae*)

maritimum	CArn EBWF GPoy NLar SPlb WJek

Crocosmia ✿ (*Iridaceae*)

'Alistair'	ECtt
'Anniversary'	IBlr
'Apricot'	CTca ECrc IBal
'Apricot Surprise'	ELon
aurea misapplied	see *C.* × *crocosmiiflora* 'George Davison' Davison
aurea ambig.	EShb GCal
aurea (Pappe ex Hook.f.) Planch.	CDes CPne CPou ECtt IBlr NHol
- subsp. ***aurea***	CTca IBlr
- - 'Maculata'	ECrc IBlr
- subsp. ***pauciflora***	IBlr
'Auricorn'	IBlr NCot NHol
'Auriol'	IBlr NCot
'Aurora'	CHVG NGdn
'Beth Chatto'	CPrp CTca ECrc IBal MAvo
Bressingham Beacon = 'Blos'	EBrs IBlr WRHF
'Bressingham Blaze'	CBre CMHG CPrp CTca EBee EBla EBrs ECrc ECtt GKir IBlr LRHS NBre NGdn NHol WCot WHil
Bridgemere hybrid	ECrc NHol
Bright Eyes = 'Walbreyes'	LRHS
'Cadenza'	IBal IBlr NCot NHol
'Carnival'	ECtt IBlr
'Cascade'	IBal IBlr NCot
'Chinatown'	IBal IBlr MAvo NCot NHol WHil
'Citronella' misapplied	see *C.* × *crocosmiiflora* 'Honey Angels'
'Comet' Knutty	CPrp CTca EBrs ECrc GCal IBlr MAvo NCot NHol WMoo
§ × ***crocosmiiflora***	CHEx CTca CTri EBee IBlr LAst LRHS MCot NBPC NHol SEND SPlb SRms WBrk WCot WFar WMoo WShi
- 'A.E.Amos'	ECrc ECtt
- 'A.J. Hogan'	CPrp CTca GBin IBal IBlr NHol SMrs SUsu
- 'African Glow'	CTca ECrc IBal
- 'Amber Sun'	IBlr
- 'Amberglow'	CBgR CElw CPrp ECho EWoo GKir IBal IBlr NBre NHol NPer WFar
- 'Apricot Queen'	CTca IBlr NHol
- 'Autumn Gold'	IBlr
- 'Baby Barnaby'	CBre CDes CTca EBee ECtt IBlr NHol WPGP
- 'Babylon'	Widely available
- 'Best of British'	CHVG
- 'Bicolor'	CPrp CTca IBal IBlr NHol WHil
- 'Burford Bronze'	CPrp CTca IBal IBlr MAvo NHol
- 'Buttercup'	CSam CTca EBee ECrc EPfP ERCP EWll GKev IBal IBlr IKil MAvo MCot MLLN NBre NHol SBfd SRkn SRot STes WBor WFar WMoo WWEG
- 'Canary Bird'	CPne CPrp CRow CSam CYeo EBee ECho ECtt GAbr GMac IBal IBlr MNFA NBPC NGdn NHol WBrk WRHF
- 'Cardinale'	IBlr
§ - 'Carmin Brillant' Ψ^{H3-4}	Widely available
- 'Carminea'	STes
- 'Challa'	CTca EBee ECrc
- 'Citrina'	CTca GKir
- 'Citronella' J.E. Fitt	CBgR CPLG CPrp CSam CTri EBee EBla EBrs ECha ECrc EPfP GMaP GQue LBMP LRHS MLLN MRav NCob NGdn NHol SAga WBVN WBrk WCot
§ - 'Coleton Fishacre'	Widely available
§ - 'Columbus'	CAvo CPar CPrp CSam CTca EBee ECrc EPfP EWld GBin IBal IBlr LHop LRHS MAvo MSCN NHol SGar WBor WFar WMnd WWEG
- 'Colwall'	IBal IBlr MAvo NCot
- 'Constance'	CBgR CElw CPrp CSam CTca EBee EBrs ECrc GGar GKir IBal IBlr LRHS MAvo MBri NBid NGdn NHol SRGP SRos WBrk WFar WHil
- 'Corona'	CPrp CTca IBal IBlr MAvo NHol
- 'Corten'	IBlr
§ - 'Croesus'	CTca ECrc IBal IBlr MAvo MRav
- 'Custard Cream'	CPrp CSpe CTca ECrc ECtt IBlr MAvo NHol SRos WCon WFar
- 'D.H. Houghton'	IBlr
- 'Debutante'	CDes CPrp CTca EBee EBrs ECrc ECtt IBal IBlr LRHS MAvo NHol SUsu WHoo WPGP WSHC
§ - 'Diadème'	CSam CTca LEdu NHol
- 'Dusky Maiden'	Widely available
- 'Dwarf Gold' **new**	IBal
§ - 'E.A. Bowles'	CPou CPrp CTca EBee EBrs ECrc IBlr WCot
- 'Eastern Promise'	CBre CPrp CTca ELon IBal IBlr MAvo NCot SMrm WHil
- 'Eclatant'	IBlr
- 'Elegans'	CBre CElw EBrs ECrc ECtt IBal IBlr LRHS
§ - 'Emily McKenzie'	Widely available
- 'Etoile de Feu'	IBlr
- 'Fantasie'	CBgR ECrc IBal
- 'Festival Orange'	ECrc IBlr
- 'Fire Jumper'	CDes CTca EBee MAvo WPGP
- 'Firebrand'	IBlr NCot
- 'Fireglow'	CTca ECho ECtt GKir IBal IBlr IFFs NCot WFar WPer
- 'Flamethrower'	IBlr MAvo
- 'George Davison' misapplied	see *C.* × *crocosmiiflora* 'Golden Glory' ambig., 'Sulphurea'
§ - 'George Davison' Davison	Widely available
- 'Gloria'	CTca ECrc IBal IBlr MAvo SUsu WHil
- 'Golden Glory' misapplied	see *C.* × *crocosmiiflora* 'Diadème'
§ - 'Golden Glory' ambig.	CPLG CWCL EHrv ELan IBal IBlr LSou MSwo NBir NHol SPlb SRos WCot WFar

	- 'Goldfinch'	CPrp CTca ECrc IBlr NCot NHol SMrm WHil WWEG
	- 'Goldie'	CTca ECrc MAvo
	- 'Hades'	CPrp CTca IBlr MAvo
	- 'Harvest Sun'	IBlr
	- 'Heligan'	EPfP
	- 'His Majesty'	CPne CPrp CSam CSpe CTca CYeo ECrc ECtt IBal IBlr NHol SDys WFar WHil WPer
	- 'Hoey Joey'	ECrc GMac
§	- 'Honey Angels'	Widely available
	- 'Honey Bells'	CElw ECrc WBrk
	- 'Irish Dawn'	CPrp ECrc IBal IBlr NBre NCot NHol
§	- 'Jackanapes'	CPne CPrp CRow CTca CWCL EBee EBrs ECtt EHrv ELan ELon GCal GGar GKir IBal IBlr LRHS MBri MGos MLHP NHol SBfd SDys SUsu WFar WPGP
	- 'Jackanapes VI' **new**	IBal
	- 'James Coey' misapplied	see *C.* × *crocosmiiflora* 'Carmin Brillant'
	- 'James Coey' J.E. Fitt	CHar COIW CPrp CRow EAEE EBee EBla ECha EHoe EHrv EPfP EPla IFoB MLHP MWhi NDov NGdn NHol SPhx SRGP SWvt WFar WMoo
	- 'Jesse van Dyke'	IBlr
§	- 'Jessie'	CElw CTca ECrc IBlr MAvo SMrm WPer
	- 'Judith'	CTca ECrc IBlr NCot
	- 'Kapoor'	IBlr
	- 'Kiautschou'	CHVG CTca CWCL EBee EBrs ECtt GMac IBal IBlr MAvo NBre NHol SDys
	- 'Lady Hamilton'	Widely available
	- 'Lady McKenzie'	see *C.* × *crocosmiiflora* 'Emily McKenzie'
	- 'Lady Oxford'	CPrp CTca ECrc IBlr LRHS MAvo NHol SMrm WHil
	- 'Lambrook Gold'	CAvo ECrc IBlr SUsu
	- 'Lord Nelson'	CPrp CTca IBal NHol
	- 'Loweswater'	ECrc MAvo SUsu
	- 'Lutea'	EBee ECtt IBal IBlr NCob NHol
	- 'Marjorie'	ECrc
	- 'Mars'	CElw CPrp EBla ECrc EWes EWll GAbr GGar GMac IBal IBlr IFoB LPio LRHS MAvo MLLN MWhi NHol SBfd SMrm SPlb SRGP SRkn SRot WFar WPGP WPer WWEG
	- 'Mephistopheles'	CPrp CTca IBlr MAvo NHol
	- 'Merryman'	ECrc GAbr GMac IBal MAvo
	- 'Météore'	CBgR CPrp EPot GAbr GGar IBal LRHS MBNS MSpe NBre NHol NPri SWal WCon WPrP WWEG
	- 'Morgenlicht'	CTca ECtt IBal IBlr NHol WBrk WCot
	- 'Moses'	CTca ECrc
	- 'Mount Usher'	CFir CMdw CPrp CTca ECrc ECtt GCal IBal IBlr MAvo NHol SGar WFar WOut
	- 'Mrs David Howard'	SApp
§	- 'Mrs Geoffrey Howard'	CDes CPrp CSam CTca EBrs ECtt GGar IBal IBlr LEdu MAvo NHol SHar SUsu WBrk WCru WPGP
	- 'Mrs Morrison'	see *C.* × *crocosmiiflora* 'Mrs Geoffrey Howard'
	- Newry seedling	see *C.* × *crocosmiiflora* 'Prometheus'
	- 'Nigricans'	ECrc
	- 'Nimbus'	CPrp CTca EBee IBal IBlr WHil
§	- 'Norwich Canary'	CBgR CMHG COIW CPrp CTca EBee EBla ECha EPfP EShb GCra IBal IBlr LEdu LRHS MRav NBir NGdn NHol NPri NSti SMrm SUsu WBrk WCot WHil WMoo WSpi WWEG
	- 'Olympic Fire'	CTca ECrc IBlr MAvo NCot NHol
	- 'Olympic Sunrise' **new**	CTca
	- 'Pepper'	ECrc IBlr
	- 'Ping Pong' **new**	CTca
	- 'Plaisir'	CTca IBal IBlr MAvo NBid NHol WFar WPrP WWEG
	- 'Polo'	CBgR CSam CTca
	- 'Princess'	see *C. pottsii* 'Princess'
§	- 'Princess Alexandra'	IBlr
	- 'Prolificans'	IBlr
§	- 'Prometheus'	CPrp CTca IBal IBlr NHol WHil
	- 'Queen Alexandra' misapplied	see *C.* × *crocosmiiflora* 'Princess Alexandra'
§	- 'Queen Alexandra' J.E. Fitt	CTca ECha IBlr LEdu NHol SPer WHal WMoo WPer
	- 'Queen Charlotte'	CPrp CTca ECrc IBal IBlr
	- 'Queen Mary II'	see *C.* × *crocosmiiflora* 'Columbus'
	- 'Queen of Spain'	CPrp CTca EBrs GKir IBal IBlr LRHS MDKP MLLN NHol WHil
	- 'Rayon d'Or'	CDes ECrc IBlr MAvo WPGP
	- 'Red King'	CPrp EBee EBla EBrs EPfP EPot IBal IBlr LHop LRHS MBri MWea NLar SGar WBrk WFar WHil WRHF WSpi WWEG
	- 'Red Knight'	CBgR CHVG CMMP GAbr IBlr NHol
	- 'Rheingold' misapplied	see *C.* × *crocosmiiflora* 'Diadème'
	- 'Rose Queen'	IBlr
	- 'Saint Clements'	ECrc IBlr NCot NHol
	- 'Saracen'	CBcs CMac CTca EAEE EBee ECtt EShb GAbr GCal GGar GKir GMac IBal IBlr LAst LLWG MAvo MBNS MCot NBre NCob NGdn NLar SKHP SMrm WBrk WCot WEas WFar WMoo
	- 'Severn Seas'	ECrc
	- 'Sir Mathew Wilson'	CDes EBee EBrs GKir IBal IBlr WCot WPGP
	- 'Solfatare' ♀H3	Widely available
	- 'Solfatare Coleton Fishacre'	see *C.* × *crocosmiiflora* 'Coleton Fishacre'
	- 'Star of the East' ♀H3	Widely available
	- 'Starbright'	IBlr
	- 'Starfire'	ECrc ECtt
	- 'Sultan'	CDes CElw CYeo ECrc IBlr WFar WMoo WPGP
	- 'Venus'	CBgR CBre CPou CPrp CTca EBee EBrs ECtt EShb EWll IBal IBlr IFFs LRHS MAvo NBre NHol NLar NPla SRGP SRos WFar WHil WMoo WPrP
	- 'Vesuvius'	ECrc GCal IBlr NCGa WFar WSHC
	- 'Vic's Yellow'	ECrc SGar SMrm
	- 'Voyager'	CPrp CTca EBee ECtt ELon EPot ERCP GAbr IBal IBlr LHop LRHS MBri NHol SGar WBor WHil WPer
	- Wasdale strain	ECrc
	- 'Zeal Tan'	CElw CMHG CPar CPrp CSam CTca EBee ECGP ECtt ELan ELon GCal GKir IBal IBlr MAvo MBNS MCot MNFA NEgg SBfd SMrm SUsu WBrk WCot WOut
§	× ***crocosmioides***	CTca IBlr WHil
	- 'Castle Ward Late'	CBgR CPou CRow CTca EAEE ECha ECrc GAbr GCal GCra GGar IBal IBlr LHop MAvo NBre NCGa NDov NHol SMrm SUsu WMoo WOut
	- 'Mount Stewart Late'	IBlr
§	- 'Vulcan' Leichtlin	CTca IBlr LRHS NHol WHil
	'Cylvia'	ECrc

'Darkleaf Apricot'	see *C.* × *crocosmiiflora* 'Coleton Fishacre'
'Doctor Marion Wood'	EBee ECrc
'Eldorado'	see *C.* × *crocosmiiflora* 'E.A. Bowles'
'Elegance'	EBee IBlr
'Elizabeth'	NHol
'Ellenbank Canary'	CBgR CTca GMac MAvo
'Ellenbank Firecrest'	CBgR CDes CTca EBee MAvo NCGa WOut WPGP
'Ellenbank Skylark'	CBgR GMac MAvo
'Emberglow'	Widely available
'Fandango'	IBal IBlr NCot NHol
'Fernhill'	ECrc IBlr
* 'Feuerser'	ECtt
'Fire King' misapplied	see *C.* × *crocosmiiflora* 'Jackanapes'
'Fire King' ambig.	CBgR EBee ECrc ERCP GAbr IBal IFFs MBri NBPC NLar WHil WSpi
'Fire Sprite'	IBlr
'Firefly'	IBlr NHol
'Fireworks'	NCot
'Flaire'	IBlr
'Fleuve Jaune'	CPne CTca EBrs ECrc ECtt LRHS
fucata	IBlr
- 'Jupiter'	see *C.* 'Jupiter'
fucata* × *paniculata	CPrp CTca IBal NHol
'Fugue'	IBlr
'Fusilade'	IBlr
'Gold Sprite'	IBlr NCot
'Golden Ballerina'PBR	CPrp EBee EWes IBal LRHS LSou SGSe SPoG
'Golden Dew'	CBcs CBre CTca EBee ECrc ECtt GAbr GKir GQue IBal LSou MBNS NCGa NEgg SBfd SKHP WCot WGor WOut
Golden Fleece *sensu* Lemoine	see *C.* × *crocosmiiflora* 'Coleton Fishacre'
'Harlequin'	CElw CTca MAvo
'Harmonia' **new**	CDes CTca
'Hellfire'	CBgR CSam CSpe ECtt ELon GAbr IBal LRHS MAvo MBNS MTis NDov NGdn SMad WCot WCra WFut
'Highlight'	ECrc IBal IBlr MAvo NHol
'Hill House'	MAvo
'Irish Flame'	ECrc GKir NHol
'Irish Sunset'	GKir NHol
'Jennine'	EBee EBrs ECrc IBal NCot NHol SRGP WHil
'Jenny' **new**	MAvo
Jenny Bloom = 'Blacro'PBR	COlW CPrp EBrs ECrc GKir NBir NChi NLar SMHy SMrs
'John Boots'	CPrp EBee ECtt EHrv ELon GAbr IBal IBlr LPio LRHS MCot NBid NHol NLar SMrm SRGP WFar WHil
§ 'Jupiter'	CBre CPou CPrp CSam CTca CWCL CYeo EBrs GCal GMac IBal IBlr MAvo MRav NCGa NHol SApp WFar WHil
'Kathleen'	ECrc
'Krakatoa'	CPrp EBee ECrc EPfP IBal LLHF MWea SGSe SKHP SRkn WMoo
'Lady Wilson' misapplied	see *C.* × *crocosmiiflora* 'Norwich Canary'
'Lana de Savary'	CPrp CTca EBee EBrs EWes GBin GCal IBal IBlr NBid NHol
'Late Cornish'	see *C.* × *crocosmiiflora* 'Queen Alexandra' J.E. Fitt
'Late Lucifer'	CHEx CTca CTri GCal IBlr LSRN SDix SMHy
× ***latifolia***	see *C.* × *crocosmioides*
'Limpopo'	CBgR CMac CTca EBee ECha ECtt ELon GAbr GMac GQue LRHS MAvo MBNS NCot NEgg NPnk SHar SMrm SPer WCot WCra WFut
'Lucifer' ♀H4	Widely available
'Malahide Castle Red' **new**	CTca
'Mandarin'	ECrc IBlr
'Marcotijn'	CTca ECtt GGar IBal IBlr IGor LPio NHol WOut
masoniorum ♀H3	Widely available
- from Satan's Nek **new**	CTca
- 'African Dawn'	ECrc ECtt GQue MAvo
- 'Amber'	IBlr
- 'Dixter Flame'	ECtt IBlr IFoB LPio SDix WOut
- 'Firebird'	EBrs GCra IBlr IGor MAvo MBri NBre NHol SRos
- 'Flamenco'	IBlr
- 'Golden Swan'	ECtt
- Holehird strain	ECrc
- 'Kiaora'	ECrc IBlr SMrm
- 'Moira Reid'	ECrc IBlr NHol
- red-flowered	IBlr
- 'Rowallane Apricot'	IBlr
- 'Rowallane Orange'	CTca GAbr IBlr NHol
- 'Rowallane Yellow' ♀H3-4	CDes CTca EBrs ECtt GAbr GCal GKir GMac IBlr IGor IMou ITim MBri MMuc NHol SMHy SMrm SRos SUsu WCot WOut
- Slieve Donard selection	CTca ECrc IBal
- 'Tropicana'	IBlr
mathewsiana	IBlr
mathewsiana* × *paniculata **new**	CTca
'Mex'	MAvo WCot
'Minotaur'	IBlr
'Mistral'	CBgR CMea CPrp CTca EBee EBrs EPfP EPot GMac IBal IBlr MLLN MSpe NBre NHol NLar SBfd WBor WFar WMoo
'Moorland Blaze'	WMoo
'Mount Stewart'	see *C.* × *crocosmiiflora* 'Jessie'
'Mr Bedford'	see *C.* × *crocosmiiflora* 'Croesus'
'Mullard Pink'	CTca ECrc
'Okavango'PBR	CBgR CBre CMac CTca CYeo EBee ECGP ECtt ELon GAbr GQue IBal LSou MAvo MBNS MCot MNrw NBPC NCot NGdn NLar SHar SKHP SMrm WCot WRHF
Old Hat	see *C.* 'Walberton Red'
'Orange Devil'	CBre ECtt IBal IBlr MBNS MBri MNFA MWea SMrm
'Orange Lucifer'	NBre WPrP
'Orange River'	WCot
'Orange Spirit'	WFar
'Orangeade'	CTca EBrs ECtt GBin IBal IBlr NCot NHol SMrm SMrs SUsu
'Out of the West'	ECrc WOut
'Pageant'	ECrc
§ ***paniculata***	CMac CPne CPou CTca EBla EBrs ECtt GAbr GGar LPla MNFA NBid NHol SAPC SBfd SPet WBor WBrk WCot WMoo WOut WPen WShi WTin
- from Howick **new**	CTca
- from Kologha **new**	CTca
- brown/orange-flowered	IBlr
- 'Cally Greyleaf'	EWld GCal
- 'Cally Sword'	GCal
- 'Major'	CTri IBlr
- 'Natal'	CPrp CTca ECtt IBal NHol WFar
- red-flowered	CTca IBlr SWvt
- triploid	IBlr
aff. ***paniculata***	ECtt IBlr

	'Paul's Best Yellow'	CDes CMea CSam CTca ECGP ECtt EWes GAbr IBal LLWG MAvo MBNS MTis NSti SHar SUsu WCot WFut
	pearsei	CTca IBlr
	'Phillipa Browne'	CTca EBee ECtt IBal LSou NEgg SRGP WCot WMoo
§	***pottsii***	CBgR CHVG CRow CSev CTca ECtt EPla GBin IBal IBlr NHol NLar WFar WOut WPtf WWEG
	- CD&R 109	CPou
	- 'Culzean Pink'	CBgR CHVG CPrp CTca EBee GAbr GBin GCal GMac IBal IBlr MAvo MLHP MRav NBir NCob NCot NHol NLar SMrm SMrs WCot WOut WPGP WPtf WWEG
	- deep pink-flowered	IBlr IGor WMoo
	- 'Grandiflora'	IBlr
§	- 'Princess'	ECrc IBal MAvo
	- tall **new**	CTca
	'Quantreau'	ECrc IBlr NCot
	'R.W. Wallace'	CPrp ECrc IBal NHol
	'Red Devils'	NHol
	'Red Star'	IBal
	'Roman Gold'	IBlr
	rosea	see *Tritonia disticha* subsp. *rubrolucens*
	'Rowden Bronze'	see *C.* × *crocosmiiflora* 'Coleton Fishacre'
	'Rowden Chrome'	see *C.* × *crocosmiiflora* 'George Davison' Davison
	'Ruby Velvet'	IBlr
	'Rubygold'	CPrp IBlr
	'Sabena'	MAvo
	'Saffron Queen'	IBlr
	'Salsa'	WCot
	'Saturn'	see *C.* 'Jupiter'
	'Scarlatti'	CTca GAbr IBal IBlr NHol
	'Severn Sunrise' 🏆H3-4	Widely available
	'Shocking'	ECrc IBlr NCot NHol
	'Son of Lucifer'	WFar
	'Sonate'	CTca NHol SPlb
	'Spitfire'	CBot CHVG CPne CPrp CSam CTca EBee EBla EBrs ECha ECtt ELan GAbr GGar GMac IBal IBlr LHop LRHS MArl MAvo MRav NHol NLar SGSe SRkn SRos SWvt WFar
§	'Sulphurea'	CPou CPrp CSam ECtt EPfP IBal IBlr MAvo MSpe NHol SDix WBrk WCot WEas WHal WPer
	'Sunzest'	CTca ECrc MAvo WFar
	'Tamar Glow' **new**	CTca
	'Tangerine'	ECrc
	'Tangerine Queen'	CTca EBrs ECrc ECtt IBal IBlr NCot NHol SUsu WHil WMoo
	'Tiger'	CElw CTca ECrc IBlr MAvo
	'Vulcan' Leichtlin	see *C.* × *crocosmioides* 'Vulcan' Leichtlin
I	'Vulcan' A. Bloom	CPrp CTca CYeo EBrs ECtt GAbr GGar IBal IBlr MAvo NHol SAga WCot WFar
§	'Walberton Red'	CBgR CTca ECrc EWes IBal IBlr MAvo MBri SAga SApp SKHP SMHy SMad SUsu WCot WHil
	Walberton Yellow = 'Walcroy'PBR	LRHS MAsh SApp SMHy SUsu WCot
	'Zambesi'PBR	CDes CKno CTca CYeo EBee ECtt EHrv ELon GAbr GBin GQue IBal LHop LSou MAvo MBNS MCot MNrw MTis NBPC NCGa NCot NLar SBfd SKHP SPer WCot WPGP
	'Zeal Giant'	CRow CTca ECrc ECtt IBlr MAvo NHol
	'Zeal Remembrance' **new**	CTca
	Zeal unnamed	CPrp CTca EBee ECrc GMac IBal IBlr NHol WFar

Crocus ✿ (*Iridaceae*)

	abantensis	ECho WWst
	- 'Sky Blue' **new**	WWst
	'Advance'	ECho EPfP EPot ERCP LAma LRHS MBri SPer
	alatavicus	ECho WWst
	albiflorus	see *C. vernus* subsp. *albiflorus*
	'Alionka'	WWst
	ancyrensis	ECho EPot LAma
	- 'Golden Bunch'	EBrs ECho EPfP LRHS SDeJ WShi
§	***angustifolius*** 🏆H4	EBrs ECho SDeJ
	- 'Berlin Gold'	ECho
	- bronze-tinged	NMin
	- 'Minor'	ECho
	antalyensis	ECho
	'Ard Schenk'	ECho EPot GKev LAma LRHS
	asturicus	see *C. serotinus* subsp. *salzmannii*
	asumaniae	ECho
	'Aubade'	CMea ECho EPot
	aureus	see *C. flavus* subsp. *flavus*
	banaticus 🏆H4	ECho EPot GKev LLHF MSSP NHar NMen WWst
	baytopiorum	ECho NMen
	biflorus	ECho
	- subsp. ***biflorus***	ECho
	- 'Bowles's Blue'	ECho
	- subsp. ***crewei***	ECho
	- subsp. ***isauricus***	ECho
	- subsp. ***melantherus***	ECho WWst
	- 'Miss Vain'	ECho EPfP EPot ERCP LAma MBri SPhx
	- 'Serevan'	NMin
	- subsp. ***tauri***	ECho WWst
	- subsp. ***weldenii***	ECho
	- - 'Albus'	ECho EPot LAma
	- - 'Fairy'	ECho LAma
	'Blue Bird'	ECho EPot LAma LRHS
	'Blue Pearl' 🏆H4	CAvo CFFs EBrs ECho EPfP EPot GKev LRHS MBri NBir SBch SDeJ SPer SPhx WShi
	boryi	ECho LLHF WCot
	cambessedesii	ECho SCnR
§	***cancellatus*** subsp. ***cancellatus***	ECho GKev LAma
	- var. ***cilicicus***	see *C. cancellatus* subsp. *cancellatus*
	- subsp. ***lycius***	ECho
	- subsp. ***mazziaricus*** large-flowered	WWst
	- - 'Rendina'	WWst
	- subsp. ***pamphylicus***	ECho
	candidus	ECho WWst
	- var. ***subflavus***	see *C. olivieri* subsp. *olivieri*
	cartwrightianus 🏆H4	ECho GKev LRHS SPhx
	- CE&H 613	WWst
	- 'Albus' misapplied	see *C. hadriaticus*
N	- 'Albus' Tubergen 🏆H4	ECho EPot SDeJ
	- 'Halloween'	WWst
	- white-flowered clone	WWst
	chrysanthus 'Blue Peter'	ECho
	- 'Cream Beauty' 🏆H4	CAvo CFFs CMea EBrs ECho EPfP EPot GKev LAma LRHS MBri NBir SDeJ SPhx
	- 'E.A. Bowles' 🏆H4	ECho
	- 'E.P. Bowles'	LAma MBri
	- 'Early Gold'	ECho WWst
	- var. ***fuscotinctus***	ECho EPfP EPot LAma MBri SDeJ
	- 'Milea'	ECho

	- 'Moonlight'	LAma
	- 'Skyline'	ECho
	- 'Sunspot'	EPot
	- 'Uschak Orange'	WWst
	- 'Warley'	ECho
	- 'Zwanenburg Bronze' ♀^{H4}	ECho EPfP LAma LRHS SPhx
	'Cloth of Gold'	see *C. angustifolius*
	clusii	see *C. serotinus* subsp. *clusii*
	corsicus ♀^{H4}	ECho EPot WWst
	cvijicii	ECho
	- white-flowered	ECho
	dalmaticus	ECho EPot
	- 'Petrovac'	ECho
	'Dorothy'	ECho EPot LAma
	'Dutch Yellow'	see *C.* × *luteus* 'Golden Yellow'
	'Ego'	ECho WWst
	etruscus 'Rosalind'	ECho
	- 'Zwanenburg'	ECho EPot LAma SDeJ
	flavus	ECho WWst
§	- subsp. ***flavus*** ♀^{H4}	ECho EPot LAma WShi
	fleischeri	EBrs ECho EPot LAma LRHS
	gargaricus	SCnR WWst
	- subsp. ***gargaricus***	EPot
	'Golden Mammoth'	see *C.* × *luteus* 'Golden Yellow'
	'Goldilocks'	ECho GKev LAma LRHS SDeJ
	goulimyi ♀^{H4}	EBrs ECho EPot GKev LAma LRHS SDeJ WCot
	- 'Albus'	see *C. goulimyi* subsp. *goulimyi* 'Mani White'
§	- subsp. ***goulimyi*** 'Mani White' ♀^{H4}	ECho SCnR
	- subsp. ***leucanthus*** HOA 0183	WWst
	'Gypsy Girl'	CAvo ECho EPot ERCP LAma MBri SPhx
§	***hadriaticus*** ♀^{H4}	ECho EPot LAma
	- var. ***chrysobelonicus***	see *C. hadriaticus*
	- 'Crystal'	WWst
	- 'Elysean Pearl'	WWst
	- 'Indian Summer'	WWst
	'Herald'	CAvo EPot LAma SPhx
	imperati subsp. ***suaveolens***	EPot
	- - 'De Jager'	ECho ERCP LAma
	'Janis Ruksans'	WWst
	'Jeanne d'Arc'	CAvo CFFs EBrs ECho EPfP EPot LAma MBri NBir SDeJ WShi
	'Jeannine'	ECho EPot
	× ***jessoppiae***	ECho WWst
	karduchorum	ECho LAma
	korolkowii	CGrW ECho LAma
	- 'Golden Nugget'	EPot
	- 'Kiss of Spring'	EBrs ECho EPot LRHS
	- 'Lemon Queen'	ECho
	kosaninii	ECho EPot NMin
	- CH 801	WWst
	kotschyanus ♀^{H4}	ECho LRHS NRya SPer
	- HKEP 9205	WWst
	- 'Albus'	ECho SDeJ
§	- subsp. ***kotschyanus***	ECho EPot LAma SDeJ
	- var. ***leucopharynx***	ECho LRHS
	- 'Reliance'	ECho WWst
	- stoloniferous HKEP 9317	WWst
	kotschyanus × ***ochroleucus***	ECho WWst
	'Ladykiller' ♀^{H4}	CAvo CFFs ECho EPot ERCP GKev LAma LRHS MBri SPhx WShi
	laevigatus ♀^{H4}	ECho
	- HOA 0138	WWst
	- 'Fontenayi'	ECho EPot ERCP
	- white-flowered	ECho
	'Large Yellow'	see *C.* × *luteus* 'Golden Yellow'
	ligusticus	ECho
	'Little Amber'	WWst
	longiflorus ♀^{H4}	ECho GEdr LLHF SPhx WWst
	- HOA 9703	WWst
§	× ***luteus*** 'Golden Yellow' ♀^{H4}	CAvo CFFs EBrs EPfP LAma WShi
§	- 'Stellaris'	ECho
	malyi ♀$^{H2-4}$	ECho NMin
	- 'Ballerina'	ECho WWst
	- 'Sveti Roc'	EPot
	mathewii	ECho EPot WCot
	- HKEP 9291	WWst
	medius ♀^{H4}	EPot LAma
	michelsonii	WWst
	minimus	ECho EPot ERCP LAma
	'Nida'	WWst
	niveus	ECho EPot LAma
	- pale blue-flowered	WWst
	nudiflorus	ECho EPot GKev LAma NMen
	ochroleucus ♀^{H4}	ECho EPot SDeJ SPhx
	olivieri	ECho
	- subsp. ***balansae***	ECho
	- - 'Zwanenburg'	CMea ECho EPot
§	- subsp. ***olivieri***	ECho
	- - 'Little Tiger'	ECho WWst
	oreocreticus	ECho
	pallasii	ECho
	- subsp. ***pallasii***	ECho
	pelistericus	WWst
	pestalozzae	ECho WWst
	- var. ***caeruleus***	ECho SCnR
	- - CRO 401	WWst
	'Prins Claus'	EBrs ECho EPfP EPot LAma LRHS MBri SDeJ SPer
	'Prinses Beatrix'	ECho
	pulchellus ♀^{H4}	EBrs ECho EPot ERCP LAma LRHS NWCA SPhx WCot
	- ***albus***	ECho EPot
	- 'Inspiration'	ECho
	- 'Michael Hoog'	ECho
	'Purpureus'	see *C. vernus* 'Purpureus Grandiflorus'
	reticulatus	ECho WWst
	- subsp. ***reticulatus***	ECho EPot
	'Romance'	CAvo CFFs EPot GKev LAma LRHS MBri SDeJ SPer
	'Ruby Giant'	CAvo EBrs ECho EPfP EPot LAma LRHS MBri NBir SDeJ SPer SPhx WShi
	rujanensis	ECho WWst
	salzmannii	see *C. serotinus* subsp. *salzmannii*
	sativus	CArn CAvo CBod CGrW CPrp CTca EBrs ECho ELan EOHP EPot ERCP GPoy LAma LRHS MMHG NBir NGHP SDeJ SPer
	'Saturnus'	EPot LAma
	scardicus	WWst
	scepusiensis	see *C. vernus* subsp. *vernus*
§	***serotinus*** subsp. ***clusii***	ECho LAma LRHS
	- - 'Poseidon'	WWst
§	- subsp. ***salzmannii***	ECho LAma
	- - HOA 9911	WWst
	- - KPW 9425	WWst
	- - f. ***albus***	ECho
	- - 'Atropurpureus'	LRHS
	- - 'Erectophyllus'	ECho WWst
	sibiricus	see *C. sieberi*
§	***sieberi*** ♀^{H4}	EPot
§	- 'Albus' ♀^{H4}	CAvo CFFs ECho EPot GKev LRHS MBri SDeJ
	- subsp. ***atticus***	ECho LAma LRHS

- - 'Firefly'	ECho EPot GKev LAma LRHS SDeJ SPhx
- 'Bowles' White'	see *C. sieberi* 'Albus'
- 'Hubert Edelsten' ♀H4	ECho LAma
- 'Ronald Ginns'	EPot
- subsp. ***sublimis*** 'Tricolor' ♀H4	CAvo CTca EBrs ECho EPfP EPot GKev LAma MBri NBir SDeJ
- 'Violet Queen'	ECho LAma MBri
'Snow Bunting' ♀H4	CAvo CFFs CTca ECho EPfP EPot LAma LRHS NBir SDeJ SPer SPhx WShi
speciosus ♀H4	CAvo CTca EBrs EPot LAma LRHS MLHP NBir SDeJ SPer WCot WHoo WShi
- 'Aino'	ECho WWst
- 'Aitchisonii'	CGrW ECho EPot LAma LRHS SPhx
- 'Albus' ♀H4	CAvo EBrs ECho EPot GKev LRHS SPhx
- 'Artabir'	ECho EPot GKev LRHS SDeJ
- 'Cassiope'	ECho EPot GKev LAma LRHS SDeJ
- 'Conqueror'	EBrs ECho EPot GKev LAma LRHS SDeJ WBor
- 'Lithuanian Autumn'	WWst
- 'Oxonian'	ECho EPot GKev LAma LRHS SPhx
- subsp. ***speciosus***	ECho
- subsp. ***xantholaimos***	WWst
× ***stellaris***	see *C.* × *luteus* 'Stellaris'
susianus	see *C. angustifolius*
suterianus	see *C. olivieri* subsp. *olivieri*
thomasii BM 7589	WWst
tommasinianus ♀H4	CAvo CFFs CGrW CMea CTca EBrs ECho EPot LAma LLWP LRHS MBri MRav NBir SDeJ SPhx SRms WShi
- 'Albus'	EPot LAma LRHS WShi
- 'Barr's Purple'	ECho EPot LAma LRHS SDeJ
- 'Claret'	ECho
- 'Eric Smith'	ECho
- 'Lilac Beauty'	ECho EPfP EPot LAma SPer
- 'Pictus'	ECho EPot LAma NMen WShi
- 'Roseus'	CAvo CMea ECho EPot ERCP LAma NMen SPhx WCot
- 'Whitewell Purple'	CAvo CFFs ECho EPot ERCP GKev LAma MBri NBir SDeJ SPhx WShi
tournefortii ♀H2-4	ECho SCnR
* - 'Albus'	ECho
'Vanguard' ♀H4	EPot LAma LRHS SBch SDeJ
veluchensis	ECho WWst
veneris	ECho
§ ***vernus*** subsp. ***albiflorus***	ECho EPot
- 'Fantasy'	ECho
- 'Flower Record'	EPfP GKev LAma MBri NBir
- 'Graecus'	ECho EPot WWst
- 'Grand Maître'	CAvo CFFs CMea LAma LRHS MBri SDeJ
- 'Haarlem Gem'	ECho
- 'King of the Striped'	EBrs ECho LAma SPer
- 'Michael's Purple'	ECho
- 'Negro Boy'	EPot LAma
- 'Pickwick'	CAvo CFFs EPfP EPot LAma LRHS MBri NBir SDeJ WShi
§ - 'Purpureus Grandiflorus'	EPot SDeJ
- 'Queen of the Blues'	CAvo CFFs EPot WShi
- 'Remembrance'	EBrs EPfP EPot LAma NBir SDeJ WShi
- 'Tatra Shades'	WWst
- Uklin strain	ECho WWst
§ - subsp. ***vernus***	ECho
- - 'Grandiflorus'	see *C. vernus* 'Purpureus Grandiflorus'
- - Heuffelianus Group	EPot WWst
- - - 'Dark Eyes'	WWst
- - 'Oradea'	WWst
versicolor	ECho
- 'Picturatus'	EBrs ECho EPot ERCP GKev LAma LLHF SDeJ
vitellinus	ECho EPot
'White Triumphator'	LAma
'Yalta'	ECho ERCP
'Yellow Mammoth'	see *C.* × *luteus* 'Golden Yellow'
'Zenith'	ECho EPot
'Zephyr' ♀H4	ECho EPot LAma LRHS
zonatus	see *C. kotschyanus* subsp. *kotschyanus*

Croomia (*Stemonaceae*)

heterosepala	WCru

Crotalaria (*Papilionaceae*)

laburnifolia	CCCN

Crowea (*Rutaceae*)

exalata × ***saligna***	CPLG

Crucianella (*Rubiaceae*)

stylosa	see *Phuopsis stylosa*

Cruciata (*Rubiaceae*)

§ ***laevipes***	NMir

Crusea (*Rubiaceae*)

coccinea	WSHC
- B&SWJ 10254	WCru

Cryptanthus (*Bromeliaceae*)

bromelioides	MBri

Cryptocarya (*Lauraceae*)

alba	EBee IArd

Cryptogramma (*Adiantaceae*)

crispa	EBee WHer WRic

Cryptomeria (*Cupressaceae*)

fortunei	see *C. japonica* var. *sinensis*
japonica ♀H4	CDul CMen CSpr CTho ELau GKir IFFs MMuc SEND STre WEve
- Araucarioides Group	EHul NLar
- 'Atawai'	NLar
- 'Bandai'	LBuc
- 'Bandai-sugi' ♀H4	CKen CMac CMen ECho EHul EPfP EPot GKir IFFs LRHS MGos NHol SCoo SLim WGor
- 'Barabits Gold'	MGos WEve
- 'Birodo' **new**	CKen
- 'Black Dragon' **new**	SLim
- 'Compressa'	CDoC CKen ECho EHul EPfP LBee MAsh MGos SCoo SLim WAbe WGor
§ - 'Cristata'	CBcs CDoC CMac ECho ELan LRHS MGos NPal SCoo SLim SPoG
- 'Dacrydioides'	CDoC SLim
- Elegans Group	CBcs CDoy CDul CMac CSBt ECrN EHul ELan EPfP GKir LAst LRHS MBri MGos MMuc NEgg NWea SBfd SCoo SEND SLim SPer SPoG WBVN WDin WFar
- 'Elegans Aurea'	CBcs CTri ECho ECrN EHul MAsh STre WDin WEve
- 'Elegans Compacta' ♀H4	CDoC CMac CSBt CWib ECho EHul ELan GBin LBee LRHS MAsh MBri MMuc SCoo SEND SLim SPoG WBVN WEve
- 'Elegans Nana'	IFFs LBee LRHS NEgg SRms

	- 'Elegans Viridis'	ELan LRHS NEgg SCoo SLim SPer SPoG
	- 'Globosa Nana' ♀H4	ECho EHul EPfP ERom LAst LBee LRHS MAsh MBri MGos NEgg SAPC SArc SCoo SLim SPoG WFar WGor
	- 'Golden Promise'	LRHS MAsh NHol SCoo SLim SPer SPoG WEve WGor
	- Gracilis Group	CDoC
	- 'Jindai-sugi'	ECho NLar
	- 'Karl Fuchs' **new**	SLim
	- 'Kilmacurragh'	CKen EHul NWea SLim WThu
	- 'Knaptonensis' (v)	MGos WEve
	- 'Kohui-yatsubusa'	CKen
*	- 'Konijn-yatsubusa'	CKen
	- 'Koshiji-yatsubusa'	MGos
	- 'Koshyi'	CKen
	- 'Little Champion'	CDoC CKen NLar SCoo SLim
	- 'Little Diamond'	CKen
	- 'Littleworth Dwarf'	see *C. japonica* 'Littleworth Gnom'
§	- 'Littleworth Gnom'	NLar
	- 'Lobbii Nana' hort.	see *C. japonica* 'Nana'
§	- 'Mankichi-sugi'	MBri NHol WEve
	- 'Monstrosa Nana'	see *C. japonica* 'Mankichi-sugi'
	- 'Mushroom'	MGos WFar
§	- 'Nana'	CDoC CMac CTri EHul EPfP WFar
	- 'Osaka-tama'	CKen
	- 'Pipo'	CKen NLar
	- 'Pygmaea'	MGos NHol SCoo SRms
	- 'Rasen'	IArd IFFs
	- 'Rasen-sugi'	LRHS MBri MGos NLar NPal SCoo SLim SMad SPoG
	- 'Rein's Dense Jade' **new**	SLim
	- 'Sekkan-sugi'	CBcs CCVN CDoC CDul CMac ECho EHul EPfP ESwi GBin IArd LAst LBee LRHS MAsh MGos NHol NLar SBfd SCoo SLim SPer SPoG WEve WFar
	- 'Sekka-sugi'	see *C. japonica* 'Cristata'
§	- var. ***sinensis***	CMCN
§	- 'Spiralis'	CDoC CKen CMac ECho EHul EPfP IFFs IVic LAst LBee LRHS MAsh MGos NEgg NHol NPal SCoo SLim SPer SPoG WEve WFar
§	- 'Spiraliter Falcata'	NLar
§	- 'Tansu'	CKen ECho MGos NHol
	- 'Tenzan-sugi'	CDoC CKen LRHS MGos SLim WThu
	- 'Tilford Cream'	ECho
	- 'Tilford Gold'	ECho EHul EPot IFFs MGos NEgg NHol WEve WFar WGor
	- 'Toda'	CKen
	- 'Vilmorin Gold'	CKen MGos NHol WFar
	- 'Vilmoriniana' ♀H4	CDoC CKen CMen CTri ECho EHul EPfP EPla GKir IFFs LBee MGos NEgg NHol SCoo SLim SPer SPoG WDin WEve WFar WMoo
	- 'Viminalis'	NHol
	- 'Winter Bronze'	CKen
	- 'Yatsubusa'	see *C. japonica* 'Tansu'
	- 'Yore-sugi'	see *C. japonica* 'Spiralis', 'Spiraliter Falcata'
	- 'Yoshino'	CKen LRHS SLim
	sinensis	see *C. japonica* var. *sinensis*

Cryptostegia (*Asclepiadaceae*)

grandiflora	CCCN

Cryptotaenia (*Apiaceae*)

japonica	CHby CPou MHer MNHC WHer WJek
- f. ***atropurpurea***	CArn CPla CSpe CSpr EBee EHoe EWTr GGar LEdu MNrw SDix SGSe WFar

Ctenanthe (*Marantaceae*)

	lubbersiana ♀H1	XBlo
§	***oppenheimiana***	XBlo

Ctenitis (*Dryopteridaceae*)

subglandulosa **new**	WRic

Cucubalus (*Caryophyllaceae*)

baccifer	EWld NLar WPer WPrP

Cudrania see *Maclura*

cumin see *Cuminum cyminum*

Cuminum (*Apiaceae*)

cyminum	CArn ELau MNHC SIde SVic

Cunninghamia (*Cupressaceae*)

	konishii	CPLG
§	***lanceolata***	CBcs CDTJ CDoC CDul CGHE CKen CMCN CMac CTho ECho EPla GKir IArd IDee IFFs LRHS MBlu NMun SBfd SCoo SLim SMad SPoG SSpi SSta STre WBor WEve WPGP WSpi
	- 'Glauca'	CPLG CTho WPGP
	- 'Grounded'	STre
	- 'Little Leo'	CDoC CKen ECho
	sinensis	see *C. lanceolata*
	unicaniculata	see *C. lanceolata*

Cunonia (*Cunoniaceae*)

capensis	CPLG CTrC EShb GKir

Cuphea (*Lythraceae*)

	blepharophylla	EBee
	caeciliae	SGar WWlt
*	***compacta***	LAst
	cyanea	CMHG SDix SOWG SUsu WWlt
	'Firecracker' **new**	NPri
	hirtella	SOWG
	hyssopifolia ♀H1	CHII EShb SBfd SOWG SWvt
	- 'Alba'	CCCN SBfd SOWG SWvt
	- Lemon Squash = 'Kkcuphls'	SVil
	- pink-flowered	CCCN SBfd
	- red-flowered	CCCN
	- 'Rosea'	SEND SWvt
§	***ignea*** ♀H1	MBri SOWG SUsu WWlt
	- 'Variegata' (v)	SOWG
§	***llavea*** 'Georgia Scarlet'	CCCN LAst LSou WWlt
	- 'Tiny Mice'	see *C. llavea* 'Georgia Scarlet'
I	***macrophylla*** hort.	CHII
	platycentra	see *C. ignea*
	'Torpedo' **new**	LSou
	'Vienco Lavender' **new**	LAst
	viscosissima	CSpe MCot

× *Cupressocyparis* see × *Cuprocyparis*

Cupressus (*Cupressaceae*)

	arizonica var. ***arizonica***	MGos MREP
	- - 'Arctic'	CDoC SLim
	- 'Conica Glauca'	WEve
§	- var. ***glabra***	WBor WPGP
	- - 'Angaston' **new**	SLim
	- - 'Aurea'	CMac ECho EHul LRHS MGos NPCo SLim WBor WFar
	- - 'Blue Ice' ♀H3	CBcs CDul CMac CTho ECho EHul LRHS MAsh MGos NPCo SCoo SLim SPer SPoG SWvt WEve WFar

	- - 'Compacta'	CKen
	- - 'Conica'	CKen
I	- - 'Fastigiata'	CCVT CDoC ECrN EHul EPfP LMaj SBfd SCoo
	- - 'Glauca'	ECho EPfP IFFs MBlu WBVN
*	- - 'Lutea'	ECho SPoG
	- var. ***nevadensis***	GAuc
	- 'Pyramidalis' ♀H3	ECrN EPfP MMuc SEND WEve
I	- 'Sulfurea'	MAsh
	atlantica **new**	SLim
	cashmeriana ♀H2	CBcs CDTJ CDoC CTho ELan ERea LRHS NPCo SLim WFar
	glabra	see *C. arizonica* var. *glabra*
	lusitanica	CKen LRHS SLim
	'Brice's Weeping'	
	- 'Glauca Pendula'	CKen EPfP WEve
	- 'Pygmy'	CKen
	macrocarpa	CBcs CCVT CDoC CDul CTho EHul IFFs SEND
	- 'Compacta'	CKen
	- 'Conybearii Aurea'	NPCo
	- 'Gold Spread'	ECho EHul SCoo SLim SPoG WFar
	- 'Goldcrest' ♀H3	CBcs CCVT CDoC CDul CMac CSBt ECho ECrN EHul ELan IFFs LBee LRHS MBri MGos NBir NPri SBfd SLim SPer SPoG STre SWvt WCFE WDin WEve WFar
	- 'Golden Cone'	CKen CSBt ECho NPCo WEve
	- 'Golden Pillar' ♀H3	CDoC CMac EHul SWvt WDin WFar
	- 'Golden Spire'	WFar
	- 'Greenstead Magnificent'	ECho LRHS MAsh SCoo SLim
	- 'Horizontalis Aurea'	EHul
	- 'Lohbrunner'	CKen
	- 'Lutea'	CDoC ECho NPCo WFar
I	- 'Pendula'	SLim
	- 'Pygmaea'	CKen
	- 'Sulphur Cushion'	CKen
	- 'Wilma'	CSBt ECho EHul LAst LBee LRHS MAsh MGos NEgg SBfd SCoo SLim SPoG SWvt
	- 'Woking'	CKen
	sempervirens	CDul CMCN EAmu ECrN EHul ELan ERom ETod LRHS NPri SBfd SPlb STrG WEve WFar
	- 'Agrimed'	LMaj
	- 'Bolgheri'	SBig
	- 'Garda'	CDoC
	- 'Green Pencil'	CKen EPfP WEve
	- 'Pyramidalis'	see *C. sempervirens* Stricta Group
	- var. ***sempervirens***	see *C. sempervirens* Stricta Group
§	- Stricta Group ♀H3	CArn CBcs CCVT CKen CMCN CSWP CTho ECho EHul EPfP EWTr MAsh MREP NLar SAPC SArc SBfd SCoo WCFE WEve
	- 'Swane's Gold'	CBcs CDoC CKen ECho EHul EPfP LRHS NPCo SCoo SLim SPoG WCFE WEve WFar
	- 'Totem Pole'	CCVT CKen CSBt CTho CTri ECho ECrN EHul EPfP LAst LBee LRHS MGos NEgg NPla SCoo SEND SLim SPer SPoG WEve

× *Cuprocyparis* ✿ (*Cupressaceae*)

§	***leylandii*** ♀H4	CBcs CCVT CChe CDoC CDul CMac CTri EHul EPfP LBuc LSRN MAsh MBri MGos MMuc NEgg NWea SBfd SLim SPer SPoG SWvt WDin WEve WHar WMou
I	- '2001'	CDoC WMou
§	- 'Castlewellan'	CBcs CCVT CChe CDoC CDul CMac CTri EHul EPfP ERom LBuc LRHS LSRN MAsh MBri MGos MMuc NWea SBfd SEND SLim SPer SPoG SWvt WDin WEve WFar WHar WMou
	- 'Galway Gold'	see × *C. leylandii* 'Castlewellan'
	- 'Gold Rider' ♀H4	CDoC EHul LTen MAsh MGos MMuc NEgg NWea SCoo SEND SPer SPoG STre SWvt WDin WEve WHar
§	- 'Harlequin' (v)	CBcs CMac SEND SWvt
	- 'Herculea'	CDoC MAsh
	- 'Leighton Green'	WMou
	- 'Naylor's Blue'	CMac
	- 'Olive's Green'	EHul SWvt
	- 'Robinson's Gold' ♀H4	CMac EHul GQui LRHS MMuc NWea SLim WFar WMou
	- 'Silver Dust' (v)	WFar
	- 'Winter Sun'	WCFE
	- 'Variegata'	see × *C. leylandii* 'Harlequin'
	ovensii	EHul

Curculigo (*Hypoxidaceae*)

capitulata	XBlo
crassifolia B&SWJ 2318	WCru

Curcuma ✿ (*Zingiberaceae*)

alismatifolia	EPfP
longa	CArn
roscoeana	LAma
zedoaria	LAma
- 'Bicolor Wonder'	CCCN
- 'Pink Wonder'	CCCN
- 'White Wonder'	CCCN

Curtonus see *Crocosmia*

Cussonia (*Araliaceae*)

paniculata	CDTJ CPne CWit EBee EShb SPad SPoG WCot
- subsp. ***paniculata*** **new**	MAvo
spicata	CDTJ EShb
transvaalensis	EShb

custard apple see *Annona cherimola*, *A. reticulata*

Cyananthus (*Campanulaceae*)

	incanus	GKev
	integer misapplied	see *C. microphyllus*
	lobatus ♀H4	CPla ECho GKev GMaP
	- 'Albus'	EPot EWes WAbe
	- dark	WAbe
	- 'Dark Beauty'	ECho
	- giant	EPot GEdr
	- 'Midnight'	GEdr
	lobatus* × *microphyllus	NWCA WAbe
	longiflorus	GKev
	macrocalyx	GKev
§	***microphyllus*** ♀H4	CPla ECho EPot GEdr GJos GMaP IFoB NSla WAbe
	sherriffii	GJos IFoB WAbe WFar

Cyanella (*Tecophilaeaceae*)

alba 'Biedouw' **new**	ECho
lutea	ECho
orchidiformis	ECho

Cyathea (*Cyatheaceae*)

atrox	CDTJ
australis	CBty CDTJ CKel EAmu ESwi ETod IDee LPal LRHS MAsh MGos NPal WFib WPGP WRic
brownii	WRic

	cooperi	CDTJ CKel EAmu EFtx GBin LRHS WFib WRic
*	- 'Brentwood'	WRic
	cunninghamii	CDTJ EAmu EFtx
	dealbata	CDTJ CKel CTrC EAmu EUJe LPal MGos WRic
	dregei	SPlb WRic
	incisoserrata	WRic
	medullaris	CDTJ CKel CTrC EAmu EFtx EUJe GBin LRHS MGos WRic
	milnei	CDTJ WRic
	robusta	WRic
	smithii	CDTJ CKel CTrC EAmu WRic
	tomentosissima	CDTJ CKel EFtx WRic

Cyathodes (*Epacridaceae*)

	colensoi	see *Leucopogon colensoi*
	fasciculata	see *Leucopogon fasciculatus*
	fraseri	see *Leucopogon fraseri*
	juniperina	see *Leptecophylla juniperina*
	parviflora	see *Leucopogon parviflorus*
	parvifolia	see *Leptecophylla juniperina* subsp. *parvifolia*

Cybistetes (*Amaryllidaceae*)

	longifolia	WCot

Cycas (*Cycadaceae*)

	circinalis	LPal
	media	LPal SBst
	panzhihuaensis	CBrP LPal SPlb
	revoluta ♀H1	CAbb CBrP CCCN CDoC CHEx CTrC EAmu EPfP EUJe LPal MBri MMuc MREP NLar NPal SAPC SArc SBfd SBst SChr SEND SMad STrG WCot
	revoluta × ***taitungensis***	CBrP
§	***rumphii***	CBrP LPal
	taitungensis	CBrP
	thouarsii	see *C. rumphii*

Cyclamen ✿ (*Primulaceae*)

	africanum	ECho EDAr EJWh ITim LAma LRHS MAsh NWCA STil WCot
	africanum × ***hederifolium***	CWCL ECho
§	***alpinum***	ECho EJWh EPot GKev LAma LLHF LRHS MAsh SDeJ STil
	balearicum	CPBP ECho EJWh LAma LRHS MAsh NMen STil
	cilicium ♀H2-4	ECho EJWh EPot ERCP LAma LRHS MAsh MHer MTho NMen STil WCom WFar WHoo WIvy WPat WShi
	- f. ***album***	ECho EJWh EPot GKir LAma LRHS MAsh NMen STil WCom WCot
	- patterned-leaved	ECho NBir
	colchicum	ECho MAsh STil
§	***coum*** ♀H4	Widely available
	- var. ***abchasicum***	see *C. coum* subsp. *caucasicum*
§	- subsp. ***caucasicum***	MAsh STil
	- subsp. ***coum***	ECho MAsh
	- - f. ***albissimum***	WCom
	- - - 'George Bisson'	MAsh
	- - - 'Golan Heights'	MAsh STil WIvy
	- - f. ***coum*** Nymans Group	MAsh WFar
	- - - Pewter Group ♀H2-4	CBel CPMA ECGP ECho ELon GKev MAsh MTho WCom WFar WIvy
	- - - - bicoloured	EJWh
	- - - - 'Blush'	CPMA STil
	- - - - 'Maurice Dryden'	CBel CLAP CPMA ECGP ECho EHrv LAma LRHS MAsh STil WHoo
	- - - - red-flowered	LAma WPat
	- - - - 'Tilebarn Elizabeth'	CBel EHrv MAsh NBir STil WHoo
	- - - - white-flowered	MAsh
	- - - plain-leaved, red-flowered	STil
	- - - 'Roseum'	STil
	- - - Silver Group	CPMA ECho EHrv GEdr GKir LHop LRHS NPnk NRya NSla WCot WFar WHoo WPGP
	- - - - red-flowered	CAvo EPot MTho STil WHoo
	- - magenta-flowered	CWCL WHoo
	- - f. ***pallidum*** 'Album'	CAvo CBel CPMA ECho EPot GKev LAma MAsh SDeJ SMrm SPer STil WHoo WPat WSpi
	- - - 'Marbled Moon'	MAsh STil
	- dark pink-flowered	CAvo CLAP ECho WHoo
	- hybrid	ERCP
	- marble-leaved	CBel CWCL ECho LHop WHoo
	- plain-leaved	CBel CLAP EBla EPot WCom
	- red-flowered	CLAP ECho
I	- 'Rubrum'	GKev
	- 'Tilebarn Graham'	MAsh
	creticum	ECho EJWh MAsh STil
	cyprium	ECho EJWh LRHS MAsh STil WIvy
	- 'E.S.'	ECho MAsh STil WFar
	× ***drydeniae***	CPMA
	elegans	EJWh STil
	europaeum	see *C. purpurascens*
	fatrense	see *C. purpurascens* subsp. *purpurascens* from Fatra, Slovakia
	graecum	ECho EDAr EJWh EPot GKev LRHS MAsh NMen STil WCot WIvy
	- subsp. ***anatolicum***	MAsh STil
	- subsp. ***candicum***	MAsh STil
	- subsp. ***graecum*** f. ***album***	ECho EJWh EPot LRHS MAsh STil
	- - f. ***graecum*** 'Glyfada'	STil
§	***hederifolium*** ♀H4	Widely available
	- SL 175/1	WCot
	- 'Amaze Me'	EWTr
	- arrow-head	CLAP ECho
	- var. ***confusum***	MAsh STil WCot
	- var. ***hederifolium***	CAvo CBel CSWP CSam CStu CTri
	f. ***albiflorum***	ECho EDAr EHrv EPot GKev LAma MBri NHol NMen NMyG NPnk SDeJ SPhx STil WCom WCot WHoo WPat WPnP
	- - - 'Album'	EBrs
	- - - Bowles's Apollo Group	WCom
§	- - - - 'Artemis'	MAsh STil
	- - - - 'White Bowles's Apollo'	see *C. hederifolium* var. *hederifolium* f. *albiflorum* (Bowles's Apollo Group) 'Artemis'
	- - - 'Daley Thompson'	WCot
	- - - 'Linnett Stargazer'	WCot
	- - - 'Nettleton Silver'	see *C. hederifolium* var. *hederifolium* f. *albiflorum* 'White Cloud'
	- - - 'Perlenteppich'	GMaP
	- - - 'Tilebarn Helena'	STil
§	- - - 'White Cloud'	CBel CLAP EBla ECho EPot MAsh NSla STil WCot WHoo WIvy
	- - f. ***hederifolium*** Bowles's Apollo Group	CHid CLAP ECGP MAsh STil WCom
	- - - 'Fairy Rings'	MAsh
	- - - 'Rosenteppich'	GMaP
	- - - 'Ruby Glow'	CBel LRHS MAsh NBir WCot WPat WThu
	- - - 'Silver Cloud'	CBel CHid CLAP EHrv MAsh NBir STil WCom WCot WHoo WIvy WPGP WPat

- - - 'Silver Shield'	MAsh
- - - 'Stargazer'	MAsh WCot
- - 'Tilebarn Silver Arrow'	CPMA MAsh STil
- long-leaved	CPMA WCom
- 'Pewter Mist'	LAma
- 'Rose Pearls'	SRot
- 'San Marino Silver'	GEdr
- scented	NHol STil WCom
- Silver-leaved Group	CAvo CPMA EBla EBrs ECGP ECho ELon EPot LHop LRHS MAsh NWCA SRot STil WFar
- 'Turkish Delight'	EDAr
ibericum	see *C. coum* subsp. *caucasicum*
intaminatum	ECho EJWh GKir LAma LRHS MAsh NMen STil WIvy
- patterned-leaved	CBel EJWh MAsh STil
- pink-flowered	MAsh NMen STil
- plain-leaved	MAsh STil WThu
latifolium	see *C. persicum*
libanoticum	CBel CPBP ECho EJWh LAma LRHS MAsh NMen STil WFar
mirabile ♀H2-3	CBel CPBP ECho EJWh EPot LAma LRHS MAsh NMen SDeJ STil WIvy WThu
- f. ***mirabile*** 'Tilebarn Anne'	MAsh STil
- - 'Tilebarn Nicholas'	CBel ECho MAsh STil
- f. ***niveum***	EJWh
- - 'Tilebarn Jan'	CPMA ECho MAsh STil
neapolitanum	see *C. hederifolium*
orbiculatum	see *C. coum*
parviflorum	EJWh MAsh STil
§ ***persicum***	CWCL ECho EJWh LRHS MAsh STil
- CSE 90560	STil
- var. ***persicum*** f. ***puniceum*** from Lebanon	STil
- - - 'Tilebarn Karpathos'	MAsh STil
persicum white-flowered	ECho MAsh
pseudibericum ♀H2-3	CBel CPBP ECho EJWh EPot LAma LHop LRHS MAsh SDeJ STil
- AC&W 664	ITim
- f. ***roseum***	MAsh NMen STil
§ ***purpurascens*** ♀H4	ECho EJWh EPot GKir LLHF MAsh NMen NWCA STil WHoo WIvy WPat
- var. ***fatrense***	see *C. purpurascens* subsp. *purpurascens* from Fatra, Slovakia
- 'Lake Garda'	MAsh WPGP
- silver-leaved	STil
§ - subsp. ***purpurascens*** from Fatra, Slovakia	STil
repandum	CAvo CDes CWCL ECho EHrv EJWh LAma LRHS MAsh NMen STil WHer
- 'Pelops' misapplied	see *C. rhodium* subsp. *peloponnesiacum*
- subsp. ***repandum*** f. ***album***	CLAP EJWh MAsh STil
rhodium ♀H2-3	EJWh MAsh WCot
§ - subsp. ***peloponnesiacum***	ECGP STil
- - white-flowered	STil
- subsp. ***rhodium***	MAsh STil
- subsp. ***vividum***	MAsh STil
rohlfsianum	ECho EJWh LRHS MAsh STil WThu
× ***saundersiae***	EJWh MAsh STil
trochopteranthum	see *C. alpinum*
× ***wellensiekii***	MAsh STil

Cyclea (*Menispermaceae*)

polypetala KWJ 12157 new	WCru

Cyclosorus (*Thelypteridaceae*)

esquirolii new	WRic
tottoides new	WRic

Cydonia ✿ (*Rosaceae*)

japonica	see *Chaenomeles speciosa*
oblonga (F)	ECrN GKev LMaj
- 'Agvambari' (F)	SKee
- 'Aromatnaya' (F)	ERea
- 'Champion' (F)	CAgr CBcs ECrN ERea GTwe LBuc MCoo NEgg NLar SKee SVic
- 'Early Prolific' (F)	ECrN LAst
- 'Ekmek' (F)	SKee
- 'Isfahan' (F)	SKee
- 'Krymsk' (F)	CAgr
- 'Leskovac' (F)	CAgr ERea NLar
§ - 'Lusitanica' (F)	CAgr ECrN ERea GTwe MCoo NLar SKee SPer
- 'Meech's Prolific' (F)	CAgr CDul CLnd CTho CTri ECrN EMil ERea GTwe IFFs LAst MBlu MBri MGos MRav MWat NLar SDea SFam SKee SLim SPer SPoG WClo
- pear-shaped (F)	ECrN MCoo NEgg SPer
- Portugal	see *C. oblonga* 'Lusitanica'
- 'Rea's Mammoth' (F)	NLar
- 'Serbian Gold' (F)	GTwe LRHS MAsh MBri WHar
- 'Shams' (F)	SKee
- 'Sobu' (F)	SKee
- 'Vranja' (F) ♀H4	Widely available

Cymbalaria (*Scrophulariaceae*)

aequitriloba 'Alba'	GGar
§ ***hepaticifolia***	WPer
§ ***muralis***	EBWF ECho ECtt EWll LBMP LRHS MHer MSCN NPri WCom WGor
- 'Albiflora'	see *C. muralis* 'Pallidior'
- 'Kenilworth White'	WMoo
- 'Nana Alba'	EPot MMuc NPri SPhx WPer
§ - 'Pallidior'	ECho
§ ***pallida***	CPBP MMuc NSla SBch SPlb WMoo WPer
- 'Alba'	EWTr
§ ***pilosa***	ECtt NLar

Cymbopogon (*Poaceae*)

citratus	CArn CBod CCCN COld ERea GPoy MNHC NGHP SBfd SHDw SIde SPoG SVic WJek
flexuosus	CCCN ELau MHer WJek
martini	CArn GPoy
nardus	CArn GPoy

Cymophyllus (*Cyperaceae*)

§ ***fraserianus***	CDes CHEx GBin

Cynanchum (*Asclepiadaceae*)

acuminatifolium	GCal
ascyrifolium new	EBee

Cynara (*Asteraceae*)

cardunculus ♀H3-4	Widely available
- ACL 380/78	SWat
I - 'Cardy'	CBot EBee LRHS NBre NCGa SWat WBrE
- dwarf	SMHy
- var. ***ferocissima***	EBrs LRHS
I - 'Florist Cardy'	IGor NLar
- 'Gobbo di Nizza'	EBee ELau ERea WHer
- 'Grosse Grün' new	WSpi

§ - Scolymus Group	Widely available
- - 'Carciofo Violetto Precoce'	WHer
- - 'Gigante di Romagna'	WHer
- - 'Gros Camus de Bretagne'	MAvo WCot
- - 'Gros Vert de Lâon'	CBcs ECha ELan ELau WCot WPGP
- - 'Imperial Star'	ELau
- - 'Large Green'	NLar
- - 'Monica Lynden-Bell' **new**	WCot
- - 'Purple Globe'	CArn CPrp ELau SMrm
- - 'Romanesco'	EBee ELau SVic
- - 'Vert Globe'	CBod CBot CFox CHar CPrp CSBt CSev ELau ERea IFoB MWat NPer SMrm SVic SWal
- - 'Violet de Provence'	CFox CSBt ELau SWal
- - 'Violetto di Chioggia'	CSev EBee ELau ERea WHer
scolymus	see *C. cardunculus* Scolymus Group

Cynodon (*Poaceae*)

aethiopicus	EBee EHoe EPPr GBin LEdu SBfd SGar SHDw SWal WCot

Cynoglossum (*Boraginaceae*)

***amabile* f. *roseum* 'Mystery Rose'**	WPGP
coelestinum	WCot
dioscoridis	CBot SPhx
nervosum	CBot EBee ECtt ELan EPfP GKir LAst LHop LRHS MCot MLHP MMuc MRav NChi NEgg NGdn NWCA SPer SPhx SWat WCAu WCot WFar WWEG
officinale	CArn EBWF MHer WHer WSFF

Cynosurus (*Poaceae*)

cristatus	EBWF NMir
- viviparous	CNat

Cypella (*Iridaceae*)

aquatilis	LLWG
herbertii	CPom EDif EWTr
peruviana	WHil
plumbea	see *Phalocallis coelestis*

Cyperus (*Cyperaceae*)

§ ***albostriatus***	CCCN CHEx EShb MBri
alternifolius misapplied	see *C. involucratus*
alternifolius L.	CBen EAmu LPBA MSKA SAPC WMAq
- 'Compactus'	see *C. involucratus* 'Nanus'
'Chira'	EKen MBNS NWsh WGwG
§ ***cyperoides***	MBri
diffusus misapplied	see *C. albostriatus*
§ ***eragrostis***	CArn CPom CWit EHoe GCal MCCP MWts NSti SDix SPlb SWat WAbb WGrn WMAq WMoo
esculentus	CArn
fuscus	EKen MDKP WFar WHal WMoo
glaber	EBee EUJe MBNS MMuc NBre WWEG
haspan misapplied	see *C. papyrus* 'Nanus'
haspan L.	EShb MSKA
§ ***involucratus*** ♀H1	CHEx EBak EHon EShb EUJe LPBA MBri MSKA MWts SArc SGSe SMad SWat WFar WMnd WMoo
- 'Gracilis'	EBak MBri
§ - 'Nanus'	LPBA
longus	CBen CWat EHoe EHon EPPr GCal LPBA MMuc MWts NNor NPer NSti NWsh SEND SWal SWat WFar WHal WMAq WPnP WPrP
papyrus ♀H1	CDTJ CHEx CKno EAmu ERea EUJe GKir MBri MSKA SAPC SArc SBig SMad XBlo
§ - 'Nanus' ♀H1	CHEx LPal XBlo
prolifer	LLWG
rotundus	MCCP SBch WTou
sumula hort.	see *C. cyperoides*
ustulatus	CKno MDKP
vegetus	see *C. eragrostis*

Cyphomandra (*Solanaceae*)

betacea (F)	CCCN SVic

Cypripedium (*Orchidaceae*)

acaule	WWst
Aki gx	GEdr NLAp WWst XFro
- 'Pastel'	GEdr NLAp WWst XFro
Axel gx	NLAp
× ***barbeyi***	see *C.* × *ventricosum*
calceolus	CFir EHrv NLAp WWst
- from Korea	NLAp
- from Kurilen Island	NLAp
- from Lake Baikal	NLAp
calceolus* × *macranthos* f. *albiflorum **new**	NLAp
calcicola	NLAp
californicum	GEdr NLAp
× ***columbianum*** **new**	WWst
cordigerum	NLAp
corrugatum	see *C. tibeticum*
debile	GEdr NLAp
Dietrich gx **new**	NLAp
Emil gx	GEdr NLAp WWst XFro
fargesii	GEdr
fasciolatum	GEdr NLAp
fasciolatum* × *flavum **new**	NLAp
flavum	GBin GEdr NLAp
- white-flowered	GEdr
- white-flowered × ***reginae*** **new**	GEdr
- yellow-flowered **new**	GEdr
formosanum	GEdr LAma NLAp SKHP WWst
franchetii	GEdr
franchetii* × *macranthos **new**	NLAp WWst
franchetii* × *parviflorum **new**	NLAp WWst
Gisela gx	GCrs GEdr LAma WWst XFro
- 'Pastel'	GCrs GEdr NLAp WWst
- 'Yellow'	LAma
guttatum	GEdr NLAp WWst
- var. ***yatabeanum***	see *C. yatabeanum*
Hank Small gx	GCrs GEdr NLAp WWst XFro
Hans Erni gx **new**	NLAp
henryi	GEdr LAma NLAp
himalaicum	NLAp
Inge gx	GEdr NLAp WWst XFro
Ingrid gx	GEdr NLAp WWst XFro
japonicum	GBin GEdr NLAp WWst
kentuckiense	CCCN CFir GEdr NLAp
Kristi Lyn gx **new**	NLAp WWst XFro
lichiangense	GEdr
lichiangense* × *reginae **new**	GEdr
macranthos	EHrv GEdr NLAp WWst
- from Lake Baikal	NLAp
- f. ***albiflorum***	NLAp

macranthos var. ***hotei-atsumorianum* × *tibeticum*** new	NLAp
Maria gx	NLAp XFro
Michael gx	GEdr NLAp WWst XFro
montanum	NLAp WWst
parviflorum	GCrs NLAp
- var. ***makasin***	NLAp
- var. ***parviflorum***	NLAp
§ - var. ***pubescens***	GBin GEdr LAma NLAp
- var. ***pubescens* × *reginae***	GEdr
Philipp gx	GEdr NLAp WWst XFro
plectrochilum	GEdr
Princess gx	NLAp
pubescens	see *C. parviflorum* var. *pubescens*
Rascal gx	GEdr
reginae	CCCN EBee EHrv EWes GCrs GEdr GKev LAma MREP NLAp SKHP WClo WHlf
- f. ***albolabium***	GEdr
- f. ***album*** new	GEdr WWst
- 'Red Pouch' new	GEdr
***reginae* × Tilman gx** new	GEdr
Sabine gx	GEdr NLAp WWst XFro
- pastel-flowered new	WWst
Sebastian gx	GEdr NLAp WWst XFro
segawae	LAma
§ ***tibeticum***	NLAp
Ulla Silkens gx	EBee GCrs GEdr GKev LAma NLAp WWst XFro
Ursel gx new	NLAp WWst XFro
§ × ***ventricosum***	GEdr NLAp WWst XFro
- dark-flowered new	WWst
- 'Pastel'	NLAp WWst XFro
- red-flowered	NLAp
- white-flowered	GEdr NLAp WWst
Victoria gx new	NLAp WWst
§ ***yatabeanum***	GEdr
yunnanense	GEdr

Cyrilla (*Cyrillaceae*)

racemiflora	CMac MBri

Cyrtanthus (*Amaryllidaceae*)

from high altitude	WCot
'Alaska'	ECho
§ ***brachyscyphus***	CSpe EBee ECho EShb GGar WCot
breviflorus	CAby CDes EBee ECho NMen WPGP
'Edwina'	CCCN ECho EShb
§ ***elatus*** ♀H1	CPne CSpe CStu CTca ECho EShb EWll LAma LEdu LRHS MCCP SEND SMrm WCot WGwG
- 'Cream Beauty'	ECho WCot
- 'Pink Diamond'	ECho
'Elizabeth'	CCCN ECho
falcatus ♀H1	CLak EBee
mackenii	CPne EBee ECho WGwG WPGP
- cream-white-flowered	CCCN
- 'Himalayan Pink'	CCCN EBee
- red-flowered	CCCN EBee
montanus	EBee ECho WCot
parviflorus	see *C. brachyscyphus*
purpureus	see *C. elatus*
rhodesianus	GCal
sanguineus	ECho WCot WPGP
smithiae	ECho
speciosus	see *C. elatus*

Cyrtomium (*Dryopteridaceae*)

§ ***caryotideum***	CLAP EBee ISha WRic WWEG
§ ***falcatum*** ♀H3	Widely available
- 'Rochfordianum'	CBcs CBty CCCN EBee ISha LRHS WFib WRic
§ ***fortunei*** ♀H4	Widely available
- var. ***clivicola***	CBty CEnt CKel CPrp CWCL EBee EPfP EShb GCal ISha LRHS MGos MRav NHol NLar NMoo SBfd SPad WRic
hookerianum new	WRic
macrophyllum	CLAP GLin

Cystopteris ✿ (*Woodsiaceae*)

bulbifera	CLAP MNFA
diaphana	WRic
dickieana	CLAP GBin NHol SRms WCot WFib WRic
fragilis	EBee ECha EFer SRms WFib
- from Chilean new	WRic
moupinensis	WRic
- B&SWJ 6767	WCru
tennesseensis	WRic

Cytisus (*Papilionaceae*)

albus misapplied	see *C. multiflorus*
albus Hacq.	see *Chamaecytisus albus* (Hacq.) Rothm.
'Amber Elf'^PBR	MBri SRms
'Andreanus'	see *C. scoparius* f. *andreanus*
'Apricot Gem'	LRHS MGos NLar SPoG WFar
battandieri ♀H4	Widely available
- 'Yellow Tail' ♀H4	CEnd EBee EPfP LRHS MBri
× ***beanii*** ♀H4	SKHP CDul EBee ELan EPfP GKir LRHS MAsh SLon SRms WDin WFar
'Boskoop Glory'	NLar
'Boskoop Ruby' ♀H4	CDoC CSBt CWit EPfP EWTr GGar GKir LBMP LRHS LSRN MAsh NEgg NPri SBfd SPer SPoG SWvt WBor WFar WHar
'Burkwoodii' ♀H4	CBcs CDoC CDul CWSG EBee ELan EPfP GKir LAst LRHS LSRN MRav MSwo MWat NEgg NHol SBfd SPoG WFar
canariensis	see *Genista canariensis*
'Compact Crimson'	CDoC EBee LRHS SBfd
'Darley Dale Red'	EWTr
§ ***decumbens***	MAsh
'Donard Gem'	CDoC EBee SBfd SLim
'Dorothy Walpole'	WFar
'Dukaat'	EBee GKir
'Firefly'	CBcs CMac NBro
'Fulgens'	CMac EPfP
'Golden Cascade'	CBcs CDoC EBee ELan LRHS MAsh NEgg SBfd SLim
'Golden Sunlight'	CSBt EBee EPfP MSwo
'Goldfinch'	CChe CDoC CSBt EBee ELan GKir LRHS MAsh MBri MNHC MSwo NLar SPad SWal
hirsutus	see *Chamaecytisus hirsutus*
'Hollandia' ♀H4	CBcs CDoC CSBt CTsd CWSG EBee EPfP GKir LBMP MAsh MGos MMuc MRav NBro NHol NPri SPer WDin WFar
× ***kewensis*** ♀H4	CMac CWSG EBee ELan EPfP GKir LRHS MAsh MGos MRav NHol SRms WDin WSpi
- 'Niki'	EBee EPfP LRHS MAsh MGos MMuc SEND SPoG
'Killiney Red'	ELan MBri MGos MMuc
'Killiney Salmon'	GGar LRHS LSRN MRav WFar
'La Coquette'	CDoC EBee EPfP LRHS MAsh SBfd SPlb

	'Lena' ♀H4	CDoC CHar CMac CSBt EBee EPfP GGar GKir LRHS LSRN LTen MAsh MBri MGos MMuc MWat NBir NCGa NEgg NHol NLar NPri SLim WBor WClo WFar WHar
	leucanthus	see *Chamaecytisus albus* (Hacq.) Rothm.
	'Luna'	EBee WFar
	maderensis	see *Genista maderensis*
	'Maria Burkwood'	MGos NLar
	'Minstead'	CDoC ELan EPfP GGar LBuc LRHS NEgg SLim
	monspessulanus	see *Genista monspessulana*
	'Moonlight'	NBro
	'Moyclare Pink'	CMHG
	'Mrs Norman Henry'	NLar
§	***multiflorus*** ♀H4	SRms
	nigricans	WPGP
	- 'Cyni'	CTsd ECrN ELan ELon IArd LAst LRHS MAsh MMuc SEND SPer SPoG SSpi
	'Palette'	MMuc
	'Porlock'	see *Genista* 'Porlock'
	× ***praecox***	CMac EWTr LAst LRHS MAsh NEgg SPlb SPoG WFar WHar
	- 'Albus'	CDoC CDul CHar CMac CSBt EBee ECrN ELan EPfP GGar GKir LAst LRHS LSRN MAsh MGos MRav NHol NPri SBfd SPer WFar WHar
	- 'Allgold' ♀H4	Widely available
	- 'Canary Bird'	see *C.* × *praecox* 'Goldspeer'
	- cream-flowered	MMuc
	- 'Frisia'	NBro WFar
§	- 'Goldspeer'	CWit MMuc SEND
	- 'Warminster' ♀H4	EBee EPfP MBri MRav MWat NWea SBfd SEND SPer SRms
	purpureus	see *Chamaecytisus purpureus*
	- 'Atropurpureus'	see *Chamaecytisus purpureus* 'Atropurpureus'
	racemosus	see *Genista* × *spachiana*
	Red Favourite	see *C.* 'Roter Favorit'
	'Red Wings'	NHol SPer
§	'Roter Favorit'	EPfP LTen MGos MNHC NPla WGor
	scoparius	CArn CDul CRWN NWea SRms WDin
§	- f. ***andreanus*** ♀H4	CDoC EPfP MGos NWea SPer WFar
	- 'Cornish Cream'	CDoC CDul CSBt EPfP GKir LRHS SPer WFar
§	- subsp. ***maritimus***	MCoo SLPl
	- Monarch strain	GJos SWal
	- var. ***prostratus***	see *C. scoparius* subsp. *maritimus*
	× ***spachianus***	see *Genista* × *spachiana*
	supinus	see *Chamaecytisus supinus*
	'Windlesham Ruby'	CDoC CPLG EBee ELan EPfP GKir LRHS LSRN NLar SBfd SLim SPad SPer WBVN WDin WFar
	'Zeelandia' ♀H4	CMac EBee EPfP GKir LRHS LTen MRav MWat NEgg NHol NPri SPer WFar

D

Daboecia ✿ (*Ericaceae*)

§	***cantabrica***	MMuc
§	- f. ***alba***	CSBt MBri NHol SHeS SPer SRms SWhi
	- - 'Alba Globosa'	CCCN SHeS
	- - 'Bellita'	IVic SHeS
	- - 'Creeping White'	SHeS
	- - 'David Moss' ♀H4	MMuc SHeS
I	- - 'Early Bride'	SHeS
	- - 'Snowdrift'	SHeS
	- - 'White Carpet'	SHeS
	- 'Arielle' ♀H4	IVic SHeS
	- 'Atropurpurea'	CCCN CSBt NHol SHeS SPer SWhi
	- 'Barbara Phillips' ♀H4	SHeS
	- 'Bicolor' ♀H4	IVic SHeS
	- 'Blueless'	SHeS
	- f. ***blumii*** 'Pink Blum'	SHeS
	- - 'Purple Blum'	SHeS
	- - 'White Blum'	SHeS
	- 'Bubbles'	SHeS
	- 'Celtic Star'	SHeS
	- 'Chaldon'	SHeS
	- 'Charles Nelson' (d)	SHeS
	- 'Cherub'	SHeS
	- 'Cinderella'	SHeS
	- 'Cleggan'	SHeS
	- 'Clifden'	SHeS
	- 'Covadonga'	SHeS
	- 'Cupido'	CTsd SHeS
§	- 'Donard Pink'	SHeS
	- 'Eskdale Baron'	SHeS
	- 'Eskdale Blea'	SHeS
	- 'Eskdale Blonde'	SHeS
	- 'Glamour'	SHeS
I	- 'Globosa Pink'	SHeS
	- 'Harlequin'	SHeS
	- 'Heather Yates'	SHeS
	- 'Heraut'	SHeS
	- 'Hookstone Purple'	CCCN NHol SHeS
	- 'Irish Shine'	SHeS
I	- 'Joanna' **new**	IVic
	- 'Johnny Boy'	SHeS
	- 'Lilac Osmond'	SHeS
	- 'Pink'	see *D. cantabrica* 'Donard Pink'
	- 'Pink Lady'	SHeS
	- 'Polifolia'	SHeS SRms
	- 'Porter's Variety'	SHeS
	- 'Praegerae'	CCCN CTri SHeS SWhi
	- 'Purpurea'	SHeS
	- 'Rainbow' (v)	SHeS SWhi
	- 'Rodeo' ♀H4	SHeS
	- 'Rosea'	SHeS
	- 'Rubra'	SHeS
	- subsp. ***scotica*** 'Bearsden'	SHeS
	- - 'Ben'	SHeS
	- - 'Cora'	SHeS
	- - 'Golden Imp'	SHeS
	- - 'Goscote'	MGos SHeS
	- - 'Jack Drake' ♀H4	GGar MBri SHeS SWhi
	- - 'Katherine's Choice'	CBcs SHeS
	- - 'Red Imp'	SHeS
	- - 'Robin'	SHeS
	- - 'Silverwells' ♀H4	CBcs MBri SHeS SWhi
	- - 'Tabramhill'	SHeS
	- - 'William Buchanan' ♀H4	GGar MBri NHol SHeS SWhi
	- - 'William Buchanan Gold' (v)	CCCN MBri SHeS
	- 'Tom Pearce'	CCCN
	- 'Waley's Red' ♀H4	IVic NHol SHeS SWhi
	- 'Wijnie'	SHeS

Dacrycarpus (*Podocarpaceae*)

§	***dacrydioides***	CBcs ECou LEdu
	- 'Dark Delight'	ECou

Dacrydium (*Podocarpaceae*)

	bidwillii	see *Halocarpus bidwillii*
	cupressinum	CBcs CDoC CTrC SMad SPlb

franklinii	see *Lagarostrobos franklinii*
laxifolium	see *Lepidothamnus laxifolius*

Dactylis (*Poaceae*)

glomerata	WSFF
- 'Variegata' (v)	EBee EPPr LTen MCCP MMuc NBid NHol SBfd SEND SHDw WCot WFar

Dactylorhiza (*Orchidaceae*)

sp. **new**	NDav
from China **new**	NLAp
alpestris	CFir EBee MDun NLAp SKHP
aristata	EFEx NLAp WWst
- f. ***alba*** **new**	NLAp WWst
× ***braunii***	ECha
§ ***elata*** ♀H4	GAbr IBlr LAma MBri NLAp SMrm SUsu WWst
- 'Lydia'	GCra
§ ***foliosa*** ♀H4	CCCN CTsd EBee GCra GKir IBlr LLWG MDun MNrw MTho NLAp WFar WOld WWst
foliosa × ***incarnata*** subsp. ***coccinea*** **new**	NLAp
§ ***fuchsii***	CCCN CMil CPrp EBee EBla EPot GKev MAvo MDun MNrw NLAp NMen NRya NSla SKHP SUsu WCot WFar WHer WPnP WTin
- 'Bressingham Bonus'	GCrs
- pink-flowered	CFir
- white-flowered	CFir MNrw NLAp
× ***grandis***	EBla IBlr SCnR SUsu
hybrids	GKir NLAp
incarnata	CPrp EBee EBla MDun MREP NBid NLAp WPnP WSpi WWst
- subsp. ***coccinea*** **new**	NLAp
- subsp. ***ochroleuca*** **new**	NLAp
lapponica **new**	NLAp
§ ***maculata***	CFir CHid EBee EBla EHrv ELan EPfP GAbr GKir LAma MDun MREP NLAp NMen WBor WCot WFar WHer WHlf WPnP
- subsp. ***ericetorum***	NLAp WWst
maderensis	see *D. foliosa*
§ ***majalis***	CLAP CPrp EBla EPot LAma MDun MREP NLAp WFar WPnP WWst
- subsp. ***sphagnicola***	EBee MDun NLAp WCot WWst
mascula	see *Orchis mascula*
praetermissa	CCCN CFir CLAP CPBP CPrp EBee EBla GKev MDun MREP NLAp NMen SKHP WCot WFar WPnP WWst
- 'Copenhaven'	NLAp
- subsp. ***praetermissa*** hybrid	NLAp SKHP WWst
purpurella	CLAP CPrp EBee EBla MDun MREP NLAp NMen NRya WCot WFar WPnP WWst
- 'Palmengarten'	NLAp
romana subsp. ***georgica*** **new**	NLAp
sambucina	EBee NLAp
traunsteineri	EBee NLAp

Dahlia ✿ (*Asteraceae*)

NJM 05.008	WPGP
NJM 05.085	WPGP
'Abba' (SD)	ECtt
'Abbie' (SD) **new**	NHal
'Admiral Rawlings' (SD)	MWea WHal WWlt
'Aitara Caress' (MinC) **new**	NHal
'Aitara Cloud' (MinC)	NHal
'Akita' (Misc)	CSut EPfP MCot SPer
'Alauna Clair-Obscur' (MC/Fim)	ERCP
'Alfred Grille' (MS-c)	LRHS SPer
'Allan Snowfire' (MS-c)	LAyl NHal
'Alloway Candy' **new**	ERCP
'Alloway Cottage' (MD)	NHal
'Alstergruss' (Col)	CBgR
'Alva's Doris' (SS-c) ♀H3	LAyl
'Alva's Regalia' (MD) **new**	LRHS
'Alva's Supreme' (GD) ♀H3	LAyl NHal
'Amber Festival' (SD)	NHal
'Amberglow' (MinBa)	LAyl
'Ambition' (SS-c)	ERCP
'American Dream' (MS-c) **new**	ERCP
'Amira' (SBa)	NHal
'Amy Cave' (SBa) **new**	NHal
'Andrea Clark' (MD)	NHal
'Andrea Lawson'	NHal
'Andrew Mitchell' (MS-c)	NHal
'Andries' Orange' (MinS-c)	LYaf
'Ann Breckenfelder' (Col) ♀H3	ECtt EHrv ERCP LOck LRHS NEgg NHal SDix SMrm WCot
'Anniversary Ball' (MinBa)	LAyl
'Apache' (MS-c/Fim)	ERCP LRHS SPer WClo
'Apache Blauw'	ERCP
'April Heather' (Col)	NHal
'Arabian Night' (SD)	Widely available
'Asahi Chohje' (Anem) ♀H3	EBee
'Aspen' (Dwf)	MWea NBPC
'Audacity' (MD)	LAyl
'Aurora's Kiss' (MinBa)	LYaf NHal
'Aurwen's Violet' (Pom)	LAyl NHal
australis	EBee WPGP
- B&SWJ 10208	WCru
- B&SWJ 10358	WCru
- B&SWJ 10389	WCru
'Autumn Choice' (MD)	LAyl
'Autumn Fairy' (D)	ERCP
'Avoca Comanche' (SS-c)	NHal
'Avoca Salmon' (MD)	NHal
'B.J. Beauty' (MD)	LAyl NHal
'Babette' (S-c)	LYaf
'Babylon' (GD)	EPfP
'Babylon Bronze'	CSut
'Bantling' (MinBa)	ECtt ERCP
'Barbarry Banker' (MinD)	LAyl
'Barbarry Bluebird' (MinD)	NHal
'Barbarry Riviera' (MinD)	LRHS
'Barberry Maverick' **new**	GBin
'Baret Joy' (LS-c)	NHal
'Bargaly Blush' (MD)	NHal
'Barton Memory' (S-c)	LAyl NHal
'Bayou'PBR (Misc)	LRHS
'Bednall Beauty' (Misc/DwB) ♀H3	CBgR CHVG CHll CMoH COIW CSpe EBee ECtt EHrv ELan EShb EWes GBin LHop LRHS LSRN MBri MRav NEgg SAga SBfd SDnm SDys SMrm SUsu WClo WCot WHil WSpi WWEG
'Bell Boy' (MinBa)	ECtt
'Berger's Rekord' (S-c)	CSut EPfP ERCP
'Berliner Kleene' (MinD/DwB)	SBfd
'Berwick Wood' (MD)	NHal
'Beth's Chaplet'	WCot
'Bishop of Auckland'PBR (Misc)	CBgR CSpe EBee ECtt ERCP GKir LPio LRHS MAvo MCot NEgg SMrm WBrk WCot WWEG WWlt
'Bishop of Canterbury'PBR (Misc)	EBee ECtt EPfP GKir LRHS MBri NGdn NHal
'Bishop of Dover'	EBee

'Bishop of Lancaster' (Misc)	EBee LPio
'Bishop of Leicester' (Misc)	CSpe ECtt EPfP LPio LRHS LSou MBri MNrw MWea SPet
'Bishop of Llandaff' (Misc) 🏆^{H3}	Widely available
'Bishop of Oxford' (Misc)	CSpe EBee EPfP GKir LPio LRHS LSou MBri MWea NBPC NGdn SAga SPet
'Bishop of York' (Misc)	CAvo CFFs CSpe EBee ECtt EPfP EPot GKir LPio LRHS LSou MBri MWea NBPC NGdn SPet
'Bishop Peter Price' (Sin)	CHar
'Bishop's Children'	CSpr
'Black Barbara' (D) **new**	ERCP
'Black Fire' (SD)	LAyl
'Black Monarch' (GD)	NHal
'Black Narcissus' (MC)	CHVG EPfP SMrm SPer WClo WWlt
'Black Touch' **new**	ERCP
'Black Wizard' (MS-c)	EPfP
'Blackberry Ripple' (S-c) **new**	ERCP
'Bloommaster' (MinD)	NHal
'Blue Record' **new**	MCot
'Bluesette' (SD)	LRHS
'Blyton Lady in Red' (MinD)	NHal
'Blyton Softer Gleam' (MinD)	NHal
'Bodacious' **new**	WHlf
'Bonaventure' (GD)	LRHS NHal
'Boogie Woogie' (Anem)	CSut
'Boy Scout' (MinBa)	ERCP
'Bracken Ballerina' (SWL)	GBin NHal
'Brackenridge Ballerina' (SWL)	CSam LAyl
'Brantwood' (Sin) **new**	CSam
Braveheart = 'VDTG67' (Dark Angel Series) (Sin) **new**	LRHS
'Brian's Dream' (MinD)	LAyl NHal
'Bride's Bouquet' (Col)	ERCP
'Bridge View Aloha' (MS-c) 🏆^{H3}	EPfP WClo
'Brookfield Delight' (Sin/Lil) 🏆^{H3}	SUsu
'Bryn Terfel' (GD)	NHal
'Café au Lait' (GD)	IPot LRHS SEND SPer WSpi
'Camano Phantom' (SD) **new**	NHal
'Cameo' (WL)	CSam LAyl LYaf NHal
* 'Canary Fubuki' (MD)	ERCP
I 'Candlelight' (GD)	NHal
Candy Eyes = 'Zone 10' (Sin/DwB)	CChe EBee EKen EPfP GBin LRHS LSRN LSou MGos NPri SBfd WClo
'Candy Keene' (LS-c)	NHal
'Caribbean Fantasy'	EBee NGdn SPer
'Caribbean Sunset'	LRHS SMrm
'Carolina Moon' (SD)	CSam LAyl NHal
'Carstone Ruby' (SD)	NHal
'Carstone Suntan' (MinC)	NHal
'Carstone Valliant' (MinBa) **new**	NHal
'Catherine Deneuve' (Misc)	ECtt
'Charlie Briggs' (SBa)	NHal
'Charlie Dimmock' (SWL) 🏆^{H3}	NHal
'Charlie Two' (MD)	NHal
'Chat Noir' (MS-c)	CAvo CFFs EBee ERCP LRHS SPhx
'Cherwell Goldcrest' (SS-c)	NHal
'Cherwell Skylark' (SS-c) 🏆^{H3}	NHal
'Chic' (MinBa)	EBee ECtt LRHS
'Chic en Rouge'	NBPC
'Chimborazo' (Col)	LAyl SDix
'Christine' (SD)	LRHS SPer
'Christmas Carol' (Col)	ECtt
'Christopher Taylor' (SWL)	NHal
'Citizen'	ERCP
'City of Alkmaar' (SC)	LRHS SMrm
'City of Leiden' (MinS-c)	LRHS
'City of Rotterdam'	LRHS
'Clair de Lune' (Col) 🏆^{H3}	CWCL EBee ECtt ERCP LAst LOck LRHS MAvo MCot MWea NHal SMrm WBrk WCot WHoo WHrl WSpi
'Clarion' (MS-c)	CSpe LRHS
'Clarion'	NPri SBfd
'Clarion 79' (DwB)	SUsu
'Classic Rosamunde'^{PBR} (Misc)	CBgR NGdn NHal
'Classic Summertime' (Misc)	CBgR
'Classic Swanlake'^{PBR} (Misc)	ERCP
'Classic Thaïs'^{PBR} (Misc) **new**	CBgR
'Clearview Irene' (MS-c)	NHal
'Clearwater David' (SD) **new**	GBin
coccinea (B)	CBgR CGHE CHll CSpe EBee EHrv EPfP GBin GCal LPio MCot SDix SUsu WCot WPGP
- B&SWJ 9126	WCru
- NJM 05.072	WPGP
- var. ***palmeri***	CAvo EBee LPio SUsu WPGP
coccinea × ***merckii*** (B)	EWes
'Confection' (MinD) **new**	NHal
'Cornel' (SBa)	LAyl LYaf NHal
'Cornel Brons' (MinBa)	ERCP
'Cornish Ruby' **new**	CFir
'Craigowan' (MS-c) **new**	NHal
'Czardas'	GCal
'Daleko Jupiter' (GS-c)	NHal
'Dark Desire'^{PBR} (Sin/DwB)	CAvo CBct CBgR CFir CSpe CWCL ECtt GBin LAst LHop MWea SCoo SDnm SUsu WCot WHil
'David Digweed' (SD)	NHal
'David Howard' (MinD) 🏆^{H3}	Widely available
'Dawn Sky' (SD)	LAyl
'Deborah's Kiwi' (SC)	NHal
'Debra Anne Craven' (GS-c)	NHal
dissecta	WPGP
- F&M 191	WPGP
'Doctor John Grainger' (MinD)	CHVG
'Don Hill' (Col) 🏆^{H3}	NHal
'Doris Day' (SC)	LYaf NHal
'Doris Knight' (SC)	LYaf
'Dovegrove' (Sin) **new**	CSam
'Downham Royal' (MinBa)	ERCP
'Duet' (MD)	ECtt EPfP LRHS
'Eastwood Moonlight' (MS-c)	NHal
'Edge of Joy'	LRHS
'Edinburgh' (SD)	ERCP SWal
'Electric Haze'	NGdn
'Elga'	ERCP
'Elise' (MinD)	SPer
'Ellen Huston' (Misc/DwB) 🏆^{H3}	CBgR EBee ECtt ERCP LOck LPio LRHS NHal SBfd SMrm WCot
'Elma E' (LD)	LAyl NHal
'Embrace' (SC)	LAyl NHal
'Engelhardt's Matador' (MD)	CBgR EBee ECtt LAst LOck LRHS MCot SBfd WCot WHrl
'Eveline' (SD)	CBgR EPfP ERCP MBri

	excelsa (B)	CHll WPGP
	- B&SWJ 10233	WCru
	- B&SWJ 10238	WCru
	'Excentrique' (Misc)	ECtt SUsu
	'Exotic Dwarf' (Sin/Lil)	EBee ECtt LOck LRHS NGdn NHal WCot WHoo
	'Explosion' (SS-c)	LRHS
	'Eye Candy'	EBee LRHS SBfd
	'Fabula' (Col)	LRHS
	'Fairfield Frost' (Col)	NHal
	'Fairway Spur' (GD)	NHal
	'Famoso' (Col)	ERCP
	'Fantastico' (Col)	ERCP
	'Fascination' ambig.	CFox ERCP
I	'Fascination' (Misc)	SPet
	'Fascination' (SWL/DwB) 🏆H3	CBcs CHVG CHar COIW CSam EBee ECtt EPfP EWll LAyl LPio LRHS LSou MCot MWea NEgg NGdn SBfd WHoo WSpi WWEG
	'Fashion Monger' (Col)	EBee ECtt EHrv ERCP LOck NEgg NGdn NHal WClo WCot
	'Ferncliffe Illusion' (LD)	ERCP LRHS
	'Festivo' (Col)	LRHS
	'Fidalgo Supreme' (MD)	LAyl
	'Finchcocks' (SWL) 🏆H3	LAyl
	'Fire and Ice'	LRHS
	'Fire Mountain' (MinD)	CSam NHal WCot
	'Firebird' (MS-c)	see *D.* 'Vuurvogel'
	'Fleur' (MinD/Fim)	SMrm SPer
	'Florence Li Tim-Oi' (Sin)	CHar
	'Forncett Furnace' (B)	GCal
	'Fortuna' (Col)	ERCP
	'Franz Kafka' (Pom)	ECtt ERCP
§	'Freya's Paso Doble' (Anem) 🏆H3	LAyl
*	'Friquolet'	CSut ERCP
	'Fusion' (MD) 🏆H3	WCot
	'Fuzzy Wuzzy' (MD)	CSut
	'Gainesville' (MinD) **new**	EPfP
	(Gallery Series) 'Gallery Art Deco'PBR (SD) 🏆H3	ERCP GKir LRHS NHal SBfd
	- 'Gallery Art Fair'PBR (MinD) 🏆H3	GKir LRHS NHal
	- 'Gallery Art Nouveau'PBR 3 (MinD) 🏆H	ERCP GKir LOck LRHS NHal SBfd WCot
	- 'Gallery Cézanne'PBR (MinD)	LRHS
	- 'Gallery Matisse'PBR (SD)	LRHS
	- 'Gallery Renoir'PBR (SD) 🏆H3	LRHS NHal
	- 'Gallery Salvador'PBR (SD)	ERCP
	'Garden Festival' (SWL)	ERCP
	'Garden Party' (MC/DwB) 🏆H3	LAyl
	'Garden Wonder' (SD)	EPfP SBfd
	Gateshead Festival	see *D.* 'Peach Melba' (SD)
	'Gay Princess' (SWL)	LAyl
	'Geoffrey Kent' (MinD) 🏆H3	NHal
	'Gerrie Hoek' (SWL)	CSam IPot LYaf MWea WSpi
	'Gina Lombaert' (MS-c)	SEND
	'Giraffe' (DblO)	ERCP
	'Giselle'	SPer SPet
	'Glorie van Heemstede' (SWL) 🏆H3	CSam ERCP LAyl LPio LYaf MWte NHal SEND WHrl
	'Glorie van Noordwijk' (MinS-c)	ERCP
	'Go American' (GD)	NHal
	'Gold Crown' (LS-c)	EPfP
	'Golden Emblem' (MD)	ECtt SWal
	'Golden Jubilee' (D)	EPfP
	'Good Earth' (MC)	ERCP SMrm
	'Gracie S' (MinC)	NHal
	'Grenadier' (SWL) 🏆H3	CBgR EBee ECtt LRHS LSou SDix SDys WCot WWEG
	'Grenidor Pastelle' (MS-c)	NHal
	'Gurtla Twilight' (Pom)	NHal
	'Gypsy Boy' (LD)	LAyl
	'Hamari Accord' (LS-c) 🏆H3	LAyl
	'Hamari Bride' (MS-c) 🏆H3	LAyl
	'Hamari Girl' (GD)	NHal
	'Hamari Gold' (GD) 🏆H3	NHal
	'Hamari Rosé' (MinBa) 🏆H3	NHal
	'Hamari Sunshine' (LD) 🏆H3	NHal
	'Hanny Polle' **new**	ERCP
	(Happy Single Series) Happy Single First Love = 'HS First Love'PBR (Sin)	ERCP LSou WHil
	- Happy Single Juliet = 'HS Juliet'PBR (Sin)	ERCP
	- Happy Single Kiss = 'HS Kiss'PBR (Sin)	LSou
	- Happy Single Party = 'HS Party'PBR (Sin)	ERCP LSou
	- Happy Single Romeo = 'HS Romeo'PBR (Sin)	LSou NPri WHil
	- Happy Single White = 'HS White' (Sin) **new**	MWea WHil
	- Happy Single Wink = 'HS Wink'PBR (Sin)	EPfP LRHS LSou NPri
	'Haresbrook' (Sin)	EShb NGdn WSpi
§	'Harvest Samantha' (Sin/Lil) 🏆H3	NHal
	'Hayley Jayne' (S-Sc)	ERCP
	'Helga' (MS-c)	ECtt ERCP
	'Herbert Smith' (D)	SEND
	'Hillcrest Delight' (MD)	NHal
	'Hillcrest Desire' (SC) 🏆H3	LAyl
	'Hillcrest Hannah' (MinD)	NHal
	'Hillcrest Kismet' (MD)	LAyl NHal
	'Hillcrest Royal' (MC) 🏆H3	NHal SDix
	'Holland Festival' (GD)	LRHS
	'Honka' (SinO) 🏆H3	CBgR ERCP LAyl LRHS MCot WCot WWlt
	'Honka Red' (Misc)	ERCP
	'Honka Surprise' (Misc)	EPfP ERCP WCot
	'Honka White' (Misc)	ERCP
	'Hot Chocolate' (MinD)	EPfP WBrk WCot WHoo
	'Hugs and Kisses'	EPfP SMrm
	imperialis (B)	CDTJ CFir CHEx CHll CSpe EUJe EWes LRHS SBig WBVN WHal
	- B&SWJ 8997	WCru
	- 'Alba' (B)	CFir
I	- 'Tasmania' (B)	GCal
	'Inca Dambuster' (GS-c)	NHal
	'Indian Summer' (SC)	NHal
	'Ivanetti' (MinBa)	EPfP NHal
	'Jan van Schaffelaar' ambig.	ERCP
	'Janal Amy' (GS-c)	NHal
	'Jean Fairs' (MinWL) 🏆H3	LYaf
	'Jeanne d'Arc' (GC)	EPfP
	'Jescot Jess' (MinD)	LYaf
	'Jescot Julie' (Db/O)	ERCP GBin LAyl
	'Jessica Willows' (SWL) **new**	NHal
	'Jill Day' (SC)	LYaf
	'Jim Branigan' (LS-c)	NHal
	'Jocondo' (GD)	NHal
	'Johann' (Pom)	NHal
	'John Street' (SWL) 🏆H3	WSpi
	'Jomanda' (MinBa) 🏆H3	GBin LYaf NHal
	'Jo's Choice' (MinD)	LYaf
	'Judy Tregidden' (MWL)	CSam

	Name	Suppliers
	'Jules Dyson' (Misc)	SDys
	'Jura' (SS-c)	EPfP ERCP
	'Karenglen' (MinD) ♀H3	GBin LYaf NHal
	'Karma Amanda' (SD)	LRHS
	'Karma Choc'PBR (SD) **new**	MSCN MWea SWal WHlf
	'Karma Fuchsiana' (SD)	ERCP SBfd
	'Karma Lagoon'PBR (SD)	LRHS SBfd
	'Karma Naomi'PBR (SD)	LRHS
	'Karma Prospero'PBR (SD)	SBfd
	'Karma Royal Sea'PBR **new**	ERCP
	'Karma Sangria'PBR (SC)	LRHS
	'Karma Ventura'PBR (SD)	LRHS SBfd
	'Katie Dahl' (MinD)	NHal
	'Kea Magic' (GD) **new**	NHal
	'Keith's Choice' (MD)	NHal
	'Keith's Pet' (Sin) **new**	SUsu
	'Kelsea Carla' (SS-c) ♀H3	NHal
	'Kenn Emerland' (MS-c)	EPfP
	'Kenora Challenger' (LS-c)	NHal
	'Kenora Jubilee' (LS-c)	NHal
	'Kenora Macop-B' (MC/Fim)	CSut LRHS
	'Kenora Sunset' (MS-c) ♀H3	LAyl LYaf NHal
	'Kenora Superb' (LS-c)	NHal
	'Kenora Valentine' (LD) ♀H3	LAyl NHal
	'Ken's Choice' (SBa)	NHal
	'Kidd's Climax' (GD) ♀H3	ERCP
	'Kilmorie' (SS-c)	NHal
	'Kiss Me' (SD)	EPfP LRHS
	'Kiwi Gloria' (SC)	NHal
	'Knock Out' (MS-c) **new**	CChe
I	'Knockout' (Sin)	EPfP GBin LRHS LSRN LSou MGos MWea SBfd
	'L.A.T.E.' (MinBa)	GBin NHal
	'La Rouvre' (SS-c) **new**	GBin
	'Lady Linda' (SD)	LYaf NHal
	'Lambada' (Anem)	LRHS
	'L'Ancresse' (MinBa)	GBin LAyl NHal
	'Lauren's Moonlight'	see *D.* 'Pim's Moonlight'
	'Lavender Line' (SS-c)	NHal
	'Lavender Perfection' (GD)	LRHS
	'Le Baron' (SD)	ERCP
	'Lemon Elegans' (SS-c) ♀H3	LYaf NHal
	'Lemon Zing' (MinBa)	LAyl NHal
	'Lilac Marston' (MinD) ♀H3	GBin NHal
	'Lilac Taratahi' (SC) ♀H3	CSam LAyl
	'Lilac Time' (MD)	ERCP
	'Lilian Alice' (Col)	NHal
	'Linda's Chester' (SC)	LYaf
	'Lismore Canary' (SWL)	CSam
	'Lismore Carol' (Pom)	GBin NHal
	'Lismore Moonlight' (Pom)	LAyl NHal
	'Lismore Robin' (MinD)	NHal
	'Lismore Willie' (SWL) ♀H3	LYaf
	'Little Robert' (MinD)	EPfP
	'Little Treasure'	EPfP
I	'Little William' (MinBa)	LRHS
	'Loretta' (SBa)	GBin
	'Lorona Dawn' (SinO) **new**	ERCP
	'Ludwig Helfert' (S-c)	ERCP SEND
	'Mabel Ann' (GD)	LAyl NHal
	'Madame de Rosa' (LS-c)	NHal
	'Madame J. Snapper'	WSpi
	'Madame Simone Stappers' (WL)	LPio LRHS MMHG
	'Madame Vera' (SD)	LYaf
	'Magenta Magic' (Sin/DwB)	NHal
	'Magenta Star' (Sin) **new**	GBin
	'Maggie C' (MS-c) **new**	NHal
	'Malvina' **new**	MCri SMrm
	'Marble Ball' (MinD)	ERCP WClo
	'Margaret Haggo' (SWL)	CSam NHal
	'Margareth Kleene' (MD)	LRHS
	'Martina' (SD)	NHal
	'Martin's Yellow' (Pom)	NHal
	'Mary Eveline' (Col)	ECtt LAyl LRHS NHal
	'Mary Hammett' (MinD)	WSpi
	'Mary's Jomanda' (SBa) ♀H3	GBin NHal
	'Matilda Huston' (SS-c)	NHal
	'Maxine Bailey' (MinBa) **new**	GBin
	'Maya' (SD)	IPot
	'Megan Dean' (MInBa)	NHal
	'Melody Harmony'PBR (SD) **new**	EPfP
	merckii (B)	CBgR CFir CGHE CMdw CSpe EWes LPio LRHS MCot MNrw MRav SMad SUsu WCom WPGP WSHC
	- F&M 222	WPGP
	- ***alba*** (B)	CSpe LPio SUsu WCom WCru
	- compact (B)	WPGP
	'Mermaid of Zennor' (Sin)	CFir
	'Mingus Randy' (LS-c) **new**	SPer
	'Minley Carol' (Pom) ♀H3	LAyl NHal
	'Mistral' (MS-c/Fim)	ECtt
	'Molly Trotter' (Sin)	CHar
	'Mom's Special' (LD)	LRHS
	'Moonfire' (Misc/DwB) ♀H3	Widely available
	'Moonglow' (LS-c)	ERCP
	'Moor Place' (Pom)	NHal
	'München' (MinD)	NGdn
	'Murdoch'	CBgR EBee ECtt LOck LRHS SDys WCot WHrl WSpi
	'Murillo'	LAyl WCot
	'Musette' (MinD)	ECtt
	'My Beverley' (MS-c/Fim)	LAyl NHal
	'My Love' (SS-c)	CSut EPfP ERCP LAst LRHS MWea SEND SMrm
	'Myama Fubuki' (MS-c) **new**	ERCP
	'Mystery Day' (MD)	CBgR ECtt EPfP ERCP NBPC NGdn SBfd
	Mystic Desire	see *D.* 'Scarlet Fern'
	Mystic Mars	see *D.* 'Scarlet Fern'
	'Nargold' (MS-c/Fim)	LAyl
	'Narrow's Tricia' (MS-c) **new**	NHal
	'Natal' (MinBa)	ECtt EPfP ERCP
	'Nepos' (SWL)	GBin
	'Nescio' (Pom)	EPfP ERCP
	'New Baby' (MinBa)	ERCP
	'New Dimension' (SS-c)	EPfP ERCP
	'New Millennium' (Col) **new**	SMrm
I	'Night Queen' (Pom)	EPfP ERCP
	'Nippon' (Sin)	EBee LRHS NGdn
	'Nonette' (SWL)	CBgR EBee ECtt LAst LOck LRHS NEgg WClo WCot
	'Noreen' (Pom)	NHal
*	'Nuit d'Eté' (MS-c)	CAvo EBee EPfP ERCP LAst LPio LRHS MNrw MWea SEND
	'Oakwood Diamond' (SBa)	LYaf
	'Onesta' (SD)	CSam ERCP
	'Orange Fubuki' (SD)	LRHS SPer
	'Oreti Bliss' (SC) **new**	NHal
	'Oreti Classic' (MD)	NHal
	'Orfeo' (MC)	ECtt ERCP MNrw
	'Osirium' (SD)	LRHS
	'Otto's Thrill' (LD)	SMrm
	'Pablo'	LRHS
	'Pacific Argyle' (SD)	NHal
	'Painted Girl' (D) **new**	ERCP
	'Palm Springs' (SD)	EPfP LRHS
	'Pam Howden' (SWL)	NHal

	'Park Princess' (SC/DwB)	NGdn NHal SMrm
	'Paso Doble' misapplied	see *D.* 'Freya's Paso Doble'
	'Patricia' (Col)	NHal
	'Peach Brandy' (MinWL) **new**	SMrm
	'Peach Cupid' (MinBa) ♀H3	LYaf
§	'Peach Melba' (SD)	NHal
	'Peaches and Cream' PBR (MinD)	SBfd
	'Pearl of Heemstede' (SD) ♀H3	NHal
	'Pembroke Levenna' (MinBa) **new**	NHal
	'Pembroke Pattie' (Pom)	NHal
	'Penelope' (MS-c) **new**	IPot
	'Peter' (MinD)	ECtt
I	'Peter' (SS-c)	EPfP
§	'Pim's Moonlight' (MS-c)	NHal
	'Pinelands Pixie' (MinC/Fim)	NHal
	'Pink Giraffe' (DblO) ♀H3	ERCP
	'Pink Jupiter' (GS-c)	NHal
	'Pink Pastelle' (MS-c) ♀H3	NHal
	'Pink Shirley Alliance' (SC)	LAyl
	'Pink Skin' (MD)	ERCP LRHS
	pinnata B&SWJ 10240	WCru
	'Piper's Pink' (SS-c/DwB)	LAyl
	'Poème'	CSpe MWea
	'Pontiac' (SC)	LAyl
	'Pooh' (Col)	LAyl NHal
	'Porcelain' (SWL) ♀H3	LYaf WSpi
	'Preference' (SS-c)	ERCP
	'Preston Park' (Sin/DwB) ♀H3	CSam LAyl NHal
	Pretty Woman = 'VDTG43' (Dark Angel Series) (Sin) **new**	LRHS
	Pride of Berlin	see *D.* 'Stolz von Berlin'
	'Primrose Pastelle' (MS-c)	NHal
	'Procyon' (SD)	CBgR EPfP ERCP MWea
	'Promise' (MS-c/Fim)	ECtt ERCP
	'Pumpkin Pie'	CBgR WCot
	'Purple Gem' (SS-c)	ERCP LRHS
	'Purple Puff' (Anem)	LRHS
	aff. ***purpusii*** B&SWJ 10321	WCru
	'Radiance' (MC)	ERCP
	'Raffles' (SD)	LAyl
	'Ragged Robin' (Misc)	CBgR CSpe CWCL EBee ECtt ERCP LOck LRHS MCot MNrw WCot WWlt
	'Raiser's Pride' (MC)	NHal
	'Red Bird'	CMoH
	'Red Diamond' (MD)	NHal
	'Reginald Keene' (LS-c)	NHal
	'Requiem' (SD)	ERCP
	'Rhonda' (Pom)	NHal
	'Richard S' (LS-c)	NHal
	'Rip City' (SS-c)	CSpe ERCP MCot
	'Rocco' (MinBa)	ERCP
	'Romeo'	LRHS
	'Rose Jupiter' (GS-c)	NHal
	'Rosella' (MD)	EPfP
	'Rossendale Natasha' (MinBa)	NHal
	'Rothesay Robin' (SD)	GBin
I	'Roxy' (Sin/DwB)	CBcs CBgR CFox CMMP COIW CSam EBee ECtt EHrv ELan EPfP ERCP GKir LAst LAyl LRHS MAvo MNrw NEgg NGdn NHal NVic SBfd SMrm SPav WCot WHoo WSpi WWEG

	'Ruskin Andrea' (SS-c)	NHal
	'Ruskin Charlotte' (LS-c)	LAyl NHal
	'Ruskin Diana' (SD)	LYaf NHal
	'Ruskin Marigold' (SS-c)	LAyl LYaf NHal
	'Ruskin Michelle' (MS-c) **new**	GBin
	'Ruskin Myra' (SS-c)	LAyl NHal
	'Ruskin Penelope' (SS-c)	CAvo CFFs
	'Ruskin Splendour' (MS-c) **new**	NHal
*	'Ruskin Tangerine' (SBa)	NHal
	'Ryecroft Claire' (MinD)	NHal
	'Ryecroft Delight' (MinBa)	NHal
	'Ryecroft Gem' (MinBa)	NHal
	'Ryecroft Jan' (MinBa) ♀H3	NHal
	'Ryecroft Jim' (Anem) **new**	NHal
	'Ryecroft Laura' (MinBa) **new**	NHal
	'Ryecroft Magnum' (MD)	NHal
	'Ryecroft Marge' (Anem) ♀H3 **new**	NHal
	'Ryecroft Zoe' (SS-c)	NHal
	'Sabrina' (SD) **new**	IPot
	'Saint-Saëns' (S-c)	ERCP SEND
	'Sakura Fubuki'	ERCP
	'Sam Hopkins' (SD)	CSam NHal
	'Samantha'	see *D.* 'Harvest Samantha'
	'Sandra' ambig.	ERCP
	'Santa Claus' (MD)	SPer
	'Sarah' (MinS-c) **new**	LRHS WHil
	'Sarah G' (LS-c)	NPri
	'Sascha' (SWL) ♀H3	LAyl NHal
	'Scarborough Fair' (MS-c)	NHal
§	'Scarlet Fern' (Sin)	CChe EBee LSRN MGos MWea
	'Scaur Swinton' (MD)	LAyl NHal
	'Sean C' (Col)	NHal
	'Seattle' (SD)	CSut WClo
	'Seduction' (MinD)	ERCP
	'Shandy' (SS-c)	LAyl NHal
	sherffii	MWea
	'Shooting Star' (LS-c)	CSut
	'Siberia' PBR (MinD)	ERCP
	'Silver City' (LD)	NHal
	'Sir Alf Ramsey' (GD)	LAyl NHal
	'Small World' (Pom) ♀H3	LAyl NHal
	'Smokey'	EPfP SEND
	'Sneezy' (Sin)	ELan LRHS
	'Snowflake' (SWL)	ERCP LRHS SMrm
	'Snowstorm' (MD)	SBfd
	'So Dainty' (MinS-c) ♀H3	LAyl
	'Sorbet' (MS-c)	LAyl NHal
	'Soulman' (Anem)	CSpe LRHS
	'Spartacus' (LD)	IPot LAyl NHal
	'Staleen Condesa' (MS-c) ♀H3	NHal
	'Starburst'	LRHS
	'Star's Favourite' (MC)	ERCP
§	'Stolz von Berlin' (MinBa)	ECtt EPfP ERCP
	'Stoneleigh Cherry' (Pom)	LAyl
	'Suffolk Punch' (MD)	ERCP LAyl LYaf
I	'Summer Night' (SC)	ECGP LAyl MCot NHal
I	'Sunshine' (Sin)	ECtt LAyl LRHS
	'Susan Gilliott' (MS-c) **new**	NHal
	'Swan Lake' (SD)	EShb SPet
	'Sweetheart' (SD)	ERCP
I	'Sylvia' (SBa)	EPfP LRHS
	'Tally Ho' (Misc) ♀H3	CMMP CSam EBee ECtt EHrv EPfP LRHS MRav SDys WCot WWEG
	'Tam Tam'	WClo
	'Taratahi Ruby' (SWL) ♀H3	GBin LAyl LYaf NHal
	'Tartan' (MD)	WHlf
	'Taxi Driver'	CMoH

	'Teesbrooke Audrey' (Col)	ECtt LAyl NHal
	'Teesbrooke Red Eye' (Col) 🏆H3	NHal
	tenuicaulis	CDTJ CFir EBee SBig
	- F&M 99	WPGP
	- F&M 355	WPGP
	'Terracotta' (DwB) **new**	NHal
	'The Phantom' (Anem)	ERCP
	'Thomas A. Edison' (MD)	EPfP ERCP
	'Tioga Spice' (MS-c/Fim)	NHal
	'Tiptoe' (MinD)	LAyl NHal
	'Tomo' (SD)	LAyl NHal
	'Top Totty' (MinD)	NHal
	'Toto' (Anem)	ERCP SBfd
	'Trelyn Kiwi' (SS-c) 🏆H3	NHal
	'Trengrove Millennium' (MD)	NHal
	'Tropical Sunset' (SD)	EPfP
	'Troy Dyson' (Misc)	SDys
	'Tsuki-ytori-no-shisha' (MC)	IPot
	'Tudor 1' (DwB)	NHal
	'Twyning's After Eight' (Sin) 🏆H3	CAvo CPLG CSam CSpe EBee ECtt EPfP ERCP ETod LRHS MBri MCot MMHG NEgg SDix SMad SMrm SPer SUsu WBor WClo WCot WCra WHoo
	'Twyning's Aniseed' (Sin)	EPfP ETod
	'Twyning's Chocolate' (Sin) 🏆H3	CSam ETod
	'Twyning's Pink Fish' (Col) 🏆H3	ETod
	'Tyrell' **new**	SMrm
	'Vancouver' (Misc)	CSut ERCP NBPC
§	'Vuurvogel' (MS-c)	ERCP
	'Wanda's Aurora' (GD)	NHal
	'War of the Roses'	SGar SWal WHer
	'Weston Pirate' (MinC) 🏆H3	NHal
	'Weston Spanish Dancer' (MinC) 🏆H3	LAyl LYaf NHal
	'White Alva's' (GD) 🏆H3	LAyl NHal
	'White Ballerina' (SWL)	CSam LAyl NHal
	'White Ballet' (SD) 🏆H3	LAyl
	'White Charlie Two' (MD)	NHal
	'White Knight' (MinD)	NHal
	'White Linda' (SD)	NHal
	'White Moonlight' (MS-c)	LAyl NHal
	'White Perfection' (LD)	ECtt EPfP WSpi
	'White Star' (MS-c)	ERCP
	'White Swallow' (SS-c)	NHal
	'Willo's Borealis' (Pom)	NHal
	'Willo's Surprise' (Pom)	NHal
	'Willo's Violet' (Pom)	NHal
	'Willowfield Matthew' (MinD)	NHal
	'Winholme Diane' (SD)	NHal
	'Winston Churchill' (MinD)	LYaf WSpi
	'Winter Springs' (S-Sc)	ERCP
	'Wittem' (MD)	LRHS
	'Witteman's Superba' (SS-c) 🏆H3	NHal SDix
	'Woodside Finale' (MinD) **new**	NHal
	'Wootton Impact' (MS-c) 🏆H3	NHal
	'Worton Blue Streak' (SS-c)	ERCP
	'Yellow Hammer' (Sin/DwB) 🏆H3	LAyl NHal
	'Yellow Star' (MS-c)	ERCP LRHS
	'Yelno Enchantment' (SWL)	LAyl
	'York and Lancaster' (MD)	CBgR IGor
I	'Yvonne' (MWL)	GBin
	'Zorro' (GD) 🏆H3	ERCP NHal

Dais (*Thymelaeaceae*)

	cotinifolia	EShb

Daiswa see *Paris*

Dalea (*Papilionaceae*)

	candida	EBee
	purpurea	EBee

Dalechampia (*Euphorbiaceae*)

	dioscoreifolia	CCCN
	spathulata	CCCN

damson see *Prunus insititia*

Danae (*Ruscaceae*)

§	***racemosa***	CBcs CTri EBee ECrN ELan EPfP EPla GKir MGos MRav SAPC SArc SEND SPer SRms SSpi SWvt WCFE WCot WCru WDin WPGP WPat WSpi

Daphne ✿ (*Thymelaeaceae*)

	DJHC 98164 from China	WCru
	acutiloba	CPMA ECho GKev WPGP WSHC
	- 'Fragrant Cloud'	CPLG CPMA EWes SChF
	albowiana	CPMA EWes LLHF LRHS SAga SCoo WSpi
	alpina	CPMA GKev NEgg
	altaica	CPMA
	arbuscula 🏆H4	CPMA ECho EPot LLHF MWat NMen WThu
	- subsp. ***arbuscula*** f. ***albiflora***	CPMA
	- 'Diva'	CPMA
	- 'Muran Pride'	CPMA
	- f. ***radicans***	CPMA
	arbuscula × ***cneorum*** var. ***verlotii***	CPMA
	arbuscula × 'Leila Haines'	see *D.* × *schlyteri*
	arisanensis B&SWJ 6983	WCru
	bholua	CAbP CHll CPMA EPfP GGal LRHS MGos SReu SSpi SSta WAbe WCru WSpi
I	- 'Alba'	CBcs CLAP CMac CPMA ECho ELan EPfP GGGa LRHS MGos SCoo WGob WPGP
	- 'Darjeeling'	CBcs CLAP CPLG CPMA EPfP LRHS NLar SChF SCoo WGob WPGP
	- var. ***glacialis*** 'Gurkha'	CGHE CPLG CPMA EBee ELan EPfP IRar SChF SKHP SSpi WPGP WSpi
	- 'Glendoick'	EPfP GGGa
	- 'Jacqueline Postill' 🏆H3	Widely available
	- 'Limpsfield'	LRHS SCoo SSta
	- 'Peter Smithers'	CLAP CPLG CPMA GGGa LRHS LSRN SChF SCoo SReu SSta WGob WPGP
	- 'Winter Bliss'	MWya
	blagayana	CPMA ECho NBir SRms WPGP WPat WThu
	- 'Brenda Anderson'	CPMA WAbe
	'Bramdean'	see *D.* × *napolitana* 'Bramdean'
	× ***burkwoodii*** 🏆H4	CMea LSRN SAga WDin
	- 'Albert Burkwood'	CPMA
	- 'Astrid' (v)	CBcs CBow CPMA GKir LRHS MGos MWea NLar WClo WDin
§	- 'Carol Mackie' (v)	CPMA
	- 'G.K. Argles' (v) 🏆H4	CPMA MAsh
I	- 'Gold Sport'	CPMA SChF
	- 'Gold Strike' (v)	CPMA
	- 'Golden Treasure'	CPMA SChF

	- 'Lavenirei'	CPMA
	- 'Somerset'	CBcs CPMA ELan EPfP MRav MSwo NWea SAga SLim WDin
§	- 'Somerset Gold Edge' (v)	CPMA
§	- 'Somerset Variegated' (v)	WThu
	- 'Variegata' broad cream edge	see *D.* × *burkwoodii* 'Somerset Variegated'
	- 'Variegata' broad gold edge	see *D.* × *burkwoodii* 'Somerset Gold Edge'
	- 'Variegata' narrow gold edge	see *D.* × *burkwoodii* 'Carol Mackie'
	calcicola 'Gang-ho-ba'	CPMA
	- 'Sichuan Gold'	CPMA
	caucasica	CPMA
	circassica	CPMA SChF
	cneorum	CBcs CPMA IVic MGos MWya NMen WDin
	- f. ***alba***	CPMA SChF
	- 'Benaco'	CPMA
	- 'Blackthorn Triumph'	CPMA WAbe
	- 'Eximia' ♀H4	CPMA ECho EPot SRms WAbe
	- 'Klaus Patzner'	CPMA
	- 'Lac des Gloriettes'	CPMA
	- 'Puszta'	CPMA SAga WAbe
	- var. ***pygmaea***	CPMA EPot WAbe
	- - 'Alba'	CPMA
	- 'Ruby Glow'	CPMA EPot
	- 'Variegata' (v)	CPMA EPot WAbe
	- 'Velký Kosir'	CPMA SChF WAbe
	- var. ***verlotii***	EPot
	collina	see *D. sericea* Collina Group
	× ***eschmannii*** 'Jacob Eschmann'	CPMA
	'Forarch'	CPMA
	genkwa	CPMA SKHP
	giraldii	CPMA EPot
	aff. ***giraldii***	NMen
	gnidioides	CPMA
	'Guardsman' **new**	CPMA SChF
	× ***hendersonii***	CPMA
	- 'Appleblossom'	CPMA ECho SChF WAbe
	- 'Aymon Correvon'	CPMA
	- 'Blackthorn Rose'	CPMA
	- 'Ernst Hauser'	CPMA ECho LLHF WAbe WThu
	- 'Fritz Kummert'	CPMA WAbe WThu
	- 'Jeanette Brickell'	CPMA WAbe
	- 'Kath Dryden'	CPMA SChF
	- 'Marion White'	CPMA SChF
	- 'Rosebud'	CPMA WThu
	- 'Solferino'	CPMA
	'Hinton'	CPMA WAbe
	× ***houtteana***	CPMA ECho MWya NBir
	× ***hybrida***	CPMA
	japonica 'Striata'	see *D. odora* 'Aureomarginata'
	jasminea	CPMA ECho NMen WAbe
	jezoensis	CPMA LRHS SSta WCru
	× ***jintyae*** 'Pink Cascade'	CPMA
	juliae	CPMA
	kamtschatica	CPMA
	'Kilmeston Beauty'	CPMA
	kosaninii	CPMA GKev
	× ***latymeri*** 'Spring Sonnet'	CPMA SChF
	laureola	CBcs CPMA CSWP EPfP GBin GKev GPoy MBri MMHG NBir NPer WCFE WPGP
	- 'Kingsley Green'	CPMA
	- 'Margaret Mathew'	CPMA EPfP SChF
	- subsp. ***philippi***	CBgR CMac CPMA CWSG EBee ELan EPfP EWTr LHop LRHS MBlu MBri NMen SKHP SSta WPat WSpi
	'Leila Haines'	CPMA
	longilobata	GKev

	× ***mantensiana*** 'Audrey Vockins'	CPMA SChF
	- 'Manten'	CPMA ECho
	× ***mauerbachii*** 'Perfume of Spring'	CPMA ECho SChF
	'Meon'	see *D.* × *napolitana* 'Meon'
	mezereum	CBot CSBt CTri EBee ECho GGal GKev GKir IFFs IFoB ITim MBri MGos NChi NPri NWea SBfd SLim SWvt WDin WFar WHar WPGP
	- f. ***alba***	CLAP CPMA ECho ELon GKev GKir MGos NChi SRms SWvt WAbe WCFE WSpi
	- - 'Bowles's Variety'	CBot CPMA EPot GAbr
	- 'Rosea'	ECho SRms
	- var. ***rubra***	CBcs CMac CPMA CWSG CWib ECho ELan EWTr GKir LRHS LSou MGan MGos MRav MSwo SPer WAbe WDin WFar
	× ***napolitana*** ♀H4	CBcs CPMA ECho EPfP GKev MWya SChF SPer WPat
§	- 'Bramdean'	CPMA ECho WThu
§	- 'Meon'	CPMA ECho EPot MAsh WAbe WThu
	odora	CBcs CPMA EBee EPfP EWTr LRHS LSRN MSwo NMen SLim SSta WDin WSpi
§	- f. ***alba***	CCCN CMac CPMA ECho GKir NLar SPer
	- - 'Sakiwaka'	CCCN CLAP CPLG CPMA ECho EWes MWya SKHP
§	- 'Aureomarginata' (v) ♀H3-4	Widely available
	- 'Clotted Cream' (v)	CPMA
	- 'Geisha Girl' (v)	CPMA ELan MAsh MGos MWya SPoG
	- var. ***leucantha***	see *D. odora* f. *alba*
	- 'Limelight'	CPMA
	- 'Mae-jima' (v)	CPLG CPMA ELan EPfP LLHF LRHS MAsh NLar SLon SPoG
	- 'Marginata'	see *D. odora* 'Aureomarginata'
	- 'Rebecca' (v) **new**	LRHS
	- var. ***rubra*** (v)	CCCN CFir CLAP CPMA ECho LLHF NLar WGob
	- 'Walberton' (v)	EPfP LRHS MGos
	oleoides	CPMA GKev
	papyracea	CPLG GGGa
	petraea	CPMA
	- 'Cima Tombea'	CPMA
	- 'Corna Blacca'	CPMA
	- 'Garnet'	CPMA WAbe
	- 'Grandiflora'	CPMA SChF WAbe
	- 'Lydora'	CPMA WAbe
	- 'Michele'	CPMA
	- 'Persebee'	CPMA
	- 'Punchinello'	CPMA
	- 'Tuflungo'	CPMA
	petraea × ***sericea*** Collina Group	SSta
	'Pink Star'	CPMA
	pontica ♀H4	CBcs CGHE CPMA ECho EOHP EPfP GCrs GKev GKir LRHS MAsh MBri NLar NMen NWCA SDix SKHP SPer SSpi WPGP
	pseudomezereum	WCru
	retusa	see *D. tangutica* Retusa Group
	'Richard's Choice'	CPMA
	× ***rollsdorfii*** 'Arnold Cihlarz'	CPMA EPot WAbe
	- 'Wilhelm Schacht'	CPMA ECho EPot MWya SAga SChF SKHP WAbe
	'Rossetii'	CPMA
	'Rosy Wave'	CPMA SChF

§	× ***schlyteri***	CPMA
	- 'Lovisa Maria'	CPMA WAbe
	sericea	CPMA
§	- Collina Group	CPMA EPfP IRar SRms WThu
	'Spring Beauty'	CPMA
	'Spring Herald'	CPMA
	'Stasek' (v)	CPMA
	× ***susannae*** 'Anton Fahndrich'	CPMA EPot WAbe
	- 'Cheriton'	CPMA ECho EPfP EPot LRHS SChF WAbe
	- 'Tage Lundell' new	CPMA
	- 'Tichborne'	CPMA MAsh NMen SChF WAbe WThu
	tangutica ♀H4	Widely available
	- compact	MAsh
§	- Retusa Group ♀H4	CPLG CPMA ECho ELan ELon EPot GBin GEdr GGar GKir GMaP LHop MAsh NMen NRya NWCA SPer SRms WAbe WCru WSHC WSpi
	× ***thauma***	NMen WAbe
	× ***transatlantica*** 'Beulah Cross' (v)	CAbP CPMA ELan LLHF LRHS MAsh MBri SChF SPoG SSpi
	- Eternal Fragrance = 'Blafra'PBR	CAbP CLAP ELan EPfP EPot GAbr LLHF LRHS LSqu MAsh MBri MGos MWya SKHP SLon SPer SPoG SSpi WPat
	- 'Jim's Pride'	SChF
	'Valerie Hillier'	CPMA GKir IRar LRHS
	velenovskyi	CPMA
	× ***whiteorum*** 'Beauworth'	CPMA ECho LLHF WAbe
	- 'Kilmeston'	CPMA NMen
	- 'Warnford'	CPMA
	wolongensis 'Kevock Star'	CPLG GKev

Daphniphyllum (*Daphniphyllaceae*)

	aff. ***angustifolium*** B&SWJ 8225 new	WCru
	calycinum B&SWJ 4058	WCru
	glaucescens	WCru
	subsp. ***oldhamii*** var. ***kengii*** B&SWJ 6872	
	- - - B&SWJ 7119	WCru
	- - var. ***oldhamii*** B&SWJ 7056	WCru
	humile	see *D. macropodum* var. *humile*
	aff. ***longeracemosum*** B&SWJ 11788 new	WCru
	macropodum	CBcs CCCN CGHE CHEx CWib EBee EPfP EPla IArd LRHS MBri NLar SAPC SArc SDix SKHP SSpi WCru WFar WPGP WSpi
	- B&SWJ 581	WCru
	- B&SWJ 2898	WCru
	- B&SWJ 6809 from Taiwan	WCru
	- B&SWJ 8507 from Ulleungdo, South Korea	WCru
	- B&SWJ 8763 from Cheju-do, Korea	WCru
	- dwarf	WCru
§	- var. ***humile*** B&SWJ 11232	WCru
	paxianum B&SWJ 9755	WCru
	pentandrum B&SWJ 6888	WCru
	teijsmannii B&SWJ 11110 from Japan	WCru
	- B&SWJ 11112	WCru
	- B&SWJ 11358 from Japan	WCru

Darlingtonia (*Sarraceniaceae*)

	californica ♀H1	CSWC EFEx MCCP NChu SHmp WSSs

Darmera (*Saxifragaceae*)

	peltata ♀H4	Widely available
	- 'Nana'	CHEx EBee ECha NBid NHol NLar SWat WFar WMoo

Darwinia (*Myrtaceae*)

	fascicularis	SOWG
	taxifolia	SOWG

Dasylirion (*Dracaenaceae*)

§	***acrotrichum***	CDTJ SAPC SArc SChr
	berlandieri NJM 05.048	WPGP
	cedrosanum	CDTJ
	glaucophyllum	EAmu MREP
	gracile Planchon	see *D. acrotrichum*
	leiophyllum	WPGP
	longissimum	CAbb CBrP CTrC EAmu EShb ETod EUJe SChr WCot
	miquihuanense F&M 321	WPGP
	- NJM 05.062	WPGP
	quadrangulatum NJM 05.064	WPGP
	serratifolium	EAmu ERom EUJe
	texanum	CTrC LEdu
	wheeleri ♀H1	CBrP CTrC EAmu SChr SPlb WCot

Dasyphyllum (*Asteraceae*)

	diacanthoides	WPGP

date see *Phoenix dactylifera*

Datisca (*Datiscaceae*)

	cannabina	CArn CDTJ CDes CFir EBee ECha EPPr GBin GCal IMou LPla NChi NLar SDix SMHy SMad SMrm SPhx SUsu WMoo WPGP

Datura (*Solanaceae*)

	arborea	see *Brugmansia arborea*
	chlorantha	see *Brugmansia chlorantha*
	cornigera	see *Brugmansia arborea*
	rosea	see *Brugmansia* × *insignis* pink-flowered
	rosei	see *Brugmansia sanguinea*
	sanguinea	see *Brugmansia sanguinea*
	stramonium	CArn MNHC
	suaveolens	see *Brugmansia suaveolens*
	versicolor	see *Brugmansia versicolor* Lagerh.
	- 'Grand Marnier'	see *Brugmansia* × *candida* 'Grand Marnier'

Daubenya (*Hyacinthaceae*)

	alba	ECho
	aurea	ECho
	- var. ***coccinea***	ECho
	marginata	ECho
	namaquensis	ECho

Daucus (*Apiaceae*)

	carota	CArn CRWN EBWF MNHC NMir NSco SVic WSFF

Davallia (*Davalliaceae*)

	canariensis ♀H1	ISha
	mariesii ♀H3	CMen CTsd ISha SMad WAbe WCot
	- var. ***stenolepis***	CMen WRic
	tasmanii	WRic
	trichomanoides	CMen
	- f. ***barbata***	CMen

Davidia (*Cornaceae*)

involucrata $\mathbb{Y}^{H4}$	Widely available
- 'Sonoma'	MBlu
- var. ***vilmoriniana*** $\mathbb{Y}^{H4}$	CBcs CDoC CWCL EBee ELan EPfP GKir LRHS MAsh MBlu MCCP MGan MGos SBfd SLim SPer

Daviesia (*Papilionaceae*)

cordata new	SPlb
* ***ovalifolia***	SPlb
pectinata	SPlb

Debregeasia (*Urticaceae*)

longifolia WWJ 11686	WCru

Decaisnea (*Lardizabalaceae*)

fargesii	Widely available
- B&SWJ 8070	WCru
insignis	WPGP

Decodon (*Lythraceae*)

verticillatus new	LLWG

Decumaria (*Hydrangeaceae*)

barbara	CBcs CMac EBee NLar NSti SLim SSta WCru WFar WSHC
- 'Vicki'	EBee NLar
sinensis	EBee EPfP LRHS MAsh SKHP SLon SPoG SSpi WCru WSHC

Deinanthe (*Hydrangeaceae*)

bifida	CDes CLAP CMil EWes GEdr LEdu WCru WPGP
- B&SWJ 5436	EWld GEdr SBig
- B&SWJ 5551	WCru
- B&SWJ 5659	WCru
- 'Pink-Kii'	WCru
- 'Pink-Shi'	CLAP EWld WCru
bifida × ***caerulea***	CLAP WCru
'Blue Blush'	WCru
caerulea	CLAP CMil EBee GEdr IGor IMou LEdu NLar NPnk SKHP WCru WPGP
- 'Blue Wonder'	CLAP CPLG EBee EPPr
- pale-flowered	GEdr

Delairea (*Asteraceae*)

§ ***odorata***	CFee

Delonix (*Caesalpiniaceae*)

regia	SOWG SPlb

Delosperma (*Aizoaceae*)

from Graaf Reinet, South Africa new	EPot
from Sani Pass, South Africa new	EPot
§ ***aberdeenense*** $\mathbb{Y}^{H1}$	CHEx
ashtonii	CCCN EDAr GEdr
basuticum	NSla
'Basutoland'	see *D. nubigenum*
congestum	CCCN CMea CStu ECho EDAr EPot EWll GEdr NWCA WClo
- 'Gold Nugget'	LRHS
cooperi	CBgR CCCN CTri ECho ECtt EDAr EPfP EPot EWll ITim LRHS MSCN SBfd SEND SPlb WBor WFar WNew WPer WPnn
ecklonis	GKev
harazianum	CPBP EDAr
karrooicum new	NWCA
lineare	NBir
lydenburgense	SChr
§ ***nubigenum***	CStu CTri ECho ECtt EDAr ELan EPfP EPot GEdr GGar GKev ITim LRHS MSCN SEND SPlb SPoG WFar WNew WPer
'Ruby Coral' new	EPot
sphalmanthoides new	GEdr
sutherlandii	ECho EDAr EWll GGar NWCA
- 'Peach Star'	EDAr NWCA
Table Mountain = 'John Proffitt' new	CCCN GKev

Delphinium ✿ (*Ranunculaceae*)

sp.	SVic
CC 5584	GKev
HWJK 2179 from Nepal	WCru
HWJK 2263 from Nepal	WCru
from Nepal	GKir
'After Midnight'	CNMi
'Ailsa'	CNMi
'Alice Artindale' (d)	EWes EWld IFoB MWte SAga SMrm WCot WPGP
'Alie Duyvensteyn'	EBee WSpi
ambiguum	see *Consolida ajacis*
'Angela Harbutt'	CNMi
'Ann Woodfield'	CNMi
'Anne Kenrick'	CNMi
'Ariel' ambig.	LRHS WSpi
Astolat Group	CBcs CBot CSBt CTri CWCL CWib EBee ELan EPfP GKir GMaP LBMP LRHS MBri MGos MLHP MWat NBPC NBir NCob NLar NPri SBfd SMrm SPer SPoG WCAu WFar WHoo WWEG
'Atholl' $\mathbb{Y}^{H4}$	ELar
'Atlantic Blue'	LSou
(Aurora Series) 'Aurora Dark Blue' new	LRHS
- 'Aurora Deep Purple' new	LRHS
- 'Aurora Lavender' new	LRHS
Belladonna Group	ELan IFoB
- 'Atlantis' $\mathbb{Y}^{H4}$	EBee ECha ELar LRHS NLar SMrm WCot WSpi
- 'Balaton'	ELar
- 'Ballkleid'	WSpi
- 'Blue Shadow'	CWCL
- 'Capri'	EBee
- 'Casa Blanca'	EBee ELar EPfP GMaP NLar SBfd SMrm
- 'Cliveden Beauty'	EBee EPfP GMaP LHop NLar SBfd SMrm WSpi WWEG
- 'Delft Blue'^{PBR}	EBee NMoo
§ - 'Janny Arrow'^{PBR}	LRHS
- 'Moerheimii'	SMrm WSpi
- 'Piccolo'	ECha NLar
- 'Pink Sensation'	see *D.* × *ruysii* 'Pink Sensation'
- 'Völkerfrieden' $\mathbb{Y}^{H4}$	ELar MRav WCot WSpi
Bellalightblue = 'Barfifteen'^{PBR}	LRHS
× ***bellamosum***	CBot EPfP NLar SBfd WPer WSpi WWEG
'Beryl Burton'	CNMi
Black Knight Group	Widely available
'Black Velvet'	CBcs
'Blauwal'	GBin WSpi
'Blue Arrow'	see *D.* 'Blue Max Arrow', *D.* (Belladonna Group) 'Janny Arrow', *D.* 'Kings Blue Arrow'
Blue Bird Group	CBcs CSBt CTri CWCL EBee ELan EPfP GMaP LBMP LRHS MGos MRav MWat NBPC NLar NMir NPri

		SBfd SPer SPoG WCAu WFar WHoo WWEG
	'Blue Butterfly'	see *D. grandiflorum* 'Blue Butterfly'
	'Blue Dawn' ♀^{H4}	CNMi ELar
	Blue Fountains Group	CSBt EPfP GKir LSRN SPer SPet SPoG SRms
	'Blue Hex'	WCot
	'Blue Jay'	CBcs CTri EBee ECtt EPfP GKir LRHS LSRN MWat NBir NLar NPri SBfd SMrm SPer WWEG
	'Blue Lace' **new**	WSpi
§	'Blue Max Arrow'	LRHS
	'Blue Mirror'	SRms
	'Blue Nile' ♀^{H4}	CNMi
	'Blue Oasis'	CNMi
	Blue River	CBcs
	'Blue Skies'	ECtt GKir NLar
	Blue Springs Group	NGdn NLar
	'Blue Tit'	CNMi
	'Bruce' ♀^{H4}	CNMi ELar WCFE
	brunonianum	WThu
	bulleyanum	GAuc
	'Butterball'	ELar
	Cameliard Group	CBcs CSBt EBee ECtt ELan EPfP GKir LBMP LRHS MWat NBPC NLar NPri SPer SPoG WRHF WWEG
	'Can-Can' ♀^{H4}	CNMi ELar
	cardinale	EHrv
	caucasicum	see *D. speciosum*
	'Centurion Sky Blue' (Centurion Series) ♀^{H4}	LRHS
	ceratophorum var. ***ceratophorum*** BWJ 7799	WCru
	'Chelsea Star'	CNMi
	'Cher'	CNMi
	'Cherry Blossom'	EPfP NLar
	'Cherub' ♀^{H4}	ELar
	chinense	see *D. grandiflorum*
	'Christel'	LRHS LSRN WSpi
	'Christine Harbutt'	ELar
	'Clack's Choice'	CNMi
	'Claire' ♀^{H4}	CNMi ELar
	Clear Springs Series	SGar
	- 'Clear Springs Mid Blue'	GAbr
	'Clifford Sky' ♀^{H4}	ELar LRHS MBri
	Connecticut Yankees Group	SMrm
	'Conspicuous' ♀^{H4}	CNMi ELar
	'Constance Rivett' ♀^{H4}	ELar
	'Coral Sunset'^{PBR} (d)	LBuc NMoo
	'Crown Jewel'	ELar WCFE
	'Cupid'	ELar
	'Darling Sue'	CNMi
	'Darwin's Blue Indulgence'^{PBR}	EPfP
	delavayi B&SWJ 7796	WCru
	'Delphi's Power' **new**	WSpi
	'Delphi's Saffier' **new**	WSpi
	'Delphi's Surprise' **new**	WSpi
	'Diamant'^{PBR}	LRHS WSpi
	'Dreaming Spires'	SRms
	drepanocentrum HWJK 2263	WCru
	'Dunsden Green'	CNMi
	Dusky Maidens Group	IFoB STes
	dwarf, dark blue-flowered	LRHS
	dwarf, lavender-flowered	LRHS
	'Eelkje'	EBee WSpi
	elatum	GCal NGdn SRms
	- 'Double Innocence' (New Millennium Series) (d)	SMrm
	'Elisabeth Sahin' ♀^{H4}	CNMi ELar
	'Elizabeth Cook' ♀^{H4}	CNMi ELar
	'Elmfreude'	LRHS WSpi
	'Elmhimmel'	GKir
	'Emily Hawkins' ♀^{H4}	CNMi
	'Fanfare'	CNMi ELar
	'Faust' ♀^{H4}	CNMi ELar WSpi
	'Fenella' ♀^{H4}	CNMi ELar WCFE
	'Finsteraarhorn'	EBee GBin LRHS WSpi
	'Florestan'	CNMi
	'Foxhill Nina' ♀^{H4}	CNMi ELar
	'Franjo Sahin'	ELar
	Galahad Group	Widely available
	'Galahad' (Pacific Hybrids Series)	GJos MGos
	'Galileo' ♀^{H4}	CNMi
	'Gemma'	CNMi
	'Gillian Dallas' ♀^{H4}	ELar
	glaciale HWJK 2299	WCru
	'Gordon Forsyth'	CNMi
	'Gossamer'	CNMi IKil WSpi
§	***grandiflorum***	CWCL GKev
§	- 'Blauer Zwerg'	SPoG
§	- 'Blue Butterfly'	CBot CSpe EBur EPfP LRHS MBNS SCoo SPlb SPoG WSHC
	- Blue Dwarf	see *D. grandiflorum* 'Blauer Zwerg'
	- 'Delfix'	LRHS
	- (Summer Series) 'Summer Blues'	LRHS SRot
	- - 'Summer Nights' **new**	LRHS
	- - 'Summer Stars' **new**	LRHS
	'Green Twist' (New Millennium Series)	NBre STes
	(Guardian Series) 'Guardian Blue'	LRHS NPri
	- 'Guardian Lavender'	LRHS NPri
	- 'Guardian White'	LRHS NPri
	Guinevere Group	CBcs CSBt CWCL CWib EBee ECtt EPfP LBMP LRHS MBri MWat NBPC NBir NLar NPri SBfd SPad SPer SPoG WCAu WFar WWEG
	'Guy Langdon'	CNMi
	hansenii	LLHF
	'Harlekijn'	NLar
	'Heavenly Blue'	NLar
I	'Independence'	LRHS WSpi
	Ivory Towers Group	ECtt
	'Jenny Agutter'	CNMi
	'Jill Curley' ♀^{H4}	CNMi ELar
	'Kathleen Cooke'	CNMi
	'Kestrel' ♀^{H4}	CNMi ELar
	King Arthur Group	CBcs CSBt EBee ECtt ELan EPfP LBMP LHop LRHS LSRN MGos MRav MWat NBPC NLar NPri SBfd SMrm SPer SPoG WCAu WFar WWEG
§	'Kings Blue Arrow'^{PBR}	LRHS
	'Lady Guinevere'	MGos
§	'Langdon's Royal Flush' ♀^{H4}	CNMi ELar
	'Lanzenträger'	LRHS WSpi
	'Leonora'	CNMi ELar
	'Lily Radley'	ELar
	'Loch Leven' ♀^{H4}	CNMi GBin
	'Lord Butler' ♀^{H4}	CNMi ELar LRHS
	'Lucia Sahin' ♀^{H4}	CNMi
	maackianum	EWld GAuc GCal WCot
	Magic Fountains Series	CSam IFoB LRHS MRav SPlb SPoG WFar WGor WRHF

- 'Magic Fountains Cherry Blossom' SBfd SPoG WFar
- 'Magic Fountains Dark Blue' EPfP GMaP LSRN NEgg NLar SBfd SPoG STes WFar
- 'Magic Fountains Deep Blue' NLar SBfd
- 'Magic Fountains Lavender' EPfP SBfd
- 'Magic Fountains Lilac Pink' SBfd SPoG
- 'Magic Fountains Lilac Rose' NLar NVic WFar WGor
- 'Magic Fountains Pure White' EPfP NEgg NLar SBfd WFar
- 'Magic Fountains Sky Blue' EPfP NVic SBfd SPoG STes WFar

'Margaret' ELar
'Merlin' ambig. LRHS LSRN WSpi
'Michael Ayres' ♀H4 CNMi ELar
micropetalum CNDS 031 WCru
'Mighty Atom' CNMi
'Min' ♀H4 CNMi ELar
'Misty Mauves' (New Millennium Series) (d) SMrm
'Moonbeam' ELar
'Morgentau' **new** LRHS
'Mrs Newton Lees' IKil LRHS
'Ned Wit' IKil
New Century hybrids CBcs
'Nicolas Woodfield' CNMi
'Nobility' ELar
nudicaule CBot ECho
- NNS 06-183 GKev
- 'Laurin' ECho LRHS NWCA WFar
'Olive Poppleton' ♀H4 CNMi SAga
'Oliver' ♀H4 CNMi ELar
'Our Deb' ♀H4 ELar
Pacific hybrids CWCL EPfP LHop LRHS LSRN MHer MLHP NLar SBfd SPet SRms SWal SWvt WFar
'Pagan Purples' (d) IFoB
'Pandora' CNMi
'Patricia Johnson' ELar
Percival Group NLar
Pink River = 'Barfourtythree'PBR CBcs
'Pink Ruffles' CNMi ELar
'Plagu Blue'PBR **new** WCot
Princess Caroline = 'Odabar'PBR CBcs
'Purple Passion' (New Millennium Series) STes
'Purple Ruffles' EPfP
'Purple Velvet' ♀H4 CNMi ELar
'Red Caroline' CBcs
requienii CBgR CBot CSpe EWld NSti
'Rona' CNMi
'Rosemary Brock' ♀H4 ELar
Round Table Group CTri
'Royal Aspirations' (New Millennium Series) STes
'Royal Flush' see *D.* 'Langdon's Royal Flush'
§ × ***ruysii*** 'Pink Sensation' CBot NCGa NLar WPGP WSpi
'Sandpiper' ♀H4 CNMi
'Sarita' SUsu
'Secret'PBR LRHS
§ ***semibarbatum*** CBot
'Sentinel' CNMi
siamense B&SWJ 7278 WCru
'Silver Jubilee' CNMi ELar
'Sky Sensation' NLar
'Snow Crown' **new** WSpi
'Snow Queen Arrow' LRHS
'Sommerabend' LRHS
§ ***speciosum*** GKev
'Spindrift' ♀H4 CNMi ELar
stapeliosmum B&SWJ 2954 WCru
staphisagria CArn ECGP EOHP
'Starlight'PBR WSpi
'Starmaker' EPfP
'Strawberry Fair' CNMi
Summer Skies Group CBcs CSBt CTri EBee ECtt ELan EPfP LBMP LHop LRHS MBri MWat NBir NLar NPri SBfd SPer SPoG WBrE WCAu WFar WHoo WWEG
'Summer Wine' ELar
'Summerfield Miranda' ♀H4 CNMi
'Summerfield Oberon' CNMi ELar WCot
'Sungleam' ♀H4 ELar IKil NLar WSpi
'Sunkissed' ♀H4 CNMi ELar
sutchuenense EWld NCGa WWlt
- BWJ 7867 WCru
tatsienense IFoB SRms WCru
tenii BWJ 7693 WCru
'Tiddles' ♀H4 ELar
'Tiger Eye' CNMi ELar
'Tiny Tim' CNMi
'Vanessa Mae' CNMi
vestitum ECtt EWld
viscosum HWJK 2268 WCru
'Walton Beauty' CNMi
'Walton Benjamin' CNMi
'Walton Gemstone' ♀H4 CNMi ELar
White River CBcs
'White Swan' EPfP
Woodfield strain WHrl
'Yvonne' LRHS LSRN NLar
zalil see *D. semibarbatum*
'Zauberflöte' **new** LRHS

Dendranthema see *Chrysanthemum*

pacificum see *Ajania pacifica*

Dendriopoterium see *Sanguisorba*

Dendrobenthamia see *Cornus*

Dendrocalamus (*Poaceae*)

asper XBlo
calostachys SPlb
giganteus XBlo
§ ***strictus*** XBlo

Dendromecon (*Papaveraceae*)

rigida CBcs EPfP LRHS MBri NLar SAga SKHP SMad WCot WPGP WSHC

Dendropanax (*Araliaceae*)

trifidus B&SWJ 11230 WCru

Dennstaedtia (*Dennstaedtiaceae*)

punctilobula CLAP WCot WRic

Dentaria see *Cardamine*

pinnata see *Cardamine heptaphylla*
polyphylla see *Cardamine kitaibelii*

Dermatobotrys (*Scrophulariaceae*)

saundersii ECre

Derwentia see *Parahebe*

Deschampsia (*Poaceae*)

	cespitosa	CKno COlW CRWN CSam CWib EBWF EPPr EPfP GFor LBMP LRHS MWat SMrm SPlb WCFE WCot WDin WGwG WMnd WMoo WPnP WTin WWEG
	- subsp. ***alpina***	LEdu
	- Bronze Veil	see *D. cespitosa* 'Bronzeschleier'
§	- 'Bronzeschleier'	Widely available
	- brown-leaved	SApp
	- 'Fairy's Joke'	see *D. cespitosa* var. *vivipara*
	- 'Fose'	SApp
	- Gold Dust	see *D. cespitosa* 'Goldstaub'
	- Golden Dew	see *D. cespitosa* 'Goldtau'
	- Golden Pendant	see *D. cespitosa* 'Goldgehänge'
	- Golden Shower	see *D. cespitosa* 'Goldgehänge'
	- Golden Veil	see *D. cespitosa* 'Goldschleier'
§	- 'Goldgehänge'	CSam EHoe EHul EPfP EPla MMHG NBir WWEG
§	- 'Goldschleier'	CPrp CSam CSpe EBee EBrs ECha EPPr EPla GCal GGar GKir GMaP GQue LEdu LRHS NGdn NWsh SApp SBfd SPhx WMoo WPGP
§	- 'Goldstaub'	EPPr
§	- 'Goldtau'	Widely available
	- 'Morning Dew'	WFar
	- 'Northern Lights' (v)	CWCL EBee ELan EPfP GGar GKir LEdu LRHS MAvo MBri MMuc MWhi SApp SBfd SLim SPer SPoG SRms SWvt WPGP WWEG
	- 'Schottland'	EBee EPPr GBin
	- 'Tardiflora'	EBee
	- 'Tauträger'	EBee
§	- var. ***vivipara***	EHoe EPPr EPla NBro NHol SGSe
	- 'Waldschatt'	EBee
	- 'Willow Green'	GCal MRav SCoo
	flexuosa	COlW EHoe GFor NBir NWsh SMrm
	- 'Tatra Gold'	Widely available
	media	EHoe

Desfontainia (*Loganiaceae*)

§	***spinosa*** ♀H3	Widely available
	- 'Harold Comber'	CMac WCru
	- f. ***hookeri***	see *D. spinosa*

Desmodium (*Papilionaceae*)

	callianthum	CMac EBee EPfP WSHC
	canadense	CPom NLar
§	***elegans*** ♀H4	CBcs CHEx CPLG EBee ELan EPfP MBri NLar WHer WPGP WSHC
	paniculatum new	CPom
	praestans	see *D. yunnanense*
	tiliifolium	see *D. elegans*
§	***yunnanense***	CHEx CPLG EPfP WSHC

Deuterocohnia (*Bromeliaceae*)

	brevifolia ♀H1	WPGP
	longipetala RCB/Arg L-5 new	WCot

Deutzia ✿ (*Hydrangeaceae*)

	CC 4548	CPLG
	CC 4550	CPLG
	calycosa	GQui WPat
	- BWJ 8007	WCru
	- 'Dali'	CDoC CPLG SDys
	aff. ***calycosa*** SIN 1878 new	GLin
	chunii	see *D. ningpoensis*
	compacta	SLon WFar WPGP
	- GWJ 9202	WCru
	- 'Lavender Time'	CDoC CMac CPLG EBee NLar WCFE
	cordatula B&SWJ 6917	WCru
	coreana BWJ 8588	WCru
	corymbosa	CDoC
	crenata B&SWJ 8896	WCru
	- 'Flore Pleno'	see *D. scabra* 'Plena'
	- var. ***heterotricha*** B&SWJ 5805	WCru
	- var. ***nakaiana***	WPat
	- - B&SWJ 8879	WCru
	- - 'Nikko'	see *D. gracilis* 'Nikko'
§	- 'Pride of Rochester' (d)	CBcs CMCN CWib EBee ECrN GKir IFFs LRHS LSou LTen MGos MMuc MRav NLar SLim SPad SPoG SWvt WDin WGrn
	'Dark Eyes'	GGGa
	discolor 'Major'	CPLG
	× ***elegantissima***	SRms
	- 'Fasciculata'	EBee EPfP LRHS SPer
	- 'Rosealind' ♀H4	CBar CBcs CMac CPLG CTri EBee EPfP EWTr LHop LRHS MGos MMuc MRav NCGa SEND SPoG SRms SSpi SWvt WCFE WCom WKif WSHC WSpi
	glabrata B&SWJ 617	GQui WCru
	glomeruliflora BWJ 7742	WCru
	gracilis	CDoC CDoy CSBt EBee ELan EPfP EWTr GGal GQui LTen MAsh MGos MRav MSwo SPad SPer SPoG WDin WFar WSpi
	- B&SWJ 8927	WCru
	- 'Aurea'	CBcs EPfP
	- 'Carminea'	see *D.* × *rosea* 'Carminea'
§	- 'Marmorata' (v)	CBow CPMA SLon WCom WCot
§	- 'Nikko'	CBcs CMCN CMac CPBP CPLG CTri EBee ECho EWes LBMP LRHS MGos MHer MMuc MWhi NHol NLar SPlb SPoG WDin WKif WSHC
	- var. ***ogatae*** B&SWJ 8911	WCru
	- 'Rosea'	see *D.* × *rosea*
	- 'Variegata'	see *D. gracilis* 'Marmorata'
	hookeriana	LLHF WFar
	× ***hybrida*** 'Contraste'	CMac SPer
	- 'Joconde'	CPLG GKir WFar WKif
	- 'Magicien'	CDoC CDul CMHG CMac CPLG CSBt CSam CWib EBee ECrN ELan EPfP GQui LHop LRHS MAsh MBri MRav MSwo NBir SLon SMrm SPer SWvt WCom WFar WPat
	- 'Mont Rose' ♀H4	Widely available
§	- 'Strawberry Fields' ♀H4	CBcs CGHE CMCN CPLG CWCL EBee ELan ELon EPla GKir IArd LAst LBMP LBuc LRHS LSRN LSou MAsh MBlu MGos NEgg NLar SLon SPad SPoG WBVN WBor WFar WKif WPGP
	'Iris Alford'	CGHE GKir LRHS SLon
	× ***kalmiiflora***	CMac CPLG CPMA CSBt CTri EBee GKir GQui LRHS MAsh MBri MMuc SLPl SPer SPoG SRms
	× ***lemoinei***	CBot GKir
	longifolia 'Veitchii' ♀H4	CDoy CSBt GQui MRav WCFE
	- 'Vilmoriniae'	CDul MRav
	× ***magnifica***	CBcs EBee ELan EPfP GQui MBri SRms WDin WSpi
	- 'Rubra'	see *D.* × *hybrida* 'Strawberry Fields'
	maximowicziana B&SWJ 11567	WCru

monbeigii	CDoC CPLG GKir WKif
- BWJ 7728	WCru
multiradiata	WPGP
§ ***ningpoensis*** 🏆^{H4}	CAbP CPLG EBee EPfP GBin GQui SLPl SMrm SPer
parviflora var. ***barbinervis*** B&SWJ 8478	WCru
'Pink Pompon'	see *D.* 'Rosea Plena'
pulchra	CAbP CDoC CMCN CPom EBee EPfP GKir GMac LRHS MRav SLon SMrm SPer SSpi WFar WPGP WSpi
- B&SWJ 3870	WCru
- B&SWJ 6908	WCru
purpurascens BWJ 7859	WCru
§ × ***rosea***	CDul CWib CWit EBee EPfP LAst LRHS SPoG SRms WFar WKif
- 'Campanulata'	CPLG EPfP MSwo
§ - 'Carminea'	SPlb SRms WCom WDin WFar WPat
§ 'Rosea Plena' (d)	CDoC CMac CPLG CSBt CWib EBee ECrN EPfP LRHS MAsh MGos MMuc NEgg NLar SLim SPoG WCom WFar WPat WRHF
scabra	CDul CTri IFFs
- B&SWJ 8924	WCru
§ - 'Candidissima' (d)	CMac GKir GMac GQui MRav NLar SPer WPat
- 'Codsall Pink'	MRav
§ - 'Plena' (d)	CPLG EBee ECrN ECtt ELan EPfP GKir SPer WCFE
- 'Pride of Rochester'	see *D. crenata* 'Pride of Rochester'
- 'Punctata' (v)	EBee EHoe MMuc SRms WFar
- 'Robert Fortune'	SPlb
- 'Variegata' (v)	CDul CMac
setchuenensis	CMac EPfP GQui SSpi WPat WSHC
- var. ***corymbiflora*** 🏆^{H4}	CBcs CBot CDoC CDul CGHE CPLG CSam CTri EBee EPfP GKir IDee LHop LRHS MBri MSwo SPoG WCom WFar WKif WPGP
taiwanensis	EBee
- B&SWJ 6858	WCru
- CWJ 12459	WCru
'Tourbillon Rouge'	EBee EQua LRHS SBfd WDin WSpi
* ***vidalii***	GGal
× ***wellsii***	see *D. scabra* 'Candidissima'
× ***wilsonii***	SRms

Dianella ✿ (*Phormiaceae*)

brevicaulis	ECou LEdu
caerulea	CHid CMac ECha ECou ELan IFoB IGor IMou LEdu NBir SOWG
- Breeze = 'Dcnco'^{PBR}	ECou ELan IFFs LTen NOak
- Cassa Blue = 'Dbb03'^{PBR}	EBee ELan EWes GEdr GGar IFFs LAst LBMP LEdu LHop LRHS LTen MMHG NOak SHar
- 'Kulnura'	ECou
- Little Jess = 'Dcmp01'^{PBR}	CPLG EBee EPla GEdr GGar IFFs LEdu LRHS LTen MMHG NOak
- 'Variegata'	see *D. tasmanica* 'Variegata'
ensifolia	LEdu
intermedia	CTrC EBee EWld IBlr SMad
- 'Variegata' (v)	IBlr
nigra	CBcs CHid CPLG CPou CTrC EBee ECou IFro IMou LEdu WFar
- 'Margaret Pringle' (v)	CBcs CPLG CTrC GGar NOak
- 'Taupo'	ECou
prunina Utopia = 'Dp3031'	CBow ESwi NOak
revoluta	CFir ECou
- 'Baby Bliss'	CKno EBee ECou NOak
- 'Baby Blue'	WClo
- 'Hartz Mountain'	ECou
- Little Rev = 'Dr5000'^{PBR}	EBee ELan EPfP ESwi GEdr GGar IFFs LHop MMHG MMuc MSCN NOak SMrm WCot
'Silver Streak' (v) **new**	ESwi
tasmanica	Widely available
- from Logan **new**	GCal
- 'Emerald Arch'	ELan ESwi NOak
- 'Prosser'	ECou
- Tasred = 'Tr20'^{PBR}	CPLG EBee ELan EPfP ESwi GBin GEdr IFFs LHop LRHS LTen MCot MMHG NOak SHar WAul WClo
§ - 'Variegata' (v)	CBct CBod CCCN CDTJ CFir CPLG CSpe CStu EAmu EBee ECou ELan LHop SGSe WCot

Dianthus ✿ (*Caryophyllaceae*)

sp.	ECtt SVic
AC&W 2116	GEdr
'Acton's Propellor'	WEas
'Admiral Crompton' (pf)	CNMi
'Alan Titchmarsh' (p)	EBee ECtt EPfP EWll LRHS LSRN MGos MMHG MTis NCGa NEgg NPri SPoG SWvt
'Aldridge Yellow' (b)	SAll
'Alegro' (pf)	SAll
'Alfriston' (b) 🏆^{H4}	SAll
'Alice' (p)	LSRN SAll
'Alice Lever' (p)	WAbe
'Allspice' (p)	MRav SBch WEas WHoo
Allwoodii Alpinus Group (p)	SRms WFar
'Allwood's Crimson' (pf)	SAll
alpinus 🏆^{H4}	ECho GJos LRHS NMen NWCA SRms WFar WNew
- 'Albus'	ECho NHol WAbe
- 'Joan's Blood' 🏆^{H4}	ELon EPot LSRN NHol SMad WAbe WCom WFar WHoo
- 'Rax Alpe'	EPot
'Alyson' (p)	SAll
amurensis	ECho EDAr EPPr GCal GKev MLHP NDov SPhx SSvw
anatolicus	CTri ECho MHer NGdn NWCA WCom WPer
'Andrew Morton' (b)	SAll
'Angelo' (b)	SAll
'Ann Franklin' (pf) 🏆^{H1}	CNMi
'Annabelle' (p)	ECho
'Anne Jones' (b)	EPfP
'Annette' (p)	EBee ECho ECtt EWTr GKev LRHS LSRN MWat SWvt
'Annie Claybourne' (pf)	CNMi
'Apricot Sue' (pf)	CNMi
'Arctic Star' (p)	CMea CTri EBee ECho GMaP NEgg SPet SPoG SRot SSvw SWvt WFar
arenarius	EDAr EWTr GKev SPlb SSvw
- 'Little Maiden' **new**	NDov SPhx
- 'Snow Flurries' **new**	ITim
'Argus'	IGor SSvw
armeria	CBgR WHer WOut
arpadianus	GEdr
'Arthur Leslie' (b)	SAll
§ × ***arvernensis*** (p) 🏆^{H4}	ECha ECho EPot
- 'Albus'	ECho
'Audrey Robinson' (pf)	CNMi
'Aurora' (b)	SAll
'Auvergne'	see *D.* × *arvernensis*
'Averiensis'	see *D.* 'Berlin Snow'
'Baby Treasure' (p)	ECho ECtt SRot
'Badenia' (p)	ECha
'Bailey's Celebration' (p)	EPfP MTis MWat SRGP
§ 'Bailey's Daily Mail' (p) 🏆^{H4}	CBcs SPoG
'Barbara Norton' (p)	ECtt
barbatus	GAuc

- Barbarini Series **new** WGor
- 'Black Adder' CSpe
- Nigrescens Group (p,a) Υ^{H4} CBre CMea CSpe SAga SPhx
I - 'Sooty' (p,a) EBee ELan EWld MCot NGdn WCFE WFar
- 'Tuxedo Black' MWea
§ 'Bat's Double Red' (p/d) IGor SAll SSvw
'Becky Robinson' (p) Υ^{H4} SAll
'Bedfordshire Belle' (b) SAll
§ 'Berlin Snow' (p) CPBP ECho ELan EWes ITim LRHS SAll WPat
'Betty Miller' (b) SAll
'Betty Morton' (p) Υ^{H4} ECtt IFoB MWea SSvw WFar WKif
'Betty's Choice' (pf) CNMi
'Blue Hedgehog' ECtt
'Blue Hills' (p) ECho MWea
'Blue Ice' (b) SAll
'Blush' see *D.* 'Souvenir de la Malmaison'
'Bobby' (p) SAll
'Bob's Highlight' (pf) CNMi
'Bombardier' (p) ECtt ELon
'Bookham Gleam' (b) SAll
'Bookham Grand' (b) SAll
'Bookham Heroine' (b) SAll
'Bookham Lad' (b) SAll
'Border Special' (b) SAll
'Bouquet Purple' (p) CSpe
'Bovey Belle' (p) Υ^{H4} CBcs SAll
'Bressingham Pink' (p) ECtt
'Brian Tumbler' (b) Υ^{H4} SAll
'Bridal Veil' (p) SAll SBch SSvw WHer
'Brigadier' (p) ECho ECtt
'Brilliance' (p) ECho WMoo
'Brilliant' see *D. deltoides* 'Brilliant'
'Brilliant Star' (p) Υ^{H4} ECho ECtt LBee LRHS SPet SWvt WWFP
'Brympton Red' (p) ECha MRav SAll WCom WEas
'Bryony Lisa' (b) Υ^{H4} SAll
caesius see *D. gratianopolitanus*
callizonus LLHF NMen
'Calypso' (pf) CTri
'Calypso Star' (p) Υ^{H4} EBee ECho ECtt GMaP SPet SPoG STes
'Camilla' (b) WCom
'Can-can' (pf) ECho ECtt
'Candy Clove' (b) SAll
Candy Floss = 'Devon Flavia'PBR (Scent First Series) (p) ECtt GKir LBMP LRHS MTis MWat NEgg SBfd SPoG WHil
'Candy Spice'PBR (p) MRav
'Carmine Letitia Wyatt'PBR (p) Υ^{H4} EBee ECtt SPoG
carthusianorum CAby CArn CKno EWTr IGor LPla MCot NDov SAga SAll SGSe SGar SPhx SPlb SSvw STes SWat WCom WOut WPGP WPer WSHC
I - 'Rupert's Pink' EDAr
caryophyllus CArn ELau GBar MNHC
'Casser's Pink' (p) SBch WCom
'Charles' (p) SAll
'Charles Edward' (p) SAll
'Charles Musgrave' see *D.* 'Musgrave's Pink'
'Chastity' (p) WHoo
Cheddar pink see *D. gratianopolitanus*
'Cheerio' (pf) Υ^{H2} SAll
'Cherly' LSRN
'Cherry Clove' (b) SAll
'Cherry Pie' (p) ECtt EPfP LRHS SPoG WMnd
'Cheryl' see *D.* 'Houndspool Cheryl'
'Chianti' (pf) NGdn
'Chianti Double' (p) SAll
chinensis (p,a) CArn
- 'Black and White' CSpe
'Chris Crew' (b) Υ^{H4} SAll
'Christopher' (p) SAll
'Clara' (pf) CNMi
'Clara's Lass' (pf) CNMi
'Clare' (p) SAll
'Claret Joy' (p) Υ^{H4} CBcs ECtt EPfP MMuc NEgg SAll SEND
§ 'Cockenzie Pink' (p) IGor SAll SSvw WEas
'Coconut Sundae' (p) ECtt EWTr EWll LBMP LRHS MTis SBfd SMrm SRot WBor WRHF
'Constance' (p) SAll
'Constance Finnis' see *D.* 'Fair Folly'
'Consul' (b) SAll
'Conwy Silver' NMen WAbe
'Conwy Star' CPBP NMen WAbe
'Copperhead' (b) SAll
'Coral Reef' (p) ECtt LRHS SPoG WHil WRHF
'Coronation Ruby' (p) Υ^{H4} SAll
'Cosmic Swirl Pink' (p) **new** SVil
'Cosmic Swirl Red' (p) **new** SVil
'Coste Budde' (p) IGor WEas WSHC
'Cover Story' **new** NWCA
'Cranmere Pool' (p) Υ^{H4} CBcs CMea EBee ECtt ELan EPfP LRHS NPri SBfd SPoG SWvt WFar WMnd WWEG
cretaceus NWCA
'Crimson Chance' (p) EPot NSla
'Crimson Tempo'PBR (pf) SAll
'Crock of Gold' (b) SAll
'Crompton Classic' (pf) CNMi
'Crompton Princess' (pf) CNMi
cruentus NDov SMHy SPhx SSvw WPer WWEG
'D.D.R.' see *D.* 'Berlin Snow'
'Dad's Favourite' (p) CEnt IGor SAll SRms SSvw WEas
'Daily Mail' see *D.* 'Bailey's Daily Mail'
'Dainty Dame' (p) Υ^{H4} CPBP CSpe CTri EBee ECho LRHS MNHC MWea SPoG SRot WFar
'Damask Superb' (p) IGor
Dancing Queen = 'Wp07 Verity' (p) **new** MTis
'Daphne' (p) SAll
'Dark Star' (p) ECho
'Dartington Double' (p) ECho
'David' (p) LSRN SAll
'David Russell' (b) Υ^{H4} SAll
'David Saunders' (b) Υ^{H4} SAll
'Dawlish Joy' (p) EBee SPoG SRGP
'Dawn' (b) SAll
'Dawn' (pf) ECho
'Dedham Beauty' WCot
deltoides Υ^{H4} CArn CEnt CSev EBWF ECha ECho EPfP GBar MMuc NSco SPlb SRms WFar WJek WNew
- 'Albus' ECha EPfP EWTr GBar LRHS MNHC NGdn NPri NWCA WMoo
- 'Arctic Fire' CWib ECho EPfP LRHS NGdn WFar WMoo
- 'Bright Eyes' ECho MTis MWat
§ - 'Brilliant' CChe CTri ECho EPau GJos LAst MDun MNHC NPri NVic SAll SRms WCom WFar WGor WRHF WWEG
- 'Canta Libra' SWal
- 'Dark Eyes' (p) EWes
- 'Erectus' EPfP
- Flashing Light see *D. deltoides* 'Leuchtfunk'
§ - 'Leuchtfunk' ECho ECtt EPfP GGar LAst LRHS MWat NBPC NChi NGdn NNor SPoG WFar WMoo WWEG

I	- 'Luneburg Heath Maiden Pink'	SSvw
	- 'Microchip'	WClo WFar WMoo
	- 'Nelli' (p)	ECho MBNS SSvw
	- red-flowered	SVic
	- 'Shrimp'	NGdn
	'Denis' (p)	LSRN SAll
	'Desert Song' (b)	SAll
	'Desmond'	EPfP
	'Devon Blush' (p)	ECtt
	'Devon Cream'PBR (p)	EAEE EBee ECtt LRHS MWat NEgg NPnk SPoG WMnd
	'Devon Dove'PBR (p) ♀H4	CMea CSBt EAEE EBee ECtt EPfP MRav MWat NCGa NDov NEgg SBfd SPoG WWFP
§	'Devon Flores' (p)	LRHS
	'Devon General'PBR (p)	CTri EBee ECtt SBfd SPoG
	'Devon Glow' (p) ♀H4	EBee EPfP SPoG
	'Devon Magic'PBR (p)	EBee ECtt ELan SPoG WFar
	'Devon Pearl'PBR (p)	WMnd
	'Devon Wizard'PBR (p) ♀H4	CMea CSBt EAEE EBee ECtt EPfP LRHS MMuc MRav MSpe NCGa NDov NEgg SBfd SPoG WFar
	'Dewdrop' (p)	CMea CTri EBee ECho ECtt EPfP MHer MMuc NBir NGdn SAll SEND WFar
	'Diana'	see *D.* Dona
	'Diane' (p) ♀H4	EBee ECtt ELan EPfP GKir LRHS MWat NEgg SAll SPoG SWvt WMnd
*	'Diane Cape'	SAll
	'Diplomat' (b)	SAll
§	Dona = 'Brecas' (pf)	EAEE LSRN SRGP
	'Dora' (p)	LRHS
	'Doris' (p) ♀H4	Widely available
	'Doris Allwood' (pf)	CNMi CSBt EMal SAll
	'Doris Elite' (p)	SAll
	'Doris Galbally' (b)	SAll
	'Doris Majestic' (p)	SAll WFar
	'Doris Ruby'	see *D.* 'Houndspool Ruby'
	'Doris Supreme' (p)	SAll
	'Double North'	ELon NWCA
	'Dubarry' (p)	CTri CWan ECho ECtt WGor WPat WPer
	'Duchess of Fife' (p)	ECtt EPfP
	'Duchess of Roxburghe' (pf) **new**	SAll
	'Duchess of Westminster' (M)	EMal SAll
	'Duke of Norfolk' (pf)	EMal
	'Earl of Essex' (p)	SAll
	'Edenside Scarlet' (b)	SAll
	'Edenside White' (b)	SAll
	'Edna' (p)	SAll
	'Edward Allwood' (pf)	SAll
	'Eileen' (p)	SAll
	'Eileen Lever' (p)	CPBP WAbe WFar
	'Eleanor Parker' (p)	WAbe
	'Eleanor's Old Irish' (p)	ELon LRHS MWhi WCot WHoo WTin WWEG
	'Elfin Star' (p)	ECho SPet
	'Elizabeth' (p)	CEnt WEas
	'Elizabethan' (p)	CDes CFee GMac MCot
*	'Elizabethan Pink' (p)	SAll
	'Emile Paré' (p)	WCom
	'Emma James' (b)	SAll
	'Emperor'	see *D.* 'Bat's Double Red'
*	***erectaceaus***	GAuc
	erinaceus	ECho SRot WAbe WPat
	- var. ***alpinus***	EPot ITim
	'Erycina' (b)	SAll
	'Ethel Hurford' (p)	WHoo
	'Eva Humphries' (b)	SAll
	'Evening Star' (p) ♀H4	CHVG CTri ECho LBee NEgg SPet SPoG SWvt
	'Exquisite' (b)	SAll
§	'Fair Folly' (p)	SAll SSvw
	'Fanal' (p)	NBir
	'Farida'PBR (pf)	SAll
	'Farnham Rose' (p)	SAll SSvw
	'Fenbow Nutmeg Clove' (b)	MBrN SDix WMnd
	'Fettes Mount' (p)	MWhi WCom WCot
	'Feuerhexe' (p)	EPot
	'Fimbriatus' (p)	WHoo
	'Fiona' (p)	SAll
	'Fireglow' (b)	SAll
	'Firestar' (p)	CTri LBee LRHS MWat SPet SRot SWvt
	'First Lady' (b)	ECho SAll
	Fizzy = 'Wp08 Ver03' (Early Bird Series) (p/d)	EWTr MWat SBfd
	'Flanders' (b) ♀H4	SAll
	'Fleur' (p)	SAll
	'Forest Princess' (b)	SAll
	'Forest Sprite' (b)	SAll
	'Forest Treasure' (b)	SAll
	'Forest Violet' (b)	SAll
	'Fortuna' (p)	SAll
	'Fountain's Abbey' (p)	IGor
	'Fragrant Ann' (pf) ♀H1	CNMi
	'Frances Isabel' (p)	SAll
	'Frank Bruno' (pf) **new**	CNMi
	'Freda' (p)	SAll
	'Freda Woodliffe' (p) **new**	WAbe
	freynii	ECho EWes GKev WAbe
*	- var. ***nana***	GKev
N	fringed pink	see *D. superbus*
	'Fusilier' (p)	CElw CMea CPBP CTri ECho ECtt EDAr EPfP GMaP LHop LRHS MAsh NWCA SAll SRot SWvt WFar
	'Gail Graham' (b)	SAll
	'Gail Tilsley' (b)	SAll
	'Garland' (p)	CMea CTri WGor
	'Gaydena' (b)	SAll
	giganteus	CSpe MWea WSHC
	'Gingham Gown' (p)	ECtt EPot NBir SAll SPoG
	'Glebe Cottage White' (p)	CPou
	'Gold Flake' (p)	SBch
	'Gold Fleck'	ECtt EPot
	'Golden Cross' (b) ♀H4	SAll
	'Grandma Calvert' (p)	SAll
	graniticus	EPot
	'Gran's Favourite' (p) ♀H4	CEnt CMea CSBt CTri EAEE EBee ECtt EPfP EWTr LAst LHop LRHS LSRN MCot MMuc MTis MWat NEgg NPri SAll SBfd SEND SPlb SPoG SRGP SRms SWvt WEas WFar
§	***gratianopolitanus*** ♀H4	CArn CBod CTri EPfP EPot GJos GKev MHer MNHC MRav NBid NChi NWCA SRms WAbe WGwG
	- 'Albus'	EPot MHer
	- dwarf	NWCA
	- 'Emmen' (p)	ELon
	- 'Grandiflorus'	WFar
§	- 'Tiny Rubies' (p)	NWCA
	'Gravetye Gem' (b)	SRms
	'Green Lane' (p)	CHll
	'Grenadier' (p)	ECho
	'Grey Dove' (b) ♀H4	SAll
	'Greytown' (b)	GCal
	'Gypsy Star' (p)	EBee ECho GMaP SPet SPoG
	haematocalyx	EPot NMen WCom WFar
	- 'Alpinus'	see *D. haematocalyx* subsp. *pindicola*
§	- subsp. ***pindicola***	GAuc GKev LLHF NMen

	'Hannah Gertsen' (p/d) **new**	SAll
	'Harkell Special' (b)	SAll
	'Harlequin' (p)	WPer
	'Haytor Rock' (p) Ψ^{H4}	EBee EPfP
	'Haytor White' (p) Ψ^{H4}	CBcs CWib EPfP GKir MRav MWhi SAll SRms WCot WEas WWEG
	'Hazel Ruth' (b) Ψ^{H4}	SAll
	'Heidi' (p)	EPot
	'Helen' (p)	ELon LSRN SAll
	'Helena Hitchcock' (p)	SAll
	'Helix' (pf)	SAll
	'Hereford Butter Market' (p)	EBee
	'Hidcote' (p)	CTri LRHS MWat NMen WFar
	'Hidcote Red'	ECho LBee MWat
	'Highland Fraser' (p)	SRms WKif
	'Hope' (p)	SAll
	'Horsa' (b)	SAll
	'Hot Spice'^{PBR} (p) Ψ^{H4}	SPoG
§	'Houndspool Cheryl' (p) Ψ^{H4}	CTri EBee EPfP SAll SBfd SRGP SRms WFar
§	'Houndspool Ruby' (p) Ψ^{H4}	CBcs EPfP LSRN SAll SBfd WEas
	'Ian' (p)	LSRN SAll
	'Iceberg' (p)	ECho
	Iced Gem = 'Wp06 Fatima'^{PBR} (Scent First Series) (p/d)	MTis MWat SBfd SPoG SRot
	'Icomb' (p)	SRms WHoo WPer
	'Imperial Clove' (b)	SAll
	'Ina' (p)	SRms
	'Inchmery' (p)	SAll SSvw WEas WHoo
	'India Star'^{PBR} (p) Ψ^{H4}	CTri EBee ECho LRHS NEgg WPat
	'Inglestone' (p)	CTri NHol WPer
	'Inshriach Dazzler' (p) Ψ^{H4}	CPBP ECho ECtt EPot GAbr GGar GMaP LBee LRHS MAsh MHer NEgg NHar NHol NRya NWCA SRot WCom
	'Inshriach Startler' (p)	CMea WNew
	'Ipswich Pink' (p)	MNHC SRms
I	'Ivonne' (pf)	SAll
	'Ivonne Orange' (pf)	SAll
	'Jacqueline Ann' (pf) Ψ^{H1}	CNMi
	'James Portman' (p)	EBee ELon WMnd
	'Jane Austen' (p)	WPer
	'Janelle Welch' (pf)	CNMi
	'Janet Walker' (p)	GMaP
	japonicus f. ***albiflorus***	GKev
	'Jess Hewins' (pf)	CNMi SAll
*	'Jewel'	ECho ECtt
	'Joan Schofield' (p)	ECho SBch SPoG
	'Joanne's Highlight' (pf)	CNMi
	'Joe Vernon' (pf)	CNMi
	'Joy' (p) Ψ^{H4}	EBee ECho ECtt EPfP GKir LAst SAll SPoG SSvw
	'Julian' (p)	SAll
	'Julie Ann Davis' (b)	SAll
	'Kathleen Hitchcock' (b) Ψ^{H4}	SAll
	'Kessock Charm'	MNrw
	'Kesteven Chamonix' (p)	WPer
	'Kesteven Kirkstead' (p) Ψ^{H4}	CSWP MNrw
	kitaibelii	see *D. petraeus* subsp. *petraeus*
	knappii	EBee EWTr SRms SSvw WMoo WPer
	- 'Yellow Harmony' (p,a)	GJos SGar
	'La Bourboule' (p) Ψ^{H4}	CMea CTri ECho EDAr EPot GAbr LRHS MWat NHol NMen NPri NWCA SBch SRms WCom WFar WPat
	'La Bourboule Alba' (p)	CTri ECho ECtt EDAr EPot WFar WGor
	'Laced Hero' (p)	IGor
	'Laced Joy' (p)	SAll
	'Laced Monarch' (p)	CBcs EAEE EBee ECtt EPfP GCra GKir MMuc NCGa NDov NEgg SAll SEND SMrm SPlb SPoG SSvw WWEG
	'Laced Mrs Sinkins' (p)	SAll
	'Laced Prudence'	see *D.* 'Prudence'
	'Laced Romeo' (p)	SAll
	'Laced Treasure' (p)	SAll
	'Lady Granville' (p)	IGor SAll SBch SSvw
	Lady in Red = 'Wp04 Xanthe'^{PBR} (p)	CSBt EAEE EBee ECtt LRHS MTis MWat NDov
	'Lady Madonna' (p)	MTis SSvw
	'Lady Wharncliffe' (p)	IGor SBch
	'Lancing Monarch' (b)	SAll
	'Lancing Supreme' (p/d) **new**	SAll
	langeanus NS 255	NWCA
	'Laura' (p)	SAll
	'Lemsii' (p) Ψ^{H4}	ECho ECtt NMen WPer
	'Leslie Rennison' (b)	SAll
	'Letitia Wyatt' (p) Ψ^{H4}	CMea EBee EPfP MRav MWat SBfd SPoG SRGP
	'Leuchtkugel'	ECho LLHF NMen
	'Liberty' (pf)	SAll
	'Lily Lesurf' (b)	SAll
I	'Lily the Pink' (p)	LRHS MTis
	'Linfield Annie's Fancy' (pf)	CNMi
	'Linfield Doreen Ashmore' (p) **new**	SAll
	'Linfield Dorothy Perry' (p) Ψ^{H4}	SAll
	'Linfield Isobel Croft' (p)	SAll
	'Linfield Julie' (p)	SAll
	'Linfield Kathy Booker' (p) Ψ^{H4} **new**	SAll
	'Lionheart' (p)	LRHS
	'Little Ben' (p)	SAll
	'Little Jock' (p/d)	ECho ECtt EDAr LRHS MHer MWat SAll SPlb SPoG SRms WFar
	'Little Miss Muffet' (p)	CHll
	'London Brocade' (p)	SAll
	'London Glow' (p)	SAll
	'London Lovely' (p)	SAll SSvw
	'London Poppet' (p)	SAll
	'Loveliness' (p,a)	CBre
	lumnitzeri	ECho LLHF WPer
	'Lustre' (b)	SAll
	'Madonna' (pf)	EPfP SSvw
	'Maggie' (p)	LSRN
	'Maisie Neal' (b) Ψ^{H4}	SAll
	'Mambo' (pf) Ψ^{H4}	SAll
	'Mandy' (p)	SAll
	'Marjery Breeze'	SAll
	'Marmion' (M)	EMal SAll
	'Mars' (p)	ECho ECtt
	'Matthew' (p)	WHoo
	'Maudie Hinds' (b)	SAll
	'Maybole' (b)	SAll
	'Maythorne' (p)	SRms
	'Melody' (pf)	LRHS
	'Mendip Hills' (b)	SAll
	Mendlesham Minx = 'Russmin'^{PBR} (p)	EBee ECho EDAr GGar LRHS MWea SAll SBfd SWvt
	'Merlin' Ψ^{H4}	NEgg
	'Messines Pink' (p)	SAll
	'Michael Saunders' (b) Ψ^{H4}	SAll
	microlepis	ECho ITim NBre NGdn WAbe
	- ED 791562	NGdn
	- 'Leuchtkugel'	ECho WAbe
	- var. ***musalae***	ECho EPot ITim LLHF NMen
	'Mike Briggs' (b)	SAll

	'Miss Sinkins' (p)	CTri IFoB SPet
	monadelphus subsp. ***pallens***	GAuc
	'Monica Wyatt' (p) ♀H4	CBcs EAEE EBee ECtt EPfP GKir LRHS MTis NCGa NEgg SPoG WWEG
	monspessulanus	GKev WMoo
	- subsp. ***sternbergii***	ITim
	'Montrose Pink'	see *D.* 'Cockenzie Pink'
	Morning Star = 'Devon Winnie'PBR (p)	ECtt LBee LRHS
	'Moulin Rouge' (p) ♀H4	EBee ECtt EPfP GCra MTis MWat SPhx SPoG SSvw WWEG WWFP
	'Mrs Clark'	see *D.* 'Nellie Clark'
	'Mrs Macbride' (p)	SAll
	'Mrs Perkins' (b)	SAll
	'Mrs Roxburgh' (p)	CSam
	'Mrs Sinkins' (p)	Widely available
	'Murray Douglas' (p)	SSvw
	'Murray's Laced Pink' (p)	MWhi
N	'Musgrave's Pink' (p)	CHid ECha MRav SAll SBch SSvw WEas
	'Musgrave's White'	see *D.* 'Musgrave's Pink'
	myrtinervius	ECho EPot GKev MHer SRms WHoo
	'Mystic Star'	CMea ELan SBfd SSvw
	'Napoleon III' (p)	SAll SSvw WCom
	nardiformis	SPhx
	'Nautilus' (b)	SAll
	neglectus	see *D. pavonius*
§	'Nellie Clark' (p)	ECho MWat
	'Nelson'PBR	SAll
	'Neon Star'PBR (p) ♀H4	CTri EBee ECho EDAr ELan GKev LRHS NPri SPoG WFar
	'Night Star' (p) ♀H4	EBee ECho ELan EPfP GMaP LSou NEgg SPet SRot SSvw WFar WPtf
	nitidus	NBir NWCA
	nivalis	EPot GKev
	noeanus	see *D. petraeus* subsp. *noeanus*
	'Northland' (pf)	CNMi EMal SAll
	'Nyewoods Cream' (p)	CMea CTri ECho EPot MHer NMen NPri WPer
§	'Oakington' (p)	CTri LRHS MRav NPri NWCA
	'Oakington Rose'	see *D.* 'Oakington'
	'Old Blush'	see *D.* 'Souvenir de la Malmaison'
	'Old Dutch Pink' (p)	IGor
	'Old Irish' (p)	IGor
	'Old Mother Hubbard' (p)	CFee CHll
	'Old Red Clove' (p)	CFee WCot
§	'Old Square Eyes' (p)	MNrw SAll SSvw WCom WEas WFar
	'Old Velvet' (p)	GCal MNrw SAll
	'Oliver' (p)	SAll
	'Orange Maid' (b)	SAll
	'Oscar' (b)	SAll
	oschtenicus **new**	GKev
	'Painted Lady' (p)	IGor SAll
	'Paisley Gem' (p)	SAll SSvw
	Passion = 'WP Passion' (Scent First Series) (p)	EWTr LRHS MTis SBfd SPoG WCot
§	***pavonius*** ♀H4	EWTr EWes NBre NGdn NWCA WPer
	'Pax' (pf)	SAll
	'Peach' (p)	SEND
§	***petraeus***	EWes
§	- subsp. ***noeanus***	EPot GKev LHop LLHF WHal WPer
§	- subsp. ***petraeus***	WPer
	'Petticoat Lace' (p)	SAll
	'Pheasant's Eye' (p)	SAll SSvw WHer
	'Pike's Pink' (p/d) ♀H4	CSpe CTri EBee ECho ECtt EDAr ELan EPfP EWTr LHop LRHS MHer MMuc MRav MWat NBir NMen SAll SEND SPet SPoG SRms WClo WCom

	pindicola	see *D. haematocalyx* subsp. *pindicola*
	pinifolius	NBre
	'Pink Devon Pearl'PBR	SAll
	'Pink Fantasy' (b)	SAll
	'Pink Jewel' (p)	CMea CPBP ECho ECtt EPot NMen SAll WEas
	'Pink Mrs Sinkins' (p)	ECha MHer MLHP SAll
	'Pixie Star'PBR (p) ♀H4	ECho EPfP SPoG SRot
	plumarias 'Ipswich Pinks'	GJos
	plumarius	CArn MLHP SAll SRms SSvw WHer WMoo
	- 'Sonata'	GJos
	Popstar = 'Wp04 Esther' (p)	EWll LRHS STes
	'Prado' (pf) ♀H4	SAll
	'Pretty Lady' (p)	ECho
	'Prince Charming' (p)	ECho ECtt EPot NPri SRms
	'Princess of Wales' (M)	EMal SAll
	'Priory Pink' (p)	SAll
§	'Prudence' (p)	SAll
	'Pudsey Prize' (p)	CPBP EPot WAbe
	'Pummelchen' (p)	CPBP ITim
	'Purple Jenny' (p)	SAll
	'Queen of Hearts' (p)	CTri ECho MMuc NWCA SEND
§	'Queen of Henri' (p)	ECho ECtt LRHS MHer WBVN WFar
	'Queen of Sheba' (p)	SAll SSvw WKif
	'Rachel' (p)	ECtt
	'Rainbow Loveliness' (p,a)	SAll SRms
	'Ralph Gould' (p)	ECho
	'Raspberry Ripple' (p)	WHil
	'Raspberry Sundae' (p)	ECtt EWTr LBMP LRHS MTis MWat SBfd SPoG WHil
	'Rebecca' (b)	SAll
	'Rebekah' **new**	MWat
	'Red Star'PBR (p) ♀H4	ELan GGar LRHS NPri SRot
	'Reine de Henri'	see *D.* 'Queen of Henri'
	'Richard Pollak' (b)	SAll
	'Rivendell' (p)	ECho NMen WAbe
	'Robert Allwood' (pf)	SAll
	'Robin Ritchie' (p)	WHoo
	'Romance' (p) **new**	LRHS MTis MWat SBfd
	'Rose de Mai' (p)	CSam SAll SBch SSvw WHoo
	'Rose Devon Pearl'PBR	EAEE EPfP
	'Rose Joy' (p) ♀H4	EBee EPfP
	'Roysii' (p)	WPer
	rubicunda var. ***rubicundus***	GKev
	'Rubin' (pf)	WEas
	'Ruby'	see *D.* 'Houndspool Ruby'
	'Ruby Doris'	see *D.* 'Houndspool Ruby'
	'Ruby Wedding' (p)	LSRN
	'Sam Barlow' (p)	SAll SSvw
	sanguineus	NDov
	'Santa Claus' (b)	SAll
	seguieri	WHrl
	serotinus	EPot WCot
	shinanensis	GKev
	Shooting Star	see *D.* 'Devon Flores'
	'Shot Silk' (pf)	SAll
	'Show Aristocrat' (p)	SAll
	'Show Beauty' (p)	ECtt SAll
	Show Girl = 'Hilshow' (pf) **new**	MTis
	'Show Glory' (p)	SAll
	'Show Harlequin' (p)	SAll
	'Show Satin' (p)	ECtt SAll
	'Shrimp' (b)	CWib
*	'Six Hills'	WCom WPat
	Slap 'n' Tickle = 'Wp 05 Pp 22'PBR (Scent First Series) (p)	ECtt LRHS LSRN MTis SBfd SPoG SRot

	'Snowflake' (p)	ECho
	'Snowshill Manor' (p)	WPer
	'Solomon' (p)	SSvw
	'Sops-in-wine' (p)	CSam ECha ECtt MSCN SAll
	'Southmead' (p)	ECho
§	'Souvenir de la Malmaison' (M)	EMal SAll
	'Spangle' (b)	SAll
	'Spencer Bickham' (p)	MNrw
	spiculifolius	CMea EDAr EPot EWTr GAuc ITim MBNS NBre NWCA SPhx WFar
	'Spirit' (pf)	SAll
	'Spring Star' (p)	ECtt MSCN SRot WJek
	'Square Eyes'	see *D.* 'Old Square Eyes'
	squarrosus	ECho EPot NHol NWCA
*	- ***alpinus***	ECho
	- 'Nanus'	see *D.* 'Berlin Snow'
	'Starburst'	CMea LRHS SBfd
	Starlight = 'Hilstar'	CMea EWTr LRHS
	'Starry Eyes' (p) $\mathbb{Y}^{H4}$	ELan EPfP GBin GMaP LRHS MWat MWea NEgg NPri SBch SRot STes SWvt WFar
	'Storm' (pf)	CNMi EMal SAll
	'Strawberries and Cream' (p)	CBcs EAEE EBee ECtt GKir LRHS NEgg SPoG WMnd
	subacaulis	EDAr NGdn NWCA
	- subsp. ***brachyanthus***	EPot NMen WAbe
	- - 'Murray Lyon'	NMen WThu
	suendermannii	see *D. petraeus*
	'Suffolk Hussar' (p)	LRHS
	Sugar Plum = 'Wp08 Ianthe' (Scent First Series) (p)	EWTr MTis SBfd
	'Summerfield Adam' (p)	SAll
	'Summerfield Amy Francesca' (p)	SAll
	'Summerfield Blaze' (p)	SAll
	'Summerfield Debbie' (p)	SAll
	'Summerfield Emma Louise' (p)	SAll
	'Summerfield Rebecca' (p)	SAll
	'Sunflor Odessa Purple' (Sunflor Series)	SGar
	'Sunray' (b)	SAll
	'Sunstar' (b)	SAll
§	***superbus***	GBBs LHop MBNS SPhx WHer WMoo WRHF
	- 'Crimsonia'	MBrN
I	- 'Primadonna'	GQue NBre
	- subsp. ***speciosus***	GKev
	'Susan' (p)	SAll
	'Susannah' (p)	SAll
*	'Susan's Seedling' (p)	SAll
	'Swanlake' (p)	SAll
	'Sweet Sophie' (pf)	CNMi
	'Sweet Sue' (b)	SAll
	'Sweetheart Abbey' (p)	IGor SSvw
I	'Sweetness Mix' (p)	GJos
	sylvestris dwarf	EPot
	'Tamsin Fifield' (b) $\mathbb{Y}^{H4}$	SAll
	'Tatra Blush' (p)	GCal
	'Tatra Fragrance' (p)	CMdw GCal SAll
	'Tatra Ghost' (p)	GMac SAll
	'Tayside Red' (M)	EMal SAll
	'Tempo' (pf) $\mathbb{Y}^{H1}$	SAll
	'Thomas' (p)	SBch
	'Thora' (M)	EMal SAll
	Tickled Pink = 'Devon PP 11' (Scent First Series) (p)	EBee ECtt ELan GKir LBMP LRHS LSRN MTis MWat SBfd SPoG WClo
	'Tiny Rubies'	see *D. gratianopolitanus* 'Tiny Rubies'
	'Tony's Choice' (pf)	CNMi

	'Treasure' (p)	ECho
	'Trevor' (p)	SAll
	turkestanicus	NBir WPtf
	Tyrolean trailing carnations	SAll
	'Uncle Teddy' (b) $\mathbb{Y}^{H4}$	SAll
	'Unique' (p)	MNrw SAll SBch SSvw WHoo
	'Ursula Le Grove' (p)	IGor SSvw
	'Valda Wyatt' (p) $\mathbb{Y}^{H4}$	CBcs EAEE EBee ELan EPfP GKir LAst LRHS MWat NCGa NEgg SAll SBch SBfd SPoG SRGP SWvt WMnd
	'Vic Masters'	SPhx
	'Violet Clove' (b)	SAll
	'W.A. Musgrave'	see *D.* 'Musgrave's Pink'
	'W.H. Brooks' (b)	SAll
	'Waithman Beauty' (p)	CTri ECtt GMaP SAll WHoo WPer WTin
	'Waithman's Jubilee' (p)	MWhi SAll SRms
	'Warden Hybrid' (p)	CMea CTri ECho ECtt EPfP GMaP LAst LRHS MWea SPoG SWvt WAbe WFar
	'Waterloo Sunset' (p)	CMea CSBt LRHS MWat SBfd
	'Wedding Bells' (pf)	SAll
	'Weetwood Double' (p)	CFee MWhi SBch
	weyrichii	ECho
	'Whatfield Anona' (p)	SAll
	'Whatfield Beauty' (p)	ECho ECtt ELan EWTr NWCA
	'Whatfield Brilliant' (p)	ECho
	'Whatfield Cancan' (p) $\mathbb{Y}^{H4}$	CElw CMea ECho ECtt EWTr GMaP LHop LRHS MNHC MWat NEgg NPri SAll SBch SMrm SPoG SWvt WJek WNew WWFP
	'Whatfield Cream Lace' (p)	NWCA
	'Whatfield Cyclops' (p)	ECho EWTr SAll
	'Whatfield Dawn' (p)	ECho EWTr
	'Whatfield Dorothy Mann' (p)	ECho SAll
	'Whatfield Fuchsia Floss' (p)	SAll
	'Whatfield Gem' (p)	ECho ECtt ELan EPfP EWTr GEdr LRHS MWat NPri SAll SPoG SWvt WClo WFar WNew WPer
	'Whatfield Joy' (p)	ECho ECtt ELan EPfP EWTr LBee LRHS MHer NMen SAll SPoG WFar WHoo
	'Whatfield Magenta' (p) $\mathbb{Y}^{H4}$	ECho ELan EPfP EPot EWTr LBee LRHS MWat NMen NWCA SAll SPoG WAbe WEas
	'Whatfield Mini' (p)	EWTr SAll SRms WPer
	'Whatfield Miss' (p)	EWTr SAll
	'Whatfield Misty Morn' (p)	ECho EWTr SAll
	'Whatfield Peach' (p)	SAll
	'Whatfield Polly Anne' (p)	EWld
	'Whatfield Pretty Lady' (p)	ECho SAll
	'Whatfield Rose' (p)	ECho EPot
	'Whatfield Ruby' (p)	ECho ELan EWTr NWCA SAll WFar
	'Whatfield Supergem' (p)	ECho ECtt
	'Whatfield White' (p)	ECho ECtt EWTr SAll SRms
	'Whatfield White Moon' (p)	ECho
	'Whatfield Wisp' (p)	CPBP CTri ECho EPfP EPot GEdr MRav NBir NMen NWCA SPoG WNew
	'White and Crimson' (p)	SAll
	'White Joy'PBR (p) $\mathbb{Y}^{H4}$	MRav
	'White Ladies' (p)	ELan MRav SAll
	'Whitecliff' (b)	SAll
	'Whitehill' (p) $\mathbb{Y}^{H4}$	ECho EPot MHer NMen
	'Whitesmith' (b) $\mathbb{Y}^{H4}$	SAll
	'Widecombe Fair' (p) $\mathbb{Y}^{H4}$	CTri EBee ECtt ELan EWTr SAll SBfd SPoG SRms
	'Winnie Lesurf' (b)	SAll
	'Yorkshireman' (b)	SAll
	'Zebra' (b)	SAll

zederbaueri	NWCA
zonatus	NWCA

Diapensia (*Diapensiaceae*)

lapponica var. ***obovata***	NHar WAbe

Diarrhena (*Poaceae*)

americana	GFor
japonica	EPPr GFor MMoz
* ***mandschurica***	EPPr
obovata	EPPr

Diascia ✿ (*Scrophulariaceae*)

'Alice Cap'	SBch
'Andrew'	SBch
'Appleby Appleblossom'	SBch
'Apricot'	see *D. barberae* 'Hopleys Apricot'
Apricot Delight = 'Codicot' (Sun Chimes Series)	WFar
barberae	WPtf
- 'Belmore Beauty' (v)	ECtt EWes LIMB WWEG
- 'Blackthorn Apricot' 🏆$^{H3-4}$	CBar CBot EAEE ECha ECho ECtt ELan EPfP EShb GMaP LRHS MRav MWte NDov SMrm SPav SPer SPlb SPoG SWvt WFar WWEG
§ - 'Fisher's Flora' 🏆$^{H3-4}$	EPyc NDov WFar
- 'Fisher's Flora' × 'Lilac Belle'	ECtt
§ - 'Hopleys Apricot'	EPfP MSCN
§ - 'Ruby Field' 🏆$^{H3-4}$	CBar CMea ECha ECho ECtt ELan EPfP LHop LRHS LSRN MRav NEgg SPer SPoG SWvt WFar WHil WWEG
Blue Bonnet = 'Hecbon'	ECtt GBee SBch SWvt WFar
'Blush'	see *D. integerrima* 'Blush'
Blush Delight = 'Codiush' (Sun Chimes Series)	WFar
'Candy Floss'	SBch
'Coldham'	CMdw
Coral Belle = 'Hecbel'^{PBR} 🏆$^{H3-4}$	ECho ECtt EPfP EWes LHop LSou SBfd SMrm SPav WFar
cordata misapplied	see *D. barberae* 'Fisher's Flora'
cordifolia	see *D. barberae* 'Fisher's Flora'
'Denim Blue' **new**	WHil WHlf
Eclat = 'Heclat'	ECtt WFar
elegans misapplied	see *D. fetcaniensis*, *D. vigilis*
'Elizabeth' 🏆$^{H3-4}$	MWea WHrl
'Emma'	SWvt
felthamii	see *D. fetcaniensis*
§ ***fetcaniensis***	CMHG CMea EPfP EShb LRHS MHer MWea NEgg WBrk WCFE WClo WHal WKif WWEG
- 'Daydream'	LBuc WHrl
flanaganii misapplied	see *D. vigilis*
(Flying Colours Series) Flying Colours Appleblossom = 'Diastara'	EPfP SPoG
- Flying Colours Apricot = 'Diastina'	EPfP SPoG
- Flying Colours Coral = 'Diastis'^{PBR}	SPoG
- Flying Colours Red = 'Diastonia'^{PBR}	EPfP SPoG WGor
'Frilly' 🏆$^{H3-4}$	ECtt
'Hector Harrison'	see *D.* 'Salmon Supreme'
Ice Cracker = 'Hecrack'	CMea ECho ECtt ELan LHop LRHS SBch SPav
Ice Cream = 'Icepol'	LHop SCoo
Iceberg = 'Hecice'^{PBR}	SWvt
§ ***integerrima*** 🏆$^{H3-4}$	CSam ECha ELan ELon LLWP
- from Lesotho	SAga
- 'Alba'	see *D. integerrima* 'Blush'
§ - 'Blush'	CSpe
- 'Ivory Angel'	see *D. integerrima* 'Blush'
integrifolia	see *D. integerrima*
'Isabel'	SBch
'Jacqueline's Joy'	CMea NPer SBch WFar
'Joyce's Choice' 🏆$^{H3-4}$	ECho EWes LRHS WFar
'Katherine Sharman' (v)	ECtt EWes SAga
'Lady Valerie' 🏆$^{H3-4}$	EWes WPer
'Lilac Belle' 🏆$^{H3-4}$	CMea ECho ECtt ELan EPfP LHop LRHS NBir NEgg NGdn SBch SPlb SPoG WFar
'Lilac Gem'	SBch
'Lilac Mist' 🏆$^{H3-4}$	NPer
lilacina × ***rigescens***	GBee
Little Dancer = 'Pendan'^{PBR}	LAst LSou MSCN NLar SBfd SCoo SMrm SVil
'Little Dazzler' **new**	SVil
Little Dreamer = 'Pender'^{PBR}	LAst NLar SBfd SVil
Little Drifter	LSou NLar SVil WGor
Little Maiden = 'Penmaid'^{PBR}	LSou NLar SVil WGor
Little Tango	LHop LSou NLar SBfd SMrm SVil WRHF
(Miracle Series) 'Miracle Carmine'	LSou
- 'Miracle Orange' **new**	LSou
- 'Miracle Rose-Pink' **new**	LSou
- 'Miracle White' **new**	LSou
patens	CHll
personata	CHll CPrp CSpe LPla SAga SBch SDys SMHy SUsu WCot WEas
- 'Hopleys' **new**	LHop MAvo
Pink Delight = 'Codiink'	WFar
Pink Panther = 'Penther'	ECtt NLar SCoo SPav SWvt
'Pink Queen'	ECtt
'Pink Spires'	CElw
Red Ace = 'Hecrace'^{PBR}	EPfP LAst LHop NPer SPav SWvt
Redstart = 'Hecstart'	ECtt EPfP NGdn SWvt WFar
rigescens 🏆^{H3}	CBot CHEx COIW CPrp CSpe CWCL ECtt ELan EPfP EShb GEdr GGar MHer MRav MWte NPer SAga SPlb SPoG SWvt WBor WCFE WClo WCom WFar WHlf WPGP WSHC WSpi
§ - 'Anne Rennie'	ECtt LRHS SWvt
- pale-flowered	see *D. rigescens* 'Anne Rennie'
'Ruby Field'	see *D. barberae* 'Ruby Field'
'Rupert Lambert' 🏆$^{H3-4}$	EWes NDov SBri WPer
§ 'Salmon Supreme'	ECho ECtt ELan EPfP GBee LAst LRHS NGdn NPer SPoG WFar WMoo WPer
'Sunchimes Denim' (Sun chimes Series)	LAst
Susan = 'Winsue'^{PBR}	WFar
tugelensis	WFar
'Twinkle' 🏆$^{H3-4}$	CBar ECtt EPfP LAst LRHS NBir NGdn NPer WFar
* 'Twins Gully'	EWes GCal SMrm
§ ***vigilis*** 🏆^{H3}	CBot CMHG CMea CPLG ECha ECho EPfP GBee LHop LRHS MCot NBro SBch WCom WHal
- 'Jack Elliott'	MRav
(Whisper Series) Whisper Apricot Improved = 'Balwhisaptim'^{PBR}	NPri SCoo
- Whisper Cranberry Red = 'Balwhiscran'^{PBR}	LAst SCoo
- Whisper Pumpkin = 'Balwhispum'	LAst SGar
- Whisper Salmon Red = 'Balwhisred' **new**	LAst

- Whisper Tangerine = 'Balwhistang'	LSou
- Whisper White = 'Balwhiswhit'^{PBR}	LAst NPri SGar
White Belle = 'Penbel'	LSou SMrm

Dicentra ✿ (*Papaveraceae*)

CC 4452	CPLG
'Adrian Bloom'	CPLG EBee ECtt EHrv EPfP GBin MLLN MWat NBPC NPri SCoo SMrm SPer SWvt WFar WMoo WWEG
'Bacchanal' ♀H4	Widely available
'Boothman's Variety'	see *D.* 'Stuart Boothman'
'Bountiful'	CMac EBee MRav NDov NGdn SWvt WWEG
'Brownie'	CMoH
'Burning Hearts' new	CWGN EBee IPot MAsh WHil
canadensis	CLAP EBee EPot MAvo MTho NLar WAbe WCot WCru WHal
'Candy Hearts'^{PBR}	CBct EBee ECtt ELan EPfP LAst LHop MAsh NBPC NBro NGdn NLar SMrm WFar WHil
'Cherub'	EWld
'Coldham'	ELon WSHC
cucullaria	CElw CLAP CMea CRow CStu CTca CWCL EBee ECho EPot GCrs GGar LRHS MRav MTho NLar NMen NWCA SMrm WAbe WBVN WCru WFar
- 'Pittsburg'	CDes EBee EPPr MNrw SCnR WCot
* 'Dark Stuart Boothman'	ECho
'Double Decker'	MCot
eximia misapplied	see *D. formosa*
eximia ambig.	CChe
eximia (Ker Gawl.) Torr.	EBee
- 'Alba'	see *D. eximia* 'Snowdrift'
- 'Percy Picton'	EBee
§ - 'Snowdrift'	CLAP EBee ECtt EHrv ELan EPfP MCot MDun NGdn SMrm SRms WFar WMoo WPrP WWEG
§ ***formosa***	CBcs CTri EBee ECha EHrv ELan EPfP GGar IFro LAma LAst LBMP MLHP NBPC NBro NCob NGdn NMen NPri SPlb SRms WBrE WEas WFar WMoo WWEG
- alba	CSev CTri ECha GCra GMaP NBir NCGa SRms WCru WFar
- 'Aurora'	EBee ECtt ELon EPfP GBin LAst LRHS MRav NBPC NGdn NSti SBfd SPer SPet SPoG SWvt WCAu WFar WMoo WPnP
- 'Cox's Dark Red'	CLAP CPLG EBee EWes GAbr GBin LLHF NMen SKHP
- dark-flowered	WMoo
- 'Furse's Form'	CMoH
- subsp. ***oregana***	CLAP EBee EPPr GGar NBre NChi NMen SKHP WHal
- - 'Rosea'	EPPr
- 'Spring Gold'	ECha ELon WMoo
'Ivory Hearts'^{PBR}	CWGN EBee ECtt ELan EPfP LAst LHop LRHS LSRN MAsh MAvo NBPC NBro NCGa NGdn NLar SMrm SPer WHil WWEG
'Katy'	EPPr
'King of Hearts'	Widely available
'Langtrees' ♀H4	CMac CMil CRow CSam CSev EBee ECha EPau EPfP LHop MLHP MRav MWte NBro NCob SGSe SGar SMad SMrm SRms SWvt WCru WEas WFar WMoo WOut WPtf WSpi WWEG
lichiangensis	WCru WSHC
'Luxuriant' ♀H4	CBcs CSBt EBee ECtt ELan EPfP EShb LRHS MCot MGos MRav NBPC NCob NPri SBfd SPer SPoG SRms SRot SWvt WBor WFar WMoo WPnP WWEG
macrantha	CDes CEnt CLAP CMoH EBee ECha EPfP EWld GCra LAma LHop MNrw MTho SMad WCru WPGP WSHC
macrocapnos	CFir CRow EBee EPfP GCal GQui IFoB IFro MDKP MTho WCru WTou
'Paramount'	GBin
'Pearl Drops'	CElw CRow EHrv ELan GAbr GGar GMaP MCot MMoz MRav NBid NGdn NMen SRms WAbb WHil WMoo
peregrina	GEdr WAbe WWst
- alba	GEdr WWst
- 'Yubae'	WWst
'Red Fountain' new	LRHS MAsh
§ ***scandens***	CRHN CRow CSam CSpe ECho EPfP GCal ITim LAst MCCP MNrw MSCN MTho NCob NLar SGSe SUsu WSHC
- GWJ 9438	WCru
- 'Shirley Clemo'	CPLG
'Silver Beads'	EBee ECho ELon
Snowflakes = 'Fusd'	EBee EWes MRav
spectabilis ♀H4	Widely available
- 'Alba' ♀H4	Widely available
- 'Gold Heart'^{PBR}	CBcs CBow EPfP MAsh MGos MRav SBfd SPoG WCot
'Spring Morning'	CElw CMHG CMoH CSam EAEE ECtt EHrv EPPr LBMP NSti WRHF
§ 'Stuart Boothman' ♀H4	Widely available
thalictrifolia	see *D. scandens*
torulosa	WTou
- B&SWJ 7814	WCru
ventii	EWld
- GWJ 9376	WCru

Dichelachne (*Poaceae*)

crinita new	SMea

Dichelostemma (*Alliaceae*)

§ ***capitatum*** NNS 95-213	WCot
congestum	CAvo CFFs EBee ECho GAuc WCot
§ ***ida-maia***	CAvo CFFs CGrW CTca EBee EBrs ECho EPot GAuc MCot MWea SDeJ
- 'Pink Diamond'	EBee EBrs ECho SDeJ
multiflorum	WCot
pulchellum	see *D. capitatum*
volubile	CTca EBee ECho WCot

Dichondra (*Convolvulaceae*)

argentea 'Silver Falls'	CFox CSpe EShb LAst LSou NPri SCoo SGar SPoG
§ ***micrantha***	EShb
repens misapplied	see *D. micrantha*

Dichopogon (*Anthericaceae*)

strictus	ECou

Dichorisandra (*Commelinaceae*)

thyrsiflora	EUJe

Dichroa (*Hydrangeaceae*)

febrifuga	CAbb CBcs CDoC CHEx CHGN CHll CMil CPLG CTsd CWGN CWib EBee ELan EWes LRHS SOWG WCot WCru WPGP
- B&SWJ 2367	WCru
- HWJK 2430	WCru

- pink-flowered	CHEx
hirsuta B&SWJ 8207 from Vietnam	WCru
aff. ***hirsuta*** B&SWJ 8371 from Lao	WCru
versicolor B&SWJ 6565	WCru
- B&SWJ 6605 from Thailand	WCru
aff. ***versicolor*** Guiz 48	WPGP
aff. ***yunnanensis*** B&SWJ 9734	WCru

Dichromena see *Rhynchospora*

Dicksonia ✿ (*Dicksoniaceae*)

antarctica ♀H3	Widely available
berteriana	WRic
fibrosa ♀H3	CDTJ CKel CTrC EAmu EFtx GBin GLin IDee LTen MAsh SPoG WRic
sellowiana	CDTJ CKel WRic
squarrosa ♀H2	CBty CCCN CDTJ CKel CTrC EAmu MGos NMoo SAPC SPoG WRic

Dicliptera (*Acanthaceae*)

§ ***sericea***	CDes CHll CMdw EBee EShb GCal IKil LHop MSCN MWea SEND SMrm SRkn WCom WCot WFar WHil WPGP WSHC
suberecta	see *D. sericea*

Dicoma (*Asteraceae*)

anomala	SPlb

Dicranostigma (*Papaveraceae*)

leptopodum	CSpe

Dictamnus ✿ (*Rutaceae*)

albus	Widely available
- var. ***albus*** ♀H4 new	NPnk
§ - var. ***purpureus*** ♀H4	Widely available
* - var. ***roseus***	NBPC
* - ***turkestanicus***	GCal
caucasicus	SMHy
fraxinella	see *D. albus* var. *purpureus*

Didymochlaena (*Dryopteridaceae*)

lunulata	see *D. truncatula*
§ ***truncatula***	WRic XBlo

Dierama ✿ (*Iridaceae*)

adelphicum	EBee GAbr
ambiguum	EBee GAbr
'Aphrodite' new	NFir
argyreum	CBgR CCCN CElw CMac CPla CWCL EBee GAbr GEdr MCot NExo NFir SGSe SPoG SUsu SWal WPtf
'Ariel'	IBlr
'Ballerina'	ECho
'Ballyrogan Red'	IBlr
'Black Knight'	CPLG CPrp IBlr
'Blue Belle' new	CWGN EBee IBal LBuc LRHS SUsu
'Blush'	IBlr
'Buckland White'	WPGP
'Candy Stripe'	CBcs CPla CRow CSpe EBee STes
'Cherry Chimes'	MGos
cooperi	CElw CPou CPrp CTca CYeo EBee IBlr NBir SPoG WWEG
'Coral Bells'	CDes EBee GCal WPGP
'Cosmos'	CPLG EDAr EOHP GAbr MAvo MWhi NChi NExo WSHC
'Delicacy'	IBlr
'Desire'	IBlr
dissimile	EBee NFir
'Donard Legacy'	IBlr
§ ***dracomontanum***	Widely available
- JCA 3.141.100	WPGP
- dwarf, pale pink-flowered	LRHS
- Wisley Princess Group	MBri
dracomontanum* × *pulcherrimum	SMad
dubium	EBee IBlr
ensifolium	see *D. pendulum*
erectum	CBcs CBgR CCCN CHid CMac CWCL EBee GAbr GEdr IBlr LRHS MAvo NExo SBfd SGSe SUsu
'Fairy Bells'	CPen EBee NCob
'Fireworks'	CWCL EBee GEdr NExo
floriferum	EBee IBlr
formosum	CFir CGHE EBee WPGP
galpinii	CCCN CGHE CPla CWCL CYeo EBee ELan GAbr GBin GEdr LLHF LRHS NExo NFir STes WPGP
grandiflorum	CPBP CPou CYeo ECho IBlr NExo
'Guinevere'	Widely available
igneum	Widely available
- CD&R 278	CPou
insigne	CCCN CHid
'Iris'	IBlr
jucundum	EBee MLLN
'Knee-high Lavender'	CDes EPla SAga WPGP
'Lancelot'	Widely available
latifolium	CGHE CHid IBlr LRHS MGos NExo NFir
luteoalbidum	EBee GAbr WPGP WThu
'Mandarin'	CDes IBlr WPGP
medium	CGHE CPen EBee ELon LPio NCGa SUsu SWat WCot WPGP WWEG
'Milkmaid'	CPLG CPrp IBlr NCot
'Miranda'	CAbP CPen CSpe CYeo EBee ECtt GEdr GQue IBal LRHS MBNS MNrw NCGa NCob NEgg NGdn NPnk NSti SDix SDnm SMrm SPad WCot WCra WPtf WSpi
mossii	CBcs CCCN CDul CFir CHid CMac CPLG CPrp CWCL CYeo EBee ELan GBin GEdr IBlr LHop LRHS MCot NBre NExo NLar SBfd SGSe SPlb SPoG WPGP WSpi
nixonianum	EBee IBlr
'Oberon'	MRav
'Painted Lady' new	LBuc
'Pamina'	CPLG CPrp IBlr
'Papagena'	IBlr
'Papageno'	IBlr
pauciflorum	CBgR CCCN CFir CGHE CHid CPLG CPrp CWCL CWib CYeo EBee ECho EDAr GEdr LPio MHer NBir NExo NFir NLar SMrm SRot SUsu SWat WAbe WPGP WSHC WWEG
- CD&R 197	CPBP MDKP
§ ***pendulum***	CBen CBot CFee CRHN EBee ELan EPfP GAbr GBBs GEdr GGar IBlr LRHS LSRN MCCP MGos MNrw MRav NHol SMrm SWal SWvt WCot WFar WPnP WSpi WWEG
- var. ***pumilum***	CMoH
'Petite Fairy'	CPen
pictum	EBee IBlr
Plant World hybrids	ELon GGar SGSe
Plant World Jewels new	NExo
'Pretty Flamingo'	CPLG CPrp IBlr
'Puck'	CDes EBee GCal IBlr IGor MRav WPGP

pulcherrimum	Widely available
- var. ***album***	CBcs CCCN CGHE CLAP CSpr CYeo EBee ECho ELan GEdr IBlr ITim LPio MHer MNrw MWhi NCGa NCob NExo NHol STes WHil WPGP WSpi WWEG
- 'Blackbird'	Widely available
- dark pink-flowered	SGSe
- dwarf	ELon IPot
- 'Falcon'	IBlr
- 'Flamingo'	IBlr
- lilac-flowered	LHop
- 'Merlin'	Widely available
- pale-flowered **new**	ECha
- 'Pearly Queen'	CRow EBee
- 'Peregrine'	WPGP
- 'Redwing'	IBlr
- Slieve Donard hybrids	CLAP CWCL EBee ECho ECtt EDAr ITim LAst LHop MCot MHer NEgg SBfd SMad SPet WFar WHil WHrl WMnd WSpi WWEG
pumilum misapplied	see *D. dracomontanum*
'Purple Passion'	CPen NCGa
'Queen of the Night'	IBlr
reynoldsii	Widely available
robustum	CDes CGHE CPLG CPou GAbr IBlr NExo NFir WBVN WPGP
'Sarastro'	CPLG CPrp IBlr
'September Charm'	IBlr
sertum	EBee
'Spring Dancer'	CWCL EBee EHoe GEdr NExo NHol SGSe
'Tamino'	IBlr
'Tiny Bells'	CDes EBee ECha EDAr GCal WPGP
'Titania'	IBlr
trichorhizum	CBgR CCCN CFir CGHE CPBP CPLG CPla CPrp CWCL CYeo EBee ECho EKen ELan GAbr IBlr LHop MCot NExo NFir SBfd SGSe SPoG WPtf WWEG
'Tubular Bells'	IBlr
tyrium	EBee NFir
'Violet Ice'	IBlr
'Westminster Chimes'	CDes IBlr WPGP
'Zulu Bells'	ELon

Diervilla ✿ (*Caprifoliaceae*)

lonicera	CHar WHil
middendorffiana	see *Weigela middendorffiana*
rivularis 'Troja Black'	NLar
§ ***sessilifolia***	CBcs CHGN CHar CMac CWit EBee GAuc LAst MAsh MRav NLar SGar SLon WBVN WCot WFar WMoo
- 'Butterfly'	CMac EPPr NLar WMoo
× ***splendens***	CAbP CMHG CPLG CWib EBee EHoe ELan EPPr EPfP LHop LRHS MBNS MBlu MGos MRav MSwo NHol SEND SGar SLPl SPer SPoG WDin

Dietes (*Iridaceae*)

bicolor	CAbb CBod CDes CHEx CPLG CPen CPne CPrp CTca ERea EShb LEdu LPio LSou SChr SDnm SGSe SHom
butcheriana **new**	CDes
grandiflora	CAbb CArn CDes CFee CMdw CPLG CPen CPne CPrp CTca EBee ECho ERea EShb GBin LEdu LPio SBch SGSe SHom WBor WCot WPrP WSHC WThu
- 'Silver Sword' (v) **new**	CPen
§ ***iridioides***	CDes CPne CPrp CSWP CStu CTca EBee ECho EShb GBin LPio WCot WPGP
robinsoniana **new**	CSpe

Digitalis ✿ (*Scrophulariaceae*)

sp.	SVic
RCB/TQ 059 from İkizdere	WCru
ambigua	see *D. grandiflora*
apricot hybrids	see *D. purpurea* 'Sutton's Apricot'
cariensis	EBee GAbr GKev SPav
ciliata	EBee ELan GCal SPav
davisiana	CBot CPLG GAbr MCot MNHC SPav SPhx WMoo
dubia	CBot EPfP NBir NBre SDnm SPav
'Elsie Kelsey'	CEnt ECtt EShb LRHS NBir SDnm SWvt
eriostachya	see *D. lutea*
ferruginea ♀H4	Widely available
- 'Gelber Herold'	CBot EBee GAbr GMaP LBMP NBre NLar SMrm
- 'Gigantea'	EBee GQue LRHS MBri NBPC NPri SWat WAul WBox WCot WWEG
- subsp. ***schischkinii***	SDnm SPav
* ***floribunda***	NBir SPav
fontanesii	CEnt EBee GKev NBir
'Foxley Primrose'	NPri
'Foxtrot' **new**	LRHS
× ***fulva***	NBir
'Glory of Roundway'	CBot CDes EBee EBla MHer WCot
§ ***grandiflora*** ♀H4	Widely available
- 'Carillon'	CWan EBee EPau EPfP GAbr IFoB LAst LBMP LRHS NBir NGHP NLar SGSe SRot WGor
- 'Cream Bell'	EPfP LRHS
- 'Dwarf Carillon'	ECtt EWld
heywoodii	see *D. purpurea* subsp. *heywoodii*
'John Innes Tetra'	EBee EShb WPGP
kishinskyi	see *D. parviflora*
laevigata	CBot CFir CSam EBee EBla EBrs EPfP GKev LRHS MCot MWea NBro NGHP SDnm SEND SPav SPet WBox WCot WMnd WMoo WPer
lamarckii misapplied	see *D. lanata*
lamarckii Ivanina	NBPC
§ ***lanata***	CArn CBot EBee ECtt ELan EPfP GKev LAst LBMP LRHS MBNS MNHC NCob NGHP NGdn NPri SBfd SGSe SPav SPer SPlb SRms WCot WFar WMnd WPer WWEG
- 'Café Crème'	CSpr LRHS MNHC NBPC
§ ***lutea***	Widely available
§ - subsp. ***australis***	EBla SDnm
- 'Flashing Spires' (v)	CBow CPla LRHS
- 'Yellow Medley'	EBee
× ***mertonensis*** ♀H4	Widely available
- 'Summer King'	ECtt LRHS LSRN NBre
micrantha	see *D. lutea* subsp. *australis*
nervosa	SPav
obscura	CBot EBee ECho EHrv GKev IFoB LBMP MCot NBir NCob NGHP SDnm SIde SPav SPet WMnd
orientalis	see *D. grandiflora*
§ ***parviflora***	Widely available
- 'Milk Chocolate'	CBcs CMHG ECtt EPfP GKir GQue LRHS LSRN LSou MCot MHer MNHC NBPC NBre NEgg SBHP SGSe SIde SKHP SPet WFar
purpurea	CArn EBWF EBee ECtt EDAr EPfP GKir GPoy MHer MLHP

	MMuc MNHC NCob NLan NMir NPri SBfd SEND SIde SMrm SPlb SPoG WBrk WClo WJek WMoo WWFP
- 'Alba'	see *D. purpurea* f. *albiflora*
§ - f. ***albiflora***	Widely available
- - 'Anne Redetzky' PBR	CBow IFoB LRHS MGos WMnd
- - unspotted	CWan
- Camelot Series	LRHS NGHP WHil WRHF
- - 'Camelot Cream'	EAEE EPfP LRHS NLar NPri SWvt
- - 'Camelot Lavender'	EPfP LRHS NEgg NLar NPri SWvt
- - 'Camelot Rose'	EPfP LRHS NEgg NLar NPri SWvt
- - 'Camelot White'	EPfP LRHS MGos NEgg WBor
- 'Candy Mountain'	EWll
- Excelsior Group	CBcs CBot CSBt CSam CTri EAEE ECtt EPfP GJos GKir GMaP LAst LRHS MBri NMir NVic SBfd SPer SPoG SRms SWvt WFar WGor WWEG
- - (Suttons; Unwins) 🏆H4	ECtt MRav
- Foxy Group	CBot CWib ECtt EHrv EPfP LRHS SBfd SPet SPoG WFar WWEG
- - 'Foxy Apricot'	CBcs SWvt
- Giant Spotted Group	CBot ECtt EHrv EPfP LRHS MAsh SCoo
- Glittering Prizes Group	SWat
- Gloxinioides Group	ELan NCob WFar
- - 'Isabellina'	CBot
- - 'The Shirley' 🏆H4	ECtt SGar WGor WMoo
§ - subsp. ***heywoodii***	CBot EBee ELan MGos SDnm SPav SPhx WMoo WWEG
- - 'Silver Fox'	ECtt LRHS LSRN
- 'Jellito's Apricot'	CSam
- subsp. ***mariana***	GKev
- subsp. ***nevadensis***	CBot
- 'Pam's Choice'	CBar CPLG CSpe EBee EBla EBrs ECtt EPfP LAst LBMP LHop LRHS LSRN MAsh MGos MWat NBPC NEgg NGBl NPnk SBfd SMrm SPer SRGP WFar WHrl WMnd WMoo WWEG WWlt
- 'Primrose Carousel'	ECtt LRHS NEgg
- 'Snow Thimble'	EBee EBrs ECtt LBMP LRHS MAvo MBNS MBri NLar NPnk NVic SMrm WWEG
§ - 'Sutton's Apricot' 🏆H4	Widely available
* - 'Sutton's Giant Primrose'	CBot
- 'Torpedo Lilac Rose'	LRHS
- 'Virtuosa' **new**	WGor
purpurea* × *thapsi	CBot WWEG
'Red Skin'	CPom SGSe WMoo
'Saltwood Summer'	IFoB LRHS
× ***sibirica***	EBee
'Spice Island' PBR	EBee LRHS LSou MAvo MTis SPoG WCot WFut WWlt
* ***stewartii***	ECtt ELan EWes GAbr GCra NBPC SPad SPav WHil WKif WMoo
thapsi	CArn ECtt EPfP GAbr LRHS NBPC NPri SDnm SIde SPav SPhx WBrk WClo WMoo WPer WWFP
- JCA 410.000	EBee
- 'Spanish Peaks'	LRHS LSou
trojana	CSpr EBee ECtt IFoB SGar
- 'Helen of Troy'	NBPC SKHP SPad WSpi
viridiflora	CPLG ECtt MCot NBro NChi SGar SPav WFar

dill see *Anethum graveolens*

Dimorphotheca (*Asteraceae*)

cuneata white-flowered **new**	WCot

Dionaea ✿ (*Droseraceae*)

muscipula	CHew CSWC MCCP NChu SHmp SKHP SPlb WSSs
- 'Akai Ryu'	CSWC EECP NChu SHmp WSSs
- 'Red Piranha'	NChu
- 'Royal Red'	CHew CSWC NChu WSSs
- shark-toothed	CSWC EECP NChu
- 'Spider'	CSWC EECP NChu

Dionysia (*Primulaceae*)

'Annielle'	WAbe
aretioides 🏆H2	EDAr WAbe
- 'Bevere'	WAbe
- 'Gravetye'	ECho
- 'Phyllis Carter'	ECho
bazoftica	WAbe
bryoides	WAbe
'Charlson Jake'	WAbe
'Charlson Primrose'	WAbe
'Charlson Terri'	WAbe
curviflora	WAbe
'Emmely'	WAbe
'Eric Watson'	WAbe
'Ewesley Iota'	WAbe
'Ewesley Kappa'	WAbe
gaubae	WAbe
involucrata white-flowered	WAbe
janthina	WAbe
'Judith Bramley' **new**	WAbe
'Monika'	WAbe
'Schneeball'	WAbe
tapetodes	WAbe
- farinose	ECho
'Yellowstone'	WAbe

Dioon (*Zamiaceae*)

califanoi	CBrP
caputoi	CBrP
edule 🏆H1	CBrP LPal SBst SChr
- var. ***angustifolium***	CBrP
mejiae	CBrP LPal
merolae	CBrP
rzedowskii	CBrP LPal
spinulosum	CBrP LPal SBig

Dioscorea (*Dioscoreaceae*)

CC 5622	EWld
araucana	LSou
batatas	LEdu
caucasica 'Zojugre'	EBee
deltoidea	CPLG
japonica	CAgr EShb WBVN
villosa	CArn

Diosma (*Rutaceae*)

ericoides	MMuc SEND SWvt
- 'Pink Fountain'	EBee SPoG
- 'Sunset Gold'	CBod CWGN EBee MAsh SCoo SPoG

Diosphaera (*Campanulaceae*)

asperuloides	see *Trachelium asperuloides*

Diospyros (*Ebenaceae*)

austroafricana	SPlb
* ***hyrcanum***	EGFP NLar
kaki (F)	CBcs CMCN CTho EBee EPfP ERom MREP WDin WPGP
- 'Fuyu'	CAgr
- 'Kostata'	CAgr

- 'Mazelii'	CAgr
lotus	CAgr CBcs CMCN CMac CTho IVic LEdu NLar SPlb
- (f)	CAgr
- (m)	CAgr
lycioides	EShb SPlb
'Nikita's Gift'	CAgr
'Russian Beauty'	CAgr
virginiana (F)	CAgr CBcs CMCN CTho NLar SSpi

Dipcadi (*Hyacinthaceae*)

ciliare	CLak
marlothii	ECho
'Bloemfontein' **new**	
serotinum	ECho ITim
- subsp. ***lividum***	WPGP
viride **new**	CLak
white-flowered	CLak

Dipelta (*Caprifoliaceae*)

floribunda ♀H4	CBcs CBot CDoy CDul CMCN CMac CPLG CPMA ELan EPfP GKir MBlu MBri MWya NLar WCFE WPGP WPat
ventricosa	CAbP CBcs CGHE CPLG CPMA EPfP LRHS MAsh MBlu MBri NLar SLon SSpi WPGP WPat
yunnanensis	CPLG CPMA EBee ELan EPfP MBri NLar SSpi SSta WPGP WPat

Diphylleia (*Berberidaceae*)

cymosa	CAby CLAP ECha GEdr MRav SPhx WCot WCru WTin
- red-marked **new**	CDes
grayi	CLAP EBee GEdr WCru
sinensis	CPLG GEdr WCru

Dipidax see *Onixotis*

Diplacus see *Mimulus*

Dipladenia see *Mandevilla*

Diplarrhena (*Iridaceae*)

§ ***latifolia***	CFir GBBs GCal GGar GMac IBlr LRHS SGSe
- Helen Dillon's form	IBlr
moraea	CAbP CMac CMea CPen CWCL EBee ECha ECho GAbr GBBs GBin GCal GKir IBlr IFoB IKil ITim MCot MSCN NCGa NLBP WAbe WBrE WPGP WSHC
- ***minor***	IBlr
- 'Slieve Donard'	IBlr
- West Coast form	see *D. latifolia*

Diplazium (*Woodsiaceae*)

wichurae	EBee

Diplolaena (*Rutaceae*)

dampieri	SOWG

Diplostephium (*Asteraceae*)

alveolatum B&SWJ 10686	WCru

Diplotaxis (*Brassicaceae*)

muralis	CArn ELau WJek
tenuifolia	ELau MNHC NGHP NPri

Dipsacus (*Dipsacaceae*)

§ ***fullonum***	CArn CMac CPrp CWan EBWF EPfP GAbr GBar GPWP IFro MBri MHer MMuc MNHC NMir NPri SBch SEND SIde WHer WJek WSFF
inermis	CSam ECha NBid NLar WFar
japonicus	CArn SPhx
- HWJ 695	WCru
pilosus	CPom EBWF
sativus	GAbr GPWP NLar
strigosus	SPhx
sylvestris	see *D. fullonum*

Dipteracanthus see *Ruellia*

Dipteronia (*Aceraceae*)

sinensis	CGHE CMCN EBee EPla IArd MBri NLar WPGP

Disa (*Orchidaceae*)

Kewensis gx	NDav
tripetaloides	CDes

Disanthus (*Hamamelidaceae*)

cercidifolius ♀H4	CAbP CBcs CMCN CMac CPMA EPfP GKir IArd LRHS MAsh MBlu MBri NLar SPer SPoG SSpi WClo WPGP
- 'Ena-nishiki' (v)	NLar

Discaria (*Rhamnaceae*)

chacaye	LEdu WPGP

Diselma (*Cupressaceae*)

archeri	CDoC CKen SCoo
- 'Read Dwarf'	CKen

Disphyma (*Aizoaceae*)

crassifolium	SChr

Disporopsis (*Convallariaceae*)

B&SWJ 229 from Taiwan	WCru
B&SWJ 1864 from Taiwan **new**	WCru
aspersa	CDes CLAP CSpe EBee ECho EPPr EWld IMou LEdu MAvo WCon WCru WPGP
- tall	CBct WCru
fuscopicta	CBct CLAP EBee EHrv EPPr MAvo WCru WTin WWEG
longifolia	CLAP
- B&SWJ 5284	WCru
* ***luzoniensis***	CBct CPLG GEdr
- B&SWJ 3891	WCru
'Min Shan'	ELon
* ***nova***	EPPr WHil
§ ***pernyi***	Widely available
- B&SWJ 1864	CBct EPPr
- 'Bill Baker'	EBee LEdu MAvo
taiwanensis	CBct
- B&SWJ 3388	WCru
undulata	LEdu NBid WCru WPrP

Disporum (*Convallariaceae*)

austrosinense B&SWJ 9777	WCru
bodinieri	CDes CPLG LEdu WPnP
- BWJ 8128	WCru
- DJHC 765	WCru
aff. ***bodinieri***	WPGP
cantoniense	CDes CFir CLAP CPom EBee EPPr GEdr IFoB LEdu SKHP WCru WFar WPGP WPrP WWst
- B&L 12512	CLAP

	- B&SWJ 1424	WCru
	- B&SWJ 9715	WCru
	- DJHC 98485	CDes MMoz
I	- 'Aureovariegata'	CBct CDes EBee LEdu WCot WPGP
	- var. ***cantoniense*** f. ***brunneum*** B&SWJ 5290	WCru
	- 'Green Giant'	CDes CLAP CPLG EBee IFoB LEdu SSvw WFar WPGP WPnP
	- var. ***kawakamii*** B&SWJ 350	WCru
	- - RWJ 10103	WCru
	- var. ***multiflorum*** B&SWJ 11252	WCru
	- - B&SWJ 11291	WCru
	- 'Night Heron'	CDes CLAP CPLG EBee IFoB IPot MWea WCot WFar WPnP
	- var. ***sikkimense*** B&SWJ 2337	WCru
*	***flavum***	CAby CAvo EBrs ECho GKir SUsu
	hookeri	CLAP CPom EBee ECho GGar GKir MAvo NMen WCru
	- var. ***oreganum***	EPPr IBlr IFoB WCru
	lanuginosum	CBct EBee EPPr GEdr IMou LEdu MAvo WCot WCru
	leschenaultianum B&SWJ 9484	WCru
	- B&SWJ 9505	WCru
	leucanthum	WFar
	- B&SWJ 2389	WCru
	longistylum	IMou
	- B&SWJ 2859	WCru
	- L 1564	WCru
	lutescens	EBee EPot WCru
	maculatum	CAby CBct CLAP IFoB IMou MNrw WCru
	megalanthum	CLAP CPLG EBee EHrv IFoB MMoz WCru WPnP
	- CD&R 2412B	EPPr
	nantouense	IFoB LEdu WCot WFar WPGP
	- B&SWJ 359	CBct WCru
	- B&SWJ 6812	WCru
	sessile	EBee ECho GGar LEdu WCru
	- AGSJ 146	NMen
	- B&SWJ 2824	WCru
I	- 'Aureovariegatum' (v)	ECho MAvo WCru
	- 'Cricket'	EBee GEdr WFar
	- 'Kinga' (v)	EBee GEdr
	- f. ***macrophyllum*** B&SWJ 4316 **new**	WCru
I	- 'Robustum Variegatum'	EBee MAvo
	- variegated (v)	CBct EBee
	- 'Variegatum' (v)	Widely available
	- var. ***yakushimense***	ECho
	shimadae B&SWJ 399	WCru
	smilacinum	NLar WCru WFar
	- B&SWJ 713	WCru
*	- 'Aureovariegatum' (v)	LEdu WCot WCru
	- double-flowered (d)	EBee GCrs GEdr
	- 'Kino-tsukasa'	EBee
	- pink-flowered	WCru
	smithii	CBct CPom CStu EBee ECho EPfP EPot GAbr GEdr GGar GKev GKir LEdu NBir NMen WCot WCru WFar WPGP
	taiwanense B&SWJ 1513	WCru
	- B&SWJ 2018	WCru
	tonkinense B&SWJ 11814 **new**	WCru
	trabeculatum	IMou WCru
	- 'Nakafu'	LEdu WCru
	trachycarpum	CLAP
	uniflorum	CBct CDes CGHE CLAP CPom EBee ECho EPfP EPla GKir IFoB LEdu NBid SBch SMHy WFar WPGP WPnP WSHC WTin
	- B&SWJ 651	WCot WCru
	- B&SWJ 872	WCru
	- B&SWJ 4100	WCru
	viridescens	CBct EBee LEdu SKHP WCru
	- B&SWJ 4598	WCru

Distictis (*Bignoniaceae*)

buccinatoria	SOWG
'Mrs Rivers'	SOWG

Distylium (*Hamamelidaceae*)

myricoides	CMCN NLar WFar
racemosum	CBcs CMac EBee EPfP MBlu MBri NLar SLPl SReu SSta WSHC

Diuranthera see *Chlorophytum*

Dizygotheca see *Schefflera*

Dobinea (*Podoaceae*)

vulgaris B&SWJ 2532	WCru

Dodecatheon (*Primulaceae*)

	alpinum	NHar SRms WAbe
	- subsp. ***alpinum*** NNS 04-128	GKev
	- subsp. ***majus***	EBee
	amethystinum	see *D. pulchellum*
	'Aphrodite'PBR	EBee EKen MBri NBPC NLar
	austrofrigidum	EBee GKev NCGa NHar
	clevelandii	MDKP
	- subsp. ***insulare***	EBee LLHF NWCA
	- subsp. ***patulum***	ECho LRHS
	conjugens	GKev
	cusickii	see *D. pulchellum* subsp. *cusickii*
	dentatum ♀H4	CElw EBee GCrs GEdr GKev LEdu MDKP NHar WAbe WFar
	frigidum	WAbe
§	***hendersonii*** ♀H4	EPot GAuc NMen SRms
	integrifolium	see *D. hendersonii*
§	***jeffreyi***	EBee ECho EPPr GEdr GKev LEdu LRHS MBri MNFA MNrw NBPC NLar NMen NPnk WAbe WBor WFar
	- NNS 05-250	NWCA
	- 'Rotlicht'	SRms
*	× ***lemoinei***	WAbe
§	***meadia*** ♀H4	Widely available
	- from Cedar County, USA	WAbe
	- f. ***album*** ♀H4	CSWP CTri EBee ECho ELan EPfP EPot GAuc GEdr GGar GKev LAma LEdu LHop LRHS MTho NHol NMen NMyG NPnk NWCA SKHP SPer SRms SWvt WPnP WSpi
	- 'Aphrodite'	GEdr LSou WBor
*	- 'Goliath'	EBee
	- membranaceous	WAbe
	- 'Queen Victoria'	EBee ECho GEdr LEdu NLar NPnk SKHP SRGP WCot WFar WPnP
	- red shades	SMrm
	pauciflorum misapplied	see *D. pulchellum*
	pauciflorum (Dur.) E. Greene	see *D. meadia*
	poeticum	EBee NCGa
§	***pulchellum*** ♀H4	EBee ECho EDAr GCrs GEdr GKev LHop LLWG LRHS MNrw NMen NWCA SBfd
§	- subsp. ***cusickii***	LEdu SRms

- subsp. ***monanthum*** new GKev
- subsp. ***pulchellum*** 'Red Wings' EBee EBla ECho EPot LLHF MDKP NBir NLar NMen NPnk SKHP SPoG WFar WHoo WPnP
- ***radicatum*** see *D. pulchellum*
- 'Sooke's Variety' CStu WAbe

radicatum see *D. pulchellum*
redolens EBee
tetrandrum see *D. jeffreyi*

Dodonaea (*Sapindaceae*)

viscosa CArn CTrC ECou SPlb
- (f) ECou
- (m) ECou
- 'Purpurea' CAbb CBcs CDoC CHGN CPLG CTrC CWit EAmu EBee ECou EHoe ELon EShb EUJe EWTr GBin IVic LRHS LTen MAsh SLim
- - (f) ECou
- - (m) ECou

Doellingeria (*Asteraceae*)

scabra see *Aster scaber*

Dolichandra (*Bignoniaceae*)

cynanchoides RCB RA Q-4 WCot

Dolichos (*Papilionaceae*)

purpureus see *Lablab purpureus*

Dombeya (*Sterculiaceae*)

burgessiae IDee SOWG
calantha CCCN
× ***cayeuxii*** CCCN
wallichii CCCN

Dondia see *Hacquetia*

Doodia (*Blechnaceae*)

aspera WRic
§ ***caudata*** WAbe WRic
media CBty CDes GBin ISha LLHF MGos WAbe WRic
squarrosa see *D. caudata*

Doronicum (*Asteraceae*)

austriacum NBid NBre
cataractarum NBre
caucasicum see *D. orientale*
§ ***columnae*** CBcs GKev
cordatum see *D. columnae*
§ × ***excelsum*** 'Harpur Crewe' CPrp EBee LEdu MRav NBre NPer NVic
'Finesse' CAby GCal LRHS NBre SPoG SRms SRot
'Little Leo' EBee ELan EPfP GJos LRHS LSRN MAvo NBPC NLar NPri NVic SBfd SPet SPoG SRGP WBrE WWEG
§ ***orientale*** CWan EBee EPfP GJos GKir NBid SEND SPer SPoG SWat
- 'Goldcut' NBre NGdn
- 'Magnificum' CSBt EPfP GMaP MAvo MBri NBPC NEgg NGBl NMir SPoG SRms SWal WFar WWEG

pardalianches CMea ECha MMuc NBre NSco WRHF WSpi
- 'Goldstrauss' EBee

plantagineum 'Excelsum' see *D.* × *excelsum* 'Harpur Crewe'

Doryanthes (*Doryanthaceae*)

excelsa CHEx CTrC
palmeri CBrP CHEx

Dorycnium see *Lotus*

Doryopteris (*Adiantaceae*)

nobilis new ISha
pedata MBri

Douglasia see *Androsace*

vitaliana see *Vitaliana primuliflora*

Dovea (*Restionaceae*)

macrocarpa CCCN SPlb

Dovyalis (*Flacourtiaceae*)

caffra (F) XBlo

Doxantha see *Macfadyena*

Draba (*Brassicaceae*)

aizoides ECho GKev LRHS MWat SPlb SRms WFar
aizoon see *D. lasiocarpa*
athoa EDAr
bruniifolia EBur ECho EWes LRHS
- subsp. ***olympica*** WFar

bryoides see *D. rigida* var. *bryoides*
compacta see *D. lasiocarpa* Compacta Group
crassifolia ECho
cretica ECho NMen
cusickii GKev
cuspidata EPot
dedeana ECho EWes
densifolia GAuc
dubia EDAr
glacialis EDAr
hispanica EDAr
hoppeana EDAr
§ ***lasiocarpa*** SGar
§ - Compacta Group ECho NWCA
longisiliqua ♀H2 ITim WAbe
- EMR 2551 EPot

mogadanensis GAuc
mollissima EPot NWCA WAbe
oligosperma subsp. ***subsessilis*** NWCA
ossetica WAbe
parnassica EDAr GAuc
polytricha GAuc WAbe
§ ***rigida*** var. ***bryoides*** ECho WThu
- var. ***imbricata*** f. ***compacta*** EPot

rosularis GAuc
× ***salomonii*** EPot
scardica see *D. lasiocarpa*
ventosa WAbe

Dracaena ✿ (*Dracaenaceae*)

congesta see *Cordyline stricta*
draco ♀H1 CArn CTrC EShb XBlo
fragrans MBri
- (Compacta Group) 'Compacta Purpurea' MBri
- - 'Compacta Variegata' (v) MBri
- Deremensis Group XBlo
- - 'Lemon Lime' (v) ♀H1 MBri
- - 'Warneckei' (v) ♀H1 MBri
- - 'Yellow Stripe' (v) ♀H1 MBri

* - ***glauca*** MBri
- 'Janet Craig' MBri
- 'Massangeana' (v) ♀H1 MBri

indivisa see *Cordyline indivisa*
'Lemon Lime Tips' XBlo

	marginata (v) Υ^{H1}	MBri XBlo
	- 'Colorama' (v)	MBri
	- 'Tricolor' (v) Υ^{H1}	XBlo
	sanderiana (v) Υ^{H1}	MBri
*	***schrijveriana***	MBri
	steudneri	MBri
	stricta	see *Cordyline stricta*

Dracocephalum (*Lamiaceae*)

	sp.	LLHF
	argunense	CAby SPhx SRms WCom WPat
	- 'Fuji Blue'	CEnt CPLG EBee EPfP EWes GKev LRHS LSRN NBre NLar
	- 'Fuji White'	CEnt CPLG EBee GKev LSRN SPhx
	botryoides	LLHF
	forrestii	GKev
	aff. ***forrestii***	LLHF
	grandiflorum	CBod CEnt GKev GKir LLHF MMHG SBHP SPhx WFar
	- 'Altai Blue'	CMea
	hemsleyanum	LLHF WPat
	mairei	see *D. renatii*
	moldavica	SIde
	nutans	NLar
	prattii	see *Nepeta prattii*
§	***renatii***	LLHF SPhx
	rupestre	EBee MBri NBre
	ruyschiana	ELan EWes GEdr MRav NLar NWCA SPhx
	- 'Blue Moon'	NBPC NBre
	sibiricum	see *Nepeta sibirica*
	virginicum	see *Physostegia virginiana*
	wendelboi	NBir

Dracunculus (*Araceae*)

	canariensis	CStu WCot
	muscivorus	see *Helicodiceros muscivorus*
§	***vulgaris***	CArn CHid CPom EBee ECho EHrv EPot ERCP EUJe LEdu LRHS MCCP MRav SDix SEND SMad SPad SPlb WCot WFar WPnP
	- white-flowered	WPnP

Dregea (*Asclepiadaceae*)

	sinensis	CBot CCCN CHll CRHN CWGN EBee ELan EPfP ERea EWes LRHS MAsh MRav SEND SKHP SOWG SPer WCot WPGP WSHC
	- 'Brockhill Silver'	SKHP WSHC
	- 'Variegata' (v)	CCCN EShb EWes WCot

Drepanostachyum (*Poaceae*)

§	***falcatum***	GKir
	falconeri J.J.N. Campbell. ex D. McClintock	see *Himalayacalamus falconeri*, *Himalayacalamus falconeri* 'Damarapa'
	hookerianum	see *Himalayacalamus hookerianus*
§	***khasianum***	CDTJ CGHE CPLG WPGP
§	***microphyllum***	IMou WJun WPGP

Drimia (*Hyacinthaceae*)

	angustifolia ambig.	ECho
	anomala	CLak
	elata new	CLak
	involuta new	CLak
	mzimvubuensis new	CLak
	sphaerocephala new	CLak
	uniflora new	CLak

Drimiopsis (*Hyacinthaceae*)

	maculata	CStu LToo WCot

Drimys (*Winteraceae*)

	sp.	CPla
	aromatica	see *D. lanceolata*
	colorata	see *Pseudowintera colorata*
	granadensis	WCru
	var. ***grandiflora*** B&SWJ 10777	
	granatensis	CGHE WPGP
§	***lanceolata***	Widely available
	- (f)	CTrC ECou GGar NCGa SPer
	- (m)	CDoC CTrC ECou GGar SPer
	- 'Inverewe Prolific' (f)	GGar
	- 'Mount Wellington'	GCal
	- 'Suzette' (v)	LRHS MBlu MGos
*	***latifolia***	CBcs CHEx
	winteri Υ^{H4}	Widely available
	- var. ***andina***	CPLG EBee EPfP WPGP
§	- var. ***chilensis***	CPLG EPfP GGar LRHS SSpi WCru WPGP
	- Latifolia Group	see *D. winteri* var. *chilensis*

Drosanthemum (*Aizoaceae*)

	hispidum	ECho ELan EPfP EPot GMaP ITim LRHS MTho NMen NWCA SBHP SPlb SPoG WNew
	speciosum	ECho
*	***sutherlandii***	ECho

Drosera ✿ (*Droseraceae*)

	admirabilis	CHew CSWC
	aliciae	CHew CSWC EECP NChu SHmp
	andersoniana	EFEx
	androsacea	CHew
	anglica	CSWC NChu
	ascendens	CHew
	binata	CHew EECP SHmp
	- var. ***binata*** new	CSWC
§	- subsp. ***dichotoma***	CHew CSWC
	- 'Extrema'	CHew
	- 'Multifida'	CHew MCCP
	browniana	EFEx
	bulbigena	EFEx
	bulbosa subsp. ***bulbosa***	EFEx
	- subsp. ***major***	EFEx
	callistos	CHew
	capensis	CHew CSWC MCCP NChu SHmp SPlb
	- 'Albino'	CHew EECP MCCP SHmp
	- red	CSWC NChu
	cuneifolia	CHew
	dichotoma	see *D. binata* subsp. *dichotoma*
	dichrosepala	CHew EECP
	echinoblastus	CHew
	enodes	CHew
	ericksoniae	CHew
	erythrorhiza	EFEx
	- subsp. ***collina***	EFEx
	- subsp. ***erythrorhiza***	CHew EFEx
	- subsp. ***magna***	EFEx
	- subsp. ***squamosa***	EFEx
	filiformis	NChu
	- var. ***filiformis***	CHew CSWC EECP
	gigantea	EFEx
	graniticola	EFEx
	helodes	CHew
	heterophylla	EFEx
	× ***hybrida*** new	CSWC
	lasiantha	CHew
	leioblastus	CHew
	loureiroi	EFEx
	macrantha	EFEx

- subsp. ***macrantha***	EFEx
macrophylla	EFEx
subsp. ***macrophylla***	
madagascariensis new	SHmp
mannii	CHew
marchantii	EFEx
subsp. ***prophylla***	
menziesii	EFEx
subsp. ***basifolia***	
- subsp. ***menziesii***	EFEx
- subsp. ***thysanosepala***	EFEx
modesta	EFEx
nidiformis	CHew
orbiculata	EFEx
paleacea	CHew
subsp. ***trichocaulis***	
peltata	EFEx
platypoda	EFEx
pulchella	CHew
pycnoblasta	CHew
pygmaea	CHew
ramellosa	EFEx
roseana	CHew
rosulata	EFEx
rotundifolia	CSWC SHmp WHer
salina	EFEx
sargentii	CHew
scorpioides	CHew CSWC EECP SHmp
slackii	CHew CSWC NChu
spatulata	CSWC SHmp
stelliflora	CHew
stolonifera	EFEx
subsp. ***compacta***	
- subsp. ***humilis***	EFEx
- subsp. ***porrecta***	EFEx
- subsp. ***rupicola***	EFEx
- subsp. ***stolonifera***	EFEx
tubaestylus	EFEx
zonaria	EFEx

Drosophyllum (*Droseraceae*)

lusitanicum	CHew

Dryandra (*Proteaceae*)

formosa	LTen SPlb WCot

Dryas (*Rosaceae*)

drummondii	ECho LLHF WAbe WFar
grandis	GKev
§ ***integrifolia***	CMea NMen
- 'Greenland Green'	WAbe
octopetala 𝕐H4	CMea ECho EPfP EPot GJos LHop LRHS MWat NChi NLAp SPoG SRms WAbe
- 'Harry Bush'	GJos
- subsp. ***hookeriana***	LLHF
- 'Minor' 𝕐H4	ECho NMen WAbe
× ***suendermannii*** 𝕐H4	EPfP EPot GEdr GMaP NHar NMen SRot WAbe WBVN
tenella Pursh	see *D. integrifolia*

Dryopteris ✿ (*Dryopteridaceae*)

from Emei Shan, China	WPGP
aemula	EFer SRms WRic
§ ***affinis*** 𝕐H4	CBty CLAP EBee ECha EPfP GMaP IFFs LBuc LPBA MAsh MCot MGos MLLN MMoz MRav NHol NMoo SRms WFib WRic WShi WWEG
§ - subsp. ***borreri***	SRms
- subsp. ***cambrensis*** 'Crispa Barnes'	WPGP
- - 'Insubrica'	EFer
- 'Congesta'	CLAP EBee WWEG
- 'Congesta Cristata'	CFee CLAP CWCL EFer EPfP GMaP LPBA MAsh NHol SRot WBrE
- Crispa Group	CLAP EHon GBBs LAst MMoz WWEG
§ - 'Crispa Gracilis' 𝕐H4	CKel CLAP EFtx ELan GBin ISha MAvo MCCP MMoz NBir NEgg NMyG WRic WWEG
* - 'Crispa Gracilis Congesta'	CBty GEdr NGdn NHol SBfd SGSe WFib WPat
§ - 'Cristata' 𝕐H4	Widely available
- 'Cristata Angustata' 𝕐H4	CBty CChe CLAP EBee EFer ELan EPfP ETod GBin LRHS MAsh MMoz NBid NGdn NHol SRms WFib WMoo WPGP WRic WSpi
- 'Cristata The King'	see *D. affinis* 'Cristata'
- 'Grandiceps Askew'	EFer SRms WFib
- 'Pinderi'	CBty CLAP EBee EFer ELan EUJe GBin MMuc NHol NMyG SEND SRms WRic WWEG
- Polydactyla Group	CLAP SPer WFar
- - 'Polydactyla Dadds'	CBty CLAP EFtx EQua LLHF NLar NMyG WWEG
- - 'Polydactyla Mapplebeck' 𝕐H4	CLAP GBin LPBA NBid NHol SRms WFib WRic
- 'Revoluta'	SGSe
- 'Revolvens'	CLAP EFer NWsh SRms
atrata misapplied	see *D. cycadina*
atrata	CDTJ CKel CWCL EWTr MAsh MMuc NMoo SBfd SPoG
× ***australis***	CLAP EBee ISha WRic
austriaca	see *D. dilatata*
bissetiana	ISha WRic
blanfordii	WPGP WRic
borreri	see *D. affinis* subsp. *borreri*
buschiana	CBty CDTJ CLAP EBee EFtx MRav NLar
carthusiana	CLAP EBee EFer GBin NLar SRms STre WPtf WRic
- 'Cristata'	EFer
celsa	ISha WRic
championii	CCCN CLAP EBee ISha LRHS WRic
clintoniana	CLAP EBee EFer GBin LRHS NMyG WPGP WRic
× ***complexa*** new	ISha
- 'Stablerae'	CLAP EFtx GBin WFib WPGP WRic
- 'Stablerae' crisped	NMyG WFib
coreanomontana	EBee NMyG
costalisora new	WRic
crassirhizoma	CCCN CKel CLAP EBee GBin WRic
cristata	CLAP CWCL EBee EPfP WMoo WRic
§ ***cycadina*** 𝕐H4	CHEx CLAP EBee EFer EFtx ELan EPfP EShb GBin LPBA LRHS MAsh MBri MCCP MGos MMoz MWat NBid NBir NHol NWsh WFib WMoo WPnP WRic
dickinsii	GLin
§ ***dilatata*** 𝕐H4	CBgR CRWN ECha EFer EFtx ELan EPfP EUJe LRHS MAsh MRav NHol SGSe SRms WFib WHal WRic WShi
- 'Crispa Whiteside' 𝕐H4	CBgR CBty CLAP CWCL EBee EFer EFtx EPfP GEdr MAsh MBri NHol NLar NMyG SBfd SPlb SRms WFib WMoo WPGP WRic WWEG
- 'Grandiceps'	CLAP EFer NHol WFib
- 'Jimmy Dyce'	CLAP ISha
- 'Lepidota Crispa Cristata'	CLAP EBee
- 'Lepidota Cristata' 𝕐H4	CBty CChe CLAP CMHG CWCL EFtx ELan GBin LTen MAsh

	NGdn NHol NMyG NVic NWsh SGSe SRms WFar WFib WMoo WPrP WRic
- 'Lepidota Grandiceps'	CLAP
* - 'Recurvata'	CBty CLAP EBee ISha LLHF NLar WRic
erythrosora ♀H4	Widely available
- 'Brilliance'	CCCN CLAP EBee ISha LRHS LSou NLar WRic
§ - var. ***prolifica*** ♀H4	CBty CChe CKel CLAP EBee EFtx GMaP LRHS MAsh MGos MMoz NBir NEgg NHol NLar WCot WFib WRic WWEG
expansa	EBee
filix-mas ♀H4	Widely available
- 'Barnesii'	CLAP CWCL CWit EBee EFer GBin ISha MAsh MMuc NLar NMoo NWsh SEND SPlb SPoG WRic WWEG
- 'Crispa'	CBty CLAP EBee EHon LRHS NHol SRms WFib
- 'Crispa Congesta'	see *D. affinis* 'Crispa Gracilis'
- 'Crispa Cristata'	CBgR CBty CLAP CWCL EBee EFer EFtx ELan EPfP GMaP IKil LHop LRHS MAsh MBri MMuc NBid NBir NHol SEND SGSe SPoG SRms SWat WFib WGor WRic WWEG
- 'Cristata' ♀H4	CLAP EBee EFer ELan EPfP GKir MMoz NMyG SRms SWat WBVN WMoo
- Cristata Group	EFer WRic
* - - 'Cristata Grandiceps'	EFer
- - 'Cristata Jackson'	CLAP SPlb
- - 'Cristata Martindale'	CLAP NBid NHol SRms WFib
- - 'Fred Jackson'	CLAP NHol WFib
- 'Depauperata'	CLAP WPGP
- 'Euxinensis'	CLAP
- 'Furcans'	CLAP WRic
- 'Grandiceps Wills' ♀H4	NBid NHol WFib
- 'Linearis'	CMHG EBee EFer EHon ELan ISha LAst LPBA MCot MGos NHol NWsh SGSe SRms WFib
- 'Linearis Congesta'	WPGP
- 'Linearis Cristata'	WRic
- 'Linearis Polydactyla'	CBgR CBty CLAP CWCL EBee EFer EFtx EPfP GBin GKir LBMP LRHS MAsh MMoz MMuc NGdn NHol NMoo NMyG SEND SPoG WAbe WFar WIvy WMoo WPnP WPtf
- 'Parsley'	CLAP ISha
* - Polydactyla Group	MGos MRav MWat NEgg
I ***fllix-mas*** 'Revolvens'	WFib
formosana	WRic
fuscipes	WRic
goldieana	CDTJ CFwr CLAP CMHG EBee EFer EFtx EWTr GBin GMaP LRHS NBid NBir NCob NGdn NLar NMyG WCot WFar WFib WMoo WPnP WRic WSpi WWEG
hirtipes misapplied	see *D. cycadina*
hondoensis	EFtx WRic
intermedia	ISha WRic
labordei new	CBty EBee ISha
lacera	ISha WRic
lepidopoda	EBee EFtx GLin WAbe WRic
ludoviciana	EBee EFtx ISha WRic
marginalis	CDTJ CKel CLAP EBee EKen GBin LRHS MMoz NHol NLar NMyG SBfd WMoo WRic
oreades	SRms
pacifica	CLAP
paleacea	CLAP
pseudofilix-mas	ISha WRic
pseudomas	see *D. affinis*
pycnopteroides	EFtx WRic
× ***remota***	EBee ISha SRms WRic
scottii new	WRic
× ***separabilis*** new	ISha
sieboldii	CBty CEnt CFir CHEx CLAP CPrp CWCL EBee EFer ELan EShb GEdr LRHS MAvo NBid NBir NGdn NHol NLar NMyG SBfd SGSe SRms WBor WMoo WPGP WRic WWEG
sordidipes new	WRic
stewartii	CLAP GBin LLHF NLar NMyG WRic WWEG
sublacera new	EFtx
tokyoensis	CDTJ CDes CFwr CKel CLAP EBee EFtx GBin ISha MMoz NHol NLar NMyG WPGP WRic WSpi
uniformis	CLAP ELan
wallichiana ♀H4	Widely available
- F&M 107	WPGP

Duchesnea (*Rosaceae*)

chrysantha	see *D. indica*
§ ***indica***	CSWP GAbr IGor LEdu MRav SEND WMoo WOut
§ - 'Harlequin' (v)	CPLG EBee GBar MCCP
* - 'Snowflake' (v)	EBee WMoo
- 'Variegata'	see *D. indica* 'Harlequin'

Dugaldia (*Asteraceae*)

hoopesii	see *Hymenoxys hoopesii*

Dulichium (*Cyperaceae*)

arundinaceum	GKir LLWG LSRN
- 'Tigress' new	LLWG

Dunalia (*Solanaceae*)

australis	see *Iochroma australe*
- blue-flowered	see *Iochroma australe* 'Bill Evans'
- white-flowered	see *Iochroma australe* 'Andean Snow'

Duranta (*Verbenaceae*)

§ ***erecta***	CCCN CHll EShb
§ - 'Geisha Girl'	CCCN EShb
- 'Sapphire Swirl'	see *D. erecta* 'Geisha Girl'
- 'Variegata' (v)	CCCN EShb
plumieri	see *D. erecta*
repens	see *D. erecta*
serratifolia	CCCN

Duvernoia see *Justicia*

Dyckia (*Bromeliaceae*)

frigida	EBee WCot
leptostachya	WCot WGrn
marnier-lapostollei	WCot
'Morris Hobbs'	WCot
remotiflora	CBrP SChr
velascana	CHEx

Dymondia (*Asteraceae*)

margaretae	CFee CPBP CStu WAbe
* ***repens***	WHil

Dypsis (*Arecaceae*)

§ ***decaryi***	CCCN EAmu LPal XBlo
decipiens	CBrP
lutescens ♀H1	LPal MBri XBlo

Dysosma see *Podophyllum*

E

Ecballium (*Cucurbitaceae*)

elaterium	CArn CDTJ LEdu SGar SIde WPGP

Eccremocarpus (*Bignoniaceae*)

scaber	CBcs CDul CRHN ELan EPfP LBMP LRHS MBri MNrw NPer SBfd SEND SGar SLim WBrE WTou
- 'Aureus'	EPfP GKev WPtf
- 'Carmineus'	EPfP EWld GGar SGar
- coral-red-flowered	GKev
- orange-flowered	GKev SPoG
I - 'Roseus'	NLar
- 'Tresco Cream'	CSpe
- Tresco Series	CTsd GKev

Echeandia (*Anthericaceae*)

formosa B&SWJ 9147	WCru

Echeveria ✿ (*Crassulaceae*)

agavoides ♀H1	MRav
* 'Black Prince'	CAbb CBow CDoC CStu NPer SMrm SRot WCom WCot WDyG WEas WFar
'Blue Waves'	WCot
* ***cana***	CBct CDoC EWll SRot
coccinea	ELan
'Crûg Ice'	WCru
derenbergii ♀H1	STre
× ***derosa***	EPfP
- 'Worfield Wonder' ♀H1	MWte STre WEas
'Doris Taylor' **new**	MSCN
'Duchess of Nuremberg'	CDoC CHVG SMrm SPlb SRot WCot WFar WNew
elegans ♀H1	CDoC CHEx EPfP GAbr LSou SAPC SPlb WBrE WCom WCot WDyG WGwG WNew
§ ***gibbiflora*** var. ***metallica*** ♀H1	EPfP WEas
* × ***gilva*** 'Red' ♀H1	WCot WEas
glauca Baker	see *E. secunda* var. *glauca*
harmsii ♀H1	CDoC CSWP STre WGwG
'Hens and Chicks'	CHEx
lilacina **new**	SMrm SRot
'Mahogany'	MAvo MSpe SUsu WCot WGrn
'Mauna Loa'	WCot
maxonii B&SWJ 10396	WCru
'Meridian'	CHEx
montana B&SWJ 10277	WCru
multicaulis	MSCN
nodulosa	WCot
peacockii	EOHP MSCN SMrm SPet SPlb WNew
'Perle d'Azur'	CHEx WCom WCot
'Perle von Nürnberg' ♀H1	CAbb SMad SPet
'Pinky'	WCot
prolifica	STre
pulidonis ♀H1	EPfP WCot
I ***pulvinata*** 'Rubra' **new**	MSCN
rosea	WCot
runyonii 'Topsy Turvy'	CDoC CHEx CStu EOHP EPfP SPet
secunda	CAbb STre SWal
§ - var. ***glauca*** ♀H1	CDTJ CDoC CHEx CTsd EAmu EBee ELan EPfP EShb ETod GAbr LPJP NBir SArc STre SUsu WCom WCot
* - - 'Gigantea'	NDov NPer
setosa ♀H1	EPfP MSCN
- var. ***ciliata***	EShb
shaviana	CBow CStu
'Violet Queen'	CAbb

Echinacea ✿ (*Asteraceae*)

§ 'After Midnight' (Big Sky Series)	CPar EBee EBrs IPot LRHS NGHP NLar WCra WFut
angustifolia	CArn CBod EBee EBla EPfP GMac GPoy LPio LRHS MHer MMuc NGHP WJek
§ 'Art's Pride'PBR	Widely available
'Emily Saul'	see *E.* 'After Midnight'
'Evan Saul'PBR	see *E.* 'Sundown'
'Green Envy'PBR	Widely available
'Green Jewel' **new**	NDov SPhx
§ 'Harvest Moon'PBR (Big Sky Series)	Widely available
'Hot Papaya' (d) **new**	SBfd WCot WHlf
'Katie Saul'	see *E.* 'Summer Sky'
laevigata	NGdn
Mango Meadowbrite = 'CBG Cone3'	CWCL EBee NPnk
'Matthew Saul'	see *E.* 'Harvest Moon'
'Minstrel' **new**	LRHS
Orange MeadowbritePBR	see *E.* 'Art's Pride'
pallida	Widely available
- 'Hula Dancer'	CAby CSam EBee EPfP GMac NDov NPri SPhx WHil WWEG
paradoxa	Widely available
- 'Yellow Mellow'	EPfP LSRN
Pixie Meadowbrite = 'CBG Cone 2'	CAbP CDes CKno CWGN EBee EBrs ECtt IKil LRHS MTis NDov NSti WCot WCra
§ ***purpurea***	Widely available
- 'After Midnight'	CBcs ECtt LSou NCGa WCot
- 'Alaska'PBR	EBee LRHS NGdn NLar
- 'Alba'	EBla ECtt EShb GKir LBMP LRHS MNHC NVic
- 'Augustkönigin'	EBee EHrv NBir
- 'Avalanche'	LRHS MWea SBfd
- 'Baby Swan White'	CSam EBrs ELon LRHS MWea NLar STes WCot WHil WWEG
- Bressingham hybrids	EBla ELan LRHS MRav NCGa SPer SPhx WFar
- 'Coconut Lime'PBR	CBcs CBod CWGN EBee ECtt EPfP GKir LRHS LSou MWea NGHP NGdn NPnk SBfd SPhx SPoG SRkn SUsu WCAu WCot WCra WHlf
- Doppelganger	see *E. purpurea* 'Doubledecker'
§ - 'Doubledecker'	EBee ECtt EPfP LBMP LLHF LRHS MBNS MDKP NGHP NGdn SBfd SMad STes SWat WFar WHil WWEG
- Elton Knight = 'Elbrook' ♀H3	CKno CWCL EBee EKen IPot LFCN LRHS LSRN MBNS MBri MWea NGHP SDix SKHP SRkn SWvt WClo WCra
- 'Fancy Frills'	EBee EBla ECtt GAbr IPot LSou NGHP NGdn WCot
- 'Fatal Attraction'PBR	Widely available
- 'Fragrant Angel'PBR	CHid CKno CMac CWGN EBee EBla ECtt ELon EPfP GMac IPot LRHS LSRN LSou MAvo MCot MLLN MTis MWea NGHP SKHP SMrm SPhx SPoG SUsu SWat SWvt WCot WCra
- 'Hope'PBR	EBee IPot LRHS
- 'Indiaca'	NGHP SMrm WSpi
- 'Jade'	CKno CMea CWGN EBee EBrs ECtt EHrv EPfP GQue LPio LRHS LSRN LSou MBNS MCot NCGa NDov NEgg NGdn NPnk SPhx SUsu SWat WCAu WCot WWlt

- 'Kim's Knee High'^{PBR}	Widely available
- 'Kim's Mop Head'	CKno CMac EBee EBla EBrs ECtt EHrv ELon EPfP EWes GKir LRHS LSou MAsh MRav NLar NPnk SPoG WCot WFar WWEG
§ - 'Leuchtstern'	CKno EBee LRHS NBir NBre NGHP NGdn SWat WHal WMnd WWEG
- 'Lilliput'	LFCN
- 'Little Giant'	EBee
- 'Little Magnus'^{PBR}	EBee
- 'Magnus' ♀^{H4}	Widely available
- 'Mars' **new**	IPot
- 'Maxima'	CAbP EBee EBrs ECtt EHrv LPio LRHS MTis NDov WCot WFut WWEG
- 'Pica Bella'	EBee EBrs EPfP LRHS NDov NGdn NLar
- 'Pink Double Delight'^{PBR}	LHop LRHS MRav NCGa NGHP NGdn SWat WHlf WWEG
- 'Pink Glow' **new**	NDov
- 'Pink Poodle' **new**	SBfd
- 'Pink Shuttles'^{PBR}	SPhx
- 'Prairie Frost' (v)	NGHP
- 'Prairie Splendor'	EPfP SPoG
- 'Primadonna Deep Rose'	EBee ECGP NBre NGBl NGHP
- 'Primadonna White' **new**	CChe GMac
- 'Razzmatazz'^{PBR} (d)	Widely available
- 'Robert Bloom'	CAbP EBee EBla ECtt EHrv GQue LHop MCot MLLN MNFA NBir NGdn SMrm SWvt WCot WWEG
- 'Rubinglow'	CDes CElw CHar CWCL EBee EBla ECtt EHrv IBal IPot LSou MDKP NBir NDov NGHP NGdn NLar SPer SWvt WCot WCra
- 'Rubinstern' ♀^{H4}	Widely available
- 'Ruby Giant' ♀^{H4}	Widely available
- 'Sparkler' (v)	CWGN ECtt MBNS NLar WCot WFut
- 'The King'	EBee ECtt IBal MAvo NGHP NGdn
- 'Verbesserter Leuchtstern'	NBre NGHP NLar
- 'Vintage Wine'^{PBR}	Widely available
- 'White Lustre'	EBee ECha EPfP LPio NBre NMoo SPav SRms WFar
- White Natalie = 'Norwhinat'	NGHP
- 'White Swan'	Widely available
'Raspberry Tart'	IPot LRHS NLar SBfd
simulata	WCot
'Starlight'	see *E. purpurea* 'Leuchtstern'
§ 'Summer Sky' (Big Sky Series)	CPar CWCL CWGN EBrs ECtt GKir IPot LRHS LSou MBNS MTis NCGa NDov NGHP NPnk SPhx STes SUsu WCot WCra WFut
§ 'Sundown'^{PBR} (Big Sky Series)	Widely available
'Sunrise'^{PBR} (Big Sky Series)	Widely available
'Sunset'^{PBR} (Big Sky Series)	Widely available
tennesseensis	CArn WPGP
- 'Rocky Top'	CBcs CMac CMea EBee ECtt EHrv EPfP GMac IBal LRHS LSRN MNFA NBre NGHP NGdn SBfd SKHP SPhx SUsu WCot
'Tiki Torch'	CCVN CPar CWCL CWGN EBrs ECtt EWes IPot LRHS LSou MAvo MCot MTis NCGa NDov NSti SBfd SPoG STes SUsu WCot WCra WFut
'Tomato Soup' **new**	CWGN LSou MCot MTis NSti SBfd SPoG WFut
'Twilight'^{PBR} (Big Sky Series)	CPar CWCL EBee ECtt EPfP GQue IPot LFCN LRHS LSou MLLN MWea NDov NGHP NPnk SPhx SRkn WClo WCra WFut
'Virgin' **new**	IPot MAsh NDov SPhx

Echinocystis (*Cucurbitaceae*)

lobata **new**	CArn

Echinops (*Asteraceae*)

RCB AM -14	WCot
albus	see *E.* 'Nivalis'
babatagensis	EBee
§ ***bannaticus***	CBcs CSBt EBee GKir NBid WFar WWEG
* - 'Albus'	EPfP LAst MMuc NBre NGdn
- 'Blue Globe'	CMHG CSev EBee EHoe ELon EPfP EShb GCal GKir GMaP LAst LRHS LSRN MBri MGos NBPC NChi NGdn SBfd SCoo SMrm SPoG STes WFar WMnd WWEG
- 'Star Frost' **new**	GQue NBre
- 'Taplow Blue' ♀^{H4}	Widely available
commutatus	see *E. exaltatus*
§ ***exaltatus***	LPla NBir NBre
maracandicus	EBee GCal
§ 'Nivalis'	CBre EBee SEND WCAu
* ***perringii***	GCal
ritro misapplied	see *E. bannaticus*
§ ***ritro*** L. ♀^{H4}	Widely available
- subsp. ***ruthenicus*** ♀^{H4}	ECGP ELan IGor MRav NBre SUsu WPGP
- - 'Platinum Blue'	EBee GKir GQue LRHS NBPC NEgg NLar SPad SPet WCAu WMnd WPer
- 'Sea Stone'	EBee
- 'Veitch's Blue' misapplied	see *E. ritro* L.
- 'Veitch's Blue'	Widely available
sphaerocephalus	NBid NBir NBre SMrm SPlb
- 'Arctic Glow'	CMac CPou CSam EBee ECha ECtt EHoe ELan EPfP EShb GKir LAst LRHS MWhi NBro NGdn NLar NPri NVic SMrm SPer SPlb SWvt WCAu WFar WMnd WWEG
strigosus	EBee NBre
terscheckii	EAmu
tjanschanicus	CMea EWTr LRHS NBPC NMoo WWEG
tournefortii	GBin

Echium (*Boraginaceae*)

acanthocarpum	XPde
aculeatum	XPde
- 'Bicolor'	XPde
- 'Rosea'	XPde
amoenum	NWCA
'Blue Steeple' **new**	GKev WHil
boissieri	CCCN ELan XPde
brevirame	XPde
callithyrsum	XPde
§ ***candicans*** ♀$^{H2-3}$	CAbb CBcs CCCN CFir CHEx CTrC CTsd ECre EShb GGal IDee SAPC SArc WFar WSpi XPde
- 'Ciel'	XPde
- 'Death Star' (v)	CSpe
- 'Marine'	XPde
- 'Rouge'	XPde
decaisnei subsp. ***decaisnei***	XPde
famarae	XPde
fastuosum	see *E. candicans*
gentianoides	XPde
- 'Dark Globe'	XPde
- 'Maryvonne'	XPde
- 'Pablina'	XPde
giganteum	CHll XPde
handiense	XPde

italicum	CArn CCCN NLar SIde XPde
lusitanicum	CCCN
- subsp. ***polycaulon***	XPde
onosmifolium	CHll XPde
pininana 🏆H2-3	CAbb CBcs CDoC CHEx CPla CTrC CTsd CWit EAmu EBee ECre ELan EWll GAuc GGal IDee NVic SAPC SArc SBfd SBst SChr SDnm SEND SGar SIde SMad SPav XPde
- 'Snow Tower'	CCCN CDTJ CPla CTsd ELan SBst SMad XPde
'Pink Fountain'	CCCN CDTJ CPla ECre ELan MCot NLar SBst SMad XPde
plantagineum	CCCN XPde
rosulatum	CCCN XPde
russicum	CAby CCCN CSpe CTsd EBee GAuc IDee IFro LHop NBPC NChi NLar SDnm SIde SPad SPav SPhx SPlb WCot WPer XPde
simplex	CCCN WSpi XPde
strictum	CCCN XPde
sventenii	XPde
tuberculatum	CCCN SPhx WMoo XPde
vulgare	CArn CCCN EBWF ELan EOHP GPWP MHer MNHC NLar NMir NPri NSco SBch SIde WBrE WHer WHfH WJek
- 'Blue Bedder'	WSFF
- Drake's form	SGar SPhx
webbii	MMHG XPde
wildpretii 🏆H2-3	CBow CCCN CDTJ CPla ELan SBfd SMad XPde
- subsp. ***wildpretii***	SPav

Edgeworthia (*Thymelaeaceae*)

§ ***chrysantha***	CBcs CHGN CHll CPMA CWib EBee EPfP GBin GKir IDee LRHS MBri MGos NPal SBig SPer WCot WSHC WSpi
I - 'Grandiflora'	CPMA GBin IRar MBri MGos NLar NPal
§ - 'Red Dragon'	CPMA NLar
- f. ***rubra*** hort.	see *E. chrysantha* 'Red Dragon'
papyrifera	see *E. chrysantha*

Edraianthus (*Campanulaceae*)

croaticus	see *E. graminifolius*
dalmaticus	GKev
dinaricus	NMen WAbe
§ ***graminifolius***	ECho GKev NMen WFar WPat
owerinianus	CPBP GKev WAbe
§ ***pumilio*** 🏆H4	ECho GKev NMen SRms WAbe
§ ***serpyllifolius***	ECho NMen WPat
- 'Major'	NMen WAbe
tenuifolius	NBre
wettsteinii	GKev

Egeria (*Hydrocharitaceae*)

§ ***densa***	CBen

Ehretia (*Boraginaceae*)

anacua	CBcs
dicksonii	CBcs CHEx IArd WPGP

Ehrharta (*Poaceae*)

thunbergii	EPPr

Eichhornia (*Pontederiaceae*)

crassipes	CBen CWat LPBA MSKA MWts SCoo
- 'Major'	NPer

Elaeagnus ✿ (*Elaeagnaceae*)

angustifolia	CAgr CBcs CBot CDul EBee EMac EPfP LMaj MBlu MCoo MGos NLar NWea SPer SRms WDin WFar
- Caspica Group	see *E.* 'Quicksilver'
argentea	see *E. commutata*
§ ***commutata***	CBcs CBot CMac EBee ECrN EHoe EPfP EWTr LEdu LHop MBlu MMuc MWhi NLar SPer WDin WPen WSpi
- 'Zempin'	ECrN MAsh
§ × ***ebbingei***	Widely available
- 'Coastal Gold' (v)	CAbP CBcs CDoC CDul CSBt EBee EQua IVic LRHS LSRN MAsh MGos SLim SRms
- 'Gilt Edge' (v) 🏆H4	Widely available
* - 'Gold Flash'	LAst
- Gold Splash = 'Lannou' (v)	CDoC CTrC CWSG EBee EPfP EQua LRHS MAsh MBri SPoG SWvt
- 'Lemon Ice' (v)	NLar
- 'Limelight' (v)	Widely available
- 'Salcombe Seedling'	CCCN NLar
ebbingii 'Moonlight'	LRHS MBri
glabra	EPfP GGal
- 'Reflexa'	see *E.* × *reflexa*
macrophylla	CMac EPfP WMoo
multiflora	CDul NLar SPer
parvifolia	CCCN EBee
pungens	ERom NBir
- 'Argenteovariegata'	see *E. pungens* 'Variegata'
- 'Aureovariegata'	see *E. pungens* 'Maculata'
- 'Dicksonii' (v)	CBow CWib EBee LRHS NLar SLon SPer SRms WFar
- 'Forest Gold' (v)	ELan EPfP LRHS MAsh
- 'Frederici' (v)	CBcs CDoC CMHG CMac CTrC CWit EBee ECrN EHoe ELan EPfP EPla LAst LBMP LHop LRHS MAsh MRav SPer SPoG SWvt WAbe WBor WDin WPat
- 'Goldrim' (v) 🏆H4	EPfP MGos SLim WDin WMoo
- 'Hosuba-fukurin' (v)	LLHF LRHS SLon SPoG
§ - 'Maculata' (v)	Widely available
§ - 'Variegata' (v)	CBcs CMac EPla EQua NBir SPer
§ 'Quicksilver' 🏆H4	Widely available
§ × ***reflexa***	CBcs EPla WPGP
× ***submacrophylla***	see *E.* × *ebbingei*
umbellata	CBcs CPLG EBee EMac EPfP EWTr MAsh MBlu NLar SPer WSHC
- 'Big Red' (F)	CAgr
- var. ***borealis*** 'Polar Lights'	MBri NLar
- 'Brilliant Rose' (F)	CAgr
- 'Hidden Springs' (F)	CAgr
- 'Jewel' (F)	CAgr
- 'Newgate' (F)	CAgr
- 'Red Cascade' (F)	CAgr
- 'Sweet 'n' Tart' (F)	CAgr

Elatostema (*Urticaceae*)

rugosum	CHEx

elderberry see *Sambucus nigra*

Elegia (*Restionaceae*)

capensis	CAbb CBct CCCN CDTJ CDoC CFir CHEx CPen CTrC EAmu EBee ESwi ETod GBin IDee LTen MAvo SPlb WDyG WPGP
spathacea	CFir

Eleocharis (*Cyperaceae*)

acicularis	CWat MSKA WPnP
palustris	CRWN EBWF

Eleorchis (*Orchidaceae*)

japonica new — NLAp WWst
* - f. ***alba*** new — WWst

Elettaria (*Zingiberaceae*)

cardamomum — CArn EOHP EShb GPoy LEdu SBfd SHDw WJek

Eleutherococcus (*Araliaceae*)

aff. ***cissifolius*** BWJ 7713 — WCru
hypoleucus B&SWJ 5532 — WCru
nakaianus B&SWJ 5027 — WCru
pictus — see *Kalopanax septemlobus*
senticosus — GPoy
- B&SWJ 4568 — WCru
septemlobus — see *Kalopanax septemlobus*
sessiliflorus B&SWJ 4528 — WCru
- B&SWJ 8457 — WCru
sieboldianus — CBcs MGos MMuc MRav SEND WDin WFar
- 'Variegatus' (v) — CBcs CBot EBee EHoe ELan ELon EPfP EQua GBin LAst MGos MRav NEgg NLar NMun WHer WSHC
trifoliatus RWJ 10108 — WCru

Elingamita (*Myrsinaceae*)

johnsonii — ECou

Elisena (*Amaryllidaceae*)

longipetala — see *Hymenocallis longipetala*

Elliottia (*Ericaceae*)

bracteata — see *Tripetaleia bracteata*
* ***paniculata latifolia*** — IVic

Ellisiophyllum (*Scrophulariaceae*)

pinnatum — CDes EBee WBor WCot WPGP
- B&SWJ 197 — WCru WPrP

Elmera (*Saxifragaceae*)

racemosa — EDif

Elodea (*Hydrocharitaceae*)

canadensis — MSKA NBir WMAq
crispa — see *Lagarosiphon major*
densa — see *Egeria densa*

Elsholtzia (*Lamiaceae*)

fruticosa — CArn
stauntonii — CArn CBcs CBot CMHG EBee ECha GBin IDee IVic LRHS MHer MMuc SBch SEND SPer SPoG WBor
- 'Alba' — CArn CBot

Elymus (*Poaceae*)

arenarius — see *Leymus arenarius*
canadensis — CRWN EHoe EPPr WBox
- f. ***glaucifolius*** — CFir GCal
cinereus from Washington State, USA — EBee WPGP
elongatus — SApp
glaucus misapplied — see *E. hispidus*
§ ***hispidus*** — CMoH EHoe EPPr EPau MBlu MBri MLHP MMoz SPer WCFE WCot
§ ***magellanicus*** — Widely available
- 'Blue Sword' — LRHS MGos NBPC SRms WPtf
riparius — EPPr
sibiricus — EPPr
solandri — EHoe EWes GFor
- JCA 5.345.500 — WPGP
villosus — EPPr MAvo
- var. ***arkansanus*** — EPPr
virginicus — EBee EPPr

Elytrigia (*Poaceae*)

atherica — EBWF

Embothrium ✿ (*Proteaceae*)

coccineum — CBcs CDoy CGHE CPne CTri EBee EPfP GKev MGos MPhe SPlb WBrE WPGP WPat
- Lanceolatum Group — CAby CDoC CDul CEnd CHid EBee ELan ELon EPfP GGar GKev LRHS MBlu MDun MMuc SAPC SArc SBfd SLim SMad SPer SSpi SSta WAbe WDin
- - 'Inca Flame' — CBcs CCCN CDoC CPMA ELan ELon EPfP MAsh MGos NCGa NLar SBfd SPoG SSta SWvt
* - - 'Inca King' — EBee
- - 'Ñorquinco' ♀^{H3} — CBcs CDoC GGal GGar
- Longifolium Group — CCCN GGal IBlr MMHG WPGP

Eminium (*Araceae*)

albertii — ECho

Emmenopterys (*Rubiaceae*)

henryi — CBcs CCCN CGHE EBee EPfP EWTr IArd IFFs MBlu NLar WPGP

Empetrum (*Empetraceae*)

nigrum — GAuc GPoy WThu
rubrum 'Tomentosum' — WThu

Empodium (*Hypoxidaceae*)

plicatum — ECho

Enantiophylla (*Apiaceae*)

B&SWJ 10318 from Guatemala — WCru
heydeana B&SWJ 9114 — WCru

Enceliopsis (*Asteraceae*)

covillei NNS 04-136 — WCot

Encephalartos ✿ (*Zamiaceae*)

altensteinii — CBrP
caffer — CBrP
cycadifolius — CBrP LPal
ferox — CBrP
friderici-guilielmi — CBrP
ghellinckii — LPal
horridus — CBrP
kisambo — LPal
lanatus — CBrP
lebomboensis — CBrP
lehmannii — CBrP LPal
natalensis — CBrP LPal
senticosus — LPal
umbeluziensis — CBrP
villosus — CBrP LPal

Endymion see *Hyacinthoides*

Enkianthus ✿ (*Ericaceae*)

campanulatus ♀^{H4} — Widely available
- var. ***campanulatus*** f. ***albiflorus*** — CBcs LTen NLar
I - 'Hollandia' — CBcs MBri
- var. ***palibinii*** — CBcs EPfP GGGa MAsh MGos NLar SSpi SSta WBrE

	- 'Red Bells'	CBcs CDoC CDul CMac EPfP GBin GKev IArd LRHS MAsh MGos MMHG NLar SPoG SSpi SSta SWvt WFar
	- 'Red Velvet'	CBcs IArd NLar
	- 'Ruby Glow'	CBcs IVic MBri NLar
	- var. ***sikokianus***	EPfP GGGa NLar
	- 'Tokyo Masquerade'	CPMA
*	- 'Variegatus' (v)	LRHS MAsh SPoG
	- 'Venus'	CBcs IArd NLar
	- 'Victoria'	CBcs NLar
	- 'Wallaby'	CBcs NLar WAbe
	cernuus	GKir
	- f. ***rubens*** ♀H4	CBcs EPfP GBin GGGa NBea NLar WDin
	chinensis	EPfP GGGa LRHS MAsh
	deflexus	CMCN MAsh SSpi WPGP
	- GWJ 9225	WCru
	perulatus ♀H4	CDul CMac EBee EPfP GBin GKir IFFs LRHS MGos MRav SSpi WFar

Ensete (*Musaceae*)

	gilletii	XBlo
	glaucum	CDTJ EAmu EUJe GCal NExo SBst WCot
	superbum	NExo
§	***ventricosum*** ♀H1+3	CBot CCCN CDTJ CDoC CHll EAmu EUJe LPal LSou NExo SAPC SArc SBst SChr SEND XBlo
	- from Uganda	GCal
§	- 'Maurelii'	CBrP CCCN CDTJ CDoC CHEx CHll CSpe CTsd EAmu ESwi EUJe LRHS NPla SAPC SArc SDix SEND SPad SPer SPoG WCot WPGP
	- 'Montbeliardii'	EAmu EUJe
	- 'Rubrum'	see *E. ventricosum* 'Maurelii'
	- 'Tandarra Red'	CAbb CDoC CWit EBee EUJe LSou

Entelea (*Tiliaceae*)

arborescens	CHEx ECou EShb

Eomecon (*Papaveraceae*)

chionantha	CAby CDes CFir CHEx CHid CPLG CSam CSpe CYeo EBee ECho EHrv GAbr GCal GCra LEdu MLHP MRav MWhi NBid SMad SMrm WFar WHer WMoo WPGP WWEG

Epacris (*Epacridaceae*)

longiflora	SOWG
paludosa	ECou
serpyllifolia	ECou WThu

Ephedra (*Ephedraceae*)

	sp.	SAPC SArc
	chilensis 'Mellow Yellow'	EBee
	- 'Quite White'	EBee
	distachya	GPoy
	equisetina	IFro
	gerardiana	EBee GEdr IFro
	- var. ***sikkimensis***	WOld
	intermedia RCB/TQ K-1	WCot
§	***major***	WHer
	minima	GEdr NWCA WThu
	minuta	CKen MSCN
	nebrodensis	see *E. major*
	nevadensis	CArn GPoy NMun
	sinica	CArn GEdr GPoy
	viridis	CArn

Epigaea (*Ericaceae*)

gaultherioides	GGGa

Epilobium (*Onagraceae*)

	angustifolium	see *Chamerion angustifolium*
	- f. ***leucanthum***	see *Chamerion angustifolium* 'Album'
	californicum misapplied	see *Zauschneria californica*
	canum	see *Zauschneria californica* subsp. *cana*
	dodonaei	see *Chamerion dodonaei*
	garrettii	see *Zauschneria californica* subsp. *garrettii*
N	***glabellum*** misapplied	CSpe MWat NSla SPhx SUsu WCFE WEas WWlt
	hirsutum	EBWF
	- 'Album'	WAlt
	- 'Caerphilly Castle' (d)	WAlt
	- 'Spring Lime'	WAlt
	- 'Well Creek' (v)	WAlt WHrl
	microphyllum	see *Zauschneria californica* subsp. *cana*
	rosmarinifolium	see *Chamerion dodonaei*
	septentrionale	see *Zauschneria septentrionalis*
	villosum	see *Zauschneria californica* subsp. *mexicana*

Epimedium ✿ (*Berberidaceae*)

sp.	IFoB
from Yunnan, China	CDes CLAP CPom
acuminatum	CDes CElw CFir CGHE CLAP CMoH CPLG EBee EFEx LEdu LPio MNrw SUsu WPGP WSHC
- L 575	EHrv
- 'Galaxy'	CDes CLAP CMil CPMA EBee
'Akakage'	CLAP EBee
'Akebono'	CDes CLAP CMil CPMA EBee EPPr IFoB NLar WCon
alpinum	CMac EBee EBla EPPr GEdr GKir NHol WMoo
'Amanogawa'	CDes CLAP CPMA CPom IFoB
'Amber Queen' PBR	CLAP EBee EPPr EWTr GEdr LLHF LPio NCob NPnk SMHy SPhx WCAu
'Arctic Wings' new	EBee GEdr
'Asiatic hybrid'	CElw CLAP CPMA WHal WPnP
'Beni-kujaku'	CDes CLAP CPMA EBee GEdr
'Beni-yushima'	GEdr
'Black Sea'	CLAP CPMA CSpe EBee EHrv LHop MAvo MNrw NCGa NLar
brachyrrhizum	CDes CLAP CMil CPLG CPMA CPom EBee GEdr LLHF WPGP
brevicornu	CLAP CPMA CPom WPGP
- Og 82.010	EBee
'Buckland Spider'	CDes CLAP EBee EPPr MNrw WPGP
campanulatum	CGHE CPMA LLHF
× ***cantabrigiense***	CMac ECtt EPla GEdr GGar GMaP MRav NBre NHol SPur WPnP WWEG
chlorandrum	CDes CLAP EBee IFoB LEdu SUsu WPGP
creeping yellow	MBri MSCN
cremeum	see *E. grandiflorum* subsp. *koreanum*
davidii	CDes CGHE CMoH CPLG CPMA EBee GEdr LEdu MNFA MNrw NLar SKHP WFar WHal WPGP WSHC
- EMR 4125	CElw CLAP EHrv
diphyllum	CAby CGHE CPom EBee EHrv ELan NDov WBVN WHal
- 'White Splash'	GEdr
dolichostemon	CElw CLAP CPMA

ecalcaratum	CAby CDes CLAP CMil CPLG CPMA CPom EBee MNrw WPGP
elongatum	CLAP GEdr
'Emperor' **new**	CDes
'Enchantress'	CLAP CMil CPMA CPom ECha EHrv EWld IFoB MNrw SAga SKHP WHal
epsteinii	CAby CDes CLAP CMil CPLG CPMA CPom EBee EPPr LLHF MNrw WPGP
fangii	CPLG
fargesii	CDes CMil CPLG EBee EHrv GEdr MNrw WCot WPGP
- 'Pink Constellation'	CDes CLAP CPMA CPom EBee SBch WPGP
'Fire Dragon'PBR	CLAP EPPr EPfP GEdr LLHF
flavum	CDes CLAP CPMA EBee EHrv SKHP WPGP
franchetii	CFir CGHE CPLG SKHP
- 'Brimstone Butterfly'	CDes CLAP CPLG CPMA EBee EPPr MAvo WHoo WPGP
'Fukujuji'	CLAP EBee GEdr
'Golden Eagle'	CBow CDes CLAP CPLG CPMA CPom EBee EWes EWld MNrw
§ ***grandiflorum*** ♀H4	CBcs CElw CPla CTri CYeo EBee EHrv ELan ELon EPfP EWTr GEdr GKir LBMP NBir NLar NMen NPnk SPer WFar WPnP WPtf WWEG
- 'Album'	CLAP EBee
- 'Beni-chidori'	CLAP EBee GEdr
- 'Crimson Beauty'	CLAP CPMA MRav WHal WHoo WSHC
- 'Crimson Queen'	CBow CDes IFoB WPGP
- 'Freya'	CDes
§ - var. ***higoense***	CDes CPMA EBee GEdr WHal
- 'Jennie Maillard'	SUsu
- 'Koji'	CLAP NLar WSHC
§ - subsp. ***koreanum***	CLAP CPla ECha EFEx
- 'La Rocaille'	CDes CLAP EBee
- lilac-flowered	CLAP WFar WHal
- lilac-pink-flowered **new**	SMHy
- 'Lilafee'	Widely available
- 'Mount Kitadake'	CLAP
- 'Nanum' ♀H4	CDes CMil CPMA CPom EBee ECho EHrv EWld GCrs GKir MNrw NMen NWCA WAbe WPGP
- pink-flowered	EHrv
- 'Purple Prince'	CDes CLAP
- 'Queen Esta'	CDes CLAP CPMA MAvo MNrw WPGP
- 'Red Beauty'	CLAP NLar SBfd
- 'Rose Queen' ♀H4	CAby CMMP CSam EBee ECha EHrv ELan EPfP GEdr GGar GMaP MAvo MBri MRav NBir NMyG NSti SPoG SUsu SWvt WMoo WWEG
- 'Roseum'	CLAP CMac CMil NMen SGSe SWvt
- 'Rubinkrone'	EBee GEdr GMaP MNrw
- 'Sirius'	CLAP CPMA EBee MNrw
- f. ***violaceum***	CLAP CPMA WSHC
- 'White Beauty'	WSHC
- 'White Queen' ♀H4	CElw CFir CPMA EBee EHrv EPPr MRav NMyG SMHy WHal
- 'Wildside Red'	CPMA
- 'Yellow Princess'	CDes CElw CLAP CPMA
- 'Yubae'	EBee GEdr IFoB WWst
'Hagoromo'	EBee
'Hakubai'	EBee GEdr
'Harugasumi' **new**	GEdr
higoense	see *E. grandiflorum* var. *higoense*
ilicifolium	CDes EBee WPGP
'Jean O'Neill'	CDes EBee LEdu WPGP
'Jenny Pym'	EBee
'Kaguyahime'	CBow CLAP CMil CPMA EHrv EPPr IFoB WCon
'Koki'	EBee GEdr
latisepalum	CAby CBow CDes CLAP CMil CPMA CPom EBee EHrv GEdr LEdu MNrw NLar WCot WPGP
leptorrhizum	CAby CDes CElw CGHE CLAP CPLG CPMA EBee EHrv EPPr EWTr GCrs MAvo MNFA MNrw NCGa NHar NMyG SKHP SUsu WCom WHal WSHC
- 'Mariko'	CDes CLAP CMil CPMA CPom
lishihchenii	CDes CLAP WPGP
'Little Shrimp'	CPMA CTri EBee LLHF MNFA MNrw NLar SUsu WPat
macranthum	see *E. grandiflorum*
membranaceum	CFir CGHE CLAP CPMA EBee EPPr GEdr LLHF SUsu WHal WPGP
mikinorii	CPom
myrianthum	CBow CDes CPMA WPGP
ogisui	CAby CDes CLAP CMil CPLG CPMA CPom EBee EHrv SKHP SMHy WPGP WThu
§ × ***omeiense*** 'Akame'	CAby CBow CDes CGHE CLAP CMil CPLG CPMA EBee EPPr WPGP
- 'Emei Shan'	see *E.* × *omeiense* 'Akame'
- 'Myriad Years'	CLAP
- 'Pale Fire'	EWld
- 'Pale Fire Sibling'	CDes CPMA CPom
- 'Stormcloud'	CDes CGHE CLAP CMil CPLG CPMA CPom EBee EPPr MNrw WPGP
pauciflorum	CHid CLAP CPMA EPPr NHar NMyG
× ***perralchicum*** ♀H4	CMac CPMA CTri ECha GKev GKir LRHS MLHP NLar SGar SLPl WBVN WPnP WSHC
- 'Fröhnleiten'	Widely available
- 'Lichtenberg'	CDes SUsu
- 'Wisley'	CElw CPMA CSam EHrv EWes
perralderianum	CHEx CMac CSam EBee ELan GEdr GMaP MCot MLLN MNrw SMrm SRms WHal WHoo WPnP
- 'Weihenstephan'	MMoz WPnP
'Pink Elf'PBR	EBee EPfP EWTr LLHF NBPC NCob NPnk NSti
pinnatum	ECho GMaP WHal
§ - subsp. ***colchicum*** ♀H4	CLAP CMac CPMA CPom CWCL EBee ELan EPfP EUJe EWTr GAbr GBBs GEdr LRHS MCot MRav NGdn NHol NLar NWsh SBfd SDix SPoG WCot WFar WHoo WPGP WPnP WTin WWEG
- - L 321	CDes
- ***elegans***	see *E. pinnatum* subsp. *colchicum*
platypetalum	CBow CLAP CPMA SMHy WCot WPGP
pubescens	CMil CPMA EBee EHrv IFoB
pubigerum	CPMA CSam EBee ECha EHrv EWTr GAbr GEdr GKir NHol NMRc NMyG NPri SBfd SWvt WCAu WHal WPtf WSpi WWEG
rhizomatosum	CAby CLAP EBee EPPr LLHF WCot WPGP WSHC
- Og 92.114	CPMA
× ***rubrum*** ♀H4	Widely available
sagittatum	CLAP EFEx
'Sakura-maru'	EBee GEdr
'Sasaki'	CLAP EBee GEdr MBri NHar NLar NMyG
sempervirens	CLAP CPMA EBee WHal
- 'Cream Sickle'	EBee

- 'Okuda's White' **new**	CDes
- var. ***sempervirens***	CLAP
× ***setosum***	CPMA CPom EBee ECha EHrv NLar WHal
stellulatum 'Wudang Star'	CDes CGHE CLAP CMil CPLG CPMA CPom EHrv EWes GEdr IFoB IMou WPGP WSpi
sutchuenense	CLAP
'Suzuka'	CBow GEdr LEdu
'Tama-no-genpei'	CPMA CPom
× ***versicolor***	CBow CPLG LRHS
- 'Cherry Tart' **new**	CLAP
- 'Cupreum'	CLAP CPMA CPom EBee SBfd WCAu
§ - 'Discolor'	CDes CLAP CPom EBla ECha EHrv EPPr EWld NBir SMHy
- 'Neosulphureum'	CDes CLAP CMMP EBee EPPr SLPl WPGP WThu
- 'Sulphureum' ♀H4	Widely available
- 'Versicolor'	see *E.* × *versicolor* 'Discolor'
× ***warleyense***	Widely available
- 'Orangekönigin'	CElw CMoH CPom CWCL EBee EBla ELon GBBs LBMP LHop LPio LSRN MBri MCot MMuc MNrw MRav NBro NLar NMyG NSti SBfd SEND WBor WCAu WFar WHal WPnP
'William Stearn'	CLAP CPMA
wushanense	CLAP CMil CPMA EPPr LEdu
- 'Caramel'	CAby CBow CDes CLAP CMil CPLG CPMA CPom EBee EHrv LEdu WPGP WSHC
× ***youngianum***	CMac NEgg
- 'Merlin'	CLAP CMil CPMA EBee ECha EHrv EPfP GEdr IFoB MBri NLar NMyG NSti WHal
- 'Niveum' ♀H4	Widely available
- 'Roseum'	Widely available
- 'Shikinomai'	CLAP CPMA
- 'Tamabotan'	CBow CDes CLAP EBee MNrw MRav
§ - 'Typicum'	CLAP EBee WSHC
- white-flowered	NMen
- 'Yenomoto'	CLAP CPMA
- 'Youngianum'	see *E.* × *youngianum* 'Typicum'

Epipactis (*Orchidaceae*)

gigantea	Widely available
gigantea × ***veratrifolia***	see *E.* Lowland Legacy gx
helleborine	WHer
§ **Lowland Legacy gx**	NLAp
- 'Irène'	WWst
mairei	WWst
palustris	CPrp EBee EBla ECho GEdr MREP NDav NLAp NLar NPnk NWCA WHer WPnP WPrP
Renate **gx**	GCrs WWst
royleana	CAby
Sabine gx	CAby GEdr NLAp WFar WWst
- 'Frankfurt'	NMen
thunbergii	EBee EFEx GEdr NLAp WWst
- yellow-flowered	GEdr WWst
veratrifolia	WWst

Epipremnum (*Araceae*)

§ ***aureum*** ♀H1	MBri
§ ***pinnatum***	MBri
- 'Marble Queen' (v)	XBlo

Episcia (*Gesneriaceae*)

dianthiflora	SRms WDib
'San Miguel'	WDib

Equisetum ✿ (*Equisetaceae*)

arvense	CArn
'Bandit' (v)	CBow CNat MSKA SMad WMoo
× ***bowmanii***	CNat
* ***camtschatcense***	CBgR CDes EBee EPPr ETod SBig SMad
× ***dycei***	CNat
fluviatile	CNat EBee MSKA NLar
hyemale	CChe CKno CTrC EHoe EPfP EPla MSCN MSKA MWts NOak NPer NSti SAPC SArc SPlb WDyG WFar WMoo WPnP WPrP
§ - var. ***affine***	CBgR CHid CNat CRow EBee ELan EPla EWll LEdu LSou MBlu MSKA MWts NPnk NVic SMad WMAq WOld
- var. ***robustum***	see *E. hyemale* var. *affine*
pratense	CNat
ramosissimum	CNat
- var. ***japonicum***	EBee LEdu LPBA MCCP NPla SWat WPnP
robustum	CTrC
scirpoides	CTrC EBee EFer EHoe EPfP LPBA MCCP MSKA NHol NLar NPer SPlb SWat WMAq WMoo WPnP WPrP
sylvaticum	CNat
telmateia	CNat SMad
variegatum	EBee EFer EWll

Eragrostis (*Poaceae*)

sp.	EBee
RCB/Arg S-7	WCot
airoides misapplied	see *Agrostis montevidensis*
airoides ambig.	CHar EKen GAbr WMnd WMoo
chloromelas	EPPr WPGP
curvula	Widely available
- S&SH 10	WPGP
- 'Totnes Burgundy'	CAby CDes CKno CPLG CPen CWCL EBee ECha EHoe EPPr LEdu MAvo MMoz MNrw NOak SMea SPhx SRms SUsu WHal WHrl WMoo WPGP WPrP WWEG
elliottii	CKno CWit EBee ECha EPPr GFor LBMP LHop LRHS MAvo MMuc MWea NBPC NCGa SBfd SEND SHDw SMea WFar WHrl WWEG
- 'Wind Dancer'	EPPr
'Silver Needles'	see *Agrostis canina* 'Silver Needles'
spectabilis	CFir CKno CSBt EBee EBrs EPfP GFor LBMP LRHS MDKP MMHG MMuc MWea MWhi NBPC NGdn NLar SBfd SMad SMrm SPur SWal WClo WFar WMoo WWEG
trichodes	CFir CKno EBee EHoe LEdu LRHS NBPC NBre SMad SUsu WHrl WPer

Eranthemum (*Acanthaceae*)

pulchellum ♀H1	ECre

Eranthis (*Ranunculaceae*)

cilicica	see *E. hyemalis* Cilicica Group
§ ***hyemalis*** ♀H4	Widely available
§ - Cilicica Group	ECho EHrv ELan EPot ERCP GKev GMaP LAma LRHS NLar SDeJ SPhx WRHF
- 'Flore Pleno' (d)	ECho
- 'Grünling' **new**	ECho
- 'Schwefelglanz' **new**	ECho EPot
§ - Tubergenii Group	ECho EPot WAbe WWst
- - 'Guinea Gold' ♀H4	CTca ECho
pinnatifida	ECho EFEx GEdr WCru WWst

	× ***tubergenii***	see *E. hyemalis* Tubergenii Group

Ercilla (*Phytolaccaceae*)

	volubilis	CPLG CRHN CWGN EBee EWes LHop NSti WCru WSHC

Eremophila (*Myoporaceae*)

	bignoniiflora	SOWG
§	***debilis***	ECou
	glabra 'Burgundy'	SOWG
	- orange-flowered	ECou
	'Kilbara Carpet'	ECou SOWG
	longifolia **new**	SPlb
	maculata	ECou
	- var. ***brevifolia***	SOWG
	- pale pink-flowered	SOWG
	- 'Peaches and Cream'	SOWG
*	'Summer Blue'	SOWG
	'Yellow Trumpet'	ECou

Eremurus (*Asphodelaceae*)

	altaicus JCA 0.443.809	WCot
	'Brutus'	EBee LAma
	bungei	see *E. stenophyllus* subsp. *stenophyllus*
	cristatus JCA 0.444.029	WCot
	'Disco'	EBee
	'Emmy Ro'	EBee LAma WCot
	fuscus JCA 0.444.043	WCot
	'Grace' **new**	LAma
	'Helena'	EBee LAma MNrw
	himalaicus	CAvo CBot CMea CTca EBee EHrv ELan EPot ERCP LAma LAst MHer NLar SDeJ SPer SPhx WWEG
	'Image'	EBee LRHS
	× ***isabellinus*** 'Cleopatra'	CAvo CMea CSWP CTca CWGN EBee EBrs EHrv ELon EPot ERCP GMaP LAma LRHS MBNS MGos MHer NMoo SBfd SDeJ SPad SPoG WWEG
	- 'Obelisk'	EBee ELan ERCP LAma
	- 'Pinokkio'	CAvo CMea EBee EBrs EPot LAma LRHS MHer SDeJ SPer
	- Ruiter hybrids	CMea CSWP EBee ELan EPfP GMaP LAma LAst LRHS MGos MNrw MWat SPer SPet SPhx SPoG WBVN WClo WFar
	- Shelford hybrids	CAvo CBcs EBee ELan LAma MNrw SDeJ SPhx WBVN
	- 'Tropical Dream'	EBee
	'Jeanne-Claire'	EBee LAma NLar
	'Joanna'	EBee LAma LSRN NLar WCot
	lactiflorus	EBee
	'Line Dance'	EBee ELon LAma
	'Luca Ro'	EBee
	'Moneymaker'	EBee LAma LRHS
	'Oase'	CTca EBee EHrv ELan EWll LAma WWEG
	'Paradiso'	EBee LRHS
	regelii JCA 444.083	WCot
	'Rexona'	EBee EWll LAma MBNS SDeJ
	robustus ♀^{H4}	CAvo CBcs CBot CMea CTca EBee EBrs EHrv ELan EPot ERCP EWTr LAma LAst LRHS MAvo MHer MNrw NLar SDeJ SPhx SPlb WFar WWEG
	'Roford'	EBee LAma MNrw NMoo
	'Romance'	CAvo CTca EBee ELon EPot ERCP EWll LAma LRHS MBNS MNrw NLar NMRc SPhx WWEG
	'Rumba'	CMea EBee LAma NLar
	'Samba'	EBee LAma
	sogdianus	EBee
	spectabilis	EBee
	stenophyllus ♀^{H4}	CTca CTri CWib EPot ERCP LHop MWat SBfd SDeJ SMrm SPhx SPoG WCot WFar WWEG
§	- subsp. ***stenophyllus***	CAvo CBcs CFox EBee EHrv EPfP GMaP LAma LRHS MHer MNrw NBPC NLBP NPer NPri SPer WBVN WFar
	'Tap Dance'	EBee LAma
	'Yellow Giant'	EBee
	zenaidae	WCot

Erianthus see *Saccharum*

Eriastrum (*Polemoniaceae*)

	densifolium 'Tetra Riesen' NNS 05-271	WCot

Erica ✿ (*Ericaceae*)

	abietina subsp. ***aurantiaca***	CDes
	aestiva **new**	SPlb
	'African Fanfare'	SHeS
	× ***afroeuropaea***	SHeS
	alopecurus	SPlb
	arborea	GAbr IRar SPlb
	- var. ***alpina*** ♀^{H4}	CDoC CTri EPfP LRHS NHol SHeS SPer SPoG SRms SSpi SWhi
§	- - 'Albert's Gold' ♀^{H4}	CBcs CSBt CTri ELan EPfP LRHS MAsh MBri MGos MSwo NHol SHeS SPer SPoG SRms SWhi WFar
	- 'Arbora Gold'	see *E. arborea* var. *alpina* 'Albert's Gold'
	- 'Arnold's Gold'	see *E. arborea* var. *alpina* 'Albert's Gold'
	- 'Estrella Gold' ♀^{H4}	CBcs CDoC CSBt CTri ELan EPfP IVic MAsh MGos NHol SBfd SHeS SLon SPer SPoG SRms SWhi
	- 'Great Star'	SBfd
	- 'Picos Pygmy'	SHeS
	- 'Spanish Lime'	SHeS
	- 'Spring Smile'	SHeS
	australis f. ***albiflora*** 'Mr Robert' ♀^{H3}	EPfP SHeS
	- 'Castellar Blush'	SHeS
	- 'Holehird'	SHeS
	- 'Riverslea' ♀^{H4}	CTri GCal GGar LRHS SHeS SPoG SWhi
	caffra	SHeS SPlb
	canaliculata ♀^{H3}	CBcs SHeS
	carnea	ELan
	- 'Accent'	SHeS
	- 'Adrienne Duncan' ♀^{H4}	NHol SHeS
	- 'Alan Coates'	SHeS
	- f. ***alba*** 'C.J. Backhouse'	SHeS
	- - 'Cecilia M. Beale'	SHeS
	- - 'Golden Starlet' ♀^{H4}	CSBt CTri EPfP MGos NHol NPri SHeS SPer SRms SWhi
	- - 'Ice Princess' ♀^{H4}	EPfP NHol SCoo SHeS SPer SRms SWhi
	- - 'Isabell' ♀^{H4}	CBcs EPfP NPri SCoo SHeS SRms SWhi
	- - Madame Seedling	see *E. carnea* f. *alba* 'Weisse March Seedling'
	- - 'Romance'	SHeS
	- - 'Rosalinde Schorn'	SHeS
	- - 'Schneekuppe'	SHeS
	- - 'Schneesturm'	SHeS SRms
	- - 'Snow Prince'	SHeS
	- - 'Snow Queen'	SHeS
	- - 'Springwood White' ♀^{H4}	CSBt CTri EPfP MGos MSwo NHol SHeS SPer SRms SWhi

§ - - 'Weisse March Seedling'	SHeS
- - 'Whitehall'	NHol SHeS SRms SWhi
- - 'Winter Snow'	CSBt SCoo SHeS SRms
I - 'Alba'	SHeS
- 'Amy Doncaster'	see *E. carnea* 'Treasure Trove'
- 'Ann Sparkes' ♀H4	CSBt CTri EPfP MSwo NHol SHeS SRms SWhi
- 'Atrorubra'	SHeS
- f. ***aureifolia*** 'Altadena'	SHeS
- - 'Aurea'	NHol SHeS SRms
- - 'Barry Sellers'	SHeS
§ - - 'Bell's Extra Special'	EPfP SHeS
- - 'Foxhollow' ♀H4	CBcs CTri EPfP IArd MGos MSwo NHol SHeS SRms SWhi
- - 'Gelber Findling'	SHeS
- - 'Gelderingen Gold'	SHeS
- - 'Hilletje'	SHeS SRms
- - 'January Sun'	SHeS
- - 'Moonlight'	SHeS
- - 'Netherfield Orange'	SHeS
- - 'Sunshine Rambler' ♀H4	SHeS
- - 'Tybesta Gold'	SHeS
- - 'Westwood Yellow' ♀H4	CSBt MGos NHol SHeS SPer SRms SWhi
- - 'Winter Gold'	SHeS
- 'Beoley Pink'	SHeS
I - 'Carnea'	SHeS
- 'Catherine Kolster'	SHeS
- 'Challenger' ♀H4	EPfP MGos NHol SCoo SHeS SPer SRms SWhi
- 'Christine Fletcher'	SHeS
- 'Clare Wilkinson'	SHeS
- 'David's Seedling'	SHeS
- 'December Red'	CSBt EPfP MSwo NHol SHeS SPer SRms SWhi
- 'Diana Young' **new**	SWhi
- 'Dømmesmoen'	SHeS
- 'Dwingeloo Pride'	SHeS
- 'Early Red'	SHeS
- 'Eileen Porter'	NHol SHeS
- 'Eva'	CBcs IVic SHeS
- 'Foxhollow Fairy'	SHeS SRms
- 'Gracilis'	SHeS
- 'Hamburg'	SHeS
- 'Heathwood'	NHol SCoo SHeS SRms
- 'Jack Stitt'	SHeS
- 'James Backhouse'	CTri SHeS
- 'Jason Attwater'	SHeS
- 'Jean'	SHeS
- 'Jennifer Anne'	SHeS
- 'John Kampa'	NHol SHeS
- 'John Pook'	SHeS
- 'King George'	CTri NHol SHeS SWhi
§ - 'Kramer's Rubin'	SHeS
- 'Lake Garda'	SHeS
- 'Late Pink'	SHeS
- 'Lena'	see *E. × darleyensis* 'Lena'
- 'Lesley Sparkes'	CSBt SHeS
- 'Little Peter'	SHeS
- 'Lohse's Rubin'	IVic NHol SHeS
- 'Lohse's Rubinfeuer'	SHeS
- 'Lohse's Rubinschimmer'	SHeS
- 'Loughrigg' ♀H4	CSBt CTri NHol SHeS SRms
- 'March Seedling'	EPfP NHol NPri SHeS SRms SWhi
- 'Margery Frearson'	SHeS
I - 'Martin'	SHeS
- 'Mrs Sam Doncaster'	SHeS
- 'Myretoun Ruby' ♀H4	CBcs CSBt CTri EPfP MGos NHol NPri SHeS SPer SRms SWhi
- 'Nathalie' ♀H4	CSBt IVic MSwo NHol SCoo SHeS SRms SWhi
- 'Oriënt'	SHeS SRms
- 'Pallida'	SHeS
- 'Pink Beauty'	see *E. carnea* 'Pink Pearl'
- 'Pink Cloud'	SHeS
- 'Pink Mist'	SHeS SPer SRms SWhi
§ - 'Pink Pearl'	SHeS
- 'Pink Spangles' ♀H4	CBcs CSBt CTri MGos MSwo NHol SHeS SRms SWhi
- 'Pirbright Rose'	SHeS SRms
- 'Polden Pride'	SHeS
- 'Porter's Red'	SHeS
- 'Praecox Rubra' ♀H4	EPfP NHol SHeS
- 'Prince of Wales'	SHeS
- 'Queen Mary'	SHeS
- 'Queen of Spain'	SHeS
- 'R.B. Cooke' ♀H4	EPfP SCoo SHeS SRms
- 'Red Rover'	SHeS
- 'Robert Jan'	SHeS
- 'Rosalie' ♀H4	CBcs EPfP IArd MMuc MSwo SCoo SHeS SPer SRms SWhi
- 'Rosantha'	IVic SHeS SRms
- 'Rosea'	SPlb
- 'Rosy Gem'	SHeS
- 'Rosy Morn'	SHeS
- 'Rotes Juwel'	SHeS
- 'Rubinteppich'	SHeS SRms
- 'Ruby Glow'	MSwo NHol SHeS
- 'Scatterley'	SHeS
- 'Schatzalp'	SHeS
- 'Sherwood Creeping'	SHeS
- 'Smart's Heath'	SHeS
- 'Sneznik'	SHeS
- 'Spring Cottage Crimson'	SHeS
- 'Spring Day'	MSwo SHeS
- 'Springwood Pink'	CSBt CTri NHol SHeS SRms SWhi
I - 'Startler'	NHol SHeS
- 'Thomas Kingscote'	SHeS
§ - 'Treasure Trove'	SHeS
- 'Viking'	NHol SHeS
- 'Vivellii' ♀H4	CSBt CTri NHol SHeS SRms SWhi
- 'Vivellii Aurea'	SHeS
- 'Walter Reisert'	SHeS
- 'Wanda'	SHeS
- 'Wentwood Red'	SHeS
- Whisky	see *E. carnea* 'Bell's Extra Special'
- 'Winter Beauty'	NHol SHeS
- 'Winter Melody'	SHeS
- Winter Rubin	see *E. carnea* 'Kramer's Rubin'
- 'Winter Sport'	SHeS
- 'Winterfreude'	SHeS
- 'Wintersonne'	CBcs EPfP SHeS SRms SWhi
ciliaris f. ***albiflora*** 'Stoborough' ♀H4	SHeS
- - 'White Wings'	SHeS
- f. ***aureifolia*** 'Aurea'	SHeS SRms
- 'Bretagne'	SHeS
- 'Camla'	SHeS
- 'Corfe Castle'	SHeS
- 'David McClintock'	SHeS
- 'Fada das Serras'	SHeS
- 'Globosa'	SHeS
- 'Mawiana'	SHeS
- 'Mrs C.H. Gill' ♀H4	SHeS
- 'Ram'	SHeS
- 'Rotundiflora'	SHeS
- 'Stapehill'	SHeS
- 'Wych'	SHeS
cinerea f. ***alba*** 'Alba Major'	CSBt SHeS
- - 'Alba Minor' ♀H4	NHol SHeS SWhi
- - 'Celebration'	NHol SHeS SWhi
- - 'Doctor Small's Seedling'	SHeS
- - 'Domino'	SHeS
- - 'Geke'	SHeS

	Name	Suppliers
	- - 'Godrevy'	SHeS
	- - 'Honeymoon'	SHeS
	- - 'Hookstone White' ♀H4	SHeS SWhi
	- - 'Jos' Honeymoon'	SHeS
	- - 'Marina'	SHeS
	- - 'Nell'	SHeS
	- - 'Snow Cream'	SHeS
	- - 'White Dale'	SHeS
	- 'Alette'	SHeS
	- 'Alfred Bowerman'	SHeS
	- 'Angarrack'	SHeS
	- 'Anja Bakker'	SHeS
	- 'Anja Blum'	SHeS
	- 'Anja Slegers'	SHeS
	- 'Apple Blossom'	SHeS
	- 'Aquarel'	SHeS
	- 'Ashdown Forest'	SHeS
	- 'Ashgarth Garnet'	SHeS
	- 'Atropurpurea'	SHeS
	- 'Atrorubens'	SHeS SRms
	- 'Atrorubens, Daisy Hill'	SHeS
	- 'Atrosanguinea Reuthe's Variety'	SHeS
	- 'Atrosanguinea Smith's Variety'	SHeS
I	- 'Aurea'	MMuc
	- f. ***aureifolia*** 'Alice Ann Davies'	SHeS
	- - 'Ann Berry'	SHeS
	- - 'Apricot Charm'	CSBt MSwo SHeS
	- - 'Constance'	SHeS
	- - 'Fiddler's Gold' ♀H4	NHol SHeS
	- - 'Golden Charm'	NHol SHeS SWhi
	- - 'Golden Drop'	CSBt NHol SHeS
	- - 'Golden Hue' ♀H4	NHol SHeS
	- - 'Golden Sport'	SHeS
	- - 'Golden Striker'	SHeS
	- - 'Golden Tee'	SHeS
	- - 'Goldilocks'	SHeS
	- - 'Jack London'	SHeS
	- - 'John Eason'	SHeS
	- - 'Jos' Golden'	SHeS
	- - 'Robert Michael'	SHeS
	- - 'Rock Pool'	NHol SHeS
	- - 'Screel'	SHeS
	- - 'Summer Gold'	SHeS SWhi
	- - 'Windlebrooke' ♀H4	NHol SHeS
	- 'Baylay's Variety'	SHeS
	- 'Bemmel'	SHeS
	- 'Blossom Time'	SHeS
	- 'Bucklebury Red'	SHeS
	- 'C.D. Eason' ♀H4	CBcs CSBt CTri EPfP IVic NHol SHeS SRms SWhi
§	- 'C.G. Best' ♀H4	SHeS
	- 'Cairn Valley'	SHeS
	- 'Caldy Island'	SHeS
	- 'Cevennes'	SHeS SWhi
	- 'Champs Hill' ♀H4	SHeS
	- 'Cindy' ♀H4	NHol SHeS
	- 'Coccinea'	SHeS
	- 'Colligan Bridge'	SHeS
	- 'Contrast'	SHeS
	- 'Crimson Glow'	SHeS
	- 'Discovery'	SHeS
	- 'Duncan Fraser'	SHeS
	- 'Eden Valley' ♀H4	NHol SHeS SRms
	- 'Eline'	SHeS
	- 'England'	SHeS
	- 'Felthorpe'	SHeS
	- 'Flamingo'	SHeS
	- 'Foxhollow Mahogany'	SHeS
	- 'Frances'	SHeS
	- 'Frankrijk'	SHeS
	- 'Fred Corston'	SHeS
	- 'G. Osmond'	SHeS
	- 'Glasnevin Red'	SHeS
	- 'Glencairn'	NHol SHeS SWhi
	- 'Graham Thomas'	see *E. cinerea* 'C.G. Best'
	- 'Grandiflora'	SHeS
	- 'Guernsey Lime'	SHeS
	- 'Guernsey Pink'	SHeS
	- 'Guernsey Plum'	SHeS
	- 'Guernsey Purple'	SHeS
	- 'Hardwick's Rose'	SHeS
	- 'Harry Fulcher'	SHeS
	- 'Heatherbank'	SHeS
	- 'Heathfield'	SHeS
	- 'Heidebrand'	SHeS
	- 'Hermann Dijkhuizen'	SHeS
	- 'Hookstone Lavender'	SHeS
	- 'Hutton's Seedling'	SHeS
	- 'Iberian Beauty'	SHeS
	- 'Janet'	SHeS
	- 'Jersey Wonder'	SHeS
	- 'Jiri'	SHeS
	- 'John Ardron'	SHeS
	- 'Joseph Murphy'	SHeS
	- 'Josephine Ross'	SHeS
	- 'Joyce Burfitt'	SHeS
	- 'Katinka'	CBcs MSwo NHol SHeS SWhi
	- 'Kerry Cherry'	SHeS
	- 'Knap Hill Pink' ♀H4	SHeS
	- 'Lady Skelton'	SHeS
	- 'Lavender Lady'	SHeS
	- 'Lilac Time'	SHeS
	- 'Lilacina'	SHeS
	- 'Lime Soda' ♀H4	SHeS
	- 'Lorna Anne Hutton'	SHeS
	- 'Michael Hugo'	SHeS
	- 'Miss Waters'	SHeS
	- 'Mrs Dill'	SHeS
	- 'Mrs E.A. Mitchell'	NHol SHeS SPlb
	- 'Mrs Ford'	SHeS
	- 'My Love'	SHeS SWhi
	- 'Neptune'	SHeS
	- 'Newick Lilac'	SHeS
	- 'Next Best'	SHeS
	- 'Novar'	SHeS
	- 'Old Rose'	SHeS
	- 'P.S. Patrick' ♀H4	SHeS SWhi
	- 'Pallas'	SHeS
	- 'Pallida'	SHeS
	- 'Paul's Purple'	SHeS
	- 'Peñaz'	SHeS
	- 'Pentreath' ♀H4	SHeS
	- 'Pink Foam'	SHeS
	- 'Pink Ice' ♀H4	CTri EPfP MSwo NHol SHeS SWhi
	- 'Plummer's Seedling'	SHeS
	- 'Promenade'	SHeS
	- 'Prostrate Lavender'	SHeS
	- 'Providence'	SHeS
	- 'Purple Beauty'	SHeS SWhi
	- 'Purple Robe'	SHeS
	- 'Purple Spreader'	SHeS
	- 'Purpurea'	SHeS
	- 'Pygmaea'	SHeS
	- 'Red Pentreath'	SHeS
	- 'Rock Ruth'	SHeS
	- 'Romiley'	SHeS
	- 'Rose Queen'	SHeS
	- 'Rosea'	SHeS
I	- 'Rosea Splendens'	SHeS
	- 'Rosy Chimes'	SHeS
	- 'Rozanne Waterer'	SHeS

	- 'Ruby'	SHeS
	- 'Sandpit Hill'	SHeS
	- 'Schizopetala'	SHeS
	- 'Sea Foam'	SHeS
	- 'Sherry'	NHol SHeS SWhi
	- 'Smith's Lawn'	SHeS
	- 'Spicata'	SHeS
	- 'Splendens'	SHeS
	- 'Startler'	SHeS
	- 'Stephen Davis' ♀^{H4}	NHol SHeS SWhi
	- 'Strawberry Bells'	SHeS
	- 'Sue Lloyd'	SHeS
	- 'Tilford'	SHeS
	- 'Tom Waterer'	SHeS
	- 'Underwood Pink'	SHeS
	- 'Uschie Ziehmann'	SHeS
	- 'Velvet Night' ♀^{H4}	CSBt NHol SHeS SRms SWhi
	- 'Victoria'	SHeS
I	- 'Violacea'	SHeS
	- 'Violetta'	SHeS
	- 'Vivienne Patricia'	SHeS SWhi
	- 'W.G. Notley'	SHeS
	- 'West End'	SHeS
	- 'Wine'	SHeS
	- 'Yvonne'	SHeS
	cooperi **new**	SPlb
	curviflora	SHeS SPlb
	× ***darleyensis*** 'Alba'	see *E.* × *darleyensis* 'Silberschmelze'
	- f. ***albiflora*** 'Ada S. Collings'	SHeS
	- - 'Dunreggan'	SHeS
	- - 'N.R. Webster'	SHeS
§	- - 'Silberschmelze'	CSBt CTri EPfP MGos MMuc MSwo NHol NPri SHeS SPer SRms SWhi
	- - 'White Glow'	CTri SHeS
	- - 'White Perfection' ♀^{H4}	CBcs CSBt EPfP IArd IVic NHol NPri SBfd SCoo SHeS SRms SWhi
	- 'Archie Graham'	SHeS
	- 'Arthur Johnson' ♀^{H4}	CSBt CTri NHol SHeS SRms SWhi
§	- f. ***aureifolia*** 'Eva Gold'^{PBR}	NHol SHeS SRms SWhi
	- - 'Jack H. Brummage'	CSBt CTri IArd MGos MSwo NHol SHeS SRms SWhi
	- - 'Mary Helen'	CSBt EPfP NHol SCoo SHeS SPer SRms SWhi
	- - 'Moonshine'	NHol SWhi
	- - 'Tweety'	CBcs SHeS
	- 'Aurélie Brégeon'	SHeS SRms
	- 'Cherry Stevens'	see *E.* × *darleyensis* 'Furzey'
§	- 'Darley Dale'	CSBt EPfP MMuc NHol NPri SBfd SCoo SHeS SPer SRms SWhi
	- 'Epe'	SHeS
	- 'Erecta'	SHeS
	- 'Eva'^{PBR}	see *E.* × *darleyensis* f. *aureifolia* 'Eva Gold'
§	- 'Furzey' ♀^{H4}	CSBt EPfP MGos NHol SCoo SHeS SPer SRms SWhi
	- 'George Rendall'	CSBt CTri EPfP NHol SCoo SHeS
	- 'Ghost Hills' ♀^{H4}	CSBt EPfP MSwo NHol NPri SBfd SCoo SHeS SPer SRms SWhi
	- 'J.W. Porter' ♀^{H4}	EPfP MMuc SCoo SHeS SRms SWhi
	- 'James Smith'	SHeS
	- 'Jenny Porter' ♀^{H4}	CSBt EPfP SHeS SWhi
	- 'Kramer's Rote' ♀^{H4}	CBar CBcs CSBt CTri EPfP MGos MMuc NHol NPri SBfd SHeS SRms SWhi
§	- 'Lena'	SHeS
	- 'Margaret Porter'	EPfP SHeS SWhi
	- Molten Silver	see *E.* × *darleyensis* f. *albiflora* 'Silberschmelze'
	- 'Mrs Parris' Red'	SHeS
	- 'Pink Perfection'	see *E.* × *darleyensis* 'Darley Dale'
	- 'Spring Surprise'^{PBR}	EPfP NPri SHeS
	- 'W.G. Pine'	SHeS
	- 'White Fairy'	SHeS
	discolor	SHeS
	erigena f. ***alba*** 'Alba'	SHeS
	- - 'Brian Proudley'	SHeS
	- - 'Golden Lady' ♀^{H4}	CSBt MSwo NHol SCoo SHeS SWhi
	- - 'Ivory'	SHeS
	- - 'Mrs Parris' White'	SHeS
	- - 'Nana Alba'	SHeS
I	- - 'Nana Compacta'	SHeS
	- - 'W.T. Rackliff' ♀^{H4}	CBcs CSBt EPfP MGos MSwo NHol SCoo SHeS SPer SRms SWhi
	- - 'W.T. Rackliff Variegated' (v)	SHeS
	- f. ***aureifolia*** 'Thing Nee'	SHeS
	- 'Brightness'	CSBt EPfP MSwo NHol SCoo SHeS
	- 'Coccinea'	SHeS
	- 'Ewan Jones'	SHeS
	- 'Glauca'	SHeS
	- 'Hibernica'	SHeS
	- 'Hibernica Alba'	SHeS
	- 'Irish Dusk' ♀^{H4}	CBcs CSBt CTri EPfP MGos NHol SCoo SHeS SRms SWhi
	- 'Irish Salmon'	SHeS
	- 'Irish Silver'	SHeS
	- 'Maxima'	SHeS
	- 'Mrs Parris' Lavender'	SHeS
	- 'Nana'	SHeS
	- 'Rosea'	SHeS
	- 'Rosslare'	SHeS
	- 'Rubra'	SHeS
	- 'Superba'	SHeS SRms SWhi
	× ***garforthensis*** 'Tracy Wilson'	SHeS
	'Ghislaine'	SHeS
	glauca var. ***elegans***	CDes
	- var. ***glauca***	SPlb
	gracilis	SPoG
	× ***griffithsii*** 'Ashlea Gold'	SHeS
	- 'Elegant Spike'	SHeS
§	- 'Heaven Scent'	SHeS SWhi
	- 'Jacqueline'	NHol SHeS SRms SWhi
	- 'Valerie Griffiths'	NHol SCoo SHeS SRms SWhi
	'Heaven Scent'	see *E.* × *griffithsii* 'Heaven Scent'
	'Hélène'	SHeS
	holosericea	CDes
	× ***krameri*** 'Otto'	SHeS
	- 'Rudi'	SHeS
	lusitanica ♀^{H3}	LRHS SHeS SPoG
	- f. ***aureifolia*** 'George Hunt'	ELan EPfP LRHS NHol SHeS SLon SPer SPoG
	- 'Sheffield Park'	ELan EPfP LRHS SHeS SPoG SSpi
	mackayana subsp. ***andevalensis***	SHeS
	- - f. ***albiflora***	SHeS
	- 'Donegal'	SHeS
	- f. ***eburnea*** 'Doctor Ronald Gray'	SHeS
	- - 'Shining Light'	SDys SHeS
	- 'Errigal Dusk'	SHeS
	- 'Galicia'	SHeS
	- 'Lawsoniana'	SHeS
	- f. ***multiplicata*** 'Ann D. Frearson' (d)	SHeS
	- - 'Maura' (d)	SHeS
	- - 'Plena' (d)	SHeS
	- 'William M'Calla'	SHeS
	mammosa	SPlb
	manipuliflora 'Aldeburgh'	SHeS
§	- 'Cascades'	SHeS

	- 'Corfu'	SHeS
	- 'Don Richards'	SHeS
	- 'Ian Cooper'	SHeS
	- 'Korçula'	SHeS
	- 'Toothill Mustard'	SHeS
	- 'Waterfall'	see *E. manipuliflora* 'Cascades'
	mediterranea	see *E. erigena*
	multiflora f. ***alba*** 'Formentor'	SHeS
	× ***oldenburgensis*** 'Ammerland'	SHeS
	- 'Oldenburg'	SHeS
	patersonii	CDes SPlb
	plukenetii	CDes
	racemosa	SHeS
	scoparia subsp. ***azorica***	SHeS
	- subsp. ***maderincola*** 'Madeira Gold'	SHeS
	- subsp. ***platycodon***	SHeS
§	- 'Minima'	SHeS
	- 'Pumila'	see *E. scoparia* 'Minima'
	sphaerocephala **new**	CDes
	spiculifolia	WPat WThu
	- f. ***albiflora***	SHeS
	- 'Balkan Rose'	GCal SHeS
	'Spring Field White'	MMuc
	straussiana	SPlb
I	× ***stuartii*** 'Charles Stuart'	SHeS
	- 'Connemara'	SHeS
	- 'Irish Lemon' 🏆H4	CSBt EPfP GGar MSwo NHol SHeS SWhi
	- 'Irish Orange'	CSBt NHol SHeS SWhi
	- 'Irish Rose'	SHeS
	- 'Nacung'	SHeS
	- 'Pat Turpin'	SHeS
	subdivaricata	SHeS
	taxifolia **new**	CDes
	terminalis 🏆H4	SHeS SRms
	- 'Golden Oriole'	SHeS
	- 'Thelma Woolner'	SHeS
	tetralix	SRms
	- f. ***alba*** 'Bartinney'	SHeS
	- - 'Dee'	SHeS
	- - 'Hailstones'	SHeS
	- - 'Melbury White'	SHeS
§	- - 'Ruby's Variety'	SHeS
	- 'Alba'	SHeS
	- 'Alba Mollis' 🏆H4	CSBt GGar NHol SHeS SWhi
	- 'Alba Praecox'	SHeS
	- 'Allendale Pink'	SHeS
	- 'Ardy'	SHeS
	- f. ***aureifolia*** 'Renate'	SHeS
	- - 'Ruth's Gold'	NHol SHeS
	- - 'Swedish Yellow'	SHeS
	- 'Bala'	SHeS
	- 'Con Underwood' 🏆H4	CSBt MSwo NHol SHeS SRms SWhi
	- 'Curled Roundstone'	SHeS
	- 'Dänemark'	SHeS
	- 'Daphne Underwood'	SHeS
	- 'Darleyensis'	SHeS
	- 'Delta'	SHeS
	- 'Foxhome'	SHeS
	- 'George Fraser'	SHeS
	- 'Gratis'	SHeS
	- 'Hookstone Pink'	MSwo SHeS
	- 'Humoresque'	SHeS
	- 'Jos' Creeping'	SHeS
	- 'Ken Underwood'	SHeS
	- 'L.E. Underwood'	NHol SHeS
	- 'Mary Grace'	SHeS
	- 'Morning Glow'	see *E.* × *watsonii* 'F. White'
	- 'Pink Glow'	SHeS
	- 'Pink Pepper' (v)	SHeS
	- f. ***racemosa*** 'Terschelling'	SHeS
	- 'Riko'	SHeS SRms
	- 'Rosea'	SHeS
	- 'Rubra'	SHeS
	- 'Ruby's Velvet'	see *E. tetralix* f. *alba* 'Ruby's Variety'
	- 'Salmon Seedling'	SHeS
	- 'Samtpfötchen'	IVic SHeS
	- 'Silver Bells'	CSBt SHeS
	- f. ***stellata*** 'Helma'	SHeS
	- - 'Helma Variegated' (v)	SHeS
	- - 'Pink Star' 🏆H4	NHol SHeS SRms SWhi
	- 'Stikker'	SHeS
	- 'Tina'	SHeS
	- 'Trixie'	SHeS
	- 'White House'	SHeS
	umbellata	SHeS
	- f. ***albiflora*** 'Anne Small'	SHeS
	- 'David Small'	SHeS
	vagans f. ***alba***	MMuc
	- - 'Bianca'	SHeS
	- - 'Cornish Cream' 🏆H4	EPfP NHol SHeS SWhi
	- - 'Cream'	SHeS
	- - 'Diana's Gold'	SHeS
	- - 'French White'	SHeS
	- - 'Golden Triumph'	SHeS SWhi
	- - 'Kevernensis Alba' 🏆H4	SHeS
	- - 'Leucantha'	SHeS
§	- - 'Nana'	SHeS
	- - 'Valerie Proudley' 🏆H4	CSBt MGos NHol SHeS SRms
	- - 'White Lady'	GGar SHeS
	- - 'White Rocket'	SHeS
	- - 'White Spire'	SHeS
	- 'Alba Nana'	see *E. vagans f. alba* 'Nana'
	- f. ***aureifolia*** 'Yellow John'	CBcs SHeS SWhi
	- 'Birch Glow' 🏆H4	EPfP SHeS SWhi
	- 'Carnea'	SHeS
	- 'Charm'	SHeS
	- 'Chittendenii'	SHeS
	- 'Diana Hornibrook'	SHeS
	- 'Fiddlestone'	SHeS
	- 'George Underwood'	SHeS
	- 'Grandiflora'	SHeS
	- 'Holden Pink'	SHeS
	- 'Hookstone Rose'	SHeS
	- 'Ida M. Britten'	SHeS
	- 'J.C. Fletcher'	SHeS
	- 'Lilacina'	SHeS
	- 'Lyonesse' 🏆H4	CTri MGos MMuc MSwo NHol SHeS SRms SWhi
	- 'Miss Waterer'	SHeS
	- 'Mrs D.F. Maxwell' 🏆H4	CSBt CTri MGos MSwo NHol SHeS SPer SRms SWhi
	- 'Mrs Donaldson'	SHeS
	- 'Pallida'	SHeS
	- 'Peach Blossom'	SHeS
	- 'Pyrenees Pink'	SHeS
	- 'Rosea'	SHeS
	- 'Rubra'	SHeS
	- 'Saint Keverne'	CSBt CTri IArd IVic NHol SHeS SWhi
	- 'Summertime'	SHeS
	- 'Valerie Smith'	SHeS
	- 'Viridiflora'	SHeS
	× ***veitchii*** 'Brockhill'	SHeS
	- 'Exeter' 🏆H3	CDoy CSBt ELan EPfP LRHS NHol SHeS SWhi WFar
	- 'Gold Tips' 🏆H4	CSBt EPfP LRHS NHol SHeS SWhi
	- 'Pink Joy'	SHeS
	ventricosa	IRar

versicolor SPlb
verticillata SHeS
viridescens SHeS
× ***watsonii*** 'Cherry Turpin' SHeS
- 'Dawn' ♀H4 SHeS
- 'Dorothy Metheny' SHeS
- 'Dorset Beauty' SHeS
§ - 'F. White' SHeS
- 'Gwen' SHeS
- 'H. Maxwell' SHeS
- 'Mary' IVic SHeS
- 'Pink Pacific' SHeS
- 'Rachel' SHeS
- 'Truro' SHeS
× ***williamsii*** 'Cow-y-Jack' SHeS
- 'Croft Pascoe' SHeS
- 'David Coombe' SHeS
- 'Gew Graze' SHeS
- 'Gold Button' SHeS
- 'Gwavas' SHeS
- 'Jean Julian' SHeS
- 'Ken Wilson' SHeS
- 'Lizard Downs' SHeS
- 'Marion Hughes' SHeS
- 'P.D. Williams' ♀H4 SHeS
'Winter Fire' SHeS
woodii new SPlb

Ericameria (*Asteraceae*)

discoidea NNS 06-209 WCot

Erigeron (*Asteraceae*)

from Big Horn, USA NMen
acris MNHC
'Adria' EBee EBla ECtt LLHF LRHS MBNS SPer WFar WMnd
§ ***alpinus*** NLAp
annuus NDov
aurantiacus EPfP MBNS NBre NBro NPri
§ ***aureus*** NWCA
- 'Canary Bird' ♀H4 EPfP NBir NMen NSla WAbe
- 'The Giant' CPBP
'Azure Beauty' EBee EPfP
Azure Fairy see *E.* 'Azurfee'
§ 'Azurfee' CSBt EBee ELan EPfP GKir GMaP LRHS LSqH MBNS MWat NBir NLar NPri SGSe SGar SPer SPhx SPoG SWvt WMoo WPer WWEG
Black Sea see *E.* 'Schwarzes Meer'
bloomeri var. ***bloomeri*** NNS 05-274 NWCA
'Blue Beauty' CMac LRHS
borealis GKev
'Charity' MRav WBrE WBrk
chrysopsidis ECho LHop LLHF LRHS NWCA
'Grand Ridge' WAbe
compactus var. ***consimilis*** CPBP
compositus CPBP CTri SRms
§ - var. ***discoideus*** EBur GKev NBre NMen SPlb
- 'Rocky' ECho SRot
Darkest of All see *E.* 'Dunkelste Aller'
deep pink-flowered CHEx
'Dignity' EBee EBla EKen ELan LLHF MBrN MRav MWat NBro SMrm SPoG SUsu WBrk WCot WFar WWEG
'Dimity' CMea ECha NBir NBre SAga WAbe WBrk WClo WFar WHal WSFF
'Dominator' EBee GBin WCot
I 'Dunkelste Aller' ♀H3 CMea CSam EBee EBla ELan EPfP GMaP LBMP LHop MAvo MRav NMRc SPoG SRms SWvt WCAu WEas WFar WWEG
elegantulus CMea
* ***ereganus*** NBre WBrk
'Felicity' EBee
flettii EDAr WPat
'Foersters Liebling' ♀H4 EBee EBla EPfP GBin MNrw NGdn WWEG
formosissimus GBin
'Four Winds' CAbP ECtt ELan EWes GKev MRav NGdn NMen WPer WWEG
frigidus NMen
'Gaiety' NBre WBrk
glaucus CCCN CSBt EBee EWll GBee GGar GJos LRHS MBNS MRav NBre NGdn NVic SEND SMad WBrk WFar WHoo
- 'Albus' LHop MBNS SAga SMad WFar WPer
- 'Elstead Pink' CElw CTri EBee ECtt ELan SAga WFar WSHC
- 'Roger Raiche' MRav SMrm
- 'Roseus' CBcs SEND
- 'Sea Breeze' CCCN COIW CPrp GGar GMaP IFFs LAst LHop MBNS MBri NBre NCGa NPri SBfd SPoG WNew
howellii EBee NBre
humilis EDAr
§ ***karvinskianus*** ♀H3 Widely available
leiomerus EPot GKev LBee LLHF
linearis LLHF NBre NMen
'Mrs F.H. Beale' EBee EBla ECtt SRGP WSpi
mucronatus see *E. karvinskianus*
multiradiatus GCal
'Nachthimmel' EBla ECtt NBre NGdn
ochroleucus var. ***scribneri*** LLHF
'Offenham Excellence' WCot
§ ***peregrinus*** subsp. ***callianthemus*** CPBP
philadelphicus CElw IGor NBir NBro
'Pink Beauty' SKHP
Pink Jewel see *E.* 'Rosa Juwel'
pinnatisectus CPBP GKev
'Profusion' see *E. karvinskianus*
pumilus CDes
pygmaeus LLHF
pyrenaicus misapplied see *E. alpinus*
pyrenaicus Rouy see *Aster pyrenaeus*
'Quakeress' CElw CPrp EBee EBla EBrs ECtt EPfP EShb GMaP GMac IKil LBMP LEdu LHop LRHS MCot MNrw MRav MSpe NBro NGdn SBfd SMrm SUsu WBrk WEas WFar WWEG
§ 'Rosa Juwel' CSBt CTri EBee ECtt ELan EPfP GMaP LBMP LRHS LSqH MBNS MRav NBir NPri SPer SPoG SRms SWvt WClo WMnd WMoo WPer
'Rosenballett' WCot
'Rotes Meer' CMac EBee EBla ELan MRav WCot WFar
rotundifolius 'Caerulescens' see *Bellis caerulescens*
salsuginosus misapplied see *Aster sibiricus*, *E. peregrinus* subsp. *callianthemus*
§ 'Schneewittchen' EBee EBla ELan EPfP GMac MRav MSpe MWat NCGa NVic SBfd SPet SPoG SWvt WCAu WWEG
§ 'Schwarzes Meer' EBee NGdn WFar
scopulinus CPBP ITim LLHF WPat
simplex ECho LRHS
'Sincerity' WFar
'Snow Queen' WFar
Snow White see *E.* 'Schneewittchen'

'Sommerabend'	EBee
'Sommerneuschnee'	EBee ECha GBin LPla NDov WMnd
speciosus NNS 07-195	GKev
- 'Grandiflora'	NBre
'Strahlenmeer'	EBee MAvo NBre NGdn WFar
trifidus	see *E. compositus* var. *discoideus*
uniflorus	LLHF SRms
'Unity'	LRHS
untermannii NNS 06.214	CPBP
vagus	LLHF
'Wayne Roderick'	EBee SRGP
'White Quakeress'	CMea EBee MRav WBrk WCot
'Wuppertal'	EBee MRav NBro NGdn

Erinacea (*Papilionaceae*)

§ ***anthyllis*** ♀H4	WThu
pungens	see *E. anthyllis*

Erinus (*Scrophulariaceae*)

alpinus ♀H4	CTri ECho ECtt EPfP GAbr GJos GKev LBMP LRHS MLHP MMuc MWat NHol NPri NWCA SPet SRms WCom WEas WFar WPer
- var. ***albus***	ECho GJos NHol NLAp NMen SRms WHoo WPer
- 'Doktor Hähnle'	ECho EDAr GMaP NMen SRms WFar WHoo WSpi
- 'Mrs Charles Boyle'	NMen

Eriobotrya (*Rosaceae*)

'Coppertone'	see × *Rhaphiobotrya* 'Coppertone'
deflexa	CHEx
japonica (F) ♀H3	Widely available
- 'Baffico' (F) **new**	CAgr
- 'BB' (F) **new**	CAgr
- 'Gold Nugget' (F) **new**	XBlo
- 'Ottaviana' (F) **new**	CAgr

Eriocapitella see *Anemone*

Eriocephalus (*Asteraceae*)

africanus	SPlb WJek

Eriogonum (*Polygonaceae*)

cespitosum NNS 03-254	GKev
fasciculatum **new**	NBre
flavum	GEdr
jamesii	WPat
latifolium	MWts
umbellatum	ECho NBre
- subsp. ***covillei***	CMea
- var. ***humistratum***	WPat
- var. ***porteri*** NNS 06-230	NWCA
- var. ***torreyanum***	CMea GEdr
- var. ***umbellatum***	LBee

Eriophorum (*Cyperaceae*)

angustifolium	CBen CRWN CWat EBWF EHoe EHon LPBA MCCP MSKA MWts SPlb SWat WAbe WMAq WMoo WPer WPnP WSFF
latifolium	GFor LPBA MSKA SGSe
rousseauianum **new**	MSKA
vaginatum	CRow EHoe GFor LLWG MSKA NSco SGSe WSFF

Eriophyllum (*Asteraceae*)

lanatum	EBee ECha EPfP MDKP MWat NBid NBre NGBl SAga WCom WWEG

Eriospermum (*Liliaceae*)

paradoxum **new**	ECho

Erodium (*Geraniaceae*)

absinthoides	EPot LRHS
- var. ***amanum***	see *E. amanum*
§ ***acaule***	LLHF WClo WFar
§ ***amanum***	EWes
'Ardwick Redeye'	GCal SUsu
balearicum	see *E.* × *variabile* 'Album'
'Bidderi'	EPot NWCA WAbe
'Caroline'	CMea WHoo
carvifolium	CElw NWCA WFar
§ ***castellanum***	EBee LLHF NBro NMen
- 'Dujardin'	SPhx
'Catherine Bunuel'	NMen
celtibericum	EPot
chamaedryoides	see *E. reichardii*
- 'Roseum' hort.	see *E.* × *variabile* 'Roseum'
cheilanthifolium 'David Crocker'	EPot NMen
chrysanthum	Widely available
- pink-flowered	CSpe EPot LHop NMen SMrm SRot
corsicum	EBee EBur ECho MTho NMen NWCA
- 'Album'	EBee ECho LLHF NMen
'County Park'	CMea EBee ECha ECou MLHP NLAp SHar SRms WCom
daucoides misapplied	see *E. castellanum*
daucoides Boiss.	EBee
'Eileen Emmett'	EPot
'Florida'	MAga
foetidum	MSpe NMen
- 'Couvé'	NMen
'Fran's Delight'	CMea ECtt EPot GMaP MLHP NMen WHoo
'Fripetta'	WAbe
N ***glandulosum*** ♀H4	CMea EBee ECho EPfP LHop MMuc SEND SRms SRot WCom WFar WKif WPat WSHC
'Grey Blush' **new**	SMHy
gruinum	EBee SPhx SWal
guttatum misapplied	see *E.* 'Katherine Joy'
N ***guttatum*** (Desf.) Willd.	ECho EPot EWTr LHop MWat NLar NMen SRms WNew
hymenodes L'Hér.	see *E. trifolium*
'Julie Ritchie'	CMea WHoo
§ 'Katherine Joy'	EBee EPot EWes MHer SRGP SRot
× ***kolbianum***	SMHy WAbe WCot WFar WHoo
- 'Natasha'	CMHG EBee ECtt EHoe EPot EWes GGar GKir GMaP LBee MHer NLAp NMen NSla SPoG SRGP WAbe WFar WKif
'Las Meninas'	SUsu
× ***lindavicum***	ECha
- 'Charter House'	CMoH
macradenum	see *E. glandulosum*
manescavii	Widely available
'Marchants Mikado'	SMHy
'Maryla'	NMen
'Merstham Pink'	CMHG CMoH EBee GMaP NLAp SRms
'Mesquita'	CMea
moschatum	ECho
'Nunwood Pink'	NWCA
'Pallidum'	CSam
pelargoniiflorum	CBot CSpe EBee EPfP EWTr GGar ILis LBMP LPio LRHS MCot NBro NLar SEND SMrm SRms WFar WHil WKif WPer WPnP WWFP
'Peter Vernon'	NWCA
petraeum subsp. ***petraeum***	EPot
'Pickering Pink'	EBee LIMB NLAp NMen

	'Pippa Mills'	CElw CMea
	'Princesse Marion'	MLHP
*	'Purple Haze'	EBee MSCN SMrm SRms SRot WFar
§	***reichardii***	CTri ECho ECtt LRHS MBrN MHer MTho NLAp NWCA SPet SPoG SRms WCFE
	- 'Album'	CEnt ECho GEdr NMen SGar SMrm SPet SPoG WCom WFar WHoo
	- 'Bianca'	EBee SUsu
	- 'Pipsqueak'	NWCA
*	- 'Rubrum'	CElw ECho
	'Robertino'	NMen WAbe
	'Robespierre'	SPhx
	rodiei	EPfP EWes
	romanum	see *E. acaule*
§	***rupestre***	CBot EBee ECho ECtt GMaP MWea NWCA SRms SRot WPat
	sebaceum 'Polly'	NWCA
	'Spanish Eyes'	NEgg NLAp SRot WCot WFar WKif
	'Stephanie'	CMHG EBee ECho EPot EWes GMaP LBee LRHS LSRN MHer NMen SUsu SWal
	supracanum	see *E. rupestre*
	'Tiny Kyni'	NLAp WFar
	trichomanifolium L'Hér.	EWes LBee LRHS
§	***trifolium***	ECho ELan EPfP MHer NSla SGar
	× ***variabile***	ECtt NLAp
§	- 'Album'	CMea CYeo EBee ECho EDAr EPfP EPot GKev LRHS MHer MMuc MTho NEgg NPri NSla NWCA SRms SRot WAbe WBrk WFar WNew WPer
I	- 'Bishop's Form'	Widely available
	- 'Candy'	GEdr GJos MHer
	- 'Derek'	ECho
	- 'Flore Pleno' (d)	CYeo EBee ECho EDAr ELan EPfP EWes ITim LRHS NMen SMrm SRms WBrk WFar WPer
	- 'Red Rock'	CTri EBee
§	- 'Roseum' 🏆H4	CBot ECho ECtt EDAr ELan EPfP GGar MMuc NSla NWCA SPlb SRms WBrk WFar WPer
I	'Westacre Seedling'	EWes
	'Whitwell Superb'	CDes CElw NWCA WPGP
	× ***willkommianum***	NWCA

Erpetion see *Viola*

Eruca (*Brassicaceae*)

	vesicaria	CWan
	- subsp. ***sativa***	CSpe ELau GPoy MHer MNHC NGHP SIde

Eryngium ✿ (*Apiaceae*)

	F&M 208	WPGP
	PC&H 268	EKen
§	***agavifolium***	Widely available
	alpinum 🏆H4	CBcs CSpe EBee ECha ECho ECtt ELan ELon EPfP GKir GMaP LAst LHop MGos MLLN MRav MSCN NBir SKHP SPer SPet SRms SRot WCAu WFar WTou
	- 'Amethyst'	EBee IPot LRHS LSRN NBro SMrm WEas
	- 'Blue Jacket'	NSti WBrE
	- 'Blue Star'	CBot CHar CPLG CSpe EBee EBla ECtt EHrv ELan EPfP GAbr GMac MCot MWat NGBl NHol NLar SMrm SPer STes WCot WPer WSpi WTin WWEG
	- 'Holden Blue'	MAvo
	- 'Slieve Donard'	see *E.* × *zabelii* 'Donard Variety'
	- 'Superbum'	CBot CChe CSpe ECtt EHrv GJos GLog LRHS MNrw NCob NLar SRms SWat WGwG WTou
	amethystinum	CBot CMac CMdw EBee EBla EHrv EPfP LPio MCot WPer WTou WWEG
	biebersteinianum	see *E. caeruleum*
	'Blue Jackpot'	EBee EHrv EWes NMoo
	'Blue Steel'	EBee LLHF MDKP NChi SBfd SPoG
	bourgatii	Widely available
	- Graham Stuart Thomas's selection	Widely available
	- 'Oxford Blue' 🏆H4	CEnt EBee EHrv GCrs GMaP GMac LAst MHer NLar SGSe SGar SKHP SWvt WEas
	- 'Picos Amethyst'	CBcs CKno CMac CWCL CWGN EBee EKen LHop LRHS LSRN NLar NSti SCoo SGSe SKHP SVil
	- 'Picos Blue' PBR	Widely available
	bromeliifolium misapplied	see *E. agavifolium*, *E. eburneum*
§	***caeruleum***	MNrw
	campestre	CArn CBot EWll MDKP NLar WFar WPer WWEG
	caucasicum	see *E. caeruleum*
	'Cobalt Star'	GMac MAvo MDKP
	creticum	NBro
	cymosum B&SWJ 10267	WCru
	decaisneanum misapplied	see *E. pandanifolium*
	deppeanum	SSvw
	- NJM 05.031	WPGP
	Dove Cottage hybrid	NDov
	ebracteatum	CSpe EBla IGor LPio MCot
	- var. ***poterioides***	LPla SMHy SPhx
§	***eburneum***	CBcs CBot CFir CGHE CWit EBee EBrs ECha EPfP EWes GCal GMaP LPio LRHS MAvo MLLN MSpe NBPC NBro NChi NHol NSti SBfd SKHP SMad SPad WFar WSpi
	aff. ***eburneum***	CMac WPGP
	'Electric Haze'	ECtt IPot NCGa NDov
	elegans var. ***elegans*** CDPR 3076	WPGP
	foetidum	CArn
§	***giganteum*** 🏆H4	Widely available
	- 'Silver Ghost' 🏆H4	CHar CMea CPLG CSam CSpe EBee ECtt EHrv EWll GAbr LHop LPio LRHS NChi NDov NGdn SBfd SGar SKHP SMad SWat SWvt WCot WFar WSpi WWEG
	gracile B&SWJ 10205 **new**	WCru
	- B&SWJ 10441	WCru
	'Green Jade'	ECtt LRHS
	guatemalense	CGHE WPGP
	- B&SWJ 8989	WCru
	- B&SWJ 10322	WCru
	- B&SWJ 10420	WCru
	horridum misapplied	see *E. eburneum*
	horridum ambig.	EWes GGar GKir LEdu LPio MNrw NChi SAPC SArc WFar WMnd WPGP
	horridum Malme	WCot
	humile B&SWJ 10464	WCru
	'Lapis Blue' **new**	GMac
	maritimum	CArn CBot CPou EBee GPoy ITim MDKP MHer NLar SPlb WAbe WFar WWEG
	Miss Willmott's ghost	see *E. giganteum*
	monocephalum	WPGP
	× ***oliverianum*** 🏆H4	Widely available
	palmatum	NChi
§	***pandanifolium*** 🏆H4	CFir CHEx CMHG EBee EPfP EWes GBin GCal LEdu LPio MAvo NBPC SAPC SArc SEND SGSe SGar SKHP

		SMad SMrm SPlb SPoG SWvt WCot WCru WMnd WPGP WWEG
	- 'Physic Purple'	CAby SPhx WCot
	paniculatum	WPGP
	planum	Widely available
	- 'Bethlehem' ♀H4	EBee NLar SWat WSpi
§	- 'Blauer Zwerg'	CKno EBee GQue MGos WFar WSpi
	- 'Blaukappe'	CBot CHar CMea EBee EBrs ELon EPfP LRHS NLar SEND SKHP SMrm SPet SPhx WAul WWEG
*	- 'Blue Candle'	EBee WFar
	- Blue Dwarf	see *E. planum* 'Blauer Zwerg'
	- 'Blue Glitter'	LRHS NLar
	- 'Blue Hobbit'	CChe CPLG EAEE EPfP GKir IPot LBuc LRHS NGdn NLBP NLar SPoG
	- 'Blue Ribbon'	CKno EBee EBla LAst LRHS LSou MRav NGdn
	- 'Flüela'	EBee EBla EPPr EWes LRHS LSRN MLLN NBro NEgg SCoo SWat
	- 'Hellas'	EBee
	- 'Jade Frost'PBR (v)	CAbP CDes CWGN EBee ECtt ELon EWes LHop LLHF LOck LPio LRHS LSou MAvo MBNS MLLN MPnt MTis NLar NSti SKHP SPoG WClo WCot WCra WFut WSpi
	- 'Paradise Jackpot'PBR	EBee MNrw NGdn SPer
	- 'Seven Seas'	CFir EBee EBla ECtt LRHS MBNS MBri MLLN NEgg NGdn WPer
	- 'Silver Stone'	EBee EBla ECtt GMaP LRHS MDKP NGdn NPri SMrm
	- 'Tetra Blau'	LRHS
	- 'Tetra Petra'	CBcs LRHS MAvo NEgg WPer
	- 'Violet Blue'	GCal
	proteiflorum	CWit EBee EBrs ECre EPfP GBin GCal IPot LPio MAvo MDKP NBPC SKHP SPlb WHil
	- F&M 224	WPGP
	'Sapphire Blue' **new**	CWGN LRHS LSRN SRkn
	serbicum	GCal MAvo WCot WWEG
	serra	EBee EBrs EDAr EWes LRHS MAvo NChi SEND
	- RB 90454	MDKP
	spinalba	CBot
	strotheri B&SWJ 9109	WCru
	- B&SWJ 10392	WCru
	tricuspidatum	EBrs ECtt GKir LRHS WPer WSpi WWEG
	× ***tripartitum*** ♀H4	Widely available
*	***umbelliferum***	EDAr GBin GCal GKir LAst MBNS MDKP NBPC NBre NChi NPri SKHP SPoG WClo WFar
	variifolium	Widely available
	venustum	CDes CPom EBee EBrs LPio LRHS MAvo MCot SBfd SMrm WFar WOut WTou
	yuccifolium	CArn CKno EBee EBla EBrs EPfP EWes GCal GKir LBMP LEdu LPio NHol NLar SBfd SDix SDnm SPhx SPlb SWvt WBrE WFar WHoo WTin
	× ***zabelii***	ECha GMac LPio NBir NChi WPGP
	- 'Blaue Ritter'	SKHP SWat
§	- 'Donard Variety'	EBla ECtt GCal IPot ITim LRHS MDKP NLar SWat WHoo WWEG
	- 'Forncett Ultra'	GCal GMac MAvo WPGP
	- 'Jewel'	MAvo SApp SUsu SWat
	- 'Jos Eijking'PBR	CSpe EBrs ECtt EKen ELon GKir GMac IPot LBMP LRHS LSRN MCot MMuc MRav MTis NCGa NDov NHol NLar SEND SMad SPer SPoG SUsu WBor WClo WCot
	- 'Violetta'	ECha ELan GMac IGor MAvo MBri NLar SWat WFar WHoo

Erysimum ✿ (*Brassicaceae*)

	from Madeira	CPLG
	amoenum	LLHF WAbe
	'Anthony Hicks'	CHll
	'Apricot Delight'	see *E.* 'Apricot Twist'
§	'Apricot Twist'	Widely available
	arkansanum	see *E. helveticum*
	asperum	GJos IFro
	bicolor	GGar
	'Bowles's Mauve' ♀H3	Widely available
	'Bowles's Purple'	SRms SWvt WBVN
	'Bowles's Yellow'	WCot
	'Bredon' ♀H3	EPfP NPer WHoo WKif WSpi
	brevistylum	GKev
	'Butterscotch'	CFee MMHG WCom WHoo WTin
	cheiri	CArn MHer NSco
	- 'Bloody Warrior' (d)	CBot CElw ECtt WCom
	- 'Deben'	CBot
	- 'Harpur Crewe' (d)	CBot CFee CHll CTri ECtt ELan ELon EPfP EShb GMaP MMuc MTho NPer SRms SUsu WCot
	- 'Orange Bedder' (Bedder Series)	NBir
	- Rysi Gold = 'Innrysigol'PBR	WCot
	'Chelsea Jacket'	ECtt EPfP SUsu
	'Constant Cheer'	Widely available
	'Cotswold Gem' (v)	CElw EBee ECtt EHoe ELan ELon EPPr EPfP EShb LBMP LSou MAsh MHer MMuc NBPC NPer SAga SBfd SBri SEND SLim SMrm SWvt WCot WWEG
	'Dawn Breaker'	CWGN EBee ECtt EWes LRHS LSou MAsh MWea NBPC SOkt SUsu WCot WWEG
	'Devon Sunset'	SAga
	'Dorothy Elmhirst'	see *E.* 'Mrs L.K. Elmhirst'
	dwarf, lemon-flowered	WHoo
	'Ellen Willmott'	CEnt GBin
	'Emm's Variety'	ECtt EPot
	'Gold Rush'	GJos
	'Gold Shot'	GJos
	'Golden Gem'	WCom
	'Golden Jubilee'	ECho ECtt ELon GGar LIMB WFar
	grandiflorum	GAuc
	'Hector's Gatepost'	EBee LRHS LSRN LSou NBPC SRGP SRkn
§	***helveticum***	CSpr ECho IFro MMuc SAga SEND SRms
	- var. ***drenowskyi*** **new**	GKev
	'Jacob's Jacket'	ECha ECtt EPot MBNS MHer NPer WBVN
	'Jenny Brook'PBR	EBee WHlf
	'Joan Adams'	LHop
	'John Codrington'	LHop NPer SUsu WKif WSpi WWFP
	'Joseph's Coat'	LIMB
	'Jubilee Gold'	WWEG
	'Julian Orchard'	CHll SSth
	kotschyanum	CPBP ECho ECtt EPot GEdr LBee LRHS NMen SRms WAbe WCom WPat
	linifolium	EBur SRms WFar WGor
	- 'Little Kiss Lilac'	GJos
§	- 'Variegatum' (v)	CArn CCCN CSBt CWan EBee ECtt ELan EPfP GBee GGar LRHS NEgg NLar NPer NPri SBfd SPer SPoG SRot WPGP
	- 'Variegatum' peach-flowered (v)	MBNS NLBP

	'Moonlight'	ECtt EPot GMaP MHer MTho NBir NCGa SRms WBVN WHoo
§	'Mrs L.K. Elmhirst'	ECtt ELon MMHG NDov NPer WHoo WWFP
	mutabile	CBgR CTri EBee EPfP MAsh MRav SIde SPhx SUsu WHal
	- 'Variegatum' (v)	WCom
	'My Old Mum'	CWGN EAEE EBee ECtt LSRN MAsh MBNS MRav MWea NDov WCra
	'Orange Flame'	CMea ECha ECho ECtt ELon EPot LHop LRHS MHer MMuc NPer NWCA SEND WCom WNew WPer
	'Parish's'	CMdw CSpe ECtt MRav SAga
	'Parkwood Gold'	CYeo EDAr EPot GJos
	'Pastel Patchwork'	CSpe EBee LRHS LSou NBPC SBfd SUsu SWal
	Perry's hybrid	NPer
	'Perry's Peculiar'	NPer
	'Perry's Surprise' **new**	NPer
	'Perry's Variegated' (v) **new**	NPer
	'Plant World Lemon'	CHGN CPLG ECtt LSou MBri NLar SDnm
	'Poppet' **new**	CSpe
§	***pulchellum***	ECha SMrm
	- 'Variegatum' (v)	WBrE
	aff. ***pulchellum***	SEND
	pumilum DC.	see *E. helveticum*
	pusillum **new**	WAbe
	'Roddy's Own' **new**	EDif
	rupestre	see *E. pulchellum*
	'Ruston Royal'	ECha
	'Rysi Bronze'	LSou NLar
	scoparium	ECha EDif
	'Sissinghurst Variegated'	see *E. linifolium* 'Variegatum'
	'Sprite'	CMea CTri ECtt EPot MMuc NPer SEND
	'Starbright'	CWCL EBee LRHS LSou SPoG SUsu
	'Stars and Stripes' (v)	CWGN EBee EPfP LBuc LRHS LSou MGos SBfd SPoG
	'Sunshine'	SWal
	'Sweet Sorbet'	EBee ECtt EPfP GMaP MBri NBPC NDov NEgg NLar NPri SPav SRkn SWal SWvt WHil
	'Valerie Finnis'	WCom
	Walberton's Fragrant Sunshine = 'Walfrasun'	CHll EPfP LRHS SBfd SCoo SPoG
	'Wenlock Beauty'	GBin SRms
	'Winter Joy'	CBow LLHF LRHS LSou MBNS NLar SUsu WCot
	'Winter Sorbet'	CBow ECtt LAst LSou NCGa NLar SMrm
	'Yellow Bird'	EPfP
	'Yellow Flame' **new**	WPer

Erythraea see *Centaurium*

Erythrina (*Papilionaceae*)

	arborescens **new**	SPlb
	× ***bidwillii***	CCCN
	crista-galli	CBcs CBot CCCN CDTJ CSpe EAmu EBee ELan EPfP EUJe GQui IDee LRHS MWea SOWG SPlb WCot WPGP WPat WSHC
	- 'Compacta'	MBri SMad
§	***humeana***	CDTJ
	latissima	CDTJ
	lysistemon	SPlb
	princeps	see *E. humeana*

Erythronium ✿ (*Liliaceae*)

	albidum	CLAP EBee ECho GAuc GGar IBlr LAma MMoz NMen
	americanum	CAby CArn CLAP EBee ECho EPot IBlr LAma MMoz MSSP NHol NMen WAbe
	'Apple Blossom'	ECho
	'Beechpark'	IBlr
	'Blush'	ECho IBlr
	'Californian Star'	IBlr
	californicum ♀H4	CAby CFir CLAP ECho EPot IBlr ITim SCnR WAbe
	- J&JA 13216	CLAP
	- JCA 1.350.200	WWst
*	- var. ***candidum*** MS 01/009	WWst
	- 'Harvington Snowgoose'	CLAP EBee EHrv LRHS MAsh MBri SKHP WCra WWst
	- Plas Merdyn form	IBlr
	- 'White Beauty' ♀H4	Widely available
	californicum × ***hendersonii***	IBlr
	caucasicum	CLAP
	citrinum	MSSP NMen
	- J&JA 13462	CLAP WWst
	citrinum × ***hendersonii***	CAvo IBlr
	'Citronella'	CFir CLAP CMil EHrv GEdr GKev IBlr ITim MSSP NMen WAbe
	cliftonii hort.	see *E. multiscapoideum* Cliftonii Group
	dens-canis ♀H4	Widely available
	- JCA 470.001	CLAP
	- from Slovenia	CLAP
	- 'Charmer'	CMil ECho GCrs GEdr MNrw WWst
	- 'Frans Hals'	CLAP CMil EBee ECho EPot GEdr GGar IPot LRHS MNrw MTho SKHP WAbe WHal
	- 'Lilac Wonder'	EBee ECho EPot GEdr GKev GMaP IPot LAma LEdu LRHS MNrw MTho NHol SDeJ WWst
*	- 'Moerheimii' (d)	CMil EBee ECho GKev IBlr WWst
	- var. ***niveum***	EPot IBlr NEgg
	- 'Old Aberdeen'	CLAP EBee IBlr LRHS MNrw WWst
	- 'Pink Perfection'	EBee ECho EPot GEdr GGar LEdu LRHS MNrw NHol SDeJ
	- 'Purple King'	EBee ECGP ECho EPot GEdr GMaP IPot LAma LRHS MMoz MNrw NHol SDeJ WAbe
	- 'Rose Queen'	CAby CFir CMil EBee ECho EPot GGar GKev GMaP IPot LAma LRHS MAvo MTho NHol SDeJ SPhx WHal
*	- 'Semi-plenum' (d)	IBlr
	- 'Snowflake'	CLAP CTca EBee ECha ECho EPot GCrs GEdr GGar GKev IPot LAma LRHS MMoz MNrw NBir NMen SDeJ SPhx WAbe
	- 'White Splendour'	ECho IBlr MNrw WWst
	- white-flowered, from Serbia	ECho
	elegans	ECho EHrv GCrs WWst
	'Flash'	IBlr
§	***grandiflorum***	CLAP ECho MSSP NMen
	- M&PS 007	CLAP
	- M&PS 96/024	NMen
	- subsp. ***chrysandrum***	see *E. grandiflorum*
	helenae	CLAP ECho GAuc IBlr WAbe
	- J&JA 11678	WWst
	hendersonii	CLAP CPom ECho EHrv GAuc LRHS MSSP SKHP WAbe WWst
	- J&JA 12945	CLAP
	howellii	CLAP
	- J&JA 13428	WWst
	- J&JA 13441	CLAP
	japonicum	CBcs EBee ECho EFEx EPot GAuc GEdr LAma MNrw NHol NMen WCru WFar WWst
	'Jeanette Brickell'	CLAP IBlr WWst

	'Jeannine'	GEdr IBlr
	'Joanna'	IBlr MNrw NMen WWst
	klamathense	EPot
	'Kondo'	CFir CTri EBee ECho EPfP EPot GEdr GGar GMaP IBlr IFro ITim LAma LEdu LRHS MTho NBir NHol NLar NMen SMrm SPer WAbe WClo WCot WHil
	'Margaret Mathew'	CLAP IBlr WAbe WWst
	'Minnehaha'	WWst
	montanum	ECho EHrv WWst
§	***multiscapideum***	CLAP ECho WCot
	- JCA 1.352.100	WWst
	- NNS 99-163	WWst
§	***multiscapoideum*** Cliftonii Group	CLAP WAbe
	'Oregon Encore'	IBlr
	oregonum	CLAP EBee ECho EHrv EPot GAuc GGar IBlr LRHS MNrw MSSP SKHP
	- subsp. ***leucandrum***	CLAP WWst
	- - JCA 4.352.400	WWst
	- subsp. ***oregonum***	WCot
I	- 'Sulphur Form'	CLAP
	'Pagoda' ♀H4	Widely available
	purdyi	see *E. multiscapideum*
	revolutum ♀H4	CAby CLAP CMea CPom CWCL EBee ECho EHrv EPot GAuc GCrs GEdr GGar GKev GMaP IBlr LAma LRHS MNrw MSSP NMen SCnR SKHP SRot WAbe WBVN WCru
	- from God's Valley	WWst
	- 'Guincho Splendour'	IBlr
	- Johnsonii Group	EBee ECho WAbe WCru WWst
	- 'Kinfauns'	WWst
	- 'Knightshayes'	CAvo EBee LRHS MAsh MBri SKHP WCra
	- 'Knightshayes Pink'	CLAP EHrv IBlr NBir WShi WWst
	- 'Pink Beauty'	EBee GKev
	- Plas Merdyn form	IBlr
	- 'Rose Beauty'	CMil ECho NMen
	- 'Wild Salmon'	CLAP LRHS MAsh MBri WCra
	'Rippling Waters'	IBlr
	'Rosalind'	IBlr SCnR
	sibiricum	ECho NMen WWst
*	- subsp. ***altaicum***	WWst
	- white-flowered	WWst
	'Sundisc'	CAby ECha ECho GEdr IBlr MSSP MTho NMen WAbe WWst
	'Susannah'	WWst
	taylorii	WWst
	tuolumnense ♀H4	CFir CLAP CTca CWCL EBee ECho EHrv EPot GAuc GCrs GEdr GGar GKev GMaP IBlr LAma LRHS MCot MNrw NMen SDeJ WAbe WBVN
	- EBA clone 2	WAbe WWst
	- EBA clone 3	WAbe
	- 'Edgar Klein'	WWst
	- Plas Merdyn form	IBlr
	- 'Spindlestone'	IBlr WWst
	umbilicatum	IBlr MSSP WWst

Escallonia ✿ (*Escalloniaceae*)

	'Alice'	EBee SLPl SPer
	'Apple Blossom' ♀H4	Widely available
§	***bifida*** ♀H3	CAlb CDoC CDul CHGN EQua WFar WPat WSHC
	'C.F. Ball'	CBcs CSBt CTri EBee ELan LBuc LRHS MAsh MGan MMuc MSwo NEgg NPla NWea SEND SPad SRms WBVN WDin WFar WMoo
	'Compacta Coccinea'	CBcs LRHS
	'Dart's Rosy Red'	LBMP NHol SLPl
	'Donard Beauty'	NEgg SRms
	'Donard Radiance' ♀H4	CBcs CDoC CDul CMac CSBt CSam CWib EBee ELan EPfP LHop LRHS LSRN NHol NWea SLim SPer SPoG SRms SWvt WDin WFar WMoo
	'Donard Red'	GGal
	'Donard Seedling'	CBcs CDoC CDul CSBt CWit ECrN ELan EPfP LAst LBuc LRHS MAsh MGan MGos MSwo NHol NPer NWea SBfd SLPl SLim SPer SRms SWvt WFar WMoo
	'Donard Star'	CWib EBee EPfP NWea SLPl WCFE
	'Donard White'	SPoG
	'Edinensis'	CWit EBee EPfP GGar NLar SBch SLim WDin WFar WMoo WSpi
	'Erecta'	EPfP
	'Everest'	LBuc LRHS NEgg SLon SPoG
	× ***exoniensis***	SRms
	'Gwendolyn Anley'	SLPl WFar
	'Hopleys Gold'PBR	see *E. laevis* 'Gold Brian'
	illinita	EBee GQui LLHF NLar
	'Iveyi' ♀H3	Widely available
	'Jamie' **new**	EShb LSRN
§	***laevis***	LRHS WFar
§	- 'Gold Brian'PBR	CDul CMHG EHoe ELan EPau EPfP GGar LRHS LSRN MAsh MGos MWat SCoo SPer SPoG SWal WFar WHar
	- 'Gold Ellen' (v)	CChe CSBt CTri CWSG EBee EHoe ELan EPfP LAst LBMP LRHS LSRN MAsh MGos MRav MSwo NEgg NHol NLar SAga SBfd SCoo SEND SLim SPer SPoG SRms SWvt WMoo
	'Langleyensis' ♀H4	CBcs CDoy CMac CTri CWib GGal NWea WDin WFar WHar
	mexicana	CBot WFar
	montevidensis	see *E. bifida*
	organensis	see *E. laevis*
	'Peach Blossom' ♀H4	CAlb CBar CBcs CDoC CDul CSam CWib EBee ELan ELon EPfP GGar LHop LRHS MAsh MBri MLHP MMuc MSwo NBir SBfd SCoo SEND SLPl SLim SPer SPoG SRms WFar
	'Pink Elf'	MSwo
	'Pink Pyramid'	LRHS
	'Pride of Donard' ♀H4	CBcs CDoC CPLG CSBt EBee EPfP LRHS LTen MGan MGos SRms
	punctata	see *E. rubra*
	Red Carpet = 'Loncar'	CSBt SLon WHar
	'Red Dream'	CSBt CWSG EBee EPfP LBMP LRHS MAsh MBlu MBri MGos MSwo NHol NLar SAga SBfd SCoo SPoG SRms SWvt WFar
	'Red Elf'	CMac EBee ELan EPfP GGar LAst LRHS MBri MGos MSCN MWat NEgg NHol SCoo SLPl SPer SPlb SPoG SRms SWvt WClo WFar
	'Red Hedger'	CDoC CSBt CTsd CWib ELan GGal MRav SBfd SCoo SRms WMoo
	'Red Robin'	GGar SPoG
	resinosa	CPLG SAPC SArc SPlb WJek
	revoluta	CTri
§	***rubra***	MLHP
	- 'Crimson Spire' ♀H4	Widely available
	- 'Ingramii'	CWib MMuc NWea SEND
	- var. ***macrantha***	Widely available
*	- - ***aurea***	NPla
	- 'Pygmaea'	see *E. rubra* 'Woodside'
§	- 'Woodside'	ECho EPfP LLHF MLHP NHol SRms
	'Silver Anniversary'	MSwo
	'Slieve Donard'	CMac EBee EPfP MRav NEgg NHol NWea SLPl SLim SLon SRms WFar

tucumanensis	SPlb

Eschscholzia (*Papaveraceae*)

californica ♀H4	GKir
- 'Jersey Cream'	CSpe
'Great Dane' new	IVic
lobbii	CSpe

Espeletia (*Asteraceae*)

aff. ***summapacis*** B&SWJ 10766	WCru

Esterhuysenia (*Aizoaceae*)

alpina	CPBP

Eucalyptus ✿ (*Myrtaceae*)

	aggregata	MWya SAPC SArc
	alpina	SPlb
	amygdalina	SPlb
	archeri	CCVT CDTJ CDoC CTho ECrN EPfP GQui LRHS MMuc MWhi MWya NLar SBfd
	botryoides	GLin
	caesia	SPlb
	camaldulensis	SPlb
	camphora	CCCN CTho MMuc
	cinerea	GQui SBig SPlb
	citriodora	CArn CTsd EOHP GQui MHer MNHC SPlb
	coccifera	CBcs CCVT CDoC CSBt CTho ELan EPfP GGar LMaj LRHS LTen MMuc MWya NEgg NPer SBig SPlb SPoG WDin
	cordata	CCVT CDul
	crenulata	CTrC GLin GQui
	crucis subsp. ***crucis***	SPlb
	curtisii new	SPlb
	cypellocarpa	SPlb
	dalrympleana ♀H3	CBcs CCVT CDoC CMHG CMac EBee ECrN ELan EPfP EWTr EWes IFFs LRHS LSRN MGos MMuc MSwo NBea NLar NPer SBig SEND SLim SPer SPoG SRms WClo WDin
	debeuzevillei	see *E. pauciflora* subsp. *debeuzevillei*
	delegatensis	CMHG GLin NPer
	- subsp. ***tasmaniensis***	GGar
	divaricata	see *E. gunnii* subsp. *divaricata*
	erythrocorys	SPlb
	eximia	SPlb
*	- 'Nana'	SPlb
	ficifolia	CDTJ
	fraxinoides	SPlb
	gamophylla	SPlb
	glaucescens	CMHG CTho CWCL ELan EPfP ETod EWes GQui LRHS SAPC SArc SBfd SPer WBVN WPtf
	globulus	CArn IFFs MNHC SPlb WFar
	goniocalyx	EPfP
§	***gregsoniana***	CDoC CTho EPfP GGal SPlb
	gunnii ♀H3	Widely available
	- Azura = 'Cagire' new	LRHS MAsh SBfd SLon
	- 'Blue Ice' new	CTho
§	- subsp. ***divaricata***	CCVT EPfP GQui MBri
	- 'Silbertropfen' new	MAsh
	johnstonii	CDul CTrC ECrN IFFs NLar SPer
	kruseana	SPlb
	kybeanensis	CCVT GQui
§	***lacrimans***	MWya
	lehmannii	SOWG
	leucoxylon subsp. ***megalocarpa***	SPlb
*	- - 'Rosea'	MCot
	'Little Boy Blue'	CWib LSRN
	macrocarpa	SPlb
*	***moorei nana***	CDTJ
	neglecta	GLin MWya
	nicholii	CBcs CCVT CDul EBee EPfP EWes GQui LRHS MGos MWya NLar SCoo SEND SLim SPoG
	niphophila	see *E. pauciflora* subsp. *niphophila*
	nitens	CCVT CDTJ CDul EGFP SBig SEND SPlb
	parviflora	IFFs WBVN
	parvifolia ♀H4	CCCN CCVT CDoC CDul CLnd CMHG CMac EPfP LRHS LTen MMuc MWhi SCoo SEND
	pauciflora	CCCN CDoC CSBt CTho ELan MGos MMuc NLar SPer
§	- subsp. ***debeuzevillei***	CDoC CTho EPfP EWes GQui LMaj MGos SAPC SArc SBig
	- var. ***nana***	see *E. gregsoniana*
§	- subsp. ***niphophila*** ♀H4	Widely available
	- - 'Pendula'	see *E. lacrimans*
	- subsp. ***pauciflora***	MMuc
	perriniana	Widely available
	phoenicea	SOWG
	pulverulenta	CMac ETod SPlb
	- 'Baby Blue'	IFFs LRHS MGos SWvt
	rodwayi	GGar
	rossii new	SPlb
	rubida	CCCN CMHG
	sideroxylon	SPlb
	- 'Rosea'	SPlb
	subcrenulata	EPfP GLin GQui
	tetraptera	SPlb
	torquata	SPlb
	urnigera	CCVT CDoC LHop LRHS WDin
	vernicosa	CCVT
	viminalis	CArn LRHS MWya WDin

Eucharidium see *Clarkia*

Eucharis (*Amaryllidaceae*)

§	***amazonica*** ♀H1	CCCN ECho EShb LAma SPav
	grandiflora misapplied	see *E. amazonica*

Eucodonia (*Gesneriaceae*)

'Adele'	EABi

Eucomis ✿ (*Hyacinthaceae*)

	'African Beauty'	LRHS
	'African Bride'	CTca
	autumnalis misapplied	see *E. zambesiaca*
§	***autumnalis*** (Mill.) Chitt. ♀H2-3	CAvo CBgR CDes CFFs CHEx CPou CPrp CSWP EBee ECho EPot ERCP IVic LAma LPio MCCP SDnm SPav SPer SPhx SPlb SWal WBrE WGwG WHil WPGP WTin
	- subsp. ***amaryllidifolia***	WPGP
	- subsp. ***autumnalis***	WPGP
	- - 'Peace Candles'	CPen
	- subsp. ***clavata***	CTca
	bicolor ♀H2-3	Widely available
	- 'Alba'	CAvo CBgR CPLG CTca EAmu EBee ECho EPot LAma LPio LRHS SDnm WHil
	- 'Stars and Stripes'	WCru
	'Cabernet Candles'	CPen
§	***comosa***	CAvo CBgR CFFs CHEx CHll CPrp CSam CStu CTca CTrC EBee ERCP EShb GAbr LAma LEdu LPio SDnm SMad SPav SPhx WHil WTin WWEG
	- 'Cornwood'	CAvo CFFs CTca WHil

- 'First Red'	CDes CPou WPGP
- green-leaved	CTca
- 'Kilimanjaro'	CTca EBee SPhx
- 'Oakhurst' **new**	EUJe
- purple-leaved	CTca EShb
- 'Sparkling Burgundy'	Widely available
- var. ***striata*** **new**	CDes
- 'Tarzan's Tail'	WHil
'Frank Lawley'	CDes
humilis	CPen CTca
- 'Twinkle Stars'	WHil
hybrid	SDix
'John Treasure'	WHil
'Joy's Purple'	CPar CPen CTca LRHS
montana	CBgR CFwr CPen CPrp CTca EBee ERCP LAma WPGP
pallidiflora ♀H4	CAvo CDes CGHE CHEx LEdu SMHy WHil WPGP
pole-evansii	CDes CFir CPLG CPen CPne CTca CTrC EAEE EAmu EBee ECGP ELan ERCP EShb EUJe EWld IVic LAma LPio LRHS MLLN MMHG MRav SMrm WPGP WTin WWEG
I - 'Purpurea'	EBee GCal
punctata	see *E. comosa*
regia	WCot
* ***reichenbachii***	CDTJ WHil
'Swazi Pride'	CTca WHil
undulata	see *E. autumnalis* (Mill.) Chitt.
vandermerwei	CAvo CDes CFwr CPLG CPen CTca EBee EPot ERCP LAma SKHP WHil WPGP WTin WWst
- 'Octopus'	CKno CPen CPrp CSpr CTca EAmu EBee ELan ELon EPfP EShb ESwi GAbr IPot LRHS LSou MAvo MGos SBfd SMad SPoG SUsu WBrE WCot WFut WHil WPrP WWEG
§ ***zambesiaca***	CMea CPen CTca EWld GCal LPio SMHy WHil WWEG
- 'White Dwarf'	CStu ECho EShb LRHS SPer WClo
'Zeal Bronze'	CDes CGHE CMHG CMil CTca ELan EPfP GCal LPio LRHS NSti WHrl WPGP

Eucommia (*Eucommiaceae*)

ulmoides	CCCN CDul CMCN EBtc EPfP GKir IDee IVic NLar WPGP

Eucrosia (*Amaryllidaceae*)

bicolor	EBee LAma WCot

Eucryphia ✿ (*Eucryphiaceae*)

cordifolia	CAbP CBcs CDul CGHE CMac CWib GKir LAst NMun SSpi WDin
- Crarae hardy form	GGGa
§ ***cordifolia*** × ***lucida***	CBcs CCCN ELan GGal MSnd SLdr SPer SRot WDin WPat
glutinosa ♀H4	CBcs CCCN CDul CTho EBee EPfP GKev MBri SSpi WDin WFar
- 'Miniature' **new**	SChF
- Plena Group (d)	WPat
× ***hillieri***	WSpi
- 'Winton'	CMHG GQui
× ***intermedia***	CMac CPLG CTrC CWSG EBee ELan GGGa LRHS NLar NPal SLdr SPer SRms SSpi WDin WFar
- 'Rostrevor' ♀H3	CBcs CMHG CMac CPLG CPMA CSBt CTho EBee ELan EPfP GAbr GBin GQui IFFs IVic LHyd LRHS LSRN MAsh MBlu MDun MGos NLar SReu SSta WFar WSHC WSpi
'Leatherwood Cream'	WSpi
lucida	CCCN CDoC CTrC CTsd EBee ELan GGar IArd NLar WFar WSpi
- 'Ballerina'	CMHG CMac CPMA CTho ELon GGGa LRHS MAsh MGos SCoo SPoG SRot SSpi SSta WAbe WFar
- 'Dumpling'	CGHE CPLG EBee WPGP
- 'Gilt Edge' (v)	CBcs CTrC CWGN LLHF LRHS MMHG
- 'Pink Cloud'	Widely available
- 'Pink Whisper'	see *E. milliganii* subsp. *pubescens* 'Pink Whisper'
- 'Spring Glow' (v)	CTrC CWGN LLHF LRHS MAsh SPoG SSta
milliganii	CAbP CBcs CDoC CMac CTrC EBee ELan EPfP GGGa GGar GQui LHop LRHS MRav NPal SRms SSpi SSta WAbe WPGP WSpi
§ - subsp. ***pubescens*** 'Pink Whisper'	SSpi WPGP
moorei	CBcs CCCN CMac CPLG GQui MMuc NMun SSpi
× ***nymansensis***	CWib LSRN SAPC SArc SDnm SReu SRms SSpi
- 'George Graham'	GGGa
- 'Nymans Silver' (v)	ELan LLHF LRHS MAsh SPoG SSpi
- 'Nymansay' ♀H3	Widely available
- 'Nymansay Variegated' (v)	CPMA
'Penwith' misapplied	see *E. cordifolia* × *lucida*
'Penwith' ambig.	CDoC CTsd GQui MMuc SPer WBrE WDin WFar

Eugenia (*Myrtaceae*)

uniflora	CCCN

Eunomia see *Aethionema*

Euodia (*Rutaceae*)

daniellii	see *Tetradium daniellii*
hupehensis	see *Tetradium daniellii* Hupehense Group

Euonymus ✿ (*Celastraceae*)

B&L 12543	EPla EWes
- CC 4522	CPLG
alatus ♀H4	Widely available
- B&SWJ 8794	WCru
- var. ***apterus***	EPfP
- Chicago Fire	see *E. alatus* 'Timber Creek'
- 'Compactus' ♀H4	Widely available
§ - 'Fire Ball'	CPMA EPfP
- Little Moses = 'Odom'	NLar
* - 'Macrophyllus'	CPMA EPfP
- 'Rudy Haag'	CPMA EPfP NLar
- 'Select'	see *E. alatus* 'Fire Ball'
- 'Silver Cloud'	CPMA EPfP
§ - 'Timber Creek'	CPMA EPfP NLar WPat
americanus	EPfP MBlu NLar
- 'Evergreen'	EPfP
- narrow-leaved	EPfP
atropurpureus	EPfP
'Benkomoki'	EMil
bungeanus	EPfP WPat
- 'Dart's Pride'	CPMA EPfP NLar
- 'Fireflame'	CPMA EPfP
* - var. ***mongolicus***	EPfP
- 'Pendulus'	CPMA EPfP MBlu SCoo
- var. ***semipersistens***	CPMA
carnosus	CPMA EPfP
chibae B&SWJ 11159	WCru
cornutus var. ***quinquecornutus***	CPMA ELan EPfP GKev GKir IDee MBlu NLar WCot WPGP WPat
'Den Haag'	CPMA EPfP NLar

	echinatus	EPfP EPla
	europaeus	Widely available
	- f. ***albus***	CBot CPMA CTho EPfP EQua NLar
	- 'Atropurpureus'	CMCN CTho EPfP
	- 'Atrorubens'	CPMA
	- 'Aucubifolius' (v)	CMac EPfP
*	- 'Aureus'	CNat
	- 'Brilliant'	CPMA EPfP NLar
*	- f. ***bulgaricus***	EPfP
	- 'Chrysophyllus'	EPfP MBlu
	- 'Howard'	EPfP
	- var. ***intermedius***	CPMA EPfP MBlu MBri NLar
	- 'Miss Pinkie'	CEnd GKir
	- 'Red Cascade' ♀^{H4}	Widely available
	- 'Scarlet Wonder'	CPMA EPfP
	- 'Thornhayes'	CTho EPfP NLar
I	- 'Variegatus'	EPfP
	europeaus 'Pumilis'	EPfP
	farreri	see *E. nanus*
	fimbriatus	CPMA EPfP
	fortunei	LEdu NHol
	- Blondy = 'Interbolwi'^{PBR} (v)	CAbP CDoC CDul CSBt CTri CWSG CWib CWit EBee ELan EPfP GKir IFoB LAst LRHS MAsh MBri MGos MRav MSwo NEgg NHol NPri SBfd SCoo SLim SPer SPoG WDin
	- 'Canadale Gold' (v)	EBee EPfP EPla EQua LRHS MAsh MGos NHol SPoG WDin
	- 'Coloratus'	CMac EBee EPfP MBlu MSwo NHol SEND SPer WDin
	- 'Dart's Blanket'	CDul ELan EPPr MMuc MRav WDin WFar
	- 'Emerald Cushion'	CDul
	- 'Emerald Gaiety' (v) ♀^{H4}	Widely available
	- 'Emerald 'n' Gold' (v) ♀^{H4}	Widely available
	- 'Emerald Surprise' (v) ♀^{H4}	EBee EPfP SRGP
	- 'Gold Spot'	see *E. fortunei* 'Sunspot'
	- 'Gold Tip'	see *E. fortunei* Golden Prince
	- 'Golden Harlequin' (v)	CSBt EGxp EMil LRHS MAsh SPoG
§	- 'Golden Pillar' (v)	EHoe EPla WFar
§	- Golden Prince (v)	CMac EHoe EPfP EPla MGos MRav MSwo SLim SRms WGor
	- 'Harlequin' (v)	CBar CBcs CMac CSBt CWSG EBee EHoe ELan ELon EPfP LAst LBMP LBuc LRHS LSRN MAsh MBlu MGos MMuc MNHC MRav NBir SAga SBfd SLim SPer SRms SWvt WFar WFoF
	- 'Hort's Blaze'	EPPr
	- 'Kewensis'	CDoC CMac CWib EBee EPfP GCal LRHS MWhi SAPC SArc SPoG WCru
	- 'Minimus'	CTri EPPr EPla MGos NHol WFar
*	- 'Minimus Variegatus' (v)	ECho EPPr SPlb
	- 'Perrolino'	EBee
§	- var. ***radicans***	MGan
	- 'Sheridan Gold'	CMac CTri EPla MRav
	- 'Silver Gem'	see *E. fortunei* 'Variegatus'
	- 'Silver Pillar' (v)	CPLG EBee EHoe WFar
	- 'Silver Queen' (v)	Widely available
	- 'Silverstone'^{PBR} (v)	EPfP LRHS NHol SPoG
	- 'Sunshine' (v)	CAbP ELan EPfP LRHS MAsh MGos SLon SPoG
§	- 'Sunspot' (v)	CBcs CMac EBee ECrN ELan LBMP MGos MSwo NHol SLim SRms WDin WFar WHar
	- 'Tustin' ♀^{H4}	EPPr LTen SLPl
§	- 'Variegatus' (v)	SRms STre WDin
	- var. ***vegetus***	EPla
	- 'Wolong Ghost'	CDoC MGos SKHP WCot
	frigidus	EPfP WPGP
	grandiflorus	CPMA EPfP GKir NLar SCoo SPur WFar
	- 'Red Wine'	CPMA CTho EPfP LHop LRHS NLar SKHP WPGP WPat
	- f. ***salicifolius***	CPMA EPfP
	hamiltonianus	CMCN EBtc EPfP SSpi
I	- 'Calocarpus'	CPMA SCoo
	- 'Fiesta'	CPMA EPfP NLar
	- subsp. ***hians***	see *E. hamiltonianus* subsp. *sieboldianus*
	- 'Indian Summer'	CPMA EBee EPfP GKir LRHS MBri MMHG NLar SCoo SKHP SPur SSpi WPGP WPat
	- 'Koi Boy'	CPMA GKir MAsh MGos SPur
	- 'Miss Pinkie'	CDul CPMA EPfP GKir MAsh MGos NLar SCoo SPur SSpi WPat
	- 'Pink Delight'	CPMA EPfP
	- 'Poort Bulten'	CPMA EPfP NLar
	- 'Popcorn'	CPMA EPfP WPat
	- 'Rainbow'	CPMA EPfP MBri
	- 'Red Chief'	CPMA EPfP
	- 'Red Elf'	CPMA EPfP
	- 'Rising Sun'	CPMA EPfP MBri NLar
§	- subsp. ***sieboldianus***	CDul CMen CPLG CPMA CTho EPfP GAuc MAsh MRav NPCo SLPl WFar WPat
	- - B&SWJ 10941	WCru
	- - 'Calocarpus'	EPfP
	- - 'Coral Charm'	CPMA EPfP NLar
	- - Semiexsertus Group	EPfP
*	- - var. ***yedoensis*** f. ***koehneanus***	EPfP
	- 'Snow'	CPMA EPfP MBri MWya NLar WPat
	- 'Winter Glory'	CPMA EPfP GKir MMHG WPat
	- var. ***yedoensis***	see *E. hamiltonianus* subsp. *sieboldianus*
	japonicus	CBcs CCVT CDoC CDul CMac ECrN EPfP MMuc SAPC SArc SBfd SEND SPer WDin
	- 'Albomarginatus'	CBcs CChe CTri EPfP MMuc SEND SRms
	- 'Aureopictus'	see *E. japonicus* 'Aureus'
	- 'Aureovariegatus'	see *E. japonicus* 'Ovatus Aureus'
§	- 'Aureus' (v)	CBcs CDoC CFee CSBt CWib EBee ECrN LAst LTen NPri SCoo SLon SPer WDin WHar
	- 'Benkomasaki'	EPfP
	- 'Bravo'	CDoC CDul EBee ECrN EHoe EPfP IVic LRHS LTen MGos MWea NLar SCoo SLim SPer SPoG SWvt WDin WFar
	- 'Chollipo' ♀^{H4}	ELan EPfP EPla LRHS MAsh MGos MMuc SPoG
	- 'Compactus'	SArc SCoo
	- 'Duc d'Anjou' misapplied	see *E. japonicus* 'Viridivariegatus'
	- 'Duc d'Anjou' Carrière (v)	CBcs EBee EHoe ELan EPfP EPla EWes MRav SBfd SEND SPoG
	- Exstase = 'Goldbolwi'^{PBR} (v)	SPoG
	- 'Extase' (v)	WCot
	- 'Golden Maiden'	ELan EPfP LRHS MAsh SLim SLon SPoG SWvt
	- 'Golden Pillar'	see *E. fortunei* 'Golden Pillar'
	- 'Green Rocket'	EPfP LRHS SBfd SPoG
	- 'Green Spider'	SPoG
	- 'Grey Beauty'	EBee ELon NLar
	- 'Hibarimisake'	EPfP
	- 'Kathy'^{PBR}	EPfP LRHS MGos SPoG SRGP
§	- 'Latifolius Albomarginatus'	CDul ELan EPfP MRav MSwo SBfd SPer WDin
	- 'Luna'	see *E. japonicus* 'Aureus'
	- 'Macrophyllus Albus'	see *E. japonicus* 'Latifolius Albomarginatus'
	- 'Maiden's Gold'	CSBt EBee

- 'Marieke'	see *E. japonicus* 'Ovatus Aureus'
- 'Microphyllus'	CDoC MRav SBfd STre WFar
§ - 'Microphyllus Albovariegatus' (v)	CBcs CChe CDoC CDul CMac CMea CSBt CTri CWSG ELan EPfP EPla LAst LRHS MGos NHol SBfd SLim SPoG SRms SWvt WDin WFar
§ - 'Microphyllus Aureovariegatus' (v)	CDoC CMea ELan EPfP LRHS MGos NLar SBfd SPoG
- 'Microphyllus Aureus'	see *E. japonicus* 'Microphyllus Pulchellus'
§ - 'Microphyllus Pulchellus' (v)	CBcs CDoC CMac CSBt EBee ECrN EPfP EPla LRHS LTen MGos NHol SBfd SPoG SWvt WDin
- 'Microphyllus Variegatus'	see *E. japonicus* 'Microphyllus Albovariegatus'
§ - 'Ovatus Aureus' (v) ♀H4	CBar CChe CDoC CDul CPLG CSBt CTri CWSG EBee ELon EPfP LAst LRHS MGos MMuc MRav NPri SBfd SLim SPer SPlb SPoG SRms SWvt WDin WFar
- 'Président Gauthier' (v)	CBar CDoC EBee ECrN EQua LTen MGos MWea SBfd SCoo SLim SPer SWvt WCFE WDin
- 'Pulchellus Aureovariegatus'	see *E. japonicus* 'Microphyllus Aureovariegatus'
I - 'Pyramidatus'	EPfP
- 'Robustus'	EPfP EPla
- 'Silver King'	CMac
- 'Silver Krista' (v)	SPoG
- 'Susan' (v)	CDoC EPla EQua MAsh SRGP
§ - 'Viridivariegatus' (v)	LRHS
kachinensis	WCru
B&SWJ 11668 **new**	
kiautschovicus	EPfP
- 'Berry Hill'	EPfP NLar
- 'Manhattan'	EPfP NLar
latifolius	CMCN CPMA EPfP GKir WPat
lucidus	CBcs CHII CPLG IRar SSpi WFar
maackii	MMHG
macropterus	CPMA EPfP
maximowiczianus	EPfP WPat
morrisonensis	EPfP
- B&SWJ 3700	WCru
myrianthus	CPMA EPfP EWes MAsh MBlu NLar
§ ***nanus***	CWib EPfP MAsh NHol NLar WThu
- var. ***turkestanicus***	EPfP LHop SLon SRms WClo WFar
obovatus	EPfP NLar
occidentalis	EPfP
oresbius	CPMA EPfP
oxyphyllus	CMCN CPMA EPfP GKir IArd MBri NLar SCoo SSpi WCru WDin
- 'Angyo Elegant' (v)	EPfP
- 'Waasland'	CPMA EPfP
pauciflorus	EPfP
phellomanus ♀H4	CDul CEnd CTho EBee EPfP EWTr GKir IDee LHop LRHS MBlu MGos MPkF MRav NLar SCoo SKHP WDin WFar WPGP WPat
- 'Silver Surprise' (v)	CPMA EPfP WPat
Pierrolino = 'Heespierrolino'PBR	EGxp LRHS SCoo SPoG
§ ***planipes*** ♀H4	Widely available
- 'Dart's August Flame'	CPMA EPfP
- 'Gold Ore'	EPfP
- 'Sancho'	CPMA EPfP IArd WPat
quelpaertensis	EPfP
radicans	see *E. fortunei* var. *radicans*
'Rokojō'	CStu LLHF NWCA WPat
'Rokojō Variegated' (v) **new**	LLHF
rongchuensis	CPMA EPfP
rosmarinifolius	see *E. nanus*
sachalinensis misapplied	see *E. planipes*
sacrosanctus	CPMA EPfP NLar
sanguineus	CPMA EPfP NLar SSpi
sieboldianus	WCru
var. ***sanguineus*** B&SWJ 11140	
spraguei	CFee EPfP
tingens	CPMA EPfP GKir NLar
trapococcus	EPfP
vagans	EPfP
- L 551	EPla
velutinus	EPfP
verrucosus	CPMA EPfP EPla GKir NLar
vidalii	EPfP
wilsonii	MAsh
yedoensis	see *E. hamiltonianus* subsp. *sieboldianus*

Eupatoriadelphus see *Eupatorium*

Eupatorium ✿ (*Asteraceae*)

B&SWJ 9052 from Guatemala	WCru
album L.	NBid SWat
altissimum	CBot SRms
aromaticum	see *Ageratina aromatica*
atrorubens	see *Bartlettina sordida*
cannabinum	CArn CWan EBWF EBee EHon ELan GBar GGar GPWP GPoy IFoB LPBA MBNS MHer MLLN MMuc MNHC MRav NBir NGHP NMir NPer SGSe SMrm SPav SWat WBVN WHfH WPer WSFF
§ - f. ***albiflorum***	SPhx
- 'Album'	see *E. cannabinum* f. *albiflorum*
- f. ***cannabinum*** 'Flore Pleno' (d)	CAby CMac CPrp CSev EBee ECha ECtt ELan ELon EPfP LHop MHer MLLN MRav NBir NEgg NGdn SAga SPhx SWat WAul WCom WCot WFar WMnd WPtf WSFF WTin
- - 'Spraypaint' (v)	WSFF
capillifolium ♀H3	CAby CSpe EBee ECtt EShb ESwi EWes GBin LEdu LHop LSou MDKP SAga SDix SDys SHar SMad SMrm SPhx SUsu WCot WPGP WSFF WWEG
coelestinum	see *Conoclinium coelestinum*
dubium 'Baby Joe' **new**	MBri
- 'Little Joe' **new**	EBee
fistulosum	NGdn
- f. ***albidum*** 'Bartered Bride'	CKno EBee ECtt EWes GCal
- - 'Joe White'	WSFF
- - 'Massive White' ♀H4	CFir EBee GCal NBir NDov NSti SMad WSpi
- 'Berggarten'	EBee GCal
- 'Carin'	WSFF
fortunei	CArn
- 'Fine Line' (v)	CBow CKno EBee EPPr LSou MHer WCot WPGP WSFF
glechonophyllum	see *Ageratina glechonophylla*
japonicum	GPoy
ligustrinum	see *Ageratina ligustrina*
lindleyanum	CKno
maculatum	EHrv MDKP NGHP NGdn NLar STes WHrl
- Atropurpureum Group ♀H4	Widely available
- - 'Ankum's August'	NDov
- - 'Gateway'	CRow EBee EBrs GCal NBPC NBre NCGa SPhx WHil WHoo WPtf WSFF WTin
- - 'Glutball'	CHVG CKno EBee EBrs ELon GCal LBMP LPla LRHS MNrw NChi SMad
- - 'Little Red'	WSFF

- - 'Orchard Dene' ♀H4	SPur
- - 'Phantom'	EBee ECtt GQue IPot MBri NLar SPoG SSvw
- - 'Purple Bush' ♀H4	CKno CSam EBee ECha ELon EPPr GCal MDKP NBre NCGa NDov NEgg SMad SPhx SSvw WSFF WWEG
- - 'Riesenschirm' ♀H4	Widely available
makinoi var. ***oppositifolium***	EBee
- - B&SWJ 8449	WCru
micranthum	see *Ageratina ligustrina*
occidentale	see *Ageratina occidentalis*
perfoliatum	CArn CKno EBee GPoy MNrw NBre NLar SPav SPhx
purpureum	Widely available
- 'Album'	CTri MLLN SPhx
rugosum	see *Ageratina altissima*
- ***album***	see *Ageratina altissima*
variabile	EWes WWEG
'Golders Green' (v)	
weinmannianum	see *Ageratina ligustrina*

Euphorbia ✿ (*Euphorbiaceae*)

'Abbey Dore'	MAvo WCot
altissima	ITim
ambovombensis	LToo
amygdaloides	CTca EBla ECtt GKir SWat SWvt
- 'Bob's Choice'	EWes
- 'Craigieburn'	CDes EBla EWes GCal GCra LBMP LBuc LRHS MAsh MGos MRav NDov SUsu WCom WPGP WWEG
§ - 'Purpurea'	Widely available
§ - var. ***robbiae*** ♀H4	Widely available
- - dwarf	EWes
- - 'Pom Pom'	EBee ELon LSou WPGP
- - 'Redbud'	EBee EPla EWes LSou SLPl
- 'Rubra'	see *E. amygdaloides* 'Purpurea'
- 'Winter Glow'	CSpe
- yellow-leaved	WCot
ankarensis	LToo
baselicis	CBow CPla CPom CTca EBee GAbr LPio WPer
biglandulosa Desf.	see *E. rigida*
Blackbird = 'Nothowlee'PBR	Widely available
'Blue Dome' new	CSpe
'Blue Haze'	CDes MAvo NWit WCot
bupleurifolia new	LToo
canariensis	EPfP
capitulata	EWes MTho
cashmeriana	NWit
- CC&McK 607	EWes
- CC&McK 724	GBin
ceratocarpa	EBee EPPr EWes GMaP LRHS LSou NEgg NWit SEND SMad WClo WCot WPGP WSHC
characias	CBcs CBot CHEx CMac EBee EBla ECtt EPfP GKir LRHS MCot MLHP MRav NPer NVic SBfd SMrm SPer SRms SWvt WBrk WCom WCot WMnd WPer WWEG
I - 'Best Yet'	WCot
- 'Black Pearl'	CBcs CCVN CTca EBee EBrs ECtt EPfP GKir LAst LRHS LSou MAvo MCCP MGos NBPC NCGa NEgg SBfd SDnm SEND SMrm SPer SWvt WFar
- 'Blue Wonder'	CMac CSpe EBee EBrs ECtt EHrv ELan EPfP GAbr GMaP LRHS LSou MAvo MCCP MGos MTis NEgg NLar NSti NWit SDnm SPad WCot WHoo WWEG
- subsp. ***characias***	CPrp EHrv GMaP MGos SEND
- - 'Blue Hills'	ECtt
- - 'Burrow Silver' (v)	CFir EBee GMaP LSRN MAvo MRav NEgg SDnm SMrm SWvt WFar
- - 'H.E. Bates'	NBir
- - 'Humpty Dumpty'	Widely available
- - 'Perry's Winter Blusher'	ECtt
- 'Dwarf Black Pearl'	CBar ECtt WWEG
- 'Forescate'	CSev CTca EBee EPfP GMaP LHop LPio LRHS LSRN NBPC SBfd SDnm WWEG
- 'Goldbrook'	CMac EBla ECtt EHoe MRav WCra
- 'Kestrel' (v)	WCom WCot
- 'Portuguese Velvet' ♀H4	Widely available
- Silver Swan = 'Wilcott'PBR (v)	CBcs CMac CSpe CWGN EBee ECtt EHoe ELan EPfP EWes IFoB LAst LBMP LBuc LRHS LSRN LSou MAsh MGos MRav NSti SDix SHeu SKHP SPoG SUsu SWvt WClo WCot WFar
- 'Spring Splendour'	EWes
- 'Starbright'	EBee GBin
- 'Tasmanian Tiger' (v)	CSpe CWGN EBrs EWes LRHS NCGa SBfd SKHP
- subsp. ***wulfenii*** ♀H3-4	Widely available
- - 'Bosahan' (v)	CBcs CPLG GCra
- - dwarf	WOut
- - 'Emmer Green' (v)	CBow CPLG CSpe EBee EHrv EPfP EWes GAbr GCal GMaP LRHS MLLN MMHG MTis NPnk NWit SMrm WClo WCot WFoF WWEG
- - 'Jayne's Golden Giant'	SMad
- - 'Jimmy Platt'	SRms WCom WCot
§ - - 'John Tomlinson' ♀H3-4	CMoH EBee EHrv EWes GBin LSRN MRav SUsu WCot WSpi
- - Kew form	see *E. characias* subsp. *wulfenii* 'John Tomlinson'
- - 'Lambrook Gold' ♀H3-4	CSam CTca CWCL ECtt EPfP GCra GMaP MRav MWat NLar NPer SMad WCot WFar WMnd WSpi WWEG
- - 'Lambrook Gold' seed-raised	see *E. characias* subsp. *wulfenii* Margery Fish Group
- - 'Lambrook Yellow'	EBee GCal NWsh
§ - - Margery Fish Group	CMac CSev EBee LBMP NBir SPer
- - 'Perry's Tangerine'	EWes NPer NWit
§ - - 'Purple and Gold'	EBee EWes GMaP MAvo NLar NWit SMad SWvt WSpi WWEG
- - 'Purpurea'	see *E. characias* subsp. *wulfenii* 'Purple and Gold'
- - 'Thelma's Giant'	NWit
clavarioides var. ***truncata***	WCot
'Copton Ash'	CSpe EBee EPPr EWes MAvo NWit SKHP
corallioides	EBee ECha IFro LRHS NPer NSti SPav WBrE WHer WPnP
§ ***cornigera*** ♀H4	EBee ECha EPfP GBin GMac LPio LRHS MCot MMuc MRav MSpe NBid NGdn NWit SEND SMHy SPhx SWat WCru WPGP WPen WPnP
- 'Goldener Turm'	CMoH EBee ECtt GBin GCal LSou NDov SMrm SPer WCot
corollata	EBee
croizatii	LToo
cylindrifolia var. ***tubifera***	LToo
cyparissias	CArn CBcs EBee ECha ELan LRHS MLHP MRav NBir NGdn NMen SBfd SMrm SPav SRms WBrk WEas WFar WFoF WPer WTin
- 'Baby'	WFar

- 'Betten'	see *E.* × *gayeri* 'Betten'
- 'Bushman Boy'	SMrm
- 'Clarice Howard'	see *E. cyparissias* 'Fens Ruby'
§ - 'Fens Ruby'	Widely available
- 'Orange Man'	CTca EBee EBla ECtt EPfP EPla EWes GBin LBMP LRHS NBro NEgg NGdn NHol SPoG SWat SWvt WBrk WFar WOut
- 'Purpurea'	see *E. cyparissias* 'Fens Ruby'
- 'Red Devil'	NWit SMrm
- 'Tall Boy'	EWes SMrm
decaryi var. ***cap-saintemariensis*** new	LToo
- var. ***spirosticha*** new	LToo
deflexa	EBee EWes MAvo
dendroides	WCot
§ ***donii***	EBee EWes IFoB NDov NWit SDix WCot
- HWJK 2405	WCru
- 'Amjillasa'	SAga SDix SMHy SUsu
dulcis	CBre CStu ECtt NBro NWit
- 'Chameleon'	Widely available
'Efanthia' PBR	CEnd CSev EBee EPfP EWes LHop LRHS LSou MBri NLar NPri SPoG STes
enopla	EPfP
epithymoides	see *E. polychroma*
esculenta new	LToo
esula Baker's form	NWit
Excalibur = 'Froeup' PBR 🏆H4	CWCL EBee ELan ELon GBin LHop LRHS MBNS MBri MCCP MMuc MRav NBir NEgg NHol SBfd SEND SPer SPoG WFar
flavicoma	GCal
fragifera	EBee NWit SUsu
'Garblesham Enchanter'	EPPr
§ × ***gayeri*** 'Betten'	EBee LPla
glauca	CFir ECou MAvo NWit SKHP
'Golden Foam'	see *E. stricta*
gottlebei	LToo
griffithii	CHll GGal IFoB NBro SPav SWat WFar WMoo
- 'Dixter' 🏆H4	Widely available
- 'Dixter Flame'	IFoB NWit
- 'Fern Cottage'	CElw CWCL EBee EHrv EWes GAbr MSpe WMnd WWEG
- 'Fireglow'	Widely available
- var. ***griffithii*** new	GKev
- 'King's Caple'	EBee ELon EWes GBin SBfd SPoG WCru
- 'Wickstead'	EBee GAbr GBin MLHP NLar
'Helena' PBR (v)	CHVG EBee EPfP LHop LSRN MAsh NLar NPri SHeu SRot WClo WCot WHil WWEG
hyberna	LLHF NMen NWit SWat
hypericifolia Diamond Frost = 'Inneuphe' PBR	CCVN CFox CSpe CWit EPfP ESwi LHop LSou MWea SRkn SVil
ingens	NPla
jacquemontii	EBee IFoB LPio MRav NChi NDov NWit
'Jade Dragon'	SBfd WWEG
'Jessie'	MAvo NCGa
jolkinii SDR 4307	GKev
Kalipso = 'Innkalff'	EPfP NLar SHeu
knuthii new	LToo
'Lambrook Silver'	SRkn
lathyris	CArn CBre CTca MHer MLHP NHol NLar NPer NWit SRms SVic WEas
longifolia misapplied	see *E. cornigera*
longifolia D. Don	see *E. donii*
longifolia Lam.	see *E. mellifera*
margalidiana	EWes
× ***martini*** 🏆H3	Widely available
- 'Aperitif' PBR	CBow EBee EPfP SMrm
- 'Baby Charm'	CWCL EAEE EBee EPPr GBBs IPot LRHS LSRN MAvo NDov SMrm WCot
- 'Cherokee' new	WCot
- dwarf	CFir CSpr
- 'Helen Robinson'	CDes MAvo WCot WPGP
- Helena's Blush = 'Inneuphhel' (v)	EPfP LRHS
- 'Kolibri'	EBee EPfP LSou SPoG
- Rudolph = 'Waleuphrud'	LRHS
- 'Tiny Tim'	EPfP GKir LRHS LSRN MAsh MWat SBfd SPoG SWvt
- 'Walberton's Rudolf'	MAsh SPoG
§ ***mellifera*** 🏆H3	Widely available
milii 🏆H1	EBak LRHS
moratii	LToo
myrsinites 🏆H4	Widely available
nereidum	EWes NWit
nicaeensis	CPom EBee GCal LRHS SEND SPer WPGP WSHC
- subsp. ***glareosa***	NWit
oblongata	EWes NWit SEND
pachypodioides	LToo
palustris 🏆H4	Widely available
- 'Walenburg's Glorie'	CMHG CWCL EBee EBla ECha ELan GBin MBri MNrw MRav NCGa NSti NWit SMad SWat WSpi
- 'Zauberflöte'	SRms WFar
× ***paradoxa***	NWit
paralias	WCot WHer
× ***pasteurii***	CDTJ CFir CPom ECGP EWes LSou MAvo MSpe NBir NWit SMad WPGP WSpi
- 'Devil's Honey'	CHid CSpe WCot
- 'John Phillips'	CMHG CPLG LRHS SBfd SChF SMad WPGP WSpi
pekinensis	SKHP
pilosa 'Major'	see *E. polychroma* 'Major'
piscatoria	WPGP
pithyusa	CBot EBee ECha ECtt ELan EPfP LHop MAvo MRav NGdn SEND WCom WCot
platyclada new	LToo
§ ***polychroma*** 🏆H4	Widely available
- 'Bonfire' new	NDov
§ - 'Candy'	CBot CWCL EBee EBrs ECha ECtt EHrv ELan EPfP MCCP MMuc WCom WFar WMnd
- compact	NWit
- 'Emerald Jade'	WPGP
- 'First Blush' (v)	CWGN EWes NBre
- 'Golden Fusion'	LRHS MAsh WFar
§ - 'Lacy' (v)	CDoC EBee ECtt EHrv EWes GCal LAst MCCP MRav NBir NGdn NWit SKHP WFar
§ - 'Major' 🏆H4	CPLG SAga WCom WCot WKif
- 'Midas'	GBin NWit
- 'Purpurea'	see *E. polychroma* 'Candy'
* - 'Senior'	MAvo MGos MWat NWit
- 'Sonnengold'	EWes WSHC
- 'Variegata'	see *E. polychroma* 'Lacy'
portlandica	NWit WHer
§ × ***pseudovirgata***	NWit
'Purple Preference'	EPPr
Redwing = 'Charam' PBR 🏆H4	CBcs EBee ELan EPfP IKil LBuc LRHS LSou MAsh MBri MGos MRav MWea NDov NLar NWit SCoo SLim SPer SPhx SPoG SRkn SWvt
reflexa	see *E. seguieriana* subsp. *niciciana*

§ ***rigida*** ♀H4	CAby CBot CDes CTca EBee ECGP EHoe EHrv ELan EPfP EPyc EWes GKir ITim LPio LRHS NSti SMrm SPhx SUsu WCot WFar WPGP WSpi WWEG
- 'Sardis'	NWit
robbiae	see *E. amygdaloides* var. *robbiae*
'Rosies Surprise'	LLHF
rothiana GWJ 9479a	WCru
'Roundway Titan'	SSpi WSHC
'Royal Velvet'	CBow
sarawschanica	ECha GBBs GBin GQue LPla LRHS NWit SMad SMrm SPhx
schillingii ♀H4	CAby CMea CSam EBee EBrs EHoe ELan EPfP GCra GMaP LHop LPio LRHS MCot MRav MSCN SDix SPer SPoG SUsu WCru WFar WHoo WPGP WSpi WTin WWEG
seguieriana	ECha NLar WPer
§ - subsp. ***niciciana***	CBot CBow CMoH GBin IMou NWsh WHoo
serrulata Thuill.	see *E. stricta*
sikkimensis ♀H4	CBot CBow CMHG CPLG CPom CSam CWCL EBee ECha ELan GCal GKev LPio LRHS MAvo NEgg NPer SMrm SRms WCom WCot WCru WEas WFar WHoo WPnP
- GWJ 9214	WCru
- 'Crûg Contrast' new	WCru
soongarica	NWit
spinosa	NWit SPlb
§ ***stricta***	WTin
stygiana	CFir CMil CPLG CSam CSpe CWCL EBee ELon EUJe EWes GBin GCal ITim LPio MAvo MTis SAga SMrm SPlb WCot WCru WPGP
symmetrica	LToo
Thalia = 'Innthal'	EPfP LTen
tirucalli	EShb
tortirama new	LToo
triangularis new	SPlb
umfoloziensis	LToo
uralensis	see *E.* × *pseudovirgata*
valdevillosocarpa	CPom CTca WPer
'Velvet Ruby'	EWes LSou MAvo NDov NWit SPoG WCot
verrucosa	NWit WFar
viguieri ♀H1	LToo
villosa Waldst. & Kit. ex Willd.	NWit
§ ***virgata***	EWes NWit SPav
× ***waldsteinii***	see *E. virgata*
wallichii misapplied	see *E. donii*
wallichii Kohli	see *E. cornigera*
wallichii ambig.	NPnk
wallichii Hook. f.	CPLG EBee EPfP GCal GKir MGos SKHP WPGP
- 'Lemon and Lime'	CWib LSou WFar
'Whistleberry Garnet'	EBee LLHF LRHS LSou MWea SDix SKHP SPoG

Euptelea (Eupteleaceae)

franchetii	see *E. pleiosperma*
§ ***pleiosperma***	EBee NLar SSpi
polyandra	EPfP MBri NLar WPGP

Eurya (Theaceae)

japonica	WPGP
- 'Moutiers' (v)	WPat
- 'Variegata' misapplied	see *Cleyera japonica* 'Fortunei'

Euryops (Asteraceae)

abrotanifolius	CCCN CTca CTrC
§ ***acraeus*** ♀H4	CMea CSBt ECho EPfP EPot EWes LRHS MWat NMen NWCA SAga WAbe WCom WFar
candollei	CTrC
§ ***chrysanthemoides***	CCCN CHEx CSam EShb MREP
- 'Sonnenschein'	EBee SPet
evansii	see *E. acraeus*
lateriflorus	SPlb
pectinatus ♀H2	CBcs CCCN CDTJ CDoC CHEx CPLG CSam CTca CTrC CTri EBee EPfP EShb GBin GGal GGar IVic LAst MMuc MNrw MRav NPri SGar SOWG SWvt WCFE WHer
spathaceus	CTrC
tenuissimus	CTrC
tysonii	CTca CTrC EBee EWes GCal GEdr SPlb WCot
virgineus	CCCN CHVG CPLG CTrC GGar

Eustachys (Poaceae)

§ ***distichophylla***	CAby NWsh WCot WPrP

Eustrephus (Philesiaceae)

latifolius	ECou

Eutaxia (Papilionaceae)

obovata	ECou

Euthamia (Asteraceae)

gymnospermoides	EWes

Eutrochium see *Eupatorium*

Ewartia (Asteraceae)

planchonii	NSla WAbe

Exochorda (Rosaceae)

alberti	see *E. korolkowii*
giraldii	CWit
- var. ***wilsonii***	CMac CPLG CSam EBee EPfP GBin LHop LRHS MBlu NLar SLim SSta SWvt
§ ***korolkowii***	LRHS
× ***macrantha***	CSpe EBee LRHS
- 'Irish Pearl'	CPLG
- 'The Bride' ♀H4	Widely available
racemosa	EPfP MMuc NLar SPer WDin
serratifolia	EPfP GAuc LRHS
- 'Snow White'	CMHG CPMA EBee EWes IArd MBlu NLar SBfd SLon

F

Fabiana (Solanaceae)

imbricata	CAbP EPfP LLHF LRHS SAga SLon SPer
- 'Prostrata'	EBee EPfP LRHS SSpi WAbe
- f. ***violacea*** ♀H3	CBcs CSBt CTri EBee EPfP LLHF LRHS MMuc SEND SPer WKif
nana	WAbe

Fagopyrum (Polygonaceae)

cymosum	see *F. dibotrys*
§ ***dibotrys***	CArn EBee ECha ELan EWld LEdu WMoo
- 'Variegatum' (v)	CBow

Fagus ✿ (*Fagaceae*)

§	***crenata***	CMen WDin
	- 'Mount Fuji'	SBir
	engleriana	CMCN SBir
	grandifolia	SBir
	subsp. ***mexicana***	
	japonica	SBir
	- var. ***multinervis***	SBir
	orientalis	CMCN ECrN SBir
	- 'Iskander'	MBlu
	sieboldii	see *F. crenata*
	sylvatica ♀H4	Widely available
§	- 'Albomarginata' (v)	CMCN
	- 'Albovariegata'	see *F. sylvatica* 'Albomarginata'
	- 'Ansorgei'	CEnd CMCN MBlu NLar
	- 'Arcuata'	SBir
N	- Atropurpurea Group	Widely available
	- - 'Friso'	CEnd
	- - 'Swat Magret'	CDul
	- 'Aurea Pendula'	CEnd CMCN ECrN MBlu SBir
	- 'Bicolor Sartini'	MBlu
	- 'Birr Zebra'	CEnd
	- 'Black Swan'	CMCN CPMA CWit EBee ECrN GKir IArd MBlu MGos NEgg NLar NPCo SBir SLon WClo
	- 'Cochleata'	CMCN
	- 'Cockleshell'	CDul MBlu MBri SBir SMad
	- 'Comptoniifolia'	see *F. sylvatica* var. *heterophylla* 'Comptoniifolia'
	- 'Cristata'	MBlu
N	- Cuprea Group	NWea
§	- 'Dawyck' ♀H4	CBcs CDoC CDul CLnd CMCN CMac CSBt CTho EBee ECho ECrN ELan EPfP GKir LAst LMaj MAsh MBri MGos NEgg NLar NPCo NWea SBir SLau SLim SPer WDin
	- 'Dawyck Gold' ♀H4	Widely available
	- 'Dawyck Purple' ♀H4	Widely available
	- 'Eugen'	SBir
	- 'Fastigiata' misapplied	see *F. sylvatica* 'Dawyck'
	- 'Felderbach'	MBlu SBir
	- 'Franken' (v)	MBlu SBir
	- 'Grandidentata'	CMCN
	- 'Greenwood'	MBlu
	- var. ***heterophylla***	CLnd CSBt CTho ECho NWea
	- - 'Aspleniifolia' ♀H4	CBcs CDoC CDul CEnd CMCN CMac EBee ECrN ELan EPfP EWTr GKir LRHS MBlu MBri MGos NPCo SBir SCoo SLau SPer SPoG WClo WDin WFar WMou
§	- - 'Comptoniifolia'	SBir
	- - f. ***laciniata***	GKir MBlu
	- 'Horizontalis'	MBlu
	- 'Incisa'	MBlu
	- 'Luteovariegata' (v)	CEnd CMCN CPMA
	- 'Mercedes'	CDoC CMCN MBlu NPCo WPat
N	- 'Pendula' ♀H4	CBcs CDoC CDul CEnd CMCN CSBt CTho EBee ECho ECrN ELan EPfP GKir LMaj LRHS MGos MSwo NEgg NPCo NWea SLau SPer SPoG WClo WDin WHar WMou
	- 'Prince George of Crete'	CDul CMCN SBir
	- 'Purple Fountain' ♀H4	CDoC CDul CEnd CMCN CPMA CWit EBee ELan GKir LAst LHop LRHS LTen MAsh MBlu MBri MGos NLar SBir SLau SLim WClo WFar WPat
	- Purple-leaved Group	see *F. sylvatica* Atropurpurea Group
	- 'Purpurea Latifolia'	LMaj
	- 'Purpurea Nana'	NPri
	- 'Purpurea Pendula'	Widely available
§	- 'Purpurea Tricolor' (v)	CDul CEnd CMCN CPMA ECrN MAsh MBlu MGos MWya NBea NWea SBir SCoo SPer WClo WDin
	- 'Quercifolia'	MBlu
I	- 'Quercina'	SBir
	- 'Red Obelisk'	see *F. sylvatica* 'Rohan Obelisk'
	- 'Riversii' ♀H4	CBcs CDoC CDul CEnd CLnd CMCN CSBt CTho CTri CWib EBee ECrN ELan EPfP LAst LRHS MAsh MBri MGos NEgg NWea SLim SPer SPoG WDin WFar WHar
	- 'Rohan Gold'	CDul CEnd CMCN EBee MBlu
§	- 'Rohan Obelisk'	CDul CEnd CMCN CTho EBee ELan IArd MBlu MGos NLar SBir
I	- 'Rohan Pyramidalis'	CEnd
	- 'Rohan Trompenburg'	CMCN MBlu
	- 'Rohan Weeping'	MBlu SBir
	- 'Rohanii'	CBcs CDoC CDul CEnd CLnd CMCN CTri EBee ECho ELan EPfP LHop NPCo SBir SCoo SLau SPer WDin WFar WHar
	- 'Roseomarginata'	see *F. sylvatica* 'Purpurea Tricolor'
	- 'Rotundifolia'	CDoC CDul MBlu SBir
	- 'Spaethiana'	EWTr
	- 'Striata'	LLHF NPCo SBir
	- 'Sychrov'	SBir
	- 'Tortuosa Purpurea'	CDul MBlu
	- 'Tricolor' misapplied	see *F. sylvatica* 'Purpurea Tricolor'
	- 'Tricolor' ambig. (v)	SLau WFoF
	- 'Tricolor' (v)	CBcs CLnd CMac CSBt CWib EBee ELan NEgg WDin
	- 'Viridivariegata' (v)	CMCN
	- 'Zlatia'	CBcs CDul CLnd CMCN CSBt CWib EBee ELan EPfP GKir MBlu MBri MGos MSwo SBir SCoo SLau SPer WClo WDin
	× ***taurica*** new	SBir

Fallopia (*Polygonaceae*)

	aubertii	see *F. baldschuanica*
§	***baldschuanica***	Widely available
	- Summer Sunshine = 'Acofal'PBR	CBcs
	× ***bohemica*** 'Spectabilis' (v)	CBow CRow
§	***japonica*** var. ***compacta***	CRow NLar WFar WMoo
	- - 'Fuji Snow'	see *F. japonica* var. *compacta* 'Milk Boy'
§	- - 'Milk Boy' (v)	CBow CRow
	- - f. ***rosea*** hort.	WSpi
	- - 'Variegata' misapplied	see *F. japonica* var. *compacta* 'Milk Boy'
	- 'Crimson Beauty'	CRow
§	***multiflora***	CArn EOHP NPnk
	- var. ***hypoleuca***	EBee MCCP SCoo SLim SPoG
	- - B&SWJ 120	WCru
	sachalinensis	NLar

Farfugium (*Asteraceae*)

§	***japonicum***	CHEx EPPr LRHS MTho
	- B&SWJ 884	WCru
	- 'Argenteum' (v)	CFir SMad WCom WCot WFar
§	- 'Aureomaculatum' (v) ♀H1	CFir CHEx EBee LEdu MCCP MTho SDnm WFar
	- 'Crispatum'	CAbP CBct CBow CFir EBee ECtt ELan EPPr EPfP EWll LAst LEdu MCCP NSti SDnm SMad WCot WFar WWEG
	- double-flowered (d)	WCru
	- var. ***formosanum*** B&SWJ 7125	WCru

	- var. ***giganteum***	CHEx WCot
	- 'Kagami-jishi' (v)	EPPr WCot
	- 'Kaimon Dake' **new**	WCot
	- 'Kinkan' (v)	WCot
I	- 'Nanum'	CHEx
	- 'Ryuto'	EBee EPPr SMad WCot
I	- 'Tsuwa-buki'	WCot
	tussilagineum	see *F. japonicum*

Fargesia (*Poaceae*)

	from Jiuzhaigou, China	CEnt EPfP ETod MBri MMoz MMuc NLar SEND WJun
	adpressa	EPla WJun
	angustissima	CDTJ CEnt ENBC EPla MMuc MWht SBig WJun WPGP
	'Baby'	STre
	confusa	CDTJ
	denudata	CDTJ CEnt EBee ENBC EPla SBig WJun
	- L 1575	CGHE MMoz MWht WPGP
	- Xian 1	CDTJ EPla MMoz WPGP
	- Xian 2	EPla
	dracocephala	CAbb CDoC CEnt CGHE EBee EPfP EPla ESwi GBin LEdu MAvo MBrN MBri MMoz MMuc MWht NGdn SBig SEND SLPl SPoG WDyG WJun WMoo WPGP
	ferax	EPla WJun WPGP
	fungosa	EPla ESwi WJun WPGP
§	***murielae*** 🏆H4	Widely available
	- 'Amy'	NLar NMoo
	- 'Bimbo'	CEnt EBee EPfP EPla ESwi ETod GBin LAst LRHS MWht NLar NPal NWsh STre WJun WMoo WPGP
	- 'Grüne Hecke'	EBee MWht SBig
	- 'Harewood'	CWSG GBin MGos MMoz MWht NMoo SWvt WFar WPGP
	- 'Joy'	GBin NLar WMoo WPnP
	- 'Jumbo'	CEnt CHEx CSBt EAmu ELan ELon ENBC EPfP EPla ESwi GBin LPal LRHS MAvo MBri MGos MMoz MWht NGdn NWsh SBig SPoG SRms SWvt WFar WJun
	- 'Kranich'	NLar
	- 'Lava'	MBri
	- 'Mae'	CDTJ MWht
	- 'Novecento'	ELan
	- 'Pinocchio'	EBee MBri
	- 'Simba' 🏆H4	Widely available
	- 'Vampire'	LRHS MBri MGos SBig
	- 'Willow'	EBee MBri
	murieliae 'Dana Jumbo'	LRHS
*	***nepalensis***	CDTJ ESwi
§	***nitida***	Widely available
*	- from Jiuzhaigou, China	CDTJ EPla GBin MWht NWsh SBig WDyG WPGP
	- 'Anceps'	MWht
	- 'Chennevières'	EPla
	- 'Eisenach'	EBee GKir MMoz WFar WMoo
	- Gansu 2	CGHE
	- 'Great Wall'	EBee GBin MBlu MBri MGos MWhi MWht
	- 'Jiuzhaigou 1'	EPla WJun
	- 'Jiuzhaigou 2'	EPla WJun
	- 'Jiuzhaigou 4'	EPla WPGP
	- 'Jiuzhaigou Genf' **new**	WPGP
	- 'Nymphenburg' 🏆H4	CEnd CPMA GKir MBri MMoz MWhi MWht NLar NMoo SBig WFar WMoo WPGP
	- 'Wakehurst'	MWht NLar
	nujiangensis	EPla
	perlonga	EPla WJun
	- Yunnan 95/6	MMoz WPGP
	robusta	CAbb CDTJ CEnd CEnt EBee ENBC EPfP EPla ETod GCal LPal MAvo MBrN MBri MMoz MMuc MWht NGdn NLar NMoo SBig SEND SLPl WDyG WJun
	- 'Ming Yunnan'	LEdu WJun
	- 'Pingwu'	CDTJ CEnt EBee ENBC ETod GBin MGos MWht NLar SBig WJun
	- 'Red Sheath'	CEnt EPla MMoz MWht NPal NPla WJun WPGP
	- 'Wolong'	CDoC EBee EPla ETod GBin MMoz MWht WJun WPGP
	rufa	CAbb CEnt EBee ENBC EPPr EPfP EPla EShb GCal LMaj LRHS LSRN MAvo MBrN MCCP MGos MMoz MMuc MWhi MWht NLar NPal SBig SEND WDyG WJun WPGP
	- variegated (v)	EPla
	spathacea misapplied	see *F. murielae*
	utilis	CEnt EBee EPla ETod LEdu MMoz MMuc MWht NLar SEND WDyG WJun WPGP
	yulongshanensis	EPla MWht WJun
	aff. ***yulongshanensis***	EPla

Farsetia (*Brassicaceae*)

	clypeata	see *Fibigia clypeata*

Fascicularia (*Bromeliaceae*)

	andina	see *F. bicolor*
§	***bicolor***	Widely available
§	- subsp. ***bicolor*** **new**	CPne SArc
§	- subsp. ***canaliculata***	CHEx EBee EPla IBlr LEdu LPio SBfd SChr SKHP SPad WCot WFut WPGP
	kirchhoffiana	see *F. bicolor* subsp. *canaliculata*
	litoralis	see *Ochagavia litoralis*
	pitcairniifolia misapplied	see *F. bicolor* subsp. *bicolor*
	pitcairniifolia (Verlot) Mez	see *Ochagavia litoralis*

× *Fatshedera* (*Araliaceae*)

	lizei 🏆H3	CAlb CBcs CChe CDoC CDul CHEx CMac CTri EBee EPfP EPla LRHS MAsh MMuc MRav NEgg SAPC SArc SBfd SDix SEND SPer SPlb SPoG SWvt WCFE WDin
§	- 'Annemieke' (v) 🏆H3	CAlb CBcs CBow CDoC CHEx CMac EBee ELan EPfP LHop LRHS MMuc MRav NEgg SBfd SEND SMad SPer SPoG WBor
§	- 'Aurea' (v)	ELan MAsh SEND
	- 'Aureopicta'	see × *F. lizei* 'Aurea'
	- 'Lemon and Lime'	see × *F. lizei* 'Annemieke'
	- 'Maculata'	see × *F. lizei* 'Annemieke'
	- 'Variegata' (v) 🏆H3	CHEx CMac EBee ELan EPfP LAst LRHS LTen MAsh MGos MMuc NEgg SBfd SEND SPer SWvt WCFE WDin

Fatsia (*Araliaceae*)

§	***japonica*** 🏆H4	Widely available
	- 'Annelise' (v)	EGxp
	- 'Golden Handshake'	CBow
	- 'Moseri'	CAbP CMdw CSam CTrC EBee ECtt ESwi EUJe LHop NGdn NLar SWvt WCot WGwG
	- 'Spider's Web' (v)	CBow EUJe LHop LSou NGdn WCot
	- 'Variegata' (v) 🏆H3	CBcs CMac EAmu EGxp EPfP LRHS MBri MGos MMuc MRav SEND SLim SPer

	papyrifera	see *Tetrapanax papyrifer*
	polycarpa	CDTJ EAmu WPGP
	- B&SWJ 7144	WCru
	- RWJ 10133	WCru

Faucaria (*Aizoaceae*)

	felina **new**	SWal
	tigrina ♀H1	EPfP

Fauria see *Nephrophyllidium*

Feijoa see *Acca*

Felicia (*Asteraceae*)

	aethiopica	GFai
§	***amelloides***	CCCN CFox CHEx EShb LAst MCot SBfd SEND SGar SPlb
	- 'Astrid Thomas'	see *F. amelloides* 'Read's Blue'
	- 'Blue Eyes' **new**	LAst
§	- 'Read's Blue'	SDnm SGar
	- 'Read's White'	SDnm SEND
	- 'Santa Anita' ♀H3	CTri ERea
§	- variegated (v)	CFox CMoH ECtt ELon LAst MBri MCot NPer SBfd SPet
§	***amoena***	CTri SRms
	- 'Variegata' (v)	CCCN CTri
	capensis	see *F. amelloides*
	coelestis	see *F. amelloides*
	echinata	CCCN
	erigeroides	GFai
	filifolia	SPlb
	- blue-flowered	LAst
	fruticosa	CHll
	natalensis	see *F. rosulata*
	pappei	see *F. amoena*
§	***petiolata***	CMea CTri EBee NSti WEas WWFP
§	***rosulata***	CMea CPBP ECho GCrs LRHS MBrN MHer MTho NBro SFgr SRms SRot
	uliginosa	ECho EWes GEdr GGar MTho

fennel see *Foeniculum vulgare*

fenugreek see *Trigonella foenum-graecum*

Ferraria (*Iridaceae*)

§	***crispa***	ECho WPrP
	- var. ***nortieri***	WCot
	undulata	see *F. crispa*

Ferula (*Apiaceae*)

	assa-foetida	CArn
	chiliantha	see *F. communis* subsp. *glauca*
§	***communis***	CArn CMea CSpe EBee ECGP ECha ELan EPfP EWTr GCra LPio NBPC NLar NSti SDix SDnm SEND SMad SPav SPhx SPlb WCAu WCot WFar WJek WPtf
	- 'Gigantea'	see *F. communis*
§	- subsp. ***glauca***	EWes SDix SGar SMHy WCot WHal WPGP
	'Giant Bronze'	see *Foeniculum vulgare* 'Giant Bronze'
	tingitana 'Cedric Morris'	ECha GCra LPio SDix WSHC

Festuca (*Poaceae*)

	amethystina	CKno CWCL CWib EBee ECrN EHoe GFor LEdu LRHS NGdn NHol SEND SRot WMoo WTin WWEG
	- 'Aprilgrün'	EPPr
	arenaria	EBWF
	arundinacea	CRWN EBWF MMoz SEND
	californica	CKno EPPr
	coxii	GBin MAvo WCot
	curvula subsp. ***crassifolia***	EPla EShb NHol
	'Eisvogel'	EBee
	elegans	EPPr
	eskia	EAEE EBee EHoe EHul EPPr LRHS NHol WDyG
	'Fromefield Blue'	EHul
§	***gautieri***	EBee EGxp EPPr GBin GFor NGdn
	- 'Pic Carlit'	EBee GBin
	gigantea	EBee GFor SEND
	glauca Vill.	Widely available
I	- 'Auslese'	CPLG EPPr GFor NGdn
	- 'Azurit'	EBee EHoe EPPr EWes LAst NHol NWsh SPad SPoG
§	- 'Blaufuchs' ♀H4	EAEE EBee EBrs EHon EHrv EPPr EPfP EWes GGar GKir GMaP LRHS MAsh MAvo MBlu MGos MMoz MRav NHol SBfd SLim SPer SPlb SWvt WFar WWEG
§	- 'Blauglut'	EAEE EBee EHul EPPr EPfP LRHS MBri MRav NHol SRms WFar
	- Blue Fox	see *F. glauca* 'Blaufuchs'
	- Blue Glow	see *F. glauca* 'Blauglut'
	- 'Elijah Blue'	Widely available
	- 'Euchre'	LSRN
	- 'Golden Toupee'	CPla EBee ECha ELan EPfP EWes GKir LAst LRHS MAsh MBlu MGos MRav NBir NEgg NHol NSti SGSe SLim SPer SPlb SWvt WDin WFar WWEG
	- 'Harz'	EBee EHoe EHul SApp
*	- ***minima***	CCCN WWEG
	- 'Pallens'	see *F. longifolia*
	- Sea Urchin	see *F. glauca* 'Seeigel'
§	- 'Seeigel'	EHoe EPPr GKir LRHS NHol NLar
	- Select	see *F. glauca* 'Auslese'
	- 'Seven Seas'	see *F. valesiaca* 'Silbersee'
	- 'Silberreiher'	EBee EPPr WWEG
	- 'Uchte'	CWCL EBee EPPr WPtf
	'Hogar'	EHoe EPPr
	idahoensis	EShb
	- 'Tomales Bay' **new**	CKno
§	***longifolia***	EBee EPPr
	mairei	CKno EBee ECha EHoe EPPr GFor GQue NWsh SPhx
	novae-zelandiae	CWCL
	ovina	CWan EBWF EPfP GFor LRHS WSFF
	- var. ***gallica***	NWsh
	- 'Söhrewald'	EPPr
*	- 'Tetra Gold'	SWvt
	paniculata	CKno EHoe EPPr NWsh SMHy
	punctoria	GFor SEND
	rubra	CRWN EBWF WSFF
	- subsp. ***rubra***	CRWN
	scoparia	see *F. gautieri*
	'Siskiyou Blue'	CKno CMea EBee EPPr
	tatrae	WCot
	valesiaca var. ***glaucantha***	CWib EPPr GFor NGdn NLar WWEG
§	- 'Silbersee'	EBee EHoe EPPr LRHS NHol NWsh SRms WFar WSpi
	- Silver Sea	see *F. valesiaca* 'Silbersee'
	violacea	CSpr EBee EPPr SWal
	vivipara	CPrp EBWF EHoe LEdu NBid NHol
*	'Willow Green'	SLim SPlb

Fibigia (*Brassicaceae*)

§	***clypeata***	SGar
I	- 'Select'	CSpe

Ficus ✿ (*Moraceae*)

	afghanistanica	ERea
	benjamina ♀^{H1}	SEND SRms
	carica (F)	CCCN ETod LMaj MBri MNHC MREP SArc SLon SPad
	- 'Abicou' (F)	ERea
	- 'Adam' (F)	ERea
	- 'Alma' (F)	ERea
	- 'Angélique' (F)	ERea
	- 'Archipel' (F)	ERea
	- Bayernfeige Violetta = 'Violetta'^{PBR} (F)	GKir LRHS MBri
	- 'Beall' (F)	ERea
	- 'Black Ischia' (F)	ERea
	- 'Black Jack' (F)	ERea
	- 'Black Neck Lady' (F) **new**	LRHS
	- 'Boule d'Or' (F)	ERea
	- 'Bourjassotte Grise' (F)	ERea SDea
	- 'Brogiotto' (F)	CCCN
	- 'Brown Turkey' (F) ♀^{H3}	Widely available
	- 'Brunswick' (F)	CAgr CCCN CHll ELan ELon EPfP ERea GTwe MCoo NGHP SEND SLim WCot
	- 'Castle Kennedy' (F)	ERea GTwe
	- 'Colummaro Black Apulia' (F)	CCCN
	- 'Colummaro White Apulia' (F)	CCCN
	- 'Conandria' (F)	ERea
	- 'Continental' (F) **new**	LRHS
	- 'Dalmatie' (F)	CCCN ELan ERea SEND
§	- 'Desert King' (F)	ERea
I	- 'Digitata' (F)	MBlu
	- 'Drap d'Or' (F)	ERea
	- 'Figue d'Or' (F)	ERea
	- 'Filacciano' (F)	CCCN
	- 'Goutte d'Or' (F)	ERea SDea
	- 'Grise de Saint Jean' (F)	ERea
	- 'Ice Crystal' (F) **new**	LRHS MAsh MBri
	- 'Kadota' (F)	CCCN ERea SBfd
	- 'King'	see *F. carica* 'Desert King'
*	- 'Laciniata' (F)	MBri SMad
	- 'Lisa' (F)	ERea
	- 'Little Yellow Wonder' (F)	ERea
	- 'LSU Purple' (F)	ERea
	- 'Malcolm's Giant' (F)	ERea
	- 'Malta' (F)	GTwe
	- 'Marseillaise' (F)	GTwe SDea
	- 'Melanzana' (F)	CCCN
	- 'Nazaret' (F)	LRHS
	- 'Negro Largo' (F)	ERea
	- 'Nero' (F)	ELon
	- 'Newlyn Harbour' (F)	ELon
	- 'Noir de Provence'	see *F. carica* 'Reculver'
	- 'Noire de Carombe' (F)	ERea
	- 'Osborn's Prolific' (F)	ECrN ERea SEND SWvt
	- 'Panachée' (F)	ERea
	- 'Pastilière' (F)	ERea
	- 'Peter's Honey' (F)	ERea
	- 'Petite Nigra' (F)	ERea
	- 'Pinet' (F)	LRHS
	- 'Pittaluse' (F)	ERea
	- 'Porthminster' (F)	CHEx
	- 'Précoce de Dalmatie' (F)	ERea NLar WPGP
	- 'Précoce Ronde de Bordeaux' (F)	ERea SEND
§	- 'Reculver' (F)	ERea SEND
	- 'Rouge de Bordeaux' (F)	CCCN ERea SDea SPlb
	- 'Saint Johns' (F)	ERea
	- 'San Pedro Miro' (F)	ERea
	- 'Sollies Pont' (F)	ERea
	- 'Sugar 12' (F)	ERea
	- 'Sultane' (F)	ERea
	- 'Tena' (F)	ERea
	- 'Texas Everbearing' (F)	ERea
	- 'Violette Dauphine' (F)	EPfP ERea
	- 'Violette de Sollies' (F)	ERea
	- 'Violette Normande' (F)	SEND
	- 'Violette Sepor' (F)	ERea
	- 'White Genoa'	see *F. carica* 'White Marseilles'
	- 'White Ischia' (F)	ERea
§	- 'White Marseilles' (F)	CAgr CCCN CWib ECrN EPfP ERea MBri MCoo NGHP SDea SEND
	pubigera	CPLG
	pumila ♀^{H1}	CHEx
	- 'Minima'	CFee
	- 'Variegata' (v)	CHEx
	retusa (F)	STre

fig see *Ficus carica*

filbert see *Corylus maxima*

Filipendula ✿ (*Rosaceae*)

	alnifolia 'Variegata'	see *F. ulmaria* 'Variegata'
	camtschatica	CFir CRow EBee ECha ELan LEdu MCot NBid NLar SMrm WFar WPGP
	- B&SWJ 10828	WCru
	- 'Rosea'	LHop MRav SMad
	digitata 'Nana'	see *F. multijuga*
	formosa B&SWJ 8707	WCru
	hexapetala	see *F. vulgaris*
	- 'Flore Pleno'	see *F. vulgaris* 'Multiplex'
	'Kahome'	CPrp CRow EBee ELon EPPr EPla EShb GKir GMaP IFoB LAst LLWG NBPC NBir NGdn NLar NMir SPer SPhx SWat WFar WHoo WMoo WPnP WWEG
	kiraishiensis B&SWJ 1571	EBee WCru
§	***multijuga***	CRow EBee GCal GGar IFoB LRHS NHol WFar WMoo
	palmata	ECha MLHP NBre SWat WMoo
	- 'Digitata Nana'	see *F. multijuga*
	- dwarf	CDes CLAP MLHP
	- 'Elegantissima'	see *F. purpurea* 'Elegans'
	- 'Nana'	see *F. multijuga*
	- 'Rosea'	CMac NBir
	- 'Rubra'	CTri GCra MRav NGdn
	purpurea ♀^{H4}	CKno CRow CSBt ECha ELon EPfP EWTr GGar IBlr LPBA MBri MMuc SEND WCru WFar WMoo WPnP
	- f. ***albiflora***	EBee MBri NPri WMoo
§	- 'Elegans'	CRow EBee ECha ELon GGar LAst MLHP NBPC NBid NHol NSti SPer SPet SWat WHlf WMoo WPnP WSpi
	- 'Nephele'	EBee GMac
	- 'Pink Dreamland'	EBee SPhx
*	- 'Plena' (d)	NLar
	'Queen of the Prairies'	see *F. rubra*
§	***rubra***	CRow IFro LAst LSRN WSFF
§	- 'Venusta' ♀^{H4}	Widely available
	- 'Venusta Magnifica'	see *F. rubra* 'Venusta'
	rufinervis B&SWJ 8611	WCru
§	***ulmaria***	CArn CBen CHby COld CRWN CWan EBWF EBee EHon ELau GBar GMaP GPoy MCot MHer MNHC NHol NLan NMir SIde SWat WHfH WJek WMoo WSFF WShi
	- 'Aurea'	CArn CMac CRow EBee EBrs ECha ECtt EHoe ELan GAbr GBar GMaP MLHP MRav NBid NLar NPri SGar SMad SRms WEas WFar WMoo WSHC WTin WWEG

- 'Flore Pleno' (d)	CBre CRow EBee EBrs LHop LLWG LRHS MRav NBPC NBid NBre NGdn SIde SPer SWat WCot WFar
- 'Rosea'	CDes EBee IBlr MHer MLLN WPGP
§ - 'Variegata' (v)	CArn CBen CFee CPrp CRow EBee ECtt EHoe ELan GBar IFoB LBMP NBPC NBid NGdn NLar SPer SPoG WBor WFar WHfH WHoo WMoo WPGP WPnP WTin WWEG WWFP
§ ***vulgaris***	CArn CFee CRWN CTri CWan EBWF ECtt GBar GKir MLHP MMuc MNHC NBro NMir SBfd SWat WHfH WJek WPer WWEG
- 'Alba'	EBee
- 'Flore Pleno'	see *F. vulgaris* 'Multiplex'
- 'Grandiflora'	CBre GKir
§ - 'Multiplex' (d)	CMac EBee ECha ELan EWTr GGar GKir GMaP LLWG MHer MLLN MMuc MRav NBid NBir NPri NRya NSti SEND SPer SRms WAul WEas WFar WMoo WTin
- 'Plena'	see *F. vulgaris* 'Multiplex'
- 'Rosea'	NBre

Firmiana (*Sterculiaceae*)

simplex	CHEx EShb EUJe IDee WPGP

Fitzroya (*Cupressaceae*)

cupressoides	CBcs CDoC CMac CTho GBin GKir IFFs LRHS NMun SCoo SLim WThu

Fockea (*Asclepiadaceae*)

edulis	EShb

Foeniculum (*Apiaceae*)

vulgare	Widely available
- 'Bronze'	see *F. vulgare* 'Purpureum'
- var. ***dulce***	CSev SIde
§ - 'Giant Bronze'	EBee ELan EWTr SPhx WSpi
- green-flowered	SEND
§ - 'Purpureum'	Widely available
- 'Smokey'	ECha MRav

Fontanesia (*Oleaceae*)

phillyreoides	CBcs

Fontinalis (*Fontinalaceae*)

sp.	LPBA

Forsythia (*Oleaceae*)

'Arnold Dwarf'	ECrN GKir NBir NLar SRms
'Beatrix Farrand' ambig.	CTri CWSG EBee MGos MWat SEND SPer SRms
'Beatrix Farrand' K. Sax	GKir MMuc NLar SEND
'Fiesta' (v)	CPMA CWSG EPfP LAst LRHS MAsh MGos MRav MSwo NWea SBfd SLim SPoG WCom WCot WDin WFar
giraldiana	GKir MSwo SLon SRms WSpi
Gold Tide^{PBR}	see *F.* Marée d'Or
'Golden Bells'	WHar
'Golden Nugget'	CMac EBee ELan EPfP LBuc LRHS MAsh SCoo SLon SPoG WCFE
'Golden Times' (v)	CMac EWes LAst LBuc LSRN MGos NLar NWea SCoo SPoG SWvt WDin WFar
× ***intermedia*** 'Arnold Giant'	MBlu
- 'Casque D'Or'	see *F.* × *intermedia* 'Courdijau'
§ - 'Courdijau'	MAsh
- 'Goldrausch'	LRHS MAsh MGos NLar
- 'Goldzauber'	NWea
- 'Josefa' (v)	ELan
- 'Lynwood Variety' $\mathbb{Y}^{H4}$	Widely available
- 'Lynwood Variety' variegated (v)	CWib
- Minigold = 'Flojor'	CSBt EPfP MGos MSwo MWat NLar SRms WBVN
- 'Spectabilis'	CDul EBee EMac EPfP LBuc NWea SCoo SLim WDin WFar
- 'Spectabilis Variegated' (v)	CBow CMHG MBNS
- 'Spring Glory'	MHer WSpi
- 'Variegata' (v)	WCom WGwG
- Week-End = 'Courtalyn'^{PBR} $\mathbb{Y}^{H4}$	CWSG EBee EPfP LBuc LRHS LSou MAsh MBri MGos MMuc NLar SEND SLPl SLim SLon SPlb WDin WFar
§ Marée d'Or = 'Courtasol'^{PBR} $\mathbb{Y}^{H4}$	CWSG IVic LRHS MAsh MGos MRav NLar NWea SLon SPoG WDin
Mêlée d'Or = 'Courtaneur'	LRHS MAsh SCoo SPer
Melissa = 'Courtadic'	NLar NWea
ovata 'Tetragold'	EBee NWea
'Paulina'	NLar
suspensa	CArn CMac CTri CWib EOHP EPfP GKir MGos NWea SPlb SRms WSpi
- f. ***atrocaulis***	NWea WSpi
- 'Nymans'	EPfP GKir MBri MRav NSti SEND
§ - 'Taff's Arnold' (v)	CPLG CPMA EBee
- 'Variegata'	see *F. suspensa* 'Taff's Arnold'
'Tremonia'	NEgg NLar WGwG
viridissima	NWea
- 'Bronxensis'	CMac ECho GEdr LLHF MAsh NBir NLar WPat
- var. ***koreana*** 'Kumsom' (v)	EMil GKir LRHS MAsh
- 'Weber's Bronx'	IVic NLar NWea WAbe

Fortunella (*Rutaceae*)

'Fukushu' (F) $\mathbb{Y}^{H1}$	ERea
§ ***japonica*** (F)	EPfP
§ ***margarita*** (F)	CDoC LRHS LSRN

Fothergilla (*Hamamelidaceae*)

gardenii	CBcs CPMA ELan EPfP EWTr MBlu MBri MGos MRav NLar SPer SSpi SWvt WDin
- 'Blue Mist'	CAbP CDoC CEnd CPLG CPMA EBee ELan ELon EPfP GQue IVic MPkF NLar SBfd SKHP SMad SPer SReu SSta WDin WFar WPat
- 'Harold Epstein'	NLar
- 'Suzanne'	NLar
- 'Zundert'	NLar
'Huntsman'	CCCN EBee WFar
× ***intermedia*** Beaver Creek = 'Klmtwo'	NLar
- 'Blue Shadow'	CBcs CPMA ESwi LSRN MGos MPkF NLar SKHP
- 'Mount Airy'	CMCN CPMA EBee EPfP GBin IArd LRHS NLar SKHP SSpi
- 'Red Licorice'	CPMA NLar
- 'Sea Spray'	CPMA
- 'Windy City'	CPMA
major $\mathbb{Y}^{H4}$	CBcs CDul CEnd CPMA CWib EBee ELan EPfP LRHS LSRN MAsh MBlu MBri MGos NEgg NLar NPri SPer SPoG SReu SSpi SWvt WDin WFar WPat WSpi
- 'Bulkyard'	IArd
- Monticola Group	CDoC CEnd CPMA CSBt ELan EPfP LRHS MAsh MGos MMuc NPal SBfd SLim SPer SSpi SSta WBrE WFar

Fouquieria (*Fouquieriaceae*)

diguetii new	SPlb

Fragaria (*Rosaceae*)

from Taiwan	WHer
alpina	see *F. vesca* 'Semperflorens'
- 'Alba'	see *F. vesca* 'Semperflorens Alba'
× ***ananassa*** 'Albion'PBR (F)	CSut MCoo WClo
- 'Alice'PBR (F) ♀H4	CSut ERea LBuc MCoo
- 'Aromel' (F) ♀H4	CAgr EPfP GTwe LBuc LRHS SDea SEND WClo
- 'Bogota' (F)	LRHS
- 'Bolero' (F)	LRHS MBri
- 'Calypso'PBR (F)	CAgr CSBt LBuc LRHS SDea SEND
- 'Cambridge Favourite' (F) ♀H4	CAgr CSBt CTri EMil EPfP ERea GTwe LBuc LRHS MBri MCoo MGan MGos NEgg NGHP NPri SDea SPlb WClo
- 'Cambridge Vigour' (F)	GTwe LRHS SDea
- 'Christine' (F)	CSut EMil
- 'Elsanta'PBR (F)	CFox CSBt CTri EMil EPfP GKir GTwe IArd LBuc LRHS MGan NEgg NPri SBfd SDea SEND SPer WClo
- 'Elvira' (F)	EPfP LRHS
* - 'Emily' (F)	CAgr CFox WClo
- 'Eros'PBR (F)	CFox GTwe LBuc WClo
- 'Everest'PBR (F)	LBuc
- 'Flamenco'PBR (F)	ERea LRHS NGHP
- 'Florence'PBR (F)	CSBt CTri EMil ERea GTwe LBuc LRHS MBri SPer
- Fraise des Bois	see *F. vesca*
- 'Fruitful Summer' (F)	LRHS
- 'Hapil' (F) ♀H4	CTri EMil EPfP ERea GTwe LBuc NGHP
- 'Honeoye' (F) ♀H4	CAgr CFox CSBt EMil EPfP GTwe LBuc LRHS MBri MCoo NGHP SEND SPer
- 'Judibell'PBR (F)	LRHS
- 'Loran' (F)	LRHS
- 'Malling Opal'PBR (F)	GTwe
- 'Malling Pearl' (F)	EMil GTwe
- 'Pegasus'PBR (F) ♀H4	CSBt EPfP GTwe LRHS NGHP NPri
- Pink Panda = 'Frel'PBR (F)	CBcs CTri EAEE EBee ELan LBuc LRHS MGos MRav NEgg NHol NLar SPer WCAu WEas WJek WWFP
- pink-flowered (F)	CFee
- 'Rabunda' (F) new	LRHS
- Red Ruby = 'Samba'PBR	EAEE EBee ECGP LHop LRHS MNrw NEgg NGdn NLar SPer SPoG WCAu
- 'Redgauntlet' (F)	EPfP GTwe LRHS
- 'Rhapsody' (F) ♀H4	GTwe LBuc
- 'Rosie'PBR (F)	SDea
- 'Royal Sovereign' (F)	CTri GTwe LRHS MGan NBir SVic
- 'Senga Sengana' (F)	SVic
- 'Sonata'PBR (F)	CSut
- 'Sophie'PBR (F)	EMil LRHS
- 'Symphony'PBR (F) ♀H4	CAgr CFox CSBt EPfP LBuc LRHS MBri SEND
- 'Totem' (F)	GTwe LRHS
§ - 'Variegata' (v)	CArn CMea CTri EAEE EBee EPla LHop LRHS MRav SPer SPoG WCom WMoo
'Bowles's Double'	see *F. vesca* 'Multiplex'
chiloensis (F)	ILis LEdu
- 'Chaval' (F)	CHid ECha EHrv EPPr IMou MRav WMoo
- 'Variegata' misapplied	see *F.* × *ananassa* 'Variegata'
daltoniana	GCra
indica	see *Duchesnea indica*
'Lipstick'	NLar WSpi
moschata	CAgr
nubicola	CAgr GPoy
- 'Mount Omei'	EBee
'Roman'	LRHS
'Variegata'	see *F.* × *ananassa* 'Variegata'
§ ***vesca*** (F)	CAgr CArn CRWN CWan EBWF EPfP GPoy MHer MNHC NGHP NMir NPri SIde SPlb SVic WGwG WJek WSFF WShi
- 'Alexandra' (F)	CArn CBod CPrp ELau ERea GAbr NVic SIde
- 'Baron Solemacher' (F)	SBfd SHDw WHer
- 'Delicious' (F) new	EWTr
- 'Flore Pleno'	see *F. vesca* 'Multiplex'
- 'Fructu Albo' (F)	CAgr CArn CBre CRow CWan EBee NLar WMoo
- 'Golden Alexandra'	EBee ECha EHoe ELau ERea EWes MHer WHer WMoo
- 'Golden Surprise'	SBfd SHDw
- 'Monophylla' (F)	CRow IGor SIde WCom WHer
§ - 'Multiplex' (d)	CRow CSev ILis MRav NChi NGHP NHol NLar WAlt WBor WCom WHer WOut
§ - 'Muricata'	CBre CRow IGor ILis LEdu WAlt WCom WHer
- 'Pineapple Crush' (F)	WHer
- 'Plymouth Strawberry'	see *F. vesca* 'Muricata'
- 'Rügen' (F)	IGor
§ - 'Semperflorens' (F)	ILis WAlt
§ - 'Semperflorens Alba' (F)	CAgr
- 'Variegata' misapplied	see *F.* × *ananassa* 'Variegata'
* - 'Variegata' ambig. (v)	EHoe EHrv NEgg NGHP WFar WHrl WWEG
virginiana	CAgr
- subsp. ***glauca***	EPPr
viridis	CAgr

Franchoa (*Saxifragaceae*)

Francoa (*Saxifragaceae*)

appendiculata	CAbP EBla GAbr GQui MDKP MMuc SGar SWal WFar WHer WMoo WPnP
- red-flowered	CDes EBee
Ballyrogan strain	IBlr
'Confetti'	CKno CPLG ELan LPio LRHS MAvo NCob SMrm SWal WCot WFar WPGP
'Purple Spike'	see *F. sonchifolia* Rogerson's form
ramosa	CCVN CTri EHrv EWld IBlr MHav MNrw NBro SDix SPav WFar WKif WMoo
* - 'Alba'	CSpe
sonchifolia	Widely available
- 'Alba'	MDKP SUsu WFar WMoo
- 'Culm View Lilac'	CCVN
- 'Doctor Tom Smith'	WCot
- 'Lynda Windsor'	MAvo
- 'Molly Anderson'	EBee LPio MAvo SUsu
- 'Pink Giant' new	GBin GGar
§ - Rogerson's form	Widely available

Frangula (*Rhamnaceae*)

§ ***alnus***	CArn CCVT CDul CLnd CRWN CTri ECrN EMac IDee LBuc MBlu NWea STre WDin WFar WMou WSFF
- 'Aspleniifolia'	EBee EPfP MBlu MBri MMuc MPkF NLar WDin WFar WPat
- 'Columnaris'	SLPl
- 'Minaret'	MBri

Frankenia (*Frankeniaceae*)

laevis	SRms
thymifolia	CTri ECho LRHS MHer MWat NPri SPlb WFar WTin

Franklinia (*Theaceae*)

alatamaha	CBcs IMou LHyd MBlu MBri SEND WFar

Fraxinus ✿ (*Oleaceae*)

americana	CDul CMCN EPfP EWTr IFFs NEgg WDin
- 'Autumn Purple'	CDul CEnd CMCN CTho CWit EBee ECrN EPfP MAsh MBlu WMou
- 'Rosehill'	CTho
angustifolia	CMCN EGFP IFFs
§ - subsp. ***oxycarpa***	SEND
- 'Raywood' 🏆H4	Widely available
* - 'Variegata' (v)	MGos
bungeana	EGFP
caroliniana new	EGFP
chinensis	CLnd CMCN EGFP
elonza	CLnd
excelsior	CBcs CCVT CDoC CDul CLnd CMac CRWN CSBt CTho CTri CWib EBee ECrN EMac EPfP GKir IFFs LAst LBuc MAsh MBri MGos MMuc NWea SBfd SEND SLim STre WDin WMou
- 'Aurea Pendula'	CCVT CDul CEnd CMac CWib EBee ECrN MBlu MGos NPal SPoG
- 'Crispa'	MBlu MBri NLar WCom
- f. ***diversifolia***	CDul CLnd
- 'Jaspidea' 🏆H4	Widely available
- 'Nana'	LMaj WPat
- 'Pendula' 🏆H4	CCVT CDoC CDul CEnd CLnd CMac EBee ECrN ELan LAst LMaj MBlu NEgg NPal NWea SLim SPer SPoG WDin WMou
- 'R.E. Davey'	CDul CNat
- variegated (v)	CMac ECrN WPat
- 'Westhof's Glorie' 🏆H4	CCVT CDoC CDul CLnd EBee ECrN LMaj SBfd WDin WFar
hopeiensis	MBlu
insularis var. ***henryana***	CDul
latifolia	CLnd CMCN
mariesii	see *F. sieboldiana*
nigra	CMCN
- 'Fallgold'	CEnd
ornus 🏆H4	CArn CCVT CDul CLnd CMCN CMac CTri EBee ECrN ELan EMac EPfP EWTr GKir IFFs LAst LMaj MMuc MSnd MSwo NPal NWea SEND SPer WDin WFar WMoo
- 'Arie Peters'	CDul
- 'Mecsek'	MBlu
- 'Obelisk'	EBee LMaj LRHS MBlu NLar
- 'Rotterdam'	EBee
oxycarpa	see *F. angustifolia* subsp. *oxycarpa*
pennsylvanica	CDul CLnd
- Cimmaron = 'Cimmzam'	CDul
- 'Variegata' (v)	CLnd EBee GKir WPat
quadrangulata	EGFP WDin
richardi	CDul
§ ***sieboldiana***	CDoC CDul CLnd CMCN CPMA EPfP MBlu MBri SSpi WPat
velutina	CDul CLnd SLPl
xanthoxyloides	MBlu NEgg
- var. ***dumosa***	EBee WPGP

Freesia (*Iridaceae*)

alba Foster	see *F. lactea*
alba (G.L. Mey.) Gumbl.	CYeo
double mixed (d)	SWal
fucata	ECho
grandiflora	see *Anomatheca grandiflora*
§ ***lactea***	CDes ECho
laxa	see *Anomatheca laxa*
Rainbow mixture new	SWal
refracta 'Worcester' new	ECho
xanthospila	EBee WCot

Fremontodendron (*Sterculiaceae*)

'California Glory' 🏆H3	Widely available
californicum	CDoy CTri CWib EBee ELan MBri NLar SEND SLim SOWG SPlb WDin WFar
'Pacific Sunset'	EPfP LHop LSRN MGos MRav NEgg SPer WFar
'Tequila Sunrise'	CBcs CDoC CWGN EBee GBin LLHF MBlu MGos NLar SBfd WBrE

Freylinia (*Scrophulariaceae*)

cestroides	see *F. lanceolata*
densiflora	GFai
§ ***lanceolata***	CBcs CCCN CTrC CWib CWit EBee SPlb
tropica	CHII GFai
visseri	GFai SOWG

Fritillaria ✿ (*Liliaceae*)

acmopetala 🏆H4	CAvo CFFs CFox CHid CPom CWCL ECho EPot ERCP GKev ITim LAma LRHS MSSP MTho NMen SDeJ SPhx WCot
- 'Brunette'	ECho SPhx WWst
- subsp. ***wendelboi***	ECho EPot LAma SPhx WCot
- - 'Zwanenburg'	WWst
affinis	CWCL ECho EPot GBin GGar GKev ITim LAma MSSP NMen WCot WWst
- 'Limelight'	ECho
- 'Sunray'	ECho EPot GCrs GEdr ITim WWst
§ - var. ***tristulis***	NMen NWCA
- 'Vancouver Island'	ECho
alburyana	ECho WWst
alfredae subsp. ***glaucoviridis***	ECho WCot WWst
arabica	see *F. persica*
ariana	WWst
armena	ECho
- MP 8146	WWst
assyriaca	EPfP EPot MWea
- subsp. ***melanthera*** new	WWst
aurea	ECho NMen WCot WWst
- 'Golden Flag'	ECho EPfP EPot GKev LLHF SPhx WHil
biflora	ECho EPot GEdr
- 'Martha Roderick'	ECho GKev ITim LAma MSSP NMen SDeJ
§ ***bithynica***	ECho EPot GEdr ITim LAma MSSP WWst
- from Turkey	WCot
bucharica	EBee ECho EPot GKev WWst
- 'Nurek Giant'	ECho WWst
camschatcensis	CAvo CPom CWCL ECha ECho EFEx EPfP EPot ERCP GAbr GAuc GCrs GEdr GGar GKir GMaP LAma MSSP MTho NBir NHar NLar NMen NWCA SDeJ SPhx WAbe WBVN WCru

	- from Alaska	GCrs
I	- ***alpina aurea***	GEdr
	- 'Aurea'	ECho GCrs NHar NMen SPhx WWst
	- black-flowered	ECho
	- double-flowered (d)	CFir ECho LAma NMen
	- f. ***flavescens***	ECho EFEx GEdr LAma
	- green-flowered	MSSP NMen
	carduchorum	see *F. minuta*
	carica	ECho EPot GEdr MSSP NMen
	- brown-flowered	ECho
	- subsp. ***serpenticola***	WWst
	- tall clone	WWst
	caucasica	ECho GAuc NMen WWst
	chlororhabdota	GAuc
	cirrhosa	ECho GEdr GKir WWst
	- brown-flowered	ECho GEdr NMen WWst
	- green-flowered	ECho GEdr NMen WWst
	citrina	see *F. bithynica*
	conica	NMen WCot WWst
	crassifolia	ECho LAma
	- subsp. ***crassifolia***	WWst
§	- subsp. ***kurdica***	ECho EPot ITim NMen WCot WWst
	davidii	ECho SCnR
	davisii	ECho EPot GAuc GEdr LAma LRHS NMen NWCA WCot
	delphinensis	see *F. tubiformis*
	drenovskii	WWst
	eastwoodiae	WCot
	eduardii	ECho ERCP WCot WWst
	ehrhartii	WWst
	elwesii	ECho EPot ERCP GEdr ITim NMen SPhx WCot WWst
	euboeica **new**	WWst
	ferganensis	see *F. walujewii*
	fleischeriana	WWst
	forbesii	WWst
	frankiorum	WCot WWst
	gentneri	WCot
	glauca	LAma MSSP
*	- 'Golden Flag'	ECho
	- 'Goldilocks'	ECho NMen SDeJ
	graeca	ECho EPot GKev LRHS MTho NMen NMin SDeJ
	- subsp. ***ionica***	see *F. graeca* subsp. *thessala*
§	- subsp. ***thessala***	ECho ITim MSSP MTho NMen WCot WWst
	- - HOA 8964	WWst
	gussichiae	ECho NMen WWst
	hermonis	WWst
	- subsp. ***amana***	CTca CWCL ECho EPot ERCP GKev ITim LAma LLHF LPio MSSP NMen NMin WCot
	- - 'Cambridge' ♀H4	WCot
	- - yellow-flowered	EPot
	hispanica	see *F. lusitanica*
	imperialis	ECGP GKir MBri WTin
	- 'April Flame' **new**	LAma
	- 'Aureomarginata' (v)	EBee ELon LAma
	- 'Aurora'	EBee EBrs EPot ERCP GKev LAma LRHS NLar NPer SDeJ SPer WClo WFar
	- Crown Upon Crown	see *F. imperialis* 'Kroon op Kroon'
	- 'Garland Star'	EBee EBrs LAma LRHS NLar SPoG
	- 'Grenadier' **new**	EBee LAma NLar
	- var. ***inodora***	EBee ERCP LAma
	- 'Inodora Purpurea'	CTca EBee
§	- 'Kroon op Kroon' **new**	CTca
	- 'Lutea'	CAvo CTca EBee EBrs ELan EPfP ERCP GKev LRHS NBPC SPoG WFar
	- 'Maxima'	see *F. imperialis* 'Rubra Maxima'
	- 'Maxima Lutea' ♀H4	ELan EPfP EPot ERCP GAbr LAma NLar SDeJ SPer
	- 'Orange Brilliant'	EBee LAma
	- 'Prolifera'	CTca EBee ECho LAma NLar WHer
	- 'Rubra'	CTca EBee EBrs ECho ERCP GAbr GKev LAma NLar SMrm SPer WClo WFar
§	- 'Rubra Maxima'	CTca EBee ELan EPfP EPot ERCP LAma LRHS SDeJ
	- 'Slagzwaard'	EBee
	- 'Striped Beauty'	CTca LAma
	- 'Sulpherino'	EBee LAma
	- 'The Premier'	EBee ECho LAma SDeJ
	- 'William Rex'	CAvo CFFs EBee EPot ERCP LAma LRHS SDeJ
	- yellow-flowered	CFFs
	involucrata	ECho WCot
	ionica	see *F. graeca* subsp. *thessala*
	japonica var. ***koidzumiana***	ECho EFEx GEdr WWst
	karadaghensis	see *F. crassifolia* subsp. *kurdica*
I	***karelinii***	ECho
	kotschyana	ECho EPot GEdr NMen WCot WWst
	- subsp. ***grandiflora*** **new**	WCot
	lanceolata	see *F. affinis* var. *tristulis*
	latakiensis	ECho EPot GEdr WCot WWst
§	***latifolia***	ECho GAuc GEdr NMen
	- var. ***nobilis***	see *F. latifolia*
§	***lusitanica***	MSSP NMen
	macedonica **new**	WWst
	maximowiczii	ECho
	meleagris	Widely available
	- 'Mars'	ECho
	- var. ***unicolor*** subvar. ***alba*** ♀H4	CSam ECho ERCP GKev LAma LRHS MBri MMHG MSSP NHol SDeJ SMrm SPer SPhx WAul WPnP WShi
	- - - 'Aphrodite'	EPot NBir
	meleagroides	WWst
§	***messanensis***	MSSP
	- subsp. ***gracilis***	ITim MSSP WCot
	michailovskyi ♀H2	CAvo CFFs CHid CTri EBrs ECho EPfP EPot ERCP GEdr GKev LAma LRHS MNrw MTho NHol NMen SDeJ SRms WFar
	minima	ECho
§	***minuta***	ECho EPot ERCP GAuc LAma NMen NMin
	montana	ECho NMen WWst
	nigra Mill.	see *F. pyrenaica*
	obliqua	WCot WWst
	olivieri GBK 82	WWst
§	***orientalis***	ECho MSSP WWst
	pallidiflora ♀H4	CAvo CLAP CTca EBee ECho EPot ERCP GAbr GKev ITim LAma LPio LRHS MSSP MTho NBid NBir NMRc NMen SPhx WPnP
	pelinaea **new**	WWst
§	***persica***	EBee EBrs ECha ECho ECtt EHrv EPfP EPot ERCP GAbr LAma LHop LRHS MBri MNrw NBPC NMen SGar SPad SPhx SPoG WFar
	- 'Adiyaman' ♀H4	CAvo ELan LRHS SDeJ
	- 'Chocolate' **new**	CWCL
	- 'Ivory Bells'	CAvo ECho EPot ERCP LAma LRHS NLar SDeJ WWst
*	- 'Senkoy'	ECho WWst
	pinardii	ECho EPot NMen
	- MPR 7921	WWst
	pontica ♀H4	CLAP CWCL ECho EPot ERCP GAbr GAuc GEdr GKev ITim LAma LPio LRHS MNrw MSSP MTho NMen SDeJ SPhx WCru WPnP

	pudica	ECho GEdr GKev ITim LAma MSSP MTho NMen WAbe WCot
*	- 'Fragrant'	ECho NMen
	- 'Giant'	ECho EPot NMin
	- 'Richard Britten'	NMen
	purdyi	ECho
§	***pyrenaica*** $\mathbb{Y}^{H4}$	CLAP CTca ECho GAbr GCra GEdr LAma LPio MSSP NMen SPhx WCot WCru WTin WWst
	- 'Cedric Morris'	MSSP WCot
	raddeana	CAvo EBee EBrs ECho EPot ERCP LAma LRHS NLar SPhx WCot WWst
	recurva	ECho
	- NNS 00-179	WCot
	regelii	WWst
	rhodia new	WWst
	rhodocanakis	ECho EPot NMen NMin WCot WWst
	- subsp. ***argolica***	ECho NMen
	rixii	GAuc WWst
	rubra major	see *F. imperialis* 'Rubra Maxima'
	ruthenica	ECho NMen
	sewerzowii	ECho GAuc LAma WCot WWst
	- 'Brown Eyes' new	WWst
	sibthorpiana	ECho WWst
	sinica	WCot
	sororum	GAuc
	spetsiotica	WWst
	sphaciotica	see *F. messanensis*
	stenanthera	ECho EPot LAma NMen WWst
	stribrnyi	ECho NWCA WWst
	tachengensis	see *F. yuminensis*
	tenella	see *F. orientalis*
	theophrasti	WCot
	thunbergii	EBee ECho EPot GEdr GKev NMen SMrm WCot
	tortifolia	NMen
§	***tubiformis***	ECho GAuc GEdr MSSP
	tuntasia subsp. ***tuntasia***	WCot WWst
	uva-vulpis	CAby CMea CTca EBrs ECtt EPfP EPot ERCP GEdr GGar GKev LAma LHop LPio LRHS MNrw MTho NBir NMen SDeJ SPad SPhx WCot WCru WFar WHil
	verticillata	EBee ECha ECho EHrv EPot GEdr LAma LRHS MTho NMen SPhx WCru WWst
§	***walujewii***	MSSP WCot
	whittallii	ECho EPot MSSP NMen
	- PW 72-64B	WWst
	- 'Green Light'	NMin
§	***yuminensis***	ECho WCot

Fuchsia ✿ (*Onagraceae*)

	'A.M. Larwick'	CSil EBak SRiF
	'A.W. Taylor'	EBak
	'A1' (d)	CTsd
	'Aalt Groothuis' (d)	SRiF WPBF
	'Aaltje'	WPBF
	'Aandenken Bert Pelgrims' (d)	WPBF
	'Aart Verschoor' (d)	WPBF
	'Abbé Farges' (d)	CDoC CLoc CSil CWVF EBak EPts SPet SRiF SVic WFuv WRou
	'Abbigayle Reine' (v)	SRiF
	'Abigail' ambig.	CWVF SRiF WRou
	'Abigail Storey'	CSil
	'Abundance'	CSil
	'Acclamation' (d)	WPBF
	'Achievement' $\mathbb{Y}^{H4}$	CDoC CLoc CSil LCla MJac SPet SRiF SVic WPBF
	'Adagio' (d)	CLoc
	'Adalbert Bogner' (d)	CDoC WPBF
	'Adelaide Hoodless'	WRou
	'Adinda' (T)	CDoC EPts LCla SLBF SRiF WRou
	'Admiration'	CSil
	'Adrienne' (d)	MHav SRiF
	'Agnes de Ridder' (d)	WPBF
	'Aiguillette'	WPBF
	'Ailsa Garnett' (d)	EBak
	'Aintree'	CTsd CWVF
	'Airedale'	CWVF
	'Aisen'	WRou
	'Ajax' (d)	SRiF
	'Aladna's Sander' (d)	CWVF SRiF WPBF
	'Alan Ayckbourn'	CWVF SRiF
	'Alan Titchmarsh'	CDoC EPts LCla MHav SLBF SRiF
	'Alaska' (d)	CLoc EBak SRiF SVic
	'Albertina'	SRiF SVic WFuv WRou
	'Albertus Schwab'	LCla
	'Alde'	CWVF SRiF
	'Alderford'	SLBF WPBF
	'Alf Thornley' (d)	CTsd CWVF SRiF WPBF
	'Alfie' (d)	SRiF
	'Alfred Rambaud' (d)	CDoC CSil SRiF
	'Alice Ashton' (d)	EBak
	'Alice Blue Gown' (d)	CWVF
	'Alice Doran'	CDoC CSil LCla SRiF
	'Alice Hoffman' (d) $\mathbb{Y}^{H3-4}$	Widely available
	'Alice Mary' (d)	EBak
	'Alice Sweetapple' (d)	CWVF SRiF
	'Alice Travis' (d)	EBak
	'Alipat'	EBak
	'Alisha Jade'	SRiF
	'Alison Ewart'	CLoc CWVF EBak MJac SPet SRiF SVic
	'Alison Patricia' $\mathbb{Y}^{H3}$	CWVF EBak MJac SLBF SRiF SVic WFuv WPBF WRou
	'Alison Reynolds' (d)	CWVF SRiF WPBF
	'Alison Ruth Griffin' (d)	MJac
	'Alison Ryle' (d)	EBak
	'Alison Sweetman' $\mathbb{Y}^{H1+3}$	CSil CWVF MJac
	'Allure' (d)	CWVF
	'Alma Hulscher' (d)	SRiF
	Aloha = 'Sanicomf'PBR (Sunangels Series)	SLBF SRiF
	'Alpengluhn'	WPBF
	alpestris	CDoC CSil EBak LCla LPio SRiF SVic WPBF
	'Alsa Garnet' (d) new	SRiF
	'Alton Waters' (d/v)	SRiF
	'Alwin' (d)	CWVF SRiF
	'Alyce Larson' (d)	CTsd CWVF EBak MJac SRiF SVic
	'Amanda Bridgland' (d)	SRiF
	'Amanda Jones'	SRiF
	'Amaranth'	WPBF
	'Amazing Grace' (d) new	MJac
	'Amazing Maisie' (d)	SLBF WPBF
	'Ambassador'	CTsd EBak MHav SRiF SVic
	'Ambiorix'	WFuv
	'Amelie Aubin'	CLoc CWVF EBak SVic
	'America'	CWVF
	'Americana Elegans'	WPBF
	'Amethyst Fire' (d)	CSil SRiF
	'Amigo' ambig.	EBak SRiF
§	***ampliata***	CDoC LCla
	'Amy'	MJac
	'Amy Lye'	CLoc CSil EBak SVic
	'Amy Ruth'	CWVF
§	'Andenken an Heinrich Henkel' (T)	CDoC CLoc CWVF EBak SRiF WRou
	'André Le Nostre' (d)	CWVF EBak SRiF SVic
	'Andreas Schwab'	LCla
	andrei	CDoC LCla SRiF

'Andrew'	EBak SRiF
'Andrew Carnegie' (d)	CLoc
'Andrew George'	MJac
'Andrew Hadfield'	CWVF SRiF SVic WRou
'Andrew Ryle'	SRiF
'Andromeda' De Groot	CSil
'Andy Jordens' (d)	WFuv
'Angel Kiss' (E)	CDoC
'Angela Dawn'	WPBF WRou
'Angela Leslie' (d)	CLoc CWVF EBak SRiF SVic
'Angela Rippon'	CWVF MJac
'Angelika Fuhrmann' (d)	WPBF
'Angel's Flight' (d)	EBak SRiF
'Anita' (d)	CCCN CLoc CWVF EPts LAst MHav MJac SLBF SRiF SVic WFuv WGor WPBF WRou
'Anjo' (v)	CWVF SLBF SRiF
'Ann Howard Tripp'	CDoC CLoc CWVF MBri MJac SRiF SVic WFuv WPBF WRou
'Ann Lee' (d)	EBak SRiF
'Anna of Longleat' (d)	CCCN CTsd CWVF EBak LAst MJac SPet SRiF WFuv
'Anna Silvena'	LSou MHav
'Annabel' (d) ♀H3	CCCN CDoC CLoc CTri CTsd CWVF EBak EPts LAst MBri MJac SLBF SPet SRiF SVic WFuv WPBF WRou
'Annabelle Stubbs' (d)	SRiF
'Anne Strudwick' (d)	SRiF
'Anneke de Keijzer'	CDoC LCla
'Annie Den Otter'	WPBF
'Annie Earle'	SRiF
'Annie Geurts'	WPBF
'Annie M.G. Schmidt'	EPts WPBF
'Another Little Cracker'	WRou
'Another Storey'	CSil SRiF
'Anouchka de Weirdt' (d)	WPBF
'Ant and Dec' (d/v)	MHav MJac
'Anthea Day' (d)	CLoc
'Anthony Heavens'	SRiF
'Antigone'	SLBF SRiF WPBF
'Aphrodite' (d)	CLoc CWVF EBak SRiF
'Applause' (d)	CLoc CWVF EBak EPts SPet SRiF SVic
aprica misapplied	see *F.* × ***bacillaris***
aprica Lundell	see *F. microphylla* subsp. *aprica*
'Apricot Ice'	CLoc SVic
'Aquarius'	SRiF
'Arabella'	CWVF
'Arabella Improved'	CWVF SRiF SVic
arborea	see *F. arborescens*
§ ***arborescens***	CBcs CDoC CHEx CLoc CSil CWVF EBak EWld LCla LPio SDys SRiF SVic WRou WWlt
- B&SWJ 10475	WCru
'Arcadia Gold' (d)	CWVF SRiF SVic
'Arcady'	CLoc CWVF
'Archie Owen' (d)	SRiF
'Arels Arjen'	WPBF
'Arend Moerman' (d)	WPBF
'Aretha' (Diva Series)	MHav
'Ariel' (E)	CDoC CSil SVic WCom WRou
'Arkie' **new**	MJac
'Arlendon' (d)	CWVF
'Army Nurse' (d) ♀H4	CDoC CLoc CSil CWVF EPts GKir LAst LRHS MBri MGos NBir SLBF SPet SRiF SVic WFuv
'Aronst Hoeck'	WPBF
'Art Deco' (d)	SRiF WPBF
'Arthur Baxter'	EBak
'Artosa' (d)	WPBF
'Ashley'	CDoC CTsd LCla

'Ashley and Isobel'	CWVF SRiF
'Ashtede'	SLBF
'Atahualpa' (T)	CDoC WPBF
'Athela'	EBak SRiF
'Athene' **new**	SRiF
'Atlantic Star'	CWVF MJac SRiF WPBF
'Atlantis' (d)	CWVF MJac
'Atlas'	SRiF
'Atomic Glow' (d)	EBak SRiF SVic
'Aubergine'	see *F.* 'Gerharda's Aubergine'
'Aubrey Harris' (d)	SRiF
'Audray'	SRiF
'Audrey Booth' (d)	SRiF
'Audrey Dahms'	SRiF
'Audrey Hepburn'	CWVF
'Aunt Juliana' (d)	EBak SRiF
'Auntie Jinks'	CCCN CDoC CWVF EBak LAst LCla MJac SPet SRiF SVic WFuv WRou
'Auntie Kit'	SRiF
'Aurora Superba'	CLoc CTsd CWVF EBak MHav SLBF SRiF WRou
'Australia Fair' (d)	CWVF EBak SRiF
§ ***austromontana***	EBak SRiF
'Autumnale' ♀H1+3	CCCN CDoC CHEx CLoc CWVF EBak EPts LAst LCla NVic SBfd SLBF SMrm SPet SPoG SVic WFuv WPBF WRou
'Avalanche' ambig. (d)	CDoC CLoc CSil EBak SLBF
'Avocet'	CLoc EBak SRiF
'Avon Celebration' (d)	CLoc
'Avon Gem'	CLoc CSil SRiF
'Avon Glow' (d)	CLoc
'Avon Gold'	CLoc
ayavacensis	CDoC LCla
'Azure Sky' (d)	MJac WPBF
'Babette' (d)	SRiF
'Baby Blue' **new**	MHav
'Baby Blue Eyes' ♀H3-4	CDoC CSil CWVF ELon GKir LRHS MAsh MBri WFuv WRou
'Baby Blush'	CSil
'Baby Bright'	CWVF SLBF SRiF WRou
'Baby Chang'	SRiF WPBF
'Baby Face' ambig.	SRiF
'Baby Girl'	WFuv
'Baby Love'	SRiF WPBF
'Baby Pink' (d)	CWVF
'Baby Thumb' (v)	EPts SRiF
'Baby van Eijk'	WPBF
'Babyface' Tolley (d)	SVic
§ × ***bacillaris*** (E)	CChe CDoC CDul CEnt CHGN CSil EBak EWes GCal ITim MBlu SBfd SEND SLBF SPoG SRms WPBF
§ - 'Cottinghamii' (E)	CDoC CSil EWld IDee SPlb WSHC
- 'Oosje'	see *F.* 'Oosje'
§ - 'Reflexa' (E)	CAbP CCCN CTrC GKir GQui LSou
'Baden Powell' (E)	SRiF SVic
'Bagworthy Water'	CLoc
'Bahia'	WPBF
'Baker's Tri' (T)	EBak
'Balkonkönigin'	CLoc CWVF EBak SRiF WFuv
'Ballerina'	CDoC
'Ballerina Girl' (E) **new**	SLBF
'Ballet Girl' (d) ♀H1+3	CDoC CLoc CWVF EBak SLBF SRiF
'Balmoral' (d)	SRiF
'Bambini'	CWVF EPts SRiF
'Banks Peninsula'	GBin GQui
'Barbara'	CLoc CSil CTsd CWVF EBak EPts MJac SPet SRiF SVic WFuv WPBF WRou
'Barbara Evans'	SLBF SRiF
'Barbara Pountain' (d)	CWVF
'Barbara Windsor'	CWVF MJac SRiF

'Barnet Belle'	SLBF
'Baron de Ketteler' (d)	CSil CTsd SRiF
'Baroncelli' (d)	WPBF
'Barry M. Cox'	WPBF
'Barry's Queen'	see *F.* 'Golden Border Queen'
'Bart Comperen' (d)	WPBF
'Bart-Els' (d)	WPBF
'Bartje'	SLBF WPBF
'Bashful' (d)	CDoC CSil EPts LCla SPet SRiF SVic WPBF
'Basketfull' (d)	SRiF
'Beacon'	CDoC CLoc CSil CWVF EBak EPfP EPts LAst LBMP LRHS MBri MJac MWat SPet SPoG SRiF SVic WFuv WRou
'Beacon Rosa'	CCCN CDoC CLoc CSil CWVF ELon EPts LAst LRHS MBri MJac SLBF SPet SPoG SRiF SVic WFuv WPBF WRou
'Beacon Superior'	CSil
'Bealings' (d)	CLoc CWVF MBri MHav SRiF SVic WFuv
'Beansweyr' (d)	WPBF
'Beau Nash'	CLoc
'Beauty of Bath' (d)	CLoc EBak
'Beauty of Bexley' (d)	SRiF
'Beauty of Clyffe Hall' Lye	CSil EBak
'Beauty of Exeter' (d)	CWVF EBak SRiF
'Beauty of Meise' (d)	WPBF
'Beauty of Prussia' (d)	CLoc CSil CWVF
'Beauty of Swanley'	EBak SRiF
'Beauty of Trowbridge'	CWVF LCla
'Beckey' (d)	SRiF WPBF
'Becky Jane'	CSil
'Becky Reynolds'	SRiF
'Belinda Jane'	WPBF
'Bella Forbes' (d) ♀$^{H1+3}$	CLoc CSil EBak
'Bella Harris' (d)	SRiF
'Bella Rosella' (California Dreamers Series) (d)	CCCN EPts LAst MJac SCoo SRiF WFuv WPBF
'Bellbottoms'	SRiF
'Belle de Spa'	SRiF
'Belsay Beauty' (d)	CWVF MJac SRiF SVic
'Belvoir Beauty' (d)	CLoc
'Ben de Jong'	CDoC CTsd LCla SRiF WRou
'Ben Jammin'	CDoC CLoc CSil CWVF EPfP EPts LAst LRHS LSou MJac SPoG SRiF SVic WFuv WRou
'Ben Jiggins' (d)	SRiF
'Ben Turner' (d)	SRiF
'Beninkust'	WPBF
'Béranger' Lemoine, 1897 (d)	CSil EBak
'Berba's Coronation' (d)	WPBF
'Berba's Happiness' (d)	CWVF
'Berba's Trio'	SRiF
'Bergnimf'	CTsd SRiF
'Berliner Kind' (d)	CSil CWVF EBak SRiF
'Bermuda' (d)	CWVF SRiF
'Bernadette' (d)	CWVF
'Bernie's Big-un' (d)	MJac
'Bernisser Hardy' ♀$^{H3-4}$	CDoC CSil EPts LCla LRHS SLBF SRiF
'Bert de Jong'	WPBF
'Beryl Shaffery'	WPBF
'Beryl's Choice' (d)	SRiF
'Beryl's Jewel'	WPBF
'Berys Elizabeth'	SRiF
'Bessie Girl'	WPBF
'Bessie Kimberley' (T)	CDoC LCla WPBF
'Beth Robley' (d)	CWVF SRiF
'Betsy Huuskes'	WPBF
'Betsy Ross' (d)	EBak
'Bette Sibley' (d)	SRiF
'Betty Jean' (d)	WPBF
Betty = 'Shabetty'^{PBR} (Shadowdancer Series)	LAst
'Beverley'	CSil CWVF EBak EPts SRiF
'Beverley Sisters' (d)	MJac
'Bewitched' (d)	EBak
'Bianca' (d)	CWVF SRiF SVic WPBF
'Bicentennial' (d)	CCCN CLoc CTsd CWVF EBak EPts MJac SPet SRiF SVic WFuv WPBF
'Big David' (d)	WPBF
'Big Slim'	SRiF WPBF
'Bill Gilbert'	SRiF
'Bill Stevens' (d)	CTsd
'Billy'^{PBR}	CDoC
'Billy Green' (T) ♀$^{H1+3}$	CDoC CLoc CWVF EBak EPts LCla MHer MJac SLBF SRiF SVic WFuv WPBF WRou
'Billy P' **new**	LAst
'Bishop's Bells' (d)	CWVF SVic
'Bits' (d)	CTsd
'Bittersweet' (d)	SVic
'Black Beauty' (d)	CWVF
'Black Country 21' **new**	SLBF
'Black Prince'	CDoC CWVF MHav SRiF SVic WFuv WPBF
'Blackmore Vale' (d)	CWVF
'Blacky' (d)	CCCN EBak LAst LSou MHav MSCN SGar SPet SRiF SVic
I 'Blanche Regina' (d)	CWVF MJac
'Bland's New Striped'	CDoC EBak EPts LAst SLBF SRiF
'Blauer Engel'	WPBF
'Blaze Away' (d)	LAst MBri MJac SRiF WGor
'Bliss' (d)	WPBF
'Blober'	WPBF
'Blood Donor' (d)	MJac SRiF
'Blowick'	CDoC CWVF MBri MJac SPet SRiF
'Blue Beauty' (d)	CSil EBak SRiF
'Blue Boy' (d)	WFuv WPBF
'Blue Bush'	CBgR CSil CWVF EPts MJac SRiF SVic
'Blue Butterfly' (d)	CWVF EBak SRiF SVic
'Blue Eyes' (d)	CDoC SPet SRiF
'Blue Gown' (d)	CDoC CLoc CSil CWVF EBak GKir LRHS MGos SPet SRiF SVic WPBF WRou
'Blue Lace' (d)	CSil WFuv
'Blue Lagoon' ambig. (d)	CWVF
'Blue Lake' (d)	CWVF
'Blue Mink'	EBak SRiF
'Blue Mirage' (d)	CLoc CTsd CWVF MHav SRiF SVic WFuv
'Blue Mist' (d)	EBak
'Blue Pearl' (d)	CWVF EBak MHav SRiF
'Blue Pinwheel'	CWVF EBak
'Blue Sails'	SRiF WPBF
'Blue Satin' (d)	LAst
'Blue Sleighbells'	WPBF
'Blue Tit'	CSil LCla SRiF
'Blue Veil' (d)	CCCN CLoc CTsd CWVF MHav MJac SCoo SRiF SVic WFuv
'Blue Waves' (d)	CLoc CSBt CTsd CWVF EBak MJac SPet SRiF SVic
'Blueberry Fizz' (d) **new**	SRiF
'Blush o' Dawn' (d)	CLoc CTsd CWVF EBak EPts SPet SRiF SVic
'Blythe' (d)	SRiF
'Bob Bartrum'	SLBF
'Bob Pacey'	CWVF
'Bob Paisley' (d)	SRiF
'Bobby Boy' (d)	EBak

	'Bobby Dazzler' (d)	CWVF SRiF
	'Bobby Shaftoe' (d)	EBak SRiF WPBF
	'Bobby Wingrove'	EBak
	'Bobby's Girl'	EPts
	'Bobolink' (d)	EBak SRiF
	'Bob's Best' (d)	CWVF EPts MJac SRiF
	'Boerhaave'	EBak SRiF
	'Bohémienne'	WPBF
	boliviana Britton	see *F. sanctae-rosae*
	boliviana ambig.	CTsd IDee LPio
§	***boliviana*** Carrière	CDoC CHEx CLoc CWVF EBak LCla SRiF WRou
§	- var. ***alba*** 🏆H1+3	CDoC CLoc EBak EPts LCla LPio SRiF SVic WRou
	- var. ***boliviana***	CRHN SVic
	- var. ***luxurians*** 'Alba'	see *F. boliviana* Carrière var. *alba*
	- f. ***puberulenta*** Munz	see *F. boliviana* Carrière
	'Bon Accorde'	CLoc CWVF EBak EPts SLBF SRiF SVic WFuv
	'Bon Bon' (d)	CTsd CWVF EBak SRiF SVic
	'Bonita' (d)	CWVF SVic
	'Bonnie Bambini'	SRiF
	'Bonnie Lass' (d)	EBak
	'Bonzai Overijsel'	WPBF
	'Bora Bora' (d)	CTsd CWVF EBak SRiF SVic
	'Borde Hill' (d)	EPts
	'Border Princess'	EBak SRiF
	'Border Queen' 🏆H3-4	CDoC CLoc CSil CTsd CWVF EBak EPts EWes MJac SPet SRiF SVic WRou
	'Border Reiver'	CWVF EBak SVic
	'Börnemann's Beste'	see *F.* 'Georg Börnemann'
	'Bosom Pals' **new**	SRiF
	'Boson's Norah'	SRiF
	'Boswinning'	WPBF
	'Bouffant'	CLoc SVic
	'Bountiful' Lye **new**	SRiF
	'Bountiful' Munkner (d)	CLoc CWVF
	'Bouquet' (d)	CDoC CSil SRiF
	'Bow Bells'	CDoC CLoc CWVF MJac SPet SRiF SVic WFuv
	'Boy Marc' (T)	LCla SRiF WPBF
	'Braamt's Glorie'	WPBF
	bracelinae	CDoC CSil
	'Bram Verdonk' (d)	WPBF
	'Brancaster'	SRiF
	'Brandt's 500 Club'	CLoc EBak SRiF
	'Brann's Blossom'	SRiF
	'Breakaway'	SRiF
	'Brechtje'	WPBF
	'Breckland'	EBak SRiF
	'Breeders' Delight'	CSil CWVF MBri SRiF WFuv
	'Breeder's Dream' (d)	EBak
	'Breevis Arion' (d)	WPBF
	'Breevis Electo' (d)	WPBF
	'Breevis Evelien' (d)	WPBF
	'Breevis Hector' (d)	WPBF
	'Breevis Homerus' (d)	WPBF
	'Breevis Ilia' (d)	WPBF
	'Breevis Iris' (d)	WPBF
	'Breevis Karna' (d)	WPBF
	'Breevis Lucina' (d)	WPBF
	'Breevis Minimus'	SLBF
I	'Breevis Nobilis' (d)	WPBF
	'Breevis Panclione' (d)	WPBF
	'Breevis Pomona' (d)	WPBF
	'Breevis Rubi' (d)	WPBF
	'Breevis Selene' (d)	WPBF
	'Breevis Varuna' (d)	WPBF
	'Breevis Zagreus' (d)	WPBF
	'Brenda' (d)	CLoc CWVF EBak
	'Brenda Megan Hill' **new**	SRiF

'Brenda Pritchard' (d)	SRiF
'Brenda White'	CDoC CLoc CWVF EBak SRiF SVic WRou
'Brentwood' (d)	EBak
brevilobis	CSil WPBF
'Brian C. Morrison' (T)	LCla SRiF
'Brian G. Soanes'	EBak SRiF
'Brian Kimberley' (T)	LCla
'Bridal Pink' (d)	CTsd SRiF
'Bridal Veil' (d)	EBak SRiF
'Bridesmaid' (d)	CWVF EBak SPet SRiF SVic
'Brigadoon' (d)	EBak
'Bright Lights'	WPBF
'Brightling'	WPBF
'Brighton Belle' (T)	CDoC CWVF SRiF
'Brilliant' ambig.	CWVF MBri MHav WFuv
'Brilliant' Bull, 1865	CDoC CLoc CSil EBak LCla
'Briony Caunt'	CSil
'British Jubilee' (d)	CWVF SVic
'British Sterling' (d)	SRiF
'Brixham Orpheus'	CWVF
'Broadbent' (d) **new**	SRiF
'Brodsworth'	CSil
'Bronze Banks Peninsula'	CDoC CSil
'Brookwood Belle' (d)	CTsd CWVF EPts LCla MJac SLBF SRiF
'Brookwood Joy' (d)	CWVF MJac SRiF
'Brutus' 🏆H4	CDoC CLoc CSil CWVF EBak EPfP EPts GKir LRHS MAsh MBri MWat SPet SPoG SRiF SVic WFuv
'Bryan Breary' (E)	LCla SRiF
'Bubble Hanger'	SRiF
'Buddha' (d)	EBak
'Bugle Boy'	LCla SRiF
'Bunny' (d)	CWVF EBak SLBF SRiF SVic
'Burning Bush'	CTsd
'Burstwick'	CSil
'Burton Brew'	MJac
'Buster' (d)	LCla SRiF
'Buttercup'	CLoc CTsd CWVF EBak MHav SVic
'C.J. Howlett'	CSil EBak SRiF
'Caballero' (d)	EBak
'Cabaret' (d) **new**	SRiF
'Cable Car' (d)	SRiF
'Caesar' (d)	CWVF EBak SRiF
'Caitlin'	WPBF
'Caledonia'	CSil EBak SRiF
'Callaly Pink'	CWVF
'Cambridge Louie'	CWVF EBak MBri SPet SRiF
'Camelot'	SRiF
campos-portoi	CDoC CSil CTsd LCla WPGP
'Candlelight' (d)	CLoc CTsd EBak
'Candy Bells' (d)	CSBt
'Candy Kisses' (d)	SRiF
'Candy Stripe'	CLoc
canescens misapplied	see *F. ampliata*
'Cannell's Gem'	SRiF
'Cannenburgh Floriant' (d)	SRiF
'Canny Bob'	MJac
'Canopy' (d)	CWVF
'Capri' (d)	CTsd CWVF EBak SRiF
'Captivating Kelly' **new**	SRiF
'Cara Mia' (d)	CLoc CTsd SPet SRiF
'Caradela' (d)	CLoc MJac
'Cardinal'	CLoc CTsd WPBF
'Cardinal Farges' (d)	CLoc CSil CWVF MHav SLBF SPet SRiF SVic WFuv
'Careless Whisper'	LCla SLBF WPBF
'Carioca'	EBak
'Carisbrooke Castle' (d)	SRiF
'Carl Drude' (d)	CSil CTsd SRiF SVic
'Carl Wallace' (d)	SRiF

'Carla Johnston' 🏆H1+3	CDoC CLoc CWVF EPts MBri MJac SVic WFuv WPBF WRou
'Carla Knapen' (d)	WPBF
'Carlisle Bells'	WPBF
'Carl's Brummagem Beauty' **new**	MJac
'Carmel Blue'	CCCN CDoC CLoc CTsd LAst MSCN SBfd SPet SRiF SVic WFuv WGor
'Carmen' ambig.	WPBF
'Carmen' Lemoine (d)	CDoC CSil
'Carmine Bell'	CSil
'Carnea'	CSil CWib
'Carnival' (d)	CTsd SRiF
'Carnoustie' (d)	EBak
'Carol Grace' (d)	CLoc
'Carol Lynn Whittemore' (d)	SRiF
'Carol Nash' (d)	CLoc
'Caroline'	CLoc CWVF EBak EPts SRiF SVic WFuv WPBF WRou
'Caroline's Joy'	LAst MHav MJac SBfd SCoo SPet SRiF
'Carol's Choice'	WPBF
'Caron Keating'	WPBF
'Cascade'	CCCN CDoC CLoc CWVF EPts MBri MJac SPet SRiF WFuv WPBF
'Caspar Hauser' (d)	CWVF SLBF SRiF SVic
'Catharina' (T)	CDoC SRiF
'Catherine Bartlett'	CWVF WPBF
'Catherine Law' (d)	WPBF
'Cathie MacDougall' (d)	EBak
'Cecil Glass'	SRiF
'Cecile' (d)	CCCN CDoC CTsd CWVF EPts LAst MJac SRiF SVic WFuv WPBF WRou
'Celadore' (d)	CWVF SRiF SVic
'Celebration' (d)	CLoc CWVF SRiF
'Celia Smedley' 🏆H3	CCCN CDoC CLoc CTsd CWVF EBak EPts LCla MBri MJac SLBF SPet SRiF SVic WFuv WPBF WRou
'Centenary' (d) **new**	SRiF
'Centerpiece' (d)	EBak
'Ceri'	CLoc
'Cerrig'	SVic
'Chameleon'	SRiF
'Champagne Celebration'	CLoc
'Champagne Gold'	SRiF
'Champion'	SRiF
'Chancellor' (d)	CWVF
'Chandleri'	CWVF SLBF SRiF SVic
'Chang' 🏆H1+3	CDoC CLoc CTsd CWVF EBak LCla SLBF SRiF SVic WPBF
'Chantal Lavrijsen' (d)	WPBF
'Chantry Park' (T)	LCla SRiF
'Charisma'	SVic
§ 'Charles de Gaulle'	SRiF WPBF
'Charles Edward' (d)	CSil SRiF
'Charles Lester'	SRiF
'Charles Welch'	EPts
Charlie Dimmock = 'Foncha' PBR (d)	CLoc LAst SRiF WPBF
'Charlie Gardiner'	CWVF EBak
'Charlie Girl' (d)	EBak SRiF SVic
'Charlie Pridmore' (d)	SRiF
'Charlotte' **new**	SRiF
'Charlotte Clyne'	SRiF
'Charm of Chelmsford' (d)	WPBF
'Charming'	CDoC CLoc CSil CWVF EBak LRHS MAsh MJac SPet SVic WRou
'Chartwell'	WPBF
'Chase Delight' (v)	CDoC
'Chase Royal'	CTsd
'Chatt's Delight'	SLBF
'Checkerboard' 🏆H3	CCCN CLoc CSil CTsd CWVF EBak EPts LCla MJac MSCN SLBF SPet SVic WEas WFuv WPBF
'Cheeky Chantelle' (d)	SLBF WPBF
'Cheers' (d)	CWVF WFuv
'Chelsea Louise'	EPts
'Chenois Godelieve'	WPBF
'Cherry' PBR Götz	LAst WPBF
'Chessboard'	CLoc
'Chillerton Beauty' 🏆H3	CLoc CSil CTri CWVF ELon EPts LAst LRHS MJac SLBF SPer SPet SVic WMnd WPBF WRou
'China Doll' (d)	CWVF EBak SRiF SVic
'China Lantern'	CLoc CSil CTsd CWVF EBak SRiF SVic
'Chomal' (d)	SRiF
'Chor Echo'	CDoC WPBF
'Chris'	WPBF
'Chris Coleman' **new**	SRiF
'Chris Nicholls' (d)	CSil
'Chris Tarrant' (d) **new**	EPts
'Christa Lehmeier'	WPBF
'Christel Poelmans'	WPBF
'Christina Becker'	SRiF SVic
'Christine Bamford'	CDoC CSil CTsd CWVF SRiF
'Christine Rogers'	CDoC
'Christine Truman' (d) **new**	SRiF
'Christmas Gem' (T)	WPBF
'Chriwito'	WPBF
'Churchtown'	CWVF SRiF
'Cicely Ann' **new**	SRiF
cinerea	CDoC LCla
'Cinnabarina' (E)	CLoc SRiF
'Cinnamon' (d)	SRiF WPBF
'Cinque Port Liberty' (d)	SLBF SRiF
'Cinvenu'	LCla
'Cinvulca'	LCla
'Circe' (d)	CWVF EBak SVic
'Circus'	EBak
'Circus Spangles' (d)	CLoc LAst
'Citation'	CLoc CWVF EBak SVic
'City Lights'	SLBF
'City of Adelaide' (d)	CLoc SRiF
'City of Leicester'	CWVF MHer SPet
'Clair de Lune'	CDoC CWVF EBak MHav SRiF SVic WRou
'Claire Evans' (d)	CWVF
'Claire Oram'	CLoc
'Clare Frisby'	WPBF
'Claudia' (d)	CDoC LAst LCla MJac WFuv WPBF WRou
'Cliantha' (d)	CDoC MJac SRiF WFuv WRou
'Clifford Gadsby' (d)	CTsd EBak SRiF
'Cliff's Hardy'	CDoC CSil LCla SRiF
'Cliff's Own'	SVic
'Cliff's Unique' (d)	CWVF EPts
'Clifton Beauty' (d)	CTsd CWVF MJac SRiF
'Clifton Belle' (d)	CWVF
'Clifton Charm'	CSil EPts LCla MJac SVic WPBF
'Clipper'	CSil CWVF
'Cloth of Gold'	CLoc CWVF EBak MJac SPet SRiF SVic
'Cloverdale Jewel' (d)	CDoC CTsd CWVF EBak MHav SPet SRiF SVic
'Cloverdale Joy'	EBak SRiF
'Cloverdale Pearl'	CTsd CWVF EBak EPfP SPet SVic WPBF
'Coachman' 🏆H4	CLoc CWVF EBak EPts LCla SLBF SPet SRiF SVic WFuv WRou
'Cobalt'	SLBF

	coccinea	CDoC CSil CTsd LCla
	'Codringtonii'	CSil
	'Coen Bakker' (d)	WPBF
	× ***colensoi***	CDoC CSil ECou LCla
	'Colibri'	SRiF
	'Colin Chambers' (d)	SRiF
	'Collingwood' (d)	CLoc CWVF EBak SRiF
	'Colne Fantasy' (v)	CDoC SRiF
	'Come Dancing' (d)	CDoC CTsd CWVF MHav SPet SRiF SVic
	'Comet' ambig.	SRiF
	'Comet' Banks	CWVF
I	'Comet' Tiret (d)	CDoC CLoc EBak SPet
	'Comperen Alk'	WPBF
	'Comperen Groenling'	WPBF
	'Comperen Havik' (d)	WPBF
	'Comperen Lineola' (d)	WPBF
	'Comperen Lutea' (d)	WPBF
	'Conchilla' (d)	EBak SRiF
	'Condor'	WPBF
	'Confection' (d)	CTsd
	'Connie' (d)	CSil EBak SRiF SVic WPBF
	'Conspicua' ♀$^{H3-4}$	CSil CWVF EBak SRiF SVic
	'Constable Country' (d)	CWVF SRiF
	'Constance' (d)	CDoC CLoc CSil CTsd CWVF LCla MJac SLBF SPet SRiF SVic WPBF WRou
	'Constance Comer'	MJac SRiF WRou
	'Constellation' ambig.	CTsd CWVF
	'Constellation' Schnabel, 1957 (d)	CLoc EBak
	'Consuelo' (d)	WPBF
	'Continental' (d)	SRiF WFuv
	'Contraste' (d)	SBfd
	'Coombe Park'	MJac
	'Copycat'	CSil
	'Coquet Bell'	CWVF EBak SRiF WPBF
	'Coquet Dale' (d)	CWVF EBak SRiF
	'Coquet Gold' (d/v)	SRiF
	'Cor Spek' (d)	WPBF
	'Coral Baby' (E)	LCla
	'Coral Rose' (d)	SVic
	'Coral Seas'	EBak
	'Coralle' (T)	CCCN CDoC CLoc CWVF EBak EPts LBMP LCla MHer MJac MSCN SLBF SRiF SVic WFuv WRou
	'Corallina' ♀$^{H3-4}$	CDoC CLoc CSil CTsd EBak ELon MHav SBfd SPet SRiF SVic WFar WPnn
I	'Corallina Variegata' (v)	CSil WPBF
*	***cordata*** B&SWJ 9095	WCru
	- B&SWJ 10325	WCru
	cordifolia misapplied	see *F. splendens*
	'Core'ngrato' (d)	CLoc CWVF EBak SRiF
	'Corneel Cornelis' (d)	WPBF
	'Cornelia Smith' (T)	CDoC LCla
	'Cornwall Calls' (d)	EBak
	'Corrie Barten' (d)	WPBF
	'Corsage' (d)	CWVF SVic
	'Corsair' (d)	EBak SRiF SVic
	corymbiflora misapplied	see *F. boliviana* Carrière
	corymbiflora Ruíz & Pav.	CDoC EBak SVic
	'Cosmopolitan' (d)	EBak SRiF
	'Costa Brava'	CLoc EBak
	'Cotta Bright Star'	CDoC CWVF LCla
	'Cotta Carousel'	LCla WRou
	'Cotta Christmas Tree'	CDoC LCla SLBF SRiF
	'Cotta Fairy'	CWVF
	'Cotta Vino'	SRiF SVic
	'Cottinghamii'	see *F.* × *bacillaris* 'Cottinghamii'
	'Cotton Candy' (d)	CLoc CWVF SRiF SVic
	'Countdown Carol' (d)	EPts
	'Countess of Aberdeen'	CLoc CSil CWVF EBak SLBF SRiF WFuv
	'Countess of Maritza' (d)	CLoc CWVF
	'County Park'	CTsd ECou
	'Court Jester' (d)	CLoc EBak SRiF
	'Cover Girl' (d)	EBak EPts MJac SPet SRiF WPBF
	'Coxeen'	EBak
I	'Cracker' (d) **new**	SRiF
	'Crackerjack'	CLoc EBak SRiF
	'Creampuff' (d)	CDoC CTsd SRiF
	'Crescendo' (d)	CLoc CWVF
	'Crinkley Bottom' (d)	EPts MJac SLBF SRiF WFuv
	'Crinoline' (d)	EBak SRiF
	'Crosby Serendipity'	CLoc
	'Crosby Soroptimist'	CWVF MJac SRiF WRou
	'Cross Check'	CWVF MBri MJac WFuv
	'Crusader' (d)	CWVF SRiF
	'Crystal Aniversary' (d)	SRiF
	'Crystal Blue'	EBak SRiF SVic
	'Crystal Stars' (d)	SVic
	'Cupid'	CSil EBak
	'Curly Q'	EBak SPet SRiF SVic
	'Curtain Call' (d)	CLoc CTsd CWVF EBak SRiF SVic
	'Cutie Karen' (d)	SRiF
	cylindracea misapplied	see *F.* × *bacillaris*
	cylindracea Lindl. (E)	CSil LCla SRiF WPBF
	- (E/f) B&SWJ 10294	WCru
	'Cymon' (d)	CWVF SRiF
	'Cymru' (d)	SVic
	'Cyndy Robyn' (d)	SRiF WPBF
	'Cyril Holmes'	SRiF
	cyrtandroides	CSil
	'Dainty'	EBak
	'Dainty Lady' (d)	EBak
	'Daisy Bell'	CDoC CLoc CTsd CWVF EBak LCla MJac SPet SRiF SVic WRou
	'Dalton'	EBak
	'Dana Samantha'	EPts
	'Dancing Bloom'	EPts SRiF
	'Dancing Elves' (d)	WPBF
	'Dancing Flame' (d) ♀$^{H1+3}$	CCCN CLoc CTsd CWVF EBak EPts LAst LBMP MBri MJac SLBF SPet SRiF SVic WFuv WPBF
	'Daniel Reynolds'	WPBF
	'Danielle'	SRiF WPBF WRou
	'Danielle Frijstein'	WPBF
	'Danish Pastry'	CTsd CWVF SPet SRiF
	'Danny Boy' (d)	CLoc CWVF EBak SRiF SVic WFuv WPBF
	'Danny Kaye' (d)	WPBF
	'Danson Belle' (d)	SRiF
	'Dark Eyes' (d) ♀^{H4}	CCCN CLoc CSil CTsd CWVF EBak LAst MBri MJac SBfd SLBF SPet SRiF SVic WFuv WPBF
	'Dark Mystery' (d)	SRiF
	'Dark Night' (d)	CSil
	'Dark Secret' (d)	EBak
	'Dark Treasure' (d)	CDoC CTsd SRiF
	'Darreen Dawn' (d)	WPBF
	'Daryn John Woods'	CDoC LCla SRiF
	'Dave's Delight'	WPBF
	'David' ♀$^{H3-4}$	CDoC CLoc CSil CWVF ELon EOHP EPts LAst LCla LSRN SLBF SRiF WFuv WGor WPBF WRou
	'David Alston' (d)	CLoc CWVF EBak
	'David Lockyer' (d)	CLoc CWVF SVic
	'David Savage' (d)	LCla
	'David Ward' (d)	NEgg WPBF
	'Dawn'	EBak SRiF
	'Dawn Carless' (d)	SRiF WPBF
	'Dawn Fantasia' (v)	CLoc EPts MHav SRiF WPBF
	'Dawn Mist' (d)	WFuv

'Dawn Redfern' (d)	CWVF
'Dawn Sky' (d)	EBak
'Dawn Star' (d)	CTsd CWVF MHav MJac SVic WFuv
'Dawn Thunder' (d)	CTsd SVic
'Day by Day'	CSil
'Day Star'	EBak
'Daytime Live'	SRiF
'De Berckt' **new**	SRiF
'De Groot's Beauty'	WPBF
'De Groot's Black Beauty' (d)	WPBF
'De Groot's Floriant' **new**	LCla
'De Groot's Kattiensnor'	WPBF
'De Groot's Lady'	WPBF
'De Groot's Moonlight'	SRiF WPBF
'De Groot's Parade'	WPBF
'De Groot's Regenboog'	WPBF
'De Groot's Tricolore'	SRiF
'De Lemmentjes' (d)	WPBF
'De Mijnlamp' (d)	WPBF
'De Zeveraar' (d)	WPBF
'Deal Marine' (d)	SRiF
'Debby' (d)	EBak SRiF
'Deben Petite' (E)	LCla
'Deben Rose'	CTsd SRiF
'Deborah Jane'	SLBF
'Deborah Louise' **new**	SRiF
'Deborah Street' (d)	CLoc
§ ***decussata*** Ruíz & Pav.	CDoC EBak
'Dee Copley' (d)	EBak
'Dee Star' (d)	SVic
'Deep Purple' (d)	CCCN CDoC CLoc CWVF LAst MJac SCoo SRiF WFuv WPBF
'Delia Smith' (d) **new**	EPts
'Delilah' (d)	CWVF
'Delta's Angelique'	WPBF
'Delta's Bride'	SLBF
'Delta's Dream'	CTsd CWVF SRiF WPBF
'Delta's Drop'	SLBF SRiF SVic WPBF
'Delta's Groom'	LCla SRiF WRou
'Delta's Ko' (d)	SRiF SVic
'Delta's Paljas'	SRiF WPBF
'Delta's Parade' (d)	CDoC EPts SRiF
'Delta's Pim'	SRiF WPBF
'Delta's Prelude'	SRiF
'Delta's Rien'	SRiF SVic
'Delta's Sara'	CDoC LAst LRHS MJac NPri SPoG SRiF WPBF
'Delta's Song'	SRiF WPBF WRou
'Delta's Sprinkler'	SRiF
'Delta's Star'	WPBF
'Delta's Symphonie' (d)	CWVF
'Delta's Trick'	SRiF
'Delta's Wonder'	CSil SRiF SVic
'Demi van Roovert'	WPBF
§ ***denticulata***	CDoC CLoc CWVF EBak EPts LCla MHer SLBF SRiF SVic WPBF WRou
'Depardieu' (d)	WPBF
'Derby Imp'	CWVF SRiF
'Desperate Daniel'	EPts
'Devonshire Dumpling' (d)	CCCN CDoC CLoc CTsd CWVF EBak EPts LAst MBri MJac SLBF SPet SRiF SVic WFuv WPBF
'Diablo' (d)	EBak SRiF
'Diament' **new**	SRiF
'Diamond Celebration' (d)	SRiF
'Diamond Wedding'	SRiF SVic
'Diana' (d)	EBak SRiF
'Diana Princess of Wales'	LAst MJac SBfd SVil WFuv WPBF
'Diana Simpson' **new**	SRiF
'Diana Wills' (d)	CWVF
'Diana Wright'	CDoC CSil LPla SRiF
'Diane Brown'	CWVF WFuv WPBF
'Diane Stephens' **new**	SLBF
'Dick Swinbank' (d)	SRiF
'Didgeridoo' (d)	WPBF
§ 'Die Schöne Wilhelmine'	SLBF SVic WFuv WPBF
'Dijk van Tuin' (d)	WPBF
'Dilly-Dilly' (d)	CWVF SRiF
'Dimples' (d)	CSil MBri SRiF
'Diny Hetterscheid' (T)	WPBF
'Dipton Dainty' (d)	CLoc EBak SRiF SVic
'Display' ♀H4	CCCN CDoC CLoc CSil CWVF EBak EPts LAst LBMP LCla LRHS MBri MJac NPer SLBF SPet SPoG SRiF SVic WFar WFuv WPBF WRou
'Doc'	CDoC CSil EPts MHav SPet SRiF SVic WFuv WPBF
'Docteur Topinard'	CLoc EBak
'Doctor'	see *F.* 'The Doctor'
'Doctor Foster' ♀H4	CDoC CLoc CSil CTri EBak EPfP SRiF SVic
'Doctor Mason'	CWVF
'Doctor Olson' (d)	CLoc EBak SRiF
'Doctor Robert'	CWVF EPts MBri MJac SRiF SVic WFuv WPBF
'Dodo'	WPBF
§ 'Dollar Prinzessin' (d) ♀H4	CCCN CDoC CLoc CSil CWVF EBak EPfP EPts GKir LAst LCla LRHS MAsh MBri MJac MWat NPer NPri SLBF SPet SPlb SRiF SVic WFar WFuv WPBF
'Dollie Pausch'	WPBF
'Dolly Harris' **new**	SRiF
'Dominyana'	CSil CTsd EBak LCla
'Don Peralta'	EBak
'Dopy' (d)	CDoC EPts SPet SRiF SVic WFuv WPBF
'Doreen Redfern'	CLoc CTsd CWVF MHav MJac SPet SRiF SVic WRou
'Doreen Stroud' (d)	CWVF
'Doretteke'	WPBF
'Dorian Brogdale'	SRiF
'Doris Coleman' (d)	SRiF
'Doris Deaves'	SLBF
'Doris Joan'	SLBF SRiF WPBF
'Doris Yvonne' (d) **new**	SRiF
'Dorking Blue' (d)	SRiF
'Dorking Delight'	SRiF
'Dorothea Flower'	CLoc CSil CWVF EBak SRiF
'Dorothy'	LCla SLBF SPet SRiF
'Dorothy Ann'	LCla SLBF WPBF
'Dorothy Cheal'	CWVF
'Dorothy Clive' **new**	MHav
'Dorothy Day' (d)	CLoc
'Dorothy Hanley' (d)	CAlb CBgR CCCN CLoc CSil EPts LAst LRHS LSRN LSou MAsh MBri MJac SLBF SPet SPoG SRiF SVic WFuv WPBF WRou
'Dorothy Oosting' (d)	WPBF
'Dorothy Shields' (d)	CWVF MHav MJac SRiF
'Dorrian Brogdale' (T)	LCla WPBF
'Dorset Abigail'	CWVF
'Dorset Delight' (d)	CWVF SRiF
'Dot Woodage'	SRiF
'Double Trouble' (d)	WPBF
'Douglas Boath' (d)	WFuv
'Dovercourt Pride'	SRiF
'Dragon Fang'	WPBF
'Dragon Moon' (d)	WPBF
'Drake 400' (d)	CLoc
'Drama Girl' (d)	CWVF SRiF
'Drame' (d)	CDoC CSil CWVF EBak LCla SPet SRiF SVic WRou

	'Drum Major' (d)	EBak
	'Du Barry' (d)	EBak
	'Duchess of Albany'	CLoc EBak SRiF
	'Duchess of Cornwall' (d)	CSil EPts SRiF
	'Duet' (d)	CTsd SRiF SVic
	'Duke of Wellington' Haag, 1956 (d)	CLoc
	'Dulcie Elizabeth' (d)	CWVF EBak MJac SPet SRiF
	'Dunrobin Bedder'	CSil WPBF
	'Dusky Beauty'	CWVF SRiF SVic
	'Dusky Blue' **new**	SRiF
	'Dusky Rose' (d)	CLoc CWVF EBak MHav MJac SVic
	'Dusted Pink' (d)	SRiF
	'Dutch Flamingo' **new**	SRiF
	'Dutch Mill'	CLoc CWVF EBak SRiF
	'Duyfken'	CTsd CWVF SRiF
	'Dying Embers'	CLoc WRou
	'Dymph Werker van Groenland' (E)	LCla WPBF
	'Earre Barré'	SRiF WPBF
	'East Anglian'	CLoc EBak SRiF
	'Easter Belle' **new**	LRHS
	'Easter Bonnet' (d)	CLoc CWVF
	'Ebb 'n' Flow'	EBak SRiF
	'Ebbtide' (d)	CLoc EBak
	'Echo'	CWVF SRiF
	'Ectors Nursery'	WPBF
	'Ed Largarde' (d)	EBak SRiF
	'Eden' **new**	SRiF
	'Eden Lady'	CDoC CLoc CTsd SPet SRiF
	'Eden Princess'	CWVF MJac SRiF
	'Eden Rock' (d)	MHav WGor
	'Edie Lester'	SRiF
	'Edith' ambig.	EPts WRou
	'Edith' Banks	SRiF
	'Edith' Brown (d)	CSil LCla SLBF
	'Edith Emery' (d)	SPet SRiF
	'Edna May'	CWVF
	'Edna W. Smith'	CWVF
	'Eileen Drew'	SLBF
	'Eileen Raffill'	EBak
	'Eileen Saunders'	CSil EBak
	'Eisleban'	SRiF
	'El Camino' (d)	CWVF SRiF
	'El Cid'	CLoc CSil EBak SRiF SVic
	'Elaine Ann'	EPts MJac
	'Elaine Taylor' (d)	MJac WPBF
	'Eleanor Clark'	WPBF
	'Eleanor Leytham'	CWVF EBak SRiF SVic WRou
	'Eleanor Rawlins'	CSil EBak SRiF
	'Elf'	CSil
	'Elfin Glade'	CLoc CSil CWVF EBak SRiF
	'Elfrida' (d)	CSil WPBF
	'Elfriede Ott' (T)	CLoc EBak LCla SRiF WPBF
	'Elisabeth Schnedl' (d)	WRou
	'Elizabeth' ambig.	CTsd SRiF
I	'Elizabeth' Tiret, 1970 (d)	WPBF
	'Elizabeth' Whiteman, 1941	EBak
	'Elizabeth Honnorine'	SVic
	'Elizabeth Travis' (d)	EBak
	'Ellen Morgan' (d)	CWVF EBak SRiF
	'Ellen White' (d) **new**	SRiF
	'Elma'	LCla WPBF
	'Elsa' (d)	CWVF SPet SRiF SVic
	'Elsie Maude' (d)	CWVF SRiF
	'Elsie Mitchell' (d)	CTsd CWVF SPet SRiF WRou
	'Elsie Vert' (d)	SRiF WPBF
	'Elsstar' (d)	SRiF WPBF
	'Elysée'	CSil
§	'Emile de Wildeman' (d)	CWVF EBak SPet SRiF WFuv
	'Emile Zola'	CSil SRiF
	'Emily'	WPBF
	'Emily Austen'	CWVF SRiF
	'Emily Bright' **new**	SRiF
	'Emma Alice' (d)	CWVF
	'Emma Louise' (d)	SRiF
	'Emma Margaret'	SLBF SRiF
	'Emma Massey'	SRiF
	'Empress of Prussia' 🏆^{H4}	CDoC CLoc CSil CWVF EBak EPts SLBF SPet SRiF SVic WMnd WPBF WRou
	'Enchanted' (d)	CWVF EBak
	encliandra **new**	IFoB
	- subsp. ***encliandra*** (E)	CDoC WRou
*	- var. ***gris*** (E)	CSil
§	'Enfant Prodigue' (d)	CDoC CLoc CSil LPla SDix SLBF SRiF SVic WMnd
	'English Rose' (d)	CWVF WPBF
	'Enstone'	see *F. magellanica* var. *molinae* 'Enstone'
	'Erica Julie' (d)	SRiF
	'Eric's Hardy' (d)	CDoC
	'Eric's Majestic' (d)	MJac SRiF
	'Erika Köth' (T)	LCla SRiF
	'Ernest Rankin'	CSil SRiF SVic
	'Ernie'^{PBR}	LAst SLBF
	'Ernie Bromley'	CSil CWVF SRiF
	'Ernie Wise' (d)	MJac SCoo SRiF
	'Eroica'	SVic
	'Eruption'	CDoC WPBF
	'Esmerelda'	MJac
	'Estafette' (d)	SRiF
	'Estelle Marie'	CLoc CWVF EBak MBri SPet SRiF SVic WFuv
	'Eternal Flame' (d)	CTsd CWVF EBak EPts MBri SRiF SVic WFuv
	'Ethel' ambig.	WPBF
	'Ethel May' (d)	MJac
	'Ethel May Lester' (d) **new**	SRiF
	'Ethel Wilson'	CSil
	'Eureka Red' (Californian Dreamers Series) (d)	SRiF
	'Eurofuchsia' (d)	WPBF
	'Eurofuchsia 2007 Denmark' (d)	WPBF
	'Eusebia' (d)	CTsd SRiF SVic
	'Eva Boerg'	CCCN CLoc CSil CTri CWVF EBak LAst LCla MBri SPet SRiF SVic WFuv WKif WPBF
	'Evelyn Stanley' (d)	CWVF
§	'Evelyn Steele Little'	EBak SRiF
	'Evening Sky' (d)	EBak SRiF
	'Evensong'	CLoc CTsd CWVF EBak SRiF SVic WFuv
	'Everbeur' (d)	WPBF
	excorticata	CBcs CDoC CPLG CSil CTsd SPlb
	'Exmoor Woods'	CSil SRiF
	'Expo '86' (d)	SRiF WFuv
	'Eynsford' (d)	SRiF
	'Fabian Franck' (T)	CDoC LCla SRiF
	'Falklands' (d)	CSil SLBF SRiF
	'Falling Stars'	CLoc CTsd CWVF EBak SRiF SVic
	'Fan Dancer' (d)	EBak
	'Fancy Free' (d)	MBri
	'Fancy Pants' (d)	CLoc CWVF EBak SVic
	'Fanfare'	CDoC EBak LCla SVic WPBF WRou
	'Farningham'	SRiF
	'Fascination'	see *F.* 'Emile de Wildeman'
	'Fashion' (d)	EBak
	'Fasna 1100'	WPBF
	'Favourite'	EBak SRiF
	'Felicity Kendal' (d)	MJac SCoo
	'Feltham's Pride'	CWVF
	'Fenman'	CWVF SRiF SVic

'Fergie' (d)	SRiF
'Ferre Peeters' (d)	WPBF
'Festival Lights' (E)	SLBF
'Festoon'	EBak
'Fey' (d)	CWVF SRiF WFuv
'Ffion'	CDoC EPts SRiF
'Fiery Spider'	EBak SRiF SVic
'Finn'	CWVF EPts MHav
'Fiona'	CDoC CLoc CWVF EBak MHav SPet SRiF SVic
'Fiorelli Flowers' (d)	WPBF
'Fire Mountain' (d)	CLoc SRiF SVic
'Firecracker'^{PBR}	see *F.* 'John Ridding'
'Firefly'	SRiF SVic
'Firelite' (d)	EBak SRiF
'Firenza' (d)	CWVF SRiF
'First Kiss' (d)	CWVF
'First Lady' (d)	CTsd CWVF SRiF
'First Lord'	CWVF SRiF
'First of the Day'	SRiF
'First Success' (E)	CDoC CTsd CWVF LCla SRiF SVic WRou
'Flair' (d)	CLoc CWVF SRiF
'Flame'	EBak
'Flamenco Dancer' (California Dreamers Series) (d)	CLoc
'Flament Rose'	WPBF
'Flamingo' (d)	SVic
'Flash' 𝕐$^{H3-4}$	CBgR CLoc CSil CTri CWVF EBak EPfP EPts LCla MJac SLBF SPet SPoG SRiF SVic WFuv WRou
'Flashlight'	CDoC CSil CWVF EPfP EWld LAst MHav MJac SRiF WPBF
'Flashlight Amélioré'	CSil
'Flat Jack o' Lancashire' (d)	CSil SLBF SRiF
'Flavia' (d)	EBak
'Fleur de Picardie'	SLBF
'Flirtation Waltz' (d)	CLoc CTsd CWVF EBak MJac SRiF SVic WFuv
'Flocon de Neige'	CSil EBak
'Flogman'	WPBF
'Flor Izel' (d)	WPBF
'Floral City' (d)	CLoc EBak
'Floren Kennes' (d)	WPBF
'Florence Mary Abbott'	WPBF
'Florence Taylor' (d)	CWVF
'Florence Turner'	CSil EBak SRiF
'Florencio' (d)	WPBF
'Florentina' (d)	CLoc CWVF EBak SRiF SVic
'Florrie Lester' (d)	SRiF
'Florrie's Gem' (d)	SLBF
'Flowerdream' (d)	CWVF
'Flyaway' (d)	EBak SRiF
'Fly-by-night' (d)	CWVF
'Flying Cloud' (d)	CDoC CLoc CSil CWVF EBak MBri SRiF SVic
'Flying Scotsman' (d)	CCCN CDoC CLoc CTsd CWVF EBak EPts MJac SCoo SRiF SVic WFuv WRou
'Fokkos Katrientje'	WPBF
'Folies Bergères' (d)	EBak
'Foline'	SVic
'Foolke'	CSil EBak SRiF
'Forfar's Pride' (d)	CSil SRiF
'Forget-me-not'	CLoc CSil CWVF EBak SVic WPBF
'Forgotten Dreams'	WPBF
'Fort Bragg' (d)	CWVF EBak SRiF
'Forward Look'	SRiF WPBF
'Fountains Abbey' (d)	CWVF
'Four Farthings' (d)	EPts
'Foxgrove Wood' 𝕐$^{H3-4}$	CSil CWVF EBak EPts SLBF SRiF
'Foxtrot' (d)	CWVF
'Foxy Lady' (d)	CWVF SRiF WPBF
'Frances Haskins'	CSil SRiF WRou
'Frank Sanford' (d)	SRiF
'Frank Saunders'	CWVF LCla SLBF WPBF
'Frank Unsworth' (d)	CWVF EPts MJac SPet SRiF WFuv WPBF
'Frankfurt 2006' **new**	MJac
'Frankie's Magnificent Seven' (d)	EPts
'Frank-Marlyse' (d)	WPBF
'Franz von Zon'	LCla
'Frau Hilde Rademacher' (d)	CDoC CSil CWVF EBak EPts MHav SLBF SRiF SVic WPBF
'Frauke'	SVic
'Fred Hansford'	CDoC CSil CWVF SRiF
'Fred Shepherd'	SRiF
'Fred Swales' (T)	WPBF
'Fred's First' (d)	CDoC CSil SRiF
'Freefall'	EBak
'Freunden Tanzer' (d)	WPBF
'Frida Cox' (d)	WPBF
'Friendly Fire' (d)	CLoc SRiF
'Friendship' (d)	SRiF
'Frosted Flame'	CCCN CLoc CTsd CWVF EBak LAst LCla MJac SPet SRiF
'Frozen Tears'	SRiF
'Frühling' (d)	CSil EBak
'Fuchsiade'	WRou
'Fuchsiade '88'	CLoc CSil CTsd CWVF EBak SRiF WPBF
'Fuchsiarama '91' (T)	CWVF WRou
'Fuji-san'	CDoC ELon EPts SRiF
'Fuksie Foetsie' (E)	CDoC CSil SRiF
fulgens 𝕐$^{H1+3}$	CDoC GCal LCla MRav WPBF WRou
* - 'Variegata' (T/v)	CDoC CLoc EPts LCla SRiF WRou
'Fulpila'	LCla SLBF SRiF
'Für Elise' (d)	EBak
'Gala' (d)	EBak SRiF
'Galadriel'	WPBF
'Garden News' (d) 𝕐$^{H3-4}$	CDoC CLoc COlW CSil CWVF EPfP EPts LAst LCla LRHS MAsh MBri MJac MSCN NPer NPri SLBF SPet SRiF SVic WFar WMnd WPBF WRou
'Garden Week' (d)	CDoC CTsd CWVF SRiF SVic
'Gartenbauverein Eupen' (d)	WPBF
'Gartenmeister Bonstedt' (T) 𝕐$^{H1+3}$	CCCN CDoC CLoc CWVF EBak EWld LCla SRiF SVic
'Gary Rhodes' (d)	EBak MJac SBfd SCoo SRiF WFuv
'Gay Fandango' (d)	CLoc CTsd CWVF EBak SPet SRiF
'Gay Parasol' (d)	CLoc LAst MJac SRiF SVic WFuv WRou
'Gay Paree' (d)	EBak
'Gay Senorita'	EBak
'Gay Spinner' (d)	CLoc
'Geeskie Guskie'	SRiF
gehrigeri	EBak
'Gemma Fisher' (d)	EPts
Gene = 'Goetzgene'^{PBR} (Shadowdancer Series)	LAst LSou SCoo
'Général Charles de Gaulle'	see *F.* 'Charles de Gaulle'
'Général Monk' (d)	CDoC CSil CTsd CWVF EBak EPts LAst MBri SRiF SVic WPBF
'Général Voyron'	CSil
'General Wavell' (d)	CTsd SRiF SVic
'Genii' 𝕐^{H4}	Widely available
'Geoff Oke'	CDoC WPBF
'Geoffrey Smith' (d)	CSil EPts SRiF
§ 'Georg Börnemann' (T)	CLoc EBak SRiF WPBF
'Georgana' (d)	SRiF
'George Allen White' (d)	CDoC CWVF WPBF

	'George Barr'	SRiF WPBF
	'George Johnson'	CDoC CTsd SRiF
	'George Travis' (d)	EBak SRiF
	'Gerald Drewitt'	CSil
§	'Gerharda's Aubergine'	CDoC CLoc CSil CWVF SRiF
	'Gerharda's Kiekeboe'	WPBF
	'Gerharda's Panache'	WPBF
	'Gesneriana'	CDoC CLoc EBak SRiF WWlt
	'Ghislaine' (d)	SRiF
	'Giant Pink Enchanted' (d)	CLoc EBak
	'Gilda' (d)	CWVF MJac SVic
	'Gillian Althea' (d)	CTsd CWVF SRiF WFuv
	'Gilt Edge' (v)	CLoc
	'Gimlie'	WPBF
I	'Gina'	WPBF
	'Gina Bowman' (E)	CDoC LCla SLBF
	Ginger = 'Goetzginger'PBR (Shadowdancer Series)	LAst LSou SCoo
	'Gingham Girl' (d)	SRiF
	'Giovanna and Wesley' (d)	SRiF
	'Gipsy Princess' (d)	CLoc
	'Girls' Brigade'	CWVF SRiF
	'Gitana'	WPBF
	'Gladiator' (d)	EBak SRiF SVic
	'Gladys Godfrey'	EBak
	'Gladys Lorimer'	CDoC CWVF EPts LRHS
	'Gladys Miller'	CLoc
	glazioviana	CDoC CSil CTsd CWVF LCla MHer SLBF SRiF SWal WGwG WRou
	'Glenby' (d)	CWVF SRiF
	'Glendale'	CWVF
	'Glitters'	CWVF EBak
§	'Globosa'	CAgr CSil EBak SRiF
	'Glow'	CSil EBak SRiF WPBF
	'Glowing Embers'	EBak SRiF
	'Glowing Lilac' (d)	EPts WFuv
	'Gold Brocade'	CSil SPet SRiF
	'Gold Crest'	EBak SRiF
	'Gold Leaf'	CWVF SRiF
	'Golden Amethyst' (d)	SRiF
	'Golden Anniversary' (d)	CLoc CWVF EBak MJac SRiF SVic WFuv WPBF
	'Golden Arrow' (T)	CDoC LCla SRiF SVic
§	'Golden Border Queen'	CLoc CSil EBak SPet
	'Golden Dawn'	CLoc CWVF EBak SPet SRiF SVic
	'Golden Girl'	SLBF
	'Golden Herald'	CSil SLBF
	'Golden la Campanella' (d/v)	CLoc MBri
	'Golden Lena' (d/v)	CSil CWVF
	'Golden Marinka' (v) ♀H3	CCCN CLoc EBak LSou MBri SPet SRiF SVic WPBF
	'Golden Melody' (d)	SRiF
	'Golden Peppermint Stick' (d)	CTsd SRiF
	'Golden Swingtime' (d)	CTsd MBri MHav MJac SPet SRiF SVic WFuv
	'Golden Treasure' (v)	CLoc CSil CWVF MBri SRiF
	'Golden Vergeer' (v)	SLBF
	'Golden Wedding'	SRiF SVic
	'Goldsworth Beauty'	CSil SRiF
	'Golondrina'	CSil CWVF EBak
	'Goody Goody'	EBak SRiF SVic
	'Gooseberry Hill'	SRiF
	'Goosebery Belle'	SRiF WRou
	'Gordon Boy' (d)	CSil
	'Gordon Thorley'	CSil
	'Gordon's China Rose'	LCla
	'Gota'	SLBF WPBF
	'Göttingen' (T)	EBak SRiF WPBF
	'Gouden Pater' (d)	WPBF
	'Governor Pat Brown' (d)	EBak SRiF
	'Grace Darling'	CWVF EBak SRiF
	gracilis	see *F. magellanica* var. *gracilis*
	'Graf Witte'	CDoC CSil CWVF SPet SRiF SVic
	'Granada' (d)	SRiF
	'Grand Duchess' (T)	WPBF
	'Grand Duke' (T/d)	CWVF
	'Grand Prix' (d)	CTsd SVic
	'Grand Slam' (d)	CTsd SVic
	'Grandad Fred' (d)	SRiF
	'Grandad Hobbs' (d)	LCla SLBF
	'Grandma Hobbs'	LCla
	'Grandma Sinton' (d)	CLoc CTsd CWVF MBri SRiF
	'Grandpa George' (d)	LCla SRiF
	'Grandpa Jack' (d)	SLBF
	'Granny Charlton' **new**	WCFE
	'Grasmere'	SRiF
	'Grayrigg'	CDoC CSil CTsd EPts LCla SRiF
	'Great Ouse' (d)	EPts
	'Great Scott' (d)	CLoc CTsd
	'Green 'n' Gold'	EBak
	'Greenpeace'	CDoC CTsd SRiF SVic WPBF
	'Greg Walker' (d)	SRiF
	'Greta' (T)	SRiF WPBF
	'Gretna Chase'	MBri SRiF
	'Grey Lady' (d)	CSil SRiF SVic
	'Grietus Luisman' (d)	WPBF
	'Gris'	SRiF
	'Groene Boelvaar' (d)	WPBF
	'Groene Kan's Glorie'	CTsd SVic WPBF
	'Groovy'	WPBF
	'Grumpy'	CWVF EPts MHav SPet SVic WFuv WPBF
	'Gruss aus dem Bodethal'	CLoc CWVF EBak EPts SRiF
	'Guinevere'	CWVF EBak
	'Gustave Doré' (d)	CDoC CSil EBak SRiF
	'Guy Dauphine' (d)	EBak
	'Guy-Ann Mannens'	WPBF
	'Gwen Dodge'	SRiF SVic WPBF
	'Gwend-a-ling'	SRiF
	'Gwendoline Clare'	WPBF
	'Gypsy Girl' (d)	CWVF SRiF
	'H.G. Brown'	CSil EBak SRiF
	'Habanero' (d)	WPBF
	'Hagelander'	WPBF
	'Halsall Beauty' (d)	MBri
	'Halsall Belle' (d)	MBri SRiF
	'Halsall Pride' (d)	MBri
	'Hamadryad' (d)	WPBF
	'Hampshire Blue'	CDoC CWVF SRiF SVic WFuv
	'Hanna Improved'	SRiF
	'Hannah Louise' (d)	EPts
	'Hans Callaars'	LCla
	'Hansi'	WPBF
	'Happiness' (d)	SVic
	'Happy'	CDoC CSil CTsd CWVF EPts LCla MHav SPet SRiF SVic WFuv WPBF
	'Happy Anniversary'	CLoc SVic WPBF
	'Happy Fellow'	CDoC CLoc CSil EBak MHav SRiF
	'Happy Wedding Day' (d)	CLoc CWVF EPts LAst MJac SCoo SPet SRiF SVic WFuv
	'Hapsburgh'	EBak SRiF
	'Harbour Lites'	SLBF WPBF WRou
	'Harlow Car'	CDoC CWVF EPts SRiF
	'Harlow Perfection'	CDoC
	'Harmony' Niederholzer, 1946	EBak
	'Harnser's Flight'	SRiF
	'Harold Smith'	SRiF
	'Harriet Lye' **new**	SRiF
	'Harriett' (d)	WPBF
	'Harry Dunnett' (T)	EBak

'Harry Gray' (d)	CCCN CLoc CTsd CWVF EBak EPts LAst MBri MJac SPet SVic WFuv
'Harry Pullen'	EBak
'Harry Taylor' (d)	EPts SRiF
'Harry's Sunshine'	SLBF
'Harti's Olivia'	WPBF
hartwegii	CDoC CSil LCla MHer
'Harvey's Reward'	SLBF
'Hathersage' (d)	EBak
hatschbachii	CDoC CSil CTsd ECre ELon EWes GCal LCla MHer SDix SPlb SPoG SRiF WPnn
'Haute Cuisine' (d)	CLoc SVic
'Hawaiian Sunset' (d)	CLoc CWVF EPts SLBF SRiF WFuv WPBF
'Hawkshead' ♀H3-4	Widely available
'Hazel' (d)	CWVF MHav SRiF SVic
'Hazerland'	WPBF
'Heart Throb' (d)	EBak
'Heather Rose' (d) **new**	SRiF
'Heavenly Hayley' (d)	SLBF SRiF
'Hebe'	EBak SRiF
'Heemaeer'	WPBF
'Heidi Ann' (d) ♀H3	CCCN CDoC CLoc CSil CWVF EBak EPts LAst LRHS MAsh MBri MSCN SLBF SPet SRiF SVic WFuv WPBF
'Heidi Blue' (d)	SLBF
'Heidi Joy'	CSil
§ 'Heidi Weiss' (d)	CDoC CLoc CSil CWVF MBri SPet WFuv WPBF
'Heinrich Henkel'	see *F.* 'Andenken an Heinrich Henkel'
'Helen Clare' (d)	CLoc CWVF EBak
'Helen Gair' (d)	CWVF SRiF
'Helen Nicholls' (d)	WPBF
'Hellen Devine'	CWVF
'Hello Moideer'	SRiF
'Hemsleyana'	see *F. microphylla* subsp. *hemsleyana*
'Henk Kaspers' (d)	WPBF
'Henkelly's Athena'	WPBF
'Henkelly's Consivia'	WPBF
'Henkelly's Diana'	WPBF
'Henkelly's Elisabeth'	WPBF
'Henkelly's Jasmine'	WPBF
'Henkelly's Tim'	WPBF
'Henning Becker' ♀H3	CBgR CWVF ELon
'Henri Poincaré'	EBak SRiF
'Henrieke Dimi' (d)	WPBF
'Henriette Ernst' **new**	SRiF
'Herald' ♀H4	CDoC CSil CWVF EBak MAsh MHav SLBF SRiF SVic WFuv
'Herbé de Jacques'	see *F.* 'Mr West'
'Heri Arapaima'	WPBF
'Heri Candiru'	WPBF
'Heri Leng'	WPBF
'Heri Mochara' (d)	WPBF
'Heri Panga' (d)	WPBF
'Heri Shusui' (d)	WPBF
'Heri Snapper' (d)	WPBF
'Heritage' (d)	CLoc CSil EBak SRiF
'Herman de Graaff' (d)	WPBF
'Hermiena'	CLoc CTsd CWVF EPts MHav SLBF SRiF SVic WFuv WPBF
'Hermienne'	WRou
'Heron'	CSil EBak SRiF
'Herps Baljurk'	WPBF
'Herps Bazuin'	WPBF
'Herps Bongo'	WPBF
'Herps Cornu'	WPBF
'Herps Helicopter'	WPBF
'Herps Kwikstep'	WPBF

'Herps Pierement'	SLBF
'Herps Schalmei'	WPBF
'Herps Trailer'	WPBF
'Herps Tweespan'	WPBF
'Hertogin van Brabant' (d)	WPBF
'Hessett Festival' (d)	CWVF EBak SRiF WFuv
'Heston Blue' (d)	CWVF SRiF
'Heydon'	CWVF SRiF
'Hi Jinks' (d)	EBak SRiF SVic
hidalgensis	see *F. microphylla* subsp. *hidalgensis*
'Hidcote Beauty'	CLoc CTsd CWVF EBak LCla MHav SLBF SPet SRiF SVic WPBF
'Hidden Treasure'	WPBF WRou
'Highland Pipes'	LCla SVic
'Hilda May Salmon'	CWVF
'Hindu Belle'	EBak SRiF
'Hinnerike' (E)	CSil CWVF LCla SVic WPBF
'Hiroshige' (T)	LCla SRiF
'His Excellency' (d)	EBak SRiF
'Hobo' (d)	CSil SRiF
'Hobson's Choice' (d)	CWVF SLBF SRiF
'Holly's Beauty' (d)	CDoC CLoc EPts LAst SRiF WFuv
'Hollywood' (d)	SRiF
'Hollywood Park' (d)	EBak
'Hot Coals'	CWVF EPts MCot MJac SRiF SVic WPBF WRou
'Howard's Own' **new**	SRiF
'Howerd Hebden'	CDoC
'Howlett's Hardy' ♀H3-4	CDoC CLoc CSil CWVF EBak GKir LRHS MHav NLar SRiF SVic WMnd WRou
'Huet's Akabar'	WPBF
'Huet's Almandien'	WPBF
'Huet's Amaril' (d)	WPBF
'Huet's Andalusiet' (d)	WPBF
'Huet's Baraketh'	WPBF
'Huet's Calamijn' (d)	WPBF
'Huet's Draviet'	WPBF
'Huet's Heliotroop' (d)	WPBF
'Huet's Kwarts'	WPBF
'Huet's Parelmoer' (d)	WPBF
'Huet's Topaas'	WPBF
'Huet's Turkoois'	WPBF
'Huet's Uvardiet' (d)	WPBF
'Hugh Morgan' (d)	SRiF
'Hula Girl' (d)	CDoC CTsd CWVF EBak MJac SPet SRiF
'Humboldt Holiday' (d)	SRiF
'Huntsman' (d)	CCCN CDoC MHav MJac SRiF WPBF
'Huygen Ireen' (d)	WPBF
'Ian Leedham' (d)	CTsd EBak SRiF
'Ian Storey'	CDoC CSil WPBF
'Ice Cream Soda' (d)	EBak SRiF
'Ice Maiden' ambig. (d)	WPBF
'Iceberg'	CWVF EBak SVic
'Icecap'	CWVF MBri SVic
'Iced Champagne'	CLoc CWVF EBak MHav MJac
'Ichiban' (d)	CLoc CTsd SRiF
'Icicle' (d)	WPBF
'Ida' (d)	EBak SRiF
'Ien Van Adrichem' (d)	WPBF
'Igloo Maid' (d)	CLoc CWVF EBak SPet SRiF SVic WFuv
'Ijzerwinning' (d)	WPBF
'Illusion'	WPBF
'Impala' (d)	CWVF WPBF
'Imperial Fantasy' (d)	CWVF SRiF
'Impudence'	CLoc CWVF EBak SPet SRiF
'Impulse' (d)	CLoc
'Independence' (d)	SRiF SVic

'Indian Maid' (d)	CDoC CWVF EBak SRiF
'Ingram Maid'	WPBF
'Insulinde' (T)	CDoC CTsd CWVF EPts LCla MJac SLBF SRiF
'Intercity'	WPBF
'Interlude' (d)	EBak
'Iolanthe' (T)	CWVF WPBF
'Irene L. Peartree' (d)	CWVF LCla
'Irene Sinton' (d)	MJac
'Iris Amer' (d)	CLoc CWVF EBak
'Irving Alexander' (d)	WPBF
'Isabel Ryan'	CSil
'Isis' Lemoine	CSil
'Isle of Mull'	CDoC CSil SPet
'Isle of Purbeck'	SRiF SVic
'Italiano' (d)	CWVF MJac SVic
'Ivy Grace'	CSil
'Ixion'	SRiF
'Jack Acland'	CWVF SRiF
'Jack Coast'	SRiF
'Jack King'	SRiF
'Jack Rowlands' (d)	SRiF
'Jack Shahan' ♀^{H3}	CCCN CDoC CLoc CSil CTsd CWVF EBak LAst LCla MBri MJac SPet SRiF WFuv WPBF
'Jack Stanway' (v)	CDoC CWVF SRiF WPBF
'Jack Wilson'	CSil
'Jackie Bull' (d)	CWVF EBak
'Jackpot' (d)	EBak
'Jackqueline' (T)	CWVF SRiF
'Jacky' **new**	SRiF
'Jacq Puts'	WPBF
'Jadi Femke'	WPBF
'Jamboree' (d)	EBak SRiF
'James Eve' (d)	SRiF
'James Hammond'	SRiF
'James Lye' (d)	CWVF EBak SRiF
'James Shaffery' (d)	WPBF
'James Travis' (E/d)	CDoC CSil EBak LCla SRiF
'Jan Bremer'	SVic
'Jan Murray'	SLBF SRiF
'Jandel'	CWVF SRiF
'Jane Amanda' (d)	SRiF
'Jane Humber' (d)	CWVF SRiF
'Jane Lye'	EBak SRiF
'Janet Williams' (d)	CSil
'Janice Ann'	LCla WPBF
'Janice Perry's Gold' (v)	CLoc MHav MJac SLBF SRiF
'Janie' (d)	EPfP MAsh SRiF
'Janneke Brinkman-Salentijn'	SRiF
'Janske Vermeulen'	WPBF
'Jap Vantveer' (T)	LCla WPBF
'Jaspers Kameleon'	WPBF
'Jaspers Vlammetje' (T)	WPBF
'Jaunty Jack'	SLBF
'Jayess Helen' (d)	SRiF
'Jean Baker'	CDoC CSil
'Jean Campbell'	EBak
'Jean de Fakteur' (d)	WPBF
'Jean Frisby'	CLoc
'Jean Taylor' **new**	MHav
'Jean Webb' (v) **new**	WCot
'Jef van der Kuylen' (d)	WPBF
'Jelle Veemen'	WPBF
'Jennie Rachael' (d)	SRiF WFuv
'Jennifer'	EBak MJac SRiF
'Jennifer Ann'	SLBF
'Jennifer Hampson' (d)	CSil
'Jennifer Lister' (d)	CSil
'Jenny May'	CLoc EPts
'Jenny Sorensen'	CWVF SRiF WFuv WPBF

'Jess'	LCla SLBF SRiF
'Jessica Reynolds'	SRiF WPBF
'Jessie Pearson'	CWVF
'Jessimae'	CWVF SPet SRiF
'Jester' Holmes (d)	CLoc CSil
'Jet Fire' (d)	EBak
'Jezebel' (d)	SRiF SVic WPBF
'Jiddles' (E)	LCla SRiF WRou
'Jill Holloway' (T)	SLBF WPBF
'Jill Whitworth'	CDoC WPnn
'Jim Coleman'	CWVF SRiF SVic
'Jim Dodge' (d)	EPts
'Jim Hawkins'	EBak SRiF
'Jim Missin' (d/v)	SRiF
'Jim Muncaster'	CWVF
'Jim Todd'	SRiF
'Jim Watts'	CDoC CTsd WPBF
jimenezii	CDoC LCla WPBF
'Jimmy Cricket' (E)	CDoC
'Jingle Bells'	CTsd SRiF
'Joan Barnes' (d)	CTsd CWVF SRiF
'Joan Cooper'	CLoc CSil CWVF EBak SLBF SRiF SVic
'Joan Gilbert' (d)	SRiF
'Joan Goy'	CWVF MJac SRiF SVic WFuv
'Joan Knight'	CLoc
'Joan Leach'	CSil
'Joan Margaret' (d)	MJac
'Joan Morris'	SLBF
'Joan Pacey'	CDoC CWVF EBak SRiF
'Joan Pawley' **new**	SRiF
'Joan Smith'	EBak SRiF
'Joan Waters' (d)	CWVF
'Joanna Lumley' (d)	EPts MHav MJac
'Jo-Anne Fisher' (d)	EPts
'Joan's Delight'	WPBF
'Jock Buchanan' (d)	WPBF
'Jody Goodwin'	WPBF
'Joe Kusber' (d)	CWVF EBak SRiF WFuv
'Joel'	CLoc WPBF
'Joergen Hahn'	WPBF
'Johannes Nowinski'	SRiF
'John Bartlett'	CLoc
'John E. Caunt' ♀$^{H3-4}$	CSil
'John Grooms' (d)	CLoc SRiF SVic WFuv WRou
'John Lockyer'	CLoc CWVF EBak SRiF
'John Maynard Scales' (T)	CDoC CWVF LCla MJac SRiF WPBF WRou
§ 'John Ridding'^{PBR} (T/v)	CLoc EPts LAst SPoG SVil WPBF
'John Shead'	WPBF
'John Suckley' (d)	EBak
'John Wright'	CSil LCla
'Joke's Albino'	WPBF
'Jolanda Weeda'	WPBF
'Jomam' ♀^{H3}	CLoc CWVF
'Jon Oram'	CLoc CWVF
'Jonny Wilkinson' **new**	MJac
'Jorma van Eijk' (d)	WPBF
'Jose Tamerus' (d)	WPBF
'Jose's Joan' (d)	CWVF SVic
'Joy Patmore'	CLoc CTsd CWVF EBak MBri SLBF SPet SRiF WFuv WPBF
'Joyce'	WPBF
'Joyce Adey' (d)	CWVF SRiF
'Joyce Forward'	SRiF
'Joyce Sinton'	CLoc CWVF MBri SRiF WFuv
'Joyce Wilson' (d)	EPts
'Jubie-Lin' (d)	WPBF
'Jubilee Quest'	WPBF
'Judith Coupland'	CWVF
'Jülchen'	CWVF
'Jules Daloges' (d)	EBak SRiF

	'Julia' (d)	WPBF
	'Julie'	SRiF
	'Julie Ann'	SRiF
	'Julie Ann Goodwin'	WPBF
	'Julie Horton' (d)	WPBF
	'Julie Marie' (d)	CWVF MJac
	'June Gardner'	CWVF SRiF
	'Jungle'	LCla SLBF SRiF
I	'Juno' Kennett	EBak
	juntasensis	SRiF
	'Jupiter Seventy'	EBak SRiF
	'Jus' For You'	MJac
	'Just Pink' (E) **new**	CDoC
	'Just William'	SRiF
	'Justin's Pride'	CDoC CSil SRiF
	'Kalang Talinga' (d) **new**	SRiF
	'Kaleidoscope' (d)	EBak SRiF
	'Kareeloven' (d)	WPBF
	'Karen Isles' (E)	CDoC LCla STre WRou
	'Karen Louise' (d)	CLoc
	'Karin de Groot'	SVic WFuv
	'Karl Hartness'	SRiF
	'Kate Harriet' (d)	SRiF
	'Kate Taylor' (d)	SLBF WPBF
	'Kath van Hanegem'	SLBF SRiF WPBF WRou
	'Kathleen Galea'	SRiF
	'Kathleen van Hanegan'	CLoc
	'Kathryn Maidment'	SVic
	'Kathy Louise' (d)	SRiF WPBF
	'Kathy's Sparkler' (d)	SRiF
	'Katie Coast' **new**	SRiF
	'Katie James' **new**	SRiF
	'Katie Reynolds' (d)	SRiF
	'Katie Rogers'	EPts
	'Katie Susan'	SLBF
	'Katinka' (E)	CDoC CWVF LCla SLBF WPBF
	'Katjan'	CSil LCla SLBF SRiF WPBF
	'Katrien Michiels'	SRiF
	'Katrina' (d)	CLoc EBak SRiF
	'Katrina Thompsen'	CLoc CWVF EPts SRiF WFuv
	'Katy Flynn' **new**	SLBF
	'Katy M'	WPBF
	'Keepsake' (d)	CLoc EBak
	'Kees van Eijk' (d)	WPBF
	'Keesje'	CTsd
	'Kegworth Carnival' (d)	CWVF SRiF
	'Kelly Jo'	SRiF
	'Ken Goldsmith' (T)	CWVF
	'Ken Jennings'	CWVF
	'Ken Shelton'	SRiF
	'Kenny Dalglish' (d)	CSil SRiF
	'Kenny Holmes'	CWVF
	'Kenny Walkling'	LCla SLBF
	'Kentish Maid' **new**	SRiF
	'Kernan Robson' (d)	CLoc CWVF EBak SRiF
	'Keystone'	EBak SRiF
	'Kim de Groot'	WPBF
	'Kim Wright' (d)	SRiF
	'Kimberly' (d)	EBak SRiF WPBF
	'King George V'	SRiF
	'King of Bath' (d)	EBak
	'King of Hearts' (d)	EBak SRiF
	'King's Ransom' (d)	CLoc CTsd CWVF EBak SPet SRiF SVic
	'Kiss 'n'Tell'	CWVF MJac SRiF
	'Kit Oxtoby' (d)	CDoC CWVF LCla MJac SRiF WFuv WPBF
	'Kiwi' (d)	EBak SRiF
	'Knockout' (d)	CWVF SVic
	'Kobold'	WPBF
	'Kolding Perle'	CWVF MHav SPet SRiF
	'Komeet'	CDoC SBfd

	'Kon-Tiki' (d)	CLoc CTsd SPet
	'Koog Aan de Zaan'	WPBF
	'Kuniko Atarashi' (d) **new**	EPts
	'Kwintet'	CWVF EBak MJac SPet SRiF
	'La Bianca'	EBak
	'La Campanella' (d) $\mathbb{Y}^{H3}$	CCCN CDoC CLoc CWVF EBak EPts LAst MBri MJac MSCN NVic SBfd SPet SRiF SVic WPBF
	'La Fiesta' (d)	EBak
	'La France' (d)	EBak SRiF
	'La Neige' ambig.	CTsd CWVF
	'La Neige' Lemoine (d)	EBak
	'La Porte' (d)	CLoc CWVF
	'La Rosita' (d)	EBak SLBF SRiF
I	'La Traviata' Blackwell (d)	EBak SRiF
	'Lace Petticoats' (d)	EBak SRiF SVic
	'Lady Bartle Frere' (d)	SRiF
	'Lady Beth' (d)	SRiF SVic
	'Lady Boothby'	Widely available
	'Lady Edwards' (d) **new**	SRiF
	'Lady Framlingham' (d)	EPts
	'Lady Heytesbury'	SRiF
	'Lady in Grey' (d)	MJac SRiF SVic WPBF
	'Lady Isobel Barnett'	CLoc CTsd CWVF EBak MBri MJac SPet SRiF SVic WFuv WPBF
	'Lady Kathleen Spence'	CWVF EBak SPet SVic
	'Lady Lupus'	EPts SRiF
	'Lady Patricia Mountbatten'	CWVF SRiF SVic WRou
	'Lady Ramsey'	EBak SRiF
	'Lady Rebecca' (d)	CLoc
	'Lady Thumb' (d) $\mathbb{Y}^{H3}$	Widely available
	'Laepines'	WPBF
	'Laing's Hybrid'	CWVF EBak SRiF
	'Lakeland Princess'	EBak
	'Lakeside'	EBak SRiF
	'Lambada'	LAst SRiF WPBF WRou
	'Lancambe'	CSil
	'Lancashire Lad' (d)	CTsd
	'Lancashire Lass'	CWVF MBri SRiF
	'Lancelot'	EBak SRiF
	'Langsford'	SRiF
	'Lapshead White'	CPLG
	'Lark' (T)	CWVF SRiF WPBF
	'Lassie' (d)	CDoC CLoc CWVF EBak SRiF
	'Last Chance' (E)	SLBF
	'Laura' ambig.	CWVF SVic WFuv WRou
I	'Laura' (Dutch)	CLoc EPts LCla SLBF SRiF
	'Laura Biolcati-Rinaldi' (d)	WPBF
	'Laura Cross' (E)	CDoC
	'Lauren' **new**	MHav
	'Laurena'	WPBF
	'Lavaglut'	WPBF
	'Lavender Beauty' (d)	SRiF
	'Lavender Heaven' (d)	WPBF
	'Lavender Kate' (d)	CLoc CWVF EBak
	'Lazy Lady' (d)	CWVF EBak SRiF
	'Lechlade Apache'	CDoC LCla SRiF
	'Lechlade Bullet'	LCla
	'Lechlade Chinaman'	CDoC SRiF SVic
	'Lechlade Debutante'	CDoC LCla SLBF SRiF
	'Lechlade Fire-eater' (T)	CDoC LCla SRiF
	'Lechlade Gorgon'	CDoC CWVF LCla SLBF
	'Lechlade Magician'	CDoC CSil CTsd EPts LCla MHav SPet SRiF SVic
	'Lechlade Maiden'	CDoC CWVF LCla SRiF
	'Lechlade Martianess'	LCla SRiF SVic
	'Lechlade Potentate'	LCla
	'Lechlade Rocket' (T)	WPBF
	'Lechlade Tinkerbell' (E)	CDoC LCla SLBF SRiF
	'Lechlade Violet' (T)	CSil LCla SRiF SVic
	'Leendert Beije'	WPBF
	lehmanii	LCla

	'Len Bielby' (T)	CDoC CWVF LCla SRiF
	'Lena' (d) ♀H3	CDoC CLoc CSil CTri CTsd CWVF EBak EPts MBri MJac SMrm SPer SPet SPlb SRiF SVic WPBF
	'Lena Dalton' (d)	CLoc CWVF EBak SRiF SVic
	'Leonhart von Fuchs'	WPBF
	'Leonie Boffe' (d)	WPBF
	'Leonora'	CDoC CLoc CTsd CWVF EBak MBri SPet SRiF SVic WFuv WRou
	'Lesley' (T)	CWVF LCla SRiF WPBF
	'Lett's Delight' (d)	CWVF EPts SRiF
	'Letty Lye'	EBak SRiF
	'Leverhulme'	see *F.* 'Leverkusen'
§	'Leverkusen' (T)	CDoC CLoc EBak LCla MJac SRiF WRou
	'Li Kai Lin'	CSil SRiF
I	'Liebesträume' Blackwell (d)	EBak
	'Liebriez' (d) ♀H3-4	CSil CTsd EBak SPet SRiF SVic
	'Liemers Lantaern'	CWVF
	'Likalin'	CWVF
	'Lilac'	CSil EBak
	'Lilac Dainty' (d)	CSil
	'Lilac Lustre' (d)	CLoc CWVF EBak SPet SRiF SVic
	'Lilac Princess'	SRiF
	'Lilac Queen' (d)	EBak
	'Lilac Tint'	WPBF
	'Lilian'	SRiF
	'Lillian Annetts' (d)	CCCN CDoC CWVF LCla MJac SLBF SRiF WFuv WPBF WRou
	'Lillibet' (d)	CDoC CLoc CWVF EBak SRiF
	'Lillydale' (d)	SRiF
	'Lilo Vogt' (T)	SRiF
	'Lime Lite' (d)	MJac
I	'Limelight' Weston	SLBF
	'Linda Goulding'	CTsd CWVF EBak SVic WFuv
	'Linda Grace'	MJac
	'Linda Rosling' (d)	CDoC
	'Lindisfarne' (d)	CLoc CWVF EBak MJac SPet WPBF
	'Lindsey Victoria' (d)	SVic
	'Lionel'	CSil SRiF WPBF
	'Lisa' (d)	CDoC EPts SPet SRiF WPBF
	'Lisa Ashton'	SRiF
	'Lisa Rowe' (d)	WPBF
	'Little Baby'	SRiF
	'Little Beauty'	CDoC CSil CWVF SVic WPBF
	'Little Boy Blue'	EPts SRiF
	'Little Brook Gem'	SLBF
	'Little Catbells' (E)	SLBF
	'Little Gene'	EBak
	'Little Giant'	LPla
	'Little Jewel'	CTsd SPet SRiF
	'Little Orphan Annie'	SRiF
	'Little Ouse' (d)	CWVF
	'Little Ronnie' (d)	SRiF WPBF
	'Little Scamp'	SLBF WRou
	'Little Snow Queen'	WPBF
	'Little Witch'	SLBF SRiF
	'Liz' (d)	CSil EBak SRiF WPBF
	Liza = 'Goetzliza' PBR (Shadowdancer Series)	CDoC LAst LSou
	'Liza Todman' (d)	SRiF
	'Lochinver' (d)	CWVF
	'Loeky'	CLoc CWVF EBak SPet SRiF SVic WPBF
	'Logan Garden'	see *F. magellanica* 'Logan Woods'
	'Lolita' (d)	CWVF EBak SRiF
	'London 2000'	CDoC LCla MJac SLBF SRiF WPBF WRou
	'London in Bloom'	SLBF WPBF
	'Lonely Ballerina' (d)	CLoc CWVF SRiF
	'Long Distance' (T)	LCla WPBF
	'Long John'	WPBF
	'Long Wings'	SRiF SVic
	'Longfellow' Hoag	WPBF
	'Lonneke'	WPBF
	'Loraja' **new**	SLBF
	'Lord Byron'	CLoc EBak SRiF
	'Lord Derby'	CSil
	'Lord Jim'	CDoC LCla
	'Lord Lonsdale'	CWVF EBak EPts LCla MSCN SRiF SVic WFuv WPBF WRou
	'Lord Roberts'	CLoc CSil CWVF SLBF
	'Lorelei'	CDoC
	'Lorentz Schwab'	WPBF
	'Lorna Fairclough'	MJac
	'Lorna Florence'	SLBF
	'Lorna Swinbank'	CLoc CWVF SRiF SVic
	'Lorraine's Delight' (d)	SVic
	'Lottie Hobby' (E) ♀H1+3	CDoC CLoc CMac CSil CTrC CTsd CWVF EPfP EPts LCla MLHP SPet SRiF SVic WFuv WRou
	'Louise Emershaw' (d)	CWVF EBak MJac SRiF SVic
	'Louise Nicholls'	MJac SLBF SRiF
	'Loulabel'	SVic
	'Lovable' (d)	EBak
	'Loveliness'	CLoc CWVF EBak SRiF SVic
	'Lovely Les' (d)	SRiF
	'Lovely Linda'	SRiF
	'Love's Reward' ♀H1+3	CLoc CWVF MJac SLBF SRiF SVic WFuv WPBF WRou
	'Lower Raydon'	EBak SRiF
I	'Loxensis'	CDoC CWVF EBak SVic WAbe WCot
	loxensis misapplied	see *F.* 'Speciosa', *F.* 'Loxensis'
	loxensis Kunth	SRiF
	'Loxhore Herald'	CSil
	'Loxhore Lullaby' (E)	CSil LCla
	'Loxhore Mazurka' (T)	SRiF WPBF
	'Loxhore Minuet' (T)	CDoC LCla SRiF WRou
	'Loxhore Posthorn' (T)	CDoC LCla
	'Lucinda'	CWVF SRiF
	'Lucky Strike' (d)	CLoc EBak SRiF
	Lucy = 'Goetzlucy' (Shadowdancer Series)	EBak SRiF WPBF
	'Lucy Locket'	MJac
	'Lukas'	WPBF
	'Lunter's Klokje'	WPBF
	'Lunter's Trots' (d)	SRiF WPBF
	'Luscious Lisa'	WPBF
	'Lustre'	CWVF EBak SVic
	'Lut' (d)	WPBF
	'Lutz Bogemann'	SRiF
	'Luuk van Riet' (d)	WPBF
	lycioides misapplied	see *F.* 'Lycioides'
§	***lycioides*** Andrews	EBak
I	'Lycioides'	LCla
	'Lydia'	WPBF
	'Lye's Elegance'	CSil SRiF
	'Lye's Excelsior'	EBak SRiF
	'Lye's Own'	EBak SPet SRiF
	'Lye's Unique' ♀H1+3	CDoC CLoc CSil CWVF EBak EPts LCla MJac SLBF SPet SRiF SVic WFuv
	'Lynette' (d)	CLoc
	'Lynn Cunningham'	CDoC
	'Lynn Ellen' (d)	CDoC CTsd CWVF EBak
	'Lynne Marshall'	CSil
	'Lynne Patricia' (d)	EPts
	'Maartje'	SRiF
	'Mabel Greaves' (d)	CWVF
	'Mac Wagg'	WRou
	'Machu Picchu'	CLoc CWVF EPts LCla SRiF SVic WPBF WRou

	macrophylla	CDoC WMoo
	'Madame Aubin'	CSil
	'Madame Butterfly' (d)	CLoc
	'Madame Cornélissen' (d) 🏆^{H3}	CDoC CLoc CSBt CSil CTri CWVF EBak EBee EPfP EPts GKir LRHS MAsh MRav SCoo SLim SPer SPet SPoG SRiF SVic WFar WFuv WRou
	'Madame Eva Boye'	EBak SRiF
	'Madeleine Sweeney' (d)	MBri
	'Maes-y-Groes'	CSil
	'Maet Suycker'	WPBF
	'Magda Cerules' (d)	WPBF
	magellanica	CDoC COld CSil CTsd CWib GGar GKir LBMP MLHP MSCN NPer NWea SPer SVic WFar WPnn
	- 'Alba'	see *F. magellanica* var. *molinae*
I	- 'Alba Aureovariegata' (v)	CBgR CDoC CMac CTrC CWan EPfP SPer SVic WFar
	- 'Alba Variegata' (v)	CSil
	- 'Americana Elegans'	CDoC CSil WPBF
	- 'Angel's Teardrop' **new**	CDoC
	- 'Comber'	CSil
	- var. ***conica***	CDoC CSil
	- var. ***discolor***	CSil
	- 'Duchy of Cornwall'	CDoC
	- 'Exmoor Gold' (v)	CSil
§	- var. ***gracilis*** 🏆^{H3}	CAgr CDoC CHEx CLoc CSil CTri CWVF EPfP MLHP NBro SCoo SVic WGwG WPnn WSpi
	- - 'Aurea' 🏆$^{H3-4}$	CBcs CBot CDoC CMac CSil CTsd CWVF EBee ELan EPfP GGar GQui LCla LRHS MHer MRav SAga SCoo SDix SLBF SPer SPet SPoG WCom WFar WRou WSpi
	- - 'Purple Mountain' **new**	LRHS
§	- - 'Tricolor' (v) 🏆^{H3}	CDoC CSil CTsd EPfP EPts EWes LBMP LCla LRHS NLar SEND SLBF SRiF SRms WCFE WPnn WRou
	- - 'Variegata' (v) 🏆^{H3}	CDoC CSil EBak EPfP GGar LCla LRHS MGos MRav SAga SBfd SDix SPet SRiF WCom WFuv WPnn WSpi
	- 'Guiding Star'	CDoC
	- 'Lady Bacon'	CBgR CDoC CSil ELon EPts EWes GCal GGar MCot SDys SLBF SMHy SRiF WSHC
§	- 'Logan Woods'	CDoC CSil ELon EQua SLBF SMrm
	- 'Longipedunculata'	CDoC CSil SLPl WPBF
	- 'Lyonesse Lady'	CDoC
	- var. ***macrostema***	CSil
§	- var. ***molinae***	Widely available
§	- - 'Enstone' (v)	CBgR EHoe ELon LAst SRiF
	- - 'Golden Sharpitor' (v)	CBgR CCCN LAst MDKP MHav SBfd WAbe
§	- - 'Sharpitor' (v)	CBcs CBgR CDoC CSil EBak EHoe ELan EPfP GQue IFro LRHS MAsh NPer SAga SBfd SCoo SRiF SVic WCom WFar WKif WMoo WPBF WRou WSHC
	- var. ***myrtifolia***	CDoC CSil CTsd
*	- var. ***prostrata***	CSil
	- var. ***pumila***	CBgR CDoC CEnt CSil EWes GCal GGar GKir ITim LRHS MHer MLHP SAga SCoo SMHy SRot SVic WAbe
	- ***purpurea***	LRHS
	- 'Red Mountain' **new**	EWes
	- 'Sea King'	CDoC
	- 'Sea Spray'	CDoC
	- 'Seahorse'	CDoC
§	- 'Thompsonii' 🏆$^{H3-4}$	CDoC CSil ECGP LPla SBch SMHy SRiF
§	- 'Versicolor' (v)	Widely available
	'Magenta Flush'	CDoC CTsd CWVF

	'Maggie Rose'	SLBF
	'Magic Flute'	CLoc CWVF MJac SVic
	'Maharaja' (d)	EBak SRiF
	'Maid Marion'	SLBF
	'Maik Luijten' (d)	WPBF
	'Majebo' (d)	SRiF
	'Major Heaphy'	CWVF EBak SRiF WPBF
	'Making Waves'	WRou
	'Malibu Mist' (d)	CWVF SRiF WPBF
	'Mama Bleuss' (d)	EBak SRiF WFuv
	'Mancunian' (d)	CTsd CWVF SRiF
I	'Mandarin' Schnabel	EBak SRiF
	'Mandi Oxtoby' (T)	LCla SRiF
	'Manfried Kleinau' (d)	WPBF
	'Mantilla' (T)	CDoC CLoc CWVF EBak MJac SVic
	'Maori Maid'	SRiF WPBF
	'Maori Pipes' (T)	SRiF WPBF
	'Marbled Sky'	SVic
	'Marcel Michiels' (d)	WPBF
	'Marcia'PBR (Shadowdancer Series)	CLoc LAst LSou
	'Marcus Graham' (d)	CLoc CTsd CWVF EBak MSCN SCoo SRiF SVic WFuv WPBF WRou
	'Marcus Hanton' (d)	CWVF SRiF
	'Mardi Gras' (d)	CTsd EBak SRiF
	'Margaret' (d) 🏆^{H4}	CDoC CLoc CSil CTri CTsd CWVF EBak EPts GKir SEND SPet SRiF SVic WFuv
	'Margaret Berger' (d)	SRiF
	'Margaret Bird'	LCla
	'Margaret Brown' 🏆^{H4}	CDoC CLoc CSil CTri CWVF EBak LCla LRHS SLBF SMrm SPet SRiF SVic WRou
	'Margaret Davidson' (d)	CLoc
	'Margaret Hazelwood'	SRiF
	'Margaret Pilkington'	CTsd CWVF SRiF SVic
	'Margaret Roe'	CDoC CSil CWVF EBak MJac SPet SRiF WPBF
	'Margaret Rose'	SRiF
	'Margaret Susan'	EBak
	'Margarite Dawson' (d)	CSil SRiF
	'Margery Blake'	CSil EBak SRiF
	'Margharita' (d)	SRiF
	'Margrit Willimann'	WPBF
	'Maria Landy'	CWVF LCla MJac SRiF WRou
	'Maria Mathilde' (d)	SLBF
	'Maria Merrills' (d)	MHav SRiF
	'Mariah' (Diva Series)	MHav SRiF
	'Marie Elizabeth' (d)	WPBF
	'Marielle van Dummelen' (d)	WPBF
	'Marie-Louise Luyckx' (d)	WPBF
	'Marietta' (d)	SRiF
	'Marilyn Olsen'	CWVF SRiF
	'Marin Belle'	EBak SRiF
	'Marin Glow' 🏆^{H3}	CLoc CWVF EBak SLBF SPet SRiF SVic WFuv
	'Marina Kelly'	WRou
	'Marinka' 🏆^{H3}	CCCN CLoc CWVF EBak EPts LAst LCla MBri MJac SLBF SPet SRiF SVic WFuv WPBF
	'Marja' **new**	SRiF
	'Mark Kirby' (d)	CWVF EBak SRiF
	'Marlea's Marlot' (d)	WPBF
	'Marlea's Schouwpijpke'	WPBF
	'Marlies de Keijzer' (E)	CDoC LCla SLBF WPBF
	'Marry Perry'	WRou
	'Mart'	WPBF
	Martha = 'Goetzmart' (Shadowdancer Series) **new**	LAst
	'Martien A. Soeters'	WPBF
	'Martin Beije'	WPBF

	'Martina'	SLBF
	'Martin's Choice'	WPBF
	'Martin's Delight 2002' (d)	WPBF
	'Martin's Double Delicate' (d)	WPBF
	'Martin's Inspiration'	CDoC LCla
	'Martin's Little Beauty'	WPBF
	'Martin's Yellow Surprise' (T)	LCla SLBF SRiF SVic
	'Martinus' (d)	WPBF
	'Marty' (d)	EBak SRiF
	'Mary' (T) ♀H1+3	CDoC CLoc CWVF EPts LCla SLBF SRiF SVic WPBF
	'Mary Lockyer' (d)	CLoc CTsd EBak SRiF
	'Mary Poppins'	CWVF SRiF SVic
	'Mary Reynolds' (d)	CWVF
	'Mary Sturman' (E)	SRiF
	'Mary Thorne'	CSil EBak SRiF
	'Mary's Millennium'	CWVF
	'Masquerade' (d)	EBak SVic
	'Maud Murphy'	WPBF
	'Mauve Beauty' (d)	CSil CWVF SLBF
	'Mauve Lace' (d)	CSil SRiF
	'Mauve Wisp' (d)	SVic
	'Max Jaffa'	CWVF SRiF
I	'Maxima'	EPts LCla SRiF WFuv WPBF
	'Maxima's Baby'	WPBF
	'Maxima's Girl'	WPBF
	'Maybe Baby'	SRiF WPBF
	'Mayblossom' (d)	CWVF SPet
	'Mayfayre' (d)	CLoc
	'Mayfield'	CWVF
	'Maytime' (d)	SRiF
	'Mazda'	CWVF SRiF
	'Meadowlark' (d)	CTsd CWVF EBak SRiF
	'Mechtildis de Lechy'	SRiF WPBF
	'Medard's Botsaert' (d)	WPBF
	'Medard's Hersinde'	WPBF
	'Medard's Koning Nobel'	WPBF
	'Medard's Krieke Putte'	WPBF
	'Medard's Reinaertsland'	WPBF
	'Medard's Tiecelijn' (d)	WPBF
	'Meditation' (d)	CLoc CSil
	'Megeti'	WPBF
	'Melanie'	CDoC CTsd MHav SRiF SVic WFuv WPBF
	'Melissa Heavens'	CWVF
	'Melody'	EBak SPet SRiF SVic
	'Melody Ann' (d)	EBak SRiF
	'Melting Moments' (d)	MHav SCoo SRiF WFuv
	'Mendocino Mini' (E)	WPBF
	'Mendocino Rose'	SVic
	'Menna'	WPBF
	'Mephisto'	CSil CWVF
	'Mercurius'	CSil
	'Merlin'	CDoC CSil LCla SRiF
	'Merry England' (d)	WPBF
	'Merry Mary' (d)	CWVF EBak
	'Meteor Storm' **new**	SRiF
I	'Mexicali Rose' Machado	CLoc
	'Michael' (d)	CWVF EPts SRiF
	'Michael Barker' (d)	WPBF
	'Michael Wallis' (T)	LCla SLBF SRiF WPBF
	'Michelle Wallace'	SLBF SVic
	michoacanensis misapplied	see *F. microphylla* subsp. *aprica*
	loxensis Sessé & Moç. (E) B&SWJ 9027	WCru
	- B&SWJ 9148	WCru
	- F&M 356	WPGP
	'Micky Goult' ♀H1+3	CDoC CLoc CWVF EPts LCla MJac SPet SRiF SVic WFuv WPBF WRou
	'Microchip' (E)	CSil LCla
	microphylla (E)	CBcs CBgR CDoC CElw CHid CLoc CPLG CSil CTsd CWVF EBak ELon GCal GGar MSCN NBro STre SVic WBor
	- B&SWJ 10331	WCru
§	- subsp. ***aprica*** (E)	CDoC LCla
	- - B&SWJ 9101	WCru
	- - 'Dolly's Dress' **new**	WCru
	- 'Cornish Pixie'	CDoC
§	- subsp. ***hemsleyana*** (E)	CDoC CPLG CSil LCla SRiF WOut
	- - B&SWJ 10478	WCru
	- - 'Silver Lining' **new**	WCru
§	- subsp. ***hidalgensis*** (E)	CDoC CSil LCla
	- subsp. ***microphylla*** (E)	CSil
§	- subsp. ***minimiflora***	SVic
	- subsp. ***quercetorum*** (E)	CDoC CSil LCla
	- 'Sparkle' (E/v)	WCot
	- 'Variegata' (E/v)	EWes MCCP
	'Midas'	CWVF MBri
	'Midnight' (Diva Series)	MHav
	'Midnight Sun' (d)	CWVF EBak SRiF
	'Midwinter'	CWVF SRiF SVic WPBF
	'Mieke Meursing' ♀H1+3	CDoC CLoc CWVF EBak MJac SPet SRiF
	'Mieke Sarton'	WPBF
	'Mien Kuypers'	WPBF
	'Mien van Oirschot' (d)	WPBF
	'Miep Aalhuizen'	CDoC LCla SRiF SVic WRou
	'Mike Oxtoby' (T)	CWVF
	'Millennium'	CLoc EBak EPts MJac SCoo SRiF
	'Millie'	SRiF
	'Millie Butler'	CWVF
	'Ming'	CLoc CTsd SRiF
	'Mini Skirt' (d)	SRiF
	'Miniature Jewels' (E)	SLBF
	minimiflora misapplied	see *F.* × ***bacillaris***
	minimiflora Hemsl.	see *F. microphylla* subsp. *minimiflora*
	'Minirose'	CDoC CWVF EPts SRiF WFuv WRou
	'Minnesota' (d)	EBak
	'Mipam'	SLBF
	'Miramere'	EPts
	'Mirjana'	SRiF
	'Mischief'	CSil SVic
	'Miss California' (d)	CDoC CLoc CWVF EBak LAst MBri SRiF
	'Miss Debbie' (d)	SRiF WFuv
	'Miss Grace' (d) **new**	SRiF
	'Miss Great Britain'	CWVF SRiF
	'Miss Lye'	CSil SRiF
	'Miss Marilyn'	SRiF
	'Miss Muffett' (d)	CSil EPts SRiF
	'Miss Vallejo' (d)	CTsd EBak SRiF
	'Mission Bells'	CDoC CLoc CSil CTsd CWVF EBak EPts MHav SPet SRiF
	'Mistoque'	CTsd SRiF
	'Misty Blue' (d)	SVic
	'Misty Haze' (d)	CWVF SRiF SVic
	'Misty Pink' (d)	WPBF
	'Molenkerk' (d)	WPBF
	'Molesworth' (d)	CWVF EBak MJac SPet
	'Mollie Beaulah' (d)	SRiF
	'Molly Bellamy' **new**	SRiF
	'Monarch Mammoth' **new**	SRiF
	'Money Spinner'	CLoc EBak SRiF
	'Monica' (d) **new**	SRiF
	'Monica Dare' (T)	WPBF
	'Monique Comperen'	WPBF
	'Monsieur Thibaut' ♀H4	CSil MGos SPer SRiF
	'Monte Rosa' (d)	CWVF SRiF
	'Monterey'	SRiF

'Montevideo' (d)	CWVF
'Montrose' **new**	SRiF
'Monument' (d)	CSil SRiF
'Mood Indigo' (d)	CTsd CWVF SLBF SRiF SVic WFuv
'Moody Blues' **new**	SRiF
'Moonbeam' (d)	CLoc SRiF
'Moonglow'	CTsd MJac SRiF WFuv WPBF
'Moonlight'	CCCN
'Moonlight Sonata'	CLoc CWVF EBak SPet
'Moonraker' (d)	CWVF SRiF SVic
'More Applause' (d)	CLoc SRiF
'Morning Cloud' (d)	SRiF
'Morning Light' (d)	CLoc EBak SPet SRiF SVic
'Morning Mist'	EBak SRiF
'Morning Star'	MBri
'Morrells' (d)	EBak SRiF
'Moth Blue' (d)	CWVF EBak MHav SPet SRiF
'Mother's Day'	SVic
'Mount Edgcumbe'	CTsd
'Mountain Mist' (d)	CWVF SVic
'Moyra' (d)	CWVF
'Mr A. Huggett'	CLoc CSil CWVF EPts SLBF SRiF
'Mr W. Rundle'	EBak SRiF SVic
§ 'Mr West' (v)	LSou MCot SPet WRou
'Mrs Churchill'	CLoc
'Mrs Hobhouse' (d) **new**	SRiF
'Mrs John D. Fredericks'	CSil
'Mrs Lawrence Lyon' (d)	EBak
'Mrs Lee Belton' (E)	CDoC LCla SLBF
'Mrs Lovell Swisher' ♀H4	CTsd CWVF EBak LCla SPet SRiF SVic WFuv
'Mrs Marshall'	CWVF EBak SLBF SPet SRiF
'Mrs Popple' ♀H3	Widely available
'Mrs Susan Brookfield' (d)	SRiF
'Mrs W. Castle'	CDoC CSil CTsd SVic
'Mrs W.P. Wood' ♀H3	CBgR CDoC CLoc CSil CWVF ELon LRHS MSCN SRiF SVic WFuv WRou
'Mrs W. Rundle'	CLoc CTsd CWVF EBak SLBF SPet
'Muriel' (d)	CLoc CWVF EBak SRiF
'Murru's Pierre Marie' (d)	SLBF
'My Dear' (d)	WPBF
'My Delight'	CWVF
'My Fair Lady' (d)	CLoc CWVF EBak SPet SRiF
'My Little Cracker'	CDoC WPBF
'My Mum'	LCla SLBF SRiF WFuv
'My Pat'	SLBF
'My Reward' (d)	CWVF
'Naaldwijk 800'	WPBF
'Nananice'	SRiF
'Nancy Lou' (d)	CDoC CLoc CWVF LAst MJac SLBF SPet SRiF SVic WFuv WRou
'Nanny Ed' (d)	CWVF MBri
'Natal Bronze'	SRiF
'Natalie Jones'	SRiF
'Natasha Sinton' (d)	CCCN CLoc CTsd CWVF LAst MBri MJac SPet WPBF WRou
'Native Dancer' (d)	CWVF EBak WPBF
'Naughty Nicole' (d)	SRiF WPBF
'Nautilus' (d)	EBak
'Navy Blue'	CSil SRiF
'Neapolitan' (d)	CDoC MHav SLBF
'Nell Gwyn'	CLoc CWVF EBak SRiF SVic
'Nellie Nuttall' ♀H3	CLoc CWVF EBak EPts SPet SRiF SVic WFuv
'Neon White' (Diva Series)	MHav
'Neopolitan' (E)	CLoc CSil EPts MHav SVic WPBF
'Nettala'	CDoC SRiF SVic WPBF
'Neue Welt'	CSil CWVF EBak
'New Fascination' (d)	EBak
'New Millennium'	CDoC
'Niagara Falls' (d)	WPBF
'Nice 'n' Easy' (d)	MBri MJac SRiF

'Nicki Fenwick-Raven' (E)	LCla
'Nicki's Findling'	CDoC CTsd CWVF EPts LCla MJac SRiF WFuv WRou
'Nicky Veerman'	WPBF
'Nicola'	EBak
'Nicola Claire'	MHav
'Nicola Jane' (d)	CDoC CSil CTsd CWVF EBak EPts LCla MBri MJac SHar SLBF SPet SRiF SVic WFuv WRou
'Nicolette'	CWVF MJac
'Niek' (d)	WPBF
'Nightingale' (d)	CLoc EBak WPBF
§ ***nigricans***	CDoC
'Nikki' **new**	SRiF
'Nimue'	SRiF
'Nina Wills'	EBak
'Niobe' (d)	EBak
'Niula'	CDoC LCla SRiF
'No Name' (d)	EBak
'Noel Freeman' **new**	SRiF
'Noel van Steenberghe' (d)	WPBF
'Nonchalance' (T)	LCla WPBF
'Nora' (d)	WPBF
'Norfolk Belle' (d)	SRiF
'Norfolk Ivor' (d)	SRiF WPBF
'Norman Greenhill'	SRiF
'Normandy Bell'	EBak SVic
'North Cascades' (d)	WPBF
'Northilda'	SVic
'Northumbrian Belle'	EBak SRiF
'Northumbrian Pipes'	LCla
'Northway'	CLoc CWVF MJac SPet SRiF SVic
'Norvell Gillespie' (d)	EBak SRiF
'Novato'	CTsd EBak SRiF
'Novella' (d)	CWVF EBak SRiF
'Noyo Star' (d)	SRiF
'Nuance'	LCla WPBF
'Nunthorpe Gem' (d)	CDoC CSil MHav SRiF
'O Sole Mio'	SVic
obconica (E)	CDoC CSil LCla
'Obcylin' (E)	CDoC LCla SRiF WRou
'Obergärtner Koch' (T)	CDoC SLBF SRiF
'Ocean Beach'	CDoC CTsd EPts SRiF WPBF
'Oddfellow' (d)	SRiF
'Oetnang' (d)	CTri SCoo
'Oklahoma' (d) **new**	SRiF
'Old Lottie Hobby' **new**	SRiF
'Old Rose' **new**	SRiF
'Old Somerset' (v)	CCCN CDoC CTsd SRiF SVic WPBF
'Oldbury'	SRiF
'Oldbury Gem'	SRiF
'Oldbury Pearl'	SRiF
'Olga Storey'	CDoC
'Olive Moon' (d)	WPBF
'Olive Smith'	CWVF EPts LCla MJac SRiF WPBF WRou
'Olympic Lass' (d)	EBak
'Olympic Sunset'	SVic
'Omeomy'	SRiF
'Onward'	CSil WPBF
'Onward Dingle' **new**	SRiF
§ 'Oosje' (E)	CDoC CSil LCla SLBF SRiF SVic WPBF WRou
'Opalescent' (d)	CLoc CWVF SVic
'Orange Crush'	CCCN CLoc CTsd CWVF EBak MHav MJac SPet WFuv
'Orange Crystal'	CCCN CWVF EBak MJac SVic WPBF
'Orange Drops'	CLoc CTsd CWVF EBak EPts SRiF SVic WFuv
'Orange Flare'	CLoc CWVF EBak MHav SLBF SRiF SVic WFuv WRou
'Orange Heart'	LCla

'Orange King' (d)	CLoc CWVF
'Orange Mirage'	CLoc CTsd CWVF EBak LAst SPet SVic WFuv WPBF WRou
'Orange Queen' **new**	SRiF
'Orange Star' (E)	CDoC
'Orangeblossom'	MHav SLBF SRiF
'Oranje van Os'	CWVF
'Orient Express' (T)	CDoC CLoc CWVF MJac SRiF SVic WFuv WPBF
'Oriental Lace'	SRiF
'Oriental Sunrise'	CWVF
'Ornamental Pearl' (v)	CLoc CWVF EBak SRiF
'Ortenburger Festival'	WFuv
'Orwell' (d)	CWVF
'Oso Sweet'	CWVF SRiF
'Other Fellow'	CWVF EBak EPts LCla MJac SLBF SPet SRiF SVic WFuv
'Oulton Empress' (E)	LCla SLBF
'Oulton Fairy' (E)	SLBF
'Oulton Painted Lady'	WRou
'Oulton Red Imp' (E)	LCla SLBF
'Oulton Travellers Rest' (E)	SLBF
'Our Boys'	WPBF
'Our Darling'	CWVF SRiF
'Our Hilary'	SLBF
'Our Joyce' **new**	SRiF
'Our Nan' (d)	MJac
'Our Nell' **new**	SRiF
'Our Pamela'	MJac
'Our Spencer' **new**	SLBF
'Our Ted' (T)	EBak EPts SRiF WPBF
'Our William'	WPBF
'Overbecks'	see *F. magellanica* var. *molinae* 'Sharpitor'
'P.J.B.' (d)	WPBF
'Pabbe's Kirrevaalk'	WPBF
'Pabbe's Klompnoagel'	WPBF
'Pabbe's Kopstubber' (d)	WPBF
'Pabbe's Loug'	WPBF
'Pabbe's Lutjemaid'	WPBF
'Pabbe's Primeur'	WPBF
'Pabbe's Pronkjewail' (d)	WPBF
'Pabbe's Siepeltrien'	WPBF
'Pabbe's Torreldöve'	WPBF
'Pabbe's Wikwief'	WPBF
'Pacemaker'	MGos
'Pacific Grove' Greene	see *F.* 'Evelyn Steele Little'
'Pacific Grove' Niederholzer (d)	EBak
'Pacific Queen' (d)	EBak
'Pacquesa' (d)	CDoC CTsd CWVF EBak SPet SRiF SVic
'Padre Pio' (d)	CWVF EBak MJac
'Pagona Fuhrmann' (d)	WPBF
'Pale Flame' (d)	SRiF
'Pallas'	CSil
'Palm Springs' (d)	SRiF
'Pam Plack'	CDoC CSil LCla SLBF SRiF
'Pamela Hutchinson'	SRiF
'Pamela Knights' (d)	EBak
'Pamela Wallace'	SLBF
'Pam's People'	LCla
'Pan' (T)	SRiF WPBF
'Pan America' (d)	EBak
'Panache' (d)	LCla
'Pangea' (T)	LCla WPBF
paniculata (T) 🏆$^{H1+3}$	CBot CCCN CDoC CFee CRHN CTsd CWVF EBak EPts IDee LCla LPio MHer SLBF SRiF WCru WPBF
'Panique'	CDoC LCla
'Pantaloons' (d)	EBak
'Pantomine Dame' (d)	CWVF SRiF

'Panylla Prince'	CDoC LCla SRiF WRou
'Papa Bleuss' (d)	CWVF EBak SRiF
'Papoose' (d)	CDoC CSil EBak LCla SEND SRiF SVic
'Paramour'	SRiF
'Parasol'	WPBF
'Parkstone Centenary' (d)	CWVF
'Party Frock'	CDoC CLoc CTsd CWVF EBak
'Party Time' (d)	CWVF
parviflora misapplied	see *F.* × *bacillaris*
parviflora Lindl.	see *F. lycioides* Andrews
'Pastel'	EBak SRiF
'Pat Meara'	CLoc EBak SRiF
'Pat Rogers' (d)	WPBF
'Pathétique' (d)	CLoc
'Patience' (d)	CDoC CWVF EBak SRiF
'Patio King'	EBak
'Patio Princess' (d)	CCCN CLoc CWVF EPts LAst MBri WFuv
'Patricia' Wood	EBak SRiF
'Patricia Hodge'	WRou
'Pat's Smile'	SLBF
'Patty Evans' (d)	CWVF EBak SRiF
'Patty Sue' (d)	MBri SRiF WRou
'Paul Berry' (T)	LCla WPBF
'Paul Cambon' (d)	EBak SRiF
'Paul Fisher'	CDoC
'Paul Kennes'	WPBF
'Paul Meredith' **new**	SRiF
'Paul Pini' (d)	SRiF
'Paul Roe' (d)	MJac
'Paul Storey'	CDoC CSil SRiF WPBF
'Paula Jane' (d)	CCCN CDoC CTsd CWVF LAst LCla LRHS MBri MJac SLBF SRiF SVic WFuv WGor WPBF WRou
'Pauline Rawlins' (d)	CLoc EBak SRiF
'Paulus'	WPBF
'Peace' (d)	EBak SRiF
'Peachy' (California Dreamers Series) (d)	CCCN CDoC CLoc LAst MJac SCoo SRiF WFuv WPBF
'Peachy Keen' (d)	EBak SRiF
'Peacock' (d)	CLoc
'Pearly Gates'	SRiF
'Pearly Queen' (d)	WPBF
'Pee Wee Rose'	CSil EBak SRiF SVic WPBF
'Peggy Burford' (T)	LCla
Peggy = 'Goetzpeg'^{PBR} (Shadowdancer Series)	CDoC LAst LSou SCoo SRiF
'Peggy King'	CDoC CSil CTsd EBak SPet SRiF SVic WPBF
'Peloria' (d)	CLoc EBak
'Pennine'	MBri WFuv
'People's Princess'	MJac SRiF
'Peper Harow'	EBak SRiF
'Pepi' (d)	CLoc CWVF EBak SPet SRiF
'Peppermint Candy' (d)	CDoC CWVF MJac
'Peppermint Stick' (d)	CDoC CLoc CWVF EBak MBri SPet SVic WFuv
'Percy Thorpe' **new**	SRiF
'Periwinkle' **new**	SRiF
'Perky Pink' (d)	CWVF EBak EPts SPet SRiF
'Perry Park'	CWVF EBak MBri MJac SRiF SVic
'Perry's Jumbo'	NBir NPer
perscandens	CBcs CPLG CSil LCla WGwG
'Personality' (d)	EBak SRiF
'Peter Bielby' (d)	CWVF SRiF
'Peter Crookes' (T)	CWVF SRiF
'Peter Grange'	EBak
'Peter Hornby'	SRiF
'Peter James' (d)	CSil SRiF
'Peter Lemmen' (d)	WPBF
'Peter Pan'	CSil CWVF SRiF

	Name	Suppliers
	'Peter Peeters' (d)	WPBF
	petiolaris	CDoC LCla
	'Petit Four'	CWVF SRiF WPBF
	'Petit Point'	SRiF
	'Petite' (d)	EBak
	'Petronella' (d)	SRiF
	'Pfaffenhutchen' (d)	WPBF
	'Phaidra'	CDoC LCla
	'Pharaoh'	CLoc
	'Phénoménal' (d)	CSil CWVF EBak SRiF WPBF
	'Philippe'	WPBF
	'Phillip Taylor'	MJac WPBF
	'Phryne' (d)	CSil EBak SRiF SVic
	'Phyllis' (d) ♀H4	CAgr CBgR CDoC CLoc CSil CTsd CWVF EBak ELon EPts GKir LCla LRHS MJac SLBF SPet SRiF SVic WFar WFuv WRou
	'Piet G. Vergeer'	WRou
	'Piet van der Sande'	CDoC LCla
	'Piggelmee'	WPBF
	'Pinch Me' (d)	CWVF EBak MHav SPet SRiF SVic
	'Pink Aurora'	CLoc SRiF
	'Pink Ballet Girl' (d)	CLoc EBak SVic
	'Pink Bon Accord'	CLoc CTsd CWVF SVic WPBF
	'Pink Cascade'	CTsd
	'Pink Cloud'	CLoc CTsd EBak SRiF
	'Pink Cornet'	LCla SRiF
	'Pink Darling'	CLoc EBak SRiF
	'Pink Dessert'	CTsd EBak
	'Pink Domino' (d)	CSil
	'Pink Fairy' (d)	EBak SPet SRiF
	'Pink Fandango' (d)	CLoc
	'Pink Fantasia'	CDoC CLoc CWVF EBak EPts LAst LCla MJac SRiF SVic WFuv WPBF
	'Pink Flamingo' (d)	EBak SRiF
	'Pink Frills' **new**	SRiF
	'Pink Galore' (d)	CCCN CLoc CTsd CWVF EBak LAst MBri MJac SPet SRiF SVic WFuv WPBF
	'Pink Goon' (d)	CDoC CSil LCla SLBF SRiF SVic
	'Pink Haze'	CSil SRiF SVic
	'Pink Jade'	CWVF EBak
	'Pink la Campanella'	CWVF EBak MBri SRiF WGor
	'Pink Lace' (d)	CSil SPet
	'Pink Marshmallow' (d) ♀H1+3	CCCN CDoC CLoc CWVF EBak MJac SLBF SPet SRiF SVic WFuv WPBF
	'Pink Panther' (d)	SRiF SVic
	'Pink Pearl' ambig.	SRiF
	'Pink Pearl' Bright (d)	CSil EBak
	'Pink Princess' **new**	SRiF
	'Pink Profusion'	EBak SRiF
	'Pink Quartet' (d)	CLoc CWVF EBak MHav SPet SRiF
	'Pink Rain'	CWVF MJac SRiF WFuv WPBF WRou
	'Pink Slippers'	CLoc
	'Pink Spangles'	CCCN CWVF MBri SVic
	'Pink Surprise' (d)	CTsd
	'Pink Temptation'	CLoc CWVF EBak LAst SVic
	'Pinto de Blue' (d)	MHav SRiF WPBF
	'Pinwheel' (d)	CLoc EBak SRiF
	'Piper' (d)	CDoC CWVF SRiF
	'Piper's Vale' (T)	CDoC MJac SLBF SRiF
	'Pippa Rolt'	SRiF
	'Pirbright'	CWVF
	'Pixie'	CDoC CLoc CSil CTsd CWVF EBak MHav MJac SLBF SPet SRiF SVic
	'Playboy' (d)	SVic WPBF
	'Playford'	CWVF EBak SRiF
	'Plenty'	CSil EBak SVic
	'Plumb Bob' (d)	CWVF
	'Pol Jannie' (d)	SRiF WPBF

	Name	Suppliers
	'Pole Star'	CSil SRiF
	'Polskie Fuksji'	CDoC
	'Pop Whitlock' (v)	CWVF MCot SPet SRiF SVic
	'Poppet'	CWVF
	'Popsie Girl'	CDoC SLBF SRiF WPBF WRou
	'Port Arthur' (d)	CSil EBak SRiF
	'Postiljon'	CTsd CWVF EBak SRiF
	'Postman'	CDoC SRiF
	'Powder Puff' ambig.	CWVF MBri WFuv
	'Powder Puff' Hodges (d)	CLoc SVic
I	'Powder Puff' Tabraham (d)	CSil
	'Prelude' ambig.	SVic
	'Prelude' Blackwell	CLoc CSil
I	'Prelude' Kennett (d)	EBak
	'President'	CDoC CSil EBak SRiF
	'President B.W. Rawlins'	EBak SRiF
§	'President Elliot'	CSil SRiF
	'President George Bartlett' (d)	CDoC CLoc CSil EPts LCla MJac SLBF SRiF WFuv WPBF WRou
	'President Jim Muil'	SLBF WPBF
	'President Joan Morris' (d)	SLBF
	'President Leo Boullemier'	CSil CWVF EBak MJac SPet SRiF SVic WPBF
	'President Margaret Slater'	CLoc CTsd CWVF EBak LCla MHav SPet SRiF SVic WPBF
	'President Moir' (d)	SLBF SRiF WPBF
	'President Norman Hobbs'	CWVF
	'President Roosevelt' (d)	CDoC WPBF
	'President Stanley Wilson' (d)	CWVF EBak EPts SRiF
	'President Wilf Sharp' (d)	SRiF SVic
	'Preston Guild' ♀H1+3	CDoC CLoc CSil CTsd CWVF EBak NPer SDys SLBF SPet SRiF SVic WPBF WRou
	'Pride of Ipswich'	SRiF WPBF
	'Pride of Roualeyn'	WRou
	'Pride of the West'	EBak SRiF
	'Prince of Orange'	CLoc CSil CWVF EBak SRiF SVic WPBF
	'Prince of Peace' (d)	SRiF
	'Prince Syray'	SRiF
	'Princess Dollar'	see *F.* 'Dollar Prinzessin'
	'Princess Pamela' (d)	SLBF
	'Princessita'	CTsd CWVF EBak MHav SPet
	procumbens	CBcs CCCN CDoC CLoc CPLG CSil CTrC CWVF EBak ECou EPfP EPts EWld GCal GGar IDee ITim LCla LPio MCot MHer NWCA SLBF SRiF SWal WPBF WPtf WRou
	- 'Argentea'	see *F. procumbens* 'Wirral'
	- 'Variegata'	see *F. procumbens* 'Wirral'
§	- 'Wirral' (v)	CDoC CLoc CSil CTrC CTsd ELon EQua SRiF WBor WPBF WPrP
	'Prodigy'	see *F.* 'Enfant Prodigue'
	'Profusion' ambig.	SVic
	'Profusion' Wood	SRiF
	'Prosperity' (d) ♀H3	CDoC CLoc CSil CWVF EBak EPfP EPts LCla LRHS MJac MRav SPet SRiF SVic WFuv WRou
	'Pumila'	CMac CPLG CWib ELan EPfP EPts SDix SLBF SPet SRiF SVic WPBF WPat WRou
	'Purbeck Mist' (d)	CWVF
	'Purperklokje'	CSil CWVF EBak SRiF SVic WPBF
	'Purple Emperor' (d)	CLoc
	'Purple Heart' (d)	CLoc EBak SRiF
	'Purple Lace'	CSil SRiF SVic
	'Purple Patch'	MBri
	'Purple Pride'	MBri
	'Purple Rain'	EPts WFuv WPBF WRou
	'Purple Showers'	SRiF
	'Purple Splendour' (d)	CDoC CSil SRiF

'Pussy Cat' (T)	CLoc CWVF EBak SRiF SVic
'Putney Pride'	EPts
'Put's Folly'	CWVF EBak MJac SPet SRiF WFuv
putumayensis	CSil EBak SRiF
'Quasar' (d)	CCCN CDoC CLoc CTsd CWVF EPts LAst MJac SLBF SPet SRiF SVic WFuv WPBF WRou
'Queen Esther'	CTsd SRiF
'Queen Mabs'	EBak SRiF
'Queen Mary'	CLoc CSil EBak SRiF
'Queen of Bath' (d)	EBak SVic
'Queen of Derby' (d)	CSil CTsd CWVF SRiF
'Queen of Hearts' Kennett (d)	SVic
'Queen Victoria' Smith (d)	SRiF
'Queen's Park' (d)	EBak
'Query'	CSil EBak SRiF SVic
'R.A.F.' (d)	CCCN CLoc CTsd CWVF EBak EPts SLBF SPet SRiF SVic WFuv
'Rachel Sinton' (d)	MBri SRiF WRou
'Radcliffe Bedder' (d)	CSil
'Radings Gerda' (E)	LCla SLBF
'Radings Inge' (E)	CDoC LCla
'Radings Karin'	CDoC
'Radings Mapri'	WPBF
'Radings Michelle'	CSil CWVF
'Rahnee'	CWVF SRiF
'Rainbow'	CWVF
'Raintree Legend' (d)	SRiF
'Rakastava' (d)	WPBF
'Ralph Oliver' (d)	WPBF
'Ralph's Delight' (d)	CTsd CWVF SRiF WFuv
'Ram'	WPBF
'Rambling Rose' (d)	CLoc CWVF EBak MJac SRiF
'Rambo' (d)	SRiF
'Rams Royal' (d)	CDoC CWVF SRiF
'Raspberry' (d)	CLoc CTsd CWVF EBak SRiF SVic WFuv
'Raspberry Punch' (d)	WFuv
'Raspberry Red'	SRiF
'Raspberry Sweet' (d)	CWVF SRiF
'Ratae Beauty'	CWVF
'Ratatouille' (d)	CTsd SRiF SVic WFuv WPBF
ravenii	CSil LCla
'Ravensbarrow'	CSil
'Ravenslaw'	CSil
'Ray Redfern'	CWVF
'Razzle Dazzle' (d)	EBak SRiF
'Reading Show' (d)	CSil CWVF EPts SRiF
'Rebecca Williamson' (d)	CWVF MJac SRiF WPBF
'Rebeka Sinton' (v)	CLoc CTsd EBak MBri SRiF
'Red Ace' (d)	CSil WPBF
'Red Imp' (d)	CSil
'Red Jacket' (d)	CWVF EBak SRiF
'Red Petticoat'	CWVF SRiF
'Red Rain'	CWVF LCla SRiF WPBF WRou
'Red Ribbons' (d)	EBak
'Red Rover'	SRiF WRou
'Red Rum' (d)	SPet
'Red Shadows' (d)	CLoc CWVF EBak
'Red Spider'	CCCN CLoc CTsd CWVF EBak LAst SCoo SPet SVic WFuv WPBF
'Red Sunlight'	WPBF
'Red Wing'	CLoc
'Reflexa'	see *F.* × *bacillaris* 'Reflexa'
'Reg Gubler'	SLBF
'Regal'	CLoc
'Regal Robe' (d)	CDoC
regia	CSil
- var. ***radicans***	CSil
- subsp. ***regia***	CDoC CSil CTsd LCla SRiF
- subsp. ***reitzii***	CSil EQua EWes LCla
- subsp. ***serrae***	CDoC CSil
'Remember Eric'	CSil WPBF WRou
'Remember Tommy Struck'	WPBF
'Remembrance' (d)	CSil EPts LCla SLBF
'Remus' (d)	SVic
'Remy Kind' (d)	SRiF
'Rene Schwab'	LCla
'Requiem'	CLoc
'Reverend Doctor Brown' (d)	EBak
'Reverend Elliott'	see *F.* 'President Elliot'
'Revival'	SRiF
'Rhapsody' ambig.	SVic
I 'Rhapsody' Blackwell (d)	CLoc
'Rhombifolia'	CSil
'Rianne Foks'	SRiF
'Riant' (d)	SRiF
'Riccartonii' ♀H3	Widely available
'Richard John' (v)	SRiF SVic
'Richard John Carrington'	CSil
'Ridestar' (d)	CLoc CWVF EBak SRiF
'Rigoletto'	SVic
'Rijs 2001' (E)	CDoC SLBF SRiF
'Rik Knapen'	WPBF
'Ringwood Gold'	SVic
'Ringwood Market' (d)	CSil CWVF EPts MJac SCoo SPet SRiF SVic
'Rita Mary'	SRiF
'Rivendell' **new**	EPts
'Riverdancer Liam'	WPBF
'Riverside' (d)	SRiF
'Robbie'	SRiF WPBF
'Robert Lutters'	SVic
'Robin Hood' (d)	CSil SRiF
'Rocket'	WPBF
'Rocket Fire' (California Dreamers Series) (d)	MJac SRiF WFuv
'Roesse Auriga' (d)	WPBF
'Roesse Belinda' (d)	WPBF
'Roesse Bianca' (d)	WPBF
'Roesse Blacky'	CDoC WFuv WPBF
'Roesse Callisto'	CDoC WPBF
'Roesse Cancer'	WPBF
'Roesse Cetus' (d)	WPBF
'Roesse Charon'	WPBF
'Roesse Cressida' (d)	WPBF
'Roesse Crux' (d)	WPBF
'Roesse Franklin' (d)	WPBF
'Roesse Gauss'	WPBF
'Roesse Hydrus' (d)	WPBF
'Roesse Indus' (d)	WPBF
'Roesse Juliet'	CDoC WPBF
'Roesse Lacerta' (d)	WPBF
'Roesse Larissa' (d)	WPBF
'Roesse Littrow'	WPBF
'Roesse Peacock' (d)	CDoC WPBF
'Roesse Pictor' (d)	WPBF
'Roesse Piscus' (d)	WPBF
'Roesse Sextans'	WPBF
'Roger de Cooker' (T)	CLoc LCla LPio SRiF WPBF
'Rohees Alioth' (d)	WPBF
'Rohees Izar'	SRiF
'Rohees King'	WPBF
'Rohees Lava'	SLBF
'Rohees Leada' (d)	SLBF SRiF
'Rohees Merope'	SRiF
'Rohees Naos' (d)	SRiF
'Rohees New Millennium' (d)	SLBF SRiF WPBF
'Rohees Nunki'	WPBF
'Rohees Reda' (d)	SRiF
'Rohees Tethys' (d)	SLBF

'Rolla' (d)	CWVF EBak SRiF WPBF
'Rollezenger'	WPBF
'Rolt's Bride' (d)	SRiF
'Rolt's Ruby' (d)	CSil CWVF SRiF SVic
'Roman City' (d)	CLoc SRiF SVic
'Romance' (d)	CWVF SRiF WFuv
'Romany Rose'	CLoc SRiF
'Ron Ewart'	WFuv WRou
'Ron Holmes'	SRiF
'Ronald L. Lockerbie' (d)	CLoc CTsd CWVF SRiF SVic
'Rondo'	MJac
'Ronnie Barker' (d)	MHav MJac
'Ronny Bogaert' (d)	WPBF
'Ron's Ruby'	CSil SRiF
'Roos Breytenbach' (T)	CCCN CDoC LAst LCla MJac SRiF WPBF WRou
'Rosamunda' (d)	CLoc
'Rose Aylett' (d)	EBak
'Rose Bower'	WPBF
'Rose Bradwardine' (d)	EBak SRiF
'Rose Churchill' (d)	MBri MJac
'Rose Fantasia'	CCCN CDoC CLoc CWVF EPts LAst LCla MJac SLBF SRiF WFuv WPBF
'Rose Marie' (d)	CLoc
'Rose of Castile'	CDoC CLoc CSil CTsd EBak LCla MJac SVic WFuv WRou WWlt
'Rose of Castile Improved' 🏆^{H4}	CSil CWVF EBak LCla MJac SPet SRiF WPBF
'Rose of Denmark'	CCCN CLoc CSil CTsd CWVF EBak MBri MJac SCoo SPet SRiF WFuv WGor WPBF
'Rose Reverie' (d)	EBak
'Rose van der Bergh'	SRiF WPBF
'Rose Winston' (d)	LAst SCoo
rosea misapplied	see *F.* 'Globosa'
rosea Ruíz & Pav.	see *F. lycioides* Andrews
'Rosebud' (d)	EBak SRiF
'Rosecroft Beauty' (d)	CSil CWVF EBak SRiF SVic
Rosella = 'Goetzrose'^{PBR} (Shadowdancer Series)	LAst WPBF
'Rosemarie Higham'	MJac SCoo
'Rosemary Day'	CLoc
'Rosemoor' (T)	SRiF
'Roslyn Lowe' (d)	CDoC
'Ross Lea' (d)	CSil
'Roswitha'	SLBF SRiF WPBF
'Rosy Bows'	CWVF SRiF
'Rosy Frills' (d)	CWVF MJac SRiF SVic WFuv
'Rosy Morn' (d)	CLoc EBak
'Rothbury Beauty'	CTsd SRiF
'Rough Silk'	CLoc CWVF EBak SRiF
'Roy Castle' (d)	CWVF
'Roy Walker' (d)	CLoc CWVF SRiF WFuv
'Royal Academy' (d)	EPts WRou
'Royal and Ancient'	CWVF
'Royal Mosaic' (California Dreamers Series) (d)	CCCN CDoC MJac SRiF WFuv
'Royal Orchid'	EBak
'Royal Purple' (d)	CSil EBak MBri SPet
'Royal Ruby'	SRiF
'Royal Serenade' (d)	CWVF
'Royal Touch' (d)	EBak
'Royal Velvet' (d) 🏆^{H3}	CCCN CLoc CTsd CWVF EBak EPts MAsh MJac SLBF SPet SRiF SVic WFuv WRou
'Royal Wedding'	SRiF
'Royal Welsh'	WRou
'Rozientje'	SRiF
'Rubra Grandiflora'	CWVF EBak LCla SDys SLBF SRiF WRou
'Ruby' (d)	SRiF
'Ruby Wedding' (d)	CWVF SLBF SRiF WPBF
'Ruddigore'	CWVF SRiF
'Ruffles' (d)	CWVF EBak SRiF
'Rufus' 🏆$^{H3-4}$	CDoC CLoc CSil CTsd CWVF EBak EPfP EPts LCla MJac SLBF SPet SRiF SVic WFar WFuv WRou
'Rusty' (d)	WPBF
'Ruth'	CSil SRiF SVic
'Ruth Brazewell' (d)	CLoc
'Ruth King' (d)	CWVF EBak MHav SRiF
'Rutland Water'	CDoC SRiF
'S'Wonderful' (d)	CLoc EBak SRiF
'Sabrina'	MHav WFuv WRou
'Sailor'	EPts SVic
'Sally Ann' (d)	SRiF
'Sally Bell'	CSil
'Salmon Cascade'	CTsd CWVF EBak EPts LCla MJac SLBF WFuv WRou
'Salmon Glow'	CWVF MJac SVic
'Salmon Perfection'	WPBF
'Salmon Queen'	WPBF
'Sam' (d)	WPBF
'Sam Sheppard'	SLBF
'Samantha Reynolds'	SRiF
'Samba' (d)	LAst
'Sammy Girl'	SRiF
'Sam's Song' (d)	SRiF
'Samson' (d/v)	EBak SRiF
'San Diego' (d)	CTsd CWVF
'San Francisco'	EBak
'San Leandro' (d)	EBak
'San Mateo' (d)	EBak
§ ***sanctae-rosae***	CDoC CTsd EBak LCla SRiF
'Sandboy'	CWVF EBak
'Sanguinea'	CSil
'Sanrina'	CDoC
'Santa Cruz' (d)	CSil CTsd CWVF EBak MHav SLBF SRiF SVic
'Santa Lucia' (d)	CLoc EBak
'Santa Monica' (d)	EBak SRiF WPBF
'Santorini Sunset'	WPBF
'Sapphire' (d)	EBak SRiF
'Sara Helen' (d)	CLoc EBak
'Sarah Brightman' (d)	MHav MJac
'Sarah Eliza' (d)	MHav SCoo WFuv
'Sarah Jane' (d)	CSil EBak SVic
'Sarah Louise'	CWVF
'Sarina'	SRiF
'Sarong' (d)	EBak
'Satellite'	CLoc CWVF EBak SRiF
'Saturnus'	CBgR CSil CWVF EBak ELon LRHS MAsh SLBF SPet SPoG SRiF WRou
'Saxondale Sue'	SRiF SVic
'Scabieuse'	CSil
scabriuscula	CDoC LCla SRiF
scandens	see *F. decussata* Ruíz & Pav.
'Scarborough Rosette' (d)	SRiF
'Scarcity'	CDoC CSil CWVF EBak SRiF SVic
'Schiller' ambig.	WPBF
'Schlosz Bentheim'	WPBF
'Schneeball' (d)	CDoC CSil EBak SRiF SVic
'Schneekoppen' (d) **new**	SRiF
'Schneewitcher'	CDoC EPts SRiF
'Schneewittchen' Hoech	CSil
'Schneewittchen' Klein	CSil EBak
'Schönbrunner Schuljubiläum' (T)	EBak
'Schone Hanaurin'	SLBF
'Schöne Wilhelmine'	see *F.* 'Die Schöne Wilhelmine'
'Scion of Longleat' **new**	SRiF
'Scotch Heather' (d)	CWVF SRiF
'Sea Shell' (d)	CWVF EBak SRiF
'Seaforth'	EBak SRiF

'Sealand Prince'	CDoC CSil CTsd CWVF LCla SRiF SVic WPBF
'Sebastopol' (d)	CLoc
'Selma Lavrijsen'	WPBF
serratifolia Hook.	see *F. austromontana*
serratifolia Ruíz & Pav.	see *F. denticulata*
'Seventh Heaven' (d)	CCCN CLoc CTsd CWVF LAst MHav MJac SCoo SRiF SVic WPBF
'Shady Blue'	CWVF
'Shangri-La' (d)	EBak
'Shania' (Diva Series)	MHav SRiF
'Shanley'	CWVF SVic WPBF
'Sharon Allsop' (d)	CWVF SRiF
'Sharon Caunt' (d)	CSil
'Sharon Leslie'	WRou
'Sharpitor'	see *F. magellanica* var. *molinae* 'Sharpitor'
'Shawna Ree' (E)	CDoC
'Sheila Crooks' (d)	CDoC CWVF EBak MHav SRiF
'Sheila Kirby'	CWVF
'Sheila Purdy' **new**	SRiF
'Sheila Steele' (d)	CWVF SRiF
'Sheila's Love'	MJac
'Sheila's Surprise' (d)	SRiF WPBF
'Shelford'	CDoC CLoc CWVF EBak EPts MJac SLBF SRiF SVic WRou
'Shell Pink'	SVic
'Shelley Lyn' (d)	SRiF WPBF
'Shirley Halladay' (d)	LCla SRiF WPBF
'Shirley' PBR (Shadowdancer Series)	CDoC GKev LAst LSou SCoo SLBF SRiF
'Shooting Star' (d)	EBak SRiF
'Showfire'	EBak
'Showtime' (d)	CWVF
'Shrimp Cocktail'	CLoc MSCN SRiF
'Shuna Lindsay'	LCla WPBF
'Shy Lady' (d)	CTsd SRiF
'Siberoet' (E)	CDoC LCla SLBF
'Sierra Blue' (d)	CDoC CLoc CWVF EBak MHav SRiF
'Silver Anniversary' (d)	SRiF SVic
'Silver Dawn' (d)	MHav SRiF
'Silver Dollar'	SVic WPBF
'Silver Pink'	CSil
'Silver Wedding' (d) **new**	SRiF
'Silverdale'	CDoC CSil EPts SRiF
'Simon J. Rowell'	LCla SRiF
'Simonne Bosmans' (d)	WPBF
'Simple Simon'	SRiF
simplicicaulis	CDoC EBak LCla WPBF
- pale-flowered **new**	GCal
'Sincerity' (d)	CLoc
'Sinton's Standard'	MBri
'Siobhan'	CWVF
'Siobhan Evans' (d)	SLBF
'Sipke Arjen'	WRou
'Sir Alfred Ramsey'	CWVF EBak
'Sir David Attenborough' (d)	MJac
'Sir David Jason'	MJac WFuv
'Sir Ian Botham' (d)	MJac
'Sir Matt Busby' (d)	CTsd EPts LAst MHav MJac SRiF WPBF WRou
'Sir Steve Redgrave' (d)	MJac
'Sir Thomas Allen'	SLBF
'Siren' Baker (d)	EBak
'Sister Ann Haley'	EPts SRiF
'Sister Sister' (d)	SLBF
'Sjan Schilders' (d)	WPBF
'Sleedoorn' (d)	WPBF
'Sleepy'	CDoC CSil CTsd EPts MHav SPet SRiF SVic WFuv WPBF
'Sleigh Bells'	CLoc CTsd CWVF EBak SPet SRiF SVic
'Small Pipes'	CWVF SRiF WFuv WPBF
'Smokey Mountain' (d)	SRiF SVic WFuv
'Sneezy'	EPts MHav SRiF SVic WFuv WPBF
'Snow Burner' (California Dreamers Series) (d)	CCCN CDoC CLoc LAst MHav SRiF
'Snow Pearls'	WPBF
'Snow White' (d)	SRiF SVic WPBF
'Snowbird' (d)	SLBF
§ 'Snowcap' (d) ♀H3-4	CCCN CDoC CLoc CSil CTsd CWVF EBak EPts GKir LAst LCla LRHS MAsh MBri MGos MJac MWat NPer SBfd SCoo SGar SLBF SPet SPoG SRiF SVic WFar WFuv WRou
'Snowdon' (d)	CWVF SRiF
'Snowdrift' ambig.	SRiF
'Snowdrift' Colville (d)	CLoc
'Snowdrift' Kennett (d)	EBak
'Snowfall'	CWVF
'Snowfire' (d)	CLoc CWVF SCoo SRiF SVic WFuv WPBF
'Snowflake' (E)	CDoC LCla SLBF WBor WRou
'Snowstorm' (d)	SRiF WPBF
'So Big' (d)	SRiF
'Softpink Jubelteen'	WPBF
'Software' (d)	SRiF WPBF
'Sombrero' (d) **new**	SRiF
'Son of Thumb' ♀H4	CDoC CLoc CSil CTsd CWVF EPfP EPts LAst LBMP LRHS MAsh MGos MJac SLBF SLim SPet SRiF SVic WFar WFuv WPBF WRou
'Sonata' (d)	CLoc CWVF EBak SRiF SVic
'Sophie Louise'	CWVF EPts SRiF WFuv WPBF WRou
'Sophie's Silver Lining' (d)	MJac
'Sophie's Surprise' (T)	WPBF
'Sophisticated Lady' (d)	CLoc CWVF EBak EPts SPet SRiF SVic
'Soroptimist International'	SRiF
'South Gate' (d)	CLoc CTsd CWVF EBak EPts LAst MBri MJac MSCN SPet SRiF SVic WPBF
'South Lakeland'	CSil SRiF
'South Seas' (d)	EBak SVic
'South Today' (d) **new**	SRiF
'Southern Pride'	SLBF
'Southlanders'	EBak
'Southwell Minster'	SRiF
'Space Shuttle'	CLoc LCla LPio SLBF SRiF
'Sparky' (T)	CLoc CWVF EPts LCla SRiF WRou
§ 'Speciosa'	CDoC EBak LCla LPio SRiF WRou
'Spice of Life' (d)	SRiF
'Spion Kop' (d)	CCCN CDoC CTsd CWVF EBak LAst SPet SRiF WFuv WGor
§ ***splendens*** ♀H1+3	CBcs CCCN CDoC CLoc CSil EBak IDee LCla MCot MHer NPer SLBF SMrm SRiF WRou
- B&SWJ 10469	WCru
- 'Karl Hartweg'	CDoC
'Spotlight' **new**	SRiF
'Spring Bells' (d)	SRiF
'Spring Classic' (d)	SRiF
'Squadron Leader' (d)	CWVF EBak EPts SRiF
'Square Peg' (d)	SRiF
'Stad Genk' (d)	WPBF
'Stals Kevin' (T)	WPBF
'Stan'	WPBF
'Stanley Cash' (d)	CLoc CTsd CWVF SPet SRiF SVic WFuv
'Star Wars'	CDoC CLoc EPts MBri MJac SRiF WPBF WRou
'Stardust'	CDoC CWVF EBak MHav MJac
'Steeley' (d)	SVic
'Steirerblut' (T)	SRiF WPBF

'Stella Ann' (T)	CWVF EBak EPts LCla SRiF WFuv WPBF
'Stella Marina' (d)	EBak
'Stevie Doidge' (d)	WPBF
'Stewart Taylor'	MJac
'Stolze von Berlin' (d)	SRiF
'Stoney Creek' (d)	SRiF
'Straat Bali'	WPBF
'Straat Cook'	LCla
'Straat Cumberland'	LCla
'Straat Fiji'	LCla
'Straat Flores'	WPBF
'Straat Fuknoka'	CDoC LCla
'Straat Futami' (e)	CDoC EPts LCla
'Straat Kobe' (T)	CDoC LCla WPBF
'Straat La Plata'	LCla
'Straat Magelhaen'	LCla
'Straat Malakka'	SRiF
'Straat Messina'	LCla
'Straat Moji'	WPBF
'Straat of Plenty'	CDoC LCla
'Strawberry Daiquiri' (d)	WPBF
'Strawberry Delight' (d)	CLoc CWVF EBak MHav MJac SPet SVic WFuv
'Strawberry Fizz' (d)	MHav SRiF
'Strawberry Sundae' (d)	CLoc CWVF EBak SRiF
'Strawberry Supreme' (d)	CSil
'String of Pearls'	CLoc CWVF MJac SLBF SPet SRiF SVic
'Stuart Joe'	CWVF
'Stuart Martin' **new**	SRiF
'Sue'	CTsd SLBF SRiF
'Suffolk Punch' **new**	SRiF
'Suffolk Splendour' (d) **new**	EPts
'Sugar Almond' (d)	CWVF
'Sugar Blues' (d)	EBak SRiF
'Summerdaffodil'	SRiF WPBF
'Summerwood' (d)	SRiF
(Sunbeam Series) 'Sunbeam Ernie'	WPBF
- 'Sunbeam Hillary'	WPBF
'Sunkissed' (d)	EBak
'Sunlight Path'	WPBF
'Sunningdale' (T)	CWVF LCla
'Sunny'	SRiF
'Sunny Jim'	SVic
'Sunny Smiles'	CSil CWVF SPet SRiF
'Sunray' (v)	CBar CChe CDoC CLoc COlW CWVF EBak ELon GKir LBuc MAsh MGos MWat NEgg SBfd SCoo SLim SPoG SRiF WCot WPBF
'Sunset'	CLoc CWVF EBak SPer SRiF
'Sunset Boulevard' (d)	SRiF WPBF
'Supersport' (d)	SVic
'Superstar'	CWVF EPts SRiF SVic
'Susan' (d)	SRiF
'Susan Ford' (d)	CWVF SPet SRiF
'Susan Green'	CSil CWVF EBak MJac SRiF
'Susan McMaster'	CLoc
'Susan Olcese' (d)	CWVF EBak SRiF
'Susan Skeen'	WPBF WRou
'Susan Travis'	CLoc CSil CWVF EBak SRiF SVic
'Susanna D. Dijkman'	WPBF
'Suzanna'	WPBF
'Swanley Gem' ♀H3	CLoc CWVF EBak SLBF SPet SRiF SVic
'Swanley Pendula'	CLoc MHav
'Swanley Yellow'	CWVF EBak SRiF SVic
'Sweet Lavender' (d) **new**	SRiF
'Sweet Leilani' (d)	EBak
'Sweet Sixteen' (d)	CLoc
'Sweetheart' ambig.	SRiF
I 'Sweetheart' van Wieringen	EBak
'Swingtime' (d) ♀H3	CCCN CLoc CTsd CWVF EBak EPts LAst LCla MGos MJac SLBF SPet SRiF SVic WFuv WPBF
sylvatica misapplied	see *F. nigricans*
sylvatica Benth.	CDoC
'Sylvia' Veitch (d)	SRiF
'Sylvia Barker'	CWVF LCla SRiF WFuv WPBF WRou
'Sylvia Gale' **new**	SRiF
'Sylvia Rose' (d)	CWVF SRiF
'Sylvia's Choice'	EBak
'Symphony'	CLoc CWVF EBak
'T.C. Grootenboer Droger'	WPBF
'T. Heivrouwke' (d)	WPBF
'T.S.J.' (E)	CDoC LCla
'T'Vöske' (d/v)	SRiF WPBF
'Taatje'	SRiF
'Taco'	CDoC LCla SRiF
'Taddle'	CWVF SLBF
'Taffeta Bow' (d)	CLoc SRiF SVic
'Taffy' (d)	EBak
'Tam O'Shanter' (d)	CTsd SRiF WFuv
'Tamara Balyasnikova' (d)	WPBF
'Tamerus Hop' (d)	WPBF
'Tamerus Nandoe'	WPBF
'Tamerus Toerako'	WPBF
'Tammy'	SRiF
'Tamworth'	CLoc CTsd CWVF EBak MJac SVic
'Tangerine'	CLoc CWVF EBak MHav SRiF SVic WCot WRou
'Tania Leanne'	SRiF
'Tanja's Blue Bells' (d)	WPBF
'Tantalising Tracy' (d)	WPBF
'Tanya'	CLoc
'Tanya Bridger' (d)	EBak SRiF
'Tarra Valley'	LCla SRiF SVic WPBF
'Task Force'	CWVF SRiF SVic
'Tausendschön' (d)	CLoc
'Ted Perry' (d)	CWVF
'Ted Stiff' (d) **new**	SRiF
'Ted's Tribute'	SRiF WPBF
'Television' (d)	CTsd SRiF
'Temptation' ambig.	CTsd CWVF SPet
'Temptation' Peterson	CLoc EBak
'Tennessee Maiden' (d) **new**	SRiF
'Tennessee Waltz' (d) ♀H3	CDoC CLoc CSil CTsd CWVF EBak EPts SLBF SPet SRiF SVic WFuv WRou
'Tequila Sunrise'	SRiF WPBF
'Teresa' (d) **new**	SRiF
'Tessa Jane'	CSil
tetradactyla misapplied	see *F. × bacillaris*
'Texas Longhorn' (d)	CLoc CWVF EBak SRiF SVic WPBF
'Thalia' (T) ♀H1+3	Widely available
'Thamar'	CDoC CLoc CWVF EPts SRiF SVic WPBF WRou
'That's It' (d)	EBak SVic WPBF
'The Aristocrat' (d)	CLoc EBak SRiF
'The Boys'	WPBF
'The Cannons' (d)	SRiF
§ 'The Doctor'	CLoc CSil CWVF EBak SRiF
'The Jester' (d)	EBak
'The Madame' (d)	CTsd CWVF EBak SRiF
'The Marvel' **new**	SRiF
'The Speedbird' **new**	SRiF
'The Tarns'	CSil CWVF EBak SRiF SVic
'Thelma Vint'	CDoC WPBF
'Thérèse Dupois'	CSil SRiF
'Théroigne de Méricourt'	EBak SRiF
'Thilco'	CDoC CSil
'Think Pink'	CTsd SRiF
'This England' (d)	SRiF

	'Thistle Hill' (d)	CDoC CSil
	'Thomas' (d)	EPts
	'Thomas Berge'	WPBF
	'Thomas Pips'	WPBF
	'Thomas Ritchie'	SRiF
	'Thompsonii'	see *F. magellanica* 'Thompsonii'
	'Thornley's Hardy'	CSil MRav SPet SRiF SVic WPBF
	'Three Cheers'	CLoc EBak SRiF
	'Three Counties'	EBak SRiF
	'Thumbelina'	WPBF
	'Thunderbird' (d)	CLoc CWVF EBak SRiF
	thymifolia (E)	CWVF EBee GCra GQui LRHS MHer SMHy WBor WKif
	- subsp. ***minimiflora*** (E)	CSil LCla
	- subsp. ***thymifolia*** (E)	CDoC CSil LCla
	'Tiara' (d)	EBak
	'Tickled Pink'	WRou
	'Tiffany' ambig.	SRiF
	'Tiffany' Reedstrom (d)	EBak
	'Tillingbourne' (d)	CSil SLBF
	'Time After Time'	CLoc MHav WRou
	'Timlin Brened' (T)	CWVF EBak SRiF WPBF
	'Timothy Titus' (T)	LCla SLBF SRiF
	'Ting-a-ling'	CLoc CTsd CWVF EBak SPet SRiF SVic WFuv WPBF
	'Tinker Bell' ambig.	SRiF WPBF
	'Tinker Bell' Hodges	EBak SVic WPBF
I	'Tinker Bell' Tabraham	CSil
	'Tintern Abbey'	CWVF
	'Tiny Whisper'	WPBF
	'Titania' (d)	WPBF
	'Tjinegara'	CDoC LCla
	'Toby Bridger' (d)	CLoc EBak SRiF
	'Toby Foreman'	SLBF
	'Tolling Bell'	CTsd CWVF EBak SPet WPBF
	'Tom Boy' **new**	SRiF
	'Tom Goedeman'	LCla
	'Tom H. Oliver' (d)	EBak SRiF
	'Tom Knights'	EBak SPet SRiF
	'Tom Thorne'	EBak
	'Tom Thumb' ♀H3	Widely available
	'Tom West' misapplied	see *F.* 'Mr West'
	'Tom West' Meillez (v)	CDoC CHEx CLoc CMHG CSBt CSil CWVF CWib EBak EHoe EPts LAst LCla LHop MAsh MHer MJac MSCN NVic SAga SBfd SDix SLBF SRiF WFar WFuv WHil WPBF
	'Tom Woods'	CWVF SRiF
	'Tommy Struck' (d)	WPBF
	'Tommy Tucker'	SRiF
	'Ton Ten Hove'	CDoC LCla
	'Tony Galea'	SRiF
	'Tony Porter' (d)	SRiF
	'Tony's Treat' (d)	EPts
	'Toon's Tuinklokje'	WPBF
	'Toos'	SVic
	'Topaz' (d)	CLoc EBak
	'Topper' (d)	CWVF SRiF
	'Torch' (d)	CLoc CWVF EBak SRiF SVic
	'Torchlight'	CWVF EPts LCla WFuv
	'Torvill and Dean' (d)	CCCN CLoc CTsd CWVF EPts LAst MJac SLBF SPet WFuv WGor WRou
	'Tosca'	CWVF SRiF
	'Town Crier'	SLBF
	'Tracid' (d)	CLoc CSil
	'Tracie Ann' (d)	SRiF
	'Trail Blazer' (d)	CLoc CWVF EBak MJac SPet SRiF
	'Trailing King'	WPBF
	'Trailing Queen'	EBak MJac SRiF
	'Trase' (d)	CDoC CSil CTsd CWVF CWib EBak MHav SRiF SVic WPBF
	'Traudchen Bonstedt' (T)	CDoC CLoc CWVF EBak LCla SLBF SRiF SVic WPBF
	'Traviata'	see *F.* 'La Traviata' Blackwell
	'Treasure' (d)	EBak
	'Tresco'	CSil SRiF
	'Treslong'	WPBF
	'Tric Trac'	WPBF
	'Tricolor'	see *F. magellanica* var. *gracilis* 'Tricolor'
	'Trident' **new**	SRiF
	'Trientje'	LCla SLBF
	'Trimley Bells'	EBak SRiF
	'Trio' (d)	CLoc
	triphylla (T)	EBak MHer
	'Trish's Triumph'	EPts
	'Tristesse' (d)	CLoc CWVF EBak SRiF
	'Troika' (d)	EBak SRiF
	'Troon'	CWVF SRiF
	'Tropic Sunset' (d)	CTsd MBri SRiF WPBF
	'Tropicana' (d)	CLoc CWVF EBak SRiF SVic WPBF
	'Troubador' Waltz (d)	CLoc
	'Troubadour' Bland (d)	SRiF
	'Troutbeck'	CSil
	'Trudi Davro'	LAst MJac SCoo SRiF
	'Trudy'	CDoC CSil CWVF EBak SRiF SVic
	'Truly Treena' (d)	SLBF SRiF
	'Trumpeter' ambig.	CDoC CWVF SRiF WFuv
	'Trumpeter' Fry	SRiF SVic
	'Trumpeter' Reiter (T)	CLoc EBak EPts LCla MJac
	'Tsjiep'	SRiF WPBF
	'Tubular Bells' (T)	LCla SLBF SRiF
	'Tuonela' (d)	CLoc CWVF EBak WPBF
	'Turandot'	WPBF
	'Turkish Delight'	SRiF WRou
	'Tutone' (d)	SRiF
	'Tutti-frutti' (d)	CLoc
	'Twiggy' **new**	SRiF
	'Twinkling Stars'	CWVF MJac SVic
	'Twinny'	CWVF EPts SRiF
	'Twirling Square Dancer' (d)	WPBF
	'Twister' **new**	SRiF
	'Two Tiers' (d)	CSil CWVF SRiF WPBF
	'Twydale'	SRiF
	'U.B.' (d)	SRiF
	'U.F.O.'	CTsd CWVF SVic
	'Ullswater' (d)	CWVF EBak SRiF
	'Ultramar' (d)	EBak SRiF
	'Uncle Charley' (d)	CDoC CLoc CSil EBak SRiF SVic
	'Uncle Jinks'	SPet SRiF
	'Uncle Steve' (d)	CTsd EBak SRiF SVic
	'University of Liverpool'	CLoc MJac SRiF WPBF
	'Upward Look'	EBak SRiF
	'Valda May' (d)	CWVF
	'Vale of Belvoir'	SRiF
	'Valentine' (d)	EBak
	'Valerie'	WFuv
	'Valerie Ann' (d)	EBak SPet SVic
	'Valerie Bradley' **new**	EPts
	'Valiant'	EBak SRiF
	'Van Eijk Bello' (a)	WPBF
	'Van Eijk Sheltie' (d)	WPBF
	'Vanessa Jackson'	CLoc CWVF MHav MJac SRiF SVic
	'Vanity Fair' (d)	CLoc EBak SRiF
	'Variegated Lottie Hobby' (E/v)	CSil CTsd SRiF WPBF
	'Variegated Pink Fantasia' (v)	WFuv
	'Variegated Pixie' (v)	CSil SRiF
	'Variegated Procumbens'	see *F. procumbens* 'Wirral'
	'Variegated Superstar' (v)	MBri
	'Variegated Swingtime' (v)	EBak LAst SRiF
	'Variegated Triphylla' (T/v)	SRiF

'Variegated Vivienne Thompson' (d/v)	MBri
'Variegated Waveney Sunrise' (v)	MBri
'Veenlust'	EBak SRiF WPBF WRou
'Vendeta'	CDoC LCla
'Venus Victrix'	CSil EBak SRiF WPBF
venusta	CDoC CTsd EBak LCla
'Vermeulen Rani'	WPBF
'Versicolor'	see *F. magellanica* 'Versicolor'
'Vespa'	SRiF
'Victorian' (d)	SRiF SVic
'Victory' Reiter (d)	EBak
'Vielliebchen'	CDoC CSil WPBF
'Vienna Waltz' (d)	WFuv
'Vincent van Gogh' (T)	SRiF WPBF
'Vintage Dovercourt'	LCla
'Violet Bassett-Burr' (d)	CLoc EBak SRiF
'Violet Gem' (d)	CLoc
'Violet Lace' (d)	CSil
'Violet Rosette' (d)	CTsd CWVF EBak SRiF SVic
Violetta = 'Goetzviol' (Shadowdancer Series)	CDoC LAst LSou SCoo SVil WPBF
'Violette Szabo' **new**	SRiF
'Viva Ireland'	EBak SRiF
'Vivien Colville'	CLoc
'Vlasberg 39' (d)	WPBF
'Vobeglo'	CWVF
'Vogue' (d)	EBak SRiF
'Voltaire'	CSil EBak SRiF
'Voodoo' (d)	CCCN CDoC CLoc CWVF EBak EPts LAst SCoo SLBF SRiF SVic WPBF WRou
'Vrens Louisa'	WPBF
vulcanica André	CDoC LCla SRiF WPBF
'Vuurwerk'	SRiF WPBF
'Vyvian Miller'	CWVF
'W. Grootenboer' (d)	WPBF
'W.P. Wood'	CDoC CSil
'Waanrode Bloemendorp'	WPBF
'Wagtails White Pixie'	CSil EBak EPfP
'Waldfee' (E)	CCVN CDoC CSil LCla WPBF
'Waldis Alina'	WRou
'Waldis Geisha' (d)	SLBF SRiF
'Waldis Junella' (d)	SLBF
'Waldis Maja'	WPBF
'Waldis Marion'	WPBF
'Waldis Ovambo'	SLBF
'Waldis Simon'	WPBF
'Waldis Spezi'	CDoC LCla SRiF
'Waldis Speziella'	SLBF
'Wally Yendell' (v)	SRiF WPBF
'Walsingham' (d)	CWVF EBak SRiF WPBF
'Walton Jewel'	EBak SRiF
'Waltz Harp'	MHav
'Waltzing Matilda' (d)	SRiF
'Walz Banjo'	WPBF
'Walz Bella'	LCla SRiF WFuv WPBF
'Walz Blauwkous' (d)	CWVF SRiF
'Walz Bombardon'	SRiF
'Walz Cello'	WPBF
'Walz Cimbaal'	SRiF
'Walz Cocktail'	WPBF
'Walz Doedelzak'	SRiF
'Walz Dreumes'	WPBF
'Walz Duimelot'	SRiF
'Walz Epicurist'	WPBF
'Walz Fagot'	SRiF
'Walz Fanclub'	LCla SRiF WPBF
'Walz Fluit'	MJac WPBF WRou
'Walz Fonola'	SRiF WPBF
'Walz Freule'	CWVF MJac
'Walz Harp'	CWVF SRiF SVic WPBF
'Walz Hoorn'	WPBF
'Walz Jubelteen'	CAlb CDoC CLoc CTsd CWVF ELon EPts LCla MJac MSCN SLBF SRiF SVic WFuv WPBF WRou
'Walz Kattesnoor'	WPBF
'Walz Klarinet'	SRiF WPBF
'Walz Klokkenspel'	WFuv
'Walz Lucifer'	CWVF LCla SRiF WPBF
'Walz Luit'	SRiF
'Walz Mandoline' (d)	CWVF SVic
'Walz Nugget'	SRiF
'Walz Orgelpijp'	WPBF
'Walz Panfluit'	LCla WPBF
'Walz Polka'	CDoC LCla SLBF SRiF
'Walz Rail' **new**	SRiF
'Walz Ratel' (d)	WPBF
'Walz Saxofoon'	WPBF
'Walz Sitar'	WPBF
'Walz Spinet'	WPBF
'Walz Sprietje'	CDoC
'Walz Triangel' (d)	SVic WPBF
'Walz Trombone'	WPBF
'Walz Trompet'	WPBF
'Walz Tuba'	CDoC SRiF WPBF
'Walz Viool'	WPBF
'Walz Waterval'	WPBF
'Walz Wipneus'	WPBF
'Walz Xylofoon'	WPBF
'Wapenveld 150'	LCla
'Wapenveld's Bloei'	CDoC LCla SLBF
'War Paint' (d)	CLoc CTsd EBak SRiF
'Warke' (d)	WPBF
'Warton Crag'	CWVF SRiF SVic
'Water Nymph'	CLoc SLBF SRiF SVic WPBF
'Wattenpost'	SLBF
'Wave of Life'	CWVF SRiF
'Waveney Gem'	CDoC CLoc CWVF EBak LCla MJac SLBF SPet SRiF WFuv WPBF
'Waveney Queen'	CWVF SVic
'Waveney Sunrise'	CTsd CWVF MHav MJac SPet SRiF SVic
'Waveney Unique'	CWVF
'Waveney Valley'	CWVF EBak MJac
'Waveney Waltz'	CWVF EBak SRiF
'Waxen Beauty' (d)	WPBF
'Wedding Bells' ambig.	SRiF SVic WFuv
'Welsh Dragon' (d)	CLoc CWVF EBak SRiF
'Wendy' Catt	see *F.* 'Snowcap'
'Wendy van Wanten'	WPBF
'Wendy's Beauty' (d)	CCCN CLoc EBak EPts MHav MJac SRiF WFuv WRou
'Wentworth'	CWVF SRiF SVic WPBF
'Wessex Belle' (d/v)	CWVF SRiF
'Wessex Hardy'	CSil
'Westham'	LCla SRiF
'Westminster Chimes' (d)	CLoc CWVF SPet SRiF SVic
'Wharfedale' ♀H3	CSil ELon MJac SLBF SRiF SVic
'Whickham Blue'	CWVF
'Whirlaway' (d)	CLoc CWVF EBak SRiF SVic
'White Ann'	see *F.* 'Heidi Weiss'
'White Clove'	CDoC CSil MHav SRiF SVic WPBF
'White Fairy' (d)	SRiF WPBF
'White Galore' (d)	CWVF EBak SRiF SVic
'White Général Monk' (d)	CDoC CSil MHav
'White Gold' (v)	EBak SRiF
'White Haven'	SVic
'White Heidi Ann' (d)	CSil CTsd SRiF
'White Joy'	EBak SRiF
'White King' (d)	CLoc CTsd CWVF EBak SPet SRiF SVic WFuv WRou
'White Lace'	CSil SRiF

'White Pixie' ♀$^{H3-4}$	CDoC CSil EPts MHav MJac SLBF SPer SPet SRiF SVic
'White Princess'	SRiF
'White Queen' ambig.	CWVF
'White Queen' Doyle	EBak
'White Spider'	CLoc CWVF EBak SRiF SVic
'White Veil' (d)	CWVF
'White Wafer' (d)	SRiF
'Whiteknights Amethyst'	CDoC CSil
'Whiteknights Blush'	CChe CDoC CMdw CPLG CSil EWes GCal GGar GQui NLar SMrm SRiF WPBF
'Whiteknights Cheeky' (T)	CWVF EBak EPts LCla SRiF SVic
'Whiteknights Green Glister'	CDoC CSil EPfP
'Whiteknight's Pearl' ♀$^{H1+3}$	CDoC CSil CTsd CWVF ECha EPfP EPts LCla LRHS SEND SLBF SMHy SPet SRiF SVic WFuv WPBF
'Whiteknights Ruby' (T)	LCla SRiF
'Whitney' (Diva Series)	MHav SRiF
'Whitton Starburst'	CDoC LCla
'Wicked Queen' (d)	CSil SVic WPBF
'Widow Twanky' (d)	CWVF WPBF
'Wiebke Becker'	SRiF
'Wigan Pier' (d)	EPts SLBF SRiF WPBF WRou
'Wight Magic' (d)	MJac SRiF WFuv
'Wild and Beautiful' (d)	CTsd CWVF SRiF SVic
'Wilf Langton'	SLBF SRiF WPBF WRou
'Wilhelmina Schwab'	CDoC LCla
'Willeke Smit' (d)	WPBF
'Willie Tamerus'	SRiF WPBF
'Willy Winky'	CSil
'Wilma van Druten'	CDoC LCla
'Wilma Versloot'	SRiF WPBF
'Wilson's Colours'	EPts
'Wilson's Joy'	MJac
'Wilson's Pearls' (d)	CWVF SLBF SPet SRiF
'Wilson's Sugar Pink'	EPts LCla MJac SRiF
'Win Oxtoby' (d)	CWVF
'Windhapper'	LCla WFuv WPBF
'Windmill'	CWVF
'Wine and Roses' (d)	EBak SRiF
'Wingrove's Mammoth' (d)	SRiF SVic
'Wings of Song' (d)	CWVF EBak SRiF
'Winifred'	SRiF
'Winston Churchill' (d) ♀^{H3}	CCCN CLoc CTsd CWVF EBak LAst MBri MJac SBfd SCoo SPet SPlb SRiF SVic WFuv WPBF
'Winter Yellow'	WPBF
'Winter's Touch'	SRiF WPBF
'Witchipoo'	SLBF
'Witte Van Munster'	WPBF
'Woodnook' (d)	CWVF SRiF
'Woodside' (d)	CSil SVic
'Wrotham' (d) **new**	SRiF
'Xmas Tree'	WPBF
'Y Me'	SRiF
'Yellow Heart'	WPBF
'Ymkje'	EBak
'Yolanda Franck'	CDoC LAst WRou
'York Manor'	CDoC MHav WRou
'Yours'	SRiF
'Yuletide' (d)	SRiF
'Yvonne Priest'	SRiF
'Yvonne Schwab'	CDoC LCla SRiF
'Zara'	SRiF
'Zeebrook'	SRiF SVic
'Zellertal'	WPBF
'Zeta'	WPBF
'Zets Alpha'	SRiF
'Zets Bravo'	CDoC CTsd SRiF
'Ziegfield Girl' (d)	EBak SRiF SVic
'Zifi'	SLBF
'Zulu King'	CDoC CSil SRiF SVic
'Zulu Queen'	SVic
'Zus Liebregts' (d)	WPBF
'Zwarte Dit'	WPBF
'Zwarte Snor' (d)	CWVF WPBF
'Zyzy' **new**	SRiF

Fumaria (*Papaveraceae*)

lutea	see *Corydalis lutea*
officinalis	CArn

Furcraea (*Agavaceae*)

bedinghausii	see *F. parmentieri*
§ ***foetida***	CCCN SBig
§ - var. ***mediopicta*** (v)	SBig
- 'Variegata'	see *F. foetida* var. *mediopicta*
gigantea	see *F. foetida*
guatemalensis **new**	MAga
longaeva misapplied	see *F. parmentieri*
longaeva ambig.	CAbb CBcs CDTJ CFir CHEx CHGN CPen CPne CTrC CTsd EAmu GBin GGar LEdu SAPC SArc SBst SChr SPlb WCot WPGP
macdougalii **new**	MAga
§ ***parmentieri***	CBct CCCN CHll CMdw EAmu LEdu MAga WPGP
- NJM 05.081	WPGP
selloa	MAga
- var. ***marginata*** (v)	CDoC CHEx EAmu MAga

G

Gahnia (*Cyperaceae*)

sieberiana	SPlb

Gaillardia (*Asteraceae*)

aristata 'Granada'	LRHS
- 'Maxima Aurea'	EBee EBla EPfP MSpe NBre NPri NVic SPhx WCAu
- 'Primavera' **new**	SMrm
'Arizona Sun'	CChe EBee ECtt GKir LSou MHer NPri WRHF
'Bijou'	CMea EBee NBre NLar NVic SWvt
'Dwarf Goblin'	NGBl SPet
§ 'Fackelschein'	EBee NBre SRms
'Fanfare'^{PBR}	CMac EBee ECtt ELon LBuc LHop LRHS LSou MGos MWea NDov SCoo SPer SPoG
Goblin	see *G.* × *grandiflora* 'Kobold'
× ***grandiflora***	CSam EBee GMac LLHF LRHS
'Amber Wheels'	NGdn NPri SBfd WWEG
- 'Bremen'	EBee MSpe WWEG
- 'Burgunder'	Widely available
- 'Dazzler' ♀^{H4}	CMac CSBt EAEE EBee EBla ECtt ELan EPfP LAst LBMP LRHS NBPC NLar NVic SMrm SPer SPoG WCAu WMoo WWEG
- Gallo Series **new**	LRHS
§ - 'Kobold'	CBcs CMac COIW CSBt EBee EBla ECtt ELon EPfP GJos GKir GMaP LAst LHop LRHS MBri MWat NBre NEgg NLar NPri SMrm SPad SPer SPlb SPoG SRms SWvt WWEG
- Monarch Group	WSpi
- 'Summer's Kiss'^{PBR}	EBee
- (Sunburst Series)	LRHS
Sunburst Burgundy Picotee = 'Granretip' **new**	

	- - Sunburst Burgundy Silk = 'Granbur' **new**	LRHS
	- - Sunburst Scarlet Halo **new**	LRHS
	- - Sunburst Tangerine = 'Granoran' **new**	LRHS
	- - Sunburst Yellow = 'Granyel' **new**	LRHS
	- 'Tokajer'	EBee EPfP LBMP LRHS NBre NLar SMrm SPhx
	'Mandarin'	SRms
*	new giant hybrids	WFar
§	'Oranges and Lemons'PBR	EBee ECtt EGxp EWll GKir LHop LRHS LSou MBri MWea NLar SHar SPoG SUsu WCAu WCra
	'Red Kiwi' **new**	WHlf
	'Red Ribbons' **new**	CSpe
	Saint ClementsPBR	see *G.* 'Oranges and Lemons'
	Torchlight	see *G.* 'Fackelschein'

Galactites (*Asteraceae*)

	tomentosa	CSpe EHrv ELan EPfP EPyc EWTr MWea SDnm SGar SPav WEas
	- white-flowered	CPla

Galanthus ✿ (*Amaryllidaceae*)

	× ***allenii***	WIvy
	alpinus	CLAP ECho
	- var. ***alpinus***	ECho MTho NMen
	angustifolius	WCot
	'Annette'	ECho LAma NMyG
	'Armine'	CAvo CElw CSna IFoB
	'Atkinsii' ♀H4	CAvo CBel CBgR CElw CFFs CLAP ECha ECho EHrv EPot GCrs GEdr GKev IFoB LAma LRHS MAsh MAvo MHom MRav NBir NCot NDov NMyG WCom WCot WHoo WShi WTin
	'Barbara's Double' (d)	CLAP LRHS
	'Benhall Beauty'	CAvo CBel WTin
	'Benton Magnet'	CBel
	'Bertram Anderson'	GCrs MAsh WCot
	'Bess' **new**	IFoB
	'Bill Bishop'	CAvo CBel CDes ECha IPot LRHS MAsh
	'Brenda Troyle'	CBel CElw CLAP CSWP ECha EHrv ELon EPot GCrs GEdr IGor IPot LRHS MAsh MHom NCot NMyG WCot WFar WIvy WPnP
	byzantinus	see *G. plicatus* subsp. *byzantinus*
	'Castlegar'	IFoB
	caucasicus misapplied	see *G. elwesii* var. *monostictus*
	caucasicus (Bak.) Grossh.	see *G. alpinus* var. *alpinus*
	caucasicus ambig.	ECho GCrs IFoB
	- 'Comet'	see *G. elwesii* 'Comet'
	- var. ***hiemalis*** Stern	see *G. elwesii* var. *monostictus* Hiemalis Group
	- 'Mrs McNamara'	see *G. elwesii* 'Mrs McNamara'
	cilicicus	WCot
	'Clare Blakeway-Phillips'	CLAP
	'Colesborne'	EHrv
	corcyrensis spring-flowering	see *G. reginae-olgae* subsp. *vernalis*
	'Cordelia' (d)	CLAP IFoB IPot LRHS MAvo
	'Cowhouse Green'	EHrv
	'Curly'	CDes
	'Desdemona' (d)	CLAP EPot LRHS NMyG WCot WIvy
	'Ding Dong'	CAvo
	'Dionysus' (d)	CBgR CLAP CPLG ECha EHrv EPot GCrs GEdr LRHS MHom NBir NMyG WBrk WTin
	'Drummond's Giant'	IFoB

§	***elwesii*** ♀H4	CTca CTri CWCL EBrs ECho ELan ELon EPfP EPot ERCP EWTr GCrs GKev IFoB IGor ITim LAma LRHS MAsh MWat NBir SDeJ SMrm SRms WCot WHoo WPnP WShi
	- 'Abington Green' **new**	CSna
	- 'Cedric's Prolific'	CBel ECha IFoB
§	- 'Comet'	CBel CElw ECho ELon IFoB LRHS MAsh NCot
	- 'David Shackleton'	EHrv IFoB
	- Edward Whittall Group	CLAP
	- var. ***elwesii*** 'Fenstead End'	CAvo
	- - 'Kite'	MAsh
	- - 'Magnus'	CLAP NBir
	- - 'Maidwell L'	CAvo CSna EHrv MAsh
	- - 'Pat Mason' **new**	CBel
	- - 'Sibbertoft Magnet' **new**	IFoB
	- (Hiemalis Group) 'Barnes'	EHrv WCot
	- 'J. Haydn'	ECho LAma NCot NMyG WWst
	- 'Kyre Park'	LRHS
	- 'Long 'drop'	IFoB
§	- var. ***monostictus*** ♀H4	CAvo ECho EHrv IFoB LRHS MAsh WBrk WFar WIvy
	- - 'G. Handel'	ECho LAma NCot NMyG WWst
	- - 'H. Purcell'	CElw ECho LAma NCot WWst
§	- - Hiemalis Group	CBel ECha EHrv EPot LRHS WCot
	- - 'Warwickshire Gemini'	CDes
§	- 'Mrs McNamara'	CBel CDes IFoB
	- 'Penelope Ann' **new**	LRHS
	- poculiform **new**	CBel
	- 'Sickle'	CDes
	- 'Sir Edward Elgar' **new**	LAma
	- 'Washfield Colesbourne'	see *G.* 'Washfield Colesbourne'
	- 'Zwanenburg'	LRHS
	'F63'	IFoB
	'Faringdon Double' (d)	EHrv
	fosteri	ECho EHrv GCrs LRHS SCnR
	'G71' (d)	IFoB
	'Galatea'	CBel CLAP CSna ECha EHrv GCrs LRHS MAsh MHom WIvy
	'Gill Gregory'	MNrw
	'Ginns'	CBel CDes CLAP CSWP IFoB LRHS
§	***gracilis***	CAvo CLAP CPLG LRHS MTho
	- 'Highdown'	CElw CLAP IFoB LRHS MHom
	- 'Vic Horton'	WThu
	graecus misapplied	see *G. gracilis*
	graecus Orph. ex Boiss.	see *G. elwesii*
	'Grande Juge'	IFoB
	'Grayling'	see *G. plicatus* 'Percy Picton'
	Greatorex double (d)	CLAP
	'Greenfields'	CBel CStu IFoB LRHS
	'Hawkshead' **new**	CSWP
	'Heffalump' (d)	LRHS
	'Hill Poë' (d)	CBel CDes CElw CLAP IFoB IGor IPot MHom NMyG
	'Hippolyta' (d)	CAvo CElw CLAP ECha ECho EHrv ELon EPot GEdr IFoB LAma LRHS MAsh MHom NMyG SKHP WCot WFar WIvy
	× ***hybridus*** 'Merlin'	CBel CBro CElw IFoB IGor LRHS MAsh MHom NCot WCot WIvy WTin
	- 'Robin Hood'	CFee CLAP EHrv IFoB WFar
	'Icicle'	CAvo
§	***ikariae*** Bak.	CElw ECho EPfP EPot IGor LRHS SGar WFar WWst
	- Latifolius Group	see *G. platyphyllus*
	- subsp. ***snogerupii***	see *G. ikariae* Bak.
	'Imbolc'	CAvo
	'Jacquenetta' (d)	CBel CDes CElw CFee CLAP CStu EHrv IFoB ITim MHom WTin

'James Backhouse'	CBel ECha WHoo
'John Gray'	CBel CSna IFoB LRHS MAsh
'Ketton'	CElw LRHS MAsh NRya WIvy
'Kingston Double' (d)	CBgR CLAP
'Lady Beatrix Stanley' (d)	CAvo CElw CLAP ECha EHrv EPot GEdr IFoB LLWP LRHS MAsh MHom MTho NDov NMyG WFar WTin
lagodechianus	ECho MPhe
'Lapwing'	CSna
latifolius Rupr.	see *G. platyphyllus*
'Lavinia' (d)	CAvo CElw CFee CLAP MHom WFar
'Lerinda'	EHrv IFoB
'Limetree'	CBel CBgR CElw CLAP EHrv MHom
'Little Ben'	GCrs
'Little John'	EHrv WBrk
'Longstowe'	LRHS
lutescens	see *G. nivalis* Sandersii Group
'Lyn'	CBel CBro EHrv NBir
'Magnet' $\mathbb{Y}^{H4}$	CAvo CBel CBgR CElw CFFs CFee CLAP ECha ECho ELon EPot GCrs GEdr IGor LAma LRHS MAsh MHom NBir NDov NMyG SKHP WBrk WCot WFar WHoo WShi
'Maidwell'	IFoB
'Mighty Atom'	CBel CDes CFee CLAP EHrv WBrk
'Moccas'	CBgR CElw
'Modern Art'	CSna IFoB
'Mrs Backhouse No 12'	EHrv
'Mrs Thompson'	CAvo CBel CDes ECha EHrv LRHS WIvy
'Neill Fraser'	GCrs LRHS
nivalis $\mathbb{Y}^{H4}$	Widely available
- 'Anglesey Abbey'	CAvo CBel GCrs IFoB LRHS MAsh MHom
- 'April Fool'	MHom WTin
- 'Bitton'	CLAP GCrs
- 'Blonde Inge'	CBel IFoB
- 'Chedworth'	CElw WBrk
- 'Dreycott Greentip'	IFoB
- dwarf	GAbr
- 'Greenish'	CAvo CDes CSna
- subsp. ***imperati***	CPLG LRHS
- 'Lutescens'	see *G. nivalis* Sandersii Group
- 'Major Pam' **new**	IFoB
- 'Maximus'	WShi
- f. ***pleniflorus*** (d)	CTca ECha GKev MAsh NDov WAbe WBVN
- - 'Bagpuize Virginia' (d)	CAvo CSna
- - 'Blewbury Tart' (d)	CAvo CBro CLAP CSna IFoB LRHS WBrk
- - 'Flore Pleno' (d) $\mathbb{Y}^{H4}$	CPLG CStu CTri CWCL EPfP EPla EPot ERCP IFoB LAma LHop LLWP LRHS MMuc NCot NRya SDeJ SEND SGar SMrm SPer SRms WBrk WCot WFar WHoo WPnP WShi
- - 'Hambutt's Orchard' (d)	CFee
- - 'Lady Elphinstone' (d)	CAvo CBgR CDes CFee CLAP CRow CSna EHrv IFoB LRHS MAsh MTho NRya WIvy
- - 'Pusey Green Tip' (d)	CElw CLAP EPot GEdr IFoB IPot LRHS MAsh MHom NMyG WCot WTin
- - 'Walrus' (d)	LRHS MAsh
§ - - 'Wonston Double' (d)	CAvo IFoB
- Poculiformis Group	CLAP GCrs LRHS
§ - Sandersii Group	CDes IFoB
§ - Scharlockii Group	CAvo CBel CBgR CElw IGor LRHS NCot WBrk
- 'Tiny'	MHom NBir
- 'Tiny Tim'	ITim NRya
- 'Virescens'	CLAP IFoB
- 'Viridapice'	CAvo CBgR CElw CPLG ECha ECho EPot GEdr GKev IFoB LAma LRHS MAsh MWat NBir NMen SDeJ SKHP WCot WFar WHoo WShi WTin
- 'Warei'	CDes
'Nothing Special'	LRHS
'Ophelia' (d)	CAvo CBel EPot GCrs IGor LRHS MAsh MHom NDov SKHP WBrk WFar WHoo
'Orion'	CDes
'Peardrop' **new**	LRHS
'Peg Sharples'	CSna IFoB
peshmenii	ECho EPot SCnR
- HOA 0201	WWst
§ ***platyphyllus***	CPLG NHol
plicatus $\mathbb{Y}^{H4}$	CAvo CBel CElw CFee ECho EHrv EPot GEdr LRHS MCot MHom NMen NMyG WBrk WCot WFar WHoo WShi WTin
- from Coton Manor **new**	MCot
- 'Augustus'	CAvo CBel CDes CElw CFee CSna EHrv ELon IFoB ITim LRHS MAsh MAvo MHom WBrk WFar WIvy WTin
- 'Baxendale's Late'	CAvo CLAP MAsh
- 'Beth Chatto' **new**	LRHS
- 'Bolu Shades'	WWst
- 'Bowles's Large'	CElw
§ - subsp. ***byzantinus***	MHom WThu
- 'Colossus'	CBel IFoB
- 'Diggory'	CSna MAsh
- 'Edinburgh Ketton'	CSna EHrv
- 'Florence Baker'	EHrv
- 'Gerard Parker'	CSna IFoB
- late flowering	WWst
- 'Oreanda' **new**	IPot
§ - 'Percy Picton'	CAvo
- 'Sally Pasmore'	CAvo
- 'Sophie North'	CLAP IFoB
- 'The Pearl'	EHrv IFoB
- 'Three Ships'	CAvo EHrv
- 'Trym'	CLAP WFar
- 'Warham'	EHrv EPot GEdr IFoB LRHS MHom NMyG
- 'Wendy's Gold'	CDes CSna IFoB LRHS MAsh WFar
'Primrose Warburg'	IFoB
reginae-olgae	CAvo EBrs EHrv GKev MAsh WThu
- HOA 0165	WWst
- subsp. ***reginae-olgae*** $\mathbb{Y}^{H2-4}$	ECho WCot
- - 'Cambridge'	MAsh
§ - subsp. ***vernalis***	ECho IFoB
- - 'John Marr'	LRHS
'Richard Ayres' (d) **new**	IFoB
rizehensis	CAvo CLAP EHrv IFoB
- Baytop 34474 **new**	IFoB
'S.Arnott' $\mathbb{Y}^{H4}$	Widely available
'Saint Anne's'	CElw CSna IFoB LRHS MAsh WIvy
'Scharlockii'	see *G. nivalis* Scharlockii Group
'Seagull'	CSna
'Silverwells'	CElw CSna EHrv GEdr IFoB LRHS
§ 'Straffan'	CAvo CBel CElw EPot GCrs GEdr IFoB IGor LRHS MAsh MHom NMyG WBrk WCot WFar
'Sutton Courtenay'	CDes CSna
'The Apothecary'	EHrv
'The O'Mahoney'	see *G.* 'Straffan'
'Titania' (d)	EHrv ELon GCrs IFoB LRHS WFar
'Trotter's Merlin'	CSna

'Tubby Merlin' CAvo CBel CDes CElw CLAP CSna IFoB MCot WIvy
× ***valentinei*** CBro
'Compton Court'
§ 'Washfield Colesbourne' LRHS
'Washfield Warham' CBel CSna ECha ITim LRHS MAsh
'White Admiral' **new** SKHP
'White Dreams' WFar
'White Wings' CSna
'William Thomson' CSna LRHS
'Winifrede Mathias' CElw CLAP
'Wisley Magnet' LRHS
'Wonston Double' see *G. nivalis* f. *pleniflorus* 'Wonston Double'
woronowii 🏆H4 CElw CHid CLAP CTca ECho GKev IFoB ITim LAma LRHS MAsh MHom MWat NBir NMyG SDeJ WAbe WBrk WCot WFar

Galax (*Diapensiaceae*)

aphylla see *G. urceolata*
§ ***urceolata*** GCrs IBlr MNrw

Galega (*Papilionaceae*)

bicolor MLLN NBir NBre NChi SRms SWat WFar
'Duchess of Bedford' EBee GBin
× ***hartlandii*** CPLG LRHS
- 'Alba' 🏆H4 EBee EHrv ELon EWes IBlr MArl MCot MRav SMHy SPhx SWat WBox WCot WHoo WPrP WSHC
- 'Candida' NBir
- 'Lady Wilson' 🏆H4 CElw CPom EBee ECtt ELon EWes EWld MArl MLHP WAul WCom WCot WFoF WHoo WOut WPen
- 'Spring Light' (v) EWes LSou
'Her Majesty' see *G.* 'His Majesty'
§ 'His Majesty' CKno ECtt ELon IFro MArl MCot MDKP MLHP MRav NBre NCob SMrm WBox WCom WCot WFar WHoo WHrl WPGP
officinalis Widely available
- 'Alba' 🏆H4 CPom CPrp ECtt ELan EPfP MBrN MHer MNHC NCob NPnk SMrm SPoG WFar WHer WHrl WMoo WOut WSpi
- Coconut Ice = 'Kelgal' (v) CAbP LRHS NCob WHer
- 'Lincoln Gold' EBee
orientalis CDes ECha ECtt EWes LEdu MArl MCot MLLN SPhx WAbb WCot WMoo WPGP WSHC

Galeobdolon see *Lamium*

Galeopsis (*Lamiaceae*)

tetrahit WSFF

Galium (*Rubiaceae*)

boreale EBWF
cruciata see *Cruciata laevipes*
mollugo CArn CRWN EBWF NSco SIde
§ ***odoratum*** Widely available
palustre EBWF
verum CArn CRWN EBWF EBee GJos GPWP GPoy MCoo MHer NLan NMir NMun NSco SIde WFar WHer

Galtonia (*Hyacinthaceae*)

candicans 🏆H4 Widely available
- 'Moonbeam' (d) CTca EBee ERCP
princeps CDes CSam CTca ECha GCra WHil WPGP WTin
regalis CPLG CTca WPGP
viridiflora CAvo CBct CBot CHar CTca EBee ECha ECho ELan EPPr EPot ERCP GBin GCal GGal GKir IFro LEdu LRHS MNrw NChi NWCA SDnm WBVN WFar

Galvezia (*Scrophulariaceae*)

speciosa WHil

Garcinia (*Clusiaceae*)

mangostana CCCN

Gardenia (*Rubiaceae*)

augusta see *G. jasminoides*
florida L. see *G. jasminoides*
grandiflora see *G. jasminoides*
§ ***jasminoides*** 🏆H1 CBcs CCCN EBak MBri
- 'Kleim's Hardy' Widely available
- 'Star' SOWG
magnifica SOWG
thunbergia EShb SPlb

garlic see *Allium sativum*

garlic, elephant see *Allium ampeloprasum* 'Elephant'

Garrya ✿ (*Garryaceae*)

F&M 215 WPGP
congdonii NLar
elliptica CBcs CDul CMac EBee ECrN EPfP GGal LSRN MBri MGos NHol NPri NWea SBfd SEND SPlb WFar WHar WPat
- (f) MSwo SWvt
- (m) CDoC CSBt CTri LAst LRHS MAsh MBlu MGan MMuc NLar SLim
- 'James Roof' (m) 🏆H4 Widely available
fremontii NLar
× ***issaquahensis*** 'Glasnevin Wine' CAbP CDul CHGN CPMA EBee ELan EPfP IArd LRHS MAsh MBri MGos NSti SCoo SLim SPoG WFar WSpi
- 'Pat Ballard' (m) EPfP NLar
× ***thuretii*** CBcs CDul MBri MGos NLar WDin WFar

× *Gasteraloe* (*Aloaceae*)

hybrid (***Aloe descoingsii*** × ***Gasteria brevifolia***) MAga

Gasteria ✿ (*Aloaceae*)

brachyphylla STre
carinata var. ***verrucosa*** EShb MSCN
nitida var. ***nitida*** variegated (v) WCot

× *Gaulnettya* see *Gaultheria*

Gaultheria ✿ (*Ericaceae*)

sp. MGan MGos
adenothrix NMen WThu
antarctica WThu
antipoda 'Adpressa' WThu
cardiosepala GEdr
- CLD 1351 GEdr
cumingiana B&SWJ 1542 WCru
cuneata 🏆H4 ECho GKir LRHS NHar WThu
- 'Pinkie' ECho
depressa var. ***novae-zelandiae*** NHol

	forrestii	CPLG
	hispidula	ECho
	hookeri	IBlr
	itoana	ECho GEdr GKev GKir NHar
	'Jingle Bells'	MGos
	miqueliana	WThu
§	***mucronata***	CDul EPfP GKir NWea WDin WFar
	- (m)	CDoC CMac CSBt CTri CWSG EPfP LRHS MGos NEgg NHol SPer SPoG SRms
	- 'Alba' (f)	MGos
	- 'Bell's Seedling' (f/m) $\mathbb{Y}^{H4}$	CBcs CDoC CDul CTri CWSG EPfP GKir LRHS MMuc NBir NEgg SPer SPoG
	- 'Cherry Ripe' (f)	CMac MMuc
	- 'Crimsonia' (f) $\mathbb{Y}^{H4}$	CBcs CMac EPfP SPer SRms
	- 'Indian Lake'	NHol
	- 'Lilacina' (f)	CBcs CMac
	- 'Lilian' (f)	CSBt CWSG EPfP NHol
	- Mother of Pearl	see *G. mucronata* 'Parelmoer'
	- 'Mulberry Wine' (f) $\mathbb{Y}^{H4}$	CSBt CTri EPfP MGos NEgg NHol SPer SPoG
§	- 'Parelmoer' (f)	CSBt LAst NEgg SPer SPoG
	- 'Pink Pearl' (f) $\mathbb{Y}^{H4}$	SRms
	- 'Rosea' (f)	MGos
§	- 'Signaal' (f)	CBcs CMac EPfP LAst MGos NEgg NHol SPer
	- Signal	see *G. mucronata* 'Signaal'
§	- 'Sneeuwwitje' (f)	CBcs CWSG EPfP LAst NBir SPer SPoG
	- Snow White	see *G. mucronata* 'Sneeuwwitje'
	- 'Thymifolia' (m)	EPfP
	- white-berried (f)	MMuc
	- 'Wintertime' (f) $\mathbb{Y}^{H4}$	CMac MGos SRms
§	***myrsinoides***	GKev WThu
	nummularioides	GEdr GGar NHol NLar
	'Pearls'	NHar NHol WThu
	procumbens $\mathbb{Y}^{H4}$	Widely available
	- 'Very Berry' **new**	EShb
	prostrata	see *G. myrsinoides*
	pumila	GAbr LEdu NHar NHol
	- 'E.K. Balls'	NHol
	schultesii	WThu
	shallon	CAgr CBcs CDul CSBt EBee EPfP IFFs MGos SPer SRms SWvt WDin WFar
	sinensis	NHar
	- lilac-berried	NHar WThu
	tasmanica	ECou GAbr
	tetramera	CPLG
	trichophylla	NHar
	× ***wisleyensis***	LRHS SLon SRms SSta
	- 'Pink Pixie'	ECho GKir LRHS MAsh NLar SSta
	- 'Ruby'	CMac
	- 'Wisley Pearl'	CBcs EBee GGar IBlr NLar SCoo SReu WFar
	yunnanensis	CPLG SReu

Gaura (*Onagraceae*)

	lindheimeri $\mathbb{Y}^{H4}$	CMac CMea COIW CSBt CSpe CWib EBee EBrs ECha ELan EPfP EShb EWTr LAst LHop LRHS MCot MHer MRav NEgg SMrm SPer SPhx SUsu WCAu WFar WHoo WMnd WMoo WPer
	- 'Ballerina Blush'	LAst
	- 'Ballerina Rose'	LAst SGar SPet
	- Belleza Series **new**	MWea WHil
	- Cherry Brandy = 'Gauchebra'^{PBR}	EBee ECtt EPfP EWes LBMP LHop LRHS SPur SWvt WFar
	- 'Corrie's Gold' (v)	CMac CWSG EAEE EBee ECha ECtt EHoe ELan EPfP EShb EWTr LRHS MGos MHer SBfd SGar SPer SPet WCFE WMnd WWEG
	- 'Crimson Butterflies'^{PBR}	EBee ECtt ELon EPfP LRHS MAvo NDov
§	- 'Heather's Delight'	MRav
	- 'Heaven's Harmony'	LRHS MGos
	- In the Pink	see *G. lindheimeri* 'Heather's Delight'
	- 'Jo Adela' (v)	ELan EPfP
	- Karalee Petite = 'Gauka'	CWCL EBee EPfP SCoo
	- Karalee Petite Improved	see *G. lindheimeri* Lillipop Pink
	- Karalee Pink	LSRN MBri
	- Karalee White = 'Nugauwhite'^{PBR}	CFox CSpe CWCL CWit EPfP LAst LHop LRHS LSRN LSou MBri NLar SBfd SCoo SPoG
§	- Lillipop Pink = 'Redgapi'	CWCL CWit ECtt EPfP EWll LAst LHop LRHS LSou MBrN MBri MWea NEgg NLar NPri SBfd SMrm SPoG STes SVil
	- 'Madonna' (v)	CBow
	- 'My Melody'^{PBR} (v)	CWCL EBee LBMP LRHS SBfd SPoG
	- 'Passionate Blush'^{PBR}	CChe CMac EBee EPfP LRHS LSRN LSou MGos NDov SPoG
	- 'Passionate Pink'^{PBR}	CBcs
	- 'Passionate Rainbow'^{PBR} (v)	EBee EPfP LSou SPoG
	- 'Pink Dwarf'	CMac CSpr EPfP LRHS
	- 'Rosyjane' **new**	CKno EBee GKir LAst LRHS LSou MWea SHar SOkt SPoG
	- short	LSou SGar
	- 'Siskiyou Pink'	CBcs CSBt CWCL EBee EBrs ECha ECtt EHoe ELan EPfP EShb LBMP LLWG LRHS LSRN MWat NDov SBfd SMad SMrm SPer SWat SWvt WCFE WFar WMnd WWEG
	- 'Snowstorm' **new**	CBar
	- 'Summer Breeze' **new**	EDif SBfd SPhx
	- 'Sunset Dreams'	EPPr SPad
	- 'The Bride'	CEnt CTri EBee ECtt EPfP GCal LLWG LRHS LSRN LSou MMuc MRav MWat NDov SPav SPet SRGP STes SWal SWvt WMnd
	- 'Tutti Frutti' **new**	MPnt
	- 'Vanilla' **new**	MPnt
	- 'Whirling Butterflies'	CKno CSpe CWCL EBee ECtt ELan EPfP GMaP LRHS MAvo MWat NBPC SMad SMrm SPav SPer SWat SWvt WMnd WWEG
	- 'White Dove'	EPfP
	- 'White Heron'	MNrw
	sinuata	CAby SHar
I	'Variegata' (v)	CWCL

Gaylussacia (*Ericaceae*)

	baccata (F)	NLar

Gazania (*Asteraceae*)

	'Aztec' $\mathbb{Y}^{H1+3}$	CCCN SUsu
	'Bicton Orange'	CCCN COIW LSou MAJR SCoo
	'Blackberry Ripple'	CCCN COIW GGar LAst MAJR SAga SCoo SMrm
	'Blackcurrant Ice'	MCot
	'Caledon Giants'	SGar
	'Christopher'	SCoo
	'Christopher Lloyd'	CCCN COIW LAst MAJR SMrm
	'Cornish Pixie'	CCCN
	'Cream Beauty'	MCot
	Daybreak Series	MPet WFar
	- 'Daybreak Red Stripe'	NGBl
	- 'Daybreak Rose Stripe' **new**	NGBl
	Gazoo Series	SPoG

'Jamaica Ginger' SMrm
krebsiana CCCN
linearis WClo
'Magic' CCCN MAJR NPri SCoo
Nahui = 'Suga119' (PLA Sunbathers Series) SVil
'Northbourne' ♀H1+3 GGar
'Orange Beauty' CHEx ELan
'Red Velvet' CHEx SAga
§ ***rigens*** MPet
- var. ***uniflora*** 'Variegata' (v) CBot
- 'Variegata' (v) ♀H1+3 CBow CCCN COlW ELan
Rumi = 'Suga116' (PLA Sunbathers Series) SVil
'Silver Beauty' CBot
splendens see *G. rigens*
Sunset Jane = 'Sugaja'PBR CCCN
'Talent' SEND
Talent Series ♀H3 MPet
'Tiger Eye' CCCN LAst LSou
'Torbay Silver' CHEx
Totonaca = 'Suga212' (PLA Sunbathers Series) SVil

Geissorhiza (*Iridaceae*)

aspera ECho
bracteata new ECho
brehmii 'Rawsonville' new ECho
darlingensis new ECho
imbricata ECho
- subsp. ***bicolor*** new ECho
inequalis ECho
inflexa ECho
monanthos ECho
ornithogaloides new ECho
- subsp. ***marlothii*** new ECho
radians ECho
rosea new ECho
splendidissima ECho

Gelasine (*Iridaceae*)

azurea see *G. coerulea*
§ ***coerulea*** WSHC

Gelidocalamus (*Poaceae*)

fangianus see *Drepanostachyum microphyllum*

Gelsemium (*Loganiaceae*)

rankinii EBee
sempervirens ♀H1-2 CArn CCCN CHll CRHN EBee EShb LRHS LSRN SLim SOWG SPoG

Genista (*Papilionaceae*)

aetnensis ♀H4 CBcs CCVT CDul ELan EPfP EWTr MMuc NLar SAPC SArc SEND SPer SRms WDin WPat WSpi
§ ***canariensis*** CPLG CWib WBrE
cinerea WCFE
decumbens see *Cytisus decumbens*
delphinensis see *G. sagittalis* subsp. *delphinensis*
'Emerald Spreader' see *G. pilosa* 'Yellow Spreader'
fragrans see *G. canariensis*
hispanica CBcs CDul CSBt CTri CWit EBee ECrN ELan EPfP GGal MGos NWea SEND SLim SPer SRms SWvt WCFE WDin WFar WHar
humifusa see *G. pulchella*
lydia ♀H4 Widely available
§ ***maderensis*** EWes LRHS SMrm
§ ***monspessulana*** ECho
pilosa CTri EPot NMen
- 'Goldilocks' LRHS MMuc
- 'Lemon Spreader' see *G. pilosa* 'Yellow Spreader'
- var. ***minor*** NLar NMen WAbe
- 'Procumbens' CMea MDKP MHer WPat
- 'Vancouver Gold' CBcs ELan EPfP GGar GKir MGos MRav SMad SPer SRms WDin WFar WGor
§ - 'Yellow Spreader' CBcs CMHG GEdr MMuc MSwo
§ 'Porlock' ♀H3 CAlb CBcs CBod CDoC CDul CMac CPLG CSBt CSPN CTri CWSG CWib EBee ELon GGal GGar LRHS MAsh MBri MMuc MRav NCGa SBfd SEND SLim WDin
§ ***pulchella*** CTri
sagittalis CTri EBee LRHS MMuc NBir SPer WTin WWFP
§ - subsp. ***delphinensis*** ♀H4 GKir NMen
- ***minor*** see *G. sagittalis* subsp. *delphinensis*
§ × ***spachiana*** ♀H1 CTri SBfd SPoG
tenera 'Golden Shower' SLPl
tinctoria CArn EOHP GBar GPoy ILis MHer SIde WHer
§ - 'Flore Pleno' (d) ♀H4 ECho GEdr MGos NMen
- 'Humifusa' EPot GEdr NWCA
- 'Plena' see *G. tinctoria* 'Flore Pleno'
- 'Royal Gold' ♀H4 CWSG CWib EPfP MGos MRav SPer SPlb
villarsii see *G. pulchella*

Gentiana ✿ (*Gentianaceae*)

§ ***acaulis*** ♀H4 CMea CPla CWCL ECho ELan EPfP EPot GEdr GKev GMaP LHop LRHS MWat NCGa NGdn NHar NHol NMen NRya SPlb SRms SRot WAbe WCFE WFar WPat
- f. ***alba*** WThu
- - 'Snowstorm' GKev
- 'Belvedere' NMen WAbe
- 'Coelestina' WThu
- 'Dinarica' see *G. dinarica*
- 'Holzmannii' IVic NMen WAbe
- 'Krumrey' EPot GKev
- 'Max Frei' NHar
I - 'Maxima Enzian' GCrs
- 'Rannoch' GEdr GKev NMen
- 'Stumpy' EPot GEdr
- 'Trotter's Variety' EPot WAbe
- 'Undulatifolia' EPot
- 'Velkokvensis' EPot IVic
affinis LHop
'Alex Duguid' GEdr IVic
'Amethyst' GCrs GEdr GMaP LRHS WAbe
angulosa misapplied see *G. verna* 'Angulosa' hort.
angustifolia WAbe
I - 'Alba' new GKev
'Ann's Special' GEdr
asclepiadea ♀H4 Widely available
- 'Alba' CBot CLAP EBee GBee GCal GEdr GGar GKev IGor MDKP MTho NBid SGSe SRms WHoo WTin
- 'Knightshayes' CLAP EBee GKev GKir LLHF
I - 'Nana' EBee GKev
- pale blue-flowered WPGP
- 'Phyllis' EBee GKev
- 'Pink Cascade' GEdr GKev SGSe
- 'Pink Swallow' CLAP GAbr GBBs GKev GMac NLar WHoo WWEG
- 'Rosea' GKev GMaP MDKP MNrw WPGP
- 'Whitethroat' GKev

	'Balmoral'PBR	GMaP
	'Barbara Lyle'	WAbe
	bavarica var. ***subacaulis***	SPlb
	× ***bernardii***	see *G.* × *stevenagensis* 'Bernardii'
	'Berrybank Dome'	CSam GEdr GMaP NHar NHol
	'Berrybank Sky'	GEdr GMaP NHol
	'Berrybank Star'	GEdr GMaP
	bisetaea	SRms
	'Blauer Stern' **new**	IVic
	'Blue Heaven'	GEdr
	'Blue Sea'	LRHS
	'Blue Silk'	EWes GCrs GEdr GKev IVic LRHS NHar NHol WAbe
	brachyphylla	WAbe
	- subsp. ***favratii***	WAbe
	'Braemar'PBR	GMaP
	'Cairngorm'	GAbr GCrs GEdr LRHS
	'Carmen'	GEdr
	× ***caroli***	WAbe
	clusii	NMen WAbe
	- purple-flowered	WAbe
	'Compact Gem'	GEdr NHar NHol WAbe
§	***cruciata***	EBee ITim LHop MMHG MTho NLar
§	***dahurica***	EBee ECho GEdr NGdn NHol
	'Dark Hedgehog'	GEdr
	depressa	EPot MTho WAbe
	'Devonhall'	GEdr IVic NHol WAbe
	'Diana'PBR	LRHS
§	***dinarica***	ECho EPot NHar NMen
	- 'Colonel Stitt'	GEdr WThu
	- 'Frocheneite'	EPot
	'Dumpy'	CPBP GEdr WAbe
	'Elehn'	NHar
	'Elizabeth'	GEdr
	'Ettrick'	GEdr IVic NHol
	'Eugen's Allerbester' (d)	CCVN GCrs GEdr GKev GMaP IVic LRHS NHar NHol SPer WAbe
	'Eugen's Bester'	NHar
	farreri	WAbe
	- 'Duguid'	GEdr WAbe
	- hybrids	WAbe
	fetissowii	see *G. macrophylla* var. *fetissowii*
	gelida	LLHF
	'Gellerhard'	GEdr NHar
	'Gewahn'	IVic NHar
	Glamis strain	GEdr NHar
	'Glen Isla'	EWes
	'Glen Moy'	GEdr
	'Glendevon'	GEdr WAbe
§	***gracilipes***	ECho GKev MWat SPlb SRms
	- 'Yuatensis'	see *G. macrophylla* var. *fetissowii*
	× ***hascombensis***	see *G. septemfida* var. *lagodechiana* 'Hascombensis'
	'Henry'	GEdr WAbe
	hexaphylla SDR 5003	GKev
	'Indigo'	WAbe
	Inshriach hybrids	LRHS
	'Inverleith' ♀H4	EWes GAbr GEdr LRHS NHol SPlb
	'Iona'PBR	GMaP
	'Joan Ward'	LRHS SPer
	'Kirriemuir'	EWes
	kochiana	see *G. acaulis*
	kurroo	LHop
	- var. ***brevidens***	see *G. dahurica*
	lagodechiana	see *G. septemfida* var. *lagodechiana*
	'Little Diamond'PBR	LRHS NLar
	'Lucerna'	GEdr GKev LRHS NHol
	lutea	EBee ECho GAbr GKev GPoy NBid NChi SMad SRms WPer
	- SDR 3502	GKev

	- SDR 3522	GKev
	× ***macaulayi*** ♀H4	CPla SRms
	- 'Blue Bonnets'	GEdr
	- 'Elata'	IVic NHol
	- 'Kidbrooke Seedling'	CTri EWes GCrs GEdr GMaP LRHS NHol WAbe
	- 'Kingfisher'	CPla CTri GKev IVic LRHS NBir WAbe
§	- 'Praecox'	GEdr
§	- 'Wells's Variety'	WAbe
§	***macrophylla*** var. ***fetissowii***	EBee GKev LHop LLHF
	makinoi 'Marsha'PBR	LRHS SPoG
	- 'Royal Blue'	GCal WWEG
	'Margaret'	GEdr WAbe
	'Maryfield'	GEdr
	'Melanie'	GEdr NHol
*	***nepaulensis***	GAuc
	occidentalis	EPot
	olgae	EBee LHop
	Olga's pale	GCrs
	olivieri	LLHF
	paradoxa	GCrs GKev LLHF NSla WAbe WPat
	- 'Blauer Herold'	MWat
	phlogifolia	see *G. cruciata*
	pneumonanthe	LRHS SPlb
	prolata	NHar
	pumila subsp. ***delphinensis***	WAbe WPat
	purdomii	see *G. gracilipes*
	'Robyn Lyle'	WAbe
	'Saphir Select'	GEdr NHol
	saxosa	GKev ITim LRHS NBir WAbe
	scabra	LRHS
	- 'Zuikorindo'	EBee NLar
	'Selektra' **new**	IVic
	'Sensation'	GEdr NHar
	septemfida ♀H4	GAbr GEdr GKev GKir LBee LHop LRHS MBri MTho NBir NWCA SPlb SRms WHoo WKif
	- 'Alba'	GKir NBir
§	- var. ***lagodechiana*** ♀H4	EPot GKir LRHS NMen SRms WFar
§	- - 'Hascombensis'	ECho
	'Serenity'	GEdr IVic LRHS NHol WAbe
	'Shot Silk'	CSam CTri EWes GCrs GEdr GGar GJos GKev GMaP IVic LRHS MGos NBir NHol WAbe
	'Silken Giant'	GEdr WAbe
	'Silken Night'	WAbe
	'Silken Seas'	GEdr NHol WAbe
	'Silken Skies'	GEdr WAbe
	'Silken Surprise'	WAbe
	sino-ornata ♀H4	CPla CTri EBee ECho EMil GAbr GGar GKev GKir LRHS LSRN MBri MGos MWat NMen SPer SRms WAbe WFar
	- CLD 476B	GEdr
	- 'Alba'	CPla NHol WFar
	- 'Angel's Wings'	GEdr LRHS NHol
	- 'Bellatrix'	GEdr IVic NHar NHol
	- 'Blautopf'	IVic
	- 'Brin Form'	SRms WAbe
	- 'Downfield'	GCrs GKev GMaP LRHS NHol SPer
	- 'Edith Sarah'	GEdr IVic SRms
	- 'Mary Lyle'	GEdr WAbe
	- 'Oha'	IVic
	- 'Praecox'	see *G.* × *macaulayi* 'Praecox'
	- 'Purity'	GEdr WAbe
	- 'Starlight'	NHar
I	- 'Trotter's Form'	EWes
	- 'Weisser Traum'	GEdr IVic LRHS NHol
	- 'White Wings'	EWes

'Sir Rupert'	IVic NHar
'Soutra'	GEdr
× ***stevenagensis*** ♀H4	CPla CTri LRHS
§ - 'Bernardii'	GEdr IVic WAbe
- dark-flowered	WAbe
stipitata subsp. ***tizuensis***	GKev
straminea	GCrs LLHF MDKP
'Strathmore' ♀H4	CSam CSpr CTri EWes GAbr GCrs GEdr GGar GKev GMaP IVic LRHS NBir NHar NHol SPer SPlb WAbe
'Suendermannii'	GKev LLHF
syringea	WAbe
ternifolia 'Cangshan'	GEdr WAbe
- 'Dali'	GEdr NBir NHar NHol
tianschanica	LHop
tibetica	CArn CPla EBee EWld GAuc GEdr GPoy LEdu MWat NMun WAul WEas WPer WTin
triflora	GKev LHop WFar WPGP
- 'Alba'	GKev
- f. ***horomuiensis***	GCal
- var. ***japonica***	WWEG
- 'Royal Blue'	EBee WCot
verna	CWCL EBee ECho EPfP EPot EWes LHop LRHS LSRN NMen NSla SPoG SRot WAbe WFar WPat
- 'Alba'	NSla WAbe WPat
§ - 'Angulosa' hort. ♀H4	GCrs ITim
- subsp. ***balcanica***	SRms WPat
- subsp. ***oschtenica***	WAbe
- subsp. ***tergestina***	ITim
villosa	LHop
'Violette'	GCrs GEdr LRHS NHol
waltonii	ECho EWes
wellsii	see *G.* × *macaulayi* 'Wells's Variety'
wutaiensis	see *G. macrophylla* var. *fetissowii*

Geranium ✿ (*Geraniaceae*)

from Bambashata Altai Mountains	NCot
from Pamirs, Tadzhikistan	WPnP
aconitifolium misapplied	see *G. palmatum*
aconitifolium L'Hér.	see *G. rivulare*
'Alan Mayes'	CElw CMac CSev EBee EBla ECtt EPPr LRHS MWea NGdn SRGP
'Alan's Blue' new	EBee
albanum	CElw EBee EPPr GAbr LLWP MMuc MNrw NWsh SDix SRGP WMoo
albiflorum	EPPr WMoo WPnP
anemonifolium	see *G. palmatum*
'Ann Folkard' ♀H4	Widely available
'Ann Folkard' × ***psilostemon***	LSRN
'Anne Thomson' ♀H4	Widely available
× ***antipodeum*** 'Chocolate Candy' PBR	EPfP LRHS MGos
§ - Crûg strain	CMoH EHrv NGdn NWCA
- 'Elizabeth Wood'	SMrm
- (*G. sessiliflorum* subsp. *novae-zelandiae* 'Nigricans' × *G. traversii* var. *elegans*)	SRms
- 'Kahlua'	EHrv EPfP
- 'Pink Spice' PBR	EBla ECtt LBuc LRHS MGos
- 'Sea Spray'	CMHG ECtt GCra MCot NBro WMnd
- 'Stanhoe'	ECtt SRot WBrk
antrorsum	ECou
aristatum	CDes EBee EBla EPPr EWes GCal GGar MNFA MNrw MRav NBir NCot SBch SRGP STes WCru WMoo WPnP WPtf
- NS 649	NWCA
armenum	see *G. psilostemon*
'Arnoldshof'	EPPr
asphodeloides	CBre CElw CHid IFro LLWP MBNS MNrw MWhi NBid NBir NCot SPav SRGP WBrk WFar WMnd WMoo WPnP WTin
- subsp. ***asphodeloides*** 'Prince Regent'	EBee WCra WPnP
- - white-flowered	CSpr EBla SRGP STes WCra WFar WMoo
- 'Starlight'	CMoH NBid
atlanticum Hook. f.	see *G. malviflorum*
'Aussie Gem'	EBee WWEG
'Baby Blue'	see *G. himalayense* 'Baby Blue'
'Benjamin Browne'	CSev
'Bertie Crûg'	CFox EBee EBla ECtt EHrv GQue LAst LLHF NBir NMoo SBfd SPoG SRms SRot SWat SWvt WCru WFar
biuncinatum	IFro
'Blue Cloud' ♀H4	Widely available
'Blue Pearl'	EBee EPPr MNFA NBir NSti SRGP SVil WCra WMoo WPnP
§ Blue Sunrise = 'Blogold' PBR ♀H4	Widely available
'Bob's Blunder'	CMHG CSam CSpe CWit EBee EBla ECtt LRHS LSRN MBNS MNrw NBPC NLar SMrm SPoG SRGP SWvt WCot WFar WHoo
bohemicum	EBla NCot SRGP WHer
- 'Orchid Blue'	EPfP SWvt WFar
'Brookside' ♀H4	Widely available
'Buckland Beauty'	CDes CElw CPLG SBch
'Buxton's Blue'	see *G. wallichianum* 'Buxton's Variety'
caeruleatum	EBee EBla EPPr GCal
caespitosum new	LLHF
caffrum	CPla SRGP WOut
canariense	see *G. reuteri*
candicans misapplied	see *G. lambertii*
§ × ***cantabrigiense***	CMac CSBt ECtt EShb LRHS MHer MNrw NBid NBir NBro NPer NSti SGar SRms WBrk WCru WFar WMoo
- 'Berggarten'	CDes CElw EBee EPPr GBin SBch SRGP WPtf
- 'Biokovo'	Widely available
- 'Cambridge'	Widely available
- 'Harz'	EPPr NCot
- 'Karmina'	CElw EBee EBla EPPr EPfP EPla GKir LRHS MNFA MWhi SWat WBrk WCom WHoo WMoo WPnP WWEG
- 'Rosalina'	EPPr NCot
- 'Show Time'	EBla
- 'St Ola'	Widely available
- 'Vorjura'	EPPr NCot
- 'Westray' PBR	CHVG CHid COIW EBee EPPr EShb GAbr GQue LAst LRHS LSou MCCP MMuc NCot NGdn SBfd SEND SMrm SPoG SRkn SRms STes SVil SWvt WBrk WCra
'Chantilly'	EBee EBla ECGP ECtt EPPr MAvo MNFA MNrw MWea NBir NCGa SBch WCra WCru WMoo WPnP WPtf
christensenianum B&SWJ 8022	WCru
cinereum	EBla ECho
- 'Album'	GKir NChi
- 'Apple Blossom'	see *G.* × *lindavicum* 'Apple Blossom'
- 'Ballerina'	see *G.* (Cinereum Group) 'Ballerina'
- 'Elizabeth'	ECtt LPio LSRN

- 'Hidgate's Emily' EBla
- 'Sateene'PBR EBee EBla EPPr NCGa NMoo NSti SPoG SRot WCra
- 'Souvenir de René Macé' EPPr LBuc
- subsp. ***subcaulescens*** var. ***ponticum*** see *G. ponticum*
(Cinereum Group) 'Alice'PBR EBee EBla EPPr IPot LLHF LSRN MBNS NCGa NDov NGdn NHar NLar NSti WCra
§ - 'Ballerina' ♀H4 Widely available
- 'Carol' CDes EAEE EBee EBla EPPr EWes GKir LRHS LSRN LSou MBNS MBri NDov NHar NLar NSti SRkn SWvt WCra WFar
I - 'Heather' EBla EPPr
- 'Lambrook Helen' CPLG EBla
- 'Laurence Flatman' Widely available
- 'Lizabeth'PBR EPPr LSou NCGa NHar WCra
- 'Prima Ballerina' NLar
- 'Purple Pillow' Widely available
- René Macé = 'Progera' LRHS MGos SRkn
- Rothbury Gem = 'Gerfos'PBR ♀H4 CMac CWGN EBee EBla EBrs EKen EPPr LLHF LRHS MWea NChi NSti SKHP SUsu SWvt
- 'Signal' EBee EBla GEdr NHar NLar SBfd
'Claridge Druce' see *G.* × *oxonianum* 'Claridge Druce'
clarkei 'Kashmir Pink' Widely available
§ - 'Kashmir White' ♀H4 Widely available
- 'Mount Stewart' CPLG EBee GCal WCru WPGP
- (Purple-flowered Group) 'Gulmarg' NCot
- - 'Kashmir Purple' Widely available
clarum B&SWJ 10246 **new** WCru
collinum EPPr MNrw NBir NCot SRGP
'Colour Carousel' **new** IPot
'Coombland White' CDes CFir CPLG CSam EBee EBla ECtt EPPr LAst LPio LSou MAvo MCot MNFA MNrw NBPC NGdn NLar NSti NWsh SBfd SKHP SRGP SVil WCot WHoo WMoo
'Criss Canning' EPPr
Crûg strain see *G.* × *antipodeum* Crûg strain
'Cyril's Blue' **new** EBee
'Cyril's Fancy' EBee EBla EPPr LPio MAvo WPtf
dahuricum WCru
dalmaticum ♀H4 Widely available
- 'Album' CYeo EBee EBla ECho ECtt ELan EPPr EPot LRHS MRav MTho NRya SRGP SRms SWat WAbe WCom WCru WFar
- 'Bressingham Pink' EPPr WPnP
- 'Bridal Bouquet' EBee LLHF NChi NMen NSla WAbe WHil
- 'Croftlea' GKir
- 'Stades Hellrosa' EPPr NCot
dalmaticum × ***macrorrhizum*** see *G.* × *cantabrigiense*
delavayi misapplied see *G. sinense*
'Devon Pride' **new** EBee
'Dilys' ♀H4 CElw CPrp EBee EBla ELan EPPr LPio MAvo MCot MLHP MNrw NBir NChi NGdn NLar SBfd SRGP SUsu WCru WFar WHal WMoo WPnP
dissectum CHll
'Distant Hills' CDes EBee EBla EPPr MAvo SRGP SUsu WPtf
'Diva' CSam EBee EBla EPPr EPfP LLHF MAvo SRGP WCru WPnP
'Double Jewel' (d) see *G. pratense* 'Double Jewel'
'Dragon Heart' EBee ECtt EPPr LSRN MAsh MBri NLar NSti SKHP SPoG WCra
'Dusky Crûg' CChe CDes CElw CLAP CSBt CSam EAEE EBee ECtt EHoe EHrv EPPr EPfP EShb ETod LAst LRHS MCot MNrw MSCN NBPC NEgg SBfd SPoG SWvt WCot WCru WFar WHoo WMnd
'Dusky Gem' SUsu
'Dusky Rose' CBod CLAP CMoH CPrp CSpe EBee ELan EPfP LAst MGos SRGP SRot WFar
'Eleanor Fisher' SUsu
'Elizabeth Ross' LPio MAvo WHoo
'Elke' Widely available
'Ella' CWGN
'Elworthy Dusky' CElw
'Elworthy Eyecatcher' CDes CElw EPPr MAvo SBch SRGP SUsu WPGP
'Elworthy Tiger' CElw
'Emily' SRGP
endressii ♀H4 CBre CElw CSev EBee EBla ECha ECho EHrv EPfP GAbr GKir GLog GMaP MBNS MCot MHer MMuc NBro NPer SEND SGar SPlb SRGP SRms SWvt WFar WMoo WWEG
- 'Album' see *G.* 'Mary Mottram'
- 'Castle Drogo' ♀H4 EBee EBla EPPr SRGP
- 'Prestbury White' see *G.* × *oxonianum* 'Prestbury Blush'
- 'Rose' MAvo WPer
- 'Wargrave Pink' see *G.* × *oxonianum* 'Wargrave Pink'
- white-flowered WPtf
erianthum GMaP IMou MLHP NBre NCGa NLar SRGP STes WCot WCru WMoo WPnP
- 'Axeltree' **new** SUsu
- 'Cally Pearl' **new** GCal
- 'Calm Sea' EBla SUsu WCru WMoo WPnP
- f. ***leucanthum*** 'Undine' SUsu WCot
- 'Neptune' MNFA SUsu WCru WPnP WWEG
eriostemon Fischer see *G. platyanthum*
'Eva' EBee WPnP
'Expression'PBR see *G.* 'Tanya Rendall'
'Farncombe Cerise Star' CElw EBee EPPr GCal NCot
§ ***farreri*** CPLG EBla ECho LHop LLHF LRHS NBir WEas
'Foundling' **new** NDov
fremontii EWld
goldmannii SKHP
gracile EBee GMaP LSou MNrw NBir NBre SRGP WBrk WMoo WPnP
- 'Blanche' CElw EBee EPPr SMrs
- 'Blush' CElw EBee EPPr LPla MNFA
grandiflorum see *G. himalayense*
'Grasmere' ECtt
guatemalense LAst
'Gwen Thompson' WOut
gymnocaulon EBee EBla EBrs EPPr LRHS MAvo NLar SRGP WCru
gymnocaulon × ***platypetalum*** EBee NCot
'Harmony' EBee EPPr
harveyi CDes CElw CMea EBla EPPr EWes EWld GCal NChi SPhx SRGP WCru WKif WPGP WPat WSpi
hayatanum WPnP
- B&SWJ 164 WCru WMoo
§ ***himalayense*** Widely available
- CC 1957 from Tibetan border EPPr
- from Tibetan border CPLG
- ***alpinum*** see *G. himalayense* 'Gravetye'

§	- 'Baby Blue'	CElw EBee EBla EBrs EPPr GCal GCra IFro MAvo MNFA MNrw NCot NGdn NLar NSti SBch SRGP SUsu WBrk WCAu WCra WCru WMoo WPnP WPtf
	- 'Birch Double'	see *G. himalayense* 'Plenum'
	- 'Derrick Cook'	CDes CElw EBee EPPr MAvo MNFA MWhi NCot SUsu WBrk WCra WPtf
	- 'Devil's Blue'	EBee EPPr SRGP WPtf
§	- 'Gravetye' 🏆^{H4}	Widely available
	- 'Irish Blue'	CElw EBee EBla ECtt EPPr GCal GCra MNFA NCot NLar NSti SRGP WCra WCru WMoo WPnP WPtf WTin
	- ***meeboldii***	see *G. himalayense*
	- 'Pale Irish Blue'	EBee GCal
§	- 'Plenum' (d)	Widely available
	hispidissimum	CFee
	ibericum misapplied	see *G.* × *magnificum*
	ibericum Cav.	CSBt CTri EBla NBre NLar SPav SRGP STes WFar
	- 'Blue Springs'	ECtt
	- subsp. ***ibericum***	CMac EBee EPPr
	- subsp. ***jubatum***	EBla EPPr MNFA MNrw NCot SRms WCru WPnP
	- - 'White Zigana'	CPrp EBee ECtt EPPr GCal MWea SBfd WCra WPnP
	- subsp. ***jubatum*** × ***renardii***	SWvt
	- var. ***platypetalum*** misapplied	see *G.* × *magnificum*
	- var. ***platypetalum*** Boissier	see *G. platypetalum* Fisch. & C.A. Mey.
§	- 'Ushguli Grijs'	EBee EBla NChi NLar WPnP
	ibericum × ***libani***	CDes
	incanum	CAbP CHll CMHG EBee EShb EWes MNrw NBir SGar SMrm SRGP WNew
	- white-flowered	SRGP
	'Ivan' 🏆^{H4}	CElw CEnt CLAP CMoH EBee EBla EBrs ECtt EPPr GMac LPio LRHS MNFA NChi NCob NCot NGdn NLar SRGP WCra WCru WMoo WPnP
	'Jean Armour'	CDes EBee ECtt EPPr GGar LRHS MWea NGdn SPoG SRGP WPGP
	'Johnson's Blue' 🏆^{H4}	Widely available
	'Jolly Bee'^{PBR} 🏆^{H4}	Widely available
	'Joy'	CAby EBee EBla ECtt EPPr LPio LSqH MAvo MCot MMuc MNFA MNrw MRav NBPC NBir NCGa NCot NEgg NLar NSti SBfd SPhx SRGP STes WCot WCra WMoo WPnP
§	'Kanahitobanawa'	CDes EBee
	'Karen Wouters' **new**	EBee
	'Kashmir Blue'	CPLG EBee ECtt EPPr EPfP GMaP LRHS MAvo NCot NGdn NLar NPnk SBch SMrs SWat WFar WMoo WPnP WPtf WWEG
	'Kashmir Green'	EBee ECtt EPPr GBin MNFA MWea WMoo WPnP
	'Kashmir Light Blue' **new**	EBee
§	'Kate'	EBla
	'Kate Folkard'	see *G.* 'Kate'
§	'Khan'	EBee EBla EPPr IFro IPot MAvo NCot SDys SMHy SRGP SUsu WBrk WCon WCru
	'Kirsty'	EBee EPPr
	kishtvariense	EBee EBla EPPr GCal MNrw MRav NCot NSti WCru
	koraiense	CDes CPLG EBla NBre WMoo
	- B&SWJ 797	WCru
	- B&SWJ 878	EBee WCru
	koreanum ambig.	CPLG CPla EBee EBla WFar WMoo
	- B&SWJ 602	WCru
§	***kotschyi*** var. ***charlesii***	EBla EPPr
	krameri	CPLG EBla IMou
	- B&SWJ 1142	EBla WCru
§	***lambertii***	CSpr EBla EWes GCal NBir
	- 'Swansdown'	EBla GMac WCru WPtf WSHC
I	***libani***	EBee ELon EPPr GKir LLWP MCot NBid NChi NCot NSti WBrk WCot WCra WCru WEas WPnP WTin
	- RCB RL B-2	WCot
	libani × ***peloponnesiacum***	CDes EBee
	'Libretto'	WCru
§	× ***lindavicum*** 'Apple Blossom'	CMea CMoH EBla EBrs EPPr LRHS NMen WAbe WSpi
	- 'Lissadell'	EPot
	linearilobum subsp. ***transversale***	EPPr NCot SRot WCru WPnP
I	- - 'Laciniatum'	NCot WWst
	- - 'Rose Foundling'	WWst
§	'Little David'	EBee NLar SUsu
	'Little Devil'	see *G.* 'Little David'
	'Little Gem'	CMea EBla EBrs EPPr LRHS NChi NLar WAbe WFar WMoo WPnP
	lucidum	WPtf WSFF
	'Luscious Linda'^{PBR}	EBee NGdn NLar WFar WPnP
	'Lydia'	NCot SRGP
§	***macrorrhizum***	CArn CFee CSBt EBee ECrN ELon EPfP GKir IFro LEdu MBNS MCot MRav MWat MWhi NBro NCGa NHol NPnk SRms SWat WBrE WFar WGor WWEG
	- AL & JS 90179YU	CHid EPPr
	- 'Album' 🏆^{H4}	Widely available
	- 'Bevan's Variety' 🏆^{H4}	Widely available
	- 'Bulgaria'	EPPr LAst
	- 'Cham-ce'	EPPr WBrk
	- 'Czakor'	Widely available
I	- 'De Bilt'	EBee EWes
	- 'Freundorf'	EBee EPPr EWes GCal WCra
	- 'Ingwersen's Variety' 🏆^{H4}	Widely available
	- 'Lohfelden'	CDes EBee EPPr EWes GCal SRGP WCru WPGP
	- 'Mount Olympus'	see *G. macrorrhizum* 'White-Ness'
	- 'Mytikas' 🏆^{H4}	EBee EPPr NCot WPtf
	- 'Pindus'	CBod CPrp CYeo EAEE EBee EBla ECGP EPPr GAbr LRHS MBNS NBre NCot NSti SRGP WCru WFar WPtf
	- 'Prionia'	EPPr NCot
	- 'Purpurrot'	WWEG
	- 'Ridsko'	CFee EPPr GCal LPla NBro NCot SRGP WCru
	- ***roseum***	see *G. macrorrhizum*
	- 'Rotblut'	EPPr SRGP
	- 'Sandwijck'	EPPr NCot
	- 'Snow Sprite'	CBod CEnt CMea CPla CSpr EPPr EPyc MCCP NCot STes WHrl
	- 'Spessart'	CBar EBee EBla ELan ELon EPPr EPfP GMaP LAst LBMP LRHS MBri MGos NLar SBfd SPer WBVN WBrk WCra WFar WPnP WRHF WWEG
	- 'Variegatum' (v)	EBee EBla EHrv ELan GMaP MHer MNFA NBPC NBir SPer SRGP SRms WCom WCot WFar WHil WMnd WSHC WWEG WWFP
	- 'Velebit'	NCot SRGP WCru
§	- 'White-Ness' 🏆^{H4}	Widely available
	- 'Witoscha'	EBee LRHS
	macrostylum	WBVN WCot WCru WPer
	- MP 8103D	EBee

I	- 'Caeruleum' **new**	WPtf
	- 'Leonidas'	EBee EPPr NCot WCot WPnP
	- 'Marocco'	NCot
	- 'Talish'	EPPr NCot
	- 'Uln Oag Triag'	EPPr
	maculatum	CElw CSev EPfP EWTr LLWP LRHS MAvo MNrw MRav NSti NWCA SRGP SWat WCra WCru WHal WPnP
	- from Kath Dryden	EBee EPPr
	- f. ***albiflorum***	CElw CLAP EBee EBla EPPr EWTr MNFA MNrw MWhi MWte NBid NChi NLar NSti SRGP STes WBrk WCru WMoo WPnP
	- 'Beth Chatto'	Widely available
	- 'Elizabeth Ann'[PBR] ♀[H4]	Widely available
	- 'Espresso'	Widely available
	- 'Shameface'	EBee EPPr SBch SDys SGar WMoo
	- 'Silver Buttons'	CDes EBee
	- 'Smoky Mountain'	EBee EPPr
	- 'Spring Purple'	CElw EBee EPPr MAvo NCot NLar
	- 'Sweetwater'	EPPr
	- 'Vickie Lynn'	CLAP EBee EPPr NChi
	maderense ♀[H2]	Widely available
	- 'Guernsey White'	CFir GCal NCot SPhx
	- white-flowered	CSpe WCot
	maderense × ***palmatum***	WCru
§	× ***magnificum*** ♀[H4]	Widely available
	- 'Blue Blood'	CElw CLAP CSev CWGN EBee ECtt EKen EPPr IPot LSou MCot MTis MWea NBPC NCob NCot NDov NGdn NPnk NSti SBfd SMrm SRGP WClo WCot WCra WFar
	- 'Hylander'	EBee EPPr
	- 'Peter Yeo'	EPPr MNFA SRGP WPtf
	- 'Rosemoor'	CElw CHid EBee EBla EHrv ELan EPPr EPfP GCal IKil LHop SBfd WCot WCra WMnd WPtf
	- 'Vital'	EBee
	magniflorum	EWes MRav NBid NGdn
	'Maître Hugo'	EBee
§	***malviflorum***	CMHG ECha ELan EPPr LLWP MNFA MNrw NCot SBch WAul WCom WCot WCru WFar WPnP
	- from Spain	EWes
	- pink-flowered	EBee EPPr
§	'Mary Mottram'	CElw EPPr LPio NBir WCot WEas WPnP
	'Mavis Simpson' ♀[H4]	Widely available
	maximowiczii	CElw SBch WPtf
	'Melinda'	EBee EPPr MBri NMir SBfd WCra
	'Mellow Yellow' **new**	SUsu
	'Memories'[PBR]	CPar EBee ECtt EPPr LRHS LSRN MBNS NCGa NDov NSti WFar
	'Menna Bach'	MAvo
	'Meryl Anne'	SRGP WPtf
	microphyllum	see *G. potentilloides*
	molle	NBir WSFF
	- white-flowered	NBir
	× ***monacense***	CPrp EBee EBla ELan EPla IFoB LEdu LRHS MBNS SBfd SRGP SWat WBrk WCru WMoo WPnP WPtf
	- var. ***anglicum***	CFir EBla ECtt EPPr GMaP LRHS MRav MTis MWhi WMoo WPnP
	- 'Anne Stevens'	EBee NCot WPtf
	- 'Claudine Dupont'	CElw CMoH EBee EPPr IFro MAvo MNFA NCot WCot WCra WPtf
	- dark-flowered	WMoo WPtf
	- var. ***monacense***	EBla NEgg WFar
	- - 'Breckland Fever'	EBee EPPr MAvo NChi SRGP
§	- - 'Muldoon'	EBee EBla EPPr LRHS MLLN MTis NBir SRGP STes WFar WMoo WPnP

	'Monita Charm'	CMoH
	moupinense	NCot
	'Mourning Widow'	see *G. phaeum* 'Lady in Mourning'
	'Mrs Jean Moss'	EBee EPPr EWes
	napuligerum misapplied	see *G. farreri*
	'Natalie'	EBee EBla EBrs EPPr LRHS LSRN MAvo NChi SUsu
	nepalense	SRGP SRms
	'Nicola'	CElw EBee EBla EPPr IFro MAvo MNFA NCob NHaw NLar SBch SRGP
	'Nimbus' ♀[H4]	Widely available
	nodosum	Widely available
	- dark-flowered	see *G. nodosum* 'Swish Purple'
	- 'Darkleaf' **new**	MAvo
	- 'Hexham Big Eyes'	EBee
	- 'Hexham Freckles' **new**	EBee
	- 'Julie's Velvet'	CDes MAvo SMrs WBor WHoo WPGP WTin
	- pale-flowered	see *G. nodosum* 'Svelte Lilac'
	- 'Pascal'	EPPr
	- 'Saucy Charlie'	SBch
	- 'Silverwood'	CElw EBee EPPr MAvo MNFA SBch SUsu
	- 'Simon'	EBee SRGP
§	- 'Svelte Lilac'	CElw EAEE EBee EBla EPPr EPfP LRHS MNFA NHol SRGP SWat WCot WCra WCru WFar WMoo WPnP
§	- 'Swish Purple'	CElw EBee EBla EPPr MAvo MNFA NLar SRGP WCra WCru WFar WMoo WPGP WPnP
	- 'Whiteleaf'	CElw CMea EBee EBla EPPr MAvo MNFA NChi SBch SMrs SRGP WCom WCru WFar WHal WMoo WPnP
	- 'Whiteleaf' seedling	CElw EBla
	'Nora Bremner'	NChi SUsu
	'Nunnykirk Pink'	EWes SUsu
	'Nunwood Purple'	EBee EPPr MAvo WPtf
	'Old Rose'	GKir SRGP WCru WPnP
	oreganum	CMoH
§	***orientalitibeticum***	Widely available
	'Orion' ♀[H4]	Widely available
	'Orkney Blue'	EPPr WCru WPnP
	'Orkney Cherry'	CWGN EBee EPPr EPfP LAst LLHF LRHS MWea NLar NSti SHar SPoG SRkn WMoo
	'Orkney Dawn'	NHaw WCru WPnP
	'Orkney Pink'	CMac EBee EBla ECtt EPPr EPfP GKir LAst LSRN MLHP MMuc NHol NSti NWCA SBfd SPer SPoG SRGP SRkn SWat WCom WFar WHoo
	× ***oxonianum***	NCot WMoo
	- 'A.T. Johnson' ♀[H4]	CBcs EBee EBla ECtt ELan EPfP GKir LAst LBMP LRHS MRav MWat MWhi NBir NCot NEgg NGdn NSti SBfd SPer SRGP SRms SWat WBrk WCru WMnd WMoo WWEG
	- 'Andy's Star'	NCot
	- 'Ankum's White'	NDov
	- 'Anmore'	EPPr SRGP
	- 'Beholder's Eye' ♀[H4]	CHid CPrp EBee EBla EPPr GAbr GKir NBre SBch SRGP WPnP WPtf WWEG
	- 'Breckland Sunset'	EPPr MAvo SBch SRGP WPnP
	- 'Bregover Pearl'	CBre CElw EBee EBla EPPr SRGP WMoo
	- 'Bressingham's Delight'	EBla ECtt LRHS SRGP
	- 'Buttercup'	EBee EPPr SRGP
I	- 'Cally Seedling'	EBee EBla EWes GCal
	- 'Chocolate Strawberry'	EWes

§	- 'Claridge Druce'	Widely available
	- 'Coronet'	CFir GCal SRGP WMoo
	- 'David Rowlinson'	EPPr
	- 'Diane's Treasure'	NCot NHaw
	- 'Dirk Gunst'	CElw
	- 'Elsbeth Blush'	EBla
	- 'Elworthy Misty'	CElw EBla EPPr NCot SBch SRGP
	- 'Frank Lawley'	CElw EBee EBla LLWP NBid SBch SRGP WBrk WMoo
§	- 'Fran's Star' (d)	EBee EBla SRGP WBrk WCru
	- 'Frilly Gilly'	EBee EPPr
	- 'Hexham Pink'	EPPr EWes NChi SBch SRGP
	- 'Hollywood'	EBee EBla ELan EPPr EPfP NCot NLar NPer SRGP SRms WBrk WCra WFar WMoo WPnP WPtf WWEG
	- 'Julie Brennan'	CHVG GAbr SMrs
	- 'Kate Moss'	EBee EBla EPPr EWes NSti SRGP WCra
	- 'Katherine Adele'	CBod EBee EBla ECtt EPPr EPfP EWes LPla LSou MAsh MSpe MWea NCGa NCot NLar NSti SBfd SRGP SRms WCra WFar
§	- 'Kingston'	CElw EBee EPPr
	- 'Klaus Schult'	EPPr LPio
	- 'Königshof'	EPPr EWes NLar
	- 'Kurt's Variegated'	see *G.* × *oxonianum* 'Spring Fling'
	- 'Lace Time'	CBod CBre CElw CFir CSev EBee EBla ECtt EPPr LBMP LRHS LSRN MBri MSpe NCot NEgg NGdn NHol SBch SBfd SPer SRGP SRms WCAu WMnd WMoo WPnP
	- 'Lady Moore'	EBee EBla EPla MNrw NBro NCot SRGP WHoo WMoo WPnP
	- 'Lambrook Gillian'	EBee EPPr SBch SRGP WBrk WPnP WPtf
	- 'Lasting Impression'	EBee EPPr SRGP
	- 'Laura Skelton'	CElw NCot NHaw
	- 'Little John'	EWes
	- 'Maid Marion'	EWes
	- 'Miriam Rundle'	CElw EPPr LRHS NCot SRGP WCru WMoo WPnP WWEG
	- 'Moorland Jenny'	CElw WMoo
	- 'Moorland Star'	WMoo
	- 'Music from Big Pink'	EWes
	- 'Pale Walter's Gift'	GCal
	- 'Pat Smallacombe'	EBla NCot WMoo
	- 'Patricia Josephine'	WCAu
	- 'Pearl Boland'	EBee EPPr SRGP
	- 'Phantom'	EBee EPPr
	- 'Phoebe Noble'	CBre CElw EBla EPPr MNrw NCob NCot NLar SMad SRGP WCra WMoo WPnP WPtf
	- 'Phoebe's Blush'	EBee EBla EPPr GCal SRGP
	- 'Pink Cluster'	CLAP
	- 'Pink Lace'	LSou
§	- 'Prestbury Blush'	CBre CElw EPPr SRGP
	- 'Prestbury White'	see *G.* × *oxonianum* 'Prestbury Blush'
	- 'Raspberry Ice'	EBee EBla EWes
	- 'Rebecca Moss'	CPrp EBee EBla ECtt EPPr GAbr GCra GMac LRHS NCot NSti SBch SRGP WCra WCru WFar WPnP WPtf WWEG
	- 'Robin's Ginger Nut'	EBee EWes
	- 'Rodbylund'	EBee
	- 'Rose Clair'	CFir CTca EBee EBla EPfP GKir LRHS MLLN MWhi NBir NLar SBfd SGar SRGP WCru WEas WMnd WMoo WWEG
	- 'Rosemary'	SBch
	- 'Rosemary Verey'	SBch
	- 'Rosenlicht'	EBee EBla ECGP EPPr LRHS MNFA MRav NGdn NLar SRGP WCAu WCra WCru WMnd WMoo WPnP WPrP WPtf
	- 'Rosewood'	SRos
	- 'Sandy' **new**	EWes
§	- 'Spring Fling' (v)	EBee EBla ECtt EHrv EPPr EWes LPla NGdn NSti SRGP WFar WSpi
	- 'Stillingfleet Keira'	EBee NSti SRGP
	- 'Summer Surprise'	EBee EPPr EWes NCob NLar WCru WPnP
	- 'Susan'	EBee EBla EPPr EWes
	- 'Susie White'	CElw EPPr MAvo SRGP WCru
§	- f. ***thurstonianum***	Widely available
	- - 'Armitageae'	EPPr NCot SRGP
	- - 'Breckland Brownie'	CElw EBee EBla EPPr EWes MAvo SRGP
	- - 'Crûg Star'	WCru
	- - 'David McClintock'	SBch SRGP WFar WMoo
	- - 'Peter Hale'	CMea
	- - 'Red Sputnik'	EBee EPPr SRGP
	- - 'Sherwood'	EBee EBla ECtt EPPr GCal GQue MLLN MSpe MTho NBro NCob NEgg NSti NVic SApp SBch SGar SMrm SRGP WCAu WFar WMoo WPnP WPtf
	- - 'Southcombe Double' (d)	CElw CPla CSev EBla ECtt EHrv EPPr EPfP GCra LAst LRHS MBri MLLN NBPC SMrm SPer SRGP SRms WBrk WCru WFar WMoo WWEG
§	- - 'Southcombe Star'	EBee EBla EPPr GAbr GCal LRHS MTis NBro NGdn SRGP WCru WFar WMoo WPer WPnP
	- - 'Sue Cox'	EPPr NCot NLar
	- 'Trevor's White'	CLAP EBla EPPr EWTr LLWP MNFA SBch SRGP WCru
	- 'Wageningen' Υ^{H4}	CBre EBee EPPr GCal GMac LPla LRHS MBri MMuc MNFA NGdn SBfd SEND SMrm SRGP SRms WCot WCra WCru WHer WMoo WPtf
	- 'Walter's Gift'	EBee EBla ECtt EPPr EPla EShb LBMP LLWP LRHS MAvo MLLN MRav MTho MTis MWhi NBir NBro NCob NHol NPer NSti SGar WBrk WClo WCru WFar WHoo WMoo WPnP
§	- 'Wargrave Pink' Υ^{H4}	Widely available
	- 'Waystrode'	EBla EPPr SRGP
	- 'Westacre White'	EWes
	- 'Whitehaven'	SRGP
	- 'Whiter Shade of Pale' **new**	EPPr
	- 'Winscombe'	EBee EPfP GCal LLWP MRav NCob SRGP WFar WMnd WMoo WWEG
	× ***oxonianum*** × ***sessiliflorum*** subsp. ***novae-zelandiae*** 'Nigricans'	EHrv
§	***palmatum*** Υ^{H3}	Widely available
	palustre	CElw EBee EBla EPPr MNFA MNrw NHol SRGP WFar WMoo
	papuanum	WCru
	Patricia = 'Brempat' Υ^{H4}	Widely available
	peloponnesiacum	EAEE EBee EPPr EWes LRHS MAvo MNFA SBch WFar WMoo WPtf
	- NS 660	CElw
	'Perfect Storm'	CWGN EBee ECtt EPPr LLHF LSou MBri MWea NLar WCra
	phaeum	Widely available
	- 'Album'	Widely available
	- 'Alec's Pink'	EBla EPPr LLWP SHar WOut WPtf
	- 'All Saints'	EBee EPPr LEdu SRGP
	- 'Angelina'	NCot

	- 'Aureum'	see *G. phaeum* 'Golden Spring'
	- 'Blauwvoet'	EBee EPPr MAvo NCot
	- 'Blue Shadow'	CDes CElw EBee EBla EPPr LLWP MAvo NCot SRGP WPtf
	- 'Caborn Lilac'	LLWP
	- 'Calligrapher'	CElw EBla EPPr LLHF LPio MAvo NChi NCot SBch SMrs SRGP SUsu WMoo WPtf
	- 'Chocolate Chip'	EBla
	- 'Conny Broe' (v)	CLAP EBee NCot
	- 'Countess of Grey'	SMrs
	- 'David Bromley'	EBla NCot WCru WPtf
	- 'David Martin'	NCot
	- 'Enid'	EPPr
	- 'George Stone'	EBee EBla EPPr LLHF
	- 'Golden Samobor'	CElw EBla EPPr NCot
§	- 'Golden Spring'	CElw EBee EBla EPPr MAvo NCot SRGP
	- 'Hannah Perry'	CMoH EBla EPPr LLWP MTis WPtf
	- 'Hector's Lavender'	EBee SRGP
	- var. ***hungaricum***	EBee EPPr LLWP SRGP WPtf
	- 'James Haunch'	EBla EPPr
	- 'Klepper'	EBee EPPr GBin NCot
	- 'Lady in Black'	NCot
§	- 'Lady in Mourning'	CMoH CPLG EPPr EShb GCal GKir MCot MNFA NChi NCob NCot SRGP SRms SWat WCru WMoo
	- 'Lavender Pinwheel' **new**	WHil
	- 'Lily Lovell'	Widely available
	- 'Lisa'	EBee EPPr MNrw NCot SMHy
	- 'Little Boy'	EBee EBla EPPr NGdn
	- var. ***lividum***	CBgR CBre CFee CPrp GMaP LLWP LRHS MAvo MRav NCot NHol SRGP SRms STes WFar WPnP
	- - 'Joan Baker'	CBgR CBre CSam EBee EPPr LPla MAvo MNFA NChi NCot NGdn NSti SRGP WCra WCru WFar WMoo WPnP WPtf WWEG
	- - 'Majus'	CElw EBee ECtt EPPr EPfP EPyc LLWP LPla LRHS WFar WMoo
	- 'Maggie's Delight' (v)	SRGP
	- 'Marchant's Ghost'	MAvo NGdn SMHy
	- 'Margaret Hunt'	NLar
	- 'Margaret Wilson' (v)	Widely available
	- 'Mierhausen'	CElw EBee EBla EPPr EShb MAvo NCot WPtf
	- 'Moorland Dylan'	EBla EPPr WMoo WOut
	- 'Moortown Pink'	NCot
	- 'Mourning Widow'	see *G. phaeum* 'Lady in Mourning'
	- 'Mrs Charles Perrin'	CBgR CElw CSpr EBee EBla EPPr MAvo STes WPtf
	- 'Mrs Withey Price'	EPPr
	- 'Night Time'	EBee EPPr SBch WPtf
	- 'Nightshade'	EBla
	- 'Our Pat' ♀H4	EBee EPPr NChi NCot WPtf
	- var. ***phaeum***	MMuc SBch SEND SGar WOut
	- - 'Langthorns Blue'	CElw CMoH CSev EBee EBrs ELan EPPr EWes GKir LEdu LRHS MAvo MNrw NBre NCot SRGP SWvt WPtf
	- - 'Samobor'	Widely available
I	- 'Ploeger de Bilt'	EPPr WPtf
	- purple-flowered	NPnk
	- 'Rachel's Rhapsody'	CElw EBee EBla EPPr MAvo NCot WPtf
	- 'Raven'	EBee EPPr NCot SUsu WHlf WPtf
	- red-flowered	MRav
	- 'Rise Top Lilac'	EBee NCot WPGP WPtf
	- 'Rose'	LRHS SEND
	- 'Rose Air'	EBee EPPr MAvo NCot SRGP WMoo WPnP WPtf
	- 'Rose Madder'	CBgR CElw CFir EBee EBla EPPr EPyc GCal LEdu LLWP LPio LPla MNrw NChi NCot NMRc SBch SMrs SRGP SUsu WCru WMoo WPnP
	- 'Saturn'	EPPr
	- 'Séricourt'	EBee WCot WCra
	- 'Slatina'	EBla EPPr WPtf
	- 'Small Grey'	EBla EPPr
	- 'Springtime' PBR	CBod CElw EBee EPPr EPfP LLHF MBNS NChi NCot NGdn NSti WCra
	- 'Stillingfleet Ghost'	CBow EBee EBla EPPr GKir LEdu LRHS MNrw NChi NCot NSti
	- 'Taff's Jester' (v)	CElw EBee EWes LPla NHol SApp SRGP WCot WHil
§	- 'Variegatum' (v)	CBre CElw CMac EBee EHoe ELan EPPr EShb GKir GMaP IFro LBMP LRHS MCot MNrw MRav NBir NBro NCot NEgg SGSe SRGP WAbb WCru WFar WHer WMoo WSpi WTin
	- 'Walküre'	EBee EPPr EWes MAvo WPtf
	'Philippe Vapelle'	Widely available
	'Pink Carpet' **new**	SBfd
	'Pink Delight'	CElw EBla LPio MAvo MNrw
	'Pink Ghost'	CBow
	'Pink Penny'	EBee EPPr EPfP IPot MAvo MWea SRGP WCra WPnP
	'Pink Splash'	LSou WPtf
§	***platyanthum***	EPPr MNrw MWhi NBre SRGP WCru
	- var. ***reinii***	WCru
	- 'Russian Giant'	EPPr SGar
	platypetalum misapplied	see *G.* × *magnificum*
	platypetalum Franch.	see *G. sinense*
§	***platypetalum*** Fisch. & C.A. Mey.	EPPr LRHS NBid NBir NBre SRGP WCru
	- 'Genyell'	EBee
	- 'Georgia Blue'	WCru WFar WPtf
§	***pogonanthum***	GLog IFro NBir NChi
§	***ponticum***	NSti
§	***potentilloides***	GCal NBir SRGP WMoo
	pratense	Widely available
I	- 'Alboroseum'	WCot
	- 'Bittersweet'	EBee EBla EPPr
	- Black Beauty = 'Nodbeauty' PBR	CBcs CPLG CPar CSBt CSpe CWGN CWit EBee ECtt EPPr EPfP EWes LRHS LSou MGos MWea NCGa NPri SBfd SDnm SPer SRkn SRot SUsu WFar
	- 'Blue Lagoon'	EPPr EWll
*	- 'Blue Skies'	LSou
	- 'Cluden Sapphire'	CSev EBla EPPr GKir MWhi NBre NGdn NHol WCru
§	- 'Double Jewel'	CWGN EPfP IPot LLHF MAsh MBNS NMRc WCra WHlf
	- 'Else Lacey' (d)	EBee
	- 'Feebers Double' (d)	CFee
	- 'Flore Pleno'	see *G. pratense* 'Plenum Violaceum'
I	- 'Himalayanum'	NLar
	- 'Hocus Pocus'	EBee ECtt EHrv ELan EPfP LPio LRHS MAvo MBNS MBri MWea NBro NLar NMoo NSti SBfd SMrm
	- 'Ilja'	EBee
	- 'Janet's Special'	CBod CSev WHoo
	- 'Lichtenstein'	NCot
	- Midnight Reiter strain	CBcs CBct CHVG CHar CPLG CSev CSpe CWGN CWit EBee EPfP GGar GKir IFoB LRHS NBro NChi NGdn NLar NPnk SBfd SGSe SWat SWvt WCru WFar WPnP
	- 'Mrs Kendall Clark' ♀H4	Widely available
	- 'New Dimension'	CBcs EBee ELan EPPr EPfP LHop MWea NBre NSti
	- 'Okey Dokey'	EBee

- pale-flowered	WPnP
- 'Picotee'	EBee
- 'Plenum Album'	CAby CBod CBre CLAP CSev ECtt ELan EPPr EWes LLHF MAvo MNrw NBPC NCob NEgg NGdn NLar SPer WGwG WPtf WWEG
- 'Plenum Caeruleum' (d)	CHar CMHG ECtt EPPr GAbr GCra GMaP MRav NBid NEgg NGdn NHol NLar STes SWat WFar WPnP WSHC
§ - 'Plenum Violaceum' (d) ♀H4	Widely available
- var. ***pratense*** f. ***albiflorum***	CBot CElw CSam EPPr GCra GMaP IFro LRHS MNrw NBid NCot SBfd SPer WClo WCom WCot WCra WMnd WMoo WPtf
- - - 'Galactic'	EBee EPPr GKir MTis NBir NBre SPhx WCot WCra WCru WMoo WPnP
- - - 'Laura' (d) **new**	CSpr EPPr LRHS LSou MWea NSti SPoG
- - - 'Plenum Album' (d)	CDes EBee EPPr MTis NSti STes WCot WPnP
- - - 'Silver Queen'	CBre EBee EBla ECtt EPPr MLLN MNrw NBir NBre SRGP WFar WMoo WPGP WPtf
- 'Purple Heron'	CDes EBee EBla LSRN MCCP MNrw WFar
* - 'Purple-haze'	CPla CSpr CTca MCCP MCot NCob NLar STes WBVN WHrl WMoo WTou
- 'Rectum Album'	see *G. clarkei* 'Kashmir White'
§ - 'Rose Queen'	EBee EBla EPPr MNrw MRav NBir NHol NLar SRGP WCom WCru
- 'Roseum'	see *G. pratense* 'Rose Queen'
- 'Splish-splash'	see *G. pratense* 'Striatum'
- 'Stanton Mill'	NBid
- var. ***stewartianum***	MRav
- - 'Elizabeth Yeo'	EBee EBla ECtt EPPr MNFA MWea NCot NLar WCra WCru
- - 'Purple Silk'	EPPr
§ - 'Striatum'	Widely available
- 'Striatum' dwarf	WCru
- 'Striatum' pale-flowered	CBre
- variegated, white-flowered (v) **new**	WCot
§ - Victor Reiter Junior strain	CElw CPrp CSev CSpe EBee EHrv ELan EShb GKir GMac MLHP MMHG MNFA MWhi NBPC NBir NCob NGdn SMrm SPoG SRot WCot WCru WFar WPnP WPtf
- 'Wisley Blue'	EBee EBla EPPr SBch SRGP SUsu WHal
- 'Yorkshire Queen'	EBee EPPr NCob NGdn WCru WPtf
'Prelude'	CBre CDes CElw EBee ELon EPPr LPio MNFA NBir NCot NLar SRGP SUsu WCra WPtf
procurrens	CBre CElw COlW CSev CTri EBee EPPr EShb GCal GGar LLWP NBid NChi NGdn WBor WBrk WCru WFar WMoo
§ ***psilostemon*** ♀H4	Widely available
- 'Bressingham Flair'	CFir EBee EBla ECtt EPfP GAbr GCra LHop LRHS MNFA MRav NBid NGdn NHol SPer SRms WCAu WCru WFar WMoo WSHC
- 'Coton Goliath'	EPPr EWes NCot SUsu WCot
- 'Fluorescent'	NCot
- hybrid	CElw
- 'Jason Bloom'	EBrs GKir LRHS
- 'Madelon'	CElw EBee MAvo NCot
- 'Moorland Jack'	WMoo
- 'Sumela'	NCot
pulchrum	CHid CSpe EBee EWes EWld SGar SRGP WCot WPer
punctatum hort.	see *G.* × *monacense* var. *monacense* 'Muldoon'
- 'Variegatum'	see *G. phaeum* 'Variegatum'
pylzowianum	EBee GGar MRav NBid NRya SBch WFar WMoo
pyrenaicum	CRWN EBWF GAbr NBre NHol NSti
- f. ***albiflorum***	EBla GAbr IFro MNrw NBir SAga SRGP WBrk WPer WPnP
- 'Barney Brighteye'	SRGP
- 'Bill Wallis'	Widely available
- 'Bright Eyes'	LLWP NCot
- 'Isparta'	EBee EPPr IFro NCot SBch SPhx SRGP WBrk WTou
- 'Summer Sky'	GBin SPav SRGP
- 'Summer Snow'	CFir NLar
'Rachel'	CBow
'Rainbow'PBR	MBNS WCra
Rambling Robin Group	CBow ECre ECtt EHoe EPPr EWes MCCP MWhi NLBP SMad WHil
'Ray's Pink'	CPla
rectum	EPPr NBre NCot WCru
- 'Album'	see *G. clarkei* 'Kashmir White'
'Red Admiral'	CWGN EAEE EBee ECtt EPPr EWll GCal GGar LBMP LRHS MAvo NCGa NCot NDov NLar NSti SPoG SRGP SUsu WCra WFar WPtf
'Red Propellers'	CSpr
reflexum	EBla EPPr NCot WFar WPrP
refractum	CPLG
regelii	CSam EBee EPPr GAuc LEdu NCot WCru WMoo WPnP
renardii ♀H4	Widely available
- 'Beldo'	EBee MAvo
- blue-flowered	see *G. renardii* 'Whiteknights'
- 'Tcschelda'	CMHG EBee EBla ECha ECtt GAbr LBMP LPio LRHS MAsh NBir SBfd SMrm SRms SUsu WCra WFar WMoo WPnP
§ - 'Whiteknights'	CMoH EBee EBla NBir WCru
- 'Zetterlund'	CPrp EAEE EBee EBla ECGP EHrv EPPr EPfP EWTr GKir LHop LPio LRHS MWat NEgg SBfd WBrk WFar WMnd WMoo
§ ***reuteri***	CPla CTsd SChr SDnm SGar SRGP WCru WPnP
'Richard Nutt'	EBee NChi
richardsonii	EBee EBla EPPr EPfP GCal MNrw NBir SRGP WCra WCru
- pink-flowered **new**	MAvo
× ***riversleaianum*** 'Russell Prichard' ♀H4	Widely available
§ ***rivulare***	EBla NBre WMnd WPtf
- 'Album'	CSpr EBla
robertianum	CArn EBWF EPPr LLHF MHer SRms WSFF
§ - 'Album'	EBla EPPr SHar SRGP SRms WAlt
- f. ***bernettii***	see *G. robertianum* 'Album'
- 'Celtic White'	CBre EPPr GCal IFro MHer SPav SRGP WAlt WOut
- subsp. ***celticum***	WAlt
robustum	EPPr GGar MGos MNrw NBir NBro SPav SRGP WCot WFar WHal WPGP WSHC
- Hannays' form	WPGP
'Rosetta'PBR	EPfP
'Rosie Crûg'	SWvt
rosthornii	WCru
'Rothbury Red'	NChi
Rozanne = 'Gerwat'PBR ♀H4	Widely available

	rubescens	see *G. yeoi*
	rubifolium	WCru
§	'Ruprecht'	WWEG
	ruprechtii misapplied	see *G.* 'Ruprecht'
	ruprechtii (Grossh.) Woronow	EPPr GAuc MNrw NBre SRGP WPer WPtf
	Sabani Blue = 'Bremigo'[PBR]	CMac CSpe EBee EPPr EWes LHop LRHS NChi NLar NSti SMHy SOkt SPer SPoG SRkn WCot WCra WHlf WPtf
	'Salome'	Widely available
	'Sandrine'[PBR]	CBcs CDes CSev CSpe CWGN CWit EBee EPPr EPfP GAbr GBin GQue LLHF MAvo MNrw MTis MWea NBPC NBre NCGa SPoG WClo WCot WFut WPnP WPtf
	sanguineum	Widely available
	- Alan Bloom = 'Bloger'[PBR]	EBrs LRHS WCra
	- 'Album' 🏆[H4]	Widely available
	- 'Alpenglow'	EPPr SBch SRGP
	- 'Ankum's Pride' 🏆[H4]	CMMP CPrp EBee EBla ECGP EPPr LPio MNFA MTis NCot NDov NGdn NHar NSti SBch SRGP SUsu SWat WAbe WBrk WCra WCru WFar WMoo WPnP WPtf
	- 'Apfelblüte'	EBee EPPr IPot MAsh MSCN NLar SSvw WCra WFar
	- 'Aviemore' 🏆[H4]	EBee EPPr GBin GCal SBch
	- 'Barnsley'	CElw CPrp EPPr NBro WHrl
	- 'Belle of Herterton'	EBee EPPr MAvo NBid SBch SUsu WCru
	- 'Bloody Graham'	EBee EPPr MAvo NHaw SBch WMoo
	- 'Candy Pink'	EPPr
	- 'Canon Miles'	EBee EPPr LRHS SRGP
	- 'Catforth Carnival'	EPPr
	- 'Cedric Morris'	CElw CYeo EBla ECha EPPr GCra LPio LRHS MAvo NBid SMrs SRGP WCru WPnP
	- 'Compactum'	EBee
§	- 'Droplet'	SRGP
	- 'Elsbeth'	CElw CPrp EBee EBla ECha ECtt EPPr EWes GCal NCot NGdn NSti SBfd SPoG SRGP WBrk WCra WCru WFar WHal WMoo WPnP WWEG
	- 'Feu d'Automne'	EBee EPPr
	- 'Fran's Star'	see *G.* × *oxonianum* 'Fran's Star'
	- 'Glenluce'	CElw CMea CPrp EBee EBla ECtt EPPr EPot GGar GKir LBMP LHop LRHS MNFA MRav NDov SGar SMrm SRGP SRms SUsu SWat WBrk WCra WFar WHal WMnd WPer WPnP WTin
	- 'Hampshire Purple'	see *G. sanguineum* 'New Hampshire Purple'
	- 'Holden'	CElw EPPr NCot
	- 'Inverness'	EBee EPPr
	- 'Joanna'	MAvo SBch
	- 'John Elsley'	CPrp EAEE EBee EBla ECtt EHoe EPPr GKir LAst LLWP MNFA MSCN MSpe NBro NCot NGdn NLar SRGP SWat WCra WMnd WPer WWEG
	- 'John Innes'	EBee EPPr MAsh
	- 'Jubilee Pink'	EBla GCal WCru
	- 'Kristin Jacob'	EPPr
	- var. ***lancastrense***	see *G. sanguineum* var. *striatum*
	- 'Leeds Variety'	see *G. sanguineum* 'Rod Leeds'
§	- 'Little Bead' 🏆[H4]	EBla ECho GKir NHol
	- 'Max Frei'	Widely available
	- 'Minutum'	see *G. sanguineum* 'Droplet'
	- 'Nanum'	see *G. sanguineum* 'Little Bead'
§	- 'New Hampshire Purple'	CLAP CPrp EBee ECtt EPPr GGar MNFA NBro NGdn NLar NSti SSvw
	- 'Nyewood'	CPrp EAEE EBee ECGP ECtt EPPr MLLN MMuc SEND SRGP WCra WCru
I	- 'Plenum' (d)	EPPr
	- 'Pride of Coombland' **new**	SMrs
	- var. ***prostratum***	see *G. sanguineum* var. *striatum*
	- 'Purple Flame'	see *G. sanguineum* 'New Hampshire Purple'
§	- 'Rod Leeds'	CLAP EBee LPio MWea SRGP WFar
	- 'Sara'	MAvo WPnP
	- 'Shepherd's Warning' 🏆[H4]	CMea CTri EBee EBla ECtt EPPr GCal GKir MMuc NBir NLar SEND SRGP SUsu SWat WCra WCru WFar WHoo WSpi WTin
	- 'Shooting Star'	EBee NCot
	- 'South Nutfield'	MAvo NCot SUsu
§	- var. ***striatum*** 🏆[H4]	Widely available
	- - deep pink-flowered	CSBt MSwo SWvt
	- - 'Mottisfont' **new**	SBch
	- - 'Reginald Farrer'	WCru
	- - 'Splendens' 🏆[H4]	CElw CSev CWib EBla ELan EPPr LBee LHop LRHS NBid NChi NCot WCra WCru WEas WTin
	- 'Vision Light Pink'	SGar WPtf WWEG
	- 'Vision Violet'	COIW EBee EBla IFoB MAvo NHol SWvt WFar WPer
	- 'Westacre Poppet'	EPPr EWes
	saxatile	EPPr
	schlechteri	CBod CSpr
	'Sea Pink'	EDAr
	'Sellindge Blue'	MNFA
	sessiliflorum	ECou
I	- subsp. ***novae-zelandiae*** 'Nigricans'	EBla ECha ECho EHrv ELan EPfP GAbr GGar MCot MHer NLar NMoo NWCA SBch SRGP SWal WBrE WFar
§	- - 'Porters Pass'	CBow EBee ECho EHoe EWes MCCP MNrw NBir SBch SPlb WCom WHoo
	- - red-leaved	see *G. sessiliflorum* subsp. *novae-zelandiae* 'Porters Pass'
	'Sheilah Hannay'	CSpe
	shikokianum	CLAP CSpr GMac MCCP NLar SGar SPer SRGP WHrl WPtf
	- var. ***kaimontanum***	EBla WCru
	- var. ***quelpaertense***	CDes EBee EBla MAvo WPtf
	- - B&SWJ 1234	WCru
	- var. ***yoshiianum*** B&SWJ 6147	WCru
	'Shocking Blue'	EBee NSti WCra
	'Shouting Star'	see *G.* 'Kanahitobanawa'
	'Silva'	CElw CMoH EBee ECtt EPPr MAvo MNFA MNrw MRav SWat WCru
*	'Silver Shadow'	MCot SPhx
§	***sinense***	CFir CPLG EBee EBla ECtt EPPr EPfP GCal GGar LBMP LPio MCot MNrw NGdn NSti SPhx SRGP STes WCra WMnd WPnP
	'Sirak' 🏆[H4]	Widely available
	soboliferum	EBee EBla ELan EPPr GKir LRHS NBir NChi NWCA SBch SMad SRGP SUsu WCru WMoo WPtf
	- Cally strain	CDes GCal MAvo
	- var. ***kiusianum***	CElw MWea
	- 'Starman'	CPar CWGN EBee EPPr LSou MWea NLar SOkt SPoG WCra WHlf
	'Southcombe Star'	see *G.* × *oxonianum* f. *thurstonianum* 'Southcombe Star'
	'Southease Celestial'	SMHy SSth
	'Spinners'	Widely available

stapfianum var. ***roseum*** see *G. orientalitibeticum*
'Stephanie' CDes CElw EBee EPPr EPfP EWes LBMP LPio MAsh MBNS MNFA MWea NChi NGdn NLar NSti WCra WPnP
'Storm Chaser' CSpe EPPr MWea NSti SPoG WCra
'Strawberry Frost' EBla LLHF
subcaulescens ♀H4 Widely available
- 'Giuseppii' ♀H4 CPLG CYeo EAEE EBee EBla ECtt EShb GEdr GGar GKir LRHS LSou MHer MNFA MRav NBro NCot NDov NPri SBfd SMrm SRGP SRot SWvt WBrE WCra WFar WPnP
- 'Splendens' ♀H4 CSpe CTri EAEE EBee EBla ECtt EPPr EPfP LHop LRHS MCot MHer NEgg NPri NSla SRms SWat WClo WFar WPat
'Sue Crûg' Widely available
'Sue's Sister' WCru
'Summer Cloud' EBla EPPr MNFA SRGP
Summer Skies = 'Gernic'PBR (d) Widely available
suzukii WPtf
- B&SWJ 016 WCru
'Sweet Heidy'PBR CWGN EBee ECtt EKen EPPr LLHF MWea NMoo NSti SOkt SPoG WBor WCra WWlt
sylvaticum CMMP CRWN EBWF EBee EBla NBid NGdn NMir WMoo WShi
- 'Afrodite' EPPr
- f. ***albiflorum*** CBot CBre CElw EBee ELan NSti WCru
- 'Album' ♀H4 Widely available
- 'Amanda' EPPr
- 'Amy Doncaster' Widely available
- 'Angulatum' CElw EBee EPPr MNFA WMoo
- 'Birch Lilac' CElw CSam EBee EBla EPPr GCal LRHS MAvo NPnk WFar WMoo WPnP
- 'Birgit Lion' EBee
- 'Ice Blue' EBla EPPr GBin MNFA
- 'Immaculée' EPPr MRav
- 'Kanzlersgrund' CElw EPPr
- 'Lilac Time' EBla EPPr
- 'Mayflower' ♀H4 Widely available
- 'Meran' EPPr
- 'Nikita' EPPr
- f. ***roseum*** EPPr GGar NBre NLar WPtf
- - 'Baker's Pink' CElw EBee EBla EPPr GCra MNFA MNrw MRav NBir SBch SRGP WCra WCru WFar WMoo WPnP
- subsp. ***sylvaticum*** var. ***wanneri*** EBee EPPr SBch WCru
§ 'Tanya Rendall'PBR CMHG CSam CWit EBee ECGP ECtt ELon EPPr GAbr GBin GQue LOck LRHS MBNS MBri MWea NBPC NMoo SPer WCot WFar WPnP WRHF WWEG WWFP
'Terre Franche' EBee EPPr SBch SMrs SSvw WFar WWEG
§ ***thunbergii*** CFir CHid EBla EWes EWld LSou SRGP WMoo WPnP
- dark-flowered WSpi
- 'Jester's Jacket' (v) CPla EBee EKen EPPr LRHS MCCP MGos MLLN MNrw SGar SRGP WFar WHrl
- pink-flowered SRGP
- white-flowered EPPr SRGP
thurstonianum see *G.* × *oxonianum* f. *thurstonianum*
'Tinpenny Mauve' WHoo WTin
'Tiny Monster' CDes EBee EBla EPPr EWes GBin IKil LSou MAvo MNFA MNrw MWhi NGdn NLar NMoo NSti SBfd SPhx WBrk WCra WFar
transbaicalicum EBee EPPr GBin NHaw
traversii CWib GGar
- var. ***elegans*** CFee CSpe CWib ECtt LRHS WBrk WEas
tuberosum CElw CHid EBla ECha ECho ELan EShb MRav NBir NBro NCot NGdn NLBP SBch SGar SKHP WFar WPnP WSpi
- var. ***charlesii*** see *G. kotschyi* var. *charlesii*
- subsp. ***linearifolium*** WCru
'Ushguli Grijs' see *G. ibericum* Cav. 'Ushguli Grijs'
'Vera May' SUsu
'Verguld Saffier'PBR see *G.* Blue Sunrise
versicolor CElw CMac CMea COIW CRWN EBWF EBee EBla EPfP GAbr GGar LRHS MBri MHer MLLN MNrw MTho SRms WBrk WCAu WFar WMoo WPnP
- 'Kingston' see *G.* × *oxonianum* 'Kingston'
§ - 'Snow White' CElw ECtt EPPr MNrw NBre SRGP WCru WMoo WPnP
- 'The Bride' CMea ECtt
- 'White Lady' see *G. versicolor* 'Snow White'
'Victor Reiter' see *G. pratense* Victor Reiter Junior strain
violareum see *Pelargonium* 'Splendide'
viscosissimum EBla SRGP WMnd
- var. ***incisum*** MCCP NBre
- rose pink-flowered NBir
wallichianum CMac CPou EBee IFro NBir NSti WCot WMoo
§ - 'Buxton's Variety' ♀H4 Widely available
- 'Chadwell's Pink' EBee
- 'Chris' EWes NCot SRGP SUsu
- 'Crystal Lake' CSpr CWGN EBee EKen EPfP IPot MBNS MBri MWea NBir NSti WCra WHlf
- from RBGE **new** SMHy
- pale blue-flowered CElw
- 'Pink Buxton' EBee EWes GMac NLar
- pink-flowered CSpr EBla GCal GKev WCru
- 'Rosie' SRGP
- 'Syabru' CMea EBla MNrw NCot NLar SMHy WFar WMoo WPnP
- 'Wisley Jewel' EBee
'Wednesday's Child' WFar
wilfordii misapplied see *G. thunbergii*
Wisley hybrid see *G.* 'Khan'
wlassovianum Widely available
- 'Blue Star' IPot MRav SRGP WCon WCra WFar
- 'Zellertal' NCot
§ ***yeoi*** CSpe EPPr MSpe NBir NBro NDov NSti SRGP WCru WOut
yesoense EBla EPPr NBir NSti SRGP
- var. ***nipponicum*** NCot WCru
yoshinoi misapplied see *G. thunbergii*
yoshinoi Makino MWhi WPtf
yunnanense misapplied see *G. pogonanthum*
yunnanense ambig. CFir

Gerbera (Asteraceae)

(Everlast Series) Everlast Carmine = 'Amgerbcar' CWit LBuc LHop LRHS LSou SBfd SPoG STes SUsu WHil WHlf
- Everlast Pink = 'Amgerbpink' CWit LBuc LRHS SBfd SHar SPoG STes WHil WHlf
- Everlast White = 'Amgerbwhi' CSpe CWit LBuc LHop LRHS SBfd SHar SMrm SPoG STes WHil WHlf

Gerrardanthus (*Cucurbitaceae*)

macrorhizus	ERea

Gesneria (*Gesneriaceae*)

cardinalis	see *Sinningia cardinalis*
* ***macrantha*** 'Compacta'	EShb

Gethyllis (*Amaryllidaceae*)

afra 'Paarl' **new**	ECho
barkerae	ECho
- 'Nardouwsberg' **new**	ECho
- subsp. ***paucifolius*** **new**	ECho
britteniana 'Rietputs' **new**	ECho
ciliaris	ECho
- 'Porterville'	ECho
grandiflora	ECho
gregoriana	ECho
hallii 'Komiesberg' **new**	ECho
linearis 'Piketburg'	ECho
oligophylla 'Moedverloor' **new**	ECho
transkarooica 'Waboomsberg'	ECho
verticillata	ECho
- 'Pikenierskloof'	ECho
villosa	ECho

Gethyum (*Alliaceae*)

atropurpureum	EBee WCot

Geum ✿ (*Rosaceae*)

from India	GCal
'Abendsonne'	CDes CElw MAvo MSpe SBri SUsu
aleppicum	CFee NBre
alpinum	see *G. montanum*
andicola	NBre
'Beech House Apricot'	CAby CBre CElw CLAP CSev EBee EBla ECtt EPPr GCra LRHS MNFA MNrw MRav NCGa NChi NHol NLar SApp SBri WMoo WPnP WPrP WTin WWEG
'Bell Bank'	Widely available
'Birkhead's Creamy Lemon'	CElw MAvo
'Blazing Sunset' (d)	Widely available
N 'Borisii'	Widely available
'Bremner's Nectarine'	CElw MAvo MSpe NChi
bulgaricum	CElw EBee GKir MRav NBir NLar NRya WPrP WTin
'Butterscotch'	EBee
calthifolium	EPPr GKir MCCP MRav NBre NBro
capense	NBre SPlb
- JJ&JH 9401271	EBee
§ ***chiloense***	EBla LEdu
- 'Farncombe'	NCot
- 'Red Dragon'	CMac CWCL EBee LLHF LSRN NBPC NBre SGSe SPoG SWvt WRHF
'Chipchase'	GJos MAvo NCGa NChi SHar
coccineum misapplied	see *G. chiloense*
coccineum ambig.	EBla
coccineum Sibth. & Sm. 'Ann'	EPPr
- 'Cooky'	CElw CSam EBla EPfP EWll GJos GKir LRHS MMuc MSCN NGBl NPri SBfd SPad SPoG SRms SWal SWvt WClo WFar WHil WPer WWEG
- 'Eos'	CDes CElw CWCL EBee EBla EWes LEdu MAvo SPoG WCot
- 'Queen of Orange'	WRHF
- 'Werner Arends'	CMHG EBee EBla GAbr GCal MAvo MBri MNrw MRav NBro NDov SBri WCot WCra WFar WMoo
'Coppertone'	CDes CElw CLAP CPla CWGN EBee EBla ECtt EHrv ELan MAvo MRav MSpe NBir NBro NCGa NChi NRya SBri WAul WCom WHoo WMoo WPrP WTin
'Dingle Apricot'	CElw ECtt GAbr GBin MAvo MNrw MRav MSpe NBir SBri WWEG
'Dolly North'	EBee EBla EPyc GAbr GKir GMac MArl MAvo MNrw MRav MSpe NBro NGdn WCAu WHal WPrP WWEG
elatum	EBee EBla
'Fancy Frills' **new**	MDKP
'Farmer John Cross'	CAby CBre CDes CElw CLAP EBee EBla ECtt GBin GJos LPla MAvo MNrw MSpe NCGa NCob NCot NLar SBri WCra WHal WMoo WWEG
fauriei × ***kamtschatica***	EBla
'Feuerball'	NBre NCob NGdn
'Feuermeer'	EBee EBla MSpe NLar SBri
'Fire Opal' ♀H4	CDes CElw EBee EWes MAvo NBir NBre SBri SUsu WGwG WMoo WWEG
'Flames of Passion'^{PBR}	CCVN CHar CWCL CWGN EBee EBla ECtt GMac GQue LLWG LSou MAvo MBNS MLLN NBPC NCob NDov NLar SRGP STes WAul WCAu WCra WHil WWEG
'Fresh Woods'	WPGP
'Georgeham'	CPla
'Georgenberg'	Widely available
'Hannay's'	MAvo MSpe SBri
'Herterton Primrose'	CElw CFir CWCL EBla ECtt EPPr GCal LLHF LLWG MAvo MSpe MTis MWte NCGa NCob SBri SUsu WHal WHoo WWEG
'Hilltop Beacon'	CElw SBri WHoo WPrP
hispidum	SGar
* ***hybridum luteum***	NSti SBri
× ***intermedium***	CBre EBla EPPr NGdn NLar SBri WFar WMoo WWEG
- 'Diane'	CDes GJos MAvo MSpe NBre NChi SUsu WHoo
- 'Hofrennydd' **new**	WAlt
I ***japonicum*** 'Variegatum' (v)	CBow
'Karlskaer'	CElw EBee EBla EBrs ECtt EWTr EWes GBin GQue LRHS MAvo MBri MNrw MSpe MTis NCob NGdn NLar SAga SBri SMrm WCot WFar WMoo WNew WPnP WPtf WWEG
'Kashmir'	LRHS MAvo SBri
'Lady Stratheden' ♀H4	Widely available
'Lemon Drops'	Widely available
'Lionel Cox'	Widely available
'Lisanne'	CSam EBee MAvo NCGa NCot SBri SMHy SUsu
macrophyllum	EBee GAuc GBar
- var. ***sachalinense***	GAuc
magellanicum	EBla EWes NBre NLar
'Mandarin'	CDes CElw CFir EBla GAbr GCal MAvo
'Mango Lassi' **new**	MAvo WCAu
'Marmalade'	EBee EBla ECtt ELon GAbr GJos LLWG MAvo MNrw MSpe NBre NCGa NLar NPnk SDys SMHy SUsu WHrl WKif WMoo WOut WWEG
§ ***montanum*** ♀H4	CEnt EBla ECho EDAr GAuc GCra GGar GKir NBir NBro NGdn NPri NRya SPet SRms WMoo WWEG

	- 'Diana'	EBla MNrw NCot NLar SBri SUsu WWEG
	'Moorland Sorbet'	NCot SBri WFar WMoo WPtf WWEG
	'Mrs J. Bradshaw' 🏆^{H4}	Widely available
	'Mrs W. Moore'	Widely available
	'Nordek'	EAEE EBee ECtt GAbr GCal GJos MAvo MNFA MRav NCob NDov NEgg NGdn SBri WSpi WWEG
*	'Orangeman'	MAvo MNrw
	parviflorum	NBre NBro
	'Paso Doble'	CElw
	pentapetalum	see *Sieversia pentapetala*
	- 'Flore Pleno' (d)	WAbe
	'Pink Frills'	CDes CElw EBee EBla ECtt EWes GAbr GQue LLWG LPla MAvo MRav MSpe NCGa NCot NLar SBri SMHy SMrm STes WClo WPrP WWEG
	'Poco'	SBri
	ponticum	GAuc WOut
	'Present'	CElw EBee EBla ECtt MAvo MSpe NBre NCGa NChi SBri WPrP WWEG
	'Primrose'	GAbr GJos GQue NGdn NLar SBri
	'Prince of Orange'	CElw EBla GAbr IGor MNrw MRav NBre WFar WHrl
	'Prinses Juliana'	Widely available
	pyrenaicum	EBla NBre
	quellyon	see *G. chiloense*
I	'Rearsby Hybrid'	MAvo MRav MSpe SPlb SUsu WHoo
	'Red Wings'	EBee EBla GCal MAsh MRav NBir NCGa SBri SUsu
§	***reptans***	GBin NCob
	rhodopeum	LLHF
	'Rijnstroom'	EBee EBla ELan MAvo MSpe MWea NBPC WPtf
	rivale	Widely available
	- 'Album'	Widely available
	- 'Barbra Lawton'	EBla MAvo MDKP MSpe SBri WCra
	- 'Cream Drop'	EBla LLWG NCGa NChi NPnk SBri SMrm WWEG
	- cream-flowered, from Tien Shan, China	CFee
	- 'Larch Cottage Flame'	CElw MAvo NLar
	- 'Leonard's Double' (d)	CPrp CSev WFar WHil WNew WWEG
	- 'Leonard's Variety'	Widely available
	- 'Marika'	CCVN CHid CRow EBee EBla EBrs LRHS MSpe NBre NCGa NCot SBri SMrm SRGP WMoo WWEG
	- 'Marmalade'	EBla NBPC NChi SBri SUsu WCra
	- 'Oxford Marmalade'	CElw SApp
	- 'Snowflake'	MAvo NChi
	'Rubin'	CElw EBla ECtt EPPr EPyc NBre NBro NDov SBri SUsu
	'Sigiswang'	CDes CElw EBee GAbr GJos GMac MAvo MNrw MRav NBre NCob SBri WWEG
I	'Starker's Magnificum'	MAvo WCot
	'Tangerine'	EBla LSou MAvo MRav MSpe SBri
	'Tinpenny Orange'	CElw MAvo SBri WTin
	× ***tirolense***	EBee EBla NBre NCGa
	'Totally Tangerine' new	LRHS
	triflorum	CAby CElw EBee EBla EHrv EShb MCCP MNrw NLar NPnk SPhx STes WFar WTin
	- var. ***campanulatum***	CFir NChi WWEG
	urbanum	CArn EBWF GBar GJos GPWP NLan NPri NSco SWat WHer WHfH WMoo
	- from Patagonia	EBla MAvo MDKP
	'Wallace's Peach'	SBri SWal

Gevuina (*Proteaceae*)

	avellana	CBcs CHEx EBee WPGP

Gilia ✿ (*Polemoniaceae*)

	aggregata	see *Ipomopsis aggregata*
	caespitosa	CPBP

Gillenia (*Rosaceae*)

	stipulata	CLAP EBee LEdu NDov NLar SPhx SUsu
	trifoliata 🏆^{H4}	Widely available
	- 'Pixie'	EBee WPGP

Ginkgo (*Ginkgoaceae*)

	biloba 🏆^{H4}	Widely available
	- B&SWJ 8753	WCru
	- 'Anny's Dwarf'	MAsh
	- 'Autumn Gold' (m)	CBcs CEnd CMCN EBee MBlu MGos MPkF NLar SBig SLim SPoG
I	- 'Barabits Nana'	SBig
	- 'Beijing Gold'	MBlu NLar
	- 'California Sunset'	NLar SMad
	- 'Chi-chi'	MPkF SBig SLim
	- 'Chotek'	SBig
	- 'Chris' Dwarf' new	MAsh
	- 'Doctor Causton' (f)	CAgr
	- 'Doctor Causton' (m)	CAgr
	- 'Elmwood'	NLar
	- 'Elsie'	SBig
	- 'Fairmount' (m)	CMCN MBlu SBig
	- 'Fastigiata' (m)	CLnd CMCN EPfP MBlu MGos
	- 'Gnome'	ESwi LSRN MGos MPkF
	- 'Golden Globe'	ESwi MPkF NLar WBor
	- 'Horizontalis'	CLnd CMen MBlu SBig
	- 'Jade Butterflies'	CBcs MAsh MBlu MBri MPkF NLar SLim
	- 'King of Dongting' (f)	CAgr CMCN MBlu SBig
	- 'Mariken'	ESwi MAsh MBri MGos MPkF NLar NPal SBig SLim SPoG
	- 'Mayfield' (m)	SBig
	- Ohazuki Group (f)	CAgr SBig
	- Pendula Group	CEnd CMCN CTho ECrN EPfP ESwi MAsh MBlu MPkF NPal NPri SLim
	- 'Princeton Sentry' (m)	EBee SBig SMad
	- 'Robbie's Twist'	MPkF
	- 'Saratoga' (m)	CBcs CDoC CEnd CLnd CMCN CPMA CTho EPfP MAsh MBri MGos MPkF SBig SLim SMad SSpi
	- 'Tit'	CEnd CMCN CMen EPfP MGos NLar SBig
	- 'Tremonia'	CMCN CWit EBee EPfP MBlu MPkF NLar SBig SLim
	- 'Troll'	MBlu SBig SCoo SLim SMad
	- 'Tubifolia'	CMCN CMen MBlu NLar SBig SLim
	- 'Umbrella'	SBig
	- Variegata Group (v)	CBcs CMCN CMen CPMA EBee ESwi MGos MPkF NLar SBig SLim SPoG

ginseng see *Panax ginseng*

Gladiolus (*Iridaceae*)

	abyssinucus	GCal
	acuminatus	WCot
	'Akuta' (M/E) new	CGrW
	alatus	ECho LPio
	- white-flowered	WCot
	'Alba' (N)	CGrW
	'Alexandra' (P)	WCot
	'Allosius' (S)	CGrW
	'Alpen Glow' (L) new	CGrW

'Amanda Mahy' (N)	LAma
'Amsterdam' (G)	CGrW
'Andre Viette'	LLHF WCot
angustus	CGrW WCot
antakiensis	CPou
'Antica' (L)	CGrW
'Antique Lace' (L)	CGrW
'Antique Rose' (M)	WCot
'Anyu S' (L)	CGrW
'Atom' (S/P)	CAvo CBgR CGrW EBee ECho LAma WCot WHil
atroviolaceus	IPot
aureus	WCot
Barnard hybrids	CGrW
'Beautiful Angel'	CGrW
'Beauty Bride' (L)	CGrW
'Beauty of Holland' PBR (L)	CGrW
'Big Boss' (G) **new**	CGrW
'Bizar'	EPfP WCot
'Black Jack'	EPfP
'Blackbird' (S)	CGrW
'Blue Clouds' (L)	CGrW
'Blue Tropic'	CSut
'Bonfire' (G)	CGrW
'Boone'	CDes SMrm
× ***brenchleyensis***	CPen
brevifolius 'Somerset West' **new**	ECho
'Brittania' (L)	CGrW
'Bronze Tiger' (M/E)	WCot
byzantinus	see *G. communis* subsp. *byzantinus*
caeruleus 'Saldanha' **new**	ECho
callianthus	see *G. murielae*
cardinalis	CDes CPne CPrp GBin GCal GGar IBlr LEdu SAga SChr SKHP WCot WCru
carinatus	CDes CGrW ECho GGar WCot
carinatus × ***huttonii*** 'Purple Spray' **new**	WCot
carinatus × ***orchidiflorus***	WCot
'Carine' (N)	LAma LRHS
carmineus	CGrW CPen EBee ECho WCot WHil
carneus	CGrW CPen CPou EBee ECho EPot GCal LPio SDeJ WHil
'Carquirenne' (G)	CGrW
caryophyllaceus	CGrW CPou
'Charlotte' PBR	LRHS
'Charm' (N/Tub)	CPrp EBee LAma
'Charming Beauty' (Tub)	ECho LAma LRHS WHil
'Charming Lady' (Tub)	CElw ECho LAma
'Chartreuse Ruffles' (S)	CGrW
'Chocolate Smores' (E)	CGrW
'Cindy' (B)	ECho
citrinus	see *G. tribonemifolius*
'Claudia' (N)	CGrW LRHS
× ***colvillii***	CMea CPne IBlr
- 'Albus'	LPio
- 'The Bride' ♀H3	CAvo CElw CFFs CMea CPrp EBee ECho EPot GKev LAma LEdu LPio LSRN MCot SDeJ
'Comet' (N)	CAvo LPio
§ ***communis*** subsp. ***byzantinus*** ♀H4	Widely available
'Contessa Queen'	CGrW
'Coral Dream' (L)	CGrW
'Costa' PBR (L) **new**	CGrW
'Cotton Queen' (L) **new**	CGrW
'Cream Perfection' (L)	CGrW
'Creamy Yellow' (S)	CGrW
'Cristabel'	WCot
§ ***dalenii***	CGrW CPou EBee ECho IBlr LPio WCot
- subsp. ***dalenii***	CPrp IBlr
- green-flowered	IBlr
- orange-flowered	CDes
* - f. ***rubra***	IBlr
- yellow-flowered	CDes EBee
'Daydreamer' (L)	CGrW
'Day's End' (S)	CGrW
densifolius **new**	ECho
dichrous **new**	CDes
'Drama' (L)	CGrW
ecklonii 'Mount Thomas' **new**	ECho
'Elderberry Wine' (E)	CGrW
'Elegance' (G)	CGrW
'Elvira' (N)	EBee ECho LAma
'Emerald Spring' (S)	CGrW WCot
'Emily' PBR	LRHS
equitans	CGrW
'Essential' (M) **new**	CGrW
'Esta Bonita' (G)	CGrW
'Extasy' PBR (L) **new**	CGrW
'Felicta' (L)	CGrW
ferrugineus	LPio
'Finishing Touch' PBR (L)	CGrW
flanaganii	CDes CPBP CPLG CSpe ECho GBin GCal GCrs ITim LLHF LPio NSla SChr SKHP WAbe WCot WHil
- JCA 261.000	EBee
'Flevo Cosmic' (Min)	CGrW LPio SMrm
'Flevo Dancer' (S)	CGrW
'Flevo Eclips' PBR (G)	CGrW
'Flevo Eyes' PBR (L)	CGrW
'Flevo Focus' **new**	CGrW
'Flevo Jive' (S)	CGrW
'Flevo Junior' (S)	CGrW
'Flevo Libre' PBR (L) **new**	CGrW
'Flevo Primo' (S) **new**	CGrW
'Flevo Smile' (S)	CGrW WCot
'Flevo Souvenir' PBR (L)	CGrW
'Flevo Sunset' PBR (L)	CGrW
'Flevo Vito' (Min) **new**	CGrW
floribundus hort.	ECho
floribundus Jacq.	EBee
fourcadei	ECho
'Frangine' (L) **new**	CGrW
'French Silk' (L)	CGrW
garnieri	CDes
geardii	WCot WHil
Glamini Series	LRHS
- 'Glamini Christopher'	LRHS
- 'Glamini Eva'	LRHS
- 'Glamini Zoë'	LRHS
'Gold Struck' (L)	CGrW
gracilis	ECho WCot
grandis	see *G. liliaceus*
'Green Star' (L)	CGrW EPfP
'Green Woodpecker' (M)	EBee
gueinzii 'Mossel Bay' **new**	ECho
'Halley' (N)	CGrW ECho LAma
hirsutus	CGrW ECho
'Hunting Song' (L)	LRHS
'Huron County' (L) **new**	CGrW
'Huron Frost' (L)	CGrW
'Huron Jewel' (M)	CGrW
'Huron Pleasure'	CGrW
'Huron Silk' (L)	CGrW
huttonii	CDes CGrW ECho WCot
huttonii × ***tristis***	CPou
huttonii × ***tristis*** var. ***concolor***	CDes WCot

'Ibadan'PBR (L) **new**	CGrW
illyricus	CGrW CPen CSam ECho GCal WBVN
imbricatus	CGrW EBee ECho
'Impressive' (N)	LAma WHil
inflatus	CGrW ECho
- 'Ceres' **new**	ECho
'Inspector's Choice' (M)	CGrW
involutus **new**	CGrW
- 'Mossel Bay' **new**	ECho
'Irish Blessing' (S)	CGrW
§ ***italicus***	CGrW CHid CPen CTca EBee ELan GCal SKHP
'Jayvee' (S)	CGrW
'Jessica' (L)	LRHS
'Jester' (L)	CSut LRHS
'Jim S' (G)	CGrW
kotschyanus	ECho
'Lady Eleanor' (P)	WCot
'Lady Lucille' (M)	CGrW
'Lavender Flare' (S)	CGrW
'Lemon Zest' (M)	CGrW
leptosiphon **new**	CGrW
- 'Molenaars River' **new**	ECho
§ ***liliaceus***	CDes CGrW ECho WCot
- 'Caledon' **new**	ECho
'Little Rainbow' (P)	WCot
'Little Wiggy' (P)	CGrW
longicollis **new**	ECho
'Loulou' (G)	CGrW
'Lowland Queen' (L)	CGrW
'Lucifer'PBR **new**	CGrW
'Magenta Queen' (L)	CGrW
'Marj S' (L)	CGrW
meliusculus	ECho
'Mexico'	CSut
'Mileesh' (L)	CGrW
miniatus	CDes
'Mirella' (N)	CAvo CFFs LAma MRav WHil
'Mon Amour'PBR	CGrW
montanus	CPen
monticola	EBee
mortonius	GCal
§ ***murielae*** 🏆H3	CAvo CFFs CGrW CMea CSWP CStu EBee ECho EPfP ERCP EWll LAma LEdu LPio LRHS MCot SCoo SPad SPer SPet SPhx SPlb STes WGwG WHal WHil WHoo WPtf
'Murieliae'	see *G. murielae*
'My Treasure' (L)	CGrW
natalensis	see *G. dalenii*
'Nathalie' (N)	CGrW EBee SDeJ WHil
'New Wave'PBR (L)	CGrW
'Nymph' (N)	CAvo CFFs CMea EBrs EPot ITim LAma LEdu LPio SDeJ WBor
'Oasis'PBR (G)	CGrW
ochroleucus	EBee
'Of Singular Beauty' (G)	CGrW
§ ***oppositiflorus***	CDes CPou EBee SChr
- subsp. ***salmoneus***	see *G. oppositiflorus*
orchidiflorus	CGrW ECho
palustris	CDes
papilio	Widely available
- 'David Hills'	CSWP NCGa WCot WHal WPrP
§ - Purpureoauratus Group	CSam EBee IBlr SRms
- 'Ruby'	CAby CDes CMea CPen CPne CPou CPrp CTca GMac IPot LSRN NCGa NChi SMHy SMad SUsu WCot WHil WPrP
- yellow-flowered	CMdw SMad SUsu
pappei	EBee
'Parade' (G)	CGrW
'Peach Royale' (L)	CGrW
'Peggy' (P)	CGrW
permeabilis	EBee
'Perth Pearl' (M)	CGrW
'Phyllis M' (L)	CGrW
Pilbeam hybrids	CGrW
'Pink Elegance' (L)	CGrW
'Pink Lady' (L)	CGrW
'Powerful Lady' (L) **new**	CGrW
primulinus	see *G. dalenii*
'Prins Claus' (N)	CGrW CTca GKev LAma
'Prinses Margaret Rose'	CSut
priorii 'Dasberg' **new**	ECho
'Priscilla' (L)	MLHP
pritzelii **new**	CGrW
- 'Quaggasfontein' **new**	ECho
'Purple Prince' (M)	CGrW WCot
purpureoauratus	see *G. papilio* Purpureoauratus Group
quadrangularis	CGrW ECho
recurvus	CGrW ECho
'Red Deer' (L) **new**	CGrW
'Robinetta' (*recurvus* hybrid) 🏆H3	CBgR CElw ECho EPfP GGar LAma
'Roma' (L)	CGrW
'Rose Flame' (L)	CGrW
'Royal Spire'	CGrW
'Rusty Red' (P)	CGrW
'Ruth Ann'	CGrW
'San Remo'PBR (L)	CGrW
saundersii	EBee GCal GMac
'Scarlet Lady' (P)	CGrW
scullyi	CGrW
- 'Ceres Karoo' **new**	ECho
segetum	see *G. italicus*
sericeovillosus	IBlr
'Sharkey' (G)	CGrW
'Show Star' (L)	CGrW
'Show Stopper' (G)	CGrW
'Sirael' (L/E)	CGrW WCot
'Smoke Stack' (L)	CGrW
'Solveiga' (L/E)	CGrW
'Sophie'PBR	CGrW
splendens	CDes CGrW WCot WPGP
- 'Roggeveld' **new**	ECho
'Spring Green'	LRHS
'Spring Thaw' (L/E)	CGrW
stefaniae	CGrW
'Stiena' (L)	CGrW
'Sunrise' (L)	CGrW
symonsii	EBee
'Tan Royale' (P)	CGrW
'Tante Ann' (M)	CGrW
'Terry' (G) **new**	CGrW
'Trader Horn' (G)	LRHS
§ ***trichonemifolius***	CGrW ECho
tristis	CAby CAvo CDes CElw CGHE CGrW CMea CPen CPne CPou CPrp EBee ECha ECho EDif ELan ELon GBin GCal GGar IPot LPio NCGa SAga SDix SUsu WFar WHal WPGP WSHC
- var. ***concolor***	CGrW CPou CPrp EBee LPio WCot
undulatus	CDes CGrW ECho WCot
uysiae	CGrW ECho
- 'Gannaga' **new**	ECho
vandermerwei	CGrW ECho
venustus	CGrW ECho
'Video' (L)	CGrW
'Violetta' (M)	CGrW ECho
virescens	CGrW
- 'Ceres' **new**	ECho

watermeyeri	CGrW
watsonioides	CPou SKHP
'Wax Ruffles' (L/E) **new**	CGrW
'White Prosperity' (L)	CSut
'Wind Song' (L)	CSut LRHS
'Ziporra' (S) **new**	CGrW

Glandularia see *Verbena*

Glaucidium (*Glaucidiaceae*)

palmatum ♀H4	CPLG EBee EFEx EPot EWld GCrs GEdr GKev NSla WBVN WCru WHal WPtf
- 'Album'	see *G. palmatum* var. *leucanthum*
§ - var. ***leucanthum***	EFEx GBin GEdr GKev NSla

Glaucium (*Papaveraceae*)

§ ***corniculatum***	CAbP CBot CSpe EBee LRHS SEND SPhx WEas
flavum	CArn CSpe ECha ELan MHer SPav
- ***aurantiacum***	see *G. flavum* f. *fulvum*
§ - f. ***fulvum***	ECha IFro LRHS SDix WCot WHil
- orange-flowered	see *G. flavum* f. *fulvum*
- red-flowered	see *G. corniculatum*
grandiflorum	SWal
phoenicium	see *G. corniculatum*

Glaux (*Primulaceae*)

maritima	EBWF WPer
- dwarf	NWCA

Glebionis (*Asteraceae*)

coronaria	MNHC
§ ***segetum***	MNHC

Glechoma (*Lamiaceae*)

hederacea	CArn EBWF GBar GPoy MHer NMir NSco WHer
- 'Barry Yinger Variegated' (v)	EBee
- 'Rosea'	GBar WAlt
§ - 'Variegata' (v)	CFox SPer SPet

Gleditsia (*Caesalpiniaceae*)

caspica	CArn SMad
japonica	EPfP NLar
macrantha	EGFP
triacanthos	CDul CWib ECrN EMac LEdu SEND SPlb WDin
- 'Calhoun'	CAgr
- 'Elegantissima' (v)	SPer
- 'Emerald Cascade'	CBcs CEnd EBee MBri
- f. ***inermis*** Spectrum = 'Speczam'	EBee LRHS MBri
- 'Millwood'	CAgr
- 'Rubylace'	CBcs CDul CEnd CLnd CMCN CMac CSBt EBee ECrN ELan EPfP EWTr IVic LAst LSRN MAsh MBlu MGos MRav MSwo NLar SKHP SLim SMad SPer WBor WCot WDin WFar
- 'Skyline'	LMaj
- 'Sunburst' ♀H4	Widely available

Globba ✿ (*Zingiberaceae*)

marantina	ECho LAma WWst
winitii 'Mount Everest' **new**	LAma
I - 'Pink Dancing Girl'	ECho

Globularia (*Globulariaceae*)

bellidifolia	see *G. meridionalis*
bisnagarica	CElw GKev
cordifolia ♀H4	EBee ECho EDAr EPot GEdr GKev MTho NBir NLAp NMen WCom WFar WPat
§ ***meridionalis***	CElw CFee ECho EPot EWes GMaP MWat NLAp NMen NWCA SAga WHal WPat
- SDR 5444	GKev
- 'Blue Bonnets'	GEdr NHar
- 'Hort's Variety'	NMen WAbe WPat
nana	see *G. repens*
nudicaulis	GEdr
punctata	CSpe NBre SMrm SRms
pygmaea	see *G. meridionalis*
§ ***repens***	CPBP EPot MTho NMen WAbe WPat
trichosantha	CFee ECho SRms WFar
valentina	GEdr

Gloriosa (*Colchicaceae*)

lutea	see *G. superba* 'Lutea'
rothschildiana	see *G. superba* 'Rothschildiana'
superba ♀H1	MBri
- 'Carsonii'	LAma
- 'Greenii' **new**	LAma WWst
§ - 'Lutea'	LAma
§ - 'Rothschildiana'	CBcs CRHN CStu ECho EGxp LAma LRHS SOWG SPer SRms
- 'Simplex' **new**	CLak
- 'Verschuurii' **new**	CLak

Glottiphyllum (*Aizoaceae*)

grandiflorum	WHil

Gloxinia (*Gesneriaceae*)

sp.	EABi
nematanthodes 'Evita'	CDes
sylvatica	EShb WDib

Glumicalyx (*Scrophulariaceae*)

flanaganii	EBee GKev WCom
- HWEL 0325	NWCA
montanus	CFee

Glyceria (*Poaceae*)

aquatica variegata	see *G. maxima* var. *variegata*
maxima	CRWN EBWF GFor MMuc MSKA NMir NPer SPlb
§ - var. ***variegata*** (v)	CBcs CBen CWat EBee ECha EHoe EHon ELan EPfP GCra GMaP LHop LPBA LRHS MBlu MMoz MMuc MWhi NGdn SMrm SPer SRms SVic SWal SWat WFar WMAq WMoo WPnP WWEG
notata	SVic
spectabilis 'Variegata'	see *G. maxima* var. *variegata*

Glycyrrhiza (*Papilionaceae*)

echinata	CArn NLar
§ ***glabra***	CArn CBod CCCN CHby EBtc ELau GPWP GPoy MBri MHer MNHC NLar SIde WJek
glandulifera	see *G. glabra*
uralensis	CArn ELau GPoy MHer
yunnanensis	MHer

Glyptostrobus (*Cupressaceae*)

pensilis	CGHE CPLG EGFP WPGP

Gmelina (*Verbenaceae*)

hystrix	CCCN

Gnaphalium (*Asteraceae*)

	'Fairy Gold'	see *Helichrysum thianschanicum* 'Goldkind'
	mackayi	WAbe
	trinerve	see *Anaphalis trinervis*

Godetia see *Clarkia*

Gomphocarpus (*Asclepiadaceae*)

§	***physocarpus***	CArn CDTJ CEnt SBfd WCot

Gomphostigma (*Buddlejaceae*)

	virgatum	CDes CPLG CSpe EPPr MNFA SMrm SPlb SSvw WCFE WCot WHrl WOut WPGP WSHC
	- 'White Candy'	EBee NLar

Gomphrena (*Amaranthaceae*)

	globosa	CCCN

Goniolimon (*Plumbaginaceae*)

	collinum 'Sea Spray'	CSpr EBee EDAr NBre SMad WClo WHil
§	***incanum***	SMrm
	- 'Blue Diamond'	EBee
	speciosum	LLHF
§	***tataricum***	NBre NLar
§	- var. ***angustifolium***	EBee SEND SRms WPer
	- 'Woodcreek'	NLar

Goniophlebium (*Polypodiaceae*)

§	***subauriculatum*** 'Knightiae'	WRic

Goodenia (*Goodeniaceae*)

	heteromera	ECou

Goodia (*Papilionaceae*)

	lotifolia	CCCN

Goodyera (*Orchidaceae*)

	biflora	EFEx
	pubescens	EFEx
	schlechtendaliana	EFEx

gooseberry see *Ribes uva-crispa*

Gordonia (*Theaceae*)

	axillaris	see *Polyspora axillaris*

Gossypium (*Malvaceae*)

	herbaceum	CCCN

granadilla see *Passiflora quadrangularis*

granadilla, purple see *Passiflora edulis*

granadilla, sweet see *Passiflora ligularis*

granadilla, yellow see *Passiflora laurifolia*

grape see *Vitis*

grapefruit see *Citrus* × *paradisi*

Graptopetalum (*Crassulaceae*)

	bellum ♀H1	CPBP CStu
	filiferum	EWII SPlb
	pachyphyllum	MSCN
§	***paraguayense***	SEND

× *Graptoveria* (*Crassulaceae*)

	'Doctor Phillips Pink'	STre

Gratiola (*Scrophulariaceae*)

	officinalis	CArn CWan EHon LLWG MHer MSKA

Greenovia (*Crassulaceae*)

§	***aurea***	ESem SPlb
	diplocycla 'Gigantea' **new**	SPlb

Grevillea ✿ (*Proteaceae*)

	alpina	CPLG SOWG
	- 'Olympic Flame'	CBcs CCCN CDoC CPLG CSBt CWSG CWib EBee EPfP GBin LRHS MMuc SCoo SEND SOWG SPoG SRms WBor WFar WGrn
	aquifolium	SOWG
	arenaria	SOWG
	- subsp. ***canescens***	SOWG
	baileyana	SOWG
	banksii 'Canberra Hybrid'	see *G.* 'Canberra Gem'
	- var. ***forsteri***	SOWG
	banyabba	SOWG
	barklyana	SOWG
	baueri	SOWG
	beadleana	SOWG
	bedggoodiana	SOWG
	bipinnatifida	SOWG
	'Bonnie Prince Charlie'	CPLG SOWG
	'Bronze Rambler'	SOWG
§	'Canberra Gem' ♀H3-4	Widely available
	'Clearview David'	CCCN CMac CPLG CTrC CWGN EBee EUJe LBuc LRHS LSRN SCoo SLim SOWG SSpi
	confertifolia	SOWG
	'Copper Crest'	SOWG
	'Cranbrook Yellow'	CDoC CPLG EBee EPfP SOWG
	crithmifolia	SOWG SPlb
	'Desert Flame'	WClo
	diffusa subsp. ***evansiana***	SOWG
	drummondii subsp. ***pimeleoides***	SOWG
	'Elegance' red-flowered	SOWG
	endlicheriana	SOWG
	'Evelyn's Coronet'	SOWG
	'Fanfare'	SOWG
	fulgens	SOWG
	× ***gaudichaudii***	SOWG
	'Honey Gem'	SOWG
	iaspicula	SOWG
	johnsonii	CMac CTrC CWSG EUJe SOWG
	juniperina	CBcs CCCN CMac CPLG CTsd EBee EPfP LRHS MGos SLim
	- 'Molonglo'	CPLG
	- f. ***sulphurea***	CCCN CDoC CHII CPLG CTrC EPfP IDee SOWG SPlb SPoG SSpi WAbe WPat WSHC
	lanigera	CPLG ECou
I	- 'Lutea'	SOWG
	- 'Mount Tamboritha'	CBcs CCCN CDoC CMac CPLG CTrC CWGN EBee GGar IDee LRHS SBfd SPoG SSpi WBrE WFar
	- prostrate	ECou MAsh SOWG WAbe WGrn WPat
	leucopteris	SPlb
	levis	SOWG
	longistyla	SOWG
	'Mason's Hybrid'	SOWG
	'Misty Red'	LRHS
	'Moonlight'	SOWG

nudiflora	SOWG
obtusifolia 'Gingin Gem'	SOWG
olivacea **new**	LRHS
- 'Apricot Glow'	SOWG
'Orange Marmalade'	SOWG
paniculata	SOWG SPlb
parvula	SOWG
'Pink Lady'	CWit ECou ELon LRHS SCoo SOWG
'Pink Parfait' **new**	EUJe
'Pink Surprise'	SOWG
'Poorinda Constance'	SOWG
'Poorinda Peter'	CPLG SOWG
'Poorinda Rondeau'	CPLG
pteridifolia	SOWG
quercifolia	SOWG
'Red Dragon' (v)	LBuc LRHS
repens	SOWG
rhyolitica	SOWG
robusta ♀H1+3	CTsd EShb EUJe SOWG SPlb SSta WCot
- 'Red Salento'PBR	LRHS WCot
'Robyn Gordon'	EUJe SOWG
'Rondeau'	CCCN EBee
rosmarinifolia ♀H3	CAbb CDoC CHll CMac CPLG CSBt CTrC CTri CWSG CWib EBee EPfP EShb GGar IDee MWat SArc SCoo SLim SLon SOWG SPer SPlb SSta WAbe WCot WFar WGrn
- 'Desert Flame'	CPLG
- 'Jenkinsii'	CDoC CPLG CSBt EBee ELon EPPr LAst LRHS SBfd SLim SSpi WClo
'Sandra Gordon'	SOWG
'Scarlet Sprite'	SOWG
§ × ***semperflorens***	CBcs CPLG CTrC CWib EBee LRHS MMuc SCoo SEND SOWG SPlb WGrn
sericea	SOWG
shiressii	SOWG
'Sid Reynolds'	CPLG
'Spider Man'	LRHS
'Splendour'	SOWG
thelemanniana 'Silver'	CPLG
- Spriggs' form	SOWG
thyrsoides	GGal
tolminsis	see *G.* × *semperflorens*
venusta	SOWG
victoriae	CDoC CPne CWGN EBee EPfP GGar SCoo SOWG SSpi WCot
- subsp. ***victoriae***	CPLG
- yellow-flowered	LRHS
williamsonii	ECou LRHS SCoo SOWG WPat

Greyia (*Greyiaceae*)

sutherlandii	CTrC SGar SOWG SPlb WCot

Grindelia (*Asteraceae*)

§ ***camporum***	CWCL GBar IMou NBre SPlb WPer
chiloensis	CAbb ECha SMad WCot
integrifolia	EBee
robusta	see *G. camporum*
squarrosa	GBar WHil
stricta	CArn

Griselinia ✿ (*Griseliniaceae*)

littoralis ♀H3	Widely available
- 'Bantry Bay' (v)	CAbP CCCN CDoC CTsd CWSG EBee EHoe ELan ESwi LRHS NCGa SEND SLim SPer SWvt WFar
- 'Brodick Gold'	CPLG EQua GGar
- 'Crinkles'	CPMA
- 'Dixon's Cream' (v)	CBcs CCCN CDul CMac CSBt EBee EPfP GQui IArd IFoB LRHS SAga SLon SPoG
- 'Green Jewel' (v)	CBcs CCCN CPMA CTrC CWib NLar
- 'Variegata' (v) ♀H3	Widely available
scandens	WSHC

guava, common see *Psidium guajava*

guava, purple or strawberry see *Psidium littorale* var. *longipes*

Gunnera ✿ (*Gunneraceae*)

chilensis	see *G. tinctoria*
cordifolia	CPne
densiflora **new**	GEdr
dentata	CPla CPne
flavida	CPla CSpr CStu GGar NWCA WGwG
hamiltonii	CPla CPne CSpr CStu ECha EWld GAbr LLWG MAvo NBir NWCA WMoo
magellanica	Widely available
- 'Muñoz Gamero'	WShi
- 'Osorno'	EBee MMoz
manicata ♀H3-4	Widely available
× ***mixta***	CPne
monoica	CPne GGar
perpensa	CBcs CCCN IMou WCot
prorepens	CFee CMac CPLG CPla CStu EBee ECha ECou GEdr GGar LLWG NBir SBfd SWat WCon WFar WMoo WWEG
scabra	see *G. tinctoria*
§ ***tinctoria*** ♀H4	Widely available

Gymnadenia (*Orchidaceae*)

camtschatica **new**	NLAp
* - f. ***alba*** **new**	WWst
conopsea	ECho EFEx NLAp WWst
odoratissima **new**	NLAp
- white-flowered **new**	NLAp

Gymnocarpium (*Woodsiaceae*)

dryopteris ♀H4	CLAP EFer EFtx GGar GMaP LEdu MMoz NLar NWCA SGSe SRms WAbe WFib WPnP WPtf WRic WShi
- 'Plumosum' ♀H4	CBty CKel CLAP CWCL EBee EFtx EPfP EPla GBin NBid NHar NHol NLar SMad WFib WHal WMoo WWEG
fedtschenkoanum	WAbe WRic
oyamense	CLAP EFer EFtx SKHP WRic
robertianum	EFer EWld

Gymnocladus (*Caesalpiniaceae*)

chinensis	EGFP
dioica	CBcs CDul CLnd CMCN EBee EBtc ELan EPfP LRHS MBlu MBri SPer SSpi WDin WPGP

Gymnospermium (*Berberidaceae*)

§ ***albertii***	ECho WWst
sylvaticum	WWst

Gynandriris (*Iridaceae*)

setifolia	ECho
sisyrinchium	CStu EBee ECho
* - ***purpurea***	ECho

Gynerium (*Poaceae*)

	argenteum	see *Cortaderia selloana*

Gynostemma (*Cucurbitaceae*)

	pentaphyllum	CAgr
	- B&SWJ 570	WCru

Gypsophila (*Caryophyllaceae*)

	acutifolia	EBee ELan
	aretioides	ECho EPot LRHS NMen
§	- 'Caucasica'	CPBP EBur ECho EPot GEdr LLHF
	- 'Compacta'	see *G. aretioides* 'Caucasica'
	briquetiana	EPot WPat
	cerastioides	CTri ECho ECtt EDAr EPfP EWTr GAbr GGar LBMP LHop LRHS MMuc MRav NLar NMen NWCA SPlb SRms WAbe WHoo WNew WPat WPer WPnn
	dubia	see *G. repens* 'Dubia'
	fastigiata 'Silverstar'	EBee LRHS LSou SPoG
	(Festival Series) 'Festival'PBR	ECtt SRot
	- 'Festival Pink'	EBee ECtt GBee LRHS SHar SPoG WFar
	gracilescens	see *G. tenuifolia*
	'Jolien' (v)	CBow EBee ELan NBPC
	muralis 'Garden Bride'	SWvt
	- 'Gypsy Pink' (d)	SWvt
	- 'Pink Sugardot'	SBch
	nana 'Compacta'	CPBP
	'Pacific Rose'	MRav
	pacifica	EBee MWea NBre NLar SBfd WPer
	paniculata	CMea EBee EPfP LAst MGos NBre NEgg SMrm SRms
	- 'Bristol Fairy' (d) 🏆H4	CSBt CTri EBee ECha ECtt ELan EPfP GKir GMaP LRHS MAvo NLar SPoG SWvt WCAu WWEG
	- 'Compacta Plena' (d)	EBee ECtt ELan EPfP GMaP LAst LHop LRHS MLHP MRav NEgg SRms
	- 'Fairy Perfect'	EBee IPot
	- Festival Star = 'Danfestar'PBR (Festival Series) **new**	LAst
	- 'Flamingo' (d)	CBcs EBee ECha IPot LHop MWea NLar
	- My Pink = 'Dangypink' **new**	LRHS
	- 'Perfekta'	CBcs EBee SPer
	- 'Pink Star' (d)	EBee
§	- 'Schneeflocke' (d)	EBee EPfP EShb GMaP LRHS NBre NLar SPhx SRms WWEG
	- Snowflake	see *G. paniculata* 'Schneeflocke'
	repens 🏆H4	ECtt EPfP GJos MWat SBch SPlb SWvt WFar WPer
	- 'Dorothy Teacher'	CMea ECho ECtt LBee LRHS WGor
§	- 'Dubia'	ECha ECho ECtt EDAr EPot MHer MMuc SEND SPoG SRms WPer WSHC
	- 'Fratensis'	ECho ECtt ELan LLHF NMen
	- Pink Beauty	see *G. repens* 'Rosa Schönheit'
§	- 'Rosa Schönheit'	EBee ECha EPot NLar SPer
	- 'Rose Fountain'	ECho
	- 'Rosea'	CPBP CTri CWib EBee ECho ECtt EDAr EPfP EShb GJos GMaP LBMP MMuc MWat NWCA SEND SPoG SRms SWvt WFar WHoo
	- 'Silver Carpet' (v)	WPer
	- white-flowered	CMea CWib EBee ECho ELan EPfP LRHS SWvt WPer
§	'Rosenschleier' (d) 🏆H4	CMea EBee ECha ECtt ELan EPfP IPot LAst LRHS MCot MRav NDov NEgg SBch SPer SRms SRot SWvt WHoo WSHC WTin WWEG
I	'Rosenschleier Variegata' (v)	MAvo WWEG
	'Rosy Veil'	see *G.* 'Rosenschleier'
§	***tenuifolia***	ECho EPot LBee NMen WPat
	Veil of Roses	see *G.* 'Rosenschleier'
	'White Festival'PBR (Festival Series) (d)	EBee GMac LRHS SPoG WFar

Gyptis (*Asteraceae*)

	commersonii	LHop

H

Haberlea (*Gesneriaceae*)

	ferdinandi-coburgii	CLAP ECho NMen NWCA
	- 'Connie Davidson'	GEdr NMen
	rhodopensis 🏆H4	CDes CElw CFee CStu EBee ECho GEdr GGar GKev NMen NSla SRms WAbe WCom WKif WPGP WTin
	- 'Virginalis'	CElw CLAP CStu NMen NSla NWCA WAbe WThu

Habranthus ✿ (*Amaryllidaceae*)

	andersonii	see *H. tubispathus*
	'Argentine Pink'	EDif
	brachyandrus	GCal SRms WPrP
	gracilifolius	WThu
	howardii	ECho
	martinezii	CPBP CStu ECho EPot NWCA
	'Pinky'	WHil
§	***robustus*** 🏆H1	CCCN CPLG CPne EBee ECho EPot EShb LAma LHop LRHS NLBP WCot WPGP
§	***tubispathus*** 🏆H1	CGHE CStu CYeo EBee ECho EDif EPot GCal ITim NWCA WCot WPrP

Hacquetia (*Apiaceae*)

	epipactis 🏆H4	Widely available
§	- 'Thor' (v)	CBow CDes CLAP EBee EWes GCrs GEdr LLHF MAvo NMen SUsu WAbe WCom WCot WFar WPGP
	- 'Variegata'	see *H. epipactis* 'Thor'

Haemanthus (*Amaryllidaceae*)

	albiflos 🏆H1	CHEx CPrp CSpe CStu CTca CTsd ECho EOHP LAma LToo SRms STre WCot
	amarylloides subsp. ***amarylloides***	CLak
	- subsp. ***polyanthes***	CLak ECho
	barkerae	CLak ECho
	carneus **new**	ECho
	coccineus 🏆H1	CLak ECho
	crispus	ECho
	humilis	ECho
	katherinae	see *Scadoxus multiflorus* subsp. *katherinae*
	lanceifolius	ECho
	montanus	CLak ECho
	natalensis	see *Scadoxus puniceus*
	pauculifolius	ECho
	pubescens subsp. ***leipoldtii***	CLak ECho
	sanguineus	ECho

Hakea (*Proteaceae*)

§	***drupacea***	CBcs CTrC

	epiglottis	CTrC ECou
	laurina	SPlb
	lissocarpha	CTrC
§	***lissosperma***	CDoC CWit ECou EPfP SPlb WPGP
	microcarpa	ECou
	nodosa	CCCN
	platysperma	SPlb
§	***salicifolia***	CCCN EBee IDee SPlb
	- 'Gold Medal' (v)	CTrC EBee
	saligna	see *H. salicifolia*
	sericea misapplied	see *H. lissosperma*
	sericea Schrad. & J.C.Wendl.	ECou
	- pink-flowered	SPlb
	suaveolens	see *H. drupacea*
	teretifolia	CTrC

Hakonechloa ✿ (*Poaceae*)

	macra	CAby CEnt CGHE CKno CPla CSam EBee EBrs EHoe EPPr EPla EShb GCal GKir MAvo MLLN MMoz MRav NDov SApp SMad SPhx SPoG WCot WDyG WPGP WSHC
§	- 'Alboaurea' ♀H4	CBcs CChe CFee CKno CPLG CWGN EBee EBrs ELan EPfP EShb GFor GKir LAst LRHS LSRN MGos MRav NCGa NPla NWCA SAga SApp STre WFar
	- 'Albovariegata' (v)	CKno CWan EPPr GCal LEdu MAsh MAvo WDyG WSpi
	- 'All Gold'	EBee EPPr EWes GBin LEdu SBfd SMad WWEG
	- 'Aureola' ♀H4	Widely available
*	- 'Mediopicta' (v)	SApp
	- 'Mediovariegata' (v)	CGHE CWCL EBee EPPr EPla WPGP
	- 'Naomi' (v)	CWGN EBee LRHS WCot
	- 'Nicolas'	CMea CSam CSpe EBee ELon EWes GBin LLHF LRHS LSou MLLN NDov NLBP SMad SMrm SPad SPoG WCot WFut
	- 'Stripe It Rich' (v) **new**	EBee EWes MAsh SBfd
	- 'Variegata'	see *H. macra* 'Alboaurea'

Halenia (*Gentianaceae*)

	elliptica	EBee
	- SDR 4640	GKev

Halesia (*Styracaceae*)

§	***carolina***	Widely available
	- Wedding Bells = 'Uconn Wedding Bells'	CPMA MBlu
	diptera	CBcs MBlu NEgg SKHP
	- var. ***magniflora***	EPfP LRHS MBlu SSpi
	monticola	CBcs CDul CMCN ELan EPfP GBin IFFs IVic MMuc NLar SPur SSpi SWvt
	- var. ***vestita*** ♀H4	CDoC CDul CPMA CTho EBee EPfP LRHS MAsh MBlu MBri MGos MRav NLar NVic SPer SPoG SSpi WBrE WDin WFar WGob WPGP WPat
	- - f. ***rosea***	CBcs CPMA EPfP MBlu
	tetraptera	see *H. carolina*

× *Halimiocistus* (*Cistaceae*)

	algarvensis	see *Halimium ocymoides*
§	'Ingwersenii'	CBcs CDoC EBee ELan EWes MMuc SBfd SPer SPoG SRms
	revolii misapplied	see × *H. sahucii*
§	***sahucii*** ♀H4	CBcs CBgR CDoC CSBt CTri EBee ECha ELan EPfP LBMP LRHS LTen MAsh MBNS MRav MSwo MWat NPri SBfd SDys SPer SPoG SRms SWvt WDin WFar
	- Ice Dancer = 'Ebhals'PBR (v)	CDoC EBee EPfP LAst MAsh SBfd SPer SWvt WClo
	'Susan'	see *Halimium* 'Susan'
§	***wintonensis*** ♀H3	CBcs CDoC EBee ELan EPfP GMaP LRHS MAsh SLon SPer SRms WHar WSHC
§	- 'Merrist Wood Cream' ♀H3	CBcs CBgR CDoC CMac CSBt EBee ELan EPfP LAst LRHS MAsh MMuc MRav MSwo NBir SBfd SEND SPer SPoG SSpi SWvt WAbe WCom WDin WFar WPat WSHC

Halimium (*Cistaceae*)

§	***calycinum***	CChe CDoC EBee ELan EPfP GKev IVic LRHS MAsh MBri MMuc SAga SBfd SCoo SEND SLim SPer SPoG SWvt WAbe WCFE WClo WDin WGob
	commutatum	see *H. calycinum*
	formosum	see *H. lasianthum* subsp. *formosum*
N	***halimifolium*** misapplied	see *H.* × *pauanum*
§	***lasianthum*** ♀H3	CBcs CMac CSBt CWib ELan EPfP LRHS MRav SBfd SLim WEas WKif
	- 'Concolor'	CWib EBee LRHS MSwo NPri SWvt WDin
§	- subsp. ***formosum***	GGar
	- - 'Sandling'	EBee ELan EPfP LRHS MMuc SLon SRms
	libanotis	see *H. calycinum*
§	***ocymoides*** ♀H3	CBcs CChe CDoC CWib ELan EPfP IVic MMHG MSwo NPri WHar
§	× ***pauanum***	EBee MMuc
	'Sun Spot'	LRHS
§	'Susan' ♀H3	CBgR CDoC EBee ELan EPfP MMHG SCoo SLim SPer SPoG WAbe
§	***umbellatum***	EBee EPfP MMuc SEND SPer WKif
	wintonense	see × *Halimiocistus wintonensis*

Halimodendron (*Papilionaceae*)

	halodendron	CArn CBcs CDul EBee MBlu SPer WDin

Halleria (*Scrophulariaceae*)

	lucida	CCCN EBee

Halocarpus (*Podocarpaceae*)

§	***bidwillii***	CDoC ECou

Haloragis (*Haloragaceae*)

	erecta 'Rubra'	WCot WPer
	- 'Wellington Bronze'	CBow CEnt CPLG CSpe EBee ECtt EHoe GGar LEdu MBNS MCCP MLHP SDys WBox WCon WEas WHer WMoo

Hamamelis ✿ (*Hamamelidaceae*)

	'Amethyst'	NLar
	'Brevipetala'	CBcs GKir NHol NLar
	'Danny'	CPMA
	'Doerak'	CPMA MBlu
	'Girard Orange'	EPfP
	× ***intermedia*** 'Advent'	CPMA NLar
	- 'Angelly' ♀H4	CPMA MBlu MBri MGos NLar SBir
	- 'Aphrodite' ♀H4	CPMA EPfP GKir LRHS MAsh MBlu MBri MGos MRav NCGa NLar SBir SSpi
	- 'Arnold Promise' ♀H4	Widely available
	- 'Aurora' ♀H4	CPMA GKir LRHS MBlu MBri NLar
	- 'Barmstedt Gold' ♀H4	CPMA EBee EPfP GKir LRHS LSRN MAsh MGos MRav NHol NLar SPoG SReu SRms SSpi SSta

	– 'Bernstein' **new**	IVic
	– 'Carmine Red'	CMac CPMA MGos NLar
	– 'Copper Beauty'	see *H.* × *intermedia* 'Jelena'
	– 'Diane' ΨH4	Widely available
§	– 'Feuerzauber'	CEnd CMac CSBt CTri LBuc MSwo NLar SBir SPer SRms WDin
	– Fire Cracker	see *H.* × *intermedia* 'Feuerzauber'
	– 'Frederic'	CPMA LRHS MAsh SBir
	– 'Gimborn's Perfume'	NLar
	– 'Gingerbread'	CPMA LRHS MAsh
	– 'Glowing Embers'	CPMA LRHS MAsh SPoG
	– 'Harlow Carr'	LRHS
	– 'Harry'	CPMA GKir LRHS MAsh MBri NLar SBir SSpi
§	– 'Jelena' ΨH4	Widely available
	– 'John'	MBri
	– 'Limelight'	CPMA MBlu NLar
	– 'Livia'	CPMA LRHS MAsh MBri NLar SBir SPoG SSpi
	– Magic Fire	see *H.* × *intermedia* 'Feuerzauber'
	– 'Moonlight'	CPMA NLar
	– 'Nina'	LRHS MAsh NLar SBir SPoG
	– 'Orange Beauty'	CBcs LRHS MBlu MGos SCoo
	– 'Orange Peel'	EPfP LRHS MAsh MBri NLar SBir SPoG
	– 'Ostergold'	NLar
	– 'Pallida' ΨH4	Widely available
	– 'Primavera'	CPMA CWSG EBee IArd NLar NPCo SBfd SLim
	– 'Ripe Corn'	CPMA EPfP LRHS MAsh MBri SPoG
	– 'Robert'	CPMA LRHS MAsh MBri SPoG
	– 'Rubin'	CPMA GKir LRHS MAsh MBri NLar SPoG SSpi
	– 'Rubinstar'	CPMA
	– 'Ruby Glow'	CBcs CMac CWib EBee ECho EGxp LMaj LSRN MGos NLar NPCo NWea SBfd SCoo SLim SPer WDin
	– 'Savill Starlight'	CPMA
	– 'Spanish Spider' **new**	MBlu
	– 'Strawberries and Cream'	CPMA
	– 'Sunburst'	EPfP LRHS MGos NLar
	– 'Twilight'	CPMA
	– 'Vesna' ΨH4	CMac CPMA EPfP LRHS MAsh MBlu NLar SBir SPoG
	– 'Westerstede'	CPMA CWSG EBee EPfP IArd LAst LSRN MGos MRav NLar NPla NWea SBfd SCoo SLim WDin WHar
	– 'Wiero'	CPMA
	– 'Zitronenjette'	CPMA
	japonica	WFar
	– 'Pendula'	CPMA MBlu NLar
	– 'Rubra'	NPCo
	– 'Zuccariniana'	NLar
	mollis ΨH4	Widely available
	– 'Boskoop'	NLar
	– 'Coombe Wood'	CPMA LRHS
	– 'Goldcrest'	CPMA
	– 'Jermyns Gold' ΨH4	CPMA EPfP LRHS
	– 'Wisley Supreme'	CAbP CPMA ELan EPfP LRHS MAsh MBri SPoG SSpi
	'Rochester'	CPMA NLar NPCo SBir
	vernalis	WDin
	– 'Lombarts' Weeping'	NLar
	– purple	MBlu NLar
	– 'Sandra' ΨH4	CBcs CMCN EBee ELan EPfP GKir LRHS MAsh MBlu MGos MRav NLar SLon SPer SPoG SReu SSpi SSta
	virginiana	CAgr ECrN GPoy IDee LLHF MMuc NWea WDin
	– 'Mohonk Red'	CPMA

Hamelia (*Rubiaceae*)

	patens	CCCN EShb

Hanabusaya (*Campanulaceae*)

§	***asiatica***	NCGa NChi WFar

Haplocarpha (*Asteraceae*)

	rueppellii	CFee NBro SRms SRot

Haplopappus (*Asteraceae*)

	brandegeei	see *Erigeron aureus*
	coronopifolius	see *H. glutinosus*
§	***glutinosus***	EBee ECha ECho ECtt EPot GEdr MMuc MTho NLar NWCA SEND SPlb SRms WCom
	lyallii	see *Tonestus lyallii*
	prunelloides	NWCA
	– var. ***mustersii***	WCot
	rehderi	MWat WCon

Hardenbergia (*Papilionaceae*)

	comptoniana ΨH1	CPLG WCot
	– 'Rosea'	ERea
	violacea ΨH1	CBcs CCCN CHII CRHN CSPN CTrC CTsd EBee EGxp ELan ERea LRHS MHer SEND SLim SPer WCot
	– f. ***alba***	CBcs ECou GGar IDee LRHS SLim
	– – 'White Crystal'	EBee ERea SPer WPGP
	– – 'White Wanderer' **new**	CCCN
	– dwarf	ECou
	– 'Happy Wanderer'	CCCN ERea LRHS SChF SOWG WPGP
	– f. ***rosea***	CBcs CCCN EBee GGar LRHS SLim SPer

Harpephyllum (*Anacardiaceae*)

	caffrum (F)	XBlo

Haworthia ✿ (*Aloaceae*)

	attenuata	EShb
	'Black Prince'	EPfP
	cooperi	STre
	cymbiformis	EPfP STre
	fasciata	EPfP SEND SWal
	glabrata var. ***concolor***	EPfP EShb
	pumila ΨH1	SEND
	radula	EPfP
	tesselata	see *H. venosa* subsp. *tesselata*
§	***venosa*** subsp. ***tesselata*** ΨH1 **new**	SEND

hazelnut see *Corylus*

Hebe ✿ (*Scrophulariaceae*)

	albicans ΨH4	CMac ECou ELan EPfP GGar GKir IFFs IFoB LAst LRHS LSRN MBri MGos MRav SBfd SCoo SPer SPoG STre SWal WClo WFar
	– 'Cobb'	ECou
	– prostrate	see *H. albicans* 'Snow Cover'
*	– 'Snow Carpet'	CCCN LRHS
§	– 'Snow Cover'	EWes LRHS
	– 'Snow Drift'	see *H. albicans* 'Snow Cover'
§	– 'Sussex Carpet'	STre
§	'Alicia Amherst'	CDoy LRHS SPer SRms SWal
	allanii	see *H. amplexicaulis* f. *hirta*
	'Amanda Cook' (v)	MCCP NPer SPoG
	'Amethyst'	SBfd
	amplexicaulis clone 4	STre
§	– f. ***hirta***	NHol

§	'Amy'	ELon GGal LRHS NPer SPer WCom WOut
	× ***andersonii***	CDul EPfP LRHS
§	- 'Andersonii Variegata' (v)	LRHS SBfd SRms
	- 'Argenteovariegata'	see *H.* × *andersonii* 'Andersonii Variegata'
	'Andressa Paula'	CCCN LRHS
	anomala misapplied	see *H.* 'Imposter'
	anomala (Armstr.) Cockayne	CCCN LRHS
	'Aoira'	see *H. recurva* 'Aoira'
§	***armstrongii***	ECho GGar MGos WDin
	'Arthur'	ECou
	astonii	ECho
	'Autumn Glory'	CSBt CWSG ECho ELan EPfP GKir LAst LRHS MAsh MGos MLHP MSwo NBir NPri SBfd SGar SPer SPlb SPoG SWal SWvt WDin
	azurea	see *H. venustula*
	'Azurens'	see *H.* 'Maori Gem'
	'Baby Blush' PBR	LRHS
	'Baby Marie'	CAbP CChe CSBt ECho ECou ELan EPfP GKir LRHS LSRN MGos MSwo NMen NPer NPri SBfd SCoo SPoG SRGP SRms SRot SWvt
	'Beverley Hills' PBR	CSBt LRHS NLar WHar
	'Bicolor Wand'	CCCN CTsd LRHS
	bishopiana	ECou EPfP MGos SCoo
	'Black Night' **new**	LRHS
	'Black Panther'	LBuc
	'Blue Clouds' ♀H3	LAst LLHF LRHS MSwo SPer WCFE
§	'Blue Gem'	CTrC MGos SBfd
	Blue Star = 'Vergeer 1' PBR	CBgR LRHS LSou MAsh NLar SLon SPoG
	bollonsii	GGar
	'Boscawenii'	CTsd MGos MMuc
	'Bouquet' PBR	NEgg
§	'Bowles's Hybrid'	CCCN LEdu LRHS MRav MSwo SEND SRms STre
	brachysiphon	CTrC CTri EPfP MGos MRav SEND SPer WDin
	brevifolia	LRHS
	'Bronzy Baby' PBR (v)	SPoG
	buchananii	ECho GGar GKir MGos MHer NPer STre
§	- 'Fenwickii'	ECho NWCA
	- 'Minima'	ECho
	- 'Minor' Hort N.Z.	ECho GBin NBir NWCA
	buxifolia misapplied	see *H. odora*
	buxifolia (Benth.) Andersen	CMac ELan MMuc NHol NWea SEND SWal WDin WHar
§	'Caledonia' ♀H3	CCCN CSBt EPfP LBMP LRHS LSRN MAsh MBri MGos NPer SBfd SCoo SPoG WCom WFar
§	***canterburiensis***	ECou GGar
N	'Carl Teschner'	see *H.* 'Youngii'
	'Carnea Variegata' (v)	EPfP LRHS MGos MSCN SPer SPoG WOut
	carnosula	GGar MGos NBir SPer WHar
	catarractae	see *Parahebe catarractae*
	'Celine'	GGar MGos SBfd SPoG SRGP
I	'Chalk's Buchananii'	WCom
	'Champagne'	CCCN LAst LRHS LSRN NHol SBfd SCoo
	Champion = 'Champseiont' PBR	EKen LRHS LSou LTen NLar SCoo WClo
	'Charming White'	CChe EQua LRHS LSRN MGos SBfd SPoG
	chathamica	ECou GGar LRHS
	'Christabel'	LRHS
	'Claymoddie Blue Seedling'	GGal
	'Clear Skies' PBR	ECou LRHS NEgg
	'Colwall'	ECho
	'Conwy Knight'	WAbe
*	'Coral Pink'	LRHS
	'County Park'	ECou EWes NHol NMen
	'Cranleighensis'	CTsd SBfd
	'Cupins'	NWCA SWal
	cupressoides	IRar WDin
	- 'Boughton Dome'	CTri ECho EPfP MGos MHer MTho NMen SWal WAbe WCFE WHoo WPer
	'Dazzler' (v)	CAbP
	decumbens	EWes GGar MGos NHol
	'Denise'	LRHS
	'Diamond'	LRHS LSRN
	dieffenbachii	GGar
	diosmifolia	CAbP CBot CDoC ELan LRHS WAbe WFar
	- 'Marie'	SWal
	divaricata	ECou
*	- 'Marlborough'	ECou
	- 'Nelson'	ECou
	'Dorothy Peach'	see *H.* 'Watson's Pink'
	'E.A. Bowles'	ECou WBVN
	'E.B. Anderson'	see *H.* 'Caledonia'
	'Early Blue'	NBir
	'Edington'	LRHS SPer WCFE
	'Ellie'	LRHS
	elliptica	CDul ECou MGos SBfd
	- 'Kapiti'	ECou
	- 'Variegata'	see *H.* 'Silver Queen'
	'Emerald Dome'	see *H.* 'Emerald Gem'
§	'Emerald Gem' ♀H3	CMac CTri ECho EPfP GKev GKir LRHS LSRN MAsh MBri MGos MHer MMuc MSwo NHol NLar NMen NWCA SBfd SCoo SPer SPlb SPoG SWal WCom WPat
	'Emerald Green'	see *H.* 'Emerald Gem'
	epacridea	ECho EWes
§	'Eveline'	CSBt CTri LRHS MGos NBir SPer
	evenosa	GGar
	'Eversley Seedling'	see *H.* 'Bowles's Hybrid'
	'Fairfieldii'	IRar
	'First Light' PBR	CWSG GGar LRHS MGos NPri SCoo WHar
	'Fragrant Jewel'	CWib LRHS SEND SPhx
	× ***franciscana***	ECou
	- 'Blue Gem' misapplied	see *H.* × *franciscana* 'Lobelioides'
	- 'Blue Gem' ambig.	ECho ELan EPfP LRHS MRav NBir NPer SBfd SEND SPer SPlb SPoG SRms SWal WHar
§	- 'Lobelioides'	GGar
	- 'Purple Tips' misapplied	see *H. speciosa* 'Variegata'
	- 'Variegata'	see *H.* 'Silver Queen'
I	- 'White Gem'	SRms
	- yellow-variegated (v)	SPer
	'Franjo'	ECou
	Garden Beauty Blue = 'Cliv' PBR	LBuc LRHS MGos
	Garden Beauty Pink = 'Lowink'	LBuc LRHS
	Garden Beauty Purple = 'Nold' PBR	LBuc LRHS
	'Gauntlettii'	see *H.* 'Eveline'
	'Gibby'	LRHS
	glaucophylla 'Clarence'	ECou GGar
I	'Glaucophylla Variegata' (v)	CTri EPfP LRHS NBir SCoo SPer WKif
	'Glengarriff'	NHol
§	'Gloriosa'	CEnt
	'Godefroyana'	see *H. pinguifolia* 'Godefroyana'
	'Goethe'	SEND
	'Gold Beauty' (v)	LRHS NPri

	'Golden Nugget'	LRHS
	'Goldrush' PBR (v)	LBuc LRHS MGos SPoG
	'Gran's Favourite'	CCCN LRHS
	'Great Orme' ♀H3	Widely available
	'Green Globe'	see *H.* 'Emerald Gem'
	'Greensleeves'	GGar LRHS
	'Grethe'	SPoG
	'Gruninard's Seedling'	GGar
	haastii	NLar
	'Hadspen Pink'	LRHS
	'Hagley Park'	EPfP LRHS SWal
§	'Hartii'	LRHS MRav SBfd
	'Heartbreaker' PBR (v)	CWSG EGxp ELan GGar LBuc LRHS MCCP MGos NPri SBfd SCoo SPoG
	'Hielan Lassie'	LRHS
	'Highdownensis'	LRHS
	'Hinderwell'	NPer
	'Hinerua'	GGar
	'Hobby'	LRHS
	'Holywell'	SWal
	hookeriana	see *Parahebe hookeriana*
	hulkeana ♀H3	CBot CTri LRHS LSou MHer SAga SSpi SWal WCom WEas WKif WPat
§	'Imposter'	SRms
	'Inspiration'	GGar LRHS
	insularis	ECho ECou
	'James Stirling'	see *H. ochracea* 'James Stirling'
	'Jane Holden'	LRHS
	'Janet'	SGar
	'Jean Searle'	LAst
	'Joanna'	ECou
§	'Johny Day'	LRHS
	'Judy'	LRHS
	'Kirkii'	CDul EPfP SBfd SCoo SPer SWal
	'Knightshayes'	see *H.* 'Caledonia'
	'La Séduisante'	CTri ECou GGal LRHS MLHP SEND WKif WOut
	'Lady Ann' PBR (v)	CSBt CWSG GGar LRHS NEgg NLar SPoG WHar
	'Lady Ardilaun'	see *H.* 'Amy'
	laevis	see *H. venustula*
	latifolia	see *H.* 'Blue Gem'
	'Lavender Spray'	see *H.* 'Hartii'
	'Lilac Wand'	CTsd
	'Lindsayi'	ECou LRHS
	'Lisa'	EPfP
§	'Loganioides'	GGar
	'Lopen' (v)	ECou
	'Louise'	LIMB SGar
	lyallii	see *Parahebe lyallii*
	lycopodioides	EWes WThu
	- 'Aurea'	see *H. armstrongii*
	'Lynash'	LRHS
	mackenii	see *H.* 'Emerald Gem'
	macrantha ♀H3	EPfP GGar LRHS SRms WAbe WCom
	macrocarpa	ECou LRHS
	- var. ***latisepala***	ECou LRHS
§	'Maori Gem'	GGar SBfd
	'Margery Fish'	see *H.* 'Primley Gem'
	'Margret' PBR ♀H4	CSBt CWCL EPfP GKir LAst LRHS LSRN MAsh MGos NPri SBfd SCoo SPer SPoG SRGP
	'Marie Antoinette'	GGar LRHS
	'Marjorie'	CDul CMac CTrC ELan EPfP LAst LRHS MGos MRav MSwo NLar NPer NWea SBfd SPer SPoG SRms WDin
	matthewsii	WPat
	'Mauve Queen'	LRHS
	'Mauvena'	SPer
	'McKean'	see *H.* 'Emerald Gem'
	'Megan'	ECou
	'Mercury'	ECou
	'Mette' **new**	LLHF
	'Midnight Sky'	LBuc LRHS
	'Midsummer Beauty' ♀H3	CWCL ECou EPfP LAst LRHS MGos MLHP MRav NBir SBfd SEND SMad SPer SPlb SPoG SWvt WDin WHar WOut WSFF
	'Milmont Emerald'	see *H.* 'Emerald Gem'
*	***minima*** 'Calvin'	ECho
	'Misty'	CCCN
§	'Mohawk' PBR	LBuc LRHS MGos
	'Monica'	WOut
*	'Moppets Hardy'	SPer
§	'Mrs Winder' ♀H4	Widely available
	'Mystery'	ECou ELan SWal
	'Nantyderry'	CCCN LRHS SWal WOut
§	'Neil's Choice' ♀H4	CCCN ECou ELon SWal
	'Neopolitan'	LRHS
	'Nicola's Blush' ♀H4	Widely available
	ochracea	LRHS MGos SWal
§	- 'James Stirling' ♀H4	CBcs CSBt ECho ELan EPfP GKev GKir LRHS LSRN LTen MAsh MBri MGos MSwo NBir NLar SBfd SCoo SLim SPer SPlb SPoG SRGP SWvt WDin WFar
	'Oddity'	LRHS
§	***odora***	ECou EPfP GGar MGos MMuc SEND STre
I	- 'Nana'	EPfP
	- 'New Zealand Gold'	GKir LRHS MAsh MGos MMuc NHol SCoo SEND SWal
	- 'Summer Frost'	LRHS NHol NWCA
	'Oratia Beauty' ♀H4	MGos MMuc MRav SBfd SEND
	'Orphan Annie' PBR (v)	CWSG LRHS MGos SPoG
	parviflora misapplied	see *H.* 'Bowles's Hybrid'
§	***parviflora*** (Vahl) Cockayne & Allan	GGar
	- var. ***angustifolia***	see *H. stenophylla*
	- var. ***arborea***	see *H. parviflora* (Vahl) Cockayne & Allan
	- 'Holdsworth'	LRHS SDys
	- 'Palmerston'	ECou
	'Pascal' ♀H4	CCCN ECou ELan EPfP LRHS LSRN MBri MGos MRav SBfd SCoo SLon SPer SPoG
	'Pastel Elegance' **new**	LRHS
	'Patti Dossett'	see *H. speciosa* 'Patti Dossett'
	pauciramosa	SRms
	'Paula'	LRHS
	'Pearl of Paradise' PBR	MGos SPoG
	perfoliata	see *Parahebe perfoliata*
	'Perry's Rubyleaf'	NPer
	'Petra's Pink'	CCCN LRHS
	'Pewter Dome' ♀H4	CMac CSBt ECou EPfP GKir LHop LRHS MGos MNHC MRav NHol SBfd SDix SPer SRms STre SWal WBrE WCom
	'Pimeba'	WCom
	pimeleoides	ECou NHol
	- 'Glauca'	NPer
	- 'Glaucocaerulea'	ECou
	- 'Quicksilver' ♀H4	CSBt CTri ECou EDAr ELan EPfP GGar LAst LRHS LSRN MGos MMuc MRav MSCN MSwo NBir NHol NPer SBfd SCoo SPer STre SWal WHar WPat
	- 'Red Tip'	ECho
	pinguifolia	ECou SPlb
	- 'Dobson'	LRHS
§	- 'Godefroyana'	SWal
	- 'Pagei' ♀H4	Widely available

	- 'Sutherlandii'	CBcs CDoC ECho GGar IFFs LEdu LRHS LSRN LTen MGos SCoo WFar
	'Pink Elegance' new	LRHS
	'Pink Elephant' (v) ♀H3	ELan EPfP LBuc LRHS MAsh SBfd SPoG WCom
	'Pink Fantasy'	CChe LRHS MGos MRav NHol
	'Pink Goddess'	LRHS MGos SRGP
	'Pink Lady'PBR	SPoG
	'Pink Paradise'PBR	CAbP ELan EPfP LRHS LSou MGos NHol SPoG
	'Pink Payne'	see *H.* 'Eveline'
	'Pink Pearl'	see *H.* 'Gloriosa'
	'Pink Pixie'	LBuc LRHS MBri MGos SCoo
	'Pink Princess'	LRHS
	'Pink Wand'	CTsd
	'Porlock Purple'	see *Parahebe catarractae* 'Delight'
§	'Primley Gem'	CCCN EQua LRHS
	propinqua	NMen
I	'Prostrata'	CSBt
	'Purple Emperor'	see *H.* 'Neil's Choice'
	'Purple Paradise'PBR	EPfP LSou MBri NEgg SPoG
	'Purple Picture'	ELon
	'Purple Pixie'PBR	see *H.* 'Mohawk'
	'Purple Princess'	LRHS
	'Purple Queen'	ELan EPfP EShb LIMB LRHS SPoG
	Purple Shamrock = 'Neprock'PBR (v)	EPfP LAst LBuc LRHS LSRN MBri MGos NEgg NLar SBfd SCoo SPer SPoG WClo WHar
	'Purple Tips' misapplied	see *H. speciosa* 'Variegata'
	'Rachel'	LSRN
	rakaiensis ♀H4	Widely available
	ramosissima	GGar
	raoulii	NMen WAbe
	'Raven'	LRHS
	recurva	CSam CTri EPfP LAst MGos MMuc NHol SEND SRms SWal WCom WCot WDin
§	- 'Aoira'	ECou
	- 'Boughton Silver' ♀H3	ELan EPfP LRHS
	- 'White Torrent'	ECou
	'Red Edge' ♀H4	Widely available
	'Red Rum'	ELan
	'Red Ruth'	see *H.* 'Eveline'
	rigidula	LRHS MMuc NHol
	'Ronda'	ECou
	'Rose Elegance' new	LRHS
	'Rosie'PBR	CSBt EPfP LAst LBuc LRHS LSRN NMen SCoo SPer
*	'Royal Blue'	LRHS
	'Royal Purple'	see *H.* 'Alicia Amherst'
	salicifolia	CCCN CChe CMac CTca ECou ELan EPfP GGar LAst LRHS MDun MGos MRav NHol SBfd SCoo SEND SPlb SRms WFar
	- BR 30	GGar
	- 'Snow Wreath'	see *H.* 'Snow Wreath'
	'Sandra Joy'	CCCN
	'Sapphire' ♀H4	ECou EPfP GKir LRHS MAsh MGos MWea NPri SBfd SCoo WFar
	'Sarana'	CCCN ECou LRHS
	selaginoides hort.	see *H.* 'Loganioides'
	'Shiraz'	LRHS
	'Silver Dollar' (v)	CCCN CMac CSBt CSam ELan EPfP LBuc LRHS LTen MGos MMuc NEgg SPer SPoG SWal WSpi
§	'Silver Queen' (v) ♀H2	CMac CSBt ECou ELan EPfP LRHS MGos NEgg NLar NPer SBfd SEND SPer SPoG SWal WOut
	'Simon Délaux'	CEnt ECou LRHS SEND
§	'Snow Wreath' (v)	WCom
I	'Southlandii'	ECho LAst MWhi
	speciosa	ECho
	- 'Johny Day'	see *H.* 'Johny Day'
§	- 'Patti Dossett'	LRHS
	- 'Rangatira'	ECou
§	- 'Variegata' (v)	NPer WEas
	'Spender's Seedling' misapplied	see *H. stenophylla*
	'Spender's Seedling' ambig.	MCot MMuc
	'Spender's Seedling' Hort.	ECou EPfP LRHS MRav SEND SPoG SRms STre
	'Spring Glory'	LRHS
§	***stenophylla***	ECou EShb GGal MSCN SAPC SArc SBfd SDix
	- 'White Lady'	GGar
	stricta	ECou LRHS
	- var. ***egmontiana***	ECou LRHS
	- var. ***macroura***	ECou
	'Stuart Fraser' new	SWal
	subalpina	CSBt ECho LTen NHol
	'Summer Blue'	EPfP LRHS MMuc MRav
	'Super Red'	CSBt LRHS
	'Sussex Carpet'	see *H. albicans* 'Sussex Carpet'
	'Sweet Kim' (v)	CMac LBuc LRHS MGos NPri
	'Tina'	ECou
	'Tom Marshall'	see *H. canterburiensis*
	topiaria ♀H4	CAbP CChe CSBt CSam ECho ECou EPfP GGar GKir LAst LHop LRHS LTen MBrN MMuc MRav MSwo NHol SBfd SCoo SEND SPer SPoG STre SWal WAbe WCom WFar
	- 'Doctor Favier'	LRHS
	townsonii	ECou LHop LRHS SCoo
	traversii	ECou NHol SRms
	- 'Mason River'	ECou
	- 'Woodside'	ECou
	'Tricolor'	see *H. speciosa* 'Variegata'
	'Trixie'	CCCN ECou LRHS
	'Trudi'	LRHS
	'Twisty'	ELan
	'Valentino'PBR	LRHS NEgg
	'Veitchii'	see *H.* 'Alicia Amherst'
§	***venustula***	ECou GGar IArd LRHS MGos MMuc
	- 'Patricia Davies'	ECou
	vernicosa ♀H3	CChe CDul ECho EPfP GKir LAst LRHS MGos MHer NHol SBfd SCoo SPer SPlb SRot STre SWvt WAbe WCom WFar
	'Violet Wand'	LRHS
	'Vogue'	EPfP
	'Waikiki'	see *H.* 'Mrs Winder'
	'Warley Pink'	LRHS
§	'Watson's Pink'	MWea SPer WKif
	'White Gem' (*brachysiphon* hybrid) ♀H4	CCCN CWCL ECou LRHS MGos NPer SPer WFar
	'White Heather'	LRHS MGos NBir SBfd
	'White Paradise'PBR	SPoG
	'Willcoxii'	see *H. buchananii* 'Fenwickii'
	'Wingletye' ♀H3	CCCN ECho ECou LRHS WCom
	'Winter Glow'	CCCN LRHS MGos SBfd SCoo
	'Wiri Blush'	LRHS SWvt
	'Wiri Charm'	CAbP CBcs CMac CSBt EPfP GGar LAst LRHS MGos MMuc MRav MSwo NEgg SBfd SEND SPoG SWal WBVN WClo
	'Wiri Cloud' ♀H3	CMac EPfP GGar LRHS LSou MGos MMuc MSwo SBfd SEND SWal
	'Wiri Dawn' ♀H3	ELan EPfP EWes LRHS LSou MGos MMuc SBfd SEND SWvt WHrl
	'Wiri Desire'	CCCN LRHS
	'Wiri Gem'	LRHS MRav
	'Wiri Icing Sugar'	LRHS
	'Wiri Image'	CBcs CSBt LRHS MMuc SEND SPoG
	'Wiri Joy'	LRHS MMuc SEND SPoG

	'Wiri Mist'	CTrC GGar LRHS MGos SBfd SCoo SPoG SWal WFar
	'Wiri Prince'	LRHS SPoG
	'Wiri Splash'	CTrC LRHS MGos SPoG
	'Wiri Vision'	CSBt LRHS MMuc SEND
§	'Youngii' ƳH3-4	CSBt CTri ELan EPfP GKir LAst LRHS MGos MHer MMuc MRav NBir NMen NPri SBfd SEND SPer SPlb SPoG SRms STre SWvt WBVN WCFE WHoo

Hebenstretia (*Scrophulariaceae*)

	dura	CPBP
	- 'Jeanie'	SDys
*	***quinquinervis***	LSou

Hechtia (*Bromeliaceae*)

	F&M 188	WPGP

Hedeoma (*Lamiaceae*)

	hyssopifolia	SPhx

Hedera ✿ (*Araliaceae*)

§	***algeriensis***	CDoC SAPC SArc WFib
	- 'Bellecour'	WFib
§	- 'Gloire de Marengo' (v) ƳH3	Widely available
§	- 'Gloire de Marengo' arborescent (v)	SPer
	- 'Marginomaculata' (v) ƳH3	CDoC EPfP LRHS MAsh SBfd SMad WFib
	- 'Montgomery'	LRHS LSRN MWht SBfd
	- 'Ravensholst' ƳH3	CMac MRav WFib
§	***azorica***	WFar WFib
	- 'Pico'	EPfP WFib
	canariensis hort.	see *H. algeriensis*
	- var. ***azorica***	see *H. azorica*
	- 'Cantabrian'	see *H. maroccana* 'Spanish Canary'
	- 'Gloire de Marengo'	see *H. algeriensis* 'Gloire de Marengo'
	- 'Variegata'	see *H. algeriensis* 'Gloire de Marengo'
	chinensis	see *H. sinensis* var. *sinensis*
	- typica	see *H. sinensis* var. *sinensis*
§	***colchica*** ƳH4	CDul EPfP SPer WCFE WDin WFar WFib
	- 'Batumi'	MBNS WFib
	- 'Dentata' ƳH4	EHoe MRav MWhi NEgg WFib
	- 'Dentata Aurea'	see *H. colchica* 'Dentata Variegata'
§	- 'Dentata Variegata' (v) ƳH4	Widely available
	- 'My Heart'	see *H. colchica*
	- 'Paddy's Pride'	see *H. colchica* 'Sulphur Heart'
§	- 'Sulphur Heart' (v) ƳH4	Widely available
	- 'Variegata'	see *H. colchica* 'Dentata Variegata'
	cristata	see *H. helix* 'Parsley Crested'
§	***cypria***	EShb EWld WFib
	helix	CArn CCVT CMac CRWN CTri GKir MGos NWea WDin WHer WSFF
	- 'Adam' (v)	CWib EBee LAst LSRN MBri WFib
	- 'Amberwaves'	MBri WFib
	- 'Angularis Aurea' ƳH4	EPfP MWht NBir WFib
	- 'Anita'	GBin WFib WGwG
§	- 'Anna Marie' (v)	CMac MBri SRms WFib
	- 'Anne Borch'	see *H. helix* 'Anna Marie'
	- 'Arborescens'	EBee MGos WDin WSFF
	- 'Ardingly' (v)	MWhi WFib
	- 'Asterisk'	WFib
	- 'Atropurpurea'	EPPr GBin WDin WFib
	- 'Baby Face'	WFib
	- var. ***baltica***	WFib
	- 'Barabits' Silver' (v)	EPla
	- 'Bill Archer'	GBin WFib
	- 'Bird's Foot'	see *H. helix* 'Pedata'
	- 'Blarney'	WFib
	- 'Blue Moon'	WFib
	- 'Boskoop'	WFib
	- 'Bowles's Ox Heart'	WFib
	- 'Bredon'	MRav
	- 'Brimstone' (v)	WFib
§	- 'Brokamp'	MWht SLPl WFib
	- 'Bruder Ingobert' (v)	WHrl
	- 'Buttercup'	CBcs CDul CMac CTri EBee EHoe ELan EPfP EShb LAst LRHS LSRN MAsh MBri MGos MWhi NBea NBid NHol SAga SBfd SLim SPer SPoG WCFE WDin WFar WFib WTin
	- 'Buttercup' arborescent	MAsh
	- 'Caecilia' (v) ƳH4	EPfP EQua LRHS MSwo SPer SWvt WCot WFib
N	- 'Caenwoodiana'	see *H. helix* 'Pedata'
	- 'Caenwoodiana Aurea'	WFib
	- 'Calico' (v)	WFib
	- 'California Gold' (v)	WFib
	- 'Calypso'	WFib
	- 'Carolina Crinkle'	CBgR GBin MWhi WFib
	- 'Cathedral Wall'	WFib
§	- 'Cavendishii' (v)	SRms WFib WRHF
	- 'Cavendishii Latina'	WCot
	- 'Celebrity' (v)	WFib
§	- 'Ceridwen' (v) ƳH4	MBri SPlb WFib
	- 'Chalice'	WFib
	- 'Cheap Thrills'	WFib
	- 'Cheeky'	WFib
	- 'Cheltenham Blizzard' (v)	CNat
	- 'Chester' (v)	LRHS MAsh WFib
	- 'Chicago'	CWib WFib
	- 'Chicago Variegated' (v)	WFib
	- 'Chrysophylla'	MSwo
	- 'Clotted Cream' (v)	CMac ECGP ELon LRHS MAsh MWat WFib
	- 'Cockle Shell'	WFib
	- 'Colin'	GBin
§	- 'Congesta' ƳH4	CMac EPla GCra NBir SRms STre WFib
	- 'Conglomerata'	CBcs ELan EPla NBir SRms WDin WFib
	- 'Conglomerata Erecta'	MAsh SRms WCFE WFib
	- 'Courage'	WFib WGwG
	- 'Crenata'	WFib
	- 'Crispa'	MRav
	- 'Cristata'	see *H. helix* 'Parsley Crested'
	- 'Curleylocks'	see *H. helix* 'Manda's Crested'
	- 'Curley-Q'	see *H. helix* 'Dragon Claw'
	- 'Curvaceous' (v)	WCot WFib
	- 'Cyprus'	see *H. cypria*
	- 'Dainty Bess'	CWib
	- 'Danish Crown'	WFib
	- 'Dead Again'	GBin WCot
§	- 'Dealbata' (v)	CMac WFib
	- 'Delft'	WFib
	- 'Deltoidea'	see *H. hibernica* 'Deltoidea'
	- 'Discolor'	see *H. helix* 'Minor Marmorata', *H. helix* 'Dealbata'
§	- 'Donerailensis'	MBlu WFib
	- 'Don's Papillon'	CBgR CNat WAlt
	- 'Dovers'	WFib
§	- 'Dragon Claw'	WFib
	- 'Duckfoot' ƳH4	CBgR CDoC EShb GBin MWhi WFib WOut
	- 'Egret'	WFib
	- 'Eileen' (v)	WFib
	- 'Elfenbein' (v)	WFib
	- 'Emerald Jewel'	WFib

	- 'Erecta' ♀H4	CBgR CDul CTca EPPr EPfP EPla GCal LAst MBlu MGos NHol SBfd SPer SPlb WDin WFar WFib
	- 'Erin'	see *H. helix* 'Pin Oak'
	- 'Ester' (v)	CBar EQua LAst SRGP WFib
§	- 'Eva' (v)	MGos WDin WFib
	- 'Fanfare'	WFib
	- 'Fantasia' (v)	EShb MBri WFib
	- 'Feenfinger'	WFib WGwG
	- 'Ferney'	WFib
	- 'Filigran'	NLar WFib WHer
	- 'Flashback' (v)	WFib
	- 'Flavescens'	WFib
	- 'Fluffy Ruffles'	WFib
	- 'Forking Hell'	WAlt
I	- 'Francis Ivy'	WFib
	- 'Frizzle'	WFib
	- 'Frosty' (v)	WFib
	- 'Funny Girl'	WFib
	- 'Garland'	WFib
	- 'Gavotte'	MWht WFib
	- 'Ghost'	WFib
	- 'Gilded Hawke'	WFib WGwG
	- 'Glache' (v)	WFib
	- 'Glacier' (v) ♀H4	Widely available
	- 'Glymii'	GBin WCFE WFar WFib WTin
	- 'Gold Harald'	see *H. helix* 'Goldchild'
	- 'Gold Ripple'	NLar SEND
§	- 'Goldchild' (v) ♀H3-4	CBar CBcs CDoC CMac CSam EBee EHoe EPfP LAst LOck LRHS LTen MAsh MGos MRav MSwo NBir NEgg NHol SAga SBfd SLim SPer SPoG SWvt WDin WFib
	- 'Goldcraft' (v)	WFib
	- 'Golden Ann'	see *H. helix* 'Ceridwen'
*	- 'Golden Arrow'	ELan LRHS MAsh
	- 'Golden Curl' (v)	CMac EPfP LRHS MAsh
	- 'Golden Ester'	see *H. helix* 'Ceridwen'
	- 'Golden Gate' (v)	LAst WFib
	- 'Golden Girl'	WFib
	- 'Golden Ingot' (v) ♀H4	ELan EQua MAsh MWhi SBfd WFib WGwG
	- 'Golden Jytte' (v)	WFib
	- 'Golden Kolibri'	see *H. helix* 'Midas Touch'
	- 'Golden Mathilde' (v)	GBin
	- 'Golden Pittsburgh' (v)	WFib
	- 'Golden Snow' (v)	WFib
	- 'Goldfinch'	MBri WFib
	- 'Goldfinger'	MBri WFib
	- 'Goldheart'	see *H. helix* 'Oro di Bogliasco'
	- 'Goldstern' (v)	MRav MWhi WFib
	- 'Gracilis'	see *H. hibernica* 'Gracilis'
	- 'Green Finger'	see *H. helix* 'Très Coupé'
	- 'Green Ripple'	CBcs CTri EBee GKir LRHS MAsh MGos MRav MSwo MWht NBro NPri SEND SPer SPlb SRms WDin WFar WFib
	- 'Greenman'	WFib WGwG
	- 'Halebob'	MBri WFib WGwG
	- 'Hamilton'	see *H. hibernica* 'Hamilton'
	- 'Harald' (v)	CTri CWib WDin WFib
*	- 'Hazel' (v)	WFib
	- 'Hedge Hog'	WFib
	- 'Heise' (v)	WFib
	- 'Heise Denmark' (v)	WFib
	- 'Helvig'	see *H. helix* 'White Knight'
	- 'Henrietta'	WFib
	- 'Hester'	WFib
	- 'Hispanica'	see *H. iberica*
	- 'Hite's Miniature'	see *H. helix* 'Merion Beauty'
	- 'Holly'	see *H. helix* 'Parsley Crested'
	- 'Hullavington'	CNat
	- 'Humpty Dumpty'	CPLG
	- 'Imp'	see *H. helix* 'Brokamp'
	- 'Ingelise' (v)	WFib
	- 'Ingrid' (v)	WFib
	- 'Itsy Bitsy'	see *H. helix* 'Pin Oak'
	- 'Ivalace' ♀H4	CBcs EBee ECha EPfP LTen MGos MSwo MWhi MWht SRms WDin WFib WTin
	- 'Jake'	MBri WFib
	- 'Jasper'	WFib
	- 'Jersey Doris' (v)	WFib
	- 'Jerusalem'	see *H. helix* 'Schäfer Three'
	- 'Jester's Gold'	EBee ELan EPfP MBri MGos SBfd WDin WRHF
	- 'Jubilee' (v)	WCFE WFib
	- 'Kaleidoscope'	WFib
	- 'Kevin'	WFib
	- 'Kloster's Joy'	WFib
	- 'Knülch'	WFib
	- 'Kolibri' (v)	CDoC CRHN CWan EBee EPfP LAst LRHS MBri MGos MWht SBfd WFib
§	- 'Königer's Auslese'	CDul WFib
	- 'Lalla Rookh'	MRav WFib WGwG WHrl
	- 'Lemon Swirl' (v)	WFib
	- 'Leo Swicegood'	CBgR MWhi WFib
	- 'Light Fingers'	EBee EPfP LRHS WFib WGwG WHrl
	- 'Limey'	WFib
	- 'Little Diamond' (v)	CDoC CMac CTri ELan EPfP LRHS LTen MAsh MBri MWht NHol SLon SWvt WDin WFib WHrl WTin
	- 'Little Luzii'	WFib
	- 'Liz'	see *H. helix* 'Eva'
	- 'Lucille'	WFib
	- 'Luzii' (v)	EBee MGos WFib WGwG
	- 'Maculata'	see *H. helix* 'Minor Marmorata'
§	- 'Manda's Crested' ♀H4	CDul CSWP NLar WFib WGwG
	- 'Maple Leaf' ♀H4	GBin WFib
	- 'Maple Queen'	MBri
	- 'Marginata' (v)	SRms
	- 'Marginata Elegantissima'	see *H. helix* 'Tricolor'
	- 'Marginata Minor'	see *H. helix* 'Cavendishii'
I	- 'Marmorata' Fibrex	WFib
	- 'Masquerade' (v)	WFib WGor
	- 'Mathilde' (v)	EBee MWht SBfd WFib
	- 'Melanie' ♀H4	ECha SRGP WFib WGwG
	- 'Meon'	WFib
§	- 'Merion Beauty'	WFib
§	- 'Midas Touch' (v) ♀H3-4	CWib EPfP MBri WFib
	- 'Mini Ester' (v)	EPfP MBri
	- 'Mini Heron'	LAst MBri
	- 'Mini Pittsburgh'	LAst
	- 'Minikin' (v)	WCot WFib
	- 'Minima' misapplied	see *H. helix* 'Spetchley'
	- 'Minima' Hibberd	see *H. helix* 'Donerailensis'
	- 'Minima' M.Young	see *H. helix* 'Congesta'
§	- 'Minor Marmorata' (v) ♀H4	CWan WSHC
	- 'Mint Kolibri'	EHoe LAst MBri
	- 'Minty' (v)	MWht WFib
	- 'Misty' (v)	WFib
	- 'Mon Premier'	WFib
	- 'New Ripples'	MWht
	- 'Niagara Falls'	LRHS MAsh
	- 'Nigra Aurea' (v)	WFib
	- 'Obovata'	WFib
N	- 'Oro di Bogliasco' (v)	CDul CMac CTri EBee EPfP GKir LRHS MAsh MBri MMuc MRav MSwo NBea NHol NLar NPri NWea SBfd SPer SPlb SPoG SRms STre SWvt WDin WFar WFib WPat
	- 'Ovata'	WFib

§	- 'Parsley Crested' ♀H4	CMac EBee EPfP EQua LRHS MAsh MGos NBid SRms WBVN WFib WGwG
	- 'Patent Leather'	WFib
N	- 'Pedata'	CDul MSwo WFib
	- 'Perkeo'	WFib
	- 'Persian Carpet'	WFib
	- 'Peter' (v)	WFib
	- 'Peter Pan'	WFib WGwG
	- 'Phantom'	WFib
§	- 'Pin Oak'	WDin
	- 'Pink 'n' Curly'	WFib
	- 'Pink 'n' Very Curly'	WCot
§	- 'Pittsburgh'	LTen MGos SBfd WFib
	- 'Plume d'Or'	WFib
§	- f. ***poetarum***	EPla MBlu WFib WPat
	- - 'Poetica Arborea'	ECha SDix
	- 'Poetica'	see *H. helix* f. *poetarum*
	- 'Professor Friedrich Tobler'	EBee
	- 'Raleigh Delight' (v)	WCot
	- 'Ray's Supreme'	see *H. helix* 'Pittsburgh'
	- subsp. ***rhizomatifera***	WFib
	- 'Richard John'	WFib
	- 'Ritterkreuz'	WFib WGwG
	- 'Romanze' (v)	WFib WGwG
	- 'Rotunda'	WFib
	- 'Russelliana'	WFib
	- 'Sagittifolia' misapplied	see *H. helix* 'Königer's Auslese'
	- 'Sagittifolia' ambig.	MAsh MMuc
	- 'Sagittifolia' Hibberd	see *H. hibernica* 'Sagittifolia'
	- 'Sagittifolia Variegata' (v)	MBri NBea WFib WRHF
	- 'Saint Agnes'	MAsh
	- 'Sally' (v)	WFib
	- 'Salt and Pepper'	see *H. helix* 'Minor Marmorata'
§	- 'Schäfer Three' (v)	CWib WFib
	- 'Seabreeze'	WFib
	- 'Shadow'	WFib
	- 'Shamrock'	EPfP MWht WFib
	- 'Shannon'	WFib
	- 'Silver Butterflies' (v)	WFib
	- 'Silver Ferny'	WFib
	- 'Silver King' (v)	MRav MWht WFib WGwG
	- 'Silver Queen'	see *H. helix* 'Tricolor'
	- 'Spectre' (v)	WHer
§	- 'Spetchley' ♀H4	CMac EPla EPot GCal GGar GKev MRav MWhi NHol NPer SMad WCot WFib WGwG WHrl WPtf WTin
	- 'Spinosa'	WFib
	- 'Splashes'	WFib
	- 'Stuttgart'	WFib
	- 'Sunrise'	WFib
	- 'Suzanne'	see *H. nepalensis* 'Suzanne'
	- 'Tanja'	WFib
	- 'Teardrop'	WFib
	- 'Telecurl'	WFib
	- 'Temptation' (v)	WFib
	- 'Tenerife' (v)	WFib
	- 'Tiger Eyes'	WFib
	- 'Topazolite' (v)	WFib
§	- 'Très Coupé'	CBgR CDoC LRHS MAsh SAPC SArc WDin
§	- 'Tricolor' (v)	CMac CTri EBee EPfP LRHS MAsh MCot MGos MWht WCFE WFib
	- 'Trinity' (v)	WFib
	- 'Tripod'	WFib WGwG
	- 'Triton'	EPfP WFib
	- 'Troll'	WFib WPat
	- 'Tussie Mussie' (v)	WFib
	- 'Ursula' (v)	EShb WFib
	- 'Very Merry'	EPPr WFib
*	- 'Vitifolium'	WFib
§	- 'White Knight' (v) ♀H4	WFib
	- 'White Mein Herz' (v)	WFib
	- 'White Ripple' (v)	WFib
	- 'White Wonder'	WFib
	- 'William Kennedy' (v)	WFib
	- 'Williamsiana' (v)	WFib
	- 'Woeneri'	MWht WFib
	- 'Wonder'	WFib
	- 'Yellow Ripple'	LAst MBri WDin WFib
	- 'Zebra' (v)	WFib
	hibernica ♀H4	CCVT CDul CSBt EPfP IFFs LBuc MRav MSwo MWhi NWea SBfd SPer SRms WDin WFib
	- 'Anna Marie'	see *H. helix* 'Anna Marie'
	- 'Aracena'	EPla SLPl
I	- 'Arbori Compact' **new**	EPfP
	- 'Betty Allen'	WFib
§	- 'Deltoidea' ♀H4	EPla MWht WCFE WFib
I	- 'Digitata Crûg Gold'	WCru
	- 'Ebony'	WFib
	- 'Glengariff'	WFib
§	- 'Gracilis'	WFib
§	- 'Hamilton'	WFib
	- 'Harlequin' (v)	WFib
	- 'Lobata Major'	SRms
	- 'Maculata' (v)	SLPl WSHC
	- 'Palmata'	WFib
	- 'Rona'	WFib WGwG
§	- 'Sagittifolia'	CTri EPfP GBin LBMP SBfd SRms WDin
	- 'Sulphurea' (v)	WFib
	- 'Variegata' (v)	MGos WFib
§	***iberica***	WFib
	maderensis	WFib
	maroccana 'Morocco'	WFib
§	- 'Spanish Canary'	WFib
	nepalensis	WFib
	- 'Marble Dragon'	see *H. sinensis* var. *sinensis* 'Marble Dragon'
§	- 'Suzanne'	WFib
	pastuchovii	WFib
	- from Troödos, Cyprus	see *H. cypria*
	- 'Ann Ala'	EBee EPfP GBin WCot WFib WGwG
	- 'Lagocetti'	WFib
§	***rhombea***	WCot WFib
	- 'Eastern Dawn'	WFib
	- 'Japonica'	see *H. rhombea*
I	- f. ***pedunculata*** 'Maculata'	CWib
	- var. ***rhombea*** 'Variegata' (v)	WFib
§	***sinensis*** var. ***sinensis***	MWht WFib
§	- - 'Marble Dragon'	WFib

Hedychium ✿ (*Zingiberaceae*)

	B&SWJ 3110	WPGP
	B&SWJ 7155	WPGP
	'Anne Bishop'	SEND WPGP
	aurantiacum	CBcs CBct CHEx EAmu EBee ETod LAma LEdu NPla SBig SEND SPoG SSwd
	brevicaule B&SWJ 7171	WCru
	chrysoleucum	CCCN EShb LAma LTen SBst
	coccineum ♀H1	CDTJ CTsd EAmu EBee ECho EPfP EShb ETod EUJe IKil MNrw SBig SPlb SSwd
	- B&SWJ 5238	WCru
	- var. ***angustifolium***	CDes CGHE CRHN EPfP WPGP
	- 'Disney'	CDTJ
	- 'Tara' ♀H3	CBct CDes CDoC CGHE CHEx CPLG CPne CRHN CSam EAmu

	EBee EPfP EUJe IBlr IGor LEdu LPJP MNrw SAPC SArc SBfd SBst SChr SUsu WCru WPGP
coronarium	CBct CCCN CDTJ CDes CFee CTsd EAmu EBee EPfP EShb EUJe GBin IKil LEdu MWea SBig WPGP XBlo
- 'Gold Spot'	EUJe SSwd
- var. ***maximum***	ETod
- 'Orange Spot'	EAmu
- var. ***urophyllum***	IBlr
- - HWJ 604	WCru
coronarium* × *gardnerianum	SPer SSwd
'Daniel Weeks'	EBee
densiflorum	CBct CCCN CDTJ CDes CHEx CHll CPLG CPne CSpe EAmu EBee ECha EPfP ETod EUJe GBin IBlr LEdu MLLN NPla SDix SSpi WCom WCru WPGP
- 'Assam Orange'	Widely available
- 'Sorung'	CPLG LEdu SChr
- 'Stephen'	CAvo CBct CCCN CDTJ CDes CFir CGHE CHEx CPLG CPne CSam EAmu EBee EPfP EUJe LEdu MNrw NPal SChr SPlb WPGP
'Devon Cream'	CCCN CDTJ CPLG EAmu NPal
'Doctor Moy' (v)	CDTJ EBee SPoG
'Double Eagle'	WPGP
'Elizabeth'	CDes EBee LEdu WPGP
ellipticum	CDTJ CHEx CRHN EAmu EBee ETod EUJe LAma LEdu LRHS MNrw SBig SPoG SSwd
- B&SWJ 8354	WCru
'Filigree'	CDes CPLG EBee LEdu WPGP
flavescens	CBcs CBct CDTJ CStu EAmu EBee EPfP EShb EUJe LAma LEdu MNrw SChr SSwd WCru WPGP
flavum Roxb.	EBee
forrestii misapplied	CTrC
forrestii Diels	CDes CPLG EAmu EBee EShb ETod EUJe GCal IBlr LPJP MNrw MREP SAPC SArc SPlb WPGP
gardnerianum ♈H1	Widely available
'Gold Flame'	CDes CMdw EBee LEdu MNrw SChr WPGP
gracile	EAmu EUJe LEdu WCru
greenii	CBct CDoC CFir CHEx CPne CRHN CSam CTsd EBee ECho EPfP EShb EUJe GBin LEdu MNrw NPla SBfd SBig SChr SDix SHaC SPoG SSwd WBor WCru WPGP
griffithianum	CSpe EAmu EBee EPfP ETod EUJe IKil MNrw SBig SSwd
- white-flowered	CCCN
'Hardy Exotics 1'	CHEx
I × ***kewense***	SSwd
'Kinkaku'	WDyG WPGP
'Luna Moth'	WPGP
luteum	CBcs
maximum	EAmu SChr SSwd WDyG WPGP
- B&SWJ 8261A	WCru
- HWJ 810	WCru
'Pink Flame'	EBee LEdu
'Pink V'	EBee WPGP
pink-flowered	CDes SSwd
'Pradhan'	CFir
× ***raffillii***	MNrw SBig
'Shamshiri'	CCCN
spicatum	CDTJ CDes CFir CHEx CPLG CRHN EBee EUJe GCal GPoy IBlr LEdu MNrw SPoG SSwd WCFE
- B&SWJ 2303	WPGP
- B&SWJ 7231	WCru
- BWJ 8116 from Sichuan, China **new**	WCru
- P.Bon. 57188	WPGP
- from Salween Valley, China	CPLG
- var. ***acuminatum***	EBee WPGP
- 'Liberty' **new**	WCru
- 'Singalila'	CDes WCru
'St Martin's'	CCCN ELon GBin SPoG
stenopetalum B&SWJ 7155	WCru
'Tahitian Flame' (v) **new**	EUJe
thyrsiforme	EAmu EBee EShb ETod EUJe LEdu SBig SSwd WCru
villosum	CDTJ EBee ECho
wardii	CHEx CPLG WPGP
yunnanense	CDes CFir CPLG CRHN CSam EBee IBlr LEdu MNrw SBig WPGP
- B&SWJ 9717	WCru
- BWJ 7900	WCru

Hedysarum (*Papilionaceae*)

coronarium	CArn CSpe EHrv ELan EPfP MCot SMrm SPhx WAul WCot WKif
hedysaroides	IKil
multijugum	CBcs EBee MBlu NPal SPer
tauricum **new**	SPhx

Heimia (*Lythraceae*)

salicifolia	CArn ECre EOHP IDee MBlu NMun SGar

Helenium ✿ (*Asteraceae*)

'Autumn Lollipop'	EBee IBal MCCP NLar SPav
autumnale	CSBt CSam CTri EPPr GKir LSRN MLHP MNHC NChi SMrm SPet SWvt WClo WFar WGwG WMoo
- 'All Gold'	NBPC SWvt
I - 'Cupreum'	SBch
- Helena Series	SWvt
- - 'Helena Gold'	CEnt EBee EPfP NBre SBfd WPer
- - 'Helena Rote Töne'	CChe CSpr EBee EPfP LBMP MWhi SBfd WPer
'Baronin Linden'	CSam MAvo MSpe
'Baudirektor Linne' ♈H4	CSam EBee WSpi
'Biedermeier'	CPrp CSam CWCL EBee EBla ECtt EShb MRav MSpe NCob NEgg NGdn SPhx SPoG WCAu WHlf
bigelovii	EBrs
'Blütentisch' ♈H4	CHVG CMHG CMea COlW CSam EBee GMaP MSpe MTis NCGa NLar NVic WHal WMnd
'Bressingham Gold'	CSam LRHS MAvo MNrw MSpe WBrk WHrl
'Bruno'	CAby CHar CWCL EBee EBrs ELan ELon GKir LRHS MArl MSpe MTis NLar WSpi
'Butterpat' ♈H4	EBee EBrs ECtt EHrv EPfP GBee GCra GKir GMaP GMac LRHS MArl MRav MSpe NCGa NPri NSti SBfd SMrm WWEG
'Can Can'	CSam MAvo MSpe
'Chelsey'	CPrp EBee EHrv ELan EPfP IBal LHop LRHS LSRN LSou MSpe MTis NBPC NChi NLar NMoo NPri NSti WWlt
'Chipperfield Orange'	CElw CSam ECtt MArl MRav MSpe MTis NBre NGdn NVic WOld WWEG
'Coppelia'	CSam EBrs LRHS MAsh MRav MSpe NBir NGdn
Copper Spray	see *H.* 'Kupfersprudel'
'Crimson Beauty'	ECtt ELan MRav WSpi

Dark Beauty	see *H.* 'Dunkelpracht'
'Dauerbrenner'	CSam MAvo MSpe
'Die Blonde'	EBee MSpe NBre SMHy
'Double Trouble'^{PBR}	EBee EBrs EHrv EPfP IKil LLHF LSou MAvo MBNS MSpe NBPC NPri SBfd SOkt SPoG STes WCot WWlt
§ 'Dunkelpracht'	CAby CElw CMHG CSam CWGN EBee ECtt EHrv EWll LAst LSRN MCot MSpe NBPC NCob NDov NEgg NGdn NLar SPoG WBrk WCot WFar WOld WWEG
'El Dorado'	CSam MSpe
'Fata Morgana'	EBee ECtt LLHF NBre SPoG WCAu
'Feuersiegel' 🏆^{H4}	CSam EBee ECtt MSpe NBre WOld
'Fiesta'	CAby CSam EBee MSpe
'Flammendes Käthchen'	CSam EBee EBrs IPot LRHS MAsh MAvo MSpe NBre NDov SMrm
'Flammenrad'	CSam EBee MSpe SDys
'Flammenspiel'	EBee EBrs ECtt LRHS MAsh MCot MNrw MSpe MTis WSpi
flexuosum	EBee NBre SPhx
'Gartensonne' 🏆^{H4}	CSam MSpe NBre SMrm
'Gay-go-round'	CSam MSpe
Gold Fox	see *H.* 'Goldfuchs'
'Gold Intoxication'	see *H.* 'Goldrausch'
Golden Youth	see *H.* 'Goldene Jugend'
§ 'Goldene Jugend'	CElw CMea CSam ECtt ELan MRav MSpe WCot WEas WWEG
§ 'Goldfuchs'	CSam CWCL MSpe SDys WCot
§ 'Goldlackzwerg'	EBee EBrs GKir GMac LRHS MAvo NBre
§ 'Goldrausch'	CHar CSam CWCL EBee EBla ECtt GBee GCra LRHS MDKP MSpe MTis MWat NBre NGdn SPhx WOld WSpi WWEG
'Goldreif'	CSam
'Hartmut Reiger'	CSam MSpe
'Helena'	NLar WPer
hoopesii	see *Hymenoxys hoopesii*
'Indianersommer'	CElw CSam CWCL EBee EBla ECtt EHrv GMaP IBal LRHS MDun MTis NBPC NCGa NDov NLar NMRc SGSe SMrm SPer SUsu WCAu WClo WFar WHoo
'Jam Tarts'	MSpe WCot
'July Sun'	NBir
'Kanaria'	CAby CPrp EBee EBrs EWll GKev GQue LRHS MAsh MLLN MSpe NCob NEgg NLar SMrm SPhx WMnd WOld WSpi
'Karneol' 🏆^{H4}	CSam MSpe NBre SUsu
'Kleiner Fuchs'	CSam EHrv MSpe NLar
'Kokarde'	CSam MAvo MSpe
'Königstiger'	CSam EBee EBrs ECtt GQue LRHS MAsh MNrw MSpe MWea NBre NCGa NDov WFar
'Kugelsonne'	EBee NBre
'Kupfersiegel'	CSam MSpe
§ 'Kupfersprudel'	CSam MAvo
'Kupferzwerg'	CSam CWCL EBee ELan IPot NBre NDov
'Loysder Wieck'	EBee NDov WHil
'Luc'	CSam MSpe
'Mahagoni'	CSam GBin MSpe
'Mahogany'	see *H.* 'Goldlackzwerg'
Mahogany	see *H.* 'Mahogany'
'Mardi Gras'	ECtt LSou NDov SPoG
'Margot'	CSam CWCL MAvo MSpe MTis NBre SDys SUsu
'Marion Nickig'	CSam MSpe NDov
'Meranti'	CMea CSam MAvo MSpe NDov WHlf

'Moerheim Beauty' 🏆^{H4}	Widely available
'Moth' **new**	MSpe
'Orange Beauty'	EBee
'Patsy'	MSpe
Pipsqueak = 'Blopip'	ECtt GKir LLHF LRHS MSpe NBre
'Potter's Wheel'	CSam IPot MAvo MSpe NDov
puberulum	WHil
'Pumilum Magnificum'	CHar CSam CWCL EBee EPfP GQue LEdu LHop LRHS MSpe SPer WFar WPGP
'Ragamuffin'	CSam MSpe SUsu
'Rauchtopas'	CDes CSam EBee IBal IPot MAvo MSpe NCGa NDov SDys SUsu WPGP
Red and Gold	see *H.* 'Rotgold'
'Red Army'	CPrp EKen ELan GKir GMac IBal LRHS MAvo MNrw MSCN MSpe NCGa NGdn
'Red Glory'	EBee EHrv GMac
'Red Jewel'	CDes CWGN EBee ELon ITim LLHF LPla LRHS LSou MSpe MTis NBPC NDov NEgg NGdn NSti SMad SMrm SPoG SUsu WBrk WCot WCra WWEG
'Ring of Fire' 🏆^{H4}	CSam IPot MSpe SMHy
'Riverton Beauty'	CSam LLHF MSpe MTis SUsu WCot WHoo
'Riverton Gem'	CSam ECtt EHrv LLHF MNrw MSpe MTis NBre NChi WHoo
§ 'Rotgold'	CMea ECtt LRHS LSRN MSpe NBre NChi SGar SRms WFar WMoo WPer WWEG
'Rotkäppchen'	CSam
'Rubinkuppel'	CAby NCGa
'Rubinzwerg' 🏆^{H4}	Widely available
§ 'Ruby Thuesday'	CAby CMac EBee EHrv EPPr EPfP GMac GQue IKil LLHF LRHS LSRN LSou MBNS MHer MNrw MSpe NBPC NDov NEgg NGdn NLar NSti SBfd SHar SPoG WBrk WCot WCra WWEG
'Ruby Tuesday'	see *H.* 'Ruby Thuesday'
'Sahin's Early Flowerer' 🏆^{H4}	Widely available
'Samtjuwel' **new**	MSpe
'Septemberfuchs'	LEdu MCot NBre NDov WWEG
'Sonnenwunder'	EBee ECha LEdu MLHP MSpe NBre
'Summer Circle' 🏆^{H4}	CSam
'Sunshine'	MSpe
'The Bishop'	COIW CSam EBee EBla ECtt ELon EPPr EPfP GMac LAst LEdu LRHS MDKP MRav MSCN MSpe NBro NPri SPer SPet SRGP SWvt WCAu WFar WMnd WWEG
'Tip Top'	EBee LBMP MSpe SBfd WHil
'Vicky' **new**	MAvo MSpe
'Vivace'	CSam MSpe
'Wagon Wheel'	WCot
'Waltraut' 🏆^{H4}	Widely available
'Wesergold' 🏆^{H4}	EBee EBla GBBs LLHF LSou MHer NDov NLar
'Wonnadonga'	MSpe
'Wyndley'	Widely available
'Zimbelstern'	CDes CElw CMdw EBee ECha ECtt ELon LHop LRHS MAsh MCot MNFA MRav MSpe MTis SMrm SPhx WAul WFar WPGP WWEG
'Zonnedam' **new**	ECtt

Heliamphora ✿ (*Sarraceniaceae*)

minor	SHmp
nutans	SHmp

Helianthella (*Asteraceae*)

§	***quinquenervis***	CDes EBee GBin GCal LLHF NLar SPer
	uniflora NNS 06-272	WCot

Helianthemum ✿ (*Cistaceae*)

	SDR 5508	GKev
	'Albert's Brick'	LIMB
	'Albert's Gold'	LIMB
	'Alice Howarth'	LIMB WHoo
	alpestre serpyllifolium	see *H. nummularium* subsp. *glabrum*
	'Amabile Plenum' (d)	EPfP GAbr GCal LIMB
	'Amy Baring' ♀H4	CTri ECho ECtt GAbr LIMB LRHS NHol WCom WPer
	'Annabel' (d)	ECho ECtt GAbr IGor LRHS NHol WCom WPer
	apenninum	LLHF SRms
	- var. ***roseum***	ECho
	'Apricot'	CTri LIMB SPer
	'Apricot Blush'	LIMB WAbe
	'Baby Buttercup'	CMea GAbr LIMB
	'Banwy Copper'	LIMB WBVN
	'Banwy Velvet'	LIMB WBVN
	'Beech Park Red'	CTri ECho ECtt LIMB MHer SDix WAbe WFar WHoo WKif
	'Ben Afflick'	ECho ECtt LHop LIMB LRHS SPer SRms WFar
	'Ben Alder'	ECho ECtt GAbr LIMB MHer
	'Ben Attow'	LIMB
	'Ben Dearg'	CMea ECho ECtt LIMB SRms
	'Ben Fhada'	CBcs CMea COlW CTri ECho ECtt EPfP GAbr GKev GKir GMaP LBee LIMB LRHS MAsh MHer NEgg SBfd SEND SPer SPoG SRGP SRms WAbe WFar WPer
	'Ben Heckla'	CSam ECho ECtt EPfP GAbr LHop LIMB LRHS WPer
	'Ben Hope'	CTri ECho ECtt EPfP LIMB NHol SMrm SPer SRGP
§	'Ben Ledi'	CBcs COlW ECho ECtt EPfP GAbr GMaP LHop LIMB MHer MSCN NHol NSla SBfd SPer SPoG SRms SRot WAbe WClo WFar WNew WPer
	'Ben Lomond'	ECho GAbr LIMB
	'Ben Macdhui'	ECtt GAbr LIMB
	'Ben More'	CBar CBcs CMea COlW ECho ECtt ELon EPfP GAbr GJos GMaP LHop LIMB LRHS MSCN MSwo NBir SBfd SEND SPer SPoG SRGP SRms SRot WFar WHoo
	'Ben Nevis'	CTri ECho ECtt LIMB SPer SRms WFar
	'Ben Vane'	ECho ECtt LIMB LRHS
	'Big Orange'	LIMB
	'Birch Double' (d)	LIMB
	'Blutströpfchen'	LIMB
	'Boughton Double Primrose' (d)	CPBP ECho ELan GMaP LHop WEas WHoo WSHC WTin
	'Braungold'	LIMB
	'Bronzeteppich'	LLHF
	'Broughty Beacon'	ECtt GAbr LIMB WGor
	'Broughty Orange'	LIMB
	'Broughty Sunset'	CSam ECtt LIMB NBir NHol WHoo
	'Bunbury'	COlW ECtt ELon LHop LIMB MBrN NBir SDix SPoG SRms WRHF
I	'Butter and Eggs'	LIMB
	'Captivation'	GAbr LIMB
I	'Carminium Plenum'	LIMB
	'Cerise Queen' (d)	CTri ECha ECho ECtt GAbr LHop LIMB MMHG MSwo NCGa SDix SEND SPer SRms WCom WHoo
	chamaecistus	see *H. nummularium*
	'Cheviot'	CMea ECtt GAbr LIMB NBir WEas WHoo WSHC
	'Chichester'	LIMB
I	'Chloe's Variegata' (v) **new**	EWes
	'Chocolate Blotch'	ECho ECtt GAbr GCra LHop LIMB LRHS NHol SEND SRms WPer
	'Cornish Cream'	ECho ECtt EWTr GAbr LBee LIMB
	croceum	LLHF
	cupreum	GAbr
	'David'	LIMB
	'David Ritchie'	LIMB LLHF WHoo
	'Diana'	CMea LIMB
	'Dompfaff'	LIMB
	'Dora'	LIMB
	double apricot-flowered (d)	GAbr LIMB
	double cream-flowered (d)	ECho
	double orange-flowered (d)	LHop
	double primrose-flowered (d)	CHVG CMea GAbr LIMB
	double red-flowered (d)	NChi
	'Eisbar'	LIMB
	'Elfenbeinglanz'	LIMB
	'Ellen' (d)	CMea LIMB
	'Etna'	LIMB NHol STre
	'Everton Ruby'	see *H.* 'Ben Ledi'
	'Fairy'	ECho EPfP GAbr LIMB LLHF
	'Feuerbraund'	LIMB
§	'Fire Dragon' ♀H4	CMea ECho ECtt EPfP GAbr GMaP GQue LIMB LRHS MGos NBir NWCA SEND SRms WAbe WCom
	'Fireball'	see *H.* 'Mrs C.W. Earle'
	'Firegold' (v)	LIMB WAbe WFar
	'Flame'	LIMB
	'Frau Bachtaler'	LIMB
	'Georgeham'	CMea ECho ECtt ELon EPfP GAbr LBee LIMB NBir SAga SRms WEas WGor WHoo WPer
§	'Golden Queen'	ECho ECtt EPfP GAbr LIMB MSwo NCGa WFar WPer
	'Hampstead Orange'	CTri
	'Hartshorn'	LIMB
	'Hartswood Ruby'	GMaP LRHS MBNS
	'Henfield Brilliant' ♀H4	CHVG CPLG ECho ECtt EPfP GAbr LHop LIMB LRHS MRav MSCN NBir NHol SBfd SDix SMad SPer SRms WCot WEas WHoo WPer
	'Highdown'	GAbr SRms
	'Highdown Apricot'	ECho ECtt LHop LIMB LLHF SPoG WFar WRHF
	'Honeymoon'	ECtt EPfP GAbr LIMB NHol
	'Ilna's Master' (d)	LIMB
	'Ilona' (d/v)	LIMB
	'Jubilee' (d) ♀H4	CTri ECho ECtt ELan EPfP GAbr LHop LIMB MBNS NBir NChi NPri SPoG SRms WEas WFar WKif
I	'Jubilee Variegatum' (v)	ECtt GAbr LIMB
	'Karen's Silver'	LIMB WAbe
	'Kathleen Druce' (d)	ECho ECtt EWes GAbr LIMB NHol WHoo
	'Kathleen Mary'	CMea LIMB
	'Lawrenson's Pink'	ECho ECtt GAbr LIMB LRHS SRGP WPer
	'Lemon Queen'	LIMB
	'Lucy Elizabeth'	ECtt GAbr LIMB
	lunulatum	CMea ECho ECtt GKir LIMB LLHF LRHS NMen WAbe WPat
	'Magnificum'	MWat
	'Marianne'	LIMB

	'Mette'	LIMB
§	'Mrs C.W. Earle' (d) ♀H4	CBar COlW CTri ECho ECtt ELan EPfP GCra LIMB LRHS MBNS MLLN NEgg NHol SRms WFar WPer
	'Mrs Clay'	see *H.* 'Fire Dragon'
	'Mrs Croft'	LIMB
	'Mrs Hays'	GAbr LIMB
	'Mrs Jenkinson'	LIMB
	'Mrs Lake'	GAbr LIMB
	'Mrs Moules'	LIMB SRms
	mutabile	SPlb
§	***nummularium***	EBWF GPoy MHer MNHC NMir NSco WAbe WPat WSFF
§	- subsp. ***glabrum***	GAbr NHol WPat
	- subsp. ***pyrenaicum***	NWCA
§	- subsp. ***tomentosum***	GAbr NHol
I	'Oblongatum'	LIMB
	oelandicum	GAbr NHol NWCA SRms WAbe
	- subsp. ***alpestre***	NMen
	- subsp. ***piloselloides***	WAbe
	'Old Gold'	ECtt GAbr LIMB NHol SRms WAbe
	'Orange Phoenix' (d)	ECtt EPfP GAbr LIMB MBNS NHol NPri WFar
	'Orange Surprise'	LIMB
	'Ovum Supreme'	LIMB
	'Peach'	LIMB
	'Pershore Orange'	LIMB
	'Pink Angel' (d)	CBow ECtt LIMB MBNS WPer
	'Pink Beauty'	LIMB
	'Pink Glow'	GAbr LIMB WPer
	'Praecox'	CMea CTri ECho GAbr LBee LIMB SRms WHoo
	'Prima Donna'	EPfP NBir
	'Prostrate Orange'	LIMB SRms
	'Raspberry Ripple'	CBow ECho ECtt ELan EPfP EPot LIMB LRHS NHol SPoG SRms WAbe WFar
	'Razzle Dazzle' (v)	CBow ECtt GKev LIMB LLHF SBfd SRms WFar
	'Red Dragon'	ECtt EPot LIMB WAbe
	'Red Orient'	see *H.* 'Supreme'
	'Regenbogen' (d)	GCal LIMB SEND
§	'Rhodanthe Carneum' ♀H4	Widely available
§	'Rosakönigin'	ECho ECtt GAbr LIMB MHer WAbe
	'Rose of Leeswood' (d)	CMea CTri LBee LIMB NChi NEgg SAga SPoG SRms WClo WEas WFar WHoo WKif WSHC
	Rose Queen	see *H.* 'Rosakönigin'
	'Roxburgh Gold'	SRms
	'Rubin' (d)	LIMB
	'Rushfield's White'	LIMB
	'Ruth'	LIMB
	'Saint John's College Yellow'	CSam ECho GAbr LIMB LRHS
	'Salmon Queen'	ECho ECtt GAbr LHop LIMB LRHS SEND SRms WPer
*	***scardicum***	CMea
	'Schnee' (d)	LIMB
	serpyllifolium	see *H. nummularium* subsp. *glabrum*
	'Shot Silk'	ECtt EWes
	'Snow Queen'	see *H.* 'The Bride'
	'Southmead'	ECho LIMB
	'Sterntaler'	GAbr LIMB LLHF SRms
	'Sudbury Gem'	CTri ECha ECho GAbr GKir LIMB LRHS
	'Sulphur Moon'	ECho LHop LLHF LRHS
	'Sulphureum Plenum' (d)	ECtt EPfP LIMB
	'Sunbeam'	CSam ECho LIMB SRms
	'Sunburst'	LIMB
§	'Supreme'	ECho ELan EPfP EWes LIMB SRms
	'Tangerine'	ECtt GAbr LIMB NHol
§	'The Bride' ♀H4	Widely available
	'Tigrinum Plenum' (d)	EWes LIMB
	'Tomato Red'	NSla SEND
	tomentosum	see *H. nummularium* subsp. *tomentosum*
	umbellatum	see *Halimium umbellatum*
	'Venustum Plenum' (d)	LIMB WEas
	'Victor' (d)	LIMB
	'Voltaire'	ECho ECtt EPfP LIMB LLHF NHol
	'Watergate Rose'	ECho ECtt LIMB MWat NBir
	'Welsh Flame'	LIMB WAbe WFar
	'Windmill Gold'	LIMB
	'Wisley Pink'	see *H.* 'Rhodanthe Carneum'
	'Wisley Primrose' ♀H4	Widely available
	'Wisley Rose'	WCom
	'Wisley White'	CTri ECha ECho ECtt EPfP GAbr LIMB
	'Wisley Yellow'	ECtt GKir
	'Yellow Queen'	see *H.* 'Golden Queen'
I	'Zonatus'	LIMB

Helianthus (*Asteraceae*)

	sp.	WBor
	RCB/Arg CC-3	WCot
	angustifolius	WFar
	atrorubens	EBee LHop MRav NBPC NBro
	- 'Giganteus' **new**	MAvo
	'Bitter Chocolate'	WCot
	'Capenoch Star' ♀H4	CElw CPrp EBee ECha ECtt GMaP LEdu LPio LRHS MAvo MRav NBPC NBro NLar SDix SMrm WCAu WFar WOld WWEG
	'Capenoch Supreme'	EBrs ECtt LRHS NBPC
	'Carine'	MAvo MNrw WCot
	decapetalus	CHar CMac MLLN WHal
	- Morning Sun	see *H.* 'Morgensonne'
	divaricatus	NBre
	giganteus	CAby CBre CElw EBee IPot LHop
	'Sheila's Sunshine'	NBPC NDov WOld
	gracilentus	NBre
	'Gullick's Variety' ♀H4	CAby CBre EBee ECtt LLWP NBro NChi NLar STes WOld WWEG
	'Happy Days'	EBee MAvo WCot
	'Hazel's Gold'	ECtt NBre
	hirsutus	EBee NBre
	× ***kellermanii***	EBee NBre NDov SAga SPhx
§	× ***laetiflorus***	EBee ELan GAbr LPio MWhi NBre NLar WPer
§	'Lemon Queen' ♀H4	Widely available
	'Limelight'	see *H.* 'Lemon Queen'
	'Loddon Gold' ♀H4	CHar EBee ECtt ELan EPfP EShb LRHS MAvo MLLN MRav MSCN NBPC NBir NVic SAga SRGP WBrk WCot WFar WWEG
§	***maximiliani***	CSam EBee ELon EWll LPio MDKP SPav SPhx WPer
	microcephalus	CSam EBee NDov
	'Miss Mellish' ♀H4	CAby EBee MSCN WBrk WCot WHoo
	mollis	CSam EBee NBre SPav WPer
	'Monarch' ♀H4	CMea CSam EBee GBee MDKP MLLN MRav NBre NCGa SDix SMad SMrm WCot WMoo WOld
§	'Morgensonne'	CPrp ECtt EHrv MTis MWat WCot WFar
	× ***multiflorus*** 'Meteor'	EBrs ECtt LRHS NBre NChi WWEG
	occidentalis	CSam EBee WPer
	orgyalis	see *H. salicifolius*
	quinquenervis	see *Helianthella quinquenervis*
	rigidus misapplied	see *H.* × *laetiflorus*
§	***salicifolius***	Widely available
	- 'Low Down' PBR	EBee LRHS MCCP NLar NMoo

- 'Table Mountain'	EBee
scaberrimus	see *H.* × *laetiflorus*
'Soleil d'Or'	EBee ECtt EWll IPot WHal WWEG
strumosus	WCot
'Triomphe de Gand'	MRav MWat NDov WFar WOld
tuberosus	CArn EBee GPoy SVic
- 'Fuseau'	LEdu NHol SVic
- 'Garnet'	LEdu
- 'Sugarball'	LEdu

Helichrysum (*Asteraceae*)

from Drakensberg Mountains, South Africa	GAbr NWCA
adenocarpum	SPlb
aggregatum	MSCN
alveolatum	see *H. splendidum*
ambiguum	EPfP WCom
amorginum Ruby Cluster = 'Blorub' PBR	EBee LRHS LSou NPri SPer WCot
angustifolium	see *H. italicum*
- from Crete	see *H. microphyllum* (Willd.) Cambess.
- 'Nanum'	SEND
arenarium	ECho
§ ***arwae***	CPBP EPot IRar WAbe
basalticum	WAbe
bellidioides	see *Anaphalioides bellidioides*
bellum	NWCA
'Coco'	see *Xerochrysum bracteatum* 'Coco'
coralloides	see *Ozothamnus coralloides*
'County Park Silver'	see *Ozothamnus* 'County Park Silver'
'Dargan Hill Monarch'	see *Xerochrysum bracteatum* 'Dargan Hill Monarch'
depressum	EPot
'Elmstead'	see *H. stoechas* 'White Barn'
fontanesii	WHer
frigidum	CPBP WAbe
heldreichii NS 127	NWCA
hookeri	see *Ozothamnus hookeri*
§ ***hypoleucum***	GGar SDix
§ ***italicum*** ♀H3	CArn CPrp CWan ECha GPoy MHer MMuc MNHC NGHP NPri SBfd SEND SPet SPoG SRms WCom WDin WGwG WHfH WJek
- from Crete	NWCA
- 'Dartington'	EBee EOHP NGHP SIde WJek
I - 'Glaucum'	CWib
- 'Korma' PBR	CAbP EBee EHoe ELan EPfP EWTr GBin LRHS LSRN LSou MAsh MGos NGHP NPri SIde SLon SPoG WJek
- subsp. ***microphyllum***	see *H. microphyllum* (Willd.) Cambess.
- 'Nanum'	see *H. microphyllum* (Willd.) Cambess.
§ - subsp. ***serotinum***	CBcs EBee EHoe EPfP GGar GPoy MCot MRav SBfd SLim SMad SPer SRms STre SWal SWvt WDin WPer
lanatum	see *H. thianschanicum*
ledifolium	see *Ozothamnus ledifolius*
marginatum misapplied	see *H. milfordiae*
§ ***microphyllum*** (Willd.) Cambess.	GBar MHer MNHC SIde WJek
§ ***milfordiae*** ♀H2-3	ECho EPot GEdr NSla SRms WAbe WPat
orientale	EPot IRar
pagophilum	CPBP EPot
petiolare ♀H2	EBak ECtt MCot SBfd SGar SPer SPoG
- 'Aureum'	see *H. petiolare* 'Limelight'
- 'Goring Silver' ♀H2-3	SPet SPoG
§ - 'Limelight' ♀H2	ECtt MCot NPri SBfd SPer SPet SPoG
- 'Variegatum' (v) ♀H2	ECtt LAst MCot NPri SBfd SPet SPoG
populifolium misapplied	see *H. hypoleucum*
rosmarinifolium	see *Ozothamnus rosmarinifolius*
§ 'Schwefellicht'	EBee ECha EPPr EPfP EShb MLHP MNFA SPer WEas WKif WSHC WWEG
selago	see *Ozothamnus selago*
serotinum	see *H. italicum* subsp. *serotinum*
sessilioides	EPot WAbe
§ ***sibthorpii***	ECho IRar NWCA
'Skynet'	see *Xerochrysum bracteatum* 'Skynet'
§ ***splendidum*** ♀H3	EPfP LRHS NBro SKHP SLon WBrE WCom WDin WPer
stoechas	CArn
§ - 'White Barn'	CSpe EBee WCot
Sulphur Light	see *H.* 'Schwefellicht'
§ ***thianschanicum***	EDAr SRms
- Golden Baby	see *H. thianschanicum* 'Goldkind'
§ - 'Goldkind'	EPfP NBir
thyrsoideum	see *Ozothamnus thyrsoideus*
trilineatum	see *H. splendidum*
tumidum	see *Ozothamnus selago* var. *tumidus*
virgineum	see *H. sibthorpii*
wightii B&SWJ 9503	WCru
woodii	see *H. arwae*

Helicodiceros (*Araceae*)

§ ***muscivorus***	CHid CStu EBee WCot

Heliconia ✿ (*Heliconiaceae*)

caribaea 'Burgundy'	see *H. caribaea* 'Purpurea'
§ - 'Purpurea'	XBlo
'Golden Torch'	XBlo
indica 'Spectabilis'	XBlo
latispatha 'Orange Gyro'	XBlo
* - 'Red Gyro'	XBlo
metallica	XBlo
psittacorum	CCCN
rostrata	CCCN XBlo

Helictotrichon (*Poaceae*)

pratense	EHoe
§ ***sempervirens*** ♀H4	Widely available
I - 'Pendulum'	EBee GBin MAvo
- 'Saphirsprudel'	CMdw EBee LRHS WCot WPGP

Heliophila (*Brassicaceae*)

longifolia	CSpe

Heliopsis (*Asteraceae*)

Golden Plume	see *H. helianthoides* var. *scabra* 'Goldgefieder'
helianthoides	MLHP NBre
- 'Limelight'	see *Helianthus* 'Lemon Queen'
- Loraine Sunshine = 'Helhan' PBR (v)	EBee LLWG LRHS LSou NSti SPoG WClo WCot WFut
- var. ***scabra***	CMac MDKP NBPC SRot WMnd WWFP
- - 'Asahi'	EBee EBla ECtt ELan EPPr MAvo MCCP NBPC NDov NLar NPri WHoo
- - Ballerina	see *H. helianthoides* var. *scabra* 'Spitzentänzerin'
- - 'Benzinggold' ♀H4	LSou MRav
- - Golden Plume	see *H. helianthoides* var. *scabra* 'Goldgefieder'

§	- - 'Goldgefieder' 🏆H4	EBee EBla EPfP NBPC NBre WFar
	- - Goldgreenheart	see *H. helianthoides* var. *scabra* 'Goldgrünherz'
§	- - 'Goldgrünherz'	EBee LRHS NBre
	- - 'Hohlspiegel'	EBee NBre
	- - 'Incomparabilis'	MRav
	- - 'Karat'	EBee
	- - 'Mars'	EBee
	- - 'Patula'	EBee
	- - 'Prairie Sunset'PBR	EBee ECtt GGar MBri MWea NBPC
§	- - 'Sommersonne'	CSBt EBee ECtt GKir MSpe MWhi NGBl NPer NPri SPer SRms WMnd WWEG
	- - 'Sonnenschild'	EBee
§	- - 'Spitzentänzerin' 🏆H4	EBee EBla MAvo NBre
	- - 'Summer Nights'	CMac CMea CSam EBee EBrs EPPr GMac LBMP LSou MBri MDKP MNFA MSpe NBPC SPhx
	- - Summer Sun	see *H. helianthoides* var. *scabra* 'Sommersonne'
	- - 'Venus'	EBee EBla ECtt MAvo MBri NBPC NLar NSti WCAu WCra WFar
	- 'Super Dwarf'	LSou SPoG

Heliotropium ✿ (*Boraginaceae*)

§	***amplexicaule***	SDys
	anchusifolium	see *H. amplexicaule*
§	***arborescens***	CArn EPfP EShb MAJR MCot MHom
	- 'Chatsworth' 🏆H1	CAby CCCN CSev CSpe ECre ECtt ERea EShb MAJR MHom SDnm WFar
	- 'Chequerboard'	ERea MAJR
	- 'Dame Alice de Hales'	ERea MAJR MHom
	- 'Florence Nightingale'	MAJR
	- 'Fowa'	ERea
	- 'Gatton Park'	MAJR MHom SMrm
	- 'Lord Roberts'	ERea MAJR MHom WWlt
	- 'Marine'	CFox ECtt SPav WGor
	- 'Mary Fox'	ERea MAJR MHom
	- 'Mrs J.W. Lowther'	MAJR MHom
	- 'Netherhall White'	ERea
	- 'President Garfield'	ERea MAJR MHom WFar
	- 'Princess Marina' 🏆H1	EPfP LAst LSou MAJR NLar SDys SPav
	- 'Reva'	MAJR MHom
	- 'Seifel'	ERea
	- 'The Queen'	ECtt ERea MAJR
	- 'The Speaker'	ERea MAJR MHom
	- 'White Lady'	CCCN CSpe ECtt ERea MAJR MHom NLar
	- 'White Queen'	ECtt MAJR MHom
	- 'Woodcote'	MAJR MHom
	'Baby Blue'	LAst NPri
	peruvianum	see *H. arborescens*

Helleborus ✿ (*Ranunculaceae*)

	abruzzicus WM 0227	MPhe
	abschasicus	see *H. orientalis* Lam. subsp. *abchasicus* (A. Braun) B. Mathew
	'Angel Glow' **new**	LRHS SPoG
§	***argutifolius*** 🏆H4	Widely available
	- from Italy	EHrv
	- 'Janet Starnes' (v)	MAsh
	- mottled-leaved	see *H. argutifolius* 'Pacific Frost'
§	- 'Pacific Frost' (v)	CBow CLAP CPla EBla EBrs EWes LRHS MAsh WWEG
	- 'Red Riding Hood'	LRHS
	- 'Silver Lace'	CBod CBow CFir CHid CSpe CWCL EBee EBrs ELan ELon EPfP GKev GKir LRHS LSRN MCCP MGos MLLN NBir NLar NSti SKHP SPer SPoG WCom WPtf
	atrorubens misapplied	see *H. orientalis* Lam. subsp. *abchasicus* Early Purple Group
	atrorubens ambig.	EWTr
	atrorubens Waldst. & Kit.	CDes MRav WAbe WPGP
	- WM 9028 from Slovenia	MPhe
	- WM 9805 from Croatia	MPhe
	- WM 9825	WWst
	- from Slovenia	CBel
	- spotted form	MPhe
	× ***ballardiae***	CLAP WAbe WFar
	bocconei	WWst
	- subsp. ***bocconei***	see *H. multifidus* subsp. *bocconei*
	'Briar Rose' **new**	MAsh
	colchicus	see *H. orientalis* Lam. subsp. *abchasicus* (A. Braun) B. Mathew
	corsicus	see *H. argutifolius*
	croaticus	WFar
	- WM 9313	MPhe
	- WM 9810 from Croatia	MPhe
	cyclophyllus	GBin GEdr GKir GMaP MAsh MHom MPhe SPer WFar
	- HOA 8934	WWst
	- HOA 9144	WWst
	dumetorum	CBel EBee GKir WFar
	- WM 0023	WWst
	- WM 9209 from Hungary	MPhe
	- WM 9209 from Slovenia	MPhe
	- WM 9627 from Croatia	MPhe
	- WM 9832	WWst
§	× ***ericsmithii***	Widely available
	- 'Bob's Best'	CBel MAvo MNrw NPnk SPoG WCot
	- 'HGC Silvermoon'PBR	LRHS NLar SPoG
	- 'Ruby Glow'	EPfP LRHS
	- 'Winter Moonbeam'	EPfP LRHS MAsh NCGa
	foetidus 🏆H4	Widely available
	- 'Chedglow'	CNat WCom
	- 'Gold Bullion'	CBow CPla CSpe MAsh SBfd WFar WWEG
	- 'Harvington Pewter'	LRHS SPoG
	- 'Pewter'	CLAP
	- 'Sopron'	CLAP
	- sweet-scented	MHom
	- Wester Flisk Group	CMac CPLG EBee EBla EHrv EPPr EPfP GKir IFoB LRHS MAsh MBri MGos MNrw MRav MSwo NPer NPnk SBfd SPer SPoG SWal WCAu WFar WHoo WPGP WTin
	- 'Yorkley'	LSRN
	'HGC Jericho'PBR **new**	IVic
	'HGC Josef Lemper'PBR	IVic LRHS
N	× ***hybridus***	Widely available
	- anemone-centred	CHid CLAP EHrv IFoB LHel LRHS MNrw NRar SPoG WFar
	- 'Antique Shades'	WFar
	- 'Apple Blossom'	EHrv WFar
	- apricot-flowered	CLAP EHrv WFar WTin
	- Ashwood Garden hybrids	CPMA EBrs EHrv EPPr EPfP LRHS MAsh MGos MMuc MRav SCoo SEND SPoG SRms WSpi WWEG
	- Ashwood Garden hybrids, anemone-centred	CPMA MAsh
	- Ashwood Garden hybrids, double-flowered (d)	MAsh
	- Ballard's Group	CLAP EBee EBrs GEdr MWat NCGa NRar SPer WFar WMnd WPnP WSpi
	- 'Black Beauty'	MWea NEgg NPnk NPri WHlf WSpi
	- black-flowered	CBel CLAP EHrv GMaP SSth WFar WHoo WTin
	- 'Blue Lady' (Lady Series)	CBcs COlW EBee EBla EPfP GAbr GBin GEdr IFoB LRHS MBNS MGos

	MNrw MWat MWea NGdn NMoo SMad SMrm SPer STes WSpi
- 'Blue Metallic Lady' (Lady Series)	COlW CPLG CSpe CWit EAEE EBee EPfP GAbr GEdr LAst LRHS MBNS MWat NCGa NEgg NPri WSpi
- blue-grey-flowered	CBel EHrv
- Bradfield hybrids	EHrv MCot
- Bradfield hybrids, anemone-centred	EHrv
- Bradfield Star Group	EHrv
- Caborn hybrids	LLWP
- 'Cheerful'	NBir
- 'Clare's Purple'	GBin LSRN SCoo
- 'Cosmos'	MBNS
- cream-flowered	CBel CLAP CPMA MCCP WFar WTin
- dark purple-flowered	LHel SBfd
- dark red-flowered	LHel
- 'David's Star' (d)	CFir
- deep red-flowered	CBel CLAP NHol WFar WTin
- double (d)	CBel CLAP CMea CSpe LHop MDun MNrw NPnk NRar WFar
- Double Ladies, mixed (d)	GAbr MWat
- double pink-flowered	LHel LRHS SSth
- 'Double Vision' (d)	EPPr WWEG
- double, black-flowered (d)	CPLG IFoB NRar
- double, purple-flowered (d)	LHel
- double, red-flowered (d)	CPLG MDun WSpi
- double, white-flowered (d)	CPLG IFoB LHel SSth
- double, yellow-flowered (d)	CPLG IFoB LHel MDun
- Draco strain	NChi
- Farmyard anemone-centred	WFar
- 'Farmyard Appleblossom'	WFar
- Farmyard apricot	WFar
- Farmyard black	WFar
- Farmyard cream	WFar
- Farmyard cream, dark-eyed	WFar
- Farmyard cream, spotted	WFar
- Farmyard dark pink	WFar
- Farmyard double apricot (d)	WFar
- Farmyard double black (d)	WFar
- Farmyard double cream (d)	WFar
- Farmyard double cream spotted (d)	WFar
- Farmyard double pink (d)	WFar
- Farmyard double pink spotted (d)	WFar
- Farmyard double primrose (d)	WFar
- Farmyard double primrose spotted (d)	WFar
- Farmyard double red (d)	WFar
- Farmyard double slate-grey (d)	WFar
- Farmyard double white (d)	WFar
- Farmyard double white spotted (d)	WFar
- Farmyard green	WFar
- Farmyard green spotted	WFar
- Farmyard picotee	WFar
- Farmyard pink	WFar
- Farmyard pink spotted	WFar
- Farmyard plum	WFar
- Farmyard primrose	WFar
- Farmyard primrose dark-eyed	WFar
- Farmyard primrose spotted	WFar
- Farmyard red	WFar
- Farmyard slate spotted	WFar
- Farmyard slate-grey	WFar
- Farmyard veined	WFar
- Farmyard white	WFar
- Farmyard white dark-eyed	WFar
- Farmyard white splash	WFar
- Farmyard white spotted	WFar
- 'Farmyard Woodland'	WFar
- 'Green Ripple'	WFar
- green-flowered	LHel WFar
- 'Günther Jürgl' (d)	WFar
- 'Harvington Apricots'	EBee NBir NLar SKHP WCra
- Harvington double pink (d)	EBee SKHP SPoG WCra
- Harvington double purple (d)	EBee NBir NLar SKHP SPoG
- Harvington double red (d)	EBee GKir NBir NLar SPoG WCra
- Harvington double white (d)	EBee NBir NLar SKHP SPoG WCra
- Harvington double yellow (d)	EBee NBir NLar SKHP SPoG WCra
- Harvington double, lime-green (d)	LRHS
- Harvington picotee	EBee GKir LRHS MGos NBir NLar SKHP SPoG WCra
- Harvington pink	EBee GKir LRHS MGos MHer NLar SPoG WCra
- Harvington pink speckled	EBee GKir MGos NLar SPoG
- Harvington red	EBee GKir LRHS MGos MHer NLar SPoG WCra
- 'Harvington Shades of the Night'	EBee GKir LRHS MGos MHer NLar SKHP SPoG WCra WSpi
- 'Harvington Smokey Blues'	SKHP
- 'Harvington Smokey Double' (d)	EBee
- Harvington speckled	EBee LRHS MHer
- Harvington speckled white	EBee SKHP SPoG
- Harvington white	EBee GKir LRHS MGos MHer NLar SKHP SPoG WSpi
- Harvington yellow	EBee GKir LRHS MGos MHer NLar SKHP SPoG
- Harvington yellow speckled	EBee LRHS MGos MHer NLar SPoG WSpi
- 'Helen Ballard'	GKev
- 'Hidcote Double' (d)	NRar
- Hillier hybrids, burgundy	LRHS MGos
- - clear-white	LRHS MGos
- - double red	LRHS
- - double yellow	LRHS
- - purple	LRHS MGos
- - slate	LRHS
- - spotted, double yellow (d)	LRHS
- - spotted, double-pink (d)	LRHS
- - spotted, green	LRHS
- - spotted, pink	LRHS MGos
- - spotted, white	LRHS
- - 'Spring Romance'	LRHS MGos
- - yellow	LRHS
- - yellow, magenta eye	LRHS
- 'Ian Raithby'	WSpi
- ivory-flowered	WFar
- Joy hybrids	SPoG
- Kaye's garden hybrids	EPfP NBPC WMnd
- 'Lady Macbeth'	EWes
- Lady Series	NSum
- large, pink-flowered	WTin
- maroon-flowered	NRar WFar
- 'Monita Nightshades'	CMoH
- 'Mrs Betty Ranicar' (d)	EPfP EWes GEdr IFoB LRHS MBNS MGos NCGa NLar NSum WBVN WFar WWEG
- nearly black-flowered	CBel
- pale pink-flowered	LHel
- 'Pamina'	EHrv IFoB
§ - Party Dress Group (d)	CHid EBla EHrv ELan ELon EPfP IFoB SPoG WFar

	- Picotee Group	CBel SSth WTin
	- 'Picotee'	CLAP EGxp EHrv IFoB LHel NRar WCru WFar WHoo
	- 'Picotee' double-flowered (d)	LHel
	- 'Pink Lady' (Lady Series)	CWit EBee EPfP GQue MGos MWat NEgg NGdn NPri SMrm SPer
	- 'Pink Upstart'	IFoB
	- pink-flowered	CLAP CPMA GAbr LHel MBNS MCCP MMuc NRar SSth WFar WHoo WTin
	- plum-flowered	CBel CLAP EHrv MMuc SSth WFar WTin
	- 'Pluto'	WFar
	- primrose-flowered	CLAP ECGP ELan EWTr MMuc NEgg NRar SBfd SEND WFar WTin
	- purple-flowered	CBel CLAP CPMA NHol NRar SEND SGSe SSth WBor WFar WHoo
*	- 'Purpurascens'	MCCP
	- 'Queen of the Night'	CLAP CPLG EPfP IBal MWhi SPad
	- 'Red Lady'	CBcs COlW CPLG CWit EAEE EBee EBla EPfP EPot GAbr GBin GQue IBal LAst LHop LRHS MBNS MGos MWat MWea NEgg NMoo NPri SMrm SPer WHil
	- 'Red Spotted'	EPfP GEdr
	- 'Red Upstart'	IFoB
	- 'Shades of Night'	EHrv
	- slaty blue-flowered	CBel CLAP EHrv IFoB LHel SSth WFar
	- slaty purple-flowered	NRar WFar
	- 'Smokey Blue'	EGxp EWTr LRHS SEND
	- smokey purple-flowered	ELan MMuc SBfd SEND WFar
	- 'Snow Queen'	EHrv
	- 'Speckled Draco'	CPLG
§	- spotted	CLAP EPfP GMaP MCCP NEgg SBfd SWal WCot WCru WHoo WTin WWEG
	- - cream	CBel CLAP NBir SSth WTin
	- - green	CLAP WFar WTin
	- - ivory	CLAP
	- - pink	CLAP LHel LRHS MBNS NBir NHol NRar SEND WFar WHoo WTin
	- - primrose	CLAP ELan WFar WTin
	- - white	EBla LHel MMuc NBir NRar SEND SSth WFar WTin
	- - yellow	LHel LRHS
	- - double, pink (d)	SSth
	- - - white (d)	GBin LHel
	- 'Spotted Lady'	GBin
	- Sunshine selections	GKev IBal
	- 'Swirling Skirts'	EBla
	- 'Tricastin'	CHid SPad
	- 'Tutu'	EGxp LBuc LRHS NCGa SPoG
	- 'Ushba'	CLAP
	- Washfield double-flowered (d)	EPfP LRHS MGos MNrw SBfd SPer SPoG SRkn SWal WBor WHil WSpi
	- - white (d)	IFoB
	- 'White Lady' (Lady Series)	COlW CPLG CWit EBee EBla GEdr GQue IFoB LAst MBNS MGos MWat MWea NEgg NPri SMrm SPer
	- 'White Lady Spotted' (Lady Series)	CHVG COlW EBee EPfP GEdr GQue NEgg SMad
	- white-flowered	CBel LHel NRar SSth WCFE WFar WHoo WTin
	- white-veined	WFar
	- Winter Queen strain	WWEG
	- 'Yellow Lady' (Lady Series)	CBcs CWit EBee EPfP EPot GEdr GQue LHop LRHS MBNS MWat MWea NEgg NPri SPer
	- yellow-flowered	CBel CBow GMaP IFoB LHel SSth WFar WHoo WTin

	- Zodiac Group	EBla
§	Ivory Prince = 'Walhelivor'	EPfP LBuc LRHS MAsh
	'Kiwi Black Velvet' **new**	IBal
	Lenten Booty Mix **new**	CWit
	liguricus WM 0230	MPhe
	lividus ♀$^{H2-3}$	CAby CEnt CLAP CSpe ECho EPfP EWes GKev GKir LHop LRHS MMuc MPhe NBir SDeJ SKHP SWal SWat WFar
	- subsp. ***corsicus***	see *H. argutifolius*
	- 'Silver Edge'	EPfP
	- 'White Marble' **new**	GKev
	'Moonshine'^{PBR}	EKen NHol NLar
	multifidus	EBee EPPr NBir WFar
§	- subsp. ***bocconei***	EBee EHrv MAsh MHom WFar
	- - WM 9719 from Italy	MPhe
	- - WM 9905 from Sicily	MPhe
	- subsp. ***hercegovinus***	EHrv WFar
	- - WM 0020	MPhe
	- - WM 0622	MPhe
	- subsp. ***istriacus***	MAsh WFar
	- - WM 9322	MPhe
	- - WM 9324	MPhe
	- subsp. ***multifidus***	EHrv MAsh MHom
	- - WM 9529	MPhe
	- - WM 9748 from Croatia	MPhe
	- - WM 9833	MPhe
	niger ♀^{H4}	Widely available
	- Ashwood strain	CLAP MAsh
	- Blackthorn Group	CBow CLAP EHrv
	- 'David' **new**	IVic
	- double-flowered (d)	ELan
	- 'Eifelturm' **new**	IVic
	- Harvington hybrids	EHrv GKir LRHS MHer
	- 'HGC Jacob'^{PBR}	IVic LBuc LRHS
	- 'HGC Joshua'^{PBR} **new**	IVic
	- 'Ivory Prince'	see *H.* Ivory Prince
§	- subsp. ***macranthus***	EBee NMoo
	- ***major***	see *H. niger* subsp. *macranthus*
	- 'Marion' (d)	IFoB
	- 'Maximus'	CLAP EBee EWes WFar
	- 'Potter's Wheel'	CDes CLAP CMoH CPMA EBee ELan EPfP GKir LRHS MRav NBir
	- 'Praecox'	CWan EBee EPPr EPfP EWes LRHS
	- 'Ras Buis'	NMoo
	- 'Schneeball' **new**	IVic
	- 'White Christmas'	LRHS
	- 'White Magic'	CPMA MGos MNrw
	× ***nigercors*** ♀^{H4}	CDes CElw CEnt CMac CSam CSpe EBrs ECha ECtt EHrv GKir GMaP LHop LRHS MBri MCot SPoG WAbe WCot WFar WPGP
	- double-flowered (d)	EHrv IBal LSou
	- 'HGC Green Corsican'^{PBR}	LRHS
	- 'Pink Beauty'	LBuc
	× ***nigristern***	see *H.* × *ericsmithii*
	odorus	CBel EHrv EWes GMaP IFoB MAsh MPhe SPer WFar WPGP
	- WM 0312 from Bosnia	MPhe
	- WM 9415	MPhe
	- WM 9728 from Hungary	MPhe
N	***orientalis*** misapplied	see *H.* × *hybridus*
	orientalis ambig.	CBar ECho LAst
	orientalis Lam.	CBcs CBel CChe EPot EWTr EWes LRHS MPhe MSwo STre
§	- subsp. ***abchasicus***	EBee GEdr MAsh SRms WFar
§	- - Early Purple Group	CBre CTri GCal MRav WFar
	- subsp. ***guttatus*** misapplied	see *H.* × *hybridus* spotted
	- subsp. ***guttatus*** (A. Braun & Sauer) B. Mathew	EBee EWTr NChi NHol SRkn

- subsp. ***orientalis*** from the Caucasus	WWst
'Pink Beauty'PBR	EPfP LRHS MAsh MBri MGos NLar SPoG
'Pink Ice' **new**	MAsh
'Pirouette' **new**	LBuc LRHS
purpurascens	CBel EBee EHrv EPPr EPfP GEdr GMaP IFoB MAsh MRav NBir SMad SPer WAbe WBrE WFar WPnP
- WM 0815 from Romania **new**	MPhe
- WM 9211 from Hungary	MPhe
- WM 9412	MPhe
- WM 9922	WWst
'Silver Dollar' **new**	SPoG
Snowdon strain	WSpi
× ***sternii***	CBcs CSpe CTri EBla ECho ELan EPfP EUJe EWTr GKir GMaP IFro LRHS MCot MGos MNrw MWat NEgg NHol NLar NMRc SGar SPer SPoG WAbe WFar WMnd WMoo WTin
- Aberconwy strain	CLAP
- Ashwood strain	MAsh
- 'Beatrice le Blanc'	MAsh
- Blackthorn Group ♀H3-4	CBcs CPMA EHrv ELon EPfP GAbr IFoB LRHS MBNS MRav NCGa SBfd SPoG SWal WBrk WFar WPGP
- Blackthorn dwarf strain	CLAP EBee MCot WBor
- 'Boughton Beauty'	CLAP CMea EBee EHrv ELan MAsh MTho NSum WSpi
- Bulmer's blush strain	WSpi
- dwarf	WFar
- 'Joy's Purple'	EBla LAst
- pewter-flowered	CAby CSpe
thibetanus	CFir CLAP CPLG EBee EFEx EHrv EPot EWes GEdr LAma MAsh MPhe
torquatus	CBel EBee EBla EHrv MAsh MPhe MTho SPer WFar WTin
- HOA 9115	WWst
- LD 308 from Serbia	WWst
- WM 0609 from Montenegro	MPhe
- WM 0617 from Serbia	MPhe
- WM 9106 from Montenegro	MPhe
- WM 9745	EHrv
- WM 9820 from Bosnia	MPhe
- Caborn hybrids	LLWP
- 'Dido' (d)	CPLG WFar
- double-flowered, from Montenegro (d)	WFar
- - WM 0620	MPhe
- - hybrids (d)	WFar
- hybrids	ECGP EHrv WFar
- Party Dress Group	see *H.* × *hybridus* Party Dress Group
- semi-double-flowered (d)	WFar
- Wolverton hybrids	WFar
'Verboom Beauty'	LRHS
vesicarius	EHrv EWes MAsh
viridis	EBee EHrv EPfP GKir GPoy IFoB SRms WFar WTin
- WM 0444	MPhe
- subsp. ***occidentalis***	EHrv MHom
- - WM 9401	MPhe
- - WM 9502 from Germany	MPhe
- subsp. ***viridis*** WM 9723 from Italy	MPhe
'Walberton's Ivory Prince' **new**	SPoG
'Walberton's Rosemary' **new**	LBuc LRHS SPoG
'White Beauty'PBR	CBcs EPPr EPfP EWes LBuc LRHS MAsh MBri MGos MRav NLar SPoG

Helonias (*Melanthiaceae*)

bullata	EBee GEdr WCot

Heloniopsis (*Melanthiaceae*)

acutifolia	CDes GEdr
- B&SWJ 218	WCru
- B&SWJ 6817	WCru
japonica	see *H. orientalis*
§ ***kawanoi***	CDes EBee EPot GEdr NMen SKHP WCot WCru
§ ***orientalis***	CLAP ECho GCal GEdr GGar NMen WCot WCru
- B&SWJ 6380 from Japan	WCru
- from Korea	EBee GEdr SKHP
- var. ***breviscapa***	EBee GEdr WCru WPGP
- - B&SWJ 5873	WCru
- - 'A-so' **new**	WCru
- variegated (v)	GEdr WCru
- var. ***yakusimensis***	see *H. kawanoi*
tubiflora B&SWJ 4173 **new**	WCru
- B&SWJ 822	WCru
- 'Temple Blue' **new**	WCru
umbellata	CDes CLAP CPom EBee GEdr SKHP
- B&SWJ 1839	WCru
- B&SWJ 6836	WCru
- B&SWJ 6846	WCru
- B&SWJ 7117	WCru

Helwingia (*Helwingiaceae*)

chinensis	NLar SSpi WBor WPat
himalaica	CGHE WPGP
japonica	CBot CHGN EFEx WFar

Helxine see *Soleirolia*

Hemerocallis ✿ (*Hemerocallidaceae*)

'Aabachee'	CBgR SApp
'Above the Clouds' **new**	EWoo
'Absolute Treasure'	CFwr SBrk
'Absolute Zero'	CFwr SBrk SPol SRos WAul
'Adah'	SDay
'Added Dimensions'	SApp
'Addie Branch Smith'	EGol SDay
'Admiral'	CHar
'Admiral's Braid'	EWoo
'Adoration'	SPer
'Aerea'	EMar
'Africa'	SBrk
'African Chant'	ELan
'Age of Miracles'	SPol
'Ah Youth'	SApp
'Ahoya'	CBgR SRos
'Alabama Jubilee'	WNHG
'Alan'	EBrs ECtt LRHS MRav SRos
'Alaqua'	CFir EMar LAst MBNS MNrw SApp SBrk SPer WFar
'Alec Allen'	SBrk SDay SRos
'Alejandro Pavlos'	SApp
'Alien Encounter'	SPol
'All American Baby'	CWat EMar MBNS SBrk SPol
'All American Chief'	SBrk
'All American Magic'	SPol
'All American Plum'	CWCL EMar EPfP GBin IPot MBNS SBrk WAul WHrl
'All American Tiger'	SBrk SDay SRos
'All American Windmill'	EMar EWoo SRos
'All Fired Up'	CFwr EMar SBrk SPol SRos
'All the Magic'	CFwr
'Allegiance'	WNHG

'Alma Atha' (d)	EMar
'Almond Puff' **new**	SDay
'Almost Paradise' **new**	SPol
'Alpine Mist'	SDay
'Alpine Rhapsody'	SPol
'Alpine Snow'	EWoo SBrk SRos
altissima	CHEx EBee LPla MNrw SPhx
'Always Afternoon'	CKel EBee EBla EMar EWoo LRHS MBNS MNrw MSpe NCGa SApp SBrk SPol SRos WAul WCAu WHrl WWEG
'Amadeus'	LRHS SApp
'Ambassador'	CBgR
'Amber Classic'	SApp
'American Original'	SRos
'American Revolution'	Widely available
'Amersham'	MNFA SApp
'Amerstone Amethyst Jewel'	SApp SRos
'Amy'	WWEG
'Anastasia' **new**	SBrk
'Andrew Christian'	SPol
'Android' **new**	EWoo
'Angel Artistry'	SApp SDay
'Angel Curls'	EGol
'Angel Rodgers'	SApp
'Angel Unawares'	SApp WTin
'Angels Sigh' **new**	EMar
'Ann Blocher'	CFwr
'Ann Kelley'	SApp SBrk SDay SRos
'Anna Warner'	SEND
'Annie Golightly'	SDay
'Annie Welch'	ELon EPfP EPla MBNS NBre
'Antarctica'	SApp SPol
'Antique Rose'	CKel EMar SBrk SDay
'Anzac'	COIW ECha ECtt EHrv EPla GMac LRHS MBNS NBre NGdn NHol NPri SAga SApp SPav SRos SWvt WMoo
'Apache Bandana' **new**	EWoo
'Apache Beacon' **new**	EWoo
'Apache Uprising'	SBrk SRos
'Apollodorus'	EMar SBrk
'Apple Court Chablis'	SApp SPol
'Apple Court Champagne'	SApp SPol
'Apple Court Damson'	SApp SPol
'Apple Court Ruby'	SApp SPol
'Apple Crisp'	SApp
'Apple Of My Eye'	EWoo
'Après Moi'	EBla EKen EMar MBNS NLar WBrE WCAu
'Apricot Angel'	SApp
'Apricot Beauty' (d)	CPrp ECho EMar MBNS WSpi
'Apricotta'	WCot WPnP
'Aquamarine'	SDay WCon
'Aquamarine Seedling'	SApp
'Arachnephobia' **new**	EWoo
'Arctic Snow'	CBgR CMac EBee ELon EMar EWoo GMac LAst LRHS LTen MBNS MNrw NBPC NLar SBrk SDnm SRos SUsu WAul WClo WCon WPnP
'Arms to Heaven' **new**	EWoo
'Arpeggio'	WHrl
'Arriba'	MNFA NBro
'Arthur Vincent'	SPol
'Artistic Gold'	WTin
'Asian Artistry'	WNHG
'Asiatic Pheasant'	SPol
'Asterisk'	SRos
'Aten'	CBgR CSpr SBfd WAul
'Athlone' **new**	EWoo
'Atlanta Bouquet'	SBrk SRos
'Atlanta Fringe Benefit' **new**	SApp SDay
'Atlanta Full House'	SDay
'August Frost'	CBgR SRos
'August Orange'	MNFA
'Augusto Bianco'	SApp SRos
'Autumn Minaret'	EMar EWoo
'Autumn Red'	CBcs EBla EMar MBNS MMuc MNrw NBir SEND SPol WCot
'Autumn Wood'	SDay
'Ava Michelle'	SApp SDay
'Avant Garde'	SApp SPol
'Avon Crystal Rose'	WNHG
'Awakening Dream'	SBrk SRos
'Awash With Color'	SRos
'Awesome Blossom'	EMar GBin LSou MBNS MNrw NMoo SMrm SRos WCAu
'Awesome Candy'	EWoo LSRN
'Aztec Firebird' **new**	EWoo
'Baby Blues'	SDay SPol
'Baby Darling'	WCon
'Baby Red Eyes'	CFwr
'Baby Talk'	CFir SMrm
'Badge of Honor'	SApp
'Baja'	MNFA WFar
'Bald Eagle'	WWEG
'Bali Hai'	COIW GBee GBin LRHS MBNS MSCN SRms WHrl WSpi
'Ballerina Girl'	SBrk SRos
'Ballerina on Ice'	CFwr
'Bambi Doll'	CFwr
'Bamboo Blackie'	EMar EWoo SPol
'Bamboo Ruffles'	EMar
'Banbury Cinnamon'	MBNS
'Bangkok Belle'	CWat SDay
'Banned in Boston'	EWoo MSpe
'Banzai'	CFwr
'Barbara Mitchell'	CFwr EWTr MBNS MNFA MNrw NMoo SApp SBrk SDay SHar SRos WAul
'Barbary Corsair'	SApp
'Barnegat Light' **new**	EWoo
'Baronet's Badge'	SPol
'Baroni'	ECha
'Bathsheba'	SBrk SPol SRos
'Battle Hymn'	WCAu
'Bayou Bride'	SRos
'Beat the Barons'	SBrk SPol SRos
'Beautiful Edgings'	EMar EWoo SBrk SDay SPol SRos
'Beauty to Behold'	SApp SBrk SDay SRos
'Becky Lynn'	ECtt MBNS SApp
'Beijing'	SBrk
'Bejewelled'	EGol EPla NMoo SApp SBrk WTin
'Bela Lugosi'	Widely available
'Belconto'	CFwr
'Bellini'	SBrk SRos
'Ben Adams'	SRos
'Ben Lee'	SDay
'Benchmark'	EMar MNFA SApp SBrk SRos WCon
'Benedict' **new**	SBrk
'Bengal Bay'	EWoo
'Berlin Lemon' $\mathbb{Y}^{H4}$	LRHS MNFA
'Berlin Maize'	SApp
'Berlin Oxblood'	WAul
'Berlin Red' $\mathbb{Y}^{H4}$	CPrp EBee EBla ECha EMar EPla GBee LBMP MNFA MNrw SApp SRos WFar
'Berlin Red Velvet' $\mathbb{Y}^{H4}$	MNFA
'Berlin Tallboy'	SApp SBrk SDay
'Berlin Watermelon'	MBNS
'Berliner Premiere'	MNFA
'Bernard Thompson'	EMar SApp SRos
'Bertie Ferris'	MSpe NLar SRos
'Bess Ross'	CMHG MNFA
'Bess Vestale'	MWat NHol

'Best Kept Secret'	EWoo SPol
'Bette Davis Eyes'	CBgR CWat EMar SApp SBrk SPol SRos
'Betty Benz'	SBrk SRos
'Betty Jenkins'	SBrk SDay SRos
'Betty Lyn'	SApp
'Betty Warren Woods'	SBrk SDay SRos
'Betty Woods' (d)	SBrk SDay SRos
'Betty's Pick' **new**	EWoo
'Beyond 2000'	SApp
'Bible Story'	CFwr
'Big Apple'	EMar SApp SBrk SDay SPol SRos
'Big Bird'	CPar EWoo GMac LSRN MBNS MWea NCGa SApp SBrk WAul
'Big Blue'	EWoo
'Big City Eye'	MBNS SApp SBrk
'Big Golden'	WWEG
'Big Kiss' **new**	SPol
'Big Smile'	CWCL CWGN EBee EMar IPot MBNS MNrw MWea NBPC NBro NMoo SBrk WFar
'Big Snowbird'	CFwr EMar SBrk SRos
'Big Time Happy'	MBNS SBfd SBrk
'Bill Norris'	SApp SBrk SDay SRos
'Bird Bath Pink'	SPol
'Birdwing Butterfly' **new**	SPol
'Bitsy'	EGol ELon SPet WCot WMnd WWEG
'Black Ambrosia'	CFwr SDay
'Black Briar Bay'	EMar SRos
'Black Emmanuella'	CPLG EBee ECho EMar ERCP IKil LAst MBNS MNrw MWhi SBch
'Black Eye'	SDay WNHG
'Black Eyed Stella'	CKel MBNS WCot WSpi
'Black Eyed Susan'	MBNS SBrk
'Black Ice'	EWoo SPol
'Black Knight'	NLar SRms
'Black Magic'	CHar CTri CWat EBee EBla EGol ELan EPla EWTr GMaP GMac LRHS LSRN MHer MLLN MRav MSpe NBir NEgg NGdn NHol SAga SGSe SPer SPoG WHer WHrl WMoo
'Black Moon'	CFwr
'Black Passion' **new**	SRos
'Black Plush'	EWoo SPol SRos
'Black Prince'	CBgR CFir EBee EWll MBNS NBre NBro WAul
'Blackberry Candy'	CSam EMar EWoo MBNS MNrw SBrk WAul WCAu
'Blackberry Sherbert'	CBgR
'Blackthorne'	CFwr
'Blessing'	SBrk SDay SPol SRos
'Blonde Is Beautiful'	SBrk SDay SRos
'Blood Stream' **new**	EWoo
'Blue Diana'	SRos
'Blue Moon'	SApp
'Blue Sheen'	CBgR CFir CMac CPar EBee ECtt EGol GMaP MBNS MCCP NGdn WFar WMoo WSpi
'Blueberry Candy'	ECtt EWoo MBNS SApp SBrk WAul WHrl
'Blueberry Cream'	CWCL EPfP MBNS MMHG MNrw MWea SBrk SPad
'Blueberry Sundae' **new**	EMar
'Blue-eyed Butterfly'	SPol
'Blue-eyed Chris' **new**	WCot
'Blushing Belle'	CMil EBla ECGP EMar LRHS MBNS NBro NEgg SApp
'Blushing Valentine'	SRos
'Bogie and Becall' **new**	SPol
'Bold Encounter'	CFwr
'Bold One'	CMHG SPol SRos
'Bold Ruler'	SPol
'Bold Tiger'	EMar SDay
'Bonanza'	Widely available
'Boney Maroney'	EWoo SApp SBrk SRos
'Booger'	SBrk SRos
'Boogie My Woogie Baby' **new**	EWoo
'Bookmark'	EMar
'Boom Town'	EMar
'Booroobin Magic'	EWoo
'Border Baby'	ECtt SBrk
'Border Lord'	EWoo
'Born Yesterday'	SApp
'Boulderbrook Serenity'	SDay
'Bourbon Kings'	EBee EGol MBNS MSpe NBre SPav WCon WHrl
'Bowl of Roses'	SApp
'Bradley Bernard'	SPol
'Brand New Lover'	SApp
'Brass Buckles'	see *H.* 'Puddin'
'Breed Apart'	SPol
'Brenda Newbold'	SPol
'Brer Rabbit's Baby' **new**	EWoo
'Bridget'	ELan
'Bright Banner'	WCAu
'Bright Beacon'	SPol
'Bright Spangles'	SApp SRos WEas
'Brilliant Circle'	SApp
'Bristol Fashion'	SApp
'Broadway Bold Eyes' **new**	MMoz SPol
'Broadway Image'	SBrk SRos
'Broadway Valentine'	SApp SBrk SRos
'Brocaded Gown'	ELan SApp SBrk SDay SRos
'Brookwood Wow'	SApp
'Brown Exotica' **new**	EWoo
'Brown Witch' **new**	EWoo
'Brunette'	SApp
'Bruno Müller'	MNFA SApp
'Brutus'	EMar
'Bubbling Brown Sugar'	SDay SRos
'Bubbly'	SApp SDay SRos
'Buc Crête de Coq'	EMar
'Buc Soleil Couchant'	EMar
'Buckyballs' **new**	SDay
'Bud Producer'	SPol
'Buffy's Doll'	EBee EMar MBNS MNFA SApp SBrk SRos WGob
'Bumble Bee'	CWat ECtt EMar GKir MBNS NBre SApp SBfd
'Burlesque'	SPol WCot
'Burning Daylight' ♀H4	EBee EBrs ECtt EHrv EMar EPfP EPla LRHS MNFA MNrw MRav MWat NBre NEgg NHol SMad SPer SRms SRos WCFE WCon WCot WFar WWHy
'Burning Embers'	SApp
'Burning Inheritance'	SRos
'Bus Stop'	SApp SPol
'Butter Curls'	SRos
'Butterfly Ballet'	SBrk SRos
'Butterfly Charm'	CWat
'Butterfly Garden' **new**	SRos
'Butterscotch'	WFar
'Butterscotch Ruffles'	SDay
'Buzz Bomb'	CWat ECtt EHrv EMar GBee LRHS LSRN MBNS NCob NEgg NGdn SApp SPer SPoG SRos WFar WWEG
'By Myself'	CFwr
'Cage' **new**	SBrk
'Calico Spider'	SBrk SRos
'California Sunshine'	SApp SRos
'Camden Glory'	SApp

'Camden Gold Dollar'	EGol SApp SBrk SRos
'Camelot Green'	WNHG
'Cameron Quantz'	SApp
'Campfire Embers'	GBin
'Canadian Border Patrol'	CWCL EMar EPfP EWoo IBal IPot LRHS MBNS MNrw MSCN MWea NLar SApp SBrk SPer SPol SRos WCAu WFar WHrl
'Canary Feathers'	SApp
'Canary Glow'	CTri SMrm SRos WFar
'Canary Wings'	CBgR
'Candide'	SApp SDay
'Cantique'	SApp SPol
'Cap and Bells'	EMar
'Cape Romain Harbor'	CFwr
'Capernaum Cocktail'	SPol
'Captain Ahab'	SApp
'Captive Audience'	SBrk SRos
'Capulina' **new**	EWoo
'Cara Mia'	CBgR LAst MBNS NBir SPol WFar
'Caramba'	EMar
'Caribbean Jack Dolan'	EWoo
'Carmine Monarch'	SRos
'Carolicolossal'	EWoo SDay SPol
'Carolina Cranberry'	ELan
'Carolina Ruffles'	CFwr
'Caroline Taylor'	WHrl
'Carolipiecrust'	SApp
'Carrot'	CFwr
'Cartwheels' ♀H4	EBee EBla EHrv EMar EPfP EPla EShb GMaP LRHS MBNS NBro SBch SPer SRos WCAu WCon WFar WMoo WTin
'Casino Gold'	SBrk SRos
'Castle Strawberry Delight'	SPol
'Catherine Neal'	SBrk SPol SRos
'Catherine Woodbery'	Widely available
'Cathy's Sunset'	CKel CSam EBee EBla ECtt EMar EPla EWTr LRHS MBNS MSpe MWat NBre NBro NEgg NGdn SMrm SRGP
'Cedar Waxwing'	EGol MNrw
'Cee Tee'	SBrk SRos
'Celebration of Angels'	SApp
'Celtic Christmas'	CFwr SPol
'Cenla Crepe Myrtle'	EWoo
'Cerulean Star'	EWoo SApp
'Challenger'	EMar
'Champagne Memory'	SApp
'Chance Encounter'	MBNS
'Charles Johnston'	CBgR CKel CMMP EMar LAst MBNS MNrw SApp SBrk SRos WAul
'Charlie Pierce Memorial'	EMar MSpe SBrk SPol SRos
'Chartreuse Magic'	CMHG EGol EPla
'Chasing the Sun'	CFwr
'Chateau Defleur' **new**	EMar
'Cheerful Note'	WNHG
'Cherry Brandy'	EWoo
'Cherry Cheeks'	CEnt CFir EBrs ECtt EGol ELan EPfP LRHS MBNS MBri MLLN MNrw MRav NBPC NHol SApp SBrk SMrm SRos WAul WCAu WCon WCot WFar WGob WWEG
'Cherry Eyed Pumpkin'	EMar EWoo SBrk SRos
'Cherry Kiss'	SBrk SRos
'Cherry Ripe'	EQua MNFA
'Cherry Smoke'	SApp
'Cherry Tiger'	MBNS
'Cherry Valentine'	CBcs EBee MBNS SApp SBrk
'Chesières Lunar Moth'	ELon SApp SPol SRos
'Chester Cyclone'	SDay
'Chestnut Lane'	SApp SBrk SRos
'Chewonki'	EMar
'Chicago Apache'	CFir EBee EMar EPfP MBNS MNFA MWea NBir NHol SApp SBch SBrk SPer SPol SRos SUsu WAul WCon WSpi
'Chicago Aztec'	SRos
'Chicago Blackout'	CFir CWat ECtt EGol EPfP MSCN NHol SApp WCAu WCot
'Chicago Brave' **new**	WAul
'Chicago Cattleya'	CFir EGol SApp WAul
'Chicago Cherry'	WNHG
'Chicago Fire'	EGol EPfP GKir MBNS NBPC SHar
'Chicago Heirloom'	CFir EGol EWTr MBNS WAul WCAu
'Chicago Jewel'	CFir EGol NSti WAul
'Chicago Knobby'	EMar MBNS SDay
'Chicago Knockout'	CFir EGol ELan EPfP EWoo LPio SPer WAul WCAu WWEG
'Chicago Mist'	WNHG
'Chicago Peach'	NBir WCAu
'Chicago Petticoats'	EGol NHol SApp WAul
'Chicago Picotee Lace'	EGol NGdn SApp WCAu WWEG
'Chicago Picotee Memories'	MBNS WCAu
'Chicago Picotee Promise'	WNHG
'Chicago Picotee Queen'	SApp SMrs
'Chicago Princess'	EGol
'Chicago Queen'	GKir SDay WMnd WNHG
'Chicago Rainbow'	CBgR MBNS WAul
'Chicago Rosy'	EGol
'Chicago Royal Crown'	ECtt EMar LRHS
'Chicago Royal Robe'	CWCL CWat EBrs EGol ELon EPla EWll LLWP MBNS MNFA NBid NCGa SMrm SWal SWat WCot WTin
'Chicago Ruby'	SApp SBrk SRos WWHy
'Chicago Silver'	CFir EGol MBNS WAul WCAu
'Chicago Star'	SRos WNHG
'Chicago Sugar Plum'	SDay
'Chicago Sunrise'	CBgR EBee EBla EBrs EGol EMar EPla GKir GMaP LPio MBNS MBri MLLN MRav NGdn NHol NMoo SApp SBrk SPet SRos SWvt WCot WPer WWEG
'Chicago Weathermaster'	EMar
'Chief Sarcoxie' ♀H4	SApp SRos
'Child of Fortune'	SApp SDay
'Children's Festival'	EBee EBrs ECtt EGol EWTr GKir GMaP LPBA LRHS MBNS MRav MSpe NLar SApp SBrk SGSe SRos SWvt WCon WFar WMoo
'China Bride'	EWoo SApp SBrk SDay SRos
'China Grove Plantation'	CFwr
'China Lake'	EMar
'Chinese Autumn'	SApp SBrk SRos
'Chinese Cloisonne'	SApp
'Chinese Imp'	NLar
'Chocolate Candy'	CWGN EPfP MBNS
'Chocolate Cherry Truffle'	SApp
'Chokecherry Mountain' **new**	EWoo
'Chorus Line'	SApp SBrk SPol SRos WNHG
'Chorus Line Kid'	SPol
'Chosen Love'	CFwr SApp
'Christine Lynn'	WNHG
'Christmas Carol'	SApp
'Christmas Is'	CBgR CMac COIW CWGN EBee EBla EGol ELon EMar GBin LSou MBNS MCot MNFA MNrw NBre NMoo SApp SBrk SDay SDnm SMrm SPav SPol WAul WCAu WCot WGob WHrl WWEG
'Christmas Ribbon' **new**	EWoo

'Christmas Tidings'	SApp
'Ciao'	EMar SApp
'Ciel d'Or'	GKir
'Cimarron Knight'	EWoo SBrk SPol
'Cindy's Eye'	WCot
'Circle of Beauty'	SBrk SPol
'Circles and Stripes' **new**	EMar
citrina	CBgR CHid CMac CPLG EBee EWTr GQue IMou LRHS MCot NGdn WCot WHrl WTin
citrina × (× ***ochroleuca***)	SMHy WCot
'Civil Law'	SDay
'Civil Rights'	SBrk SRos
'Classic Caper'	WNHG
'Classic Spider'	SApp
'Claudine'	SApp
'Cleopatra'	CPar EWoo SPol SRos WAul
'Clockwork' **new**	SBrk
'Clothed in Glory'	EWoo MBNS NMoo SApp WCot WWEG
'Coburg Fright Wig'	EMar EWoo
'Colonial Dame'	WTin
'Colour Me Yellow'	SApp
'Comanche Eyes'	SApp SDay
'Comet Flash'	SPol
'Coming Up Roses'	CPar SApp SBrk SRos
'Commandment'	EMar
'Condilla' (d)	CFwr SApp SBrk SPol
'Conspicua'	EMar
'Contessa'	EBrs GBin SPer
'Cool It'	CEnt CKel EBee EMar IPot MBNS NBre NCGa NHol NMoo SApp WCAu WHrl
'Cool Jazz'	EMar SApp SBrk SPol SRos
'Copper Dawn'	NChi SApp
'Copper Windmill'	EMar SPol SRos
'Copperhead'	SPol
'Coral Crab'	EWoo SApp
'Coral Eye Shadow' **new**	EWoo
'Coral Mist'	MBNS NBre
'Coral Sparkler'	WNHG
'Coral Spider'	ECtt EMar SPol
'Coral Taco' **new**	EWoo
'Corky' ♀H4	Widely available
'Cornwall'	EMar
'Corryton Pink'	SPol
'Corsican Bandit'	CMMP SDay
'Cosmic Hummingbird'	EWoo MSpe SApp
'Cosmopolitan'	MBNS MCot SBrk
'Country Club'	EGol GMaP MBNS NHol SApp SPol WWEG
'Country Melody'	SDay SRos
'Court Cavalcade' **new**	SBrk
'Court Magician'	EMar EWoo MDun MSpe SApp SBrk SRos WCra
'Court Troubadour'	SPol
'Coyote Moon'	SDay SRos
'Crackling Rosie'	EMar
'Cranberry Baby'	CWan EMar SBrk SDay SRos WHoo WNHG WTin
'Cranberry Coulis'	CWat MBNS
'Crawleycrow'	EMar
'Crazy Pierre'	EMar SPol WHrl
'Cream Drop'	CPrp EBee EBla ECtt EGol GMaP GMac LRHS MCot MHer MLLN MRav MSpe NBro NGdn NLar NSti SApp SBrk SDnm SPav WAul WCot WHrl WMoo WTin
'Creative Art'	SRos
'Creative Edge'	EWoo SDnm WAul
'Creature of the Night'	SApp
'Crimson Icon'	GMac WTin
'Crimson Pirate'	CBgR CBre EBee ELon EMar EPPr GKev GKir LSRN MBNS MSpe NBir NHol NMoo SApp SBfd SBrk SMrm SPer SPlb SPol SWat WAul WCon WHrl WTin
'Crimson Wind'	SApp
'Cripple Creek' **new**	EWoo
'Croesus'	NHol SRms
'Crystal Pinot' **new**	IPot
'Crystalline Pink'	SBrk SRos
'Cupid's Bow'	EGol
'Cupid's Gold'	SBrk SDay SRos
'Curls'	LRHS MBNS SDay
'Curly Brick Road'	SRos
'Curly Cinnamon Windmill'	SDay SRos
'Curly Ripples'	SApp
'Curly Rosy Posy'	EMar SRos
'Custard Candy'	CWCL MBNS MBri MSpe NBir NMoo SApp SBfd SBrk SRos SUsu WAul WCAu
'Cynthia Mary'	ECtt EMar EQua LHop LRHS MBNS MNFA MSpe NBro SRGP WFar
'Dad's Best White'	EMar WTin
'Daggy' **new**	SBrk
'Daily Bread'	EMar
'Daily Dollar'	EBla LRHS MBNS NGdn SApp
'Dainty Pink'	EGol
'Dallas Spider Time'	MNFA
'Dallas Star'	EMar SApp SPol
'Dan Mahony'	MBNS
'Dan Tau'	CKel SDay
'Dance Ballerina Dance'	EBee SBrk SRos
'Dancing Dwarf'	SApp WCon
'Dancing Lions' **new**	EWoo
'Dancing Shiva'	SApp SBrk SDay
'Dancing Summerbird'	SApp SPol SRos
'Daring Deception'	CFir CKel ECtt ELon EMar IPot LAst MBNS MNrw MSpe MWea NCGa NMoo SApp SMrm WCAu WCon WFar WHrl
'Daring Dilemma'	MSpe SPol
'Daring Reflection'	SDay
'Darius'	WNHG
'Dark and Handsome'	MBNS
'Dark Avenger'	EBee MBNS SBrk
'Dark Elf'	SApp WCon
'Dark Star'	SDay
'Darker Shade'	SBrk SRos
'Darkest Night'	SApp SBrk
'Darla Anita' **new**	SBrk
'David Holman'	WNHG
'David Kirchhoff'	CFwr IPot SApp WAul
'Davidson Update'	WNHG
'Dazzle'	SApp
'De Colores'	SRos
'Debussy'	EWoo
'Decatur Ballerina'	WNHG
'Decatur Captivation'	WNHG
'Decatur Cherry Smash'	SDay
'Decatur Dictator'	WNHG
'Decatur Imp'	EGol WHrl
'Decatur Rhythm'	WNHG
'Decatur Supreme'	WNHG
'Decatur Treasure Chest'	WNHG
'Dee Dee Mac'	SApp
'Deep Fire'	SRos
'Delicate Design'	SApp SPol
'Delightsome'	SBrk SRos
'Demetrius'	CWat MNFA MWea SApp
'Denali' **new**	SBrk
'Derrick Cane' **new**	SPol
'Desdemona'	CMil SPol

'Desert Bandit'	SApp
'Desert Dreams' **new**	WCot
'Desert Icicle' **new**	EWoo
'Designer Gown'	SApp
'Designer Jeans'	SBrk SPol SRos
'Desperado Love' **new**	SRos
'Destined to See'	Widely available
'Devil's Footprint'	SDay SPol
'Devon Cream'	SPer
'Devonshire'	SApp SBrk SDay SRos
'Dewberry Candy'	SRos
'Diabolique' **new**	EWoo
'Diamond Dust'	CKel EBee ECtt EPla EWTr GBee MBNS MSpe NLar SApp SMrm SPer WSpi WTin
'Dido'	CTri
'Dipped in Ink'	SPol SRos
'Distant Star' **new**	EWoo
'Diva Assoluta'	SApp
'Divertissment'	CBgR ELon EMar EWoo SApp SDay SRos
'Do You Know Doris'	SDay SRos
'Doll House'	SBrk SRos
'Dominic'	CPar EBee SApp SBrk SRos WCot WMoo
'Don Stevens'	EMar
'Donnie Delight' **new**	SBrk
'Dorethe Louise'	SBrk SPol SRos
'Dorothy McDade'	COlW EWoo
'Dot Paul'	ELan
'Double Action' (d)	SPol
'Double Coffee' (d)	SApp SPav SPol
'Double Corsage' (d)	SApp SPol
'Double Cream' (d)	WCot
'Double Cutie' (d)	EMar NBre NLar SDay WAul
'Double Delicious' (d)	WCot
'Double Dream' (d)	EMar WHrl
'Double Entendre'	EMar
'Double Firecracker' (d)	CCVN CWCL CWat EGxp EMar IBal MBNS MDun NBro NLar NMoo SBrk SMrm
'Double Grapette' (d)	SApp
'Double Layer'	CFwr
'Double Oh Seven' (d)	ELon SApp SPol
'Double Passion' (d)	MBNS
'Double Peach Schnapps' (d) **new**	SBrk
'Double Red Royal' (d)	EMar
'Double River Wye' (d)	CBgR CFir COlW CWat EBee ECtt EGol EMar EPfP GMac LRHS MBNS MHer MNrw NGdn NPri SApp SHar SPol SRos SWat WAul WCot WHoo WHrl WMnd WTin WWEG
'Doublecious' **new**	CWGN
§ 'Doubloon'	COlW NHol
'Dover Plantation'	CFwr
'Dragon Dreams'	SApp SPol
'Dragon Heart'	EWoo
'Dragon King'	EMar SPol
'Dragon Lore'	MBNS SBrk
'Dragon's Eye'	CFwr CWat EMar EWoo MSpe SDay SPol
'Dragon's Orb'	CKel
'Dream Baby'	NBre
'Dream Catcher' **new**	EWoo
'Dream Keeper' **new**	EWoo
'Dream Legacy'	CFwr
'Dreamy Cream'	SBrk SRos
'Dresden Doll'	SPer
'Driven Snow'	SApp
'Droopy Drawers' **new**	SRos
'Druid's Chant'	EWoo LRHS MSpe

'Duke of Durham'	MBNS MNFA MSpe SApp SPhx
dumortieri	CAvo CSam ECha EGol EHrv ELan GGar LRHS MCoo MCot MRav NBid NBir NHol NSti SPer WCot WHrl WTin WWEG
- B&SWJ 1283	WCru
'Dune Needlepoint'	EMar SPol
'Dutch Beauty'	EMar EPla WFar
'Dutch Gold'	MNrw NBro
'Dynasty Pink'	SApp
'Earl Barfield'	EMar
'Earl of Warwick'	CBgR
'Earlianna'	SPol
'Early to Bed' **new**	SBrk
'Earth Angel'	SApp SPol
'Easy Ned'	EMar EWoo SBrk SPol SRos WTin
'Echo Canyon' **new**	EWoo
'Ed Kirchhoff'	EMar
'Ed Murray'	GBin MNFA SRos WAul WCAu
'Edelweiss'	EWTr
'Edgar Brown'	EWoo MBNS SBrk
'Edge Ahead'	CMac ECtt EMar LRHS MBNS MSpe SBrk SMrm
'Edge of Darkness'	CKel CWGN EPfP IPot MBNS MWea NBro NLar NSti SApp SDnm WAul WCAu WFar
'Edna Spalding'	CFwr GMac LRHS SApp SRos
'Eenie Allegro'	ECtt EGol IBal MBNS SPer WCon WMnd
'Eenie Fanfare'	EGol LRHS MBNS NBir WAul WCon WWEG
'Eenie Weenie'	CFee EBla ECtt EGol EPla GKev GKir IBal MBNS NBro SApp SPer SRms WPer WWEG
'Eenie Weenie Non-stop'	CMoH ECha
'Eggplant Escapade'	EMar SPol SRos
'Egyptian Ibis'	EWoo WMnd WNHG
'Egyptian Queen'	EMar SRos
'El Desperado'	Widely available
'El Glorioso'	CWat EMar
'El Padre'	SApp
'Elaine Farrant'	SDay
'Elaine Strutt'	MBNS MNFA MNrw NMoo SApp SDay SRos SWvt WCot WSpi
'Elegant Candy'	CKel CMac EBee MBNS NCGa NMoo SApp SBrk SRos WCon WGob
'Eleonor'	CWGN EPfP MBNS SApp WFar
'Elfin Daydream'	SPol
'Elfin Illusion' **new**	EMar
'Elf's Cap'	SDay
'Elizabeth Anne Hudson'	SBrk
'Elizabeth Salter'	CWCL IPot MBNS NLar NMoo SApp SBrk SPol SRos SUsu WCAu
'Elizabeth Yancey'	EGol
'Elsie Spalding'	GKir
'Elva White Grow'	SDay
'Embuscade'	EMar
'Emerald Enchantment'	SApp
'Emerald Lady'	SRos
'Emily Anne'	SApp
'Emily Jaye'	SApp
'Emmaus'	SApp
'Emperor Butterfly'	SApp
'Emperor's Dragon'	EMar
'Enchanting Blessing'	SRos
'English Cameo'	SRos
'English Toffee'	SApp
'English Vermilion' **new**	EMar
'Enjoy'	SBrk SRos
'Entransette'	GMac SApp SBrk
'Entrapment'	CWGN MBNS SBrk SMrm

'Erin Prairie'	SApp
esculenta	SMad
'Etched Eyes'	EWoo SPol
'Eternal Blessing'	SPol SRos
'Ethel Smith'	SApp
'Etruscan Tomb'	SBrk SPol
'Etrusque'	EMar
'Evelyn Claar'	CMac
'Evelyn Lela Stout'	SApp
'Evening Bell'	SApp
'Evening Enchantment'	SBrk SRos
'Evening Glow'	SApp SRos
'Evening Gown'	SPol
'Ever So Ruffled'	SBrk SRos
'Exotic Love'	SDay
'Eye Catching'	EWoo
'Eye of Round'	CFwr
'Eye-yi-yi'	SPol
'Ezekiel'	EMar WHrl
'Fabergé'	SApp SBrk
'Fabulous Paradise'	EMar
'Fabulous Prize'	SApp SRos
'Fairest Love'	EBee EMar MBNS MSpe
'Fairy Charm'	SApp SDay
'Fairy Finery' **new**	SBrk
'Fairy Summerbird'	SApp SBrk SRos
'Fairy Tale Pink'	MNFA SApp SBrk SDay SPol SRos
'Fairy Wings'	SPer
'Faith Nabor'	EMar SBrk SPol SRos
'Falcon' **new**	SPol
'Fall Farewell'	WNHG
'Fall Guy'	SApp
'Fama'	GKir SBrk SRos
'Fan Club'	EMar GKir
'Fan Dancer'	EGol
'Fandango'	SPer
'Farmer's Daughter'	EWoo SApp SBrk SRos
'Fashion Model'	SApp WPer
'Feather Down'	SPol
'Feathered Fascination'	SApp
'Feelings'	SApp
'Femme Osage'	SBrk SRos
'Ferengi Gold'	CFwr
'Ferris Wheel'	SApp
'Festive Art'	SBrk SPol SRos
'Final Touch'	GMac LTen MBNS MLLN MSCN MSpe MWea NBro SBrk SPol WGob
'Finlandia'	MNFA
'Fire and Fog'	CFwr MAsh MAvo MBNS
'Fire Dance'	SRos
'Fire from Heaven'	SApp
'Fire Tree'	SPol
'Firestorm'	EWoo SApp SPol
'First Formal'	SMrm SPer
'Flames of Fantasy'	SRos
'Flaming Sword'	LRHS NHol WRHF
flava	see *H. lilioasphodelus*
'Fleeting Fancy'	SBrk SRos
'Flight of the Dragon'	SApp
'Flip Flop'	CFwr
'Flower Pavilion'	SPol
'Floyd Cove'	SBrk SDay SRos
'Flutterbye'	SRos
'Fly Catcher'	EMar SBrk SRos
'Flyaway Home'	SPol
'Foggy London Town'	CFwr
'Fol de Rol'	EWoo SRos
'Fooled Me'	EBee LRHS MBNS MSpe MWea SBrk SPad SPol SRos
'Forbidden Dreams'	EWoo
'Forever Red'	SRos
'Forgotten Dreams'	EBee MBNS MSpe MWea SBrk

	forrestii	CPLG
	'Forsyth Lemon Drop'	SDay
	'Forsyth Tangerine Ruffles'	GKir
	'Forsyth White Sentinel'	CFwr SBrk SRos
	'Forty Second Street'	CFir EBee LRHS MBNS MLLN NMoo SApp WCon WFar
	'Fragrant Bouquet'	SBrk SRos
	'Fragrant Pastel Cheers'	SDay SRos
	'Fragrant Treasure' **new**	ERCP
	'Frances Fay'	SPol SRos WAul
	'Francois Verhaert'	EWoo SBrk
	'Frandean'	MNFA
	'Frank Gladney'	MNFA SApp SBrk SRos
	'Frans Hals'	Widely available
	'Fred Ham'	SBrk SRos
	'French Doll'	SApp
	'Frilly Bliss'	CFwr
	'Frosted Encore'	SApp
	'Frosty White'	SDay
	'Frozen Jade'	SBrk SRos
	'Fuchsia Dream'	EMar
	'Fuchsia Fashion'	SApp
	fulva	CTri ELan NBir NBre SGar SPol SRms WBrk WHrl
N	- 'Flore Pleno' (d)	Widely available
N	- 'Green Kwanso' (d)	CBgR CPLG CSWP ECGP ECha EPla LBMP MMHG NVic SMad WAul WFar WPnP WTin
	- 'Kwanso' ambig. (d)	LRHS SBrk
	- var. ***kwanso*** B&SWJ 6328	WCru
	- var. ***littorea***	CMac EPla
	- var. ***rosea***	SMHy SPol WCot
§	- 'Variegated Kwanso' (d/v)	CBot CBow CRow CStu EPPr GCal GCra MAvo MRav MTho NBir SMad SUsu WBor WCot WFar WHer WHil WHoo WHrl
	'Fun Fling'	SPol
	'Funky Fuchsia'	SPol
	'Gadsden Goliath'	SPol
	'Gadsden Light'	SDay SPol
	'Gala Gown'	SApp
	'Garden Crawler' **new**	CBgR
	'Garden Portrait'	CMil EWoo SPol SRos
	'Gaucho'	MNFA
	'Gauguin'	EMar
	'Gay Music'	LRHS MBNS
	'Gay Octopus'	EMar SPol SRos
	'Gay Rapture'	SPer
	'Gemini'	SBrk SRos
	'Geneva Firetruck'	CFwr
	'Gentle Country Breeze'	SApp SBrk SPol SRos
	'Gentle Rose'	SBrk SDay
	'Gentle Shepherd'	Widely available
	'George Cunningham'	ECtt EGol EHrv ELan MRav NBir SMrs SPol SRos SUsu WFar
	'George David'	WHrl
	'George Jets On' **new**	SBrk
	'Georgetown Lovely'	SRos
	'Georgette Belden'	EBla ECGP ECtt EMar LRHS MBNS MBri MMHG MSpe MWea NHol SPol WTin
	'Georgia Cream' (d)	NLar
	'Georgia Peach' **new**	CWGN
	'German Ballerina'	SPol
	'Get All Excited'	SPol
	'Giant Moon'	CBgR CMHG EBee EBrs ECtt ELan EMar EPla LRHS MBNS NCGa NHol SPer SRms WFar WHal WWlt
	'Giddy Go Round'	EWoo SPol
	'Gingerbread Man'	SApp SBrk
	'Girl Scout'	SApp SRos
	'Glacier Bay'	CWat MBNS NCGa

'Glacier Gleam' **new**	MSpe
'Glazed Heather Plum'	SApp SBrk
'Gleber's Top Cream'	SApp
'Glomunda'	SApp
'Glory's Legacy'	SBrk SRos
'Glowing Heart'	SApp
'Going Bananas' **new**	WCot
'Gold Dust'	SRos
'Gold Imperial'	NBre
'Golden Bell'	NGdn NHol
'Golden Change'	CFwr
'Golden Chimes' 🏆H4	Widely available
'Golden Empress'	SApp
'Golden Ginkgo'	MBri MSpe SApp
'Golden Orchid'	see *H.* 'Doubloon'
'Golden Peace'	SBrk SRos
'Golden Prize'	EPla GQue MNFA NGdn NPri SApp SBrk SRos WCot WFar
'Golden Scroll'	SApp SBrk SRos
Golden Zebra = 'Malja'PBR (v)	CWGN ECtt ELan EPfP LBuc LRHS MBNS MGos MRav NLar NSti SDnm SPoG WCon WCot WSpi
'Goldeneye'	SApp
'Golliwog'	CBgR
'Good Looking'	EGol
'Good Morning America'	SRos
'Gothic Window' **new**	SDay
'Grace and Favour'	SDay SPol
'Graceful Eye'	SApp SBrk SRos
'Graceland'	EMar
'Grain de Lumière'	EMar
'Grand Masterpiece'	CMMP NGdn SPet WAul
'Grand Palais'	EMar SApp SBrk SRos
'Grandiose' **new**	SBrk
'Grandma Kissed Me'	SPol
'Grape Magic'	EGol SRos WCot WTin
'Grape Velvet'	CHar CPar CSpe EGol MCCP MNFA MSpe NBre NSti SApp SBch SBrk SRms SRos WAul WCAu WMnd WWEG
'Great Northern'	SApp
'Green Dolphin Street'	SBrk SDay SRos
'Green Drop'	WFar
'Green Eyed Giant'	MNFA
'Green Eyed Lady'	SDay SRos
'Green Flutter' 🏆H4	CFwr EBee EPfP GCal LPio LPla LRHS LSRN MBNS MNFA NBir NBre NGdn NSti SApp SPhx SPol SRos WCot WSpi WWEG
'Green Gold'	CMHG
'Green Morning Glow'	EMar
'Green Nautilus'	SRos
'Green Puff'	NBir SDay
'Green Spider'	CBgR SDay SRos
'Green Valley'	MNFA
'Green Warrior' **new**	EWoo
'Green Widow'	EWoo SDay
'Groovy Green'	SDay
'Grumbly'	ELan WPnP
'Guardian Angel'	WCFE WTin
'Gypsy Ballerina'	SApp
'Gypsy Cranberry'	SPol
'Gypsy Prince' **new**	MNFA
'Hail Mary'	WCon
'Happy Hopi'	SApp
'Happy Returns'	CBgR CHid CSBt CTri EBee EBla EBrs ECha EGol ELan EMar EPla EWoo IBal LAst LRHS LSRN MBNS MBri MNFA NBPC NEgg NGdn SApp SBrk SRGP SRms SRos WTin WWEG
'Harbor Blue'	SApp SDay
'Havana Banana'	SApp
'Hawaiian Punch'	EGol
'Hawaiian Purple'	EGol
'Hawk'	SApp SPol
'Hazel'	SRos
'Hazel Monette'	EGol
'Heady Wine' **new**	SDay
'Heather Green'	SApp
'Heavenly Treasure'	SApp SBrk SPol SRos
'Heidi Eidelweiss'	CPLG
'Heirloom Lace'	WFar
'Helen Boehm'	EMar
'Helix' **new**	SRos
'Helle Berlinerin' 🏆H4	EMar MNFA SApp SPol SRos
'Helter Skelter'	EMar SPol
'Hemlock'	GMac
'Her Majesty's Wizard'	EWoo MBNS MHer NBro SPol
'Hercules'	NBre
'Heron's Cove'	EWoo
'Hey There'	SBrk SRos
'High Energy'	SApp
'High Mogul'	EMar
'High Tor'	GBin GQui SPol SRos WTin
'Highland Belle'	SApp
'Highland Lord' (d)	EPfP MBNS MWea SApp
'Highland Summerbird'	SApp
'His Majesty's Wizard' **new**	SBrk
'Holiday Delight'	MBNS
'Holiday Mood'	ELan SApp
'Holly Dancer'	EWoo SPol
'Homeward Bound'	SDay
'Honey Jubilee'	SPol
'Honey Redhead'	SRos
'Honky Tonk Blues'	CFwr
'Honky Tonk Dream' **new**	EMar
'Hope Diamond'	SDay SRos WCAu
'Hornby Castle'	EBrs LRHS NHol
'Hot Cakes' **new**	SBrk
'Hot Chocolate'PBR	CFwr EBee SRGP
'Hot Ticket'	SApp SBrk SRos
'Hot Town'	ELan EMar
'Hot Wheels'	EMar SBrk SRos
'Hot Wire'	EMar SBrk SRos
'Houdini'	EGol MSpe WCAu WMnd
'House of Orange'	SApp SPol
'Howard Goodson'	MNFA
'Howdy'	CFwr
'Humdinger'	SBrk SRos WCot
'Hymn'	SDay WCon
'Hyperion'	CBgR CMac COlW CPrp CSev CTri EBee ECha ECtt EGol EPfP LAst LEdu MNFA MRav MSpe NGdn NHol SApp SMrs SPer SPoG SRos SUsu WCot WWEG
'Ice Carnival'	CKel ELon EPfP GMac LAst MBNS NBre NGdn SApp SPet WSpi
'Ice Castles'	CTri SApp SBrk WHrl
'Ice Cool'	SApp SRos
'Icecap'	WAul WFar WMoo WPnP
'Icy Lemon'	SBrk SRos
'Ida Duke Miles'	SBrk SDay SRos
'Ida Munson'	EGol
'Ida's Magic'	SApp SBrk WFar
'If'	EMar
'Imperator'	CBen LPBA NHol
'Imperial Lemon'	SApp
'In Depth' (d)	EPfP MBNS NBro NCGa NLar SWal WCot WHrl
'In Search of Angels'	CFwr
'In Strawberry Time'	WNHG
'Indian Fires'	CFwr
'Indian Giver'	SPol

	'Indian Paintbrush'	EWoo MBri NBir SBfd SPol WAul WCAu
	'Indian Sky'	SRos
	'Indigo Moon'	SApp SPol
	'Indy Envy'	CFwr
	'Inky Fingers'	SApp
	'Inner View'	ECtt MBNS MSpe NLar SApp WMnd
	'Inspired Word'	SBrk SRos
	'Invicta'	SRos
	'Invitation to Immortality'	EWoo
	'Iridescent Jewel'	SDay
	'Irish Elf'	ELon SApp SHar WTin
	'Iron Gate Glacier'	CSpr MBNS
	'Iron Gate Maiden'	WCom
	'Isle of Capri'	SRos
	'Isle of Dreams'	SPol
	'Isleworth'	EWoo
	'Itsy Bitsy Spider' **new**	CBgR EWoo
	'Ivelyn Brown'	SPol SRos
	'Jake Russell'	MBNS MNFA
	'Jamaican Jammin"	SPol
	'Jamaican me Crazy' **new**	SBrk
	'James Clark'	EWoo
	'James Marsh'	CBgR EPfP EWes MBNS MBri MNFA MNrw SApp SRos WAul WCAu WCot WMnd
	'Jan Kay'	SDay
	'Janet Gordon'	SBrk SPol SRos
	'Janice Brown'	CKel CWCL EMar EWoo LAst LSou MBNS MNFA MSpe MWea NLar NMoo SApp SBrk SDay SPol SRos WCAu
	'Jan's Twister'	EMar MNrw SApp SBrk SPol SRos
	'Jason Salter'	EWoo NCGa SApp SBrk SDay WAul
	'Jay Turman'	SApp SDay
	'Jazz Diva'	EMar
	'Jean'	SDay
	'Jean Swann'	MBNS SBrk
	'Jedi Dot Pierce'	CFwr SApp SBrk SRos
	'Jedi Irish Spring'	SApp
	'Jedi Rose Frost'	SApp
	'Jellyfish Jealousy' **new**	SRos
	'Jenny Wren'	EBee EBla EMar EPPr EPla ETod EWoo MBNS MSpe NBre NBro NHol SRGP WAul WWEG
	'Jersey Spider'	EMar SDay
	'Jerusalem'	SBrk SDay SRos
	'Jesse James'	SApp SPol
	'Jessica Lilian'	SBrk SRos
	'Jewel Case'	WNHG
	'Joan Senior'	Widely available
	'Jocelyn's Oddity'	SApp
	'Jockey Club' (d)	ECtt EMar MBNS
	'Joe Marinello'	SPol
	'John Allen'	CFwr
	'John Bierman'	SBrk SRos
	'John Robert Biggs'	SApp
	'Joie de Vivre'	EWoo
	'Jolly Red Giant' **new**	EWoo
	'Jolyene Nichole'	SApp SBrk SRos
	'Journey's End'	SDay
	'Jovial'	SApp SBrk SDay SRos
	'Judah'	SApp SDay SRos
	'Judge Roy Bean'	EWoo SPol SRos
	'Julie Newmar' **new**	IPot
	'Jungle Beauty'	SPol
	'Justin George'	SPol
	'Karen's Curls'	EWoo SBrk SPol SRos
	'Kasia'	WHrl
	'Kate Carpenter'	SBrk SDay SPol SRos
	'Kathleen Salter'	EWoo SDay SRos
	'Kathryn June Wood' **new**	EWoo SRos
	'Kathy Macartney' **new**	EWoo
	'Katie Elizabeth Miller'	SBrk SDay SRos
	'Kazuq'	SApp SBrk
	'Kecia'	EMar MNFA
	'Kelly's Girl'	SBrk SDay SPol SRos
	'Kempion'	EMar
	'Kent's Favorite Two'	SBrk SRos
	'Kevin Michael Coyne'	EWoo
	'Kindly Light'	EMar EWoo MNFA SPol SRos
	'King Haiglar'	EGol SApp SBrk SRos
	'Kiowa Sunset'	MSpe
	'Knights in White Satin' **new**	SRos
N	'Kwanso Flore Pleno'	see *H. fulva* 'Green Kwanso'
N	'Kwanso Flore Pleno Variegata'	see *H. fulva* 'Variegated Kwanso'
	'La Peche'	LRHS SDay
	'Lace Cookies'	EWoo
	'Lacy Marionette'	EMar EWoo SApp SPol SRos
	'Lady Cynthia'	CKel
	'Lady Fingers'	EMar MNFA SDay SPol SRos
	'Lady Hillary'	SApp
	'Lady Inara'	CFwr
	'Lady Inma'	SApp
	'Lady Liz'	EMar MNFA
	'Lady Mischief'	SApp
	'Lady Neva'	CBgR CPar SApp SBrk SRos
	'Ladykin'	SApp SBrk SPol SRos
	'Lake Norman Spider'	EWoo MNFA SApp
	'Lake Norman Sunset'	CFwr
	'Land of Cotton'	EMar
	'Lark Song'	EBrs EGol LRHS SRos WFar WHrl
	'Laughing Feather' **new**	EWoo
	'Laughton Tower'	SMHy
	'Lauren Leah'	SRos
	'Laurena' **new**	EWoo SPol
	'Lavender Arrowhead'	SApp
	'Lavender Bonanza'	CFwr
	'Lavender Deal'	EBee LRHS MNrw WNHG
	'Lavender Dusk'	CFwr
	'Lavender Flushing'	SApp
	'Lavender Handlebars' **new**	SBrk
	'Lavender Illusion'	CSev SApp
	'Lavender Light' **new**	EWoo
	'Lavender Memories'	SDay
	'Lavender Rainbow'	CFwr
	'Lavender Silver Cords'	SPol
	'Lavender Spider'	SApp
	'Leebea Orange Crush'	EMar
	'Lemon Bells' ♀H4	CWat EBee EBla ECGP ECha EMar EPfP EWoo GKev GMaP LRHS MBNS NBro NGdn SApp SDay SRos WCAu WSpi
	'Lemon Dessert'	SBrk SRos
	'Lemon Mint'	EGol SBrk SRos
	'Lemon Starfish'	SApp
	'Lemonora'	SDay
	'Lenox'	SBrk SDay SRos
	'Leonard Bernstein'	SApp SBrk SDay SPol SRos
	'Lesmona'	CFwr
	'Let It Rip' **new**	EWoo
	'Lexington Avenue' **new**	SPol
	'Licorice Candy'	CFwr SBrk SRos
	'Light the Way'	ECha GBin
	'Light Years Away'	ELon MBNS MNrw NBro SApp SMrm
	'Lil Ledie'	SApp
§	***lilioasphodelus*** ♀H4	Widely available
	- 'Rowden Golden Jubilee' (v)	CRow
	'Lillian Frye'	EGol
	'Lilly Dache' **new**	EWoo
	'Lilting Belle'	SBrk SPol SRos

'Lilting Lady'	SApp SDay SPol
'Lilting Lady Red'	SApp
'Lilting Lavender'	WCot
'Lime Frost'	EMar SBrk SPol SRos
'Lime Painted Lady' **new**	CBgR
'Limited Edition' **new**	EWoo
'Limoncello'	SApp
'Linda'	MNFA MRav NHol SRos
'Linda Agin'	EWoo
'Lines of Splendor'	SRos
'Lipstick Print'	SBrk SRos
'Little Angel'	SApp
'Little Audrey'	SApp
'Little Bee'	NBre
'Little Beige Magic'	EGol
'Little Big Man'	SDay WCon
'Little Bugger'	CMoH ELon NLar WWEG
'Little Bumble Bee'	CFir COIW EGol MBNS SApp WWEG
'Little Business'	MBNS SApp WAul
'Little Cadet'	MNFA
'Little Cameo'	EGol
'Little Carpet'	MBNS SPer SPet
'Little Cranberry Cove'	EGol
'Little Dandy'	EGol
'Little Deeke'	COIW SApp SBrk SDay SRos WHrl
'Little Fantastic'	EGol
'Little Fat Cat'	SApp
'Little Fat Dazzler'	SApp SBrk SPol SRos
'Little Fellow'	MBNS
'Little Fruit Cup'	SApp
'Little Grapette'	COIW EGol EPfP ERCP GCra GGar GQue LPla MBNS MSpe NLar NSti SApp SBrk SMrs SRos WAul WBrk WCAu WTin WWEG
'Little Greenie'	EMar SDay
'Little Gypsy Vagabond'	CWat EMar SBrk SDay SRos
'Little Heavenly Angel'	COIW SPol
'Little Lavender Princess'	EGol
'Little Maggie'	SApp SDay SPol
'Little Missy'	CBgR COIW CWat EMar LAst MBNS MSCN NBPC NBre SPet WGob WHoo
'Little Monica'	SApp
'Little Orange Slices'	CFwr
'Little Pumpkin Face'	EGol
'Little Rainbow'	EGol WWEG
'Little Red Hen'	CSam EBla ECGP EMar LRHS MBNS MSpe NBro NEgg NGdn SUsu WFar
'Little Show Stopper'	EWoo MBNS NBro NLar NMRc NMoo
'Little Sweet Sue'	MNFA
'Little Sweet Talk'	SBrk SRos
'Little Toddler'	SApp
'Little Violet Lace'	SDay
'Little Wart'	EGol SDay WHrl
'Little Wine Cup'	Widely available
'Little Wine Spider'	SApp
'Little Women'	MBNS SDay
'Little Zinger'	GMac SDay
'Littlest Angel'	SDay
'Littlest Clown'	SDay
'Lobo Lucy'	SRos
'Lochinvar'	MRav SRos
'Lois Burns' **new**	EWoo SBrk
'Lola Branham' **new**	SRos
'Lonesome Dove'	SBrk SPol
'Long John Silver'	SRos
'Long Stocking'	EWoo SPol SRos WCot
'Longfield's Beauty'	MBNS MSpe NCGa SBrk
'Longfield's Glory'	MBNS NBre NMoo WGob
'Longfield's Mandy'	MSpe
'Longfield's Maxim' (d)	MBNS
'Longfield's Pearl'	SBrk
'Longfield's Pride'	ECho MBNS SRms WBor
'Longfield's Purple Eye'	NCGa NLar NMoo
'Longfield's Tropica'	MBNS
'Longfield's Twins'	EKen MBNS NBPC NMoo WCot
longituba B&SWJ 4576	WCru
'Look at Me'	ELan
'Lord Camden' **new**	MNFA
'Lori Goldston'	EWoo MBNS
'Love Glow'	CFir
'Loving Memories'	SApp
'Lowenstine'	SApp
'Lucille Lennington'	WNHG
'Lucretius'	MNFA
'Luke Senior Junior'	SApp
'Lullaby Baby'	CWat EGol ELan GMac MBNS NLar SApp SDay SPol SRos
'Luscious Honeydew'	WNHG
'Lusty Lealand'	EGol EMar MBNS MNFA SBrk SRos
'Luverne'	SBrk SRos
'Luxury Lace'	CPrp CSpe CWat EBla ECho ECtt EGol ELan EMar EPfP EPla LRHS MSpe NBir NGdn NPri SPer SPol SRos WAul WCAu WFar WHrl WMoo WPnP WTin
'Lydia Bechtold'	SBrk SRos
'Lyn Wright'	EWoo
'Lynn Hall'	ECtt EGol EMil MBNS NLar WSpi
'Lyric Opera'	SDay
'Mabel Fuller'	MRav SPer SRos WHrl
'Macbeth'	EPfP MBNS SBrk SPad
'Mad Max'	EWoo SPol
'Mae Graham'	SApp
'Maestro Puccini' **new**	SDay
'Maggie Fynboe'	SPol SRos
'Magic Carpet Ride'	EMar SBrk SPol
'Magic Lace'	EWoo SBrk SRos
'Magnificent Eyes'	EMar
'Magnificent Rainbow'	CBcs SApp SRos
'Mahogany Magic'	SBrk SRos
'Make Believe Magic'	CFwr
'Malachite Prism' **new**	CWGN
'Malaysian Masquerade'	SApp
'Malaysian Monarch'	SBrk SRos WMnd WNHG
'Malaysian Spice'	WNHG
'Maleny Mite'	EWoo
'Maleny Piecrust'	EWoo
'Maleny Tapestry'	MSpe
'Maleny Think Big'	EWoo
'Mallard'	CBgR CWat ECGP ECtt EGol EHrv EMar EPla LLWP LRHS MBNS MNFA MRav MSpe SApp SBrk SPer SRos SWat WCot WCra
'Man on Fire'	CBcs MBNS
'Manchurian Apricot'	SBrk SRos
'Mandalay Bay Music'	EWoo
'Marble Faun'	SApp SBrk SDay SRos
'Margaret Perry'	CFee CPrp GBin MNrw WAul
'Margo Reed Indeed' **new**	SRos
'Marion Caldwell'	SPol
'Marion Vaughn' ♀H4	CSev EBee ECtt EHrv ELan EPfP EWoo GMaP LBMP LHop LRHS MLLN MNFA NSti SBch SBrk SDix SPer SPhx SRGP SRos SSpi WCot WFar WPtf
'Mariska'	SApp SBrk SDay SRos WNHG
'Mark My Word'	SApp
'Marked by Lydia'	SPol SRos
'Marse Connell'	MSpe SRos
'Martha Adams'	SDay
'Martie Everest' **new**	EWoo

'Martina Verhaert'	CWGN
'Mary Ethel Anderson'	EWoo MSpe
'Mary Todd'	EGol MBNS SApp WCAu WMnd
'Mary's Gold'	SBrk SPol SRos
'Mask Ball'	SBrk SRos
'Matt'	CFwr SBrk SRos
'Mauna Loa'	CSBt CWGN EBee EMar GQue MBNS MNFA MNrw MWea NBre SApp SBrk WAul WCAu WCot
'May Colvin'	LRHS
'May May'	SApp SPol
'Mayan Poppy'	EWoo
'Meadow Mist'	CBgR EGol
'Meadow Sprite'	SBrk SRos WCot
'Meadow Sweet'	CFwr
'Medicine Feather'	EWoo SRos
'Medieval Guild'	SApp
'Mega Stella'	SApp
'Melody Lane'	EGol
'Ménage Enchanté'	EMar
'Meno'	EGol
'Mephistopheles'	EWoo
'Merlot Rouge'	WAul
'Metallica'	EMar
'Metaphor'	EMar SApp SBrk SRos
'Michele Coe'	CMMP EBee EBla ECtt EGol EHrv EMar EQua LPla LRHS MBNS MNFA MSpe NBre NBro NCGa NEgg NGdn SApp SRGP SRos WHrl WMoo
middendorffii	CAvo CMac EBee GMaP LRHS MCoo NSti SMrm WFar WHrl WSpi
- 'Major'	CFee
'Midnight Dynamite'	MBNS SBrk
'Midnight Love'	EWoo
'Midnight Magic'	EMar EWoo SRos
'Midnight Mantis'	SPol
'Midnight Raider'	EWoo
'Mighty Mogul' **new**	MNFA
'Mikado'	CBgR CMac
'Milady Greensleeves'	EWoo SBrk SPol SRos
'Milanese Mango'	EWoo MSpe
'Mildred Mitchell'	CFwr CWat EBee MBNS NLar NMRc SApp SBrk
'Millie Schlumpf'	EMar SApp SBrk SDay SPol SRos
'Mimosa Umbrella'	SPol
'Ming Porcelain'	CMil EMar SApp SBrk SDay SPol SRos
'Mini Pearl'	CMMP COIW EGol ELon MBNS MBri SApp SBrk SPer SRos WPer
'Mini Stella'	ECtt GGar IBal MBNS NBPC NBre SBrk SPet WAul WFar
miniature hybrids	SRms
'Minnie Wildfire'	SPol
minor	EBrs EGol GBin GKev LRHS NGdn SRms
- B&SWJ 8841	WCru
'Miracle Maid'	WNHG
'Miss Amelia'	SRos
'Miss Jessie'	EWoo MNFA SDay SPol SRos
'Missenden' ♀H4	CBgR MNFA MNrw SApp SRos
'Mission Moonlight'	EGol
'Missouri Beauty'	MBNS SApp
'Missouri Memories'	SBrk SRos
'Mokan Cindy'	EMar
'Moment of Truth'	NBre
'Monica Marie'	SBrk SRos
'Monita Gold Stripe'	CMoH
'Mont Royal Demitasse'	SPol
'Moon Witch'	SBrk SDay SPol SRos
'Moonbeam'	SApp
'Moonlight Masquerade'	CWat EBee ECtt EPfP MMuc NLar SApp SEND SRms
'Moonlight Mist'	SApp SBrk SPol SRos
'Moonlit Caress'	EBee EMar IPot MBNS NBro SApp SBrk SRos WFar
'Moonlit Crystal'	SApp SPol
'Moonlit Masquerade'	CPar CWGN EMar EWoo GBin GMac MBNS MBri MCCP MLLN MNrw MSCN MSpe NCGa SBch SBrk SDnm SEND SPer SPet SPol SRos WAul WCAu WHrl
'Moonlit Pirouette'	SApp
'Moonlit Summerbird' **new**	SPol
'Moonstruck Madness'	CFwr
'Moontraveller'	WCot
'Mormon Spider'	SApp SPol SRos
'Morning Dawn'	WWEG
'Morning Sun'	EMar MBNS NBre NLar WCot
'Morocco'	SPol
'Morocco Red'	CMdw CTri ELan EPla NBre WWEG
'Morrie Otte'	SPol
'Moses' Fire'	ECtt EPfP MAsh MBNS NLar
'Mount Echo Sunrise' **new**	EWoo
'Mount Joy'	SPer
'Mountain Laurel'	EBee ECGP ECtt EMar LRHS LSRN MBNS MCot MRav MSpe NEgg SApp SBrk SPol WFar
'Mountain Top Experience' **new**	SDay
'Mountain Violet'	SApp
'Mrs David Hall'	CMdw
'Mrs Hugh Johnson'	CSev EBee EWTr GCra LAst NHol WHrl
'Muffet's Little Friend'	SPol
'Mulberry Truffle' (d)	EMar
multiflora	MNFA NHol
'Murphy's Law' **new**	SRos
'My Belle'	SBrk SRos
'My Darling Clementine'	SBrk SDay SRos
'My Kind'	CFwr
'My Melinda'	SDay
'My Sweet Rose'	SBrk SRos
'Mynelle's Starfish'	CPar EMar SBrk SPol SRos
'Mysterious Veil'	EGol
'Nairobi Dawn'	SBrk SRos
nana	CFir EPot
'Nanuq'	SApp SBrk SDay SRos
'Naomi Ruth'	EGol MBNS SApp WTin
'Nashville'	ELan WHrl
'Nashville Lights'	CBgR SPol
'Nathan Sommers' **new**	EWoo
'Natural Veil'	SPol
'Navajo Princess'	CBcs CWat EPfP MBNS MNrw SBrk
'Navajo Rodeo' **new**	EWoo
'Neal Berrey'	SApp SBrk SDay SRos
'Nefertiti'	CBgR ELon MBNS NBir NCGa SAga SPer WAul WCAu WTin
'Neon Rose'	EBla MWat SBrk SRos
'Netsuke'	SApp SMrm
'New Direction'	EWoo
'New Swirls'	SApp
'New York Follies' **new**	SBrk
'Newberry Borrowed Time'	CFwr
'Neyron Rose' ♀H4	CHar EGol EMar EPfP EPla GQue LAst LHop LRHS MBNS MWea NBre NEgg NGdn SRos WCAu WMoo
'Nick's Faith'	WHrl
'Night Beacon'	CBgR CFwr ECho ECtt EGol ELon EWes EWoo GMac IBal MBNS MBri MNFA MNrw MSpe NLar NMoo SApp SBrk SDay SPol SRos SWal WCAu WGob WHrl
'Night Embers'	EWoo

'Night Raider'	EMar SApp SBrk SRos
'Night Wings'	EWoo SApp
'Nigrette'	CBen LPBA NHol
'Nile Crane'	CBgR CFwr LRHS MBNS MNrw SApp SBrk SDay SHar SPer WAul
'Nile Plum'	SApp
'Nina Winegar'	SRos
'Nivia Guest'	SApp SDay
'Nob Hill'	CMdw EGol EPla GBin MNFA SApp SRos WHrl
'Nona's Garnet Spider'	SApp SPol SRos
'Nordic Night'	EMar SPol
'North Star'	SApp
'Northbrook Star' **new**	MNFA
'Norton Beauté'	WCot
'Norton Eyed Seedling'	WNHG
'Norton Orange'	MNFA WCon WFar
'Nosferatu'	EMar
'Nova' ♀H4	CPrp SApp SRos
'Nuit Parisienne' **new**	EMar
'Nuka'	EMar
'Numinous Moments'	SDay
'Nutmeg Elf'	EWoo SBrk
'Obsidian'	MNrw
'Ocean Rain'	EMar SApp SBrk SRos
'Octopus Hugs'	SBrk SRos
'Old Tangiers'	EMar SBrk SRos
'Old-fashioned Maiden'	EMar SRos
'Olive Bailey Langdon'	EGol MNFA SApp SBrk SPol SRos WCot
'Oliver Billingslea'	EWoo
'Olive's Odd One'	EMar
'Olympic Showcase'	SBrk SRos
'Omomuki'	SApp SBrk SRos
'On and On'	LHop MBNS
'On Silken Thread'	SPol SRos
'On the Web'	SApp
'Oom Pah Pah'	ECha
'Open Hearth'	EMar SBrk SDay SPol SRos
'Orange Dream'	SDay
'Orange Exotica' **new**	CBgR
'Orange Velvet'	SApp SBrk SRos
'Orangeman' hort.	EBla EPla MBNS NGdn NHol
'Orchard Sprite'	SApp
'Orchid Beauty'	ECha MLHP WMoo
'Orchid Candy'	MBNS NBir SBrk SPol WAul
'Orchid Corsage'	SApp
'Orchid Moonrise' **new**	EWoo
'Oriental Ruby'	EGol MNFA SRos
'Orion Sky'	CFwr
'Ostrich Plume'	SRos
'Ottis Leonard'	CFwr
'Ouachita Beauty'	SPol
'Our Kirsten' **new**	SDay
'Out of Darkness'	EWoo
'Outrageous'	CFwr SApp SBrk SRos WNHG
'Over the Top'	MBNS
'Paige Parker'	EGol
'Paige's Pinata'	CFwr EBee MBNS NBPC SApp SBrk SRos
'Paint Your Wagon'	SApp
'Painted Lady'	MNFA SApp
'Painted Trillium'	CMil
'Painter Poet'	EMar
'Palace Garden Beauty'	SApp
'Palace Guard'	MNFA
'Palantir'	SApp
'Pamela Williams'	EMar
'Panama Hattie'	EMar SBrk
'Pandora's Box'	Widely available
'Pantaloons'	SApp
'Pantherette'	SApp SPol

'Paper Butterfly'	EMar SBrk SPol SRos
'Paradise Prince'	EGol
'Pardon Me'	CBro CMHG CMMP ECho EGol ELan ELon EMar GMaP LRHS MBNS MNFA NBPC NCGa NGdn NHol SApp SBrk SPol SRGP SRos SWal WAul WBor WCAu
'Pardon Me Boy'	SPol
'Parfait'	CBgR EMar EWoo SPol
'Party Queen'	SDay
'Pas de Deux'	SApp
'Pastel Ballerina'	SBrk SDay SRos
'Pastel Classic'	SApp SBrk SRos
'Pastilline'	SPol
'Pat Mercer'	SApp SDay
'Patchwork Puzzle'	EWoo SBrk SPol SRos
'Patricia'	EPfP MBNS SPoG
'Patricia Fay'	MNFA SApp SRos
'Patricia Gentzel Wright'	EWoo
'Patsy Bickers'	EWoo SApp
'Patty Ann Warren' **new**	SRos
'Paul Weber'	SApp
'Pawn of Prophecy' **new**	MAvo SDay
'Peach Float' **new**	EWoo
'Peach Jubilee'	SPol
'Peach Petticoats'	SBrk SRos
'Peach Pudding' **new**	MAsh
'Peacock Curls' **new**	EWoo
'Peacock Maiden'	EMar EWoo SApp SBrk SPol SRos
'Pear Ornament'	SBrk SRos
'Pearl Lewis'	EMar SBrk SDay SRos
'Peggy Jeffcoat'	CFwr SBrk
'Penelope Vestey'	EBla EMar MBNS MNFA NCGa SApp SPol SRGP SRos
'Penny's Worth'	EBrs EGol MBNS WAul WCot WFar WHoo
'Perfect Pleasure'	MBNS
'Persian Ruby'	SPol
'Persian Shrine'	SPol
'Petite Ballerina'	SDay
'Piano Man'	EMar MBNS MWea NLar NMoo SBrk WAul WGob WNHG
'Piccadilly Princess'	SBrk SDay SRos WAul
'Pink Ambrosia'	EWoo
'Pink Attraction'	SApp
'Pink Ballerina'	EGol
'Pink Charm'	CBen CMac COlW EBee ECha ECtt EMar EPPr GMaP LPBA LRHS MBNS NBro NGdn NHol SPol SRos WCAu
'Pink Circle' **new**	SDay
'Pink Cotton Candy'	EWoo SBrk SDay SPol SRos
'Pink Crinkles' **new**	SBrk
'Pink Damask' ♀H4	Widely available
'Pink Dream'	EMar EQua MBNS NBir NBre NHol SPol WCAu
'Pink Grace'	SPol
'Pink Heaven'	EGol
'Pink Lady'	MNrw MRav SRms WCon
'Pink Lavender Appeal'	EGol WCAu
'Pink Monday'	WNHG
'Pink Picotee Deluxe' **new**	SBrk
'Pink Picotee Elite' **new**	SBrk
'Pink Prelude'	EMar GBee LRHS MBNS MWat NBro SMrm
'Pink Puff'	MBNS NBir NBre NLar WGob
'Pink Ruffled Love'	CFwr
'Pink Salute'	SRos
'Pink Spider'	SDay
'Pink Sundae'	ECha WHrl
'Pink Super Spider'	EWoo MNFA SBrk SRos
'Pink Tranquillity' **new**	SRos
'Pink Windmill'	EWoo SDay SPol SRos

'Pinocchio'	NMoo
'Pirate Treasure'	MBNS
'Pirate's Patch'	EMar SBrk SDay SPol SRos WCot
'Pixie Parasol'	WMnd WNHG WSpi
'Pixie Pipestone'	SApp
'Pixie Pleasure'	CFwr
'Pizza'	SDay
'Platinum and Gold'	CFwr
'Plum Beauty'	NLar
'Pocket Size'	SApp
'Poetic Dance' **new**	EWoo
'Pojo'	CFwr SDay
'Polish Cocktail' **new**	EMar
'Pompeian Purple'	EGol
'Pony'	CWat EGol SBrk SPol SRos
'Ponytail Pink'	EGol
'Pookie Bear'	SApp
'Porcelain Pleasure'	SDay
'Prague Spring'	EMar MNFA SPol SRos WCAu
'Prairie Belle'	CBcs CSWP MBNS NBre NLar SApp SPol WCAu WFar
'Prairie Blossoms'	CFwr
'Prairie Blue Eyes'	ECha ECho ECtt EGol GBin MBNS NMoo NPri SApp SBfd SPlb SPol SRos WAul WCAu WCot WHrl WMnd WWEG
'Prairie Charmer'	MMuc SEND WHrl
'Prairie Moonlight'	SRos
'Prairie Sunset'	WCAu
'Prelude to Love'	EMar
'Pretty Miss'	ECtt EMar LRHS MBri
'Pretty Peggy'	MNFA
'Preview Party'	WNHG
'Primal Scream'	SApp SBrk WCot
'Primrose Mascotte'	NBir
'Prince of Purple'	EMar SRos
'Prince Redbird'	SBrk SRos
'Princess Blue Eyes'	SPol
'Princess Ellen'	SApp
'Princess Lilli'	MBNS
'Princeton Eye Glow'	SDay
'Princeton Point Lace'	SApp
'Princeton Silky'	SRos
'Priscilla's Rainbow'	EMar
'Prissy Frills'	SPol
'Prize Picotee Deluxe'	SPol SRos
'Prize Picotee Elite'	EMar SPol SRos WTin
'Protocol'	SDay SPol WCon
'Ptarmigan'	SDay
'Pterodactyl Eye'	SRos
§ 'Puddin'	CWat NHol SDay WAul
'Pudgie'	SApp
'Pug Yarborough'	SPol
'Pumpkin Kid'	SApp SPol SRos
'Puppet Lady'	SApp
'Puppet Show'	SDay
'Pure and Simple'	CFwr SDay SPol SRos
'Pure Country'	CFwr
'Purple Bicolor'	WHrl
'Purple Corsage'	SApp
'Purple Grasshopper' **new**	EWoo
'Purple Oddity'	EWoo SPol
'Purple Pinwheel'	EWoo SPol
'Purple Rain'	CWat LRHS MBNS MWea SApp SPol SRos SWvt
'Purple Rain Dance'	SPol
'Purple Waters'	EMar EPfP EWll MBNS NBre NPri SPol WPnP
'Pursuit of Excellence'	EMar SBrk SRos
'Pyewacket'	SApp
'Pygmy Plum'	SBrk SDay SRos
'Queen Lily'	WNHG
'Queen of May'	MNrw SApp WCot
'Queens Delight' **new**	SBrk
'Queens Fancy'	SApp
'Queen's Gift'	SApp
'Queensland'	SApp
'Quick Results'	SApp SBrk SRos
'Quilt Patch'	SRos
'Quinn Buck'	EMar
'Ra Hansen'	SApp SBrk SDay SRos
'Radiant'	CBcs
'Radiant Greetings'	MNFA
'Radiant Moonbeam'	SRos
'Raging Tiger'	EMar
'Rags to Riches'	CFwr
'Rainbow Candy'	CWGN LLHF MBNS NMoo SBrk SPad
'Rainbow Drive'	CFwr
'Rainbow Spangles' **new**	SRos
'Raindrop'	EGol
'Rajah'	CBgR CMac EMar MBNS MSpe NBro SPer WHrl
'Randall Moore'	SPol
'Raspberry Candy'	ECho EMar GCra MBNS MNrw NBro NCGa NHol SApp SBrk SRms SRos WCAu WGob WHrl
'Raspberry Pixie'	EGol SPol
'Rave On'	SApp SBrk
'Raven Woodsong' **new**	EWoo
'Real Wind'	CFwr EMar SApp SBrk SPol SRos
'Red Admiral'	EBrs LRHS
'Red Joy'	SApp
'Red Precious' ♀H4	EGol EMar MNFA MNrw SApp SMHy SRos WCot
'Red Rain'	EMar EWoo
'Red Ribbons'	EWoo SDay SPol SRos
'Red Ruby'	ERCP
'Red Rum'	EWll NBro SBfd SMrm WCon WMoo WPnP
'Red Suspenders'	EMar MBNS
'Red Twister'	SBrk
'Red Volunteer'	EMar SBrk SPol SRos
'Reflections'	WCon
'Regal Finale'	SDay
'Regal Vision'	SApp
'Regency Dandy'	SApp SDay SPol
'Regency Masquerade' **new**	SDay
'Renee'	MNrw
'Respighi'	SApp SBrk SRos
'Return Trip'	SPol
'Revolute'	SDay
'Rhapsody in Time'	EMar
'Rhode Island Red'	CFwr
'Ribbonette'	MBNS MSpe NMoo
'Rigamarole' **new**	SPol
'Right on Red'	CFwr
'Ringlets'	LRHS MNFA
'Riptide'	SApp
'Robert Coe'	SRos
'Rocket City'	ELan SRos
'Rococo' **new**	SBrk SDay
'Rodeo Sweetheart'	CFwr
'Roger Grounds'	SApp SPol SRos
* 'Romantic Rose'	EBee EMar MBNS NLar
'Ron Rousseau'	SApp
'Root Beer'	SRos WTin
'Rose'	SDay
'Rose Corsage'	EWoo
'Rose Emily'	SApp SBrk SDay SPol SRos
'Rose Fever'	EWoo
'Rose Roland'	NBre
'Roseate Spoonbill' **new**	EWoo
'Rosella Sheridan'	SBrk SRos

'Roses in Snow'	MBNS SBrk
'Rosewood Dawn' **new**	SRos
'Rosewood Flame'	SRos
'Rosewood Rainbow End'	SRos
'Rosewood Snowflakes'	SRos
'Roswitha'	CWat SApp SPol
'Rosy Lights' **new**	EWoo
'Rosy Returns'	MBNS MWea NLar NMoo SBrk SHar
'Round Midnight'	SPol
'Royal Braid'	EPfP MBNS MNrw MSpe NCGa NLar SApp SBrk SPer WAul WCot
'Royal Celebration' **new**	WCot
'Royal Charm'	SRos
'Royal Corduroy'	SBrk SRos
'Royal Crown'	CSev
'Royal Hunter'	CFwr
'Royal Occasion'	SRos
'Royal Palace Prince'	EMar GAbr
'Royal Parade' **new**	SDay
'Royal Prestige'	SApp
'Royal Robe'	CTri
'Royal Saracen'	SDay
'Royal Thornbird'	CBgR
'Royalty'	GCra
'Ruby Sentinel'	SDay
'Ruby Spider'	EWoo SBrk SDay SPol SRos
'Rue Madelaine' **new**	SPol
'Ruffled Apricot'	CKel LBMP LRHS MBNS MNFA SBrk SDay SRos WNHG
'Ruffled Carousel'	WNHG
'Rumble Seat Romance'	WNHG
'Russian Easter'	SBrk SRos
'Russian Rhapsody'	CKel SApp SBrk SPol SRos
'Sabie'	SApp
'Sabine Baur'	CWat EBee EWoo IBal IPot MBNS MNrw MSpe MWea NLar SApp SBrk SRos WAul WFar
'Sabra Salina'	SBrk SRos
'Sachsen Little Gold'	CFwr
'Sachsen Rustic'	CFwr
'Sachsen White Gigant'	CFwr
'Saffron Glow'	SDay
* 'Sagamore'	SApp
'Saintly'	EWoo
'Salmon Sheen'	SDay SPer SRos
'Sammy Russell'	Widely available
'Samuel Bell'	EWoo
'Sandra Walker'	EGol
'Sangre de Cristo'	CFwr
'Santiago'	SPol
'Satin Clouds'	EGol
'Satin Glass'	EBrs MNFA
'Satin Glow'	ECha MLHP
'Scarlet Flame'	ECha WMoo
'Scarlet Oak'	MBri SBrk SRos WAul
'Scarlet Orbit'	EMar EWoo SApp SBrk SHar SPol SRos
'Scarlet Prince'	WNHG
'Scarlet Ribbons'	SPol
'Scarlock'	SDay
'Scatterbrain'	CKel SPol
'Schnickel Fritz'	NCGa
'School Girl'	EBrs LRHS
'Scorpio'	CBgR EMar SPol
'Scotland'	IBal SApp
'Screaming Demon'	SPol
'Searcy Marsh'	EGol
'Sebastian'	MNFA SApp SBrk SRos
'Secret Splendor'	SPol
'Segramoor'	SApp
'Selma Longlegs'	SRos
'Seminole Blood'	SBrk
'Seminole Wind'	EWoo SBrk SPol
'Serena Dark Horse'	SRos
'Serena Sunburst'	CFwr SBrk SPol SRos
'Serene Madonna'	CFir GBin MWea SBfd
'Serenity Morgan'	EPfP MBNS
'Shadowed Pink'	WNHG
'Shady Lady'	SDay
'Shaman'	EMar SApp SBrk SPol SRos
'Shelly Victoria' **new**	SDay
'Sherry Lane Carr'	SPol SRos
'Shimek September Morning'	SPol
'Shimmering Elegance'	CFwr SRos
* 'Shocker'	EWoo
'Shogun'	MBNS
'Shotgun'	SPol SRos
'Show Amber'	SApp SRos
'Significant Other'	SApp
'Silent Sentry'	EWoo SApp
'Silken Fairy'	EGol SDay
'Silken Touch'	SApp SBrk SPol SRos
'Siloam Amazing Grace'	SApp SBrk SDay SRos
'Siloam Baby Talk'	EGol ELon EMar GMac NBir SApp SRos WAul WHoo WMoo WPnP WTin
'Siloam Bertie Ferris'	MBNS
'Siloam Bo Peep'	EGol SApp SRos WAul
'Siloam Brian Hanke'	SRos
'Siloam Button Box'	EGol MBNS WAul WHrl
'Siloam Bye Lo'	EGol EWoo SBrk SRos
'Siloam Cinderella'	EGol SBrk SRos
'Siloam David Kirchhoff'	EMar MBNS MSpe SDay SRos
'Siloam Doodlebug'	CBgR CWat EGol SBrk SRos
'Siloam Double Classic' (d)	EGol EMar SBrk SPol SRos
'Siloam Dream Baby'	MBNS NCGa
'Siloam Edith Sholar'	EGol
'Siloam Ethel Smith'	EGol SApp SBrk SPol SRos
'Siloam Fairy Tale'	CWat EGol
'Siloam French Doll'	MBNS NLar SApp
'Siloam French Marble'	SBrk SDay SRos
'Siloam Frosted Mint'	SApp SBrk
'Siloam Gold Coin'	SApp SDay
'Siloam Grace Stamile'	CFir EMar MBNS SApp SRos WGob
'Siloam Harold Flickinger'	SBrk SRos
'Siloam Helpmate'	WNHG
'Siloam Jim Cooper'	MSpe SBrk SRos
'Siloam Joan Senior'	EGol MBNS
'Siloam John Yonski'	SDay
'Siloam June Bug'	CBgR EGol ELan SApp WCAu WCot
'Siloam Justine Lee'	MBNS
'Siloam Kewpie Doll'	EGol
'Siloam Little Angel'	EGol SApp SPol
'Siloam Little Girl'	CWat ECtt EGol SBrk SDay SRos
'Siloam Mama'	SApp SBrk SRos
'Siloam Merle Kent'	EMar EWoo SApp SBrk SPol SRos
'Siloam New Toy'	EGol
'Siloam Nugget'	SApp
'Siloam Orchid Jewel'	EGol
'Siloam Paul Watts'	SApp SBrk SPol SRos
'Siloam Peewee'	EGol
'Siloam Penny'	SApp
'Siloam Pink Glow'	EGol SWat WAul
'Siloam Pink Petite'	EGol
'Siloam Plum Tree'	EGol SApp
'Siloam Pocket Size'	EGol SApp
'Siloam Powder Pink'	SApp
'Siloam Prissy'	EGol SApp
'Siloam Purple Plum'	EGol
'Siloam Queen's Toy'	SPol
'Siloam Ra Hansen'	SApp
'Siloam Red Ruby'	EGol
'Siloam Red Toy'	EGol

'Siloam Red Velvet'	EGol
'Siloam Ribbon Candy'	EGol SApp SDay WNHG
'Siloam Rose Dawn'	SApp SBrk SPol SRos
'Siloam Royal Prince'	EGol EPfP NHol SApp
'Siloam Shocker'	EGol
'Siloam Show Girl'	CWGN EGol EMar EWoo MBNS MNFA NCGa SApp
'Siloam Spizz' **new**	SBrk
'Siloam Sugar Time'	EGol
'Siloam Sunburst'	EMar
'Siloam Tee Tiny'	EGol
'Siloam Tinker Toy'	EGol
'Siloam Tiny Mite'	EGol SDay WHrl
'Siloam Toddler'	EGol
'Siloam Tom Thumb'	EGol EMar MBNS WGob
'Siloam Ury Winniford'	CMac CWan ECho EGol EMar EMil MBNS MCCP MNFA NBre NLar NMoo SApp SBrk WAul WHoo WHrl WPnP WTin
'Siloam Virginia Henson'	EGol NCGa SApp SBrk SRos WWEG
'Silver Ice'	SApp SBrk SPol SRos
'Silver King' **new**	GBin
'Silver Lance'	SPol SRos
'Silver Quasar'	SBrk SRos
'Silver Trumpet'	EGol WWEG
'Silver Veil'	WFar
'Sinbad Sailor'	EMar NLar
'Singing in the Sunshine' **new**	EWoo
'Sir Blackstem'	ELon EMar GCal SApp SBrk SRos
'Sir Modred'	SPol SRos
'Sirius'	NHol
'Sirocco'	WTin
'Sixth Sense'	ELon EMar MBNS SBrk SPad WHrl
'Skinwalker' **new**	EWoo
'Slapstick'	SDay
'Slender Lady'	SBrk SRos
'Smith Brothers'	SPol
'Smoky Mountain Autumn'	EMar EWoo SApp SBrk SPol SRos
'Smoky Mountain Bell'	SApp
'Smuggler's Gold'	ECtt EMar SApp
'Snappy Rhythm'	MNFA
'Snowed In'	EWoo SBrk SRos
'Snowy Apparition'	EBla ECtt EMar EWTr GKir LHop LRHS MBNS MNFA MSpe MWea MWhi NHol SApp SMrm SPol
'Snowy Eyes'	CHid EGol EMar MBNS NCGa NHol SApp SWat WAul WHrl
'So Excited'	SBrk SDay
'So Lovely'	SApp
'So Many Stars'	CFwr
'Soft Summer Night' **new**	SRos
'Solano Bull's Eye'	MLHP
'Solid Scarlet'	SRos
'Someone Special'	SBrk SPol SRos
'Someplace Special' **new**	SBrk
'Song In My Heart'	EWoo
'Song Sparrow'	GMac SApp WPer
'Sounds of Silence'	SRos
'South Seas'	LRHS
'Southern Charmer' **new**	SBrk
'Southern Prize' **new**	SDay
'Sovereign Queen'	EGol WNHG
'Spacecoast Scrambled'	CBcs CWGN EPfP MBNS NLar SBrk
'Spacecoast Starburst'	CBcs EMar MAvo MBNS NBro SApp SBrk WCAu WCon WCot WFar
'Spanish Glow'	SBrk SRos
'Spanish Sketch'	SRos
'Sparkling Dawn'	SBrk
'Speak of Angels'	SApp SBrk
'Spider Breeder'	SApp
'Spider Man'	MNFA SApp SBrk SDay SPol SRos WCAu
'Spider Miracle'	MNFA SBrk SDay SPol
'Spider Red'	CWGN MAsh
'Spider Spirits'	EMar
'Spilled Milk'	SPol
'Spindazzle'	CBgR SPol SRos
'Spinne in Lachs'	SBrk SRos
'Spiral Charmer'	SApp
'Splendid Touch' **new**	SRos
'Spode'	SApp SDay
'Spooner'	CBgR
'Spray of Pearls'	CFwr
'Spring Ballerina'	SApp
'Spring Willow Song'	SDay
'Squash Dolly'	EWoo
'Stafford'	Widely available
'Staghorn Sumac'	EBla EMar LEdu LRHS MBNS MSpe NHol WCAu WCon
'Star of Fantasy'	EMar
'Star Twister' **new**	EWoo
'Starling'	CFir CPar EGol MNFA SApp WAul WSpi WWEG
'Starman's Quest'	SPol SRos
'Stars and Stripes'	MNFA
'Starstruck'	WNHG
'Startle'	CFir CWGN ELon EPfP MBNS MNrw SApp SBrk WCot
'Startling Creation'	CFwr
'Statuesque'	WCon WFar
'Stella de Oro'	Widely available
'Stinnette'	WCot
'Stoke Poges' ♀H4	CAvo CBgR EBee EBla EMar EPfP EPla GBin LAst LBMP LHop LRHS LSRN MBNS MNFA MSpe NGdn SApp SPer SRos STes SWat
'Stoplight'	CBgR EBla ELon EMar SApp SDay SPol SRos
'Strawberry Candy'	Widely available
'Strawberry Fields Forever'	EWoo LRHS MBNS MSpe NLar SBrk SHar SPol SRos
'Strawberry Swirl'	MNFA
I 'Streaker' B. Brown (v)	WCot
'Street Urchin'	SPol
'Strider Spider'	SApp
'Strutter's Ball'	EWoo IPot MBNS MNFA MSCN NGdn SApp SBfd SBrk SDay SPer SPol SRos SWat WAul WCAu WHoo WMnd
'Sugar Cookie'	EWoo SApp SBrk SPol SRos
'Summer Dragon'	MBNS NMoo SBrk
'Summer Interlude'	WMoo
'Summer Jubilee'	SApp
'Summer Wine'	Widely available
'Sun King' **new**	SBrk
'Sunday Gloves'	EGol SBrk SRos WNHG
'Sunday Morning'	SRos
'Sungold Candy'	SApp
'Sunray Brilliance' **new**	EWoo
'Super Purple'	CKel SApp
'Superlative'	SApp SBrk SRos
'Susan Weber'	SApp SBrk SPol SRos
'Suzie Wong'	MNFA SRos
'Svengali'	SPol
'Sweet Hot Chocolate'	MBNS
'Sweet Pea'	EGol
'Sweet Sugar Candy'	EWoo
'Swirling Spider'	CBgR EMar EWoo
'Tahitian Waterfall'	CFwr
'Taj Mahal'	ELon EWoo SApp WFar
'Tall Boy'	SApp
'Tang'	CHid MBNS MMuc NMoo WCAu

'Tangerine Tango'	EWoo
'Tango Noturno'	SApp SPol
'Tapestry of Dreams'	EWoo
'Tarantula'	ELon SApp
'Taruga' **new**	EWoo
'Tasmania'	SPer
'Tchao Pantin' **new**	EMar
'Techny Breeze' **new**	SBrk
'Techny Peach Lace'	SRos
'Techny Spider'	SBrk SRos
'Tejas'	CElw EBee ELon NBre SPer
'Ten to Midnight'	SApp
'Tender Shepherd'	EGol
'Tennessee Flycatcher'	EMar EWoo SPol
'Tet Set'	WNHG
'Tetraploid Stella de Oro'	SDay
'Tetrina's Daughter' ♀H4	CBgR EPfP LRHS NHol SApp SBrk SGSe SRos WCAu
'Texas Sunlight'	WAul
'Texas Toffee'	SRos
'Thanks a Bunch'	SBrk SPol
'Theresa Hall'	WCon WFar
'Three Diamonds'	SPol
'Thumbelina'	ECha WMoo
§ ***thunbergii***	CAvo ECha GCal MCoo
- 'Ovation'	MBNS
'Thundering Ovation'	MWea SBrk
'Thy True Love'	SApp
'Tigereye Spider' **new**	EWoo
'Tigerling'	EWoo SRos
'Tiger's Eye' **new**	SBrk
'Tigger'	CFwr
'Time Lord'	EMar SApp
'Time to Believe'	SPol
'Timeless Fire'	SApp SBrk SRos
'Tinker Bell'	SRos
'Tiny Talisman'	SApp
'Tis Midnight'	WNHG
'Tom Collins'	SBrk SRos
'Tom Wise'	SBrk SPol SRos
'Tomorrow's Song'	SApp SPol
'Tone Poem'	WNHG
'Tonia Gay'	SApp SBrk SPol SRos
'Too Much Fun'	CFwr
'Toothpick'	EMar EWoo SPol
'Tootsie Rose'	SBrk SPol SRos
'Top Honors'	SPol
'Torpoint'	CBgR EBla GBee MBNS MRav NCob NEgg SBfd
'Total Eclipse' **new**	SBrk
'Totally Tropical' **new**	SBrk
'Touched by Magic'	CFwr
'Towhead'	EGol MRav WCot
'Toyland'	EGol EMar EPfP MBNS NBir NGdn NLar NPri SPol
'Trahlyta'	CBgR CPar EWoo SApp SBrk SDay SPol SRos WTin
'Treasure of Love'	EWoo
'Tremor'	CFwr
'Trevi Fountain'	EWoo
'Trog'	EMar
'Tropic Sunset' **new**	SBrk
'Tropical Heat Wave'	SApp
'Troubled Sleep'	EWoo
'True Gertrude Demarest'	EMar
'True Glory'	SApp
'True Grit'	SApp SBrk
'True Pink Beauty'	EWoo
'Tune the Harp'	SPol
'Tuolumne Fairy Tale'	SPol
'Turandot's Tiara'	SRos
'Turkish Turban'	SPol
'Tuscawilla Blackout'	EMar SApp SBrk SRos
'Tuscawilla Tiger'	LRHS
'Tuscawilla Tigress'	ECho EMar GMac IKil MBNS MWea NCGa SBrk SMad SRos WAul WHrl
'Tuxedo'	SApp SPol
'Twenty Third Psalm'	WHal
'Twilight Secrets'	MBNS
'Twist of Lemon'	EWoo SRos
'Two Faces of Love'	SPol
'Two Part Harmony'	CFwr
'Tylwyth Teg'	SPol
'Unchartered Waters'	MBNS SBrk
'Unforgetable Fire'	EWoo
'Uniquely Different'	SPol
'Upper Class Peach'	SBrk SRos
'Uptown Girl'	SBrk SRos
'Valiant'	EMar MBNS WHrl
'Valley Monster'	EMar
'Vanessa Arden'	SApp
'Vanilla Candy'	SBrk SRos
'Varsity'	CPLG CSpr CWat EBrs EGol GMac LRHS NBir SBrk SPer SRos
'Velvet Shadows'	SDay
'Vendetta'	WNHG
'Vera Biaglow'	SApp SBrk SDay SPol SRos
'Very Berry Ice'	SPol
'Vespers'	CAbP WFar
vespertina	see *H. thunbergii*
'Veuve Joyeuse'	EMar
'Vi Simmons'	SBrk SRos
'Victoria Elizabeth Barnes'	WNHG
'Victorian Collar'	SApp SBrk SRos
'Victorian Lace'	EWoo
'Victorian Ribbons'	SPol
'Victorian Violet'	SDay
'Video'	SApp SBrk SRos
'Vino di Notte'	EMar SRos
'Vintage Bordeaux'	ELan SApp WAul
'Vintage Burgundy'	WNHG
'Violet Hour'	SDay
'Viracocha'	SApp WMnd WNHG
'Virgin's Blush'	SPer
'Vision of Beauty'	SApp
'Vohann'	SApp SBrk SRos
'Waiting in the Wings'	SBrk SRos
'Walking on Sunshine'	SApp SBrk SRos WCot
'Wally Nance'	SApp
'War Paint'	SDay
'Water Witch'	CWat EGol SApp SRos STes
'Watermelon Man' **new**	EWoo
'Watership Down'	EWoo
'Wayside Green Imp'	EGol MNrw SApp
'Weaver's Art'	CFwr SPol
'Web Browser'	SRos
'Wedding Band'	SBrk SRos
'Wee Chalice'	EGol
'Welchkins'	WAul
'Welfo White Diamond'	SApp SPol
'Wendy Glawson'	SApp
'Westward Wind' **new**	EWoo
'When Fortune Smiles' **new**	SBrk
'When I Dream' **new**	SBrk
'Whichford' ♀H4	CBgR CMMP CSam EBee EBrs ECGP ECha ECtt EGol ELan EPla LRHS MBNS MNFA MSpe NCob NEgg SMrm SPer SPhx SRos WAul
'Whirling Fury'	SApp
'Whiskey on Ice'	SApp
'White Coral'	LRHS LSRN MBNS MNFA NBro WFar
'White Dish'	EGol
'White Edged Madonna'	EMar SBch WHrl

'White Lemonade' SApp
'White Pansy' SBrk SDay SRos
'White Perfection' EWoo SRos
'White Temptation' CFir CMMP EGol EPfP EWoo GBin MLLN MNFA MWea NCGa NGdn SApp SBrk SRos WAul WHoo WMnd WNHG
'White Tie Affair' SApp SBrk SDay SRos
'White Zone' EWoo SRos
'Whooperee' EMar SBrk SDay SRos
* 'Wide Eyed' EPla GBin
'Wild about Sherry' SPol
'Wild and Wonderful' CWGN SRos
'Wild Horses' CWGN EMar LRHS SBrk SPol WHrl
'Wild Mustang' MBNS SBrk
'Wild One' SApp
'Wild Rose Fandango' **new** EWoo
'Wildest Dreams' EWoo SRos
'Wildfire Tango' SApp
'Will Return' CFwr
'Wilson Spider' SApp SPol
'Wind Beneath My Sails' **new** EMar
'Wind Frills' EMar SApp SBrk SPol
'Wind Song' SApp SBrk SRos
'Windmill Yellow' SBrk
'Window Dressing' EGol SBrk
'Winds of Love' **new** EWoo
'Windsor Castle' SApp
'Wine Bubbles' EGol SApp
'Wine Delight' SDay
'Wineberry Candy' EWoo LHop MBNS MLLN NLar SApp WAul WCAu
'Wings on High' SApp
'Winnie' EMar
'Winsome Lady' ECha ECtt EMar EWTr MBNS MSpe WHrl
'Wisest of Wizards' EMar MBNS MNrw NCGa WHrl
'Wishing Well' WCot
'Women's Work' SApp
'Wood Duck' SApp
'Woodland Spider' SDay
'Xia Xiang' SBrk SRos
'Xochimilco' WNHG
'Ya Ya Girl' **new** EWoo
'Yabba Dabba Doo' EMar SApp SPol SRos
'Yazoo Green Octopus' **new** EWoo
'Yearning Love' SApp
'Yellow Angel' ELon SApp SPol WCot
'Yellow Explosion' SApp SRos
'Yellow Lollipop' SApp SBrk SDay SRos
'Yellow Rain' WCot
'Yellow Spider' SApp
'Yellow Submarine' MBNS SBrk
'Yesterday Memories' SBrk SRos
'You Angel You' MBNS SApp SBrk
'Yuma' WNHG
'Zagora' WCAu
'Zampa' CBgR SDay
'Zara' SPer
'Zarahemla' EMar
'Zuni Thunderbird' **new** EWoo

Hemionitis (*Adiantaceae*)

arifolia WRic

Hepatica (*Ranunculaceae*)

acutiloba CBgR EBee ECho EPot GBBs GEdr GKir LAma MHom NBir NHol NLar NMen NSla WAbe WCra
- blue-flowered MAsh
- white-flowered MAsh
americana EBee ECho EHrv ELan LHop MAsh NBir NPnk WCra
angulosa see *H. transsilvanica*
henryi EBee LAma MAsh
insularis MAsh
- B&SWJ 859 WCru
maxima GEdr MAsh
- B&SWJ 4344 WCru
× ***media*** WCom
- 'Ballardii' GEdr GKir IBlr MNFA
- 'Harvington Beauty' CLAP EBee EHrv IBlr LRHS MAsh MHom NBir WSHC
§ ***nobilis*** ♀H4 Widely available
- var. ***asiatica*** MAsh
- blue-flowered ECho GEdr IFoB MAsh NSla WAbe WGwG
- 'Cobalt' CLAP ECho NSla WAbe
- 'Cremar' GCrs MAsh
- dark blue-flowered CLAP
- dwarf white GKir IFoB
- var. ***japonica*** EPfP EWes LAma LHop MAsh NBir NHol
- - 'Akane' ECho GEdr
- - 'Akebono' (9/d) GEdr
- - 'Akanezora' (b/d) GEdr
- - 'Anjyu' (9/d) GEdr
- - 'Asahi' (7/d) GEdr
- - 'Asahizuru' (6/d) GEdr
- - 'Benikanzan' GEdr
- - 'Benioiran' GEdr
- - 'Benisuzume' (1) GEdr
- - 'Bojyou' (SA/d) **new** GEdr
- - 'Dewa' (9/d) GEdr
- - 'Echigobijin' GEdr
- - 'Ensyu' (9/d) GEdr
- - 'Fujimusume' **new** GEdr
- - 'Goshozakura' (SA/d) GEdr
- - 'Gyousei' EBee ECho GEdr
- - 'Hakurin' (6/d) GEdr
- - 'Haruka' **new** GEdr
- - 'Harukaze' (5A/d) GEdr
- - 'Haruno-awajuki' (9/d) GEdr
- - 'Hohobeni' (9/d) GEdr
- - 'Houkan' (9/d) GEdr
- - 'Isaribi' (1) EBee ECho GEdr
- - 'Kagura' (5A/d) GEdr
- - 'Kasumino' ECho GEdr
- - 'Kimon' (9/d) GEdr
- - 'Koshino-maboroshi' GEdr
- - 'Kouetsu' **new** GEdr
- - 'Kougyoku' (9/d) GEdr
- - 'Kousei' (9/d) GEdr
- - 'Koushirou' GEdr
- - 'Kuukai' (8/d) GEdr
- - f. ***magna*** MAsh
- - - double, blue-flowered (d) EBee
- - - 'Murasaki-shikibu' (7/d) GEdr
- - - 'Seizan' (9/d) GEdr
- - - 'Taeka' (9/d) GEdr
- - 'Mangekyou' GEdr
- - 'Miwaku' (1) **new** GEdr
- - 'Miyuki' (9/d) GEdr
- - 'Murasaki-sakama' (1) **new** GEdr
- - 'Odoriko' (9/d) GEdr
- - 'Okina' (9/d) **new** GEdr
- - 'O-mwasaki' ECho GEdr
- - 'Orihime' (9/d) GEdr
- - 'Ryokurei' (5A/d) **new** GEdr
- - 'Ryokusetsu' (9/d) GEdr
- - 'Ryokuun' (9/d) GEdr

- - 'Ryougetsu' (1) GEdr
- - 'Sadobeni' (1) GEdr
- - 'Saichou' (7/d) GEdr
- - 'Sakuragari' EBee GEdr
- - Sandan Group (7/d) **new** GEdr
- - 'Sansetsu' (7/d) GEdr
- - 'Sawanemidori' (6/d) EBee GEdr
- - 'Sayaka' (1) GEdr
- - 'Senhime' (9/d) GEdr
- - 'Shikouden' (9/d) GEdr
- - 'Shikouryuu' (9/d) GEdr
- - 'Shirayuki' (9/d) GEdr
- - 'Shirin' (d) GEdr
- - 'Shiun' (9/d) GEdr
- - 'Shoujyouno-homare' (9/d) GEdr
- - 'Sougetsu' ECho GEdr
- - 'Subaru' (9/d) GEdr
- - 'Suien' (9/d) GEdr
- - 'Tae' (5A/d) **new** GEdr
- - 'Tamahime' (8/d) GEdr
- - 'Tamakujyaku' GEdr
- - 'Tamamushi' (9/d) GEdr
- - 'Tamao' (1) EBee GEdr
- - 'Tamasaburou' EBee GEdr
- - 'Tenjinbai' (1) **new** GEdr
- - 'Tensei' (9/d) GEdr
- - 'Toki' (9/d) GEdr
- - 'Touryoku' (9/d) GEdr
- - 'Toyama-chiyoiwai' GEdr
- - 'Usugesyou' (9/d) GEdr
- - 'Wakakusa' (9/d) **new** GEdr
- - 'Yahiko' **new** GEdr
- - 'Yahikomuasaki' EBee GEdr
- - 'Yoshinosato' (9/d) GEdr
- - 'Yukishino' GEdr
- - 'Yumegokochi' GEdr
- - 'Yuunami' (1) EBee GEdr
- - 'Yuzuru' (8/d) GEdr
- lilac-flowered MTho
- mottled leaf ECho EHrv MTho
- pink-flowered CLAP ECho GKir MAsh
- var. ***pubescens*** MAsh
* - var. ***pyrenaica*** LEdu MAsh WThu
* - - 'Apple Blossom' CLAP GCrs MAsh NBir WAbe
* - - white-flowered GCrs
- 'Pyrenean Marbles' CLAP GKir
- red-flowered ECho GKir WAbe
- Rene's form WFar
- var. ***rubra*** CLAP ECho NMen NSla
- 'Rubra Plena' (d) GKir MAsh MHom NSla SCnR WPnP
- 'Tabby' ECho
- violet-flowered MAsh
- white-flowered CLAP ECho MAsh NMen NSla WAbe
'Sakaya' ECho
§ ***transsilvanica*** ♀H4 CLAP EBee ECho GAbr GKir LAma MAsh MCot NHol NMen NPnk WAul WHal WTin
- 'Ada Scott' GCrs GEdr
- 'Blue Eyes' EBee ECho GEdr MHom
- 'Blue Jewel' CBgR CFir CLAP EBee ECho EPot GBBs GEdr MCot MHom NCGa NLar NMen WPnP
- blue-flowered IBlr MAsh
- 'Buis' CAvo CBgR CLAP EBee ECho GCrs GEdr GKev MHom NLar SPhx WPnP
- 'Eisvogel' CLAP ECho GEdr NMen
- 'Elison Spence' (d) GEdr IBlr
- 'Lilacina' ECho GEdr MAsh NSla
- 'Loddon Blue' IBlr
- pink-flowered CLAP ECho MAsh
- 'Sieben Bergen' **new** IBlr
- white-flowered ECho MAsh
triloba see *H. nobilis*
'Wakana' GEdr
yamatutai EBee
aff. ***yamatutai*** MAsh

Heptacodium (*Caprifoliaceae*)

jasminoides see *H. miconioides*
§ ***miconioides*** Widely available

Heptapleurum see *Schefflera*

Heracleum (*Apiaceae*)

lehmannianum NBPC WCot
maximum 'Washington Limes' (v) EWes
sphondylium 'Hoggin' the Limelight' WAlt

Herbertia (*Iridaceae*)

§ ***lahue*** CDes CStu ECho WPGP

Hereroa (*Aizoaceae*)

glenensis ECho EDAr SPlb

Hermannia (*Sterculiaceae*)

flammea SPlb
pinnata CPBP NMen WAbe
pulchella NWCA WAbe
stricta CPBP NWCA WAbe WPat

Hermodactylus (*Iridaceae*)

§ ***tuberosus*** CArn CAvo CHid CPrp CTri CWCL EBee EBrs ECGP ECha ECho EPfP ERCP GKev LAma LRHS MAvo MCot NWCA SBch SDeJ SMrm WCot WTin
- BS 348 WCot
- MS 76 WCot
- MS 729 WCot
- MS 731 WCot
- MS 821 WCot
- MS 964 WCot
- PB WCot

Herniaria (*Illecebraceae*)

glabra CArn GBar GPoy NGHP

Herpolirion (*Anthericaceae*)

novae-zealandiae ECou

Hertia see *Othonna*

Hesperaloe (*Agavaceae*)

F&M 311.1 **new** WPGP
parviflora CTrC EAmu EUJe LEdu SBig SChr SPlb WCot

Hesperantha (*Iridaceae*)

§ ***baurii*** ECho GBin GGar LLHF NMen
buhrii see *H. cucullata* 'Rubra'
coccinea see *Schizostylis coccinea*
cucullata EBee ECho
* - 'Rubra' NWCA
falcata ECho
grandiflora ECho
huttonii EBee ECho LLHF MSCN NBir
mossii see *H. baurii*
oligantha 'Kamiesberg' **new** ECho
pauciflora ECho

§ ***radiata***	GGar
tysonii	see *H. radiata*

Hesperis (*Brassicaceae*)

lutea	see *Sisymbrium luteum*
matronalis	Widely available
- ***alba***	see *H. matronalis* var. *albiflora*
§ - var. ***albiflora***	CFox CPrp CSpe CTri EBee ELau EPfP GMaP LRHS MAvo MCot MMuc NGHP NGdn NPnk SIde SMrm SPer STes SWat WBrk WCAu WFar WMnd WMoo
- - 'Alba Plena' (d)	CAbP EBee ECtt ELan ELon MCot MNrw NBir NCob WBrk WCot WFar WHer WSHC
- double-flowered (d)	NGdn
- 'Frogswell Doris'	CBow
- 'Lilacina'	SWat
I - 'Variegata' (v)	CBow

Hessea (*Amaryllidaceae*)

breviflora	ECho
incana	ECho
'Pendoornhoek' **new**	
mathewsii	ECho
pulcherrima	ECho
speciosa	ECho
stellaris	ECho

Heteromorpha (*Apiaceae*)

arborescens	CPLG SPlb

Heteropyxis (*Myrtaceae*)

natalensis	EShb

Heterotheca (*Asteraceae*)

camporum var. ***glandulissimum***	IMou
mariana	see *Chrysopsis mariana*
pumila	NWCA
§ ***villosa***	EPPr NBre WCot
- 'Golden Sunshine'	MWea

Heuchera ✿ (*Saxifragaceae*)

'Alan Davidson' **new**	MPnt
'Amber Waves' PBR	CPLG EBee EHrv ELan EPfP EUJe LRHS LSRN MGos MPkF NBPC NBro NGdn NHol SBfd SDnm SPer SPoG SRGP SWvt WFar
§ ***americana***	CEnt ECha GBar MRav NBir SWvt
- var. ***americana***	MPnt
- Dale's strain	CBar EBee EHoe IFoB LBMP NLar SPlb SPur SWvt WClo WHrl WMnd WPnP
- 'Eco-magnififolia'	CLAP
- 'Harry Hay'	CDes CLAP EBee EPPr MPnt NDov SUsu WCot WPGP WSHC
- 'Ring of Fire'	EBee ECtt EPfP GKir LHop LSRN MPkF NPri SApp SBfd SDnm SPav SWvt WClo WFar WWEG
'Amethyst Myst'	CFox CLAP CMMP COIW EBee ECtt EPfP LRHS LSRN MAsh MGos MPkF NPla NPri SBfd SDnm SLim SMrm SPav SPer SRkn SRot WClo WFar
'Autumn Haze' PBR	MPnt NHol
'Baby's Breath'	ECho MPnt
'Beaujolais'	CBow CWGN ESwi GCai LSou MBNS MPnt MTis NSti SHeu WCot
'Beauty Colour'	CMac CWCL CWGN EBee ECtt ELan ELon EPfP GKir GMaP LAst LHop LRHS LSRN LSqH MAsh MRav NGdn NHol NMyG SBfd SMrm SPer SPoG SWvt WClo WCot WFar WMnd
* 'Black Velvet'	EPfP NBre
'Blackberry Jam' **new**	CWit ECtt MPnt SHeu WGor
'Blackbird' ♀H4	CMac EBee LFCN MBNS MPnt SApp SDnm SHeu SPav SRkn SWvt WMnd
'Blackout' **new**	MAsh MCot MPnt MTis WCot
'Blood Red'	LSou MAsh MPkF MPnt SHeu SLim
'Blood Vein'	CBow NBre NHol SHeu
'Bressingham Glow' **new**	MPnt
Bressingham hybrids	CWib GJos IFoB LRHS MLHP MMuc NBir SBfd SEND SPer SRms WFar WPer WWEG
'Bronze Beauty' **new**	MPnt
'Brownfinch'	SMHy SUsu WKif
'Brownies'	CBow CLAP MBNS MPnt SHeu
'Burgundy Frost' ♀H4	WCot
'Cafe Ole'	EBee GCai MPnt SHeu WHer
'Can-can' ♀H4	CTri CWCL EBee EBrs ECtt ELon EPfP GBin GKir LAst LRHS LSRN LSou MGos NBir NEgg NGdn NHol NLar NPri SBfd SHar SRot SWvt WBrk WCFE WCot WSpi WWEG
'Canyon Duet'	EAEE EBee LRHS MBNS MPnt SHeu
'Canyon Pink'	NSti
'Cappuccino'	EBee ECtt ELan EPfP LSqH MRav NBro NGdn NPri SBfd SDnm SPav SWvt WFar WWEG
'Caramel' PBR	Widely available
'Cascade Dawn'	CWCL EBee ECtt EPfP LAst LSRN LSou LSqH MRav NBir NHol SBfd SPer SWvt WBrk WClo WFar
'Champagne Bubbles' PBR	EBee SHeu
'Chatterbox' **new**	MPnt
'Cherries Jubilee' PBR	CAbP CFir CLAP EBee EBla ELon EUJe GMaP LBMP LRHS LSRN LSou NHol SLim SUsu WFar
'Chiqui'	MPnt
chlorantha	MPnt NBre
'Chocolate Ruffles' PBR	Widely available
'Chocolate Veil' ♀H4	EPfP LSRN WWEG
'Christa'	EBee MPnt SHeu
'Cinnabar Silver' PBR	MPkF SBfd SHeu
'Citronelle'	CBow CWCL GCai LSou MBNS MPnt MTis MWea NDov NMoo NPnk SHeu WCot
'City Lights'	LSou SHeu
'Color Dream' PBR	EBee GKir MAsh
coral bells	see *H. sanguinea*
'Coral Bouquet'	LAst MBNS SHar SHeu
'Coral Cloud'	MPnt MRav
Crème Brûlée = 'Tnheu041' (Dolce Series)	Widely available
'Crème Caramel'	CPLG IFoB MPnt SBfd SHar
'Crimson Curls'	CLAP EBee GKir LBuc LRHS MAsh SBfd SHeu SRms SWvt
'Crispy Curly'	NBre SHeu
cylindrica	EBee EPfP LLWP MBNS MPnt MRav NBre
- var. ***alpina***	GKev NWCA
- 'Francis' **new**	EBee
- 'Greenfinch'	CWan EBee ECha ELan EPfP EWTr GKev GMaP LSRN MRav MWhi NBir SMrm SPer SWat WFar WMnd
'Dark Beauty' PBR	CLAP ECtt EWll GJos GKev LRHS LSRN LSou MBNS NHol NLar NPri SBfd SHeu SMrm SPoG
'Dark Secret' **new**	MAsh MPnt

'David'	CBow MPnt
'Dennis Davidson'	see *H.* 'Huntsman'
'Dingle Mint Chocolate'	ECtt
Ebony and Ivory = 'E and I'PBR	Widely available
'Eden's Aurora'	WMnd
'Electra' **new**	MPnt SHeu
elegans NNS 05-372	WCot
'Emperor's Cloak'	ECGP ELon LEdu MWhi NLar SHeu SWvt WMoo
'Encore'	EBee MPnt
'Fantasia'PBR	CBow NHol SHeu
'Firebird'	MPnt NBir NVic
Firefly	see *H.* 'Leuchtkäfer'
'Fireworks'PBR ♀H4	CAbP CBow EBee ECtt LAst LBMP LRHS MBNS NLar NPri SLim SPer SRot WClo WFar WGor
'Florist's Choice'	MNFA
'Frosted Violet'PBR	see *H.* 'Frosted Violet Dream'
§ 'Frosted Violet Dream'PBR	CBow CLAP EBee EBrs ECtt EPfP GKir LRHS LSRN MAsh NCGa NDov SBfd SHeu WWEG
'Georgia Peach'	CBow CWCL CWit ECtt ELon ESwi GBin GCai GKir LBMP LHop LRHS LSqH MAsh MBri MPkF MPnt NHol NPla NPnk SBfd SHeu SPoG SRkn WCot
'Ginger Ale'PBR	CHar CWCL EBee ECtt EUJe EWes GCai LHop LRHS LSou MAsh MBNS MPnt NHol NPnk SBfd SHeu WCot
glabra	MPnt
glauca	see *H. americana*
'Green Ivory'	EAEE MPnt MRav SBch WBrk
'Green Spice'	CWCL EBee ECtt EWll GBin LBMP LHop LRHS LSou MPkF MPnt NCGa NDov NHol NPla NPnk SBfd SPer SPoG SRkn SRot SUsu SWvt WClo WGor WSpi
'Green Spire'	CLAP
'Guardian Angel'	EBee SHeu SRGP
'Gypsy Dancer'PBR (Dancer Series)	ECtt MAsh MGos MPkF MPnt SBfd SHeu
'Hailstorm' (v)	MPnt
'Helen Dillon' (v)	CBow EBee GMaP NBir NPnk SRGP SWvt WFar WWEG
'Hercules'PBR	ECtt EPfP MAsh
'Hollywood'PBR	CBow CWCL EPfP LRHS LSou NCGa SBfd SHeu WFar
§ 'Huntsman'	ELan MBNS MRav WFar WMnd
'Jade Gloss'PBR	EBee EPfP LRHS MAsh SBfd SHeu
'Jubilee'	EBee
Key Lime Pie = 'Tnheu042'PBR (Dolce Series)	Widely available
'Lady in Red'	NBre
§ 'Leuchtkäfer'	CWat EBee ECtt EPfP GJos GMaP LAst LHop LRHS MHer MRav MWat MWhi NBir NEgg NMir SBfd SPad SPer SPlb SRms STes SWal WClo WFar WMnd WMoo WPer WPtf WWEG
Licorice = 'Tnheu044'PBR (Dolce Series)	CBod CWCL EAEE ECtt EWll GCai GKir LRHS MBNS MBri MGos NLar NPnk NPri SBfd SDnm SHeu SLim SRot SVil SWvt WFar WHoo
'Lime'	NBir
'Lime Marmalade' **new**	MPnt SHeu
'Lime Rickey'PBR (Rainbow Series)	Widely available
'Little Tinker'	NBir STes
'Magic Color'PBR	CBow EBee NMoo
'Magic Wand'PBR ♀H4	CAbP EBee ECtt ELon MBNS NEgg SHeu WCot
'Mahogany'	GCai LSou MAsh MPkF MPnt SBfd SHeu SLim STes
'Marmalade'PBR	Widely available
'Mars'	EBee EPfP MPnt SHeu WCot
'Melting Fire'	ETod LRHS MAsh MPkF MPnt MWhi SHeu SLim
'Mercury'	NMoo
'Metallica'	NGBl SHeu SWal WMoo
micans	see *H. rubescens*
micrantha	GCal MLHP SRms
- var. ***diversifolia*** misapplied	see *H. villosa*
- 'Martha's Compact'	WCot
§ - 'Ruffles'	ECha
'Midnight Rose'	Widely available
'Mini Mouse'	EWes MPnt
'Mint Frost'PBR	CWCL EBee EBrs ELan EPfP GAbr LAst LSou MGos MRav NGdn NHol NPri SDnm SMrm SPoG SWvt WFar WWEG
'Miracle'	MAsh MPnt SHeu
'Mocha'	CBod CBow CLAP CWGN EBee GCai LFCN MBNS MNrw MPnt MWea NMoo SBfd SHeu SPoG STes SWvt
'Molly Bush' ♀H4	EBee NCGa NMoo
'Monita Lime'	CMoH
'Montrose Ruby'	NBre
'Mother of Pearl'	MPnt
'Neptune'	EPfP NMoo
'Oakington Jewel'	EBee ELan LRHS WSpi
'Obsidian'PBR	Widely available
'Paris' **new**	MPkF MPnt
parishii NNS 93-384	NWCA
'Peach Flambé'PBR	Widely available
'Peppermint Spice'PBR (21st Century Collection Series)	EBee LSou MPnt NPnk SHeu
'Persian Carpet'	CHEx CWCL ECtt EHrv GMaP MPnt NBir NGdn NHol NPri SDnm SHeu SPer SWvt WFar WPtf
(Petite Series) 'Petite Marbled Burgundy'	EBee ECtt EHoe GKir LAst LLHF LRHS MPnt NDov NGdn SHeu SWvt WAul WCot WCra WFar
- 'Petite Pearl Fairy'	CAbP CBow EBee EHoe ELan MPnt NGdn SHeu SWvt WFar
- 'Petite Pink Bouquet'	EBee ECtt EHoe SHeu
'Pewter Moon'	CBcs EBee ELan EPfP GMaP LAst LTen MGos MRav NBir SDnm SHeu SPer WFar WTin
'Pewter Veil'PBR	EBee EPfP LAst NPri SHeu WFar WMnd WWEG
pilosissima	NBre
'Pinot Gris'	CWGN ECtt MPnt MTis SHeu WCot
'Pinot Noir' **new**	MAsh MPnt SHeu SMrm
'Pistache'	CBow ECtt GCai LSou MAvo MBNS MPnt NPnk SHeu SMrm WCot WFut
§ 'Pluie de Feu'	CFir EBee EBrs ECtt EPPr EPfP GKir LRHS MPnt MRav SMrm WFar WSpi
'Plum Pudding'PBR	Widely available
'Plum Royale' **new**	MAsh MPnt SBfd
'Prince'	CBod EBee EBrs ELan EPfP GCai LFCN LRHS LSRN MAsh MBNS NMRc NMoo SApp SHeu SPoG SRkn SWvt WClo WPtf
'Prince of Silver'	CBod MBNS NMoo SMrm
pringlei	see *H. rubescens*
pubescens	EBee ECho MPnt
pulchella	CBow CPBP EBee LLHF MHer MWat SRms

	- JCA 9508	NMen
	'Purple Mountain Majesty'	CBcs EBee ECtt LFCN SHeu WFar
	'Purple Petticoats' ♀H4	EBee ECtt EPfP LAst LRHS LSou MLHP MNFA MPkF NBre NGdn NHol NLar NPnk NPri SHar SLim SMrm SRot WFar WSpi
	'Quick Silver'	EBla MNFA NBir SHeu SWvt WFar
	'Rachel'	CAbP CWCL EBee EBrs ECtt ELan EPfP GCal GMaP IFoB LRHS LSRN MPnt MRav MWat NBir NDov NPnk SRGP SWvt WAul WBrk WFar WTin
	Rain of Fire	see *H.* 'Pluie de Feu'
	'Raspberry Ice'PBR	GKir
	'Raspberry Regal' ♀H4	ECtt GAbr MLLN MRav NBir NSti SHeu SWvt WAul WFar
	'Rave On'PBR	Widely available
	'Red Spangles'	EBee EPfP LRHS NBir
	'Regina' ♀H4	CAbP EBee ECtt EPfP LSRN MPnt NBro SBfd SHeu SWvt WFar
	richardsonii	MNrw
	'Rickard' **new**	MPnt
	Rosemary Bloom = 'Heuros'PBR	EBrs LRHS MBNS
§	***rubescens***	CAbP ECho NBro NMen WPer WThu
	'Ruby Veil'	EBee
	'Ruffles'	see *H. micrantha* 'Ruffles'
§	***sanguinea***	CMac CSBt MRav NBir WPer
	- 'Alba' ♀H4	EPPr SMHy
	- 'Geisha's Fan'	CBow CWCL EBee LSou MPkF MPnt MSpe NEgg NHol NPla SBfd SHeu SPer SUsu SWvt
	- 'Monet' (v)	CBow EBee EPfP MLHP MPnt SHeu
	- var. ***pulchra***	CPBP
	- 'Ruby Bells'	CChe EAEE EPfP LRHS MBNS MCot NLar NPri SHeu
	- 'Sioux Falls'	EWes MBNS NBre SHeu
	- 'Snow Storm' (v)	CBow CMoH ELan EPfP MAsh MGos MRav SPlb STes WFar WMnd
	- 'Taff's Joy' (v)	CBow EWes
	- 'White Cloud' (v)	EBee EPfP NBre SHeu SRms WPer
	'Sashay' ♀H4	MPkF MPnt SHeu
	'Saturn'	LRHS MBNS MPnt NMoo SWvt
	'Scarlet Flame'	EBee
	'Schneewittchen'	EBee EPfP EWTr MPnt MRav
	'Scintillation' ♀H4	CMoH NBre
	'Shamrock'	NBre
	'Shenandoah Mountain'	WWEG
	'Silver Indiana'PBR	EBee LSRN SPoG
	'Silver Light'PBR	EPfP LRHS SHeu
	'Silver Lode'PBR	EBee SBfd SHeu
	'Silver Scrolls'PBR	Widely available
	'Silver Shadows'	MBrN SHeu
	'Silver Streak'	see × *Heucherella* 'Silver Streak'
	'Snow Angel'	EPfP GCai MAsh WCot
	'Snowfire' (v)	MPnt
	'Southern Comfort'	MAsh MPkF MPnt SBfd SHeu SLim
	'Sparkling Burgundy'	CWCL ECtt GCai LSou MPkF MPnt SBfd SHeu SVil SWvt
	'Starry Night'PBR	MPnt SBfd SHeu
	'Steel City'	EBee
	'Stormy Seas'	CMHG CSpe EBee ELan EPfP GCra LRHS MLHP MRav NBir NWsh SBfd SWvt WBrk WFar WPtf
	'Strawberries and Cream' (v)	EHrv
	'Strawberry Candy'PBR	CBcs CBow CMac CWCL CWGN EAEE EBee ELon GBin GJos LAst LBMP LRHS LSRN LSou MMHG MPnt MWea NHol NLar SHeu SLim SPer SPoG SRkn
	'Strawberry Swirl'	CElw EBee EBla ECtt GMaP LRHS MGos MPnt MRav NBir NLar NPri NSti SBfd SWvt WFar WWEG
	Sugar Frosting = 'Pwheu0104'PBR	CWit ECtt EWll LAst LBMP LRHS MPnt NCGa SHeu SRot SVil SWvt WClo WFar
	'Swirling Fantasy'PBR	CBow EPfP EShb GJos LRHS MAsh MBNS MLLN MPnt NMoo SHeu SMrm
	'Tara' **new**	MPnt
	'Tiramisu'	CBod CWCL CWGN ECtt ESwi GCai LFCN LRHS LSqH MAsh MAvo MBNS MNrw MPnt MTis NCGa NPnk NSti SHeu SMrm SPer SPoG SUsu SWvt WCot WFut
	'Van Gogh'	SHeu
	'Vanilla Spice'	LRHS MPnt NHol SHeu
	'Veil of Passion'	NBre
	'Velvet Cloak'	GKir
	'Velvet Night'	CBow EBee EPfP EUJe LRHS MNHC NBir NBre NHol SHeu WFar WMnd WPtf WWEG
	'Venus'	CBod CMea CWGN EBrs ECtt ELon EPfP EShb LRHS MBNS MLLN MNrw NCGa NGdn NMRc NSti SHeu SPer SPur WBrE WBrk WCot WCra WHoo WWEG
	'Vesuvius'PBR	MPnt
§	***villosa***	ECha GKev MRav
	- 'Autumn Bride'	EBee ECtt SHeu
	- Bressingham Bronze = 'Absi'PBR	EBee EBrs LRHS SHeu SPer WFar
	- 'Chantilly'	EBee
	- var. ***macrorhiza***	EShb LBMP NBre WClo WMnd WPnP
N	- 'Palace Purple'	Widely available
	- 'Palace Purple Select'	CBcs CMac CTri CWat CWib LAst MCot NEgg SBfd SLim SWvt WFar
	- 'Royal Red'	ECha WSpi
	'White Spires'	EBrs LRHS SHar
	'William How' **new**	MPnt
	'Winter Red'	EAEE EBee LRHS MBNS NEgg SPur
	'Zabeliana'	GBee MPnt

× *Heucherella* (*Saxifragaceae*)

	'Alabama Sunrise'	CWCL EBee ELon GCai MPkF MPnt NHol SBfd SHeu SUsu
	alba 'Bridget Bloom'	EAEE EBee ECha ELan EPfP GMaP LBMP LRHS MRav SBfd SPer SRms WCAu WFar
§	- 'Rosalie'	CBow EBee ECha GJos GKev GKir LRHS MPnt MRav NBir NBro NPnk SMrs SPlb WFar WSHC
	'Birthday Cake'	EBee SHeu
	'Burnished Bronze'PBR	CBow CMoH EBee ECtt GKev LRHS LSou MPkF NBro NEgg NGdn NHol NLar NPla SBfd SDnm SMrm SPoG SRot SWvt WCot WFar
	'Chocolate Lace'PBR	EBee SHeu
	'Cinnamon Bear'	SHeu
	'Dayglow Pink'PBR	EBla EShb GKev GMaP LBMP LFCN LSRN MBri MPkF MPnt NBro NHol NLar SHar SHeu SMrm SPoG SRkn SRot WFar WGor
	Gold Strike = 'Hertn041'PBR	CBow EWll GJos LAst LRHS MBNS MPnt SHeu SPoG
	'Golden Zebra' **new**	MPnt
	'Heart of Darkness'PBR	EBee SBfd SHeu WWEG
	'Kimono'PBR ♀H4	CWCL EBee ECtt EHrv EKen EPfP EUJe GAbr GCai GMaP LAst LBMP LFCN LPla LRHS LSRN LSou MLLN MPkF MPnt NBro NCGa NGdn

	NHol NLar NPri SBfd SHar SRot WFar
'Ninja'PBR	see *Tiarella* 'Ninja'
'Party Time'PBR	SHeu
Pink Whispers = 'Hertn042'PBR	CBow LAst MPnt SHeu WFar
'Quicksilver'	CBcs EBee EHrv GMaP LAst NGdn SHeu SWvt WCAu WFar WWEG
'Ring of Fire'	CMac CMoH WFar
§ 'Silver Streak'	CBow EBee GAbr MRav NBro SHeu SWvt WFar WWEG
'Stoplight'PBR	Widely available
'Sunspot'PBR (v)	ECtt EKen EPfP EUJe MGos NBro NSti SHar SHeu WHer
'Sweet Tea' **new**	MPnt SHeu
'Tapestry' **new**	LSou MPkF MPnt NSti SBfd SHeu SRkn
tiarelloides ♀H4	CMac EPfP WMnd
§ 'Viking Ship'PBR	CElw CMHG CMMP EAEE EBee EBla EBrs ECha ECtt GKev LAst LBMP LRHS MPnt MRav NBir NGdn NPla SHar SHeu SRkn SUsu WFar WWEG

Hexastylis see *Asarum*

Hibanobambusa (*Poaceae*)

'Kimmei'	MMuc SEND
tranquillans	CEnt EPla MBrN MMoz MMuc MWht SEND WDyG WJun WPGP
- 'Shiroshima' (v) ♀H4	CAbb CDTJ CDoC CEnt CGHE EAmu EBee ENBC EPfP EPla LPal MAvo MBrN MBri MCCP MMoz MMuc MWhi MWht NMoo NPal NVic SApp SBfd SBig SEND WDyG WJun WPGP

Hibbertia (*Dilleniaceae*)

aspera	CBcs CCCN CDoC CRHN EBee ECre IVic LRHS WCFE WCot WFar WSHC
§ ***cuneiformis***	CCCN
pedunculata	WAbe
procumbens	WAbe
§ ***scandens*** ♀H1	CCCN CHll CRHN CTsd ECou ELan SEND SOWG
tetrandra	see *H. cuneiformis*
volubilis	see *H. scandens*

Hibiscadelphus (*Malvaceae*)

distans **new**	WCot

Hibiscus ✿ (*Malvaceae*)

acetosella 'Red Shield'	CSpe
'Amarilla' **new**	WHer
Blue Chiffon = 'Notwoodthree'	LBuc MGos SPoG
coccineus	EShb SMad SOWG
fallax	CHll
'Fantasia'PBR **new**	CWGN
hamabo	ELan SLim
huegelii	see *Alyogyne huegelii*
'Kopper King'PBR	CWGN MAsh WHlf
leopoldii	SRms
'Moesiana'	MBri
moscheutos	CArn CFir EBee SVic
- 'Carolina Mix'	NExo
- 'Galaxy'	EShb NExo WHil
- Southern Belle Group	CHEx
mutabilis	SOWG
'Naranja' **new**	WHer
'Old Yella'PBR **new**	CWGN
paramutabilis	EWes SMad
'Pyranees Pink'	EMil SPoG
'Rojo' **new**	WHer
rosa-sinensis	EBak EShb MBri MREP SOWG
- 'Big Tango' **new**	SOWG
- 'Bimbo'	SOWG
- 'Byron Metts' **new**	SOWG
- 'Candy' **new**	SOWG
- 'Carmen Keene' **new**	SOWG
- 'Casablanca'	MBri
- 'Cockatoo'	SOWG
- 'Cooperi' (v) ♀H1	SOWG
- 'Courier Mail' **new**	SOWG
- 'Dorothy Brady' **new**	SOWG
- 'Enid Lewis' **new**	SOWG
- 'Expo' **new**	SOWG
- 'Gina Marie'	SOWG
- 'Great White'	SOWG
- 'Gwen Mary' **new**	SOWG
- 'Helene'	LSRN
- 'Holiday'	MBri
- 'Holly's Pride' **new**	SOWG
- 'June's Joy' **new**	SOWG
- 'Kardinal'	MBri
- 'Königer'	MBri
- 'Lady Flo'	SOWG
- 'Lemon Chiffon' (d)	SOWG
- 'Linda Pear' **new**	SOWG
- 'Love' **new**	SOWG
- 'Mrs Andreasen'	SOWG
- 'Norman Lee'	SOWG
- 'Pink Mist'	SOWG
- 'Rhinestone' **new**	SOWG
- 'Silver Rose' **new**	SOWG
- 'Spanish Lady' **new**	SOWG
- 'Sprinkle Rain'	SOWG
- 'Tarantella'	SOWG
- 'The Path' **new**	SOWG
- 'Thelma Bennell'	SOWG
- 'Tivoli'	MBri
- 'Weekend'	SOWG
schizopetalus ♀H1	CCCN EShb SOWG
sinosyriacus 'Lilac Queen'	CPLG IVic LRHS SKHP WPGP
- 'Ruby Glow'	CPLG IVic LRHS MGos SKHP WPGP
syriacus	MNHC WFar
- 'Admiral Dewey' (d)	EBee EGxp
- 'Aphrodite'	CPMA EBee EPfP SEND
- 'Ardens' (d)	CEnd CSBt EBee ELon EPfP LAst MGos NLar
- Blue Bird	see *H. syriacus* 'Oiseau Bleu'
- 'Boule de Feu' (d)	CWGN EBee ELan SEND
- 'Caeruleus Plenus' (d)	MGos
- China Chiffon = 'Bricutts'	EBee EMil MAsh
- 'Diana' ♀H4	EBee EPfP EQua LRHS LSRN MAsh MGos MRav SCoo SKHP SLon
- 'Dorothy Crane'	CEnd EBee LRHS MGos SKHP
- 'Duc de Brabant' (d)	CSBt EBee EGxp ELon EMil EPfP MBlu SPer
- 'Elegantissimus'	see *H. syriacus* 'Lady Stanley'
- 'Eleonore'PBR	EMil
- 'Freedom'	EBee
- 'Hamabo' ♀H4	CDul CSBt CTri EBee EMil EPfP LAst LRHS LSRN MAsh MBri MGos MWat NLar NPri SBfd SCoo SLim SPer SPoG SWvt WDin WFar
- 'Helene'	ELan EQua LSRN MAsh MBlu MRav
- 'Jeanne d'Arc' (d)	EMil MAsh
§ - 'Lady Stanley' (d)	CMac CSBt EBee MAsh MGan SCoo SEND SPer
- Lavender Chiffon = 'Notwoodone'PBR ♀H4	EBee ELan EPfP EWes LRHS MAsh MGos NLar SCoo SEND SPer SPoG

- 'Leopoldii'	EBee EQua SBfd SKHP
- 'Marina'	EBee EPfP EWTr MAsh MBlu MRav NLar SBfd
- 'Meehanii' misapplied	see *H. syriacus* 'Purpureus Variegatus'
- 'Meehanii' (v) ♀H4	CEnd CSBt EMil EPfP LRHS MAsh MGos SCoo SKHP SPer SPoG
- 'Monstrosus'	EBee NLar
§ - 'Oiseau Bleu' ♀H4	Widely available
- Pastelrose = 'Minpast'^{PBR}	MAsh
- Pink Giant = 'Flogi'	EBee ELan EPfP EQua LAst MAsh MBri MGos SPad SPer
§ - 'Purpureus Variegatus' (v)	CMac CSBt LAst LRHS MGos SPoG
- 'Red Heart' ♀H4	CEnd CMac CPMA CSBt CTri EBee ELan EPfP LAst LRHS MAsh MBri MCCP MMuc MRav NLar SEND SKHP SLim SPad SPer SPoG SRms SWvt WCFE WDin
- Rosalbane = 'Minrosa'	EBee EMil
- 'Roseus Plenus' (d)	WDin
- Russian Violet = 'Floru'	CBcs CEnd EBee ELan EMil EPfP LAst LRHS MAsh MGos SEND SKHP
- 'Sanchon Yo'	EPfP LRHS
- 'Souvenir de Charles Breton'	MAsh
- 'Totus Albus'	CMac CSBt SPoG
- 'Variegatus'	see *H. syriacus* 'Purpureus Variegatus'
- 'Violet Clair Double' (d)	CMac
- White Chiffon = 'Notwoodtwo'^{PBR} (d) ♀H4	EBee ELan EMil EPfP EWes LRHS LSRN LTen MAsh MGos MRav NLar SCoo SEND SPer SPoG
- 'William R. Smith' ♀H4	CDul CPMA EBee ELan EMil LAst LRHS MSwo SBfd SEND SPer WDin
- 'Woodbridge' ♀H4	Widely available
trionum	CSpe EBee SBch WKif WTou
- 'Sunny Day'	ELan

hickory, shagbark see *Carya ovata*

Hieracium (*Asteraceae*)

aurantiacum	see *Pilosella aurantiaca*
brunneocroceum	see *Pilosella aurantiaca* subsp. *carpathicola*
§ ***glaucum***	WEas
§ ***lanatum***	ECho MDKP NBir WEas
maculatum	see *H. spilophaeum*
pilosella	see *Pilosella officinarum*
praecox	see *H. glaucum*
scullyi	EPPr
§ ***spilophaeum***	EHoe GGar NBid NPer WOut
- 'Leopard'	CEnt SGar
umbellatum	EBWF WOut
villosum	CPBP EBee ECho EHoe NBro WHer
waldsteinii	MDKP
welwitschii	see *H. lanatum*

Hierochloe (*Poaceae*)

odorata	EPPr GBin GPoy MBNS WHfH

hildaberry see *Rubus* 'Hildaberry'

Himalayacalamus (*Poaceae*)

asper	CDTJ CGHE WJun WPGP
cupreus	WJun
* ***equatus***	EPla
§ ***falconeri***	CDTJ CEnt EPfP EPla MAsh MMoz SDix WPGP
§ - 'Damarapa'	CDTJ CEnt EPla MMoz WDyG WJun
§ ***hookerianus***	CPLG EAmu EBee EPla IMou SBst WJun
- 'Himalaya Blue'	CDTJ CTrC MGos
- 'Jim Dawe'	ESwi
porcatus	CDTJ CGHE WJun WPGP

Himantoglossum (*Orchidaceae*)

hircinum	NLAp

× *Hippeasprekelia* (*Amaryllidaceae*)

'Red Beauty'	WCot
'Red Star'	CCCN

Hippeastrum (*Amaryllidaceae*)

× ***acramannii***	GCal WCot
advenum	see *Rhodophiala advena*
'Alfresco'^{PBR}	LAma
'Amputo'	LAma
'Apple Blossom'	EBrs LAma LRHS MBri SDeJ SGar
aulicum	CPne
'Baby Star'	EBrs SDeJ
'Balentino' new	WHlf
'Benfica'	LAma
bifidum	see *Rhodophiala bifida*
'Black Beauty' new	LAma
'Black Pearl'	LRHS
'Blossom Peacock' (d)	LAma
'Bogota'	LAma
'Bolero' new	LAma
'Bouquet'	LAma
'Britney'^{PBR}	LAma
'Charisma'	LRHS
'Chico'	LAma
'Christmas Gift'	LAma
'Dancing Queen'	LAma
'Emerald'	LAma LRHS
'Estella'	EBrs LAma
'Fairytale'	MBri SDeJ
'Ferrari' new	LAma
'Flaming Peacock'	LAma
gracile 'Pamela'	CStu LAma
'Grandeur'	LAma
'Green Goddess'	EBrs LAma
'Helios'^{PBR} new	WHlf
'Hercules'	LRHS MBri
'Inca'	LAma
'Jewel' (d)	EBrs MBri
× ***johnsonii***	CPLG WCot
'La Paz'	LAma
'Lady Jane'	LRHS MBri
'Lemon Lime'	EBrs LAma
'Liberty'	SDeJ
'Lima'	LAma LRHS
'Lovely Garden'	LAma
'Loyalty'^{PBR}	LAma
'Merengue'	LAma
'Minerva'	LRHS
'Misty'	LAma
'Mount Blanc' Goedert	LRHS
'Mrs Garfield' new	LAma
'Naughty Lady'	LAma
'Orange Souvereign' ♀H1	EBrs
papilio ♀H1	CTca EBrs EGxp LAma LRHS MMHG
'Papillon'	EBrs
pardinum CDPR 3001	WPGP
'Pasadena'	EBrs
'Philadelphia' (d)	LRHS
'Picotee'	EBrs LAma LRHS SDeJ
'Pink Floyd'	LAma
puniceum	LAma
'Quito'	EBrs LAma
'Rebecca'	LAma
'Red Lion'	EBrs LAma LRHS

'Red Peacock' (d)	LAma LRHS
'Red Rascal' **new**	WHlf
'Rembrandt van Rijn'	LAma
'Rilona'	LAma SDeJ
'Roma'	EBrs LRHS
'Rosario'	LAma
'Royal Velvet'	LAma
'Ruby Meyer'	LAma LRHS WCot
'San Antonio Rose'	CDes EBee WCot WPGP
'Santiago'	LAma
'Santos'	EBrs
striatum	WCot
'Sumatra'[PBR]	LRHS
'Sweet Surrender'	EBrs LAma
'Tango'	LAma
'Toughie'	CAby CDes CMdw CSpe EBee LLHF WCot WPGP
'Vera'	LRHS
vittatum	LAma
'White Christmas'	LAma
'White Dazzler'	LAma
'White Peacock' (d)	LRHS

Hippocrepis *(Papilionaceae)*

§ ***comosa***	CRWN EBWF SSpi
§ ***emerus***	CBcs CCCN CMHG CPLG EBee ELan EPfP LAst LHop MGos MMuc NLar SEND STre WSHC WSpi

Hippophae *(Elaeagnaceae)*

rhamnoides 🏆H4	CAlb CArn CBcs CCVT CDul CLnd CMac CRWN CSBt CSpe CTri EBee ECrN EHoe ELan EMac EPfP IFFs LBuc MBlu MCoo NWea SEND SPlb WDin WFar
- 'Askola' (f)	MGos
- 'Dorana' **new**	MCoo
- 'Frugna' (f)	CAgr
- 'Hergo' (f)	CAgr MCoo
- 'Juliet' (f)	CAgr
- 'Leikora' (f)	CAgr ELan EPfP IVic MBlu MCoo MGos NCGa NLar SPer
- 'Orange Energy' (f/F)	CAgr MCoo
- 'Pollmix' (m)	CAgr ELan EPfP IVic MBlu MCoo MGos NCGa NLar SPer
- 'Pollmix 3' (m)	MCoo
- 'Sirola' **new**	MCoo
salicifolia	CAgr
- GWJ 9221	WCru

Hippuris *(Hippuridaceae)*

vulgaris	CBen CWat EHon MSKA NPer WMAq

Histiopteris *(Dennstaedtiaceae)*

incisa	WRic

Hoheria ✿ *(Malvaceae)*

§ ***angustifolia***	ECou EPfP SSpi
'Borde Hill'	CMHG CMac CPMA EBee ECou EPfP EWTr IVic LRHS SKHP SLim SPer SPur SSpi WCFE WKif WPat WSpi
'County Park'	ECou
glabrata	CBcs ECou EPfP GBin GGal GGar GKir NBir NPal SKHP WPGP
- 'Silver Stars'	EPfP
'Glory of Amlwch' 🏆H3	CAbb CDul CPMA CSam EBee ECou EPfP GQui SKHP SMad SSpi WPGP WSpi
'Hill House'	CHll
'Holbrook'	CSam
§ ***lyallii*** 🏆H4	CBcs CCCN CDoC CPLG CWit EBee ECou ELan EPfP IDee LRHS LSRN SPer SSpi WDin
- 'Chalk Hills'	ECou
- 'Swale Stream'	ECou
microphylla	see *H. angustifolia*
populnea	CBcs CCCN SGar
- 'Alba Variegata' (v)	CTrC ECou
- 'Moonlight'	CHGN
- 'Purple Shadow'	ECou
- 'Variegata' (v)	ECou
'Purple Delta'	ECou
sexstylosa	CAbb CDoC CDul CHEx CHid CMHG CTho CTri ECou ELan EPfP EWTr LHop LRHS MGos NEgg SEND SPer SPur SSta SWvt
- 'Pendula'	CBcs WDin
- 'Stardust' 🏆H4	Widely available

Holarrhena *(Apocynaceae)*

pubescens	CCCN

Holboellia *(Lardizabalaceae)*

angustifolia	MBri NLar WCru
- subsp. ***linearifolia*** BWJ 8004 **new**	WCru
- subsp. ***obtusa*** DJHC 506	WCru
brachyandra HWJ 1023	WCru
aff. ***chapaensis*** B&SWJ 7250 **new**	WCru
coriacea	CBcs CHll CRHN CSam EBee ELan EPfP IDee MGos MRav NLar SAPC SKHP SOWG SPer WBor WCot WCru
- B&SWJ 2818	WCru
fargesii **new**	EBee LRHS SKHP
latifolia	Widely available
- HWJK 2014	WCru
- HWJK 2213	WCru
- dark-flowered HWJK 2213 **new**	WCru

Holcus *(Poaceae)*

lanatus	EBWF WSFF
mollis 'Albovariegatus' (v)	CBen CWCL EBee ECha EHoe ELan EPPr EPfP GMaP LBMP MWhi NBid NBro NGdn NPer NSti SPlb SRms WEas WFar WMoo WTin WWEG
- 'Jackdaw's Cream' (v)	EPPr MAsh
- 'White Fog' (v)	CChe EBee EHul EPPr IVic MMuc NHol SApp SEND WFar

Holmskioldia *(Verbenaceae)*

* ***lutea***	CCCN
sanguinea	CCCN EShb

Holodiscus *(Rosaceae)*

discolor	CBcs CDul EBee ELan EPfP EWes IDee LRHS MAsh MBlu MBri MMuc MRav NLar SCoo SEND SKHP SLon SPer SPlb SPoG SSpi WDin
- var. ***ariifolius***	EBee EPfP LRHS
dumosus	EBee NLar WPGP

Homalocladium *(Polygonaceae)*

§ ***platycladum***	EShb

Homeria *(Iridaceae)*

bifida 'Roggeveld' **new**	ECho
breyniana	see *H. collina*
- var. ***aurantiaca***	see *H. flaccida*
britteniae **new**	ECho

§ ***collina***	ECho
elegans new	ECho
§ ***flaccida***	ECho
- 'Roggeveld' new	ECho
hantamensis 'Calvinia' new	ECho
ochroleuca	ECho
rogersii 'Roggeveld' new	ECho
speciosa 'Tanqua' new	ECho

Homoglossum see *Gladiolus*

Hordeum (*Poaceae*)

chilense	EBee
jubatum	CKno CSpe CWCL EHoe EWes MSCN MWat MWhi NChi NGdn NHol SApp SEND SPhx SUsu WHil
- from Ussuri	NGBl
- 'Early Pink' new	NDov

Horkeliella (*Rosaceae*)

purpurascens NNS 98-323	WCot

Horminum (*Lamiaceae*)

pyrenaicum	CAby CPrp EBee EBrs ECho GAbr LBMP MMuc SEND SRms WFar WMoo WOut WPer WPtf WTin
- dark-flowered	ECho GCal
- pale blue-flowered	MDKP
- 'Rubrum' new	EDif

horseradish see *Armoracia rusticana*

Hosta ✿ (*Hostaceae*)

sp.	WPGP
AGSJ 302	CDes
'A Many-Splendored Thing'	EMic IBal
'Abba Dabba Do' (v)	EBee ECtt EGol EMic LBuc LPla NBPC NEgg NHol SApp
'Abba Showtime'	IBal
'Abby' (v)	EGol EMic EPGN IBal NMyG SApp
'Abiqua Ariel'	EMic SApp
'Abiqua Blue Crinkles'	EMic IBal NBir SApp
'Abiqua Blue Edger'	EMic
'Abiqua Delight' (v)	IBal
'Abiqua Drinking Gourd'	EBee EGol EMic EPGN GBin GKir IBal MHom NMyG SApp WWEG
'Abiqua Ground Cover'	EGol IBal
'Abiqua Moonbeam' (v)	CFir EMic EPGN IBal MSwo NGdn NMyG SApp
'Abiqua Recluse'	EGol SApp
'Abiqua Trumpet'	EGol EMic IBal NGdn NLar NMyG NNor SApp
'Academy Blushing Recluse' (v) new	IBal
'Ada Reed' new	IBal
aequinoctiiantha	EGol
'Alan Titchmarsh'	EPGN
albomarginata	see *H. sieboldii* 'Paxton's Original'
§ 'Albomarginata' (*fortunei*) (v)	CBcs CMac EGol EQua GKir MNrw NBir SEND SGSe SPoG SWvt WBrE
'Alex Summers'	EMic IBal WFar
alismifolia	IBal
'All That Jazz' (v) new	EMic IBal
'Allan P. McConnell' (v)	EGol EMic EPGN GCra IBal MHom NMyG SPoG WHal WWEG
'Allegan Emperor' (v)	IBal
'Allegan Fog' (v)	EBee EGol EMic EPGN IBal
'Alligator Shoes' (v)	EGol EMic IBal
'Alpine Aire'	EMic
'Alpine Dream'	IBal
'Alternative'	IBal
'Alvatine Taylor' (v)	EGol EMic IBal LAst
'Amanuma'	EGol EMic IBal MHom
'Amazing Grace' (v)	IBal
'Amber Maiden' (v)	EGol
'Amber Tiara'	EMic IBal
'American Dream' (v)	EGol EMic EPGN IBal NMyG
'American Halo'	EBrs EMic IBal LRHS NBPC NLar NMRc
'American Icon'	EMic IBal
'American Sweetheart'	EMic IBal SApp
'Americana' (v) new	IBal
'Amy Elizabeth' (v)	EGol EMic IBal NMyG
'Angel Feathers' (v)	EGol
'Anglo Saxon' (v)	IBal
'Ann Kulpa' (v)	EMic EPGN IBal
'Anne' (v)	EGol IBal LSRN NMyG
'Anne Arett' (*sieboldii*) (v)	EPGN
'Ansly' (v)	IBal
'Antioch' (*fortunei*) (v)	EGol EMic GQue IBal LPla MRav NBPC NLar NMyG WFar
'Aoba Tsugaru'	IBal
'Aoki' (*fortunei*)	EMic NHol
'Aphrodite' (*plantaginea*) (d)	EBee EGol EHrv IBal LSou MBNS MCot NCob NGdn NLar NMoo SApp SMrm WCot WGwG WWEG
'Apollo'	NNor
'Apple Court'	SApp
'Apple Green'	EMic IBal
'Apple Pie'	SApp
'Aqua Velva'	EGol IBal
'Arc de Triomphe'	EMic IBal SApp
'Archangel'	EGol
'Arctic Blast' new	EMic IBal
'Argentea Variegata' (*undulata*)	see *H. undulata* var. *undulata*
'Aristocrat' (Tardiana Group) (v)	EBrs EGol EMic EPGN IBal LRHS SApp WFar
'Asian Beauty'	EGol
'Aspen Gold' (*tokudama* hybrid)	EMic SApp
'Athena' (v)	IBal
'Atlantis'PBR (v)	EMic IBal
'August Beauty'	EMic IBal
'August Moon'	Widely available
aureafolia	see *H.* 'Starker Yellow Leaf'
'Aureoalba' (*fortunei*)	see *H.* 'Spinners'
'Aureomaculata' (*fortunei*)	see *H. fortunei* var. *albopicta*
'Aureomarginata' ambig. (v)	GKir MMuc SCoo SEND
'Aureomarginata' (*montana*) (v)	CMac EGol EHoe ELan EMic EPGN GCal GMaP IBal MMuc NCGa NEgg NGdn NHol NLar NWsh SApp SEND SGSe WFar WTin WWEG
'Aureomarginata' (*rohdeifolia*) (v)	EMic
§ 'Aureomarginata' (*ventricosa*) (v) ♀H4	ECha EGol EMic EPfP IBal MWat NGdn NMyG SApp WFar WTin
'Aureostriata' (*tardiva*)	see *H.* 'Inaho'
'Aurora Borealis' (*sieboldiana*) (v)	EGol IBal
'Austin Dickinson' (v)	EGol EMic IBal LBuc LRHS NEgg WPtf
'Avalanche'	IBal
'Avocado'	IBal
'Azure Mediterranean'	IBal
'Azure Snow'	EGol IBal
'Babbling Brook'	EGol
'Baby Blue' (Tardiana Group)	EMic
'Baby Blue Eyes'	IBal
'Baby Bunting'	EGol EMic EPGN IBal IFoB NBro NLar
'Ballerina'	EGol IBal

'Banana Boat' (v)	EGol IBal
'Banana Muffins'	IBal
'Banana Sundae' (v)	IBal
'Band of Gold'	IBal
'Banyai's Dancing Girl'	EGol EMic
'Barbara Ann' (v)	EMic EPGN IBal MBri NMyG WWEG
'Barbara May'	IBal
'Barbara White'	EGol IBal
'Beauty Little Blue'	EGol IBal
'Beauty Substance'	EGol EMic EPGN IBal NMyG NNor
'Beckoning'	EMic IBal
'Bedford Blue'	EMic IBal
'Bell Bottom Blues'	IBal
bella	see *H. fortunei* var. *obscura*
'Bennie McRae'	EGol
'Betcher's Blue'	EGol EMic
'Betsy King'	CMac EBee EGol MRav NHol NMyG
'Bette Davis Eyes'	EGol
'Betty'	EGol IBal
'Bianca'	SApp
'Biddy's Blue'	IBal
'Big Boy' (*montana*)	EGol
'Big Chance'	IBal
'Big Daddy' (*sieboldiana* hybrid) (v)	Widely available
'Big Mama'	EGol EUJe NLar NPnk SApp
'Big Top'	IBal
'Bigfoot'	EGol
'Biggie'	IBal SApp
'Bill Brinka' (v)	EGol EMic
'Bill Dress's Blue'	IBal
'Birchwood Blue'	EGol
'Birchwood Blue Beauty'	IBal NMyG
'Birchwood Elegance'	NMyG SApp
'Birchwood Gem'	IBal
§ 'Birchwood Parky's Gold'	CFir CMHG CMoH EBee EGol EMic EPfP EWTr GMaP IBal LBMP LRHS MBNS NCob NGdn NHol NNor SApp
'Birchwood Ruffled Queen'	EGol EMic IBal
'Bitsy Gold'	EGol EMic IBal
'Bitsy Green'	EGol
'Bix Blues' **new**	IBal
'Bizarre'	EMic IBal
'Black Beauty'	EGol IBal
'Black Hills'	EGol EMic IBal NMyG
'Black Pearl'	IBal
'Blackfoot'	EGol EMic
'Blackjack' (*sieboldiana*) **new**	IBal NMyG SApp
'Blaue Venus'	EGol IBal
'Blaues Boot' **new**	IBal
'Blauspecht'	IBal
'Blaze of Glory' **new**	IBal
'Blazing Saddles' (v)	EMic IBal MBNS
'Blonde Elf'	EGol EMic IBal NEgg NGdn NHol NMyG NNor SApp WWEG
'Blue Angel' misapplied	see *H. sieboldiana* var. *elegans*
'Blue Angel' (*sieboldiana*) ♀H4	CBar COlW CWit ECtt EGol EHoe ELan EMic EPGN EPfP GBBs GBin GKev GMaP IBal LEdu MHer MHom MSwo NBPC NBid NBir NEgg NGdn NMyG NNor NPri WAul WFar WMnd
'Blue Arrow'	EGol IBal NNor SApp
'Blue Baron'	EMic IBal
'Blue Beard'	IBal
'Blue Belle' (Tardiana Group)	EGol EMic IBal NGdn WHoo WTin
'Blue Blush' (Tardiana Group)	EGol EMic IBal NGdn

'Blue Boy'	EGol EMic EWes NHol NMyG NNor
'Blue Cadet'	CBcs CMac EGol EMic IBal IFoB LPBA LRHS MLHP NBir NGdn NLar NMyG SApp SMrm WFar WMnd WWEG
'Blue Canoe'	EMic IBal SApp
'Blue Chip'	EMic EPGN IBal SApp
'Blue Clown'	IBal
'Blue Cup' (*sieboldiana*)	MRav
'Blue Danube' (Tardiana Group)	EGol EMic IBal MHom NMyG
'Blue Diamond' (Tardiana Group)	EGol EMic NNor WFar WWEG
'Blue Dimples' (Tardiana Group)	ECtt EGol EMic IBal NMoo
'Blue Edger'	EMic IBal NBir
'Blue Eyes'	IBal
'Blue Flame'	EMic IBal
'Blue Frost' **new**	IBal
'Blue Haired Lady'	IBal
'Blue Hawaii'	EMic IBal
'Blue Heart' (*sieboldiana*)	ECha EMic IBal
'Blue Ice' (Tardiana Group)	EGol EPGN IBal
'Blue Impression'	EMic
'Blue Ivory' (v) **new**	IBal NMyG
'Blue Jay' (Tardiana Group)	EGol EMic IBal SApp
'Blue Lady'	EMic IBal
'Blue Mammoth' (*sieboldiana*)	EGol EMic IBal SApp
'Blue Maui'	EMic IBal
'Blue Monday'	EMic
'Blue Moon' (Tardiana Group)	CMea EGol EMic EPfP IBal NGdn NHol NNor WAul
'Blue Mountains'	IBal LBuc
'Blue Mouse Ears'	EGol EMic EPGN EPfP GBin GEdr GQue IBal LLWG MBNS MHom NGdn NHar NMyG SApp WWEG
'Blue River' (v)	EMic SApp
'Blue Seer' (*sieboldiana*)	EGol
'Blue Shadows' (*tokudama*) (v)	EMic ESwi NLar SApp WFar
'Blue Skies' (Tardiana Group)	EGol IBal MHom SApp
'Blue Splendor' (Tardiana Group)	IBal
'Blue Umbrellas' (*sieboldiana* hybrid)	CMoH EGol ELan EMic EPGN EPfP IBal MHom NGdn NHol NLar NMyG SApp SMrm
'Blue Veil'	EGol
'Blue Vision'	EMic EPGN SApp
'Blue Wedgwood' (Tardiana Group)	EBee EGol ELan EMic GKir IBal LPBA MGos MMuc NGdn NHol SApp SEND SPoG WClo WHil WWEG
'Blue Wonder' **new**	IBal
'Blueberry Tart'	IBal
'Blütenwunder'	SApp
'Bob Deane' (v)	EMic IBal
'Bob Olson' (v)	EGol IBal
'Bobbie Sue' (v)	EGol IBal
'Bodacious Blue'	IBal
'Bold Edger' (v)	EGol
'Bold Intrigue' (v)	IBal
'Bold Ribbons' (v)	EGol EMic GAbr IBal WTin
'Bold Ruffles' (*sieboldiana*)	EGol SApp
'Bolt out of the Blue'	EMic
'Bonanza'	EMic
'Border Bandit' (v)	EGol IBal
'Border Favorite'	EMic IBal
§ 'Borwick Beauty' (*sieboldiana*) (v)	EGol EMic EPGN IBal NBPC NCGa NGdn NLar NMyG NPnk SApp SPer WAul WWEG

'Bottom Line' (v) **new**	IBal
'Bountiful'	EGol EMic
'Bouquet'	EGol
'Brandywine'	IBal
'Brash and Sassy'	IBal
'Brass Ring' (v)	IBal
'Bread Crumbs'	IBal
'Brenda's Beauty' (v)	EGol EMic IBal
'Bressingham Blue'	EBee EBrs ECtt EGol EMic GQue IBal LRHS MRav NLar NMyG NNor SApp SWvt WFar WMnd
'Bridal Veil'	IBal
'Bridegroom'	EGol EMic
'Bridgeville'	IBal
'Brigadier'	EGol
'Brigham Blue' **new**	IBal
'Bright Glow' (Tardiana Group)	EGol EMic
'Bright Lights' (*tokudama*) (v)	EGol EMic EPGN GBBs IBal NGdn SApp WFar
'Brim Cup' (v)	EBee EGol ELon EMic EPGN IBal LAst LSou MBNS MBri NBro NGdn SApp SBfd SMrm WWEG
'Brooke'	EGol EMic GKir IBal NMyG WWEG
'Brother Ronald' (Tardiana Group)	EGol EMic IBal SApp
'Brother Stefan'	EMic IBal SApp
'Bruce's Blue'	EGol
'Bubba'	IBal
'Buckshaw Blue'	EGol EPGN IBal MDKP NBir NGdn
'Buckwheat Honey'	IBal
'Bunchoko'	IBal NNor
'Burke's Dwarf'	IBal
'Butter Rim' (*sieboldii*) (v)	EGol
'Cadillac' (v)	EMic
'Caliban'	SApp
'Cally Atom'	GCal IBal
'Calypso' (v)	EGol EMic EPGN IBal LBuc WWEG
'Camelot' (Tardiana Group)	EGol EMic IBal LRHS MNHC NGdn
'Cameo'	EGol EMic IBal SApp
'Camouflage'	IBal
'Canadian Blue'	EMic
'Candy Hearts'	CMHG CSam EGol EMic MHom MWat NNor WTin
capitata B&SWJ 588	WCru
'Captain Kirk' (v)	EMic IBal NMyG SApp
caput-avis	see *H. kikutii* var. *caput-avis*
'Carder Blue'	EMic
'Carnival' (v)	EGol EMic EPGN IBal NBPC NEgg SApp
'Carol' (*fortunei*) (v)	EGol EMic IBal MLLN NEgg NLar NMyG NNor NWsh SApp WHal
'Carolina Blue'	IBal
'Carousel' (v)	EGol IBal
'Carrie' (*sieboldii*) (v)	EGol
'Cascades' (v)	EGol EMic EPGN IBal
'Cat and Mouse' **new**	IBal
'Cathedral Windows' (v) **new**	EMic IBal
'Catherine'	IBal LLWG
'Cat's Eyes' (*venusta*) (v)	EGol EMic EPGN IBal SApp
'Celebration' (v)	EBrs EGol ELan EMic LRHS MDKP WHal WWEG
'Celestial'	IBal
'Center of Attention'	EBee EMic IBal SApp
'Cha Cha Cha'	IBal
'Chain Lightning' (v) **new**	IBal
'Challenger'	EMic
'Change of Tradition' (*lancifolia*) (v)	EMic
'Chantilly Lace' (v)	EGol EMic NMyG SApp WTin
'Chariots of Fire' (v)	IBal
'Chartreuse Waves'	EGol
'Chartreuse Wiggles' (*sieboldii*)	IBal
'Cheatin' Heart'	EGol EMic IBal WWEG
'Chelsea Babe' (*fortunei*) (v)	EGol
'Cherish'	EGol EMic EPGN IBal
'Cherry Berry' (v)	CMHG EGol EMic EPGN GBin IBal LRHS MBNS MLLN MMuc NBro NCob NEgg NGdn NLar NMyG SApp SBfd SMrm SPoG WAul WBor WCAu WFar WWEG
'Cherry Tart' **new**	IBal
'Cherub' (v)	EGol IBal
'Chesapeake Bay'	EMic IBal
'Chesterland Gold' **new**	IBal
'Chickadee' (v) **new**	EMic
'Chinese Sunrise' (v)	CWCL EBee EGol EMic EPGN IBal LBuc MHom NMyG NNor SRms WHal
'Chionea' (v)	IBal
'Chiquita'	EGol
'Chodai Ginba'	IBal
§ 'Chōkō Nishiki' (*montana*) (v)	EGol EMic EPGN EQua IBal LRHS NGdn NMyG NNor SApp SBfd
'Choo Choo Train'	EGol EMic SApp
'Chopsticks'	IBal
'Christmas Candy'[PBR]	EMic EPGN IBal NCob
'Christmas Cookies'	IBal
'Christmas Lights' (v)	IBal
'Christmas Pageant' (v)	EMic IBal
'Christmas Tree' (v)	CMMP EGol EMic EPGN IBal IFoB IPot LPla LRHS NBPC NEgg NGdn NMyG SApp WMoo WWEG
'Cinderella'	IBal
'Cinnamon Sticks'	IBal
'Citation' (v)	EGol
'City Lights'	EGol EMic NEgg
'City Slicker' (v)	IBal
clausa var. ***normalis***	CMoH EGol GQui NBir NGdn NLar NMyG
'Clear Fork River Valley'	IBal
'Cleopatra' (v)	IBal
'Clifford's Forest Fire'	EMic EPGN IBal LRHS NLar NMyG WFar
'Clifford's Stingray' (v)	EMic IBal LLWG
'Climax' (v)	EMic IBal
'Cloudburst'	IBal
'Clovelly' **new**	IBal
'Cody'	IBal
'Collector's Banner'	EGol
'Collector's Choice'	EGol IBal
'Color à la Mode' (v) **new**	IBal
'Color Glory'	see *H.* 'Borwick Beauty'
'Colossal'	EGol EMic
'Columbus Circle' (v)	EGol EMic
'Cookie Crumbs' (v)	EGol EMic EPGN IBal SApp
'Coquette' (v)	EGol EMic IBal NMyG
'Corkscrew'	EMic SApp
'Corn Belt' (v) **new**	IBal
'Cotillion' (v)	EGol EMic SApp
'Country Mouse' (v)	IBal
'County Park'	EGol EMic IBal
'Cowrie' (v) **new**	IBal
'Cracker Crumbs' (v)	EGol EMic EPGN IBal MHom NHar NMyG NNor SApp
'Craig's Temptation'	IBal NMyG
'Crater's Heart' (*venusta*) (v)	IBal
'Cream Cheese' (v)	EGol IBal
'Cream Delight' (*undulata*)	see *H. undulata* var. *undulata*
'Crepe Soul' (v)	EGol IBal

'Crepe Suzette' (v)	EGol EPGN NNor
'Crested Reef'	CMoH EGol EMic NMyG
'Crested Surf' (v)	EGol EMic EPGN IBal
'Crinoline Petticoats'	EGol
§ ***crispula*** (v) 🏆H4	CBot EGol EMic EPfP MCot MHom MRav NChi NCob NMyG
'Crown Jewel' (v)	EPGN IBal
'Crown Prince' (v)	EGol IBal
§ 'Crowned Imperial' (*fortunei*) (v)	CWat EMic NHol
'Crumples' (*sieboldiana*)	EGol
'Crusader' (v)	EGol ELon EMic EPGN IBal LRHS NMyG SApp WFar WWEG
'Crystal Chimes'	IBal
'Crystal Dixie' **new**	IBal SApp
'Cupboard Love'	SApp
'Cupid's Dart' (v)	EGol
'Curlew' (Tardiana Group)	EGol IBal
'Curls' **new**	IBal
'Curtain Call'	IBal
'Cutting Edge'	IBal
'Dab a Green'	IBal
'Daisy Doolittle' (v)	IBal SApp
'Dance with Me' (v)	EMic IBal
'Dancing in the Rain' (v)	CWGN EBee EMic EPGN MAvo NBro NMyG SApp SMrm WFar
'Dark Shadows'	EMic EPGN IBal
'Dark Star' (v)	EGol EMic EPGN IBal SApp
'Dark Victory'	IBal
'Dawn'	EGol EMic IBal NMyG
'Dawn's Early Light' **new**	EMic
'Dax' **new**	IBal
'Daybreak'	EGol EMic EPGN IBal LAst MBri NBro SApp
'Day's End' (v)	EGol EMic IBal
'Deane's Dream'	EMic IBal
decorata	EGol EMic
'Deep Blue Sea'	EMic IBal SApp
'Deep Pockets'	IBal
'Déjà Blu' (v)	EMic IBal
'Delia' (v)	EPGN
'Delta Dawn' (v)	EBrs EMic IBal LRHS
'Delta Desire'	IBal
'Deluxe Edition'	IBal
'Designer Genes'	EMic IBal SApp
'Devon Blue' (Tardiana Group)	EGol EMic IBal NMyG NNor
'Devon Desire' (*montana*)	NLar
'Devon Discovery'	IBal
'Devon Giant'	EMic IBal NNor SApp
'Devon Gold'	EMic IBal
'Devon Green'	ELan EMic EPGN GBin IBal IPot LRHS MHom MLLN MMuc NBro NCob NEgg NGdn NLar NMyG SApp SBfd SEND SPoG WAul WFar WHal WWEG
'Devon Hills'	IBal
'Devon Mist'	IBal NNor
'Devon Tor'	IBal
'Dew Drop' (v)	EGol EMic IBal SGSe WWEG
'Diamond Tiara' (v)	EGol EMic EPGN IBal LRHS NBir NGdn NMyG WWEG
'Diana Remembered'	EGol EMic EPGN IBal WBor
'Dick Ward'	EMic IBal
'Dilithium Crystal' **new**	IBal
'Dillie Perkeo'	IBal
'Dilys'	EMic MNrw
'Dimple'	EMic IBal
'Dinky Donna'	IBal
'Dixie Chick' (v)	EGol EMic IBal SApp
'Dixieland Heat'	IBal
'Doctor Fu Manchu'	IBal
'Domaine de Courson'	EMic EPGN SApp WFar
'Don Stevens' (v)	EGol IBal
'Donahue Piecrust'	EGol
'Dorothy'	EMic IBal
'Dorset Blue' (Tardiana Group)	EGol EMic EPGN IBal SApp SBfd
'Dorset Charm' (Tardiana Group)	EGol EMic
'Dorset Flair' (Tardiana Group)	EGol EMic IBal
'Doubloons'	EGol EMic
'Dragon Tails'	EMic IBal LRHS
'Dragon Wings'	IBal
'Dream Queen' (v)	ECtt EMic IBal
'Dream Weaver' (v)	EBee EGol EMic EPGN IBal LRHS MHom MNrw NBro NGdn NMyG SApp SPer SPoG WFar WWEG
'Dress Blues'	CMac EMic IBal
'Drummer Boy'	EGol EMic IBal WWEG
'Duchess' (*nakaiana*) (v)	IBal
'DuPage Delight' (*sieboldiana*) (v)	EGol EMic IBal NGdn NLar
'Dust Devil' (*fortunei*) (v)	EGol IBal
'Eagle's Nest' (v)	IBal
'Earth Angel' (v)	EGol EMic IBal NGdn NMyG SApp
'Ebb Tide' (*montana*) (v)	IBal
'Edge of Night'	EGol EMic
'Edwin Bibby'	EMic
'El Capitan' (v)	EGol EMic EPGN IBal
'El Niño'[PBR] (Tardiana Group) (v)	CWGN EGol EMic IBal MHom MNrw NBro NGdn NMyG SApp WFar WWEG
§ 'Elata'	EGol EMic SApp
'Elatior' (*nigrescens*)	EMic IBal
'Eldorado'	see *H.* 'Frances Williams'
'Eleanor Lachman' (v)	EGol EMic IBal
'Eleanor Roosevelt'	IBal
'Elegans'	see *H. sieboldiana* var. *elegans*
'Elegans Alba' (*sieboldiana*)	GKir
'Elfin Power' (*sieboldii*) (v)	EGol
'Elisabeth'	EMic GBin IBal LSRN NMyG
'Elizabeth Campbell' (*fortunei*) (v)	EGol EMic IBal
'Elkheart Lake'	EMic
'Ellen'	EMic
'Ellerbroek' (*fortunei*) (v)	EGol EMic IBal
'Ellie Bee'	IBal
'Elsley Runner'	EGol IBal
'Elvis Lives'	EGol EMic EPGN GBin IBal LAst NEgg NGdn NLar NMyG NNor
'Embroidery' (v)	EPGN
'Emerald Carpet'	EGol IBal
'Emerald Crown' **new**	IBal
'Emerald Necklace' (v)	EGol
'Emerald Ruff Cut'	EMic IBal SApp
'Emerald Skies'	EGol
'Emerald Tiara' (v)	EGol EMic EPGN LRHS MLHP NLar NMyG SApp SBfd WTin WWEG
'Emeralds and Rubies'	EGol EMic IBal
'Emily Dickinson' (v)	EBee EGol EMic IBal LRHS MMuc NNor SApp SEND SPad WWEG
'Empress Wu' **new**	IBal
'Encore'	IBal
'English Sunrise' (Tardiana Group)	IBal
'Enterprise'	EMic IBal LLWG SApp
'Eos' **new**	NLar
'Eric Smith' (Tardiana Group)	EGol EMic IBal MHom NMyG WFar
'Eric's Gold'	EPGN IBal
'Erie Magic' (v)	EGol IBal

	'Eskimo Pie' (v)	EBee EMic IBal NMyG SApp SMrm WFar
	'Essence of Summer'	EMic EPfP IBal SApp
	'Eternal Flame'	EMic IBal
	'Evelyn McCafferty' (*tokudama* hybrid)	EGol
	'Evening Magic' (v)	EGol
	'Eventide' (v)	EGol
	'Everlasting Love' (v)	EGol
	'Excitation'	EGol EMic
	'Extasy' (v) **new**	EMic IBal
	'Extreme' **new**	IBal
	'Eye Candy' (v)	IBal
	'Eye Catcher'	EMic
	'Eye Declare' (v)	IBal
	'Fair Maiden' (v)	IBal
	'Faith' **new**	EMic
	'Faithful Heart' (v)	IBal
	'Fall Bouquet' (*longipes* var. *hypoglauca*)	EGol
	'Fall Emerald'	EMic
	'Fallen Angel'	IBal
	'Falling Waters' (v)	EGol IBal
	'Fan Dance' (v)	EGol IBal
	'Fantabulous' (v)	EPGN IBal
	'Fantastic' (*sieboldiana* hybrid)	EGol
	'Fantasy Island' (v)	EMic IBal
	'Fatal Attraction'	IBal
	'Feather Boa'	EGol EMic IBal NHar NMyG WWEG
	'Fenman's Fascination'	EMic
	'Fiesta' (v)	IBal
	'Fire and Ice' (v)	Widely available
	'Fire Island'	EGol EMic EPGN GBin IBal MHom SApp
	'Fireworks' (v)	EBee EGol EMic EPGN GBin IBal MBNS NBro NGdn NMyG SApp SMrm
	'First Frost' (v)	EMic IBal LRHS NGdn SApp WWEG
	'First Mate' (v)	EMic IBal
	'Five O'Clock Shadow' (v)	IBal
	'Five O'Clock Somewhere' (v)	IBal
	'Flame Stitch' (*ventricosa*) (v)	EGol IBal
	'Flemish Sky'	EMic IBal NGdn SApp
	'Floradora'	EGol EMic IBal NMyG
	'Flower Power'	EGol NNor
	'Fool's Gold' (*fortunei*)	EMic IBal
	'Forest Fireworks' (v) **new**	IBal
	'Forest Shadows'	IBal
	'Formal Attire' (*sieboldiana* hybrid) (v)	EGol EMic IBal LRHS
	'Forncett Frances' (v)	EGol IBal
	'Fortis'	see *H. undulata* var. *erromena*
	fortunei	EGol EMic NHol NNor WEas WFar
§	- var. ***albopicta*** (v) ♀H4	Widely available
	- - f. ***aurea*** ♀H4	CMHG CMac ECha EGol EHoe ELan EMic EPla GBin MRav NEgg NLar NMyG SRms WFar WHal
	- - - dwarf	EMic
§	- var. ***aureomarginata*** (v) ♀H4	Widely available
	- var. ***gigantea***	see *H. montana*
	- var. ***hyacinthina*** ♀H4	EBrs EGol EMic EPfP IBal LRHS MGos MRav NGdn NLar SApp WPtf
	- - variegated	see *H.* 'Crowned Imperial'
§	- var. ***obscura***	EGol EMic IBal LRHS
	- var. ***rugosa***	EMic IBal
	- 'Shaman' **new**	SApp
	'Fountain of Youth' (*kikutii*)	IBal
	'Fourth of July'	EGol
	'Fragrant Blue'	EBee EGol EMic GBBs IBal LRHS NBro NGdn NMyG SApp SCoo SPoG
	'Fragrant Bouquet' (v)	CMHG EGol ELan EMic EPGN GAbr IBal LAst LRHS LSRN MMuc NCGa NGdn NHol NLar NMyG SEND WPtf WWEG
	'Fragrant Dream'	EGol EMic EPfP IBal NLar WWEG
	'Fragrant Fire'	EMic IBal SApp
	'Fragrant Gold'	EGol EMic IBal
	'Fragrant King'	IBal
	'Fragrant Star'	EMic IBal SApp
	'Fragrant Surprise' (v)	IBal
	'Fran Godfrey'	EPGN IBal
	'Francee' (*fortunei*) (v) ♀H4	Widely available
§	'Frances Williams' (*sieboldiana*) (v) ♀H4	Widely available
	'Frances Williams Improved' (*sieboldiana*) (v)	EGol EPfP MWat
	'Fresh' (v)	EGol EPGN IBal SApp
	'Fried Bananas'	EGol EMic EWll SApp WWEG
	'Fried Green Tomatoes'	EGol EMic GBin NLar NMyG NNor SApp
	'Fringe Benefit' (v)	EGol GAbr GKir SApp WWEG
	'Frosted Dimples'	EMic IBal
	'Frosted Jade' (v)	EBee EGol EMic EPGN IBal NLar SApp SBfd SRGP WTin
	'Frosted June' **new**	IBal
	'Frosted Mouse Ears' **new**	EMic
	'Frozen Margarita'	EMic IBal
	'Frühlingsgold' (v)	IBal
	'Fujibotan' (v)	EGol EMic IBal SApp
	'Fulda'	EGol EMic
	'Gaiety' (v)	EGol EMic EPGN
	'Gaijin' (v)	EGol IBal SApp
	'Garden Party' (v)	IBal
	'Garden Treasure'	EGol
	'Garnet Prince'	EGol IBal
	'Gay Blade' (v)	EGol IBal SApp
	'Gay Feather' (v)	EMic IBal NMyG SApp
	'Gay Search' (v)	EPGN IBal
	'Geisha' (v)	EGol EPGN IBal LRHS MCCP NGdn NMyG NNor SApp WHal WWEG
	'Geisha Satin Ripples'	IBal
	'Gemini Moon' (v)	IBal
	'Gemstone'	IBal
	'Gene's Joy'	EPGN IBal
	'Ghost Spirit'	IBal SApp WFar
	'Ghostmaster' (v)	IBal LRHS
	'Gig Harbor' **new**	IBal
	'Gigantea' (*sieboldiana*)	see *H.* 'Elata'
	'Gilt by Association'	IBal
	'Gilt Edge' (*sieboldiana*) (v)	CWat EMic NMyG WWEG
	'Gingee'	IBal
	'Ginko Craig' (v)	Widely available
	'Ginrei'	IBal
	'Ginsu Knife' (v)	EMic IBal
	'Glass Hearts'	EMic IBal
	glauca	see *H. sieboldiana* var. *elegans*
	'Glitter'	EMic IBal
	'Glockenspiel'	EGol EMic
I	'Gloriosa' (*fortunei*) (v)	EGol IBal LRHS WFar
	'Glory'	EGol
	'Goddess of Athena' (*decorata*) (v)	EGol
	'Gold Drop' (*venusta* hybrid)	EGol EMic NHol WWEG
	'Gold Edger'	CBcs CMac CPrp EGol EHoe ELan EMic EPfP GKev GMaP IBal MLLN MRav NBir NGdn NHol NLar NMyG NNor NSti SApp WFar WTin WWEG
	'Gold Edger Surprise' (v)	EMic

'Gold Flush' (*ventricosa*)	EMic
§ 'Gold Haze' (*fortunei*)	EGol EMic EPGN IBal MHom NBir NCGa NHol NMyG WWEG
'Gold Leaf' (*fortunei*)	EGol
'Gold Regal'	EBee EGol EMic EPGN GBin IBal LRHS MHom NMyG SMrm WFar WMnd
'Gold Rush'	EMic NMyG
'Gold Standard' (*fortunei*) (v)	Widely available
'Goldbrook' (v)	EGol EMic IBal WTin
'Goldbrook Galleon'	EGol IBal
'Goldbrook Gayle' (v)	EGol
'Goldbrook Gaynor'	EGol IBal
'Goldbrook Genie'	EGol IBal
'Goldbrook Ghost' (v)	EGol
'Goldbrook Girl'	EGol IBal
'Goldbrook Glamour' (v)	EGol IBal
'Goldbrook Glimmer' (Tardiana Group) (v)	EGol IBal LRHS
'Goldbrook Glory' **new**	EGol EMic
'Goldbrook Gold'	EGol IBal
'Goldbrook Grace'	EGol
'Goldbrook Gratis' (v)	EGol IBal
'Goldbrook Grayling'	EGol EMic IBal
'Goldbrook Grebe'	EGol IBal
'Goldbrook Greenheart'	IBal
'Golden Age'	see *H.* 'Gold Haze'
'Golden Anniversary'	EGol IBal NHol
'Golden Bullion' (*tokudama*)	EGol
'Golden Fascination'	EGol
'Golden Fountain'	EMic
'Golden Friendship'	EGol
'Golden Gate'	EGol
'Golden Goal' **new**	IBal
'Golden Guernsey' (v)	EMic
'Golden Isle'	EGol EMic IBal
'Golden Meadows' PBR (*sieboldiana*)	EMic EPGN IBal MAvo NCob
'Golden Medallion' (*tokudama*)	CMHG EBrs EGol ELan IBal LRHS NEgg NGdn NHol NMyG WFar
'Golden Nakaiana'	see *H.* 'Birchwood Parky's Gold'
'Golden' (*nakaiana*)	see *H.* 'Birchwood Parky's Gold'
'Golden Oriole'	EGol EMic IBal NMyG NNor WWEG
'Golden Prayers' (*tokudama*)	ECtt EGol EHoe ELan EMic IBal MRav NBir NBro NEgg NGdn NHol NLar WFar WHal WSHC
'Golden Scepter'	EGol EMic EPGN IBal LRHS NHol NMyG NNor SApp WFar
'Golden Sculpture' (*sieboldiana*)	EGol EMic
'Golden Spider'	EGol EMic WWEG
'Golden Sunburst' (*sieboldiana*)	CPrp EGol ELan IBal NEgg NGdn NHol NLar WFar
'Golden Tiara' (v) ♀H4	Widely available
'Golden Tusk' **new**	IBal
'Golden Waffles'	CMHG EMic NEgg
'Goldsmith'	EGol SApp
'Gone Fishin'' (v)	IBal
'Goober'	IBal
'Good as Gold'	EMic EPGN IBal NMyG
'Gorgon'	IBal
'Gosan Leather Strap'	IBal
'Gosan' (*takahashii*)	EGol
gracillima	EPGN IBal NRya
'Granary Gold' (*fortunei*)	EGol EPGN
'Grand Canyon'	EMic SApp
'Grand Finale'	IBal
'Grand Forks'	IBal
'Grand Marquee' (v)	EMic GBin IBal NLar SApp WFar
'Grand Master'	EGol IBal MDKP SApp

'Grand Prize' (v)	IBal
'Grand Slam'	EGol
'Grand Tiara' (v)	EGol EMic EPGN IBal NMyG SApp
'Grand Total'	IBal
'Grant Park'	IBal
'Gray Cole' (*sieboldiana*)	EGol EMic IBal NMyG
'Great Arrival'	EMic IBal
'Great Escape' (v)	EMic IBal
'Great Expectations' (*sieboldiana*) (v)	Widely available
'Great Lakes Gold'	IBal
'Green Acres' (*montana*)	EMic IBal LEdu WFar
'Green Angel' (*sieboldiana*)	EGol
'Green Dwarf'	NWCA WFar
'Green Eyes' (*sieboldii*) (v)	EGol EMic IBal
'Green Fountain' (*kikutii*)	EGol EMic NMyG WWEG
'Green Gold' (*fortunei*) (v)	EMic
'Green Lama'	IBal
'Green Mouse Ears'	EMic IBal
'Green Piecrust'	EGol NNor
'Green Sheen'	EGol EMic EPGN NMyG
'Green Velveteen'	EGol
'Green with Envy' (v)	EGol EMic EPGN IBal NNor SApp
'Greensleeves' (v) **new**	IBal
'Grey Ghost'	EMic IBal
'Grey Piecrust'	EGol IBal
'Ground Cover Trompenburg'	SApp
'Ground Master' (v)	CMHG CMac EBee ECtt EGol ELan EPfP GCra GMaP IBal IFoB LPBA MRav MSwo NBro NGdn NHol NNor NSti SPer WFar WMoo WWEG
'Ground Sulphur'	EGol
'Grünherz'	IBal
'Grunspecht' (Tardiana Group)	IBal
'Guacamole' (v)	CBcs ECha EGol EMic EPGN EPfP GBin GMac IBal IPot LRHS NGdn NLar NMyG NNor NPnk SApp WAul WTin WWEG
'Guardian Angel' (*sieboldiana*)	EGol EMic EPGN IBal NLar
'Gum Drop'	EMic NNor
'Gun Metal Blue'	EGol IBal
'Gypsy Rose'	EMic EPGN EPfP IBal NMyG SApp WFar
'Hacksaw' **new**	EMic IBal
'Hadspen Blue' (Tardiana Group)	Widely available
'Hadspen Hawk' (Tardiana Group)	EGol IBal NMyG SApp
'Hadspen Heron' (Tardiana Group)	EGol IBal MHom MWat NMyG WCot
'Hadspen Nymphaea'	EGol IBal
'Hadspen Rainbow'	IBal
'Hadspen Samphire'	EGol EMic EPGN MHom NBir NMyG
'Hadspen White' (*fortunei*)	EMic IBal NLar
'Haku-chu-han' (*sieboldii*) (v)	IBal
'Hakujima' (*sieboldii*)	EGol IBal
'Hakumuo' (v) **new**	IBal
§ 'Halcyon' (Tardiana Group) ♀H4	Widely available
'Halo'	EGol
'Hampshire County' (v)	EMic IBal
'Hanky Panky' (v)	EMic EPGN IBal NMyG NSti
'Happily Ever After' (v) **new**	IBal
'Happiness' (Tardiana Group)	EGol EHoe EMic MHom MRav NMyG
'Happy Camper' (v)	IBal
'Happy Hearts'	EGol EMic

'Happy Valley' (v)	IBal
'Harlequin'	SApp
'Harmony' (Tardiana Group)	EGol EMic
'Harpoon' (v)	EMic IBal
'Harriette Ward'	IBal
'Harry van de Laar'	EMic IBal SApp
'Harry van Trier'	EMic GBin
'Hart's Tongue'	IBal
'Harvest Dawn'	IBal
'Harvest Glow'	EGol
'Harvest Moon'	GKir
'Hawkeye' (v)	IBal
'Hazel'	EMic IBal
'Heart Ache'	EGol
'Heart and Soul' (v)	EGol EMic IBal SApp
'Heart Broken'	IBal
'Heart of Chan'	IBal
'Heart Throb' **new**	EMic
'Heartbeat' (v)	IBal
'Heartleaf'	EMic
'Heart's Content' (v)	EGol IBal
'Heartsong' (v)	EGol EMic NMyG
'Heat Wave' (v)	EMic EPGN IBal SApp
'Heavenly Beginnings' (v)	IBal
'Heavenly Tiara' (v)	IBal
'Heideturm'	EGol
'Helen Doriot' (*sieboldiana*)	EGol EMic
'Helen Field Fischer' (*fortunei*)	CPrp IBal
helonioides misapplied f. ***albopicta***	see *H. rohdeifolia*
'Herifu' (v)	EGol EMic
'Herkules'	EMic IBal
'Hertha' (v)	EMic
'Hidden Cove' (v)	EGol IBal
'High Kicker'	EGol IBal NMyG
'High Society' (v)	CBcs EMic EPGN EPfP GBin IBal MHom MNrw NGdn NMyG SApp WClo
'High Tide'	IBal
'Hi-ho Silver' (v)	EMic EPGN IBal
'Hilda Wassman' (v)	EGol
'Hillbilly Blues' (v)	IBal
'Hippodrome' (v)	IBal
'Hirao Elite'	IBal
'Hirao Majesty'	EGol
'Hirao Splendor'	EGol NMyG
'Hirao Supreme'	EGol EMic
'His Honor' (v)	IBal
'Holly's Honey'	EGol
'Hollywood Lights' (v)	EMic IBal
'Holstein'	see *H.* 'Halcyon'
'Holy Molé' (v)	IBal
'Holy Mouse Ears' **new**	EMic
'Honey Moon'	EGol NNor
'Honeybells' ♀H4	CBcs CMHG CMac CTri EBee ECha EGol ELan EMic EPGN EPfP GBin LHop LPBA LRHS MCot MRav NBid NCob NGdn NHol NMyG NNor NSti SApp SPer WClo WFar WPtf WWEG
'Honeysong' (v)	EBee EGol EMic EPGN NMyG NNor
'Hoosier Dome'	EMic
'Hoosier Harmony' (v)	EGol EMic
'Hoosier Homecoming'	SApp
'Hope' (v)	EGol IBal SApp
'Hotcakes' **new**	IBal
'Hotspur' (v)	EGol EMic IBal SApp
'Hush Puppie'	EMic IBal
'Hyacintha Variegata' (*fortunei*) (v)	CMHG CMac NNor

'Hydon Gleam'	EGol EMic IBal
'Hydon Sunset' (*nakaiana*)	CMHG CMMP CMea ECtt EGol EMic EPGN GCra GKir IBal NBir NHol NMyG NRya NSti NWCA SApp SBch SGSe WHal WMnd WPtf WTin WWEG
hypoleuca	EGol EMic
'Hyuga Urajiro' (v)	EMic IBal SApp
'Ice Age Trail' (v)	IBal
'Ice Cream' (*cathayana*) (v)	EGol
'Iced Lemon' (v)	EMic IBal
'Illicit Affair'	EGol EMic IBal SApp
'Ilona' (v)	EGol
'Imp' (v)	EMic IBal
§ 'Inaho'	EGol LRHS
'Inca Gold'	EGol IBal
'Independence' (v)	EBee EMic EPGN IBal NBro NMyG SApp WFar
'Indigo'	IBal
'Innisjade'	IBal
'Inniswood' (v)	ECtt EGol EMic EPGN EPfP IBal IPot MBNS NBro NGdn NLar NSti SApp SPoG WFar WMnd WWEG
'Invincible'	EBee EGol EMic GBin IBal LAst NBid NEgg NGdn NLar NMyG NNor SApp SPoG WPtf WTin WWEG
'Iona' (*fortunei*)	EGol EMic EPGN NMyG NNor
'Irische See' (Tardiana Group)	EGol
'Irish Eyes' (v)	IBal
'Iron Gate Delight' (v)	NNor
'Iron Gate Glamour' (v)	EGol IBal
'Iron Gate Special' (v)	EMic
'Iron Gate Supreme' (v)	EMic
'Island Charm' (v)	EBrs EGol EMic EPGN IBal MBNS NLar NMyG SApp
'Island Forest Gem'	IBal
'Itsy Bitsy Spider'	IBal
'Ivory Necklace' (v)	IBal
'Iwa Soules'	EGol
'Jack of Diamonds'	IBal
'Jade Cascade'	CFir EGol ELan EMic GBin IBal NBir NEgg NHol NLar SApp SMrm WWEG
'Jade Scepter' (*nakaiana*)	EGol EMic
'Jadette' (v)	EGol GBin
'Janet Day' (v)	EMic SApp
'Janet' (*fortunei*) (v)	EBee EGol EMic GMaP IBal NGdn NNor
'Janet's Green Sox'	IBal
'Japan Girl'	see *H.* 'Mount Royal'
'Jaz'	IBal
'Jerry Landwehr'	IBal
'Jester'	SApp
'Jewel of the Nile' (v)	EMic IBal SApp
'Jim Mathews'	IBal
'Jimmy Crack Corn'	EBrs EGol EMic IBal LRHS SApp
'Jingle Bells'	IBal
'John Wargo'	EGol
'Joker' (*fortunei*) (v)	NNor
'Jolly Green Giant' (*sieboldiana* hybrid)	EMic
'Joseph'	EGol EMic IBal
'Josephine' (v)	NNor
'Journeyman'	EGol EMic IBal LRHS
'Journey's End' (v)	EMic IBal SApp
'Joyce Trott' (v)	EMic IBal
'Joyful' (v)	IBal
'Jubilee' (v) **new**	IBal
'Judy Rocco'	IBal
'Juha' (v)	EMic IBal SApp

	'Julia' (v)	EGol EMic IBal
	'Julie Morss'	EGol EMic EPGN GMaP IBal MHom MWat NEgg NMyG SApp WWEG
	'Jumbo' (*sieboldiana*)	EMic
	'June'PBR (Tardiana Group) (v) ♀H4	Widely available
	'June Beauty' (*sieboldiana*)	NWsh
	'June Fever'PBR (Tardiana Group)	EMic ESwi GBin GKir IBal LLWG NBro NLar NMoo SApp SMrm SPoG
	'Jurassic Park'	EMic IBal
	'Just So' (v)	EGol EMic IBal
	'Kabitan'	see *H. sieboldii* var. *sieboldii* f. *kabitan*
	'Kabuki'	IBal
	'Kalamazoo' (v)	EMic IBal
	'Karin'	EGol EMic
	'Katherine Lewis' (Tardiana Group) (v)	ECtt EMic IBal LSRN NHol NMyG
	'Kath's Gold'	EMic
	'Katie Q' (v)	EMic IBal
	'Katsuragawa-beni' (v)	EMic IBal
	'Kelsey'	EGol EMic
	'Key Lime Pie'	EMic IBal SApp
	'Ki Nakafu Otome' (*venusta*)	IBal
§	'Kifukurin Hyuga' (v)	IBal
	'Kifukurin' (*kikutii*)	see *H.* 'Kifukurin Hyuga'
	'Kifukurin Ko Mame' (*gracillima*) (v)	EMic
	'Kifukurin' (*pulchella*) (v)	EGol
	'Kifukurin Ubatake' (*pulchella*) (v)	EGol EPGN IBal
	'Kifukurin' (*venusta*) (v) **new**	EMic
	kikutii	EGol EMic IMou NWCA WTin
§	- var. ***caput-avis***	EGol EMic
	- var. ***kikutii*** f. ***leuconota***	SApp
	- var. ***polyneuron***	EGol SApp
	- var. ***pruinosa***	SApp
§	- var. ***yakusimensis***	CPBP EGol EMic GBin GKir IBal SMad
	'Kinbotan' (v)	EGol EMic IBal
	'King James'	IBal
	'King of Spades'	IBal
	'King Tut'	EMic
	'Kingfisher' (Tardiana Group)	EGol IBal
§	'Kirishima'	EMic
	'Kisuji'	see *H.* 'Mediopicta'
	'Kitty Cat'	EMic EPGN IBal SApp
	'Kiwi Black Magic'	EGol IBal
	'Kiwi Blue Baby'	EGol IBal
	'Kiwi Blue Ruffles'	IBal
	'Kiwi Blue Sky'	IBal
	'Kiwi Canoe'	IBal
	'Kiwi Cream Edge' (v)	EMic
	'Kiwi Fruit'	SApp
	'Kiwi Full Monty' (v)	IBal
	'Kiwi Gold Rush'	IBal
	'Kiwi Hippo'	EGol IBal
	'Kiwi Jordan'	IBal
	'Kiwi Kaniere Gold'	IBal
	'Kiwi Minnie Gold'	IBal
	'Kiwi Parasol'	IBal
	'Kiwi Skyscraper'	IBal
	'Kiwi Spearmint'	IBal
	'Kiwi Sunlover'	IBal
	'Kiwi Sunshine'	IBal
	'Kiwi Treasure Trove'	IBal
	kiyosumiensis	NMyG
	'Klopping Variegated' (v)	EGol EMic
	'Knight's Journey'	IBal

	'Knockout' (v)	EGol IBal MBNS MNrw MRav NBPC NBro NEgg NGdn NLar NMyG NNor SApp
	'Komodo Dragon'	EMic IBal SKHP WTin
	'Kong'	IBal
	'Konkubine' **new**	EMic
	'Korean Snow'	IBal
I	'Koreana Variegated' (*undulata*)	EMic
	'Koriyama' (*sieboldiana*) (v)	EMic IBal
	'Krossa Cream Edge' (*sieboldii*) (v)	IBal
	'Krossa Regal' ♀H4	Widely available
	'Krugerrand'	IBal
	'Lacy Belle' (v)	CSBt EGol EMic IBal NBro NGdn NMyG SBfd SPoG
	'Lady Godiva'	IBal
	'Lady Guineverre'	EMic IBal
	'Lady Helen'	EMic
	'Lady Isobel Barnett' (v)	EMic IBal NMyG SApp
	laevigata	EGol SApp
	'Lake Hitchock'	EGol IBal
	'Lakeside Accolade'	EGol IBal NMyG
	'Lakeside April Snow' (v)	EMic
	'Lakeside Baby Face' (v)	IBal
	'Lakeside Beach Captain' (v)	EMic IBal
	'Lakeside Black Satin'	EMic IBal LRHS SApp
	'Lakeside Blue Cherub'	EMic IBal
	'Lakeside Butter Ball'	IBal SApp
	'Lakeside Cha Cha' (v)	EGol EMic
	'Lakeside Cindy Cee' (v)	IBal
	'Lakeside Coal Miner'	EMic IBal
	'Lakeside Contender'	IBal
	'Lakeside Cranberry Relish' (v)	IBal
	'Lakeside Cricket' (v)	IBal
	'Lakeside Cupcake' (v)	EMic IBal
	'Lakeside Dividing Line' (v)	IBal
	'Lakeside Down Sized' (v)	EMic IBal
	'Lakeside Dragonfly' (v)	EMic EPfP IBal MAvo
	'Lakeside Elfin Fire'	EMic IBal
	'Lakeside Feather Light' (v)	IBal
	'Lakeside Hoola Hoop' (v)	IBal
	'Lakeside Iron Man'	IBal
	'Lakeside Kaleidoscope'	EGol EMic IBal
	'Lakeside Legal Tender'	IBal
	'Lakeside Lime Time'	IBal
	'Lakeside Little Gem'	IBal
	'Lakeside Little Tuft' (v)	IBal
	'Lakeside Lollipop'	EGol EMic EPGN IBal SApp
	'Lakeside Looking Glass'	EMic IBal NMyG
	'Lakeside Love Affaire'	EGol EMic IBal
	'Lakeside Maestro' **new**	NLar
	'Lakeside Meadow Ice' (v)	IBal
	'Lakeside Meter Maid' (v)	IBal
	'Lakeside Miss Muffett' (v)	IBal
	'Lakeside Missy Little' (v)	IBal
	'Lakeside Neat Petite'	EGol IBal
	'Lakeside Ninita' (v)	EGol EMic EPGN IBal NMyG
	'Lakeside Old Smokey' **new**	IBal
	'Lakeside Party Dress'	IBal
	'Lakeside Premier'	EGol EMic IBal
	'Lakeside Prophecy'	IBal
	'Lakeside Rhapsody' (v)	EMic IBal
	'Lakeside Ring Master' (v)	IBal
	'Lakeside Ripples'	IBal
	'Lakeside Rocky Top' (v)	IBal
	'Lakeside Roy El' (v)	IBal
	'Lakeside Shadows' (v)	IBal
	'Lakeside Shockwave' (v)	IBal

'Lakeside Shoremaster' (v)	EMic IBal
'Lakeside Sir Logan'	IBal
'Lakeside Sparkle Plenty' (v)	IBal
'Lakeside Spellbinder' (v)	IBal
'Lakeside Spruce Goose' (v)	IBal
'Lakeside Symphony' (v)	EGol EMic
'Lakeside Tycoon'	IBal
'Lakeside Zinger' (v)	EMic IBal
lancifolia ♀^{H4}	CMHG CMac EBee ECha EGol EHrv ELan EMic GMaP MRav NGdn NHol NMyG NSti SApp SGSe SRms WAul WGwG WKif WSHC WTin
'Last Dance' (v)	IBal
'Laura Z' **new**	IBal
'Lavender Doll'	IBal
'Lavender Lace'	IBal
'Leading Lady'	IBal
'Leather Sheen'	EGol EMic IBal
'Leatherneck'	IBal
'Lederhosen'	EMic IBal
'Lee Armiger' (*tokudama* hybrid)	EGol
'Lemon Delight'	EGol EMic EPGN IBal NMyG
'Lemon Frost'	IBal
'Lemon Lime'	EGol EMic GBin IBal MHom MNrw NMyG WPat WTin WWEG
'Lemonade'	GBin
'Leola Fraim' (v)	EGol EMic IBal LRHS NMyG
'Let Me Entertain You'	EMic
'Leviathan'	EMic
'Libby'	IBal
'Liberty'^{PBR} (v)	CBcs CWGN EGol EMic GBin IBal LRHS NBro NGdn NMyG NNor SApp WFar
'Li'l Abner' (v)	IBal
* ***lilacina***	WFar
'Lily Pad'	EPGN IBal
'Lime Fizz'	EMic IBal SApp
'Lime Piecrust'	EGol
'Lime Shag' (*sieboldii* f. *spathulata*)	EGol
'Limey Lisa'	EGol EMic EPGN IBal NMyG
'Linda Sue' (v)	IBal
'Little Aurora' (*tokudama* hybrid)	EGol EMic IBal WWEG
'Little Black Scape'	EGol EMic EPGN EWTr GBin IBal LSRN MHom NCob NEgg NGdn NHol NLar NMyG
'Little Blue' (*ventricosa*)	EGol EMic
'Little Bo Beep' (v)	EGol
'Little Boy'	IBal
'Little Caesar' (v)	EGol EMic EPGN IBal
'Little Doll' (v)	EGol
'Little Jay' (v)	EMic IBal SApp
'Little Miss Magic'	IBal
'Little Razor'	EGol
'Little Red Joy'	EMic IBal
'Little Red Rooster'	EMic EPGN IBal NGdn NMyG WWEG
'Little Stiffy'	EMic SApp
'Little Sunspot' (v)	EGol EMic IBal
'Little Town Flirt' (v)	IBal
'Little White Lines' (v)	EGol EMic EPGN IBal
'Little Wonder' (v)	EGol EMic EPGN IBal
'Lizard Lick'	IBal
'Lochness Monster' (v)	EMic
'Lollapalooza' (v)	IBal
'London Fog' (v)	IBal
'Lonesome Dove' (v)	EMic IBal
longipes	EGol SApp
- B&SWJ 10806	WCru
longissima	CMHG WCru
'Lothar the Giant' **new**	IBal
'Love Pat' ♀^{H4}	CFir EBee EGol EMic EPGN EPfP GAbr GBin GKev IBal LSRN MRav NGdn NLar NMyG NNor SApp WCAu
'Lovely Loretta'	IBal
'Loyalist'^{PBR} (v)	EBrs EMic LRHS NLar SApp WFar WWEG
'Lucy Vitols' (v)	EGol EMic IBal
'Lullabye'	EMic
'Lunar Eclipse' (v)	CHid EGol EMic NEgg SApp WWEG
'Machete'	IBal
'Mack the Knife'	IBal
'Maekawa'	EGol EMic
'Magic Fire'^{PBR} (v)	EMic EPGN EPfP IBal MNrw
'Majesty'	EGol EMic IBal NGdn WClo
'Mama Mia' (v)	CWat EGol EMic EPGN EQua IBal MBNS MMuc NBro NGdn NHol NMyG SBfd SRGP
'Manhattan'	EMic
'Maraschino Cherry'	EGol EMic EWTr GBin IBal NEgg NMyG SApp
'Marble Rim' (v)	EGol
'Mardi Gras' (v)	EMic SApp
'Marge' (*sieboldiana* hybrid)	EMic
'Margin of Error' (v)	EGol EPGN IBal NMyG
'Marginata Alba' misapplied	see *H.* 'Albomarginata' (*fortunei*), *H. crispula*
'Marginata Alba' ambig. (v)	ECha GKir LPBA NNor
'Marilyn'	EGol EMic
'Marilyn Monroe'	EMic IBal
'Marmalade on Toast' **new**	EMic
'Marquis' (*nakaiana* hybrid)	EGol
'Maruba' (*longipes* var. *latifolia*)	EGol
'Mary Joe'	EMic IBal
'Mary Marie Ann' (*fortunei*) (v)	EGol EMic EPGN IBal NMyG
'Masquerade' (v)	EGol EMic EPGN IBal NHar NWCA SApp SMHy WFar WHal WThu
'Maui Buttercups'	IBal SApp
'May'	EMic IBal
'Maya' (*fortunei*) (v)	IBal
§ 'Mediopicta' (*sieboldii*)	EMic
'Mediovariegata' (*undulata*)	see *H. undulata* var. *undulata*
'Medusa' (v)	EGol EMic IBal
'Memories of Dorothy'	EMic IBal
'Mentor Gold'	EGol
'Merlin' (v)	IBal
'Mesa Fringe' (*montana*)	EMic
'Mid Afternoon'	IBal
'Midas Touch'	EGol GBin NEgg NHol NLar NNor
'Middle Ridge'	EMic
'Midnight Ride'	IBal
'Midwest Gold'	MHom SApp
'Midwest Magic' (v)	EGol EMic IBal NLar SApp
'Mieke' (v)	IBal
'Mikawa-no-yuki'	EGol IBal
'Miki'	IBal
'Mildred Seaver' (v)	EGol EMic GAbr IBal LRHS NMyG
'Millennium'	EMic SApp
'Millie's Memoirs' (v)	EGol IBal
'Ming Jade'	SApp
'Ming Treasure' (v)	IBal
'Minnie Bell' (v)	EGol IBal
'Minnie Klopping'	EMic
minor f. ***alba*** misapplied	see *H. sieboldii* var. *alba*
§ ***minor*** Maekawa	EBee EGol EPGN EWTr GEdr GGar GKir ITim MTho NHol NMyG WCot WFar

	– B&SWJ 1209 from Korea	WCru
	– from Korea	EGol IBal
	– Goldbrook form	EGol IBal
	'Minor' (*ventricosa*)	see *H. minor* Maekawa
	'Mint Candy'	IBal
	'Mint Julep' (v)	IBal
	'Minuet' (v)	IBal
	'Minuteman' (*fortunei*) (v)	CFir ECtt EMic EPGN EPfP IBal IPot LAst MBNS MMuc NBPC NGdn NLar NNor NPnk SApp SBfd SEND SPoG WClo WFar WGor WTin WWEG
	'Miss Ruby' **new**	EMic IBal
	'Miss Saigon' (v)	IBal
	'Miss Tokyo' (v)	EMic IBal
	'Mississippi Delta'	EMic
	'Mister Watson'	EMic IBal SApp
	'Misty Waters' (*sieboldiana*)	EMic
	'Moerheim' (*fortunei*) (v)	EBee EGol EMic EPGN GBee IBal NHol WHal WWEG
	'Mohegan' **new**	EMic
N	***montana***	EGol EMic GBin NHol WBrE
	– B&SWJ 4796	WCru
	– B&SWJ 5585	WCru
	– 'Kinkaku'	EPGN
	– f. ***macrophylla***	EGol IBal
	'Moon Glow' (v)	EGol EMic
	'Moon River' (v)	EGol EMic EPGN NMyG SApp
	'Moon Shadow' (v)	EGol
	'Moon Waves'	EGol
	'Moonbeam'	EShb
	'Moonlight' (*fortunei*) (v)	EGol EMic EPGN GMaP IBal LRHS NMyG SApp
	'Moonlight Sonata'	EGol EMic
	'Moonstruck'[PBR] (v)	ECtt EGol EMic EPGN IBal
	'Moorheim'	LRHS
	'Morning Light'[PBR]	EBee EGol EMic EPGN EPfP IBal MAvo MBNS MBri MNHC NBro NGdn NLar NMoo NMyG NPnk SApp SRkn WBor WClo WCra
	'Moscow Blue'	EGol EMic
	'Mount Everest'	EMic IBal
	'Mount Fuji' (*montana*)	EGol IBal
	'Mount Hope' (v)	EGol
	'Mount Kirishima' (*sieboldii*)	see *H.* 'Kirishima'
§	'Mount Royal' (*sieboldii*)	NHol
	'Mount Tom' (v)	EGol EMic IBal
	'Mountain Fog' (v)	IBal
	'Mountain Snow' (*montana*) (v)	CWat EGol NMyG SApp
	'Mountain Sunrise' (*montana*)	EGol
	'Mourning Dove' (v)	EMic IBal
	'Mr Big'	IBal
	'Mrs Minky'	EMic EPGN
	'Muffie' (v)	EMic IBal
	'Munchkin' (*sieboldii*)	WPat
	'My Claire' (v)	IBal
	'My Cup of Tea' **new**	IBal
	'My Friend Nancy' (v)	EGol
	'Mystic Star' **new**	IBal
	'Naegato'	SApp
	nakaiana	EBee EMic
	'Nakaimo'	NHol
	'Nameoki'	NHol
	'Nana' (*ventricosa*)	see *H. minor* Maekawa
	'Nancy'	EMic IBal
§	'Nancy Lindsay' (*fortunei*)	CTri EGol EMic NGdn NLar SApp
	'Nancy Minks'	EMic IBal
	'Neat and Tidy'	IBal
	'Neat Splash' (v)	CWCL NBir NHol WWEG

'Nemesis' (v) **new**	IBal
'New Wave'	EGol
'Niagara Falls'	CFir EGol EMic IBal NGdn
'Nicola'	EGol EMic EPGN IBal MHom NMyG
'Night before Christmas' (v)	CFir CHid CMMP CWGN EBee EGol EMic EPGN IPot LPBA LRHS MNrw NBro NCGa NEgg NGdn NHol NMyG NNor NPnk SApp SPad WCAu WHoo WWEG
'Night Life'	EMic IBal
nigrescens	EBee EGol EMic EPGN LRHS NMyG WBVN
– 'Cally White'	GCal IBal NCGa
'Nokogiryama'	EMic
'None Lovelier' (v)	EMic IBal
'Nor'easter' (v) **new**	IBal
'North Hills' (*fortunei*) (v)	CMoH EAEE EBee EGol EMic IBal LRHS NBir NCob NGdn NMyG SWvt WCAu WWEG
'Northern Exposure' (*sieboldiana*) (v)	CFir EGol EMic IBal MAvo NGdn NMyG SApp WClo
'Northern Halo' (*sieboldiana*) (v)	EGol EMic NMyG
'Northern Lights' (*sieboldiana*)	EGol
'Northern Sunray' (*sieboldiana*) (v)	IBal
'Nougat' (v)	IBal
'Nouzang'	IBal
'Nutty Professor' (v)	IBal
'Obscura Marginata' (*fortunei*)	see *H. fortunei* var. *aureomarginata*
'Obsession'	EGol IBal
'Ocean Isle' (v)	IBal
'Oder'	IBal
'O'Harra'	EGol EMic
'Old Faithful'	EGol EMic
'Old Glory'[PBR] (v)	EGol EMic IBal
'Olga's Shiny Leaf'	EGol EMic
'Olive Bailey Langdon' (*sieboldiana*) (v)	EMic IBal SApp
'Olive Branch' (v)	EGol EMic IBal
'Olympic Edger'	EMic IBal
'Olympic Glacier' (v)	EMic IBal SApp
'Olympic Gold Medal' **new**	IBal
'Olympic Silver Medal' **new**	EMic IBal
'Olympic Sunrise' (v)	EMic IBal
'On Stage'	see *H.* 'Choko Nishiki'
'On the Border' (v)	IBal
'One Man's Treasure'	EMic EPGN GBin IBal MLLN NMyG SApp
'Ooh La La' (v)	IBal
'Ophir'	EMic IBal
'Ops' (v)	IBal
'Orange Crush' (v)	IBal SApp
'Orange Marmalade' (v)	EMic EPGN IBal LLWG NMyG SApp SBfd
'Orange Slices'	IBal
'Oriana' (*fortunei*)	EGol IBal
'Orion's Belt' (v) **new**	IBal
'Osprey' (Tardiana Group)	EGol
'Oxheart'	EMic
pachyscapa	EMic
'Pacific Blue Edger'	CFir CMMP EGol EMic MMuc NGdn NPri SApp SEND WAul WWEG
'Pamela Lee' (v)	EMic IBal
'Pandora's Box' (v)	EGol EPGN GBin GEdr IBal NHar SApp WCot
'Paradigm' (v)	EBee EGol EMic EPGN IBal LRHS NMyG SApp
'Paradise Backstage' (v)	EMic IBal

'Paradise Beach'	EMic IBal
'Paradise Expectations' (*sieboldiana*) (v)	EMic IBal SApp
'Paradise Glory'	EMic IBal
'Paradise Gold Line' (*ventricosa*) (v)	IBal
'Paradise Island' (v)	EMic IBal SApp
'Paradise Joyce'^{PBR}	EGol EMic EPGN IBal LRHS NLar NMyG NNor SApp WWEG
'Paradise Ocean' **new**	EMic
'Paradise on Fire' (v)	EMic IBal SApp
'Paradise Parade' (v) **new**	IBal
'Paradise Passion' (v)	IBal
'Paradise Power'^{PBR}	EGol EMic
'Paradise Puppet' (*venusta*)	EMic EPGN IBal SApp
'Paradise Red Delight' (*pycnophylla*)	EMic IBal
'Paradise Sandstorm' **new**	IBal
'Paradise Standard' (d)	EMic IBal
'Paradise Sunset'	EGol EMic IBal
'Paradise Sunshine' **new**	EMic
'Paradise Surprise' (v) **new**	IBal
'Parhelion' **new**	EMic
'Pastures Green'	EGol IBal
'Pastures New'	EGol EMic EQua MHom NHol NMyG SApp
'Pathfinder' (v)	EGol EMic IBal SApp
'Patricia'	EMic
'Patrician' (v)	EGol EMic EPGN IBal NMyG
'Patriot' (v)	Widely available
'Patriot's Fire' (v)	IBal
'Patriot's Green Pride'	IBal
'Paul Revere' (v)	IBal
'Paul's Glory' (v)	EGol EMic EPGN EQua GAbr GBin GMaP IBal LPBA LRHS MBri NBir NGdn NMyG NNor SApp WFar WWEG
'Peace' (v)	EGol EMic EPGN IBal
'Peacock Strut'	IBal
'Peanut'	EMic IBal
'Pearl Lake'	EBee EGol EMic EPGN GBin IBal MHom MWat NBir NCob NEgg NGdn NHol NLar NMyG NNor SApp SMrm SRGP WTin
'Peedee Absinth'	EMic
'Peedee Gold Flash' (v)	NMyG
'Peedee Laughing River' (v)	IBal
'Pelham Blue Tump'	EGol EMic
'Peppermint Cream' (*cathayana*)	IBal
'Peppermint Ice' (v)	EGol IBal
'Percy'	EMic IBal
'Permanent Wave'	EGol
'Perry's True Blue'	EMic
'Peter Pan'	EGol EMic IBal
'Peter the Rock'	IBal
'Pete's Dark Satellite'	EMic IBal
'Pewterware'	EMic IBal
'Phantom'	IBal SApp
'Philadelphia'	IBal
'Phoenix'	EGol EMic NLar SApp
'Photo Finish' (v)	EGol EMic
'Phyllis Campbell' (*fortunei*)	see *H.* 'Sharmon'
'Picta' (*fortunei*)	see *H. fortunei* var. *albopicta*
'Piecrust Power'	EGol
'Piedmont Gold'	CHid EBrs EGol EMic EPGN IBal LRHS NBPC SApp WPtf
'Pilgrim' (v)	EBee EBrs EGol ELan EMic EPGN IBal LRHS NBPC NBro NMyG SApp WFar
'Pineapple Poll'	EGol EMic EPGN NMyG NNor WTin WWEG
'Pineapple Upside Down Cake' (v)	EMic EPGN IBal NBro NLar NMyG WCot WFar
'Pinky'	IBal
'Pinwheel' (v)	IBal
'Pizzazz' (v)	EGol EMic IBal LRHS MHom NGdn NHol NLar NMyG SApp WFar WHil WWEG
plantaginea	EGol EMic IBal LEdu LPla LRHS MHom NMyG SSpi WCru WFar WKif WSpi
- var. ***grandiflora***	see *H. plantaginea* var. *japonica*
§ - var. ***japonica*** 🏆^{H4}	CBot CDes ECha EHrv EPGN IBal MRav NLar SApp SGSe SMrm WCFE WFar WPGP WWEG
'Platinum Tiara' (v)	EGol EMic IBal NBir NMyG
'Plug Nickel'	EMic IBal
'Polar Moon' (v)	IBal
'Pooh Bear' (v)	EGol
'Popcorn'	EMic IBal SApp
'Popo'	EGol EMic EPGN IBal SApp
'Porky's Prize' (v)	EGol
'Potomac Pride'	EGol EMic EPGN NMyG SApp
'Powder Blue' (v)	IBal
'Powderpuff'	IBal
'Prairie Glow'	IBal
'Prairie Sky'	CWGN EMic IBal
'Praying Hands' (v)	EGol EMic EPGN EPfP GBin IBal IPot MBNS NMyG WWEG
'Pretty Flamingo'	EMic IBal
'Primavera Primrose'	SApp
'Prince of Wales'	EMic IBal LRHS LSqu SApp SPoG SRkn
'Princess Anastasia' (v) **new**	IBal
'Puck'	EGol
'Punky' (v)	IBal
'Purple Boots'	EMic IBal
'Purple Dwarf'	EGol EMic NGdn NHol NLar WHal
'Purple Glory'	EMic
'Purple Haze' **new**	IBal
'Purple Lady Finger'	WWEG
'Purple Passion'	EGol EMic
'Purple Profusion'	EGol EMic
pycnophylla	EGol
'Quarter Note' (v)	IBal
'Queen Josephine' (v)	EGol EMic EPGN IBal IPot LRHS MBNS MBri MHom MMuc NCGa NGdn NMyG SApp SBfd SEND SRGP WFar
'Queen of the Seas'	EMic IBal SApp
'Quill'	EMic
'Quilting Bee'	EGol EMic
'Radiant Edger' (v)	EGol EMic EPGN GCra IBal NHol SBfd WWEG
'Radio Waves'	EMic IBal
'Rain Forest'	EMic IBal
'Rainbow's End' (v)	EMic IBal
'Rainforest Sunrise' (v)	EMic IBal LLWG SApp
'Raleigh Remembrance'	EGol
'Rascal' (v)	EGol EMic
'Raspberries and Cream' (v)	IBal
'Raspberry Sorbet'	EGol EMic EPGN IBal
rectifolia	NHol NNor
- 'Kinbuchi Tachi' (v)	IBal
- 'Ogon Tachi' (v)	EMic IBal
'Red Cadet'	EMic IBal
'Red Dragon'	IBal
'Red Hot Flash' (v)	IBal
'Red Hot Poker' **new**	IBal
'Red Neck Heaven' (*kikutii* var. *caput-avis*)	EGol IBal SApp WTin
'Red October'	EBee EBrs EGol EMic EPGN EPfP GAbr GBin GKir IBal LRHS LSou

		MBNS MBri NGdn NLar NMoo NMyG NPnk SPoG WCAu WCot WFar WFut WWEG
	'Red Salamander'	EGol EMic IBal
	'Red Stepper'	IBal
	'Regal Chameleon'	IBal
	'Regal Rhubarb'	EGol IBal
	'Regal Splendor' (v)	EGol EMic EPGN GBin IBal LRHS MHom NBro NCGa NGdn NHol NMyG SApp WAul WHoo WMnd
	'Reginald Kaye'	EMic
	'Remember Me' PBR	CWCL CWGN EBrs EDAr EGol ELan ELon EMic EPGN IBal LLWG LRHS LSRN MBNS MCCP NCob NGdn NHol NLar NMyG NNor SApp SMrm WFar WGor WWEG
	'Reptilian'	EGol EMic
	'Resonance' (v)	GBee GKir NGdn NLar
	'Restless Sea'	EMic IBal
	'Reversed' (*sieboldiana*) (v)	EBee EGol ELan EMic EPGN LRHS MDKP MGos NBro NGdn NNor NWsh WHal
	'Revolution' PBR (v)	CWGN EBee EBrs EGol EMic EPGN GKev GKir IBal IPot LRHS LSRN MBri MMuc NBPC NBro NCob NEgg NGdn NHol NLar NMyG SApp WAul WFar WWEG
	'Rhapsody' (*fortunei*) (v)	EGol EMic
	'Rhapsody in Blue'	EGol
	'Rheingold' (v)	IBal
	'Rhythm and Blues'	IBal
	'Rich Uncle'	IBal
	'Richland Gold' (*fortunei*)	EGol EMic EPGN NMyG
	'Rickrack'	IBal
	'Rim Rock'	EMic
	'Rippled Honey'	EGol EMic EPGN IBal NCob NMyG SApp
	'Rippling Waves'	EGol EMic
	'Risa' **new**	IBal
	'Rise and Shine' (v)	EGol
	'Rising Sun'	EGol
	'Risky Business' (v)	IBal
	'Robert Frost' (v)	EGol EMic IBal WTin
	'Robin Hood'	EMic IBal SApp
	'Robusta' (*fortunei*)	see *H. sieboldiana* var. *elegans*
	'Robyn's Choice' (v)	EMic
	'Rock Island Line' (v)	IBal
	'Rock Princess'	IBal
§	***rohdeifolia*** (v)	LRHS
	- f. ***albopicta***	EGol ELan NHol
	'Roller Coaster Ride'	IBal
	'Ron Damant'	EPGN IBal
	'Rootin'-Tootin'' (v) **new**	IBal
	'Rosedale Golden Goose'	IBal
	'Rosedale Knox'	IBal
	'Rosedale Lost Dutchman' **new**	IBal SApp
	'Rosedale Melody of Summer' (v)	IBal
	'Rosedale Misty Magic' (v)	IBal
	'Rosedale Richie Valens'	IBal
	'Rosemoor'	EGol IBal
	'Rotunda'	EGol
	'Rough Waters'	SApp
	'Roxsanne'	EMic
	'Roy Klehm' (v) **new**	IBal
	'Royal Charm' **new**	IBal
	'Royal Flush' (v)	IBal
	'Royal Golden Jubilee'	EMic EPGN IBal NMyG
§	'Royal Standard' ♀H4	Widely available
	'Royal Super' **new**	EPGN
	'Royal Tapestry' (v)	IBal

	'Royal Tiara' (*nakaiana*) (v)	EGol IBal
	'Royalty'	EGol
	rupifraga	EGol
	'Rusty Bee'	IBal
	'Ryan's Big One'	IBal NMyG
§	'Sagae' (v) ♀H3-4	CMoH CWat EBee EBrs EGol EMic EPGN EPfP IBal IPot LRHS MBri MHom MNrw NGdn NMyG NNor NPnk SApp SDix SPoG WAul WClo WFar WHoo WWEG
	'Saint Elmo's Fire' (v)	CHid EGol EMic EPGN IBal LRHS SApp
	'Saint Paul'	EMic IBal
	'Saishu Jima' (*sieboldii* f. *spathulata*)	EMic WCru
	'Saishu Yahite Site' (v)	EGol
	'Salute' (Tardiana Group)	EGol EMic
	'Samual Blue'	EGol
	'Samurai' (*sieboldiana*) (v)	EGol EMic IBal IPot MRav NBir NBro NGdn NLar NNor SApp
	'Sandhill Crane' (v)	IBal
	'Sarah Kennedy' (v)	EPGN
	'Satisfaction' (v)	EMic
	'Savannah'	EGol IBal
	'Sazanami' (*crispula*)	see *H. crispula*
	'Schwan'	GBin
	'Scooter' (v)	EGol NMyG
	'Sea Beacon' (v)	EGol
	'Sea Bunny'	EGol
	'Sea Dream' (v)	EGol EMic LRHS NEgg NMyG
	'Sea Drift'	EGol
	'Sea Fire'	EGol
	'Sea Frolic'	EGol
	'Sea Gold Star'	EGol NMyG
	'Sea Gulf Stream'	EMic
	'Sea Hero'	EGol
	'Sea Lotus Leaf'	EGol LLWP NLar NMyG
	'Sea Monster'	EGol IBal
	'Sea Octopus'	EGol
	'Sea Sapphire'	EGol
	'Sea Sunrise'	EPGN
	'Sea Thunder' (v)	EGol EMic EPGN IBal NMyG
	'Sea Yellow Sunrise'	EGol EMic IBal SApp
	'Second Wind' (*fortunei*) (v)	EGol EMic EPGN IBal NMyG SApp
	'Secret Love' PBR	EMic IBal
	'See Saw' (*undulata*)	EGol SApp
	'September Sun' (v)	EGol EMic IBal LRHS NMyG
	'Serena' (Tardiana Group)	IBal SApp
	'Serendipity'	EGol EMic MHom
	'Shade Beauty' (v)	EGol
	'Shade Fanfare' (v) ♀H4	EBrs EGol ELan EMic EPfP IBal LAst LBMP LPla LRHS MBNS MBri MRav MWhi NBir NGdn NLar NMyG NSti SApp SPer WFar WMnd WTin WWEG
	'Shade Finale' (v)	IBal
	'Shade Master'	EGol EMic NHol
	'Shamoa'	SApp
§	'Sharmon' (*fortunei*) (v)	EGol ELon EMic EPGN MBNS NEgg NHol NLar NMyG SApp SBfd
	'Sharp Dressed Man'	IBal
	'Shazaam'	IBal
	'Sheila West'	EMic IBal
	'Shelleys' (v)	EGol IBal
	'Sherborne Profusion' (Tardiana Group)	EMic IBal
	'Sherborne Songbird' (Tardiana Group)	EGol IBal
	'Sherborne Swan' (Tardiana Group)	EGol IBal
	'Sherborne Swift' (Tardiana Group)	EGol EMic LRHS

	'Shere Khan' (v)	EGol
	'Shining Tot'	EGol LLHF
	'Shiny Penny' (v)	EGol EMic IBal
	'Shirley Vaughn' (v)	EGol
	'Shogun' (v)	EGol
	'Showboat' (v)	EGol EMic IBal LRHS NMyG
	sieboldiana	CMac CSBt ECha EGol ELan EMic EPfP GCra GMaP LLWP LTen MRav MSwo NChi NHol SPlb SRms WFar WGwG WWEG
§	- var. ***elegans*** ♀H4	Widely available
	- 'George Smith'	EMic IBal SApp
	- var. ***mira***	EMic
	- var. ***sieboldiana***	GAuc
	sieboldii	CWat MRav
§	- var. ***alba***	EGol IBal
§	- 'Paxton's Original' (v) ♀H4	EGol EHrv MGos SGSe SRms WWEG
§	- var. ***sieboldii*** f. ***kabitan*** (v)	EGol EPGN SApp WTin WWEG
	- - f. ***shiro-kabitan*** (v)	EGol EMic EPGN
	- f. ***spathulata***	EMic
	'Silberpfeil'	EMic
	'Silk Kimono' (v)	EGol
	'Silver Bay'	EMic
	'Silver Bowl'	EGol
	'Silver Crown'	see *H.* 'Albomarginata'
	'Silver Lance' (v)	EGol EMic NMyG
	'Silver Lining'	IBal
	'Silver Lode' (v) **new**	IBal
	'Silver Parade' **new**	IBal
	'Silver Shadow' (v)	CHid EMic EPGN GBin IBal NBir NCob NGdn NHol NMyG SApp WClo WPtf
	'Silver Spray' (v)	EGol IBal
	'Silver Threads and Gold Needles' (v)	IBal
	'Silvery Slugproof' (Tardiana Group)	LRHS NMyG SApp
	'Singin' the Blues'	IBal
	'Singing in the Rain' (v) **new**	IBal
	'Sitting Pretty' (v)	EGol EPGN
	'Sky Dancer'	EMic IBal
	'Sleeping Beauty'	CWGN EMic EPGN GQue IBal MAvo NGdn NMyG SApp
	'Slick Willie'	EGol
	'Small Parts'	EMic IBal
	'Small Sum'	IBal
	'Smooth Sailing' (v)	IBal
	'Snow Cap' (v)	EBee EGol EMic IBal MBri NGdn NLar NMoo NMyG NNor SApp WCra WWEG
	'Snow Crust' (v)	EGol EMic
	'Snow Flakes' (*sieboldii*)	CMac EGol EPGN EPfP EWTr GKir NBro NGdn NHol NLar NMyG WFar WWEG
	'Snow Mound'	IBal
	'Snow White' (*undulata*) (v)	EGol IBal
	'Snowbound' (v)	IBal
	'Snowden'	CPrp ECha EGol EMic EPGN ETod GMaP IBal LRHS MWat NBir NCob NGdn NHol NNor SApp SSpi WAul WCru WWEG
	'Snowstorm' (*sieboldii*)	NHol
	'Snowy Lake' (v) **new**	IBal
	'So Sweet' (v)	CAby EBee EGol EHoe ELan EMic EPGN EPfP LBMP LPBA LRHS MHom MSwo NBro NGdn NHol NMyG NNor SApp SBfd SPad SPoG SRGP WSpi WWEG
	'Solar Flare'	EGol IBal
	'Something Blue'	EMic
	'Something Different' (*fortunei*) (v)	EGol EPGN
	'Sophistication' (v)	EGol
	'Southern Gold'	EMic
	'Sparkling Burgundy'	EGol IBal
	'Sparky' (v)	EGol EMic IBal
	'Spartacus' (v) **new**	EMic IBal
	'Spartan Glory' (v)	IBal
	'Special Gift'	EGol EMic WWEG
	'Spellbound' (v)	IBal
	'Spilt Milk' (*tokudama*) (v)	EGol EMic EPGN IBal SApp SPoG WHoo
§	'Spinners' (*fortunei*) (v)	ECha EGol EMic GKir NNor
	'Spinning Wheel' (v)	EGol IBal
	'Spring Fling'	EMic IBal
	'Spritzer' (v)	EGol EMic IBal MNrw NMyG SApp
	'Squash Casserole'	EGol
	'Squiggles' (v)	EGol
	'Stained Glass'	CBcs EGol ELon EMic EPGN IBal NGdn NMyG SApp WFar
	'Star Kissed'	IBal
	'Starburst' (v)	EGol
	'Starburst' stable (v)	IBal
	'Stardust' **new**	IBal
	'Stargate' **new**	IBal
§	'Starker Yellow Leaf'	EMic
	'Starship' (v) **new**	IBal
	'Stenantha' (*fortunei*)	EMic
	'Stenantha Variegated' (*fortunei*) (v)	NHol
	'Step Sister'	EMic IBal
	'Stepping Out' (v)	EMic IBal
	'Stetson' (v)	EGol
	'Stiletto' (v)	Widely available
	'Stirfry'	EGol EMic
	'Stitch in Time' (v) **new**	IBal
	'Stolen Kiss' (v)	IBal
	'Stonewall'	IBal
	'Striker' (v)	EGol IBal
	'Striptease' (*fortunei*) (v)	CMac EGol EMic EPGN GBin GQue IBal LRHS MBNS MNrw NGdn NHol NLar NMyG NPnk SApp WFar WHoo WWEG
	'Sugar and Cream' (v)	CMMP CWat EGol EMic IBal LRHS MWat NGdn NNor
	'Sugar and Spice' (v)	EMic IBal
	'Sugar Daddy'	EMic IBal
	'Sugar Plum Fairy' (*gracillima*)	EGol
	'Sultana' (v)	EMic IBal WWEG
	'Sum and Substance' ♀H4	Widely available
	'Sum Cup-o-Joe' (v)	EMic
	'Sum it Up' (v)	EMic
	'Summer Breeze' (v)	EGol EMic IBal
	'Summer Fragrance'	ECtt EGol EMic GBin IBal LRHS NMyG
	'Summer in Georgia'	IBal
	'Summer Lovin'' (v) **new**	IBal
	'Summer Music' (v)	CWCL EGol EMic EPGN IBal MBri NMyG SApp WWEG
	'Summer Serenade' (v)	EGol EMic IBal SApp
	'Sun Catcher'	EMic
	'Sun Glow'	EGol
	'Sun Kissed' (v)	IBal
	'Sun Power'	EGol EMic EPfP GBin IBal LRHS MBNS NBro NGdn NLar NSti SApp SBfd SDix SMrm
	'Sun Worshipper'	EMic IBal SApp
	'Sundance' (*fortunei*) (v)	EGol
	'Sunlight Child'	IBal
	'Sunnybrook' (v)	IBal
	'Sunshine Glory'	EGol EMic

	'Super Bowl'	EGol
	'Super Nova' (v)	EGol EMic IBal SApp
	'Surf and Turf'	IBal
	'Surprised by Joy' (v)	EGol EMic IBal SApp
	'Susy'	IBal
	'Sutter's Mill'	IBal
	'Suzuki Thumbnail'	EMic
	'Sweet Bo Beep'	EGol LRHS
	'Sweet Bouquet'	EMic
	'Sweet Home Chicago' (v)	EGol EMic IBal
	'Sweet Innocence' (v)	EMic IBal
	'Sweet Marjorie'	EGol
	'Sweet Standard'	NMyG
	'Sweet Sunshine'	EGol
	'Sweet Susan'	EGol EMic GBin LPla LSRN LTen MBNS SApp SPer SWvt
	'Sweet Tater Pie'	EGol EMic
	'Sweetie' (v)	EGol EMic IBal LRHS SApp WWEG
	'Sweetness'	IBal
	'Swirling Hearts'	EGol
	'Swizzle Sticks'	IBal
	'T. Rex'	EMic SApp
	'Tall Boy'	CSev ECha EGol NBir NNor
	'Tamborine' (v)	CWat EGol EPGN IBal LRHS NMyG SApp
	'Tango'	EMic IBal
	'Tappen Zee' (v) **new**	IBal
	Tardiana Group	EGol ELan MHom NGdn NHol
	tardiflora	EGol EPGN SApp WCot WPGP
	tardiva	GKir
	'Tattoo'PBR (v)	CWGN EGol EMic EPGN LSRN MBNS MNrw NLar NMoo NMyG SApp WWEG
	'Tea and Crumpets' (v)	EPGN IBal
	'Tea at Betty's' **new**	EPGN
	'Teaspoon'	EMic IBal SApp
	'Teatime' (v) **new**	IBal
	'Teeny-weeny Bikini' (v)	EMic IBal
	'Templar Gold'	IBal
	'Temple Bells'	EGol
	'Temptation'	EMic IBal SApp
	'Tenryu'	EGol
	'Tequila Sunrise'	IBal
	'Terracotta' **new**	MCri
	'Terry Wogan'	EPGN NNor
	'Tet-a-Poo'	IBal
	'Thai Brass' **new**	SApp
	'The Leading Edge' (v) **new**	IBal
	'The Razor's Edge' **new**	IBal
	'The Shining'	IBal
	'The Twister'	EGol IBal NMyG
	'Theo's Blue'	EMic IBal
	'Thomas Hogg'	see *H. undulata* var. *albomarginata*
	'Three Sisters' (v)	IBal
	'Thumb Nail'	ECha EGol EMic IBal SApp SCnR
	'Thumbelina'	EMic IBal
	'Thunderbolt'PBR (*sieboldiana*)	EGol EMic EPGN IBal MBNS NCob NLar NMyG SApp WFar
	'Tick Tock' (v)	IBal
	'Tidewater'	IBal
	'Time Tunnel'PBR (*sieboldiana*) (v)	EMic IBal
	'Tiny Tears'	CStu EGol IBal IFoB
	'Titanic'PBR	EMic IBal
	'Toasted Waffles'	WFar
	tokudama	EGol EMic IBal MHom NBir NGdn NHol NNor NSti SApp WFar
§	- f. ***aureo-nebulosa*** (v)	EGol EMic EPGN IBal NGdn NSti SRms WMnd
	- f. ***flavocircinalis*** (v)	CPrp EGol EMic EPGN GMaP IBal NBPC NBro NMyG SApp WFar WHoo WMnd
	'Tom Rex'	IBal
	'Tom Schmid' (v)	EGol EMic IBal
	'Tom Thumb'	EMic IBal SApp
	'Topaz'	IBal
	'Topscore'	NNor
	'Torchlight' (v)	EGol EMic IBal
	tortifrons	EMic IBal
	'Tortilla Chip'	IBal
	'Tot Tot'	EGol IBal
	'Touch of Class'PBR (v)	EMic IBal NMyG NNor WWEG
	'Touchstone' (v)	IBal LRHS NMyG SApp SWvt WWEG
	'Toy Soldier'	EMic IBal SApp
	'Tremors'	EMic
	'Trill'	SApp
	'Trixi' (v)	IBal
	'True Blue'	EGol EMic IBal SApp WWEG
	'Tsugaru Komachi'	EMic
	'Tsugaru Komachi Kifukurin' (v)	IBal
	'Turning Point'	EGol
	'Tutu'	EGol
	'Twiggie'	EMic
	'Twilight' (*fortunei*) (v)	EGol EKen EMic EPGN IBal LRHS MBNS NLar NMyG SApp SWvt WClo WWEG
	'Twilight Time'	IBal
	'Twinkle Toes'	EGol EMic
	'Twist of Lemon'	GBin
	'Twist of Lime' (v)	EGol EMic IBal
	'Ultramarine'	IBal
	'Ultraviolet Light'	EGol
	'Unchained Melody'	IBal
	undulata	MGos NNor WFar
§	- var. ***albomarginata***	Widely available
§	- var. ***erromena*** ♀H4	EBrs EMic GMaP IBal LPBA LRHS NHol
§	- var. ***undulata*** (v) ♀H4	CBot EBee EHrv ELan EPGN EPfP GMaP IBal LPBA LRHS MCot MRav MSwo NEgg NGdn NLar NMyG NVic SPer SPoG WFar WWEG
	- var. ***univittata*** (v) ♀H4	ECha EGol EMic LAst MHom MWhi NBir WBrk WFar WMoo
	'Unforgettable'	EMic IBal NMyG SApp
	'Upper Crust' (v) **new**	IBal
	'Urajiro Hachijo' (*longipes* var. *latifolia*)	EGol IBal
	'Urajiro' (*hypoleuca*)	EGol
	'Valentine Lace'	EGol EMic IBal
	'Valley's Chute the Chute'	EMic IBal
	'Valley's Vanilla Sticks'	EMic IBal
	'Van Wade' (v)	EGol EMic IBal
	'Vanilla Cream' (*cathayana*)	EGol EMic
	'Variegata' (*gracillima*)	see *H.* 'Vera Verde'
	'Variegata' (*tokudama*)	see *H. tokudama* f. *aureo-nebulosa*
	'Variegata' (*undulata*)	see *H. undulata* var. *undulata*
	'Variegata' (*ventricosa*)	see *H.* 'Aureomarginata' (*ventricosa*)
	'Variegated' (*fluctuans*)	see *H.* 'Sagae'
	'Velvet Moon' (v)	IBal
	ventricosa ♀H4	CBcs CMac EGol EMic EPfP GMaP LPBA MWhi NHol SGar WBrk WFar
	- BWJ 8160 from Sichuan	WCru
	- var. ***aureomaculata***	EGol EMic LRHS NBir NNor NSti WFar
I	'Venucosa'	EGol LAst
	'Venus' (d)	CAby IBal LRHS MLLN NGdn SApp SMrs SPer SPoG WClo WCot
	'Venus Star'	EGol EMic IBal NMyG
	venusta ♀H4	CDes CFir EBee EBrs ECho EDAr EGol EMic EPGN GCra GEdr IBal LRHS MHer MRav NBid NBir NMen

	NMyG NRya NSti SApp SRot WCot WEas WTin WWEG
- B&SWJ 4389	WCru
- dwarf	CSWP
- 'Kin Botan' (v)	GEdr
- 'Porter'	IBal
- 'Red Tubes'	IBal
- ***yakusimensis***	see *H. kikutii* var. *yakusimensis*
§ 'Vera Verde' (v)	GCra GQui IBal MHom NBir NMyG
'Verdi Valentine'	IBal
'Verkade's No 1'	IBal
'Verna Jean' (v)	EGol EMic IBal
'Veronica Lake' (v)	EGol EMic IBal LRHS NMyG WHal
'Victory'	IBal
'Viking Ship' **new**	EMic
'Vilmoriniana'	EGol IBal
'Vim and Vigor' **new**	IBal
'Vina' **new**	IBal
'Viridis Marginata'	see *H. sieboldii* var. *sieboldii* f. *kabitan*
'Vulcan' (v) **new**	EMic IBal
'Wagtail' (Tardiana Group)	EGol EMic IBal
'Wahoo' (*tokudama*) (v)	EGol
'Wakey-Wakey'	EGol
'War Paint'	EMic IBal
'Warwick Ballerina'	EGol
'Warwick Comet' (v)	EMic IBal SApp
'Warwick Curtsey' (v)	EGol EMic IBal
'Warwick Delight' (v)	EGol EMic IBal
'Warwick Edge' (v)	EGol IBal
'Warwick Essence'	EGol EMic
'Warwick Sheen'	IBal
'Waving Winds' (v)	EGol IBal
'Waving Wuffles'	EMic NMyG
'Wayside Blue'	EMic
'Wayside Perfection'	see *H.* 'Royal Standard'
'Website'	IBal
'Weihenstephan' (*sieboldii*)	EGol EMic
'Weser'	EGol
'Wheaton Blue'	EMic IBal
'Whirligig' (v)	EMic
'Whirling Dervish' (v)	IBal
'Whirlwind' (*fortunei*) (v)	CBcs EGol EMic EPGN GBin GQue IBal IPot MBri MNrw MRav NBro NEgg NGdn NMyG NNor SApp SMad SMrm SPad WAul WMnd WWEG
'Whirlwind Tour' (v)	EGol IBal SApp
'Whiskey Sour'	IBal
'White Bikini' (v)	IBal
'White Christmas' (*undulata*) (v)	EGol EMic EPGN EQua IBal
'White Dove' (v) **new**	EMic IBal
'White Fairy' (*plantaginea*) (d)	EMic IBal
'White Feather' (*undulata*)	CHid CWGN ELon MSCN NBir NGdn NMyG NNor
'White Gold'	EGol NMyG
'White Knight'	IBal
'White On' (*montana*)	EMic IBal
'White Triumphator' (*rectifolia*)	EGol EMic GBin IBal NMyG
'White Trumpets'	EMic
'White Vision'	EGol IBal
'Wide Brim' (v) ♀H4	Widely available
'Wiggle Worms' (v) **new**	IBal
'William Lachman' (v) **new**	NLar
'Wily Willy'	IBal
'Wind River Gold'	EGol EMic
'Windsor Gold'	see *H.* 'Nancy Lindsay'
'Winfield Blue'	CMHG EGol EMic IBal
'Winfield Gold'	EGol EMic IBal
'Winfield Mist' (v)	IBal
'Winsome' (v)	EGol IBal
'Winter Lightning' (v) **new**	NNor
'Winter Snow' (v)	EMic IBal SApp
'Wintergreen' (v)	IBal
'Wogon' (*sieboldii*)	CMMP EMic GBin GEdr GKev GMaP NHol NMen NSti
'Wogon's Boy'	EGol EMic EPGN IBal LRHS WWEG
'Wolverine' (v)	EBee ECGP ECtt EGol EHoe EMic EPGN GAbr IBal ITim LPla LSou MBNS MHom NGdn NLBP NMyG SWvt WClo WCot WWEG
'Woolly Mammoth' (v)	IBal
'Wooly Bully'	NMyG SApp
'Woop Woop' (v)	IBal
'World Cup'	IBal
'Worldly Treasure'	IBal
'Wrinkles and Crinkles'	EGol EMic IBal
'Wylde Green Cream'	EGol IBal
'Xanadu' (v)	IBal
'X-rated' (v)	IBal
'Yakushima-mizu' (*gracillima*)	EGol EMic IBal NMyG
* ***yakushimana***	NMen
'Yang'	IBal
'Yankee Blue'	IBal
'Yellow Boa'	EGol EMic
'Yellow Edge' (*fortunei*)	see *H. fortunei* var. *aureomarginata*
'Yellow Edge' (*sieboldiana*)	see *H.* 'Frances Williams'
'Yellow River' (v)	EGol EMic GBin IBal MBri NGdn NMyG SApp
'Yellow Splash' (v)	CMoH ECha EMic EPGN LRHS MHom NMyG NNor
'Yellow Splash Rim' (v)	EGol NCGa
'Yellow Splashed Edged' (v)	EMic
'Yellow Submarine'	IBal
'Yesterday's Memories' (v)	EMic
'Yin' (v)	EMic IBal SApp
yingeri	EGol SApp WPGP
- B&SWJ 546	WCru
'Yucca Ducka Do' (v)	EGol
'Zager Blue'	EMic
'Zager Green'	EMic
'Zager White Edge' (*fortunei*) (v)	EGol EMic IBal NMyG SApp WTin
'Zitronenfalter'	EGol IBal
'Zodiac' (*fortunei*) (v)	IBal
'Zounds'	CBot CMHG EBee EBrs ECtt EGol ELan EMic EPfP EShb GBin GKir IBal LRHS MRav NHol NLar NMyG NSti SApp SBfd SRms WBor WFar WWEG

Hottonia (*Primulaceae*)

palustris	CBen CWat EHon ELan LPBA MSKA MWts NPer NSco SWat WPnP

Houstonia (*Rubiaceae*)

caerulea misapplied	see *H. michauxii*
caerulea L.	ECho NPri
- var. ***alba***	SPlb
longifolia	EWes
michauxii 'Fred Mullard'	EWes
serpyllifolia	ECho

Houttuynia (*Saururaceae*)

cordata	GBar GKev GPoy SBfd SDix SWat WFar
§ - 'Boo-Boo' (v)	CMac EPfP EPla LBMP NBro SBfd WFar WWEG
§ - 'Chameleon' (v)	Widely available

- 'Fantasy'	EBee
- 'Flame' (v)	CBcs CMac CWCL LRHS MBri NPri SBfd SMrm WWEG
- 'Flore Pleno' (d)	CBen CMac CRow CWat EBee ECha EHon ELan EPfP EPla GBar LPBA MCCP MRav MSCN NBir NPer NVic SGar SIde SPer SPlb SRms SWat WFar WPnP
- 'Joker's Gold'	CMac EBee ECtt EPPr EPfP EPla LBMP NBro NVic SMrm SPoG
- 'Pied Piper'	CDoC EBee EWll SBfd SPad
- 'Sunshine'	EBee
- 'Tequila Sunrise'	CHEx
- 'Terry Clarke'	see *H. cordata* 'Boo-Boo'
- 'Tricolor'	see *H. cordata* 'Chameleon'
- Variegata Group (v)	GBar LPBA NBro

Hovea (*Papilionaceae*)

celsii	see *H. elliptica*
§ ***elliptica***	SPlb
montana **new**	SPlb

Hovenia (*Rhamnaceae*)

dulcis	CAgr CBcs CMCN EPfP IVic LEdu NLar WBVN
- B&SWJ 11024	WCru

Howea (*Arecaceae*)

§ ***belmoreana*** ♀H1	LPal
§ ***forsteriana*** ♀H1	CCCN LPal NPla XBlo

Hoya (*Asclepiadaceae*)

§ ***australis***	SOWG
bella	see *H. lanceolata* subsp. *bella*
carnosa ♀H1	CBcs CRHN EBak EOHP SEND SRms SWal WWFP
- 'Compacta Regalis' (v)	NPer
- 'Krinkle 8'	NPer
- 'Tricolor' (v)	NPer
cinnamomifolia	SOWG
* ***compacta*** 'Tricolor'	NPer
darwinii misapplied	see *H. australis*
lacunosa	CCCN
§ ***lanceolata*** subsp. ***bella*** ♀H1	CBcs EShb SRms
linearis	SOWG
multiflora	SOWG

huckleberry, garden see *Solanum scabrum*

Huernia (*Asclepiadaceae*)

barbata **new**	LToo
confusa	see *H. insigniflora*
hystrix **new**	LToo
§ ***insigniflora***	LToo
longituba **new**	LToo
namaquesis **new**	LToo
quinta **new**	LToo
zebrina **new**	LToo

Huerniopsis (*Asclepiadaceae*)

atrosanguinea **new**	LToo

Hugueninia (*Brassicaceae*)

tanacetifolia subsp. ***suffruticosa***	NBre

Humata (*Davalliaceae*)

tyermannii	CMen ISha WFib WRic

Humea see *Calomeria*

elegans	see *Calomeria amaranthoides*

Humulus (*Cannabaceae*)

lupulus	CArn CBcs CRWN EPfP GBar GPoy ILis NGHP NLar NMir SIde WDin WHer
- 'Aureus' ♀H4	Widely available
- 'Aureus' (f)	CRHN ELon EOHP GBar GCal GGar GKev MCCP SPoG WCot WWFP
- 'Aureus' (m)	MCCP
* - ***compactus***	GPoy
- 'Fuggle'	CAgr GPoy SDea
- 'Golden Showers'	MCCP
- 'Golden Tassels' (f)	CDul EBee ELon EPfP LBuc LHop LRHS MBri MGos NGHP SBfd SLim SPer SPoG
- (Goldings Group) 'Cobbs'	SDea
- - 'Mathons'	CAgr SDea
- 'Hallertauer'	SDea
- 'Prima Donna'	CAgr CDul EBee EGxp GBin LHop MCoo NLar SBfd SCoo SEND SIde SPer SPoG SWvt
- 'Taff's Variegated' (v)	EWes MAvo NGHP WSHC
- 'Wye Challenger'	CAgr GPoy MHer
- 'Wye Northdown'	CAgr SDea

Hunnemannia (*Papaveraceae*)

fumariifolia	CSpe

Huodendron (*Styracaceae*)

biaristatum	WPGP
tibeticum	WPGP

Hutchinsia see *Pritzelago*

Hyacinthella (*Hyacinthaceae*)

acutiloba	ECho WCot
dalmatica 'Grandiflora'	ECho WWst
glabrescens	WCot WWst
heldreichii	ECho WCot
leucophaea	ECho WWst
lineata	WCot
millingenii	ECho
pallens	ECho

Hyacinthoides (*Hyacinthaceae*)

aristidis	ECho
§ ***hispanica***	ECho NBir SEND
- 'Alba'	ECho
- 'Dainty Maid'	ECho
- 'Excelsior'	ECho
- 'Miss World'	ECho WCot
- 'Mount Everest'	ECho
- 'Queen of the Pinks'	ECho WCot
- 'Rosea'	ECho
- 'White City'	ECho WCot
§ ***italica*** ♀H4	CPom ECho WCot WShi
- BS 380	WCot
mauritanica **new**	WCot
§ ***non-scripta***	Widely available
- 'Alba'	ECho MMuc NBir SEND
- 'Bracteata'	CNat
- 'Rosea'	ECho MMuc SEND
- 'Wavertree'	ECho
'Stuart Williams'	CAvo
§ ***vicentina***	ECho WCot

Hyacinthus ✿ (*Hyacinthaceae*)

amethystinus	see *Brimeura amethystina*
azureus	see *Muscari azureum*
comosus 'Plumosus'	see *Muscari comosum* 'Plumosum'
multi-flowered blue	CAvo EBrs SDeJ
multi-flowered pink	EBrs SDeJ

	multi-flowered white	CAvo EBrs SDeJ
	orientalis 'Aiolos'	LRHS SPer
	- 'Amethyst'	ERCP LAma
	- 'Anastasia' **new**	SPhx
	- 'Anna Liza'	MBri
	- 'Anna Marie' ♀H4	EBrs LAma MBri SDeJ
	- 'Apricot Passion' **new**	EPfP
	- 'Ben Nevis' (d)	LAma
	- 'Blue Festival'	LRHS
	- 'Blue Giant'	LAma LRHS SDeJ
	- 'Blue Jacket' ♀H4	EBrs LAma LRHS MBri SDeJ
	- 'Blue Magic'	SDeJ
	- 'Blue Star'	LAma SPhx
	- 'Carnegie'	CAvo CFox EBrs EPfP ERCP LAma SPhx
	- 'China Pink'	SDeJ SPer
	- 'City of Haarlem' ♀H4	CAvo CFox EPfP LAma LRHS MBri SDeJ SPhx
	- 'Crystal Palace' (d)	LAma
	- 'Delft Blue' ♀H4	CAvo CFox EBrs EPfP LAma LRHS MBri SDeJ SPer SPhx
	- 'Fondant'	CFox LAma SDeJ
	- 'General Köhler' (d)	LAma
	- 'Gipsy Princess'	LAma
	- 'Gipsy Queen' ♀H4	EBrs EPfP LAma LRHS MBri SDeJ SPer
	- 'Hollyhock' (d)	EBrs LAma SDeJ
	- 'Jan Bos'	CFox EBrs EPfP LAma MBri SDeJ SPer SPhx
	- 'Lady Derby'	CFox EBrs
	- 'L'Innocence' ♀H4	CFox EPfP
	- 'Miss Saigon' **new**	ERCP
	- 'Odysseus'	LAma LRHS
	- 'Ostara' ♀H4	EPfP LAma MBri
	- 'Peter Stuyvesant'	EBrs EPfP ERCP LAma
	- 'Pink Festival'	LRHS SPer
	- 'Pink Pearl' ♀H4	EBrs EPfP LAma LRHS MBri SDeJ SPhx
	- 'Pink Royal' (d)	LAma
	- 'Purple Sensation' PBR	SPhx
	- 'Red Magic'	LAma SDeJ
	- 'Rosette' (d)	LAma
	- 'Sky Jacket'	LRHS
	- 'Splendid Cornelia'	CFox ERCP LRHS SDeJ SPer
	- 'White Festival'	LRHS SPer
	- 'White Pearl'	LAma MBri SDeJ
	- 'Woodstock'	CAvo CFox EBrs EPfP ERCP LAma LRHS SDeJ SPer SPhx

Hydrangea ✿ (*Hydrangeaceae*)

	BWJ 8120 from Sichuan, China	WCru
	angustipetala	see *H. scandens* subsp. *chinensis* f. *angustipetala*
	anomala subsp. ***anomala*** B&SWJ 2411	WCru
	- - BWJ 8052 from China	WCru
	- - 'Winter Glow'	WCru
	- subsp. ***glabra*** B&SWJ 6804	WCru
	- - 'Crûg Coral'	WCru
§	- subsp. ***petiolaris*** ♀H4	Widely available
	- - B&SWJ 5996 from Yakushima	WCru
	- - B&SWJ 6081	WCru
	- - B&SWJ 6337	WCru
§	- - var. ***cordifolia***	NLar SHyH
	- - - B&SWJ 11487	WCru
§	- - - 'Brookside Littleleaf'	EQua IDee NLar WFar
	- - dwarf	see *H. anomala* subsp. *petiolaris* var. *cordifolia*
*	- - var. ***minor*** B&SWJ 5991	WCru
	- - 'Mirranda'	CBcs EBee NBro SMad SPoG
*	- - var. ***tiliifolia***	EBee SHyH WFar WSHC
	- - - B&SWJ 8497	WCru
	- - 'Yakushima'	WCru WPGP
*	- subsp. ***quelpartensis*** B&SWJ 8799	WCru
	- - B&SWJ 8846	WCru
	- Semiola = 'Inovalaur'	LRHS MAsh SBfd
§	***arborescens***	CArn CPLG MRav WFar WPGP
	- 'Annabelle' ♀H4	Widely available
	- 'Bounty'	MAsh
§	- subsp. ***discolor***	WCru WPat
	- - 'Sterilis'	GGGa SHyH WPGP
	- 'Grandiflora' ♀H4	CBcs CBot ELan EPfP EQua LSRN MRav NBro NEgg WDin WPGP
	- 'Hayes Starburst'	CMil CWGN GGGa LRHS MAsh SHyH SMad SPoG SSpi
	- 'Hills of Snow'	IVic NLar
	- 'Picadilly'	NLar
	- 'Pink Pincushion'	NLar
	- 'Puffed Green'	NLar
	- subsp. ***radiata***	CAbP LRHS MAsh MRav SPoG SSpi WFar WPGP
	- 'Vasterival'	NLar
	- 'Wesser Falls' **new**	CMil
	- White Dome = 'Dardom' PBR	NBro WCot
	aspera	CMac CTri EUJe MGos SHyH SLon SSpi SSta WCom WCru WKif WPGP
	- HWJCM 452	WCru
	- from Gongshan, China	CMil CPLG WPGP
	- 'Anthony Bullivant'	IArd LRHS MAsh MBri NLar SHyH SSpi WPat
	- Kawakamii Group	CGHE CHEx CMil CPLG CSpe EPla NLar WCru WPGP
	- - B&SWJ 1420	WCru
	- - B&SWJ 3456	WCru
	- - B&SWJ 3462	WCru
	- - B&SWJ 6702	WCru
	- - B&SWJ 6714	WCru
	- - B&SWJ 6827	WCru
	- - B&SWJ 7025	WCru
	- - B&SWJ 7101	WCru
	- - 'August Abundance'	WCru
	- - 'Maurice Mason'	CPLG
	- - 'September Splendour'	WCru
	- - × ***involucrata***	GGGa WPGP
	- 'Macrophylla' ♀H3	CWib EPfP EWTr GCal IVic MRav NPal SMad WCru WFar WPGP WSpi
	- 'Mauvette'	CMil EPfP LRHS LTen MAsh MBlu NBro NLar NPal SSpi WCru WPGP
	- 'Peter Chappell'	CMil CPLG LRHS SSpi WPGP
§	- subsp. ***robusta***	CPLG SLPl WCru WPGP WSpi
	- - WWJ 11888	WCru
	- 'Rocklon'	NLar WPGP
	- 'Rosthornii'	see *H. aspera* subsp. *robusta*
	- 'Sam MacDonald'	CPLG GKir LRHS NLar SHyH SSpi WPGP WSpi
§	- subsp. ***sargentiana*** ♀H3	Widely available
	- - large-leaved	WCot WCru
	- subsp. ***strigosa***	CDul CPLG EPfP SHyH SSpi WCru WPGP
	- - B&SWJ 8201	WCru
	- - HWJ 653	WCru
	- - HWJ 737	WCru
	- - from Gong Shan, China	CGHE
	- 'Taiwan'	EQua
	- 'Taiwan Pink'	EPfP IArd NLar
	- 'Velvet and Lace'	LBuc LRHS NLar
§	- Villosa Group ♀H3	Widely available
	cinerea	see *H. arborescens* subsp. *discolor*
	'Cohhii'	ECre

	glandulosa B&SWJ 4031	WCru
	aff. ***gracilis*** B&SWJ 3942 **new**	WCru
§	***heteromalla***	CGHE CMHG GGal GKir SLPl SSpi WPGP
	- HWJCM 180	WCru
	- BWJ 7657 from China	WCru
	- B&SWJ 2142 from India	WCru
	- B&SWJ 2602 from Sikkim	WCru
	- HWJK 2127 from Nepal	WCru
	- Bretschneideri Group	EPfP GQui SHyH WCru WFar
	- 'Fan Si Pan'	WCru
	- 'Nepal Beauty'	IVic
	- 'Snowcap'	EPfP GQui IArd LRHS NLar SHyH SLPl SSpi WPGP
*	***heterophylla***	MGos
	hirta B&SWJ 5000	WCru
	- B&SWJ 11022	WCru
	indochinensis	CPLG
	- B&SWJ 8307	WCru
	- B&SWJ 11717	WCru
	integerrima	see *H. serratifolia*
	integrifolia	NLar WPGP
	- B&SWJ 022	WCru
	- B&SWJ 6967	WCru
	involucrata	EPfP LLHF LRHS MMHG SHyH WDin
	- dwarf	WCru
	- 'Hortensis' (d) 🏆$^{H3-4}$	CMil EPfP MGan MRav NLar SMad SSpi WCru WKif WPGP WSHC WSpi
	- 'Mihara-kokonoe'	CPMA
	- 'Plena' (d)	CLAP LRHS MRav NLar SSta WCru WFar WPGP
	- 'Sterilis'	EPfP
	- 'Viridescens'	LLHF LRHS MBri WCru WPGP WSpi
	- 'Yokudanka' (d)	GQui NLar
	lobbii	see *H. scandens* subsp. *chinensis*
	longifolia CWJ 12413 **new**	WCru
	longipes	CPLG GQui WCru WPGP
	- var. ***fulvescens*** B&SWJ 8188	WCru
	luteovenosa	WCru WPGP
	- B&SWJ 5602	WCru
	- B&SWJ 5647	WCru
	- B&SWJ 5929	WCru
	macrophylla (H)	GGal LRHS
	- 'AB Green Shadow'^{PBR}	MAsh MMHG SPoG
	- 'Adria' (H)	GGGa IFFs NLar
	- 'Aduarda'	see *H. macrophylla* 'Mousmée'
	- 'All Summer Beauty' (H)	CMil MAsh
	- Alpen Glow	see *H. macrophylla* 'Alpenglühen'
§	- 'Alpenglühen' (H)	CBcs CPLG CSBt CSpr ELan IVic LRHS SLim SRms
	- 'Altona' (H) 🏆$^{H3-4}$	CBcs EPfP GGGa IArd LRHS MAsh MGos MRav NBir NLar NPri SHyH SPer
	- 'Amethyst' (H/d)	CGHE
	- 'Ami Pasquier' (H) 🏆$^{H3-4}$	CDoC CMac CSBt CTri CWit EBee ELan EPfP GGal GKir IVic LRHS LSRN MMuc MRav MSwo NEgg SCoo SEND SGar SHyH SLim SSpi SWvt
*	- 'Aureomarginata' (v)	EPfP WCot
	- 'Aureovariegata' (L/v)	ELan
	- 'Ave Maria' (H)	EQua GGGa MAsh
§	- 'Ayesha' (H)	Widely available
	- 'Bachstelze' (Teller Series) (L)	MAsh SSpi
	- 'Beauté Vendômoise' (L)	CGHE CMil LRHS NLar SSpi WPGP
	- 'Bela'^{PBR} (H)	LRHS
	- 'Benelux' (H)	CBcs
	- 'Bicolor'	see *H. macrophylla* 'Harlequin'
§	- 'Blauer Prinz' (H)	CSam MAsh MMuc SHyH
	- 'Blauer Zwerg' (H)	MGos
§	- 'Bläuling' (Teller Series) (L)	CDoC EPfP LSRN MGos SBfd SHyH
§	- 'Blaumeise' (Teller Series) (L)	CDoC CMHG CMil ELon EPfP EQua GGGa GKir LRHS LTen MAsh MBri MDKP MGos MRav NEgg SCoo SHyH SLim SLon SPoG SSpi SWvt WDin WPGP WSpi
	- 'Blue Bonnet' (H)	CChe CSpr EPfP LRHS LSRN MRav SHyH SPer
	- Blue Butterfly	see *H. macrophylla* 'Bläuling'
	- Blue Prince	see *H. macrophylla* 'Blauer Prinz'
	- Blue Sky	see *H. macrophylla* 'Blaumeise'
	- Blue Tit	see *H. macrophylla* 'Blaumeise'
	- 'Blue Wave'	see *H. macrophylla* 'Mariesii Perfecta'
	- 'Bluebird' misapplied	see *H. serrata* 'Bluebird'
	- Bluebird	see *H. macrophylla* 'Bläuling'
	- 'Blushing Bride' (H)	see *H. macrophylla* Endless Summer Blushing Bride
	- 'Bodensee' (H)	LTen MBri MMuc SEND SHyH
	- 'Bouquet Rose' (H)	CWib ECtt GKir LBMP MMuc SEND
	- 'Brestenburg' (H) **new**	MAsh
	- 'Bridal Bouquet' (H)	CDoC
	- 'Brügg' (H)	LRHS MAsh SHyH SLim SPer WPGP
	- 'Buchfink' (Teller Series) (L)	SSpi
	- Cardinal	see *H. macrophylla* 'Kardinal' (Teller Series)
§	- 'Cardinal Red' (H)	ECre EPfP
	- 'Chaperon Rouge' (H)	LRHS
	- 'Colour Fantasy' (H)	MBrN
	- 'Cordata'	see *H. arborescens*
	- 'Dandenong' (L)	GQui MAsh
	- 'Dart's Song'	NLar
	- 'Deutschland' (H)	CTri
	- 'Doctor Jean Varnier' (L)	MAsh
	- 'Domotoi'	see *H. macrophylla* 'Setsuka-yae'
	- Dragonfly	see *H. macrophylla* 'Libelle'
*	- 'Dwaag Pink'	MRav
	- 'Eldorado' (H)	SHyH
	- Endless Summer = 'Bailmer' (H)	EBrs EMil EPfP LBuc LRHS MAsh MGos NPri
§	- Endless Summer Blushing Bride = 'Blushing Bride' (H)	LRHS MAsh
§	- 'Enziandom' (H)	CBcs CPLG CSBt GGal MAsh WPGP
	- Eternity = 'Youmetwo'^{PBR} (H/d)	LRHS
	- 'Etoile Violette'	EQua MAsh
	- 'Europa' (H) 🏆$^{H3-4}$	CBcs CPLG LRHS MGos SHyH
§	- 'Fasan' (Teller Series) (L)	EQua MAsh
	- Firelight	see *H. macrophylla* 'Leuchtfeuer'
	- Fireworks	see *H. macrophylla* 'Hanabi'
	- Fireworks Blue	see *H. macrophylla* 'Jōgasaki'
	- Fireworks Pink	see *H. macrophylla* 'Jōgasaki'
	- Fireworks White	see *H. macrophylla* 'Hanabi'
	- Forever and Ever = 'Early Sensation' (Forever and Ever Series) (H)	CMac CWit LBuc LRHS SPoG
	- 'Forever Pink' (H)	MAsh NLar
§	- 'Frau Fujiyo' (Lady Series) (H)	CPLG
§	- 'Frau Katsuko' (Lady Series) (H)	SPer
§	- 'Frau Mariko' (Lady Series) (H)	MRav
§	- 'Frau Taiko' (Lady Series) (H)	SPer
	- 'Frillibet' (H)	CAbP EPfP MRav NLar
	- 'Gartenbaudirektor Kühnert' (H)	SHyH

§ - 'Générale Vicomtesse de Vibraye' (H) ♀H3-4 — CChe CDoC CEnd CMHG CTri EBee EPfP GGal GKir LRHS MAsh SDix SEND SHyH SLim SPer SSpi
- Gentian Dome — see *H. macrophylla* 'Enziandom'
- 'Geoffrey Chadbund' — see *H. macrophylla* 'Möwe'
- 'Gertrud Glahn' (H) — SHyH WFar
- 'Gimpel' (Teller Series) (L) — MAsh
- 'Glowing Embers' (H) — IArd MBNS
- Goldrush = 'Nehyosh' (v) — CMil CWGN LRHS MAsh NEgg SBfd SLim SPoG
- 'Goliath' (H) — EPfP GGar
§ - 'Grant's Choice' (L) — EQua GGGa NBro
- Great Star = 'Blanc Bleu' — EPfP LRHS LSRN MAsh SBfd SLim SPur
- 'Hamburg' (H) — CEnd CTri EBee ECtt EPfP LAst MGos SDix SLim WFar
§ - 'Hanabi' (L/d) — CBcs CDoC CLAP CMil ECre EQua GGal MBlu NLar SHyH WSpi
§ - 'Harlequin' (H) — CMac WCot
- 'Harrow's Blue' (L) **new** — GKir
- 'Harry's Red' (H) — MAsh
- 'Hatsu-shime' (L) — NLar
- 'Heinrich Seidel' (H) — CBcs CTri WMoo
- 'Hobella'[PBR] (Hovaria Series) — CBcs
- 'Holehird Purple' — MAsh
- 'Homigo'[PBR] (Hovaria Series) (H) — SHyH
- 'Izu-no-hana' (L/d) — CAlb CBcs CLAP CMil ELon LEdu LHop MAsh MBlu NLar SHyH SPoG SSpi SUsu WBor WPGP
- 'James Grant' — see *H. macrophylla* 'Grant's Choice'
- 'Jofloma' — EQua NLar
§ - 'Jōgasaki' (L/d) — CBcs CLAP CMil CPLG MAsh MBlu NLar SHyH WPGP WSpi
- 'Joseph Banks' (H) — CBcs CTri
- 'Kardinal' — see *H. macrophylla* 'Cardinal Red'
§ - 'Kardinal' (Teller Series) (L) — MAsh
- 'King George' (H) — CBar CBcs CDoC CDul CSBt EBee LAst LBMP LRHS MGos NEgg SBfd SHyH SLim SPer SPoG SWvt WFar WMoo
§ - 'Klaveren' — CMil GGGa MAsh NBro NMun
- 'Kluis Superba' (H) — CBcs CTri GGal SHyH
- 'La France' (H) — CTri EBee IVic SBfd SHyH SLim WFar
- 'Lady Fujiyo' — see *H. macrophylla* 'Frau Fujiyo'
- 'Lady in Red' (L) — CMil
- Lady Katsuko — see *H. macrophylla* 'Frau Katsuko'
- 'Lady Mariko' — see *H. macrophylla* 'Frau Mariko'
- 'Lady Taiko Blue' — see *H. macrophylla* 'Frau Taiko'
- 'Lady Taiko Pink' — see *H. macrophylla* 'Frau Taiko'
* - 'Lanarth' blue-flowered — GGal
- 'Lanarth White' (L) ♀H3-4 — CBar CBcs CDoC CPLG CSBt CTri ELan EPfP GGal LBMP LRHS MAsh MMuc MSwo NLar SEND SHyH SLPl SLim SPer SRms SSpi WBor WKif WPGP
- 'Lemon Wave' (L/v) — NLar
§ - 'Leuchtfeuer' (H) — LRHS MGos SHyH WMoo
§ - 'Libelle' (Teller Series) (L) — CBcs CDoC CWit EPfP GGGa LBMP MGos MRav NEgg NLar NMun SBfd SHyH SLim SPer SSpi WSpi
- 'Lilacina' — see *H. macrophylla* 'Mariesii Lilacina'
- 'Love You Kiss'[PBR] (Hovaria Series) (L) — CBcs CMil LBuc LRHS NLar SCoo SHyH SPoG SRGP
§ - 'Maculata' (L/v) — ELan GQui MSCN
- 'Madame A. Riverain' (H) — NLar SHyH
- 'Madame Emile Mouillère' (H) ♀H3-4 — Widely available
- 'Magical Pearl' **new** — WHlf
- 'Maréchal Foch' (H) — CTri GGal NLar
- 'Mariesii' (L) — CDoy CMHG CTri CTsd CWit ELan GGal MSwo NLar NMun SDix SHyH SPer WKif
§ - 'Mariesii Grandiflora' (L) ♀H3-4 — CAlb CSpr CTsd EPfP GGal LRHS MMuc NBro SEND SPer SRms WDin WFar WMoo
§ - 'Mariesii Lilacina' (L) ♀H3-4 — CSpr EPfP MMuc SEND SLon SPer SSpi WKif WMoo
§ - 'Mariesii Perfecta' (L) ♀H3-4 — Widely available
- 'Mariesii Variegata' (L/v) — CWib
- 'Masja' (H) — CBar EBee IArd IVic LAst MAsh MGos MRav MSwo NBro SHyH WBor
- 'Mathilde Gütges' (H) — CDoC GGal
- 'Max Löbner' (H) — SHyH
- 'Merveille Sanguine' (H) — CDoC CGHE CMHG CMil CPLG CSpe EMil EPfP EQua GCal GGGa GGal IArd IVic LRHS MBri MMuc MRav NCGa NLar SEND SHyH SPoG WCot WGrn WPGP WPat
- 'Messalina' (L) — MAsh MGos SHyH
- 'Mirai'[PBR] (H) — CBcs SCoo SHyH
- 'Miss Belgium' (H) — CMac CTri EQua MAsh
§ - 'Mousmée' (L) — IArd SSpi
- 'Mousseline' (H) — GGGa MAsh
§ - 'Möwe' (L) ♀H3-4 — CBcs CDoC CEnd CMil CPLG EBee ECtt ELon EPfP GGal LHop LSRN MAsh MMuc NLar SCoo SDix SEND SHyH SLim SPer SRms SSpi SSta WPat
- 'Mrs W.J. Hepburn' — CSBt SHyH SPer
§ - 'Nachtigall' (Teller Series) (L) — CMil GGal MAsh
- 'Nanping'[PBR] (Sturdy Series) (L) **new** — EPfP
- 'Niedersachsen' (H) — CDoC CTri MRav SHyH
- Nightingale — see *H. macrophylla* 'Nachtigall'
- 'Nigra' (H) ♀H3-4 — CBcs CMac CMil CPLG CWib EBee ELan EPfP GGGa IFoB LRHS MAsh MBri MGos MMuc MRav MSCN NBro NLar SDix SEND SHyH SLim SPer WClo WFar WGrn WPGP WPat WSpi
- 'Nikko Blue' (H) — CBcs CTsd EPfP MHav
- var. ***normalis*** (L) — CPLG
§ - 'Nymphe' (H) — SHyH
- 'Oregon Pride' (H) — GGGa LRHS MAsh WPGP
- 'Otaksa' (H) — NLar
- 'Papagei' (Teller Series) — SPer
- 'Parzifal' (H) ♀H3-4 — CDul GGGa
- 'Pax' — see *H. macrophylla* 'Nymphe'
- 'Pfau' (Teller Series) (L) — ELon MAsh SHyH
- Pheasant — see *H. macrophylla* 'Fasan'
- 'Pia' (H) — CBgR CDoC CMil CPLG CPla CStu ELan GGGa LBuc MAsh MGos MRav SMad SRms WBor WClo WCom WCru WFar
- Pigeon — see *H. macrophylla* 'Taube'
- 'Pink Wave' (L) — LRHS NPri
- 'Pirate's Gold' — CMil MAsh WClo WHar
- 'Prinses Beatrix' (H) — SHyH
- 'Quadricolor' (L/v) — CMac CMil CPLG EHoe GCal GGal MRav SDix SGar SHyH SLim SPer SPlb SRms WCot WSHC
- 'R.F. Felton' (H) — CBcs SHyH
- 'Red Baron' — see *H. macrophylla* 'Schöne Bautznerin'
- 'Red Red' (H) — MAsh
- Redbreast — see *H. macrophylla* 'Rotkehlchen'
- 'Regula' (H) — SHyH

	- 'Renate Steiniger' (H)	CWit LTen MGos MMuc MRav SHyH
	- 'Romance'	LBuc
	- 'Rosea' **new**	MCri
	- 'Rosita' (H)	IFFs LRHS MAsh MWya NBir WFar
§	- 'Rotkehlchen' (Teller Series) (L)	CDoC EPfP GKir NEgg SCoo SLim SPlb SWvt WDin
	- 'Rotschwanz' (Teller Series) (L)	CMil EQua LRHS MAsh SHyH SSpi WPGP
	- 'Sabrina'PBR (H)	CBcs MBri MGos SPoG
	- 'Saint Claire' (H)	CBcs SHyH
	- 'Sandra' (Dutch Ladies Series) (L)	CBcs ELon
	- 'Schneeball' (H)	MAsh MGos SHyH
§	- 'Schöne Bautznerin'	LRHS MWea NCGa SHyH WClo WMoo
	- 'Sea Foam' (L)	NLar
	- 'Selina'	CBcs EPfP LSRN MDKP MGos SPoG
	- 'Selma'PBR (Dutch Ladies Series) (L)	CBcs MBri
§	- 'Setsuka-yae' (L/d)	CMil NLar
	- 'Sheila' (Dutch Ladies Series) (L)	CBcs EPfP LSRN MBri MGos SPoG
	- 'Sibilla' (H)	CBcs SPlb
	- Sister Therese	see *H. macrophylla* 'Soeur Thérèse'
§	- 'Soeur Thérèse' (H)	CBar MAsh MGos NLar SEND SWvt
	- 'Soraya'PBR (Dutch Ladies Series) (L)	CBcs
	- 'Sumida-no-hanabi' (L/d)	WPGP
*	- 'Sunset' (L)	CBcs
§	- 'Taube' (Teller Series) (L)	CBcs CDoC CMHG CPLG EPfP GGal GQui MAsh SCoo SHyH SWvt
	- 'Teller Pink'	see *H. macrophylla* 'Taube'
	- 'Teller Red'	see *H. macrophylla* 'Rotkehlchen'
N	- Teller variegated	see *H. macrophylla* 'Tricolor'
N	- Teller Weiss	see *H. macrophylla* 'Libelle'
	- var. ***thunbergii***	see *H. serrata* var. *thunbergii*
	- 'Tokyo Delight' (L) 🏆H3-4	CGHE CLAP CMil CPLG CTsd EBee GGGa LRHS MAsh SHyH WPGP
	- 'Tovelit' (H)	GGGa MWya
§	- 'Tricolor' (L/v)	CBcs CBot CDoC CDul CTri CWit ELon EMil EQua LAst LRHS MGos MLLN SHyH SLon SPer SPoG WFar WKif WMoo
	- 'Variegata'	see *H. macrophylla* 'Maculata'
	- 'Veitchii' (L) 🏆H3-4	CBcs CBot CDoy CDul CMHG CPLG CSBt EPfP EWTr GGal LRHS MGos MRav MSwo SDix SGar SHyH SSpi WPGP WSpi
	- 'Vicomte de Vibraye'	see *H. macrophylla* 'Générale Vicomtesse de Vibraye'
	- 'Westfalen' (H) 🏆H3-4	CMac IArd SDix
I	- 'White Lace' (L)	ELan SHyH
	- white lacecap (L)	CSpr
	- 'White Mop' (H)	CWib
	- 'White Wave'	see *H. macrophylla* 'Mariesii Grandiflora'
	- 'Zaunkoenig' (L)	MAsh
	- 'Zebra'PBR (H) **new**	MGos SPoG WCot
	- 'Zhuni Hito'	NLar
	- 'Zorro'PBR	CBcs EPfP LRHS MAsh SCoo SPoG SSpi
	aff. ***mangshanensis*** BWJ 8120	WCru
	paniculata	CMCN WBor
	- B&SWJ 3556 from Taiwan	WCru
	- B&SWJ 5413 from Japan	WCru
	- 'Ammarin'	GQui LLHF NLar WPat
	- Angel's Blush	see *H. paniculata* 'Ruby'
	- 'Big Ben'	EPfP GGGa GQui MBri NLar
	- 'Brussels Lace'	CAbP EBee EPfP GKir LEdu LRHS LSRN MBri MRav NLar SHyH SLon SPoG SSpi WGrn WPat
	- 'Burgundy Lace'	CBcs EQua GGGa MBlu MBri NLar
	- 'Chantilly Lace'	CMil LRHS
	- Dart's Little Dot = 'Darlido'PBR	IVic LLHF LSRN MAsh NLar WPat
	- 'Dharuma'	LLHF LRHS MAsh
	- 'Dolly'	GGGa GQui
	- 'Everest'	CAbP CMil EPfP LRHS MAsh SHyH SPoG
	- 'Floribunda'	CGHE ELan EPfP LRHS MAsh SHyH WPGP
	- 'Goliath'	NLar
	- 'Grandiflora' 🏆H4	Widely available
	- 'Great Escape'	NLar
	- 'Greenspire'	EPfP LRHS MAsh MBlu MRav SHyH WFar
	- 'Harry's Souvenir'	NLar
	- 'Kyushu' 🏆H4	Widely available
	- 'Last Post'	GQui
	- 'Limelight'PBR	Widely available
	- 'Mathilde'	NLar
	- 'Mega Pearl'	LSRN NLar
	- 'Melody'	NLar
	- 'Mount Aso'	GQui NBro WPGP
	- 'October Bride'	GQui MBri NLar WPGP
	- 'Papillon'	WPat
	- 'Pee Wee'	LLHF NLar
	- 'Phantom'	CBcs CMil EPfP GGGa LRHS LSRN LSqu MAsh MBri MDKP MRav NCGa NLar SHyH SPoG WCot WPGP WPat WSpi
	- 'Pink Beauty'PBR	LSRN
	- Pink Diamond = 'Interhydia' 🏆H4	Widely available
	- 'Pink Jewel'	CWib LLHF WPat
	- Pinky-Winky = 'Dvppinky'PBR	CWGN EGxp GQui IVic LLHF LRHS MBlu MGos NLar SPoG
	- 'Praecox'	GQui MRav WKif WPat
	- 'Rosy Morn' **new**	LRHS
§	- 'Ruby'	CBcs NPal
	- 'Silver Dollar'	EPfP GGGa LRHS LSRN MBri
	- 'Tardiva'	CBcs CBot CChe CDoC CWit EBee EPfP GQui LRHS MGos MRav NBro SDix SHyH SPer SRms WDin WFar WPGP WPat
	- 'Tender Rose'	NLar
	- 'Unique' 🏆H4	CBcs CDoC CGHE CSpe EBee EPfP GQui LEdu LHop LRHS LSRN MAsh MMuc MRav NBro NCGa NLar SHyH SPer SPoG SSpi WBor WClo WDin WFar WGrn WGwG WPGP WPat
	- Vanille Fraise = 'Renhy'PBR	CAlb CBcs CDoC CWGN CWit EPfP GGGa LRHS LSRN MAsh MBri MWya NCGa SBfd SHyH SPoG WGrn
	- 'Waterfall'	CLAP
	- 'White Goliath'	GQui
	- 'White Lace'	CBcs NLar
	- 'White Lady'	CBcs
	- 'White Moth'	CAbP CBcs CWGN EBee EPfP EQua GGGa LLHF MAsh NBro NLar SHyH WPat
	- 'Yuan-Yang' **new**	WCru
	peruviana × ***seemanii*** **new**	IArd
	petiolaris	see *H. anomala* subsp. *petiolaris*
	'Preziosa' 🏆H3-4	Widely available
*	***quelpartensis***	CRHN GQui WCom
	- B&SWJ 4400	WCru

quercifolia ♀H3-4	Widely available
- 'Alice'	CPMA EPfP EPla GGGa LRHS MAsh SSpi WPGP
- 'Alison'	EPfP
- 'Burgundy'	CBcs CPMA EPfP IVic MBri NLar WPGP
- 'Flore Pleno'	see *H. quercifolia* Snowflake
- 'Harmony'	CMil CPMA EPfP ESwi EWTr GKir IArd LRHS NLar SSta WPGP WPat
- 'Lady Anne'	MRav WPGP
- 'Little Honey' **new**	SSpi
- Little Honey = 'Brihon'	CAbP EPfP LRHS MAsh SHyH SPoG
* - 'Pee Wee'	CAbP CBcs CDoC CMil CPMA EBee EPfP LRHS MAsh NLar SHyH SLon SPoG SReu SSta WPGP WPat
- 'Sike's Dwarf'	CPMA EBee IVic LTen MGos MPkF MRav WPat WSpi
- 'Snow Giant'	CPMA IVic NLar
- Snow Queen = 'Flemygea'	CBcs CDoC CDul CKno CMac CPMA EBee ELan EPfP IVic LRHS MAsh MBri MGos MPkF MRav NCGa NLar SHyH SLim SPer SPoG SWvt WClo WFar WPGP WPat WSpi
- 'Snowdrift'	CPMA
§ - Snowflake = 'Brido' (d)	CAbP CBcs CDoC CEnd CMil CPMA CSPN CWGN EBee ELan EPfP GKir LRHS MAsh MGos MRav NLar SHyH SLon SPer SPoG SSpi SSta WPGP WPat
- 'Stardust'	MMHG
- 'Tennessee Clone'	CPMA EBee NLar
sargentiana	see *H. aspera* subsp. *sargentiana*
scandens B&SWJ 5448	WCru
- B&SWJ 5481	WCru
- B&SWJ 5496	WCru
- B&SWJ 5523	WCru
- B&SWJ 5602	WCru
- B&SWJ 5893	WCru
- B&SWJ 5929	WCru
- B&SWJ 6159	WCru
- B&SWJ 6317	WCru
§ - subsp. ***chinensis***	CBcs CPLG WFar
- - B&SWJ 1488	WCru
- - B&SWJ 3214	WCru
- - B&SWJ 3420	WCru
- - B&SWJ 3410 from Taiwan	WCru
- - B&SWJ 3423	WCru
- - B&SWJ 3487	WCru
- - BWJ 8000 from Sichuan	WCru
§ - - f. ***angustipetala***	WPGP
- - - B&SWJ 3454	WCru
- - - B&SWJ 3553	WCru
- - - B&SWJ 3667	WCru
- - - B&SWJ 3733	WCru
- - - B&SWJ 3814	WCru
- - - B&SWJ 6038 from Yakushima	WCru
- - - B&SWJ 6041 from Yakushima	WCru
- - - B&SWJ 6056 from Yakushima	WCru
- - - B&SWJ 6787	WCru
- - - B&SWJ 6802	WCru
- - - B&SWJ 7121	WCru
- - - B&SWJ 7128	WCru
- - f. ***formosana***	NLar
- - - B&SWJ 1488	WCru
- - - B&SWJ 3271	WCru
- - - B&SWJ 7058	EQua WCru
- - - B&SWJ 7097	WCru
- - f. ***macrosepala*** B&SWJ 3423	WCru
- - - B&SWJ 3476	WCru
- - f. ***obovatifolia*** B&SWJ 3487b	WCru
- - - B&SWJ 3683	WCru
- - - B&SWJ 7121	WCru
- subsp. ***liukiuensis***	WCru
- - B&SWJ 6022	WCru
- 'Splash' (v)	CMil
seemannii	Widely available
serrata	CPLG CTri CWib WDin WKif
- B&SWJ 4817	WCru
- B&SWJ 6241	WCru
- 'Acuminata'	see *H. serrata* 'Bluebird'
- 'Aigaku' (L)	CLAP CPLG
- 'Aka Beni-yama'	GQui
- 'Akabe-yama'	NBro NLar
- Amacha Group	CGHE
- - 'Amagi-amacha' (L)	CMil GQui NBro NLar
- - 'Ō-amacha'	CMil GQui
- 'Amagyana' (L)	CGHE CPLG
- Avelroz = 'Dolmyf' **new**	SBfd
- 'Belladonna'	GQui
- 'Belle Deckle'	see *H. serrata* 'Blue Deckle'
- 'Beni-gaku' (L)	CLAP CMil CPLG CTsd EBee EGxp GGGa IVic LRHS MAsh NBro NLar SHyH WPGP
- 'Beni-yama' (L)	CGHE CMil GQui WPGP
- 'Blue Billow' (L)	GGGa NBro NLar
§ - 'Blue Deckle' (L)	CMHG CMac EQua GGal MAsh MRav NBro SHyH WPGP
§ - 'Bluebird' (L) ♀H3-4	CBcs CDul EBee ELan ELon EPfP GKir GQui LAst LRHS MAsh MBlu MGos MMuc MRav MSwo NEgg SDix SEND SHyH SLim SPer SPoG SWvt WBVN WBrE WFar WHar WMoo WSpi
- 'Chiba Cherry-lips' **new**	WCru
- 'Chiri-san Sue' **new**	WCru
- 'Diadem' (L) ♀H3-4	CMil CPLG EBee EPfP EQua GGGa GQui LRHS MMuc NBro SDix SHyH WPGP
- dwarf white-flowered (L)	WCru
- 'Forget Me Not'	GQui
- Fuji Snowstorm	see *H. serrata* 'Fuji-no-shirayuki'
- 'Fuji Waterfall'	see *H. serrata* 'Fuji-no-taki'
§ - 'Fuji-no-shirayuki' (L/d)	CMil
§ - 'Fuji-no-taki' (L/d)	CAbP ELon LLHF NCGa NEgg SMad WBor WFar
- 'Golden Showers' (L)	GGGa MAsh NBro
- 'Golden Sunlight'PBR (L)	CDoC GGGa GQui SLim SWvt
- 'Graciosa' (L)	MAsh WPGP
- 'Grayswood' (L) ♀H3-4	CBcs CEnd CMac CPLG CSBt EPfP EQua GGal GKir GQui LRHS MAsh MRav NBro SDix SGar SHyH SLim SPer SSpi WBor WKif WPGP
- 'Hakucho' (L/d)	NBro
- 'Hallasan' misapplied	see *H. serrata* 'Maiko', 'Spreading Beauty'
- 'Hallasan' ambig.	CMil
- 'Hallasan' R. & J. de Belder (L)	CMil
- 'Hime-benigaku' (L)	CLAP CMil MAsh
- 'Impératrice Eugénie' (L)	GQui
- 'Intermedia' (L)	CPLG NBro
- 'Isusai-jaku' (L)	GQui
- 'Kiyosumi' (L)	CDoC CEnd CGHE CLAP CMil CPLG ECre ELon GGGa GGal GQui MAsh NBir SHyH WBor WCot WCru WPGP WPat WSpi
- 'Klaveren'	see *H. macrophylla* 'Klaveren'
- 'Koreana' (L)	EQua GGGa MAsh

- 'Kurenai' (L) NBro NLar
- 'Kurenai-nishiki' (L/v) CMil
- 'Kurohime' (L) NBro
- 'Macrosepala' (L) MAsh SHyH
§ - 'Maiko' (L) IArd
- 'Midora' CPLG
- 'Midori' (L) SHyH
- 'Mikata Yae' CMil
- 'Miranda' (L) ♀H3-4 CBow CPLG CSam EPfP LRHS MAsh NBro NLar SHyH SSpi WFar
- 'Miyama-yae-murasaki' (L/d) CGHE CLAP CMil CPLG EQua MAsh WCom WPGP
- 'Momo Beni Yama' CMil
- 'Pretty Maiden' see *H. serrata* 'Shichidanka'
- 'Professeur Iida' (L) WPGP
§ - 'Prolifera' (L/d) CGHE CMil WPGP WPat
- 'Pulchella' see *H. serrata* 'Prolifera'
- 'Ramis Pictis' (L) EQua GQui NBro NLar WPGP
- 'Rosalba' (L) ♀H3-4 CLAP CPLG ECre EPfP GGal IVic NBro WFar WSHC
- 'Sapphirine' (L) GQui
§ - 'Shichidanka' (L/d) NBro
- 'Shichidanka-nishiki' (L/d/v) CDoC CGHE CPLG ECre GQui SHyH WBor
- 'Shinonome' (L/d) CLAP CMil CPLG GQui WPGP
- 'Shirofuji' (L/d) CLAP CMil MAsh WPGP WPat
- 'Shiro-gaku' (L) MAsh NBro NLar
- 'Shirotae' (L/d) CPLG GGGa WPGP
- 'Shōjō' CMil MAsh
§ - 'Spreading Beauty' (L) CMil WPGP
§ - var. ***thunbergii*** (L) GQui WFar
* - - 'Plena' (L/d) GQui WCru
- 'Tiara' (L) ♀H3-4 CAbb CMil CPLG GGGa GGal IVic LRHS LSRN MAsh NBir NBro NLar SDix SHyH SSpi WPGP
- 'Uzu-azisai' WPGP
- 'Yae-no-amacha' (L/d) CPLG NBro SHyH WPGP
- subsp. ***yezoensis*** GQui NLar
§ ***serratifolia*** CHEx CPLG EPfP EPla IArd IDee SSpi SSta WCru WFar WPGP
- HCM 98056 WCru
sikokiana CLAP
- B&SWJ 5035 WCru
- B&SWJ 5855 WCru
'Silver Slipper' see *H. macrophylla* 'Ayesha'
tiliifolia see *H. anomala* subsp. *petiolaris*
villosa see *H. aspera* Villosa Group
xanthoneura see *H. heteromalla*
'You and Me' CMil MGos SCoo
'Zambia' **new** MGos SPoG

Hydrastis (*Ranunculaceae*)
canadensis CArn COld GPoy LEdu

Hydrocharis (*Hydrocharitaceae*)
morsus-ranae CBen CRow CWat EHon LPBA MSKA MWts NPer NSco SWat WPnP

Hydrocleys (*Limnocharitaceae*)
nymphoides XBlo

Hydrocotyle (*Apiaceae*)
asiatica see *Centella asiatica*
sibthorpioides CBow
- 'Crystal Confetti' (v) EPPr LLWG MWts
vulgaris CWat EBWF

Hydrophyllum (*Hydrophyllaceae*)
canadense EBee IMou
'Spring Silver' **new** SKHP

Hylomecon (*Papaveraceae*)
* ***hylomecoides*** WCru
§ ***japonica*** CLAP EBee ECho ELan GBBs GCra GCrs GEdr GKir NBir NMen NRya WCru WFar

Hylotelephium see *Sedum*

Hymenanthera see *Melicytus*

Hymenocallis (*Amaryllidaceae*)
'Advance' ECho LAma
§ ***caroliniana*** ECho
× ***festalis*** ♀H1 CCCN ECho EPfP LAma LRHS SPav WCot WFar WPrP
- 'Zwanenburg' CGrW ECho WHil
harrisiana CCCN ECho LRHS WPrP
littoralis 'Variegata' SPoG
§ ***longipetala*** ECho WPrP
occidentalis see *H. caroliniana*
'Sulphur Queen' ♀H1 CGrW ECho SPav

Hymenolepis (*Asteraceae*)
parviflora see *Athanasia parviflora*

Hymenosporum (*Pittosporaceae*)
flavum EShb EUJe SOWG

Hymenoxys (*Asteraceae*)
§ ***hoopesii*** CMHG EBee EBla EGxp EHrv ELan EPfP EShb GAbr GKir GMaP LHop LRHS MLLN NBPC NBir NChi NEgg NPri SPer SRms WClo WCot WFar WMnd WPer WWEG

Hyophorbe (*Arecaceae*)
lagenicaulis LPal
verschaffeltii LPal

Hyoscyamus (*Solanaceae*)
niger CArn GPoy MNHC

Hypericum ✿ (*Clusiaceae*)
CC 4131 CPLG
CC 4544 CPLG
acmosepalum WPGP
aegypticum CPBP ECho ECtt EPot MHer NMen NWCA WAbe WCom WFar WPer
androsaemum CArn CRWN ECha ELan MHer MRav MSwo NPer NSco WDin WHfH WMoo WOut
§ - 'Albury Purple' ELan EShb MRav WCom WHrl WMoo
- 'Autumn Blaze' CBcs
§ - 'Dart's Golden Penny' SPer
- 'Excellent Flair' NLar
§ - f. ***variegatum*** 'Mrs Gladis Brabazon' (v) NBir NLar NPla WCom WHrl
athoum NBir WAbe WThu
atomarium WPGP
balearicum CMea EHrv MTho WAbe WPGP
barbatum WFar
§ ***beanii*** GAuc
bellum EBee GCal SLon
buckleyi WAbe
calycinum CBcs CDul CMac CTri CWan EBee ECho ECrN ELan ELon EPfP LBuc MGos MMuc MRav MWat NWea SBfd SEND SPer SPoG SWvt WDin WGwG WMoo
- 'Brigadoon' LRHS MAsh SPoG

- 'Senior'	LAst
cerastioides	CMea CTri CWib EDif SMrm SRms WFar WPat WPer
coris	ECho EWes MWat NMen SRms
cuneatum	see *H. pallens*
× ***cyathiflorum*** 'Gold Cup'	CMac LRHS MAsh
× ***dummeri*** 'Peter Dummer'	NLar WSpi
'Eastleigh Gold'	CMac
'Elite Baby Green' **new**	EPfP
'Elite Mayor' **new**	EPfP
'Elite Sweet Lion' **new**	EPfP
elodes	CWat LLWG MSKA
empetrifolium	ECho SEND
- 'Prostatum'	see *H. empetrifolium* subsp. *tortuosum*
§ - subsp. ***tortuosum***	ECho EWes IRar
forrestii ♀H4	EBee EPfP MMuc SEND WFar WPGP
- B&L 12469	WPGP
- Hird 54	WPGP
N ***fragile*** misapplied	see *H. olympicum* f. *minus*
frondosum 'Buttercup'	NLar
- 'Sunburst'	EBee EPfP
N 'Gemo'	ECrN
'Gold Penny'	see *H. androsaemum* 'Dart's Golden Penny'
'Golden Beacon'	CBow CBre CSpe EBee LAst LRHS LSou MBri NEgg NLar SBfd SMad SPad SPoG WCot
grandiflorum	see *H. kouytchense*
henryi	MSnd
- L 753	SRms
'Hidcote' ♀H4	Widely available
'Hidcote Variegated' (v)	CBow LRHS MAsh MCCP SLim SRms WFar
hirsutum	EBWF NMir
× ***inodorum*** 'Albury Purple'	see *H. androsaemum* 'Albury Purple'
- 'Autumn Surprise'PBR	NEgg NHol WHar
- 'Dream'	NLar
- 'Elstead'	EBee ECrN ECtt ELan EPfP MGos MMHG MRav MWat NHol WDin WSpi
- 'Hysan'	GGar
- 'Rheingold'	LRHS MAsh
- 'Ysella'	MRav
japonicum	ECho EWes
kalmianum	EWes
kamtschaticum	ECho
§ ***kiusianum*** var. ***yakusimense***	MTho
§ ***kouytchense*** ♀H4	CDul CMCN CWit EBee ELon EPfP EQua EWes GQui LRHS MAsh MMuc MRav SEND SPoG WCFE WClo WHrl WPat WSpi
lancasteri	EBee EPfP LRHS MAsh SPoG
leschenaultii misapplied	see *H.* 'Rowallane'
linarioides	EBee
maclarenii	EWes
Magical Beauty = 'Kolmbeau'PBR	NHol NLar NPnk SPoG
Magical Red = 'Kolmred'PBR	NLar SPoG
'Miracle Summer' **new**	EPfP
× ***moserianum*** ♀H4	CBar CDul CMac EBee EPfP LRHS MRav NPer SLon SPer SRms WDin
- 'Daybreak'	LRHS MAsh SPoG
§ - 'Tricolor' (v)	Widely available
- 'Variegatum'	see *H.* × *moserianum* 'Tricolor'
'Mrs Brabazon'	see *H. androsaemum* f. *variegatum* 'Mrs Gladis Brabazon'
nummularium	NBir NMen WAbe
oblongifolium	CPLG WAbe WCot
olympicum ♀H4	CEnt CTri ECha ECho ELan EPfP EPot GJos LRHS MBrN MMuc MWat SEND SPer SRms WAbe WDin WFar WNew
- 'Grandiflorum'	see *H. olympicum* f. *uniflorum*
§ - f. ***minus***	CTri ECho ECtt SPlb SRms WCom WHrl WPer
§ - - 'Sulphureum'	CBgR CBot CChe CPrp ECho ELon EWes GMaP LRHS MLHP NBir SPer SRms WCFE
- - 'Variegatum' (v)	CBow CWan EWes LBee NBir SPoG WPat
§ - f. ***uniflorum***	ECho LRHS NBro NVic
- - 'Citrinum' ♀H4	CMea ECha ECtt EPfP LBee LRHS MRav MWat NBro SRot WAbe WCot WEas WHoo WKif WPat
orientale	EWes
§ ***pallens***	ECho NMen WAbe
patulum var. ***henryi*** Veitch ex Bean	see *H. beanii*
perforatum	CArn CBod CHby CWan EBWF EBee EPfP GBar GPoy MHer MNHC NMir NMun SEND SIde WHer WHfH WJek WMoo WSFF
polyphyllum	see *H. olympicum* f. *minus*
- 'Citrinum'	see *H. olympicum* f. *minus* 'Sulphureum'
- 'Grandiflorum'	see *H. olympicum* f. *uniflorum*
prolificum	ECtt MMHG WCFE
pseudopetiolatum var. ***yakusimense***	see *H. kiusianum* var. *yakusimense*
quadrangulum L.	see *H. tetrapterum*
reptans misapplied	see *H. olympicum* f. *minus*
reptans Dyer	CMea ECho EWes
§ 'Rowallane' ♀H3	CTri EPfP GCal SDix SMrm SSpi
stellatum	WFar
subsessile	CPLG
'Sungold'	see *H. kouytchense*
§ ***tetrapterum***	CArn EBWF NSco
trichocaulon	EWes
uralum HWJ 520	WCru
xylosteifolium	SLon
yakusimense	see *H. kiusianum* var. *yakusimense*

Hypocalymma (*Myrtaceae*)

angustifolium	SOWG

Hypocalyptus (*Papilionaceae*)

sophoroides	SPlb

Hypochaeris (*Asteraceae*)

maculata	WHer
radicata	EBWF NMir

Hypocyrta see *Nematanthus*

Hypoestes (*Acanthaceae*)

aristata	CPLG EShb
§ ***phyllostachya*** (v) ♀H1	EShb WHil
sanguinolenta misapplied	see *H. phyllostachya*

Hypolepis (*Dennstaedtiaceae*)

ambigua	WRic
millefolium	GGar WCot
punctata	EFer
rufobarbata	WRic

Hypoxis (*Hypoxidaceae*)

hemerocallidea 'Bloemfontein' **new**	ECho

hirsuta CPen ECho WCot
hygrometrica ECho ECou NMen WAbe WThu
iridiflora see *H. obtusa*
krebsii ECho LLHF
§ ***obtusa*** LLHF
- 'Harrismith' **new** ECho
parvula CFee CTca NMen
- var. ***albiflora*** ITim
§ - - 'Hebron Farm Biscuit' CCCN ECho EWes GEdr WAbe WFar
- pink-flowered CYeo
rigidula 'Harrismith' **new** ECho
villosa ECho

Hypoxis × *Rhodohypoxis* see × *Rhodoxis*

H. parvula × ***R. baurii*** see × *Rhodoxis hybrida*

Hypsela (*Campanulaceae*)

sp. CFee
longiflora see *H. reniformis*
§ ***reniformis*** ECho EDAr GGar LBee LLWG LRHS MRav NWCA WFar
- 'Greencourt White' ECho

Hyptis (*Lamiaceae*)

emoryi CArn

Hyssopus ✿ (*Lamiaceae*)

officinalis CArn CHby CSev ECha ELan ELau EPfP GKir GPoy LBuc LHop MBri MCot MHer MLHP MNHC MRav NBir NGHP SBfd SEND SGar SIde SPlb SPoG SVic WHfH WJek WPer WSHC
- f. ***albus*** CWan EBee ECha ELau EPfP GPoy MHer MNHC NGHP SGar SIde SPlb WHfH WJek WPer
- subsp. ***aristatus*** CArn EBee ECho ELau ELon EPfP GPoy LLWP LRHS MHer MNHC NChi SIde SPoG WJek
- 'Blaue Wolke' GBin
- 'Roseus' CEnt EBee ECha ELau EPfP GPoy LLWP MHer MNHC NGHP SBch SEND SIde SPoG WJek WPer WSHC

Hystrix (*Poaceae*)

patula CKno CSam EHoe EPPr EShb GFor LLWP MCCP MMoz MNrw MWhi NHol SBch SPlb WPer WTin

I

Iberis (*Brassicaceae*)

aurosica 'Sweetheart' GEdr WFar
candolleana see *I. pruitii* Candolleana Group
commutata see *I. sempervirens*
'Dick Self' LRHS
gibraltarica ECho SRms WGor
- 'Betty Swainson' SMrm SPhx SUsu
§ ***pruitii*** Candolleana Group ECho GEdr WAbe WFar
saxatilis ECho GKev LRHS
semperflorens WCFE WCom WWEG
§ ***sempervirens*** ♀H4 CMea CTri CWib ECho ELan EPfP GKir IFoB LAst MMuc MWat NBro NVic SEND SRms SWal WBrE WCFE WClo WFar WHoo WPer
- 'Compacta' ECho
- 'Elfenreigen' GCal
- 'Fischbeck' **new** SRot
- 'Golden Candy'PBR EHoe LRHS MAvo SPoG WFar
- 'Little Gem' see *I. sempervirens* 'Weisser Zwerg'
- 'Pygmaea' ECho NMen
- Schneeflocke see *I. sempervirens* 'Snowflake'
- 'Snow Cushion' GEdr WWEG
§ - 'Snowflake' ♀H4 CBar ECho ELon EPfP GEdr IFoB LAst MWat NBre NPri SBch SPer SPoG SWvt WFar WRHF
§ - 'Weisser Zwerg' CMea ECha ECho ECtt ELan GEdr LAst LBee MHer MRav MWat NMen NRya SBch SPoG SRms WHoo

Idesia (*Flacourtiaceae*)

polycarpa CAbP CBcs CDul CMCN EBee EPfP LHop MMuc NLar SSpi WBVN WDin WFar WPGP WPat

Ilex ✿ (*Aquifoliaceae*)

N × ***altaclerensis*** SHHo WFar
- 'Atkinsonii' (m) SHHo WWHy
- 'Balearica' (f) SHHo
- 'Barterberry' (f) WWHy
- 'Belgica' (f) GKir SHHo
§ - 'Belgica Aurea' (f/v) ♀H4 CAlb CBcs CDoC CPMA CSBt CTho EBee EPfP EQua GKir MBri MSwo NHol NWea SHHo WFar WWHy
- 'Camelliifolia' (f) ♀H4 CAlb CDul CMac CSBt CTho EBee ELan EPfP GKir LMaj MBlu MBri MWat NEgg NLar NPCo NWea SHHo WFar WSpi WWHy
- 'Golden King' (f/v) ♀H4 Widely available
- 'Hendersonii' (f) NPCo SHHo WWHy
- 'Hodginsii' (m) ♀H4 CTri MRav SHHo WFar WWHy
- 'Howick' (f/v) SHHo
- 'James G. Esson' (f) SHHo
- 'Jermyns' (m) SHHo
- 'Lady Valerie' (f/v) SHHo WWHy
- 'Lawsoniana' (f/v) ♀H4 Widely available
- 'Maderensis Variegata' see *I. aquifolium* 'Maderensis Variegata'
- 'Marnockii' (f) SHHo WWHy
- 'Moorei' (m) SHHo
- 'Mundyi' (m) SHHo
- 'N.F. Barnes' (f) SHHo
- 'Purple Shaft' (f) EQua MRav SHHo
- 'Ripley Gold' (f/v) LRHS MAsh MBri NHol SHHo WWHy
- 'Silver Sentinel' see *I.* × *altaclerensis* 'Belgica Aurea'
- 'W.J. Bean' (f) SHHo WWHy
- 'Wilsonii' (f) EBee EPfP NPCo SHHo WWHy
aquifolium ♀H4 Widely available
- 'Alaska' (f) CAlb CCVT CDoC CDul CMCN CPMA ECrN GKir IFFs LAst LBuc LRHS MAsh NHol NLar NSti SBfd SHHo SWvt WFar WGob WWHy
- 'Amber' (f) ♀H4 CTri EQua NPCo SHHo SMad WWHy
- 'Angustifolia' (f) LRHS MAsh WCFE WFar WWHy
- 'Angustifolia' (m or f) EPfP MWat SHHo SPoG WBVN WFar
- 'Angustimarginata Aurea' (m/v) NPCo SHHo
- 'Argentea Longifolia' (m/v) WWHy
§ - 'Argentea Marginata' (f/v) ♀H4 Widely available
§ - 'Argentea Marginata Pendula' (f/v) CDoC CMac CTri ELan EPfP GKir LRHS MAsh MRav NHol NLar NWea SHHo SPer SRms WFar WPat WWHy
- 'Argentea Pendula' see *I. aquifolium* 'Argentea Marginata Pendula'

	- 'Argentea Variegata'	see *I. aquifolium* 'Argentea Marginata'
	- 'Atlas' (m)	CBcs CDoC LBuc WWHy
	- 'Aurea Marginata' (f/v)	CAlb CMac CTho EBee EPfP LBuc LRHS MGos NHol NPCo NWea SCoo SHHo WCFE WDin WFar WPat
	- 'Aurea Marginata Pendula' (f/v)	CDoC NHol WPat
	- 'Aurea Marginata Stricta' (f/v)	WWHy
	- 'Aurea Regina'	see *I. aquifolium* 'Golden Queen'
	- 'Aureovariegata Pendula'	see *I. aquifolium* 'Weeping Golden Milkmaid'
	- 'Aurifodina' (f)	NPCo SHHo WWHy
	- 'Bacciflava' (f)	Widely available
	- 'Bella' (f)	SHHo
	- 'Bokrijk' (f/v)	SHHo WWHy
	- 'Bowland' (f/v)	NHol
	- 'Chris Whittle'	NHol
	- 'Cookii' (f)	SHHo WWHy
	- 'Crassifolia' (f)	CWib IArd SHHo SMad WWHy
	- 'Crispa' (m)	EBee NHol SHHo WWHy
§	- 'Crispa Aurea Picta' (m/v)	SHHo WWHy
	- 'Crispa Aureomaculata'	see *I. aquifolium* 'Crispa Aurea Picta'
	- 'Elegantissima' (m/v)	CPMA LRHS SCoo SHHo WWHy
	- 'Fastigiata Sartori'	NLar
	- 'Ferox' (m)	CDul ELan EPfP LRHS SHHo SPer SPoG WDin WWHy
	- 'Ferox Argentea' (m/v) ♀H4	Widely available
*	- 'Ferox Argentea Picta' (m/v)	WFar WWHy
	- 'Ferox Aurea' (m/v)	CDoC CPMA CSBt CWib EBee ELan ELon EPfP EPla GKir MAsh NEgg NHol NPCo SHHo SPer WWHy
§	- 'Flavescens' (f)	CBot EBee EPfP EQua MBlu NHol NPCo SHHo
	- 'Frogmore Silver' (m/v)	EQua SHHo
	- 'Gold Flash' (f/v)	EBee GKir LRHS MBri MGos NEgg NHol NLar SHHo WClo WDin WWHy
I	- 'Golden Hedgehog'	SHHo SPoG WWHy
	- 'Golden Milkboy' (m/v)	CAlb CMac ELan EPfP GKir MGos SHHo WDin WPat WWHy
§	- 'Golden Queen' (m/v) ♀H4	CDoC CMac CWSG CWib EBee IArd MGos NBir NHol NPCo SHHo SRms WPat WWHy
	- 'Golden Tears' (f/v)	SHHo WWHy
	- 'Golden van Tol' (f/v)	Widely available
	- 'Green Minaret' **new**	IVic
§	- 'Green Pillar' (f)	EPfP SHHo WWHy
	- 'Green Spire'	see *I. aquifolium* 'Green Pillar'
	- 'Handsworth New Silver' (f/v) ♀H4	Widely available
	- 'Harpune' (f)	IArd SHHo WWHy
§	- 'Hascombensis'	CDoC GKir LHop MGos NHol NMen NWea WWHy
	- 'Hastata' (m)	CWib IArd IDee MRav WWHy
	- 'Ingramii' (m/v)	SHHo WWHy
	- 'Integrifolia' (f)	WWHy
	- 'J.C. van Tol' (f) ♀H4	Widely available
	- 'Latispina' (f)	SHHo WWHy
	- 'Laurifolia' (m) **new**	IArd
	- 'Laurifolia Aurea' (m/v)	SHHo
	- 'Lichtenthalii' (f)	IArd IFFs IVic NPCo SHHo
	- 'Madame Briot' (f/v) ♀H4	Widely available
§	- 'Maderensis Variegata' (f/v)	SHHo
	- 'Monstrosa' (m)	GKir SHHo
	- moonlight holly	see *I. aquifolium* 'Flavescens'
	- 'Myrtifolia' (f)	NEgg NPCo
	- 'Myrtifolia' (m)	ELan EPfP GCal MGos NEgg NLar NPCo SCoo SHHo SMad WFar WMoo WWHy
	- 'Myrtifolia Aurea' (m/v)	GKir NEgg SWvt WFar WGob
	- 'Myrtifolia Aurea Maculata' (m/v) ♀H4	CDoC CPMA CSBt CSam EBee ELan EPfP LRHS MAsh NEgg NHol NPCo NWea SHHo SMad SPer SPoG SWvt WBVN WFar WPat WWHy
	- 'Ovata' (m)	WWHy
	- 'Ovata Aurea' (m/v)	SHHo WWHy
	- 'Pendula' (f)	EPfP GKir MRav SHHo
	- 'Pendula Mediopicta'	see *I. aquifolium* 'Weeping Golden Milkmaid'
	- 'Pyramidalis' (f) ♀H4	CDoC CDul CMac CSBt CTri EBee ELan GKir LRHS MAsh MBri MGos NHol NLar NPCo NWea SHHo SRms WDin WFar WMoo WWHy
	- 'Pyramidalis Aureomarginata' (f/v)	CDoC MBri MGos NLar SHHo
	- 'Pyramidalis Fructu Luteo' (f) ♀H4	MAsh SHHo
	- 'Recurva' (m)	CMac SHHo WWHy
	- 'Rederly' (f)	WWHy
	- 'Rubricaulis Aurea' (f/v)	NHol NLar NPCo SHHo WGob WWHy
	- 'Scotica' (f)	GKir NWea SHHo WWHy
	- Siberia = 'Limsi'PBR (f)	EBee IVic SHHo WWHy
	- 'Silver King'	see *I. aquifolium* 'Silver Queen'
	- 'Silver Lining' (f/v)	SHHo
	- 'Silver Milkboy' (f/v)	ELan MBlu MGos WFar WWHy
	- 'Silver Milkmaid' (f/v)	CDoC CWSG EBee EPfP GKir LAst LRHS NEgg NHol SHHo SLim SPer SWvt WGob WMoo WWHy
§	- 'Silver Queen' (m/v) ♀H4	Widely available
	- 'Silver Sentinel'	see *I.* × *altaclerensis* 'Belgica Aurea'
	- 'Silver van Tol' (f/v)	CDoC ELan LAst MAsh NEgg NHol NLar NPCo NPer NWea SHHo WFar WWHy
	- 'Somerset Cream' (f/v)	CPMA CWib NLar WWHy
	- 'Sterntaler' **new**	IVic
§	- 'Watereriana' (m/v)	SHHo
	- 'Waterer's Gold'	see *I. aquifolium* 'Watereriana'
§	- 'Weeping Golden Milkmaid' (f/v)	MRav SHHo WPat
	- 'White Cream' (m/v) **new**	IVic MBri
	- 'Wichtel' **new**	IVic
	- 'Yellow Star' (f/v) **new**	IVic
	× ***aquipernyi***	SHHo
	- Dragon Lady = 'Meschick' (f)	CAlb CDoC NLar NPCo SHHo WWHy
	- 'San Jose' (f)	CMCN SHHo
	× ***attenuata***	WFar
	- 'Sunny Foster' (f/v)	CDoC CMCN EPfP EPla SHHo SPoG WFar
§	***bioritsensis***	CMCN CTri GKir NWea
	'Brilliant' (f)	NPCo
	cassine L. non Walt.	GKir
	China Boy = 'Mesdob' (m)	LMaj SHHo
	China Girl = 'Mesog' (f)	SHHo
	ciliospinosa	GKir WPGP
	cinerea HWJ 916 **new**	WCru
	'Clusterberry' (f)	NPCo
	colchica	CMCN SHHo
	corallina	CBcs
	cornuta	EPfP ERom SHHo WFar
	- B&SWJ 8756	WCru
	- 'Anicet Delcambre' (f)	SHHo
*	- 'Aurea'	SHHo
	- 'Burfordii' (f)	SHHo
§	- 'Dazzler' (f)	SHHo
	- 'Fine Line' (f)	SHHo
	- 'Ira S. Nelson' (f/v)	IArd SHHo

	- 'O. Spring' (f/v)	SHHo WSpi
	- 'Rotunda' (f)	SHHo
	crenata	CMCN CTri ERom GCra GKir MGos NWea SAPC SHHo STrG WDin WFar
*	- 'Akagi'	WFar
	- 'Aureovariegata'	see *I. crenata* 'Variegata'
	- 'Convexa' (f) 🏆^{H4}	CAlb EPfP GKir IFFs MAsh MRav MSwo NEgg NHol NPCo NWea WFar WGwG WPat
	- 'Convexed Gold' (f/v)	MBri NHol SPoG
	- 'Dwarf Pagoda' (f) **new**	IVic
	- 'Fastigiata' (f)	CDoC ECrN EPfP GKir LRHS MAsh MBri MGos NLar SCoo SHHo SLim SPer SPoG WFar
*	- 'Glory Gem' (f)	CBcs
	- 'Golden Gem' (f/v) 🏆^{H4}	CAlb CDoC CDul CSBt CTri EBee ELan EPfP GKir IVic LAst LRHS LTen MAsh MGos NHol NWea SCoo SLim SPer SPoG SWvt WDin WFar WGwG WPat WWHy
*	- 'Green Hedge'	CAlb
	- 'Helleri' (f)	EPfP WPat
	- 'Hetzii' (f)	NLar
	- 'Ivory Tower' (f)	NEgg NPCo
	- var. ***latifolia*** (m)	GKir
	- 'Luteovariegata'	see *I. crenata* 'Variegata'
	- 'Mariesii' (f)	CMac EBee MBlu
	- 'Obovata' **new**	GKir
I	- 'Pyramidalis' (f)	MRav NHol NWea
	- 'Rotundifolia' (m)	CAlb
§	- 'Shiro-fukurin' (f/v)	CMCN CMHG ELan EPfP GKir GQue LRHS SHHo
	- 'Snowflake'	see *I. crenata* 'Shiro-fukurin'
	- 'Stokes' (m)	NHol NLar
§	- 'Variegata' (v)	CMac EPfP EPla LRHS
	'Dazzler'	see *I. cornuta* 'Dazzler'
	dimorphophylla	CBcs CDoC CMac SHHo SMad
	- 'Somerset Pixie' (f)	SHHo
	dipyrena	CBcs
	'Doctor Kassab' (f)	CMCN SHHo
	'Drace' (f)	SHHo
	'Elegance' (f)	MBlu WFar
	ficoidea	CMCN
	aff. ***gagnepainiana*** HWJ 946	WCru
	glabra	SHHo
	'Good Taste' (f)	CDoC SHHo WFar WWHy
	hascombensis	see *I. aquifolium* 'Hascombensis'
	hookeri	CDoC
	'Indian Chief' (f)	NPCo SMad WFar
	insignis	see *I. kingiana*
	'John T. Morris' (m)	SHHo
§	***kingiana***	WFar WPGP
	× ***koehneana***	CBot CDul ELan
	- 'Chestnut Leaf' (f) 🏆^{H4}	CCVT CDoC CLnd CMCN EBtc EPfP EQua GKir MRav NPCo SHHo SMad WFar WGrn WMou WPGP WWHy
	- 'Wirt L. Winn' (f)	WWHy
	latifolia	CBcs CHEx CMCN NLar SHHo SMad WPGP
*	'Little Diamond'	LSRN
	'Lydia Morris' (f)	CSam SHHo WFar
	'Mary Nell' (f)	SHHo
	maximowicziana var. ***kanehirae***	CBcs WWHy
	× ***meserveae***	SHHo
	- 'Blue Angel' (f)	CBcs CDoC CDul CMac CWit EBee ELan EPfP IFoB MBri MRav MWat NEgg NHol NLar NPCo NWea SHHo SPoG SRms WDin WFar WMoo WWHy
	- Blue Bunny = 'Meseal' (f) **new**	IVic
	- Blue Maid = 'Mesid' (f)	EWTr NPCo WWHy
	- Blue Prince (m)	CBcs CDoC CMac EBee ELan IFFs LBuc LRHS MBlu NEgg NHol NLar NPri NWea SHHo SLim SPer SPoG WDin WFar WWHy
	- Blue Princess = 'Conapri' (f)	CBcs CMac ELan EPfP GKir LBuc LRHS MBlu MRav NHol NLar NPCo NPri NSti NWea SCoo SHHo SLim SPer SPoG WDin WMoo WWHy
	- Blue Stallion = 'Mesan' (m)	CAlb CDoC
	- Castle Spire = 'Hachfee'^{PBR} **new**	IVic
	- Castle Wall = 'Hecken Star'^{PBR} **new**	IVic
	- Golden Girl = 'Mesgolg' (f)	WWHy
	- 'Goliath' (f)	WWHy
	- 'Heckenpracht'^{PBR} **new**	IVic
	myrtifolia	CMac MAsh MRav NPri
	'Nellie R. Stevens' (f)	CAlb CDoC LMaj LTen NLar NWea SCoo WWHy
	opaca	CMCN
	perado subsp. ***perado***	CBcs GKir NPCo
	- subsp. ***platyphylla***	CBcs CHEx CMCN MBlu SAPC SArc SHHo WWHy
	pernyi	CDoC CMCN CMac CTri EPfP GKir LRHS MAsh SHHo SLon SPoG WFar WWHy
	- var. ***veitchii***	see *I. bioritsensis*
	rugosa	WWHy
	'September Gem' (f)	CMCN NPCo
	serrata	CMac CMen
	- 'Koshobai' **new**	CMen
	- 'Leucocarpa'	CMen
	spinigera **new**	CBcs
	suaveolens	CMCN
	verticillata	CMCN LRHS NEgg WDin WFar
	- (f)	CBcs EPfP NLar NWea WFar
	- (m)	EPfP NLar
	- 'Christmas Cheer' (f)	WFar
	- 'Maryland Beauty' (f)	CPMA
	- 'Southern Gentleman' (m)	CPMA
	- 'Winter Gold' (f)	CPMA
	- 'Winter Red' (f)	CMCN CPMA EBee LTen
	vomitoria	CMCN EBtc EShb SHHo
	× ***wandoensis***	CMCN SHHo WWHy
	'Washington' (f)	SHHo WWHy
	yunnanensis	GQui SHHo

Iliamna see *Sphaeralcea*

Illicium (*Illiciaceae*)

	anisatum	CBcs CMac CPLG EPfP NLar SSpi WFar WPGP WPat WSHC
	floridanum	CBcs CPne EPfP MBri NLar SSpi WPat
	- f. ***album***	EPfP
I	- 'Compactum'	WPGP
	- 'Halley's Comet'	NLar
	henryi	CDoC CGHE CMHG CPLG CWib EBee EPfP NLar SSpi WPGP WSHC
	aff. ***henryi***	CBcs
	simonsii	CPLG MBlu WPat
	- BWJ 8024	WCru

Ilysanthes see *Lindernia*

Impatiens ✿ (*Balsaminaceae*)

CC 4980	CPLG
DJHC 98415	CDes WPGP

apiculata	GCal WPrP
arguta	CDes CFir CLAP CPLG CPom CSpe EBee EPPr EShb GCal MCCP MDKP WCot WPGP WPrP
auricoma	CSpe WCot
- 'Jungle Gold'	EShb
auricoma* × *bicaudata	EShb WDib
balfourii	EHrv
congolensis	CCCN
flanaganae	CFir WPGP
forrestii	CLAP
aff. ***forrestii***	WPrP
gomphophylla	CFir
(Harmony Series) Harmony Dark Red = 'Danhardkrd'	WGor
- Harmony Orange Star new	WGor
- Harmony Pink Smile	WGor
- Harmony Salmon = 'Danharsal'	WGor
- Harmony Violet = 'Danharvio'	WGor
keilii	WDib
kerriae B&SWJ 7219	WCru
kilimanjari subsp. ***kilimanjari***	CSpe GCal
- 'Pink Candy' new	CSpe
kilimanjari* × *pseudoviola	CDoC CFee CSpe EBee
langbianensis HWJ 1054	WCru
'Linda's White'	GCal
macrophylla B&SWJ 10157	WCru
namchabarwensis	CDes CSpe WCot WPGP
niamniamensis	CHll EBak EShb WCot WDib
- 'Congo Cockatoo'	CDTJ CDoC CHEx CTsd EOHP ERea GCal NPer SRms
- 'Golden Cockatoo' (v)	CDTJ CDoC EBak ERea EShb
noli-tangere	WSFF
omeiana	CCCN CDes CFir CHEx CLAP CPom EBee EPPr ESwi EWld GCal LEdu MCCP MNrw NLar SBch SBig SUsu WBor WCot WCru WHil WPGP WPrP WPtf WSHC
- DJH C98492	WCru
- 'Ice Storm' new	GCal
- silver-leaved	CDes CHEx CLAP MCCP MDKP WCru WPGP WPrP
parasitica	WDib
platypetala B&SWJ 9722	WCru WPrP
pseudoviola	SDix
puberula	CDes CFir EBee WPrP
- HWJK 2063	WCru
repens ♀H1 new	WDib
rothii	CFir EBee EShb GCal
scabrida	CSpe
sodenii	CDTJ CSpe EShb GCal SBHP
stenantha	CFir
tinctoria	CDoC CFir CGHE CHEx CHll CPLG CPom CSpe CWit EBee EShb GCal GCra LPio MCCP MNrw SMrm WCot WPGP WPrP WWlt
- subsp. ***elegantissima***	CFee
- subsp. ***tinctoria***	IFro
tuberosa	EShb WDib
ugandensis	GCal
uniflora	CDes CFir EBee GCal MCCP
Velvetea = 'Secret Love'PBR	CCCN
walleriana (Fiesta Series) Fiesta Olé Salmon = 'Balolesal' (d)	LAst
- - 'Pink Ruffle'PBR (d)	LAst LSou
- - Fiesta Sparkler Cherry = 'Balfiespary' (d)	LSou
- - Fiesta Stardust Lavender = 'Balfiesala'PBR (d)	LSou
- Spellbound Pink = 'Imtrarepu'PBR (Spellbound Series)	WGor

Imperata (*Poaceae*)

cylindrica	CMen
- 'Red Baron'	see *I. cylindrica* 'Rubra'
§ - 'Rubra'	Widely available

Incarvillea (*Bignoniaceae*)

SDR 6104	GKev
arguta	CBot LLHF LPio SGSe
brevipes	see *I. mairei*
compacta	GCrs GKev
- BWJ 7620	WCru
delavayi	Widely available
- 'Alba'	see *I. delavayi* 'Snowtop'
- 'Bees' Pink'	CMea EBee ECho EDAr GGar GKir LRHS LSou NLar
- 'Rose'	LRHS
§ - 'Snowtop'	CBot CMea EBee ECho ELan ELon EPfP EPot GCal GMaP LTen NBPC NBir NLar SBfd SGSe SPer SWvt WBrE WCot WFar WHil WPGP WWEG
forrestii	EBee ECho LPio
grandiflora	EBee ELan GCrs GKev
himalayensis 'Frank Ludlow'	EBee GKev
lutea BWJ 7784	WCru
§ ***mairei***	CTsd EBee ECho EDAr EPfP GEdr GKir LPio LRHS NLar WHil WPer
- SDR 1812	GKev
- var. ***mairei*** f. ***multifoliata***	see *I. zhongdianensis*
- pink-flowered	GCal GKir
olgae	EBee EPfP LPio NLar
younghusbandii	GEdr
§ ***zhongdianensis***	CPBP EBee GEdr GKev MDKP NWCA
- BWJ 7692	WCru
- BWJ 7978	WCru

Indigofera (*Papilionaceae*)

amblyantha ♀H4	CBcs CPLG CWit EBee ELon EPfP LRHS MAsh MBlu MBri MMuc NLar SEND SPlb SSpi WCot WDin WKif WSHC WSpi
australis	MHer SOWG
balfouriana	WSHC
- BWJ 7851	WCru
cassioides	WCru
decora f. ***alba***	EPfP
dielsiana	CWGN EBee EPfP MWea WKif WPGP
'Dosua'	SLPl
gerardiana	see *I. heterantha*
hebepetala	EPfP WPGP WSHC
§ ***heterantha*** ♀H4	Widely available
- from China new	MBri
himalayensis	CMHG CPLG WSHC
- Yu 10941	WPGP
- 'Silk Road'	LBuc LRHS MBri MGos
kirilowii	EPfP MBri SOWG WPGP WSHC

	pendula	CMHG CPLG EBee EPfP LRHS SEND SOWG SSpi WKif WPGP WSHC
	- B&SWJ 7741	WCru
	potaninii	CMac CPLG EPfP SOWG WHer
	pseudotinctoria	CCCN EPfP SEND SRms
	subverticillata	EBee WPGP WSHC
	tinctoria	CArn

Indocalamus (*Poaceae*)

	latifolius	EPPr EPla MMoz MMuc MWht NLar SEND WJun
	- 'Hopei'	EPla
	longiauritus	EPla
	solidus	see *Bonia solida*
§	***tessellatus*** ♀H4	CAbb CDoC CEnt CGHE CHEx EAmu EBee ELon ENBC EPfP EPla GKir MBri MCCP MMoz MMuc MWht NGdn NLar NMoo SEND SMad WDyG WFar WJun WMoo WPGP WPnP
	- f. ***hamadae***	EPla MMoz MWht WDyG WJun

Inula (*Asteraceae*)

	acaulis	WCot
	afghanica	EBee
	barbata	NBre
	britannica var. ***chinensis***	NBre
	crithmoides	WHer
	dysenterica	see *Pulicaria dysenterica*
	ensifolia	CBcs ELan GJos LEdu MBNS MDKP MNFA NBro SLPl WWEG
	- 'Compacta'	ECho GCal
	- 'Gold Star'	CMac EBee ECho GKir MRav MWat NBPC NBid NBir NEgg SPet WFar WMnd WPer WRHF
	glandulosa	see *I. orientalis*
	'Golden Beauty'	see *Buphthalmum salicifolium* 'Golden Wonder'
	helenium	CArn CHby COld CPrp CSev EBWF EBee ELau GAbr GBar GPoy ILis LEdu LPBA MHer MLLN MNHC NBPC NBid NBir NLar NMir SPoG SRms WGwG WHer WHfH WJek WMoo WPer
	- 'Goliath'	MLLN SMrm
	hirta	EBee NBre WPer
	hookeri	Widely available
	- GWJ 9033	WCru
	macrocephala misapplied	see *I. royleana*
	magnifica	Widely available
	- 'Sonnenstrahl' ♀H4	SEND SPhx
	oculus-christi	CDes EBee EWes NBre WCot
	- MESE 437	EPPr
§	***orientalis***	CMea EBee EPfP GJos MBri MNFA NBre NGBl NLar SGSe SPad SPoG WBrE WFar WJek WMnd WPGP WPer WWEG
	racemosa	CTca EPPr EPla EWes GBin GCal IBlr MNrw NBid NChi SMrm SPlb WFar
	- 'Sonnenspeer'	EBee GMac NBid NBre NLar SLPl SMad WPer WPtf
	rhizocephala	ECho MDKP WPer
§	***royleana***	CEnt GCal MDKP MNrw MRav NBre
	salicina	EBee
	verbascifolia	ECho

Iochroma (*Solanaceae*)

§	***australe***	CHll CSpe EWld LRHS SGar SMrm SOWG WCom
§	- 'Andean Snow'	CHll CPLG EShb
§	- 'Bill Evans'	CPLG EShb
	cyaneum	CCCN CDoC CHll EWld SOWG WHil
	- purple-flowered	CHll
	gesnerioides new	WCot
	- 'Coccineum'	CCCN CDoC CHll
	- - B&SWJ 10255	WCru
§	***grandiflorum***	CCCN CDoC CHEx CHll CSev SGar SOWG
	warscewiczii	see *I. grandiflorum*

Iostephane (*Asteraceae*)

§	***heterophylla***	MMuc

Ipheion ✿ (*Alliaceae*)

	'Alberto Castillo'	Widely available
	dialystemon	CStu EBee ECho EPot LLHF LPio WAbe
	hirtellum	GKev WCot
	'Jessie'	CBgR CMea CPom CPrp EBee ECho EPot ERCP LAma LHop LLHF LRHS MNrw NHol NMin SPhx WCot WHil
	'Rolf Fiedler' ♀H2-3	Widely available
	sellowianum	MAsh SCnR WCot
	sessile	EBee ECho
§	***uniflorum***	CStu CTri EBee ECha ECho LAma LEdu MNrw MRav NMen NWCA SBch SEND SGSe SMrm SPer SRms WAbb WAul WCot WFar WPer WPnP WTin
	- 'Album'	CBgR CPom CPrp EBee ECha ECho EPPr EPot ERCP EWes LEdu LPio LRHS MAsh MRav MTho SPhx WCot WHal WHil
	- 'Charlotte Bishop'	Widely available
	- 'Froyle Mill' ♀H4	Widely available
	- subsp. ***tandiliense*** new	CDes
	- 'Wisley Blue' ♀H4	Widely available
	yellow-flowered	CDes

Ipomoea (*Convolvulaceae*)

	acuminata	see *I. indica*
	alba	CCCN EShb
	batatas 'Blackie'	EShb ESwi LPio WFar
	- 'Margarita'	ESwi
	- 'Sweet Caroline Light Green'PBR	SVil
	- 'Sweet Caroline Purple'PBR	CSpe SVil
	'Black Tone' new	LAst
	bolusiana new	LToo
	carnea	CCCN SOWG
	coccinea var. ***hederifolia***	see *I. hederifolia*
§	***hederifolia***	CCCN
	× ***imperialis*** 'Sunrise Serenade'	CCCN
§	***indica*** ♀H1	CCCN CHEx CHll CRHN EShb MREP SOWG
	learii	see *I. indica*
§	***lobata***	CSpe LSou SBch SGar
	'Milky Way'	CCCN
	muellerii	CCCN
	× ***multifida***	CSpe
	purpurea 'Kniola's Purple-black'	CSpe SBch
	quamoclit	CSpe
	tuberosa	see *Merremia tuberosa*
	versicolor	see *I. lobata*

Ipomopsis (*Polemoniaceae*)

§	***aggregata***	GKev

- NNS 06-283	GKev
- subsp. ***aggregata*** NNS 07-277	GKev

Iresine (*Amaranthaceae*)

herbstii	EBak ERea EShb
- 'Aureoreticulata'	EShb
- 'Brilliantissima'	CBow
'Shiny Rose Purple'	LBuc

Iris ✿ (*Iridaceae*)

AGSJ 431	EWoo
CLD 1399	NHol
AC 4413 from Tibet	GAuc
AC 4450 from Tibet	GAuc
AC 4471 from Tibet	GAuc
AC 4490 from Tibet	GAuc
AC 4623 from Tibet	GAuc
AC 4674 from Tibet	GAuc
'Abbey Chant' (IB) **new**	CIri WCAu
'Abbey Road' (TB)	WViv
'Ablaze' (MDB)	WViv
'About Town' (TB)	WCAu
'Above the Clouds' (TB) **new**	WViv
'Abracadabra' (SDB)	SMrm
'Ace' (MTB)	ESgI
'Acoma' (TB)	EWoo WViv
'Action Front' (TB)	EAEE EBee EBla EHrv EIri ESgI ETod IPot LFCN LHop LRHS NGdn SBfd SDnm WWEG
'Actress' (TB)	CWGN EAEE EBla ECGP ETod IPot LBuc LRHS LSRN
acutiloba subsp. ***lineolata***	WWst
'Adobe Rose' (TB)	ESgI WViv
'Adventuress' (TB) **new**	WViv
'African Wine' **new**	WAul
'After Dark' (TB)	CKel
'After the Storm' (TB)	ECho
'Afternoon Delight' (TB)	CWCL ESgI EWoo WCAu WViv
'Agatha Christie' (IB)	WCAu
'Age of Innocence' (TB) **new**	WCAu
'Aggressively Forward' (TB)	WCAu
'Ahwahnee Princess' (SDB) **new**	EWoo
'Aichi-no-kagayaki' (SpH)	CBow WCot
'Alabaster Unicorn' (TB)	ESgI
'Albatross' (TB)	SMrm
albicans ♀H4	CMea ECho LEdu SEND WWst
albomarginata	ECho WWst
'Alcazar' (TB)	ESgI EWoo LSRN NMoo SWat WMnd WWEG
'Aldo Ratti' (TB)	ESgI
'Alene's Other Love' (SDB)	WCAu
'Alenette' (TB)	WCAu
'Alerte Rose' (TB)	WViv
'Alexia' (TB) ♀H4	CKel
'Alice Harding' (TB)	ESgI
'Alida' (Reticulata)	ECho ERCP GKev LAma
'Alizes' (TB) ♀H4	ESgI EWoo WCAu WViv WWEG
'All Night Long' (TB)	CIri
'Allegiance' (TB)	WCAu
'Allison Elizabeth' (BB) ♀H4	WAul
'Already' (MDB)	ECho
'Alsterquelle' (SDB)	WTin
'Always a Mystery' (Spuria) **new**	CIri
'Amadora' (TB)	CKel EIri
'Amas' (TB)	WCAu
'Ambassadeur' (TB)	EBee
'Amber Queen' (DB)	EBee EBla ECtt ELan NBir NGdn NMen SPer
'Ambersand' (IB)	SIri
'Ambroisie' (TB) ♀H4	ESgI ETod WViv
'Amelia Bedeila' (IB) **new**	SIri
'American Patriot' (IB)	CKel WCAu
'America's Cup' (TB)	WCAu
'Amethyst Dancer' (TB)	WCAu
'Amethyst Flame' (TB)	ECho ESgI NBre SRms WCAu
'Amherst Blue' (IB)	SIri
'Amherst Bluebeard' (SDB)	SIri
'Amherst Glacier' (IB) **new**	WCAu
'Amherst Jester' (BB)	SIri WAul
'Amherst Moon' (SDB)	SIri
'Amherst Mustard' (SDB)	SIri
'Amherst Purple Ribbon' (SDB)	SIri WCAu
'Amherst Sweetheart' (SDB)	SIri
'Amigo' (TB)	ESgI EWoo
'Amiguita' (CH)	WCom
'Ancient Echoes' (TB)	ESgI
'Andalou' (TB) ♀H4	CWCL ESgI EWoo SCoo WViv
'Angel Unawares' (TB)	WCAu
'Angel's Tears'	see *I. histrioides* 'Angel's Tears'
'Angel's Touch' (TB)	ESgI
anglica	see *I. latifolia*
'Anna Belle Babson' (TB)	ESgI
'Annabel Jane' (TB)	CKel COIW CWan WCAu
'Annikins' (IB) ♀H4	CKel SBch
'Anniversary Celebration' (TB)	CKel
'Announcement' (TB)	CIri
'Antarctique' (IB)	CBgR ESgI WViv
'Anvil of Darkness' (TB)	EWoo
'Aphrodisiac' (TB) **new**	WViv
aphylla	GBin WCAu WThu
- subsp. ***fieberi***	WCot
'Apollo' (Dut)	CAvo SPhx
'Apparent Secret' (TB)	WAul
'Appointer' (SpH)	GBin NChi
'Apricorange' (TB) ♀H4	CKel
'Apricot Drops' (MTB) ♀H4	ESgI WAul WCAu
'Apricot Frosty' (BB)	ESgI WCAu
'Apricot Silk' (IB)	CWGN SBfd SEND WWEG
'Apricot Topping' (BB)	WAul WCAu
'Aqua Taj' (IB) **new**	WAul
'Arab Chief' (TB)	CKel
'Arabi Pasha' (TB)	ESgI
* 'Arabic Night' (IB)	WCAu
'Arc de Triomphe' (TB)	ESgI
'Archie Owen' (Spuria)	WCAu
'Arctic Age' (TB) **new**	WViv
'Arctic Express' (TB)	ESgI
'Arctic Fancy' (IB) ♀H4	CKel
'Arctic Sunrise' (TB)	ESgI
'Arctic Wine' (IB)	WCAu
'Argument' (J)	WWst
'Argus Pheasant' (SDB)	WCAu
'Armageddon' (TB)	ESgI
'Arnold Sunrise' (CH) ♀H3	GAbr
'Around Midnight' (TB)	LRHS SPoG WCAu
'Art Deco' (TB)	SIri WViv
'Art School Angel' (TB)	CIri
'As de Coeur' (TB)	ESgI
'Ascension Crown' (TB)	ESgI
'Ask Alma' (IB)	ESgI WAul WViv
'Astrid Cayeux' (TB)	ESgI EWoo WViv
* 'Atlantique' (TB)	CKel
'Attention Please' (TB)	CKel ELan WWEG
attica	CPBP ECho LLHF MAsh NRya WThu
- J&JA 583.900	NWCA

	– lemon-flowered	CPBP WThu
§	***aucheri*** ♀H2	ECho EPot GKev NMin WWst
	– indigo-flowered	WWst
N	– 'Leylek Ice'	GAuc
N	– 'Leylek Lilac'	WWst
N	– 'Snow Princess'	ECho WWst
N	– 'Snow White'	ECho GAuc WWst
N	– 'Turkish Ice'	WWst
	'Aunt Corley' (TB)	CIri
	'Aunt Josephine' (TB)	ESgI
	'Aurean' (IB)	CKel
	'Aurelie' (TB)	SIri WViv
	'Austrian Sky' (SDB)	CAby CMac EBee EBla ECtt LHop SPhx STes WAul WCot
	'Autumn Apricot' (TB)	EWoo
	'Autumn Circus' (TB)	EWoo WAul WCAu WViv
	'Autumn Echo' (TB)	ESgI
	'Autumn Embers' (SDB) **new**	WCAu
	'Autumn Encore' (TB)	COIW EWoo MHer WBor
	'Autumn Leaves' (TB)	ESgI WCAu
	'Autumn Maple' (SDB)	ESgI
	'Autumn Tryst' (TB)	ESgI EWoo
	'Avalon Sunset' (TB)	EIri ESgI WViv
	'Avanelle' (IB)	GBin NBre
	'Awesome Blossom' (TB)	ESgI
	'Az Ap' (IB)	CHid EBee ELon WCAu
	'Aztec Sun' (TB)	SIri WViv
	'Babbling Brook' (TB)	ESgI
	'Baboon Bottom' (BB)	CIri
	'Baby Bengal' (BB)	EWoo
	'Baby Blessed' (SDB)	WCAu
	'Baby Prince' (SDB)	ESgI
	'Baccarat' (TB)	WCAu
	'Back in Black' (TB)	CKel
	'Badlands' (TB) **new**	WCAu
	'Baie Rose' (IB)	CBgR
	'Bajazzo' (La)	WCAu
	'Bal Masqué' (TB)	WViv
	baldschuanica	WWst
	'Ballerina' (TB)	NBir
	'Ballistic' (SDB) **new**	WCAu
	'Ballyhoo' (TB)	WCAu
	'Banbury Beauty' (CH) ♀H3	MAvo
	'Banbury Melody' (CH)	CFee MAvo
	'Banbury Ruffles' (SDB)	ESgI NMen SBch WAul WViv
	'Bandera Waltz' (TB)	WCAu
	'Bang' (TB)	CKel
	'Bangles' (MTB) ♀H4	ESgI WCAu
	'Bar de Nuit' (TB)	ESgI
	'Barbara My Love' (TB) **new**	WCAu
	'Barbara's Kiss' (Spuria)	CIri
	barbatula BWJ 7663	WCru
	'Baria' (SDB)	GEdr
	'Baroque Prelude' (TB)	CKel
	'Batik' (BB)	WCAu WCot WViv
	'Baubles and Beads' (MTB)	ESgI
	'Bayberry Candle' (TB)	ESgI MWea WAul WCAu
	'Be Happy' (SDB)	WViv
	'Be My Baby' (BB)	WCAu
	'Beatrice Cherbuy' (TB) **new**	WViv
	'Bedtime Story' (IB)	EBee SSvw SWat WCot WViv WWEG
	'Bee Wings' (MDB)	WViv
	'Bee's Knees' (SDB) ♀H4	SIri
	'Before the Storm' (TB)	CKel ELon ESgI GBin WCAu
	'Beguine' (TB)	ESgI
	'Being Busy' (SDB)	ESgI
	'Bel Avenir' (TB) **new**	WViv
	'Bel Azur' (IB)	CBgR ESgI WViv
	'Bel Esprit' (TB)	ESgI
	'Belise' (Spuria) ♀H4	WCot
	'Belle de Nuit' (TB) **new**	WViv
	'Belvi Queen' (TB)	MNrw
	'Ben a Factor' (MTB)	ESgI
	'Benton Caramel'	EMal EWoo
	'Benton Cordelia' (TB)	EMal
N	'Benton Daphne' (TB)	EMal
	'Benton Dierdre' (TB)	CBgR ELon SRms
	'Benton Evora' (TB)	EMal
	'Benton Nigel' (TB)	EMal WCAu
	'Benton Sheila' (TB)	CBgR CFee ECha
	'Berkeley Gold' (TB)	CSBt EBee EBla ECtt ELan EPfP EShb EWTr EWes GKir LRHS SBfd SCoo SPer SWat WWEG
	'Berlin Tiger' (SpH) ♀H4	CRow EPPr EPfP GBin LLWG MWts SApp WCAu WHil
	'Best Bet' (TB)	ESgI EWoo WCAu
	'Bethany Claire' (TB)	ESgI WCAu
	'Betty Chatten' (TB)	EPot
	'Betty Cooper' (Spuria)	WAul WCAu
	'Betty Simon' (TB)	CKel CWCL ESgI ETod EWoo WViv
	'Beverly Sills' (TB)	CWGN EPfP ESgI GBin LSou MRav SRGP WAul WCAu WViv
	'Bianco' (TB)	WCAu WWEG
	'Bibury' (SDB) ♀H4	WCAu
	'Big Dipper' (TB)	ECtt ESgI EWoo WViv
	'Big Melt' (TB)	CKel
	'Big Squeeze' (TB)	WCAu WViv
	biglumis	see *I. lactea*
	'Billie the Brownie' (MTB)	ESgI
	'Bishop's Robe' (TB)	SSvw
N	'Black Beauty' (Dut)	EPfP LRHS
	'Black Beauty' (TB)	MWat SPer
	'Black Dragon' (TB)	CHid SHar SPad
	'Black Gamecock' (La)	CFir CWCL ELan LPBA MBNS MNrw MSCN MWts NBro NLar NMoo SKHP SMrm SSvw WCAu WMAq
	'Black Hills' (TB)	EBee WCAu
	'Black Ink' (TB)	COIW
	'Black Knight' (TB)	EWll MRav NGdn WKif
	'Black Night' (IB)	MWea SRGP WBor WWEG
	'Black Sergeant' (TB) ♀H4	CKel
	'Black Stallion' (MDB)	ESgI
	'Black Suited' (TB)	CIri
	'Black Swan' (TB)	CAby CMac EBla ECha ECtt ELan EPfP ESgI EShb EWoo GCal LAst LFCN LPio LRHS LSRN MCot NBre NGdn SBfd SDnm SMrm SPer SPoG STes WCAu WCot WEas
	'Black Taffeta' (TB)	CKel
	'Black Tie Affair' (TB)	ESgI EWoo WCAu WViv
	'Blackbeard' (BB) ♀H4	CKel WCAu
	'Blackcurrant' (IB)	WAul
	'Blackout' (TB)	ESgI SIri
	'Blaeberry Pie' **new**	CIri
	'Blast' (IB)	CKel WViv
	'Blatant' (TB)	ESgI EWoo WCAu
	'Blazing Light' (TB)	ESgI
	'Blazing Sunrise' (TB)	ESgI
	'Blenheim Royal' (TB)	ESgI WCAu WPen WViv
	'Blessed Assurance' (IB)	GKir
	'Blitzen' (IB)	WCAu
	'Blowing Bubbles' (TB) **new**	CIri
	'Blue Beret' (MDB)	WViv
	'Blue Bossa' (CH) ♀H4	WAul
	'Blue Crusader' (TB)	WViv
	'Blue Denim' (SDB)	ECho ECtt EPfP GCal MRav NBir NMoo NPnk WCot WTin WWEG
	'Blue Eyed Blond' (IB)	MWea WCAu
	'Blue Eyed Brunette' (TB)	ESgI WCAu
	'Blue Flirt' (IB)	WAul

	'Blue Gown' (TB) **new**	EWoo
	'Blue Hendred' (SDB)	NBir WCAu
	'Blue Lamp' (TB)	CKel
	'Blue Line' (SDB) ♀H4	NBre
	'Blue Luster' (TB) ♀H4	ESgI
	'Blue Meadow Fly' (Sino-Sib)	EBee SMrm
*	'Blue Mystery'	WWst
	'Blue Note Blues' (TB)	WCAu
	'Blue Pigmy' (SDB)	CPBP CWat EBla ECtt NGdn NMen SBfd SPer
	'Blue Pools' (SDB)	NBir WTin
	'Blue Reflection' (TB)	CMac ESgI
	'Blue Rhythm' (TB)	CAby CKel EAEE EBla ELan ELon EPfP EWoo GMaP LRHS MRav NBre NMoo SBfd SCoo SMrm SPer SPhx SSvw WAul WCAu WMnd WWEG
	'Blue Sapphire' (TB)	ESgI WCAu
	'Blue Shimmer' (TB)	CSBt CWGN EAEE EBee EBla ECha ELan EPfP ESgI ETod EWoo LRHS LSRN MAvo MCot NGdn SBch SBfd SPer SPoG SWat WCAu
	'Blue Staccato' (TB)	CKel ESgI WCAu
	'Blue Suede Shoes' (TB)	ESgI LSRN WViv
	'Blue Warlsind' (J)	WWst
	'Bluebird Wine' (TB)	WCAu
	'Bob Nichol' (TB) ♀H4	CKel
	'Bockingford' (MTB) **new**	SIri
	'Bohemia Sekt' (TB)	CKel
	'Bohemian' (TB)	CWCL WViv
	'Bold Fashion' (TB) **new**	WViv
	'Bold Gold' (TB)	WViv
	'Bold Look' (TB)	ESgI
	'Bold Pretender' (La)	ELan EPfP MBNS NLar SKHP WHil
	'Bold Print' (IB)	CWan EAEE EBee EBla ELon LAst LRHS LSRN SBfd SPoG WAul WCAu WWEG WWlt
	'Bollinger'	see *I.* 'Hornpipe'
	'Bonbon Acidulé' (TB)	WViv
	'Bonnie Davenport' (TB)	CIri
	'Bonus Bucks' (TB)	CKel
	'Boo' (SDB)	CKel CPBP WCAu
	'Bouzy Bouzy' (TB)	ESgI
	bracteata	CPBP
	- NNS 04-223	WCot
	'Braggadocio' (TB)	CWCL WViv
	'Braithwaite' (TB)	CAby CKel CWGN EAEE EBee EBla ELan ESgI IPot LRHS NBre SBch SBfd SPer SPur SRms SWat WAul WCAu
	'Brannigan' (SDB)	NBir SMrm WPen
	'Brasero' (TB)	CWCL ECtt WViv
	'Brash' (SDB)	WViv
	'Brasilia' (TB)	NBir NBre
	'Brassie' (SDB)	GAbr GKir MBNS NMoo NPnk WWEG
	'Brave New World' (TB) ♀H4	CIri
	'Breakers' (TB) ♀H4	CKel ESgI EWoo SBfd WCAu
§	'Bride' (DB)	WMnd
	'Bride's Blush' (TB) **new**	CIri
	'Bride's Halo' (TB)	EWoo LSRN WCAu WViv
*	'Brigantino' (BB)	ESgI
	'Bright Button' (SDB)	CBgR CKel ESgI EWoo
	'Bright Chic' (SDB)	ESgI
	'Bright Fire' (TB)	EIri EWoo WViv
	'Bright Spring' (DB)	WViv
	'Bright Vision' (SDB)	ESgI
	'Bright White' (MDB)	CKel ECho NMen SMrm
N	'Bright Yellow' (DB)	MRav
	'Brighteyes' (IB)	SRms
	'Brindisi' (TB)	ESgI
	'Brise de Mer' (TB)	ESgI
	'Broad Shoulders' (TB)	WCAu
	'Broadleigh Angela' (CH)	GKir
	'Broadleigh Lavinia' (CH)	MAvo MRav NHol
	'Broadleigh Mitre' (CH)	CElw GMac
	'Broadleigh Nancy' (CH)	MAvo
	'Broadleigh Peacock' (CH)	CElw EShb MAvo WSHC
N	'Broadleigh Rose' (CH)	CElw EHrv EPyc GKir MAvo MBrN MRav MWte NHol SApp SMrm WSHC
	'Broadleigh Sybil' (CH)	GCrs GKir NHol
	'Broadway Baby' (IB)	ESgI WAul WViv
	'Bronzaire' (IB) ♀H4	CKel EIri ESgI WCAu WGwG
	'Bronze Beauty' (Dut)	LAma SBch SPer
	'Bronze Beauty' van Tubergen (*boogiana* hybrid)	EPfP LRHS MWat NBir SDeJ
	'Bronzed Aussie' (TB)	CIri
	'Bronzed Violet' (TB)	CKel
N	'Brown Chocolate' (TB)	WCAu
N	'Brummit's Mauve' (TB)	WCAu
	'Bruno' (TB)	LSRN
	'Brussels' (TB)	ESgI
	bucharica misapplied	see *I. orchioides* Carrière
	bucharica ambig.	CAvo CTca EBla ECho ELon IFro MNrw MWat NCGa SDeJ SMrm WBor WWst
§	***bucharica*** Foster ♀H3-4	CBgR CSam EBee ECho EPfP EPot GKev LAma
N	- 'Baldschuan Yellow' (J)	WWst
	- 'Princess'	ECho WWst
N	- 'Sanglok'	WWst
N	- 'Top Gold'	ECho WWst
	bucharica × ***orchioides***	ECho WWst
	bucharica × ***warleyensis*** **new**	WWst
	'Buckwheat' (TB)	SIri WViv
	'Buisson de Roses' (TB)	ESgI WViv
	bulleyana	ECho GAuc GKev NWCA SRms WCot
	- ACE 2296	EBee
	- BWJ 7912	WCru
	- CLD 495	NHol
	- black-flowered	CPLG EBee GKev GKir
	- - SDR 1792	GKev
	- - SDR 2714	GKev
	- - SDR 4775	GKev
	'Bumblebee Deelite' (MTB) ♀H4	CKel CPMA WCAu
	bungei	GAuc
	'Burgermeister' (TB) **new**	WViv
	'Burgundy Party' (TB)	ESgI
	'Burka' (TB)	ESgI
	'Burning Bright' (TB) **new**	WViv
	'Burnt Toffee' (TB)	ESgI WAul WViv
	'Burst' (TB)	CKel WCAu
	'Buto' (TB) **new**	EWoo
	'Butter Pecan' (IB)	WCAu
	'Buttercup Bower' (TB)	WCAu
	'Buttermere' (TB)	SRms
	'Butterpat' (IB)	ESgI
	'Butterscotch Carpet' (SDB)	WCAu
	'Butterscotch Kiss' (TB)	EAEE EBee EBla ELan LHop LRHS MRav MWea NBir NLar SDnm SPer
	'Bye Bye Blues' (TB)	ESgI
	'Cabaret Royale' (TB)	ESgI WCAu
	'Cable Car' (TB)	CKel CWCL ECtt ESgI EWoo SMrm WViv
	'Cache of Gold' (SDB) **new**	EWoo
	'Cajun Rhythm' (TB) **new**	WViv
	'Caliente' (TB)	COlW CWGN EKen EPfP ESgI EWll MCot MHer MRav MWhi WCAu

	'California Dreamin'' (TB)	CIri
	'California Gold' (TB)	WWEG
	'California Style' (IB)	ESgI WViv
§	Californian hybrids	CAby CElw CPBP EPot GCra MCot NBir WCFE WCot
	'Caliph' (TB) **new**	WViv
	'Calm Stream' (TB) ♀^{H4}	CKel WCAu
	'Calypso Beat' (TB) **new**	WViv
	'Cambridge Blue'	see *I.* 'Monspur Cambridge Blue'
	'Cameo Blush' (BB)	EWoo
	'Cameo Queen' (SDB) ♀^{H4}	CIri
	'Cameo Wine' (TB)	CPMA ECtt ESgI WViv
	'Cameroun' (TB)	ESgI EWoo
	'Campbellii'	see *I. lutescens* 'Campbellii'
	canadensis	see *I. hookeri*
	'Canadian Streaker' (TB/v)	WCot
	'Candle' (IB) **new**	WCAu
	'Candy Rock' (IB) **new**	CIri EWoo WCAu
	'Candylane' (MTB)	CKel
	'Cannington Apricot' (IB)	CBgR CKel
	'Cannington Bluebird' (TB)	WCAu
	'Cannington Skies' (IB)	CKel
	'Cantab' (Reticulata)	CAvo ECho EPot ERCP GBin GKev LAma LRHS SDeJ SPhx
	capnoides	WWst
	capnoides × ***orchioides*** (J)	WWst
	'Caprice' (TB) **new**	EWoo
	'Capricious' (TB)	ESgI
	'Captain Indigo' (IB)	CKel ESgI
	'Caption' (TB)	ESgI
	'Carenza' (BB)	CKel
	'Caribbean Dream' (TB)	WViv
	'Carnaby' (TB)	EAEE EBla ESgI EShb LAst LRHS MBri MRav MWea SBfd STes WCAu WViv WWEG
	'Carnival Song' (TB)	WCAu
	'Carnival Time' (TB)	CMac CWGN EAEE EBee EBla ECGP ECtt EShb IPot LBuc LFCN LRHS MAvo MCot MWea SBfd SMrm SPer STes WAul
	'Carnton' (TB)	WEas
	'Carolyn Rose' (MTB) ♀^{H4}	NBre SMrm
*	'Caronte' (IB)	ESgI
	'Carriwitched' (IB)	CKel
	'Cascade Rhythm' (TB) **new**	WCAu
	'Cascade Springs' (TB) **new**	WViv
	'Cascade Sprite' (SDB)	SRms
	'Cat's Eye' (SDB)	WViv
	caucasica	CMac
	'Cayenne Capers' (TB)	ESgI
N	'Cedric Morris'	EWes MWat
	'Cee Jay' (IB) ♀^{H4}	EWoo WCAu WViv
	'Cee Tee' **new**	EWoo
	'Celebration Song' (TB)	CWCL ESgI SIri WAul WCAu WViv
	'Celestial Glory' (TB)	WCAu
	'Celtic Glory' (TB)	WAul
	'Cercle Bleu' (TB) **new**	WViv
	'Cerdagne' (TB)	ESgI
	'Cerf-Volant' (TB) **new**	SIri WViv
	'Chalkhill' (SDB) **new**	WCAu
	chamaeiris	see *I. lutescens*
	'Champagne Elegance' (TB)	ECtt EIri ESgI EWoo NBir WCAu WViv
	'Champagne Encore' (IB)	ESgI EWoo
	'Champagne Music' (TB)	WCAu
	'Champagne Waltz' (TB)	CWCL WViv
	'Chance Beauty' (SpH) ♀^{H4}	LLWG WViv
	'Change of Pace' (TB)	ESgI WCAu WViv
	'Changing Winds' (TB) **new**	WViv
	'Chanted' (SDB)	ESgI WCAu WViv

	'Chantilly' (TB)	EAEE EBee EBla ECGP ELan EPfP EWoo LPio LRHS MRav NBir NGdn NLar SDnm SPer SWat WFoF
	'Chapeau' (TB)	ESgI WCAu
	'Chapel Bells' (TB)	CKel
	'Charlotte Maria' (TB)	CKel
	'Chartreuse Ruffles' (TB)	ECtt EWoo SIri
	'Char-true' (Spuria)	WCAu
	'Chasing Rainbows' (TB)	WCAu
	'Chaste White' (TB)	ESgI
	'Château d'Auvers-sur-Oise' (TB) **new**	SIri WViv
	'Chelsea Bleu' (TB) **new**	WViv
	'Cher' (TB)	LSRN WViv
N	'Cherished' (TB)	EBee GBin WWEG
	'Cherokee Lace' (Spuria)	WTin
	'Cherry Garden' (SDB)	Widely available
	'Cherub's Smile' (TB)	ESgI
	'Cheryl Ann O'Leary' (TB) **new**	CIri
	'Chevalier de Malte' (TB)	ESgI WViv
	'Chickee' (MTB) ♀^{H4}	CKel
	'Chicken Little' (MDB)	NMoo
	'Chief Moses' (TB)	WCAu
I	'Chieftain' (SDB)	MRav
	'China Dragon' (TB)	SWat
	'China Nights' (TB)	ESgI
	'China Seas' (TB)	NBre
	'Chinese Treasure' (TB)	WAul
	'Chinook Winds' (TB)	ESgI
	'Chivalry' (TB)	ESgI WTin
	'Chocolate Marmalade' (TB)	ECtt WViv
	'Chocolate Moose' (TB)	CIri
	'Chocolate Vanilla' (TB)	ESgI WCAu
	'Chorus Girl' (TB)	CKel
	'Chou Bleu' (TB) **new**	WViv
	'Christmas Angel' (TB)	WCAu
	Chrysofor Group	CAby
	chrysographes ♀^{H4}	CHid CMac CWCL EBee EBla EPfP EWll GKir GMac IKil IPot LAst LRHS MCCP MLHP MLLN MMuc MRav MSCN NBPC NPnk NPri NSti SPoG SRot SWal WCAu WCFE WFar WPtf
	- NNS 00-423	NWCA
	- SDR 2873	GKev
I	- 'Black Beauty'	CFir ECho EPfP
	- 'Black Gold'	ITim
I	- 'Black Knight'	CBot CMdw CPLG EDAr ELon EPfP GCal GCra GGar ITim LHop MDun MHer NCGa NChi NLar SMad SWat WBor WGwG WMnd
	- black-flowered	Widely available
*	- 'Ellenbank Nightshade'	CBgR GMac
N	- 'Inshriach'	IMou LEdu WAbe
N	- 'Kew Black'	CPLG ECho EShb LEdu NBir WHer WWEG
	- 'Mandarin Purple'	CBgR GCal GMac MBri MSpe SWat WMoo
	- red-flowered	ECho
	- 'Rob'	ECho
§	- 'Rubella'	CRow ECho GCra GMac WFar WPrP
*	- 'Rubens'	GCal
	- 'Rubra'	see *I. chrysographes* 'Rubella'
N	- 'Tsiri'	NWCA
	- yellow-flowered	GKir WFar
	chrysographes × ***forrestii***	GBin GKir NBir
	chrysophylla NNS 04.225	CPBP
	- NNS 05-387	WCot

	'Chubby Cheeks' (SDB)	CKel WCAu
	'Chuckwagon' (TB)	ESgI
	'Church Stoke' (SDB)	WCAu
N	'Cider Haze' (TB)	CKel
	'Ciel et Mer' (TB)	WViv
	'Cimarron Rose' (SDB)	ESgI WAul WCAu WViv
	'Cimarron Strip' (TB)	EPfP WWEG
	'Cinnabar Red' (Spuria)	WAul
	'Cinnamon Apples' (MDB)	ESgI
	'Cinnamon Roll' (Spuria)	WCAu
	'Cirrus Veil' (SDB) **new**	WCAu
	'Citronnade' (TB) **new**	WViv
	'City Lights' Harrell (TB)	WCAu
	'Claire Doodle' (MTB)	ESgI
	'Clairette' (Reticulata)	ECho LAma LRHS NMin SDeJ
	'Clara Garland' (IB) ♀H4	CKel WCAu
	'Clarence' (TB)	CKel ESgI EWoo WCAu
	clarkei	CPLG CPrp GKir WCon WCot WFar
	- B&SWJ 2122	WCru
	- CC 2751	NWCA WWst
	- SDR 3819	GKev
	'Classic Edition' (TB) **new**	WViv
	'Classic Hues' (TB)	ESgI
	'Classic Look' (TB)	ESgI WViv
	'Clay's Caper' (SDB)	NBre
N	'Cleo' (TB)	CKel NBir
	'Cleo Murrell' (TB)	ESgI EWoo
	'Cliffs of Dover' (TB)	CKel EIri EKen ESgI GCal MCot SGar SRms
N	'Climbing Gold'	ECho
	'Close Shave' (TB)	CIri
	'Cloud Mistress' (IB)	ESgI WViv
	'Cloud Pinnacle' (IB)	CKel
	'Cloudcap' (TB)	SRms
	'Clown Around' (TB) **new**	CIri
	'Clownerie' (TB) **new**	EWoo WViv
	'Clyde Redmond' (La) ♀H4	WAul WMAq
	'Coalignition' (TB)	ETod EWoo WCAu
	'Cocktail' (TB) **new**	WViv
	'Codicil' (TB)	EIri ESgI EWoo WCAu WViv
	'Coeur d'Or' (TB) **new**	WViv
	'Colette Thurillet' (TB)	ESgI WCAu WViv
	collettii	ECho WWst
	'Color Glory' (TB) **new**	WViv
	'Color Me Blue' (TB) **new**	WCAu
	'Colorific' (La)	EPfP NBro NLar NMoo WBor WHil
	'Combo' (SDB)	CKel
	'Coming Up Roses' (TB)	WCAu
	'Con Fuoco' (TB)	ESgI
	'Concertina' (IB)	CIri EWoo WCAu
	'Condottiere' (TB)	WViv
	'Confetti' (TB)	MBri
	confusa ♀H3	CHEx CPla CSev EWld IFro LEdu SAPC SArc SBig SEND SGSe SGar SMad WBrk WFar WWst
N	- 'Martyn Rix'	CBct CDes CFwr CGHE CHEx CHid CPou EBee ELon EPfP GCal IGor MLHP SChr SGSe WCot WFar WGwG WHer WMnd WPGP WPer
	'Congo Bongo' (BB)	WAul
	'Conjuration' (TB)	ESgI EWoo WCAu WViv
	'Constant Wattez' (IB)	CKel EBee ESgI NLar
	'Copatonic' (TB)	ESgI WCAu
	'Copper Classic' (TB)	ESgI WCAu WViv
	'Cops' (SDB)	ESgI
	'Coquetterie' (TB)	ESgI WViv
	'Coral Carpet' (SDB) **new**	WCAu
	'Coral Point' (TB)	EWoo WCAu
	'Coral Sunset' (TB) **new**	WViv
	'Cordoba' (TB)	WCAu
	'Corps de Ballet' (TB)	CIri
	'Côte d'Or' (TB)	WViv
	'Count Dracula' (TB)	CIri
	'Country Charm' (TB) **new**	WViv
	'County Town Red' (TB)	SIri
	'Coup de Soleil' (TB) **new**	WViv
	'Court Magician' (SDB)	SIri
	'Cozy Calico' (TB)	ESgI
	'Crackles' (TB)	CKel
	'Crackling Caldera' (TB)	CIri WAul
	'Cranapple' (BB) ♀H4	WAul
	'Cranberry Ice' (TB)	ELon EWoo
	'Cranberry Sauce' (TB)	CIri
	'Cranbrook' (IB) ♀H4	SIri
	'Cream and Peaches' (SDB)	SIri WViv
	'Cream Beauty' (Dut)	EBrs GKev LAma LRHS SPhx
	'Cream Soda' (TB) ♀H4	CKel
	'Crème d'Or' (TB)	ESgI
	'Crème Glacée' (TB)	ESgI WViv
	cretensis	see *I. unguicularis* subsp. *cretensis*
	'Crimson Snow' (TB)	LRHS WCAu
	'Crinoline' (TB)	CKel
	'Crisis' (TB) **new**	CIri
	'Crispette' (TB)	WCAu
	cristata ♀H4	CPBP LLHF NHar NLar SRms
	- 'Alba'	GCal GCrs LLHF NWCA WAbe
	cristata* × *lacustris	NMen
	crocea ♀H4	GBin
	'Croftway Lemon' (TB)	COlW ELon
	'Cross Current' (TB)	WCAu
	'Crowned Heads' (TB)	CKel ESgI WCAu WViv
	'Crownette' (SDB)	CKel
	'Crushed Velvet' (TB)	WCAu
	'Crystal Glitters' (TB)	ESgI WViv
	'Cumulus' (TB) **new**	WViv
	cuniculiformis	ECho GAuc
	'Cup Race' (TB)	WCAu
	'Cupid's Cup' (SDB)	ESgI
	'Curio' (MDB)	WViv
	'Curlew' (IB)	WCAu
	'Cutie' (IB)	ESgI WCAu WViv WWEG
	'Cyanea' (DB)	ECho GEdr
	cycloglossa	CPBP ECho EPot GKev WCot WWst
	'Dance Away' (TB)	ESgI WCAu WViv
	'Dancer's Veil' (TB)	CHar CKel ECtt ELon ESgI IPot LRHS MRav NBre SPer WCAu
	'Dancing Lilacs' (MTB)	ESgI
	'Dandy' (TB)	ESgI
	danfordiae	CAvo CFFs CFox ECho EPfP EPot ERCP GKev LAma LRHS NHol SDeJ SGar SMrm WFar WGwG WRHF
	'Danger' (TB)	ESgI
	'Dante's Inferno' (TB)	EWoo
	'Dardanus' (AB)	ECho EPot ERCP SDeJ WCot
	'Dark Chocolate' (TB) **new**	EWoo
	'Dark Crystal' (SDB)	ESgI EWoo
	'Dark Rosaleen' (TB) ♀H4	NBre
	'Dark Spark' (SDB)	WCAu
	'Dark Vader' (SDB)	ESgI WAul WCAu WViv
	'Darkness' (IB) **new**	SIri
	darwasica	GAuc WWst
	'Dash Away' (SDB)	ESgI SIri WViv
	'Dauber's Delight' **new**	CIri
	'Daughter of Stars' (TB)	ESgI
	'Dauntless' (TB)	ESgI
	'David Guest' (IB)	CKel
	'Dawn of Fall' (TB)	ESgI
	'Dawning' (TB) ♀H4	ESgI EWoo WViv
	'Dazzle Me' (SDB)	WCAu
	'Dazzling Gold' (TB)	ESgI WCAu WViv
	'Death by Chocolate' (SDB)	ESgI
§	***decora***	NWCA
	'Deep Black' (TB)	CKel CPar CWGN EAEE EBla EHrv ELan EPfP GBin IPot LAst LRHS

		LSRN MAvo MBNS MCot MRav MWat NLar SBfd SDnm SPer SPhx SPoG SWat WAul WCAu WCot
	'Deep Caress' (TB)	ESgI
	'Deep Pacific' (TB)	MBri WCAu
	'Deep Space' (TB)	WCAu
	'Deft Touch' (TB)	CKel WCAu WViv
	delavayi $\mathbb{Y}^{H4}$	CPLG ECho EWes GAuc GMaP IBlr MLLN WPrP WRHF
	- SDR 50	GKev
N	- 'Didcot'	EBrs LRHS
	'Delicate Lady' (IB) $\mathbb{Y}^{H4}$	CKel
	'Delirium' (IB)	WAul WViv
	'Delta Blues' (TB)	EWoo WViv
	'Delta Butterfly' (La)	WMAq
	'Demelza' (TB)	CKel
	'Demon' (SDB)	CKel CPMA
	'Denys Humphry' (TB)	CKel WCAu
	'Deputé Nomblot' (TB)	ESgI
	'Derwentwater' (TB)	SRms WCAu
	'Desert Dream' (AB)	GGar
I	'Desert Dream' (Sino-Sib)	GAbr
	'Desert Echo' (TB)	COIW MHer
	'Desert Orange' (SDB)	WViv
	'Desert Song' (TB)	CKel WCAu
	'Destination' (Spuria) $\mathbb{Y}^{H4}$	CIri
	'Devil David' (TB)	CIri
	'Devil May Care' (IB)	CIri WAul
	'Devilish Nature' (SDB)	CIri
	'Devil's Lake' (TB) **new**	WViv
	'Devil's Spoon' (TB)	CIri
	'Devonshire Cream' (TB)	CIri WCAu
	'Diabolique' (TB)	WViv
	'Diligence' (SDB) $\mathbb{Y}^{H4}$	CKel
	'Disco Jewel' (MTB)	ESgI
	'Ditto' (MDB)	WViv
	'Diversion' (TB)	ESgI
	'Divine' (TB)	CKel
	'Dixie Darling' (TB)	ESgI
	'Dixie Pixie' (SDB)	WCAu WTin
	'Dogrose' (TB) **new**	EWoo
	'Dolce Acqua' (TB)	CIri
	dolichosiphon	GAuc
	aff. ***dolichosiphon***	GAuc
	'Doll' (IB)	EWoo
	'Dolly Madison' (TB)	ESgI
	'Don Juan' (TB)	ESgI
	'Donegal' (IB)	WViv
	'Don't Touch' (TB)	CIri
	'Doodads' (TB)	ESgI
	'Dorothy' (TB) **new**	SBch
	'Double Bubble' (TB) **new**	EWoo
	'Double Espoir' (TB)	ESgI WViv
	'Double Mini' **new**	EWoo
	'Double Shot' (TB) **new**	EWoo
	'Double Vision' (TB) **new**	EWoo
	'Double Your Fun' (IB) **new**	WAul
	'Doublemint' (TB)	CIri
	'Douce Reverie' (TB) **new**	WViv
	douglasiana $\mathbb{Y}^{H4}$	ECho GCal GKev NWCA WFar WWEG
	- 'Cape Ferrelo' **new**	SKHP
	'Dovedale' (TB) $\mathbb{Y}^{H4}$	WCAu
	'Dover Beach' (TB)	SGar SIri
	'Draco' (TB)	ESgI
	'Drake Carne' (TB)	CKel
	'Drama Queen' (TB)	CIri
	'Dream Express' (TB) **new**	WViv
	'Dream Indigo' (IB)	CKel EWoo WCAu
	'Dream Lover' (TB)	ESgI
	'Dreamsicle' (TB)	SIri WViv
	'Dresden Candleglow' (IB)	WCAu

	'Dualtone' (TB)	CKel
	'Dude Ranch' (TB)	CIri
	'Dunlin' (MDB)	ECho NBir NMen
	'Dural Snowflake' (TB) **new**	WCAu
	'Dural White Butterfly' (La)	CHid CSpe LAst LPBA
	'Durham Dream' (TB) **new**	CIri
	'Dusky Challenger' (TB)	CKel CPMA ESgI EWoo SCoo WCAu WViv
	'Dusky Evening' (TB)	ESgI
	'Dutch Chocolate' (TB)	ESgI ETod EWoo WCAu WViv
	'Dwight Enys' (TB) $\mathbb{Y}^{H4}$	CKel
	'Dyonisos' (TB) **new**	WViv
	'Eagle's Flight' (TB)	CKel
	'Earl of Essex' (TB)	WCAu
	'Early Frost' (IB)	CKel WViv
	'Early Light' (TB) $\mathbb{Y}^{H4}$	ESgI WCAu
	'East Indies' (TB)	WCAu
	'Easter' (SDB) **new**	SIri
	'Easter Tide' (La)	WCAu
	'Eastertime' (TB)	ECtt ESgI WViv
	'Easy Grace' (TB) **new**	EWoo
	'Eau Vive' (TB) **new**	WViv
	'Ebony Echo' (TB) **new**	EWoo
	'Echo de France' (TB)	ESgI EWoo
	'Ecstatic Echo' (TB)	ESgI WViv
	'Edge of Winter' (TB)	CKel SIri
	'Edith Wolford' (TB)	CWCL ECtt ESgI EWll EWoo GBin MWea SRGP WBor WViv WWEG
N	'Ed's Blue' (DB)	ELan
	'Edward' (Reticulata)	ECho EPfP EPot GKev LAma LRHS MWat SDeJ SMrm
	'Edward of Windsor' (TB)	ELan GMaP LPio NLar SDnm SRGP WCAu WMnd
	'Effervescence' (TB) **new**	WViv
	'Eggnog' (TB)	EWoo
	'Eileen Louise' (TB) $\mathbb{Y}^{H4}$	WCAu
	'El Torito' (SDB) $\mathbb{Y}^{H4}$	CIri
	'Eleanor Clare' (IB) $\mathbb{Y}^{H4}$	CKel
	'Eleanor Hill' (Spuria)	WAul
	'Eleanor Roosevelt' (IB) **new**	EWoo
	'Eleanor's Pride' (TB)	CKel ESgI WCAu
	'Electrique' (TB)	WCAu
	'Elegans' (TB)	MCot
	'Elegant Lass' (BB) $\mathbb{Y}^{H4}$	CIri
	elegantissima	see *I. iberica* subsp. *elegantissima*
	'Elizabeth Arden' (TB)	CKel
	'Elizabeth of England' (TB)	COIW CSpr EWll GKev SRGP WWEG
	'Elizabeth Poldark' (TB)	ESgI
	'Ella' (IB)	CSpr
	'Ellen Manor' (TB)	WCAu
*	'Ellenbank Damselfly'	CBgR GMac
	'Elsa Sass' (TB)	ESgI
	'Elsie Petty' (IB) **new**	SIri
	'Empress of India' (TB)	EBee SEND
	'Encre Bleue' (IB)	CBgR ESgI WViv
	'Endless Love' (TB)	EIri WViv
	'English Charm' (TB)	ESgI EWoo WAul WCAu WViv
	'English Cottage' (TB)	COIW ELon GBin GCal LSRN LTen MWat NLar SMrm WCAu WWEG
	'Ennerdale' (TB)	SRms
	'Ennoble' (TB)	ESgI
	'Enriched' (MTB) $\mathbb{Y}^{H4}$	SIri
§	***ensata*** $\mathbb{Y}^{H4}$	CBcs CHEx COIW CWat ELan EPfP EWTr GKev GKir LPBA LRHS MMuc MNrw NBro NCob NGdn NLar SPlb SRms SWat WCFE WClo WFar
N	- 'Activity'	CRow GBin NBro SHar WFar WPrP WWEG
	- 'Agrippine'	SKHP

	- 'Alba'	ECha
	- 'Aldridge Prelude'	WAul
	- 'Aldridge Snow Maiden' 𝕐H4	WAul
	- 'Aldridge Visitor' 𝕐H4	WAul
	- 'Alpine Majesty' 𝕐H4	CIri
	- 'Apollo'	CBen CRow
	- 'Artist'	NBro
	- 'Asian Warrior'	CElw GGar NLar
	- 'August Emperor'	EKen LAst SMrm
	- 'Azuma-kagami'	CFir EBee EKen ELan EPfP GMac MNrw WCon
	- 'Azure'	CSpr
N	- 'Barnhawk Sybil'	SKHP
	- 'Barr Purple East' 𝕐H4	CHid CPrp CRow
	- 'Beni-tsubaki'	WAul
I	- 'Blue King'	NBro SMrm SPet WAul
I	- 'Blue Peter'	CBen CRow
	- 'Blue Pompon'	NMoo WViv
	- 'Blue Prince'	CBen
N	- 'Blush'	NBro
	- 'Butterflies in Flight'	CRow
	- 'Caprician Butterfly' 𝕐H4	CMHG CSpr EPfP GBin MBri NMoo WAul
N	- 'Carnival Prince'	CFir NBro WFar WMoo WPnP
	- 'Cascade Crest'	SWat WAul
	- 'Cascade Spice'	WAul
	- 'Center of Interest'	MSCN NBir NCGa
N	- 'Charm'	LRHS
*	- 'Chico Geisho'	WAul
	- 'Chitose-no-tomo'	CRow
	- 'Chiyodajō'	CKel
	- 'Continuing Pleasure' 𝕐H4 new	WAul
	- 'Crepe Paper'	WFar
N	- 'Cry of Rejoice'	EBee ECho ECtt EWll GMac NBre NBro SWat WAul WFar
	- 'Crystal Halo'	CIri NMoo SMrm
	- 'Dace'	GAbr GBin
	- 'Dancing Waves'	CRow
I	- 'Darling'	CRow EBee ECho EPfP MBri NBro NLar SRGP SWat WAul WCon WFar WMoo WWEG
	- 'Diamant' new	GBin
	- 'Dramatic Moment'	WFar WWEG
I	- 'Dresden China'	CRow
N	- 'Eden's Blue Pearl'	CHid EBee
N	- 'Eden's Blush'	EBee MLHP WAul
N	- 'Eden's Charm'	ELan EPfP GBin LPBA NHol
N	- 'Eden's Delight'	NHol
N	- 'Eden's Harmony'	WAul
N	- 'Eden's Paintbrush'	ELan EPfP SPer WHil
N	- 'Eden's Picasso'	CFir EBee ELan EPfP IPot
N	- 'Eden's Purple Glory'	CHid GBin WCot WTin
N	- 'Eden's Starship'	CFir EBee
	- 'Electric Rays'	WAul
I	- 'Emotion'	CMac EBee NBro WAul WFar WPnP
	- 'Epimetheus'	WViv
	- 'Evening Episode'	WViv
	- 'Exstase'	WViv
I	- 'Fortune'	EHrv WAul
	- 'Fractal Blue'	CIri
	- 'Freckled Geisha'	CElw CIri ELon NBir
	- 'Frilled Enchantment' 𝕐H4	WAul
*	- 'Galathea'	CPrp EBee
	- 'Geisha Gown'	WViv
N	- 'Gipsy'	EBee WAul
	- 'Gold Bound'	NMoo SKHP
N	- 'Gracieuse'	EBee ELan EPfP GBin LRHS MSCN NBro NLar SUsu SWat WAul WFar WMoo WPnP WPrP WWEG
	- 'Gusto'	CMHG EBee ELon EPfP IPot MBri MNrw MWts NBro NMoo SMrm SWat WBor
	- 'Haru-no-umi'	CKel
	- 'Hegira'	WAul
	- 'Hercule'	CHid CPLG CRow GAbr NBir
	- Higo white	SPer
*	- 'Himatsuri'	CMHG
	- 'Hokkaido'	CBen CRow
	- 'Hue and Cry' 𝕐H4	WAul
	- hybrids	EHon ESgI
*	- 'Innocence'	CKel EHrv EWll NBre NLar SMrm SWat WAul WFar WMoo
	- 'Iso-no-nami'	CDes EBee NBro WAul WPrP
*	- 'Jacob's Coat'	NCot
N	- 'Jitsugetsu'	CFir CMHG NLar NMoo
N	- 'Jodlesong'	WFar
	- 'Kalamazoo'	WFar
	- 'Katy Mendez' 𝕐H4	WAul
N	- 'Kiyo-tsura'	CKel
*	- 'Kiyo-zuru'	EPfP
N	- 'Kogesho'	EBee EPfP MNrw NBro NLar NMoo WAul
N	- 'Koh Dom'	SPer
	- 'Kongo San'	WFar
	- 'Kuma-funjin'	CPLG CRow
	- 'Kumo-no-obi'	CMHG CSpr EBee EBla NBro NPnk SPoG SWat WAul
*	- 'Kunshikoku'	NLar
	- 'Lace Ruff'	EBee MBri WBor
	- 'Lady in Waiting'	GBin MBri NLar SWal WBor WHil
	- 'Landscape at Dawn'	CRow
N	- 'Laughing Lion'	EBee EBla ECtt GKir MBri NBro WAul WFar WMoo WWEG
	- 'Light at Dawn'	CEnt CMHG EPfP NBPC NBro WAul WBor WFar WMoo
N	- 'Lilac Blotch'	SPer
I	- 'Loyalty'	EBla ECho SRGP WFar
	- 'Mancunian' 𝕐H4	CKel
I	- 'Mandarin'	CBen CRow
	- 'Midnight Stars'	WAul
	- 'Midnight Whisper'	WAul
	- 'Midsummer Reverie'	CRow WViv
N	- 'Momozomo'	EBee LLHF NBro NLar
§	- 'Moonlight Waves'	CHid CMHG CPLG CPrp CRow EAEE EBee EBla ELan EPPr EPfP EShb GAbr GCra GGar GMaP GMac LRHS MWts NBro NGdn NHol SMrm SPoG SWat WAul WFar
	- 'Murasame' 𝕐H4	CMHG WAul
	- 'Ocean Mist'	CHid CMHG EBee ECtt NBro NMoo WViv
	- 'Oku-banri'	CHEx CPLG CPrp EShb
	- 'Ol' Man River' 𝕐H4	WAul
	- 'Oriental Eyes'	GBin NGdn NLar NMoo WAul
	- pale mauve-flowered	NBir SPer
	- 'Pastel Princess'	WAul
	- 'Pin Stripe'	MBri NLar NMoo SMrm SUsu SWat WAul WMoo
	- 'Pink Frost'	CRow EBee ELan EPPr EPfP EWll GCal GMac LBMP LRHS NBro NHol WAul WFar WTin
	- 'Pinkerton'	CIri
	- 'Pleasant Earlybird'	WAul
	- 'Pleasant Journey'	ECtt EHrv
	- 'Prairie Frost'	EPfP NLar SMrm
	- 'Prairie Noble'	EBee NBro NLar
N	- 'Purple Glory'	ELan
	- purple-flowered	SPer
	- 'Queen's Tiara' new	ELon
	- 'Rakka-no-Utage' new	SMrm
	- 'Ranpo'	CRow

I	– 'Red Dawn'	CBen
	– 'Reign of Glory'	WAul
	– 'Returning Tide' ♀H4	WAul
I	– 'Reveille'	EBee NBro SWat WAul WPtf
	– 'Rivulets of Wine'	CIri
§	– 'Rose Queen' ♀H4	Widely available
	– 'Rowden Amir'	CRow
	– 'Rowden Autocrat'	CRow
	– 'Rowden Begum'	CRow
	– 'Rowden Caliph'	CRow
	– 'Rowden Consul'	CRow
	– 'Rowden Dauphin'	CRow
	– 'Rowden Dictator'	CRow
	– 'Rowden Emperor'	CRow
	– 'Rowden King'	CRow
	– 'Rowden Knave'	CRow
	– 'Rowden Knight'	CRow
	– 'Rowden Mikado'	CRow
	– 'Rowden Naib'	CRow
	– 'Rowden Nuncio'	CRow
	– 'Rowden Pasha'	CRow
	– 'Rowden Prince'	CRow
	– 'Rowden Queen'	CRow
	– 'Rowden Shah'	CRow
	– 'Rowden Sultana'	CRow
I	– 'Royal Banner'	EBee MBri NBro WAul WCon WFar
	– 'Royal Crown'	ECho
	– 'Royal Pageant'	CMHG EBee NBPC NBro
I	– 'Ruby King'	LEdu WAul
	– 'Ruffled Dimity'	CBcs EBee GMac IPot MWts NBPC
	– 'Sandsation'	CIri
	– 'Sapphire Star'	CKel
	– 'Sennyo-no-hora'	CPrp
I	– 'Sensation'	CMHG CWCL ECho ECtt EWll GBin GMac MBri SMrm SWat WAul WPrP WWEG
	– 'Shiro-nihonkai'	NMoo
I	– 'Snowflake'	LRHS
	– 'Snowy Hills'	WAul
	– 'Sorcerer's Triumph'	GBin GGar WFar WViv
	– var. ***spontanea***	SWat WAbe
	– – B&SWJ 1103	WCru
	– – B&SWJ 8699	WCru
	– 'Springtime Melody'	WAul
I	– 'Star'	CBen
	– 'Summer Snowflake'	WViv
	– 'Summer Storm' ♀H4	CKel SPer
	– 'Taga-sode'	WViv
	– 'The Great Mogul' ♀H4	CKel CRow
	– 'Tropic Showers'	WViv
	– 'Umi-kaze'	NLar
	– 'Variegata' (v) ♀H4	Widely available
N	– 'Velvety Queen'	CPrp WAul
	– 'Waka-murasaki'	NBro
I	– 'White Ladies'	CSBt EWll SWat WWEG
I	– 'White Pearl'	CRow
	– white-flowered	WFar
	– 'Wine Ruffles'	CMHG EBee LSRN SIri
	– 'Worley Pink'	WViv
	– 'Yako-no-tama'	CRow WMoo
	– 'Yamato Hime'	CMHG EPfP NLar NMoo
N	– 'Yedo-yeman'	WFar
	– 'Yezo-nishiki'	GBin NBro
	'Entertainer' (TB)	EWoo
	'Entice' (TB)	CIri
	'Eramosa Miss' (BB)	WCAu
	'Eramosa Skies' (SDB)	WCAu
	'Erect' (IB)	CKel
	'Esoteric' (SDB)	ESgI
	'Etched Apricot' (TB)	WCAu
	'Eternal Bliss' (TB)	EWoo WViv
	'Evening Pond' (MTB)	CKel
N	'Evening Shade' (J)	WWst
	'Ever After' (TB)	ECtt ESgI EWoo WViv
	'Evergreen Hideaway' (TB)	CIri
	'Everything Plus' (TB)	ESgI WCAu
	'Exclusivity' (TB)	ESgI
	'Exotic Isle' (TB)	ECtt ESgI WViv
	'Extra' (BB)	LLHF WViv
	'Eye Magic' (IB) ♀H4	CKel
	'Eye of Tiger'	see *I.* 'Tigereye'
	'Eye Shadow' (SDB)	WCAu
	'Eyebright' (SDB) ♀H4	WCAu
	'Fabuleux' (TB) **new**	SIri WViv
	'Fade to Black' (TB)	CIri
	'Faenelia Hicks' (La)	WMAq
	'Falcon's Crest' (Spuria) ♀H4	CIri
	'Fall Empire' (TB) **new**	EWoo
	'Fall Enterprise' (TB) **new**	CIri
	'Fall Fiesta' (TB)	ESgI WViv
	'Fancy Brass' (TB) **new**	SIri
	'Fancy Dress' (TB) **new**	SIri WViv
	'Fanfaron' (TB)	ESgI
	'Fanfreluche' (TB) **new**	WViv
	'Fashion Holiday' (IB)	SIri
	'Fashion Lady' (MDB)	ECho
	'Fashion Statement' (TB)	WViv
	'Fashionably Late' (TB) **new**	WViv
	'Fast Forward' (IB)	WAul
	'Fathom' (IB) **new**	WCAu
	'Feature Attraction' (TB)	WViv
	'Feminine Charm' (TB)	MRav WCAu
	fernaldii	GAuc
	'Festive Skirt' (TB)	CKel WCAu
	'Feu du Ciel' (TB) ♀H4	ESgI WViv
	'Fierce Fire' (IB) ♀H4	CKel
	'Fiesta Time' (TB)	CWCL ECtt EWoo WViv
	'Filibuster' (TB) **new**	WCAu
	filifolia var. ***latifolia***	NMin
	'Film Festival' (TB)	ESgI
	'Finalist' (TB)	WAul WViv
	'Firebeard' (TB)	CIri WAul
	'Firebug' (IB)	ESgI WViv
	'Firecracker' (TB)	MRav WCAu
	'First Interstate' (TB)	CWCL ESgI WViv
	'First Movement' (TB)	ESgI
	'First Romance' (SDB)	LSRN SIri WViv
	'First Violet' (TB)	WCAu
	'Fit the Bill' (TB) **new**	WViv
	'Flaming Victory' (TB)	ESgI
	'Flareup' (TB)	WCAu
	flavescens	ESgI EWoo SBch WCAu
	'Fleur Collette Louise' (La)	CIri
	'Flight of Fantasy' (La)	CKel
	'Flight to Mars' (TB)	CIri
	'Flirting' (SDB)	WViv
	'Flirting Again' (SDB) ♀H4	SIri WViv
	'Floating World' (CH) ♀H4	SIri
§	'Florentina' (IB/TB) ♀H4	CArn CHby COIW ECGP EOHP ESgI EWll EWoo GCal GPoy ILis MNHC MRav NBid NBir SEND SIde WCAu
	'Flumadiddle' (IB)	CKel
	'Flushed Delight' (TB)	CIri
	'Flute Enchantée' (TB) **new**	CIri
	foetidissima ♀H4	Widely available
	– 'Aurea'	GQue WCot
	– ***chinensis***	see *I. foetidissima* var. *citrina*
§	– var. ***citrina***	CBre CFir CRow ECGP EPfP EPla EWld GAbr GCal GCra GKir IBlr NBid SChr SUsu SWal WCot WEas WHil WWEG
	– 'Fructu Albo'	GBin GQue NSti WCot

	- var. ***lutescens***	CHid EPPr
N	- 'Moonshy Seedling'	CSWP
	- 'Variegata' (v) ♀H4	CElw CHar CSpe ECtt EHrv EPfP GBar MAvo MCCP MSCN NBir NCob NPer WBor WCot WWEG WWFP
	- yellow-seeded	GCal WTin
	'Foggy Dew' (TB)	ECGP EShb LRHS MWea NPnk
	'Folie Douce' (TB) **new**	WViv
	'Fondation Van Gogh' (TB)	ESgI
	'Foolish Fancy' (TB)	EWoo SIri
	'Footloose' (TB) **new**	SIri WViv
	'Forest Light' (SDB)	ESgI
	'Forever Blue' (SDB)	WCAu WViv
	'Forever Gold' (TB)	EWoo
*	'Forever Trevor' (CH)	SPhx
	'Forever Yours' (TB)	WAul
	'Forge Fire' (TB)	ESgI
	formosana	ECho
	- B&SWJ 3076	WCru
	forrestii ♀H4	CHid CPLG ECho GAbr GAuc GBin GCal GCra GGar GKev GKir ITim LEdu LPBA LRHS MBri MHer MMuc NBPC NBir NBro NCob NGdn SBfd SPhx SPoG SRot WAbe
	'Fort Apache' (TB)	ESgI EWes EWoo
	'Fortune Teller' (TB)	CKel
	fosteriana	NWCA
	'Fourfold Blue' (SpH)	GBin
	'Foxy Lady' (TB)	ESgI EWoo
	'Framboise' (TB) **new**	WViv
	'Frances Iva' (TB) **new**	EWoo
	'Frank Elder' (Reticulata)	ECho EPot LAma LLHF LRHS MRav MTho NMen SDeJ
	'Frans Hals' (Dut)	GKev MMHG MNrw
	'Freedom Flight' (TB)	CIri
	'French Can Can' (TB)	EWoo SIri WViv
	'French Horn' (TB) **new**	CIri
	'French Rose' (TB)	CKel WCAu
	'Fresno Calypso' (TB)	ESgI WCAu
	'Fringe Benefits' (TB)	ESgI
	'Frinousse' (TB)	ESgI WViv
	'Frison-roche' (TB)	CWCL ESgI WViv
	'Frisounette' (TB)	ESgI
	'Fritillary Flight' (IB) ♀H4	CKel
	'Frontier Lady' (TB)	CIri
	'Frontier Marshall' (TB)	NMoo
	'Frost and Flame' (TB)	CAby EAEE EBla ECtt ELan EWll LBMP LBuc LRHS MCot MRav NBir NGdn NLar SBfd SPer SPoG SWat WAul WCAu WWEG
	'Frost Echo' (TB) **new**	EWoo
	'Frosted Biscuit' (TB) ♀H4	CKel
	'Frosted Fantasy' (TB)	CIri
	'Frosted Velvet' (MTB)	WCAu
	'Frosty Jewels' (TB)	ESgI
	'Fruit Cocktail' (IB)	CKel WViv
	'Full Impact' (TB)	CIri
	'Full Tide' (TB)	WCAu
	fulva ♀H3	CBgR CDes CPrp CRow EBee GCal MWts NBir NBro NSti WBor WCot WTin
	- 'Marvell Gold' (La)	CRow
	× ***fulvala*** ♀H4	CDes CFir EPPr EWes GBin NBir NSti WTin
	'Fumo negli Occhi' (TB)	ESgI
	'Funambule' (TB) **new**	WViv
	'Furnaceman' (SDB)	MBri
	'Futuriste' (TB) **new**	SIri WViv
	'Gai Luron' (TB)	WWEG
	'Gala Gown' (TB)	WCAu
	'Gallant Moment' (TB)	ECtt EWoo SIri WViv

	'Galleon Gold' (SDB)	CKel
	'Galway' (IB)	SIri WViv
	'Garnement' (TB) **new**	WViv
	'Gay Parasol' (TB)	WViv
N	'Gelbe Mantel' (Sino-Sib)	CBot CHid EBee NBir NBro NGdn NHol NSti WFar WPrP
	'Gemstar' (SDB)	WViv
	'Gemstone Walls' (TB)	ESgI
	'Gentius' (TB)	WMnd
	'Gentle' (SDB)	WCAu
	'Gentle Grace' (SDB)	ESgI
	'George' (Reticulata) ♀H4	CAvo CFFs EBrs ECho EPfP EPot ERCP GAbr GCrs GKev LAma LRHS NHol NMin SPhx WBrk WHoo
	'George Smith' (TB)	ESgI
	'Gerald Darby'	see *I.* × *robusta* 'Gerald Darby'
	'Gérard Brière' (TB)	WViv
	germanica ♀H4	MGos MMuc SEND WCAu
	- var. ***florentina***	see *I.* 'Florentina'
N	- 'Mel Jope'	NBir
§	- 'Nepalensis'	WCAu
	- 'The King'	see *I. germanica* 'Nepalensis'
	'Gertrude' (TB) **new**	EWoo
	'Ghost Train' (TB)	EWoo WViv
	'Gingerbread Man' (SDB)	CMea EHrv ESgI MBrN MWea NMen WCAu
	'Glacier' (TB)	ECho
	'Glad Rags' (TB)	ESgI
	'Glory Bound' (TB) **new**	WViv
	'Gnus Flash' (TB)	CIri
	'Godfrey Owen' (TB)	CKel WCAu
	'Godsend' (TB)	CKel
	'Going Home' (TB) ♀H4 **new**	SIri
	'Going My Way' (TB)	ESgI EWoo LSou SIri WCAu WViv WWEG
	'Gold Country' (TB)	ESgI
	'Gold Galore' (TB)	WViv
	'Gold of Autumn' (TB)	CKel SMrm
	'Goldberry' (IB)	WCAu
	'Golden Alien' (TB)	CIri
	'Golden Alps' (TB)	SRms WCAu
	'Golden Child' (SDB)	ESgI
	'Golden Encore' (TB)	CKel WCAu
	'Golden Fair' (SDB)	NBir
	'Golden Forest' (TB)	EAEE GBin MWea WCAu
	'Golden Immortal' (TB)	EWoo WViv
	'Golden Panther' (TB)	CIri
	'Golden Planet' (TB)	CKel
	'Golden Violet' (SDB)	ESgI
	goniocarpa	WAbe
	- KR 3739	GEdr
	'Good Looking' (TB)	ESgI WCAu
	'Good Show' (TB)	EWoo WAul WViv
	'Good Vibrations' (TB)	SIri WViv
	'Goodbye Heart' (TB)	ESgI EWoo LSRN WViv
	'Gordon' (Reticulata)	CAvo CFFs ECho EPfP EPot ERCP GKev LAma LRHS MWat SMrm
	gormanii	see *I. tenax*
	'Gosh' (SDB)	CBgR CKel
	'Got Milk' (TB) **new**	WViv
	'Gracchus' (TB) **new**	WCAu
	gracilipes	GKev WAbe
	gracilipes × ***lacustris***	GAuc GEdr WAbe
	graeberiana	ECho EPot GKev SDeJ WWst
	- white fall	WWst
	- yellow fall	ECho WWst
	graminea ♀H4	CAvo CHid CMac CPrp CRow EBee ECha ECho EHrv ELan EPPr EPfP IFro LLWP LRHS NBir NCot NMen NSti NWCA SBch SEND SPer WAbe WAul WCom WCot

	- var. ***pseudocyperus***	GCal NMRc SDys
	graminifolia	see *I. kerneriana*
	'Granada Gold' (TB)	SRms
	'Grand Amiral' (TB) **new**	WViv
	'Grand Circle' (TB) **new**	CIri EWoo
	'Grape Jelly' (TB)	WViv
	'Grapelet' (MDB)	WCAu WViv
	'Grapeshot' (TB)	CIri
	'Great Gatsby' (TB)	CKel
	'Great Lakes' (TB)	ESgI EWoo
	'Grecian Skies' (TB)	ESgI
	'Green Ice' (TB)	CKel MRav
	'Green Prophecy' (TB)	CKel
	'Green Spot' (SDB) ♀^{H4}	CAby CBgR CKel CWGN EBee EBla ECho ECtt EHrv ELan EPfP GEdr MRav NBir NHol NLar NMen NWCA SDeJ SPer SPhx WAul WCFE WWEG
	'Green Streak' (TB)	CIri
	'Grenade' (TB)	WViv
	'Gringo' (TB)	WCAu
	'Guatemala' (TB)	CIri
	'Gwyneth Evans' (BB) ♀^{H4}	CKel
	'Gypsy Beauty' (Dut)	CAvo EPfP LAma LRHS SBch SPer
	'Gypsy Jewels' (TB)	CKel ESgI LTen
	'Gypsy Romance' (TB) ♀^{H4}	EIri ESgI EWoo SIri WCAu WViv
	'Habit' (TB)	WAul WCAu
	'Hafnium' (SDB)	CKel
	halophila	see *I. spuria* subsp. *halophila*
	'Handshake' (TB) ♀^{H4}	WViv
	'Happenstance' (TB)	ESgI WViv
	'Happy Again' (TB) **new**	WViv
	'Happy Birthday' (TB)	ESgI
	'Happy Mood' (IB) ♀^{H4}	NBre WCAu
	'Harbor Blue' (TB)	CKel MWat SWat WCAu WWEG
*	'Hareknoll'	NWCA
	'Harlow Gold' (IB)	ESgI
	'Harmony' (Reticulata)	CAvo CFFs ECho EPfP EPot GKev LAma LRHS MBri NHol SMrm SPhx
	'Harriette Halloway' (TB)	CSam EBee EBla EPfP EShb ETod EWTr LPio LRHS LSRN NLar SMrm SRGP WCot
	hartwegii	ECho
	- NNS 05-394	WCot
	- subsp. ***hartwegii***	GAuc
	- subsp. ***pinetorum***	EPot GAuc
	'Harvest King' (TB)	ECtt ESgI WViv
	'Harvest of Memories' (TB)	ESgI WWEG
	'Haut les Voiles' (TB)	CWCL WViv
	'Haute Couture' (TB)	WViv
	'Haviland' (TB)	WViv
	'Headcorn' (MTB) ♀^{H4}	SIri WAul
	'Headline Banner' (BB) **new**	EWoo WCAu
	'Headway' (Spuria) **new**	WCAu
	'Heartbeat Away' (TB) **new**	CIri
	'Heartbreak Point' (TB) **new**	EWoo
	'Heather Carpet' (SDB)	WCAu
	'Heather Hawk' (TB)	WCAu
	'Heather Sky' (TB)	CIri
	'Heavenly Days' (TB)	WCAu
	'Heaven's Edge' (TB) **new**	WCAu
	'Helen Boehm' (TB)	ESgI EWoo WViv
	'Helen Collingwood' (TB)	ESgI EWoo
	'Helen Dawn' (TB)	CIri
	'Helen McGregor' (TB)	CKel ESgI EWoo
	'Helen Proctor' (IB)	ESgI WCAu WCot
	'Helene C.' (TB) **new**	EWoo WViv
	'Helge' (IB)	COlW ECho NBre SWat
	'Hellcat' (IB)	EWoo WAul WCAu WViv
	'Hello Darkness' (TB) ♀^{H4}	ESgI EWoo WCAu WCot WViv
	'Hell's Fire' (TB)	EWoo GBin WCAu
	'Hemstitched' (TB)	EWoo
	'Hercules' (Reticulata)	ECho LAma LRHS NMin
	'Here Comes The Sun' (TB) **new**	WCAu
	'Heure Bleue' (TB)	EWoo WViv
	hexagona	GAuc
	'Hey There' (MDB)	WViv
	'Hi' (IB)	CIri
	'High Barbaree' (TB)	EWoo WCAu
	'High Blue Sky' (TB)	WCAu
	'High Command' (TB)	CKel SMrm
	'High Ho Silver'	ESgI
	'High Impact' (TB) **new**	EWoo
	'High Peak' **new**	WCAu
	'High Roller' (TB) ♀^{H4}	CIri
	'High Stakes' (TB) **new**	WViv
	'Highline Amethyst' (Spuria)	WAul
	'Hildegarde' (Dut)	SDeJ
	'His Royal Highness' **new**	WCAu
	'Hissy-Fit' (IB)	CKel
	histrio	ECho GAuc
	- subsp. ***aintabensis***	ECho EPot LAma
	histrioides	ECho GAuc WAbe
§	- 'Angel's Tears' (Reticulata)	CAvo ECho GKev NMen NMin WWst
	- 'Halkis' (Reticulata)	EPot LAma NMin
	- 'Lady Beatrix Stanley'	ECho EPot ERCP GBin LAma LRHS NHol NMen NMin
N	- 'Major'	CDes ECho GKev LAma NMin SPhx WWst
N	- 'Michael Tears'	ECho WWst
	- var. ***sophenensis***	ECho
	'Hocus Pocus' (SDB)	ECho EWoo WAul WViv
	'Holden Clough' (SpH) ♀^{H4}	Widely available
	'Holden's Child'	LLWG MWts WHil
	× ***hollandica*** hort.	LRHS NBir
	'Holy Fire' (TB)	CIri
	'Holy Night' (TB)	CKel
	'Honey Behold' (SDB)	CKel
	'Honey Glazed' (IB)	ESgI WAul WCAu WViv
	'Honeymoon Suite' (TB) **new**	EWoo WViv
	'Honeyplic' (IB) ♀^{H4}	SIri WAul
	'Honington' (SDB)	WCAu
	'Honky Tonk Blues' (TB)	CKel ESgI LSRN WViv
	'Honky Tonk Hussy' (BB)	CKel
	'Honorabile' (MTB)	SMrm WCAu
	hoogiana ♀^{H3}	ECho EPot GKev LRHS WWst
	- 'Purpurea'	ECho WWst
§	***hookeri***	CPBP ELan GAuc GBBs GBin GEdr GKev GMac IGor LEdu MGos NBPC SGSe SMrm WAbe WCot
	hookeriana	MMuc
	'Horizon Bleu' (TB)	EWoo
	'Horned Rosyred' (TB) **new**	EWoo
§	'Hornpipe' (TB)	WCAu
	'Hortensia Rose' (TB) **new**	SIri
	'Hot Spice' (IB)	WCAu
	'Hot to Trot' (TB)	ESgI
	'Howard Weed' (TB)	SPad
	'Huckleberry Fudge' (TB)	WAul
	'Hugh Miller' (TB)	WCAu
	'Hula Doll' (MDB)	NMen
	'Hula Moon' (TB)	ESgI
	hyrcana	ECho
	'I Repeat' (TB)	ESgI
	'I Seek You' (TB)	ESgI
	iberica	ECho GAuc
§	- subsp. ***elegantissima***	ECho WWst
	- subsp. ***iberica***	WWst
§	- subsp. ***lycotis***	WWst

	'Ice and Indigo' (SDB) new	WCAu
	'Ice Dancer' (TB) ♀H4	CKel
	'Iced Tea' (TB) ♀H4	CIri
	'Ida' (Reticulata)	ECho LAma
	'Idol' (TB) new	WCAu
	illyrica	see *I. pallida*
	imbricata	GKev
	'Imbue' (SDB)	ESgI WViv
	'Immortality' (TB)	CKel CWGN EKen ESgI EWll WCAu WCot WWEG
	'Imperator' (Dut)	ECho
	'Imperial Bronze' (Spuria)	WAul WCAu
	'Impetuous' (BB) ♀H4	CKel
	'Imprimis' (TB)	ESgI
	'In Limbo' (IB)	CKel
	'In Reverse' (TB)	WViv
	'In Town' (TB)	ESgI EWoo
	'Incentive' (TB)	ECtt EWoo
*	'Incoscente' (TB)	ESgI
	'Indeed' (IB)	CBgR
	'Indian Chief' (TB)	CWCL EPfP ESgI EWoo GBin LAst LTen MRav SPur WCAu WWEG
	'Indian Idyll' (IB)	CKel EWoo
	'Indian Jewel' (SDB)	ECho
	'Indian Pow Wow' (SDB)	CSev
N	'Indiana Sunset' (TB)	CKel
	'Indigo Flight' (IB)	CKel
	'Indigo Princess' (TB)	CKel WViv
	'Indiscreet' (TB)	WViv
	'Infernal Fire' (TB)	CIri
	'Inferno' (TB)	EWoo WViv
	'Infinite Grace' (TB)	ESgI
	'Infinity Ring' (IB) new	WCAu
	'Inner Vision' (TB) new	WViv
	'Innocent Devil' (TB)	CIri
	'Innocent Pink' (TB)	ESgI
	innominata	CAvo ECha ECho EPot GAbr GAuc IBlr LHop LRHS NBir NBro NMen NWCA SRms WCot WWEG
	- JCA 1:460:800	GEdr
	- NNS 01-407	WCot
	- apricot-flowered	IBlr
	- Ballyrogan hybrids	IBlr
	- bronze-flowered	MMuc SEND
	- 'Peacock' new	GEdr
	- yellow-flowered	NMen NRya
	'Inscription' (SDB)	ECho
	'Instant Hit' (TB) new	WCAu
	'Interpol' (TB)	ESgI EWoo
	'Intrepid' (TB)	CWCL WViv
	'Invicta Daybreak' (IB)	SIri
	'Invicta Gold' (SDB) new	SIri
	'Invitation' (TB)	ESgI
	'Irisades' (TB)	WViv
	'Irish Chant' (SDB) new	WCAu
	'Irish Doll' (MDB)	WCAu
	'Irish Moss' (SDB)	WViv
	'Irish Tune' (TB)	ESgI
	'Island Dancer' (TB) new	EWoo WViv
	'Island Sunset' (TB)	ESgI SIri WViv
	'Isoline' (TB)	ESgI
	'J.S. Dijt' (Reticulata)	CAvo CFFs ECho EPfP EPot ERCP GKev LAma LRHS MBri MGos SPhx
	'Jabal' (SDB)	SIri WViv
	'Jacquessiana' new	EWoo
	'Jade Mist' (SDB)	ECho
	'Jaguar Blue' (TB) new	EWoo WCAu
	'Jane Phillips' (TB) ♀H4	Widely available
	'Janet Lane' (BB)	CKel
	'Janine Louise' (TB) ♀H4	CKel
	japonica ♀H3	CHEx CPLG ECho EHrv EPfP NLar NPer WAul WOut
	- B&SWJ 8921	WCru
	- 'Bourne Graceful'	CAby CPLG
	- 'Ledger'	CAby CDes CHll CMac CPLG CPrp CSpe ECha EHrv ELan EPfP IGor MRav SEND SGSe SHom SMad WWFP
	- f. ***pallescens***	SGSe
N	- 'Rudolph Spring'	GCal WWFP
§	- 'Variegata' (v) ♀H3	CBgR CBot CBow CChe CDes CHEx CKel CPrp ECha EHrv ELan ELon ESwi GGar MHer NBro NPer SAPC SAga SArc SBfd SMad WAul WEas WHil WWFP
	'Jasper Gem' (MDB)	ECho NBir
	'Java Bleue' (TB) new	WViv
	'Jay Kenneth' (IB)	CBgR
	'Jayceetee' (TB) new	CIri
	'Jazz Festival' (TB)	EWoo SIri WCAu WViv
	'Jazzamatazz' (SDB)	ESgI WViv
	'Jazzed Up' (TB)	WViv
	'Je l'Adore' (TB) new	WViv
	'Jean Cayeux' (TB)	ESgI EWoo
	'Jean Guymer' (TB)	ESgI NBir
	'Jeanne Price' (TB)	LSRN SCoo WCAu WViv
	'Jelly Belly' (SDB) new	EWoo
	'Jennie Grace' (SDB)	SIri
	'Jeremy Brian' (SDB) ♀H4	WCAu
	'Jesse Lee' (SDB)	CKel
	'Jesse's Song' (TB)	ESgI WCAu
	'Jet-Setter' (TB) new	CIri
	'Jeunesse' (TB)	ESgI
	'Jewel Baby' (SDB)	CKel
	'Jeweler's Art' (SDB)	EWoo WViv
	'Jigsaw' (TB)	ESgI
	'Jitterbug' (TB)	EHrv WCAu
	'Joanna' (TB)	LSRN NLar WWEG
	'Joanna Taylor' (MDB)	NMen WCAu
	'John' (IB)	CKel LSRN
	'Joli Coeur' (TB)	ESgI EWoo WViv
	'Joseph Henry' (TB) new	WCAu
	'Joy Boy' (SDB)	ESgI
	'Joyce' (Reticulata)	ECho EPot GKev LAma LRHS MBri NLar SDeJ SGar SMrm SPhx
	'Joyce Terry' (TB)	CWan ESgI SPad
	'Joyful' (SDB)	ESgI WViv
	'Jubilant Spirit' (Spuria)	EWes
	'Jubilation' (TB) new	EWoo
	'Jubilé Rainier III' (TB)	WViv
	'Jubilee Gem' (TB)	CKel
	'Jud Paynter' (TB)	CKel
	'Julia Vennor' (TB)	CKel
	'Juliet' (TB)	ESgI
	'Jump Start' (IB) new	EWoo WCAu
	'June Prom' (IB)	EAEE LRHS SRGP WCAu
	'Jungle Fires' (TB)	WCAu
	'Jungle Shadows' (BB)	CIri EWoo MRav NBir WCAu
	'Jungle Warrior' (SDB)	CKel
	'Jurassic Park' (TB)	ESgI EWoo WAul WCAu
	'Juris Prudence' (TB)	ESgI
	'Jus d'Orange' (TB)	WViv
	'Just Before Dawn' (TB) new	WViv
	'Just Dance' (IB)	ESgI
	'Just Jennifer' (BB)	WAul WCAu
	kaempferi	see *I. ensata*
	'Kangchenjunga' (TB)	ESgI
	'Karen' (TB)	LSRN WViv
	kashmiriana	CBcs ECre
	'Katharine Hodgkin' (Reticulata) ♀H4	Widely available
	'Katie-Koo' (IB) ♀H4	CKel
	'Katy Petts' (SDB)	ESgI WCAu

	'Kayleigh-Jayne Louise' (TB)	CKel
	'Keep the Peace' (IB) **new**	WCAu
	'Kelway Renaissance' (TB)	CKel
	kemaonensis	GAuc
	'Ken's Choice' (TB) ♀H4	CKel
	'Kent Blackguard' (IB) **new**	SIri
	'Kent Compote' (IB)	SIri
	'Kent Pride' (TB)	CSBt CWGN EAEE EBee EBla ECha ECtt EPfP ESgI EShb ETod EWTr EWoo GBin LRHS MCot MRav MWat SBfd SGar SMrm SPer SPoG SWat WAul WCAu WTin
	'Kentucky Bluegrass' (SDB)	WCAu
	'Kentucky Derby' (TB)	WViv
§	***kerneriana*** ♀H4	LRHS MLLN NBir WPen
	'Kharput' (IB)	EWoo
	'Kildonan' (TB)	WCAu
	'Kind Word' (TB) **new**	WViv
	'King's Jester' (TB) **new**	EWoo
	'Kirkstone' (TB)	WCAu
	kirkwoodii	ECho WWst
	'Kiss of Summer' (TB) ♀H4	ESgI
	'Kissing Circle' (TB)	ESgI EWoo SBfd
	'Kiwi Slices' (SDB)	CPBP ESgI
	'Knick Knack' (MDB)	CAby CMea CPBP EBee EBla ECho ELan EPfP GAbr LBee MRav NMen NWCA SBfd SDnm SMrm SMrs SPhx SPoG
	kolpakowskiana	NMin WWst
	'Kona Nights' (BB)	ESgI
	koreana	GAuc
	korolkowii	ECho EPot WWst
	'La Belle Aube' (TB)	ESgI
	'La Meije' (TB) **new**	SIri WViv
	'La Nina Rosa' (BB)	WCAu
	'La Senda' (Spuria)	WCot
	'La Vie en Rose' (TB)	ESgI WViv
	'Lace Legacy' (TB)	ECtt EWoo LSRN WViv
	'Laced Cotton' (TB)	ESgI WCAu
	'Laced Lemonade' (SDB)	MBri
§	***lactea*** ♀H4	GAuc NWCA
	- var. ***lactea***	GAuc
	lacustris ♀H4	NMen NWCA WAbe
	'Lacy Snowflake' (TB)	COlW LHop
	'Lady Essex' (TB)	EWoo
	'Lady Friend' (TB)	ESgI WCAu WViv
	'Lady Gale' (IB)	CKel
	'Lady Ilse' (TB)	WCAu
	'Lady in Red' (SDB)	ESgI WCAu
	'Lady Mohr' (AB)	CKel WCAu
	'Lady of Fatima' (TB)	ESgI
	'Lady R' (SDB)	ECho
	laevigata ♀H4	CRow ECha ECho EHon ELan EPfP GAuc ITim LPBA MMuc MRav MWts NBro NPer SEND SGar SPer SWat WFar WMAq WMoo WPnP WShi
	- var. ***alba***	CBen CRow ECha ECho EHon ELan EPfP GAuc LPBA MMuc MRav SWat WAbe WFar WMoo
	- 'Albopurpurea'	SGSe
	- 'Atropurpurea'	CRow
	- blue-flowered	MMuc
	- 'Colchesterensis'	CRow NGdn NPer SWat WMAq
I	- 'Dorothy'	LPBA NGdn
N	- 'Dorothy Robinson'	LRHS SWat
	- 'Elegant'	see *I. laevigata* 'Weymouth Elegant'
*	- 'Elgar'	WMAq
	- 'Liam Johns'	CRow
	- 'Midnight'	see *I. laevigata* 'Weymouth Midnight'
	- 'Mottled Beauty'	CRow
	- 'Rashomon'	CRow
	- 'Regal'	CWat
	- 'Richard Greaney'	CRow
	- 'Rose Queen'	see *I. ensata* 'Rose Queen'
	- 'Rowden Seaspray'	CRow
	- 'Rowden Starlight'	CRow
I	- 'Snowdrift'	CBen CRow CWat LPBA LRHS NBir NGdn NLar NPer SPer SWat WFar WMAq WPnP
	- 'Variegata' (v) ♀H4	CBen CBow CRow CWat EAEE ECha ECho EHoe EHon EPfP EPla LLWG LPBA MWts NBro NGdn NPer SPer SWat WMAq WMoo WPnP WTin
	- 'Violet Garth'	CRow
	- 'Weymouth'	see *I. laevigata* 'Weymouth Blue'
§	- 'Weymouth Blue'	CBen CRow
§	- 'Weymouth Elegant'	CRow
§	- 'Weymouth Midnight'	CBen CMil CRow LPBA SWat
N	'Langport Chapter' (IB)	CBgR CKel ESgI
N	'Langport Chief' (IB)	CKel
N	'Langport Claret' (IB)	CBgR CKel ESgI
N	'Langport Curlew' (IB)	CBgR CKel ESgI
N	'Langport Duchess' (IB)	ESgI WTin
N	'Langport Fairy' (IB)	CBgR CKel ESgI
N	'Langport Finch' (IB)	NBir
N	'Langport Flame' (IB)	CBgR CKel CMac ESgI WTin
N	'Langport Haze' (IB)	ESgI
N	'Langport Hope' (IB)	CKel ESgI
N	'Langport Jane' (IB)	CKel
N	'Langport Lady' (IB)	CKel
N	'Langport Lord' (IB)	ESgI
	'Langport Minstrel' (IB)	CKel ESgI
N	'Langport Pearl' (IB)	CKel
	'Langport Phoenix' (IB)	CKel
N	'Langport Pinnacle' (IB)	CKel
N	'Langport Robe' (IB)	ESgI
N	'Langport Smoke' (IB)	CKel
	'Langport Snow' (IB)	CKel
N	'Langport Song' (IB)	CKel ESgI
N	'Langport Star' (IB)	CKel ESgI
	'Langport Storm' (IB)	CKel EAEE EBee EBla ESgI GKir MRav WAul WTin
N	'Langport Sun' (IB)	CBgR CKel ESgI SMrm
N	'Langport Swift' (IB)	CKel
	'Langport Sylvia' (IB)	CBgR CKel
N	'Langport Tartan' (IB)	CKel
N	'Langport Violet' (IB)	CBgR CKel ESgI
	'Langport Vista' (IB)	CKel
	'Langport Warrior' (IB)	CKel
	'Langport Wren' (IB) ♀H4	CAby CBgR CKel ECGP EPfP ESgI EShb GCal GQue MBri MCot NBir SBch SPhx WAul WEas WKif WPen WTin WWEG
	'Lark Ascending' (TB) **new**	WViv
	'Lark Rise' (TB) ♀H4	CKel
	'Larry Gaulter' (TB)	WCAu
	'Las Vegas' (TB)	WCAu
§	***latifolia*** ♀H4	ECho MMuc SEND WShi
	- 'Duchess of York'	ECho WCot
	- 'Isabella'	EBee ECho GKev
	- 'King of the Blues'	ECho GKev
	- 'Mansfield'	EBee ECho GKev
	- 'Montblanc'	EBee ECho
	- 'Queen of the Blues' (Eng)	ECho
	- wild-collected	GCal
	'Latin Lady' (TB)	ESgI
	'Latin Lark' (TB)	ESgI
	'Latin Rock' (TB)	WCAu
	'Laura Jean' (TB) **new**	EWoo
	'Laura Louise' (La)	MAsh SKHP
	'Lava Moonscape' (TB) **new**	CIri

	'Lavender Park' (TB)	ESgI
	lazica 🏆^{H4}	CAbP CBct CBgR CMac CPrp CRow CSpe EAEE EBee EPPr EPfP EPot ESgI GKev IBlr LEdu LFCN LRHS MRav NBir NCGa NSti NWCA NWsh SEND WAbe WCot WSHC WSpi
	- 'Joy Bishop'	CPMA WCot
*	- 'Richard Nutt'	CPMA ELon WCot
N	- 'Turkish Blue'	CPrp GBin IBlr
	'Leda's Lover' (TB)	ESgI
	'Legato' (TB)	ESgI
N	'Lemon Beauty' (TB)	LHop
	'Lemon Brocade' (TB)	ESgI EWoo MBri WCAu WViv
	'Lemon Fever' (TB)	ESgI
	'Lemon Flare' (SDB)	EIri MRav SRms
	'Lemon Flurry' (IB)	SBch
	'Lemon Ice' (TB)	CAby EAEE EBee EBla LAst LBuc LFCN LRHS MWea SBfd SMrm SPer
	'Lemon Lyric' (TB)	ESgI
	'Lemon Mist' (TB)	ESgI
*	'Lemon Peel' (IB)	CKel
	'Lemon Pop' (IB)	WCAu
	'Lemon Puff' (MDB)	WCAu
	'Lemon Tree' (TB)	WCAu
	'Lemon Whip' (IB)	EWoo
	'Lenna M' (SDB)	CKel CPBP ECho
	'Lenora Pearl' (BB)	ESgI EWoo
	'Lent A. Williamson' (TB)	GMaP WWEG
	'Lenten Prayer' (TB)	WViv
	'Leprechaun's Delight' (SDB)	CKel
	'Leprechaun's Purse' (SDB)	WCAu WViv
	'Let's Elope' (IB)	ESgI WCAu
	'Licorice Fantasy' (TB)	ESgI
	'Light Cavalry' (IB)	ESgI EWoo
	'Light Laughter' (IB)	WCAu
	'Light Rebuff' (TB) **new**	EWoo
	'Lightning Streak' (TB)	WViv
	'Lightshine' (TB) **new**	WViv
	'Lilac Times' **new**	EWoo
	'Lilli-white' (SDB)	CKel CWat EBee EBla EHrv ELan GEdr MBNS MRav SBfd SPhx SPoG WCAu WWEG
	'Lima Colada' (SDB)	NBre SMrm
	'Limbo' (SpH)	CRow
	'Lime Fizz' (TB)	ESgI
	'Limelight' (TB)	SRms
	'Lingering Love' (TB)	WCAu
N	'Little Amoena'	NMen
	'Little Black Belt' (SDB)	SIri WWEG
	'Little Blackfoot' (SDB)	ESgI WCAu
	'Little Blue-eyes' (SDB)	ESgI WCAu
	'Little Bluets' (SDB)	ESgI
	'Little Dandy' (SDB)	ECho
	'Little Dogie' (SDB)	ECho
	'Little Dream' (SDB)	WCAu
	'Little Episode' (SDB)	ESgI
	'Little Firecracker' (SDB)	WCAu
	'Little Paul' (MTB)	ESgI
	'Little Rosy Wings' (SDB)	CPBP
	'Little Sapphire' (SDB)	GEdr
	'Little Shadow' (IB)	MRav SRms WWEG
	'Little Sheba' (AB)	WCAu
	'Little Showoff' (SDB)	ESgI
	'Little Tilgates' (CH) 🏆^{H3}	WCot
	'Living Legacy' (TB)	WAul
	'Llanthony' (SDB)	WCAu
	'Local Color' (TB)	ESgI WViv
	'Local Hero' (IB) **new**	WCAu
	'Lodore' (TB)	SRms WCAu
	'Logo' (IB)	WCAu

	'Lohengrin' (TB) **new**	EWoo
	'Lollipop' (SDB)	ESgI SIri WViv
	longipetala	EWes NBir
	'Lookingglass Eyes' (Spuria)	CIri
	'Loop the Loop' (TB)	CMac EBee EWll EWoo LAst MWea NBre SCoo SPoG SWat WViv
	'Loose Valley' (MTB) 🏆^{H4}	SIri
	'Lord Warden' (TB)	CSam EAEE EBla ECtt LRHS MCot MWea SMrm SPur WAul
	'Loreley' (TB)	ESgI
	'Lorenzaccio de Médicis' (TB)	ESgI EWoo
	'Lorilee' (TB)	ESgI
	'Lothario' (TB)	WCAu WFoF
	'Lotus Land' (TB) **new**	WCAu
	'Louis d'Or' (TB) 🏆^{H4}	WViv
	'Louvois' (TB)	ESgI NLar
	'Love the Sun' (TB)	ESgI
	'Lovely Again' (TB)	MRav WCAu
	'Lovely Dawn' (TB)	WCAu
	'Lovely Leilani' (TB)	ESgI
	'Lovely Light' (TB)	MBri
	'Lovely Señorita' (TB) **new**	WCAu WViv
	'Lover's Charm' (TB)	WCAu
	'Love's Tune' (IB)	EAEE EBla LBuc LRHS SRGP SWat
	'Low Ho Silver' (IB)	WCAu
	'Loyalist' (TB)	EWoo SIri WViv
	'Lucky Charm' (MTB)	CMea
	'Lucky Devil' (Spuria) 🏆^{H4}	CIri
	'Lucy's Gift' (MTB) 🏆^{H4}	SRGP WAul
	'Lugano' (TB)	ESgI EWoo
	'Luli-Ann' (SDB) 🏆^{H4}	CKel
	'Lullaby of Spring' (TB)	CKel
	'Lumarco' (TB) **new**	EWoo WViv
	'Lumière d'Automne' (TB)	ESgI
	'Luminosity' (TB)	ESgI
	'Luna di Miele' (BB)	ESgI
	'Lunar Frost' (IB)	SIri WViv
	'Lure of Gold' (IB) **new**	WCAu
§	***lutescens*** 🏆^{H4}	ECho EPot GCra NSla WAbe
§	- 'Campbellii'	ECho NMen
	lycotis	see *I. iberica* subsp. *lycotis*
	'Lyrique' (BB)	CKel WAul
	'Ma Mie' (IB)	ESgI EWoo WViv
	maackii from Ussuri River	GAuc
	'Madame Cheseau' **new**	EWoo
	'Madeira Belle' (TB)	ESgI EWoo WCAu WViv
	'Madeleine Frances' (SDB) **new**	SIri
	'Magharee' (TB)	ESgI
	'Magic Kingdom' (TB)	CIri
	'Magic Man' (TB)	EBee
	'Magical Encounter' (TB) **new**	EWoo WViv
	magnifica 🏆$^{H3-4}$	ECho ELon GKev
N	- 'Agalik'	ECho GAuc GKev
	- 'Alba'	ECho GKev
N	'Mahogany Mix' (Dut)	LAma
	'Maisie Lowe' (TB)	ESgI EWoo
	'Majestic Ruler' (TB) **new**	WCAu
	'Making Eyes' (SDB)	ESgI EWoo WCAu
	'Mallow Dramatic' (TB)	WCAu WViv
	'Man About Town' (TB) **new**	WCAu
I	'Mandarin' (TB)	ESgI WViv
	'Mandarin Purple' (Sino-Sib)	EBee GGar NGdn NHol WPrP
	mandshurica	CPBP
	'Many Mahalos' **new**	WAul
	'Maple Treat' (TB)	WViv
	'Mara' (IB)	CKel
	'Marbre Bleu' (TB) **new**	WViv

	'Marcel Turbat' (TB)	ESgI WViv
	'Marche Turque' (TB)	ESgI EWoo
	'Margrave' (TB)	WViv
	'Marguérite' (Reticulata/v)	ECho ERCP
	'Marie José Nat' (TB) **new**	WViv
	'Mariposa Autumn' (TB) **new**	EWoo SIri WViv
	'Mariposa Skies' (TB)	ESgI
	'Mariposa Wizard' (IB) **new**	WAul
	'Marmalade Skies' (BB)	WCAu
	'Maroon Caper' (IB)	SBch
	'Martyn Rix'	see *I. confusa* 'Martyn Rix'
	'Mary Constance' (IB) ♀H4	CKel
	'Mary Frances' (TB)	ESgI LSRN WCAu WViv
	'Mary McIlroy' (SDB) ♀H4	CKel WTin
	'Maslon' (MTB)	ESgI
	'Master Plan' (TB) **new**	WViv
	'Master Touch' (TB)	ELon
	'Matinata' (TB)	CKel
	'Maui Moonlight' (IB) ♀H4	CKel ESgI WAul WCAu
	'Mauvelous' (TB)	CIri
	'May Melody' (TB)	WCAu
	'Maya Mint' (MDB)	LLHF
	'Meadow Court' (SDB)	CKel WCAu WWEG
	'Media Luz' (Spuria)	WCAu
	'Medici Prince' (TB) **new**	EWoo WCAu
	'Medway Valley' (MTB) ♀H4	SIri WCAu
	'Megabucks' (TB) **new**	WViv
	'Meg's Mantle' (TB) ♀H4	CKel
	'Melbreak' (TB)	WCAu
	mellita	see *I. suaveolens*
	'Melon Honey' (SDB)	CKel ECho ELon WCAu
	'Memphis Blues' (TB)	EWoo
	'Men in Black' (TB)	WCAu
	'Menton' (SDB)	CKel
	'Mer du Sud' (TB) ♀H4	EIri ESgI WCot WViv
*	'Merebrook Blue Lagoon' (La)	WMAq
	'Merebrook Jemma J' (La)	WMAq
*	'Merebrook Lemon Maid' (La)	WMAq
	'Merebrook Malvern Shadow' (La)	WMAq
	'Merebrook Purpla' (La)	WMAq
*	'Merebrook Rusty Red' (La)	WMAq
*	'Merebrook Snowflake' (La)	WMAq
	'Merebrook Sunnyside Up' (La)	WMAq
	'Merry Dance' (SDB)	CKel
	'Mesmerizer' (TB)	ESgI EWoo WViv
	'Metaphor' (TB)	WCAu
	'Mezza Cartuccia' (IB)	ESgI
	'Michael Paul' (SDB) ♀H4	ESgI
	'Midday Blue' (J) **new**	WWst
I	'Midnight Blue' (MDB) **new**	CBro
	'Midnight Caller' (TB)	ESgI EWoo
	'Midnight Mango'	see *I.* 'Midnight Web'
	'Midnight Oil' (TB)	WAul WCAu WViv
§	'Midnight Web' (IB) ♀H4	CKel
	'Midsummer Night's Dream' (IB)	WAul WViv
	'Mighty Mouse' **new**	EWoo
	milesii ♀H4	CPLG CPou EWld IGor NBir WSHC
	- CC 4590	CHid
	'Millennium Falcon' (TB)	WAul
	'Millennium Sunrise' (TB)	WCAu
	'Ming' (IB)	WCAu
	'Mini Big Horn' (IB)	CIri
	'Miss Carla' (IB)	NBre
	'Miss Nellie' (BB)	CKel
	'Mission Ridge' (TB)	SBfd
	'Mission Sunset' (TB)	EHrv
	missouriensis ♀H4	CAvo CMac EBee IGor NBid
	'Mister Matthew' (TB) ♀H4	CKel
	'Mister Roberts' (SDB)	ESgI
	'Mistigri' (IB)	CBgR WViv
	'Mme Chéreau' (TB)	ESgI WCAu
	'Mme Louis Aureau' (TB)	ESgI
	'Modern Classic' (TB)	EWoo
	'Monet's Blue' (TB) **new**	WViv
	monnieri	GAuc NLar
	'Monsieur-Monsieur' (TB)	ESgI
	Monspur Group	WCot
§	'Monspur Cambridge Blue' (Spuria) ♀H4	WCAu
	'Monty's Sweet Blue' (TB)	CIri
	'Moon Journey' (TB)	SIri WAul WViv
	'Moon Sparkle' (IB)	CKel
	'Moonbeam' (TB)	CKel
	'Moonlight Waves'	see *I. ensata* 'Moonlight Waves'
	'Moonlit Waves' (TB)	CKel
	'Moonstruck' (TB)	EWoo
	'Morning Show' (IB)	CWGN SBfd
	'Morning Sky' (J)	WWst
	'Morning's Blush' (SDB) ♀H4	CIri
	'Morwenna' (TB) ♀H4	CKel WCAu
	'Mote Park' (MTB)	SIri WAul
	'Mother Earth' (TB)	ESgI EWoo WAul
	'Mountain Majesty' (TB)	ESgI
	'Mountain Music' **new**	EWoo
	'Mousquetaire' (IB) **new**	WViv
	'Mrs Horace Darwin' (TB)	CFir SWat WMnd
	'Mrs Nate Rudolph' (SDB)	EBee WCAu
	'Mrs Tait' (Spuria)	NChi
	'Mukaddam' (TB)	CIri
	'Mulberry Rose' (TB)	CFee NChi
	'Mulled Wine' (TB)	ESgI
	'Muriel Neville' (TB)	WCAu
	'Murmuring Morn' (TB)	WCAu
	'Must Unite' (TB) **new**	WCAu
	'My Honeycomb' (TB)	WCAu
	'My Kayla' (SDB)	ESgI
N	'My Seedling' (MDB)	NMen
	'Myra' (SDB)	ESgI
	'Mysterieux' (TB) **new**	SIri WViv
	'Mystic Beauty' (Dut)	LAma SBch
	'Naivasha' (TB)	CKel
	'Nancy' (TB)	SApp
	'Nancy Hardy' (MDB)	ECho NMen
	'Naples' (TB)	ESgI WViv
	narbutii (J)	WWst
	narbutii* × *maracandica	WWst
	narcissiflora	WCot
	'Nassk' **new**	EWoo
	'Natascha' (Reticulata)	ECho EPot LAma LRHS NHol SDeJ SPhx
	'Natchez Trace' (TB)	MWea
	'Navajo Code' (TB) **new**	CIri
	'Navajo Jewel' (TB)	ESgI EWoo WCAu
	'Nectar' (IB)	ESgI
	nectarifera	WWst
	'Needlecraft' (TB)	NBre
	'Needlepoint' (TB)	ESgI
	'Negro Modelo' (SDB) **new**	WCAu
	'Neige de Mai' (TB)	ESgI WViv
	nepalensis	see *I. decora*
	nertschinskia	see *I. sanguinea*
	'Neutron Dance' (TB) **new**	WViv
N	'New Argument' (J)	WWst
	'New Centurion' (TB)	EWoo WViv
	'New Day Dawning' (TB)	CIri
	'New Idea' (MTB)	ESgI WCAu

	'New Leaf' (TB)	WCAu
	'New Snow' (TB)	WCAu
	'Nibelungen' (TB)	CPMA ELon MWea NBre WFar WGwG
	'Nice 'n' Nifty' (IB)	WTin
	'Nicola Jane' (TB) Υ^{H4}	CKel
	nicolai	ECho WWst
	'Night Edition' (TB)	CPMA ESgI
	'Night Game' (TB)	WViv
	'Night Owl' (TB)	CKel COIW ELan ELon ESgI LAst LHop MCot MHer SBfd SPoG
	'Night Ruler' (TB)	ESgI EWoo WCAu WViv
	'Night Shift' (IB)	NBre WViv
	'Nightfall' (TB)	EBee
	'Nightmare' (TB) **new**	CIri
	'Nights of Gladness' (TB)	ESgI
	'Noble Lady' (TB) **new**	CIri
*	'Noces Blanches' (IB)	ESgI
	'Noctambule' (TB) **new**	WViv
	'Noon Siesta' (TB)	ESgI
	'Nora Eileen' (TB) Υ^{H4}	CKel
	'Nordica' (TB)	ESgI WViv
	'Norfolk Belle' (TB) Υ^{H4}	WAul
	'North Downs' (BB)	SIri
	'Northern Jewel' (IB)	SIri WViv
	'Northwest Pride' (TB)	WCAu WViv
	'Nuit de Noces' (TB) **new**	WViv
	'Oasis Angel' (TB) **new**	CIri
	'Oasis Dragon' (TB) **new**	CIri
	'Obsidian' (TB)	CIri
	'Ocean Depths' (TB)	ESgI
	'Ocelot' (TB)	ESgI
	'Ochraurea' (Spuria)	NGdn SMrm
	'Ochre Doll' (SDB)	CKel
	ochroleuca	see *I. orientalis* Mill.
	'O'Cool' (IB)	CKel
	'October Storm' (IB)	EWoo
	'Oh Jamaica' (TB) **new**	WCAu
	'Oh So Cool' (MTB)	ESgI
	'Oiseau Lyre' (TB)	ESgI
	'Oklahoma' (TB) **new**	EWoo
	'Oktoberfest' (TB)	ESgI
	'Ola Kalá' (TB)	EAEE EBla ECGP ESgI EWll GMaP LRHS NBre NLar SPer WCAu WWEG
	'Old Black Magic' (TB)	ESgI
	'Olympiad' (TB)	ESgI
	'Olympic Challenge' (TB)	ESgI MRav WCAu
	'Olympic Torch' (TB)	ESgI WCAu
	'Ominous Stranger' (TB)	ESgI WCAu
	'Once Again' (TB) **new**	EWoo
	'Open Sky' (SDB)	SIri WViv WWEG
	'Opposing Forces' (TB) **new**	WCAu
	'Orageux' (IB)	CBgR CWCL ESgI WViv
	'Orange Caper' (SDB)	EAEE EBla ECtt EPfP ESgI GEdr MRav NGdn NLar SBfd SMrm
	'Orange Embers' (TB) **new**	WViv
	'Orange Encore' (SDB) **new**	WAul
	'Orange Harvest' (TB)	EWoo LRHS
	'Orange Order' (TB)	WCAu
N	'Orange Plaza'	ECho NMen
	'Orange Pop' (BB)	WAul
	'Orange Tiger' (SDB)	WViv
	'Orchardist' (TB)	CKel
	'Orchidarium' (TB)	CKel
	'Orchidea Selvaggia' (TB)	ESgI
	orchioides misapplied	see *I. bucharica* Foster
§	***orchioides*** Carrière	ECho ELan MLHP
	- 'Aktash' **new**	WWst
	- deep yellow-flowered	WWst
	- dwarf	WWst
N	- 'Urungachsai'	EPot WWst
	orchioides* × *warleyensis **new**	WWst
	'Oregon Skies' (TB)	ESgI ETod EWoo WViv
	'Oreo' (TB)	CIri
N	'Oriental Argument' (J)	WWst
	'Oriental Baby' (IB)	CKel EWoo
	'Oriental Beauty' (Dut)	CAvo GKev LAma LRHS SBch SPer SPhx WCot WFar
	'Oriental Glory' (TB)	WCAu
	'Oriental Touch' (SpH)	CRow
	orientalis Thunb.	see *I. sanguinea*
	- 'Alba'	see *I. sanguinea* 'Alba'
	orientalis ambig.	CAvo ELan EPyc
§	***orientalis*** Mill. Υ^{H4}	CBot EPPr EWTr GCal SGar WCAu WDyG
	'Orinoco Flow' (BB) Υ^{H4}	CHar CKel ESgI WCAu
	'Orloff' (TB)	ESgI
	'Oro Antico' (TB)	CIri
	'Osage Buff' (TB)	CKel
	'Osay Canuc' (TB)	CIri
	'Ostrogoth' (TB)	CIri
	'Oulo' (TB)	ESgI
	'Our House' (TB)	ESgI
	'Ouragan' (TB) **new**	WViv
	'Out Yonder' (TB)	WCAu
	'Ovation' (TB)	ESgI
	'Over Easy' (SDB)	CKel
	'Overjoyed' (TB)	WCAu
	'Overnight Sensation' (TB)	EWoo WViv
	'O'What' (SDB)	ESgI
	'Owyhee Desert' (TB)	WCAu
	'Oxford Tweeds' (SDB)	ESgI
	'Ozone Alert' (TB)	CIri
	Pacific Coast hybrids	see *I.* Californian hybrids
	'Pacific Gambler' (TB)	SMrm
	'Pacific Mist' (TB)	WCAu WViv
	'Pacific Panorama' (TB)	ESgI
	'Pagan Pink' (TB)	CIri
	'Pagan Princess' (TB)	WCAu
	'Paint It Black' (TB)	ETod EWoo WViv
	'Pale Primrose' (TB)	WCAu
	'Pale Shades' (IB) Υ^{H4}	CKel
	'Palissandro' (TB)	ESgI
§	***pallida***	EBee ESgI GMaP MCCP MRav MWat SEND SRms WCAu WMnd
§	- 'Argentea Variegata' (TB/v)	CSBt CWCL CWGN EBee ECha ECho EHoe EHrv EPfP EShb GMaP LAst LRHS MAsh MBrN MBri MCot MNFA MRav NBir SBfd SPer SPhx SPoG WAul WKif WWEG
	- 'Aurea'	see *I. pallida* 'Variegata' Hort.
	- 'Aurea Variegata'	see *I. pallida* 'Variegata' Hort.
	- subsp. ***cengialtii***	NWCA
	- var. ***dalmatica***	see *I. pallida* subsp. *pallida*
§	- subsp. ***pallida*** Υ^{H4}	CBot CKel CWan EAEE ECGP ECha ELan GCal LRHS MBri SDix SPer
	- 'Variegata' misapplied	see *I. pallida* 'Argentea Variegata'
§	- 'Variegata' Hort. (v) Υ^{H4}	Widely available
	'Palm Springs' (IB)	NMin
	'Palomino' (TB)	WCAu
	'Paltec' (IB)	CPou
	'Pane e Vino' (TB)	ESgI
	'Pansy Top' (SDB)	SIri
	'Paradise' (TB)	CKel
	'Paradise Bird' (TB) Υ^{H4}	WCAu
	paradoxa	ECho WWst
	'Parisien' (TB)	CWCL EIri WViv
	'Parts Plus' (IB) **new**	CIri
	'Party Dress' (TB)	CMac CSam CWGN EBee EBla ELan EPfP LRHS MRav MWhi NBir NGdn NLar SBfd SMrm SPer SPoG SRms STes SWat WCFE WCot

	'Passport' (BB)	ECho
	'Pastel Charm' (SDB)	NPnk WMnd
	'Patches' (TB)	ESgI
	'Patina' (TB)	ECtt EIri ESgI ETod EWoo WAul WCAu WViv
	'Patterdale' (TB)	NBir NBre
	'Paul Black' (TB)	CIri
	'Pauline' (Reticulata)	CAvo ECho EPfP EPot ERCP GKev LAma LRHS MWat SMrm
	'Peaceful Waters' (TB)	ECtt EWoo WViv
	'Peach Eyes' (SDB)	CKel
	'Peach Picotee' (TB)	ESgI WViv
	'Peach Spot' (TB)	CPMA
	'Peacock Pavane' (CH) 🏆^{H4}	SIri
	'Pearls of Autumn' (TB)	WCAu
	'Pearly Dawn' (TB)	EBee EBla ECtt LRHS SPer SRGP SWat WWEG
	'Peau de Pêche' (TB)	WViv
N	'Pêche Melba' (TB)	ESgI
	'Pegaletta' (La)	NBro
	'Peggy Chambers' (IB) 🏆^{H4}	CSpr SMrm
	'Pele' (SDB)	ESgI
	'Penny a Pinch' (TB)	WWEG
	'Pepita' (SDB)	SIri WViv
	'Perfect Interlude' (TB)	ECtt EIri EWoo WViv
	'Perfume Shop' (IB)	CKel WCAu
	'Persian Berry' (TB)	WCAu
	'Persian Gown' (TB) **new**	EWoo
	'Persian Wood' (IB)	WAul
	'Pétillant' (TB) **new**	WViv
	'Petit Caprice' (TB) **new**	WViv
	'Petit Tigre' (IB)	CBgR WViv
	'Petite Monet' (MTB)	ESgI
	'Phaeton' (TB)	WCAu
	'Pharaoh's Daughter' (IB)	SIri
	'Phil Keen' (TB) 🏆^{H4}	CKel
	'Phyllis Emily' (IB) **new**	WCAu
N	'Picadee'	EBla EPfP MWea
	'Piero Bargellini' (TB)	ESgI
	'Pigmy Gold' (IB)	EBee
	'Pinewood Amethyst' (CH)	CAby
	'Pinewood Poppet' (CH)	SUsu
	'Pinewood Sunshine' (CH)	MAvo SUsu
	'Pink Angel' (TB)	EWoo
	'Pink Attraction' (TB)	ESgI
	'Pink Bubbles' (BB)	WAul
	'Pink Charm' (TB)	CAby CWGN EAEE EBla EPfP LBuc LRHS SBfd SMrm SPlb WAul
	'Pink Confetti' (TB)	ESgI EWoo WViv
	'Pink Fawn' (SDB)	ESgI
	'Pink Formal' (TB)	ESgI
	'Pink Horizon' (TB)	EPfP
	'Pink Kitten' (IB)	WCAu WGwG
N	'Pink Lavender' (TB)	ELon
	'Pink Parchment' (BB) 🏆^{H4}	CKel
	'Pink Pele' (IB)	ESgI WAul
	'Pink Pussycat' (TB)	MBri
	'Pink Reprise' (BB)	WAul
	'Pink Revelry' (SDB) **new**	WCAu
	'Pink Rose' (TB) **new**	WViv
	'Pink Swan' (TB)	ESgI WViv
	'Pink Taffeta' (TB)	ESgI
	'Pinnacle' (TB)	CKel ESgI GCal SWat WCAu
	'Pipes of Pan' (TB)	ESgI WCAu
	'Pirate's Patch' (SDB)	ESgI
	'Pirate's Quest' (TB)	ESgI EWoo WViv
	'Piroska' (TB) 🏆^{H4}	ESgI SGar WViv
*	'Piu Blue' (TB)	ESgI
	'Pixie' (DB)	GKev
	'Pixie' (Reticulata) 🏆^{H4}	ECho ELan EPot LAma LRHS NLar SDeJ
	planifolia	CMea ECho
*	- f. ***alba***	ECho GKev
	'Platinum' (TB) **new**	WCAu
	'Pledge Allegiance' (TB)	ECtt ESgI EWoo WCAu WViv
	plicata	WCAu
	'Pluie d'Or' (TB)	ESgI
	'Plum Fun' (TB) **new**	WViv
	'Plum Lucky' (SDB)	SIri WViv
	'Plum Wine' (SDB)	CKel
	'Poem of Ecstasy' (TB)	WCAu
	'Poesie' (TB) **new**	WViv
	'Pogo' (SDB)	CWGN EBla ECho ECtt ELan EPfP EPot ETod EWoo GMaP LRHS MMHG MRav NBir NWCA SBfd SDeJ SMrm SRms
	'Polished Manners' (TB) **new**	WViv
	'Pond Lily' (TB)	ESgI
	'Pookanilly' (IB)	CPMA WViv
	'Poppa John' (TB) **new**	CIri
	'Portfolio' (TB)	ESgI
	potaninii	GAuc
	'Powder Blue Cadillac' (TB)	CKel
	'Power Point' (TB)	CIri
	'Power Surge' (TB)	EWoo
	'Precious Heather' (TB) 🏆^{H4}	CKel
	'Presence' (TB)	SIri WViv
	'Pretender' (TB)	WCAu
	'Pretty Please' (TB)	ESgI
	'Prince Indigo' (TB)	MRav
	'Prince of Burgundy' (IB) 🏆^{H4}	WCAu
	'Princess Beatrice' (TB)	WCAu
	'Princess Bride' (BB) 🏆^{H4}	CIri WCAu
	'Princess Sabra' (TB) 🏆^{H4}	CKel
	'Princesse Caroline de Monaco' (TB)	CWCL ESgI EWoo WViv
	prismatica	GKev
	- ***alba***	IGor
N	- 'Quartz'	ITim
	'Private Treasure' (TB) **new**	WViv
	'Prodigy' (MDB)	WViv
	'Professor Blaauw' (Dut) 🏆^{H4}	CAvo EPfP LRHS SPhx
	'Prosper Laugier' (IB)	CBgR WCAu
	'Protocol' (IB)	CKel WViv
	'Prototype' (TB)	CIri
	'Proud Tradition' (TB)	SIri WCAu WViv
	'Provençal' (TB)	CKel CPMA CWCL ECtt ESgI ETod EWoo WAul WCAu WViv
	'Prudy' (BB) 🏆^{H4}	CKel
	'Prunelle' (IB)	CBgR WViv
	pseudacorus 🏆^{H4}	Widely available
	- B&SWJ 5018 from Japan	WCru
	- from Korea	CRow
	- 'Alba'	CPrp EBee GBin GCal LAst MRav MWts NGdn SWat
	- var. ***bastardii***	CBgR CRow CWat EBee ECha ELon EPfP ESgI IGor LPBA MSKA NPer SLon SMHy SPer SWat WBrk WFar WMoo WPnP WTin WViv
	- 'Beuron'	CRow
	- cream-flowered	NBir SWat WAul
N	- 'Crème de la Crème'	ELon GBin LLWG NSti WHil
	- 'Esk'	GBin GCal
N	- 'Flore Pleno' (d)	CBgR CBot CPrp CRow EBee ECho ESgI GCra LPBA MSKA NLar NPer WBrk WCot WFar WPnP WWEG
N	- 'Golden Daggers'	CRow
I	- 'Golden Fleece'	SPer
	- 'Golden Queen'	CRow IGor
	- 'Ilgengold'	CRow

N	- 'Ivory'	CRow
	- 'Krill' **new**	WHil
	- 'Mandchurica' **new**	XBlo
*	- ***nana***	CRow
	- 'Roccapina'	GBin
	- 'Roy Davidson' $\mathbb{Y}^{H4}$	CBgR CPrp CRow GBin GCal IBlr LPBA NLar WFar WHil WPtf WTin WViv
N	- 'Sulphur Queen'	CBgR WCot
	- 'Sun Cascade'	CRow
N	- 'Tiger Brother'	SIri WBrk
	- 'Tiggah'	CRow
N	- 'Turnipseed'	WCot WTin
	- 'Variegata' (v) $\mathbb{Y}^{H4}$	Widely available
	- white-flowered, from Lake Michigan	WTin
*	***pseudocapnoides*** (J)	WWst
	pumila	CPBP LRHS MCot MWat NHol NMen NWCA
	- 'Alba' (DB)	CPBP
	- ***atroviolacea***	CBgR CKel ESgI SMrm WMnd
	- blue-flowered	SWal
*	- 'Caerulea'	GAuc
N	- 'Gelber Mantel'	NBir
N	- 'Lavendel Plicata'	NBro NGdn
	- 'Nicola' **new**	NWCA
	- 'Violacea' (DB)	SRms
	- yellow-flowered	SWal
	'Pumpin' Iron' (SDB) $\mathbb{Y}^{H4}$	CKel CPMA ESgI
	'Punch' (BB)	WAul
	'Punchline' (TB)	CWCL ECtt WViv
	'Punk' (MDB)	CIri WCAu
	'Puppet Baby' (MDB)	WViv
	'Pure As Gold' (TB)	CWCL ESgI EWoo WViv
	'Purple Gem' (Reticulata)	ECho EPfP EPot LAma MCot SPhx
	'Purple People Eater' (TB)	CIri
	'Purple Sensation' (Dut)	ECho SDeJ
	'Quaker Lady' (TB)	ESgI SIri WCAu
	'Quantum Leap' (TB) **new**	CIri
	'Quark' (SDB)	CKel CPBP
	'Quechee' (TB)	CWCL EBee EBla ECGP EPfP ESgI ETod EWoo GMaP IPot LBuc LRHS LSRN MCot MRav MWat NLar SMrm SPer STes SWat WAul WSpi
	'Queen in Calico' (TB)	ESgI WCAu WViv
	'Queen of May' (TB)	ESgI
	'Queen's Circle' (TB) $\mathbb{Y}^{H4}$	CIri
	'Queen's Ivory' (SDB)	SMrs
	'Queen's Prize' (SDB)	SIri WViv
	'Quito' (TB) **new**	WCAu
	'Rabbit's Foot' (SDB)	LSRN WViv
	'Radiant Apogee' (TB)	ECtt EIri ESgI WViv
	'Radiant Burst' (IB)	SIri
	'Rain Dance' (SDB) $\mathbb{Y}^{H4}$	ESgI
	Rainbow Grand Mixture **new**	SDeJ
	'Rainbow Rim' (SDB)	ESgI
	'Rajah' (TB)	CAby CSam EBee EBla EHrv ELan EPfP ESgI EShb GMaP LFCN LPio LRHS LSRN MCot MLHP MMHG MRav SBfd SPer SPoG SPur WMnd
	'Ramblin' Rose' **new**	WViv
	'Rameses' (TB)	ESgI EWoo
	'Rancho Rose' (TB)	CKel
	'Rapture in Blue' (TB)	EWoo WViv
	'Rare Edition' (IB)	CKel ESgI EWoo NBir NBre WAul WViv
	'Rare Quality' (TB)	WAul WViv
	'Raspberry Acres' (IB)	MRav WCAu
	'Raspberry Blush' (IB) $\mathbb{Y}^{H4}$	CAby CKel CPar EAEE EBla EIri EPfP GBin LBMP LRHS MAsh MRav NBre SPur STes SWat WAul WCAu WWFP
	'Ravenous' (TB) **new**	WViv
	'Ravissant' (TB) **new**	WViv
	'Razoo' (SDB)	CKel
	'Re La Blanche' (TB) **new**	WViv
	'Real Coquette' (SDB)	SIri WViv
	'Realm' (TB)	ESgI
	'Rebecca Perret' (TB)	EWoo WCAu WViv
	'Rebus' (SDB) **new**	SIri
	'Red at Night' (TB)	WAul
	'Red Atlast' (MDB)	ESgI
	'Red Canyon Glow' (TB)	CIri
	'Red Flash' (TB)	ESgI
	'Red Hawk' (TB)	WViv
	'Red Heart' (SDB)	ESgI GEdr MRav WTin WWEG
	'Red Orchid' (IB)	ELan NBre SRms WCAu WWEG
	'Red Revival' (TB)	MRav WCAu
N	'Red Rum' (TB)	CKel
	'Red Spot' (SDB)	ECho
	'Red Tornado' (TB)	ESgI
	'Red Zinger' (IB)	CPMA ESgI EWoo WAul WViv
	'Reflets Safran' (TB) **new**	WViv
	'Reg Wall' (TB) $\mathbb{Y}^{H4}$	CIri
	'Regal Surprise' (SpH) $\mathbb{Y}^{H4}$	CBgR CRow WAul
	'Regards' (SDB)	GEdr
§	***reichenbachii***	CPBP EPot LLHF NWCA WThu
	'Reincarnation' (TB)	EWoo
	'Reminiscence' (MTB)	ESgI
	'Renewal' (TB) **new**	EWoo
	'Renown' (TB)	ESgI EWoo
	'Repartee' (TB)	ESgI EWoo
	reticulata $\mathbb{Y}^{H4}$	CFox EBrs ECho ELan EPfP LRHS SBch SDeJ SPer WGwG
	- var. ***bakeriana***	ECho NMin
	- 'Spring Time'	ECho LAma LRHS NHol SDeJ
N	- 'Violet Queen'	ECho
	'Return to Bayberry' (TB)	CIri
	'Return to Sender' (TB) **new**	EWoo
	'Rime Frost' (TB)	WCAu
	'Ringer' (SDB)	ESgI WViv
	'Ringo' (TB)	CKel ESgI LSRN MRav WCAu
	'Rio de Oro' (TB) **new**	WViv
	'Rip City' (TB)	ESgI EWoo WViv
	'Ripple Chip' (SDB)	WTin
	'Rippling River' (TB) **new**	WViv
	'Rippling Waters' (TB)	ESgI
	'Rising Moon' (TB)	EWoo SIri WViv
	'Ritz' (SDB)	WWEG
	'Rive Gauche' (TB)	ESgI
	'River Avon' (TB) $\mathbb{Y}^{H4}$	WCAu
	'Riverbuds' **new**	WCAu
	'Robe d'Eté' (TB)	CWCL WViv
§	× ***robusta*** 'Dark Aura' $\mathbb{Y}^{H4}$	MAvo MWts WCot WTin WViv
§	- 'Gerald Darby' $\mathbb{Y}^{H4}$	Widely available
	- 'Mountain Brook'	CRow LLWG
	- 'Nutfield Blue'	WTin
N	— 'Purple Fan'	LLWG
§	'Rocket' (TB)	EBla EPfP GMaP LBuc LRHS MRav MWea NBir NBre SMrm SPer WAul
	'Rocket Master' (TB)	ESgI
	'Roman Carnival' (TB) **new**	EWoo
	'Roman Rhythm' (TB)	EWoo
	'Romance' (TB)	EWoo WViv
	'Romantic Evening' (TB)	EIri ESgI WCAu WViv
	'Romantic Mood' (TB)	CKel WViv
	'Romney Marsh' (IB)	SIri
	'Ron' (TB)	EWoo
	'Rondo' (TB)	ECtt
	'Rosalie Figge' (TB)	ESgI EWoo WCAu WCot WViv
	'Rosé' (TB)	LSRN WViv
	'Rose Queen'	see *I. ensata* 'Rose Queen'
	'Rosemary's Dream' (MTB)	ESgI NBre
	rosenbachiana	ECho GKev WWst

	– deep purple-flowered	WWst
N	– 'Harangon'	ECho WWst
I	– 'Sina'	WWst
N	– 'Varzob'	WWst
	'Roseplic' (TB)	ESgI WViv
	'Rosette Wine' (TB)	ESgI WCAu
	rossii	WWst
	'Rosy Wings' (TB)	ECho ESgI
	'Roucoulade' (TB) **new**	SIri WViv
	'Rouge Gorge' (TB) **new**	WViv
	'Rougissant' **new**	WViv
	'Roulette' (TB)	MBri
N	'Roy Elliott'	NMen
	'Royal Courtship' (TB)	ESgI
	'Royal Crusader' (TB)	CMdw CPMA EWoo
	'Royal Elegance' (TB)	EWoo SIri WViv
	'Royal Intrigue' (TB)	SIri WViv
	'Royal Magician' (SDB)	WTin
	'Royal Satin' (TB)	CHid EWoo SPad WGwG
	'Royal Tapestry' (TB)	NBre
	'Royalist' (TB)	CKel
	'Rubacuori' (TB)	ESgI EWoo
	'Ruban Bleu' (TB)	ESgI EWoo WViv
	'Rubistar' (TB)	ESgI
	'Ruby Chimes' (IB)	ESgI WCAu
	'Ruby Contrast' (TB)	WCAu
	'Ruby Eruption'	WViv
	rudskyi	see *I. variegata*
	'Ruée vers l'Or' (TB)	ESgI
	'Ruffled Goddess' (TB) **new**	WViv
	'Ruffled Revel' (SDB)	GKir
	'Russet Crown' (TB)	CKel
	'Rustic Cedar' (TB)	ESgI WCAu WViv
	'Rustic Royalty' (TB)	WViv
	'Rustle of Spring' (TB)	CIri
	'Rustler' (TB)	ESgI WAul WCAu
	'Rusty Beauty' (Dut)	LAma SBch
	'Rusty Magnificence' (TB)	WViv
	'Ruth Rowlands' (TB) **new**	EWoo
	ruthenica	ECho GBin NMen WCot
	– var. ***nana***	CPLG
	'Ryan James' (TB)	CKel
	'Sable' (TB)	CSam EAEE EBee EBla EHrv ELan EPfP ESgI ETod GMaP LBuc LRHS LSRN MCot MRav MWat NGdn NLar SCoo SEND SMrm SPer WAul WCAu WWEG
	'Sable Night' (TB)	CHar CKel ESgI
	'Sager Cedric' (TB)	WCAu
	'Sailor' (IB) **new**	WCAu
	'Saint Crispin' (TB)	EAEE EPfP GBee GCra GMaP LRHS MRav SBfd SPer SPoG
	'Sally Jane' (TB)	WCAu
	'Salonique' (TB)	NBre NLar WCAu
	'Saltwood' (SDB)	NBre SIri
	'Sam Carne' (TB)	WCAu
	'San Leandro' (TB)	MBri
	'San Leon' (DB) **new**	GBin
	'Sandro' (TB)	WViv
	'Sandstone Sentinel' (BB)	CIri
	'Sandy Caper' (IB)	WCAu WTin
	'Sangone' (IB)	ESgI
§	***sanguinea*** ♀H4	CMCN LEdu WBVN
§	– 'Alba'	IBlr
	– 'Nana Alba'	GBin IBlr
§	– 'Snow Queen'	CAvo CBcs EBee ELan EPfP EPla EShb GBin GGar GKir GMaP GMac LPBA LRHS MBri MGos MSCN NGdn NHol NMoo NPri NSti SGSe SPer STes SWat WMnd WMoo WWEG
	'Santana' (TB)	ECtt
	'Sapphire Beauty' (Dut)	EPfP LRHS SDeJ
	'Sapphire Gem' (SDB)	CKel ESgI LSRN WAul WCAu WViv
	'Sapphire Hills' (TB)	WCAu WViv
	'Sapphire Jewel' (SDB)	EPPr
	'Sarah Taylor' (SDB) ♀H4	ECho EWoo WCAu
N	'Sarajaavo' (AB)	CKel
	sari	ECho WWst
	'Sass with Class' (SDB)	CKel WTin
	'Saturday Night Live' (TB)	ESgI
	'Scene Stealer' (TB) **new**	WViv
	schachtii	CPBP
	– J&JA 596.802	NWCA
	'Scintillation' (TB)	WCAu
	'Scribe' (MDB)	NBir WCAu
	'Sea Double' (TB)	WWEG
	'Sea Monster' (SDB)	CPMA SIri
	'Sea Wisp' (La)	NBro SKHP
	'Seakist' (TB) **new**	WViv
	'Season Ticket' (IB)	ESgI WViv
	'Seastone' (SDB) **new**	WCAu
	'Second Wind' (TB)	ECtt EWoo
	'Secret Melody' (TB)	WViv
	'Secret Rites' (TB)	CIri
	'Secret Service' (TB)	LRHS WCAu
	'Self Evident' (MDB)	LLHF
	'Semola' (SDB)	ESgI
	'Senlac' (TB)	EPfP NLar WMnd
	'September Replay' (TB)	EWoo
	serbica	see *I. reichenbachii*
	'Serene Moment' (TB)	SIri WViv
	'Serenity Prayer' (SDB)	WCAu WViv
	setosa ♀H4	CMac CTri CWCL EBee ECho EKen EPfP GAuc GCra GKev GMaP IGor LEdu LPBA LRHS MHer MNrw NLAp SBfd WSpi
	– ***alba***	NLar NWCA
	– var. ***arctica***	LEdu MHer NMen NWCA WHoo WPer
	– subsp. ***canadensis***	see *I. hookeri*
	– 'Kosho-en'	MBri
	– var. ***nana***	see *I. hookeri*
	'Severn Side' (TB) ♀H4	CKel
	'Shakespeare's Sonnet' (SDB)	ESgI
	'Shameless' (IB)	NBre
	'Shampoo' (IB)	CKel SIri SMrm WCAu
	'Share the Spirit' (TB) **new**	WCAu
	'Sharper Image' (TB) **new**	WCAu
	'Shaun Emmerson' (TB)	CIri
	'Sheer Class' (SDB)	WViv
	'Sheila Ann Germaney' (Reticulata)	ECho EPot LAma LLHF NHol NMen NMin WCot WWst
	'Shelford Giant' (Spuria) ♀H4	NEgg
	'Shepherd's Delight' (TB)	WCAu
	'Sherbet Lemon' (IB) ♀H4	CKel WCAu
	'Shirley Chandler' (IB) ♀H4	SIri
	'Shocking Blue'	WWst
	'Short Distance' (IB)	EWoo SIri WViv
	shrevei	see *I. virginica* var. *shrevei*
	'Shurton Brook' (TB)	CKel
	'Shurton Inn' (TB)	CKel WCAu
	sibirica ♀H4	Widely available
	– 'Ahrtalwein' **new**	GBin
	– 'Ann Dasch'	EBee WAul
	– 'Annemarie Troeger' ♀H4	GMac NBre SMrm
	– 'Atlantic Crossing'	SIri WAul
	– 'Atoll'	WViv
	– 'Baby Sister'	CMHG EBla GAbr GBin GGar GKir GMac LRHS LSRN NBre NBro SRGP SWat WAul WViv
	– 'Banish Misfortune' **new**	CIri WAul

	– 'Berlin Bluebird'	SMHy
	– 'Berlin Purple Wine'	WViv
	– 'Berlin Ruffles' ♀^{H4}	CIri EWes GBin WViv
	– 'Berlin Sky'	ESgI EWes
	– 'Berliner Overture'	GBin
	– 'Bickley Cape'	GKir WWEG
	– 'Blaue Milchstrasse' ♀^{H4}	GBin
	– 'Blaumacher'	WViv
	– 'Blue Burgee'	ECha
I	– 'Blue Butterfly'	ELan EPfP LLWG MNrw MSCN NGdn WHil
	– 'Blue King'	CHid CKel EBee EBla ELan EPfP GBin GMaP MRav NBro NGdn NMoo SMrm SPer WMnd WMoo WWEG
	– 'Blue Mere'	MCot WAul
	– 'Blue Moon'	EBee EWll GBin LTen MSCN WFar
	– 'Blue Pennant'	GBin
	– 'Blue Reverie'	EPPr ESgI WViv
N	– 'Blue Sceptre'	IBlr
	– 'Blue Seraph'	GBin
	– 'Blueberry Fair'	CIri
	– 'Bournemouth Ball Gown'	SIri
	– 'Bracknell'	WBor
	– 'Bridal Jig'	EBee
	– 'Butter and Sugar' ♀^{H4}	Widely available
	– 'Caesar'	CRow SDys SRms
	– 'Caesar's Brother'	CFir CHid EBee ECGP ELan EPfP GBin IBlr LRHS MNFA NBro SMrm SPer SPet SWal SWat WCAu WHoo WNew WWEG
	– 'Cambridge' ♀^{H4}	CAby EBee EBla ECGP EIri GBin MNFA NBre SWat WAul WFar WHoo WWlt
	– 'Chandler's Choice'	EWes
	– 'Chartreuse Bounty'	EBee EWes GAbr GBin GQue ITim MLLN NBPC NLar NMoo NSti WPtf WViv
N	– 'Chartreuse Belle'	WBrE
	– 'Circle Round'	CSpe MWte
	– 'Cleedownton' ♀^{H4}	WAul
	– 'Cleve Dodge'	ESgI SIri WViv
	– 'Contrast in Styles' **new**	LLWG
	– 'Coquet Waters'	NBid
	– 'Coronation Anthem'	WAul WViv
	– 'Dance Ballerina Dance'	CFir CHid CRow CWCL EBee EPfP GGar GQue LLWG NBPC NMoo SBfd SMrm SPoG SPur WFar WPtf
	– 'Dancing Nanou'	EBee NBre SBfd SWat
	– 'Dark Desire'	MRav WAul
	– 'Dear Delight'	EBee EPPr LLHF WFar
	– 'Dear Dianne'	CHid CKel ECha NBre
	– 'Dirigo Black Velvet'	CIri
	– 'Double Standards'	CIri
	– 'Dreaming Green'	EBee
	– 'Dreaming Orange'	EBee ECtt WViv
	– 'Dreaming Spires' ♀^{H4}	ESgI SIri WCot WViv
	– 'Dreaming Yellow' ♀^{H4}	Widely available
	– 'Dunkler Wein'	EBee EWes
	– 'Ego'	CAvo CHid EBee ECha GAbr GBin MGos NBro SGSe SWat WMoo WPen WPrP WViv
	– 'Ellenbank Sapphire' **new**	GBin
	– 'Ellesmere'	NGdn
	– 'Emma Ripeka'	WAul
	– 'Emperor'	CRow CWat NBre NSti SWat
	– 'Eric the Red'	IBlr
	– 'Erste Sahne' **new**	GBin
	– 'Ewen'	CHid CPou CRow GBin GKir GMaP IBlr LEdu MNrw NGdn SGSe SMrm SWat WCot WFar WPrP WWEG WWlt
	– 'Exuberant Encore' ♀^{H4}	WCAu
	– 'Flight of Butterflies'	Widely available
	– 'Fourfold Lavender'	EWes NLar WAul
	– 'Fourfold White'	ESgI MWte
N	– 'Gerbel Mantel'	EWll GBin GMac MSpe SPet WFar
	– 'Golden Edge'	WViv
N	– 'Goldkind'	WAul
	– grey-flowered	SApp
	– 'Gull's Wing'	LHop
	– 'Harpswell Hallelujah'	SBch
	– 'Harpswell Happiness' ♀^{H4}	CPrp EBee EPfP GCra SBch SWat WAul WCon WMoo WViv
	– 'Harpswell Haze'	ECha WMoo WViv
	– 'Heavenly Blue'	SPer
	– 'Helen Astor'	CRow CTri EBee EShb MRav SApp SWal SWat
N	– 'Himmel von Komi'	GBin
	– 'Hohe Warte' ♀^{H4}	GBin
	– 'Höhenflug' **new**	GBin
	– 'Hubbard'	CEnt EBee EShb GBin LLWG MNrw NBro NCGa NHol SBch
	– 'Illini Charm'	CHid EWll NBro SSvw WFar WMoo
	– 'Isabelle' **new**	LSRN
	– 'Jac-y-do'	EWes
	– 'Jewelled Crown'	WFar
	– 'Kabluey'	CIri
	– 'Kathleen Mary' ♀^{H4}	WAul
	– 'Kent Arrival'	SIri
	– 'Lady Vanessa'	CPou GAbr GBin GMac MRav NBro NMoo NSti SBfd SMrm WAul
§	– 'Lake Niklas'	EBee ELon GBin NCGa
	– 'Langthorns Pink'	CMdw ELan MRav
	– 'Laurenbuhl'	CPLG
	– 'Lavendelwein' ♀^{H4}	GBin
	– 'Lavender Bounty'	CHid EBla NBre NBro SPet WCAu WViv
	– 'Lavender Fair' **new**	CIri
	– 'Limeheart'	CPou CSev ELan LLHF LRHS
	– 'Little Blue'	EBee WAul
N	– 'Little Twinkle Star'	GBin WFar
	– 'Marilyn Holmes'	WCot
	– 'Marshmallow Frosting'	WFar
§	– 'Melton Red Flare'	CMHG EBee EBla EHon ELan EPPr EShb GBin LRHS MSpe SBfd SDys SMrm SPoG WFar
	– 'Memphis Memory'	EBee ELan GBin GCra MNrw MSCN NGdn NLar SBch SPer
	– 'Mesa Pearl'	CIri
	– 'Moon Silk'	EBee ECtt GBin LLHF LLWG WCot WFar
	– 'Mountain Lake'	CAby CSam EBee EPPr EShb GBin LRHS MSpe SVic SWat WCAu WCot WFar WSpi
	– 'Mrs Rowe'	CFee CPou CRow EBla EIri LLWP MRav MWat SWat WAul WCAu WFar WPtf
	– 'Mrs Saunders'	WAul
	– 'Navy Brass'	NBre WViv
	– 'Night Breeze'	SIri WViv
	– 'Niklas Sea'	see *I. sibirica* 'Lake Niklas'
	– 'Nottingham Lace'	LLHF SWat
	– 'Oban' ♀^{H4}	ESgI
	– 'Orville Fay'	WCot WFar
	– 'Other Worlds' **new**	WAul
	– 'Ottawa'	CPou CRow CWat EBee ECGP ELan LRHS MBNS SWat WFar
	– 'Outset'	SSvw WWEG
I	– 'Pageant'	WCot
I	– 'Painted Desert'	GKir
	– 'Papillon'	CSev CTri EBee EBla EBrs ECtt ELan ELon GAbr GGar LAst LHop LPio LRHS MWat NBir NBro NCob NGdn

		NHol NSti SApp SMrm SPer STes SWat WBor WFar WPnP
N	– 'Pearl Queen'	MCot WFar
	– 'Peg Edwards'	EBee
	– 'Percheron'	ESgI SIri WViv
	– 'Perfect Vision' $\mathbb{Y}^{H4}$	CIri
	– 'Perry's Blue'	Widely available
I	– 'Perry's Favourite'	CFee CRow
	– 'Persimmon' misapplied	see *I. sibirica* 'Tycoon'
	– 'Persimmon' ambig.	CFir CHid EBee EBla ECtt GCra LRHS MWat NMoo SVic SWat WFar WMoo
	– 'Peter Hewitt' $\mathbb{Y}^{H4}$	CIri WAul
	– 'Pink Haze'	CRow EBee EPfP ESgI GBin MLLN MMuc NBro NMoo WViv
	– 'Pirate Prince'	NPer
	– 'Plissee' $\mathbb{Y}^{H4}$	GBin
	– 'Polly Dodge'	LRHS
	– 'Pounsley Purple'	CPou
	– 'Primrose Cream'	WCot
	– 'Prussian Blue' $\mathbb{Y}^{H4}$	CIri GBin
	– 'Purple Mere'	WAul WFar
N	– 'Red Flag'	NHol
	– 'Reddy Maid'	WCAu
	– 'Redflare'	see *I. sibirica* 'Melton Red Flare'
N	– 'Regality'	CWCL EBee GBin MHer MMuc NBro
	– 'Regency Belle' $\mathbb{Y}^{H4}$	SIri
	– 'Regency Buck'	MSCN SBch WCot
	– 'Rikugi-sakura'	EBee EBla GBin LLHF NBPC NBro WCot
	– 'Roanoke's Choice'	CElw EBee EWes GAbr GBin NCGa WBor WFar
	– 'Roaring Jelly'	EBee EWes NLar WCot WViv
	– 'Roger Perry'	CFee
	– 'Rosselline' $\mathbb{Y}^{H4}$	GBin
I	– 'Royal Blue'	ECha SWat
	– 'Ruby Wine'	CFir LEdu NLar
	– 'Ruffled Velvet' $\mathbb{Y}^{H4}$	Widely available
	– 'Ruffles Plus'	WCot
	– 'Salamander Crossing' **new**	CIri
	– 'Savoir Faire'	ECha
	– 'Sea Horse'	WAul
	– 'Sea Shadows'	ESgI NBir WCAu
	– 'Shaker's Prayer' $\mathbb{Y}^{H4}$	CIri CPrp EBee EWes GAbr WAul
	– 'Shall We Dance' $\mathbb{Y}^{H4}$	CIri EWes WAul
	– 'Shirley Pope' $\mathbb{Y}^{H4}$	EBee EWes GAbr GBin GKir LRHS MBri MNFA NCGa NMoo NSti WAul WCot WFar WMoo WNew WWEG
	– 'Shirley's Choice'	GKir SIri WViv
	– 'Showdown'	ECtt GKir GMaP NHol SAga SWat WCAu WFar
	– 'Shrawley'	WCAu
	– 'Silver Edge' $\mathbb{Y}^{H4}$	Widely available
	– 'Simple Gifts' $\mathbb{Y}^{H4}$	CIri
	– 'Sky Wings'	CRow ECha GKir GQue MArl WMoo
	– 'Snow Prince'	WAul
	– 'Snow Queen'	see *I. sanguinea* 'Snow Queen'
	– 'Snowcrest'	CBre SBfd
	– 'Soft Blue' $\mathbb{Y}^{H4}$	NBre WAul
N	– 'Southcombe White'	CRow GBin NGdn SIri WWEG
	– 'Sparkle' **new**	WAul
	– 'Sparkling Rosé'	Widely available
	– 'Star Cluster'	WFar
	– 'Stephen Wilcox' **new**	WAul
	– 'Steve'	CPar EWes GMac LPio NBro SWat
	– 'Steve Varner'	WFar WViv
	– 'Strawberry Fair' $\mathbb{Y}^{H4}$	CIri
	– 'Summer Revels' **new**	LLWG
	– 'Summer Sky'	CBre LEdu MSCN NCGa SWat WAul WCAu WCot WPrP WTin
	– 'Super Ego'	WTin WViv
	– 'Sutton Valence'	SIri WAul
	– 'Swank'	WAul
	– 'Taldra'	WAul
	– 'Tal-y-Bont'	WAul WFar
	– 'Tanz Nochmal'	GBin
	– 'Teal Velvet'	ECha WCAu WFar WViv
	– 'Temper Tantrum'	CEnt CKel CPrp MBNS
	– 'Tropic Night'	Widely available
§	– 'Tycoon'	EBrs EShb GBin GKir IBlr LRHS NHol SPer SVic
	– 'Velvet Night'	ECtt WBrE
	– 'Vi Luihn'	CBcs ECha WAul WMoo
	– 'Viel Creme' $\mathbb{Y}^{H4}$	GBin
	– 'Viel Schnee' **new**	GBin
N	– 'Violet Skies'	GBin
	– 'Visual Treat'	SIri
	– 'Wall Street Blues' **new**	WAul
	– 'Waterloo' **new**	WAul
	– 'Wealden Butterfly' $\mathbb{Y}^{H4}$	SIri WAul
	– 'Wealden Carousel' **new**	SIri
	– 'Wealden Mystery'	SIri WAul
	– 'Wealden Skies'	SIri WAul
	– 'Welcome Return'	CElw GAbr GBin GQue IPot MBNS MMuc NBro NLar NMoo NPri SUsu SWat WFar WMoo
N	– 'Welfenfürstin'	GBin
	– 'Welfenprinz' $\mathbb{Y}^{H4}$	WAul
I	– 'White Queen'	EBla ESgI SWat WBrE
	– 'White Swirl' $\mathbb{Y}^{H4}$	Widely available
	– 'White Triangles'	SIri
	– 'Wisley White'	GMac NBre
	– 'Yankee Consul'	WAul
	– 'Zakopane' $\mathbb{Y}^{H4}$	EWes
	– 'Zweites Hundert'	GMac NBre WFar
	'Sibirica Alba'	CMac ECha EPfP EShb GBBs LLWP SWat WBrk WCFE WFar
	'Sibirica Baxteri'	CFee WAul
	'Sibtosa Princess' (SpH)	WViv
	sichuanensis	CPLG
	sieboldii	see *I. sanguinea*
	'Sierra Blue' (TB)	ESgI
	'Sierra Grande' (TB)	EWoo WViv
	'Sierra Nevada' (Spuria)	SMrm
	'Silent Strings' (IB)	MBri
	'Silicon Prairie' (TB)	ESgI
	'Silkirim' (TB)	CKel
	'Silver Shower' (TB)	EWoo WViv
	'Silverado' (TB)	CKel ECtt ESgI EWoo WCAu WViv
	'Silvery Beauty' (Dut)	LAma LRHS NBir SBch SDeJ SPer
	'Simple Dreams' (TB) **new**	CIri
	sindjarensis	see *I. aucheri*
	'Sindpers' (Juno) $\mathbb{Y}^{H3}$	WWst
	'Sinister Desire' (IB)	EWoo WViv
	sintenisii $\mathbb{Y}^{H4}$	CHid CPBP ECho WTin WWst
	'Sir Michael' (TB)	ESgI EWoo GBBs
	'Siva Siva' (TB)	MRav
	'Six Pack' (TB)	CIri
	'Sixteen Candles' (IB) **new**	EWoo
	'Sixtine C' (TB)	SIri WViv
	'Skating Party' (TB)	CKel ESgI EWoo WViv
	'Skiers' Delight' (TB)	NBre
	'Skydancer' (SDB) **new**	WCAu
	'Skyfire' (TB)	CWCL ESgI MWea SBfd WViv WWEG
	'Skylark's Song' (TB)	EIri EWoo WViv
	'Skyline' (TB) **new**	EWoo
	'Skyline' (J)	WWst
	'Slap Bang' (SDB)	ESgI
	'Sleepy Time' (MDB)	WViv
	'Slovak Prince' (TB)	CIri
	'Smart' (SDB) **new**	WCAu

	'Smart Aleck' (TB)	ECtt EWoo WViv
N	'Smart Girl' (TB)	CKel EIri
	'Smart Move' (TB)	CWCL WViv
	'Smiling Angel' (TB) **new**	EWoo WViv
	'Smiling Faces' (TB) **new**	WCAu WViv
	'Smitten Image' (IB) **new**	WCAu
	'Smokey Dream' (TB)	CKel
	'Smokey Salmon' (TB)	CKel
	'Sneezy' (TB)	WCAu
	'Snow and Wind' (TB)	WAul
	'Snow Cloud' (TB)	EWoo
	'Snow Job' (TB) **new**	WCAu
	'Snow Plum' (IB)	SIri WViv
	'Snow Season' (SDB)	WViv
	'Snow Tracery' (TB)	EAEE MBri NPnk
	'Snow Troll' (SDB)	WCAu
	'Snowcone' (IB)	ESgI
	'Snowdrift' (*laevigata*)	see *I. laevigata* 'Snowdrift'
	'Snowmound' (TB)	CKel ESgI EWoo WCAu
	'Snowy Owl' (TB) $\mathbb{Y}^{H4}$	CKel WCAu
	'Snugglebug' (SDB) **new**	EWoo
	'Social Event' (TB)	ESgI
	'Social Graces' (TB) **new**	WCAu
	'Socialist' (TB) **new**	WCAu
	'Soft Return' **new**	EWoo
	'Solar Fire' (TB)	CIri
	'Solent Breeze' **new**	SBch
	'Solid Mahogany' (TB)	MRav
	'Somerset Blue' (TB) $\mathbb{Y}^{H4}$	CKel WCAu
N	'Somerset Vale' (TB)	SMrm
	'Somerton Brocade' (SDB)	CKel
	'Somerton Dance' (SDB)	CBgR CKel
	'Son of Sun' (Spuria)	CIri
	'Song of Norway' (TB)	ECtt EIri ESgI WCAu WViv
	'Sopra il Vulcano' (BB)	ESgI
	'Sortilege' (TB) **new**	WViv
	'Sostenique' (TB)	ESgI
	'Southern Clipper' (SDB)	MBri
	'Souvenir de Madame Gaudichau' (TB)	EWoo
	'Sparkplug' (SDB)	ESgI
	'Spartan' (TB)	CKel
	'Special Feature' (TB)	WViv
	'Speck So' (MTB)	ESgI
	'Spellbreaker' (TB)	ESgI EWoo WViv
	'Spiced Cider' (TB) **new**	WViv
	'Spiced Custard' (TB)	CKel EIri ESgI EWoo WCAu
	'Spicy Cajun' (La) **new**	WHil
	'Spinning Wheel' (TB)	SIri
	'Spirit World' (TB) **new**	WViv
	'Splashacata' (TB)	WCAu WViv
	'Splashdown' (Sino-Sib)	SWat
	'Spreckles' (TB)	ESgI
	'Spring Festival' (TB)	WCAu
	'Spring Kiss' (TB) **new**	SIri WViv
	'Spun Gold' (TB)	ESgI
	spuria	CMac CPou WCot
§	- subsp. ***halophila***	GAuc GKev
	- subsp. ***ochroleuca***	see *I. orientalis* Mill.
	- subsp. ***spuria***	GAuc
	× ***squalens***	WCAu
	'St Louis Blues' (TB)	ESgI
	'St Petersburg' (TB) **new**	EWoo WViv
	'Stairway to Heaven' (TB)	ESgI WCAu
	'Staplehurst' (MTB) $\mathbb{Y}^{H4}$	SIri WAul
	'Star Prince' (SDB)	ESgI
	'Star Shine' (TB)	CKel ESgI WCAu
	'Starcrest' (TB)	ESgI EWoo WViv
	'Stardate' (SDB)	CKel
	'Stardock' (TB) **new**	EWoo
	'Starlette Rose' (TB) **new**	WViv
	'Starring' (TB)	CIri EWoo WAul WCAu
	'Starship' (TB)	ESgI
	'Starship Enterprise' (TB)	CIri
	'Starwoman' (IB)	WAul
	'Staten Island' (TB)	ESgI SEND SRms WCAu WTin
	'Stella Polaris' (TB)	CWan ELon
	'Stellar Lights' (TB)	EIri EWoo WCAu
	'Stepping Out' (TB) $\mathbb{Y}^{H4}$	CAby CMac CPar CWGN EAEE EBee EBla EPfP ESgI EWll GBin IPot LBMP LRHS MCot MWea NBre SBfd WAul WBor WCAu
	'Stinger' (SDB) $\mathbb{Y}^{H4}$	CIri
	'Stingray' (TB)	CIri ESgI
	'Stitch in Time' (TB)	EIri EWoo WViv
	'Stockholm' (SDB)	CKel
	stolonifera	ECho WWst
	- 'Zwanenburg Beauty'	ECho
	'Storm Center' (TB)	EWoo
	'Stormy Circle' (SDB)	WCAu
	'Strange Brew' (TB) **new**	WCAu
	'Strawberry Love' (IB) $\mathbb{Y}^{H4}$	CKel
	'Striking' (TB)	EWoo WViv
	stylosa	see *I. unguicularis*
§	***suaveolens***	CPou ECho NMen
*	- var. ***flavescens***	WWst
*	- var. ***violacea***	ECho GCal NMen NWCA WWst
	'Succès Fou' (TB) **new**	EWoo SIri WViv
	'Sudden Impact' (TB) **new**	WViv
	'Sugar' (IB)	WCAu
	'Sugar Magnolia' (TB) **new**	EWoo WViv
	'Sultan's Palace' (TB)	CWCL ECho ESgI EWll EWoo LTen NBPC WSpi WViv WWEG
	'Sumatra' (TB)	ESgI
	'Summer's Smile' (TB)	ESgI EWoo
	'Summertime Blues' (TB) **new**	EWoo
	'Sun Ada Beach' (TB)	CIri
	'Sun Doll' (SDB) $\mathbb{Y}^{H4}$	CKel
	'Sundown Red' (IB)	NBir
	'Sunny and Warm' (TB)	CKel
	'Sunny Dawn' (IB) $\mathbb{Y}^{H4}$	CKel WViv
	'Sunny Side Up' **new**	WWst
	'Sunnyside Delight' (TB) **new**	WCAu
	'Sunset Colors' (Spuria) $\mathbb{Y}^{H4}$	CIri
	'Sunshine Boy' (IB)	CKel
	'Superstition' (TB) $\mathbb{Y}^{H4}$	EIri ELan ESgI EWoo GBin MRav MWhi SMrm SSvw WCAu WViv WWEG
	'Supreme Sultan' (TB)	ESgI ETod EWoo WCAu WViv
	'Susan Bliss' (TB)	CKel EBee ELan EPfP ESgI GBBs NBre WCAu
	'Susan Gillespie' (IB) $\mathbb{Y}^{H4}$	CKel
	'Suspicion' (TB)	CIri WViv
	svetlanae	WWst
	'Swain' (TB)	ESgI
	'Swazi Princess' (TB)	CKel ESgI WCAu
	'Sweet Kate' (SDB) $\mathbb{Y}^{H4}$	WCAu
	'Sweet Lena' (TB)	ESgI
	'Sweet Musette' (TB)	WCAu WViv
	'Sweeter than Wine' (TB)	ESgI EWoo MRav WCAu WViv
	'Swingtown' (TB)	WCAu
	'Swiss Majesty' (TB) **new**	WCAu
	'Sybil' (TB)	GBin GCra NHar
	'Sylvia Murray' (TB)	WCAu
	'Symphony' (Dut)	ECho NBir SDeJ
	'Syncopation' (TB)	CKel ESgI WViv
	'Tabac Blond' (TB) **new**	WViv
	'Taco Supreme' (TB) **new**	EWoo
	'Tall Chief' (TB)	WCAu
N	'Tanex'	ECho
	'Tangerine Sky' (TB)	EWoo WCAu WViv

	'Tangfu' (IB)	ESgI
	'Tango Music' (SpH) 🏆H4	GBin
	'Tantara' (SDB)	WTin
	'Tantrum' (IB) **new**	WCAu
	'Tanzanian Tangerine' (TB)	WCAu
	'Tarheel Elf' (SDB)	ESgI WTin
	'Tarn Hows' (TB)	ESgI SRms WCAu
	'Tchin Tchin' (IB)	WViv
	tectorum	CMdw CSWP GAuc GBin NWCA WAul
	- BWJ 8191	WCru
	- 'Alba'	WThu
	- 'Variegata' misapplied	see *I. japonica* 'Variegata'
	- 'Variegata' (v)	EBee NSti SGSe SPoG
	'Tell Fibs' (SDB)	CKel CPBP
	'Temple Gold' (TB)	CKel NPer
	'Temple Meads' (IB)	ESgI WCAu
	'Templecloud' (IB) 🏆H4	CBgR CHar CKel
	'Tempting Fate' (TB)	EWoo WViv
§	***tenax***	CPBP ECho GAuc GEdr GKir NWCA SMrm
	'Tennison Ridge' (TB)	WCAu
	tenuissima	CPBP GAuc NMen WAbe
	subsp. ***tenuissima***	
	'Terre de Couleur' (TB) **new**	WViv
	'Terre de Feu' (TB)	ESgI WViv
	'Thaïs' (TB)	ESgI
	'The Bride'	see *I.* 'Bride'
	'The Citadel' (TB)	ELon
	'The Red Douglas' (TB)	ESgI
	'The Rocket'	see *I.* 'Rocket'
	'Theatre' (TB)	ESgI
	'This and That' (IB) **new**	WCAu
	thompsonii J&JA 1.461.800	NWCA
	- NNS 05-416	WCot
	'Thornbird' (TB) 🏆H4	ECtt EIri ESgI EWoo WCAu WViv
	'Three Cherries' (MDB)	ECho WViv
	'Thriller' (TB)	ESgI WCAu
	'Throb' (TB)	WViv
	thunbergii	see *I. sanguinea*
	'Thunder Echo' (TB)	ESgI WViv
	'Thundering Hills' (TB)	CKel
	'Tide's In' (TB)	ECtt ESgI EWoo WViv
	'Tiffany' (TB)	WTin
	'Tiger Butter' (TB)	ESgI
	'Tiger Honey' (TB)	CIri WViv
	'Tiger Shark' (TB) **new**	CIri
	'Tiger Eye' ambig.	EPfP
§	'Tigereye' (Dut)	GKev LAma SBch
	tigridia	CPLG
	'Tiki Bird' (Sino-Sib)	SIri
	'Time Piece' (TB)	CKel
	tingitana var. ***fontanesii***	EBee WPGP
	'Tinkerbell' (SDB)	CPBP ECGP GMaP LRHS MAvo NBir NGdn SDeJ
	'Tintinara' (TB) 🏆H4	CKel
	'Titan's Glory' (TB) 🏆H4	ESgI EWoo LEdu MRav WCAu WCot WViv
	'Toile de Jouy' (TB) **new**	WViv
	'Tollong' 🏆H4	IKil
	'Tom Johnson' (TB) 🏆H4	EWoo
	'Tom Tit' (TB)	WCAu
	'Tomingo' (SDB)	WCAu
	'Tomorrow's Child' (TB)	ESgI WViv
	'Toni Lynn' (MDB)	ECho
	'Toots' (SDB)	ECho WTin
	'Top Flight' (TB)	ELan SPer SRms
	'Top Gun' (TB) **new**	CPMA WViv
N	'Topolino' (TB)	CKel GBin SAga
	'Topsy Turvy' (MTB)	NBre
	'Torchlight' (TB)	SEND
	'Torero' (TB) **new**	SIri WViv
	'Total Eclipse' (TB)	SRms
	'Totally Cool' (SDB)	LSRN WViv
	'Toucan Tango' (TB)	CIri
	'Touch of Mahogany' (TB)	WCAu
	'Tourbillon' (TB) **new**	WViv
	'Tracy Tyrene' (TB)	ESgI WViv
	'Trade Secret' (TB)	CIri
	'Trails West' (TB)	ESgI WViv
	'Trapel' (TB)	ESgI
	'Treccia d'Oro' (TB)	ESgI
	'Trencavel' (TB)	ESgI
	'Trenwith' (TB)	CKel
	'Trillion' (TB)	CIri
	'Triple Whammy' (TB)	ESgI
	'Triplicate' (SDB)	SMrm
	'Tropical Magic' (TB) **new**	WViv
	'True Navy' (SDB)	WViv
	tubergeniana (J)	WWst
	tuberosa	see *Hermodactylus tuberosus*
	'Tumblers Hill' (CH) **new**	SIri
	'Tumultueux' (TB)	ESgI EWoo WViv
	'Tunnel Vision' **new**	EWoo
	'Tut's Gold' (TB)	ECtt ESgI WCAu WViv
*	'Twin'	WWst
	'Two Sided Coin' (TB) **new**	WCAu
	typhifolia	GAuc
	'Tyrian Dream' (IB)	WCAu
	'Ultimate' (SDB)	CIri
	'Unfinished Business' (TB) **new**	WCAu
§	***unguicularis*** 🏆H4	Widely available
	- 'Abington Purple'	CPMA EIri
	- 'Alba'	CAvo CBct CPLG ECha ECho ESgI
N	- 'Bob Thompson'	CAvo SAga
	- subsp. ***carica*** J&JA 600.416	NWCA
§	- subsp. ***cretensis***	CAby ECho NMen SKHP WAbe WHil
	- - HOA 017	WWst
	- 'Diana Clare'	CPMA WCot
	- ex Lady Gibson	GEdr
N	- 'Marondera'	CAvo CPMA WSHC
	- 'Mary Barnard' 🏆H4	CAvo CBct CFee CHar CPMA CPou ECGP ECha ECho EHrv GEdr IBlr NBir NCot NMen WAbe WHil WMnd
N	- 'Oxford Dwarf'	EBee ECho LLHF
N	- 'Palette'	ELan
§	- 'Walter Butt'	CAvo CPMA EBee ECGP ECho NBir SMad WFar
	uromovii	MArl
	'Ursula Warleggan' (TB)	CKel
	'Vague à l'Ame' (TB)	ESgI WViv
	'Val de Loire' **new**	EWoo
	'Vamp' (IB)	CKel SIri SMrm WViv
	'Vandal Spirit' (TB)	ESgI EWoo
	'Vanilla Skies' (TB) **new**	WCAu
	'Vanity' (TB) 🏆H4	ESgI WViv
	'Vanity's Child' (TB)	WCAu
§	***variegata*** 🏆H4	EShb WCAu WCot
	- var. ***reginae***	WCAu
	'Vegas Heat' (BB)	CIri
	'Velvet Purple' **new**	XBlo
	'Verdissant' (IB)	CBgR WViv
	'Verity Blamey' (TB)	CKel
	verna	NHol
	versicolor 🏆H4	CArn CBen CRow CWat EBee EHon GBin GKir GMaP IBlr LPBA MGos MMuc MNHC MNrw MWts NWCA SPlb SRms SWat WBrk WFar WMAq WPnP WShi WSpi WTin WViv
	- 'Between the Lines'	CRow WViv

	- 'Candystriper'	WViv
	- 'China West Lake'	CRow
	- 'Claret Cup'	CPou WWEG
	- 'Dottie's Double'	CRow
N	- 'Georgia Bay'	CRow
	- 'Kermesina'	CRow CWat EBee ECha EHon ELan ESgI GBin GGar IBlr LLWG LPBA MBri MGos MWts NPer NSti SRms SWat WBrk WFar WMAq WMoo WPnP
I	- 'Mint Fresh'	WViv
	- 'Mysterious Monique'	CMdw CWat LLWG
	- 'Party Line'	SIri
	- 'Rosea'	CRow
	- 'Rowden Allegro'	CRow
	- 'Rowden Aria'	CRow
	- 'Rowden Cadenza'	CRow
	- 'Rowden Calypso'	CRow
	- 'Rowden Cantata'	CRow
	- 'Rowden Concerto'	CRow
	- 'Rowden Harmony'	CRow
	- 'Rowden Lullaby'	CRow
	- 'Rowden Lyric'	CRow
	- 'Rowden Mazurka'	CRow
	- 'Rowden Melody'	CRow
	- 'Rowden Nocturne'	CRow
	- 'Rowden Pastorale'	CRow
	- 'Rowden Prelude'	CRow
	- 'Rowden Refrain'	CRow
	- 'Rowden Rondo'	CRow
	- 'Rowden Sonata'	CRow
	- 'Rowden Symphony'	CRow
	- 'Rowden Waltz'	CRow
	- 'Silvington'	CRow
	- 'Whodunit'	CRow
	'Vert Galant' (TB)	ESgI
	'Via Domitia' (TB)	ESgI
	'Vibrant' (TB)	ESgI WCAu
	'Vibrations' (TB)	ESgI WCAu
	vicaria	ECho WWst
	- RM 8269	WWst
N	- 'Hodji-obi-Garm'	WWst
N	- 'Prominence'	WWst
I	- 'Sina'	WWst
	'Victoria Falls' (TB)	ESgI EWoo WCAu
	'Vin Nouveau' (TB) **new**	WViv
	'Vinho Verde' (IB) ♀^{H4}	CKel
	'Vino Rosso' (SDB)	ESgI
	'Violet Beauty' (Reticulata)	ECho ERCP GKev LAma LRHS NHol SPhx
	'Violet Classic' (TB)	WCAu
	'Violet Harmony' (TB)	ESgI
	'Violet Icing' (TB) ♀^{H4}	CKel
	'Violet Rings' (TB)	WCAu WViv
N	'Violet Tiara'	LHop
	'Viper' (IB)	CIri EWoo
	virginica	LLWG
	- 'De Luxe'	see *I.* × *robusta* 'Dark Aura'
I	- 'Pink Butterfly'	LLWG NMoo
	- 'Pond Crown Point'	CRow
	- 'Pond Lilac Dream'	CRow
N	- 'Purple Fan'	CRow
§	- var. ***shrevei***	CRow WViv
	'Visual Arts' (TB)	WViv
	'Vitafire' (TB)	ECtt EWoo WViv
	'Vitality' (IB)	ELon ESgI
	'Vitrail' (IB)	CBgR WViv
	'Vive la France' (TB)	ESgI EWoo WViv
	'Vizier' (TB)	WCAu
	'Voilà' (IB)	ESgI
	'Volts' (SDB)	CKel
	'Voluminous' (TB)	CIri
	'Volute' (TB)	ESgI WViv
I	'Vonnies Wedding Iris'	ELon
	'Voyage' (SDB)	EWoo
	'Wabash' (TB)	ELan ESgI WBor WCAu WTin
	'Walter Butt'	see *I. unguicularis* 'Walter Butt'
	'War Chief' (TB)	ESgI MRav WCAu
	'War Sails' (TB)	SIri WCAu WViv
	warleyensis	ECho WWst
	'Warlsind' (J)	WWst
	wattii	CPLG GCal WCot
	'Waxen Image' (IB) **new**	WAul
	'Way to Go' (TB)	CIri
	'Wealden Canary' (Spuria)	WAul
	'Wealden Elegance' (Spuria)	WAul
	'Wealden Sunshine' (Spuria)	WAul
	'Wedding Candles' (TB)	WCAu
	'Wedding Vow' (TB)	CKel EIri
	'Wedgwood' (Dut)	NBre
	'Welch's Reward' (MTB) ♀^{H4}	CKel ESgI
	'Well Suited' (SDB)	EWoo WCAu WViv
	'Wench' (TB) **new**	WCAu
	'Westar' (SDB) ♀^{H4}	CBgR CKel EIri
	'Westpointer' (TB) **new**	CIri
	'Westwell' (SDB)	WCAu
	'Wheels' (SDB)	WTin
	'Whispering Spirits' (TB)	WAul
	'White City' (TB)	EAEE EBla ECGP EPfP ESgI EWTr GMaP LPio LRHS MCot MRav MWat MWhi NPer SBfd SCoo SDnm SMrm SPer SRms SWat WCAu WMnd
	'White Excelsior' (Dut)	ECho WBor
	'White Knight' (TB)	EBee ELan EPfP NBre WMnd WWEG
	'White Reprise' (TB)	ESgI
	'White van Vliet' (Dut)	SDeJ
	'White Wine' (MTB)	WCAu
	'Whiteladies' (IB) ♀^{H4}	WCAu
	'White-Wave' **new**	XBlo
	'Whole Cloth' (TB)	ESgI
N	'Wild Echo' (TB)	CKel
	'Wild Jasmine' (TB)	ECtt WCAu WViv
	'Wild Ruby' (SDB)	CKel
	'Wild West' (TB)	CKel
	'Wild Wings' (TB)	MCot NCGa SBfd STes WCAu WViv WWEG
	willmottiana	ECho WWst
	- 'Alba'	ECho GKev WWst
	wilsonii ♀^{H4}	CPLG GAuc GKev GKir WBVN
	'Windjammer Seas' (TB)	WAul
	'Winemaster' (TB)	ECtt EWoo SIri
	'Wings of Peace' (TB)	CIri
	'Winner's Circle' (TB) **new**	SMrm
	winogradowii ♀^{H4}	ECho EPot GCrs LAma LLHF NMen NMin WAbe WWst
	'Winter Crystal' (TB) ♀^{H4}	CKel
	'Winter Olympics' (TB)	EAEE EBee ESgI EShb LBuc LRHS MRav STes
	'Wintry Sky' (TB) **new**	WCAu
	'Wise' (SDB) **new**	WCAu
	'Wishful Thinking' (TB)	SIri WViv
	'Wisteria Sachet' (IB)	WCAu
	'Wizard of Id' (SDB)	WTin
	'Wondrous' (TB)	ESgI
	'World Premier' (TB) **new**	WViv
	'Worlds Beyond' (TB)	WCAu
	'Wow' (SDB)	ECho
	'Wrangler' (IB) **new**	SIri
	'Xillia' (IB)	CKel

xiphioides see *I. latifolia*
xiphium ECho
'Yaquina Blue' (TB) ESgI EWoo WCAu WViv
'Yellow and White' GAbr
'Yellow Flirt' (MTB) **new** WCAu
'Yellow Moon' (J) **new** WWst
'Yes' (TB) CPMA ESgI WViv
'Yippy Skippy' (SDB) **new** WCAu
'Yo-yo' (SDB) GEdr STes
'Yvonne Pelletier' (TB) WCAu
'Zantha' (TB) ESgI WCAu
zenaidae 'Flagship' **new** WWst
'Zero' (SDB) ♀^{H4} CKel WViv
'Zinc Pink' (BB) WCAu
'Zing Me' (IB) WViv
'Zipper' (MDB) WCAu

Isatis (*Brassicaceae*)

tinctoria CArn CBod CHby COld CRWN CSev EBWF EOHP GJos GPoy ILis MHer MNHC NPnk SIde SPav WHfH WJek
- var. ***indigotica*** CArn

Ischyrolepis (*Restionaceae*)

§ ***subverticillata*** CAbb CHEx CTrC

Ismene see *Hymenocallis*

Isodon (*Lamiaceae*)

calycinus SPlb
effusus B&SWJ 11027 WCru
longitubus WCot

Isolepis (*Cyperaceae*)

§ ***cernua*** CBen CMil CWat EBee EHoe LRHS MBri MMuc MSKA MWts NOak SBfd SCoo SHDw WFar WMAq

Isoloma see *Kohleria*

Isomeris see *Cleome*

Isoplexis (*Scrophulariaceae*)

canariensis CAbb CBcs CBot CCCN CDTJ CHEx CHll CRHN CSpe EBee EWll MAsh SAga SEND SGar SPlb SPoG WBox WCFE WWlt
isabelliana CCCN CDTJ EShb
sceptrum CAbb CBot CCCN CDTJ CHEx CHll CPLG CRHN IDee SAPC SPlb WPGP

Isopogon (*Proteaceae*)

anemonifolius SPlb
anethifolius SPlb

Isopyrum (*Ranunculaceae*)

biternatum NLar
nipponicum CDes CLAP EBee WCru WPGP
stoloniferum WCru
thalictroides LLHF WAbe

Isotoma (*Campanulaceae*)

sp. LAst SWvt
§ ***axillaris*** CSpe LAst NPer SCoo SPer SPet SPoG
- 'Fairy Carpet' SRms
'Fairy Footsteps' EPfP
fluviatilis NLar

Itea (*Escalloniaceae*)

chinensis CPLG
ilicifolia ♀^{H3} Widely available
* - 'Rubrifolia' LRHS MAsh SLon SPoG
japonica 'Beppu' SLPl SSpi
virginica CAbP CBcs CMCN CWit EBee ELan MBlu MRav NPal SLim SLon SPer WBVN WFar
§ - 'Henry's Garnet' CAbP CDoC CEnd CMCN CMac CPMA CSBt CWSG CWit EBee EPfP GBin LAst LEdu LRHS MAsh MBlu MBri MGos NCGa NLar SLim SPoG SRGP SSpi SWvt WDin WGwG
- Little Henry = 'Sprich'^{PBR} CBgR CHGN CMac CSBt EBee ELan ELon IVic LAst LRHS NLar NPri
- 'Long Spire' CPMA IArd NLar WDin
- 'Merlot' CPMA EBee IVic MBlu NLar
- 'Sarah Eve' CMCN CPMA NLar SRGP
- 'Saturnalia' NLar WDin
- 'Shirley's Compact' NLar
- Swarthmore form see *I. virginica* 'Henry's Garnet'
yunnanensis CPLG NLar SSpi

Ixia (*Iridaceae*)

aurea 'Saldanha' **new** ECho
'Blue Bird' CBgR CFir CTca ECho LAma MCot WHil
capillaris 'Citrusdal' **new** ECho
'Castor' CAvo CBgR CPne CPrp ECho WHil
curta ECho
dubia ECho
flexuosa ECho
'Gemini' **new** CBgR ECho
'Giant' CAvo CBgR CTca ECho WHil
'Hogarth' CPrp ECho LAma MCot WHil
'Holland Glory' ECho
hybrids SMrm
latifolia var. ***latifolia*** ECho
longituba 'Citrusdal' **new** ECho
lutea ECho
'Mabel' CAvo CBgR ECho WCot WHil
maculata ECho
'Marquette' ECho
metelerkampiae ECho
monadelpha ECho
orientalis ECho
paniculata ECho
'Panorama' CPne ECho WHil
polystachya ECho
- var. ***longistylis*** ECho
- var. ***lutea*** ECho
purpureorosea 'Saldanha' ECho
rapunculoides var. ***rigida*** ECho
- var. ***subpendula*** ECho
'Rose Emperor' CPrp ECho LAma SDeJ WHil
scillaris ECho
var. ***subundulata*** **new**
'Spotlight' CBgR ECho WHil
thomasiae WCot
trifolia ECho
'Venus' CBgR CFir CPne CTca ECho LAma MCot WHil
versicolor ECho
viridiflora CBow CPne ECho WCot
- var. ***minor*** **new** ECho
'Vulcan' CPrp ECho
'Yellow Emperor' CAvo CBgR CPne CTca ECho MCot WHil

Ixiolirion (*Ixioliriaceae*)

montanum CHid EBee ECho
pallasii see *I. tataricum*

§	***tataricum***	ECho LAma SBch
	- Ledebourii Group	CAvo CFFs EBee

Ixora (*Rubiaceae*)

	chinensis 'Apricot Queen'	SOWG
	'Golden Ball'	SOWG
	'Pink Malay'	SOWG

J

Jaborosa (*Solanaceae*)

	integrifolia	CDes CFir CPLG CStu EBee ELan LRHS SSvw SUsu WAul WCom WCon WCot WPGP

Jacaranda (*Bignoniaceae*)

	acutifolia misapplied	see *J. mimosifolia*
§	***mimosifolia***	CBcs CCCN CHII ELan ERea EShb EWTr GQui MREP SOWG SPlb

Jacobinia see *Justicia*

Jamesbrittenia (*Scrophulariaceae*)

	Britney Series **new**	LAst
	Sumatra Indigo = 'Yagemon'	MNrw

Jamesia (*Hydrangeaceae*)

	americana	NLar

Jasione (*Campanulaceae*)

§	***heldreichii***	NBir SRms
	jankae	see *J. heldreichii*
§	***laevis***	ECho GAbr GKev SRms WWFP
§	- 'Blaulicht'	CMHG EBee ECha EPfP GGar LRHS MBNS MMuc NBPC NEgg NLar SBfd SMrm SPhx SPlb WMoo
	- Blue Light	see *J. laevis* 'Blaulicht'
	montana	EBWF EBee ECho MNHC WFar WPnn WSFF
	perennis	see *J. laevis*

Jasminum (*Oleaceae*)

	CC 4728	CPLG
	adenophyllum	SOWG
	affine	see *J. officinale* f. *affine*
	angulare ♀H1	CPLG CRHN EBee ERea EShb SEND SOWG
	azoricum ♀H1	CCCN CDoC CRHN CTrC ELan EPfP ERea EShb NPal
	beesianum	Widely available
	bignoniaceum	WSHC
	blinii	see *J. polyanthum*
	dispermum	CRHN
	diversifolium	see *J. subhumile*
	farreri	see *J. humile* f. *farreri*
	floridum	EWes
	fruticans	EBee ELon EPfP LRHS
	giraldii hort.	see *J. humile* f. *farreri*
	grandiflorum misapplied	see *J. officinale* f. *affine*
	grandiflorum L.	IDee
	- 'De Grasse' ♀H1	CRHN ERea EShb SOWG
	heterophyllum	see *J. subhumile*
	humile	CEnt CPLG EQua GAuc MGos SEND WFar WKif
§	- f. ***farreri***	MBri
	- var. ***glabrum***	see *J. humile* f. *wallichianum*
§	- 'Revolutum' ♀H4	Widely available
§	- f. ***wallichianum*** B&SWJ 2559	WCru
§	***laurifolium*** f. ***nitidum***	ERea EShb SOWG
§	***mesnyi*** ♀H2-3	CCCN CDoy CEnt CMac CPLG CRHN CSBt CTri CWib EBak EBee ELan EPfP ERea IGor IVic MAsh MRav SAga SBfd SEND SOWG SPer STre WSHC
	multiflorum	SOWG
	multipartitum	EShb
	- bushy	CSpe
	nitidum	see *J. laurifolium* f. *nitidum*
§	***nudiflorum*** ♀H4	Widely available
	- 'Argenteum'	see *J. nudiflorum* 'Mystique'
	- 'Aureum'	EBee ELan EPfP EPla LBMP LRHS MAsh MBNS MRav NHol NSti SLim SPer SPoG SRms WCot
*	- 'Compactum'	MAsh
§	- 'Mystique' (v)	ELan LRHS MAsh NLar SLon SPer SPoG WClo WCot WPat
	odoratissimum	ERea EShb SOWG
	officinale ♀H4	Widely available
§	- f. ***affine***	CBcs CCCN CRHN CSPN CSam CTri CWSG CWib EBee ELan ELon EPfP LAst LRHS MAsh MGan MRav NHol SCoo SDix SLim SRms WCru WFar
§	- 'Argenteovariegatum' (v) ♀H4	Widely available
	- 'Aureovariegatum'	see *J. officinale* 'Aureum'
§	- 'Aureum' (v)	CBot CChe CDoC CHby CMac CWSG CWib EBee ECtt ELan EPfP LBMP LRHS MAsh MBri MHer MREP MSCN NBir NHol SBfd SCoo SLim SLon SMad SPer SRms WPat
	- 'Clotted Cream' PBR	see *J. officinale* 'Devon Cream'
	- 'Crûg's Collection'	WCru
§	- 'Devon Cream' PBR	CBcs CCCN CDul CSBt CWGN EBee EPfP EShb EWTr LAst LBuc LRHS LSRN MAsh MBri MGos MREP MWea NHol NLar NPri SBfd SCoo SLim SPer SPoG WCot WPat
	- Fiona Sunrise = 'Frojas' PBR	Widely available
	- 'Grandiflorum'	see *J. officinale* f. *affine*
	- 'Inverleith' ♀H4	CCCN CDoC CMac CWSG EBee ELan EPfP IArd LAst LBMP LHop LRHS MAsh MBNS MBri MCCP MGos MRav SBfd SCoo SLim SMad SPad SPer SPoG WFar WGrn WSHC
	- 'Variegatum'	see *J. officinale* 'Argenteovariegatum'
	parkeri	CBcs CCCN CMea CTri EBee ECho EPfP EPot GEdr GMaP LRHS MAsh MBNS NLar NMen WFar WPat
§	***polyanthum*** ♀H1-2	CArn CBcs CPLG CRHN CSBt CTrC CTri EBak EBee ELan EPfP ERea ERom EShb LAst LOck LRHS MBri NEgg NPal SBfd SEND SLim SOWG SPer SRms
	- dark red-leaved	CPLG IVic WPGP
	primulinum	see *J. mesnyi*
	reevesii hort.	see *J. humile* 'Revolutum'
	sambac ♀H1	CCCN CDoC CHII CRHN EAmu ELan EPfP EShb MWya SOWG
	- 'Bangkok Peony' (d)	ERea
	- 'Grand Duke of Tuscany' (d)	ERea SOWG
	- 'Maid of Orleans' (d) ♀H1	ERea SOWG
	sieboldianum	see *J. nudiflorum*
	stenalobium	SOWG
	× ***stephanense***	Widely available

§ ***subhumile*** **new**	IRar

Jatropha (*Euphorbiaceae*)

integerrima	CCCN
multifida	SPlb

Jeffersonia (*Berberidaceae*)

diphylla	CArn CDes CLAP EBee ECho EHrv ELon EPPr GAbr GGar GKir LAma LEdu LRHS MNrw MTho NBir NLar NMen NMyG SMad WAbe WCru WFar WPnP
dubia	CFir CLAP EBee ECho EWes GCrs GEdr GKev LEdu LRHS MNrw NBir NHar NMen WAbe WCom WCru
- 'Alba'	EHrv

jostaberry see *Ribes* × *culverwellii*

Jovellana (*Scrophulariaceae*)

punctata	CCCN CDoC CMac CPLG EBee WGob
repens	CFir
sinclairii	CHll CPLG EBee ECou LLHF SMrm SUsu
violacea ♀H3	CAbP CAbb CBcs CCCN CDoC CEnt CMac CPLG CTrC CTsd CWib EBee EPfP GCal GGar IMou ITim LRHS SAPC SArc SMad SUsu WCru WPGP WSHC WWlt

Jovibarba ✿ (*Crassulaceae*)

§ ***allionii***	CMea CTri CWil EDAr LAst LBMP LBee LRHS MAsh MHer MSCN NHol NPri WAbe WCom WFar WHal WHoo WIvy WPer WTin
- 'Oki'	CWil ECho
allionii × ***hirta***	CWil MSCN NMen SDys SFgr
§ ***arenaria***	CWil GAbr NMen
- from Passo di Monte Croce Carnico	CWil
'Autumn Fires' **new**	MSCN
'Emerald Spring'	NMen SFgr
§ ***heuffelii***	ECho NHol NMen WIvy WPer
- 'Aga'	NHol WIvy
- 'Aiolos'	NHol
- 'Alemene'	NHol
- 'Almkroon'	NHol
- 'Angel Wings'	CWil LRHS NHol NMen WHoo
§ - 'Apache'	CWil
- 'Aquarius'	CWil WIvy
- 'Artemis'	NHol
- 'Aurora'	NHol
- 'Be Mine'	CWil
- 'Beacon Hill'	CWil WIvy
- 'Belcore'	CWil WIvy
- 'Benjamin'	CWil NHol
- 'Bermuda'	WIvy
- 'Bermuda Sunset'	NHol
- 'Big Red'	NHol
- 'Blaze'	CWil
- 'Brandaris'	NHol SDys
- 'Brocade'	MSCN NHol WIvy
- 'Bronze Ingot'	CWil WCot
- 'Bronze King'	WIvy
- 'Bulgarien'	CWil
- 'Cakor'	NHol
§ - 'Cherry Glow'	CWil NHol
- 'Chocoleto'	WTin
- 'Cleopatra'	NHol
- 'Copper King'	CWil WIvy
- 'Dunbar Red'	NHol
- 'Fandango'	CWil MHom WIvy
- 'Gento'	NHol
- 'Geronimo'	NHol
- 'Giuseppi Spiny'	MHom NHol WIvy WTin
- var. ***glabra***	LBee LRHS WHoo
- - from Anabakanak	CWil MHom NHol WTin
- - from Anthoborio	CWil NMen WIvy WTin
- - from Backovo	NHol
- - from Galicica	NHol
- - from Haila, Montenegro/ Kosovo	CWil NHol NMen SFgr WIvy
- - from Jakupica, Macedonia	CWil WIvy
- - from Ljuboten	CWil NHol NMen WTin
- - from Osljak	CWil
- - from Pasina Glava	CWil
- - from Rhodope	CWil MHom NHol
- - from Treska Gorge, Macedonia	CWil NMen WTin
- - from Vitse, Greece	WIvy
§ - - 'Cameo'	NHol WIvy
- 'Gold Rand'	NHol
- 'Grand Slam'	CWil
- 'Green Land'	CWil
- 'Greenstone'	CMea CWil MHom NHol NMen WAbe WIvy WTin
- 'Harmony'	CWil NHol
- 'Henry Correvon'	CWil
- 'Hot Lips'	CWil
- 'Hot Stuff' **new**	ESem
- 'Hystyle'	WIvy
- 'Ikaros'	NHol
- 'Inferno'	MHom NHol
§ - 'Inge'	ESem
- 'Iole'	WIvy
- 'Ithaca'	NHol
- 'Iuno'	CWil NHol
- 'Jade'	CWil NMen WIvy
- 'Kapo'	WIvy
- var. ***kopaonikensis***	CWil LRHS MHom NMen
- 'Mary Ann'	MHom WIvy
- 'Miller's Violet'	CWil WIvy WTin
- 'Mink'	CWil
- 'Minuta'	CWil NHol NMen WIvy WTin
- 'Mystique'	CMea CWil LBee LRHS NMen WIvy
- 'Nannette'	CWil
- 'Nobel'	NHol
- 'Opele'	NHol
- 'Orion'	CWil NHol NMen
- 'Pink Skies'	CWil WIvy
- 'Prisma'	CWil WIvy WTin
- 'Purple Haze'	WIvy
- 'Red Rose'	CWil WIvy
- 'Serenade'	CWil
- 'Springael's Choice'	CWil
- 'Sundancer'	WIvy
- 'Sungold'	NHol
- 'Suntan'	CWil NHol WIvy
- 'Sylvan Memory'	CWil
- 'Tan'	CWil NHol WTin
- 'Torrid Zone'	WAbe WIvy WTin
- 'Tuxedo'	CWil
- 'Vesta'	CWil
- 'Violet'	SDys WIvy
§ ***hirta***	CWil EDAr NHol NMen SFgr STre WPer
- from Wintergraben	SPlb
§ - subsp. ***borealis***	CWil ESem NHol
- subsp. ***glabrescens***	EPot
- - from Belianske Tatry	CWil
- - from Smeryouka	CWil
I - 'Glauca'	SFgr
- 'Hedgehog'	SFgr

	- var. ***neilreichii***	ECho LRHS MHom
	- 'Preissiana'	LBee NHol NMen SFgr WIvy WTin
	- 'Purpurea' **new**	ESem
	- 'Rax'	SFgr
§	***sobolifera***	CHEx CWil EDAr EPot NHol NMen SFgr SPlb WAbe WHal WIvy WPer
	- 'August Cream'	LBee LRHS
	- 'Bronze Globe'	SFgr
	- 'Green Globe'	ECho LRHS SDys WTin
	- 'Miss Lorraine'	SFgr

Juanulloa (*Solanaceae*)

	aurantiaca	see *J. mexicana*
§	***mexicana***	ERea SOWG

Jubaea (*Arecaceae*)

§	***chilensis***	CBcs CBrP CPHo EAmu EUJe IDee LPJP LPal SBig SChr
	spectabilis	see *J. chilensis*

Juglans ✿ (*Juglandaceae*)

§	***ailanthifolia***	CMCN EGFP
	- var. ***cordiformis*** 'Brock' (F)	CAgr
	- - 'Campbell Cw3' (F)	CAgr
	- - 'Fodermaier' seedling	CAgr
	- - 'Rhodes' (F)	CAgr
	ailanthifolia* × *cinerea	see *J.* × *bixbyi*
§	× ***bixbyi***	CAgr
	cinerea (F)	CMCN LMaj
	- 'Beckwith' (F)	CAgr
	- 'Booth' seedlings (F)	CAgr
	- 'Craxezy' (F)	CAgr
	- 'Kenworthy' seedling	CAgr
	- 'Myjoy' (F)	CAgr
	hindsii	CMCN EBtc
	mandshurica BWJ 8097 from China	WCru
	- RWJ 9905 from Taiwan	WCru
*	- subsp. ***sieboldiana*** B&SWJ 11026	WCru
	microcarpa	CMCN
	nigra (F) 🏆H4	Widely available
	- 'Bicentennial' (F)	CAgr
	- 'Emma Kay' (F)	CAgr
	- 'Laciniata'	EPfP ERea MBlu MBri WPat
	- 'Purpurea'	WPat
	- 'Thomas' (F)	CAgr
	- 'Weschke' (F)	CAgr
	regia (F) 🏆H4	Widely available
	- 'Axel' (F)	CAgr
	- 'Broadview' (F)	CAgr CDul CEnd CSBt CTho ELan ERea GTwe LAst LRHS MBlu MBri MCoo MGos NEgg SCoo SDea SKee SPoG SVic
	- 'Buccaneer' (F)	CAgr CDul CTho ECrN GTwe SDea SKee WHar
	- 'Chandler' (F)	CAgr
	- 'Corne du Périgord' (F)	CAgr
	- 'Ferjean' (F)	CAgr
	- 'Fernette'[PBR] (F)	CAgr
	- 'Fernor' (F)	CAgr
	- 'Franquette' (F)	CAgr ECrN EMil GTwe MCoo WDin
	- 'Hansen' (F)	CAgr
	- 'Hartley' (F)	CAgr
	- 'Jupiter' (F)	CAgr CMac
	- 'Laciniata'	CDul WPat
	- 'Lara' (F)	CAgr GTwe
	- 'Mayette' (F)	CAgr ECrN EMil WDin
	- 'Meylannaise' (F)	CAgr
	- number 16 (F)	CAgr
	- 'Parisienne' (F)	CAgr
	- 'Plovdivski' (F)	CAgr
	- 'Proslavski' (F)	CAgr CDul
	- 'Purpurea'	CMCN MBlu MBri
	- 'Rita' (F)	CAgr LBuc
	- 'Ronde de Montignac' (F)	CAgr
	- 'Saturn' (F)	CAgr
	- 'Soleze' (F)	CAgr
	- 'Sorrento' (F)	CCCN
	sieboldiana	see *J. ailanthifolia*

jujube see *Ziziphus jujuba*

Juncus (*Juncaceae*)

	acutiflorus	EBWF NSco
	acutus	EBWF GFor
	articulatus	EBWF
*	***balticus*** 'Spiralis'	ECho
	bulbosus	CNat CRWN EBWF
	conglomeratus	EBWF
	'Curly Gold Strike' (v)	ELon LRHS MAsh MSKA SBfd
§	***decipiens*** 'Curly-wurly'	CFee CSpe EBee EHoe EPfP EPla EWes GFor LPBA LRHS NOak SWal SWat WHal WPnP
	- 'Spiralis'	see *J. decipiens* 'Curly-wurly'
I	- 'Spiralis Nana'	NWCA
	effusus	CHEx CRWN CWat EBWF EHon GFor LPBA MSKA NPer NSco SBfd SWat WMAq
	- 'Carman's Japanese'	CKno
	- 'Gold Strike' (v)	CWat LLWG
§	- f. ***spiralis***	CBen CFee CRow CSpe CWat EHoe EHon ELan EPfP GAbr GFor LPBA LRHS LTen MAsh NBir NLar NOak NWsh SBfd SEND SLim SPer SPlb WFar WHal WMAq WPGP WPnP
§	- - 'Unicorn'[PBR]	CWit EBee EPPr LRHS SApp SBfd SPoG WWEG
	- - 'Yellow Line'[PBR] (v)	LRHS WWEG
	ensifolius	CKno CRow CWat EBee EHoe EWes LPBA MAvo MMHG MSKA NHol NPer WWEG
	filiformis 'Spiralis'	EBee SApp WWEG
	gerardii	EBWF
	inflexus	CBen CRWN CWat EBWF EHon GFor MSKA NHol NSco SEND SWat
	- 'Afro'	EBee ELan EPfP MCCP NBro NOak SPlb WHal WWEG
	pallidus	EPPr GCal NBid
	patens 'Carman's Gray'	CFee CKno CWCL EBee EBrs EPPr EPla GCal GQue LRHS MAvo MCCP MMoz NGdn NHol NNor NOak NWsh SApp WCot WMoo WPtf WWEG
	- 'Elk Blue'	CKno WWEG
	'Silver Spears'	MCCP
	squarrosus	EBWF
	'Unicorn'[PBR]	see *J. effusus* f. *spiralis* 'Unicorn'
	xiphioides	EHoe EPla NHol

Junellia (*Verbenaceae*)

	azorelloides F&W 9344	WAbe
	odonnellii	WAbe
	wilczekii	WFar

Juniperus ✿ (*Cupressaceae*)

	chinensis	CMen
	- 'Aurea' 🏆H4	CBcs CMac EHul LRHS MGos
§	- 'Blaauw' 🏆H4	CDoC CMac CMen EHul MGos SCoo STre WEve WFar
	- 'Blue Alps'	EHul GKir IFFs LRHS MGos MMuc NEgg NHol NLar SBfd SCoo SEND SLim WDin WEve WFar

	- 'Blue Point'	MGos
	- 'Densa Spartan'	see *J. chinensis* 'Spartan'
	- 'Echiniformis'	CKen
	- 'Expansa Aureospicata' (v)	CDoC CKen ECho EHul EPfP MGos SEND SLim SPoG SRms
§	- 'Expansa Variegata' (v)	CDoC CWib ECho EHul EPfP GKir MAsh MGos SCoo SRms WDin WFar WMoo
	- 'Ferngold'	CDoC MGos
	- 'Itoigawa'	CMen
	- 'Japonica Variegata' (v)	EPla
§	- 'Kaizuka' Υ^{H4}	EHul GKir LBee NLar SCoo SLim SMad STre
	- 'Kaizuka Variegata'	see *J. chinensis* 'Variegated Kaizuka'
	- 'Kuriwao Gold'	see *J.* × *pfitzeriana* 'Kuriwao Gold'
	- 'Obelisk' Υ^{H4}	EHul MGos WClo
	- 'Oblonga'	EHul
§	- 'Parsonsii'	STre WCFE
	- 'Plumosa Aurea' Υ^{H4}	EHul WDin WFar
	- 'Plumosa Aureovariegata' (v)	CKen
	- 'Pyramidalis' Υ^{H4}	CDoC EHul EPfP GKir NPri SCoo SRms WDin WFar
	- 'Robust Green'	GKir LRHS NLar
	- 'San José'	CMen EHul MAsh SCoo WDin
§	- var. ***sargentii***	CMen STre
	- 'Shimpaku'	CKen CMen NLar
§	- 'Spartan'	EHul
	- 'Stricta'	CSBt EHul LBee LRHS MAsh MGos SLim WDin
	- 'Sulphur Spray'	see *J.* × *pfitzeriana* 'Sulphur Spray'
	- 'Torulosa'	see *J. chinensis* 'Kaizuka'
§	- 'Variegated Kaizuka' (v)	ECho EHul WFar
	communis	CArn CDul CRWN EHul GKir GPoy MHer MNHC NWea SIde WAbe
	- (f)	SIde
	- 'Arnold'	CDul MGos SBfd
	- 'Arnold Sentinel'	CKen
	- 'Atholl'	CKen
	- 'Barton'	MGos NHol NLar
	- 'Berkshire'	CKen NHol WThu
	- 'Brien'	CDoC CKen
	- 'Brynhyfryd Gold'	CKen
	- 'Compressa' Υ^{H4}	Widely available
§	- 'Constance Franklin' (v)	EHul STre
	- 'Corielagan'	CKen MBri NLar WAbe
	- 'Cracovia'	CKen
	- var. ***depressa***	GPoy
	- 'Depressa Aurea'	CKen CSBt ECho EHul EPla GKir IFFs LBee MGos WFar
	- 'Depressed Star'	ECho EHul
	- 'Derrynane'	EHul
	- 'Effusa'	CKen
	- 'Gelb'	see *J. communis* 'Schneverdingen Goldmachangel'
	- 'Gold Ball'	LBee
	- 'Gold Cone'	CKen ECho EHul EPfP EPla GKir LBee LRHS MAsh MGos NHol SLim SPoG WDin WFar
	- 'Golden Showers'	see *J. communis* 'Schneverdingen Goldmachangel'
	- 'Goldenrod'	MGos
	- 'Green Carpet' Υ^{H4}	CDoC CKen CMen ECho EHul EPfP EPla GKir IFFs LBuc LRHS MAsh NEgg NHol SCoo SLim SPoG WCFE WDin
	- 'Haverbeck'	CKen
	- 'Hibernica' Υ^{H4}	CDul CSBt CTri ECho EHul EPfP GKir LAst LRHS MGos NWea SBfd SLPl SLim SPer SPoG WDin WEve
	- 'Hibernica Aurea' **new**	CMac
	- 'Hibernica Variegata'	see *J. communis* 'Constance Franklin'
	- 'Hornibrookii' Υ^{H4}	EHul MGos NWea SRms WDin
	- 'Horstmann'	NLar
I	- 'Horstmann's Pendula'	CDoC
	- 'Kenwith Castle'	CKen
	- 'Prostrata'	WFar
	- 'Pyramidalis'	SPlb
	- 'Repanda' Υ^{H4}	CBcs CDoC CMac CSBt CWib ECho EHul EPfP GGar GKir IFFs LAst MGos SBfd SCoo SLim SPer SPoG SRms WBVN WDin WEve WFar
§	- 'Schneverdingen Goldmachangel'	EPla MGos NHol NLar SLim SPoG
	- 'Sentinel'	EHul EPfP GKir LRHS SLim WCFE WDin WEve
	- 'Sieben Steinhauser'	CKen
	- 'Silver Mist'	CKen
	- 'Spotty Spreader' (v)	GKir SLim SPoG
	- Suecica Group	EHul NLar NWea SLPl
	- - 'Suecica Aurea'	EHul
	- 'Wallis'	NHol
	- 'Zeal'	CKen
	conferta	see *J. rigida* subsp. *conferta*
	- var. ***maritima***	see *J. taxifolia*
	davurica	EHul
	- 'Expansa'	see *J. chinensis* 'Parsonsii'
	- 'Expansa Albopicta'	see *J. chinensis* 'Expansa Variegata'
	- 'Expansa Variegata'	see *J. chinensis* 'Expansa Variegata'
	excelsa subsp. ***polycarpos***	CMen
	'Fitz Kukuri Gold'	MMuc
	foetidissima	CMen
	× ***gracilis*** 'Blaauw'	see *J. chinensis* 'Blaauw'
	'Grey Owl' Υ^{H4}	ECho EHul ELan EPfP MAsh NWea SBfd SCoo SLim SRms STre WDin WFar
	horizontalis	GKir NWea
§	- 'Andorra Compact'	ECho NLar SCoo
	- 'Bar Harbor'	CKen CMac EHul GKir MGos NWea
§	- 'Blue Chip'	ECho EHul ELan EPfP EPla GKir LBee LRHS MGos NBir SCoo SLim SPer SPoG WDin
	- 'Blue Moon'	see *J. horizontalis* 'Blue Chip'
	- 'Blue Pygmy'	CKen
	- 'Blue Rug'	see *J. horizontalis* 'Wiltonii'
	- 'Douglasii'	CKen EHul
	- 'Emerald Spreader'	CKen ECho EHul ELan GKir
	- 'Glacier'	CKen
	- Glauca Group	EHul GKir MGos NWea SPoG WDin
	- 'Glomerata'	CKen
	- 'Golden Carpet'	ECho ELan EPfP GKir LBuc MGos NLar SPoG
	- 'Golden Spreader'	CDoC
	- 'Grey Pearl'	CKen EHul
	- 'Hughes'	EHul LBee MGos NWea
	- Icee Blue = 'Monber'	CKen LRHS NLar SLim SPoG
	- 'Jade River'	EHul GKir MGos SPoG
	- 'Limeglow'	CDoC CKen ECho EPfP LRHS MAsh MGos NEgg NLar SCoo SLim SPer SPoG
	- 'Mother Lode'	CKen
	- 'Neumann'	CKen
	- 'Plumosa Compacta'	see *J. horizontalis* 'Andorra Compact'
	- 'Prince of Wales'	EHul GKir IFFs MAsh MGos NLar SCoo SPoG WEve
	- 'Turquoise Spreader'	CSBt ECho EHul GKir SCoo
	- 'Venusta'	see *J. virginiana* 'Venusta'
	- 'Villa Marie'	CKen

§	- 'Wiltonii' ♀H4	EHul MGos
	- 'Winter Blue'	LBee LRHS SLim SPer
	- 'Youngstown'	GKir IFFs MGos WFar
	- 'Yukon Belle'	CKen
N	× ***media***	see *J.* × *pfitzeriana*
§	× ***pfitzeriana***	CDul WEve
	- 'Armstrongii'	EHul
	- 'Blaauw'	see *J. chinensis* 'Blaauw'
	- 'Blue and Gold' (v)	CKen ECho EHul
	- 'Blue Cloud'	see *J. virginiana* 'Blue Cloud'
§	- 'Carbery Gold'	CBcs CDoC CDul CMac CSBt ECho EHul EPla GKir LBee LRHS MAsh MGos NHol SCoo SLim SPoG WEve WFar
	- 'Daub's Frosted'	SLim
	- 'Gold Coast'	CDoC CKen CSBt ECho EHul EPfP LBee MAsh MBri MGos NHol NLar SLim SPer WDin WEve
	- Gold Sovereign = 'Blound'PBR	GKir LBee MAsh MGos NHol
*	- 'Golden Joy'	LRHS SCoo SLim SPoG
	- 'Golden Saucer'	SCoo
	- 'Goldkissen'	MGos NLar
	- 'King of Spring'	SLim
§	- 'Kuriwao Gold'	CMac EHul GKir MGos NHol NLar NPri SCoo SEND STre WFar
	- 'Milky Way' (v)	SCoo
	- 'Mint Julep'	CSBt ECho EHul GKir LTen MGos SBfd SCoo SLim WDin WEve WFar WMoo
	- 'Mordigan Gold'	WEve
	- 'Old Gold' ♀H4	CKen ECho EHul EPfP LBee MGos NEgg NHol NPri NWea SBfd SCoo SLim SPlb SPoG SRms WDin WEve WFar
	- 'Old Gold Carbery'	see *J.* × *pfitzeriana* 'Carbery Gold'
	- 'Pfitzeriana'	see *J.* × *pfitzeriana* 'Wilhelm Pfitzer'
	- 'Pfitzeriana Aurea'	ECho EHul EPfP GKir MGos NWea WDin WEve WFar
	- 'Pfitzeriana Compacta' ♀H4	EHul SCoo
	- 'Pfitzeriana Glauca'	EHul SCoo
§	- 'Sulphur Spray' ♀H4	CSBt CWib ECho EHul EPla GKir LAst MAsh MGos MMuc NHol SEND SLim SRms WBVN WCFE WDin WEve WFar WMoo
§	- 'Wilhelm Pfitzer'	EHul EPfP NWea
§	***pingii*** 'Glassell'	CDoC GKir NLar
	- 'Hulsdonk Yellow' **new**	SLim
§	- var. ***wilsonii***	CDoC CKen NLar
	procera	WPGP
	procumbens 'Bonin Isles'	LRHS SPoG
	- 'Nana' ♀H4	CDoC CKen CMac CSBt ECho EHul EPfP EPla LAst LBee LRHS MAsh MGos NEgg NHol SCoo SLim SPoG WCFE WDin WEve WFar
	recurva	CDoC GKir
	- 'Castlewellan'	CDoC MGos NLar
	- var. ***coxii***	CDoC CMac ECho EHul GGGa GKir MGos NHol SRms WCFE
§	- 'Densa'	CDoC CKen EHul NHol
	- 'Nana'	see *J. recurva* 'Densa'
	rigida	CMen GKir NLar
§	- subsp. ***conferta***	CMac GKir IFFs LBee SEND WEve
	- - 'All Gold'	SLim
*	- - 'Blue Ice'	CKen WFar
	- - 'Blue Pacific'	EHul GKir MBri NLar WFar
	- - 'Blue Tosho'	ECho GKir NLar SPoG
	- - 'Emerald Sea'	EHul
	- - 'Schlager'	SLim
	- - 'Silver Mist'	CKen
	sabina	NWea
§	- 'Blaue Donau'	ECho EHul
	- Blue Danube	see *J. sabina* 'Blaue Donau'
	- 'Broadmoor'	EHul
	- 'Buffalo'	EHul
	- 'Knap Hill'	see *J.* × *pfitzeriana* 'Wilhelm Pfitzer'
	- 'Mountaineer'	see *J. scopulorum* 'Mountaineer'
	- 'Rockery Gem'	EHul LRHS SLim SPoG WGor
	- 'Skandia'	CKen
	- 'Tamariscifolia'	CBcs CWib EHul LBee LRHS LTen MGos NWea SEND SLim SPer SPoG WCFE WDin WEve WFar
	- 'Variegata' (v)	EHul
	sargentii	see *J. chinensis* var. *sargentii*
	scopulorum	CKen
	- 'Blue Arrow'	CDoC CDul CKen CSBt CWib ECho ECrN ELan EPfP EPla GKir LAst LBee LRHS MAsh MBri MGos NEgg NHol NLar NPCo SCoo SLim SPer WBor WDin WEve WFar
	- 'Blue Banff'	CKen
	- 'Blue Heaven'	EHul SRms
	- 'Blue Pyramid'	EHul
	- 'Boothman'	EHul
	- 'Moonglow'	EHul
§	- 'Mountaineer'	EHul
	- 'Mrs Marriage'	CKen
	- 'Repens'	MGos
	- 'Silver Star' (v)	EHul MGos
	- 'Skyrocket'	CBcs CCVT CDul CMac CSBt CTri CWib ECho ECrN EHul EPfP GGal GKir LAst LBee MGos NPCo NWea SEND SPlb WBVN WBor WCFE WDin WEve WFar
	- 'Snow Flurries' **new**	SLim
	- 'Springbank'	EHul WCFE
	- 'Wichita Blue'	EHul EPfP WEve
§	***squamata***	WBVN
	- 'Blue Carpet' ♀H4	Widely available
	- 'Blue Spider'	CKen LRHS SCoo SLim
	- 'Blue Star' ♀H4	Widely available
	- 'Blue Star Variegated'	see *J. squamata* 'Golden Flame'
	- 'Blue Swede'	see *J. squamata* 'Hunnetorp'
	- 'Chinese Silver'	EHul SLim
	- 'Dream Joy'	CKen LRHS NHol NLar SCoo SLim SPoG
	- var. ***fargesii***	see *J. squamata*
	- 'Filborna'	CKen LBee SLim
	- 'Glassell'	see *J. pingii* 'Glassell'
§	- 'Golden Flame' (v)	CKen
	- 'Holger' ♀H4	CDoC CDul CMac CSBt ECho EHul EPfP EPla GEdr GKir LAst LBee LRHS MAsh MBri MGos SBfd SCoo SLim SPoG WEve
§	- 'Hunnetorp'	MGos NHol
	- 'Loderi'	see *J. pingii* var. *wilsonii*
	- 'Meyeri'	CBcs ECho EHul GKev GKir IFFs NWea SCoo STre WDin WFar
	- 'Wilsonii'	see *J. pingii* var. *wilsonii*
§	***taxifolia***	CSBt GGar LBee
§	***virginiana*** 'Blue Cloud'	EHul LTen SLim WGor
	- 'Burkii'	EHul
	- 'Frosty Morn'	CKen EHul WFar
	- 'Glauca'	CSWP EHul NWea
	- 'Golden Spring'	CKen
	- 'Helle'	see *J. chinensis* 'Spartan'
	- 'Hetzii'	ECho EHul NLar NWea WDin WFar
	- 'Hillspire'	EHul
	- Silver Spreader = 'Mona'	CKen EHul
	- 'Staver'	EHul
	- 'Sulphur Spray'	see *J.* × *pfitzeriana* 'Sulphur Spray'

§ – 'Venusta' CKen

Jussiaea see *Ludwigia*

Justicia (*Acanthaceae*)

adhatodoides new WHil
americana new LLWG
aurea ERea EShb
§ **brandegeeana** ♀H1 CCCN EShb SOWG
– 'Lutea' see *J. brandegeeana* 'Yellow Queen'
– variegated (v) EShb WHil
§ – 'Yellow Queen' EShb WHil
§ **carnea** CHll EBak ERea EShb SAga SMad SOWG WCot
– 'Alba' CCCN EShb
guttata see *J. brandegeeana*
'Penrhosiensis' ERea EShb
pohliana see *J. carnea*
rizzinii ♀H1 CCCN CHll ERea SMad SOWG WHil
scheidweileri EShb
spicigera ERea EShb WHil
suberecta see *Dicliptera sericea*

K

Kadsura (*Schisandraceae*)

coccinea B&SWJ 11793 WCru
japonica CBcs EShb WPGP
– B&SWJ 1027 WCru
– B&SWJ 4463 from Korea WCru
– B&SWJ 11109 from Japan WCru
– 'Fukurin' (v) IArd NLar
– 'Variegata' (v) CBcs CCCN EBee EPfP LRHS WSHC
– white fruit CBcs EPfP
§ **verrucosa** HWJ 664 WCru

Kaempferia ✿ (*Zingiberaceae*)

rotunda CCCN LAma WWst

Kalanchoe (*Crassulaceae*)

beharensis ♀H1 CAbb CCCN CDTJ EShb LToo
– 'Fang' CDTJ
– 'Rusty' CDTJ CSpe
daigremontiana EShb SRms STre
§ **delagoensis** CCCN EShb STre
fedtschenkoi EShb STre
humilis EShb
laciniata EShb
laetivirens EShb
marmorata ♀H1 EShb
orgyalis EShb
'Partridge'PBR LRHS STre
pinnata EShb
porphyrocalyx EOHP
pubescens EShb
pumila ♀H1 EShb EWoo SBch SPet STre WEas
rhombopilosa EShb
sexangularis EShb
'Tessa' ♀H1 SRms STre WCot
thyrsiflora EShb STre
– 'Bronze Sculpture' CAbb EWll
tomentosa ♀H1 EShb WCom WCot WEas
tubiflora see *K. delagoensis*

Kalimeris (*Asteraceae*)

§ **incisa** EBee MMuc MRav WBor WTin
– 'Alba' EBee ECha LHop NLar SSvw WFar
– 'Blue Star' EBee ECha EWll LHop LRHS MWea NLar WFar WPtf WSHC
– 'Charlotte' EBee EWes NBre NDov
– 'Madiva' CSam EBee ECha LHop NDov
– 'Nana Blue' new NDov
integrifolia WTin
intricifolia NBre
§ **mongolica** CDes EBee ECha GAuc NBre WFar WPer WSHC
– 'Antonia' new NDov
§ **pinnatifida** EBee EPPr
– 'Hortensis' ECtt NBPC
§ **yomena** 'Shogun' (v) CMoH EBee ECha EHoe ELan EPfP LRHS NBir NBre NLar NPri SAga SMrm SPer WCom WFar WSHC WWEG
– 'Variegata' see *K. yomena* 'Shogun'

Kalmia ✿ (*Ericaceae*)

angustifolia ♀H4 SRms WDin WFar
– f. **rubra** ♀H4 CBcs CDoC CDul EBee ELan EPfP LRHS MAsh MGos NLar NPri SBfd SPer SPoG SReu WFar WPat WSpi
I – 'Rubra Nana' new CMac
latifolia ♀H4 CBcs CEnd CWit ELan EPfP LRHS LSou MGos MMuc NPri NWea SPer SSpi SWvt WBrE WDin WFar WSpi
– 'Alpine Pink' WSpi
– 'Bigboy' GGGa
– 'Carousel' CBcs ECho EPfP GGGa NLar WFar WGob
– 'Clementine Churchill' CMac
– 'Elf' CEnd ECho EPfP IVic MAsh MGos MLea MPkF NLar SLim WFar
– 'Freckles' ♀H4 ECho ELan EPfP GGGa NPCo SPoG WFar
– 'Fresca' ECho NPCo WGob
– 'Galaxy' GGGa
– 'Kaleidoscope' new IVic
– 'Little Linda' ♀H4 ECho GGGa
– 'Madeline' GGGa
– 'Minuet' CBcs CDoC CEnd CWSG CWit ECho EPfP GGGa GKev LRHS MGos MLea MMuc MPkF NPCo SLim SPoG SSpi SWvt WBrE WFar
– 'Mitternacht' GGGa
– f. **myrtifolia** ECho WFar WGob
– 'Nancy' WFar
– 'Nipmuck' CMac
– 'Olympic Fire' ♀H4 CEnd EPfP GGGa IVic MGos MPkF MRav NHol NLar SLim
– 'Ostbo Red' CDoC CDul CMac ECho EPfP IVic LRHS MGos MLea MPkF NCGa NPCo SPer SPoG SReu SSpi SSta SWvt WFar
– 'Peppermint' EBee GGGa IVic MPkF SLim
– 'Pink Charm' ♀H4 ECho IVic
– 'Pink Frost' ECho NLar NPCo WFar
– 'Pinwheel' CEnd MPkF NLar SLim
– 'Quinnipiac' MPkF
– 'Raspberry Glow' GGGa
– 'Richard Jaynes' ECho WFar
– 'Sarah' ECho MLea NPCo
– 'Snowdrift' CWit ECho NLar WFar
polifolia CBcs ECho EPfP NHar NLAp NMen SPer WThu
– var. **compacta** WSHC
– f. **leucantha** NLAp NMen WPat WThu

× *Kalmiothamnus* (*Ericaceae*)

ornithomma 'Cosdon' WAbe WThu
– 'Haytor' ITim WAbe

'Sindelberg'	ITim WAbe

Kalopanax (*Araliaceae*)

pictus	see *K. septemlobus*
§ ***septemlobus***	CBcs CDul ELan EPfP EUJe GBin MMuc NLar WBVN
- subsp. ***lutchuensis*** B&SWJ 5947	WCru
- f. ***maximowiczii***	CDoC EBee EPfP IVic MBlu WCot

Kelseya (*Rosaceae*)

uniflora	WAbe

Kennedia (*Papilionaceae*)

beckxiana	SOWG
coccinea	CCCN
nigricans	CCCN ERea SOWG
prostrata	SPlb
rubicunda	CCCN CRHN ERea

Kentia (*Arecaceae*)

belmoreana	see *Howea belmoreana*
forsteriana	see *Howea forsteriana*

Kentranthus see *Centranthus*

Kerria (*Rosaceae*)

japonica misapplied single	see *K. japonica* 'Simplex'
japonica (d)	see *K. japonica* 'Pleniflora'
- 'Albescens'	CBot WFar
- 'Golden Guinea' ♀H4	CMac CPLG CWSG EBee ECtt ELan EPfP GGal IFro LRHS MAsh MGos MNrw MRav MSwo SBfd SCoo SPer SRms SWvt WDin WFar
§ - 'Picta' (v)	CDul CWib EBee ECrN ELan EPfP LRHS MGos MRav MSwo SBfd SGar SLim SLon SPer SPoG SRms WDin WFar WSHC
§ - 'Pleniflora' (d) ♀H4	Widely available
§ - 'Simplex'	CMac CPLG CSBt GGal NWea WDin WFar
- 'Variegata'	see *K. japonica* 'Picta'

Khadia (*Aizoaceae*)

acutipetala	CCCN

Kirengeshoma (*Hydrangeaceae*)

palmata ♀H4	Widely available
- Koreana Group	CFir CLAP CPLG CSpe EBee EHrv ELan EPPr EPfP GCal IPot LAst LEdu MRav NBPC NBid NBir NHol NLar NPnk SMad SPer WCot WCru WFar WGwG WHil WPnP WWEG WWlt

Kitaibela (*Malvaceae*)

vitifolia	CPLG CSpe EBee ELan EWld GCal MLLN NBid SDnm SEND SGSe SGar SPav SPlb WPer

Kitchingia see *Kalanchoe*

kiwi fruit see *Actinidia deliciosa*

Kleinia (*Asteraceae*)

articulata	see *Senecio articulatus*
repens	see *Senecio serpens*
senecioides	WEas

Knautia (*Dipsacaceae*)

§ ***arvensis***	CArn CHll CMac CRWN EBWF EPfP MHer MMuc MNHC NLan NLar NMir NPnk NSco SEND SGSe SPer WFar WHer WMoo WSFF
- 'Rachael'	CElw
dipsacifolia	SHar
'Jardin d'en Face' **new**	LRHS WCot
§ ***macedonica***	Widely available
- 'Crimson Cushion'	CSpe ECtt LSou MBNS WCot WFar
- 'Mars Midget'	CHll CPLG CSam CSpe EBee ELan EPfP EShb ETod GKir GQue LAst LBMP LRHS LSRN LSou MGos NBPC NLar SAga SPoG STes SUsu SWvt WFar WHoo WSHC WWEG
- Melton pastels	COlW CPLG EBee EPfP EShb GJos LBMP LLWG LRHS LSRN LSou MGos NBPC NCob NLar NPer SPet SRot SWat SWvt WClo WFar WWEG
- pink-flowered	CSam WCom
- 'Red Knight'	EPfP MSCN SGSe
- red-flowered	CWib NCob
- short	CAbP ECtt EHrv ELon LLWG NCob SPad
- tall, pale-flowered	SPhx
sarajevensis	EBee MAvo SUsu
§ ***tatarica***	NBre

Knightia (*Proteaceae*)

excelsa	CBcs CWit EUJe IDee

Kniphofia ✿ (*Asphodelaceae*)

sp.	SVic
'Ada'	EBee EBla EBrs EWTr EWes LRHS SGSe SMrm
albescens	CAbb SGar
'Alcazar'	CBcs CDes CElw EBee EBla ECtt EPfP LPio LSRN MBri MHer NPri SBfd SGSe SPer SRkn SWvt WBrE WCot WFar WMnd WSpi WWEG
'Amber'	NBre
'Ample Dwarf'	WCot
'Amsterdam'	EBee MWat SHar
angustifolia	SPlb
'Apricot'	EBrs EPla LRHS
'Apricot Souffle'	SGSe SMrm WCot
'Apricots and Cream' **new**	WCot
'Atlanta'	SBfd SGSe
'Barton Fever'	WCot
baurii	CPLG MSpe
'Beauty of Wexford'	EBla
'Bees' Flame'	EBee
'Bees' Jubilee'	WHoo
'Bees' Lemon'	Widely available
'Bees' Sunset' ♀H4	CAvo CDes GCra MNFA MNrw SGSe SMrm SUsu WCot WPrP WSpi WWEG
'Bengal Fire' **new**	LRHS
'Bicolor'	EBee ECtt MSpe NSti WPrP
'Bitter Chocolate'	WCot
'Bob's Choice'	WCot
'Border Ballet'	EDAr EWTr LBMP LHop LRHS NBir NBre NBro NLar SWat WFar
brachystachya	EBee ELon GAbr GBin GCal SPlb WCot
'Bressingham Comet'	EBee EBla EBrs ECtt GKir LRHS MAvo MBri MRav NBir SRms
'Bressingham Gleam'	EBrs LRHS WCot
Bressingham hybrids	GKir IFoB
Bressingham Sunbeam = 'Bresun'	EBee EBla EBrs LRHS NBir SMrm WCot WWEG
'Bressingham Yellow'	EPPr
Bridgemere hybrids	WFar
'Brimstone' ♀H4	Widely available
buchananii	CDes

'Buttercup' ♀H4	CAvo LSRN WSHC WSpi WTin
'C.M. Prichard' misapplied	see *K. rooperi*
'C.M. Prichard' Prichard	EBee WCot
'Candlelight'	CDes CMdw COIW EBee ECtt LPio LRHS NBre SDys SGSe SUsu
'Candlemass'	CTca EBee LPio SBfd
'Carole's Crush' new	WCot
caulescens ♀H3-4	Widely available
- from John May	CKno EBee ECtt LRHS SPad WCot
- 'Cally Compact' new	GCal
- 'Coral Breakers'	CMac CTca EBee ECtt GBin LRHS NEgg SBfd SDix SKHP SMad SPer WCot
- early-flowering	LRHS
- short	ECha
'Chichi'	WCot
citrina	CFir EBee EDAr EPfP GCra LAst LRHS MAvo MBrN NBre NChi NLar NPri WCot WHil
'Cobra'	EBee EBla EBrs GBin LRHS MRav SBfd SMrm SUsu WCot WHil
'Comet'	ECtt
'Coral Flame'	LRHS
'Coral Sceptre'	LPla WCot
'Corallina'	EBee WFar
'Dingaan'	CAbb CSam EBee ECtt GBin GMac GQue MAvo MLLN MNrw NBir NEgg SAga SDnm WBrk WCot WFar
'Dorset Sentry'	CAbP CAbb CChe CMdw EBee EBla ECtt ELon EPfP GAbr GCal LAst LPio MCot MGos MLLN MNrw NBir NCGa NEgg NLar SAga SBfd SGSe SKHP SMrm WCAu WCot WFar WWEG
'Dropmore Apricot'	LSRN
'Drummore Apricot'	CKno CMHG EAEE EBee ECha ELan GCal GGar GKir LAst LRHS LSRN LSou MAsh MLLN MNFA MRav NBir NEgg NSti SDnm SEND SMrm SPoG WCot WFar WPrP WPtf
I 'Earliest of All'	EBee GMac
'Early Buttercup'	CTca MRav SBfd WCot WFar
ensifolia	ECtt NGdn SRms WMnd
'Ernest Mitchell'	EBee MRav WCot
Express hybrids	NBre NLar
'Fairyland'	LRHS NGBl SGar WBrk WFar WTin
'False Maid'	SMHy
'Feuerkerze' new	EBee
'Fiery Fred'	EBla EBrs ELan LRHS MRav NBre SBfd SGSe SMrm WCot
'First Sunrise' PBR	EBee ECtt EWll NCGa
'Flamenco'	CChe COIW CWan EBee EDAr EWll GKir LRHS NBre NGdn NWsh SBfd SPet WRHF WWEG
foliosa Hochst.	SMrm
'Frances Victoria'	WCot
galpinii misapplied	see *K. triangularis* subsp. *triangularis*
galpinii ambig.	WWEG
galpinii Baker ♀H4	CBot MAvo MMuc MRav NBre SEND SRms
'Gilt Bronze'	EBee WCot
'Gladness'	ECtt MRav NBir NBre NSti SGSe WCot WPrP WWEG
'Goldelse'	NBir WCot
'Goldfinch'	CMdw CSam MRav SGSe SMHy
gracilis	LEdu
'Green and Cream'	MNrw
'Green Goddess'	SGSe
'Green Jade'	Widely available
'Green Lemon'	NBre
'H.E. Beale'	GCal SMrm WCot
'Hen and Chickens'	EBee ECtt MAvo MNrw WCot
hirsuta	CFir CSam EBrs EShb GBin LPio LRHS SKHP SPad WCot WSHC
- 'Traffic Lights'	GBin
'Hollard's Gold'	WCot
'Ice Queen'	CAvo CFir CPar CSev EBee ECha ECtt ELon EPPr LAst LPio LRHS MAvo MMuc MRav NChi NGdn NLar SBfd SEND SGSe SMad SRms SSvw SWvt WBrE WCAu WCot WTin WWEG
ichopensis	CDes WPGP
'Incandesce'	WCot
'Ingénue'	WCot
'Innocence'	EBee EBla EBrs LRHS NBre SMrm
'Jane Henry'	CDes EBee MAvo
'Jenny Bloom'	Widely available
'Jess's Delight' new	WCot
'John Benary'	Widely available
'Johnathan'	WCot
laxiflora	EBee WPGP
'Lemon Ice'	WCot
'Light of the World'	see *K. triangularis* subsp. *triangularis* 'Light of the World'
linearifolia	CDes CTrC EBee GCra GGar MNrw SGSe SGar SPlb WCot
'Little Elf'	SDys
'Little Maid'	Widely available
littoralis	SGSe
'Lord Roberts'	CDes EBee GCal LPio MRav SBfd SDix SGSe SMad WCot
'Luna'	WCot
'Lye End'	SMrm
macowanii	see *K. triangularis* subsp. *triangularis*
'Maid of Orleans'	CRow WCot
'Mermaiden'	CFir CMHG CRow CSam EBee ECtt LAst LSou MNrw NCob WCot WFar
'Minister Verschuur'	EBee EBla EBrs ECtt GQue LRHS MBri NBre WCAu WFar WMnd WSpi
'Moonstone'	WCot
'Mount Etna'	EBee SMrm WCot
multiflora	CTca ECtt WCot
'Nancy's Red'	Widely available
nelsonii Mast.	see *K. triangularis* subsp. *triangularis*
'Nobilis'	see *K. uvaria* 'Nobilis'
northiae ♀H4	Widely available
- JCA 3.462.600	WCot
'November Glory'	WCot WPnP
'Old Court Seedling'	EBee GGal SGSe WCot
'Olympic Torch' new	WCot
'Painted Lady'	CAbP CAvo CSam CTca CTri CYeo EBee ECGP ECtt EPfP GAbr GMaP GMac MBri MNFA MNrw MRav MSpe MTis NCGa NLar SMHy SMrm WBrk WCot WPrP
pauciflora	SDys WCot WPrP
'Percy's Pride'	Widely available
'Pfitzeri'	SRms
× ***praecox***	MAvo SGSe SGar WCFE WCot
'Primulina' Bloom	LRHS
'Prince Igor' misapplied	see *K. uvaria* 'Nobilis'
'Prince Igor' Prichard	EBee GAbr LRHS MAsh MLHP MRav MWea NBir SGSe SMad WCot
pumila	LLHF
'Raging Inferno'	WCot
'Rich Echoes'	EBee MAvo WCot
ritualis	LSou SKHP
§ ***rooperi*** ♀H4	Widely available
- 'Cally Giant'	GCal
- 'Cally Torch'	GCal

I	- 'Torchlight'	CPne CTca
	'Royal Castle'	CFwr GMaP LRHS MHav MRav NBir WFar WWEG
	'Royal Standard' ♀^{H4}	CBcs CMac EBee EBla ELan EPfP EShb LAst LRHS LSRN MCot MRav NLar SBfd SPer SPoG SWvt WCot WFar WMnd WSpi WWEG
	rufa Baker	LHop SUsu
	- CD&R 1032	SGar
	'Safranvogel'	EBee LRHS MAvo SGSe SMad SMrm WCot
	'Samuel's Sensation' ♀^{H4}	CFir EBee EBla EBrs ELan LRHS MAsh MLLN MRav NLar SEND SGSe SMrm SRGP WCot WWEG
	sarmentosa	CTrC EBee MAvo SGSe SGar SPlb WCot
	'September Sunshine'	MRav
	'Sherbet Lace' **new**	CAbP
	'Sherbet Lemon'	CHid CTca CYeo ECtt GQue MLLN MNrw SMrm STes WCot
	'Shining Sceptre'	CSam EBee EBrs ECha ECtt LRHS MRav MSCN MWat MWte NLar SBfd SGSe SGar SMad SWvt WAul WEas WWEG
	splendida	CDes EBee SMrm
	'Springtime'	WCot
	'Star of Baden Baden'	CDes EBee MMuc NBir SEND SMad WCot WWEG
	'Strawberries and Cream'	CAvo CBcs CFir CMoH COIW CPen CTca CWCL CYeo EBee EBla EPfP GBin GQue LAst LPio SAga SBfd SMrm SPer WCot
	stricta	WCot
	'Sunbeam'	NBir
	'Sunningdale Yellow' ♀^{H4}	CDes CMdw COIW EBee EBla ECha EHrv EPfP GMaP MLHP MWat MWte SMHy SMrm SRms WCot WEas WHoo WWEG
	'Tawny King'	Widely available
	'Tetbury Torch'^{PBR}	CWGN EAEE EBee EBla ECGP ECtt GBin LHop LRHS MAsh MAvo NCGa NLar SGSe WAul WCAu WClo WPtf WWEG
	thomsonii	GCal MAvo SMrm
	- var. ***snowdenii*** misapplied	see *K. thomsonii* var. *thomsonii*
	- var. ***snowdenii*** ambig.	CPLG SMad WPGP
§	- var. ***thomsonii***	CBot CDes CEnt ECGP LPio SAga SMHy SUsu WCot WHal
	'Timothy'	Widely available
	'Toffee Nosed' ♀^{H4}	Widely available
	'Torchbearer'	NBre WCot WFar
	'Torchlight'	SGSe
	triangularis	EPfP EShb WFar
§	- subsp. ***triangularis***	COIW EBee EPfP GCal LAst LRHS LSRN MAsh MRav SMrm SRms SWat WBrE WCot
§	- - 'Light of the World'	CBcs CDes CHar CMac CSpe CTca EBee ECtt EHrv LAst LPio LSou MAvo NBPC NBir NLar SGSe SMad SMrm SRms SUsu SWvt WBrk WCot WFar WGrn WGwG
	'Tubergeniana'	WCot
	'Tuckii'	SRms
	typhoides	CDes NBir WCot
	tysonii	SPlb
	uvaria	CTrC EBrs LRHS NBir NVic SEND SRms WCot WMnd WPnP
	- 'Grandiflora'	MWhi SBfd WFar WSpi
§	- 'Nobilis' ♀^{H4}	Widely available
	'Vanilla'	CFir EBee GBin LAst LRHS LSRN MAvo MMuc MRav NGdn NLar SBfd SEND SGSe SMrm WAul WWEG
	'Vesta'	LRHS
	'Victoria'	LRHS SGSe
	'Vincent Lepage'	EBee NLar
	'White Trust' **new**	WCot
	'Wol's Red Seedling'	CAby CAvo CBct CEnt CSam EBee EBla ECtt ELon EWTr GAbr LSou MAvo MNFA MNrw NBPC NCGa NEgg NLar SBfd SPoG SUsu WCot WGrn WGwG WHoo WRHF
	'Wrexham Buttercup'	Widely available
	'Yellowhammer'	CSam EBee MMuc NBre SEND WFar WPrP
	'Zululandii'	WCot WHil

Knowltonia (*Ranunculaceae*)

	sp. **new**	CDes
	filia	CPLG

Koeleria (*Poaceae*)

	cristata misapplied	see *K. macrantha*
	glauca	Widely available
§	***macrantha***	GFor NBre NLar SPhx
	vallesiana	EBee EHoe

Koelreuteria (*Sapindaceae*)

	bipinnata	CMCN LEdu
	paniculata ♀^{H4}	Widely available
	- 'Coral Sun'^{PBR}	CGHE CPLG EBee MBlu MBri MGos NLar WPGP WPat
	- 'Fastigiata'	CMCN EBee EPfP MBlu MBri SCoo SSpi WHar
	- 'Rosseels'	NLar
	- 'September'	MBlu

Kohleria (*Gesneriaceae*)

	'Cybele'	EABi WDib
	'Dark Velvet'	WDib
	eriantha ♀^{H1}	CDoC EShb WDib
	hirsuta	WDib
	'Jester' ♀^{H1}	EABi WDib
	'Marquis de Sade'	EABi
	'Red Ryder'	EABi
	'Ruby Red'	WDib
§	'Sunrise'^{PBR}	WDib
	'Sunshine'^{PBR}	see *K.* 'Sunrise'
	warscewiczii ♀^{H1}	EABi WDib

Kolkwitzia (*Caprifoliaceae*)

	amabilis	CDoy CPLG CSBt CTri ECGP ELan EPfP GKir GQue MGan MGos MMuc NWea SPlb SRms WCFE WClo WDin WHar WMoo WRHF
	- 'Maradco'	CMac CPMA EPfP MRav NLar SCoo WPat WSpi
	- 'Pink Cloud' ♀^{H4}	Widely available

kumquat see *Fortunella*

Kunzea (*Myrtaceae*)

	ambigua	EBee ECou ESwi SOWG SPlb
	- pink-flowered	ECou
	- prostrate	ECou
	baxteri	ECou ESwi SOWG
	capitata	SOWG
	ericifolia	SPlb
§	***ericoides***	CTsd ECou GGar SOWG
	- 'Auckland'	ECou
	- 'Bemm'	ECou
	parvifolia	ECou SOWG
	pomifera	ECou

L

Lablab (*Papilionaceae*)

§	***purpureus***	LSou SHDw
	- 'Ruby Moon'	CSpe

+ *Laburnocytisus* (*Papilionaceae*)

	'Adamii'	CDul CLnd CMac CPMA EBee ECrN ELan EPfP LAst LSRN MGos MPkF MRav NLar SMad

Laburnum ✿ (*Papilionaceae*)

	alpinum	EPfP GGar NWea SPlb
	- 'Pendulum'	CDoC CDul CLnd CWit ELan EMil GKir LSRN MAsh MBri MGos MHav MRav NEgg SCrf SLim SPer SPoG
§	***anagyroides***	CDul CWib CWit EMac GKir LMaj MMuc NMun NWea SEND SRms WBVN WDin
	- var. ***alschingeri***	MGos
	vulgare	see *L. anagyroides*
	× ***watereri*** 'Vossii' ♀H4	Widely available

Lachenalia (*Hyacinthaceae*)

	alba 'Nieuwoudtville' **new**	ECho
	algoensis	ECho
§	***aloides***	CBow CDoC CGrW CTca ECho NMen
	- var. ***aurea*** ♀H1	CTca ECho SBch WCot
I	- var. ***luteola***	ECho
	- 'Nelsonii'	ECho WCot
	- 'Pearsonii'	ECho
	- var. ***quadricolor*** ♀H1	CGrW CPrp CTca ECho WCot
	- var. ***vanzyliae*** ♀H1	WCot
	angelica 'Agterkop' **new**	ECho
	anguinea **new**	ECho
	arbuthnotiae	ECho
	'Somerset West' **new**	
	attenuata	ECho
	barkeriana	ECho
	bolusii	ECho
§	***bulbifera*** ♀H1	CTca ECho WCot
	- 'George' ♀H1	ECho
	capensis	ECho
	carnosa	ECho
	cernua 'Goudini' **new**	ECho
	comptonii **new**	ECho
	congesta 'Roggeveld' **new**	ECho
	contaminata ♀H1	CPrp ECho EPfP WCot
	doleritica	ECho
	elegans	ECho
	- var. ***membranacea*** **new**	ECho
	- var. ***suaveolens*** **new**	ECho
	fistulosa	ECho
	- 'Klein Drakenstein' **new**	ECho
	framesii	ECho
	'Fransie' PBR	ECho
	gillettii	ECho
	glaucophylla	ECho
	hirta	ECho
	juncifolia	ECho
	- var. ***juncifolia*** **new**	ECho
	kliprandensis	ECho
	'Kliprand' **new**	
	lactosa	ECho
	latimerae	ECho
	leipoldtii **new**	ECho
	'Lemon Ripple'	WCot
	liliiflora	CGrW ECho
	longibracteata	ECho
	longituba **new**	WCot
	marginata **new**	ECho
	mathewsii	ECho
	maximilianii	ECho
	'Cederberg' **new**	
	mediana	ECho
	montana	ECho
	muirii 'Bredasdorp' **new**	ECho
	multifolia	ECho
	mutabilis	CTca ECho WCot
	'Namakwa' (African Beauty Series)	CTca ECho
	namaquensis	ECho
	namibiensis	ECho
	nardoubergensis	ECho
	neilii	ECho
	nervosa	ECho
	obscura	ECho WCot
	orchioides var. ***glaucina***	ECho WCot
	orthopetala	ECho WCot
	pallida	ECho
	peersii 'Betty's Bay' **new**	ECho
	pendula	see *L. bulbifera*
	polyphylla	ECho
	polypodantha	ECho
	'Varsputs' **new**	
	purpureocoerulea	ECho
	'Darling' **new**	
	pusilla	ECho WCot
	pustulata ♀H1	CPrp CTca ECho WCot
	- blue-flowered	CGrW ECho
	- 'Meerlust' **new**	ECho
	- yellow-flowered	CTca ECho
	reflexa	ECho
	'Robijn'	CPrp ECho WCot
	'Rolina'	ECho
	'Romaud'	CPrp ECho WCot
	'Romelia' PBR	ECho WCot
	'Ronina' (African Beauty Series)	ECho WCot
	'Rosabeth'	CPrp ECho WCot
	rosea	ECho
	rubida	CGrW ECho WCot
	'Rupert' (African Beauty Series)	CPrp ECho WCot
	salteri 'Elim' **new**	ECho
	splendida	ECho
	stayneri	CLak
	thomasiae	ECho
	trichophylla	ECho
	tricolor	see *L. aloides*
	unicolor	ECho WCot
	unifolia	ECho
	variegata 'Mamre' **new**	ECho
	violacea	ECho
	- var. ***glauca***	ECho
	viridiflora ♀H1	CTca ECho GKev SBch WCot
	xerophila	ECho
	youngii 'Humansdorp' **new**	ECho
	zebrina	ECho
	- f. ***densiflora***	ECho
	'Tanqua' **new**	
	zeyheri	ECho WCot

Lactuca (*Asteraceae*)

	alpina	see *Cicerbita alpina*
	lessertiana	EBee
	perennis	CPom CSpe CWan EHoe EPPr LRHS MTho NLar WCot WHer WHrl
	tenerrima	WCot
	virosa	CArn

Lagarosiphon (*Hydrocharitaceae*)

§ ***major*** CBen EHon MSKA SVic WMAq

Lagarostrobos (*Podocarpaceae*)

§ ***franklinii*** CBcs CDoC STre
- 'Fota' (f) WThu
- 'Picton Castle' (m) WThu

Lagerstroemia (*Lythraceae*)

indica ♀H1 CCCN CMen EGxp EPfP ERom EShb LRHS MWya SPlb SSpi WSHC
- 'Berlingot Menthe' IFFs SEND
- Dynamite = 'Whit II' **new** LRHS SSpi
- Little Chief hybrids EShb
- 'Nana Lavendula' **new** LRHS
- 'Red Imperator' SEND
- 'Rosea' CBcs SEND
- 'World's Fair' **new** LRHS

subcostata CWJ 12352 WCru

Lagunaria (*Malvaceae*)

patersonii CHll WPGP

Lagurus (*Poaceae*)

ovatus ♀H3 CKno EHoe GJos NGBl SBch SEND

Lallemantia (*Lamiaceae*)

canescens CPBP

Lamiastrum see *Lamium*

Lamium ✿ (*Lamiaceae*)

album CArn EBWF MWat NMir
- 'Friday' (v) CBow NBir WHer WWEG

flexuosum EBee EPPr

§ ***galeobdolon*** CArn CTri CWib EBWF LRHS MHer NSco SRms WAlt WBrE WHer
- 'Dark Angel' WAlt
- 'Hermann's Pride' EBee ECtt EHoe EPfP GKir GMaP LBMP LRHS MMuc MNFA NBir NCob NDov NMir SMrm SPer SPoG SRms SWvt WAul WFar WHoo WMoo WWEG
- 'Kirkcudbright Dwarf' EBee EWes GBin NBre
- § - subsp. ***montanum*** 'Florentinum' (v) CMac CWan EBee ECha EPfP GKir MMuc MRav WCAu WFar WPer WWEG
- § - 'Silberteppich' ECha ELan MRav
- Silver Carpet see *L. galeobdolon* 'Silberteppich'
- 'Variegatum' see *L. galeobdolon* subsp. *montanum* 'Florentinum'

garganicum WSpi
- subsp. ***garganicum*** CPom EWes LPla

luteum see *L. galeobdolon*

maculatum CArn EPot MMuc NChi SEND SRms WClo WFar
- 'Album' EBee ELan EPfP LBMP LRHS SHar SPer SRms WClo
- 'Anne Greenaway' (v) CBow EBee EWes SPet WWEG
- § - 'Aureum' CArn ECha EHoe ELan SMrm SPet SWvt WFar
- 'Beacon Silver' CArn CMac CWib EBee ECha ELan EPfP GGar GKir LRHS LTen MGos MHer MLHP MSCN MWhi NBir NCob SPer SPet SPlb SPoG SRGP SRms SWvt WEas WFar
- 'Beedham's White' NBir
- 'Brightstone Pearl' EWes MAvo
- 'Cannon's Gold' EBee ECtt ELan EWes SWvt WWEG
- 'Chequers' ambig. CMac EBee LBMP NBPC NBre SPer
- 'Elaine Franks' CSam
- 'Elisabeth de Haas' (v) CBow EBee EWes NBre
- 'Forncett Lustre' EBee EWes
- 'Forncett White Lustre' NBre
- 'Gold Leaf' see *L. maculatum* 'Aureum'
- Golden Anniversary = 'Dellam'^{PBR} (v) ELan LAst LSRN NBro SPoG SWvt WFar WRHF
- 'Golden Nuggets' see *L. maculatum* 'Aureum'
- 'Ickwell Beauty' (v) EBee WWEG
- 'James Boyd Parselle' CBow CMea CSam EBee NBre WHal
- 'Margery Fish' SRms
- 'Orchid Frost' CHid EWll
- Pink Chablis = 'Checkin' SVil
- 'Pink Nancy' CBot CSpe GKir SWvt WCFE
- 'Pink Pearls' CSBt LRHS NBre SHar SMrm SPet WFar WMoo WWEG
- 'Pink Pewter' EBee ECGP ECha ECtt EHoe ELan ELon EPfP EShb GGar LBMP LRHS MMuc SPer SPlb SPoG SUsu WBrE WWEG
- 'Red Nancy' EBee GCal SWvt
- § - 'Roseum' CWib EBee ELan EPfP GGar LBMP LRHS LTen MRav MWat NChi SGar SPer WCAu
- 'Shell Pink' see *L. maculatum* 'Roseum'
- 'Silver Shield' EWes
- 'Sterling Silver' CSam EBee GQue NBre
- 'White Nancy' ♀H4 Widely available
- 'Wootton Pink' MBri MHer NBir NLar SSvw SWvt WEas

orvala Widely available
- 'Album' CBod CBot CDes CLAP CPrp EBee EHrv ELan EPPr LEdu LRHS MAvo NBir NLar SGar SHar SMrm WHer WPGP WPtf WTin
- pink-flowered CLAP CSpe
- 'Silva' CCVN CDes CLAP CSam EBee EPPr EPfP GBin IMou LEdu LRHS NBre WCot WSHC

sandrasicum CPBP

Lampranthus (*Aizoaceae*)

sp. EDAr NWCA WClo

aberdeenensis see *Delosperma aberdeenense*

aurantiacus CBcs CHEx SPet

'Bagdad' CHEx

blandus CBcs CCCN

'Blousey Pink' CHEx

§ ***brownii*** CBcs CBgR CCCN ECho ELan ELon SEND SPet SPlb WPnn

coccineus SPet

deltoides see *Oscularia deltoides*

edulis see *Carpobrotus edulis*

glaucus SEND

mauve-flowered **new** CStu

multiradiatus SEND

oscularis see *Oscularia deltoides*

purple-flowered **new** CStu

roseus CCCN CHEx ECho IRar LRHS SPet WClo WNew

spectabilis CBcs CCCN CTri ELon SAPC SArc SPet WBrE WNew WPnn
- orange-flowered CStu
- 'Tresco Apricot' CCCN ECho
- 'Tresco Brilliant' CCCN CHEx CStu SEND SPet SWvt WCom WPnn
- 'Tresco Fire' CBgR CCCN CDoC CStu CTca ELon
- 'Tresco Orange' CCCN WPnn
- 'Tresco Peach' CCCN CStu
- 'Tresco Red' CCCN ELon SEND SWvt WPnn
- white-flowered CStu WPnn
- yellow-flowered **new** WNew WPnn

'Sugar Pink' CHEx SEND

Lamprothyrsus (*Poaceae*)

hieronymi	EPPr
- RCB RA K2-2	WCot

Lancea (*Scrophulariaceae*)

tibetica	NWCA

Lantana (*Verbenaceae*)

'Aloha' (v)	LSou
camara	CArn ELan EPfP EShb SRms WFar
- 'Kolibri'	WHil
- Lucky Honey Blush = 'Baluclush' **new**	LAst
- Lucky Red Hot **new**	LAst
- orange-flowered	CCCN
- pink-flowered	CCCN EShb
- red-flowered	CCCN
- variegated (v)	EShb
- white-flowered	CCCN EShb
- yellow-flowered	EShb
Lucky Pot of Gold = 'Balugold'PBR **new**	LAst
§ ***montevidensis***	EShb WHil
- RCB/Arg AA-1	WCot
* - ***alba***	EShb
sellowiana	see *L. montevidensis*
'Spreading Sunset'	SOWG

Lapageria ✿ (*Philesiaceae*)

rosea ♀H3	CBcs CCCN CPLG CPne CRHN CTsd EPfP EShb MDun NLar WFar WPGP
- var. ***albiflora***	CRHN
- 'Avalanche'	CBcs WCot
- 'Flesh Pink'	CPLG CRHN
- 'Pink Panther'	CBcs
- 'Tierra del Fuego'	CBcs WCot
- 'Torres del Paine'	CBcs

Lapeirousia (*Iridaceae*)

anceps	CPBP ECho
corymbosa **new**	ECho
cruenta	see *Anomatheca laxa*
divaricata	ECho
fabricii 'Grey's Pass' **new**	ECho
fastigiata **new**	ECho
jacquinii 'Gilberg' **new**	ECho
laxa	see *Anomatheca laxa*
montana 'Danielskuil' **new**	ECho
plicata 'Nieuwoudtville' **new**	ECho
pyramidalis 'Worcester' **new**	ECho

Lapiedra (*Amaryllidaceae*)

martinezii	ECho WCot

Lapsana (*Asteraceae*)

communis 'Inky'	CNat WAlt

Larix ✿ (*Pinaceae*)

decidua ♀H4	CBcs CCVT CDoC CDul CMen CRWN CSBt ECrN ELan EMac EPfP EWTr GKir MGos MMuc NEgg NWea SPer SPlb WDin WEve WFar WMou
- 'Autumn Gold Weeping'	NHol
- 'Corley'	CKen ECho MBlu NLar SLim
- 'Croxby Broom'	CKen SLim
§ - var. ***decidua***	WFar
- 'Globus'	LRHS NHol NLar SLim
- 'Grott'	NLar
- 'Horstmann Recurved'	ECho GKir LRHS NLar SCoo SLim
- 'Kornik'	NLar
- 'Krejci'	MAsh NLar SLim
- 'Little Bogle'	CKen MAsh NHol NLar
- 'Oberförster Karsten'	CKen ECho NLar
- 'Pendula'	CBcs ECho WFar
- 'Puli'	CEnd EBee ECho GKir LRHS MAsh MBlu MGos NHol NLar NPri SCoo SLim SPer SPoG WFar
- 'Schwarzenburg'	NLar
× ***eurolepis***	see *L.* × *marschlinsii*
europaea Lam. & DC.	see *L. decidua* var. *decidua*
gmelinii var. ***olgensis***	NLar
- var. ***principis-rupprechtii***	GKir
- 'Tharandt'	CKen ECho SLim
griffithii	GKir
§ ***kaempferi*** ♀H4	CCVT CDoC CDoy CDul CLnd CMen CTri ECrN ELan EMac EPfP GKir LBuc LMaj LRHS MAsh MMuc NWea SCoo SLim SPer STre WDin WEve WFar WMou
- 'Bambino'	CKen
- 'Bingman'	CKen
- 'Blue Ball'	CKen NLar SLim WEve
- 'Blue Dwarf'	CKen GKir LRHS MGos SCoo SLim SPoG WEve WFar
- 'Blue Haze'	CKen
- 'Blue Rabbit'	CKen
- 'Blue Rabbit Weeping'	GKir LRHS MGos SCoo SLim SPoG WDin
- 'Cruwys Morchard'	CKen
- 'Cupido'	NHol SLim
- 'Diane'	CEnd CKen ECho EPfP LRHS MAsh MBlu MGos NHol NLar SLim SPoG WFar
- 'Elizabeth Rehder'	CKen ECho
- 'Grant Haddow'	CKen
- 'Grey Green Dwarf'	NHol
- 'Grey Pearl'	CKen ECho NLar WFar
- 'Hanna's Broom'	LRHS SLim
- 'Hobbit'	CKen
* - 'Jakobsen's Pyramid'	CDoC CMen LRHS MAsh NHol SCoo SLim SPoG WEve WFar
- 'Lobby Dosser' **new**	LRHS
- 'Nana'	CKen ECho LRHS NLar SLim WFar
I - 'Nana Prostrata'	CKen
- 'Pendula'	CDul CEnd EBee ECho EPfP MAsh MBlu MGos NHol NLar SPer SPoG
- 'Peve Tunnis'	NLar
- 'Pulii'	ECho GKir
- 'Stiff Weeping'	CTri GKir LRHS MAsh MBlu NLar NPCo SCoo SLim
- 'Swallow Falls'	CKen
- 'Varley'	CKen
- 'Wehlen'	CKen
- 'Wolterdingen'	CKen ECho LRHS MBlu NLar SLim
- 'Yanus Olieslagers'	CKen
laricina 'Arethusa Bog'	CKen ECho NLar SLim
- 'Bear Swamp'	CKen SLim WFar
- 'Bingman'	CKen
- 'Hartwig Pine'	CKen ECho
- 'Newport Beauty'	CKen ECho
leptolepis	see *L. kaempferi*
§ × ***marschlinsii***	CCVT GBin GKir MMuc NWea
- 'Domino'	CKen ECho SLim
- 'Gail'	CKen
- 'Julie'	CKen
'Varied Directions'	SCoo SLim

Laserpitium (*Apiaceae*)

§	***siler***	CArn EBee MAvo NLar SPlb WSHC WSpi

Lasiagrostis see *Stipa*

Lasiospermum (*Asteraceae*)

	bipinnatum	SPlb

Lastreopsis (*Dryopteridaceae*)

	glabella	WRic
	hispida	ESwi WRic
	microsora	WRic

Latania (*Arecaceae*)

	loddigesii	LPal
	verschaffeltii	LPal

Lathyrus ✿ (*Papilionaceae*)

§	***aureus***	Widely available
	- 'Cally Variegated' (v)	GCal
	azureus misapplied	see *L. sativus*
	chilensis	CFir
	chloranthus	SPav
	cirrhosus	CDes EBee MPet WPGP
	cyaneus misapplied	see *L. vernus*
	cyaneus (Steven) K.Koch	SAga
	davidii	CDes EBee EWes EWld GCal LLHF WSHC
	fremontii hort.	see *L. laxiflorus*
§	***gmelinii***	EBee NLar
	grandiflorus	CSev CTri ECGP NLar SSvw SWat WCom WCot
	heterophyllus	CSpe EBee SGSe
	incurvus	MPet
	inermis	see *L. laxiflorus*
	japonicus	EBee
	'Lamorna's Love'	WViv
	latifolius 🏆H4	CArn CRHN CRWN EBee EPfP GBar LAst MWat MWhi NPer SDnm SPoG SRms SVic SWal WBVN WBrk WEas WFar WHer WPer
§	- 'Albus' 🏆H4	CBot CTri EBee ELan SGSe SPav SRms WCom WEas
	- deep pink-flowered	MHer NLar NSti
	- pale pink-flowered	NSti
	- Pink Pearl	see *L. latifolius* 'Rosa Perle'
	- 'Red Pearl'	ECtt ELan EPfP GAbr LBuc LRHS MBri MCot MMuc NPri SEND SPav SPer SPlb SPoG SSvw WPer
§	- 'Rosa Perle' 🏆H4	CBcs CTri EBee ECha ECtt EWTr LBMP LHop LRHS MBri MCot MLHP MNHC MRav NBir NLar NPer NPri SGSe SPer SSvw WCAu WHil WMoo WWEG
	- Weisse Perle	see *L. latifolius* 'White Pearl'
	- 'White Pearl' misapplied	see *L. latifolius* 'Albus'
§	- 'White Pearl' 🏆H4	ECha EPfP GAbr GCal GKir LBMP LRHS MBri MCot MHer MNHC MRav MWat NBir NLar NPer NPri NSti SPer SPoG SSvw WBor WCAu WFar WPer
§	***laxiflorus***	CDes CPom EBee MCCP MTho NChi SSvw WPGP WSHC
	linifolius	EBee NLar WHfH WPGP
	luteus (L.) Peterm.	see *L. gmelinii*
	maritimus	NLar
	montanus	GPoy
	nervosus	CSpe EBee EWes MTho SEND SRms WCom
	neurolobus	CDes CPom EBee
	nevadensis	WHil
	niger	CSpe EBee GMac LHop LRHS LSou MCot MHer MMHG NLar SSvw WFar WWEG
	odoratus	CArn SVic
	- 'Dancing Queen'	MPet
	- 'Mammoth Mixed'	MPet
	- 'Matucana'	CSpe MWat SBch WBrk
	- Winter Elegance Series	MPet
	palustris	EBee NLar
	polyphyllus	EBee MPet NSti
	pratensis	EBWF EBee NMir NSco WSFF
	pubescens	CRHN EBee MPet
	roseus	GCal WSHC WViv
	rotundifolius 🏆H4	EBee GLog MNrw MTho WCom WFar WHoo WSHC
	- 'Tillyperone'	SSvw
§	***sativus***	CHid CSpe ECho ELan
	- var. ***azureus***	see *L. sativus*
	sylvestris	CMac EBWF EBee NLar SBch SEND SMrs WBrk
	tingitanus	CSpe CStu
I	- 'Albus' **new**	CSpe
	- 'Roseus'	CSpe
	transsylvanicus	CPom EBee
	tuberosus	CArn EBee WCot WSHC
	'Tubro'	EBee
	venetus	CPom EBee GCal MNrw MWea WSHC
§	***vernus*** 🏆H4	Widely available
	- 'Alboroseus' 🏆H4	Widely available
	- var. ***albus***	CDes CLAP ECho WCot WPGP
	- ***aurantiacus***	see *L. aureus*
	- 'Caeruleus'	CLAP ECGP MNFA WHoo WPGP
*	- 'Cyaneus'	SAga SWat WCom WCot
I	- 'Filifolius'	CSpe
	- 'Flaccidus'	CAby WCom WCot WKif WTin
*	- 'Gracilis'	WViv
	- 'Madelaine' **new**	WCot
	- purple-flowered	LRHS MMuc SEND
	- 'Rainbow'	CLAP GAbr LRHS NWCA SMrm WFar WHil WWEG
	- 'Rosenelfe'	CBot CMea EBee MCot MDKP NPri SMrm SPhx WCot WHal WPGP
	- f. ***roseus***	EBee ECha GAbr LRHS MMuc MRav NBir NCGa SEND SRms WBrk WCot
	- 'Spring Beauty'	CLAP
	- 'Spring Delight'	GKir LRHS
	- 'Spring Melody'	EBee GCrs MRav WCot WPat
	- 'White Wisps' **new**	WCot

Laurelia (*Monimiaceae*)

§	***sempervirens***	CBcs CTrC EBee WPGP
	serrata	see *L. sempervirens*

Laureliopsis (*Monimiaceae*)

	philippiana	EBee

Laurentia see *Isotoma*

Laurus (*Lauraceae*)

§	***azorica***	CBcs
	canariensis	see *L. azorica*
	nobilis 🏆H4	Widely available
	- f. ***angustifolia***	CMac CSWP CTsd EOHP GGal LRHS MBlu MHer MRav NLar SAPC SArc SEND SPoG
	- 'Aurea' 🏆H4	CBcs CDul CMac CWit EBee ELan EPfP LHop LRHS MBlu MGos MHer MMuc NEgg NLar SBfd SEND SLim SLon SPer SPoG SWvt WDin WFar WMoo WPat

– clipped pyramid	GKir LSRN MGos
– 'Crispa'	MRav
– 'Sunspot' (v)	WCot
– variegated (v) **new**	CMac

Lavandula ✿ (*Lamiaceae*)

'After Midnight'	see *L.* 'Avonview'
'Alba'	see *L. angustifolia* 'Alba', *L.* × *intermedia* 'Alba'
'Alba' ambig.	CSev CWib SIde SPer SWat WEas WPer
'Alexandra'PBR	SBfd
× ***allardii*** (Gaston Allard Group) 'African Pride'	CPbn GBar
§ ***angustifolia***	CArn CBar CBcs CCVT CWCL CWib EBee ELau EPfP EWTr GKir GPoy LBuc LRHS MBri MGos MHer MREP MWat NPer NPri SAll SBfd SLim SPlb SVic WClo WFar
– 'Alba' misapplied	see *L. angustifolia* 'Blue Mountain White'
§ – 'Alba'	CChe CPbn EPfP GPoy LBuc LSRN LTen MHer MRav MSwo NMen SBch SLon SPlb WDin WFar WJek
– 'Alba Nana'	see *L. angustifolia* 'Nana Alba'
– 'Arctic Snow'	CBcs CChe CEnt GKir LRHS LSRN MHer MSwo MWat NBPC NDov NGHP NGdn NLLv NPri SDnm SDow SIoW SPoG WLav
– 'Ashdown Forest'	CPbn CWan EBee GBar LRHS LSou MHer MLHP MNHC NGHP SBch SDow SIde SIoW SPer WHoo WJek WLav WSpi
– 'Beechwood Blue' ♀H4	CPbn SDow WLav
– 'Betty's Blue'	SDow
– Blue Cushion = 'Lavandula Schola'PBR	EPfP LRHS LSRN MAsh SDow WFar WLav
– Blue Ice = 'Dow3'	CWSG LSou MTis NBPC NGHP SDow SLim WLav
– 'Blue Mountain'	GBar
§ – 'Blue Mountain White'	NLLv SDow WLav
– 'Blue Rider'	EWTr LRHS MTis SWal
– 'Blue River'PBR	WFar
– Blue Scent = 'Syngablusc'	LRHS
– 'Bowles's Grey'	see *L. angustifolia* 'Bowles's Early'
– 'Bowles's Variety'	see *L. angustifolia* 'Bowles's Early'
§ – 'Bowles's Early'	CPbn GBar NGHP SAga WFar
– 'Cedar Blue'	CPbn CSev CWan ELau EPfP GBar MHer NGHP SBfd SDow SHDw SIde SIoW WFar WJek WLav
– 'Coconut Ice'PBR	CWCL CWSG NLLv SIoW SPoG WLav WSpi
– 'Compacta'	CPbn SDow WLav
– 'Crystal Lights'PBR	SIoW
– 'Dwarf Blue'	CPbn EPfP LSRN MBrN WFar
– 'Eastgrove Dome'	WEas
– 'Elizabeth'	LRHS LSRN SDow SPoG SRGP WClo WLav
– 'Ellagance Ice'	LRHS
– 'Folgate'	CArn CBar CPbn CWCL EBee ECtt ELau EPfP GBar LSou MHer MNHC NGHP SAll SDow SIde SIoW WFar WHoo WJek WLav WMnd
– 'Fring A'	SDow
– Garden Beauty = 'Lowmar'	LBuc LRHS NPri
– 'Granny's Bouquet'	LSRN LSou SBfd SIoW WSpi
§ – 'Hidcote' ♀H4	Widely available
– 'Hidcote Pink'	CEnt CPbn CWCL CWib EBee EPfP GBar LSRN LSou MHer MNHC MRav NGHP SDow SPer SWat WFar WMnd WPer
– 'Hidcote Superior'	LBMP
– 'Imperial Gem' ♀H4	Widely available
– 'Jean Davis'	see *L. angustifolia* 'Rosea'
– 'Lady'	NPer SBfd SHDw WPer
– 'Lady Ann'	CWCL NLLv SDow SIoW WLav
– 'Lavenite Petite'PBR	EPfP LLHF LRHS LSRN NBPC NGHP NLLv NLar SDow SIoW SPoG SVil WLav
– Little Lady = 'Batlad'	EBee ECtt EPfP LAst LRHS LSRN MAsh MSwo NBPC NGHP NLLv NLar SAll SIoW WLav
– Little Lottie = 'Clarmo' ♀H4	CPbn CWCL EBee ELon EPfP GBar LSRN MHer SCoo SDow SIde SWvt WLav
– 'Loddon Blue' ♀H4	CEnt CPbn EBee EPfP GBar GKir LRHS NGHP SDow SIde SIoW WLav
§ – 'Loddon Pink' ♀H4	CPbn CWan EBee ELan EPfP GBar GKir GMaP LAst LRHS MAsh MLHP MMuc MNHC MRav NGHP SEND WEas WFar WLav
– 'Maillette'	CPbn NGHP SDow SIde SIoW SPet SWal WLav
– 'Mellisa Lilac'PBR	CBcs CSBt GKir LRHS LSRN LSou MGos MHer SDow SIoW SPoG SRkn WLav
– 'Miss Donnington'	see *L. angustifolia* 'Bowles's Early'
– 'Miss Katherine'PBR ♀H4	CWCL EBee ECtt ELan EPfP LHop LRHS LSRN MAsh NBPC NGHP NLar SDow SEND SIoW SPer SPoG WLav
– Miss Muffet = 'Scholmis' ♀H4	CWCL EBee LLHF SDow WLav
– 'Munstead'	Widely available
§ – 'Nana Alba' ♀H4	CArn CMea CPbn CWan EBee ECha ELan ELon EPfP GBar GMaP GPoy LAst LRHS MAsh MHer MNHC MWat NGHP SDow SPer SWvt WEas WHoo WJek
– 'No 9'	SDow
– 'Pacific Blue'	GKir LRHS
– 'Peter Pan'	CPbn CWCL ECtt ELau LSRN MHer NDov NGHP NGdn SBch SDow SIoW WLav
– 'Princess Blue'	CPbn EBee ELan GBar LRHS MAsh SAga SDow SIde SIoW WFar WLav WPer
– 'Rêve de Jean-Claude'	WLav
§ – 'Rosea'	Widely available
– 'Royal Purple'	CBcs CPbn EBee EWes GBar LRHS LSou NGHP SDow SIde SIoW SWvt WLav WRHF
– 'Royal Velvet'	SDow
– 'Saint Jean'	CPbn SDow
– 'Silver Mist'	EPfP GGar LTen WHer
– 'Thumbelina Leigh'PBR	SDow
– 'Twickel Purple'	CWCL EBee EPfP GKir LAst LHop LRHS LSRN MAsh MNHC MRav NGHP SBfd SDow SIde SPer SWat SWvt WFar WLav
– 'Walberton's Silver Edge'	see *L.* × *intermedia* Walberton's Silver Edge
– 'Wendy Carlile' ♀H4	EPfP SIoW WClo WLav
– 'White Horse'	NGHP
aristibracteata	MHer WLav
§ 'Avonview'	CBcs CWCL GBar MHer NGHP SDow WHoo WLav
'Badsey Starlite'	WLav
'Ballerina'	CWCL SDow
§ 'Bee Brilliant'PBR	LRHS WLav
§ 'Bee Cool'PBR	MHer NLLv WLav
§ 'Bee Happy'	CWCL NBir NLLv WJek WLav
§ 'Bee Pretty'	LRHS

	'Blue Star'	EBee EPfP GBar LRHS NGHP SAll WFar WGwG
	'Bowers Beauty'	LRHS
	buchii var. ***buchii***	CPbn SDow WLav
	- var. ***gracilis***	CSpe
	Butterfly Garden = 'Avenue'PBR	CWSG SIoW
	canariensis	MHer SDow SPet WLav
	× ***chaytoriae*** 'Gorgeous'	SDow
	- 'Richard Gray' ♀H3-4	CArn EBee GBar LSRN MHer MNHC NCGa NGHP SBfd SDnm SDow SLim SSvw WAbe WLav WMnd
§	- 'Sawyers' ♀H4	Widely available
	- 'Silver Sands'	LSRN LSou SBfd SPoG
	× ***christiana***	CArn CPbn EBee GBar LRHS MGos NGHP SBfd SDow SHDw WJek WKif WLav
	'Cornard Blue'	see *L.* × *chaytoriae* 'Sawyers'
	dentata	CEnt CPbn CSev EBee GBar GCal MNHC MRav SEND SGar SMrm WJek
§	- var. ***candicans***	CSev EBee GBar MHer MNHC NLLv SAga SBch SBfd SDow WJek WLav
	- var. ***dentata*** 'Dusky Maiden'	CPbn CWCL SDow WLav
	- - 'Linda Ligon' (v)	CBow CPbn GBar WGwG WLav
	- - 'Ploughman's Blue'	CPbn CWCL WGwG WLav
	- - f. ***rosea***	SDow WLav
	- - 'Royal Crown' ♀H2-3	CPbn MHer WFar WLav
	- - 'Serenity'	WClo
	- - 'Silver Queen'	WLav
	- silver-leaved	see *L. dentata* var. *candicans*
	'Devonshire Compact'	CAlb CSBt CWCL LRHS WJek
	'Devonshire Compact White'	CWCL
	'Fathead'	CBcs CChe CPbn CWCL EBee ECtt ELan EPfP EWTr GBar LRHS LSRN LSou MGos MHer MNHC MTis NBir NEgg NGHP NPri SCoo SDow SIoW SLim SPet SPoG WBrE WJek
	× ***ginginsii*** 'Goodwin Creek Grey'	CPbn CSpe MHer NLLv SDow WGwG WLav
	'Hazel'	EPfP LRHS
	'Helmsdale'PBR	Widely available
	heterophylla misapplied	see *L.* × *heterophylla* Viv. Gaston Allard Group
§	***heterophylla*** Viv. Gaston Allard Group	GBar NGHP NLLv WLav
	'Hidcote Blue'	see *L. angustifolia* 'Hidcote'
§	× ***intermedia***	WFar
	- 'Abrialii'	GBar NLLv SDow WLav
§	- 'Alba' ♀H4	CArn CBot CMea CPbn EPfP GBar MHer MMuc MNHC SAga SDow SEND
*	- 'Alexis'	WLav
	- 'Arabian Night'	see *L.* × *intermedia* 'Impress Purple', 'Sussex'
	- 'Chaix'	GBar
§	- Dutch Group	CArn CSBt CWan CWib EBee EPfP GBar MAsh MRav MSwo SBfd SCoo SDow SLim SPer SPoG SWat WFar WPer
	- 'Edelweiss'	CBar CPbn CWan EBee EPfP GKir LRHS LSou MRav MTis NEgg NGHP NLLv SAll SDow SWal WClo WLav
	- 'Fragrant Memories'	CPbn EBee EPfP GBar NGHP SDow SIde WLav
	- Goldburg = 'Burgoldeen' (v)	CBow EPfP MCCP MGos MRav MWat WLav
	- 'Grappenhall' misapplied	see *L.* × *intermedia* 'Pale Pretender'
	- 'Grey Hedge'	CPbn CWan NGHP SAga WLav

	- 'Gros Bleu'	CPbn SDow WLav
	- 'Grosso'	Widely available
	- 'Hidcote Giant' ♀H4	CArn CPbn EPfP GBar LRHS NPer SDow WKif WLav
§	- 'Impress Purple'	CPbn GBar MNHC NLLv SDow WLav
	- 'Lullingstone Castle'	CBod CPbn GBar NGHP SDow SIoW WGwG WJek WLav
	- 'Old English' misapplied	see *L.* × *intermedia* 'Seal'
	- 'Old English'	CPbn GBar SDow WCom
	- Old English Group	CArn CBod ELau MMuc MNHC SEND WHoo WJek WLav
§	- 'Pale Pretender'	CArn CPbn CSBt CSam CTri EBee GBar GKir LRHS LSou MHer MSwo NGHP SDow SPer SWal WFar WJek WMnd WPnn
§	- 'Seal'	CArn CPbn ELau GBar GMaP MNHC NGHP SDow SPoG WFar WJek WMnd
	- 'Sumian'	WLav
§	- 'Sussex' ♀H4	CPbn GBar SDow WLav
	- 'Twickel Purple'	CPbn CWib ECtt EWes LSRN NGHP SWat WJek WMnd
§	- Walberton's Silver Edge = 'Walvera' (v)	CBow CPbn CSBt EPfP LBuc LRHS MGos MWat NEgg SBfd SCoo SDow SIde SIoW SLim SPoG
	'Jamboree'	WLav
	'Jean Davis'	see *L. angustifolia* 'Rosea'
	lanata ♀H3	CBot ECha GPoy MHer WJek WLav
§	***latifolia***	CArn NHol
I	'Lavender Lace'	CWSG LSRN NGHP SCoo
	'Loddon Pink'	see *L. angustifolia* 'Loddon Pink'
	'Madrid Blue'	see *L.* 'Bee Happy'
	'Madrid Pink'	see *L.* 'Bee Pretty'
	'Madrid Purple'PBR	see *L.* 'Bee Brilliant'
	'Madrid White'PBR	see *L.* 'Bee Cool'
	'Marshwood'PBR	CTri EBee EPfP SCoo SDow SIde SIoW SLim
	minutolii	CPbn SDow
	multifida	CPbn CSev MHer NLLv WLav
	- 'Blue Wonder'	CPbn IFro
	officinalis	see *L. angustifolia*
	'Passionné'	CWSG LRHS MGos WClo WLav
§	***pedunculata*** subsp. ***pedunculata*** ♀H3-4	Widely available
	- - 'James Compton'	CWib ECha LRHS MAsh NBir
	- - 'Wine'	CBcs WLav
	- subsp. ***sampaiana*** 'Purple Emperor'	LRHS WLav
	- - 'Roman Candles'	WLav
	pinnata	CPbn CSev EPfP GBar LRHS MHer MNHC SDow SPoG
	'Pink Perfume'	CPbn
	'Pippa White'	NLLv
	'Pretty Polly'	CBcs LRHS LSou NBPC NGHP NLLv SDow SIoW SRkn WLav
	'Pukehou'	EPfP GBar LRHS NLLv SCoo SDow SIoW WLav
	'Regal Splendour'PBR	CSBt CWCL CWit ECtt ELan EPfP LRHS LSRN LSou MAsh MGos MHer MNHC NGHP NLLv NPri SCoo SDow SIoW SLim SPoG WClo WLav
	Rocky Road = 'Fair09'PBR	CPbn LRHS LSRN MAsh MGos NBPC NGHP NLLv SDow SIoW SRkn WLav
	'Rosea'	see *L. angustifolia* 'Rosea'
	rotundifolia	MHer SDow
	'Roxlea Park'	CWCL WLav
	'Russian Anna'	LSRN
	'Saint Brelade'	CPbn CWCL EPfP GBar LRHS NLLv SDow WLav

	'Silver Edge'	see *L.* × *intermedia* Walberton's Silver Edge
	'Somerset Mist'	WLav
N	***spica*** nom. rejic.	see *L. angustifolia*, *L. latifolia*, *L.* × *intermedia*
	- 'Hidcote Purple'	see *L. angustifolia* 'Hidcote'
	stoechas 🏆$^{H3-4}$	Widely available
	- var. ***albiflora***	see *L. stoechas* subsp. *stoechas* f. *leucantha*
	- 'Anouk'^{PBR}	LRHS SPoG
	- 'Antibles' (Provençal Series)	SVil
	- 'Arles' (Provençal Series)	SVil
	- 'Avignon' (Provençal Series)	SVil
	- (Barcelona Series) 'Barcelona Pink'	CPbn
	- - 'Barcelona Rose'	CPbn CWCL
	- - 'Barcelona White'	CPbn CWCL
	- 'Blueberries and Cream'	LRHS LSou NGHP
	- 'Blueberry Ruffles' (Ruffles Series)	SIoW
	- 'Boysenberry Ruffles' (Ruffles Series)	LRHS LSRN SIoW
	- 'Lace'	LSRN WLav
	- Lilac Wings = 'Prolil'^{PBR}	EPfP LLHF LRHS LSRN NGHP WLav
	- (Little Bee Series) Little Bee Blue and White = 'Florvendula Blue White' **new**	MTis
	- - Little Bee Lilac = 'Florvendula Lilac'	CWSG LRHS MTis
	- - Little Bee Rose = 'Florvendula Rose'	CWSG LRHS MHer MTis
	- subsp. ***luisieri*** 'Tickled Pink'^{PBR}	CWCL ECtt ELan NGHP SDnm
	- 'Madrid Rose'	NLLv
	- 'Mulberry Ruffles' (Ruffles Series)	SIoW WClo WHlf
	- 'Night of Passion' **new**	LRHS SDow
	- 'Papillon'	see *L. pedunculata* subsp. *pedunculata*
	- 'Peachberry Ruffles' (Ruffles Series)	SIoW
	- subsp. ***pedunculata***	see *L. pedunculata* subsp. *pedunculata*
	- 'Purley'	CWan
	- 'Raspberry Ruffles' (Ruffles Series)	SIoW
	- 'Rocky Red'	LSRN
	- 'Silver Anouk' **new**	LRHS
§	- subsp. ***stoechas*** f. ***leucantha***	CArn CBot CPbn CSev CWCL CWan CWib ECha EPfP GBar LRHS MNHC MSwo MWat SBfd SDow SPer WClo WFar
	- - - 'Snowman'	CBcs CChe CPbn CSBt EBee EGxp EPfP LRHS MHer MWat NBPC NGHP SBfd SCoo SIoW SLim SPer SPoG SWvt WDin WFar
	- - 'Liberty'	CWCL NLLv SDow WLav
	- - 'Provençal'	LRHS
	- - 'Purple Wings'	CPbn EPfP LRHS LSou MAsh MGos SLim SRkn
	- - f. ***rosea*** 'Kew Red'	CBcs CMea CTri CWCL CWan EBee GGar LBMP LSRN MGos MHer MNHC NBPC NGHP SDnm SDow SIoW SLim SPet SPoG SWvt WGwG WJek WLav
	- 'Sugarberry Ruffles' (Ruffles Series)	SIoW
	- 'Victory'	LRHS SPoG
	- 'With Love'	LRHS SDow

	'Sugar Plum'	WLav
	Tiara = 'Fair 10'	CPbn CSBt EPfP LRHS LSRN NBPC NGHP NLLv NPri SCoo SDow SIoW SLim SPoG WLav
	'Van Gogh'	SDow
	vera misapplied	see *L.* × *intermedia* Dutch Group
	vera DC.	see *L. angustifolia*
	viridis	CArn CChe CPbn CPla ELan ELau ELon EPfP MHer MNHC NLLv NPer SDow WAbe WJek WLav
	'Whero Iti'	SDow
	'Willow Vale' 🏆$^{H3-4}$	CMea CPbn CTri CWCL EBee EPfP GBar LRHS LSRN MAsh MHer MLHP NLLv SAga SDow SIoW SWvt WJek
	'Willowbridge Calico'^{PBR}	SIoW WClo WLav

Lavatera (*Malvaceae*)

	arborea	CArn SChr SEND WHer
	- 'Rosea'	see *L.* × *clementii* 'Rosea'
	- 'Variegata' (v)	CBow ELan NPer NSti SDix SEND SGar WCom WCot WEas WHil WTou
	bicolor	see *L. maritima*
	cachemiriana	CBod EQua MLLN NBir NPer WPer
	Chamallow = 'Inovera'^{PBR}	CWit EBee EPfP LBuc LRHS LSRN LSou MGos SPoG
	× ***clementii*** 'Barnsley'	Widely available
	- 'Barnsley Baby'	EBee LBuc LRHS NLar NPer NPri SPer
	- 'Blushing Bride'	CDoC CWCL EBee ELon EPfP GKir LBMP LRHS LSRN MAsh MBri MGos NLar SBfd SEND SPer SPoG
	- 'Bredon Springs' 🏆$^{H3-4}$	CBar CDoC CDul CSBt CWCL CWSG EBee ECha ECtt EPfP LHop LRHS LSRN MAsh MMuc MSwo NHol NLar SEND SLim SPer SWvt WFar WHar
	- 'Burgundy Wine' 🏆$^{H3-4}$	Widely available
	- 'Candy Floss' 🏆$^{H3-4}$	CAlb CWCL EBee EPfP LRHS MAsh MGos NBir NLar NPer WDin
	- 'Kew Rose'	CDoC CTri EBee EPfP LRHS MMuc MSwo NPer SEND SLim SRms
	- 'Lavender Lady'	ECtt GKir LHop NPer SEND
	- 'Lisanne'	LRHS MSwo NHol
	- 'Mary Hope'	EPfP LRHS MAsh
	- Memories = 'Stelav'	CHid EBee EPfP GBin LRHS LSRN NLar SLim
	- 'Pavlova'	CPLG
§	- 'Rosea' 🏆$^{H3-4}$	CBcs CDul CMac CWSG EBee ECtt EPfP GGar GKir LAst LRHS LSRN MAsh MGos NBir NEgg NHol NPri SBfd SLon SPer SPoG SWvt WBVN WDin WFar
	- 'Shorty'	WFar
§	- 'Wembdon Variegated' (v)	NPer
	'Dorothy'	MCot
	'Grey Beauty'	LHop MAsh
§	***maritima*** 🏆$^{H2-3}$	CBot CDoC CMHG CMac CPLG CRHN EBee ECtt ELan EPfP LHop LRHS MCot SBfd SEND SPer SPoG SUsu SWvt WCFE WCom WFar WKif WSHC
	- 'Princesse de Lignes'	MGos
	oblongifolia	CBot
N	***olbia***	CTri SPlb SRms
	- 'Eye Catcher'	CWit EBee IVic LRHS MSwo NLar SPer SPoG SWal
	- 'Lilac Lady'	EBee ECha ELan EPfP LRHS LSou MAsh MCCP MGos MWte SLim SPer WFar WKif WSHC

§	- 'Pink Frills'	CBot EBee MGos SMrm SWvt WCot WSHC WWlt
	'Peppermint Ice'	see *L. thuringiaca* 'Ice Cool'
	'Pink Frills'	see *L. olbia* 'Pink Frills'
	'Rosea'	see *L.* × *clementii* 'Rosea'
	'Sweet Dreams'PBR	NLar
N	***thuringiaca***	GCal NNor WFar
§	- 'Ice Cool'	CBot ECha ECtt GCal MGos NDov SWvt WFar
	- Red Rum = 'Rigrum'PBR	CChe CMac EBee EPfP GBin LAst LBuc LLHF LRHS LSRN MAsh NEgg NHol NLar NPri SEND SHar SLim SPoG SWvt WFar WHar
	'Variegata'	see *L.* × *clementii* 'Wembdon Variegated'
	'White Angel'PBR	NDov

Ledebouria (*Hyacinthaceae*)

	adlamii	see *L. cooperi*
	concolor misapplied	see *L. socialis*
§	***cooperi***	CDes CYeo EBee ECho EDAr ELan ITim LEdu LHop SUsu WBor WHil WPGP WPrP
	ovalifolia new	ECho
§	***socialis***	CBgR CSWP ECho LToo MCot SBHP SBch SPet STre
	violacea	see *L. socialis*

× *Ledodendron* (*Ericaceae*)

§	'Arctic Tern' ♀H4	CDoC CSBt CTri ECho GGar GQui LMil LRHS MGos MLea NHol NWCA SPer

Ledum (*Ericaceae*)

	glandulosum SIN 1828	GLin
§	***groenlandicum***	GGar MLea NLar SPer WBVN WDin WFar WSHC
	- 'Compactum'	EBee IVic NLar SPoG WFar
	- 'Helma'	IVic NLar
	- 'Lenie'	NLar
	palustre	COld GGGa GPoy NLar WThu

Legousia (*Campanulaceae*)

	pentagonica 'Midnight Stars'	CSpe

Leiophyllum (*Ericaceae*)

	buxifolium ♀H4	EPfP NLar SSpi WThu
	- var. ***hugeri***	GBin GGar GKev
	- 'Maryfield'	WAbe

Lembotropis see *Cytisus*

Lemna (*Lemnaceae*)

	gibba	NPer
	minor	CWat LPBA MSKA NPer SWat
	trisulca	CWat EHon LPBA MSKA NPer SWat

lemon see *Citrus limon*

lemon balm see *Melissa officinalis*

lemon grass see *Cymbopogon citratus*

lemon verbena see *Aloysia citridora*

Leonotis (*Lamiaceae*)

	leonitis	see *L. ocymifolia*
	leonurus	CBcs CBod CCCN CDTJ CHEx CHGN CHll CTrC ECre EPfP EShb EWes LRHS SGar SMad SPoG WHil
	- var. ***albiflora***	CCCN EShb
	nepetifolia	CCCN SDnm SPav
	var. ***nepetifolia*** 'Staircase'	
§	***ocymifolia***	CCCN CPLG LSou SMrm WPGP
	- var. ***raineriana***	CHll

Leontice (*Berberidaceae*)

	albertii	see *Gymnospermium albertii*

Leontochir (*Amaryllidaceae*)

	ovallei	CCCN

Leontodon (*Asteraceae*)

	autumnalis	EBWF NMir
	hispidus	EBWF NMir
§	***rigens***	EBee MLHP MMuc MNrw NBid NBir SDix SMad SMrm WFar WMoo WPrP
	- 'Girandole'	see *L. rigens*

Leontopodium (*Asteraceae*)

	alpinum	CTri CWib ECho EPfP GAbr GKir LRHS NPri NWCA SPlb SPoG SRms WPer WTou
	- 'Mignon'	CMea ECho EWes GEdr GMaP WAbe WClo WFar WHoo
	- subsp. ***nivale***	GKev
	coreanum	EBee GKev
	kamtschaticum	ECho
§	***ochroleucum*** var. ***campestre***	MDKP NLar
	palibinianum	see *L. ochroleucum* var. *campestre*

Leonurus (*Lamiaceae*)

	artemisia	see *L. japonicus*
	cardiaca	CArn CWan EBWF GBar GPWP GPoy MHer MNHC SIde WHfH
§	***japonicus***	CArn MMuc
	macranthus	EFEx
	- var. ***alba***	EFEx
	sibiricus misapplied	see *L. japonicus*
	sibiricus L.	CArn CWit GCal SSvw
	turkestanicus	EBee

Leopoldia (*Hyacinthaceae*)

	comosa	see *Muscari comosum*
	spreitzenhoferi	see *Muscari spreitzenhoferi*
	tenuiflora	see *Muscari tenuiflorum*

Lepechinia (*Lamiaceae*)

	bella	SDys
	chamaedryoides	CHll CPLG CSpe WHil
	floribunda	CSev
	fragans new	WHil
	hastata	CDoC CMdw CPom CSpe IMou MSpe MWea SBHP WJek WWlt
	salviae misapplied	see *S. hastata*
	salviae Lindl. (Epling)	CDTJ EPPr SEND SUsu

Lepidium (*Brassicaceae*)

	campestre	CArn
	latifolium	CArn LEdu

Lepidothamnus (*Podocarpaceae*)

§	***laxifolius***	WThu

Lepidozamia (*Zamiaceae*)

	peroffskyana	CBrP LPal

Leptecophylla (*Epacridaceae*)

§	***juniperina***	ECou
	- 'Nana'	WThu

§ - subsp. ***parvifolia***	ECou

Leptinella (*Asteraceae*)

§ ***atrata***	ECho
- subsp. ***luteola***	EBee ECho EPfP GEdr
'County Park'	ECho ECou EDAr MMuc
dendyi	ECho ECou EWes GEdr MHer NMen NSla WOut
dioica	CTrC GBin
filicula	ECou
hispida	see *Cotula hispida* (DC.) Harv.
§ ***minor***	ECou EDAr WMoo
pectinata subsp. ***villosa*** CC 475	NWCA
§ ***potentillina***	CTri EBee ECha ECho EHoe GBin GEdr MBNS NLar NRya SRms WMoo WPer WPtf
§ ***pyrethrifolia***	EBee ECho EDAr GEdr GGar NMen
- 'Macabe'	ECou
§ ***rotundata***	ECou
§ ***serrulata***	ECho
§ ***squalida***	ECha ECho EDAr EPPr GBin MWat NLar NRya STre WMoo
§ - 'Platt's Black'	Widely available
traillii	GGar MMuc

Leptocarpus (*Restionaceae*)

similis	ECou
- BR 70	GGar

Leptocodon (*Campanulaceae*)

gracilis	EWld IGor
- HWJK 2155	WCru

Leptopteris (*Osmundaceae*)

hymenophylloides	WRic
superba	WRic

Leptospermum ✿ (*Myrtaceae*)

argenteum	CBcs
'Centaurus'	CTrC WFar
citratum	see *L. petersonii*
'Confetti'	ECou
'Copper Sheen'	CBcs CTrC
'County Park Blush'	ECou ELon
cunninghamii	see *L. myrtifolium*
'Electric Red' (Galaxy Series)	CTrC CWit IVic LRHS SLim
ericoides	see *Kunzea ericoides*
flavescens misapplied	see *L. glaucescens*
flavescens Sm.	see *L. polygalifolium*
§ ***glaucescens***	ECou SPlb
§ ***grandiflorum***	CTrC ELan EPfP GGar SOWG SSpi WSHC
grandifolium	ECou
'Havering Hardy'	ECou
humifusum	see *L. rupestre*
juniperinum	CTrC SPlb
'Karo Pearl Star'	CBcs
'Karo Spectrobay' PBR	CBcs
laevigatum 'Yarrum'	ECou
§ ***lanigerum***	CBcs CMHG CPLG CTrC CTri ECou EPfP GAbr SOWG SPoG
- 'Cunninghamii'	see *L. myrtifolium*
- 'Wellington'	ECou
liversidgei	CChe ECou IVic
macrocarpum	SOWG
minutifolium	ECou
morrisonii	ECou
§ ***myrtifolium***	CTrC CTri ECou EPla EWes SOWG SPer WPat
- 'Newnes Forest'	ECou
myrtifolium × ***scoparium***	ECou
nitidum	CTrC ECou SOWG SPlb
- 'Cradle'	ECou
§ ***petersonii***	CArn ECou EOHP EShb MHer SOWG
- 'Chlorinda'	ECou
phylicoides	see *Kunzea ericoides*
'Pink Surprise'	ECou SOWG
§ ***polygalifolium***	CTrC ECou SPlb SRms
prostratum	see *L. rupestre*
pubescens	see *L. lanigerum*
'Red Cascade'	SWvt
rodwayanum	see *L. grandiflorum*
rotundifolium	CTrC ECou
§ ***rupestre*** ♀H4	CDoC CTrC CTri ECou EPot NHar SPlb SRms WFar WSHC
rupestre × ***scoparium***	ECou
scoparium	CArn CTsd ECou ELau ERom EUJe GPWP MNHC SPlb WDin WJek
- 'Adrianne'	ELan EPfP LRHS MRav
- 'Album'	CTrC
- 'Appleblossom'	CTrC SLim
- 'Autumn Glory'	CWSG EBee SLim
- 'Avocet'	ECou
- 'Big Red'	MMuc
- 'Black Robin'	SOWG
- 'Blossom' (d)	CBcs CMac CTrC ECou SOWG
- 'Burgundy Queen' (d)	CBcs CMac CSBt CTrC ECou
- 'Chapmanii'	CMHG EBee GGar
- 'Coral Candy'	CBcs CWit MMuc SEND SOWG
- 'County Park Pink'	ECou
- 'County Park Red'	ECou
- 'Crimson Glory' (d)	CSBt CWit
- 'Dove Lake'	WAbe
- 'Elizabeth Jane'	GGar
- 'Essex'	ECou
- 'Fantasia'	ECou
- 'Fred's Red'	NLAp WPat
- 'Gaiety Girl' (d)	CSBt
- var. ***incanum***	CTrC ECou SOWG
'Keatleyi' ♀H3	
- - 'Sherryl Lee' **new**	CTrC
- - 'Wairere'	ECou
- 'Jubilee' (d)	CBcs CMac SEND SLim
- 'Kerry'	CAbP
- 'Lambethii'	MAsh
- 'Leonard Wilson' (d)	CTri ECou
- 'Lyndon'	ECou
- 'Martini'	CDoC CMac CSBt CTrC EPfP GAbr LRHS SOWG WGwG
- 'McLean'	ECou
- 'Moko'	ECou
- (Nanum Group) 'Kea'	CBcs ECou MHer MMuc MRav SEND
- - 'Kiwi' ♀H3	CAbP CCCN CDoC CDul CSBt CTrC CWSG ECou ELan ELon EPfP EWes GQui LRHS MAsh SLim SPad WFar
- - 'Nanum'	ECou NMen
- - 'Pipit'	EWes ITim WAbe
- - 'Tui'	CSBt CTrC ECou
- 'Nichollsii' ♀H3	CTrC GQui SOWG WSHC
- 'Nichollsii Nanum' ♀H2-3	ITim NLAp SRms WAbe WPat WThu
- 'Pink Cascade'	CBcs CMac CTrC CWib GAbr SEND SLim
- 'Pink Damask'	IVic SLim SWvt
- 'Pink Falls'	ECou
- 'Pink Frills'	ECou
- 'Pink Queen'	LRHS
- 'Pink Splash'	ECou
- 'Pom Pom'	LRHS

- var. ***prostratum*** hort.	see *L. rupestre*
- 'Red Damask' (d) ΨH3	CBcs CChe CDoC CDul CMac CPLG CTrC CTri CWSG CWib EBee EHoe ELan EPfP GAbr GGal GQui LRHS LSRN MDun MRav NPCo SOWG SPlb SPoG SRms SWvt WBrE WFar WSHC
- 'Red Falls'	CBcs CPLG CTrC ECou SOWG
- 'Redpoll'	ECou
- 'Roseum'	MRav
* - 'Ruby Wedding'	ELan EPfP LRHS LSRN MAsh SPoG
- var. ***scoparium***	EPot GGar
- 'Silver Spire'	SOWG
- 'Snow Flurry'	CBcs CTrC CWSG CWit EBee EPfP GAbr LRHS MMuc SEND SLim SPoG
- 'Snow White'	LRHS
- 'Wingletye'	ECou
- 'Winter Cheer' (d)	CBcs LRHS
- 'Wiri Joan' (d)	CBcs
- 'Wiri Linda'	CMac
- 'Zeehan'	ECou
sericeum	ECou SOWG
'Silver Sheen' ΨH3	CEnd ECou ELan EPfP LRHS MAsh NLar SPoG WPGP
'Snow Column'	ECou
spectabile	SOWG
sphaerocarpum	ECou
squarrosum	CTrC
turbinatum	ECou
- 'Thunder Cloud'	ECou
'Wellington Dwarf'	ECou

Leschenaultia (*Goodeniaceae*)

biloba	ECou
- 'Big Blue'	SOWG
- 'Sky Blue'	ECou
* 'Eldorado'	SOWG
formosa 'Scarlett O'Hara'	SOWG
hirsuta	SOWG

Lespedeza (*Papilionaceae*)

bicolor	CCCN CWit EBee ELon EWTr LRHS MMuc NPal SEND WDin WFar WSHC
buergeri	EPfP MMHG NLar WSHC
japonica	SPlb
thunbergii ΨH4	Widely available
- 'Albiflora'	CAbP EBee EPfP LRHS MWea SPoG WPGP WSHC
- 'Avalanche'	NLar
- 'Summer Beauty'	CBcs EBee EPPr EPfP LRHS MGos
- 'White Fountain'	LRHS
tiliifolia	see *Desmodium elegans*

Lesquerella (*Brassicaceae*)

alpina	GKev
arizonica new	GKev

Leucadendron (*Proteaceae*)

argenteum	CBcs CCCN CHEx CTrC SPlb
daphnoides	SPlb
discolor	SPlb
eucalyptifolium	CTrC SPlb
galpinii	CTrC
'Inca Gold'	CBcs CTrC SOWG
laureolum	CCCN
'Maui Sunset'	CTrC
'Mrs Stanley'	CTrC SOWG
'Safari Sunset'	CBcs CCCN CDoC CTrC EAmu SBig WCot
'Safari Sunshine'	CTrC
salicifolium	SPlb
salignum	CBcs CCCN
- 'Early Yellow'	CTrC
- 'Fireglow'	CDoC CTrC SOWG
strobilinum	CDoC CTrC

Leucanthemella (*Asteraceae*)

§ ***serotina*** ΨH4	Widely available
- 'Herbststern'	NLar

Leucanthemopsis (*Asteraceae*)

§ ***alpina***	ECho
hosmariensis	see *Rhodanthemum hosmariense*

Leucanthemum ✿ (*Asteraceae*)

'Angel'	NPri SPoG SVil
atlanticum	see *Rhodanthemum atlanticum*
catananche	see *Rhodanthemum catananche*
graminifolium	EPfP LRHS WPer
hosmariense	see *Rhodanthemum hosmariense*
mawii	see *Rhodanthemum gayanum*
maximum misapplied	see *L.* × *superbum*
§ ***maximum*** (Ramond) DC.	MMuc NBro NPer WSpi
- ***uliginosum***	see *Leucanthemella serotina*
nipponicum	see *Nipponanthemum nipponicum*
'Sunshine Peach' new	LBuc MWea
§ × ***superbum***	CMac MHer MLHP MMuc NVic SEND WFar
- 'Aglaia' (d) ΨH4	Widely available
- 'Alaska'	CAni CPLG CWCL EBee EBla EPfP GKir LAst LEdu LHop LRHS MCot NGdn SBfd SPer SPur SWvt WFar WPer WWEG
- 'Amelia'	NBre NLar SRGP
- 'Andernach' new	CAni
- 'Anita Allen' (d)	CAni CElw CFee CPrp EBee EBla MAvo NBre WCot WFar WPer WWEG
- 'Anna Camilla'	CAni
- 'Antwerp Star'	NBre NLar
- 'Banwell'	CAni
- 'Barbara Bush' (v/d)	EBee ECtt ELan NBir NCob SRGP SWvt
§ - 'Beauté Nivelloise'	CAni CBgR CCVN CPrp CWCL EBee EBla ECtt EPfP GBin MAvo MDKP MMuc MSpe NBPC NBre NCGa SWat WFar WPer WPrP WPtf WSpi WWEG
- 'Becky'	CMdw CWan EBee EBrs ECha ELon EPfP EWes LLHF LRHS LSou MAvo NBre SPoG SRGP SSvw WWEG
- 'Bishopstone'	CAni CSam EBee ELan LBMP LEdu MSpe NBre NCGa WEas WPer WWEG
- 'Brightside'	EBrs GQue LRHS
- Broadway Lights = 'Leumayel'PBR	EGxp LRHS SUsu WGrn
- 'Christine Hagemann'	CAni CPrp EBee EWes GBin MAvo MDKP MRav NCGa WWEG
- 'Cobham Gold' (d)	CAni CPrp CWCL NBre SUsu
- 'Coconut Ice'	WPer WWEG
- 'Colwall'	CAni WWEG
- 'Crazy Daisy'	CAni CMMP CTri CWib EBee LRHS NBre NLar NPri SWal SWvt WHrl WSpi WWEG
- 'Crazy Daisy Butterfly' new	LAst
- 'Devon Mist'	CAni
- 'Dipsy Daisy'	WPer

	- 'Droitwich Beauty'	CAni CBgR LLHF MAvo WBrk WCFE WHoo WWEG
	- 'Duchess of Abercorn'	CAni CSam
	- 'Dwarf Snow Lady'	NBre NLar
	- 'Easton Lady'	CAni CBgR
	- 'Eclipse'	CAni MAvo
	- 'Edgebrook Giant'	CAni MAvo WWEG
	- 'Edward VII'	CAni
	- 'Eisstern'	CDes EBee LEdu MAvo WWEG
	- 'Elworthy Sparkler'	CElw MAvo WWEG
	- 'Esther Read' (d)	Widely available
	- 'Etoile d'Anvers'	EBee
§	- 'Everest'	CAni CSam EBee NBre SRms WWEG
	- 'Exhibition'	NBre WWEG
	- 'Fiona Coghill' (d)	CAni CElw CPrp EAEE EBee EBla ECtt EPfP GBin LBMP LRHS MAvo MDKP MHer MSpe NBir NCGa NEgg NGdn NVic SPoG WCot WHoo WWEG
	- 'Firnglanz'	CAni GBin MAvo WWEG
	- 'Flore Pleno' (d) **new**	SPlb
	- 'Goldrausch'PBR	Widely available
	- 'Gruppenstolz'	CAni EBee GBin
	- 'H. Seibert'	CAni CBgR CPrp EBla MArl MAvo WWEG
	- 'Harry'	CAni
	- 'Highland White Dream'PBR	LRHS WFar
	- 'Horace Read' (d)	CAni CBgR CElw ELan NBir SAga SBch SWvt WEas WPer WSpi WWEG
	- 'Jennifer Read'	CAni CBgR MAvo MSpe WCot WWEG
§	- 'John Murray' (d)	CAni EShb EWes LSou MAvo MDKP MTis NBir SMrm WAbb WCot WWEG
	- 'Little Miss Muffet'	CBgR CSBt CWGN EAEE EBee EBla ECtt LAst LBMP LLHF LRHS MBNS NCGa WWEG
	- 'Little Princess'	see *L.* × *superbum* 'Silberprinzesschen'
	- 'Majestic'	CAni
	- 'Manhattan'	CAni CBgR CMdw EBee EBla EBrs EWes GBin NBre
	- 'Margaretchen'	CAni CDes EBee MAvo WWEG
	- 'Marion Bilsland'	CAni MDKP MSpe MTis NCGa NChi WBrk
	- 'Marion Collyer'	CAni
	- 'Mayfield Giant'	CAni CTri WPer
	- 'Mount Everest'	see *L.* × *superbum* 'Everest'
	- 'Octopus'	CAni MAvo WWEG
	- 'Old Court'	see *L.* × *superbum* 'Beauté Nivelloise'
	- 'Phyllis Smith'	Widely available
	- 'Polaris'	EBee EShb LRHS MBNS NBre WMoo WSpi
	- 'Rags and Tatters'	CAni EBee ECtt EWes MAvo WWEG
	- 'Rijnsburg Glory'	WPer
	- 'Schneehurken'	CAni CMac EBee EBla LLHF LSou MAvo MTis NCGa SPoG STes SUsu WCot WWEG
	- 'Schwabengruss'	CAni
	- 'Shaggy'	see *L.* × *superbum* 'Beauté Nivelloise'
§	- 'Silberprinzesschen'	CAni COlW CSBt EBee EBla EBrs EPfP GKir LRHS NEgg NPri SBfd SPlb SRms WFar WMoo WPer WWEG
	- 'Silver Spoon'	EPfP WPer
	- 'Snow Lady'	EBee EShb NEgg NPer NPri SBfd SRms WFar
	- 'Snowcap'	CHid CMac EBla EBrs ECha EPfP LRHS MBri MRav NEgg NGdn SPer SWvt WCAu WTin
	- 'Snowdrift'	CAni CBgR CMMP GKir MAvo NBre NLar SBfd WCot WPer WWEG
§	- 'Sonnenschein'	Widely available
	- 'Starburst' (d)	SPhx SRms
	- 'Stina'	EBee GBin MAvo
	- 'Summer Snowball'	see *L.* × *superbum* 'John Murray'
	- 'Sunny Killin'	CAni WTin
	- 'Sunny Side Up'PBR	EBee ECtt GMac MBri NBPC NCGa NLar WWEG
	- Sunshine	see *L.* × *superbum* 'Sonnenschein'
	- 'T.E. Killin' (d) 🏆H4	CElw CKno CPrp CSam EBee EBla ECha ECtt EPfP GKir GMaP LBMP LRHS MBri MRav SPoG WCot WFar WSpi WWEG WWlt
	- 'White Iceberg' (d)	CAni WPer
	- 'Wirral Pride'	CAni CBgR CCVN CHar EBee ELon EPfP MAvo MSpe WBrk WMnd WWEG
	- 'Wirral Supreme' (d) 🏆H4	Widely available
	'Tizi-n-Test'	see *Rhodanthemum catananche* 'Tizi-n-Test'
§	***vulgare***	CArn CMac CRWN EBWF EPfP GBar LEdu MHer MNHC NLan NMir NSco SBch SIde WHer WJek WMoo WSFF WShi
	- 'Avondale' (v)	NGdn
	- 'Filigran'	EBee EBrs EShb LRHS SIde
§	- 'Maikönigin'	EBee WHrl
	- May Queen	see *L. vulgare* 'Maikönigin'
	- 'Sunny'	CBre EBla EWes WAlt
	'White Knight'	EBee LRHS MBri MCCP NBre NPri

Leucochrysum (*Asteraceae*)

§	***albicans***	GGar

Leucocoryne (*Alliaceae*)

	alliacea	ECho
	'Andes'	CCCN ECho
	'Caravelle'	ECho
	hybrids	CGrW ECho
	ixioides	ECho
*	- ***alba***	ECho
	purpurea 🏆H1	CGrW ECho

Leucogenes (*Asteraceae*)

grandiceps	NSla WAbe
leontopodium	GGar NSla WAbe
tarahaoa	WAbe

Leucogenes × *Raoulia* see × *Leucoraoulia*

Leucojum ✿ (*Amaryllidaceae*)

aestivum	CBcs CBgR CFee CFox CMac CTri EBee ECGP ECho EPfP GCal LAma LHop LRHS MCot MMuc NEgg NHol SEND SMrm SPad SPer SRms WBor WCot WEas WFar WShi
- 'Gravetye Giant' 🏆H4	Widely available
autumnale	see *Acis autumnalis*
longifolium	see *Acis longifolia*
roseum	see *Acis rosea*
tingitanum	see *Acis tingitana*
trichophyllum	see *Acis trichophylla*
valentinum	see *Acis valentina*
vernum 🏆H4	Widely available
- var. ***carpathicum***	CLAP ECha ECho EHrv GEdr MRav NMen WAbe
- var. ***vagneri***	CLAP EBee ECha EHrv GEdr LRHS WSHC WTin

Leucophyllum (*Scrophulariaceae*)

frutescens	SOWG

Leucophysalis (*Solanaceae*)

sinense BWJ 8093	WCru

Leucophyta (*Asteraceae*)

§ ***brownii***	WCot

Leucopogon (*Epacridaceae*)

§ ***colensoi***	MBri WPat WThu
ericoides	GKev
§ ***fasciculatus***	ECou
§ ***fraseri***	ECou GEdr NHar WPat WThu
- bronze-leaved **new**	NHar
§ ***parviflorus***	ECou

× *Leucoraoulia* (*Asteraceae*)

hybrid (***Raoulia hectorii*** × ***Leucogenes grandiceps***)	GKev
§ ***loganii***	NWCA WAbe

Leucosceptrum (*Lamiaceae*)

canum	CPLG
- GWJ 9424	WCru
japonicum B&SWJ 10981	WCru
- 'Golden Angel'	WCot
stellipilum	EWld
var. ***formosanum***	
- - B&SWJ 1804	WCru
- - RWJ 9907	WCru
- var. ***tosaense*** B&SWJ 8892	WCru

Leucospermum (*Proteaceae*)

cordifolium	SOWG
'Scarlet Ribbon'	CCCN

Leucothoe (*Ericaceae*)

axillaris 'Curly Red' PBR	CBcs CWSG EBee ELan EPfP GKir IVic LBuc LRHS MAsh MCCP MGos MMHG NCGa NLar SBfd SPoG SWvt
- 'Scarletta'	see *L.* Scarletta
Carinella = 'Zebekot'	EPfP MGos NLar SBfd SPoG
davisiae	EPfP
§ ***fontanesiana*** ♀H4	CMCN CMac EPfP GGal GKir
- 'Rainbow' (v)	Widely available
- 'Rollissonii' ♀H4	MRav SRms
keiskei	EPfP
- 'Royal Ruby'	EPfP LSou MGos NEgg NLar SLim SPoG WDin WFar WMoo
Lovita = 'Zebonard'	EBee EPfP IVic LRHS MBri MGos MRav NHol NLar SBfd SCoo
populifolia	see *Agarista populifolia*
Red Lips = 'Lipsbolwi' PBR	CDoC EBee ELan EPfP IVic MGos NPla
§ Scarletta = 'Zeblid'	Widely available
walteri	see *L. fontanesiana*

Leuzea (*Asteraceae*)

centaureoides	see *Stemmacantha centaureoides*

Levisticum (*Apiaceae*)

officinale	CArn CBod CFox CHby CPrp CSev ELau EPfP GAbr GBar GGar GPoy LEdu MHer MNHC NGHP NPri SBfd SDix SEND SIde SPlb SVic SWat WHer WHfH WJek WPer

Lewisia ✿ (*Portulacaceae*)

'Archangel'	NRya
Ashwood Carousel hybrids	ECho LRHS MAsh NHar
'Ashwood Pearl'	MAsh
'Ben Chace'	MAsh
Birch strain	CBcs ECho ELan
brachycalyx ♀H2	ECho EWes LLHF MAsh MTho WPer
- pink	MAsh
brachycalyx × ***nevadensis*** 'Rosea'	GKev
cantelovii	MAsh
columbiana	MAsh NWCA WPer
- 'Alba'	GCrs MAsh WCom
- subsp. ***columbiana*** NNS 07-430	NWCA
- 'Rosea'	GKev NSla WGor
- subsp. ***rupicola***	LLHF MAsh NWCA
- subsp. ***wallowensis***	MAsh NMen NWCA
congdonii	MAsh
'Constant Comment'	SEND
cotyledon ♀H4	CWCL ECho EDAr GAbr GKev GKir LLHF LRHS WBrE WFar
- J&JA 12959	NWCA
- f. ***alba***	GKev MAsh NWCA
- - 'Snowstorm'	LLHF
- 'Ashwood Ruby'	MAsh
- Ashwood strain	ECho EPfP EWes LBee LRHS LSou MAsh SRms WGor
- 'Brannan Bar' **new**	MAsh
- 'Bright Eyes'	GKev
- var. ***cotyledon*** NNS 05-430 **new**	NWCA
- Crags hybrids	SRms
- double-flowered (d) **new**	GKev
- 'Fransi'	NLar
- var. ***howellii***	LLHF SRms WGor
- hybrid	ECho EPot GGar LHop SPoG SWal WCom WGor
- 'John's Special'	MAsh
- magenta-flowered	ECho MAsh WGor
§ - 'Regenbogen'	NWCA WGor WPer
- Sunset Group ♀H4	ECho EPfP LAst MHer NLar NWCA SBfd SRms SWal WClo WNew WPer WRHF
- violet-flowered	GKev
'George Henley'	ECho EPfP EPot EWes LLHF MAsh NMen NRya WAbe WCom WGor
leeana	MAsh
'Little Peach'	CPBP GCrs GGar GKev ITim WGor WPer
'Little Plum'	CMea CPBP ECho EDAr EPfP GCrs GGar GKev ITim LBMP LRHS MDKP NLar NRya NWCA WGor WPer
§ ***longipetala***	ECho
§ ***nevadensis***	ECho EDAr EPot GEdr GGar ITim LRHS MAsh MTho NMen NRya NWCA SRms WHoo WPer
I - 'Alba' **new**	GKev
- ***bernardina***	see *L. nevadensis*
- 'Rosea'	MAsh NWCA
oppositifolia	EDAr MAsh
- 'Richeyi'	GKev
'Phyllellia'	MAsh
'Pinkie'	CPBP EPot LLHF MAsh NMen
pygmaea	CWCL ECho EWes GCrs GEdr GGar ITim LAst LRHS MAsh MHer MWat NBir NMen NRya WPer
- subsp. ***longipetala***	see *L. longipetala*

Rainbow mixture	see *L. cotyledon* 'Regenbogen'
'Rawreth'	LLHF
rediviva	ECho EPot EWes GEdr GKev LLHF MAsh WAbe
- NNS 03.369	CPBP
'Rose Gem' **new**	EPot
sierrae	WPer
'Trevosia'	MAsh
tweedyi ♀[H2]	ECho EPfP EPot LHop LRHS MAsh NWCA WGor
- 'Alba'	MAsh WAbe
- 'Elliott's Variety'	MAsh NWCA WGor
- lemon-flowered **new**	NWCA
- 'Rosea'	ECho LHop LRHS NWCA WGor

Leycesteria (*Caprifoliaceae*)

crocothyrsos	CAbP CArn CBcs CHid CWib EBee ELan EPfP GAbr GKev LAst MDKP NLar SMad
formosa ♀[H4]	Widely available
- brown-stemmed	IFoB
- Golden Lanterns = 'Notbruce'[PBR]	CDoC CSBt EBee ELan EPfP EQua LBuc LRHS LSRN LTen MAsh MBri MGos MMHG MMuc NEgg NHol NLar SBfd SCoo SLim SPoG SWvt WBor WFar WMoo
- 'Golden Pheasant' (v)	CPMA EHoe MDun NExo
- 'Lydia' **new**	CWit
- 'Purple Rain'	CAlb EBee EQua EWes LBuc LRHS LTen NLar SBfd
'Gold Leaf'	CBow MDKP
'Smouldering Embers'	WGrn

Leymus (*Poaceae*)

from Falkland Islands	EPPr
§ ***arenarius***	Widely available
hispidus	see *Elymus hispidus*
'Niveus'	EHul

Lhotzkya see *Calytrix*

Liatris (*Asteraceae*)

aspera	EBee NBre NLar WPer
cylindracea	EBee
elegans	EBee EPfP NBre NLar SPlb WPer
ligulistylis	EBee NBPC NBre NLar WPer
mucronata	EBee NLar
punctata	EBee NBre NLar
pycnostachya	CRWN EBee NLar SRms WPer
scariosa 'Alba'	CMea NLar WPer
§ ***spicata***	Widely available
- 'Alba'	CMac CPrp CSBt CSpe EBee ECha ECtt ELan EPfP GKir LAma LAst LEdu LSRN MNFA MNrw NBPC NBre NGdn NLar SBfd SPer SPlb STes WBrE WPer
- ***callilepis***	see *L. spicata*
- 'Floristan Violett'	CFox CTri EBee EHrv EPfP GMaP LBMP LRHS MHer MLLN NEgg NLBP NLar NPri SCoo SPlb SPoG SUsu SWal SWvt WFar WGwG WMnd WMoo WPer WWEG
- 'Floristan Weiss'	CArn CFox CTri EBee EHrv EPPr EPfP GKir GMaP LBMP LRHS MHer MRav MWhi NBPC NCGa NLar NPri SPoG SWal SWvt WClo WFar WGwG WMnd WMoo WPer WWEG
- Goblin	see *L. spicata* 'Kobold'
§ - 'Kobold'	Widely available

Libanotis (*Umbelliferae*)

montana	see *Seseli libanotis*

Libertia ✿ (*Iridaceae*)

sp.	WPGP
HCM 98.089	CDes EBee
'Amazing Grace'	CDes EBee GCal GMac SBch WPGP
'Ballyrogan Blue'	CDes
* ***breunioides***	CDes CPLG EBee WPGP
caerulescens	CBgR CCCN CCVN COIW CPLG EBee ECho EPla EShb GGar GKev IFoB IGor LPio LRHS NBid NBir NCGa SGar SMad SMrm WCot WFar WHer WMoo WPGP
chilensis	see *L. formosa*
elegans	CPLG
§ ***formosa***	Widely available
- brown-stemmed	IFoB
grandiflora ♀[H4]	Widely available
- stoloniferous	GGar
ixioides	CBcs CBgR CHid CKno EBee ECha ECho ECou EShb GKev IFFs LEdu MCot NGdn NSti SBfd WPGP WRHF WSpi
- 'Goldfinger' (v)	CBgR CKno CMac CPLG CTrC CWit EBee EShb EWll LHop LRHS LSou MMHG MPkF NHol NOak NSti SBfd SGSe SHar SKHP SMad SRkn SWvt WClo WCot WGrn WHer WMoo
- hybrid	SDix
- 'Tricolor'	CPen EBee ECho GAbr GGar GKev MMuc WMoo WPat
'Nelson Dwarf'	EBee ECho GCal
paniculata	CPLG WSHC
peregrinans	Widely available
- 'Gold Leaf'	CBcs CBgR CBod CBow CCCN CChe CElw CPrp CSpe CTri CTsd CWGN EHrv ELon IFFs LAst LHop LRHS MRav NOak SMad SWvt WFar WHoo WMoo WViv
- 'Gold Stripe'	CHar EPPr
* ***procera***	CDes CSpe EBee LEdu LRHS SKHP WPGP WSHC
pulchella	EBee
- from Tasmania	ECho
sessiliflora	CElw CFee CPLG EBee ECho NBir WFar WPGP
- RB 94073	SMad
Shackleton hybrid	WFar
'Taupo Blaze'	CBcs CKno CMac CSpe CWGN EBee EWll IFFs LRHS LSRN LSou NCGa NHol SBfd SHar SKHP SPad SUsu
'Taupo Sunset'[PBR]	CCCN CMil CPLG EBee ELon ETod EWes GBin IVic LSou MBNS MLLN MPkF NBir NOak NPnk SBfd SKHP SWvt WClo WCot WSpi

Libocedrus (*Cupressaceae*)

chilensis	see *Austrocedrus chilensis*
decurrens	see *Calocedrus decurrens*

Libonia see *Justicia*

Licuala (*Arecaceae*)

spinosa	LPal

Ligularia ✿ (*Asteraceae*)

amplexicaulis GWJ 9404	WCru
'Britt Marie Crawford'[PBR]	Widely available
calthifolia	EBee
'Cheju Charmer'	ELon LEdu WCru WWEG
clivorum	see *L. dentata*

§	***dentata***	CRow CWit EBee ECtt GAuc GGal LBMP MMuc NBro NLar SBfd SRms SWat WFar
	- 'Dark Beauty'	CBcs EWll MMuc MWhi NBre WMnd
	- dark-leaved	WWEG
	- 'Desdemona' 𝕐^{H4}	Widely available
	- 'Enkelrig'	EBee
	- 'Megamona'	EBee
	- 'Midnight Lady' **new**	NBre
	- 'Orange Princess'	NPer WPer
	- 'Orange Queen'	NBre WFar
	- 'Othello'	Widely available
	- 'Sommergold'	ECha
	- 'Twilight'	ECtt MBNS
§	***fischeri***	CBct ECha LEdu NBre SGSe WPer
	- B&SWJ 1158	WFar
	- B&SWJ 2570	WCru
	- B&SWJ 4478	WCru
	'Gold Torch' **new**	ECtt
§	'Gregynog Gold' 𝕐^{H4}	CBct EBee EBrs ECha ECtt EPfP GAbr GKir GMaP LRHS LTen MRav MWhi MWts NBro NCGa NCob NGdn NLar SDnm SPav SPer WFar WWEG WWlt
	× ***hessei***	EBee GMaP LRHS MMuc NLar SWat WFar
	hodgsonii	CKno EBee EBla EPPr GKir LEdu WPer
	- B&SWJ 10855	WCru
	intermedia	WFar
	- B&SWJ 606a	WCru
	japonica	CHar CLAP CRow ECha GCra LEdu LMaj LRHS MWhi NLar WFar
	- B&SWJ 2883	WCru
	- 'Rising Sun'	CLAP CPLG WCru
	'Laternchen'^{PBR}	EBee GGar IBal LRHS MAsh MBri NBPC NMoo
	'Little Rocket'^{PBR}	EBee ECtt EKen GBin MAsh MBNS MBri NBro NLar
	macrophylla	CRow WFar
	'Osiris Café Noir' **new**	EBee MAsh
	'Osiris Fantaisie'	CAbb COIW CPLG EBee ECtt GBin ITim LLHF MAsh NMyG NSti SMad SUsu WBor WCot WCra WFut WRHF WWEG
	× ***palmatiloba***	see *L.* × *yoshizoeana* 'Palmatiloba'
§	***przewalskii*** 𝕐^{H4}	Widely available
	- 'Light Fingered'	NBre
	sibirica	CSam GAbr NLar WFar WMoo WPer WWEG
	- B&SWJ 5806	WCru
	- B&SWJ 5841	WCru
	- var. ***speciosa***	see *L. fischeri*
	smithii	see *Senecio smithii*
	speciosa	see *L. fischeri*
	stenocephala	EBee EBrs GKir LRHS MCot NBro NLar SWat WFar
	- B&SWJ 283	WCru
	'Sungold'	CBct CMac CSam EBee EBla EBrs ECtt GBin GKir LRHS NCGa NGdn
	tangutica	see *Sinacalia tangutica*
	'The Rocket' 𝕐^{H4}	Widely available
	tussilaginea	see *Farfugium japonicum*
	- 'Aureo-maculata'	see *Farfugium japonicum* 'Aureomaculatum'
	veitchiana	CBct CDoy CFir CRow EBee EBla EBrs EPfP GAbr GCal GGar LAst LEdu NCob SDnm SPav SWat WFar
	vorobievii	CSpr EBee GAbr GCal NLar
	'Weihenstephan'	GCal GKir
	wilsoniana	CBct CFir CHEx CRow EBee ECtt LLWG MMuc MRav NBre NMun SDnm SPav SWat WCAu WFar
§	× ***yoshizoeana*** 'Palmatiloba'	CHEx EBee EBla EBrs ELan ELon EPla GBee GCal GKir LEdu MRav SBfd SDnm SPhx SWat WCot WFar WWEG
	'Zepter'	CMHG EBee EBla ECtt GCal GQue LLWG MBNS MWhi NEgg NLar SMrm WFar WWEG

Ligusticum (*Apiaceae*)

	daucoides	WPrP
	lucidum	CMCN EBee EPfP IVic SPhx WPGP
	porteri	CArn
§	***scoticum***	CArn CElw EOHP EWTr EWes GBar GKir GPoy ILis ITim MCot MDKP MHer NBPC NLar NPnk NSti SGSe SPhx WFar WHrl WJek WPtf
	striatum B&SWJ 7259	WCru

Ligustrum ✿ (*Oleaceae*)

	chenaultii	see *L. compactum*
§	***compactum***	MBri NLar
§	***delavayanum***	CPLG EBtc EPfP EQua ERom MGos NLar SAPC SArc STrG WFar WSpi
	ibota	EBtc NLar
	ionandrum	see *L. delavayanum*
	japonicum	CHEx ECrN LRHS LTen SPer WDin WFar
I	- 'Aureum'	MGos
	- 'Coriaceum'	see *L. japonicum* 'Rotundifolium'
*	- 'Coriaceum Aureum'	EMil LRHS
	- 'Macrophyllum'	EPfP MAsh
§	- 'Rotundifolium'	CAbP CBcs CDoC CDul CFee CHEx CMac CPLG CSam EBee ELan EMil EPfP IDee IVic LRHS MAsh MGos MRav NLar SCoo SMad SPer SPoG WCFE WClo WFar
	- 'Silver Star' (v)	CPMA EBee MGos NLar SLon
§	- 'Texanum'	CAlb EWes NLar WCFE
	- 'Variegatum' (v)	LMaj
	lucidum 𝕐^{H4}	CCVT CDoC CDul CSBt CTri EBee ECrN ELan EWTr IDee LAst MGos MMuc MRav MSwo NLar SAPC SArc SBfd SEND SPer SWvt WDin WFar
	- Guiz 296	CPLG
	- 'Excelsum Superbum' (v) 𝕐^{H4}	CAbP CDul CLnd CPMA ECrN ELan EPfP LAst LHop MGos SSpi WCot
	- 'Golden Wax'	CAbP CPMA MRav SSpi
	- 'Tricolor' (v)	CPMA ELan EPfP LRHS MAsh NLar SPer SPoG SSpi SWvt WDin WFar
	obtusifolium 'Dart's Perfecta'	SLPl
	ovalifolium	Widely available
§	- 'Argenteum' (v)	CBcs CCVT CDoC CDul CTri CWib EBee ECrN EHoe GKir IFFs LBuc LRHS MAsh MMuc MWat NEgg NHol NLar SBfd SEND SLim SPer SPoG SWvt WDin WFar
	- 'Aureomarginatum'	see *L. ovalifolium* 'Aureum'
§	- 'Aureum' (v) 𝕐^{H4}	Widely available
	- 'Lemon and Lime' (v)	EHoe EPfP SCoo SWvt WPat WRHF
	- 'Variegatum'	see *L. ovalifolium* 'Argenteum'
	quihoui 𝕐^{H4}	CHGN CTri EBee ECre ELan EPfP IDee LRHS MBri MWea NLar SDix SKHP SLon SMad SPer SSpi WFar WPat
	sempervirens	EPfP IArd
	sinense	CMCN EPfP GLin IFFs MRav SBfd WFar

- 'Multiflorum'	CWib WFar
- var. ***stauntonii***	NLar
- 'Variegatum' (v)	CBgR CPMA EBee EPla EWes LHop MMuc MRav SPer
- 'Wimbei'	WFar
strongylophyllum	CDoC CPLG WFar
texanum	see *L. japonicum* 'Texanum'
tschonoskii	NLar
undulatum 'Lemon Lime and Clippers'	EBee LRHS MAsh MWea NLar SDix SLim
'Vicaryi'	CPMA EBee ELan EPfP EPla EQua EWTr IArd MGos NHol SEND SPer WFar
vulgare	CBcs CCVT CDul CMac CRWN CTri CWan EBWF ECrN EMac EPfP IFFs LAst LBuc MSwo NWea SEND SWvt WDin WMou WSFF
- 'Atrovirens'	EMac
- 'Aureovariegatum' (v)	CNat
- 'Lodense'	EBtc
walkeri	GAuc

Lilium ✿ (*Liliaceae*)

'Acapulco' (VII-/d)	LAma MCri NGdn SDeJ SPet
African Queen Group (VI-/a) ♀H4	LAma LRHS NLar SCoo SPer SRms
- 'African Queen' (VIb-c/a)	MCri WCot
albanicum	see *L. pyrenaicum* subsp. *carniolicum* var. *albanicum*
'Algarve' (VIIIa-b/c)	MBri
'Altari' (VIIIa-b/b)	MCri
amabile (IXc/d)	GAuc
- var. ***luteum*** (IXc/d)	GAuc MCri
'Anastasia' (VIIIb-c/b-d) **new**	LAma
'Apeldoorn' (Ia/b)	MCri NNor
'Apollo' (Ia-b) ♀H4	GKev LAma SDeJ
'Arena' (VIIa/b)	EPfP MCri SCoo SPer WFar
'Ariadne' (Ic-d)	CDes
Asiatic hybrids (I)	LAma NGdn SGar
auratum (IXb/c)	CDoy EBee ECho EFEx EPfP GAuc GKev LRHS WGwG
- 'Gold Band'	see *L. auratum* var. *platyphyllum*
§ - var. ***platyphyllum*** (IXb/c)	GAuc MCri NNor
- - B&SWJ 4824	WCru
- var. ***virginale*** (IXb/c)	GAuc MCri
'Avignon' (Ia/b)	MCri
'Bach' (VIIIa-b/b)	MBri
Backhouse hybrids	see *L.* × *dalhansonii* Backhouse Group
bakerianum (IXc/b)	LAma
- var. ***aureum*** (IXc/b)	GAuc
- var. ***delavayi*** (IXc/b)	GAuc
'Barbaresco' (VIIa-b/b)	SCoo SPer
'Barcelona' (Ia/b-c)	NNor
Bellingham Group (IVc/d)	GEdr
'Bergamo' (VIIb/b)	EPfP SCoo WFar
'Bianco Uno'	LRHS
'Black Beauty' (VIIIb-c/d)	CAvo CFFs EPfP GKev LAma LRHS MCri SDeJ
'Black Dragon'	see *L. leucanthum* var. *centifolium* 'Black Dragon'
'Black Tie' (VIIa-b/b)	MCri
bolanderi (IXb-c/a)	GAuc
'Bright Star' (VIb-c/c)	LAma MCri
brownii (IXb-c/a)	EBee ECho GAuc LAma MCri WWst
bulbiferum (IXa/b)	ECho GAuc
- var. ***croceum*** (IXa/b)	ECho GAuc
'Burgundy Splash' (I) **new**	LAma
'Butter Pixie' PBR (Ia/b)	NNor WGor
callosum (IXc/d)	GAuc
§ ***canadense*** (IXc/a)	CDes GAuc LAma WCru
- var. ***flavum***	see *L. canadense*
candidum (IXb/a) ♀H4	CArn CAvo CBcs CTca CTri EBee EBrs ECha ECho EHrv ELan EPfP EPot ERCP GAuc GKev LAma LAst LRHS MCri MHer NGHP SDeJ SEND SPer SRms WBrE WSpi
'Capuchino' (Ia-b/c)	LAma LRHS MCri
carniolicum	see *L. pyrenaicum* subsp. *carniolicum*
'Casa Blanca' (VIIb/b-c) ♀H4	CAvo CFFs EPfP GKev LAma LRHS MCri NBir NLar NNor SCoo SDeJ SPer WFar
'Casa Rosa'	see *L.* × *parkmanii* 'Rote Horn'
'Centerfold' (Ia-b/b)	LAma LRHS NNor
cernuum (IXc/d)	CAvo EBee EBrs ECho GAuc LAma LRHS MCri SPer
* - 'Album'	ECho GAuc SPer
chalcedonicum (IXb-c/d)	GAuc
Citronella Group (Ic/d)	CAvo ECho LAma MCri SDeJ WFar
Cobra = 'Zantricob' PBR (VIIa/b)	LRHS
columbianum (IXc/d)	ECho GAuc NMen WHal
- B&SWJ 9564	WCru
- dwarf (IXc/d)	ECho GAuc NMen
'Con Amore' (VIIb/b)	SCoo SPer WFar
'Conca d'Or' PBR (VIIIb/b)	LAma
concolor (IXa/c)	GAuc
- var. ***pulchellum*** (IXa/c)	GAuc
- var. ***stictum*** (IXa/c)	GAuc
'Connecticut King' (Ia/b)	EPfP LAma MCri
'Corina' (Ia/b)	NNor SGar
'Côte d'Azur' (Ia/b-c)	CSut GKev LAma NNor WGor
'Crimson Pixie' (Ia/b)	ECho NGdn
× ***dalhansonii*** (IIc/d)	SPhx WCot
§ - Backhouse Group (IIc/d)	CAvo
§ - 'Marhan' (IIc/d)	ECho
- 'Mrs R.O. Backhouse' (IIc/d)	EBrs ECho GEdr
§ ***dauricum*** (IXa/b)	GCrs
davidii (IXc/d)	CPLG EBee ECho GAuc GEdr GKev LAma MCri WCru
§ - var. ***willmottiae*** (IXc/d)	GAuc MCri WCot
'Dimention' (I) **new**	LAma
distichum (IXb-c/d)	GAuc
- B&SWJ 794	WCru
'Dizzy' (VIIa-b/b-c)	MCri
duchartrei (IXc/d)	CDes CPLG EBee ECho GAuc GCrs GEdr LAma NSla WAbe WCru
- from Gansu, China	GAuc
'Ebony' (Ic/d) **new**	LAma
'Electric' (Ia/b-c)	MCri NNor
'Elodie' PBR (1a/b)	CAvo CFFs ECho LAma LRHS
euxanthum (IX)	GAuc
'Eyeliner' PBR **new**	LAma
'Fancy Joy' (Ia/b-c)	MBri
'Fangio' (VIIIa/b)	NNor
fargesii (IXc/d)	GAuc
'Fata Morgana' (Ia/b) ♀H4	EPfP LAma LRHS NNor SCoo
'Feuerzauber' (Ia-b/b)	SPer
'Fire King' (Ib/d)	EPfP LAma LRHS MCri SCoo SDeJ SRms WFar
formosanum (IXb/a)	ECho GAuc LRHS MCri MMuc NChi WCot
- RWJ 10005	WCru
- var. ***pricei*** (IXb/a)	CWCL EBee ECho ELan EPot GAuc GEdr GGar LRHS MHer NMen NWCA SPoG WPer
- - 'Snow Queen' (Vb/a)	SDeJ
'Fresco' (VII)	ECho
'Garden Party' (VIIb/b) ♀H4	LSou NLar SDeJ WFar
'Gerrit Zalm' PBR (VIIIa/c)	LRHS
'Gibraltar' (Ia/b)	MCri

	'Glossy Wings' (VIIIa-b/b)	NNor
	'Gold Lode' (Ia/b-c)	MCri
	'Golden Joy' (Ia/-)	MBri
	Golden Splendor Group (VIb-c/a) ♀H4	LAma LRHS MCri SCoo SDeJ SPer
	'Golden Stargazer' (VIIa-b/b)	CSut LRHS
	'Graffity' (I) **new**	LAma
	'Gran Paradiso' (Ia/b)	MCri SRms
	'Grand Cru' (Ia/b) ♀H4	MCri NNor SDeJ
	Green Magic Group (VI-/a)	NNor
	hansonii (IXb-c/d)	EBee ECho GAuc GEdr LAma MCri
	- B&SWJ 8506	WCru
	- B&SWJ 4756 from Aomori, Japan	WCru
	henrici (IXb-c/a-c)	GAuc
	henryi (IXc/d) ♀H4	CAvo CFFs CSWP EBee ECho EPfP GAuc LAma LRHS MCri NLar SDeJ WCot WCru
	- var. ***citrinum***(IXc/d)	ECho GAuc
	'Hit Parade' (VII)	SDeJ
	× ***hollandicum*** (Ia/b)	MCri
	'Honey Bee' (I)	LRHS
	'Hot Lips' (VIIb/b-d)	EPfP SPer
	humboldtii (IXc/d)	GAuc
	- subsp. ***ocellatum*** (IXc/d)	GAuc
	'Ibarra' (Ia/b)	MCri
	'Ivory Pixie' (Ia/b)	SPet
	'Jacqueline'	GKev
	japonicum (IXb/a)	EFEx
	- 'Albomarginatum' (IXb/a/v)	GEdr
	'Journey's End' (VIIb/c)	LAma
§	'Joy' (VIIa-b/b) ♀H4	LAma MCri
	kelleyanum (IXc/d)	GAuc
	- NNS 98-373	WCot
	kelloggii (IXc/d)	ECho GAuc WCot
	kesselringianum (IXc/c-d)	GAuc
	'King Pete' (Ib/b-c) ♀H4	SDeJ
	'Lady Alice' (VI-/d)	LRHS WGwG
§	***lancifolium*** (IXc/d)	CArn CHid EPot GBin WBrk WFar
	- B&SWJ 539	WCru
*	- ***album***	WBor
	- Farrer's form	WCot
	- var. ***flaviflorum*** (IXc/d)	GAuc MCri
	- 'Flore Pleno' (IXc/d)	CSWP EBee EPPr EUJe GAuc GCal GGar GKir LHop LRHS MHer MMHG NBir WCot WCru WFar WHil WTin
*	- var. ***forrestii*** (IX)	GAuc MCri
	- Forrest's form (IX)	LRHS
	- var. ***fortunei*** (IXc/d)	GAuc GCal SDix
	- - B&SWJ 4352	WCru
	- pink-flowered **new**	SDeJ
	- 'Splendens' (IXc/d) ♀H4	EBee ECGP ECho EPfP GAuc GKev LAma MCri NBid SDeJ SPhx
*	- ***viridulum***	GAuc
	'Landini'PBR (Ia/b)	LRHS
	lankongense (IXc/d)	CDes EBee EPot GAuc GEdr LAma MCri WAbe
	'Latvia' (Ia/b)	ECho MCri
	'Le Rêve'	see *L.* 'Joy'
	ledebourii (IXc/d)	GAuc
	leichtlinii (IXc/d)	EBee ECho EPot GAuc GCrs MCri
	- B&SWJ 4519	WCru
	- 'Iwashimiza' (IX)	MCri
	- var. ***maximowiczii*** (IXc/d)	GAuc
	'Lemon Pixie'PBR (Ia/b)	LAma
	leucanthum (IXb-c/a)	EBee GAuc LAma
	- var. ***centifolium*** (IXb-c/a)	GAuc MCri WBVN WCru
§	- - 'Black Dragon' (IXb-c/a)	MCri
	lijiangense (IXc/d)	GAuc GEdr MCri
	'Little John' (VIIa-b/b)	MBri
	Lollypop = 'Holebibi' (Ia/b)	ECho EPfP LRHS MBri NNor SCoo SPet
	longiflorum (IXb/a) ♀H2-3	EBee ECho GAuc LAma MCri SCoo
	- B&SWJ 11376	WCru
	- 'Memories'	MBri
§	- 'White American' (Vb/a)	CSWP ECho EPfP SPer
	- 'White Heaven'PBR (Vb/a)	EPfP WGor
	lophophorum (IXc/b)	EBee EPot GAuc LAma
	- var. ***linearifolium*** (IXc/b)	GAuc
	'Lovely Girl' (VII-/b)	CSut LRHS SDeJ
	'Luxor' (Ib)	MCri NBir SPer
	mackliniae (IXc/a)	CWCL EBee ECho EPot GAuc GCal GCra GCrs GEdr GGGa GMaP GMac ITim NBir NMen WAbe WHal
	- deep pink-flowered	GCrs GGGa
	- robust habit	GGar WWst
	'Mambo'PBR (VII) **new**	LAma
	Marco Polo	see *L.* 'Vedea'
	'Marhan'	see *L.* × *dalhansonii* 'Marhan'
	martagon (IXc/d) ♀H4	Widely available
	- var. ***albiflorum*** (IXc/d)	GAuc
	- var. ***album*** (IXc/d) ♀H4	CAvo CSWP EBee EBrs ECha ECho EHrv ELan EPfP EPot GAuc GEdr GMaP LAma NBir NChi SDeJ WCom WCot WPtf WShi
	- var. ***cattaniae*** (IXc/d)	EPot GAuc MCri WCot
	- var. ***daugavense*** (IXc/d)	WWst
	- var. ***pilosiusculum*** (IXc/d)	EBee GAuc
	- 'Plenum' (IXc/d)	WBor WCot WKif
	- var. ***sanguineo-purpureum*** (IXc/d)	GAuc
	medeoloides (IXc/d)	EBee ECho EFEx GAuc NMen
	'Mediterrannee' (VIIb/d)	NNor
	'Menton' (Ia/c)	MCri
	michiganense (IXc/d)	CSWP GAuc
	'Milano' (Ia/b)	MCri
	'Miss Feya' (VIII) **new**	LAma
	'Miss France' (VIIb/b-c) **new**	EPfP
	'Miss Lucy'PBR (VIIa-b/b-c)	CHid LAma LRHS
	'Miss Rio' (VII)	SCoo
	'Mona Lisa' (VIIb/b-c)	EPfP LAma LSou MBri MCri NGdn NNor SDeJ WFar WGor
§	***monadelphum*** (IXc/d)	ECho EPot GAuc GCra LAma NLar SDeJ
	'Monte Negro' (Ia/b)	ECho LRHS MCri NGdn
	'Montreux' (Ia/b-c)	LAma
	'Muscadet'PBR (VIIa-b/b)	CSut EPfP LAma LRHS NGdn SDeJ
§	***nanum*** (IXc/b)	ECho GAuc GEdr GGGa LAma NMen WAbe WCru WHal WWst
	- AGS/ES	WWst
	- EMAK 670	WWst
	- from Bhutan (IX)	ECho GAuc NMen WCru
	- var. ***flavidum*** (IXc/b)	ECho GEdr NMen WWst
	- - hybrids	WWst
	nepalense (IXc/a)	CAby CBcs CFir CHid CPLG CSWP CTca EBee EBla ECho EPot ERCP GAuc GEdr GGar GKir GMac LAma LRHS MCot MCri MDun NCob WCot WCru WFar WPnP
	- B&SWJ 2985	WCru
	- CC 3663	WCot
	'Nerone' (Ia/b)	CHid
	'Netty's Pride' (Ia/b-c)	CAvo CHid EPfP ERCP LRHS MCri
	nobilissimum (IXa-b/a)	EFEx

'Nove Cento' (Ia/b) ♀H4	MCri SDeJ
'Odeon' (VI-/a)	MCri
'Olivia' (Ia)	EBrs ECho LAma MCri
Olympic Group (VI-/a)	MCri
'Orange Electric' (Ia/b) **new**	SDeJ
'Orange Pixie' (Ia/b)	EPfP MCri NNor SCoo SPet WGor
'Orange Triumph' (Ia/-)	EPfP
'Orange Twinkle' (Ib-c/b) **new**	SDeJ
* Oriental Superb Group	NGdn
§ ***oxypetalum*** (IXb-c/b)	ECho GAuc WWst
- var. ***insigne*** (IXb-c/b)	ECho GAuc GBin GCrs GEdr GGGa GGar NMen WAbe WCru WHal WWst
papilliferum (IXc/d)	ECho LAma
pardalinum (IXc/d) ♀H4	CWCL ECho ELan ERCP GAuc MCot SUsu WBor WCru WHal WPnP
- var. ***giganteum*** (IXc/d)	EPfP MCri MNrw SPer WTin
- subsp. ***pardalinum*** (IXc/d) NNS 00-488	WWst
- - NNS 02=228	WWst
- subsp. ***shastense*** (IXc/d)	NMen WWst
- - NNS 98-374	WWst
- subsp. ***shastense*** × ***pardalinum*** subsp. ***vollmeri***	WWst
§ - subsp. ***wigginsii*** (IXc/d)	GAuc MCri
§ - subsp. ***vollmeri*** (IXc/d)	GAuc GCrs NMen WCru WWst
- - JCA 1.500.901	WWst
- - NNS 00-490	EBee
× ***parkmanii*** Imperial Silver Group (VIIb/c)	LAma
§ - 'Rote Horn' (VIIIb/a)	MCri
- 'Sam' (VIIb/c) ♀H4	EPfP
parryi (IXb-c/a)	EBee ECho GAuc WHal WWst
- NNS 03-384	WWst
parvum (IXa-b/a)	ECho GAuc
* - var. ***hallidayi***	GAuc
'Patricia's Pride' **new**	MCri
'Peach Pixie' (Ia/b)	NBir SCoo
pensylvanicum	see *L. dauricum*
philadelphicum (IXa/b)	GAuc
- var. ***andinum*** (IXa/b)	GAuc
philippinense (IXa-b/a)	CDes EBee LAma MCri WPGP
'Pink Heart'	LRHS
Pink Perfection Group (VIb/a) ♀H4	CAvo CFFs EPfP ERCP LAma LRHS MCri NNor SCoo SPer WFar
'Pink Pixie' PBR (Ia/b)	SPet
'Pink Tiger' (VIIIb/c)	CAvo GKev MCri NNor WGor
poilanei HWJ 681	WCru
pomponium (IXc/d)	EBee GAuc
primulinum var. ***burmanicum*** (IXc/a)	GAuc
- var. ***ochraceum*** (IXc/a)	GAuc LAma MCri WCru WWst
§ ***pumilum*** (IXc/d) ♀H4	EBee ECho ERCP GAuc GKev LAma MCri MTho WAul
'Purple Prince' (VIIIa-b/a-b)	LRHS
pyrenaicum (IXc/d)	CAby ECho GAuc GKir IBlr MCri WPGP WShi WWst
§ - subsp. ***carniolicum*** (IXc/d)	ECho GAuc MCri
§ - - var. ***albanicum*** (IXc/d)	GAuc
- - var. ***bosnaicum*** (IX)	GAuc
- - var. ***carniolicum*** (IXc/d) **new**	GAuc
- - var. ***jankae*** (IX) **new**	GAuc
'Quinta' PBR (Ia/b)	ECho
Red Band Group (VII-/b)	WFar
'Red Carpet' (Ia/b)	MCri NBir NNor SDeJ WGor
'Red Dutch' (VIIIa-b/c)	ERCP
Red Rum = 'Zanlorum'	MBri
'Red Star'	LRHS
regale (IXb/a) ♀H4	CArn CAvo CDoy CFFs CFir CMea CTca EBee EBrs ECha EHrv ELan EPfP ERCP GAuc GGar GKev LAma LEdu LRHS MCot MCri NLar NNor SDeJ SPer WBVN WBrE WCot WFar
- 'Album' (IXb/a)	CAvo CSWP EBee ERCP GAuc LAma MCri NLar NNor SCoo SDeJ SGar WCot WFar WGwG
§ - 'Royal Gold' (IXb/a)	GAuc MCri
'Reinesse' (Ia/b)	MBri
'Robert Swanson'	LAma
'Robina' (VIIIa-b/b-c)	LAma WCot
'Rodolfa' PBR (VIIa-b/-)	LRHS LSou
'Roma' (Ia/b)	NBir
'Rosefire' (Ia/b)	NNor
'Rosemary North' (Ic/d)	CDes
'Rosita' (Ia/b-c)	MCri WFar
rosthornii (IXc/d)	CPLG GAuc GEdr LAma WCot WCru
'Royal Fantasy' (VIII)	NNor
'Royal Gold'	see *L. regale* 'Royal Gold'
rubellum (IXb/a)	EFEx GAuc
rubescens (IXa/a)	GAuc
* 'Rubina'	MCri
'Ruud' (VIIb/b-c)	EPfP LAma
sachalinense (IXa/b)	GAuc
- RBS 0235	EPPr
'Salmon Twinkle' (Ib-c/c)	SDeJ WFar
sargentiae (IXb-c/a)	GAuc GCrs GGGa MCri NMen WCot
- Cox 7099	WWst
'Scheherazade' (VIIIc/d)	LAma MCri
sempervivoideum (IXb-c/b)	ECho GAuc
'Set Point' (VIIb/b) **new**	SDeJ
'Silly Girl' (Ia/-)	MCri NNor
§ 'Snow Crystal' (Ia/b)	EPfP
'Sorbonne' (VIIa-b/b-c)	LRHS
souliei (IXc/a-b)	GAuc
'Souvenir' PBR	NGdn
'Space Star' (VIIa/b-c)	LRHS
'Spark'	NNor
speciosum (IXb-c/d)	GAuc
- B&SWJ 4847	WCru
- var. ***album*** (IXb-c/d)	EBee ECho EPfP GAuc LEdu MCri NBir SDeJ
- var. ***gloriosoides*** (IXb-c/d)	GAuc LAma
- var. ***rubrum*** (IXb-c/d)	EBee EBrs ECha ECho EPfP GAuc LAma MCri NBir SPer SRms
§ - 'Uchida' (IXb-c/d)	CPLG EPfP GAuc MCri
Sphinx = 'Holecaca' (Ia/c-d)	NNor WCot
'Spring Pink' (Ia)	ERCP
'Staccato' (Ia/c)	MCri
'Star Gazer' (VIIa/c)	CSut ELan LAma LRHS MCri MHav NNor SCoo SDeJ SPer WFar WGor
'Starburst Sensation' (VIIIb/a)	LRHS
'Starfighter' (VIIa-b/c)	EPfP MCri SDeJ SPet
'Sterling Star' (Ia/b)	EPfP MCri NNor
Stones = 'Holebobo' (Ia/b)	LRHS NNor
'Sulphur King'	WCot
sulphureum (IXb-c/a)	GAuc LAma MCri WWst
'Sumatra' (VIIb/b) **new**	LAma
'Sun Ray' (Ia/b)	MCri
superbum (IXc/d)	EBee ECho GAuc GEdr LAma WCot WCru WPGP
'Sweet-kiss' (Ia-b/b)	MBri NLar
'Sweet Surrender' (Ib-c/c-d)	EPfP LRHS MCri NNor SDeJ
szovitsianum	see *L. monadelphum*

taliense (IXc/d)	ECho GAuc GEdr LAma MCri WCru WWst
tenuifolium	see *L. pumilum*
'Tiger Woods' (VII) **new**	LAma
tigrinum	see *L. lancifolium*
'Time Out'PBR (VIIa-b/b-c)	EPfP
'Tom Pouce' (VIIa/b)	EPfP MCri
'Touch' (VIIb/-)	MCri
Triumphator = 'Zanlophator'PBR (VIIIb/a-b)	EPfP LRHS MCri NNor
tsingtauense (IXa/c)	GAuc MCri
- B&SWJ 519	WCru
- B&SWJ 4263	WCru
'Uchida Kanoka'	see *L. speciosum* 'Uchida'
§ 'Vedea' (VIIb/b)	SCoo SDeJ WFar
'Vermeer' (Ia-b/b-c)	LRHS WFar
'Victory Joy'	MBri
'Vivaldi' (Ia/b)	SDeJ
vollmeri	see *L. pardalinum* subsp. *vollmeri*
wallichianum (IXb/a)	EBee ECho EPot GAuc LAma
wardii (IXc/d)	CPLG
washingtonianum (IXb/a)	GAuc
- var. ***purpurascens*** (IXb/a-b)	GAuc
'White American'	see *L. longiflorum* 'White American'
'White Dwarf' (Ia/b)	GKev
'White Mountain' (VIIa-b/c)	SPer
'White Paradise' (V)	SCoo
White Pixie	see *L.* 'Snow Crystal'
'White Twinkle' (Ia-b/b)	CAvo SDeJ
wigginsii	see *L. pardalinum* subsp. *wigginsii*
- NNS 00-493	WWst
willmottiae	see *L. davidii* var. *willmottiae*
wilsonii (IXa/b)	GAuc
xanthellum var. ***luteum*** (IXb-c/d)	CDes
Yellow Blaze Group (Ia/b)	EPfP

lime see *Citrus aurantiifolia*

lime, djeruk see *Citrus amblycarpa*

lime, Philippine see × *Citrofortunella microcarpa*

Limnanthes (*Limnanthaceae*)

douglasii ♀H4	CArn EPfP SIde
- subsp. ***rosea*** **new**	CSpe

Limonium (*Plumbaginaceae*)

bellidifolium	CMea ECha EDAr MWat WAbe WHoo WPer WTin
- 'Dazzling Blue'	WHrl
binervosum	EBWF
'Blauer Diamant'	EBee NBre
chilwellii	EBee ECGP LRHS
cosyrense	CMea GEdr MHer NMen WAbe WPer
dumosum	see *Goniolimon tataricum* var. *angustifolium*
gmelinii	MLLN SPlb WClo WPer
* - subsp. ***hungaricum***	NLar
gougetianum	LLHF WPer
latifolium	see *L. platyphyllum*
minutum	WHoo
paradoxum	WAbe
perezii	CFir EShb WPer
§ ***platyphyllum***	Widely available
- 'Robert Butler'	CPrp EBee GCal GKir
- 'Violetta'	EBee ECGP ECha ELan EPfP GCal GKir LAst LRHS MBri MRav SPer SPoG WHoo
speciosum	see *Goniolimon incanum*
tataricum	see *Goniolimon tataricum*
vulgare	WHer

Linaria (*Scrophulariaceae*)

aeruginea 'Neon Lights' **new**	EDif SBch
- subsp. ***nevadensis*** 'Gemstones'	SBch
alpina	CSpe ECho ECtt NRya NSla SRms WEas
anticaria 'Antique Silver'	EBee LSou MRav WPGP WWEG
Blue Lace = 'Yalin'	LSou
cymbalaria	see *Cymbalaria muralis*
§ ***dalmatica***	EBee ECha ELan EPPr GGar IFro MWea NBid NBre SBch WCot WKif WMoo WPer WWEG
dalmatica × ***purpurea***	WCot
× ***dominii*** 'Carnforth'	NBre SBch SGar WCot WWEG
- 'Yuppie Surprise'	CHid EBee NBir SWvt WPGP
genistifolia	MDKP
- subsp. ***dalmatica***	see *L. dalmatica*
hepaticifolia	see *Cymbalaria hepaticifolia*
* ***lobata alba***	ECho SPlb
nevadensis 'Grenada Sol'	MWea
origanifolia	see *Chaenorhinum origanifolium*
pallida	see *Cymbalaria pallida*
pilosa	see *Cymbalaria pilosa*
purpurea	CBgR COIW CTri EBWF EBee EHoe EHrv ELan EPfP IFoB LRHS MHer MMuc MNHC NBPC NBro NPer NPri NVic SEND SPhx SRms WClo WCot WHil WMoo WPer WSFF
- 'Alba'	see *L. purpurea* 'Springside White'
- 'Canon Went'	Widely available
- pink-flowered	CSpe
- 'Radcliffe Innocence'	see *L. purpurea* 'Springside White'
§ - 'Springside White'	CBgR CElw EBee ECha ECtt LBMP LRHS MBri NBir NPri SBch SPhx WAul WCot WPer
- 'Thurgarton Beauty'	MDKP
repens	CPom MNrw WCot WHer
× ***sepium***	WCot
triornithophora	CFir ECha IGor LBMP LRHS MMuc MWea WKif WMoo
- 'Pink Budgies'	LSou
- purple-flowered	ELan WMoo
tristis	CEnt
vulgaris	CArn EBWF MDKP MHer MNHC NMir NSco WHer WHfH WJek
- 'Peloria'	MDKP WCom
'Winifrid's Delight'	EPfP NBre

Lindelofia (*Boraginaceae*)

anchusoides misapplied	see *L. longiflora*
anchusoides (Lindl.) Lehm.	EPPr NBid
§ ***longiflora***	CDes EBee GCal GCra GMaP

Lindera (*Lauraceae*)

benzoin	CBcs CMac EPfP GKir LRHS NLar SSpi WDin
erythrocarpa	CBcs EPfP NLar SSpi
- B&SWJ 6271	WCru
- B&SWJ 8730	WCru
megaphylla	CBcs CHEx
obtusiloba ♀H4	CAbP EPfP SSpi WPat
- B&SWJ 8723	WCru
praecox	EPfP

- B&SWJ 10802	WCru
- B&SWJ 10953 from north Japan **new**	WCru
- B&SWJ 11125 from north Japan	WCru
reflexa	CGHE EPfP NLar
sericea B&SWJ 11141	WCru
- var. ***lancea*** B&SWJ 11118 **new**	WCru
strychnifolia	EPfP
triloba	SSpi
- B&SWJ 5570	WCru
- B&SWJ 11121	WCru
umbellata var. ***membranacea*** B&SWJ 6227	WCru

Lindernia (*Scrophulariaceae*)

grandiflora	EBee LLWG

Linnaea (*Caprifoliaceae*)

borealis	ILis WAbe
- subsp. ***americana***	NHar NWCA

Linum (*Linaceae*)

africanum	EShb
arboreum ♀H4	CMea LLHF WAbe WPat
- NS 529	NWCA
austriacum	EBee
campanulatum	WThu
- 'Sulphur'	LRHS
capitatum	GKev WAbe WPat
dolomiticum	WPat
elegans **new**	GKev
flavum	EPfP GKev GKir
- 'Compactum'	CMea EBee ECho GGar LLHF SPad SRms WCot
'Gemmell's Hybrid' ♀H4	ECho EWes GKev MDKP NBir NMen WAbe WPat
monogynum	ECou
§ - var. ***diffusum***	ECou
- 'Nelson'	see *L. monogynum* var. *diffusum*
narbonense	CMdw CSam CSpr EBee LBMP SBch
- 'Heavenly Blue'	GKir
§ ***perenne***	CArn CRWN EBee ECha ELan EPfP GKir GMaP LRHS MHer MNHC NBro NLar NMun SIde SPer SPoG WJek WPer WWEG
- 'Album'	EBee ECha ELan EPfP NLar SPer WJek WPer
- subsp. ***alpinum***	CMea
I - subsp. ***biokovoensis***	EBee
§ - 'Blau Saphir'	EBee GQue LRHS MWat NLar SWal
- Blue Sapphire	see *L. perenne* 'Blau Saphir'
- 'Diamant'	EBee LRHS
- 'Himmelszelt'	LBMP NLar
- subsp. ***lewisii***	NBir
- 'Nanum Diamond'	NLar
- 'Nanum Sapphire'	see *L. perenne* 'Blau Saphir'
- 'White Diamond'	SPoG
sibiricum	see *L. perenne*
suffruticosum	WPat
subsp. ***salsoloides*** 'Nanum'	
uninerve	WAbe
usitatissimum	CRWN MHer SIde

Liparis (*Orchidaceae*)

makinoana	WWst
'Kuro Suzu' **new**	

Lippia (*Verbenaceae*)

sp.	SWvt
canescens	see *Phyla nodiflora* var. *canescens*
chamaedrifolia	see *Verbena peruviana*
citriodora	see *Aloysia citrodora*
dulcis	CArn EOHP GPWP
nodiflora	see *Phyla nodiflora*
repens	see *Phyla nodiflora*

Liquidambar ✿ (*Hamamelidaceae*)

acalycina	CDul CLnd CPMA EBee ELan EMil EPfP LRHS MGos MRav NLar SBir SCoo SPoG SSpi SSta WPGP WPat
- 'Burgundy Flush'	CPMA NLar
- 'Spinners'	SSpi
formosana	CDul CEnd CMCN CMac EBee EPfP IArd LAst MGos MSnd NPCo SBir SSta WPGP
- B&SWJ 6855	WCru
- 'Afterglow' **new**	CPMA
- 'Ellen' **new**	CPMA
- Monticola Group	CPMA EPfP SBir SSta
orientalis	CDul CMCN CPMA EPfP EWTr LLHF NPCo SBir SSta
styraciflua	Widely available
- 'Andrew Hewson'	CAbP CLnd CPMA EBee EMil EPfP LRHS MAsh NLar SBir SSta
- 'Anja'	CPMA MBlu SBir SSta
- 'Anneke'	CPMA SBir SSta
- 'Aurea'	see *L. styraciflua* 'Variegata' Overeynder
- 'Aurea Variegata'	see *L. styraciflua* 'Variegata' Overeynder
- 'Aurora'	CPMA SBir SLim
- 'Brodsman'	NLar
- 'Burgundy'	CPMA CTho LLHF MBlu NHol SBir SSta WPGP WPat
- 'Elstead Mill'	CAbP
- 'Festeri'	CEnd SBir SSta WPat
- 'Festival'	CPMA MBlu SSta
- 'Frosty' (v)	CPMA
- 'Globe'	see *L. styraciflua* 'Gum Ball'
- 'Golden Treasure' (v)	CBcs CMCN CPMA LRHS MAsh MBri MGos NLar SMad SPer WPat
- 'Goldmember' **new**	CPMA
- 'Granary Sunset' **new**	SSta
§ - 'Gum Ball'	CEnd CLnd CMCN CPMA EBee ELon EPfP ERom EWes LLHF MGos NLar NPCo SBir SMad SSta WPat
- Happidaze = 'Hapdell'	CEnd CPMA NLar SSta WPat
- 'Jennifer Carol'	CPMA NLar
- 'Kia'	CAbP CEnd CPMA LLHF NLar SBir WPat
- 'Kirsten'	CPMA
- 'Lane Roberts' ♀H4	Widely available
- 'Manon' (v)	CDoC CEnd CPMA EMil SBir SPoG
- 'Midwest Sunset'	CPMA MBlu WPGP WPat
- 'Moonbeam' (v)	CEnd CPMA EBee NLar SBir SLim SSta WPat
- 'Moraine'	CPMA SBir
- 'Naree'	CPMA NLar SBir
- 'Oconee'	CEnd EPfP WPat
- 'Paarl' (v)	CPMA
- 'Palo Alto'	CEnd CPMA EBee LLHF LRHS MAsh MBlu NHol NPal SBir SCoo SSta WPGP WPat
- 'Parasol'	CAbP CEnd CPMA NLar NPCo SBir SSta
- 'Pendula'	CLnd CPMA MBlu SBir SSta
- 'Penwood'	CPMA NLar SSta

	- 'Rotundiloba'	CMCN CPMA EPfP LLHF SBir SSta WPat
	- 'Schock's Gold'	CPMA SSta
	- 'Silver King' (v)	CLnd CMCN CMac CPMA CWit EBee ECrN EMil MBri MGos NLar NPCo SCoo SLim SMad SPer SSta WFoF WPat
	- 'Slender Silhouette'	CAbP CPMA EBee EPfP LLHF LRHS MAsh MBlu SBir SCoo SPoG SSpi WMou WPat
	- 'Stared'	CDul CEnd CLnd CPMA EBee LRHS LTen MAsh MBlu MBri NLar SBir SCoo SPoG WPGP WPat
	- 'Thea'	CAbP CPMA EMil EPfP LRHS MAsh MBlu SBir SSta
§	- 'Variegata' Overeynder (v)	CBcs CBot CLnd CMac CPMA EBee ELan EMil EPfP LRHS MGos SLim SPoG SSta WDin WPat
	- 'White Star' (v)	CPMA
	- 'Woorby Rose' **new**	SSta
	- 'Worplesdon' Υ^{H4}	Widely available

Liriodendron ✿ (*Magnoliaceae*)

	'Chapel Hill'	MBlu
	chinense	CBcs CDul CGHE CLnd CMCN CTho EPfP MBlu WFar WPGP WPat
	chinense × ***tulipifera***	WPGP
	'Doc Deforce's Delight'	MBlu
	tulipifera Υ^{H4}	Widely available
	- 'Ardis'	CMCN NLar
	- 'Aureomarginatum' (v) Υ^{H4}	Widely available
	- 'Fastigiatum'	CDoC CDul CEnd CLnd CMCN CMac CTho CWit EBee ECrN ELan EPfP LRHS MAsh MBlu MBri MGos NLar SSta WPat
	- 'Glen Gold'	CEnd CMCN MBlu NLar SMad
	- 'Purgatory'	MBlu
	- 'Roodhaan'	NLar

Liriope ✿ (*Convallariaceae*)

	HWJ 590 from Vietnam	WPGP
	from Vietnam	WPGP
	'Big Blue'	see *L. muscari* 'Big Blue'
§	***exiliflora***	CEnd CLAP NLar WCot WWEG
	- 'Ariaka-janshige' (v)	WWEG
	- Silvery Sunproof misapplied	see *L. spicata* 'Gin-ryu', *L. muscari* 'Variegata'
§	***gigantea***	CLAP EPPr MBNS SWat
	graminifolia misapplied	see *L. muscari*
	hyacinthifolia	see *Reineckea carnea*
	koreana	EBee EPPr GCal
	- B&SWJ 8821	WCru
	'Majestic'	CBct CHar CLAP EBee WFar WHoo
	'Minnow'	WCot
	minor	CMac
§	***muscari*** Υ^{H4}	Widely available
	- B&SWJ 561	WCru
	- 'Alba'	see *L. muscari* 'Monroe White'
	- Amethyst = 'Liptp' **new**	NPri
§	- 'Big Blue'	CBct CBgR CKno CLAP CMac CPLG EBee ECtt ELon EPPr EPfP EShb LEdu LHop LRHS LSRN MRav MSwo NLar SBfd SEND SUsu SWvt WCFE WMoo WPnP WWEG
	- 'Christmas Tree'	CLAP EBee EPPr WHoo WMoo
	- 'Evergreen Giant'	see *L. gigantea*
	- 'Gold-banded' (v)	CLAP EBee EPfP LHop LRHS NSti SPer WCot WFar WWFP
	- 'Goldfinger'	CPLG EBee EPla WPGP
	- 'Ingwersen'	CBgR CPLG EBee ECho ELon EPPr EPfP LRHS NMRc WGrn WPnP
	- 'John Burch' (v)	CBct CBgR CLAP CPLG EBee ELon EShb MCCP NLar NOak SMad WGrn WSpi WWEG
	- 'Majestic' misapplied	see *L. exiliflora*
	- 'Moneymaker'	EBee ECtt EPPr
§	- 'Monroe White'	CBct CBgR CLAP CMac CPLG EBee EBla ECha ECho EHrv ELon EPfP EShb GKir LAst LEdu LRHS MRav NLar NOak SPet WAul WFar WSpi WWEG
	- 'Okina' (v)	CSpe EBee ECtt ELon EWes MAvo SMad WCot WFut
	- 'Paul Aden'	EPfP WPGP
	- 'Pee Dee Ingot'	CWGN EBee ECtt EShb NLar WPnP
	- 'Royal Purple'	CBct CHar CLAP EBee EPPr EPfP GQue LRHS NBPC NGdn NLar SBfd WClo WCot WGrn
	- 'Silver Ribbon'	CLAP CMoH CWGN EBee EBla EPfP LAst LBMP LRHS LSRN MGos NOak NSti SBch WOut WPGP WWEG
	- 'Superba'	WCot
§	- 'Variegata' (v)	Widely available
	- variegated, white-flowered (v)	CBcs CDes CFir ECho
	- 'Webster Wideleaf'	EBee
	'New Wonder'	EHrv LEdu
	platyphylla	see *L. muscari*
	'Samantha'	EBee ECha NOak SBch
	spicata	EBee ECho SWat WWEG
	- 'Alba'	ECho MRav MTho WTin
§	- 'Gin-ryu' (v)	CBct CLAP CMac CPLG CPrp EBee ECho ECtt EPPr EWes LEdu LSRN MCCP MRav NLar SLPl SMad SPer WClo WCot WPGP
	- 'Silver Dragon'	see *L. spicata* 'Gin-ryu'
	- 'Small Green'	WWEG

Listera (*Orchidaceae*)

	ovata	WHer

Litchi (*Sapindaceae*)

	chinensis	CCCN

Lithocarpus ✿ (*Fagaceae*)

	edulis	CGHE CHEx CPLG SAPC SArc SKHP WPGP

Lithodora (*Boraginaceae*)

§	***diffusa***	ECho MWat SRot
	- 'Alba'	CTri ECho EPfP GEdr GKev MGos SPer SPoG WCom WFar
	- 'Baby Barbara'	GKev
	- 'Cambridge Blue'	ECho SPer
	- 'Compacta'	CWCL ECho EWes NLAp WAbe WPat
§	- 'Grace Ward' Υ^{H4}	ECho EPfP MMuc NLAp WAbe WFar WPat
§	- 'Heavenly Blue' Υ^{H4}	Widely available
	- 'Inverleith'	ECho EWes LLHF
I	- 'Minima' **new**	EPot
	- 'Pete's Favourite'	WAbe WPat
	- 'Picos'	CMea CPBP ECho GGar GKev NLAp NLar NMen WAbe WCom WFar WPat WThu
	- 'Star'^{PBR}	CMHG EPfP GGar GKev GKir LRHS MAvo NHol NLar SCoo SPer SPoG SRot SWvt
	fruticosa	CArn
	× ***intermedia***	see *Moltkia* × *intermedia*
§	***oleifolia*** Υ^{H4}	ECho EPot LLHF LRHS MWat NBir NMen
	rosmarinifolia	CMoH CSpe WCFE

zahnii	ECho EPot LLHF WFar WPat
- 'Azureness'	CPBP WAbe

Lithophragma (*Saxifragaceae*)

heterophyllum	EBee
parviflorum	CAby EWes MTho NLar NWCA WAbe

Lithospermum (*Boraginaceae*)

diffusum	see *Lithodora diffusa*
doerfleri	see *Moltkia doerfleri*
'Grace Ward'	see *Lithodora diffusa* 'Grace Ward'
'Heavenly Blue'	see *Lithodora diffusa* 'Heavenly Blue'
officinale	CArn EBWF GBar GPoy NMir
oleifolium	see *Lithodora oleifolia*
purpureocaeruleum	see *Buglossoides purpurocaerulea*

Litsea (*Lauraceae*)

glauca	see *Neolitsea sericea*

Littonia (*Colchicaceae*)

modesta	CRHN ECho

Livistona (*Arecaceae*)

australis	EAmu EUJe LPal
chinensis ♀H1	CPHo EAmu EUJe LPal SBig SChr
decora	CPHo CTrC EAmu LPal
mariae	EAmu LPal
nitida	SChr
saribus	EAmu

Lloydia (*Liliaceae*)

serotina	GAuc

Loasa (*Loasaceae*)

triphylla var. ***volcanica***	EWes GCra WSHC

Lobelia (*Campanulaceae*)

B&SWJ 8220 from Vietnam	WCru
aberdarica	CHEx
angulata	see *Pratia angulata*
bequeartii	GCal
bridgesii	CBow CDTJ CPLG EWes EWld EWll GCal GGar LLHF NGBl NLar WKif WMoo WPGP
§ ***cardinalis*** ♀H3	CArn CBen CHEx CMac CRWN EBla EHon EPfP GAbr GKir GMaP LPBA LRHS MMuc NLar NPer SPer SPet SPlb SRms SWat SWvt WFar WMAq
- 'Bee's Flame'	CFir CPrp CWGN EBee EPla GGar LRHS MCot MRav MSpe NBre NEgg SAga SPhx SUsu SWat
§ - 'Elmfeuer'	CMHG CWit EBee EHoe EPfP EShb LAst MWat NLar NPri SBfd SMrm SPad SPlb SWvt WFar
- 'Eulalia Berridge'	CAby CSam EBee ECtt LRHS NPnk SMrm WFar WSHC
- subsp. ***graminea*** var. ***multiflora***	CFir
§ - 'Queen Victoria' ♀H3	Widely available
N - 'Russian Princess' misapplied	EGxp MAsh NPnk SUsu SWvt WWEG WWlt
chinensis	LLWG
'Cinnabar Deep Red'	see *L.* × *speciosa* (Fan Series) 'Fan Tiefrot'
'Cinnabar Rose'	see *L.* × *speciosa* (Fan Series) 'Fan Zinnoberrosa'
Compliment Blue	see *L.* × *speciosa* (Kompliment Series) 'Kompliment Blau'
Compliment Deep Red	see *L.* × *speciosa* (Kompliment Series) 'Kompliment Tiefrot'
Compliment Purple	see *L.* × *speciosa* (Kompliment Series) 'Kompliment Purpur'
Compliment Scarlet	see *L.* × *speciosa* (Kompliment Series) 'Kompliment Scharlach'
dortmanna	GAuc
Elizabeth Strangman selection **new**	NDov
erinus Big Blue = 'Weslobigblue'PBR	LAst
- 'Kathleen Mallard' (d)	CCCN ECtt LAst SWvt
- 'Purple Star'	LSou SVil
- 'Richardii'	see *L. richardsonii*
- 'Sailor Star'	LAst
- (Waterfall Series) 'Waterfall Deep Blue With Eye' **new**	SVil
- - 'Waterfall Light Blue With Eye' **new**	SVil
excelsa	EShb GGar SGar SPav SUsu WFar WSHC
- B&SWJ 9513	WCru
Fan Deep Red	see *L.* × *speciosa* (Fan Series) 'Fan Tiefrot'
Fan Deep Rose	see *L.* × *speciosa* (Fan Series) 'Fan Orchidrosa'
Fan Salmon	see *L.* × *speciosa* (Fan Series) 'Fan Lachs'
'Flamingo'	see *L.* × *speciosa* 'Pink Flamingo'
'Forncett Merry'	NBre
fulgens	see *L. cardinalis*
- Saint Elmo's Fire	see *L. cardinalis* 'Elmfeuer'
× ***gerardii***	see *L.* × *speciosa*
gibberoa	CDTJ CHEx
grandidentata F&M 133	WPGP
'Hadspen Purple'PBR	see *L.* × *speciosa* 'Hadspen Purple'
'Hot Tiger' **new**	LAst SVil
inflata	CArn EOHP GPoy
kalmii	WPer
- 'Blue Shadow'	EBla
laxiflora	CHid CHll SAga SHom SPet
- B&SWJ 9064	WCru
- F&M 71	GCal
- var. ***angustifolia***	CDTJ CHEx CPrp CSam EBee ECtt EPfP EShb EWld GCal MSpe SDnm SMrm SPav SPoG SRms SUsu WBox WCot WPrP WWlt
linnaeoides	SPlb
'Lipstick'	WWEG
'Martha'	EBee
montana **new**	EWld
pedunculata	see *Pratia pedunculata*
'Pink Passion'	LBuc LRHS
polyphylla	ECtt MSCN WBox
'Queen Victoria'	see *L. cardinalis* 'Queen Victoria'
§ ***richardsonii*** ♀H1+3	CFox ECtt SWvt
'Royal Velvet'	CSpr IPot LRHS
seguinii B&SWJ 7065	WCru
sessilifolia	CPLG EBee GMac LPBA WCot WPer
- B&SWJ 8875	WCru
siphilitica	Widely available
- 'Alba'	CEnt CSam EBee EBla EPfP GCal LPBA LRHS SBfd SPav SRms SWat SWvt WBor WFar WHoo WHrl WMnd WMoo WPer
- blue-flowered	CSpe MMuc NCGa NLar SGSe SWat SWvt
- 'Rosea'	MNrw

'Sonia'	SWat
§ × ***speciosa***	CEnt IKil MHer NBre SMHy SMrm SVic SWat WBor WFar WMoo WSHC
- 'Butterfly Blue'	EBee WWEG
- 'Butterfly Rose'	SRot
- 'Cherry Ripe'	CPrp GCra LLHF NHol WEas
- 'Dark Crusader'	CPrp CWGN EBee EBrs ECGP ECtt ELan LAst LBMP LRHS MCot MSCN MWhi NHol SAga SWat WMnd
- (Fan Series) 'Fan Blau'	EPfP NBir WWEG
- - 'Fan Burgundy'	CEnt EPfP LRHS NLar SBfd SPet WHil WWEG
§ - - 'Fan Lachs'	EPfP NBPC SAga SBfd SPet
§ - - 'Fan Orchidrosa' ♀H3-4	EBee EPfP LRHS NBir NGdn SGSe SPet SRot WHil WWEG
- - 'Fan Scharlach' ♀H3-4	CChe EBee EPfP LRHS MAvo MGos NBir NLar SGar SHar SRot SWvt WCFE WDyG WHil WShi WWEG
§ - - 'Fan Tiefrot' ♀H3-4	EPfP MSCN MWea SAga SMrm SPet SRms SWat SWvt WPer
§ - - 'Fan Zinnoberrosa' ♀H3-4	CEnt CFir CMMP EBee SRms SRot SWvt WMoo WPer
- 'Grape Knee-high'	EBee EPfP GCra LLHF LSRN SWat
§ - 'Hadspen Purple'PBR	CFox CMHG CSpe CWGN EBee ELan EPfP LRHS LSRN MAsh MBri MCCP MCot MWea NCGa NCob NHol NSti SGSe SHar SPoG SWat SWvt
- 'Kimbridge Beet'	CMac SGSe
- Kompliment Series	WWEG
§ - - 'Kompliment Blau'	CFir CWat SPet SWvt WPer
* - - 'Kompliment Pale Pink'	EShb
§ - - 'Kompliment Purpur'	MNrw SPet SWvt
§ - - 'Kompliment Scharlach' ♀H3-4	EBee EPfP LHop MNrw NHol NPer SPad SPer SPet SWvt WFar WMnd WPer WWEG
§ - - 'Kompliment Tiefrot'	CWat MMuc MNrw NCGa NLar SPet SWvt WPer
- 'Monet Moment'	CBow EBee EBla EWes GCal SWvt WSpi
- 'Pauline'	ECtt
- 'Pink Elephant' ♀H4	CBow CSWP GCra MDKP NBre SHar SMrs WFar WWEG
§ - 'Pink Flamingo'	CMMP EBee EBla NLar SPer SWat WFar WMoo WShi
- 'Purple Towers'	NBre
- red-flowered	MMuc
- 'Rosenkavalier'	EBee ECtt MCot WFar
- 'Rosy Pink'	SMrm
- 'Ruby Slippers'	CBcs EBee EBrs ECtt ELan EPfP IPot LAst LRHS LSRN NCGa SMrs SWat WFar WWEG
N - 'Russian Princess' purple-flowered	CFir CPrp CSam CTri CWCL EAEE EBee ECtt EHoe ELan LAst LBMP LPBA LSou MBri MCCP MCot MHer MSCN NCGa NHol SAga SBfd SMrm SPer WFar WMnd WMoo
- 'Sparkle deVine'	WFar
- 'Sparkling Ruby' **new**	LBuc
- 'Tania'	Widely available
§ - 'Vedrariensis'	Widely available
- 'Wildwood Splendor'	WFar
- 'Will Scarlet'	LRHS SAga
'Star Sky'	LAst LSou
treadwellii	see *Pratia angulata* 'Treadwellii'
tupa	Widely available
- Archibald's form	CPLG GCra WCot
- dark orange-flowered	SGSe
urens	WPGP
valida	SGar SWvt WFar
- 'True Blue'	CWGN SWvt
vedrariensis	see *L.* × *speciosa* 'Vedrariensis'
villosa	SGSe
(Waterfall Series) Waterfall Light Lavender = 'Balwalila'	SVil
- Waterfall White Sparkle = 'Balobwablu'PBR **new**	LAst SVil
wollastonii **new**	SPlb

Loeselia (*Polemoniaceae*)

mexicana	CHll

loganberry see *Rubus* × *loganobaccus*

Lomandra (*Lomandraceae*)

confertifolia	ECou
- 'Wingarra'	EHoe NOak
filiformis Savanna Blue = 'Lfm500'	EPPr ESwi NOak SVil
hystrix	SPlb
longifolia	ECou GCal LEdu SPlb
- 'Kulnura'	ECou
- 'Orford'	ECou
- Tanika = 'Lm300'PBR	EBee EPPr ESwi GBin LRHS LTen MWea NOak WBor

Lomaria see *Blechnum*

Lomatia (*Proteaceae*)

sp. **new**	CWit
dentata	LRHS
ferruginea	CBcs CDoC CPLG EPfP GBin GGal SAPC SArc SKHP SSpi WCru WPGP
fraseri	EBee EPfP LRHS SSpi
hirsuta	SKHP
longifolia	see *L. myricoides*
§ ***myricoides***	CBcs CCCN CDoC CPLG CTsd EBee ELan EPfP IDee LRHS MBri NLar SAPC SKHP SLon SPer SSpi
silaifolia	EPfP
tinctoria	CBcs CDoC CPLG EBee EPfP IDee NLar SAPC SArc SSpi

Lomatium (*Apiaceae*)

foeniculaceum subsp. ***fimbriatum*** NNS 06-349	WCot
grayi	SPhx

Lonicera ✿ (*Caprifoliaceae*)

sp.	CMen
B&SWJ 2654 from Sikkim	WCru
F&M 207	WPGP
KR 291	ELon
SDR 6044	GKev
§ ***acuminata***	CFir EBee LRHS WGwG
- B&SWJ 3480	WCru
alberti	EBee MBNS MMuc NLar WGwG
alseuosmoides	EBee IArd LRHS NLar SEND SKHP SLon SPoG WCru WPGP WSHC
× ***americana*** misapplied	see *L.* × *italica* Tausch
§ × ***americana*** (Miller) K. Koch	CBcs CRHN EPfP MAsh MGos MRav MSwo MWhi NLar NWea SEND SGar SKHP SLim SRms WBor WGwG
§ × ***brownii*** 'Dropmore Scarlet'	Widely available
- 'Fuchsioides' misapplied	see *L.* × *brownii* 'Dropmore Scarlet'
- 'Fuchsioides' K. Koch	WSHC
caerulea	MRav STre
- var. ***altaica***	LEdu
- var. ***edulis***	CAgr LEdu MCoo
- subsp. ***kamtschatica***	CAgr NLar

§	***caprifolium*** 🏆^{H4}	CDoC CRHN EBee ELan EPfP LRHS MAsh NBea NLar SPer
	- 'Anna Fletcher'	CRHN CSPN LSRN NHaw WCFE
	- f. ***pauciflora***	see *L.* × *italica* Tausch
	chaetocarpa	MRav WSHC
	chamissoi	NLar
	'Clavey's Dwarf'	see *L.* × *xylosteoides* 'Clavey's Dwarf'
	'Copper Beauty'^{PBR}	CAlb EPPr LBuc LSRN LSou SLim
	crassifolia	MBri WCot
	- 'Little Honey'	EPPr MGos MMHG MRav WCot
	deflexicalyx	EPfP NLar
	'Early Cream'	see *L. caprifolium*
	elisae	CAbP CMac EPfP ERea MGos NLar SSpi WPat WSHC
	etrusca	CFir LAst MRav
	- 'Donald Waterer' 🏆^{H4}	CRHN EBee EPfP LSRN MAsh NLar WFar WGor
	- 'Michael Rosse'	EBee ELan IArd LRHS MAsh MBNS SKHP SRms
	- 'Superba' 🏆^{H4}	CRHN EBee ECtt ELan EPfP LRHS MAsh NLar SEND SLim SPer SPoG WFar WSHC
	'Fire Cracker' **new**	SLon
	flexuosa	see *L. japonica* var. *repens*
	fragrantissima	Widely available
	giraldii misapplied	see *L. acuminata*
	giraldii Rehder	CBot EBee EPfP MAsh MRav SLim
	glabrata	SCoo SLim
	- B&SWJ 2150	WCru
	glehnii	GAuc
	'Golden Trumpet'	CWGN EBee LRHS LSRN
	grata	see *L.* × *americana* (Miller) K. Koch
	× ***heckrottii***	CDoC CRHN CSBt EBee ECtt MGan MGos NBea NLar NSti WDin
§	- 'American Beauty'	EBee
	- 'Gold Flame' misapplied	see *L.* × *heckrottii* 'American Beauty'
	- 'Gold Flame' ambig.	CChe LSRN LTen NLar
	- 'Gold Flame' hort.	CDul CMac EBee ELan EPfP GKir LAst LBuc LRHS MAsh MBri MGos MRav NBea NHol SBfd SLim SPer SRms WDin WFar WMoo WSHC
§	***henryi***	Widely available
	- B&SWJ 8109	WCru
	- Sich 1489	WPGP
	- 'Copper Beauty'	CFir CWit EBee EQua LAst LHop LRHS LSRN MAsh MGos MRav NCGa NLar SLon SOkt SPoG WDin WPGP
	- var. ***subcoriacea***	see *L. henryi*
	hildebrandiana	CCCN CHll CPLG CRHN ERea EShb LRHS MAsh SKHP SOWG WPGP
	'Hill House'	CHll
	'Honey Baby'^{PBR}	ELon EPfP LLHF LRHS MAsh MBlu MBri NHol WRHF
	insularis	see *L. morrowii*
	involucrata	CFee CMCN CMHG CPLG CPMA CWib EPPr GQui LHop MBNS MBlu MMuc NChi NHol SEND SPer WCFE WDin WFar
	- var. ***ledebourii***	CBgR EBee ELan EPfP GKir LAst LLHF LRHS MRav SDys SKHP WGob
	- 'Orange Dwarf' **new**	SKHP
	× ***italica*** ambig.	NPer SEND SPer
§	× ***italica*** Tausch 🏆^{H4}	CRHN CSam CTri ECtt LRHS MBNS MSwo NEgg NPer NSti SCoo SKHP SLim WClo WDin WFar WPnn
§	- Harlequin = 'Sherlite'^{PBR} (v)	CBot CMac CSPN EGxp EHoe EPfP LAst LRHS LSRN MAsh MGos NBea NSti SLim SPlb SRms SWvt WCot

	japonica	CMen
§	- 'Aureoreticulata' (v)	CDul CMac CWib EBee ECrN EHoe ELan ELon EPfP LRHS LSRN MBri MGos MRav MWhi NPer SGar SPer SPet SRms STre WDin WEas WFar
	- 'Cream Cascade'	COlW EBee LRHS MGos MSwo NLar SCoo
	- 'Dart's Acumen'	CRHN
	- 'Dart's World'	CAlb EBee LRHS MBri WFar
	- 'Halliana' 🏆^{H4}	Widely available
	- 'Hall's Prolific'	Widely available
	- Honeydew = 'Hinlon'	SPoG
§	- 'Horwood Gem' (v)	EBee ECtt LSRN MGos NLar SCoo SLim WFar
	- 'Maskerade'	EBee LLHF NBro NLar
	- 'Mint Crisp'^{PBR} (v)	CBow CMac CSBt CWGN CWSG CWit EBee ECrN ELan EPfP LAst LRHS LSRN LSou MBri MGos NLar SBfd SLim SPad SPer SPoG SWvt WDin WFar
	- 'Peter Adams'	see *L. japonica* 'Horwood Gem'
	- 'Red World'	EBee
§	- var. ***repens*** 🏆^{H4}	Widely available
	- 'Variegata'	see *L. japonica* 'Aureoreticulata'
	korolkowii	CBot CPMA EBee EPPr EPfP MBNS MMuc NBir NLar SEND SPoG WCFE WGrn WSHC
	- 'Blue Velvet'	MCoo NLar
	- var. ***zabelii*** misapplied	see *L. tatarica* 'Zabelii'
	- var. ***zabelii*** (Rehder) Rehder	ELan
	lanceolata BWJ 7935	WCru
	maackii	CHll CMCN CPMA EBee EPPr EPfP MRav NLar WCFE
	- f. ***podocarpa***	SPoG
*	***macgregorii***	CMCN
	macrantha WWJ 11606	WCru
	'Mandarin'	CDoC EBee ELan GKir LRHS MBlu MGos MRav NLar SCoo SLim SWvt WSHC WSpi
	maximowiczii var. ***sachalinensis***	NLar
§	***morrowii***	CMCN GAuc
	myrtillus	GAuc NLar
	nitida	CAlb CBar CBcs CCVT CDul CMac CMen CSBt CTri ECrN EMac EPfP IFFs NWea SBfd SPer STre SWal WDin WFar WHar
	- 'Baggesen's Gold' 🏆^{H4}	Widely available
	- Edmée Gold = 'Briloni'^{PBR}	EPfP LRHS MAsh WPat
	- 'Elegant'	LBuc STre WDin
	- 'Fertilis'	SPer
	- 'Lemon Beauty' (v)	Widely available
	- 'Lemon Queen'	CWib ELan MSwo
	- 'Lemon Spreader'	CBcs
§	- 'Maigrün'	CAlb CBar CBcs CDul EPfP MSwo SBfd SPer SWvt WDin WFar
	- Maygreen	see *L. nitida* 'Maigrün'
	- 'Red Tips'	EBee EHoe EMil EPPr EPfP EPla MGos NHol SCoo WDin WFar WMoo
	- 'Silver Beauty' (v)	CDul CMac CWib EBee ECrN EHoe EPfP LAst LHop MAsh MGos MLHP MRav MSwo NEgg NHol SAga SBfd SGar SPer SPlb SRms SWvt WCom WDin WFar WMoo
*	- 'Silver Cloud'	NHol
	- 'Twiggy' (v)	CAlb CDoC CElw CSBt EDAr EHoe EMil LBuc LRHS MAsh NEgg NHol NLar SBfd WGrn

	periclymenum	CArn CDul CRWN CTri GKir GPoy MHer MLHP MRav NLar NMir NSco NWea SPlb WDin WPnn WSFF
	- 'Belgica' misapplied	see *L.* × *italica* Tausch
	- 'Belgica'	Widely available
	- Caprilia Imperial = 'Inov86' **new**	SBfd
	- 'Florida'	see *L. periclymenum* 'Serotina'
	- 'Graham Thomas' ♀H4	Widely available
	- 'Harlequin' PBR	see *L.* × *italica* Harlequin
	- 'Heaven Scent'	LBuc LSRN MGos MNHC NLar WFar WGwG WPnn
	- 'Honeybush'	CDoC CPMA CSPN CWGN LRHS MAsh MBri MGos NHol NPri SLim WMoo
	- 'La Gasnérie'	EBee SLim WPnn
	- 'Munster'	WPnn WSHC
	- 'Purple Queen'	CChe
	- 'Red Gables'	CWan EBee ELon LSRN MBNS MGos NLar SCoo SEND SLim WClo WCot WGor WKif WPat WPnn
	- 'Scentsation' PBR	CMac CSBt CWGN EPfP LAst LBuc LRHS MAsh MBri NLar SCoo SLon SPoG
N	- 'Serotina' ♀H4	Widely available
*	- ***sulphurea***	WFar
	- 'Sweet Sue'	COIW CRHN CSPN EBee ECtt ELan ELon EPfP LAst LBuc LOck LRHS LSRN MAsh MBNS MBri MGos MLHP MSwo NEgg NHol NSti SCoo SPoG SWvt WFar WMoo
	- 'Winchester'	EBee
	- yellow	NEgg
	pileata	Widely available
	- 'Moss Green'	CBar CDoC
	- 'Pilot'	SLPl
	- 'Silver Lining' (v)	EPla SAga
	- 'Stockholm'	SLPl
	× ***purpusii***	CBgR CDoC CMac CRHN CTri CWSG CWib EBee ECrN EPfP GKir IFFs LSRN MBNS MGos MLHP MWat NBea SBfd SPer SPoG SRms WCFE WFar WSHC
	- 'Spring Romance'	CMac
	- 'Winter Beauty' ♀H4	Widely available
	ramosissima	NLar
	saccata	CPMA EPfP
	sempervirens ♀H4	CBot CMac CRHN CSBt EPfP MBNS MRav WFar WSHC
	- 'Cedar Lane'	LRHS MAsh
	- 'Dropmore Scarlet'	see *L.* × *brownii* 'Dropmore Scarlet'
	- 'Leo'	CSPN CWGN
N	- f. ***sulphurea***	EBee EPfP NBea WSHC
	- - 'John Clayton'	LRHS MAsh SKHP
	setifera	CBot
	- 'Daphnis'	EPfP WBVN
	similis var. ***delavayi*** ♀H4	CBot CChe CRHN CSPN CWGN EBee ECrN ELan EPfP LRHS MAsh MBri MMuc MNHC MRav NBea NEgg NSti SBfd SDix SEND SLPl SPoG SRms WCot WFar WGwG WPGP WSHC
	'Simonet'	EBee
	splendida	CBot WSHC
	'Spring Bouquet'	LRHS
	standishii	CTri EBee MGos WDin WFar
	- 'Budapest'	LLHF LRHS MAsh MBlu MBri MGos NLar WPat
	subaequalis	SKHP

	- Og 93.329	WPGP
	Sweet Isabel = 'Genbel'	CWit EPfP LBuc LRHS MAsh NCGa
	syringantha	CArn CRHN CSam EBee ECrN ELan EPfP GGar GKir LAst LEdu MAsh MBri MGos MMuc MNrw MRav MWhi NBea NEgg NHol NLar SEND SLPl SPer WCFE WClo WDin WFar WSHC
	- 'Grandiflora'	GQui
	tatarica	CMCN CWib EBee MRav WFar
	- 'Alba'	CPMA
	- 'Arnold Red'	CBcs EBee ELan EPfP MAsh MBlu NLar SEND WDin
	- 'Hack's Red'	CWib EBee EPfP LHop LRHS LSou MRav SAga SCoo SKHP SPer SWvt WCot WDin WFar
	- 'Rosea'	WCot
§	- 'Zabelii'	EPfP
	× ***tellmanniana***	Widely available
	- 'Joan Sayers'	EBee LSRN SCoo SLim WCFE
	thibetica	SPer WFar
	tianschanica	GAuc
	tragophylla ♀H4	CDoC CDoy CSBt EBee ELan EPfP LRHS LSRN MAsh MBNS MBri MRav SCoo SEND SLim SMad SPer SPoG SSpi SWvt WDin WSHC
	- 'Maurice Foster'	EBee ELan EPfP MBNS
	- 'Pharaoh's Trumpet'	EPfP LRHS MAsh SLon
	webbiana	ELan
	× ***xylosteoides***	WFar
§	- 'Clavey's Dwarf'	EBee LLHF NHol
	xylosteum	CArn EBee NLar WFar

Lophomyrtus (*Myrtaceae*)

§	***bullata***	CAbP CDTJ CTrC CTsd GQui SPer WFar
	- 'Matai Bay'	CBcs CTrC EBee
§	× ***ralphii***	MHer
	- 'Black Pearl' **new**	EShb LBuc LRHS SBfd
	- 'Gloriosa' (v)	CDoC CTrC EPfP
	- 'Kathryn'	CBcs CDoC EBee ELan EMil EPfP LRHS NLar SPoG SRGP SSpi
	- 'Little Star' (v)	CBcs CDoC CTrC LRHS MAsh SPoG WPat
	- Logan's form (v)	CBcs LRHS
	- 'Multicolor' (v)	CBcs CTrC EBee LRHS SLim
	- 'Pixie'	CAbP CBcs CDoC CTrC EBee EPfP LRHS MAsh SPoG WPat
	- 'Red Dragon'	CBcs CTrC CTsd CWSG EBee IDee LRHS LSou MAsh WFar WPat
	- 'Red Pixie'	CDoC
	- 'Red Wing'	LRHS
§	- 'Traversii' (v)	MGos SPoG
	- 'Tricolor' (v)	WFar
	- 'Variegata' (v)	MHer
	- 'Wild Cherry'	CBcs CTrC EBee GGar LRHS

Lophosoria (*Dicksoniaceae*)

	quadripinnata	CBty CDTJ CFir CKel SBig WPGP WRic

Lophospermum (*Scrophulariaceae*)

	'Cream Delight' **new**	CCCN
§	***erubescens*** ♀H2-3	CBot CRHN SBch SGar
	- 'Bridal Bouquet'	CPla
	'Magic Dragon'	CPla LSou
§	'Red Dragon'	CCCN CPla EShb SBch SGar
§	***scandens***	CCCN CRHN ELan
§	- 'Pink Ice'	SOWG
	'Wine Red' **new**	LAst

loquat see *Eriobotrya japonica*

Loropetalum (*Hamamelidaceae*)

chinense	CWib IMou
- Black Pearl = 'Pearl' new	CWSG
- 'China Pink'	CBcs
- 'Ming Dynasty'	CAbP MAsh MGos SSta
- 'Rose Blush' new	ECho SHeu
- f. ***rubrum***	CBcs CMen CPLG CWib WCot
- - 'Blush'	CPMA EBee SBfd SSpi
- - 'Burgundy'	CTrC MPkF
- - 'Daybreak's Flame'	CPMA CPen CWit EGxp LRHS SSta WGob
- - 'Fire Dance'	CAbP CBcs CBgR CCCN CDoC CHll CPMA CPen CTrC EBee EGxp EPfP IDee LRHS MGos SBfd SEND SHeu SPoG SSpi SWvt WBrE WFar WGwG WPat
- - 'Fire Glow' new	IDee LRHS
- - 'Pipa's Red'	MGos
- 'Snowdance'	CAbP
- 'Tang Dynasty'	CBgR CTrC ESwi LRHS MGos MMuc SSta

Lotus (*Papilionaceae*)

berthelotii	CCCN CDTJ CHEx ECtt ELan EOHP MCot SBfd SPet SPoG
- deep red-flowered ♀H1+3	SBfd SWvt
berthelotii* × *maculatus ♀H1+3	CCCN MSCN
corniculatus	CArn EBWF MCoo MHer MMuc MNHC NLan NMir NSco SEND SIde WAbe WSFF
- 'Plenus' (d)	NLar WPer
'Gold Flash'	LAst SBfd
hirsutus ♀H3-4	Widely available
- 'Brimstone' (v)	CWSG CWib ECtt LHop LRHS MAvo SBfd SPer SPoG SWvt
- Little Boy Blue = 'Lisbob'PBR	CSBt EBee EPfP LRHS LSou LSqu MAsh SBfd SSpi
- 'Lois'	EBee EPfP LHop LRHS MDKP SPoG WPGP
maculatus	EOHP SOWG SPet
maritimus	CPom SRot
pedunculatus	see *L. uliginosus*
pentaphyllus	NLar
'Red Flash'	LAst
tetragonolobus	SRot SVic
§ ***uliginosus***	EBWF MCoo NMir NSco WSFF

lovage see *Levisticum officinale*

Loxostigma (*Gesneriaceae*)

kurzii GWJ 9342	WCru

Ludwigia (*Onagraceae*)

uruguayensis	LPBA

Luetkea (*Rosaceae*)

pectinata	NRya WAbe

Luma (*Myrtaceae*)

§ ***apiculata*** ♀H3	Widely available
§ - 'Glanleam Gold' (v) ♀H3	Widely available
- 'Penlee'	WJek
- 'Saint Hilary' (v)	GGar LRHS MNHC SBfd WJek
- 'Variegata' (v)	CMHG CTri NHol SAga SLim
§ ***chequen***	CBcs CFee EBee GGar IDee LEdu LRHS MHer NLar WBrE WFar WJek WMoo

Lunaria (*Brassicaceae*)

§ ***annua***	MNHC NPri SIde SWat WHer WJek WSFF
- var. ***albiflora*** ♀H4	EWTr MMuc NBir SEND SWat WCot
I - - 'Alba Variegata' (v)	CSpe WBrk WHil WTin
- 'Chedglow'	CNat
- 'Corfu Blue'	CSpe
- 'Ken Aslet'	NHol
- 'Munstead Purple'	CSpe
- 'Pennies in Bronze' new	WHil
- 'Variegata' (v)	NBir SWat WCom WEas WHer
- violet-flowered	NBir
biennis	see *L. annua*
rediviva	CDes CSpe EBee ECGP ECha EPPr EPla EWTr GAbr GBin GCal GCra GGar IBlr IFro LPio MMuc NBid NChi NPer NSti WCot WEas WFar WHer WPGP
- 'Partway White'	WCot

Lunathyrium (*Woodsiaceae*)

pycnosorum	ISha WRic

Lupinus ✿ (*Papilionaceae*)

B&SWJ 10309 from Guatemala	WCru
'African Sunset'	CWCL
albus	CArn
'Animal'	CWCL
arboreus ♀H4	Widely available
- 'Barton-on-Sea'	WClo
- 'Blue Boy'	ELan LSRN
- blue-flowered	CHar CWCL CWib EBrs GGar MCot MLHP MWat NBPC SBfd SPer SPlb SPoG SWvt WBrE WClo WFar WHlf
- 'Chelsea Blue' new	LRHS
- mixed	CArn
- prostrate	MDKP MMHG
- 'Rhubarb and Custard' new	CWCL
- 'Snow Queen'	CWCL LRHS SPer SPoG WClo
- 'Sulphur Yellow'	SWvt
- white-flowered	CSpe CWib GCal GGar
- yellow and blue-flowered	NBir SRkn
- yellow-flowered	GGar MCot MLHP WClo WWEG
arboreus* × *variicolor	CHid
arcticus	CSpe
Band of Nobles Series ♀H4	ECtt WFar
'Beefeater'	CWCL
'Bishop's Tipple'	CWCL EWes
'Blossom'PBR	CWCL LSRN MBri WSpi
'Blue Streak'	CWCL
bogotensis B&SWJ 10761	WCru
'Brimstone'	CWCL
'Bruiser'	CWCL
'Bubblegum'	CWCL
'Camelot Blue'	EPfP
'Carmen'	CWCL
'Chameleon'	CWCL WSpi
chamissonis	CHll CPla CSpe CWCL EBee EHrv EWes LHop MCot SMrm SPer WClo WCom WFar
'Chandelier' (Band of Nobles Series)	CBcs CSBt CTri EBee ECtt ELan EPfP GKir LRHS MBri MCot MNHC MWat NBir NGBl NPri SBfd SMrm SPad SPer SPoG SWal SWvt WBVN WCAu WClo WFar WMnd
costaricensis B&SWJ 10487	WCru
'Desert Sun'	CWCL

	Dwarf Gallery hybrids	GKir WMoo
	'Dwarf Lulu'	see *L.* 'Lulu'
	Gallery Series	CSBt MAvo SCoo SGar SPlb WFar
	- 'Gallery Blue'	ECtt EPfP GKir LRHS LSRN NLar NNor NPri NVic SCoo SMrm SPer SPoG WClo WFar
	- 'Gallery Pink'	EPfP GKir LRHS NLar NPri SCoo SMrm SPer SPoG WFar
	- 'Gallery Red'	ECtt EPfP GKir LRHS NLar NPri NVic SCoo SMrm SPer SPoG WClo WFar
	- 'Gallery Rose'	GKir LSRN SPer SPoG
	- 'Gallery White'	EPfP GKir LRHS NLar NPri NVic SCoo SPer SPoG WClo WFar
	- 'Gallery Yellow'	ECtt EPfP LRHS NLar NPri NVic SCoo SMrm SPer SPoG WClo
	'Gladiator'	CWCL
	'Heathcliffe Blue' **new**	WOut
	'Imperial Robe'	CWCL
	'Inspiration'	CWCL
	'Ivory Chiffon'	GBin
	'Le Gentilhomme' (Band of Nobles Series)	MCot
	'Lindy Lou'	CWCL
§	'Lulu'	ECtt EPfP LRHS SBfd SPer SPoG STes SWvt WFar WMoo
	'Manhattan Lights'	CWCL MBri
	'Masterpiece'	CWCL GBin LRHS MBri MWea WHlf WSpi
	Minarette Group	CTri ECtt SPet SRms WClo WFar
	'Morello Cherry'	CWCL EWTr
	'Mrs Perkins'	SMrm
	'My Castle' (Band of Nobles Series)	CBcs CSBt CTri EBee ECtt ELan EPfP GKir LRHS LSRN MBri MGos MNHC MWat NGBl NPri SBfd SMrm SPad SPer SPoG SWal SWvt WBVN WBor WCAu WClo WFar WMnd WMoo
	'Neptune'	CWCL
	'Noble Maiden' (Band of Nobles Series)	CBcs CPrp CSBt CTri EBee ECtt ELan EPfP GAbr GKir LRHS LSRN MBri MCot MNHC MWat NGBl NPri SBfd SMrm SPad SPer SPoG SWal SWvt WBVN WCAu WFar WMnd WMoo
	nootkatensis	GKir GLog GMac WWEG
	'Pauly'	CWCL
	'Pen and Ink'	CWCL
	'Persian Slipper' PBR	CWCL GBin LRHS MBri WSpi
	'Plummy Blue'	MWea
	'Pluto'	CWCL
	'Polar Princess'	EWes GBin LRHS SWat
	polyphyllus	MWhi WOut
	propinquus	CEnt SPhx
	'Red Arrow'	CWCL
	'Red Rum' PBR	CWCL GBin LRHS MBri
	'Redhead'	CWCL
	'Rote Flamme'	CPrp EWes GBin SMrm
	Russell hybrids	CSBt EPfP LAst MHer MLHP MWat SBfd SEND SGar SPet SPlb SRms SVic SWvt WFar
	'Saffron'	CWCL GBin LRHS LSRN
	'Saint Andrew'	CWCL
	'Salmon Star' PBR	CWCL GBin WSpi
	'Sand Pink'	EWes
	'Snowgoose'	CWCL
	'Tequila Flame'	CWCL GBin
	'Terracotta'	CWCL
	texensis	CSpe
	'The Chatelaine' (Band of Nobles Series)	CBcs CSBt EBee ECtt ELan EPfP GBin GKir LAst LRHS LSRN MBri MCot MNHC MWat NBir NGBl NPri SBfd SMrm SPer SPoG SWal SWvt WBVN WCAu WClo WFar WMnd WMoo
	'The Governor' (Band of Nobles Series)	Widely available
	'The Page' (Band of Nobles Series)	CBcs EBee ELan EPfP GKir LRHS LSRN MBri MCot MNHC MWat NPri SBfd SMrm SPer SPoG SWal SWvt WBVN WCFE WFar WMnd WMoo
	'Thunder'	CWCL
	'Thundercloud'	CAby CDes SMrm
	'Towering Inferno'	CWCL
	'Tutti Frutti'	LAst
	variicolor	CArn CHid SGar SMad

Luzula (*Juncaceae*)

	alpinopilosa	EPPr GFor MMHG
	× ***borreri***	EPPr
	- 'Botany Bay' (v)	ECtt EPPr EPla GBin NHol WMoo WWEG
	campestris	EBWF
	forsteri	EBWF IMou
	lutea	GFor
	luzuloides	GFor GQui WPtf
	- 'Schneehäschen'	GBin GCal NWsh WPrP
	maxima	see *L. sylvatica*
	multiflora	EBWF
	nivalis	GAbr GKir
	nivea	Widely available
	- 'Lucius'	LTen SGar
	- 'Schattenkind'	EBee
	pilosa	EBWF EPla GCal
	- 'Igel'	EBee GBin LEdu NBid SLPl WWEG
	purpureosplendens	LEdu
	rufa	ECou
§	***sylvatica***	CHEx CRWN CRow CSWP EBWF ELan EPPr EPfP EPla GKir LEdu LRHS MLLN MMoz MMuc MRav NBro NMir SBfd SEND WDin WFar WHer WPGP WShi WWEG
	- 'A. Rutherford'	see *L. sylvatica* 'Taggart's Cream'
	- 'Aurea'	CHEx CKno CSWP EBrs ECha EHul EPPr EPfP EPla LAst LBMP LRHS MMoz MRav NBid NOak NSti SApp SGSe SMad STre WCom WCot WFar WGrn WMoo WPtf
	- 'Aureomarginata'	see *L. sylvatica* 'Marginata'
I	- 'Auslese'	EPPr EPfP GFor WMoo
	- 'Barcode' (v)	CNat
	- 'Bromel'	EBee SGSe
	- 'Hohe Tatra'	Widely available
§	- 'Marginata' (v)	Widely available
*	- f. ***nova***	ELon EPPr
	- 'Onderbos'	EBee
	- 'Schattenlicht' **new**	EBee
§	- 'Taggart's Cream' (v)	CElw EBee EBrs EHoe EPla GGar LRHS MBNS NBid NHol SApp WGrn WMoo WPrP WWEG
	- 'Tauernpass'	EBee EHoe EPPr EPla GCal NHol
	- 'Wäldler'	EPPr MBNS NHol
	- 'Wintergold' **new**	EBee
	ulophylla	ECou EDAr GBin GFor NWCA

Luzuriaga (*Philesiaceae*)

	polyphylla HCM 98202	WCru
	radicans	CCCN CFee IBlr WCru WSHC
	- RH 0602	WCru

Lychnis (*Caryophyllaceae*)

	alpina	CMac EBee ECho EDAr EPfP GKir GMaP MSCN NVic SGar WFar

– 'Alba'	GKir NBir
– 'Rosea'	NBir
– 'Snow Flurry'	EDAr NLar
§ × ***arkwrightii***	ECha ELan LRHS NBre SRot WFar
– 'Orange Zwerg'	CMea CSpr CWCL LAst MBNS NBre SMrm SPoG WHal
– 'Vesuvius'	CBcs CMac EAEE EBee EUJe GKir LAst LRHS MNrw MWat NBPC NBir NPnk SMrm SPad SPer SPoG SRms STes WMnd WPer WWEG WWlt
chalcedonica ♀H4	Widely available
– var. ***albiflora***	EBee LAst NBro SMrm SPer WBrk WCAu WFar WMoo WPer
– – 'Snow White'	ECtt SGSe WClo
– 'Carnea'	CAby EBrs EShb LRHS MBNS NBre SMrm SPhx WBrk WPer WWEG
– 'Dusky Salmon'	MDKP NBPC WOut
– 'Flore Pleno' (d)	EBee ELan EShb GCal MLLN NLar WFar
– 'Morgenrot'	MCCP MLLN NBPC
– 'Pinkie'	ELan NLar SGSe
– 'Rauhreif'	EShb MWat NBre SPhx
– 'Rosea'	EBee EPfP LRHS NBir WFar WHrl WMoo WPer
* – 'Salmonea'	ECtt NBir SRms WCAu
cognata	CDes EBee GMac MDKP
– B&SWJ 4234	WCru
§ ***coronaria*** ♀H4	Widely available
– 'Abbotswood Rose'	see *L.* × *walkeri* 'Abbotswood Rose'
– 'Alba' ♀H4	Widely available
– 'Angel's Blush'	CSpr MDKP NBir SPav SPer SRkn WRHF WTou
– Atrosanguinea Group	CBre EBee EBrs GMaP IBlr LRHS MLLN MRav MSCN MSpe NEgg NPri SMrm SPer WClo
– 'Blood Red' **new**	CSpe
– 'Cerise'	MArl MCot MDKP NBir
– 'Dancing Ladies'	WMnd
– Gardeners' World = 'Blych' (d)	CBcs CDes CSpe EBee EBrs ECtt ELon EWes LOck LRHS LSou MBNS MLLN MTis NBPC NGdn NSti SMrm SPer SSvw SUsu WBor WBrk WClo WCot WFar
– 'Hutchinson's Cream' (v)	NBir
– Oculata Group	CMHG CSpe EBee ECtt EPfP LEdu MCot SMrm SPav SPlb SWal WCom WFar WKif WMoo WTin WWEG
§ ***coronata*** var. ***sieboldii***	MWea NBre
dioica	see *Silene dioica*
flos-cuculi	CArn CBen CEnt CPom CRWN CWat EBWF EBee ECho EHon EHrv EPfP GKir LEdu LPBA MHer MMuc MNHC NLan NMir NPri WHer WMAq WMoo WPnP WSFF
– var. ***albiflora***	CBre GBar LPBA MSKA NBro NLar WAlt WHer WMnd WMoo WOut
– Jenny = 'Lychjen'PBR (d)	CMac CSam CWGN EBee EBrs ELan GQue LAst LLWG LOck LRHS MBNS MTis NBPC NPnk NSti SBfd SHar SPoG SRkn STes SUsu WCot WPnP
– 'Little Robin'	ECho EDAr LLWG NHol
– 'Nana'	CBre ECho EDAr GAbr IFro MMuc MSKA NLar SBch
– pink-flowered **new**	WAlt
– 'White Robin'	CBen CBod CBre CEnt EPPr EWTr GMac GQue IFro IKil LBMP LRHS MBNS NPri SBfd SPoG WAul WClo WFar WPtf
flos-jovis ♀H4	ECha EPfP GJos LRHS NBir NLar SBch SEND SGSe SRms WMoo
– 'Alba'	WPtf
– 'Hort's Variety'	EBrs GKir LRHS MRav NBir
– 'Minor'	see *L. flos-jovis* 'Nana'
§ – 'Nana'	LRHS MSCN
– 'Peggy'	EBee EShb NBre NLar
fulgens	NBre
× ***haageana***	EBee NBre NLar SRms WSpi
'Hill Grounds'	CDes EBee WCot
lagascae	see *Petrocoptis pyrenaica* subsp. *glaucifolia*
miqueliana	NBre SPhx WGwG WMoo
'Molten Lava'	EBee ECho LAst LRHS MRav NBre NLar SGSe WPer WWEG
'Rollie's Favorite'	EBee ECtt NDov SPoG WHil
* ***sikkimensis***	EBee NBre
'Terry's Pink'	EBee WFar
§ ***viscaria***	CArn EBWF ECha GCra GJos SBch SGar WFar WMoo WTin
– 'Alba'	EBee ECha NBre NBro SBch
– ***alpina***	see *L. viscaria*
§ – subsp. ***atropurpurea***	ECtt EShb EWes LSou NBre SBHP SRms WHrl WPtf
– 'Feuer'	CSpr EBee EWes GJos MBNS NLar NVic WMoo
– 'Firebird'	EWes GKir NBre
– 'Plena' (d)	NBir SRkn
– 'Schnee'	CSpr LRHS MBNS NEgg
– 'Splendens'	EPfP LRHS MNFA NBPC SPad SPet
– 'Splendens Plena' (d) ♀H4	EBee GMac MArl NBre NBro SUsu WFar
§ × ***walkeri*** 'Abbotswood Rose' ♀H4	IBlr
§ ***yunnanensis***	EBee GKev NBid SBHP SGSe SPhx WPtf
– ***alba***	see *L. yunnanensis*

Lycianthes (*Solanaceae*)

quichensis B&SWJ 10395	WCru
rantonnetii	see *Solanum rantonnetii*

Lycium (*Solanaceae*)

barbarum	CAgr CCCN CSpe EBee ECrN EPfP EWes LBuc LRHS MCoo MMuc SEND SMad SVic
chinense	CArn CMen NLar

Lycopodium (*Lycopodiaceae*)

clavatum	GPoy

Lycopsis see *Anchusa*

Lycopus (*Lamiaceae*)

americanus	CArn
europaeus	CArn EBWF ELau GBar GPoy LLWG MNHC WGwG WHer
virginicus	COld SDys

Lycoris (*Amaryllidaceae*)

albiflora	ECho WCot
aurea	EBee ECho
incarnata	ECho
radiata	CCCN EBee ECho GBin
sanguinea	ECho
sprengeri	ECho
squamigera	ECho
straminea	WCot

Lygodium (*Schizaeaceae*)

japonicum	ISha NBid WFib WRic

Lyonia (*Ericaceae*)

ligustrina	NLar

Lyonothamnus (*Rosaceae*)

floribundus	CCCN CDoC CGHE CPLG EBee
subsp. ***aspleniifolius***	EUJe NLar SAPC SArc SGar SSpi WBor WFar WPGP

Lysichiton (*Araceae*)

sp.	GGal
americanus Υ^{H4}	Widely available
americanus* × *camtschatcensis	ECha
camtschatcensis Υ^{H4}	Widely available

Lysimachia ✿ (*Primulaceae*)

albescens	CDes CPLG EBee GKev SGar
§ ***atropurpurea***	CHar CSpe EBee EBrs ELan EPfP GJos LAst LBMP LHop SBfd SMrm SPer SPlb WMnd WSpi WWEG
- 'Beaujolais'	ECGP EShb GJos GKir GQue LAst LRHS LSRN NBPC NPri NSti SPav SRkn WBor WCom WHil
- 'Geronimo'	CSpe
barystachys	GMac LPla LRHS MLLN MRav NPnk SHar WFar WOut WWEG
Candela = 'Innlyscand'^{PBR}	SMrm SPoG
candida	EBee WCot
ciliata	CMHG CMac EBee ECha EHoe ELan GMaP MNrw NBir NGdn SWat WBor WCAu WCot WFar WMnd
§ - 'Firecracker' Υ^{H4}	Widely available
- 'Purpurea'	see *L. ciliata* 'Firecracker'
clethroides Υ^{H4}	Widely available
- 'Geisha' (v)	CBow EBee ECtt EWes LLHF WCot
- 'Lady Jane'	CFir CSpr SRms
§ ***congestiflora***	LAst NPer SPet
- HWJ 846	WCru
- 'Golden Falls'	LAst LSou
- 'Outback Sunset'^{PBR} (v)	ECtt LAst
ephemerum	Widely available
fortunei	EBee EWld MWat
henryi	EPPr
japonica* var. *minutissima	CFee CStu
lichiangensis	CPLG EBee EDAr GKev GKir IMou NBir SGar WMoo
lyssii	see *L. congestiflora*
'Midnight Sun'	LAst LSou
minoricensis	CEls CFir EBee EHrv ELan MBNS SWat WSpi
nemorum	EBWF
- 'Little Sun'	WAlt
- 'Pale Star'	CBre CDes EBee WAlt
nummularia	COlW CSBt CTri CWat EBWF ECtt EHon EPfP GPoy LPBA MMuc NBir SWat WBrk WHfH
- 'Aurea' Υ^{H4}	Widely available
paridiformis	WCot
- var. ***stenophylla***	CPLG EBee EPPr WCot WPGP
- - DJHC 704	CDes
punctata misapplied	see *L. verticillaris*
punctata L.	Widely available
§ - 'Alexander' (v)	Widely available
- 'Gaulthier Brousse'	MAvo MTis WCot WWEG
- Golden Alexander = 'Walgoldalex'^{PBR} (v)	CBct MBNS MBri MLLN MMuc MTis NHol NLar SBfd SPoG WFar WWEG
- 'Golden Glory' (v)	MAvo WCot
- 'Hometown Hero'	EBee
- 'Ivy Maclean' (v)	EBee SWvt WCot WWEG
- 'Sunspot'	NBre
- 'Variegata'	see *L. punctata* 'Alexander'
- ***verticillata***	see *L. verticillaris*
'Purpurea'	see *L. atropurpurea*
pyramidalis	WPtf WWEG
quadrifolia	EBee
serpyllifolia	ECtt
Snow Candles = 'L9902'	CCVN COlW EBee LHop
thyrsiflora	CBen CWat EBee EHon GAuc NPer SWat WMAq
§ ***verticillaris***	CTri WCot
vulgaris	CArn CRWN GBar LPBA MSKA NSco SIde WFar WJek WMoo
- subsp. ***davurica***	WCot
- - B&SWJ 8632	WCru

Lysionotus (*Gesneriaceae*)

gamosepalus B&SWJ 7241	WCru
aff. ***kwangsiensis*** HWJ 643	WCru
'Lavender Lady'	CSpe SEND
pauciflorus	CDes WAbe WSHC
- B&SWJ 189	WCru
- B&SWJ 303	WCru
- B&SWJ 335	WCru
serratus	MWea
- HWJK 2426	WCru

Lythrum (*Lythraceae*)

alatum	NDov
anceps	NBre NLar
salicaria	Widely available
- 'Blush' Υ^{H4}	Widely available
§ - 'Feuerkerze' Υ^{H4}	CAby CKno CMea CPrp EAEE EBee ECtt ELan ELon EPfP GKir LAst LBMP LHop LRHS MBri MCot MRav MSpe MWts NBir NCob NEgg NHol NSti NVic SPer WFar WWEG
- Firecandle	see *L. salicaria* 'Feuerkerze'
- 'Happy'	ELon
- 'Lady Sackville'	EBee ECtt ELon EPPr GBin GMaP LRHS MCot NDov SMrm
- 'Little Robert'	LRHS NPri
- 'Morden Pink'	CChe EBee MBri MDKP MMuc NCob NLar SEND SPhx SSvw WFar WPtf
- 'Prichard's Variety'	CAby CKno EBee WPGP
- 'Robert'	Widely available
- 'Robin'	EBee LLHF LRHS MCot SRot SWvt
- 'Rose'	ELan NBir SWvt
- 'Rosencaule'	EBee
- 'Stichflamme'	NCob SMrm
- 'Swirl'	EBee ECtt LLWG MDKP NBre NDov SHar SMrm WFar
- 'The Beacon'	CMHG EBee LRHS MDKP NLar SGSe SRms
- 'Zigeunerblut'	CElw CKno CMHG EBee ELon LRHS MAvo MDKP MRav MWte NLar SMrm SPhx SSvw SWat WHil
virgatum	CAby CMHG NDov SMHy SPhx SSvw SUsu WMoo WOut WSHC
- 'Dropmore Purple'	CHar CSam EBee ECtt ELon EPPr EPfP LAst LBMP LHop LLWG LRHS LSRN MAsh MBri MCot MDKP MRav MSpe NCob NDov NEgg SAga SPhx WCAu WFar WPnP WPtf
- 'Rose Queen'	ECha ECtt GKir MDKP MRav NDov SMHy WFar WPer
- 'Rosy Gem'	CMMP EBee ECtt EPfP GMaP LAst LRHS MWat MWhi NBPC NBid NBro SGSe SRms SWvt WClo WFar WPer WWEG
- 'The Rocket'	CAby CMMP CSam CTri EBee EPfP GBee LAst LRHS MRav MSpe NBro NCob SPer SWvt

Lytocaryum (*Arecaceae*)

§ ***weddellianum*** ♀H1 — LPal

M

Maackia (*Papilionaceae*)

amurensis — CBcs CDul CHGN ELan EPfP GKir IArd IDee IVic LRHS MBri MWea SPur WSHC
- var. ***buergeri*** — CDul
chinensis — MBlu MBri

Macbridea (*Lamiaceae*)

caroliniana — WPGP

mace, English see *Achillea ageratum*

Macfadyena (*Bignoniaceae*)

uncata — SOWG
§ ***unguis-cati*** — CCCN CRHN EShb

Machaeranthera (*Asteraceae*)

bigelovii — NBre

Machaerina (*Cyperaceae*)

rubiginosa 'Variegata' (v) — CKno LLWG
sinclairii — ECou

Machilus see *Persea*

Mackaya (*Acanthaceae*)

§ ***bella*** ♀H1 — CHII ERea EShb SOWG WHil

Macleaya (*Papaveraceae*)

cordata misapplied — see *M.* × *kewensis*
§ ***cordata*** (Willd.) R. Br. ♀H4 — CArn COIW EBee ELan EPfP LHop LRHS MBri MSCN MWhi NBPC NBir NPri NWsh SBfd SPer SPlb SRms WCAu WCot WFar WMnd WMoo
- 'Celadon Ruffles' — GBin
§ × ***kewensis*** — CWan MGos WHoo WPGP
- 'Flamingo' ♀H4 — CPrp EBee EBrs ECha ECtt GQue LAst LBMP LRHS MBNS MLLN MNFA NGdn SWvt WWEG
§ ***microcarpa*** — SGar SWat
- 'Kelway's Coral Plume' ♀H4 — Widely available
- 'Spetchley Ruby' — EBee GBin MRav SPhx SUsu WCom WCot WPGP WWEG
'Plum Tassel' — WCot

Maclura (*Moraceae*)

pomifera — CArn CBcs EBee IVic NLar SPlb WDin WFar
- 'Pretty Woman' — NLar

Macrodiervilla see *Weigela*

Macropiper (*Piperaceae*)

§ ***excelsum*** — CHEx ECou

Macrozamia (*Zamiaceae*)

communis — CBrP LPal
diplomera — CBrP
dyeri — see *M. riedlei*
glaucophylla — CBrP
johnsonii — CBrP
lucida — CBrP
miquelii — CBrP
moorei — CBrP LPal
mountperiensis — CBrP
§ ***riedlei*** — CBrP LPal

Maddenia (*Rosaceae*)

hypocleuca — NLar

Madia (*Asteraceae*)

elegans — WHer

Maesa (*Myrsinaceae*)

japonica — CPLG
montana — CPLG

Magnolia ✿ (*Magnoliaceae*)

acuminata — CBcs CDul CLnd CMCN EPfP LMaj NLar WDin
- 'Blue Opal' **new** — CBcs
- 'Golden Glow' — CBcs
* - 'Kinju' — CEnd CPMA NLar
- 'Koban Dori' — CBcs CPMA ECho
- large yellow-flowered — CBcs NLar
- 'Moegi Dori' — NLar
- 'Patriot' — SKHP
- 'Patriot' × (× ***brooklynensis*** 'Yellow Bird') **new** — CPMA
- 'Seiju' **new** — CPMA
§ - var. ***subcordata*** — NLar
- - 'Miss Honeybee' — CBcs CPMA
- - 'Mister Yellowjacket' **new** — CPMA
'Advance' — CBcs CPMA
'Albatross' — CBcs CDoC CEnd WPGP
'Alex' **new** — CPMA
'Alixeed' — CPMA
'Amber' — CPMA
'Ambrosia' — CBcs CPMA
amoena — CTho
- 'Multiogeca' — CBcs CWib EGxp
'Anilou' — CPMA
'Ann' ♀H4 — CBcs CPLG CSdC MGos NLar SSpi
'Anna' **new** — CPMA
'Anticipation' — CEnd CPMA CSdC
'Apollo' — CBcs CDoC CPMA GGGa LSRN SKHP SSpi WPat
'Archangel' **new** — CPMA
ashei — see *M. macrophylla* subsp. *ashei*
'Asian Artistry' — CPMA
'Athene' — CBcs CDoC CPMA
'Atlas' — CBcs CDoC CEnd CPMA CTho GGGa LMil SSpi WPGP
'Aurora' **new** — CBcs CDoC
'Banana Split' — CPMA
'Betty' ♀H4 — CBcs CDoC CDul CMac CSdC EPfP LRHS LSRN MGos NLar NMun NPla SKHP SLim SSta WDin WFar
'Big Dude' — CBcs CEnd CPMA IArd LSRN
biondii — CBcs CSdC LSRN NLar WPGP
'Black Beauty' — CBcs CPMA
Black Tulip = 'Jurmag1' PBR — EBee ELan EPfP GGGa LBuc LRHS MGos SCoo
'Blushing Belle' — CPMA
'Brenda' — CPMA
× ***brooklynensis*** — NPal
- 'Evamaria' — CBcs CTho
- 'Golden Joy' **new** — CDoC
- 'Hattie Carthan' — CBcs CPMA NLar
- 'Woodsman' — CBcs NLar

- 'Yellow Bird'	CBcs CDoC CEnd CMCN CPMA CTho EBee EPfP IArd LSRN MBlu MGos NCGa NEgg NHol NLar NPal SKHP SSpi WDin
'Butterbowl'	CBcs CPMA
'Butterflies'	CBcs CDoC CEnd CMac CPMA CTho EBee ELan EMil EPfP GGGa GKir LHyd LRHS LSRN MBlu MDun MGos NLar SKHP SLim SSpi SSta WBVN WFar WGob WPGP WSpi
'Caerhays Belle'	CBcs CPMA ECho NLar SKHP SSpi
'Caerhays New Purple'	CLnd ECho
'Caerhays Surprise'	CBcs CPMA SKHP SSpi
campbellii	CBcs CMCN ELan EPfP SKHP SSpi WFar
- Alba Group	CBcs CEnd MGos WFar WPGP
- - 'Sir Harold Hillier'	CPMA
- 'Betty Jessel'	CPMA
- 'Darjeeling'	CBcs CDoC CPMA ECho LRHS
- 'Lamellan Pink'	CTho
- 'Lamellan White'	CTho
- subsp. ***mollicomata***	CEnd CHEx EPfP WFar
- - 'Lanarth'	CBcs CEnd LRHS
- - 'Maharanee'	CBcs
- - 'Peter Borlase'	CBcs CDoC
- - 'Werrington'	CBcs
- (Raffillii Group) 'Charles Raffill'	CBcs CDoC CDul CLnd EBee ELan EPfP LRHS MGos SLim WDin WPGP
- - 'Kew's Surprise'	CDoC CPMA SSpi
- 'Sidbury'	CBcs
'Candy Cane'	CBcs CPMA
'Carlos'	CBcs CPMA
cathcartii HWJ 874	WCru
'Cecil Nice'	CBcs CCVT CDoC
Chameleon	see *M.* 'Chang Hua'
champaca	CCCN ERea
§ 'Chang Hua'	CPMA NLar
chapensis	CBcs IArd SKHP
- HWJ 621	WCru
'Charles Coates'	CPMA CSdC EPfP NLar WPGP
chevalieri HWJ 533	WCru
'China Dream'	EGxp
China Town = 'Jing Ning'	CBcs CPMA NLar
'Chinese Magic'	EGxp
'Columbus'	CPMA CSdC SSpi WPGP
'Columnar Pink' **new**	NLar
compressa	CCCN EBee EPfP ERea
'Coral Lake'	CPMA SKHP
cordata	see *M. acuminata* var. *subcordata*
'Cotton Rose'	EGxp
'Crystal Chalice' **new**	CPMA
'Cup Cake'	CPMA
'Curly Locks' **new**	CPMA
cylindrica misapplied	see *M.* 'Pegasus'
cylindrica ambig.	CBcs IArd
cylindrica E.H.Wilson	EPfP IArd
- 'Bjuv'	CPMA
'Daphne'	CBcs CPMA NLar SKHP
'Darrell Dean'	CPMA
'David Clulow'	CBcs CPMA ECho SKHP
dawsoniana	CBcs EPfP NLar WSpi
- 'Barbara Cook' **new**	CPMA
- 'Chyverton Red'	CBcs
'Daybreak'	CBcs CPMA NPal SSpi
delavayi	CBcs CBrP CDul CHEx CMCN EPfP IArd SAPC SArc SSpi WPGP
§ ***denudata*** ♀H3-4	CBcs CMCN CTho CWib EGxp EPfP IArd LMaj LRHS MBlu MGos NLar SSpi WDin WFar
- 'Double Diamond'	CPMA
- 'Dubbel'	CBcs

- 'Forrest's Pink'	CBcs LRHS
- Fragrant Cloud = 'Dan Xin'	CBcs CPMA CWib EGxp MBri NLar
- 'Gere'	CBcs CPMA
- 'Ghost Ship'	CPMA
- 'Rubiflora' **new**	SSta
- Yellow River = 'Fei Huang'	CBcs CEnd CPMA CWib EGxp LSou MBri NLar NPal SPoG
doltsopa	CBcs CCCN CGHE CHEx CPLG EPfP SKHP SSpi SSta WPGP
- 'Silver Cloud'	CBcs CDoC CPLG
'Early Rose'	CPMA
'Eleanor May'	CPMA
'Elegance'	CPMA
'Elisa Odenwald'	CPMA
'Elizabeth' ♀H4	CBcs CDoC CDul CMCN CPMA CTho ECho ELan EPfP LAst LMil LRHS LSRN MAsh MBlu MDun MGos NLar NPal SKHP SPer SPoG SSpi SSta SWvt WPGP
§ ***ernestii***	CPLG CWib
'Eskimo'	CPMA SKHP SSpi
'Felicity'	CPMA
Felix Jury = 'Jurmag2'PBR	ELan EPfP SSpi
figo	CBcs CCCN CDoC CPLG EBee EPfP ERea IVic SKHP SSpi SSta WPGP
- var. ***crassipes***	CBcs
figo × ***laevifolia*** **new**	SKHP
'Fireglow'	CBcs CPMA CTho
'Flamingo'	CPMA
aff. ***floribunda*** var. ***tonkinensis*** DJHV 06 105	WCru
fordiana	CBcs CPLG
§ ***foveolata***	CBcs CWib SSpi
'Frank Gladney'	CPMA CTho
'Frank's Masterpiece'	CPMA SKHP
fraseri	CBcs SKHP
- var. ***pyramidata***	SKHP
'Galaxy' ♀H4	CBcs CDoC CDul CEnd CMac CPMA CSdC ECho EPfP EWTr GGGa IArd LMil LRHS MAsh MBri MGos NLar SLim SSpi SSta WBrE WDin WGob WPGP
'Genie' **new**	CBcs CDoC
'George Henry Kern'	CBcs CDoC CDul CWit EMil GKir IArd IDee LRHS MBri MGos NEgg NLar NMun NPCo SLdr SSpi SSta WCFE WClo WDin WFar WGob
'Gladys Carlson' **new**	CPMA
globosa	CBcs CPLG EGFP WFar WGob WPGP
- AC 5294	CSdC
'Gold Crown'	CBcs CPMA SSpi
'Gold Star'	CBcs CDoC CEnd CPMA CSdC CTho EMil EPfP GGGa LRHS MBri MGos NCGa NLar SKHP SSpi
'Golden Endeavour'	CBcs CPMA
'Golden Gala' **new**	CPMA
'Golden Gift'	CPMA SSpi
'Golden Pond'	CBcs CPMA
'Golden Rain' **new**	CPMA
'Golden Sun'	CBcs CPMA NLar
'Goldenship'	EGxp
'Goldfinch'	CBcs CPMA
× ***gotoburgensis*** clone 2 **new**	CPMA
grandiflora	CMCN CWib EGxp EPfP ESwi GKir LAst LEdu LRHS LSRN MGos MRav NEgg NLar SAPC SBfd WDin WFar
- 'Blanchard'	CBcs CPMA
- 'Charles Dickens'	CPMA

	- 'Edith Bogue'	CDul CPMA CWit ECho EQua MGos NEgg NLar NPCo SLdr WBVN WGob
	- 'Exmouth' ♀H3-4	Widely available
	- 'Ferruginea'	CBcs CPMA EBee MGos
	- 'François Treyve'	EPfP EQua LRHS LTen SBfd
	- 'Galissonnière'	CBcs CCVT CWib ECrN EPfP ERom LMaj LRHS LTen MGos MREP SBfd SKHP SLim SSpi SWvt WDin WFar WPGP
I	- 'Gallissonnière Nana'	LMaj
	- 'Goliath'	CBcs CDul CEnd CHEx ELan EPfP LRHS SBfd SKHP SLdr SLim SMad SSpi WPGP
	- 'Harold Poole'	CBcs CPMA
	- 'Kay Paris'	CPMA EPfP LRHS SKHP SSpi
	- 'Little Gem'	CBcs CDoC CPMA ELan EPfP MGos SSpi
	- 'Mainstreet'	CBcs CPMA
	- 'Monlia'	CBcs CPMA
	- 'Nannetensis'	CPMA EQua
	- 'Overton'	CBcs CPMA
	- 'Russet'	CPMA
	- 'Saint Mary'	CBcs CPMA
	- 'Samuel Sommer'	CPMA SSpi
	- 'Symmes Select'	CBcs CPMA
	- 'Treyvei' **new**	CPMA
	- 'Victoria' ♀H3-4	CBcs CDoC CDul CPMA CTho ELan ELon EPfP IDee LHyd LMil LRHS LSRN MAsh MBlu MGos MWat NLar SEND SLim SPer SPoG SReu SSpi SSta WFar WGob WPGP
	'Green Bee'	CBcs CPMA
	'Green Mist'	CBcs CPMA SSpi
	'Heaven Scent' ♀H4	Widely available
	'Helen Fogg'	CPMA
	heptapeta	see *M. denudata*
	'Honey Flower' **new**	CPMA NLar
§	'Hong Yur'	CEnd CPMA NPal
	'Hot Flash'	CBcs CPMA
	'Hot Lips'	CPMA
	hypoleuca	see *M. obovata* Thunb.
	'Ian's Red'	CBcs CDoC CPMA
§	***insignis***	CBcs CHEx CPLG IMou SKHP SSpi WPGP
	'Iolanthe'	CBcs CDoC CEnd CGHE CMCN CPMA CSdC CTho ECho ELan LRHS MAsh MGos NHol NLar SPer SSpi SSta WFar WPGP
	'Iufer'	CPMA
	'J.C. Williams'	CBcs CDoC CPMA CTho
	'Jack Fogg'	MPkF SKHP
	'Jane' ♀H4	CDoC CMac CPMA CSdC ELan EPfP LMil LRHS MAsh MGos MRav SPer
	'Jersey Belle'	CPMA
	'Joe McDaniel'	CPMA CSdC SKHP SSpi
	'Joli Pompom' **new**	CPMA
	'Judy'	NLar
	'Kate Brook' **new**	NLar
	× ***kewensis*** 'Wada's Memory'	see *M. salicifolia* 'Wada's Memory'
	kobus	CBcs CDoy CDul CLnd CMCN CSBt CTho CTsd EMil EPfP IFFs LMaj MBlu NLar NMoo SLdr SPoG WDin WFar WGob
	- var. ***borealis***	CPMA
	- 'Esveld Select'	CPMA SSpi
	- 'Janaki Ammal'	CPMA
§	- 'Norman Gould'	CDoC CPMA EPfP MBri NLar NPla SSta WDin
	- 'White Elegance' **new**	CPMA
§	***laevifolia***	SKHP
	- arborescent **new**	SKHP
	- 'Dali Velvet' **new**	CPLG
	- 'Gail's Favourite' **new**	LRHS SSpi
	- 'Kneehigh' **new**	SSpi
	- 'Willow Leaf' **new**	SKHP
	'Laura Saylor'	CPMA
	'Leda'	CPMA
	'Legacy'	CBcs CPMA NLar
	'Legend'	CPMA EPfP
	'Lennarth Jonsson' **new**	CPMA
§	***liliiflora***	CBcs
I	- 'Darkest Purple' **new**	CPMA
	- 'Holland Red'	CBcs
§	- 'Nigra' ♀H4	Widely available
*	'Limelight'	CBcs CPMA CSdC MBri SSpi
	× ***loebneri***	CBcs NEgg
	- 'Ballerina'	CDoC EMil NLar
	- 'Donna'	CBcs CPMA EPfP LRHS MGos NLar SKHP SSpi SSta
	- 'Encore'	CPMA
	- 'Leonard Messel' ♀H4	Widely available
	- 'Lesley Jane'	CPMA
	- 'Merrill' ♀H4	Widely available
	- 'Neil McEacharn'	CPMA
	- 'Pink Cloud'	CPMA
	- 'Powder Puff'	CPMA
	- 'Raspberry Fun'	CPMA
	- 'Snowdrift'	CPMA NLar SSta
	- 'Star Bright'	CPMA
	- 'White Stardust' **new**	CPMA
	- 'Wildcat'	CPMA NLar
	- 'Willow Wood'	CPMA
	'Lois'	CBcs CPMA EPfP GGGa LSRN NLar SKHP SSpi
	'Lombardy Rose'	NLar
	lotungensis	NLar
	'Lotus'	CPMA
	'Lucy Carlson'	CPMA
	macclurei	CBcs SSpi
	macrophylla	CBcs CBrP CMCN CMac EPfP GKir IDee LRHS MBlu MPkF NLar SAPC SArc SKHP WPGP
§	- subsp. ***ashei***	SKHP SSpi
	- subsp. ***ashei*** × ***virginiana***	CPMA
	macrophylla × ***macrophylla*** subsp. ***ashei***	SKHP
	macrophylla × ***sieboldii*** **new**	CPMA
	'Mag's Pirouette'	CBcs SKHP
	'Malin' **new**	CPMA
	'Manchu Fan'	CBcs CPMA CSdC ECho EMil EPfP IArd LRHS LSRN LTen NLar SSpi
	'Margaret Helen'	CBcs CDoC CPMA ECho
	'Marj Gossler'	CPMA
	'Mark Jury'	SKHP
	'Mary Nell' **new**	CPMA
	'Maryland'	CPMA CWib EQua SKHP SSpi
§	***maudiae***	CBcs CDoC CGHE CPLG EPfP NLar SKHP SSpi WPGP
	'Maxine Merrill'	CPMA IDee
	'May to Frost'	CBcs CPMA
	'Milky Way' ♀H4	CBcs CDoC CGHE CMHG CPMA CTho MGos SKHP SSpi WPGP
	'Moondance'	CPMA
	'Nimbus'	SKHP SSpi
	nitida	CBcs
	obovata Diels	see *M. officinalis*
§	***obovata*** Thunb. ♀H4	CAlb CBcs CMCN CPMA CTho EPfP IFFs MGos NLar SSpi SSta WDin WPGP

odora	CWib
§ ***officinalis***	CBcs EPfP NLar WBVN WFar
- var. ***biloba***	CGHE EPfP NLar WPGP
'Old Port' new	CBcs
'Olivia'	CBcs CPMA
'Peachy'	CBcs CPMA NLar
§ 'Pegasus'	CEnd CPMA GGGa SKHP SSpi WDin
'Peppermint Stick'	CBcs CSdC ECho MGos SSta
'Peter Smithers'	CPMA CTho WFar
'Phelan Bright'	CPMA CSdC
'Phillip Tregunna'	CBcs CTho SKHP
'Phil's Masterpiece'	CPMA
'Pickard's Stardust'	EPfP
'Pickard's Sundew'	see *M.* 'Sundew'
'Piet van Veen'	CPMA
'Pink Cecile Nice'	CBcs
'Pink Delight'	CPMA
'Pink Goblet'	LRHS
'Pink Surprise' new	CPMA
'Pinkie' ♀H4	CBcs CPMA EMil EPfP LSRN MGos NEgg NLar SSpi SSta WGob
'Pirouette'	CPMA EPfP GGGa LLHF LRHS SSpi
'Porcelain Dove'	CPMA SSpi
'Pretty Lee'	EGxp
'Princess Margaret'	CBcs CDoC CPMA ECho
× ***proctoriana***	CAbP CDoC CGHE CSdC LMil LRHS NLar SKHP WPGP
- Gloster form	NLar
- 'Robert's Dream'	CPMA SSpi SSta
- 'Slavin's No 44'	CPMA
'Purple Globe'	CPMA SKHP
'Purple Platter'	CBcs
'Purple Sensation'	CBcs CPMA
quinquepeta	see *M. liliiflora*
'Randy'	EPfP MGos
'Raspberry Ice'	CBcs CDoC CMHG CMac CSam CSdC CTho EPfP LMil LRHS MAsh NLar SLim WFar WGob
'Raspberry Swirl' new	SSta
'Red as Red'	CDoC
'Red Lion'	CBcs CPMA
'Ricki'	CBcs CPMA CSdC EMil EPfP LSRN MBlu MGos MHav NLar NMun WFar
'Roseanne' new	CPMA
rostrata	CBcs CGHE ELan SKHP WPGP
'Rouged Alabaster'	CBcs CDoC
'Royal Crown'	CBcs CDoC CSdC CWit EMil EQua IDee LRHS MRav NEgg NLar NPCo SLim
'Ruby'	CBcs CPMA MGos
'Ruth'	CBcs
salicifolia ♀H3-4	CBcs CMCN EPfP GGal SSpi SSta WSpi
- var. ***concolor***	CPMA
- 'Jermyns'	CPMA
- 'Louisa Fete' new	CPMA
* - 'Rosea'	CPMA
- upright	WPGP
- 'Van Veen'	CPMA
§ - 'Wada's Memory' ♀H4	CAlb CDoC CDul CMCN CPLG CPMA CTho ELan EMil EPfP EWTr GKir IFFs LMil LRHS MAsh MBri NLar SEND SKHP SLdr SSpi SSta WDin WFar WGob
- 'Windsor Beauty'	CPMA MBri MWya
sargentiana	CBcs
- 'Broadleas' new	CPMA
- var. ***robusta***	CBcs CEnd CLnd CMCN ELan EPfP LMil MGos NLar SPer SSpi SSta WDin WFar
- - 'Blood Moon'	CPMA
'Satisfaction'	CDul CPMA NLar NPal
'Sayonara' ♀H4	CBcs CPMA CSdC ECho EPfP SSpi WDin
'Schmetterling'	see *M.* × *soulangeana* 'Pickard's Schmetterling'
'Serene'	CBcs CEnd CPMA ECho EPfP MGos SSpi SSta WPat
'Shirazz'	CBcs CDoC CPMA SKHP
sieboldii	Widely available
- B&SWJ 4127	WCru
- from Korea, hardy	GGGa
- 'Colossus'	CPMA SKHP
- 'Genesis'	CPMA
- 'Genesis' × ***tripetala***	CPMA
- 'Michiko Renge'	CPMA NLar
- 'Min Pyong-gal'	CPMA
- 'Pride of Norway'	CBcs CPMA
- subsp. ***sinensis***	CBcs CDoC CLnd CPMA CTho ELan EPfP GCra GGGa MBlu NLar WDin WPGP
'Sir Harold Hillier'	CBcs WPGP
'Snow Goose'	CPMA
'Solar Flair'	CBcs
× ***soulangeana***	Widely available
- 'Alba Superba'	CBcs CDoC CSBt CTri EPfP MBlu MGos MRav NMun SLim SPer WFar WSpi
- 'Alexandrina'	CBcs EPfP NLar
- 'Amabilis'	SBfd
- 'Brozzonii' ♀H3-4	CBcs CDoC CMac CWit EPfP GGGa GKir LRHS MBri MGos MWya NEgg NLar NPCo WBVN
- 'Burgundy'	CBcs CBot CDoC MGos NPCo WFar
- 'Fukuju' new	CPMA
- 'Lennei' ♀H3-4	CBcs CDoC CDul CMCN CMac CSBt EBee EPfP LRHS MAsh MBri MGos MSwo NBea NHol NLar SLim SPer SRms WFar
- 'Lennei Alba' ♀H3-4	CBcs CDoC CMCN CMac CSdC SPer WFar WGob WSpi
- 'Nigra'	see *M. liliiflora* 'Nigra'
- 'Pickard's Ruby'	SLim
§ - 'Pickard's Schmetterling'	CDoC CSdC LMil LRHS MAsh
- 'Pickard's Snow Queen'	CPMA
- 'Pickard's Sundew'	see *M.* 'Sundew'
- 'Picture'	CBcs CDoC CMac CTri NLar WDin WGob
- Red Lucky	see *M.* 'Hong Yur'
- 'Rosea'	LMaj
- 'Rubra' misapplied	see *M.* × *soulangeana* 'Rustica Rubra'
§ - 'Rustica Rubra' ♀H3-4	Widely available
- 'San José'	LMil LRHS MAsh MBri NLar WFar
- 'Speciosa'	NMun
- 'Superba'	CMac NMun SBfd
- 'Verbanica'	CAlb CCVT LMil LRHS MAsh SPoG
'Spectrum'	CBcs CDoC CEnd CPMA CSdC EMil GGGa LRHS MBri MGos NLar SKHP SLdr SSpi
sprengeri	CWib
- 'Copeland Court'	GGGa
- var. ***diva***	CBcs CEnd CPLG EPfP NLar SKHP WPGP
- - 'Burncoose'	CBcs CDoC
- - 'Claret Cup'	GGGa
- - 'Dark Diva' new	CPMA
- - 'Diva'	GGal WPGP
- - 'Eric Savill'	CPMA SKHP SSpi SSta WPGP
- - 'Lanhydrock'	CPMA WPGP
- - 'Westonbirt'	WPGP
- var. ***elongata***	CPMA

	- 'Marwood Spring'	CMHG SKHP
	'Spring Rite'	CPMA
	'Star Wars' Υ^{H4}	CBcs CDoC CEnd CPLG CPMA CSdC CTho ECho ELan EMil EPfP GGGa LMil LRHS LTen MAsh MBri MGos NLar SKHP SSpi SSta WPGP WPat
	'Stellar Acclaim'	CBcs CPMA
	stellata Υ^{H4}	Widely available
	- 'Centennial'	CDoC CPMA CTho GGGa MBri NLar WFar
	- 'Chrysanthemumiflora'	CPMA EGxp EPfP
	- 'Dawn'	CPMA
	- 'Jane Platt'	CPMA ELan EPfP EWes LMil LRHS MBri MGos SKHP SPoG SSpi
	- f. ***keiskei***	CBcs CEnd CPMA EPfP NHol NLar
	- 'Kikuzaki'	CPMA
	- 'King Rose'	CBcs CDoC CPMA CTsd EPfP MAsh
	- 'Massey'	CPMA
	- 'Norman Gould'	see *M. kobus* 'Norman Gould'
	- 'Rosea'	CBar CMCN CPMA CTho ELan GKev IVic LMil MDun MGos MRav MSwo NEgg NLar SBfd WDin
I	- 'Rosea Massey'	WFar
	- 'Royal Star'	Widely available
	- 'Scented Silver'	CPMA CSdC LRHS
	- 'Shi-banchi Rosea'	CPMA
	- 'Waterlily' Υ^{H4}	CBcs CMCN CMac CPMA CTho ELan ELon EMil EPfP GKev GKir LRHS LSRN LTen NLar NPCo SKHP SLim SPer SPoG SSpi SSta WDin WFar WGob WGwG WPGP
	- 'Wisley Stardust'	SSpi
	'Summer Solstice'	CBcs CPMA
	'Sun Ray'	CPMA
	'Sunburst'	CBcs CPMA
	'Sundance'	CBcs CPMA MGos NLar
§	'Sundew'	CDoC CMac CTsd EBee EPfP EQua IArd LMil MGos NLar NPCo WBVN
	'Sunrise' **new**	CBcs
	'Sunsation'	CBcs CDoC CPMA
	'Sunspire'	CBcs NLar
	'Suntown'	CPMA
	'Susan' Υ^{H4}	Widely available
	'Susanna van Veen'	CBcs CDoC WPGP
	'Swedish Star'	CPMA
	'Sweet Merlot' **new**	CBcs CDoC
	'Sweet Valentine'	CBcs CPMA
	'Sweetheart'	CPMA SSpi
	'Theodora'	CBcs NLar
	× ***thompsoniana***	CMCN EPfP IDee NLar SSpi
	'Thousand Butterflies'	CBcs CPMA
	'Tina Durio'	SKHP
	'Todd Gresham'	CPMA WPGP
	'Todd's Forty Niner'	CBcs CPMA
	'Touch of Pink'	CBcs NLar
	'Tranquility'	CBcs CPMA SKHP
	'Trewidden Belle'	CEnd
	tripetala	CBcs CMCN CPLG CTri ELan EPfP MDun NLar SKHP SSpi SSta WDin WPGP
	- 'Bloomfield' **new**	CPMA
	'Ultimate Yellow'	CBcs CPMA NLar
	× ***veitchii***	CBcs CDul EPfP
	- 'Isca'	CDoy
	- 'Peter Veitch'	CDoy CTho
	virginiana	CMCN CPMA EPfP IArd NLar SBig SKHP SSpi WBVN WDin WPGP
	- 'Havener'	SKHP
	- 'Henry Hicks'	CPMA SSpi
	- 'Moonglow'	CPMA
	- 'Pink Halo'	CPMA
	- 'Satellite'	CBcs CPMA
	'Vulcan'	CBcs CDoC CEnd CPMA CTho ELan EPfP MBri NHol SSpi
	× ***watsonii***	see *M.* × *wieseneri*
§	× ***wieseneri***	CBcs CGHE CPMA EBee ELan EPfP ERea GKir IArd LRHS MBlu MWya NLar SKHP SPer SSpi WFar WPGP
	- 'Aashild Kalleberg'	CBcs CPMA SKHP SSpi
	wilsonii Υ^{H4}	Widely available
	- 'Gwen Baker'	CEnd
	'Yaeko' **new**	CPMA
	'Yellow Fever'	CBcs CMCN CPMA CTho ECho
	'Yellow Garland' **new**	CPMA
	'Yellow Lantern'	CAbP CBcs CDoC CEnd CPMA CSdC EPfP LMil LRHS LSRN MAsh MBlu NBea NLar SPoG SSpi SSta
	'Yellow Sea'	CPMA
	yunnanensis	CCCN MBri MPkF SSpi WPGP WSHC
	yuyuanensis	CBcs
	zenii	CBcs
	- 'Pink Parchment'	CPMA

× *Mahoberberis* (*Berberidaceae*)

	aquisargentii	EBee ECrN EMil EPfP GCal LRHS MMuc MRav NHol SEND SKHP SPoG WFar
	'Dart's Desire'	NLar
	'Dart's Treasure'	EPla
	'Magic'	NLar
	miethkeana	LRHS SRms WDin
	neubertii **new**	NLar

Mahonia ✿ (*Berberidaceae*)

	F&M 178	WPGP
	F&M 193	WPGP
§	***aquifolium***	CBcs CDul CMac EBee ECrN EMac GKir IFFs MGan MGos MMuc MRav NWea SPer SPlb SReu WDin
	- 'Apollo' Υ^{H4}	CMac CSBt CWib EBee ECrN ELan EPfP EUJe GKir LAst LHop LRHS LSRN MAsh MGos MRav MWat NEgg NLar NPri SCoo SEND SPer SPoG WDin
	- 'Atropurpurea'	CMac CSBt ELan EPfP EPla GKir NLar SPer WDin
	- 'Cosmo Crawl'	GKir LRHS
	- 'Euro'	NLar
	- 'Fascicularis'	see *M.* × *wagneri* 'Pinnacle'
	- 'Green Ripple'	CPMA EPfP NLar
	- 'Orange Flame'	CPMA EPfP NLar
	- 'Smaragd'	CDoC CMac ELan EPfP LRHS LSRN MBlu MGos MRav SLPl
	- 'Versicolor'	EPla MBlu
	bealei	see *M. japonica* Bealei Group
	bodinieri	NLar
	'Bokrafoot' PBR	EPfP MAsh
	chochoco	WPGP
	confusa	CDoC CGHE EPla LLHF LRHS NLar SKHP SMad SSpi WFar WPGP
	eutriphylla	see *M. trifolia*
	fortunei	CBcs MBlu NLar WSHC
	- 'Winter Prince'	NLar
	gracilipes	CGHE EPfP EPla GCal MBlu MDun NLar SKHP SLon SPoG SSpi WPGP
	gracilis	WPGP
	japonica Υ^{H4}	Widely available
§	- Bealei Group	CAlb CBcs CDul CSBt EBee ELan ELon EPfP EPla GKir LAst LRHS MAsh MGos MRav MSwo NHol NPer NPla NWea SBfd SCoo SKHP SLim SWvt WClo WDin WFar WGwG

	- 'Gold Dust'	CMac NLar NWea
	- 'Hiemalis'	see *M. japonica* 'Hivernant'
§	- 'Hivernant'	EBee EPfP LTen MGos NEgg NWea
	lanceolata	WPGP
	leschenaultii B&SWJ 9535	WCru
	lomariifolia ♀H3	CBcs CBot CHEx EBee EPfP EWes GCal LRHS MAsh SAPC SArc SBfd SKHP SPer SSpi SSta WSpi
	× ***media*** 'Buckland' ♀H4	CAlb CBcs CDul CMac CSBt CSam CTrC CWSG CWit EBee EPfP LAst MRav NCGa NEgg SBfd SDix SPer SRms WPat WRHF
	- 'Charity'	Widely available
	- 'Lionel Fortescue' ♀H4	CAlb CBcs CEnd CMac CSBt CSam CTrC EBee ELan EPfP LHop LRHS MAsh MCoo MGos MRav NCGa NEgg SBfd SDix SKHP SPer SPoG SSpi WBVN WClo
	- 'Underway' ♀H4	CSam EPfP
	- 'Winter Sun' ♀H4	Widely available
	nervosa	CMac EPfP MBlu NEgg NLar WCru WDin
	- B&SWJ 9562	WCru
	nitens	CBcs
*	***nitida***	WPGP
	oiwakensis B&SWJ 371	WCru
	- B&SWJ 3660	WCru
	pallida	SKHP SSpi WPGP
	pinnata misapplied	see *M.* × *wagneri* 'Pinnacle'
	pinnata ambig.	EPfP
	pumila	WCru
	repens	GCal NLar
	× ***savilliana***	EPla WPGP
	- 'Commissioner'	CWib
	Sioux = 'Bokrasio'PBR	LRHS MAsh SPoG
§	***trifolia***	GCal
	trifoliolata var. ***glauca***	CEnd CPMA NLar
	× ***wagneri*** 'Fireflame'	GCal WSpi
	- 'Hastings Elegant'	CPMA NLar
	- 'Moseri'	EBee NLar SSpi WCot WPat
§	- 'Pinnacle' ♀H4	EBee ELan EPfP EPla LRHS MAsh MGos NLar SPer SPoG WDin
	- 'Sunset'	CPMA MBlu NLar
	- 'Undulata'	EPfP LRHS MBlu NLar SPer SRms

Maianthemum (*Convallariaceae*)

	amoenum	LEdu
	- B&SWJ 10390	WCru
	atropurpureum	WCru
	bicolor	CDes LEdu SWat
	bifolium	CBct CDes CHid EBee ECho GCra LEdu MAvo MNrw MTho NBro NMen SBch SRms WCru WPGP WPnP WTin WWEG
§	- subsp. ***kamtschaticum***	CBct CLAP EBee ECha EHrv EPPr EPot LEdu MAvo NLar NRya WCot WTin
	- - B&SWJ 4360	WCru WPrP
	- - CD&R 2300	WCru
*	- - var. ***minimum***	GCal GEdr
	canadense	CBct EBee ECho EPot GCal GCrs GGar GKir MNrw NBid NMen WCru WPnP
*	***chasmanthum***	EBee EBrs EPPr LRHS
	comaltepecense B&SWJ 10215	WCru
	dilatatum	see *M. bifolium* subsp. *kamtschaticum*
	flexuosum	LEdu
	- B&SWJ 9069	WCru
	- B&SWJ 9150	WCru
	- B&SWJ 9255	WCru
	aff. ***flexuosum*** B&SWJ 9026	WCru
	- B&SWJ 9055	WCru
	formosanum	EPPr WCot
	- B&SWJ 349	WCru
	forrestii	WCru
	fuscum	GBin WCru
	- var. ***cordatum***	WCru
	gigas B&SWJ 10470 **new**	WCru
	henryi	CBct EBee ECho GEdr LEdu WCru
	japonicum	EBee ECho LEdu
	- B&SWJ 1179	WCru
	- B&SWJ 4714	WCru
	oleraceum	CBct CPLG EBee ECho GBin GEdr LEdu WCot WFar
	- B&SWJ 2148	WCru
	paniculatum	EBee
	- B&SWJ 9137	WCru
	- B&SWJ 9140	WCru
	pendent, B&SWJ 10305 from Guatemala	WCru
	purpureum G-W&P 150	EPPr
	racemosum ♀H4	Widely available
	- subsp. ***amplexicaule***	GBin GCal WPrP
	- - 'Emily Moody'	CBct CDes CPLG CPou EBee EPla SKHP SMad WPGP
	- dwarf	ECho
	- 'Wisley Spangles'	LRHS
	aff. ***salvinii*** B&SWJ 9000	WCru
	- B&SWJ 9088	WCru
	- B&SWJ 10402	WCru
	scilloideum B&SWJ 10407 **new**	WCru
	stellatum	CAvo CBct EBee ECha ECho EPPr EPfP EPla EPot GAuc GBBs GBin GCal GGar GKev LEdu LHop MAvo MLLN NChi NLar NMyG SMad WCru WFar WPnP WTin
	szechuanicum	WCru
	tatsienense	CBct CPLG ECho GCrs WCru WFar
	trifolium	ECho

Maihuenia (*Cactaceae*)

poeppigii	SPlb WCot

Maireana (*Chenopodiaceae*)

georgei	SPlb

Malacothamnus (*Malvaceae*)

fremontii	MDKP

Malus ✿ (*Rosaceae*)

§	'Adirondack'	CWSG EBee EPfP GKir LRHS MAsh MBlu MBri MGos MMuc MWat NLar SCoo SEND SLim SPoG WJas
	'Admiration'	see *M.* 'Adirondack'
	× ***adstringens*** 'Almey'	ECrN
	- 'Hopa'	CDul
	- 'Simcoe'	CLnd CTho EBee LLHF
	'Aldenhamensis'	see *M.* × *purpurea* 'Aldenhamensis'
	× ***arnoldiana***	LMaj
	× ***atrosanguinea*** 'Gorgeous'	CCAT CDul CLnd CTho CWSG EBee ECrN GKir GTwe LRHS MAsh MGos MSwo NLar SCoo SKee SLim SPer SPoG WDin WJas WMou
	baccata	CDul CMCN CTho EBee GTwe MMuc NWea SCoo SEND SPlb SSpi
	- 'Dolgo'	CTho SKee
	- 'Lady Northcliffe'	CLnd SFam
	- var. ***mandshurica***	CTho
	- 'Street Parade'	LMaj
	aff. ***baccata***	NWea

- MF 96038	SSpi
§ ***bhutanica***	CDul CLnd EPfP MAsh SCrf
brevipes	CLnd CTho EBee GKir LRHS MBri SCoo SPoG
- 'Wedding Bouquet'	MAsh MWat NLar
'Butterball'	CDul CLnd CTho EBee ECrN EPfP GKir LAst LMaj LTen NWea SCoo SLim SPer WDin WHar WJas
'Candymint Sargent'	CLnd
'Cave Hill'	CLnd
* 'Cheal's Weeping'	CMac LAst MMuc NBea NEgg
Coccinella = 'Courtarou'	MMuc SEND WDin
'Comtessa de Paris'	EBee GKir LTen MAsh
'Coralburst'	MBri
coronaria	CDul CLnd EBee EPfP SPer SPur
var. ***dasycalyx*** 'Charlottae' (d)	
- 'Elk River'	EBee LRHS SCoo
'Crimson Brilliant'	CLnd
'Crittenden'	CLnd EBee ECrN MRav SLim
* 'Directeur Moerlands'	CCVT CDoC EBee ECrN EPfP GKir IArd MGos SBfd SPur WDin WJas
domestica (F)	ECrN IFFs
- 'Acklam Russet' (D)	SKee
- 'Acme' (D)	ECrN MCoo SDea
- 'Adams's Pearmain' (D)	CCAT CTho ECrN ERea GBut GKir GTwe LRHS MCoo SDea SFam SKee
- 'Admiral' (D)	ECrN
- 'Akane' (D)	SDea
- 'Alfriston' (C)	CAgr SKee
§ - 'Alkmene' (D) ♀^{H4}	CAgr ECrN SDea SKee
- 'All Doer' (D/C/Cider)	CCAT CTho LBuc
- 'Allen's Everlasting' (D)	GTwe SDea SKee
- 'Allington Pippin' (D)	CSBt CTho CTri ECrN IFFs LRHS SDea SKee
- Ambassy = 'Dalil'^{PBR} (D)	SLon
- 'American Mother'	see *M. domestica* 'Mother'
- 'Ananas Reinette' (D)	ECrN SKee
- 'Anna Boelens' (D)	SDea
- 'Annie Elizabeth' (C)	CAgr CCAT CTho CWib ECrN GKir GTwe IFFs LAst LRHS MCoo MGan SDea SFam SKee SVic WBVN WHar WJas
- 'Anniversary' (D)	SDea
- 'Apache'	CSut
- 'Api Rose' (D)	WJas
- 'Ard Cairn Russet' (D)	ECrN IFFs SDea SKee WGwG
- 'Aromatic Russet' (D)	SKee
- 'Arthur Turner' (C) ♀^{H4}	CCAT CCVT CDoC CTri ECrN GBut GKir GTwe IFFs LAst LBuc MWat SCrf SDea SFam SKee WJas
- 'Ashmead's Kernel' (D) ♀^{H4}	CAgr CCAT CDul CSBt CTho CTri CWib ECrN EPfP ERea GBut GKir GTwe IFFs LBuc LRHS MAsh MCoo MRav MWat NWea SCrf SDea SFam SKee SLim SVic WHar WJas
- 'Ashton Bitter' (Cider)	CCAT CTho GTwe
- 'Ashton Brown Jersey' (Cider)	CCAT
- 'Autumn Pearmain' (D)	SDea WHar
- 'Baker's Delicious' (D)	ECrN GKir SDea SKee
- 'Ball's Bittersweet' (Cider)	CCAT CTho ERea
- 'Ballyfatten' (C)	IFFs
- 'Ballyvaughan Seedling' (D)	IFFs
- 'Balsam'	see *M. domestica* 'Green Balsam'
- 'Banana Pippin'	CEnd
- 'Banns' (D)	ECrN ERea SKee
- 'Bardsey' (D)	CAgr ERea LBuc WDol WGwG
- 'Barnack Beauty' (D)	CTho SKee
- 'Barnack Orange' (D)	SKee
- 'Baumann's Reinette' (D)	SKee

- 'Baxter's Pearmain' (D)	ECrN ERea SDea SKee
- 'Beauty of Bath' (D)	CAgr CCAT CCVT CDoC CDul CTho CTri CWib ECrN GBut GKir GTwe IFFs LAst LBuc SDea SFam SKee SPer WHar WJas
- 'Beauty of Hants' (D)	ECrN
- 'Beauty of Kent' (C)	SDea SKee
- 'Beauty of Moray' (C)	GBut GKir GQui SKee
- 'Bedwyn Beauty' (C)	CTho
- 'Beeley Pippin' (D)	GTwe SDea SKee
- 'Bell Apple' (Cider/C)	CCAT CTho
- 'Belle de Boskoop' (C/D) ♀^{H4}	CAgr CCAT ECrN GTwe MCoo SDea SKee WGwG
- 'Belvoir Seedling' (D/C)	SKee
- 'Bembridge Beauty' (F)	SDea
- 'Ben's Red' (D)	CAgr CCAT CEnd CTho
- 'Bess Pool' (D)	MCoo SDea SFam
- 'Bewley Down Pippin'	see *M. domestica* 'Crimson King' (Cider/C)
- 'Bickington Grey' (Cider)	CTho
- 'Billy Down Pippin' (F)	CTho
- 'Bismarck' (C)	CCAT ECrN SKee
- 'Black Dabinett' (Cider)	CCAT CEnd CTho
- 'Black Tom Putt' (C/D)	CTho
- 'Blenheim Orange' (C/D) ♀^{H4}	Widely available
- 'Bloody Butcher' (C)	IFFs
- 'Bloody Ploughman' (D)	ECrN GBut GKir GTwe SKee WHar
- 'Blue Pearmain' (D)	SDea
- 'Blue Sweet' (Cider)	CTho
- Bolero = 'Tuscan'^{PBR} (D/Ball)	MCoo SDea SKee
- 'Boston Russet'	see *M. domestica* 'Roxbury Russet'
- 'Bountiful' (C)	CAgr CCAT CDoC CDul CSBt CTri CWib ECrN GKir GTwe LRHS LSRN MAsh MBri NLar SDea SKee SLim WBVN WHar
- 'Braddick Nonpareil' (D)	SKee
- 'Braeburn' (D)	CAgr CCAT CDul CSut ECrN ERea LAst LBuc LRHS MAsh SCrf SDea SFam SKee SPoG WHar WJas
- 'Braintree Seedling' (D)	ECrN SKee
- 'Bramley's Seedling' (C) ♀^{H4}	Widely available
- 'Bramley's Seedling' clone 20	CDoC CMac MAsh MBri NLar SCoo SDea SLim SPoG WHar
- 'Bread Fruit' (C/D)	CEnd CTho
- 'Breakwell's Seedling' (Cider)	CCAT CTho WDol
- 'Bridgwater Pippin' (C)	CCAT CTho
- 'Broad-eyed Pippin' (C)	SKee
- 'Broadholm Beauty'	MAsh
- 'Brookes's' (D)	WHar
- 'Broom Apple' (Cider)	WDol
- 'Brown Crofton' (D)	IFFs
- 'Brown Snout' (Cider)	CCAT CTho
- 'Brownlees Russet' (D)	CAgr CCAT CTho CTri GTwe MCoo NEgg NWea SDea SFam SKee
- 'Brown's Apple' (Cider)	CAgr CCAT GTwe
- 'Broxwood Foxwhelp' (Cider)	CCAT
- 'Burn's Seedling' (D)	CTho
- 'Burrowhill Early' (Cider)	CTho
- 'Bushey Grove' (C)	SDea
- 'Buttery Do'	CCAT CTho
- 'Cadbury'	CCAT
- 'Calville Blanc d'Hiver' (D)	SKee
- 'Cambusnethan Pippin' (D)	GBut GQui SKee
- 'Camelot' (Cider/C)	CCAT LBuc
- 'Cap of Liberty' (Cider)	CCAT

	- 'Captain Broad' (D/Cider)	CCAT CEnd CTho
	- 'Captain Kidd' (D)	SKee
	- 'Captain Smith' (F)	CEnd
	- 'Carlisle Codlin' (C)	GBut GKir GTwe NLar NWea SDea
	- 'Caroline' (D)	ECrN
	- 'Carswell's Orange' (D)	SKee
	- 'Catherine' (C)	ECrN
	- 'Catshead' (C)	CAgr CCAT ECrN GKir GQui SDea SKee
	- 'Cellini' (C/D)	SDea
	- 'Channel Beauty' (D)	WDol
	- 'Charles Ross' (C/D) ♀H4	Widely available
	- 'Charlotte'^{PBR} (C/Ball)	SDea SKee
	- 'Chaxhill Red' (Cider/D)	CCAT CTho
	- 'Cheddar Cross' (D)	CAgr CCVT CTri ECrN
	- 'Chelmsford Wonder' (C)	SKee
	- 'Chips'	SKee
	- 'Chisel Jersey' (Cider)	CAgr CCAT CTri SKee
	- 'Chivers Delight' (D)	CAgr CCAT CSBt ECrN ERea GKir GTwe LRHS MCoo SDea SKee WJas
	- 'Chorister Boy' (D)	CTho
	- 'Christmas Pearmain' (D)	CAgr CTho ECrN GTwe SDea SFam SKee WClo
	- 'Cider Lady's Finger' (Cider)	CCAT SKee
	- 'Cissy' (D)	WDol WGwG
	- 'Claygate Pearmain' (D) ♀H4	CAgr CCAT CTho CTri ECrN GTwe LRHS MCoo SDea SFam SKee SVic WBVN
	- 'Clopton Red' (D)	ECrN
	- 'Clydeside'	GBut GKir GQui
	- 'Coat Jersey' (Cider)	CCAT
	- 'Cobra'	LBuc LRHS MCoo
	- 'Cockle Pippin' (D)	CAgr CTho SDea
	- 'Coeur de Boeuf' (C/D)	SKee
	- 'Coleman's Seedling' (Cider)	CTho
	- 'Collogett Pippin' (C/Cider)	CCAT CEnd CTho
	- 'Colonel Vaughan' (C/D)	SKee
	- 'Cornish Aromatic' (D)	CAgr CCAT CTho GTwe IFFs SCrf SDea SFam SKee WClo
	- 'Cornish Gilliflower' (D)	CAgr CCAT CDul CTho ECrN LRHS MCoo SDea SFam SKee WBVN
	- 'Cornish Honeypin' (D)	CEnd CTho
	- 'Cornish Longstem' (D)	CAgr CEnd CTho
	- 'Cornish Mother' (D)	CEnd CTho
	- 'Cornish Pine' (D)	CEnd CTho SDea
	- 'Coronation' (D)	SDea
	- 'Corse Hill' (D)	CCAT CTho
	- 'Costard' (C)	GTwe SKee WClo
	- 'Cottenham Seedling' (C)	SKee
	- 'Coul Blush' (D)	GBut SKee
	- 'Court of Wick' (D)	CAgr CCAT CTho ECrN GKir SKee SVic WHar
	- 'Court Pendu Plat' (D)	CAgr CCAT CTho GKir LBuc MWat NWea SDea SFam SKee WHar WJas
	- 'Court Royal' (Cider)	CCAT
	- 'Cow Apple' (C)	CCAT
	- 'Cox Cymraeg' (D)	WGwG
	- 'Cox's Orange Pippin' (D)	CBcs CCAT CCVT CDul CMac CSBt CTri CWib ECrN ERea GTwe IFFs LAst LRHS LSRN MAsh MGos MMuc MWat NLar NPri SBfd SCrf SDea SFam SKee SLim SPer SWvt WJas
	- 'Cox's Pomona' (C/D)	GBut SDea SKee WHar
	- 'Cox's Rouge de Flandres' (D)	SKee
	- 'Cox's Selfing' (D)	CDoC CTri CWSG CWib EPfP GKir GTwe LBuc LRHS MAsh MBri MGan MGos MNHC SCrf SDea SKee SPer SPoG WHar WJas
	- 'Craigflower Classic'	GKir
	- 'Crawley Beauty' (C)	CAgr CCAT GTwe SDea SFam SKee
	- 'Crimson Beauty of Bath' (D)	CAgr
	- 'Crimson Bramley' (C)	CCAT LAst
	- 'Crimson Cox' (D)	SDea
§	- 'Crimson King' (Cider/C)	CAgr CCAT
	- 'Crimson King' (D)	CAgr
	- 'Crimson Queening' (D)	WHar
	- 'Crimson Victoria' (Cider)	CTho
	- Crispin	see *M. domestica* 'Mutsu'
§	- 'Crowngold' (D)	GTwe
	- 'Cutler Grieve' (D)	SDea
	- Cybèle = 'Delrouval'	LRHS
	- 'Dabinett' (Cider)	CAgr CCAT CTho CTri ERea GKir GTwe LBuc SCrf SDea SKee
	- 'D'Arcy Spice' (D)	CAgr CCAT ECrN EPfP ERea MCoo MWat SDea SFam SKee
	- 'Deacon's Blushing Beauty' (C/D)	SDea
	- 'Deacon's Millennium'	SDea
	- 'Decio' (D)	SKee
	- Delbarestivale = 'Delcorf' (red) (D) ♀H4	LRHS
	- 'Devon Crimson Queen' (D)	CTho
	- 'Devonshire Buckland' (C)	CEnd CTho
	- 'Devonshire Crimson Queen' (D)	SDea
	- 'Devonshire Quarrenden' (D)	CAgr CCAT CDul CEnd CTho GBut GKir LRHS SDea SFam SKee SVic WJas
	- 'Diamond' (D)	WGwG
	- 'Discovery' (D) ♀H4	Widely available
	- 'Doctor Harvey' (C)	ECrN ERea SFam SKee
	- 'Doctor Kidd's Orange Red'	see *M. domestica* 'Kidd's Orange Red'
	- 'Don's Delight' (C)	CTho
	- 'Dove' (Cider)	CCAT
	- 'Dredge's Fame' (D)	CTho
	- 'Duchess's Favourite' (D)	SKee
	- 'Dufflin' (Cider)	CCAT CTho
	- 'Duke of Cornwall' (C)	CTho
	- 'Duke of Devonshire' (D)	CTho CTri SDea SFam SKee
N	- 'Dumeller's Seedling'	see *M. domestica* 'Dummellor's Seedling'
§	- 'Dummellor's Seedling' (C) ♀H4	CCAT SDea SKee
	- 'Dunkerton Late Sweet' (Cider)	CCAT CCVT CTho LBuc
	- 'Dunn's Seedling' (D)	SDea
§	- 'Dutch Mignonne' (D)	ECrN SKee
	- 'Dymock Red' (Cider)	CCAT LBuc
	- 'Early Blenheim' (D/C)	CCAT CEnd CTho
	- 'Early Bower' (D)	CEnd
	- 'Early Julyan' (C)	GBut GKir GQui SKee
	- 'Early Victoria'	see *M. domestica* 'Emneth Early'
	- Early Windsor	see *M. domestica* 'Alkmene'
	- 'Early Worcester'	see *M. domestica* 'Tydeman's Early Worcester'
	- 'East Lothian Pippin' (C)	GBut GQui
	- 'Easter Orange' (D)	GTwe
	- 'Ecklinville' (C)	SDea
	- 'Eden'	LBuc
	- 'Edith Hopwood' (D)	ECrN
	- 'Edward VII' (C) ♀H4	CCAT CDoC GKir GTwe SCrf SDea SFam SKee

- 'Egremont Russet' (D) 🏆H4	Widely available
- 'Ellis' Bitter' (Cider)	CCAT CTho GTwe SKee SVic
- 'Ellison's Orange' (D) 🏆H4	CAgr CCAT CDul CMac CSBt CTri CWib ECrN EPfP ERea GBut GKir GTwe IFFs LAst LBuc LRHS MMuc MWat NWea SDea SFam SKee SVic WHar WJas
- 'Elstar' (D) 🏆H4	CCVT CWib ECrN GKir GTwe IFFs LAst LRHS SDea SKee
- 'Elton Beauty' (D)	SDea SKee
§ - 'Emneth Early' (C) 🏆H4	CAgr ECrN ERea GKir GTwe IFFs SDea SFam SKee WJas
- 'Empire' (D)	LAst SKee
- 'Encore' (C)	SDea
- 'Endsleigh Beauty' (D)	CEnd
- 'English Codlin' (C)	CCAT CTho CTri ERea
- 'Epicure'	see *M. domestica* 'Laxton's Epicure'
- 'Ernie's Russet' (D)	SDea
- 'Eros' (D)	ECrN
- 'Essex Pippin' (D)	ECrN
- 'Evening Gold' (C)	SDea
- 'Eve's Delight' (D)	SDea
- 'Excelsior' (C)	ECrN
- 'Exeter Cross' (D)	CCAT ECrN GKir SDea SFam
- 'Fair Maid of Devon' (Cider)	CAgr CCAT CEnd CTho
- 'Fairfield' (D)	CTho
- 'Falstaff'[PBR] (D) 🏆H4	CAgr CCAT CDoC CDul ECrN EPfP GKir GTwe LSRN MGos SCoo SDea SKee WClo WJas
- 'Farmer's Glory' (D)	CAgr CTho
- 'Fiesta'[PBR] (D) 🏆H4	Widely available
- 'Fillbarrel' (Cider)	CCAT
- 'Firmgold' (D)	SDea
- 'Flame' (D)	ECrN
- 'Flamenco'[PBR]	see *M. domestica* 'Obelisk'
§ - 'Flower of Kent' (C)	SCrf SDea SKee
- 'Forfar'	see *M. domestica* 'Dutch Mignonne'
- 'Forge' (D)	CAgr SDea
- 'Fortune'	see *M. domestica* 'Laxton's Fortune'
- 'Forty Shilling' (D)	GBut
- 'Foulden Pearmain' (D)	ECrN
- 'Foxwhelp' (Cider)	LBuc SKee
- 'Francis' (D)	ECrN
- 'Frederick' (Cider)	CCAT CTho WDol
- 'French Crab' (C)	SDea
- 'Freyberg' (D)	SKee
- 'Fuji' (D)	SDea SKee
- 'Gala' (D)	CMac CSBt GTwe LAst SCoo SCrf SDea SFam SKee SLim WHar
- 'Galloway Pippin' (C)	GBut GKir GQui GTwe SKee
- 'Garnet' (D)	ECrN
- 'Gascoyne's Scarlet' (D)	CCAT GKir SDea SFam SKee WHar WJas
- 'Gavin' (D)	CAgr GBut SDea SKee
- 'Genesis II' (D/C)	SDea
- 'Genet Moyle' (C/Cider)	CCAT CTri
- 'George Carpenter' (D)	SDea
- 'George Cave' (D)	CTho ECrN GBut GTwe IFFs MCoo SDea SFam SKee WJas
- 'George Neal' (C) 🏆H4	CAgr SDea SFam
- 'Gibbon's Russet' (D)	IFFs
- 'Gilliflower of Gloucester' (D)	CTho
- 'Gin' (Cider)	CCAT
- 'Gladstone' (D)	CAgr CTho
- 'Glansevin' (D)	WDol
§ - 'Glass Apple' (C/D)	CCAT CEnd CTho
- 'Gloria Mundi' (C)	SDea SKee
- 'Gloster '69' (D)	SDea
- 'Gloucester Royal' (D)	CTho
- 'Gloucester Underleaf'	CTho
- 'Golden Ball'	CTho
- 'Golden Bittersweet' (D)	CAgr CTho
- 'Golden Delicious' (D) 🏆H4	CDul CSBt CWib ECrN EPfP LAst MMuc SBfd SCrf SDea SKee SPoG SVic WHar
- 'Golden Glow' (C)	SDea
- 'Golden Harvey' (D)	CAgr CCAT
- 'Golden Jubilee'	CEnd
- 'Golden Knob' (D)	CCAT CTho SKee
- 'Golden Noble' (C) 🏆H4	CAgr CCAT CDoC CTho CTri ECrN ERea GKir GTwe IFFs MCoo SDea SFam SKee
- 'Golden Nugget' (D)	CAgr SKee
- 'Golden Pippin' (C)	CAgr CCAT GBut WHar
- 'Golden Reinette' (D)	GTwe SKee
- 'Golden Russet' (D)	CAgr ECrN GTwe SDea SKee WHar
- 'Golden Spire' (C)	IFFs MCoo SDea SKee
- 'Gooseberry' (C)	LSRN
- 'Goring' (Cider)	CTho
- 'Granny Smith' (D)	CBcs CDul CLnd CWib ECrN GTwe LAst LSRN SCrf SDea SKee SPer SVic WHar
- 'Gravenstein' (D)	CCAT GKir GQui SDea SFam SKee
§ - 'Green Balsam' (C)	CTri
- 'Green Kilpandy Pippin' (C)	GQui
- 'Green Roland'	ECrN ERea
- 'Greensleeves'[PBR] (D) 🏆H4	CAgr CCAT CDoC CDul CMac CSBt CTri CWSG CWib ECrN EPfP GKir GTwe IFFs LAst LRHS MGos MMuc NLar SDea SKee SLim WBVN WHar WJas
- 'Grenadier' (C) 🏆H4	CAgr CCAT CDoC CSBt CTri ECrN GBut GKir GTwe IFFs LRHS MGos MMuc SDea SKee SVic WJas
- 'Hagloe Crab'	LBuc
- 'Halstow Natural' (Cider)	CAgr CTho
- 'Hambledon Deux Ans' (C)	SDea SKee
- 'Hangy Down' (Cider)	CCAT CTho
- Harmonie = 'Delorina'	LRHS
§ - 'Harry Master's Jersey' (Cider)	CAgr CCAT CTho CTri ERea SDea SKee
- 'Harvester' (D)	CTho
- 'Harvey' (C)	SDea
- 'Hawthornden' (C)	GKir GQui GTwe SKee
- 'Hector MacDonald' (C) **new**	SKee
- 'Herefordshire Redstreak'	ERea LBuc
- 'Herefordshire Russet'[PBR]	CDul GKir LBuc LRHS MAsh MBri MCoo SKee SLim WHar WJas
- 'Herring's Pippin' (D)	GTwe SDea
- 'High View Pippin' (D)	SKee
- 'Hoary Morning' (C)	CCAT CTho ECrN SDea SKee
- 'Hocking's Green' (C/D)	CAgr CCAT CEnd CTho
- 'Holland Pippin' (C)	WHar
- 'Hollow Core' (C)	CAgr CTho
- 'Holstein' (D)	CTho SDea SKee
- 'Honey Pippin' (D)	ECrN SKee
- 'Honey String' (F) **new**	CCAT
- 'Hood's Supreme' (D)	GBut
- 'Horneburger Pfannkuchen' (C)	SKee
- 'Horsford Prolific' (D)	ECrN ERea SKee
- 'Horsham Russet' (D)	ERea
- 'Howgate Wonder' (C)	CAgr CCAT CCVT CDoC CDul CSBt CWib ECrN ERea GBut GKir GTwe IFFs LAst LBuc LRHS MAsh MMuc SCrf SDea SFam SKee SPer SVic WBVN WHar WJas
- 'Hubbard's Pearmain' (D)	ECrN SKee

	- 'Hunter's Majestic' (D/C)	ECrN
	- 'Hunt's Duke of Gloucester' (D)	CTho SKee
	- 'Idared' (D) ♀H4	CCAT CWib ECrN GKir SDea SKee SVic
	- 'Improved Dove' (Cider)	CCAT
	- 'Improved Keswick' (C/D)	CEnd CTho
	- 'Improved Lambrook Pippin' (Cider)	CCAT CTho CTri
	- 'Improved Redstreak' (Cider)	CTho
	- 'Ingrid Marie' (D)	SDea SKee
	- 'Irish Peach' (D)	CAgr CCAT ECrN GBut GKir GTwe IFFs LRHS MCoo SDea SFam SKee WHar
	- 'Isaac Newton's Tree'	see *M. domestica* 'Flower of Kent'
	- 'Isle of Wight Pippin' (D)	SDea
	- 'Isle of Wight Russet' (D)	SDea
	- 'Jackson's'	see *M. domestica* 'Crimson King' (Cider/C)
	- 'James Grieve' (D) ♀H4	Widely available
	- 'Jerseymac' (D)	SDea
	- 'Jester' (D)	ECrN GTwe SDea SKee
	- 'Joaneting' (D)	CAgr
	- 'Joeby Crab'	WDol
	- 'John Standish' (D)	CAgr CCAT CTri ERea GTwe SCrf SDea
	- 'John Toucher's'	see *M. domestica* 'Crimson King' (Cider/C)
	- 'Johnny Andrews' (Cider)	CAgr CTho
	- 'Johnny Voun' (D)	CEnd CTho
	- 'Jonagold' (D) ♀H4	CTri CWib ECrN GTwe SCrf SDea SFam SKee SPer SVic WJas
	- 'Jonagold Crowngold'	see *M. domestica* 'Crowngold'
§	- 'Jonagored'^{PBR} (D)	SDea SKee
	- 'Jonared' (D)	GTwe
	- 'Jonathan' (D)	CMac SDea SKee
	- 'Jordan's Weeping' (C)	ERea SDea
	- 'Josephine' (D)	SDea
	- 'Joybells' (D)	GKir
	- 'Jubilee'	see *M. domestica* 'Royal Jubilee'
	- 'Julie's Late Golden' (F) **new**	CTri
	- 'Jumbo'	LRHS MBri MCoo SKee WJas
	- 'Jupiter'^{PBR} (D) ♀H4	CAgr CCAT CSBt CTri CWib ECrN GKir GTwe LAst LSRN MAsh SDea SKee WJas
	- 'Kandil Sinap' (D)	SKee
	- 'Kapai Red Jonathan' (D)	SDea
	- 'Karmijn de Sonnaville' (D)	SDea SKee
§	- 'Katja' (D)	CAgr CCAT CCVT CDoC CMac CTri CWib ECrN ERea GBut GKir GTwe IFFs LBuc LRHS MAsh MMuc NEgg NLar SBfd SCoo SDea SKee SPer WHar WJas
	- Katy	see *M. domestica* 'Katja'
	- 'Kenneth' (D)	WDol
	- 'Kent' (D)	ECrN ERea GTwe MCoo NLar SCrf SDea
	- 'Kentish Fillbasket' (C)	SKee
	- 'Kentish Pippin' (C/Cider/D)	SKee
	- 'Kerry Pippin' (D)	IFFs SKee
	- 'Keswick Codlin' (C)	CTho ECrN GBut GKir GTwe MBri MCoo NEgg NLar NWea SDea SKee WJas
§	- 'Kidd's Orange Red' (D) ♀H4	CAgr CCAT CMac CTri ECrN EPfP GQui GTwe LBuc LRHS MWat SBfd SCrf SDea SFam SKee WBVN WHar
	- 'Kilkenny Pearmain' (D)	IFFs
	- 'Kill Boy'	CTho
	- 'Killerton Sharp' (Cider)	CTho
	- 'Killerton Sweet' (Cider)	CTho
	- 'King Byerd' (C/D)	CCAT CEnd CTho
	- 'King Luscious' (D)	SDea
§	- 'King of the Pippins' (D) ♀H4	CCAT CTho CTri ECrN GBut GTwe MCoo SCrf SDea SFam SKee SVic WHar
	- 'King Russet' (D) ♀H4	SDea
	- 'King's Acre Pippin' (D)	CCAT SDea SFam
	- 'Kingston Bitter' (Cider)	CTho
	- 'Kingston Black' (Cider/C)	CCAT CEnd CTho CTri ECrN GTwe LBuc SDea SKee
	- 'Kirton Fair' (D)	CTho
	- 'Knobby Russet' (D)	SKee
	- 'Lady Henniker' (D)	CCAT CTho ECrN GTwe SDea SKee
	- 'Lady of the Wemyss' (C)	GKir GQui SKee
	- 'Lady Sudeley' (D)	CTho SDea SKee
	- 'Lady's Finger' (C/D)	CEnd GKir
	- 'Lady's Finger of Lancaster' (C/D)	SKee
	- 'Lady's Finger of Offaly' (D)	SDea
	- 'Lake's Kernel' (D)	CTho
	- 'Lane's Prince Albert' (C) ♀H4	CAgr CCAT CSBt ECrN GKir GTwe MGos MRav MWat NWea SCoo SCrf SDea SFam SKee SVic WHar WJas
	- 'Langley Pippin' (D)	SDea
§	- 'Langworthy' (Cider)	CCAT CTho
	- 'Lass o' Gowrie' (C)	GBut GKir GQui SKee
§	- 'Laxton's Epicure' (D) ♀H4	CAgr CDul ECrN GBut GTwe LAst SDea SFam SKee
§	- 'Laxton's Fortune' (D) ♀H4	CCAT CMac CSBt CTri CWib ECrN GBut GKir GTwe LAst SCrf SDea SFam SKee WHar WJas
	- 'Laxton's Pearmain' (D)	MCoo
	- 'Laxton's Royalty' (D)	SDea
§	- 'Laxton's Superb' (D)	Widely available
	- 'Leathercoat Russet' (D)	CAgr CCAT SKee
	- 'Lemon Pippin' (C)	CCAT ECrN SDea
	- 'Lemon Pippin of Gloucestershire' (D)	CTho
	- 'Liberty' (D)	GKir SDea
	- 'Limberland' (C)	CTho
	- 'Limelight' (D)	ERea LBuc LRHS MAsh MBri MCoo NLar SBfd SCoo SKee SLim WHar
	- 'Link Wonder'	CEnd
	- 'Lodi' (C)	SDea
	- 'London Pearmain' (D)	ECrN
	- 'London Pippin' (C)	CAgr CTho
	- 'Longkeeper' (D)	CAgr CEnd CTho
	- 'Longney Russet'	LBuc
	- 'Longstem' (Cider)	CTho
	- 'Lord Burghley' (D)	SDea
	- 'Lord Derby' (C)	CAgr CCAT CDul CMac CTho CWib ECrN GBut GKir GTwe IFFs LRHS SCrf SDea SFam SKee SVic
	- 'Lord Grosvenor' (C)	SKee WHar
	- 'Lord Hindlip' (D)	LRHS SDea SFam
	- 'Lord Lambourne' (D) ♀H4	CAgr CCAT CDoC CDul CMac CSBt CTri CWib ECrN EPfP GKir GTwe IFFs LAst LRHS MCoo MGos MWat SCrf SDea SFam SKee SPer WBVN WHar WJas
	- 'Lord of the Isles' (F)	CAgr CCAT
	- 'Lord Stradbroke' (C)	ECrN SKee
	- 'Lord Suffield' (C)	CTri ECrN SKee
	- 'Lough Tree of Wexford' (D)	IFFs
	- 'Lucombe's Pine' (D)	CAgr CCAT CEnd CTho ECrN SVic
	- 'Lucombe's Seedling' (D)	CTho
	- 'Lynn's Pippin' (D)	ECrN
	- 'Mabbott's Pearmain' (D)	SDea

	Cultivar	Suppliers
	– 'Machen' (D)	WDol
	– 'Maclean's Favourite' (D)	ECrN
	– 'Madresfield Court' (D)	SDea
	– 'Maggie Sinclair' (D)	GBut GQui
	– 'Maid of Kent'	CCAT
	– 'Major' (Cider)	CCAT
	– 'Maldon Wonder' (D)	ECrN
	– 'Malling Kent' (D)	ERea SDea SFam
	– 'Manaccan Primrose' (C/D)	CEnd
	– 'Manks Codlin' (C)	GBut
	– 'Mannington's Pearmain' (D)	SKee
	– 'Marged Nicolas' (D)	WDol
	– 'Margil' (D)	CCAT SDea SFam SKee WHar
	– 'Maxton' (D)	ECrN
	– 'May Queen' (D)	SDea SFam
	– 'Maypole'^{PBR} (D/Ball)	MAsh MGos SDea WJas
	– 'McIntosh' (D)	SKee
	– 'Médaille d'Or' (Cider)	SKee
	– 'Melon' (D)	SDea
	– 'Melrose' (D)	ECrN SVic
	– 'Merchant Apple' (D)	CCAT CTho CTri
	– 'Mère de Ménage' (C)	GKir SFam WHar
	– 'Meridian'^{PBR} (D)	CAgr CDoC ECrN EMil LRHS SDea
	– 'Merton Knave' (D)	SDea SFam
	– 'Merton Russet' (D)	SDea
	– 'Merton Worcester' (D)	ECrN SDea SKee
	– 'Michaelmas Red' (D)	GTwe NEgg SKee
	– 'Michelin' (Cider)	CAgr CCAT CTri ERea GKir GTwe SDea SKee
	– 'Miller's Seedling' (D)	SKee
	– 'Millicent Barnes' (D)	GKir SDea
	– 'Mollie's Delicious' (D)	SKee
	– 'Monarch' (C)	CAgr CCAT CTri ECrN GBut GTwe SDea SFam SKee
	– 'Monidel'^{PBR}	ECrN
	– 'Monmouthshire Green' (D)	WDol
	– 'Montfort' (D)	ECrN
	– 'Morgan's Sweet' (C/Cider)	CCAT CEnd CTho CTri SDea SKee WDol
	– 'Moss's Seedling' (D)	SDea
§	– 'Mother' (D) ♀H4	CAgr CCAT CDoC CTri ECrN GTwe SCrf SDea SKee
§	– 'Mutsu' (D)	CCAT CTri ECrN SCrf SDea SKee
	– 'Nant Gwrtheyrn' (D)	WGwG
	– 'Nettlestone Pippin' (D)	SDea
	– 'Newton Wonder' (D/C) ♀H4	CAgr CCAT CDoC CDul CSBt CTho CTri CWib ECrN GTwe IFFs LAst LRHS MCoo MGos SCrf SDea SFam SKee WJas
	– 'Newtown Pippin' (D)	SDea
	– 'Nine Square' (D)	CCAT CTho
	– 'Nittany Red' (D)	SDea
	– 'No Pip' (C)	CTho
	– 'Nolan Pippin' (D)	ECrN
	– 'Nonpareil' (D)	SKee WHar
	– 'Norfolk Beauty' (C)	ECrN ERea SKee
	– 'Norfolk Beefing' (C)	ECrN ERea SDea SFam SKee
	– 'Norfolk Royal' (D)	CDoC ECrN ERea GTwe SDea SKee
	– 'Norfolk Royal Russet' (D)	ECrN ERea GBut GKir LRHS SKee WBVN
	– 'Norfolk Summer Broadend' (C)	SKee
	– 'Norfolk Winter Coleman' (C)	ERea SKee
	– 'Northcott Superb' (D)	CTho
	– 'Northern Greening' (C)	SKee
§	– 'Northwood' (Cider)	CCAT CTho SKee
	– 'Nutmeg Pippin' (D)	CCAT ECrN SDea
	– Nuvar Freckles (D)	SKee
	– Nuvar Golden Elf	SKee
	– Nuvar Golden Hills (D)	SKee
	– Nuvar Home Farm (D)	SKee
	– Nuvar Melody (D)	SKee
	– 'Oaken Pin' (D)	CCAT CTho
§	– 'Obelisk'^{PBR} (D)	LRHS MAsh MCoo NPri SDea SKee
	– 'Old Pearmain' (D)	SDea WHar
	– 'Old Somerset Russet' (D)	CCAT CTho
	– 'Opal'^{PBR} (D)	ECrN
	– 'Opalescent' (D)	SKee
	– 'Orin' (D)	SKee
	– 'Orkney Apple' (F)	SKee
	– 'Orleans Reinette' (D)	CAgr CCAT CTho CTri CWib ECrN GBut GTwe IFFs LBuc LRHS MWat NEgg SCrf SDea SFam SKee WJas
	– 'Oslin' (D)	GBut GKir SKee
	– 'Otava'^{PBR}	SKee
	– 'Owen Thomas' (D)	CTri
	– 'Paignton Marigold' (Cider)	CTho
	– 'Pascoe's Pippin' (D/C)	CTho
	– 'Payhembury' (C/Cider)	CAgr CTho CTri
	– 'Pear Apple' (D)	CAgr CEnd CTho
	– 'Pearl' (D)	ECrN SDea
	– 'Peasgood's Nonsuch' (C) ♀H4	CAgr CCAT CDoC ECrN ERea GBut GKir GTwe IFFs NEgg SCrf SDea SFam SKee SLon
	– 'Pen Caled' (Cider)	WDol
	– 'Pendragon' (D)	CTho
	– 'Penhallow Pippin' (D)	CTho
	– 'Perthyre' (Cider)	WDol
	– 'Peter Lock' (C/D)	CAgr CCAT CEnd CTho
	– 'Peter's Pippin' (D)	SDea
	– 'Peter's Seedling' (D)	SDea
	– 'Pethyre' (Cider)	CCVT
	– 'Pig Aderyn' (C)	WDol WGwG
	– 'Pig Yr Wydd' (C)	WDol
	– 'Pig's Nose Pippin' (D)	CEnd
	– 'Pig's Nose Pippin' Type III (D)	CAgr CCAT CTho
	– 'Pig's Snout' (Cider/C/D)	CCAT CEnd CTho
	– 'Pine Apple Russet'	CAgr ERea
	– 'Pinova'^{PBR} (D)	CAgr SKee
	– 'Pitmaston Pine Apple' (D)	CCAT CTho CTri ECrN ERea GBut LAst LRHS MCoo MWat SCrf SDea SFam SKee
	– 'Pixie' (D) ♀H4	CCAT CWib GTwe LRHS MWat SDea SFam SKee WJas
	– 'Plum Vite' (D)	CAgr CTho CTri
	– 'Plympton Pippin' (C)	CEnd CTho CTri
	– Polka = 'Trajan'^{PBR} (D/Ball)	SDea SKee
	– 'Polly' (C/D)	CEnd
	– 'Polly Whitehair' (C/D)	CCAT CTho SDea
	– 'Poltimore Seedling'	CTho
	– 'Pomeroy of Somerset' (D)	CCAT CTho CTri
	– 'Ponsford' (C)	CAgr CCAT CTho
	– 'Port Allen Russet' (C/D)	GBut GKir GQui
	– 'Port Wine'	see *M. domestica* 'Harry Master's Jersey'
	– 'Porter's Perfection' (Cider)	CCAT ERea
	– 'Pren Glas' (D)	WDol
	– 'Princesse'	ECrN GKir SDea SKee
	– 'Profit'	CTho
	– 'Puckrupp Pippin' (D)	LBuc
	– 'Quarry Apple' (C)	CTho
	– 'Queen' (C)	CAgr CTho ECrN SKee
	– 'Queen Cox' (D)	CTri ECrN SDea SKee SLon
	– 'Queen Cox' self-fertile	CSut CWib ERea LSRN SDea SWvt WClo

- 'Queens' (D)	CTho
- 'Quench' (D/Cider)	CTho
- 'Radford Beauty'	MCoo
- 'Rajka' (D)	GBut SKee
- 'Red Alkmene' (D)	MBri
- 'Red Belle de Boskoop' (D)	CAgr
- 'Red Blenheim' (C/D)	SKee
- 'Red Bramley' (C)	CWib GKir
- 'Red Charles Ross' (C/D)	SDea
- 'Red Delicious' (D)	SCrf SKee
- 'Red Devil' (D)	CAgr CMac CTri CWSG ECrN GBut GKir GTwe LAst LRHS MAsh MBri SBfd SCoo SDea SKee SLim WHar WJas
- 'Red Ellison' (D)	CTho CTri ERea GTwe SDea
- 'Red Falstaff'^{PBR} (D)	CAgr CCAT CCVT CDoC CDul CMac ECrN EPfP ERea GKir LBuc LRHS LSRN MAsh MBri MCoo NLar SKee SLim SPer SPoG WBVN WHar
- 'Red Fuji' (D)	SDea
- 'Red James Grieve'	GKir LSRN
- 'Red Jersey' (Cider)	CCAT
- 'Red Joaneting' (D)	SKee WHar
- 'Red Jonagold'^{PBR}	see *M. domestica* 'Jonagored'
- 'Red Jonathan' (D)	SDea
- 'Red Miller's Seedling' (D)	ECrN SCrf SDea
- 'Red Rattler' (D)	CTho
- 'Red Roller' (D)	CTho
- 'Red Ruby' (F)	CTho
- 'Red Victoria' (C)	GTwe
- 'Red Windsor' (F)	CMac GBut GKir LBuc LRHS MAsh NLar SCoo SKee SLim SPoG WHar WJas
- 'Redcoat Grieve' (D)	GKir SDea
- 'Redsleeves' (D)	CAgr ECrN GTwe SDea SKee
- 'Redstrake' (Cider)	CCAT
- Regali = 'Delkistar'^{PBR} (F)	LRHS
- 'Reine des Reinettes'	see *M. domestica* 'King of the Pippins'
- 'Reinette Descardre' (D)	SVic
- 'Reinette d'Obry' (Cider)	CCAT
- 'Reinette du Canada' (D)	SKee
- 'Reinette Rouge Etoilée' (D)	SDea
- 'Reverend Greeves' (C)	SDea
- 'Reverend McCormick' (F)	CTho
- 'Reverend W. Wilks' (C)	CAgr CDoC CDoy CSBt CTri ECrN GKir IFFs LAst LRHS MBri SCrf SDea SFam SKee WJas
- 'Ribston Pippin' (D) ♀^{H4}	CCAT CTho CTri CWib ECrN ERea GBut GTwe LBuc LRHS MCoo MWat SCrf SDea SFam SKee WHar WJas
- 'Rival' (D)	CAgr SDea
- 'Robert Blatchford' (C)	ECrN
- 'Rome Beauty' (D)	SDea
- 'Rosemary Russet' (D) ♀^{H4}	CAgr CCAT CTho GBut GKir GTwe MCoo SCrf SDea SFam SKee
- 'Ross Nonpareil' (D)	CAgr GTwe IFFs SDea SKee
- 'Rosy Blenheim' (D)	ECrN
- 'Rough Pippin' (D)	CCAT CEnd
- 'Roundway Magnum Bonum' (D)	CAgr CTho SDea
§ - 'Roxbury Russet' (D)	SKee
- 'Royal Gala' (D) ♀^{H4}	ECrN LAst LBuc SDea SLon
§ - 'Royal Jubilee' (C)	CCAT
- 'Royal Russet' (C)	CEnd ECrN SDea
- 'Royal Somerset' (C/Cider)	CCAT CTho CTri
- 'Rubinette' (D)	ECrN SDea
- Rubinette Rosso = 'Rafzubex'^{PBR} (F) **new**	LRHS
- 'Rubinola'^{PBR}	SKee
- 'Saint Cecilia' (D)	SDea WDol WGwG
§ - 'Saint Edmund's Pippin' (D) ♀^{H4}	CTho ECrN ERea GTwe LRHS MCoo SCrf SDea SFam SKee WBVN WGwG
- 'Saint Edmund's Russet'	see *M. domestica* 'Saint Edmund's Pippin'
- 'Saltcote Pippin' (D)	SKee
- 'Sam Young' (D)	CAgr SKee
- 'Sandlands' (D)	SDea
- 'Sandringham' (C)	ECrN ERea
- 'Sanspareil' (D)	CAgr SKee
- 'Santana' (D)	SKee
- 'Saturn' (D)	CAgr CCVT CTri ERea GTwe SDea SKee
- 'Saw Pits' (F)	CAgr CEnd
- 'Scarlet Crofton' (D)	IFFs
- 'Scarlet Nonpareil' (D)	SDea
- 'Scotch Bridget' (C)	GBut GKir NBid SCoo SKee
- 'Scotch Dumpling' (C)	GBut GKir GTwe LRHS MCoo
- 'Scrumptious'^{PBR} (D)	CAgr CDoC CDul CMac EPfP ERea GKir LBuc LRHS LSRN MAsh MBri NLar NPri NWea SBfd SCoo SKee SLim SPer SPoG WHar WJas
- 'Seabrook's Red' (D)	ECrN
- 'Seaton House' (C)	GBut GKir
- 'Sercombe's Natural' (Cider)	CTho
- 'Severn Bank' (C)	CCAT CTho
- 'Sheep's Nose' (C)	CCAT CTho SDea
- 'Shenandoah' (C)	SKee
- 'Sidney Strake' (C)	CAgr CEnd
- 'Sir Isaac Newton's'	see *M. domestica* 'Flower of Kent'
- 'Sir John Thornycroft' (D)	SDea
- 'Slack Ma Girdle' (Cider)	CCAT CTho
- 'Smart's Prince Arthur' (C)	SDea
- 'Snell's Glass Apple'	see *M. domestica* 'Glass Apple'
- 'Somerset Lasting' (C)	CCAT CTri
- 'Somerset Redstreak' (Cider)	CCAT CTho CTri GTwe
- 'Sops in Wine' (C/Cider)	CCAT CTho SVic
- 'Sour Bay' (Cider)	CAgr CTho
- 'Sour Natural'	see *M. domestica* 'Langworthy'
- 'Spartan' (D)	CCAT CCVT CDoC CMac CSBt CTri CWib ECrN GKir GTwe IFFs LAst LRHS MAsh MCoo MGan MGos NPri SBfd SCrf SDea SFam SKee SPer SVic WHar WJas
- 'Spencer' (D)	CTri ECrN
- 'Spotted Dick' (Cider)	CTho
- 'Spout Apple'	LBuc
- 'Stable Jersey' (Cider)	CCAT
- 'Stamford Pippin' (D)	SDea
- 'Stanway Seedling' (C)	ECrN
- 'Star of Devon' (D)	CCAT CEnd SDea
- 'Stark' (D)	SDea
- 'Starking' (D)	ECrN
- 'Stark's Earliest' (D)	SVic
- 'Stembridge Cluster' (Cider)	CCAT
- 'Stembridge Jersey' (Cider)	CCAT
- 'Steyne Seedling' (D)	SDea
- 'Stirling Castle' (C)	CAgr GBut GKir GQui SKee
- 'Stobo Castle' (C)	GBut GKir GQui SKee
- 'Stockbearer' (C)	CTho
- 'Stoke Red' (Cider)	CCAT CTho SKee
- 'Strawberry Pippin' (D)	CTho
- 'Striped Beefing' (C)	ECrN ERea

	– 'Sturmer Pippin' (D)	CCAT CSBt CTri ECrN GTwe IFFs MWat SCrf SDea SFam SKee WHar
*	– 'Sugar Apple'	CTho
	– 'Sugar Bush' (C/D)	CTho
	– 'Sugar Loaf'	see *M. domestica* 'Sugar Apple'
	– 'Summer Golden Pippin' (D)	SKee
	– 'Summer Stubbard' (D)	CCAT
	– 'Summerred' (D)	ECrN EMil
	– 'Sunburn' (D)	ECrN
	– 'Sunnydale' (D/C)	SDea
	– 'Sunrise'PBR (D)	SKee
	– 'Sunset' (D) ♀H4	Widely available
	– 'Suntan' (D) ♀H4	CCAT CMac CWib ECrN LAst SDea SKee
	– 'Superb'	see *M. domestica* 'Laxton's Superb'
	– 'Surprise' (D)	GTwe
	– 'Sussex Mother' (C/D) **new**	SKee
	– 'Sweet Alford' (Cider)	CCAT CTho ECrN
	– 'Sweet Bay' (Cider)	CAgr CTho
	– 'Sweet Caroline' (D)	ECrN
	– 'Sweet Cleave' (Cider)	CTho
	– 'Sweet Coppin' (Cider)	CCAT CTho CTri
	– 'Sweet Society' (D)	LBuc LRHS MCoo WHar WJas
	– 'Tale Sweet' (Cider)	CCAT CTho
	– 'Tamar Beauty' (F)	CEnd
	– 'Tan Harvey' (Cider)	CCAT CEnd CTho
	– 'Taunton Cross' (D)	CAgr
	– 'Taunton Fair Maid' (Cider)	CCAT CTho
	– 'Taylor's' (Cider)	CCAT SDea
	– 'Ten Commandments' (D/Cider)	CCAT SDea
	– 'Tewkesbury Baron' (D)	CTho
	– 'The Rattler' (F)	CEnd
	– 'Thomas Rivers' (C)	SDea
	– 'Thorle Pippin' (D)	GBut SKee
	– 'Tidicombe Seedling' (D)	CTho
	– 'Tinyrwydd' (C)	WDol
	– 'Tom Putt' (C)	CAgr CCAT CCVT CTho CTri CWib ECrN GKir GTwe LBuc SDea SKee WJas
	– 'Tommy Knight' (D)	CAgr CCAT CEnd CTho
	– 'Topaz'PBR (D)	SKee
	– 'Totnes Apple' (D)	CTho
	– 'Tower of Glamis' (C)	GBut GKir GQui GTwe SKee
	– Town Farm Number 59 (Cider)	CTho
	– 'Transparent Codlin'	LBuc
	– 'Tregonna King' (C/D)	CCAT CEnd CTho
	– 'Tremlett's Bitter' (Cider)	CAgr CCAT CTho SDea SKee SVic
	– 'Trwyn Mochyn' (C)	WGwG
	– 'Twyn y Sherriff' (Cider)	WDol
§	– 'Tydeman's Early Worcester' (D)	CAgr CLnd CWib ECrN GBut GTwe SDea SKee SVic
	– 'Tydeman's Late Orange' (D)	CMac ECrN EMil ERea GTwe LAst LRHS MCoo SDea SFam SKee
	– 'Uncle John's Cooker' (C)	IFFs
	– 'Upton Pyne' (C/D)	CCAT CTho SDea
	– 'Vallis Apple' (Cider)	CCAT CTho
	– 'Veitch's Perfection' (C/D)	CTho
	– 'Venus Pippin' (C/D)	CEnd
	– 'Vicar of Beighton' (D)	ECrN ERea
	– 'Vicary's Late Keeper'	CTho
	– 'Vickey's Delight' (D)	SDea
	– 'Vileberie' (Cider)	CCAT
	– 'Vista-bella' (D)	ECrN SDea SKee
	– 'Wagener' (D)	ECrN SDea SKee
	– 'Waltham Abbey Seedling' (C)	ECrN
	– Waltz = 'Telamon'PBR (D/Ball)	SDea SKee
	– 'Warner's King' (C) ♀H4	CCAT CTho CTri GKir SCrf SDea SKee
	– 'Warrior' (F)	CCAT CTho
	– 'Wealthy' (D)	SDea
	– 'Wellington' (C)	see *M. domestica* 'Dummellor's Seedling'
	– 'Wellington' (Cider)	CAgr CTho
	– 'Welsh Russet' (D)	SDea
	– 'Wern' (C)	WDol
	– 'West View Seedling' (D)	ECrN
	– 'Wheeler's Russet' (D)	LBuc
	– 'White Alphington' (Cider)	CTho
	– 'White Close Pippin' (Cider)	CTho
	– 'White Jersey' (Cider)	CCAT
	– 'White Joaneting' (D)	CCAT GBut
	– 'White Melrose' (C)	GBut GKir GTwe IFFs LRHS MCoo SDea SKee
	– 'White Paradise'PBR (C)	GKir
	– 'White Transparent' (C/D)	SDea
	– 'Whitpot Sweet' (F)	CEnd
	– 'Wick White Styre' (Cider)	CTho
	– 'William Crump' (D)	CCAT CTho ECrN SDea SFam SKee
	– 'Winston' (D) ♀H4	CAgr CCAT CCVT CMac CSBt CTri ECrN GTwe LRHS MCoo NWea SCrf SDea SFam SKee SVic WHar
	– 'Winter Banana' (D)	ECrN LRHS SDea SKee SVic
	– 'Winter Gem' (D)	CAgr CCVT CDoC CDul ECrN EMil ERea LAst LBuc MAsh SDea SKee WHar WJas
	– 'Winter Lawrence' (F)	CTho
	– 'Winter Lemon' (C/D)	GQui
	– 'Winter Majetin' (C)	ECrN ERea
	– 'Winter Peach' (D/C)	CAgr CEnd CTho ECrN
	– 'Winter Pearmain' (D)	SKee WHar
	– 'Winter Quarrenden' (D)	SDea
	– 'Winter Queening' (D/C)	SDea
	– 'Winter Stubbard' (C)	CTho
	– 'Woodbine'	see *M. domestica* 'Northwood'
	– 'Woodford' (C)	ECrN
	– 'Woolbrook Pippin' (D)	CAgr CCAT CEnd CTho
	– 'Woolbrook Russet' (C)	CCAT CEnd CTho ECrN
	– 'Worcester Pearmain' (D) ♀H4	Widely available
	– 'Worcester Woodsil' (F) **new**	SKee
	– 'Wormsley Pippin' (D)	ECrN
	– 'Wyatt's Seedling'	see *M. domestica* 'Langworthy'
	– 'Wyken Pippin' (D)	CCAT ECrN GTwe SDea SFam SKee
	– 'Yarlington Mill' (Cider)	CAgr CCAT CTho CTri SDea SKee SVic
	– 'Yellow Ingestrie' (D)	LRHS MCoo SFam SKee WHar WJas
	– 'Yellow Styre' (Cider)	CTho
	– 'Zabergäu Renette' (D)	SKee
	'Donald Wyman'	CLnd EBee EPfP LRHS SCoo
	'Echtermeyer'	see *M.* × *gloriosa* 'Oekonomierat Echtermeyer'
	'Evelyn'	EBee GKir LRHS
§	'Evereste' ♀H4	Widely available
	florentina	CLnd CTho EBee EPfP GKir LLHF LRHS SSpi
	– 'Rosemoor'	EBee
	– 'Skopje' **new**	EPfP
	floribunda ♀H4	Widely available
	'Gardener's Gold'	CEnd CTho
§	× ***gloriosa*** 'Oekonomierat Echtermeyer'	GKir SDea WDin
	'Golden Gem'	EBee EMil EPfP GTwe SLim SPer
	'Golden Hornet'	see *M.* × *zumi* 'Golden Hornet'

'Harry Baker'	CCVT EBee EMil EPfP ERea LRHS MAsh MBlu MBri NLar SCoo SLim SPoG WJas
'Hillieri'	see *M.* × *scheideckeri* 'Hillieri'
hupehensis ♀H4	CCAT CDul CEnd CLnd CMCN CSBt CTho EBee ECrN EPfP GKir LHop MBlu MGos MRav SCrf SFam SPer WPat
'Hyde Hall Spire'	SCoo
'John Downie' (C) ♀H4	Widely available
'Kaido'	see *M.* × *micromalus*
kansuensis	CLnd EPfP
'Laura'	CDul EBee ECrN EPfP GKir LRHS LSRN MAsh MBri MGos NLar SCoo SKee SLim SPoG WJas
'Lisa'	CLnd
'Louisa'	CWSG EBee GKir LRHS MAsh NWea SCoo
× ***magdeburgensis***	CCVT CDul CLnd CSBt
'Marshal Ōyama'	CTho
'Mary Potter'	CLnd CTho
§ × ***micromalus***	NLar
× ***moerlandsii***	CLnd
- 'Liset'	CDul CEnd CLnd CSBt CWib EBee ECrN MRav NEgg SCoo SFam SPer SPoG WFar
§ - 'Profusion'	CBcs CDul CLnd CMac CTri EBee ECrN ELan EWTr LAst LRHS MGos MMuc MRav MSwo NPri NWea SBfd SCrf SEND SPer SWvt WBVN WDin WFar WJas
- 'Profusion Improved'	CEnd CSBt CWSG GKir MWat SCoo SWvt WHar
'Mokum'	LMaj LTen
'Molten Lava'	CLnd
niedzwetzkyana	see *M. pumila* 'Niedzwetzkyana'
Nuvar Carnival	SKee
Nuvar Dusty Red	SKee
Nuvar Marble	SKee
Nuvar Red Lantern	SKee
orthocarpa	CLnd
Perpetu	see *M.* 'Evereste'
'Pink Glow'	CLnd CSBt EBee LRHS MBlu NLar SBfd SCoo SLim SPer SPoG WHar
'Pink Mushroom'	NLar
'Pink Perfection'	CDoC CEnd EBee ECrN GKir
Pom'Zaï = 'Courtabri'	CDoC
'Pond Red'	CLnd
'Prairie Fire'	CDul EBee GKir LRHS MAsh MBri SCoo SLim SPoG
prattii	CTho EPfP
'Princeton Cardinal'	CLnd EBee EMil GKir LRHS MAsh SCoo SLim
'Professor Sprenger'	see *M.* × *zumi* 'Professor Sprenger'
'Profusion'	see *M.* × *moerlandsii* 'Profusion'
prunifolia	MBlu
- 'Pendula'	MGan
pumila 'Cowichan'	ECrN GKir
- 'Dartmouth'	CDul CLnd CSBt CSam CTri ECrN NEgg NPCo SFam
- 'Montreal Beauty'	CLnd GKir WJas
§ - 'Niedzwetzkyana'	CLnd CTho
§ × ***purpurea*** 'Aldenhamensis'	CLnd SDea WDin WSpi
- 'Eleyi'	CDul CLnd ECrN LAst NWea WDin
- 'Lemoinei'	CLnd ECrN
- 'Neville Copeman'	CCVT CDoC CDul CLnd EBee ECrN EWTr MGos SBfd SPur WJas
- 'Pendula'	see *M.* × *gloriosa* 'Oekonomierat Echtermeyer'
'R.J. Fulcher'	CTho
'Ralph Shay'	CLnd
'Red Ace'	CDul
'Red Barron'	CLnd
'Red Glow'	CLnd EBee ECrN MMuc WJas
'Red Jade'	see *M.* × *scheideckeri* 'Red Jade'
'Red Obelisk'	LRHS MAsh MBri SCoo SPoG
'Red Peacock'	CLnd
'Robinson'	CLnd
§ × ***robusta***	CLnd GTwe LSRN NWea SBfd SCrf SLon
- 'Red Sentinel' ♀H4	Widely available
- 'Red Siberian'	ECrN SDea SPer
- 'Yellow Siberian'	CLnd
rockii	GAuc
'Royal Beauty' ♀H4	CDoC CDul CWib EBee EMil EPfP GKir GTwe LAst LRHS MBri MGos MSwo SBfd SCoo SCrf SPer WDin WHar
'Royalty'	CBcs CDul CLnd CMac CSBt EBee ECrN ELan GKir GTwe LAst LBuc LRHS MGos MRav MSwo MWat NBea NEgg NPla SBfd SCrf SEND SPer SPoG WDin WHar WJas
'Rudolph'	CCVT CDul CLnd EBee ECrN EWTr GKir LBuc LMaj MAsh MGos SCoo SLim SPer SPoG WHCr WJas
'Ruth Ann'	CLnd
sargentii	CLnd CTho ECrN LAst MGos NWea SFam
- 'Tina'	CLnd
'Satin Cloud'	CLnd
§ × ***scheideckeri*** 'Hillieri'	CDul CLnd ECrN SFam
§ - 'Red Jade'	CDul CMCN CTri CWib EBee ECrN ELan EPfP GKir GTwe LAst LRHS MGos MMuc MRav MSwo MWat NEgg NPri NWea SBfd SEND SPer WDin WFar WJas
Siberian crab	see *M.* × *robusta*
sieboldii	see *M. toringo*
- 'Wooster'	CLnd
'Silver Drift'	CLnd
'Snowcloud'	CDul CLnd EBee ECrN SLim SPer
spectabilis	CLnd
'Street Parade'	CLnd
× ***sublobata***	CLnd
'Sun Rival'	CCVT CDoC CDul CEnd CLnd CSBt EPfP GKir GTwe MBri MGos SBfd SCoo SLim SPoG WHar WJas
sylvestris	CArn CCVT CDul CLnd CRWN ECrN EMac EPfP GKir LBuc MMuc MRav NLar NWea SEND SPer WDin WMou
§ ***toringo***	CCAT CLnd CTho ECrN EPfP LMaj MBlu MBri WSHC
I - var. ***arborescens***	CLnd CTho
- 'Browers'	LMaj
- 'Scarlett'	IArd LRHS MAsh MBri NLar SCoo SLim SPoG WJas
- 'Wintergold'	EWTr MMuc SEND
toringoides	see *M. bhutanica*
- 'Mandarin'	GKir MBri NLar SCoo
transitoria ♀H4	CDoC CDul CEnd CLnd CTho EBee ELan EMil EPfP GKir LRHS MBlu MBri NWea SCoo SSpi WMou WPGP
- 'Thornhayes Tansy'	CTho EBee GKir LRHS SLim WSpi
trilobata	CCAT CLnd CTho EBee EMil EPfP LMaj MBlu MGos MMuc SCoo SEND SPoG
- 'Guardsman'	EBee GKir LRHS MBri NLar SPoG SSpi

tschonoskii ♀H4	Widely available
'Van Eseltine'	CDul CSBt CWib EBee ECrN EPfP GKir GTwe MAsh MMuc MWat NBea SFam WHar WJas WPat
'Veitch's Scarlet'	CDoy CDul CLnd CSBt GKir GTwe NEgg NPCo SFam
Weeping Candied Apple = 'Weepcanzam'	CLnd
'White Star'	CCVT CDoC CDul CLnd CSBt EBee ECrN SBfd SCoo SLim
'Winter Gold'	CDul CLnd EBee LMaj MMuc SCrf SEND
'Wisley Crab'	CLnd EBee GKir GTwe SDea SFam
yunnanensis	EPfP GAuc GKir
- var. ***veitchii***	CTho
× ***zumi*** var. ***calocarpa***	CTho
§ - 'Golden Hornet' ♀H4	Widely available
§ - 'Professor Sprenger'	CLnd CSam EBee EPfP LMaj MBri SCoo

Malva (*Malvaceae*)

alcea var. ***fastigiata***	CMac EBee ECGP EShb NBro SPer SRms WFar WPer
bicolor	see *Lavatera maritima*
moschata	CArn CBcs CPrp CRWN EBee ECtt ELan EPfP GJos GPoy MHer MMuc MNHC NBPC NLar NMir SIde SPer SPlb SWat WCom WGwG WHer WJek WMoo
- f. ***alba*** ♀H4	Widely available
- 'Appleblossom' new	CSpr
- 'Pink Perfection'	EShb LRHS
- 'Romney Marsh'	see *Althaea officinalis* 'Romney Marsh'
- ***rosea***	EPfP GMaP NBPC NEgg NPer SBfd SPoG SWvt
- 'White Perfection'	ELon LRHS
pusilla	CCCN
'Sweet Sixteen'	EBee ECtt NBPC
sylvestris	CArn NBro NSco SEND SWat WFar WHfH WJek WMoo
- 'Bardsey Blue'	WGwG
- 'Blue Fountain'[PBR]	NBPC
- 'Brave Heart'	GJos SPav SWvt
- Marina = 'Dema'[PBR]	EBee ELan NLar WFar
- subsp. ***mauritiana***	NPer WMoo
- - 'Bibor Fehlo'	CSpe CSpr
- 'Mystic Merlin'	SPav
- 'Perry's Blue'	NPer
- 'Primley Blue'	CBot EBee ECtt ELan EPfP GMaP GQue MRav NBPC NPer SPer WCom WFar WNew WSpi
- 'Windsor Castle'	NBPC
- 'Zebrina'	CSpr EBee EPfP NPer SWvt WFar WMoo

Malvastrum (*Malvaceae*)

lateritium	Widely available

Malvaviscus (*Malvaceae*)

arboreus	CHII

mandarin see *Citrus reticulata*

mandarin, Cleopatra see *Citrus reshni*

Mandevilla (*Apocynaceae*)

§ × ***amabilis***	CCCN MWya
- 'Alice du Pont' ♀H1	CCCN CSpe ELan ERea EShb LRHS SOWG
× ***amoena***	see *M.* × *amabilis*
boliviensis ♀H1	CCCN CRHN ELan LRHS SOWG
§ ***laxa*** ♀H2	CBot CCCN CHEx CHGN CHII CRHN CSpe EBee ECre ELan ERea EShb IDee IRar LRHS SAga SOWG WCot WHrl WPGP WSHC
- 'Snowbird'	ERea
sanderi	CCCN ERea EShb
- 'Rosea'	CSpe ERea NPla
splendens ♀H1	CCCN CHII EPfP SOWG
suaveolens	see *M. laxa*
Sundaville Pink = 'Sunmandecripi'[PBR] new	LSou
'Sundaville Red'	LAst LSou

Mandragora (*Solanaceae*)

autumnalis	WCot
caulescens	WSpi
§ ***officinarum***	CArn CEls EBee GCal GPoy NGHP WCot

Manettia (*Rubiaceae*)

inflata	see *M. luteorubra*
§ ***luteorubra***	CCCN ELan WCot

Manfreda see *Agave*

× *Mangave* see *Agave*

Mangifera (*Anacardiaceae*)

indica (F)	CCCN

Manglietia see *Magnolia*

yunnanensis	see *Magnolia insignis*

mango see *Mangifera indica*

Manihot (*Euphorbiaceae*)

carthaginensis new	SPlb

Maranta (*Marantaceae*)

leuconeura var. ***erythroneura*** ♀H1	EShb XBlo
- var. ***kerchoveana*** ♀H1	EShb XBlo

Marattia (*Marattiaceae*)

salicina	WRic

Marchantia (*Marchantiaceae*)

polymorpha new	CArn

Margyricarpus (*Rosaceae*)

§ ***pinnatus***	CFee GEdr NWCA WCom WPer
setosus	see *M. pinnatus*

Mariscus see *Cyperus*

marjoram, pot see *Origanum onites*

marjoram, sweet see *Origanum majorana*

marjoram, wild, or oregano see *Origanum vulgare*

Marrubium (*Lamiaceae*)

sp.	SEND
§ ***bourgaei*** var. ***bourgaei*** 'All Hallow's Green'	CFee EBee ECha ECtt LHop LRHS MRav NEgg SPoG WOut
libanoticum	WPer
supinum	CArn

vulgare CArn CPrp GBar GPoy MHer MNHC SIde WJek
- 'Green Pompon' NLar

Marshallia (*Asteraceae*)

grandiflora CDes EBee SUsu
mohrii EBee
trinerva ELon

Marsilea (*Marsileaceae*)

quadrifolia MSKA
- variegated (v) LLWG

Mascarena see *Hyophorbe*

Massonia (*Hyacinthaceae*)

depressa ECho
- 'Branvlei Dam' new ECho
- 'Reitfontein Gamoep' new ECho
echinata CStu ECho WCot
aff. ***echinata*** CStu ECho WCot
jasminiflora ECho
pustulata CStu ECho WCot
pygmaea subsp. ***kamiesbergensis*** ECho
- subsp. ***pygmaea*** ECho

Mathiasella (*Apiaceae*)

bupleuroides CHid LPio LSou
- 'Green Dream' CAbP CAby CBcs CBod CBre CMea CSpe EBee ECtt EWll GBin IPot LOck LRHS MLLN MPnt NCGa NPnk SDix SMrm SUsu WClo WCot WCra

Matricaria (*Asteraceae*)

chamomilla see *M. recutita*
parthenium see *Tanacetum parthenium*
§ ***recutita*** CArn GPoy MNHC

Matteuccia (*Woodsiaceae*)

orientalis CBty CDTJ CKel CLAP EBee EFer EPfP GCal GGar GMaP NLar NMyG SPad WFar WMoo WPnP WRic WWEG
pensylvanica CLAP EBee WRic
struthiopteris ♀H4 Widely available
* - 'Depauperata' CLAP
- 'Jumbo' CBty CCCN CLAP EBee ISha LRHS
- 'The King' new WCot

Matthiola (*Brassicaceae*)

fruticulosa 'Alba' CDes WPGP
- subsp. ***perennis*** NSti SEND WHal
incana EBee LRHS MArl SPad WCFE WFar WKif WRHF
- ***alba*** ECha ELan LSou NCGa SEND SMad SPav WCot WSpi
- purple-flowered SEND SWal
montana new LLHF
white-flowered perennial CArn CSev CSpe MAvo MLHP MSCN NPer SEND SPhx SWal WCom WEas WTou

Maurandella (*Scrophulariaceae*)

§ ***antirrhiniflora*** EWld

Maurandya (*Scrophulariaceae*)

§ ***barclayana*** CBot CDTJ CHll MBri SGar
- ***alba*** CBot
'Bridal Bouquet' CCCN LSou
erubescens see *Lophospermum erubescens*
lophantha see *Lophospermum scandens*
lophospermum see *Lophospermum scandens*
'Pink Ice' see *Lophospermum scandens* 'Pink Ice'
'Red Dragon' see *Lophospermum* 'Red Dragon'
§ 'Victoria Falls' SOWG

Maytenus (*Celastraceae*)

boaria CMCN EBee EPfP GBin GGal IArd IDee IFFs LEdu MBri MGos NLar SAPC SArc SEND WPGP WSHC
disticha (Hook.f.) Urb. LEdu
magellanica WFar

Mazus (*Scrophulariaceae*)

miquelii EBee ECho
novae-zeelandiae CTrC
radicans ECho
reptans EBee ECho EDAr EPfP EPot GEdr LRHS MSKA NLar NPer NWCA
- B&SWJ GEdr
- 'Albus' EBee ECho EPfP GEdr GGar LLWG MSKA NLar SPlb
- 'Blue' LLWG
surculosus ECho

Mecardonia (*Scrophulariaceae*)

'Goldflake' CCCN LSou

Meconopsis ✿ (*Papaveraceae*)

aculeata GKev
baileyi see *M. betonicifolia*
Ballyrogan form GEdr
× ***beamishii*** GKev
§ ***betonicifolia*** ♀H4 Widely available
- var. ***alba*** CSpr EBee ELan GCra GGGa GKev GKir GMac LRHS NCob NGdn NLar NSum
- 'Glacier Blue' GCra
- 'Hensol Violet' CSpr EBee EPot GCra GGGa GKev GMac ITim NLar NSum
- violet-flowered ITim
cambrica CMac CPLG CTri EBee EHrv ELan EPfP GGar GJos MMuc NCot NHol NPri SGar WBrk WCom WFar WHer WPnP
- 'Anne Greenaway' (d) WCot
- var. ***aurantiaca*** SBch WCom WFar
- ***flore-pleno*** (d) MTho WCot WFar
- - orange-flowered (d) NBir WCot
§ - 'Frances Perry' EWld GCal WCom WCot WFar
- 'Muriel Brown' (d) GCal
- 'Rubra' see *M. cambrica* 'Frances Perry'
chelidoniifolia EWld GBee GCra GKir IGor NBid WCru WFar
× ***cookei*** GEdr GMac
- 'Old Rose' GCrs GGGa GMaP
- 'Satin' new GCrs
N Fertile Blue Group ITim
N - 'Blue Ice' see *M.* (Fertile Blue Group) 'Lingholm'
N - 'Lingholm' Widely available
forrestii GKev
§ George Sherriff Group GCal GCra GCrs GEdr NBir
- 'Ascreavie' GCrs GEdr GMaP
- 'Barney's Blue' new GCrs
- 'Branklyn' ambig. CGHE GEdr WFar WPGP
- 'Dalemain' GMaP
- 'Huntfield' GBin GCrs GEdr GMaP
- 'Jimmy Bayne' GBin GCrs GEdr GGGa GKir GMaP
gracilipes GKev
N ***grandis*** misapplied see *M.* George Sherriff Group

N	***grandis*** ambig.	CHar CPla EBee GEdr GLin WFar WSpi
	grandis Prain PS&W	GCrs
	- Balruddery form	GGGa
	- GS 600	see *M.* George Sherriff Group
	- 'Tromso' **new**	GEdr
	horridula	GGGa
	- SDR 6119	GKev
	- var. ***racemosa***	see *M. racemosa* var. *racemosa*
	- Rudis Group	GKev
	(Infertile Blue Group) 'Bobby Masterton'	GCra GEdr
	- 'Crarae'	GGGa GKev
	- 'Crewdson Hybrid'	GEdr GMaP
	- 'Dawyck'	see *M.* (Infertile Blue Group) 'Slieve Donard'
	- 'Maggie Sharp' **new**	GEdr
	- 'Mrs Jebb'	GCra GCrs GEdr GMaP
§	- 'Slieve Donard' ♀H4	GCal GCra GCrs GEdr GKev GMaP ITim LRHS
	integrifolia	EPot GEdr GGGa WFar
	- SDR 6032	GKev
	latifolia	GKev
	'Marit' **new**	GCrs
	'Mop-head' **new**	GEdr
N	***napaulensis*** misapplied	CAby EBee GCra GEdr GKev GKir ITim LHop MDun NHol NLar WMoo
	- pink-flowered	GBin GGar GKev NGdn WFar WPGP
	- red-flowered	CBcs ITim MDun
	- scarlet-flowered	GKev
	- white flowered	GKev
	nudicaulis	see *Papaver nudicaule*
	paniculata	GAbr GGGa GKev ITim
	- from Bhutan	GCra
	- from Ghunsa, Nepal	CLAP WAbe
	- ginger foliage	CSpr
	pseudointegrifolia	GGGa
	punicea	GCrs GGGa WAbe
	quintuplinervia ♀H4	CLAP GCra GGGa IGor NBir NHar NSla WHal
§	***racemosa*** var. ***racemosa***	GKev
	- - SDR 5917	GKev
	regia misapplied	WMoo
	- hybrids	GGGa
	× ***sarsonsii***	GKev
	× ***sheldonii*** misapplied (fertile)	see *M.* Fertile Blue Group
	× ***sheldonii*** misapplied (sterile)	see *M.* Infertile Blue Group
	× ***sheldonii*** ambig.	CBcs CBow CHar CWCL EBee GAbr GKir ITim MBri MCot MDun NBPC NBir NLar NPer WFar
	simplicifolia	GGGa
	'Stewart Annand' **new**	GEdr
	superba	GGGa GKev
	villosa	CSpr GCra GGGa WFar
	wallichii misapplied	see *M. wallichii* Hook.
§	***wallichii*** Hook.	GGGa GKev
	'Willie Duncan'	GKir GMaP

Medicago (*Papilionaceae*)

arborea	CArn SEND SPlb
lupulina	EBWF
sativa	NLar WHer WSFF

Medinilla (*Melastomataceae*)

magnifica ♀H1	CCCN MBri

Meehania (*Lamiaceae*)

cordata	CDes EBee
fargesii	CDes CLAP
urticifolia	EPPr EWld GCal WSHC
- B&SWJ 1210	WCru
- 'Japanblau'	IMou
- 'Wandering Minstrel' (v)	WCot

medlar see *Mespilus germanica*

Melaleuca (*Myrtaceae*)

	acerosa	SOWG
	acuminata	SPlb
	alternifolia	CArn CCCN CTsd CWit ECou EOHP GPWP GPoy MHer SEND SOWG SPlb WHer WHfH
	armillaris	CCCN CDoC CStu SEND SGar SOWG SPlb
	- pink-flowered	SOWG
	blaeriifolia	ECou
	bracteata	ECou SEND
	citrina	SOWG
	coccinea	SOWG
	cuticularis	SPlb
	decora	SOWG
	decussata	ECou SOWG SPlb
§	***diosmatifolia***	CPLG
	elliptica	SOWG
	ericifolia	CTri CTsd GLin SOWG SPlb
	erubescens	see *M. diosmatifolia*
	filifolia	SOWG
	fulgens	SOWG SPlb
	- apricot-flowered	SOWG
*	- 'Hot Pink'	SOWG
	- purple-flowered	SOWG
	gibbosa	CPLG EBee ECou EUJe IDee LRHS LSou SEND SOWG WSHC
	holosericea misapplied	see *M. smartiorum*
	huegelii	SOWG
	hypericifolia	CPLG CTrC ECou SOWG SPlb
	incana	EBee EUJe SOWG
	lateritia	ECou SOWG
	linariifolia	CCCN ECou SPlb
	nesophila	CTsd ECou EShb SOWG SPlb
	pentagona var. ***subulifolia***	ECou
	platycalyx	SOWG
	pulchella	ECou SOWG
	pungens	SPlb
	pustulata	ECou EShb SOWG
	radula	SOWG
*	***rosmarinifolia***	SOWG
§	***smartiorum***	SOWG
	spathulata	SOWG
	squamea	CWit EBee GGar IDee SEND SPlb
*	***squarmania***	SOWG
	squarrosa	CPLG CTrC ECou IDee SOWG SPlb
	thymifolia	ECou LRHS SOWG SPlb WAbe
	viridiflora	GQui
	wilsonii	ECou SOWG

Melandrium see *Vaccaria*

rubrum	see *Silene dioica*

Melanoselinum (*Apiaceae*)

§	***decipiens***	CAbb CArn CHEx CSpe EWes GGar IMou LEdu WCot WPGP

Melasphaerula (*Iridaceae*)

	graminea	see *M. ramosa*
§	***ramosa***	CBre ECho WPrP

Melastoma (*Melastomataceae*)

sp.	CCCN

	malabathricum	SOWG

Melia (*Meliaceae*)

§	***azedarach***	CArn CBcs CCCN CMCN EBee EPfP EShb GPoy
	- B&SWJ 7039	WCru
	- var. ***japonica***	see *M. azedarach*

Melianthus (*Melianthaceae*)

	comosus	CDTJ EAmu EBee ELan EShb EWes LPio NLar SCoo SPlb WCot
	major ♀H3	Widely available
	minor	CFir CHid LPio
	villosus	CBow CFir CHGN EWes LPio LRHS MCCP SGar SPlb WOut WPGP

Melica (*Poaceae*)

	altissima 'Alba'	EHoe MLHP
	- 'Atropurpurea'	CWCL EBee ECha EHoe EPPr GFor LEdu LHop LLWP LRHS MCot MMoz MNrw MWat MWhi NBid NLar SEND SGar SPlb WBox WFar WFoF WMnd WMoo WWEG
	ciliata	EBee EHoe GFor MMoz MWhi SSvw WMnd WWEG
	macra	EHoe EPPr SApp
	nutans	CWCL EBee EHoe EPPr EPla EShb GFor NWsh SBch SMHy SMrm
	penicillaris	EPPr
	transsilvanica	GFor
	- 'Atropurpurea'	EBee MMuc
	- 'Red Spire'	CWib EShb MBNS MWhi SBfd SHDw SMea SMrm WMoo
	uniflora	GFor IMou NOak
	- f. ***albida***	ECha EHoe EPPr MAvo NDov SLPl SMHy SUsu WCot
	- 'Variegata' (v)	CBre ECGP ECha EHoe ELon EPPr EPla EShb MMoz NGdn SUsu WCot WMoo WTin WWEG

Melicope (*Rutaceae*)

	ternata	ECou

Melicytus (*Violaceae*)

	alpinus	ECou
	angustifolius	ECou
	crassifolius	ECou WFar
	obovatus	ECou NLar
	ramiflorus	CHEx ECou

Melilotus (*Papilionaceae*)

	officinalis	CArn GPoy NSco SIde WHer
	- subsp. ***albus***	CArn

Melinis (*Poaceae*)

	nerviglumis	CKno LEdu MAvo
§	- 'Savannah'	CWib

Meliosma (*Meliosmaceae*)

	cuneifolia	CBcs NLar
	dilleniifolia subsp. ***tenuis***	CBcs CPLG
	myriantha	SSpi

Melissa ✿ (*Lamiaceae*)

	officinalis	CArn CPbn CTri CWan ELau GJos GKir GMaP GPoy MBri MHer MNHC NBir SBfd SEND SIde SPlb SVic WHfH WJek
	- 'All Gold'	CArn CBre CPbn CSev ECha EHoe ELan ELau EOHP GBar MNHC NBid NVic SPer SPoG
§	- 'Aurea' (v)	CArn CFee CPLG CPrp CSev CWan ELan ELau GBar GCra GMaP GPoy MBri MHer MMuc MNHC MRav NBid NBir NBro NPri SBfd SIde SPer SPoG SRms WFar WJek WMnd WMoo
*	- 'Compacta'	CPbn GPoy
	- 'Gold Leaf'	WPtf
	- 'Lime Balm'	CPbn EOHP
	- 'Quedlinburger Niederliegende'	CArn CPbn
N	- 'Variegata' misapplied	see *M. officinalis* 'Aurea'

Melittis (*Lamiaceae*)

	melissophyllum	CArn CLAP CMea CPom CSev CSpe EBee IMou LEdu LPio LRHS LSou MAvo MNrw MRav MWea NChi NMen NSti SMrm SRms SSvw SUsu WCot
	- subsp. ***albida***	EBee LPio
	- pink-flowered	CDes CLAP SUsu WCom
	- 'Royal Velvet Distinction' PBR	EBee MRav

Melliodendron (*Styracaceae*)

	xylocarpum	CPLG

Menispermum (*Menispermaceae*)

	canadense	CTri GPoy
	davuricum	NLar

Menstruocalamus (*Poaceae*)

	sichuanensis	WPGP

Mentha ✿ (*Lamiaceae*)

	SJ 2075 **new**	WCot
	from Jamaica **new**	CArn
	angustifolia Corb.	see *M.* × *villosa*
	angustifolia Host	see *M. arvensis*
	angustifolia ambig.	CPbn SIde
	aquatica	CArn CBen CPbn CRow CWat EBWF EHon EPfP GPWP GPoy LPBA MHer MNHC MWts NMir NPer NSco SIde SPlb SVic SWat WHer WMAq WMoo WPnP WSFF
§	- var. ***crispa***	CPbn SIde
	- krause minze	see *M. aquatica* var. *crispa*
	- 'Mandeliensis'	CPbn
§	***arvensis***	CArn CPbn ELau MHer NSco SIde
	- 'Banana'	CPbn MHer MNHC NGHP SIde WJek
	- var. ***piperascens***	MHer SIde WJek
§	- - 'Sayakaze'	CArn ELau
	- var. ***villosa***	CPbn
	asiatica	CPbn ELau MHer SIde
	'Berries and Cream'	WJek
	'Betty's Slovakian'	CPbn
	Bowles's mint	see *M.* × *villosa* var. *alopecuroides* Bowles's mint
*	***brevifolia***	CPbn SIde WHer
	cervina	CArn CBen CPbn CWat EHon LPBA MHer MSKA NLar SIde SWat WJek
*	- ***alba***	CPbn LPBA MHer NLar WMAq
I	'Chocolate Peppermint'	LLWG NBir WHer
	citrata	see *M.* × *piperita* f. *citrata*
	'Clarissa's Millennium'	CPbn SIde
	cordifolia	see *M.* × *villosa*
	corsica	see *M. requienii*
	crispa L. (1753)	see *M. spicata* var. *crispa*
	crispa L. (1763)	see *M. aquatica* var. *crispa*
	crispa ambig. × (× ***piperita***)	CArn CPbn GBar

	'Dionysus'	CPbn SIde
	× ***dumetorum***	CPbn
	'Eau de Cologne'	see *M.* × *piperita* f. *citrata*
	eucalyptus mint	CPbn ELau GBar GPWP MHer NGHP WGwG
	gattefossei	CArn
	× ***gentilis***	see *M.* × *gracilis*
§	× ***gracilis***	CArn CHby CPbn ELau GBar NGHP NPri SIde
	- 'Aurea'	see *M.* × *gracilis* 'Variegata'
§	- 'Variegata' (v)	CPbn CSev CWan ECha ELau GGar GPoy ILis MCot MHer MNHC NPri NVic SPlb SWal WFar WHer WPer
	haplocalyx	CArn ELau SIde
*	'Hillary's Sweet Lemon'	CPbn ELau MHer SIde
	'Julia's Sweet Citrus'	CPbn MHer SIde
*	***lacerata***	SIde
	lavender mint	ELau GBar GPWP GPoy MHer MNHC NGHP WJek
§	***longifolia***	CPbn CWan ELau GBar MMuc SEND SIde SPlb WEas WHer WPer
	- Buddleia Mint Group	CArn CPbn EBee ELau GGar GPWP MHer MRav NGHP SIde WJek WOut
	- - variegated (v)	GPWP WJek
	- dwarf	CPbn
	- subsp. ***schimperi***	MHer SIde WJek
	- silver-leaved	CArn CPbn ELau MHer MMuc MNHC NLar SEND WJek
*	- 'Variegata' (v)	CPbn ELau GBar
	Nile Valley mint	CArn ELau SHDw SIde
	× ***piperita***	CArn CHby CPbn CSev CWan ECha EHoe ELau GAuc GBar GGar GJos GPoy ILis LHop MBri MCot MHer MNHC NGHP NPri NVic SPlb WPer
	- 'Black Mitcham'	CArn CPbn GBar
	- black peppermint	CHby CPbn EPfP GKir GPWP LLWG MMuc MNHC NBir NGHP NHol NLar SEND SWal WGwG WJek
§	- f. ***citrata***	Widely available
	- - from Portugal	CPbn
*	- - 'Basil'	CPbn CWan ELau GBar GPWP MHer MNHC MRav NGHP NHol SBfd SHDw SIde WGwG WJek
	- - 'Bergamot'	CPbn
	- - 'Chocolate'	CArn CPbn CWan ELau EOHP EPfP GBar GGar GJos GPWP ILis MHer MNHC NGHP SBfd SHDw SIde WGwG WJek
	- - 'Grapefruit'	CPbn CWan GBar LSou MNHC NGHP SWal WGwG WJek
	- - 'Lemon'	CPbn CWan ELau GBar GGar GKir GPWP GPoy MBri MHer MNHC NGHP SBfd SHDw SIde WGwG WJek WPer
	- - 'Lime'	CPbn CWan GBar GPWP ILis LBuc LSou MHer NGHP SBfd SHDw SIde SPlb WGwG WJek
	- - 'Orange'	CPbn GBar MHer MMuc MNHC NGHP SEND WHil WJek
	- - 'Reverchonii'	CPbn SIde
	- - 'Swiss Ricola'	MHer SIde
	- 'Logee's' (v)	CPbn GBar NHol SIde WHer
	- f. ***officinalis***	CPbn ELau SIde
	- var. ***ouweneellii*** Belgian mint	CPbn SIde
	- 'Reine Rouge'	CPbn SIde
	- 'Swiss'	NGHP NLar WJek
	- Swiss mint	CArn CPbn GPWP WGwG WOut
*	- white-flowered	CArn CPbn GBar WGwG
	'Polynesian Mint'	CPbn

	pulegium	CArn CHby CPbn CRWN CSev CTri CWan EBWF ELau GBar GPWP GPoy LLWG MHer MNHC NPri SIde SPlb SRms SVic WHer WHfH WJek WPer
	- 'Upright'	CArn CPbn GBar GPoy MHer SBfd SHDw SIde WJek WPer
§	***requienii***	Widely available
	rotundifolia misapplied	see *M. suaveolens*
	rotundifolia (L.) Hudson	see *M.* × *villosa*
	rubra var. ***raripila***	see *M.* × *smithiana*
	'Russian' curled leaf	CPbn
	'Russian' plain leaf	CPbn
	'Sayakaze'	see *M. arvensis* var. *piperascens* 'Sayakaze'
§	× ***smithiana***	CArn CPbn CWan ELau GBar GPWP GPoy MHer MNHC MRav NBir NGHP WHer WJek WPer
	- 'Capel Ulo' (v)	ELau
	'South of France'	CPbn
§	***spicata***	CArn CHby COlW CPbn CPrp CSev CTri CWan ELau GBar GJos GKir GPoy ILis MBri MCot MHer MMuc MNHC NGHP NHol NPri SEND SPlb SRms SWal WClo WHer WJek WPer
	- Algerian fruity	CPbn SIde
	- 'Austrian'	CPbn
*	- 'Brundall'	CPbn ELau ILis SIde
	- 'Canaries'	CPbn
*	- var. ***crispa***	CArn CPbn CWan ECha ELau GBar GGar GPWP LEdu LHop MHer MMuc MNHC NGHP NHol NPri SBfd SIde SPlb WJek WPer
	- - 'Moroccan'	CArn CPbn CPrp CSev ELau EOHP GAbr GBar GGar GJos GPWP GPoy LEdu MHer MMuc MNHC NGHP NPri NVic SBfd SEND SHDw SIde STre WClo WJek
	- - 'Persian'	CPbn
	- 'Guernsey'	CPbn SBfd SHDw SIde
	- 'Irish'	CPbn
	- 'Kentucky Colonel'	CPbn
	- 'Mexican'	CArn CPbn
	- 'Newbourne'	CPbn ELau SIde
	- 'Pharaoh'	CArn CPbn
	- 'Rhodos'	CPbn
	- 'Russian'	NGHP NHol SIde
	- 'Small Dole' (v)	SBfd SHDw
	- 'Spanish'	GPWP
	- 'Spanish Furry'	CPbn MHer SIde
	- 'Spanish Pointed'	CPbn ELau SIde WJek
	- 'Tashkent'	CArn CHby CPbn ELau EOHP GKir LEdu MHer MNHC NGHP SBfd SHDw SIde WGwG WJek
	- subsp. ***tomentosa***	CPbn
*	- 'Variegata' (v)	CPbn SBfd SHDw WGwG
	- 'Verte Blanche'	CPbn
§	***suaveolens***	CArn CHby CPbn CWan ELau GBar GJos GMaP GPWP GPoy ILis MBri MHer MLHP MNHC NGHP NPri SBfd SIde SPlb SVic SWal WJek WPer WSFF
*	- 'Grapefruit'	GPWP NGHP NPri
	- 'Jokka'	CPbn EBee
*	- 'Mobillei'	CPbn SIde
*	- 'Pineapple'	GKir LBuc WGwG WJek
	- subsp. ***timija***	CPbn ELau SIde WJek
	- 'Variegata' (v)	Widely available
	sylvestris L.	see *M. longifolia*
*	***verona***	CPbn
	× ***verticillata*** new	WJek

§ × ***villosa***	CArn CPbn MMuc SEND SIde
§ - var. ***alopecuroides*** Bowles's mint	CBre CPbn CPrp ELau GBar GGar GPWP GPoy ILis MHer MNHC NBir NGHP SBfd SIde STre SWat WGwG WHer WJek
viridis	see *M. spicata*

Mentzelia (*Loasaceae*)

decapetala	CSpe

Menyanthes (*Menyanthaceae*)

trifoliata	CBen CRow CWat EHon GBar GPoy LLWG LPBA MCCP MMuc MSKA MWts NLar NPer NSco WBVN WFar WHal WMAq WSFF

Menziesia (*Ericaceae*)

alba	see *Daboecia cantabrica* f. *alba*
ciliicalyx 'Honshu Blue'	GGGa
- ***lasiophylla***	see *M. ciliicalyx* var. *purpurea*
- var. ***multiflora***	EPfP
- 'Plum Drops'	GGGa
§ - var. ***purpurea***	GGGa
- 'Slieve Donard'	CMac
polifolia	see *Daboecia cantabrica*
'Spring Morning'	WAbe
'Ulva'	GGGa

Mercurialis (*Euphorbiaceae*)

perennis	EBWF GPoy NSco WHer WHfH WSFF WShi

Merendera (*Colchicaceae*)

attica	ECho
eichleri	see *M. trigyna*
filifolia	ECho
§ ***montana***	CPBP ECho WIvy
pyrenaica	see *M. montana*
raddeana	see *M. trigyna*
robusta	WWst
sobolifera	WCot
§ ***trigyna***	ECho
- bright pink-flowered	WWst
- white-flowered clone	WWst

Merremia (*Convolvulaceae*)

§ ***tuberosa***	SOWG

Mertensia (*Boraginaceae*)

ciliata	CMdw CPom GKir SWat
lanceolata	GKev
§ ***maritima***	CBot CMea CSpe CWCL ECho GBee GEdr GKev GKir GPoy LEdu LRHS NBir NWCA SMrm SPlb WCom WFar WWEG
- subsp. ***asiatica***	see *M. maritima*
primuloides	GAuc LLHF
pterocarpa	see *M. sibirica*
pulmonarioides	see *M. virginica*
§ ***sibirica***	CLAP CSpe GKir NLar SPlb WCom
§ ***virginica*** ♀H4	CArn CBot CLAP EBee ECho ECtt ELan EPfP EWTr GKir LAma LEdu LRHS MAvo NBid NBir NLar NPnk NPri NWCA SRms WFar

Merwilla (*Hyacinthaceae*)

§ ***plumbea***	WCot

Merxmuellera see *Rytidosperma*

Meryta (*Araliaceae*)

sinclairii	CWit

Mesembryanthemum (*Aizoaceae*)

'Basutoland'	see *Delosperma nubigenum*
brownii	see *Lampranthus brownii*

Mespilus (*Rosaceae*)

germanica (F)	CBcs CDul CLnd CMCN CTri EBee ECrN ELan IDee IVic LMaj LTen MWat NEgg NPla SDnm SLon WDin WFar WMou WPat
- 'Bredase Reus' (F)	SKee
- 'Dutch' (F)	ERea SDea SFam SKee
- 'Large Russian' (F)	CAgr ERea
- 'Macrocarpa' (F)	SKee
- 'Monstrous' (F)	SDea
- 'Nespoli del Giappone' (F)	WSpi
- 'Nottingham' (F)	Widely available
- 'Royal' (F)	CAgr ERea LRHS MBri MCoo SCoo SKee
- 'Westerveld' (F)	NLar SKee
germanicus 'Iranian' (F)	SKee

Metapanax (*Araliaceae*)

davidii	SLon
delavayii	SBig

Metaplexis (*Asclepiadaceae*)

japonica B&SWJ 8459	WCru

Metarungia (*Acanthaceae*)

longistrobus	GFai

Metasequoia ✿ (*Cupressaceae*)

glyptostroboides ♀H4	Widely available
- 'All Bronze' **new**	NLar
- 'Emerald Feathers'	ECho SLim
- 'Fastigiata'	see *M. glyptostroboides* 'National'
- 'Gold Rush'	Widely available
- 'Golden Dawn'	NLar SLim
- 'Green Mantle'	ECho EHul
- 'Little Creamy' **new**	NLar
- 'Little Giant'	MBlu
- 'Matthaei Broom'	LRHS NLar SLim SPoG
- 'McCracken's White' (v)	NLar SLim
- 'Miss Grace'	NLar SLim
§ - 'National'	ECho MBlu
- 'Sheridan Spire'	CEnd MBlu
- 'Spring Cream'	ECho NLar
- 'Waasland'	LRHS MBlu SLim
- 'White Spot' (v)	ECho MBlu NPCo SLim WEve

Metrosideros (*Myrtaceae*)

carminea	CCCN CTrC CTsd
§ ***excelsa***	CHEx CHll CTrC CTsd EBak ECou ESwi EUJe SAPC
- 'Aurea'	ECou
- 'Fire Mountain'	CTrC
- 'Maori Princess'	CWit
- 'Parnell'	CBcs CCCN
- 'Scarlet Pimpernel'	SOWG
- 'Vibrance'	CCCN CTrC EBee
kermadecensis	ECou
- 'Red and Gold'	CBcs CDoC CTrC
- 'Twisty' (v)	CBcs
- 'Variegata' (v)	CBcs CDoC CTrC ECou EPfP SMrm
'Lord Howe Island' **new**	CTrC
lucida	see *M. umbellata*
'Moon Maiden'	SOWG
'Pink Lady'	CTrC
robusta	CCCN CHEx MREP
- ***aureovariegata***	CCCN EShb
§ 'Springfire'	CBcs CCCN CTrC EBee SOWG

× ***subtomentosa*** 'Mistral'	ECou
'Thomasii'	see *M.* 'Springfire'
tomentosa	see *M. excelsa*
§ ***umbellata***	CBcs CCCN CDul CHEx CTrC CTsd EBee ECou GGar
villosa	SOWG

Meum (*Apiaceae*)

athamanticum	CArn CSpe EBee EBrs EDAr EHrv GCal GPoy ILis LPla MAvo MCot MRav NSti SPhx WFar WPer WPrP WTin

Michauxia (*Campanulaceae*)

campanuloides	EBee GKev
tchihatchewii	CCCN CDTJ CSpe EBee GKev MWea NGBl

Michelia see *Magnolia*

chingii	see *Magnolia maudiae*
fulgens	see *Magnolia foveolata*
wilsonii	see *Magnolia ernestii*
yunnanensis	see *Magnolia laevifolia*

Microbiota (*Cupressaceae*)

decussata ♀H4	CBcs CDoC CKen CMac CSBt ECho EHul EPla GKir IFFs LAst LBee LRHS MGos MMuc MWat NHol NWea SLim SPoG WCFE WEve WFar
- 'Gold Spot'	CDoC SLim SPoG
- 'Jakobsen'	CDoC CKen
- 'Trompenburg'	CKen

Microcachrys (*Podocarpaceae*)

tetragona	CDoC ECho ECou EHul EPla SCoo WThu

Microcoelum see *Lytocaryum*

weddellianum	see *Lytocaryum weddellianum*

Microlaena see *Ehrharta*

Microlepia (*Dennstaedtiaceae*)

speluncae	EShb
strigosa	CBty CCCN CLAP LLHF LRHS WRic

Micromeria (*Lamiaceae*)

sp.	GPWP
corsica	see *Acinos corsicus*
croatica	NMen
fruticosa	CArn WJek
graeca	CArn
rupestris	see *M. thymifolia*
§ ***thymifolia***	NMen SPlb

Microseris (*Asteraceae*)

ringens hort.	see *Leontodon rigens*

Microsorum (*Polypodiaceae*)

diversifolium	see *Phymatosorus diversifolius*

Microtropis (*Celastraceae*)

petelotii HWJ 719	WCru

Mikania (*Asteraceae*)

araucana	LSou

Milium (*Poaceae*)

effusum	COld GKir
- 'Aureum' ♀H4	Widely available
- var. ***esthonicum***	EPPr
- 'Yaffle' (v)	CBre CKno EBee ECha EPPr EPfP EPla EShb GKir LEdu MWat SGar SPoG SSvw SUsu WCot WGrn WPnP

Millettia (*Papilionaceae*)

japonica 'Hime Fuji'	NLar
murasaki-natsu-fuji	see *M. reticulata*
§ ***reticulata***	CMCN CPLG

Mimosa (*Mimosaceae*)

pudica	CCCN CDTJ

Mimulus (*Scrophulariaceae*)

sp.	SVic
'Andean Nymph'	see *M. naiandinus*
§ ***aurantiacus*** ♀H2-3	CBot CElw CFee CMac CSpe CTri EBak ECtt LHop MAsh NBir NPer SAga SBch SBfd SDnm SGar SMrm SPlb SPoG SUsu WCom
- 'Rosea'	CFee
× ***bartonianus***	see *M.* × *harrisonii*
bifidus 'Trish'	CSpe SAga SUsu
- 'Verity Buff'	MAsh
§ - 'Verity Purple'	EDif MAsh
- 'Wine'	see *M. bifidus* 'Verity Purple'
× ***burnetii***	ECho LPBA SRms
cardinalis ♀H3	CAby CEnt EBee ELan EPfP GAbr LPBA MNrw MSKA MTho NBir SMrm SPer WFar WMoo WWEG
- 'Dark Throat'	SGar
- gold-flowered **new**	WHil
- 'Red Dragon'	CSpr SBHP WHrl
cupreus 'Minor'	ECho
- 'Whitecroft Scarlet' ♀H4	ECho ECtt ELan EPfP LSou SRms
'Eleanor'	ECtt LSou SGar SHom SUsu SWal
'Firedragon'	GKir
'Frost' **new**	EDif
glutinosus	see *M. aurantiacus*
- ***atrosanguineus***	see *M. puniceus*
- ***luteus***	see *M. aurantiacus*
§ ***guttatus***	NMir NPer NSco SRms WMoo WPnP
§ - 'Richard Bish' (v)	CBow MCCP
§ × ***harrisonii***	EBee EPfP EWes LSou SAga
'Highland Orange'	ECho EPfP GKir SPlb SPoG WGor
'Highland Pink'	ECho EPfP SPlb SPoG WGor
'Highland Pink Rose'	WFar
'Highland Red' ♀H4	ECho ECtt EPfP GGar GKev GKir LLWG LPBA SPlb SPoG SRms WFar WNew
'Highland Yellow'	ECho ECtt GKir LPBA SPlb SPoG WFar
hose-in-hose (d)	NPer
'Inca Sunset'	EWes
langsdorffii	see *M. guttatus*
lewisii ♀H3	CHll SRms
longiflorus	CBot MAsh
- 'Santa Barbara'	MWte
'Lothian Fire'	CWat
luteus	CBen CWat EHon EPfP GAbr LPBA NHol NPer SPlb WBrk WFar WMAq WRHF
§ - 'Gaby' (v)	LPBA
- 'Variegatus' misapplied	see *M. guttatus* 'Richard Bish'
- 'Variegatus'	see *M. luteus* 'Gaby'
- 'Variegatus' ambig. (v)	NPer
'Malibu Orange'	EPfP
minimus	ECho
moschatus	EBee LLWG
§ ***naiandinus*** ♀H3	CEnt EBee SPlb SRms
'Orange Glow'	EPfP LLWG WHal

	orange hose-in-hose (d)	NBir
	'Orkney Lemon'	NSti
	'Popacatapetl'	CSpe EDif LHop MAsh SBHP SUsu WCom
	'Prairie Caramel'	EDif
	'Prairie Cerise'	EDif
	'Prairie Citron'	EDif
	'Prairie Coral'	EDif
	'Prairie Lilac Frost'	EDif
	'Prairie Peach'	EDif
	'Prairie Sunshine'	EDif
	primuloides	ECho EWes LLWG SPlb
	- var. ***linearifolius***	GKev
	'Puck'	ECho ECtt GKir SPoG
§	***puniceus***	CBot CTri EDif LHop MAsh SBHP SHom SRkn WCom
	'Quetzalcoatl'	LHop SMrm
	ringens	CBen CWat EBee EDif EHon LPBA MSKA NBir NPer SPlb SRms WFar WMAq WMoo WWEG
	'Threave Variegated' (v)	EBee MRav NBir WFar
	tilingii	CPBP ECho
	'Vortex' **new**	LSou
	'Wine Red'	see *M. bifidus* 'Verity Purple'
	'Wisley Red'	ECho SRms
	'Yellow Velvet'	ECho

Mina see *Ipomoea*

mint, apple see *Mentha suaveolens*

mint, Bowles's see *M. × villosa* var. *alopecuroides*

mint, curly see *M. spicata* var. *crispa*

mint, eau-de-Cologne see *M. × piperita* f. *citrata*

mint, ginger see *M. × gracilis*

mint, horse or long-leaved see *M. longifolia*

mint, pennyroyal see *M. pulegium*

mint (peppermint) see *M. × piperita*

mint, round-leaved see *M. suaveolens*

mint (spearmint) see *M. spicata*

Minuartia (*Caryophyllaceae*)

	capillacea	ECho
	caucasica	see *M. circassica*
§	***circassica***	NWCA
	juniperina	GKir
	laricifolia	GKir
	parnassica	see *M. stellata*
§	***stellata***	EPot NMen WPat
§	***verna***	ECho EDAr NMen
	- subsp. ***caespitosa***	CTri ECho
	- - 'Aurea'	see *Sagina subulata* var. *glabrata* 'Aurea'

Mirabilis (*Nyctaginaceae*)

	jalapa	CArn CPLG CWCL EPfP EShb LAma LEdu LRHS SEND SPad SRms WHil WTou
	- 'Buttermilk'	CCCN
	- red-flowered	SEND SGSe WTou
	- white-flowered	CSpe WTou
	- yellow-flowered	WTou
	longiflora	WHil

Miscanthus ✿ (*Poaceae*)

	sp.	MBNS
	'Abundance' **new**	CKno
	capensis	SPlb
	chejuensis B&SWJ 8803	WCru
	'Dronning Ingrid'	CKno EBee EPPr
	'Elfin' **new**	CKno
	flavidus B&SWJ 6749	WCru
	floridulus misapplied	see *M. × giganteus*
	floridulus ambig.	CFir EBee MMuc MNrw SEND SPlb WFar WPrP
	floridulus (Labill.) Warb. ex K. Schum. & Lauterb. WJ 522	WCru
§	× ***giganteus***	CHar CKno EHoe ELon EPPr EUJe GAbr GCal GKev GQue MCCP MMoz MMuc MNrw MWat NDov NVic NWsh SApp SDix SEND SGSe SMad SVic WCot WFar WPGP WSpi WWEG
	- 'Gilt Edge' (v)	CBow CKno EPPr MAvo NWsh SApp
	- 'Gotemba' (v)	EBee ELon EPPr EWes NWsh SApp
	'Golden Bar'	EPla LRHS WCra
	'Gotemba Gold'	SApp
	'Mount Washington'	SApp
	nepalensis	CAby CBod CDes CElw CEnt CHVG CKno CPLG CSam EBrs ECha ECre EHoe EPGN EWes GCal LEdu LRHS MAvo MNrw MWte NOak SDix SGSe SUsu WTin
	- 'Shikola'	WCru
	oligostachyus	IMou NGdn SMrm
§	- 'Afrika'	CHar CKno EPPr LHop LRHS MAvo
I	- 'Nanus Variegatus' (v)	CKno EBee EHoe EWes LEdu LRHS MAvo MMoz WCot WPGP WWEG
	'Pos'	SApp
§	'Purpurascens'	CKno CWCL CWit ECha EHoe EHrv EHul EShb LBMP LPla LRHS LSRN MAvo MMoz MMuc MWhi NOak SApp SEND SGSe SPer WCot WMoo WSpi WTin
	sacchariflorus misapplied	see *M. × giganteus*
	sacchariflorus ambig.	CBcs CDul CHEx CKno EBee ECha EHrv ELan EPfP EPla EShb LPBA LRHS MBrN MMuc SBfd SEND SPer SWal WFar WMoo WSpi
	sacchariflorus (Maxim.) Hack.	EUJe MMuc MWhi WWEG
	- 'Robustus'	CHVG
	sinensis	CEnt CHEx CTri EBla GFor LEdu MMoz NGBl NOak SVic WDin WMoo WWEG
	- from Yakushima	GKir SGSe
	- 'Adagio'	CBod CHar CKno EAEE EBee EBrs EHoe EPPr GBin GQue LBMP LEdu LRHS LTen MWhi NDov SBfd SHDw SLPl SMHy SMea WCot WPrP
	- 'Afrika'	see *M. oligostachyus* 'Afrika'
	- 'Andante'	CKno
	- 'Arabesque'	EBee EBrs EPPr LRHS MMoz NLar SApp WWEG
	- 'Augustfeder'	CHar EBee EBrs EPPr LEdu LRHS SMea WWEG
	- 'Autumn Light'	CKno EBee EBrs EPPr LRHS SMea
	- 'Ballerina'	CHar
	- 'Blütenwunder'	CHar CKno EBee EPfP
	- 'China'	CDes CFir CHar CKno EAEE EBee EBla EHoe EPPr EPla EShb EWes GBin IPot LEdu LRHS MAsh MAvo

		MNrw MSpe NCGa NWsh SAga SApp SBfd SHDw SWat WMoo WPGP WWEG
	- var. ***condensatus***	EBrs LSou SMHy
	- - 'Cabaret' (v)	Widely available
	- - 'Central Park'	see *M. sinensis* var. *condensatus* 'Cosmo Revert'
§	- - 'Cosmo Revert'	EBee LEdu MMoz NWsh WDyG WSpi
	- - 'Cosmopolitan' (v) ♀H4	Widely available
	- - 'Emerald Giant'	see *M. sinensis* var. *condensatus* 'Cosmo Revert'
	- 'David'	EAEE EBee EPPr LEdu LRHS MAvo MBNS
	- 'Dixieland' (v)	CHar CKno EHoe ELan EPPr IFoB IMou LEdu LRHS MBri MMoz NWsh SApp WWEG
	- 'Emmanuel Lepage'	CHar CKno EBee EPPr LPla
	- 'Etincelle'	CKno EBee
	- 'Federriese'	LRHS
	- 'Ferner Osten'	Widely available
	- 'Flamingo' ♀H4	Widely available
	- 'Flammenmeer'	CHar
	- 'Gaa'	SApp
	- 'Gearmella'	CBod EBrs EPPr GKir LEdu MAsh NWsh
	- 'Gewitterwolke' ♀H4	CHar EWes SMHy
	- 'Ghana' ♀H4	CHar CKno EBee ELon IMou LHop MAvo NLar SMHy SUsu
	- 'Giraffe'	CDTJ CDes CHar CKno EBee EWes LEdu LRHS WPGP WWEG
	- 'Gnome'	CKno EAEE EBee EPPr IMou LRHS MMHG NDov NLar WWEG
	- 'Gold Bar' (v)	Widely available
	- 'Goldfeder' (v)	EBrs EHoe LRHS
	- 'Goliath'	CHar CKno EAEE EBee EBrs EHoe ELan ELon EPPr GQue IPot LBMP LEdu LRHS MBNS NWsh WFar WPrP WWEG
	- 'Gracillimus'	Widely available
	- 'Gracillimus Nanus'	CKno
	- 'Graziella'	Widely available
	- 'Grosse Fontäne' ♀H4	CFir CWCL EBee EBla EHoe ELan EPPr GKir LEdu LSRN NWsh SGSe SMHy SMad WAul WCot WMoo WWEG
	- 'Gutenberg Gold' **new**	EBee
	- 'Haiku'	CHar CKno EPPr LEdu NDov WPrP
	- 'Helga Reich'	EBee EBrs SApp
	- 'Hercules'	MAvo MMoz SApp
	- 'Hermann Müssel'	CHar CKno EBee EBrs EPPr EWes GBin IMou LEdu LPla NDov SMHy SMea WPrP
	- 'Hinjo' (v)	CElw CHGN CHar EBee ECGP ECha ECtt ELon EPPr EUJe GBin GQue LBMP LEdu LRHS LSou NGdn NLar NWsh SApp SPoG WCot WCra WFar WPGP WPrP WWEG
I	- 'Jubilaris' (v)	EBee EPPr EWes
	- 'Juli'	EBrs LRHS WPrP WSpi
	- 'Kaskade' ♀H4	CHar CKno CWCL EBee EBrs EHoe EPPr IPot LEdu LRHS MAsh MMoz MMuc MWhi NDov SApp SUsu WFar WMoo WWEG
	- 'Kirk Alexander' (v)	MAvo SApp
	- 'Kleine Fontäne' ♀H4	Widely available
	- 'Kleine Silberspinne' ♀H4	Widely available
	- 'Krater'	CHar CKno EBee EBrs EHoe EPPr LEdu LRHS MAsh MBrN SGSe SGar SMea SWat
	- 'Kupferberg'	CHar
§	- 'Little Kitten'	CHar CKno EBee LEdu LPla NWsh SGSe SMad SMea WMoo WPGP WWEG
	- 'Little Zebra' (v)	CKno EBee EPPr EPfP EShb LHop LSRN MAsh MGos NOak NWsh SRms
	- 'Malepartus'	Widely available
	- 'Morning Light' (v) ♀H4	Widely available
	- 'Mysterious Maiden' (v) **new**	EPPr
	- new hybrids	EHul NPla
	- 'Nippon'	CBow CDes CElw CFir CKno CPrp CWCL EAEE EBee EBla EHoe EPPr GKir LEdu LRHS MCCP MMoz MWhi NDov NGdn NWsh SDys SMrm SPer WPGP WSpi WWEG
	- 'Nishidake'	CHar EBee
	- 'November Sunset'	EBrs EPPr EWes IPot LRHS MMoz
	- 'Poseidon'	EPPr MAvo NChi SDys SMad
	- 'Positano'	CKno LRHS MMoz WPGP
	- 'Professor Richard Hansen'	CHar CKno GBin NDov SMHy SMrm WPrP
	- 'Pünktchen' (v)	CHar CKno CWCL EAEE EAmu EBee EBrs ECha EHoe EPPr EUJe GBin LBMP LEdu LRHS MAvo NOak SApp SBfd SHDw SMHy SMad SMrm SRms WFar WMoo WPnP WTin WWEG
	- var. ***purpurascens*** misapplied	see *M.* 'Purpurascens'
	- 'Red Chief'	EPPr
	- 'Rigoletto' (v)	EPPr SApp
	- 'Roland'	CHar CKno EBee GBin NWsh SPhx
	- 'Roterpfeil'	CHar EBee MBri
	- 'Rotfeder'	EPPr GKir
	- 'Rotfuchs'	CHar EBee LPla SAga WFar
	- 'Rotsilber'	Widely available
I	- 'Russianus'	NWsh
	- 'Samurai'	CEnt CHar EPPr GMaP GQue MAvo SMrm
	- 'Sarabande'	CHar CKno EBee EHoe EHul ELan EPPr IPot LRHS NDov NWsh SApp SMHy SMrm WFar WGwG WMoo
	- 'Septemberrot' ♀H4	CHVG CHar CPrp CWCL EBee LEdu MMuc SEND
§	- 'Silberfeder' ♀H4	Widely available
	- 'Silberpfeil' (v)	EHoe NWsh
	- 'Silberspinne'	CMdw EBla EBrs EPla LEdu MCCP MWat NDov NGdn SApp SBfd SMHy SMea SPlb WAul WDin
	- 'Silberturm'	CHar EBee EPPr LPla LRHS
	- Silver Feather	see *M. sinensis* 'Silberfeder'
	- 'Silver Sceptre' **new**	SMHy
	- 'Silver Stripe'	EPPr
	- 'Sioux'	CEnt CHar CKno EBee EHoe EPPr EPfP EShb GBin LBMP LEdu LRHS MBNS MMoz MWhi NWsh SPer SUsu WTin WWEG
	- 'Sirene'	CFir CHar EAEE EBee EBrs EHoe EPPr GQue LRHS MBNS MBlu MBri MSpe SMrm WFar WPrP
	- 'Spätgrün'	CHar
	- 'Strictus' (v) ♀H4	Widely available
	- 'Tiger Cub' (v)	CWCL MAvo SApp SGSe
	- 'Undine' ♀H4	CFir CHar CKno CMea CPrp EBee EBla EBrs ECha EHoe EHrv ELan EPPr LEdu LRHS MLLN MMoz MSnd NWsh SLPl WMoo WPrP
	- 'Variegatus' (v)	Widely available
	- 'Vorläufer'	CHar EBee EHoe EPPr NWsh

- 'Westacre Wine' new	EWes
- 'Wetterfahne'	CHar LEdu LRHS
§ - 'Yaku-jima'	CHar CSam EBee ECha EPPr LHop MWhi SMea
- 'Yakushima Dwarf'	Widely available
- 'Zebrinus' (v) ♀^{H4}	Widely available
- 'Zwergelefant'	CHar LRHS MMoz SMHy
I 'Spartina'	SApp
tinctorius 'Nanus Variegatus' misapplied	see *M. oligostachyus* 'Nanus Variegatus'
transmorrisonensis	CDes CHar CKno EBee EBrs EHoe ELan EPPr GFor LRHS MAvo MLLN MMoz NOak NWsh SApp SMHy SWal WBox WCot WTin WWEG
- B&SWJ 3697	WCru
yakushimensis	see *M. sinensis* 'Yaku-jima', *M. sinensis* 'Little Kitten'

Mitchella (*Rubiaceae*)

repens	EBee GBin WCru
undulata B&SWJ 10928	WCru
* - f. ***quelpartensis*** B&SWJ 4402	WCru

Mitella (*Saxifragaceae*)

breweri	CFir CHid CMac ECha GCal GGar MRav NHol SBch SRms WEas WFar WMoo WPnP WTin
caulescens	ECha NBro NHol WMoo WPrP
diphylla	EPPr
formosana	EPPr
- B&SWJ 125	WCru
× ***inami*** B&SWJ 11122 new	WCru
japonica B&SWJ 4971	WCru
kiusiana	CLAP
- B&SWJ 5888	WCru
makinoi	CLAP EBee
- B&SWJ 4992	WCru
ovalis	EBee EPPr
pauciflora B&SWJ 6361	WCru
stylosa B&SWJ 5669	WCru
yoshinagae	GEdr WMoo
- B&SWJ 4893	CHid WCru WPrP WPtf

Mitraria (*Gesneriaceae*)

coccinea	CBcs CCCN CEnt CMac CPLG CStu CTsd CWib ECho ELan LBMP LSou MAsh MBlu MDun NMun SArc SLon SPer SPlb SSpi
- Clark's form	CSam CTrC LAst NLar WBor
- 'Lake Caburgua'	CBgR CCCN CSpe CWit EBee ELon EWld GCal GGal GGar IArd IDee NLar NSti
- 'Lake Puyehue'	CBcs CCCN CDoC CFee CPLG EBee EMil EPfP ERea GQui LHop LRHS MAsh MGos SPoG SWvt WAbe WCru WFar WGwG WSHC

Moehringia (*Caryophyllaceae*)

muscosa	WCot

Molinia (*Poaceae*)

altissima	see *M. caerulea* subsp. *arundinacea*
caerulea	CRWN CWib EBWF EHul EPPr GFor GKir MBlu NChi NGBl
§ - subsp. ***arundinacea***	CKno CWCL ECha EPPr GFor LRHS MMuc NLar SApp SLPl WWEG
- - 'Bergfreund'	CKno CSam EBee EHoe EPPr MAvo NWsh SApp SMHy SUsu WDyG WMoo WTin
- - 'Cordoba'	CKno EBee EPPr SMHy SPhx
- - 'Fontäne'	CSam EBee EHoe EPPr GCal GQue LEdu LPla LRHS NDov NWsh SApp SGSe SPhx
- - 'Karl Foerster'	Widely available
- - 'Skyracer'	CCVN CChe CKno COIW CPrp CSam EBee EBla EBrs EHoe EPPr EPfP GCal GQue LRHS MAvo MMoz MWhi NVic NWsh SMHy SMad SPhx WCot WFar WGrn WMoo WWEG
- - 'Staefa'	EHoe
- - 'Transparent'	Widely available
- - 'Windsaule'	CKno EBee EPPr SPhx
- - 'Windspiel'	CKno CRow CSam EAEE EBee ECha EHoe EPPr IKil LEdu LPio LRHS MAvo MBri MNrw NDov NWsh SApp SMrm SPhx SPoG SWal WCot WMoo WPGP WTin
- - 'Zuneigung'	CKno CSam EBrs EPPr LPla LRHS MAvo SApp SPhx
- subsp. ***caerulea***	EHoe EPPr MAvo SApp SUsu WHal
'Carmarthen' (v)	WPnP WPrP WWEG
- - 'Claerwen' (v)	ECha EPPr GCal SMHy SPhx WMoo
- - 'Coneyhill Gold' (v)	EPPr
- - 'Dauerstrahl'	CKno EBee EPPr GBin GCal GQue LPla MAvo MNrw NDov NHol
- - 'Edith Dudszus'	CKno CWCL EAEE EBee ECha EHoe EPPr GQue LPio LPla LRHS MAvo MBrN MBri MMoz MNFA NDov NGdn NHol NWsh SApp SMHy SPer WCot WGrn WMoo WPGP WWEG
- - 'Heidebraut'	EAEE EBee EBla EHoe EPPr GBin GQue MBri MRav NBro NDov SApp SBfd SPhx WFar WMoo WWEG
- - 'Moorflamme'	CKno CSam EBee EHoe EPPr MAvo NDov SPhx
- - 'Moorhexe'	Widely available
- - 'Overdam'	MMuc MNrw SEND
- - 'Strahlenquelle'	CBod CKno CSam EBee ELan EPPr GCal GQue LPla MAvo MMoz MNFA NBro NDov NHol SPhx WPGP WWEG
- - 'Variegata' (v) ♀^{H4}	Widely available
- 'Heiliger Hain'	SMHy
- 'Poul Petersen'	CHar CKno EPPr NDov SPhx
- 'Winterfreude'	NDov
litoralis	see *M. caerulea* subsp. *arundinacea*

Molopospermum (*Apiaceae*)

peloponnesiacum	CSpe GCal IMou LEdu LPio NChi NLar SAga SMHy SPhx WCru WSHC

Moltkia (*Boraginaceae*)

§ ***doerfleri***	GCal NBir NChi
§ × ***intermedia*** ♀^{H4}	CMea IRar SAga SBch WAbe WCom WFar WPat
petraea	LLHF MWat WFar

Moluccella (*Lamiaceae*)

laevis 'Pixie Bells'	CSpe

Monachosorum (*Adiantaceae*)

henryi	WRic

Monadenium (*Euphorbiaceae*)

lugardiae	MBri
'Variegatum' (v)	MBri

Monarda (*Lamiaceae*)

'Adam'	EBee GCal LRHS LSRN NBre NLar WSHC

	'Amethyst'	ECtt EWes SIde
	'Aquarius'	CAby EBee EPPr IKil LRHS MSpe NCob NDov NGHP NHol SHar WCAu WWlt
	austromontana	see *M. citriodora* subsp. *austromontana*
	'Baby Spice'	EBee NCob
§	'Balance'	EBee ECtt EPfP GCal MCot MRav MSpe NBro NCob NDov NGHP NGdn NHol SMrm WCAu WFar WPGP WSHC WWEG WWlt
	'Beauty of Cobham' ♀H4	CAby CHar CPrp CWCL EBee ECha ELan EPfP EWTr GKir GMaP MBri MCot MHer NHol NLar SBch SMad SPer SPhx WHlf WWEG WWlt
	'Blaukranz'	NBre
§	'Blaustrumpf'	CElw EBee ECtt EPfP EWes GBBs GQue LRHS NCob NLar SPer
	Blue Stocking	see *M.* 'Blaustrumpf'
	Bowman	see *M.* 'Sagittarius'
	bradburyana	NBre NLar
	'Cambridge Scarlet' ♀H4	Widely available
	'Capricorn'	NBre WWEG
	'Cherokee'	WCon WFar
	'Chippawa'	LRHS
	citriodora	CArn ECtt GPoy LRHS NSti SIde SRms SWat WBox
§	- subsp. ***austromontana***	CSpe NBir SBch SGar SIde SVic WBox WFar
	- - 'Bee's Favourite'	SPad
	'Comanche'	EBee EHrv EWes NCob NDov WFar
	'Croftway Pink' ♀H4	Widely available
I	'Dark Ponticum'	LRHS
	didyma	CArn CHar CWan EPfP GKir NBro NGHP SBfd SWat WBrE WJek
	- 'Coral Reef'	EBrs EWes LRHS WWEG
	- 'Duddiscombe'	CAby CSam CWCL
	- 'Goldmelise'	NBre WMoo
	- 'Pink Lace'[PBR]	LSou MAsh MBri MNrw NLar
	'Earl Grey'	EBee GAbr NDov
	'Elsie's Lavender'	CAby EBee LPla NDov NLar WWEG
	'Elworthy'	CElw
§	'Feuerschopf'	EBee
	'Fireball'[PBR]	CPrp CWCL EBee ECtt LLHF LRHS LSou MNrw MTis NBPC NCob NHol NLar NPri SBfd SPoG WBor
	Firecrown	see *M.* 'Feuerschopf'
§	'Fishes'	EAEE EBee ECtt EHrv ELan EPPr EWes IKil LRHS MCot MRav MSpe NCob NDov NGHP NGdn NHol NLar SMrm STes WFar WSHC WWEG WWlt
	fistulosa	CArn CPrp CWan GPoy MHer MNHC WJek WMoo
	'Gardenview Scarlet' ♀H4	CAby CBar CPrp CSam CWCL EBee EBrs ECtt EWes GCal GCra GKir GQue IKil LRHS MBri MCot MDKP MWat NDov NHol NLar NSti SMrm SPhx SWal WPer WWEG WWlt
	Gemini	see *M.* 'Twins'
	'Gewitterwolke'	CAby CSam EBee SDys
	'Hartswood Wine'	EWes SMad SMrm WWEG
	'Heidelerche'	EBee EPPr LRHS
	'Jacob Cline'	EBrs EPPr GBin IPot LRHS MAsh NBre NCGa NCob NDov SMrm SPhx STes WPtf WWEG
	'Kardinal'	EBee GBin LRHS NDov
	Libra	see *M.* 'Balance'
	'Loddon Crown'	CHar COIW CPrp ECtt GQue LRHS MBri MDKP NCob NHol NLar SBfd SHar SIde WCAu WSHC WWEG
	'Mahogany'	CPrp EBee ELan GMaP IKil LRHS MNrw MRav NCob SMad SPer WSHC WSpi WWEG
	'Marshall's Delight' ♀H4	CPrp EBee ECtt EPPr EWes LRHS LSou MRav NCob NLar SGar WFar
	'Melissa'	EBee LSRN NBre
	menthifolia	CArn EBee GCal LSou MCot SMrm
	'Mohawk'	CAby CPrp CWCL EAEE EBee ECtt EHrv EPPr LRHS MWat NCob NHol WWEG
	'Mrs Perry'	EWes
	'Neon'	NDov SPhx
	'Night Rider'	EWes
	'On Parade'	EAEE EBee ECtt LRHS MMHG MTis NDov NHol
	'Othello' **new**	NDov
	'Ou Charm'	EBee EWes LRHS MMHG NLar SMrm WFar
	'Panorama'	ECtt NLar SPet SPlb WMoo
	'Panorama Red Shades' (Panorama Series)	CWib MNHC MSCN SPet WCFE WClo
	'Pawnee'	LRHS NDov
	Petite Delight = 'Acpetdel'	CBcs EBee ECtt EHoe ELan EPfP LHop MAsh MLLN NCob NGHP NHol NLar SMad WFar WWEG
	'Petite Pink Supreme'	EBee EPfP
	'Pink Supreme'[PBR]	EPfP GAbr GQue LSou MGos MTis NCob NGHP NLar NPri SBfd
	'Pink Tourmaline'	EBee NDov NHol SMad SMrm WWEG
	Pisces	see *M.* 'Fishes'
	'Poyntzfield Pink'	GPoy
	Prairie Night	see *M.* 'Prärienacht'
§	'Prärienacht'	CAby CHar CPrp CSBt CSam EBee ECha ELan EPfP MHer MLLN NBPC NBro NGdn NHol SPer SPlb SRms STes SWvt WCom WEas WFar WPer WSHC WWEG
	punctata	CArn EBee ELan EWTr LBMP MCot NGdn SDnm SGSe SWat WFar
	'Raspberry Wine'	EBrs ECtt EPPr
	'Ruby Glow'	CAby CWCL EBee EHrv LRHS LSRN MArl MBri MMHG NDov NGdn NHol SMad SMrm SPhx
§	'Sagittarius'	EAEE EBee MMHG MSpe NCob NGdn NHol NSti SPur
	'Saxon Purple'	NDov NLar
§	'Schneewittchen'	CWCL EBee ECha ECtt EHrv ELan EPfP LRHS MGos MHer MRav NBro NGHP NGdn NHol NSti SIde SPer SWvt WBVN WCAu WFar WWEG
	'Scorpion'	CWCL EBee ECtt EHrv ELan EPPr GGar LEdu LRHS MCot MRav MSpe NBPC NBir NCob NEgg NGdn NHol SMrm SPhx SWvt WPGP WSHC WWlt
	'Shelley'	ECha
	'Sioux'	EBee EHrv EWes WFar
	'Snow Maiden'	see *M.* 'Schneewittchen'
	'Snow Queen'	EBee ECtt EPPr LRHS MSpe MWat NCob NHol NLar SHar SMrm SPur STes
	Snow White	see *M.* 'Schneewittchen'
	'Squaw' ♀H4	Widely available
	'Talud' ♀H4	EBee NDov
§	'Twins'	CWCL EBee EPPr LSRN NGHP NHol SWvt WSHC WWEG
	'Velvet Queen'	LSou
	'Vintage Wine'	CAby CWCL ECtt NCob NDov WCon WFar
	'Violacea'	NHol

'Violet Queen' 🏆H4	CWCL EAEE EBee EBrs ECtt ELan EWes GQue LRHS MLLN NBre NCob SCoo SMrm WFar WHil WWlt

Monardella (*Lamiaceae*)

macrantha	CPBP
- subsp. ***hallii***	CPBP
nana subsp. ***tenuiflora***	CPBP
odoratissima	CArn
villosa new	WBox
viridis	CPBP
subsp. ***saxicola*** new	

Monochoria (*Pontederiaceae*)

§ ***hastata***	LLWG MSKA

Monstera (*Araceae*)

deliciosa (F) 🏆H1	MBri XBlo
- 'Variegata' (v) 🏆H1	MBri

Montbretia see *Crocosmia*

Montia (*Portulacaceae*)

perfoliata	see *Claytonia perfoliata*
sibirica	see *Claytonia sibirica*

Moraea (*Iridaceae*)

alpina	GCrs
alticola	CPne EBee ECho GGar WCot WPGP
§ ***aristata***	CDes ECho WCot
§ ***bellendenii***	ECho WCot
bipartita	WCot
calcicola	ECho
ciliata	ECho WCot
citrina new	ECho
comptonii	CPBP
elegans	CPBP
fergusoniae	ECho
'Swellendam' new	
fugacissima new	ECho
gigandra	ECho WCot
glaucopsis	see *M. aristata*
huttonii	CCCN CFir CPBP CSpe CTca EDif EPPr GAbr LPio SGSe WBVN WCot WHil WPrP WSHC
inclinata 'Howick' new	ECho
incurva new	ECho
iridioides	see *Dietes iridioides*
longiaristata	ECho
'Caledon' new	
loubseri	EBee WCot
lurida	WCot
- 'Bredasdorp' new	ECho
macronyx 'Komsberg' new	ECho
marlothii	ECho
mediterranea new	ECho
neglecta new	ECho
papilionacea	WCot
- 'Gordon's Bay' new	ECho
pavonia var. ***lutea***	see *M. bellendenii*
polystachya	CGrW ECho
robusta	EBee GCal
serpentina	ECho
setifolia	ECho
spathacea	see *M. spathulata*
§ ***spathulata***	CPLG CTca ECho GCal LEdu WCot WKif WPrP
tortilis 'Nababeep' new	ECho
tricolor	CPBP ECho WCot
trifida 'Sentinel Peak' new	ECho
tripetala 'Riverlands' new	ECho
tulbaghensis	EBee WCot
unibracteata	ECho
'Sentinel Peak' new	
vegeta	CPBP CTca ECho ERea WCot
versicolor 'Paarl' new	ECho
villosa	ECho WCot

Morella (*Myrtaceae*)

quercifolia new	EUJe

Moricandia (*Brassicaceae*)

arvensis	WCot

Morina (*Morinaceae*)

* ***afghanica***	GAbr
alba	EBee GCra
- SDR 2937	GKev
longifolia	Widely available
persica	EWes EWld LPio
polyphylla	EBee GPoy

Morinda (*Rubiaceae*)

umbellata WWJ 11688	WCru

Morisia (*Brassicaceae*)

hypogaea	see *M. monanthos*
§ ***monanthos***	CPla EPot NWCA SRot WFar
- 'Fred Hemingway'	ECho ECtt ITim LRHS NMen NSla WAbe WThu

Morus ✿ (*Moraceae*)

alba	CAgr CArn CBcs CCVT CDul CLnd CMCN CTho CWib EBee ECrN ELan EPfP ERea GTwe IFFs LBuc LHop LMaj MGos SMrm WDin WFar
- 'Chaparral'	EBee MAsh
- 'Issai'	LRHS
- 'Laciniata'	EBee
- 'Macrophylla'	CMCN NLar
- 'Nana'	NLar
- 'Pendula'	CDoC CDul CEnd CLnd CMac CTho CTri EBee ECrN ELan ERea GTwe LAst LRHS MAsh MBlu MBri NLar SBfd SCoo SLim SPer WDin
- 'Platanifolia'	LMaj MBlu
- var. ***tatarica***	CAgr LEdu NLar
§ ***bombycis***	IFFs MMuc SEND
'Capsrum' (F)	CAgr
'Carmen' (F)	CAgr
'Illinois Everbearing' (F)	CAgr ECrN ERea
'Italian' (F)	CAgr
'Ivory' (F)	CAgr
kagayamae	see *M. bombycis*
latifolia 'Spirata'	EMil MMuc NLar SEND
nigra (F) 🏆H4	Widely available
§ - 'Chelsea' (F)	CDul CEnd CTho CTri EBee ECrN EPfP ERea GTwe LRHS MAsh MBri MGan MGos NWea SCoo SKee SPer SPoG WHar WPGP
- 'Jerusalem' (F)	CTho LRHS MCoo
- 'King James'	see *M. nigra* 'Chelsea'
- 'Wellington' (F)	CAgr CEnd ECrN NPri
rubra	CAgr NLar
- 'Nana'	MBri NLar

Mosla (*Lamiaceae*)

dianthera	EBee EWld GCal MAvo MNrw WSHC

Muehlenbeckia (*Polygonaceae*)

astonii	EBee ECou LRHS
australis	ECou
axillaris misapplied	see *M. complexa*

§	***axillaris*** Walp.	CBcs CTri ECou GGar SBig
	- 'Mount Cook' (f)	ECou
	- 'Ohau' (m)	ECou
§	***complexa***	CBcs CDoC CHEx CHll CMac CTrC CTri CWib EBee ECou EPfP EShb ETod LRHS LTen MCCP MMuc NLBP NSti SAPC SArc SEND SLim SLon SPer SPoG SWvt WCFE WPGP WSHC
	- (f)	ECou
	- 'Nana'	see *M. axillaris* Walp.
	- small leaved **new**	ETod
	- 'Spotlight'PBR (v)	EShb
	- var. ***trilobata***	CHEx CTrC EBee EPla ESwi GCal SSta WDyG
	- 'Ward' (m)	ECou
	ephedroides	ECou
	- 'Clarence Pass'	ECou
*	- var. ***muricatula***	ECou
	gunnii	ECou
	platyclados	see *Homalocladium platycladum*

Muhlenbergia (*Poaceae*)

	capillaris	CAby EBee EPPr GCal IMou MAvo SBfd SHDw SMrm WBox
	dubia	WPGP
	dumosa	CKno IMou
	emersleyi	SMHy
	glomerata **new**	WBox
	japonica	EHoe EPPr LEdu SBfd SHDw
	'Cream Delight' (v)	
	lindheimeri	CBod EPPr GCal WCot
	mexicana	GFor LEdu SRms
	rigens	CKno GCal SApp WPGP

Mukdenia (*Saxifragaceae*)

	acanthifolia	CDes CLAP WCru
	rossii	CAby CLAP EBee ELon EPla GCal IFro ITim LEdu NBid NLar NMyG NPnk SGSe SMad WCom WCru WPGP WPrP WSHC WThu WTin
	- 'Crimson Fans'	see *M. rossii* 'Karasuba'
	- dwarf	CDes CLAP GCal
§	- 'Karasuba'	CLAP EBee GEdr LSou MAsh MAvo NLar NMyG SPoG
	- 'Ōgon'	CLAP
	- 'Shishiba'	GEdr
	- variegated (v)	MAvo WWEG

mulberry see *Morus*

Murraya (*Rutaceae*)

*	***elliptica***	SOWG
	exotica	see *M. paniculata*
	koenigii	EOHP GPoy
§	***paniculata***	CArn EShb GPoy

Musa ✿ (*Musaceae*)

	from Yangtze Valley, China **new**	LPJP
	from Yunnan, China	see *M. itinerans* 'Yunnan'
§	***acuminata***	MBri
	- 'Siam Ruby' (AA Group) (F) **new**	EAmu
§	- 'Dwarf Cavendish' (AAA Group) (F) ♀H1	EAmu ELan EShb LRHS LTen NPla SBst SPer SPlb XBlo
	- 'Grand Nain'	EAmu
	× ***acuminata*** 'Zebrina'	
	- 'Williams' (AAA Group) (F)	EAmu XBlo
	- 'Zebrina' ♀H1+3	CDTJ EAmu EShb SBst WFut XBlo
	balbisiana	EAmu SBst
	basjoo ♀H3-4	Widely available
I	- 'Rubra'	CCCN EAmu ESwi NPla
	cavendishii	see *M. acuminata* 'Dwarf Cavendish'
§	***coccinea*** ♀H1	XBlo
	ensete	see *Ensete ventricosum*
	'Helen'	EAmu LPJP WCot
	hookeri	see *M. sikkimensis*
*	***iterans glaucum***	CDTJ
	itinerans	NExo WCot
§	- 'Yunnan'	EAmu
	lasiocarpa	CBct CDTJ CDoC CHEx CHll CMHG EAmu EShb ESwi ETod EUJe LRHS MBri NPal NPla SBfd SBig SBst SMad SPlb WCot WGwG
	mannii	EAmu
	nana misapplied	see *M. acuminata* 'Dwarf Cavendish'
	nana Lour.	see *M. acuminata*
	ornata ♀H1	CCCN XBlo
	× ***paradisiaca***	CCCN EAmu
	'Ney Poovan' (AB Group) (F)	
	- 'Orinoco' (ABB Group) (F)	EAmu
	- 'Rajapuri' (AAB Group) (F)	EAmu
§	***sikkimensis***	CDTJ CDoC EAmu ELan ESwi ETod EUJe EWes LPJP SBig SBst SChr WFar XBlo
	- 'Red Tiger'	CCCN CDTJ CDoC EAmu
	'Tropicana'	CWit XBlo
	uranoscopus misapplied	see *M. coccinea*
	velutina ♀H1+3	CCCN CDoC EAmu NExo SBig SBst

Muscari ✿ (*Hyacinthaceae*)

	PF	NWCA
	'Aleyna'	ECho NMin
	ambrosiacum	see *M. muscarimi*
	anatolicum	ECho
	armeniacum ♀H4	CFox CTri EBrs ECho EPfP LRHS MBri MCot MMuc SEND SRms WCot WFar WShi
	- 'Argaei Album'	ECho EPot GAuc LAma
	- 'Atlantic'	ECho ERCP LRHS
	- 'Blue Pearl'	ECho GKev LRHS
	- 'Blue Spike' (d)	CMea CTca EBla ECho EPfP ERCP GKev LAma LRHS MBri NBir NEgg SDeJ SPer WCot WFar WGwG
	- 'Bright Eyes' **new**	GKev
	- 'Cantab'	ECho GKev SDeJ
	- 'Christmas Pearl' ♀H4	ECho SPhx WCot
	- 'Côte d'Azur'	GKev LRHS
	- 'Dark Eyes'	ECho EPfP LRHS SMrm SPer WFar WHil
	- 'Early Giant'	ECho SDeJ
	- 'Fantasy Creation'	CStu EBla ECho EPot LRHS SDeJ WBrk
	- 'Gul'	WCot
	- 'Heavenly Blue'	ECho
	- 'New Creation'	ECho
	- 'Peppermint'	CTca ECho ERCP LAma NMin SPhx WCot
	- 'Saffier' ♀H4	ECho LAma SPhx WCot
	- 'Valerie Finnis'	Widely available
	aucheri ♀H4	ECho GKev LAma NRya
*	- var. ***bicolor***	WCot
	- 'Blue Magic'	ECho EPot ERCP LAma
	- 'Ocean Magic'	ECho LAma NLar
§	- 'Tubergenianum'	ECho
	- 'White Magic'	CAvo ECho ERCP LAma LRHS WCot
§	***azureum*** ♀H4	CAvo CBgR CTca ECho ELan EPfP ERCP EWTr GMaP LAma LEdu LRHS NLar NMen NWCA SPhx WCot

	– 'Album'	CBgR EBla ECho EWTr LAma SPhx WBrk WCot
	'Baby's Breath'	see *M.* 'Jenny Robinson'
	'Big Smile'	GKev WCot
	'Blue Dream'	ECho
	'Blue Eyes'	ECho WCot
	'Blue Star'	ECho LRHS
	botryoides	ECho LAma LEdu
	– 'Album'	CAvo CFFs CFox CTca CTri EBla EBrs ECho EPfP GKev LAma MBri NChi SDeJ SMrm SPer SRms WBor WCot WShi
	caucasicum	ECho WCot
	chalusicum	see *M. pseudomuscari*
	commutatum	ECho
	– HOA 0130	WWst
§	***comosum***	CArn CBgR CFox ECho EPfP ERCP LEdu LRHS MCot MWea NEgg NWCA SEND SMrm WCot
*	– 'Album'	ECho
	– 'Monstrosum'	see *M. comosum* 'Plumosum'
	– 'Pinard'	ECho WWst
§	– 'Plumosum'	CAvo EBla ECho EPfP EPot LAma LEdu LRHS MBri SDeJ WAul WCot WHil
	'Cupido'	ECho
	dionysicum	ECho
	– HOA 8965	EBee WCot WWst
	discolor	WWst
	grandifolium	CDes ECho NWCA
	– JCA 689.450	WCot
	inconstrictum	ECho WWst
	'Ivor's Pink'	WCot
§	'Jenny Robinson' ♀H4	CMil EBla ECho EHrv IFoB SCnR SMad WCot
	latifolium ♀H4	CAby CBgR CFox CTca EBla EBrs ECho EPfP EPot ERCP GAuc GGar LAma LRHS MWat NChi NEgg NLar SBch SDeJ SGSe SMrm SPer SPhx WBor WClo WCot WTin
*	– 'Blue Angels'	NBir
§	***macrocarpum***	CAvo CTca EBee ECha ECho EPot GAuc LAma WAbe WCot
	– 'Golden Fragrance'PBR	CBgR CHid CMil CPom ECho EPot ERCP IFoB LAma LRHS MCot MNrw MWea NMin SDeJ WClo WCot WHil
	mirum	ECho
	moschatum	see *M. muscarimi*
	'Mount Hood'	CTca EBla EBrs ECho ERCP MWea SDeJ WBor
§	***muscarimi***	CAvo CFFs CTca ECho ERCP IFoB LAma LEdu NLar NWCA SDeJ WCot
	– var. ***flavum***	see *M. macrocarpum*
§	***neglectum***	ECho ITim LAma NLar SEND WCot WShi WWst
	pallens	ECho LRHS NMin NWCA WCot
	paradoxum	see *Bellevalia paradoxa*
	parviflorum	ECho WWst
§	***pseudomuscari*** ♀H4	ECho WCot
	racemosum	see *M. neglectum*
	'Sky Blue'	ECho LRHS WCot
§	***spreitzenhoferi***	ECho
	– HOA 0119	WWst
	– HOA 0120	WWst
	'Superstar'	ECho LEdu WCot
§	***tenuiflorum***	ECho WCot
	aff. ***tenuiflorum*** JCA 0.691.251 **new**	WCot
	tubergenianum	see *M. aucheri* 'Tubergenianum'
	'White Beauty'	ECho

Muscarimia (*Hyacinthaceae*)

	ambrosiacum	see *Muscari muscarimi*
	macrocarpum	see *Muscari macrocarpum*

Musella see *Musa*

Mussaenda (*Rubiaceae*)

	'Tropic Snow'	CCCN

Musschia (*Campanulaceae*)

	wollastonii	CPla ECre

Mutisia (*Asteraceae*)

	retusa	see *M. spinosa* var. *pulchella*
§	***spinosa*** var. ***pulchella***	GGal

Myoporum (*Myoporaceae*)

	debile	see *Eremophila debilis*
	laetum	CPLG CTrC

Myosotidium (*Boraginaceae*)

§	***hortensia***	CBcs CBct CGHE CPla CSpe CYeo EBee ECre EHrv ELan EPfP EUJe EWes GAbr GBin GCal GGar GKev IDee IKil LOck LRHS MCot NCGa NCob NWCA WCot WCru WPGP WWlt
	– 'True Blue' **new**	CHid
	– white-flowered	CPla
	nobile	see *M. hortensia*

Myosotis (*Boraginaceae*)

	from Eyre Mountains, New Zealand	GEdr NWCA
	alpestris 'Ruth Fischer'	NBir NMen
*	***aquatica***	NSco
	australis	CSpr
	capitata	EWTr
	colensoi	ECou NMen NWCA
	explanata	NMen
	macrantha	GBin
	Masha strain	CNat
	My Oh My = 'Myomark'PBR	ECtt LSou
	palustris	see *M. scorpioides*
	pulvinaris	ECou WAbe
	rakiura	SBch
§	***scorpioides***	CBen CRow CWat EBWF EHon LPBA MMuc MNrw MSKA MWts NMir SCoo SPer SPlb SRms SWat WBrk WMAq WMoo WPnP
	– 'Alba'	LPBA MSKA
	– 'Ice Pearl'	CBen ECha LLWG
	– Maytime = 'Blaqua' (v)	LLWG NBir
	– 'Mermaid'	CBen CRow CWat ECha GAbr LLWG LPBA SBch SDix SWat WPer WPnP
	– 'Pinkie'	CBen CWat LPBA MSKA SWat
	– 'Snowflakes'	CWat SWat
	– variegated (v)	MSKA
	sylvatica	CRWN EBWF MMuc NMir
	– 'Ultramarine' ♀H4	GJos
	'Unforgettable' (v)	CBow NBro NCob

Myrica (*Myricaceae*)

	californica	GKir LEdu NLar
	cerifera	CArn MBri NLar
	gale	CAgr CRWN EBee GPoy GQue IVic MBri MCoo MGos NLar SWat WDin WFar WGwG WHfH WSpi
	pensylvanica	EBee GAuc IVic LEdu MBri NLar
	rubra **new**	CAgr

Myricaria (*Tamaricaceae*)

germanica	NLar

Myriophyllum (*Haloragaceae*)

aquaticum	LLWG
propinquum 'Red Stem'	LPBA
spicatum	EHon MSKA NSco WMAq
verticillatum	CWat SCoo

Myrrhidendron (*Apiaceae*)

glaucescens B&SWJ 10699	WCru

Myrrhis (*Apiaceae*)

odorata	CArn CBod CBre CHby COIW CSev CSpe CWan EBWF EBee ECha ELau GBar GPWP GPoy IFro ILis MHer MNHC NBPC NPri SBfd SIde SPer WAul WHer WJek WPer WPtf WWFP
- 'Forncett Chevron'	GCal LEdu

Myrsine (*Myrsinaceae*)

africana	CWib IDee
aquilonia	ECou
divaricata	CTrC ECou
nummularia	WThu

Myrteola (*Myrtaceae*)

§ ***nummularia***	GAbr NHar NMen WAbe WThu

Myrtus (*Myrtaceae*)

apiculata	see *Luma apiculata*
bullata	see *Lophomyrtus bullata*
chequen	see *Luma chequen*
communis ♀H3	Widely available
- 'Flore Pleno' (d)	ELau EOHP
- 'Jenny Reitenbach'	see *M. communis* subsp. *tarentina*
- 'Merion'	WJek
- 'Microphylla'	see *M. communis* subsp. *tarentina*
- 'Nana'	see *M. communis* subsp. *tarentina*
- 'Pyewood Park'	WJek
§ - subsp. ***tarentina*** ♀H3	Widely available
- - 'Compacta'	LRHS NLar
- - 'Microphylla Variegata' (v)	CBcs GBar GQui MHer MNHC NGHP SBfd SPer WJek
I - - 'Variegata' (v)	EOHP EPfP SEND
- 'Tricolor'	see *M. communis* 'Variegata'
§ - 'Variegata' (v)	Widely available
dulcis	see *Austromyrtus dulcis*
'Glanleam Gold'	see *Luma apiculata* 'Glanleam Gold'
lechleriana	see *Amomyrtus luma*
luma	see *Luma apiculata*
nummularia	see *Myrteola nummularia*
* ***paraguayensis***	CTrC
× ***ralphii***	see *Lophomyrtus* × *ralphii*
'Traversii'	see *Lophomyrtus* × *ralphii* 'Traversii'
ugni	see *Ugni molinae*

N

Nananthus (*Aizoaceae*)

vittatus	WAbe

Nandina (*Berberidaceae*)

domestica ♀H3	Widely available
- B&SWJ 4923	WCru
- B&SWJ 11113	WCru
- 'Fire Power' ♀H3	Widely available
- 'Gulf Stream'	CBcs GBin
- 'Harbor Dwarf'	CDoC CEnd EBee MAsh SBfd SLim WFar
- var. ***leucocarpa***	NLar
- 'Nana'	see *N. domestica* 'Pygmaea'
- 'Nana Purpurea'	EPla GCal
- 'Orhime'	NLar
- Plum Passion = 'Monum' **new**	LRHS MAsh SPoG
§ - 'Pygmaea'	CMen WDin
- 'Richmond'	CBcs CEnd EBee ELan EPfP IFFs LAst LRHS MAsh MGos MHav NLar SBfd SLim SPer SPoG SRkn SWvt WCFE WFar WPat

Nannorrhops (*Arecaceae*)

ritchiana	EUJe LPal

Napaea (*Malvaceae*)

dioica	WCot

Narcissus ✿ (*Amaryllidaceae*)

'Abba' (4) ♀H4	CQua
'Aberfoyle' (2) ♀H4	CQua NMin
'Abstract' (11a)	CQua
'Accent' (2) ♀H4	CQua
'Accomplice' (3)	IRhd
'Achduart' (3)	CQua
'Achentoul' (4)	CQua
'Achnasheen' (3)	CQua NMin
'Acropolis' (4)	CQua EBrs EPfP SDeJ
'Actaea' (9) ♀H4	CFox CQua CTca EBrs ECho EPfP MBri SDeJ
'Acumen' (2)	CQua
'Admiration' (8)	CQua
'Advocat' (3)	CQua
'African Sunset' (3)	IRhd
'Agnes Mace' (2)	IRhd
'Ahwahnee' (2)	CQua IRhd
'Ainley' (2)	CQua
'Aintree' (3)	CQua
'Aircastle' (3)	CQua NMin
'Akepa' (5)	CQua
'Albatross' (3)	CQua
'Albus Plenus Odoratus'	see *N. poeticus* 'Plenus' ambig.
'All Rounder' (3) **new**	IRhd
'Alpine Glow' (1)	CQua
'Alpine Winter' (1)	IRhd
'Alston' (2)	IRhd
'Alto' (2)	IRhd
'Altruist' (3)	CQua ERCP
'Altun Ha' (2)	CQua IRhd NMin
'Amazing Grace' (2)	IRhd
'Amber Castle' (2)	CQua
'Ambergate' (2)	CQua LAma
'Ambergris Caye' (1) **new**	CQua
'American Goldfinch' (7) **new**	CQua
'American Heritage' (1)	CQua IRhd
'American Robin' (6)	CQua
'American Shores' (1)	CQua IRhd
'Amstel' (4)	CQua
'Andalusia' (6)	CQua
'Andrew's Choice' (7) **new**	CQua
'Angel' (3)	CQua NMin
'Angel Face' (3)	CQua IRhd
'Angelito' (3) ♀H4	IRhd
Angel's tears	see *N. triandrus* subsp. *triandrus* var. *triandrus*
'Angel's Wings' (2)	CQua
'Angkor' (4)	CQua

	'An-gof' (7)	CQua
	'Ann Sonia' (4)	IRhd
	'Anna Panna' (3)	IRhd
	'Annequin' (3) **new**	CQua
	'Apotheose' (4)	CQua LRHS SDeJ
	'Applins' (2)	IRhd
	'Apricot Blush' (2)	CQua
	'Apricot Whirl' (11a) **new**	CQua
	'April Love' (1)	CQua
	'April Snow' (2)	CQua
	'April Tears' (5) ♀H4	NMin
	'Aranjuez' (2)	CQua
	'Arctic Gem' (3)	CQua
	'Arctic Gold' (1) ♀H4	CQua LAma
	'Ardress' (2)	CQua
	'Areley Kings' (2)	CQua
	'Argosy' (1)	CQua
	'Arid Plains' (3)	IRhd
	'Arish Mell' (5)	CQua
	'Arkle' (1) ♀H4	CQua NMin SDeJ
	'Arleston' (2)	IRhd
	'Armidale' (3)	IRhd
	'Armoury' (4)	CQua
	'Arndilly' (2)	CQua
	'Arpege' (2)	CQua
	'Arran Isle' (2)	IRhd
	'Arrowhead' (6) **new**	NMin
	'Arthurian' (1)	IRhd
	'Articol' (11a)	CQua
	'Arwenack' (11a)	CQua
	'Ashmore' (2)	CQua IRhd
	'Ashton Wold' (2)	CQua
	'Asila' (2)	IRhd
	'Assertion' (2)	IRhd
§	***assoanus*** (13)	ECho EPot LAma MNrw MSSP NHol NMen NMin SPhx WWst
	'Astropink' (11a)	CQua
§	***asturiensis*** (13) ♀H3-4	CSam ECho MNrw NMin
	- giant form	see *N. asturiensis* 'Wavertree'
§	- 'Navarre' (1)	WCot
§	- 'Wavertree' (1)	CQua
	asturiensis* × *cyclamineus	NMen
	'Atlas Gold'	see *N. romieuxii* 'Atlas Gold
	'Atricilla' (11a)	IRhd
	'Auchrannie' (2)	IRhd
	'Audubon' (2)	CQua SDeJ
	'Aunt Betty' (1)	CQua
	'Auntie Eileen' (2)	CQua
	'Auspicious' (2)	IRhd
	'Avalanche' (8) ♀H3	CQua EBrs NMin SDeJ
	'Avalanche of Gold' (8)	CQua
	'Avalon' (2)	CQua
	'Azocor' (1)	IRhd
	'Baby Boomer' (7)	LAma NMin
	'Baby Moon' (7)	CQua CTca EBrs EPfP EPot ERCP GEdr GKev LAma MBri NHol NMin SDeJ SPhx
	'Back Flash' (2) **new**	CQua
	'Badanloch' (3)	CQua
	'Badbury Rings' (3) ♀H4	CQua
	'Bala' (4)	CQua
	'Balalaika' (2)	CQua
	'Baldock' (4)	CQua
	'Ballydorn' (9)	IRhd
	'Ballygarvey' (1)	CQua
	'Ballygowan' (3)	IRhd
	'Ballynichol' (3)	CQua
	'Ballyrobert' (1)	CQua
	'Baltic Shore' (3)	IRhd
	'Balvenie' (2)	CQua
	'Bandesara' (3)	CQua IRhd
	'Bandit' (2)	CQua
	'Banker' (2)	CQua
	'Banstead Village' (2)	CQua
	'Bantam' (2) ♀H4	CQua NMin
	'Barbary Gold' (2)	CQua
	'Barlow' (6)	CQua
	'Barnesgold' (1)	IRhd
	'Barnham' (1)	CQua
	'Barnsdale Wood' (2)	CQua
	'Barnum' (1) ♀H4	IRhd
	'Barrett Browning' (3)	EBla SDeJ
	'Barrii' (3)	CQua
	'Bartley' (6)	CQua
	'Bath's Flame' (3)	CAvo CQua WShi
	'Bear Springs' (4)	IRhd
	'Beautiful Dream' (3)	CQua
	'Bedruthan' (2)	CQua
	'Beersheba' (1)	CQua
	'Belbroughton' (2)	CQua
	'Belcanto' (11a)	CQua SDeJ
	'Belfast Lough' (1)	IRhd
	'Belisana' (2)	SDeJ
	'Bell Rock' (1)	CQua
	'Bell Song' (7)	CAvo CFFs CQua EPfP ERCP LSou SDeJ WShi
	'Belzone' (2)	CQua
	'Ben Aligin' (1)	CQua
	'Ben Hee' (2) ♀H4	CQua
	'Berceuse' (2)	CQua IRhd
	'Bere Ferrers' (4)	CQua
	'Bergerac' (11a)	CQua
	'Bernardino' (2)	CQua
	'Beryl' (6)	CQua ECho EPot NMin
	'Best Seller' (1)	SPer
	'Bethal' (3)	CQua
	'Betsy MacDonald' (6)	CQua
	'Biffo' (4)	CQua
*	'Big Cycla' (6)	ECho
	'Bikini Beach' (2)	IRhd
	'Bilbo' (6)	CQua
	'Billy Graham' (2) **new**	CQua
	'Binkie' (2)	CQua
	'Birchwood' (3)	CQua
	'Birdsong' (3)	CQua
	'Birma' (3)	LAma SDeJ
	'Bishops Light' (2)	CQua
	'Bittern' (12)	CQua SDeJ
	'Blair Athol' (2)	CQua
	'Blarney' (3)	CQua
	'Blisland' (9)	CQua
	'Blossom' (4)	CQua
	'Blue Danube' (1)	CQua
	'Blushing Maiden' (4)	CQua
	'Bob Spotts' (2)	CQua
	'Bobbysoxer' (7)	CQua MTho
	'Bobolink' (2)	CQua
	'Bodelva' (2)	CQua
	'Bodwannick' (2)	CQua
	'Bold Prospect' (1)	CQua
	'Bon Viveur' (11a)	IRhd
	'Bosbigal' (11a)	CQua
	'Boscastle' (7)	CQua
	'Boscoppa' (11a)	CQua
	'Boslowick' (11a) ♀H4	CQua
	'Bosmeor' (2)	CQua
	'Bossa Nova' (3)	CQua
	'Bossiney' (11a)	CQua
	'Bosvale' (11a)	CQua
	'Bosvigo' (11a)	CQua
	'Boulder Bay' (2) ♀H4	CQua
	'Bouzouki' (2)	IRhd
	'Bowles's Early Sulphur' (1)	CRow

	'Boyne Bridge' (1)	IRhd
	'Brackenhurst' (2)	EBrs
	'Brandaris' (11a)	CQua
	'Bravoure' (1) ♀^{H4}	CQua SDeJ
	'Brentswood' (8)	CQua
	'Bridal Crown' (4) ♀^{H4}	EPfP LAma LRHS SPer
	'Bright Flame' (2)	CQua
	'Bright Spot' (8)	CQua
	'Brilliancy' (3) **new**	CQua
	'Brindaleena' (2)	IRhd
	'Brindle Pink' (2)	IRhd
	'Broadland' (2)	CQua
	'Broadway Star' (11b)	LAma SDeJ
	'Brodick' (3)	CQua IRhd
	'Bronzewing' (1)	IRhd
	'Brookdale' (1)	CQua
	'Brooke Ager' (2) ♀^{H4}	IRhd
	'Broomhill' (2) ♀^{H4}	CQua
	broussonetii (13)	ECho
	'Brunswick' (2)	CQua
	'Bryanston' (2) ♀^{H4}	CQua
	'Bryher' (3)	CQua
	'Budock Bells' (5)	CQua
	'Budock Water' (2)	CQua
	'Bugle Major' (2)	CQua
	bulbocodium (13) ♀$^{H3-4}$	CStu GKev ITim LBee LEdu LRHS NWCA SBch SMrm SPer SRms
	- from Atlas Mountains, Morocco	MSSP
§	- subsp. ***bulbocodium*** (13)	LPio
§	- - var. ***citrinus*** (13)	LPio SSpi
	- - MS 577	MSSP
	- - var. ***conspicuus*** (13)	CArn CHar CPMA CQua CTca ECho EPfP EPot ERCP GEdr LAma LRHS MSSP NHol NMen NMin NRya SDeJ SGar WCot
§	- - var. ***graellsii*** (13)	NSla
	- - var. ***nivalis*** (13)	ECho WWst
	- - var. ***pallidus*** (13)	GEdr
§	- - var. ***tenuifolius*** (13)	EPot NMen
*	- - var. ***filifolius***	MSSP
§	- Golden Bells Group (10)	CAvo CHid CQua CTri CWCL EBrs ECho EPot GKev GKir LRHS MBri NHol SDeJ
	- var. ***mesatlanticus***	see *N. romieuxii* subsp. *romieuxii* var. *mesatlanticus*
	- subsp. ***obesus*** (13)	ECho MSSP WCot
§	- - 'Diamond Ring'	CQua EPot LAma MSSP NMin
	- subsp. ***praecox*** (13)	CBro ECho LRHS WCot
	- - var. ***paucinervis*** (13)	ECho
	- subsp. ***tananicus***	see *N. cantabricus* subsp. *tananicus*
	- subsp. ***vulgaris***	see *N. bulbocodium* subsp. *bulbocodium*
	bulbocodium* × *romieuxii	WCot
	'Bunchie' (5)	CQua
	'Bunclody' (2)	CQua
	'Bunting' (7) ♀^{H4}	CQua
	'Burning Bush' (3)	IRhd
	'Burntollet' (1)	CQua
	'Burravoe' (1)	CQua
	'Busselton' (3)	IRhd
	'Butterscotch' (2)	CQua
	'C.J. Backhouse' (2)	CQua
	'Cabernet' (2)	IRhd
	'Cacatua' (11a)	IRhd
	'Cadgwith' (2)	CQua
	'Cairntoul' (3)	CQua
	'Calamansack' (2)	CQua
I	***calcicola*** 'Idol' (7)	CQua EPot NMin
	'California Rose' (4)	CQua IRhd
	'Camaraderie' (2) **new**	IRhd
	'Camelot' (2) ♀^{H4}	CQua EPfP SDeJ SPer
	'Cameo Angel' (2)	CQua
	'Cameo King' (2)	CQua
	'Cameo Marie' (3) **new**	CQua
	'Camoro' (10)	MSSP NMen
	'Campernelli Plenus'	see *N.* × *odorus* 'Double Campernelle'
	'Campion' (9)	CQua IRhd
	'Canaliculatus' (8)	CArn CFox CQua CTri EBrs ECho EPfP ERCP GKev LAma LRHS MBri SDeJ SMrm SPer WGwG
	canaliculatus Gussone	see *N. tazetta* subsp. *lacticolor*
	'Canary' (7)	CQua
	'Canarybird' (8)	CQua WShi
	'Canasta' (11a)	CQua
	'Candida' (4)	CQua
	'Canisp' (2)	CQua
	'Cantabile' (9) ♀^{H4}	CQua
	cantabricus (13)	ECho WWst
	- subsp. ***cantabricus*** (13)	LPio NMin NRya
	- - var. ***foliosus*** (13) ♀^{H2}	ECho EPot GKev NMen SCnR WCot
	- - var. ***petunioides*** (13)	ECho
	- subsp. ***monophyllus*** (13)	WWst
§	- subsp. ***tananicus*** (13)	ECho EPot
	cantabricus* × *romieuxii (13)	LPio
	'Cantatrice' (1)	CQua
	'Canticle' (9)	IRhd
	'Capax Plenus'	see *N.* 'Eystettensis'
	'Cape Cornwall' (2)	CQua
	'Cape Helles' (3)	IRhd
	'Cape Point' (2)	IRhd
	'Capisco' (3)	CQua
	'Caramba' (2)	CQua
	'Carbineer' (2)	CQua SDeJ
	'Carclew' (6)	CQua
	'Cardiff' (2)	CQua
	'Cardinham' (3)	CQua
	'Cargreen' (9)	CQua
	'Carib Gipsy' (2) ♀^{H4}	CQua IRhd NMin
	'Caribbean Snow' (2)	CQua
	'Carlton' (2) ♀^{H4}	CQua EBrs EPfP LAma LRHS SDeJ
	'Carnearny' (3)	CQua
	'Carnkeeran' (2)	CQua
	'Carnkief' (2)	CQua
	'Carnyorth' (11a)	CQua
	'Carole Lombard' (3)	CQua
	'Carwinion' (2)	CQua
	'Cassata' (11a)	EBrs EPfP LAma NBir SDeJ
	'Castanets' (8)	IRhd
	'Casterbridge' (2)	CQua IRhd
	'Catalyst' (2)	IRhd
	'Catistock' (2)	CQua
	'Causeway Sunset' (2)	IRhd
	'Causeway Sunshine' (1)	IRhd
	'Cavalryman' (3)	IRhd
	'Cawdron' (2) **new**	CQua
	'Caye Chapel' (3)	CQua
	'Cazique' (6)	CQua
	× ***cazorlanus*** (13)	MSSP NSla
	'Ceasefire' (2)	IRhd
	'Cedar Hills' (3)	CQua
	'Cedric Morris' (1)	CDes CLAP ECha EHrv
	'Celestial Fire' (2)	CQua
	'Celtic Gold' (2)	CQua
	'Centannées' (11b)	EBrs
	'Centrefold' (3)	CQua
	'Cernuus Plenus' (4)	CQua
	'Cha-cha' (6)	CQua
	'Changing Colors' (11a)	CQua
	'Chanson' (1) ♀^{H4}	IRhd

'Chanterelle' (11a)	EBla LAma
'Chantilly' (2)	CQua
'Chapman's Peak' (2)	IRhd
'Charity May' (6) ♀H4	CQua
'Charleston' (2)	CQua
'Charlie Connor' (1) **new**	CQua
'Chasseur' (2)	IRhd
'Chaste' (1)	CQua IRhd
'Chat' (7)	CQua
'Cheer Leader' (3)	CQua
'Cheerfulness' (4) ♀H4	CAvo CFFs CQua LAma LRHS MBri SDeJ
'Cheesewring' (3)	CQua
'Cheetah' (1)	CQua IRhd
'Chelsea Girl' (2)	CQua
'Cheltenham' (2)	CQua
'Chenoweth' (2)	CQua
'Chérie' (7)	CQua
'Cherish' (2)	CQua
'Cherry Glow' (3)	IRhd
'Cherrygardens' (2)	CQua IRhd
'Chesapeake Bay' (1)	CQua
'Chesterton' (9) ♀H4	CQua
'Chickadee' (6)	CQua
'Chicken Hill' (1) **new**	CQua
'Chickerell' (3)	CQua
'Chief Inspector' (1)	IRhd
'Chiloquin' (1)	CQua
'China Doll' (2)	CQua
'Chinchilla' (2)	CQua IRhd
'Chingah' (1)	IRhd
'Chinita' (8)	CQua
'Chipper' (5)	CQua NMin
'Chit Chat' (7) ♀H4	CQua EPot LRHS NMin
'Chiva'	CHid LRHS NMin
'Chobe River' (1)	CQua IRhd
'Chorus Line' (8)	IRhd
'Chromacolor' (2) ♀H4	LRHS
'Churchfield Bells' (5) **new**	CQua
'Churston Ferrers' (4)	CQua
'Chy Noweth' (2)	CQua
'Chysauster' (2)	CQua
'Cinco de Mayo' (2) **new**	CQua
'Cisticola' (3)	IRhd
citrinus	see *N. bulbocodium* subsp. *bulbocodium* var. *citrinus*
'Citron' (3)	CQua
'Citronita' (3)	CQua
'Clare' (7)	CQua IRhd NMin
'Claverley' (2)	CQua
'Clearbrook' (2)	CQua
'Clouded Yellow' (2)	CQua IRhd
'Clouds Rest' (2)	IRhd
'Codlins and Cream'	see *N.* 'Sulphur Phoenix'
'Coldbrook' (2)	CQua
'Colin's Joy' (2)	CQua
'Coliseum' (2)	IRhd
'Colleen Bawn' (1)	CQua NMin
'Colley Gate' (3)	CQua
'Colliford' (2)	CQua
'Colorama' (11a)	CQua
'Colourful' (2)	IRhd
'Columbus' (2)	CQua
'Colville' (9)	CQua
'Comal' (1)	CQua
'Compressus'	see *N.* × *intermedius* 'Compressus'
'Compton Court' (3)	IRhd
concolor	see *N. triandrus* subsp. *triandrus* var. *concolor*
'Conestoga' (2)	CQua IRhd
'Congress' (11a)	CQua
'Conly' (3) **new**	CQua
'Conowingo' (11a)	CQua
'Conspicuus' ambig.	CQua LAma
'Content' (1)	CQua
'Cool Autumn' (2)	CQua
'Cool Crystal' (3)	CQua
'Cool Evening' (11a)	CQua IRhd
'Cool Pink' (2)	CQua
'Cool Shades' (2)	CQua
'Coolmaghery' (2)	IRhd
'Coombe Creek' (6)	CQua
'Copper Nob' (2)	IRhd
'Copper Rings' (3)	CQua
'Copperfield' (2)	CQua
'Coral Fair' (2)	CQua
'Corbiere' (1)	CQua IRhd NMin
'Corbridge' (2)	CQua
'Corky's Song' (2) **new**	CQua
'Cornell' (3) **new**	NMin
'Cornet' (6)	CQua
'Cornish Chuckles' (12) ♀H4	CBgR CQua
'Cornish Sun' (2)	CQua
'Cornish Vanguard' (2) ♀H4	CQua
'Coroboree'	IRhd
'Corofin' (3)	CQua
'Coromandel' (2)	IRhd
'Corozal' (3)	CQua
'Cosmic Dance' (3)	IRhd
'Cotinga' (6)	CQua NMin
'Countdown' (2)	CQua
'Coverack Glory' (2)	CQua
'Crackington' (4) ♀H4	CQua IRhd
'Cragford' (8)	SDeJ
'Craig Stiel' (2)	CQua
'Creag Dubh' (2)	CQua
'Creed' (6)	CQua
'Crenver' (3)	CQua
'Crevenagh' (2)	IRhd
'Crewenna' (1)	CAvo CQua
'Crill' (7)	CQua
'Crimson Chalice' (3)	CQua IRhd
'Cristobal' (1)	CQua NMin
'Crock of Gold' (1)	CQua
'Croesus' (2)	CQua
'Crofty' (6)	CQua
'Croila' (2)	CQua
'Crowndale' (4)	CQua IRhd
'Crugmeer' (11a)	CQua
'Cryptic' (1)	CQua IRhd
'Crystal Star' (2)	CQua
cuatrecasasii var. ***segimonensis*** (13)	LPio
'Cudden Point' (2)	CQua
'Cul Beag' (3)	CQua
'Culmination' (2)	CQua
'Cultured Pearl' (2)	CQua NMin
'Cum Laude' (11a) **new**	ERCP
'Curlew' (7) ♀H4	CQua SDeJ
'Curly' (2)	SDeJ
cyclamineus (13) ♀H4	CDes CStu MAsh MSSP NMen SCnR SKHP SRms
'Cyclope' (1)	CQua
cypri (8)	CQua
'Cyros' (1)	CQua
'Dailmanach' (2)	CQua IRhd
'Dailmystic' (2)	IRhd
'Dallas' (3)	CQua
'Dambuster' (4)	IRhd
'Damson' (2)	CQua
'Dan du Plessis' (8)	CQua
'Dancing Queen' (2)	IRhd
'Dardanelles' (2)	IRhd

'Dateline' (3) CQua
'David Alexander' (1) CQua
'David Mills' (2) CQua
'Dawn Call' (2) IRhd
'Dawn Run' (2) IRhd
'Dawn Sky' (2) CQua
'Daydream' (2) ♀H3 CQua EBrs
'Daymark' (8) CQua
'Dayton Lake' (2) CQua
'Debutante' (2) CQua
'December Bride' (11a) CQua
'Decision' (2) IRhd
'Defence Corps' (1) IRhd
'Delia' (6) IRhd
'Dell Chapel' (3) CQua
'Delnashaugh' (4) CQua ERCP LAma
'Delos' (3) CQua
'Delphin Hill' (4) IRhd
'Delta Flight' (6) EBrs IRhd
'Demand' (2) CQua
'Demeanour' IRhd
'Demmo' (2) CQua
'Dena' (3) IRhd
'Denali' (1) IRhd
'Derryboy' (3) IRhd
'Descant' (1) IRhd
'Desdemona' (2) ♀H4 CQua SDeJ
'Desert Bells' (7) CQua NMin
'Desert Orchid' (2) CQua
'Dewy Dell' (3) IRhd
'Diamond Ring' see *N. bulbocodium* subsp. *obesus* 'Diamond Ring'
'Dick Wilden' (4) CQua EBla
'Dickcissel' (7) ♀H4 CQua
'Dignitary' (2) IRhd
'Dimity' (3) CQua
'Dimple' (9) CQua
'Disquiet' (1) **new** CQua
'Diversity' (11a) IRhd
'Doctor Hugh' (3) ♀H4 CQua IRhd NMin
'Doctor Jazz' (2) CQua
'Dolly Mollinger' (11b) EBla
'Doombar' (1) CQua
'Dora Allum' (2) CQua
'Dorchester' (4) CQua IRhd NMin
'Dorneywood' (1) **new** IRhd
'Double Campernelle' see *N.* × *odorus* 'Double Campernelle'
double pheasant eye see *N. poeticus* 'Plenus' ambig.
double Roman see *N.* 'Romanus'
'Double Smiles' (4) LRHS
'Double White' (4) CQua
'Doubleday' (4) CQua IRhd
'Doublet' (4) CQua
'Doubtful' (3) CQua
'Dove Wings' (6) ♀H4 CQua
'Dover Cliffs' (2) CQua
'Downlands' (3) CQua
'Downpatrick' (1) CQua
'Dragon Run' (2) CQua
'Drama Queen' (11a) IRhd
'Dream Catcher' (2) IRhd
'Dreamlight' (3) **new** CQua
'Drumlin' (1) ♀H4 IRhd
dubius (13) ECho EPot
'Duiker' (6) IRhd
'Dulcimer' (9) CQua
'Dunadry Inn' (4) IRhd
'Dunkeld' (2) CQua
'Dunkery' (4) CQua IRhd
'Dunley Hall' (3) CQua IRhd
'Dunmurry' (1) CQua
'Dunskey' (3) CQua
'Dupli Kate' (4) IRhd
'Dusky Lad' (2) IRhd
'Dusky Maiden' (2) IRhd
'Dutch Delight' (2) IRhd
'Dutch Lemon Drops' (5) ♀H4 **new** CQua
'Dutch Master' (1) ♀H4 CQua EBrs LAma SDeJ SPer
'Early Bride' (2) CQua
'Early Flame' (2) LRHS
'Early Splendour' (8) CQua
'Earthlight' (3) CQua
'Easter Bonnet' (2) EBla
'Easter Moon' (2) CQua
'Eastern Dawn' (2) CQua SDeJ
'Eastern Promise' (2) CQua
'Eaton Song' (12) ♀H4 CQua
'Ebony' (1) **new** CQua
'Eddy Canzony' (2) CQua
'Edenderry' (1) IRhd
'Edgbaston' (2) CQua
'Edge Grove' (2) CQua
'Editor' (2) IRhd
'Edward Buxton' (3) CQua
'Egard' (11a) CQua
'Egmont King' (2) CQua
'Eland' (7) CQua
'Elburton' (2) CQua
'Electrus' (11a) IRhd
elegans (13) ECho
'Elegant Lady' (1) **new** NMin
'Elf' (2) CQua
'Elfin Gold' (6) CQua
'Elizabeth Ann' (6) CQua
'Elka' (1) CAvo CBgR CMea CQua MSSP NMin
'Ella D' (2) CQua
'Ellen' (2) LRHS
'Elphin' (4) CQua
'Elrond' (2) CQua
'Elven Lady' (2) CQua
'Elvira' (8) CQua WShi
'Emcys' (6) NMin
'Emerald Pink' (3) CQua
'Emily' (2) NMin
'Eminent' (3) CQua
'Emperor' (1) CQua
'Emperor's Waltz' (6) IRhd
'Empress of Ireland' (1) ♀H4 CQua IRhd
'English Caye' (1) CQua
'Ensemble' (4) CQua
'Enterprise' (4) CQua
'Epona' (3) CQua
'Erlicheer' (4) CQua SDeJ
'Escapee' (2) IRhd
'Estrella' (3) CQua
'Ethereal Beauty' (2) IRhd
'Ethos' (1) IRhd
eugeniae (13) EPot WCot
'Euryalus' (1) CQua
'Eve Robertson' (2) CQua
'Evening' (2) CQua
'Evesham' (3) IRhd
'Exotic Beauty' (4) EBrs
'Eyeglass' (3) CQua IRhd
'Eyelet' (3) CQua IRhd
'Eype' (4) IRhd
'Eyrie' (3) CQua IRhd
§ 'Eystettensis' (4) ECha IBlr
'Fair Head' (9) CQua
'Fair Prospect' (2) CQua
'Fair William' (2) CQua
'Fairgreen' (3) CQua
'Fairlawns' (3) CQua

'Fairmile' (3)	CQua
'Fairy Chimes' (5)	CQua
'Fairy Footsteps' (3)	CQua IRhd
'Fairy Island' (3)	CQua
'Fairy Spell' (3)	IRhd
'Fairy Tale' (3)	CQua
'Falconet' (8) 𝕐H4	CQua EPfP LRHS SPer
'Falmouth Bay' (3)	CQua
'Falstaff' (2)	CQua
'Fanline' (11a)	CQua
'Far Country' (2)	CQua
I 'Fashion' (11b)	CQua
'Fashion Model' (2)	IRhd
'Fastidious' (2)	CQua
'February Gold' (6) 𝕐H4	CAvo CFFs CQua CTri EBrs EPfP EPot ERCP LAma LRHS MBri NBir SDeJ SGar SPer SPhx SRms WShi
'February Silver' (6)	EPot ERCP LAma SDeJ
'Felindre' (9)	CQua
'Feline Queen' (1)	IRhd
'Feock' (3)	CQua
fernandesii (13)	ECho GEdr NMin SCnR WCot WThu
- var. ***cordubensis*** (13)	ECho GEdr
- var. ***cordubensis* × *jonquilla***	NMin
'Ferndown' (3)	CQua IRhd
'Ferral' (4)	IRhd
'Fertile Crescent' (7) **new**	CQua
'Ffitch's Ffolly' (2)	CQua
'Filoli' (1)	CQua IRhd
'Finchcocks' (2)	CQua
'Fine Gold' (1)	CQua
'Fine Romance' (2)	CQua
'Finland' (2)	CQua
'Fiona Linford' (3)	IRhd
'Fiona MacKillop' (2)	IRhd
'Fire Tail' (3)	CQua WShi
'First Born' (6)	CQua NMin
'First Formal' (3)	CQua
'First Hope' (6)	CQua
'Flambards Village' (4)	CQua
'Flirt' (6)	CQua
'Florida Manor' (3)	IRhd
'Flower Record' (2)	LAma
'Flusher' (2) **new**	CQua
'Flycatcher' (7)	CQua
'Flying Colours' (4)	IRhd
'Flying High' (3)	CQua
'Foff's Way' (1)	CQua
'Foresight' (1)	CQua
'Forge Mill' (2)	CQua
'Fortescue' (4)	IRhd
'Fortune' (2)	CQua LAma LRHS MBri SDeJ
'Fossie' (4)	CQua
'Foundling' (6) 𝕐H4	CQua
'Foxfire' (2)	CQua
'Foxhunter' (2)	CQua
'Fragrant Breeze' (2)	SDeJ
'Fragrant Rose' (2)	CQua IRhd
'Francolin' (1)	IRhd
'Frank' (9)	IRhd
'Freedom Rings' (2)	CQua
'Freedom Stars' (11a) 𝕐H4	IRhd
'Fresco' (11a)	IRhd
'Fresh Field' (2) **new**	CQua
'Fresh Lime' (1)	CQua
'Fresno' (3)	IRhd
'Frigid' (3)	CQua
'Frogmore' (6)	CQua
'Front Royal' (2)	CQua
'Frosted Pink' (2)	IRhd
'Frostkist' (6)	CQua
'Frosty Morn' (5)	NMin
'Frou-frou' (4)	CQua
'Frozen Jade' (1)	CQua
'Fruit Cup' (7)	CQua EPfP LRHS SDeJ
'Fuco' (1)	CQua NMin
'Full House'	SDeJ
'Fulwell' (4)	CQua
'Furbelow' (4)	CQua
'Furnace Creek' (2)	IRhd
'Fynbos' (3)	IRhd
'Gamebird' (1)	IRhd
'Garden News' (3)	IRhd
'Garden Opera' (7) 𝕐H4 **new**	CQua
'Garden Treasure' (2)	IRhd
'Gatecrasher' (1)	IRhd
'Gay Cavalier' (4)	CQua
'Gay Kybo' (4) 𝕐H4	CQua NMin
'Gay Song' (4)	CQua
gayi (13)	CQua WShi
'Geevor' (4)	CQua
'Gellymill' (2)	CQua
'Gemini Girl' (2)	CQua
'George Leak' (2)	CQua
'Georgie Girl' (6)	CQua
'Geranium' (8) 𝕐H4	CQua EBrs EPfP ERCP LAma SDeJ SPer WShi
'Gettysburg' (2)	CQua
'Gillan' (11a)	CQua
'Gin and Lime' (1) 𝕐H4	CQua
'Gipsy Moon' (2)	CQua
'Gipsy Queen' (1)	CBgR CQua GCrs NMin
'Gironde' (11)	CQua
'Glacier' (1)	CQua
'Glasnevin' (2)	CQua
'Glen Cassley' (3)	CQua
'Glen Clova' (2)	CQua
'Glendermott' (2)	CQua
'Glenside' (2)	CQua
'Glissando' (2)	CQua
'Gloriosus' (8)	CQua
'Glover's Reef' (1)	CQua
'Glowing Pheonix' (4)	CQua
'Glowing Red' (4)	CQua
'Goff's Caye' (2)	CQua IRhd
'Golant' (2)	CQua
'Gold Bond' (2)	CQua IRhd
'Gold Cache' (11a) **new**	CQua
'Gold Charm' (2)	CQua
'Gold Convention' (2) 𝕐H4	CQua IRhd
'Gold Ingot' (2) 𝕐H4	IRhd
'Gold Medallion' (1)	CQua
'Gold Top' (2)	CQua
'Golden Amber' (2)	CQua
'Golden Anniversary'	CQua
'Golden Aura' (2) 𝕐H4	CQua
'Golden Bear' (4)	CQua
'Golden Bells'	see *N. bulbocodium* Golden Bells Group
'Golden Cheer' (2)	CQua
'Golden Dawn' (8) 𝕐H3	CQua EPfP LRHS
'Golden Ducat' (4)	CQua LAma LRHS MBri NBir
'Golden Flute' (2)	IRhd
'Golden Gamble' (11a)	IRhd
'Golden Goal' (2)	IRhd
'Golden Halo' (2)	CQua
'Golden Harvest' (1)	CQua LAma
'Golden Incense' (7)	CQua
'Golden Jewel' (2) 𝕐H4	CQua
'Golden Joy' (2)	CQua
'Golden Lion' (1)	CQua EPfP

'Golden Marvel' (1)	CQua
'Golden Orbit' (4)	CQua
'Golden Phoenix' (4)	CQua
'Golden Rain' (4)	CQua
'Golden Rapture' (1) 🏆H4	CQua
'Golden Sheen' (2)	CQua
'Golden Splash' (11a)	IRhd
'Golden Spur' (1)	CQua LAma
'Golden Torch' (2)	CQua
'Golden Vale' (1) 🏆H4	CQua
'Goldfinger' (1) 🏆H4	CQua IRhd NMin
'Goldhanger' (2)	CQua
'Golitha Falls' (2)	CQua
'Good Fella' (2)	CQua
'Good Measure' (2)	CQua
'Goonbell' (2)	CQua
'Gorran' (3)	CQua
'Gossmoor' (4)	CQua
'Grace Note' (3)	CQua
graellsii	see *N. bulbocodium* subsp. *bulbocodium* var. *graellsii*
'Grand Monarque'	see *N. tazetta* subsp. *lacticolor* 'Grand Monarque'
'Grand Opening' (4)	IRhd
'Grand Primo Citronière' (8)	CQua
'Grand Prospect' (2)	CQua
'Grand Soleil d'Or' (8)	CQua ERCP LAma SDeJ
'Great Expectations' (2)	CQua
'Greatwood' (1)	CQua
'Greek Surprise' (4)	IRhd
'Green Chartreuse' (2)	CQua
'Green Howard' (3)	ECho
'Green Island' (2)	SDeJ
'Green Lodge' (9)	IRhd
'Greenodd' (3)	CQua
'Greenpark' (9)	IRhd
'Grenoble' (2)	CQua
'Gresham' (4)	CQua IRhd
'Gribben Head' (4)	CQua
'Groundkeeper' (3)	IRhd
'Gulliver' (3)	CQua
'Gunwalloe' (11a)	CQua
'Guy Wilson' (2)	CQua
'Gwennap' (1)	CQua
'Gwinear' (2)	CQua
'Hacienda' (1)	CQua
'Half Moon Caye' (2)	CQua
'Halley's Comet' (3)	CQua IRhd
'Halloon' (3)	CQua
'Halzephron' (2)	CQua
'Hambledon' (2) 🏆H4	CQua
'Hampton Court' (2)	CQua
'Happy Dreams' (2)	IRhd
'Happy Fellow' (2)	CQua
'Happy Valley' (2)	IRhd
'Harbour View' (2)	IRhd
'Harmony Bells' (5)	CQua
'Harp Music' (2)	IRhd
'Harpers Ferry' (1)	CQua
'Hartlebury' (3)	CQua
'Hawangi' (3)	IRhd
'Hawera' (5) 🏆H4	CAvo CFFs CFox CHid CMea CQua CTca CTri EBrs EPfP EPot ERCP GKev LAma LRHS LSou MBri SDeJ SPer SPhx WShi
'Heamoor' (4) 🏆H4	CQua
hedraeanthus (13)	ECho EPot WCot
'Helford Dawn' (2)	CQua
'Helford Sunset' (2)	CQua
'Helios' (2)	CQua
hellenicus	see *N. poeticus* var. *hellenicus*
henriquesii	see *N. jonquilla* var. *henriquesii*
'Henry Irving' (1)	CQua
'Hero' (1)	CQua
'Heslington' (3)	CQua
'Hexameter' (9)	CQua
'Hexworthy' (3)	CQua
'Hibernian' (4)	IRhd
'Hicks Mill' (1)	CQua
'High Society' (2) 🏆H4	CQua EBrs
'Highfield Beauty' (8) 🏆H4	CQua
'Highgrove' (1)	CQua
'Highlite' (2)	CQua
'Hihitahi' (2) **new**	CQua
'Hilda's Pink' (2)	CQua
'Hill Head' (9)	IRhd
'Hillstar' (7) 🏆H4	CQua LRHS SDeJ
hispanicus (13)	ECho
'Hocus Pocus' (3)	IRhd
'Hollypark' (3)	IRhd
'Holme Fen' (2)	CQua
'Home Fires' (2)	CQua
'Homestead' (2) 🏆H4	IRhd
'Honey Pink' (2)	CQua
'Honeybird' (1)	CQua
'Honeyorange' (2)	IRhd
'Hoopoe' (8) 🏆H4	CQua LRHS
'Horace' (9)	CQua
'Horn of Plenty' (5)	CBgR CQua
'Hornpipe' (1)	IRhd
'Hospodar' (2)	CQua
'Hot Affair' (2)	IRhd
'Hot Gossip' (2)	CQua
'Hotspur' (2)	CQua
'Hugh Town' (8)	CAvo CQua
'Hugus' (7) **new**	CQua
'Hullabaloo' (2)	IRhd
humilis misapplied	see *N. pseudonarcissus* subsp. *pseudonarcissus* var. *humilis*
'Hunting Caye' (2)	CQua
'Huntley Down' (1)	CQua
'Ice Chimes' (5)	CQua
'Ice Dancer' (2)	CQua
'Ice Diamond' (4)	CQua
'Ice Follies' (2) 🏆H4	CQua EBrs EPfP LAma MBri NBir SDeJ SPer
'Ice King' (4)	EBla LRHS NBir SDeJ
'Ice Wings' (5) 🏆H4	CAvo CFFs CQua EPot NMin WShi
'Idless' (1)	CQua
'Immaculate' (2)	CQua
'Inara' (4)	CQua
'Inca' (6)	CQua
'Inchbonnie' (2)	CQua
'Independence Day' (4)	CQua
'Indian Maid' (7) 🏆H4	CQua IRhd
'Indora' (4)	CQua
'Inner Glow' (2)	IRhd
'Innisidgen' (8)	CQua
'Innovator' (4)	CQua
'Innuendo' (2) **new**	IRhd
'Inny River' (1)	IRhd
'Interim' (2)	CQua
× ***intermedius*** (13)	CQua WAbe WCot
§ - 'Compressus' (8)	CQua
'Intrigue' (7) 🏆H4	CQua LRHS
'Invercassley' (3)	CQua
'Ireland's Eye' (9)	CQua
'Irene Copeland' (4)	CQua
'Irish Fire' (2)	CQua
'Irish Light' (2)	CQua
'Irish Luck' (1)	CQua
'Irish Minstrel' (2) 🏆H4	CQua
'Irish Mist' (2)	CQua
'Irish Rum' (2) **new**	CQua

'Irish Wedding' (2)	CQua
'Isambard' (4)	CQua
'Island Pride' (8) **new**	CQua
'Islander' (4)	CQua
'Ita' (2)	IRhd
'Itzim' (6) ♀H4	CQua EBrs ECho SDeJ
jacetanus (13)	MSSP NMin
'Jack Snipe' (6) ♀H4	CAvo CFFs CHid CQua EBrs ECho EPfP EPot LAma LRHS MBri SDeJ WShi
'Jack Wood' (11a)	CQua
'Jackadee' (2)	CQua IRhd
'Jake' (3)	IRhd
'Jamage' (8)	CQua
'Jamaica Inn' (4)	CQua
'Jamboree' (2)	CQua
'Jammin' (3) **new**	IRhd
'Janelle' (2)	CQua
'Jantje' (11a)	CQua
'Jauno' (1)	IRhd
'Javelin' (2)	CQua
'Jeanine' (2)	CQua
'Jeanne Bicknell' (4)	CQua
'Jedna' (2)	CQua
'Jenny' (6) ♀H4	CMea CQua CTca EBla EBrs ECho EPot ERCP LAma MCot NBir SDeJ WShi
'Jersey Carlton' (2)	CQua
'Jersey Lace' (2) **new**	CQua
'Jersey Roundabout' (4)	CQua
'Jersey Sun'	LRHS
'Jersey Torch' (4)	CQua
'Jetfire' (6) ♀H4	CFox CQua EBrs ECho EPfP EPot ERCP GKev LAma LRHS LSou SDeJ SPer WShi
'Jimmy Noone' (1)	CQua
'Jim's Gold' (2)	CQua
'Jingle Bells' (4) **new**	CQua
'Jodi' (11b)	IRhd
'Jodi's Sister' (11a)	IRhd
'John Daniel' (4)	CQua
'John Lanyon' (3)	CQua
'John Philip Sousa' (2) **new**	CQua
'John's Delight' (3)	CQua
× ***johnstonii***	see *N.* × *taitii*
jonquilla (13) ♀H4	CQua EPot LAma LEdu NMin WShi
§ - var. ***henriquesii*** (13)	CQua ECho NMin SCnR
'Joppa' (7)	CQua
'Joy Bishop'	see *N. romieuxii* 'Joy Bishop'
'Joybell' (6)	CQua
'Juanita' (2)	EPfP LRHS SDeJ
'Jules Verne' (2)	CQua
'Julia Jane'	see *N. romieuxii* 'Julia Jane'
'Jumblie' (12) ♀H4	CQua EPfP EPot GGar LAma LRHS MBri SDeJ
'Jumbo Gold' (1)	CTri
juncifolius Req. ex Lag.	see *N. assoanus*
'June Lake' (2)	CQua IRhd
'Junior Miss' (12)	NMin
'Kabani' (9)	CQua
'Kaka Point' **new**	IRhd
'Kalimna' (1)	CQua
'Kamau' (9)	IRhd
'Kamms' (1)	CQua
'Kamura' (2)	CQua
'Kanchenjunga' (1)	CQua
'Katherine Jenkins' (7) **new**	CQua
'Kathy A' **new**	IRhd
'Kathy's Clown' (6)	CQua
'Katie Heath' (5)	ECho ERCP LRHS SDeJ
'Katrina Rea' (6)	CQua
'Kaydee' (6) ♀H4	CQua IRhd LRHS SPhx WShi
'Kea' (6)	CQua
'Keats' (4)	CQua NMin
'Kebaya' (2)	CQua
'Kedron' (7) **new**	ERCP
'Kelly Bray' (1)	CQua
'Kenellis' (10)	CQua EPot GEdr
'Kernow' (2)	CQua
'Kidling' (7)	CQua ECho EPot NMin
'Killara' (8)	CQua
'Killigrew' (2)	CQua
'Killivose' (3)	CQua
'Kilmood' (2)	CQua
'Kiltonga' (2)	IRhd
'Kilworth' (2)	CQua
'Kimmeridge' (3)	CQua
'King Alfred' (1)	CQua EPfP GKir SDeJ SPer
'King Size' (11a)	CQua
'Kinglet' (7)	CQua
'King's Grove' (1) ♀H4	CQua
'Kings Pipe' (2)	CQua
'Kingscourt' (1) ♀H4	CQua
'Kingsleigh' (1)	IRhd
'Kingsmill Lake' (2) **new**	CQua
'Kirklington' (2)	CQua
'Kissproof' (2)	EBla
'Kit Hill' (7)	CQua CTca
'Kitten' (6)	CQua
'Kiwi Magic' (4)	CQua IRhd
'Kiwi Solstice' (4)	CQua
'Kiwi Sunset' (4)	CQua
'Knightsbridge' (1) **new**	CQua
'Knocklayde' (3)	CQua
'Knowehead' (2) **new**	CQua
'Knowing Look' (3)	IRhd
'Kokopelli' (7) ♀H4	CQua LRHS NMin
'Koomooloo' (2) **new**	CQua
'Korora Bay' (1)	IRhd
'La Riante' (3)	CQua
'La Vella' (2)	CQua
'Ladies' Choice' (7)	IRhd
'Ladies' Favorite' (7)	IRhd
'Lady Alice' (7) **new**	CQua
'Lady Ann' (2)	IRhd
'Lady Be Good' (2)	CQua
'Lady Diana' (2)	CQua
'Lady Emily' (2)	CQua
'Lady Eve' (11a)	IRhd
'Lady Hilaria' (2) **new**	CQua
'Lady Margaret Boscawen' (2)	CQua
'Lady Serena' (9)	CQua
'Lake District' **new**	IRhd
'Lake Tahoe' (2)	IRhd
'Lalique' (3)	CQua
'Lamanva' (2)	CQua
'Lamlash' (2)	IRhd
'Lancaster' (3)	CQua
'Landewednack Lady' (4) **new**	CQua
'Langarth' (11a)	CQua
'Lapwing' (5)	IRhd
'Larkelly' (6)	CQua
'Larkhill' (2)	CQua
'Larkwhistle' (6) ♀H4	LAma SDeJ
'Las Vegas' (1)	LRHS
'Latchley' (2)	CQua
'Lauren' (3)	IRhd
'Laurens Koster' (8)	CQua
'Lava Flow' (3) **new**	IRhd
'Lavender Lass' (6)	CQua
'Lavender Mist' (2)	CQua
'Lazy River' (1)	CQua

'Leading Light' (2)	CQua
'Lee Moor' (1)	CQua
'Lemon Beauty' (11b)	CQua EBla SDeJ
'Lemon Drizzle' (2) **new**	CQua
'Lemon Drops' (5)	CMea EBrs ECho EPot ERCP LRHS SDeJ SPhx
'Lemon Grey' (3)	IRhd
'Lemon Haze' (2) **new**	CQua
'Lemon Silk' (6)	CMea CQua ECho LPio NMin SPhx
'Lemon Snow' (2)	IRhd
'Lemonade' (3)	CQua
'Lennymore' (2)	CQua IRhd
'Lewis George' (1)	CQua
'Libby' (2)	IRhd
'Liberty Bells' (5)	CQua ECho LAma MBri
'Liebeslied' (3)	CQua
'Life' (7)	CQua
'Lifeline' (1) **new**	IRhd
'Lighthouse' (3)	CQua
'Lighthouse Reef' (1)	CQua IRhd
'Lilac Charm' (6)	CQua IRhd
'Lilac Mist' (2)	CQua
'Lilliput' ambig.	CQua
'Limbo' (2)	CQua IRhd
'Limehurst' (2)	CQua
'Limequilla' (7) **new**	CQua
'Limpopo' (3)	IRhd
'Lindsay Joy' (2)	CQua
'Lintie' (7)	CQua
'Lisbarnett' (3)	IRhd
'Lisnamulligan' (3)	IRhd
'Lisnaruddy' (3)	IRhd
'Little Beauty' (1) ♀H4	CBgR CQua ECho LAma NMin
'Little Dancer' (1)	CQua
'Little Dorr' (4)	IRhd
'Little Gem'	see *N. minor* 'Little Gem'
'Little Jewel' (3)	CQua
'Little Karoo' (3)	IRhd
'Little Rosie' (2)	IRhd
'Little Rusky' (7)	CQua NMin
'Little Sentry' (7)	CQua
'Little Soldier' (10)	CQua NMin
'Little Spell' (1)	CQua
'Little Tyke' (2) **new**	CQua
'Little Witch' (6)	CQua ECho EPfP EPot LAma SDeJ SPhx WShi
'Littlefield' (7)	CQua
'Livelands' (1) **new**	CQua
'Liverpool Festival' (2)	CQua
lobularis (Haw.) Schult. & Schult. f.	CArn CAvo CFFs CQua CTca CTri EBrs ECho EPot MBri SDeJ SPer SPhx
lobularis misapplied	see *N. nanus*
'Loch Alsh' (3)	CQua IRhd
'Loch Assynt' (3)	CQua
'Loch Brora' (2)	CQua
'Loch Coire' (3)	CQua
'Loch Fada' (2)	CQua
'Loch Hope' (2)	CQua
'Loch Leven' (2)	CQua
'Loch Loyal' (2)	CQua
'Loch Lundie' (2)	CQua
'Loch Maberry' (2)	CQua
'Loch Naver' (2)	CQua
'Loch Owskeich' (2) ♀H4	CQua
'Loch Stac' (2)	CQua
'Logan Rock' (7)	CQua
'Longitude' (1)	IRhd
'Lordship' (1)	CQua
'Lorikeet' (1)	CQua
'Loth Lorien' (3) **new**	NMin
'Lothario' (2)	LAma MBri
'Lough Gowna' (1)	IRhd

'Love Call' (11a) **new**	CQua
'Loveny' (2)	CQua
'Lubaantun' (1)	CQua
'Lucifer' (2)	CQua WShi
'Lucky Chance' (11a)	IRhd
'Lundy Light' (2)	CQua
'Lynher' (2)	CQua
'Lyrebird' (3)	CQua
'Lyric' (9)	CQua
'Lysander' (2)	CQua
× ***macleayi*** (13)	NMin
'Madam Speaker' (4)	CQua
'Madison' (4)	CQua
'Magic Moment' (3) **new**	CQua
'Magician' (2)	CQua IRhd
'Magna Carta' (2)	CQua
'Magnet' (1)	LAma
'Magnificence' (1)	CQua
'Mai's Family' (6)	CQua
'Majestic Star' (1)	CQua
'Mallee' (11a) ♀H4	IRhd
'Malpas' (3)	CQua
'Malvern City' (1)	CQua LRHS
'Mamma Mia' (4)	IRhd
'Manaccan' (1)	CQua
'Mangaweka' (6)	CQua
'Manly' (4) ♀H4	CQua ERCP
'Mantle' (2)	CQua
'Marabou' (4)	CQua
'Maria Pia' (11a)	IRhd
'Marie Curie Diamond' (7) **new**	CQua
'Marieke' (1)	LAma
'Marilyn Anne' (2)	CQua
'Marjorie Hine' (2)	CQua
'Marjorie Treveal' (4)	CQua
'Marlborough' (2)	CQua
'Marlborough Freya' (2)	CQua
'Marshfire' (2)	CQua
'Martha Washington' (8)	CQua
'Martinette' (8)	CQua CTca MBri SDeJ
'Martinsville' (8)	CQua
marvieri	see *N. rupicola* subsp. *marvieri*
'Mary Copeland' (4)	CQua
'Mary Kate' (2)	CQua IRhd
'Mary Lou' (6)	IRhd
'Mary Rosina' **new**	CQua
'Mary Veronica' (3)	CQua
'Marzo' (7)	CQua IRhd NMin
'Matador' (8)	CQua IRhd
'Mawla' (1)	CQua
'Max' (11a)	CQua
'Maximus Superbus' (1) **new**	CQua
'Maya Dynasty' (2)	CQua
'Mazzard' (4)	CQua
'Media Girl' (2)	IRhd
× ***medioluteus*** (13)	CQua NMin
'Melancholy' (1)	CQua
'Melbury' (2)	CQua
'Meldrum' (1)	CQua
'Memento' (1)	CQua
'Menabilly' (4)	CQua
'Měn-an-Tol' (2)	CQua
'Menehay' (11a) ♀H4	CQua
'Mereworth' (2) **new**	CQua
'Merlin' (3) ♀H4	CQua LAma NMin SDeJ
'Merry Bells' (5)	CQua
'Merrymeet' (4)	CQua
'Mersing' (3)	CQua
'Merthan' (9)	CQua
'Michaels Gold' (2)	CQua

	'Midas Touch' (1)	CQua
	'Midget'	see *N. nanus* 'Midget'
	'Mike Pollock' (8)	CQua
	'Milan' (9)	CQua
	'Millennium Sunrise' (2)	CQua
	'Millennium Sunset' (2)	CQua
	'Millgreen' (1)	LRHS
	'Milly's Magic' (2)	CQua
	Minicycla Group (6)	ECho MSSP
	minimus misapplied	see *N. asturiensis*
	'Minnow' (8) ♀H3	CAvo CFFs CFox CMea CQua CStu EBrs ECho EPfP ERCP GKev LAma LRHS MBri NBir SDeJ SPer SPhx
	minor (13) ♀H4	CQua ECha ECho EPot GKev LAma LRHS NMin WCot WShi
§	- 'Little Gem' (1) ♀H4	CQua CTri EBrs EPfP LAma LRHS SPhx
	- var. ***pumilus*** 'Plenus'	see *N.* 'Rip van Winkle'
	- Ulster form	IBlr MSSP
	'Mint Julep' (3) ♀H4	EBrs SPhx
	'Minute Waltz' (6)	CQua
	'Mirar' (2)	CQua
	'Misquote' (1) **new**	CQua
	'Miss Klein'	CQua NMin
	'Miss Muffit' (1)	CAvo CBgR CFFs CQua
	'Mission Bells' (5) ♀H4	CQua IRhd
	'Mission Impossible' (11a)	CQua
	'Misty Glen' (2) ♀H4	CQua NMin
	'Misty Moon' (3)	CQua
	'Mite' (6) ♀H4	CMea CQua EBrs EPot LAma NMin
	'Mithrel' (11a)	CQua
	'Mitylene' (2)	CQua
	'Mitzy'	NMin
	'Modern Art' (2)	CQua
	'Mondragon' (11a)	CQua LRHS
	'Mongleath' (2)	CQua
	'Monks Wood' (1)	CQua
	'Monksilver' (3)	CQua
	'Montclair' (2)	CQua
	'Montego' (3)	CQua
	'Montroig' **new**	IRhd
	'Moon Dream' (1)	CQua
	'Moon Ranger' (3)	CQua IRhd
	'Moon Shadow' (3)	CQua
	'Moon Valley' (2)	IRhd
	'Moonstruck' (1)	CQua
	'Morab' (1)	CQua
	'Moralee' (4)	IRhd
	'Morvah Lady' (5)	CQua
	'Morval' (2)	CQua
	moschatus (13) ♀H4	CQua ECho EPot LAma LRHS NMin SPhx WCot WShi
	'Motmot'	CQua
	'Mount Fuji' (2)	CQua
	'Mount Hood' (1) ♀H4	EBrs EPfP ERCP GKev LAma LRHS NBir SDeJ SPer SPhx
	'Mount Rainier' (1)	CQua
	'Movie Star' (2)	IRhd
	'Mowser' (7)	CQua
	'Mr Julian' (6)	CQua
	'Mrs Langtry' (3)	CQua WShi
	'Mrs R.O. Backhouse' (2)	CQua EBla WShi
	'Mullion' (3)	CQua
	'Mulroy Bay' (1)	CQua IRhd
	'Murlough' (9)	CQua
	'Muscadet' (2)	CQua
	'My Story' (4)	LRHS
	'My Sunshine' (2)	CQua
	'My Sweetheart' **new**	CQua
	'Mystic' (3)	CQua
	'Naivasha' (2)	IRhd
	'Namraj' (2)	CQua
	'Nancegollan' (7)	CQua
	'Nangiles' (4)	CQua
	'Nanpee' (7)	CQua
	'Nansidwell' (2)	CQua
	'Nanstallon' (1)	CQua
§	***nanus***	CWCL
§	- 'Midget' (1)	CQua EBrs ECho EPot ERCP GKev LAma SKHP
	'Narrative' (2)	IRhd
	'Navarre' Gathorne-Hardy	see *N. asturiensis* 'Navarre'
	'Nederburg' (1)	IRhd
	'Neon Light' (2) **new**	CQua
	'Nether Barr' (2)	CQua
	nevadensis (13)	EPot SKHP
	'New Hope' (3)	CQua
	'New Life' (3)	CQua
	'New Paris' (2) **new**	CQua
	'New Penny' (3)	CQua IRhd NMin
	'New World' (2)	CQua
	'New-Baby' (7)	CQua CTca EPfP LRHS NMin WClo
	'Newcastle' (1)	CQua
	'Newcomer' (3)	CQua
	'Night Music' (4)	CQua IRhd
	'Nightcap' (1)	CQua
	'Niveth' (5)	CQua
§	***nobilis*** (13)	CQua EPot
	- var. ***leonensis*** (13)	ECho
	- var. ***nobilis*** (13)	NMin
	'Nonchalant' (3)	CQua IRhd
	'Norma Jean' (2)	CQua
	'North Liberty' (2) **new**	CQua
	'North Rim' (2)	CQua
	'Noss Mayo' (6)	CQua
	'Notre Dame' (2) ♀H4	CQua IRhd
	'Numen Rose' (2)	IRhd
	Nylon Group (10)	ECho EPot GEdr LPio MSSP WCot
	- yellow-flowered (10)	ECho EPot
	'Oadby' (1)	CQua
	'Obdam' (4)	EBla SDeJ
	'Obelisk' (11a)	CQua
	'Obsession' (2)	CQua
	obvallaris (13) ♀H4	CAvo CFFs CQua CTca ECho EPfP EPot ERCP LRHS NHol SDeJ SGar SPer SPhx WHer WShi
	'Ocarino' (4)	CQua
	'Ocean Blue' (2)	IRhd
	'Odd Job'	CQua
	× ***odorus*** (13)	LRHS WShi
§	- 'Double Campernelle' (4)	CQua ECho SDeJ WShi
	- 'Plenus' (d) **new**	ERCP
	'Oecumene' (11a)	CQua
	'Ohau Lights' (1) **new**	CQua
	old pheasant's eye	see *N. poeticus* var. *recurvus*
	'Ombersley' (1) **new**	CQua
	'Orange Queen' (3)	EBrs
	'Orange Tint' (2) **new**	CQua
	'Orange Walk' (3)	CQua IRhd
	'Orangery' (11a)	EBla LAma
	'Orbital Pink' (3)	IRhd
	'Orchard Place' (3)	CQua
	'Oregon Bells' (7) **new**	CQua
	'Oregon Lights' (2) **new**	NMin
	'Oregon Pioneer' (2)	IRhd
	'Oregon Snow' (2) ♀H4	LRHS
	'Orkney' (2)	CQua
	'Ormeau' (2) ♀H4	CQua
	'Oryx' (7) ♀H4	CQua
	'Osceola' (2) **new**	CQua
	'Osmington' (2)	CQua
	'Ouma' (1)	CQua
	'Outline' (2)	IRhd
	'Ouzel' (6)	CQua

	'Owyhee' (2) **new**	CQua
	'Oykel' (3)	CQua
	'Oz' (12)	CQua
	pachybolbus	ECho NMin SPhx
	'Pacific Coast' (8) 🏆^{H4}	CQua ECho EPfP LAma LRHS NMin
	'Pacific Mist' (11a)	CQua
	'Pacific Rim' (2)	CQua IRhd
	'Painted Desert' (3)	CQua
	'Palace Pink' (2)	IRhd
	'Pale Sunlight' (2)	CQua
	pallidiflorus (13)	ECha
	'Palmares' (11a)	CQua LEdu SDeJ
	'Pamela Hubble' (2)	CQua
	'Pamela Joan' (2) **new**	CQua
	'Pampaluna' (11a)	CQua
	'Panache' (1)	CQua
	'Pandemonium' (3)	IRhd
	panizzianus	CQua
	'Panorama Pink' (3)	IRhd
	'Paper White'	see *N. papyraceus*
	'Paper White Grandiflorus' (8)	CQua EPfP MBri SPer WClo
	'Papillon Blanc' (11b)	EBrs ERCP
	'Papua' (4) 🏆^{H4}	CQua
§	***papyraceus*** (13)	CFox CQua CStu CTca EBrs ECho GKev LAma LRHS
	'Paradigm' (4)	IRhd
	'Paramour' (4)	IRhd
	'Parisienne' (11a)	EBla
	'Park Springs' (3)	CQua NMin
	'Parkdene' (2)	CQua
	'Party Time' (2)	IRhd
	'Passionale' (2) 🏆^{H4}	CQua LAma NBir
	'Pastiche' (2)	CQua
	'Patabundy' (2)	CQua
	'Pathos' (3)	IRhd
	'Patois' (9)	CQua IRhd
	'Patrick Hacket' (1)	CQua
	'Pay Day' (1)	CQua
	'Peach Prince' (4)	CQua
	'Peaches and Cream' (2)	LRHS
	'Pearl Wedding' (3)	CQua
	'Pearlshell' (11a)	CQua
	'Peeping Tom' (6) 🏆^{H4}	ECho ERCP LAma SDeJ SRms
	'Peggy's Gift' (3)	IRhd
	'Pemboa' (1)	CQua
	'Pencrebar' (4)	CAvo CHid CQua EPot LAma NMin SDeJ WShi
	'Pend Oreille' (3)	CQua
	'Pengarth' (2)	CQua
	'Penjerrick' (9)	CQua
	'Penkivel' (2) 🏆^{H4}	CQua
	'Pennance Mill' (2)	CQua
	'Pennine Way' (1)	CQua
	'Penny Perowne' (7) **new**	CQua
	'Pennyfield' (2)	CQua
	'Penpol' (7)	CQua
	'Penril' (6)	CBgR CQua
	'Penstraze' (7)	CQua
	'Pentewan' (2)	CQua LRHS
	'Pentille' (1)	CQua
	'Pentire' (11a)	CQua
	'Penvale'	CQua
	'Peppercorn' (6)	CQua
	'Percuil' (6)	CQua
	'Perdredda' (3)	CQua
	perez-chiscanoi (13)	SKHP
	'Perimeter' (3)	CQua
	'Peripheral Pink' (2)	CQua
	'Perky' (1970) (6) **new**	NMin
	'Perlax' (11a)	CQua
	'Perpetuation' (7) **new**	CQua
	'Personable' (2)	CQua
	'Petanca' (5)	IRhd
	'Petit Four' (4)	EBla LAma SDeJ
	'Petrel' (5)	CQua EBrs EPot ERCP LRHS SDeJ SPhx
	'Phalarope' (6)	CQua
	'Phantom' (11a)	CQua
	'Phil's Gift' (1)	CQua
	'Phinda' (2)	IRhd
	'Phoenician' (2)	CQua
	'Piano Concerto' (2) **new**	NMin
	'Picatou' (3)	IRhd
	'Picoblanco' (2)	CQua NMin
	'Pigeon' (2)	CQua
	'Pineapple Prince' (2) 🏆^{H4}	CQua
	'Pink Angel' (7)	CQua
	'Pink Champagne' (4)	CQua
	'Pink Charm' (2)	CQua
	'Pink China' (2) **new**	CQua
	'Pink Clover' (2) **new**	CQua
	'Pink Evening' (2)	CQua
	'Pink Formal' (11a)	CQua
	'Pink Gilt' (2)	IRhd
	'Pink Glacier' (11a)	CQua
	'Pink Holly' (11a)	CQua
	'Pink Ice' (2)	CQua
	'Pink Pageant' (4)	CQua IRhd
	'Pink Paradise' (4)	CQua IRhd
	'Pink Parasol' (1) **new**	SDeJ
	'Pink Perry' (2)	IRhd
	'Pink Sapphire' (2)	CQua
	'Pink Silk' (1)	CQua
	'Pink Smiles' (2)	SPer
	'Pink Surprise' (2)	CQua
	'Pink Tango' (11a)	CQua
	'Pinza' (2) 🏆^{H4}	CQua
	'Pipe Major' (2)	CQua EPfP SPer
	'Pipers Barn' (7)	CQua
	'Piper's End' (3)	CQua
	'Piper's Gold' (1)	CQua
	'Pipestone' (2)	CQua
	'Pipit' (7) 🏆^{H4}	CAvo CFFs CMea CQua ECho EPfP ERCP GKev LAma MBri MNrw NBir SDeJ SPer WClo WShi
	'Piraeus' (4)	IRhd
	'Pismo Beach' (2)	CQua
	'Pitchroy' (2)	CQua
	'Pitt's Diamond' (3)	CQua
	'Pixie's Sister' (7) 🏆^{H4}	CQua NMin
	'Pledge' (1)	NMin
	poeticus (13)	CAvo WHer
§	– var. ***hellenicus*** (13)	CQua
	– old pheasant's eye	see *N. poeticus* var. *recurvus*
	– var. ***physaloides*** (13)	CQua ECho SPhx
	– 'Plenus' misapplied	see *N.* 'Tamar Double White'
§	– 'Plenus' ambig. (4)	CQua ERCP GKir GQui SDeJ WShi
§	– var. ***recurvus*** (13) 🏆^{H4}	CArn CFFs CFox CQua CTca EBrs ECho EPfP ERCP LAma NBir SDeJ SPhx WShi
	'Poet's Way' (9)	CQua
	'Pol Crocan' (2)	CQua IRhd
	'Pol Dornie' (2)	CQua
	'Pol Voulin' (2)	CQua IRhd
	'Polonaise' (2) **new**	CQua
	'Polar Ice' (3)	LAma SDeJ
	'Polar Morn' (3) **new**	CQua
	'Polgooth' (2)	CQua
	'Polly's Pearl' (8)	CQua
	'Polwheveral' (2)	CQua
	polyanthus from Morocco	WCot
	'Pooka' (3)	IRhd
	'Poppy's Choice' (4)	CQua

	'Pops Legacy' (1)	CQua IRhd
	'Porthchapel' (7)	CQua
	'Portloe Bay' (3)	CQua
	'Portrush' (3)	CQua
	'Potential' (1)	CQua
	'Powerstock' (2)	IRhd
	'Praecox' (9) **new**	CQua
	'Prairie Fire' (3)	CQua IRhd
	'Pratincole' (3)	IRhd
	'Preamble' (1)	CQua
I	'Precocious' (2) ♀H4	CQua LRHS
	'Premiere' (2)	CQua
	'Presidential Pink' (2)	CQua
	'Pretty Baby' (3)	CQua
	'Pride of Cornwall' (8)	CQua
	'Primrose Beauty' (4)	CQua
	'Princeps' (1)	CQua
	'Princess Zaide' (3)	CQua
	'Princeton' (3)	CQua
	'Printal' (11a)	SDeJ
	'Prism' (2)	CQua
	'Problem Child' (2)	IRhd
	'Probus' (1)	CQua
	'Professor Einstein' (2)	EPfP SDeJ
	'Prologue' (1)	CQua
	'Prototype' (6)	IRhd
	'Proud Fellow' (1)	IRhd
	'Proverbial Pink' (2)	IRhd
	'Prussia Cove' (2)	CQua
	pseudonarcissus (13) ♀H4	CFox CQua CRow LAma SPhx WHer WShi
	- subsp. ***nobilis***	see *N. nobilis*
	- subsp. ***pseudonarcissus*** (4) **new**	CQua
§	- - var. ***humilis*** (13)	ECho
§	- 'The O'Mahoney' **new**	WCot
	'Pueblo' (7)	CQua EBrs LRHS SDeJ
	'Pulsar' (2)	IRhd
	pumilus (13)	see *N. dubius*; *N. minor* var. *pumilus*
	pumilus ambig.	CQua ECho EPot NMin SDeJ WShi
	'Punchline' (7) ♀H4	CQua
	'Puppet' (5)	CQua
	'Purbeck' (3) ♀H4	CQua IRhd
	'Quail' (7) ♀H4	CQua CTca EPfP LAma LRHS LSou MBri SPer
	'Quasar' (2) ♀H4	CQua
	Queen Anne's double daffodil	see *N.* 'Eystettensis'
	'Queen Juliana' (1)	CQua
	'Queen Mum' (1)	CQua
	'Queen of Spain' (10)	CQua
	'Queen's Guard' (1)	IRhd
	'Quick Step' (7)	CQua
	'Quiet Day' (2)	CQua
	'Quiet Hero' (3)	IRhd
	'Quiet Man' (1)	IRhd
	'Radiant Gem' (8)	CQua
	radiiflorus var. ***poetarum*** (13)	CQua
	'Radjel' (4)	CQua
	'Rainbow' (2) ♀H4	CQua
	'Rame Head' (1)	CQua
	'Rameses' (2)	CQua
	'Ransom' (4)	IRhd
	'Rapid Stride' (6) **new**	IRhd
	'Rapture' (6) ♀H4	CQua IRhd NMin
	'Rashee' (1)	CQua
	'Raspberry Ring' (2)	CQua
	'Rathowen Gold' (1)	CQua
	'Ravenhill' (3)	CQua
	'Rebekah' (4)	CQua
	'Recital' (2)	CQua
	'Red Coat' (2)	CQua
	'Red Devon' (2) ♀H4	CBgR CQua SDeJ
	'Red Era' (3)	CQua
	'Red Legend' (2) **new**	CQua
	'Red Lips' (2) **new**	CQua
	'Red Reed' (1)	IRhd
	'Red Socks' (6)	CQua
	'Red Spartan' (2)	CQua
	'Refrain' (2)	CQua
	'Regal Bliss' (2)	CQua
	'Reggae' (6) ♀H4	CQua ERCP LRHS
	'Rembrandt' (1)	CQua
	'Rendezvous Caye' (2)	CQua
	'Replete' (4)	CQua EBla EBrs
	'Reprieve' (3)	CQua
	requienii	see *N. assoanus*
	'Resistasol' (1)	IRhd
	'Reverse Image' (11a)	CQua
	'Ribald' (2)	IRhd
	'Ridgecrest' (3)	IRhd
	rifanus	see *N. romieuxii* subsp. *romieuxii* var. *rifanus*
	'Rijnveld's Early Sensation' (1) ♀H4	CAvo CFFs CMea CQua EBrs ECha ERCP
	'Rikki' (7)	CQua NMin
	'Rima' (1)	CQua
	'Rimmon' (3)	CQua
	'Ring Fence' (3)	IRhd
	'Ringhaddy' (3)	IRhd
	'Ringing Bells' (5)	CQua
	'Ringleader' (2)	CQua
	'Ringmaster' (2)	CQua
	'Ringmer' (3)	CQua
	'Rio Bravo' (2)	IRhd
	'Rio Gusto' (2)	IRhd
	'Rio Lobo' (2)	IRhd
	'Rio Rondo' (2)	IRhd
	'Rio Rouge' (2)	IRhd
§	'Rip van Winkle' (4)	CAvo CFox CQua CSWP CTca CWCL EBla EBrs EPfP EPot ERCP IFro LAma LRHS MBri SDeJ WShi
	'Rippling Waters' (5) ♀H4	CQua EPot LAma
	'Ristin' (1)	CQua
	'Rival' (6)	CQua
	'River Dance' (2)	IRhd
	'River Queen' (2)	CQua IRhd
	'Rockall' (3)	CQua
	'Rockery White' (1)	NMin
	'Rocoza' **new**	IRhd
	'Roger' (6)	CQua
	'Rogue' (2) **new**	CBro
	'Romance' (2) ♀H4	EBrs LAma
§	'Romanus' (4)	CQua
	romieuxii (13) ♀H2-3	CDes CPBP EPot ITim LPio LRHS MSSP SCnR WCot
	- JCA	WWst
	- JCA 805	EPot WWst
	- SB&L 237	WCot
	- SF 370	WCot
	- subsp. ***albidus*** (13)	ECho EPot WCot
	- - SF 110	WCot
§	- - var. ***zaianicus*** (13)	ECho SPhx
	- - - SB&L 82	MSSP WCot
I	- - - f. ***lutescens*** (13)	GEdr
§	- 'Atlas Gold' (10)	EPot GEdr SCnR
§	- 'Joy Bishop' (10)	EPot GEdr NMen SCnR
§	- 'Julia Jane' (10)	EBrs ECho EPot GEdr GKev LPio NMin SCnR SPhx WCot
	- subsp. ***romieuxii*** (13)	GKev
§	- - var. ***mesatlanticus*** (13)	ECho WCot
§	- - var. ***rifanus*** (13)	ECho SPhx

	- - - B 8929	WCot
§	- 'Treble Chance' (10)	EPot GEdr
	'Rory's Glen' (2)	CQua
	'Rosannor Gold' (11a)	CQua
	'Roscarrick' (6)	CQua
	'Rose of May' (4)	CQua WShi
	'Rose of Tralee' (2)	CQua
	'Rose Royale' (2)	CQua
	'Rose Sheen' (2) **new**	CQua
	'Rose Villa' (2) **new**	CQua
	'Rosemerryn' (2)	CQua
	'Rosemoor Gold' ♀H4	CQua
	'Rosemullion' (4) **new**	CQua
	'Rosevine' (3)	CQua
	'Roseworthy' (2)	EBla
	'Rosy Wonder' (2)	CQua
	'Roxton' (4)	IRhd
	'Royal Armour' (1)	LRHS
	'Royal Ballet' (2)	CQua
	'Royal Connection' (8)	CQua
	'Royal Marine' (2)	CQua
	'Royal Princess' (3)	CQua LRHS
	'Royal Regiment' (2)	CQua
	'Rubh Mor' (2)	CQua
	'Ruby Red' (2) **new**	CQua
	'Ruby Rose' (4)	IRhd
	'Ruby Wedding' (2)	IRhd
	'Rubythroat' (2)	CQua
	'Ruddy Duck' **new**	IRhd
	'Ruddy Rascal' (2)	IRhd
	'Rugulosus' (7) ♀H4	CQua ECho
*	'Rugulosus Flore Pleno' (d)	ECho LRHS
	'Rumpus' (3)	IRhd
	'Runkerry' (4) **new**	IRhd
	rupicola (13)	CQua EBrs ECho EPot MSSP NMen NMin NSla NWCA SCnR WWst
§	- subsp. ***marvieri*** (13) ♀H2	EPot
§	- subsp. ***watieri*** (13)	CQua ECho EPot ITim LLHF NMin WCot
	'Rustom Pasha' (2)	CQua
	'Rytha' (2)	CQua
	'Saberwing' (5)	CQua
	'Sabine Hay' (3)	CQua EBrs ERCP
	'Sabrosa' (7)	CQua NMin
	'Sacré Coeur' (2)	IRhd
	'Sagana' (9)	CQua
	'Sailboat' (7) ♀H4	CQua LRHS
	'Saint Agnes' (8)	CQua
	'Saint Budock' (1)	CQua
	'Saint Day' (5)	CQua
	'Saint Dilpe' (2)	CQua
	'Saint Keverne' (2) ♀H4	CQua EPfP LRHS SDeJ
	'Saint Keyne' (8)	CQua
	'Saint Patrick's Day' (2)	CQua EBla LAma SDeJ SPer
	'Saint Peter' (4)	CQua
	'Saint Petroc' (9)	CQua
	'Saint Piran' (7)	CQua
	'Salakee' (2)	CQua
	'Salcey Forest' (1)	CQua
	'Salmon Trout' (2)	CQua
	'Salome' (2) ♀H4	CQua EBla EPfP LAma LRHS NBir SDeJ
	'Salute' (2)	CQua
	'Samantha' (4)	CQua
	'Sancerre' (11a)	CQua
	'Sandycove' (2)	CQua
	'Santa Claus' (4)	CQua
	'Sarah Dear' (2)	CQua
	'Sargeant's Caye' (1)	CQua
	'Satchmo' (1)	CQua
	'Satsuma' (1)	CQua
	'Saturn' (3)	CQua
	'Savoir Faire' (2)	IRhd
	scaberulus (13)	ECho EPot
	'Scarlet Chord' (2)	CQua
	'Scarlet Elegance' (2)	CQua
	'Scarlet Gem' (8)	SDeJ
	'Scarlett O'Hara' (2)	CQua
	'Scented Breeze' (2)	IRhd
	'Scilly Spring' (8)	CAvo
	'Scilly White' (8)	CQua
	'Scorrier' (2)	CQua
	'Scrumpy' (2)	CQua
	'Sea Dream' (3)	CQua
	'Sea Green' (9)	CQua
	'Sea Legend' (2)	CQua
	'Sea Princess' (3)	CQua
	'Sea Shanty' (2)	IRhd
	'Seagull' (3)	CAvo CQua ECho LAma WShi
	'Sealing Wax' (2)	CQua
	'Segovia' (3) ♀H4	CMea CQua EBla EBrs EPot LAma LRHS NMin SCnR SPer SPhx
	'Sempre Avanti' (2)	LAma MBri SDeJ
	'Seraglio' (3)	CQua
	'Serena Beach' (4)	IRhd
	'Serena Lodge' (4) ♀H4	CQua IRhd
	serotinus L. (13)	ECho EPot WCot
	- MK 6374	WWst
	'Sextant' (6)	CQua
	'Shangani' (2)	IRhd
	'Sheelagh Rowan' (2)	CQua IRhd
	'Sheer Joy' (6)	CQua IRhd
	'Shepherd's Hey' (7)	CQua EPfP
	'Sherborne' (4) ♀H4	CQua NMin
	'Sherpa' (1)	IRhd
	'Sheviock' (2)	CQua
	'Shindig' (2)	IRhd
	'Shining Light' (2)	CQua
	'Shockwave' (2) **new**	CQua
	'Shortcake' (2)	CQua
	'Shrimp Boat' (11a)	IRhd
	'Sidhe' (5)	CQua
	'Sidley' (3)	CQua IRhd
	'Signorina' (2)	IRhd
	'Silent Pink' (2)	NMin
	'Silent Valley' (1) ♀H4	CQua NMin
	'Silk Cut' (2)	CQua
	'Silkwood' (3)	CQua
	'Silver Bells' (5)	CQua
	'Silver Chimes' (8)	CAvo CQua CTca EBrs ECho EPfP LAma NBir SDeJ WClo
	'Silver Convention' (1)	CQua
	'Silver Crystal' (3)	IRhd
	'Silver Kiwi' (2)	CQua
	'Silver Minx' (1)	CQua
	'Silver Plate' (11a)	CQua
	'Silver Shell' (11a)	CQua
	'Silver Smiles' (7) **new**	SPhx
	'Silver Standard' (2)	CQua
	'Silver Surf' (2)	CQua IRhd
	'Silversmith' (2)	CQua
	'Silverthorne' (3)	CQua
	'Silverwood' (3)	CQua IRhd
	'Singing Pub' (3)	IRhd
	'Sinopel' (3)	LAma SDeJ
	'Sir Samuel' (2)	CQua
	'Sir Watkin' (2)	CQua
	'Sir Winston Churchill' (4) ♀H4	CQua EPfP LAma SDeJ SPer
	'Sissy' (6) **new**	CQua
	'Skerry' (2)	CQua
	'Skilliwidden' (2) ♀H4	CQua
	'Skookum' (3)	CQua
	'Skywalker' (2)	IRhd

'Slieveboy' (1)	CQua
'Slipstream' (6)	IRhd
'Small Fry' (1)	CQua
'Small Talk' (1)	CQua NMin
'Smiling Maestro' (2)	CQua
'Smokey Bear' (4)	CQua
'Smooth Sails' (3)	CQua
'Snipe' (6)	CQua NMin
'Snoopie' (6)	CQua
'Snowcrest' (3)	CQua
'Snowshill' (2)	CQua
'Soft Focus' (2)	IRhd
'Solar System' (3)	IRhd
'Solar Tan' (3)	CQua
'Soleil d'Or' (8)	CQua
'Solera' (2)	IRhd
'Solferique' (2)	CQua
'Soloist' (2)	IRhd
'Sonata' (9)	CQua
'Songket' (2)	CQua
'Sophie Girl' (2) **new**	CQua
'Soprano' (2)	CQua IRhd
'Sorcerer' (3)	CQua
'South Street' (2)	CQua
'Southease' (2)	CQua
'Spaniards Inn' (4)	CQua
'Sparkling Tarts' (8)	CQua
'Sparnon' (11a)	CQua
'Sparrow' (6)	CQua
'Special Envoy' (2) ♀H4	CQua
'Speenogue' (1)	IRhd
'Spellbinder' (1) ♀H4	CQua MBri
'Spencer Tracy'	CQua
'Spin Doctor' (3)	IRhd
'Spindletop' (3) ♀H4	IRhd
'Spirit of Rame' (3)	CQua
'Split Image' (2)	IRhd
'Split Vote' (11a)	IRhd
'Sportsman' (2)	CQua NMin
'Spring Dawn' (2)	EPfP LRHS LSou SPer
'Spring Morn' (2)	IRhd
'Spring Sunset' (2) **new**	IRhd
'Spun Honey' (4)	CQua
'Stadium' (2)	LAma
'Stainless' (2)	EBrs SPhx
'Stann Creek' (1)	CQua
'Stanway' (3)	CQua
'Star Glow' (2)	CQua
'Star Quality' (3)	IRhd
'Starfire' (7)	CQua
'State Express' (2)	CQua
'Steenbok' (3)	IRhd
'Stella' (2)	WShi
'Stella Glow' (3)	IRhd
'Stenalees' (6)	CQua
'Step Child' (6) **new**	CQua
'Step Forward' (7)	CQua
'Stilton' (9)	CQua
'Stinger' (2)	CQua
'Stint' (5) ♀H4	CQua
'Stocken' (7)	CPBP CQua MSSP NMin
'Stoke Charity' (2)	CQua
'Stoke Doyle' (2)	CQua
'Stormy Weather' (1)	CQua
'Stratosphere' (7) ♀H4	CQua NMin
'Strines' (2)	CQua NMin
'Suave' (3)	CQua
'Subtle Shades' (2)	IRhd
'Sugar and Spice' (3)	CQua
'Sugar Bird' (2)	IRhd
'Sugar Cups' (8)	CQua
'Sugar Loaf' (4)	CQua

	'Sugarbush' (7)	WShi
	'Suisgill' (4)	CQua
§	'Sulphur Phoenix' (4)	CQua WShi
	'Summer Solstice' (3)	IRhd
	'Sumo Jewel' (6)	CQua
	'Sun Disc' (7) ♀H4	CMea CQua CTri ECho EPot LAma LSou MBri NMin SDeJ SPer WClo WShi
	'Sunday Chimes' (5)	CQua
	'Sundial' (7)	CQua ECho EPot LAma NMin
	'Sunrise' (3)	CQua
	'Sunstroke' (2)	CQua
	'Suntory' (3)	CQua
	'Suntrap' (2)	IRhd
	'Surfside' (6) ♀H4	CQua LRHS
	'Surprise Packet' (2)	IRhd
	'Surrey' (2)	CQua
	'Suzie Dee' (6)	IRhd
	'Suzie's Sister' (6)	IRhd
	'Suzy' (7) ♀H4	SDeJ
	'Swaledale' (2)	CQua
	'Swallow' (6)	CBgR CQua LAma SDeJ
	'Swallow Wing' (6)	IRhd
	'Swanpool' (3)	CQua
	'Swanvale' (1)	CQua
	'Swedish Fjord' (2)	CQua
	'Sweet Blanche' (7)	CQua
	'Sweet Lorraine' (2)	CQua
	'Sweet Memory' (2) **new**	CQua
	'Sweet Sue' (3)	CQua NMin
	'Sweetness' (7) ♀H4	CAvo CFFs CQua LAma SPer WPtf WShi
	'Swift Arrow' (6) ♀H4	CQua
	'Swing Wing' (6)	CQua
	'Sydling' (5)	CQua
I	'Sylph' G.E. Mitsch (1)	CQua
	'Taffeta' (10)	ECho WCot
	'Tahiti' (4) ♀H4	CQua EPfP LAma SDeJ
§	× ***taitii***	CAvo CQua ECho NMin
	'Talgarth' (2)	CQua
§	'Tamar Double White' **new**	CBro CTca
	'Tamar Fire' (4) ♀H4	CQua
	'Tamar Lad' (2)	CQua CTca
	'Tamar Lass' (3)	CQua CTca
	'Tamar Snow' (2)	CQua
	'Tamara' (2)	CQua
	'Tangent' (2)	CQua
	'Tarnished Gold' (2) **new**	CQua
	'Tasgem' (4)	CQua
	'Taslass' (4)	CQua
	'Tater-du' (5)	CQua
	tazetta (13)	EBrs ECho
§	- subsp. ***lacticolor*** (13)	CQua ERCP LAma SDeJ
§	- - 'Grand Monarque' (8)	CQua
	- subsp. ***ochroleucus*** (13) **new**	CQua
*	- var. ***odoratus***	CQua WPtf
	'Teal' (1)	CQua
	'Tehidy' (3)	CQua
§	'Telamonius Plenus' (4)	CAvo CQua EBrs IGor WCot WShi
	'Temba' (1)	IRhd
	'Temple Cloud' (4)	IRhd
	tenuifolius	see *N. bulbocodium* subsp. *bulbocodium* var. *tenuifolius*
	'Terracotta' (2)	CQua IRhd
	'Terrapin' (3)	IRhd
	'Tête-à-tête' (12) ♀H4	CAvo CFFs CFox CHar CQua CTca CWCL EBrs EPfP EPot ERCP GKir LAma LRHS LSou MBri MNHC SDeJ SPer WClo WMoo WPtf
	'Texas' (4)	CQua

'Thalia' (5)	CAvo CFFs CFox CMea CQua CTca EBrs EPfP ERCP LAma LRHS MBri MCot NBir SDeJ SPer SPhx WClo WShi
'The Alliance' (6) ♀H4	CQua
'The Grange' (1)	CQua
'The Knave' (6)	CQua
'The O'Mahoney'	see *N. pseudonarcissus* 'The O'Mahoney'
'Thistin' (1)	IRhd
'Thoresby' (3)	CQua
'Thoughtful' (5)	CQua
'Tibet' (2)	CQua
'Tideford' (2)	CQua
'Tidy Tippet' (2)	IRhd
'Tiercel' (1)	CQua
'Tiffany Jade' (3)	CQua
'Tiger Moth' (6)	CQua
'Timolin' (3)	CQua
'Tinderbox' (2)	IRhd
'Tinhay' (7) **new**	CQua
'Tiritomba' (11a)	CQua
'Titania' (6)	CQua
'Tittle-tattle' (7)	CQua
'Toby' (2)	SDeJ
'Toby the First' (6)	CAvo CQua
'Tommora Gold' (2)	CQua
'Tommy White' (2)	CQua EBrs
'Top Hit' (11a)	CQua
'Topolino' (1) ♀H4	CAvo CFFs CFox CMea CQua EBrs EPot LAma SGar
'Toretta' (3)	IRhd
'Torianne' (2) ♀H4	CQua
'Torridon' (2)	CQua
'Toto' (12) ♀H4	CMea CQua EBrs ERCP LRHS MBri
'Tracey' (6) ♀H4	CQua LAma SPhx
'Treasure Hunt' (2)	IRhd
'Trebah' (2) ♀H4	CQua
'Treble Chance'	see *N. romieuxii* 'Treble Chance'
'Treble Two' (7)	CQua
'Trecara' (3)	CQua
'Trefusis' (1)	CQua
'Trehane' (6)	CQua
'Trelawney Gold' (2)	CQua
'Trelissick'	CQua
'Tremough Dale' (11a)	CQua
'Trena' (6) ♀H4	CQua ERCP NMin
'Trendy Trail' (3)	IRhd
'Trepolo' (11b) **new**	ERCP
'Tresamble' (5)	CQua LAma SDeJ
'Trevaunance' (6)	CQua
'Treverva' (6)	CQua
'Treviddo' (2)	CQua
'Trevithian' (7) ♀H4	CQua EBla LAma SDeJ SPhx WShi
'Trewarvas' (2)	CQua
'Trewirgie' (6)	CQua
'Trewoon' (4)	CQua
triandrus var. ***albus***	see *N. triandrus* subsp. *triandrus* var. *triandrus*
§ - subsp. ***triandrus*** var. ***concolor*** (13)	ECho
§ - - var. ***triandrus*** (13)	CQua ECho
'Tricollet' (11a)	SDeJ
'Trident' (3)	CQua
'Trielfin' (5)	IRhd
'Trigonometry' (11a) ♀H4	CQua
'Tripartite' (11a) ♀H4	CQua NMin SDeJ
'Triple Crown' (3) ♀H4	CQua IRhd
'Tristram' (2)	CQua
'Tropic Isle' (4)	CQua
'Tropical Heat' (2)	IRhd
'Trousseau' (1)	CQua
'Troutbeck' (3)	CQua
'Tru' (3)	CQua
'Truculent' (3) **new**	CQua
'Trueblood' (3)	IRhd
'Trumpet Warrior' (1) ♀H4	CQua IRhd
'Tryst' (2)	CQua
'Tudor Minstrel' (2)	CQua
'Tuesday's Child' (5) ♀H4	CQua
'Tullynagee' (3)	IRhd
'Turncoat' (6)	CQua
'Tutankhamun' (2)	CQua
'Tweeny' (2)	CQua
'Twink' (4)	CQua
'Tyee' (2)	CQua
'Tyrian Rose' (2)	CQua IRhd
'Tyrone Gold' (1) ♀H4	CQua IRhd
'Tyrree' (1)	IRhd
'Tywara' (1)	CQua
'Ulster Bank' (3)	CQua
'Ulster Bride' (4)	CQua
'Ultimus' (2)	CQua
'Uncle Bill' (1) **new**	CQua
'Uncle Duncan' (1)	CQua IRhd NMin
'Unique' (4) ♀H4	CQua EBla LAma SDeJ
'Unsurpassable' (1)	CQua LAma
'Upalong' (12)	CQua
'Upshot' (3)	CQua
'Urchin' (2)	IRhd
'Utiku' (6)	CQua
'Val d'Incles' (3)	CQua IRhd
'Valdrome' (11a)	CQua EBla
'Valinor' (2)	CQua
'Valley Dew' (2) **new**	CQua
'Valley Glow' (2) **new**	CQua
'Van Sion'	see *N.* 'Telamonius Plenus'
'Vanellus' (11a) ♀H4	IRhd
'Vaticaan' (1) **new**	SDeJ
'Velvet Spring' (2) **new**	CQua
'Veneration' (1)	CQua
'Verdin' (7)	CQua
'Verger' (3)	LAma MBri SDeJ
'Vernal Prince' (3) ♀H4	CQua
'Verona' (3) ♀H4	CQua LRHS NMin
'Verran Rose' (2)	IRhd
'Vers Libre' (9)	CQua
'Version' (1) **new**	IRhd
'Vice-President' (2) ♀H4	CQua
'Victoria' (1)	CQua
'Victorious' (2)	CQua
'Vigil' (1) ♀H4	CQua
'Viking' (1) ♀H4	CQua
'Violetta' (2)	CQua
'Virginia Waters' (3)	CQua
'Volare' (2)	CQua
'Volcanic Rim' (3)	IRhd
'Vulcan' (2) ♀H4	CQua
'W.P. Milner' (1)	CAvo CBgR CQua EBla EBrs EPfP EPot ERCP LAma NMin SDeJ SMrm SPhx WShi
'Wadavers' (2)	CQua
'Waif' (6)	CQua
'Waldon Pond' (3)	CQua
'Waldorf Astoria' (4)	CQua IRhd
'Walton' (7)	CQua
'War Dance' (3)	IRhd
'Warbler' (6) ♀H4	CQua LAma NMin
'Warm Day' (2)	IRhd
'Warm Welcome' (2) **new**	IRhd
'Warmington' (3)	CQua
'Watamu' (3)	IRhd
'Waterperry' (7)	LAma
'Watership Down' (2)	CQua

'Watersmeet' (4)	CQua
watieri	see *N. rupicola* subsp. *watieri*
'Wave' (4) **new**	CQua
'Wavelength' (3)	IRhd
'Wavertree'	see *N. asturiensis* 'Wavertree'
'Waxwing' (5)	CQua
'Wayward Lad' (3)	IRhd
'Wee Bee' (1)	CQua
'Weena' (2)	CQua
'Welcome' (2)	CQua
'West Post' (3)	IRhd
'Westward' (4)	CQua
'Whang-hi' (6)	CQua
'Wheal Bush' (4)	CQua
'Wheal Coates' (7) ♀H4	CBgR CQua
'Wheal Honey' (1)	CQua
'Wheal Jane' (2)	CQua
'Wheal Kitty' (7)	CQua
'Wheal Rose' (4)	CQua
'Wheatear' (6)	CQua IRhd NMin SPhx
'Whetstone' (1)	CQua
'Whisky Galore' (2)	CQua
'Whisky Mac' (2)	CQua
'White Emperor' (1)	CQua
'White Empress' (1)	CQua
'White Ideal' (1) **new**	CQua
'White Lady' (3)	CAvo CQua LAma WShi
'White Lion' (4) ♀H4	CFox CQua LAma LRHS
'White Majesty' (1)	CQua
'White Marvel' (4)	CQua EBrs
'White Medal' (4)	EBrs
'White Nile' (2)	CQua
'White Prince' (1)	CQua
'White Star' (1)	CQua
'White Tea' (2) **new**	CQua
'White Tie' (3)	CQua
'Wicklow Hills' (3)	CQua
'Widgeon' (2)	CQua
'Wild Honey' (2)	CQua
'Will Scarlett' (2)	CQua
'Williamsburg' (2)	NMin
willkommii (13)	CQua EBrs ECho MSSP NMin
'Wimbledon County Girl' (2) **new**	CQua
'Wind Song' (2)	CQua
'Winged Victory' (6)	CQua
'Winholm Jenni' (3)	CQua
'Winifred van Graven' (3)	CQua
'Winter Waltz' (6)	CQua
'Witch Doctor' (3)	IRhd
'Witch Hunt' (4)	IRhd
'Woodcock' (6)	CQua
'Woodland Prince' (3)	CQua
'Woodland Star' (3)	CQua
'Woodley Vale' (2)	CQua
'Woolsthorpe' (2)	CQua
'World Class' (5) **new**	CQua
'Xit' (3)	CAvo CQua NMin
'Xunantunich' (2)	CQua IRhd
'Yellow Belles' (5)	IRhd
'Yellow Cheerfulness' (4) ♀H4	CQua EBrs EPfP LAma LRHS MBri SDeJ
'Yellow Minnow' (8)	CQua
'Yellow River' (1)	LAma
'Yellow Wings' (6)	ECho
'Yellow Xit' (3)	CQua NMin
'Yoley's Pond' (2)	CQua
'York Minster' (1)	CQua IRhd NMin
'Young American' (1)	CQua
'Young Blood' (2)	CQua IRhd
'Your Grace' (2)	CQua NMin
'Yum-Yum' (3)	IRhd
zaianicus	see *N. romieuxii* subsp. *albidus* var. *zaianicus*
'Zekiah' (1)	CQua
'Zion Canyon' (2)	CQua
'Ziva' (8)	CAvo CFFs ERCP SDeJ
'Zwynner' (2)	IRhd

Nardostachys (*Valerianaceae*)

grandiflora	GPoy

Nardus (*Poaceae*)

stricta	CRWN EBWF EBee

Nassella (*Poaceae*)

cernua	WPGP
formicarum (Delile) Barkworth	EBee
poeppigiana	see *Stipa poeppigiana*
pulchra	WPGP
tenuissima	see *Stipa tenuissima*
trichotoma	CKno CMea EHoe EPPr MCCP SLim WHal WPGP

Nasturtium (*Brassicaceae*)

'Banana Split'	CCCN
officinale	MSKA SVic SWat

Natal plum see *Carissa macrocarpa*

Nauplius (*Asteraceae*)

sericeus	CSpe

nectarine see *Prunus persica* var. *nectarina*

Nectaroscordum (*Alliaceae*)

sp.	WFoF
koelzii	EBee
§ ***siculum***	CArn CAvo CBre CFFs CMea CTri CWCL EBee EBrs ECho ELan ERCP GCra LLWP LRHS MCot NBPC NBir NChi NLar SDeJ SGar SMrm SPad SPer SPhx WBor WFar WHoo
§ - subsp. ***bulgaricum***	CAby CTca EBee ECha EPfP EPot IBlr IPot ITim LRHS MMoz MNrw NLar SPhx WAbb WBrE WCot WTin
tripedale	CMea EBee ECho WWst

Neillia (*Rosaceae*)

affinis	CDul EBee ECrN EPfP EWTr IDee LLHF LRHS NBid NLar SCoo SWvt WBVN WDin
longiracemosa	see *N. thibetica*
sinensis	CMac NLar
§ ***thibetica***	Widely available
thyrsiflora var. ***tunkinensis*** HWJ 505	WCru

Nelumbo (*Nelumbonaceae*)

nucifera	XBlo

Nematanthus (*Gesneriaceae*)

'Apres'	WDib
'Black Magic'	WDib
'Christmas Holly'	WDib
'Freckles'	WDib
§ ***gregarius*** ♀H1	EBak WDib
§ - 'Golden West' (v)	WDib
- 'Variegatus'	see *N. gregarius* 'Golden West'
'Lemon and Lime'	WDib
radicans	see *N. gregarius*
'Tropicana' ♀H1	WDib

Nemesia (*Scrophulariaceae*)

Amelie = 'Fleurame'PBR	EPfP GKir SPoG
(Aromatica Series)	LAst LSou
Aromatica Royal = 'Balaroyal'PBR	
- Aromatica Compact White = 'Balarcomwit'	NPri
- Aromatica Rose Pink = 'Balarropi'PBR	LAst
- Aromatica True Blue = 'Balartublue'	NPri
Berries and Cream = 'Fleurbac'	EPfP LBuc LSou MSCN MWea NPri SPoG SVil
'Blue Button'	LAst LSou
'Bluebird'	see *N.* Bluebird = 'Hubbird'
§ Bluebird = 'Hubbird'PBR	CHll
Blue Lagoon = 'Pengoon'PBR (Maritana Series)	LSRN MGos SBfd SCoo
§ ***caerulea***	ECtt WPer
N - 'Joan Wilder' (clonal)	ECtt
§ ***denticulata*** 🏆H3-4	CPrp ECtt EPfP GBee LHop LRHS MGos NEgg SAga SCoo SPoG WBrE WFar WFoF WHlf
- 'Confetti'	see *N. denticulata*
- 'Maggie'	LBuc LRHS
'Fleurie Blue'	SPoG
foetens	see *N. caerulea*
'Fragrant Cloud'	ELan EPfP LSou MNrw
'Fragrant Gem'	LSRN
fruticans misapplied	see *N. caerulea*
Golden Eye = 'Yateye'PBR	EPfP LRHS LSRN LSou MPnt
Honey Girl = 'Penhon'PBR (Maritana Series)	LSRN MGos SBfd SCoo
'Innocence' 🏆H3	CPrp LAst MArl SCoo SPoG
(Karoo Series)	LSou SCoo
Karoo Blue = 'Innkablue'PBR	
- Karoo White = 'Innkarwhi'PBR (Karoo Series)	LSou SMrm
'Lemon Drop'	LAst
Maritana Sky Lagoon = 'Pensky' (Maritana Series)	SCoo
Melanie = 'Fleuron' 🏆H3	EPfP
Nemesis Orange = 'Wesneo'	LAst
(Nuvo Series)	LSou WGor
'Nuvo Blue' new	
- 'Nuvo Blue Bicolour' new	LSou
- 'Nuvo Carmine' new	LSou SVil WGor
- 'Nuvo Lavender' new	SVil
- 'Nuvo Purple Bicolor' new	SVil
- 'Nuvo Rose' new	LSou WGor
- 'Nuvo White' new	SVil
Candy Girl = 'Pencand'PBR (Maritana Series)	SCoo
'Orchard Blue'	EPfP
'Pippa Manby'	ECtt
'Provencal Dusky Blue' new	EPfP
'Provencal Dusky Pink' new	EPfP
Pure Lagoon = 'Penpur'PBR	LHop SBfd
'Rose Wings'	EPfP
Sugar Girl = 'Pensug'PBR (Maritana Series)	EPfP LHop LSRN
'Sugar Plum'PBR	EPfP LRHS SLon
(Sunsatia Series)	LHop SBfd SCoo
Sunsatia Blackberry = 'Inuppink'PBR	
- Sunsatia Cranberry = 'Intraired'PBR	SCoo
- Sunsatia Lemon = 'Intraigold'PBR	ESwi SCoo
- Sunsatia Mango = 'Inupyel'PBR	ESwi LHop
- Sunsatia Peach = 'Inupcream'PBR	SCoo SVil
sylvatica	CSpe
'Utopia Painted Face' (Utopia Series)	MGos
Vanilla Mist = 'Grega'PBR	CChe EPfP LRHS LSou SLon SPoG
'White Wings'	EPfP
'Wisley Vanilla'	EPfP LRHS SPoG

Nemophila (*Hydrophyllaceae*)

menziesii	CFox
- 'Penny Black'	CFox CSpe

Neodypsis (*Arecaceae*)

decaryi	see *Dypsis decaryi*

Neolepisorus (*Polypodiaceae*)

lancifolius	CPLG

Neolitsea (*Lauraceae*)

glauca	see *N. sericea*
§ ***sericea***	CBcs SSpi WSHC

Neomarica ✿ (*Iridaceae*)

caerulea	CDes EBee WCot
gracilis	CLak

Neopanax (*Araliaceae*)

§ ***arboreus***	CDoC CHEx CTrC ECou LEdu SBig
colensoi	CTrC
§ ***laetus***	CDoC CHEx CTrC ECou LEdu SAPC SArc SBig

Neoregelia (*Bromeliaceae*)

carolinae (Meyendorffii Group) 'Meyendorffii'	XBlo
'Hojo Rojo'	XBlo
'Marconfos'	XBlo

Neoshirakia (*Euphorbiaceae*)

japonica	EPfP MBlu WPGP
- B&SWJ 8744	WCru

Neotinea (*Orchidaceae*)

tridentata new	NLAp
ustulata	ECho

Neottia (*Orchidaceae*)

ovata new	NLAp

Neottianthe (*Orchidaceae*)

cucullata	EFEx

Nepenthes ✿ (*Nepenthaceae*)

alata	CSWC NChu
alata × ***ventricosa***	SHmp
bongso	SHmp
copleandii new	CSWC
densiflora	SHmp
diatas	SHmp
ephippiata	SHmp
fusca	SHmp
fusca × ***maxima***	SHmp
glabrata	SHmp
× ***hookeriana***	SHmp
izumiae	SHmp

lowii	SHmp
macfarlanei	SHmp
maxima mixta	SHmp
maxima* × *talangensis new	SHmp
mikei	SHmp
muluensis* × *lowii	SHmp
ovata new	SHmp
rajah	SHmp
ramispina	SHmp
'Rebecca Soper'	SHmp
sanguinea	SHmp
sibuyanensis	SHmp
singalana	SHmp
spectabilis	SHmp
tobaica	SHmp
truncata highland form	SHmp
ventricosa	SHmp

Nepeta ✿ (*Lamiaceae*)

RCB/TQ-H-6	WCot
from China new	EWes
from Ethiopia	GCal
'Blue Beauty'	see *N. sibirica* 'Souvenir d'André Chaudron'
* ***buddlejifolium***	NBre NLar
* - 'Gold Splash'	NBre
camphorata	NBre SIde
cataria	CArn CPrp CTri CWan EBWF ELau GBar GJos GPoy MHer MNHC NBro NGHP NPri SBfd SIde SVic WHfH WJek WMoo
§ - 'Citriodora'	CArn CBot CHar EBee ELan GBar GPWP GPoy MHer NGHP SIde SPhx WClo WJek WTou
citriodora Dum.	see *N. cataria* 'Citriodora'
clarkei	EBee EPPr GMaP IFro LEdu MDKP MMuc MNFA NDov SBfd SEND SIde SWat WFar WHil WHrl WMoo WSpi
'Dropmore'	EBee
§ ×***faassenii*** ♀H4	Widely available
- 'Alba'	COlW CSpr EBee ECtt EPfP GBar LAst MMuc NBPC NBre NGHP NLar SBfd SEND WFar WHil WJek WWEG
- 'Blauknirps'	NBre
- 'Blue Wonder' new	WHlf
- 'Kit Cat'	CPrp CSpe EBee GCal LHop LSRN MNrw NDov SPoG WFar
- 'Select'	WPtf
glechoma 'Variegata'	see *Glechoma hederacea* 'Variegata'
govaniana	Widely available
grandiflora	MMuc NBre SIde WFar WHrl
- 'Blue Danube'	NDov SIde
- 'Bramdean'	CElw CMea EBee ECtt EPfP EWes LRHS MCot SAga SBch SPhx WClo WWEG
- 'Dawn to Dusk'	Widely available
- 'Pool Bank'	EBee ECtt EWes GCal LPla MAvo NBre SGar SIde SMrm
- 'Wild Cat'	EBee EPfP MAvo MBri SPur WFar
hederacea 'Variegata'	see *Glechoma hederacea* 'Variegata'
italica	EBee SIde
kubanica	IMou LPla
lanceolata	see *N. nepetella*
latifolia	NBre SIde
- 'Super Cat'	EBee
'Lilac Cloud'	NBir
* ***longipes*** hort.	CPrp CSam EBee EPfP LAst LEdu LHop LRHS MCot MNFA MRav NGdn NSti SMrm SPer SWat WAul WCAu WClo WCom WFar WHal WMnd WPer WWEG
macrantha	see *N. sibirica*
melissifolia	SBch WPer
mussinii misapplied	see *N.* × *faassenii*
mussinii Spreng.	see *N. racemosa*
§ ***nepetella***	NBir WFar
nervosa	CSpe EBee ECha ELan EPfP GKir LAst MCot MHer MNHC NBPC NBro NLar NPri NSti SBfd SPer WClo WFar WJek WMnd WSHC WSpi WWEG
- 'Blue Carpet'	CSpe NEgg
- 'Blue Moon'	EAEE EBee EPfP EWes GJos LRHS NBid SMrm WFar
- 'Forncett Select'	CSam MRav NBre SDys SMrm
- 'Pink Cat'	EPfP GKir LRHS MDKP NLar SRot WHil WRHF WWEG
§ ***nuda***	CSam EBee ECha ECtt EPPr MDKP SHar SIde WFar WHil WHrl
- 'Accent'	EBee GBin
- subsp. ***albiflora***	ECha
* - 'Anne's Choice'	EBee GBin SIde
* - 'Grandiflora'	NBre NLar WMoo
- 'Isis'	EBee
- 'Purple Cat'	EBee EPfP GBin LLHF LSou SIde WFar
- 'Snow Cat'	EBee GBin SIde SPhx
pannonica	see *N. nuda*
parnassica	CElw EBee ECtt GAbr LRHS MLLN MMuc MWhi NBPC NLar SEND SIde SMad SMrm SPav WBox WFar WHil WHrl WMnd WMoo WPtf
phyllochlamys	CBot CPBP
Pink Candy	EWll WHil
'Porzellan'	EBee LPla SMrm
§ ***prattii***	CSpe MWat NLar SIde WSpi WWEG
§ ***racemosa*** ♀H4	CArn CBot CHby CMac CPbn CSev CWan CWit ELau EPfP GBBs GBar GJos GKir LRHS MCot MLHP MNHC MRav MSCN SGar SIde WClo WMoo
- RCB AM 3	WCot
- ***alba***	WFar
- 'Blue Ice'	SIde
- 'Grog'	EBee SIde WSpi
- 'Little Titch'	CBod CPrp EAEE EBee ECtt EPfP EShb GCra LRHS LSRN MAsh MCot NLar SIde SMrm SPoG SWat WFar WSpi WWEG
- 'Snowflake'	CBcs CMea CPrp EAEE EBee ELan ELon EPfP EShb GMaP LRHS MAsh MCot MHer MTis NBir SAga SIde SMrm SPer SPoG SWvt WCAu WClo WCom WFar
- 'Superba'	NBre WCot WFar
- 'Walker's Low'	Widely available
* 'Rae Crug'	ECtt EWes
reichenbachiana	see *N. racemosa*
§ ***sibirica***	COlW EBee ECha ELan EPfP GMac LEdu MHer MMuc MRav MSCN NBid NBro NLar NPri SBch SBfd SRkn WCom WCot WFar WHal WJek WPer WPtf
§ - 'Souvenir d'André Chaudron'	CPrp CSam CWCL EBee ECtt EHrv ELan EPfP EWTr GKir GMaP LAst LHop LRHS MBri MCot MRav NCob NVic SMrm SPer SPoG WCAu WClo WCot WEas WFar WHil WSpi WWEG
sintenisii	NBre
'Six Hills Giant'	Widely available

stewartiana LLHF MRav NLar WMoo
- BWJ 7999 WCru
subsessilis CBot CHar EBee ECtt EHrv ELan EPfP EShb GAbr GMaP GMac ITim LAst LEdu LRHS MCot MNrw MRav NBid NBir NGdn SPhx SPoG WCom WCru WFar WMnd WPer WSpi WWEG
- 'Blue Dreams' LBMP NLar SHar SPhx WHil WHrl
- 'Candy Cat' EBee EHrv EPfP MDKP NBPC NBre SBHP SPoG
- 'Cool Cat' EBee EPfP LSRN MDKP NBre NLar SIde SPoG WFar
- Nimbus = 'Yanim'PBR CCVN EBee LRHS MPnt SPoG
- 'Pink Dreams' ELon EPfP GBee GJos LBMP LRHS SHar WHil
- pink-flowered ECha MLLN SMrm WWEG
- 'Sweet Dreams' CHar CKno EAEE EBee ECtt EPfP EWTr LBMP LEdu LHop LRHS MCot MDKP MRav NCGa NLar NSti SPoG WCom WFar WMnd
- 'Washfield' CAby IPot LHop SAga
tenuifolia CArn
transcaucasica NBre NLar WMnd WMoo WWEG
'Blue Infinity'
troodii MDKP SIde
tuberosa CArn CBod CSpe ECha EKen ITim MAvo MHer MRav SBch SBfd SIde SPav STes WBox WCot WMnd WMoo
'Veluws Blauwtje' EBee
'Veluwse Wakel' IMou
yunnanensis EBee EPPr LEdu LPla SMrm WHil WOut WPGP

Nephrolepis (*Oleandraceae*)

auriculata **new** WRic
cordifolia WRic
duffii EShb WRic
falcata EShb WRic
pendula WRic

Nephrophyllidium (*Menyanthaceae*)

crista-galli IBlr

Nerine ✿ (*Amaryllidaceae*)

Smee 275 CDes
'Afterglow' EBee ECho LAma SGar WCot
'Albivetta' CBgR EBee ECho LPio WCot
alta see *N. undulata* Alta Group
§ ***undulata*** Alta Group WCot
angustifolia CPen
'Aries' WCot
'Aurora' ECho WCot
'Baghdad' ECho WCot
'Belladonna' WCot
'Bennett-Poë' WCot
'Berlioz' WCot
'Blanchefleur' WCot
bowdenii ♀H3-4 Widely available
- 'Alba' CBgR CFir CMea CPrp CTca EBee ECho ELan EPot ERCP GAbr LPio SCoo SMHy WCot
- 'Chris Sanders' WCot
- 'Codora' see *N.* 'Codora'
- 'E.B.Anderson' EBee WCot
- Irish clone WCot
- 'Linda Vista' **new** WCot
- 'Manina' CMdw WCot
- 'Marjorie' EMal
- 'Mark Fenwick' CBcs CDes EBee ECha ECho WCot WOld
- 'Marnie Rogerson' CPne EBee SMHy WCot
§ - 'Mollie Cowie' (v) CMdw CPrp EBee GCal IBlr LPio LRHS NCGa WCot WCru WHil WSHC
- 'Ostara' CBgR CPrp EBee SPhx WCot
- pale pink, striped darker CDes
- 'Pink Surprise' **new** WCot
- 'Pink Triumph' misapplied CAbP CBcs CBgR CFox EBee EBla ECho ELon EShb GQui IBlr LAma LHop LRHS SPer WCot WHoo
- 'Porlock' EBee
§ - 'Quinton Wells' CDes CPrp CTca EBee SCnR SPhx WCot WHil
- 'Rowie' CBgR CPrp EPot
- 'Ted Allen's Early' EBla
- 'Variegata' see *N. bowdenii* 'Mollie Cowie'
- Washfield form SMHy
- 'Wellsii' see *N. bowdenii* 'Quinton Wells'
'Canasta' WCot
'Cardinal' WCot
'Carolside' **new** WCot
'Caryatid' **new** WCot
'Catherine' WCot
'Catkin' ECho WCot
'Clent Charm' WCot
'Codora' CCCN CFox CPen EBee ECho LHop LRHS LSou SPer WCot
'Cordoba' CWGN
'Corlette' WCot
corusca 'Major' see *N. sarniensis* var. *corusca*
'Cranfield' **new** WCot
'Diana Oliver' **new** WCot
'Doris Vos' WCot
'Druid' WCot
'Elspeth' WCot
'Eve' WCot
'Evelyn Emmett' **new** WCot
'Exbury Red' WCot
filamentosa misapplied see *N. filifolia*
filamentosa ambig. CLak ECho
§ ***filifolia*** CPBP CPen ECho EPot GKev ITim MTho WAbe
flexuosa see *N. undulata* Flexuosa Group
'Fucine' CDes EBee WCot
'Gloaming' WCot
gracilis ECho WCot
'Grilse' WCot
'Harlequin' WCot
'Hera' SPhx WCot
'Hertha Berg' **new** WCot
* ***hirsuta*** ECho
humilis ECho
- Breachiae Group CStu SBch
huttoniae CLak ECho
'Iman' **new** WCot
'Isobel' EPot
'Janet' WCot
'Jenny Wren' WCot
'Kashmir' CDes WCot
'Killarney' WCot
'King Leopold' WCot
'King of the Belgians' ECho LAma WCot
'Kinn McIntosh' CDes WCot
krigei CPen ECho
'Kyoto' WCot
'Lady Cynthia Colville' WCot
'Lady Eleanor Keane' WCot
'Lady Havelock-Allen' CDes WCot
'Lady Llewellyn' WCot
'Lady St Aldwyn' **new** WCot
laticoma ECho WCot
'Leila Hughes' WCot

'Lyndhurst Salmon'	WCot
'Mansellii'	WCot
'Maria'	CBgR WCot
masoniorum	CPen ECho MTho NMen SBch WCot WHil WThu
'Miss E. Cator'	WCot
'Miss Frances Clarke'	WCot
'Mrs Dent Brocklehurst'	WCot
'Nikita'	CBgR CPen EBee ECho EPot LRHS SPhx
'November Cheer'	ECho
peersii	WCot
'Pink Frostwork' new	WCot
'Plymouth'	SChr
pudica	CLak SBch
- pink-flowered	EBee WCot
'Purple Prince'	CDes
pusilla	CLak
'Red Pimpernel'	ECho LAma
'Regina'	WCot
'Rushmere Star'	CBgR CDes EBee SChr WCot
'Ruth'	WCot
sarniensis ♀H2-3	CPne EBee ECha ECho EPot WCot
* - 'Alba'	LPio WCot
§ - var. ***corusca***	LAma
- - 'Major'	ECho SChr WCot
- var. ***curvifolia*** f. ***fothergillii***	CAvo ECho WCot
- late, dull red-flowered	CDes
'Snowflake'	WCot
'Stephanie'	CBgR CCCN CTca CWGN EBee ECho EShb LAma LHop LRHS LSou SPer SPhx WCot WFar WHoo
'Timoshenko'	WCot
§ ***undulata***	CBgR CCCN CPen CPne CTca EBee ECha ECho EPot LAma LSou SPer WCot WHil
* - 'Alba'	ECho
§ - Alta Group	WCot
§ - Flexuosa Group	CPne ECho MRav
- - 'Alba'	CBgR CDes CPen EBee ECha ECho EWTr EWll MRav WAbe WCot
'Variegata' (v)	CWGN
'Vicky'	WCot
'Virgo'	CMdw ECho LAma
'White Swan'	ECho
'Wolsey'	ECho WCot
'Zeal Giant' ♀H3-4	CAvo CPne ECho GCal WCot
'Zeal Grilse'	CDes CPne
'Zeal Silver Stripe'	CFir

Nerium ✿ (*Apocynaceae*)

oleander misapplied	see *N. oleander* 'Soeur Agnès'
oleander L.	CAbb CArn CBcs CEls CHll CTri EBak ELan EShb EUJe LRHS MMuc NLar SArc SChr SEND SPad SPer SPlb SPoG SRms SWal
- 'Album'	CEls CTri
- 'Album Plenum' (d)	CEls
- 'Alsace'	CEls
- 'Altini'	CEls
- 'Angiolo Pucci'	CEls
- 'Bousquet d'Orb'	CEls
§ - 'Carneum Plenum' (d)	CEls
- 'Cavalaire' (d)	CEls
* - 'Clare'	SOWG
- 'Cornouailles'	CEls
- 'Docteur Golfin'	CEls
- 'Emile Sahut'	CEls
- 'Emilie'	CEls
- 'Flavescens Plenum' (d)	CEls EShb
- 'Géant des Batailles' (d)	CEls SOWG
- 'Hardy Red'	CEls
- 'Hawaii'	CEls
- 'Isle of Capri'	SOWG
- 'J.R.'	CEls
- 'Jannoch'	CEls
- 'Louis Pouget' (d)	CEls
- 'Madame Allen' (d)	CEls EShb
- 'Maresciallo Graziani'	CEls
- 'Margaritha'	CEls
- 'Marie Gambetta'	CEls
- 'Mont Blanc' (d)	CEls
- 'Mrs Roeding'	see *N. oleander* 'Carneum Plenum'
- 'Nana Rosso'	CEls
- 'Oasis' (d)	CEls
- subsp. ***oleander***	CEls
- 'Papa Gambetta'	CEls
- 'Petite Pink'	CEls
- 'Petite Red'	CEls
- 'Petite Salmon'	CEls
- 'Professeur Granel' (d)	CEls
- 'Provence' (d)	CEls SOWG
- 'Rosario' (d)	EShb
- 'Rose des Borrels' (d)	CEls
- 'Rosée du Ventoux' (d)	CEls SOWG
- 'Roseum'	CEls
- 'Roseum Plenum' (d)	CEls CRHN SEND
- 'Rosita'	CEls
- salmon-flowered	SEND
- 'Sealy Pink'	CEls
* - 'Snowflake'	SOWG
§ - 'Soeur Agnès'	CEls
- 'Soleil Levant'	CEls
- 'Souvenir d'Emma Schneider'	CEls
- 'Souvenir des Iles Canaries'	CEls
- 'Splendens' (d)	SOWG
- 'Splendens Giganteum' (d)	CEls EShb
- 'Splendens Giganteum Variegatum' (d/v)	CEls
- 'Tito Poggi'	CEls
- 'Vanilla Cream'	MWea
- 'Variegatum' (v) ♀H1+3	CBot CHll EShb LRHS
- 'Variegatum Plenum' (d/v)	CBow
- 'Villa Romaine'	CEls
- 'Ville de Carpentras' (d)	CEls
- white-flowered	SEND

Nertera (*Rubiaceae*)

balfouriana	ECou

Neviusia (*Rosaceae*)

alabamensis	NLar

Nicandra (*Solanaceae*)

physalodes	CArn CHby GBee ILis NBir NVic SMrm WSFF
- 'Splash of Cream' (v)	CCCN
- 'Violacea'	CSpe SRms SWvt WTou

Nicotiana (*Solanaceae*)

alata	CFox EPfP WSFF
glauca	CCCN CDTJ CHGN CHll CSpe EShb EWTr SDnm SPav
'Hopleys'	CSpe
knightiana	CDTJ CSpe WTou
langsdorffii ♀H3	CSpe LPio SDnm SPav
- 'Cream Splash' (v)	CPla
- 'Hot Chocolate' new	CSpe WHil
'Lime Green' ♀H3	CFox CSpe
mutabilis	CHll CSpe EBee MWea SBch SPhx

rustica	WTou
suaveolens	CBre CSpe
sylvestris ♀H3	CDTJ CFox CSpe CWSG ELan EPfP NPri SBfd SDnm SEND SPav SPoG SWvt WTou
tabacum	CArn SPav
- var. ***macrophylla***	CDTJ
'Tinkerbell'	CSpe

Nidularium (*Bromeliaceae*)

innocentii	XBlo

Nierembergia (*Solanaceae*)

caerulea	see *N. linariifolia*
frutescens	see *N. scoparia*
hippomanica	see *N. linariifolia*
§ ***linariifolia*** ♀H1	EBee EHrv
§ ***repens***	CDoy EBee ECho EDAr NLar
rivularis	see *N. repens*
§ ***scoparia***	CSpr
- 'Mont Blanc'	CFox

Nigella (*Ranunculaceae*)

papillosa 'African Bride'	CSpe
- 'Midnight'	CSpe

Nigritella see *Gymnadenia*

Nipponanthemum (*Asteraceae*)

§ ***nipponicum***	CDes CSam CWan EBee ECho GBin GCal IVic LAst LPio NSti SRms WBrk WCot
* - ***roseum***	LPio

Noccaea see *Thlaspi*

Nolina (*Dracaenaceae*)

F&M 333	WPGP
bigelovii	WPGP
longifolia	EAmu EUJe
microcarpa	WCot
nelsonii	EAmu WPGP
parryi subsp. ***wolfii***	WPGP
parviflora NJM 05.010	WPGP
texana	CTrC NWCA

Nomocharis (*Liliaceae*)

aperta	CPLG EBee ECho EHrv GCra GCrs GEdr GGar GKir GLin LAma WCru
- ACE 2271	GCrs WWst
- CLD 229	WWst
- CLD 524	WWst
farreri	ECho
× ***finlayorum***	EBee ECho GEdr WWst
mairei	see *N. pardanthina*
meleagrina	EBee ECho GAuc LAma WAbe WWst
nana	see *Lilium nanum*
oxypetala	see *Lilium oxypetalum*
§ ***pardanthina***	GAuc GGGa GGar GMac WAbe
- CLD 1490	EHrv WWst
- f. ***punctulata***	GGGa WCru WWst
saluenensis	ECho GCrs WAbe WWst

Nonea (*Boraginaceae*)

lutea	LSou NSti WHal

Nothochelone see *Penstemon*

Nothofagus ✿ (*Fagaceae*)

§ × ***alpina***	CBcs CDul CMCN GBin GKir IFFs NWea WDin
antarctica	CBcs CCVT CDul CLnd CMCN CTho ECrN ELan EPfP EWTr GKir IFFs IVic LRHS LTen MBlu MBri MGos NPal NWea WDin WSHC
betuloides	CBcs CMCN GBin IDee IFFs SPlb WPGP
cunninghamii	CDul GKir IArd IFFs
dombeyi	CBcs CDoC CDul CLnd CMCN EPfP GBin GKir IArd IFFs LHyd LRHS MBlu NWea SAPC SArc WPGP WSpi
fusca	CDoC MGos
glauca	CBcs CDul IFFs
menziesii	CTrC IDee IFFs
nitida	CBcs GBin IArd IDee IFFs WPGP
obliqua	CBcs CDul CLnd CMCN GAbr GBin NWea WDin
procera misapplied	see *N.* × *alpina*
pumilio	CBcs GBin
solanderi	GGar
- var. ***cliffortioides***	NMun

Notholaena see *Cheilanthes*

Notholirion (*Liliaceae*)

bulbuliferum	EBee EBrs ECho GAuc GCra
- Cox 5074	WWst
campanulatum	EBee ECho GAuc WWst
macrophyllum	EBee ECho GAuc GKev WWst
thomsonianum	ECho WWst

Nothoperanema (*Dryopteridaceae*)

squamisetum new	WRic

Nothoscordum (*Alliaceae*)

sp.	GCal
gracile	CFir WPrP
montevidense	WWst
neriniflorum	see *Caloscordum neriniflorum*
ostenii	SCnR
strictum	EBee ECho

Nuphar (*Nymphaeaceae*)

advenum	LPBA
japonica	CRow NLar
var. ***variegata*** (v)	
lutea	CBen CRow EHon LPBA MMuc NSco SCoo SWat

Nuxia (*Buddlejaceae*)

congesta	EShb
floribunda	EShb

Nylandtia (*Polygalaceae*)

spinosa	SPlb

Nymphaea ✿ (*Nymphaeaceae*)

alba (H)	CBen CRWN CRow CWat EHon LPBA MSKA NBir NSco SCoo SVic SWat WMAq WPnP
'Alba Plenissima' (H)	WPnP
'Albatros' misapplied	see *N.* 'Hermine'
§ 'Albatros' Latour-Marliac (H)	CWat LPBA MSKA NPer SWat WPnP
'Albatross'	see *N.* 'Albatros' Latour-Marliac, *N.* 'Hermine'
* 'Albida'	WMAq XBlo
'Almost Black' (H)	CBen MSKA
'Amabilis' (H)	CBen CRow LPBA MSKA SWat WMAq
'American Star' (H)	CBen CWat SWat WMAq
'Andreana' (H)	CBen CWat LLWG LPBA MSKA SWat
'Arc-en-ciel' (H)	CBen LPBA SCoo SWat WMAq

	'Arethusa' (H)	LPBA
	'Atropurpurea' (H)	CBen LLWG LPBA MSKA NPer SWat WMAq
	'Attraction' (H)	CBen CRow EHon LPBA MSKA NPer SCoo SVic SWat WMAq XBlo
	'Aurora' (H)	CBen LPBA SVic SWat WMAq WPnP
	'Barbara Davies' (H)	LLWG
	'Barbara Dobbins' (H)	CBen LLWG LPBA MSKA
	'Bateau' (H)	CBen LLWG
	'Bernice Ikins' (H)	MSKA
	'Berthold' (H)	CBen
	'Brakeleyi Rosea' (H)	CBen LPBA MSKA WMAq
	'Burgundy Princess' (H)	CWat LLWG MSKA NPer
	candida (H)	CBen EHon MSKA NPer WMAq
	'Candidissima' (H)	SWat
§	***capensis*** (T/D)	XBlo
	'Carolina Sunset' (H)	LLWG
	'Caroliniana Nivea' (H)	CBen EHon
	'Caroliniana Perfecta' (H)	CBen LPBA MSKA SWat
	'Celebration' (H)	LLWG MSKA
	'Charlene Strawn' (H)	CWat LLWG LPBA WMAq
	'Charles de Meurville' (H)	CBen CRow LPBA MSKA NPer SVic WMAq WPnP
	'Château le Rouge' (H)	LLWG
	'Clyde Ikins' (H)	MSKA
	'Colonel A.J. Welch' (H)	CBen EHon LPBA MSKA NPer SCoo SWat WMAq
	'Colorado' (H)	CBen LLWG MSKA NPer
	colorata	see *N. capensis*
	'Colossea' (H)	CBen CWat LPBA MSKA NPer WPnP
	'Comanche' (H)	CBen MSKA NPer WMAq
	'Conqueror' (H)	CBen IArd LPBA MSKA NPer SCoo SVic SWat
§	'Darwin' (H)	CBen CWat LPBA MSKA NPer SLon SWat WMAq WPnP
	× ***daubenyana*** (T/D)	ECho
	'David' (H)	CBen LLWG
	'Denver' (H)	LLWG MSKA
	'Ellisiana' (H)	CBen LLWG LPBA MSKA NPer SWat
	'Escarboucle' (H) Υ^{H4}	CBen CRow CWat EHon LPBA MSKA NLar NPer SCoo SVic SWat WMAq WPnP XBlo
	'Esmeralda' (H)	SWat
§	'Fabiola' (H)	CBen CRow EHon LPBA MSKA NPer SCoo WMAq
	'Fiesta'	CBen MSKA
	'Fire Crest' (H)	CBen LPBA MSKA NPer SCoo SVic SWat WMAq
	'Fireball' (H)	MSKA
	'Fritz Junge' (H)	CBen
	'Froebelii' (H)	CBen CRow CWat EHon LPBA MSKA NPer SWat WMAq WPnP
	'Fulva' (H)	LLWG
	'Galatée' (H)	CBen MSKA
	'Geisha Girl'	MSKA
	'Georgia Peach' (H)	LLWG MSKA
	'Gladstoniana' (H) Υ^{H4}	CBen CRow EHon LPBA MSKA NPer SCoo SWat WMAq
	'Gloire du Temple-sur-Lot' (H)	CBen EHon NPer SWat WMAq
	'Gloriosa' (H)	CBen LPBA NPer SCoo SWat WPnP
	'Gold Medal' (H)	CBen LLWG MSKA
	'Gonnère' (H) Υ^{H4}	CBen CRow CWat EHon LPBA MSKA NPer SLon SWat WMAq WPnP
	'Graziella' (H)	CBen LPBA MSKA WMAq WPnP
	'Gypsy' (H)	LLWG
	'Hal Miller' (H)	LLWG
	'Hassell' (H)	LLWG
	'Helen Fowler' (H)	SWat WMAq
	× ***helvola***	see *N.* 'Pygmaea Helvola'
§	'Hermine' (H)	CBen MSKA NPer SWat WMAq
	'Highlight'	LLWG
	'Hollandia' misapplied	see *N.* 'Darwin'
	'Hollandia' Koster (H)	SWat
	'Indiana' (H)	CBen LPBA MSKA NPer WMAq
	'Inner Light'	LLWG MSKA
	'James Brydon' (H) Υ^{H4}	CBen CHid CRow CWat EHon LPBA MSKA NLar NPer SCoo SLon SVic SWat WMAq WPnP
	'Jean de Lamarsalle' (H)	LLWG
	'Jerusalem Dawn'	MSKA
§	'Joanne Pring' (H)	SWat
	'Joey Tomocik' (H)	CBen CWat LLWG LPBA MSKA SCoo WMAq WPnP
	'King of the Blues' (T/D)	MSKA
	'Lactea' (H)	CBen LLWG
	'Laydekeri Fulgens' (H)	CBen LPBA MSKA SWat WMAq
	'Laydekeri Lilacea' (H)	CBen CRow LPBA SWat WMAq
	'Laydekeri Purpurata' (H)	CBen LPBA SWat
	'Laydekeri Rosea' misapplied	see *N.* 'Laydekeri Rosea Prolifera'
§	'Laydekeri Rosea Prolifera' (H)	CBen LPBA
	'Lemon Chiffon' (H)	CBen MSKA
	'Lemon Mist'	LLWG MSKA
	'Lily Pons' (H)	CBen MSKA
	'Limelight'	SWat
	'Liou' (H)	CBen LLWG MSKA
	'Little Sue' (H)	LLWG MSKA
	'Livingstone' (H)	LLWG
	'Lucida' (H)	CBen LPBA MSKA SWat WMAq
	'Madame Wilfon Gonnère' (H)	CBen CWat EHon LPBA MSKA NPer SVic SWat WMAq
	'Marliacea Albida' (H)	CBen CWat EHon LPBA MSKA NPer SWat WMAq WPnP XBlo
	'Marliacea Carnea' (H)	CBen CRow EHon LPBA MSKA NPer SCoo SWat WMAq
§	'Marliacea Chromatella' (H) Υ^{H4}	CBen CHid CRow CWat EHon LPBA MSKA NLar SCoo SVic SWat WMAq WPnP XBlo
	'Marliacea Rosea' (H)	CBen MSKA SWat WMAq XBlo
	'Marliacea Rubra Punctata' (H)	LPBA
	'Mary' (H)	LLWG
	'Masaniello' (H)	CBen CRow EHon LPBA MSKA SWat WMAq
	'Maurice Laydeker' (H)	CBen LLWG
	'Maxima'	see *N.* 'Odorata Maxima'
	'Mayla'	CBen LLWG LPBA MSKA NPer
§	'Météor' (H)	CBen CWat MSKA WMAq
	mexicana	MSKA
	'Millennium Pink'	MSKA
	'Moorei' (H)	CBen LPBA MSKA SWat WMAq
	'Mrs Richmond' misapplied	see *N.* 'Fabiola'
	'Mrs Richmond' Latour-Marliac (H)	SWat XBlo
	'Neptune' (H)	LLWG
	'Newchapel Beauty'	WMAq
	'Newton' (H)	CBen LLWG MSKA SWat WMAq
	'Nigel' (H)	CBen LLWG MSKA SWat
	'Norma Gedye' (H)	CBen CWat LPBA MSKA SWat WMAq
	'Odalisque' (H)	CBen
§	***odorata*** (H)	CBen CRow EHon LPBA MSKA SCoo WMAq
§	- var. ***minor*** (H)	CBen CRow LPBA MSKA SWat WMAq
	- 'Pumila'	see *N. odorata* var. *minor*
	- subsp. ***tuberosa*** (H)	CBen LPBA
	'Odorata Alba'	see *N. odorata*

§ 'Odorata Maxima' (H)	WMAq
'Odorata Sulphurea' (H)	CBen EHon SWat WPnP
§ 'Odorata Sulphurea Grandiflora' (H)	CBen CRow LPBA MSKA SCoo SWat XBlo
§ 'Odorata Turicensis' (H)	LPBA MSKA
'Odorata William B. Shaw'	see *N.* 'W.B. Shaw'
'Pam Bennett' (H)	CBen LLWG
'Panama Pacific' (T/D)	XBlo
'Patio Joe'	LLWG MSKA
'Paul Hariot' (H)	CWat LPBA MSKA NPer SWat WMAq WPnP
'Peace Lily'	LLWG MSKA
'Peach Glow'	LLWG MSKA
'Peaches and Cream' (H)	MSKA
Pearl of the Pool (H)	SWat
'Perry's Baby Red' (H)	CBen CWat LLWG MSKA MWts NPer SCoo WMAq
'Perry's Crinkled Pink' (H)	CBen
'Perry's Double White' (H)	MSKA NPer WPnP
'Perry's Double Yellow'	MSKA WPnP
'Perry's Dwarf Red' (H)	MSKA
'Perry's Fire Opal' (H)	MSKA NPer
'Perry's Orange Sunset'	MSKA
'Perry's Pink' (H)	SWat WMAq
'Perry's Red Beauty' (H)	CBen
'Perry's Red Bicolor' (H)	LLWG
'Perry's Red Glow' (H)	MSKA
'Perry's Red Wonder' (H)	CBen
'Perry's Viviparous Pink' (H)	CBen
'Perry's White Star' (H)	LLWG
'Perry's Yellow Sensation'	see *N.* 'Yellow Sensation'
'Peter Slocum' (H)	CBen SWat
'Phoebus' (H)	CBen SWat
'Picciola' (H)	LLWG
'Pink Domino'	MSKA
'Pink Grapefruit' (H)	XBlo
'Pink Opal' (H)	CBen CWat LPBA
'Pink Peony' (H)	MSKA
'Pink Pumpkin' (H)	LLWG
'Pink Sensation' (H)	CBen LLWG MSKA NPer SLon SWat WMAq
'Pink Sparkle' (H)	LLWG
'Pink Sunrise' (H)	MSKA
'Pöstlingberg' (H)	LLWG LPBA
'Princess Elizabeth' (H)	CBen EHon LLWG LPBA
'Pygmaea Alba'	see *N. tetragona*
§ 'Pygmaea Helvola' (H) ♀H4	CBen CHid CRow CWat LPBA MSKA MWts NLar NPer SCoo SLon SVic SWat WMAq WPnP
'Pygmaea Rubis' (H)	CRow LPBA SWat WMAq
'Pygmaea Rubra' (H)	CBen CWat MSKA MWts NLar NPer SCoo SVic WMAq WPnP
'Ray Davies' (H)	CBen LLWG
'Red Paradise' (H)	MSKA
'Red Spider' (H)	LPBA MSKA NPer SVic
'Rembrandt' misapplied	see *N.* 'Météor'
'Rembrandt' Koster (H)	LPBA
'René Gérard' (H)	CBen CWat EHon LPBA MSKA NPer SWat WMAq WPnP
'Rosanna Supreme' (H)	LLWG SWat
'Rose Arey' (H)	CBen EHon LPBA MSKA NPer SCoo SVic SWat WMAq
'Rose Magnolia' (H)	CWat SWat
'Rosea' (H)	CBen LPBA
'Rosennymphe' (H)	CBen LPBA MSKA NPer SWat WMAq WPnP
'Rosy Morn' (H)	CBen LLWG MSKA
'Shady Lady'	MSKA
'Sioux' (H)	CBen EHon LPBA MSKA NPer SVic WMAq XBlo
'Sirius' (H)	CBen LLWG LPBA MSKA SWat
'Snow Princess'	LPBA WPnP
'Solfatare' (H)	LLWG
'Splendida' (H)	WMAq
'Starbright'	LLWG
'Starburst' (H)	MSKA
'Steven Strawn' (H)	LLWG
'Sultan' (H)	MSKA
'Sunny Pink'	LLWG MSKA
'Sunrise'	see *N.* 'Odorata Sulphurea Grandiflora'
§ ***tetragona*** (H)	CBen CRow CWat LPBA MWts NPer WMAq
- 'Alba'	see *N. tetragona*
- 'Johann Pring'	see *N.* 'Joanne Pring'
'Texas Dawn' (H)	CBen CWat LLWG MSKA SLon WMAq
'Thomas O'Brian'	LLWG
'Tuberosa Flavescens'	see *N.* 'Marliacea Chromatella'
'Tuberosa Richardsonii' (H)	CBen EHon MSKA NPer WPnP
'Turicensis'	see *N.* 'Odorata Turicensis'
'Vésuve' (H)	LLWG MSKA SWat
'Virginalis' (H)	CBen LLWG LPBA MSKA NPer SWat WMAq
'Virginia' (H)	LLWG
§ 'W.B. Shaw' (H)	CBen EHon LPBA MSKA NPer SWat WMAq
'Walter Pagels' (H)	CBen LLWG MWts WMAq
'Weymouth Red' (H)	CBen
'White Sultan' (H)	CWat LLWG MSKA
'William Doogue' (H)	MSKA
'William Falconer' (H)	CBen CWat LPBA MSKA NPer SWat
'Wow' (H)	MSKA
'Yellow Queen' (H)	MSKA
§ 'Yellow Sensation' (H)	CBen
'Yul Ling' (H)	LLWG MSKA SWat
'Zeus'	MSKA

Nymphoides (*Menyanthaceae*)

indica	XBlo
peltata	CBen CWat MSKA NLar NPer NSco SCoo SVic WMAq WPnP
§ - 'Bennettii'	LPBA

Nyssa ✿ (*Cornaceae*)

aquatica	CBcs SBir SSta
leptophylla **new**	SSta
sinensis ♀H4	CAbP CBcs CDoC CDul CMCN ELan EPfP IDee LRHS MAsh MBlu SBir SPer SReu SSpi SSta
- 'Jim Russell'	SSta
- Nymans form	EPfP SBir
sylvatica ♀H4	Widely available
- 'Autumn Cascades'	EPfP LRHS MBlu NLar SMad SSpi SSta WPGP
- var. ***biflora***	SSta
- 'Dirr' **new**	SSpi
- 'Haymen's Red'	see *N. sylvatica* Red Rage
- 'Isobel Grace'	LRHS MAsh MBri SBir SSpi
- 'Jermyns Flame'	CAbP EPfP LRHS MAsh SBir SPoG SSpi SSta
- 'Miss Scarlet' (f)	NLar SSta
- 'Pendula' **new**	SSta
§ - Red Rage = 'Haymanred'	LRHS SSpi
- 'Red Red Wine'	CGHE EPfP NLar SBir SMad SSta WPGP
- 'Sheffield Park'	CAbP EPfP LRHS MAsh SBir SLim SSpi
- 'Wildfire'	SSpi
- 'Windsor'	EPfP LRHS MAsh SBir
- 'Wisley Bonfire' (m)	CAbP CGHE EBee ECrN EPfP LRHS MAsh NLar SBir SSpi SSta WPGP
ursina	CBcs

O

Oakesiella see *Uvularia*

Ochagavia (*Bromeliaceae*)

sp.	NPal SAPC
carnea	EBee
- RCB RA S-2	LSou
§ ***litoralis***	SMad
* ***rosea***	CHEx SPlb

Ochna (*Ochnaceae*)

serrulata	CCCN

Ocimum (*Lamiaceae*)

'African Blue'	CArn CBod ELau EOHP GPoy LSou MHer NGHP NPri SPoG SVil
§ ***americanum***	NGHP WJek
- 'Meng Luk'	see *O. americanum*
basilicum	CArn CSev ELau GPoy NPri SBfd SIde SWat WJek
- 'Anise'	see *O. basilicum* 'Horapha'
- 'Ararat'	ELau NGHP
- ***camphorata***	see *O. kilimandscharicum*
- 'Cinnamon'	ELau MNHC NGHP SBfd SHDw WJek
- 'Cuban'	GPoy
- 'Gecofure' **new**	ELau
- 'Genovese'	ELau MHer MNHC NGHP NVic
- 'Genovese Special Select' **new**	ELau
- 'Glycyrrhiza'	see *O. basilicum* 'Horapha'
- 'Green Globe'	MNHC NGHP
- 'Green Ruffles'	ELau EPfP MNHC WJek
- 'Holy'	see *O. tenuiflorum*
§ - 'Horapha'	CArn ELau MHer MNHC NGHP SIde WJek
* - 'Horapha Nanum'	NGHP WJek
- 'Magic Michael' **new**	ELau
- 'Magic White'	NGHP
- 'Mexican' **new**	ELau
- 'Mrs Burns'	NGHP WJek
- 'Napolitano'	CBod ELau NGHP SIde SWat WJek
- 'New Guinea'	ELau
- 'Osmin'PBR **new**	ELau
- 'Pistou' **new**	ELau
- 'Purple Delight' **new**	ELau
- var. ***purpurascens***	CArn CSev SIde
- - 'Dark Opal'	CBod MNHC NGHP SBfd SHDw
- - 'Purple Ruffles'	EPfP MNHC SIde SWat WJek
- - 'Red Rubin'	MHer MNHC WJek
- var. ***purpurascens*** × ***kilimandscharicum***	CSpe GPoy
- 'Queenette' **new**	ELau
- 'Sweet Genovase'	SVic
- 'Thai'	see *O. basilicum* 'Horapha'
canum	see *O. americanum*
× ***citriodorum***	CArn MNHC NGHP SBfd SHDw SIde WJek
- 'Lime'	MNHC NGHP
- 'Pesto Perpetuo'	NGHP
- 'Siam Queen'	ELau MHer NGHP WJek
gratissimum	ELau
§ ***kilimandscharicum***	ELau GPoy
minimum	CArn CBod CSev ELau MHer MNHC NGHP SBfd SIde WJek
sanctum	see *O. tenuiflorum*
'Spice'	ELau NGHP
'Spicy Globe'	ELau
§ ***tenuiflorum***	CArn ELau GPoy MNHC NGHP SBfd SHDw SIde WJek

Odontonema (*Acanthaceae*)

schomburgkianum	CCCN
tubaeforme	CCCN

Oemleria (*Rosaceae*)

cerasiformis	CBcs CHGN CMac CPMA EBee EBtc EPfP EPla LRHS NLar SSpi WCot WEas WSHC

Oenanthe (*Apiaceae*)

fistulosa	LLWG
javanica 'Flamingo' (v)	CWat ELan EPfP GCal GGar LEdu LPBA MWts NBro WFar WMAq WSHC
lachenalii	EBWF LLWG

Oenothera ✿ (*Onagraceae*)

§ ***acaulis***	CBot CPBP CSpe CSpr GKev MNrw SBch SBri SGar SPhx WPGP
- ***alba***	MDKP WCot
'Apricot Delight'	EBee EHoe GJos STes WMnd WMoo
§ ***biennis***	CArn COld CSev CWan EBWF ELan GAbr GPoy MHer NBro NGHP SBfd SGar SIde SPhx WBrk WEas WFar WHer WJek WSFF
'Blood Orange'	CBow MDKP SMrm
caespitosa	GKev
childsii	see *O. speciosa*
cinaeus	see *O. fruticosa* subsp. *glauca*
'Cold Crick'	EBee LRHS
'Colin Porter'	EBur MDKP WHrl WMoo
'Copper Canyon'	SGSe STes
'Crown Imperial'	CChe CMac EBee LEdu LRHS LSou MArl MCCP NHol SHar SLon SPoG
Crown of Gold = 'Lishal'	ELan LLHF LRHS
§ ***elata*** subsp. ***hookeri***	EWes NBre
erythrosepala	see *O. glazioviana*
'Finlay's Fancy'	WCru
§ ***fruticosa***	NLar SEND SPlb
- 'African Sun'PBR	EBee EWes SRot
- 'Camel' (v)	MDKP SMrm WHrl WWEG
- Fireworks	see *O. fruticosa* 'Fyrverkeri'
§ - 'Fyrverkeri' ♀H4	CBcs CMac CMea CPrp EBee ECtt ELan EShb GKir GMaP LEdu LHop LRHS MRav NGdn NHol NVic SPer SWvt WAul WBVN WCAu WMnd WWEG
§ - subsp. ***glauca*** ♀H4	CElw CEnt EPfP MDKP MNrw MWhi NBPC SBfd SRms WJek WPer
- - 'Erica Robin' (v)	CBct CChe CMea CPrp EBee EBrs ECtt EHoe LRHS LSou MNrw MRav NEgg NGdn SAga SMad SMrm SPoG SRot SWvt WCot WHoo WPGP WWEG
- - 'Frühlingsgold' (v)	CMac ECtt EShb SPoG
- - 'Longest Day'	MBrN
- - Solstice	see *O. fruticosa* subsp. *glauca* 'Sonnenwende'
§ - - 'Sonnenwende'	CBre CElw CEnt EBee EBrs LRHS MAvo NLar SPad WMoo WWEG
- Highlight	see *O. fruticosa* 'Hoheslicht'
§ - 'Hoheslicht'	EBee
- 'Lady Brookeborough'	MRav
- 'Michelle Ploeger'	NBre SUsu
- 'Silberblatt' (v)	CBow EBee
- 'W. Cuthbertson'	EBee
- 'Yellow River'	CElw EBee

- 'Youngii'	CWan EPfP LEdu MCCP MLLN WJek WPer WWEG
glabra misapplied	ECha NSti
glabra Miller	see *O. biennis*
§ ***glazioviana***	CWan MNHC NBir SVic
- 'Black Magic' **new**	WOut
hookeri	see *O. elata* subsp. *hookeri*
kunthiana	CEnt ECha ECho MDKP MHer NWCA WMnd WMoo
- 'Glowing Magenta'	SPoG
lamarckiana	see *O. glazioviana*
'Lemon Sunset'	CCVN LSou MBNS SWal WMoo
linearis	see *O. fruticosa*
§ ***macrocarpa*** ♀H4	Widely available
- subsp. ***fremontii*** 'Silver Wings'	EBee ECtt NLar SMrm
- subsp. ***incana***	CMea CSpe NBre WHoo
- 'Yellow Queen'	GJos
* ***minima***	MDKP
missouriensis	see *O. macrocarpa*
muricata	NBre
oakesiana	SPhx
odorata misapplied	see *O. stricta*
odorata Hook. & Arn.	see *O. biennis*
odorata Jacquin	CArn
- cream-flowered	CSpe
organensis	CDes EBee WPGP
pallida 'Innocence'	CBot NBre
'Penelope Hobhouse'	CBct
§ ***perennis***	CEnt EBee NBre SRms WBVN WEas WPer
pumila	see *O. perennis*
rosea	CMea
'Rosie Baby'	GJos
'Silky Orchid'	ELon
§ ***speciosa***	CMHG EBee NBre SEND WFar WJek
* - 'Alba'	EBee EWes
- var. ***childsii***	see *O. speciosa*
- 'Pink Petticoats'	ECha NPer SWat
- 'Rosea'	CBot ECho LEdu LRHS SPlb SWat
- 'Siskiyou'	CSpe EAEE EBee ECtt EPfP EShb EWld GKir LBMP LEdu LRHS LSou SCoo SGar SMrm SPer SRot SUsu
- Twilight = 'Turner01'PBR (v)	EBee LRHS SHar
- 'Woodside White'	ELon SMrm
§ ***stricta***	CHar CMea GCal WBrk
* - 'Moonlight'	SGar
- 'Sulphurea'	CHar CMHG CMea ECGP ELan EWld GCal GKev GMaP IFro LBMP MNFA NPer SBch SGar SMrm SPhx WAbb WCom WCot
'Summer Sun'	EAEE EBee ECGP LRHS NBre
taraxacifolia	see *O. acaulis*
tetragona	see *O. fruticosa* subsp. *glauca*
- var. ***fraseri***	see *O. fruticosa* subsp. *glauca*
versicolor	CSev WCFE
- 'Sunset Boulevard'	CPom CSpe EBee GCal LRHS MBNS MMuc SGar SPer WFar WMoo

Olea (*Oleaceae*)

europaea (F)	Widely available
- subsp. ***africana***	CTrC WPGP
- 'Aglandau' (F)	CAgr
- 'Arbequina' (F)	ETod SBig
- 'Bouteillan' (F)	CAgr
- 'Cailletier' (F)	CAgr
- 'Chelsea Physic Garden' (F)	CDoC CDoy WPGP
§ - 'Cipressino' (F)	ERea ESwi SBfd SBig
- 'Cornicabra' (F) **new**	ETod
- 'El Greco' (F)	CBcs
- subsp. ***europaea*** var. ***sylvestris***	SEND
- 'Fastigiata'	SBfd
- 'Frantoio' (F)	CAgr CDoy ETod SBfd SBig
- 'Hojiblanca' (F)	SBig
- 'Leccino' (F)	CDoy SBig
- 'Manzanillo' (F)	ETod
- 'Maurino' (F)	SBig
- 'Peace' **new**	CDoy
- 'Pendolino' (F)	SBig
- 'Picual' (F)	ETod SBig
- 'Pyramidalis'	see *O. europaea* 'Cipressino'
- 'Serrana' **new**	ETod
- 'Villalonga'	ETod

Olearia ✿ (*Asteraceae*)

albida misapplied	see *O.* 'Talbot de Malahide'
albida Hook. f.	GGar
- var. ***angulata***	CTrC CTsd
algida	ECou GGar
angustifolia **new**	GGar
arborescens	GGar
argophylla	CPLG ECou GGar
avicenniifolia	CBcs CMac ECou GGar SEND
bullata	ECou
canescens	CPne
× ***capillaris***	CDoC EBee ECou GGar
chathamica	GGar IFFs
§ ***cheesemanii***	CBcs CDoC CMHG CPLG CTrC GGal GGar LRHS NLar
coriacea	ECou GGar
'County Park'	ECou
erubescens	CDoC CPLG
floribunda	GGar
frostii	GGar
furfuracea	ECou SEND
glandulosa	ECou GGar
gunniana	see *O. phlogopappa*
× ***haastii***	Widely available
- 'McKenzie'	ECou ELon
'Havering Blush'	ECou
hectorii	ECou
§ 'Henry Travers'	CBcs CCCN CPLG EPfP GGar GQui NMun
ilicifolia	CDoC EBee EPfP GGar IFFs LRHS NLar
insignis	see *Pachystegia insignis*
ledifolia	GGar
lepidophylla	ECou
- 'Silver Knight'	NLar
- silver-leaved	ECou
lirata	ECou GGar
macrodonta ♀H3	Widely available
- 'Intermedia'	GGar
- 'Major'	CCCN GGal GGar LTen NLar
- 'Minor'	CBcs CCCN CDoC CMac CTrC ELan EPfP GBin GGar GQui SPlb WSpi
§ × ***matthewsii***	GGar
× ***mollis*** misapplied	see *O.* × *matthewsii*
× ***mollis*** (Kirk) Cockayne	CMac GQui LRHS
- 'Zennorensis' ♀H3	CBcs CCCN CDoC EBee EPfP GGar IArd IDee IFFs NLar SOWG WDin WEas WPGP
moschata	GGar NLar
moschata × ***nummularifolia*** var. ***cymbifolia***	GGar
myrsinoides	CPLG
nummularifolia	CBcs CCCN CDoC CHll CTrC CTri EBee ECou ELan EPfP EPla GGar GKir IVic LRHS NLar SPer STre SWvt WDin WFar
- var. ***cymbifolia***	ECou

	- hybrids	ECou
	- 'Little Lou'	ECou
	odorata	CPLG ECou NLar WFar
	oleifolia	see *O.* 'Waikariensis'
	paniculata	CBcs CDoC CMHG CTrC CTri CTsd EBee EPfP GGar IFFs IVic LRHS
§	***phlogopappa***	CTri ECou GGar WBrE WKif
	- 'Comber's Blue'	CBcs CCCN EBee ELan EPfP GGal GGar GKir IVic LSRN SCoo SPer
§	- 'Comber's Pink'	CBcs CCCN CDoC CPLG CWan EBee ELan ELon EPfP GGar GKir LRHS LSRN MAsh NPer SAga SCoo WEas WGrn WSHC
	- 'Rosea'	see *O. phlogopappa* 'Comber's Pink'
	- 'Sawtooth'	GGar
	- Splendens Group	WFar
I	- var. ***subrepanda*** (DC.) J.H.Willis	CTrC GGal GGar LEdu WAbe
	- 'Tournaig Titch'	GGar
	ramulosa	CCCN CDoC CPLG EBee
	- 'Blue Stars'	ECou
	- var. ***ramulosa***	ECou
	rani misapplied	see *O. cheesemanii*
	rani Druce	IFFs
*	***rossii***	CTrC
	× ***scilloniensis*** misapplied	see *O. stellulata* DC.
	× ***scilloniensis*** ambig.	CBcs IFFs SGar SPoG WFar WKif
	× ***scilloniensis*** Dorrien-Smith ♀H3	CCCN CTsd GGar MRav
	- 'Compacta'	CBcs
	- 'Master Michael'	CBot CCCN CDoC CTri ELon EPfP IVic LRHS NPri SOWG SPer SPoG WCFE WEas WGrn WSHC
	semidentata misapplied	see *O.* 'Henry Travers'
	solandri	CCCN CDoC CMac CTsd CWit EBee ECou EHoe GGar LRHS SDix SEND SPer STre
	- 'Aurea'	CBcs GQui
	'Stardust'	CTrC CWit WClo
	stellulata misapplied	see *O. phlogopappa*
§	***stellulata*** DC.	CBot CPLG CSBt CWSG CWib ECou EPfP GGal LRHS SAga SCoo SDix SLim SOWG SPer WDin WEas WFar WSHC
	- 'Michael's Pride'	CPLG
	- var. ***rugosa***	ECou
§	'Talbot de Malahide'	GGar
	traversii	CBcs CBod CCCN CDoC CMHG CSBt CTrC CTsd EBee GGal GGar IFFs LRHS SBfd SEND WHer
	- 'Tweedledee' (v) **new**	CChe
	- 'Tweedledum' (v)	CBod CBow CCCN CDoC CTrC CWib ECou GGar LAst SBfd WCom
	- 'Variegata' (v)	CBcs CTsd GGar
	virgata	CCCN CHEx ECou GBin GGar GQui IFFs LEdu MCot WCot
	- var. ***laxiflora***	CTrC WHer
	- var. ***lineata***	CDoC CPLG ECou GGar NLar SEND WDin WSHC
	- - 'Dartonii'	CBcs CBod CDoC EBee ECou EPfP GGar LRHS SLPl SPoG
§	'Waikariensis'	CBot CMHG CMac CPLG CTrC EBee ECou GGar IDee IVic LRHS MSCN SEND SLon WCFE WClo WDin

Oligoneuron see *Solidago*

Oligostachyum (*Poaceae*)

lubricum	see *Semiarundinaria lubrica*
oedogonatum	WPGP

olive see *Olea europaea*

Olsynium (*Iridaceae*)

§	***douglasii*** ♀H4	EPot LLHF NMen NRya WAbe WCot
	- 'Album'	ELon EPot GAbr GBin GCrs GEdr LLHF NHar NMen NRya NSla WHal
	- dwarf	GEdr
	- var. ***inflatum***	EWes
§	***filifolium***	GAbr NWCA WHil
§	***junceum***	MDKP WPGP
	- JCA 12289	MTho
	scirpoideum	LLHF
	trinerve B&SWJ 10459	WCru

Omphalodes ✿ (*Boraginaceae*)

	cappadocica ♀H4	CElw CEnt EBee EShb IFoB LBMP LEdu LRHS MMuc NBro NCob NPer NSum NWCA SRms SWat WBrk WFar WKif WPat
	- 'Anthea Bloom'	NEgg
	- 'Blue Rug'	NBPC
	- 'Blueberries and Cream' (v)	CBow
	- 'Cherry Ingram' ♀H4	Widely available
	- 'Lilac Mist'	CLAP EBee EPot LLWP MRav NCob SBch SRms SSvw SWat SWvt WGwG WTin WWEG
	- 'Parisian Skies'	CDes CLAP
	- 'Starry Eyes'	Widely available
§	***linifolia*** ♀H4	CMea CSpe MCot NMen SBch
	- ***alba***	see *O. linifolia*
	luciliae	CLAP WThu
	- var. ***cilicica***	WFar
	nitida	CSpe EWld GGar IMou MMuc NLBP NRya WWEG
	verna	Widely available
	- 'Alba'	Widely available
	- 'Elfenauge'	CMil EBee NBir NLar NRya SMrm SSvw WCot WWEG
	- ***grandiflora***	WCot

Omphalogramma (*Primulaceae*)

delavayi SDR 5167	GKev

Oncostema see *Scilla*

onion see *Allium cepa*

Onixotis (*Colchicaceae*)

stricta	CLak WCot

Onobrychis (*Papilionaceae*)

viciifolia	EBWF EBee

Onoclea (*Woodsiaceae*)

sensibilis ♀H4	Widely available
- copper-leaved	CHEx CPMA CRow WPGP
- 'Rotstiel'	EBee

Ononis (*Papilionaceae*)

repens	CArn EBWF NMir
rotundifolia	CPom
spinosa	EBWF EBee MHer SMrm SPhx WFar WPer WSpi

Onopordum (*Asteraceae*)

acanthium	CArn CBct EBee EBrs ECha ELan EPfP GAbr GBar GKir GMaP LRHS MHer MSpe MWat NBid NEgg NVic SBfd SIde WCAu WCot WFar WHer WMnd WSpi

arabicum	see *O. nervosum*
§ ***nervosum*** ♀H4	CSpe NBPC SEND

Onosma (*Boraginaceae*)

alborosea	CMdw EBee ECha GCal GCra SAga SEND WEas WKif WPGP WPat WSHC
nana	WAbe
taurica ♀H4	CMdw

Onychium (*Adiantaceae*)

contiguum	WAbe
japonicum	EFer EFtx GQui SMad SRms WAbe WRic
lucidum	WCot

Ophiopogon ✿ (*Convallariaceae*)

ACE 2362	NMen
BWJ 8244 from Vietnam	WCru
from India	GCal
'Black Dragon'	see *O. planiscapus* 'Nigrescens'
bodinieri	CBct ECho EShb EWes LEdu
- B&L 12505	CLAP EBee EPPr EPla
caulescens B&SWJ 8230	WCru
- B&SWJ 11813	WCru
aff. ***caulescens*** HWJ 590	WCru
chingii	EBee EPPr GCal LEdu SCnR
clarkei new	MMoz
formosanus	CPrp GBin
- B&SWJ 3659	WCon WCru
'Gin-ryu'	see *Liriope spicata* 'Gin-ryu'
graminifolius	see *Liriope muscari*
intermedius	CBct EBee EPPr GGar NLar WAbe WCot WPGP
- GWJ 9387	WCru
§ - 'Argenteomarginatus'	ECho EWes WPGP
- 'Variegatus'	see *O. intermedius* 'Argenteomarginatus'
§ ***jaburan***	CMac EBee ECho EShb LBMP LEdu NHol STre WMoo
- 'Variegatus'	see *O. jaburan* 'Vittatus'
§ - 'Vittatus' (v)	ECho EHoe ELan EPfP EShb EWes LEdu MCCP MGos MTis WCot WFar WSpi
japonicus	CMac ECho EPPr EPfP EPla EShb LEdu
- B&SWJ 1871	WCru
- 'Albus'	CLAP ECho NHol
- 'Compactus'	CDoC EBee WPGP
- 'Gyoku-Ryu' new	GCal
- 'Kigimafukiduma'	CMac CMoH EBee GGar LRHS MRav WCot WSpi
- 'Kyoto'	EBee EPPr ESwi
- 'Minor'	CBct CChe CEnd CKno ELon EPPr EPfP EPla NLar WPGP WWEG
- 'Nanus Variegatus' (v)	CDes EBee NChi
- 'Nippon'	CPrp EBee ECho EHoe EPPr GGar LAst LRHS NGdn
- 'Tama-ryu'	WPat
* - 'Tama-ryu Number Two'	ECho EPPr
* - 'Variegatus' (v)	CDTJ CKno CMac CPrp ECho LEdu SLPl
longifolius 'Takashi-shimomura' (v)	WCot
parviflorus GWJ 9387	WCru
- HWJK 2093	WCru
planiscapus	CEnd CFee CKno CMHG CPLG CSWP CSam CSev EBee ECho EPPr EPla GAbr MWat NBro SPad STre WMoo
* - 'Albovariegatus'	WFar
- 'Black Beard' new	MAsh
- 'Green Dragon'	ELan
- 'Kansu'	SBfd
- ***leucanthus***	EPPr SLPl WCot
- 'Little Tabby' (v)	CBow CDes CLAP EBee ECho EPla MDKP MMoz MWhi WAbe WCot WDyG WGrn WHal WPGP WTin WWEG
* - ***minimus***	ECho
§ - 'Nigrescens' ♀H4	Widely available
- 'Silver Ribbon'	ECho MDKP SGar
scaber B&SWJ 1842	WCru
'Spring Gold'	EShb

Ophrys (*Orchidaceae*)

apifera	CFir NLAp WHer
- subsp. ***trollii***	NLAp
apifera × ***holoserica***	NLAp
apifera × ***scolopax***	NLAp
araneola	NLAp
bombyliflora	NLAp
fuciflora	NLAp
heldreichii	NLAp
holoserica	NLAp
insectifera	NLAp
reinholdii new	NLAp
speculum	NLAp
sphegodes	NLAp
strausii new	NLAp

Oplopanax (*Araliaceae*)

horridus B&SWJ 9551	WCru

Opopanax (*Apiaceae*)

chironium	LEdu

Opuntia (*Cactaceae*)

sp. new	SArc
compressa	see *O. humifusa*
erinacea var. ***utahensis*** × ***polycantha***	WCot
§ ***humifusa***	CDTJ EAmu EGxp ETod SChr SMad WCot
§ ***polyacantha***	SChr SPlb
rhodantha	see *O. polyacantha*

orange, sour or Seville see *Citrus aurantium*

orange, sweet see *Citrus sinensis*

Orbea (*Asclepiadaceae*)

cooperi new	LToo
halipedicola new	LToo
knobelii new	LToo
lugardii new	LToo
pulchella new	LToo
speciosa new	LToo
§ ***variegata*** ♀H1	EShb LToo STre

Orchis (*Orchidaceae*)

anthropophora	EFEx
elata	see *Dactylorhiza elata*
foliosa	see *Dactylorhiza foliosa*
fuchsii	see *Dactylorhiza fuchsii*
laxiflora	see *Anacamptis laxiflora*
maculata	see *Dactylorhiza maculata*
maderensis	see *Dactylorhiza foliosa*
majalis	see *Dactylorhiza majalis*
§ ***mascula***	ECho NLAp WHer
militaris	GAuc NLAp WHer
morio	see *Anacamptis morio*
purpurea	NLAp
simia	NLAp

oregano see *Origanum vulgare*

Oreomyrrhis (*Apiaceae*)

argentea	EBee GKev NMen

Oreopteris (*Thelypteridaceae*)

§ ***limbosperma***	SRms WRic

Oreorchis (*Orchidaceae*)

patens	WWst

Origanum ✿ (*Lamiaceae*)

from Kalamata **new**	SEND
amanum ♀H2-3	CPBP EBee ECho EWes MDKP NBir NMen WAbe WCom WPat
- var. ***album***	EBee ECho LLHF NSla WAbe
× ***applii***	ELau
'Barbara Tingey'	CPBP EBee ECho ELan EWes ITim LBee MNrw MTho NWCA SEND SPhx WAbe WCFE
'Bristol Cross'	GBar MHer
'Buckland'	CPrp CWCL EBee ECho ECtt EPot MHer NMen NWCA SPhx WAbe WCom WSHC
caespitosum	see *O. vulgare* 'Nanum'
§ ***calcaratum***	EBee ECho LLHF MTho SUsu WPat
'Carol's Delight'	MHer
creticum	see *O. vulgare* subsp. *hirtum*
dictamnus	CArn CEls CMea EBee ECho GPoy LLHF MHer SBfd SHDw WJek
'Dingle Fairy'	CMMP CWCL EBee ECho EDAr ELon EPot EWes GBar MHer MNrw MTho NBir SBch SIde SRot WGwG WMoo
'Emma Stanley'	WAbe
'Frank Tingey'	EBee ECho LLHF
'Gold Splash'	CPbn EPfP GBar SIde WMoo
heracleoticum L.	see *O. vulgare* subsp. *hirtum*
'Hot and Spicy'	CPbn GBar LBuc MHer WJek
§ × ***hybridinum***	WCom
'Ingolstadt'	SPhx
'Kent Beauty'	Widely available
'Kent Beauty Variegated' (v)	ECho
laevigatum ♀H3	CArn CMHG ECho ELan EPfP GBee MHer NBro NMir NPer NWCA SEND SGar SIde SUsu WCom WKif WMoo WPer WSHC
- 'Herrenhausen' ♀H4	Widely available
- 'Hopleys'	Widely available
- 'Purple Charm'	EBee EDAr MNHC NBre SIde WSpi
majorana	CArn CFox CPbn CSev ELan ELau MHer MNHC SIde SWat WJek WPer
I - 'Aureum'	SWal
- Pagoda Bells = 'Lizbell'PBR	SIde WHoo
'Marchants Seedling'	SMHy SPhx
microphyllum	CFee CPbn EDAr GBar NMen
minutiflorum	EBee ECho LLHF
'Norton Gold'	CBre EBee ECha ECtt GBar LRHS MHer NBre NHol NPer SIde SMrm
'Nymphenburg'	CFee EBee LSou MHer NCob SIde WHer WSpi
onites	CArn CFox CHby CPbn CWan ELau GBar ILis LBuc MHer MNHC SBfd SIde SPlb WBrk WGwG WJek WPer
Overseas Farm hybrid **new**	MHer
pulchellum	see *O.* × *hybridinum*
'Rosenkuppel'	CMea CPbn EBee ECha ECtt ELan EPot GCal LAst LHop MHer MLHP MRav NGHP SPer SPhx SPlb WJek WMoo WPnn WSpi WTin WWEG
'Rotkugel'	CAby CHVG CMHG ELon LRHS WCFE WWEG
rotundifolium ♀H4	CMea EBee ECho ELan LLHF MDKP MHer NBir SBch WAbe WCom
- hybrid	MDKP
scabrum	CArn
- subsp. ***pulchrum*** 'Newleaze'	SBch WHoo
syriacum	CArn
'Tinpenny Pink'	WTin
tournefortii	see *O. calcaratum*
villosum	see *Thymus villosus*
virens	CArn GBar ILis MCCP
vulgare	Widely available
- from Israel	ELau
- 'Acorn Bank'	CArn CBod CPbn CPrp EBee ELau EWes GBar GGar MNHC NHol NLar SAga SIde SPoG WGwG WHer WJek
- var. ***album***	CElw ELau WAlt
- 'Aureum' ♀H4	Widely available
- 'Aureum Crispum'	CPbn CPrp CWan ECha ELau GBar GPoy ILis NBid SBch SBfd SIde SWat WJek
- 'Compactum'	CArn CMea CPbn CPrp CSev EBee ECha ELau GBar GCal GGar GPoy ILis LEdu MHer MNHC NBir NCob NGHP SIde SPlb SWat WGwG WJek WMoo WPer WTin
- 'Corinne Tremaine' (v)	NBir WHer
- 'Country Cream' (v)	Widely available
- ***formosanum*** B&SWJ 3180	WCru
§ - 'Gold Tip' (v)	CEnt CMea CPbn CSev EBee ELau GBar MCot MHer MNHC SBfd SIde SPlb SWat WFar WHer WJek WWEG
- 'Golden Shine'	CMMP EHoe EWes SIde
§ - subsp. ***hirtum***	CArn CHby CPbn GPoy SPlb WJek WPer
- - 'Greek'	CBod CEnt CPrp CWan ELau MHer MNHC NGHP SBfd SEND WGwG
§ - 'Nanum'	ECho GBar WJek
- 'Nyamba'	GPoy
- 'Polyphant' (v)	CPbn CSev GBar LSou NBir WBrE WJek
- subsp. ***prismaticum***	GBar
- 'Thumble's Variety'	CElw CMea CPrp EAEE EBee ECha EHoe EPfP GBar GCal LHop LRHS MAsh MBri MHer MRav NCob NHol SIde SSvw SWat WEas WMnd WMoo WSpi WWEG
- 'Tomintoul'	GPoy
- 'Variegatum'	see *O. vulgare* 'Gold Tip'
- 'White Charm'	CPbn NHol SIde
'Z'Attar'	MHer SIde WJek

Orixa (*Rutaceae*)

japonica	CBot CPLG EBee GAuc MBri NLar WFar WPGP
- 'Variegata' (v)	EPfP LLHF NLar

Orlaya (*Apiaceae*)

grandiflora	CBre CFir CSpe LBMP LPio MWea SBch SUsu WCot WFar WHal WWFP

Ornithogalum (*Hyacinthaceae*)

algeriense	ECho
arabicum	CFir CHid CStu ECho LAma LRHS MBri
arcuatum	WCot

	arianum	EBee ECho SPhx
	balansae	see *O. oligophyllum*
	caudatum	see *O. longibracteatum*
	chionophilum	EBee ECho
	comosum	ECho
	dubium ♀H1	CStu ECho LRHS MAvo MWea WCot
	exscapum	ECho
	fimbriatum	EBee ECho
	graminifolium	ECho
	'Soutpan' **new**	
	hispidum	ECho
	lanceolatum	ECho WCot
§	***longibracteatum***	CHEx CStu EBee ECho GAuc SChr WGwG WPrP
	maculatum	ECho
	magnum	CAvo CFFs CMea EBee ECho ERCP GAuc GMac LRHS MCot MNrw SPad SPhx
	- 'Saguramo'	ECho
	montanum	ECho
	'Mount Everest'	ECho ERCP
	'Mount Fuji'	ECho
	multifolium	ECho
	'Loeriesfontein' **new**	
	nanum	see *O. sigmoideum*
	narbonense	EBee EBrs ECho GAuc LRHS MMHG SPhx WCot
	nutans ♀H4	CAvo CFFs CHid CPrp CTca EBee ECho EPfP EPot GCal LAma LRHS MCot MNrw NBir NMRc NMen NWCA SDeJ SEND SPhx WCot WFar
§	***oligophyllum***	EBee ECho EPfP EPot MMHG MNrw NWCA
§	***orthophyllum***	ECho
	- HOA 9405	EBee
	ponticum	ECho
	pyramidale	CPom EBee ECho EPot GAuc GMac LRHS MNrw SPhx
	- short	SMHy
	pyrenaicum	ECha WShi
	reverchonii	EBee ECho
	saundersiae	CHid EBee ECho
	sibthorpii	see *O. sigmoideum*
§	***sigmoideum***	EBee ECho
	sintenisii	EBee ECho
	suaveolens 'Saldanha' **new**	ECho
	tenuifolium	see *O. orthophyllum*
	- subsp. ***aridum***	ECho WWst
	thyrsoides ♀H1	CBgR CCCN CStu ECho EPfP ERCP LAma LRHS
	ulophyllum	EBee ECho
	umbellatum	CAvo CFFs CTca CTri EBrs ECho EPfP GKev GPoy LAma LRHS MBri MCot MNrw NMen SDeJ SEND SMrm SPer SRms WBVN WFar WHil WPer WShi
	unifolium	ECho

Ornithoglossum (*Colchicaceae*)

	viride **new**	CLak

Orontium (*Araceae*)

	aquaticum	CBen CWat EHon LLWG LPBA MSKA MWts NLar NPer SWat WMAq WPnP

Orostachys (*Crassulaceae*)

	furusei	WCot WFar
§	***spinosa***	EWes GKev NMen NWCA SPlb WFar

Orthrosanthus (*Iridaceae*)

	chimboracensis	CFir EWld MDKP MGos MWea NLar WFar WPGP WPer
	- JCA 13743	CPou
	- RCB/Eq	EBee
	laxus	CFir CHid EBee ECou EPau GMac LLHF SEND SHom SMad WMoo WNew WPrP WWEG
	multiflorus	CDes CSpe EBee WPGP
	polystachyus	CCVN CSpe CTsd CWCL CYeo EWld MWea SGSe SMrm WSHC

Orychophragmus (*Brassicaceae*)

	violaceus	CCCN WHil

Oryzopsis (*Poaceae*)

	lessoniana	see *Anemanthele lessoniana*
	miliacea	CKno CSpe EBee ECha EHoe EPPr GFor MMoz NDov NWsh SEND SMHy SUsu WCot WPGP WWEG
	paradoxa	EPPr

Oscularia (*Aizoaceae*)

§	***deltoides*** ♀H1-2	CCCN CHEx NWCA WCot WEas

Osmanthus (*Oleaceae*)

	armatus	CAbP CBcs CMac EBee EPfP NLar SPur WFar
§	× ***burkwoodii*** ♀H4	Widely available
§	***decorus***	CBcs CMac CTri EBee ELan EPfP GKir MGos MRav MWea NLar NWea SPer WDin WFar WSpi
	delavayi ♀H4	Widely available
	- 'George Gardner' **new**	CMac
	- 'Latifolius'	CPMA LRHS MAsh SLon SPer SPoG WFar
	forrestii	see *O. yunnanensis*
	× ***fortunei***	CPLG EBee EPfP LLHF LRHS SEND WFar
	fragrans	CBcs CDoC CMCN GBin MBri SLon
	- f. ***aurantiacus*** **new**	GBin
	- 'Fudingzhu' **new**	GBin
	- 'Latifolius'	CBcs
	- f. ***thunbergii***	CBcs GBin
§	***heterophyllus***	CBcs CDul CMac EBee ECrN EPfP MGos MRav NLar SPer SReu SRms SSta WDin WFar
§	- all gold	CAbP CDoC EBee IVic SPer
	- 'Argenteomarginatus'	see *O. heterophyllus* 'Variegatus'
§	- 'Aureomarginatus' (v)	CBcs CDoC CMHG CSBt CTsd EBee EHoe ELon EPfP NWea SLon SPer
	- 'Aureus' misapplied	see *O. heterophyllus* all gold
	- 'Aureus' Rehder	see *O. heterophyllus* 'Aureomarginatus'
§	- 'Goshiki' (v)	Widely available
N	- 'Gulftide' ♀H4	CDul EBee EPfP IFFs LRHS MGos NLar SCoo WFar
	- 'Kembu' (v)	NLar
	- 'Myrtifolius'	CMac NLar
	- 'Ogon'	EPfP
	- 'Purple Shaft'	CAbP ELan EPfP LRHS MAsh
	- 'Purpureus'	CAbP CBcs CBot CDoC CDul CMHG CMac CWib EBee EHoe ELon EPfP MBri MGos MSwo NHol NLar SCoo SEND SLim SLon SPer SSpi WCFE WDin
	- 'Rotundifolius'	CBcs CMac EBee NLar
	- Tricolor	see *O. heterophyllus* 'Goshiki'
§	- 'Variegatus' (v) ♀H4	Widely available
	ilicifolius	see *O. heterophyllus*

	rigidus	NLar
	serrulatus	CBot NLar
	suavis	GKir NLar
§	***yunnanensis***	CBcs CMHG EBee EPfP MBlu MBri NLar SAPC SArc WFar WPGP WPat

× *Osmarea* see *Osmanthus*

Osmaronia see *Oemleria*

Osmitopsis (*Asteraceae*)

asteriscoides	GFai

Osmorhiza (*Apiaceae*)

aristata B&SWJ 1607	WCru

Osmunda ✿ (*Osmundaceae*)

sp.	CCCN
cinnamomea ♀H4	CBty CCCN CFwr CKel CLAP CWCL EBee EWes GBin GCal ISha LRHS NLar NMyG SGSe WPGP WRic
claytoniana ♀H4	CLAP CMil EBee EFer GBin GLin ISha LRHS NHol NLar NMyG WCru WPnP WRic
japonica	CLAP GBin ISha NMyG
regalis ♀H4	Widely available
- from southern USA	CLAP
- 'Cristata' ♀H4	CBty CFwr CLAP EBee ELan EPfP GBin LRHS MBri MRav NBid NLar NMyG SWvt WFib WPGP WRic
- 'Purpurascens'	Widely available
- var. ***spectabilis***	CCCN CLAP ISha LRHS WRic
- 'Undulata'	NHol WFib

Osteomeles (*Rosaceae*)

subrotunda	MBri

Osteospermum (*Asteraceae*)

	'African Queen'	see *O.* 'Nairobi Purple'
	'Almach'PBR (Springstar Series)	LSou MBNS
	'Arusha'PBR (Cape Daisy Series)	LSou
	(Astra Series)	SVil
	'Astra Cream' **new**	
	- 'Astra Dark Copper' **new**	SVil
	- 'Astra Light Copper' **new**	SVil
	- 'Astra Outback Purple' **new**	SVil
	- 'Astra Peach Ice' **new**	SVil
	- 'Astra Pink Silver' **new**	SVil
	- 'Astra Purple Spoon'	WGor
	- 'Astra Violet' **new**	LAst
	Banana Symphony = 'Sekiin47' (Symphony Series)	CCCN CWCL LAst MBNS SMrm SPoG
	barberae misapplied	see *O. jucundum* (Phillips) Norlindh
	'Blue Streak'	CCCN
	'Brickell's Hybrid'	see *O.* 'Chris Brickell'
	'Buttermilk' ♀H1+3	CCCN CTsd ELan WWlt
	'Cannington John'	GCra LSRN
	'Cannington Roy'	CBar CBcs CCCN COlW CSam EBee ECtt ELan EPfP GAbr LSRN SPoG WNew
	caulescens misapplied	see *O.* 'White Pim'
§	'Chris Brickell'	GCal
	compact white-flowered	CHEx
	ecklonis	CBcs CCCN CDTJ CHll CTri EBee GGar GMaP NBro NGdn WPer
	- var. ***prostratum***	see *O.* 'White Pim'
	'Edna Bond'	WEas
	'Giles Gilbey' (v)	CCCN MBNS
	'Gold Sparkler' (v)	SEND SMrm
	'Gweek Variegated' (v)	CCCN
	'Helen Dimond'	LBuc LRHS
	'Hopleys' ♀H3-4	MHer SEND
	'Iced Gem'	LBuc
	'Irish'	EPot IGor LSou SMrm
§	***jucundum*** (Phillips) Norlindh ♀H3-4	CChe CEnt CMea CTri CWCL ECha EPfP LRHS LSRN MAvo MLHP MRav NBir NGdn NHol NPer SEND SMrm SPlb SRms WBVN WBrk
	- 'Blackthorn Seedling' ♀H3-4	CMea CWGN GGar IVic MWte NGdn SAga
	- var. ***compactum***	CHEx CPBP ELan ELon EPfP EShb GCal LAst LRHS MBri NPer SMrm SPer SPoG SPur SWvt WAbe WCom WHoo WNew WPat
	- 'Killerton Pink'	WPer
	- 'White Moon'	GGar
	Kalanga Rosy = 'Aksinto'PBR (Cape Daisy Series)	LRHS
	'Keia'PBR (Springstar Series)	CCCN LSou
	'La Mortola'	GCal
§	'Lady Leitrim' ♀H3-4	CBar CCCN CWGN EBee ECGP ECha ELan ELon EPfP EShb GCra GGar GKev LHop LRHS LSRN MGos MSpe NPer SAga SPer SWvt WFar WNew WPtf
	'Lemon Symphony'PBR (Symphony Series)	CBcs
	Milk Symphony = 'Seiremi' (Symphony Series)	CCCN CWCL
	'Mirach' (Springstar Series)	LSou MBNS
§	'Nairobi Purple'	CCCN CFee CHEx COlW CWGN EBee ELan ESwi MBri NPri SEND SMrm SWvt WHil WNew
	Nasinga Cream = 'Aknam'PBR (Cape Daisy Series)	CCCN
	Nasinga Purple = 'Aksullo' (Cape Daisy Series)	EPfP
	oppositifolium	CCCN
	Orange Symphony = 'Seimora'PBR (Symphony Series)	CBcs CCCN CWCL LAst MBNS SMrm SPoG
	'Pale Face'	see *O.* 'Lady Leitrim'
	'Peggyi'	see *O.* 'Nairobi Purple'
I	'Pink Superbum'	CHEx
	'Pink Whirls' ♀H1+3	CCCN
	'Pollux' (Springstar Series)	MBNS
	'Port Wine'	see *O.* 'Nairobi Purple'
	'Seaside'PBR (Side Series)	EPfP
	'Silver Sparkler' (v) ♀H1+3	CCCN CDTJ ELan MBNS MHer WBrE
	'Snow Pixie'	CSpe CWGN LHop NPri SWvt WHil
	Sonja = 'Sunny Sonja'PBR	EPfP
	'Sparkler'	CCCN CHEx
	Springstar Series	CBcs
	'Stardust'PBR	EPfP LBuc LRHS NPer SCoo SPoG
	'Sunny Amanda'PBR	LSou
	'Sunny Dark Florence'	LSou
	'Sunny Dark Martha'	EPfP LAst
	'Sunny Davina'	LSou WGor
	'Sunny Mary'PBR	MCot
	'Sunny Serena'PBR	LSou WGor
	'Sunny Sheila'	LSou WGor
*	'Superbum'	CHEx
I	'Superbum' × 'Lady Leitrim'	CHEx
	'Tauranga'	see *O.* 'Whirlygig'

'Tresco Peggy'	see *O.* 'Nairobi Purple'
'Tresco Pink'	CCCN
'Tresco Purple'	see *O.* 'Nairobi Purple'
Warembo Arwen = 'Sakcadwar'PBR (Cape Daisy Series)	LRHS
'Weetwood' 🏆$^{H3-4}$	CBar CCCN CWGN EBee ECtt ELan EPot EShb GCal LRHS MBNS MHer MLHP SAga SPer SPoG SWvt WEas WFar
§ 'Whirlygig' 🏆$^{H1+3}$	CCCN CSpr
§ 'White Pim' 🏆$^{H3-4}$	CDTJ CHll ELan ELon LRHS MAvo NPer SDix SEND SMrm SPer SUsu
'Wine Purple'	see *O.* 'Nairobi Purple'
'Wisley Pink'	EPyc NEgg
'Zaurak'PBR (Springstar Series)	CCCN CWCL MBNS
'Zulu' (Cape Daisy Series)	CCCN

Ostrowskia (*Campanulaceae*)

magnifica	MTho WCom WWst

Ostrya (*Corylaceae*)

carpinifolia	CBcs CDul CLnd CMCN CTho CWib EBee ECrN EMil EPfP EWTr GKir IFFs MBlu MMuc NLar NWea SWvt
japonica	CDul NLar
virginiana	EPfP IArd

Othonna (*Asteraceae*)

cheirifolia	CBot CCCN CSpe EHoe ELan EWes NBir SEND WEas WPer WSHC WWEG

Othonnopsis see *Othonna*

Ourisia (*Scrophulariaceae*)

× ***bitternensis*** 'Cliftonville Canary' **new**	WAbe
- 'Cliftonville Lemon'	WAbe
- 'Cliftonville Ling' **new**	WAbe
- 'Cliftonville Pink' **new**	WAbe
- 'Cliftonville Roset'	WAbe
caespitosa	NMen
- var. ***gracilis***	NMen
coccinea	EBee GAbr GCra GEdr GGar GKev GKir GMac NBir NMen NWCA WAbe
crosbyi	GEdr LRHS
'Loch Ewe'	CPLG CPla GAbr GBin GGar GKir MMuc WPGP
macrophylla	EBee GGar IGor LLHF
microphylla	WAbe
- f. ***alba***	WAbe
modesta	GBin
polyantha 'Cliftonville Scarlet'	WAbe WFar
ruelloides **new**	WAbe
'Snowflake' 🏆^{H4}	GAbr GBin GEdr NBir NLBP NMen WAbe

Oxalis (*Oxalidaceae*)

sp.	NMen
from Mount Stewart	WMoo
acetosella	CRWN EBWF MHer NMir NSco WHer WShi
- var. ***rosea***	WAlt
- var. ***subpurpurascens***	IFro MMHG WCot
adenophylla 🏆^{H4}	CElw CMea CPLG CTri EBrs ECho EPfP EPot GGar GKev GKir GMaP ITim LAma LHop LRHS NEgg NHol NLar NMen NWCA SDeJ SPoG WBrE WFar WHoo WPer
- dark	MTho
adenophylla × ***enneaphylla***	see *O.* 'Matthew Forrest'
anomala	ECho WCot
arenaria F&W 10584	WCot
§ ***articulata***	CArn LRHS MTho NPer SEND WCot WSHC
- 'Alba'	SEND WCot
- 'Aureoreticulata'	MTho
I - f. ***crassipes*** 'Alba'	WCot
- 'Festival'	WCot
- 'Jesse's Pink Treasure' (v) **new**	WCot
§ - subsp. ***rubra***	EBee WBrE
'Beatrice Anderson'	EPot GCrs ITim MTho
'Black Velvet' (Xalis Series)	ECtt SMrm WCot
bowiei	CPBP ECho EPot
- 'Amarantha'	EBee ECho
'Bowles's White'	MTho
brasiliensis	CPBP CStu ECho EPot MTho NMen
'Burgundy Wine' (Xalis Series)	ECtt
corniculata var. ***atropurpurea***	MTho
'Dark Eye'	GCrs
deppei	see *O. tetraphylla*
§ ***depressa***	CStu CTri EBee ECho EPot EWes GEdr LLHF MTho NBir NLAp NMen NRya NSla SRms WBrE WFar
eckloniana	ECho
- var. ***sonderi***	EBee ECho WCot
enneaphylla 🏆^{H4}	CElw ECho ELon EPot GAbr GCrs GGar LRHS MTho NMen NRya SBch WCom WFar
- 'Alba'	CPBP ECho GCrs GEdr GGar NMen NSla NWCA WCom
- subsp. ***ibari***	ECho EPot GEdr NMen
- 'Minutifolia'	GCrs LLHF MTho NMen NRya WCom
- 'Rosea'	CBgR ECho EPot GKev ITim MTho NLar NRya NSla
- 'Sheffield Swan'	ECho GEdr LLHF NMen NSla
falcatula	WCot
'Fanny'	CStu EBee ECho
flava	CGrW ECho WCot
floribunda misapplied	see *O. articulata*
fourcadei	ECho WCot
glabra	CPBP WAbe
griffithii	WWst
- double-flowered (d)	GEdr WWst
'Gwen McBride'	CPBP GCrs NMen
hedysaroides	CCCN GCal
'Hemswell Knight'	NMen
hirta	CPBP EPot MTho
- 'Gothenburg'	CPBP EBee ECho MTho NMen
imbricata	CPBP ECho EPot LLHF
inops	see *O. depressa*
'Ione Hecker' 🏆^{H4}	CBgR CPBP ECho ELon EPot GCrs GEdr GGar GKev ITim LRHS MTho NHar NMen NRya NSla NWCA WCom
'Irish Mist' (v)	CHid CStu EBee ECho WCot
* ***karroica***	CStu EBee ECho NMen WCot
§ ***laciniata***	ECho GCrs GKev MTho NHar NMen NSla WCom
- hybrid seedlings	NHar
lactea double-flowered	see *O. magellanica* 'Nelson'
lasiandra	CCCN EBee ECho
§ ***latifolia*** **new**	CPBP
loricata	ECho NMen

	magellanica	CRow CSpe CTri ECho EDAr GGar IMou LBee LRHS MTho SPlb WFar WMoo WPer
	- 'Flore Pleno'	see *O. magellanica* 'Nelson'
§	- 'Nelson' (d)	CRow CSpe CStu EBee ECho EWes GCal GGar GMac LBee NBir NPer WMoo WPer WPnP WPrP
	mallobolba 'Citrino'	WAbe
	massoniana	CPBP EBee ECho EPot NMen WAbe WCot
§	'Matthew Forrest'	EPot NMen WCot
§	***megalorrhiza***	CHEx SChr
§	***melanosticta***	CPBP CStu EBee ECho EPot LLHF SDeJ WCot
	monophylla	ECho
	namaquana	ECho
	obtriangulata	ECho
	obtusa	CBgR ECho MTho NMen SCnR WCom
	- apricot-flowered	WCot
	oregana	CBgR CDes CHid CMac CRow EBee ECho ELon GGar GMac NChi SPhx WCot WCru WPGP WPrP WSHC
	- 'Klamath Ruby' new	WSHC
	- f. ***smalliana***	EWes IMou WCru
	palmifrons	CPBP ECho EPot LLHF MTho
	perdicaria	CPBP EBee ECho EWes LRHS MTho WAbe WFar
	pes-caprae	CGrW
	polyphylla	EBee ECho
	- var. ***pentaphylla***	CPBP EPot
§	***ptychoclada***	CSpe
§	***purpurea***	ECho MWea WAbe
	- 'Ken Aslet'	see *O. melanosticta*
	regnellii	see *O. triangularis* subsp. *papilionacea*
	rosea misapplied	see *O. articulata* subsp. *rubra*
	semiloba	ECho GCal NCGa WCot
	speciosa	see *O. purpurea*
	spiralis	CCCN LSou SDix WDyG
	subsp. ***vulcanicola***	
	- - 'Burgundy'	NPri
	- - 'Zinfandel'	SVil
	squamata	LLHF WPat
	squamosoradicosa	see *O. laciniata*
	stipularis	ECho LLHF
	succulenta misapplied	see *O. ptychoclada*
	succulenta Barnéoud	see *O. megalorrhiza*
	succulenta ambig.	CHll
	'Sunny'	ECho
	'Sunset Velvet'	WCot
	'Superstar'	NMen
§	***tetraphylla***	CPLG EBee ECho LAma MTho NPer
*	- ***alba***	ECho
	- 'Iron Cross'	CFox CHEx CHid CStu EBee ECho EPot LAma MCot MLLN NBir NPnk SDeJ SWal WBVN WPer
	'Tina'	CPBP
	triangularis	CCCN CFox CHEx CPLG ECho EOHP EPot LAma MAvo NBir NPer WBrE WFar
	- 'Birgit'	EBee ECho
	- 'Cupido'	EBee ECho GGar WPer
	- 'Mijke'	EBee ECho
§	- subsp. ***papilionacea*** 🏆H1	EBee ECho LAma MMHG
	- - 'Atropurpurea'	CSpe EBee ECGP LHop SDeJ WBVN
*	- - ***rosea***	WCot
	- subsp. ***triangularis***	CHid EBee ECho EUJe NCGa
	tuberosa	GGar GPoy ILis LEdu
	'Ute'	CPBP GEdr NMen NSla
	valdiviensis	MDKP
	versicolor 🏆H1	CPBP CStu EBee EBrs ECho EPot MTho NBir NMen SCnR WAbe WCom WCot
	vespertilionis Zucc.	see *O. latifolia*
I	'Waverley Hybrid'	NMen
	zeekoevleyensis	WCot

Oxycoccus see *Vaccinium*

Oxydendrum ✿ (*Ericaceae*)

	arboreum	CAbP CBcs CDoC CDul CEnd CMCN EBee EPfP EWTr IDee IFFs IVic LRHS MAsh MBri MMuc NLar SCoo SPer SSpi SSta WDin WFar WPGP
	- 'Chameleon'	SPoG SSta

Oxylobium (*Papilionaceae*)

	ellipticum	GAbr GGar

Oxypetalum (*Asclepiadaceae*)

	caeruleum	see *Tweedia caerulea*
	solanoides	EBee

Oxyria (*Polygonaceae*)

	digyna	GGar

Oxytropis (*Papilionaceae*)

	purpurea	LLHF
	shokanbetsuensis	LLHF

Ozothamnus (*Asteraceae*)

	antennaria	WSHC
§	***coralloides*** 🏆H2-3	ECou EPot NHar WAbe
§	'County Park Silver'	EWes GEdr ITim MDKP NLAp NWCA WPat
§	***hookeri***	CBcs CDoC EBee ECou GGar LRHS MBrN MRav SPer WJek WPat
§	***ledifolius*** 🏆H4	CBcs CDoC EBee ELan EPfP GGar MBri NBir SLon SPer WAbe WDin WPat
§	***rosmarinifolius***	CBcs CDoC CTsd EBee ELan EPfP EUJe GGar LRHS MSwo SBfd SPer WDin WEas WFar
	- 'Kiandra'	ECou
	- 'Silver Jubilee' 🏆H3	CBcs CDoC CEnd CEnt CSBt EBee ECrN ELan EPfP GBin GCal GGar LRHS MAsh MBri MGos MRav MSwo NSti SAga SLim SLon SPer SPlb SPoG SRkn WDin
	scutellifolius	ECou
	secundiflorus	GGar
§	***selago***	ECou WCot WPat WThu
§	- var. ***tumidus***	ITim WPat WThu
	'Sussex Silver'	CDoC GGar
	'Threave Seedling'	CDoC EBee ELan GBin IVic MAsh SPer
§	***thyrsoideus***	WFar

P

Pachyphragma (*Brassicaceae*)

§	***macrophyllum***	CPom CSev EBee ECGP ECha EHrv ELan GCal IBlr IMou NCGa NLar NMRc NSti WCot WCru WMoo WPGP WSHC

Pachyphytum (*Crassulaceae*)

	oviferum	SChr

Pachypodium (*Apocynaceae*)

geayi ♀H1	EAmu
lamerei ♀H1	EAmu LToo
succulentum	LToo

Pachysandra (*Buxaceae*)

axillaris	CLAP EBee GCal SKHP
- BWJ 8032	WCru
- 'Crûg's Cover'	WCru
procumbens	CLAP EBee EHrv EPla LHop NLar SKHP WCot WCru
- 'Angola' (v)	WCot
stylosa	MRav NLar SMad
terminalis	Widely available
- 'Green Carpet' ♀H4	Widely available
- 'Green Sheen'	ECha EPPr EPfP LRHS MBri WCon WFar
- 'Variegata' (v) ♀H4	Widely available

Pachystachys (*Acanthaceae*)

lutea ♀H1	CCCN EShb

Pachystegia (*Asteraceae*)

§ ***insignis***	LRHS

Pachystima see *Paxistima*

Paederia (*Rubiaceae*)

scandens	WSHC

Paederota (*Scrophulariaceae*)

lutea	NWCA WAbe

Paeonia ✿ (*Paeoniaceae*)

'Age of Gold' (S)	GBin WCAu
'Age of Victoria' **new**	GBin
albiflora	see *P. lactiflora*
'Alley Cat'	WAul
'America'	GBin WCAu
'Angelo Cobb Freeborn'	WCAu
'Anna Marie' (S)	GBin
anomala	CFir EBee GEdr GKev MHom MPhe NLar NSla WCot WWst
§ - var. ***anomala***	GBin
- var. ***intermedia***	EBee GCal
'Argosy'	WCAu
arietina	see *P. mascula* subsp. *arietina*
'Athena'	GBin
aurelia **new**	MNrw
'Auten's Red'	WCAu
banatica	see *P. officinalis* subsp. *banatica*
'Banquet' (S)	GBin WCAu
§ 'Bartzella' (d)	CKel GBin WCAu WHlf
beresowskii	EBee WWst
'Black Monarch'	WCAu
'Black Panther' (S)	GBin WCAu
'Black Pirate' (S)	CKel WCAu
'Blaze'	GMaP LRHS MNrw MSCN NSti WCAu
Blue and Purple Giant	see *P. suffruticosa* 'Zi Lan Kui'
'Border Charm'	GBin WHlf
'Boreas' (s) **new**	GBin
'Bravura'	GBin
'Bridal Icing'	WCAu
'Bride's Dream'	GBin
'Brocaded Gown' (S)	GBin
broteroi	SKHP WCot
brownii	EPot
'Buckeye Belle' (d)	CKel EBee EPfP GBin LPio LSRN MHom MNrw MRav MWea SMrm SWat WCAu WCot WWEG
'Burma Midnight'	GBin
'Burma Ruby'	GBin WCAu
californica	WCot
'Callie's Memory'	CKel GBin WCAu WHlf
cambessedesii ♀H2-3	CSpe EBee EPot GKev LRHS MTho NBir NMen NSla NWCA SSpi SUsu WAbe WCot WKif
- dwarf **new**	EPot
'Canary Brilliant'PBR	GBin WCAu
'Cardinal's Robe'	GBin
'Carina'	GBin
'Carol'	WCAu
caucasica	see *P. mascula* subsp. *mascula*
'Chalice'	GBin
× ***chamaeleon***	EBee SKHP
'Cheddar Royal'	GBin
'Cherry Ruffles'	GBin WCAu
'Chinese Dragon' (S)	CKel WCAu
'Chocolate Soldier'	GBin
'Claire de Lune'	CKel GBin MBri SHar WCAu
'Claudia'	WCAu
'Command Performance' **new**	GBin
'Copper Kettle' **new**	CKel WCAu
'Cora Louise'	CKel GBin WCAu WHlf
'Coral Charm'	CKel GBin SHar SKHP WCot
'Coral Fay'	GBin WCAu
'Coral 'n' Gold'	WCAu
'Coral Sunset'	CKel GBin NCGa NLar SMrm SPoG
'Coral Supreme'	GBin
corallina	see *P. mascula* subsp. *mascula*
coriacea	EBee WWst
'Court Jester'	GBin
Crimson Red	see *P. suffruticosa* 'Hu Hong'
'Crusader'	WCAu
'Cytherea'	MHom WCAu
'Dancing Butterflies'	see *P. lactiflora* 'Zi Yu Nu'
'Daredevil' (S) **new**	GBin
daurica	see *P. mascula* subsp. *triternata*
'Dawn Glow'	WCAu
decomposita	MPhe
decora	see *P. peregrina*
'Defender'	WCAu
delavayi (S) ♀H4	Widely available
- BWJ 7775	WCru
- SDR 4327	GKev
- from China (S)	MPhe
- var. ***angustiloba*** f. ***alba*** (S)	CPLG
§ - - f. ***angustiloba*** (S)	EPot SSpi WCot
- - - 'Coffee Cream' (S)	CKel
§ - - f. ***trollioides*** (S)	CPLG WCAu
§ - var. ***delavayi*** f. ***lutea*** (S)	CDul CMea CSpe EBee EPfP GAbr GAuc GKev IFro LEdu LRHS MAsh MGos NBir NEgg SLon SPhx SPoG SRms STre SUsu WAul WFar WHar WHoo WTin
- var. ***lutea***	see *P. delavayi* var. *delavayi* f.
- 'Mrs Colville' (S)	GBin GCal
- 'Mrs Sarson' (S)	CHid CSpe ELan EWes EWll GBin NCGa NHol NLar SWat
- Potaninii Group	see *P. delavayi* var. *angustiloba* f. *angustiloba*
- 'Tapestry' **new**	CSpe
- Trollioides Group	see *P. delavayi* var. *angustiloba* f. *trollioides*
- 'Yellow Queen' (S)	GKev
delavayi × ***suffruticosa***	LSRN
delavayi var. ***delavayi*** f. ***delavayi*** × ***delavayi*** var. ***delavayi*** f. ***lutea***	ELan
'Diana Parks'	CKel GBin

	Drizzling Rain Cloud	see *P. suffruticosa* 'Shiguregumo'
	'Early Bird'	GBin LRHS
	'Early Glow'	GBin
	'Early Scout'	GBin MHom WCAu WCot
	'Early Windflower'	WCAu
	'Eastgrove Ruby Lace'	WEas
	'Echt Klasse' **new**	GBin
	'Eden's Perfume'	GBin LRHS
	'Elizabeth Foster'	GBin WCAu
	'Ellen Cowley'	GBin WCAu
	emodi	CAvo CDes LPio
	'Etched Salmon'	GBin
	'Ezra Pound' (S)	GBin
	'F. Koppius'	CKel
	'Fairy Princess'	GBin WAul WCAu
	'Firelight'	GBin WCAu
	'First Arrival'	CKel GBin WCAu WHlf
	'First Dutch Yellow'	see *P.* 'Garden Treasure'
	'Flame'	CKel EBee EWTr GBin GKir MHom MNrw MWea NLar WAul WCAu WCot
	'Fuchsia Cuddles'	GBin
§	Gansu Group (S)	CKel MHom MPhe
	- 'Bai Bi Fen Xia' (S)	MPhe
	- 'Bai Bi Lan Xia' (S)	MPhe
	- 'Bai Zhang Bing' (S)	IPPs
	- 'Bing Shan Xue Lian' (S)	IPPs MPhe
	- 'Cheng Xin' (S)	MPhe
	- 'Fen He' (S)	IPPs MPhe
	- 'Fen Jin Yu Zhu' (S)	MPhe
	- 'Feng Xian' (S)	MPhe
	- 'He Hua Deng' (S)	MPhe
	- 'He Ping Lian' (S)	MPhe
	- 'Hei Feng Die' (S)	MPhe
	- 'Hei Tian E' (S)	MPhe
	- 'Hei Xuan Feng' (S)	MPhe
	- 'Hong Lian' (S)	IPPs MPhe
	- 'Hong Xia Ying Xue' (S)	MPhe
	- 'Huang He' (S)	MPhe
	- 'Hui He' (S)	MPhe
	- 'Jiao Rong' (S)	MPhe
	- 'Jin Cheng Ming Yue' (S)	MPhe
	- 'Ju Hua Fen' (S)	MPhe
	- 'Lan Hai Yiu Bo' (S)	MPhe
	- 'Lan He' (S)	IPPs MPhe
	- 'Lan Tian Meng' (S)	MPhe
	- 'Li Xiang' (S)	MPhe
	- 'Lian Chun' (S)	MPhe
	- 'Long Yuan Hong' (S)	MPhe
	- 'Mei Gui Sa Jin' (S)	IPPs
	- 'Mo Hai Yin Bo' (S)	MPhe
	- 'Mo Hai Yin Zhou' (S)	MPhe
	- 'Shu Sheng Peng Mo' (S)	MPhe
	- 'Tao Hua Nu' (S)	MPhe
	- 'Tie Mian Wu Si' (S)	MPhe
	- 'Xiang Lu Zi Yan' (S)	MPhe
	- 'Xiong Mao' (S)	MPhe
	- 'Xue Hai Bing Xin' (S)	IPPs MPhe
	- 'Xue Hai Dan Xin' (S)	IPPs
	- 'Xue Lian' (S)	MPhe
	- 'Ye Guang Bei' (S)	MPhe
	- 'Yu Ban Xiu Qiu' (S)	MPhe
	- 'Yu Guan Lan Dai' (S)	MPhe
	- 'Yu Lu Lian Dan' (S)	MPhe
	- 'Yu Rong Dan Xin' (S)	MPhe
	- 'Zi Ban Bai' (S)	IPPs
	- 'Zi Die Ying Feng' (S)	MPhe
	- 'Zi Guan Yu Zhu' (S)	IPPs
	- 'Zi Hai Yin Bo' (S)	MPhe
	- 'Zi He' (S)	IPPs
	- 'Zong Ban Bai' (S)	MPhe
	Gansu Mudan Group	see *P.* Gansu Group

§	'Garden Treasure'	GBin WCAu WHlf
	'Gauguin' (S)	WCAu
	'Gerry' **new**	WCAu
	'Gold Standard'	GBin WAul
	'Golden Bowl'	CKel GBin
	'Golden Dream'	see *P.* 'Bartzella'
	'Golden Glow' Glasscock	WCAu
	'Golden Isles'	CKel
	'Golden Thunder'	CKel
	'Golden Wings'	GBin
	'Grace Root'	GBin
	Green Dragon Lying on a Chinese Inkstone	see *P. suffruticosa* 'Qing Long Wo Mo Chi'
	'Hei Hua Kui'	see *P. suffruticosa* 'Hei Hua Kui'
	'Hephestos' (S) **new**	GBin
	'Heritage'	GBin
	'Hesperus' (S)	WCAu
	'Hillary'	CKel GBin WCAu
	'Ho-gioku'	GBin
	'Honor'	WCAu
	'Horizon'	GBin WCAu
	humilis	see *P. officinalis* subsp. *microcarpa*
	'Illini Belle'	GBin
	'Illini Warrior'	WAul WCAu
	'In the Mood' **new**	GBin
	intermedia	WCot
	'Isani Gidui'	see *P. lactiflora* 'Isami-jishi'
	japonica misapplied	see *P. lactiflora*
	japonica ambig.	GEdr
	japonica (Makino) Miyabe & Takeda	EBee
	'Jay Cee' **new**	GBin
	'Jean E. Bockstoce'	WCAu
	jishanensis	MPhe
	'Joseph Rock'	see *P. rockii*
	'Joyce Ellen'	GBin WCAu
	'Jubilation' **new**	GBin
	'Julia Rose'	CKel GBin WCAu WHlf
	'Kamikaze'	CKel
	'Kathryn Ann' **new**	GBin
	kavachensis	EBee GCal WWst
	'Kinkaku'	see *P.* × *lemoinei* 'Souvenir de Maxime Cornu'
	'Kinko'	see *P.* × *lemoinei* 'Alice Harding'
	'Kinshi'	see *P.* × *lemoinei* 'Chromatella'
	'Kintei'	see *P.* × *lemoinei* 'L'Espérance'
	'Koikagura'	CKel
	'Kokamon'	CKel
§	***lactiflora***	EBee EHrv GCal GKev MLLN MPhe MRav WCot WWst
	- 'Abalone Pearl'	GBin
	- 'Adolphe Rousseau'	CBcs CKel EBee WCAu
*	- 'Afterglow'	CKel
	- 'Agida'	CSam GBin LRHS MRav
	- 'Agnes Mary Kelway'	CKel
	- ***alba***	WBor
	- 'Albert Crousse'	CBcs CKel GBin MRav NBir SWat WCAu
	- 'Alexander Fleming'	CFox EBee EWTr MBNS MWea NBir SMrm SWat WBrE WCAu
	- 'Algae Adamson'	CKel
	- 'Alice Harding'	GBin WCAu
	- Amibilis'	WCAu
	- 'Amo-no-sode'	WCAu
	- 'Angel Cheeks'	CKel GBin WCAu
	- 'Anna Pavlova'	CKel MRav
	- 'Antwerpen'	MBri WCAu
	- 'Arabian Prince'	CKel
	- 'Argentine'	EBee WCAu
	- 'Asa Gray'	CKel
	- 'Auguste Dessert'	CKel GBin MWea WCAu WCFE WCot

§ – 'Augustin d'Hour' CKel
– 'Aureole' CKel MRav
– 'Avalanche' CKel EBee EPfP GBin NBPC NLar SHar SMrm
– 'Ballerina' CKel MRav
– 'Barbara' CKel WCAu
– 'Baroness Schröder' EBee ELan GBin
– 'Barrington Belle' EPfP GBin MBri WAul
– 'Barrymore' CKel
– 'Beacon' CKel
– 'Beatrice Kelway' CKel
– 'Belle Center' GBin WCAu
– 'Bernice Carr' **new** GBin
– 'Best Man' NGdn WCAu
– 'Bethcar' CKel
– 'Better Times' WCAu
– 'Bev' GBin
– 'Big Ben' GBin NCGa WCAu
– 'Bing Qing' IPPs
– 'Blaze of Beauty' CKel
– 'Blenheim' EBee
– 'Bluebird' CKel
– 'Blush Queen' ELan WCAu
– 'Border Gem' MRav
– 'Bouchela' EBee
– 'Boule de Neige' EWll NLar
– 'Bower of Roses' CKel
– 'Bowl of Beauty' ♀H4 Widely available
– 'Bowl of Cream' CKel EBee GBin SMrm SWat SWvt WCAu
– 'Bracken' CKel
– 'Break o' Day' WCAu
– 'Bridal Gown' GBin WCAu
– 'Bridal Veil' CKel
– 'Bridesmaid' CKel MRav
– 'British Beauty' CKel
– 'Bunker Hill' CKel EBee GBin SBfd SPer SWvt WCAu
– 'Bu-te' **new** GBin
– 'Butter Bowl' GBin MBri WCAu
– 'Canarie' MBri
– 'Candeur' CKel EBee
– 'Cang Long' CKel
– 'Captivation' CKel
– 'Carnival' CKel
– 'Caroline Allain' CKel
– 'Carrara' GBin
– 'Cascade' CKel
– 'Catherine Fontijn' CKel EBee GBin SHar WCAu
– 'Charles' White' CKel EBee EPfP GBin NBPC WCAu
– 'Charm' GBin WCAu
– 'Cheddar Charm' GBin MBri WAul WCAu
– 'Cheddar Gold' ♀H4 GKir
– 'Cheddar Supreme' GBin
– 'Cherry Hill' WCAu
– 'Chestine Gowdy' CKel
– 'Chief Wapello' GBin
– 'Chippewa' GBin
– 'Chun Xiao' CKel
– 'Circus Circus' GBin
– 'Claire Dubois' CKel GBin WCAu
– 'Cornelia Shaylor' WCAu
– 'Couronne d'Or' GBin WCAu
– 'Crimson Glory' CKel
– 'Crinkles Linens' GBin
– 'Dandy Dan' WCAu
– 'Dawn Crest' CKel EBee
– 'Dayspring' CKel
– 'Daystar' MRav
– 'Decorative' CKel
– 'Delachei' CKel
– 'Denise' MRav
– 'Dinner Plate' GBin MBri SPer WCAu WCot
– 'Do Tell' GBin NGdn NLar SPer WCAu
– 'Docteur H. Barnsby' CKel
– 'Doctor Alexander Fleming' CKel NCGa STes SWat SWvt WHoo
– 'Dominion' CKel
– 'Don Juan' CKel
– 'Doreen' CFir CKel EBee GBin MBri NCGa SHar WCAu
– 'Doris Cooper' WCAu
– 'Dorothy Welsh' CKel
– 'Dragon' CKel
– 'Dresden' WCAu
– 'Duchesse de Nemours' ♀H4 Widely available
– 'Duchesse d'Orléans' WCAu
– 'Edouard Doriat' WCAu
– 'Edulis Superba' CKel EBee ELan GBin LRHS LSRN MBNS MRav NMoo NPer SPer WCAu
– 'Elizabeth Stone' CKel
– 'Ella Christine Kelway' CKel
– 'Elsa Sass' GBin WCAu
– 'Emma Klehm' GBin WCAu
– 'Emperor of India' CKel
– 'Enchantment' CKel
– 'English Princess' CKel
– 'Ethereal' CKel
– 'Evelyn Tibbets' GBin
– 'Evening Glow' CKel
– 'Evening World' CKel
– 'Fairy's Petticoat' WCAu
– 'Fashion Show' CKel
– 'Félix Crousse' ♀H4 CBcs CFox CKel CMac CTri ELan GBin GMaP LRHS LSRN MBNS MRav MSCN NBir NWsh SPer SWat WCAu
– 'Felix Supreme' GBin
– 'Fen Chi Jin Yu' CKel
– 'Fen Yu Nu' IPPs
– 'Festiva Maxima' ♀H4 CKel CSBt CTri EBee ELan EPfP GBin GKir LRHS MAvo NBir NEgg NLar SBfd SPer SRkn SRot SWat SWvt WAul WCAu WHoo WWEG
– 'Festiva Supreme' **new** GBin
– 'Florence Nicholls' GBin
– 'France' CKel
– 'Fuji-no-mine' GBin
– 'Garden Lace' GBin
– 'Gardenia' CKel EBee EPfP GBin NLar
– 'Gay Paree' CKel GBin NCGa NLar SPer WCAu
– 'Gayborder June' CKel WCAu
– 'Gene Wild' GBin WCAu
– 'Général Joffre' MRav
– 'Général MacMahon' see *P. lactiflora* 'Augustin d'Hour'
– 'General Wolfe' CKel
– 'Germaine Bigot' CKel GBin MRav WCAu
– 'Gertrude' GBin
– 'Gilbert Barthelot' WCAu
– 'Gladys McArthur' GBin
– 'Gleam of Light' CKel
– 'Globe of Light' GBin
– 'Gloriana' WCAu
– 'Glory Hallelujah' WCAu
– 'Glowing Candles' WCAu
– 'Go-Daigo' GBin
– 'Golden Fleece' WCAu
– 'Goldmine' GBin
– 'Great Sport' MRav
– 'Green Lotus' WAul
– 'Guidon' WCAu

- 'Gypsy Girl'	CKel
- 'Hakodate'	CKel
- 'Heartbeat'	CKel
- 'Helen Hayes'	GBin WCAu
- 'Henri Potin'	GBin
- 'Henry Bockstoce'	CKel GBin
- 'Her Grace'	CKel
- 'Herbert Oliver'	CKel
- 'Hermione'	CKel GBin WCAu
- 'Hiawatha'	WCAu
- 'Hit Parade'	WCAu
- 'Honey Gold'	CKel ELan GBin GKir LPio NCGa SPoG WAul WCAu
- 'Huang Jin Lun'	CKel IPPs
- 'Hyperion'	CKel
- 'Immaculée'	CKel EBee EPfP GBin LPio LSRN MBri NCGa SPoG WSpi
- 'Inspecteur Lavergne'	CKel EBee LRHS MBri MSCN MWea SPer STes WAul WCAu WCot WWEG
- 'Instituteur Doriat'	CKel GBin MBri WCAu
§ - 'Isami-jishi'	GBin
- 'Jacorma'	CFir GBin WHoo
- 'Jacques Doriat'	CKel
- 'Jadwigha'	EBee
- 'James Kelway'	GBin
- 'James Pillow'	WCAu
- 'Jan van Leeuwen'	CKel EBee EPfP GBin SPer WCAu WCot WSpi
- 'Jappensha-Ikhu'	GBin
- 'Jeanne d'Arc'	CKel
- 'Jin Chi Yu'	CKel
- 'Jin Dai Wei'	IPPs
- 'John Howard Wigell'	WCAu
- 'Joy of Life'	CKel
- 'Judith Eileen'	GBin
- 'June Morning'	CKel
- 'June Rose'	WCAu
- 'Kakoden'	GBin
- 'Kansas'	CFox CKel EBee ELan EPfP GBin GKir LRHS MBri NBir NGdn NLar NMoo SMrm SPoG WCAu WCot WFar
- 'Karen Gray'	GBin WCAu
- 'Karl Rosenfield'	CKel CSBt EBee EPfP GKir LRHS LSRN MNrw MRav NEgg SBfd SHar SPer SPoG SRms STes SWvt WBor WFar WHoo WWEG
- 'Kathleen Mavoureen'	CKel
- 'Kelway's Betty'	CKel
- 'Kelway's Brilliant'	CKel
- 'Kelway's Circe'	CKel
- 'Kelway's Daystar'	CKel
- 'Kelway's Exquisite'	CKel
- 'Kelway's Glorious'	CKel EBee EPfP GBin GKir LPio MBNS MRav NLar WCAu WGwG
- 'Kelway's Lovely'	CKel GBin
- 'Kelway's Lovely Lady'	CKel
- 'Kelway's Majestic'	CKel MRav
- 'Kelway's Scented Rose'	CKel
- 'Kelway's Supreme'	CKel SWat
- 'King of England'	GBin
- 'Knighthood'	CKel
- 'Kocho-jishi'	CKel
- 'Königswinter'	GBin
§ - 'Koningin Wilhelmina'	EBee GBin MNrw
- 'Krinkled White'	CKel EBee EWTr GBin LRHS MHom MRav NLar NSti SHar SKHP SUsu WAul WCAu WCot WWEG
- 'La Belle Hélène'	CKel EBee
- 'La France'	GBin
- 'La Lorraine'	CKel
- 'Lady Alexandra Duff' ♀H4	CKel EBee EPfP GBin GKir LRHS MRav MWea NBir NCGa NGdn SCoo SMrm SWvt WCAu WWEG
- 'Lady Kate'	WCAu
- 'Lady Ley'	CKel
- 'Lady Mayoress'	CKel
- 'Lady Orchid'	EPfP MSCN NGdn WCAu
- 'Lady Romilly'	MRav
- 'Lancaster Imp'	GBin WAul
- 'Langport Triumph'	CKel
- 'Laura Dessert' ♀H4	CKel EBee EPfP GBin GKir MWea NCGa SPer WCAu
- 'Le Cygne'	GBin
- 'L'Éclatante'	CKel EBee GBin LRHS WGwG
- 'Legion of Honor'	CKel WCAu
- 'Lemon Ice'	CKel
- 'Lemon Queen'	GBin
- 'L'Étincelante'	GBin
- 'Lian Tai'	IPPs
- 'Lights Out'	GBin
- 'Lillian Wild'	GBin WCAu
- 'Little Medicineman'	EBee GBin WBor
- 'Lois Kelsey'	GBin WCAu
- 'Longfellow'	CKel GBin
- 'Lora Dexheimer'	WCAu
- 'Lord Calvin'	WCAu
- 'Lord Kitchener'	CKel GBin
- 'Lorna Doone'	CKel
- 'Lotus Queen'	GBin SHar WCAu
- 'Louis Barthelot'	WCAu
- 'Louis Joliet'	ELan
- 'Louis van Houtte'	CKel NEgg SBfd
- 'Lowell Thomas'	WCAu
- 'Lyric'	CKel
- 'Madame Calot'	WCAu
- 'Madame de Verneville'	WCAu
- 'Madame Ducel'	CKel WCAu
- 'Madame Emile Debatène'	CKel MBNS NMoo WBor WCAu
- 'Madame Gaudichau'	MAvo WCot
- 'Madame Jules Dessert'	EBee WCAu
- 'Madelon'	CKel WCAu
- 'Maestro'	GBin
- 'Magic Orb'	CKel
- 'Mandarin's Coat' **new**	GBin
- 'Margaret Truman'	CKel WCAu
- 'Marguérite Gerard'	WCAu
- 'Marie Crousse'	WCAu
- 'Marie Lemoine'	CKel EBee GBin LRHS WCAu WCot
- 'Marietta Sisson'	WCAu
- 'Mary Brand'	WCAu
- 'Mary Elizabeth'	GBin
- 'Masterpiece'	CKel MRav
- 'May Treat'	GBin WCAu
- 'Merry Mayshine'	GBin WCAu
- 'Midnight Sun'	GBin MBri WCAu
- 'Minnie Shaylor'	WCAu
- 'Mischief'	MRav WCAu
- 'Miss America'	EPfP GBin MBri WCAu WCot
- 'Miss Eckhart'	CKel EBee GBin WCAu
- 'Miss Mary'	EPfP LAst
- 'Missie's Blush'	GBin
- 'Mister Ed'	GBin WCAu
- 'Mistral'	CKel MBri
- 'Mo Zi Ling'	WCAu
- 'Monsieur Jules Elie' ♀H4	CKel EBee EPfP GBin LPio MBri MHom MSCN NBPC NGdn SBfd SPer WAul WCAu WHoo WWEG
- 'Monsieur Martin Cahuzac'	CFir GBin LRHS WCAu
- 'Moon River'	EPfP GBin WHoo
- 'Moonglow'	WCAu
- 'Mother's Choice'	CKel GBin LSRN NGdn NLar WCAu
- 'Mr G.F. Hemerik'	CKel EBee GBin WCAu WCot

	– 'Mr Thim'	WCAu
	– 'Mrs Edward Harding'	WCAu
	– 'Mrs F.J. Hemerik'	WCAu
	– 'Mrs Franklin D. Roosevelt'	GBin WCAu
	– 'Mrs J.V. Edlund'	EBee GBin WCAu
	– 'Mrs Livingston Farrand'	WCAu
	– 'My Pal Rudy'	GBin WCAu
	– 'Myrtle Gentry'	GBin
	– 'Nancy Nicholls'	WCAu
	– 'Nancy Nora'	NGdn SPer
	– 'Neomy Demay'	CKel GBin
	– 'Neon'	NCGa
	– 'Nice Gal'	WCAu
	– 'Nick Shaylor'	CKel GBin WCAu
	– 'Nippon Beauty'	EBee GBin SKHP
	– 'Norma Volz'	GBin
	– 'Orlando Roberts'	GBin
	– 'Ornament'	CKel
	– 'Orpen'	CKel
	– 'Paola'	CKel
	– 'Paul Bunyan'	GBin
	– 'Paul M. Wild'	CKel WCAu
	– 'Pêche'	EBee
*	– 'Pecher'	CKel LPio NLar NMoo NPer WSpi
	– 'Peter Brand'	CKel GBin NBPC
	– 'Philippe Rivoire'	WCAu
	– 'Philomèle'	WCAu
	– 'Pico'	WCAu
	– 'Pillow Talk'	CKel GBin MBri NCGa SPer WCAu
	– 'Pink Cameo'	EBee NLar WCAu WCot
	– 'Pink Giant'	WCAu
	– 'Pink Lemonade'	WCAu
	– 'Pink Parfait'	GBin LRHS SPer WCAu
	– 'Pink Princess'	GBin MBri WCAu
	– 'Plainsman'	GBin
	– 'Polar King'	WCAu
	– 'Port Royale'	CKel
	– 'President Franklin D. Roosevelt'	SWat WCAu
	– 'Président Poincaré'	CKel MRav SWat
	– 'President Taft'	see *P. lactiflora* 'Reine Hortense'
	– 'Primevère'	CKel EBee EPfP EWll GBin GKir LAst LPio MWea NBir NCGa NLar NMoo SHar SMrm SPer WCAu WWEG
	– 'Qi Hua Lu Shuang'	CKel IPPs
	– 'Qing Wen'	CKel
	– 'Queen of Sheba'	WCAu
	– 'Queen Victoria'	GBin
	– 'Queen Wilhelmina'	see *P. lactiflora* 'Koningin Wilhelmina'
	– 'Raoul Dessert'	WCAu
	– 'Raspberry Sundae'	CKel ELan GBin MRav NLar STes WCAu WCot
	– 'Ray Payton'	GBin
	– 'Red Dwarf'	CKel
	– 'Red Emperor'	WCAu
	– 'Red Rover'	CKel
	– 'Red Sarah Bernhardt'	ELan SMrm WWEG
§	– 'Reine Hortense'	CKel GBin MRav WCAu WWEG
	– 'Renato'	GBin WCAu
	– 'Richard Carvel'	WCAu
	– 'Ruth Cobb'	WCAu
	– 'Sante Fe'	EPfP NCGa WCAu
	– 'Sarah Bernhardt' ♀H4	Widely available
	– 'Scarlet O'Hara'	CMac GBin NGdn SHar SPer WCAu
	– 'Schaffe'	GBin
	– 'Sea Shell'	EPfP GBin GMaP LRHS
	– 'Sha Jin Guan Ding'	IPPs
	– 'Shawnee Chief'	GBin WCAu
	– 'Shen Tao Hua'	CKel
	– 'Shimmering Velvet'	CKel
	– 'Shi-pen Kue'	EBee
	– 'Shirley Temple' (d)	CKel EBee ELan GBin GKir LTen MAvo MBNS MBri MRav NBir NGdn SBfd SPoG WCAu WWEG
	– 'Silver Flare'	CKel
	– 'Soft Salmon Joy'	GBin
	– 'Solange'	CKel GBin LPio NLar WCAu
	– 'Sorbet'	CKel EBee EPfP GKir LPio NBPC NBir NCGa NLar NMoo NPer SBfd SMrm STes WBor WCAu WWEG
	– 'Spellbinder'	GBin
	– 'Starlight'	CKel GBin STes WCAu WCot
	– 'Strephon'	CKel
	– 'Surugu'	EBee
	– 'Sweet Melody'	GBin WCAu
	– 'Sweet Sixteen'	WCAu
	– 'Sword Dance'	CKel EBee EWll GBin SPoG WSpi
	– 'Taff'	WBor
	– 'Tamate-boko'	WCAu
	– 'The Mighty Mo'	GBin
	– 'The Nymph'	NBir WWEG
	– 'Thérèse'	WCAu
	– 'Tom Eckhardt'	EKen GBin SPer
	– 'Top Brass'	CBot CKel EBee GBin MRav NLar WCAu WWEG
	– 'Topeka Garnet'	GBin
	– 'Toro-no-maki'	WCAu
	– 'Translucient'	CKel
	– 'Victoire de la Marne'	CKel EBee LRHS
	– 'Violet Dawson'	GBin
	– 'Vivid Rose'	GBin
	– 'Vogue'	CKel GBin MRav NCGa SWvt WCAu
	– 'Walter Faxon'	GBin
	– 'West Elkton'	GBin
	– 'Westerner'	GBin WCAu
	– 'White Ivory'	MBri WCAu
	– 'White Rose of Sharon'	CKel
	– 'White Sands' **new**	GBin
	– 'White Wings'	CBcs CKel CMac CTri EBee ELan EPfP EWTr GBin GKir LPio LRHS MWea NBPC NLar SWat SWvt WAul WCAu WCot
	– 'Whitleyi Major' ♀H4	GKir MPhe
	– 'Wiesbaden'	WCAu
	– 'Wilbur Wright'	GBin WCAu
	– 'Wine Red'	GBin
	– 'Wladyslawa'	EBee GBin LRHS NLar WCot
	– 'Wu Hua Long Yu'	IPPs
	– 'Xue Feng'	CKel
	– 'Yan Fei Chu Yu'	CKel
	– 'Yan Zi Dian Yu'	CKel IPPs
	– 'Yu Cui He Hua'	IPPs
	– 'Zhong Sheng Feng'	GBin
	– 'Zhu Sha Dian Yu'	CKel
	– 'Zi Die Xian Jin'	IPPs
	– 'Zi Feng Chao Yang'	IPPs
§	– 'Zi Yu Nu'	LRHS LSRN WCAu
	– 'Zuzu'	GBin WAul WCAu
	'Lafayette Escadrille' (S) **new**	WCAu
	'Late Windflower'	CKel GCra LPio MHom
	'Leda' (S)	GBin
	'Legion of Honour' **new**	GBin
	× ***lemoinei*** (S)	GBin WHal
§	– 'Alice Harding' (S)	CKel WCAu
§	– 'Chromatella' (S)	CKel LAma
	– 'High Noon' (S)	CKel MPhe NBPC SKHP SWat WCAu
§	– 'L'Espérance' (S)	LAma WCAu
	– 'Marchioness' (S)	CKel WCAu
§	– 'Souvenir de Maxime Cornu' (S)	CKel EPfP LAma MGos SKHP SPer WCAu

'Lemon Dream'PBR new	CKel
'Lilith' (S)	GBin
lithophila	see *P. tenuifolia* subsp. *lithophila*
'Little Joe'	WCAu
'Little Red Gem' new	GBin
lobata 'Fire King'	see *P. peregrina*
'Lois Arleen'	WCAu
'Lovebirds' new	GBin
ludlowii (S) 𝕐H4	Widely available
lutea	see *P. delavayi* var. *delavayi* f. *lutea*
macrophylla	MPhe
'Magenta Gem'	WAul
'Mai Fleuri'	WCAu
mairei	CFir CPLG MPhe
'Many Happy Returns' new	GBin
mascula	EBee EPfP GKev LLHF NBir WCot WWEG WWst
- from Sicily	MPhe
§ - subsp. ***arietina***	GKev MWat WCot WEas
- - 'Northern Glory'	LRHS WCAu
- subsp. ***bodurii***	WWst
- subsp. ***hellenica*** from Sicily	MPhe
§ - subsp. ***mascula***	EBee GBin WCot
- - from Georgia	MPhe
§ - subsp. ***russoi***	WCot WThu WWst
- - from Sardinia	MPhe
- - 'Picotee' new	GBin
§ - subsp. ***triternata***	CWit EBee GBin GKev LRHS MPhe WCot
- - RS 125/80	WWst
'Mikuhino-akebono'	CKel
mlokosewitschii 𝕐H4	Widely available
- 'Pearl Rose'	GBin
mollis	see *P. officinalis* subsp. *villosa*
'Montezuma'	WCAu
'Moonrise'	WCAu
'Morning Lilac' new	WCAu
'Murad of Hershey Bar' (S)	GBin
'My Love'	GBin
'Nova' new	GBin
'Nymphe'	CKel EBee EPfP GKir LPio MRav NLar WAul WCAu
obovata 𝕐H4	CFir GAuc GKir MPhe WCot
- var. ***alba*** 𝕐H4	CPLG GBin GEdr GKev LLHF WAbe WCot WEas WThu
- 'Grandiflora'	GKir LRHS
- var. ***willmottiae***	CPLG MPhe
officinalis	EBee GAuc GCra NWsh WCot
- WM 9821 from Slovenia	MPhe
- from NW Croatia	WWst
- 'Alba Plena'	CPou EBee GKir LRHS MRav NEgg SWvt WCAu WWEG
- 'Anemoniflora Rosea' 𝕐H4	EBee EPfP GBin GKir LRHS MBri MHom MNrw SWvt WCAu
§ - subsp. ***banatica***	EBee EPPr MHom MPhe WCAu WCot
- 'China Rose'	GBin WCAu
- subsp. ***humilis***	see *P. officinalis* subsp. *microcarpa*
- 'Lize van Veen'	GBin WCAu
§ - subsp. ***microcarpa***	WAbe
- 'Mutabilis Plena'	IBlr WCAu
- 'Rosea Plena' 𝕐H4	CKel CMac EBee ECtt EPfP GBin GKir GMaP LAst LRHS MRav NEgg SPer SWat SWvt WCAu WCot WFar WWEG
- 'Rosea Superba Plena'	WCAu
- 'Rubra Plena' 𝕐H4	CPou CTri EBee ECtt EPfP GAbr GBin GCra GKir GMaP LAst LHop LRHS MBri MHom MMuc MRav NEgg NGdn SEND SPer SRms SWat SWvt WAul WCAu WCot WFar
§ - subsp. ***villosa***	CKel ELan GBin GKev SEND WCAu WFar
'Old Faithful'	GBin
'Old Rose Dandy' new	GBin
'Oriental Gold'	CKel
ostii (S)	CKel CPLG EPfP MPhe SKHP
§ - 'Feng Dan Bai' (S)	CKel GBin IPPs MPhe WCAu WSpi
'Pageant' new	GBin
'Paladin'	GBin
papaveracea	see *P. suffruticosa*
paradoxa	see *P. officinalis* subsp. *microcarpa*
'Pastel Splendor' new	CKel GBin WCAu
'Paula Fay'	CKel EPfP GBin MRav STes WCAu WCot
'Peachy Rose'	GBin
§ ***peregrina***	CKel EBee ECho GBin GEdr LRHS MPhe NLar NSla SKHP SSpi WAbe WCAu WCom WCot
§ - 'Otto Froebel' 𝕐H4	EWll GBin GCra NLar WCAu WSpi
- 'Sunshine'	see *P. peregrina* 'Otto Froebel'
'Pink Hawaiian Coral'	CKel GBin NLar SPoG WCot
'Pink Vanguard' new	GBin
'Postilion'	GBin WCAu
potaninii	see *P. delavayi* var. *angustiloba* f. *angustiloba*
'Prairie Charm'	GBin
'Prairie Moon'	GBin WCot
qiui new	MPhe
'Red Charm'	CKel EBee GBin LPio MBNS MBri NCGa WCAu WSpi
'Red Glory'	GBin
'Red Magic'	NBPC NLar SMrm WFar WSpi
'Red Red Rose'	WCAu
'Renown' (S)	CKel
'Requiem'	GBin WCAu
'Robert W. Auten'	WCAu
§ ***rockii*** (S)	CBcs CKel CSpe EBee EPfP GAuc GBin LRHS MPhe NLar WCot WSpi
- from Tianshui, Gansu new	MPhe
- from Wenshian, Gansu new	MPhe
- 'Hong Guan Yu Dai'	IPPs
- hybrid	see *P.* Gansu Group
- subsp. ***linyanshanii*** (S)	MPhe
- 'Tian Bai Xue'	IPPs
aff. ***rockii*** (S)	GAuc
'Roman Gold'	CKel
romanica	see *P. peregrina*
'Rose Garland'	GBin WCAu
'Roselette'	GBin WCAu
'Roselette's Child' new	GBin
Rouge Red	see *P. suffruticosa* 'Zhi Hong'
'Roy Pehrson's Best Yellow'	GBin
ruprechtiana	WCot WWst
russoi	see *P. mascula* subsp. *russoi*
'Scarlet Heaven'	CKel GBin WCAu WHlf
Shandong Red Lotus	see *P. suffruticosa* 'Lu He Hong'
'Shimano-fuji'	CKel
'Shining Light' new	GBin
'Show Girl' new	GBin
'Showanohokori'	CKel
'Silver Dawn'	GBin
sinensis	see *P. lactiflora*
sinjianensis	see *P. anomala* var. *anomala*
'Soshi'	GBin
'Spring Carnival' (S)	GBin
'Squirt' new	GBin
'Stardust'	WCAu
sterniana	EBee
steveniana	EBee MHom MPhe NLar WCot WWst
§ ***suffruticosa*** (S)	CWib ELan GKev IPPs MGos SSpi WBVN

	- 'Akashigata' (S)	CKel
	- 'Alice Palmer' (S)	CKel
	- 'Bai Yu' (S)	CBcs
	- 'Bai Yulan' (S)	LLHF
	- Best-shaped Red	see *P. suffruticosa* 'Zhuan Yuan Hong'
I	- 'Better Than Peach Blossom' (S) new	LRHS
	- Bird of Rimpo	see *P. suffruticosa* 'Rimpo'
	- Black Dragon Brocade	see *P. suffruticosa* 'Kokuryū-nishiki'
	- Black Flower Chief	see *P. suffruticosa* 'Hei Hua Kui'
	- Brocade of the Naniwa	see *P. suffruticosa* 'Naniwa-nishiki'
	- 'Burgundy Wine' (s) new	GBin
	- 'Cardinal Vaughan' (S)	CKel
	- Charming Age	see *P. suffruticosa* 'Howki'
	- 'Dou Lu' (S)	CBcs CKel IPPs
	- Double Cherry	see *P. suffruticosa* 'Yae-zakura'
	- 'Duchess of Kent' (S)	CKel
	- 'Duchess of Marlborough' (S)	CKel
	- 'Er Qiao' (S)	CBcs CKel
	- Eternal Camellias	see *P. suffruticosa* 'Yachiyo-tsubaki'
	- 'Fen Qiao' (S)	CBcs
	- 'Feng Dan Fen' (S)	IPPs
	- 'Feng Dan Zi' (S)	IPPs
	- Flight of Cranes	see *P. suffruticosa* 'Renkaku'
	- Floral Rivalry	see *P. suffruticosa* 'Hana-kisoi'
	- 'Frost on Peach Blossom' (S)	LRHS
	- 'Fuji Zome Goromo' (S)	CKel
*	- 'Glory of Huish' (S)	CKel
	- 'Godaishu' (S)	CKel GBin LAma SKHP SPer
	- 'Guardian of the Monastry' (S) new	GBin
§	- 'Hakuo-jisi' (S/d)	CKel EPfP WCAu
§	- 'Hana-daijin' (S)	LAma WCAu
§	- 'Hana-kisoi' (S)	CKel GBin LAma WCAu
	- 'Haru-no-akebono' (S)	CKel
§	- 'Hei Hua Kui' (S)	IPPs
§	- 'Higurashi' (S)	EPfP
§	- 'Howki' (S)	WCAu
§	- 'Hu Hong' (S)	LTen WCAu WSpi
§	- 'Huang Hua Kui' (S)	CKel
	- 'Hu's Family Red' (S)	LRHS
	- Jewel in the Lotus	see *P. suffruticosa* 'Tama-fuyo'
	- Jewelled Screen	see *P. suffruticosa* 'Tama-sudare'
	- 'Jia Ge Jin Zi' (S)	CKel
	- 'Jitsugetsu-nishiki' (S)	CKel
	- 'Jiu Zui Yang Fei' (S)	IPPs
	- 'Joseph Rock'	see *P. rockii*
	- Kamada Brocade	see *P. suffruticosa* 'Kamada-nishiki'
§	- 'Kamada-fuji' (S)	CKel WCAu
§	- 'Kamada-nishiki' (S)	CKel
§	- 'Kaow' (S)	CKel WCAu
	- King of Flowers	see *P. suffruticosa* 'Kaow'
	- King of White Lions	see *P. suffruticosa* 'Hakuo-jisi'
	- 'Kinkaku'	see *P.* × *lemoinei* 'Souvenir de Maxime Cornu'
	- 'Kinshi'	see *P.* × *lemoinei* 'Alice Harding'
	- 'Kokucho' (S)	CKel
§	- 'Kokuryū-nishiki' (S)	CKel GBin LAma LRHS SKHP SPer
	- 'Koshi-no-yuki' (S)	CKel
	- 'Lan Bao Shi' (S)	IPPs
	- 'Lan Hu Die' (S)	IPPs
§	- 'Lu He Hong' (S)	WCAu
	- Magnificent Flower	see *P. suffruticosa* 'Hana-daijin'
	- 'Montrose' (S)	CKel
*	- 'Mrs Shirley Fry' (S)	CKel
	- 'Mrs William Kelway' (S)	CKel
§	- 'Naniwa-nishiki' (S)	CKel
	- 'Nigata Akashigata' (S)	CKel
	- Pride of Taisho	see *P. suffruticosa* 'Taisho-no-hokori'
	- 'Princess Chiffon' (S) new	GBin
§	- 'Qing Long Wo Mo Chi' (S)	CKel IPPs WCAu
	- 'Reine Elisabeth' (S)	CKel
§	- 'Renkaku' (S)	CKel SKHP SPer WCAu
§	- 'Rimpo' (S)	CKel EPfP GBin LAma SKHP SPer
	- subsp. ***rockii***	see *P. rockii*
	- 'Rou Fu Rong' (S)	LTen WCAu WSpi
	- 'Sheng Hei Zi' (S)	CBcs
§	- 'Shiguregumo' (S)	CKel
	- 'Shimadaigin' (S)	CKel
	- 'Shimane-chojuraku' (S)	CKel GBin
	- 'Shimane-hakugan' (S)	CKel
	- 'Shimane-seidai' (S)	CKel
	- 'Shimanishiki' (S)	CKel SKHP SPer
	- 'Shin Shima Kagayaki' (S)	CKel
	- 'Shintoyen' (S)	CKel
	- 'Sumi-no-ichi' (S)	CKel
	- 'Superb' (S)	CKel
§	- 'Taisho-no-hokori' (S)	CKel WCAu
§	- 'Taiyo' (S)	CKel EPfP LAma SKHP SPer
§	- 'Tama-fuyo' (S)	CKel
§	- 'Tama-sudare' (S)	CKel WCAu
	- The Sun	see *P. suffruticosa* 'Taiyo'
	- Twilight	see *P. suffruticosa* 'Higurashi'
	- Wisteria at Kamada	see *P. suffruticosa* 'Kamada-fuji'
	- 'Wu Jin Yao Hui' (S)	CBcs WCAu
	- 'Wu Long Peng Sheng' (S)	CKel GBin WCAu WSpi
	- 'Xiao Tao Hong' (S)	CBcs
	- 'Xue Ta' (S)	CKel LRHS
§	- 'Yachiyo-tsubaki' (S)	CKel LAma SKHP WCAu
§	- 'Yae-zakura' (S)	LAma WCAu
	- 'Yan Long Zi Zhu Pan' (S)	CKel
	- 'Yin Hong Qiao Dui' (S)	CKel
	- 'Yoshinogawa' (S)	CKel EPfP
	- 'Yu Ban Bai' (S)	IPPs
	- 'Zha Sha Lei' (S)	GBin
	- 'Zhao Fen' (S)	IPPs LRHS NBPC NPer
§	- 'Zhi Hong' (S)	CKel
	- 'Zhu Sha Lei' (S)	CKel IPPs WSpi
*	- 'Zhuan Yuan Hong' (S)	WSpi
	- 'Zi Er Qiao' (S)	CKel IPPs
§	- 'Zi Lan Kui' (S)	CKel
	'Sunshine'	see *P. peregrina* 'Otto Froebel'
	'Taiheko'	CKel
	'Ten' i'	CKel
	tenuifolia	CAby CBot CPMA CWit EBee EPot EWll GAuc GBin GCal GKev GKir LPio LRHS MHom MWea NMen NSla SKHP SMad WCAu WCot WSpi
	- subsp. ***carthalinica***	MPhe
§	- subsp. ***lithophila***	MHom MPhe WWst
	- 'Plena'	EPot GEdr MHom
	- 'Rosea'	GBin
	'Thunderbolt' (S)	WCAu
	tomentosa	MHom MPhe
	'Tria' (S) new	GBin
	turcica	GBin
	'Vanilla Twist'	WAul
	veitchii	CAvo EBee EPfP GAuc GCal GEdr GKev GKir GMaP LPio MHom MTho NBid NLar NMen SSpi WCAu WSpi
	- from China	MPhe
	- 'Alba'	LPio SPhx
	- pale-flowered	GCal
	- var. ***woodwardii***	EBee ECho EPot GBin GCra GCrs GKev GKir LPio MTho NSla NWCA SSpi WCAu WCot WSpi WWst
	'Vesuvian'	CKel WCAu

'Viking Full Moon' GBin WCAu
'Walter Mains' WCAu
'White Emperor' **new** WCAu
White Phoenix see *P. ostii* 'Feng Dan Bai'
'Wine Angel' GBin
wittmanniana CBot EBee GBin GCal WCAu WCot
'Xiang Yu' LRHS
§ 'Yao Huang' (S) CBcs IPPs WCAu
Yao's Yellow see *P.* 'Yao Huang'
'Yellow Crown' CKel GBin NCGa SHar WCAu
'Yellow Dream' GBin WCAu
'Yellow Emperor' GBin WCot
Yellow Flower of Summer see *P. suffruticosa* 'Huang Hua Kui'
'Yellow Gem' GBin

Paesia (*Dennstaedtiaceae*)

scaberula CDes CLAP GGar NBir SSpi WAbe

Paliurus (*Rhamnaceae*)

spina-christi CArn CBcs EBee IDee NLar SLon SMad

Pallenis (*Asteraceae*)

§ ***maritima*** CCCN NWCA

Pamianthe (*Amaryllidaceae*)

peruviana ERea

Panax (*Araliaceae*)

ginseng GPoy
japonicus EBee GPoy WCru
- BWJ 7932 WCru
quinquefolius MMuc

Pancratium (*Amaryllidaceae*)

maritimum CArn EBee ECho GKev SDeJ

Pandanus (*Pandanaceae*)

utilis EAmu LPal

Pandorea (*Bignoniaceae*)

jasminoides CCCN CHII CRHN CTri CTsd EBak EBee EPfP EShb SOWG
§ - 'Charisma' (v) CBcs CBow CCCN CHII EAmu EBee EPfP ERea EShb LSou SEND SLim SOWG SPer
- 'Lady Di' CCCN ERea SOWG
- 'Rosea' CCCN
- 'Rosea Superba' ♀^{H1} CBcs CHEx CRHN EBee ERea SEND SLim SPer
- 'Variegata' see *P. jasminoides* 'Charisma'
lindleyana see *Clytostoma calystegioides*
pandorana CRHN ERea SLim
- 'Golden Showers' CBcs CCCN CRHN EBee ERea EShb MRav SEND SLim SOWG
- 'Ruby Heart' ERea

Panicum (*Poaceae*)

amarum 'Dewey Blue' CKno EPPr
bulbosum CKno EHoe EPPr EPla
clandestinum EBee EHoe EPPr EWes GFor IMou MCCP MWhi SMea
miliaceum EBrs LRHS
- 'Purple Majesty' CWib
- 'Violaceum' CKno CSpe LRHS
virgatum CRWN CSpe CTri GFor LRHS SMrm WMnd WPer WWEG
- 'Blue Tower' CKno EBrs ELon EPPr LRHS MAvo SApp SGSe SMea
- 'Cloud Nine' CKno CMea EBee EPPr LRHS MAvo MSnd NOak SApp SGSe SMHy SUsu WHal WRHF
- 'Dallas Blues' CDes CKno CPrp CSpe EAEE EBee EBla ECha EHoe EPPr EWes LEdu LHop LRHS MAvo MRav NOak NWsh SApp SGSe SHDw SMHy SPer WFar WMoo WPGP
- 'Farbende Auslese' EBee MAvo
- 'Hänse Herms' CBod CKno EBee EBrs EHoe EPPr LPio MAvo MWhi SApp SBfd SMea WFar WTin WWEG
- 'Heavy Metal' Widely available
- 'Heiliger Hain' CHar EBee EPPr LHop MAvo MWea
I - 'Kupferhirse' CKno EBee EPPr
- 'Northwind' CKno EBee EBrs EPPr MAvo SApp SMHy SPhx WFar
- 'Pathfinder' SApp SGSe
- 'Prairie Sky' CKno CWCL EAEE EBee EBrs EHoe ELon EPPr LEdu LPio LRHS MAvo MBri NLar SDix SGSe SMHy SMea SUsu WFar WPGP WTin
- 'Purple Haze' EBrs LRHS
- 'Red Cloud' CKno SMHy
- 'Red Metal' IPot
- 'Rehbraun' EBee EBrs EHoe EPPr EPfP LEdu LHop LPio LRHS LTen NGdn NMRc NOak NWsh SAga SApp WCAu WFar WTin WWEG
- 'Rotstrahlbusch' CKno CPrp CWib EBee EBla EHoe EPPr GMaP LRHS MAvo MWhi NBea NOak SPer SWal WCot WMnd WMoo WPGP WWEG
- 'Rubrum' CKno ECha EHoe ELan EPPr EPfP LRHS MAvo MRav MWat SApp SBfd SDix STes WMoo
- 'Shenandoah' Widely available
- 'Squaw' Widely available
- 'Strictum' CSpe EBee EBrs EHoe EHul EPPr EWes GQue LEdu LPla LRHS NLar SApp SMHy SPhx SUsu WMoo
I - 'Strictum Compactum' CBod
- 'Warrior' Widely available
- 'Wood's Variegated' (v) WCot

Papaver ✿ (*Papaveraceae*)

aculeatum CTca
alboroseum ECho LRHS
'Alpha Centauri' (SPS) LLHF SWat WHoo
alpinum L. CSpe ECho GJos GKev LRHS SPet SWal SWat WFar
- 'Flore Pleno' (d) NBir
amurense SWat
anomalum album CSpe
apokrinomenon ELan
atlanticum NBro SPlb
- 'Flore Pleno' (d) CSpe IFro MCCP NBro WFar
'Aurora' (SPS) SWat
'Beyond Red' (SPS) SWat
bracteatum see *P. orientale* var. *bracteatum*
'Bright Star' (SPS) SWat
burseri SRot
'Cathay' (SPS) SWat
commutatum ♀^{H4} CSpe ELan SWat
corona-sancti-stephani SWat
'Danish Flag' NNor
'Eccentric Silk' (SPS) SWat
fauriei GKev
§ 'Fire Ball' (d) ECha GCal IGor LHop NBid NBro SWat WMnd WWEG
'Heartbeat'^{PBR} (SPS) MAsh SWat
heldreichii see *P. pilosum* subsp. *spicatum*
hybridum 'Flore Pleno' (d) LRHS NSti SWat
'Jacinth' (SPS) CDes EBee LLHF SWat WCot WHoo
lateritium CHid CPou SRms

	- 'Nanum Flore Pleno'	see *P.* 'Fire Ball'
	'Lauffeuer'	ELon SWat
	'Matador'[PBR] ♀H4	NNor WBor
	'Medallion' (SPS)	CDes EBee LLHF SSvw SWat WCot WHoo
§	***miyabeanum***	CSpe ECho ELan GKev LRHS MMuc NWCA SRot WFar WPer
	- ***album***	ECho
	- ***tatewakii***	see *P. miyabeanum*
	nanum 'Flore Pleno'	see *P.* 'Fire Ball'
§	***nudicaule***	ELan GKir LRHS
	- Champagne Bubbles Group	NNor SWat WFar
	- - 'Champagne Bubbles Orange'	NPri
	- - 'Champagne Bubbles Pink'	NPri
	- - 'Champagne Bubbles White'	NPri
	- - 'Champagne Bubbles Yellow'	NPri
	- var. ***croceum*** 'Flamenco'	NNor
	- Garden Gnome Group	see *P. nudicaule* Gartenzwerg Group
§	- Gartenzwerg Group ♀H4	COlW CSpe EPfP LAst LRHS MBri MHav SBfd SPet SPlb SRot WFar WGor WWEG
	- Hazy Days Group	GJos
	- 'Matador'	GAbr GGar NLar
	- 'Pacino'	EWll LRHS NLar SPet SPoG WFar
	- 'Summer Breeze Orange' ♀H4	NPri
	- 'Summer Breeze Yellow'	LRHS NPri
	- Wonderland Series	EHrv NNor SPet
N	***orientale***	CBcs EPfP LAst LRHS SRms SWat WFar WPer
	- 'Abu Hassan'	SWat
	- 'Aglaja' ♀H4	CElw CKno COlW CWit EBee ECtt ELon GBin LAst LPio LRHS NEgg NGdn NSti SAga SMad SMrm SMrs SUsu SWat WClo WCot WHoo
	- 'Aladin'	SWat
	- 'Ali Baba'	GCra SWat
	- 'Alison'	SWat
	- 'Allegro'	CMea CSBt EBee EBrs ECtt EPfP GAbr GKir GMaP LAst LRHS MBNS MBri MHer NGdn NVic SBfd SPer SPlb SVic SWat SWvt WWEG
	- 'Arwide'	SWat
	- 'Aslahan'	ECha ELon MRav SWat
	- 'Atrosanguineum'	SWat
	- 'Avebury Crimson'	MWat SWat
	- 'Baby Kiss'[PBR]	ECtt NLar SWat
	- 'Ballkleid'	ECha ELon SWat
	- 'Beauty Queen'	EAEE EBee ECha GMac LPio LRHS MRav NGdn SDix SWat
	- 'Bergermeister Rot'	SWat
	- 'Big Jim'	SWat
	- 'Black and White' ♀H4	CSpe ECha EHrv ELan EPfP GMaP LRHS MNrw MRav NBPC NEgg SApp SMrm SWat
	- 'Blackberry Queen'	ECtt SWat
	- 'Blickfang'	SWat
	- 'Blue Moon'	WHal
	- 'Bolero'	EBee ECtt NCGa NLar
	- 'Bonfire'	EHrv LSou NCob
	- 'Bonfire Red'	EBee SWat WCAu
§	- var. ***bracteatum*** ♀H4	NBir SMHy SWat WMoo
	- 'Brilliant'	EBee GJos LRHS LTen MWat NBre NGdn SWat WFar WMoo
	- 'Brooklyn' (New York Series)	ECtt IPot LPio LRHS LSRN MAvo SPad SWat
	- 'Burning Heart'	EBee ECtt LRHS NLar SPer SPoG
	- 'Carmen'[PBR]	MNrw MSCN NBPC NCGa WCot
*	- 'Carneum'	NBre NLar WWEG
	- 'Carnival'	EBee NBre SWat
	- 'Casino'	NGdn
	- 'Catherina'	NBre SWat
	- 'Cedar Hill'	EBee ECtt EWes GCal GMac MRav NBre SMrm SWat
	- 'Cedric Morris' ♀H4	ECha ELan EPPr GMaP LPio MArl MRav SMrm SWat WCot WHoo WMnd
	- 'Central Park' (New York Series)	EBee WFar
I	- 'Charming' pink-flowered	EAEE EBee ECtt NGdn SMrm SWat
	- 'Charming' red-flowered	LRHS
	- 'Checkers'	CTri LRHS MHav MLHP NBPC SEND
	- 'China Boy'	EBee SWat WHrl
	- 'Choir Boy'	CEnt CSpr ECtt ELon LRHS MSpe SGar SWat WMoo
	- 'Clochard'	CElw EBee SWat WCot
	- 'Coral Reef'	EBee MHer MLHP SAga SWat WHer WMoo WRHF
	- 'Corrina'	SWat
	- 'Curlilocks'	CPar EAEE EBee ECtt ELan ELon EPfP LRHS MRav MWat SBfd SMrs SPer SPoG SRms SWat SWvt WHoo WWEG
	- 'Derwisch'	ELon SWat
*	- 'Diana'	SWat
	- 'Double Pleasure'	EBee ECtt MSCN NBre NMoo SWat WHrl
	- double red shades (d)	NGdn
	- 'Doubloon' (d)	EBee LRHS NBre NGdn SWat
	- 'Dwarf Allegro'	WMnd
	- 'Dwarf Allegro Vivace'	LRHS
	- 'Earl Grey' **new**	SWat WCot
	- 'Effendi' ♀H4	EBee MAvo SUsu SWat WCot
	- 'Elam Pink'	SWat WCot
	- 'Erste Zuneigung'	ECha ELon SWat
	- 'Eskimo Pie'	SWat
	- 'Fancy Feathers'[PBR]	ECtt LAst NBPC NGdn SWat
	- 'Fatima'	CDes NBre SWat WHrl
	- 'Feuerriese'	SWat
	- 'Feuerzwerg'	SWat
	- 'Fiesta'	ELon GKir NBre SWat
	- 'Flamenco'	CBcs ECtt ELon NGdn SWat
	- 'Flamingo'	ELon MSCN SWat
N	- 'Flore Pleno' (d)	NGdn
	- 'Forncett Summer'	CPar EAEE EBee ECtt ELon GMac LPio MRav NBre NGdn NLar SMrs SPer STes SWat WHoo WHrl WTin WWEG
	- 'Frosty' (v)	SHar
	- 'Fruit Punch'	GJos SWal
	- 'Garden Glory'	EAEE EBee ECtt ELon GCra GMac LRHS LSRN MArl NBre SMrs SWat WCAu
	- 'Glowing Embers'	ECtt SWat
	- 'Glowing Rose'	ELon MDKP NBre SWat
	- Goliath Group	EAEE ECha ELan ELon LRHS MRav NBro NVic SDix SRms SWat WFar WMnd WWEG
	- - 'Beauty of Livermere'	Widely available
§	- - 'Beauty of Livermere' clonal **new**	WCot
	- 'Graue Witwe'	ELon SApp SMHy SWat WHrl WTin
	- 'Guardsman'	see *P. orientale* (Goliath Group) 'Beauty of Livermere' clonal
	- 'Halima'	NBre SWat
	- 'Harlem' (New York Series)	CElw CSpe EBee EPfP IPot MAvo MWea NGdn NPnk SWat WCAu WHrl

- 'Harvest Moon' (d)	CMac EBee ECtt LRHS NPer SMrm SPhx SWat WCAu WHal WWEG
- 'Heidi'	SWat
- 'Hewitt's Old Rose'	NBre
- 'Hula Hula'	ECha ELon SWat
- 'Indian Chief'	CWCL EBee EPfP GMac IPot LPio MLLN NBPC NLar NMoo NPer NPri SMrm WFar WWEG
- 'Joanne'	NLar
- 'John III' ♀H4	LPio SPhx SWat
- 'John Metcalf'	EBee ECtt EPPr LPio LRHS MAvo NBre NSti SMrs SWat WCot WSpi
- 'Juliane'	ECha ECtt ELon GMac NSti SWat WCot WTin
- 'Karine' ♀H4	CDes CElw CSam CSpe CWCL EBee EBrs ECha ELan EPfP GMaP GMac LPio LRHS MNrw MWte NLar NPri SMHy SPhx SPoG SWat WCAu WHoo WPtf WTin
- 'Khedive' (d) ♀H4	CWCL EBee SWat
- 'King George'	SWat
- 'King Kong'	IPot NBPC
- 'Kleine Tänzerin'	CSam ECtt GMac LRHS LSou MAvo MLLN MMuc MRav MSCN NBre NGdn NPri NSti SAga SMrm SMrs SWat WCAu WCot
- 'Kollebloem'	NBre SWat
- 'Lady Frederick Moore'	GMac LPio LRHS NBre NLar SWat WWEG
- 'Lady Roscoe'	NBre SWat
- 'Ladybird'	EPfP LRHS NBre
- 'Lambada'	SWat
- 'Lauren's Lilac'	CMdw EAEE EBee ECtt ELon LBMP LRHS LSRN MSpe NBre SMrs SPhx SWat WAul
- 'Leuchtfeuer' ♀H4	CDes ECha NBre SMHy SWat
- 'Lighthouse' ♀H4	CWCL SWat WCAu
- 'Lilac Girl'	CMac EBee ECha ECtt ELon GMaP NLar SApp STes SWat WHrl
- 'Little Candyfloss' PBR **new**	NLar SWat
- 'Louvre'	COlW EBee ECtt EHrv ELon MAvo NLar SMrs SPoG SWat WCot WFar
- 'Maiden's Blush'	ECtt NBre NSti SWat
- 'Mandarin' PBR	EBee NMoo
- 'Manhattan' (New York Series)	CElw CSam CSpe EBee EBrs ECtt EPfP EWes GMac IPot MNrw NCob NEgg NGdn NPnk NPri NSti SMrs SPer SPoG SSvw STes SWat WCot WHrl
- 'Marcus Perry'	EAEE EBee ECtt EWes GMaP LRHS MSpe NEgg SBfd SPoG SWat WCAu WFar
- 'Mary Finnan'	CTca EAEE EBee NBre SWat WCAu
- 'Master Richard'	SWat
- 'May Queen' (d)	EWes IBlr MRav NBre NBro NLar NSti SWat WCot WHrl WPnn
- 'May Sadler'	EBee NBre NLar SWat
- 'Midnight'	EBee ELon NBre SWat
- 'Miss Piggy' PBR	EBee ECtt IKil IPot LLHF NGdn SPer WCot
- 'Mrs H.G. Stobart'	SWat
- 'Mrs Marrow's Plum'	see *P. orientale* 'Patty's Plum'
- 'Mrs Perry'	CMac CMea CSBt CSam EBee ECtt ELan GMaP IFro LRHS MDun MLLN MWat NGdn NPer NPri SMad SPer SRms SRot SWat WBrk WCAu WFar WMnd WTin
- 'Nanum Flore Pleno'	see *P.* 'Fire Ball'
- 'Noema'	SWat
- 'Olympic Flame' (d) **new**	SWat
- 'Orange Glow'	EBee NMoo SWat WMoo
- 'Orangeade Maison'	NBre SWat
- 'Oriana'	NBre SWat
- 'Oriental'	SWat
- 'Pale Face'	SWat
- 'Papillon' PBR	EBee GKir WFar WPtf
§ - 'Patty's Plum'	Widely available
- 'Perry's White'	Widely available
- 'Peter Pan'	ELon NBPC NBre SWat
- 'Petticoat'	ECtt ELan NBre SWat
- 'Picotée'	CBcs EBee EBrs ECtt EHrv ELan EPfP LPio LRHS MRav NBPC NCGa NCob NEgg NGdn NLar NMoo NPri SPer SPhx SRot SWat SWvt WCAu WFar WHil WMoo WWEG
- 'Pink Lassie'	NBre SWat
- 'Pink Panda'	SWat
- 'Pink Pearl' PBR	NBPC SWat WBor
- 'Pink Ruffles' PBR	EBee LRHS SWat
- 'Pinnacle'	CDes EBee ELon NBPC NGdn SMrm SWat WFar
- 'Pizzicato'	CEnt CWib EHrv LBMP LRHS MBri NPer SBfd SGar SPet SWal SWat WClo WFar WMoo WRHF WWEG
- 'Place Pigalle' (Parisienne Series)	COlW CSpe EBee EHrv ELon EPfP LSou MAvo MLLN MWea NBPC NEgg NGdn NPri SMad SPer SPhx SPoG SWat WClo WCot WHil
- 'Polka'	SWat
- 'Prince of Orange'	SWat WHlf WWEG
- Princess Victoria Louise	see *P. orientale* 'Prinzessin Victoria Louise'
- 'Prinz Eugen'	EAEE EBee ELon GMaP NBre SWat
§ - 'Prinzessin Victoria Louise'	CSWP EBee EPfP GMaP LAst LRHS MLLN NGdn NLar NNor SPoG SWat WBrk WFar WPer WRHF WWEG
- 'Prospero'	NBre
- 'Queen Alexandra'	CSpr EHrv LBMP LRHS NGdn NLar WWEG
- 'Raspberry Queen'	CDes CFir CMea EBee ECtt ELan ELon GMaP MArl MLLN MRav MWat NBPC NLar NSti SApp SMrm STes SWat WClo WCot WFar WHal WHoo WMnd WTin WWEG
- 'Raspberry Ruffles'	NBre SWat
- 'Rembrandt'	EBee EHrv MDKP NBre NMoo SMrm SWat WPer
- 'Rose Queen'	NBre WCot
- 'Rosenpokal'	EAEE EBee NGdn SWat
- 'Roter Zwerg'	ECha ELon SWat
- 'Royal Chocolate Distinction'	CElw CSpe CWCL EBee ECtt ELon EPPr EPfP MAvo MWea NBPC NLar NMoo NPri NSti SMrm SMrs SPoG SWat WCAu
- 'Royal Wedding'	Widely available
- 'Ruffled Patty'	EBee ECtt MAsh SMrm WHlf
* - 'Saffron'	SWat
- 'Salmon Glow' (d)	GKir SWat WFar WPer WWEG
- 'Salome'	GKir SWat
- 'Scarlet King'	CMac LRHS SWat
- scarlet-flowered	NCot
- 'Scarlett O'Hara' PBR (d)	ECtt EPfP LLHF NPri SWat WBor WFar
- 'Showgirl'	EBee ELon MLLN NBre SWat
* - 'Silberosa'	SWat
- 'Sindbad'	ECtt ELon GMac MRav NEgg SWat
- 'Snow Goose'	EBee ELon SWat WCot WHoo
- 'Soho' (New York Series)	NGdn SPoG
- 'Spätzünder'	NBre SWat
- 'Springtime'	ELon EWes GMac LAst MRav NGdn SWat WCAu WTin
- 'Staten Island' (New York Series)	EBee ECtt MAvo MNrw
- Stormtorch	see *P. orientale* 'Sturmfackel'

§	- 'Sturmfackel'	NBre SWat
	- 'Suleika'	SWat
	- 'Sultana'	EBee ECha ELon GMac MArl MWat SMrs SWat
	- 'Sunset'PBR **new**	SWat
	- 'The Promise'	NBre SWat
	- 'Tiffany'	CBow COIW CSpe EBee ECtt ELon GAbr GMac LPio LSRN MAvo MCot MTis NCGa NEgg NGdn SMrm SPer SSvw STes SWat WCot WWEG
	- 'Trinity'	SWat
	- 'Türkenlouis'	EBee EBrs ECGP ECtt ELon EPfP GAbr GCra GKir GMaP GMac LAst LRHS LSRN MRav MSCN NBPC NLar SMrm SPad STes SWat WCAu WCot WFar WHil WHoo WTin WWEG
	- 'Turkish Delight'	EBee ECtt ELon EPfP GCra GKir GMaP GMac LRHS LSRN MAvo MLLN MMuc MRav MWat NBir NLar NPri SBfd SPoG STes SWat SWvt WFar WMnd WWEG
	- 'Tutu'	SWat
	- 'Victoria Dreyfuss'	SWat
	- 'Viola'	SWat
	- 'Violetta'	SWat
	- 'Walking Fire'	MNrw
	- 'Water Babies'	SWat
	- 'Watermelon'	ECtt GKir IPot LRHS MAvo NBPC NLar SMrm SPer STes SWat WFar WHoo
	- 'White Karine'	GMac
	- 'White King'	GMac NBre
	- 'White Ruffles' **new**	ECtt IKil SWat
	- 'Wild Salmon'	NBre
	- 'Wisley Beacon'	ELon SWat
	- 'Wunderkind'	EBee ECtt GKir SWat
	'Party Fun'	CSpe SWal
	paucifoliatum	WHrl
	pilosum	SGSe SWat WTin
§	- subsp. ***spicatum***	CFir CMea CSev ECha ELon LHop LSou NBir STes SUsu WClo WCot WFar WMoo
	radicatum	GKev
	'Rhapsody in Red' (SPS)	SWat
	rhoeas	CArn EBWF GJos GPoy MNHC NNor WJek
	- Angels' Choir Group (d)	NNor SWat
	- Mother of Pearl Group	CSpe MCot SWat
	- Shirley Group	NNor
	'Ruffled White'	WHlf
	rupifragum	CArn CEnt ECha LEdu MSCN SGar WCot WEas WFar WPer WPnn
	- 'Double Tangerine Gem'	see *P. rupifragum* 'Flore Pleno'
§	- 'Flore Pleno' (d)	CSpe LRHS MHer NDov WBrk WFar WHrl WMoo
	- 'Tangerine Dream'	MCCP SPet
	'Serena' (SPS)	SWat
	'Shasta' (SPS)	LLHF SSvw SWat WCot
	'Snow White' (SPS) **new**	SWat
	somniferum	CArn ELau GPoy SWat
	- 'Blackcurrant Fizz' (d) **new**	WHer
	- (Laciniatum Group) 'Crimson Feathers' **new**	NNor
	- - 'Swansdown' (d)	CSpe
	- Paeoniiflorum Group (d)	CWCL SWat
	- - 'Black Beauty' (d)	CSpe SWat
	- - 'Black Paeony' (d)	CWCL
	- 'Pink Chiffon'	SWat WEas
	- subsp. ***setigerum*** **new**	NNor
	- single white-flowered	CSpe
	- 'White Cloud' (d)	CWCL GJos SWat
	'Tequila Sunrise' (SPS)	CDes EBee SWat
	'The Cardinal'	NBre
	'The Falklands' (SPS)	SWat
	triniifolium	CSpe SPhx
	- RCB AM -10	WCot
	'Vesuvius' (SPS)	SWat
	'Viva' (SPS)	SWat
*	'Witchery'	MAvo

papaya (paw paw) see *Carica papaya*

Parabenzoin see *Lindera*

Parachampionella see *Strobilanthes*

Paradisea (*Anthericaceae*)

	liliastrum ♀H4	CHid EBee ECho EPPr GCal GKir IGor LRHS NBid NChi
	- 'Major'	ECho SPhx
	lusitanica	CAvo CDes CHid CMHG CPom CPrp CSam CSpe CTca EBee ECho GCal IBlr IFro LEdu MCot SGSe SWal WCot WHoo WPGP WThu WTin

Parahebe (*Scrophulariaceae*)

	'Angela' **new**	MSCN
	'Betty'	GGar
	× ***bidwillii***	GJos MHer NWCA SRms SRot
	- 'Kea'	CFee ECou ECtt MDKP SRot WPer
	canescens	ECou
§	***catarractae***	CHar CMHG CPLG CTri CWib EBee ECho ECou EPfP GCra GGar MLHP MRav MSCN MWat NBir NBro SUsu WBrE WCom WFar WKif WMnd WPer
	- from Chatham Island	EWes
	- 'Baby Blue'	CAbP EPfP
	- blue-flowered	CDoC CHar GKir SPer
	- 'County Park'	ECou
	- 'Cuckoo'	ECou NHol
§	- 'Delight' ♀H3	CPLG ECho ECou EWes GCal GGar GMaP GQue LHop LRHS MHer NHol NPer SDix SRot WFar
	- subsp. ***diffusa***	ECho ECou NPer WCom
	- - 'Annie'	ECou NHol
	- subsp. ***martinii***	ECou
	- 'Miss Willmott'	NPri SBch SPer SPlb WBVN WPer
	- 'Porlock'	CBar GKev
	- 'Porlock Purple'	see *P. catarractae* 'Delight'
	- 'Rosea'	ECho WFar
	- white-flowered	CBot CSpe ECho IRar MLHP WPer
	densifolia	see *Chionohebe densifolia*
	formosa 'Aspley White'	ECou
	- erect	GGar
	'Gillian'	SWal WPer
	'Greencourt'	see *P. catarractae* 'Delight'
§	***hookeriana***	GGar
§	- var. ***olsenii***	ECou GGar
	'Jean'	GGar
	'Joy'	EWes
	'Julia'	GGar
	linifolia	CTri
§	***lyallii***	CBot EBee ECho EPfP GJos GKir GMaP LAst MCot MHer MMuc MRav MSwo MWat NHol NWCA SEND SPlb SRms WCom WKif
	- 'Baby Pink'	EPfP
	- 'Glacier'	ECou
	- 'Julie-Anne' ♀H3	EPfP GCal LRHS
	- 'Rosea'	CTri WPer
	- 'Summer Snow'	ECou

'Mervyn'	CTri MDKP WPer
olsenii	see *P. hookeriana* var. *olsenii*
§ ***perfoliata*** ♀H3-4	Widely available
- 'Pringle'	EPfP
'Snow Clouds'	CBar GKev LHop LRHS SBch SDix SRot SUsu SWal WFar
'Snowcap'	CDoC EPfP LAst LRHS MRav SPlb

Parajubaea (*Arecaceae*)

cocoides	LPal
torallyi var. ***microcarpa***	EUJe
- var. ***torallyi***	EAmu

Parakmeria see *Magnolia*

Paraquilegia (*Ranunculaceae*)

adoxoides	see *Semiaquilegia adoxoides*
§ ***anemonoides***	CPLG WAbe
grandiflora	see *P. anemonoides*

Parasenecio (*Asteraceae*)

delphiniifolius	EBee GEdr IMou
- B&SWJ 5789	WCru
- B&SWJ 11189	WCru
farfarifolius	WCru
var. ***bulbifer*** new	
mortonii GWJ 9419	WCru
- HWJK 2214	WCru
tebakoensis B&SWJ 11167 new	WCru
aff. ***yatabei*** B&SWJ 11117	WCru

Paraserianthes (*Mimosaceae*)

distachya	see *P. lophantha*
§ ***lophantha*** ♀H1	CDTJ CHEx CPLG CRHN CSpr CWit EBak ELan ELon EShb SOWG

Parasyringa see *Ligustrum*

Parathelypteris (*Thelypteridaceae*)

beddomei new	WRic

× *Pardancanda* (*Iridaceae*)

norrisii	EBee EWes WWEG
- 'Dazzler'	MLLN SBfd SPad

Pardanthopsis (*Iridaceae*)

dichotoma	EWes

Parietaria (*Urticaceae*)

judaica	GPoy WHer WSFF

Paris ✿ (*Trilliaceae*)

Chen Yi 8	WCot
chinensis	WCru
- B&SWJ 265 from Taiwan	WCru
cronquistii	CLAP
delavayi	WCru
fargesii	GAuc LAma WCru
- var. ***brevipetalata***	WCru
- var. ***petiolata***	WCru
forrestii	WCru
incompleta	CLAP GCal GCrs WCot WCru
japonica	GCrs LAma WCru WWst
lancifolia B&SWJ 3044 from Taiwan	WCru
mairei	WCru
polyphylla ♀H4	CArn CBct CFir CLAP EBee ECho GAuc GBin GEdr LAma MNrw SPhx WAbe WCot WCra WCru WFar WPnP WSHC WShi WSpi WWst
- B&SWJ 2125	WCru
- Forrest 5945	GCal
- HWJCM 475	WCru
- var. ***alba***	CFir
- var. ***stenophylla***	CFir EBee LAma WCru WWst
* - var. ***yunnanensis alba***	GCal
quadrifolia	CFir CLAP ECho GCal GPoy NLar NMen NMyG SPhx SSpi WCru WHer WPGP WPnP WShi WTin
- SDR 2828	GKev
tetraphylla	EBee GEdr WCru WWst
thibetica	CFir EBee WCru
- var. ***apetala***	WCru
verticillata	CLAP EBee GAuc GEdr LAma WCru WWst
- 'Ryokutei' (d)	WCru

Parkinsonia (*Caesalpiniaceae*)

florida new	EGFP

Parochetus (*Papilionaceae*)

§ ***africanus*** ♀H2	CHid CStu ELon
communis misapplied	see *P. africanus*
communis ambig.	CFee CFir CPLG MSCN NPer
communis (Buch.-Ham.) D. Don from Himalaya	GCra
- B&SWJ 7215 from the Golden Triangle	WCru
* - 'Blue Gem'	CCCN CSpe
- dark-flowered	GGar

Paronychia (*Illecebraceae*)

argentea	WPat
§ ***capitata***	CTri LRHS SRms
kapela	SMad SPlb
- 'Binsted Gold' (v)	CBow WPer
§ - subsp. ***serpyllifolia***	GBin NRya
nivea	see *P. capitata*
serpyllifolia	see *P. kapela* subsp. *serpyllifolia*

Parrotia (*Hamamelidaceae*)

persica ♀H4	Widely available
- 'Biltmore'	CPMA
- 'Burgundy'	CPMA NLar
- 'Felicie'	CPMA EPfP NLar
- 'Globosa'	NLar
- 'Jodrell Bank'	CPMA MBlu NLar
§ - 'Lamplighter' (v)	CPMA
- 'Pendula'	CMCN CPMA EPfP
- 'Summer Bronze'	LRHS MAsh SSpi
- 'Vanessa'	CBcs CDoC CMCN CPMA EPfP EWes GBin LRHS LTen MAsh MBlu MBri MGos NLar NPal SLPl SPoG SPur WDin WFar WMou
- 'Variegata'	see *P. persica* 'Lamplighter'

Parrotiopsis (*Hamamelidaceae*)

jacquemontiana	CBcs CPMA IVic MBlu NLar SSpi

Parrya (*Brassicaceae*)

menziesii	see *Phoenicaulis cheiranthoides*

parsley see *Petroselinum crispum*

Parsonsia (*Apocynaceae*)

capsularis	ECou
heterophylla	ECou

Parthenium (*Asteraceae*)

integrifolium	CArn EBee GKir GPoy IMou NBre SPhx
* ***virginicum***	SPhx

Parthenocissus (*Vitaceae*)

§	***henryana*** 🏆H4	Widely available
	himalayana	CBcs
	- 'Purpurea'	see *P. himalayana* var. *rubrifolia*
§	- var. ***rubrifolia***	CMac CWCL EBee ELan LRHS LTen MAsh MRav NLar SBfd SEND SLim SLon SPoG WCru WFar WGrn
	inserta ambig.	CMac CTsd NLar
	laetevirens	NLar
§	***quinquefolia*** 🏆H4	Widely available
	- var. ***engelmannii***	CBcs EBee LAst LBuc MGos SBfd SPer WCFE
	- 'Guy's Garnet'	WCru
	- Star Showers = 'Monham' (v)	EBee EPfP LRHS MGos NLar
	semicordata B&SWJ 6551	WCru
	striata	see *Cissus striata*
	thomsonii	see *Cayratia thomsonii*
§	***tricuspidata*** 🏆H4	CCVT CWib EBee ECtt EHoe EPfP GKir LAst MGos MMuc SPer SReu WDin WFar
	- 'Beverley Brook'	EBee LBuc LOck LRHS MBri NLar SPer SRms WFar
	- 'Crûg Compact'	CGHE WCru
	- 'Fenway Park'	EBee MGos MRav NLar
	- 'Green Spring'	CBcs EBee IArd MGos NLar
	- 'Lowii'	CMac EBee EPfP LRHS MAsh MBlu MGos MRav NLar SEND SLon SPer SPoG
	- 'Minutifolia'	EBee
	- 'Purpurea'	EBee
	- 'Robusta'	CHEx EBee EPfP SBfd
§	- 'Veitchii'	Widely available

Pasithea (*Anthericaceae*)

	caerulea	CAvo WCot

Paspalum (*Poaceae*)

	glaucifolium	LEdu
	quadrifarium	CKno CMHG EHoe EPPr WCot WPrP

Passerina (*Thymelaeaceae*)

	montana	NWCA

Passiflora ✿ (*Passifloraceae*)

	RCB/Arg R-7	WCot
	actinia	CRHN
	'Adularia'	CCCN
	alata (F) 🏆H1	CCCN EGxp
	× ***alatocaerulea***	see *P.* × *belotii*
	'Alexia'	NExo
	'Allardii'	CCCN EShb
§	'Amethyst' 🏆H1	CCCN CRHN CSBt CSPN EAmu LHop LRHS LSRN MAsh MREP MRav NExo SPad SPoG WFar WPGP WPat
	amethystina misapplied	see *P.* 'Amethyst'
§	***amethystina*** Mikan	CBcs ECre ERea
	'Anastasia'	CCCN
	'Andy'	CCCN
	'Angelo Blu'	CCCN
	antioquiensis misapplied	see *P.* × *exoniensis*
	antioquiensis ambig.	CBcs CDoC CTsd EShb SEND SOWG
	antioquiensis ambig. × ***exoniensis*** 'Hill House'	CHll
	antioquiensis ambig. × ***mixta***	CTrC
	antioquiensis Karst 🏆H2	CHll CRHN EBee GGal
	× ***atropurpurea***	CCCN
§	***aurantia***	CTsd LRHS
	banksii	see *P. aurantia*
§	× ***belotii***	CCCN CRHN EAmu EBee EQua EShb SLim SPad
	- 'Impératrice Eugénie'	see *P.* × *belotii*
	'Betty Myles Young' **new**	CRHN
	'Blue Bird'	CCCN
	'Blue Moon'	CCCN
	'Byron Beauty'	CCCN
§	***caerulea*** 🏆H3	Widely available
	- RCB/Arg R-7	WCot
	- 'Clear Sky'PBR	LRHS
	- 'Constance Elliott'	Widely available
	- ***rubra***	CSBt MGos WFar
	× ***caeruleoracemosa***	see *P.* × *violacea*
	× ***caponii***	CCCN
	chinensis	see *P. caerulea*
	citrifolia	CCCN EGxp
	citrina	EBee EShb LRHS SLim SOWG
	× ***colvillii***	CHll
	'Coordination'	CCCN
	'Crimson Trees'	CCCN
	× ***decaisneana*** (F)	CCCN
	Eden = 'Hil Pas Eden'PBR	CCCN CSBt EAmu EBee LRHS MBri SCoo SLim SPoG SRkn
	edulis (F)	CAgr CBcs CCCN ELau SVic
	- 'Crackerjack' (F)	ERea
	'Empress Eugenie'	see *P.* × *belotii*
§	× ***exoniensis*** 🏆H1	CBot CHll CRHN CSBt ECre
	'Fairylights'	CCCN
	'Flying V'	CCCN
	foetida	SOWG
	gibertii	EShb
	hahnii	EAmu
	incarnata (F)	CAgr CArn SPlb
	'Incense' (F) 🏆H1	CCCN SPlb WFar
	'Jelly Joker'	CCCN
*	***jureia*** × ***amethystina*** 'Santa Teresa'	EShb
	'Justine Lyons' **new**	CRHN
	× ***kewensis***	CCCN
	'Lady Margaret'	EGxp LRHS
	'Lambiekins' **new**	CRHN
§	***ligularis*** (F)	CBcs
	'Lilac Lady'	see *P.* × *violacea* 'Tresederi'
	lowei	see *P. ligularis*
	maliformis (F)	CHll
	'Maria'	CCCN
	'Mary Jane'	CCCN
I	***matthewsii*** 'Alba' **new**	CRHN
	'Mavis Mastics'	see *P.* × *violacea* 'Tresederi'
	mayana	see *P. caerulea*
	membranacea (F)	NExo
	'Mini Lamb'	CRHN
	mixta (F)	CCCN EBee SEND
	mollissima misapplied	see *P. tarminiana*
	mollissima ambig. (F)	CBcs CCCN CHll CTsd EShb SOWG SPlb
	mollissima (Kunth) L.H. Bailey (F) 🏆H1	CRHN EUJe
	morifolia	EShb
	murucuja	CCCN
	naviculata RCB/Arg P-12	WCot
	onychina	see *P. amethystina* Mikan
	'Peter Lawerence'	CCCN
	'Pink Festival'	NExo
	× ***piresiae***	CCCN
	'Purple Haze'	CBar CCCN CRHN CWib EBee EPfP NEgg NLar
	quadrangularis (F) 🏆H1	CCCN CHll CWSG ERea

	quinquangularis	CBcs
	racemosa ♀H2	CTsd EBee ERea LAst MNHC SOWG
	rubra	CCCN EBee SLim
	'Simply Red'	CCCN
	'Smythiana'	EShb
	'Star of Bristol' ♀H2	EBee SLim
	'Star of Surbiton'	CRHN
	'Sunburst'	CCCN CHEx
§	***tarminiana*** (F)	CSBt
	tetrandra	CPLG ECou
	× ***tresederi***	see *P.* × *violacea* 'Tresederi'
	trifasciata	CCCN EShb
	tulae	LRHS
	umbilicata	WCru
§	× ***violacea*** ♀H1	CBcs CRHN ERea LHop NExo SGar WFar
	- 'Eynsford Gem'	CCCN EAmu
	- 'Lilac Lady'	see *P.* × *violacea* 'Tresederi'
§	- 'Tresederi'	CTsd SEND WFar
	- 'Victoria'	CSBt EBee NLar SLim
	vitifolia (F)	SOWG
	'White Lightning'	LBuc LOck LRHS LSqu MAsh SBfd SLim SPoG SWvt

passion fruit see *Passiflora*

passion fruit, banana see *Passiflora mollissima*

Pastinaca (*Apiaceae*)

sativa	EBWF SVic

Patersonia (*Iridaceae*)

occidentalis	SPlb

Patrinia (*Valerianaceae*)

	gibbosa	GEdr LRHS MLHP MLLN SGSe WFar WMoo WPat WPnP
	- B&SWJ 874	WCru
	scabiosifolia	CAby CDes CHll CKno CSpe EBee ECha ECtt GAbr GCal LRHS MNFA NBir NLar NPri SGSe SPhx SPoG SUsu WAul WFar WHoo WMoo WPGP
	- B&SWJ 8740	WCru
	- 'Nagoya'	MNrw
	triloba	CPla CSpe ECho GCal GEdr GKir LSou SUsu WBVN WFar WMoo WPnP WWFP
*	- 'Minor'	ECho
	- var. ***palmata***	EBee GCrs GKev WDyG WFar WMoo WPnP
	villosa	CPLG EBee GCal IMou LRHS NGdn NLar SSvw

Paulownia (*Scrophulariaceae*)

catalpifolia	EBee EGFP LLHF MBri NLar
elongata	CBcs EGFP LLHF NLar WBVN
fortunei	CBcs IVic MBlu NLar SEND SPlb WBVN
- Fast Blue = 'Minfast'	CHGN CPLG EBee EPfP ESwi IVic LHop LLHF LRHS LSRN MWya SBfd SLim WHar WPGP
kawakamii B&SWJ 6784	WCru
taiwaniana B&SWJ 7134	WCru
tomentosa ♀H3	Widely available
- 'Coreana'	CHll
- - B&SWJ 8503	WCru

Pavonia (*Malvaceae*)

	× ***gledhillii***	ERea EShb
*	***littoralis*** new	MWya
	missionum	CSpe
	multiflora ambig.	CCCN
	praemorsa	CBot CSpe
	strictiflora	CCCN
*	***volubilis***	CCCN

paw paw (false banana) see *Asimina triloba*

paw paw (papaya) see *Carica papaya*

Paxistima (*Celastraceae*)

canbyi	WPat WThu

peach see *Prunus persica*

pear see *Pyrus communis*

pear, Asian see *Pyrus pyrifolia*

pecan see *Carya illinoinensis*

Pedicularis (*Scrophulariaceae*)

SDR 2931	GKev
SDR 5513	GKev
SDR 5901	GKev
superba SDR 1960	GKev

Peganum (*Zygophyllaceae*)

harmala	CArn

Pelargonium (*Geraniaceae*)

	'A.M. Mayne' (Z/d)	WFib
	'Abb and Mab' (Sc) new	MBPg
	'Abba' (Z/d)	WFib
	'Abbie Hillier' (R)	LDea
	'Abel Carrière' (I/d)	SKen SPet
	abrotanifolium (Sc)	EWoo LPio MBPg MHer SSea WFib WGwG WPen
	'Abundance' (Sc)	CSev LDea
	acetosum	CSev EWoo GCal LPio MHer
*	- 'Variegatum' (v)	LPio
	'Acushla by Brian' (Sc)	MBPg
	'Ada Green' (R)	LDea WFib
	'Ada Sutterby' (Dw/d)	SKen
	'Adam's Quilt' (Z/C)	SKen WEas
	'Adele' (Min/d)	ESul
	'Ade's Elf' (Z/St)	NFir SSea
	'Aerosol' (Min)	ESul
	'Ailsa' (Min/d)	ESul SKen
	'Ainsdale Beauty' (Z)	SSea WFib
	'Ainsdale Duke' (Z)	NFir
	'Ainsdale Eyeful' (Z)	WFib
	'Ainsdale Happiness' (Z/d)	SSea
	'Akela' (Min)	ESul
	'Alan Shellard' (Z/d/v) new	ESul
	'Alan West' (Z/St)	SSea
	Alba = 'Fisalb' (Z/d)	SKen
	'Alberta' (Z)	SKen
	album	EWoo
	alchemilloides	CRHN LPio
	'Alcyone' (Dw/d)	ESul SKen WFib
	'Alde' (Min)	NFir SKen SSea WFib
	'Aldenham' (Z)	WFib
	'Aldham' (Min)	ESul WFib
	'Aldwyck' (R)	ESul LDea WFib
	'Alex' (Z)	SKen
	'Alex Kitson' (Z)	WFib
	'Alex Mary' (R)	ESul
	'Algenon' (Min/d)	ESul WFib
I	'Alice' (Min)	WFib
	'Alice Greenfield' (Z)	NFir

'Alison' (Dw)	ESul
'Alison Field' (R) **new**	LDea
'Alma' (Dw/C)	ESul
'Altair' (Min/d)	ESul
I 'Amalfi' (R)	EWoo
'Amari' (R)	WFib
'Amazon' (R)	ESul
'Ambrose' (Min/d)	ESul WFib
Amelit = 'Pacameli'PBR (I/d)	LAst NPri SSea WGor
'American Prince of Orange' (Sc)	MBPg
'Amethyst' (R)	ESul LDea SCoo SPet WFib
§ Amethyst = 'Fisdel'PBR (I/d) ♀H1+3	ECtt SKen
'Amour' (R)	ESul
I 'Amy' (Dw)	WFib
'Andrew Salvidge' (R)	LDea
'Androcles' (A)	LDea
'Angela' (R)	ESul LDea
'Angela Read' (Dw)	ESul
'Angela Thorogood' (R)	ESul
'Angela Woodberry' (Z)	WFib
(Angeleyes Series) Angeleyes Bicolor = 'Pacbicolor'PBR (A)	LAst NPri
- Angeleyes Burgundy = 'Pacburg'PBR (A)	LAst SSea
- Angeleyes Orange = 'Paccrio' (A)	EWoo LSou MWea SUsu
- Angeleyes Randy (A)	SSea
- Angeleyes Velvet Duet (A)	LAst
'Angelique' (Dw/d)	ESul NFir WFib
'Anglia' (Dw)	ESul
'Ann Field' (Dw/d)	ESul
'Ann Hoystead' (R) ♀H1+3	ESul NFir WFib
'Ann Redington' (R)	ESul
'Anna' (Dw)	ESul
'Anna Scheen' (Min)	ESul
'Anne' (I/d)	WFib
'Annsbrook Aquarius' (St)	ESul NFir
'Annsbrook Beauty' (A/C)	ESul NFir WFib
'Annsbrook Capricorn' (St/d)	ESul
'Annsbrook Fruit Sundae' (A)	LDea
'Annsbrook Jupitor' (Z/St)	ESul NFir
'Annsbrook Mars' (St/C)	ESul
'Annsbrook Peaches' (Min)	ESul
'Annsbrook Pluto' (Z/St)	ESul
'Annsbrook Venus' (Z/St)	ESul
'Anthony Ayton' (R)	ESul
Anthony = 'Pacan'PBR (Z/d)	LAst
(Antik Series) Antik Pink = 'Tikpink'PBR (Z)	MWea
- Antik Violet = 'Tikvio'PBR (Antik Series) (Z)	MWea
'Antoine Crozy' (Z × I/d)	WFib
'Antoinette' (Min)	ESul
'Antonnia Scammell' (St/d)	ESul
'Apache' (Z/d) ♀H1+3	WFib
'Aphrodite' (Z)	ECtt
'Apollo' (R)	ESul
appendiculatum	LPio
'Apple Betty' (Sc)	EWoo MBPg WFib
'Apple Blossom Rosebud' (Z/d) ♀H1+3	CStu ECtt EShb ESul MBri MCot MHer NEgg SKen SSea WBrk WFib
'Appleblossom' (Angeleyes Series)	LAst
'Appledram' (R)	LDea

'Apri Parmer' (Min)	ESul
'Apricot' (Z/St)	ESul LAst SKen WGor
'Aprika'	WGor
'April Hamilton' (I)	WFib
'April Showers' (A)	LDea WFib
'Aquarell' (R)	ESul
'Arctic Frost'	WFib
§ 'Arctic Star' (Z/St)	CSpe ESul MCot NFir SAga SKen SSea WBrk WFib
'Ardens'	CHll CSev CSpe EBee ESul EWoo LOck LPio LSou MCot MHer NCob NFir SMrm SSea SUsu SWvt WCot WFib WGwG
'Ardwick Cinnamon' (Sc)	ESul EWoo LDea MBPg MHer NFir WFib
aridum	LPio WCot
(Aristo Series) Aristo Apricot = 'Regapri' (R)	LAst
- Aristo Beauty = 'Regbeauty'PBR (R)	LSou
- Aristo Clara Schumann (R)	LAst
- Aristo Clarina = 'Regli'PBR (R) **new**	LAst
- Aristo Red Velvet = 'Regvel'PBR (R)	LAst
- Aristo Schoko = 'Regschoko' (R)	LAst
- Aristo Velvet (R)	LSou
'Arizona' (Min/d)	SKen
'Arnside Fringed Aztec' (R)	LDea WFib
'Aroma' (Sc)	EWoo MBPg
'Arthington Slam' (R)	LDea
'Ashby' (U/Sc)	CWCL EWoo MBPg MHer NFir SBch SSea
'Ashfield Jubilee' (Z/C)	NFir SKen
'Ashfield Monarch' (Z/d) ♀H1+3	NFir
'Ashfield Serenade' (Z) ♀H1+3	SKen SSea WFib
'Ashley Stephenson' (R)	WFib
'Askham Fringed Aztec' (R) ♀H1+3	ESul LDea MHer WFib
'Askham Slam' (R)	LDea
asperum Ehr. ex Willd.	see *P.* 'Graveolens'
'Astrakan' (Z/d)	SSea
'Athabasca' (Min)	ESul
'Atlantic Burgundy'	CWCL MCot
§ 'Atomic Snowflake' (Sc/v)	CArn CFee ESul LDea MBPg MCot MHer MNHC SDnm SIde SKen SPet SSea WFib
'Atrium' (U)	MHer WFib
'Attar of Roses' (Sc) ♀H1+3	CArn CHby CRHN ERea ESul GBar LDea MBPg MCot MHer NFir NPri SBch SDnm SIde SKen SSea WBrk WFib WGwG
'Attraction' (Z/Ca/d)	SSea
'Aubusson' (R)	ESul
'Audrey Clifton' (I/d)	SKen
'Augusta'	SAga
'Auntie Billie' (A)	LDea
'Aurelia' (A)	LDea
'Aurora' (Z/d)	LAst LSou SKen SSea
australe	CRHN CSpe EWoo LPio MCot SBch SChr WFib
- pink-flowered **new**	EWoo
'Australian Bute' (R)	ESul
'Australian Mystery' (R/Dec)	CSpe ESul LPio NFir SAga WFib
'Autumn Colours' (Min)	ESul
'Autumn Haze' (R)	ESul

'Aztec' (R) $\heartsuit^{H1+3}$ ESul LDea NFir WFib
'Baby Bird's Egg' (Min) ESul WFib
'Baby Brocade' (Min/d) ESul WFib
'Baby Harry' (Dw/v) WFib
'Baby Helen' (Min) ESul
'Baby James' (Min) ESul
'Baby Snooks' (A) ESul LDea
'Babylon' (R) ESul
'Badley' (Dw) ESul
Balcon Imperial see *P.* 'Roi des Balcons Impérial'
'Balcon Lilas' see *P.* 'Roi des Balcons Lilas'
'Balcon Rose' see *P.* 'Hederinum'
'Balcon Rouge' see *P.* 'Roi des Balcons Impérial'
'Balcon Royale' see *P.* 'Roi des Balcons Impérial'
I 'Ballerina' (Min) WFib
'Ballerina' (R) see *P.* 'Carisbrooke'
'Bandit' (Min) ESul
'Bantam' (Min/d) ESul WFib
'Barbara Houghton' (Dw/d) WFib
§ 'Barbe Bleu' (I/d) ECtt NFir SKen SSea WFib
'Barcelona' (R) ESul
'Barham' (Min/d) ESul
'Barking' (Min/z) ESul NFir
'Barnston Dale' (Dw/d) ESul NFir
'Bath Beauty' (Dw) CSpe SKen WEas
'Baylham' (Min) ESul
'Beacon Hill' (Min) ESul
'Beatrice Cottington' (I/d) SKen WFib
'Beau Geste' (R) ESul
Beau Jangles Tom (I) NPri
'Beauty of Eastbourne' misapplied see *P.* 'Lachskönigin', *P.* 'Eastbourne Beauty'
'Beauty of El Segundo' (Z/d) SKen
'Beckwith's Pink' (Z) SKen
'Beidermeier' (R) ESul
'Belinda Adams' (Min/d) $\heartsuit^{H1+3}$ NFir SSea
Belladonna = 'Fisopa' (I/d) ECtt SCoo
'Belle Ville Red Star' MCot
'Belvedere' (R) ESul
'Bembridge' (Z/St/d) SSea WFib
'Ben Franklin' (Z/d/v) $\heartsuit^{H1+3}$ ESul NFir SSea
'Ben Matt' (R) ESul WFib
'Ben Nevis' (Dw/d) ESul
'Ben Picton' (Z/d) WFib
'Bentley' (Dw) ESul
'Berkswell Beacon' (A) **new** LDea
'Berkswell Blush' (A) LDea
'Berkswell Bonanza' (A) **new** LDea
'Berkswell Calypso' (A) LDea
'Berkswell Carnival' (A) LDea
'Berkswell Champagne' (A) LDea
'Berkswell Charm' (A) LDea
'Berkswell Dainty' (A) LDea
'Berkswell Debonair' (A) LDea
'Berkswell Fondant' (A) **new** LDea
'Berkswell Gaiety' (A) LDea
'Berkswell Gipsy' (A) **new** LDea
'Berkswell Jester' (A) LDea
'Berkswell Lace' (A) LDea MHer
'Berkswell Nocturne' (A) **new** LDea
'Berkswell Petticote' (A) **new** LDea
'Berkswell Pixie' (A) LDea
'Berkswell Rosette' (A) LDea
'Berkswell Sparkler' (A) LDea
'Berkswell Trinket' (A) **new** LDea
'Berkswell Windmill' (A) LDea
'Berliner Balkon' (I) SKen
Bernardo = 'Guiber'PBR (I/d) LAst
'Bernice Ladroot' ESul LDea
'Beromünster' (Dec) ESul EWoo MHer NFir SAga WFib
'Bert Pearce' (R) ESul LDea WFib
'Beryl Read' (Dw) CWCL ESul
'Beryl Reid' (R) ESul LDea WFib
'Berylette' (Min/d) ESul SKen
'Bess' (Z/d) ESul SKen
'Bett Rickaby' (R) **new** LDea
'Bette Shellard' (Z/d/v) NFir
'Betty Merry' (R) LDea
'Betty Read' (Dw) ESul
'Betty West' (Min/d) ESul
betulinum EWoo LPio WFib
'Betwixt' (Z/v) SKen SSea
'Bianca' (Min/d) ESul
'Big Apple' (Sc) MBPg
'Bildeston' (Dw/C) ESul WFib
'Bill West' (I) SSea WFib
'Billie Read' (Dw/d) ESul
'Bingo' (Min) ESul
'Bird Dancer' (Dw/St) $\heartsuit^{H1+3}$ CSpe ESul MHer MNHC NFir SBch SKen SSea SWal WBrk
(Birdbush Series) MBPg
'Birdbush Andy Pandy' (Sc)
- 'Birdbush Beautiful' (Sc) MBPg
- 'Birdbush Belinda' (Sc) MBPg
- 'Birdbush Bella' (Sc) MBPg
- 'Birdbush Betty' (Sc) **new** MBPg
- 'Birdbush Billy' (Sc) MBPg
- 'Birdbush Blanco' (Sc) MBPg
- 'Birdbush Blush' (Sc) MBPg
- 'Birdbush Bobby' (Sc) MBPg
- 'Birdbush Bold and Beautiful' (Sc) MBPg
- 'Birdbush Bolero' (Sc) **new** MBPg
- 'Birdbush Bonny' (Sc) **new** MBPg
- 'Birdbush Bountiful' (Sc) MBPg
- 'Birdbush Bramley' (Sc) MBPg
- 'Birdbush Brandy' (Sc) MBPg
- 'Birdbush Brilliant' (Sc) MBPg
- 'Birdbush Chloe' (St) MBPg
- 'Birdbush Claire Louise' (Sc) MBPg
- 'Birdbush Dawndew' (Sc) MBPg
- 'Birdbush Eleanor' (Z) MBPg WFib
- 'Birdbush Julie Anne' (Sc) MBPg
- 'Birdbush Kay Lye' (Sc) MBPg
- 'Birdbush Lemonside' (Sc) MBPg
- 'Birdbush Limey' (Sc) MBPg
- 'Birdbush Linda Creasey' (Sc) MBPg
- 'Birdbush Marion Louise' (Sc) MBPg
- 'Birdbush Matty' MBPg
- 'Birdbush Miriam' (Sc) MBPg
- 'Birdbush Nutty' (Sc) MBPg
- 'Birdbush Pink and Perky' (U) MBPg
- 'Birdbush Pinky' (Sc) MBPg
- 'Birdbush Sweetness' (Sc) MBPg
- 'Birdbush Tiny Tot' (Sc) MBPg
- 'Birdbush Too Too O' (Sc) MBPg
- 'Birdbush Velvet' (Sc) MBPg
- 'Birdbush Victoria' (Sc) MBPg
'Birthday Girl' (R) WFib
'Bitter Lemon' (Sc) ERea ESul MBPg
'Black Butterfly' see *P.* 'Brown's Butterfly'
'Black Knight' (R) CSpe EShb EWoo MHer

'Black Knight' Lea (Dw/d/C)	ESul NFir
'Black Moth' **new**	EWoo
'Black Night' (A)	ESul
'Black Prince' (R/Dec)	EWoo NFir WFib
'Black Top' (R)	ESul
'Black Velvet' (R)	ESul EWoo LDea MCot
'Black Vesuvius'	see *P.* 'Red Black Vesuvius'
'Blackberry Yhu' (Dec/R) **new**	ESul
'Blackcurrant Yhu' (Dec)	NFir
'Blackdown Delight' (Z)	NFir
'Blackdown Sensation' (Dw/Z)	NFir
'Blakesdorf' (Dw)	ESul
Blanca = 'Penwei'PBR (Dark Line Series) (Z/d)	LAst
Blanche Roche = 'Guitoblanc' (I/d)	LAst LSou NPri SCoo
§ 'Blandfordianum' (Sc)	EWoo LDea LPio MHer
'Blandfordianum Roseum' (Sc)	LDea
'Blaze Away'	SSea
'Blazonry' (Z/v)	SKen SSea WFib
'Blendworth' (R)	LDea
'Blue Beard'	see *P.* 'Barbe Bleu'
'Blue Orchid' (R)	ESul
'Blue Peter' (I/d)	SKen
Blue Sybil = 'Pacblusy'PBR (I/d)	LAst LSou NPri
Blue Wonder = 'Pacbla'PBR (Z/d)	LAst WGor
Blue-Blizzard = 'Fisrain'PBR (I)	SCoo
'Blush Petit Pierre' (Min)	ESul
'Blushing Bride' (I/d)	SKen
'Blushing Emma' (Dw/d)	ESul
'Bob Hall' (St)	ESul
'Bob Newing' (Min/St)	ESul WFib
'Bobberstone' (Z/St)	WFib
'Bold Appleblossom' (Z)	WFib
'Bold Carmine' (Z/d)	NFir
'Bold Carousel' (Z/d)	WFib
'Bold Dawn' (Z)	NFir
'Bold Flame' (Z/d)	WFib
'Bold Limelight' (Z/d)	WFib
'Bold Melody' (Z)	SSea
'Bold Pixie' (Dw/d)	WFib
'Bold Sunrise' (Z/d)	NFir
'Bold Sunset' (Z/d)	NFir WFib
'Bold White' (Z)	NFir
'Bolero' (U) ♀H1+3	NFir WFib
'Bon Bon' (Min/St)	WFib
'Bonito' (I/d)	SSea
'Bonnie Austin' (St)	ESul
'Bonny' (Min/St)	ESul
'Bosham' (R)	ESul LDea WFib
'Both's Snowflake' (Sc/v)	GBar MBPg
bowkeri	WFib
'Brackenwood' (Dw/d) ♀H1+3	ESul NFir
'Bramford' (Dw)	ESul
Bravo = 'Fisbravo'PBR (Z/d)	WFib
'Break o' Day' (R)	LDea
'Bredon' (R) ♀H1+3	ESul
'Brenda' (Min/d)	ESul WFib
'Brenda Hyatt' (Dw/d)	ESul WFib
'Brettenham' (Min)	ESul
'Brian West' (Min/St/C)	ESul WFib
'Briarlyn Beauty' (A)	LDea MBPg
'Briarlyn Moonglow' (A)	ESul LDea
'Bridesmaid' (Dw/d)	ESul NFir SKen
'Bright Eyes' ambig. (Dw)	WFib
'Brightstone' (Z/d)	WFib
'Brightwell' (Min/d)	ESul
'Brilliant' (Dec)	WFib
'Brilliantine' (Sc)	CSev ESul EWoo MBPg MHer WFib WGwG
'Bristol' (Z/v)	SSea
'Britannia' (R)	LDea
'Brixworth Pearl' (Z)	WFib
'Brockbury Scarlet' (Ca)	WFib
'Bronze Corinne' (Z/C/d)	SKen SPet
'Bronze Velvet' (R)	LDea
'Brook's Purple'	see *P.* 'Royal Purple'
'Brookside Betty' (Dw/C/d)	ESul
'Brookside Bolero' (Z)	ESul
'Brookside Candy' (Dw/d)	ESul
'Brookside Champagne' (Min/d)	ESul
'Brookside Fiesta' (Min/d)	ESul
'Brookside Flamenco' (Dw/d)	ESul WFib
'Brookside Free Spirit' (Min/D)	ESul
'Brookside Melody' (Min/D)	ESul
'Brookside Polka' (Dw/D)	ESul
'Brookside Primrose' (Min/C/d)	ESul NFir SKen WFib
'Brookside Rosita' (Min)	ESul
'Brookside Serenade' (Dw)	ESul WFib
'Brookside Spitfire' (Dw/d)	ESul
'Brookside Tango' (Min/D)	ESul
§ 'Brown's Butterfly' (R)	ECtt EShb ESul LPio NFir WFib
'Brunswick' (Sc)	ESul EWoo LDea MHer WFib
'Bucklesham' (Dw)	ESul
'Bullfinch' (R)	ESul
'Bumblebee' (Dw)	ESul
'Burgenlandmädel' (Z/d)	SKen
'Burns Country' (Dw)	NFir
'Burstall' (Min/d)	ESul
'Bushfire' (R) ♀H1+3	ESul EWoo WFib
'Butley' (Min)	ESul
'Butterfly' (Min/v)	ECtt
'Butterfly Brian West' (Min/St)	WFib
Butterfly = 'Fisam'PBR (I)	NFir NPri SCoo
'Button 'n' Bows' (I/d)	WFib
caffrum	LPio
'Cal'	see *P.* 'Salmon Irene'
Calais = 'Paclai'PBR	LAst
'Caledonia' (Z)	SKen
'California Brilliant' (U)	MHer
'Calignon' (Z/St)	WFib
'Camphor Rose' (Sc)	ESul GPWP LDea MBPg NFir SSea
'Can-can' (I/d)	WFib
'Candy' (Min/d)	ESul
'Candy Kisses' (D)	ESul
Candy Rose = 'Pacdy'PBR	LAst
canescens	see *P.* 'Blandfordianum'
'Cape Beauty'	EWoo
'Capel' (Dw/d)	ESul
capitatum	CArn LPio MBPg MHer MNHC WFib
'Capri' (Sc)	MBPg WFib
'Capricorn' (Min/d)	ESul
'Captain Starlight' (A)	CRHN ESul EWoo LDea MBPg MHer NFir SSea WFib
'Caravan' (A)	LDea
'Cardinal'	see *P.* 'Kardinal'
'Cardington' (St/Dw)	ESul
'Carefree' (U)	LPio NFir WFib
§ 'Carisbrooke' (R) ♀H1+3	ESul LDea WFib

'Carl Gaffney'	LDea
'Carmel' (Z)	WFib
'Carnival' (R)	see *P.* 'Marie Vogel'
carnosum	MHer
'Carol' (R)	ESul
'Carol Gibbons' (Z/d)	NFir WFib
'Carol Helyar' (Z/d)	WFib
'Caroline' (Dec)	ESul
'Caroline Plumridge' (Dw)	ESul
'Caroline Schmidt' (Z/d/v)	CFox LAst MCot NFir SKen SSea WBrk WFib
'Carolyn' (Dw)	ESul
'Carolyn Dean' (St)	NFir
'Carolyn Hardy' (Z/d)	WFib
Cascade Lilac	see *P.* 'Roi des Balcons Lilas'
Cascade Pink	see *P.* 'Hederinum'
'Catford Belle' (A) ♀H1+3	ESul LDea
'Cathay' (Z/St)	ESul NFir
'Cathy' (R)	NFir
caucalifolium	LPio MHer
subsp. ***caucalifolium***	
- subsp. ***convolvulifolium***	LPio WFib
'Cayucas' (I/d)	SKen
'Celebration' (Z/d)	ESul
'Cerise' (I/d)	SSea
'Cézanne' (R)	ESul LDea MCot WFib
'Chantilly Claret' (R)	LDea
'Chantilly Lace' (R)	ESul
'Charity' (Sc) ♀H1+3	EOHP ESul LDea MBPg MCot MHer NFir WBrk WFib
'Charlie Boy' (R)	LDea
'Charlotte Amy' (R)	LDea
'Charlotte Bidwell' (Min)	ESul
'Charlotte Bronte' (Dw/v)	WFib
'Charm' (Min)	ESul
'Charmay Alf' (A)	LDea
'Charmay Aria' (A)	LDea
'Charmay Bagatelle' (A)	LDea
'Charmay Electra' (A)	LDea
'Charmay Marjorie' (A)	LDea
'Charmay Snowflake' (Sc/v)	ESul MBPg
'Chattisham' (Dw/C)	ESul NFir
'Chelmondiston' (Min/d)	ESul
'Chelsea Gem' (Z/d/v) ♀H1+3	SKen SSea WFib
'Chelsea Morning' (Z/d)	WFib
'Chelsworth' (Min/d)	ESul
'Cherie' (R)	ESul
'Cherie Bidwell' (Dw/d/v)	ESul
'Cherie Maid' (Z/v)	SSea
'Cherry' (Min)	WFib
'Cherry Baby' (Dec)	NFir
'Cherry Cocktail' (Z/d/v)	NFir
'Cherry Hazel Ruffled' (R)	ESul LDea
'Cherry Orchard' (R)	ESul LDea WFib
'Cherry Sundae' (Z/d/v)	ESul
'Cheryldene' (R)	LDea
'Chew Magna' (R)	WFib
'Chi-Chi' (Min)	ESul
'Chieko' (Min/d)	WFib
'Chime' (Min/d)	ESul
'China Doll' (Dw/d)	WFib
'Chinz' (R)	CSpe NFir
§ 'Chocolate Peppermint' (Sc)	CRHN CSev ESul LDea MBPg MHer MNHC NFir SIde SKen SSea SWal WBrk WFib
'Chocolate Tomentosum'	see *P.* 'Chocolate Peppermint'
'Chrissie' (R)	ESul WFib
'Christina Beere' (R)	LDea
'Christopher Ley' (Z)	SKen
'Cindy' (Dw/d)	ESul WFib
'Citriodorum' (Sc) ♀H1+3	LDea MBPg MCot MHer WFib

'Citronella' (Sc)	CRHN LDea MBPg SSea WFib WGwG
citronellum (Sc)	LPio MBPg
'City of Bath'	CWCL
'Clara Read' (Dw)	ESul NFir
'Claret Rock Unique' (U)	EWoo MBPg SKen SSea WFib
'Clarissa' (Min)	ESul
'Clatterbridge' (Dw/d)	ESul NFir
'Claude Read' (Dw)	ESul
'Claudette' (Min)	ESul
'Claudius' (Min)	ESul
'Claydon' (Dw/d)	ESul NFir
'Claydon Firebird' (R)	ESul
'Clorinda' (U/Sc)	CRHN EShb ESul EWoo MBPg MCot MHer MNHC SIde SKen SSea SWal WFib WGwG
'Clovelly Rose'	CWCL
'Clown' (R)	ESul
'Coconut Ice' (Dw)	ESul
Coco-Rico (I)	SKen
'Coddenham' (Dw/d)	ESul WFib
§ 'Colonel Baden-Powell' (I/d)	WFib
'Colwell' (Min/d)	WFib
'Concolor Lace'	see *P.* 'Shottesham Pet'
'Confetti' (R)	ESul
'Contrast' (Z/C/v)	CWCL MBri NEgg SCoo SKen SPoG SSea WFib
'Cook's Peachblossom'	WFib
'Copdock' (Min/d)	ESul
'Copthorne' (U/Sc) ♀H1+3	CRHN CSpe ESul EWoo LDea MBPg MCot MHer NFir SKen SSea WFib WPen
'Coral Frills' (Min/d)	ESul
cordifolium	CRHN EWoo WFib
- var. ***rubrocinctum***	ESul NFir
coriandrifolium	see *P. myrrhifolium* var. *coriandrifolium*
'Cornell' (I/d)	ECtt WFib
cortusifolium	MHer
'Corvina' (R)	WFib
'Cottenham Beauty' (A)	ESul LDea NFir
'Cottenham Belle' (A)	ESul
'Cottenham Bliss' (A)	ESul SUsu
'Cottenham Charm' (A)	ESul LDea
'Cottenham Cheer' (A)	ESul
'Cottenham Cynthia Haird' (A)	ESul
'Cottenham Delight' (A)	ESul LDea NFir
'Cottenham Gem' (A)	ESul
'Cottenham Glamour' (A)	ESul MHer NFir
'Cottenham Harmony' (A)	ESul LDea
'Cottenham Jubilee' (A)	ESul LDea MHer
'Cottenham Magic' (A) **new**	ESul
'Cottenham Mervyn Haird' (A)	ESul
'Cottenham Star' (A)	ESul
'Cottenham Surprise' (A)	ESul LDea NFir
'Cottenham Treasure' (A)	ESul LDea
'Cottenham Triumph' (A) **new**	ESul
'Cottenham Wonder' (A)	ESul NFir
'Cotton Candy' (Min/d)	ESul
'Cottontail' (Min)	ESul WFib
cotyledonis	WFib
'Countess Mariza'	see *P.* 'Gräfin Mariza'
'Countess of Scarborough'	see *P.* 'Lady Scarborough'
'Country Girl' (R)	SPet
'Cover Girl' (Z/d)	WFib
'Cowes' (St/Min/d)	ESul
'Cramdon Red' (Dw)	SKen WFib
'Cransley Blends' (R)	ESul
'Cransley Star' (A)	LDea WFib
'Cream 'n' Green' (R/v)	NFir

	'Creamery' (d)	WFib
	'Creamy Nutmeg' (Sc/v)	CArn EShb ESul EWoo GBar LDea MHer NFir SSea WBrk
	'Creeting St Mary' (Min)	ESul
	'Creeting St Peter' (Min)	ESul
	'Crescendo' (I/d)	ECtt
	'Crimson Fire' (Z/d)	MBri
	'Crimson Unique' (U) ♀H1+3	CSpe EWoo MCot MHer SKen SSea WFib
§	***crispum*** (Sc)	GBar GPoy MBPg NEgg
§	- 'Golden Well Sweep' (Sc/v)	MBPg WFib
	- 'Major' (Sc)	ESul MCot SKen WFib
	- 'Peach Cream' (Sc/v)	ESul MBPg WFib
	- 'Prince Rupert' (Sc)	MBPg
	- 'Variegatum' (Sc/v) ♀H1+3	CRHN GBar GPoy LDea MBPg MCot MHer NFir SIde SPet SSea WCom WFib
	crithmifolium	MHer
	'Crocketta' (I/d/v)	NFir SKen
	'Crocodile' (I/C/d)	ECtt ERea EShb MHer NFir SKen SSea WBrk WFib
	'Crowfield' (Min/d)	ESul WFib
	'Crowfoot Rose' (Sc)	GBar
	'Crown Jewels' (R)	LDea
	'Crystal Palace Gem' (Z/v)	SKen SSea WFib
	'Crystal West' (Min/St)	ESul
	cucullatum	ESul LPio SSea WFib
	- 'Flore Pleno'	MHer WFib
	- subsp. ***strigifolium***	EWoo
	'Culpho' (Min/C/d)	ESul
	'Cupid' (Min/Dw/d)	WFib
	'Cyril Read' (Dw)	ESul
§	'Czar' (Z/C)	SCoo
	'Dainty Lassie' (Dw/v)	ESul
	'Dainty Maid' (Sc)	CSpe ESul EWoo MBPg NFir SAga SSea
	'Dale Queen' (Z)	WFib
	'Dallimore' (Dw)	ESul
	'Danielle Marie' (A)	LDea
	'Danton' (Z/d)	WFib
I	'Daphne' (Dec)	SKen
	'Dark Ascot' (Dec)	ESul
	'Dark Red Irene' (Z/d)	SKen WFib
	'Dark Secret' (R)	CSpe ESul LDea WFib
	'Dark Venus' (R)	ESul EWoo LDea WFib
	Dark-Red-Blizzard = 'Fisblizdark' (I)	CWCL EWoo
	'Darmsden' (A) ♀H1+3	ESul LDea NFir SSea
	'David John' (Dw/d)	ESul
	'David Mitchell' (Min/Ca/d)	ESul
	'Davina' (Min/d)	ESul WFib
	'Dawn Star' (Z/St)	ESul NFir
	'Deacon Arlon' (Dw/d)	ESul SKen
	'Deacon Avalon' (Dw/d)	WFib
	'Deacon Barbecue' (Z/d)	ESul SKen WFib
	'Deacon Birthday' (Z/d)	ESul WFib
	'Deacon Bonanza' (Z/d)	ESul SSea WFib
	'Deacon Clarion' (Z/d)	ESul SKen WFib
	'Deacon Constancy' (Z/d)	ESul
	'Deacon Coral Reef' (Z/d)	ESul WFib
	'Deacon Finale' (Z/d)	ESul
	'Deacon Fireball' (Z/d)	ESul SKen WFib
	'Deacon Flamingo' (Z/d)	ESul
	'Deacon Gala' (Z/d)	ESul WFib
	'Deacon Golden Bonanza' (Z/C/d)	ESul WFib
	'Deacon Golden Gala' (Z/C/d)	ESul SKen
	'Deacon Golden Lilac Mist' (Z/C/d)	ESul WFib
	'Deacon Jubilant' (Z/d)	ESul SKen
	'Deacon Lilac Mist' (Z/d)	ESul SKen SSea WFib
	'Deacon Mandarin' (Z/d)	ESul SKen WFib
	'Deacon Minuet' (Z/d)	ESul NFir SKen WFib
	'Deacon Moonlight' (Z/d)	ESul
	'Deacon Peacock' (Z/C/d)	ESul WFib
	'Deacon Picotee' (Z/d)	ESul SKen WFib
	'Deacon Regalia' (Z/d)	ESul SKen WFib
	'Deacon Romance' (Z/d)	ESul SKen
§	'Deacon Summertime' (Z/d)	ESul WFib
	'Deacon Sunburst' (Z/d)	ESul SKen
	'Deacon Suntan' (Z/d)	ESul SKen
	'Deacon Trousseau' (Z/d)	ESul WFib
	'Dean's Delight' (Sc)	LDea MBPg
	'Debbie' (A)	LDea
	'Debbie Parmer' (Dw/d)	ESul
	'Debbie Thrower' (Dw)	ESul
	'Deborah Miliken' (Z/d)	ESul NFir WFib
	'Decora Lavender'	see *P.* 'Decora Lilas'
§	'Decora Lilas' (I)	ECtt LAst NPri SKen SPet
	'Decora Mauve'	see *P.* 'Decora Lilas'
	'Decora Pink'	see *P.* 'Decora Rouge'
	'Decora Red'	see *P.* 'Decora Rouge'
§	'Decora Rose' (I)	ECtt LAst NPri SPet
§	'Decora Rouge' (I)	ECtt SKen SPet
	'Decora Scarlet' (I)	SKen
	'Decora Stellena' (I/v) new	LAst
	'Deerwood Darling' (Min/v/d)	WFib
	'Deerwood Lavender Lad' (Sc)	CSev ESul EWoo LDea MBPg MHer SSea WFib
	'Deerwood Lavender Lass'	ESul LDea LPio MBPg MHer
	'Deerwood Pink Puff' (St/d)	WFib
	'Delightful' (R)	WFib
	'Delli' (R)	MHer NFir NPer SMrm WFib
	'Delta' (Min/d)	ESul
	'Denebola' (Min/d)	ESul
	'Dennis Hunt' (Z/C)	NFir
	denticulatum	GBar MHer SKen SSea
§	- 'Filicifolium' (Sc)	CRHN EShb ESul EWoo LDea LPio MBPg MHer SSea WFib
	'Diana Hull'	MBPg
	'Diana Palmer' (Z/d)	SKen
	'Diane' (Min/d)	ESul
	'Diane Louise' (d)	SSea
	'Dibbinsdale' (Z)	ESul NFir
	dichondrifolium (Sc)	CSev LPio MBPg MHer NFir SSea WFib
	dichondrifolium* × *reniforme (Sc)	ESul NFir
	'Didi' (Min)	SKen
	'Dinky' (Min/d)	ESul
	'Display' ambig. (Dw/v)	WFib
	'Distinction' (Z)	ERea MHer NFir SKen SPoG SSea WFib
	'Dollar Bute' (R)	ESul
	'Dollar Princess' (Z/C)	SKen
	'Dolly Read' (Dw)	ESul
	'Dolly Varden' (Z/v) ♀H1+3	ESul LDea NFir SKen SSea WFib
	'Don's Carosel' (Z/v)	SSea
	'Don's Helen Bainbridge' (Z/C)	NFir
	'Don's Mona Noble' (Z/C)	NFir SKen
	'Don's Richard A. Costain' (Z/C)	NFir
	'Don's Seagold' (Z/C)	NFir
	'Don's Silva Perle' (Dw/v)	SKen
	'Don's Southport' (Z/v)	NFir
	'Don's Swanland Girl' (Min)	ESul
	'Don's Wensleydale' (Dw/C)	ESul

'Dorcas Brigham Lime' (Sc) CSpe
'Dorcus Bingham' (Sc) GBar MBPg
'Doris Frith' (R) LDea
'Doris Hancock' (R) WFib
'Doris Shaw' (R) ESul
'Dorothy May' (A) LDea
'Dot Fowler' (R) **new** LDea
'Double Bird's Egg' (Z/d) SKen
'Double Grace Wells' (Min/d) ESul
'Double Lilac White' (I/d) SKen
'Double Orange' (Z/d) SKen
'Double Pink' (R/d) WFib
'Dovedale' (Dw/C) ESul WFib
'Dovepoint' (Dw/2) NFir
'Downlands' (Z/d) WFib
'Dresden China' (R) ESul LDea
'Dresden Pippa Rosa' (Z) SKen
'Dresden White' (Dw) WFib
Dresdner Apricot = 'Pacbriap'[PBR] (I/d) NPri
'Drummer Boy' (Z) SKen
'Dryden' (Z) SKen
'Dubonnet' (R) LDea
'Duchess of Devonshire' (U) EWoo WFib
'Duke of Edinburgh' see *P.* 'Hederinum Variegatum'
'Dulcie' (Min) ESul
'Dunkery Beacon' (R) ESul WFib
'Dusty Rose' (Min) ESul
'E. Dabner' (Z/d) SKen WFib
'Earl of Chester' (Min/d) ♀H1+3 WFib
'Earliana' (Dec) ESul LDea SUsu
'Earlsfour' (R) LDea
'East Sussex' (Dw/C) ESul
§ 'Eastbourne Beauty' (I/d) SKen
'Easter Promise' (R) ESul
echinatum CSpe EWoo LPio MHer
- 'Album' LPio SSea WFib
'Eclipse' (Dw/d) SKen
'Eclipse' (I/d) SKen
'Eden Gem' (Min/d) WFib
'Edith Stern' (Dw/d) ESul
'Edmond Lachenal' (Z/d) WFib
'Edward Humphris' (Z) SKen
'Edwards Michael' (A) LDea
'Eileen' (Min/d) ESul
'Eileen Nancy' (Z) NFir
'Eileen Postle' (R) ♀H1+3 WFib
'Eileen Stanley' (R) LDea
'Elaine' (R) LDea
'Elaine Thompson' (R) LDea
Elbe Silver = 'Pensil' (I) LAst NFir SCoo
'Electra' (Z/d) SKen
elegans ERea
'Elizabeth Angus' (Z) SKen WFib
'Elizabeth Read' (Dw) ESul
'Ella Martin' (St) ESul
'Elmfield' (St/Min/d) ESul
'Elmsett' (Dw/C/d) ESul NFir SSea WFib
'Elna' (Min) ESul
'Els' (Dw/St) ESul SKen WBrk
'Elsi' (I × Z/d/v) WFib
'Elsie Gillam' (St) ESul WFib
'Elsie Hickman' (R) ESul LDea
'Elsie Portas' (Z/C/d) ESul SKen
'Embassy' (Min) ESul WFib
'Emerald' (I) SKen
Emilia = 'Pactina'[PBR] LAst WGor
'Emma Game' (Z/St) WFib
'Emma Hössle' see *P.* 'Frau Emma Hössle'
'Emma Jane Read' (Dw/d) ESul NFir WFib
'Emma Louise' (Z) SKen
'Emmy Sensation' (R) LDea
'Emperor Nicholas' (Z/d) SKen SSea
'Empress' (Z) SKen
'Ena' (Min) ESul
'Enchantress' (I) SKen
'Encore' (Z/d/v) SSea
endlicherianum LPio NWCA WCot WWFP
'Endsleigh' (Sc) MBPg SBch
'Enid Brackley' (R) ESul
'Erwarton' (Min/d) ESul NFir
'Escapade' (Min/d) ESul
'Eskay Gold' (A) WFib
'Eskay Jewel' (A) WFib
'Eskay Ruby' (A) **new** MHer
'Eskay Sugar Candy' (A) WFib
'Eskay Verglo' (A) WFib
'Evka'[PBR] (I/v) CWCL LAst SCoo SSea SWal
exstipulatum EShb EWoo SSea WEas
'Fabiola' LAst
'Fair Dinkum' (Z/v) ESul
'Fair Ellen' (Sc) ESul LDea MBPg MHer WFib
'Fairlee' (DwI) WFib
'Fairy Lights' (Dw/St) ESul NFir
'Fairy Orchid' (A) ESul LDea WFib
'Fairy Queen' LDea MHer
'Falkenham' (Min) ESul
'Falkland Brother' (Z/C/v) WFib
'Falkland Hero' (Z/v) NFir
'Fallen Angel' (Z/St) WFar
'Fandango' (Z/St) ESul NFir WFib
'Fanny Eden' (R) CWCL EWoo WFib
'Fantasia' white-flowered (Dw/d) ♀H1+3 ESul WFib
'Fareham' (R) ♀H1+3 LDea WFib
'Feneela' (Dw/d) ESul
'Fenland' (R) ESul
'Fenland Queen' (A) **new** ESul
'Fenton Farm' (Dw/C) ESul NFir
'Festal' (Min/d) ESul
'Feuerriese' (Z) SKen
'Fiat' (Z/d) SKen
'Fiat Queen' (Z/d) SKen WFib
'Fiat Supreme' (Z/d) SKen
'Fiery Sunrise' (R) ESul LDea
'Fiesta' (I/d) LDea
'Fifth Avenue' (R) ESul LPio WFib
'Filicifolium' see *P. denticulatum* 'Filicifolium'
'Fir Trees Audrey B' (St) NFir
'Fir Trees Celebration' (Sc) NFir
'Fir Trees Echoes of Pink' (A) EWoo
'Fir Trees Eileen' (St) NFir SMrm
'Fir Trees Ele' (A/v) NFir
'Fir Trees Fantail' (Min) NFir
'Fir Trees Flamingo' (Dw) NFir
'Fir Trees Jack' (Z/Dw) NFir
'Fir Trees Janet' (Dw) **new** NFir
'Fir Trees Jennifer' (R/Dec) **new** NFir
'Fir Trees John Grainger' (Z/v) NFir
'Fir Trees Mark' (R/Dec/v) NFir
'Fir Trees Nan' (R/Dec) NFir
'Fir Trees Pink Pom-Pom' (Dw/St/C)(d) **new** NFir
'Fir Trees Ruby Wedding' (C) NFir
'Fir Trees Silver Wedding' (Z/C/d) NFir
'Fir Trees Sparkler' (Min/C) NFir
'Fir Trees Val' (Z) **new** NFir

'Fire Dancer' (R)	ESul
'Fire Dragon' (Z/St/d)	SKen SSea
'Firefly' (Min/d)	ESul
'Firestone' (Dw)	ESul
(Fireworks Series)	LAst SBfd
Fireworks Cherry = 'Fiwocherry'PBR (Z)	
- Fireworks Cherry-white = 'Fiwocher'PBR (Z)	LAst SSea
- Fireworks Light Pink = 'Fiwopink'PBR (Z/St)	SBfd
- Fireworks Red-white = 'Fiworewhi'PBR (Z)	SBfd
- Fireworks White = 'Fiwowit'PBR (Z)	SBfd
'First Blush' (R)	WFib
'First Love' (Z)	NFir
'Flakey' (I/d/v) Υ^{H1+3}	ESul SKen
'Flaming Katy' (Min)	ESul NFir
'Flarepath' (Z/C/v)	NFir
'Flash' (Min)	ESul
'Flecks' (Min/St)	ESul
'Fleur-de-lys' (A)	LDea
'Fleurette' (Min/d)	ESul SKen
'Fleurisse' (Z)	WFib
'Flirt' (Min)	WFib
'Floral Cascade' (Fr/d)	SSea
'Florence Hunt' (R)	NFir
'Floria Moore' (Dec)	ESul EWoo NFir SAga SSea
'Flower Basket' (R/d)	ESul EWoo LDea
(Flower Fairy Series)	LSou
Flower Fairy Rose = 'Swero'PBR (Z)	
- Flower Fairy White Splash = 'Swewhi' (Z)	LAst LSou
'Flower of Spring' (Z/v) Υ^{H1+3}	SKen SSea
'Flowton' (Dw/d)	ESul
'Foxhall' (Dw)	ESul
Foxy = 'Pacfox'PBR (Z)	LSou
Fragrans Group (Sc)	CRHN CSev ESul EWoo GBar GPoy MBPg MCot MHer SDnm SKen SMrm SPet SSea WFib WGwG
§ - 'Fragrans Variegatum' (Sc/v)	CSev ESul MBPg NFir SKen SWal WBrk WFib
- 'Snowy Nutmeg'	see *P.* (Fragrans Group) 'Fragrans Variegatum'
'Fraiche Beauté' (Z/d)	WFib
'Francis Gibbon' (Z/d)	WFib
'Francis James' (Z)	WFib
'Francis Kelly' (R)	ESul
'Francis Parrett' (Min/d) Υ^{H1+3}	ESul SKen WFib
'Francis Read' (Dw/d)	ESul
'Frank Headley' (Z/v) Υ^{H1+3}	CFox ERea EShb ESul LAst MCot MWea NPer NVic SAga SCoo SDnm SIde SKen SSea WFib
§ 'Frau Emma Hössle' (Dw/d)	ESul WFib
'Freak of Nature' (Z/v)	ESul MHer NFir SKen SSea WFib
'Frensham' (Sc)	ESul LDea MBPg MHer WFib
'Freshfields Suki' (Dw)	NFir
'Freshwater' (St/C)	ESul SSea WFib
'Freston' (Dw)	ESul
'Friary Wood' (Z/C/d)	ESul NFir WFib
'Friesdorf' (Dw/Fr)	ESul MCot MHer NFir SKen WBrk WFib
'Frills' (Min/d)	ESul
'Fringed Angel' (A)	CFee
'Fringed Apple' (Sc)	LDea MBPg
'Fringed Aztec' (R) Υ^{H1+3}	CWCL ESul LDea NFir SPet WFib
'Fringed Jer'Ray' (A)	LDea SSea
'Frosty' misapplied	see *P.* 'Variegated Kleine Liebling'
'Frosty Petit Pierre'	see *P.* 'Variegated Kleine Liebling'
'Frühlingszauber Lila' (R)	ESul
'Fruity' (Sc)	MBPg
fruticosum	EShb EWoo LPio WFib
'Fuji' (R)	NFir
fulgidum	CSpe ESul EWoo LPio MCot WFib
'Funny Girl' (R)	ESul
'Fynn' (Dw)	ESul
'Gabriel' (A)	ESul EWoo LDea
'Gaiety Girl' (A) **new**	ESul
'Galilee' (I/d) Υ^{H1+3}	SKen
Galleria Sunrise = 'Sunrise' (R)	ESul LDea SKen
'Galway Star' (Sc/v) Υ^{H1+3}	MBPg MHer WBrk WFib
'Garland' (Dw/d)	ESul
'Garnet' (Z/d)	ESul
'Garnet Rosebud' (Min/d)	ESul NFir WFib
'Gartendirektor Herman' (Dec)	ESul EWoo NFir WFib
'Gaudy' (Z)	WFib
'Gay Baby' (DwI)	ESul
'Gay Baby Supreme' (DwI)	ESul
'Gemini' (Z/St/d)	CWCL NFir WFib
'Gemma' (R)	ESul NFir
'Gemma Jewel' (R) Υ^{H1+3}	ESul
I 'Gemstone' (Min)	ESul
'Gemstone' (Sc) Υ^{H1+3}	CSev LDea MBPg MHer WBrk
'Genie' (Z/d)	SKen WFib
'Gentle Georgia' (R)	WFib
'Geofbar' (R)	ESul
'Geoff May' (Min)	ESul
'Georgia' (R)	WFib
'Georgia Mai Read'	ERea
'Georgia Peach' (R)	ESul WFib
'Georgie' (R)	LDea
'Georgina Blythe' (R) Υ^{H1+3}	WFib
'Gerald Portas' (Dw/C)	ESul
'Gerald Wells' (Min)	ESul
'Geraldine' (Min)	ESul
'Gesa'	LAst
'Gess Portas' (Z/v)	ESul
'Giant Butterfly' (R)	ESul
'Giant Oak' (Sc)	ESul MBPg
gibbosum	EWoo LPio MHer SSea WFib WGwG
'Gilbert West' (Z)	SKen
'Gilda' (R/v)	LDea
'Gill' (Min/Ca)	ESul
'Ginger Frost' (Sc/v)	WFib WGwG
'Ginger Rogers' (Z)	NFir
'Glacier Claret' (Z)	WFib
'Glacier Crimson' (Z)	SKen
'Glacis'PBR (Quality Series) (Z/d)	CFox LSou SSea
'Gladys Evelyn' (Z/d)	WFib
'Gladys Stevens' (Min/d)	ESul
'Gladys Weller' (Z/d)	WFib
glaucum	see *P. lanceolatum*
'Glen Sheree' (R)	ESul
'Gloria Pearce' (R)	ESul LDea
'Glowing Embers' (R)	ESul LDea
§ ***glutinosum***	WFib
'Goblin' (Min/d)	ESul SKen WFib
'Godshill' (R)	LDea
Golden AngelPBR	see *P.* 'Sarah Don'
'Golden Baby' (Dw/I/C)	ESul LDea WFib
'Golden Brilliantissimum' (Z/v)	ESul SSea WFib
'Golden Butterfly' (Z/C)	ESul
'Golden Chalice' (Min/v)	ESul NFir WFib
'Golden Clorinda' (U/Sc/C)	CRHN LDea MBPg NFir SSea

'Golden Crest' (Z/C)	SKen
'Golden Ears' (Dw/St/C)	ESul NFir NPer WFib
'Golden Edinburgh' (I/v)	WFib
'Golden Everaarts' (Dw/C)	ESul
'Golden Fleece' (Dw/C/d)	ESul
'Golden Gates' (Z/C)	ESul SKen
'Golden Harry Hieover' (Z/C) ♀$^{H1+3}$	ESul MBri SSea
'Golden Lilac Gem' (I/d)	WFib
'Golden Lilac Mist'	SKen
'Golden Oldie' (Sc) **new**	MHer
'Golden Petit Pierre' (Min/C)	ESul SSea
'Golden Princess' (Min/C)	WFib
'Golden Roc' (Min/C)	ESul
'Golden Square' (Dw/St)	WFib
'Golden Staphs' (Z/St/C)	ESul MHer NFir SSea WFib
'Golden Stardust' (Z/St)	ESul
'Golden Wedding' (Z/d/v)	NFir
'Golden Well Sweep'	see *P. crispum* 'Golden Well Sweep'
'Goldilocks' (A)	ESul
'Gooseberry Leaf'	see *P. grossularioides*
'Gordano Midnight' (R)	EWoo LDea
'Gordon Quale' (Z/d)	WFib
'Gosbeck' (A)	SSea WFib
'Gothenburg' (R)	ESul
'Gottweig' (Z)	ESul
'Grace' (A)	LDea
'Grace Thomas' (Sc) ♀$^{H1+3}$	CSev LDea MBPg MHer WFib
'Grace Wells' (Min)	ESul WFib
§ 'Gräfin Mariza' (Z/d)	SKen
'Grand Slam' (R)	CWCL ESul LDea NFir WFib
'Grandad Mac' (Dw/St)	ESul NFir SSea
grandiflorum	EWoo LPio MCot MHer WFib
'Grandma Ross' (R)	ESul
'Grandma Thompson' (R)	ESul
'Granny Hewitt' (Min/d)	ESul
graveolens	LDea LPio SBch WFib
sensu J.J.A. van der Walt	
§ 'Graveolens' (Sc)	ESul GBar GPoy MBPg MHer SSea WBrk WFib
'Great Bricett' (Dw/d)	ESul
'Green Ears' (Z/St)	ESul
'Green Eyes' (I/d)	MHer SKen
'Green Goddess' (I/d)	SKen
'Green Gold Petit Pierre' (Min)	ESul
'Green Silver Galaxy' (St)	ESul
§ 'Greengold Kleine Liebling' (Min/C/v)	ESul SKen
'Greengold Petit Pierre'	see *P.* 'Greengold Kleine Liebling'
'Greetings' (Min/v)	ESul MBri SSea WFib
'Grey Lady Plymouth' (Sc/v)	ESul EWoo LDea MBPg MCot MHer WFib
'Grey Sprite' (Min/v)	ESul WFib
§ ***grossularioides***	EOHP MBPg MHer
- 'Coconut'	MBPg
'Grozser Garten' (Dw)	ESul
'Grozser Garten Weiss' (Dw)	ESul
'Guardsman' (Dw)	ESul
'Guernsey Flair' (Z)	CSpe LAst LSou MCot
'Gustav Emich' (Z/d)	SKen
'Gwen' (Min/v)	NFir
'H. Rigler' (Z)	SKen
'Hadleigh' (Min)	ESul
'Halo' (R)	ESul
§ 'Hannaford Star' (Z/St)	WFib
'Hannah West' (Z/C)	SSea
'Hansen's Pinkie' (R)	EWoo
'Hansen's Wild Spice' (Sc)	GBar LPio MBPg
'Happy Appleblossom' (Z/v/d)	NFir SKen
(Happy Face Series)	NPri
Happy Face Amethyst = 'Penrad'^{PBR} (I)	
- Happy Face Mex = 'Pacvet'^{PBR} (I)	LAst NPri
- Happy Face Scarlet = 'Penhap'^{PBR} (I)	LAst
- Happy Face Velvet Red = 'Pachafvel'^{PBR} (I)	LAst NPri
- Happy Face White = 'Pacfali' (I)	LAst NPri
'Happy Thought' (Z/v) ♀$^{H1+3}$	ESul MBri MCot NFir NVic SCoo SKen SSea WFib
'Happy Valley' (R)	ESul
'Harbour Lights' (R)	ESul LDea WFib
'Harewood Slam' (R)	ESul LDea WFib
'Harkstead' (Dw)	ESul
'Harlequin' (Dw)	ESul
'Harlequin Mahogany' (I/d)	SKen
§ 'Harlequin Miss Liver Bird' (I)	SKen
'Harlequin Picotee' (I/d)	SKen
'Harlequin Pretty Girl' (I × Z/d)	WFib
'Harlequin Rosie O'Day' (I)	SKen WFib
'Harriet Le Hair' (Z)	SKen
'Harvard' (I/d)	WFib
'Havenstreet' (Dw/St)	ESul
havlasae	ECou
'Hazel' (R)	MSCN WFib
'Hazel Barolo' (R)	LDea
'Hazel Burtoff' (R)	ESul LDea
'Hazel Candy' (R)	ESul
'Hazel Carey' (R)	LDea
'Hazel Cherry' (R)	CWCL ESul LDea WFib
'Hazel Chick' (R)	ESul
'Hazel Choice' (R)	ESul LDea NFir
'Hazel Glory' (R)	LDea
'Hazel Gowland' (R)	LDea
'Hazel Gypsy' (R)	ESul LDea NFir
'Hazel Harmony' (R)	ESul LDea
'Hazel Henderson' (R)	LDea
'Hazel Herald' (R)	ESul
'Hazel Orchid' (R)	ESul
'Hazel Perfection' (R)	NFir
'Hazel Ripple' (R)	ESul
'Hazel Rose' (R)	LDea
'Hazel Satin' (R)	LDea
'Hazel Star' (R)	ESul WFib
'Hazel Stardust' (R)	ESul NFir
§ 'Hederinum' (I)	LSou SKen
§ 'Hederinum Variegatum' (I/v)	MCot NFir SPet WFib
'Heidi' (Min/d)	ESul
'Helen Christine' (Z/St)	ESul NFir WFib
'Hemingstone' (A)	LDea
'Hemley' (Sc)	LDea
'Henhurst Gleam' (Dw/d)	ESul
'Henley' (Min/d)	ESul
'Henry Weller' (A)	ESul MBPg NFir WFib
'Hermione' (Z/d)	WFib
'High Fidelity' (R)	ESul
'High Tor' (Dw/C/d)	SKen
'Highfields Appleblossom' (Z)	SKen
'Highfields Attracta' (Z/d)	SKen WFib
'Highfields Candy Floss' (Z/d)	NFir
'Highfields Choice' (Z)	SKen

'Highfields Comet' (Z) SKen
'Highfields Contessa' (Z/d) SKen WFib
'Highfields Delight' (Z) WFib
'Highfields Fancy' (Z/d) NFir SKen
'Highfields Festival' (Z/d) NFir SKen WFib
'Highfields Joy' (Z/d) SKen
'Highfields Melody' (Z/d) WFib
'Highfields Paramount' (Z) SKen
'Highfields Pride' (Z) SKen WFib
'Highfields Prima Donna' (Z/d) SKen
'Highfields Promise' (Z) SKen
'Highfields Snowdrift' (Z) SKen
'Highfields Sugar Candy' (Z/d) SKen WFib
'Highfields Symphony' (Z) WFib
'Hilbre Island' (Z/C/d) NFir
'Hildegard' (Z/d) SKen
'Hills of Snow' (Z/v) MBri MHer SKen SSea WFib
'Hillscheider Amethyst'PBR see *P.* Amethyst = 'Fisdel'
'Hindoo' (R × U) CSpe EWoo NFir SAga SSea WFib
'Hindoo Rose' (U) NFir
'Hintlesham' (Min) ESul
hirtum LPio
hispidum LPio MHer
'Hitcham' (Min/d) ESul WFib
'Holbrook' (Dw/C/d) ESul NFir WFib
'Holt Beauty' **new** EWoo
'Honeywood Lindy' (R) ESul LDea
'Honeywood Lindy Variegated' (R/V) ESul
'Honeywood Margaret' (R) ESul
'Honeywood Suzanne' (Min/Fr) ESul NFir SKen
'Honne Frühling' (Z) SKen
'Honneas' (Dw) ESul
'Honnestolz' (Dw) ESul SKen
'Hope Valley' (Dw/C/d) ♀H1+3 ESul NFir SKen
'Horace Parsons' (R) ESul WFib
'Horace Read' (Dw) ESul
'Horning Ferry' (Dw) ESul
'House and Garden' (R) NFir
'Hula' (R × U) EWoo MHer
'Hulda Conn' (Z/Ca/d) WFib
'Hulverstone' (Dw/St) ESul
'Hunter's Moon' (Z/C) NFir
'Hurdy-gurdy' (Z/d/v) ESul
'Ian Read' (Min/d) ESul
'Ibiza' (Dw/C) ESul
'Icecrystal'PBR (Sweetheart Series) (Z/d) CFox
'Icing Sugar' (I/d) ESul WFib
'Immaculatum' (Z) WFib
'Imperial'PBR (R) LAst
'Imperial Butterfly' (A/Sc) CRHN ESul EWoo LDea NFir SKen SSea WFib
'Inca' (R) ESul
'Inspiration' (R) ESul
ionidiflorum CSpe EShb LPio MBPg MCot MHer MNHC SAga SPhx
'Ipswich Town' (Dw/d) ESul
'Irene' (Z/d) ♀H1+3 SKen WFib
'Irene Collet' (R) LDea
'Irene Picardy' (Z/d) SKen
'Irene Toyon' (Z) ♀H1+3 SKen WFib
'Isidel' (I/d) ♀H1+3 SKen WFib
'Islington Peppermint' (Sc) LPio MBPg NFir SBch WFib
'Isobel Eden' (Sc) LDea MBPg
'Italian Gem' (I) SKen
'Ivalo' (Z/d) WFib
'Ivory Snow' (Z/d/v) ESul NFir SKen WFib
'Jack of Hearts' (I × Z/d) WFib
'Jack Simmons' (Z/d/Dw) ESul
'Jack Wood' (Z/d) NFir WFib
§ 'Jackie' (I/d) EShb EWoo MBri SKen WFib
'Jackie Gall' see *P.* 'Jackie'
'Jackie Totlis' (Z/St) WFib
'Jackpot Wild Rose' (Z/d) WFib
'Jacqueline' (Z/d) SKen
'Jacqui Caws' (Dw) ESul
'Jake Brougham' (St) ESul
'Jane Biggin' (Dw/C/d) ESul SKen
'Janet Dean' (R) LDea
'Janet Hofman' (Z/d) WFib
'Janet Kerrigan' (Min/d) ESul WFib
'Jasmin' (R) ESul
'Jaunty' (Min/d) ESul
'Jayne' (Min/d) ESul
'Jayne Eyre' (Min/d) ESul WFib
'Jazzy' (Min/St) ESul
'Jean Bart' (I) SSea
'Jean Caws' (Z/St) WFib
'Jean Marion' (R) **new** LDea
'Jean Oberle' (Z/d) SKen
'Jeanetta' (R) LDea
'Jeanie Hunt' (Z/C/d) NFir
'Jeanne' (Z) WFib
§ 'Jeanne d'Arc' (I/d) SKen WFib
'Jenifer Read' (Dw) ESul
'Jennifer' (Min) ESul
'Jennifer Strange' (R) ESul
'Jericho' (Z/St/v) ESul
'Jer'Ray' (A) ESul EWoo LDea NFir SSea WFib
'Jessel's Unique' (U) MHer SPet
'Jewel'PBR (R) ESul
'Jimbar' (R) ESul
'Jinny Reeves' (R) LDea
'Jip's Freda Burgess' (Z/C/d) NFir
'Jip's Nippy' (Dw) NFir
'Jip's Pip' (Z/C/d) **new** NFir
'Jip's Rosy Glow' (Min/d) ESul NFir
'Jip's Twink' (Iv/v) NFir
'Joan Cashmere' (Z/d) ESul
'Joan Fontaine' (Z) WFib
'Joan Hayward' (Min) ESul
'Joan Morf' (R) ESul EWoo NFir WFib
'Joan of Arc' see *P.* 'Jeanne d'Arc'
'Joan Sharman' (Min) ESul
'Joanna Pearce' (R) LDea
'John Thorp' (R) LDea
'John's Pride' (Dw) MBri NFir
'Joseph Haydn' (R) ESul LDea
'Joseph Wheeler' (A) ESul LDea
'Joy' (R) ♀H1+3 CSpe ESul EWoo LDea NFir SKen WFib
'Joy' (I) SPet
I 'Joy' (Z/d) LAst SKen
'Joy Lucille' (Sc) ESul LDea MBPg
'Joyful' (Min) ESul
'Jubilant' (R) ESul
'Judy Read' (Dw) ESul
'Julia' (R) ♀H1+3 LDea
'Juliana' (R) LAst LDea
'Julie Bannister' (R) ESul
'Julie Smith' (R) ESul WFib
'Julie's Delight' (Sc) **new** MHer
'June Filbey' (R) LDea
'Jungle Night' (R) ESul
'Juniper' (Sc) MBPg
'Jupiter' (Min/d) SKen
'Jupiter' (R) ESul
'Just Bella' (d) NFir

'Just Beth' (Z/C/d) NFir
'Just Joss' (Dw/d) NFir
'Just Rita' (A) SSea
'Just William' (Min/C/d) ESul WFib
'Kamahl' (R) ESul WFib
§ 'Kardinal' (Z/d) SPet
'Karen' (Dw/C) **new** LSou
'Karl Hagele' (Z/d) SKen WFib
'Karl Offenstein' (R) ESul
'Karmin Ball' WFib
'Karrooense' see *P. quercifolium*
'Kathleen' (Min) ESul
'Kathleen Gamble' (Z) SKen WFib
'Kathryn' (Min) ESul
'Kathryn Portas' (Z/v) ESul SKen
'Kathy Kirby' (R) ESul
'Katie' (R) EWoo
'Katie Hillier' (R) LDea
'Katrine' CWCL LAst NPri
'Kayleigh Aitken' (R) CWCL
'Kayleigh West' (Min) ESul SSea
'Keepsake' (Min/d) ESul WFib
'Keith Vernon' (Z) NFir
'Kelly Brougham' (St/dw) ESul
'Ken Lea' (Z/v) ESul
'Ken Salmon' (Dw/d) ESul
'Kenny's Double' (Z/d) WFib
'Kensington' (A) LDea
'Kerensa' (Min/d) ESul SKen WFib
'Kershy' (Min) ESul
'Kesgrave' (Min/d) ESul WFib
'Kettlebaston' (A) Y^{H1+3} LDea WFib
'Kewense' (Z) EShb
'Kimono' (R) ESul NFir
'Kinder Gaisha' (R) NFir
'King Edmund' (R) ESul LDea NFir
'King of Balcon' see *P.* 'Hederinum'
'King of Denmark' (Z/d) WFib
'King Solomon' (R) LDea WFib
'Kirton' (Min/d) ESul
§ 'Kleine Liebling' (Min) ESul WFib
'Knaves Bonfire' (R) ESul
'Krista' (Min/d) ESul WFib
'Kyoto' (R) NFir
'Kyra' (Min/d) ESul WFib
'L.E. Wharton' (Z) SKen
'La France' (I/d) Y^{H1+3} LDea MCot WFib
'La Paloma' (R) ESul WFib
Laced Red Mini Cascade = 'Achspen' (I) NFir SKen
Lachsball (Z/d) SKen
§ 'Lachskönigin' (I/d) SPet WFib
'Lady Ilchester' (Z/d) SKen WFib
'Lady Love Song' (R) ESul NFir WFib
'Lady Mary' (Sc) ESul EWoo MBPg MCot MHer
'Lady Mavis Pilkington' (Z/d) WFib
'Lady Plymouth' (Sc/v) Y^{H1+3} CRHN CSpe CStu EPfP ERea EShb ESul LDea LPio MBPg MCot MHer MNHC MSCN NEgg NFir SBfd SKen SPet SSea SWal WFib WGwG
§ 'Lady Scarborough' (Sc) ESul EWoo LPio MBPg MHer WFib
'Lady Woods' (Z) SSea
laevigatum MHer
'Lakeland' (I) ESul SKen SSea
'Lakis' (R) LDea
'Lamorna' (R) ESul LDea
'Lancastrian' (Z/d) WFib
§ ***lanceolatum*** LPio MHer
'Langley' (R) ESul
'Lanham Royal' (Dw/d) ESul
'Lara Aladin' (A) LDea
'Lara Ballerina' NFir SBch
'Lara Candy Dancer' (Sc) Y^{H1+3} CRHN ESul LDea MBPg SBch WFib
'Lara Jester' (Sc) EWoo WFib
'Lara Maid' (A) Y^{H1+3} WFib
'Lara Nomad' (Sc) LDea MBPg
'Lara Starshine' (Sc) Y^{H1+3} ESul EWoo LPio MHer NFir SSea WFib
'Lara Waltz' (R/d) WFib
'Lark' (Min/d) ESul
'Larkfield' (Z/v) SSea
N 'Lass o' Gowrie' (Z/v) ESul NFir SKen
'Lateripes' (I) SKen
'Latte Coffee' (R) ESul
'Laura Parmer' (Dw/St) ESul
'Laura Wheeler' (A) ESul LDea
'Laurel Hayward' (R) WFib
'Lauren Alexandra' (Z/d) WFib
Lauretta = 'Pacamla'^{PBR} (Quality Series) (Z/d) LAst
Lavenda = 'Penlava'^{PBR} (Dark Line Series) (Z/d) LAst
'Lavender Grand Slam' (R) Y^{H1+3} ESul LDea NFir
'Lavender Harewood Slam' (R) ESul LDea
'Lavender Mini Cascade'^{PBR} see *P.* Lilac Mini Cascade
'Lavender Sensation' (R) WFib
'Lawrenceanum' ESul EWoo LPio WFib
'Layham' (Dw/d) ESul
'L'Élégante' (I/v) Y^{H1+3} EWoo MCot MHer SKen SSea SWal WEas WFib
'Lemon Air' (Sc) ESul MBPg
'Lemon Crisp' see *P. crispum*
'Lemon Fancy' (Sc) LDea MBPg MCot MHer NFir WFib
'Lemon Kiss' (Sc) CSpe EWoo MBPg
'Lemon Meringue' (Sc) MBPg
'Lemon Toby' (Sc) MBPg
'Len Chandler' (Min) ESul
'Lenore' (Min/d) ESul
'Leo' (Min) ESul
'Leonie Holbrow' (Min) ESul
'Lesley Judd' (R) ESul
'Leslie William Burrows' EWoo
Lila Compakt-Cascade see *P.* 'Decora Lilas'
Lilac Cascade see *P.* 'Roi des Balcons Lilas'
'Lilac Domino' see *P.* 'Telston's Prima'
'Lilac Elaine' (R) LDea
'Lilac Gem' (Min/I/d) MCot
'Lilac Gemma' (R) ESul
'Lilac Jewel' (R) ESul
'Lilac Joy' (R) ESul
§ Lilac Mini Cascade = 'Lilamica'^{PBR} (I) ESul LAst NFir
'Lili Marlene' (I) SKen SPet
'Lilian' (Min) ESul
'Lilian Pottinger' (Sc) CArn CRHN CSev ESul EWoo GBar LDea MBPg MHer NFir SKen SSea
'Lilian Woodberry' (Z) WFib
Lilly = 'Paclill'^{PBR} NPri
'Limoneum' (Sc) CSev MBPg MHer
'Linda' (R) ESul
'Lindsey' (Min) ESul
'Lindy Portas' (I/d) SKen
'Lipstick' (St) WFib
'Lisa' (Min/C) ESul WFib WGor
'Lisa Jo' (St/v/Dw/d) WFib
'Little Alice' (Dw/d) Y^{H1+3} ESul NFir WFib
'Little Blakenham' (A) ESul LDea SSea
'Little Fi-fine' (Dw/C) ESul
'Little Gem' (Sc) EWoo LDea MBPg MHer SSea WFib
'Little Jim' (Min/d) NFir

'Little Jip' (Z/d/v)	NFir WFib
'Little Lisa' (Dw)	ESul
'Little Margaret' (Min/v)	ESul
'Little Primular' (Min)	ESul
'Little Rascal' (A)	LDea
'Little Spikey' (St/Min/d)	ESul WFib
'Lively Lady' (Dw/C)	ESul
'Liverbird'	see *P.* 'Harlequin Miss Liver Bird'
'Lizzie Hillier' (R)	LDea
lobatum	LPio
longicaule	LPio MBPg
longifolium	LPio
'Lord Baden-Powell'	see *P.* 'Colonel Baden-Powell'
'Lord Bute' (R) ♀H1+3	CSpe ECtt ERea ESul EWoo LAst LDea MCot MHer MSCN NFir NPer SBch SDnm SGar SIde SKen SPet SSea SUsu WEas WFib WGwG WPen
'Lord Constantine' (R)	LDea
'Lord de Ramsey'	see *P.* 'Tip Top Duet'
'Lord Roberts' (Z)	WFib
'Loretta' (Dw)	ESul
'Lorna' (Dw/d)	ESul LAst
'Lorraine' (Dw)	ESul
'Lotta Lundberg' (Dw/Z/St/d) **new**	ESul
Lotus = 'Floscala' (Z/d)	LAst
'Lotusland' (Dw/St/C)	NFir SSea WFib
'Louise' (Min)	ESul
I 'Louise' (R)	ESul NFir
'Louise Waddington' (Min/St)	ESul
'Love Song' (R/v)	ESul LDea NFir WFib
'Love Story' (Z/v)	ESul
'Loveliness' (Z)	WFib
* 'Loverly' (Min/d)	ESul
'Lovesdown' (Dw/St)	ESul
'Lowood' (R)	ESul
'Lucie Caws' (St/d)	ESul
'Lucilla' (Min)	ESul
'Lucinda' (Min)	ESul
'Lucy' (Min)	ESul
'Lucy Gunnett' (Z/d/v)	ESul NFir
'Lucy Jane' (R)	ESul
luridum	WCot
'Lustre' (R)	ESul
'Lyewood Bonanza' (R)	CWCL ESul WFib
'Lynne Valerie' (A)	LDea
'Lyric' (Min/d)	ESul WFib
'Mabel Grey' (Sc) ♀H1+3	CRHN CSev CSpe ESul EWoo LPio MBPg MHer MNHC NFir NPer SBch SIde SKen SSea WFib
§ 'Madame Auguste Nonin' (U/Sc)	ESul MHer NFir SKen WFib
'Madame Butterfly' (Z/d/v)	ESul NFir SKen
'Madame Crousse' (I/d) ♀H1+3	WFib
'Madame Fournier' (Dw/C)	ESul
'Madame Hibbault' (Z)	SKen
'Madame Layal' (A)	EWoo MHer NFir SBch WFib
'Madame Margot'	see *P.* 'Hederinum Variegatum'
'Madame Salleron' (Min/v) ♀H1+3	LDea LSou SKen SWal
'Madame Thibaut' (R)	LDea
'Madge Taylor' (R)	NFir
'Magaluf' (I/C/d)	SSea
'Magda' (Z/d)	ESul
magenteum	CSev ESul
'Magic Lantern' (Z/C)	NFir
'Magic Moments' (R)	ESul
'Magnum' (R)	WFib
'Maid of Honour' (Min)	ESul
'Mairi' (A)	LDea WFib

'Majesta' (Z/d)	SKen
'Majorca' (Dw/C)	ESul
'Maloya' (Z)	SKen
'Mamie' (Z/d)	SKen
'Mandarin' (R)	ESul
'Mangles' Variegated' (Z/v)	WFib
'Mantilla' (Min)	ESul
'Manx Maid' (A)	ESul LDea NFir
'Maple Leaf' (Sc)	EWoo MBPg
'Marble Sunset'	see *P.* 'Wood's Surprise'
'Marchioness of Bute' (R/Dec)	LDea MHer NFir WFib
'Maréchal MacMahon' (Z/C)	SKen SSea
'Margaret Harris' (A)	ESul
'Margaret Parmenter' (I/C)	ESul
'Margaret Pearce' (R)	LDea
'Margaret Salvidge' (R)	LDea
'Margaret Soley' (R) ♀H1+3	LDea WFib
'Margaret Waite' (R)	ESul WFib
'Margery Stimpson' (Min/d)	ESul WFib
'Maria Wilkes' (Z/d)	WFib
'Marie Rober' (R)	ESul
'Marie Rudlin' (R)	SSea
'Marie Thomas' (Sc)	LDea MBPg SBch SSea
§ 'Marie Vogel' (R)	ESul
Marimba = 'Fisrimba'[PBR]	SCoo
'Marion' (Min)	ESul
'Mariquita' (R)	ESul WFib
'Marja' (R)	LDea
'Mark' (Dw/d)	WFib
'Marmalade' (Min/d)	ESul WFib
'Marquis of Bute' (R/v)	ESul NFir
'Martha Parmer' (Min)	ESul
'Martin Parrett' (Min/d)	WFib
'Martin's Splendour' (Min)	ESul
'Martlesham' (Dw)	ESul
'Mary' (R)	ESul
'Mary Caws' (Dw/Z/d)	ESul
'Mary Ellen Tanner' (Min/d)	ESul
'Mary Harrison' (Z/d)	WFib
'Mary Read' (Min)	ESul
'Mary Webster' (Min)	ESul
'Masquerade' (R)	ESul SPet
'Masquerade' (Min)	ESul
'Master Paul' (Z/v)	ESul
'Masterpiece' (Z/C/d)	SKen
'Maureen' (Min)	ESul NFir
'Mauve Beauty' (I/d)	SKen WFib
(Maverick Series)	LAst
'Maverick Red' (Z) **new**	
- 'Maverick Violet' (Z) **new**	LAst
- 'Maverick White' (Z) **new**	LAst
'Maxime Kovalevski' (Z)	WFib
'Maxine' (Z/C)	NFir
'May Day' (R)	LDea WFib
'May Magic' (R)	ESul NFir WFib
'Mayfield County Girl' (R)	ESul
'Meadowside Dark and Dainty' (St)	NFir SKen WFib
'Meadowside Harvest' (Z/St/C)	NFir WFib
'Meadowside Julie Colley' (Dw)	NFir
'Meadowside Midnight' (St/C)	MHer WFib
'Medallion' (Z/C)	SSea
'Meditation' (Min)	ESul
'Medley' (Min/d)	WFib
'Megan Hannah' (Dw/c/d)	NFir
'Meike' (R)	ESul
'Melanie' (R)	ESul LDea

	'Melanie' (Min)	ESul
	'Melanie Day' (St)	NFir
*	'Melissa' (Min)	ESul
	'Melissa' (R)	ESul
	'Melody'[PBR] (Tempo Series) (Z/d)	LAst
	Melosilver = 'Penber' (Tempo Series) (Z/d/v)	CFox SPoG
	'Memento' (Min/d)	ESul WFib
	'Mendip' (R)	WFib
	'Mendip Anne' (R)	NFir
	'Mendip Barbie' (R)	NFir
	'Mendip Blanche' (R)	NFir
	'Mendip Candy Floss' (R)	ESul
	'Mendip Lorraine' (R)	ESul NFir
	'Mendip Louise' (R)	NFir
	'Mendip Sarah' (R)	NFir
	'Menorca' (Dw/C/d)	ESul WFib
	'Meon Maid' (R)	ESul LDea WFib
	'Mere Casino' (Z)	WFib
	'Mere Greeting' (Z/d)	WFib
	'Mere Seville' (Z)	WFib
	'Mere Sunglow' (R)	LDea
	'Merle Seville' (Z/d)	SKen
	'Mexica Tomcat' (I/d)	LAst
	'Mexically Rose' (R)	ESul
	'Mexican Beauty' (I)	WFib
	'Mexicana'	see *P.* 'Rouletta'
	'Mexicanerin'	see *P.* 'Rouletta'
	'Michael' (A)	ESul LDea MHer NFir SUsu
	'Michelle' (Min/C)	LDea
	'Michelle West' (Min)	ESul WFib
	'Midas Touch' (Dw/C/d)	ESul
	'Mikado' (R)	ESul
	'Milden' (Dw/Z/C)	ESul NFir
	'Millbern Clover' (Min/d)	ESul
	'Millbern Sharna' (Min/d)	ESul
	'Millfield Gem' (I/d)	SKen WFib
	'Millfield Rose' (I/d)	EWoo
	'Mimi' (Dw/C/d)	ESul
	'Mina Lorenzen' (R)	ESul
	'Mini-Czech' (Min/St)	ESul WBrk
	'Minnie' (Z/d/St)	WBrk
	'Minstrel Boy' (R)	CSpe ESul EWoo LDea SSea WFib
	'Minx' (Min/d)	WFib
	'Miranda' (Dw)	ESul
	'Miriam' (A) <u>**new**</u>	ESul
	'Miss Australia' (R/v)	LDea MBPg
	'Miss Burdett Coutts' (Z/v)	ESul MHer SKen SSea WFib
	'Miss Liverbird' (I/d)	WBrk
	'Miss McKinsey' (Z/St/d)	NFir
	'Miss Muffett' (Min/d)	WFib
§	'Miss Stapleton'	EWoo LPio MHer WFib
	'Miss Wackles' (Min/d)	ESul
	'Misterioso' (R)	EWoo WFib
	'Misty Morning' (R)	EWoo WFib
	'Modesty' (Z/d)	SKen WFib
	'Mohawk' (R)	ESul LDea NFir WFib
	'Mole'	see *P.* 'The Mole'
	mollicomum	WCot
	'Mollie' (R)	CSpe
	'Mona Lisa'[PBR]	ESul
	'Monarch' (Dw/v)	ESul
	'Monica Bennett' (Dw)	ESul SKen
	'Monkwood Charm' (R)	ESul
	'Monkwood Rhapsody' (R)	ESul
	'Monkwood Rose' (A)	LDea NFir
	'Monkwood Sprite' (R)	ESul LDea
	'Monsal Dale' (Dw/C/d)	ESul SKen
	'Monsieur Ninon' misapplied	see *P.* 'Madame Auguste Nonin'
§	'Monsieur Ninon' (U)	CRHN WFib
	'Mont Blanc' (Z/v)	ESul WFib
	'Montague Garabaldi Smith' (R)	WFib
	'Moon Maiden' (A)	CSpe ESul EWoo LDea WFib
	'Moor' (Min/d)	ESul
	'Moppet' (Min/d)	ESul
	'Morello'[PBR] (R)	ESul
	'More's Victory' (U/Sc)	SSea
	'Morning Cloud' (Min/d)	ESul
	'Morse' (Z)	SKen
	'Morval' (Dw/C/d) ♀[H1+3]	ESul SKen WFib
	'Morwenna' (R)	ESul LDea LPio MHer NFir SKen SMrm WFib
	'Mosaic Gay Baby' (I/v/d)	WFib
	'Mountie' (Dw)	ESul
	'Mozart' (R)	ESul
	'Mr Everaarts' (Dw/d)	ESul
	'Mr Henry Cox' (Z/v) ♀[H1+3]	ESul MHer NFir SKen WFib
	'Mr Wren' (Z)	SKen SSea WFib
	'Mrs A.M. Mayne' (Z)	SKen
	'Mrs Cannell' (Z)	WFib
	'Mrs Dumbrill' (A)	ESul LDea
	'Mrs Farren' (Z/v)	MCot SKen
	'Mrs G.H. Smith' (A)	ESul LDea MBPg NFir SSea WFib
	'Mrs Innes Rogers' (R)	ESul
	'Mrs J.C. Mappin' (Z/v) ♀[H1+3]	SKen
	'Mrs Kingsbury' (U)	WFib
	'Mrs Langtry' (R)	LDea
	'Mrs Lawrence' (Z/d)	SKen
	'Mrs Martin' (I/d)	WFib
	'Mrs McKenzie' (Z/St)	WFib
	'Mrs Parker' (Z/d/v)	ESul NFir SKen WFib
	'Mrs Pat' (Dw/St/C)	NFir
	'Mrs Pollock' (Z/v)	CFox LAst MCot MWea NEgg NVic SCoo SKen SSea WBrk WFib
	'Mrs Quilter' (Z/C) ♀[H1+3]	MBri NVic SKen SMrm SSea WBrk WFib
	'Mrs Salter Bevis' (Z/Ca/d)	ESul WFib
	'Mrs Strang' (Z/d/v)	SKen SSea
	'Mrs Taylor' (Sc)	MBPg
	'Mrs W.A.R. Clifton' (I/d)	LDea WFib
	multicaule	LPio
	mutans	EWoo WFib
§	'Mutzel' (I/v)	NFir
	'My Chance' (Dec)	NFir WFib
	'My Choice' (R)	LDea
	myrrhifolium	LPio
§	- var. ***coriandrifolium***	LPio MHer NFir WFib
	'Mystery' (U) ♀[H1+3]	CWCL LPio NFir SSea WFib
	'Nacton' (Min)	ESul
	'Nancy Grey' (Min)	ESul
	'Nancy Mac' (St)	ESul
	'Narina' (I)	SCoo
	'Natalie' (Dw)	ESul
	'Naughton' (Min)	ESul
	Nealit 2 = 'Pennea'[PBR] (I/d)	NPri
	'Needham Market' (A)	ESul LDea WFib
	'Neene' (Dw)	ESul
	'Neil Clemenson' (Sc)	WFib
	'Neil Jameson' (Z/v)	SKen
	'Nell Smith' (Z/d)	WFib
	'Nellie' (R)	ESul LDea
	'Nellie Green' (R)	LDea
	'Nellie Nuttall' (Z)	WFib
	'Nervosum' (Sc)	ESul MBPg
	'Nervous Mabel' (Sc) ♀[H1+3]	ESul LDea LPio MHer WBrk WFib
	'Nettlecombe' (Min/St)	ESul
	'Nettlestead' (Dw/d)	ESul

'Nettlestone' (Dw/d)	ESul
'Nettlestone Star' (Min/St)	ESul
'Neville West' (Z)	SSea
'New Day' (A)	LDea
'New Life' (Z)	ESul NFir
'Newbridge' (St/Min/d)	ESul
'Newtown' (Min/St)	ESul
'Nicola Buck' (R)	LDea NFir
'Nicor Star' (Min)	ESul WFib
'Nikki' (A)	LDea
'Nimrod' (R)	LDea
'Noche' (R)	ESul LDea SKen
'Noel' (Z/Ca/d)	WFib
'Noele Gordon' (Z/d)	WFib
'Nono' (I)	WFib
'Notting Hill Beauty' (Z)	SKen
oblongatum	LPio NFir
'Occold Embers' (Dw/C)	ESul NFir
'Occold Lagoon' (Dw/d)	ESul
'Occold Orange Tip' (Min/d)	ESul
'Occold Profusion' (Dw/d)	ESul NFir
'Occold Shield' (Dw/C/d)	ESul LAst NEgg NFir SDnm SSea WBrk WFib
'Occold Tangerine' (Z)	WFib
'Occold Volcano' (Dw/C/d)	WFib
odoratissimum (Sc)	ESul EWoo GBar GPoy LDea MBPg MHer NFir SKen SSea WFib WGwG
'Odyssey' (Min)	WFib
'Offton' (Dw)	ESul
'Old Orchard' (A)	LDea
'Old Rose' (Z/d)	WFib
'Old Spice' (Sc/v)	ESul EWoo GBar LDea MBPg MCot NFir SWal WFib WGwG
'Oldbury Duet' (A/v)	ESul LAst LDea MBPg MHer NFir SSea
'Olga Shipstone' (Sc)	MBPg
'Oliver Welfare' (Dw/C)	ESul
'Olivia' (R)	WFib
'Onalee' (Dw)	ESul WFib
'Opera House' (R)	WFib
'Orange Fizz' (Sc)	ESul EWoo MHer NFir SDnm WBrk
'Orange Fizz' (Z/d)	LDea
'Orange Imp' (Dw/d)	ESul
'Orange Parfait' (R)	WFib
I 'Orange Princeanum' (Sc)	MBPg
'Orange Ricard' (Z/d)	SKen
'Orange Ruffy' (Min)	ESul
'Orange Splash' (Z)	SKen
'Orangeade' (Dw/d)	SKen WFib
'Orchid Clorinda' (Sc)	MBPg WFib
'Orchid Paloma' (Dw/d)	ESul SKen
'Oregon Hostess' (Dw)	ESul
'Oriental Delight' (R)	ESul
'Orion' (Min/d)	ESul SKen SSea WFib
'Orsett' (Sc) ♀H1+3	LDea
'Osna' (Z)	SKen
'Otto's Red' (R)	NFir
'Our Amy' (Z/d) **new**	SSea
'Our Gynette' (Dec)	EWoo SSea
'Overchurch' (Dw)	NFir
'Oyster' (Dw)	ESul
PAC cultivars	see under selling name
'Paddie' (Min)	ESul
'Page Boy' (Dw/Z/d/v) **new**	ESul
'Pagoda' (Z/St/d)	ESul MHer SKen WFib
'Paisley Red' (Z/d)	NFir WFib
'Palais' (Z/d)	SKen
'Pam Craigie' (R)	LDea
'Pamela' (R)	ESul
'Pamela Vaughan' (Z/St)	WFib
'Pampered Lady' (A)	LDea NFir
panduriforme	LPio WFib
papilionaceum	CHEx CRHN EWoo LPio MCot MHer SSea WEas WFib
'Parisienne' (R)	ESul EWoo LDea WFib
'Parmenter Pink' (Min)	ESul
'Party Dress' (Z/d)	SKen WFib
'Pascal' (Z)	SKen
'Pat Hannam' (St)	WFib
'Paton's Unique' (U/Sc) ♀H1+3	CRHN EShb EWoo MBPg MCot MHer NFir SPet SSea WCot WFib
'Patricia Andrea' (T)	ESul NFir NPer WFib
'Patricia O'Reilly' (R)	LDea
'Patricia Read' (Min)	ESul
'Patsy 'Q'' (Z/C)	SKen
'Paul Crampel' (Z)	MCot MHer SSea WFib
'Paul Gotz' (Z)	SKen
'Paul West' (Min/d)	CFee ESul
'Pauline' (Min/d)	ESul SSea
'Pauline Harris' (R)	LDea
'Pax' (R)	LDea
'Peace' (Min/C)	ESul WFib
'Peace Palace' (Dw)	ESul
'Peach Princess' (R)	ESul NFir
'Peaches and Cream' (R)	MBPg
'Peacock'	LDea
Pearl Necklace	see *P.* 'Perlenkette'
'Peggy Clare' (Dw/St)	ESul
'Peggy Sue' (R)	ESul LDea
PELFI cultivars	see under selling name
peltatum	LPio WFib
'Penny' (Z/d)	SKen WFib
'Penny Dixon' (R)	NFir
'Penny Lane' (Z)	WFib
'Penny Serenade' (Dw/C)	ESul SKen
'Pensby' (Dw)	ESul NFir
'Peppermint Lace' (Sc)	CSev EWoo MBPg
'Peppermint Scented Rose' (Sc)	MBPg MSCN
'Peppermint Star' (Z/St)	ESul SSea
'Percy Hunt' (R)	NFir
'Perfect' (Z)	SKen WFib
§ 'Perlenkette' (Z/d)	MHer
Perlenkette Orange = 'Orangepen'^{PBR} (Quality Series) (Z/d)	LAst
Perlenkette Sabine (Quality Series) (Z/d)	LAst
'Pershore Princess'	WBrk
'Persian King' (R)	LDea
'Persian Ruler' (Min)	ESul
'Persimmon' (Z/St)	WFib
'Petals' (Z/v)	SKen
'Peter Beard' (Dw/d)	ESul
'Peter Godwin' (R)	ESul LDea WFib
'Peter Read' (Dw/d)	ESul
'Peter's Choice' (R)	ESul LDea WFib
'Peter's Luck' (Sc) ♀H1+3	ESul MBPg
'Petit Pierre'	see *P.* 'Kleine Liebling'
'Petite Blanche' (Dw/d)	SSea WFib
'Philomel' (I/d)	SPet
'Phlox New Life' (Z)	ESul
'Phyllis' (Z)	MCot
'Phyllis' (U/v)	ESul EWoo MBPg MHer NFir SAga SSea
'Phyllis Brooks' (R)	ESul
'Phyllis Read' (Min)	ESul
'Phyllis Richardson' (R/d)	ESul
'Phyllis Variegated' (v)	MSCN WCot
'Picotee'	MHer
'Pin Mill' (Min/d)	ESul
'Pink Aura' (Min/St)	ESul SSea
'Pink Aurore' (U)	WFib

	'Pink Blush' (Min/St)	ESul
	'Pink Bonanza' (R)	ESul NFir WFib
	'Pink Bouquet' (R)	ESul
	'Pink Capitatum'	see *P.* 'Pink Capricorn'
§	'Pink Capricorn' (Sc)	CHVG CRHN ESul EWoo MBPg SBch SDnm WFib
	'Pink Carnation' (I/d)	SKen
	'Pink Cascade'	see *P.* 'Hederinum'
	'Pink Champagne' (Sc)	CRHN ESul MCot MHer
	'Pink Countess Mariza' (Z)	SKen
	'Pink Dolly Varden' (Z/v)	SSea WFib
	'Pink Flamingo' (R)	LDea
	'Pink Fondant' (Min/d)	ESul WFib
	'Pink Gay Baby'	see *P.* 'Sugar Baby'
	'Pink Golden Ears' (Dw/St/C)	ESul SKen
	'Pink Golden Harry Hieover' (Z/C)	ESul
	'Pink Happy Thought' (Z/v)	MSCN SDnm SSea SWal WFib
	'Pink Hindoo' (Dec)	EWoo
	'Pink Ice' (Min/d)	ESul NFir
	'Pink Margaret Pearce' (R)	ESul
	'Pink Mini Cascade'	see *P.* 'Rosa Mini-cascade'
	'Pink Needles' (Min/St)	ESul WFib
	'Pink Paradox' (Sc)	LDea
	'Pink Rambler' (Z/d)	SKen WFib
	'Pink Raspail' (Z/d)	SSea
	'Pink Rosebud' (Z/d)	SSea WFib
	'Pink Snow' (Min/d)	ESul
	'Pink Sparkler' (Dw/St/C)	ESul
	'Pink Splash' (Min/d)	ESul
	'Pink Tiny Tim' (Min)	ESul
	'Pippa' (Min/Dw)	ESul NFir
	'Pixie' (Min)	ESul
	'Playmate' (Min/St)	ESul WFib
	'Plum Rambler' (Z/d)	EShb SKen SSea WFib
	'Poetesse' (A)	LDea
	'Polestar' (Min/St)	ESul
	'Polka' (U)	ESul EWoo MBPg MHer NFir WFib
	'Pompeii' (R)	ESul NFir WFib
	'Poquita' (Sc)	MBPg MSCN
	'Porchfield' (Min/St)	ESul
	'Portsmouth' (R)	ESul
	'Potpourri' (Min)	SKen
	'Potter Heigham' (Dw)	ESul
	'Powder Puff' (Dw/d)	WFib
	'Praeludium Scarlet'	WGor
	'Presto' (Dw/St)	ESul
	'Preston Park' (Z/C)	SKen WFib
	'Pretty Girl' (I)	MCot
	'Pretty Petticoat' (Z/d)	WFib
	'Pretty Polly' (Sc)	LDea WFib
	'Pride of Exmouth'	CStu
	'Prim' (Dw/St/d)	ESul WFib
	'Prince of Orange' (Sc)	CArn CRHN CSev ESul EWoo GBar GPoy LDea MBPg MCot MHer MWea NFir SBch SIde SPet SSea SWal WFib WGwG
	'Princeanum' (Sc) 𝕐$^{H1+3}$	MBPg WFib
	'Princess Abigail' (Dw/d) **new**	NFir
	'Princess Alexandra' (Z/d/v)	ESul NFir
	'Princess Anne' (Z)	CSpe
	'Princess Josephine' (R)	LDea MCot WFib
	'Princess of Balcon'	see *P.* 'Roi des Balcons Lilas'
	'Princess of Orange' (Sc/v)	NFir
	'Princess of Wales' (R)	ESul LDea WFib
	'Princess Virginia' (R/v)	ESul LDea WFib
	'Priory Salmon' (St/d)	EShb ESul
	'Priory Star' (St/Min/d)	ESul WFib
	'Prosperity' (Sc)	LDea MBPg
	pseudoglutinosum	WFib
	'Purple Ball'	see *P.* Purpurball
	'Purple Emperor' (R)	ESul LDea WFib
	'Purple Flare' (St)	ESul
	'Purple Heart' (Dw/St/C)	ESul NFir
	'Purple Rambler' (Z/d)	ESul
	'Purple Rogue' (R)	WFib
	'Purple Unique' (U/Sc)	EShb ESul EWoo MCot MHer NFir SSea WFib
§	Purpurball (Z/d)	SKen
	Purpurball 2 = 'Penbalu'^{PBR} (Quality Series) (Z/d)	LAst
	'Pygmalion' (Z/d/v)	SSea WFib
	'Quakeress' (R)	ESul
	'Quakermaid' (Min)	ESul
	'Quantock' (R)	ESul WFib
	'Quantock Angelique' (A)	NFir
	'Quantock Beauty' (A)	ESul LDea
	'Quantock Blonde' (A)	CWCL LDea
	'Quantock Candy' (A)	EWoo NFir
	'Quantock Clare' (A)	NFir
	'Quantock Classic' (A)	EWoo NFir
	'Quantock Darren' (A)	NFir
	'Quantock Jayne' (A)	ESul
	'Quantock Kendy' (A)	CWCL ESul LDea NFir
	'Quantock Kirsty' (A)	EWoo LDea NFir
	'Quantock Louise' (A)	NFir
	'Quantock Marjorie' (A)	CWCL ESul LDea MBPg NFir SSea
	'Quantock Matty' (A)	ESul LDea NFir
	'Quantock May' (A)	LDea NFir
	'Quantock Medoc' (A)	ESul LDea
	'Quantock Millennium' (A)	CWCL ESul LDea
	'Quantock Mr Nunn' (A)	NFir
	'Quantock Perfection' (A) **new**	NFir
	'Quantock Philip' (A)	ESul
	'Quantock Rory' (A)	LDea
	'Quantock Rory Paul' (A) **new**	NFir
	'Quantock Rose' (A)	CWCL ESul LDea
	'Quantock Sapphire' (A)	LDea
	'Quantock Sarah' (A)	ESul
	'Quantock Shirley' (A)	ESul LDea
	'Quantock Star' (A)	CWCL LDea NFir
	'Quantock Ultimate' (A)	ESul NFir
	'Quantock Victoria' (A)	ESul
	'Queen of Denmark' (Z/d)	SKen WFib
	'Queen of Hearts' (I × Z/d)	WFib
	'Queen of Sheba' (R)	LDea
	'Queen of the Lemons'	EWoo
N	***quercifolium*** (Sc)	CRHN CSev GPoy LPio MBPg NFir SKen WFib
	- variegated (v)	MBPg SKen
	quinquelobatum	CSpe LPio MCot
	'R.A.Turner' (Z/d)	WFib
	'Rachel' (Min)	ESul
	radens (Sc)	EPfP LPio WFib
	'Rads Star' (Z/St)	ESul NFir WFib
	'Radula' (Sc) 𝕐$^{H1+3}$	CSev ESul GBar LDea MBPg MHer MNHC SBch SSea SWal WFib
	'Radula Roseum' (Sc)	EWoo MBPg SSea WFib
	'Ragamuffin' (Dw/d)	ESul
	'Rager's Pink' (Dw/d)	ESul
	'Rager's Star' (Dw)	ESul
	'Rager's Veri-Star' (Min/C)	ESul
	'Rakastani' (Z)	SKen
	'Raphael' (A)	LDea
	'Raspberry Ripple' (A)	ESul LDea NFir WFib
	'Raspberry Surprise' (R)	ESul SSea
	'Raspberry Yhu' (R)	ESul
	'Ray Bidwell' (Min)	ESul NFir WFib
	'Raydon' (Min)	ESul

	'Reba'	ESul
	'Rebecca' (Min/d)	ESul WFib
	'Red Admiral' (Min/d/v)	ESul SKen
§	'Red Black Vesuvius' (Min/C)	ESul SKen SSea WFib
	'Red Cactus' (St)	NFir
	'Red Capri' (Sc)	MBPg
	'Red Cascade' (I) Υ^{H1+3}	WFib
	'Red Gables'	WEas
	'Red Glitter' (Dw/St)	ESul
	'Red Ice' (Min/d)	ESul NFir
	'Red Magic Lantern' (Z/C)	SKen
	'Red Pandora' (z)	NFir WFib
	'Red Rambler' (Z/d)	ESul SKen WBrk WFib
	'Red Robin' (R)	WCot
	'Red Silver Cascade'	see *P.* 'Mutzel'
	'Red Spider' (Dw/Ca)	ESul MHer WFib
	'Red Starstorm' (Dw/St)	ESul
	'Red Startel' (Z/St/d)	SKen WFib
	'Red Susan Pearce' (R)	ESul WFib
	Red Sybil = 'Pensyb'^{PBR} (I/d)	LAst NPri
	'Red Witch' (Dw/St/d)	ESul MHer SSea WBrk WFib
	Red-Blizzard = 'Fizzard'^{PBR} (I)	MCot SCoo
§	Red-Mini-Cascade = 'Rotemica' (I)	ESul LAst SKen WFib
	'Redondo' (Dw/d)	ESul WFib
	'Reflections' (Z/d)	WFib
	'Reg 'Q'' (Z/C)	NFir
	'Regina' (Z/d)	SKen WFib
	'Rembrandt' (R)	WFib
	'Renate Parsley'	CDes ESul LPio MBPg MCot MHer NFir SSea WFib
	'Rene Roué' (Dw/d/v)	ESul NFir
	reniforme	GBar LPio MBPg MHer SSea SUsu SWal WFib
	'Retah's Crystal' (Z/v)	ESul
	'Rhian Harris' (A)	LDea
	Rhodonit = 'Paccherry'^{PBR} (I/d)	LAst
	'Richard Gibbs' (Sc)	LDea MBPg MHer
	'Richard Key' (Z/d/C)	WFib
	'Ricky Black Velvet' (A) **new**	LDea
	'Ricky Cheerful' (A)	LDea
	Ricky = 'Pacric'	LAst NPri
	'Ricky Promise' (A)	LDea
	'Ricky Ruby' (A)	LDea
	'Ricky Susan' (R) **new**	LDea
	'Rietje van der Lee' (A)	ESul WFib
	'Rigel' (Min/d)	ESul NFir SKen
	'Rigi' (I/d)	MBri SKen
	'Rimey' (St)	NFir
	'Rimfire' (R)	CWCL ESul EWoo LDea MHer NFir WFib
	'Rimfire Dark' (R)	ESul
	'Rio Grande' (I/d)	MHer NFir SKen SPet WFib
	'Rising Sun'	NFir
	'Rita Scheen' (A/v)	ESul SSea
	'Ritchie' (R)	ESul
	'Robbie Hare' (R)	ESul
	'Robe'^{PBR} (Quality Series) (Z/d)	LAst
	'Rober's Lemon Rose' (Sc)	CRHN ESul GBar LDea MBPg MCot MHer SIde SKen SSea WBrk
	'Rober's Salmon Coral' (Dw/d)	ESul
	'Robert Fish' (Z/C)	ESul SCoo
	'Robert McElwain' (Z/d)	WFib
	'Robin' (Sc)	LDea MBPg
	'Robin' (R)	LDea SSea
	'Robin's Unique' (U)	EWoo MHer WFib

	'Robyn Hannah' (St/d)	NFir
	rodneyanum	CDes WAbe
	'Rogue' (R)	WFib
	'Roi des Balcons'	see *P.* 'Hederinum'
	'Roi des Balcons Des Rameaux' (I)	SKen
§	'Roi des Balcons Impérial' (I) Υ^{H1+3}	SKen
§	'Roi des Balcons Lilas' (I) Υ^{H1+3}	WFib
	'Roi des Balcons Mauve' (I)	SKen
	'Roi des Balcons Rose'	see *P.* 'Hederinum'
	'Roller's Echo' (A)	ESul LDea WFib
	'Roller's Pioneer' (I/v)	EWoo SAga SKen
	'Roller's Satinique' (U) Υ^{H1+3}	LPio MHer
	'Roller's Shadow' (A)	ESul LDea
	'Rollisson's Unique' (U)	MHer SSea WFib
	'Romeo' (R)	CSpe EWoo
	Romy (I)	LDea
	'Rookley' (St/d)	ESul NFir
§	'Rosa Mini-cascade' (I)	ESul LAst NFir SKen
	'Rosaleen' (Min)	ESul
	'Rosalie' (R)	ESul
	'Rose Bengal' (A)	CRHN ESul LDea WFib
	'Rose Jewel' (R)	ESul
	'Rose of Amsterdam' (Min/d)	ESul WFib
	'Rose Paton's Unique' (U/Sc)	SMrm
	'Rose Silver Cascade' (I)	MCot MHer
	'Rose Startel' (Z/St)	SKen
	'Rosebud Supreme' (Z/d)	ESul WFib
	'Rosette' (Dw/d)	SKen
	'Rosina Read' (Dw/d)	ESul
	'Rosmaroy' (R)	ESul LDea WFib
	'Rospen' (Z/d)	SKen
	'Rosy Dawn' (Min/d)	WFib
	'Rosy Morn' (R)	NFir
	'Rote Mini-cascade'	see *P.* Red-Mini-Cascade
§	'Rouletta' (I/d)	ECtt LAst SKen WFib
	'Rousillon' (R)	LDea
	'Royal Ascot' (R)	ESul LDea NFir SPet SSea
	'Royal Black Rose'	LAst MCot MWea
	'Royal Carpet' (Min/d)	ESul
	'Royal Celebration' (R)	ESul
	'Royal Court' (R)	LDea
	'Royal Decree' (R)	LDea
	'Royal Hussar' (R)	ESul
	'Royal Knight' (R)	ESul
	'Royal Magic' (R)	ESul LDea
	'Royal Majesty' (R)	ESul
	'Royal Norfolk' (Min/d)	ESul NFir SKen
	'Royal Oak' (Sc) Υ^{H1+3}	CRHN CSev ESul GBar LDea MBPg MCot MHer MNHC MWea SBch SGar SPet SSea SWal WFib
	'Royal Pride' (R)	LDea
	'Royal Prince' (R)	ESul
§	'Royal Purple' (Z/d)	SKen WFib
	'Royal Sovereign' (Z/C/d)	LDea
	'Royal Star' (R)	LDea
	'Royal Surprise' (R)	ESul EWoo NFir
	'Royal Wedding' (R)	ESul
	'Royal Winner' (R)	LDea
	'Ruben' (d)	LAst LSou
	'Rubin Improved' (Z/d)	SKen
	'Ruby' (Min/d)	ESul WFib
	'Ruby Orchid' (A)	LDea
	'Ruby Wedding' (Z)	ESul
	'Ruffled Velvet' (R)	EWoo
	'Rushmere' (Dw/d)	ESul WFib
	'Rusty' (Dw/C/d)	ESul

'Saint Elmo's Fire' (St/Min/d)	SSea WFib
'Saint Helen's Favourite' (Min)	ESul
Saint Malo = 'Guisaint' (I)	NFir
'Sally Munro' (R)	LDea
'Sally Read' (Dw/d)	ESul
'Salmon Beauty' (Dw/d)	WFib
'Salmon Black Vesuvius' (Min/C)	ESul
§ 'Salmon Irene' (Z/d)	WFib
Salmon Princess = 'Pacsalpri'PBR	LAst LSou WGor
'Salmon Queen'	see *P.* 'Lachskönigin'
salmoneum	SSea
'Saltford' (R)	ESul
'Samantha' (R)	ESul WFib
'Samantha Stamp' (Dw/d/C)	WFib
Samelia = 'Pensam'PBR (Dark Line Series) (Z/d)	LAst WGor
'Sammi Caws' (St)	ESul
'Sancho Panza' (Dec) 🏆H1+3	CSpe ESul LDea SKen SSea WFib
'Sandford' (Dw/St)	ESul
'Sandown' (Dw/d)	ESul
'Sandra Lorraine' (I/d)	WFib
'Sanguineum'	CSev CSpe
'Santa Maria' (Z/d)	SKen
'Santa Paula' (I/d)	ECtt SKen
§ 'Sarah Don'PBR (A/v)	WFib
'Sarah Hunt' (Min/d)	NFir
'Sarah Jane' (Sc)	MBPg
'Sassa'PBR (Quality Series) (Z/d)	LAst
'Satsuki' (R)	ESul NFir
'Scarborough Fair' (A)	NFir
'Scarlet Gem' (Z/St)	WBrk WFib
'Scarlet Pet' (U)	CFee CRHN ESul MBPg NFir SMrm
'Scarlet Pimpernel' (Z/C/d)	ESul
'Scarlet Rambler' (Z/d)	EShb SSea WFib
'Scarlet Unique' (U)	CRHN SKen SMHy SSea SUsu WFib
schizopetalum	WFib
§ 'Schneekönigin' (I/d)	ECtt SKen
'Schottii'	LPio MHer NFir WFib
'Scottow Star' (Z/C)	WFib
'Seale Star' (Dw/St/C)	SSea
'Seaview Silver' (Min/St)	WFib
'Seaview Sparkler' (Z/St)	WFib
'Secret Love' (Sc)	LDea MBPg
'Seeley's Pansy' (A)	EWoo LDea MHer WFib
'Sefton' (R) 🏆H1+3	ESul LDea WFib
'Selena' (Min)	LDea
'Semer' (Min)	ESul SKen
* 'Serre de la Madone' (Sc)	WEas
'Shalfleet' (Min/St)	ESul
'Shanks' (Z)	NFir
'Shannon'	SBch WFib
'Sharon' (Min/d)	ESul
'Sheila' (Dw)	ESul
'Shelley' (Dw)	ESul SKen
'Shirley Ash' (A)	LDea WFib
'Shirley Gillam' (Z/St/v)	ESul
Shocking Pink = 'Pensho'PBR (Quality Series) (Z/d)	LAst
Shocking Violet = 'Pacshovi'PBR (Quality Series) (Z/d)	LAst
'Shogan' (R)	NFir
'Shorwell' (Dw/C/d)	ESul
§ 'Shottesham Pet' (Sc)	ESul EWoo MBPg MHer
'Shrubland Pet' (U/Sc)	LPio SKen SSea
'Shrubland Rose' (Sc)	LPio SSea
sidoides	CSpe EBee ESul EWoo LPio MBPg MCot MHer MWea NFir SBch SMHy SMrm SPhx SSea WCom WCot WEas WFib WGwG
- black-flowered	CTca
- 'Sloe Gin Fizz'	CSpe LPio
Sidonia = 'Pensid'PBR (Dark Line Series) (Z/d)	LAst WGor
'Sienna' (R)	ESul NFir
'Sil Claudio'PBR (Z)	LAst
'Sil Falko'PBR (I)	LSou WGor
'Sil Frauke'PBR (Z)	LAst
'Sil Friesia'PBR (Z)	LAst
'Sil Hero'PBR (Z)	LAst WGor
'Sil Linus'PBR (Z) **new**	LSou
'Sil Malaika' (I) **new**	LSou
'Sil Okka'	LAst
'Sil Pia'PBR (I)	LAst LSou
'Sil Raiko'PBR	LAst
'Sil Renko'PBR (Z)	LAst
'Sil Rumika'PBR	LAst
'Sil Sören'	LAst
'Sil Tedo'PBR (Z)	LAst
'Sil Teske'PBR (I)	LAst WGor
'Sil Tomke'PBR (I)	LAst LSou
'Sil Wittje'PBR (I)	LAst
'Silver Anne' (R/v)	ESul NFir
'Silver Dawn' (Min/St)	ESul
'Silver Delight' (v/d)	WFib
'Silver Dusk' (Min/St)	ESul
'Silver Glitter' (Dw/St)	ESul
'Silver Kewense' (Dw/v)	ESul NFir WFib
'Silver Leaf Rose' (Sc)	MBPg
'Silver Rimfire' (R)	ESul
'Silver Snow' (Min/St/d)	ESul WFib
'Silver Wings' (Z/v)	ESul NFir SSea
'Simon Read' (Dw)	ESul
'Sir Colin' (Z)	SSea
'Skelly's Pride' (Z)	SKen WFib
'Skies of Italy' (Z/C/d)	MBri SKen SSea WFib
'Small Fortune' (Min/d)	ESul SKen
'Smuggler' (R)	LDea
'Snape' (Min)	ESul
'Sneezy' (Min)	ESul NFir
'Snow Cap' (MinI)	NFir
'Snow Flurry' (Sc)	WBrk
Snow Queen	see *P.* 'Schneekönigin'
'Snow White' (Min)	ESul
'Snowbaby' (Min/d)	ESul
'Snowberry' (R)	ESul
'Snowbright' (St/d)	ESul
'Snowdrift' (I/d)	WFib
'Snowflake' (Min)	see *P.* 'Atomic Snowflake'
'Snowstorm' (Z)	SKen WFib
'Snowy Baby' (Min/d)	WFib
'Sofie'	see *P.* 'Decora Rose'
'Solent Waves' (R)	ESul
'Solferino' (A)	ESul LDea
Solidor (I/d) 🏆H1+3	NFir
'Somersham' (Min)	ESul WFib
'Something Special' (Z/d)	NFir WFib
'Sonata' (Dw/d)	ESul
'Sophia' (Z) **new**	LAst
'Sophie' (R)	ESul
Sophie Casade	see *P.* 'Decora Rose'
'Sophie Caws' (St)	ESul
'Sophie Dumaresque' (Z/v)	MBri NFir SKen SSea WFib
'Sorcery' (Dw/C)	ESul SKen
'Sound Appeal' (A)	ESul LDea

	'South American Bronze' (R) ♀H1+3	ESul SMrm WFib
	'South American Pink' (R)	ESul
	'Southern Belle' (A)	LDea SSea
	'Southern Belle' (Z/d)	WFib
	'Southern Charm' (Z/v)	NFir
	'Southern Cherub' (A)	LDea
	'Southern Damsel' (R)	ESul
	'Southern Fairy' (A)	ESul
	'Southern Festival' (Dw)	ESul
	'Southern Flamenco' (R)	ESul
	'Southern Frills' (A)	ESul
	'Southern Galaxy' (Min/St)	ESul
	'Southern Gem' (Min/d)	ESul
	'Southern Michaela' (A)	ESul
	'Southern Peach' (Min/d)	ESul
	'Southern Posy' (Dw)	ESul
	'Southern Purity' (Min)	ESul
	'Southern Rosina' (Dw)	ESul
	'Southern Scheen' (A) **new**	ESul
	'Southern Siewigy' (Dec)	ESul
	'Southern Starlight' (A)	ESul
	'Souvenir' (R)	ESul LDea
	'Souvenir de Prue'	EWoo
	'Spanish Angel' (A) ♀H1+3	CWCL ESul LDea MHer NFir SSea WFib
	'Spanish Banks' (Z/St/v)	ESul
	'Spellbound' (R)	WFib
	'Spital Dam' (Dw/d)	ESul NFir
	'Spitfire' (Z/Ca/d/v)	ESul WFib
	'Spithead Cherry' (R)	LDea
§	'Splendide'	CRHN CSpe ESul LPio MBPg MHer MSCN NFir SPoG SSea SWvt WCom WEas WFib
	'Splendide' white-flowered	LPio MBPg
	'Spot-on-bonanza' (R)	ESul NFir WFib
	'Spring Bride' (R)	LDea
	'Spring Park' (A)	ESul MHer SSea WFib
I	'Springfield Alba' (R)	ESul
	'Springfield Black' (R)	ESul LDea MCot
	'Springfield Joy' (R)	ESul
	'Springfield Pearl' (R)	ESul
	'Springfield Purple' (R)	ESul
	'Springfield Unique' (R)	ESul
	'Springtime' (Z/d)	SKen WFib
I	'Springtime' (R)	ESul
	'Sproughton' (Dw)	ESul
	'Stacey' (R)	ESul
	'Stadt Bern' (Z/C)	LAst MBri NFir SKen
	'Stan Shaw' (R)	LDea
	'Staplegrove Fancy' (Z)	SKen
	× ***stapletoniae***	see *P.* 'Miss Stapleton'
	'Star Flair' (St/Min/d)	ESul
	'Star Flecks' (St)	NFir
	'Star of Persia' (Z/Ca/d)	WFib
	'Star Storm' (St/d)	ESul
	'Starlet' (Ca)	WFib
	'Starlight' (R)	WFib
	'Starlight Magic' (A) ♀H1+3	ESul LDea
	'Starry Eyes' (Dw)	ESul
	'Startel Salmon' (Z/St)	MHer
	'Stella Read' (Dw/d)	ESul
	'Stellar Arctic Star'	see *P.* 'Arctic Star'
	'Stellar Cathay' (Z/St/d)	SSea
	'Stellar Hannaford Star'	see *P.* 'Hannaford Star'
	'Stephen Read' (Min)	ESul
	'Stewart Meehan' (R)	LDea
	'Stolen Kisses' (Min/D)	ESul
	'Strawberries and Cream' (Z/St)	NFir
	'Strawberry Fayre' (Dw/St)	WFib
	'Strawberry Sundae' (R)	ESul LDea WFib

	'Stringer's Delight' (Dw/v)	ESul
	'Stringer's Souvenir' (Dw/d/v)	SSea
	'Stuart Mark' (R)	LDea
	'Stutton' (Min)	ESul
	'Suffolk Agate' (R)	ESul
	'Suffolk Amethyst' (A)	ESul
	'Suffolk Coral' (R)	ESul
	'Suffolk Emerald' (A)	ESul
	'Suffolk Garnet' (Dec)	ESul
	'Suffolk Jade' (Min)	ESul
	'Suffolk Jet' (Min)	ESul
	'Suffolk Salmon' (R)	ESul
§	'Sugar Baby' (DwI)	ECtt ESul LAst MBri MHer SKen WFib
	'Summer Cloud' (Z/d)	WFib
	'Summertime' (Z/d)	see *P.* 'Deacon Summertime'
	'Sun Rocket' (Dw/d)	WFib
	'Sundridge Moonlight' (Z/C)	WFib
	'Sundridge Surprise' (Z)	WFib
	'Sunny Jim' (Z) **new**	SSea
	'Sunraysia' (Z/St)	WFib
	'Sunridge Moonlight' (Dw)	NFir
	'Sunset Snow' (R)	ESul NFir WFib
	'Sunspot' (Min/C)	NFir
	'Sunspot Kleine Liebling' (Min)	SSea WFib
	'Sunspot Petit Pierre' (Min/v)	WFib
	'Sunstar' (Min/d)	ESul WFib
	'Super Rose' (I)	SKen SPet
	'Supernova' (Z/St/d)	ESul SKen WFib
	'Surcouf' (I)	EWoo WFib
	'Surfing Purple'	LSou SVil
	'Surfing Red'	LSou SVil
	'Susan Hillier' (R)	LDea
	'Susan Payne' (Dw/d)	ESul MHer
	'Susan Pearce' (R)	ESul LDea
	'Susan Read' (Dw)	ESul
	'Susie 'Q'' (Z/C)	SKen SSea
	'Sussex Delight' (Min)	SPet
	'Sussex Gem' (Min/d)	ESul SKen WFib
	'Sussex Lace'	see *P.* 'White Mesh'
	'Swanland Lace' (I/d/v)	WFib
	'Swedish Angel' (A)	ESul LDea NFir WFib
	'Sweet Lady Mary' (Sc)	LDea MBPg
	'Sweet Mimosa' (Sc) ♀H1+3	CHVG CRHN ESul EWoo GBar MCot MHer MWea NEgg NFir SDnm SKen SSea SWal WBrk WFib WGwG
	'Sweet Miriam' (Sc)	GBar LDea MBPg
	'Sweet Sixteen'	WFib
	'Sweet Sue' (Min)	ESul
	'Swilland' (A)	LDea WFib
	'Sybil Bradshaw' (R)	LDea
	'Sybil Holmes' (I/d)	ECtt LAst MBri SKen SPet WFib
	'Sylbar' (R)	ESul
	'Sylvia' (R)	ESul
	'Sylvia Gale' (R)	ESul
	'Sylvia Marie' (d)	NFir SKen
	'Taffety' (Min)	ESul WFib
	'Tamie' (Dw/d)	ESul NFir
	'Tammy' (Dw/d)	ESul
	'Tangerine' (Min/Ca/d)	ESul WFib
	'Tangerine Elf' (St)	WFib
	'Tanzy' (Min)	ESul
	'Tapriz' (R)	ESul
	'Tara Caws' (Z)	ESul
	'Taspo' (R)	ESul
	'Tattingstone' (Min)	ESul
	'Tattoo' (Min)	ESul

	'Tazi' (Dw)	ESul
	'Ted Dutton' (R)	ESul
	'Telstar' (Min/d)	ESul SKen
§	'Telston's Prima' (R)	ESul LDea
	'Tenderly' (Dw/d)	ESul
	'Tenerife Magic' (MinI/d)	ESul
	tetragonum	CRHN EWoo MBPg MHer SSea WFib
	'The Alde'	EWoo
	'The Axe' (A)	LDea
	'The Barle' (A) ♀$^{H1+3}$	LDea WFib
	'The Boar' (Fr) ♀$^{H1+3}$	EShb EWoo MCot WFib
	'The Bray' (A)	LDea
	'The Creedy' (A)	LDea
	'The Culm' (A)	ESul EWoo LDea SSea WFib
	'The Czar'	see *P.* 'Czar'
	'The Dart' (A)	LDea
	'The Heddon' (A)	LDea
	'The Joker' (I/d)	WFib
	'The Kenn-Lad' (A)	LDea
	'The Lowman' (A)	LDea
	'The Lyn' (A)	ESul LDea
§	'The Mole' (A)	ESul LDea MHer SKen WFib
	'The Okement' (A)	LDea
	'The Otter' (A)	ESul LDea
	'The Tamar' (A)	CFee EWoo LDea MHer
	'The Tone' (A) ♀$^{H1+3}$	LDea
	'The Yar' (Z/St)	WFib
	'Thomas' (Sc)	MBPg
	'Thomas Earle' (Z)	WFib
	'Thomas Gerald' (Dw/C)	ESul SKen
	'Tilly' (Min)	NFir
	'Tim' (Min)	ESul
	'Timothy Clifford' (Min/d)	ESul
	'Tinkerbell' (A)	LDea
§	'Tip Top Duet' (A) ♀$^{H1+3}$	ESul EWoo LDea MHer NFir SKen SMrm SSea WFib
	'Tirley Garth' (A)	WFib
	'Tomcat'^{PBR} (I/d)	NPri SSea
	tomentosum (Sc) ♀$^{H1+3}$	CArn CHEx CRHN CSev CSpe EShb ESul EWoo GBar GPoy LDea LPio MBPg MCot MHer MNHC NFir SBch SKen SSea WFib WGwG
	- 'Chocolate'	see *P.* 'Chocolate Peppermint'
	'Tomgirl' (A)	NPri
	Tomgirl = 'Pactomgi'^{PBR} (IxZ/d)	SSea
	'Tommay's Delight' (R)	LDea
	'Tony' (Min)	ESul
	'Topan' (R)	ESul
	'Topcliffe' (Dw/St)	ESul
	'Topscore' (Z/d)	SKen WFib
	'Tornado' (R)	CWCL ESul NFir WFib
	'Torrento' (Sc)	ESul GBar LDea MBPg MHer WFib
	'Tortoiseshell' (R)	WFib
	'Toscana Okka' (Toscana Series) (I)	LAst LSou
	'Tracy' (Min/d)	ESul NFir
	transvaalense	EWoo LPio NFir
	'Treasure Chest' (Z)	SKen
	'Treasure Trove' (Z/v)	NFir
	tricolor misapplied	see *P.* 'Splendide'
	tricolor Curt.	CPla NFir
	tricuspidatum	CSpe EWoo LPio WCot
	trifidum	EWoo LPio MBPg SSea WFib
	'Trimley' (Dw/d)	ESul
	'Trinket' (Min/d)	WFib
	'Triomphe de Nancy' (Z/d)	WFib
	triste	EWoo LPio SSea SUsu WCot WFib WGwG
	'Trudie' (Dw/Fr)	ESul MHer SKen WBrk WFib
	'Trulls Hatch' (Z/d)	SKen

	'Tu Tone' (Dw/d)	ESul
	'Tuddenham' (Min/d)	ESul
	'Tuesday's Child' (Dw/C)	ESul SKen
	'Tunias Perfecta' (R)	ESul
	'Turkish Coffee' (R)	CWCL ESul NFir WFib
	'Turkish Delight' (Dw/C)	ESul NFir WFib
	'Turtle's Surprise' (Z/d/v)	SKen
	'Tuyo' (R)	WFib
	'Tweedle-Dum' (Dw)	ESul
	'Tweenaway' (Dw)	ESul
	'Twinkle' (Min/d)	ESul WFib
	'Tyabb Princess' (R)	EWoo
	'Ullswater' (Dw/C)	ESul
	'Unique Aurore' (U)	MHer SKen
	'Unique Mons Ninon'	see *P.* 'Monsieur Ninon'
	'Urban White' (Dec)	CSpe WFib
	urbanum	EShb
	'Urchin' (Min/St)	ESul NFir WFib
	'Ursula Key' (Z/c)	SKen WFib
	'Ursula's Choice' (A)	WFib
	'Val Merrick' (Dw/St)	WFib
	'Valencia' (R)	ESul
	'Valentina' (Min/d)	ESul
	'Valentine' (Z/C)	ESul WFib
	'Valerie Susan' (R) **new**	LDea
	'Vancouver Centennial' (Dw/St/C) ♀$^{H1+3}$	ESul GKir MBri MCot MHer NEgg NFir SCoo SDnm SKen SPoG SSea WFib
	'Vandersea'	EWoo
	'Variegated Attar of Roses' (Sc/v)	MBPg
	'Variegated Clorinda' (Sc/v)	WFib
	'Variegated Fragrans'	see *P.* (Fragrans Group) 'Fragrans Variegatum'
	'Variegated Giroflée' (I/v)	SSea
	'Variegated Joy Lucille' (Sc/v)	MBPg
§	'Variegated Kleine Liebling' (Min/v)	ESul SSea WFib
	'Variegated Madame Layal' (A/v) ♀$^{H1+3}$	WFib
	'Variegated Petit Pierre' (Min/v)	MHer WFib
	'Variegated Wootton's Unique' **new**	EWoo
	'Vasco da Gama' (Dw/d)	ESul
	'Vectis Blaze' (I)	EWoo
	'Vectis Cascade'	EWoo
	'Vectis Dream' (St)	ESul
	'Vectis Fanfare' (St/d)	ESul
	'Vectis Finery' (St/d)	ESul NFir
	'Vectis Glitter' (Z/St)	ESul NFir SSea WBrk WFib
	'Vectis Pink' (Dw/St)	WFib
	'Vectis Purple' (Z/d)	WFib
	'Vectis Sparkler' (Dw/St)	ESul NFir
	'Vectis Spider' (Dw/St)	ESul
	'Vectis Starbright' (Dw/St)	WFib
	'Vectis Volcano' (Z/St)	WFib
	'Velvet Duet' (A) ♀$^{H1+3}$	LDea NFir SKen
	'Venus' (Min/d)	ESul
	'Vera Dillon' (Z)	SKen
	'Verdale' (A)	LDea WFib
	'Verity Palace' (R)	ESul WFib
	'Verona' (Z/C)	MBri SKen SSea
	'Verona Contreras' (A)	CWCL ESul LDea NFir WFib
	'Veronica' (Z/d)	SKen
	'Vic Claws' (Dw/St)	NFir
	'Vicki Town' (R)	WFib
	'Vicky Claire' (R)	ESul LDea NFir SKen WFib
	Vicky = 'Pacvicky'^{PBR} (I)	LAst NPri
	'Vickybar' (R)	ESul

Victor = 'Pacvi'PBR (Quality Series) (Z/d)	LAst LSou
'Victoria' (Z/d)	SKen
'Victoria Regina' (R)	ESul LDea
'Viking' (Min/d)	SKen
'Village Hill Oak' (Sc)	ESul LDea MBPg
Ville de Dresden = 'Pendresd'PBR (I)	CFox
'Ville de Paris'	see *P.* 'Hederinum'
'Vina' (Dw/C/d)	SKen WFib
'Vincent Gerris' (A)	ESul LDea
Vinco = 'Guivin'PBR (I/d)	LAst WGor
violareum misapplied	see *P.* 'Splendide'
'Violet Lambton' (Z/v)	WFib
I 'Violetta' (R)	WFib
'Virginia' (R)	LDea SPet
'Viscossisimum' (Sc)	MHer SKen
viscosum	see *P. glutinosum*
'Vivat Regina' (Z/d)	WFib
'Voo Doo' (Dec)	ESul
'Voodoo' (U) ♀H1+3	CSpe EShb EWoo LPio MBPg MCot MHer NFir SPet SSea SUsu WBrk WCot WFib
'Wallis Friesdorf' (Dw/C/d)	ESul
'Wantirna' (Z/v)	ECtt MHer NFir SSea
'Warrenorth Coral' (Z/C/d)	WFib
'Warrenorth Red Beryl' (Dw/Z/d/v) **new**	ESul
'Warrenorth Rubellite' (Z/v)	ESul
'Warrenorth Spinel' (Min/Z/d/v) **new**	ESul
'Warrion' (Z/d)	SSea
'Washbrook' (Min/d)	ESul NFir
'Watersmeet' (R)	LDea
'Wattisham' (Dec)	LDea
'Waveney' (Min)	ESul
'Wayward Angel' (A) ♀H1+3	ESul LDea WFib
'Wedding Royale' (Dw/d)	WFib
'Welcome' (Z/d)	WFib
'Welling' (Sc)	ESul GBar LDea MBPg MHer NFir
'Wendy Anne'	SKen
'Wendy Jane' (Dw/d)	WFib
'Wendy Read' (Dw/d)	ESul WFib
'Wendy-O' (R)	LDea
'Wensum' (Min/d)	ESul
'Westdale Appleblossom' (Z/d/C)	ESul SSea WBrk WFib
'Westerfield' (Min)	ESul
'Westside' (Z/d)	WFib
'Westwood' (Z/St)	WFib
'Wherstead' (Min)	ESul
'Whisper' (R)	WFib
'White Bird's Egg' (Z)	WFib
'White Boar' (Fr)	CSpe EShb EWoo WFib
'White Bonanza' (R)	ESul WFib
'White Charm' (R)	ESul LDea
'White Chiffon' (R)	ESul
'White Christmas' (Min/St)	ESul
'White Duet' (A)	LDea
'White Eggshell' (Min)	ESul WFib
'White Feather' (Z/St)	MHer
'White Glory' (R) ♀H1+3	ESul NFir
'White Lively Lady' (Dw/C)	ESul
§ 'White Mesh' (I/v)	ECtt MBri SKen
'White Prince of Orange' (Sc)	MBPg
'White Roc' (Min/d)	ESul
'White Unique' (U)	CSpe SBch SPet SSea WFib
'White Velvet Duet' (A)	ESul
White-Blizzard = 'Fisbliz'PBR	SCoo
'Wickham Lad' (R)	LDea
Wico = 'Guimongol'PBR (I/d)	CWCL LAst WGor
'Wild Spice' (Sc)	LDea
'Wilf Vernon' (Min/d)	ESul
'Wilhelm Kolle' (Z)	WFib
'Wilhelm Langath'	SCoo SDnm
'Willa' (Dec)	WFib
'Winnie Read' (Dw/d)	ESul
'Wirral Target' (Z/d/v)	ESul
'Wispy' (Dw/St/C)	ESul
'Witnesham' (Min/d)	ESul
'Wolverton' (Z)	WFib
§ 'Wood's Surprise' (Min/I/d/v)	ESul SKen SWal
'Wootton's Unique'	CSev CSpe EWoo
'Wychwood' (A/Sc)	EWoo LDea
'Wyck Beacon' (I/d)	SKen
'Yale' (I/d) ♀H1+3	MBri SKen WFib
'Yhu' (R)	ESul NFir SMrm WFib
'Yolanda' (Dw/C)	ESul
'York Minster' (Dw/v)	SKen
'Yvonne' (Z)	WFib
'Zama' (R)	NFir
'Zena' (Dw)	ESul
'Zinc' (Z/d)	WFib
'Zoe' (A)	LDea
zonale	WFib
'Zulu King' (R)	WFib
'Zulu Warrior' (R)	WFib

Peliosanthes (*Convallariaceae*)

arisanensis B&SWJ 3639	WCru
monticola B&SWJ 5183	WCru

Pellaea (*Adiantaceae*)

andromedifolia	WRic
atropurpurea	CLAP WFib
§ ***calomelanos***	WRic
falcata	CLAP EShb MBri SEND WRic
hastata	see *P. calomelanos*
rotundifolia ♀H2	CBty CLAP EBee EShb LLHF LRHS MBri STre WRic
viridis	WPGP WRic
- var. ***macrophylla***	WRic

Pellionia see *Elatostema*

Peltandra (*Araceae*)

alba	see *P. sagittifolia*
§ ***sagittifolia***	CRow
undulata	see *P. virginica* (L.) Schott
§ ***virginica*** (L.) Schott	CRow LPBA NLar NPer SWat
- 'Snow Splash' (v)	CRow

Peltaria (*Brassicaceae*)

alliacea	CSpe LEdu

Peltiphyllum see *Darmera*

Peltoboykinia (*Saxifragaceae*)

§ ***tellimoides***	CLAP EBee GCal GEdr GKev GKir NBir WBVN WFar WMoo
watanabei	CAby CDes CLAP CSpe EBee GEdr IMou LEdu NLar WCot WCru WMoo WPGP

Pennantia (*Icacinaceae*)

baylisiana	ECou
corymbosa	ECou
- 'Akoroa'	ECou
- 'Woodside'	ECou

Pennellianthus see *Penstemon*

Pennisetum ✿ (*Poaceae*)

§	***alopecuroides***	CEnd CHar CWCL EBee EHoe EHrv EPfP GFor GKir LRHS MBrN MLLN NGdn SAPC SApp SEND SLim SPer SPlb SWat SWvt WDin WFar WWEG
	- Autumn Wizard	see *P. alopecuroides* 'Herbstzauber'
	- 'Black Beauty'	CSpe IFro SMHy
	- 'Cassian's Choice'	CKno CSam EBee EHoe ELon EWes SMrm
	- 'Caudatum'	CKno EBee SApp
	- f. ***erythrochaetum***	EBee
	- - 'Ferris'	WCru
	- 'Foxtrot'	EBee IPot
	- 'Gelbstiel'	EBee EPPr
	- 'Hameln'	Widely available
§	- 'Herbstzauber'	CFir CKno CMdw CSam EBee EBrs EHoe EPfP LEdu LHop
	- 'Little Bunny'	CKno CPrp CWCL CWib EBee EBrs EHoe ELan EPPr EPfP EQua GCal IVic LRHS LTen NGdn NLar SApp SMea SWvt WDin WFar WWEG
	- 'Little Honey' (v)	CKno EBee MBNS MBri NLar
	- 'Magic'	ELon EPPr MAvo MDKP WWEG
	- 'Moudry'	CKno CPLG CSam EBee EHoe ELon EPPr EPfP LRHS MAvo MBri NSti SBfd SHDw
	- 'National Arboretum'	CKno EBee EHoe EPPr LEdu SApp WCot
	- 'Red Head'	CKno CMea CSam CSpe ELon EWes IPot LSou MAvo MLLN NBPC SMrm WCot
	- f. ***viridescens***	CKno COlW EBee EBrs ECha EHoe ELan EPPr EPfP EShb GFor LEdu LRHS MMoz MRav MWhi NWsh SApp SDix SMrm WPer WWEG
	- 'Weserbergland'	CKno CSam EBee EBrs EHoe SApp WWEG
	- 'Woodside'	CKno CSam CWCL EBee EHoe EPPr EQua LEdu LRHS MBNS SApp SMad
	compressum	see *P. alopecuroides*
	divisum RCB RL 15 **new**	WCot
	'Fairy Tails'	CKno SMHy
	flaccidum	CSam EBee EHul EPPr
	glaucum 'Purple Baron'	SBfd
	- 'Purple Majesty'	CMea MNrw NGBl NPri SBfd SCoo SMad SMrm
	incomptum	EHoe LRHS WHal
	- purple-flowered	CFir MMoz
	longistylum misapplied	see *P. villosum*
	macrourum	Widely available
	- 'Tail Feathers' **new**	CPrp
	massaicum 'Red Bunny Tails'	ELon LRHS
	- 'Red Buttons'	see *P. thunbergii* 'Red Buttons'
	orientale ♀H3	Widely available
	- 'Karley Rose' PBR	CKno EBee EHoe EHrv EWes IPot LHop LRHS MAvo MWhi NDov NPnk SBfd SPhx SSvw SUsu WGrn WWEG
I	- 'Robustum'	CDes EPPr SApp
	- 'Shenandoah'	SApp
	- 'Shogun'	CKno EBee EPPr MAvo WCot
	- 'Tall Tails'	CAby CHar CKno CWit EBee EBrs ECGP ECha EHoe EPPr EWes IPot LEdu LRHS MAvo MWhi NBPC NPnk NSti SMea WWEG
	'Paul's Giant'	CKno SApp
	rueppellii	see *P. setaceum*
§	***setaceum*** ♀H3	CKno CWib MNrw SBfd SHDw SIde
	- 'Eaton Canyon'	CKno LRHS
	- 'Emelia Mae'	SBfd SHDw
	- 'Rubrum' ♀H4	CAbb CBcs CKno CPLG CSam CWCL EBee EShb LAst LHop LRHS LSRN MGos SAga SBfd SCoo SDix SGar SHDw SMad SMrm SPoG SRkn SRot SWvt WCon WCot
§	***thunbergii*** 'Red Buttons'	CAby CBod CKno ECha EHoe EPPr LEdu MAvo MDKP MSCN SBfd SHDw SMHy SMea SUsu WGrn
§	***villosum*** ♀H3	Widely available
	- 'Cream Falls' **new**	LRHS

pennyroyal see *Mentha pulegium*

Penstemon ✿ (*Scrophulariaceae*)

	sp.	SVic
	P&C 150	CFee
	'Abberley'	MBNS WPer
	'Abbey Dore'	SLon
	'Abbotsmerry'	EBee ECtt EPfP MBNS MCot SAga SGar SLon
	'Agnes Laing'	LPen MBNS SLon SPlb
§	'Alice Hindley' ♀H3	Widely available
§	'Andenken an Friedrich Hahn' ♀H4	Widely available
§	***angustifolius***	MNrw SRms
	'Apple Blossom' misapplied	see *P.* 'Thorn'
	'Apple Blossom' ♀H3-4	Widely available
	arizonicus	see *P. whippleanus*
	'Ashton'	LPen MBNS SLon WHrl
	attenuatus	GKev
	'Audrey Cooper'	CChe MBNS SLon
	'Axe Valley Pixie'	SAga
	azureus	CFir EBee
	- NNS 02-065	NWCA
	- subsp. ***azureus***	CFir
	- - NNS 05-527	GKev
	'Baby Lips'	LLHF
	'Barbara Barker'	see *P.* 'Beech Park'
§	***barbatus***	CAby CArn CBot CFee EHrv ELan EPfP SRms WFar
	- 'Cambridge Mixed'	LAst
	- subsp. ***coccineus***	CFir EBee LPen MBNS NChi NLar SPhx
	- 'Iron Maiden'	LRHS NBPC SGSe
	- 'Jingle Bells'	EAEE EPfP LPen MDKP NBPC SAll SMrm SPav
	- 'Navigator'	LRHS
	- orange-flowered	SPlb
	- 'Peter Catt'	MDKP
	- Pinacolada Series	LRHS
	- var. ***praecox***	CBot EPfP MBNS SRot WPer
	- - f. ***nanus***	SRms
	- - - 'Rondo'	LRHS NLar WBrE
	barrettiae	LLHF
	'Beckford'	EBee EPfP EShb LLHF MBNS
§	'Beech Park' ♀H3	EBee ECtt EPfP EWes IGor LPen LRHS MBNS NBir
§	***berryi***	EPot
	'Bisham Seedling'	see *P.* 'White Bedder'
	'Blackbird'	Widely available
	'Blueberry Fudge' (Ice Cream Series)	WHlf
	'Blue Spring' misapplied	see *P. heterophyllus* 'Blue Spring'
	'Bodnant'	LAst LLHF LSou MBNS WHoo WPer WWEG
	bradburii	see *P. grandiflorus*
	'Bredon'	ECtt MBNS SAga WBrk
	bridgesii	see *P. rostriflorus*

	'Bubblegum' (Ice Cream Series)	WHlf
	'Burford Purple'	see *P.* 'Burgundy'
	'Burford Seedling'	see *P.* 'Burgundy'
	'Burford White'	see *P.* 'White Bedder'
§	'Burgundy'	CMac CPrp CSam CWCL CWit EBee ECtt ELon GBBs GMaP LLWP LPen LRHS MCot NBir NPer NPri SAga SGar SMrm SPer SPoG SRms WFar WPer
	caeruleus	see *P. angustifolius*
	californicus	WFar
	calycosus	EBee
§	***campanulatus***	ECtt EPfP EPot EWes GEdr MHer NMen SAga SRms WFar WPer
	- PC&H 147	CFee
	- PC&H 148	SGar
	- ***pulchellus***	see *P. campanulatus*
	- ***roseus*** misapplied	see *P. kunthii*
	'Candy Pink'	see *P.* 'Old Candy Pink'
	cardwellii	EWes
	- NNS 07-385	GKev
	cardwellii × ***davidsonii***	WAbe
	'Carolyn Orr' (v)	CBow ECtt
	'Castle Forbes'	EPyc GMac LPen MBNS SRms WPer
	'Cathedral Rose'	EPfP
	'Catherine de la Mare'	see *P. heterophyllus* 'Catherine de la Mare'
	'Centra'	MBNS
	'Charles Rudd'	CWCL EBee ECtt ELon LPen LSRN MBNS MLLN SRGP SRms STes SWal SWvt WCot
§	'Cherry' ♀H3	GBee GMac LPen LRHS MBNS SGar SHar SMrm SPlb WBVN WPer WWEG
	'Cherry Ripe' misapplied	see *P.* 'Cherry'
§	'Chester Scarlet' ♀H3	CWCL ECtt GMac LPen LRHS MBNS MRav SDix SGar SLon WPer
	'Choirboy'	EWes
	cinicola	LLHF
	cobaea	EBee GKev LRHS WPer
	'Comberton'	ECtt MBNS SAga
	confertus	CTri CWGN EBee ECho EPot LPen MBNS NChi NMen SGar SRms WCot WPer
	- NNS 94-95	NWCA
	- RCB/MO A-7	WCot
	'Connie's Pink' ♀H3	ECtt LPen MBNS SGar SLon SRms WWEG
	'Cottage Garden Red'	see *P.* 'Windsor Red'
§	'Countess of Dalkeith'	CBcs CHVG ECtt ELan EWes GKir LLWP LPen LRHS MLLN MRav SGar SPer SPlb SRms SUsu SWvt WCot WFar
	crandallii	CPBP
§	- subsp. ***taosensis***	MRav SMrm
	cristatus	see *P. eriantherus*
*	***cyananthus*** var. ***utahensis*** **new**	WCot
	cyaneus	EBee GKev
	davidsonii	ECho EWes NMen WAbe WFar WPat
	- var. ***davidsonii***	GKev
	- var. ***menziesii*** 'Microphyllus'	LLHF NHar WAbe
	- var. ***praeteritus***	MDKP
	'Dazzler'	CMMP CWCL LPen MBNS SAga SMrm SWvt WPer
	'Devonshire Cream'	CWCL ECtt LPen LRHS MBNS SAga
	diffusus	see *P. serrulatus*
	digitalis	CRWN GCal LPen LRHS MBNS NWCA SHar WFar WPer
§	- 'Husker Red'	Widely available
	- 'Joke'	IPot
	- 'Mystica'	EDif EWll
	- 'Purpureus'	see *P. digitalis* 'Husker Red'
	- 'Ruby Tuesday'	EBee EWes SUsu WPGP
	- white-flowered	SPhx SRms
	discolor pale lavender-flowered	NBir WFar
§	'Drinkstone Red'	ECtt EPfP LPen LRHS MBNS NChi SAga SDix WPer
	'Drinkwater Red'	see *P.* 'Drinkstone Red'
	eatonii	NBPC
	- subsp. ***undosus***	WCot
	- - NNS 04-326	WCot
	'Edithae'	LPen MWte
	'Ellenbank Amethyst'	GMac
	'Ellenbank Cardinal'	GMac
	'Ellwood Red Phoenix'	LRHS MBNS
	'Elmley'	EPfP MBNS WCot
§	***eriantherus***	LLHF
	Etna = 'Yatna'	EAEE ECtt EPfP GKev GKir LHop LRHS MAvo MBNS NEgg SAll SBfd SMrm SPad SRms WClo WHlf
	euglaucus	EBee LLHF
§	'Evelyn' ♀H4	CMac CTri EBee ECha ECtt ELan EPfP GKir LRHS MBNS MCot MHer MRav NBir NEgg SBfd SPer SPet SPlb SPoG SRGP SRms SWvt WCot WFar WKif WSHC WWEG
	'Evelyn' × 'Papal Purple'	LPen
	'Fanny's Blush'	CWGN SAga
	'Firebird'	see *P.* 'Schoenholzeri'
	'Flame'	LPen LRHS MBNS SAga SLon WPer WWEG
	'Flamingo'	CBar CWCL EBee ECtt EPfP EWes GBBs LAst LPen LRHS LSRN MBNS NBir NLar NPri SAga SBfd SGar SMrm SPet SPoG SRms STes SWvt WFar WHoo WWEG
	fruticosus	WAbe WFar
	- var. ***fruticosus*** **new**	GKev
§	- var. ***scouleri*** ♀H4	MAsh
	- - f. ***albus*** ♀H4	CSpe WAbe WThu
	- - 'Amethyst'	WAbe
	- var. ***serratus*** 'Holly'	NMen
	Fujiyama = 'Yayama'PBR	CWCL CWGN ECtt EPfP GKir LBMP LHop LRHS MAvo SAll SBfd SMrm SPad SRms STes WFar WHlf
	'Garden Red'	see *P.* 'Windsor Red'
	'Garnet'	see *P.* 'Andenken an Friedrich Hahn'
	gentianoides B&SWJ 10271	WCru
	'Geoff Hamilton'	CElw CWGN EBee ECtt EPfP LPen LSRN MBNS SAga SPoG
	'George Elrick'	LPen WHoo
§	'George Home' ♀H3	CWCL ECtt ELon EWes LPen LRHS MBNS SRms WBVN
	'George Moon' **new**	LRHS
	'Ghent Purple'	CFee
	'Gilchrist'	ECtt SLon SPhx
	glaber	CEnt CMHG CMac CMea GBee GMac LHop LLWP LPen LRHS LSRN SPlb WKif WPer
	- 'Roundway Snowflake'	CWGN SHar SPhx
	- white-flowered	SGar
	globosus	GKev
	'Gloire des Quatre Rues'	MBNS
	gormanii	SGar
	gracilis	WPer
§	***grandiflorus***	CFir EBee EShb GMac SPhx
	- 'Prairie Snow'	EBee
	'Great Witley'	WPer
	grinnellii	WFar

	hallii	EPot EWes WPat
	harbourii	CPBP
	hartwegii ♀H3-4	EPyc LPen WPer
	- 'Albus'	LPen SGar SHar
	- 'Picotee Red'	CWCL LRHS
	- 'Tubular Bells Rose'	LRHS NGBl SPet
	'Helenetti'	SDys
	heterodoxus	SGar
	- NNS 93-564	NWCA
§	***heterophyllus***	CMea LPen MNrw MSCN NBir NGBl NGdn SPet SRkn SRms WCot WEas WPer
	- 'Blue Eye'	MBrN
	- 'Blue Fountain'	LPen
	- 'Blue Gem'	CTri GKir LRHS
§	- 'Blue Spring'	CBot CSpe EBee ECtt EPfP LPen LRHS MRav NBir NLar SPoG WAbe WWEG
§	- 'Catherine de la Mare' ♀H4	EBee ELan GKir LPen LRHS LSRN MHer MMuc MWat NBir SBch SPer SRGP SWal SWvt WEas WFar WHrl WKif WSpi WWEG
	- 'Electric Blue'	LRHS MCCP SGar SWal
	- 'Heavenly Blue'	Widely available
	- 'Jeanette'	CMea WCot
	- 'Misty Blue Shades' **new**	LRHS
	- subsp. ***purdyi***	EPyc
	- 'Roundway White' **new**	WCot
	- 'True Blue'	see *P. heterophyllus*
	- 'Züriblau'	CFir EBee EPfP GAbr SGSe SPlb
§	'Hewell Pink Bedder' ♀H3	CHar EAEE EBee ECtt EPfP LPen LRHS MBNS MLLN NLar SGar SMad SMrm SRms SWvt WFar WMnd WPer
	'Hewitt's Pink'	CBcs ECtt SLon
	'Hidcote Pink' ♀H3-4	Widely available
	'Hidcote Purple'	CElw SHar WHoo
*	'Hidcote White'	LIMB MHer SWvt WWEG
	'Hillview Pink'	SLon
	'Hillview Red'	MBNS
§	***hirsutus***	CEnt SGSe SGar WFar WPer
	- var. ***pygmaeus***	CMea EBee ECho EShb MHer NMen NWCA SAll SGar SPlb WHoo
*	- - f. ***albus***	NWCA WHoo
	'Hopleys Variegated' (v)	CBow CWGN LRHS MBNS NBir SWvt
	idahoensis	CPBP EDAr
	isophyllus ♀H3-4	EPfP LPen MMuc SEND WFar WPer
	'James Bowden'	MBNS
	jamesii	EBee
	Jean Grace = 'Penbow'	CSpe EBee LRHS NDov NPri WHlf
	'Jessica'	CWGN SAga
	'Jingle Bells'	LRHS NLar
	'John Booth'	MBNS
	'John Nash' misapplied	see *P.* 'Alice Hindley'
	'John Nash'	ECtt MHer SAga SRkn SRms
	'John Spedan Lewis'	SLon
	'Joy'	ECtt EPyc LPen MBNS SAga WPer
	'Juicy Grape' (Ice Cream Series)	MTis WHlf
	'June'	see *P.* 'Pennington Gem'
	'Kate Gilchrist'	SLon
	Kilimanjaro = 'Yajaro'	EPfP LRHS SBfd SRms
	'King George V'	Widely available
	'Knight's Purple'	ECtt LPen MBNS
	'Knightwick'	LPen MBNS WPer
§	***kunthii***	CAby EBee LLWP LPen MAsh MDKP WPer
	- upright	SGar
§	***laetus*** subsp. ***roezlii***	ECho EPot GGar LHop LRHS
§	'Le Phare'	LPen LRHS MBNS WPer
	'Lilac and Burgundy'	LPen LRHS MBNS SMrm SRms SWvt WFar WWEG
	'Lilac Frost'	EBee ECtt LLHF LRHS MWhi WPer
	'Lilliput'	EPfP GKev LHop LIMB NPri SBfd SMrm SPet WHoo
	linarioides	SAga WPat
	- 'Marilyn Ross'	ECtt MBNS SLon
	- subsp. ***sileri***	WAbe
	'Little Witley'	WPer
	'Lord Home'	see *P.* 'George Home'
	'Lucinda Gilchrist'	SLon
	lyallii	EHrv ELan LPen LSou MCCP WPer
	'Lynette'	LPen LRHS MBNS SPlb WPer
	'Macpenny's Pink'	ECtt EPyc LPen MBNS SAga
	'Madame Golding'	CWCL GBee GMac LPen LRHS MBNS SGar SPlb WPer
	'Malvern Springs'	MBNS
	'Margery Fish' ♀H3	CElw ECtt EPyc EWes LPen LRHS WPer WWEG
	'Martley'	WPer
	'Maurice Gibbs' ♀H3	CBcs CMMP CWCL EAEE ECtt EPfP EPyc EWes LPen LSRN MBNS MLLN NBPC SAga SGar SRGP SRms SWal WBrE WMnd WWEG
	'Melting Candy' (Ice Cream Series)	WHlf
	mensarum	GBee GMac
	Mexicali hybrids	LPen MLLN WFoF
	× ***mexicanus*** 'Sunburst Amethyst' **new**	LRHS SBfd WPer
	- 'Sunburst Ruby'	LRHS SBfd
	'Midnight'	CSam ECtt ELan EPfP GBBs LPen MBNS MMuc MRav SAga SEND SGar STes SWvt WCot WMnd WPer WWEG
	'Mint Pink'	SAga
	'Modesty'	EPfP LPen LRHS MBNS SAga SRms WPer
	'Mother of Pearl'	CBcs CFir CWCL EHrv EPfP EShb GMaP GMac LHop LPen LRHS LSRN MBNS MCot MSwo MWat NBPC SAga SGar SPer SPlb SPoG SRkn SRms SWvt WFar WMoo WPer WWEG WWlt
	'Mrs Miller'	ECtt LPen MBNS
	'Mrs Morse'	see *P.* 'Chester Scarlet'
	'Mrs Oliver'	EWes
	multiflorus	LPen
§	'Myddelton Gem'	LPen LRHS MWat SRms WCot WFoF
	'Myddelton Red'	see *P.* 'Myddelton Gem'
	newberryi ♀H4	SAga
	- subsp. ***berryi***	see *P. berryi*
	- f. ***humilior***	EPot
§	- subsp. ***sonomensis***	GEdr WAbe WFar
*	'Newbury Gem'	LSRN MBNS SRGP SWvt WFar
	'Oaklea Red'	ECtt EPyc SEND
§	'Old Candy Pink'	CFee LPen MBNS SWvt WPer
	'Osprey' ♀H3	CMac COlW CWCL EBee ECtt ELan EPfP EShb EWes GKir LBMP LPen MBNS NBPC NBir SBfd SPer SRkn SRms STes SWvt WBrE WHoo WMnd WPer WWEG WWlt
	ovatus	CFir CMac CSpe EBee ELan EWTr GBBs LPen NBre NLar SGar SPhx SRms
	'Overbury'	EBee ECtt LPen MBNS NChi SAga SRms
	pallidus	EBee
	palmeri	WHil
	'Papal Purple'	LLWP LPen LRHS MAsh MBNS MHer NBir NChi SAga SLon SPhx SRms WFar

'Patio Bells Pink'	LPen MLHP SBfd
Patio Bells Red = 'Yapbred'	SBfd
'Patio Bells Shell'	LHop SLon SMrm WHlf
'Patio Coral'	SMrm
'Patio Wine'	SLon
paysoniorum	EBee
'Peace'	LPen LRHS MBNS MRav SLon
§ 'Pennington Gem' ♀H3	CPrp CWCL ELan GMac GQue LLWP LPen LRHS MHer MSCN NBir SGSe SPer SRms SWvt WPer WWEG WWlt
'Pensax'	WPer
'Pensham Amelia Jane'	CCVN CWGN EAEE ECtt EPfP LHop LRHS LSRN LSou MAsh MBNS MSCN MTis MWea SAga SAll SPer SRGP SRkn SWal WClo WHlf
'Pensham Arctic Fox'	ECtt LHop LRHS MWea SAga SLon
'Pensham Arctic Sunset'	ECtt SAga SLon WHrl
'Pensham Avonbelle'	MBNS SRms
'Pensham Bilberry Ice'	ECtt EPyc MBNS WMnd
'Pensham Blackberry Ice'	CWGN ECtt EPfP EPyc LRHS LSou MBNS MBri MWea SAll SRms WMnd
'Pensham Blueberry Ice'	CWGN ECtt EPyc LRHS LSou MBNS MBri SAga SAll WFar WMnd
'Pensham Bow Bells'	SAga
'Pensham Capricorn Moon'	ECtt NLar SAga SLon SRGP
'Pensham Charlotte Louise'	ECtt LRHS MTis NLar SAll SWal
'Pensham Claret'	WFar
'Pensham Czar'	CCVN ECtt EPfP LHop LRHS LSou MAsh MAvo MBNS MCot MTis MWea NPla SAga SAll SLon SPer SRkn SRms WClo WHil WHlf
'Pensham Dorothy Wilson'	EPyc SRGP
'Pensham Edith Biggs'	CHVG CWCL ECtt EPfP WFar WMoo
'Pensham Eleanor Young'	ECtt LSou MBNS MTis MWea SAll SRGP SUsu SWal WClo WHlf
'Pensham Freshwater Pearl'	CElw MLLN SAga SRms WHoo
'Pensham Great Expectations'	EBee SAga
'Pensham Jessica Mai'	ECtt LRHS LSou MTis SPer WHil
'Pensham Just Jayne'	CWGN ECtt EPfP EPyc LRHS LSRN MBNS MLLN NPla SAll SLon SRGP SRms WHoo WMnd WSpi
'Pensham Kay Burton'	EPfP EPyc SRGP WMnd
'Pensham Laura'	CCVN CWGN EAEE ECtt EPfP LHop LRHS LSRN MAsh MBNS MBri MLLN MTis MWea SAga SAll SPer SRGP SRkn WClo WHil WHlf
'Pensham Loganberry Ice'	LSou MBNS MBri SLon
'Pensham Marjorie Lewis'	WMnd
'Pensham Miss Wilson'	SAga SRms
'Pensham Petticoat'	EBee SUsu
'Pensham Plum Dandy'	SAga
'Pensham Plum Jerkum'	CWGN ECtt EPyc LHop LRHS LSou MBNS MBri MCot MWea NLar NPla SAga SAll SPer SWal WClo WHil WMnd WMoo
'Pensham Raspberry Ice'	CElw MBNS MBri SAga WMnd
'Pensham Saint James's'	MLLN
'Pensham Son of Raven'	SAga
'Pensham Tayberry Ice'	ECtt EPyc MBNS SAga SGar WMnd
'Pensham Tiger Belle Coral'	NChi SAga
'Pensham Tiger Belle Rose'	SAga
'Pensham Victoria Plum'	CElw MHer SHar WHoo
'Pensham Wedding Bells'	SRms WFar
'Pensham Wedding Day'	CWCL LSRN LSou MBNS MBri NLar SAga SAll SPer SPoG SRGP WHlf
'Pershore Carnival'	SAga SRms WHrl
'Pershore Fanfare'	LPen SAga WHrl
'Pershore Festival'	SAga

'Pershore Pink Necklace'	CWCL ECtt LPen LRHS SAga SRms SWvt WCot WWEG
'Phare'	see *P.* 'Le Phare'
'Phyllis'	see *P.* 'Evelyn'
pinifolius ♀H4	CEnt CFir CMea CTri ECho ECtt EDAr EPot GAbr GKev GKir LHop LRHS MLLN NHar SGar SPoG WFar WHoo WPat
- 'Mersea Yellow'	CFir CMea EBee ECho ECtt EDAr EPfP EPot GEdr GKir LHop LRHS NHar NWCA SPlb SPoG WFar WPat WPer
- 'Wisley Flame' ♀H4	ECho EPfP EWes GEdr GKir MBNS MHer MWat NRya NWCA
'Pink Bedder'	see *P.* 'Hewell Pink Bedder', 'Sutton's Pink Bedder'
'Pink Endurance'	LPen MBNS SRkn WHal WPer
'Port Wine' ♀H3	CElw CMea CSam CTri CWCL ELon EPfP GMaP LPen LRHS LSRN MCot MWat NBPC NBir NChi SEND SPer SPoG SRms SWal WBrE WMnd WPer WWEG
'Powis Castle'	ECtt EWes SAga WPer
'Pretty Petticoat'	IPot
'Primrose Thomas'	SAga
'Priory Purple'	MBNS WPer
procerus	ECho WPer
§ - var. ***formosus***	GEdr NMen WAbe WFar
- - NNS 01-345	NWCA
§ - 'Roy Davidson' ♀H4	CMea EPot LBee LHop LRHS NHar NMen WAbe WFar WPat
- var. ***tolmiei***	CElw EPot GCal GEdr GKev NMen
pubescens	see *P. hirsutus*
pulchellus Greene	see *P. procerus* var. *formosus*
pulchellus Lindl.	see *P. campanulatus*
'Purple and White'	see *P.* 'Countess of Dalkeith'
'Purple Bedder'	CHar COlW EBee EPfP LPen LRHS LSRN MLHP MWat NBir SBfd SMrm SPoG SRkn SRms SWal SWvt WCFE WFar WGor
'Purple Passion'	CElw EBee EBrs EHrv EPfP EWes LPen LRHS WCAu WWEG
'Purple Pixie'	WCot
'Purple Sea'	SGar
'Purpureus Albus'	see *P.* 'Countess of Dalkeith'
purpusii	LLHF
§ ***putus***	SGSe
'Rajah'	LPen
'Raven' ♀H3	Widely available
'Razzle Dazzle'	LPen LRHS MBNS SPlb SRms WCot WPer
'Red Emperor'	ECtt LPen SPlb WPer WWEG
'Red Knight'	CWCL GCra LPen LRHS MBNS
'Red Riding Hood' PBR **new**	LRHS
'Red Sea'	SGar
'Rich Purple'	EPyc LRHS MBNS SPlb
'Rich Ruby'	CWCL CWGN EBee EBrs ECtt EHrv ELan EPfP EWes LLWP LPen LRHS MCot NBir SAga SPlb SRGP SWvt WCot WPer WWEG
richardsonii	WPer
- NNS 00-623	NWCA
'Ridgeway Red'	MBNS
roezlii Regel	see *P. laetus* subsp. *roezlii*
'Ron Sidwell'	SGar SLon
§ ***rostriflorus***	LLHF
'Rosy Blush'	LPen LRHS MBNS SAga SPlb
'Roundhay'	CFee
'Roy Davidson'	see *P. procerus* 'Roy Davidson'
'Royal White'	see *P.* 'White Bedder'
'Rubicundus' ♀H3	CWCL CWGN EBee ECtt EHrv ELan EPfP LPen LRHS LSRN MBNS MWte

		SAga SBfd SWvt WCot WFar WMnd WWlt
	'Ruby' misapplied	see *P.* 'Schoenholzeri'
	'Ruby Field'	EPyc GBee MSCN WCFE
	'Ruby Gem'	LPen
	rupicola ♀H4	EPot LHop LRHS NSla
	- 'Albus'	NSla
	- 'Conwy Lilac'	WAbe
	- 'Conwy Rose'	WAbe
	'Russian River'	CPrp EAEE EBee ECtt EPPr EPfP EPyc EWes LPen LRHS LSRN MBNS SGar SPlb WPer
*	Saskatoon hybrids	LHop
	Saskatoon hybrids rose-flowered	SLon
	Scarlet Queen	see *P.* 'Scharlachkönigin'
§	'Scharlachkönigin'	ECtt
§	'Schoenholzeri' ♀H4	Widely available
	scouleri	see *P. fruticosus* var. *scouleri*
§	***serrulatus***	EWes SGar
	'Shell Pink'	LPen NChi WPer
*	'Sherbourne Blue'	SAga SLon WCot WPer
	'Shock Wave'	MCCP
*	'Shrawley'	WPer
	'Sissinghurst Pink'	see *P.* 'Evelyn'
	'Six Hills'	WAbe WPat
	'Skyline'	EPfP
	smallii	CDes CEnt EBee EPPr EShb EWes GKev LPen LRHS LSRN MCCP NBPC NGdn NLar NWCA SAll SGar SPhx SRkn WPGP WPer
	'Snow Storm'	see *P.* 'White Bedder'
	'Snowflake'	see *P.* 'White Bedder'
	sonomensis	see *P. newberryi* subsp. *sonomensis*
	'Sour Grapes' misapplied	see *P.* 'Stapleford Gem'
	'Sour Grapes' ambig.	CChe CMea MCot MGos MLLN SAll STes WWEG
§	'Sour Grapes' M. Fish ♀H3-4	Widely available
	'Southcombe Pink'	LPen
	'Southgate Gem'	CWCL GBee LPen LRHS MBNS MWat SRms SWvt
	'Souvenir d'Adrian Regnier'	LPen MBNS SGar
	'Souvenir d'André Torres' misapplied	see *P.* 'Chester Scarlet'
	speciosus subsp. ***kennedyi***	CPBP
§	'Stapleford Gem' ♀H3	CBot CWCL ECtt ELan EPfP GKir LPen LRHS MCot MLHP MLLN MRav MWhi NCGa NChi SPad SPer SPet SPlb SRms SWvt WCot WFar WHlf WHoo WMnd WMoo WWEG
	'Strawberries and Cream' (Ice Cream Series)	MTis WHlf
	strictus	EAEE EBee EPPr EShb LPen MBNS MCCP SGar SRms WPer
	- 'Bandera'	WFar
	Stromboli = 'Yaboli'	LRHS
§	'Sutton's Pink Bedder'	LRHS MBNS SPlb
	'Sweet Cherry' (Ice Cream Series) **new**	MTis
	'Sylvia Buss'	LPen
	tall pink-flowered	see *P.* 'Welsh Dawn'
N	'Taoensis'	EWes MBNS SGar
	taosensis	see *P. crandallii* subsp. *taosensis*
	teucrioides	EPot
	- JCA 1717050	CPBP
	'The Juggler'	CChe ECtt EPfP LPen LRHS MBNS MLLN SUsu WFar WMnd
§	'Thorn'	CWGN EBee ECtt ELan EShb LPen LRHS MMuc MWat NBir SAga SEND SPer SPhx SRms SWvt WWEG
	'Threave Pink'	CWCL EBee ECtt LLWP LRHS MBNS MRav SEND SHar SPer SWvt
	'Thundercloud'	ECtt SAga
	'Torquay Gem'	LLHF LPen MBNS WCot WPer
	tracyi	EPot
	'True Sour Grapes'	see *P.* 'Sour Grapes' M. Fish
	tubaeflorus	SPhx
	'Tubular Bells Red'	NGBl
	utahensis	CBot GBee SAga
	'Vanilla Plum' (Ice Cream Series) **new**	MTis
	venustus	GKev SRms
	Vesuvius = 'Yasius'	EAEE ECtt EPfP EPyc GKir LRHS NEgg SBfd SMrm SPad SRms SWal WFar WHlf
	virens	CPBP WPer
	virgatus 'Blue Buckle'	EBee EShb IPot NBir SPlb WFar
	- subsp. ***putus***	see *P. putus*
	watsonii	EBee ELan
§	'Welsh Dawn'	CEnt LPen MBNS
§	***whippleanus***	MWea WAbb
§	'White Bedder' ♀H3	Widely available
	'Whitethroat' Sidwell	LPen MBNS SAga SLon
I	'Whitethroat' purple-flowered	SMrm WPer
	'Willy's Purple'	ECtt MBNS
§	'Windsor Red'	CTri EBee ECtt EPfP LPen LRHS MBNS NBPC SBfd SGar SPoG SRms SWal SWvt
	'Woodpecker'	CAby ECtt MAvo MBNS SAga SGar SRms SUsu SWal

Pentachondra (*Epacridaceae*)

	pumila	IBlr

Pentaglottis (*Boraginaceae*)

§	***sempervirens***	CArn EPfP MHer WSFF

Pentagramma (*Adiantaceae*)

	triangularis	WRic

Pentapanax see *Aralia*

Pentapterygium see *Agapetes*

Pentas (*Rubiaceae*)

	lanceolata	CCCN ELan EShb

Penthorum (*Penthoraceae*)

	sedoides	LLWG

pepino see *Solanum muricatum*

peppermint see *Mentha* × *piperita*

Perezia (*Asteraceae*)

	linearis	MAvo
	recurvata	NWCA

Pericallis (*Asteraceae*)

	aurita **new**	CRHN
	lanata ambig.	IRar
§	***lanata*** (L'Hér.) B. Nord.	CHII EShb
	- Kew form	CSpe SMrm
	Senetti Series	MGos NPer NPri SPoG
	- 'Senetti Blue Bi-color'	MGos SPoG
	- 'Senetti Magenta Bi-color'	MGos SPoG

Perilla (*Lamiaceae*)

§	***frutescens*** var. ***crispa*** ♀H2	CArn CSpe
	- green-leaved	ELau

- var. ***japonica***	GPoy
- var. ***nankinensis***	see *P. frutescens* var. *crispa*
- var. ***purpurascens***	CArn ELau WJek
- 'Shizo Green'	CSpe

Periploca (*Asclepiadaceae*)

graeca	CBcs CMac CRHN EBee SLon WSHC
purpurea	WSHC
- B&SWJ 7235	WCru
sepium	CPLG

Peristrophe (*Acanthaceae*)

speciosa	ECre

Pernettya see *Gaultheria*

mucronata	see *Gaultheria mucronata*

Perovskia (*Lamiaceae*)

atriplicifolia	CArn CBcs CBot CDul CMea ELan LRHS MHer MNHC NSti WKif WMnd WPer
- 'Blue Shadow' **new**	LRHS
- 'Little Spire' PBR	CAbP CBow CHar CMac CSpe EBee EMil EPfP EWes GBin GCra GQue LRHS LSRN MAsh MLLN NBPC NBid NLar SBfd SPer SPoG SRkn WSHC
'Blue Haze'	GCal LRHS SMHy
'Blue Spire' ♀H4	Widely available
'Filigran'	EBee LBMP LRHS MWhi NDov SMad SPoG WFar WPat WSpi
'Hybrida'	CAlb LRHS SBfd
'Longin'	LRHS NDov
scrophulariifolia	WCom

Persea (*Lauraceae*)

americana	CCCN
indica	CCCN
japonica B&SWJ 8410 **new**	WCru
lingue	CBcs EBee IDee
thunbergii	CBcs CHEx

Persicaria (*Polygonaceae*)

SDR 4566	GKev
B&SWJ 11268 from Sumatra	WCru
§ ***affinis***	CBcs CBen CSBt EBee GAbr MTho MWhi NBro NSti NVic SWat WBrk WCFE WClo WFar WMoo
- 'Darjeeling Red' ♀H4	Widely available
- 'Dimity'	see *P. affinis* 'Superba'
- 'Donald Lowndes' ♀H4	CChe CMac COIW CTri CYeo EBee ELan EPfP GBBs GKir GMaP IVic LAst LPBA LRHS LSRN MHer MNrw MRav SPer SPoG SRGP SRms SWat SWvt WCFE WFar WMoo WSpi WWEG
- 'Kabouter'	EBee GBin IPot NLar
§ - 'Superba' ♀H4	Widely available
alata	see *P. nepalensis*
alpina	CBct CDes CKno CSpe EBee ECha EHrv ELan EPPr EWTr GBin GMaP LEdu LRHS MCot MRav NCGa NDov SBch SDix SMad SPhx WCot WFar WMoo WPnP WSpi WTin WWEG
amphibia	CRow LLWG MSKA NSco SWat
§ ***amplexicaulis***	CAby CBre CHVG CKno COld CPrp CRow CSpe ELan EWes GKir GMaP MCot MHer MLLN MMuc SEND WBor WClo WCom WFar WGwG WMoo WTin
- 'Alba'	CElw CHar CKno CPrp CRow CSam EBee ECha ELon EPPr GCal GGar LBMP LRHS MCot MLLN MRav NDov SMrm SPhx SWat WBor WCAu WCom WFar WMnd WMoo WPnP WTin WWEG
- 'Arun Gem'	see *P. amplexicaulis* var. *pendula*
- 'Atrosanguinea'	CKno CMac CRow CTri EBee ECha ELan EPla GGar LRHS MMuc MNFA MRav MSpe NBir NLar NVic SEND SPer SRms SWat SWvt WCAu WFar WOld WWEG
- 'Baron'	CRow
- 'Betty Brandt'	EBee
- 'Blackfield' PBR	EPPr NDov WCot
- 'Blush Clent'	WHoo WTin
- 'Clent Charm'	NChi WWEG
- 'Cottesbrooke Gold'	CRow ECtt MAvo
- 'Dikke Floskes'	CRow
- 'Eastfield' (v) **new**	WCot
- 'Fat Domino' PBR	GBin IPot NDov
- 'Firedance'	CKno EBee EPPr GBin IPot NDov SMHy SMrm SPhx SWat WCot
- 'Firetail' ♀H4	Widely available
- 'High Society'	EBee
- 'Inverleith'	CBre CDes CHar CKno CRow EBee ECha ECtt EPPr EPla EWll GBin GGar GQue LBMP LRHS MAvo MLLN SPhx WCot WMoo WPGP WPnP
I - 'Jo and Guido's Form'	EBee NDov SUsu WCAu WFar
- 'Orange Field' **new**	EPPr
* - var. ***pendula***	CRow EBee EPPr LRHS NBir WFar WMoo
- - HWJK 2255	WCru
- 'Pink Elephant'	EPPr GBee GBin NDov WWEG
- 'Pink Lady'	CRow NLar
- 'Rosea'	Widely available
- 'Rowden Gem'	CRow WMoo
- 'Rowden Jewel'	CRow
- 'Rowden Rose Quartz'	CRow
- 'September Spires' **new**	NDov
- 'Summer Dance'	EBee EPPr NBre NDov NLar
- Taurus = 'Blotau'	CElw CKno EBee EBrs ECha EPPr GBin LRHS MBri NLar NSti SMHy WFar WPGP WPnP WTin WWEG
§ ***bistorta***	CArn CRow EBWF ELau GBar GPWP GPoy IMou MHer MMuc MNHC MWhi NBir NLar NSco SEND SRms SWat WOut
- subsp. ***carnea***	CRow EBee EBla ECha ELon GGar LLWG LPla LRHS MBNS MDKP MMuc NBir NDov SEND WFar WMoo
- 'Hohe Tatra'	CDes CRow EBrs LRHS NDov WFar WMoo
- 'Superba' ♀H4	Widely available
campanulata	CElw CRow EBee ECha ECtt EHoe GAbr GGar GMaP IFro MCot MMuc MRav NBro NEgg SPer WCom WFar WMoo WOld WOut WRHF
- Alba Group	CElw EBee GBin GGar MCot NBro WMoo
- var. ***lichiangense***	GBin
- 'Madame Jigard'	CRow GBin
- 'Rosenrot'	CBre CKno CRow LRHS NBir NHol NLar SWat WFar WOld WWEG
- 'Southcombe White'	CRow EPla LRHS WPer WWEG
§ ***capitata***	CRow LLWG SRms WMoo
- 'Pink Bubbles'	ECtt EHoe SPet SWvt
chinensis	WCru
B&SWJ 11268 **new**	

	conspicua	EBee NBre
	dshawachischwilii	SUsu
*	***elata***	CSpr LRHS
	emodi	CRow NBre
	hydropiper 'Fastigiata'	CArn
*	***kahil*** new	WCot
*	***macrophylla***	CRow EBee LRHS WFar
I	- 'Cally Strain'	GCal
	microcephala	CRow EWes
	- 'Red Dragon'[PBR]	Widely available
	- var. ***wallichii***	CRow
	milletii	CRow EBrs EWTr LRHS NLar WCru WFar WWEG
§	***mollis***	CRow EBee LRHS WDyG WPGP
	nakaii	EBee
§	***nepalensis***	CPLG CRow EBee EPPr EShb IMou
§	***odorata***	CArn ELau EOHP GPWP GPoy ILis MHer MNHC NGHP NPri SBfd SHDw SIde WJek
	orientalis	CSpe SMHy SMrm SUsu
	polystachya	see *P. wallichii*
	'Red Baron'	EPPr
§	***runcinata***	CRow EBee GGar MMuc NBir NCob NLar WFar WHer WMoo
	- Needham's form	CRow NBid
	scoparia	see *Polygonum scoparium*
	sphaerostachya Meisn.	see *P. macrophylla*
	tenuicaulis	CBre CEnt CRow ECho EHrv EPla GBin GEdr GGar MNFA NLar SBch WCru WFar WMoo
§	***tinctoria***	EOHP WSFF
§	***vacciniifolia*** ♀H4	Widely available
	- 'Ron McBeath'	CRow
§	***virginiana***	CRow EBrs ECtt GCal LRHS WMoo
	- 'Ballet' new	WCot
	- var. ***filiformis***	CHEx CSpe CWit EBee ECtt GBin GQue LBMP LPla NBPC SBfd SWvt WCot WDyG WHil WPtf WWEG
	- - 'Batwings'	ESwi GKir LRHS SGSe
	- - 'Compton's Red'	CRow EBee ECha EPPr EPfP GCal LHop LPla LRHS NCob WAul WCot WHil
	- - 'Lance Corporal'	CMac CRow EBee EHoe EPPr GBin GQue MAvo NBre NCob NLar SMrm WMnd WMoo
	- - 'Moorland Moss'	WMoo
	- Variegated Group	CBot CRow ECha EPla EShb MBNS WMoo WOld
	- - 'Painter's Palette' (v)	Widely available
	- white-flowered	EPPr NCob
	vivipara	CRow NLar
§	***wallichii***	CRow EBee GBee MMuc NBre NLar SDix SWat WCot WMoo WPtf
§	***weyrichii***	EBee GCal NBir NBro NLar WFar WMoo

persimmon see *Diospyros virginiana*

persimmon, Japanese see *Diospyros kaki*

Petalostemon see *Dalea*

Petamenes see *Gladiolus*

Petasites (*Asteraceae*)

	albus	EBee GPoy MHer NLar
	formosanus	LEdu
	fragrans	EBee ELan MHer NLar SWat WFar
§	***frigidus*** var. ***palmatus***	CRow EBee LEdu NLar
	- - JLS 86317CLOR	SMad
	- var. ***palmatus*** 'Golden Palms'	CBow EHrv EUJe
	hybridus	EBee LEdu MSKA NSco SWat WMAq WSFF
	japonicus	CBcs GPoy IDee
	- var. ***giganteus***	CArn CHEx CMac CRow ECha ELan EPfP EUJe LEdu NVic SGSe SWat
§	- - 'Nishiki-buki' (v)	CHEx CMac CRow EBee EPPr EPla EWld MLLN MSKA NBir NEgg NSti SGSe SMad WBor WCom WFar
	- - 'Variegatus'	see *P. japonicus* var. *giganteus* 'Nishiki-buki'
	- f. ***purpureus***	EPPr EWes SGSe
	palmatus	see *P. frigidus* var. *palmatus*
	paradoxus	CDes CLAP EPPr EWes EWld LEdu MLLN SMad WCot

× *Petchoa* (*Solanaceae*)

	Supercal Terracotta = 'Kakegawa S91' (Supercal Series) new	LAst

Petrea (*Verbenaceae*)

	volubilis	CCCN CHII EShb SOWG

Petrocallis (*Brassicaceae*)

	lagascae	see *P. pyrenaica*
§	***pyrenaica***	WAbe
	- ***alba***	WAbe

Petrocoptis (*Caryophyllaceae*)

	pseudoviscosa	WPat
	pyrenaica	EBur SRms
§	- subsp. ***glaucifolia***	GKev NBir NLar

Petrocosmea (*Gesneriaceae*)

	begoniifolia	WAbe
	formosa 'Crûg's Capricious'	WCru
	forrestii new	WAbe
	grandiflora	WAbe
	- 'Crème de Crûg'	WCru
	iodioides	WAbe
	kerrii	CDes WAbe
	minor	CPBP WAbe
	rosettifolia	WAbe
	sericea	WAbe

Petrophytum (*Rosaceae*)

	caespitosum	EPot WAbe
	cinerascens	NWCA WAbe
§	***hendersonii***	NHol

Petrorhagia (*Caryophyllaceae*)

	'Pink Starlets'	LHop
	saxifraga ♀H4	CSpe EBur ECho EDAr EHoe EShb LBMP LRHS NPri SRms SWal WMoo WPnn WPtf
	- 'Rosette'	MTho

Petroselinum (*Apiaceae*)

§	***crispum***	CArn GPoy ILis MNHC NGHP SBfd SIde SPoG SWal WJek WPer
	- 'Bravour' ♀H4	ELau MHer
	- 'Champion Moss Curled'	SVic
	- 'Darki'	ELau NGHP NPri
	- French	CArn CFox ELau MHer MNHC NPri NVic SPoG WJek
	- 'Hank' (v)	CNat

- 'Italian' see *P. crispum* var. *neapolitanum* plain-leaved
- 'Moss Curled' ♀H4 new CFox
§ - var. ***neapolitanum*** plain-leaved ELau SBfd SIde SPoG SVic
- 'Super Moss Curled' NVic SWal
§ - var. ***tuberosum*** MHer MNHC SIde SVic
hortense see *P. crispum*
tuberosum see *P. crispum* var. *tuberosum*

Petteria (*Papilionaceae*)

ramentacea EBtc MBri NLar

Petunia (*Solanaceae*)

Conchita Azur (Conchita Series) SVil
'Empaurea' LAst NPri
'Mini Me Pink Star' (Mini Me Series) new SVil
patagonica WAbe
(Supertunia Series) Supertunia Bordeaux = 'Lanbor'PBR SVil
- Supertunia Raspberry Blast = 'Temari' LSou SVil
- Supertunia Royal Magenta = 'Kakegawa S36'PBR SVil
- Supertunia Vista Bubblegum = 'Ustuni6001' SVil
(Surfinia Series) Surfinia Baby Pinkmorn = 'Sunbapimo'PBR LSou
- Surfinia Blue = 'Sunblu' LAst LSou NPri WGor
- Surfinia Blue Topaz = 'Sunsurfbupa' LAst
- Surfinia Blue Vein = 'Sunsolos'PBR LAst LSou WGor
- Surfinia Burgundy = 'Keiburtel' LAst NPri WGor
- Surfinia Crazy Pink = 'Sunrovein'PBR LAst NPri
- Surfinia Giant Purple = 'Sunlapur'PBR LAst
- Surfinia Hot Pink = 'Marrose'PBR LSou WGor
- Surfinia Hot Red = 'Sunhore'PBR NPri
- Surfinia Lime = 'Keiyeul'PBR LAst LSou NPri WGor
- Surfinia Pastel 2000 = 'Sunpapi'PBR WGor
- Surfinia Pink Ice = 'Hakice'PBR (v) LAst NPri WGor
- Surfinia Pink Vein = 'Suntosol'PBR ♀H3 LAst
- Surfinia Purple = 'Shihi Brilliant' ♀H3 LAst LSou NPri WGor
- Surfinia Red = 'Keirekul'PBR LAst NPri WGor
- Surfinia Rose Vein = 'Sunrove'PBR LAst WGor
- Surfinia Sky Blue = 'Keilavbu'PBR ♀H3 LAst NPri WGor
- Surfinia Sweet Pink = 'Sunsurfmomo' LSou
- Surfinia Vanilla = 'Sunvanilla'PBR LSou
- Surfinia Victorian Yellow = 'Sunpatiki'PBR LAst NPri
- Surfinia White = 'Kesupite' LAst
(Tiny Tunia Series) Tiny Tunia Bridal White new LSou
- Tiny Tunia Cerise new LSou
- Tiny Tunia Double Blue Ice = 'Mpd2' LSou
- Tiny Tunia Pink = 'Mp7' LSou
- Tiny Tunia Violet Ice new LSou
(Tumbelina Series) Candyfloss = 'Kercan'PBR (d) LSou NPri
- Cherry Ripple = 'Kerripcherry' (d) NPri
- Joanna new SVil
- Julia = 'Kerjul'PBR (d) LAst
- Melissa = 'Kermelis' (d) LAst LSou
- Priscilla = 'Kerpril'PBR (d) LAst LSou NPri
- Rosy Ripple = 'Kerryprosy' (d) LAst NPri
- Victoria = 'Kervic'PBR LAst LSou
(Veranda Series) Veranda Rose Vein = 'Kerverrovein' SVil
- Veranda Salmon = 'Kerversalm' SVil
- Veranda White = 'Kerverwhite' SVil
(Viva Series) 'Viva Amethyst' new LSou
- 'Viva Burgundy' new LSou
- 'Viva Dark Purple Vein' LAst LSou
- 'Viva Forest Fire' SVil
- 'Viva Hot Pink' new LSou
- 'Viva Red' new LSou
- 'Viva Violet' (d) new LSou

Peucedanum (*Apiaceae*)

* ***aromaticum*** IMou
japonicum B&SWJ 8816B WCru
officinale NLar
ostruthium GPoy
- 'Daphnis' (v) CDes CElw CSpe EBee EPPr LEdu LPla MMoz NChi NLar NMRc WCot WHrl WWFP
palustre EBWF
praeruptorum CArn
siamicum B&SWJ 6487 WCru
thodei SPlb
verticillare CArn CSam EBee GQue IMou ITim LRHS MAvo MCot MLLN MMuc MNFA NChi SDix SEND SKHP SMad SMrm SPhx WClo WSHC WWEG

Peumus (*Monimiaceae*)

boldus EBee EUJe IDee

Phacelia (*Hydrophyllaceae*)

sericea EBee GKev LRHS
- subsp. ***sericea*** NNS 06-467 GKev

Phaedranassa (*Amaryllidaceae*)

BKBlount 2623 WCot
carmiolii CDes WCot
cinerea ECho WCot
dubia ECho WCot
* ***montana*** ECho
tunguraguae ECho

	viridiflora	ECho WCot

Phaedranthus see *Distictis*

Phaenocoma (*Asteraceae*)

	prolifera	SPlb

Phaenosperma (*Poaceae*)

	globosa	CSam CSpe EBee EHoe EPPr EWes LEdu MAvo NWsh SPhx WBor WBox WCot WPGP WPrP

Phagnalon (*Asteraceae*)

	saxatile	WCot
	(L.) Cass. RCB RL-21	

Phaiophleps see *Olsynium*

	nigricans	see *Sisyrinchium striatum*

Phalaris (*Poaceae*)

	arundinacea	GFor MBNS MMuc SPlb SVic SWat WTin
	- cream-flowered	WWEG
	- 'Elegantissima'	see *P. arundinacea* var. *picta* 'Picta'
	- var. ***picta***	CBen CDul CHEx CTri CWCL CWib MMuc MSKA NBid NBir NPer SApp SPoG WDin WFar
	- - 'Arctic Sun' (v)	CKno EPPr LLWG
	- - 'Aureovariegata' (v)	CBcs CSWP MRav NGdn NPer SWat WMoo
	- - 'Feesey' (v)	Widely available
	- - 'Luteopicta' (v)	EBee EHoe EPPr EPfP MMuc SEND WTin
	- - 'Luteovariegata' (v)	EShb NGdn
§	- - 'Picta' (v) 𝕐H4	COlW EBee ELan EPfP EPla GFor GKir LPBA LRHS MMuc SBfd SEND SPer SWat WMoo
	- - 'Streamlined' (v)	EPPr EPla LLWG NWsh SLPl WFar
	- - 'Tricolor' (v)	EHoe EPla LLWG

Phalocallis (*Iridaceae*)

§	***coelestis***	WHil WPGP

Phanerophlebia (*Dryopteridaceae*)

	caryotidea	see *Cyrtomium caryotideum*
	falcata	see *Cyrtomium falcatum*
	fortunei	see *Cyrtomium fortunei*

Pharbitis see *Ipomoea*

Phaseolus (*Papilionaceae*)

	caracalla	see *Vigna caracalla*
	vulgaris 'Yin Yang'	LSou

Phedimus see *Sedum*

Phegopteris (*Thelypteridaceae*)

§	***connectilis***	EBee EFer EFtx SRms WAbe WRic
	decursive-pinnata	CLAP EFtx LRHS NHol NLar NMyG WAbe WFib WPnP WRic WSpi

Phellodendron (*Rutaceae*)

	amurense	CBcs CCCN CDul CMCN EBee ELan EPfP EWTr GAuc GBin IFFs IVic LEdu NLar NMun SEND WBor WDin WPGP
	- B&SWJ 11000	WCru
	- var. ***sachalinense***	CBcs
	chinense	EGFP
	japonicum	EGFP
	- B&SWJ 11175	WCru

Phenakospermum (*Strelitziaceae*)

	guianense	XBlo

Pherosphaera (*Podocarpaceae*)

	fitzgeraldii	CKen

Philadelphus ✿ (*Hydrangeaceae*)

	sp.	CPLG
	F&M 152	WPGP
	SDR 4862	GKev
	SDR 4945	GKev
	SDR 4946	GKev
	SDR 5111	GKev
	argyrocalyx	GKir
	'Avalanche'	CMHG CPLG EBee GKir NLar SEND SPer SRms WDin WFar
	'Beauclerk' 𝕐H4	CDoC CDul CTri EBee EPfP GGal GKir GQui IVic LRHS MBri MGos MRav NBro NCGa NEgg NHol SKHP SPer SRms SWvt WBVN WDin WKif WPat
	'Belle Etoile' 𝕐H4	Widely available
	'Bicolore'	EBee NLar WSpi
	'Boule d'Argent' (d)	CMHG
	'Bouquet Blanc'	EBee GKir MRav NLar SRms WPat
	brachybotrys	EPfP MRav
	'Buckley's Quill' (d)	EBee ECrN EPfP EQua EWes LRHS MAsh MRav SWvt WGrn
	'Burfordensis'	EBee EPfP LAst MRav
	aff. ***calvescens***	MRav
	- BWJ 8005	WCru
	caucasicus	WPGP
	coronarius	CBcs CDul EPfP GKir LBuc MLHP MMuc MWhi NWea SEND SPer WDin
	- 'Aureus' 𝕐H4	Widely available
	- 'Bowles's Variety'	see *P. coronarius* 'Variegatus'
§	- 'Variegatus' (v) 𝕐H4	Widely available
	'Coupe d'Argent'	MRav
	'Dainty Lady' new	LRHS
	'Dame Blanche' (d)	EWTr GKir MAsh MRav
	delavayi	CGHE EPfP GGal GKir SKHP WPGP
	- var. ***melanocalyx***	GCra GKir MRav WPGP
	- 'Nymans'	CPLG EPfP SKHP
	'Enchantement' (d)	MRav SDix
	'Erectus'	CSBt CWib EBee EPfP LEdu LRHS MGos MRav SKHP SLim SPer SPoG WDin WPat
	'Etoile Rose'	GKir WMoo
	'Frosty Morn' (d)	CBcs GKir LRHS MGos MRav NBro NCGa SEND SPer
	hirsutus	GKir
	incanus	GKir
	- B&SWJ 8616	WCru
§	'Innocence' (v)	CBot CMac CPLG CWSG CWit EBee ECrN EHoe ELan EPfP EWTr LAst LBMP LRHS MAsh MBri MGos MMuc MRav MSwo SAga SBfd SEND SKHP SPad SPer SPoG WCot WFar
	'Innocence Variegatus'	see *P.* 'Innocence'
	inodorus	GKir
	var. ***grandiflorus***	
§	***insignis***	MRav
	'Kelmarsh' new	SLPl
	× ***lemoinei***	CDul CTri ELon EWTr LBMP MGos MWat NLar WDin WFar
I	- 'Lemoinei'	NWea
	lewisii	CPLG GKir
	- L 1896	WPGP
	'Limestone'	MRav

	maculatus	GKir
	- 'Mexican Jewel'	CPLG SKHP WPGP
	madrensis	LHop MRav
	'Manteau d'Hermine' (d) 🏆H4	Widely available
	'Marjorie'	EBee NLar
	mexicanus	EBee GCal WSHC
	- B&SWJ 10253	WCru
	- 'Rose Syringa'	CGHE CPLG SKHP WPGP
	- 'Silver Storm' **new**	CSam
	microphyllus	CBot CDul CMCN EBee ELan EPfP GKir LAst MAsh MGos MRav MWhi NHol SKHP SLon SPer SSpi WClo WPat WSHC
	'Miniature Snowflake' (d)	SEND WPat
	'Minnesota Snowflake' (d)	CBcs CWit EBee ECtt EQua EWes GKir LBuc LRHS LSRN MMuc MRav NEgg NHol NLar SBfd SPur WDin WFar
	'Mont Blanc'	CBcs EBee MRav NCGa WFar
	'Mrs E.L. Robinson' (d)	CMac CWSG EBee ECtt GKir LAst LLHF LRHS NEgg NLar WBor WClo WPat
	'Natchez' (d)	CMac EBee ECtt WDin WPat
	'Oeil de Pourpre'	MRav
	palmeri	WPGP
	pekinensis	CPLG
	'Perryhill'	MRav
	'Polar Star'	ELon GBin
§	***purpurascens***	CWit EPfP EWes GQui LLHF MRav WClo WPGP WPat
	- BWJ 7540	WCru
	× ***purpureomaculatus***	GKir LLHF MRav WPat
	satsumi	SLPl
	- B&SWJ 10811	WCru
	schrenkii	NLar WPGP
	- B&SWJ 8465	WCru
§	'Silberregen'	CAlb CDul CMac CSam CWit EBee ELon EPfP GKir LRHS MAsh MGos MMuc MRav NCGa NHol NLar SLim SMad SRms SWvt WClo WFar WPat
	Silver Showers	see *P.* 'Silberregen'
	'Snow Velvet'	EBee EPfP LLHF LRHS MAsh
	'Snowbelle' (d)	EBee LBMP LRHS MAsh MBri MWea NBro NHol NLar SKHP SWvt WClo
	'Snowflake'	CWSG GKir NMoo
	'Snowgoose'	MAsh
	'Souvenir de Billiard'	see *P. insignis*
	subcanus	CPLG
	- L 524	WPGP
	'Sybille' 🏆H4	CDul CMHG EPfP EWTr GKir LHop LRHS MRav MSwo SDix SKHP SPer SRms SSpi WClo WPat WSHC WSpi
	tenuifolius	NLar SLPl
	tomentosus	CPLG GKir WPGP
	- B&SWJ 2707	WCru
	- GWJ 9215	WCru
	'Virginal' (d)	Widely available
	'Voie Lactée'	MRav
	White Icicle = 'Bialy Sopel'	CCCN WBrE
	White Rock = 'Pekphil'	CDoC CMac CPLG EBee GKir LLHF LRHS MRav NMoo SKHP SLim SPer WPat
	'Yellow Cab'	CWSG EBee NEgg NLar SLim SPoG WClo
	'Yellow Hill'	CMac EBee EPfP LRHS MAsh NEgg NLar SBfd SKHP SLim SPoG
	zeyheri **new**	SLPl

Philesia (*Philesiaceae*)

	buxifolia	see *P. magellanica*
§	***magellanica***	CPLG GGGa SSpi WAbe WCru WSHC
	- 'Rosea'	CWib EPfP IBlr SSpi

Phillyrea (*Oleaceae*)

	angustifolia	CBcs CDul CGHE CMCN EBee ELan EPfP ERom IFFs LRHS MBri MGos MMuc MRav MWya NLar SBig SEND SPer SSpi WDin WFar WPGP WSHC
	- f. ***rosmarinifolia***	CCCN CPLG EBee ELan EPfP EPla LAst NLar SLPl SMad WFar
	- - 'French Fries'	WPGP
	decora	see *Osmanthus decorus*
§	***latifolia***	CDul EBee EGFP ELan EPfP GGal LRHS MAsh MWea NLar SAPC SArc SBfd SSpi WDin WFar WPGP
I	- 'Rodrigueziensis'	WCFE
	media	see *P. latifolia*

Philodendron (*Araceae*)

	bipinnatifidum 🏆H1	EAmu SEND XBlo
	epipremnum	see *Epipremnum pinnatum*
	'Pink Princess' (v)	CBow
*	***rubrum***	XBlo
	scandens 'Mica'	XBlo
	xanadu	XBlo

Philotheca (*Rutaceae*)

	buxifolia	ECou
	- 'Cascade of Stars'	SOWG

Phlebodium (*Polypodiaceae*)

§	***aureum*** 🏆H1	CSpe EShb WRic
	- 'Mandaianum'	WRic
	pseudoaureum **new**	WCot

Phleum (*Poaceae*)

	bertolonii	CRWN EBWF
	pratense	EHoe NMir WSFF

Phlomis ✿ (*Lamiaceae*)

*	***anatolica***	LRHS NLar WClo
*	- 'Lloyd's Variety'	CAbP CSam ELan LRHS MAsh SEND SPer WClo WPen
	angustifolia	LRHS
	atropurpurea BWJ 7922	WCru
	bourgaei 'Whirling Dervish'	WCom
	bovei subsp. ***maroccana***	CBot IFro SEND WHal
	cashmeriana	CBcs CBot CFir EBee ECha EHoe EPfP GKev LRHS LSou MMuc NLar SKHP SMad SPhx WWEG WWlt
	chrysophylla 🏆H3	CAbP CBot EBee ECha ELan EPfP LRHS MAsh MRav NLar SDix SEND SPer WCFE WClo WSpi
	crinita	EBee
	'Edward Bowles'	CDul ECha LRHS LSRN MRav NBid SKHP SLPl SWvt WCom
*	'Elliot's Variety'	CPLG
	fruticosa 🏆H4	Widely available
	- white-flowered	ECrN
	grandiflora	CBot SEND
	italica	Widely available
	- 'Pink Glory'	CMac
	lanata 🏆H3-4	CAbP CBgR EBee ELan EPfP LRHS NLar SPer SPoG WClo WEas
	- 'Pygmy'	CHVG MGos
	leucophracta 'Golden Janissary'	WPGP
	longifolia	CBot EBee EPfP LHop LRHS LSou MGos MMuc MNrw NLar SEND SKHP SPer SSvw
	- var. ***bailanica***	CSam EBee WClo

lycia	SEND
macrophylla	SPhx
pratensis	EBee
purpurea	CAbP CArn CBot CPLG CSam EBee ELan EPfP LRHS MAsh MNrw NBir SBfd SEND WClo WCot WGrn
- ***alba***	CBot EBee EPfP
- subsp. ***almeriensis***	CMdw CPom
§ ***russeliana*** ♀H4	Widely available
- 'Mosaic' (v)	MAvo WCAu WCot
samia Boiss.	see *P. russeliana*
samia L.	CEnt CKno CPom CSpe EBee EWTr LBMP LHop LRHS NBPC NBir NChi NGdn NLar SKHP SPoG WCot WPtf
- 'Green Glory'	WTin
taurica	EPfP GAbr NBPC NChi
tuberosa	CArn CBcs CBot CFir CKno CPou EBee EBrs EPPr EPfP GKir LEdu LRHS LSRN MMuc NGdn NLar SBfd SGSe SMrm SPet WCot WFar WGwG WHoo WMnd WPtf
- 'Amazone'	EBee ECha EHrv EPfP LHop MLLN MRav NBid NCGa NDov NPnk NSti SAga SMad SMrm SWal WFar WMnd WSpi
- 'Bronze Flamingo'	CKno EBee ECGP EHrv EPfP LAst LRHS LSou MAvo MNrw MRav NBPC SKHP SPoG SPur WHlf WMnd WPer WSpi
viscosa misapplied	see *P. russeliana*

Phlox ✿ (*Polemoniaceae*)

adsurgens ♀H4	NCob WCom
- 'Mary Ellen'	ITim NHar
- 'Red Buttes'	ECho
- 'Wagon Wheel'	CWCL EBee ECho ECtt EWes GGar GKir ITim LAst LRHS NHar NWCA SMrm SPlb SRms SRot WCFE WClo WFar
amplifolia	EBee NBre WFar
× ***arendsii*** 'Andrew' **new**	WCot
- 'Anja'	NDov WCot
- 'Babyface'	NGdn
- 'Dougal' **new**	WCot
- 'Dylan' **new**	WCot
- 'Early Star'	EBee LSou
- 'Eyecatcher'	CPrp NBro NGdn
- 'Gary' **new**	WCot
- 'Lilac Girl'	NBre
- 'Luc's Lilac'	CPrp ECtt GBin LLHF LRHS MSpe NBro NDov NEgg NGdn SMrm SMrs SPhx SPoG STes WAul WWlt
§ - 'Miss Jill' (Spring Pearl Series)	EBee EPfP MAvo MSCN NBPC NHol SPet WCot WTin
§ - 'Miss Karen' (Spring Pearl Series)	NBro
§ - 'Miss Margie' (Spring Pearl Series)	LEdu NBir
§ - 'Miss Mary' (Spring Pearl Series)	EBrs ECtt EPfP GMaP LRHS MDKP MSpe NHol
§ - 'Miss Wilma' (Spring Pearl Series)	EPfP GMaP
- 'Paul'	WCot
- 'Ping Pong'	MSCN NBPC NBre NBro STes
- 'Pink Attraction'	CPrp MNrw NBro NCGa
- 'Purple Star'	EBee
- 'Rosa Star'	EBee NBre
austromontana	EPot GKev NHol NWCA
'Bavaria'	LLHF
bifida	ECho
- 'Alba'	ECho LLHF LSou WFar
- blue-flowered	ECho LSou SUsu
- 'Colvin's White'	ECho
- 'Frohnleiten' **new**	NHar WPer
- 'Minima Colvin'	ECho ECtt EPot GKev
- 'Petticoat'	CMea CPBP ECtt EPot MDKP NHar WFar
- 'Ralph Haywood'	CMea CWCL ECtt EPot ITim
- 'Starbrite'	WFar
- 'Starcleft'	WRHF
- 'Thefi'	ECho EWes MNrw
'Black Buttes'	GEdr
borealis	see *P. sibirica* subsp. ***borealis***
* - ***arctica***	EPot
bryoides	see *P. hoodii* subsp. ***muscoides***
caespitosa	CMea ECho EWes
- subsp. ***pulvinata***	see *P. pulvinata*
- 'Zigeunerblut'	CPBP
canadensis	see *P. divaricata*
carolina subsp. ***angusta***	GMac SUsu
- 'Bill Baker' ♀H4	Widely available
- 'Magnificence'	EBee EWes GMac MDKP NLar SMad SPhx WCot WSHC
- 'Miss Lingard' ♀H4	CSam CWCL EBee ECtt LAst LBMP LRHS MCot MMuc NBid NBir NGdn NHol NLar NSti SMrm WAul WCot WFar WRHF WWEG
'Casablanca'	NDov SMrm
'Charles Ricardo'	EWes GMac SUsu WHoo
'Chattahoochee'	see *P. divaricata* subsp. ***laphamii*** 'Chattahoochee'
§ ***condensata***	ECho WPat
covillei	see *P. condensata*
'Daniel's Cushion'	see *P. subulata* 'McDaniel's Cushion'
diffusa	WAbe
§ ***divaricata*** ♀H4	GKir SPlb
- 'Blue Dreams'	CFir ECtt EHrv LRHS MAsh MNrw NCob SUsu WFar WHal WSHC WWlt
- 'Blue Perfume'	CPrp EBee ECtt NBro NGdn NLar SMrm WFar
- 'Clouds of Perfume'	CMMP CWCL EAEE EBee ECtt GMaP LAst LRHS LSRN MSCN NCGa NCob NDov NEgg NLar NPnk SMrm SPoG STes WClo WFar WWEG
- 'Dirigo Ice'	EBee ECho EHrv LHop LRHS MWte NLar WFar WSHC
- 'Eco Texas Purple'	CPrp ECtt NCGa NCob WFar WSHC WWlt
- 'Fuller's White'	CWCL ECtt LRHS
- subsp. ***laphamii***	CBot EWes NWCA WFar
§ - - 'Chattahoochee' ♀H4	CBcs CBot CPrp CSpe CWCL EBee ECho ECtt ELan EPfP EPot EWes GMac LHop LRHS MAsh MCot MWat NBPC NLar SMrm SPoG SRot WCFE WCom WFar WHoo
§ - 'Louisiana Purple'	WSHC
- 'May Breeze'	CAby ECho EHrv GCra GKir GMaP LHop LRHS MNrw NCob SUsu WCom WFar WSHC WWEG WWlt
- 'Plum Perfect'	ECtt LLHF NBro WFar WPtf
* - 'White Perfume'	CMMP CPrp CWCL EBee EWes LAst LRHS MDKP NBro NCGa NCob NLar SMrm STes WFar WWEG
douglasii	GKir NWCA SRms
- 'Alba'	GJos
- 'Apollo'	CTri ECho ECtt EPot LLHF NHar NMen
- 'Boothman's Variety' ♀H4	ECha ECho ECtt EDAr ELan EPfP EPot MLHP MWat NMen SRms WAbe WCom

- 'Crackerjack' 🏆H4	CMea CStu CTri ECho ECtt EDAr ELan ELon EPfP EPot GAbr GJos GKev GKir GMaP LRHS MAsh MHer MLHP NBir NEgg NMen NWCA SPoG SRGP WFar
- 'Eva'	CMMP CPBP ECho ECtt EDAr EPot GMaP LRHS LSRN MSCN NBir NLar NMen NPri NWCA SRGP WCom WFar WNew
- 'Galaxy'	ECho
- 'Georg Arends'	ECtt EPot GJos
- 'Holden Variety'	ECtt
- 'Ice Mountain'	CPBP ECho ECtt ELan EPot GMaP NEgg NHol NWCA SPoG SRot WFar WNew WRHF
- 'Iceberg' 🏆H4	ECho GJos NMen
- 'J.A. Hibberson'	EPot
- 'Lilac Cloud'	CYeo ECho ECtt EDAr GJos WAbe
- Lilac Queen	see *P. douglasii* 'Lilakönigin'
- 'Lilac Wonder' **new**	CPBP
§ - 'Lilakönigin'	CTri ECho
- 'Napoleon'	CPBP ECho ECtt EPot LLHF NHol NMen WAbe
- 'Ochsenblut'	ECho EPot LLHF LRHS MHer MLHP MSCN NHar NLar WAbe
- 'Red Admiral' 🏆H4	ECho ECtt EPfP EWes GKev GKir GMaP MWat NLar NMen WCFE WFar WRHF
- 'Rose Cushion'	ECho EDAr EWes MHer NMen
- 'Rose Queen'	ECho
- 'Rosea'	ECho EDAr ELan LRHS NMen WBVN WFar WNew
- 'Silver Rose'	ECho EPot MWat NWCA
- 'Sprite'	SRms
- 'Tycoon'	see *P. subulata* 'Tamaongalei'
- 'Violet Queen'	ECho EWes WFar WPat
- 'Waterloo'	CMea ECho ECtt EPot NMen
I - 'White Admiral'	CTri CYeo ECho ECtt EPot LRHS LSRN
- 'Zeigeurnerblut' **new**	WAbe
drummondii 'Classic Cassis'	NPri SPoG WHlf
'Fancy Feelings' (Feelings Series)	NBro NCob
glaberrima 'Morris Berd'	CDes EBee
hoodii	ECho
§ - subsp. ***muscoides***	ECho
* 'Hortensia'	LRHS
'Kelly's Eye' 🏆H4	CMMP CPBP ECho ECtt EPot NBir NHar NHol NMen SPoG WCom WFar
kelseyi	ECho NWCA WAbe WPat
- 'Rosette'	ECho EPot MDKP NMen WFar WPer
Light Pink Flame = 'Bareleven'PBR	ECtt EPfP LRHS SPoG WHil
Lilac Flame = 'Barten'PBR	EPfP SPoG WHil
longifolia subsp. ***brevifolia***	CPBP
'Louisiana'	see *P. divaricata* 'Louisiana Purple'
maculata	WPer
- 'Alpha' 🏆H4	CPrp CSam CWCL EBee EBrs ECha ECtt EPfP GCal GCra GGar GKir GMaP LRHS MSpe NCGa NHol NLar SKHP SPer SWvt WAul WFar WSHC WWlt
- Avalanche	see *P. maculata* 'Schneelawine'
- 'Delta'	EBee EBrs EPPr EPfP LRHS LSou NBPC NHol NLar SBfd SPer SRkn SWvt WBor WFar
- 'Natascha'	Widely available
- 'Omega' 🏆H4	CBar CPLG CPrp EAEE EBee EBrs ECtt EWTr GGar GKir LRHS MCot MMuc NBPC NGdn NHol NLar NPnk SBfd SKHP SMad SPer SPoG SWvt WAul WCAu WFar WSHC WSpi WWEG
- 'Princess Sturdza' 🏆H4	MWte SDix
- 'Reine du Jour'	CSam GMac IVic LPla LSou MDKP NDov SAga SMrm SPhx WSHC
- 'Rosalinde'	CPrp EAEE EBee ECtt ELon LRHS MMuc NCob NHol NLar SBfd SRGP STes SWvt WCAu WFar WSHC WWEG
§ - 'Schneelawine'	GKir SPlb
'Matineus'	SPhx
'Millstream'	see *P.* × *procumbens* 'Millstream'
'Millstream Blue' **new**	EPfP
'Millstream Jupiter'	ECho
'Minnie Pearl'	EBrs LRHS NDov SKHP
muscoides	see *P. hoodii* subsp. *muscoides*
nana **new**	GKev
- 'Mary Maslin'	WCom
nivalis 'Jill Alexander'	CMea
- 'Nivea'	GJos LSou
paniculata	ECha GCra NBid NDov SDix WCot WTin
- 'Aida'	EBee
- var. ***alba***	CMoH MAvo SDix WCot WTin
- 'Alba Grandiflora' 🏆H4	EHrv GMaP MAvo MNrw NCob WCot WEas WHoo
- 'All in One'	ECtt LSou
- 'Amethyst' misapplied	see *P. paniculata* 'Lilac Time'
- 'Amethyst' Foerster	CFir CSam EBee EHrv GKev LAst LRHS MWhi NBir NLar SPet SWat WCAu WFar
I - 'Aureovariegata Undulata' (v)	WCot
- 'Balmoral'	EBee ECtt EPfP GCra GKir LRHS MLHP MRav MSpe NCob NEgg NSti SBfd SMrs SPoG SWat SWvt WSpi WWEG
- 'Barnwell'	SWat
- 'Becky Towe'PBR (v)	CBow EBee ECtt ELon LHop LLHF LOck LRHS LSou MNrw NEgg NLar WCot
- 'Bill Green'	LRHS
- 'Blauer Morgen'	IPot
- 'Blue Boy'	COIW EBee ECGP ECtt EPfP EWTr GMaP LAst LRHS MDKP NBir NBro NChi NEgg NGdn NLar SMrm WBrE WClo WCot WFar WMnd
- 'Blue Ice' 🏆H4	EBee ELan NBro
- 'Blue Paradise'	Widely available
- 'Blushing Bride'	SRms
- 'Border Gem'	CBcs CMac EBee ECtt GKir LRHS MCot MRav MSpe MWat NChi NCob NHol NLar NVic SDix SPur SWat SWvt WBrk WHrl WSHC WWEG
- 'Branklyn'	EBrs GCra GKir LRHS
- 'Brigadier' 🏆H4	CPrp CTri EBee ECtt ELan GMaP LRHS MCot MDKP MSpe MWat NCob NEgg NGdn NVic SBfd SMrm SRms WCAu WFar
- 'Bright Eyes' 🏆H4	Widely available
- 'Burgi'	SDix
- 'Candy Floss'	LLHF NCob
- 'Cardinal' **new**	NDov
- 'Caroline van den Berg'	LRHS SRms
- 'Cecil Hanbury'	NLar SRms
- 'Cherry Pink'	LRHS
- 'Chintz'	SRms

	- 'Cinderella'	EBee ECtt
	- 'Cool Best' **new**	NDov
§	- 'Cool of the Evening'	EBee WKif
	- 'Cosmopolitan'	LSou MAsh MNrw
	- Count Zeppelin	see *P. paniculata* 'Graf Zeppelin'
	- 'Danielle'	CSBt LSou MWea WHil WHlf
	- 'Darwin's Choice'	see *P. paniculata* 'Norah Leigh'
	- 'David'	Widely available
	- 'David's Lavender'	EBrs LRHS
	- 'Delilah'^{PBR}	EBee NPri
	- 'Discovery'	EBee EHrv EWes IPot LRHS MCot MRav NCob NEgg SBfd SPur STes SWat WCAu
	- 'Dodo Hanbury-Forbes' 🏆H4	GKir
	- 'Doghouse Pink'	SDix
	- 'Dresden China'	MAvo SWat
§	- 'Düsterlohe'	CElw CSBt CSam EBee ECtt NBir NDov NGdn NLar NSti SMrm SPer STes SWat WCot WHil WHoo
	- 'Eclaireur' misapplied	see *P. paniculata* 'Düsterlohe'
	- 'Eclaireur' Lemoine	SWat
	- 'Eden's Crush'	NBre NVic
	- 'Eden's Flash'	EBee ECtt LRHS MSpe
	- 'Eden's Smile'	EBee
	- 'Elisabeth' (v)	ECtt EPfP GKir LSRN SRGP WHil
	- 'Elizabeth Arden'	EBee ECtt MAvo NLar SWat
	- 'Elizabeth Campbell'	GCal
	- 'Empty Feelings' (Feelings Series)	NBro
	- 'Etoile de Paris'	see *P. paniculata* 'Toits de Paris' Symons-Jeune
	- 'Europa'	EBee ECtt ELan LRHS MCot NBir NCob NGdn NHol NLar SPer WCAu WFar
	- 'Eva Cullum'	EBee EBrs ECtt EPfP GCra GKir GMaP LHop LRHS MArl MCot NBPC NHol NLar NMoo SBfd SPer SPet SPoG SWat WCot WWEG WWlt
	- 'Eva Foerster'	EBrs LRHS
	- 'Eventide' 🏆H4	CMac CSam CWCL EBee ECGP ECtt EPfP GKir LRHS MArl MCot MNrw MRav NCob SBfd SPer SPet SPoG SWat WCot
	- 'Excelsior'	LRHS MRav
	- 'Fairy's Petticoat'	LRHS MWat
	- 'Ferris Wheel'	MBri MWea
	- 'Flamingo'	EBee ECtt EWTr LRHS NLar SWvt
	- 'Fondant Fancy'^{PBR}	NLar SPoG
	- 'Franz Schubert'	CAby CSam EBee EBrs ECtt EPfP GCra GKir LRHS MCot MLHP MRav MSpe MWat NBir NGdn NLar NSti SBfd SPhx STes SWat SWvt WCot WFar WKif WWEG WWlt
§	- 'Frau Alfred von Mauthner'	COIW ECtt SMrm
	- 'Frosted Elegance' (v)	ECtt MAvo
	- 'Fujiyama'	see *P. paniculata* 'Mount Fuji'
	- 'Giltmine' (v)	EBee
	- 'Glamis'	MWat
	- 'Goldmine'^{PBR} (v)	EBee ELan LRHS LSou MCCP MNrw NSti
§	- 'Graf Zeppelin'	ECtt ELan LRHS SRms
	- 'Grenadine Dream'	LLHF MBri NVic SPoG
	- 'Harlequin' (v)	CBcs EBee ECha ECtt EHoe ELon GMaP LAst LRHS MCCP MCot NBPC NBid NBro NEgg NLar NSti SGSe SPer SPoG WCom WCot WFar WWlt
	- 'Hesperis'	CMdw EBee ECha ELon GBin NDov NLar SMrm SPhx WFar
	- 'Inspiration'	LRHS
	- 'Iris'	CMoH SMrm SRms WCot
	- 'Judy'	LSRN NBro
	- 'Jules Sandeau'	LRHS
§	- 'Juliglut'	CSpr SWat WCot
	- July Glow	see *P. paniculata* 'Juliglut'
	- 'Junior Bouquet' **new**	MAsh
	- 'Junior Dance'	LSou NGdn NLar SRot
	- 'Junior Dream'	LSou NLar SRot
	- 'Junior Fountain'	LSou NLar
	- 'Katarina'	CElw ECtt NLar
	- 'Katherine'	CHar EBrs LRHS NLar
	- 'Kirchenfürst'	CElw IPot LRHS MSpe NBir SBfd SMrm
	- 'Kirmesländler'	EBee ECtt GBin NLar SWat
	- 'Lads Pink'	SDix
	- 'Lady Clare'	SRms
	- 'Landhochzeit'	GBin WFar
*	- 'Laura'	CMMP EBee ECtt EPfP IPot LRHS MWhi NBPC NBro NPri NVic SGSe SMrm SPet SPoG SRGP SRkn STes WFar WHoo WMnd WTin
§	- 'Lavendelwolke'	CSam GCal NBir NLar SWat
	- Lavender Cloud	see *P. paniculata* 'Lavendelwolke'
	- 'Le Mahdi' 🏆H4	ELan LRHS MRav MWat SRms SWat
	- 'Lichtspel'	SAga SPhx
§	- 'Lilac Time'	EBee ECtt EHrv LSRN MDKP MWat NLar NMoo SWat SWvt WHlf WWEG
	- 'Little Boy'	CElw EBrs ECtt LRHS LSou MDKP MNrw NLar WFar
	- 'Little Laura'	CElw CWGN EBee ECtt LRHS LSRN MCCP MWea NLar WCot
	- 'Little Princess'	ELon LLHF LRHS NLar SMrm SRGP WMnd
	- 'Little Sara' **new**	NDov
	- 'Lizzy'^{PBR}	NLar
	- 'Manoir d'Hézèques'	WCot
	- 'Mary Christine' (v)	CDes NBid
	- 'Mary Fox'	CSam LRHS
	- 'Mia Ruys'	MArl MLHP
	- 'Midnight Feelings' (Feelings Series)	LLHF NBro NLar
	- 'Mies Copijn'	GMaP WFar
	- 'Milly van Hoboken'	WKif
	- 'Miss Elie'	LAst NBre NGdn SGSe SPoG WFar
	- 'Miss Holland'	LAst MWea NBPC NGdn SPet STes WWEG
	- 'Miss Jessica'	EBrs LAst LRHS STes
	- 'Miss Jill'	see *P.* × *arendsii* 'Miss Jill'
	- 'Miss Karen'	see *P.* × *arendsii* 'Miss Karen'
	- 'Miss Kelly'	CMMP LRHS LSou MSpe MWat MWea SRGP WHoo
	- 'Miss Margie'	see *P.* × *arendsii* 'Miss Margie'
	- 'Miss Mary'	see *P.* × *arendsii* 'Miss Mary'
	- 'Miss Pepper'	CWCL ECtt ELon LSou MMuc NGdn NLar SMrm SRkn WBor WFar WHil
	- 'Miss Universe'	MCCP NBre SGSe WHil WWEG
	- 'Miss Wilma'	see *P.* × *arendsii* 'Miss Wilma'
	- 'Monica Lynden-Bell'	Widely available
	- 'Mother of Pearl' 🏆H4	EBee ECtt ELan GQue IPot LRHS MSpe MWat NCob NEgg NHol NVic SPer SUsu WFar WWEG
§	- 'Mount Fuji' 🏆H4	Widely available
	- 'Mount Fujiyama'	see *P. paniculata* 'Mount Fuji'
	- 'Mrs A.E. Jeans'	SRms
	- 'Natural Feelings'^{PBR} (Feelings Series)	ELan MCCP MWea NBro NLar
	- 'Newbird'	SRms WWEG
	- 'Nicky'	see *P. paniculata* 'Düsterlohe'
§	- 'Norah Leigh' (v)	Widely available
	- 'Orange Perfection'	see *P. paniculata* 'Prince of Orange'

	- 'Othello'	CSam EBee ECGP ECtt GKir LRHS MSpe NCob NSti SBfd SUsu WFar WMnd WWlt
	- 'Otley Choice'	EBee ECtt LRHS MRav MWat NCob NHol NLar NVic SCoo SWat
	- 'Otley Purple'	MHer
	- 'P.D. Williams'	WCot
	- 'Pastorale'	LRHS WCot
	- 'Peppermint Twist'	CWCL CWGN EBee ELon GKev LSou MAsh MBri MMuc MNrw MTis MWea NEgg NLar SMad SMrm SPur WCot WCra WFut WHil
	- 'Picasso'	ECtt LSou
	- 'Pina Colada'	LSou MAsh SPoG WCra WHil
	- Pink Eye Flame = 'Barthirtyfive'[PBR]	EPfP GKir LSou SBfd SHar SKHP WHil
	- 'Pink Perfection'	LRHS
	- 'Pink Posie' (v)	WCot
	- Pink Red Eye Flame **new**	EPfP
	- 'Pinky Hill'	CElw CSBt LSou NPri
	- 'Pixie Miracle' **new**	LRHS
	- 'Pleasant Feelings'[PBR] (Feelings Series)	NBro
	- 'Popeye'	ECtt LPla NLar
	- 'Prime Minister'	ELon
§	- 'Prince of Orange' 𝕐H4	CMac CSam EBee ECtt ELan EPfP LRHS LSRN MRav MSpe MWat NCob NEgg NGdn NHol NLar NVic SBfd SPad SPet SPoG STes SWvt WAul WBor WCot WMnd WWEG
	- 'Prospero' 𝕐H4	CHar CSam CSpe EBee EHrv LRHS MCot MSpe NBid SRkn SWat
	- Purple Eye Flame = 'Barthirtythree'[PBR]	GKir LLHF LRHS LSou SBfd SHar SKHP WHil
	- 'Purple Kiss'	LSou WHil
	- 'Rainbow'	ELon
	- 'Red Feelings' (Feelings Series)	NBro
	- 'Red Flame'	CWGN ECtt EPfP GKir LRHS LSou SKHP WCot WHil
	- 'Red Riding Hood'	EBrs ECtt LAst LRHS MSCN MWea NBPC SPet
I	- 'Reddish Hesperis'	NDov
	- 'Rembrandt'	CPLG LRHS LTen WCot
	- 'Rijnstroom'	CBcs EBee ECha ECtt ELon GAbr GKir LRHS MArl NLar SMrm WBrk WFar WSpi
	- 'Robert Poore'	ELon GBin
	- 'Rosa Pastell'	EHrv ELon IPot LPla LSou MDun SAga SMrm SUsu WCot
	- 'Rowie'	NBid
	- 'Rubymine' (v)	LLHF
	- 'San Antonio'	LRHS
	- 'Sandringham'	CMac EBee EHrv EPfP GKir LRHS MArl MLHP MRav MSpe NBir NHol SBfd SPer SPoG SWvt
§	- 'Schneerausch'	LPla SPhx
	- 'Septemberglut'	LRHS NLar
	- 'Silvermine' (v)	CBow MCCP SDnm
	- 'Sir Malcolm Campbell'	EBee
	- 'Skylight'	EBee EHrv EWTr LRHS LSRN MAvo MWhi NBre NBro NVic SBfd SDix WAul
	- 'Snow White'	NBre NVic
	- Snowdrift	see *P. paniculata* 'Schneerausch'
	- 'Speed Limit 45'	WCot
	- 'Spitfire'	see *P. paniculata* 'Frau Alfred von Mauthner'
	- 'Starburst'	EBee NBro NGdn
	- 'Starfire' 𝕐H4	Widely available
	- 'Starlight' **new**	NHar
	- 'Steeple Bumpstead'	EBee LSou WCot
	- 'Sternhimmel'	LPla
	- 'Strawberry Daiquiri' **new**	MBri
	- 'Swizzle' **new**	LSou MAsh MBri MLLN SPoG WBor
	- 'Sylvia'	LRHS
	- 'Tenor'	CDes CFir CHar CTri EBee ECtt EPfP LAst LRHS MCot MDKP NCob NGdn NHol NLar NPri SBfd SPet SPoG STes SWvt WBrE WFar WWEG
	- 'The King'	CElw EBee ECtt LRHS MAvo MDKP NBro NLar SWat WSHC WSpi
	- 'Tiara' (d) **new**	WHlf
	- 'Toits de Paris' misapplied	see *P. paniculata* 'Cool of the Evening'
	- 'Toits de Paris' ambig.	MAvo
§	- 'Toits de Paris' Symons-Jeune	WSHC
	- 'Uspekh'	COlW CSam EBee EBrs ECtt EPPr EWes LRHS MCot MDKP MDun MRav MSpe NBro NCob NGdn NHol SAga SBfd SPer SUsu WFar WWEG
	- 'Utopia'	CDes CSam ELon LPla NLar SMrm SPhx SUsu WCot
	- 'Van Gogh'	CMdw EHrv
	- 'Velvet Flame'	LSou MWea SHar SKHP WHil
	- 'Violetta Gloriosa'	ELon LPla MWte SMrm
	- 'Watermelon Punch'	LSou MBri WCra
	- 'Wendy House'	LLHF MNrw
	- 'Wenn Schon Denn Schon'	EBee GBin
	- 'White Admiral' 𝕐H4	Widely available
	- White Flame = 'Bartwentynine'[PBR]	ECtt EPPr EPfP GKir LRHS LSou SHar SKHP WHil
	- 'Wilhelm Kesselring'	EBee ECtt ELon NBre WBor
	- 'William Ramsay'	LRHS
	- 'Windsor' 𝕐H4	CBar EBee ECtt ELon EPfP GCal GKir LRHS MSpe NEgg NHol NLar SBfd SCoo SPoG SRms SWvt WCAu WFar WSpi WWEG
	Pink Flame = 'Bartwelve'[PBR]	EPfP LLHF LRHS LSou SBfd SPoG
	'Pride of Rochester'	GJos LHop LRHS
§	× ***procumbens*** 'Millstream' 𝕐H4	EPPr WClo
	- 'Variegata' (v)	ECha ECho LRHS MDKP NPri NWCA SPlb SRot SUsu
§	***pulvinata***	WAbe
	Purple Flame = 'Barfourteen'[PBR]	EPfP LRHS LSou SBfd SPoG
	× ***rugelii***	EPot
	'Sandra'	LRHS
	'Scented Pillow'	NHol SGSe
	'Sherbet Cocktail'	CSpr CWGN EBee EKen MWea NLar SPoG WCot
§	***sibirica*** subsp. ***borealis***	EDAr WAbe
	stansburyi dwarf	GKev
	stolonifera	IFro MNrw
I	- 'Alba'	EBee EPfP
	- 'Ariane'	CWCL ECha EPPr EWld LSou SBch WCFE
	- 'Blue Ridge' 𝕐H4	CPLG CWCL EBee ECha ECtt EPPr EPfP EShb GKir LRHS LSRN MRav SRms
	- 'Bob's Motley' (v)	ECtt
	- 'Fran's Purple'	ELon EWld LRHS NBro WCFE
	- 'Home Fires'	EBee ECho ECtt ELon EPPr EPfP LEdu LRHS NBro SPlb WFar
	- 'Mary Belle Frey'	CEnt
	- 'Montrose Tricolor' (v)	EBee NBre NBro
	- 'Pink Ridge'	LRHS NBir
	- 'Purpurea'	CWCL EBee EPPr EPfP LEdu LSou MMuc SGSe

- variegated (v) GKir
subulata ECho ECtt EDAr EPfP EPot LBee
'Alexander's Surprise' LRHS NBir NLar SPlb SRGP WClo
- 'Amazing Grace' CTri CWCL ECho EDAr EPfP EPot EWes GKir LAst LHop LRHS SPoG WAbe
- 'Apple Blossom' EDAr EPot LRHS SPet SPoG SRms WFar
- 'Atropurpurea' EDAr EPfP LIMB LRHS SPoG
- Beauty of Ronsdorf see *P. subulata* 'Ronsdorfer Schöne'
- 'Betty' ECtt
- 'Blue Eyes' see *P. subulata* 'Oakington Blue Eyes'
- 'Bonita' ECho ECtt EPot GJos GKir LRHS MMuc MWte NLar
- 'Bressingham Blue Eyes' see *P. subulata* 'Oakington Blue Eyes'
- 'Brightness' ECho
- 'Brilliant' ECho
- 'Candy Stripe' see *P. subulata* 'Tamaongalei'
- 'Cavaldes White' SPoG
- 'Drumm' see *P. subulata* 'Tamaongalei'
- 'Emerald Cushion' CSam CTri ECho ECtt EDAr ELon GKev GKir LRHS MDKP MWat NCGa NLar WBVN WNew
- 'Emerald Cushion Blue' CPLG CTri CYeo ECho EPfP GJos LIMB LRHS NBir NMen NPnk NPri SPlb SPoG WAbe WClo WFar WPer
- 'Fairy' WPer
- 'Fort Hill' NHar
- 'G.F. Wilson' see *P. subulata* 'Lilacina'
* - 'Holly' ECtt EPot LLHF NHol NMen
- 'Jupiter' ECho
- 'Kimono' see *P. subulata* 'Tamaongalei'
§ - 'Lilacina' CMea ECho ECtt MAvo MWat
§ - 'Maischnee' CTri ECho ECtt EPfP MWat NHol SPlb WFar
- 'Marjorie' ECho ECtt GJos LBee MHer NBir NWCA SPoG SRGP WFar WNew
- May Snow see *P. subulata* 'Maischnee'
§ - 'McDaniel's Cushion' ♀H4 Widely available
- 'Mikado' see *P. subulata* 'Tamaongalei'
- 'Moonlight' ECtt EDAr GJos WCom
- 'Nettleton Variation' (v) CYeo ECho EDAr EPfP EPot EWes GKev GKir LHop LRHS MDKP NLar SPlb SPoG
§ - 'Oakington Blue Eyes' GKir LRHS SRms
- 'Pink Pearl' EWes
- 'Purple Beauty' CMea ECho EPot GGar GJos LIMB LLHF MWte NHar SPoG STes WFar WPer WSHC
- 'Red Wings' ♀H4 ECho ECtt EPfP GKir NMen SRms
§ - 'Ronsdorfer Schöne' EPot LBee LLHF NBir
- 'Samson' EDAr LSRN MMuc
- 'Sarah' LLHF
- 'Scarlet Flame' CBar CMea CSam ECho ECtt EDAr EPfP EPot NHol NPri SRGP WFar
- 'Schneewittchen' GKir
- 'Snow Queen' see *P. subulata* 'Maischnee'
- 'Snowflake' **new** MSCN
§ - 'Tamaongalei' CMea CPBP CTri CWCL ECho EDAr ELon EPfP EWes GGar GJos GKev GKir GMaP LAst LRHS MMuc MSCN NHol SCoo SPet STes WCFE WClo WNew WPer
- 'Temiskaming' CTri ECho ECtt EDAr EWes LBee LHop LRHS MLHP NMen SPoG SRms WCom WSHC
- 'White Delight' CBar ECho ECtt EDAr EPfP GJos LAst LBee LRHS NMen SPet SPoG STes WClo WFar WPer
- 'Winifred' NEgg
- 'Zwergenteppich' LLHF MAvo WPer
'Sweet William' MSpe NCob NEgg SRGP
'Swirly Burly' GQue
'Tiny Bugles' WPat
'White Kimono' LHop LRHS

Phoenicaulis (*Brassicaceae*)

§ **cheiranthoides** LLHF

Phoenix (*Arecaceae*)

canariensis ♀H1+3 CBcs CPLG CTrC CWSG CWib EAmu EBee EPfP EUJe IVic LPJP LPal LRHS MBri MCCP MMuc MREP NMoo SAPC SArc SBfd SBst SEND SLim SPlb SPoG STrG WFar
dactylifera (F) EAmu LPal SBig
reclinata EAmu NPal XBlo
roebelenii ♀H1+3 CBrP CDTJ CDoC CTsd EBee EGxp LPal LRHS MBri SBig
- 'Multistem' XBlo
rupicola EAmu LPal
sylvestris EAmu LPal
theophrasti CPHo EAmu LPJP LPal

Phormium ✿ (*Phormiaceae*)

§ 'Alison Blackman'PBR CAlb CBcs CDoC CKno CSBt CTrC EBee ESwi IVic LHop LRHS LSRN MBri MCCP MGos MREP MRav NPla SBfd SCoo SEND SPoG SWvt WClo WCot
'Amazing Red' CTrC EBee ESwi SBfd
'Apricot Queen' (v) Widely available
'Back in Black' **new** MPnt SBfd WCot
'Black Edge' MRav
Black Velvet = 'Seivel' NPla SBfd WClo
'Bronze Baby' Widely available
'Buckland Ruby' CDoC
'Carousel' CTrC ESwi IBal
'Chocolate Fingers' CBcs WCot
colensoi see *P. cookianum*
§ **cookianum** CHEx CTrC ECre EPfP GGar GKev GKir MGos SAPC SArc SCoo SEND WFar
- 'Alpinum Purpureum' see *P. tenax* 'Nanum Purpureum'
- 'Black Adder' EUJe LRHS LSRN SBfd SPoG
- dwarf SLPl
- 'Flamingo' (v) CAlb CBcs CCCN CDTJ CSBt CTrC EBee ELan ELon EPfP ESwi EUJe GKir LRHS LSou MGos NLar SBfd SEND SLim SPer SPoG SRkn WCFE WCot WPat
- subsp. **hookeri** 'Cream Delight' (v) ♀H3-4 Widely available
- - 'Tricolor' (v) ♀H3-4 Widely available
'Copper Beauty' NMoo WDyG
'Crimson Devil' CBcs CTrC MREP NPri SBfd
'Dark Delight' CBcs CDoC
'Dazzler' (v) CBcs CDoC GKir LAst LSRN WCot
'Duet' (v) ♀H3 CCCN CDoC CTrC CWib CWit EBee EHoe ELon EPfP ESwi LHop LRHS MGos NLar SWvt
'Dusky Chief' CSBt CTrC ESwi IBal LRHS
'Dusky Princess' ESwi LRHS SPad
'Emerald Isle' CDoC
'Evening Glow' (v) CBcs CCCN CSBt CTrC EBee ELan EPfP ESwi ETod GKir LRHS LSRN MAsh MBri MGos MMuc MREP NPri SBfd SEND SPoG SRkn SWvt WCot WGrn WPat

'Firebird'	ESwi LSRN SAga SWvt
'Glowing Embers'	CTrC EAmu ELon ESwi IBal IVic
'Gold Ray'	CTrC EBee ELon ESwi GKir IBal LRHS MBri MREP NLar NPri SBfd SWvt WCot WGrn
'Gold Sword' (v)	CBcs CCCN CDoC CMHG CSBt CTrC EBee EPfP ESwi LRHS MAsh MGos NEgg SBfd
'Golden Alison'PBR	see *P.* 'Alison Blackman'
'Golden Ray' (v) **new**	LRHS
'Green Sword'	CCCN
'Jack Spratt' (v)	CWit EBee ECou EHoe ELan IBal MNHC SWvt WPrP
'Jester' (v)	Widely available
'Limelight'	NBid SBfd SPad SWvt
§ 'Maori Chief'	CSBt ELan EPfP ESwi LOck MAsh NMoo SWvt WFar WGrn WPat
§ 'Maori Maiden' (v)	CAlb CBcs CCCN CChe CDoC CDul CTrC CTri EBee EHoe EPfP ESwi GKir LAst MBri MGos MREP MRav SBfd SRkn SWvt WFar
§ 'Maori Queen' (v)	CBcs CCCN CChe CDTJ CDoC CSBt CTrC CWit EBee ELan EPfP ESwi GKir LRHS MBri MGos MMuc MSwo NBid NMoo SBfd SCoo SEND SLPl SPer SPoG SRkn SWvt WFar WPGP
§ 'Maori Sunrise' (v)	CBcs CCCN CDoC CTrC EBee ELon EPfP ESwi GKir IArd LAst LRHS LSRN MAsh MBrN MGos MRav NPla SBfd SCoo SEND SLim SPer SWvt WFar
'Margaret Jones'PBR	CBcs CCCN CKno CTrC EBee LSRN SLim
'Merlot'PBR	EGxp LBuc LRHS NPri
'Peach Melba' **new**	GKir LRHS
'Pink Panther' (v)	Widely available
'Pink Stripe' (v)	CBcs CDoC CMHG CSBt EAmu EBee EQua ESwi GGar GKir LRHS MBri MGos MLLN NPal NPri SBfd SPad SPoG SWvt WCot
'Platt's Black'	Widely available
'Rainbow Chief'	see *P.* 'Maori Chief'
'Rainbow Maiden'	see *P.* 'Maori Maiden'
'Rainbow Queen'	see *P.* 'Maori Queen'
'Rainbow Sunrise'	see *P.* 'Maori Sunrise'
'Red Sensation'	EPfP LRHS WClo
I 'Rubrum'	CTrC ESwi GKir LRHS
'Stormy Dawn'	WCot
'Sundowner' (v) 🏆H3	Widely available
'Sunset' (v)	CBcs CCCN CSBt IFoB LAst NPri SWvt WCot
'Surfer' (v)	CBcs EHoe LHop MCCP MLLN WGrn
'Surfer Boy'	CWit LAst LTen SPur
'Surfer Bronze'	CCCN CSBt EBee ETod LFCN LSou SBfd
'Surfer Green'	CCCN CTsd ESwi LFCN SBfd WHer
'Sussex Velvet'	SCoo SLim
tenax 🏆H4	Widely available
- 'All Black'PBR	LRHS MGos
- 'Atropurpureum'	CEnt CHEx EUJe GKir LAst
- 'Bronze'	CHEx MMuc SWvt
- 'Chocolate Dream'	EPfP
- 'Co-ordination'	CBcs CCCN EBee EPfP GGar SBfd
- 'Deep Purple'	CHEx
- dwarf	SLPl
I - 'Giganteum'	CHEx
* - ***lineatum***	MMuc SEND
§ - 'Nanum Purpureum'	MMuc SEND
- Purpureum Group 🏆H3-4	Widely available
- Sweet Mist = 'Phos2'	LBMP MAvo NOak
- 'Variegatum' (v) 🏆H3-4	CDTJ CDoy CSBt CTrC EBee ELon EPfP ETod EUJe IBal LPal LRHS MGos MMuc NMoo SAPC SArc SBfd SEND SPer SRms WBrE WFar
- 'Veitchianum' (v)	CDoy SPer
'Thumbelina'	CBcs CCCN ESwi IFoB MAsh WPat
'Tom Thumb'	WDin WPrP
'Wings of Gold'	ESwi ETod IBal
'Yellow Wave' (v) 🏆H3	Widely available

Photinia ✿ (*Rosaceae*)

beauverdiana	GKir IRar
- var. ***notabilis***	EPfP NLar
davidiana	CDul CMac CTri ELan EPfP MRav NLar SPer SRms WDin WFar
- 'Palette' (v)	Widely available
- var. ***undulata*** 'Fructu Luteo'	CAbP EPfP EPla GGal MMuc MRav NLar SEND WFar
- - 'Prostrata'	CMac CTri ELan EQua MRav NLar WFar
×***fraseri***	CMCN
- 'Allyn Sprite'PBR	EBee NEgg SBfd WClo
I - 'Atropurpurea Nana'	MGos
- 'Birmingham'	CMac EBee EWes GKir WDin
- 'Canivily'	CTrC EBee EMil EWes GKir IVic LBMP LRHS NLar SBfd SLim SPoG
* - 'Ilexifolium'	ESwi
- 'Little Red Robin'	CBcs CChe CSBt EGxp EShb GKir IVic LBuc LRHS LSRN MAsh MWea NHol NLar NPal SBfd SLim SPad SPoG
- Pink Marble = 'Cassini' (v)	SBfd
- 'Purple Peter'	CEnd
- 'Red Robin' 🏆H4	Widely available
- 'Red Select'	CAlb EQua WPat
- 'Robusta'	CMac CTrC EPfP LRHS MAsh SWvt
I - 'Robusta Compacta'	MWea WFar
glabra	SArc
§ - 'Parfait' (v)	CAbP ELan LRHS MAsh WFar
- 'Pink Lady'	see *P. glabra* 'Parfait'
- 'Rubens'	ELan EPfP LRHS MAsh MRav SPer SSta WPat
- 'Variegata'	see *P. glabra* 'Parfait'
glomerata misapplied	see *P. prionophylla*
lasiogyna	CMCN
lucida **new**	WCru
microphylla B&SWJ 11837	WCru
- HWJ 564	WCru
parvifolia	EPfP
§ ***prionophylla***	CHEx GKir
'Redstart'	CAbP CMac EBee EPfP LSou MGos NEgg NHol NLar SEND SLim SLon SPer SSta SWvt WMoo
§ ***serratifolia***	CBcs CBot CDul CHEx EBee ECrN EPfP GKir MBri NLar SAPC SArc SBfd SEND SPer SPoG SSpi WFar
I - 'Compacta'	WFar
- 'Jenny'	CTrC IVic LRHS LSou NEgg NLar
serrulata	see *P. serratifolia*
- Curly Fantasy = 'Kolcurl'PBR	EBee EMil IVic LRHS MGos MRav SPoG
Super Hedge = 'Branpara'PBR	CTrC LRHS LSou WHar
'Super Red'	CAlb CSBt EBee NLar WClo
villosa 🏆H4	CAbP CGHE CTho GAuc GKir
- B&SWJ 8665	WCru
- var. ***laevis***	CPLG EPfP
- - B&SWJ 8877	WCru
- f. ***maximowicziana***	EPfP GAuc
* - var. ***zollingeri*** B&SWJ 8903	WCru

Phragmites (*Poaceae*)

from Sichuan, China — EPPr
§ ***australis*** — CBen CRWN CWat EBWF GFor LPBA MSKA NLar NMir SVic SWat WMAq WPnP
- subsp. ***australis*** var. ***striatopictus*** — EPPr
- - 'Variegatus' (v) — CBen CKno CWCL CWat EBee ECGP EHoe EPPr EPla EShb LLWG LPBA MMoz MMuc MWhi NBir NLar NWsh SEND SMad WFar WWEG
- subsp. ***pseudodonax*** — EPPr MMoz
communis — see *P. australis*
karka — EPPr
- 'Candy Stripe' (v) — CBen EPPr MSKA

Phuopsis (*Rubiaceae*)

§ ***stylosa*** — CSev CTri EBee ECha ELan ELon EPfP GAbr GMaP IFoB LRHS MHer MLHP MLLN MMuc MSCN NBid NBir NBro NChi NDov SPoG SRms WCAu WCom WFar WMoo WPer
- 'Purpurea' — CElw EBee MNrw MRav NChi NDov WCom

Phygelius ✿ (*Scrophulariaceae*)

aequalis — CFee CTca MNrw MRav WMoo
- ***albus*** — see *P. aequalis* 'Yellow Trumpet'
- 'Apricot Trumpet' — GKir
- 'Aureus' — see *P. aequalis* 'Yellow Trumpet'
- Cedric Morris form — SHom
- 'Cream Trumpet' — see *P. aequalis* 'Yellow Trumpet'
- 'Indian Chief' — see *P.* × *rectus* 'African Queen'
- 'Pink Trumpet' — SCoo SMrm SPet
- 'Sani Pass' — CPrp ECtt ELon EPfP GMaP LSRN MHer MMuc MRav SCoo SHom SPet SPlb SRms SWvt WCot WSpi
- 'Trewidden Pink' ♀H4 — CWib EBee ELan ELon EPfP LAst LHop MHer MSCN NGdn SBfd SGSe SHom SLim SWvt WHoo WMnd WMoo WWEG
§ - 'Yellow Trumpet' ♀H3-4 — Widely available
(Candy Drops Series) Candy Drops Purple = 'Kerphypur'PBR **new** — MCCP SGar
- Candy Drops Yellow **new** — MCCP
- Candy Drops Salmon Orange = 'Kerphysalm'PBR **new** — MCCP
§ ***capensis*** ♀H3-4 — CDoy CDul CWib ELan EPfP GCra GGal MHer NLar SBch SGar SHom SPet SRms WFar WMnd
- ***coccineus*** — see *P. capensis*
- orange-flowered — LHop SHom
Cherry Ripe = 'Blacher'PBR — LRHS LSou
'Golden Gate' — see *P. aequalis* 'Yellow Trumpet'
'Madame Aerts' — WSHC
'Midas Touch' — CBow MAsh NLar NPri
New Sensation = 'Blaphy'PBR — LRHS MNrw SPoG SWvt
§ × ***rectus*** — EPla
§ - 'African Queen' ♀H3-4 — CFee EBee ECtt ELan EPfP GKir MLHP MMuc MRav MSwo NBir NGdn SEND SHom SMad SPlb SWvt WFar WKif WMnd WMoo WWEG
- 'Aylesham's Pride' — SHom
- 'Devil's Tears' ♀H4 — CBcs CWit EBee ELan EPfP GKir LAst LRHS MBri MMuc MNHC NEgg NLar SBfd SEND SGSe SHom SLim SPad SWvt WMnd WMoo
- 'Ivory Twist'PBR — LHop LRHS SHom WHlf
- 'Jodie Southon' — LSou SHom SUsu
* - 'Logan's Pink' — LSRN
- 'Moonraker' — CTri CWit EBee ECtt ELan EPfP LAst LHop LRHS MBri MHer MNHC MRav MWat NEgg NGdn NLar SBfd SEND SGSe SHom SMrm SPlb SRms SWal WFar WMoo
- 'Pink Elf' — ELan
- 'Raspberry Swirl'PBR — EPfP LRHS SHom
- 'Salmon Leap' ♀H4 — CBcs CTri EBee ELan EPfP GKir LAst LRHS LSRN MBNS MBri MGos MMuc MRav NEgg NLar SBfd SEND SHom SLim SMrm SPad SPlb SWal SWvt WFar WHoo WMnd WMoo WWEG
- Somerford Funfair Apricot = 'Yapapr' — SWvt
- Somerford Funfair Coral = 'Yapcor'PBR — CDoC EAEE EBee EPfP GKev MBri NEgg NLar SLim SRkn SWvt WFar
- Somerford Funfair Cream = 'Yapcre'PBR — CDoC EBee EPfP LBMP LRHS MNHC NEgg NLar NPri SGSe SGar SLim SMrm SRkn SWvt WFar
- Somerford Funfair Orange = 'Yapor'PBR — EBee GKir LBMP LRHS MBri NLar NPri SGSe SLim SPoG SWvt WFar
- Somerford Funfair Wine = 'Yapwin' — EBee ELan EPfP EShb GJos GKir LHop LRHS LSou MAsh MBNS MBri NEgg NLar NPri SBfd SGSe SGar SLim SMrm SPoG SWvt WFar
- Somerford Funfair Yellow = 'Yapyel'PBR — EBee GKir LRHS MHav SLim SPoG SWvt
- 'Sunshine' — EBee ELan MDKP SHom SMrm WCom
- 'Sweet Dreams'PBR — LRHS SHom
§ - 'Winchester Fanfare' — CSBt ECtt ELan EPfP GKir GMaP LRHS MGos MRav MWat NGdn NVic SEND SLim SMrm SPer SWvt WFar WKif WMoo WWEG
- 'Winton Fanfare' — see *P.* × *rectus* 'Winchester Fanfare'
'Rory' — LRHS

Phyla (*Verbenaceae*)

lanceolata — LLWG
§ ***nodiflora*** — CEls CStu ECha EPPr NWCA SEND WJek WPer
- 'Alba' — MMuc SEND
§ - var. ***canescens*** — WHal

× *Phylliopsis* (*Ericaceae*)

'Coppelia' ♀H4 — GCrs GEdr ITim NHar WAbe WPat
hillieri 'Askival' — WAbe WThu
- 'Pinocchio' — GKir ITim NHar WAbe WPat WThu
'Hobgoblin' — WAbe
'Mermaid' — ITim NHar WThu
'Sprite' — EBee GCrs WPat
'Sugar Plum' — CCCN CWSG EBee ITim LRHS NHar NLar SSta SWvt WAbe WThu

Phyllitis see *Asplenium*

scolopendrium — see *Asplenium scolopendrium*

Phyllocladus (*Phyllocladaceae*)

alpinus — CDoC CDul ECou NHol NLar

Phyllodoce (*Ericaceae*)

aleutica — ECho GCrs NMen SRms WThu
× ***alpina*** — GKir
caerulea ♀H4 — ECho
- var. ***japonica*** — see *P. nipponica*
- 'Murray Lyon' **new** — NHar
- 'W.M. Buchanan's Peach Seedling' — GKir NHar

	empetriformis	ECho GKir SRms WThu
	× ***intermedia*** 'Fred Stoker'	GKir
§	***nipponica*** Υ^{H4}	GKir NMen WThu
	- var. ***oblongo-ovata***	GCrs NMen

Phyllostachys ✿ (*Poaceae*)

	angusta	EPla MWht SBig WJun
	arcana	EPla GKir WJun
	- 'Luteosulcata'	CEnt CGHE EPla GBin MMoz MMuc MWht NLar NPal SEND WJun WPGP
§	***atrovaginata***	EPla WJun
	aurea Υ^{H4}	Widely available
	- 'Albovariegata' (v)	CDTJ EBee ENBC EPla WJun
	- 'Flavescens Inversa'	EPla MMuc MWht SEND WJun
	- 'Holochrysa'	CDTJ EPla MMuc MWht SEND WJun WPGP
	- 'Koi'	CDTJ CEnt CGHE EPla LPal MMoz MMuc MWht NMoo NPal SBig SEND WJun WPGP
	aureocaulis	see *P. aureosulcata* f. *aureocaulis*, *P. vivax* f. *aureocaulis*
	aureosulcata	CWib EBee ENBC EPfP EPla GKir LEdu MAsh MMoz MWht NMoo WBVN WJun WMoo
	- f. ***alata***	see *P. aureosulcata* f. *pekinensis*
	- 'Argus'	EPla
§	- f. ***aureocaulis*** Υ^{H4}	Widely available
	- 'Harbin'	EPla
	- 'Harbin Inversa'	CDTJ EBee EPla
	- 'Lama Tempel'	CDTJ EPla WPGP
§	- f. ***pekinensis***	EPla MMoz NLar SBig SPer WPGP
	- f. ***spectabilis*** Υ^{H4}	Widely available
	bambusoides	CDTJ EPla GKir MAvo SBig SDix WJun
	- 'Albovariegata' (v)	EPla
	- 'Allgold'	see *P. bambusoides* 'Holochrysa'
	- 'Castilloni Inversa'	CGHE EAmu EPla ETod EWes LEdu LPal MMoz MWht SEND WJun WPGP
	- 'Castillonii'	CBcs CEnt EAmu EBee ENBC EPla EWes GKir LEdu LPal MMoz MMuc MWht NLar NMoo NPal SAPC SBig SDix SEND WJun WPGP
	- 'Castillonis Inversa Variegata' (v)	WJun
§	- 'Holochrysa'	CDTJ CDoC CEnt EPla MGos MMoz MMuc MWht NMoo NPal SEND WJun WPGP
	- 'Katashibo'	EPla
	- 'Kawadana' (v)	EPla WJun
	- f. ***lacrima-deae***	CAgr CDTJ CTrC EPfP EPla ETod GBin IMou
	- 'Marliacea'	EPla SBig WJun
	- 'Subvariegata'	EPla WPGP
	- 'Sulphurea'	see *P. bambusoides* 'Holochrysa'
	- 'Tanakae'	CDTJ ENBC MMoz NLar NMoo SBig WPGP
	- 'Violascens'	EPla NMoo SBig
	bissetii	Widely available
	circumpilis	EPla
	congesta misapplied	see *P. atrovaginata*
	decora	EBee EPla MMoz MMuc MWht NLar NMoo NPal SEND WDyG WJun WPGP
	dulcis	CEnt EPfP EPla LPJP MMuc MWht SBig WDyG WJun WPGP
§	***edulis***	CAgr CDTJ CTrC ELon EPla MMoz MWht SAPC SArc SBig WJun WPGP
	- 'Bicolor'	WJun
§	- 'Heterocycla'	XBlo
	- f. ***pubescens***	see *P. edulis*
	fimbriligula	EPla WJun
	flexuosa	CEnt EPla GKir LRHS MWht WJun WPGP
	glauca	CDTJ EPla ETod MMoz MWht NLar NMoo NPal SBig WDyG
	- f. ***yunzhu***	EPla MWht WJun
	heteroclada	CAgr CDTJ CEnt NMoo WJun
	- 'Solid Stem' misapplied	see *P. purpurata* 'Straight Stem'
	heterocycla	see *P. edulis* 'Heterocycla'
	- f. ***pubescens***	see *P. edulis*
	humilis	CDul CEnt EBee ENBC EPla EUJe MCCP MGos MMoz MMuc MWhi MWht NLar NMoo NPal SBig SEND WJun
	incarnata	WJun
	iridescens	EPla ETod EUJe NLar SBig WJun
	kwangsiensis	EPla
	lithophila	EPla
	lofushanensis	EPla
	mannii	EPla MWht
	meyeri	EPla
	nidularia	EPla MMoz SBig WDyG WJun
	- f. ***farcta***	EPla
	nigella	EPla
	nigra Υ^{H4}	Widely available
	- 'Boryana'	CDoC CEnt CGHE EAmu EBee EPfP EPla GKir MGos MMoz MMuc MWht NMoo SBig SEND SWvt WFar WJun WMoo WPGP
	- 'Fulva'	EPla
	- 'Hale'	EPla MWht
	- f. ***henonis*** Υ^{H4}	EAmu EBee ENBC EPla EUJe LPal MMoz MMuc MREP MWht NLar NMoo SBig SEND WDyG WJun WPGP
	- 'Megurochiku'	ENBC EPla MWht WJun
	- f. ***nigra***	EPla SPer
	- f. ***punctata***	CDoC EBee ENBC EPfP EPla MAvo MMuc MWht NGdn SEND WDyG WJun WMoo WPGP
	- 'Tosaensis'	EPla
	- 'Wisley'	EPla
	nuda	EAmu EPla GKir MMoz MMuc MWht NLar NPal SEND WJun
	- f. ***localis***	EPla MWht
	parvifolia	CEnt EPla MWht WJun WPGP
	platyglossa	EPla WPGP
	praecox	EPla ETod NMoo WJun
	- f. ***notata***	EPla
	- f. ***viridisulcata***	EAmu EPla WJun
	prominens	EPla
	propinqua	CDoC CDul EPla GBin MMoz MMuc MWht NMoo WJun
	- 'Li Yu Gan'	EPla
*	***pubescens*** 'Mazel'	SPlb
§	***purpurata*** 'Straight Stem'	EPla MWht
	rubicunda	EPla WJun
	rubromarginata	CDTJ CEnt EPla MMuc MWht NLar WJun WPGP
	'Shanghai 3'	EAmu ETod
	stimulosa	EPla MWht WJun
	sulphurea	CDTJ NMoo
	- 'Houzeau'	EPla
	- 'Mitis'	LMaj
	- 'Robert Young'	EPla
§	- f. ***sulphurea***	WJun
	- 'Sulphurea'	see *P. sulphurea* f. *sulphurea*
§	- f. ***viridis***	EBee EPla MAsh NMoo SBig
	violascens	CBcs CEnt EPla MMoz MWht SBig WJun WPGP
	virella	EPla

viridiglaucescens	CBcs CDTJ EBee EPfP EPla ETod GKir MBrN MMoz MMuc MWht NLar SBig SEND WJun
viridis	see *P. sulphurea* f. *viridis*
vivax	EPfP EPla EUJe GKir GQui LEdu MMoz MWht NLar SBig SEND WJun
§ - f. ***aureocaulis*** ♀H4	Widely available
- - 'Huanwenzii'	CDTJ CGHE CTrC EAmu ENBC EPla ETod MAvo MGos MMoz MWht NMoo NPla WJun
- 'Katrin'	LEdu
* - 'Sulphurea'	EPla XBlo

× *Phyllothamnus* (*Ericaceae*)

erectus	WAbe WPat

Phymatosorus (*Polypodiaceae*)

§ ***diversifolius***	CGHE WCot WPGP

Phymosia (*Malvaceae*)

§ ***umbellata***	CBot CRHN ERea SOWG

Phyodina see *Callisia*

Physalis (*Solanaceae*)

alkekengi ♀H4	CTri EPfP GKir NBir NLar SWvt WFar
- var. ***franchetii***	Widely available
- - dwarf	LRHS NLar
- - 'Gigantea'	ECGP LRHS MNHC NGBl NLar SPlb
- - 'Gnome'	see *P. alkekengi* var. *franchetii* 'Zwerg'
- - 'Variegata' (v)	ECtt EPla EWes EWld LEdu MMuc SEND WOld
§ - - 'Zwerg'	LRHS
angulata B&SWJ 7016	LLHF WCru
campanula	EWld
- B&SWJ 10409	WCru
edulis	see *P. peruviana*
§ ***peruviana*** (F)	CBod CCCN SBfd SHDw SVic

Physaria (*Brassicaceae*)

alpestris	GKev
didymocarpa	GKev

Physocarpus (*Rosaceae*)

§ Diable D'Or = 'Mindia' PBR	CAlb CDoC EBee EMil EPfP GKir LRHS MAsh MBri NEgg NPla SBfd WMoo
malvaceus	EWes
monogynus	NLar
opulifolius	CDul IFFs
- 'Angel Gold' **new**	SBfd
- 'Center Glow' **new**	MGos
- Coppertina PBR	see *P.* Diable D'Or
- 'Dart's Gold' ♀H4	Widely available
- 'Diabolo' PBR ♀H4	Widely available
- Lady in Red = 'Tuilad' PBR	CMac CSBt CWit EBee EShb EWes LAst LHop LRHS LSqu MAsh MGos MPkF MWea NLBP NLar SHar SLon SPoG SRkn WMoo
§ - 'Luteus'	CBot CDoC CSam CWib MRav SRms WDin WFar WMoo WPat
- 'Nugget'	GKir LRHS MAsh
§ - 'Seward' PBR	EPfP EWTr EWes MGos
- Summer Wine PBR	see *P. opulifolius* 'Seward'
- 'Tilden Park'	EBee
ribesifolius 'Aureus'	see *P. opulifolius* 'Luteus'

Physochlaina (*Solanaceae*)

orientalis	CAby NLar WAul

Physoplexis (*Campanulaceae*)

§ ***comosa*** ♀H2-3	ECho EPot ITim NMen NSla

Physostegia (*Lamiaceae*)

angustifolia	GQui NBre
I 'Aquatica' **new**	LLWG
§ ***virginiana***	CSBt CTri GBar GKir GMaP LHop LRHS MBNS MLLN SBfd SGar SPoG SRms SWat WBrk WFar WRHF
- 'Alba'	CBot COIW CSBt CTri EBee EHrv ELon EPfP EShb GAbr GBar GJos GMaP LEdu LRHS NBPC NChi NLar SMrm SPet SPlb WClo WHrl
§ - 'Crown of Snow'	CFir CMMP EBee ECtt EPfP GKir MHer MRav MSCN MWat NPri SBfd SPoG SWvt WFar WHil WPer
- 'Galadriel'	EBee
- 'Grandiflora'	CFir
- 'Miss Manners'	EAEE EBee ECGP ECtt LRHS MBNS MBri MCot NBre NCGa NCob NLar SRGP SUsu
- 'Olympic Gold' (v)	MDKP MRav
- 'Red Beauty'	EBee MDKP NBPC
- 'Rose Queen'	COIW CTri MWat NBre NChi SBfd WTin
- 'Rosea'	CBot EBee GJos IFoB MDKP MMuc NBPC NBre SHar SPoG SWal SWvt WClo WFar WHrl WPer WWEG
- Schneekrone	see *P. virginiana* 'Crown of Snow'
- 'Snow Queen'	see *P. virginiana* 'Summer Snow'
- var. ***speciosa***	WFar
§ - - 'Bouquet Rose'	CPrp EBee ECGP ECha EHrv EPfP GKir LEdu LRHS MCot MNFA MRav NBir NHol NLar SPer SWvt WAul WCAu WFar WGwG WMoo WWEG
- - Rose Bouquet	see *P. virginiana* var. *speciosa* 'Bouquet Rose'
- - 'Variegata' (v)	CHar CMac COIW CSBt EBee ECha ECtt EHoe EHrv ELan EPfP EShb LHop MRav NBPC NBir NPnk SPer SRms SWat WBrk WCom WCot WFar WHil WHoo WMnd WSHC WWEG
§ - 'Summer Snow' ♀H4	CBcs CPrp EBee ECha ELan EPfP GKir LHop LRHS NHol NLar SRms SWat WBrk WCAu WCot WFar WMnd
- 'Summer Spire'	EHrv ELan LRHS NHol WFar
- 'Vivid' ♀H4	Widely available
- 'Wassenhove'	SMrm

Phyteuma (*Campanulaceae*)

balbisii	see *P. cordatum*
comosum	see *Physoplexis comosa*
§ ***cordatum***	GJos
hemisphaericum	ECho GKev
humile	EDAr
nigrum	CEnt EBee ECho LLHF NBid WBor WPGP
orbiculare	EBWF GEdr
scheuchzeri	CDes CEnt CSpe EBee ECho EPfP EWld GEdr NPri NWCA SGSe SGar SMad SRms SRot WHoo WPGP
sieberi	CPBP
spicatum	CDes NBro

Phytolacca (*Phytolaccaceae*)

acinosa	EWld GPoy NLar SWat WBox
- HWJ 647	WCru
§ ***americana***	CAby CArn COld CSev EBee ELan EPfP EWld GPoy MBNS MHer

	MNHC NLar NMun SIde SMad SRms SWat WAbb WBox WCru WFar WHil WJek WMnd WMoo WSFF
- B&SWJ 8817A	WCru
- 'Silberstein' (v)	CBct EBee ECtt MBNS MHer NLar WCot WHil
- 'Variegata'	NBir
bogotensis	WBox WHil
chilensis **new**	WBox
clavigera	see *P. polyandra*
decandra	see *P. americana*
dioica	CHEx CPLG LEdu
esculenta	LEdu LHop MMuc SEND
icosandra B&SWJ 8988	WCru
- B&SWJ 9033	WCru
- 'Laca Boom' **new**	SVil
- Purpurascens Group B&SWJ 11251	WCru
insularis **new**	WBox
japonica B&SWJ 3005	NBid
- B&SWJ 4897	WCru
'Laka Boom' **new**	WHil
octandra B&SWJ 9514	WCru
- B&SWJ 10151	WCru
§ ***polyandra***	NBid NBro SRms WBor
rivinoides B&SWJ 10264	WCru
rugosa B&SWJ 7132	WCru

Picea (*Pinaceae*)

§ ***abies***	CCVT CChe CDul CLnd CMac CSBt CTri CWib EHul EMac EPfP GKir IFFs LAst LBuc MBri MGos MMuc NEgg NWea SCoo SEND SLim SPer SPoG WBVN WDin WEve WMou
- 'Acrocona'	ECho EHul GKir IVic MAsh MBlu MBri MGos NLar SCoo WEve
- 'Archer'	CKen
- 'Argenteospica' (v)	ECho NHol NPCo
- 'Aurea'	MGos NPCo WEve
- 'Capitata'	CKen NLar
- 'Ceejay's Gem'	SCoo
- 'Clanbrassiliana'	CKen ECho MGos NLar SCoo WEve WFar
- Compacta Group	ECho LBee NPCo
I - 'Congesta'	CKen
- 'Crippsii'	CKen
I - 'Cruenta'	CKen SLim
- 'Cupressina'	CKen
- 'Diffusa'	CKen NLar SCoo
- 'Dumpy'	CKen MGos NLar
- 'Ellwangeriana'	NLar WEve
- 'Excelsa'	see *P. abies*
- 'Fahndrich'	CKen CMen
- 'Finedonensis'	MGos NHol NLar WEve
- 'Formanek'	CDoC CKen CMen ECho NLar
- 'Four Winds'	CKen NLar
- 'Frohburg'	CKen ECho GKir MGos NLar NPri
- 'Globosa'	ECho
- 'Globosa Nana'	ECho LAst MGos
- 'Goldstart'	MGos
- 'Gregoryana'	CKen CMac ECho WAbe
- 'Heartland Gem'	CKen
- 'Himfa'	NLar
- 'Horace Wilson'	CKen CMen
- 'Humilis'	CKen
- 'Hystrix'	CMen NHol NLar
- 'Inversa'	CDul CKen ECho GKir IVic MBlu MGos NLar SLim WEve
- 'J.W. Daisy's White'	see *P. glauca* 'J.W. Daisy's White'
- 'Jana'	CKen
- 'Kral'	CKen
- 'Little Gem' 🏆H4	CDoC CKen CMen ECho EHul EPla GEdr GKir LBee LRHS MAsh NHol NLar NWea SCoo SLim SPer SPoG WEve WFar
- 'Marcel'	CKen
- 'Maxwellii'	EHul
- 'Mikulasovice'	NLar
- 'Nana Compacta'	CKen CMen ECho EHul LAst LBee WFar
- 'Nidiformis' 🏆H4	CDoC CKen CMac CMen CSBt CTri ECho EHul GKir LAst LRHS NHol NPCo NWea SCoo SLim SPer SPoG SRms WDin WEve WFar
- 'Norrkoping'	CKen
- 'Ohlendorffii'	CKen ECho EHul MGos NLar SCoo
- 'Pachyphylla'	CKen
- 'Pseudomaxwellii'	NLar
- 'Pumila Nigra'	EHul LRHS MGos SLim
- 'Pusch'	CKen CMen NLar SLim
- 'Pygmaea'	CKen MGos NLar
- 'Reflexa'	ECho NHol NPCo WEve
- 'Remontii'	NWea
- 'Repens'	ECho MBlu
- 'Rydal'	CBcs CDoC CDul CKen MGos NHol NLar NWea SLim WEve
- 'Saint James'	CKen
- 'Saint Mary's Broom'	CMen
- 'Silberkugel'	NLar
- 'Sonnenberg'	NLar
- 'Starý Smolivec'	NLar
- 'Tompa'	EMil LRHS MBri NLar SLim
- 'Veitchii'	NHol
- 'Vermont Gold'	CKen NLar
- Will's Dwarf	see *P. abies* 'Wills Zwerg'
§ - 'Wills Zwerg'	GKir SCoo
ajanensis	GAuc
§ ***alcoquiana*** var. ***alcoquiana***	GKir NWea SLim
- var. ***reflexa***	MPkF
asperata	GKir NWea
bicolor	see *P. alcoquiana* var. *alcoquiana*
I - 'Prostrata'	MGos
brachytyla	GKir
breweriana 🏆H4	CCVT CDoC CDul CMac CTri ECho EHul EPfP GKir IDee LEdu MBlu MGos MMuc MRav NEgg NPCo NPri NWea SEND SLim SPoG SSta WCFE WDin WEve WFar WMou
- 'Emerald Midget'	NLar
- 'Kohout's Dwarf'	CKen
chihuahuana **new**	SLim
engelmannii	CDul GKir NWea
- 'Compact'	GKir
- subsp. ***engelmannii***	CKen GKir NPCo
- 'Jasper'	NLar
- 'Lace' **new**	NLar
glauca	CDul GKir WEve
- Alberta Blue = 'Haal'[PBR]	CKen GKir LRHS MAsh SLim WEve WFar
- var. ***albertiana*** 'Alberta Globe'	CDoC CSBt ECho EHul EPla EPot GKir LBee LRHS MAsh MBri MGos NEgg NHol SCoo SLim SPoG WEve WFar
- - 'Conica'	CBcs CDoC CDul CMac CSBt ECho EHul EPfP EPla GKev GKir LAst LBee LRHS MAsh MBri MGos NEgg NHol NWea SEND SLim SPer SPoG STre WCFE WDin WEve WFar
- - 'Gnome'	CKen WEve
- - 'Laurin'	CKen ECho EPla LRHS MAsh MGos NHol NPCo WEve
- - 'Tiny'	CKen NHol WEve WGor

	- 'Arneson's Blue Variegated' (v)	CDoC CKen LRHS MAsh SLim WFar WGor
	- 'Biesenthaler Frühling'	LAst NLar SLim
	- 'Blue Planet'	CKen MGos NLar
	- 'Coerulea'	GKir NPCo
I	- 'Coerulea Nana'	NLar
	- 'Cy's Wonder'	CKen
	- 'Echiniformis' ♀^{H4}	CKen ECho LBee MBri
	- var. ***glauca***	WEve
	- 'Goldilocks'	CKen
§	- 'J.W. Daisy's White'	CBcs CDoC CKen ECho EHul EPla GKir LRHS MAsh MGos NEgg NHol NLar SCoo SLim SPer SPoG WBor WEve WFar WGor
I	- 'Julian Potts Monstrosa'	NLar
	- 'Lilliput'	CKen ECho EHul MBri MGos NLar
§	- 'Nana'	CKen
	- 'Piccolo'	CBcs CKen ECho GKir LRHS MAsh MGos NHol NLar SLim WEve
	- 'Pixie'	CKen WEve
	- 'Rainbow's End' (v)	CKen ECho EMil LRHS MGos NLar SLim WFar
	- 'Sander's Blue'	CKen ECho EHul EPfP EPla LAst LBee LRHS MBri MGos SLim WEve WFar
	- 'Zuckerhut'	LRHS MBri
	glehnii	GKir
	- 'Sasanosei'	CKen
	- 'Shimezusei'	CKen
	jezoensis	CKen CMen GKir MGos
	- 'Aurea' new	SLim
	- subsp. ***hondoensis***	CMen GKir
	- 'Marianbad'	CKen
	- 'Yatsabusa'	CKen CMen
	koraiensis	GAuc GKir
	kosteri 'Glauca'	see *P. pungens* 'Koster'
	koyamae	GKir
	- 'Bedgebury Cascade' new	SLim
	likiangensis	CDul CMCN EPfP GKir
	- var. ***balfouriana***	see *P. likiangensis* var. *rubescens*
§	- var. ***rubescens***	GKir MGos NHol SLim
	mariana	GGar GKir NWea
	- 'Aureovariegata' (v)	ECho WFar
	- 'Austria Broom'	CKen
	- 'Fastigiata'	CKen
	- 'Nana' ♀^{H4}	CDoC CKen CMac CMen ECho EHul EPfP EPot GEdr GKir LAst LRHS MAsh MMuc NHol NWea SCoo SEND SLim SPoG WDin WEve WFar
I	- 'Pygmaea'	CKen
	× ***mariorika*** 'Gnom'	MGos
	- 'Machala'	ECho MBri MGos
	meyeri	GKir
	morrisonicola	CKen GKir
	obovata	GAuc GKir
	- var. ***coerulea***	GAuc GKir NLar NWea
	omorika ♀^{H4}	CBcs CCVT CDul CMCN EMac GKir IFFs MGos MMuc NWea SEND SPer WCFE WDin WEve WFar
I	- 'Aurea'	ECho
	- 'Bruns'	GKir
	- 'Frohnleiten'	CKen
	- 'Frondenberg'	CKen ECho
	- 'Karel'	CKen MBri NLar
	- 'Minimax'	CKen ECho
	- 'Nana' ♀^{H4}	ECho EHul GKir LRHS MAsh MGos NPCo SCoo SLim SPoG WCFE WEve WFar
	- 'Pendula' ♀^{H4}	CDoC ECho GKir LRHS MBlu NLar NPal SLim SSta WEve
	- 'Pendula Bruns'	LRHS NLar SLim SPoG

	- 'Peve Tijn'	LRHS MAsh NLar SPoG
	- 'Pimoko'	CKen GKir LRHS MGos NLar NPCo SCoo SLim
	- 'Pimpf' new	IVic
	- 'Pygmy'	CKen
	- 'Schneverdingen'	CKen
	- 'Tijn'	CKen SLim
	- 'Treblitsch'	CKen NLar
	orientalis ♀^{H4}	CDul GKir NWea WThu
	- 'Aurea' (v) ♀^{H4}	CMac ECho EHul ELan EPla GKir LRHS MBri MGos NHol NLar NPri SCoo SLim WDin
	- 'Aureospicata'	CDoC CTho ECho MBlu NLar NPCo SCoo WEve
	- 'Bergman's Gem'	CKen
	- 'Early Gold' (v)	MBri WFar
	- 'Golden Start'	LRHS MBri NLar SLim
	- 'Jewel'	CKen
	- 'Kenwith'	CKen ECho
	- 'Mount Vernon'	CKen
	- Nana Group	SCoo
	- Pendula Group	MGos
	- 'Professor Langner'	CKen MAsh SLim
	- 'Skylands'	CKen ECho ELan GKir LRHS MAsh MBri MGos NHol NLar SLim SPoG WEve
	- 'Tom Thumb'	CKen NLar SLim
	- 'Wittboldt'	MAsh
	pungens	GKir WDin WEve
	- 'Baby Blueeyes'	ECho WFar
	- 'Blaukissen'	CKen
	- 'Blue Mountain'	ECho LAst
	- 'Blue Pearl'	NLar
	- 'Blue Trinket'	GKir
	- 'Drayer'	ECho
	- 'Edith'	CKen GKir LRHS NLar NPCo SLim SPer WFar
	- 'Endtz'	ECho
	- 'Erich Frahm'	ECho GKir LRHS LTen MAsh MGos SLim WFar
	- 'Fat Albert'	CDul CWib ECho GKir LAst LRHS MGos NEgg NLar NPCo NWea SLim WFar
	- 'Frieda'	LRHS SLim
	- Glauca Group	CDul CLnd CMac EMac GKir MMuc NWea SCoo SEND SPoG WBVN WDin WEve WFar WMou
	- - 'Glauca Procumbens'	CMen NLar NWea
§	- - 'Glauca Prostrata'	ECho EHul GKir SLim WEve
	- 'Glauca Globosa'	see *P. pungens* 'Globosa'
	- 'Globe'	CKen CMen GKir
I	- 'Globosa' ♀^{H4}	CBcs CKen CSBt ECho EHul EPla GKir LBee LRHS MAsh MBri MGos NPCo NPri NWea SCoo SLim SPer SPoG SRms WEve WFar
I	- 'Globosa Viridis'	ECho
	- 'Gloria'	CKen GKir SLim
	- 'Hoopsii' ♀^{H4}	CDul CSBt ECho EHul EPfP EPla GKir IVic LAst LMaj LRHS MAsh MGos NEgg NLar NPCo NPri NWea SLim SPoG SWvt WDin WEve WFar
	- 'Hoto'	EHul GKir MGos SLim
	- 'Hunnewelliana'	EPfP
	- 'Iseli Fastigiate'	ECho GKir LRHS MAsh MBri MGos NPCo SCoo SLim SPer SPoG WEve
	- 'Iseli Foxtail'	NLar
§	- 'Koster' ♀^{H4}	CDoC CSBt ECho EHul EPfP GKir LAst MGos NEgg NPla NPri NWea SLim SPoG SRms WDin WEve WFar WMou
	- 'Koster Fastigiata'	NEgg
	- 'Lucky Strike'	CKen ECho MBri MGos NLar

- 'Maigold' (v)	CKen ECho MAsh NLar SLim
- 'Moerheimii'	ECho EHul NLar WEve
- 'Montgomery'	CKen ECho GKir NLar WEve
- 'Mrs Cesarini'	CKen NLar
- 'Nimety'	CKen
- 'Oldenburg'	GKir LAst NEgg NLar NPCo NWea SLim
- 'Procumbens'	CKen GKir
- 'Prostrata'	see *P. pungens* 'Glauca Prostrata'
- 'Prostrate Blue Mist'	WEve
- 'Rovelli's Monument'	NLar
- 'Saint Mary's Broom'	CKen NLar NPCo
- 'Schovenhorst'	ECho EHul WFar
- 'Snowkiss'	ECho NPCo WFar
- 'Spek'	ECho GKir MGos
- 'Thomsen'	ECho EHul GKir MAsh NPla
- 'Thuem'	ECho EHul EPfP MGos NLar NPCo WFar
- 'Waldbrunn'	CKen ECho LRHS MAsh WEve
- 'Wendy'	CKen
purpurea	GKir WEve
retroflexa	GAuc NWea
rubens	NLar NWea WEve
schrenkiana	CMCN GKir
sitchensis	CDul GKir IFFs NWea
- 'Nana'	ECho
- 'Papoose'	see *P. sitchensis* 'Tenas'
- 'Pévé Wiesje'	NLar
- 'Silberzwerg'	CKen ECho LRHS NLar SLim SPoG
- 'Strypemonde'	CKen
§ - 'Tenas'	CKen ECho GKir LRHS NLar SLim SPoG
smithiana	CDul EPfP GKir NLar NWea WEve
I - 'Aurea'	MGos
- 'Sunray'	SLim
wilsonii	CKen GKir NLar NWea

Picrasma (*Simaroubaceae*)

ailanthoides	see *P. quassioides*
§ ***quassioides***	EPfP WPGP

Picris (*Asteraceae*)

echioides	CArn WHer

Picrorhiza (*Scrophulariaceae*)

kurrooa	GPoy

Pieris (*Ericaceae*)

'Balls of Fire'	CMac
'Bert Chandler'	CMac SSpi WSpi
'Brouwer's Beauty'	IVic SLim
'Firecrest' ♀H4	CMHG MMuc NLar SEND SSpi
'Flaming Silver' (v) ♀H4	Widely available
'Forest Flame' ♀H4	Widely available
formosa B&SWJ 2257	WCru
- var. ***forrestii***	CDoC CWib GLin
- - 'Jermyns'	CMac MRav
- - 'Wakehurst' ♀H3	CAbP CDul CMac CTri ELon EPfP LHyd LRHS MAsh MGos MRav MSnd SPer SPoG SSpi WFar WSpi
Havila = 'Mouwsvila' (v)	CMac MAsh MGos NHol WFar
japonica	CMac GGal GKir MGos SArc SReu WDin
- 'Astrid'	IVic MGos
- 'Bisbee Dwarf'	NHol
- 'Blush' ♀H4	GKir MBri MGos NHol
- 'Bonfire'	CCCN CEnd EBee ELan EQua GAbr IVic LRHS MBri MGos MMuc NEgg NLar SBfd SLim SPoG
- 'Brookside Miniature'	NHol
- 'Carnaval' (v)	CCCN CDoC CEnd CMac CSBt CWib CWit EBee ELan ELon GAbr IFFs IVic LBuc LRHS LSRN MAsh MGos MMuc NLar NPCo SBfd SCoo SLim SPer SPoG SWvt WFar
- 'Cavatine' ♀H4	CMHG GKir IVic
§ - 'Christmas Cheer'	CMac CWit EQua GKir LSou NLar WFar WMoo
- 'Cupido'	CDoC EMil GKir IVic LRHS MGos NHol NLar SBfd SLim SPoG WFar
- 'Debutante' ♀H4	CBcs CWib CWit EBee ELan EMil EPfP GKir IFFs LRHS MAsh MBri MGos NHol NLar NPCo NPri SBfd SCoo SPoG SSpi SWvt WFar
- 'Don'	see *P. japonica* 'Pygmaea'
- 'Dorothy Wyckoff'	GKir NHol SSta
- 'Flaming Star'	SWvt
- 'Flamingo'	CMac GKev MGos NHol
- 'Grayswood' ♀H4	EPfP NHol WFar
I - 'Katsura'	Widely available
- 'Little Heath' (v) ♀H4	Widely available
- 'Little Heath Green' ♀H4	CChe CDoC CMac CSBt ELon GKir LHyd MAsh MGos MMuc NEgg NHol NPCo SBfd SPer SPoG SWvt WFar WMoo
- 'Minor'	GKev NHol WThu
- 'Mountain Fire' ♀H4	Widely available
- 'Passion' PBR	CEnd IVic MGos SBfd
- 'Pink Delight' ♀H4	CAbP CDoC CWit GKir LMil LRHS LSRN LSou MRav NEgg NMun SBfd SRms
- 'Prelude' ♀H4	CSBt CWSG EMil GKev GKir LRHS MAsh MSnd NHol NLar NMen SPad WAbe WFar
- 'Purity' ♀H4	CBcs CDoC CMHG CMac CWSG CWit GKir LRHS MGos NEgg NHol SBfd SLim SReu SSta SWvt WDin WFar WGwG WHar
§ - 'Pygmaea'	CMac NHol SSta
- 'Red Mill'	CEnd CWSG EPfP GKir MAsh MHav SLim SPer SSpi WFar
- 'Rokujo's Dwarf'	WAbe
- 'Rondo' **new**	IVic
- 'Rosalinda'	LTen MGos NLar WFar
- 'Rosea'	LHyd
- 'Sarabande' ♀H4	GKir IVic MAsh MGos MMuc NLar SPoG SSta
- 'Scarlett O'Hara'	CSBt GKir MGos
- Taiwanensis Group	EPfP GGar MMuc NLar SBfd SRms SSta WFar
- 'Temple Bells'	CSBt GKir LTen MGos SBfd
- 'Tickled Pink'	GKir
- 'Valley Rose'	CGHE CSBt ELan ELon EPfP GKir IVic LLHF MGos MHav NLar NMun SPoG SSpi WFar WSpi
- 'Valley Valentine' ♀H4	CBcs CDoC CDul CEnd CMac CSBt CWSG CWib EPfP IVic LRHS LSRN MAsh MBri MDun MGos MMuc NPCo NPri SBfd SCoo SEND SLim SPer SPoG SReu SSta SWvt WFar
- 'Variegata' misapplied	see *P. japonica* 'White Rim'
- 'Variegata' ambig.	NLar
- 'Variegata' (Carrière) Bean (v)	CMHG EPfP GKir LHyd LRHS MGos MRav NHol SBfd SPoG WDin WFar WHar
- 'Wada's Pink'	see *P. japonica* 'Christmas Cheer'
- 'White Pearl'	CAbP CMac EPfP IVic MGos
§ - 'White Rim' (v) ♀H4	CDul CMac EPfP MAsh NHol SPlb WFar
- 'William Buchanan'	NHol WThu
- var. ***yakushimensis***	NLar

	nana	WThu
	'Tilford'	CMac

Pilea (*Urticaceae*)

§	***microphylla***	EBak EShb
	muscosa	see *P. microphylla*
	peperomioides ♀H1	CSev WSpi

Pileostegia (*Hydrangeaceae*)

	sp.	GGal
	viburnoides ♀H4	Widely available
	- B&SWJ 3565	WCru
	- B&SWJ 7132	WCru
	- B&SWJ 3570 from Taiwan	WCru

Pilosella (*Asteraceae*)

§	***aurantiaca***	CArn CRWN EBWF ELan LEdu MHer MNHC NBid NPri SGar SIde WCAu WCot WFar WHer WMoo WSFF
§	- subsp. ***carpathicola***	GGar
§	***officinarum***	EBWF NRya
	× ***stoloniflora*** 'Phil Clark'	WAlt

Pilularia (*Marsileaceae*)

	globulifera	MSKA

Pimelea (*Thymelaeaceae*)

	coarctata	see *P. prostrata*
	ferruginea	ECou WAbe
	- 'Magenta Mist'	SOWG
	filiformis	ECou
	ligustrina	GGar
	oreophila new	WThu
§	***prostrata***	CBcs CTrC CTri ECho ECou EPot WPer
	- 'Misty Blue'	CTrC
	- f. ***parvifolia***	ECou
	tomentosa	ECou LRHS

Pimpinella (*Apiaceae*)

	anisum	CArn SIde SVic
	bicknellii	WPGP
	major	EBWF
	- 'Rosea'	CBow CDes CMea CPLG CSpe EBee EPPr GCal GMac LHop LPio LRHS LSou MAvo MLLN NBPC NCGa NChi NCob NDov NGdn SMrm SUsu WCot WFar WHal WPGP
	minima rosea new	NDov
	saxifraga	NBre

pineapple see *Ananas comosus*

pineapple guava see *Acca sellowiana*

Pinellia (*Araceae*)

	cordata	CPom EBee EWTr LEdu MDKP NMen SChF WCot WCru WWst
	- pink-flowered	GEdr
	pedatisecta	CDes EBee GEdr LPio MDKP MMoz SChF WCot WFar
	pinnatisecta	see *P. tripartita*
	ternata	CStu EBee GEdr LEdu NLar NMen WCot WFar WPnP
	- B&SWJ 3532	WCru
§	***tripartita***	CFee CPLG CStu EBee ECho EPPr MDKP WAbe WCot WPrP
	- B&SWJ 1102	WCru
	- 'Dragon Tails' (v)	SKHP
	- 'Purple Face'	WCru

Pinguicula (*Lentibulariaceae*)

	crassifolia	CHew
	crassifolia × ***emarginata***	SHmp
	cyclosecta	CHew CSWC SHmp
	debbertiana	SHmp
	ehlersiae	EFEx
	esseriana	CSWC EFEx
	grandiflora	CSWC EECP EFEx GCra MCCP NMen NRya NWCA
	hemiepiphytica	CHew
	heterophylla	CHew SHmp
	jaumavensis	CHew
	lauana	CHew SHmp
	longifolia subsp. ***longifolia***	EFEx
	macrophylla	CHew
	macrophylla × ***zecheri***	SHmp
	moranensis var. ***caudata***	EFEx
	- ***moreana***	EFEx
	- ***superba***	EFEx
	rotundiflora	CHew SHmp
	vulgaris	EFEx
	'Weser'	CSWC NChu

pinkcurrant see *Ribes rubrum* (P)

Pinus ✿ (*Pinaceae*)

	albicaulis 'Flinck'	CKen
	- 'Nana'	see *P. albicaulis* 'Noble's Dwarf'
	- 'No. 3'	CKen
§	- 'Noble's Dwarf'	CKen
	aristata	CDul CLnd CMen EHul GKir MAsh MGos NMun STre WDin WEve
	- 'Cecilia'	CKen
	- 'Kohout's Mini'	CKen
	- 'Sherwood Compact'	CKen GKir MAsh MBri NLar SLim
	- 'So Tight'	CKen
	armandii	CAgr CDoC CDul CMCN CTrC GKev GKir WPGP
	- 'Gold Tip'	CKen
	attenuata	GKir
	austriaca	see *P. nigra* subsp. *nigra*
N	***ayacahuite***	CKen GKir
	balfouriana dwarf	CKen
	banksiana	CDul GKir
	- 'Arctis'	NLar
	- 'Chippewa'	CKen ECho
I	- 'Compacta'	CKen
	- 'H.J. Welch'	CKen
	- 'Manomet'	CKen
	- 'Neponset'	CKen
	- 'Schneverdingen'	CKen
	- 'Schoodic'	ECho LRHS NLar SLim SPoG
	- 'Uncle Fogy'	ECho MGos NLar
	- 'Wisconsin'	CKen
	brutia var. ***eldarica***	GAuc
	bungeana	CDoC CDul CLnd CMCN EPfP MBlu SLPl WEve
	- 'Diamant'	CKen
	- 'June's Broom'	CKen
	cembra	CAgr CDul CLnd GKir NLar STre WEve
	- 'Aurea'	see *P. cembra* 'Aureovariegata'
§	- 'Aureovariegata' (v)	ECho LRHS NPCo SCoo WEve
	- 'Barnhourie'	CKen
	- 'Blue Mound'	CKen
	- 'Chalet'	CKen
	- 'Compacta Glauca'	ECho MBri
	- Glauca Group	SCoo WEve
*	- 'Griffithii'	WDin

	- 'Inverleith'	CKen
	- 'Jermyns'	CKen
	- 'King's Dwarf'	CKen
	- 'Ortler'	CKen
	- 'Roughills'	CKen
	- 'Stricta'	CKen ECho
	- witches' broom	CKen
	contorta	CBcs CDoC CDul GKir IFFs MGos NWea SPlb WDin
	- 'Asher'	CKen
	- 'Chief Joseph' **new**	CKen
I	- 'Compacta'	SCoo
	- 'Frisian Gold'	CKen SLim
	- var. ***latifolia***	CDul CLnd GKir WDin
	- 'Spaan's Dwarf'	CKen ECho LRHS MGos NLar SCoo SLim SPoG WEve
	- 'Taylor's Sunburst' **new**	CKen
	coulteri ♀H4	CDul CMCN GKir SBig SKHP SMad WThu
	densiflora	CDul CMCN CMac GAuc
	- 'Alice Verkade'	CMen ECho EHul GKir LRHS MAsh MBri NLar SCoo SLim WEve WFar
	- 'Aurea'	LRHS MGos NLar SLim
	- 'Golden Ghost'	MAsh NLar SLim
	- 'Jane Kluis'	CKen ECho EHul EPla GKir LRHS LTen MBri NLar SCoo SLim WEve WFar
	- 'Jim Cross'	CKen
	- 'Low Glow'	CKen ECho LRHS NLar NPCo SLim
	- 'Oculus-draconis' (v)	ECho GKir LRHS MGos NEgg NLar SLim WEve WFar
	- 'Pendula'	CKen ECho LRHS NEgg NLar SCoo SLim WEve WFar
*	- 'Pyramidalis'	ECho
	- 'Umbraculifera'	CMen ECho GKir MAsh MGos NLar NPCo SCoo SSta WEve WFar
I	- 'Umbraculifera Nana'	ECho
§	***devoniana***	LRHS SLim
	edulis	CAgr GAuc
	- 'Juno'	CKen
	elliottii	SBig
	- var. ***densa*** **new**	CKen
	engelmanii 'Glauca'	WFar
	engelmannii	SKHP
	fenzeliana	CKen
	flexilis	CDul NWea
	- 'Blackfoot' **new**	NLar
	- 'Firmament'	ECho LRHS NLar SLim
	- 'Glenmore Dwarf'	CKen
	- 'Nana'	CKen
	- 'Tara Mae' **new**	NLar
	- 'Tarryall'	CKen
	- 'Tinby Temple'	NLar
	- 'Vanderwolf's Pyramid'	CDoC MAsh MBri NLar
	- WB No 1	CKen
	- WB No 2	CKen
	gerardiana	GAuc GKir
	greggii	EPfP
	griffithii	see *P. wallichiana*
	halepensis	CDul GAuc
§	***heldreichii*** ♀H4	CDoC CDul ECho GKir MGos NWea SCoo WFar
	- 'Aureospicata'	NLar WEve
	- 'Compact Gem'	CDoC CKen ECho MBri MGos NLar SCoo SLim SSta WEve
	- 'Dolce Dorme'	CKen NLar
	- 'Groen'	CKen
	- 'Kalous'	NLar
	- var. ***leucodermis***	see *P. heldreichii*
	- - 'Irish Bell'	NLar
	- - 'Pirin 7'	NLar
	- 'Malink'	CKen ECho LRHS SLim
	- 'Ottocek'	CKen
	- 'Pygmy'	CKen ECho
	- 'Pyramid' **new**	NLar
	- 'Satellit'	CKen ECho EHul GKir LRHS MGos NLar NPCo SCoo SLim WEve
	- 'Schmidtii'	see *P. heldreichii* 'Smidtii'
§	- 'Smidtii' ♀H4	CDoC CKen CMen ECho GKir LRHS MAsh MGos NLar SLim WEve
	- 'Zwerg Schneverdingen'	CKen NLar NPCo
	× ***holfordiana***	CDoC CDul
	jeffreyi ♀H4	CDul CMCN CTho GAuc GKir NWea
	- 'Joppi'	CKen NLar SLim
	koraiensis	GAuc GKir LRHS MBlu
	- 'Bergman'	CKen
	- 'Dragon Eye'	CKen
	- 'Jack Corbit'	CKen
	- 'Shibamichi' (v)	CKen
	- 'Silver Lining'	MAsh NPCo
	- 'Silveray'	NLar
	- 'Silvergrey'	CKen
	- 'Winton'	CKen NLar
	leucodermis	see *P. heldreichii*
	magnifica	see *P. devoniana*
*	***meyerei***	GAuc
	monophylla	ECho
	- 'Tioga Pass'	NLar
	montezumae ambig.	SAPC
	montezumae Lamb.	SArc
	monticola 'Pendula'	CKen
	- 'Pygmy'	see *P. monticola* 'Raraflora'
§	- 'Raraflora'	CKen
	- 'Skyline'	NLar WEve
	- 'Windsor Dwarf'	CKen
	mugo	CArn CBcs CDul CMac CTri EHul GKir MGos NWea WBor WBrE WDin WEve WFar
	- 'Allgau'	CKen NLar
	- 'Amber Glow'	MAsh NLar
	- 'Benjamin'	CKen ECho EPla MAsh MGos NLar SCoo
	- 'Bisley Green'	ECho
	- 'Brownie'	CKen
	- 'Carsten'	CKen ECho MAsh MGos SCoo SLim WEve
	- 'Carsten's Wintergold'	CDoC EMil GKir LRHS MAsh MBri NLar SCoo SPoG WEve
	- 'Chameleon'	NLar
	- 'Columbo'	NLar
	- 'Corley's Mat'	CKen ECho GKir LAst NHol NLar SCoo SLim WEve
	- 'Devon Gem'	ECho NPCo
	- 'Dezember Gold'	LRHS NLar SLim
	- 'Flanders Belle'	ECho SLim
	- 'Gnom'	CDul ECho EHul GKir MBri MGos NEgg NLar NPCo SCoo WDin WEve WFar
	- 'Gold Star'	CMen EPla SLim
	- 'Golden Glow'	CKen ECho MBri NLar SCoo SLim
	- 'Heinis Triumph' **new**	MBri
	- 'Hesse'	ECho GKir SCoo
	- 'Hoersholm'	CKen ECho
	- 'Hulk'	CKen
	- 'Humpy'	CKen CMen ECho GKir LRHS MAsh MBri MGos NPCo SCoo SLim WEve WFar
	- 'Ironsides'	CKen
	- 'Jacobsen'	CKen NLar
	- 'Janovsky'	CKen ECho
	- 'Kamila'	NLar
	- 'Kissen'	CKen ECho MGos NLar SLim WEve
	- 'Kleiner Wimbachi'	NHol

	- 'Klosterkotter'	ECho MGos NLar WFar
	- 'Kobold'	ECho NEgg WFar
	- 'Krauskopf'	CKen
	- 'Laarheide'	ECho GKir WEve
	- 'Laurin'	CKen ECho
	- 'Little Lady'	NLar
	- 'Marand'	ECho NLar
	- 'March'	CKen ECho
	- 'Mini Mops'	CKen ECho NLar WEve
	- 'Minikin'	CKen MAsh
	- 'Mops' Υ^{H4}	CDul CMac CMen ECho EHul EPfP GKir LRHS LTen MAsh MBlu MBri MGos NHol NPCo NWea SCoo SLim SPer SPoG SSta WDin WEve WFar
	- 'Mops Midget'	CMen ECho MAsh MBri NPCo WEve
	- 'Mops Snezna' **new**	NLar
	- var. ***mughus***	see *P. mugo* subsp. *mugo*
§	- subsp. ***mugo***	EMac GAuc IFFs NWea WCFE WFar
	- 'Mumpitz'	CKen
	- 'Northern Lights' **new**	CKen
	- 'Ophir'	CBcs CDul CKen CMen ECho EHul EPfP EPla GKir LAst LRHS MBri MGos NLar SCoo SLim SPer SSta WDin WEve WFar
	- 'Pal Maleter' (v)	ECho GKir LRHS MAsh NLar NPCo SCoo SLim SPoG
	- 'Paradekissen'	NPCo
	- 'Paul's Dwarf'	CKen
	- 'Picobello'	LRHS MAsh NLar SLim
	- 'Piggelmee'	CKen NLar
	- Pumilio Group Υ^{H4}	CDoC CDul CLnd ECho EHul IFFs MGos MMuc NHol NWea SBfd SCoo STre WBVN WCFE WDin WFar WMoo
	- 'Pygmy'	ECho
	- var. ***rostrata***	see *P. mugo* subsp. *uncinata*
	- 'Rushmore'	CKen
	- 'Spaan'	CKen
	- 'Sunshine' (v)	CKen NLar
	- 'Suzi'	CKen
	- 'Trompenburg'	NPCo
	- 'Tuffet'	ECho MGos NLar
	- 'Uelzen'	CKen NLar
§	- subsp. ***uncinata***	GAuc LMaj NWea SLim WFar
	- - 'Grüne Welle'	CKen ECho NLar SLim
	- - 'Paradekissen'	CKen NLar
	- 'Varella'	CKen IVic LRHS NLar SCoo SLim
	- 'White Tip'	CKen ECho
	- 'Winter Gold'	CKen ECho EHul EPfP EPla LAst MGos NLar NPCo NWea SSta WEve WFar
	- 'Winter Sun'	ECho NLar
	- 'Winzig'	CKen
	- 'Zundert'	CKen ECho GKir MGos NLar WEve
	- 'Zwergkugel'	CKen
	muricata Υ^{H4}	CDoC CDul CLnd GKir MGos NWea
	nigra Υ^{H4}	CBcs CDul CLnd CMac CTri ECrN GKir LMaj LRHS MGos SBfd SCoo WBrE WDin WEve WMou
	- var. ***austriaca***	see *P. nigra* subsp. *nigra*
	- 'Bambino'	CKen
	- 'Black Prince'	CKen ECho GKir LRHS MGos NLar NPCo SCoo SLim SPoG WEve WFar WGor
	- var. ***calabrica***	see *P. nigra* subsp. *laricio*
	- var. ***caramanica***	see *P. nigra* subsp. *pallasiana*
N	- 'Cebennensis Nana'	CKen
	- var. ***corsicana***	see *P. nigra* subsp. *laricio*
*	- 'Fastigiata'	GKir NPCo

	- 'Frank'	CKen ECho NLar SLim
	- 'Globosa'	ECho
	- 'Green Tower'	NLar
	- 'Hornibrookiana'	CKen ECho NLar
	- 'Komet'	IVic NLar SCoo SLim
§	- subsp. ***laricio*** Υ^{H4}	CCVT CDoC CDul CKen CMac ECrN EMac IFFs LAst LRHS MGos MMuc NWea SEND
	- - 'Aurea'	MBlu
	- - 'Bobby McGregor'	CKen ECho GKir
	- - 'Globosa Viridis'	ECho GKir LRHS NEgg NPCo
	- - 'Goldfingers'	CKen ECho NLar
	- - 'Moseri'	CKen ECho SSta
	- - 'Pygmaea'	CKen ECho WFar
	- - 'Spingarn'	CKen ECho
	- - 'Talland Bay'	CKen ECho
	- - 'Wurstle'	CKen
	- subsp. ***maritima***	see *P. nigra* subsp. *laricio*
	- 'Molette'	GKir
	- 'Nana'	ECrN MBri NLar
§	- subsp. ***nigra***	CCVT CDoC CLnd CTho ECrN GKir IFFs LBuc MGos MMuc NLar NWea SBfd SEND WFar
	- - 'Birte'	CKen
	- - 'Bright Eyes'	ECho GKir NLar SCoo SLim SPoG WEve
	- - 'Helga'	CKen NLar SCoo
	- - 'Schovenhorst'	CKen ECho
	- - 'Skyborn'	CKen
	- - 'Strypemonde'	CKen NPCo
	- - 'Yaffle Hill'	CKen ECho NLar
	- 'Obelisk'	CKen NLar SCoo
§	- subsp. ***pallasiana***	CDul
	- - 'Pyramidalis' **new**	NLar
	- 'Pierrick Bregeon' PBR	LRHS
	- 'Richard'	CKen NLar
	- 'Rondello'	NLar
	- 'Spielberg'	NLar
	palustris	CDoC CDul CLnd MAsh SBig SKHP
	parviflora	CDul CTri GGar GKir SPlb WDin WThu
	- 'Aaba-jo' **new**	CKen
	- 'Adcock's Dwarf' Υ^{H4}	CDoC CKen ECho GKir LRHS MGos NLar NPCo SCoo SLim SPoG WEve
	- Aizu-goyo Group	ECho
	- 'Al Fordham'	CKen
	- 'Aoi'	CKen CMen
	- 'Ara-kawa'	CKen CMen
	- 'Atco-goyo'	CKen
	- Azuma-goyo Group	CKen CMen
I	- 'Baasch's Form'	CKen MGos NLar
	- 'Bergman'	CDoC MAsh NLar
	- 'Blauer Engel'	CDoC ECho MBlu MGos NLar
	- 'Blue Giant'	ECho EPla LTen MBri NLar
	- 'Blue Lou' **new**	NLar
	- 'Bonnie Bergman'	CDoC CKen ECho GKir NLar WEve
	- 'Brevifolia'	NLar
	- 'Chikusa Goten'	NLar
	- 'Dai-ho'	CKen
	- 'Daisetsusan'	CKen
	- 'Doctor Landis Gold'	CKen ECho
	- 'Dougal'	CKen
	- 'Fukai' (v)	CKen MAsh MGos NHol NLar
	- 'Fukiju'	CKen
	- Fukushima-goyo Group	CKen CMen
	- 'Fuku-zu-mi'	CKen ECho IVic WEve
	- 'Fu-shiro'	CKen
	- 'Gimborn's Ideal'	NLar
	- 'Gin-sho-chuba'	CKen
	- Glauca Group	ECho EHul MBlu MBri MGos NPCo NPal SKHP WEve WFar

I	– 'Glauca Nana'	CKen
	– 'Goldilocks'	CKen ECho GKir NLar
	– 'Green Wave'	CKen
	– 'Gyok-ke-sen'	CKen
	– 'Gyo-ko-haku'	CKen
	– 'Gyokuei'	CKen
	– 'Gyokusen Sämling'	CKen NLar
	– 'Gyo-ku-sui'	CKen CMen ECho
	– 'H2'	CKen
	– 'Hagaromo Seedling'	CKen CMen ECho MAsh NLar
	– 'Hakko'	CKen MGos
	– 'Hatchichi'	CKen
	– 'Hatsumari'	NHol NLar
	– 'Hatsumi'	NHol
	– 'Ibo-can'	CKen CMen
	– 'Ichi-no-se'	CKen
	– 'Iri-fune'	CKen
	– Ishizuchi-goyo Group	CKen
	– 'Ka-ho'	CKen ECho
	– 'Kanrico'	CKen
	– 'Kanzan'	CKen
	– 'Kin-po' **new**	NLar
	– 'Kiyomatsu'	CKen NLar
	– 'Kobe'	CKen ECho NLar WEve
	– 'Kokonoe'	CKen CMen
	– 'Kokuho'	CKen NLar
	– 'Koraku'	CKen
	– 'Kusu-dama'	CKen
	– 'Meiko'	CKen CMen ECho
	– 'Michinoku'	CKen
	– 'Momo-yama'	CKen
	– 'Myo-jo'	CKen
	– Nasu-goyo Group	CKen
	– 'Negishi'	CDoC CKen CMen GKir LRHS MAsh NLar SCoo SLim WEve
	– 'Nellie D.'	NLar
	– 'Ogon-janome'	CKen LRHS SLim SPoG
	– 'Ossorio Dwarf'	CKen
	– var. ***pentaphylla***	IVic
	– 'Regenhold'	CKen
	– 'Richard Lee'	CKen
	– 'Ryo-ku-ho'	CKen
	– 'Ryu-ju'	CKen NLar
	– 'Sa-dai-jin'	CKen
	– 'San-bo'	CKen ECho MGos
§	– 'Saphir'	CKen ECho
	– 'Schoon's Bonsai'	CDoC NLar
	– 'Setsugekka'	CKen NLar
	– 'Shika-shima'	CKen
	– 'Shimada'	CKen
	– Shiobara-goyo Group	CKen
	– 'Shirobana'	NLar
	– 'Shizukagoten'	CKen MBri
	– 'Shu-re'	CKen
	– 'Sieryoden'	CKen
	– 'Smout'	CKen
	– 'Tani-mano-uki'	CKen
	– 'Tempelhof'	GKir LMaj MAsh NHol NLar NPCo
	– 'Tenysu-kazu'	CKen
	– 'Tokyo Dwarf'	CKen
	– 'Tribune'	NLar
	– 'Walker's Dwarf'	CKen
	– 'Watnong'	CKen
	– 'Zelkova'	CMen ECho
	– 'Zui-sho'	CKen
	patula ♀H2-3	CBcs CCCN CDoC CDul CLnd CMCN EPfP GKir IDee LAst LRHS NWea SAPC SArc SBfd SBig SCoo SLim SMad SPlb SPoG WEve WPGP
	peuce	GAuc GKir GLin NLar
	– 'Arnold Dwarf'	CKen
	– 'Cesarini'	CKen
	– 'Thessaloniki Broom'	CKen
	pinaster ♀H4	CBcs CDoC CDul CLnd GKir IFFs MMuc SEND
	pinea ♀H4	CAgr CArn CCVT CDoC CDul CKen CLnd CTho ELau EPfP IDee IFFs IVic LEdu LHop LMaj LRHS MGos MMuc NPri SAPC SArc SBfd SCoo SEND SLim WEve WPGP
	– 'Queensway'	CKen
	ponderosa ♀H4	CDul CLnd GAuc GKir NWea WEve
	– var. ***scopulorum***	NWea
	pumila	CDul
	– 'Buchanan'	CKen ECho
	– 'Draijer's Dwarf'	ECho GKir LRHS SCoo SLim WEve
	– 'Dwarf Blue'	ECho MAsh NLar
	– 'Glauca' ♀H4	CKen NLar
	– 'Globe'	ECho MBri NLar SLim
	– 'Jeddeloh'	CKen
	– 'Knightshayes'	CKen
	– 'Pinocchio' **new**	CKen
	– 'Säntis'	CKen ECho
	– 'Saphir'	see *P. parviflora* 'Saphir'
	radiata ♀H3-4	CBcs CCVT CDoC CDul CLnd CMac CTrC CTri ECrN ELan GKir IFFs LRHS MMuc NWea SAPC SArc SBfd SCoo SEND SPer STre WDin WEve WFar
	– Aurea Group	CDoC CDul CKen ECho GKir LRHS MAsh MGos NEgg NPCo SCoo SLim SPoG WBor WEve WFar
	– 'Bodnant'	CKen
	– 'Isca'	CKen ECho
	– 'Marshwood' (v)	CKen ECho SLim
	resinosa 'Don Smith'	CKen
	– 'Joel's Broom'	CKen
	– 'Nana'	NLar
	– 'Quinobequin'	CKen
	rigida	CMac
	roxburghii	WPGP
	sabineana	GAuc
	× ***schwerinii***	CDoC CKen ECho MBri
	– 'Wiethorst'	CKen IDee LRHS MBri NLar SLim SPoG
	sibirica	GKir
	– 'Blue Smoke'	CKen
	– 'Mariko'	CKen
	strobiformis 'Coronado'	CKen
	– 'Loma Linda'	CKen
	strobus	CAlb CBcs CDul CLnd CMen GKir IFFs MGos MMuc NWea SEND SLim WDin WEve WFar
§	– 'Alba'	MGos SLim
	– 'Amelia's Dwarf'	CKen
	– 'Anna Fiele'	CKen
	– 'Bergman's Mini'	CKen NLar
	– 'Bergman's Pendula Broom'	CKen
I	– 'Bergman's Sport of Prostrata'	CKen
	– 'Beth' **new**	CKen
	– 'Bloomer's Dark Globe'	CKen
	– 'Blue Shag'	ECho GKir LRHS MGos NLar SCoo SLim SPer SPoG
	– 'Brevifolia' **new**	CKen
	– 'Cesarini'	CKen
	– 'Compacta'	NPCo
	– 'Densa'	CKen ECho MAsh
	– 'Dove's Dwarf'	CKen
	– 'Ed's Broom'	CKen
	– 'Elkins Dwarf'	CKen NHol
	– 'Fastigiata'	CKen ECho MBri
	– 'Golden Showers'	NLar

	- 'Green Curls'	CKen
	- 'Green Twist'	MAsh NLar
	- 'Greg'	CKen ECho
	- 'Hershey'	CKen
	- 'Hillside Gem'	CKen
	- 'Himmelblau'	IDee MBlu MBri NLar SLim
	- 'Horsford'	CKen ECho LRHS NLar SLim
	- 'Jericho'	CKen NLar
	- 'Julian Pott'	CKen
	- 'Julian's Dwarf'	CKen
	- 'Krügers Lilliput'	GKir LRHS NHol NLar SLim
	- 'Louie'	CKen LRHS MAsh NLar SLim
	- 'Macopin'	ECho EMil NLar SCoo
	- 'Mary Butler'	CKen NLar
	- 'Merrimack'	CKen ECho NLar
	- 'Minima'	CDul CKen ECho LRHS MAsh MBlu MBri MGos NLar NPCo NWea SCoo SLim SPoG WGor
	- 'Minuta'	CKen
§	- Nana Group	MGos NPri WEve
	- 'Nana'	see *P. strobus* Nana Group
	- 'Nana Compacta'	LRHS
	- 'Nivea'	see *P. strobus* 'Alba'
	- 'Northway Broom'	CKen ECho LRHS SLim
	- 'Pendula'	CKen SMad
I	- 'Pendula Broom'	CKen
	- 'Radiata'	CTri EHul LRHS NLar
	- 'Reinshaus'	CKen ECho
	- 'Sayville'	CKen
	- 'Sea Urchin'	CKen ECho SLim SPoG
	- 'Secrest'	NLar
	- 'Stowe Pillar' **new**	NLar SLim
	- 'Tiny Kurls'	NLar SLim
I	- 'Tortuosa'	NLar
	- 'Torulosa'	MBlu
	- 'Uncatena'	CKen
	- 'Verkade's Broom'	CKen
	- 'Wendy'	NLar
	sylvestris ♀H4	Widely available
	- 'Abergeldie'	CKen
	- 'Alderly Edge'	CMen WEve WFar
	- 'Andorra'	CKen MGos
§	- 'Argentea'	CMen ECho SLim
§	- Aurea Group ♀H4	CDul CKen CMac CMen ECho EHul EMil EPfP GKir LRHS MAsh MBlu MBri NEgg NHol NLar NPCo NPri NWea SCoo SLim SPer SPoG SSta WBVN WEve WFar
	- 'Aurea'	see *P. sylvestris* Aurea Group
	- 'Avondene'	CKen ECho
	- 'Bergfield'	CMen ECho NLar
	- 'Beuvronensis' ♀H4	CMen ECho GKir LRHS MGos NEgg NHol NLar NPCo SCoo SLim WEve
	- 'Blue Sky'	NLar SLim
	- 'Bonna'	CLnd GKir LRHS SCoo SLim
	- 'Brevifolia'	MGos
	- 'Buchanan's Gold'	CKen
	- 'Burghfield'	CKen CMen ECho WFar
	- 'Chantry Blue'	CMen ECho EHul GKir LAst LRHS MAsh MBri MGos NEgg NHol NLar NPCo SCoo SLim WEve WFar
	- 'Clumber Blue'	CKen
	- 'Compressa'	SLim
	- 'Corley'	ECho
	- 'Dereham'	CKen ECho
	- 'Doone Valley'	CKen ECho GKir MGos NEgg NPCo SCoo WEve WFar
	- 'Edwin Hillier'	see *P. sylvestris* 'Argentea'
	- Fastigiata Group	CDoC CDul CEnd CKen CMac CMen ECho GKir IDee LRHS MAsh MGos NPCo SCoo SLim SPoG WCFE WEve WFar
	- 'Frensham'	CKen ECho EPla MAsh MGos NHol NLar NPCo SCoo WEve WFar
	- 'Globosa'	ECho GKir NPCo
	- 'Gold Coin'	CDoC CDul CKen CMen ECho EPfP GKir LRHS MAsh MGos NEgg NHol NLar NPCo SCoo SLim SPoG WEve WFar
	- 'Gold Medal'	CKen ECho GKir SLim WEve WFar
	- 'Grand Rapids'	CKen
	- 'Gwydyr Castle'	CKen
	- 'Helsey Dwarf' **new**	NLar
	- 'Hillside Creeper'	CKen ECho GKir LRHS NLar SCoo SLim SPoG WEve
	- 'Humble Pie'	CKen
	- 'Inverleith' (v)	ECho EHul GKir MGos SCoo SLim SPoG WEve WFar
	- 'Jeremy'	CKen ECho GKir NEgg NHol NPCo SCoo SLim SPoG WEve
	- 'John Boy'	CMen ECho NLar
	- 'Kelpie'	ECho GKir LRHS SCoo
	- 'Kenwith'	CKen ECho
	- 'Kosice' **new**	NLar
	- 'Lakeside Dwarf'	CMen ECho
	- 'Lodge Hill'	CMen ECho GKir LRHS MAsh NPCo SCoo SLim WEve
	- 'Longmoor'	CKen ECho MGos NLar
	- 'Martham'	CKen CMen ECho WEve
	- 'Mitsch Weeping'	CKen
*	- 'Moseri'	ECho GKir MAsh NPCo
	- 'Mount Vernon Blue'	NLar
	- 'Munches Blue'	CKen
	- 'Nana' misapplied	see *P. sylvestris* 'Watereri'
	- 'Nana Compacta'	CMen
§	- 'Nisbet's Gem'	CKen CMen ECho
	- 'Padworth'	CMen MGos NLar
	- 'Peve Heiheks'	NLar
	- 'Peve Miba'	NLar
I	- 'Pine Glen'	CKen
	- 'Piskowitz'	CKen
	- 'Pixie'	CKen ECho MGos NLar
I	- 'Prostrata'	NPCo SCoo
	- 'Pulham'	ECho
	- 'Pygmaea'	SCoo SLim
	- 'Reedham'	ECho
	- 'Repens'	CKen
	- 'Saint George'	CKen
	- 'Sandringham'	ECho
	- 'Saxatilis'	CKen CMen ECho GKir MAsh WEve
	- subsp. ***scotica***	GQue NWea
	- 'Scott's Dwarf'	see *P. sylvestris* 'Nisbet's Gem'
	- 'Scrubby'	ECho NLar
	- 'Sentinel'	CKen ECho SLim
	- 'Skjak I'	CKen NLar
	- 'Skjak II'	CKen ECho LRHS SCoo
	- 'Skogbygdi'	NLar
	- 'Slimkin'	CKen
	- 'Spaan's Slow Column'	CKen ECho GKir LRHS SCoo SLim
	- 'Tabuliformis'	ECho
	- 'Tage'	CKen ECho
	- 'Tanya'	CKen
	- 'Tilhead'	CKen ECho
	- 'Treasure'	CKen ECho
	- 'Trefrew Quarry'	CKen
	- 'Troll Guld' **new**	SLim
	- 'Variegata' (v)	MGos
§	- 'Watereri'	ECho EHul GKir LAst LRHS LTen MAsh MBri MGos NHol NLar NPri SCoo SLim SPer WDin WFar
	- 'Westonbirt'	CKen CMen ECho EHul NLar WEve
	- 'Wishmoor'	ECho

	- 'Wolf Gold'	CKen ECho
	- 'Xawrey 1'	NLar
*	- 'Yaff Hill'	ECho GKir
	tabuliformis	CDul CMCN NMun STre
	taeda	NWea WPGP
	taiwanensis	CDul
	thunbergii	CDul CLnd CMCN CMen ELan GAuc GKir IDee IFFs MGos MMuc NWea SEND STre
	- 'Akame'	CKen CMen
	- 'Akame Yatsabusa'	CMen
	- 'Aocha-matsu' (v)	CKen CMen NLar
	- 'Arakawa-sho'	CKen CMen
	- 'Banshosho'	CKen CMen ECho GKir LRHS MGos NLar SLim WEve
	- 'Beni-kujaku'	CKen CMen
	- 'Compacta'	CKen CMen
	- var. ***corticosa*** 'Fuji'	CMen
	- - 'Iihara'	CMen
	- 'Dainagon'	CKen CMen
	- 'Eechee-nee'	CKen
	- 'Hayabusa'	CMen
	- 'Iwai'	CMen
	- 'Janome'	CMen
	- 'Katsuga'	CMen
	- 'Kotobuki'	CKen CMen GKir NLar NPCo WEve WFar
	- 'Koyosho'	CMen
	- 'Kujaku'	CKen CMen
	- 'Kyokko'	CKen CMen
	- 'Kyushu'	CKen CMen
	- 'Maijima'	NLar
	- 'Mikawa'	CMen
	- 'Miyajuna'	CKen CMen
	- 'Nishiki-ne'	CKen CMen
	- 'Nishiki-tsusaka'	CMen ECho
	- 'Oculus-draconis' (v)	CMen ECho NPCo
	- 'Ogon'	CKen CMen GKir LRHS NLar SLim
	- 'Porky'	CKen CMen
§	- 'Sayonara'	CMen ECho GKir LRHS MAsh MBri NLar SCoo SLim SPoG
	- 'Senryu'	CKen CMen
	- 'Shinsho'	CKen CMen
	- 'Shio-guro'	CKen CMen MAsh
	- 'Suchiro'	NEgg NPCo
	- 'Suchiro Yatabusa'	CKen CMen ECho
	- 'Sunsho'	CKen CMen ECho
	- 'Taihei'	CKen CMen
I	- 'Thunderhead'	CDoC CKen CMen GKir LRHS MAsh NLar SLim
	- 'W.B.' **new**	CKen
	- 'Yatsubusa'	see *P. thunbergii* 'Sayonara'
	- 'Ye-i-kan'	CKen
	- 'Yoshimura'	CMen
	- 'Yumaki'	CKen CMen ECho MGos SCoo
	torreyana	GAuc
	uncinata	see *P. mugo* subsp. *uncinata*
	- 'Etschtal'	CKen
	- 'Hexe'	NHol
	- 'Hnizdo'	NHol
	- 'Jezek'	CKen SLim
	- 'Kostelnicek'	NLar
	- 'Leuco-like'	CKen
	- 'Litomysl'	NLar
	- 'Offenpass'	CKen
	- 'Susse Perle'	CKen
	virginiana	GAuc
	- 'Wate's Golden'	CKen NLar
§	***wallichiana*** ♀H4	Widely available
	- 'Densa'	NLar SLim
	- 'Densa Hill'	LRHS
	- 'Frosty' **new**	CKen
	- 'Nana'	CKen LRHS NLar SCoo SLim SPoG WEve
	- 'Umbraculifera'	MBri
	- 'Zebrina' (v)	MAsh MBlu MGos NLar
	yunnanensis	CDoC WBor

Piper (*Piperaceae*)

auritum	GPoy
excelsum	see *Macropiper excelsum*

Piptanthus (*Papilionaceae*)

	forrestii	see *P. nepalensis*
	laburnifolius	see *P. nepalensis*
§	***nepalensis***	CBcs CBot CDul CSpe CWit EBee ELan EPau EPfP GGar GKir LHop LRHS MGos MMuc MSCN NBid NLar SEND SGar SMad SOWG SPer SPoG SRms WBVN
	tomentosus	MMHG WPGP

Pistacia (*Anacardiaceae*)

chinensis	EBtc EPfP IArd
lentiscus	CArn CBcs ERom EUJe MGos SEND

Pistia (*Araceae*)

stratiotes	CBen LPBA MSKA NPer SCoo

Pitcairnia (*Bromeliaceae*)

bergii	CHll
heterophylla	WCot

Pithecellobium (*Mimosaceae*)

flexicaule **new**	EGFP

Pittosporum ✿ (*Pittosporaceae*)

	anomalum	ECou SOWG
	- (f)	ECou
	- (m)	ECou
	- 'Falcon'	ECou
	- 'Raven' (f)	ECou
	- 'Starling' (m)	ECou
*	***argyrophyllum***	LRHS LTen
	'Arundel Green'	CDoC CWSG EBee EJRN EPfP LFCN LRHS LSRN MAsh SBfd SLim SRms SWvt
	bicolor	CTsd ECou GGal GQui WPGP
	- 'Cradle' (f)	ECou
	- 'Mount Field' (f)	ECou
	buchananii	SGar
	colensoi	ECou
	- 'Cobb' (f)	ECou
	- 'Wanaka' (m)	ECou
	'Collaig Silver'	LRHS MAsh SBfd SPoG
	crassifolium	CBcs CCCN CHEx CHGN CTrC ECou LRHS WBrE WPGP
	- 'Havering Dwarf' (f)	ECou
	- 'Napier' (f)	ECou
	- 'Variegatum' (v)	CCCN WPat
	'Crinkles' (f)	ECou
	daphniphylloides	ELan
	- B&SWJ 6789	WCru
	- RWJ 9913	WCru
	'Dark Delight' (m)	ECou
	divaricatum	ECou
	'Emerald Lake'	MGos
	'Essex' (f/v)	ECou EJRN
	eugenioides	CHEx GGar
	- 'Mini Green'	CAlb SBfd WBrE
	- 'Platinum' (v)	CBcs CCCN LRHS MGos
	- 'Variegatum' (v) ♀H3	CAlb CBty CCCN CDoC CDul CHEx CWit EBee EHoe EJRN EPfP EWTr GGar GQui IArd LRHS MBri

	MGos MMuc MREP SBfd SEND SKHP SLim SPer SPoG WGob WPGP WSHC
'Garnettii' (v) ♀H3	Widely available
heterophyllum	ECou ECrN ELan EWes SEND
- variegated (v)	EBtc ECou LRHS MAsh SEND WSHC
'Holbrook' (v)	CSam
'Humpty Dumpty'	ECou EJRN
illicioides	WCru
var. ***angustifolium*** B&SWJ 6771	
- - RWJ 9846	WCru
- var. ***illicioides*** B&SWJ 6712	WCru
× ***intermedium***	CWib ECou SWvt
- 'Craxten' (f)	CCCN ECou EJRN LRHS
lineare	ECou
michiei	ECou
- (f)	ECou
- (m)	ECou
- 'Jack' (m)	ECou
- 'Jill' (f)	ECou
'Nanum Variegatum'	see *P. tobira* 'Variegatum'
obcordatum	ECou
- var. ***kaitaiaense***	ECou
'Oliver Twist'	LRHS LSRN SBfd SCoo SMad
omeiense	ECou EWes GKir SKHP
'Peter Pan'	EJRN
pimeleoides	ECou
var. ***reflexum*** (m)	
'Purple Princess'	EJRN
ralphii	CCCN CTsd CWit EBee ECou WBVN WPGP
- 'Green Globe'	ECou SKHP
- 'Variegatum' (v)	CCCN CGHE EPla LRHS SEND SKHP SSpi WPGP
ralphii × ***tenuifolium***	ECou
'Saundersii' (v)	EQua SCoo SEND
'Tadina Gold'	GKev SEND
tenuifolium ♀H3	Widely available
- 'Abbotsbury Gold' (f/v)	CAbb CAlb CBty CCCN CDoC CMac CTri CWit EBee ECou EHoe ELan EWTr EWes LFCN LRHS MGos MMuc MREP MSwo SBfd SEND SLim SPer WGob WSHC
- 'Atropurpureum'	ELan
- 'County Park'	CCCN EUJe LRHS WFar
- 'County Park Dwarf'	CBty ECou EJRN EQua MAsh
- 'County Park Green'	ELon
- 'Deborah' (v)	ECou EJRN LSou
- 'Dixie'	ECou
§ - 'Eila Keightley' (v)	CMHG EJRN
- 'Elizabeth' (m/v)	CAbP CBcs CDoC CMac CTrC CWit EBee ECou EHoe EJRN EPfP EUJe IArd LAst LFCN LRHS LSRN MAsh MBri MGos MMuc MREP NMun SBfd SEND SLim WClo WGob
- 'French Lace'	CAlb CBcs CCCN CWSG EBee ECou EJRN ELan GBin LRHS MREP NHol NLar SBfd SEND WFar
- 'Gold Edge'	LRHS
- 'Gold Star'	CAlb CChe CDoC ECou EGxp ELan EPfP LRHS MAsh MGos NHol SBfd SCoo SLim SPer SPoG WFar WGob WMoo
- 'Golden Cut'	NLar
- 'Golden King'	CAlb CCCN CDoC CMHG CMac CSBt EBee EJRN EPfP LRHS LSou MAsh NEgg NPla SBfd SLim SRms
- 'Golden Princess' (f)	ECou EJRN
- 'Golf Ball' PBR	CBcs CDoC CTrC EUJe GBin
- 'Green Elf'	ECou EJRN
- 'Green Thumb'	CMac EBee ELan
- 'Irene Paterson' (m/v) ♀H3	Widely available
- 'James Stirling'	CCCN ECou EPfP
- 'John Flanagan'	see *P. tenuifolium* 'Margaret Turnbull'
- 'Limelight' (v)	CBcs CSBt CSPN CWGN CWSG EBtc LHop LRHS LSRN MGos MREP NHol SLim SPoG
- 'Loxhill Gold'	CAbP CCCN EBee EUJe IArd LRHS LSou MGos NPla SEND
§ - 'Margaret Turnbull' (v)	CBcs CTrC CWit ECou EJRN ELan EWes LRHS LSRN MBri MGos SEND
- 'Marjory Channon' (v)	CBty EBee ELan EPfP LRHS LSRN
- 'Mellow Yellow'	CAbP
- 'Moonlight' (v)	CAlb CBcs CTrC EBee LRHS WDin
- 'Mountain Green'	CMac MGos SBfd
- 'Nutty's Leprechaun'	CCCN EBee ELan
- 'Pompom'	CCCN EBee IVic LRHS SRms
- 'Purpureum' (m)	Widely available
- 'Silver Magic' (v)	CBcs CChe CSBt EBee EJRN EPfP LRHS MGos SBfd WGob
- 'Silver Princess' (f)	ECou EJRN
- 'Silver Queen' (f/v) ♀H3	Widely available
- 'Silver Sheen' (m)	CBcs EBee ECou LFCN LRHS MGos SBfd
- 'Stevens Island'	CBcs CTrC CWit EBee LRHS MGos
- 'Stirling Gold' (f/v)	ECou EPfP EWes
- 'Sunburst'	see *P. tenuifolium* 'Eila Keightley'
- 'Tandara Gold' (v)	CAlb CBcs CBty CCCN CDoC CDul CSBt CTrC EBee ECou EHoe EJRN ELan ELon EPfP LBMP LFCN LRHS LSRN MAsh MGos MMuc SBfd SLim SPoG WBrE WCot WFar WGob
- 'Tiki' (m)	CBcs CCCN CTrC EBee ECou LRHS
- 'Tom Thumb' ♀H3	Widely available
- 'Tresederi' (f/m)	CCCN CTrC CTsd EBee ECou WFar
- 'Variegatum' (m/v)	CAlb CBar CBcs CDoC CSBt EBee ECou EQua LAst LRHS LSRN MGos MSwo SAPC SLim SPer SPoG SWvt WGob
- 'Victoria' (v)	CBcs CCCN CDoC CTrC EBee LRHS LSRN MGos SLim SPoG WFar
- 'Warnham Gold' (m) ♀H3	CBty CDoC CMac CSBt CWib EBee ECou EJRN ELan EPfP IVic LAst LFCN LRHS MAsh MCCP MGos SBfd SLim SPer SPoG SSpi WClo WFar
- 'Wendle Channon' (m/v)	CAlb CBty CCCN CMac CSBt CWit EBee ECou EHoe EPfP EQua LRHS MAsh SLim SPer WGob WSHC
- 'Wrinkled Blue'	CBcs CTrC CWSG LFCN LRHS MAsh MRav SBfd SPoG
tobira ♀H3	Widely available
- B&SWJ 4362	WCru
* - 'Cuneatum'	CCCN CDoC CPLG CWGN EBee ELan EPfP LHop LRHS LSRN SAga SKHP
* - 'Nanum'	CAlb CBcs CCCN CDoC CMac EBee ECou ELan EPfP ERom ETod EUJe IFFs LRHS LTen MGos MWya SAPC SArc SBfd SEND SLim SOWG SPer SPoG WDin WFar
§ - 'Variegatum' (v) ♀H2-3	Widely available
truncatum	EWes
undulatum	CHEx ECou
viridiflorum	ECou EShb

Plagianthus (*Malvaceae*)

betulinus	see *P. regius*
divaricatus	CBcs CTrC ECou WPGP

lyallii see *Hoberia lyallii*
§ ***regius*** CBcs SBig

Plagiorhegma see *Jeffersonia*

Planera (*Ulmaceae*)
aquatica EGFP

Plantago (*Plantaginaceae*)
asiatica 'Ki Fu' (v) WBox
- 'Variegata' (v) NBro WBox
coronopus EBWF ELau
lanceolata EBWF NMir WHfH WSFF
- 'Golden Spears' CBre EBee
- 'Keer's Pride' (v) WCot
- 'Streaker' (v) WCot
major 'Atropurpurea' see *P. major* 'Rubrifolia'
- 'Bowles's Variety' see *P. major* 'Rosularis'
- 'Everywhere I Glow' new WAlt
- 'Frills' WBox
- 'Rosenstolz' CRow
§ - 'Rosularis' CArn CRow CSpe EBee ILis LEdu MBNS MHer MTho NBro NChi NPri SPav WBox WCom WHer
§ - 'Rubrifolia' CArn CHid CRow CSpe EBee EShb MBNS MHer NBid NBro NChi NLBP WBox WCom WHer WMoo
- 'Subtle Streak' (v) WAlt
- 'Tony Lewis' WAlt
maritima EBWF WHer
media EBWF MHer
psyllium L. CArn
rosea see *P. major* 'Rosularis'
sempervirens MTho
triandra 'Wanaka' IMou
uniflora Hook. f. WCom WCot

Platanthera (*Orchidaceae*)
chlorantha NLAp
hologlottis EFEx
metabifolia EFEx NLAp WWst

Platanus ✿ (*Platanaceae*)
× ***acerifolia*** see *P.* × *hispanica*
§ × ***hispanica*** 🏆^{H4} CBcs CCVT CDul CLnd CMCN CTho EBee ECrN EMac EPfP EWTr LAst LBuc LMaj MGos MMuc NWea SEND SPer WDin WFar WMou
- 'Pyramidalis' ECrN
- 'Suttneri' (v) WMou
mexicana F&M 065 WPGP
orientalis 🏆^{H4} CCVT CDul CLnd CMCN CTho EBee EPfP GKir LEdu NLar SLPl WDin
- 'Cuneata' ECrN IFFs
§ - f. ***digitata*** 🏆^{H4} CDoC CDul CLnd CMCN CTho EPfP GKir MBlu WFar
- 'Laciniata' see *P. orientalis* f. *digitata*
- 'Minaret' CDul
- 'Mirkovec' CDoC GKir MBri SMad SPer
racemosa new EGFP

Platycarya (*Juglandaceae*)
strobilacea CBcs CMCN NLar

Platycerium (*Polypodiaceae*)
alcicorne misapplied see *P. bifurcatum*
§ ***bifurcatum*** 🏆^{H1} CCCN MBri WRic XBlo
'Lemoinei' WRic

Platycladus (*Cupressaceae*)
§ ***orientalis*** CDoC CKen CMac CSBt CWib
'Aurea Nana' 🏆^{H4} ECho EHul EPfP GKir LBee LRHS MAsh MBri MGos NHol NWea SLim SPoG WCFE WDin WEas WEve WFar
- 'Autumn Glow' CKen MAsh SCoo WGor
- 'Beverleyensis' NLar WEve
- 'Caribbean Holiday' MAsh
- 'Collen's Gold' EHul
- 'Conspicua' CKen CSBt CWib ECho EHul
- 'Elegantissima' 🏆^{H4} ECho EHul LRHS
- 'Franky Boy' CDoC LRHS MGos NHol NLar SLim SPoG
- 'Golden Pygmy' CKen MAsh
- 'Juniperoides' EHul NHol
- 'Kenwith' CKen
- 'Lemon 'n' Lime' WEve
- 'Magnifica' EHul
- 'Meldensis' CDoC CTri EHul
- 'Minima' EHul WGor
- 'Minima Glauca' CKen
- 'Morgan' NLar
- 'Purple King' SCoo
I - 'Pyramidalis Aurea' LBee LRHS NHol SCoo WEve
- 'Raffles' NHol
- 'Rosedalis' CKen CSBt ECho EHul EPfP IFFs LBee LRHS MAsh SCoo
- 'Sanderi' WCFE
- 'Shirley Chilcott' LBee MAsh
- 'Sieboldii' EHul
- 'Southport' LBee LRHS MAsh
- 'Summer Cream' CKen EHul
- 'Westmont' (v) CKen NLar

Platycodon ✿ (*Campanulaceae*)
grandiflorus 🏆^{H4} CArn CMea CTri EBee ECha ELau EPfP GKev GKir LHop LRHS MHer SRms WHoo
- 'Albus' CMac EBee ECho EPfP LRHS SPer SWvt WHoo WPer
- Apoyama Group 🏆^{H4} ECho GKev NMen WHoo WPer
- - 'Fairy Snow' EBee ECho ELan EShb GGar LBMP NBre NPnk SMrm WEas WHoo WSHC
- (Astra Series) 'Astra Blue' CSpe ECho EPfP SPoG SRot WHoo
- - 'Astra Double Blue' (d) CSpe
- - 'Astra Pink' SPoG WHoo
- - 'Astra White' SPoG WHoo
- 'Blaue Glocke' NBre
- 'Blue Pearl' WHoo
- 'Blue Star'^{PBR} LRHS
- 'Florist Blue' SGSe
- 'Florist Rose' SGSe WOut
- 'Florist Snow' SGSe
- 'Fuji Blue' EBee ELon NLar SPad WHoo WWEG
- 'Fuji Pink' CPrp EAEE EBee ECho ELan ELon EPfP LAst LHop LRHS MRav NLar SMrm SPad SWvt WHoo WWEG
- 'Fuji White' EBee ECho ELan ELon LAst NLar SMrm WWEG
- 'Hakone' LAst MRav WHoo
- 'Hakone Blue' ECho NBre NLar SGSe SMrm
* - 'Hakone Double Blue' (d) EAEE EBee ELan MBNS SRms WCAu
- 'Hakone White' CPrp EBee ECho EPfP LAst MRav NLar NMen SGSe SMrm WHoo
- 'Mariesii' 🏆^{H4} CAby CDoy CSBt EAEE EBee ECho ECtt EPfP LAst NBir NEgg NMen SMrm SPer SPlb SRms SWvt WEas WHoo WPer WSHC WWEG WWlt
- Mother of Pearl see *P. grandiflorus* 'Perlmutterschale'
§ - 'Perlmutterschale' CPrp EAEE EBee ECho EPfP LBMP MRav WAul WHoo

- 'Pink Star'	LRHS
- pink-flowered	GKev
- ***pumilus***	GKev NChi NWCA WHoo
- ***roseus***	GKev
- 'Sentimental Blue'	CMac CWib EBee ECho GKev NLar SPet
- 'Shell Pink'	see *P. grandiflorus* 'Perlmutterschale'
- 'Zwerg'	ECho EShb LBMP NBre

Platycrater (*Hydrangeaceae*)

arguta	WCru
- B&SWJ 6266	WCru

Plectocephalus (*Asteraceae*)

varians	GCal

Plectranthus (*Lamiaceae*)

sp.	LAst
from Puerto Rico	CArn
ambiguus	EOHP
- 'Manguzuku'	EOHP
- 'Nico'	CSpe EOHP
- 'Umigoye'	EOHP
amboinicus	CArn EOHP NHor WJek
* - 'Variegatus' (v)	EOHP
- 'Well Sweep Wedgewood' (v)	EOHP
argentatus ♀H2	CDoC CMdw CPom CSev CSpe EOHP MCot MMuc SDix SEND SGar SMrs SRkn WKif WWlt
- 'Hill House' (v)	CHll CPne EOHP
australis misapplied	see *P. verticillatus*
barbatus 'Vicki'	CPne
behrii	see *P. fruticosus*
Blue Angel = 'Edelblau' (Cape Angels Series)	EOHP
caninus	NHor SPoG
ciliatus	CPne EOHP EShb SGar SRkn WWlt
- 'All Gold'	CPne
- 'Easy Gold'	EOHP
- 'Sasha' (v)	CCCN CDoC CHll ECtt EOHP EShb SPet
'Cloud Nine'	EOHP
coleoides 'Marginatus'	see *P. forsteri* 'Marginatus'
- 'Variegatus'	see *P. madagascariensis* 'Variegated Mintleaf'
Cuban oregano	EOHP
ecklonii	EOHP WDyG
- NJM 02.010	WPGP
- 'Medley Wood'	EOHP
ernstii	EOHP
excisus	CDes EOHP IMou
§ ***forsteri*** 'Marginatus'	EOHP EShb SGar
frederici	see *P. welwitschii*
'Frills'	EOHP
§ ***fruticosus***	CPne EOHP
- 'Behr's Pride'	EOHP
- 'James'	EOHP
hadiensis	EOHP
var. ***tomentosus*** 'Carnegie'	
- - 'Ernst'	EOHP
- - green-leaved	EOHP
- - 'Penge' (v)	EOHP
I - 'Variegata' (v)	CPne
- var. ***woodii***	EOHP
madagascariensis	CPne EOHP
- gold-leaved	EOHP
- 'Lothlorien' (v)	EOHP
§ - 'Variegated Mintleaf' (v) ♀H1	EOHP MNHC SPet SRms WJek
'Marble Ruffles'	EOHP EShb
menthol-scented, large-leaved	EOHP
menthol-scented, small-leaved	EOHP
mutabilis	EOHP
§ ***oertendahlii*** ♀H1	EBak EOHP
- silver-leaved	EOHP
- 'Uvongo'	CPne
ornatus	EOHP MCCP NHor NPla SWal
- 'Pee Off'	EOHP
- variegated (v)	EOHP NPla
prostratus	EOHP
purpuratus large-leaved	EOHP
- small-leaved	EOHP
rehmannii	EOHP
saccatus	GFai
- subsp. ***longitubus***	EOHP WCot
- subsp. ***pondoensis***	EOHP
'Silver Shield' **new**	WHrl
sinensis	LRHS
spicatus	EOHP
- 'Nelspruit'	EOHP
strigosus	EOHP
Swedish ivy	see *P. verticillatus*, *P. oertendahlii*
§ ***thyrsoideus***	ECre EOHP
§ ***verticillatus***	CPne EOHP
- 'Barberton'	EOHP
- 'Pink Surprise'	EOHP
Vick's plant	EOHP
§ ***welwitschii***	NHor
zatarhendii	EOHP
zuluensis	CArn CDoC CFee CMdw CPne CSpe EOHP EShb MCot SBch SRkn WBor WPen
- dark-leaved	EOHP
- 'Sky'	EOHP
- 'Symphony'	CFee

Pleioblastus (*Poaceae*)

§ ***argenteostriatus*** 'Okinadake' (v)	EBee EPla
§ - f. ***pumilus***	CDoC EHoe EPfP EPla GKir MBlu MMoz MMuc MWht SPlb WFar WJun
auricomus	see *P. viridistriatus*
- 'Vagans'	see *Sasaella ramosa*
§ ***chino***	EBee EPla
- f. ***angustifolius***	see *P. chino* 'Murakamianus'
- var. ***argenteostriatus***	see *P. argenteostriatus* 'Okinadake'
- f. ***aureostriatus*** (v)	EPla MGos MMoz
- f. ***elegantissimus***	CDoC CEnt CFir CGHE EPfP EPla MGos MMoz MMuc MWhi NLar NMoo SBig WJun WMoo WPGP WPnP
- var. ***hisauchii***	EPla WJun
- 'Kimmei'	EPla MMuc
§ - 'Murakamianus'	GBin
fortunei	see *P. variegatus* 'Fortunei'
* ***funghomii***	MMuc SEND
'Gauntlettii'	see *P. argenteostriatus* f. *pumilus*
glaber 'Albostriatus'	see *Sasaella masamuneana* 'Albostriata'
gramineus	EPla IArd
§ ***hindsii***	EPla GBin MMoz MMuc NMoo SEND
§ ***humilis***	ENBC GKir MWhi SEND
- var. ***pumilus***	see *P. argenteostriatus* f. *pumilus*
kongosanensis 'Aureostriatus' (v)	EPla
linearis	CAbb CBcs EAmu EPla LPal MMoz MWht NLar NMoo SBig WJun WMoo WPGP
longifimbriatus	see *Sinobambusa intermedia*

	oleosus	EPla
§	***pygmaeus***	CBcs CDoC CDul CSam CTri EBee EHoe EHul ELan ENBC EPla GKir LEdu MAvo MBrN MGos MMoz MMuc MWhi NBro NGdn NLar NWCA SPer SRms WFar WMoo
§	- 'Distichus'	CEnt EHul ENBC EPPr EPla MGos MMoz MMuc MWht NGdn NLar NMoo SEND WJun WMoo
§	- 'Mirrezuzume'	CPLG WFar
*	- var. ***pygmaeus*** 'Mini'	SEND WCot
§	***simonii***	EBee GBin LRHS MMoz MMuc MWht NLar SEND
	- 'Variegatus' (v)	EPla LRHS NGdn SPer WJun WPGP
§	***variegatus*** (v) ♀H4	CDoC CEnt CWSG EBee EHoe EHul ELan ELon ENBC EPfP EPla EShb LEdu LRHS MBrN MGos MWht NGdn NMoo SArc SBfd SDix SLim SPlb SWvt WDin WFar WJun WMoo XBlo
§	- 'Fortunei' (v)	EBee EPla MMuc MWhi SEND
	- 'Tsuboii' (v)	CAbb CChe CDTJ CDoC EBee EPPr EPla GQui LPal MAvo MBrN MBri MMoz MWhi MWht NLar NMoo WFar WJun WMoo WPGP WPnP
§	***viridistriatus*** ♀H4	Widely available
	- 'Chrysophyllus'	EPla MMoz
	- f. ***variegatus*** (v)	SAga SWvt WMoo
	yixingensis	EPla

Pleione ✿ (*Orchidaceae*)

	sp. **new**	NDav
	Adams gx	LYaf
	albiflora	CFwr
	Alishan gx 'Merlin'	LYaf
	- 'Mother's Day'	LYaf
	- 'Mount Fuji'	ECho LYaf
	Asama gx 'Red Grouse'	LYaf
	Askia gx	GEdr LYaf
	aurita	CFwr EPot LYaf
	Bandai-san gx	LYaf
	- 'Sand Grouse'	LYaf
	× ***barbarae***	EPot LYaf
	Barcena gx	EPot LYaf
	Berapi gx 'Purple Sandpiper'	LYaf
	Betty Arnold gx	LYaf
	Brigadoon gx	LYaf
	- 'Stonechat'	LYaf
	- 'Woodcock'	LYaf
	Britannia gx	LYaf
	- 'Doreen'	EPot LYaf
§	***bulbocodioides***	CFwr LYaf
§	- 'Yunnan'	EPot GEdr
	Captain Hook gx	EPot LYaf
	chunii	EFEx LAma LYaf
	Danan gx	LYaf
	Deriba gx	EPot LYaf
	Eastfield gx 'Purple Emperor' **new**	LYaf
	Eiger gx	LYaf
	- cream-flowered	LYaf
	El Pico gx 'Goldcrest'	EPot
	- 'Kestrel'	EPot
	- 'Pheasant'	EPot LYaf
	Erebus gx 'Redpoll'	LYaf
	formosana ♀H2	CFir ECho EFEx EPot GGar LAma LEdu WFar WPGP
	- Alba Group	CFwr ECho WFar
	- - 'Claire'	EPot LEdu LYaf
	- - 'Snow Bunting'	LEdu LYaf
	- 'Blush of Dawn'	ECho EPot LYaf
	- 'Chen'	ECho
	- 'Greenhill'	LYaf
	- 'Pitlochry'	LYaf
	- 'Polar Star' **new**	ECho
	- (Pricei Group) 'Oriental Grace'	LYaf
	- - 'Oriental Splendour'	GEdr LYaf
	- 'Red Spot'	ECho
	- 'Snow Cap'	ECho
	- 'Snow White'	LEdu LYaf
	forrestii	CFwr ECho EFEx EPot LAma
	Fuego gx	EPot
	Ganymede gx	LYaf
	Gerry Mundey gx 'Tinney's Firs'	LYaf
§	***grandiflora***	CFwr LYaf
	Harlequin gx 'Norman'	LYaf
	Hekla gx 'Locking Stumps' **new**	GEdr
	- 'Partridge'	LYaf
	hookeriana	CFwr WWst
	humilis	LYaf WWst
	Irazu gx 'Cheryl'	EPot
	Jorullo gx 'Long-tailed Tit'	LYaf
	Keith Rattray gx 'Kelty'	LYaf
	Kenya gx	LYaf
	- 'Bald Eagle'	LYaf
	Kilauea gx	LYaf
	Kohala gx	LYaf
	Krakatoa gx 'Wheatear'	LYaf
	Leda gx	LYaf
	limprichtii ♀H2	CFwr ECho EFEx EPot LYaf
	- mauve-flowered	ECho
	maculata	CFwr EFEx WWst
	Marion Johnson gx	LYaf
	Mauna Loa gx	LYaf
	- 'Glossy Starling' **new**	LYaf
	Mawenzi gx	LYaf
	Novarupta gx 'Raven'	LYaf
	Orizaba gx	LYaf
	- 'Fish Eagle'	LYaf
	Paricutin gx	LYaf
	pinkepankii	see *P. grandiflora*
	Piton gx	EPot LYaf
§	***pleionoides***	EPot LYaf
	pogonioides misapplied	see *P. pleionoides*
	pogonioides (Rolfe) Rolfe	see *P. bulbocodioides*
	praecox	CFwr WWst
	Quizapu gx 'Peregrine'	LYaf
	Rainier gx	LYaf
	Rakata gx 'Redwing'	LYaf
	- 'Rock Dove'	LYaf
	- 'Shot Silk'	LYaf
	- 'Skylark'	LYaf
	San Salvador gx	LYaf
	Sangay gx	LYaf
	Santorini gx	LYaf
	- 'Yellow Wagtail' **new**	LYaf
	saxicola	CFwr LYaf
	scopulorum	CFwr EFEx
	Shantung gx	CFir EPot LAma
	- 'Ducat'	LYaf
	- 'Gerry Mundey'	LYaf
	- 'Ridgeway'	EPot LYaf
	- 'Silver Anniversary'	LYaf
	Sharon Ann Winter gx **new**	LYaf
	Soufrière gx	LYaf
	speciosa Ames & Schltr.	see *P. pleionoides*
	Stromboli gx 'Fireball'	EPot
	Surtsey gx	EPot
	Taal gx 'Red-tailed Hawk'	LYaf
	× ***taliensis***	LYaf

Tarawera gx LYaf
Toff gx new LYaf
Tolima gx 'Moorhen' LEdu LYaf
Tongariro gx CPBP EPot
Ueli Wackernagel gx new GEdr
Versailles gx EPot
- 'Bucklebury' ♀H2 EPot LYaf
- 'Heron' LYaf
Vesuvius gx EPot
- 'Aphrodite' EPot
- 'Grey Wagtail' LYaf
- 'Leopard' LYaf
- 'Phoenix' EPot LYaf
- 'Tawny Owl' LYaf
Volcanello gx LYaf
'Honey Buzzard'
- 'Song Thrush' LYaf
Whakari gx LYaf
'Wharfedale Pine Warbler' LYaf
yunnanensis misapplied see *P. bulbocodioides* 'Yunnan'
yunnanensis ambig. LAma
yunnanensis (Rolfe) Rolfe LYaf
Zeus Weinstein gx LYaf

Pleomele see *Dracaena*

Pleurospermum (*Apiaceae*)

aff. ***album*** KWJ 12281 new WCru
aff. ***amabile*** BWJ 7886 WCru
benthamii B&SWJ 2988 WCru
calcareum B&SWJ 8008 WCru
yunnanense BWJ 7952A new WCru

plum see *Prunus domestica*

Plumbago (*Plumbaginaceae*)

§ ***auriculata*** ♀H1-2 CBcs CCCN CHEx CRHN CSBt CTri CWCL CWSG EBak EBee ELan EPfP EShb LRHS MMuc NPal SEND SMrm SOWG SPer SPoG SRms SVic
- f. ***alba*** ♀H1-2 CBcs CBot CHEx CRHN CSev EBak EBee EPfP ERea EShb SEND SOWG
* - ***aurea*** MRav
- 'Crystal Waters' CCCN ERea EShb
- dark blue-flowered CSpe
capensis see *P. auriculata*
§ ***indica*** ♀H1 CCCN EShb SOWG
- ***rosea*** see *P. indica*
larpentiae see *Ceratostigma plumbaginoides*

Plumeria (*Apocynaceae*)

sp. WSFF
rubra ♀H1 CCCN SOWG XBlo
- f. ***acutifolia*** SOWG

Pneumatopteris (*Thelypteridaceae*)

pennigera WRic

Poa (*Poaceae*)

alpina NGdn NLar
- var. ***nodosa*** SWal
chaixii EHoe EPPr EPla GFor NLar
cita GFor GMaP
colensoi CKno EBee EHoe EPPr GAbr MAvo
× ***jemtlandica*** EHoe EPPr
labillardierei CKno CWCL EBee EBrs ECha EHoe EPPr GGar LRHS MAvo MMuc NWsh SEND SPer SUsu WDyG WMoo WPrP
trivialis CRWN EBWF
I 'Variegata' (v) SApp

Podalyria (*Papilionaceae*)

calyptrata SPlb
sericea SPlb

Podistera (*Apiaceae*)

nevadensis CPBP

Podocarpus ✿ (*Podocarpaceae*)

acutifolius CBcs CDoC ECou GGar GKir STre
- (f) ECou
- (m) ECou
alpinus R. Br. ex Hook. f. NHol
andinus see *Prumnopitys andina*
'Autumn Shades' (m) ECou
'Blaze' (f) CBcs CDoC ECho ECou EMil LEdu LRHS MBrN NHol NLar SCoo SLim SPoG WFar
chilinus see *P. salignus*
'Chocolate Box' (f) ECho ECou SLim
'County Park Fire' PBR (f) CBcs CDoC CWSG ECho ECou EHul EMil EPfP IFFs LRHS MAsh MGos NEgg NHol NLar SCoo SLim SPoG SWvt WEve WFar WGor WSpi
'County Park Treasure' ECou
cunninghamii CBcs ECou
- 'Kiwi' (f) ECou MGos
- 'Roro' (m) CBcs CDoC ECou
cunninghamii × ***nivalis*** (f) ECou
dacrydioides see *Dacrycarpus dacrydioides*
elongatus CTrC IDee
- 'Blue Chip' CBcs
'Flame' CDoC ECho ECou EHul NLar NPCo SCoo
'Havering' (f) CDoC ECou MGos
henkelii CTrC EShb GGar
'Jill' (f) ECou
latifolius ECou EShb GCal
lawrencei EHul GGar WThu
lawrencei (f) ECou
- 'Alpine Lass' (f) ECou
- 'Blue Gem' (f) CDoC ECou EPla IArd IFFs LRHS MAsh MGos MMuc NHol SCoo SEND SLim WEve WFar
- 'Kiandra' ECou
- 'Kosciuszko' ECou
- 'Pine Lake' ECou
- 'Red Tip' CDoC EMil IFFs LRHS MAsh SCoo SLim STre WGor
'Lucky Lad' ECou
'Macho' (m) ECou
macrophyllus CHEx ERom SAPC SArc SMad STre WFar
- (m) ECou WFar
- 'Aureus' CBcs
'Maori Prince' (m) CDoC ECou MGos
nivalis CBcs CDul CMac CTrC ECou EPla GCal GGar GKir SCoo SRms STre
- 'Arthur' (m) ECou
- 'Bronze' CDoC ECou EPla MGos
- 'Christmas Lights' (f) CKen ECou
- 'Clarence' (m) ECou
- 'Cover Girl' LRHS SPoG
- 'Green Queen' (f) ECou
- 'Hikurangi' CDoC
- 'Jack's Pass' (m) ECho ECou WFar
- 'Kaweka' (m) ECou
- 'Kilworth Cream' (v) CBcs CDoC CMen ECho ECou EMil LRHS MAsh MGos NHol NLar SCoo SLim SWvt WGor

	- 'Little Lady' (f)	ECou
	- 'Livingstone' (f)	ECou
	- 'Lodestone' (m)	ECou
	- 'Moffat' (f)	CBcs CDoC ECou
	- 'Otari' (m)	CDoC ECho ECou NLar
	- 'Park Cover'	ECou
	- 'Princess' (f)	ECou MBrN
	- 'Ruapehu' (m)	CDoC ECou EPla
	- 'Trompenburg'	NLar
	nubigenus	CBcs
	'Orangeade' (f)	CBcs CDoC MGos NHol NLar
	'Red Embers'	CDoC ECho ECou NEgg SCoo WFar
*	'Redtip'	CMen
§	***salignus*** ℽ^{H3}	CBcs CDoC CDul CHEx CPLG EPfP EPla GGal IDee IFFs LRHS NMun SAPC SArc SLim WFar WSHC
	- (f)	ECou WFar
	- (m)	ECou
	'Soldier Boy'	ECou
	spicatus	see *Prumnopitys taxifolia*
	'Spring Sunshine' (f)	CBcs CDoC ECou EPla MGos NLar
	totara	CBcs CTrC ECou GGar IFFs LEdu WFar
	- 'Albany Gold'	CTrC
	- 'Aureus'	CBcs CDoC ECou EPla WEve WFar
	- 'Pendulus'	CDoC ECou
	'Young Rusty' (f)	CBcs CDoC ECou EPla MAsh MGos NHol WEve

Podophyllum (*Berberidaceae*)

	sp.	WBor
	aurantiocaule	CPLG GGGa
§	***delavayi***	CBct CFir CLAP CPLG EBee EBla ECho GEdr MDun NLar SKHP WAbe WCru WSpi
	difforme	CBct CLAP EBee GEdr SKHP WAbe WCru
	emodi	see *P. hexandrum*
	- var. ***chinense***	see *P. hexandrum* var. *chinense*
§	***hexandrum***	Widely available
§	- var. ***chinense***	CLAP CPLG CRow EBee EBla ECho GCal GEdr GKev IBlr LEdu WCru WWst
	- - BWJ 7908	WCru
	- - SDR 4409	GKev
	- - SDR 4620	GKev
	- 'Chinese White'	CPLG WCot
	- 'Majus'	CFir CLAP EBee LRHS SMad WCot WHal
I	- 'Nanum'	LRHS
	'Kaleidoscope' (v)	CBow CLAP EBee EUJe WCot WFut
	peltatum	CAby CArn CBct CDes CHid CLAP COld EBee EBla ECho EWld GAbr GBBs GEdr GPoy LAma LEdu NLar NMyG NSti SPhx WBor WCon WCra WCru WFar WPGP WPnP
	- var. ***peltatum*** f. ***deamii***	EBee
	pleianthum	CAby CBct CDes CLAP CSpr GEdr NLar WCot WCru
	- B&SWJ 282 from Taiwan	WCru
	- short	WCru WFar
	veitchii	see *P. delavayi*
	versipelle	CLAP EBee LEdu SKHP WCru WWst
	- 'Spotty Dotty'	CBct CLAP CPLG EBee GEdr GQue ITim LRHS MMoz MMuc NMyG NPnk NSti SHeu SUsu WCon WCot WPrP

Podranea (*Bignoniaceae*)

	brycei	CRHN
§	***ricasoliana***	CRHN EBee ERea EShb SOWG SPoG WBor

Pogonatherum (*Poaceae*)

*	***distichum*** **new**	XBlo

Pogonia (*Orchidaceae*)

	sp. **new**	NDav
	ophioglossoides	NLAp

Pogostemon (*Lamiaceae*)

	from An Veleniki Herb Farm, Pennsylvania	CArn
§	***cablin***	GPoy
	patchouly	see *P. cablin*

Polemonium ✿ (*Polemoniaceae*)

	ambervicsii	see *P. pauciflorum* subsp. *hinckleyi*
	'Apricot Beauty'	see *P. carneum* 'Apricot Delight'
N	***archibaldiae*** ℽ^{H4}	NBir SRms
	'Blue Pearl'	CMea EBee ELan EPfP LRHS MBri MLLN MNrw NBro NCob NGdn NLar NPri SBfd SGar SMrm WClo WFar
§	***boreale***	EBee ECho GKir LRHS SWvt WMoo
	- 'Heavenly Habit'	EBee GJos LRHS MWhi WJek WWEG
	brandegeei misapplied	see *P. pauciflorum*
§	***brandegeei*** Greene	CCVN
	- subsp. ***mellitum***	see *P. brandegeei* Greene
§	***caeruleum***	Widely available
	- 'Bambino Blue'	EBee GKir NBre SWvt
	- 'Blue Bell'	LRHS
	- Brise d'Anjou = 'Blanjou'^{PBR} (v)	CMMP EBee ECtt EHrv ELan EPfP EShb EWes GKir LRHS MAsh MBri NBir NCob SBfd SMad SPer SWvt WFar WWEG
	- subsp. ***caeruleum*** f. ***album***	CBre CSBt CWCL EBee ECha EHrv ELan EPfP GAbr GKev MBNS MHer MRav NBro SBfd SGar SPer SPoG SRms STes WMoo
	- 'Filigree Clouds'	LRHS MAvo NLar SMrm
	- 'Filigree Skies'	GCal LBMP LRHS NLar
	- var. ***grandiflorum***	see *P. caeruleum* subsp. *himalayanum*
§	- subsp. ***himalayanum***	CSpe GAbr MMuc WJek WMoo
	- 'Humile'	see *P.* 'Northern Lights'
	- 'Pam' (v)	CBow CDes EBee WCot
	- 'Snow and Sapphires' (v)	MBri MCCP NPer SWvt
	- white-flowered	GJos MMuc
	carneum	CTri CWan EBrs ECGP ECha GCal GKir GMaP LBMP LRHS MCCP MNrw MTho NLar SPer WFar WMoo
§	- 'Apricot Delight'	EBee GJos GMac MCCP MNrw NBir NGdn SBfd SGar SIde SPad SPoG STes WBVN WFar WHer WJek WPer WPnP WPtf WSpi WWEG
	cashmerianum	see *P. caeruleum* subsp. *himalayanum*
	chartaceum	LLHF
	'Churchills'	CBre EBee WPGP WPrP WSHC
	'Dawn Flight'	NCot WFar
	delicatum	see *P. pulcherrimum* Hook. subsp. *delicatum*
	'Eastbury Purple'	CElw CWCL
	'Elworthy Amethyst'	CElw EBee WPGP
	eximium	LLHF
	foliosissimum misapplied	see *P. archibaldiae*
	foliosissimum A. Gray	IGor
	- var. ***albiflorum***	see *P. foliosissimum* var. *alpinum*
§	- var. ***alpinum***	NBir
	- 'Cottage Cream'	WPGP
	- var. ***foliosissimum***	EWes

	'Glebe Cottage Lilac'	CHar GCra NBir SBch WPGP
	'Hannah Billcliffe'	CDes CElw EBee ECtt EWes MBrN NCot WPGP
	'Heavenly Blue'	ECtt
§	'Hopleys'	GBar GCal LHop NCot WFar
	x ***jacobaea***	EBee WCot WPGP WTin
	'Katie Daley'	see *P.* 'Hopleys'
	'Lambrook Mauve' Υ^{H4}	Widely available
	mellitum	see *P. brandegeei* Greene
	'North Tyne'	NChi
§	'Northern Lights'	CDes CSev CWCL EBee ELon EWes MCot MNrw MTis NDov SBch SPoG SSvw SUsu WCot WFar WMoo WPGP
	'Norwell Mauve'	MNrw
§	***pauciflorum***	CEnt EBee ECtt EHrv EPfP IFro MTho NBir SPer WFar WJek WMoo
§	- subsp. ***hinckleyi***	GKev LRHS NLBP SGar
§	- subsp. ***pauciflorum***	SGar SPav
	- silver-leaved	see *P. pauciflorum* subsp. *pauciflorum*
	- 'Sulphur Trumpets'	ECtt SWvt
	- subsp. ***typicum***	see *P. pauciflorum* subsp. *pauciflorum*
	'Pink Beauty'	CMac EBee ELan EPfP EWTr LBMP NBre NCob NCot NGdn WWEG
	pulchellum Salisb.	see *P. reptans*
	pulchellum Turcz.	see *P. caeruleum*
	pulcherrimum misapplied	see *P. boreale*
	pulcherrimum Hook.	GCal GKev NBro WPer
	- 'Tricolor'	see *P. boreale*
§	- subsp. ***delicatum***	MTho
	- subsp. ***pulcherrimum***	GCrs LLHF
	- - NNS 05-599	GKev
§	***reptans***	CArn GBar GPoy MHer NBro WAul WCom WFar WMoo WPtf
	- 'Album'	see *P. reptans* 'Virginia White'
	- 'Firmament'	EBee WPGP
*	- 'Sky Blue'	NBro
	- 'Stairway to Heaven'PBR (v)	Widely available
	- 'Touch of Class'	CBow EBee MAsh
§	- 'Virginia White'	CBre CDes CElw CMea CSev EBee EWes MAvo MTis NChi SUsu WFar WPGP
	- 'White Pearl'	NPri WClo
	richardsonii misapplied	see *P.* 'Northern Lights'
	richardsonii Graham	see *P. boreale*
	'Sapphire'	CBre ELan LRHS MBrN
	scopulinum	see *P. pulcherrimum* Hook. subsp. *delicatum*
	'Sonia's Bluebell'	CDes CElw CWCL EBee ECGP ECtt EWes GBin LPio MAvo MDKP MNrw MTis NDov NLar NSti SBch STes WPGP
	'Theddingworth'	WFar
	yezoense	CBre NBre NCot WClo WFar
	- var. ***hidakanum*** Bressingham Purple = 'Polbress'	CBow CSpe EBee ECtt ELan EWes GBin LHop LRHS MBNS MBri MCot NCGa NDov NLar NPri SBfd SMad SMrm SPer WFar
	- - 'Purple Rain'	Widely available

Polianthes (*Agavaceae*)

	elongata	WCot
§	***geminiflora***	WCot
	tuberosa Υ^{H1-2}	CBcs CCCN ECho EPfP LRHS WCot
	- 'The Pearl' (d)	ECho LAma WCot WHil WPGP

Poliomintha (*Lamiaceae*)

	bustamanta	NBir SPhx WSHC

Poliothyrsis (*Flacourtiaceae*)

	sinensis Υ^{H4}	EBee EPfP MBri NLar SSpi WPGP

Pollia (*Commelinaceae*)

	japonica	CBgR CWit ESwi EWes WPnP

Polygala (*Polygalaceae*)

	calcarea	ECho LLHF WPat
	- 'Lillet' Υ^{H4}	ECho EWes LHop LLHF LRHS NLAp NLar NMen NSla WFar WPat
	chamaebuxus Υ^{H4}	CBcs EBee ECho GCrs GKir LSou MAsh MDKP MGos MMuc MWea NLar NSla NWCA SPoG SRms SRot WGwG
I	- ***alba***	LBee LRHS LSou NLar SChF SRot WAbe
§	- var. ***grandiflora*** Υ^{H4}	CBcs CFir ECho EPfP EPot GAbr GCrs GEdr GGar GKev GKir IVic LBee LRHS MAsh MGos MWat NLAp NMen NSla SChF SPoG WAbe WFar WPat WSHC
	- 'Kamniski'	ECho EPot NLar
	- 'Loibl'	EPot
	- 'Purpurea'	see *P. chamaebuxus* var. *grandiflora*
	- 'Rhodoptera'	see *P. chamaebuxus* var. *grandiflora*
§	x ***dalmaisiana*** Υ^{H1}	CAbb CCCN CHEx CHll CRHN CSpe EBee EPfP MMuc SEND SGar WAbe WCFE
	myrtifolia	CCCN CTrC GFai MGos NWCA SGar SMrm SPlb
	- Bibi Pink = 'Polylap' **new**	LRHS
	- 'Grandiflora'	see *P.* x *dalmaisiana*
	'Rhubarb Rock'	GKir
	virgata	CCCN ERea

Polygonatum ✿ (*Convallariaceae*)

	ACE 1753	EPot
	acuminatifolium	EBla
	altelobatum	EBla
	- B&SWJ 286	WCru
	- B&SWJ 1886	WCru
	arisanense B&SWJ 3839	WCru
§	***biflorum***	Widely available
	- dwarf	EBla EPla
	canaliculatum	see *P. biflorum*
	cirrhifolium	CDes CFir CLAP CMdw CPom EBee EBla ELan EPot GBin GEdr GGar GKir MAvo MMoz SKHP WCot WCru WPGP WPrP
	- red-flowered	NLar WCot WFar
	commutatum	see *P. biflorum*
	'Corsley'	CPou
	cryptanthum	EBla WCru
	curvistylum	CAby CAvo CBct CFir CLAP CPom EBla ECha EHrv EPPr GEdr IFoB IMou MNFA NLar NRya SPhx WCru WFar WHil
	- CLD 761	GEdr
	cyrtonema misapplied	see *Disporopsis pernyi*
	cyrtonema Hua	IMou
	- B&SWJ 271	WCru
	desoulavyi **new**	IMou
*	- var. ***yezoense*** B&SWJ 764	WCru
	falcatum misapplied	see *P. humile*
	falcatum A. Gray	EBee EBla EPot NRya WHer WThu
	- B&SWJ 1077	WCru
	- silver-striped	CLAP GEdr
	- - B&SWJ 5101	WCru

	- 'Variegatum'	see *P. odoratum* var. *pluriflorum* 'Variegatum'
	'Falcon'	see *P. humile*
	filipes	WCru
	fuscum	IMou WCru
	geminiflorum	CBct CLAP CPom EBla WCru WFar
	- McB 2448	GEdr
	giganteum	see *P. biflorum*
	glaberrimum	CBct EBee EBla IPot WCot WFar
§	***graminifolium***	CBct CLAP CPBP CPom EBla ECho EPot GEdr NMen SCnR WCot WCru
	- G-W&P 803	IPot
§	***hirtum***	CAby CBct CLAP CPom CPrp EBla ECho EPPr EPla IFoB LEdu MAvo MMoz WCru WFar WTin
	- BM 7012	EBee
	hookeri	Widely available
	- McB 1413	GEdr
§	***humile***	CBct CLAP EBee EBla ECho EHrv EPPr EPfP GCal GCrs GGar GKir IBal LHop LRHS NGdn NLar NMen NMyG NPnk SGSe WAul WCot WCru WFar WHil
I	- 'Variegatum' (v)	CMac
§	× ***hybridum*** ♀H4	Widely available
	- 'Betberg'	CAvo CBct CFir CLAP CRow EBla ECha EHrv EPPr IMou LPio NBir WCot
	- 'Flore Pleno' (d)	CBct EBla WHer
	- 'Nanum'	CAby CBct CHid EBla WCot
	- 'Purple Katie'	MAvo
§	- 'Striatum' (v)	Widely available
	- 'Variegatum'	see *P.* × *hybridum* 'Striatum'
	- 'Wakehurst'	EBla EHrv
	- 'Weihenstephan'	EBee EBla GCal
	- 'Welsh Gold' (v)	CAvo
	inflatum	EBee EBla ECho WCru
	- B&SWJ 922	WCru
	involucratum	ECho WCru
	- B&SWJ 4285	WCru
	japonicum	see *P. odoratum*
	kingianum	EBee WHil
	- yellow-flowered B&SWJ 6545	WCru
	- - B&SWJ 6562	WCru
	'Langthorn's Variegated' (v)	ELan
	lasianthum	EBee WCru WWst
	- B&SWJ 671	WCru
	latifolium	see *P. hirtum*
	leptophyllum KEKE 844	GEdr
	maximowiczii	CPom EBee EPPr GCal WCru
	'Multifide'	EBee
	multiflorum misapplied	see *P.* × *hybridum*
	multiflorum L.	CBcs CElw CMac CPrp CRow CSBt CWCL EBee EBrs ECha ECho EPla EPot EWTr GAbr GCal MAvo MRav NLar NMyG NVic SEND SKHP SPlb SRms WBor WCAu WFar WHer WMoo
	- CC 4572	WCot
	- ***giganteum*** hort.	see *P. biflorum*
*	- 'Ramosissima'	EBla SMHy
*	***nanum*** 'Variegatum' (v)	CBcs ECho
	nodosum	EBla WCru
	obtusifolium	EBla
§	***odoratum*** ♀H4	CAby CAvo CBct CPom CRow CSWP EBee EBla ECho EHrv EPfP EPla GMaP LPio LRHS MAvo NBid NLar NPnk NRya WCru WFar WHil WPnP WWEG
	- 'Angel's Wings'	MAvo
§	- dwarf	ECho LEdu
	- 'Flore Pleno' (d) ♀H4	CDes CLAP CPom CRow EBee EBla ECha ECho EHrv EPla LEdu MAvo MMoz SCnR SMHy WCot WFar WHoo WPGP WPrP WTin
	- 'Grace Barker'	see *P.* × *hybridum* 'Striatum'
	- Kew form	EPot
	- var. ***pluriflorum***	EBee
§	- - 'Variegatum' (v) ♀H4	Widely available
	- 'Red Stem'	ECho WCru
	- 'Silver Wings' (v)	CBct CLAP EBla ECha EHrv NBir
	- 'Ussuriland'	EPPr GCal
	officinale	see *P. odoratum*
	oppositifolium	EBla WFar
	- B&SWJ 2537	WCru
§	***orientale***	CAvo CBct CHid CLAP EBla ECho ELau WFar
	pluriflorum	see *P. graminifolium*
	polyanthemum	see *P. orientale*
	prattii	EBee EBla ECho EPot
	- CLD 325	GEdr
	pubescens	CBct EBee ECho IMou LEdu WCru WThu
	pumilum	see *P. odoratum* dwarf
	punctatum	IMou LEdu WFar
	- B&SWJ 2395	CBct EBla WCru
	roseum	CDes CLAP CPom EBee EPPr GEdr GKev MAvo MMoz SGSe WHer WPGP
	sewerzowii	EBla EPPr EPla
	sibiricum	CAvo CBct CPom EBee EBla GEdr WCot WCru WFar WPGP
	- DJHC 600	CDes
	stenanthum	WWst
	- B&SWJ 5727	WCru
	stenophyllum	CAvo EBla WCru
	stewartianum	CLAP CPom EPPr NRya
	aff. ***tessellatum*** B&SWJ 9752	WCru
	tonkinense	LEdu WFar
	- B&SWJ 8246	WCru
	- HWJ 551	WCru
	- HWJ 861	WCru
	verticillatum	CBct CGHE CHid CRow EBla EBrs ECha EPfP EPla EPot GKir IFoB LBMP LEdu LRHS MNFA MNrw MRav MTho SKHP SMad WCom WCru WFar WPGP
	- CLD 1308	EPPr
	- 'Giant One'	EBee IPot
	- 'Himalayan Giant'	CHid EBla ECho WFar WPnP
*	- 'Roseum'	CAvo GKir LRHS
	- 'Rubrum'	CAby CArn CBct CLAP CRow EBee EBla EHrv EPPr EPla GEdr IPot LEdu MAvo MTho NBid NLar SPhx WCot WPrP
	- 'Serbian Dwarf'	CBct CHid EBee EBla ECho
	aff. ***verticillatum***	CSpe
	wardii new	WCot
	aff. ***wardii***	WCot
	- B&SWJ 6599	WCru
	zanlanscianense	CBct EBla IMou WCru WFar

Polygonum (*Polygonaceae*)

affine	see *Persicaria affinis*
amplexicaule	see *Persicaria amplexicaulis*
aubertii	see *Fallopia baldschuanica*
aviculare	CArn
baldschuanicum	see *Fallopia baldschuanica*
bistorta	see *Persicaria bistorta*
capitatum	see *Persicaria capitata*
compactum	see *Fallopia japonica* var. *compacta*

	filiforme	see *Persicaria virginiana*
	equisetiforme misapplied	see *P. scoparium*
	forrestii SDR 2578	GKev
	molle	see *Persicaria mollis*
	multiflorum	see *Fallopia multiflora*
	odoratum	see *Persicaria odorata*
	polystachyum	see *Persicaria wallichii*
	runciforme	see *Persicaria runcinata*
§	***scoparium***	CBcs CRow EHoe EPPr EPla ESwi SDys WFar WOld
	tinctorium	see *Persicaria tinctoria*
	vacciniifolium	see *Persicaria vacciniifolia*
	weyrichii	see *Persicaria weyrichii*

Polylepis (*Rosaceae*)

	australis	EBee EPla ESwi LEdu MBri SMad WCot WCru WPGP
	- tall	WPGP

Polymnia (*Asteraceae*)

	sonchifolia	LEdu

Polypodium ✿ (*Polypodiaceae*)

	aureum	see *Phlebodium aureum*
	- 'Glaucum'	CSpe WCot
	australe	see *P. cambricum*
§	***cambricum***	EBee EFer SGSe WCot WFib WRic WTin
	- 'Barrowii'	CBgR CLAP WAbe WFib
I	- 'Cambricum' ♀H4	CBgR CLAP GCal WAbe WRic
	- 'Cristatum'	CLAP WFib
	- (Cristatum Group) 'Grandiceps Forster'	CLAP
	- - 'Grandiceps Fox' ♀H4	WFib
	- 'Hornet'	GBin WFib
	- 'Macrostachyon'	CLAP EFer GBin NBid WFib
	- 'Oakleyae'	EFtx SMHy
	- 'Omnilacerum Oxford'	CLAP
	- 'Prestonii'	CBgR EBee WAbe WCot WFib
	- Pulcherrimum Group	CLAP WAbe WRic
	- - 'Pulcherrimum Addison'	CDes GBin WAbe WFib
	- - 'Pulchritudine'	CLAP WAbe WCot
	- 'Richard Kayse'	CDes CLAP EBee WAbe WCot WFib WPGP
	- Semilacerum Group	WRic
	- - 'Carew Lane'	WFib
	- - 'Robustum'	WFib
	- 'Whilharris' ♀H4	CLAP SMHy WAbe
I	× ***coughlinii*** bifid	WFib
	formosanum	WRic
	glycyrrhiza	CLAP GPoy WFib WRic
	- bifid	see *P.* × *coughlinii* bifid
	- 'Longicaudatum' ♀H4	CLAP GBin WAbe WCot WFib WRic
	- 'Malahatense'	CLAP
	- 'Malahatense' (sterile)	CDes WAbe
	interjectum	CBgR CLAP EFer LRHS MMoz NVic WPnP WRic
	- 'Cornubiense' ♀H4	CBgR CDes CLAP EBee GEdr MMoz NBid NBir NHol NVic WAbe WTin
	- 'Glomeratum Mullins'	WFib
	× ***mantoniae***	WFib WIvy
	- 'Bifidograndiceps'	NBid WFib WRic
	scouleri	CLAP EFer NBro
	× ***shivasiae*** new	EBee
	subauriculatum 'Knightii'	see *Goniophlebium subauriculatum* 'Knightiae'
	vulgare	Widely available
	- 'Bifidocristatum'	see *P. vulgare* 'Bifidomultifidum'
	- 'Bifidomulticeps'	WCot
§	- 'Bifidomultifidum'	CBgR CBty CLAP CWCL CWit GBin GCal GEdr LLWP MAsh MCCP MGos MRav NHol NLar SEND SGSe STes WCot WWEG
*	- 'Congestum Cristatum'	SRms
	- 'Cornubiense Grandiceps'	GCal SRms WIvy WRic
*	- 'Cornubiense Multifidum'	EBee WCot
	- 'Elegantissimum'	NBid WFib
	- 'Parsley'	WCot
	- 'Trichomanoides Backhouse'	CLAP GCal WAbe WFib
	'Whitley Giant'	WCot

Polypompholyx see *Utricularia*

Polyspora (*Theaceae*)

§	***axillaris***	CCCN EBee
	speciosa B&SWJ 11750 new	WCru

Polystichum ✿ (*Dryopteridaceae*)

	BWJ 8182 from China	WCru
	acrostichoides	CBty CDTJ CDes CFwr CKel CLAP CMHG EBee GEdr LRHS MBri NLar NMyG SBfd WPGP WRic
	aculeatum ♀H4	CLAP CRWN EBee ECha EFer ELan EPfP EShb GKir GMaP LAst LRHS MBri MCot MGos MMuc NBid NEgg NHol NLar SEND SRms SWvt WFib WMoo WRic WWEG
I	- Densum Group	EFer
	- Grandiceps Group	EFer
	- 'Portia'	WFib
	andersonii	CLAP EBee EFtx NHol WRic
	bissectum	CPLG
	braunii	CBcs CMHG CWCL EBee EFtx EGol EQua GBin GMaP IKil MMoz MMuc NBid NHol NLar SBfd SEND WFib WPnP WRic WWEG
	caryotideum	see *Cyrtomium caryotideum*
	chilense	WRic
	deltodon	WRic
	dracomontanum	WRic
	× ***dycei***	CBty EBee ISha WRic
	falcatum	see *Cyrtomium falcatum*
	fortunei	see *Cyrtomium fortunei*
	imbricans	CLAP
	interjectum	MRav
	lentum new	NBir
	lepidocaulon new	WRic
	makinoi	CBty CCCN CLAP EBee ETod LRHS NBid NHol WFib WRic
	munitum ♀H4	Widely available
	neolobatum	EFtx WFib
	- BWJ 8182	WCru
	parvipinnulum new	WRic
	piceopalaceum new	WRic
	polyblepharum ♀H4	Widely available
	- 'Jade' new	LRHS
	proliferum misapplied	see *P. setiferum* Acutilobum Group
	proliferum ambig.	CBty EUJe MAsh WPtf
	proliferum (R. Br.) C. Presl	CLAP EFtx GCal SBig WAbe WFib WPGP WRic
*	- ***plumosum***	LAst SPad SWvt
	retrorsopaleaceum	WRic
	richardii	EUJe GBin SBig WRic
	rigens	CBty CLAP CPrp EBee EFer LRHS LSou MAsh MMuc NHol NLar NMyG SBfd SGSe SRms SRot WCru WFib WRic WWEG
	setiferum ♀H4	Widely available
§	- Acutilobum Group	CBgR CFwr CLAP CMHG CPrp EBee ECha EWTr GMaP LRHS NHol SDix SMad SPer SRms

		STes WMoo WPGP WPnP WPrP WRic
	- Congestum Group	CBgR GBin MMoz NCGa NEgg NHol NLar SBfd SPer SRms WFib WRic
	- - 'Congestum'	CBty CFwr CLAP CWCL EBee EFtx ELan EPPr EPfP IKil LRHS MAsh MRav NBir NGdn NHol NMyG SPoG WGor WMoo WPrP
	- - 'Congestum Cristatum'	LAst
	- 'Cristatopinnulum'	CGHE CLAP EBee NHar WPGP
	- Cristatum Group	CLAP EHrv SRms
	- Cruciatum Group	CLAP
	- Divisilobum Group	CBcs CFee CLAP CMHG CRow EFer ELan LPBA MGos MLHP MMoz NHol SRms STre WAul WFar WFib WHoo WIvy WKif WPGP WRic WTin
	- - 'Caernarvon'	CLAP EFtx
	- - 'Dahlem'	Widely available
	- - 'Divisilobum Densum' ♀H4	CBgR CLAP EHrv EPfP MMuc NBir
	- - 'Divisilobum Iveryanum' ♀H4	CLAP EFer NHol SRms WFib
	- - 'Divisilobum Laxum'	CLAP
	- - 'Divisilobum Wollaston'	CDTJ CKel CLAP CWCL ETod GBin MRav NBid NHol NLar
	- - 'Herrenhausen'	Widely available
	- - 'Madame Patti'	MMoz
	- - 'Mrs Goffey'	CGHE WFib WPGP
	- Foliosum Group	CLAP EFer
	- 'Gracile'	MRav NBir
	- 'Grandiceps'	CGHE CLAP EBee EFer ELan WPGP
	- 'Hamlet'	WFib
	- 'Helena'	WFib
	- 'Hirondelle'	SRms
	- Lineare Group	GKir WFib
	- Multilobum Group	CLAP SRms WFib
	- 'Othello'	WFib
	- Perserratum Group	GBin NBid SMHy WFib
	- 'Plumo-Densum'	see *P. setiferum* 'Plumosomultilobum'
	- 'Plumosodensum'	see *P. setiferum* 'Plumosomultilobum'
	- Plumosodivisilobum Group	CLAP CRow ECha EGol GBin LSou NBid SGSe SMHy WFib
	- - 'Baldwinii'	CLAP WFib
	- - 'Bland'	WFib
I	- 'Plumosomultilobum'	CBty CFwr CGHE CLAP CWCL EBee EFtx EPfP EUJe GBin LAst LBMP MAsh MCot MGos MMoz NBir NLar SBfd SMad SPer WCot WFib WGwG WHoo WMoo WPat WPnP WPrP WRic
I	- - 'Plumosomultilobum Densum'	WCot WWEG
	- Plumosum Group	CBgR CGHE CLAP CMHG CSpe EBee EFer EFtx SAPC SArc SRot
	- - dwarf	CSBt MMuc
*	- ***plumosum grande*** 'Moly'	SRms
	- 'Portmeirion'	CLAP
	- Proliferum Group	see *P. setiferum* Acutilobum Group
*	- 'Proliferum Wollaston'	CBcs CBty CPrp EBee ETod MMoz WWEG
	- 'Pulcherrimum Bevis' ♀H4	CBgR CDes CHid CLAP CMea EBee ECGP ESwi GBin LRHS MAvo MRav NBid NDov NGdn NMyG SDix SMad SUsu SWvt WCot WFib WPGP WPat WPnP WRic
	- Rotundatum Group	CLAP
	- - 'Cristatum'	CLAP
	- - 'Rotundatum Ramosum'	CLAP
	- 'Smith's Cruciate'	CFwr CLAP GBin LLHF WFib
	- 'Wakeleyanum'	EFer SRms
	tsussimense ♀H4	Widely available
	vestitum	CLAP CTrC EFtx EUJe GBin MMoz SBig WRic
	xiphophyllum	WAbe
	yunnanense	WRic

Polyxena (*Hyacinthaceae*)

*	***brevifolia***	ECho
	corymbosa	ECho NMen
§	***ensifolia***	ECho LLHF
	longituba	CPBP ECho
	odorata	ECho NRya
	paucifolia	ECho
	pygmaea	see *P. ensifolia*

Pomaderris (*Rhamnaceae*)

	apetala	CPLG
	elliptica	CPLG ECou
	kumeraho	CCCN

pomegranate see *Punica granatum*

Poncirus (*Rutaceae*)

§	***trifoliata***	CAgr CArn CBcs CCCN CDoC EBee ELan EPfP GBin IDee IVic LEdu MBlu MRav NEgg NWea SAPC SArc SMad SPer SPlb SPoG SVic WBVN WDin WFar WPGP WSHC

Ponerorchis (*Orchidaceae*)

	graminifolia	LAma WWst

Pontederia (*Pontederiaceae*)

	cordata ♀H4	CBen CHEx CRow CWat EHon ELan EPfP LPBA MCCP MMuc MSKA MWts NPer SCoo SPlb SWat WFar WMAq WPnP
	- f. ***albiflora***	CRow CWat EPfP LPBA MCCP MWts NLar WMAq
	- 'Blue Spires'	MSKA
§	- var. ***lancifolia***	CBen CRow EPfP LPBA MCCP MNrw MSKA MWts NPer SWat WTin
	- 'Pink Pons'	CRow LPBA MSKA NLar
	dilatata	see *Monochoria hastata*
	lanceolata	see *P. cordata* var. *lancifolia*

Populus ✿ (*Salicaceae*)

	× ***acuminata***	WMou
	alba	CAlb CBcs CCVT CDoC CDul CLnd CMac CSBt CTho CTri CWib EBee ECrN EMac GKir IFFs LBuc NWea SBfd SPer WDin WMou
	- 'Bolleana'	see *P. alba* f. *pyramidalis*
	- 'Nivea'	SEND
§	- f. ***pyramidalis***	SRms WMou
§	- 'Raket'	CCVT CLnd CTho ELan SPer
	- 'Richardii'	EBtc GKir MAsh SPer WCom WCot WFar WMou
	- Rocket	see *P. alba* 'Raket'
§	'Balsam Spire' (f) ♀H4	CAlb CDoC CDul CLnd CTho EMac GKir NWea WDin WMou
§	***balsamifera***	CCVT CDoC CSBt CTri EMac GKir MGos NWea SBfd SPer SRms WCot WDin WFar
	- 'Vita Sackville West'	MBlu
	× ***berolinensis***	CDoC
	× ***canadensis***	ECrN

§ - 'Aurea' ♀H4	CDul CLnd CTho CWib EBee EMac IFFs MGos MRav NEgg SPer WDin WFar WMou
- 'Aurea' × ***jackii*** 'Aurora'	WDin
- 'Columbia' new	WMou
- 'Eugenei' (m)	WMou
- 'Robusta' (m)	CCVT CDoC CDul CLnd CTri IFFs LBuc NWea WDin WMou
- 'Serotina' (m)	CDoC CDul WDin WMou
× ***candicans*** misapplied	see *P.* × *jackii*
× ***canescens***	CDoC CLnd IFFs MMuc NWea WDin
× ***generosa*** 'Beaupré'	WMou
§ × ***jackii*** (f)	WDin
- 'Aurora' (f/v)	CBcs CCVT CDul CLnd CMac CSBt EBee ELan GKir LBuc LRHS MBri MGos MMuc NPri NWea SBfd SPer SRms WDin WFar WHar WMou
lasiocarpa ♀H4	CEnd CGHE CMCN CPLG CSdC CTho EBee ELan EPfP IArd MBlu MRav SLPl WMou WPGP
nigra	CDul CLnd CMac CTho EMac EPfP NWea WDin WSFF
- (f)	ECrN SLPl
- (m)	SLPl
- subsp. ***betulifolia***	CCVT CDul CLnd CWan NWea WDin WMou
- - (f)	WMou
- - (m)	WMou
§ - 'Italica' (m) ♀H4	CAlb CCVT CDoC CDul CLnd CMac CSBt CTho CTri CWib EBee ECrN ELan EMac GKir IFFs LBuc MGos NWea SBfd SPer SRms WDin WMou
- 'Italica Aurea'	see *P. nigra* 'Lombardy Gold'
§ - 'Lombardy Gold' (m)	CEnd
- 'Pyramidalis'	see *P. nigra* 'Italica'
'Serotina Aurea'	see *P.* × *canadensis* 'Aurea'
simonii 'Fastigiata'	WMou
szechuanica	WMou
§ - var. ***tibetica***	WMou
tacamahaca	see *P. balsamifera*
'Tacatricho 32'	see *P.* 'Balsam Spire'
tremula ♀H4	CCVT CDoC CDul CLnd CMac CRWN CSBt CTho CTri CWib EBee ECrN ELan EMac EWTr GKir IFFs LBuc NWea SBfd SPer WDin WHar WMou WSFF
§ - 'Erecta'	CDul CEnd CLnd CTho EBee LMaj MBlu MBri MMuc SEND SMad WFar WMou
- 'Fastigiata'	see *P. tremula* 'Erecta'
- 'Pendula' (m)	CEnd CLnd CTho ECrN GKir WDin WMou
trichocarpa	CDul LMaj NWea SPer
- 'Fritzi Pauley' (f)	CDul CTho WMou
violascens	see *P. szechuanica* var. *tibetica*
yunnanensis	WMou

Porophyllum (*Asteraceae*)

ruderale	ELau

Portulaca (*Portulacaceae*)

oleracea	CArn MHer MNHC SIde SVic WJek
- var. ***aurea***	MNHC WJek

Portulacaria (*Portulacaceae*)

afra	EShb
- 'Variegata' (v)	EShb

Potamogeton (*Potamogetonaceae*)

crispus	CBen CWat EHon MSKA NSco WMAq
natans	NSco SEND
pectinatus	CWat

Potentilla ✿ (*Rosaceae*)

CC 5226	GKev
CC 5356	EWld
alba	CTri EBee ECha ECho ELan GCal GGar GMac MLHP MNFA MRav MWat NChi WAul
alchemilloides	CMac LRHS WPer
alpicola	WPer
ambigua	see *P. cuneata*
andicola	EBee
anglica new	CArn
anserina	CArn EBWF GBar MHer WHer
- 'Golden Treasure' (v)	EBee WHer
anserinoides	WMoo WPer
arbuscula misapplied	see *P. fruticosa* 'Elizabeth'
- 'Beesii'	see *P. fruticosa* 'Beesii'
'Arc-en-ciel'	Widely available
argentea	CRWN EBWF GAuc GKir LRHS MBNS SPlb WFar
arguta	EBee NBre
argyrophylla	see *P. atrosanguinea* var. *argyrophylla*
- 'Alfred Salter'	LRHS
* - ***insignis rubra***	NWCA
atrosanguinea	Widely available
§ - var. ***argyrophylla***	CFir COlW CSam CWCL EBee ECha ELan EPfP GCal LHop MMuc NBPC NBir NBro NChi SMad SRms STes WAul WClo WCom WFar WHil WMoo
- 'Fireball' (d)	EAEE EPfP GJos GKir WPer
- var. ***leucochroa***	see *P. atrosanguinea* var. *argyrophylla*
* - 'Sundermannii'	CSpr LLHF
aurea	EBee ECho ECtt EPfP LRHS MTho NLAp NWCA WBrk WNew WPat
- 'Aurantiaca'	EWes NLar SRot
§ - subsp. ***chrysocraspeda***	NMen
§ - 'Goldklumpen'	ECtt MRav
- 'Plena' (d)	LRHS SRot
'Blazeaway'	EBee ECtt LBMP LRHS LSou MArl MAvo MBNS NGdn WFar
brevifolia	NWCA
calabra	CSpr EBee ECha EWes MMuc WHer
§ ***cinerea***	CTri ECho LBee LLHF LRHS
collina	LLHF
§ ***crantzii***	CMea EBee SRms
- 'Nana'	see *P. crantzii* 'Pygmaea'
§ - 'Pygmaea'	ECho ECtt EPfP NBir NMen
§ ***cuneata*** ♀H4	ECho GAbr MMuc MTho NWCA WPer
davurica 'Abbotswood'	see *P. fruticosa* 'Abbotswood'
delavayi	LRHS MNrw
detommasii	LLHF
- MESE 400	EBee
dickinsii	NMen
'Emilie'	CSpe EBee ECtt GAbr GCal GMac LRHS MBNS MBri MLLN MNrw NBPC NCob NLar SWvt WBor WCra WFar
§ ***erecta***	CRWN CWan EBWF GBar GPoy MHer MNHC WHfH WNew
eriocarpa	EBee ECho ECtt EPau GEdr NLAp NMen NSla WAbe WPat
- var. ***tsarongensis***	WAbe
- - CC 4627	EWld
'Esta Ann'	CMac CSpr EBee ECtt EPPr LHop MArl MBNS MCot NCGa SRGP
'Etna'	CEnt CHar CKno EBee ECtt ELan LPio LRHS MLHP MNFA MNrw

		NBir NLar NPnk WCom WMoo WPer
	'Everest'	see *P. fruticosa* 'Mount Everest'
	'Fireflame'	ECha MRav NBre NLar WMoo
	fissa	MNrw NBir NBre SPhx
	'Flambeau' (d)	EBee ECtt EShb GMac LBMP LHop LPla LRHS MArl MNFA MRav NBre NCob NGdn NLar WMoo
	'Flamenco'	CSam CTri ECtt ELon GKir GMac MArl MBNS MBri MLHP MNrw MRav NBir SUsu WAbb WCom WFar WMoo
	fragariiformis	see *P. megalantha*
	fruticosa	LBuc MGan NWea
§	- 'Abbotswood' ♀H4	Widely available
	- 'Abbotswood Silver' (v)	LAst MSwo SLim WMoo
	- 'Annette'	CMac MBrN
	- 'Apple Blossom'	CWib
	- var. ***arbuscula*** hort.	see *P. fruticosa* 'Elizabeth'
	- 'Argentea Nana'	see *P. fruticosa* 'Beesii'
	- 'Baby Bethan'PBR (d)	LLHF LRHS NHol WFar WRHF
§	- 'Beesii'	ELan EPfP GGar
	- 'Bewerley Surprise'	NBir
	- 'Chelsea Star' ♀H4	CMac LRHS LSRN MAsh MGos SBfd
	- 'Chilo' (v)	NEgg WMoo
	- var. ***dahurica*** 'Hersii'	see *P. fruticosa* 'Snowflake'
	- - 'Rhodocalyx'	WFar
	- 'Dart's Cream'	MGan
	- 'Dart's Golddigger'	CTri SEND
	- 'Daydawn'	CBcs CDoC CMac CWSG EBee ECtt ELan EPfP GKir LAst LHop LRHS MAsh MBri MLHP MRav MSwo NBir NEgg NHol NLar SLim SPer SRms SWvt WClo WDin WFar WMoo
§	- 'Elizabeth'	Widely available
	- 'Farreri'	see *P. fruticosa* 'Gold Drop'
	- 'Floppy Disc'	ELan EPfP NHol
	- 'Glenroy Pinkie'	CSam EPfP MRav NLar SCoo
§	- 'Gold Drop'	CMac NHol
	- 'Golden Spreader'	GKir LRHS
	- 'Goldfinger'	CBar CCVT CChe CDoC CMac CSBt CWSG EBee ELan EPfP GKir LHop LRHS MAsh MGos MRav MSwo MWat NEgg NHol NPri SCoo SLim SPer SPlb SPoG WDin WFar
	- Goldkugel	see *P. fruticosa* 'Gold Drop'
	- 'Goldstar'	CBar CDul EQua GKir IArd LRHS MBri MGos NHol SBfd SCoo SLon WFar
	- 'Goldteppich'	LBuc
	- 'Goscote'	MGos
	- 'Grace Darling'	CAbP ELan EPfP EWes GGar NBir NEgg NHol NLar SRGP SWvt WBrE WMoo
	- 'Groneland' ♀H4	EPfP LRHS MAsh SPoG
	- 'Haytor's Orange'	CWib
	- 'Hopleys Little Joker'	WFar
	- 'Hopleys Orange' ♀H4	CDoC EBee EPfP EWes GKir LHop LRHS MMuc MWat NHol NPri SCoo SEND WFar WGor WGwG WMoo
	- 'Jackman's Variety' ♀H4	CSam CWib LRHS MAsh SRms
	- 'Jolina'	LRHS
	- 'Katherine Dykes'	CDoC CDul CMac CTri CWib EBee EPfP GKir LAst LBMP LRHS LSRN MAsh MGos MNHC NEgg NWea SCoo SLim SPer SPoG SRms WDin WFar WHar WMoo
*	- 'King Cup' ♀H4	LRHS MAsh SPoG
§	- 'Klondike'	CBcs CSBt EBee EPfP GKir MGan NEgg NWea WHil
	- 'Kobold'	EBee
*	- 'Lemon and Lime'	LRHS NBir
	- 'Limelight' ♀H4	CSBt EBee ELan EPfP LRHS LSou MAsh MBri MRav MSwo NHol WClo WFar
	- 'Longacre Variety'	CMac CTri EQua IArd MSwo NWea
	- 'Lovely Pink'PBR	see *P. fruticosa* 'Pink Beauty'
§	- 'Maanelys'	CSBt ELan EQua MGan NHol NWea SPer SRms WDin WMoo
	- 'Macpenny's Cream'	CMac
§	- 'Manchu'	CDoC CMac MRav MWat SLPl SPer SRms WCFE
	- Mango Tango = 'Uman'PBR	CDoC CSBt CWSG EBee LRHS LSRN MNHC SPoG
§	- Marian Red Robin = 'Marrob'PBR ♀H4	CDoC CSBt CWSG CWib EBee ELan EPfP GKir LAst LRHS MAsh MBri MRav MSwo MWat NEgg NHol NPri NWea SCoo SEND SLim SLon SPer SPoG SWvt WDin
	- 'McKay's White'	NLar
	- 'Medicine Wheel Mountain' ♀H4	ELan EWes IArd LRHS MAsh MGos MRav NHol NLar SCoo SLim SPer SPoG
	- Moonlight	see *P. fruticosa* 'Maanelys'
§	- 'Mount Everest'	EQua MMuc NWea SLon SRms
	- 'Nana Argentea'	see *P. fruticosa* 'Beesii'
	- 'New Dawn'	CDoC MBri NCGa SEND WFar
	- 'Orangeade'	EPfP LRHS MAsh NLar SPoG
	- 'Peaches and Cream'	WEas
	- 'Penny White' ♀H4	EPfP
§	- 'Pink Beauty'PBR ♀H4	CDoC CSBt EBee EGxp ELan EPfP GKir LRHS LSRN MAsh MBrN MBri MRav NCGa NEgg NHol NPri SCoo SEND SPer SPoG SWvt WClo WHar WMoo
	- 'Pink Pearl'	WMoo
	- 'Pink Queen'	NLar
	- 'Pink Whisper'	CWSG WGwG
	- 'Pretty Polly'	CWSG ELan LAst LRHS MGos MSwo NHol NLar WDin WFar WMoo
	- 'Primrose Beauty' ♀H4	CDoC CDul CMac EBee ECrN ELan EPfP GKir LAst LBMP LRHS LSRN MAsh MMuc MRav MSwo NEgg NHol SCoo SEND SLPl SLim SPer SPlb WClo WDin WFar WMoo
§	- Princess = 'Blink'	CBcs CDul CWSG ELan GKir LAst LBMP LRHS MAsh MRav MSwo NEgg NHol SCoo SLim SPer SRms WBVN WDin WFar
	- var. ***pumila***	GKev
	- 'Red Ace'	Widely available
	- Red RobinPBR	see *P. fruticosa* Marian Red Robin
	- 'Royal Flush'	NHol
	- 'Snowbird'	EBee EPfP MGos SLim WFar
§	- 'Snowflake'	CBcs WMoo
	- 'Sommerflor' ♀H4	EBee EPfP EQua LRHS MAsh NCGa
	- 'Sophie's Blush'	CChe MRav NHol NWea WDin WSHC
	- 'Summer Sorbet'	LRHS NPri
	- 'Sunset'	CBcs CMac CSam CWib EBee ECrN ELan EPfP GKir LSRN MGos NBir NEgg NHol NWea SCoo SLim SPer SRms SSta WBVN WFar WMoo
	- 'Tangerine'	Widely available
	- 'Tilford Cream'	CDoC CSBt CSam CTri EBee ELan EPfP EWTr GKir LAst LBMP LRHS LSRN MSwo NBir NEgg NHol NPri SPer SRms WBVN WClo WDin WFar WMoo
	- 'Tom Conway'	CMac NLar
	- 'Valley Gold'	WClo

- var. ***veitchii***	CSBt
- 'Vilmoriniana'	CBot CTri ELan EPfP GCal LRHS MAsh MLHP MRav SPer SPoG SSpi SWvt WKif WPat WSHC WSpi
- 'Whirligig'	CMac
- 'Wickwar Beauty'	CWib
- 'Wickwar Trailer'	EPot
- 'Yellow Bird' ♀H4	LRHS MAsh MGos SPoG
'Gibson's Scarlet' ♀H4	Widely available
glandulosa	LRHS NBre SMad WBrk
'Gloire de Nancy' (d)	EBee IGor LBMP LRHS MRav NBir NChi NCob NLar WCom WPrP
'Gold Clogs'	see *P. aurea* 'Goldklumpen'
gracilis	EBee WKif
'Hamlet'	LRHS
'Helen Jane'	GBee GJos GKir LPio LRHS MHer NBir NGdn NLar SAga STes WFar WMnd
heptaphylla	NBre
'Herzblut'	NLar
× ***hopwoodiana***	Widely available
× ***hybrida*** 'Jean Jabber'	EBee GMac MRav NCob NLar SRGP
hyparctica	MDKP
- ***nana***	LBee
'Light My Fire'	EBee ECtt EKen LLHF MBNS MBri NMoo
* ***lutea***	NCob
'Mandshurica'	see *P. fruticosa* 'Manchu'
'Maynard's'	NDov
§ ***megalantha*** ♀H4	Widely available
- 'Gold Sovereign'	EAEE EBee EPfP LRHS LSou SPoG
'Melton'	EBee MNrw NBir
* 'Melton Fire'	CEnt CWan ECtt EPfP EShb GBee GJos GKir GQue LAst LEdu MMuc MNHC NBir SGar WClo WFar WMnd WMoo
'Monarch's Velvet'	see *P. thurberi* 'Monarch's Velvet'
'Monsieur Rouillard' (d)	CSam CWCL EBee ECtt GCra GKir IPot LRHS MArl MNrw MRav MWat NGdn WCom WHoo WMnd
'Mont d'Or'	MRav
montana	WPer
morefieldii new	CPBP
nepalensis	CEnt EHoe LAst MLHP NBPC NBro NChi
- 'Flammenspiel'	WFar
- 'Master Floris'	WFar WHal
§ - 'Miss Willmott' ♀H4	Widely available
- 'Ron McBeath'	Widely available
- 'Roxana'	CFir EBee ECGP ELan MRav NBro NLar SRGP WAbb WFar WMoo WPer
- 'Shogran'	COIW EBee GAbr GJos GMac GQue LAst LBMP LRHS MBNS NBPC NHol NLar NVic SPad WPtf
§ ***neumanniana***	CSpr EBWF NBir NPri
- 'Goldrausch'	LEdu MRav
§ - 'Nana'	EBee ECho ECtt EPot GGar LBee MHer MMuc MWat NLAp NLar NMen NRya SPlb SRms WFar WMoo WPat
- white-flowered	LAst
nevadensis	CTri ECho GEdr SRms
nitida	GEdr NMen SRms WAbe
- 'Alba'	ECho NCob NMen
- 'Lissadell'	EPot
- 'Rubra'	CFir ECho EDAr MWat NBir NLAp NWCA SRms WAbe WPat
nivalis	ECho
norvegica	GAuc
palustris	CWat EBWF EBee LLWG NLar WMoo
parvifolia 'Klondike'	see *P. fruticosa* 'Klondike'
pedata	LLWP NChi
pensylvanica	LLHF
'Pink Panther'	see *P. fruticosa* Princess
aff. ***polyphylla*** CHP&W 314	GKev
recta	COIW CSpr EBWF MArl NPri
- 'Alba'	CEnt GMaP LAst NBre NCob NEgg WPtf
- 'Citrina'	see *P. recta* var. *sulphurea*
- 'Macrantha'	see *P. recta* 'Warrenii'
§ - var. ***sulphurea***	CAby CEnt ECrN EWTr IGor LAst MHer MLHP MMuc MNFA MNrw NBir NBre NLar SAga SEND SPhx WBrk WCom WFar WHal WHoo WMnd WMoo WPer WTin
§ - 'Warrenii'	CSBt EBee EPla GKir GMaP LAst LRHS MRav NBPC NBir NEgg SPer SPoG SRms WFar WHal WMoo WPer
reptans	CArn CRWN EBWF
- 'Pleniflora' (d)	WAlt
'Roxanne' (d)	MHer
rupestris	CMea EBWF ECha NBPC NLar NSti SGar WCAu WFar WHal WMoo WPer WPtf
simplex	EBee NBre
speciosa	EWes IGor WMoo
sterilis	CHid EBWF WHer WSFF
* ***sundermanii***	WHrl
'Sungold'	ECho
tabernaemontani	see *P. neumanniana*
ternata	see *P. aurea* subsp. *chrysocraspeda*
thurberi	LRHS MBNS MCot MMHG MNFA MNrw NLar NMoo SPhx WMoo WSHC
§ - 'Monarch's Velvet'	Widely available
tommasiniana	see *P. cinerea*
× ***tonguei*** ♀H4	Widely available
tormentilla	see *P. erecta*
'Twinkling Star'	EBee
uniflora	LLHF
verna	see *P. neumanniana*
- 'Pygmaea'	see *P. neumanniana* 'Nana'
'Versicolor Plena' (d)	EBee NLar
villosa	see *P. crantzii*
'Volcan'	EBee ECtt ETod EWes MAvo MBri MNFA SMHy SUsu WAbb WFar WHal
'White Queen'	GMac MNrw MRav NBre NCob SHar SPur
'William Rollison' ♀H4	Widely available
willmottiae	see *P. nepalensis* 'Miss Willmott'
'Yellow Queen'	CBcs CMac CTri EPfP GMaP LHop MNrw MRav NHol NLar SPer WCAu WFar

Poterium see *Sanguisorba*

sanguisorba	see *Sanguisorba minor*

Pouteria (*Sapotaceae*)

costata	ECou

Pratia (*Campanulaceae*)

§ ***angulata***	CDoy CTrC
- 'Jack's Pass'	ECho NEgg
§ - 'Treadwellii'	ECha ECho EPfP GEdr GGar LRHS SPlb WHal
- 'Woodside'	ECho
§ ***pedunculata***	CBar CPLG CTri ECha ECho ECou ECtt EDAr ELan EPfP GGar GKir LBMP LBee LLWG LRHS MAsh

	NChi NRya SPet SPlb SRms SRot WFar WMoo WPer WPtf
– 'County Park'	CBar CEnt CSpe CTri CYeo ECha ECho ECou ECtt EDAr ELan EPfP GAbr GGar GKir LBMP LLWG LRHS MAsh MMuc SPlb SPoG SRms SRot WHoo WMoo WPer
– 'Tom Stone'	ECtt MBNS
– 'White Stars'	ECho EDAr LLWG

Premna (*Verbenaceae*)

* ***vanrensburgii***	CCCN

Preslia see *Mentha*

Primula ✿ (*Primulaceae*)

sp.	SVic
Lismore 79-26	NHol
SDR 4735 (Cy)	GKev
acaulis	see *P. vulgaris*
'Adrian Jones' (Au)	IPen NHol WAbe
advena var. ***euprepes***	see *P. euprepes*
'Alan Robb' (Pr/Prim/d)	ECtt EPfP GAbr SPer SRGP WFar
'Alexina' (*allionii* hybrid) (Au)	GKev MFie NHar
algida (Al)	ECho
– 'Sibirica' new	GKev
§ ***allionii*** (Au) ♀H2	IPen NSum WAbe
– Hartside 383/3	NHol
– HNG 12	ITim
– 'Agnes' (Au)	NMen
– 'Aire Waves'	see *P.* × *loiseleurii* 'Aire Waves'
– 'Allen Moonbeam' (Au) new	ITim
– 'Anna Griffith' (Au)	CPBP IPen MFie NWCA WAbe
– 'Anne' (Au)	IPen
– 'Aphrodite' (Au)	NHar
– 'Apple Blossom' (Au)	GAbr
– 'Archer' (Au)	IPen ITim NHol
– 'Ares' (Au)	NHar
– 'Aries Violet' (Au)	NHar
– 'Austen' (Au)	NHol
– 'Avalanche' (Au)	IPen ITim WAbe
– BC No. 4 new	CPBP
– 'Bill Martin' (Au)	EPot IPen ITim NHol
– 'Blood Flake'	IPen
– Burnley form (Au)	NHol
– 'Circe's Flute' (Au)	NHar
– 'Cissie' (Au) new	ITim
– 'Claude Flight' (Au)	MFie
– 'Crowsley Variety' (Au)	NMen NWCA
– 'Crusader' (Au)	WThu
– 'Crystal' (Au)	WAbe
– 'Duncan' (Au)	ITim
§ – 'Edinburgh' (Au)	CPBP GKev IPen ITim NHol
– 'Edrom' (Au)	IPen ITim NHol
– 'Elizabeth Baker' (Au)	IPen ITim MFie
– 'Elizabeth Burrow' (Au)	WAbe
– 'Elizabeth Earle' (Au)	EPot ITim WAbe
– 'Elliott's Large'	see *P. allionii* 'Edinburgh'
– 'Elliott's Variety'	see *P. allionii* 'Edinburgh'
– 'Eureka' (Au)	CPBP
– 'Eveline Burrow' (Au) new	WAbe
– 'Fanfare' (Au)	IPen NHar NHol
– 'Frank Barker' (Au)	NHol
– 'Gavin Brown' (Au)	IPen ITim
– 'Gilderdale Glow' (Au)	CPBP
– 'Giuseppi's Form'	see *P. allionii* 'Mrs Dyas'
– 'Grandiflora' (Au)	GKev ITim
– 'Hartside'	NHol
– 'Hartside 6' (Au)	IPen ITim NHar
– 'Hartside 12' (Au)	IPen
– 'Hazey' (Au) new	ITim
– 'Hemswell' (Au)	NHol
– 'Hocker Edge' (Au)	ITim NHol
– 'Huntsman' (Au)	MFie
– 'Io 2' (Au)	NHar
– 'Ion's Amethyst' (Au)	NHar
– 'Jenny' (Au)	EPot
– 'Joe Elliott' (Au)	IPen
– K R W	see *P. allionii* 'Ken's Seedling'
§ – 'Kath Dryden' (Au)	GKev IPen LLHF
§ – 'Ken's Seedling' (Au)	IPen NHol
– 'Little O' (Au)	NHol WAbe
– 'Lucy' (Au)	NHar
– 'Margaret Earle' (Au)	NHol WAbe
– 'Marjorie Wooster' (Au)	IPen ITim MFie NWCA
– 'Martin' (Au)	IPen ITim
– 'Mary Anne' (Au)	WAbe
– 'Mary Berry' (Au)	CPBP IPen MFie NHol
– 'Maurice Dryden' (Au)	WAbe
– 'Molly' (Au)	IPen NWCA
§ – 'Mrs Dyas' (Au)	IPen NHol WAbe
– 'Neptunes Wave' (Au)	NHar
– 'New Dawn' (Au)	NHar
– 'Pale Venus' (Au)	NHar
– 'Peggy Wilson' (Au)	EPot NLar
– 'Pennine Pink' (Au)	MFie
– 'Perkie' (Au)	IPen
– 'Phoebe's Moon' new	NHar
– 'Pink Ice' (Au)	ITim MFie NHol
– 'Pinkie' (Au)	WAbe
– 'Praecox' (Au)	IPen
– 'Raymond Wooster' (Au)	NHol
– 'Scimitar' (Au)	MFie NHol
– 'Snowflake' (Au)	CPBP GCrs GKev IPen NHol NWCA WAbe
– 'Tranquillity' (Au)	GKev ITim MFie NHar NHol
– 'Travellers' (Au)	EPot IPen
– 'William Earle' (Au)	CPBP ITim NHol
allionii × ***auricula*** 'Blairside Yellow' (Au)	ECho IPen NSum WFar
allionii × ***auricula*** 'Old Red Dusty Miller' (Au)	ECho
allionii × ***clusiana*** (Au)	ECho
allionii × ***hirsuta*** (Au)	NHol
allionii × 'Lismore Jewel' (Au)	NWCA
allionii × 'Lismore Treasure' (Au)	CPBP MFie NWCA
allionii × ***pedemontana***	see *P.* × *sendtneri*
allionii × ***pubescens*** (Au)	ECho
allionii × ***pubescens*** 'Harlow Car' (Au)	GAgs
allionii × 'Snow Ruffles' (Au)	ITim
allionii × 'White Linda Pope' (Au)	IPen MFie NHar
alpicola (Si) ♀H4	CFee CLAP CRow CSWP CWCL EBee EPfP GAbr GAuc GEdr GGar GKev IPen LPBA LRHS NBid NBro NCGa NGdn NHol NSum NWCA SBfd WBVN
– var. ***alba*** (Si)	CPla CRow CSWP EBee GAuc GEdr GGar GKev IPen LRHS MNrw NBid
§ – var. ***alpicola*** (Si)	CLAP CSWP EBee GCra GEdr GKev GKir IPen MMuc MNrw SEND
– hybrids (Si)	STes
– 'Kevock Sky' (Si)	EBee GKev
– 'La Luna' (Si)	MMuc
– var. ***luna***	see *P. alpicola* var. *alpicola*

- var. ***violacea*** (Si)	CAby CFir CLAP CPla CRow CSWP EBee GAbr GCra GGar GKev IPen MMuc MNrw NBid NHol SEND WFar WPer
'Altaica'	see *P. elatior* subsp. *meyeri*
altaica grandiflora	see *P. elatior* subsp. *meyeri*
amethystina (Am)	WAbe
- SDR 4745	GKev
- subsp. ***brevifolia*** (Am)	GKev
amoena	see *P. elatior* subsp. *meyeri*
angustifolia (Pa)	NWCA
anisodora	see *P. wilsonii* var. *anisodora*
'Annemijne'	WCot
'April Rose' (Pr/Prim/d)	NBid
× ***arctotis***	see *P.* × *pubescens*
atrodentata (De)	GKev
aurantiaca (Pf)	CFir CPla EBee GEdr GKev GKir IPen
aureata (Pe)	WAbe
auricula ambig. (Au)	CTsd GKev
auricula L. (Au) Υ^{H4}	EDAr IPen LRHS MFie MHer NBro NSla SPer SPet SPlb SPoG WAbe
- var. ***albocincta*** (Au)	NWCA
- subsp. ***bauhinii*** (Au)	GAuc
auricula misapplied (Au)	GAgs
- A74 (Au)	NCob NPri SEND STre
- K85 (Au/S)	ITim SPop
- '2nd Vic' (Au/S)	SPop WFar
- 'Abdor' (Au/St) **new**	SPop
- 'Abundance' (Au/A)	SPop
- 'Achates' (Au/A)	WAln
- 'Admiral' (Au/A)	WAln
- 'Adrian' (Au/A)	GAgs IPen MFie NBro NDro SPop WHil
- 'Aga Khan' (Au/A)	WAln
- 'Agamemnon' (Au/A)	MFie WAln WCre
- 'Alamo' (Au/A)	MFie NDro SPop WCre
- 'Alan Ball' (Au)	WCre
- 'Alan Ravenscroft' (Au/A)	MFie SPop WAln WFar WHil
- 'Alansford' (Au/A)	WAln
- 'Albert Bailey' (Au/d)	EWoo GAbr GAgs GCai IPen ITim MFie NDro NEgg SPop WCre WHil
- 'Alexandra Georgina' (Au/A)	MFie WAln
- 'Alf' (Au/A)	MFie NDro SPop WAln
- 'Alfred Charles' (Au/A)	WAln
- 'Alfred Niblett' (Au/S)	IPen
- 'Alice Haysom' (Au/S)	CWCL ELan EWoo GAbr GAgs GCai IPen MAsh NDro SDnm SPop WCre WFar WHil
- 'Alicia' (Au/A)	GAbr GAgs MFie NDro NHol SDnm SPop WCre
- 'Alison Jane' (Au/A)	MFie NDro WCre WHil
- 'Alison Telford' (Au/A)	WHil
- 'Allensford' (Au/A)	WCre
- 'Alloway' (Au/d)	WAln
- 'Almand' (Au/d)	WAln
- 'Almondbury' (Au/S)	NDro
- alpine mixed (Au/A)	EPfP GKir SRms
- 'Amber Waves' (Au)	GAbr
- 'Amicable' (Au/A)	MFie NDro NHol SPop WCre WHil
- 'Ancient Order' (Au/A)	WAln
- 'Ancient Society' (Au/A)	EWoo GAbr GAgs IPen NDro NHol SPop WFar
- 'Andrea Julie' (Au/A)	GAgs IPen MFie NDro SPop WCre WHil
- 'Andrew Hunter' (Au/A)	MFie NDro SPop WAln
- 'Andy Cole' (Au/A)	EWoo NDro SPop WAln
- 'Angel Eyes' (Au/St)	SPop
- 'Angel Islington' (Au/S) **new**	NDro
- 'Angela Gould' (Au)	GAbr MFie
- 'Angela Short' (Au/St) **new**	SPop
- 'Angostura' (Au/d)	SPop
- 'Ann Taylor' (Au/A)	IPen
- 'Anne Hyatt' (Au/d)	GAbr MAsh WAln
- 'Anne Swithinbank' (Au/d)	WAln
- 'Annie Tustin' (Au/S)	SPop
- 'Antoc' (Au/S)	SPop
- 'Anwar Sadat' (Au/A)	MFie NDro WCre WFar WHil
- 'Apple Blossom' (Au/B)	NDro WHil
- 'Applecross' (Au/A)	IPen NDro SPop WCre WFar WHil
- 'April Moon' (Au/S)	GAgs MAsh MFie NDro SPop WAln
- 'April Tiger' (Au/St)	WAln
- 'Arabian Night' (Au/A)	WAln
- 'Arctic Fox'	MFie WAln
- 'Argus' (Au/A)	GAbr GAgs MAsh MFie NDro NHol SPop WCre WHil
- 'Arlene' (Au/A)	WAln
- 'Arthur Delbridge' (Au/A)	MFie NDro WFar WHil
- 'Arundel Cross' (Au)	IPen NEgg
- 'Arundell' (Au/S/St)	EBee GAbr GAgs GCai ITim MAsh MFie NHol SPop WCre WFar WHil
- 'Arwen' (Au/A)	SPop
- 'Ashcliffe Gem' (Au/A)	NDro WAln
- 'Ashcliffe Gold' (Au/A)	WAln
- 'Astolat' (Au/S)	EBee EWoo GAbr GAgs IPen ITim NDro SDnm SPav SPop WCre WHil
- 'Athene' (Au/S)	IPen NDro SPop WAln
- 'Atlantic' (Au/S)	NDro NEgg
- 'Aubergine' (Au/B) **new**	NDro
- 'Audacity' (Au/d)	WAln
- 'Aurora' (Au/A)	EDAr MFie NDro WCre
- 'Austin' (Au/A)	IPen WAln
- 'Autumn Fire' (Au/A)	SPop
- 'Aviemore' (Au/A)	SPop
- 'Avon Carrier' (Au/d) **new**	SPop
- 'Avon Citronella' (Au)	SPop
- 'Avon Twist' (Au/d)	SPop
- 'Avril' (Au/A)	NDro SPop WAln
- 'Avril Hunter' (Au/A)	GAgs IPen MAsh MFie NDro NHol SPop WCre WHil
- 'Aztec' (Au/d)	WAln
- 'Bacchante' (Au/d)	WAln
- 'Bacchus' (Au/A)	MFie NDro SPop WHil
- 'Baggage' (Au)	MAsh SPop
- 'Balbithan' (Au/B)	GAbr GAgs
- 'Baltic Amber' (Au)	MFie SPop WHil
- 'Barbarella' (Au/S)	MAsh MFie NDro SPop
- 'Barbarian'	WFar
- Barnhaven doubles (Au/d)	GAbr NSum
- 'Barnhaven Gold' (Au)	IPen
- 'Barr Beacon' (Au/A) **new**	NDro
- 'Basilio' (Au/S)	NDro WAln
- 'Basuto' (Au/A)	IPen ITim MFie NDro SPop WCre WHil
- 'Beatrice' (Au/A)	CTri GAbr GCai IPen MFie NDro NHol SPop WCre WFar WHil
- 'Bedford Lad' (Au/A)	WCre
- 'Beechen Green' (Au/S)	EWoo GAbr GAgs GCai ITim MAsh NDro SPop WCre
- 'Behold' (Au)	WCre
- 'Belgravia Gold' (Au/B) **new**	NDro
- 'Bellamy Pride' (Au/B)	GAbr IPen MAsh NDro SPop
- 'Belle Zana' (Au/S)	EWoo GAgs IPen MAsh MFie NDro SPop WAln
- 'Ben Lawers' (Au/S)	SPop
- 'Ben Wyves' (Au/S)	NHol SPop WCre
- 'Bendigo' (Au/S)	MFie SPop WAln
- 'Bengal Rose' (Au/S)	SPop
- 'Benny Green' (Au/S)	SPop

– 'Beppi' **new**	WHil
– 'Bethan McSparron' (Au/B) **new**	NDro
– 'Bewitched' (Au/A)	MFie NDro NHol WAln
– 'Big Ben' (Au/S)	ECho
– 'Bilbo Baggins' (Au/A)	NDro SPop WAln
– 'Bill Bailey' (Au/d)	GAbr NDro SPop WCre
– 'Bilton' (Au/S)	MAsh WCre
– 'Bingley Folk' (Au/B)	SPop
– 'Bizarre' (Au)	GAgs WCre
– 'Black Ice' (Au/S)	NDro
– 'Black Jack'PBR (Au/d)	EBee LRHS
– 'Black Knight' (Au/d)	WAln
– 'Blackcurrant' (Au) **new**	GAbr
– 'Blackfield' (Au/S)	SPop
– 'Blackhill' (Au/S)	MFie SPop
– 'Blackpool Rock' (Au/St)	WAln
– 'Blairside Yellow' (Au/B)	ECho EWes LLHF NDro WAbe
– 'Blakeney' (Au/d)	GCai MFie NDro WAln
– 'Blossom' (Au/A)	GAbr MFie WFar
– 'Blue Bonnet' (Au/A/d)	EWoo GAbr GAgs NDro SPop WAln WCre
– 'Blue Boy' (Au/S) **new**	WHil
– 'Blue Chips' (Au/S)	MAsh SPop WAln WHil
– 'Blue Cliffs' (Au/S)	MAsh SPop WAln
– 'Blue Fire' (Au/S)	SPop
– 'Blue Frills' (Au)	WAln
– 'Blue Heaven' (Au/A)	NDro SPop WCre
– 'Blue Jean' (Au/S)	GAbr IPen MFie NDro SPop
– 'Blue Lace' (Au) **new**	WAln
– 'Blue Moon' (Au/S)	WAln
– 'Blue Nile' (Au/S)	NDro SPop WCre
– 'Blue Skies' (Au/St)	SPop
– 'Blue Velvet' (Au/B)	GAgs GKir IPen LLHF NBro NDro WCre WHil WPat
– 'Blue Wave' (Au/d)	MSCN
– 'Blue Yodeler' (Au/A)	GAgs NDro SPop WHil
– 'Blush Baby' (Au/St)	GAbr GAgs SPop
– 'Bob Dingley' (Au/A)	WCre
– 'Bob Lancashire' (Au/S)	GAgs IPen ITim MFie NDro NHol SPop WCre WHil
– 'Bold Tartan' (Au/St)	WAln
– 'Bollin Tiger' (Au/St)	WAln
– 'Bonafide' (Au/d)	WAln
– 'Bonanza' (Au/S)	WAln
– 'Bookham Firefly' (Au/A)	GAbr GAgs IPen MFie NDro NHol SPop WCre WFar WHil
– 'Bookham Star' (Au/S) **new**	NDro
– 'Boortree Bush' (Au)	WCre
– 'Border Bandit' (Au/B)	SPop
– 'Border Tawny' (Au/B) **new**	NDro
– 'Boromir' (Au/A)	WAln
– 'Boy Blue' (Au/S)	NDro
– 'Bradford City' (Au/A)	EBee NDro SDnm WHil
– 'Bradmore Bluebell' (Au)	GAbr
– 'Bramley Rose' (Au/B)	SPop
– 'Bran' (Au/B)	NDro
– 'Branno' (Au/S)	WAln
– 'Brasso' (Au)	MFie NDro WAln
– 'Brazen Hussy' (Au/d)	WAln
– 'Brazil' (Au/S)	EBee GAbr IPen MAsh MFie NDro NHol SPop WCre WHil
– 'Brazos River' (Au/A)	MFie WAln
– 'Breckland Joy' (Au/A) **new**	NDro
– 'Brenda's Choice' (Au/A)	IPen MFie NDro SPop WCre WFar
– 'Brentford Bees' (Au/St)	WAln
– 'Bright Eyes' (Au/A)	IPen MFie WCre
– 'Broad Gold' (Au/A)	MFie SPop WAln WCre
– 'Broadwell Gold' (Au/B)	GAbr MAsh NDro NLar SPop WCre
– 'Brookfield' (Au/S)	IPen ITim MAsh MFie NDro SPop WCre WHil
– 'Broughton' (Au/S)	MFie SPop
– 'Brown Ben' (Au)	GAgs MFie WFar WHil
– 'Brown Bess' (Au/A)	GAbr GAgs GCai IPen MFie NDro WCre WFar WHil
– 'Brownie' (Au/B)	CWCL NBir NDro SDnm SPop WHil
– 'Brownie Guider' (Au/B) **new**	NDro
– 'Buccaneer'	ECho
– 'Bucks Green' (Au/S)	GAbr NDro SPop
– 'Bunty' (Au/A)	MFie
– 'Bush Baby' (Au/B) **new**	NDro
– 'Butterwick' (Au/A)	EWoo GAbr GAgs GMaP IPen MFie NDro NEgg SPop
– 'C.G. Haysom' (Au/S)	GAbr GAgs MAsh MFie NDro SPop WCre
– 'C.W. Needham' (Au/A)	IPen MFie NDro SPop WCre
– 'Cadiz Bay' (Au/d) **new**	WAln
– 'Calypso' (Au/d)	WAln
– 'Cambodunum' (Au/A)	IPen MFie NDro SPop WCre WFar WHil
– 'Camelot' (Au/d)	EBee ECho ELan GAgs GCai MFie NBro NDro NHol SPop WCre WFar WHil
– 'Cameo' (Au/A)	WCre
– 'Cameo Beauty' (Au/d)	NDro SPop
– 'Camilla' (Au/A)	WAln
– 'Candida' (Au/d)	GAgs IPen MFie NDro SPop WCre
– 'Candy Stripe' (Au/St)	SPop
– 'Cappela' (Au/d) **new**	WAln
– 'Caramel' (Au/A)	IPen WAln
– 'Cardinal Red' (Au/d)	SPop
– 'Carioca' (Au/A)	WAln
– 'Carmel' (Au/D)	SPop
– 'Carole' (Au/A)	MFie WFar WHil
– 'Carreras' (Au)	MFie
– 'Carzon' (Au/A)	NDro
– 'Catherine Wheel' (Au/St)	WAln
– 'Ceri Nicolle' (Au/B) **new**	NDro
– 'Chaffinch' (Au/S)	EWoo GAbr GAgs IPen NDro SPop
– 'Chamois' (Au/B)	GAbr IPen MFie NDro WHil
– 'Chanel' (Au/S)	SPop
– 'Channel' (Au/S)	WAln
– 'Chantilly Cream' (Au/d)	WAln
– 'Charles Bronson' (Au/d)	MFie NDro WAln
– 'Charles Rennie' (Au/B)	NDro SPop WAln
– 'Charlie's Aunt' (Au/A)	WAln
– 'Checkmate' (Au)	MFie SPop WAln
– 'Chelsea Bridge' (Au/A)	IPen MFie NDro SPop WCre WHil
– 'Cheops' (Au/A)	MFie NDro NEgg
– 'Cherry' (Au/S)	IPen ITim NDro
– 'Cherry Picker' (Au/A)	MFie NDro SPop WCre WFar
– 'Cheyenne' (Au/S)	GAbr GAgs MAsh MFie NDro WCre WFar
– 'Chiffon' (Au/S)	EWoo IPen NDro SPop
– 'Chiquita' (Au/d)	MAsh SPop
– 'Chloë' (Au/S)	NDro
– 'Chloris' (Au/S)	WAln
– 'Chorister' (Au/S)	CPBP EBee ECho GAbr GAgs GCai IPen ITim MFie NDro NHol WHil
– 'Chyne' (Au)	EWoo
– 'Cicero' (Au/A)	MFie NDro SPop WAln
– 'Cindy' (Au/A)	ECho NDro
– 'Cinnamon' (Au/d)	GAgs ITim MAsh MFie NDro SPop WCre
– 'Cinnamon' (Au/S)	GAbr WHil
– 'Ciribiribin' (Au/A)	WAln
– 'Clare' (Au/S)	IPen MAsh MFie NDro SPop
– 'Clatter-Ha' (Au/d)	MAsh WHil
– 'Claudia Taylor' (Au)	SPop
– 'Clouded Yellow' (Au/S)	SPop WAln WHil

- 'Cloudy Bay' (Au) LRHS WCot WFar
- 'Cloverdale' (Au/d) WAln
- 'Clunie' (Au/S) IPen NDro WCre
- 'Clunie II' (Au/S) GAgs IPen WFar
- 'Cobden Meadows' (Au/A) WAln WCre
- 'Coffee' (Au/S) IPen MAsh MFie NDro WCre WFar
- 'Colbury' (Au/S) NDro SPop
- 'Colonel Champney' (Au/S) EWoo NDro SPop
- 'Comet' (Au/S) IPen NDro
- 'Connaught Court' (Au/A) EWoo WAln
- 'Conservative' (Au/S) GAbr GAgs IPen NDro WFar
- 'Consett' (Au/S) EWoo IPen MFie WHil
- 'Cooper's Gold' (Au/B) **new** NDro
- 'Coppi' (Au/A) IPen NDro SPop WAln
- 'Coral' (Au/S) NDro
- 'Coral Sea' (Au/S) MAsh
- 'Cornish Cream' (Au/B) **new** NDro
- 'Cornmeal' (Au/S) ITim MFie NDro WAln WHil
- 'Corporal Jones' (Au/S) SPop
- 'Corporal Kate' (Au/St) WAln
- 'Corrie Files' (Au/d) MFie WAln
- 'Cortez Silver' (Au/S) WAln
- 'Cortina' (Au/S) ECho EWoo GAbr GAgs GCai IPen MAsh MFie NDro SDnm SPav SPop WCre WFar WHil
- 'County Park Red' (Au/B) ECou NDro
- 'Coventry Street' (Au/S) MAsh MFie NDro
- 'Crackley Tagetes' (Au/d) ECho
- 'Craig Dhu' (Au/B) SPop
- 'Craig Vaughan' (Au/A) MFie NDro NHol SPop
- 'Cranborne' (Au/A) SPop
- 'Crecy' (Au/A) MFie SPop WAln
- 'Crimple' (Au/S) NDro
- 'Crimson Glow' (Au/d) GAbr MAsh MFie NDro SPop WAln
- 'Crinoline' (Au/S) **new** NDro SPop
- 'Cuckoo Fair' (Au/S) GAbr GAgs IPen NDro SPop WAln WCre
- 'Cuddles' (Au/A) MFie NDro WAln
- 'Curry Blend' (Au/B) GAbr GAgs NDro
- 'Cutie Pie' (Au/St) MAsh
- 'Cuttlefish' (Au/St) SPop
- 'Daftie Green' (Au/S) GAbr GAgs IPen NDro
- 'Dakota' (Au/S) MFie
- 'Dales Red' (Au/B) GAbr GAgs ITim MFie NDro NHol NLar SDnm SPop WAln WHil
- 'Dan Tiger' (Au/St) MAsh MFie SPop WAln WHil
- 'Daniel' (Au/A) NDro WAln
- 'Dark Eyes' (Au/d) GAbr MFie NDro SPop WAln
- 'Dark Lady' (Au/A) WAln
- 'Dark Red' (Au/S) IPen
- 'David Beckham' (Au/d) SPop WAln
- 'Deckchair' (Au/St) NDro SPop
- 'Dedham' (Au/d) WAln
- 'Delilah' (Au/d) GAbr GAgs ITim MAsh MFie NDro SPop WHil
- 'Denise' (Au/S) WAln
- 'Denna Snuffer' (Au/d) GAbr NDro
- 'Devon Cream' (Au/d) ECho MFie NDro SPop WFar WHil
- 'Diane' (Au/A) MFie
- 'Dick Rogers' (Au/B) **new** NDro
- 'Digby' (Au/d) NDro WAln
- 'Digit' (Au/d) WAln
- 'Dilemma' (Au/A) SPop
- * - 'Dill' (Au/A) NDro WAln
- 'Dilly Dilly' (Au/A) NDro SPop WAln
- 'Divint Dunch' (Au/A) IPen MFie NDro SPop WCre WFar WHil
- 'Doctor Duthie' (Au/S) SPop
- 'Doctor Lennon's White' (Au/B) GAgs IPen MFie NDro SPop WHil
- 'Dolly Viney' (Au/d) GAbr WAln
- 'Donhead' (Au/A) MFie NDro SPop WCre WFar
- 'Donna Clancy' (Au/S) EWoo SPop
- 'Dorado' (Au/d) WAln
- 'Doreen Stephens' (Au/A) MFie WAln WFar
- 'Doris Jean' (Au/A) MFie WFar
- 'Dorothy' (Au/S) WAln
- 'Doublet' (Au/d) ECho GAbr GAgs GCai IPen MFie NDro NHol SPop WCre WFar WHil
- 'Doubloon' (Au/d) ECho
- 'Doublure' (Au/d) GAbr GAgs NDro SPop WHil
- 'Douglas Bader' (Au/A) GAbr MFie NDro SPop WCre WHil
- 'Douglas Black' (Au/S) EWoo GAbr GAgs MFie NDro SPop WCre WHil
- 'Douglas Blue' (Au/S) WAln
- 'Douglas Green' (Au/S) CWCL IPen NDro
- 'Douglas White' (Au/S) MFie SPop
- 'Dovedale' (Au/S) NDro WAln
- 'Dowager' (Au/A) MFie
- Downtown Doubles (d) **new** SPop
- 'Doyen' (Au/d) ITim MAsh MFie WAln WFar
- 'Drax' (Au/A) WAln
- 'Dubarii' (Au/A) MFie WAln
- 'Duchess of Malfi' (Au/S) SPop
- 'Duchess of York' (Au) GAbr
- 'Duke of Edinburgh' (Au/B) **new** NDro
- * - 'Dusky' (Au) WFar
- 'Dusky Girl' (Au/A) NDro WAln
- 'Dusky Maiden' (Au/A) GAbr GAgs GCai MFie NDro SPop WCre WHil
- 'Dusky Yellow' (Au/B) ECho NDro
- 'Dusty Miller' (Au/B) EBrs ECho LRHS MRav NBir NHol
- 'Eastern Promise' (Au/A) GAgs GCai MFie NDro SPop WFar WHil
- 'Ed Spivey' (Au/A) NDro WCre
- 'Eddy Gordon' (Au/A) WAln
- 'Eden Alexander' (Au/B) MFie NDro
- 'Eden Blue Star' (Au/B) **new** SPop
- 'Eden Carmine' (Au/B) MFie
- 'Eden David' (Au/B) MFie SPop WHil
- 'Eden Moonlight' (Au/B) **new** WHil
- 'Edith Allen' (Au/A) WAln
- 'Edith Major' (Au/d) MFie WHil
- 'Edward Sweeney' (Au/S) WAln
- 'Eglinton' WCre
- 'Eileen K' (Au/S) NDro
- 'Elf Star' (Au/A) SPop
- 'Eli Jenkins' (Au) WAln
- 'Elizabeth Ann' (Au/A) GAbr GAgs NDro SPop
- 'Ellen Thompson' (Au/A) EWoo GAbr GAgs MFie NDro SPop WCre WFar
- 'Elsie' (Au/A) WCre
- 'Elsie May' (Au/A) MAsh MFie NDro SPop WCre WHil
- 'Elsinore' (Au/S) IPen MAsh NDro WCre
- 'Emberglow' (Au/d) WAln
- 'Embley' (Au/S) NDro SPop
- 'Emery Down' (Au/S) ITim NDro SPop
- 'Emmett Smith' (Au/A) NDro WAln
- 'Enlightened' (Au/A) MFie
- 'Envy' (Au/S) MFie NHol
- 'Eric Price' **new** ITim
- 'Erica' (Au/A) IPen ITim MFie NDro SPop WCre WHil
- 'Erjon' (Au/S) MFie NDro SPop WAln
- 'Error' (Au/S) MFie WAln
- 'Esso' (Au/S) NDro

- 'Ethel' (Au) NDro
- 'Etna' (Au/S) WAln
- 'Eve Guest' (Au/A) NDro
- 'Eventide' (Au/S) MAsh SPop
- 'Everest Blue' (Au/S) GAbr GAgs MAsh SPop WCre
- 'Excalibur' (Au/d) GAbr NDro SPop WAln WFar
- 'Eyeopener' (Au/A) MFie NDro SPop WAln WCre WHil
- 'Fabuloso' (Au/St) SPop
- 'Fairy' (Au/A) NDro WAln
- 'Fairy Moon' (Au/S) IPen WAln
- 'Fairy Queen' (Au/S) WAln
- 'Faliraki' (Au/A) SPop WAln
- 'Faliraki Fanciful' (Au) EWoo
- 'Faloonside' (Au) WCre
- 'Falstaff' (Au/d) WAln
- 'Fanciful' (Au/S) MFie NDro WHil
- 'Fancy Free' (Au) SPop
- 'Fandancer' (Au/A) WAln
- 'Fanfare' (Au/S) MAsh MFie NDro SPop WAln
- 'Fanny Meerbeck' (Au/S) GAbr GCai IPen MFie NDro SPop WFar WHil
- 'Faro' (Au/S) MAsh NDro WAln
- 'Favourite' (Au/S) EWoo GAbr GAgs IPen ITim MAsh MFie NDro NHol SPop WCre WFar WHil
- 'Fen Tiger' (Au/St) SPop
- 'Ferrybridge' (Au/A) IPen
- 'Fiddler's Green' (Au/d) GAbr NDro SPop
- 'Figaro' (Au/S) GAbr GAgs MAsh MFie NDro SPop WAln
- 'Finchfield' (Au/A) GAbr IPen MFie NDro NHol
- 'Firecracker' (Au) WAln
- 'Firenze' (Au/A) MFie SPop
- 'Firsby' (Au/d) MAsh SPop WAln WCre
- 'First Lady' (Au/A) WAln
- 'Fishtoft' (Au/d) MFie WAln
- 'Fitzroy' (Au/d) SPop
- 'Fleet Street' (Au/S) **new** NDro
- 'Fleminghouse' (Au/S) GAbr MAsh MFie NDro SPop
- 'Forest Burgundy' (Au/d) SPop
- 'Forest Cappuccino' (Au/d) SPop
- 'Forest Duet' (Au/d) SPop
- 'Forest Fire' (Au/d) **new** SPop
- 'Forest Lemon' (Au/d) SPop
- 'Fradley' (Au/A) IPen MFie NDro WAln WHil
- 'Frank Bailey' (Au/d) MAsh SPop WAln
- 'Frank Crosland' (Au/A) MFie NDro WCre WFar WHil
- 'Frank Jenning' (Au/A) NDro WAln
- 'Frank Taylor' (Au/S) EWoo
- 'Fred Booley' (Au/d) GAbr GAgs IPen MAsh MFie NDro NHol SPop WCre WFar WHil
- 'Fred Livesley' (Au/A) NDro WAln
- 'Fresco' (Au/A) SPop
- 'Friskney' (Au/d) WAln
- 'Frittenden Yellow' (Au/B) NDro SPop WFar
- 'Frosty' (Au/S) NDro
- 'Fuller's Red' (Au/S) MAsh SPop WCre WFar WHil
- 'Funny Valentine' (Au/d) IPen MAsh MFie SPop
- 'Fuzzy' (Au/St) WAln
- 'G.L.Taylor' (Au/A) IPen NDro
- 'Gaia' (Au/d) SPop WAln
- 'Gail Atkinson' (Au/A) SPop
- 'Galatea' (Au/S) WAln
- 'Galen' (Au/A) WFar
- 'Ganymede' (Au/d) SPop WAln
- 'Gary Pallister' (Au/A) MAsh WAln
- 'Gavin Ward' (Au/S) MAsh WAln
- 'Gay Crusader' (Au/A) GAbr GAgs MFie NDro SPop WCre WFar WHil
- 'Gazza' (Au/A) WAln
- 'Gee Cross' (Au/A) GAbr IPen NDro
- 'Geldersome Green' (Au/S) GCai NDro SPop WFar
- 'Gemini' (Au/S) GLin NDro
- 'General Champney' (Au) WCre
- 'Generosity' (Au/A) MFie SPop WHil
- 'Geordie' (Au/A) WAln
- 'George Edge' (Au/B) **new** NDro
- 'George Harrison' (Au/B) GAbr GAgs NDro SPop
- 'George Jennings' (Au/A) MFie NDro WAln
- 'George Swinford's Leathercoat' (Au/B) NDro
- 'Geronimo' (Au/S) GAbr IPen MAsh MFie NDro SPop WCre
- 'Ghost Grey' (Au) WCre
- 'Gimli' (Au/A) WAln
- 'Girl Guide' (Au/S) WAln WHil
- 'Gizabroon' (Au/S) CWCL EBee GAbr GAgs GCai MFie NDro NEgg SDnm SPav SPop WCre WFar WHil
- 'Glasnost' (Au/S) WAln
- 'Gleam' (Au/S) EBee ECho EDAr GAgs GCai LLHF MFie NDro SPop WCre WFar WHil
- 'Glencoe' (Au/S) ECho
- 'Gleneagles' (Au/S) EWoo GCai IPen NDro SPop WAln WCre
- 'Glenelg' (Au/S) EWoo GAbr GAgs ITim MAsh MFie NDro SPop WCre WHil
- 'Glenluce' (Au/S) SPop
- 'Gnome' (Au/B) GAgs IPen NDro NHol
- 'Gold Blaze' (Au/S) NDro
- 'Gold Seal' (Au/d) SPop
- 'Gold Seam' (Au/A) MFie WAln
- 'Golden Chartreuse' (Au/d) GAbr
- 'Golden Fleece' (Au/S) EWoo GAbr GAgs GCai MAsh MFie NDro SPop
- 'Golden Harvest' (Au/A) **new** SPop
- 'Golden Hill' (Au/S) MAsh SPop
- 'Golden Hind' (Au/d) EWoo GAgs MFie NBro NDro SPop WCre
- 'Golden Splendour' (Au/d) EWoo GAgs IPen ITim MAsh MFie NDro SPop WCre WFar WHil
- 'Golden Wedding' (Au/A) IPen MFie SPop WAln WHil
- 'Goldie' (Au/S) NDro
- 'Goldwin' (Au/A) WAln
- 'Gollum' (Au/A) MAsh MFie NDro SPop WAln WHil
- 'Good Report' (Au/A) EWoo GAgs MAsh MFie NDro SPop WFar WHil
- 'Goody Goody' (Au/St) **new** SPop
- 'Gorey' (Au/A) MFie NDro WHil
- 'Gorgeous George' (Au/St) **new** SPop
- 'Grabley' (Au/S) SPop WAln
- 'Grandad's Favourite' (Au/B) NDro SPop
- 'Green Elg' (Au) NHol
- 'Green Finger' (Au/S) MFie SPop WHil
- 'Green Frill' (Au) GAgs
- 'Green Goddess' (Au/St) WAln
- 'Green Isle' (Au/S) GAbr IPen MFie NDro SPop WCre WFar
- 'Green Jacket' (Au/S) IPen WCre
- 'Green Magic' (Au/S) WAln
- 'Green Meadows' (Au/S) GAgs SPop WAln
- 'Green Parrot' (Au/S) GAbr NDro SPop
- 'Green Shank' (Au/S) EWoo IPen NDro SPop WFar
- 'Greenfield's Fancy' (Au) EBee

- 'Greenfinger' (Au/S) WAln
- 'Greenheart' (Au/S) SPop
- 'Greenpeace' (Au/S) GAgs NDro SPop
- 'Greenways' (Au/S) WAln
- 'Greswolde' (Au/d) SPop
- 'Greta' (Au/S) ECho EWoo GAbr GAgs IPen ITim NDro NHol SPop WCot WFar WHil
- 'Gretna Green' (Au/S) SPop
- 'Grey Bonnet' (Au/S) SPop
- 'Grey Dawn' (Au/S) WAln
- 'Grey Edge' ECho
- 'Grey Friar' (Au/S) WAln
- 'Grey Hawk' (Au/S) IPen MFie NDro SPop
- 'Grey Lady' (Au/S) WAln
- 'Grey Lag' (Au/S) WHil
- 'Grey Monarch' (Au/S) GAbr GAgs GCai MAsh MFie NDro SPop WHil
- 'Grey Owl' (Au/S) WAln
- 'Grizedale' (Au/S) WAln
- 'Grüner Veltliner' (Au/S) NDro SPop
- 'Guinea' (Au/S) EWoo GAbr IPen NDro SPop
- 'Gwen' (Au/A) GAbr NDro SPop WAln WCre
- 'Gwen Baker' (Au/d) GAbr MFie NDro SPop WCre
- 'Gwenda' (Au/A) SPop WAln WHil
- 'Gypsy Rose Lee' (Au/A) NDro WAln
- 'Habanera' (Au/A) NDro SPop WCre WFar
- 'Haffner' (Au/S) MAsh NDro SPop
- 'Hallmark' (Au/A) MFie WAln
- 'Handsome Lass' (Au/St) SPop
- 'Harlequin' (Au/B) **new** NDro
- 'Harmony' (Au/B) MFie NBro NDro NHol
- 'Harry Hotspur' (Au/A) EWoo GAgs IPen MFie NDro SPop WFar WHil
- 'Harry 'O'' (Au/S) EWoo MFie NDro SPop WCre
- 'Harvest Glow' (Au/S) IPen NDro SPop WHil
- 'Hawkwood' (Au/S) CPBP CWCL GAbr GAgs IPen MAsh MFie NDro NEgg SDnm SPop WFar WHil

* - 'Hazel' (Au/A) IPen MFie NDro SPop WCre WHil
- 'Headdress' (Au/S) GAbr MFie SPop WCre
- 'Heady' (Au/A) EWoo MFie NDro WHil
- 'Heart of Gold' (Au/A) MAsh MFie SPop WAln
- 'Hebers' (Au) NDro SPop WAln
- 'Helen' (Au/S) GAbr IPen MFie NDro SPop WHil
- 'Helen Barter' (Au/S) MFie NDro SPop
- 'Helen Ruane' (Au/d) EBee GAgs SPop WAln WCre WFar
- 'Helena' (Au/S) IPen MAsh MFie NDro SPop WFar WHil
- 'Helena Dean' (Au/d) MAsh WAln
- 'Her Nibs' (Au/St) MAsh
- 'Hermia' (Au/A) MFie SPop
- 'Hetty Woolf' (Au/S) ECho NDro NHol SPop WCre
- 'Hew Dalrymple' (Au/S) NDro SPop
- 'High Hopes' (Au) WAln
- 'Highland Park' (Au/A) NDro SPop
- 'Hinton Admiral' (Au/S) EWoo GAgs IPen NDro SPop WAln
- 'Hinton Fields' (Au/S) CPBP CSev CWCL EBee GAbr GAgs GCai IPen MAsh MFie NDro NEgg NWCA SDnm SPop WCre WFar WHil
- 'Hoghton Gem' (Au/d) WAln
- 'Holyrood' (Au/S) GAbr GAgs IPen ITim NDro SPop
- 'Honey' (Au/d) GAbr NBro NDro NEgg SPop WAln
- 'Honeymoon' (Au/S) WAln
- 'Hopleys Coffee' (Au/d) GAbr GAgs GCai NDro SPop WAln WCre
- 'Hurstwood Midnight' (Au) MFie
- 'Iago' (Au/S) NDro SPop WAln
- 'Ian Greville' (Au/A) IPen MAsh MFie NDro SPop WAln
- 'Ibis' (Au/S) WAln WCre
- 'Ice Maiden' (Au/A) EWoo MFie NDro SPop WAln WHil
- 'Idmiston' (Au/S) ECho GAgs MAsh MFie NDro SPop WFar WHil
- 'Ilona' (Au/d) SPop
- 'Imari Stripe' (Au/St) MAsh
- 'Immaculate' (Au/A) SPop WAln WHil
- 'Impassioned' (Au/A) MFie SPop WAln WFar
- 'Impeccable' (Au/A) WAln
- 'Imperturbable' (Au/A) MFie NDro SPop WAln
- 'Indian Love Call' (Au/A) GAbr GAgs IPen ITim MFie NDro SPop WCre WFar WHil
- 'Iris Scott' (Au/A) NDro
- 'Isabel' (Au/S) WAln
- 'Isabella' (Au/A) NDro WAln
- 'Jack Dean' (Au/A) MFie NHol SPop WAln WCre WFar WHil
- 'Jack Redfern' (Au/A) **new** NDro
- 'Jack Wood' (Au/S) **new** NDro
- 'James Arnot' (Au/S) IPen MFie NDro SPop WFar
- 'Jane' (Au/S) WAln
- 'Jane Myers' (Au/d) WAln WHil
- 'Janet' (Au) ECho GEdr
- 'Janet Watts' **new** GAgs
- 'Janie Hill' (Au/A) GAbr MFie SPop WCre
- 'Jean Fielder' (Au/A) SPop
- 'Jean Jacques' (Au/A) WAln
- 'Jean Walker' (Au/B) SPop
- 'Jeanne' (Au/A) MFie
- 'Jeannie Telford' (Au/A) MFie SPop WHil
- 'Jenny' (Au/A) ECho GAgs GEdr IPen MFie NDro SPop WCre WFar
- 'Jersey Bounce' (Au/A) GAbr NDro WAln
- 'Jesmond' (Au/S) WAln
- 'Jessie' (Au/d) WAln
- 'Jilting Jessie' (Au/St) **new** SPop
- 'Joan Curtis' (Au/d) **new** SPop
- 'Joan Elliott' (Au/A) GAbr GAgs
- 'Joanne' (Au/A) GAbr MFie NDro SPop WCre
- 'Joe Perks' (Au/A) EWoo IPen MFie NDro SPop WAln WFar WHil
- 'Joel' (Au/S) EWoo GAgs IPen MFie NDro SPop WAln WCre
- 'Johann Bach' (Au/B) SPop
- 'John Stewart' (Au/A) MFie SPop
- 'John Wayne' (Au/A) MAsh MFie NDro WCre WFar WHil
- 'John Woolf' (Au/S) ECho NDro
- 'Jonathon' (Au/A) NDro WAln
- 'Jorvic' (Au/S) NDro
- 'Joy' (Au/A) ECho IPen LLHF MAsh NDro SPop WCre WFar WHil
- 'Joyce' (Au/A) GAbr GAgs IPen MFie NDro SPop WCre WFar WHil
- 'Judith' (Au/B) NDro
- 'Julia' (Au/S) MAsh
- 'Julie Nuttall' (Au/B) **new** NDro
- 'June' (Au/A) NDro SPop WAln
- 'Jungfrau' (Au/d) WAln
- 'Jupiter' (Au/S) MAsh NDro SPop WAln
- 'Just Steven' (Au/A) WAln
- 'K S' (Au/S) **new** NDro
- 'Karen' (Au) GAgs
- 'Karen Cordrey' (Au/S) EBee ECho EWoo GAbr GAgs GKev IPen ITim MAsh MFie NHol SDnm SPop WCre WFar WHil
- 'Karen McDonald' (Au/A) MFie SPop
- 'Kate Haywood' (Au/B) **new** NDro WHil
- 'Kath Dryden' see *P. allionii* 'Kath Dryden'
- 'Kelso' (Au/A) MFie
- 'Ken Chilton' (Au/A) EWoo GAgs MFie NDro WAln WFar WHil
- 'Kentucky Blues' (Au/d) SPop
- 'Kercup' (Au/A) MFie NDro SPop WCre

- 'Kerry' GAgs
- 'Kevin Keegan' (Au/A) MFie SPop WHil
- 'Key West' (Au/A) SPop WAln
- 'Khachaturian' (Au/A) NDro WAln
- 'Kilby' (Au/A) SPop
- 'Kim' (Au/A) GAbr IPen MFie NDro
- 'Kingcup' (Au/A) MFie SPop WCre
- 'Kingfisher' (Au/A) GAbr ITim MFie NDro SPop WHil
- 'Kingpin' (Au/St) **new** NDro
- 'Kintail' (Au/A) MFie
- 'Kiowa' (Au/S) SPop
- 'Kirklands' (Au/d) MFie NDro SPop WHil
- 'Kohinoor' (Au) MFie WHil
- 'Königin der Nacht' (Au/St) MFie WAln WHil
- 'Lady Daresbury' (Au/A) MFie NDro SPop WFar
- 'Lady Day' (Au/d) SPop
- 'Lady Diana' (Au/S) NDro WAln
- 'Lady Emma Monson' (Au/S) ITim NDro
- 'Lady Joyful' (Au/S) WCre
- 'Lady of the Vale' (Au/A) WAln
- 'Lady Penelope' (Au/S) WAln
- 'Lady Zoë' (Au/S) MAsh MFie NDro NHol SPop WCre
- 'Lambert's Gold' (Au) SPop
- 'Lamplugh' (Au/d) IPen WHil
- 'Lancelot' (Au/d) SPop WAln
- 'Landy' (Au/A) MFie NDro SPop WCre
- 'Langley Park' (Au/A) IPen MFie NDro SPop WHil
- 'Lara' (Au/A) MFie WAln
- 'Laredo' (Au/A) WAln
- 'Larry' (Au/A) GAgs MFie NDro SPop WAln WCre WFar
- 'Last Chance' (Au/St) SPop
- 'Lavender Lady' (Au/B) IPen NDro NEgg
- 'Lavenham' (Au/S) WAln
- 'Laverock' (Au/S) MAsh MFie NBir NBro NEgg NHol WCre WHil
- 'Laverock Fancy' (Au/S) GAbr GAgs GCai IPen MAsh NDro NHol
- 'Lazy River' (Au/A) NDro WAln
- 'Leather Jacket' (Au) GAbr WHil
- 'Lechistan' (Au/S) ECho GAbr GAgs IPen MAsh MFie NDro SPop WCre WHil
- 'Lee' (Au/A) IPen WAln WCre
- 'Lee Clark' (Au/A) MFie WAln
- 'Lee Paul' (Au/A) EWoo GAbr GAgs GCai IPen MAsh MFie NDro NHol SPop WCre WHil
- 'Lee Sharpe' (Au/A) IPen MFie NDro SPop WAln
- 'Lemmy Getatem' (Au/d) SPop
- 'Lemon Drop' (Au/S) EWoo ITim MAsh NBro NDro SPop
- 'Lemon Sherbet' (Au/B) NDro SPop WHil
- 'Lemonade' **new** ITim
- 'Lepton Jubilee' (Au/S) GAbr NDro WAln
- 'Leroy Brown' (Au/A) WAln
- 'Lester' (Au/d) SPop
- 'Letty' (Au/S) WAln
- 'Leverton' (Au/d) SPop WAln
- 'Lewis Telford' (Au/A) SPop
- 'Lich' (Au/S) NDro
- 'Lichfield' (Au/A/d) IPen SPop WAln WCre
- 'Light Hearted' (Au/A) MFie NDro WFar
- 'Light Music' (Au/d) WAln
- 'Likely Lad' (Au/St) **new** SPop
- 'Lila' (Au/S) EWoo NDro WAln
- 'Lilac Domino' (Au/S) EWoo GAbr GAgs IPen ITim MFie NDro NEgg SPop WAln WFar WHil
- 'Lillian Hill' (Au/A) WAln
- 'Lima' (Au/d) MFie WAln
- 'Limelight' (Au/A) NDro SPop WAln
- 'Limelight' (Au/S) IPen WAln
- 'Lincoln Bullion' (Au/d) SPop
- 'Lincoln Charm' (Au/D) GAbr SPop
- 'Lincoln Chestnut' (Au/d) SPop
- 'Lincoln Imp' (Au/d) SPop
- 'Lincoln Imperial' (Au/d) SPop
- 'Lincoln Major' (Au/d) **new** SPop
- 'Lindley' (Au/S) ITim MAsh
- 'Lindsey Moreno' (Au/S) WAln
- 'Ling' (Au/A) GAgs MFie NDro SPop WCre
- 'Linnet' (Au/B) NDro
- 'Lintz' (Au/B) MAsh MFie NDro
- 'Linze 2' (Au/S) MFie NDro
- 'Lisa' (Au/A) GAgs IPen MFie NDro SPop WCre WFar WHil
- 'Lisa Clara' (Au/S) EWoo GAbr GAgs GCai IPen ITim MAsh MFie NDro SPop WFar
- 'Lisa's Smile' (Au/S) EWoo GCai MFie NDro SPop WHil
- 'Little Rosetta' (Au/d) ITim NDro WAln WHil
- 'Lockyer's Gem' (Au/B/St) NDro NEgg
- 'Lofty' (Au/St) MAsh
- 'Lolita' (Au/St) **new** SPop
- 'Lord Saye and Sele' (Au/St) EWoo GAbr GAgs GCai IPen ITim MAsh MFie NEgg SPop WCre WHil
- 'Lothlorien' (Au/A) WAln
- 'Louisa Woolhead' (Au/d) SPop
- 'Lovebird' (Au/S) CPBP CWCL GAbr GAgs ITim MAsh MFie NDro SPop
- 'Lucy Locket' (Au/B) CWCL EBee GAgs IPen LRHS NDro NEgg NHol NLar WCre WHil
- 'Ludlow' (Au/S) GAbr
- 'Lupy Minstrel' (Au/S) NDro SPop
- 'Lynn' (Au/A) WAln
- 'Lynn Cooper' (Au) WFar
- 'MacWatt's Blue' (Au/B) GAbr IGor IPen MFie NDro SPop WHil
- 'Madelaine Palmer' (Au/d) SPop
- 'Maggie' (Au/S) GAbr NDro SPop WCre
- 'Magnolia' (Au/B) WCre
- 'Maid Marion' (Au/d) MAsh WCre
- 'Mandarin' (Au/A) GAgs MFie NDro SPop WCre WFar WHil
- 'Mansell's Green' (Au/S) WAln
- 'Mardi Gras' (Au/d) **new** WAln
- 'Margaret' (Au/S) GAbr
- 'Margaret Faulkner' (Au/A) GAbr GAgs GCai MFie NDro WCre
- 'Margaret Irene' (Au/A) IPen NDro SPop WAln WCre
- 'Margaret Martin' (Au/S) IPen MAsh MFie NDro SPop WAln
- 'Margery Thompson' (Au/d) **new** SPop
- 'Margot Fonteyn' (Au/A) GAbr SPop WAln WHil
- 'Marie Crousse' (Au/d) CMea CPBP GMaP MFie NDro NHol SPop WCre WFar
- 'Marigold' (Au/d) WFar
- 'Marion Howard Spring' (Au/A) MFie WAln WCre
- 'Marion Tiger' (Au/St) WAln
- 'Mark' (Au/A) GAgs IPen MAsh MFie NBro NDro SPop WCre WFar
- 'Marmion' (Au/S) EWoo GAgs IPen ITim MFie NDro SPop WAln WFar WHil
- 'Martha Livesley' (Au/A) WAln
- 'Martha's Choice' (Au/A) WAln
- 'Martin Fish' (Au) WCre
- 'Martin Luther King' (Au/S) CWCL NDro
- 'Mary' (Au/d) GAbr NDro SPop
- 'Mary Taylor' (Au/S) WAln
- 'Mary Zach' (Au/S) EWoo MFie NDro WHil
- 'Matthew Yates' (Au/d) CWCL EBee GAbr GAgs GCai IPen ITim MAsh MFie NDro NHol NPri

	SBch SDnm SPav SPop WCot WCre WHil
- 'Maureen Millward' (Au/A)	IPen MFie NDro SPop WCre
- 'May' (Au/A)	WAln WCre
- 'Mazetta Stripe' (Au/S/St)	GAbr GAgs ITim MFie NLar SPop
- 'Meadowlark' (Au/A)	GAgs ITim MFie SPop WAln WCre WFar WHil
- 'Mease Tiger' (Au/St)	GAbr WAln
- 'Megan' (Au/d)	WAln
- 'Mellifluous' (Au)	MFie WAln WCre WFar WHil
- 'Melody' (Au/S)	IPen SPop
- 'Merlin' (Au/S)	MFie WAln
- 'Merlin' (Au/A)	EBee IPen
- 'Merlin Stripe' (Au/St)	GAgs IPen SPop WCre WHil
- 'Mermaid' (Au/d)	NDro
- 'Merridale' (Au/A)	GAbr MFie WCre WHil
- 'Mersey Tiger' (Au/S)	GAgs ITim MAsh MFie NDro SPop WCre WHil
- 'Metha' (Au/A)	NDro WAln
- 'Metis' (Au/d) **new**	SPop
- 'Mexicano' (Au/A)	WAln
- 'Michael' (Au/S)	MAsh MFie SPop WAln
- 'Michael Wattam' (Au/S)	MFie WAln
- 'Mick' (Au/A)	MAsh MFie WAln WHil
- 'Midland Marvel' (Au/St)	SPop
- 'Midnight' (Au/A)	WAln
- 'Mikado' (Au/S)	IPen MAsh MFie WCre WHil
- 'Milkmaid' (Au/A)	MFie WMAq
- 'Millicent' (Au/A)	MFie WAln WFar
- 'Mink' (Au/A)	MFie NDro WFar
- 'Minley' (Au/S)	CPBP GAbr GAgs GCai ITim MFie NBir NBro NDro NEgg NHol SPop WCre
- 'Minstead' (Au/S)	SPop
- 'Minstrel' (Au/S)	MAsh MFie NDro WCre
- 'Mipsie Miranda' (Au/d)	SPop
- 'Mirabella Bay' (Au/A)	WAln
- 'Mirandinha' (Au/A)	MFie WAln
- 'Miriam' (Au/A)	SPop WAln
- 'Mish Mish' (Au/d)	NDro WHil
- 'Miss Bluey' (Au/d)	NDro SPop WAln
- 'Miss Newman' (Au/A)	SPop WAln
- 'Miss Pinky'	SPop
- 'Mojave' (Au/S)	CWCL EWoo GAbr GAgs IPen ITim MFie NDro NEgg NHol SPop WCre WHil
- 'Mollie Langford' (Au/A)	MFie SPop WAln WHil
- 'Monet' (Au/S)	WAln
- 'Moneymoon' (Au/S)	EWoo IPen NDro WCre WHil
- 'Monica' (Au/A)	MFie
- 'Monk' (Au/S)	MFie NDro WHil
- 'Monk's Eleigh' (Au/A)	WAln
- 'Monmouth Star' (Au/St) **new**	NDro
- 'Moody Cow' (Au/St)	MAsh
- 'Moon Fairy' (Au/S)	MAsh NDro SPop
- 'Moonglow' (Au/S)	MAsh NDro
- 'Moonlight' (Au/S)	WAln
- 'Moonrise' (Au/S)	NDro
- 'Moonriver' (Au/A)	EWoo NHol SPop WAln WCre WFar WHil
- 'Moonshadow' (Au/d)	WAln
- 'Moscow' (Au/S)	SPop
- 'Moselle' (Au/S)	NDro WAln
- 'Mr A' (Au/S)	NDro SPop WHil
- 'Mr Bojangles' (Au/d) **new**	SPop
- 'Mr Greenfingers' (Au)	WCre
- 'Mrs Cairn's Blue' (Au/B) **new**	NDro
- 'Mrs Dargan' (Au/d) **new**	NDro
- 'Mrs Harris' (Au/B)	WAln
- 'Mrs J.H. Watson' (Au)	WCre
- 'Mrs L. Hearn' (Au/A)	GAbr IPen NDro SPop WHil
- 'Mrs Lowry' (Au/B) **new**	NDro
- 'Mrs R. Bolton' (Au/A)	WFar
- 'Murray Lakes' (Au/A)	NDro
- 'Murray Lanes' (Au/A)	WAln
- 'Mustard Sauce' (Au/B) **new**	ITim NDro
- 'My Buddy' (Au/St)	SPop
- 'My Fair Lady' (Au/A)	MFie WAln
- 'My Friend' (Au/B) **new**	NDro
- 'Nancy Dalgetty' (Au/B) **new**	NDro
- 'Naniconan' (Au/A) **new**	NDro
- 'Nankenan' (Au/S)	MFie NDro WAln
- 'Neat and Tidy' (Au/S)	ECho GAbr GAgs MAsh MFie NDro NHol SPop WCre WFar
- 'Nefertiti' (Au/A)	IPen MFie NDro SPop WAln WHil
- 'Nessun Dorma' (Au/A)	SPop WAln
- 'Neville Telford' (Au/S)	GAbr GAgs IPen MAsh MFie NDro WFar WHil
- 'Nick Drake' (Au/d)	SPop
- 'Nickity' (Au/A)	GAbr GAgs IPen ITim MAsh MFie NDro SPop WFar WHil
- 'Nicola Jane' (Au/A)	SPop WAln
- 'Nigel' (Au/d)	GAbr MFie NDro
- 'Night and Day' (Au/S)	GAgs NDro SPop
- 'Nightwatch' (Au/S)	WAln
- 'Nightwink' (Au/S)	MFie WAln
- 'Nil Amber'	SPop
- 'Nina' (Au/A)	NDro WAln
- 'Nita' (Au/d)	WAln
- 'No 21' (Au/S) **new**	NDro
- 'Nocturne' (Au/S)	IPen NBro NDro NHol SPop
- 'Nona' (Au/d)	NDro SPop
- 'Nonchalance' (Au/A)	MFie NDro SPop WHil
- 'Norma' (Au/A)	MFie NDro
- 'Notability' (Au/A)	WAln
- 'Notable' (Au/A)	WAln
- 'Nymph' (Au/d)	EWoo MFie NDro SPop WHil
- 'Oake's Blue' (Au/S)	NDro
- 'Oakie' (Au/S)	WAln
- 'Oban' (Au/S)	NDro SPop
- 'Oikos' (Au/B)	SPop
- 'Ol' Blue Eyes' (Au/St)	WAln
- 'Old Black Isle Dusty Miller' (Au/B)	NDro
- 'Old Clove Red' (Au/B)	GAbr GAgs MFie NDro WHil
- 'Old Cottage Blue' (Au/B)	GAbr NDro WFar
- 'Old Dublin Blue' (Au/B) **new**	NDro
- 'Old England' (Au/S)	MFie SPop
- 'Old Gold' (Au/S)	GAbr IPen NDro NHol WFar
- 'Old Gold Dusty) Miller' (Au/B	NDro
- 'Old Irish Blue' (Au/B)	ECho GAgs ITim NDro NEgg
- 'Old Irish Green' (Au/B)	NDro
- 'Old Irish Scented' (Au/B)	GAbr IPen NBro NDro WHil
- 'Old Irish Yellow' (Au/B)	NDro NEgg
- 'Old Mustard' (Au/B)	NDov NDro SMHy
- 'Old Pink Dusty Miller' (Au/B)	GAbr IPen NDro
§ - 'Old Purple Dusty Miller' (Au/B)	GAbr
- 'Old Red' **new**	GAgs
- 'Old Red Dusty Miller' (Au/B)	GAbr LLHF NDro SPop WHil
- 'Old Red Elvet' (Au/S)	GAbr NDro SPop WAln
- 'Old Smokey' (Au/A)	GAgs NDro SPop WAln WHil

– 'Old Suffolk Bronze' (Au/B)	GAgs ITim NDro WHil
– 'Old Yellow Dusty Miller' (Au/B)	EWes GAbr GAgs GCai IPen NBro NDro NHol NLar NRya WHil WThu
– 'Olivia' (Au/d)	SPop
– 'Olton' (Au/A)	IPen MFie
– 'Optimist' (Au/St)	SPop
– 'Opus One' (Au/A)	WAln
– 'Orb' (Au/S)	IPen MAsh MFie NDro SPop WHil
– 'Ordvic' (Au/S)	WAln
– 'Orlando' (Au/S)	MFie NDro SPop WAln
– 'Orwell Tiger' (Au/St)	EWoo GAgs IPen SPop
– 'Osbourne Green' (Au/B)	EWoo GAbr GAgs GCai MFie NDov NDro SPop WCre WHil
– 'Ossett Saphire' (Au/A) **new**	NDro
– 'Otto Dix' (Au/A)	WAln
– 'Overdale' (Au/A)	WAln
– 'Paddlin Madeleine' (Au/A)	NDro WAln
– 'Pagoda Belle' (Au/A)	WAln
– 'Paleface' (Au/A)	GAgs IPen MFie NDro WAln WCre
– 'Pam Tiger' (Au/St)	WAln
– 'Panache' (Au/S)	WAln
– 'Papageno' (Au/St)	WAln
– 'Paphos' (Au/d)	MAsh SPop
– 'Paradise Yellow' (Au/B)	GEdr NDro NEgg SPop
– 'Paragon' (Au/A)	ITim MFie WHil
– 'Paris' (Au/S)	WAln
– 'Party Time' (Au/S)	IPen
– 'Pastiche' (Au/A)	MFie NDro WCre
– 'Pat' (Au/S)	SPop
– 'Pat Barnard' (Au)	IPen
– 'Patience' (Au/S)	ITim NDro SPop WHil
– 'Pauline' (Au/A)	MFie
– 'Pauline Taylor' (Au/d)	WAln
– 'Pavarotti' (Au/A) **new**	NDro
– 'Pegasus' (Au/d)	SPop WAln
– 'Peggy' (Au/A)	GAbr WHil
– 'Peggy's Lad' (Au/A)	WAln
– 'Pequod' (Au/A)	NDro SPop WAln
– 'Peter Beardsley' (Au/A)	WAln
– 'Peter Hall' (Au/d)	WAln
– 'Petite Hybrid' (Au)	EPot
– 'Phantom' (Au/D)	SPop WAln
– 'Pharaoh' (Au/A)	GAgs MFie NDro SPop WAln WFar
– 'Phyllis Douglas' (Au/A)	IPen MFie NDro NEgg SPop WCre WHil
– 'Piccadilly' (Au/S)	MAsh MFie
– 'Pierot' (Au/A)	IPen MFie NDro SPop WCre WHil
– 'Piers Telford' (Au/A)	CPBP CWCL EBee GAbr GAgs GCai IPen ITim MFie NDro NEgg NLar SBch SDnm SPop WCre WHil
– 'Piglet' (Au/D)	GAbr SPop
– 'Pink Fondant' (Au/d)	GAbr NDro WAln
– 'Pink Hint' (Au/B)	NDro
– 'Pink Lady' (Au/A)	MFie NBro SPop WHil
– 'Pink Lilac' (Au/A/S)	NDro
– 'Pinkie' (Au/A)	WAln WHil
– 'Pinkie Dawn' (Au/B)	NDro
– 'Pinstripe'	GAgs IPen SPop WCre WHil
– 'Pioneer Stripe' (Au/S)	GAgs IPen
– 'Pippin' (Au/A)	GAbr GAgs IPen MFie NBro NDro SPop WCre WFar WHil
– 'Pixie' (Au/A)	EWoo IPen MFie WAln
– 'Plain Jane' (Au)	MAsh
– 'Playboy' (Au/A)	NDro WAln
– 'Plush Royal' (Au/S)	WAln
– 'Polestar' (Au/A)	MFie NDro SPop WCre WFar WHil
– 'Pop's Blue' (Au/S/d)	NEgg SPop
– 'Porcelain' (Au/d) **new**	WAln
– 'Portree' (Au/S)	SPop
– 'Pot o' Gold' (Au/S)	CPBP EBee ECho EWoo GAgs IPen MAsh MFie NDro NEgg SPop WCre WFar WHil
– 'Prague' (Au/S)	GAgs IPen MAsh MFie NBir NDro NHol SPop
– 'Pretender' (Au/A)	SPop WAln
– 'Pride of Poland' (Au/S)	SPop
– 'Prince Bishop' (Au/S)	NDro WAln
– 'Prince Charming' (Au/S)	GAgs IPen ITim MFie NDro SPop
– 'Prince John' (Au/A)	MAsh MFie NBro NDro NHol SPop WCre WFar WHil
– 'Proctor's Yellow' (Au/B)	NDro
– 'Prometheus' (Au/d)	MAsh MFie NRya SPop WAln WCre WHil
– 'Prosperine' (Au/S)	MAsh
– 'Purple Dusty Miller'	see *P. auricula* 'Old Purple Dusty Miller'
– 'Purple Emperor' (Au/A)	MFie
– 'Purple Frills' (Au)	MFie
– 'Purple Glow' (Au/d)	WAln
– 'Purple Haze'	SPop
– 'Purple Lovely'	MFie
– 'Purple Promise' (Au) **new**	GAbr
– 'Purple Prose' (Au/St)	MFie SPop
– 'Purple Rain' (Au)	MAsh
– 'Purple Royale' (Au/B) **new**	NDro
– 'Purple Sage' (Au/S)	GCai MFie NDro NHol
– 'Purple Velvet' (Au/S)	CWCL GAgs IPen NDro NHol SPop
– 'Quatro' (Au/d)	SPop WAln
– 'Queen Alexandra' (Au/B)	GAbr GAgs NDro WHil
– 'Queen Bee' (Au/S)	GAbr MFie NDro WFar
– 'Queen's Bower' (Au/S)	SPop
– 'Quintessence' (Au/A)	MFie WAln WCre
– 'R.L. Bowes' (Au/A)	NDro
– 'Rab C. Nesbitt' (Au/A)	WAln
– 'Rabley Heath' (Au/A)	GAgs GCai MFie NDro SPop
– 'Rachel' (Au/A)	WAln
– 'Radiant' (Au/A)	NDro
– 'Rag Doll' (Au/S)	NDro
– 'Rajah' (Au/S)	EBee ECho GAbr GAgs IPen ITim MAsh MFie NDro NEgg NHol NLar SPop WCre WFar WHil
– 'Raleigh Stripe' (Au/St)	GAgs IPen WAln
– 'Ralenzano' (Au/A)	WAln
– 'Ralph's Tan' (Au/B) **new**	NDro
– 'Rameses' (Au/A)	IPen MFie NDro WAln WCre
– 'Rebecca Baker' (Au/d) **new**	SPop
– 'Rebecca Hyatt' (Au/d)	WAln
– 'Red Admiral' (Au)	WAln
– 'Red and White Stripe' (Au/S/St)	WFar
– 'Red Arrows' (Au)	WAln
– 'Red Baron' (Au/S) **new**	WAln
– 'Red Bordeaux' (Au/S) **new**	NDro
– 'Red Embers' (Au/S)	WAln
– 'Red Ensign' (Au/B) **new**	NDro
– 'Red Gauntlet' (Au/S)	GAbr GAgs GCai IPen MFie MRav NDro NHol SPop WFar
– 'Red Mark' (Au/A)	MFie WHil
– 'Red Sonata' (Au/S)	SPop
– 'Red Vulcan' (Au)	WCre
– 'Red Wire'	MAsh SPop
– 'Redcar' (Au/A)	MFie NDro WAln WCre
– 'Redstart' (Au/S)	IPen ITim WHil
– 'Redstart' (Au/B)	ITim
– 'Regency' (Au/A)	NDro WAln
– 'Regency Dandy' (Au/St)	SPop
– 'Regency Emperor' (Au/St)	SPop

- 'Regency Saint Clements' (Au/St) **new**	SPop
- 'Remus' (Au/S)	CPBP ECho ELan EWoo GAbr GAgs GCai IPen ITim LLHF MAsh MFie NDro NEgg NHol SPop WCre WFar WHil
- 'Renata' (Au/S)	NDro
- 'Rene' (Au/A)	GAbr IPen MFie NDro WCre
- 'Renown' (Au/A) **new**	NDro
- 'Resi' **new**	WHil
- 'Respectable' (Au/A)	WAln
- 'Reverie' (Au/d)	WAln
- 'Reynardyne' (Au/d)	SPop
- 'Riatty' (Au/d)	GAbr NDro WAln
- 'Richard Shaw' (Au/A)	IPen
- 'Ring of Bells' (Au/S)	SPop WAln
- 'Risdene' (Au)	IPen
- 'Rita' (Au/S)	WAln
- 'Robbo' (Au/B)	NDro
- 'Robert Lee' (Au/A)	WAln
- 'Roberto' (Au/S)	MAsh WAln
- 'Robin Hood Stripe' (Au/St)	NDro SPop
- 'Robinette' (Au/d)	SPop
- 'Rock Sand' (Au/S)	ECho GAgs GCai MFie NDro WFar WHil
- 'Rodeo' (Au/A)	GAbr GAgs IPen SPop WPat
- 'Rolts' (Au/S)	ECho EWoo GAbr GAgs IPen MAsh MFie NBro NDro NHol SDnm SPav SPop WCre WFar WHil
- 'Rondy' (Au/S)	MFie WHil
- 'Ronnie Johnson' (Au)	WAln
- 'Ronny Simpson'	WCre
- 'Rosalie' (Au)	SPop
- 'Rosalie Edwards' (Au/S)	MFie SPop
- 'Rose Conjou' (Au/d)	GAbr GAgs IPen MFie NDro SPop WAln WFar
- 'Rose Kaye' (Au/A)	IPen SPop
- 'Rosebud' (Au/S)	GAbr GAgs NDro
- 'Rosemarket Rackler' (Au/B)	SPop
- 'Rosemary' (Au/S)	EWoo MAsh MFie NDro SPop WCre WHil
- 'Rosewood' (Au)	WCre
- 'Rosie' (Au/S)	NDro
- 'Rothesay Robin' (Au/A)	WAln
- 'Rowena' (Au/A)	GAgs GCai IPen MFie NBro NDro SDnm SPav SPop WCre WHil
- 'Roxborough' (Au/A)	CWCL GAgs IPen WAln
- 'Roxburgh' (Au/A)	MFie NDro SPop WCre
- 'Roy Keane' (Au/A)	IPen MFie SPop
- 'Royal Mail' (Au/S)	MAsh MFie NDro SPop WAln
- 'Royal Marine' (Au/S)	MFie WAln
- 'Royal Velvet' (Au/S)	GAbr GAgs IPen NDro NHol WHil
- 'Ruby Hyde' (Au/B)	GAbr NDro
- 'Rumbled' (Au/St)	MAsh
- 'Rusty Dusty' (Au)	GAbr
- 'Rusty Red' (Au/B) **new**	NDro
- 'Ryecroft' (Au/A)	WAln
- 'Sabrina' (Au/A)	WAln
- 'Saginaw' (Au/A)	WAln
- 'Sailor Boy' (Au/S)	MFie NDro SPop WHil
- 'Saint Boswells' (Au/S)	GAbr NDro SPop WAln
- 'Saint Elmo' (Au/A)	MFie SPop
- 'Saint Quentin' (Au/S)	WAln
- 'Salad' (Au/S)	GAbr
- 'Sale Green' (Au/S)	MFie
- 'Sally' (Au/A)	WAln
- 'Sam Gamgee' (Au/A)	NDro WAln
- 'Sam Hunter' (Au/A)	NDro SPop WAln
- 'Samantha' (Au/A)	WAln
- 'Sandhills' (Au/A)	MFie WAln WCre

- 'Sandmartin' (Au/S)	MFie
- 'Sandra' (Au/A)	ECho ELan GAbr GAgs IPen MAsh MFie NDro SPop WCre WHil
- 'Sandra's Lass' (Au/A)	SPop WAln
- 'Sandwood Bay' (Au/A)	GAbr GAgs GCai MFie NBro NDro NEgg NHol SPop WCre WHil
- 'Sarah Gisby' (Au/d)	MFie SPop
- 'Sarah Lodge' (Au/d)	GAbr IPen MAsh NDro SPop
- 'Satin Doll' (Au/d)	MFie SPop
- 'Scipio' (Au/S)	NDro SPop WAln
- 'Scorcher' (Au/S)	GAgs IPen MFie NDro SPop WAln
- 'Searchlight' (Au)	WCre
- 'Second Victory' (Au)	CPBP NDro WCre WHil
- 'Serenity' (Au/S)	MFie NDro NHol WCre WHil
- 'Sergeant Wilson' (Au)	SPop WAln
- 'Shalford' (Au/d)	GAbr MFie NDro SPop WCre WFar WHil
- 'Sharman's Cross' (Au/S)	MFie WAln
- 'Sharon Louise' (Au/S)	IPen MAsh NDro WCre
- 'Sheila' (Au/S)	ECho GAbr MAsh NDro SPop WCre WFar WHil
- 'Shere' (Au/S)	EWoo MFie NDro SPop WCre
- 'Shergold' (Au/A)	MFie WCre
- 'Sherwood' (Au/S)	GAgs GCai IPen MAsh MFie NDro SPop WHil
- 'Shirley' (Au/S)	SPop WAln
- 'Shotley' (Au/A)	MFie SPop
- 'Show Bandit' (Au/St)	SPop
- 'Showman' (Au/S)	WAln
- 'Showtime' (Au/S)	NDro
- 'Sibsey' (Au/d)	CWCL MAsh SPop WAln
- 'Sidney' (Au/A)	WAln
- 'Silmaril' (Au)	SPop WAln
- 'Silver Rose' (Au)	MAsh
- 'Silverway' (Au/S)	EWoo ITim MAsh NDro SPop WHil
- 'Simply Red' (Au)	GAgs IPen MAsh MFie NDro SPop WAln WHil
- 'Sir John' (Au/A)	MAsh MFie WFar WHil
- 'Sir John Hall'	MFie
- 'Sir Robert' (Au/d)	WAln
- 'Sirbol' (Au/A)	EWoo GAgs IPen MFie NDro SPop WCre WFar WHil
- 'Sirius' (Au/A)	CWCL EWoo GAbr GAgs IPen MFie NDro NHol SPop WCre WFar WHil
- 'Skipper' (Au/d)	SPop
- 'Skylark' (Au/A)	GAbr GAgs IPen ITim SPop WAln WCre WHil
- 'Skyliner' (Au/A)	NDro
- 'Slim Whitman' (Au/A)	NDro SPop WAln
- 'Slioch' (Au/S)	ECho EWoo GAbr GAgs IPen MAsh MFie NDro NHol SPop WCre
- 'Slip Anchor' (Au/A)	WAln
- 'Smart Tar' (Au/S)	WAln
- 'Snooty Fox' (Au/A)	GAbr IPen MFie SPop
- 'Snooty Fox II' (Au/A)	MFie NDro
- 'Snowy Owl' (Au/S)	GAbr GAgs MFie NDro SPop WCre
- 'Soliloquy' (Au)	MAsh
- 'Somersby' (Au/d)	WAln
- 'Soncy Face' (Au/A)	MFie WAln WHil
- 'Sonia Nicolle' (Au/B) **new**	NDro
- 'Sonny Boy' (Au/A)	NDro WAln
- 'Sophie' (Au/d)	SPop WAln
- 'South Barrow' (Au/d)	GAbr GAgs SPop WCre WHil
- 'Sparky' (Au/A)	WAln
- 'Spartan' (Au)	WAln
- 'Spitfire' (Au/S)	MAsh MFie
- 'Spokey' (Au)	IPen
- 'Spring Meadows' (Au/S)	EWoo GAbr GAgs MAsh MFie NDro NEgg NHol SPop
- 'Springtime' (Au/A)	SPop
- 'Standish' (Au/d)	GAbr

- 'Stant's Blue' (Au/S)	GCai IPen MAsh MFie NBro NDro WFar
- 'Star Wars' (Au/S)	GAbr MAsh MFie NDro NHol SPop WAln WHil
- 'Star Wars II' **new**	GAgs
- 'Starburst' (Au/S)	WAln
- 'Starling' (Au/B)	GAgs IPen NDro SPop
- 'Starry' (Au/S)	WCre
- 'Stella Coop' (Au/d)	NDro WAln
- 'Stoke Poges' (Au/A)	WAln
- 'Stoney Cross' (Au/S)	SPop
- 'Stonnal' (Au/A)	MFie NDro SPop WHil
- 'Stormin Norman' (Au/A)	MFie NDro SPop WAln WHil
- 'Stormy Weather' (Au/St) **new**	SPop
- 'Striped Ace' (Au/St)	WHil
- 'Stripey' (Au/d)	IPen NHol WAln
- 'Stromboli' (Au/d)	SPop
- 'Subliminal' (Au/A)	WAln
- 'Sue' (Au/A)	MFie WCre WFar
- 'Suede Shoes' (Au/S)	SPop
- 'Sugar Plum Fairy' (Au/S)	GAbr GAgs NDro SPop WHil
- 'Sultan' (Au/A)	WAln
- 'Summer Sky' (Au/A)	SPop WCre
- 'Summer Wine' (Au/A)	MFie
- 'Sumo' (Au/A)	GAbr GAgs MAsh MFie NDro SPop WAln WCre WFar WHil
- 'Sunflower' (Au/A/S)	EWoo GAbr GAgs ITim MAsh MFie NDro SPop WCre
- 'Sunsplash' (Au)	WCre
- 'Sunstar' (Au/S)	NDro
- 'Super Para' (Au/S)	EWoo GAbr GAgs IPen MFie NDro SPop WHil
- 'Superb' (Au/S)	MFie NDro WAln
- 'Susan' (Au/A)	GAbr MFie NDro WCre
- 'Susannah' (Au/d)	CWCL EWoo GAbr GAgs GCai GMaP IPen MFie NDro NHol NPri SDnm SPop WCre WFar WHil
* - 'Sweet Chestnut' (Au/S)	WAln
- 'Sweet Georgia Brown' (Au/A)	SPop WAln
- 'Sweet Pastures' (Au/S)	CPBP ECho GAbr GAgs IPen MFie NDro NHol SPop WCre
- 'Swiss Royal Velvet' (Au/B) **new**	NDro
- 'Sword' (Au/d)	CWCL ECho GAbr GAgs IPen ITim MAsh MFie NDro NHol SPop WAln WCre WFar WHil
- 'Symphony' (Au/A)	ITim MFie NDro SPop WFar WHil
- 'T.A. Hadfield' (Au/A)	EWoo GAgs MFie NDro SPop WFar WHil
- 'Taffeta' (Au/S)	CWCL EBee GAgs MAsh NDro SDnm SPav WAln WHil
- 'Tall Purple Dusty Miller' (Au/B)	SPop
- 'Tally-ho' (Au/A)	NDro WAln
- 'Tamar Mist' (Au)	MAsh
- 'Tamino' (Au/S)	MFie NDro SPop WAln
- 'Tarantella' (Au/A)	MFie NDro SPop
- 'Tawny Owl' (Au/B)	GAbr NBro
- 'Tay Tiger' (Au/St)	GAbr GAgs MAsh MFie SPop WHil
- 'Teawell Pride' (Au/d)	SPop WHil
- 'Ted Gibbs' (Au/A)	MFie NDro WAln WCre WHil
- 'Ted Roberts' (Au/A)	MFie NDro SPop WCre WFar WHil
- 'Teem' (Au/S)	GAbr IPen MAsh NDro SPop
- 'Temeraire' (Au/A)	MFie WAln
- 'Tenby Grey' (Au/S)	WCre
- 'Tender Trap' (Au/A)	WAln
- 'Terpo' (Au/A)	MFie WAln WHil
- 'The Argylls' (Au/St)	SPop
- 'The Baron' (Au/S)	GAgs GCai IPen ITim MFie NDro SPop WCre WFar WHil

- 'The Bishop' (Au/S)	GAbr GAgs IPen SPop WHil
- 'The Bride' (Au/S)	MFie NDro SPop
- 'The Cardinal' (Au/d)	WAln
- 'The Czar' (Au/A)	MFie NDro SPop
- 'The Egyptian' (Au/A)	IPen NDro SPop WAln WHil
- 'The Hobbit' (Au/A)	WAln
- 'The Lady Galadriel' (Au/A) **new**	NDro
- 'The Maverick' (Au/S)	MFie
- 'The Raven' (Au/S)	EWoo GAbr GAgs ITim MAsh MFie SPop WCre
- 'The Sneep' (Au/A)	IPen MFie NDro SPop WCre WFar
- 'The Snods' (Au/S)	EBee IPen MFie NDro SPop
- 'The Wrekin' (Au/S)	WAln
- 'Thetis' (Au/A)	GAgs MFie SPop WCre WFar
- 'Thirlmere' (Au/d)	WAln
- 'Thisbe' (Au/A) **new**	NDro
- 'Three Way Stripe' (St)	GAbr GAgs WCre WHil
- 'Thunderstorm' (Au)	MAsh
- 'Thutmoses' (Au/A)	NDro WAln
- 'Tiger Tim' (Au/St)	WAln
- 'Tim' (Au)	IPen
- 'Tim's Fancy' (Au/S) **new**	NDro
- 'Tinker' (Au/S)	WAln
- 'Tinkerbell' (Au/S)	IPen MAsh MFie SPop WCre WFar
- 'Titania' (Au)	SPop
- 'Toffee Crisp' (Au/A)	IPen SPop WAln
- 'Tom Farmer' (Au)	WCre
- 'Tomboy' (Au/S)	GAgs IPen MAsh NDro SDnm SPop
- 'Toolyn' (Au/S)	NDro WAln
- 'Top Cat' (Au/d) **new**	WAln
- 'Tosca' (Au/S)	GAgs GCai IPen MAsh NDro SPop WFar WHil
- 'Trish'	GAbr
- 'Trojan' (Au/S)	MAsh WCre
- 'Trouble' (Au/d)	GAbr GAgs GMaP IPen MAsh MFie NDro SPop WCre WHil
- 'Troy Aykman' (Au/A)	MFie NDro SPop WAln
- 'Trudy' (Au/S)	EWoo GCai IPen ITim MAsh MFie NDro SPop WCre WHil
- 'True Briton' (Au/S)	IPen MFie NDro SPop WCre
- 'Trumpet Blue' (Au/S)	MFie SPop WFar WHil
- 'Tudor Rose' (Au/S) **new**	NDov NDro
- 'Tumbledown' (Au/A)	MFie SPop
- 'Tummel' (Au/A)	EWoo MFie NDro SPop WAln WHil
- 'Turnberry' (Au/S) **new**	SPop
- 'Twiggy' (Au/S)	GCai NDro SPop WAln
- 'Tye Lea' (Au/S)	WAln
- 'Typhoon' (Au/A)	EWoo IPen MFie SPop WCre
- 'Uncle Arthur' (Au/A)	MFie WAln WHil
- 'Unforgettable' (Au/A)	MFie WAln
- 'Upper Crust' (Au/St) **new**	SPop
- 'Upton Belle' (Au/S)	GAgs IPen MAsh MFie NDro SPop WAln WFar
- 'Ushba' (Au/d)	SPop
- 'Valerie' (Au/A)	IPen MFie SPop
- 'Valerie Clare'	WAln WHil
- 'Vee Too' (Au/A)	GAbr MFie NDro SPop WFar WHil
- 'Vega' (Au/A)	SPop WAln
- 'Vein' (Au/St)	WAln
- 'Velvet Moon' (Au/A)	MFie WAln WFar
- 'Venetian' (Au/A)	GAgs MFie NDro SPop WAln WFar WHil
- 'Venus' (Au/A)	WAln
- 'Vera' (Au/A)	NDro SPop
- 'Verdi' (Au/A)	WAln
- 'Vesuvius' (Au/d)	IPen SPop
- 'Victoria' (Au/S)	WAln
- 'Victoria de Wemyss' (Au/A)	MFie WCre WHil
- 'Victoria Park' (Au/A)	WAln

- 'Virginia Belle' (Au/St)	WAln
- 'Vivian' (Au/S)	WAln
- 'Vulcan' (Au/A)	ECho MAsh MFie NBro
- 'Walhampton' (Au/S)	SPop
- 'Walter Lomas' (Au/S)	WAln
- 'Walton' (Au/A)	CPBP GAbr GAgs MAsh MFie NDro SPop WCre WFar WHil
- 'Walton Heath' (Au/d)	ECho GAgs IPen MAsh MFie NDro SPop WCre WFar
- 'Waltz Time' (Au/A)	MFie
- 'Wanda's Moonlight' (Au/d)	WAln
- 'Warwick' (Au/S)	MAsh MFie NDro SPop
- 'Watchett' (Au/S)	WAln
- 'Wayward' (Au/S)	WCre
- 'Wedding Day' (Au/S)	ITim MFie NDro WAln
- 'Wentworth' (Au/A)	IPen WAln
- 'Whistle Jacket' (Au/S)	MFie NDro WAln
- 'White Ensign' (Au/S)	ECho EWoo GAbr GAgs IPen ITim NDro SPop WCre WFar WHil
- 'White Water' (Au/A)	MFie SPop WAln WHil
- 'White Wings' (Au/S)	EWoo GCai ITim MFie NDro SPop
- 'Whitecap' (Au/S)	WAln
- 'Whoopee' (Au/A)	EWoo WAln
- 'Wichita Falls' (Au/A)	NDro WAln
- 'Wide Awake' (Au/A)	NDro
- 'Wild and Grey' (Au/S) **new**	NDro
- 'Wilf Booth' (Au/A)	MFie SPop WFar
- 'William Gunn' (Au/d)	MFie SPop
- 'Wilson's Wonder' (Au)	MAsh
- 'Wincha' (Au/S)	EWoo GAgs GCai MFie NDro NEgg SPop WCre WFar
- 'Windways Mystery' (Au/B)	GAbr NDro
- 'Winifrid' (Au/A)	GAbr NDro NHol SPop WCre WFar WHil
- 'Witchcraft' (Au)	SPop
- 'Woodlands Lilac' (Au/B) **new**	NDro
- 'Woodmill' (Au/A)	EWoo IPen MFie SPop WAln WHil
- 'Wookey Hole' (Au/A)	NDro
- 'Wycliffe Harmony' (Au/B) **new**	NDro
- 'Wycliffe Midnight' (Au/B)	GAbr NDro
- 'Wye Hen' (Au/St)	SPop WAln
- 'Wye Lemon' (Au/S)	SPop
- 'X2' (Au)	WHil
- 'Yellow Hammer' (Au/S)	WAln
- 'Yellow Isle' (Au/S)	WAln
- 'Yellow Ribbon'	WAln
- 'Yitzhak Rabin' (Au/A)	WAln WHil
- 'Yorkshire Grey' (Au/S)	IPen MFie NBro
- 'Zambia' (Au/d)	ECho GAbr MFie NDro WCre
- 'Zimmer' (Au/St) **new**	SPop
- 'Zircon' (Au/S)	MAsh WAln
- 'Zoe' (Au/A)	MAsh WAln
- 'Zoe Ann' (Au/S)	WAln
- 'Zorro' (Au/St)	WAln
auriculata (Or)	EBee
'Barbara Barker' (Au)	GEdr NMen
'Barbara Midwinter' (Pr)	CDes EBee GAbr GEdr SHar WAbe WCot
Barnhaven Blues Group (Pr/Prim) ♀H4	EBee EBla GAbr NCGa NSum
Barnhaven Gold-laced Group	see *P.* Gold-laced Group Barnhaven
Barnhaven hybrids	NSum
'Beatrice Wooster' (Au)	EPot GAbr GAgs GKev GKir IPen MFie NLAp NWCA WFar
'Beeches' Pink'	GAbr NHar NSum
beesiana (Pf)	Widely available
(Belarina Series) 'Belarina Butter Yellow' (Pr/Prim/d)	CAby CWCL EPfP EWll GAbr LAst NLar NPnk SMrm SRot SVil WHil
- 'Belarina Cobalt Blue' (Pr/Prim/d)	CAby CWCL EPot EWll MFie NPnk SMrm SRot WCot WHil
- 'Belarina Cream' (Pr/Prim/d)	CAby CWCL EWll LLHF MFie NPnk SMrm SRot SVil WCot
- 'Belarina Pink Ice' (Pr/Prim/d)	CAby CWCL EWll LHop NLar NPnk SVil WHil
- 'Belarina Rosette Nectarine' (Pr/Prim/d)	CAby CWCL ECtt EPot EWll MFie NLar NPnk SMrm SVil WHil WPtf
'Belinda'	ITim
bella (Mi)	GKev
bellidifolia (Mu)	GEdr GKev IPen
§ - subsp. ***hyacinthina*** (Mu)	WAbe
beluensis	see *P.* × *pubescens* 'Freedom'
× ***berninae*** (Au) **new**	GAgs
§ - 'Windrush' (Au)	WAbe
'Bewerley White'	see *P.* × *pubescens* 'Bewerley White'
bhutanica	see *P. whitei* 'Sherriff's Variety'
'Big Red Giant' (Pr/Prim/d)	ECtt
bileckii	see *P.* × *forsteri* 'Bileckii'
'Blue Julianas' (Pr) **new**	NCGa NSum
'Blue Riband' (Pr/Prim)	CDes EBee LLHF WFar
'Blue Sapphire' (Pr/Prim/d)	CSpe GAbr MFie NDov
'Blutenkissen' (Pr/Prim)	GAbr GEdr
'Bon Accord Cerise' (Pr/Poly/d)	GAbr
'Bon Accord Purple' (Pr/Poly/d)	WFar
boothii (Pe)	NSum
- ***alba*** (Pe)	LLHF NHar
- subsp. ***repens*** (Pe)	CEnt MNrw
'Boothman's Ruby'	see *P.* × *pubescens* 'Boothman's Variety'
bracteata (Bu)	WAbe
§ ***bracteosa*** (Pe)	GKev ITim
Bressingham (Pf)	WFar
brevicula (Cy) SDR 4452	GKev
- SDR 4770	GKev
'Broadwell Milkmaid'	WAbe
'Broadwell Oliver' (Au) **new**	ITim
'Broadwell Pink' (Au)	WAbe
'Broadwell Ruby' (Au)	CPBP WAbe
'Broadwell Violet' **new**	EPot WAbe
'Broxbourne'	EPot MFie NHol
'Buckland Wine' (Pr/Prim)	CElw
× ***bulleesiana*** (Pf)	Widely available
- Moerheim hybrids (Pf)	WFar
bulleyana (Pf) ♀H4	Widely available
- SDR 4261	GKev
burmanica (Pf)	CPla EBee GAbr GEdr GGar GKir IPen MMuc NCGa NWCA SWat WFar WMoo
- SDR 5801	GKev
'Butterscotch' (Pr/Prim)	NCGa NSum
'Caerulea Plena' (Pr/Prim)	GCal NBid
calderiana (Pe)	GCrs
- subsp. ***strumosa*** (Pe)	GKev
calliantha (Cy) SDR 5168	GKev
Candelabra hybrids (Pf)	CBre ECho GAbr GGar GKir ITim LSou NBir NCob NGdn SGSe SMrm SPet SWal SWat WFar WHil WPtf
- orange-flowered (Pf)	SMrm
Candy Pinks Group (Pr/Prim)	NCGa NSum
capitata (Ca)	CMMP CMac CPla CSpe EBee ECho EPfP GCal GCrs GKev IPen MSCN

	NWCA SPer SPoG WFar WGwG WWFP
- CC 3843	GKev
- dark-flowered (Ca)	WCot
- subsp. ***mooreana*** (Ca)	CFir CLAP CPrp CTsd GKev IPen LBMP LRHS NGdn NLAp NSum SBch SMrm SPet SPlb SRot SWal WHrl
- 'Norverna Blue' (Ca)	CSpr
- subsp. ***sphaerocephala*** (Ca) SDR 3225	GKev
'Captain Blood' (Pr/Prim/d)	CDes ECtt EKen EPfP MFie WClo WFar
Carnation Victorians Group (Pr/Poly)	NCGa
carniolica (Au)	WCot
cernua (Mu)	GKev IPen
§ ***chionantha*** (Cy) ♀H4	CLAP CWCL EPfP GAuc GCra GGar GKev GKir MMuc NBPC NBir NCGa NCob NGdn NSum SBfd SEND WAbe WFar WGwG WPtf
- SDR 4610	GKev
- SDR 4847	GKev
- subsp. ***chionantha*** (Cy)	GKev IPen
- cream-flowered **new**	MMuc
§ - subsp. ***melanops*** (Cy)	GAuc
§ - subsp. ***sinopurpurea*** (Cy)	CLAP CWCL EBee GGar GKev GKir IPen MDKP NBir NCGa NLar NSum SBfd SPer WAbe WBVN
- - SDR 2747	GKev
- - SDR 4418	GKev
chungensis (Pf)	CAby CLAP CWCL EBee EPfP GCra GEdr GGar GKev GKir IPen MMuc NBPC NGdn NHol NSum SBfd SWvt WAbe WMoo WSpi
§ ***chungensis*** × ***pulverulenta*** (Pf)	CHid CLAP EBee GEdr GKir NBPC NHol NLar WMnd WWEG
× ***chunglenta***	see *P. chungensis* × *P. pulverulenta*
'Cisca' **new**	WCot
'Clarence Elliott' (Au)	CDes CPBP GCrs GKev IPen ITim MFie NHar NMen NWCA WAbe WFar
clarkei (Or)	GEdr GKev
clusiana 'Murray-Lyon' (Au)	NMen
cockburniana (Pf) ♀H4	EBee EBla GAuc GEdr GGar GKev GQui IPen MMuc NCGa NGdn SWat WAbe WFar
- hybrids (Pf)	SWat
- 'Kevock Sunshine'	EBee GEdr GKev GMac IPen
concholoba (Mu)	EBee GKev
'Corporal Baxter' (Pr/Prim/d)	EPfP LLHF WBVN
cortusoides (Co)	CLAP CPla EBee EPfP GAbr GCra GKev GKir IPen LSou NLar
Cowichan (Pr/Poly)	CElw
Cowichan Amethyst Group (Pr/Poly)	CDes EBee NCGa
Cowichan Blue Group (Pr/Poly)	NCGa NSum
Cowichan Garnet Group (Pr/Poly)	CAby CDes EWoo NCGa NSum
Cowichan Red Group (Pr/Poly)	WFar
Cowichan Venetian Group (Pr/Poly)	CDes NCGa NSum WFar
Cowichan Yellow Group (Pr/Poly)	CDes NCGa NSum
'Coy' (Au)	WAbe
Crescendo Series (Pr/Poly)	GAbr WHil
'Crimson Velvet' (Au)	GAbr IPen ITim WThu
crispa	see *P. glomerata*
cuneifolia (Cu)	GKev
- subsp. ***heterodonta*** (Cu)	GEdr
daonensis (Au)	GAgs GKev
darialica (Al)	GKev LLHF
'Dark Rosaleen' (Pr/Poly)	EBee ECGP ECtt GAbr GEdr ITim LLHF MFie MNrw NBPC NDov SSvw SUsu WCot
'David Valentine' (Pr)	EBla GAbr WAbe WCot
'Dawn Ansell' (Pr/Prim/d)	CDes CRow CSpe CWCL EBla ECtt EPfP GAbr GCrs MFie MRav NBir NDov NLar NWCA SRGP WFar WHer WHil
Daybreak Group (Pr/Poly)	NCGa
deflexa (Mu)	GKev IPen
denticulata (De) ♀H4	Widely available
- CC 4629	GKev
- var. ***alba*** (De)	CBcs CBen CTri CWCL CWat EBee ECha ECho EPfP GAbr GCra GGar GMaP LRHS MFie MLLN MWat NBid NCGa NCob NHol NLar NPri SMrm SPer SPoG WClo WMoo WPer WWEG
- blue-flowered (De)	CWCL ECho GAbr GKir NLar NPri SMrm WFar
- 'Bressingham Beauty' (De)	EBrs LRHS
- 'Glenroy Crimson' (De)	CLAP EBee LLHF SWvt WCom
- 'Karryann' (De/v)	CBow WCot
- lilac-flowered (De)	ECho EHon MWat NCob NPri SMrm WWEG
- 'Prichard's Ruby' (De)	NCob
- purple-flowered (De)	ECho WMoo
- red-flowered (De)	ECho GGar GKir MFie NBir WMoo
- 'Ronsdorf' (De)	ELon LBMP NBPC NLar
- rose-flowered (De)	GKir
- 'Rubin' (De)	CWCL CWat ECho EHon GAbr GMaP LRHS MBrN MLHP NChi NCob NLar SMrm SPer SPoG SRms WPer WWEG
- 'Rubinball' (De)	NHol
deorum (Au)	GKev
× ***deschmannii***	see *P.* × *vochinensis*
'Desert Sunset' (Pr/Poly)	NCGa
deuteronana (Pe)	GCrs
'Devon Cream' (Pr/Prim)	WFar
diantha SDR 4511 **new**	GKev
'Don Keefe' PBR	CBod CHid EBee ECGP ECtt GAbr GBin GEdr GMac LLHF LSou MBNS MFie NBPC NGdn NLar NPnk SUsu WCot WFut
'Dorothy' (Pr/Poly)	MRav
'Double Lilac'	see *P. vulgaris* 'Lilacina Plena'
'Duchess of York' (Poly) **new**	LLWP
'Duckyls Red' (Pr/Prim)	WHal
'Dusky Lady'	CLAP MBri WFar
'Early Bird' (*allionii* hybrid) (Au)	IPen ITim MFie
'Easter Bonnet' (Pr/Prim)	NBid WCot
edgeworthii	see *P. nana*
§ ***elatior*** (Pr) ♀H4	Widely available
- hose-in-hose (Pr/d)	NBid
- hybrids (Pr)	MWat SPlb
I - 'Jessica'	WCot WHil
- subsp. ***leucophylla*** (Pr)	ECho SBch
§ - subsp. ***meyeri*** (Pr)	EBee GKev GKir LLHF NSla
- subsp. ***pallasii*** (Pr)	GAuc
'Elizabeth Browning'	GAbr WCot
'Elizabeth Killelay' PBR (Pr/Poly/d)	CBct CElw CHid CMea CWCL CWGN EBee EBla ECtt ELan GEdr GMaP LSou MFie MLLN NBPC NBir NChi NDov NEgg

		NLar NPnk NSti SPer SPoG SUsu WClo WCot WFar WPnP
	'Ellen Page' (Au)	MFie
	'Ethel Barker' (Au)	IPen MFie NHol
	'Eugénie' (Pr/Prim/d)	ECtt GAbr LLHF MFie NCGa SRGP
§	***euprepes***	GKev
	'Fairy Rose' (Au)	IPen ITim NHol WAbe
	farinosa (Al)	GKir IPen NGdn NSum WFar
	fasciculata (Ar)	GEdr GKev NWCA
	- CLD 345	WAbe
	- SDR 3092	GKev
	'Fire Opal'	EBrs LRHS
	Firefly Group (Pr/Poly)	NCGa WCot
§	***firmipes*** (Si)	EBee EWes GKev IPen
§	***flaccida*** (Mu)	GAuc GEdr GGGa GKev IPen NCGa SBfd WAbe
	Flamingo Group (Pr/Poly)	NCGa
	florida (Y)	GKev NCob
	florindae (Si) ♀H4	Widely available
	- SDR 4626	GKev
	- bronze-flowered (Si)	GKir GQui NBir SWat
	- buff-flowered (Si)	GAuc
	- hybrids (Si)	CMac EHrv GAbr GEdr GKir GMaP ITim NCGa NCob NHol NSti SMrm WHil
	- Keillour hybrids (Si)	CLAP NGdn NLar
	- magenta-flowered (Si)	MDKP
	- 'Muadh' (Si)	MMuc SEND
	- orange-flowered (Si)	CSam GCal GMac IPen LLWG MDKP MNrw WFar WMoo
	- peach-flowered (Si)	MDKP
	- 'Ray's Ruby' (Si)	CHar CLAP EBee GEdr MDKP MNrw NBir NGdn SWat WWFP
	- red-flowered (Si)	CAby GBin GGar GKev IPen LLWG MMuc NBid NLar NSum WCom WFar
	- terracotta-flowered (Si)	NGdn
	Footlight Parade Group (Pr/Prim)	NCGa
	forbesii (Mo)	GKev
	- CC 4084	CPLG
	forrestii (Bu)	GAuc GKev IPen WAbe WHil
	- SDR 4304	GKev
§	× ***forsteri*** 'Bileckii' (Au)	NBir NWCA
	- 'Dianne' (Au)	EDAr GAbr GCrs NBro NRya NWCA WAbe
	'Francisca' (Pr/Poly)	Widely available
	'Freckles' (Pr/Prim/d)	SWat
	'Fritz Kummert' (Au)	WAbe
	frondosa (Al) ♀H4	EBee ECho GCra IPen NMen NWCA SBch WAbe
	'Garnet' (*allionii* hybrid) (Au)	MFie
	'Garryarde Crimson'	GEdr LLHF
	'Garryarde Guinevere'	see *P.* 'Guinevere'
	gemmifera (Ar)	GCrs GKev
	- var. ***monantha*** (Ar)	GKev
	geraniifolia (Co)	CLAP EBee GEdr GKev
§	'Gigha' (Pr/Prim)	CLAP EBee GCal GCrs
	'Gilded Ginger'	NCGa
	glaucescens (Au)	NSum
§	***glomerata*** (Ca)	ECho GKev IPen
	- GWJ 9213	WCru
	- SDR 3924	GKev
	'Glowing Embers' (Pf)	GKev LLHF NBir
	glutinosa All.	see *P. allionii*
	Gold-laced Group (Pr/Poly)	Widely available
§	- Barnhaven (Pr/Poly)	EBla GAbr GKir NBPC NBir
	- Beeches strain (Pr/Poly) ♀H4	NCob

	gracilipes (Pe)	CDes CLAP GCrs MDKP NHol WAbe
	- early-flowering (Pe)	GCra WAbe
	- late-flowering (Pe)	CLAP GCra
	- 'Major'	see *P. bracteosa*
	- 'Minor'	see *P. petiolaris* Wall.
	graminifolia	see *P. chionantha*
	Grand Canyon Group (Pr/Poly)	NCGa
	grandis (Sr)	IPen
	'Groenekan's Glorie' (Pr/Prim)	GAbr GEdr NBir NSum WFar
§	'Guinevere' (Pr/Poly) ♀H4	CSam EBee EBla EHoe GAbr GEdr GKir GMaP ITim LSou MAvo MBri MFie NBPC NBid NBir NBro NHol NSla NSum SPlb WCom WCot WFar WHil WPat
	'Hall Barn Blue' (Pr/Prim)	EPot GAbr GEdr GMaP MFie NBPC NHar NHol NMyG WCot WHil
§	***halleri*** (Al)	IPen MDKP NSum WAbe
	- 'Longiflora'	see *P. halleri*
	aff. ***handeliana*** **new**	GKev
	Harbour Lights mixture (Pr/Poly)	NCGa
	Harlow Carr hybrids (Pf)	CSWP EPfP GMac GQui LRHS NCGa NSla WMoo
	Harvest Yellows Group (Pr/Poly)	NCGa WCot
	'Hazel's White' **new**	GKev ITim
	'Helmswell Abbey' (Au)	GAgs GKev
	helodoxa	see *P. prolifera*
	'Hemswell Blush' (Au)	CSpe GKev ITim NLar WCre
	'Hemswell Ember' (Au)	CPBP GAgs NHol NLAp NRya
	heucherifolia (Co)	CPla EBee GAuc IPen
	- SDR 3224	GKev
	hidakana (R)	GEdr
	'High Point' (Au)	NMen WAbe
	hirsuta (Au)	GAgs GKev IPen MMuc SEND
	- 'Lismore Snow' (Au)	NHar
	- ***nivea*** (Au)	GKev
	- red-flowered (Au)	EBee GAgs MMuc
	hose-in-hose (Pr/Poly/d)	MNrw
	'Hyacinthia' (Au)	GAgs IPen MFie NLar WThu
	hyacinthina	see *P. bellidifolia* subsp. *hyacinthina*
	ianthina	see *P. prolifera*
	iljinskyi	GKev
	incana (Al)	GKev
	'Ingram's Blue' (Pr/Poly)	CDes GAbr WCot
	Inshriach hybrids (Pf)	CMHG LRHS WFar
	integrifolia (Au)	GEdr
§	'Inverewe' (Pf) ♀H4	CRow GBin GCra GKev GQui NBir NBre NChi NMun SUsu WCom
	involucrata	see *P. munroi*
	ioessa (Si)	EWes GCra GQui NGdn
	- var. ***hopeana*** (Si)	EBee
	'Iris Mainwaring' (Pr/Prim)	ECtt GAbr GCra GEdr GKev LLHF MCot NHol WCot
	irregularis (Pe)	WAbe
	Jack in the Green Group (Pr/Poly)	CLAP CStu MNrw WBVN WBor WFar WMoo
	- Barnhaven (Pr/Poly)	EBla
	- white-flowered (Pr/Poly) **new**	IFro
	Jackanapes Group (Pr/Poly)	EBla
	'Jackie Richards' (Au)	GCrs MFie NHol
	jaffreyana (Pu)	EPot
	japonica (Pf)	CMHG CRow CSam ECha GAuc GGar GQui IPen LPBA LRHS MSCN NBro NGdn NHol SPer SWat WAbe WBrE WFar WMoo
	- 'Alba' (Pf)	CPrp CTri EBee ECho EHrv EPfP EWTr GAuc GCal GEdr GGar GKir

		IPen MFie NGdn NPri SPer WAbe WFar WHil WWEG
	- 'Apple Blossom' (Pf)	CAby CCVN CFir COIW CWCL EBee EBrs EShb EWTr GAbr GCal GEdr GGar GKev GKir GMac IPen LBMP LRHS MBri MFie NCGa NGdn NHol NPri SBfd SWvt WFar WHoo WPnP
*	- 'Carminea' (Pf)	CHid COIW EBee GEdr GGar GKev GKir IPen MFie MSCN NBro NGdn NLar WFar WHil
	- 'Fuji' (Pf)	NBro
	- 'Fuji' hybrids (Pf)	NLar
	- hybrids (Pf)	CMac GAbr GCra GKir MRav
	- 'Jim Saunders' (Pf)	SLon
	- 'Merve's Red' (Pf)	CAby EBee SUsu WPGP
	- 'Miller's Crimson' (Pf) ♀H4	Widely available
	- 'Oriental Sunrise' (Pf)	CCVN CMil CSWP EBee GKev LLHF NSum
	- pale pink-flowered (Pf)	ITim NSum
	- 'Peninsula Pink' (Pf)	IPen
	- 'Pink Pagoda' (Pf)	ITim
	- 'Pinkie' (Pf)	IPen
	- 'Postford White' (Pf) ♀H4	Widely available
	- Redfield strain (Pf)	IPen
	- red-flowered (Pf)	IPen WAbe
	- 'Splendens' (Pf)	IPen
	- 'Valley Red' (Pf)	EBee GKev IPen ITim LRHS
	jesoana (Co)	GGar GKev LLHF
	- B&SWJ 618	WCru
	- var. ***pubescens*** (Co)	EBee GKev
	'Joan Hughes' (*allionii* hybrid) (Au)	WAbe
	'Joanna'	ECou MHer
	'Johanna' (Pu)	GAbr GEdr GKev LLHF NGdn NHar NHol NPnk NSum NWCA WAbe
	'John Fielding' (Sr × Pr)	CElw EBee GAbr GEdr MCot WCot
	'Jo-Jo' (Au)	MFie NHol WAbe
	juliae (Pr)	CPla ECho EDAr GEdr GKev LHop LRHS NBid NPnk NSum NWCA SPlb WAbe
I	- 'Millicent' (Pr)	WCot
	- white-flowered (Pr)	NSum
	'Ken Dearman' (Pr/Prim/d)	CSpe ECtt EPfP NBir NWCA SRGP WClo
	kewensis (Sp) ♀H2	WAbe
	'Kinlough Beauty' (Pr/Poly)	CAby GAbr GCrs GEdr GMaP LLHF NPnk WEas
§	***kisoana*** (Co)	CLAP EBla GKev IPen LLHF WCru
	- var. ***alba*** (Co)	CLAP EBee
	- var. ***shikokiana***	see *P. kisoana*
	- 'Velvet' (Co)	CLAP GEdr
	'Kusum Krishna'	GEdr NHar
	'Lady Greer' (Pr/Poly) ♀H4	CMac CSam EBee EDAr EPfP GAbr GEdr GKev GMaP LLWP MCot MHer NChi NGdn NHar NLar NRya NSum SAga SUsu WFar WHer WHil
	latisecta (Co)	GEdr IPen WCot
§	***laurentiana*** (Al)	CTsd GAuc GKev NMen WAbe
	'Lea Gardens' (*allionii* hybrid) (Au)	IPen MFie NHol
	'Lee Myers' (*allionii* hybrid) (Au)	IPen MFie
	leucophylla	see *P. elatior*
	'Lilac Domino' (Au)	IPen
	lilacina SDR 3088	GKev
	'Lilian Harvey' (Pr/Prim/d)	CElw CSpr SPer
	limbata <u>new</u>	GKev
	'Lindum Moonlight'	MFie
	'Lingwood Beauty' (Pr/Prim)	CSam GAbr WAbe

	'Lismore' (Au)	GAgs
	'Lismore Bay' (Au)	GKev
	'Lismore Jewel' (Au)	NMen WAbe
	'Lismore Sunshine'	NHar
	'Lismore Treasure' (Au)	NMen WAbe
	'Lismore Yellow' (Au)	CPBP NHar WAbe
	Lissadel hybrids (Pf)	NCGa
	'Little Egypt' (Pr/Poly)	NCGa NSum
	littoniana	see *P. vialii*
	× ***loiseleurii*** 'Aire Mist' (Au)	CPBP EPot GKev IPen MAsh NHar NHol NMen NRya NSum NWCA WAbe WHil WThu
§	- 'Aire Waves' (Au)	ITim NHar NHol NMen
	- 'Pink Aire Mist' (Au)	WHil
	- 'White Waves' (Au)	IPen
	longiflora	see *P. halleri*
	longipes (Cy)	GKev
	luteola (Or)	EBee ECho EWTr GGar GKev GKir LLHF NGdn NSum WFar WPer
	macrocalyx	see *P. veris*
	macrophylla (Cy)	EBee GKev
	- var. ***moorcroftiana*** (Cy)	GKev
	'MacWatt's Claret' (Pr/Poly)	GAbr LLWP
	'MacWatt's Cream' (Pr/Poly)	CSWP EBee EBla GAbr GCra GEdr GKir LRHS WCot
	magellanica (Al)	NGdn WAbe
	'Maisie Michael'	LLHF WAbe
	marginata (Au) ♀H4	CPne ECho GAbr GCrs GEdr GKir IPen LHop LRHS MFie MMuc NHol NLAp NSla NSum SBch SEND WAbe WFar
	- from the Dolomites (Au)	NHol
	- 'Adrian Evans' (Au)	ITim
	- 'Adrian Jones' <u>new</u>	ITim
	- ***alba*** (Au)	MFie NBro NHol NRya WFar WThu
	- 'Ardfearn' <u>new</u>	GAgs
	- 'Baldock's Purple' (Au)	IPen
	- 'Barbara Clough' (Au)	GEdr IPen ITim MFie WFar
	- 'Beamish' (Au) ♀H4	NBro NHol NRya WCom
	- 'Beatrice Lascaris' (Au)	GCrs MFie NRya WAbe WCom WThu
	- 'Boothman's Variety' (Au)	CTri ECho NLAp WCom
	- 'Caerulea' (Au)	EPot GKev MAsh MFie NLAp WAbe
	- 'Clear's Variety' (Au)	IPen ITim WCom
	- cut-leaved (Au)	NHol WCom
	- 'Doctor Jenkins' (Au)	IPen ITim NHol NLar NRya
	- 'Drake's Form' (Au)	IPen NLAp NLar NRya
	- dwarf (Au)	ECho GEdr LRHS MFie
	- 'Earl L. Bolton'	see *P. marginata* 'El Bolton'
§	- 'El Bolton' (Au)	IPen NHol
	- 'Elizabeth Fry' (Au)	IPen WCom
	- 'F.W. Millard' (Au)	WCom
	- 'Grandiflora' (Au)	IPen NHol
	- 'Highland Twilight' (Au)	IPen NSla WAbe
	- 'Holden Variety' (Au)	IPen ITim MFie NHol NRya WCom
	- 'Ivy Agee' (Au)	IPen NLAp NRya
	- 'Janet' (Au)	GEdr NLAp WCom
	- 'Jenkins Variety' (Au)	ECho
	- 'Kesselring's Variety' (Au)	CMMP ECho GEdr IPen MFie NLAp WAbe WCom WFar WTin
	- 'Laciniata' (Au)	ECho IPen LRHS
	- lilac-flowered (Au)	IPen
	- 'Linda Pope' (Au) ♀H4	GAgs IPen MAsh NBir NHar NHol NLAp NSla NSum WAbe WCom
	- maritime form (Au)	IPen
	- 'Millard's Variety' (Au)	IPen ITim NHol WCom
	- 'Miss Fell' (Au)	GAgs IPen
	- 'Miss Savory' (Au)	WCom
	- 'Mrs Carter Walmsley' (Au)	NRya
	- 'Mrs Gatenby' (Au)	NWCA

- 'Nancy Lucy' (Au)	WAbe
- 'Napoleon' (Au)	GCrs GEdr IPen ITim MFie MSCN
- 'Prichard's Variety' (Au) ♀H4	ECho EPot GEdr IPen ITim MFie MSCN NCob NLAp NRya NWCA WAbe WFar
- 'Rosea' (Au)	IPen
- 'Sheila Denby' (Au)	IPen ITim NLAp
- 'Snowhite' (Au)	NHar
- 'The President' (Au)	EPot GAgs ITim
- violet-flowered (Au)	ECho
- 'Waithman's Variety' (Au)	IPen NLAp NRya
- wild-collected (Au)	MFie NHol
'Maria Talbot' (*allionii* hybrid) (Au)	NWCA
'Marianne Davey' (Pr/Prim/d)	CSpr MRav WKif
'Marie Crousse' (Pr/Prim/d)	CWCL EPfP NWCA SRGP WFar WHal
Marine Blues Group (Pr/Poly)	NCGa NSum
'Maris Tabbard' (Au)	IPen NLar
'Mars' (*allionii* hybrid) (Au)	MFie NHol NRya
'Marven' (Au)	GEdr IPen MFie
'Mary Anne'	GAbr
'Mauve Mist' (Au)	MAsh
maximowiczii (Cy)	GCrs
megaseifolia (Pr)	GCrs
melanops	see *P. chionantha* subsp. *melanops*
× ***meridiana*** (Au)	NHol
§ - 'Miniera' (Au)	IPen MFie
'Mexico'	LLHF WCot
Midnight Group	NCGa
'Miniera'	see *P.* × *meridiana* 'Miniera'
minima (Au)	GCrs NBro NLar WAbe
- var. ***alba*** (Au)	GCrs NLar NRya
minima × ***wulfeniana***	see *P.* × *vochinensis*
'Miss Indigo' (Pr/Prim/d)	ECtt EPfP GAbr GMaP MFie MRav NDov NLar NWCA SGar SPer WFar
mistassinica (Al)	CPBP
- var. ***macropoda***	see *P. laurentiana*
miyabeana (Pf)	EBee EWld GKev IPen
modesta	EPot GAuc IPen NWCA
var. ***faurieae*** (Al)	
- - f. ***leucantha*** (Al)	GKev
- 'Nemuro-koza-kura' (Al/v)	CBow
mollis (Co)	ITim
'Moorland Apricot'	WMoo
moupinensis	CLAP GAbr GEdr GGGa WAbe
* 'Mrs Eagland'	GAbr
'Mrs Frank Neave' (Pr/Prim)	GEdr IPen
'Mrs McGillivray' (Pr/Prim)	GAbr
§ ***munroi*** (Ar)	CDes GEdr GKev GLin IPen WAbe
- CC 5311	EWld
- SDR 6121	GKev
§ - subsp. ***yargongensis*** (Al)	GAuc GCrs GGar GKev IPen
- - SDR 1932	GKev
- - SDR 3096	GKev
muscarioides (Mu)	GKev IPen MFie
Muted Victorians Group (Pr/Poly)	NCGa NSum
§ ***nana*** (Pe)	IPen WAbe
- 'Alba' (Pe)	WAbe
nanobella (Mi)	GKev
'Netta Dennis' (Pe)	NHar WAbe
New Pinks Group (Pr/Poly)	GAbr NCGa NSum
'Nightingale'	NHol
nipponica (Su)	GEdr

nivalis Pallas	see *P. chionantha*
nivalis ambig.	NSum
'No Eye Cow' **new**	WPGP
nutans Delavay ex Franch.	see *P. flaccida*
'Old Port' (Pr/Poly)	CElw CSam EBee GKev LLWP NMen NSum
Old Rose Victorians Group (Pr/Poly)	NSum
orbicularis (Cy)	GKev
'Oriental Sunset'	MDKP
Osiered Amber Group (Pr/Prim)	NSum
palinuri (Au)	IPen WCom
palmata (Co)	GCrs GEdr
'Paris '90' (Pr/Poly)	CDes NCGa NSum
parryi (Pa)	EBee GKev NWCA SBfd WAbe
- NNS 04-422	WCot
- NNS 04-423	WCot
- NNS 06-494	NWCA
'Peardrop' (Au)	NHol
pedemontana (Au)	EBee NWCA
- 'Alba' (Au)	WPat WThu
'Perle von Bottrop' (Pr/Prim)	GAbr
'Peter Klein' (Or)	GCrs GEdr LLHF NHol WAbe WTin
petiolaris misapplied	see *P.* 'Redpoll'
§ ***petiolaris*** Wall. (Pe)	GCra ITim NHar NSum WAbe
- Sherriff's form	see *P.* 'Redpoll'
'Petticoat'	NCGa
'Pincushion'	GEdr
'Pink Aire' (Au)	EPot MFie NMen NRya WCom
'Pink Fairy' (Au)	IPen ITim
'Pink Ice' (*allionii* hybrid) (Au)	CPBP GCrs GKev ITim MFie NHol NRya
pinnata	GKev
poissonii (Pf)	CBen CPla CTri ELan EPfP GAuc GCra GEdr GGar GKev GKir GMac GQui IBal IPen LPBA LRHS NCGa NGdn NHol SBfd SPad WAbe WGwG WHil WShi
- ACE 2030	EPot
- SDR 3201	GKev
- SDR 5126	GKev
polyanthus (Pr/Poly)	WFar
polyneura (Co)	CPla EBee GEdr GGar IGor IPen MSnd NGdn
'Port Wine' (Pr)	EBla GAbr GCra
'Powdery Pink'	EBrs LRHS
prenantha (Pf)	EBee
- SDR 3909	GKev
primulina (Mi)	GKev
§ ***prolifera*** (Pf) ♀H4	CMHG CMea CWCL EBee ECha EPfP GCra GEdr GGar GKev GKir GMac GQui IPen LPBA LRHS NCGa NGdn NHol NVic SPer SWat WAbe WGwG WMoo WPtf
§ × ***pubescens*** (Au) ♀H4	GAgs IPen NGdn WHil WPer
- 'A.E. Matthews' (Au)	NHol
- 'Apple Blossom' (Au)	GAgs IPen MFie WHil
- 'Balfouriana' (Au)	NHol
§ - 'Bewerley White' (Au)	EBee ECho EPfP GAgs IPen NDro NHol WCre WFar
- 'Blue Wave' (Au)	IPen MFie
§ - 'Boothman's Variety' (Au)	CTri ECho EPfP MFie NLAp WCom WFar WHoo WTin
- 'Carmen'	see *P.* × *pubescens* 'Boothman's Variety'
- 'Chamois' (Au)	MFie
- 'Christine' (Au)	CDes CMea GAgs IPen MFie NBir NSum WCot
- 'Cream Viscosa' (Au)	WCom
- 'Deep Mrs Wilson' (Au)	CPBP MFie WCom

	- 'Faldonside' (Au)	IPen MFie NPnk NSum WCom WHil WThu
§	- 'Freedom' (Au)	CTri ECho GAgs GKev IPen MFie NBir NHol NLAp NLar WCom
	- 'George Harrison' (Au)	MFie
	- 'Harlow Car' (Au)	CMea CPBP GQui IPen MFie NSum NWCA WFar WTin
	- 'Hazel's White' (Au)	GAgs
	- 'Henry Hall' (Au)	NWCA
	- 'Joan Danger' (Au)	IPen ITim
	- 'Joan Gibbs' (Au)	ECho IPen ITim MFie
	- 'Lilac Fairy' (Au)	IPen ITim NHol NPnk WAbe WThu
	- 'Mrs J.H. Wilson' (Au)	GEdr MFie NHol NRya
	- 'Pat Barwick' (Au)	GKir IPen MFie NDro NHol NRya WTin
	- 'Peggy Fell' (Au)	WHil
	- 'Rufus' (Au)	ECho EWes GAbr GAgs NDro WThu
	- 'S.E. Matthews' (Au)	GAgs NHol
	- 'Sid Skelton' (Au)	IPen
	- 'Snowcap' (Au)	IPen ITim
	- 'Sonya' (Au)	IPen
	- 'The General' (Au)	CTri IPen MFie SPop
§	- 'Wedgwood' (Au)	GAbr IPen MFie WHil
	- 'Winifred' (Au)	EWoo GAgs NDro NHol SPop WHil
	- yellow-flowered (Au)	IPen
	pulverulenta (Pf) 🏆^{H4}	Widely available
	- Bartley hybrids (Pf) 🏆^{H4}	CBot GMac LRHS LSou NBre NSum
	- 'Bartley Pink' (Pf)	CPla
	'Quaker's Bonnet'	see *P. vulgaris* 'Lilacina Plena'
	'Rachel Kinnen' (Au)	GAbr IPen MFie WFar
	'Ramona' (Pr/Poly)	NCGa
	'Ravenglass Vermilion'	see *P.* 'Inverewe'
§	'Redpoll' (Pe)	CLAP LLHF NHar NHol WAbe
	reidii (So)	GEdr GKev NSla
	- var. ***williamsii*** (So)	IPen
	'Reverie' (Pr/Poly)	NCGa NSum
	'Rheniana' (Au)	IPen MFie NLar NRya
	'Romeo' (Pr/Prim)	CLAP WCot
	rosea (Or) 🏆^{H4}	CAby CBot CElw EBee ECho EPfP GAuc GEdr IPen MFie MMuc NBid NBir NVic
	- 'Delight'	see *P. rosea* 'Micia Visser-de Geer'
	- 'Gigas' (Or)	NHol WFar
	- 'Grandiflora' (Or)	CMac CPrp ECho EPfP GGar GKev LPBA LRHS NCGa NWCA SBfd SPoG SRms SWal SWat WFar WHil WPer
§	- 'Micia Visser-de Geer' (Or)	WTin
§	***rotundifolia*** (Cf)	IPen
	'Rowallane Rose' (Pf)	IGor
I	'Rowena'	GCra LLHF WCot
	roxburghii	see *P. rotundifolia*
	'Roy Cope' (Pr/Prim/d)	EPfP GAbr NBir SGar SRGP WFar
	rubra	see *P. firmipes*
	rusbyi (Pa)	EBee GKev MFie NWCA
	- subsp. ***ellisiae*** (Pe)	IPen
	scandinavica (Al)	GAuc GCrs GKev
§	'Schneekissen' (Pr/Prim)	EBee GAbr GCra GEdr IPen LRHS MHer NBro NChi NGHP NMyG WHil
	scotica (Al)	GAuc GKev GPoy NSla WAbe
	secundiflora (Pf)	CLAP CPla CWCL EBee ELan GCra GGar GKev GKir LLWG LPBA MMuc NBir SBfd SPer SPlb SWat WAbe WFar WGwG WMoo
	- SDR 4401	GKev
§	× ***sendtneri*** (Au)	MFie
	× ***serrata***	see *P.* × *vochinensis*
	serratifolia (Pf)	EBee GGGa
	- SDR 5165	GKev
	sibthorpii	see *P. vulgaris* subsp. *sibthorpii*
	sieboldii (Co) 🏆^{H4}	CEnt CSpr ECho GCrs MAsh MCot MFie MLHP MNrw NMen NWCA SBch SRms SUsu WAbe WFar
	- 'Akinoysool' (Co)	WFar
	- 'Ankoan' (Co)	WFar
	- 'Asahi' (Co)	WFar
	- 'Ayanami' (Co)	WFar
	- 'Bide-a-Wee Blue' (Co)	NBid
	- 'Bijyonomai' (Co)	WFar
	- 'Blacksmith's Blue' (Co)	EBla
I	- 'Blue Lagoon' (Co)	EBee EBrs GKir LLHF LRHS MMHG NLar
	- 'Blue Shades' (Co)	IPen NMen
	- blue-flowered (Co)	CLAP CWCL ECho NMen WHil
	- 'Blush' (Co)	CLAP
	- 'Bureikou' (Co)	WFar
	- 'Carefree' (Co)	CLAP IPen LLHF NBro NLar NMen
	- 'Cherubim' (Co)	CAby CLAP CStu EBee EBrs GCra GKir LLHF LRHS MMHG WHil
	- 'Dancing Ladies' (Co)	CAby CLAP CMil CSWP EBla IPen MFie NBro WFar
	- 'Dart Rapids' (Co)	CDes
	- 'Duane's Choice' (Co)	CDes CLAP EBee WHil
	- 'Edasango' (Co)	WFar
	- 'Edomurasaki' (Co)	WFar
	- 'Frilly Blue' (Co)	EBrs LRHS
	- 'Galaxy' (Co)	NBro
	- 'Geisha Girl' (Co)	CAby CFir CLAP CSpe EBla EBrs GKir LRHS MRav NLar WAbe WFar WHil WWEG
	- 'Ginhukurin' (Co)	WFar
	- 'Godaisyo' (Co)	WFar
	- 'Hatagarasi' (Co)	WFar
	- 'Higurias' (Co)	WFar
	- 'Hinokoromo' (Co)	WFar
	- 'Hujikosi' (Co)	WFar
	- 'Hutaezuru' (Co)	WFar
	- 'Inikina White' (Co)	WFar
	- 'Inokima Minoura'	WFar
	- 'Izuto' (Co)	WFar
	- 'Jyuuyuunovtage' (Co)	WFar
	- 'Kaedegari' (Co)	WFar
	- 'Kansenden' (Co)	WFar
	- 'Karagoromo' (Co)	WFar
	- 'Kokoroiki' (Co)	WFar
	- 'Kosijimoyuki' (Co)	WFar
	- 'Kotonosirabe' (Co)	WFar
	- 'Kourohou' (Co)	WFar
	- 'Kurama' (Co)	WFar
	- 'Lacewing' **new**	WHil
	- f. ***lactiflora*** (Co)	CDes CLAP EBee IPen NBro NMen SMHy SRot WFar WPGP WTin
	- 'Lilac Sunbonnet' (Co)	CLAP EPfP LLHF NWCA WFar
	- 'Lisujyanome' (Co)	WFar
	- 'Maiougi' (Co)	WFar
	- 'Makazebeni' (Co)	WFar
	- 'Managuruma' (Co)	WFar
	- 'Manakoora' (Co)	CLAP CSWP EBee IPen NBro NSum WFar WHil
	- 'Mangetu' (Co)	WFar
	- 'Masasino' (Co)	WFar
	- 'Matunoyuki' (Co)	WFar
	- 'Mihonokoji' (Co)	WFar
	- 'Mikado' (Co)	CLAP EBee EBrs GCra GKir IPen LRHS WFar WHil
	- 'Mikininonomare' (Co)	WFar
	- 'Mitanohikari' (Co)	WFar
	- 'Miyakowakare' (Co)	WFar
	- 'Miyuki' (Co)	WFar
	- 'Musasi' (Co)	WFar
	- 'Myoutiriki' (Co)	WFar
	- 'Okinatomo' (Co)	WFar

- 'Pago-Pago' (Co)	CDes CLAP EBee IPen MFie NBro NWCA WFar WHil
- 'Pink Laced' (Co)	WFar
- pink-flowered **new**	EWld
- 'Rasyoumon' (Co)	WFar
- 'Rock Candy' (Co)	WFar
- 'Sakuragana' (Co)	WFar
- 'Sasanari' (Co)	WFar
- 'Senyuu' (Co)	WFar WHil
- 'Seraphim' (Co)	CLAP EBee EBrs GKir LRHS MMHG NLar
- 'Shirousasi' (Co)	WFar
- 'Sikoubai' (Co)	WFar
- 'Sinipukurn' (Co)	WFar
- 'Sinnkirou' (Co)	WFar
- 'Sinseiu' (Co)	WFar
- 'Siritonbo' (Co)	WFar
- 'Sitikenjin' (Co)	WFar
- 'Snowdrop' **new**	NCGa WCot
- 'Snowflake' (Co)	CLAP EBee EBrs LRHS MMHG NLar NMen NSla WAbe WFar
- 'Sotodorihime' (Co)	WFar
- 'Sousiarai' (Co)	WFar
- 'Spring Blush' (Co)	GEdr
- 'Spring Rose' (Co)	GEdr
- 'Spring Song' (Co)	GEdr
- 'Sumida No Hatu' (Co)	WFar
- 'Sumisonegawa' (Co)	WFar
- 'Sweetie' (Co)	WFar
- 'Syunkou' (Co)	WFar
- 'Syutyuka' (Co)	WFar
- 'Tagonoura' (Co)	WFar
- 'Tah-ni' (Co)	CMil NBro NSum
- 'Tatutanoy' (Co)	WFar
- 'Tidoriasobi' (Co)	WFar
- 'Tokinohina' (Co)	WFar
- 'Toyonoharu' (Co)	WFar
- 'Tukinomiyaka' (Co)	WFar
- 'Winter Dreams' (Co)	CLAP CSWP NBid NBro NSum WFar WHil
- 'Yukiguruma' (Co)	WFar
sikkimensis (Si) ♀H4	CAby CEnt EBee ECho EPot GAuc GEdr GGar GKev GKir IPen LRHS MSnd NGdn NSum SBfd SPer SPoG WFar WHoo WPnP
- CC&McK 1022	GQui
- SDR 3099	GKev
- SDR 4414	GKev
- SDR 4528 from high altitude	GKev
- SDR 4763	GKev
- SDR 4845	GKev
- SDR 4919	GKev
- SDR 5933	GKev
- from Bhutan	GCra
- var. ***pseudosikkimensis*** (Si)	IPen
- var. ***pudibunda*** (Si)	GEdr GKev
aff. ***sikkimensis*** (Si)	CBot GKir ITim NCGa
Silver-laced Group (Pr/Poly)	ECGP LBMP NLar STes SWvt WFar WPtf
'Silverwells' (Pf)	GEdr
simensis (Sp)	EBee GKev
sinopurpurea	see *P. chionantha* subsp. *sinopurpurea*
'Siobhan'	WCot
'Sir Bedivere' (Pr/Prim)	CDes GAbr WCot
smithiana	see *P. prolifera*
'Snow Carpet'	see *P.* 'Schneekissen'
'Snow Queen'	CStu
'Snow White' (Pr/Poly)	GEdr MRav
Snowcushion	see *P.* 'Schneekissen'

'Snowruffles'	ITim
sonchifolia (Pe)	CFir CLAP
sorachiana	see *P. yuparensis*
'Sorbet' **new**	NCGa
souliei (Y) SDR 4767	GKev
'Sparkling Eyes'	WCot
spectabilis (Au)	EBee GCrs GEdr GKev
- SDR 2415	GKev
Spice Shades Group (Pr/Poly)	GKir NCGa WCot
'Stonewash' **new**	LRHS
'Stradbrook Charm' (Au)	CPBP EPot MFie NHol WCre WFar WThu
'Stradbrook Dainty' (Au)	MFie NHol WFar
'Stradbrook Dream' (Au)	EPot ITim MFie WFar
'Stradbrook Gem' (Au)	EPot
'Stradbrook Lilac Lustre' (Au)	MFie
'Stradbrook Lucy' (Au)	EPot GKev IPen ITim NHol WFar
'Stradbrook Mauve Magic' (Au)	MFie
Striped Victorians Group (Pr/Poly)	NCGa NSum
'Sue Jervis' (Pr/Prim/d)	CWCL MRav NBir NDov NLar NSum SPer WGwG WHal WPrP
suffrutescens (Su)	WAbe
'Sunshine Susie' (Pr/Prim/d)	CSpr EPfP GAbr MRav SPer SRGP WBVN WHil
szechuanica (Cy)	GCrs GLin
takedana (Bu)	LLHF
'Tango' (Pr/Prim) **new**	NCGa NSum
tanneri (Pe)	GKev
'Tantallon' (Pe)	CLAP ITim LLHF NHar
'Tawny Port' (Pr/Poly)	CLAP GAbr NBro SBfd WCom
'Tie Dye' (Pr/Prim)	CDes CElw EBla ECGP GAbr GBin GEdr MNrw NBPC NLar SMrm SPoG WCot WFar
'Tinney's Moonlight' (Pe)	NHar
'Tipperary Purple' (Pr/Prim)	GAbr GEdr
'Tomato Red' (Pr/Prim)	EBee GAbr WCot
'Tony' (Au)	CPBP IPen MFie WAbe WCom
'Top Affair' (Au/d)	IPen
'Tournaig Pink' (Pf)	GGar
tyrolensis (Au)	GKev
'Val Horncastle' (Pr/Prim/d)	ECtt EPfP EWTr GMaP MFie NDov NLar SPer WCot
Valentine Victorians Group (Pr/Poly)	NCGa
× ***venusta***	GKev
'Vera Maud' (Pr) **new**	NCGa NSum
§ ***veris*** (Pr) ♀H4	Widely available
- subsp. ***columnae*** (Pr)	EBee
- feather-petalled (Pr)	WCot
- hybrids (Pr)	LBMP MLLN SGar
- 'Katy McSparron' (Pr/d)	CMea EBee GCra GKir LSou WBor WCot
- subsp. ***macrocalyx*** (Pr)	WCot
- orange-flowered (Pr)	MHer SWal WMoo
- red-flowered (Pr)	CAby CSpr NBid NGdn SPer SWal WCom WMoo
- 'Sunset Shades' (Pr)	ECGP NGHP NLar SBch WFar
vernalis	see *P. vulgaris*
verticillata (Sp)	IPen
§ ***vialii*** (So) ♀H4	Widely available
- JJH 061070	GKev
§ × ***vochinensis*** (Au)	CFee NWCA
§ ***vulgaris*** (Pr/Prim) ♀H4	Widely available
- var. ***alba*** (Pr/Prim)	CRow NSla WBrk
- 'Alba Plena' (Pr/Prim)	CRow GAbr GCal GGar IGor MBri NSum WPtf
- green-flowered	see *P. vulgaris* 'Viridis'

§	– 'Lilacina Plena' (Pr/Prim/d)	CBot CDes EBee EPfP GCal GMaP IFro LLHF MFie MRav NCGa NSum NWCA SMHy SPer WFar
§	– subsp. ***sibthorpii*** (Pr/Prim) ♀H4	CAby CMHG CSam EBee EBla EBrs ECho GAbr GEdr IPen ITim LLWP LRHS MCot MFie MHer MLHP MNrw MRav NBro NChi NDov NGHP NMyG SKHP SRms WCot WEas WHil
§	– 'Viridis' (Pr/Prim/d)	CDes CFir CRow EBla EOHP MNrw
	walshii (Mi)	WAbe
	waltonii (Si)	CCVN CLAP CMil CPla EBee EDAr GKev IPen MDKP MNrw NBPC NCGa SBch SBfd WPtf
	– hybrids (Si)	NWCA
	'Wanda' (Pr/Prim) ♀H4	CBcs CTri EBla ECho GAbr GCra LBMP LLWP MCot MFie MHer MMuc NBid NDov NPnk NVic SEND SRGP SRms WBrk WCFE WCom WCot WEas WFar WHil WTin
	Wanda Group (Pr/Prim)	ECho SPoG WCot
	'Wanda Grace' new	NPnk
	'Wanda Hose-in-hose' (Pr/Prim/d)	EBla GAbr GCra LLWP MMHG NBir NChi SSvw WBor WHer WHil
	'Wanda Jack in the Green' (Pr/Prim)	CLAP WCot WFar
	wardii	see *P. munroi*
	warshenewskiana (Or)	CLAP EBee ECtt GEdr GGar GKev NCob NHol NMen NRya NWCA WAbe WGwG
	watsonii (Mu)	EBee EWes GKev SWat WPtf
	– ACE 1402	IPen
	– SDR 1626	GKev
	– SDR 1673	GKev
	'Wedgwood'	see *P.* × *pubescens* 'Wedgwood'
	'Welsh Blue'	CSpe
	'Wharfedale Bluebell' (Au)	NBir NRya NWCA WAbe
	'Wharfedale Buttercup' (Au)	ITim NHar
	'Wharfedale Butterfly' (Au)	NHol
	'Wharfedale Crusader' (Au)	ITim NHol
	'Wharfedale Gem' (*allionii* hybrid) (Au)	ITim MFie
	'Wharfedale Ling' (*allionii* hybrid) (Au)	CPBP GCrs ITim MFie NHol NLar
	'Wharfedale Sunshine' (Au)	CPBP GKev ITim MFie
	'Wharfedale Superb' (*allionii* hybrid) (Au)	ITim NWCA
	'Wharfedale Village' (Au)	WAbe WThu
	'White Linda Pope' (Au)	GAgs MAsh NMen WCom
	'White Wanda' (Pr/Prim)	GAbr NDov
	'White Waves' (*allionii* hybrid) (Au)	ITim
§	***whitei*** 'Sherriff's Variety' (Pe)	CLAP
	wigramiana (So) CC 4940	GKev
	– CC 4941	GKev
	'William Genders' (Pr/Poly)	GAbr GEdr
	wilsonii (Pf)	CPla CSam CTri CTsd GKev GKir LLWG MDKP MSnd NBPC SGSe SWat WGwG WHoo
§	– var. ***anisodora*** (Pf)	CLAP CPla EBee GKev GKir GQui IPen ITim NGdn WHrl WPtf
	'Windrush'	see *P.* × *berninae* 'Windrush'
	'Winter White'	see *P.* 'Gigha'
	'Wisley Crimson'	see *P.* 'Wisley Red'
§	'Wisley Red' (Pr/Prim)	CElw
	aff. ***woodwardii*** new	GKev
	wulfeniana (Au)	GCrs GEdr GKev
	yargongensis	see *P. munroi* subsp. *yargongensis*
	yunnanensis (Y)	NLar
§	***yuparensis*** (Al)	EBee IPen NWCA
	– white-flowered (Al)	GKev
	zambalensis (Ar)	GKev IPen
	– SDR 1716	GKev

Prinsepia (*Rosaceae*)

sinensis	CArn CBcs CFee MBlu NLar SLon WSHC
utilis	CTrC

Prionosciadium (*Apiaceae*)

thapsoides B&SWJ 10345	WCru

Pritchardia (*Arecaceae*)

affinis	XBlo
pacifica	XBlo

Pritzelago (*Brassicaceae*)

alpina	GEdr NBre NWCA

Prosopis (*Mimosaceae*)

chilensis	IDee

Prostanthera (*Lamiaceae*)

	aspalathoides	CCCN CTsd ECou EWes SOWG
	'Badja Peak'	CTrC CTsd LRHS MAsh SOWG WAbe
	baxteri	ECou SOWG
	chlorantha	SOWG
	cuneata ♀H4	Widely available
	– 'Alpine Gold'	CMHG CWSG EBee LRHS WBrE WFar
	– Kew form	WPGP
*	***digitiformis***	CTsd ECou SOWG
	incisa	CTsd EBee SBfd SHDw
	– 'Rosea'	EOHP
	'La Provence' PBR	LRHS
	lasianthos	CCCN CDoC CHll CRHN CTsd EWes LRHS SAga SBfd SHDw SOWG SPlb WCFE WJek
	– 'Kallista Pink'	CTsd SOWG
	– var. ***subcoriacea***	CPLG
	latifolia	CTsd
	magnifica	SOWG
	'Mauve Mantle'	SOWG
	melissifolia	CArn CTsd
§	– var. ***parvifolia***	CBcs CCCN WAbe
	'Mint Royale'	LRHS
	'Mint-Ice'	LRHS
	nivea	ECou
	ovalifolia ♀H2	CCCN ECou IRar SOWG WJek
I	– 'Variegata' (v)	CBcs CCCN CHGN CMac CPLG CTrC CTsd ECou GGar LRHS SBfd SOWG WCFE WGrn
	'Poorinda Ballerina'	CAlb CDoC CTsd CWit EBee ECou EOHP GGar LRHS MGos SOWG SPoG SRkn WFar
	'Poorinda Petite'	CTsd LRHS
	rotundifolia ♀H2	CCCN CHEx CSBt CSev CTri CTsd CWSG EBee ECho EOHP ESwi MNHC MSCN NGHP SEND SOWG SPer WCFE WGrn
	– 'Chelsea Girl'	see *P. rotundifolia* 'Rosea'
§	– 'Rosea' ♀H2	CCCN CDoC CSBt CTrC CTsd EBee ECou GGar LRHS NHol SEND SOWG SPoG
	scutellarioides 'Lavender Lady'	ECou
	sericea	LRHS

sieberi misapplied	see *P. melissifolia* var. *parvifolia*
sieberi Benth.	CTrC CTsd SOWG
walteri	CCCN EBee ECou LRHS SOWG

Protea (*Proteaceae*)

aurea	SPlb
burchellii	SPlb
'Christine'	CTrC
coronata	SPlb
cynaroides	CBcs CCCN CHEx CTrC EAmu LTen SBig SOWG SPlb
effusa	SPlb
eximia	CBcs CCCN EAmu SPlb
grandiceps	CBcs CCCN SPlb
lacticolor	SPlb
laurifolia	SPlb
nana	SPlb
neriifolia	CCCN SPlb
- 'Snowcrest'	CTrC
obtusifolia	SPlb
'Pink Ice'	CTrC
repens	SPlb
subvestita	CTrC SPlb
susannae	SPlb
venusta	CTrC

Prumnopitys (*Podocarpaceae*)

§ ***andina***	GKir IDee IFFs NMun SLim WThu
elegans	see *P. andina*
§ ***taxifolia***	CDoC CTrC ECou

Prunella (*Lamiaceae*)

§ ***grandiflora***	CHby CPrp ECha GBar GKir MHav SBfd SPer SWat WFar WPGP WWEG
- 'Alba'	EBee ECha EPfP GMaP MNFA NGHP NLar SPer WFar
- 'Altenberg Rosa'	EBee
- 'Bella Deep Rose'	WFar
- 'Blue Loveliness'	GBee GKir SWvt
- 'Carminea'	EBee ECtt SPer
- light blue-flowered	GBar NLar WFar WOut
- 'Loveliness' ♀^{H4}	CDoC CMac EBee ECha ECtt GKir GMaP MLLN MNFA MRav NBro NGdn NSti NVic SPer SPlb SRGP WCAu WFar
- 'Pagoda'	CEnt CSpe NBre NLar
- 'Pink Loveliness'	CPrp SRms WWEG
- 'Rosea'	CElw EBee EPfP WOut
- 'Rubra'	GAbr NGHP NLar WPer
- violet-flowered	EPfP
- 'White Loveliness'	CMac CPrp WWEG
incisa	see *P. vulgaris*
* 'Inshriach Ruby'	GBin
§ ***vulgaris***	CArn CRWN EBWF GBar GPoy MHer MNHC NLan NMir NPri NSco WHer WHfH WJek WMoo
- f. ***leucantha***	GBar WAlt WHer
- 'Marbled White' (v)	WAlt
- variegated (v)	WAlt
- 'Voile'	WAlt
× ***webbiana***	see *P. grandiflora*
- 'Gruss aus Isernhagen'	EBee

Prunus ✿ (*Rosaceae*)

'Accolade' ♀^{H4}	Widely available
§ 'Amanogawa' ♀^{H4}	Widely available
amygdalus	see *P. dulcis*
armeniaca 'Alfred' (F)	ERea GTwe MGos SDea SKee SPer
- var. ***ansu*** 'Flore Pleno' (d)	ERea LAst
- 'Blenheim' (F)	ERea
- 'Bredase' (F)	CWib ERea SDea
- 'De Nancy'	see *P. armeniaca* 'Gros Pêche'
- 'Early Moorpark' (F)	CAgr CWib EPfP ERea GTwe IFFs LAst MBri SDea SLon
- 'Farmingdale' (F)	ERea SDea
- Flavorcot = 'Bayoto'^{PBR} (F)	CAgr CSut SPer
- 'Garden Aprigold' (F)	MGos SPoG
- 'Goldcot' (F)	CAgr ERea LRHS MBri MCoo SDea SKee WHar
- 'Golden Glow' (F)	CAgr CTho ERea GTwe LAst LRHS MBri MCoo MWat SKee
- 'Goldrich' (F)	CAgr
§ - 'Gros Pêche' (F)	SVic
- 'Hargrand' (F)	CAgr SVic
- 'Harogem' (F)	CAgr
- 'Hemskirke' (F)	SKee
- 'Hongaarse' (F)	SDea
- 'Isabella' (F)	CAgr ERea MBri MGos
- 'Moorpark' (F) ♀^{H3}	CEnd CSBt CTri CWib ERea GKir GTwe LAst LBuc MAsh MGos MMuc MRav SDea SKee SPer
- 'New Large Early' (F)	ERea SDea SEND SKee
- 'Petit Muscat' (F)	ERea
- 'Tomcot' (F)	CAgr CTho GKir LBuc LSRN MBri MCoo SFam SKee SLim SPoG WBVN
- 'Tross Orange' (F)	CWib SDea
avium ♀^{H4}	CBcs CCVT CDul CLnd CRWN CSBt CTho CTri CWib ECrN EMac EPfP GKir IFFs LBuc LMaj MGos MMuc MRav MSwo NLar NWea SBfd SFam SPer WDin WHar WMoo WMou
- 'Amber Heart' (F)	SKee
- 'Bigarreau Gaucher' (F)	SKee
§ - 'Bigarreau Napoléon' (F)	GTwe SCrf SKee SVic
- 'Birchenhayes'	see *P. avium* 'Early Birchenhayes'
- 'Black Eagle' (F)	SKee
- 'Black Elton' (F)	SKee
- 'Black Heart' (F)	CWib MMuc
- 'Black Tartarian' (F)	SKee
- 'Bottlers'	see *P. avium* 'Preserving'
- 'Bradbourne Black' (F)	ECrN SCrf SKee
- 'Bullion' (F)	CEnd CTho
- 'Burcombe' (F)	CEnd CTho
- 'Caroon' (F)	SKee
- Celeste = 'Sumpaca'^{PBR} (D)	CAgr CTri EMil GTwe LRHS MAsh MBri MCoo NLar SBfd SDea SFam SKee SLim SPoG
- 'Cherokee'	see *P. avium* 'Lapins'
- 'Colney' (F) ♀^{H4}	ERea GTwe NLar SFam SKee WJas
- 'Crown Morello' (F)	ERea
- 'Dun' (F)	CTho
§ - 'Early Birchenhayes' (F)	CEnd CTho
- 'Early Rivers' (F)	CSBt CWib ECrN GTwe LAst LSRN NLar SDea SKee SVic
- 'Elton Heart' (F)	SKee
- 'Emperor Francis' (F)	ECrN SKee
- 'Fice' (F)	CEnd CTho
- 'Florence' (F)	SKee
- 'Governor Wood' (F)	GTwe SKee
- 'Grandiflora'	see *P. avium* 'Plena'
- 'Greenstem Black' (F)	CTho
- 'Hannaford' (D/C)	CTho
- 'Hertford' (F) ♀^{H4}	SFam SKee
- 'Inga' (F)	SFam SKee
- 'Kentish Red' (F)	SKee
- 'Kordia' (D)	SFam SKee
§ - 'Lapins' (F)	CAgr CDul CTho CTri ECrN EPfP GBut GTwe LAst MAsh NLar SDea SFam SKee SPoG WHar WJas

- 'May Duke'	see *P.* × *gondouinii* 'May Duke'
- 'Merchant' (F) ♀H4	ECrN SKee
- 'Merton Favourite' (F)	SKee
- 'Merton Glory' (F)	CDul CSBt ECrN ERea GTwe IFFs MAsh MGos SCrf SFam SKee SLim WHar
- 'Merton Late' (F)	SKee
- 'Merton Marvel' (F)	SKee
- 'Merton Premier' (F)	SKee SVic
- 'Merton Reward'	see *P.* × *gondouinii* 'Merton Reward'
- 'Nabella' (F)	MAsh WJas
- 'Napoléon'	see *P. avium* 'Bigarreau Napoléon'
- 'Noble' (F)	SKee
- 'Noir de Guben' (F)	ECrN GTwe SKee
- 'Noir de Meched' (D)	SKee
- 'Old Black Heart' (F)	SKee
- 'Penny' PBR (F)	CAgr SKee
§ - 'Plena' (d) ♀H4	Widely available
§ - 'Preserving' (F)	CTho
- 'Regina' (F)	CSut SFam
- 'Ronald's Heart' (F)	SKee
- 'Roundel Heart' (F)	SKee
- 'Small Black' (F)	CTho
- 'Starkrimson' (F)	ECrN
- 'Stella' (F) ♀H4	Widely available
- 'Stella Compact' (F)	CWib ECrN LAst LSRN SDea WHar
- 'Summer Sun' (D) ♀H4	CAgr CSut CTho CTri ERea GBut GTwe LBuc LRHS MAsh MBri MCoo NLar SBfd SCoo SDea SFam SKee SLim SPoG WHar
- 'Summit' (F)	SKee
- 'Sunburst' (D)	CAgr CCVT CDul CEnd CMac CTho CTri CWib ECrN GTwe LBuc LRHS LSRN MBri SBfd SCoo SDea SFam SKee SLim SPoG SVic SWvt WBVN WClo WHar WJas
- 'Sweetheart' (F)	CAgr CDul GTwe LRHS LSRN MBri SKee SLim SPoG WHar
- 'Sylvia' (F)	CAgr SFam
- 'Turkish Black' (F)	SKee
- 'Van' (F)	CSBt ECrN GTwe SFam SKee
- 'Vega' (F)	CAgr ERea GTwe IFFs LBuc SKee WJas
- 'Waterloo' (F)	SKee
- 'White Heart' (F)	CWib ECrN SKee
- 'Zweitfrühe' (F)	GKir
'Beni-yutaka'	CEnd EBee GKir LRHS MBri SCoo SLim
besseyi	CAgr GAuc
'Blaze'	see *P. cerasifera* 'Nigra'
× ***blireana*** (d) ♀H4	CDul CEnd CTri ECrN EPfP LAst MBri MGos MMuc MRav MSwo MWat NLar NWea SBfd SCoo SEND SPer SPoG WCFE WFar WHar
- 'Saling Hall' (d)	ERea
'Blushing Bride'	see *P.* 'Shogetsu'
campanulata 'Felix Jury' **new**	EBee GKir SSpi
'Candy Floss'	see *P.* 'Matsumae-beni-murasaki'
cerasifera	CDul CRWN CTri ECrN EMac GKir IFFs LBuc MAsh NWea SEND SPer SVic WDin
- 'Cherry Plum' (F)	CTri ECrN MMuc SDea SKee
- 'Crimson Dwarf'	GKir MBri SCoo SWvt
- 'First' (F)	CAgr
- 'Golden Sphere' (F)	CAgr CTho GKir LRHS MBri SLim
- 'Gypsy' (F)	CAgr CTho GKir LRHS MBri SLim
- 'Hessei' (v)	CBow CEnd EBee MBri MGos MRav SBfd
- 'Kentish Red' (F)	SEND
§ - Myrobalan Group (F)	ECrN MRav SDea SVic
- - 'Magda Jensen' (C)	CAgr
§ - 'Nigra' ♀H4	Widely available
- 'Pendula'	CTho ECrN SWvt WFar
§ - 'Pissardii'	CWib ECrN EPfP GKir IFFs LAst LMaj LSRN MMuc NBea NWea SCoo SFam SLim SWvt WFar WJas WMou
* - 'Princess'	CWSG
- 'Spring Glow'	CCVT CEnd EBee EPfP LRHS MSwo SBfd SCoo SLim
cerasus 'Maynard'	LSRN
- 'Montmorency' (F)	SKee
- 'Morello' (C) ♀H4	Widely available
- 'Nabella' (F)	SKee
- 'Rhexii' (d)	CDul CLnd ECrN MBri MGos NEgg NPCo
'Cheal's Weeping'	see *P.* 'Kiku-shidare-zakura'
'Chocolate Ice'	see *P.* 'Matsumae-fuki'
§ × ***cistena*** ♀H4	CDul CSBt CWSG EBee ELan EPfP GKir IFFs LAst LRHS MBri MGan MGos MSwo SBfd SCoo SPlb SPoG SWvt WDin
- 'Crimson Dwarf'	see *P.* × *cistena*
'Collingwood Ingram'	EBee GKir LRHS MAsh MBri MGos SLim SPoG
conradinae	see *P. hirtipes*
'Daikoku'	EBee GKir MAsh
davidiana	SPlb
domestica 'Allgroves Superb' (D)	ERea
- 'Angelina Burdett' (D)	ERea GTwe SDea SKee
- 'Anna Späth' (C/D)	SKee
- 'Ariel' (C/D)	SDea SKee
- 'Autumn Compote' (C)	SKee
- 'Avalon' (D)	CAgr CCAT CCVT ECrN GTwe IFFs SDea SKee
- 'Beauty' (D)	CSut
- 'Belgian Purple' (C)	SKee
- 'Belle de Louvain' (C)	CDul CTho CTri ECrN GTwe SDea SKee WBVN
- 'Birchenhayes' (F)	CEnd
- 'Black Diamond'	see *P. salicina* 'Black Diamond'
- 'Blaisdon Red' (C)	CTho GTwe
- 'Blue Rock' (C/D) ♀H4	SKee
- 'Blue Tit' (C/D) ♀H4	CAgr CTho ERea GTwe SDea SKee
- 'Bonne de Bry' (D)	SKee
- 'Brandy Gage' (C/D)	SKee
- 'Bryanston Gage' (D)	CTho SKee
- 'Burbank's Giant'	see *P. domestica* 'Giant Prune'
- 'Burcombe' (F)	CEnd
- 'Cambridge Gage' (D) ♀H4	Widely available
- 'Chrislin' (F)	CAgr CTho
- 'Coe's Golden Drop' (D)	CCAT ECrN ERea GTwe IFFs LAst MBri MGos MRav SDea SFam SKee SPer
- 'Count Althann's Gage' (D)	ERea GTwe NEgg SDea SFam SKee
- 'Cox's Emperor' (C)	SKee
- 'Crimson Drop' (D)	ERea SKee
- 'Cropper'	see *P. domestica* 'Laxton's Cropper'
- 'Curlew' (C)	SDea SKee
- 'Czar' (C) ♀H4	Widely available
- 'Delikya' (D)	ERea
- 'Denbigh Plum' (D)	WGwG
- 'Denniston's Superb'	see *P. domestica* 'Imperial Gage'
- 'Diamond' (C)	SKee
- 'Dittisham Black' (C)	CAgr CTho
- 'Dittisham Ploughman' (C)	CTho SKee
- 'Dunster Plum' (F)	CAgr CTho CTri CWib

	– 'Early Favourite' (D/C)	ERea
	– 'Early Green Gage' (D)	NEgg
	– 'Early Laxton' (C/D) Y^{H4}	ECrN ERea GTwe LAst SDea SFam SKee
	– 'Early Prolific'	see *P. domestica* 'Rivers's Early Prolific'
	– 'Early Rivers'	see *P. domestica* 'Rivers's Early Prolific'
	– 'Early Transparent Gage' (C/D)	CCAT CMac CSBt CTho ECrN EMil ERea GTwe IFFs LBuc LRHS MBri MCoo SCoo SDea SFam SKee
	– 'Early Victoria' (C/D)	SDea
	– 'Edwards' (C/D) Y^{H4}	CTri CWib GTwe NEgg SDea SKee
	– 'Excalibur' (D)	CAgr GTwe IFFs LBuc SDea SKee
§	– German Prune Group (C)	MCoo SKee
§	– 'Giant Prune' (C)	CCAT ECrN GTwe SDea SKee
I	– 'Godshill Big Sloe' (F)	SDea
	– 'Godshill Blue' (C)	SDea
	– 'Godshill Minigage' (F)	SDea
	– 'Golden Transparent' (D)	CTho GTwe MCoo SFam SKee
	– 'Goldfinch' (D)	GTwe MCoo SKee
	– Green Gage Group	see *P. domestica* Reine-Claude Group
	– 'Grey Plum' (F)	CAgr CTho
	– 'Grove's Late Victoria' (C/D)	CCAT
	– 'Guinevere' (F)	LRHS MBri
	– 'Guthrie's Late Green' (D)	SKee
	– 'Hays' (C/D)	ERea
	– 'Herman' (C/D)	CAgr EMil GKir GTwe LAst LRHS MBri MCoo SDea
	– 'Heron' (F)	GTwe SKee
	– 'Impérial Epineuse' (D)	SKee
§	– 'Imperial Gage' (C/D) Y^{H4}	CAgr CCAT CSBt CTho CTri ECrN ERea GTwe LRHS MAsh MGos NLar SDea SFam SKee WHar
	– 'Italian Prune' (F)	MCoo
	– 'Jan James' (F)	CEnd
	– 'Jefferson' (D) Y^{H4}	CAgr ECrN GTwe NLar SDea SFam SKee SVic
*	– 'Jubilaeum' (D)	CAgr GTwe IFFs SCoo SKee
	– 'Kea' (C)	CAgr CTho SKee
	– 'Kirke's' (D)	CCAT CTho CTri GTwe SDea SFam SKee
	– 'Landkey Yellow' (F)	CAgr CTho
	– 'Langley Gage' (F)	CAgr SDea
	– 'Late Muscatelle' (D)	ERea SKee
	– 'Late Transparent Gage' (D)	SKee
§	– 'Laxton's Cropper' (C)	CTri GTwe MCoo SKee
	– 'Laxton's Delight' (D) Y^{H4}	GTwe
	– 'Laxton's Gage' (D)	SDea SKee
I	– 'Liegel's Apricot'	SKee
	– 'Mallard' (D) Y^{H4}	SKee
	– 'Manaccan' (C)	CAgr CTho
	– 'Marjorie's Seedling' (C) Y^{H4}	Widely available
	– 'McLaughlin' (D)	SKee
	– 'Merton Gage' (D)	SKee
	– 'Merton Gem' (C/D)	SKee
	– 'Monarch' (C)	SKee
	– Old English gage	LAst MAsh SBfd
	– 'Olympia' (C/D)	SKee
	– 'Ontario' (C/D)	SKee
	– 'Opal' (D) Y^{H4}	CAgr CCAT CCVT CDoC CDul CMac CWSG CWib ECrN ERea GBut GTwe IFFs LBuc LRHS MBri MGos MMuc MWat NLar NWea SCoo SCrf SDea SEND SFam SKee SLim SPoG WHar
	– 'Orleans' (C)	SKee

	– 'Oullins Gage' (C/D) Y^{H4}	Widely available
	– 'Pershore' (C) Y^{H4}	CAgr CDul CTho CWib GTwe LAst MAsh MBri NEgg SDea SFam SKee WHar WSpi
	– 'Pond's Seedling' (C)	CSBt SDea SKee
	– 'President' (C/D)	SDea SKee
	– 'Priory Plum' (D)	SDea
	– 'Purple Pershore' (C)	CAgr CCAT CTri CWib GTwe IFFs NEgg SDea SFam SKee WSpi
	– 'Quetsche d'Alsace'	see *P. domestica* German Prune Group
	– 'Reeves' (C) Y^{H4}	GTwe SFam SKee
	– 'Reine-Claude Dorée'	see *P. domestica* Reine-Claude Group
§	– Reine-Claude Group (C/D)	CSBt ECrN GKir GTwe MGos SDea SFam SKee SLim SPer
	– – 'Old Green Gage'	see *P. domestica* (Reine-Claude Group) 'Reine-Claude Vraie'
	– – 'Reine-Claude de Bavais' (D)	CCAT CTho CTri ERea GTwe SDea SFam SKee
	– – 'Reine-Claude de Vars' (D)	SVic
	– – 'Reine-Claude Violette' (D)	ECrN ERea SKee
§	– – 'Reine-Claude Vraie' (C/D)	CAgr CCAT CMac CSBt CWib ECrN EPfP ERea GKir LAst LRHS SPoG WJas
§	– – 'Willingham Gage' (C/D)	CMac ERea GTwe
§	– 'Rivers's Early Prolific' (C)	CAgr CCAT CSBt CTho CTri ECrN ERea GBut GTwe MCoo NWea SCoo SDea SFam SKee WHar
	– 'Royale de Vilvoorde' (D)	SKee
	– 'Sanctus Hubertus' (D) Y^{H4}	CTri ECrN EPfP GTwe SDea SKee
	– 'Severn Cross' (D)	GTwe SKee
	– 'Stanley' (C/D)	SVic
	– 'Stella'	CCVT CDul GKir LAst NEgg NPri SLim
	– 'Stella's Star' **new**	LBuc MCoo
	– 'Swan' (C)	ECrN GTwe SKee
	– 'Syston White'	MGos
	– 'Thames Cross' (D)	CSut SKee
	– 'Transparent Gage' (D)	ECrN SKee
	– 'Upright' (F)	CEnd
	– 'Utility' (D)	SKee
	– 'Verity' (D/C)	SKee
	– 'Victoria' (C/D) Y^{H4}	Widely available
	– 'Violetta'^{PBR} (C/D)	CAgr GTwe
	– 'Warwickshire Drooper' (C)	CAgr CTho CWib ERea GTwe MAsh NEgg NLar SDea SFam SKee
	– 'Washington' (D)	SDea SKee
	– 'White Magnum Bonum' (C)	SDea
	– 'Willingham'	see *P. domestica* (Reine-Claude Group) 'Willingham Gage'
§	***dulcis***	CDul CLnd CTri CWSG CWib CWit EBee EPfP EWTr LAst MGos MMuc MREP MWat NBea NWea SBfd SCoo SCrf SDea SEND SFam SVic SWvt WDin
	– 'Ai' (F)	CAgr
	– 'Ardechoise' (F)	CAgr
	– 'Ferraduel' (F)	CAgr
	– 'Ferragnes' (F)	CAgr
	– 'Lauranne' (F)	CAgr
	– 'Mandaline' (F)	CAgr
*	– 'Phoebe' (F)	CAgr
	– 'Supernova' (F)	CCCN
	– 'Tuono' (F)	CCCN
	Easter Bonnet = 'Comet'^{PBR}	CTri EPfP LRHS NPri
	Fragrant Cloud	see *P.* 'Shizuka'

	fruticosa 'Globosa'	NHol
	'Fugenzō'	CDoy CSBt GKir
	glandulosa 'Alba Plena' (d)	CEnd CMac CSBt EBee MAsh NBea SPlb SPoG SRms SWvt WCFE WDin WGrn
	- 'Rosea Plena'	see *P. glandulosa* 'Sinensis'
§	- 'Sinensis' (d)	CEnd CPLG CSBt EBee SPoG SRms WDin
§	× ***gondouinii*** 'May Duke' (F)	SKee SVic
§	- 'Merton Reward' (F)	ERea
	'Gyoikō'	CEnd EBee GKir
	'Hally Jolivette'	CEnd EBee ELan GKir MAsh NWea SPoG WDin
	'Hillieri'	MGos
	'Hillieri Spire'	see *P.* 'Spire'
	'Hilling's Weeping'	EBee
§	***hirtipes***	CEnd CLnd
	'Hokusai'	EPfP GKir
	Hollywood	see *P.* 'Trailblazer'
	'Horinji'	EBee GKir MBri SCoo
	'Ichiyo' (d) Ψ^{H4}	CDul EBee ECrN EPfP GKir LAst MBri SCoo SCrf SPer
	incisa	CTri NBea NEgg NWea SPer WSpi
	- 'Ariane'	LMaj
	- 'Beniomi'	MRav
	- 'February Pink'	CPMA MRav WDin
	- 'Fujima'	CSBt EBee LAst SBfd WSpi
	- 'Kojo-no-mai'	Widely available
	- 'Mikinori'	CEnd CMac CSBt GKir LRHS MAsh MBlu NLar SCoo WClo WFar WSpi
	- 'Oshidori' (d)	CSBt EPfP GKir LRHS MBri MGos MRav NEgg NLar SLim SPoG SRms
	- 'Paean'	NLar
	- 'Pendula'	GKir SCoo
	- 'Praecox' Ψ^{H4}	CHGN CSBt CTho CWSG EPfP GKir LRHS MWat SCoo
	- 'The Bride'	CEnd CWSG GKir LRHS MAsh MBri SCoo WClo
§	- f. ***yamadae***	CPMA LBMP MAsh MBri NLar WSpi
	insititia (F)	CRWN IFFs
	- 'Blue Violet Damson' (F)	SKee
§	- 'Bradley's King Damson' (C)	SKee
	- bullace (C)	NWea SDea
	- 'Countess' (C)	CTri
	- 'Dittisham Damson' (C)	CTho
	- 'Farleigh Damson' (C) Ψ^{H4}	CAgr CWib ECrN ERea GKir GTwe LAst LBuc LRHS MMuc NWea SDea SEND SFam SKee SPer SVic WJas
	- 'Godshill Damson' (C)	SDea
	- 'Golden Bullace'	see *P. insititia* 'White Bullace'
	- 'King of Damsons'	see *P. insititia* 'Bradley's King Damson'
	- 'Langley Bullace' (C)	CAgr CDul CTho ECrN ERea GTwe NLar SKee
	- 'Lisna' (C)	CTri
	- 'Merryweather Damson' (C)	Widely available
	- 'Mirabelle de Nancy' (C)	CAgr CTho CTri CWit ECrN ERea GTwe LAst LMaj SDea SFam SKee SLim
	- 'Mirabelle de Nancy' red (C)	SDea
§	- 'Prune Damson' (C) Ψ^{H4}	CAgr CDoC CTho CTri CWSG GBut GTwe LBuc LRHS MAsh MBri MMuc MWat NLar SDea SEND SFam SKee SPer WBVN WClo WHar WJas
	- 'Shepherd's Bullace' (C)	CAgr CTho ERea SKee
	- 'Shropshire Damson'	see *P. insititia* 'Prune Damson'
	- 'Small Bullace' (C)	CAgr SKee
§	- 'White Bullace' (C)	CAgr ERea
	- 'Yellow Apricot' (C)	ERea SKee
§	***jamasakura***	CDul
	'Jō-nioi'	CDul CEnd CTho MBri
§	'Kanzan' Ψ^{H4}	Widely available
§	'Kiku-shidare-zakura' Ψ^{H4}	Widely available
	Korean hill cherry	see *P. verecunda*
	'Kulilensis Ruby'	GKir LSRN SLPl
	'Kursar' Ψ^{H4}	CDul CLnd CSBt CTho CTri EBee EPfP GKir LSRN MBri NLar NWea SBfd SCoo SCrf SLim SPer SPoG SWvt WClo
	laurocerasus Ψ^{H4}	CBcs CCVT CChe CDul CMac CPMA CWSG EBee ECrN ELan EMac EPfP GKir IFFs LAst MGos MMuc MRav NBea NWea SEND SPer SPoG SReu WFar WMoo WMou
	- 'Angustifolia'	WDin
	- 'Aureovariegata'	see *P. laurocerasus* 'Taff's Golden Gleam'
	- 'Camelliifolia'	CMac CTri EPla EQua MBlu WCFE WCom
N	- 'Castlewellan' (v)	CAlb CBot CDoC CDul CTri EPfP EPla LAst LHop LRHS MGos MRav MSwo NHol NLar SBfd SDix SLim SPer SPoG SSta WCom WDin WFar WGrn WHar WMoo
	- 'Caucasica'	CEnd GKir LTen MGos NLar SBfd
	- 'Cherry Brandy'	GKir MRav SLPl WDin
	- Dart's Lowgreen	see *P. laurocerasus* Low 'n' Green
	- Etna = 'Anbri'[PBR]	CMac EBee EPfP IFFs LBuc LRHS LSou MAsh MBri MGos MWat SBfd SWvt WMou
	- 'Gajo'[PBR]	NLar SPer
	- 'Green Marble' (v)	CPMA CTri EBee EHoe
	- 'Herbergii'	IFFs MAsh NLar
§	- 'Latifolia'	CHEx EQua SLPl
§	- Low 'n' Green = 'Interlo'	MRav
	- 'Magnoliifolia'	see *P. laurocerasus* 'Latifolia'
	- 'Mano'	MGos NLar
	- 'Marbled White'	see *P. laurocerasus* 'Castlewellan'
	- 'Miky'	CPMA
	- 'Mischeana'	SLPl
	- 'Mount Vernon'	CTri LBuc MBlu MGos WDin
	- 'Novita'	EPfP
	- 'Otinii'	CHEx
	- 'Otto Luyken' Ψ^{H4}	CBcs CDul CMac CTri EBee EHoe ELan EPfP GKir LAst LBuc LHop LRHS LSRN LTen MAsh MCot MGos MRav MSwo MWhi NBir NEgg NHol NWea SPer SPlb WDin WFar
	- 'Prostrata'	NHol
	- 'Reynvaanii'	CPMA MBri
	- 'Rotundifolia'	Widely available
	- 'Schipkaensis'	SLPl
§	- 'Taff's Golden Gleam' (v)	CBow CPMA
	- 'Van Nes'	CPMA EBee IFFs MAsh NLar WDin
	- 'Variegata' misapplied	see *P. laurocerasus* 'Castlewellan'
	- 'Variegata' ambig. (v)	CWib SRms
	- 'Whitespot'	MMuc
	- 'Zabeliana'	CAlb CDul CMac CTri EBee EPfP GKir MGos MSwo NEgg NHol NWea SPer SRms WDin WFar
	litigiosa	CEnd EBee GKir MBri SCoo
	'Little Pink Perfection'	CDul MBri SCoo
	lusitanica Ψ^{H4}	Widely available
	- subsp. ***azorica***	CDoC CPLG EQua GKir LRHS MRav WFar WPGP
	- 'Myrtifolia'	CBar CTri EBee ECrN EPfP EQua GKir LRHS MBri MRav SWvt WCFE WDin WMoo
	- 'Variegata' (v)	Widely available

maackii	EPfP MMuc SEND SSpi WDin
– 'Amber Beauty'	CBcs CDoC CDul EBee ECrN EPfP GBin GKir LMaj LSRN MRav SBfd WDin WFar
mahaleb	IFFs
'Mahogany Lustre'	see *P. serrula* 'Mahogany Lustre'
mandshurica	EGFP ERea GKir
maritima	GAuc
§ 'Matsumae-beni-murasaki'	EBee GKir NLar SCoo
'Matsumae-beni-tamanishiki'	EBee GKir LRHS
§ 'Matsumae-fuki'	EBee GKir LRHS LSRN MBri NPal NWea SLim SPoG
§ 'Matsumae-hanagasa'	CEnd EBee GKir LRHS MBri NLar WClo
maximowiczii B&SWJ 10967	WCru
'Mount Fuji'	see *P.* 'Shirotae'
mume	CMCN CMen WDin
– 'Beni-chidori'	CEnd CMac CWib EBee EPfP IVic LRHS MBlu MBri MGos NBea NLar SCoo SLim SPoG WCot WJas
§ – 'Omoi-no-mama' (d)	CEnd CMen
– 'Omoi-no-wac'	see *P. mume* 'Omoi-no-mama'
myrobalana	see *P. cerasifera* Myrobalan Group
nipponica	CBcs CSBt GKir LRHS MAsh MBri
var. ***kurilensis*** 'Brilliant'	MGos NLar SBfd SCrf SPoG
– – 'Ruby'	CBcs CEnd GKir LSRN MBri MGos NEgg SPoG WFar
'Okamé' ♀H4	Widely available
'Okame Harlequin' (v)	EBee SLim SPoG
'Okumiyako' misapplied	see *P.* 'Shogetsu'
padus	CCVT CDul CLnd CMac CRWN CSBt CTri ECrN EMac GKir IFFs LAst LBuc MGos MMuc MSwo NBea NWea SEND WDin WMou
– 'Albertii'	CCVT EBee GKir MMuc SCoo
– 'Colorata' ♀H4	CBcs CDoC CDul CEnd CMac CSam CTho EBee ECrN ELan GKir LHop LMaj MGos NLar SCoo SPer SWvt WCot WDin WFar WPat
– 'Grandiflora'	see *P. padus* 'Watereri'
– 'Purple Queen'	CEnd ECrN EQua
§ – 'Watereri' ♀H4	CCVT CDoC CDul CEnd CLnd CMCN CMac CTho CWib EBee ECrN ELan EPfP EWTr GKir LAst LHop LMaj NWea SCoo SLim SPer SPoG WDin WMou
'Pandora' ♀H4	CDul CLnd EBee ECrN EPfP GKir LAst MBri MGos MMuc MRav MSwo NBea NPCo NWea SBfd SCoo SCrf SEND SPer SPoG WFar
pendula	SCrf
– var. ***ascendens*** 'Rosea'	EBee
§ – 'Pendula Rosea' ♀H4	CDoC CDul CEnd CTri CWib EPfP GKir MAsh SCrf SPer WFar WJas
§ – 'Pendula Rubra' ♀H4	CCVT CDoC CDul CLnd CSBt CWib EBee EPfP GKir LAst LHop LRHS MAsh MBri MGos MSwo SBfd SCoo SLim SPer SPoG WFar WPat
§ – 'Stellata'	LRHS MAsh MBri
pensylvanica	LMaj
persica 'Amsden June' (F)	CWib EBtc ERea GTwe MCoo NLar SDea SFam SKee WBVN
– 'Avalon Pride' (F)	CSut ERea LBuc MCoo
– 'Barrington' (F)	ERea
– 'Bellegarde' (F)	ERea GTwe SDea SFam
– 'Bonanza' (F)	ERea LSRN
– 'Cardinal' (F/d)	ERea
– 'Darling' (F)	SVic
– 'Dixi Red' (F)	CAgr ERea
– 'Doctor Hogg' (F)	ERea SDea
– 'Duke of York' (F) ♀H3	CTri ERea GTwe SDea SFam SKee
– 'Dymond' (F)	ERea
– 'Early Alexander' (F)	ERea
– 'Flat China' (F)	ERea
– 'Foliis Rubris' (F)	CDul LRHS
– 'Francis' (F)	SKee
– 'Garden Lady' (F)	ERea GTwe SLim SPoG
– 'Hale's Early' (F)	ERea GTwe MRav MWat SEND SFam SKee SLim SPer
– 'Hylands' (F)	ERea SDea
– 'Johnny Brack' (F)	ERea
– 'Kestrel' (F)	ERea
– 'Madison' (F)	ERea
– 'Melred' (F)	MGos
– 'Natalia' (F)	SDea
– var. ***nectarina*** Crimson Gold (F)	SDea
– – 'Early Blaze' (F)	ERea
– – 'Early Gem' (F)	ERea SDea
– – 'Early Rivers' (F) ♀H3	ERea GTwe LSRN SDea
– – 'Elruge' (F)	ERea GTwe SDea
– – 'Fantasia' (F)	ERea SDea
– – 'Fire Gold' (F)	ERea SDea
– – 'Flavortop' (F)	ERea
– – 'Garden Beauty' (F/d)	MGos SPoG
– – 'Humboldt' (F)	ERea GTwe SDea SKee
– – 'John Rivers' (F)	GTwe SDea SFam
– – 'Lord Napier' (F) ♀H3	CAgr CDoC CSBt CTri CWSG CWib EPfP ERea GKir LAst LBuc LRHS MAsh MGos MMuc MWat SDea SEND SFam SKee SLim SPer SPoG SVic WHar
– – 'Nectared' (F)	CWib ERea
– – 'Nectarella' (F)	ERea LSRN SLim
– – 'Pineapple' (F)	CAgr CTri ERea GTwe SDea SFam SKee
– – 'Red Gold' (F)	ERea
– – 'Ruby Gold' (F)	ERea SDea
– – 'Terrace Ruby' (F)	MGos SPoG
– – 'Violette Hâtive' (F)	ERea
– 'Peregrine' (F) ♀H3	CAgr CSBt CTri CWSG CWib EPfP ERea GKir GTwe IFFs LAst LBuc LRHS LSRN MAsh MBri MGos MMuc MWat SDea SEND SFam SKee SLim SPer SPoG WJas
– 'Pink Peachy' (F)	NLar
– 'Purpurea'	EBee
– 'Red Haven' (F)	CAgr CWib ERea GTwe SDea SKee SVic
– 'Redwing' (F)	CAgr ERea
– 'Reliance' (F)	SDea
– 'Robin Redbreast' (F)	SDea
– 'Rochester' (F) ♀H3	CAgr CSBt CWSG CWib ERea GTwe LAst LRHS LSRN MAsh MBri MMuc SDea SEND SFam SKee SLim SPer SPoG
– 'Royal George' (F)	GTwe SFam SPer
– 'Saturne' (F)	ERea SKee
– 'Springtime' (F)	ERea SDea
– 'Terrace Amber' (F)	MGos SPoG
– 'Terrace Diamond' (F)	MGos SPoG
– 'Terrace Garnet' (F)	MGos
– 'White Peachy' (F)	NLar
× ***persicoides*** 'Angélique' (F)	GKir
– 'Ingrid' (F)	CAgr EBtc LBuc LRHS MBri MCoo SCoo
– 'Pollardii' (F)	MMuc NWea SEND WJas
– 'Robijn' (F)	CAgr LBuc MCoo SVic
– 'Spring Glow' (F)	CDoC MBri MMuc MWea NWea SEND WJas

	'Pink Parasol'	see *P.* 'Matsumae-hanagasa'
	'Pink Perfection' Υ^{H4}	CBcs CDul CLnd CSBt CWSG CWib EBee ECrN EPfP GKir LAst LRHS MBri MGos MWat NLar SBfd SCrf SPer WDin WFar WHar WJas
	'Pink Shell' Υ^{H4}	CLnd EBee EPfP GKir MBri SFam SPur
	pissardii	see *P. cerasifera* 'Pissardii'
	'Pissardii Nigra'	see *P. cerasifera* 'Nigra'
	prostrata	GAuc
*	- var. ***discolor***	NLar
	pumila var. ***depressa***	EMil MRav NLar
	'Rebecca'	MAsh SPoG
	'Royal Burgundy' (d)	CCVT CDul CEnd CLnd CMac CWSG CWit EBee ECrN EMil EPfP GKir LAst LRHS LSRN MAsh MBri MDun MGos MWat SBfd SCoo SLim SPer SPoG SPur WFar WHar
	rufa	CDul CPMA CTho EBee EBtc SKHP SSpi
	salicina	ERea
	- 'Beauty'	ERea
§	- 'Black Diamond' (F)	SDea
	- 'Methley' (D)	ERea SPoG WHar
	- 'Satsuma' (F)	ERea
	- 'Shiro' (D)	ERea
	sargentii Υ^{H4}	Widely available
	- 'Charles Sargent'	GKir
	- 'Columnaris'	GKir MBri
	- 'Rancho'	SCoo SLim WFar
	× ***schmittii***	ECrN MAsh MMuc SCoo SPer WJas
	'Sekiyama'	see *P.* 'Kanzan'
	serotina	CDul IFFs NLar
§	***serrula*** Υ^{H4}	Widely available
	- Branklyn form	MGos
	- Dorothy Clive form	EBee GKir LSRN
§	- 'Mahogany Lustre'	WFar WPat
	- var. ***tibetica***	see *P. serrula*
	serrula × ***serrulata***	CBcs CTho
	serrulata (d)	MGos
	- 'Erecta'	see *P.* 'Amanogawa'
	- 'Grandiflora'	see *P.* 'Ukon'
	- 'Longipes'	see *P.* 'Shōgetsu'
	- 'Miyako' misapplied	see *P.* 'Shōgetsu'
N	- var. ***pubescens***	see *P. verecunda*
	- 'Rosea'	see *P.* 'Kiku-shidare-zakura'
	- var. ***spontanea***	see *P. jamasakura*
	'Shidare-zakura'	see *P.* 'Kiku-shidare-zakura'
	'Shimizu-zakura'	see *P.* 'Shōgetsu'
	'Shirofugen' Υ^{H4}	CBcs CDoC CDul CLnd CMCN CMac CSBt CTho CWSG CWib CWit EBee ECrN EPfP GKir LBuc LRHS LSRN MBri MMuc MRav MWat SBfd SCrf SEND SPer WDin WFar WHar WJas
§	'Shirotae' Υ^{H4}	Widely available
§	'Shizuka'	CWSG CWib EBee GKir LRHS MBri NLar SCoo SLim SPer SPoG WClo
§	'Shōgetsu' Υ^{H4}	CBcs CDul CEnd CLnd CSBt CTho CWSG EBee ELan EPfP GKir LAst LMaj MBri MMuc MRav NEgg NLar SBfd SCrf SEND SFam SLim SPer SPoG WClo WDin
	'Shosar'	CEnd CWib ECrN GKir LAst NLar SCoo SPer
	× ***sieboldii*** 'Caespitosa'	GKir SCoo
	'Snow Goose'	CDoC EBee GKir LAst LMaj LRHS NEgg SCoo WFar
	'Snow Showers'	CEnd CMac CWSG CWit EBee GKir LRHS MAsh MBri MMuc MWat NWea SBfd SEND SPer SPoG WClo
	spinosa	CCVT CDoC CDul CMac CRWN CTri ECrN EMac EPfP GKir LBuc LSRN MAsh MBlu NLar NWea SBfd SPer SPoG SVic WDin WFar WMou WSFF
	- 'Plena' (d)	CEnd CTho MBlu
	- 'Purpurea'	CDul CTho MBlu MBri NHol NLar WDin WFar WMou
§	'Spire' Υ^{H4}	CCVT CDoC CDul CLnd CMac CSBt CTho CWib EBee ECrN ELon EPfP GKir LAst LBuc LRHS MBlu MGos MMuc MSwo NWea SBfd SCoo SEND SPer WDin WFar WJas
	× ***subhirtella***	LAst
	- var. ***ascendens***	see *P. pendula* var. *ascendens*
	- 'Autumnalis' Υ^{H4}	Widely available
	- 'Autumnalis Rosea' Υ^{H4}	Widely available
	- 'Fukubana'	CLnd CMac EBee ECrN EPfP GKir NLar
	- 'Pendula' misapplied	see *P. pendula* 'Pendula Rosea'
	- 'Pendula Plena Rosea' (d)	CMac LAst
	- 'Pendula Rosea'	see *P. pendula* 'Pendula Rosea'
	- 'Pendula Rubra'	see *P. pendula* 'Pendula Rubra'
N	- 'Rosea'	CLnd MRav
	- 'Stellata'	see *P. pendula* 'Stellata'
	'Sunset Boulevard'	EBee GKir
	'Taihaku' Υ^{H4}	Widely available
	'Taki-nioi'	ECrN
	tenella	CAgr ELan SEND WCot
	- 'Fire Hill'	CPMA CSBt CWib ECho ELan EPfP LRHS LSRN MGos MRav SBfd SPer SSpi WCFE WCot WDin WJas WSpi
	tibetica	see *P. serrula*
	tomentosa	CAgr LLHF MAsh
§	'Trailblazer' (C/D)	CEnd CLnd CSBt ECrN IVic LAst MSwo SPer
	triloba	CBcs CWib ECrN EGxp LAst MBlu NWea SBfd WDin
	- 'Multiplex' (d)	ECho IFFs MGos SPoG SRms WJas
§	'Ukon' Υ^{H4}	Widely available
	'Umineko'	CCVT CDoC CLnd CWib ECrN GKir GQue MGos SCoo SLPl SPer WDin WHar
§	***verecunda***	CLnd NWea WJas
	virginiana 'Schubert'	CDul CLnd EBee ECrN EWTr SCoo WFar WJas WMou WPat
	'White Cloud'	CDul
	yamadae	see *P. incisa* f. *yamadae*
	× ***yedoensis***	CDul EBee LMaj MAsh MBri MRav SPer
	- 'Ivensii'	CBcs CDul CSBt CWib EBee GKir LMaj MMuc NEgg NWea SCoo SEND SPer WDin
	- 'Moerheimii'	GKir
	- 'Pendula'	see *P.* × *yedoensis* 'Shidare-yoshino'
	- 'Perpendens'	see *P.* × *yedoensis* 'Shidare-yoshino'
§	- 'Shidare-yoshino'	CCVT CDul CEnd CLnd CSBt EBee ECrN GKir LRHS MAsh MBri MGos MRav MSwo MWat NWea SBfd SLim SPoG
§	- 'Somei-yoshino' Υ^{H4}	CCVT CLnd CTho CTri ECrN EPfP GKir LAst MBri NWea SLim SPer WDin WHar WJas
	'Yoshino'	see *P.* × *yedoensis* 'Somei-Yoshino'
	'Yoshino Pendula'	see *P.* × *yedoensis* 'Shidare-yoshino'

Psacalium (*Asteraceae*)

	pinetorum B&SWJ 10269	WCru

Pseuderanthemum (*Acanthaceae*)

	carruthersii var. ***atropurpureum*** 'Rubrum'	LSou

	laxiflorum	CCCN
	reticulatum	CCCN
	orange-flowered	

Pseudocydonia (*Rosaceae*)

§	***sinensis***	CAgr CBcs CMen NLar

Pseudofumaria see *Corydalis*

	alba	see *Corydalis ochroleuca*
	lutea	see *Corydalis lutea*

Pseudogynoxys (*Asteraceae*)

§	***chenopodioides***	CCCN CSpe ELan SOWG

Pseudolarix (*Pinaceae*)

§	***amabilis*** ♀H4	CBcs CDoC CMCN CTho ECrN EHul EPfP GBin GKir GQue IFFs LRHS MBlu MBri MMuc MPkF NHol NPCo NWea SBfd SCoo SEND SKHP SLim SMad SPoG SSpi STre WFar WPGP
	kaempferi	see *P. amabilis*

Pseudomuscari see *Muscari*

	azureum	see *Muscari azureum*

Pseudopanax (*Araliaceae*)

	(Adiantifolius Group) 'Adiantifolius'	CBcs CDoC CHEx CTrC ESwi GQui
	- 'Cyril Watson' ♀H1	CBcs CDoC CHEx EBee ELan EUJe LRHS LTen SBig
	arboreus	see *Neopanax arboreus*
	chathamicus	CDoC CHEx SAPC SArc
	crassifolius	CAbb CBcs CBot CBrP CCCN CDTJ CHEx CTrC CWit EAmu EBee ESwi EUJe GBin IDee LRHS SAPC SArc SBig
	- var. ***trifoliolatus***	CHEx
	discolor	CBcs CWit ECou IDee LEdu
	ferox	CAbb CBcs CBrP CDTJ CTsd CWit EAmu ESwi EUJe GBin IDee SAPC SArc SBig SMad
	'Forest Gem'	CTrC
	laetus	see *Neopanax laetus*
	lessonii	CBcs CHEx ECou ELan
	- 'Gold Splash' (v) ♀H1	CBcs CDoC CDul CHEx CTrC EBee ELan EUJe IVic LRHS MMuc SBig SEND
	- 'Goldfinger' **new**	CBcs
	- 'Nigra'	CTrC
	- 'Rangitira'	CBcs CDoC CTrC CWit EUJe GBin LRHS SBig
	'Linearifolius'	CHEx CTrC LEdu
	'Purpureus' ♀H1	CDoC CHEx CTrC ESwi IDee MMuc SEND
	'Sabre'	CBcs CDoC CHEx CTrC EBee
	'Trident'	CDoC CHEx CTrC ECou LEdu SBig

Pseudophoenix (*Arecaceae*)

*	***nativo***	MBri
	sargentii **new**	EAmu

Pseudosasa (*Poaceae*)

	amabilis misapplied	see *Arundinaria gigantea*
§	***amabilis*** (McClure) Keng f.	CEnt EPla WFar
§	***japonica*** ♀H4	Widely available
§	- 'Akebonosuji' (v)	CEnt CGHE EPla MMoz MWht NMoo WJun WPGP
I	- var. ***pleioblastoides***	EPla MWht WPGP
	- 'Tsutsumiana'	CHEx EBee ELon EPla MMoz MWht NLar NMoo SBig WJun
	- 'Variegata'	see *P. japonica* 'Akebonosuji'
	orthotropa	see *Sinobambusa orthotropa*
	usawai	EPla WJun
	viridula	MWht NMoo

Pseudotsuga (*Pinaceae*)

§	***menziesii*** ♀H4	CBcs CDul CLnd ECrN EMac EPfP GKir IFFs MBlu MMuc NWea SEND WDin WFar
	- 'Bhiela Lhota'	CKen NLar
	- 'Blue Wonder'	CKen
	- 'Densa'	CKen
	- 'Fastigiata'	CKen
	- 'Fletcheri'	CKen SLim
	- 'Geijsteren'	NLar
	- var. ***glauca***	CDul GKir
	- 'Glauca Pendula'	CKen MGos
I	- 'Gotelli's Pendula'	CKen
	- 'Graceful Grace'	CKen
	- 'Idaho Gem'	CKen
	- 'Julie'	CKen
	- 'Knaphill'	GKir NLar
	- 'Little Jamie'	CKen
	- 'Little Jon'	NHol
	- 'Lohbrunner'	CKen
	- 'McKenzie'	CKen
	- 'Nana'	CKen
	- 'Oudemansii'	GKir NLar
	- Pendula Group	NPCo
	- 'Stairii'	CKen
	- 'Uwes Golden'	NLar
	- 'Young's Broom'	NHol
	taxifolia	see *P. menziesii*

Pseudowintera (*Winteraceae*)

§	***colorata***	CBcs CDoC CMac CPLG CPla CWib EBee GAbr GCal GGar GKir IDee LRHS MPkF MRav NLar SPoG WCru WFar
	- 'Marjorie Congreve'	IDee
	- 'Moulin Rouge' **new**	CBcs
	- 'Mount Congreve'	CBcs IArd MBri NLar
	- 'Red Glow' **new**	CBcs
	- 'Red Leopard'	LBuc LRHS

Psidium (*Myrtaceae*)

	cattleyanum	see *P. littorale* var. *longipes*
	guajava (F)	CCCN ERea XBlo
	littorale (F)	ERea MWya
§	- var. ***longipes*** (F)	CCCN ERea XBlo

Psilotum (*Psilotaceae*)

	nudum	ECou

Psoralea (*Papilionaceae*)

	glabra	SPlb
	glandulosa	CArn CMdw SPlb WSHC
*	***macrothyrsa*** **new**	EBee
	oligophylla	SPlb
	pinnata	CHEx CPLG CTrC IRar

Psychotria (*Rubiaceae*)

	capensis	CPLG EShb

Ptelea (*Rutaceae*)

	trifoliata	CArn CBcs CDul CLnd CMac CWib EBee EMil EPfP IFFs MBlu MBri SPer SRms SSpi WDin WPGP
	- 'Aurea' ♀H4	CAbP CBcs CBot CDul CEnd CLnd CMac CPLG CPMA EBee ELan EMil EPfP EWTr GBin GKir LHop LRHS MAsh MBlu MBri NLar SPer SPoG SSpi WDin WPat

- 'Fastigiata'	EPfP

Pteracanthus see *Strobilanthes*

Pteridophyllum (*Papaveraceae*)

racemosum	EBee EFEx GEdr WCru WWst

Pteris (*Pteridaceae*)

from Yunnan	CLAP
§ ***actiniopteroides***	WCot
angustipinna B&SWJ 6738	WCru
cretica 🏆H1+3	CHEx EShb SAPC SArc
- var. ***albolineata*** 🏆H1	EShb GQui SRms XBlo
- 'Ouvradii' **new**	ISha
- 'Parkeri'	EShb
- 'Rowei'	XBlo
dentata	WRic
ensiformis 'Victoriae'	EShb
gallinopes	CLAP
* ***hendersonii*** **new**	GLin
henryi	see *P. actiniopteroides*
multifida **new**	WRic
nipponica	WRic
quadriaurita	WRic
* ***staminea***	XBlo
tremula	CHEx EFtx GQui SRms WRic
tricolor **new**	WRic
umbrosa	WRic
wallichiana	CGHE CHEx CLAP WPGP

Pterocarya (*Juglandaceae*)

fraxinifolia 🏆H4	CBcs CCVT CDul CLnd CMCN ECrN EGFP EPfP GQui LMaj MBlu MBri MMuc WDin
- IDS 02	WHCr
macroptera var. ***insignis*** **new**	WPGP
× ***rehderiana***	CTho MBlu WMou
stenoptera	CBcs CDTJ CDul CMCN CTho EGFP NLar
- 'Fern Leaf'	EPfP MBlu WMou WPGP

Pterocephalus (*Dipsacaceae*)

depressus	CPBP WAbe WPat
parnassi	see *P. perennis*
§ ***perennis***	CMea ECho MHer NBir NMen NRya NWCA SRms WAbe WEas WHoo
- subsp. ***perennis***	WHrl
pinardii	NWCA WAbe

Pterodiscus (*Pedaliaceae*)

aurantiacus **new**	LToo
ngamicus	LToo

Pterostylis (*Orchidaceae*)

coccina	ECho
curta	CStu ECho LLHF SCnR
× ***toveyana***	ECho

Pterostyrax (*Styracaceae*)

corymbosa	CPMA IArd IDee MBlu MBri NLar SSpi WFar
hispida 🏆H4	CAbP CBcs CDoC CDul CEnd CHGN CMCN CMac CPMA CWib EBee EPfP EPla GBin GKir IArd IDee LRHS MBlu MBri MGos MRav NLar SPoG SSpi SSta WDin WFar WPGP

Ptilostemon (*Asteraceae*)

afer	CMdw EHrv SMrm
§ ***diacantha***	EBee ELan IFoB NBre NPri WCot WSpi
echinocephalus	GKir MDKP NBre

Ptilotrichum see *Alyssum*

Ptilotus (*Amaranthaceae*)

exaltatus	SPlb

Puccinellia (*Poaceae*)

distans	EBWF

Pueraria (*Papilionaceae*)

montana var. ***lobata***	CArn

Pulicaria (*Asteraceae*)

§ ***dysenterica***	CArn EBWF MHer NMir SIde WSFF

Pulmonaria (*Boraginaceae*)

affinis 'Margaret'	NCob
angustifolia 🏆H4	CMac EBee EPfP GKev GKir GMaP MNrw SRms WTin
* - ***alba***	IFoB
- 'Azurea'	CElw CTca EBee ELan EPPr EPfP GMaP LRHS MMuc MRav NBro NLar SBfd SEND SMrm SPer SRms WFar WMnd
- 'Blaues Meer'	CSam EBee EPfP GAbr GKir LAst LLWG WCru
- 'Munstead Blue'	CElw CLAP CMac ECha EHrv MRav MTho NCob NRya SRms
'Apple Frost'	EBee GEdr LRHS NLar NSti WWEG
'Baby Blue' **new**	SHeu
'Barfield Regalia'	CMHG EBee IGor LLHF NSti SDys WCru
'Benediction'	CDes LLHF MAvo MNrw NSti
'Beth's Pink'	ECha GAbr WFar
'Blauer Hügel'	CElw LLHF NSti
'Blauhimmel'	CElw GCra
'Blue Buttons'	CBow CFir ECtt EPla
'Blue Crown'	CElw CLAP CSev EBee EHrv EWes
'Blue Ensign'	Widely available
'Blue Moon'	see *P. officinalis* 'Blue Mist'
'Blueberry Muffin'	CSpe
'Bonnie'	CMea
'Botanic Hybrid'	WCru
Cally hybrid	CElw CLAP GCal NBre NSti SMrm
'Cedric Morris'	CElw
'Chintz'	CLAP CSam SMrm
'Cleeton Red'	NSti
'Coral Springs'	EBee GKir LLHF LRHS MAvo NLar NSti
'Corsage'	ECtt
'Cotton Cool'	CElw CGHE CLAP CMac CPrp CTca EAEE EBee ECha ECtt EHoe EShb GGar LBMP LRHS MAvo MBNS MCot MSpe MWhi NCGa NEgg NSti SBfd SPer SUsu WCAu WFar WMoo
'Crawshay Chance'	CElw SMHy
'De Vroomen's Pride' (v)	EBee WMnd
'Diana Clare'	Widely available
'Elworthy Rubies'	CElw EPPr
'Excalibur'	ECtt EHrv LRHS NLar
'Fiona'	MAvo WWEG
'Glacier'	CElw CMoH CTca EBee EPfP MNrw NSti WWEG
'Hazel Kaye's Red'	LLWP NSti
'Highdown'	see *P.* 'Lewis Palmer'
'Ice Ballet' (Classic Series)	EBee GEdr
'Joan's Red'	CElw WTin

§	'Lewis Palmer' ♀^{H4}	CElw CMHG CSam CTca EBee ECtt ELan GCal GKir GMaP LRHS MNrw NBir NDov NHol SPoG SRGP SRms WBrk WCAu WCFE WCot WCru WHoo WTin WWEG
	'Little Blue'	NSti
	'Little Star'	EBee MAvo NBre NSti SMHy SRGP SUsu WCru WFar
	longifolia	CArn CBot CFee CHar CPrp EAEE EBee ECha EHoe ELan EPfP GAbr GKev LRHS NBir NLar NSti WBrk WEas WFar
§	- 'Ankum'	CElw CLAP CSam EPfP GKir MRav NBir NSti WSHC WWEG
	- 'Ballyrogan Blue'	IBlr
	- 'Bertram Anderson'	CTca EBee ECtt ELon GKir GMaP LRHS NBir NLar NVic SBfd SPer SRGP SRms SWvt WBrk WCAu WFar WMnd WWEG
	- subsp. ***cevennensis***	CLAP EBee EPfP GKir LRHS MAsh MBri MLLN NLar NSti WPtf WWEG
	- 'Coen Jansen'	see *P. longifolia* 'Ankum'
	- 'Coral Spring'	GKir NBre
	- 'Dordogne'	CLAP GKir LRHS MAsh NBir NLar
	- 'Howard Eggins'	EBee
	'Majesté'	Widely available
	'Margery Fish' ♀^{H4}	CHar CLAP CSam EBee EPfP GKir LRHS MBNS MLLN SPer WMnd
	'Mary Mottram'	CElw ECtt ELan NBir NSti WCot WMnd
	'Matese Blue'	CLAP
	'Mawson's Blue'	CElw CLAP ECha EWes GKir GMac MRav MSpe MWat MWea NBir NChi SWvt WBrk WEas WMoo WRHF WSHC
	'May Bouquet'^{PBR}	LLHF NSti
	'Melancholia'	IBlr
	'Merlin'	CLAP SKHP
§	'Milchstrasse'	CLAP
	Milky Way	see *P.* 'Milchstrasse'
	mollis	CBot CLAP CSWP EBee ECGP GCal MNrw NSti WCru
	- 'Royal Blue'	MRav
	- 'Samobor'	CLAP
	'Moonshine'^{PBR}	NSti
	'Moonstone'	CElw CLAP
	'Mountain Magic'^{PBR}	ECtt NSti SIde
	'Mournful Purple'	EHrv ELon
	'Mrs Kittle'	CElw CFir CMMP EBee IFoB LRHS MLLN MRav NBir NSti SDys WBrk WCAu WFar WMnd WWEG
	'Netta Statham'	EBee LLHF NSti
	'Northern Lights'^{PBR}	SHar
	'Nürnberg'	WWEG
	officinalis	CArn CHby IFoB MLHP MNHC NChi NVic SIde WBrk WFar
	- 'Alba'	ELan WBrk
§	- 'Blue Mist'	CElw CLAP EBee ECha ELan GMaP MLLN NBir WBrk WCot WHoo WMnd WMoo WTin
	- 'Bowles's Blue'	see *P. officinalis* 'Blue Mist'
	- Cambridge Blue Group	EBee GMaP LRHS MRav MWat NBir WCot WPtf
*	- 'Frühlingslied'	EBee
	- 'Stillingfleet Gran'	LLHF NSti
	- 'White Wings'	CElw CLAP EBee GKir LRHS MAsh MRav SIde WFar
	- 'Wuppertal'	EBee
	'Oliver Wyatt's White'	CLAP EBee SRGP
	Opal = 'Ocupol'	Widely available
	'Pink Haze'^{PBR}	EBee ECtt GBBs LLWG LPla NSti SBfd SHeu WCot WFut
	'Polar Splash'	EBee GBin GKir SIde WFar
	'Raspberry Splash'^{PBR}	CAby CBct CLAP EBee EGxp LRHS NLar NSti SHeu SIde SMrm SPoG
	'Roy Davidson'	CLAP CSam CTca EBee ECGP ECtt EHrv GKir GMac LHop LRHS NBir NCGa NDov NSti SMHy SRGP SRms SWvt WFar WPtf
	rubra ♀^{H4}	CBcs CElw CPom CSWP ECha ELan EShb GAbr GKir LBMP LLWP MLHP MMuc MNrw MWte NBid NCob NSti SEND SRms WCAu WFar WTin
	- var. ***alba***	see *P. rubra* var. *albocorollata*
§	- var. ***albocorollata***	CBre EBee EBtc ECha EHrv GAbr MLLN NBid SHar WBrk WFar WWEG
	- 'Ann'	CLAP NMoo WFar
	- 'Barfield Pink'	ELan GCal GKir IFro MLLN NBir WCru
	- 'Bowles's Red'	CBot EBee ECtt EHrv EPfP GKir IFoB LAst LRHS MNrw MRav NBir NCGa NGdn NPnk NSti SHeu SIde SPer STes WFar WMnd
	- 'David Ward' (v)	Widely available
	- 'Rachel Vernie' (v)	CLAP CPou MAvo WBrk
	- 'Redstart'	Widely available
§	***saccharata***	ECha EHrv ELan GMaP IFro MMuc NEgg NPnk SIde SRms WFar
	- 'Alba'	CElw ECha MMuc SRms
	- Argentea Group ♀^{H4}	CSev CTri EBee ELan EPfP GMaP LRHS MLLN MRav MTho NGdn SEND WBrk WCot WWEG
	- 'Clent Skysilver'	EBee
	- 'Dora Bielefeld'	Widely available
	- 'Frühlingshimmel'	CElw EBee ECtt ELon GKir LRHS MAsh MNrw MRav NDov WFar
	- 'Glebe Cottage Blue'	CElw ECGP
	- 'Jill Richardson'	ELan
	- 'Leopard'	CElw CEnt CLAP CMac CSam CTca CWCL EBee ECtt GMaP LLWG LRHS MLLN MNrw NBir NBre NLar SApp SBfd SRGP WBrk WClo WCot WFar WHoo WWEG
	- 'Mrs Moon'	CTri CWib EBee ECtt ELon EPfP GMaP LAst LLWG LRHS LTen MBNS MHer NBPC NLar NPri SBfd SPer SRGP SWvt WCAu WMnd WWEG
	- 'Old Rectory Silver'	CLAP NBir
	- 'Picta'	see *P. saccharata*
	- 'Pink Dawn'	CMHG WMnd
	- pink-flowered	WCru
	- 'Reginald Kaye'	CElw EBee ECha EWes MNrw
	- 'Silverado'^{PBR}	EBee ECtt GEdr GKir LRHS MAsh
	- 'Stanhoe'	EWes
	'Saint Ann's'	CElw LLHF NBre NSti WCru
	'Samurai'	EBee GBin GEdr NSti SMHy WPtf
	'Silver Lance'	GKir LRHS
	'Silver Sabre'	IBlr
	'Silver Surprise'	WCot
	'Sissinghurst White' ♀^{H4}	Widely available
	'Smoky Blue'	CLAP EBee ECtt EPfP MBNS MRav NBPC NMoo SMrm SWat WFar WMnd WWEG
	'Spilled Milk'	EBee NBre NLar
	'Stillingfleet Meg'	CLAP EAEE EBee ECtt LAst LRHS MAvo MBNS MCot MLLN MNrw NCob NHol NSti SRGP WFar
	'Tim's Silver'	EBee ECtt
	'Trevi Fountain'	CAby CBct CLAP EBee EShb GJos GKev GKir LRHS NBre NSti SHar SHeu SIde SMrm SPoG WCot WPtf
	'Vera May' ♀^{H4}	EBee

'Victorian Brooch'PBR	CBct CLAP EBee GAbr GKev GKir GQue LSou MNrw NEgg NLar NSti SHeu SIde WFar WPtf WSpi WWEG
'Weetwood Blue'	CBre CLAP CTca EBee EPfP MNrw
'Wendy Perry'	CElw
'Wisley White'	CElw

Pulsatilla (*Ranunculaceae*)

alba	NWCA
albana	ECho LHop LLHF LRHS
- 'Lutea'	EBee GKev LLHF
alpina	CBot ECho SRms WPat
§ - subsp. ***apiifolia*** 𝕐H4	EBee ELan GMac IFro
- subsp. ***sulphurea***	see *P. alpina* subsp. *apiifolia*
ambigua	EBee GKev LLHF
bungeana	EBee GCrs GKev
cernua	LHop LRHS
× ***gayeri***	ECho NBir
georgica	GEdr
halleri 𝕐H4	EBee ECho GKev LRHS
- subsp. ***slavica*** 𝕐H4	GCrs GEdr LLHF NWCA
lutea	see *P. alpina* subsp. *apiifolia*
montana	LLHF NMen SPlb
multifida	GCrs
§ ***patens***	EDAr LLHF
pratensis	CDes GPoy SRms
- subsp. ***nigricans***	GCrs LHop LRHS WFar
I - 'Semiplena' new	MMoz
rubra	ECho GKev MLLN NGHP SPad SRot WGwG
sibirica new	LAst
turczaninovii	LLHF
§ ***vernalis*** 𝕐H2	ECho EPot GCrs NWCA WAbe
§ ***vulgaris*** 𝕐H4	Widely available
- 'Alba' 𝕐H4	Widely available
- 'Barton's Pink'	ECho EWes GKir LHop LLHF LRHS SRot
- 'Blaue Glocke'	GEdr MCot MWat NLar NPri SHar SMrm SWvt WFar WHil
- 'Eva Constance'	EBee ECho GKev LHop LLHF LRHS WAbe
- 'Gotlandica'	LLHF
- subsp. ***grandis***	CBot LRHS NMen
- - 'Budapest Seedling'	WCom
- - 'Papageno'	CBot CSpe EAEE EBee ECho ELon GMaP LAst LBMP LRHS NCGa NHol NLar SMrm SRot WFar WHil
- Heiler hybrids	CPrp EAEE EBee LRHS MRav NCGa NEgg NGdn WHal
- Red Clock	see *P. vulgaris* 'Röde Klokke'
§ - 'Röde Klokke'	EBee ECtt GEdr GKev MCot MWat NBPC NHol NLar NPri NWCA SHar SMrm SWvt WHil WSpi
- ***rosea***	GAbr
- Rote Glocke	see *P. vulgaris* 'Röde Klokke'
- var. ***rubra***	Widely available
§ - 'Weisse Schwan'	ECho GKir GMaP NHol NMen SRot
- 'White Bells' new	GEdr
- White Swan	see *P. vulgaris* 'Weisse Schwan'
zimmermannii	NWCA

Pultenaea (*Papilionaceae*)

juniperina new	SPlb

pummelo see *Citrus maxima*

Punica (*Lythraceae*)

granatum	CBcs CHEx CMen CTsd EAmu EPfP ERom EUJe LRHS MGos MREP MWya SDnm SLim SOWG STre SVic WBVN WSHC
- 'André le Roi' (F)	SLPl
- 'Chico'	SEND
- 'Fina Tendral'	CCCN ERea
- 'Legrelleae' (F/d)	SEND SLPl
- var. ***nana*** 𝕐H3	CAgr CArn CCCN CMen CStu EBee EBtc ELau EPfP EShb LRHS MREP SMrm SRms WPat
- f. ***plena*** (d)	CBcs LRHS MRav WCFE WPat
- - 'Rubrum Flore Pleno' (d) 𝕐H3	SEND
* - 'Striata'	SOWG

Purshia (*Rosaceae*)

aff. ***mexicana***	WSHC

Puschkinia (*Hyacinthaceae*)

scilloides	ECho NBir
- 'Aragat's Gem'	ECho WWst
§ - var. ***libanotica***	EBrs ECho EPfP EPot GKev LAma LEdu LRHS MAvo SDeJ SMrm SPer WRHF WShi
- - 'Alba'	ECho EPot LAma SPer WCot

Puya (*Bromeliaceae*)

alpestris	CBrP CCCN CTrC EAmu EBee EShb ETod EUJe SAPC SArc SBig WCot WPGP
berteroana	CBcs CCCN CDTJ CHEx EBee EShb ETod EUJe MAvo SPlb
chilensis	CAbb CBcs CCCN CDTJ CDoC CHEx CHGN EAmu EBee EUJe SAPC SPlb
coerulea	CCCN CDTJ CFir EAmu EBee ELon EUJe EWld SPlb
laxa	SChr
mirabilis	CDTJ CTrC ESwi
- RCB/Arg L-3	WCot
spathacea new	EBee
- RCB/Arg S-2	WCot
venusta	CCCN CDTJ EBee ETod MAvo SPlb

Pycnanthemum (*Lamiaceae*)

muticum	EBee
pilosum	CArn EBee ELau MHer NBre NLar NPri SIde SWal
tenuifolium	NBre NLar
virginianum	EBee GCal

Pycnostachys (*Lamiaceae*)

reticulata	EOHP EShb
urticifolia	ECre EOHP EWes

Pygmea see *Chionohebe*

Pyracantha (*Rosaceae*)

Alexander Pendula = 'Renolex'	LHop MRav MSwo SRms WFar
angustifolia	NMun WCFE
§ ***atalantioides***	SPlb WCFE
'Brilliant'	EBee EPfP SCoo
'Buttercup'	EPla
§ ***coccinea*** 'Lalandei'	CMac
- 'Red Column'	Widely available
- 'Red Cushion'	CBar MRav SRms
crenulata	WCFE
Dart's Red = 'Interrada'	CSBt EBee GKir SBfd SLim SPoG WHar
'Fiery Cascade'	LRHS SPoG SRms
gibbsii	see *P. atalantioides*
'Gold Rush'	MAsh
'Golden Charmer' 𝕐H4	EBee ECtt EPfP GKir LRHS MAsh MGan MGos MMuc MSwo NEgg

	NLar NPri NWea SBfd SCoo SEND SLPl SPer SPoG SRms SWvt WDin WFar WGwG WRHF
'Golden Glow'	SLim
'Golden Sun'	see *P.* 'Soleil d'Or'
'Harlequin' (v)	WFar
'Knap Hill Lemon'	MBlu
koidzumii 'Victory'	EBee MGos WClo WRHF
'Mohave'	CChe CMac CTri EBee ECrN ELan ELon GKir LRHS MAsh MGan MNHC MWat NPri SCoo SLim SRms SWvt WDin
'Mohave Silver' (v)	CWSG ELan LAst LBMP LOck LRHS MAsh SBfd
'Molten Lava'	MBri
'Monrovia'	see *P. coccinea* 'Lalandei'
'Mozart'	EBee
'Navaho'	EPfP GKir
'Orange Charmer'	CBar CMac CTri EBee ELan GKir LHop LRHS MGan MGos MWat NLar SPer SPlb WFar
'Orange Glow' 𝕐H4	Widely available
* 'Red Pillar'	GKir
'Renault d'Or'	LRHS SLPl
rogersiana 𝕐H4	CDul ECrN EPfP MRav WFar
- 'Flava' 𝕐H4	CDul CSBt EBee EPfP LRHS MAsh NEgg SBfd SPoG SWvt
'Rosedale'	EBee LRHS WHar
Saphyr Jaune = 'Cadaune'PBR	CAlb CBar CBcs CCVT CDoC CEnd CMac CSBt CWSG EBee ECrN EMil EPfP GKir LRHS LTen MGos MRav SCoo SPer
Saphyr Orange = 'Cadange'PBR 𝕐H4	CAlb CBar CBcs CCVT CDoC CEnd CMac CSBt CWSG CWit EBee EMil EPfP GKir LRHS LTen MBri MGos MRav NEgg SCoo SPer WClo
Saphyr Panache = 'Cadvar'PBR (v)	CWit
Saphyr Rouge = 'Cadrou'PBR 𝕐H4	CAlb CBar CBcs CCVT CDoC CEnd CMac CSBt CWSG EBee ECrN ELan EMil EPfP GKir LTen MBri MGos MMuc MRav NPri SCoo SEND SPer SWvt WClo WFar
'Shawnee'	CMac CSBt CWib EBee MSwo MWat
§ 'Soleil d'Or'	Widely available
'Sparkler' (v)	EGxp EHoe MGos SLim WFar
'Teton' 𝕐H4	CMac CWSG EBee ELan EPfP EPla GKir LAst LRHS MAsh MSwo MWat NEgg SEND SPoG SRms WDin WFar
'Ventoux Red'	SCoo
'Watereri'	NWea SLPl WFar WSpi
'Yellow Sun'	see *P.* 'Soleil d'Or'

Pyrenaria (*Theaceae*)

spectabilis	see *Tutcheria spectabilis*

Pyrethropsis see *Rhodanthemum*

hosmariense	see *Rhodanthemum hosmariense*

Pyrethrum see *Tanacetum*

Pyrola (*Ericaceae*)

minor	NMen
rotundifolia	WHer

Pyrostegia (*Bignoniaceae*)

venusta	CCCN SOWG

Pyrrosia (*Polypodiaceae*)

lingua	WRic
polydactyla	WRic

Pyrus ✿ (*Rosaceae*)

amygdaliformis var. ***cuneifolia***	CLnd EBee SCoo
betulifolia	CMCN
calleryana 'Bradford'	CLnd
- 'Capital'	LMaj
- 'Chanticleer' 𝕐H4	Widely available
- 'Chanticleer' variegated (v)	CLnd
- 'Redspire'	MWya
communis (F)	CCVT CDul CTri EMac IFFs LBuc NWea SPer SPlb WMou
- 'Abbé Fétel' (D)	SKee
- 'Baronne de Mello' (D)	CTho SFam
- 'Beech Hill' (F)	CDul CLnd EBee ECrN EPfP SPer
- 'Belle Guérandaise' (D)	SKee
- 'Belle Julie' (D)	SKee
- 'Berllanderi Green' (Perry)	WDol
- 'Berllanderi Red' (Perry)	WDol
- 'Beth' (D) 𝕐H4	CAgr CCAT CDoC CMac CSBt CTri CWib ECrN EPfP ERea GKir GTwe LAst LBuc LRHS MAsh MBri MGos NLar NPri SDea SFam SKee SLim SPer WHar
- 'Beurré Alexandre Lucas' (D)	SKee
- 'Beurré Bedford' (D)	SKee
- 'Beurré d'Amanlis' (D)	SKee
- 'Beurré d'Avalon' (D)	SKee
- 'Beurré de Beugny' (D)	SKee
- 'Beurré Diel' (D)	SKee
- 'Beurré Dumont' (D)	CAgr SFam
- 'Beurré Giffard' (D)	CAgr
- 'Beurré Hardy' (D) 𝕐H4	CAgr CCAT CCVT CDoC CDul CMac CSBt CTho CTri CWib ECrN ERea GKir GTwe IFFs LAst MBri MCoo MGan MMuc MWat NEgg NLar SBfd SDea SEND SFam SKee SPer
- 'Beurré Jean van Geert' (D)	GKir
- 'Beurré Mortillet' (D)	SKee
§ - 'Beurré Precoce Morettini' (D)	SDea
- 'Beurré Six' (D)	SKee
- 'Beurré Superfin' (D) 𝕐H4	ECrN GTwe MCoo SFam SKee
- 'Bianchettone' (D)	SKee
- 'Bishop's Thumb' (D)	SDea
- 'Black Worcester' (C)	GTwe SDea SFam SKee WJas
- 'Blakeney Red' (Perry)	SDea
- 'Blickling' (D)	SKee
- 'Brandy' (Perry)	CAgr SDea SKee
- 'Bristol Cross' (D)	CAgr GTwe SKee
- 'Calebasse Bosc' (D)	SKee
- 'Cannock' (F)	CCAT
- 'Catillac' (C) 𝕐H4	CAgr CCAT CTho GTwe SFam SKee
- 'Chapman's Orange' (Perry)	WDol
- 'Charneaux' (F)	SVic
- 'Chaumontel' (D)	SKee
- 'Clapp's Favourite' (D)	CTho ECrN SKee SVic
- 'Concorde'PBR (D) 𝕐H4	Widely available
- 'Conference' (D) 𝕐H4	Widely available
- 'Deacon's Pear' (D)	SDea
- Delbardélice = 'Delété'	LRHS
- 'Devoe' (D)	SDea
- 'Docteur Jules Guyot' (D)	CAgr ECrN SDea
- 'Doyenné d'Eté' (D)	ERea MCoo SFam SKee
- 'Doyenné du Comice' (D) 𝕐H4	Widely available

	- 'Duchesse d'Angoulême' (D)	SKee
	- 'Durondeau' (D)	ERea GTwe SDea SFam SKee
	- 'Early Saint Brides' (Perry)	WDol
	- 'Easter Beurré' (D)	SKee
	- 'Emile d'Heyst' (D)	GBut GTwe MCoo
	- 'Fertility' (D)	CLnd ERea SKee
	- 'Fertility Improved'	see *P. communis* 'Improved Fertility'
	- 'Fondante d'Automne' (D)	CAgr CTho SKee
	- 'Forelle' (D)	ERea SKee
	- 'Glou Morceau' (D)	CAgr ECrN ERea GTwe MCoo MWat SDea SFam SKee
	- 'Glow Red Williams' (D)	SFam
	- 'Gorham' (D) 🏆^{H4}	CAgr CTho ECrN GBut GTwe MCoo SFam SKee
	- 'Green Pear of Yair' (D)	SKee
	- 'Gregoire Bordillon' (D)	SKee
	- 'Gwehelog' (Perry)	WDol
	- 'Gwehelog Red' (Perry)	WDol
	- 'Hacon's Imcomparable' (D)	SKee
	- 'Harrow Delight' (D)	SDea
	- 'Harvest Queen' (D/C)	CAgr SDea
	- 'Hellen's Early' (Perry)	SKee
	- 'Hendre Huffcap' (Perry)	CCAT
	- 'Hessle' (D)	CAgr GTwe MCoo NWea SDea SFam SKee
§	- 'Improved Fertility' (D)	CAgr CDoC GTwe SDea
	- Invincible = 'Delwinor' (D/C)	CAgr CDul CSut CTho LBuc LRHS MBri MCoo SLim
	- 'Jargonelle' (D)	CAgr CTho ECrN GBut GTwe SDea SFam SKee
	- 'Jeanne d'Arc' (D)	SVic
	- 'Joséphine de Malines' (D) 🏆^{H4}	CAgr GTwe SDea SFam SKee
	- 'Kieffer' (C)	CAgr
	- 'Laxton's Foremost' (D)	CAgr SKee
	- 'Laxton's Satisfaction' (D)	SFam
	- 'Légipont' (F)	CAgr
	- 'Little Cross Huffcap'	WDol
	- 'Louise Bonne of Jersey' (D) 🏆^{H4}	CAgr CDoC CMac CTri ECrN GBut GTwe IFFs LAst MGos SDea SFam SKee
	- 'Maréchal de Cour' (D)	SKee
	- 'Marguérite Marillat' (D)	SDea
	- 'Merton Pride' (D)	CAgr CTho CTri GTwe MCoo MWat SDea SFam SKee
	- 'Monmouthshire Burgundy' (Perry)	WDol
	- 'Moonglow'	CAgr ERea GBut SDea
	- 'Moorcroft' (Perry)	SKee
	- 'Morettini'	see *P. communis* 'Beurré Precoce Morettini'
	- 'Nouveau Poiteau' (C/D)	CAgr ECrN GTwe SKee
	- 'Nye Russet Bartlett' (F)	CAgr
	- 'Onward' (D) 🏆^{H4}	CAgr CCAT CDul CLnd CTho CTri CWib ECrN GTwe MBri NEgg NLar NWea SDea SFam SKee WHar
	- 'Ovid' (D)	CAgr
§	- 'Packham's Triumph' (D)	CAgr CDoC CTri CWib ECrN GTwe LAst SDea SVic
	- 'Passe Crassane' (D)	SKee
	- 'Pear Apple' (D)	SDea
	- 'Pero Nobile'	SKee
	- 'Pitmaston Duchess' (C/D) 🏆^{H4}	ECrN GTwe MCoo SDea SFam SKee
	- 'Potato Pear' (Perry)	WDol
	- 'Red Comice' (D/C)	GTwe SKee
	- 'Red Sensation Bartlett' (D/C)	GTwe LBuc LRHS SKee
	- 'Redbald' (D)	SKee
	- 'Robin' (C/D)	ERea SDea SKee
	- 'Santa Claus' (D)	SDea SFam SKee
	- 'Seckel' (D)	SFam SKee
	- 'Sierra' (D)	CAgr
	- 'Snowdon Queen' (D)	WGwG
	- 'Souvenir du Congrès' (D)	CAgr
	- 'Terrace Pearl'	MGos SPoG
	- 'Thompson's' (D)	SFam SKee
	- 'Thorn' (Perry)	CAgr
	- 'Triomphe de Vienne' (D)	SFam
	- 'Triumph'	see *P. communis* 'Packham's Triumph'
	- 'Uvedale's St Germain' (C)	SFam SKee
	- 'Verbelu'	SKee
	- 'Vicar of Winkfield' (C/D)	GTwe SDea SKee
	- 'Welsh Gin' (Perry)	WDol
	- 'Williams' Bon Chrétien' (D/C) 🏆^{H4}	Widely available
	- 'Williams Red' (D/C)	GTwe
	- 'Winter Nelis' (D)	CAgr CTri CWib ECrN GKir GTwe LRHS SDea SFam SKee
	cordata	CDul
	elaeagnifolia	CDul CEnd GKir SLim
	var. ***kotschyana***	
	- 'Silver Sails'	CLnd EBee EMil GKir LAst LRHS MBlu MBri MGos NLar SCoo SPur SSpi
	nivalis	CDul CLnd CTho EBee ECrN EPfP LMaj MBri MRav SCoo SPer SPur
	- 'Catalia'	EBee MBri NPal SCoo
	pyraster	CDul
	pyrifolia	GAuc
	- '20th Century'	see *P. pyrifolia* 'Nijisseiki'
	- 'Chojuro' (F)	ERea MAsh
	- 'Hosui' (F)	SVic
	- 'Kosui' (F)	ERea SVic
	- 'Kumoi' (F)	LRHS MAsh SDea
§	- 'Nijisseiki' (F)	ERea SVic
	- 'Shinko' (F)	ERea
	- 'Shinseiki' (F)	CAgr CLnd ERea SDea SKee
	- 'Shinsui' (F)	SDea SKee
*	***salicifolia*** var. ***orientalis***	CTho
	- 'Pendula' 🏆^{H4}	Widely available
	ussuriensis	GAuc

Q

Qiongzhuea see *Chimonobambusa*

Quercus ✿ (*Fagaceae*)

	NJM 05.013A	WPGP
	acerifolia	EPfP
	acherdophylla new	SBir
§	***acuta***	CBcs
	acutifolia	SBir
	acutifolia × ***mexicana***	SBir
	acutissima	CBcs CDul CLnd CMCN EPfP SBir
	aegilops	see *Q. ithaburensis* subsp. *macrolepis*
	affinis	EPfP SBir
	agrifolia	CDul CMCN EBtc EGFP SBir
	ajudaghiensis	see *Q. hartwissiana*
	alba	CDul CMCN SBir WDin
	aliena	CMCN SBir
	alnifolia	CDul SBir
	arkansana	SBir
	× ***atlantica*** new	SBir
	austrina	SBir

	× ***beadlei***	see *Q.* × *saulii*
	× ***benderi*** new	SBir
	berberidifolia	CMCN SBir
	bicolor	CDul CMCN EPfP SBir WDin
	× ***bimundorum*** new	SBir
§	- 'Crimschmidt'	EPfP MBlu MBri
	borealis	see *Q. rubra*
	breweri	see *Q. garryana* var. *breweri*
	buckleyi	CMCN MBri SBir
	× ***bushii***	CMCN EPfP MBlu MBri SBir
	canariensis ♀H4	CBcs CLnd CMCN CTho EPfP GKir WPGP
	canbyi	CMCN
	castaneifolia	CDul CMCN IFFs WDin
	- 'Green Spire' ♀H4	CMCN EPfP GKir IArd MBlu SBir SEND SMad
	cerris	CBcs CCVT CDoC CDul CLnd CMCN EBee ECrN EMac EPfP EWTr GKir IFFs LAst LMaj MGos MMuc NWea SEND SPer STre WDin WFar
	- 'Afyon Lace'	MBlu MBri
§	- 'Argenteovariegata' (v)	CBcs CDul CEnd CMCN CPMA CTho EBee ELan EPfP GKir IArd MAsh MBlu MBri SBir SMad SPoG WPat
*	- 'Marmorata'	SBir
	- 'Variegata'	see *Q. cerris* 'Argenteovariegata'
	- 'Wodan'	EPfP GKir MBlu
	chenii	CMCN EGFP SBir
	chrysolepis	CMCN EPfP
	coccifera	CDul CGHE CMCN EPla SSpi WDin WPGP
	coccinea	CBcs CDul CMCN CTho CTri EBee ECrN EPfP EWTr GKir IFFs MBlu MMuc MWht NBea NEgg NWea SBir SLim SPer SPoG WDin WPat
	- 'Splendens' ♀H4	CDoC CDul CEnd CHll CMCN CPMA CTri EBee ELan EPfP EWTr LRHS MBlu MBri SMad SPer WDin WPat
	crassipes	SBir
	Crimson Spire	see *Q.* × *bimundorum* 'Crimschmidt'
	crispipilis new	SBir
	dalechampii	SBir
	× ***deamii***	SBir
	dentata	CMCN EPfP
	- 'Carl Ferris Miller'	CBcs CMCN EPfP GKir LLHF MBlu MBri SBir WPat
	- 'Pinnatifida'	CMCN EPfP GKir IDee MBlu MPkF SMad WPat
	- 'Sir Harold Hillier'	MBlu MBri
	- subsp. ***yunnanensis***	SBir
	dolicholepis new	SBir
	'Doring's Zweizack' new	SBir
	douglasii	CMCN SSpi
	- G 261	WPGP
	dumosa	CMCN
	- G 315	WPGP
	- G 316	WPGP
	elliottii	SBir
	ellipsoidalis	CMCN SBir
	- 'Hemelrijk'	CDul EPfP IArd MBlu MBri
	emoryi	CMCN
	engelmannii	CMCN
	fabrei	CMCN SBir
	faginea	EGFP
	falcata	CDul CMCN EBtc SBir
	- var. ***pagodifolia***	see *Q. pagoda*
	× ***fernaldii***	CMCN MBlu
	frainetto	CCVT CDoC CDul CLnd CMCN CTho EBee ECrN EPfP GKir IFFs LMaj NWea SEND SPer WDin WMou
	- 'Hungarian Crown' ♀H4	CMCN EPfP GKir MBlu MBri MMuc SBir
	- 'Tortworth'	MBri SMad WMou
	- 'Trump'	CLnd CMCN
	gambelii	CMCN EGFP
	garryana	CMCN
§	- var. ***breweri***	EGFP
	- var. ***fruticosa***	see *Q. garryana* var. *breweri*
	georgiana	CMCN EGFP EPfP SBir
	gilva	SBir
	glandulifera	see *Q. serrata* Thunb.
§	***glauca***	CDul CMCN EPfP SAPC SArc SBir WPGP
	graciliformis new	SBir
	gravesii	CMCN EPfP SBir
	grisea	CMCN
§	***hartwissiana***	SBir
	× ***hastingsii***	CMCN SBir
	× ***hawkinsiae***	SBir
	× ***haynaldiana***	SBir
	hemisphaerica	CDul CMCN EPfP SBir
	× ***heterophylla***	CMCN EPfP SBir
	× ***hickelii***	CMCN EPfP SBir
	hinckleyi	WDin
§	× ***hispanica***	CLnd GKir
	- 'Ambrozyana'	CDul CMCN WDin
	- 'Bloemendaal'	MBlu
	- 'Diversifolia'	CMCN EPfP IArd MBlu
	- 'Fulhamensis'	CMCN IArd MBlu SBir WMou
§	- 'Lucombeana' ♀H4	CBcs CDul CHGN CMCN CSBt CTho EPfP IArd IDee MBlu SBir SPer
§	- 'Pseudoturneri'	CBcs CDul EBee EPfP EWTr GKir IArd MBlu
	- 'Waasland'	MBri SBir
	- 'Wageningen'	CMCN EPfP MBri SBir
	hypoleucoides	EPfP
	ilex ♀H4	Widely available
	ilicifolia	CMCN EPfP SBir
	imbricaria	CDul CMCN EPfP SBir
	incana Roxb.	see *Q. leucotrichophora*
	× ***introgressa***	SBir
	ithaburensis	EPfP
§	- subsp. ***macrolepis***	CMCN LEdu SBir
	- - 'Hemelrijk Silver'	MBlu SBir
	× ***jackiana***	EPfP
	john-tuckeri G 271 new	WPGP
	kelloggii	CBcs CMCN SBir WPGP
	× ***kewensis***	CMCN LMaj SBir
	laceyi	SBir
	laevigata	see *Q. acuta*
	laevis	CMCN EPfP SBir
	'Langtry'	SBir
§	***laurifolia***	CDul CMCN EGFP EPfP SBir
	laurina	SBir
§	***leucotrichophora***	CMCN GKir SBir WCFE
	liaotungensis	see *Q. wutaishanica*
	× ***libanerris***	SBir
	- 'Rotterdam'	CMCN SBir
	libani	CMCN EPfP WDin
	lobata	CMCN EGFP LEdu
	× ***lucombeana***	see *Q.* × *hispanica*
	- 'William Lucombe'	see *Q.* × *hispanica* 'Lucombeana'
	× ***ludoviciana***	CMCN EPfP GKir SBir
	lyrata	CMCN
	macranthera	CLnd CMCN EPfP MBri SBir
	macrocarpa	CDul CMCN EPfP SMad
	- var. ***macrocarpa***	SBir
	macrolepis	see *Q. ithaburensis* subsp. *macrolepis*

	marilandica	CBcs CDul CEnd CMCN EPfP GKir IArd IFFs MBlu SBir
	'Mauri'	MBri
	mexicana	CMCN SBir
§	***michauxii***	CMCN EPfP MBlu SBir
	mongolica	GKir MBlu SBir
	- subsp. ***crispula*** var. ***grosseserrata***	CMCN
	muhlenbergii	CDul CMCN MBlu SBir
	× ***mutabilis***	SBir
	myrsinifolia	see *Q. glauca*
	myrtifolia	EPfP SBir
	nigra	CMCN NLar SBir
	- 'Beethoven'	MBlu MBri SBir
I	- 'Nyewoodii' **new**	SBir
	nuttallii	see *Q. texana*
	obtusa	see *Q. laurifolia*
	oglethorpensis	SBir
	pacifica G 301 **new**	WPGP
	- G 305	WPGP
	- G 313	WPGP
§	***pagoda***	CMCN SBir
	palustris ♀H4	CCVT CDoC CDul CLnd CMCN CSam CTho EBee ECrN EMac EPfP EWTr GKir IArd IFFs LMaj MAsh MBlu MMuc NEgg NLar NWea SBir SPer WDin
*	- 'Compacta'	EPfP
	- 'Green Dwarf'	CMCN MBlu
	- 'Pendula'	CEnd CMCN
	- 'Silhouette' **new**	SBir
	- 'Swamp Pygmy'	CMCN EPfP MBlu
	- 'Windischleuba'	MBlu
	parvula var. ***parvula*** **new**	SBir
	- var. ***shrevei*** **new**	SBir
§	× ***pauciloba***	CMCN EGFP
	pedunculata	see *Q. robur*
	pedunculiflora	see *Q. robur* subsp. *pedunculiflora*
§	***petraea*** ♀H4	CDoC CDul CLnd ECrN EMac EPfP GAbr GKir IFFs MBlu NLar NWea SPer WDin WFar WMou
	- 'Acutiloba'	SBir
§	- 'Insecata'	CDul CEnd CMCN EPfP MBlu
	- 'Laciniata'	see *Q. petraea* 'Insecata'
§	- 'Purpurea'	CMCN GKir MBlu
	- 'Rubicunda'	see *Q. petraea* 'Purpurea'
§	***phellos***	CDul CLnd CMCN EBtc ECrN EPfP MBlu MBri SBir SLPl WDin
	phillyreoides	CBcs CDul CMCN EPfP SBir SLPl
	polymorpha	CMCN
	'Pondaim'	CMCN GKir SBir
	pontica	CMCN EPfP GKir LLHF MBlu WPat
	prinoides	CMCN
	prinus misapplied	see *Q. michauxii*
§	***prinus*** L.	CMCN EPfP
	pubescens	CMCN EMac SBir
	pumila Michx.	see *Q. prinus* L.
	pumila Walt.	see *Q. phellos*
	pyrenaica	CDul CMCN CTho EBtc MBri
	- 'Pendula'	CMCN EPfP WDin
	'Red Queen' **new**	MBlu
	Regal Prince	see *Q.* × *warei* 'Long'
	rhysophylla	CDul CMCN EPfP GKir MBlu SBir WPGP
	- 'Maya'	ELan EWTr IArd IDee MBri MGos MPkF SBir
	× ***riparia***	SBir
§	***robur*** ♀H4	Widely available
	- 'Argenteomarginata' (v)	CDul CMCN MBlu WPat
	- 'Atropurpurea'	IArd MGos MPkF NWea WDin
*	- 'Compacta'	MBlu

	- 'Concordia'	CBcs CDul CEnd CLnd CMCN EBee EBtc ELan EPfP GKir LRHS MAsh MBlu MPkF NLar NWea SMad WDin
*	- ***dissecta***	CMCN
	- 'Facrist'	SBir
	- f. ***fastigiata***	CDoC CDul CLnd CTho EBee ECrN EPfP GKir IVic MGos NWea SBir SLPl SLim SPer SPoG WDin WFar
	- - 'Koster' ♀H4	CDul CMCN CMac CTri EPfP LMaj MBlu NWea SPoG
	- 'Fennesseyi'	IArd
	- 'Filicifolia' misapplied	see *Q. robur* 'Pectinata'
	- 'Filicifolia'	see *Q.* × *rosacea* 'Filicifolia'
	- var. ***haas***	CDul
	- - 'Cankiri' **new**	SBir
	- 'Irtha'	EPfP
	- 'Menhir'	LLHF MBlu WPat
§	- 'Pectinata'	EPfP GKir MBlu WDin
§	- subsp. ***pedunculiflora***	CMCN SBir
	- 'Pendula'	CEnd CMCN MBlu MGos
	- 'Purpurascens'	CEnd CMCN
	- 'Purpurea'	MBlu
	- 'Raba'	CMCN
	- 'Rita's Gold'	MBlu SMad
§	- 'Salfast'	MBlu
	- 'Salicifolia Fastigiata'	see *Q. robur* 'Salfast'
	- Sherwood oak clone	SMad
	- 'Strypemonde'	CMCN
	- 'Timuki' **new**	MBlu
	- f. ***variegata*** (v)	CPMA MGos
	- - 'Fürst Schwarzenburg' (v)	MBlu
I	- 'Zeelandia'	SBir
	robur × ***macrocarpa*** × ***virginiana***	SBir
§	× ***rosacea*** 'Filicifolia'	CEnd GKir WPat
	rotundifolia	CAgr EPfP
§	***rubra*** ♀H4	Widely available
	- 'Aurea'	CDul CEnd CMCN CPMA EBee EPfP MBlu
	- 'Boltes Gold'	CPMA MBlu
	- 'Cyrille'	SBir
	- 'Magic Fire'	EPfP MBlu NLar SBir
*	- 'Sunshine'	CMCN MBlu WPat
	rugosa	CMCN SBir
	× ***runcinata***	SBir
	sadleriana	GKir
	salicina	WPGP
	sartorii	SBir
§	× ***saulii***	CMCN SBir
	× ***schochiana***	EPfP
	× ***schuettei***	SBir
§	***serrata*** Thunb.	CMCN EGFP MBri SBir
	sessiliflora	see *Q. petraea*
	shumardii	CDul CMCN EPfP MBlu MBri NLar SBir
	sinuata subsp. ***breviloba***	SBir
	stellata	CMCN EPfP SBir
	suber	CAgr CBcs CCVT CDoC CDul CLnd CMCN CTho EBee ELan EPfP EPla IArd IFFs LEdu LMaj MGos MMuc MREP MWya SAPC SArc SEND WDin WPGP
	- 'Sopron'	EPfP MBlu
§	***texana***	CMCN EPfP SBir
	- 'New Madrid'	MBlu MBri
	trojana	CMCN SBir
	turbinella	CMCN
	× ***turneri***	CDoC CLnd CMCN CTho EPfP MBri WDin WMou WSpi
	- 'Pseudoturneri'	see *Q.* × *hispanica* 'Pseudoturneri'
	undulata Torr.	see *Q.* × *pauciloba*

variabilis	CDul CMCN EPfP
velutina	CDul CLnd CMCN CPMA CTho EPfP NLar SBir
- 'Albertsii'	MBlu
- 'Rubrifolia'	CMCN EPfP
'Vilmoriana'	GKir
virginiana	CDul CMCN SBir
× ***warburgii***	EPfP
× ***warei***	SBir
§ - 'Long'	IArd MBlu
- 'Windcandle'	MBlu SBir SMad
wislizeni	CDul CMCN SBir
- G 265	WPGP
§ ***wutaishanica***	CDul CMCN

Quillaja (*Rosaceae*)

saponaria	CArn CCCN EBee

quince see *Cydonia oblonga*

Quisqualis (*Combretaceae*)

indica	CCCN SOWG

R

Racosperma see *Acacia*

Ramonda (*Gesneriaceae*)

§ ***myconi*** ♀H4	CLAP CPBP ECho EPot EWes GEdr LLHF LSou NLar NMen NSla SChF SRms WAbe
- var. ***alba***	CLAP ECho MTho WThu
- 'Jim's Shadow'	WAbe
- 'Rosea'	CLAP ECho
nathaliae ♀H4	CLAP ECho WAbe WThu
- 'Alba'	CLAP ECho NSla WAbe
pyrenaica	see *R. myconi*
serbica	ECho WThu
- 'Alba' new	ECho

Randia (*Rubiaceae*)

formosa	CCCN

Ranunculus (*Ranunculaceae*)

abnormis	WAbe WCot
aconitifolius	EBee ECha ECho EWld GCra GKir GMaP NLar SHar SWat WCot WHal WMnd WMoo WSHC WSpi
- 'Flore Pleno' (d) ♀H4	Widely available
acris	EBWF NBir NLan NMir NPer
* - 'Citrinus'	CElw EWoo GBin LRHS MCot MMHG NCGa NRya SHar WHal WMoo
- 'Cricket' (v)	WAlt
- 'Flore Pleno' (d) ♀H4	CBgR CDes CElw CFee EBee ECha ECho EHrv ELan EPPr EPfP GBin GQue LLWG LRHS MCot MRav NBid NBro NGdn NRya SPoG SRms WCom WFar WHil WMoo WSpi
- 'Hedgehog'	EBee ECho EPPr LSou NDov WPrP
- 'Jaffa' new	WAlt
- 'Stevenii'	CFee EPPr IGor SDix WHal WSHC
- 'Sulphureus'	CBre EBee ECha WEas WFar WHal
alpestris	ECho GEdr NMen NRya
amplexicaulis	CMea EBee ELon EPot GCrs GKev GMaP NHar NMen WAbe
- 'Grandiflorus'	LRHS
aquatilis	CWat EHon MSKA MWts NSco SWat WMAq WPnP
× ***arendsii*** 'Moonlight'	SUsu WSHC
baurii	ECho
bilobus	NMen WAbe
bulbosus	NSco
§ - 'F.M. Burton'	EHrv NRya WCot
- ***farreri***	see *R. bulbosus* 'F.M. Burton'
- 'Speciosus Plenus'	see *R. constantinopolitanus* 'Plenus'
calandrinioides ♀H2-3	CBgR EBee ECho EWes NBir WAbe WCot
- SF 137	WCot
§ ***constantinopolitanus*** 'Plenus' (d)	CElw ECha GCal MBri MLLN MRav NBid NBro NRya WCot WEas WFar WMoo
cortusifolius	NCGa SWat WSHC
crenatus	CStu ECho GAuc GCrs GEdr NMen NRya WAbe
creticus	ECho
extorris 'Flore Pleno'	CDes EBee WCot
ficaria	CArn CTri EBWF ESwi GBar MHer NChi NMir NSco WHer WShi
- 'Aglow in the Dark'	CHid EBee
- var. ***albus***	CHid CSam ELon LEdu NRya WAlt
- anemone-centred	see *R. ficaria* 'Collarette'
- 'Ashen Primrose'	EBee
§ - var. ***aurantiacus***	CBgR CStu ECha ECho LRHS MRav NLar NRya SPhx SRms WAbe WFar WPtf
- 'Bowles's Double'	see *R. ficaria* 'Double Bronze', 'Picton's Double'
- 'Brambling'	CBre CHid CLAP ECho LEdu LRHS MRav NLar SBch SSvw WAlt WPrP
- 'Brazen Child'	EBee MDKP SHar
- 'Brazen Daughter'	ECho
- 'Brazen Hussy'	Widely available
- 'Broadleas Black'	ECho
- subsp. ***bulbilifer*** 'Chedglow'	MDKP WCot
- 'Cartwheel' (d)	EBee
- 'Chocolate Cream'	ECho
§ - subsp. ***chrysocephalus***	ECha ELon IFro LRHS NRya SBch WCot WFar
- 'Coffee Cream'	EBee
§ - 'Collarette' (d)	CHid CStu EBee ECho ELon EPot GBar GCrs LEdu LRHS MHer MTho NBir NLar NMen NRya WAbe WCom WFar
- 'Coppernob'	CBre CHid EBee ECha ECho ELon LRHS MDKP SBch WCot WFar
- 'Corinne Tremaine'	WHer
- 'Crowson's White' new	IFro
- 'Cupreus'	see *R. ficaria* var. *aurantiacus*
- 'Damerham' (d)	CHid LRHS
- 'Dappled Grey'	GKir WAlt
- 'Deborah Jope'	ECha SUsu
- 'Diane Rowe'	LRHS
§ - 'Double Bronze' (d)	CBgR CHid CStu EBee ECho LEdu LRHS MDKP MHer MTho NBir NLar NRya SHar
- double cream-flowered	see *R. ficaria* 'Double Mud'
§ - 'Double Mud' (d)	CBgR CBow CHid CLAP CStu ECho IFro LEdu LRHS MTho NLar NRya SHar WAbe WCom WFar WHal WSHC
- double yellow-flowered	see *R. ficaria* Flore Pleno Group
- double, green-eyed (d)	CHid GKir LEdu
- 'Dusky Maiden'	ECho NLar SBch WFar
- 'E.A. Bowles'	see *R. ficaria* 'Collarette'
- 'Elan' (d)	CDes EBee
- subsp. ***ficariiformis***	LRHS
- 'Filigree Heart' new	WAlt

§	- Flore Pleno Group (d)	CBgR CFee CHid CStu CTri EBee ECha ECho ELan ELon EPPr NRya NSti SBch SRms WAbe WCot WFar
	- 'Fried Egg'	ECho
	- 'Granby Cream'	ECho
	- 'Green Mantle'	ECho
	- 'Green Petal'	CHid CStu EBee ECho EPPr EPot GKir LEdu MCot MDKP MHer MTho NBir NLar NRya WHal WHer WHil
	- 'Holly'	see *R. ficaria* 'Holly Green'
§	- 'Holly Green'	ECho
	- 'Hyde Hall'	ECho SBch WFar WPrP
	- 'Jake Perry'	CDes EBee MNrw
	- 'Jane's Dress'	CHid
	- 'Ken Aslet Double' (d)	CDes EBee LEdu MHer NLar WHal
	- 'Lambrook Black'	WHer
	- 'Lambrook Variegated' (v)	EPPr
	- 'Lemon Queen'	CHid
	- 'Leo'	LRHS MDKP
	- subsp. ***major***	see *R. ficaria* subsp. *chrysocephalus*
	- 'Melanie Jope'	EBee
	- 'Mimsey' (d)	EBee
	- 'Mobled Jade'	CHid
	- 'Monksilver' **new**	IFro
	- 'Mud'	MDKP
	- 'Newton Abbot'	CBre
I	- 'Nigrifolia'	EBee MDKP
	- 'Old Master'	CBow NCGa WCot
	- 'Orange Sorbet'	LEdu MNrw NLar
§	- 'Picton's Double' (d)	CStu GBar MTho NRya WAbe
	- 'Primrose'	CHid MTho NLar NRya
	- 'Primrose Elf'	EBee ECha
	- 'Quantock Brown'	CBgR
	- 'Ragamuffin' (d)	CDes EBee LEdu WPrP
	- 'Randall's White'	CBgR CSWP CStu EBee EPfP MCot MRav MTho NCGa SHar WCom WFar WPtf
	- 'Richard and Val' **new**	WCot
	- 'Salad Bowl' (d)	ECho
	- 'Salmon's White'	CBre EBee ECho ELan ELon EPPr LRHS MRav NBir NLar NRya SHar WFar WHal WHer WHrl WPtf
	- 'Sheldon Silver'	CHid
	- 'Silver Collar'	LEdu
	- 'Torquay Elf'	EBee
	- 'Tortoiseshell'	CHid EBee MDKP WCom WFar WPtf
	- 'Tubby'	WAlt
	- 'Undercurrent' (v)	WAlt
	- 'Winkworth'	LRHS
	- 'Wisley Double'	see *R. ficaria* 'Double Bronze'
	- 'Wisley White'	NSti
	- 'Witchampton'	EBee
	- 'Yaffle'	CHid EBee ECho LRHS MDKP
	flammula	CBen CRow CWat EBWF EHon LPBA MSKA NSco SWat WPnP
	- subsp. ***minimus***	CRow
	gouanii	NRya
	gramineus ♀H4	CFir CSpe CWCL EBee EBrs ECho EDAr EWTr GBin GEdr GKir GMaP LBee LRHS MNrw MTho MWat NMen NRya SMrm SPhx SRms SUsu WCAu WCom WFar WHil WPer
	- 'Pardal'	SCnR WCot WFar
*	***guttatus***	NMen
	hederaceus	LLWG
	illyricus	EBee ECha EDAr EPPr NRya WAbe WHal
	kochii	EBee ECho EPot
	lanuginosus	EPPr
	lingua	COld EBWF MCCP NSco SPlb WSFF
	- 'Grandiflorus'	CBen CRow EHon LPBA MMuc MSKA NPer SWat WHal WMAq WPnP
	lyallii	GGar GKev
	macauleyi	GCrs GEdr
	millefoliatus	ECho MTho NMen WAbe
	montanus double-flowered (d)	CPBP CStu EBee LRHS SHar WCot
	- 'Molten Gold' ♀H4	CStu ECho ECtt GMaP MRav MTho NRya
	muelleri	ECou
	parnassiifolius	NMen WAbe
	platanifolius	EBrs LRHS SMHy
	pyrenaeus	NMen
	repens 'Broken Egg' (v)	WAlt
	- 'Buttered Popcorn' (v)	CBow CRow EBee LLWG NLar WMoo WSpi
	- 'Cat's Eyes' (v)	EBee WAlt
	- 'Dinah Myte' (v)	WAlt
	- 'Gloria Spale'	CBre CRow WAlt
	- 'In Vein' (v)	WAlt
	- 'Joe's Golden'	WAlt
	- 'Orkney Chocolate'	WAlt
	- var. ***pleniflorus*** (d)	CBre CRow GGar LLWG SPhx SRot WAlt WEas WFar
	- semi-double (d)	WAlt
	- 'Snowdrift' (v)	CDes EBee LEdu
	- 'Time Bomb' (v)	WAlt
	- 'Timothy Clark' (d)	CBre WAlt WSHC
	seguieri	ECho WAbe
	serbicus	EBee
	speciosus 'Flore Pleno'	see *R. constantinopolitanus* 'Plenus'

Ranzania (*Berberidaceae*)

	japonica	WCru

Raoulia (*Asteraceae*)

	australis misapplied	see *R. hookeri*
	australis Hook.f. ex Raoul	CEnt EDAr EPot GEdr GKev GKir ITim LRHS MWat NWCA WHoo
§	- Lutescens Group	ECha ECho SMad
	glabra	EPot
	haastii	ECho ECou
§	***hookeri***	ECha ECho EPot GAbr GEdr ITim NWCA SMad SPlb SRms WPat
	- var. ***laxa***	EWes
	× ***loganii***	see × *Leucoraoulia loganii*
	lutescens	see *R. australis* Lutescens Group
	petriensis	ECho WAbe
	× ***petrimia*** 'Margaret Pringle'	WAbe
	subsericea	ECho EWes NMen NWCA
	tenuicaulis	ECha EPot SPlb

raspberry see *Rubus idaeus*

Ratibida (*Asteraceae*)

	columnifera	CRWN EBee EBrs EPfP LRHS NBre SPet
	- f. ***pulcherrima***	CSpe EBee EPfP LBMP LSou NBre SGSe SPet SPhx
	- 'Red Midget'	EBrs SBfd SPhx SUsu
	pinnata	CEnt CRWN CSam CSpe EBee EPfP LRHS LSRN NBir SMHy SMad SMrs SPet SPhx SPlb WHal WMnd

Ravenala (*Strelitziaceae*)

	madagascariensis	EAmu LPal XBlo

Ravenea (*Arecaceae*)

	rivularis	CCCN EAmu EUJe LPal XBlo

Rechsteineria see *Sinningia*

redcurrant see *Ribes rubrum* (R)

Rehmannia (*Scrophulariaceae*)

	angulata misapplied	see *R. elata*
§	***elata*** ♀H2	CBot CFir CSam CSpe EBee ELan EPfP IDee LAst LBMP LHop LLWP LPio LRHS MHer MNHC SGSe SGar SWal WBor WEas WFar WWEG WWlt
	- 'White Dragon'	CSpe LPio
	piasezkii	CTsd

Reineckea (*Convallariaceae*)

§	***carnea***	CDes CFee CFir CHid CHll CPLG CStu EBee ECha ELan EPPr EPla GEdr GGar GKev IDee IMou LEdu MMuc NLar NSti SDys SEND SGSe SPlb SUsu WCru WPGP WPtf WTin
	- B&SWJ 4808	ELon WCru
	- SDR 330	GKev
	- 'Baoxing Booty'	WCon WCru
	- 'Crûg's Broadleaf'	WCru
	- 'Variegata' (v)	EShb MAvo WCot

Reinwardtia (*Linaceae*)

§	***indica***	CCCN CHll CPLG ERea EShb SMrm
	trigyna	see *R. indica*

Remusatia (*Araceae*)

	hookeriana	WWst
	pumila	EUJe WWst
	vivipara	EUJe

Reseda (*Resedaceae*)

	alba	MHer
	lutea	SIde
	luteola	CHby GBar GPoy MHer NSco WHer WHfH WSFF

Restio (*Restionaceae*)

	brunneus	EBee
	festuciformis	EHoe
	quadratus	IDee
	subverticillatus	see *Ischyrolepis subverticillata*
	tetraphyllus	CAbb CBct CFir CHid CTrC CWit EBee EHoe GBin GCal GGar IDee SPlb SPoG WDyG

Reynoutria see *Fallopia*

Rhamnus (*Rhamnaceae*)

	alaternus	WFar WPGP
	var. ***angustifolia***	
§	- 'Argenteovariegata' (v) ♀H4	Widely available
	- 'Variegata'	see *R. alaternus* 'Argenteovariegata'
	cathartica	CCVT CDul CLnd CTri ECrN EMac EPfP LBuc NLar NWea WDin WMou WSFF
	frangula	see *Frangula alnus*
	imeretina	CGHE WPGP WPat
	lycioides subsp. ***oleoides***	GAuc
	pallasii	NLar
	pumila	NLar
	taquetii	NLar

Rhaphiolepis (*Rosaceae*)

	× ***delacourii***	CMHG CMac CWib EBee ECrN ELan EPfP LAst MWea SRms
	- 'Coates' Crimson'	CDoC CTsd EBee ELan EMil EPfP IVic LAst LHop LRHS SEND SOWG WPat WSHC
	- Enchantress = 'Moness'	CMHG CSam CTsd EBee ELan EPfP LRHS MAsh MRav SLon
	- 'Pink Cloud'	CBcs EPfP LRHS
	- 'Spring Song'	SLon
	indica	ERom MMuc SEND
	- B&SWJ 8405	WCru
	- 'Coppertone'	see × *Rhaphiobotrya* 'Coppertone'
	- Springtime = 'Monme'	CBcs IVic LRHS MMuc SEND SPer SPur WDin
	umbellata ♀H2-3	CBcs CBot CFee CHEx CSam CTri CWib EBee ELan EPfP EWTr GKir IVic LAst LHop LRHS MAsh MMuc SEND SLon SOWG WFar WPGP WPat WSHC
	- f. ***ovata*** B&SWJ 4706	WCru

× *Rhaphiobotrya* (*Rosaceae*)

§	'Coppertone'	EPfP SAPC SArc SCoo

Rhaphithamnus (*Verbenaceae*)

	cyanocarpus	see *R. spinosus*
§	***spinosus***	CBcs EBee EPfP GBin GGar GKir LRHS

Rhapidophyllum (*Arecaceae*)

	hystrix	CBrP LPal NPal

Rhapis ✿ (*Arecaceae*)

§	***excelsa*** ♀H1	CCCN EAmu LPal NPal WCot XBlo
	multifida	LPal

Rhazya (*Apocynaceae*)

	orientalis	see *Amsonia orientalis*

Rheum ✿ (*Polygonaceae*)

	CC 4845	GKev
	CC 5243	EWld GKev
	GWJ 9329 from Sikkim	WCru
	HWJK 2354 from Nepal	WCru
	SDR 1863	GKev
	SDR 2817	GKev
	SDR 5004	GKev
	from India	GCal
§	'Ace of Hearts'	Widely available
	'Ace of Spades'	see *R.* 'Ace of Hearts'
	acuminatum	EBee
	- HWJCM 252	WCru
	alexandrae	EBee EWes GCal GCra LPio NCGa NChi
	- SDR 4602	GKev
	- SDR 4757	GKev
	- SDR 6031	GKev
	altaicum	LEdu
	'Andrew's Red'	GTwe
§	***australe***	CAgr CFir CRow CSpe EBee GCal LEdu LPBA LPio LRHS NBro NLar WCot WFar WHoo WMnd
N	× ***cultorum***	see *R.* × *hybridum*
	delavayi	GCal
	emodi	see *R. australe*
	forrestii	GAuc
§	× ***hybridum***	SEND
	- from Burston Hall	LRHS
	- from Isle of Ely Horticultural Institute	LRHS

- from Sherburn Park LRHS
- 'Amerikanske Kaempe' LRHS
- 'Amstel Seedling' LRHS
- 'Appleton's Forcing' GTwe LRHS
- 'Baker's All Season' GTwe LRHS
- 'Bedford Scarlet' LRHS
- 'Brandy Carr Scarlet' ECrN MRav NGHP
- 'Brown's Crimson' LRHS
- 'Brown's Red' LRHS
- 'Canada Red' GTwe LRHS
- 'Carter's Forcing' LRHS
- 'Cawood Advance' LRHS
- 'Cawood Castle' LRHS
- 'Cawood Delight' GKir GTwe LRHS
- 'Cawood Ensign' LRHS
- 'Cawood Oak' LRHS
- 'Champagne' CAgr CFox ECrN EPfP GTwe LRHS NGHP SBfd SPer SWal WSpi
* - 'Champagne Rood' LRHS
- 'Collis's Ruby' LRHS
- 'Coutt's Red Stick' LRHS
- 'Crimson Queen' LRHS
- 'Crimson Wine' LRHS
- 'Cutbush's Seedling' LRHS
- 'Dawe's Challenge' LRHS
- 'Daw's Champion' GTwe LRHS
- 'Donkere Bloedrede Zoet' LRHS
- 'Early Champagne' LRHS
- 'Early Cherry' GTwe LRHS
- 'Early Devon' LRHS
- 'Early Mitchell' LRHS
- 'Early Superb' LRHS
- 'Early Victoria' LRHS
- 'Exhibition Red' LRHS
- 'Fenton's Special' CTri GTwe LRHS MCoo MRav NGHP
* - 'Frambozenrood Limburg' LRHS
- 'Fulton's Strawberry Surprise' ♀^{H4} GTwe
- 'German Wine' LRHS
- 'Giant Grooveless Crimson' LRHS
- 'Glaskin's Perpetual' CAgr CWib LBuc MAsh SWal
- 'Goliath' LRHS
- 'Grandad's Favorite' ♀^{H4} LRHS
- 'Green Jam' LRHS
- 'Greengage' GTwe LRHS
- 'Guardsman' LRHS
- 'Hadspen Crimson' CBct WCot
- 'Hammond's Early' GTwe LRHS
- 'Harbinger' GTwe LRHS
- 'Hawke's Champagne' ♀^{H4} GTwe LRHS
- 'Holsteiner Blut' ECho EPfP LRHS
- 'Larne' LRHS
- 'Laxton's No 1' LRHS
- 'Linnaeus' LRHS
- 'Livingstone'^{PBR} EPfP LRHS
- 'Mac Red' ♀^{H4} GTwe
- 'Marshall's Early' LRHS
- 'McDonald' LRHS
- 'Merton's Banner' LRHS
- 'Merton's Broadleaf' LRHS
- 'Merton's Foremost' LRHS
- 'Merton's Yardstick' LRHS
- 'Mitchell's Early Albert' LRHS
- 'Mitchell's Royal Albert' LRHS
- 'Mrs McKenzie' LRHS
- 'Perpetual' LRHS
- 'Prince Albert' GTwe LRHS NEgg NGHP
* - 'Ras Versteeg' LRHS
- 'Raspberry Red' LRHS SBfd
- 'Red Champagne' EPfP LBuc LRHS NGHP WSpi
- 'Red Prolific' GTwe
- 'Reed's Champagne' LRHS
- 'Reed's Early Superb' ♀^{H4} GTwe LRHS
- 'Riverside Giant' LRHS
- 'Rosenhagen' LRHS
- 'Ruby' LRHS
- 'Seedling Piggot' LRHS
- 'Stein's Champagne' ♀^{H4} GTwe LRHS
- 'Stockbridge' LRHS
- 'Stockbridge Arrow' CSut CTri GTwe LRHS NEgg NGHP
- 'Stockbridge Bingo' GTwe LRHS
- 'Stockbridge Cropper' LRHS
- 'Stockbridge Emerald' GTwe LRHS
- 'Stockbridge Guardsman' GTwe
- 'Stockbridge Harbinger' LRHS
- 'Stockbridge Smith' LRHS
- 'Stott's Monarch' LRHS
- 'Strawberry' GTwe LRHS NBir
- 'Strawberry Red' LRHS
- 'Sutton's Cherry Red' GTwe LRHS
- 'The Appleton' LRHS
- 'The Sutton' CWib GTwe LRHS
- 'Timperley Early' ♀^{H4} CDoC CMac CSBt CTri CWib EMil EPfP EUJe GKir GTwe LRHS MAsh MGos MMuc MRav NEgg NGHP NPri SBfd SCoo SDea SKee SLim SPer SPoG
- 'Tingley Cherry' GTwe
- 'Valentine' LRHS
- 'Victoria' CAgr CDoC CFox CSBt CTri CWib ELau EMil EPfP EUJe GTwe LRHS MAsh MCoo MHer MNHC NGHP SBfd SLim SPoG SVic SWal WHar
- 'Vinrabarber Svenborg' LRHS
- 'Vroege Engelse' LRHS
- 'Zwolle Seedling' GTwe

kialense CBct CDes NBid NSti WPGP WPnP
moorcroftianum EBee
nobile EBee
- SDR 4750 GKev

officinale CArn CBct CHEx EBee GCal LRHS MBri SIde SWat
palmatum CArn CBcs EBee ECha ELan EPfP GCra LAst LPBA LRHS MGos MNHC MRav NGdn SWat WCot WFar
- 'Atropurpureum' see *R. palmatum* 'Atrosanguineum'
§ - 'Atrosanguineum' ♀^{H4} Widely available
- 'Bowles's Crimson' CBct GKir LRHS MBri MGos MRav NBid WCot
- 'Red Herald' CBct GKir LRHS WCot WWEG
- 'Rubrum' CBct EBee GKir LRHS MCCP NBir NHol WFar
- 'Savill' GKir LRHS MBri MRav WWEG
- var. ***tanguticum*** Widely available
- - 'Rosa Auslese' WHil

rhaponticum NLar
ribes WCot
subacaule NLar
tataricum LEdu

Rhinanthus (*Scrophulariaceae*)

minor GJos NSco

Rhodanthe (*Asteraceae*)

§ ***anthemoides*** CPBP ECou IRar SEND

Rhodanthemum (*Asteraceae*)

'African Eyes' EBee ECho EPfP LRHS MGos NPri SPoG SRkn SRot SUsu WNew

§ ***atlanticum*** ECho EWes
§ ***catananche*** CCCN ECho EPot EWes MBNS SRot
§ - 'Tizi-n-Test' ECho
- 'Tizi-n-Tichka' CPBP ECho EWes LRHS
§ ***gayanum*** CCCN ECho EWes IRar
- 'Flamingo' see *R. gayanum*
§ ***hosmariense*** ♀H4 CCCN EBee ECha ECho EDAr ELan EPfP EPot GGar GMaP LHop LRHS MCot MWat NPri SCoo SEND SPer SPoG SRms SRot WAbe WCom WHoo WPat

Rhodea (*Liliaceae*)

tonkinensis HWJ 562 **new** WCru

Rhodiola (*Crassulaceae*)

SDR 4742 GKev
SDR 4759 GKev
SDR 4901 GKev
SDR 5015 GKev
amabilis GAuc
crassipes see *R. wallichiana*
cretinii HWJK 2283 WCru
§ ***fastigiata*** EBee GCal GKev NMen NWCA
§ ***heterodonta*** ECha ELan MRav WCot
himalensis misapplied see *R.* 'Keston'
himalensis (D. Don) Fu CTri EBee
- HWJK 2258 WCru
§ ***integrifolia*** NNS 95-458 NWCA
- subsp. ***integrifolia*** **new** EDAr
§ ***ishidae*** CTri
§ 'Keston' CTri
§ ***kirilovii*** LRHS
- var. ***rubra*** EBrs LRHS
§ ***pachyclados*** EBur ECho ECtt EDAr EPot GJos GKir GMaP LBee LRHS MHer MMuc NBir NHol NRya SEND SGar SPlb SRot SWvt WAbe WCom WEas WFar WOut WPer
aff. ***purpureoviridis*** WFar
- BWJ 7544 WCru
§ ***rosea*** Widely available
semenovii NLar
sinuata HWJK 2318 WCru
- HWJK 2326 WCru
§ ***trollii*** ECho EPot LRHS SPlb WAbe
§ ***wallichiana*** MLHP NBid
- GWJ 9263 WCru
- HWJK 2352 WCru

Rhodochiton (*Scrophulariaceae*)

§ ***atrosanguineus*** ♀H1-2 CCCN CEnd CFox CSpe ELan EPfP GBee GGar IDee MAsh SGar SLon SOWG SPer SPoG WBor
volubilis see *R. atrosanguineus*

Rhodocoma (*Restionaceae*)

arida CBct CCCN
capensis CAbb CBct CCCN CFir CPen CPrp CSpe CTrC CTsd EAmu EBee GBin LRHS
foliosa IDee
fruticosa CTrC
gigantea CCCN CFir CPen CTrC EAmu ESwi ETod GBin IDee

Rhododendron ✿ (*Ericaceae*)

sp. MGos
'A. Gilbert' SHea
'A.J. Ivens' see *R.* 'Arthur J. Ivens'
'Abegail' MGos SLdr
aberconwayi LMil SReu
- 'His Lordship' GGGa LHyd LMil MSnd
acrophilum (V) GGGa
Argent 2768
'Ada Brunieres' (K) CSdC
'Addy Wery' (EA) ♀H3-4 CDoC ECho MGos
adenogynum GGGa LMil MSnd
§ - Adenophorum Group SLdr
F 20444
adenophorum see *R. adenogynum* Adenophorum Group
adenopodum GGGa
adenosum NHol
- R 18228 GGGa
'Admiral Piet Hein' SReu
'Adonis' (EA/d) CBcs CMac LMil NLar SLdr SPoG
'Adriaan Koster' (hybrid) SHea
'Advance' (EA) SLdr
aeruginosum see *R. campanulatum* subsp. *aeruginosum*
aganniphum GGGa MSnd
- var. ***flavorufum*** MSnd
- 'Rusty' MSnd
× ***agastum*** PW 98 LMil
'Aida' (R/d) CSBt SReu
'Aksel Olsen' CTri GEdr GKir LRHS MAsh
'Aladdin' (EA) CMac ECho NEgg SLdr WBrE WFar
'Aladdin' (*auriculatum* hybrid) GGGa
Aladdin Group SReu
'Albatross' LHyd
Albatross Group LMil SReu
'Albatross Townhill Pink' LMil
'Albert Schweitzer' ♀H4 CDoC CWri GGGa GKir LMil NLar SLdr SLim WFar
albrechtii (A) GGGa IVic LMil SLdr SReu
- Whitney form (A) LMil
'Album Elegans' MSnd
'Alena' GGGa
'Alex Hill' CBcs
'Alexander' (EA) ♀H4 IVic LMil LSRN MAsh MGos SLdr SReu
'Alexis' **new** IVic
'Alfred' NMun
'Alice' (EA) LHyd SLdr
'Alice' (hybrid) ♀H4 CMac CSBt LHyd LMil SHea SLdr SReu
Alison Johnstone Group CBcs GGGa LMil MSnd SLdr SReu
Alpine Gem Group GQui
§ ***alutaceum*** GGGa
var. ***alutaceum*** Globigerum Group R 11100
§ - var. ***iodes*** MSnd
§ - var. ***russotinctum*** MDun
- - R 158 SLdr
§ - - Triplonaevium Group GGGa
USDAPI 59442/R10923
amagianum (A) LMil
Amalfi Group LMil
'Amber Rain' (A) SLdr
ambiguum LMil MSnd SReu
I - 'Crosswater' LMil
- 'Golden Summit' GGGa
- 'Jane Banks' LMil
- 'Medley' **new** IVic
'Ambrosia' (EA) CSBt
'America' SHea WFar
'Amity' CSBt CWri ECho LMil MAsh MBri MSnd NPCo WFar WGwG
'Amoenum Coccineum' (EA/d) IVic SLdr SReu
Amor Group LHyd SHea

	'Amoretto'	IVic
	'Anah Kruschke'	GGGa MAsh SPoG
	'Analin'	see *R.* 'Anuschka'
	'Anchorite' (EA)	SLdr
*	'Andrae'	SReu
	'Androcles' **new**	LMil
	'Angelo'	IVic LHyd LMil
	Angelo Group	CWri LHyd LMil SReu
	'Anita Dunstan'	MLea
	Anita Group	SHea
	'Ann Callingham' (K)	CSdC
	'Ann Lindsay'	SReu
	'Anna Baldsiefen'	ELon MGos NPCo SLim SPoG SReu
	'Anna Kauser' **new**	MSnd
	'Anna Rose Whitney'	CBcs CTri CWri GKir LHyd LRHS LTen MAsh MGos MSnd NEgg NPri SLim
	'Annabella' (K) ♀H4	CSdC LMil NLar
	annae	GGGa LMil NMun
	'Anne Frank' (EA)	MGos WFar
	'Anne George'	LHyd
	'Anne Teese'	GGGa LMil
	'Annegret Hansmann'	GGGa
	'Anneke' (A)	EPfP LMil MBri NLar SLdr SReu SSta WFar
	'Anouk' (EA)	NMun
	anthopogon	LMil
	- from Marpha Meadow, Nepal	WAbe
	- 'Betty Graham'	GGGa
	- subsp. ***hypenanthum***	MDun
	- - 'Annapurna'	GGGa ITim WAbe
	'Antilope' (Vs)	CBcs CWri ECho LMil MGos MLea MMuc NEgg NHol NLar SLdr SPer SReu SSta WBVN
	'Antonio'	LMil
§	'Anuschka'	GKir LRHS MAsh MMuc
	anwheiense	CWri LHyd SHea
	aperantum F 27022	GGGa
	apodectum	see *R. dichroanthum* subsp. *apodectum*
	'Apotrophia'	SLdr
	'Apple Blossom' ambig.	CMac
	'Apple Blossom' Wezelenburg (M)	SLdr
N	'Appleblossom' (EA)	see *R.* 'Ho-o'
	'Apricot Blaze' (A)	MDun NHol
	'Apricot Fantasy'	LMil MDun
	'Apricot Nectar' (V)	MDun
	'Apricot Surprise'	CTri LMil LRHS MAsh
	'April Dawn'	GGGa
	'April Gem'	IVic
	'April Glow'	LHyd
	'April Rose'	IVic
	'April Showers' (A)	LMil
	'Aquamarin' **new**	IVic
	'Arabesk' (EA)	LMil MBri MGos SLdr WFar
	'Arabesque'	SLim
	araiophyllum KR 4029	LMil
	- KR 7483	LMil
	arborescens (A)	GGGa LHyd LMil
	- pink-flowered (A)	LMil
	arboreum	CDoC CHEx GGGa IDee LMil MDun MSnd SReu
	- 'Blood Red'	MSnd
	- subsp. ***cinnamomeum***	CDoC GGGa GGar IDee LMil MSnd SReu
	- - var. ***album***	LHyd NMun SReu
	- - var. ***roseum***	GGGa
	- - - 'Tony Schilling'	IDee LMil NLar SReu
	- subsp. ***delavayi***	GGGa IDee LMil MSnd
	- - C&H 7178	GGGa

	- - KR 3909	LMil
	- - var. ***delavayi***	GLin
	- - var. ***peramoenum*** AC 5577	GLin
	- 'Heligan'	CWri SReu
§	- subsp. ***nilagiricum***	GGGa GLin
	- var. ***roseum***	SHea
§	- subsp. ***zeylanicum***	GGGa
	'Arctic Fox' (EA)	GGGa
§	'Arctic Glow'	GKir
	'Arctic Regent' (K)	CSdC GQui
	'Arctic Tern'	see × *Ledodendron* 'Arctic Tern'
§	***argipeplum***	GGGa
	'Argosy' ♀H4	LMil SReu
	argyrophyllum	CWri GKir MSnd SLdr
	- subsp. ***argyrophyllum***	SLdr
§	- subsp. ***hypoglaucum***	GGGa LHyd
	- - JN	GGGa
	- subsp. ***nankingense***	GGGa
	- - 'Chinese Silver' ♀H4	CDoC IDee LHyd LMil MDun MSnd SLdr SReu
	arizelum	GGGa GKir IDee LMil LRHS MAsh MDun MSnd
	- R 25	GGGa
	- subsp. ***arizelum*** Rubicosum Group	LMil
	'Arkona' **new**	IVic
	armitii (V) Woods 2518	GGGa
	'Arneson Gem' (M)	CBcs CDoC GGGa LMil LRHS MAsh SLdr
	'Arpege' (Vs)	LMil MBri SLdr SReu
	'Arthur Bedford'	CBcs LHyd SLdr SReu
§	'Arthur J. Ivens'	SLdr
	'Arthur Osborn'	SSpi
	'Arthur Stevens'	MSnd SLdr
	'Asa-gasumi' (Kurume) (EA)	LHyd
	asterochnoum C&H 7051	GGGa
	Asteroid Group	SLdr
	'Astrid'	IVic LMil LSRN
	atlanticum (A)	GGGa GKev LMil
	- 'Seaboard' (A)	LMil
	atlanticum × ***canescens***	GKev
	augustinii	CWri GGGa IDee LHyd LMil MLea MSnd SLdr SSpi SSta
	- subsp. ***augustinii*** C&H 7048	GGGa
§	- subsp. ***chasmanthum***	GGGa
	- compact EGM 293	LMil
§	- Electra Group	CDoC GGGa LHyd LMil MLea SLdr
	- Exbury best form	LHyd LMil SReu
§	- subsp. ***hardyi***	GGGa
	- 'Lilastar' **new**	IVic
	- pale lilac-flowered	SLdr
§	- subsp. ***rubrum***	GGGa
*	- 'Trewithen'	IDee LMil
I	- 'Werrington'	CPLG SLdr SReu
	- white-flowered	LHyd
§	***aureum***	GGGa
	auriculatum	GGGa GKir LHyd LMil MDun MSnd SLdr SReu SSta WBVN
	- Reuthe's form	SReu
	auriculatum × ***hemsleyanum***	GGGa
	auritum	GGGa MSnd SLdr
	'Aurora' (K)	SLdr
	austrinum (A)	IDee LMil NLar
	- yellow-flowered (A)	LMil
	'Autumn Glow' (EA)	LMil
	'Autumn Gold'	SLdr
	'Avalanche' ♀H4	LMil SReu
	Avocet Group	LMil
	'Award'	LMil

'Ayah'	LMil
'Aya-kammuri' (EA)	LHyd
Azamia Group	LHyd
Azor Group	LHyd SHea SReu
'Aztec' (EA) **new**	LMil
§ 'Azuma-kagami' (Kurume) (EA)	LHyd LMil SLdr WFar
'Azurika'	IVic
'Azurro'	GGGa LMil NLar
B.B.C. Group **new**	LMil
'B. de Bruin'	SHea
'Babette'	see *R.* (Volker Group) 'Babette'
'Babuschka'	LMil
'Baden-Baden'	CMac CTri ECho GEdr GKir MAsh MGos MSnd NEgg NHol NLar NMun SLdr SPoG WFar
'Bagshot Ruby'	SHea SReu
baileyi	GGGa
* 'Baker's Lavender' (EA)	CTrh
'Balalaika'	MDun
balangense EN 3530	GGGa
'Balbina' **new**	IVic
balfourianum	GGGa
'Bali'	MDun
'Baltic Amber' (A)	GGGa
'Balzac' (K)	CDoC CSam ECho MBri MGos NEgg SLdr SPer SPur WBVN
'Bambi'	LSou
'Banana Boat' **new**	IVic
'Banana Ripe'	MDun
'Bandoola'	SReu
'Barbara Coats' (EA)	SLdr
barbatum	CDoC CHEx CWri GGGa GGar LHyd LMil MDun MSnd
- B&SWJ 2160	WCru
- B&SWJ 2237	WCru
- B&SWJ 2624	WCru
'Barbecue' (K)	LMil
'Barmstedt'	CWri MAsh
'Barnaby Sunset'	GGGa LMil LRHS
'Bashful' ♀H4	CBcs CSBt ECho EPfP LSou MGos SLdr
§ ***basilicum***	CDoC GGGa GKir IDee LMil LRHS NLar SLdr
- AC 616	MSnd
- KR 7532	LMil
- KR 7540	LMil
'Basilisk' (K)	SLdr
× ***bathyphyllum*** Cox 6542	GGGa
bauhiniiflorum	see *R. triflorum* var. *bauhiniiflorum*
beanianum	GGGa
- KC 122	GGGa
- compact	see *R. piercei*
'Beatrice Keir'	LMil MSnd SReu
'Beattie' (EA)	SLdr
Beau Brummell Group	LMil
'Beaulieu Manor'	GQui
'Beautiful Day'	MDun
'Beautiful Dreamer'	MDun
'Beauty of Littleworth'	LHyd SHea SReu
'Beefeater' × ***yakushimanum***	SLdr
beesianum	GGGa
'Beethoven' (EA) ♀H3-4	LHyd MSnd SLdr SReu
'Belkanto'	CDoC SPoG
'Belle Heller'	SLdr
'Bengal'	ECho GEdr GKir LRHS NHol SLdr SLim SReu
'Bengal Beauty' (EA)	SLdr
'Bengal Fire' (EA)	CMac
'Beni-giri' (EA)	CMac
'Bergensiana'	SReu
'Bergie Larson'	CBcs ECho IVic LMil MDun MLea MMuc NPCo SLdr WBVN
bergii	see *R. augustinii* subsp. *rubrum*
'Berg's 10'	MLea
'Berg's Yellow'	CWri ECho LMil MGos MLea MMuc MSnd WBVN WFar
'Bernstein'	LMil SPoG WFar
'Berryrose' (K) ♀H4	CBcs CMac CSBt CTri CWri ECho EPfP GKir LMil MAsh MGos MLea MMuc NLar SLdr SPer WBVN WFar
'Beryl Taylor'	GGGa
'Betty' (EA)	LHyd
'Betty Anne Voss' (EA)	ECho GKir LHyd LSRN MAsh MGos NPri SCoo SLdr SReu
'Betty Wormald'	CMac CSBt ECho GKir LHyd LMil MBri MGos MLea MMuc NMun SHea SLdr SPer
bhutanense CH&M	GGGa
- KR 8233	LMil
Bibiani Group	SHea SLdr
'Bijou de Ledeberg' (EA)	CMac
'Birthday Girl'	ECho LMil LSRN MAsh MDun MLea SPoG
Biskra Group	GGGa LMil
'Blaauw's Pink' (EA) ♀H3-4	CDoC CMac CSBt ECho EPfP GKir GQui LHyd LMil MBri MGos MMuc NPCo SLdr SPer SPlb SPoG SReu SRms WFar
'Black Hawk' (EA)	CBcs
'Black Knight' (A)	SLdr
'Black Magic'	CDoC CWri LMil
'Black Sport'	MLea
Blaue Donau	see *R.* 'Blue Danube'
'Blazecheck'	MGos SCoo
'Blewbury' ♀H4	IVic LHyd LMil SLdr SReu SSta
'Blue Bell'	SHea SLdr
'Blue Boy'	CDoC LMil
'Blue Chip'	LHyd SLdr
§ 'Blue Danube' (EA) ♀H3-4	CChe CDoC CMac CSBt CTri ECho ELon EPfP GKir IVic LHyd LMil LRHS MAsh MBri MGos MSnd NPCo NPri SLdr SLim SPer SPoG SReu SSta WFar
'Blue Diamond'	CMac CSBt ECho ELon GKir LHyd LSRN MGos NPCo SPer SPoG WGwG
Blue Diamond Group	CBcs ECho EPfP LRHS MDun MGos MSnd NHol SLdr SReu SRms
'Blue Haze'	LHyd
'Blue Monday' (EA)	SLdr
'Blue Moon'	ELon LMil LRHS SLdr
'Blue Peter' ♀H4	CSBt CWri ECho EPfP LHyd LMil LRHS MAsh MDun MGos MLea NLar SLdr SPer SReu SSta
'Blue Pool'	LMil
Blue Ribbon Group	SLdr
'Blue Star'	GGar LHyd MDun NMen
'Blue Steel'	see *R. fastigiatum* 'Blue Steel'
Blue Tit Group	CBcs CDoC CSBt EPfP GKir LHyd LRHS LSou MSnd NHol SLdr SLim SReu SSta STre
Bluebird Group	CMac CSBt MGos NHol NWCA SLdr SRms
'Bluerettia'	CDoC CWri IVic LRHS MMuc
'Blutopia'	LMil
'Bob Bovee'	NLar
'Bob's Blue'	MDun
'Boddaertianum'	LHyd SHea SLdr SReu
'Bodnant Yellow'	LMil
Bohlken's Lupinberg **new**	IVic
'Bonfire'	SHea SLdr SReu

	boothii	GGGa
	'Bo-peep'	GQui LHyd LMil
	Bo-peep Group	CBcs SLdr
	'Boskoop Ostara'	CBcs LMil MGos
	'Bouquet de Flore' (G) ♀H4	CDoC CSdC EPfP LMil MLea SReu
	'Bow Bells' ♀H4	ECho EPfP GEdr GKir LMil LRHS MAsh NHol NLar NPri SHea SLdr WFar
	Bow Bells Group	CSam LHyd MDun MGos MLea
	'Bow Street'	SHea
	brachyanthum subsp. ***hypolepidotum***	GGGa
	brachycarpum	GKev GLin
	- 'Roseum Dwarf'	GGGa
	'Brambling'	GGGa
	'Brazier' (EA)	LHyd SLdr
	'Brazil' (K)	CSBt
	'Bremen'	LMil
	'Briane' (EA)	GGGa
	'Bric-à-brac'	WThu
	Bric-à-brac Group	CBcs SLdr
	'Bridesmaid' (O)	EPfP
	'Bright Forecast' (K)	CWri IVic MLea SLdr
	'Brigitte'	CWri GGGa IVic LMil LRHS LSRN MAsh MDun SLdr
	'Brilliant' (EA)	MGos
	'Brilliant' (hybrid)	MGos NHol WFar
	'Brilliant Blue' (EA)	MAsh
	'Britannia'	CBcs CSBt CWri EPfP GKir LHyd SReu WFar
	'Brocade'	CSam LHyd LMil MSnd SHea SLdr
	'Bronze Fire' (A)	NHol SLdr SReu
	'Brown Eyes'	ECho MMuc SLdr WFar
	'Bruce Brechtbill' ♀H4	CDoC CWri ECho GGGa LMil MAsh MBri MGos MMuc NPCo SLdr SReu SSta
	'Bruce Hancock' (Ad)	CChe ECho ELon MMuc SLdr
	'Bruns Diamant' **new**	IVic
§	'Bruns Gloria'	LMil
	'Bruns Schneewitchen'	SReu
	'Buccaneer' (EA)	SLdr
	'Buketta'	GGGa
	bullatum	see *R. edgeworthii*
	bulu C&V 9503	GGGa
	'Bungo-nishiki' (EA/d)	CMac
	bureavii ♀H4	CBcs GGGa GKir GLin IDee LHyd LMil MDun MGos MSnd SReu SSta
	- 'Ardrishaig'	GGGa
	bureavii × Elizabeth Group	SReu
	bureavii × ***yakushimanum***	MSnd SReu
	bureavioides	GKir LMil MSnd SReu
	- Cox 5076	GGGa
	'Burletta'	IVic LMil
	burmanicum	GGGa MDun
	'Busuki'	LMil
	'Butter Brickle'	LMil MLea SLdr WBVN WFar
	'Butter Yellow'	ECho
	'Buttered Popcorn'	MDun
	'Butterfly'	LMil SHea
	'Buttermint'	CWri ECho GQui MGos MLea WFar
	'Buttons and Bows' (K)	GGGa
	'Buzzard' (K)	CSdC LMil
	'Caerhays Lavender' (EA)	CBcs
	caesium	SLdr
	calendulaceum (A)	GKev LMil
	- red-flowered (A)	LMil
	- yellow-flowered (A)	LMil
	Calfort Group	SLdr
	'Calico' (K)	CSdC
	caliginis (V)	GGGa
	callimorphum	GGGa LMil
	calophytum ♀H4	GGGa GKir IDee LMil LRHS MSnd SLdr
	- EGM 343	LMil
	- var. ***openshawianum*** C&H 7055	GGGa
	calostrotum	CWri NMun WAbe
	- subsp. ***calostrotum***	GKev
	- 'Gigha' ♀H4	GGGa IDee LMil MAsh MGos SLdr WAbe
§	- subsp. ***keleticum*** ♀H4	CDoC GEdr IVic MDun MGos NMun WAbe WFar
	- - F 21756	SLdr
	- - R 58	LMil
§	- - Radicans Group	GCrs GEdr MDun MLea NHol WAbe WThu
	- - - USDAPI 59182/R11188	MLea
	- subsp. ***riparium***	GLin
	- - Calciphilum Group	GGGa WThu
§	- - Nitens Group	CDoC GBin GGGa MAsh NMen WAbe
	caloxanthum	see *R. campylocarpum* subsp. *caloxanthum*
	'Calsap'	GGGa
	Calstocker Group	LMil
	camelliiflorum	GGGa
	campanulatum	LHyd LMil MDun MSnd SLdr SReu WAbe
	- CC 5124	GKev
	- HWJCM 195	WCru
§	- subsp. ***aeruginosum***	GGGa LMil MDun SLdr SReu
	- 'Knaphill'	MSnd
	campylocarpum	GGGa IDee LMil MDun MSnd SReu
	- B&SWJ 2462	WCru
	- from East Nepal	MDun
§	- subsp. ***caloxanthum***	GGGa LMil MDun
	- - KR 6152	LMil
	campylogynum ♀H4	CBcs LMil MLea NMen NMun NPCo SSpi WAbe
	- 'Album'	see *R.* 'Leucanthum'
	- black-flowered **new**	IVic
	- 'Bramble'	MDun
	- Charopoeum Group	GGGa MDun WThu
	- - 'Patricia'	ECho EPot LLHF LMil MDun NLar NWCA
§	- Cremastum Group	GGGa LHyd
	- - 'Bodnant Red'	WThu
	- Myrtilloides Group	CDoC ECho GGGa GKev GQui LHyd LMil MAsh MDun MGos MSnd NMen NMun SLdr SReu WAbe
	- pink-flowered	WAbe
	- salmon pink-flowered	ECho GEdr
	camtschaticum	GAuc GCrs GGGa LMil MBri
	- from Hokkaido, Japan	NMen
	- var. ***albiflorum***	GGGa NMen
	- red-flowered	GGGa
	canadense (A)	GGGa
	- f. ***albiflorum*** (A)	GGGa LMil
	- dark-flowered (A)	LMil
	- 'Deer Lake' (A)	SReu
	'Candy Striped Pink' **new**	IVic
	canescens (A)	LMil
	'Cannon's Double' (K/d) ♀H4	CBcs CWri LHyd LMil LRHS MBri MGos MLea NLar SLdr SPer
	'Canzonetta' (EA) ♀H4	ECho GGGa IVic LMil LRHS MAsh MGos MMuc NMun SLdr
	'Capistrano'	GGGa
	'Caprice' (EA)	SReu
	'Captain Jack'	GGGa
	'Caractacus'	WFar

	'Carat' (A)	NLar SReu
	cardiobasis	see *R. orbiculare* subsp. *cardiobasis*
	Carita Group	SHea SReu
	'Carita Golden Dream'	LMil
	'Carita Inchmery'	LHyd SHea
	'Carmen'	CWri ECho GEdr GGGa GKev GKir LHyd LMil MAsh MDun MGos MLea NHol NMun NPCo SLdr SReu SRms WBVN
	'Carmine' **new**	MSnd
	carneum	GGGa
	'Carnival' (EA)	CBcs
	'Caroline Allbrook' ♀H4	CWit CWri ECho EPfP GGGa IDee LHyd MAsh MBri MDun MGos MLea NEgg NHol NLar SLdr SPoG WBVN
	'Caroline de Zoete'	LHyd SHea
	'Caruso' **new**	IVic
	'Cary Ann'	CBcs CTri CWri GKir MAsh SLdr SReu WFar
	'Casablanca' (EA)	SLdr
	'Cassata'	LMil LRHS
	'Cassley' (Vs)	LMil
	catacosmum	GGGa
	catawbiense	GKev GLin LHyd MSnd SLdr
	'Catawbiense Album'	CTri GKir WFar
	'Catawbiense Boursault'	MAsh SLdr WFar
	'Catawbiense Grandiflorum'	CWri GKir NMun WFar
	'Catharine van Tol' **new**	LMil
	'Caucasicum Pictum'	LHyd LMil MSnd SLdr
	'Cavalcade'	GKir
	'Cayenne' (EA)	SLdr
	'Cecile' (K) ♀H4	CBcs CDoC CMac CWri ECho GKir LHyd LMil MBri MDun MGos MMuc SLdr SPer SReu WBVN
	'Celestial' (EA)	CMac
	'Centennial'	see *R.* 'Washington State Centennial'
	cephalanthum	GGGa LMil
	- subsp. ***cephalanthum*** SBEC 0751	WAbe WThu
	- - Crebreflorum Group	GGGa LMil WAbe WThu
	- - - Week's form	ITim
	- - Nmaiense Group C&V 9513	GGGa
	- subsp. ***platyphyllum***	GGGa
	cerasinum	GGGa LMil MSnd
	- 'Cherry Brandy'	MSnd
	'Cetewayo' ♀H4	CWri LMil LRHS SReu
	chaetomallum	see *R. haematodes* subsp. *chaetomallum*
	chamaethomsonii	GGGa
	chameunum	see *R. saluenense* subsp. *chameunum*
§	'Champagne' ♀H3-4	CSBt EPfP GKir LHyd LMil LRHS MAsh MDun SHea SReu
	championiae	GGGa
	'Chanel' (Vs)	MDun SReu SSta
	changii	GGGa
	'Chanticleer' (EA)	SLdr SReu
	chapaense	see *R. maddenii* subsp. *crassum*
	'Chapeau'	LMil
	'Chariots of Fire' (EA) **new**	LMil
	charitopes	GGGa LMil
	- F 25570	LMil
§	- subsp. ***tsangpoense***	GGGa GQui NHol
*	'Charlotte de Rothschild' (A)	SLdr
	Charmaine Group	NHol
	'Charme La'	GGGa

	chasmanthum	see *R. augustinii* subsp. *chasmanthum*
	'Cheer'	CWri MMuc NEgg SLdr SLim SReu WFar
	'Cheerful Giant' (K)	MGos
	'Chelsea Reach' (K/d)	CSdC SLdr
	'Chelsea Seventy'	MSnd SLdr
	'Chenille' (K/d)	SLdr
	'Cherokee' (EA)	SLdr
	'Cherries and Cream'	LMil
	'Cherry Cheesecake'	GGGa
	'Cherry Drops' (EA)	LRHS MAsh
	'Cherry Float'	MDun
	'Chetco' (K)	LMil SLdr
	'Chevalier Félix de Sauvage' ♀H4	LMil SHea SReu
	'Chiffchaff'	LHyd
	'Chikor'	CBcs CSBt ECho GGGa GKir MBri MGos MSnd NHol WFar
	'China A'	SLdr
	China Group	SReu
	'Chinchilla' (EA)	GQui
	'Chink'	CBcs SLdr
	'Chionoides'	CMac GGGa LMil SLdr
	'Chipmunk' (EA/d)	GKir LRHS MAsh
	'Chippewa' (EA)	CTri IVic LMil
	'Choremia' ♀H3	LHyd LMil MLea SHea SLdr SReu
	'Chorus Line'	MDun
	christi (V)	GGGa
	'Christina' (EA/d)	LMil NHol SReu
	'Christmas Cheer' (EA/d)	see *R.* 'Ima-shojo'
	'Christmas Cheer' (hybrid)	CBcs CDoC CMac CSBt CWri GGGa GGal GKir LHyd LMil MAsh MGos MLea MSnd NLar SLdr SReu WClo
	chrysanthum	see *R. aureum*
	chryseum	see *R. rupicola* var. *chryseum*
	chrysodoron	GGGa LMil
	ciliatum	CBcs GGGa IDee LMil SLdr
	'Cilpinense' ♀H3-4	CMac CSBt CWri ECho EPfP GEdr GGGa GKev LHyd LMil LRHS MMuc NLar NPri SHea SPoG SReu WBVN WBrE WGwG
	Cilpinense Group	CBcs MDun MMuc MSnd SLdr WFar
	cinnabarinum	LMil MDun MSnd SLdr
	- subsp. ***cinnabarinum***	MDun
	- - BL&M 234	LMil
	- - Blandfordiiflorum Group	GGGa LMil MSnd
§	- - 'Conroy'	CBcs GGGa LMil MDun MLea SReu
	- - 'Nepal'	LMil
	- - Roylei Group	GGGa LHyd LMil MDun
	- - - 'Magnificum'	MDun
	- - - 'Vin Rosé'	LMil MDun
§	- subsp. ***tamaense*** KW 21021	GGGa
	- 'Wasgau' **new**	IVic
§	- subsp. ***xanthocodon***	CBcs LMil MDun MSnd
§	- - Concatenans Group	GGGa LHyd LMil MDun MSnd SLdr
	- - - KW 5874	LMil
	- - - 'Amber'	MDun
	- - Purpurellum Group	GGGa MDun MSnd
	Cinnkeys Group	MDun
	Cinzan Group	LMil SReu
	'Circus'	MDun
	citriniflorum	LMil
	- R 108	GGGa LMil
	- Brodick form	LMil
	- var. ***citriniflorum***	LMil
	- var. ***horaeum***	SLdr
	- - F 21850*	GGGa
	'Claudine' **new**	IVic

clementinae	GGGa MSnd
- F 25705	LMil
- SDR 3230	GKev
'Cliff Garland'	GQui LMil
'Coccineum Speciosum' (G) ♀H4	CDoC CMac CSBt CSdC LMil LRHS SLdr
coeloneuron	GGGa LMil
- EGM 334	LMil
'Colin Kenrick' (K/d)	CSdC
collettianum H&W 8975	GGGa
'Colonel Coen'	CWit CWri GKir LMil MBri MGos MLea MMuc SLdr WBVN
Colonel Rogers Group	LHyd SLdr SReu
'Colyer' (EA)	SLdr
(Comely Group) 'Golden Orfe'	SLdr
- yellow-flowered	LHyd
complexum F 15392	GGGa
'Comte de Gomer' (hybrid)	CBcs
concatenans	see *R. cinnabarinum* subsp. *xanthocodon* Concatenans Group
concinnum	CWri LHyd SLdr
- Pseudoyanthinum Group	GGGa GQui MDun SLdr
'Concorde'	LHyd
'Conroy'	see *R. cinnabarinum* subsp. *cinnabarinum* 'Conroy'
'Constable'	LHyd
'Conversation Piece' (EA)	SLdr
cookeanum	see *R. sikangense* var. *sikangense* Cookeanum Group
'Coral Mist'	GGGa LMil
'Coral Reef'	SLdr SReu
'Coral Sea' (EA)	MDun SReu
'Corany' (A)	SLim
coriaceum	GGGa LMil MSnd SLdr
- R 120	MSnd
'Corinna' **new**	IVic
'Corneille' (G/d) ♀H4	CSBt LMil
Cornish Cross Group	LHyd
Cornish Early Red Group	see *R.* Smithii Group
'Cornish Red'	see *R.* Smithii Group
'Corona'	SHea
'Coronation Day'	LMil SHea SReu
coryanum	GGGa
- 'Chelsea Chimes'	MSnd
'Cosmopolitan'	CWri LMil MGos MMuc SPoG SReu WClo
'Costa del Sol'	MSnd
Cote Group (A)	SLdr
'Cougar'	MDun
'Countess of Athlone'	SLdr
'Countess of Derby'	SHea SLdr SReu
'Countess of Haddington' ♀H2	CBcs LMil SLdr
'Countess of Stair'	WFar
cowanianum	GGGa
'Cowslip' **new**	LHyd
Cowslip Group	CTri CWri LMil MAsh MDun MGos MLea MSnd SLdr SReu
coxianum C&H 475B	GGGa
'Cranbourne'	LHyd SReu
'Crane' ♀H4	EPfP GGGa GKir GQui IVic LLHF LMil LRHS MAsh NPri SLdr
crassum	see *R. maddenii* subsp. *crassum*
'Cream Crest'	GQui LMil SLdr SLim WFar
'Cream Glory'	LHyd MDun
'Creamy Chiffon'	CWri ECho MGos MLea NLar WBVN WGwG
§ 'Creeping Jenny'	ECho GGGa GGal GGar LHyd MSnd SLdr
cremastum	see *R. campylogynum* Cremastum Group
'Crest' ♀H3-4	CWri GGGa LHyd LMil MGos
'Crete' ♀H4	LMil
'Crimson Pippin'	LMil
crinigerum	GGGa IDee LMil MDun SLdr
'Crinoline' (EA)	SLdr
'Crinoline' (K)	SReu
'Croceum Tricolor' (G)	CSdC
Crossbill Group	CBcs SLdr
'Crossroads' **new**	MSnd
'Crosswater Belle'	IDee LMil LRHS
'Crosswater Red' (K)	LMil
'Csárdás' **new**	IVic
cubittii	see *R. veitchianum* Cubittii Group
cucullatum	see *R. roxieanum* var. *cucullatum*
cumberlandense (A)	GGGa IDee LMil
- 'Sunlight' (A)	LMil MBri
cuneatum	GGGa
'Cunningham's Blush'	GGGa
'Cunningham's Snow White' **new**	IVic
'Cunningham's White'	CBcs CSBt CSam CTri CWri ELan EPfP GGGa GKir LMil LTen MAsh MDun MGos MMuc MSnd NPri SLdr SLim SPoG SReu WFar
'Cupreum Ardens' (G)	CSdC
'Curlew' ♀H4	CMac CSBt EPfP GEdr GGGa GKev GKir LMil MAsh MBri MGos MSnd NHol NLar SLdr SReu SSpi WBVN WFar
cyanocarpum Bu 294	GGGa
'Cynthia' ♀H4	CBcs CMac CSBt CSam CWri ECho EPfP GGGa GKir LHyd LMil LSRN MBri MDun MGos MSnd NEgg SLdr SPer SReu SSta
'Dagmar'	IVic
'Daimio' (EA)	IVic LHyd
'Dairymaid'	SReu
dalhousieae	GGGa
§ - var. ***rhabdotum***	GGGa
Damaris Group	SLdr
'Damaris Logan'	see *R.* 'Logan Damaris'
'Damozel'	SHea SLdr
'Danger' (K)	SLdr
'Danuta' **new**	IVic
'Daphne Daffarn'	SHea
'Daphne Millais'	SHea
'Dartmoor Blush'	SReu
'Dartmoor Pixie'	SReu
'Dartmoor Rose'	SReu
dasycladum	see *R. selense* subsp. *dasycladum*
dasypetalum	MDun
dauricum 'Arctic Pearl'	GGGa
- 'Mid-winter' ♀H4	GGGa LHyd
'David' ♀H4	LHyd SHea SReu
davidii	GGGa LMil
- EN 4213	GGGa
davidsonianum ♀H3-4	GGGa IDee LMil SLdr SSpi
- Bodnant form	LMil MDun
- 'Caerhays Blotched'	SLdr
- 'Caerhays Pink'	GGGa SLdr
- 'Ruth Lyons'	LMil
'Daviesii' (G) ♀H4	CBcs CDoC CSBt CSdC CTri CWri ECho EPfP GGGa GKir GQui IDee LMil LRHS MBri MLea MMuc NPCo SLdr SPer SReu SSpi WBVN WFar
'Daviesii' hybrid **new**	GKev
* 'Day Dawn'	GKir SReu
'Day Dream'	SHea SReu
N 'Daybreak'	see *R.* 'Kirin'
'Daybreak' (K)	GQui
'Dear Grandad' (EA)	CTri LMil NPri SCoo
'Dear Grandma'	LMil

'Dearest' (EA)	LRHS MAsh NPri
'Debutante'	NHol
decorum ♀H4	CDoC GGGa LHyd LLHF LMil LRHS MDun MSnd SReu SSpi
- Bu 286	NHol
- C&H 7023	GGGa
- SDR 4208	GKev
- SDR 5026	GKev
- 'Cox's Uranium Green'	SReu
§ - subsp. ***diaprepes***	LHyd SLdr
- - 'Gargantua'	SReu
- late-flowering	LMil LRHS
- pink-flowered SDR 4209	GKev
decorum × ***yakushimanum***	SLdr SReu
degronianum	GGGa IDee
§ - subsp. ***degronianum***	LMil
- - 'Gerald Loder'	LHyd
§ - subsp. ***heptamerum***	MDun
- - 'Ho Emma'	IDee LMil MDun
- - 'Oki Island'	LMil
- 'Rae's Delight'	IDee LMil
dekatanum	GGGa
deleiense	see *R. tephropeplum*
'Delicatissimum' (O)	CBcs CDoC CWri ECho GGGa GQui MGos MLea MMuc NEgg NLar NPCo SLdr SPer WBrE WGwG
'Delta'	NLar SLim
dendricola	SLdr
- KW 20981	GGGa
dendrocharis Cox 5016	GGGa NHol WAbe
- Glendoick Gem = 'Gle002'	GGGa
* 'Denny's Rose' (A)	LMil MDun SReu
'Denny's Scarlet'	MDun SReu
'Denny's White' (A)	LMil NHol SReu
denudatum	GLin
- C&H 7118	GGGa
- EGM 294	LMil
- SEH 334	LMil
'Desert Orchid'	LHyd
desquamatum	see *R. rubiginosum* Desquamatum Group
'Dexter's Champagne'	MDun
'Dexter's Spice'	MDun
'Dexter's Springtime'	MDun
'Dexter's Vanilla'	MDun
'Diadem' (V)	IVic MAsh
Diamant Group lilac-flowered (EA)	ECho LMil MLea
- pink-flowered (EA)	ECho MGos MLea
§ - purple-flowered (EA)	ECho MGos MLea
§ - red-flowered (EA)	ECho MLea
- rosy red-flowered (EA)	ECho
- white-flowered (EA)	ECho MLea
'Diamant Purpur'	see *R.* Diamant Group purple-flowered
'Diamant Rot'	see *R.* Diamant Group red-flowered
'Diana Pearson'	LHyd
'Diane'	CMac SLdr
diaprepes	see *R. decorum* subsp. *diaprepes*
dichroanthum	GGGa LMil MDun SReu
§ - subsp. ***apodectum***	GGGa LMil
- subsp. ***dichroanthum*** SBEC 545	GGGa
§ - subsp. ***scyphocalyx***	LMil LTen NLar
- - F 24546	GGGa
- subsp. ***septentroniale*** JN 575	GGGa
didymum	see *R. sanguineum* subsp. *didymum*
'Dietrich'	WFar
dimitrum	MDun
'Diny Dee'	MGos
'Diorama' (Vs)	LMil SReu SSta
discolor	see *R. fortunei* subsp. *discolor*
'Django' **new**	IVic
'Doc'	CBcs CMac EPfP GKir MDun MGos SLdr SReu WFar
'Doctor A. Blok'	SLdr
'Doctor Ernst Schäle'	GGGa
'Doctor M. Oosthoek' (M) ♀H4	CSBt SReu
'Doctor Rieger' **new**	SLim
'Doctor Stocker'	MSnd
'Doctor V.H. Rutgers'	MDun WFar
'Dolcemente' **new**	IVic
'Don Quixote' (K)	CSdC
'Doncaster'	GKir MGos SHea WFar
'Donna Hardgrove'	MDun
'Dopey' ♀H4	CBcs CSBt CWri ECho EPfP GGGa GGar GKir LMil LRHS MAsh MBri MDun MGos MLea MSnd NEgg NHol SLdr SLim SReu WBVN
'Dora Amateis' ♀H4	CBcs CDoC ECho GGGa GKir IVic LMil LRHS MAsh MGos NHol NPri SLdr SLim SReu
Dormouse Group	CBcs ECho LMil MAsh NLar SLdr SReu WBVN WFar
'Dorothea'	SLdr
'Dörte Reich'	GGGa
'Double Beauty' (EA/d)	SReu SSta
'Double Damask' (K/d) ♀H4	SLdr
double yellow-flowered (A/d)	SLdr
'Douggie Betteridge' **new**	MSnd
'Douglas McEwan'	SLdr
'Dracula' (K)	GGGa
Dragonfly Group	SReu
'Dreamland' ♀H4	CBcs CDoC CSBt CWri ECho GKir LMil LRHS MAsh MDun MGos MLea MSnd NLar SLdr SLim SReu WClo WFar
'Drury Lane' (K)	GQui LMil
dryophyllum misapplied	see *R. phaeochrysum* var. *levistratum*
'Duchess of Teck'	SReu
'Dufthecke' PBR	see *R.* 'Rhodunter 48'
Duke of Cornwall Group **new**	SLim
'Dusky Orange'	MDun SReu
'Düsselfeuer' **new**	IVic
'Dusty Miller'	GKir LHyd LRHS MAsh MDun MGos MSnd NLar SLdr
'Earl of Athlone'	LHyd SHea SReu
'Earl of Donoughmore'	LHyd SReu
'Early Beni' (EA)	LHyd
eastmanii (A) **new**	GKev
'Ebony Pearl'	CBcs CWit ECho GBin IVic MGos MMuc SLdr WBVN WGwG
eclecteum	LMil
- Cox 6054	GGGa
'Edeltraut' (EA) **new**	IVic
§ ***edgeworthii*** ♀H2-3	CBcs GGGa SLdr WAbe
- KC 0106	GGGa
'Edith Bosley'	GGGa NLar
Edmondii Group	LHyd
'Edmund de Rothschild'	NMun
'Edna Bee' (EA)	LMil
'Egret' ♀H4	ECho GEdr GGGa GKev LMil MDun MGos MLea MSnd NLar SLdr WThu
'Eider'	GGGa SLdr SReu

	'Eileen'	LMil
	'El Camino'	ECho MMuc MSnd NPCo
	'El Greco'	SLdr
	Eldorado Group	GQui
	Eleanore Group	SLdr
	Electra Group	see *R. augustinii* Electra Group
	elegantulum	GGGa IDee LMil MDun MSnd
	'Elfin Gold'	SReu
	'Elisabeth Hobbie' 𝕐H4	ECho GEdr GGGa GKir LMil SLim
	'Eliska' **new**	IVic
N	'Elizabeth' (EA)	CMac CSBt EPfP MGos SLdr
	'Elizabeth'	CTri CWri ECho GKir IVic LRHS LSRN MGos MSnd NPri SHea
	Elizabeth Group	CBcs GGGa LHyd LMil MAsh SLdr SPer SReu WFar
	'Elizabeth Jenny'	see *R.* 'Creeping Jenny'
	'Elizabeth Lockhart'	ECho GEdr GQui MDun MGos NMun
	'Elizabeth Red Foliage'	CTri GGGa GKir LHyd LMil LRHS MAsh SPer SReu
	'Elke' **new**	IVic
	elliottii	GGGa
	Elsae Group	NMun
	'Else Frye'	GGGa
	'Elsie Lee' (EA/d) 𝕐H3-4	CSBt CTrh ECho GGGa LHyd LMil MAsh MGos NPCo
	'Elsie Pratt' (A)	NHol
	'Elsie Straver'	NHol SReu
	'Elspeth'	LHyd
	'Emasculum'	LMil SLdr SReu
	'Emerald Isle' **new**	LHyd
	Emerald Isle Group	SReu
	'Emma Williams'	CBcs
	'Endsleigh Pink'	CBcs LMil MMuc
	'Erato'	LMil
	eriocarpum 'Jitsugetsuse' (EA)	LHyd
	eriogynum	see *R. facetum*
	'Ernest Inman'	LHyd LMil SLdr
	'Eruption' **new**	IVic
	'Esmeralda'	CMac
	'Etna' (EA)	SLdr
	'Etta Burrows'	CWri GGGa MDun
	'Euan Cox'	GGGa
	euchroum	MSnd
	eudoxum	GGGa MSnd
	'Europa'	SReu
	eurysiphon	MSnd
	- Arduaine form	GGGa
	'Evelyn Hyde' (EA)	SLdr
	'Evening Fragrance' (A)	LMil SReu
	'Everbloom' (EA)	SLdr
	'Everest' (EA)	LHyd LMil SPoG
	'Everestianum'	GGGa SHea
	Everred = '851C' PBR	GGGa
	exasperatum KC 0116	GGGa
	- KC 0126	GGGa
	- KW 8250	GGGa
	Exburiense Group **new**	MMuc
	'Exbury Calstocker'	LMil
	'Exbury Lady Chamberlain'	MSnd
	'Exbury Naomi'	LHyd LMil
	'Exbury White' (K)	GQui
	excellens	IDee LMil
	- AC 146	GGGa
	eximium	see *R. falconeri* subsp. *eximium*
	'Exotic'	MDun
	'Exquisitum' (O) 𝕐H4	CBcs CDoC CWri ECho EPfP GGGa LMil MBri NLar SLdr WBVN WBrE
	exquisitum	see *R. oreotrephes* Exquisitum Group
	faberi	GGGa LMil
	'Fabia' 𝕐H3	CBcs CMac GGGa LMil LRHS MDun MSnd NMun SHea
	Fabia Group	CWri SLdr
§	'Fabia Tangerine'	MLea SReu
	'Fabia Waterer'	LMil SLdr
§	***facetum***	GGGa IDee LMil
	- KR 7593	LMil
	'Faggetter's Favourite' 𝕐H4	LMil MDun SHea SReu SSta
	Fairy Light Group	LMil
	'Falcon'	see *R.* (Hawk Group) 'Hawk Falcon'
	falconeri 𝕐H3-4	CBcs CDoC CHEx CWri GGGa LMil MDun MGos MLea MSnd NPCo SLdr SPer WBVN
	- from East Nepal	MDun
§	- subsp. ***eximium***	CDoC GGGa IDee LMil MDun NLar
	'Fanal' (K)	MBri
	'Fanny'	see *R.* 'Pucella'
	'Fantastica' 𝕐H4	CDoC CWri ELan EPfP GGGa GKev IDee LHyd LMil LRHS MAsh MBri MDun MGos MLea NPCo SLdr SLim WClo
	fargesii	see *R. oreodoxa* var. *fargesii*
	'Fashion' (EA)	SLdr
	fastigiatum	GEdr LMil MSnd NMun SLdr
	- C&H 7159	GGGa
	- SBEC 804/4869	GGGa WThu
§	- 'Blue Steel' 𝕐H4	CBcs CTri CWri ECho ELon GKir IVic LMil LRHS MAsh MDun MGos NPCo SLdr SPlb SReu WPat
	'Fastuosum Flore Pleno' (d) 𝕐H4	CBcs CMac CSBt CWri EPfP GGGa GKir LHyd LMil MDun MGos MLea MSnd NLar SHea SLdr SPer SPoG SReu SSta WFar
	'Fatima'	LMil
	faucium	GGGa
	'Favorite' (EA)	LHyd NMun
	'Fawley' (K)	SLdr
	'Fedora' (EA)	CBcs SLdr
	ferrugineum	GGGa LHyd LMil MGos
	- 'Plenum' (d)	MDun
	'Festive'	LHyd
	'Festivo'	MDun
	'Feuerwerk' (K)	IVic
	fictolacteum	see *R. rex* subsp. *fictolacteum*
	Fire Bird Group	SHea SLdr
	'Fire Rim'	GGGa
	'Fireball' (K) 𝕐H4	CBcs CDoC CSam CTri CWit CWri EPfP GGGa GKev GKir LMil LRHS MAsh MBri MGos MLea MMuc NLar NMun SLdr SPer SPoG WBrE
	Firedrake Group	SReu
	'Firefly' (EA)	see *R.* 'Hexe'
	'Fireglow' (EA)	CSBt CSdC LMil WFar
	'Firelight' (hybrid)	LMil
	'Firetail'	SHea
	'Flaming Bronze'	SReu
	'Flaming Gold'	EPfP LRHS MAsh NPri
§	***flammeum*** (A)	LMil
	'Flanagan's Daughter'	GKir LMil LRHS
	'Flautando'	IVic LMil
	Flava Group	see *R.* Volker Group
	flavidum Cox 6143	GGGa
	- 'Album'	WThu
	fletcherianum 'Yellow Bunting'	GGGa
	aff. ***flinckii*** AC 5441	GLin
	floccigerum	GGGa LMil
	'Floradora' (M)	SReu
	'Floriade'	LHyd
	'Floriade' × ***yakushimanum***	SLdr

	floribundum	LMil MSnd SLdr
	- EGM 294	LMil
	'Florida' (EA/d) ♀H3-4	CMac LMil SReu WFar
	'Flower Arranger' (EA)	LMil MAsh SCoo
	formosum	CBcs GGGa GQui SLdr
§	- var. ***formosum*** Iteaphyllum Group	GGGa
	- - 'Khasia'	GGGa
	- var. ***inaequale*** C&H 301	GGGa
	forrestii	MSnd
	- KR 6113	LMil
	- subsp. ***forrestii***	LMil
	- - Repens Group	GCrs GGGa GKev LMil
	- - - 'Seinghku'	GGGa WThu
	- Tumescens Group	GGGa WThu
	- - C&V 9517	GGGa
	Fortune Group	SLdr
	fortunei	GGGa IVic LHyd LMil MDun SLdr
§	- subsp. ***discolor*** ♀H4	GGGa LMil MSnd SLdr
	- - (Houlstonii Group) 'John R. Elcock'	LMil
	- - var. ***kwangfuense*** AC 5208 **new**	LMil
	- - 'Nymphenrose' **new**	IVic
	- 'Lu-Shan'	MDun
	- 'Mrs Butler'	see *R. fortunei* 'Sir Charles Butler'
§	- 'Sir Charles Butler'	LMil
	'Fox Hunter'	SLdr
	fragariiflorum C&V 9519	GGGa
	- LS&E 15828	GGGa
	'Fragrans' (Ad)	SLdr
	'Fragrant Star' (A)	GGGa
	'Fragrantissimum' ♀H2-3	CBcs CMac CSBt CTsd CWri GGGa GGal IDee LHyd LMil MRav NLar NMun SKHP SLdr
	'Francesca'	GGGa
	Francis Hanger Group	SLdr SReu
	'Frank Baum'	SReu
	'Frank Galsworthy' ♀H4	LMil SReu
	'Fraseri' (M)	SLdr
	'Fred Hamilton'	CWri
	'Fred Peste'	CDoC ECho GKir LMil MAsh MBri MDun MGos MLea MMuc MSnd NLar NPCo SLim SReu
	'Fred Wynniatt'	MSnd SLdr
	'Frentano' **new**	IVic
	'Freya' (R/d)	LMil
	'Fridtjof Nansen' (A) **new**	SLdr
	'Frilled Petticoats'	SReu
	'Frosted Orange' (EA)	LMil MAsh
	'Frosthexe'	GGGa
	'Frühlingsbeginn' **new**	IVic
	'Frühlingstraum'	LHyd
	'Fulbrook'	LMil
	fulgens	GGGa LMil MDun MSnd
	fulvum ♀H4	CDoC GGGa IDee LHyd LMil MDun MSnd NLar SReu SSta
	- KR 7614	LMil
	- subsp. ***fulvoides***	LMil
	- - Cox 6532	GGGa
§	'Fumiko' (EA)	CBcs CChe CSBt CWit ELon LRHS MAsh MGos MLea MMuc NLar NMun NPCo SLim WFar
	'Furnivall's Daughter' ♀H4	CMac CSBt CWri ECho EPfP GGGa GKir LHyd LMil MGos MMuc MSnd NLar SHea SLdr SPer SReu SSta WFar
	'Fusilier'	SHea SReu
	'Gabrielle Hill' (EA)	MAsh MGos SLdr
	'Gaiety' (EA)	LMil LRHS SPoG SReu
	galactinum	IDee LMil MDun
	- EN 3537	GGGa
	'Gandy Dancer'	CWri MLea
	'Garden State Glow' (EA/d)	SLdr
	'Garibaldi'	SHea
	'Garnet'	SHea SLdr
	'Gartendirektor Glocker'	CWri ECho GGGa IVic MAsh MDun MSnd SLim
	'Gartendirektor Rieger' ♀H4	CWri GGGa IVic LMil MDun SHea SReu
	'Gauche' (A)	GQui SLdr
	'Gaugin'	GQui
	'Geisha' (EA)	GKir
	'Geisha Lilac'	see *R.* 'Hanako'
	'Geisha Orange'	see *R.* 'Satschiko'
	'Geisha Pink'	see *R.* 'Momoko'
	'Geisha Purple'	see *R.* 'Fumiko'
	'Geisha Red'	see *R.* 'Kazuko'
	'Geisha White'	see *R.* 'Hisako'
	'Gena Mae' (A/d)	GGGa SLdr
	'General Eisenhower'	SHea SReu
	'General Eric Harrison'	SLdr
	'General Practitioner'	MSnd SLdr
	'General Wavell' (EA)	CMac SLdr
	'Gene's Favourite'	SReu
	genestierianum CC&H 8080	GGGa
	'Genoveva'	LMil
	'Geoffrey Millais'	LMil
	'Georg Arends' (Ad)	EPfP GKir LRHS MAsh SLdr SLim
	'George Hyde' (EA)	LRHS LSRN MAsh MGos SCoo
	'George Johnstone'	SLdr
	'George's Delight'	MSnd
	'Georgette'	LHyd
§	× ***geraldii***	SLdr
	'Germania'	LMil LRHS MAsh NPri SPoG SReu
	Gertrud Schäle Group	CDoC CTri GEdr SHea SReu
	'Gibraltar' (K) ♀H4	CBcs CDoC CMac CSBt CTri CWri EPfP GGGa GKir LMil LRHS MAsh MBri MDun MGos NLar SLdr SLim SReu SSta WFar
	Gibraltar Group	CTri
	giganteum	see *R. protistum* var. *giganteum*
	'Gilbert Mullie' (EA)	LMil LRHS SLim
	'Gill's Crimson'	SHea SReu
	'Ginger' (K)	CSBt CWri LMil LRHS
	'Ginny Gee' ♀H4	CBcs CDoC CSBt CWri ECho EPfP EPot GEdr GGGa GGar GKev GKir IVic LHyd LMil LRHS MAsh MGos MLea MMuc MSnd NEgg NHol NLar SLdr SPoG SReu SSta WFar WPat
§	'Girard's Hot Shot' (EA)	CChe ECho GQui MAsh MGos SReu WFar
	'Girard's Hot Shot' variegated (EA/v)	ECho GGGa LMil MAsh NMun
	'Glacier' (EA)	MGos
	glanduliferum C&H 7131	GGGa
	- EGM 347	LMil
	glaucophyllum	GGGa LMil MDun MSnd NMun
	- B&SWJ 2638	WCru
	- Borde Hill form	LMil
§	- subsp. ***tubiforme***	NMun
	Glendoick Butterscotch = 'Gle003'	GGGa
	Glendoick Dream = 'Gle005' (EA)	GGGa
	Glendoick Ermine = 'Gle006' (EA)	GGGa
	Glendoick Frolic = 'Gle007'	GGGa
	Glendoick Garnet = 'Gle008' (EA)	GGGa
	Glendoick Glacier = 'Gle009' (EA)	GGGa

Glendoick Goblin = 'Gle010' (EA)	GGGa
Glendoick Gold = 'Gle011'	GGGa
Glendoick Honeydew = 'Gle012'	GGGa
Glendoick Ice Cream = 'Gle013'	GGGa
Glendoick Mystique = 'Gle014'	GGGa
Glendoick Petticoats = 'Gle015'	GGGa
Glendoick Rosebud = 'Gle022' (EA)	GGGa
Glendoick Ruby = 'Gle016'	GGGa
Glendoick Silver	GGGa
Glendoick Snowflakes = 'Gle001' (EA)	GGGa
Glendoick Vanilla = 'Gle017'	GGGa
Glendoick Velvet = 'Gle018'	GGGa
'Gletschernacht'	CWri IVic
glischrum	GGGa MSnd
- subsp. ***glischroides***	GGGa LMil
- subsp. ***glischrum***	GGGa
§ - subsp. ***rude***	GGGa
- - C&V 9524	GGGa
globigerum	see *R. alutaceum* var. *alutaceum* Globigerum Group
'Glockenspiel' (K/d)	SLdr
glomerulatum	see *R. yungningense* Glomerulatum Group
'Gloria'	see *R.* 'Bruns Gloria'
'Gloria Mundi' (G)	SHea
'Glory of Littleworth' (Ad)	LMil
'Glowing Embers' (K)	CBcs CDoC CMac CSam CTri CWri ECho GKir LRHS MAsh MBri MDun MLea NHol SLdr SLim SPur SReu WBVN
'Goblin' **new**	MSnd
Goblin Group	SLdr
'Gog' (K)	CSBt
'Gold Mohur'	SReu
§ 'Goldbukett'	GGGa LHyd
'Golden Bee'	GGGa NHol
'Golden Belle'	CWri
Golden Bouquet	see *R.* 'Goldbukett'
'Golden Clipper'	LHyd
'Golden Coach'	CWri ECho MGos MSnd SLdr SPer WBVN
'Golden Eagle' (K)	CBcs CDoC CWit ECho GGar LMil MBri MDun MGos NLar SLdr WBVN WMoo
'Golden Flare' (A)	CBcs CDoC CSBt CSam CWri ECho LRHS MAsh MBri MGos MLea MMuc NEgg NMun NPCo SLdr SPoG WBrE
'Golden Fleece'	SReu
'Golden Gate'	CDoC CSBt ECho MMuc NLar NMun SReu WFar
'Golden Horn' (K)	GQui
Golden Horn Group	SLdr
'Golden Lights' (A)	CWri ECho LMil MBri MGos MLea NEgg NPCo WBVN WGwG
'Golden Orfe'	LHyd
Golden Oriole Group	NHol
§ - 'Talavera'	SSpi
'Golden Oriole Talavera'	see *R.* (Golden Oriole Group) 'Talavera'
'Golden Princess'	LMil NHol
'Golden Ruby'	ECho MGos SPer
'Golden Splendour'	LMil SLdr
'Golden Sunset' (K)	CMac CSdC ECho LMil LRHS MAsh MBri MGos MLea NHol NLar SLdr
'Golden Torch' ♀H4	CBcs CDoC CMHG CSBt CWit CWri ECho EPfP GGar GKir LHyd LMil LRHS MAsh MBri MDun MGos MLea MSnd NLar NPri SLdr SLim SPer SPoG SReu SSta WBVN WFar
'Golden Wedding'	CBcs CSBt CWit CWri ECho LHyd LMil LSRN MAsh MDun MGos MMuc NPCo SLdr SPoG WBVN
'Golden Wit'	MAsh MMHG MMuc NEgg
'Goldfinch' (K)	SLdr
'Goldfinger'	MGos
'Goldflimmer' (v)	CDoC GGGa LMil LRHS MAsh MGos MLea NPri SLim SPoG SReu WFar
'Goldfort'	SReu
'Goldika'	LMil LRHS
'Goldkollier'	IVic
'Goldkrone' ♀H4	CWri EPfP GGGa LHyd LMil MAsh MGos MLea SPoG SReu
'Goldpracht' (K) **new**	IVic
Goldschatz = 'Goldprinz'	GGGa IVic LMil
'Goldsworth Crimson'	LHyd
'Goldsworth Orange'	CSBt CWri ECho MGos MSnd SLdr
'Goldsworth Yellow'	CSBt MGos
'Goldtopas' (K)	LMil LRHS
'Golfer'	CWri GGGa LMil MLea
'Gomer Waterer' ♀H4	CDoC CMac CSBt CWri ECho EPfP GGGa GKir LHyd LMil LRHS LTen MAsh MDun MGos MMuc MSnd SLdr SPer SPoG SReu SSta WBVN WFar
gongshanense	GGGa
'Gorbella'	SLim
'Gordian'	MDun
Gowenianum Group (Ad)	LMil
'Grace Seabrook'	CSBt CTri CWit CWri ECho GGGa GKir LHyd MDun MGos MMuc MSnd NPCo SLdr SPer SReu
gracilentum (V)	GGGa
'Graciosum' (O)	SReu
'Graffito'	IVic LMil
'Graham Thomas'	LMil SReu
'Grand Slam'	ECho MLea MSnd
grande	GGGa MSnd SLdr
- pink-flowered	MSnd
'Grandeur Triomphante' (G)	CSdC
gratum	see *R. basilicum*
'Graziella'	GGGa LMil LRHS MDun
'Greensleeves'	LMil
'Greenway' (EA)	CBcs SLdr
'Grenadier'	SHea
'Greta' (EA)	LHyd
'Gretzel'	SReu
griersonianum	CBcs GGGa LHyd LMil MDun
griersonianum* × *yakushimanum	SLdr
griffithianum	GGGa SLdr
'Gristede' ♀H4	ECho LMil MGos NHol SReu WBVN
groenlandicum	see *Ledum groenlandicum*
'Grosclaude'	CMac SHea
'Grouse' × ***keiskei*** var. ***ozawae*** 'Yaku Fairy'	ECho
'Grumpy'	CBcs CSBt CWri ECho GGGa GKir LHyd LMil LRHS MAsh MGos SLdr SReu
'Gumpo' (EA)	CBcs CMac
'Gumpo Pink' (EA)	SLdr

	'Gumpo White' (EA)	LRHS MAsh MGos NLar NMun
	'Gwenda' (EA)	CTri LHyd SLdr
	'Gwillt-king'	CBcs
	habrotrichum	GGGa LMil SLdr
	'Hachmann's Anastasia'	LMil NLar
	'Hachmann's Bananaflip'	NLar
	'Hachmann's Brasilia'	MDun
	'Hachmann's Charmant'	IVic LMil SPoG
	'Hachmann's Constanze'	LMil
	'Hachmann's Diadem'	LMil
	'Hachmann's Eskimo'	LMil
	'Hachmann's Feuerschein'	LMil
	'Hachmann's Juliette' (EA) **new**	IVic
	'Hachmann's Junifeuer'	IVic LMil
	'Hachmann's Kabarett'	LMil NLar
	'Hachmann's Marianne'	LMil
	'Hachmann's Marlis' Ψ^{H4}	LHyd LMil LRHS
	'Hachmann's Pinguin' **new**	IVic
§	'Hachmann's Polaris' Ψ^{H4}	CDoC LHyd LMil MBri NLar SLdr SLim
	'Hachmann's Porzellan' Ψ^{H4}	LMil
§	'Hachmann's Rokoko' (EA)	LMil NMun
	'Hachmann's Topsi' **new**	IVic
	haematodes	GGGa IDee LHyd LMil LRHS MDun MSnd SRms
§	- subsp. ***chaetomallum***	LMil SLdr
	- - JN 493	GGGa
	- subsp. ***haematodes***	LMil
	- - SBEC 585	GGGa
	'Haida Gold'	SReu
	'Halfdan Lem'	CBcs CDoC ECho GGGa LHyd LTen MAsh MBri MGos MLea MMuc MSnd SLdr SLim SPer SReu SSta WBVN
	'Hallauer's Seedling' **new**	ESem
	'Hallelujah'	IVic
	'Halopeanum'	LMil SHea SLdr
	'Hamlet' (M)	LMil
	'Hampshire Belle'	LMil
	'Hana-asobi' (EA)	LHyd
§	'Hanako' (EA)	GKir MGos MLea
	hanceanum 'Canton Consul'	GGGa
	- Nanum Group	CBcs GGGa
	'Hanger's Flame' (A)	LMil
	'Hansel'	CDoC CWri ECho GQui LMil MAsh MDun SLdr WFar
	haofui Guiz 75	GGGa
	Happy Group	CMac ECho
	'Hardijzer Beauty' (Ad)	MSnd SLdr
	hardyi	see *R. augustinii* subsp. *hardyi*
	'Harkwood Moonlight'	LMil
	'Harkwood Premiere'	GGGa
	'Harkwood Red' (EA)	SLdr
	'Harvest Moon' (K)	GKir SCoo SLdr SReu
	'Harvest Moon' (hybrid)	CSBt MMuc SReu
	'Hatsu-giri' (EA)	CMac LHyd LMil SLdr SReu
	Hawk Group **new**	SLdr
§	- 'Hawk Falcon'	SReu
	'Heather Macleod' (EA)	SLdr
	heatheriae	IDee LMil
	- KR 6158	GGGa
	- KR 6176	LMil
	'Heidi'^{PBR} (EA) **new**	SLdr
	'Helen Close' (EA)	SLdr
	'Helen Curtis' (EA)	SLdr SReu
	'Helene Schiffner' Ψ^{H4}	GGGa LMil SReu
	heliolepis	GGGa LMil
	hemidartum	see *R. pocophorum* var. *hemidartum*
	hemitrichotum	WThu
	hemsleyanum	GGGa IDee LMil MDun MSnd SLdr
	heptamerum	see *R. degronianum* subsp. *heptamerum*
	'Herbert' (EA)	CMac SLim
	'Heureuse Surprise' (G)	SLdr
§	'Hexe' (EA)	CTrh
	'High Summer'	LMil SLdr
	'Hilda Margaret'	SReu
	'Hilda Niblett' (EA)	MGos
	'Hille'	LMil
	'Hinamayo'	see *R.* (Obtusum Group) 'Hinomayo'
	'Hino-crimson' (EA) Ψ^{H3-4}	CBcs CDoC CMac CSBt CTri LMil MAsh MBri MGos MMuc NHol SLdr SPer SPoG SReu SSta WFar
	'Hinodegiri'	CBcs CMac CSBt LHyd SLdr SReu WFar
	'Hinode-no-taka' (EA)	LHyd
	hippophaeoides	LMil MDun MSnd SLdr WAbe WFar
	- Yu 13845	LMil MDun
	- 'Bei-ma-shan'	see *R. hippophaeoides* 'Haba Shan'
	- 'Blue Silver'	EGxp GGGa IVic LMil MAsh NLar NMun
	- Glendoick Iceberg = 'Gle019'	GGGa
§	- 'Haba Shan' Ψ^{H4}	GGGa LMil MDun WThu
	- var. ***hippophaeoides*** Fimbriatum Group	NMun
	hirsutum	GGGa LMil
	- f. ***albiflorum***	GGGa SReu
	- 'Flore Pleno' (d)	ECho GCrs GEdr MDun
	hirtipes	GGGa
	- C&V 9546	GGGa
§	'Hisako' (EA)	GEdr
	hodgsonii	GGGa GKir IDee LMil MDun NHol SLdr
	'Holden'	MAsh WFar
	'Homebush' (K/d) Ψ^{H4}	CBcs CDoC CMac CTri CWri EPfP GGGa GKev LHyd LMil MAsh MBri MDun MGos NPCo SLdr SPer SPoG SSta WBVN
	'Honey Butter'	LMil SLim
	'Honeysuckle' (K)	NHol SReu
	hongkongense	GGGa
§	'Ho-o' (EA)	CBcs NLar SLdr
	hookeri	SReu
	- 'Golden Gate'	SLim
	- Tigh-na-Rudha form	GGGa
	'Hope Findlay'	LHyd
	'Hoppy'	CBcs CSBt CWit CWri GKir LMil LRHS MAsh MDun MGos MLea MMuc MSnd NLar NMun SLdr SLim SPoG WBVN
	'Horizon Monarch' Ψ^{H3-4}	CDoC CWit CWri GGGa IVic LHyd LMil LRHS MDun MLea SLdr SLim WBVN
	horlickianum	GGGa
	'Hortulanus H. Witte' (M)	CSBt SReu WFar
	'Hot Shot'	see *R.* 'Girard's Hot Shot'
	'Hot Shot Variegated' (EA/v)	CDoC NEgg SLdr
	'Hotei' Ψ^{H4}	CDoC CSBt CWri ECho EPfP GGGa GKir LHyd LMil MAsh MDun MGos NEgg NPCo NPri SLdr SReu WBVN WFar
	'Hotspur' (K)	CSBt CSam CWri ECho GBin MGos NLar SLdr
	Hotspur Group (K)	LHyd
	'Hotspur Red' (K) Ψ^{H4}	CDoC GKev LMil NEgg NPCo SReu WMoo
	'Hotspur Yellow' (K)	SReu
	huanum	LMil
	- C&H 7073	GGGa

- EGM 316	LMil
'Hugh Koster'	CSBt MGos SLdr
aff. ***huidongense*** KR 7315	LMil
'Hullaballoo'	LMil
'Humboldt'	WFar
Humming Bird Group	CBcs CMHG GEdr LHyd MDun NHol SLdr SRms
hunnewellianum	MSnd
'Hussar'	CWri
'Hyde and Seek'	GQui
'Hydie' (EA/d)	MGos SPoG
'Hydon Amethyst'	LHyd
'Hydon Ben'	LHyd
'Hydon Comet'	LHyd
'Hydon Dawn' 𝕐^{H4}	CDoC CWri GGGa GKir LHyd LMil MAsh MGos MLea MSnd SHea SLdr SReu SSta WClo
'Hydon Glow'	LHyd
'Hydon Gold'	LHyd
'Hydon Haley'	LHyd
'Hydon Hunter' 𝕐^{H4}	LHyd LMil MSnd SHea SLdr SReu SSta
'Hydon Mist'	LHyd
'Hydon Pearl'	LHyd
'Hydon Pink'	SHea
'Hydon Rodney'	LHyd
'Hydon Velvet'	IVic LHyd LMil SReu
hylaeum	MSnd
- BASEX 9659	GGGa
Hyperion Group	SReu SSta WFar
hyperythrum	GGGa LHyd NMun SLdr
hypoglaucum	see *R. argyrophyllum* subsp. *hypoglaucum*
'Ice Cube'	ECho MBri MMuc NLar SLdr WFar
'Ice Music'	GGGa
'Iceberg'	see *R.* 'Lodauric Iceberg'
'Idealist'	CWri SReu
'Ightham Gold'	SReu
'Ightham Peach'	SReu
'Ightham Purple'	SReu
'Ightham Yellow'	SHea SLdr SReu
'Igneum Novum' (G)	SReu
§ 'Ilam Melford Lemon' (A)	LMil LRHS
§ 'Ilam Ming' (A)	LMil
'Ilam Violet'	LHyd LMil
'Imago' (K/d)	CSdC LMil SLdr
§ 'Ima-shojo' (EA/d)	CMac LHyd LRHS MGos SLim
impeditum	CBcs CSBt CWib CWit ECho GGGa GKev GQui LHyd MGos MLea MMuc MSnd NWCA SLdr SPer SReu SSta WBVN WBrE WFar
- F 29268	GGGa
- 'Blue Steel'	see *R. fastigiatum* 'Blue Steel'
- 'Indigo'	LLHF MAsh MGos NPCo SLdr WAbe WGwG
- 'Pygmaeum'	GEdr WAbe WThu
- Reuthe's form	SReu
- 'Williams'	NMun
imperator	see *R. uniflorum* var. *imperator*
'Impi'	MSnd NMun SReu
Impi Group	MDun
inconspicuum (V)	SLim
§ ***indicum*** 'Macranthum' (EA)	LHyd SLdr
insigne 𝕐^{H4}	GGGa GLin LMil MSnd NLar
- Reuthe's form	SReu
insigne × ***yakushimanum***	SReu
Intrepid Group	SReu
intricatum	GGGa
Intrifast Group	GGGa LHyd
iodes	see *R. alutaceum* var. *iodes*
'Irene Koster' (O) 𝕐^{H4}	CDoC CSBt CWri EPfP GGGa LHyd LMil MBri MLea NEgg NLar SLdr SLim SSpi
'Irish Mist'	GGGa
'Irohayama' (EA) 𝕐$^{H3-4}$	CMac EPfP GQui LHyd LMil LRHS MAsh NPri SLdr
irroratum	LMil
- KR 7711	LMil
- subsp. ***irroratum*** C&H 7100	GGGa
* - subsp. ***kontumense*** var. ***ningyuenense***	GLin
- 'Polka Dot'	GGGa LHyd LMil
- subsp. ***yiliangense*** EGM 339	LMil
'Isabel'	NPri
'Isabel' (EA) **new**	MAsh
'Isabel Pierce'	CWri
Isabella Group	WFar
'Isola Bella'	GGGa
iteaphyllum	see *R. formosum* var. *formosum* Iteaphyllum Group
'Ivery's Scarlet'	GKir
'Ivette' (EA)	CMac LHyd
Iviza Group	SReu
'J.C. Williams'	CBcs
'J.G. Millais'	SLdr
'J.J. de Vink'	SHea
'J.M. de Montague'	see *R.* 'The Hon. Jean Marie de Montague'
'Jabberwocky'	LHyd
'Jack Skilton'	LHyd
'Jacksonii'	SHea
Jalisco Group	SLdr
'Jalisco Eclipse'	LMil MSnd
'Jalisco Elect'	CWri SLdr
'Jalisco Goshawk'	SHea
'Jalisco Janet'	LMil SHea SLdr
'James Barto'	LHyd SLdr
'James Burchett' 𝕐^{H4}	LMil SLdr SReu
'James Gable' (EA)	MAsh SLdr
'Jan Bee'	SLdr
'Jan Dekens'	SReu
'Janet Blair'	CWri MDun
'Janet Ward'	LHyd SReu
japonicum (A. Gray) Valcken	see *R. molle* subsp. *japonicum*
japonicum Schneider var. ***japonicum***	see *R. degronianum* subsp. *heptamerum*
- var. ***pentamerum***	see *R. degronianum* subsp. *degronianum*
javanicum (V)	GGGa
'Jean Marie Montague'	see *R.* 'The Hon. Jean Marie de Montague'
'Jeff Hill' (EA)	ECho MMuc SReu
'Jenny'	see *R.* 'Creeping Jenny'
'Jeremy Davies'	SReu
'Jervis Bay'	SReu
'Jingle Bells'	GGGa
'Joan Paton' (A)	SLdr
'Joanna'	MMuc MNHC
'Jocelyne' **new**	LMil
'Jock'	SLdr
Jock Group	CBcs CMHG
'Jock Brydon' (O)	GGGa IDee LMil
'Jock Coutts' (K)	CSdC
'Johann Sebastian Bach' (EA)	SLdr
'Johann Strauss' (EA)	GKir
'Johanna' (EA) 𝕐^{H4}	CBcs CDoC CTri EPfP GGGa GKir IVic LMil LRHS MAsh MMHG NHol NLar NPri SLdr SPer SReu

	'John Cairns' (EA)	CMac LHyd SLdr
	'John Walter'	SHea
	'John Waterer'	SHea WFar
	'Johnny Bender'	SLdr
	johnstoneanum	CBcs GGGa GGal LMil MSnd NMun SLdr
	- KW 7732	SLdr
	- 'Double Diamond' (d)	LMil
	'Jolie Madame' (Vs)	CSam CWri ECho LMil MBri MLea NLar SLdr SPur SReu
	'Joseph Baumann' (G)	CSdC SLdr
	'Joseph Hill' (EA)	ECho MGos MMuc NHol SReu
	'Josephine Klinger' (G)	CSdC SReu
	'Jubilant'	LMil SHea
	'Jubilee'	SLdr
	'June Fire' (A)	MDun SReu
	kaempferi (EA)	CBcs LHyd LMil
	- 'Damio'	see *R. kaempferi* 'Mikado'
§	- 'Mikado' (EA)	LMil SLdr SReu
	- orange-flowered (EA)	CMac
	'Kakiemon' (EA)	LHyd
	'Kalinka'	LMil LRHS MAsh NHol NLar SLdr SPoG
	'Kaponga'	MGos
	'Karen Triplett'	LMil
	'Karin'	MDun SLdr
	'Kasane-kagaribi' (EA)	LHyd
	kasoense HECC 10009	GGGa
	'Kate Waterer' ♀^{H4}	CWri MDun MGos SReu WFar
	'Kathleen' van Nes (EA)	LHyd SLdr
	'Katisha' (EA)	LHyd SLdr
	'Katy Watson'	SReu SSta
	kawakamii (V)	GGGa
§	'Kazuko' (EA)	GEdr MGos NLar SLim WFar
	'Keija' (EA)	SLdr
	keiskei	LLHF
	- var. ***ozawae*** 'Yaku Fairy' ♀^{H4}	GGGa ITim LMil WAbe WThu
	keleticum	see *R. calostrotum* subsp. *keleticum*
	'Ken Janeck' ♀^{H4}	GGGa
§	***kendrickii***	GGGa
	'Kentucky Colonel'	SLdr
	'Kermesinum' (EA)	CTri MAsh MGos NMun SLdr SLim SPlb SReu
I	'Kermesinum Album' (EA)	MGos SReu
I	'Kermesinum Rosé' (EA)	CSBt ECho GGGa LMil MGos MLea SLdr SLim SReu
	'Kerrigan's Super Red' (EA)	CTrh
	kesangiae	LMil MDun
	- AC 5343	LMil
	- CH&M 3058	GGGa
	- CH&M 3099	GGGa
	- KCSH 0347	LMil
	- var. ***album*** KCSH 0362	GGGa
	Kewense Group	CSBt LHyd
	keysii	CBcs GGGa MDun
	- EGM 064	LMil
	- KC 0115	GGGa
	'Kilian' (A)	LRHS MAsh
	'Kilimanjaro'	LMil SReu
	'Kimbeth'	GGGa
	'Kimigayo' (EA)	LHyd
	'King Fisher'	NMun
	'King George' Loder	see *R.* 'Loderi King George'
	'King George' van Nes	SReu
	kingianum	see *R. arboreum* subsp. *zeylanicum*
	'Kings Ride'	IVic LHyd
§	'Kirin' (Kurume) (EA/d)	CBcs CMac CSBt LHyd LMil SLdr
	'Kirishima' (EA)	SRms
	'Kiritsubo' (Kurume) (EA)	LHyd
	'Kirsten Begeer' **new**	IVic
	kiusianum (EA) ♀^{H4}	LHyd LMil SReu SRms
I	- 'Album' (EA)	LHyd LMil SReu
	- 'Hillier's Pink' (EA)	LMil
	'Kiwi Majic'	LMil MDun
	'Kleiner Prinz' (EA) **new**	IVic
	'Klondyke' (K) ♀^{H4}	CBcs CSBt CTri EPfP GGGa GKir LMil LRHS MAsh MGos NLar SLdr SReu
	'Kluis Sensation' ♀^{H4}	CMac CSBt LHyd MDun MSnd NHol SLdr SReu
	'Kluis Triumph'	SReu
	'Knap Hill Apricot' (K)	CSdC LMil
	'Knap Hill Red' (K)	CDoC LMil
	'Knap Hill White' (K)	CSdC
	'Kobold' (EA)	SLdr
	'Koichiro Wada'	see *R. yakushimanum* 'Koichiro Wada'
	'Kokardia'	LMil LRHS NLar
	'Kokette' **new**	IVic
	kongboense	GGGa WAbe
	- C&V 9540	GGGa
	'Königstein' (EA)	LMil
§	'Koningin Emma' (M)	LMil NLar
	'Koningin Wilhelmina' (EA) **new**	SLdr
	konori var. ***phaeopeplum*** (V)	GGGa
	'Koromo-shikibu' (EA)	GGGa GKir
	'Koromo-shikibu White' (EA)	GGGa
	'Koster's Brilliant Red' (M)	CSBt EPfP MGos SReu
§	'Kure-no-yuki' (EA/d)	EPfP LHyd LMil MAsh MMuc
	'Lackblatt'	see *R.* (Volker Group) 'Lackblatt'
	lacteum	LMil MDun
	- SBEC 345	GGGa
	'Lady Alice Fitzwilliam' ♀$^{H2-3}$	CBcs CEnd CMHG CMac GGGa IDee LHyd LMil
	'Lady Chamberlain Salmon Trout'	see *R.* 'Salmon Trout'
	'Lady Clementine Mitford' ♀^{H4}	CSBt CWri ECho EPfP GQui LHyd LMil MBri MDun MGos MLea MMuc SHea SLdr SPer SReu
	'Lady Digby'	CWri
	'Lady Eleanor Cathcart'	SHea SLdr
	'Lady Grey Egerton'	SHea
	'Lady Linda' **new**	MSnd
	'Lady Longman'	LHyd
	'Lady Louise' (EA)	SLdr
	'Lady Primrose'	SReu
	'Lady Robin' (EA)	SLdr
	'Lady Romsey' ♀^{H4}	LMil MSnd
	'Lady Rosebery' (K)	CSdC
	Ladybird Group	SReu
	laetum (V)	GGGa
	Lamellen Group	LHyd
	'Lampion'	GGGa
	'Lamplighter'	SHea SReu
	lanatoides	LMil
	- C&C 7548	GGGa
	- C&C 7574	GGGa
	- C&C 7577	GGGa
	- KR 6385	LMil
§	***lanatum***	ECho GGGa LMil MDun
	- CH&M 3080	GGGa
	- dwarf, cream-flowered	GGGa
	- Flinckii Group	see *R. lanatum*
	'Langworth'	CWit CWri ECho GQui LMil MGos MLea MSnd SLdr SReu WBVN
	lanigerum	LMil MDun MSnd SReu
	- C&V 9530	GGGa
	- KW 8251	GGGa

	'Lanzette' **new**	IVic
	lapponicum Confertissimum Group	GGGa
	- Parvifolium Group from Siberia	GGGa WAbe
	'Lapwing' (K)	SLdr
	'Laramie'	GGGa
	'Lascaux'	SReu
	'Late Love' (EA)	CDoC MGos
§	***latoucheae*** (EA) PW 86	GGGa
	laudandum var. ***temoense***	GGGa
	Laura Aberconway Group	SHea SLdr
	'Laura Morland' (EA)	LHyd
	'Lava Flow'	LHyd
	'Lavender Girl' ♀H4	CMac LHyd LMil MSnd SHea SLdr SReu SSta
	'Lavendula'	IVic
	'Le Progrès'	LMil
	'Lea Rainbow'	MLea
	'Ledifolium'	see *R.* × *mucronatum*
	'Ledifolium Album'	see *R.* × *mucronatum*
	'Lee's Dark Purple'	CSBt CWri LMil WFar
	'Lee's Scarlet'	LMil
	'Lem'	SReu
	'Lemon Cloud'	IVic
	'Lemon Dream'	LMil MDun SLim
*	'Lemon Drop' (A)	GGGa
	'Lemon Lights' (A)	LMil
	'Lemon Marmalade'	MDun
	'Lemon Meringue'	LMil
	'Lemonora' (M)	CBcs MBri
	'Lem's 45'	CWri ECho SLdr
	'Lem's Cameo' ♀H3	GGGa LHyd LMil SReu SSta
	'Lem's Monarch' ♀H4	CBcs CDoC CWri GGGa GKir LHyd LMil MBri MGos MLea MMuc SLdr SReu SSta
	'Lem's Tangerine'	CDoC LMil
	'Lemur' (EA)	ECho GEdr GGGa MAsh MLea NHol SReu WThu
	'Leni'	LRHS MAsh
	'Leny' (EA)	NHol
	'Leo' (EA)	GQui LHyd SLdr
	'Leonardslee Giles'	SLdr
	'Leonardslee Primrose'	SLdr
	Leonore Group	SReu
	lepidostylum	CBcs CMac CWri GGGa ITim LMil MDun NHol SLdr SReu WFar
	lepidotum	GGGa MDun WAbe
	- Elaeagnoides Group	GGGa
	- yellow-flowered McB 110	WThu
§	***leptocarpum***	GGGa
	Letty Edwards Group	CSBt SReu
§	'Leucanthum'	GGGa IVic WThu
	leucaspis	GGGa LHyd MDun NMun SLdr SReu WAbe
	'Leuchtpolster' **new**	IVic
	levinei	GGGa
	'Lewis Monarch'	GQui
	'Lila Pedigo'	CWri ECho MBri MGos SPer WBVN WFar
	'Lilac Time' (EA)	SLdr
	liliiflorum Guiz 163	GGGa
	'Lily Marleen' (EA)	CTri SCoo SReu
	'Linda' ♀H4	CBcs CSam CTri ECho EPfP GGGa LMil LRHS LSRN MAsh MGos MMuc SLdr
	'Linda Lee'	SLdr
	'Linda R' (EA)	NPri
	lindleyi	CBcs GQui LHyd
	- L&S	GGGa
	- 'Dame Edith Sitwell'	LMil
	'Linearifolium'	see *R. stenopetalum* 'Linearifolium'
	'Lionel's First' **new**	LMil
	Lionel's Triumph Group	LMil
	'Lissabon' **new**	IVic
	'Little Beauty' (EA)	SLdr
	'Little Ben'	ECho GEdr MDun
	'Loch Awe'	GGGa
	'Loch Earn'	GGGa
	'Loch Laggan'	GGGa
	'Loch Leven'	GGGa
	'Loch Linnhe'	GGGa
	'Loch Lomond'	GGGa
	'Loch Morar'	GGGa
	'Loch o' the Lowes'	MBri MGos WFar
	'Loch Rannoch'	MGos WFar
	'Loch Tummel'	GGGa
	lochiae misapplied	see *R. viriosum*
	'Lochinch Spinbur'	GQui
	Lodauric Group	SReu
§	'Lodauric Iceberg' ♀H3-4	LMil MSnd SReu
	'Lodbrit'	SReu
	'Loderi Fairy Queen'	SLdr
	'Loderi Fairyland'	LHyd
	'Loderi Game Chick' ♀H3-4	LHyd SLdr SReu
	'Loderi Georgette'	SLdr
	Loderi Group	SLdr
	'Loderi Helen'	SLdr
§	'Loderi King George' ♀H3-4	CBcs CDoC CMac CSBt CWit CWri ECho GGGa IVic LHyd LMil LRHS MDun MGos MLea MSnd NLar SLdr SPer SReu SSta WBVN WGwG
	'Loderi Patience'	SLdr
	'Loderi Pink Coral'	LMil SLdr
	'Loderi Pink Diamond' ♀H3-4	CDoC CWri GGGa LMil SLdr
	'Loderi Pink Topaz' ♀H3-4	LHyd SLdr
	'Loderi Pretty Polly'	CWri SLdr
	'Loderi Princess Marina'	SLdr
	'Loderi Sir Edmund'	LHyd SLdr
	'Loderi Sir Joseph Hooker'	LHyd SLdr
	'Loderi Titan'	SLdr SReu
	'Loderi Venus' ♀H3-4	CWri LHyd SLdr SReu SSta
	'Loderi White Diamond'	LHyd SLdr
	'Loder's White' ♀H3-4	CWri LHyd LMil MLea SHea SLdr SReu SSta
§	'Logan Damaris'	LHyd SReu
	longesquamatum	GGGa MSnd
	longipes	LMil SLdr
	- EGM 336	LMil
	- var. ***longipes*** C&H 7113	GGGa
	longistylum	GGGa
	'Lord Roberts' ♀H4	CBcs CDoC CMac CSBt CTri CWri ECho EPfP GGGa GKir IVic LMil MAsh MGos MLea MMuc MSnd NEgg SHea SLdr SLim SReu WFar
	'Lord Swaythling'	LHyd
	'Loreley'	IVic NLar
	'Lori Eichelser'	GEdr
	'Lorna' (EA)	LMil
	'Louis Pasteur'	SReu
	'Louisa Hill' (EA)	MGos
	'Louise Dowdle' (EA)	SLdr
	'Lovely William'	CMac LMil MSnd SLdr
	lowndesii	WAbe
	luciferum CER 9935	GGGa
	'Lucy'	NMun
	'Lucy Lou'	GGGa
	ludlowii	GGGa
	'Luisella' **new**	IVic
	'Lullaby' (EA)	GKir
	'Lunar Queen'	LHyd SLdr

	luteiflorum KW 21556	GGGa
	lutescens	CBcs LMil MDun MSnd SLdr SReu SSta WAbe
	- C&H 7124	GGGa
	- 'Bagshot Sands' ♀H3-4	GGGa IDee LHyd LMil SLdr
	- 'Exbury'	CPLG
	luteum (A) ♀H4	Widely available
	- 'Golden Comet' (A)	GGGa
	lyi KR 2962	GGGa
	× ***lysolepis***	NMun
*	'Mac Ovata'	CMac
	'Macarena' **new**	IVic
	maccabeanum ♀H3-4	CBcs CDoC CWri GGGa GGar GKev GKir IDee LHyd LMil LRHS MBri MDun MLea MSnd NLar NPCo SLdr SPer SReu SSpi SSta WBVN WFar WHer
	- SEH 27	GGGa
	- SEH 52	GGGa
	- Reuthe's form	SReu
	maccabeanum × ***sinogrande***	SReu
	maccabeanum × ***wardii***	GGGa
	macgregoriae (V) Woods 2646	GGGa
	macranthum	see *R. indicum* 'Macranthum'
	'Macranthum Roseum' (EA)	MMHG
	macrophyllum	GGGa
	macrosmithii	see *R. argipeplum*
	maculiferum	GGGa SLdr
	'Madame Ad. van Hecke' (EA)	CTri GKir IVic LMil MAsh MBri SLdr SLim WFar
	'Madame Galle'	SLim
	'Madame Masson'	CDoC CTri CWri ECho GKir LMil LRHS MAsh MBri MDun MGos MLea MMuc MSnd NLar NPCo NPri SLdr SPer SReu SSta WBVN WFar
	maddenii	CDoC LMil
§	- subsp. ***crassum***	CBcs CPLG GGGa GLin IVic SKHP SLdr
§	- subsp. ***maddenii*** Polyandrum Group	CBcs GGal GQui LHyd NMun
	'Mademoiselle Masson'	WFar
	'Maggie' **new**	IVic
	'Magic Flute' (EA)	LRHS MAsh MGos
I	'Magic Flute' (V)	LMil NPri SCoo
N	'Magnificum' (A)	SLim
	'Magnificum' (O)	SLdr
	magnificum	SReu
	'Maharani'	GGGa IVic
	'Mai-ogi' (EA) **new**	IVic
	'Maischnee' (EA) **new**	IVic
§	***makinoi*** ♀H4	GGGa GKir IDee LHyd LLHF LMil LRHS MDun SLdr SReu SSpi SSta WAbe
	- 'Fuju-kaku-no-matsu'	MGos
	'Makiyak' **new**	LMil
	'Malahat'	MSnd
	mallotum	GGGa IDee LHyd LMil LRHS MDun MSnd NMun SReu
	- BASEX 9672	GGGa
	Mandalay Group	LHyd SHea
	'Mandarin Lights' (A)	LMil MBri SLdr
	maoerense	GGGa
	'Maraschino' (EA) **new**	IVic
	'Marcel Ménard'	CDoC GGGa LMil LRHS MAsh NLar NPri SReu WFar
	'Marchioness of Lansdowne'	CWri SHea
	'Mardi Gras'	CDoC MAsh MLea NEgg NLar NPCo SLdr
	Margaret Dunn Group	CWri
	'Margaret Falmouth'	SReu
	'Margaret George' (EA)	LHyd
	'Maria Elena' (EA/d)	SLim
	'Marianne' (EA/d)	MAsh
	'Maricee'	GGGa WAbe
	'Marie Curie'	LMil SReu
	'Marie Hoffman'	LMil
	'Marilee' (EA)	CDoC ECho IVic LRHS MAsh MGos SLdr
	Mariloo Group	LMil MSnd
	'Marion Street' ♀H4	LHyd LMil SReu
	'Markeeta's Prize' ♀H4	CDoC CWit CWri ECho EPfP GGGa LMil LRHS MAsh MBri MDun MGos MLea MMuc NPri SHea SLdr SLim SReu
	'Marley Hedges'	GGGa LMil
	'Marlies' (A)	MBri SLdr
	'Marmot' (EA)	ECho MLea
	'Mars'	GGGa SLdr SReu
	'Marsalla' **new**	LMil
	'Martha Hitchcock' (EA)	SRms
	'Martha Isaacson' (Ad) ♀H4	LMil MGos SLdr SReu
	'Martine' (Ad)	MGos
	martinianum	SLdr
	aff. ***martinianum*** KW 21557	GGGa
	'Maruschka' (EA)	IVic LMil LRHS MAsh
	'Mary Helen' (EA)	LHyd LRHS MAsh SCoo SLim
	'Mary Meredith' (EA)	LHyd
	'Mary Poppins' (K)	CTri LMil LRHS MAsh NPri SCoo SLdr SLim
	'Maryke'	LMil
	'Master of Elphinstone' (EA)	SLdr
	'Matador'	LHyd LMil MSnd SHea
	Matador Group	SLdr SReu
	'Maxi' (EA) **new**	IVic
	maximum	GGGa
	- SDR 2205	GKev
§	'Maxwellii' (EA)	CMac SLdr
	'May Day' ♀H3-4	CMac MAsh NEgg NLar SHea
	May Day Group	CBcs CWri MDun MGos MSnd SLdr
	'May Glow'	MGos
	May Morn Group	SReu
	'Mayor Johnstone'	CTri MAsh NPri
	'Mazurka' (K)	SLdr
	meddianum	GGGa
	Medea Group	SLdr
	Medusa Group	SHea SLdr SReu
	megacalyx	GGGa
	'Megan' (EA)	ECho ELon MAsh MGos MMuc NLar SLdr WGwG
	megaphyllum	see *R. basilicum*
	megeratum	GGGa SLdr SReu
	- 'Bodnant'	WAbe WThu
	mekongense	GGGa
	- var. ***mekongense***	SReu
	- - Rubroluteum Group	see *R. viridescens* Rubroluteum Group
	- - Viridescens Group	see *R. viridescens*
§	- var. ***melinanthum***	SReu
	'Melford Lemon'	see *R.* 'Ilam Melford Lemon'
	'Melidioso'	LMil
	'Melina' (EA/d)	LMil
	melinanthum	see *R. mekongense* var. *melinanthum*
	'Mendosina' **new**	IVic

mengtszense	MSnd
'Merganser' $\mathbb{Y}^{H4}$	GEdr GGGa LMil MLea NHol SReu WThu
metternichii	see *R. degronianum* subsp. *heptamerum*
- var. ***pentamerum***	see *R. degronianum* subsp. *degronianum*
'Mi Amor'	LMil
'Miami' (A)	SLdr
'Michael Hill' (EA)	LHyd MAsh
'Michael Waterer'	MSnd SLdr
'Michael's Pride'	CBcs GQui LMil
micranthum	GGGa MDun
microgynum F 14242	GGGa
microleucum	see *R. orthocladum* var. *microleucum*
micromeres	see *R. leptocarpum*
'Midnight Mystique'	GGGa MDun
'Midnight Ruby'	GGGa
'Midsummer'	IVic SHea SLdr
'Midsummer Mermaid' (A)	GGGa LMil
'Mikado' (EA)	see *R. kaempferi* 'Mikado'
'Millennium' (A)	GGGa
'Milton' (R)	LMil
mimetes	GKev
'Mimi' (EA)	CMac LHyd
'Mindy's Love'	LMil MDun
'Ming'	see *R.* 'Ilam Ming'
'Minterne Cinnkeys'	MDun
minus	GQui
- SDR 2228	GKev
- SDR 2251	GKev
- var. ***minus*** (Carolinianum Group) 'Epoch'	LMil
'Miss Muffet' (EA)	SLdr
'Moerheim' $\mathbb{Y}^{H4}$	CBcs CWri ECho IVic LRHS LSou MGos NHol NPCo NPri SLdr SLim SReu WBVN WBrE
§ 'Moerheim's Pink'	LHyd LMil MSnd NHol
'Moidart' (Vs)	LMil
'Moira Salmon' (EA)	LHyd
§ ***molle*** subsp. ***japonicum*** (A)	GGGa LMil SArc SLdr
- subsp. ***molle*** (A)	LMil
- - C&H 7181	GGGa
'Mollie Coker'	CWri SLdr
Mollis orange-flowered (M)	SRms
Mollis pink-flowered (M)	SRms
Mollis red-flowered (M)	SRms
Mollis salmon-flowered (M)	GQui
Mollis yellow-flowered (M)	GQui SRms
'Molly Ann'	ECho GEdr GGGa IVic MGos MSnd NLar
'Molten Gold' (v)	LMil MAsh NPri
§ 'Momoko' (EA)	GKir MAsh
monanthum CCH&H 8133	GGGa
monosematum	see *R. pachytrichum* var. *monosematum*
montroseanum	CDoC LMil MDun SLdr
* - 'Baravalla'	GGGa
'Moon Maiden' (EA)	ECho ELon GQui NLar SLdr
'Moonshine'	SReu
'Moonshine Bright'	LHyd MDun
Moonstone Group	CWri MLea SLdr
- pink-tipped	GEdr
'Moonstone Pink'	MSnd SLdr
'Moonstone Yellow'	MSnd
'Moonwax'	CWri SLdr
§ 'Morgenrot'	GGGa IVic LSou MAsh MGos NLar SReu WFar
morii	GGGa LHyd MDun
'Morning Cloud' $\mathbb{Y}^{H4}$	ECho EPfP LHyd LMil LRHS MAsh NHol NPri SLdr SLim SReu
'Morning Magic'	LHyd MDun
Morning Red	see *R.* 'Morgenrot'
'Moser's Maroon'	CWri ECho MGos MLea NLar SLdr SPoG WBVN
'Motet' (K/d)	CSdC SLdr
'Mother of Pearl'	SReu
'Mother's Day' (EA) $\mathbb{Y}^{H4}$	CBcs CDoC CMac CSBt CTri ECho EPfP GKir GQui LHyd LMil LRHS MAsh MBri MGos MMuc MNHC NEgg NHol NPCo NPri SLdr SLim SPer SPoG SReu SSta WFar
Moulten Gold = 'Blattgold'	GGGa
'Mount Everest'	GGGa LHyd LMil SReu SSta
'Mount Rainier' (K)	SLdr SReu
'Mount Saint Helens' (A)	LMil NLar SLdr SLim
'Mount Seven Star'	see *R. nakaharae* 'Mount Seven Star'
moupinense	GGGa GLin LHyd LMil SLdr SReu
'Mrs A.C. Kenrick'	SHea SLdr
'Mrs A.T. de la Mare' $\mathbb{Y}^{H4}$	CSBt GGGa LHyd LMil MDun SHea SLdr SReu SSta
'Mrs Betty Robertson'	CMac ECho MGos MMuc SLdr SReu
'Mrs C.B. van Nes'	SReu
'Mrs Charles E. Pearson' $\mathbb{Y}^{H4}$	CSBt LMil MSnd SHea SLdr SReu
'Mrs Davies Evans' $\mathbb{Y}^{H4}$	CWri LHyd SReu SSta
'Mrs Dick Thompson'	SReu
'Mrs Donald Graham'	SReu
'Mrs E.C. Stirling'	SRms
'Mrs Emil Hager' (EA)	LHyd SLdr
'Mrs Furnivall' $\mathbb{Y}^{H4}$	CBcs CDoC CWri ECho EPfP GGGa GKir LHyd LMil MGos MLea MMuc SLdr SReu
'Mrs G.W. Leak'	CSBt CWri EPfP GGGa GKir LHyd LMil MDun MLea SHea SReu
'Mrs J.C. Williams' $\mathbb{Y}^{H4}$	LMil
'Mrs J.G. Millais'	LMil SHea
'Mrs James Horlick'	CWri
'Mrs Kingsmill'	SLdr
'Mrs Lionel de Rothschild' $\mathbb{Y}^{H4}$	CWri SReu
'Mrs P.D. Williams'	SReu
'Mrs Peter Koster' (M)	SLdr WFar
'Mrs R.S. Holford' $\mathbb{Y}^{H4}$	MSnd SHea SLdr
'Mrs T.H. Lowinsky' $\mathbb{Y}^{H4}$	CDoC CMac CSBt ECho EPfP GGGa GKir LMil MAsh MDun MGos MLea MMuc MSnd NLar SHea SLdr SLim SPer SReu SSta
'Mrs W.C. Slocock'	GKir
'Mucronatum'	see *R.* × ***mucronatum***
§ × ***mucronatum*** (EA)	CBcs LHyd SLdr SRms
mucronulatum	CBcs GGGa MSnd
- var. ***chejuense***	see *R. mucronulatum* var. *taquetii*
- 'Cornell Pink' $\mathbb{Y}^{H4}$	GGGa LHyd WFar
§ - var. ***taquetii***	GGGa
'Muncaster Hybrid'	NMun
'Muncaster Mist'	LHyd MSnd
'Munstead'	LHyd
'Nabucco' (A)	EPfP
nakaharae (EA)	MSnd SLdr SReu WAbe
- 'Mariko' (EA)	LHyd NHol WAbe WThu
§ - 'Mount Seven Star' (EA) $\mathbb{Y}^{H4}$	ECho EPot GGGa LHyd LMil MGos NHol SLdr WAbe
§ - orange-flowered (EA)	ECho LMil LRHS MAsh MGos MMuc NPri SReu
- pink-flowered (EA)	ECho IVic MGos NLar SLdr SPer SReu SSta
- red-flowered (EA)	ECho MGos
'Nakahari Orange'	see *R. nakaharae* orange-flowered

	'Nancor'	CBcs
	'Nancy Buchanan' (K)	SLdr
	'Nancy Evans' ♀H3-4	CDoC CSBt CWri ECho EPfP GGGa GKir LHyd LMil MAsh MDun MLea NLar NPCo NPri SLdr SLim SReu SSpi WFar
	'Nancy of Robinhill' (EA)	SReu
	'Nancy Waterer' (G) ♀H4	EPfP LMil NLar SPoG SReu
	'Nanki Poo' (EA)	LHyd SLdr
	'Naomi' (EA)	GQui MSnd SLdr
	Naomi Group	CWri LHyd MSnd
	'Naomi Hope'	LMil
	'Naomi Nautilus'	LMil
	'Naomi Pink Beauty'	LMil
	'Naomi Stella Maris'	LHyd
	'Narcissiflorum' (G/d) ♀H4	CSBt EPfP LHyd LMil NLar SLdr
	'Naselle'	GGGa SReu
	'Nassau' (EA/d)	LMil
	neriiflorum	GGGa MDun MSnd SReu
	- subsp. ***neriiflorum***	GKir
	- - L&S 1352	GGGa
§	- subsp. ***phaedropum***	MDun
	- - CCH&H 8125	GGGa
	nervulosum Sleumer (V)	GGGa
	'Nestor'	SReu
	'New Comet'	LHyd
	'New Moon'	SReu
	'Newcomb's Sweetheart'	LMil
	'Niagara' (EA) ♀H3-4	CMac EPfP LHyd LMil MGos SLdr SPoG
	'Nichola' (EA)	SReu
	'Nico' (EA)	CMac LRHS MAsh
	'Nicoletta'	IVic LMil LRHS
	'Night Sky'	CDoC ECho GGGa LHyd LMil LRHS MAsh MDun MGos MLea MMuc MSnd NPCo SLdr WBVN
	'Nightingale'	LMil SReu
	nigroglandulosum	GGGa
	nilagiricum	see *R. arboreum* subsp. *nilagiricum*
	'Nimbus'	LMil SLdr
	Nimrod Group	SLdr
	'Nishiki' (EA)	CMac
	nitens	see *R. calostrotum* subsp. *riparium* Nitens Group
	nitidulum var. ***omeiense***	IVic MSnd
	- - KR 185	GGGa
	nivale subsp. ***boreale*** Ramosissimum Group	GGGa
§	- subsp. ***nivale***	ITim
	niveum ♀H4	GGGa LMil MSnd SReu
	- B&SWJ 2611	WCru
	- B&SWJ 2659	WCru
	- B&SWJ 2675	WCru
	- 'Nepal'	LHyd
	nobleanum	see *R.* Nobleanum Group
	'Nobleanum Album'	GGGa GGal LHyd LMil SReu SSta
	'Nobleanum Coccineum'	GGal SReu
§	Nobleanum Group	CBcs GGGa LHyd LMil MSnd SLdr SSta
	'Nobleanum Venustum'	CSBt LHyd LMil SReu SSta
	'Nordlicht' (EA)	SLdr
	'Norfolk Candy'	LMil LRHS MDun
	'Noriko' (EA)	SLdr
N	'Norma' (R/d) ♀H4	SReu
	Norman Shaw Group	LHyd
	'Northern Hi-Lights' (A)	LMil MBri NLar SLdr SLim
	'Northern Lights'	see *R.* 'Arctic Glow'
	'Northern Star'	LHyd
	'Nova Zembla'	CBcs CDoC CTri ECho EPfP GGGa GKir LMil LRHS MAsh MGos MMuc NEgg NPri SLim SPer SPoG SReu SSta WClo
	nudiflorum	see *R. periclymenoides*
	nudipes	LMil
	nuttallii	GGGa GLin LMil
	'Oban'	GEdr ITim WAbe WThu
	Obtusum Group (EA)	LHyd SLdr
	- 'Amoenum' (EA/d)	CBcs CDoC CMac CSBt ECho LHyd LMil MGos NMun SBfd SLdr SPer WFar
N	- 'Hinomayo' (EA) ♀H3-4	CBcs CMac CTri EPfP GKir GQui LHyd LMil MSnd NMun SLdr SReu SSta
	occidentale (A) ♀H4	GGGa GGal LMil LRHS MDun SSpi
	- SIN 1830	GLin
	ochraceum	LMil
	- C&H 7052	GGGa
	- EGM 312	LMil
	'Odee Wright'	CTri CWri LRHS MAsh SLdr SReu
	'Odoratum' (Ad)	MLea
	'Oh! Kitty'	CWri ECho MLea NPCo SLdr
	'Oi-no-mezame' (EA)	LHyd
	'Old Copper'	CWri SLdr
	'Old Gold' (K)	ECho SLdr SReu
	'Old Port' ♀H4	CWri GGGa LHyd LMil NLar
	'Olga' ♀H4	CBcs IVic LHyd LMil SHea SReu SSta
	'Olga Mezzitt'	LHyd
	'Olga Niblett' (EA)	LMil MGos SReu
	oligocarpum	LMil
	- Guiz 148*	GGGa
	'Olin O. Dobbs'	IVic SReu
	'Olive'	IVic LHyd
	'Olympic Flame' (EA)	LMil
	Olympic Lady Group	LHyd MLea
	'Olympic Sunrise'	LMil
§	'One Thousand Butterflies'	MSnd SLdr
	'Ophelia'	SLdr
	'Opossum' (EA)	GGGa
	'Orange Beauty' (EA) ♀H3-4	CBcs CDoC CMac CSBt ECho GGGa GKir LHyd LMil MAsh MGos MSnd SLdr SReu WBVN WFar
	'Orange Flirt'	MDun
	'Orange King' (EA)	CTrh LMil MGos SLdr SPoG
	'Orange Sunset'	MDun
	orbiculare ♀H3-4	GGGa LHyd LMil MSnd
	- C&K 230	GGGa
§	- subsp. ***cardiobasis***	SLdr
	- Sandling Park form	SReu
	'Orchid Lights'	GKir LRHS MAsh
	'Oregon' (EA)	SLdr
	oreodoxa	LMil
§	- var. ***fargesii*** ♀H4	GGGa LHyd LMil
	- var. ***oreodoxa***	LMil
	- - EN 4212	GGGa
	oreotrephes	IDee IVic LHyd LMil MSnd SHea SLdr SReu
	- SDR 5027	GKev
	- 'Bluecalyptus'	GGGa
§	- Exquisitum Group	SLdr SReu
	- 'Pentland'	GGGa LMil
	'Orient' (K)	SLdr
§	***orthocladum*** var. ***microleucum***	GGGa WThu
	- var. ***orthocladum*** F 20488	GGGa
	'Oryx' (O)	CSdC SLdr
	'Osaraku Seedling' (EA)	EPfP LRHS SLim
	'Osmar' ♀H4	GGGa MGos MSnd NLar SReu
	'Ostara'	MDun MGos
	'Ostergold'	LMil
	'Osterschnee' **new**	IVic

	'Oudijk's Favorite'	SLdr
	'Oudijk's Sensation'	CBcs CWri ECho GQui MAsh MGos MMuc NPCo SLdr WBVN WBrE
	'Oxydol' (K)	MBri MMuc SLdr
§	***pachypodum***	GGGa
	pachysanthum ♀H4	CDoC LHyd LMil LRHS MDun MSnd NLar SLdr SReu SSpi
	- RV 72/001	GGGa
	- 'Crosswater'	IDee LMil MDun
	pachysanthum* × *yakushimanum	GGGa SReu
	pachytrichum	GGGa SLdr
§	- var. ***monosematum***	SReu
	'Pacific Gold'	MDun
	'Palestrina' (EA) ♀H3-4	CBcs CMac CSBt ECho EPfP GKir LHyd MAsh MGos MMuc NLar NPCo SLdr SPer SReu SSta WFar
	'Pallas' (G)	SReu
	paludosum	see *R. nivale* subsp. *nivale*
	'Pamela Miles' (EA)	LHyd
	'Pamela Robinson'	LHyd
	'Pamela-Louise'	LHyd
	'Pancake'	CMac
	'Panda' (EA) ♀H4	CSBt CTri ECho EPfP GGGa GKir LHyd LMil LRHS MAsh MLea SReu
	'Papaya Punch'	LMil
	'Paprika Spiced'	CWri ECho LMil MAsh MDun MGos MLea NLar NPCo SLdr WFar
	'Paris'	LHyd
	'Parkfeuer' (A)	IVic LMil
	parmulatum	LMil
	- KW 5876	LMil
	- 'Ocelot'	GGGa LHyd
	parryae	GGGa
	'Patty Bee' ♀H4	CBcs CSBt CTri CWit CWri ECho EPfP EPot GEdr GGGa GGar GKev GKir IDee LHyd LMil LRHS MAsh MDun MGos MLea NHol NPri SLdr SLim SPoG SReu SSpi SSta WFar
	patulum	see *R. pemakoense* Patulum Group
	'Pavane' (K)	SLdr
	'Peace'	GGGa
	'Peach Blossom'	see *R.* 'Saotome'
	'Pearce's American Beauty' new	IVic
	'Peep-bo' (EA)	LHyd SLdr
	'Peeping Tom'	MDun SReu
	pemakoense	CSBt GGGa MSnd NHol SLdr SReu
§	- Patulum Group	SLdr
	'Pemakofairy'	WThu
	pendulum LS&T 6660	GGGa
	Penelope Group	SReu
	'Penheale Blue' ♀H4	CWri GGGa LMil MDun NLar
	'Penjerrick Cream'	LHyd
	'Penny'	SReu
	'Penny Tomlin' new	SSta
	pentaphyllum (A)	LMil NMun
	'Peppina'	GGGa
	'Percy Wiseman' ♀H4	CBcs CDoC CSBt CWri ECho EPfP GGGa GGar GKir LHyd LMil LRHS LSou MAsh MBri MGos MLea MMuc MSnd NEgg NPri SLdr SLim SPer SPoG SReu SSta WFar
	'Perfect Lady'	LMil
§	***periclymenoides*** (A)	GGGa GKev LMil
	'Persil' (K) ♀H4	CBcs CMac CSBt CWri ECho EPfP GGGa GKev GKir LHyd LMil LRHS MAsh MBri MDun MGos MLea MMuc NLar SCoo SLdr SReu WBVN
	'Peter Alan'	LMil
	'Peter Bee'	GGGa
	'Peter Berg'	MGos
	'Peter John Mezitt'	see *R.* (PJM Group) 'Peter John Mezitt'
	'Peter Koster' (M)	SHea WFar
	'Peter Koster' (hybrid)	SLdr WFar
	petrocharis Guiz 120	GGGa
	'Petrouchka' (K)	SLdr
	phaedropum	see *R. neriiflorum* subsp. *phaedropum*
	phaeochrysum	GGGa MSnd SLdr
§	- var. ***levistratum***	SLdr SReu
	- var. ***phaeochrysum*** SDR 4237	GKev
	'Phalarope'	GEdr SReu
	'Phyllis Korn'	CWri LHyd LMil LTen SLdr
	'Piccolo' (K/d)	CSdC
§	***piercei***	LMil MSnd
	- KW 11040	GGGa
	Pilgrim Group	LMil
	'Pineapple Delight'	MDun
	pingianum	SLdr
	- KR 184	GGGa
	'Pink Cameo'	CWri
	'Pink Cherub' ♀H4	ECho MAsh SLdr SReu
	'Pink Delight'	GQui NLar
I	'Pink Delight' (A)	MBri MGos NLar
	'Pink Delight' (V)	MMuc
	'Pink Drift'	CSBt ECho LMil MGos NHol NPCo SLdr SPer WBrE
	'Pink Gin'	LMil
	'Pink Lady' ambig. (A)	SReu
	'Pink Mimosa' (Vs)	SLdr
	'Pink Pancake' (EA) ♀H4	ECho EPfP GKir LMil LRHS MAsh MGos NPri SLdr
	'Pink Pearl' (EA)	see *R.* 'Azuma-kagami'
	'Pink Pearl' (hybrid)	CBcs CMac CSBt CTri CWri ECho EPfP GGGa GKir LMil MAsh MBri MGos MMuc MSnd NPri SHea SLdr SPer SPoG SReu SSta WBVN WFar
	'Pink Pebble' ♀H3-4	CBcs CPLG LHyd MAsh MLea SLdr
	'Pink Perfection'	CMac MGos MSnd SHea SLdr SReu WFar
	'Pink Polar Bear'	LMil LRHS
	'Pink Rosette'	LMil
	'Pink Ruffles' (K)	SLdr
	'Pinkerton'	LMil
	'Pintail'	GGGa LMil LRHS MAsh
	'Pipit'	GGGa MLea
	'Pippa' (EA)	CMac
	'PJM Elite'	LHyd NLar
§	(PJM Group) 'Peter John Mezitt' ♀H4	LHyd SLdr
	'PJM Regal' new	IVic
	platypodum	GGGa
	'Pleasant White' (EA)	NMun
	'Plover'	GGGa
	pocophorum	MSnd
§	- var. ***hemidartum***	GGGa MSnd
	'Point Defiance'	CWri ECho GGGa LMil MDun MSnd NLar WBVN
	'Polar Bear' (EA)	MDun SLdr
	'Polar Bear' ♀H3-4	CBcs CSBt IVic LHyd LMil LRHS MGos SReu WBVN
	Polar Bear Group	CWri ECho GGGa LMil MLea MSnd SLdr
	'Polaris'	see *R.* 'Hachmann's Polaris'
	'Polaris' (EA)	SReu
	'Polarnacht'	CDoC IVic LMil LRHS MAsh
	poluninii KR 8231	LMil
	polyandrum	see *R. maddenii* subsp. *maddenii* Polyandrum Group
§	***polycladum*** Scintillans Group	LHyd NHol SLdr

- - 'Policy' ♀H4	GGGa SReu
polylepis	MSnd
- C&K 284	GGGa
'Polynesian Sunset'	MDun
ponticum	CBcs CDul CMac CTri CWri MGos SBfd SReu WFar
- 'Foliis Purpureis'	SReu
§ - 'Variegatum' (v)	CBcs CMac CSBt CTri EPfP GGGa LMil LRHS MAsh MDun MGos MLea MSnd NPri SBfd SLdr SLim SPoG SReu SRms SSta WFar
'Pooh-Bah' (EA)	LHyd
'Pook'	LHyd
'Popocatapetl'	SReu
poukhanense	see *R. yedoense* var. *poukhanense*
'Praecox' ♀H4	CBcs CSBt ECho ELon EPfP GGGa GKev LHyd LMil LRHS MAsh MDun MGos MMuc NHol NPri SLdr SLim SPer SPoG SReu SSta WFar
praestans	GGGa LMil MDun SLdr
praevernum	GGGa
prattii 'Perry Wood'	LMil
'Prawn'	SReu
preptum	GGGa SLdr
'President Roosevelt' (v)	CSBt EPfP GKir LRHS MAsh MDun MGos MLea NMun NPri SPer SPoG SReu WFar
'Pride of Leonardslee'	SLdr
'Pridenjoy'	LMil
primuliflorum	GGGa WAbe
- 'Doker-La'	LMil WAbe
'Prince Camille de Rohan'	LMil SHea
'Prince Henri de Pays Bas' (G)	CSdC
'Princess Alice'	CBcs LHyd WAbe
'Princess Anne' ♀H4	CBcs CMHG ECho EPfP GEdr GGGa LMil LSou MAsh MDun MGos MLea NMun SLdr SLim SPer SPoG SReu SSta
'Princess Galadriel'	SLdr
'Princess Ida' (EA)	LHyd
'Princess Juliana'	ECho MGos MMuc
'Princess Margaret of Windsor' (K)	GQui LMil
'Princess Margaret Toth'	CSdC
principis	LMil SLdr
- C&V 9547	GGGa
- 'Lost Horizon'	CDoC LMil MSnd
§ - Vellereum Group	SLdr
§ ***prinophyllum*** (A)	LMil LRHS
'Prins Bernhard' (EA)	SLdr
'Prinses Juliana' (EA)	MMuc SLdr SReu WFar
'Professor Hugo de Vries' ♀H4	SHea SLdr SReu
'Professor J.H. Zaayer'	MGos
pronum	GGGa
- R.B. Cooke form	GGGa
- Towercourt form	GGGa
prostratum	see *R. saluenense* subsp. *chameunum* Prostratum Group
proteoides	GGGa
protistum KR 1986	GGGa
§ - var. ***giganteum***	SReu
pruniflorum	GGGa
prunifolium (A)	GGGa LMil
przewalskii	GGGa
- subsp. ***dabanshanense***	GGGa
pseudochrysanthum ♀H4	GGGa IDee LHyd LMil MSnd SLdr SReu SSta
pseudociliipes	GGGa
'Psyche' (EA)	MDun
Psyche Group	see *R.* Wega Group

'Ptarmigan' ♀H3-4	ECho GEdr GGGa LHyd LMil MAsh MGos MSnd NHol SLdr SReu WFar WPat
pubicostatum	GLin LMil
'Puccini' **new**	IVic
§ 'Pucella' (G) ♀H4	CWri
pudorosum L&S 2752	GGGa
'Pulchrum Maxwellii'	see *R.* 'Maxwellii'
pumilum	GGGa GKev WAbe WThu
'Puncta'	SLdr
'Purple Cushion' (EA)	LRHS MAsh
'Purple Diamond'	see *R.* Diamant Group purple-flowered
'Purple Gem'	SLim SPoG
purple Glenn Dale (EA)	SLdr
'Purple Heart'	LMil
'Purple Queen' (EA/d)	MAsh
'Purple Splendor' (EA)	CMac MGos MMuc SLdr
'Purple Splendour' ♀H4	CBcs CSBt CWri ECho ELon EPfP LHyd LMil MGos MLea MMuc NEgg NPCo SPer SReu SSta WBVN WFar
'Purple Triumph' (EA) ♀H3	LMil SLdr SReu SSta
'Purpurtraum' (EA) ♀H4	GGGa IVic LMil
'Quail'	GGGa LMil
Quaver Group	SRms
'Queen Alice'	MDun NLar
'Queen Elizabeth II' ♀H4	LHyd
Queen Emma	see *R.* 'Koningin Emma'
'Queen Mother'	see *R.* 'The Queen Mother'
'Queen of England' (G)	CSdC
(Queen of Hearts Group) 'Queen of Hearts'	LHyd LMil SHea SLdr SReu
'Queen Souriya'	SReu
'Queenswood Centenary'	LMil
'Quentin Metsys' (R)	SLdr
quinquefolium (A)	GGGa LMil MSnd
'Raby' (A)	LMil
racemosum ♀H4	LMil MDun MSnd SLdr
- SDR 5107	GKev
- SSNY 47	GGGa
- 'Rock Rose' ♀H3-4	GGGa LHyd LMil
'Racil'	MGos
'Racine' (G)	SLdr
'Racoon' (EA) ♀H4	GGGa GKir
radicans	see *R. calostrotum* subsp. *keleticum* Radicans Group
'Radistrotum'	IVic
'Raimunde' (K) **new**	IVic
'Ramapo' ♀H4	CDoC ECho EPfP GGGa GKev LMil LRHS MAsh MGos MSnd NHol SLim SPer SReu
'Raoul Millais' **new**	LMil
'Raphael de Smet' (G/d)	SReu
'Rashomon' (EA)	LHyd
'Raspberry Ripple'	SReu
'Rasputin'	GGGa
'Razorbill' ♀H4	CDoC ECho GGGa LHyd LMil MGos SLdr SLim
recurvoides	GGGa IDee LHyd LMil MDun MSnd SLdr SReu
- Keillour form	GGGa
'Red and Gold'	GGGa
'Red Arrow'	LHyd
'Red Dawn'	LRHS MAsh
'Red Delicious'	CWri GGGa LMil WBVN
'Red Diamond'	see *R.* Diamant Group red-flowered
'Red Fountain' (EA)	ECho MGos MMuc
'Red Glow'	LHyd
'Red Jack'	CWri GGGa LMil
'Red Panda' (EA)	GGGa
'Red Pimpernel' (EA)	SLdr
'Red Sunset' (A) **new**	SLdr

'Red Velour'	MSnd SLdr
'Red Wood'	GGGa
'Redwing' (EA)	CDoC MAsh SLdr
'Reich's Charmant'	GGGa
'Rendezvous' ♀H4	LMil SLdr SReu
'Rennie' (A)	ECho MBri MGos MLea
'Renoir' ♀H4	CSBt LHyd LMil SLdr SReu
reticulatum (A)	GGGa LMil MSnd SReu
- 'Sea King' (A)	LHyd
retusum (V)	GGGa
'Reuthe's Purple'	LHyd NHol SReu WAbe WThu
'Rêve d'Amour' (Vs)	MDun SReu SSta
'Rex' (EA)	MAsh SLdr WFar
rex	CDoC GGGa IDee LMil LRHS
	MDun SLdr
- EGM 295	LMil
§ - subsp. ***fictolacteum*** ♀H3-4	CDoC GGGa IDee LMil MDun NLar
	NMun SLdr SReu
- - Miniforme Group	MDun
- subsp. ***gratum***	LMil
- yellow-flowered AC 2079	LMil
rex* × *yakushimanum	SReu
'Rexima' **new**	IVic
rhabdotum	see *R. dalhousieae* var. *rhabdotum*
§ 'Rhodunter 48'PBR **new**	IVic
'Ria Hardijzer'	LMil
'Ribera' (R)	SLdr
rigidum	GLin
* - ***album***	LMil
'Ring of Fire'	CWri ECho IVic LMil MDun MGos
	MLea MSnd WBVN
'Ripe Corn'	MSnd SLdr SReu
ripense (EA)	LHyd
'Ripples' (EA)	CTrh
ririei	GGGa LHyd LMil SReu
- AC 2036	LMil
'Robert Croux'	MSnd SLdr
'Robert Seleger'	LMil LRHS MAsh SReu
'Robert Whelan' (A)	NHol SReu
'Robin Hill Frosty' (EA)	SLdr
'Robinette'	CBcs CWri ECho MAsh
'Rocket'	CDoC CTri ECho MAsh MGos MLea
	MMuc SLdr SLim WBVN
'Roehr's Peggy Ann' (EA) **new**	IVic
'Rokoko'	see *R.* 'Hachmann's Rokoko'
Romany Chai Group	LHyd
- 'Romany Chai'	SHea
'Romany Chal'	SHea
'Rosa' (EA) **new**	LMil
'Rosa Mundi'	CSBt
Rosalind Group	CMac
'Rosalinda' (EA)	NLar SLdr
'Rosata' (Vs) ♀H4	SLdr SReu SSta
'Rose Bud'	CSBt CTri
'Rose de Flandre' (G)	SLdr
'Rose Elf'	WThu
'Rose Glow' (A)	GKir SReu
'Rose Gown'	SReu
'Rose Greeley' (EA)	CDoC ECho GQui SLdr SLim SReu
	WFar WGwG
'Rose Haze' (A)	SLdr SReu
'Rose Torch' (A)	SReu
roseatum F 17227	GGGa
'Rosebud' (EA/d) ♀H3-4	CBcs CMac LHyd MGos NHol SLdr
	SReu
'Rosenkavalier'	LHyd
roseotinctum	see *R. sanguineum* subsp.
	sanguineum var. *didymoides*
	Roseotinctum Group
roseum	see *R. prinophyllum*
'Roseum Elegans'	CDoC MAsh NPri SLdr SLim WFar
'Rosy Dream'	CWri ECho MAsh MMuc MSnd
'Rosy Fire' (A)	LMil NHol SReu
'Rosy Lea'	MLea
'Rosy Lights' (A)	CTri LMil NLar SLdr
'Rotglocke' **new**	IVic
'Rothenburg'	LHyd
rothschildii	CDoC GGGa IDee LMil
'Rotkäppchen' **new**	IVic
'Rouge'	SHea
rousei (V)	GGGa
roxieanum	IDee LMil MSnd SLdr SReu
§ - var. ***cucullatum***	GKir
- - CN&W 695	LMil
- - SBEC 350	GGGa
- var. ***oreonastes*** ♀H4	GGGa LMil MSnd SSta
- - USDAPI 59222/R11312	GGGa
- - Nymans form	SReu
- var. ***parvum***	GGGa
'Royal Blood'	LHyd SLdr
'Royal Command' (K)	CBcs CWri LMil
'Royal Lodge' (K)	SLdr
'Royal Mail'	SHea
'Royal Ruby' (K)	CWri ECho MGos MMuc SLdr
'Roza Stevenson'	LHyd LMil
'Rubicon'	CWri ECho GQui MAsh MMuc
	MSnd SLdr
rubiginosum	CBcs GGGa IDee LHyd LMil MSnd
- SDR 5142	GKev
§ - Desquamatum Group	CBcs LHyd
- pink-flowered	LMil
- white-flowered	LMil
rubineiflorum	GGGa
'Rubinetta' (EA)	LMil WFar
'Rubinstern' (EA) **new**	IVic
rubroluteum	see *R. viridescens* Rubroluteum
	Group
'Ruby F. Bowman'	CBcs SReu
'Ruby Hart'	CBcs GGGa LSRN MSnd NHol SReu
Ruddigore Group	LHyd
rude	see *R. glischrum* subsp. *rude*
rufum	GGGa
§ ***rupicola*** var. ***chryseum***	GGGa LHyd
- var. ***muliense*** Yu 14042	GGGa
russatum ♀H4	CBcs EPfP GGGa LMil MDun MSnd
	NMun SLdr SSpi WFar
- blue-black-flowered	LMil LRHS
- 'Purple Pillow'	CSBt
Russautinii Group	MSnd
russotinctum	see *R. alutaceum* var. *russotinctum*
'Ryde Heron' (EA) **new**	SLdr
'Sabina' (EA)	SLdr
'Sacko'	CWri GGGa IVic LLHF LMil MAsh
	MDun NHol SLim WBVN
'Saffron Queen'	CBcs SLdr
'Sahara' (K)	CSdC LMil
'Saint Breward'	GQui LHyd MDun MLea MSnd
	NMun SLdr
'Saint Merryn' ♀H4	CBcs ECho LHyd MDun SLdr
'Saint Minver'	SLdr
'Saint Tudy'	EPfP LHyd MDun SLdr
'Salmon Queen' (M)	WFar
'Salmon Sander' (EA)	SLdr
§ 'Salmon Trout'	LMil
'Salmon's Leap' (EA/v)	CMac CSBt GKir LHyd LMil LRHS
	MAsh NPri SLdr SReu WAbe WFar
saluenense	GGGa LMil MSnd SLdr WThu
- JN 260	GGGa
§ - subsp. ***chameunum***	GGGa SLdr
§ - - Prostratum Group	GGGa WAbe
'Sammetglut'	CWri SReu
'Samuel Taylor Coleridge' (M)	NLar

'Sanderling'	GGGa
'Sandling'	LHyd
'Sang de Gentbrugge' (G)	CSdC SReu
sanguineum	GGGa LMil MDun MSnd SLdr
§ - subsp. ***didymum***	GGGa MDun
§ - subsp. ***sanguineum*** var. ***didymoides*** Roseotinctum Group USDAPI 59038/R10903	GGGa
- - var. ***haemaleum***	CWri GGGa LMil
- - var. ***sanguineum*** F 25521	LMil
'Santa Maria' (EA)	ECho LMil LRHS MGos SLdr SReu SSta WBrE
§ 'Saotome' (EA)	LHyd SLdr
'Sapphire'	CBcs CSBt GEdr MDun SRms WThu
'Sappho'	CBcs CMac CSBt CWri ECho EPfP GBin GGGa GKir LHyd LMil MBri MDun MGos MLea MSnd NEgg NPCo SLdr SPer SReu SSta WBVN WFar WGwG
'Sapporo'	LMil
'Sarah Boscawen'	SReu
sargentianum	GGGa LMil WAbe WThu
- 'Whitebait'	GGGa WAbe
'Sarita Loder'	LHyd
Sarled Group	SRms WAbe
- 'Sarled' ♀H4	GGGa ITim LMil SHea WPat WThu
'Saroi' (EA)	SLdr
'Sarsen' (K)	CSdC
'Satan' (K) ♀H4	CSBt SReu
§ 'Satschiko' (EA) ♀H4	CBcs CSBt CWit GEdr GGGa GKir LRHS MAsh MGos NLar NMun SLim
'Satsop Surprise'	GGGa
Satsuki type (EA)	ECho
'Saxon Glow' PBR **new**	IDee
§ ***scabrifolium*** var. ***spiciferum***	GGGa NMun WAbe
'Scandinavia'	LHyd SHea
'Scarlet Wonder' ♀H4	CBcs CDoC CMHG CSBt CWri ECho EPfP GEdr GGGa GKev GKir LMil LRHS LSou MAsh MBri MGos NHol NPri SHea SLdr SPer SPoG SReu WFar
schistocalyx F 17637	MSnd
schlippenbachii (A)	CStu GGGa LMil SLdr
- 'Sid's Royal Pink' (A)	LMil
'Schneeauge' **new**	IVic
'Schneekrone' ♀H4	GGGa
'Schneeperle' (EA)	LMil
'Schneespiegel'	GGGa
scintillans	see *R. polycladum* Scintillans Group
'Scintillation'	CWri GGGa LMil LTen MAsh MGos MLea MMuc MSnd NLar SLdr
scopulorum	SLdr
- C&C 7571	GGGa
- KW 6354	GGGa
'Scotian Bells'	GGGa
scottianum	see *R. pachypodum*
'Scout' (EA)	NMun SLdr
scyphocalyx	see *R. dichroanthum* subsp. *scyphocalyx*
'Seaview Sunset'	GGGa
'Seb'	SLdr
'Second Honeymoon'	CBcs CWri ECho LMil MLea MSnd SLdr SReu WFar
'Seikai' (EA)	SLdr
seinghkuense	LMil
- CCH&H 8106	GGGa
- KW 9254	GGGa
selense	GGGa
§ - subsp. ***dasycladum***	MSnd
- subsp. ***jucundum***	GGGa
semibarbatum	GLin
semnoides	GGGa LMil SLdr
'Senator Henry Jackson'	GGGa
'Sennocke'	LHyd LMil
'September Song'	CBcs CMac CSBt CWit CWri ECho GGGa LMil MAsh MBri MDun MGos MLea MMuc NHol NPCo SLdr WFar
serotinum	GLin LHyd LMil SReu
- C&H 7189	GGGa
serpyllifolium (A)	CBcs NMun SLdr
'Sesostris' (G)	CSdC
'Sesterianum'	CMHG SLdr
'Seta'	CAbP CBcs LHyd SHea WThu
Seta Group	SReu
setosum	GGGa WAbe
'Seven Stars'	CSBt
'Shamrock'	CDoC EPfP GEdr GKir LHyd LRHS MAsh MGos MLea NEgg NMun SLdr SLim SPoG SReu WFar
'Sheila' (EA)	CSBt MAsh NPri
shepherdii	see *R. kendrickii*
sherriffii	GGGa MSnd
'Shiko' (EA)	MAsh
'Shiko Lavender' (A)	SPoG
Shilsonii Group	LMil SReu
'Shi-no-noe' (EA)	SLdr
'Shintoki-no-hagasane' (EA)	LHyd
'Shrimp Girl'	GKir LHyd MSnd SLdr SReu
sichotense	GAuc GGGa
sidereum	GGGa
siderophyllum	GLin NMun
sikangense	MSnd SLdr
- var. ***exquisitum***	GGGa GLin
§ - var. ***sikangense*** Cookeanum Group	SLdr
'Silbervelours' **new**	IVic
§ 'Silberwolke' ♀H4	IVic LMil LRHS LSou MAsh SReu WClo
Silver Cloud	see *R.* 'Silberwolke'
'Silver Edge'	see *R. ponticum* 'Variegatum'
'Silver Glow' (EA)	CMac
'Silver Jubilee' ♀H4	CBcs LHyd LMil
'Silver Moon' (EA)	SLdr
'Silver Queen' (A)	ECho ELon LMil MGos MNHC NEgg
'Silver Sixpence'	CBcs CSBt CWit ECho EPfP GKir LRHS MAsh MGos MMuc MSnd NPCo SLdr SReu
'Silver Skies'	LMil
'Silver Slipper' (K) ♀H4	CBcs GKir LHyd LMil MAsh MBri MLea NHol NLar SLdr SPoG SReu SSta WFar
'Silver Thimbles' (V)	GGGa
'Silverwood' (K)	LMil
'Silvester' (EA)	CTri LMil LRHS MAsh MBri MGos NMun SLdr SReu
'Simona'	SReu
simsii (EA)	CMac LMil SLdr
sinofalconeri	GGar LMil LRHS
- C&H 7183	GGGa
- KR 7342	LMil
- SEH 229	LMil
sinogrande ♀H3	CBcs CDoC CHEx CWri GGGa GKev LHyd LMil LRHS MBri MDun MLea NLar NMun NPCo SLdr SPer WBVN WFar
- KR 4027	LMil
'Sir Charles Lemon' ♀H3-4	CBcs CDoC CWri ECho GKir LHyd LMil MAsh MGos MLea NPCo SHea SLdr SPer SReu

'Sir Robert' (EA)	MAsh NPri SLdr
'Sir William Lawrence' (EA)	SReu
'Skookum'	MBri MGos WBVN
'Sleepy'	CBcs CSBt CWit ECho MAsh MGos MSnd SLdr
smirnowii	GGGa IDee LMil MSnd SReu
smithii	see *R. argipeplum*
§ Smithii Group	CWri SReu
'Sneezy'	CBcs CSBt CWri ECho EPfP GGGa GKir LHyd LMil LRHS MAsh MGos MSnd NHol SLdr SLim WFar
'Snipe'	CBcs CTri ECho GEdr LMil LRHS MAsh MGos NHol SLdr SLim SReu
'Snow' (EA)	SLdr
'Snow Crown' (*lindleyi* hybrid)	MLea
'Snow Hill' (EA)	GQui LHyd LMil MGos SLdr
'Snow Lady'	CBcs ECho EPfP GEdr GGar GQui MAsh MDun MGos MMuc SLdr SPoG SReu WBVN
'Snow Pearl'	MAsh
'Snow Queen'	LMil
Snow Queen Group	SReu
'Snowbird' (A)	GGal LMil SLdr
'Snowflake' (EA/d)	see *R.* 'Kure-no-yuki'
'Snowstorm'	NPCo
'Snowwhite' (EA)	LMil
'Soho' (EA)	CSdC GQui
'Soir de Paris' (Vs)	CSBt GGGa IVic LHyd LMil MBri MDun MLea MMuc NHol NLar SLdr SReu SSta WBVN WBrE WFar WGwG
'Soldier Sam'	SReu
'Solidarity'	ECho MBri MGos SLdr WBVN
'Solway' (Vs)	CSdC LMil
'Sommerduft' (A) **new**	IVic
'Son de Paris' (A)	GQui
'Sonata'	CWri GGGa MDun SReu
'Songbird'	LHyd LMil MAsh MSnd SLdr SReu
'Sophie Hedges' (K/d)	SLdr
sororium (V)	LMil
- KR 3085	LMil
souliei	GKir IDee LMil LRHS SSpi
- deep pink-flowered	GGGa
'Southern Cross'	SLdr
'Souvenir de D.A. Koster'	SLdr
'Souvenir de Doctor S. Endtz' $\mathbb{Y}^{H4}$	SHea SLdr
'Souvenir of Anthony Waterer' $\mathbb{Y}^{H4}$	SHea SReu
'Souvenir of W.C. Slocock'	SReu
'Sparkler' (Vs)	GGGa
'Spätlese' **new**	IVic
speciosum	see *R. flammeum*
'Spek's Orange' (M) $\mathbb{Y}^{H4}$	MGos
sperabile var. ***weihsiense***	GGGa SLdr
sperabiloides	GGGa
sphaeranthum	see *R. trichostomum*
sphaeroblastum	GGGa
- var. ***wumengense***	GLin
- - CN&W 968	GGGa
- - EGM 359	LMil
spiciferum	see *R. scabrifolium* var. *spiciferum*
'Spicy Lights' (A)	LMil
spilotum	GGGa
'Spinner's Glory'	MAsh
spinuliferum	GGGa
'Spitfire'	MDun NHol
'Splendens' (G)	CSdC
'Spring Beauty' (EA)	CMac SLdr SReu
'Spring Magic'	MSnd SLdr
'Spring Pearl'	see *R.* 'Moerheim's Pink'
'Spring Rose'	SLdr
'Spring Sunshine'	LMil
'Springbok'	LHyd
'Springday'	CMac
'Squirrel' (EA) $\mathbb{Y}^{H4}$	CDoC ECho GEdr GGGa GKir LHyd LMil MAsh MGos MLea SLdr SLim SReu
Stadt Essen Group	LMil
stamineum	GGGa
'Stanley Rivlin'	LHyd
'Starbright Champagne'	LMil
'Starcross'	LHyd
'Starfish'	SReu
'Statuette'	IVic MDun
§ ***stenopetalum*** 'Linearifolium' (A)	CMac LHyd LMil NMun SLdr WAbe
stenophyllum	see *R. makinoi*
stewartianum	GGGa LMil SLdr
'Stewartstonian' (EA)	CMac LHyd SReu SSta WFar
'Stoat' (EA)	GQui
'Stopham Girl' (A)	LMil
'Stopham Lad' (A)	LMil LRHS
'Strategist'	SHea SLdr
'Strawberry Cream'	GGGa MAsh
'Strawberry Ice' (K) $\mathbb{Y}^{H4}$	CBcs CDoC CSBt CWit CWri ECho EPfP GGGa GKir LMil LRHS MAsh MBri MGos MMHG MMuc NEgg SLdr SPer SReu WMoo
'Strawberry Sundae'	MLea MMuc NEgg SLdr
'Stretta' (EA) **new**	IVic
strigillosum	GGGa GLin LMil MSnd
- C&H 7035	GGGa
- EGM 338	LMil
- Reuthe's form	SReu
subansiriense C&H 418	GGGa
suberosum	see *R. yunnanense* Suberosum Group
succothii	SLdr
'Suede'	MDun
'Sui-yohi' (EA)	LHyd
sulfureum SBEC 249	GGGa
'Summer Blaze' (A)	SLdr SReu
'Summer Dawn' **new**	LMil
'Summer Flame'	SReu
'Summer Fragrance' (O) $\mathbb{Y}^{H4}$	LMil LRHS MDun SReu SSta
'Summer Snow'	IVic MDun
'Sun Chariot' (K)	CBcs LMil MMHG SReu
'Sun of Austerlitz'	SHea SLdr
'Sunbeam' (hybrid)	SReu
'Sunny' (V)	GGGa
(Sunrise Group) 'Sunrise'	MSnd SLdr
'Sunset Pink' (K)	LHyd SLdr
'Sunte Nectarine' (K) $\mathbb{Y}^{H4}$	ECho GQui IDee LHyd LMil MBri MLea MMuc NLar NPri SLdr
superbum (V)	GGGa
'Surprise' ambig. (EA)	CDoC CTri SLdr
'Surrey Heath'	CBcs CDoC CSBt CWit CWri ECho EPfP GKir LMil LRHS MAsh MDun MGos MMuc MSnd NMun SLdr SLim
'Susan' (EA) **new**	MSnd
'Susan' J.C. Williams $\mathbb{Y}^{H4}$	CSBt CWri LHyd LMil MDun SPer SReu
'Susannah Hill' (EA)	CBcs CDoC MGos SLdr
sutchuenense	GGGa IDee LMil SLdr
- var. ***geraldii***	see *R.* × *geraldii*
'Swamp Beauty'	CWri ECho MAsh MDun MGos MLea MMuc MSnd SLdr WBVN WGwG
'Swansong' (EA)	CMac SLdr

'Sweet Simplicity'	CWri SHea SLdr
'Sweet Sue'	MSnd SLdr SReu
'Swift'	ECho GEdr GGGa GQui LLHF LMil LRHS MAsh MMuc NHol NPCo SLdr SReu WBVN
'Sword of State' (K)	CWri
'Sylphides' (K)	CMac SLdr
'T.S. Black' (EA)	SLdr
taggianum 'Cliff Hanger'	LMil
'Takasago' (EA/d)	LHyd
taliense	GGGa LMil MDun
Tally Ho Group	SHea
tamaense	see *R. cinnabarinum* subsp. *tamaense*
'Tama-no-utena' (EA)	LHyd
'Tamarindos'	LMil
'Tanager' (EA/k)	SLdr
'Tangerine'	see *R.* 'Fabia Tangerine'
'Tangiers' (K)	SLdr
'Tarantella'	NEgg
'Taurus' ♀H4	CDoC CWri ECho GGGa LHyd LMil LRHS MAsh MDun MGos MLea MMuc MSnd NPCo SLdr
taxifolium (v)	GGGa
'Tay' (K)	SLdr
'Teal'	ECho GEdr MGos MLea NHol
'Teddy Bear'	CWri GGGa LMil MDun MLea
temenium var. ***gilvum*** 'Cruachan'	GGGa
'Temple Belle'	CBcs CWri ECho GKev MDun
Temple Belle Group	GEdr LHyd SLdr
§ ***tephropeplum***	GGGa
- Deleiense Group	see *R. tephropeplum*
'Tequila Sunrise'	LHyd LMil LRHS
'Terra-cotta'	LMil
'Terra-cotta Beauty' (EA)	WPat WThu
'Tessa'	CBcs ECho GKev IVic MMuc SLdr WBrE
Tessa Group	LMil MGos
'Tessa Roza' (EA) ♀H4	GGGa GKev GQui LHyd
thayerianum	GGGa
§ 'The Hon. Jean Marie de Montague' ♀H4	CWri ELon EPfP GKir LMil MAsh MBri MDun MGos MLea MSnd NLar SLdr SReu
'The Master' ♀H4	LHyd SReu
§ 'The Queen Mother'	LHyd
thomsonii	CDoC GGGa IDee LHyd LMil MDun NHol SReu
- B&SWJ 2465	WCru
- B&SWJ 2638	WCru
- SDR 3929	GKev
- subsp. ***lopsangianum***	GGGa
- subsp. ***thomsonii*** L&S 2847	GGGa
'Thor'	SReu
'Thousand Butterflies'	see *R.* 'One Thousand Butterflies'
'Thunderstorm'	LHyd SReu
'Tibet' ♀H3-4	GQui LMil MDun
'Tidbit' ♀H4	CMac GGGa LMil MGos MLea MSnd SLdr
'Timothy James'	GKir
'Tinkerbird'	GGGa
'Tinsmith' (K)	SLdr
titapuriense	GGGa
'Titian Beauty'	CBcs CDoC CSBt CWri ECho EPfP GGGa LHyd LMil LRHS MAsh MGos MMuc MNHC MSnd NEgg NPCo NPri SLdr SLim SPer WFar
'Titipu' (EA)	LHyd
'Titness Delight'	SLdr
'Tit-Willow' (EA)	GKir LHyd LRHS MAsh NPri SCoo
'Tolkien'	SReu
'Tom Hyde' (EA)	LMil
'Top Banana'	SLdr
'Topsvoort Pearl'	SReu
'Torchlight' (EA)	LMil
'Toreador' (EA)	SLdr
'Tornado'	WFar
'Torridon' (Vs)	LMil
'Tortoiseshell Champagne'	see *R.* 'Champagne'
'Tortoiseshell Orange' ♀H3-4	CBcs CSBt CWri LHyd LMil MDun SHea SLim SPoG SReu SSta
'Tortoiseshell Salome'	SHea SReu
'Tortoiseshell Scarlet'	SReu
'Tortoiseshell Wonder' ♀H3-4	CSBt EPfP LMil LRHS MAsh NPri SHea SReu
'Totally Awesome' (K)	SLdr
'Toucan' (K)	CSBt SLdr
'Tower Beauty' (A)	LHyd SLdr
'Tower Dainty' (A)	LHyd
'Tower Daring' (A)	LHyd SLdr
'Tower Dexter' (A)	LHyd
'Tower Dragon' (A)	LHyd LMil SLdr
traillianum	GGGa MSnd
'Treecreeper'	GGGa LMil SLdr
'Tregedna Red'	SReu
'Trewithen Orange'	SLdr
trichanthum	GGGa
- 'Honey Wood'	LMil SLdr
trichocladum	NMun
§ ***trichostomum***	GGGa SSpi WAbe
- Ledoides Group	LMil
- - 'Collingwood Ingram' (EA) ♀H4	LMil
triflorum	GGGa LMil
- C&V 9573	GGGa
§ - var. ***bauhiniiflorum***	CBcs GGGa MSnd SLdr
'Trilby'	SReu
trilectorum	GGGa
- HECC 56	GGGa
'Trill' (EA)	SLdr
'Trinidad'	MDun
triplonaevium	see *R. alutaceum* var. *russotinctum* Triplonaevium Group
'Tromba'	LMil
'Trude Webster'	GGGa
tsangpoense	see *R. charitopes* subsp. *tsangpoense*
tsariense	GGGa IDee LMil MSnd
- var. ***trimoense***	GGGa LMil MSnd
- - KW 8288	LMil
- 'Yum Yum'	GGGa
§ ***tsusiophyllum***	GGGa
'Tsuta-momiji' (EA)	LHyd
tubiforme	see *R. glaucophyllum* subsp. *tubiforme*
'Tuffet'	SReu
'Turaço'	GGGa LMil MGos SLdr
'Turnstone'	GGGa
'Twilight Pink'	SLdr
'Ukamuse' (EA/d)	LHyd
'Ulrike Jost'	IVic
'Umpqua Queen' (K)	MBri SLdr
ungernii	GGGa SLdr
§ ***uniflorum*** var. ***imperator*** KW 6884	GGGa
'Unique' (G)	ECho EPfP MGos MMuc NHol SLdr SPer
'Unique' (*campylocarpum* hybrid) ♀H4	CBcs GGGa LHyd MAsh MBri MSnd SHea SLdr SReu SSta
'Unique Marmalade'	ECho LMil MAsh MMuc NLar SLdr WBVN
uvariifolium	GGGa

- var. ***griseum***	LMil
- - KR 3774	LMil
- - KR 3782	LMil
- 'Reginald Childs'	LMil
- 'Yangtze Bend'	GGGa
vaccinioides (V) CCH&H 8051	GGGa
'Valentine' (EA)	GGGa
valentinianum	CBcs GGGa MSnd NMun SLdr
- F 24347	MSnd
- var. ***oblongilobatum*** C&H 7186	LMil
'Van'	LMil NLar SLim
'Van Nes Sensation'	LMil
Vanessa Group	GGal LMil SReu
'Vanessa Pastel' ♀H3-4	CMac GGGa LHyd LMil MDun SReu
vaseyi (A) ♀H3-4	CBcs GGGa GLin IVic LMil SLdr
- SDR 2209	GKev
- 'White Find'	GGGa
- white-flowered (A)	LMil
'Vayo' (A)	SLdr
veitchianum	GGGa
§ - Cubittii Group	GGGa
- - 'Ashcombe'	LHyd
- KNE Cox 9001	GGGa
'Veldtstar'	LHyd
vellereum	see *R. principis* Vellereum Group
venator	GGGa
'Venetian Chimes'	CSBt ECho MGos MSnd NMun SLdr SPoG SReu
vernicosum	GGGa MSnd
'Veryan Bay'	CBcs
'Vespers' (EA)	CTrh
vialii (A)	GGGa
'Victoria Hallett'	SLdr SReu
'Vida Brown' (EA/d)	CMac SLdr SReu WThu
'Viking' (EA)	LHyd
'Viking Silver'	GGGa
'Vinecourt Dream' (M)	MBri MLea MMuc NLar
'Vinecourt Duke' (R/d)	CWri ECho MBri MMuc NEgg NLar NPCo NPri WBVN
'Vinecourt Troubador' (K/d)	CWri LMil MAsh NPCo WBVN
'Vineland Dream' (K/d)	CWri ECho
'Vineland Fragrance'	SLdr
'Vintage Rosé' ♀H4	LMil MLea SLdr SReu
'Violet Longhurst' (EA)	LHyd
'Violetta' (EA)	SLdr
'Violette Funken' **new**	LMil
Virginia Richards Group	CWri MAsh MGos SLdr SReu
§ ***viridescens***	MSnd
- 'Doshong La'	GGGa LMil
§ - Rubroluteum Group	SLdr
§ ***viriosum*** (V) **new**	CBcs
viscidifolium	GGGa
'Viscosepalum' (G)	CSdC SLdr
viscosum (A) ♀H4	GGGa GQui IVic LMil MDun MLea MMHG SReu WBVN WBrE WGwG
- SDR 2312	GKev
- 'Grey Leaf' (Vs)	LMil
- var. ***montanum*** (A)	IBlr
- f. ***rhodanthum*** (A)	LMil
- 'Roseum' (Vs)	LMil
'Viscount Powerscourt'	SLdr
'Viscy' ♀H4	CSBt CWri ECho EPfP GGGa GQui IVic LHyd LMil LRHS MAsh MBri MDun MGos MMuc MSnd NLar SLdr WBVN WBrE
§ Volker Group	CWri LMil LRHS MAsh SReu SSta WFar
§ - 'Babette'	IVic LMil
§ - 'Lackblatt'	LMil MBri MGos MSnd
'Vulcan' ♀H4	EPfP GGGa LMil MLea
'Vulcan' × ***yakushimanum***	SReu
'Vuyk's Rosyred' (EA) ♀H4	CBcs CDoC CMac CTri GKir GQui LHyd LMil LRHS MAsh MGos NHol SLdr SPer SPoG SReu WFar
'Vuyk's Scarlet' (EA) ♀H4	CBcs CDoC CMac CSBt CTri EPfP GKir GQui LHyd LMil LRHS MAsh MGos MMuc MSnd NHol NPri SLdr SPer SPlb SPoG SReu SSta WFar
'W.E. Gumbleton' (M)	SReu
'W.F.H.' ♀H4	CWri IDee LMil MSnd SLdr SSpi
'Walküre'	LMil LRHS
wallichii	GGGa SLdr
- DM 21	LMil
- KR 8227	LMil
- Heftii Group	GLin SLdr
Walloper Group	SReu
'Wallowa Red' (K)	ECho GBin LMil MBri MLea MMuc SLdr
'Wally Miller'	CWit ECho MAsh SReu WFar
aff. ***walongense*** C&H 373	GGGa
wardii	GGGa GKir LHyd LMil MDun MSnd SHea
- KR 4913	LMil
- KR 5268	LMil
- L&S	SReu
- var. ***puralbum***	GGGa
'Ward's Ruby' (EA)	CTrh SLdr
§ 'Washington State Centennial' (A)	MBri
wasonii	GGGa LHyd LMil MSnd
- SIN 1852	GLin
- f. ***rhododactylum*** KW 1876	GGGa
- var. ***wenchuanense*** C 5046	GGGa
'Water Baby' (A)	LMil
'Water Girl' (A)	GGGa LMil
'Waterfall'	SLdr
watsonii	GGGa
- Cox 5075	GGGa
wattii	GGGa
'Waxbill'	GGGa
websterianum Cox 5123	GGGa
'Wee Bee' ♀H4	CDoC CSBt ECho EPot GEdr GGGa GGar GKir LLHF LMil MAsh MLea NHol NPCo SLdr SLim SReu
§ Wega Group	LHyd
'Wendy'	MAsh
'Westminster' (O)	LMil SLdr
'Weston's Pink Diamond' (d)	LMil
weyrichii (A)	LMil
'What a Dane'	GGGa
'Wheatear'	GGGa
'Whidbey Island'	LMil
'Whisperingrose'	GEdr LMil NLar SPoG
'White Frills' (EA)	CWit ECho NLar SLdr
White Glory Group	SLdr
'White Gold'	GGGa
'White Grandeur' (EA)	CTrh
'White Lady' (EA)	LMil
'White Lights' (A) ♀H4	EPfP GKir LMil LRHS NLar NPri
'White Perfume' (A)	MDun SReu
'White Rosebud' (EA)	SReu WFar
'White Swan' (hybrid)	CBcs SReu
'White Swan' (K)	MAsh MGos MMuc SLdr
'White Wings'	GQui
'Whitethroat' (K/d) ♀H4	CSdC CWri ECho EPfP GQui LMil MBri MMHG MMuc NEgg SLdr SPer WBVN

	'Whitney's Dwarf Red'	SLdr
	'Wigeon'	GGGa LMil NHol
	wightii	GGGa GLin MSnd
	'Wild Affair'	MDun
	'Wilgen's Ruby'	CDoC CSBt GKir LMil MGos MSnd NHol SLdr SLim WFar
	'Willbrit'	CBcs CWri ECho IVic LHyd MAsh MGos SLdr WBVN WBrE
	'William III' (G)	SLdr
	williamsianum ♀H4	CBcs CMac CWri ECho GBin GEdr GKev LMil MDun MLea SLdr SReu SRms SSpi WFar
	- 'Andrea' **new**	IVic
	- Caerhays form	CPLG LMil
	- 'Special'	GGGa
	wilsoniae	see *R. latoucheae*
	wiltonii ♀H4	GGGa IDee LHyd LMil MDun NLar SLdr
	'Windlesham Scarlet'	LHyd SLdr
	'Windsor Hawk'	CWri
	'Windsor Lad'	SReu
	'Windsor Sunbeam' (K)	CWri
	'Wine and Roses' PBR	GGGa
	'Winsome' (hybrid) ♀H3	CBcs GGGa LHyd NPri SHea SReu
	Winsome Group	CMac CWri MAsh MDun MSnd SLdr SSta
	'Winston Churchill' (M)	NHol
I	'Winter Green' (EA)	MMuc
	'Wintergreen' (EA)	GKir MMuc
	'Winterpurpur' **new**	IVic
	'Wishmoor'	SReu
	'Wisley Blush'	LMil LRHS
	'Wisley Pearl'	LRHS
	'Witchery'	GGGa
	'Wombat' (EA) ♀H4	CTri EPfP GGGa GKir LHyd LMil LRHS MAsh MGos NHol NLar NPri SLdr SReu
	wongii	GGGa GQui SLdr
	'Woodcock'	SHea SLdr
	'Wren'	ECho GEdr GGGa GKev IVic LMil LRHS MAsh MGos MLea MMuc SLdr SReu WBVN
	'Wryneck' (K)	CSdC SLdr SReu
	xanthocodon	see *R. cinnabarinum* subsp. *xanthocodon*
	xanthostephanum CCH&H 8070	GGGa
	- KR 3095	LMil
	- KR 4462	LMil
	'Yaku Angel'	IVic MDun
	'Yaku Incense'	ECho LMil MAsh MBri MLea MMuc MSnd NLar SLdr
	'Yaku Prince'	ECho MAsh MGos MMuc SLdr WFar
	yakushimanum	CBcs CMHG CSBt CWri ECho GGGa GGar GKev GKir IDee LHyd LMil MAsh MBri MDun MGos MLea MMuc MSnd NHol NLar SLdr SMad SPer SReu SSta WFar
	- 'Edelweiss' ♀H4	LMil
	- Exbury form	CMac SReu
	- Exbury form × ***roxieanum*** var. ***oreonastes***	SReu
	- FCC form	see *R. yakushimanum* 'Koichiro Wada'
§	- 'Koichiro Wada' ♀H4	CMac CPLG EPfP GGGa GKir IDee LHyd LMil LRHS MAsh MDun MGos SLdr SPoG SReu
	- 'Snow Mountain'	SReu
*	'Yaya'	SLdr
	'Yaye-hiryu' (EA)	LHyd
§	***yedoense*** var. ***poukhanense***	SLdr SReu
	'Yellow Cloud' (A)	ECho LMil MLea NPCo SLdr
	'Yellow Cloud' (K) **new**	MMuc
	'Yellow Hammer' ♀H4	CBcs CMac ECho EPfP LHyd LMil MDun NLar SLdr WBrE WFar
	Yellow Hammer Group	CWri GGGa MGos MSnd SLdr SPer SReu SSta
	'Yol'	SLdr
	yuefengense	GGGa
§	***yungningense*** Glomerulatum Group	SLdr
	yunnanense	CBcs CWri GGGa GGal GGar LMil MSnd SLdr SSpi
	- C&H 7145	GGGa
	- SDR 4217	GKev
	- SDR 4957	GKev
	- SDR 4960	GKev
	- 'Openwood' ♀H3-4	LMil
	- pink-flowered	GGGa
	- 'Red Throat'	SLdr
	- red-blotched	LMil
§	- Suberosum Group	SLdr
	- white-flowered	GGGa LMil
	zaleucum	LMil NMun
	- AC 685	MDun
	- F 15688	GGGa
	- KR 2687	GGGa
	- KR 3979	LMil
	zeylanicum	see *R. arboreum* subsp. *zeylanicum*

Rhodohypoxis ✿ (*Hypoxidaceae*)

	'Andromeda'	EWes
	baurii ♀H4	CAvo CCCN CMea CPBP ECho GAbr GCrs GEdr GKir IBal ITim LRHS MLLN MTho NBir NMen NSla NWCA SPoG SRms WAbe WFar WNew
	- 'Abigail'	EWes
	- 'Alba'	CMea ECho IBal NMen SMrm
	- 'Albrighton'	CTri ECho EWes GEdr IBal ITim LAma NHol NMen WAbe WPat
	- 'Apple Blossom'	CFwr CPen CTca ECho ELon EPot EWes IBal ITim LBee LRHS NHol NMen SCnR WAbe WFar
	- 'Badger' **new**	WAbe
	- var. ***baurii***	EWes LBee
	- 'Bridal Bouquet' (d)	EWes NHol WAbe WFar
	- 'Coconut Ice'	EWes
	- var. ***confecta***	CPen ECho EWes NHol
	- 'Daphne Mary'	EWes
	- 'David Scott'	EWes
	- 'Dawn'	CPen CYeo ECho EPot EWes GEdr IBal LAma NMen WAbe WFar
	- 'Douglas'	CPen ECho EPfP EPot EWes GEdr IBal ITim LAma NHol NMen WAbe WClo WFar
	- 'Dulcie'	CPen ECho EWes GEdr SCnR SUsu WAbe WFar
	- 'Emily Peel'	CFwr ECho EWes ITim LLHF NHol WAbe
	- 'Eva-Kate'	ECho EWes ITim LAma WAbe WFar WPat
	- 'Fred Broome'	CTca CYeo ECho EPot EWes GEdr LAma NHol NMen WAbe WFar WPat
	- 'Goliath'	EWes
	- 'Harlequin'	ECho EPot EWes GEdr IBal LAma LAst NHol NMen WAbe WFar
§	- 'Helen'	ECho EPot EWes GEdr IBal NHol WAbe WFar

- 'Jacqueline Potterton' **new**	EPot
- 'Lily Jean' (d)	CEnt CFwr CStu CTri CYeo ECho ELon EPfP EWes GEdr IBal ITim LRHS NCGa NWCA WCot WFar
- 'Luna' **new**	EWes
- 'Margaret Rose'	CTca ECho EWes IBal ITim LLHF NHol NMen WAbe WFar
- 'Mars'	EWes NHol
- 'Pearl'	ECho
- 'Perle'	ECho EWes GEdr NHol SCnR WAbe
- 'Pictus' (v)	ECho EPot EWes GEdr IBal LAma LBee NHol WAbe WFar WPat
- 'Pink Pearl'	EPot EWes IBal NHol WAbe
- 'Pink Pictus'	MSCN
- pink-flowered	ITim NLAp
- var. ***platypetala***	CYeo ECho EPfP EPot EWes GEdr IBal NHol NMen WAbe WFar
- - Burtt 6981	EWes
- var. ***platypetala*** × ***milloides***	IBal LLHF NHol WAbe
- 'Rebecca'	ECho EWes
- 'Red King'	EWes IBal
- red-flowered	ECho MSCN NLAp SPlb
- 'Ruth'	CEnt ECho EWes IBal LAma NHol WAbe WFar
- 'Susan Garnett-Botfield'	ECho EWes GEdr IBal NMen SMrm WAbe WFar
- 'Tetra Red'	CEnt ECho EPot EWes LRHS NHol NMen WAbe WFar
- 'The Bride'	EWes
- white-flowered	CTca ECho EPot NMen
'Betsy Carmine'	CPen ELon GEdr IBal WAbe WFar
'Blush' **new**	CYeo
'Bright Eyes' (d)	EWes
'Burgundy'	ITim
'Candy Stripe'	ECho EWes GEdr
'Carina'	ECho EWes
'Cayasan' **new**	WAbe
'Confusion'	EWes NHol NSla WAbe WFar
'Dainty Dee' (d)	EWes
deflexa	CPBP CPen CYeo ECho EWes GEdr GKev IBal ITim LRHS NHol NSla SCnR SMrm WAbe WFar
'Donald Mann'	ECho EWes LLHF NHol NMen WAbe
'Dusky'	CFwr ECho EWes GEdr
'E.A. Bowles'	CPen ECho EWes IBal ITim NMen NSla WAbe WFar
'Ellicks'	IBal
'Garnett'	ECho EWes IBal NMen WAbe
'Goya' (d)	ECho NWCA WPat
'Great Scot'	CYeo ECho EWes GEdr GGar ITim NMen WAbe WFar
'Hebron Farm Biscuit'	see *Hypoxis parvula* var. *albiflora* 'Hebron Farm Biscuit'
'Hebron Farm Cerise'	see × *Rhodoxis* 'Hebron Farm Cerise'
'Hebron Farm Pink'	see × *Rhodoxis hybrida* 'Hebron Farm Pink'
'Hinky Pinky'	CFwr GEdr
'Holden Rose'	ECho NHol
hybrids	CWCL ELan MWat
'Jupiter'	GEdr
'Kiwi Joy' (d)	CFwr CStu CYeo EWes GEdr GGar IBal LLHF NCGa NHol NMen WAbe WFar
'Knockdolian Red'	NHol
'Lily Fan'	WFar
'Midori'	EWes GEdr SUsu
milloides	CEnt CPla CTca ECho EPfP EPot EWes GCrs GEdr IBal ITim LBee LRHS NHol NLAp NMen NWCA WAbe WFar
- 'Claret'	CEnt CSam CStu CYeo ECho EWes IBal ITim LLHF NCGa NHol SUsu WAbe WFar WPat
- 'Damask'	CStu EWes
- 'Drakensberg Snow'	EWes
- giant	ECho WFar
'Monty'	ECho EWes GEdr ITim WAbe
'Mystery'	EWes NHol NSla WAbe
'Naomi'	ECho EWes
'New Look'	ECho EWes GEdr IBal LAst LLHF NMen WAbe WFar WGor
'Ori Zuru' **new**	GEdr
'Pearl White'	ECho
'Pink Ice'	GEdr IBal
'Pink Star'	WFar
'Pinkeen'	ECho EPot EWes GEdr IBal LLHF WAbe WFar
'Pinkie'	IBal
'Pintado'	EWes GEdr WAbe
'Raspberry Ice'	ECho NHol
'Rosie Lee'	EWes WAbe
'Shell Pink'	EWes IBal ITim NHol WAbe
'Snow'	EWes
'Snow White'	EWes NHol
'Starlett'	CYeo EWes NHol
'Starry Eyes' (d)	CStu ECho EWes
'Stella'	ECho EPot EWes GEdr IBal NHol NMen NSla WAbe WClo
'Tetra Pink'	ECho EWes IBal NHol SMrm WAbe
'Tetra Rose'	GEdr WFar
'Tetra White'	see *R. baurii* 'Helen'
thodiana	ECho EPot EWes GEdr IBal NHol NMen SCnR WAbe WFar
'Twinkle Star Mixed'	ECho LRHS
'Two Tone'	EWes
'Venetia'	CMea ECho IBal NHol NSla WAbe
'Westacre Picotee'	EWes
'Wild Cherry Blossom'	CFwr ECho EWes

Rhodohypoxis × *Rhodoxis* see × *Rhodoxis*

R. baurii × ***Hypoxis parvula***	see × *Rhodoxis hybrida*

Rhodophiala (*Amaryllidaceae*)

§ ***advena***	EPot
bagnoldii	WCot
§ ***bifida***	SCnR WCot
chilensis F&W 9700	WCot
elwesii F&W 10283	WCot
- F&W 10734	WCot
fulgens F&W 10299	WCot
'Harry Hay'	WCot
montana	CFee
rosea **new**	LAma
* ***serotina*** F&W 9586	WCot
splendens	WCot

Rhodora see *Rhododendron*

Rhodothamnus (*Ericaceae*)

sessilifolius	WThu

Rhodotypos (*Rosaceae*)

kerrioides	see *R. scandens*
§ ***scandens***	CBot CPLG CTri CWib CWit EBee ELan EPfP EPla EShb EWTr LRHS MBri MMHG MWea NHol NLar SEND SLon SPoG SSpi WCru WPat WSHC

× *Rhodoxis* ✿ (*Hypoxidaceae*)

	'Anne Crock' new	CYeo
	'Aurora'	EWes
	'Bloodstone'	EWes NHol
	'Hebron Farm Biscuit'	see *Hypoxis parvula* var. *albiflora* 'Hebron Farm Biscuit'
§	'Hebron Farm Cerise'	CCCN CYeo ELon EWes GEdr NMen NWCA WFar WNew
	'Hebron Farm Rose'	LLHF
§	***hybrida***	CPen CPne ECho EWes IBal NMen NWCA SMrm WAbe
	- 'Aya San'	CYeo EWes
§	- 'Hebron Farm Pink'	CYeo ECho EWes GEdr IBal NHol NMen SCnR WAbe WFar
	- 'Hebron Farm Red Eye'	ELon EWes GEdr NWCA SCnR WAbe WFar
	- 'Pink Stars'	CYeo
	'Little Pink Pet'	EWes

Rhoeo see *Tradescantia*

Rhopalostylis (*Arecaceae*)

	baueri	CBrP LPal
	sapida	CBrP CTrC CWit LPal
	- 'East Cape'	SBig

rhubarb see *Rheum* × *hybridum*

Rhus (*Anacardiaceae*)

	ambigua	EPfP
	- B&SWJ 3656	WCru
	- large-leaved B&SWJ 10884	WCru
§	***aromatica***	CArn EBee EBtc ELan LRHS NLar
	chinensis	CMCN EPfP NLar
	- var. ***roxburghii*** new	SSpi
	copallina	EBee EBtc ELan EPfP
	coriaria	CArn EPfP NLar
	cotinus	see *Cotinus coggygria*
	glabra	CArn CBcs CDoC EBtc EPfP MGos SPer WDin
	- 'Laciniata' misapplied	see *R.* × *pulvinata* Autumn Lace Group
	- 'Laciniata' ambig.	MMuc
	- 'Laciniata' Carrière	NLar
	glauca	EShb
N	***hirta***	see *R. typhina*
	incisa	SPlb
	integrifolia	CArn
	krebsiana	WHil
	leptodictya	WHil
	magalismontana	EShb
	potaninii	CBod EPfP GKir MAsh SBfd
§	× ***pulvinata*** Autumn Lace Group	EBee EPfP MGos WFar WPat
	- - 'Red Autumn Lace' ♀H4	GKir LBuc LRHS MBlu MBri MRav SBfd SPer SPoG
§	***radicans***	CArn COld GPoy WHer
	succedanea	CDTJ SSpi
	toxicodendron	see *R. radicans*
	trilobata	see *R. aromatica*
N	***typhina*** ♀H4	CBcs CDoC CDul CHEx CLnd CMac CTri EBee ECrN ELan EPfP GKir LRHS MAsh MGos MMuc MRav NBea NEgg NLar NWea SArc SBfd SEND SPer SPoG SSta WBrE WDin WFar
§	- 'Dissecta' ♀H4	CBcs CDoC CDul CLnd CMac EBee ECrN ELan EPfP EWTr GKev GKir LAst LRHS MBri MGan MGos MRav MWat NBea NEgg NPri SBfd SEND SPer WDin WFar
	- 'Laciniata' hort.	see *R. typhina* 'Dissecta'
	- Radiance = 'Sinrus'PBR	EBee LRHS MAsh MBlu
	- Tiger Eyes = 'Bailtiger'PBR	EBee ELan EMil EPfP GKir LBuc LRHS MAsh MBlu MBri MGos NPri SCoo SWvt
§	***verniciflua***	EGFP NLar SSpi

Rhynchelytrum see *Melinis*

Rhynchospora (*Cyperaceae*)

	alba	GAuc
	colorata	CRow LLWG NPer SHom WHal
	latifolia	CKno SBfd SHDw

Rhytidocaulon (*Asclepiadaceae*)

I	***obesum*** new	LToo

Ribes ✿ (*Grossulariaceae*)

	alpinum	CPLG EMac IFFs MRav MWht NWea SPer SRms WDin
	- 'Aureum'	CAbP EHoe NEgg WCot WDin
	- 'Schmidt'	EBee
	americanum	SBfd
	- 'Variegatum' (v)	EHoe ELan WPat
	aureum hort.	see *R. odoratum*
	'Ben Hope'PBR (B)	CAgr MAsh MCoo SWvt
	'Black Velvet' (D)	CAgr IFFs MCoo
§	× ***culverwellii*** (F)	CAgr CWib EMil GTwe IFFs LBuc LEdu LSRN MAsh NLar SDea SPoG SVic
	divaricatum	CAgr GPri LEdu
	gayanum	CPMA NLar
	glaciale new	NLar
	× ***gordonianum***	Widely available
	himalense GWJ 9331	WCru
	jostaberry	see *R.* × *culverwellii*
	laurifolium	CBcs CBgR CBot CDoC CDul CEnd CHGN CPLG CPla CTri EBee ELan EQua GKir LAst MRav NLar WBVN WDin WFar WSHC WSpi
	- (f)	CMac EPfP
	- (m)	EPfP WPat
	- 'Mrs Amy Doncaster'	WCot
	- Rosemoor form	CDoC CSam SPoG WCot WPGP
	longeracemosum	GGGa
	menziesii	CHll EWes NLBP WCot
	nigrum	LTen
	- 'Baldwin' (B)	CDoC CTri ECrN EPfP LRHS MAsh NLar SDea SKee SLim SPer SPoG
	- 'Barchatnaja' (B)	CAgr
	- 'Ben Alder'PBR (B)	CAgr CWib GKir LRHS MAsh SDea
	- 'Ben Connan'PBR (B) ♀H4	CAgr CMac CSBt CWib EMil EPfP ERea EUJe GKir GPri GTwe LRHS LSRN MAsh MBri MGos NLar NPri SCoo SDea SKee SLim SPoG SWvt WBVN
	- 'Ben Gairn'PBR (B)	CAgr CSBt MCoo
	- 'Ben Lomond'PBR (B) ♀H4	CAgr CMac CSBt CTri CWib ECrN EMil EPfP EUJe GPri GTwe LBuc LRHS MAsh MGos MMuc MRav NEgg NPri SBfd SDea SEND SKee SPer SVic
	- 'Ben More' (B)	CAgr CWib MBri SDea
	- 'Ben Nevis' (B)	CAgr CTri CWib SDea SKee
	- 'Ben Sarek'PBR (B) ♀H4	CAgr CDoC CMac CSBt CSut CTri CWib ECrN EMil EPfP ERea GTwe LBuc LRHS LSRN MAsh MGos MRav NLar NPri SBfd SDea SEND SKee SLim SPer SPoG SWvt

	- 'Ben Tirran'PBR (B)	CAgr CDoC CSBt CWib ERea EUJe GKir LBuc LRHS MAsh MBri MGos NLar SBfd SPoG SWvt
	- 'Black Reward' (B)	CAgr MCoo
	- 'Boskoop Giant' (B)	CAgr GTwe MGan NEgg SLim SPer
*	- 'Byelorussian Sweet' (B)	CAgr
	- 'Consort' (B)	CAgr
	- 'Ebony' **new**	EMil
*	- 'Hystawneznaya' (B)	CAgr
	- 'Jet' (B)	CAgr GTwe NEgg
*	- 'Kosmicheskaya' (B)	CAgr
	- 'Pilot Alexander Mamkin' (B)	CAgr
	- 'Seabrook's' (B)	CAgr MGan
	- 'Tsema' (B)	MCoo
	- 'Wellington XXX' (B)	CAgr GTwe LBuc MGan SPer
§	***odoratum***	Widely available
	- 'Crandall'	CAgr LEdu
	'Pink Perfection'	CMCN
	praecox	CBcs MMuc SEND
	rubrum 'Blanka' (W)	CAgr CSut LRHS SBfd
	- 'Cascade' (R)	CAgr
	- 'Cherry' (R)	CAgr MCoo
	- 'Hollande Rose' (P)	GTwe
	- 'Jonkheer van Tets' (R) ♀H4	CAgr CMac CSBt CWib EMil EPfP EUJe GTwe IArd IFFs LRHS LSRN MAsh MCoo NLar SDea SEND SKee SLim SPer
	- 'Junifer' (R)	CAgr GTwe SKee
	- 'Laxton's Number One' (R)	CAgr CTri GPri GTwe LRHS LSRN MAsh MGan NLar SDea SLim SPer SPoG
	- 'Laxton's Perfection' (R)	MCoo
	- 'Raby Castle' (R)	GTwe
	- 'Red Lake' (R) ♀H4	CAgr CTri CWib EPfP ERea GPri GTwe IFFs LBuc LRHS MGan MGos MMuc MNHC NEgg NLar SDea SKee SPer SPoG
	- 'Redstart' (R)	CAgr CSBt CTri CWib GKir GTwe LBuc LRHS MAsh NLar SDea SKee SPoG
	- 'Rondom' (R)	CAgr SDea SVic
	- 'Rosetta' (R)	MCoo
	- 'Rovada' (R)	CAgr CSBt CSut CWib EMil ERea EUJe GKir GTwe IFFs MAsh SBfd SKee
	- 'Roxby Red' (R)	MCoo
	- 'Stanza' (R) ♀H4	CAgr GTwe MCoo SDea SEND
	- 'Transparent' (W)	GTwe
§	- 'Versailles Blanche' (W/C)	CAgr CMac CSBt CTri CWib EPfP EUJe GTwe LBuc LRHS LSRN MAsh MBri MGan MGos MMuc NPri SDea SEND SKee SLim SPer SPoG
	- 'White Dutch' (W)	ERea MCoo
	- 'White Grape' (W) ♀H4	ERea GTwe
	- 'White Pearl' (W)	MCoo SDea SVic
	- White Versailles	see *R. rubrum* 'Versailles Blanche'
	- 'Wilson's Long Bunch' (R)	GTwe
	sanguineum	CDul CWCL EMac NEgg WBVN WFar WMoo
I	- 'Atrorubens Select'	MBri
	- 'Brocklebankii'	CAbP CMac CPLG ELan EPfP LEdu MGos MRav NHol NLar SAga SLim SPer WPat WSHC
	- double-flowered	see *R. sanguineum* 'Plenum'
	- 'Flore Pleno'	see *R. sanguineum* 'Plenum'
	- 'King Edward VII'	Widely available
	- 'Koja'	EBee GBin LBuc LRHS LSRN MGos NPri SPoG
	- 'Lombartsii'	MRav
§	- 'Plenum' (d)	CBot WCom
	- 'Poky's Pink'	CMac EWTr LLHF MRav
	- 'Pulborough Scarlet' ♀H4	Widely available
	- 'Red Bross'	SWvt
	- 'Red Pimpernel'	EBee EPfP LBMP LRHS LSRN MAsh MBNS SCoo SPoG SWvt
	- 'Tydeman's White'	CPLG CSBt ELan EPfP MGos NPri SDnm SSpi WSHC
	- var. ***variegata***	CMac
	- White Icicle = 'Ubric' ♀H4	CBcs CBot CDoC CEnd CTri CWib EBee EPfP EWTr GKir LAst LRHS MAsh MBlu MHer MRav MWat NBea NBir NLar NPri SBfd SDnm SLim SPer SPoG SSpi SWvt WFar WSpi
	speciosum ♀H3	Widely available
	uva-crispa 'Achilles' (D)	GTwe
	- 'Admiral Beattie' (F)	GTwe NEgg
	- 'Annelii' (F)	CAgr SDea
	- 'Bedford Red' (C/D)	GTwe
	- 'Bedford Yellow' (C/D)	GTwe
	- 'Beech Tree Nestling' (D)	GTwe
	- 'Blucher' (D)	GTwe
	- 'Bright Venus' (D)	GTwe
	- 'Broom Girl' (D)	GTwe
	- 'Captivator' (C)	CSBt GTwe LBuc MAsh NEgg SDea
	- 'Careless' (C/D) ♀H4	CSBt EMil GKir GTwe LRHS LSRN MAsh MGan MGos MNHC SDea SKee SPer SPoG
	- 'Catherine'	SDea
	- 'Cook's Eagle' (C)	GTwe
	- 'Cousen's Seedling' (D)	GTwe
	- 'Criterion' (D)	GTwe
	- 'Crown Bob' (C/D)	GTwe MGan
	- 'Dan's Mistake' (D)	GTwe
	- 'Drill' (D)	GTwe
	- 'Early Sulphur' (D)	GTwe SDea
	- 'Firbob' (D)	GTwe NEgg
	- 'Forester' (D)	GTwe
	- 'Freedom' (C)	GTwe
	- 'Gipsy Queen' (D)	GTwe
	- 'Glenton Green' (D)	GTwe
	- 'Golden Ball' (D)	SDea
	- 'Golden Drop' (D)	GTwe
	- 'Green Gem' (C/D)	GTwe
	- 'Green Ocean' (D)	GTwe
	- 'Greenfinch' (C) ♀H4	CAgr GTwe SDea
	- 'Guido' (F)	GTwe
	- 'Gunner' (C/D)	GTwe NEgg
	- 'Heart of Oak' (F)	GTwe
	- 'Hedgehog' (D)	GTwe
	- 'Hero of the Nile' (D)	GTwe
	- 'High Sheriff' (D)	GTwe
	- 'Hinnonmäki' (F)	CAgr LBuc MAsh SPer
	- 'Hinnonmäki Grön'	CMac CSBt EPfP
	- 'Hinnonmäki Gul' (D)	CAgr CMac CSBt CSut CTri EMil EPfP ERea GKir LBuc MAsh MGos SBfd SDea SKee SPer SPoG SVic
	- 'Hinnonmäki Röd' (C/D)	CAgr CMac CTri EMil ERea EUJe GTwe LBuc LRHS MAsh MBri MCoo SBfd SDea SPer SPoG SVic
	- 'Howard's Lancer' (C/D)	GTwe SDea
	- 'Invicta' (C/D) ♀H4	Widely available
	- 'Ironmonger' (D)	GTwe
	- 'Jubilee' (C/D)	LBuc
	- 'Keen's Seedling' (D)	GTwe
	- 'Keepsake' (C/D)	GTwe SDea
	- 'King of Trumps' (F)	GTwe
	- 'Lancashire Lad' (C/D)	GTwe
	- 'Langley Gage' (D)	GTwe MCoo NEgg
	- 'Laxton's Amber' (D)	GTwe
	- 'Leveller' (D) ♀H4	CTri EUJe GKir GTwe IFFs LAst LBuc LRHS MAsh MCoo MGan MGos SDea SPer

- 'London' (C/D)	GTwe
- 'Lord Derby' (C/D)	GTwe
- 'Martlet' (F)	CAgr GTwe LRHS MCoo MNHC SKee SLim
- 'May Duke' (C/D)	SDea
- 'Mitre' (D)	GTwe
- 'Pax'^{PBR} (D)	CAgr CDoC CSut EPfP GKir GTwe LBuc LRHS SDea SKee SLim SPoG
- 'Peru' (D)	GTwe
- 'Pitmaston Green Gage' (D)	GTwe
- 'Plunder'	GTwe
- 'Queen of Trumps' (D)	GTwe
- var. ***reclinatum*** 'Aston Red'	see *R. uva-crispa* 'Warrington'
- 'Red Champagne' (D)	GTwe
- 'Rifleman' (D)	GTwe
- 'Rokula'^{PBR} (C/D)	CDoC GTwe LRHS MBri SDea SLim
- 'Rosebery' (D)	GTwe
- 'Scotch Red Rough' (D)	GTwe
- 'Scottish Chieftan' (D)	GTwe
- 'Snow' (F)	EPfP SCoo
- 'Snowdrop' (D)	GTwe
- 'Spinefree' (C)	GTwe
- 'Surprise' (D)	GTwe
- 'Telegraph' (F)	GTwe
- 'Tom Joiner' (F)	GTwe
- 'Victoria' (C/D)	GTwe
§ - 'Warrington' (F)	GTwe
- 'Whinham's Industry' (C/D) $\mathbb{Y}^{H4}$	CMac CSBt CTri EMil GKir GPri GTwe IFFs LAst LBuc LRHS LSRN MAsh MGos MMuc MRav NEgg SDea SEND SPer
- 'White Lion' (C/D)	GTwe
- 'White Transparent' (C)	GTwe
- 'Whitesmith' (C/D)	CTri GTwe MCoo MGan SDea
- 'Woodpecker' (D)	GTwe NEgg
- 'Yellow Champagne' (D)	GTwe
valdivianum	WCot
viburnifolium	NLar
'Worcesterberry' (C)	IFFs MGos SDea SPer

Richea (*Epacridaceae*)

dracophylla	SAPC

Ricinocarpos (*Euphorbiaceae*)

pinifolius	ECou

Ricinus (*Euphorbiaceae*)

communis	CDTJ SBfd
- 'Carmencita' $\mathbb{Y}^{H3}$	MNHC SGar
- 'Carmencita Pink'	CDTJ
- 'Carmencita Red'	CDTJ EShb EUJe SBfd
- 'Dominican Republic'	CDTJ
- 'Gibsonii'	CDTJ SBst SMrm
- 'Impala'	CDTJ SBst SMrm
- 'New Zealand Black'	CDTJ CSpe
- 'Zanzibariensis'	CDTJ CSpe EShb

Riocreuxia (*Asclepiadaceae*)

torulosa	CCCN SPlb

Robinia (*Papilionaceae*)

× ***ambigua***	SSpi
§ ***boyntonii***	LSRN
§ ***hispida***	CDul CEnd CLnd CWib ECrN ELan EPfP EWTr MBlu NLar SPer WDin WJas
- 'Macrophylla'	CEnd
- 'Rosea' misapplied	see *R. boyntonii*, *R. hispida*
- 'Rosea' ambig.	CBcs CBot EBee
kelseyi	CDul EBee EWes SPer WSpi
× ***margaretta*** Casque Rouge	see *R.* × *margaretta* 'Pink Cascade'
§ - 'Pink Cascade'	CCVT CDoC CDul CEnd CLnd CMac EBee EPfP IVic LAst LMaj MAsh MBlu MGos MREP SBfd SCoo SCrf SEND SLim SPer WDin WFoF
pseudoacacia	CCVT CDul CLnd EBee ELan EMac LBuc MCoo NEgg SEND SPlb WDin WFar
- 'Bessoniana'	CDul EBee LAst LMaj SCoo
- 'Fastigiata'	see *R. pseudoacacia* 'Pyramidalis'
- 'Frisia' $\mathbb{Y}^{H4}$	Widely available
- 'Inermis' hort.	see *R. pseudoacacia* 'Umbraculifera'
§ - 'Lace Lady'^{PBR}	CSBt CWSG EBee ELan EPfP LRHS MAsh MBri MGos NLar SCoo SLim SPoG
§ - 'Pyramidalis'	EBee
- 'Rozynskiana'	CDul EBee
- 'Tortuosa'	CEnd EBee EBtc ELan LAst MBlu MGos SBfd SPer
- 'Twisty Baby'^{PBR}	see *R. pseudoacacia* 'Lace Lady'
§ - 'Umbraculifera'	CDul CLnd EMac LMaj LTen MBri MGos SCoo
- 'Unifoliola'	LMaj
× ***slavinii*** 'Hillieri' $\mathbb{Y}^{H4}$	CDoC CDul CEnd CLnd EBee ELan EPfP EWTr LRHS LSRN MBlu MBri MGos NLar SBfd SCrf SEND SPer SPoG WSpi

Rochea see *Crassula*

Rodgersia ✿ (*Saxifragaceae*)

CLD 1329	NHol
CLD 1432	NHol
aesculifolia $\mathbb{Y}^{H4}$	Widely available
- green bud	IBlr
- var. ***henrici***	CLAP CRow EBrs LPio LRHS MRav NBro NMyG SWat WHoo WMoo
- - 'Buckshaw White'	ITim
- - hybrid	CHid EBee EWTr NHol NLar WAul WWEG
- pink-flowered	SSpi
- 'Red Dawn'	IBlr
- 'Red Leaf'	GCal IFoB
'Badenweiter'	ECha
'Blickfang'	IBlr
'Bloody Mary'	CBcs EPPr
'Borodin'	EBee
Cally strain	GCal
'Die Anmutige'	CLAP CRow
'Die Schöne'	CLAP EBee GBin NLar
'Die Stolze'	EBee GBin LLWG
'Elfenbeinturm'	EBee IBlr
'Fascination'	IBlr
'Herkules'	CAby CSam EBee ECha ECtt EHoe ELon EUJe GBin GCal GMaP IFoB LHop LSou MBNS MMuc NEgg NLBP NLar SKHP SSpi WCot WCra WPnP WWEG
'Irish Bronze' $\mathbb{Y}^{H4}$	CLAP EAEE EBee EBrs GBin GKir GQue LBMP LPio LRHS MBNS NPnk SPur WAul WFar WMoo WPnP WWEG
'Koriata'	IBlr
'Kupfermond'	CRow IBlr NBir
'La Blanche'	CAby CWit EBee ECtt ELon EWTr LOck LRHS NCGa NEgg NGdn WCot WCra WPnP WWEG
'Maigrün'	IBlr
nepalensis	CLAP IBlr MDun
- HWJK 2140	WCru

'Panache'	IBlr
'Parasol'	CLAP CMac GBin IBlr NBir NHol SKHP SSpi WPGP
pinnata	Widely available
- B&SWJ 7741A	WCru
- L 1670	CLAP SSpi
- SDR 3301	GKev
- 'Alba'	GCal IBlr NHol WMAq
- 'Buckland Beauty'	CDes EBrs IBlr LRHS SSpi WPGP
- 'Cally Coffee' **new**	GCal
- 'Cally Salmon'	EWes GCal IBlr
- 'Chocolate Wing'	Widely available
- 'Crûg Cardinal'	GCal WCru
- 'Elegans'	CFir EBee EBrs EHoe ELan EPfP EPla GKir GMaP IBlr LBMP LEdu LRHS MRav NEgg NHol SGSe SPer SWvt WAul WPnP
- 'Fireworks' PBR	CFir CHid CLAP CMoH EBee ECtt ELan GBin IMou IPot MBri MSCN SPer WFar
- hybrids	LRHS
- 'Jade Dragon Mountain'	CDes IBlr SKHP
- 'Maurice Mason'	CLAP CMoH EBee GKev IBlr LTen SMHy WWEG
- 'Mont Blanc'	IBlr
- Mount Stewart form	IBlr
- 'Perthshire Bronze'	IBlr
- pink-flowered	WCru
- 'Rosea'	IBlr
- 'Superba' ♀H4	Widely available
- white-flowered	GAbr SWat WCru
pinnata × ***sambucifolia***	IBlr
podophylla ♀H4	Widely available
- SDR 5158	GKev
- WAL 10818	WCru
- 'Braunlaub'	CLAP EBee LLWG MBNS NBro SMad WFar WMoo WPnP WWEG
- 'Bronceblad'	IBlr
- Donard selection	GBin IBlr MBri WPGP
- 'Rotlaub'	CAby CDes CLAP CRow EBee EBrs GBin IBlr IMou IPot LRHS WBor WMoo WPGP
- 'Smaragd'	CDes CLAP CRow EBee EBrs GBin GCal IBlr LRHS MRav NBir NLar
purdomii hort.	CLAP EBee EBrs GCal GKir LRHS WPGP
'Reinecke Fuchs'	IBlr
'Rosenlicht'	CRow EBee
'Rosenzipfel'	IBlr
sambucifolia	CBcs CLAP CMac CRow EBee GBBs GBee GCal GKir LEdu LLWG MLHP NBir NEgg NLar NSti SWat WCAu WFar WMoo WPnP WWEG
- B&SWJ 7899	WCru
- dwarf pink-flowered	IBlr
- dwarf white-flowered	IBlr
- large red-stemmed	NBir
- 'Mountain Select'	EBee GCal WFar
tabularis	see *Astilboides tabularis*

Rohdea (*Convallariaceae*)

japonica	CHEx WCot WPGP
- B&SWJ 4853	WCru
- B&SWJ 5091	WCru
- 'Godaishu' (v)	WCot
- 'Gunjaku' (v)	WCot
- long-leaved	WCot WFar
- 'Miyakonojo' (v)	EBee WCot
- 'Talbot Manor' (v)	EBee EBla WCon WCot
- 'Tama-jishi' (v)	WCot
- 'Tuneshige Rokujo' (v)	WCot
watanabei B&SWJ 1911	WCru

Romanzoffia (*Hydrophyllaceae*)

californica	GKev
§ ***sitchensis***	CTri
suksdorfii Greene	see *R. sitchensis*
tracyi	CDes CLAP GGar NRya WCon WPrP
unalaschcensis	CLAP EBee GKev GKir NWCA SRms WPtf

Romneya (*Papaveraceae*)

coulteri ♀H4	Widely available
§ - var. ***trichocalyx***	CFir CGHE EBee WPGP
§ - 'White Cloud' ♀H4	EBee ELan SChF WPGP WSpi
× ***hybrida***	see *R. coulteri* 'White Cloud'
trichocalyx	see *R. coulteri* var. *trichocalyx*

Romulea (*Iridaceae*)

amoena 'Nieuwoudtville'	ECho
austinii 'Komsberg' **new**	ECho
§ ***autumnalis***	ECho
barkerae 'Paternoster'	ECho
biflora 'Vanrhynsdorp' **new**	ECho
bulbocodium	ECho WAbe
- var. ***clusiana***	ECho
- var. ***crocea***	ECho
* - 'Knightshayes'	SCnR
camerooniana	GCrs
citrina from Tweerivier	ECho
- 'Kamiesberg' **new**	ECho
columnae	ECho
- subsp. ***columnae***	ECho
congoensis	GCal
cruciata var. ***cruciata*** 'Riverlands' **new**	ECho
- var. ***intermedia*** 'Somerset West'	ECho
dichotoma	ECho
discifera 'Grasberg' **new**	ECho
diversiformis 'Komsberg'	ECho
eximia	ECho
flava var. ***minor*** 'Dassenberg' **new**	ECho
- 'Rawsonville' **new**	ECho
gigantea	CStu
hirsuta var. ***cuprea*** 'Rawsonville' **new**	ECho
- var. ***hirsuta*** 'Klipheuwel' **new**	ECho
- var. ***zeyheri*** 'Malmesbury' **new**	ECho
hirta	ECho
kamisensis	ECho
leipoldtii	ECho
linaresii	ECho WWst
- subsp. ***graeca***	WWst
longipes 'Coega' **new**	ECho
longituba	see *R. macowanii*
* ***luteoflora*** var. ***sanguinea***	ECho NMen
§ ***macowanii***	ECho
montana	ECho
namaquensis	ECho
nivalis	ECho
obscura var. ***blanda***	ECho
- var. ***obscura***	ECho
- var. ***subtestacea***	ECho
pratensis	ECho
ramiflora	CPBP CPLG ECho WWst
requienii	NMen
rosea	ECho
- var. ***rosea*** 'Caledon' **new**	ECho

- var. ***speciosa***	see *R. autumnalis*
sanguinalis from Tweerivier	ECho
setifolia var. ***aggregata*** 'Rawsonville' **new**	ECho
sladenii 'Gifberg' **new**	ECho
stellata 'Nardouwsberg' **new**	ECho
subfistulosa from Roggeveld	ECho
tabularis	ECho
tempskyana	CPBP ECho WWst
tetragona var. ***flavandra*** 'Matjiesfontein' **new**	ECho
tortuosa subsp. ***aurea*** 'Komsberg' **new**	ECho
- var. ***tortuosa*** 'Botuin' **new**	ECho
toximontana 'Gifberg' **new**	ECho
triflora 'Riverlands' **new**	ECho
unifolia from Roggeveld	ECho

Rondeletia (*Rubiaceae*)

amoena	SOWG

Rorippa (*Brassicaceae*)

amphibia	LLWG MSKA
nasturtium-aquaticum	WMAq

Rosa ✿ (*Rosaceae*)

A Shropshire Lad = 'Ausled'^{PBR} (S)	LRHS LStr MAus MBri NEgg SSea SWCr WClo
A Whiter Shade of Pale = 'Peafanfare'^{PBR} (HT)	ESty MAus MJon SWCr
Abbeyfield Rose = 'Cocbrose'^{PBR} (HT) 🏆^{H4}	GCoc MGan MRav SMrm SPer
Abigaile = 'Tanelaigib' (F)	LSRN MJon
Abraham Darby = 'Auscot'^{PBR} (S)	CGro CWit EBee EPfP LAst LRHS LStr MAus MBri MGan MJon MRav MWat NEgg NLar SEND SMrm SPer SPoG SWCr WClo
Absent Friends = 'Dicemblem'^{PBR} (F)	ESty IDic MWat
Absolutely Fabulous = 'Wekyossutono' (F) **new**	CSBt ECnt ESty LStr
Accademia = 'Baracc'^{PBR} (S) **new**	ECnt
acicularis	GAuc
'Adam Messerich' (Bb)	MAus SLon
Adam's Rose = 'Wekromico' (F) **new**	MJon
'Adélaïde d'Orléans' (Ra) 🏆^{H4}	CRHN LRHS MAsh MAus MBri MCot MRav SEND SFam SPer SWCr
Admirable = 'Searodney' (Min)	MJon
'Admiral Rodney' (HT)	MGan
Agatha Christie = 'Kormeita'^{PBR} (ClF)	MGos
'Aglaia' (Ra)	EBee MAus
'Agnes' (Ru) 🏆^{H4}	CGro EBee ECnt ELon EPfP EWTr GCoc IArd LRHS MAsh MAus MGan MRav NLar SPer SPoG SRGP SSea
'Agnès Schilliger'	CWit MRav
'Aimée Vibert' (N)	CSam MAus MRav NLar SEND SPer
'Alain Blanchard' (G)	CPou MAus MGan
Alan Titchmarsh = 'Ausjive'^{PBR} (S)	CSBt ESty LRHS MAus MBri MJon SCoo SPer SWCr WClo
× ***alba*** (A)	ECrN
§ - 'Alba Maxima' (A)	EWTr GCoc LRHS MAus MGan MRav NLar SEND SPer SSea SWCr
§ - 'Alba Semiplena' (A) 🏆^{H4}	LRHS MAsh MAus MGan SPer SWCr
- Celestial	see *R.* 'Céleste'
- 'Maxima'	see *R.* × *alba* 'Alba Maxima'
'Albéric Barbier' (Ra) 🏆^{H4}	CRHN CSBt CSam EBee ECnt ELan EPfP EWTr LRHS LStr MAus MBri MGan MJon MRav MWat NBir NPri NWea SEND SMad SMrm SPer SPoG SSea SWCr
'Albertine' (Ra) 🏆^{H4}	Widely available
'Alchymist' (S/Cl)	CPou EBee EPfP LRHS LTen MAus MBri MGan MRav NLar SEND SMrm SPer
Alec's Red = 'Cored' (HT)	CBcs CSBt CTri CWSG GCoc LAst LRHS LSRN LStr MAsh MAus MGan MJon MRav MWat SMrm SPer SPoG SRGP SWCr
Alexander = 'Harlex' (HT) 🏆^{H4}	CGro GCoc LStr MAus MGan MJon MRav SEND SPer SSea SWCr
'Alexander von Humboldt' (Cl)	MGan NLar
Alexander's Issie = 'Dicland' (F) **new**	IDic
'Alexandre Girault' (Ra)	CRHN LRHS MAus MBri NLar SEND SPer SWCr
'Alfred de Dalmas' misapplied	see *R.* 'Mousseline'
'Alfresco'^{PBR} (ClHT)	CSBt SSea
Alibaba = 'Chewalibaba' (Cl) **new**	ECnt ESty
'Alida Lovett' (Ra)	LRHS MAus
Alison = 'Coclibee'^{PBR} (F)	GCoc LSRN SWCr
§ 'Alister Stella Gray' (N)	EBee EPfP EWTr MAsh MAus MBri MCot MGan MMuc NEgg NLar SEND SLon SMad SPer SSea SWCr
'Allen Chandler' (ClHT)	MAus
'Allgold' (F)	GKir MGan
Alnwick Castle = 'Ausgrab'^{PBR} (S)	EPfP LRHS LStr MAus MBri MJon SCoo SSea SWCr WClo
'Aloha' (ClHT) 🏆^{H4}	CBcs CGro CTri ELon EPfP ESty LAst LRHS LStr MAsh MAus MBri MCot MGan MRav NLar SEND SMad SMrm SPer SPoG SSea SWCr
alpina	see *R. pendulina*
'Alpine Sunset' (HT)	CTri ELon ESty MAsh MRav SPer SPoG SWCr
altaica Willd.	see *R. spinosissima*
Altissimo = 'Delmur' (Cl)	MAus MGan SEND SPer SSea SWCr
'Amadis' (Bs)	MAus
Amanda = 'Beesian' (F)	ESty LSRN
'Amazing Grace' (HT)	SWCr
'Ambassador Nogami' (S)	EBls
Amber Abundance = 'Harfizz'^{PBR} (Abundance Series) (S)	ESty MRav SWCr
Amber Cover = 'Poulbambe'^{PBR} (Towne & Country Series) (GC)	SWCr
Amber Nectar = 'Mehamber'^{PBR} (F)	MAsh MJon
Amber Queen = 'Harroony'^{PBR} (F) 🏆^{H4}	CGro CSBt CTri EPfP GCoc IArd LRHS LStr MAsh MAus MBri MGan MJon MRav MWat SMrm SPer SWCr
Amber Star = 'Manstar' (Min)	MJon
amblyotis RBS 0262	NLar
Ambridge Rose = 'Auswonder' (S)	LRHS MAus

	'Amélia'	see *R.* 'Celsiana'
	Amelia = 'Poulen011'^{PBR} (Renaissance Series) (S)	ECnt SWCr
	'American Pillar' (Ra)	CGro CSBt CSam CTri CWSG ECnt ELan EPfP EWTr LRHS LStr MAsh MAus MGan MMuc MRav NLar SEND SPer SPoG SSea SWCr WBor WKif
	'Amy Robsart' (RH)	MAus MGan
	'Anaïs Ségalas' (G)	MAus
	'Andersonii' (*canina* hybrid)	MAus
	'Andrea' (ClMin)	MJon
§	'Anemone' (Cl)	EWTr
	anemoniflora	see *R.* × *beanii*
	anemonoides	see *R.* 'Anemone'
	'Angel Wings' (HT) **new**	LBuc
	Angela = 'Grifgela' **new**	LSRN
	Angela Rippon = 'Ocaru' (Min)	CSBt SPer
	'Angela's Choice' (F)	LSRN MGan
	Anisley Dickson = 'Dickimono'^{PBR} (F) 𝕐^{H4}	IDic MGan SPer
	Ann = 'Ausfete'^{PBR} (S)	LRHS MAus
	Ann Henderson = 'Fryhoncho' (F)	LSRN
	Anna Ford = 'Harpiccolo' (Min/Patio) 𝕐^{H4}	LStr MGan SPer
	Anna Livia = 'Kormetter'^{PBR} (F) 𝕐^{H4}	EBls ECnt MGos
	Anne Boleyn = 'Ausecret'^{PBR} (S)	LRHS MAsh MAus MBri NEgg SCoo
	'Anne Cocker' (F)	GCoc
	'Anne Dakin' (ClHT)	MAus
	Anne Harkness = 'Harkaramel' (F)	MAus MGan SPer
	'Anne of Geierstein' (RH)	MGan NHaw
	Aperitif = 'Macwaira'^{PBR} (HT)	ECnt ESty MJon
	Aphrodite = 'Tanetidor' (HT)	ESty
	apothecary's rose	see *R. gallica* var. *officinalis*
	'Apple Blossom' (Ra)	MGan
	'Apricot Nectar' (F)	MAus MGan NHaw SPer
	'Apricot Silk' (HT)	CTri MGan SPer
	Apricot Sunblaze = 'Savamark' (Min)	CSBt
	'Archiduc Joseph' misapplied	see *R.* 'Général Schablikine'
	'Arethusa' (Ch)	SLon
§	***arkansana*** var. ***suffulta***	GAuc
	'Arthur Bell' (F) 𝕐^{H4}	CGro CSBt EPfP ESty GKir IArd LAst LStr MAsh MAus MGan MGos MRav MWat NEgg NPri SMrm SPer SPoG SRGP SSea SWCr WBor
	'Arthur de Sansal' (DPo)	MAus
	arvensis	CCVT CRWN IFFs LBuc MAus NHaw NWea
	'Assemblage des Beautés' (G)	MAus
	'Astra Desmond' (Ra)	WTin
	Audrey Wilcox = 'Frywilrey' (HT)	CSBt
	'Auguste Gervais' (Ra)	MAus SPer
	Austrian copper rose	see *R. foetida* 'Bicolor'
	Austrian yellow	see *R. foetida*
	'Autumn Delight' (HM)	EBee
	Autumn Fire	see *R.* 'Herbstfeuer'
	'Autumn Sunlight' (c)	MGan SPer
	'Autumn Sunset' (ClS)	MJon
	'Autumnalis'	see *R.* 'Princesse de Nassau'
	'Avignon' (F)	EBee ECnt
	Avon = 'Poulmulti'^{PBR} (GC) 𝕐^{H4}	ELan EPfP GCoc MRav SPer SWCr
	Awakening = 'Probuzení' (ClHT)	EBee ECGP MGan NLar SWCr
	'Ayrshire Splendens'	see *R.* 'Splendens'
	'Baby Bio' (F/Patio)	SWCr
	'Baby Darling' (Min)	MGan
	'Baby Faurax' (Poly)	MAus
	Baby Gold Star (Min)	see *R.* 'Estrellita de Oro'
	Baby Love = 'Scrivluv'^{PBR} (yellow) (Min/Patio) 𝕐^{H4}	CTri MAus
	Baby Masquerade = 'Tanba' (Min)	MGan MGos MJon MRav SMrm SPer SWCr
	Babyface = 'Rawril'^{PBR} (Min)	ESty
	'Ballerina' (HM/Poly) 𝕐^{H4}	CGro CSBt EBee ECnt ELan EPfP ESty EWTr GCoc LRHS LSRN LStr MAsh MAus MBri MGan MJon MRav MWat NEgg NLar NPri SEND SMad SMrm SPer SSea SWCr WClo WKif
	Ballindalloch Castle = 'Cocneel'^{PBR} (F)	GCoc
	'Baltimore Belle' (Ra)	CRHN MAus
	banksiae (Ra)	CFee CPou SRms
	- ***alba***	see *R. banksiae* var. *banksiae*
§	- var. ***banksiae*** (Ra/d)	CBot CDul CPou CSBt CTri EBee ELan EPfP ERea GQui LRHS LStr MAus SEND SLon SPer WCot
	- 'Lutea' (Ra/d) 𝕐^{H3}	Widely available
	- 'Lutescens' (Ra)	ERea
	- var. ***normalis*** (Ra)	CBot CSBt LRHS MAus SKHP SLon WCot WHer
I	- 'Rosea'	NLar
	'Bantry Bay' (ClHT)	CSBt EBee ELan LSRN LStr MGan SEND SLon SPer SSea SWCr
	Barbara Austin = 'Austop'^{PBR} (S)	LRHS MAus
	Barbara Windsor = 'Ganleon' (F)	ECnt MGan SWCr
	Barkarole = 'Tanelorak'^{PBR} (HT)	CSBt ESty LStr SWCr
	'Baron de Wassenaer' (CeMo)	MGan
	'Baron Girod de l'Ain' (HP)	EBee ELon ESty EWTr LAst LRHS MAsh MAus MGan MMuc MRav NEgg NHaw NLar SEND SMrm SPer SWCr
	'Baroness Rothschild' ambig.	see *R.* Baronne Edmond de Rothschild, Baronne Edmond de Rothschild, Climbing
	'Baroness Rothschild' (HP)	see *R.* 'Baronne Adolph de Rothschild'
	'Baroness Rothschild' (HT)	see *R.* Baronne Edmond de Rothschild
§	'Baronne Adolph de Rothschild' (HP)	MAus MGan MRav
§	Baronne Edmond de Rothschild = 'Meigriso' (HT)	MGan
§	Baronne Edmond de Rothschild, Climbing = 'Meigrisosar' (ClHT)	CSBt
	'Baronne Prévost' (HP)	MAus SFam
	Baroque Floorshow = 'Harbaroque'^{PBR} (S)	CGro MRav
	Barry Stephens = 'Horcabellero' (HT) **new**	LSRN
§	× ***beanii*** (Ra)	IFro SMad
	'Beau Narcisse' (G)	MAus
	'Beauté' (HT)	MGan

Beautiful Britain = 'Dicfire'PBR (F)	LStr MGan MRav SWCr
Beautiful Sunrise = 'Bostimebide'PBR (ClPatio)	MAsh SMrm SWCr
Behold = 'Savahold' (Min)	MJon
'Bel Ange' (HT)	MGan
§ Bella = 'Pouljill'PBR (Renaissance Series) (S)	CPou EPfP
'Belle Amour' (A × D)	EBee MAus
Belle Blonde = 'Menap' (HT)	MGan SPer
'Belle de Crécy' (G) 𝕐H4	CPou CSam GKir LStr MAsh MAus MMuc SFam SMrm SPer SWCr
'Belle des Jardins' misapplied	see *R.* × *centifolia* 'Unique Panachée'
Belle Epoque = 'Fryyaboo'PBR (HT)	LStr MGan MJon SMrm SWCr
'Belle Isis' (G)	MAus MRav SPer
'Belle Poitevine' (Ru)	MCot
'Belle Portugaise' (ClT)	MAus
§ 'Belvedere' (Ra)	CPou MAus MGan SPer WBor
Benita = 'Dicquarrel' (HT)	IDic
Benjamin Britten = 'Ausencart'PBR (S)	CSBt EPfP LRHS MAsh MAus MBri MJon NEgg WClo
Benson and Hedges Gold = 'Macgem' (HT)	CWSG
Benson and Hedges Special = 'Macshana'PBR (Min)	ECGP MJon
Berkshire = 'Korpinka'PBR (GC) 𝕐H4	LStr MGan NLar SWCr
Beryl Joyce = 'Tan96145'PBR (HT)	ESty SWCr
Best of Friends = 'Pouldunk'PBR (HT)	ECnt LSRN SWCr
Best Wishes = 'Chessnut'PBR (ClHT/v)	CSBt EBls LSRN MGan
Bettina = 'Mepal' (HT)	MGan
Betty Boop = 'Wekplapic'PBR (F)	MJon SRGP
Betty Driver = 'Gandri'PBR (F)	MGan
'Betty Prior' (F)	GCoc MGan
§ Bewitched = 'Poulbella'PBR (Castle Series) (F)	ECnt EPfP SWCr
Bianco = 'Cocblanco'PBR (Patio/Min)	GCoc MAus MRav MWat SPoG
Big Purple = 'Stebigpu'PBR (HT)	ECnt ESty MJon
Birthday Boy = 'Tan97607'PBR (HT)	CGro ESty LSRN LStr MRav SWCr
Birthday Girl = 'Meilasso'PBR (F)	CSBt ESty LSRN LStr MJon MRav MWat SCoo SMrm SRGP SSea SVic SWCr
Birthday Wishes = 'Guesdelay' (HT)	CTri LRHS MBri SWCr
Bishop Elphinstone = 'Cocjolly' (F)	GCoc
Black Baccara = 'Meidebenne'PBR (HT)	CPou EGxp ESty SWCr
Black Beauty = 'Korfleur' (HT)	MAus MJon
Black Country Pride = 'Franjolil' (F) **new**	MJon
'Black Ice' (F)	CGro MGan SPer SWCr
'Black Jack' (Ce)	see *R.* 'Tour de Malakoff'
Black Jade = 'Benblack' (Min/Patio)	MJon
'Blairii Number Two' (ClBb) 𝕐H4	EPfP LRHS MAus MRav NEgg NLar SEND SPer
'Blanche Double de Coubert' (Ru) 𝕐H4	CDul CSBt CSam CTri EBee ECnt ELan EPfP GCoc LBuc LSRN LStr MAus MGan MJon NEgg NLar SEND SMrm SPer SSea SWCr WEas
'Blanche Moreau' (CeMo)	MAus MGan NHaw NLar SKHP SLon SPer
'Blanchefleur' (Ce × G)	EWTr MAus MRav
'Blesma Soul' (HT)	CSBt
'Blessings' (HT) 𝕐H4	CBcs CGro CSBt LSRN LStr MAsh MAus MGan MGos MJon MRav MWat SMrm SPer SRGP SWCr
'Bleu Magenta' (Ra) 𝕐H4	EBee EWTr IArd MAus MRav NLar SEND SMrm SWCr WKif
'Bloomfield Abundance' (Poly)	CPou ECGP EPfP MAus MGan MRav SPer SWCr WHer
'Blossomtime' (Cl)	SMad SPer
Blue for You = 'Pejamblu'PBR (F)	EBee ECnt ESty GCoc LRHS LStr MAsh MAus MBri MGan MJon NPri SMad SMrm SPoG SWCr
Blue Moon = 'Tannacht' (HT)	CGro CTri ELan GCoc MGan MGos MJon MRav NPri SMad SPer SPoG SWCr
Blue Peter = 'Ruiblun'PBR (Min)	ESty MJon MWat SEND
'Blush Hip' (A)	MAus
'Blush Noisette'	see *R.* 'Noisette Carnée'
'Blush Rambler' (Ra)	CSBt EPfP EWTr MAsh MAus MGan MMuc SPer
'Blushing Lucy' (Ra)	SMrm
Blythe Spirit = 'Auschool'PBR (S)	MAus MBri NEgg
'Bobbie James' (Ra) 𝕐H4	CWit EPfP LRHS LStr MAus MBri MGan MJon MRav NEgg NLar SEND SPer SPoG SRGP SWCr WBVN
Bonica = 'Meidomonac'PBR (GC) 𝕐H4	CSam CTri EBee ECnt ELan EPfP ESty GCoc GKir LRHS LShp LStr MAsh MAus MBri MGan MJon MRav MWat NEgg NLar NPri SEND SMrm SPer SPoG SSea SWCr WClo WKif
§ Bonita = 'Poulen009'PBR (Renaissance Series) (S)	ECnt
'Bonnie Scotland' (HT)	MGan
Boogie-Woogie = 'Poulyc006'PBR (Courtyard Series) (ClHT)	ECnt LRHS MAsh MBri SWCr
'Born Again'	MRav
'Botzaris' (D)	SFam
'Boule de Neige' (Bb)	CBcs CGro EBee ECnt ELan ELon EPfP GCoc LRHS LSRN LStr MAus MBri MGan MRav NLar SFam SMrm SPer SWCr
'Bouquet d'Or' (N)	MAus
'Bouquet Tout Fait' misapplied	see *R.* 'Nastarana'
'Bouquet Tout Fait' (N)	EBee
'Bourbon Queen' (Bb)	MAus NLar
Bow Bells = 'Ausbells' (S)	MAus
Bowled Over = 'Tandolgnil'PBR (F)	ESty MGan SWCr
§ ***bracteata***	CHII CRHN ECre EWes GQui MAus
Brass Ring	see *R.* Peek-a-boo
Brave Heart = 'Horbondsmile' (F)	MAus MRav SPoG
Breath of Life = 'Harquanne'PBR (ClHT)	CGro CSBt CTri ELan EPfP LStr MAus MGan MRav SPer SWCr
Breathtaking = 'Hargalore'PBR (HT)	SWCr
Bredon = 'Ausbred' (S)	MAus
§ 'Brenda Colvin' (Ra)	MAus
'Brian's Star' (F)	MGan

	Bride = 'Fryyearn'PBR (HT)	ESty GCoc LSRN LStr MGan MRav SWCr
	Bridge of Sighs = 'Harglowing'PBR (Cl)	ECnt ESty LRHS LStr MAsh MBri SPoG SWCr
	Bright Day = 'Chewvermillion'PBR (ClMin)	SSea
	Bright Fire = 'Peaxi'PBR (ClHT)	SPer SSea SWCr
	Bright Future = 'Kirora' (Cl)	ECnt ESty MJon SWCr
	Bright Smile = 'Dicdance' (F/Patio)	MAus MGan MRav SPer
	Brilliant Pink Iceberg = 'Probril' (F)	LStr SWCr
	'Brindis' (ClF)	MGan
	Britannia = 'Frycalm'PBR (HT)	ECnt ESty MAsh SWCr
	Broadlands = 'Tanmirsch'PBR (GC)	MGan NLar SEND SLon SWCr
	Brother Cadfael = 'Ausglobe'PBR (S)	EBls LRHS LStr MAsh MAus MBri NEgg NLar SCoo SPer SSea SWCr WClo
	Brown Velvet = 'Maccultra'PBR (F)	ESty MJon SPer SWCr
§	***brunonii*** (Ra)	CPLG EWes MAus WCot
	- CC 5147	GKev
	- 'Betty Sherriff' (Ra)	GGar
§	- 'La Mortola' (Ra)	MAus MRav SPer
	Brush-strokes = 'Guescolour' (F)	ESty SWCr
	'Buff Beauty' (HM) 🏆H4	Widely available
	'Bullata'	see *R.* × *centifolia* 'Bullata'
§	'Burgundiaca' (G)	MAus
	Burgundian rose	see *R.* 'Burgundiaca'
	Burgundy Ice = 'Prose'PBR (F)	CGro CSBt EBee EBls ECnt ESty GCoc LRHS LShp LStr MGan MGos MRav SCoo SMrm SPoG SWCr
	'Burgundy Rose'	see *R.* 'Burgundiaca'
	'Burma Star' (F)	MGan SWCr
	burnet, double pink	see *R. spinosissima* double pink-flowered
	burnet, double white	see *R. spinosissima* double white-flowered
	Bush Baby = 'Peanob'PBR (Min)	SWCr
	Buttercup = 'Ausband'PBR (S)	LRHS MAus SWCr
	Buxom Beauty = 'Korbilant'PBR (HT)	ECnt ESty GCoc LRHS MAsh MBri MGos MJon NPri SCoo SPoG SWCr
	'C.F. Meyer'	see *R.* 'Conrad Ferdinand Meyer'
	californica (S)	GAuc MAus
	- 'Plena'	see *R. nutkana* 'Plena'
	'Callisto' (HM)	CSam MAus
§	Calypso = 'Poulclimb'PBR (ClHT)	ECnt SWCr
	'Camayeux' (G)	CPou ECnt MAus NLar SPer
	Cambridgeshire = 'Korhaugen'PBR (GC)	LStr MAus SPer SSea SWCr
	Camille Pisarro = 'Destricol' (F)	LRHS MRav SPoG
	'Canary Bird'	see *R. xanthina* 'Canary Bird'
	canina (S)	CArn CCVT CDul CGro CLnd CRWN CTri ECrN EMac EPfP GKir IFFs LBuc MAus MRav NWea SPer SPoG WMou
	'Cantabrigiensis' (S) 🏆H4	CSam EBee EPfP MAus NLar SLon SPer SSea
	Canterbury = 'Ausbury' (S)	MAus
	'Capitaine Basroger' (CeMo)	MAus
	'Capitaine John Ingram' (CeMo) 🏆H4	EBee EWTr MAus SEND SLon
	'Captain Christy'	see *R.* 'Climbing Captain Christy'
	'Captain Scarlet' (ClMin)	ESty
	Caramella = 'Korkinteral'PBR (HT)	MGos
	'Cardinal de Richelieu' (G) 🏆H4	Widely available
	Cardinal Hume = 'Harregale' (S)	ESty MGan NHaw
	Carefree Days = 'Meirivouri' (Patio)	EPfP LRHS MAsh MBri NPri SPoG
	Caring for You ambig.	LSRN
	Caring for You = 'Coclust'PBR (HT)	GCoc
	'Carmenetta' (S)	NHaw
	'Carol' (Gn)	see *R.* 'Carol Amling'
§	'Carol Amling' (F)	LSRN MJon
	carolina	NHaw SLPl
	'Caroline Testout'	see *R.* 'Madame Caroline Testout'
	Cascade = 'Poulskab'PBR (ClMin)	EBee ECnt
§	Casino = 'Macca' (ClHT)	CTri CWit ELon LAst MAsh MGan MRav SPer SPoG
	'Castle Apricot'PBR	see *R.* Lazy Days
	'Castle Cream'	see *R.* Perfect Day
	'Castle Fuchsia Pink'PBR	see *R.* Bewitched
	Castle of Mey = 'Coclucid' (F)	GCoc
	'Castle Red'PBR	see *R.* Krönberg
	'Castle Shrimp Pink'PBR	see *R.* Fascination = 'Poulmax'
	'Castle Yellow'PBR	see *R.* Summer Gold
	'Catherine Mermet' (T)	MAus
§	'Cécile Brünner' (Poly) 🏆H4	CTri ELan GCoc LRHS LSRN LStr MAus MCot MGan NLar SMad SMrm SPer SSea SWCr
	Celebration 2000 = 'Horcoffitup'PBR (S)	MAus
§	'Céleste' (A) 🏆H4	EPfP EWTr GCoc LStr MAus MRav NLar SEND SFam SPer
	'Célina' (CeMo)	LSRN MGan
	'Céline Forestier' (N) 🏆H3	CPou MAus MRav NLar SEND SFam SPer SPoG
§	'Celsiana' (D)	CPou CSam EBee EWTr MAus SFam SPer
	Centenary = 'Koreledas'PBR (F) 🏆H4	MGos SPer
§	× ***centifolia*** (Ce)	CArn LRHS MAus MRav SMad
§	- 'Bullata' (Ce)	MAus
§	- 'Cristata' (Ce) 🏆H4	ECnt EPfP LRHS LStr MAus MRav NLar SEND SFam SPer SWCr WBor
§	- 'De Meaux' (Ce)	MAus MRav NLar SPer
§	- 'Muscosa' (CeMo)	GCoc LRHS LStr MAus MGan MRav SEND SFam
	- 'Parvifolia'	see *R.* 'Burgundiaca'
§	- 'Shailer's White Moss' (CeMo)	MAus MGan SEND SFam
	- 'Spong' (Ce)	MAus
§	- 'Unique' (Ce)	MAus NLar
§	- 'Unique Panachée' (Ce)	CPou MAus MGan
	'Centifolia Variegata'	see *R.* × *centifolia* 'Unique Panachée'
	Centre Stage = 'Chewcreepy'PBR (S/GC)	MAsh MAus MJon
	'Cerise Bouquet' (S) 🏆H4	MAus MGan MRav SPer WKif
	Champagne Cocktail = 'Horflash'PBR (F) 🏆H4	LRHS SPer
§	Champagne Moments = 'Korvanaber'PBR (F)	CBcs CGro CSBt EBee EBls ECnt ELan EPfP ESty GCoc LRHS LSRN LStr MAsh MAus MGan MGos MJon MRav MWat NPri SPer SPoG SSea SWCr

'Champneys Pink Cluster' (China hybrid)	LRHS MAus
Chandos Beauty = 'Harmisty'PBR (HT)	EBee ECnt ESty GCoc LRHS LStr MJon SWCr
'Chanelle' (F)	MGan SDix SPer
Chantal Merieux = 'Masmaric' (Generosa Series) (S)	MRav
Chapeau de Napoléon	see *R.* × *centifolia* 'Cristata'
'Chaplin's Pink Climber' (Cl)	MGan
Charity = 'Auschar' (S)	LRHS
Charles Austin = 'Ausles' (S)	MAus MRav
Charles Darwin = 'Auspeet'PBR (S)	MAus MBri MJon NEgg SCoo SPer SWCr WClo
Charles de Gaulle	see *R.* Katherine Mansfield
'Charles de Mills' (G) ♀H4	CSam CWit EBee ECnt ELan EPfP EWTr GCra LRHS LShp LStr MAsh MAus MBri MGan MRav NLar SEND SFam SPer SRGP SWCr
Charles Rennie Mackintosh = 'Ausren'PBR (S)	CSBt LRHS MAus MBri NEgg SWCr
Charlie's Rose = 'Tanellepa' (HT)	ESty SWCr
Charlotte = 'Auspoly'PBR (S) ♀H4	EPfP ESty LRHS LSRN MAus MBri MJon NEgg SCoo SEND SPer SSea SWCr WClo
Charmant = 'Korpeligo'PBR (Min)	LRHS MGos
Charmian = 'Ausmian' (S)	MAus
Chartreuse de Parme = 'Delviola' (S)	MRav
'Château de Clos-Vougeot' (HT)	IArd
Chatsworth = 'Tanotax'PBR (Patio/F)	MRav MWat SMrm SPer SSea SWCr
Chaucer = 'Auscer' (S)	MAus
§ Cheek to Cheek = 'Poulslas'PBR (Courtyard Series) (ClMin)	MAsh SWCr
Cheerful Charlie = 'Cocquimmer'PBR (F)	LSRN MRav
Chelsea Belle = 'Talchelsea' (Min)	MJon
Cherry Brandy '85 = 'Tanryrandy'PBR (HT)	CSBt MGan
Cheshire = 'Fryelise'PBR (HT)	GCoc MJon
Cheshire = 'Korkonopi'PBR (County Rose Series) (S)	MAus
'Cheshire Life' (HT)	MAus
Chester Cathedral = 'Franshine' (HT)	MJon
Chianti = 'Auswine' (S)	MAus MGan NLar
Chicago Peace = 'Johnago' (HT)	MGan SWCr
Child of AchievementPBR	see *R.* Bella
Child of My Heart = 'Beapeace' (HT) **new**	EBls
Childhood Memories = 'Ferho' (ClHM)	SWCr
Chilterns = 'Kortemma'PBR (GC)	SWCr
'Chinatown' (F/S) ♀H4	CGro CSBt LStr MAsh MAus MGan MRav SMrm SPer SWCr
chinensis misapplied	see *R.* × *odorata*
- 'Minima' sensu stricto hort.	see *R.* 'Pompon de Paris'
- 'Mutabilis'	see *R.* × *odorata* 'Mutabilis'
- 'Old Blush'	see *R.* × *odorata* 'Pallida'
Chloe = 'Poulen003'PBR (Renaissance Series) (S)	CPou EBee ECnt LSRN SLon SWCr
'Chloris' (A)	CPou
'Chorus Girl' (F)	MBri
Chris Beardshaw = 'Wekmeredoc' (HT) **new**	MJon
Chris = 'Kirsan'PBR (ClHT)	ECnt ESty LSRN MAus MGan MJon SWCr WGor
'Christine Gandy' (F)	MGan
Christopher = 'Cocopher' (HT)	GCoc SWCr
Christopher Columbus = 'Meinronsse' (HT)	IArd MMuc
Christopher Marlowe = 'Ausjump'PBR (S)	LRHS MAus MBri SCoo
§ 'Chromatella' (N)	MAus
Cider Cup = 'Dicladida'PBR (Min/Patio) ♀H4	CTri ESty IDic LStr MAus SWCr
'Cinderella' ambig.	SWCr
'Cinderella' (Min)	CSBt MGan
Cinderella = 'Korfobalt' (ClS)	MJon
City Lights = 'Poulgan'PBR (Patio)	CSBt
City Livery = 'Harhero 2000' (F)	LRHS
'City of Cardiff' (HT)	MGan
'City of Leeds' (F)	MAsh MGan SPer SPoG
City of London = 'Harukfore'PBR (F)	CSBt SPer SWCr
City of York = 'Direktör Benschop' (Cl)	MCot
Clair Matin = 'Meimont' (ClS)	MAus
Claire Austin = 'Ausprior' (S)	EPfP ESty LRHS MAsh MAus MBri SSea SWCr
'Claire Jacquier' (N)	EWTr MAus SPer SWCr
Claire Rayner = 'Macpandem' (F/Patio)	MJon
Claire Rose = 'Auslight'PBR (S)	CGro CWit LRHS LSRN MAus MJon MRav SMrm SPer SPoG
Claire's Dream = 'Guesideal'	SWCr
Claret = 'Frykristal' (HT)	ESty GCoc LStr MJon SWCr
Clarinda = 'Cocsummery'PBR (F)	GCoc
Claude Monet = 'Jacdesa' (HT)	LRHS MRav SPoG
Cleo = 'Beebop' (HT)	LSRN MJon
Cleopatra = 'Korverpea'PBR (HT)	MGos
'Cliff Richard' (F)	ESty LSRN SWCr
'Climbing Alec's Red' (ClHT)	ELon
'Climbing Allgold' (ClF)	SLon
'Climbing Arthur Bell' (ClF) ♀H4	CSBt CTri ESty GCoc LAst LRHS MAsh MGan SPer SPoG SSea SWCr
'Climbing Ballerina' (Ra)	CSBt MGan SWCr
'Climbing Blue Moon' (ClHT)	MGan SWCr
§ 'Climbing Captain Christy' (ClHT)	MAus
'Climbing Cécile Brünner' (ClPoly) ♀H4	CSBt CTri EBee ECnt EPfP LSRN LStr MAsh MAus MBri MGan MRav NLar SEND SPer SPoG SSea SWCr
'Climbing Château de Clos-Vougeot' (ClHT)	MAus
'Climbing Christine' (ClHT)	MAus

§	'Climbing Columbia' (ClHT)	ERea EShb SPer
	'Climbing Crimson Glory' (ClHT)	CPou MAus MBri MGan
§	'Climbing Devoniensis' (ClT)	CPou
	'Climbing Ena Harkness' (ClHT)	CTri ELon GCoc MAsh MAus MBri MGan MRav SEND SPer SPoG SSea SWCr
	'Climbing Etoile de Hollande' (ClHT) ♀H4	CSBt CSam CTri CWSG EPfP GCoc LStr MAsh MAus MBri MGan MJon MRav MWat SEND SFam SMad SPer SPoG SSea SWCr WClo
	Climbing Fragrant Cloud = 'Colfragrasar' (ClHT)	CBcs ELan MGan
	'Climbing Home Sweet Home' (ClHT)	LSRN
	'Climbing Iceberg' (ClF) ♀H4	CGro CSBt EBee ELan EPfP ESty IArd LSRN LStr MAsh MAus MGan MJon MMuc MRav MWat NEgg NLar SEND SKHP SMrm SPer SPoG SSea SWCr WClo WHlf
	'Climbing Jazz'PBR	see *R.* That's Jazz
	'Climbing Josephine Bruce' (ClHT)	MGan
	'Climbing la France' (ClHT)	MRav
§	'Climbing Lady Hillingdon' (ClT) ♀H3	ECGP EPfP LRHS MAus MBri MGan MRav NEgg NLar SEND SPer SSea SWCr WBor
	'Climbing Lady Sylvia' (ClHT)	CSBt EBee EPfP LRHS MAus MBri MGan SPer
	'Climbing Little White Pet'	see *R.* 'Félicité Perpétue'
	'Climbing Madame Abel Chatenay' (ClHT)	MAus
	'Climbing Madame Butterfly' (ClHT)	MAus MGan NLar SPer
	'Climbing Madame Caroline Testout' (ClHT)	CPou CTri EBee MAsh MAus MRav NPri SEND SMad SPer
§	'Climbing Madame Edouard Herriot' (ClHT)	MAus
	'Climbing Madame Henri Guillot' (ClHT)	MAus
	'Climbing Maman Cochet' (ClT)	MAus
	'Climbing Masquerade' (ClF)	MAus MGan MRav NEgg SEND SPer SSea SWCr
	'Climbing Mrs Herbert Stevens' (ClHT)	EBee LRHS MAus MRav SEND SPer SWCr
	'Climbing Mrs Sam McGredy' (ClHT) ♀H4	CSBt MAus MGan
	'Climbing Niphetos' (ClT)	MAus
	'Climbing Ophelia' (ClHT)	MAus SEND SPer
	Climbing Orange Sunblaze = 'Meiji Katarsar'PBR (ClMin)	SPer
§	'Climbing Paul Lédé' (ClT)	EBee LRHS MAus SEND SWCr
	'Climbing Peace' (ClHT)	SPer
§	'Climbing Pompon de Paris' (ClMinCh)	CBot CTri MAus MGan MRav SEND SLPl SMrm SPer
	'Climbing Ruby Wedding'	LSRN
	'Climbing Shot Silk' (ClHT) ♀H4	EBee MGan SPer SWCr
§	'Climbing Souvenir de la Malmaison' (ClBb)	CPou EBee MAus SPer
	'Climbing Sterling Silver' (ClHT)	MGan
	'Climbing Sutter's Gold' (ClHT)	MGan
	'Climbing White Cloud'PBR	see *R.* White Cloud = 'Korstacha'
	Clodagh McGredy = 'Macswanle'PBR (F)	MJon
	'Cloth of Gold'	see *R.* 'Chromatella'
	Cloud Nine = 'Fryextra'PBR (HT)	ECnt GCoc SWCr
	Cocktail = 'Meimick' (S)	MGan
	'Colby School' (F)	EBls
	Colchester Beauty = 'Cansend' (F)	ECnt
	Colchester Castle = 'Poulcs008'PBR (Patio)	ECnt
§	'Colonel Fabvier'	MAus
	colonial white	see *R.* 'Sombreuil'
	'Columbia'	CPou
	'Columbian'	see *R.* 'Climbing Columbia'
	'Commandant Beaurepaire' (Bb)	EBee MAus
	common moss	see *R.* × *centifolia* 'Muscosa'
	Commonwealth Glory = 'Harclue'PBR (HT)	SWCr
	'Compassion' (ClHT) ♀H4	Widely available
*	'Compassionate' (F)	MRav
	'Complicata' (G) ♀H4	CTri EPfP EWTr LRHS LStr MAus MBri MCot MGan MRav NLar SEND SFam SKHP SPer SWCr
	'Comte de Chambord' misapplied	see *R.* 'Madame Knorr'
	Comtes de Champagne = 'Ausufo'PBR (S)	LRHS MAus MBri SCoo
	'Comtesse Cécile de Chabrillant' (HP)	CPou EBee MAus
	'Comtesse de Lacépède' misapplied	see *R.* 'Du Maître d'Ecole'
§	'Comtesse de Murinais' (DMo)	MAus SFam
	Comtesse de Ségur = 'Deltendre' (S)	MRav
§	'Comtesse du Caÿla' (Ch)	MAus SSea
	ConcertPBR	see *R.* Calypso
	'Conditorum' (G)	SFam
	Congratulations = 'Korlift' (HT)	CSBt ECnt IArd LSRN LStr MAus MGan MGos MJon MRav NPri SMrm SPer SRGP SSea SVic SWCr
	Connie = 'Boselftay'PBR (F)	EGxp ESty LSRN MGan
§	'Conrad Ferdinand Meyer' (Ru)	CSBt MGan NHaw SMrm SPer
	Conservation = 'Cocdimple'PBR (Min/Patio)	GCoc SMrm SWCr
	Constance Finn = 'Hareden'PBR (F)	MRav SWCr
	'Constance Spry' (ClS) ♀H4	EBee ELan EPfP LRHS LStr MAus MBri MGan MJon MMuc MRav MWat NEgg NLar NPri SMrm SPer SWCr
§	'Cooperi' (Ra)	CAbP CWib EWTr GGal LRHS MAus MCot SPer SSea SWCr WKif WPGP
	Cooper's Burmese	see *R.* 'Cooperi'
	'Coral Cluster' (Poly)	MAus
	'Coral Satin' (Cl)	MGan
	Cordelia = 'Ausbottle'PBR (S)	LRHS MAus MBri
	'Cornelia' (HM) ♀H4	CBcs CSBt CSam CTri EBee EPfP EWTr IArd LAst LRHS LSRN LStr MAsh MAus MCot MGan MJon MRav NLar SFam SMad SPer SRGP SSea SWCr
	Coronation Street = 'Wekswetrup' (F)	MJon
	Corvedale = 'Ausnetting'PBR (S)	LRHS MAus

cottage maid — see *R.* × *centifolia* 'Unique Panachée'
Cottage Rose = 'Ausglisten'^{PBR} (S) — CGro LRHS LSRN MAus MBri MRav SEND SMrm SWCr
'Coupe d'Hébé' (Bb) — MAus
Courage = 'Poulduf'^{PBR} (HT) — ECnt
Courvoisier = 'Macsee' (F) — CSBt
'Cramoisi Picotée' (G) — MAus
'Cramoisi Supérieur' (Ch) — MAus
Crathes Castle = 'Cocathes' (F) — GCoc
Crazy for You = 'Wekroalt'^{PBR} (F) — ESty LSRN MAsh MJon SRGP SSea SWCr
Cream Abundance = 'Harflax'^{PBR} (Abundance Series) (F) — ESty LStr SWCr
Crème Anglaise = 'Ganang'^{PBR} (ClHT) — MGan
Crème Brûlée = 'Ganbru'^{PBR} (Cl) — MGan
Crème de la Crème = 'Gancre'^{PBR} (ClHT) — CSBt EBls ECnt ELon ESty GCoc MAus MGan MJon MRav SPer SPoG SWCr
'Crépuscule' (N) — MAus
Cressida = 'Auscress' (S) — MAus
crested moss — see *R.* × *centifolia* 'Cristata'
Cricri = 'Meicri' (Min) — MAus
Crimson Cascade = 'Fryclimbdown'^{PBR} (ClHT) — ESty LRHS MAsh MBri MGan MRav MWat SPer SPoG SSea SWCr
crimson damask — see *R. gallica* var. *officinalis*
'Crimson Descant' (ClHT) — ECnt SWCr
'Crimson Globe' (Mo) — MGan
'Crimson Glory' (HT) — MGan SMrm WClo
'Crimson Shower' (Ra) $\mathbb{Y}^{H4}$ — CSam EWTr LRHS MAus MBri MGan MMuc MRav NEgg SEND SMrm SPer SWCr WHer
'Cristata' — see *R.* × *centifolia* 'Cristata'
Crocus Rose = 'Ausquest'^{PBR} (S) — CWit EPfP LRHS LStr MAus MBri MGos MRav NEgg SMrm SWCr WClo
Crown Princess Margareta = 'Auswinter'^{PBR} (S) — ECnt EPfP ESty LRHS MAsh MAus MBri NEgg SCoo SPer SSea SWCr WClo
cuisse de nymphe — see *R.* 'Great Maiden's Blush'
'Cupid' (ClHT) — EWTr MAus SPer
I 'Cutie' (Patio) — ESty SWCr
Cymbeline = 'Auslean' (S) — SPer
Dacapo = 'Poulcy012'^{PBR} (Courtyard Series) (ClPatio) — ECnt
'D'Aguesseau' (G) — MAus
'Daily Mail' — see *R.* 'Climbing Madame Edouard Herriot'
'Dainty Bess' (HT) — EBee EWTr MAus SSea SWCr
× ***damascena*** var. ***bifera*** — see *R.* × *damascena* var. *semperflorens*
§ - var. ***semperflorens*** (D) — MAus MRav NLar SSea SWCr
- 'Trigintipetala' misapplied — see *R.* 'Professeur Emile Perrot'
§ - 'Versicolor' (D/d) — MAus MGan SEND SPer SSea SWCr
Dame Wendy = 'Canson' (F) — MAus MGan
Dames de Chenonceau = 'Delpabra' (S) — MRav
'Danaë' (HM) — CSam MAus
Dancing Queen = 'Fryfeston' (ClHT) — EBee ECnt GCoc LRHS MAsh MBri NPri SWCr
Danny Boy = 'Dicxcon'^{PBR} (Patio) — IDic MJon WGor
'Danse du Feu' (ClF) — CBcs CSBt CTri CWSG ELan EPfP GKir LRHS LStr MAsh MAus MGan MJon MRav NPri SMrm SPer SPoG SWCr
'Daphne Gandy' (F) — MGan
Dapple Dawn = 'Ausapple' (S) — MAus
Darcey Bussell = 'Ausdecorum'^{PBR} (S) — CSBt EPfP ESty LRHS MAsh MAus MBri SSea SWCr WClo
'Dart's Defender' (Ru) — SLPl
David Whitfield = 'Gana'^{PBR} (F) — MGan
davidii — MAus
Dawn Chorus = 'Dicquasar'^{PBR} (HT) $\mathbb{Y}^{H4}$ — CGro CSBt CWSG ECnt EPfP ESty IDic LRHS LStr MAsh MBri MGan MRav MWat SPer SPoG SWCr
'Daybreak' (HM) — CTri EBee MAus
'De Meaux' — see *R.* × *centifolia* 'De Meaux'
'De Meaux, White' — see *R.* 'White de Meaux'
§ 'De Resht' (DPo) $\mathbb{Y}^{H4}$ — CPou CTri EBee ECnt EPfP GKir LRHS MAsh MAus MCot MGan MJon MRav NLar SEND SMrm SPer SWCr
'Dearest' (F) — CBcs CSBt MGan MRav SPer SWCr
'Debbie Thomas' (HT) — MJon
Deb's Delight = 'Legsweet'^{PBR} (F) — LSRN MJon
'Debutante' (Ra) — CSam EBee EWTr LRHS MAus SMrm
'Deep Secret' (HT) $\mathbb{Y}^{H4}$ — CBcs CGro CSBt CTri CWSG EBee ECnt EPfP ESty GCoc LRHS LStr MAsh MGan MJon MRav NPri SMrm SPer SPoG SRGP SSea SWCr
'Delambre' (DPo) — MAus
Della Balfour = 'Harblend'^{PBR} (ClHT) — SWCr
Dentelle de Malines = 'Lenfro' (S) — LRHS MAus
Desert Island = 'Dicfizz'^{PBR} (F) — GCoc IDic
'Designer Sunset' (Patio) — MAsh SPoG SWCr
§ 'Desprez à Fleur Jaune' (N) — IArd LRHS MAus MGos MRav NEgg NLar SFam SPer SWCr
'Devon Maid' (ClHT) — SWCr
'Devoniensis' (ClT) — see *R.* 'Climbing Devoniensis'
Diamond Anniversary = 'Morsixty' (Min) **new** — LSRN
'Diamond Celebration' — LSRN
Diamond Days Forever = 'Fryjess' (F) — ESty LSRN SWCr
'Diamond Jubilee' (HT) — CSBt MGan SWCr
Diamond = 'Korgazell'^{PBR} (Patio) — ESty LSRN LStr MGan MGos MJon SWCr
'Diamond Wishes'^{PBR} — see *R.* Misty Hit
Dick's Delight = 'Dicwhistle' (GC) — ESty LSRN MJon SWCr
Die Welt = 'Diekor' (HT) — MJon
Dizzy Heights = 'Fryblissful'^{PBR} (ClHT) — GCoc MAsh MAus MGan MRav SMrm SPer SWCr
'Docteur Grill' (T) — MAus
Doctor Goldberg = 'Gandol' (HT) — MGan
Doctor Jackson = 'Ausdoctor' (S) — MAus
Doctor Jo = 'Fryatlanta'^{PBR} (F) — SWCr
'Doctor John Snow' (HT) — MGan
'Doctor W. Van Fleet' (Ra/Cl) — MAus
'Don Charlton' (HT) — NEgg
'Don Juan' (ClHT) — MGan SWCr
'Doreen' (HT) — LSRN
'Doris Tysterman' (HT) — CGro CTri LStr MAus MGan SPer SRGP

Dorothy = 'Cocrocket'PBR (F)	GCoc LSRN MRav
'Dorothy Perkins' (Ra)	CGro CTri GCoc LRHS MAus MGan MRav NLar NPer SPer
'Dortmund' (S) ♀H4	EPfP MAus MGan NHaw NLar SWCr
Double Delight = 'Andeli' (HT)	CGro ESty GCoc LSRN MGan MJon SPer SWCr
Dream Lover = 'Peayetti'PBR (Patio)	ESty MJon SWCr
'Dreaming Spires' (Cl)	SPer SWCr
Drummer Boy = 'Harvacity'PBR (F/Patio)	MGan SPer
§ 'Du Maître d'Ecole' (G)	ELon LRHS MAus MRav WHer
Dublin Bay = 'Macdub' (ClF) ♀H4	CSBt CTri EBee ECnt ELan EPfP GKir IArd LAst LRHS LStr MAsh MBri MGan MJon MRav NLar SEND SMrm SPer SSea SWCr
'Duc de Guiche' (G) ♀H4	CSam MAus SEND SFam SLon SPer WHer
Duchess of Cornwall = 'Tan97157' (HT)	CSBt SWCr WClo
'Duchess of Portland'	see *R.* 'Portlandica'
Duchess of YorkPBR	see *R.* Sunseeker
'Duchesse d'Angoulême' (Ce × G)	MAus SFam
'Duchesse de Buccleugh' (G)	MAus MRav SMrm
§ 'Duchesse de Montebello' (G) ♀H4	EWTr MAus NLar SFam SLon SPer
'Duchesse de Verneuil' (CeMo)	MAus SFam
'Duke of Edinburgh' (HP)	MAus
'Duke of Windsor' (HT)	MGan SPer
'Dundee Rambler' (Ra)	MAus
§ 'Duplex' (S)	MAus
'Dupontii' (S)	EWTr MAus MGan SFam SPer
'Dusky Maiden' (F)	MAus MCot SWCr
Dusty Springfield = 'Horluvdust' (F)	MGan
'Dutch Gold' (HT)	MAus MGan SPer
'E.H. Morse'	see *R.* 'Ernest H. Morse'
'Easlea's Golden Rambler' (Ra) ♀H4	EBee ECGP EPfP LRHS MAus MRav NEgg NLar SLon
'Easter Morning' (Min)	SPer
Easy Going = 'Harflow'PBR (F)	IArd MAsh MRav SWCr
'Eblouissant' (Poly)	MGan
ecae	MAus
'Eddie's Jewel' (*moyesii* hybrid)	LSRN MAus MGan
'Eden Rose' (HT)	MGan SLon
Eden Rose '88 = 'Meiviolin'PBR (ClHT)	CPou MJon SPer SWCr
Edith Holden = 'Chewlegacy'PBR (F)	ESty SPer
'Edward Hyams' (*persica* hybrid)	MAus
Edward's Rose = 'Smi73/7/97' (F) **new**	ESty
eglanteria	see *R. rubiginosa*
Eglantyne = 'Ausmak'PBR (S) ♀H4	CSBt EBls EPfP ESty GCoc LRHS MAsh MAus MBri MJon MRav SEND SMrm SPer SPoG SSea SWCr WClo
'Eleanor' (Min)	EWTr
Eleanor = 'Poulberin'PBR (S)	ECnt SLon SWCr
§ ***elegantula*** 'Persetosa' (S)	MAus NLar SKHP SPer
Elfe = 'Tanelfe' (HT)	NHaw
§ Elina = 'Dicjana'PBR (HT) ♀H4	ECnt IDic LStr MAus MGan MGos MJon MRav SPer SPoG SWCr
Elizabeth = 'Coctail'PBR (F)	GCoc

'Elizabeth Harkness' (HT)	MAus MGan SPer
Elizabeth of Glamis = 'Macel' (F)	CGro CTri GCoc MGan SPer SWCr
Elizabeth Stuart = 'Maselstu' (Generosa Series) (S)	LSRN MRav
Elle = 'Meibderos'PBR (HT)	ESty LSRN SWCr
Ellen = 'Auscup' (S)	MAus
'Ellen Poulsen' (Poly)	MGan
'Ellen Willmott' (HT)	EBee EWTr MAus MCot SPer
'Elmshorn' (S)	CBcs MGan
Eloise = 'Kirsandra' (HT)	ESty MJon
Elspeth Marshall = 'Coczefma' (HT) **new**	GCoc
Emanuel = 'Ausuel' (S)	SPer
Emilien Guillot = 'Masemgui' (Generosa Series) (S)	MRav
'Emily Gray' (Ra)	CGro CTri ECnt EPfP GKir LRHS LStr MAsh MAus MGan MRav SEND SPer SWCr
Emily Victoria = 'Boshipeacon'	MGan
'Emma Wright' (HT)	MAus
'Empereur du Maroc' (HP)	MAus MRav SMrm
Empress Michiko = 'Dicnifty'PBR (HT)	ESty IDic
'Ena Harkness' (HT)	CTri ELan LRHS MGan SRGP SWCr
§ 'Enfant de France' (HP)	MCot
§ England's Rose = 'Ausrace' (S)	MAus
English Elegance = 'Ausleaf' (S)	MAus
English Garden = 'Ausbuff'PBR (S)	CGro EPfP EWTr LRHS MAus MGos MRav SEND SLon SMrm SPer
'English Miss' (F) ♀H4	CSBt CTri CWit ECnt EPfP ESty LStr MAsh MAus MGan MJon MRav SPer SPoG SWCr
'Eos' (*moyesii* hybrid)	MAus
'Erfurt' (HM)	MAus MGan SPer SWCr
§ 'Ernest H. Morse' (HT)	CSBt CTri GCoc MGan MJon MRav SPer SPoG SSea SWCr
'Ernest May' (HT)	SSea
Escapade = 'Harpade' (F) ♀H4	MAus
Especially for You = 'Fryworthy'PBR (HT)	CSBt CTri ELon ESty GCoc LRHS LSRN LStr MAsh MBri MGan NPri SCoo SRGP SSea SWCr
Essex = 'Poulnoz'PBR (GC)	MRav SPer SPoG SWCr
§ 'Estrellita de Oro' (Min)	SPer
'Etain' (Ra)	ECnt
§ 'Étendard' (ClHT)	MGan MRav SPer SPoG SWCr
Eternally Yours = 'Macspeego'PBR (HT)	EBee ECnt MJon
'Ethel' (Ra)	CPou EBee LSRN SWCr
'Étoile de Hollande' (HT)	EBee ELan GKir LRHS NEgg NLar SLon SMrm
'Eugénie Guinoisseau' (Mo)	CPou
Euphoria = 'Intereup'PBR (GC/S)	GCoc IDic SWCr
'Europeana' (F)	MGan
'Evangeline' (Ra)	MAus
Evelyn = 'Aussaucer'PBR (S) ♀H4	CSBt EBee EPfP ESty GCoc LRHS LSRN MAus MBri MGan MJon MRav NEgg NLar SMrm SPer SWCr
§ Evelyn Fison = 'Macev' (F)	CSBt CTri ELan LSRN MAus MGan MRav SPer SWCr
Evening Light = 'Chewpechette'PBR (ClMin)	MAsh
Evening Light = 'Tarde Gris' (ClMin)	LRHS MBri SSea

'Excelsa' (Ra)	CSBt CTri EPfP GKir IArd MAsh MGan MRav NWea SMrm SPoG
Exception = 'Rotes Meer' (Ru)	EBls SEND
Eye Paint = 'Maceye' (F)	MAus
'Eyecatcher' (F)	ECnt
'F.E. Lester'	see *R.* 'Francis E. Lester'
§ 'F.J. Grootendorst' (Ru)	MAus MGan NEgg SPer
'Fabvier'	see *R.* 'Colonel Fabvier'
Fair Bianca = 'Ausca' (S)	MAus
Fairy Prince = 'Harnougette' (GC)	ESty
Fairy Queen = 'Sperien' (Poly/GC)	IDic
'Fairy Rose'	see *R.* 'The Fairy'
Fairy Snow = 'Holfairy' (S)	SWCr
Fairyland = 'Harlayalong' (Poly)	MGan
Faithful Friend = 'Beachallenge' (S) **new**	EBls
Falstaff = 'Ausverse'PBR (S)	CSBt ECnt EPfP LRHS LSRN LStr MAsh MAus MBNS MBri MGos MJon MRav NEgg SMrm SPoG SSea SWCr WClo
'Fantin-Latour' (*centifolia* hybrid) 𝕐H4	CTri EBee ECnt ELan EPfP EWTr GCoc GCra LAst LRHS LStr MAus MBri MCot MGan MRav MWat NEgg NLar SEND SFam SMad SPer SSea SWCr WKif
farreri var. ***persetosa***	see *R. elegantula* 'Persetosa'
Fascination = 'Jacoyel' (Castle Series) (HT)	LStr MBri SCoo
§ Fascination = 'Poulmax'PBR (F) 𝕐H4	CSBt CWit ECnt EPfP LRHS MGan MGos MRav MWat SPer SRGP SWCr
Father's Favourite = 'Gandoug' (F)	LSRN MGan SWCr
§ Favourite Hit = 'Poululv'PBR (Patio)	MAsh
fedtschenkoana misapplied	MAus SPer
fedtschenkoana Regel	SLPl
Fée des Neiges	see *R.* Iceberg
'Felicia' (HM) 𝕐H4	CSBt CSam CTri EBee ECnt ELan EPfP EWTr GCoc GKir LRHS LStr MAsh MAus MCot MGan MGos MJon MRav NLar SEND SFam SKHP SMad SMrm SPer SWCr WKif
'Félicité Parmentier' (A × D) 𝕐H4	EBee LRHS MAus MBri MGan MRav NLar SEND SFam SPer SWCr
§ 'Félicité Perpétue' (Ra) 𝕐H4	CBcs CSBt CWit EBee ELan EPfP GCoc GKir LRHS LShp LStr MAsh MAus MBri MGan MRav NEgg NLar SEND SFam SMrm SPer SPoG SSea SWCr
'Fellemberg' (ClCh)	MAus
Fellowship = 'Harwelcome'PBR (F) 𝕐H4	ECnt ESty LStr MAus MGan MJon MRav SCoo SSea SWCr
'Ferdinand Pichard' (Bb) 𝕐H4	CPou CSBt ECnt ELon EPfP ESty LAst LRHS MAus MBri MCot MGan MJon MRav MWat NEgg NLar SEND SKHP SPer SPoG SSea SWCr WFoF WKif
Ferdy = 'Keitoli'PBR (GC)	MRav SPer
Fergie = 'Ganfer'PBR (F/Patio)	MGan SWCr
ferruginea	see *R. glauca* Pourr.
Festival = 'Kordialo'PBR (Patio)	ESty LStr MRav SPer SPoG SWCr
Fetzer Syrah Rosé = 'Harextra'PBR (S)	ESty
Fiery Hit = 'Poulfiry'PBR (PatioHit Series) (Min)	MAsh
Fiery Sunblaze = 'Meineyta'PBR (Min)	SWCr
Fiesta = 'Macfirinlin' (Patio)	MJon
filipes	GAuc
- 'Brenda Colvin'	see *R.* 'Brenda Colvin'
§ - 'Kiftsgate' (Ra) 𝕐H4	Widely available
§ 'Fimbriata' (Ru)	CPou ECGP ELon MAus NLar SPer WBor
Financial Times Centenary = 'Ausfin' (S)	MAus
Fiona = 'Meibeluxen'PBR (S/GC)	LSRN
First Great Western = 'Oracharpam' (HT)	ESty LStr MJon SMrm SWCr
'First Love' (HT)	MGan
'Fisher and Holmes' (HP)	MAus
Fisherman's Friend = 'Auschild'PBR (S)	MAus SPer
Flashdance = 'Poulyc004'PBR (ClMin)	ECnt LRHS
'Flora' (HT) **new**	MAus
'Flora McIvor' (RH)	MGan NHaw
'Flore' (Ra)	CRHN
'Florence Mary Morse' (S)	SDix
Florence Nightingale = 'Ganflor'PBR (F)	MGan SPer
'Flower Carpet Amber'	MAsh SCoo
'Flower Carpet Coral'PBR (GC)	CGro GCoc LRHS MAsh MBri SCoo SWCr
Flower Carpet Gold = 'Noalesa'PBR (GC)	EBee ECnt GCoc LRHS MAsh MBri NPri SPoG SWCr
Flower Carpet PinkPBR	see *R.* Pink Flower Carpet
Flower Carpet Red Velvet = 'Noare'PBR (GC/S)	CGro ECnt ELan EPfP GCoc LRHS LStr MAsh MBri MGan NPri SCoo SPer SPoG SWCr
Flower Carpet Ruby (GC) **new**	LRHS MAsh SCoo
§ Flower Carpet Sunshine = 'Noason'PBR (GC)	CGro CTri ELan EPfP GCoc LRHS LStr MAsh SCoo SPer
Flower Carpet White = 'Noaschnee'PBR (GC) 𝕐H4	CGro CTri EBee ECnt ELan EPfP GCoc LRHS LStr MAsh MAus MBri MGan NPri SCoo SPer SPoG SWCr
Flower Power = 'Frycassia'PBR (Patio)	CSBt ECnt ELon ESty GCoc LRHS LStr MAsh MAus MJon MRav SPoG SWCr
§ ***foetida*** (S)	MAus NHaw
§ - 'Bicolor' (S)	CArn MAus NHaw
§ - 'Persiana' (S)	MAus MGan NHaw SPer
foliolosa	SLPl
Fond Memories = 'Kirfelix'PBR (Patio)	ESty LSRN LStr MJon SWCr
For You With Love = 'Fryjangle' (Patio)	LSRN MGan
Forever Royal = 'Franmite' (F)	ESty
Forever Young = 'Jacimgol'PBR (F)	IDic
Forget Me Not = 'Coccharm' (HT)	GCoc
forrestiana	LRHS MAus
Fortune's double yellow	see *R.* × *odorata* 'Pseudindica'
'Fountain' (HT)	MAus MGan SPer SWCr
Fragrant Cloud = 'Tanellis' (HT)	CGro CTri CWSG EPfP ESty GCoc LRHS LStr MAsh MAus MBri MGan MGos MJon MRav MWat NPri SMrm SPer SPoG SWCr
'Fragrant Delight' (F) 𝕐H4	CSBt CWit ELan GCoc LStr MAus MGan MJon MRav MWat SPer SPoG
Fragrant Dream = 'Dicodour'PBR (HT)	CGro CWit ESty IDic LStr MGan MRav SWCr

Fragrant Memories = 'Korpastato'PBR (HT) — CSBt GCoc LRHS MGos SCoo SKHP SWCr
Fragrant Plum = 'Aroplumi' (HT) — SSea
'Francesca' (HM) — LRHS LSRN MAus MGan SFam SPer
Francine Austin = 'Ausram'PBR (S/GC) — LRHS MAus MBri NEgg SPer
'Francis Dubreuil' (T) — MCot
§ 'Francis E. Lester' (HM/Ra) ♀H4 — CRHN CSam EBee EPfP EWTr LRHS MAus MBri MJon MMuc NLar SMrm SPer SRGP SSea SWCr WClo
× *francofurtana* misapplied — see *R.* 'Impératrice Joséphine'
- 'Empress Josephine' — see *R.* 'Impératrice Joséphine'
'François Juranville' (Ra) ♀H4 — CPou CRHN EPfP EWTr GGal LAst LRHS LShp LStr LTen MAus MBri MGan MMuc MRav NLar SLon SMrm SPer SWCr
§ 'Frau Karl Druschki' (HP) — MAus
'Fred Loads' (F) ♀H4 — MAus MGan MRav
Freddie Mercury = 'Batmercury' (HT) — LSRN MJon NEgg
Free Spirit = 'Fryjeru' (F) — ECnt GCoc
Freedom = 'Dicjem'PBR (HT) ♀H4 — CTri EBls ECnt GCoc LStr MAus MGan MGos MRav MWat SMrm SPer SRGP SVic
'Frensham' (F) — MGan SSea SWCr
Fresh Pink = 'Macpinderal' (Min/Poly) — MGan
Friend for Life = 'Cocnanne'PBR (F) ♀H4 — GCoc LSRN MJon MRav
Friends Forever = 'Korapriber' (F) **new** — EPfP
'Fritz Nobis' (S) ♀H4 — EBee LStr MAus MGan MRav NHaw NLar SPer
Frothy = 'Macfrothy'PBR (Patio) — ECnt MJon
'Fru Dagmar Hastrup' (Ru) ♀H4 — CDul CSBt EBee ECnt ELan EPfP GCoc LBuc LRHS LStr MAus MGan MJon NEgg NLar SEND SMad SPer SWCr WBor
'Frühlingsanfang' (PiH) — CTri
'Frühlingsduft' (PiH) — EWTr
'Frühlingsgold' (PiH) ♀H4 — CBcs ELan EPfP GCoc LRHS LStr MAus MGan MRav NLar NWea SPer SPoG WKif
'Frühlingsmorgen' (PiH) — GCoc LStr MAus MGan SLon SMad SPer
Fulton Mackay = 'Cocdana'PBR (HT) — GCoc MGan
Fyvie Castle = 'Cocbamber' (HT) — GCoc
'Gail Borden' (HT) — MGan
§ ***gallica*** (G) — IFFs
§ - var. ***officinalis*** (G) ♀H4 — CAbP CArn CPrp CSam CTri EPfP GCoc GPoy LRHS MAsh MAus MBri MGan MJon MRav NLar SFam SKHP SPer SSea SWCr
§ - 'Versicolor' (G) ♀H4 — Widely available
Galway Bay = 'Macba' (ClHT) — LRHS MAsh MGan MRav SPer SWCr
§ Garden News = 'Poulrim'PBR (HT) — ECnt
Gardeners Glory = 'Chewability' (ClHT) — ESty MJon
'Gardenia' (Ra) — EBee EWTr LRHS MAus NLar SPer
'Gardiner's Pink' (Ra) — MCot
'Garnette Carol' — see *R.* 'Carol Amling'
'Garnette Pink' — see *R.* 'Carol Amling'
'Gaujard' — see *R.* Rose Gaujard
'Gelbe Dagmar Hastrup'PBR — see *R.* Yellow Dagmar Hastrup
'Général Jacqueminot' (HP) — MAus
'Général Kléber' (CeMo) — MAus SFam
§ 'Général Schablikine' (T) — MAus
Genesis = 'Fryjuicy' (Patio) — ECnt ESty LRHS MAsh MBri MJon SWCr
N ***gentiliana*** misapplied — see *R.* 'Polyantha Grandiflora'
N ***gentiliana*** H. Lév. & Variot — see *R. multiflora* var. *cathayensis*
Gentle Hermione = 'Ausrumba'PBR (S) — LRHS MAus MBri SWCr WClo
Gentle Touch = 'Diclulu'PBR (Min/Patio) — CSBt IDic MRav SPer
Geoff Hamilton = 'Ausham'PBR (S) — EPfP ESty LRHS LStr MAsh MAus MBNS MBri NEgg SCoo SMrm SPer SSea SWCr WClo
'Georg Arends' (HP) — MAus
George Best = 'Dichimanher' (Patio) — ESty IDic LSRN MJon SWCr
'George Dickson' (HT) — MAus
'Georges Vibert' (G) — EWTr MAus
'Geranium' (*moyesii* hybrid) ♀H4 — CBcs CDul CSam ELan EPfP GCoc GKir IArd LRHS LStr MAsh MAus MBri MGan MJon MRav NLar NPla NPri SEND SPer SSea SWCr
Gerbe d'Or — see *R.* Casino
'Gerbe Rose' (Ra) — MAus
Gertrude Jekyll = 'Ausbord'PBR (S) ♀H4 — Widely available
'Ghislaine de Féligonde' (Ra/S) — CPou CSam EBee LStr MAus MCot MGan NLar SMrm SPer SWCr WPen
GhitaPBR — see *R.* Millie
Ginger Syllabub = 'Harjolina'PBR (ClHT) — ECnt ESty GCoc SKHP SPoG SWCr
Gipsy Boy — see *R.* 'Zigeunerknabe'
giraldii — GAuc
Glad Tidings = 'Tantide'PBR (F) — CSBt CWSG MGan MRav SPer SWCr
Glamis Castle = 'Auslevel'PBR (S) — CBcs CTri EPfP LRHS LStr MAsh MAus MBri NEgg NPri SCoo SMrm SPer SWCr WClo
glauca ambig. — EMac GCra IFFs MHer MLLN NLar
§ ***glauca*** Pourr. (S) ♀H4 — Widely available
'Glenfiddich' (F) — CSBt CTri CWSG GCoc LStr MAus MBri MRav NPri SPer SWCr
Glenshane = 'Dicvood' (GC/S) — MRav
Global Beauty = 'Tan 94448' (HT) — MRav SWCr
'Gloire de Dijon' (ClT) — CGro CSBt CTri CWSG EBee ECnt ELan EPfP GKir LAst LRHS LStr MAsh MAus MBri MGan MJon MRav NEgg NLar NPri SMad SMrm SPer SWCr
'Gloire de Ducher' (HP) — EWTr MAus MGan NHaw
'Gloire de France' (G) — MAus MRav WHer
'Gloire de Guilan' (D) — MAus
'Gloire des Mousseuses' (CeMo) — LRHS MAus SFam
'Gloire du Midi' (Poly) — MAus
'Gloire Lyonnaise' (HP) — SLon
'Gloria Mundi' (Poly) — NEgg
Gloriana = 'Chewpope'PBR (ClMin) — CGro ECnt ESty LRHS MAsh MAus MBri MJon MRav MWat SCoo SKHP SMrm SPer SPoG SSea SWCr
Glorious = 'Interictira'PBR (HT) — ESty IDic SWCr
'Glory of Seale' (S) — SSea
Glowing Amber = 'Manglow' (Min) — ESty MJon
glutinosa — see *R. pulverulenta*
'Goldbusch' (RH) — MGan
'Golden Anniversary' (Patio) — LRHS LStr MAsh SPer SPoG SWCr

Golden Beauty = 'Korberbeni'^{PBR} (F)	ESty MAsh MBri MGos
Golden Beryl = 'Manberyl' (Min)	MJon
Golden Celebration = 'Ausgold'^{PBR} (S) $\mathbb{Y}^{H4}$	CGro CSBt CWSG ECnt EPfP ESty GCoc LRHS LSRN LStr MAsh MAus MBri MJon MRav NLar SMrm SPer SPoG SRGP SSea SWCr WClo
'Golden Chersonese' (S)	MAus SMad
Golden Future = 'Horanymoll'^{PBR} (ClHT)	MAus SWCr
Golden Gate = 'Korgolgat'^{PBR} (ClHT)	ECnt ESty LStr MAus MGos MJon SWCr
Golden Jewel = 'Tanledolg'^{PBR} (F/Patio)	ESty MAsh MBri SPoG
Golden Jubilee = 'Cocagold' (HT)	CTri CWit GCoc MRav SWCr
Golden Kiss = 'Dicalways'^{PBR} (HT)	GCoc IDic
Golden Memories = 'Korholesea'^{PBR} (F)	CBcs CGro CSBt CWit EBls ESty GCoc LRHS LStr MAsh MGos MJon MRav SCoo SPer SWCr
§ Golden Penny = 'Rugul' (Min)	MGan MJon
'Golden Rambler'	see *R.* 'Alister Stella Gray'
'Golden Salmon' (Poly)	MGan
'Golden Showers' (Cl) $\mathbb{Y}^{H4}$	Widely available
Golden Smiles = 'Frykeyno' (F) **new**	ECnt
Golden Tribute = 'Horannfree' (F)	MGan
Golden Trust = 'Hardish'^{PBR} (Patio)	LStr
Golden Wedding = 'Arokris'^{PBR} (F)	Widely available
'Golden Wedding Celebration' (F)	ESty LSRN SPoG
'Golden Wings' (S) $\mathbb{Y}^{H4}$	CTri ELan EPfP EWTr GCoc LRHS LStr MAus MGan MJon MRav NLar SEND SKHP SPer SSea SWCr
Golden Years = 'Harween'^{PBR} (F)	ESty
'Goldfinch' (Ra)	EBee ELan EPfP LRHS LStr MAus MBri MRav NEgg NLar SPer SPoG SWCr
Goldstar = 'Candide' (HT)	ECnt MGan
Good as Gold = 'Chewsunbeam'^{PBR} (ClMin)	CSBt ECnt ESty LStr MBri MJon SPer SRGP SWCr
Good Life = 'Cococircus'^{PBR} (HT)	GCoc SCoo SPer
Good Luck = 'Burspec' (F/Patio)	SPer
Good Wishes^{PBR}	see *R.* Favourite Hit
Gordon Snell = 'Dicwriter' (F)	IDic
Gordon's College = 'Cocjabby'^{PBR} (F) $\mathbb{Y}^{H4}$	ESty GCoc MJon
'Grace Abounding' (F)	LSRN
Grace = 'Auskeppy'^{PBR} (S)	CSBt EPfP ESty LRHS LSRN LStr MAsh MAus MBri MJon NEgg SMrm SPer SRGP SSea SWCr WClo
Gracious Queen = 'Bedqueen' (HT)	GCoc SWCr
'Graciously Pink' (Min)	MAsh
Graham Thomas = 'Ausmas'^{PBR} (S) $\mathbb{Y}^{H4}$	Widely available
Grande Amore = 'Korcoluma'^{PBR} (HT)	CSBt LRHS MBri MGos

'Grandma' (F)	LSRN
Grand-mère Jenny = 'Grem' (HT)	MGan
'Grandpa Dickson' (HT)	CBcs MAsh MAus MGan MJon MRav NPri SPer SRGP
Granny's Favourite (Patio/F)	LSRN SWCr
Great Expectations ambig.	CWit
Great Expectations = 'Jacdal' (F)	EBee SPoG
Great Expectations = 'Lanican' (HT)	CBcs
Great Expectations = 'Mackalves'^{PBR} (F)	ECnt EPfP ESty GCoc IArd LStr MAsh MJon MRav SCoo SPer SWCr
§ 'Great Maiden's Blush' (A)	GCoc MRav NLar SFam
'Great News' (F)	MAus
Greenall's Glory = 'Kirmac'^{PBR} (F/Patio)	MAus MJon MRav
Greetings = 'Jacdreco'^{PBR} (F)	IDic MAsh MRav SMrm SRGP WBor
Grenadine = 'Poulgrena'^{PBR} (HT)	ECnt
Grimaldi = 'Delstror' (F)	LRHS
'Grootendorst'	see *R.* 'F.J. Grootendorst'
'Grootendorst Supreme' (Ru)	SPer
Grouse = 'Korimro'^{PBR} (S/GC) $\mathbb{Y}^{H4}$	EPfP GCoc LRHS MAus NLar SEND SLon SMrm SPer SWCr
'Gruss an Aachen' (Poly)	EPfP EWTr LStr MAus MGan NLar SPer SWCr
'Gruss an Teplitz' (China hybrid)	MAus SPer
'Guinée' (ClHT)	CSBt CWit EBee ECnt ELan ELon EPfP EWTr GKir LAst LRHS LStr MAsh MAus MGan MRav NPri SEND SMrm SPer SPoG SSea
Guletta	see *R.* Golden Penny
'Gustav Grünerwald' (HT)	MAus
Guy Savoy = 'Delstrimen'^{PBR} (F)	MRav
Gwen Mayor = 'Cocover'^{PBR} (HT)	GCoc
Gwent = 'Poulurt'^{PBR} (GC)	CSBt ELan GCoc LSRN LStr SEND SPer
§ ***gymnocarpa*** var. ***willmottiae***	MAus MGan SPer SSea
Gypsy Boy	see *R.* 'Zigeunerknabe'
'Hakuun' (F/Patio) $\mathbb{Y}^{H4}$	MAus MGan
'Hamburger Phönix' (Ra)	CGro MGan SPer
Hampshire = 'Korhamp'^{PBR} (GC)	MAus MGan
Hand in Hand = 'Haraztec'^{PBR} (Patio/Min)	MAsh SPoG
Händel = 'Macha' (ClHT) $\mathbb{Y}^{H4}$	CGro CSBt CTri CWSG ELan EPfP LAst LRHS LStr MAsh MGan MJon MRav NEgg NLar SPer SPlb SPoG SSea SWCr
Hanky Panky = 'Wektorcent'^{PBR} (F)	CGro EBls ESty GCoc LRHS MAsh MBri MJon MRav NPri SCoo SWCr
Hannah Gordon = 'Korweiso'^{PBR} (F)	EBee EBls ECnt MGan SPer SWCr
'Hansa' (Ru)	EBee ECGP EMil GCoc LBuc MAus MGan SPer SWCr
Happy Anniversary ambig.	LSRN
Happy Anniversary = 'Bedfranc'^{PBR}	LSRN MJon NPri SWCr
Happy Anniversary = 'Delpre' (F)	CGro CTri LRHS LStr MAsh MBri MRav SPoG
'Happy Birthday' (Min/Patio)	CGro CWSG ESty LSRN LStr MGan SPoG SWCr
Happy Child = 'Auscomp'^{PBR} (S)	LRHS MAus MJon

Happy Retirement = 'Tantoras'PBR (F)	CGro ESty GCoc LRHS LSRN LStr MAsh MGan MRav MWat SCoo SMrm SPoG SSea SWCr
Happy Times = 'Bedone'PBR (Patio/Min)	LRHS
§ × ***harisonii*** 'Harison's Yellow' (PiH)	MAus SPer
§ - 'Lutea Maxima' (PiH)	MAus
§ - 'Williams Double Yellow' (PiH)	GCoc MAus MGan
Harlow Carr ambig.	CWit
Harlow Carr = 'Aushouse'PBR	LRHS MAus SCoo SMrm WClo
Harlow Carr = 'Kirlyl' (F)	MBri
Harrogate Rose = 'Macmaryl' (HT) **new**	MJon
'Harry Edland' (F)	SSea SWCr
'Harry Wheatcroft' (HT)	CGro MAus MGan SPer SWCr
Harvest Fayre = 'Dicnorth'PBR (F)	CTri IDic MGan SPer
Havana Hit = 'Poulpah032'PBR (Patio)	MAsh
'Headleyensis' (S)	MAus SLon
Heart of Gold = 'Coctarlotte'PBR (HT)	ECnt ESty GCoc MRav
Heather Austin = 'Auscook'PBR (S)	LRHS MAus
Heavenly Rosalind = 'Ausmash'PBR (S)	LRHS MAus
§ 'Hebe's Lip' (DxRH)	MAus MGan
'Helen Knight' (*ecae* hybrid) (S)	MAsh MAus NPri SSea
helenae	CTri MAus MGan NLar SPer
hemisphaerica (S)	MAus
§ 'Henri Martin' (CeMo)	LRHS MAus MGan NEgg NLar SLon SMrm SPer
Henri Matisse = 'Delstrobla' (HT)	LRHS MRav SPoG
'Henry Nevard' (HP)	MAus
Her Majesty = 'Dicxotic'PBR (F)	IDic
§ 'Herbstfeuer' (RH)	CPou SPer
Heritage = 'Ausblush'PBR (S)	CGro ELan ELon EPfP GCoc LRHS LStr MAsh MAus MBri MRav NEgg NLar SLon SMrm SPer SPoG SSea
'Hermosa' (Ch)	LAst LRHS MAus MRav
Hero = 'Aushero' (S)	MAus
Hertfordshire = 'Kortenay'PBR (GC) $\mathbb{Y}^{\text{H4}}$	ELan MAus MJon MRav NPri SEND SPer SWCr
× ***hibernica***	MAus
'Hidcote Gold' (S)	MAus
§ 'Hidcote Yellow' (Cl)	EBee LRHS MAus
Hide and Seek = 'Diczodiac'PBR (F)	IDic
High Flier = 'Fryfandango'PBR (ClHT)	SWCr
High Flyer = 'Jacsat' (ClHT)	SRGP
High Hopes = 'Haryup'PBR (ClHT) $\mathbb{Y}^{\text{H4}}$	EPfP LRHS LStr MAsh MAus MGan MJon SPer SPoG SSea SWCr
'Highdownensis' (*moyesii* hybrid) (S)	ELan MAus SPer
Highfield = 'Harcomp' (ClHT)	MAus SPer
Hilda Murrell = 'Ausmurr' (S)	MAus
'Hillieri' (*moyesii* hybrid)	MAus
'Hippolyte' (G)	MAus
Hole-in-one = 'Horeagle' (F)	LSRN SWCr
holy rose	see *R.* × *richardii*
'Homère' (T)	MAus

Honey Bunch = 'Cocglen'PBR (F)	ELon MGos MRav SPer SRGP
Honey Dijon = 'Weksproulses' (F)	CSBt EBee ECnt ESty GCoc MJon SWCr
Honeybun = 'Tan98264'PBR (Patio)	ESty
'Honorine de Brabant' (Bb)	CPou LRHS MAus SPer SWCr
Hospitality = 'Horcoff'PBR (F)	ESty
Hot Chocolate = 'Wekpaltez' (F)	Widely available
Hot Stuff = 'Maclarayspo' (Min)	MJon SWCr
Hot Tamale = 'Jacpoy' (Min)	MJon
House Beautiful = 'Harbingo'PBR (Patio)	SMrm
'Hugh Dickson' (HP)	CPou MAus NLar
hugonis	see *R. xanthina* f. *hugonis*
- 'Plenissima'	see *R. xanthina* f. *hugonis*
Humanity = 'Harcross'PBR (F)	MAus MRav
Hyde Hall = 'Ausbosky'PBR	LRHS MAus SCoo
Ice Cream = 'Korzuri'PBR (HT) $\mathbb{Y}^{\text{H4}}$	CSBt CWSG CWit ECnt ESty GCoc LStr MAus MGan MGos MJon MRav SPoG SWCr
§ Iceberg = 'Korbin' (F) $\mathbb{Y}^{\text{H4}}$	CBcs CGro CSBt CTri CWSG CWit EBee ECnt EPfP ESty GCoc LAst LRHS LStr MAsh MAus MGan MGos MJon MRav MWat NPri NWea SMrm SPer SPoG SSea SWCr
'Iced Ginger' (F)	MGan SPer
'Illusion' (ClF)	SWCr
§ 'Impératrice Joséphine' $\mathbb{Y}^{\text{H4}}$	CSam LRHS MAsh MAus MRav NLar SFam
In Memory Of	LSRN
§ In the Mood = 'Wekfrancoly' (HT) **new**	MJon
Incognito = 'Briincog' (Min)	MJon
Indian Summer = 'Peaperfume'PBR (HT) $\mathbb{Y}^{\text{H4}}$	CSBt CWSG ELon GCoc LRHS MAsh MRav MWat SMrm SWCr
Indianna Mae = 'Beacrunch' (S) **new**	EBls
'Indigo' (DPo)	CPou ELon MAus
Ingrid Bergman = 'Poulman'PBR (HT) $\mathbb{Y}^{\text{H4}}$	CWit ECnt EPfP LRHS LStr MAsh MAus MBri MGan MGos MJon MRav SMrm SPoG SRGP SWCr
Innocence = 'Cocoray'PBR (Patio)	GCoc
Intrigue = 'Korlech'PBR (F)	LStr
Invincible = 'Runatru'PBR (F)	MGan
'Ipsilanté' (G)	MAus
'Irène Watts' (Ch)	CPou EBee ECre EPfP EWTr LSRN NLar SKHP SWCr
'Irene's Delight' (HT)	LSRN
Iris = 'Coczero' (HT)	ECnt
Iris = 'Ferecha' (HT)	GCoc LSRN SWCr
Irish Eyes = 'Dicwitness'PBR (F)	CBcs CWSG EPfP ESty IArd IDic LStr MAsh MBri MGan MJon MRav MWat SCoo SPer SSea SWCr
Irish Hope = 'Harexclaim'PBR (F)	SWCr
Irish Wonder	see *R.* Evelyn Fison
Irresistible = 'Tinresist' (Min/Patio)	MJon
Isabella = 'Poulisab'PBR (Renaissance Series) (S)	CPou ECnt EPfP SLon SWCr
IsisPBR (HT)	see *R.* Silver Anniversary = 'Poulari'
Isn't She Lovely = 'Diciluvit' (HT)	ECnt ESty GCoc IDic SWCr
'Ispahan' (D) $\mathbb{Y}^{\text{H4}}$	CFee ELon EPfP LRHS MAus MBri NEgg NLar SFam SLPl SLon SPer

Jack's Wish = 'Kirsil' (HT) MJon
§ × ***jacksonii*** 'Max Graf' (GC/Ru) LRHS MAus MGan NLar
- Red Max Graf^{PBR} see *R.* Rote Max Graf
Jacobite rose see *R.* × *alba* 'Alba Maxima'
§ Jacob's Ladder = 'Weksacsodor' (ClHT) MJon
Jacqueline du Pré = 'Harwanna'^{PBR} (S) $\mathbb{Y}^{H4}$ ECnt EPfP ESty EWTr GCoc MAus MCot MGan MJon MRav NLar SLon SPer SWCr
Jacquenetta = 'Ausjac' (S) MAus
N 'Jacques Cartier' misapplied see *R.* 'Marchesa Boccella'
James Galway = 'Auscrystal'^{PBR} (S) CSBt CWSG LRHS LStr MAus MBri NEgg SCoo SSea WClo
'James Mason' (G) CSam MAus
'James Mitchell' (CeMo) MAus
'James Veitch' (DPoMo) MAus
Janet = 'Auspishus'^{PBR} (S) LRHS LSRN MAus MBri SSea SWCr
'Janet's Pride' (RH) MAus
§ 'Japonica' (CeMo) MAus
§ Jardins de Bagatelle = 'Meimafris' (HT) LSRN MJon MRav
Jasmina = 'Korcentex'^{PBR} (ClHT) CPou EPfP ESty MGos MJon SWCr
'Jaune Desprez' see *R.* 'Desprez à Fleur Jaune'
Jayne Austin = 'Ausbreak'^{PBR} (S) CSBt CWSG LRHS MAus SPer
Jazz^{PBR} (Cl) see *R.* That's Jazz
Jean = 'Cocupland'^{PBR} (Patio) GCoc
Jean Kenneally = 'Tineally' (Min) MJon
'Jean Mermoz' (Poly) MAus
'Jeanne de Montfort' (CeMo) MAus
'Jenny Duval' misapplied see *R.* 'Président de Sèze'
'Jenny Wren' (F) MAus
Jenny's Rose = 'Cansit' (F) EBee ECnt LSRN MGan SWCr
'Jens Munk' (Ru) NHaw
Jillian McGredy = 'Macarnhe' (F) MJon
Jill's Rose = 'Ganjil'^{PBR} (F) LSRN MGan SWCr
'Jimmy Greaves' (HT) MGan
Joëlle Marouani = 'Masjoma' (Generosa Series) (S) MRav
John Clare = 'Auscent'^{PBR} (S) LRHS MAus
John Gibb = 'Coczorose' (F) GCoc
'John Gwilliam' **new** MAvo
'John Hopper' (HP) MAus SWCr
'Jolly Roger' (F) SMrm
'Josephine Bruce' (HT) CBcs CSBt MGan
'Joseph's Coat' (ClS) IArd LAst LStr MGan SRGP SWCr
'Journey's End' (HT) MGan
'Jubilee Celebration' (F) EPfP
Jubilee Celebration = 'Aushunter'^{PBR} (S) CSBt EPfP ESty LRHS MAus MBri SMrm SSea WClo
Jude the Obscure = 'Ausjo'^{PBR} (S) CSBt ESty LRHS MAus MBri MJon NEgg SWCr WClo
'Julia's Rose' (HT) CGro LSRN LStr MAus MGan MJon SPer SWCr
Julio Iglesias = 'Meisiastri' (F) **new** ESty LSRN
'Juno' (Ch) CPou MAus
'Just for You' (F) SWCr
Just for You = 'Moryou' (Min) LSRN
'Just Jenny' (Min) LSRN MJon
'Just Joey' (HT) $\mathbb{Y}^{H4}$ CBcs CGro CSBt CWSG ECnt ELan EPfP GCoc IArd LRHS LStr MAsh MAus MBri MGan MJon MRav MWat NEgg NPri SMrm SPer SPoG SRGP SSea SWCr WClo
'Katharina Zeimet' (Poly) CPou CTri EBee MAus MGan NLar
§ Katherine Mansfield = 'Meilanein' (HT) CSBt
'Kathleen Ferrier' (F) MGan
'Kathleen Harrop' (Bb) ELon LStr MAus MMuc NLar SEND SFam SMrm SPer SRGP SSea SWCr
Kathleen's Rose = 'Kirkitt' (F) MJon
Kathryn McGredy = 'Macauclad' (HT) ESty MJon
Kathryn Morley = 'Ausclub'^{PBR} (F) LRHS MAus
'Katie' (ClF) LSRN MGan SWCr
N 'Kazanlik' misapplied see *R.* 'Professeur Emile Perrot'
Keep Smiling = 'Fryflorida' (HT) GCoc LStr MAsh MGan MHav SRGP SWCr
Keepsake = 'Kormalda' (HT) MGan MJon
'Keith Maughan' (Cl) EBls
§ Kent = 'Poulcov'^{PBR} (Towne & Country Series) (S/GC) $\mathbb{Y}^{H4}$ CSBt CWit ECnt ELan EPfP ESty GCoc LSRN LStr MGan MJon MRav MWat NLar SEND SMrm SPer SPoG SWCr
Kew Gardens = 'Ausfence' (S) **new** MAus
'Kew Rambler' (Ra) CRHN CSam EBee MAus MMuc MRav NLar SEND SFam SLon SPer
'Kiese' (*canina* hybrid) NHaw
'Kiftsgate' see *R. filipes* 'Kiftsgate'
'Kilworth Gold' (HT) MGan
Kind Regards = 'Peatiger' (F) LSRN
King's Macc = 'Frydisco'^{PBR} (HT) MAus MGan
'King's Ransom' (HT) CSBt MGan MRav SPer SPoG SWCr
Knock Out = 'Dadler' (F) MAsh SWCr
§ 'Königin von Dänemark' (A) $\mathbb{Y}^{H4}$ CWit EBee ECnt ELon EPfP GCoc LRHS MAus MBri MRav NEgg NLar SEND SKHP SPer SSea SWCr
§ 'Kordes' Magenta' (S/F) MAus
'Kordes' Robusta' see *R.* Robusta
Korona = 'Kornita' (F) SPer
'Korresia' (F) CSBt CTri ECnt EPfP ESty GCoc LStr MAsh MAus MBri MGan MGos MJon MRav SPer SPoG SWCr
§ Krönberg = 'Poultry'^{PBR} (Castle Series) (F) EPfP
'Kronprinzessin Viktoria von Preussen' (Bb) MAus
L.D. Braithwaite = 'Auscrim'^{PBR} (S) $\mathbb{Y}^{H4}$ CBcs ELan EPfP GCoc LRHS LStr MAsh MAus MBNS MBri MGan MJon MRav MWat NLar NPri SPer SWCr WClo
'La Belle Sultane' see *R.* 'Violacea'
'La France' (HT) MAus
'La Mortola' see *R. brunonii* 'La Mortola'
'La Perle' (Ra) CRHN
'La Reine Victoria' see *R.* 'Reine Victoria'
'La Rubanée' see *R.* × *centifolia* 'Unique Panachée'
La Sévillana = 'Meigekanu' (F/GC) SPer WCot
'La Ville de Bruxelles' (D) $\mathbb{Y}^{H4}$ LRHS MAus SLon SPer
Lady Emma Hamilton = 'Ausbrother'^{PBR} (S) EPfP ESty LRHS MAsh MAus MBri SCoo SPer SWCr
'Lady Gay' (Ra) WBor
'Lady Godiva' (Ra) MAus
'Lady Hillingdon' (T) MAus SMrm

'Lady Hillingdon' (ClT)	see *R.* 'Climbing Lady Hillingdon'
'Lady Iliffe' (HT)	MGan SWCr
Lady in Red = 'Sealady' (Min)	MJon
Lady MacRobert = 'Coclent' (F)	GCoc
§ Lady Meillandina = 'Meilarco' (Min)	CSBt
Lady of Megginch = 'Ausvolume'PBR (S)	ESty LRHS MAus MBri SSea SWCr WClo
Lady of Shalott = 'Ausnyson' (S) **new**	MAus
Lady Penelope = 'Chewdor'PBR (ClHT)	CSBt MAsh MJon SSea
§ 'Lady Penzance' (RH) ♀H4	CBcs MAus MGan SPer
Lady Rachel = 'Candoodle' (F)	ECnt
Lady Rose = 'Korlady' (HT)	MAsh
Lady Sunblaze	see *R.* Lady Meillandina
'Lady Sylvia' (HT)	MAus MGan NEgg
'Lady Waterlow' (ClHT)	EWTr MAus NLar
laevigata (Ra)	MAus MMuc NLar
- 'Anemonoides'	see *R.* 'Anemone'
Laguna = 'Koradigel'PBR (Cl)	MGos MJon
L'Aimant = 'Harzola'PBR (F) ♀H4	CSBt ESty GCoc LRHS LStr MAus MGan MRav SWCr
'Lamarque' (N)	CPou MAus
Lancashire = 'Korstesgli'PBR (GC) ♀H4	ECnt ESty GCoc LSRN LStr MAus MGan MRav SMrm SWCr
Lara = 'Wekplagneze' (HT) **new**	MJon
Laura Ford = 'Chewarvel'PBR (ClMin) ♀H4	CGro CTri LRHS LStr MAsh MAus MGos MJon MRav MWat SPer SPoG SRGP SSea
'Laure Davoust' (Ra)	CPou
Lavender Ice = 'Tan04249' (F) **new**	ECnt ESty
'Lavender Jewel' (Min)	MAus
'Lavender Lassie' (HM) ♀H4	CPou CSam MAus MGan NLar SPer SSea SWCr
Lavender Parfum de Provence = 'Meibriacus'PBR (HT) **new**	ESty
Lavender Symphonie = 'Meiptima' (Patio) **new**	ESty
Lavender Symphonies	SMrm
LaviniaPBR	see *R.* Lawinia
§ Lawinia = 'Tanklewi'PBR (ClHT) ♀H4	CSBt EPfP LStr MAsh MRav SPer SWCr
'Lawrence Johnston'	see *R.* 'Hidcote Yellow'
§ Lazy Days = 'Poulkalm'PBR (F)	ECnt
'Le Vésuve' (Ch)	EWTr MAus
Lea = 'Poulren019'	ECnt
Leander = 'Auslea' (S)	MAus
Leaping Salmon = 'Peamight'PBR (ClHT)	CGro CSBt EBee ELan ELon ESty GCoc LAst LStr MAus MGan MRav SPer SWCr
'Leda' (D)	ELon MAus NLar SFam SPer
'Lemon Pillar'	see *R.* 'Paul's Lemon Pillar'
Léonardo de Vinci = 'Meideauri'PBR (F)	CSBt
'Léontine Gervais' (Ra)	CRHN LRHS MAus MBri NLar
'Leo's Eye'	CPou EPfP
Leslie's Dream = 'Dicjoon' (HT)	IDic
'Leverkusen' (ClF) ♀H4	EWTr LRHS MAus MGan MRav NLar SEND SMrm SPer SWCr
Lichfield Angel = 'Ausrelate'PBR (S)	LRHS MAus MBri SCoo WClo
Lichtkönigin Lucia = 'Korlillub' (S)	SSea
Life Begins at 40! = 'Horhohoho' (F)	LSRN SWCr
Light Fantastic = 'Dicgottago' (F)	ESty GCoc IDic
'Lilac Dream' (F)	SWCr
Lilac Rose = 'Auslilac' (S)	MAus
Lilian Austin = 'Ausli' (S)	MAus
Liliana = 'Poulsyng'PBR (S)	ECnt SLon SWCr
Lilli Marlene = 'Korlima' (F)	CSBt ECGP MGan SPer
Lincoln Cathedral = 'Glanlin'PBR (HT)	MJon SPer
Lincolnshire Poacher = 'Glareabit' (HT)	NEgg
Lion's Fairy TalePBR	see *R.* Champagne Moments
Lisa = 'Kirdisco' (F)	LSRN MJon
Little Amy = 'Battamy' (Min)	LSRN
'Little Buckaroo' (Min)	SPer
Little Cherub = 'Tan00814' (Patio)	SWCr
'Little Flirt' (Min)	MAus MGan
'Little Gem' (DPMo)	MAus MGan
Little Jackie = 'Savor' (Min)	MJon
Little Rambler = 'Chewramb'PBR (MinRa) ♀H4	CSBt ECnt ESty LRHS LStr MAus MBri MGan MGos MJon MMuc MRav MWat SCoo SMrm SPer SSea SWCr
'Little White Pet'	see *R.* 'White Pet'
Little Woman = 'Diclittle'PBR (Patio)	IDic LStr
Lochinvar = 'Ausbilda'PBR (S)	MAus
'Lolabelle'	CPou
'Long John Silver' (Cl)	MAus SSea
longicuspis misapplied	see *R. mulliganii*
longicuspis Bertol. (Ra) AC 2097	GGar
§ - var. ***sinowilsonii*** (Ra)	GCal GGar MAus
aff. ***longicuspis***	SWCr
Lord Byron = 'Meitosier' (ClHT)	LStr SSea SWCr
'Lord Penzance' (RH)	CGro MGan NHaw SPer
Lorna = 'Cocringer' (F)	GCoc
'L'Ouche' misapplied	see *R.* 'Louise Odier'
'Louis Gimard' (CeMo)	MAus SFam
'Louis XIV' (Ch)	MCot
§ 'Louise Odier' (Bb)	EBee ECnt ELon EPfP EWTr IArd LRHS LStr MAus MBri MCot MGan MJon MRav MWat NLar SFam SPer SSea SWCr WBor
Love & Peace = 'Baipeace'PBR (HT)	ELan ESty SWCr
Love Knot = 'Chewglorious'PBR (ClMin)	CSBt ECnt ESty MAsh MJon MRav SCoo SRGP SSea SWCr WGor
§ Lovely Bride = 'Meiratcan'PBR (Patio)	MAsh MBri SPoG SWCr
Lovely Fairy = 'Spevu'PBR (Poly/GC)	IDic
Lovely Lady = 'Dicjubell'PBR (HT) ♀H4	CSBt EBee EBls ECnt ESty IDic LSRN LStr MAus MGan MJon MRav MWat SRGP SSea SWCr
Lovely MeidilandPBR	see *R.* Lovely Bride
'Lovers' Meeting' (HT)	MGan MRav SPer SRGP SSea SWCr
Loving Memory = 'Korgund'PBR (HT)	CGro CSBt CWSG ECnt ESty GCoc IArd LSRN LStr MGan MGos MJon MRav MWat NPri SPer SPoG SRGP SVic SWCr
Lucetta = 'Ausemi' (S)	MAus

	luciae* var. *onoei	EPot
	'Lucky' (F)	CGro CWSG ESty LShp LStr MGan NPri SMrm
	Lucky! = 'Frylucy' (F)	CSBt ECnt GCoc LBuc LRHS LSRN MAsh MBri MJon SCoo SPoG SSea SWCr
	Lucy = 'Kirlis' (F)	LSRN MJon
	Ludlow Castle	see *R.* England's Rose
	'Lutea Maxima'	see *R.* × *harisonii* 'Lutea Maxima'
	'Lykkefund' (Ra)	EBee MAus
	'Mabel Morrison' (HP)	MAus
	Macartney rose	see *R. bracteata*, *R.* The McCartney Rose
	Macmillan Nurse = 'Beamac' (S)	ESty
	'Macrantha' (Gallica hybrid)	MAus SPer
	macrophylla	MAus
	- B&SWJ 2603	WCru
§	- 'Master Hugh' ♀H4	MAus
	'Madame Abel Chatenay' (HT)	MAus
	'Madame Alfred Carrière' (N) ♀H4	Widely available
	'Madame Alice Garnier' (Ra)	CPou SPer
	'Madame Bravy' (T)	MAus
	'Madame Butterfly' (HT)	MAus MGan SPer SSea
§	'Madame Caroline Testout' (HT)	GKir LRHS MGan SEND SMad SPoG
	'Madame de la Roche-Lambert' (DPMo)	CPou MAus
	'Madame de Sancy de Parabère' (Bs)	EWTr IArd MAus SWCr
	'Madame Driout' (ClT)	CPou EBee
	'Madame Ernest Calvat' (Bb)	CPou
	'Madame Eugène Résal' misapplied	see *R.* 'Comtesse du Cayla'
	Madame Figaro = 'Delrona' (S)	MRav
§	'Madame Grégoire Staechelin' (ClHT) ♀H4	ECnt ELan EPfP LAst LRHS LStr MAus MBri MGan MJon MRav NEgg SEND SMrm SPer SPlb SWCr
	'Madame Hardy' (ClD) ♀H4	CPou CSBt EBee ECnt EPfP GCoc LRHS LStr MAus MBri MGan MJon MRav NEgg NLar SEND SFam SMrm SPer SSea SWCr
	'Madame Isaac Pereire' (ClBb) ♀H4	CSBt CTri EBee ECnt EPfP ESty EWTr GCoc GKir LRHS LStr MAsh MAus MBri MCot MGan MRav MWat NLar SFam SMad SMrm SPer SPoG SSea SWCr
	'Madame Jules Gravereaux' (ClT)	MAus
§	'Madame Knorr' (DPo) ♀H4	CPou EBee ECnt ELon EPfP EWTr GKir LRHS MAsh MAus MCot MRav NLar SEND SPer SSea SWCr
	'Madame Laurette Messimy' (Ch)	MAus SEND
	'Madame Lauriol de Barny' (Bb)	EWTr MAus MGan MRav NHaw NLar SFam SLon
	'Madame Legras de Saint Germain' (A × N)	CPou LRHS MAus NLar SFam SPer
	'Madame Louis Lévêque' (DPMo)	NLar
	'Madame Pierre Oger' (Bb)	EBee ECnt LRHS LStr MAus MGan MRav SPer SWCr
	'Madame Plantier' (A × N)	CPou LRHS MAus MRav NHaw NLar SEND SPer
	'Madame Zöetmans' (D)	MAus
	'Madeleine Seltzer' (Ra)	ECGP MGan
	'Madge' (HM)	SDix
	'Magenta' (S/F)	see *R.* 'Kordes' Magenta' (S/F)
	Magic Carpet = 'Jaclover'PBR (S/GC) ♀H4	CWSG ELan GCoc IDic MAus MGan MGos MRav SMrm SPer SSea SWCr
	Magic Hit = 'Poulhi004' (Min)	LRHS
	'Magnifica' (RH)	LRHS MAus MGan
	'Maid of Kent'PBR (Cl)	CSBt MAus MJon SCoo SPer SWCr
	'Maiden's Blush' (A) ♀H4	CArn CTri ELan EWTr GKir LRHS MAsh MAus MGan NPri SFam SPer SSea SWCr
	'Maiden's Blush, Great'	see *R.* 'Great Maiden's Blush'
	'Maigold' (ClPiH) ♀H4	CBcs CGro CTri ECnt ELan EPfP GCoc GKir LRHS LStr MAsh MAus MCot MGan MJon MRav MWat NLar SMad SPer SPoG SWCr
	Make a Wish = 'Mehpat'PBR (Min/Patio)	ESty LStr
	Maltese rose	see *R.* 'Cécile Brünner'
	Malvern Hills = 'Auscanary'PBR (Ra)	CSBt LRHS MAsh MAus MBri MGan MJon SPer SSea SWCr WClo
	Mamma Mia! = 'Fryjolly' (HT)	ECnt ESty GCoc LRHS MAsh MBri SMrm
	Mandarin = 'Korcelin'PBR (Min)	ESty LStr MRav
	Mandy = 'Korinor' (HT) **new**	MGan
	'Manning's Blush' (RH)	MAus
	Manou Meilland = 'Meitulimon' (HT)	SSea
	Many Happy Returns = 'Harwanted'PBR (F) ♀H4	CBcs CGro CSBt CWSG ECnt ELan EPfP GCoc LRHS LSRN LStr MAsh MGan MGos MJon MRav NPri SPer SPoG SRGP SSea SVic SWCr
	'Marbrée' (DPo)	MAus
	'Märchenland' (F)	MAus
§	'Marchesa Boccella' (DPo) ♀H4	CPou CSam CTri EPfP GKir LRHS MAsh MAus MBri MCot MGan MGos NLar NPri SMrm SPer SPoG SSea SWCr WBor
	'Marcia Gandy' (HT)	MGan
	'Maréchal Davoust' (CeMo)	MAus SFam
	'Maréchal Niel' (N)	ERea EShb EWTr MAus SPer
	'Margaret' (HT)	MGan
	Margaret Merril = 'Harkuly' (F) ♀H4	CBcs CGro CSBt CTri CWSG EBee ECnt ELan ELon EPfP ESty GCoc IArd LRHS LStr MAsh MAus MBri MGan MJon MRav MWat SPer SPoG SRGP SSea SWCr WBor
	'Marguerite Hilling' (S) ♀H4	EPfP MAus MGan MRav NLar SPer
	Maria McGredy = 'Macturangu'PBR (HT)	MJon
	'Mariae-Graebnerae'	SLPl
	'Marie Louise' (D)	MAus SFam
	'Marie Pavič' (Poly)	CPou MAus
	'Marie van Houtte' (T)	MAus
	'Marie-Jeanne' (Poly)	MAus
	Marilyn Monroe = 'Weksunspat' (HT)	MJon
	Marinette = 'Auscam'PBR (S)	MAus
	Marjorie Fair = 'Harhero' (Poly/S) ♀H4	EPfP ESty MAsh MAus MGan MRav SWCr WBor
	Marjorie Marshall = 'Hardenier'PBR	MRav
	'Marlena' (F/Patio)	GCoc MAus
	Marry Me = 'Dicwonder'PBR (Patio) ♀H4	ESty IDic
	'Martian Glow' (F)	MGan NLar
	'Martin Frobisher' (Ru)	MAus NHaw
I	'Mary' (Poly)	LStr

	Name	Suppliers
	Mary Magdalene = 'Ausjolly'[PBR] (S)	LRHS MAus
	'Mary Manners' (Ru)	NLar
	Mary Rose = 'Ausmary'[PBR] (S) ΨH4	CGro CSBt CWSG EBee ELan EPfP GCoc LRHS LSRN LStr MAsh MAus MBri MCot MGan MJon MRav MWat NLar NPri SMrm SPer SPoG SSea SWCr WClo WKif
	'Mary Wallace' (Cl)	MAus
	Mary Webb = 'Auswebb' (S)	MAus
	'Masquerade' (F)	ELan MGan SMrm SPer SSea SWCr
	'Master Hugh'	see *R. macrophylla* 'Master Hugh'
	Matangi = 'Macman' (F) ΨH4	MGan
	Matawhero Magic[PBR]	see *R.* Simply the Best
	'Max Graf'	see *R.* × *jacksonii* 'Max Graf'
	'Maxima'	see *R.* × *alba* 'Alba Maxima'
	'May Queen' (Ra)	CPou LRHS MAus MBri MGan MRav NLar SEND SFam SPer SWCr
	Mayor of Casterbridge = 'Ausbrid'[PBR] (S)	LRHS MAus
	'McCartney Rose'[PBR]	see *R.* The McCartney Rose
	'Meg' (ClHT)	EBee EWTr LRHS LSRN MAus MCot MGan MMuc SPer SRGP
	'Meg Merrilies' (RH)	MAus MGan NLar
	'Megiddo' (F)	MGan
	'Meicobius'[PBR]	see *R.* Terracotta = 'Meicobuis'
	Melody Maker = 'Dicqueen'[PBR] (F)	IDic
	Memento = 'Dicbar' (F) ΨH4	MGan
	'Memoriam' (HT)	MGan
	'Memories Are Made of This' (F)	MGan
	Memory Lane = 'Peavoodoo'[PBR] (F)	SWCr
	'Mermaid' (Cl) ΨH3-4	CBcs CGro CSBt CTri ECnt ELon EPfP LHop LRHS LStr MAus MBri MGan MJon NLar SEND SMrm SPer SPoG SSea SWCr
	'Meteor' (F/Patio)	MGan
§	'Mevrouw Nathalie Nypels' (Poly) ΨH4	LRHS LStr MAus MRav NLar SPer SWCr WKif
	Michael Fish = 'Kirgale' (F)	MJon
	'Michèle Meilland' (HT)	MAus
	Michelle Chetcuti = 'Kirchief' (HT)	MJon
	× ***micrugosa***	MAus
	- 'Alba'	MAus
	Midnight Blue = 'Wekfabpur' (S)	MJon
§	Millie = 'Poulren013'[PBR] (Renaissance Series) (S)	ECnt LRHS LSRN MAsh MBri NPri SPoG SWCr
	Millie Rose = 'Wekblunez' (HT) **new**	MJon
	Millionaire = 'Peazara' (F)	LSRN
	'Mills and Boon' (F)	MGan
	'Minnehaha' (Ra)	MAus
	Minnie Pearl = 'Savahowdy' (Min)	MJon
	mirifica stellata	see *R. stellata* var. *mirifica*
	Mischief = 'Macmi' (HT)	LSRN MGan SPer
	Miss Alice = 'Ausjake'[PBR] (S)	LRHS MAus MBri SWCr
	Miss Dior = 'Harencens'[PBR] (S)	MRav
	'Miss Edith Cavell' (Poly)	MAus
	Miss Flippins = 'Tuckflip' (Min)	MJon
	Missing You = 'Horcakebread' (F)	MGan SWCr
§	'Mister Lincoln' (HT)	MGan SPer SSea SWCr
	Mistress Quickly = 'Ausky'[PBR] (S)	MAus
§	Misty Hit = 'Poulhi011'[PBR] (PatioHit Series) (Patio)	ECnt LRHS LSRN MAsh SWCr
	'Mojave' (HT)	MGan
	Molineux = 'Ausmol'[PBR] (S) ΨH4	CSBt ECnt EPfP LRHS MAsh MAus MBri SMrm SWCr WClo
§	***mollis***	MAus
	'Monique' (HT)	MGan
	Moonbeam = 'Ausbeam' (S)	MAus
	'Moonlight' (HM)	CTri ELan EWTr LRHS MAus MGan MRav SMrm SPer SWCr
	Moonshine = 'Tan97123'[PBR] (HT) **new**	ESty
	'Morgengruss' (Cl)	MGan SPer SWCr
	Moriah = 'Ganhol'[PBR] (HT)	MGan
	'Morletii' (Bs)	MRav
	'Morning Jewel' (ClF) ΨH4	GCoc MGan MJon SPer SWCr
	Morning Mist = 'Ausfire' (S)	MAus SSea
§	'Morsdag' (Poly/F)	LSRN LStr MJon SVic
	Mortimer Sackler = 'Ausorts'[PBR] (S)	LRHS MAsh MAus MBri MJon SCoo WClo
	moschata (Ra)	MAus MRav SSea
	- 'Autumnalis'	see *R.* 'Princesse de Nassau'
	- var. ***nepalensis***	see *R. brunonii*
I	'Mother's Day'	SRGP
	Mother's Day	see *R.* 'Morsdag'
	Mother's Joy = 'Horsiltrop' (F)	LSRN
	Mountain Snow = 'Aussnow' (Ra)	LRHS MAus MBri
	Mountbatten = 'Harmantelle' (F) ΨH4	CWit ELan EPfP LRHS LStr MAsh MAus MGan MJon MRav NPri SMrm SPer SPoG SSea SWCr
§	'Mousseline' (DPoMo)	CPou MAus MRav NLar SPer
	'Mousseuse du Japon'	see *R.* 'Japonica'
	moyesii (S)	CDoy CTri ELan GCra GKev GKir MAus MGan NEgg NWea SKHP SPer
	'Mr Bluebird' (MinCh)	MAus MGan
	'Mr Lincoln'	see *R.* 'Mister Lincoln'
	'Mrs Anthony Waterer' (Ru)	MAus SPer
	Mrs Doreen Pike = 'Ausdor'[PBR] (Ru)	MAus
	'Mrs Eveline Gandy' (HT)	MGan
	'Mrs John Laing' (HP)	EPfP LRHS MAus NLar SFam SLon SWCr
	'Mrs Oakley Fisher' (HT)	MAus MCot SDix SMrm SPer SWCr
	'Mrs Paul' (Bb)	MAus
	'Mrs Sam McGredy' (HT)	LRHS MGan NEgg SSea
	'Mullard Jubilee' (HT)	MGan SWCr
§	***mulliganii*** (Ra) ΨH4	EPfP MAus SPer
	multibracteata (S)	MAus
	multiflora (Ra)	IFFs LBuc MAus NHaw NWea
§	- var. ***cathayensis*** (Ra)	WBor
§	- 'Grevillei' (Ra)	EBee MAus SPer
	- 'Platyphylla'	see *R. multiflora* 'Grevillei'
	'Mum in a Million'	see *R.* Millie
	Mummy[PBR]	see *R.* Newly Wed
	mundi	see *R. gallica* 'Versicolor'
	Munstead Wood = 'Ausbernard' (d)	LRHS MAus
	'Murjami' **new**	EBls
	'Muscosa Alba'	see *R.* × *centifolia* 'Shailer's White Moss'
	'Mutabilis'	see *R.* × *odorata* 'Mutabilis'
	'My Choice' (HT)	MGan
	My Everything = 'Coccastle' (F)	ESty GCoc
	My Love = 'Cogamo' (HT)	MJon
	My Mum = 'Webmorrow'[PBR]	EGxp ESty LSRN MGan SMrm SWCr
	My Valentine = 'Mormyval' (Min)	LSRN LStr MAsh SPoG SWCr

	Myriam = 'Cocgrand' (HT)	GCoc LSRN
	Mystery Girl = 'Dicdothis' (HT)	ECnt ESty GCoc IDic
	Mystique = 'Kirmyst' (F)	EBls MJon
	Nahéma = 'Deléri' (ClHT)	MRav SMrm SWCr
	nanothamnus	WCot
	'Narrow Water' (Ra)	CPou EBee NLar SWCr
§	'Nastarana' (N)	NLar
	'Nathalie Nypels'	see *R.* 'Mevrouw Nathalie Nypels'
	'National Trust' (HT)	CBcs IArd MAsh MGan MJon SMrm SPer
	'Nelson's Pride' (F)	EBls
	'Nestor' (G)	EWTr MAus
	'Nevada' (S) $\mathbb{Y}^{H4}$	CSBt CTri ECnt ELan EPfP EWTr GCoc IArd LStr MAsh MAus MCot MGan MJon MRav NLar SEND SPer SSea SWCr
	Never Forgotten = 'Gregart' (HT)	SWCr
	New Age = 'Wekbipuhit'PBR (F)	CSBt MJon
	New Arrival	see *R.* 'Red Patio'
	'New Arrival' (Patio/Min)	MGan SWCr
	New Beginnings = 'Korprofko' (F)	GCoc SSea
§	'New Dawn' (Cl) $\mathbb{Y}^{H4}$	Widely available
	'New Home' **new**	LSRN
	New Life = 'Cocwarble' (F)	GCoc
	'New Look' (F)	MGan
	New Zealand = 'Macgenev'PBR (HT)	MJon SWCr
§	Newly Wed = 'Dicwhynot'PBR (Patio)	IDic LStr MJon
	News = 'Legnews' (F)	MAus MGan SWCr
	Nice Day = 'Chewsea'PBR (ClMin) $\mathbb{Y}^{H4}$	CGro CWSG ELon EPfP ESty LRHS LStr MAsh MRav MWat SPer SRGP SSea SWCr
	'Nicola' (F)	MGan SWCr
	Night Light = 'Poullight'PBR (Courtyard Series) (Cl)	ECnt MGan MRav SWCr
	Night Sky = 'Dicetch'PBR (F)	IDic SSea
	Nina = 'Mehnina'PBR (S)	LSRN SWCr
	Nina Nadine = 'Kirhand' (F)	MJon
	Nina = 'Poulren018' (Renaissance Series) (S)	ECnt
	nitida	EMac MAus MGan NHaw NWea SEND SLPl SPer WHer
	Noble Antony = 'Ausway'PBR (S)	LRHS LStr MAus MBri MJon
§	'Noisette Carnée' (N)	CSam EPfP GCra LRHS LStr MAus MBNS MGan MJon MRav NLar SLPl SPer SSea SWCr WClo
	Norfolk = 'Poulfolk'PBR (GC)	NLar SMrm SPer
	'Norma Major' (HT)	MJon
	Northamptonshire = 'Mattdor'PBR (GC)	MGan
	'Northern Lights' (HT)	GCoc
	'Norwich Pink' (S)	MAus
	Norwich Theatre Royal = 'Beacalm' (S) **new**	EBls
	Nostalgia = 'Savarita' (Min)	CGro MAsh MAus MGan
	Nostalgie = 'Taneiglat'PBR (HT)	CSBt EBee EBls ECnt EGxp ESty LStr MBri MJon MRav SPoG SSea SWCr
	'Nottingham Millennium' (F)	MGan
	'Nozomi' (ClMin/GC) $\mathbb{Y}^{H4}$	CGro CTri ELan ESty EWTr GCoc MAus MGan MJon MRav NLar SMad SMrm SPer
	'Nuits de Young' (CeMo) $\mathbb{Y}^{H4}$	GCoc LRHS MAus SEND SFam SKHP
	'Nur Mahal' (HM)	MAus
	nutkana (S)	MAus
§	- 'Plena' (S/D) $\mathbb{Y}^{H4}$	EPfP MAus MGan NLar SKHP
	'Nymphenburg' (HM)	SPer
	'Nyveldt's White' (Ru)	MAus
	Octavia Hill = 'Harzeal'PBR (F)	EWTr MRav SPer SWCr
§	× ***odorata***	SVic
	- 'Fortune's Double Yellow'	see *R.* × *odorata* 'Pseudindica'
§	- 'Mutabilis' (Ch) $\mathbb{Y}^{H3-4}$	CRHN ECre EPfP EWTr GCoc GGal LRHS MAus MCot MGan MRav MWat SEND SKHP SMad SMrm SPer SPoG SSea SWCr WBor WCFE WCot WKif
§	- 'Pallida' (Ch)	EPfP GCoc LRHS MAus MCot MRav SEND SPer SSea SWCr
§	- 'Pseudindica' (ClCh)	MAus
	- (Sanguinea Group) 'Bengal Crimson' (Ch)	ECGP EPfP EWTr LRHS SKHP WCot WKif
	- - 'Bob's Beauty' (Ch)	WCot
§	- 'Viridiflora' (Ch)	EBee LRHS MAus SLon SPer SSea WCot
	Odyssey = 'Franski'PBR (F)	ESty MJon
	'Oeillet Flamand'	see *R.* 'Oeillet Parfait'
§	'Oeillet Parfait' (G)	MAus
	officinalis	see *R. gallica* var. *officinalis*
	'Oklahoma' (HT)	MGan
	old blush China	see *R.* × *odorata* 'Pallida'
	old cabbage	see *R.* × *centifolia*
	Old John = 'Dicwillynilly' (F)	IDic
	old pink moss rose	see *R.* × *centifolia* 'Muscosa'
	Old Port = 'Mackati'PBR (F)	IArd MJon
	old red moss	see *R.* 'Henri Martin'
	old velvet moss	see *R.* 'William Lobb'
	'Old Velvet Rose'	see *R.* 'Tuscany' (G)
	old yellow Scotch (PiH)	see *R.* × *harisonii* 'Williams Double Yellow'
	Olympic Palace = 'Poulymp'PBR (Palace Series) (F)	ECnt
	'Omar Khayyám' (D)	EWTr MAus MRav
	omeiensis	see *R. sericea* subsp. *omeiensis*
	'One Another' (F)	MGan
	One Promise = 'Frannite'PBR	LRHS MAsh MBri NPri
	Open Arms = 'Chewpixcel'PBR (ClMin) $\mathbb{Y}^{H4}$	ESty MAus MBri MJon SPer SSea SWCr
	'Ophelia' (HT)	LRHS MAus MGan
	'Orange Sensation' (F)	CTri MAus MGan
§	Orange Sunblaze = 'Meijikatar'PBR (Min)	CSBt MGan SPer
	Oranges and Lemons = 'Macoranlem'PBR (S/F)	CGro CSBt EBee EBls ECnt ELan ESty LStr MAsh MAus MGan MJon SPoG SSea SWCr
	Othello = 'Auslo'PBR (S)	MAus SLon
	'Our Beth' (S)	EBls
	'Our Dream' (Patio)	MAsh
	Our George = 'Kirrush' (Patio)	LSRN MJon
	Our Jubilee = 'Coccages' (HT)	ESty SVic
	Our Molly = 'Dicreason' (GC/S)	IDic LSRN MGan MJon SWCr
	Oxfordshire = 'Korfullwind'PBR (GC) $\mathbb{Y}^{H4}$	LStr MRav MWat
	Paddy McGredy = 'Macpa' (F)	MGan
	Paddy Stephens = 'Macclack'PBR (HT)	MJon SWCr

	Painted Moon = 'Dicpaint' (HT)	ESty
	Panache = 'Poultop'PBR (Patio)	ECnt LRHS LStr MAsh SMrm
	'Papa Gontier' (T)	MAus
	Papa Meilland = 'Meisar' (HT)	CGro CSBt LRHS MAus MGan SPer SWCr
	Paper Anniversary (Patio)	LSRN
	Papi Delbard = 'Delaby' (ClHT)	MRav
§	'Para Ti' (Min)	MAus MGan SPer
I	'Parade' (Cl) ♀H4	CWit MAus MRav SMrm SWCr
	'Paradise' (Patio)	SPoG
	Paradise = 'Wezip' (HT)	MGan
	'Parkdirektor Riggers' (ClF)	LStr MAus MBri MGan NLar SPer SWCr
	'Parkjuwel' (CeMo)	MGan
	Parson's pink China	see *R.* × *odorata* 'Pallida'
	Partridge = 'Korweirim'PBR (GC)	MAus MGan SPer
	'Party Girl' (Min)	MJon
	parvifolia	see *R.* 'Burgundiaca'
	Pas de Deux = 'Poulhult'PBR (Courtyard Series) (ClF)	LRHS MAsh
	Pascali = 'Lenip' (HT)	CTri GCoc MAus MGan MJon MRav MWat SMrm SPer SSea
	Pat Austin = 'Ausmum'PBR (S) ♀H4	CSBt ECnt EPfP LRHS LStr LTen MAus MBNS MBri MGan MRav NEgg NLar SEND SMrm SPoG SRGP SWCr WClo
	Pathfinder = 'Chewpobey' (GC)	MJon
	Patricia = 'Korpatri' (F)	SWCr
	Paul Cézanne = 'Jacdeli' (S)	LRHS
	'Paul Crampel' (Poly)	MGan
	'Paul Lédé' (ClT)	see *R.* 'Climbing Paul Lédé'
	Paul McCartneyPBR (HT)	see *R.* The McCartney Rose
	'Paul Neyron' (HP)	EWTr MAus SPer
	'Paul Ricault' (Ce × HP)	MAus
	Paul Shirville = 'Harqueterwife'PBR (HT) ♀H4	ELan ELon MAus MGan SPer SRGP SWCr
	'Paul Transon' (Ra) ♀H4	CPou CRHN EBee EPfP EWTr LRHS MAus MBri MMuc NEgg NLar SEND SPer SWCr WClo WHer
	'Paulii Rosea' (Ru/GC)	MAus MGan
	'Paul's Himalayan Musk' (Ra) ♀H3-4	CPLG CRHN CSBt CSam CTri EBee ECnt EPfP EWTr IArd LRHS LStr MAus MBri MGan MJon MRav NEgg NLar SEND SFam SMrm SPer SPoG SSea SWCr WBVN WBor WClo WKif
§	'Paul's Lemon Pillar' (ClHT)	LAst LRHS MAus NLar SMrm SPer SSea
	'Paul's Scarlet Climber' (Cl/Ra)	CGro CSBt ELan EPfP GKir LAst LStr MAsh MAus MGan MJon MRav NPri SEND SPer SRGP SWCr
	'Paul's Single White Perpetual' (Ra)	MMuc
	'Pax' (HM)	CPou MAus WKif
	Peace = 'Madame A. Meilland' (HT) ♀H4	CGro CSBt ECnt ELan EPfP ESty GCoc LRHS LStr MAsh MAus MBri MGan MJon MRav MWat NEgg NPri SMrm SPer SPoG SRGP SSea SWCr WBor
	Peace Sunblaze (Min)	see *R.* Lady Meillandina
	Peacekeeper = 'Harbella'PBR (F)	CSBt MRav
	Peach Blossom = 'Ausblossom' (S)	MAus
	'Peach Grootendorst' (Ru)	CPou EBee EWTr
	Peachy = 'Macrelea' (HT)	MAsh

§	Pearl Abundance = 'Harfrisky'PBR (F)	ESty SWCr
	Pearl Anniversary = 'Whitston'PBR (Min/Patio)	CSBt ESty LSRN LStr MGos MRav MWat SWCr
	Pearl Drift = 'Leggab' (S)	MAus SMrm SPer SWCr
	Pearl = 'Korterschi'PBR (F)	SWCr
	PeaudoucePBR	see *R.* Elina
§	Peek-a-boo = 'Dicgrow' (Min/Patio)	MGan SPer
	Peer Gynt = 'Korol' (HT)	MGan SWCr
	Pegasus = 'Ausmoon'PBR (S)	LRHS MAus SSea
§	***pendulina***	LBuc MAus NHaw
	- 'Nana'	NHol
	'Penelope' (HM) ♀H4	CSBt CSam CTri ECnt ELan EPfP EWTr GCoc LRHS LSRN LStr MAsh MAus MBri MCot MGan MGos MJon MRav MWat NLar NPri SFam SPer SRGP SSea SWCr WKif
	Penny Lane = 'Hardwell'PBR (ClHT) ♀H4	CSBt ECnt EPfP ESty GCoc LAst LRHS LStr MAsh MAus MBri MGan MGos MJon MRav MWat NLar SCoo SPer SPoG SSea SWCr
	Pensioner's Voice = 'Fryrelax'PBR (F)	MGan
	× ***penzanceana***	see *R.* 'Lady Penzance'
	Perception = 'Harzippee'PBR (HT)	SWCr
	Perdita = 'Ausperd' (S)	ESty LRHS MAus MRav
	Perennial Blue = 'Mehv9601' (Ra)	ESty MGan SSea SWCr
	Perennial Blush = 'Mehbarbie'PBR (Ra) **new**	ESty MGan
§	Perfect Day = 'Poulrem' (F)	EBee ECnt
	Perfecta = 'Koralu' (HT)	MGan
	'Perle des Jardins' (T)	MAus
§	'Perle d'Or' (Poly) ♀H4	ECGP EPfP MAus MGan NLar SDix SLon SMad SPer SWCr
	Perpetually Yours = 'Harfable'PBR (Cl)	CGro LStr MRav MWat SCoo
	Persian yellow	see *R. foetida* 'Persiana'
	Peter Pan = 'Chewpan'PBR (Min)	MAsh MAus MJon MWat NPri SWCr
	Peter Pan = 'Sunpete' (Patio)	EPfP LRHS NPri SPoG
	'Petite de Hollande' (Ce)	EWTr MAus NLar SPer
	'Petite Lisette' (Ce × D)	MAus NLar
	'Petito' (F)	SMrm
	Phab Gold = 'Frybountiful'PBR (F)	ESty GCoc MAsh
	Pheasant = 'Kordapt'PBR (GC)	GCoc MAus MGan MJon SPer SWCr
	Phillipa = 'Poulheart'PBR (S)	ECnt LSRN SWCr
	Phoebe (Ru)	see *R.* 'Fimbriata'
	'Phyllis Bide' (Ra) ♀H4	CAbP EBee ECGP EPfP EWTr IArd LRHS LStr MAus MBri MGan MJon NLar SEND SPer SSea SWCr WKif
	Picasso = 'Macpic' (F)	MGan NHaw
	Piccadilly = 'Macar' (HT)	CGro CSBt CTri MGan MRav SPer SWCr WBor
	Piccolo = 'Tanolokip'PBR (F/Patio)	CGro ESty LStr MBri MJon MRav SWCr
	'Picture' (HT)	MAus MGan SPer
	Pigalle '84 = 'Meicloux' (F)	SWCr
	'Pilgrim'PBR	see *R.* The Pilgrim
	pimpinellifolia	see *R. spinosissima*
	- double yellow-flowered	see *R.* × *harisonii* 'Williams Double Yellow'
	- 'Harisonii'	see *R.* × *harisonii* 'Harison's Yellow'
	- 'Lutea'	see *R.* × *harisonii* 'Lutea Maxima'

Pink Abundance = 'Harfrothy' PBR (Abundance Series) (F)	ESty LStr MAus
Pink Bells = 'Poulbells' PBR (GC)	GCoc SPer
'Pink Bouquet' (Ra)	CRHN
'Pink Favorite' (HT)	CSBt MGan SPer
Pink Fizz = 'Poulycool' (ClPatio)	ECnt SWCr
§ Pink Flower Carpet = 'Noatraum' PBR (GC) ♀H4	CGro CSBt CTri ECnt ELan GCoc LRHS LStr MAsh MAus MBri MGan NPri SCoo SEND SPer SPoG SWCr
'Pink Garnette'	see *R.* 'Carol Amling'
'Pink Grootendorst' (Ru) ♀H4	EPfP LRHS MAus MGan NEgg NLar SPer SWCr
§ Pink Hit = 'Poultipe' PBR (Min/Patio)	ECnt LRHS MAsh MBri SWCr
'Pink Medley' (F)	MAsh MBri
pink moss	see *R.* × *centifolia* 'Muscosa'
'Pink Parfait' (F)	MGan SPer
Pink Peace = 'Meibil' (HT)	SWCr
'Pink Perpétué' (Cl)	CBcs CGro CSBt CTri ECnt ELan EPfP GCoc GKir LRHS LStr MAsh MAus MGan MJon MRav SEND SMrm SPer SPoG SWCr
'Pink Pins' new	GKir
'Pink Prosperity' (HM)	MAus
Pink Skyliner = 'Franwekpink' PBR (ClS)	EBls MJon
Pirouette = 'Poulyc003' PBR (Cl)	ECnt MAsh SWCr
'Plaisanterie' (HM) new	MAus
'Playboy' (F)	GCoc
Playtime = 'Morplati' (F)	MAus
Pleine de Grâce = 'Lengra' (S)	LRHS MAus
Poetry in Motion = 'Harelan' PBR (HT)	EBls
Polar Star = 'Tanlarpost' PBR (HT)	CSBt ECnt LStr MAsh MGan MRav SPer SWCr
× ***polliniana***	SLPl
'Polly' (HT)	LSRN MGan
§ 'Polyantha Grandiflora' (Ra)	MAus
pomifera	see *R. villosa* L.
'Pompon Blanc Parfait' (A)	MAus
'Pompon de Bourgogne'	see *R.* 'Burgundiaca'
'Pompon de Paris' (ClMinCh)	see *R.* 'Climbing Pompon de Paris'
§ 'Pompon de Paris' (MinCh)	SMrm WAbe
'Pompon Panaché' (G)	MAus
Port Sunlight = 'Auslofty' (HM)	LRHS MAsh MAus WClo
Portland rose	see *R.* 'Portlandica'
§ 'Portlandica' (Po)	CTri GKir LRHS MAsh MAus SPer
Portmeirion = 'Ausguard' PBR (S)	LRHS MAus SCoo
Pot o' Gold = 'Dicdivine' (HT)	SPer SWCr
Pour Toi	see *R.* 'Para Ti'
prairie rose	see *R. setigera*
'Precious Memories' (Min)	LSRN
Precious Memories = 'Dichello' (F) new	ESty GCoc IDic
'Precious Platinum' (HT)	MJon SPer
§ 'Président de Sèze' (G) ♀H4	CPou MAus NLar SFam SPer
Pretty in Pink = 'Dicumpteen' PBR (GC)	ECnt IDic SWCr
Pretty Jessica = 'Ausjess' (S)	CGro LRHS MAus MJon MRav SPer
Pretty Lady = 'Scrivo' PBR (F) ♀H4	MAus MJon
Pretty Polly = 'Meitonje' PBR (Min) ♀H4	CGro EPfP ESty LRHS LStr MAsh MBri MGan MRav MWat SMrm SPer SPoG SRGP SWCr
Pride of Cheshire = 'Wekosupalz' (HT) new	MJon
Pride of England = 'Harencore' PBR (HT)	EBls GCoc MJon SWCr
Pride of Scotland = 'Macwhitba' (HT)	GCoc MJon
'Prima Ballerina' (HT)	CGro CSBt CTri CWSG GCoc LStr MAsh MGan SPer SSea
primula (S) ♀H3-4	IFFs MAus MGan MJon NLar SPer SSea
'Prince Camille de Rohan' (HP)	MAus
Prince Caspian	see *R.* In the Mood
'Prince Charles' (Bb)	MAus NLar WKif
Prince Regent = 'Genpen' (S)	SSea
Princess Alexandra of Kent = 'Ausmerchant'	EPfP LRHS MAsh MAus MBri SSea WClo
Princess Alexandra = 'Pouldra' PBR (Renaissance Series) (S)	CTri ECnt EPfP SWCr
Princess Alice = 'Hartanna' (F)	MGan
Princess = 'Canfound' (HT) new	ECnt
Princess Nobuko = 'Coclistine' PBR (HT)	GCoc
'Princess of Wales' (HP)	EPfP
Princess of Wales = 'Hardinkum' PBR (F) ♀H4	EPfP LRHS LStr MAsh MBri MGan MRav SCoo SPer SWCr
Princess Royal = 'Dicroyal' PBR (HT)	IDic
§ 'Princesse de Nassau' (Ra)	MAus SEND
'Princesse Louise' (Ra)	CRHN MAus SFam
'Princesse Marie' misapplied	see *R.* 'Belvedere'
'Pristine' (HT)	MAus
§ 'Professeur Emile Perrot' (D)	CArn MAus SMad
'Prolifera de Redouté' misapplied	see *R.* 'Duchesse de Montebello'
'Prosperity' (HM) ♀H4	CSam CTri EBee EPfP GCoc LRHS MAus MCot MGan MJon MRav NLar SLon SPer SWCr
Prospero = 'Auspero' (S)	MAus NLar SEND
§ ***pulverulenta***	GAuc
Pure Bliss = 'Dictator' PBR (HT)	ECnt IDic MGan SWCr
Pure Gold = 'Harhappen' PBR (F)	CSBt
'Purezza' (Ra)	NLar
'Purity' (HT)	EBee
'Purple Beauty' (HT)	MGan
Purple Skyliner = 'Franwekpurp' PBR (ClS)	ESty MJon SMrm SSea
Purple Tiger = 'Jacpurr' PBR (F)	ESty IDic LStr SWCr
Quaker Star = 'Dicperhaps' (F)	IDic
quatre saisons	see *R.* × *damascena* var. *semperflorens*
Queen Elizabeth	see *R.* 'The Queen Elizabeth'
Queen Mother = 'Korquemu' PBR (Patio) ♀H4	CSBt CWit ELan EPfP GCoc LStr MAus MGan MRav SEND SPer SPoG SWCr
Queen of Denmark	see *R.* 'Königin von Dänemark'
Queen of Sweden = 'Austiger' PBR (S)	ECnt LRHS MAus MBri MJon SPer SWCr WClo

	'Rachel' ambig.	GCoc
	'Rachel' (HT)	EBls LSRN
	Rachel = 'Tangust'^{PBR} (HT)	CSBt ESty LStr MJon MRav SPoG SWCr
	Rachel's Delight = 'Beadimple' (S) **new**	EBls
	Racy Lady = 'Dicwaffle'^{PBR} (HT)	IDic MJon
	Radio Times = 'Aussal'^{PBR} (S)	ESty LRHS MAus
	'Radway Sunrise' (S)	EBls
	'Ragamuffin' (Patio)	LShp
	Rainbow Magic = 'Dicxplosion'^{PBR} (Patio)	IDic
	'Ralph Tizzard' (F)	SSea
	'Rambling Rector' (Ra) 🏆^{H4}	Widely available
	Rambling Rosie = 'Horjasper' (Ra)	EBls ECnt ESty LSRN MAus MJon SWCr
	'Ramona' (Ra)	MAus SWCr
	'Raspberry Royale' (F/Patio)	MAsh SPoG
	'Raubritter' ('Macrantha' hybrid)	ECGP EPfP LRHS MAus SPer SWCr
	Ray of Hope = 'Cocnilly'^{PBR} (F)	GCoc
	Ray of Sunshine = 'Cocclare'^{PBR} (Patio)	GCoc
	Raymond Blanc = 'Delnado' (HT)	LRHS
	'Raymond Chenault' (S)	CGro MGan SWCr
	Rebecca (Patio)	ESty LSRN
	'Rebecca Claire' (HT)	LSRN SWCr
	Rebecca Mary = 'Dicjury' (F) **new**	IDic
	Reconciliation = 'Hartillery'^{PBR} (HT)	SRGP SWCr
	Red Abundance^{PBR}	see *R.* Songs of Praise
	Red Blanket = 'Intercell' (S/GC)	GCoc MAus SPer
	Red Coat = 'Auscoat' (F)	MAus
	Red Devil = 'Dicam' (HT)	MAsh MGan MJon SCoo SPoG
	Red Eden Rose = 'Meidrason'^{PBR} (Cl)	ESty SSea SWCr
	'Red Facade' (Cl)	MAsh
	Red Finesse = 'Korvillade'^{PBR} (F)	MAsh MGos
	'Red Grootendorst'	see *R.* 'F.J. Grootendorst'
	Red Hot = 'Weksacquem' (Patio)	MJon
	'Red Max Graf'^{PBR}	see *R.* Rote Max Graf
	Red Medley = 'Noapu'^{PBR} (Min) **new**	MAsh MBri
	red moss	see *R.* 'Henri Martin'
	Red New Dawn	see *R.* 'Étendard'
§	'Red Patio' (F/Patio)	LSRN
	Red Rascal = 'Jacbed'^{PBR} (S/Patio)	CSBt ECGP IDic
	Red Romance = 'Peafelicity' (F)	SPoG
	red rose of Lancaster	see *R. gallica* var. *officinalis*
	'Red Wing' (S)	MAus
	Redouté = 'Auspale'^{PBR} (S)	LRHS MAus
	Reflections = 'Simref' (F)	SWCr
	Regensberg = 'Macyoumis'^{PBR} (F/Patio)	MAus MBri MGan MJon SPer SWCr
	'Reine des Centfeuilles' (Ce)	SFam
	'Reine des Violettes' (HP)	CGro CPou ELon EPfP GKir IArd LRHS LStr MAus MBri MCot MGan MRav NLar SPer SWCr WBor
§	'Reine Victoria' (Bb)	EBee EPfP LRHS LStr MAsh MAus MBri MCot MGan SPer SWCr
	Remember Me = 'Cocdestin'^{PBR} (HT) 🏆^{H4}	CGro CSBt CWSG ECnt ESty GCoc IArd LSRN LStr MAus MBri MGan MGos MJon MRav MWat NEgg NPri SPer SPoG SRGP SWCr
§	Remember = 'Poulht001'^{PBR} (HT)	ECnt EPfP LRHS MAsh SWCr
	Remembrance = 'Harxampton'^{PBR} (F) 🏆^{H4}	CGro CTri CWSG EBls ESty LRHS LSRN LStr MAsh MGan MJon MRav NPri SPer SPoG SRGP SWCr
	Renaissance = 'Harzart'^{PBR} (HT)	CSBt GCoc LStr MWat SWCr
	'René André' (Ra)	CPou CRHN MAus
	'René d'Anjou' (CeMo)	LRHS MAus
	'Rescht'	see *R.* 'De Resht'
	'Rêve d'Or' (N)	MAus SLon SPer
	'Réveil Dijonnais' (ClHT)	MAus
	Rhapsody in Blue = 'Frantasia'^{PBR} (S)	CGro CSBt CWSG EBee ECnt ELan ELon EPfP ESty GCoc LAst LRHS LStr MAsh MAus MBri MGan MGos MJon MRav MWat NPri SCoo SMad SMrm SPer SPoG SSea SWCr
§	× ***richardii***	MAus MGan MRav NLar
	Rick Stein = 'Tan96205'^{PBR} (HT)	LSRN LStr SWCr
	'Rival de Paestum' (T)	MAus
	'River Gardens'	NPer
	Rob Roy = 'Cocrob' (F)	GCoc MGan SPer
	Robbie Burns = 'Ausburn' (PiH)	MAus
	'Robert le Diable' (Ce × G)	MAus NLar SPer
§	Robusta = 'Korgosa' (Ru)	ECnt MGan
	Rockabye Baby = 'Dicdwarf' (Patio)	ESty IDic SWCr
	'Roger Lambelin' (HP)	MAus
	Romance = 'Tanezamor'^{PBR} (S)	MRav
	'Rosa Mundi'	see *R. gallica* 'Versicolor'
	Rosabell = 'Cocceleste'^{PBR} (F/Patio)	ESty GCoc
	Rosarium Uetersen = 'Kortersen' (ClHT)	MJon
§	'Rose d'Amour' (S) 🏆^{H4}	CFee
	'Rose de Meaux'	see *R.* × *centifolia* 'De Meaux'
	'Rose de Meaux White'	see *R.* 'White de Meaux'
	'Rose de Rescht'	see *R.* 'De Resht'
	'Rose des Maures' misapplied	see *R.* 'Sissinghurst Castle'
	'Rose du Maître d'Ecole'	see *R.* 'Du Maître d'Ecole'
	'Rose du Roi' (HP/DPo)	ELon MAus
	'Rose du Roi à Fleurs Pourpres' (HP)	MAus
§	Rose Gaujard = 'Gaumo' (HT)	MAsh MGan
	Rose of Picardy = 'Ausfudge' (S)	LRHS MAus MBri SSea
	Rose Pearl = 'Korterschi'^{PBR} (S)	MGan
	Rose-Marie = 'Ausome'^{PBR} (S)	MAus
	'Rose-Marie Viaud' (Ra)	CFee CPou CSam EBee MAus
	'Rosemary Gandy' (F)	MGan
	Rosemary Harkness = 'Harrowbond'^{PBR} (HT)	ESty LStr MRav SMrm SPer
	'Rosemary Rose' (F)	SPer
	Rosemoor = 'Austough'^{PBR} (S)	CSBt LRHS MAus MBri SSea WClo
	Rosenprofessor Sieber^{PBR}	see *R.* The Halcyon Days Rose
	'Roseraie de l'Haÿ' (Ru) 🏆^{H4}	Widely available
	Roses des Cistercians = 'Deltisse'	MRav
	Rosy Cushion = 'Interall' (S/GC) 🏆^{H4}	EWTr LRHS MAsh MAus MGan SLon SPer

Rosy Future = 'Harwaderox' (F/Patio)	CSBt SWCr
'Rosy Mantle' (ClHT)	CSBt MGan SPer SWCr
§ Rotary Sunrise = 'Fryglitzy' (HT)	CSBt MBri
§ Rote Max Graf = 'Kormax'PBR (GC/Ru)	CDul EPfP NLar
Roxanne Pallett = 'Oradal' (HT) **new**	MJon
roxburghii (S)	EPfP GAuc LEdu MAus MGan
- f. ***normalis*** (S)	CFee
- 'Plena'	see *R. roxburghii* f. *roxburghii*
§ - f. ***roxburghii*** (d/S)	MAus
'Royal Albert Hall' (HT)	GCoc
Royal Celebration = 'Wekbiphitsou' (F)	MJon
Royal CopenhagenPBR	see *R.* Remember = 'Poulht001'
'Royal Gold' (ClHT)	MGan
'Royal Occasion' (F)	SPer
Royal William = 'Korzaun'PBR (HT) ♀H4	CSBt CWSG ELan ESty GCoc LStr MAsh MAus MBri MGan MGos MJon MRav MWat SPer SWCr WBor
§ ***rubiginosa***	CArn CCVT CDul CRWN EMac EPfP GPoy IFro ILis LBuc MAus MJon MRav NWea SFam SPer WMou
rubra	see *R. gallica*
rubrifolia	see *R. glauca* Pourr.
'Rubrotincta'	see *R.* 'Hebe's Lip'
rubus (Ra)	MAus
Ruby Anniversary = 'Harbonny'PBR (Patio)	CSBt CWSG EBls ESty LRHS LSRN LStr MAsh MRav SCoo SPoG SRGP SVic SWCr
Ruby Celebration = 'Peawinner'PBR (F)	EBls ESty MJon MRav MWat SWCr
Ruby Ruby	see *R.* Ruby Slippers
§ Ruby Slippers = 'Weksactrumi' (Min)	LRHS MAsh MBri
'Ruby Wedding' (HT)	CBcs CGro CSBt CTri CWSG CWit ECnt ELan EPfP GCoc IArd LRHS LSRN LStr MAsh MAus MBri MGan MGos MJon MRav NPri SMrm SPer SPoG SSea SVic SWCr WBor WClo
'Ruby Wedding Anniversary' (F)	LSRN
rugosa (Ru)	CBar CDul CLnd CTri ECrN EMac EPfP GGar GKir IFFs LBuc LRHS MAsh MAus MBri MHer MRav NWea SBfd SPlb SVic SWCr WMou
- 'Alba' (Ru) ♀H4	CBcs CCVT CDul CTri EBee ECnt ELan EMac EPfP EWTr GBin GKir LAst LBuc LRHS LStr MAus MCot MGan MJon MRav NWea SBfd SMrm SPer SPoG SSea SVic SWCr
- 'Rubra' (Ru) ♀H4	CBcs CCVT CTri CWib EPfP GKir LAst LBuc LRHS LStr MGan SBfd SMrm SPer SPoG SVic
- Sakhalin form	MCCP
'Rugosa Atropurpurea' (Ru)	GKir SBfd
'Rural England' (Ra)	EBls
Rushing Stream = 'Austream' (GC)	MAus
'Russelliana' (Ra)	EBee MAus SFam WKif
Safe Haven = 'Jacreraz'PBR (F)	IDic
Saint Alban = 'Auschesnut'PBR (S)	MAus
Saint Boniface = 'Kormatt' (F/Patio)	CSBt
'Saint Catherine' (Ra)	CFee
Saint Cecilia = 'Ausmit'PBR (S)	LRHS LStr MAus SMrm
Saint Dunstan's Rose = 'Kirshru' (S)	MJon
Saint Edmunds RosePBR	see *R.* Bonita
Saint John = 'Harbilbo'PBR (F)	CSBt MRav
Saint John's rose	see *R.* × *richardii*
Saint Mark's rose	see *R.* 'Rose d'Amour'
'Saint Nicholas' (D)	MAus
Saint Swithun = 'Auswith'PBR (S)	EPfP LRHS MAsh MAus MBri MJon SSea WClo
'Salet' (DPMo)	EWTr MAus
'Sally Holmes' (S) ♀H4	ECnt EPfP EWTr GCoc MAus MGan MJon MRav SEND SLon SPer SSea SWCr
Sally Kane = 'Frygroovy'PBR (HT)	EBee ECnt
Sally's Rose = 'Canrem' (HT)	ECnt LSRN
SalsaPBR	see *R.* Cheek to Cheek
Salvation = 'Harlark'PBR (F)	ECnt ESty SWCr
Samaritan = 'Harverag'PBR (HT)	CSBt ESty LRHS MRav SPoG SWCr
sancta	see *R.* × *richardii*
'Sander's White Rambler' (Ra) ♀H4	CRHN CSam CTri EBee ECGP EPfP LRHS LStr MAus MBri MGan MRav NLar SPer SWCr
Sandra = 'Carsandra'	EPfP SLon
Sarah (HT)	see *R.* Jardins de Bagatelle
'Sarah van Fleet' (Ru)	CTri EBee EPfP GCoc IArd LRHS LStr MAus MCot MGan MGos MMuc MRav MWat NEgg NLar SMad SMrm SPer SPoG
Sarah, Duchess of YorkPBR	see *R.* Sunseeker
Savoy Hotel = 'Harvintage'PBR (HT) ♀H4	CGro ECnt LRHS LStr MAus MGan MRav SMrm SPer SPoG SWCr
'Scabrosa' (Ru) ♀H4	EBee ECnt GCoc GKir LAst LRHS MAsh MAus MGan MJon NLar SLon SPer SSea
Scarborough Fair = 'Ausoran' (S)	MAsh MAus MBri
Scarlet Fire	see *R.* 'Scharlachglut'
Scarlet Glow	see *R.* 'Scharlachglut'
Scarlet Hit = 'Poulmo'PBR (PatioHit Series) (P)	ECnt LRHS MAsh
Scarlet Patio = 'Kortingle'PBR (Patio)	ESty LRHS MAsh
Scarlet Queen Elizabeth = 'Dicel' (F)	CBcs MRav
'Scented Air' (F)	MGan SPer
Scented Carpet = 'Chewground'PBR (GC)	ECnt MAus MJon SWCr
Scented Memory = 'Poulht002'PBR (HT)	ECnt LRHS MBri
Scentimental = 'Wekplapep'PBR (F)	CWit ESty LStr MAsh MBri MRav SCoo SSea SWCr
Scent-sation = 'Fryromeo'PBR (HT)	CWSG GCoc LRHS LStr MAsh MBri MGan MRav SCoo SPoG SWCr
Scepter'd Isle = 'Ausland'PBR (S) ♀H4	CSBt ECnt LRHS MAus MBri SCoo SPer SSea SWCr WClo
§ 'Scharlachglut' (ClS) ♀H4	CPou LRHS MAus MCot MGan MRav SPer
* ***schmidtiana***	CFee
Schneewittchen	see *R.* Iceberg
§ 'Schneezwerg' (Ru) ♀H4	CGro EBee GCoc MAus MGan MGos MRav NLar SPer SPoG SSea SWCr
'Schoolgirl' (ClHT)	CBcs CGro CSBt CTri CWSG EBee ELan EPfP GCoc GKir LAst LRHS LStr MAsh MGan MJon MRav NEgg SPer SPoG SWCr
'Schratel'	LRHS
'Scintillation' (S/GC)	MAus

	Scotch rose	see *R. spinosissima*
	Scotch yellow (PiH)	see *R.* × *harisonii* 'Williams Double Yellow'
	'Seagull' (Ra) 🏆H4	CGro CTri CWSG EBee ECnt EPfP ESty LAst LRHS LStr MAsh MAus MGan MJon MRav MWat NLar NPri NWea SLon SMad SMrm SPer SPoG SSea SWCr WHer
	'Seale Pink Diamond' (S)	SSea
	'Sealing Wax' (*moyesii* hybrid)	NLar
	Selfridges = 'Korpriwa' (HT)	MJon
	'Semiplena'	see *R.* × *alba* 'Alba Semiplena'
	sericea (S)	CFee MAus
	- var. ***morrisonensis*** B&SWJ 7139	WCru
§	- subsp. ***omeiensis*** BWJ 7550	WCru
	- - f. ***pteracantha*** (S)	CSBt ELan EPfP EWTr GGar LRHS LTen MAus MGan MRav NLar NWea SMad SPer SPoG SSea
	- - - 'Atrosanguinea' (S)	CArn WBor
	sertata	GAuc
§	***setigera***	MAus
	setipoda (S)	MAus
	seven sisters rose	see *R. multiflora* 'Grevillei'
	Seventh Heaven = 'Fryfantasy'PBR (HT)	GCoc SWCr
	Sexy Rexy = 'Macrexy'PBR (F) 🏆H4	CGro CSBt EPfP ESty GCoc LRHS LSRN LStr MAsh MAus MBri MGan MJon MRav SMrm SPer SPoG SWCr
	'Shailer's White Moss'	see *R.* × *centifolia* 'Shailer's White Moss'
	Sharifa Asma = 'Ausreef'PBR (S)	CSBt EBee ELan ELon LRHS LStr MAus MBri MRav NEgg NLar SLon SMrm SPer SWCr
	Sheila's Perfume = 'Harsherry'PBR (F)	CGro ECnt ESty GCoc LStr MAsh MGan MJon MRav SPer SPoG SRGP SWCr
	Shine On = 'Dictalent'PBR (Patio) 🏆H4	CSBt ECnt ESty IDic LStr MAsh SPoG SWCr
	Shining Light = 'Cocshimmer'PBR (Patio)	GCoc MRav SCoo
	Shocking Blue = 'Korblue' (F)	CSBt MGan SPer
	Shona = 'Dicdrum' (F)	IDic
	'Shot Silk' (HT)	MGan
	Showtime = 'Baitime' (ClS)	MAsh
	Shrimp Hit = 'Poulshrimp'PBR (Patio)	ECnt MAsh
	'Shropshire Lass' (S)	MAus
	Silver Anniversary ambig.	LSRN
§	Silver Anniversary = 'Poulari'PBR (HT) 🏆H4	CGro CSBt CTri CWSG EBls ECnt ELan GCoc LRHS LSRN LStr MAsh MAus MGan MGos MJon MRav MWat NPri SCoo SMrm SPer SPoG SSea SVic SWCr WClo
	'Silver Jubilee' (HT) 🏆H4	CGro CSBt EPfP GCoc IArd LRHS LStr MAsh MAus MGan MJon MRav SPer SPoG SVic SWCr
	'Silver Lining' (HT)	ELon SRGP
	'Silver Moon' (Cl)	CRHN
	'Silver Wedding' (HT)	ELan GCoc IArd MAus MRav NBir NEgg SMrm SPer SRGP SVic SWCr WBor
	'Silver Wedding Celebration' (F)	CTri ESty
	Silver WishesPBR	see *R.* Pink Hit
	Simba = 'Korbelma' (HT)	MGan
	'Simplex Multiflora'	CWib
	Simply Heaven = 'Diczombie'PBR (HT)	ESty GCoc IDic
§	Simply the Best = 'Macamster'PBR (HT)	CGro CSBt CWSG CWit EBls ECnt ELan ESty GCoc LSRN LStr MAsh MAus MGan MGos MJon MRav MWat NPri SCoo SMrm SPer SPoG SRGP SWCr
§	Singin' in the Rain = 'Macivy' (F)	MJon
	sinowilsonii	see *R. longicuspis* var. *sinowilsonii*
	'Sir Cedric Morris' (Ra)	SSea
	Sir Clough = 'Ausclough' (S)	MAus
	Sir Edward Elgar = 'Ausprima'PBR (S)	MAus
I	'Sir Galahad' white-flowered (F)	MRav
	Sir John Betjeman = 'Ausvivid' **new** (S)	MAsh MAus
	'Sir Joseph Paxton' (Bb)	CAbP MAus
	Sir Paul Smith = 'Beapaul' (ClHT)	EBls
	Sir Walter Raleigh = 'Ausspry' (S)	MAus MRav SMrm
§	'Sissinghurst Castle' (G)	MAus
	Sister Elizabeth = 'Auspalette'PBR (S)	LRHS MAus MBri SCoo
	Skylark = 'Ausimple' (S)	LRHS MAus MBri WClo
	'Skyrocket'	see *R.* 'Wilhelm'
	Smarty = 'Intersmart' (S/GC)	MAus SPer
	'Smooth Angel' (HT)	MGan
	Smooth Lady = 'Hadlady' (HT)	MGan
	Smooth Melody = 'Hadmelody' (F)	LAst
	Smooth Prince = 'Hadprince' (HT)	LAst
	'Smooth Velvet' (HT)	LAst
	Snow Carpet = 'Maccarpe' (Min/GC)	MAus MJon SSea
	'Snow Dwarf'	see *R.* 'Schneezwerg'
	Snow Goose = 'Auspom'PBR (ClS)	CSBt LRHS MAus MBri SSea SWCr
	Snow Hit = 'Poulsnows'PBR (Min/Patio)	ECnt LRHS SWCr
	'Snow Queen'	see *R.* 'Frau Karl Druschki'
	Snow Sunblaze = 'Meigovin' (Min)	CSBt SPer
	Snowball = 'Macangeli' (Min/GC)	MJon
	Snowcap = 'Harfleet'PBR (Patio)	ESty SPoG
	'Snowdon' (Ru)	LRHS MAus
	'Soldier Boy' (Cl)	CPou SWCr
	Solitaire = 'Macyefre'PBR (HT)	MJon
§	Solo Mio = 'Poulen002'PBR (Renaissance Series) (S)	CTri ECnt
§	'Sombreuil' (ClT)	EBee EPfP IArd LRHS MAsh MAus MBri MRav NEgg NLar SPer SSea SWCr
	Something Special = 'Macwyo'PBR (HT)	ECnt ESty GCoc MJon SWCr
	Song and Dance = 'Frydishy' (HT)	ESty GCoc SWCr
§	Songs of Praise = 'Harkimono'PBR (Abundance Series) (F)	ESty SWCr
	Sonia	see *R.* Sweet Promise
	'Sophia'PBR	see *R.* Solo Mio
	'Sophie's Perpetual' (ClCh)	CPou MAus MGan MGos SLon SPer SWCr
	Sophy's Rose = 'Auslot'PBR (S)	ESty LRHS LSRN LStr MAus MBri MJon NEgg NPri SPer SSea SWCr

soulieana (Ra/S) Y^{H3-4}	MAus
'Soupert et Notting' (DPoMo)	LRHS MAus MRav SPer
'Southampton' (F) Y^{H4}	EPfP LSRN LStr MAsh MAus SPer SSea SWCr
'Souvenir de Claudius Denoyel' (ClHT)	MGan SPer
'Souvenir de Jeanne Balandreau' (HP)	CPou
'Souvenir de la Malmaison' (ClBb)	see *R.* 'Climbing Souvenir de la Malmaison'
'Souvenir de la Malmaison' (Bb)	EPfP GCoc MAus MCot MGan MRav NLar SEND SPer
Souvenir de Louis Amade = 'Delilac' (S)	MRav
'Souvenir de Madame Léonie Viennot' (ClT)	MAus MRav SPoG
'Souvenir de Saint Anne's' (Bb)	EWTr MAus
'Souvenir di Castagneto' (HP)	MRav
'Souvenir du Docteur Jamain' (ClHP)	CPou CSBt ECGP ELan ELon EPfP ESty EWTr LStr MAus MGan MRav NLar SFam SMrm SPer SPoG SSea SWCr WKif
Spangles = 'Ganspa'^{PBR} (F)	MGan NHaw
'Spanish Beauty'	see *R.* 'Madame Grégoire Staechelin'
Sparkler^{PBR}	see *R.* Kent
Sparkling Scarlet = 'Meihati' (ClF)	ELan MAsh
Special Anniversary = 'Whastiluc'^{PBR} (HT)	CGro CSBt EPfP ESty GCoc LRHS MAsh MBri MRav MWat NPri SCoo SMrm SPoG SRGP SWCr
Special Child = 'Taniripsa'^{PBR} (Patio)	ECnt LStr MGan SWCr
Special Event = 'Meibrelon' (HT) **new**	ESty
Special Friend = 'Kirspec'^{PBR} (Patio)	CWSG ESty GCoc LSRN LStr MGan MJon MWat SMrm SWCr
Special Occasion = 'Fryyoung'^{PBR} (HT)	ESty GCoc LRHS MBri MGos MRav MWat SMrm SWCr
'Spectabilis' (Ra)	SKHP
Spek's Centennial (F)	see *R.* Singin' in the Rain
Spellbound^{PBR}	see *R.* Garden News
'Spencer' misapplied	see *R.* 'Enfant de France'
Spice of Life = 'Diccheeky'^{PBR} (F/Patio)	IDic
§ ***spinosissima***	CDul EMac GKir IFFs LBuc MAus MGan NHaw NWea SPer SSea WCot
- 'Andrewsii' Y^{H4}	MAus MRav
§ - double pink-flowered	SKHP WBor
§ - double white-flowered	CNat ECha EWTr GCoc IGor MAus
- 'Dunwich Rose'	EPfP MAus MGan MJon NLar SKHP SPer
- 'Falkland'	ECha GCra MAus
- 'Glory of Edzell'	MAus
- 'Marbled Pink'	MAus
- 'Mary, Queen of Scots'	MAus MGan SRms
- 'Mrs Colville'	MAus
- 'Ormiston Roy'	MAus
- 'Single Cherry'	MAus SSea
- 'Variegata' (v)	CArn
- 'William III'	EWes GCra MAus SLPl
Spirit of Freedom = 'Ausbite'^{PBR} (S)	ESty LRHS MAsh MAus MBri NEgg SSea WClo
§ 'Splendens' (Ra)	EBee SLPl
St Helena = 'Canlish' (F)	ECnt
'Stanwell Perpetual' (PiH)	CSam EBee EPfP EWTr GCoc LStr MAus MCot MRav NLar SEND SFam SPer SSea SWCr
'Star Performer'^{PBR} (ClPatio)	CSBt EBee ECnt ESty MAsh MJon SMrm SPoG SRGP SSea SWCr
Stardust = 'Peavandyke'^{PBR} (Patio/F)	ESty
Starina = 'Megabi' (Min)	MGan
Starlight Express = 'Trobstar'^{PBR} (Cl)	MAsh MBri MRav MWat SCoo SMrm SPer SPoG
Starry Eyed = 'Horcoexist' (Patio)	MGan SWCr
'Stars 'n' Stripes' (Min)	MAus
Stella (HT)	LSRN MGan
stellata	MAus
§ - var. ***mirifica***	MAus MGan SSea
'Sterling Silver' (HT)	MGan
Strawberries and Cream = 'Geestraw' (Min/Patio)	ELan ESty
Strawberry Fayre = 'Arowillip'^{PBR} (Min/Patio)	ESty MRav SPoG
Strawberry Hill = 'Ausrimini'^{PBR} (S)	CSBt ECnt ESty LRHS MAus MBri SCoo SSea
Stunning = 'Poulpm004'^{PBR} (HT)	SWCr
§ Sue Hipkin = 'Harzazz'^{PBR} (HT)	SWCr
Suffolk = 'Kormixal'^{PBR} (S/GC)	CGro CSBt ELan GCoc LStr MAus MGan MRav MWat SEND SPer SSea
suffulta	see *R. arkansana* var. *suffulta*
Sugar and Spice = 'Peaallure'^{PBR} (Patio)	MAus SPoG
Sugar Baby = 'Tanabagus'^{PBR} (Patio)	ESty SWCr
Sugar 'n' Spice = 'Tinspice' (Min)	MRav
Suma = 'Harsuma' (GC)	ESty MJon SMrm
Summer Beauty = 'Kororbe'^{PBR} (F) **new**	ECnt
Summer Breeze = 'Korelasting'^{PBR} (ClS)	MGos
Summer Fever = 'Tan99106' (Patio)	SWCr
Summer Fragrance = 'Tanfudermos'^{PBR} (Castle Series) (HT)	ELon
§ Summer Gold = 'Poulreb'^{PBR} (F)	ECnt SWCr
Summer Love = 'Franluv' (F)	CBcs
Summer Memories = 'Koruteli'^{PBR} (Palace Series) (F)	MGos
Summer Snow = 'Weopop' (Patio)	MJon
Summer Song = 'Austango'^{PBR} (S)	EPfP LRHS MAus MBri MJon SWCr WClo
Summer Wine = 'Korizont'^{PBR} (Cl) Y^{H4}	CSBt ECnt GKir LRHS MAsh MGan MGos MJon SCoo SPer SPoG SWCr
Summertime = 'Chewlarmoll'^{PBR} (Patio/Cl)	CGro CSBt EBee EBls ECnt ELan GCoc LRHS LStr MAsh MAus MGan MGos MJon MRav MWat NPri SCoo SMrm SPer SPoG
Sun Hit = 'Poulsun'^{PBR} (PatioHit Series) (Patio)	CSBt ECnt LRHS MAsh MRav SWCr
'Sunblaze'^{PBR}	see *R.* Orange Sunblaze
Sunblest = 'Landora' (HT)	LRHS MAsh MRav SWCr
Sunrise = 'Kormarter'^{PBR} (Cl)	CGro ESty MBri MWat SWCr
§ Sunseeker = 'Dicracer'^{PBR} (F/Patio)	EPfP IDic LRHS MAsh MRav SPoG SWCr
Sunset Boulevard = 'Harbabble'^{PBR} (F) Y^{H4}	EBee ECnt LStr MAsh MAus MBri MGan MRav SCoo SPer SWCr

	Sunset Celebration PBR	see *R.* Warm Wishes
	'Sunshine' (Poly)	MGan
	Sunsplash = 'Cocweaver' PBR (F)	MRav SPoG
	Super Dorothy = 'Heldoro' (Ra)	LSRN MAus MJon SSea SWCr
	Super Elfin = 'Helkleger' PBR (Ra) ♀H4	LStr MAus MGan MJon MRav SMrm SPer SSea SWCr
	Super Excelsa = 'Helexa' (Ra)	ESty LRHS LStr MAsh MAus MGan MJon SSea SWCr
	Super Fairy = 'Helsufair' PBR (Ra)	ECnt LStr MAus MGan MJon MRav SMrm SPer SSea SWCr
	Super Sparkle = 'Helfels' PBR (Ra)	ECnt LStr SSea
§	Super Star = 'Tanorstar' (HT)	LStr MAus MGan MJon MRav SRGP SWCr
	Super Trooper = 'Fryleyeca' (F) **new**	CSBt ECnt ESty GCoc LStr
	'Surpasse Tout' (G)	MAus
	Surprise = 'Presur' PBR (HT)	SWCr
	Surrey = 'Korlanum' PBR (GC) ♀H4	CSBt ECnt ELan EPfP ESty LSRN LStr MAus MGan MRav MWat NLar SPer SPoG SSea SWCr
	Susan = 'Poulsue' (S)	ECnt SLon SWCr
	Sussex = 'Poulave' PBR (GC)	CSBt CWit GCoc LStr MGan MRav SMrm SPer SWCr
	'Sutter's Gold' (HT)	MGan
	Swan = 'Auswhite' (S)	MAus
	Swan Lake = 'Macmed' (Cl)	EBee ECnt ELan EPfP LStr MGan MRav NLar NPri SMrm SPer SWCr
	Swany = 'Meiburenac' (Min/GC) ♀H4	ESty LSRN MAus MGan SPer SWCr
	Sweet Dream = 'Fryminicot' PBR (Patio) ♀H4	CGro CSBt CTri ECnt ELan EPfP ESty GCoc LAst LSRN LStr MAsh MAus MBri MGan MJon MRav MWat NPri SMad SMrm SPer SPoG SRGP SSea SWCr
	'Sweet Fairy' (Min)	CSBt
	Sweet Haze = 'Tan97274' PBR (F)	CGro CSBt EPfP ESty GCoc LRHS LStr MAsh MGan MJon MRav MWat NPri SCoo SWCr
	Sweet Juliet = 'Ausleap' PBR (S)	CSBt ELon ESty LRHS MAus MCot MJon SPer SWCr
*	'Sweet Lemon Dream' (Patio)	CTri
	Sweet Magic = 'Dicmagic' PBR (Min/Patio) ♀H4	CGro CSBt CTri EPfP IDic LStr MAsh MBri MGan MJon MRav NPri SPoG SWCr
	Sweet Memories = 'Whamemo' (Patio)	CTri ECnt EPfP ESty LRHS LStr MAsh MJon MRav NPri SCoo SMrm SPer SPoG SRGP SWCr
	Sweet Parfum de Provence = 'Meiclusif' (HT) **new**	ESty
§	Sweet Promise = 'Meihelvet' (GC)	MGan SPer
	Sweet Remembrance = 'Kirr' (HT)	LStr SCoo
	'Sweet Repose' (F)	MGan
	'Sweet Revelation' PBR	see *R.* Sue Hipkin
	'Sweet Velvet' (F)	MGan
	'Sweet Wonder' (Patio)	EPfP MAsh MBri SPoG
N	Sweetheart = 'Cocapeer' (HT)	GCoc
	'Sweetie' (Patio)	ESty SWCr
	sweginzowii	GAuc MAus
	'Sylvia Dot' (F) **new**	LSRN
	'Sympathie' (ClHT)	MGan MGos SPer SSea SWCr
	Tall Story = 'Dickooky' PBR (F) ♀H4	MJon SWCr
	Tamora = 'Austamora' (S)	MAus
	Tango = 'Macfirwal' (F)	MJon
	Tango Showground = 'Chewpattens' PBR (GC)	SSea
	Tapis Jaune	see *R.* Golden Penny
	Tatoo = 'Poulyc002' PBR (ClPatio)	EBee ECnt
	Tatton = 'Fryentice' PBR (F)	EBls ESty MAus MJon MRav SMrm SWCr
	Tawny Tiger = 'Frygolly' PBR (F)	CGro GCoc SWCr
	Tea Clipper = 'Ausrover' PBR (S)	CSBt ESty LRHS MAsh MAus MBri SCoo SSea WClo
	Tear Drop = 'Dicomo' PBR (Min/Patio)	IDic LStr MGan SWCr
	Teasing Georgia = 'Ausbaker' PBR (S)	ECnt EPfP ESty LRHS LSRN MAsh MAus MBri MJon SCoo SRGP SSea SWCr WClo
	'Telstar' (F)	MGan
	Temptress = 'Korramal' (ClS)	EPfP MAsh MGos
	Tenacious = 'Macblackpo' PBR (F)	ESty LStr MJon SWCr
	'Tequila Gold'	SMrm
	Tequila Sunrise = 'Dicobey' PBR (HT) ♀H4	CGro CTri CWit EBls ECnt ELan EPfP ESty IDic LRHS LStr MAsh MAus MGan MJon MRav SMrm SPer SPoG
§	Terracotta = 'Meicobuis' PBR (HT)	ESty SWCr
	Tess of the d'Urbervilles = 'Ausmove' PBR (S)	ESty LRHS LStr MAsh MAus MBri NEgg SCoo SPer SWCr WClo
	'Tessa' (F)	LSRN MGan
	Thank You = 'Chesdeep' PBR (Patio)	ESty LStr MGan SMrm SPoG SRGP SWCr
§	That's Jazz = 'Poulnorm' PBR (Courtyard Series) (ClF)	ECnt MAsh MBri MJon MWat SMrm SWCr
	The Alexandra Rose = 'Ausday' PBR (S)	LRHS MAus SEND SSea
	The Attenborough Rose = 'Dicelope' PBR (F)	IDic
	'The Bishop' (Ce × G)	MAus
	'The Bishop of Bradford' (ClPiH)	ECnt
	The Compass Rose = 'Korwisco' PBR (S)	EPfP MGos
	The Countryman = 'Ausman' PBR (S)	ELon LRHS LStr MAus SSea
	The Dark Lady = 'Ausbloom' PBR (S)	LRHS MAus MBri NEgg SPer WClo
	'The Doctor' (HT)	MGan
	The Dove = 'Tanamola' PBR (F)	MGan
§	'The Fairy' (Poly) ♀H4	CSBt CTri EBee ECnt ELan EPfP EWTr LAst LRHS LStr MAus MCot MGan MJon MRav MWat NLar SBfd SEND SMad SMrm SPer SSea SWCr WCFE
	'The Garland' (Ra) ♀H4	CRHN EPfP EWTr LRHS MAsh MAus MBri NLar SFam SPer SWCr
	The Generous Gardener = 'Ausdrawn' PBR (S)	EPfP LRHS MAus MBri SCoo SWCr WClo
	The Gold Award Rose = 'Poulac008' (Palace Series) (Patio)	ECnt
§	The Halcyon Days Rose = 'Korparesni' PBR (F)	MGos
	The Herbalist = 'Aussemi' (S)	LRHS MAus SSea
	The Ingenious Mr Fairchild = 'Austijus' PBR (S)	LRHS MAsh MAus MBri SCoo

The Jubilee Rose = 'Poulbrido'^{PBR} (F)	ECnt SCoo
'The Lister Rose' (F)	MGan
The Maidstone Rose = 'Kordauerpa' (S)	SCoo
'The Margaret Coppola Rose'^{PBR}	see *R.* White Gold
The Mayflower = 'Austilly'^{PBR} (S)	CSBt LRHS LStr MAus MBri SSea
§ The McCartney Rose = 'Meizeli'^{PBR} (HT)	MJon SWCr
'The New Dawn'	see *R.* 'New Dawn'
The Nun = 'Ausnun' (S)	MAus
The Painter = 'Mactemaik'^{PBR} (F)	LStr MJon
§ The Pilgrim = 'Auswalker'^{PBR} (S)	CSBt EPfP ESty LRHS LStr MAus MBri MGan MJon SEND SPer SSea SWCr WClo
The Prince = 'Ausvelvet'^{PBR} (S)	LRHS MAus NLar SLon SPer
The Prince's Trust = 'Harholding'^{PBR} (Cl)	LRHS LStr MAus MJon SPoG
'The Prioress' (S)	MAus
§ 'The Queen Elizabeth' (F)	CBcs CGro CSBt CTri CWSG GCoc LStr MAsh MAus MBri MGan MJon MRav MWat NPri SEND SPer SWCr WBor
The Reeve = 'Ausreeve' (S)	MAus
The Rotarian	see *R.* Rotary Sunrise
I 'The Rugby Rose' (HT)	MGan
The Schofield Rose	see *R.* Jacob's Ladder
The Shepherdess = 'Austwist'^{PBR} (S)	LRHS MAsh MAus MBri MJon SSea WClo
The Soham Rose^{PBR}	see *R.* Pearl Abundance
The Soroptimist Rose = 'Benstar' (Patio)	MJon
The Squire = 'Ausquire' (S)	MAus
The Times Rose = 'Korpeahn'^{PBR} (F) $\mathbb{Y}^{H4}$	ECnt LStr MAus MGan MGos MJon MRav SPer SWCr
The Wedgwood Rose = 'Ausjosiah' (ClS) **new**	MAus
The Wren = 'Kormamtiza'^{PBR} (F/Patio) **new**	EPfP
'Thelma' (Ra)	MAus
'Thérèse Bugnet' (Ru)	MAus NHaw
Thinking of You = 'Frydandy'^{PBR} (HT)	EBls ESty GCoc LRHS LStr MAsh MAus MGan MHav NPri SRGP SVic SWCr
'Thisbe' (HM)	CPou EBee EWTr MAus SPer
Thomas Barton = 'Meihirvin' (HT)	LStr SWCr
'Threave' (Bb)	CPou
Three Cheers = 'Dicdomino'^{PBR} (F)	IDic
'Three Wishes'	MBri
Three Wishes = 'Poulpak038' (Patio) **new**	MAsh
threepenny bit rose	see *R. elegantula* 'Persetosa'
Thumbs Up = 'Hornothing' (S)	EBls
tibetica	GAuc
Tickled Pink = 'Fryhunky' (F)	CGro CSBt EBls ECnt EPfP ESty GCoc LRHS LSRN LShp MAsh MBri MGan MGos MJon MRav SCoo SMrm SPer SPoG SRGP SWCr
Times Past = 'Harhilt'^{PBR} (ClHT)	ELon ESty GCoc LStr MGan MJon MRav SPoG SWCr
'Tina Turner' (HT)	LSRN MJon
Tintinara = 'Dicuptight'^{PBR} (HT)	ECnt IDic
Tip Top = 'Tanope' (F/Patio)	MGan SPer
'Tipo Ideale'	see *R.* × *odorata* 'Mutabilis'
Titanic = 'Macdako'^{PBR} (F)	MJon
'Toby Tristam' (Ra)	CRHN
Together Forever = 'Dicecho'^{PBR} (F)	GCoc IDic
Too Hot to Handle = 'Macloupri' (ClS)	MJon
Top Marks = 'Fryministar'^{PBR} (Min/Patio)	CGro CSBt CTri GCoc LAst LStr MGan MJon MRav MWat NPri SCoo SPer SWCr
Topaz Jewel^{PBR}	see *R.* Yellow Dagmar Hastrup
Toprose = 'Cocgold'^{PBR} (F)	GCoc MAsh
'Topsi' (F/Patio)	SPer
§ 'Tour de Malakoff' (Ce)	CPou EWTr LRHS MAus MRav NLar SEND SFam SMrm SPer
Tower Bridge = 'Haravis' (HT)	ESty
'Trade Winds' (HT)	MGan
Tradescant = 'Ausdir'^{PBR} (S)	MAus
Tradition^{PBR}	see *R.* Tradition '95
§ Tradition '95 = 'Korkeltin'^{PBR} (ClHT) $\mathbb{Y}^{H4}$	MGos
'Treasure Trove' (Ra)	CRHN LRHS MAus MGan NLar SMrm SWCr
Trevor Griffiths = 'Ausold'^{PBR} (S)	MAus
'Tricolore de Flandre' (G)	MAus
'Trier' (Ra)	CPou MAus
'Trigintipetala' misapplied	see *R.* 'Professeur Emile Perrot'
'Triomphe de l'Exposition' (HP)	MAus
'Triomphe du Luxembourg' (T)	MAus
triphylla	see *R.* × *beanii*
Troika = 'Poumidor' (HT) $\mathbb{Y}^{H4}$	CSBt ELan EPfP LRHS LStr MAsh MAus MBri MGan MRav SMrm SPer SPoG SWCr
Troilus = 'Ausoil' (S)	MAus
'Tropicana'	see *R.* Super Star
Trumpeter = 'Mactru' (F) $\mathbb{Y}^{H4}$	CSBt CWit EBee ECnt IArd LRHS LStr MAsh MAus MBri MGan MJon MRav SPer SPoG SSea SWCr
§ 'Tuscany' (G)	GCoc MAus SPer
'Tuscany Superb' (G) $\mathbb{Y}^{H4}$	CPou CSBt CSam EBee EPfP EWTr GCra LAst LRHS MAus MBri MCot MGan MRav NChi NLar SEND SKHP SMrm SPer SSea SWCr WKif
Twenty-one Again! = 'Meinimo'^{PBR} (HT)	LSRN SWCr
Twice in a Blue Moon = 'Tan96138'^{PBR} (HT)	CGro CSBt EBee EBls ECnt ESty MAsh MBri MGan MJon MRav SCoo SMrm SPoG SSea SWCr
Twist = 'Poulstri'^{PBR} (Courtyard Series) (ClPatio)	CGro EBee ECnt ESty MAsh SWCr
Tynwald = 'Mattwyt' (HT)	LStr MGos SPer
'Ulrich Brünner'	see *R.* 'Ulrich Brünner Fils'
§ 'Ulrich Brünner Fils' (HP)	MAus
UNICEF = 'Cocjojo'^{PBR} (F)	GCoc
'Unique Blanche'	see *R.* × *centifolia* 'Unique'
Valencia = 'Koreklia'^{PBR} (HT) $\mathbb{Y}^{H4}$	ECnt MAus
Valentine Heart = 'Dicogle'^{PBR} (F) $\mathbb{Y}^{H4}$	CSBt ESty IArd IDic LRHS MAsh MAus MBri MGos MRav SPoG SRGP SWCr
Vanilla Twist = 'Dicghost' (F)	IDic

	Varenna Allen = 'Harmode'[PBR] (F)	EBee ECnt
	'Variegata di Bologna' (Bb)	EBee EPfP LRHS MAus MRav SLon SMrm SSea SWCr
	'Vatertag' (Min)	LSRN
	'Veilchenblau' (Ra) ♀H4	CRHN CSBt CSam ECnt ELan EPfP LRHS LStr MAus MGan MRav NEgg NLar NPri SEND SMrm SPer SPoG SSea SWCr WBor WKif
	'Velindre' (HT) **new**	MJon
	Velvet Abundance (F)	LRHS
	Velvet Fragrance = 'Fryperdee'[PBR] (HT)	CSBt CWSG ECnt ESty GCoc LRHS LStr MAus MGan MJon MRav SMrm SPoG SWCr
	'Venusta Pendula' (Ra)	MAus
	'Verschuren' (HT/v)	MGan MJon
	versicolor	see *R. gallica* 'Versicolor'
	Versigny = 'Masversi' (Generosa Series) (S)	MRav
	'Vick's Caprice' (HP)	EWTr MAus
	'Vicomtesse Pierre du Fou' (ClHT)	MAus
	'Victor Madeley' (F)	MGan
	Victoria Joy = 'Diciwill' (F) **new**	IDic
	Vidal Sassoon = 'Macjuliat'[PBR] (HT)	MGan MJon
	'Village Maid'	see *R.* × *centifolia* 'Unique Panachée'
	villosa misapplied	see *R. mollis*
§	***villosa*** L.	CArn
§	'Violacea' (G)	MAus
	'Violette' (Ra)	CPou CRHN EWTr LRHS LTen MAus SPer SWCr
	virginiana ♀H4	CFee GAuc GCal IFFs LBuc MAus MGan NHaw NWea SPer
	- 'Harvest Song'	NHaw
	- 'Plena'	see *R.* 'Rose d'Amour'
	'Viridiflora'	see *R.* × *odorata* 'Viridiflora'
	Waltz = 'Poulkrid'[PBR] (Courtyard Series) (ClPatio)	ECnt LRHS
	wardii var. ***culta***	MAus
	Warm Welcome = 'Chewizz'[PBR] (ClMin) ♀H4	CGro CWSG ECnt EPfP ESty LRHS LSRN LStr MAsh MAus MBri MGan MGos MJon MRav MWat SMad SMrm SPer SPoG SRGP SSea SWCr
§	Warm Wishes = 'Fryxotic'[PBR] (HT) ♀H4	CSBt ECnt ESty GCoc LRHS LSRN LStr MAsh MAus MBri MGan MGos MJon MRav SPoG SRGP SWCr WBor
	'Warrior' (F)	MGan SPer
	Warwick Castle = 'Auslian'[PBR] (S)	MAus
	Warwickshire = 'Korkandel'[PBR] (GC)	SPer
	webbiana	MAus SPer
	Wedding Celebration = 'Poulht006' (HT)	EBee ECnt SWCr
	'Wedding Day' (Ra)	Widely available
	Wee Cracker = 'Cocmarris'[PBR] (Patio)	ESty GCoc SWCr
	Wee Jock = 'Cocabest' (F/Patio)	GCoc SMrm
	'Weetwood' (Ra)	CRHN
	Weisse Wolcke[PBR]	see *R.* White Cloud = 'Korstacha'
	Welcome Home = 'Koraubala'[PBR] (F)	MGos
	Well-Being = 'Harjangle'[PBR] (S)	CSBt ELon ESty SWCr
	'Wendy Cussons' (HT)	CGro CTri GCoc MGan MRav SPer SWCr
	Wenlock = 'Auswen' (S)	MAus SPer
	'West Country Millennium' (F)	MGan
	Westerland = 'Korwest' (S) ♀H4	ECGP MGan MJon MRav SMad SWCr WCot
	Where the Heart Is = 'Cocoplan'[PBR] (HT)	ESty
	'Whisky Gill' (HT)	MGan
	Whisky Mac = 'Tanky' (HT)	CBcs CGro CSBt CTri ELan GCoc MGan MJon MRav NPri SPer SPoG
	'White Bath'	see *R.* × *centifolia* 'Shailer's White Moss'
	'White Christmas' (HT)	MGan
§	White Cloud = 'Korstacha'[PBR] (S/ClHT) ♀H4	CSBt EBee ECnt EPfP ESty LRHS MAsh MGos MJon MWat SKHP SPoG SWCr
	White Cloud = 'Savacloud' (Min)	MBri
	'White Cockade' (Cl)	EBee ESwi GCoc MGan SMrm SPer SWCr
	White Cover[PBR]	see *R.* Kent
§	'White de Meaux' (Ce)	MAus
	White Diamond = 'Interamon'[PBR] (S)	EBee ECnt IDic MGan
§	White Gold = 'Cocquiriam'[PBR] (F)	CSBt CWit GCoc MRav SPoG
	'White Grootendorst' (Ru)	LRHS
	white moss	see *R.* 'Comtesse de Murinais', *R.* × *centifolia* 'Shailer's White Moss'
	White Parfum de Provence = 'Meidiaphaz' (HT) **new**	CSBt ESty
§	'White Pet' (Poly) ♀H4	CSBt EBee ECnt EPfP EWTr GCoc LRHS LStr MAus MBri MCot MGan MJon MRav SEND SMrm SPer SWCr WKif
	white Provence	see *R.* × *centifolia* 'Unique'
	white rose of York	see *R.* × *alba* 'Alba Semiplena'
	White Skyliner = 'Franwekwhit'[PBR] (ClS)	EBls MJon
	'White Wings' (HT)	EWTr MAus MGan WKif
N	***wichurana*** (Ra)	GCal GLin MAus MGan
	- 'Cally Anemone' (d)	GCal
	- 'Variegata' (Ra/v)	CBow CSWP EPot MJon
*	- 'Variegata Nana' (Ra/v)	MRav
	'Wickwar' (Ra)	CSWP GCal GGal
	Wife of Bath = 'Ausbath' (S)	MAus
	Wild Edric = 'Aushedge'[PBR] (Ru)	LRHS MAus MBri SCoo
	Wild Rover = 'Dichirap'[PBR] (F)	ESty IDic LStr SSea SWCr
	Wild Thing = 'Jactoose' (S)	ESty IDic
	Wildeve = 'Ausbonny'[PBR] (S)	LRHS MAsh MAus MBri WClo
	Wildfire = 'Fryessex' (Patio)	ECnt ESty LRHS MAsh MAus MBri MJon SMrm SPoG SWCr
§	'Wilhelm' (HM)	MAus MRav SPer
	'Will Scarlet' (HM)	MAus
	'William Allen Richardson' (N)	MAus
	'William Cobbett' (F)	SSea
§	'William Lobb' (CeMo) ♀H4	CGro CPou CRHN EBee EPfP EWTr LRHS LStr MAus MBri MCot MGan MRav NEgg NLar SEND SPer SWCr WKif
	William Morris = 'Auswill'[PBR] (S)	CSBt LRHS MAus MBri MJon NEgg SWCr
	William Shakespeare 2000 = 'Ausromeo'[PBR] (S)	CSBt ECnt EPfP ESty LRHS LStr MAsh MAus MBNS MBri NEgg SCoo SSea SWCr
	William Shakespeare = 'Ausroyal'[PBR] (S)	LRHS SMrm SPer WClo

	'Williams' Double Yellow'	see *R.* × *harisonii* 'Williams Double Yellow'
	willmottiae	see *R. gymnocarpa* var. *willmottiae*
	Wilton = 'Eurosa'	SWCr
	Wiltshire = 'Kormuse'^{PBR} (S/GC) Υ^{H4}	CSBt ECnt ESty LSRN LStr MJon MRav SLon SSea SWCr
	Winchester Cathedral = 'Auscat'^{PBR} (S)	CGro CSBt EBee ECnt ELon EPfP ESty EWTr LRHS LSRN LStr MAsh MAus MBri MGos MRav MWat NEgg NLar SPer SPoG SSea SWCr WClo
	Windflower = 'Auscross' (S)	LRHS MAus
	Windrush = 'Ausrush' (S)	MAus MJon SPer SWCr
	Wine and Dine = 'Dicuncle' (GC)	EBls
	Winter Magic = 'Foumagic' (Min)	MJon
	Wise Portia = 'Ausport' (S)	MAus
	Wishing = 'Dickerfuffle'^{PBR} (F/Patio)	IDic MGan
	Wisley 2008 = 'Ausbreeze' (S) **new**	CSBt MAus
	Wisley = 'Ausintense'^{PBR} (S)	LRHS MJon SCoo SSea
	With All My Love = 'Coczodiac'^{PBR} (HT)	CSBt ESty GCoc LStr
	With Love = 'Andwit' (HT)	SWCr
	With Thanks = 'Fransmoov'^{PBR} (HT)	SRGP SWCr
	'Woburn Abbey' (F)	SSea
	'Wolley-Dod'	see *R.* 'Duplex'
	Woman o'th' North = 'Kirlon' (F/Patio)	MJon
	Wonderful News = 'Jonone'^{PBR} (Patio)	ESty MJon
	Wonderful = 'Poulpmt005'^{PBR} (HT)	ECnt SWCr
§	***woodsii***	MAus
	- var. ***fendleri***	see *R. woodsii*
	Worcestershire = 'Korlalon'^{PBR} (GC)	GCoc MAus MGan MJon MRav SPer SSea SWCr
	Wordly Wishes = 'Poulpah023' (Patio) **new**	MAsh
	Wymondham Abbey = 'Beadevil' (ClHT) **new**	EBls
§	***xanthina*** 'Canary Bird' (S) Υ^{H4}	Widely available
§	- f. ***hugonis*** Υ^{H4}	CTri MAus MGan NHaw SKHP SPer
	X-rated = 'Tinx' (Min)	MJon
	'Yellow Cécile Brünner'	see *R.* 'Perle d'Or'
	Yellow Charles Austin = 'Ausyel' (S)	MAus
§	Yellow Dagmar Hastrup = 'Moryelrug'^{PBR} (Ru)	MGan MJon SPer
*	'Yellow Dream' (Patio)	SPoG
	Yellow Floorshow = 'Harfully'^{PBR} (GC)	CWit MRav
	Yellow Flower Carpet^{PBR}	see *R.* Flower Carpet Sunshine
	'Yellow Mutabilis' **new**	EBls
	'Yellow Patio' (Min/Patio)	LStr MAsh SPoG SSea SWCr
	yellow Scotch	see *R.* × *harisonii* 'Williams Double Yellow'
	Yellow Sunblaze = 'Meitrisical' (Min)	CSBt
	'Yesterday' (Poly/F/S) Υ^{H4}	EWTr MAsh MAus MGan NLar SLon SMrm
	York and Lancaster	see *R.* × *damascena* 'Versicolor'
	Yorkshire = 'Korbarkeit'^{PBR} (GC)	GCoc LStr MRav MWat
	'Yorkshire Lady' (HT)	MJon NEgg
	You Are My Sunshine = 'Frykwanko' (HT) **new**	GCoc
	Young Lycidas = 'Ausvibrant' (S) **new**	CSBt LRHS MAus
	'Yvonne Rabier' (Poly) Υ^{H4}	MAus MGan MRav SLon SPer
	'Zéphirine Drouhin' (Bb)	Widely available
§	'Zigeunerknabe' (S)	ECnt ELan MAus MGan MRav NLar SPer
	'Zweibrücken' (Cl)	MGan

Roscoea ✿ (*Zingiberaceae*)

	ACE 2539	GEdr
	alpina	CAby CLAP CPLG CPrp EBee ECho EHrv EPPr GCrs GEdr GGar GKir LRHS MTho NGdn NMen NWCA WCru
	- CC 3667	GEdr
	- 'Leaping Salmon' **new**	CFir
	- pink-flowered	IBlr
	- purple-flowered	IBlr
	- short	WCru
§	***auriculata***	Widely available
	- B&SWJ 2594	WCru
	- brown-stemmed × ***purpurea***	IBlr
	- early-flowering	IBlr NCot WCru
	- 'Floriade'	CLAP EBee GMac IBlr LRHS SPoG WWst
	- green-stemmed × ***purpurea***	IBlr
	- late-flowering	WCru
	- 'Special'	CLAP
	- 'White Cap'	EBee WWst
	auriculata × ***australis***	IBlr
	auriculata × ***capitata*** **new**	IBlr
	australis	CFir ELon GEdr MNrw NMyG WCru WHil
	- pink-flowered	NCot
	- - KW 22124	IBlr
	- purple-flowered KW 22124	IBlr
	australis × ***humeana***	IBlr
	'Ballyrogan Lavender'	IBlr
	'Ballyrogan Purple'	IBlr
	'Beesiana'	Widely available
	'Beesiana' dark-flowered	ELon IBlr WAbe
	'Beesiana' pale-flowered	ECho EWld LEdu SKHP WCru
	'Beesiana' white-flowered	CBct CDes CFwr CLAP EBee EHrv ELon EPfP EPot GEdr IBlr MMHG NBir NGdn NMyG NPnk WPGP
	Blackthorn strain	IBlr WAbe
	brandisii	EBee ECho WWst
	capitata	CLAP IBlr
	cautleyoides Υ^{H4}	Widely available
	- CLD 772	IBlr
I	- 'Alba'	EUJe NGdn NLAp WCot
	- var. ***cautleyoides*** f. ***atropurpurea***	IBlr
	- - - 'Giraffe'	IBlr
	- 'Doge Purple'	IBlr
	- 'Early Purple'	CDes CLAP ECho WPGP
	- 'Early Yellow'	EBee
	- 'Himalaya'	CLAP EBee WWst
	- hybrid	ECho
	- 'Jeffrey Thomas'	CBct CBgR CFwr CLAP CSam EBee ECha ECho ELon EPPr EPot GCal GEdr IBlr MLHP NMyG SRGP WCot
	- 'Kew Beauty' Υ^{H4}	CDes CFir CLAP CMea CPLG EBee EBrs EPfP GCal GEdr GKir LRHS MMoz MTho NMyG SKHP SMHy WCom WCot WPGP
	- late, lavender-flowered	IBlr
	- late, yellow-flowered	IBlr

- 'Lemon Giraffe'	IBlr
- 'Pennine Purple'	IBlr NHar
- plum-flowered	IBlr
- var. ***pubescens***	IBlr
- 'Purple Giant'	CLAP EWll NMyG SKHP WCot WWst
- purple-flowered	CAby IBlr NHar
- 'Reinier'	CAby CLAP EBee GCal IBlr SKHP WCot
- f. ***sinopurpurea***	IBlr
- 'Vanilla'	EBee LEdu NMyG SKHP WWst
- 'Washfield Purple'	IBlr
- 'Yeti'	CLAP EBee NMyG SKHP
cautleyoides × ***humeana***	CLAP IBlr WHar WWst
cautleyoides × ***scillifolia*** f. ***atropurpurea***	IBlr
debilis var. ***debilis***	IBlr
forrestii f. ***forrestii***	IBlr
- f. ***purpurea***	IBlr
- f. ***purpurea*** × ***humeana***	IBlr
'Gestreept'	CLAP
humeana Υ^{H4}	CAby CBct CLAP CSam ECho GAuc GCrs GEdr LAma LRHS MBri NMyG WCFE WCot WHil WThu WWst
- ACE 2539	IBlr
- CC 1820	IBlr
- f. ***alba***	IBlr
- cream-flowered	WWst
- Forrest's form	IBlr
- lavender-flowered	IBlr
- 'Long Acre Sunrise'	CLAP
- f. ***lutea***	CLAP GEdr IBlr
- pink-flowered	IBlr
- 'Purple Streaker'	CAby CDes CLAP EBee WPGP
- 'Rosemoor Plum'	CDes CLAP GEdr WPGP
- 'Snowy Owl'	CLAP
- f. ***tyria***	EBee IBlr
- - 'Inkling'	WWst
'Ice Maiden'	IBlr
'Monique'	CDes CLAP EBee IBlr NHar NMyG WPGP
nepalensis **new**	WHil
'Petite Purple'	IBlr
praecox	IBlr
- BWJ 7848	WCru
procera misapplied	see *R. auriculata*
procera Wall.	see *R. purpurea*
'Purple King'	EBee WCot WWst
§ ***purpurea***	Widely available
- CC 1757	IBlr
- CC 3667	WCot
- HWJK 2020	WCru
- HWJK 2169	WCru
- HWJK 2175	WCru
- HWJK 2400	WCru
- HWJK 2401	WCru
- HWJK 2407	WCru
- KW 13755	IBlr
- MECC 2	IBlr
- MECC 10	IBlr
- f. ***alba***	GEdr
- bronze-leaved **new**	CAby
- 'Brown Peacock'	CDes CLAP IBlr NMyG SKHP WPGP WWst
- 'Dalai Lama'	WWst
- var. ***gigantea***	CLAP IBlr
- - CC 1757	MNrw
- green-stemmed **new**	WWst
- 'Himalayan Delight'	IBlr
- 'Nico'	CLAP EBee ELan IBlr SKHP WWst
- 'Niedrig'	EBee IBlr SKHP
- pale-flowered	EBla
- 'Peacock'	CLAP EBee IBlr NMyG SKHP WFar WWst
- 'Peacock Eye'	CLAP IBlr SKHP WWst
- var. ***procera***	see *R. purpurea*
- 'Red Foot' **new**	WWst
- red-stemmed **new**	WWst
- Rosemoor form	CLAP WWst
- f. ***rubra*** 'Red Gurkha'	CDes CLAP IBlr
- short	CLAP IBlr
- tall	CLAP NLAp WCru WPGP
- 'Typico'	IBlr
- 'Vannin' **new**	WCru
- 'Vincent'	EBee WCot WWst
- 'Wisley Amethyst'	CLAP GEdr IBlr LRHS MBri NCot SKHP WWst
schneideriana	IBlr MMoz WThu
- robust form	IBlr
scillifolia	CBgR CDes CFir CPBP ECho GKev GKir LAma LHop LRHS MTho NBir NGdn NMen WHar WPrP
- f. ***atropurpurea***	CPom CStu EHrv GEdr IBlr NMyG WAul WCru WPGP WThu WWEG
- f. ***scillifolia***	CYeo EBee ECho EHrv GEdr IBlr IFoB NMen NMyG WCot WCru WHar WPrP
aff. ***scillifolia*** purple-flowered	IBlr
tibetica	CFir CLAP EBee GEdr GKev IBlr LRHS WCru WThu
- ACE 2538	IBlr
- SDR 467	GKev
aff. ***tibetica***	IBlr NMyG
- f. ***albo-purpurea***	IBlr
tumjensis	CLAP EBee EWes IBlr WPGP
wardii	CPLG IBlr

Rosenia (*Asteraceae*)

humilis	CPBP

Rosmarinus ✿ (*Lamiaceae*)

* 'Compactus Albus'	WClo
corsicus 'Prostratus'	see *R. officinalis* Prostratus Group
lavandulaceus misapplied	see *R. officinalis* Prostratus Group
officinalis	Widely available
- SDR 5234	GKev
- var. ***albiflorus***	CArn CPrp CSev ELau EOHP EPfP GBar GPoy MHer MNHC SBfd SDow SHDw SLim SPlb STre WClo WGwG WJek
- - 'Lady in White'	CSBt EBee ELan EPfP GBar LRHS MHer SDow SEND SPer SPoG WGwG WJek
- 'Alderney'	GBar MHer SDow
§ - var. ***angustissimus*** 'Benenden Blue' Υ^{H4}	CSBt CWan CWib EBee EPfP GBar GPoy SBfd SDix SPer SPlb SPoG WGwG WJek WPnn WSpi
- - 'Corsican Blue'	CAlb CArn EBee ELan EPfP GBar GPoy MHer MNHC MRav SBfd SDow SHDw SIde SPad SPer WBrE WPer WRHF
* - 'Argenteovariegatus' (v)	WPGP
- 'Aureovariegatus'	see *R. officinalis* 'Aureus'
§ - 'Aureus' (v)	CBow CPla GBar WCom WJek
- 'Baby P.J.'	EOHP
- 'Barbecue'^{PBR}	ELau MHer NGHP SIde
- 'Blue Lagoon'	EBee ELau EOHP MHer MNHC MSCN NGHP SIde WGwG WHer WJek WPnn
- 'Blue Rain'	CBar CBod GPWP MHer NGHP SIde WHfH WPnn
- 'Boule'	CArn CBod ELau MHer SDow WGwG WJek

- 'Capercaillie'	SDow
- 'Collingwood Ingram'	see *R. officinalis* var. *angustissimus* 'Benenden Blue'
- 'Cottage White'	WGwG WHer
- dwarf, blue-flowered	ELau GBar
- 'Farinole'	CArn CBod ELau GBar MNHC
- 'Fastigiatus'	see *R. officinalis* 'Miss Jessopp's Upright'
- 'Fota Blue'	CArn CBod CBow CTsd CWib ELau GBar IArd IVic MHer MNHC NGHP NHol SAga SBfd SDow SHDw SIde SPoG WFar WGwG WJek WPnn
- 'Foxtail'	WJek
- 'Frimley Blue'	see *R. officinalis* 'Primley Blue'
- 'Genges Gold' (v)	ECtt MHer SBfd
- 'Golden Rain'	see *R. officinalis* 'Joyce DeBaggio'
- 'Gorizia'	CBcs GBar SDow WGwG WPnn
- 'Green Ginger'	CBod CPrp ELan ELau EOHP EPfP GBar GBin LHop LRHS MAsh MHer MNHC MRav MSCN NGHP NPer SDow SPer SPoG WGwG WJek WMnd WPnn
- 'Guilded'	see *R. officinalis* 'Aureus'
- 'Gunnel's Upright'	GBar
- 'Haifa'	CBod EBee EBtc ECtt ELau GGar NGHP NLBP SIde WJek WPnn
- 'Heavenly Blue'	GBar
- 'Henfield Blue'	SBfd SHDw
- 'Iden Blue'	SIde
- 'Iden Blue Boy'	SIde
- 'Iden Pillar'	SIde
§ - 'Joyce DeBaggio' (v)	MHer SDow WGwG WHer
- 'Lady in Blue'	WGwG
- ***lavandulaceus***	see *R. officinalis* Prostratus Group
- 'Lilies Blue'	GPoy
- 'Lockwood Variety'	see *R. officinalis* (Prostratus Group) 'Lockwood de Forest'
- 'Majorca Pink'	CBcs CSBt CSam CSpe CWan ELau GBar GGar GPWP LRHS MCot MHer MNHC NPri SDow SIde SPer WGwG WJek
- 'Marenca'	ELau MNHC
- 'McConnell's Blue' ♀H4	CAlb CArn CDoC CPrp EBee ELan ELau EShb GBar LHop LRHS MAsh MGos MNHC SBfd SDow SHDw SPoG WFar WGwG WHer WHoo WJek WPGP
* - 'Miss Jessopp's Prostrate'	GKir
§ - 'Miss Jessopp's Upright' ♀H4	Widely available
- 'Mrs Harding'	CBod
- 'Pat Vlasto'	SUsu
- 'Pointe du Raz'	CAbP EBee ELan EPfP LRHS MAsh SChF WSpi
§ - 'Primley Blue'	CArn CBcs CMea CSam CSev CTsd EBee ECtt ELau GBar LSou MNHC MRav SIde WFar WJek WPer WSpi
§ - Prostratus Group	Widely available
- - 'Capri'	CAbP CDul CSBt ECtt ELau EPfP LRHS MBrN MHer NGHP SPoG WJek
- - 'Gethsemane'	SIde WGwG
- - 'Jackman's Prostrate'	CBcs ECtt
§ - - 'Lockwood de Forest'	GBar LSou WGwG WHer
- - 'Sheila Dore' **new**	SPlb
- f. ***pyramidalis***	see *R. officinalis* 'Miss Jessopp's Upright'
- ***repens***	see *R. officinalis* Prostratus Group
- 'Rex'	ELau
- 'Roman Beauty'	CBcs LAst LRHS LSRN SPoG WSpi
- 'Roseus'	CArn CEnt CPrp CWib EBee ELan ELau EPfP GPoy LHop LRHS MAsh MHer MNHC NEgg SBfd SDow SEND SLim SPoG WClo WCom WGwG WHer WJek WMnd WPer WPnn
- 'Russell's Blue'	WFar
- 'Salem'	CBod MHer
- 'Sea Level'	CBod ELau MHer WGwG
- 'Severn Sea' ♀H4	Widely available
- 'Shimmering Stars'	SDow
- 'Silver Sparkler'	WCom WPat
- Silver Spires = 'Wolros'	MNHC WFar
- 'Sissinghurst Blue' ♀H4	CArn CDul CSev CWan EBee ECha ECrN ELan ELau EPfP GBar LAst LRHS MHer MLHP MNHC MRav SBfd SDow SIde SLim SPer SPlb SRms WClo WCom WGwG WJek
- 'Sissinghurst White'	MMuc WGwG
- 'Sorcerer's Apprentice' **new**	WGwG
- 'South Downs Blue'	SBfd SHDw
- 'Spanish Snow'	WGwG
- 'Sudbury Blue'	EBee ELau EPfP GBar MNHC SBfd SDow SHDw WEas WFar WJek WPnn
- 'Trusty'	CWan GBar
- 'Tuscan Blue'	CDoC CPLG EBee ECGP ECha ECtt ELan ELau EPfP GGar GKir LRHS MHer MNHC MSwo NEgg NPri SBfd SDow SIde SPad SPer SRms WFar WGwG WHfH WJek WPGP WPnn WSpi
- 'Variegatus'	see *R. officinalis* 'Aureus'
repens	see *R. officinalis* Prostratus Group
'Sappho' **new**	CHll

rosemary see *Rosmarinus officinalis*

Rostrinucula (*Lamiaceae*)

B&SWJ 11739 from northern Vietnam	WCru
dependens	ECre EPfP EWes NLar
sinensis	CPLG

Rosularia ✿ (*Crassulaceae*)

sp.	MWat
from Sandras Dag	CWil LBee LRHS
§ ***aizoon***	ECho LRHS
alba	see *R. sedoides* var. *alba*
alpestris from Rhotang Pass	WThu
§ ***chrysantha***	EBur ECho EDAr EPot LRHS NMen SFgr SPlb
- number 1	CWil
crassipes	see *Rhodiola wallichiana*
libanotica RCB RL 20	WCot
lineata RCB RL C-5	WCot
§ ***muratdaghensis***	EBur
pallida A. Berger	see *R. chrysantha*
pallida Stapf	see *R. aizoon*
pallida ambig.	SFgr
platyphylla misapplied	see *R. muratdaghensis*
sedoides	CWil
§ - var. ***alba***	ECho EDAr EPot GGar WNew WTin
sempervivum	CWil ECho EWes NMen
§ - subsp. ***glaucophylla***	CWil NSla WAbe WThu
spatulata hort.	see *R. sempervivum* subsp. *glaucophylla*

Rothmannia (*Rubiaceae*)

capensis	EShb SOWG

Rubia (*Rubiaceae*)

peregrina	CArn GPoy
tinctorum	CArn CHby EOHP GBar GPoy MHer SWat WHfH WSFF

Rubus ✿ (*Rosaceae*)

CC 6100	EWld
CC C755	EWld
RCB/Eq C-1	WCot
SDR 4635	GKev
alceifolius Poir.	CFee SDys
arcticus	EBee ECtt EPPr GAuc GEdr GGar MCCP NHar NLar SHar SRms SRot WCru WPat
- subsp. ***stellatus***	GAuc
× ***barkeri***	ECou
'Benenden' ♀H4	Widely available
'Betty Ashburner'	CAgr CBcs CDoC CDul EBee EPPr EWTr GQui LAst MGos MRav MWhi SLPl SPer WDin WMoo WTin
biflorus ♀H4	EPfP EWes LEdu MBlu MMuc SEND WPGP
'Black Butte'	CSut GPri SDea SVic
'Boatsberry'	SDea
boysenberry, thornless (F)	CMac EMil ERea GPri GTwe LBuc LSRN MGan NPri SDea SPer
buergeri B&SWJ 5555	WCru
calophyllus	CDul WPGP
calycinoides Hayata	see *R. rolfei*
calycinoides Kuntze	EBtc
chamaemorus	GAuc GPoy
cockburnianus (F)	CArn CBcs CTri CWib EBee ECrN ELan EPfP GCra GKir IFoB LBuc MRav MSwo NHol NLar NSti NWea SPer SPlb SRms WDin WEas WFar WSpi
- 'Goldenvale' ♀H4	Widely available
crataegifolius	LEdu MRav WPat
deliciosus	WFar
'Emerald Spreader'	GKir WMoo
fockeanus misapplied	see *R. rolfei*
formosensis B&SWJ 1798	WCru
N ***fruticosus*** agg.	WSFF
- 'Adrienne' (F)	CAgr CSBt MAsh WHar
- 'Ashton Cross' (F)	CDoC GTwe LBuc
- 'Bedford Giant' (F)	CSBt GTwe LRHS LSRN MAsh MGan MGos MMuc SEND SKee SLim SPoG WHar
- 'Black Satin' (F)	CAgr LRHS MCoo NLar NPri SDea SVic
- 'Chester' (F)	LRHS SBfd SKee
- 'Godshill Goliath' (F)	SDea
- 'Helen' (F)	CAgr CSut EMil MCoo SDea
- 'Himalayan Giant' (F)	GTwe MGan MRav NEgg NLar SDea
- 'John Innes' (F)	MCoo
- 'Kotata' (F)	MRav
- 'Loch Ness'PBR (F) ♀H4	CAgr CMac CWib GKir GTwe IArd LBuc LRHS LSRN MCoo SCoo SDea SKee WHar
- 'Loch Tay'PBR (F) **new**	SBfd
- 'Merton Thornless' (F)	CSBt CWib ERea GTwe LSRN MAsh MGan MGos WHar
- 'No Thorn' (F)	SDea
- 'Oregon Thornless' (F)	CAgr CCVT CDoC CSBt CWib ECrN EPfP GTwe LRHS LSRN MAsh MRav NEgg NLar SCoo SDea SKee SLim SPoG SRms
- 'Parsley Leaved' (F)	SDea
* - 'Sylvan' (F)	MCoo MGos MMuc
- 'Thornfree' (F)	CAgr CDoC CTri LRHS MMuc NLar SDea SKee SLim
- 'Variegatus' (v)	CBot CMac MBlu SMad WCot
- 'Waldo' (F)	CAgr CSBt CWib ECrN LBuc LSRN MAsh MBri MGos SDea
aff. ***gachetensis*** B&SWJ 10603	WCru
'Golden Showers'	CWib
henryi	CBot EBla ESwi LRHS MRav NSti SPoG WCot
- var. ***bambusarum***	EBee EPla MCCP MRav WCru
'Hildaberry' (F)	GPri
hupehensis	SLPl
ichangensis	CBcs CBot EPla LEdu
idaeus	GPoy
- 'All Gold' (F)	CAgr CSut EMil ERea GPri LRHS MAsh MNHC SBfd SPer SVic
- 'Aureus' (F)	ECha ELan EPla EWes MRav NBid WCot WFar WMoo
- 'Autumn Bliss'PBR (F) ♀H4	Widely available
- 'Black Jewel' (F) **new**	LRHS
- 'Fallgold' (F)	CWib EPfP MCoo MMuc SKee SPoG
- 'Glen Ample'PBR (F) ♀H4	Widely available
- 'Glen Clova' (F)	CAgr CSBt CTri CWib ECrN GKir GTwe LSRN MAsh MGan MGos MRav NLar SBfd SKee SLim SPer SPoG SVic WHar
- 'Glen Lyon'PBR (F)	CWib LBuc LRHS MAsh MBri SCoo
- 'Glen Magna'PBR (F)	CAgr CSBt CWSG CWib ERea MAsh MBri MNHC NLar SCoo SDea SKee SLim SPoG
- 'Glen Moy'PBR (F) ♀H4	CAgr CSBt CTri CWib ECrN EMil EPfP ERea EUJe GPri GTwe LRHS LSRN MAsh MGos NEgg NPri SCoo SDea SKee SLim WClo
- 'Glen Prosen'PBR (F) ♀H4	CAgr CSBt CWib ECrN GKir GTwe LRHS LSRN MAsh MBri MGos MRav NEgg SCoo SDea SKee SLim SPer WClo WHar
- 'Glen Rosa' (F)	ERea
- 'Heritage' (F)	CWib MAsh MGos SCoo
- Himbo Top = 'Rafzaqu'PBR (F)	GPri
- 'Joan J'PBR (F)	CMac CSut EMil ERea GPri
- 'Joan Squire' (F)	SKee
- 'Julia' (F)	GTwe MCoo
- 'Leo'PBR (F) ♀H4	CSBt CTri CWib GTwe MAsh MGos SCoo SKee SPer WHar
- 'Mac Black' (F) **new**	LRHS
- 'Malling Admiral' (F) ♀H4	CSBt CTri CWib GKir GTwe LSRN MAsh SCoo SKee SPer
- 'Malling Delight' (F)	CSBt CWib MAsh SCoo SPlb
- 'Malling Jewel' (F) ♀H4	CSBt CWib GKir GTwe LBuc LSRN MAsh MGan SDea SKee SPer WHar
- 'Malling Promise' (F)	CWib
- 'Octavia'PBR (F)	CAgr CSBt EMil LBuc LRHS MAsh MCoo NLar SLim SPoG
- 'Polka'PBR (F)	CSut GPri LRHS LSRN MAsh MCoo SKee SLim SVic WClo
- 'Summer Gold' (F)	GTwe
- 'Tulameen' (F)	CAgr CSBt CWib EMil GPri LRHS LSRN MAsh MBri NLar SBfd SCoo SKee SLim SPer SPoG SVic WClo
- 'Valentina' (F)	EMil SVic
- 'Zeva Herbsternte' (F)	CWib MAsh
irenaeus	EBla LRHS SSpi
Japanese wineberry	see *R. phoenicolasius*
'Jermyn's Jubilee'	SLPl
'Karaka Black'PBR	GPri LBuc SVic
'Kenneth Ashburner'	CDoC NLar WTin
laciniatus	EPla
leucodermis NNS 00-663	EPPr

lineatus	CBot CDTJ CDoC CSpe CWib EPfP EWes LRHS MCot NSti SKHP SMad WCru WDin WPGP
- HWJK 2045	GQui
- from Nepal	GCra
- - HWJK 2045	WCru
- B&SWJ 11261 from Sumatra	WCru
- HWJ 892 from Vietnam	ESwi WCru
× ***loganobaccus*** 'Brandywine'	SDea
- 'Ly 59' (F) ♀H4	ECrN EPfP GTwe MMuc MRav SDea SKee SPer SRms
- 'Ly 654' (F) ♀H4	CSBt GTwe LBuc MBri MGos NEgg NPri SDea SPer WHar
- thornless (F)	CAgr CTri CWSG CWib GPri GTwe MAsh MGan SBfd SDea SPoG SVic
ludwigii	WBox
'Malling Minerva' (F)	CMac CSut
'Margaret Gordon'	MRav
microphyllus 'Variegatus' (v)	MRav WPat
§ ***nepalensis***	CAgr CDoC EBee GCra LEdu
- from Nepal	GCra
nutans	see *R. nepalensis*
occidentalis 'Haut'	GPri
- 'Jewel'	GPri
odoratus	CPLG EBee ELan EPPr EPfP EWTr LEdu MBlu MRav NBid NPal SPer WBor WCot WFar WTin
'Ouachita' (F) **new**	SPer
parviflorus	CArn
- double-flowered (d)	EPPr WCru
- 'Sunshine Spreader'	EHoe WPat
parvus	GGar LEdu
pectinellus var. ***trilobus***	CFee EWld LEdu NLar WCot
- - B&SWJ 1669B	WCru
peltatus	CGHE NLar WPGP
pentalobus	see *R. rolfei*
§ ***phoenicolasius***	CAgr CCCN CHGN CMac EPfP EPla EWTr GTwe LEdu LHop LRHS MBlu MCoo MGan MRav NLar SDea SPer SPoG SVic WAbb WPGP
§ ***rolfei***	CTri EPPr
- B&SWJ 3546 from Taiwan	WCru
- B&SWJ 3878 from the Philippines	WCru
- 'Emerald Carpet'	CAgr EBee EWTr NLar
rosifolius	CSpe
- 'Coronarius' (d)	CFee CSpe ECrN ELan LSou MRav NLar WCot WFar
sachalinensis	GAuc
sanctus	CNat
setchuenensis	CFee CMCN EWes NLar
'Silvan' (F) ♀H4	GPri GTwe SEND
spectabilis	CBcs CSev CWib ELan EPPr EPla EWTr LEdu MMuc MRav WFar WSHC
- 'Flore Pleno'	see *R. spectabilis* 'Olympic Double'
§ - 'Olympic Double' (d)	Widely available
splendidissimus B&SWJ 2361	WCru
squarrosus	ECou
* ***stelleri***	GAuc
'Sunberry' (F)	CCCN GTwe SDea
swinhoei B&SWJ 1735	WCru
taiwanicola	EDAr GEdr LLHF
- B&SWJ 317	ESwi GBin WCru
Tayberry Group (F) ♀H4	CSBt CTri ECrN GTwe LSRN MAsh MGan MGos NLar NPri SPer SRms SVic WHar
- 'Buckingham' (F)	CSut EMil GTwe LBuc LRHS MAsh SVic
- 'Medana Tayberry' (F)	CAgr EPfP ERea GPri LRHS SDea SKee SPoG
§ ***thibetanus*** ♀H4	Widely available
- 'Silver Fern'	see *R. thibetanus*
treutleri B&SWJ 2139	WCru
tricolor	CAgr CBcs CDul CSBt CTri CWib EBee ECrN EPfP GKir MBlu MCoo MMuc MRav MSwo NEgg NHol NLar SDix SPer WDin WMoo
trilobus B&SWJ 9096	WCru
'Tummelberry' (F)	EMil GTwe LRHS MCoo SBfd SVic
ulmifolius	GCal MBlu MRav MSwo SDix WAbb
'Bellidiflorus' (d)	WEas WHrl
ursinus	SBfd
'Veitchberry' (F)	CDoy
xanthocarpus	NLar
'Youngberry' (F)	SDea
'Youngberry' thornless (F)	GPri

Rudbeckia ✿ (*Asteraceae*)

Autumn Sun	see *R. laciniata* 'Herbstsonne'
'Cherry Brandy' **new**	EWTr
deamii	see *R. fulgida* var. *deamii*
fulgida	GKir
- 'City Garden'	NDov
§ - var. ***deamii*** ♀H4	Widely available
- var. ***fulgida***	CMea EBee EPfP MAvo SBfd SMad
§ - var. ***speciosa*** ♀H4	CKno CMMP CSam EBee ECha ECtt ELan EPfP GAbr MMuc NBPC SBch SPlb SRms SWal WEas WFar WMoo WPer WPtf WTin WWEG
- var. ***sullivantii*** 'Goldsturm' ♀H4	Widely available
- Viette's Little Suzy = 'Blovi'	EBee EBrs GKir LRHS
gloriosa	see *R. hirta*
'Golden Jubilee'	LRHS
grandiflora	CSam SBfd
'Sundance' **new**	
- 'Sunshine' **new**	NDov
§ ***hirta***	CHar LRHS NBir
- 'Autumn Colours' (mixed)	CMea LRHS
- 'Cherokee Sunset' (d)	CSpe
- 'Chim Chiminee'	LRHS NGBl
- 'Goldilocks'	CBar LRHS
- 'Indian Summer' ♀H3	SPav
- 'Irish Eyes'	SPav
- 'Marmalade'	EPfP LBMP LRHS NGBl
- 'Prairie Sun'	ELon EPfP LRHS NGBl SAga
- 'Rustic Dwarfs'	LRHS
- 'Sonora'	LRHS NGBl WHal
- 'Toto' ♀H3	SPav SWvt
- 'Toto Rustic'	LRHS
July Gold	see *R. laciniata* 'Juligold'
laciniata	CElw CHVG CKno CMac CSam EBee EBrs ELan EPPr GCal GKir GQue LEdu LRHS MDKP MMuc NCGa NDov NGBl NLar SBfd SMHy SPhx WCot WMoo WOld WWEG
- var. ***digitata***	IMou
- 'Golden Glow'	see *R. laciniata* 'Hortensia'
- 'Goldquelle' (d) ♀H4	CMac CWCL EBee EBrs ECha ECtt ELan EPfP EShb LHop LRHS MSpe NBPC NGdn NPri SMrm SPer SPet SPoG SRms SRot STes SWvt WBor WCot WFar WMnd WWEG
§ - 'Herbstsonne' ♀H4	Widely available
§ - 'Hortensia' (d)	EBee GQue MAvo MRav WHoo WOld WWEG
§ - 'Juligold'	CPrp EBee LBMP LRHS MBNS NBre NEgg NGdn SMrm SPoG WFar WWEG

- 'Starcadia Razzle Dazzle' WCot WWEG
maxima CKno COlW CSpe EBee ECha GMac IFoB LEdu LHop LRHS MAvo MBri MCCP MSpe NCGa NLar NSti SBfd SDix SKHP SMad SMrm SPhx SPlb WBor WCot WFar WWEG
missouriensis EBee NBre NLar SBfd SUsu
mollis EBee LRHS NBre
newmannii see *R. fulgida* var. *speciosa*
nitida EBee EShb WSpi
occidentalis GKev LBMP LRHS NBre NLar
- 'Black Beauty'^{PBR} EBee EHrv EPfP GKir NMoo WMnd WSpi
- 'Green Wizard' CMac CWib EBee ECtt EHrv ELan EPfP GKir LRHS MCot MLHP NBid NChi NLar NPri NSti SGSe SGar SMad SPav SPer SPet SPoG SRms WClo WFoF WPGP WSpi WTin WWEG
* **paniculata** EBee LLHF NBre WCot
purpurea see *Echinacea purpurea*
speciosa see *R. fulgida* var. *speciosa*
subtomentosa CDes CSam EBee EBrs EWes GCal LPla LRHS MDKP MNFA NBre NDov NSti SMHy STes WOld
- 'Henry Eilers' ECtt ELan EPfP IKil LSou MWea SBfd SPoG
'Takao' CWCL EBee LSou MAvo MDKP MWea NLar SPoG
triloba 🏆^{H4} CDes CEnt CMea CSam EBee EBrs ECha ELon EPPr EPfP EShb LRHS MAvo MNrw MSpe NDov NGdn SGSe SMad SMrs SPet SPhx SUsu WCot WFar WMoo WPGP WTin

rue see *Ruta graveolens*

Ruellia (*Acanthaceae*)

amoena see *R. brevifolia*
§ **brevifolia** ECre EShb WHil
ciliata f. **depressa** CPBP
humilis EBee EPPr EShb NLar WHil
macrantha CCCN EShb
makoyana 🏆^{H1} CSev EShb MBri WHil
strepens EBee
tweediana EShb

Rumex (*Polygonaceae*)

acetosa CArn CFox CHby CSev CWan EBWF ELau GBar GPoy MCoo MHer MMuc MNHC NBir NGHP NSco SBfd SEND SIde WHer WJek WSFF
- 'Abundance' ELau
- subsp. **acetosa** 'Saucy' (v) WAlt WCot
- 'De Belleville' CPrp NPri
- 'Profusion' GPoy MHer
- subsp. **vinealis** EBee
acetosella CArn EBWF NMir WSFF
alpinus EBee LEdu SPhx WCot
crispus new ELau
flexuosus CSpe CSpr EBee GCal MDKP NLar WJek
hydrolapathum CArn EBWF LPBA MMuc MSKA SEND SPlb WSFF
patientia CArn ELau
sanguineus CTri EShb LPBA MSKA NCob NLar SPoG WFar WMAq
- var. **sanguineus** CArn CBgR CElw CRow CSev EBee ELan IFoB MHer MNHC MNrw MTho NBro NHol SGSe WHer
'Schavel' LEdu
scutatus CArn CHby CPrp CSev ELau GPoy MNHC SBfd SIde SPlb WHer WHfH WJek
- 'Silver Shield' CBod CRow ELau LEdu MHer SIde WJek

Rumohra (*Davalliaceae*)

sp. SEND
adiantiformis 🏆^{H1} CCCN EBee EFtx ISha LRHS SEND WFib WPGP WRic
- RCB/Arg D-2 WCot

Ruscus ✿ (*Ruscaceae*)

aculeatus Widely available
- (f) WFar WGrn
- (m) WCFE
- hermaphrodite EPfP EPla EWes GCal MBri SEND SMad WPGP WPat WThu
- var. **aculeatus** 'Lanceolatus' (f) GCal
- var. **angustifolius** EPla LEdu
- - (f) EPla
- 'Christmas Berry' ELan EPfP NLar
- 'John Redmond'^{PBR} Widely available
* - 'Wheeler's Variety' (f/m) CPMA MRav
hypoglossum MMuc SEND WPGP WSpi
× **microglossum** (f) CDul
racemosus see *Danae racemosa*

Ruspolia (*Acanthaceae*)

hypocrateriformis CCCN
seticalyx EShb

Russelia (*Scrophulariaceae*)

§ **equisetiformis** 🏆^{H1} CHII EShb SOWG
- 'Lemon Falls' EShb SOWG
juncea see *R. equisetiformis*

Ruta (*Rutaceae*)

chalepensis CArn
corsica CArn
graveolens CArn CWan EPfP GBar GPoy SBfd SIde WJek
- 'Jackman's Blue' CBcs CDul CPrp CSev CTri EBee EHoe ELan EOHP EPfP GKir GMaP GPoy LAst MGos MHer MNHC MRav MSwo NLar SBfd SLim SRms WMnd WSpi
- 'Variegata' (v) CBot CBow CWan ELan EOHP GBar LRHS MNHC NPer

Ruttya (*Acanthaceae*)

fruticosa CCCN

× *Ruttyruspolia* (*Acanthaceae*)

lutea CCCN
'Phyllis van Heerden' GFai SOWG

Rytidosperma (*Poaceae*)

* **arundinaceum** EShb

S

Sabal (*Arecaceae*)

§ **bermudana** EAmu
causiarum EAmu
etonia LPal
§ **mexicana** EAmu

minor	CBrP CHEx CPHo EAmu ETod EUJe LPal MREP NPal SBig SPlb
palmetto	CDoC EAmu LPal
princeps	see *S. bermudana*
rosei	LPal
texana	see *S. mexicana*
uresana	LPal

Saccharum (*Poaceae*)

arundinaceum	CKno EPPr
§ ***baldwinii***	EBee EPPr GCal GFor
brevibarbe var. ***contortum***	EPPr GCal
ravennae	EBee EPPr GFor MLLN MWhi SApp SEND SMad SMrm SPlb WCot
strictum (Baldwin) Nutt.	see *S. baldwinii*

Sadleria (*Blechnaceae*)

cyatheoides	WRic

sage see *Salvia officinalis*

sage, annual clary see *Salvia viridis*

sage, biennial clary see *Salvia sclarea*

sage, pineapple see *Salvia elegans*

Sageretia (*Rhamnaceae*)

§ ***thea***	CMen STre
theezans	see *S. thea*

Sagina (*Caryophyllaceae*)

boydii	EPot
subulata	ECho EHoe SVic
§ - var. ***glabrata*** 'Aurea'	CMea CTri ECha ECho ECtt EDAr GKir GMaP SPoG SRms WClo WEas WFar WPer

Sagittaria (*Alismataceae*)

'Bloomin Babe'	CRow
graminea **new**	LLWG
- 'Crushed Ice' (v)	CRow MWts
japonica	see *S. sagittifolia*
latifolia	COld LLWG LPBA MWts NPer SMad
* ***leucopetala*** 'Flore Pleno' (d)	NLar NPer
§ ***sagittifolia***	CBen CRow CWat EHon LLWG LPBA MSKA NSco WMAq WPnP
- 'Flore Pleno' (d)	CBen CWat LPBA WMAq
- var. ***leucopetala***	WMAq

Saintpaulia (*Gesneriaceae*)

'Aca's Pink Delight' **new**	WDib
'Aca's Red Ember' (v) **new**	WDib
'Alamo Folly' **new**	WDib
'Allegro Appalachian Trail' **new**	WDib
'Alliance' (v) **new**	WDib
'Arctic Frost' (d)	WDib
'Baby's Breath' **new**	WDib
'Bahamian Sunset' (d) **new**	WDib
'Bangle Blue'	WDib
'Beacon Trail' **new**	WDib
'Beate' **new**	WDib
'Beatrice Trail'	WDib
'Betty Stoehr'	WDib
'Blackie Bryant' **new**	WDib
'Blue Dragon' (d)	WDib
'Bob Serbin' (d)	WDib
'Buffalo Hunt' (d)	WDib
'Cactus Rose' (d) **new**	WDib
'Candy Swirls' **new**	WDib
'Cathedral' **new**	WDib
'Cherries 'n' Cream'	WDib
'Chiffon Fiesta'	WDib
'Chiffon Mist' (d)	WDib
'Chiffon Moonmoth'	WDib
'Chiffon Vesper'	WDib
'Coral Sparkle Trail' **new**	WDib
'Crimson Ice' **new**	WDib
'Deer Trail' **new**	WDib
'Delft' (d)	WDib
'Desire' **new**	WDib
'Dubois Othello' (v) **new**	WDib
'Electric Dreams'	WDib
'Emerald Love' **new**	WDib
'Falling Raindrops' **new**	WDib
'Fantinci' **new**	WDib
'Favorite Child' **new**	WDib
'Flashy Angel' (v) **new**	WDib
'Fun Trail' **new**	WDib
'Genetic Blush' **new**	WDib
'Gillian' (d)	WDib
'Golden Eye' **new**	WDib
'Golden Glow' (d)	WDib
'Grandmother's Halo' **new**	WDib
'Green Ice' **new**	WDib
'Halo's Aglitter'	WDib
'Happy Cricket' **new**	WDib
'Iceberg' **new**	WDib
'Irish Flirt' (d)	WDib
'King's Trail' (d)	WDib
'King's Treasure' **new**	WDib
'Lemon Drop' (d)	WDib
'Lemon Whip' (d)	WDib
'Lis' **new**	WDib
'Little Axel' **new**	WDib
'Little Seneca Girl' (Little Indian Series) **new**	WDib
'Lollipop' **new**	WDib
'Looking Glass' **new**	WDib
'Louisiana Lagniappe' **new**	WDib
'Love Spots'	WDib
'Lucky Lee Ann' (d)	WDib
'Luminescence' **new**	WDib
'Lyon's Plum Pudding' **new**	WDib
'Mac's Carnival Clown' **new**	WDib
'Mac's Circus Clown' **new**	WDib
'Mac's Coral Cutie' **new**	WDib
'Mac's Exquisite Extravaganza' **new**	WDib
'Mac's Just Jeff' (d/v) **new**	WDib
'Mac's Nocturne' (d) **new**	WDib
'Mair' **new**	WDib
'Ma's Corsage' **new**	WDib
'Ma's Lily Pad' **new**	WDib
'Ma's Mars' **new**	WDib
'Ma's Winter Moon' **new**	WDib
'Mermaid' (d)	WDib
'Midget Lilian' (v)	WDib
'Midnight Flame' (d)	WDib
'Midnight Magic'	WDib
'Midnight Rascal' (d) **new**	WDib
'Midnight Waltz' (d)	WDib
'Milky Way Trail' **new**	WDib
'Minstrel's Mary Ruth' **new**	WDib
'Mosaique' **new**	WDib
'Motley Crew' **new**	WDib
'Ness' Antique Red' **new**	WDib
'Ness' Blueberry Puff' **new**	WDib
'Ness' Crinkle Blue' (d)	WDib
'Ness' Midnight Fantasy' **new**	WDib

'Ness' Sno Fun' **new**	WDib
'Ness' Viking Maiden' **new**	WDib
'Newtown Ohio' **new**	WDib
'Ode to Beauty' **new**	WDib
'Okie Easter Bunny' **new**	WDib
'Otoe' (d)	WDib
'Ozio' **new**	WDib
'Paprika' **new**	WDib
'Persian Swirl' **new**	WDib
'Pink Duchess' (d) **new**	WDib
'Pinkie Winkie' **new**	WDib
'Pixie Blue' **new**	WDib
'Pixie Pink' **new**	WDib
'Pixie Show-off' **new**	WDib
'Powder Keg' (d)	WDib
'Powwow' (d/v)	WDib
'Rain Man' **new**	WDib
'Rainbow's Quiet Riot' **new**	WDib
'Ramblin' Amethyst' **new**	WDib
'Ramblin' Angel' (d) **new**	WDib
'Ramblin' Dots' **new**	WDib
'Ramblin' Lassie' **new**	WDib
'Ramblin' Magic' (d)	WDib
'Ramblin' Sunshine' **new**	WDib
'Rapid Transit' (d)	WDib
'Rare Tapestry' **new**	WDib
'Raspberry Crisp' **new**	WDib
'Raspberry Rampage' **new**	WDib
'Red Lantern' (d) **new**	WDib
'Red Summit' **new**	WDib
'Rhapsodie Clementine'	WDib
'Robert Mayer' **new**	WDib
'Rob's Bamboozle' (d)	WDib
'Rob's Blue Socks' **new**	WDib
'Rob's Calypso Beat' (d)	WDib
'Rob's Cloudy Skies' (d)	WDib
'Rob's Dandy Lion' (d/v)	WDib
'Rob's Denim Demon' (d/v)	WDib
'Rob's Dust Storm' (d)	WDib
'Rob's Gundaroo' (d)	WDib
'Rob's Hallucination' **new**	WDib
'Rob's Hopscotch' (d)	WDib
'Rob's Ice Ripples' (d)	MMuc WDib
'Rob's Jitterbug' **new**	WDib
'Rob's June Bug' (d/v)	WDib
'Rob's Loose Goose' (d)	WDib
'Rob's Love Bite' (d)	WDib
'Rob's Macho Devil' (d/v)	WDib
'Rob's Mad Cat' (d)	WDib
'Rob's Peedletuck' **new**	WDib
'Rob's Red Bug' (d/r)	WDib
'Rob's Rinky Dink' (d)	WDib
'Rob's Ruff Stuff' **new**	WDib
'Rob's Sarsparilla' (d)	WDib
'Rob's Scrumptious' **new**	WDib
'Rob's Seduction' (d/v)	WDib
'Rob's Shadow Magic' (d/v)	WDib
'Rob's Smarty Pants' (d)	WDib
'Rob's Sticky Wicket' (d)	WDib
'Rob's Toorooka' (d)	WDib
'Rob's Twinkle Blue' (d) **new**	WDib
'Rob's Vanilla Trail' (d) **new**	WDib
'Rob's Wooloomooloo' (d) **new**	WDib
'Roll Along Blue' (d) **new**	WDib
'Ruffled Red' **new**	WDib
'Santa Anita' **new**	WDib
shumensis	WDib
'Sky Bells' (v)	WDib
'Sweet Amy Sue' (d)	WDib
'Taffeta Blue' (d)	WDib
'Taffeta Petticoats' **new**	WDib
'Teen Thunder' **new**	WDib
'The Madam'	WDib
'Twist 'n' Shout' **new**	WDib
'Warm Sunshine' **new**	WDib
'Whirligig Star' **new**	WDib
'White Lace' **new**	WDib
'Wisteria' (d) **new**	WDib
'Yesterday's Child' **new**	WDib

Salicornia (*Chenopodiaceae*)

europaea	SVic

Salix ✿ (*Salicaceae*)

acutifolia	ELan IFFs WDin
- 'Blue Streak' (m) ♀H4	CEnd CWiW CWit CWon EBee EPfP EPla EWes MBlu NBir NLar SMHy SWat WFar WMou
- 'Pendulifolia' (m)	WPat
'Aegma Brno' (f) **new**	WMou
aegyptiaca	CDoC CWon EBtc MBlu NWea WMou
alba	CCVT CDul CLnd CWiW ECrN EMac GGal IFFs LBuc LMaj NWea WDin WJPR WMou
- f. ***argentea***	see *S. alba* var. *sericea*
- 'Aurea'	CLnd CTho CWon WIvy WMou
- 'Belders' (m)	IFFs
- var. ***caerulea***	CDul CLnd CWon NWea WMou
- - 'Wantage Hall' (f)	CWiW CWon
- 'Cardinalis' (f)	CWiW CWon IFFs SWat
- 'Chermesina' hort.	see *S. alba* var. *vitellina* 'Britzensis'
- 'Dart's Snake'	ELan EPfP EPla MAsh MBrN MRav NLar SCoo WCot
- 'Golden Ness'	LRHS MAsh MBlu
- 'Hutchinson's Yellow'	CDoC CTho CWon EBee MGos NLar SCoo SLim WDin
- 'Liempde' (m)	NWea
- 'Raesfeld' (m)	CWiW CWon
§ - var. ***sericea*** ♀H4	CBcs CDul CLnd CTho CWon EPfP MBlu MRav NLar NWea SPer WDin WIvy WMou
- 'Splendens'	see *S. alba* var. *sericea*
- 'Tristis' misapplied	see *S.* × *sepulcralis* var. *chrysocoma*
§ - 'Tristis' ambig.	CCVT CLnd CTri ELan GKir LAst MBri MGos MRav MSwo NLar NWea SLim SRms SWat WDin WFar WHar
- 'Tristis' Gaud.	MMuc
- var. ***vitellina*** ♀H4	CDul CTri CWon EMac EPfP GQue IFFs LBuc MBNS MBrN NLar NWea SLon SWat WDin WIvy WJPR WMoo
§ - - 'Britzensis' (m) ♀H4	Widely available
- - 'Nova'	SWat
§ - - 'Yelverton'	CWon LRHS MAsh SWat
- 'Vitellina Pendula'	see *S. alba* 'Tristis' ambig.
- 'Vitellina Tristis'	see *S. alba* 'Tristis' ambig.
§ ***alpina***	ECho NBir NHar
'Americana'	CWiW
amplexicaulis **new**	CWon
- 'Pescara' (m)	CWiW
amygdaloides	CWiW CWon
'Aokautere'	see *S.* × *sepulcralis* 'Aokautere'
apennina 'Cisa Pass'	CWon
apoda	CWon
- (m)	ECho WPer
§ ***arbuscula***	CWon ECho GAuc NLar NWCA WDin
arctica var. ***petraea***	WPat
arenaria	see *S. repens* var. *argentea*
aurita	GAuc IFFs NLar NWea
babylonica	CDul CEnd CWon WMou

	- 'Annularis'	see *S. babylonica* 'Crispa'
	- 'Bijdorp'	MBri NLar
§	- 'Crispa'	CDul CWon ELan LHop LRHS MBri MWts SMad SPoG WCom WFar
	- 'Pan Chih-kang'	CWiW NLar
	- var. ***pekinensis***	CWon
	- - 'Pendula'	NLar
	- - 'Snake'	CWon
§	- - 'Tortuosa' ♀^{H4}	Widely available
*	- 'Tortuosa Aurea'	MCCP SWvt
	× ***balfourii***	CWon
	bebbiana	CWon
	bicolor new	CWon
	'Blackskin' (f)	CWiW
	bockii	EBee EBtc ELan LLHF LRHS MMuc WFar
§	'Bowles's Hybrid'	WMou
	'Boydii' (f) ♀^{H4}	CWon EBee ECho EPfP EPot GAbr GEdr GKir ITim LEdu MGos NBir NMen NRya NSla SRms WAbe WFar WPat
§	'Boyd's Pendulous' (m)	CWib
	burjatica	CWon
	- 'Germany'	CWon
	- 'Korso'	CWon
	caesia	EMac NWCA WIvy
	× ***calodendron*** (f)	CWon
	candida	CWon GAuc
	cantabrica	CWon
	caprea	CBcs CCVT CDul CLnd CTri CWon ECrN EMac EPfP IFFs LBuc LMaj NWea SPer STre WDin WMou WSFF
	- 'Black Stem'	CDul
	- 'Curlilocks'	IVic
§	- 'Kilmarnock' (m)	Widely available
	- var. ***pendula*** (m)	see *S. caprea* 'Kilmarnock' (m)
	caprea × ***lanata***	CWon
	× ***capreola***	CWon
	cashmiriana	CWon GAuc GEdr WAbe WPat
	caspica	CWon
*	- ***rubra nana***	SWat
	× ***cernua***	NWCA
	'Chrysocoma'	see *S.* × *sepulcralis* var. *chrysocoma*
	cinerea	CBcs CDoC CWon EMac GKir IFFs LBuc NWea STre WDin WJPR WMou
	- 'Bude'	CWon
	- subsp. ***oleifolia*** × ***phylicifolia***	CWon
	- 'Tricolor' (v)	CArn
	cordata	CWon SLPl WDin
	- 'Purpurescens'	CWon
	× ***cottetii***	GAuc WDin
	daphnoides	CCVT CDoC CDul CLnd CMac CWon EBee EMac EPfP GKir IFFs LRHS MAsh MBrN MGos MMuc MSwo NWea SEND SPer SRms SWat WDin WFar WJPR WJas WMou WSFF
	- 'Aglaia' (m)	CBcs CWon GQue MGos WIvy
	- 'Continental Purple'	CWon
	- 'Lady Aldenham'	CWon
	- 'Meikle' (f)	CWiW SWat
	- 'Netta Statham' (m)	CWiW CWon
	- 'Ovaro Udine' (m)	CWiW
	- 'Oxford Violet' (m)	CWon WIvy
	- 'Pendulifolia'	CWon
	- 'Purple Heart'	CWon
	- 'Sinker'	WIvy
	- 'Stewartstown'	CWiW
	- 'Wynter Bloom'	CWon

	× ***dasyclados***	CWon
	- 'Grandis'	NWea
	discolor	CWon
§	× ***doniana*** 'Kumeti'	CWiW CWon
	'E.A. Bowles'	see *S.* 'Bowles's Hybrid'
	× ***ehrhartiana***	CNat CWon
§	***elaeagnos***	CCVT CDoC CLnd CTho CTri ECrN EPfP GKir MBrN MMuc SLon SPer SWat WClo WDin WFar WMou
§	- subsp. ***angustifolia*** ♀^{H4}	CBcs CDul CWon ELan EPfP GKir IFFs MMuc MRav MSwo NLar NPCo NWea SEND SRms STre WIvy
	- 'Angustifolia'	see *S. elaeagnos* subsp. *angustifolia*
	'Elegantissima'	see *S.* × *pendulina* var. *elegantissima*
	× ***erdingeri***	EPla
	eriocephala 'American Mackay' (m)	CWiW
	- 'Green USA'	CWon
	- 'Kerksii' (m)	CWiW CWon
	- 'Mawdesley' (m)	CWiW
	- 'Russelliana' (f)	CWiW CWon
§	'Erythroflexuosa'	CBcs CDoC CEnd CWon EBee ELan EPPr EPfP IFFs LAst LBMP LHop LRHS MAsh MGos MMuc MRav NWea SBfd SLim SMad SPer SPoG SWat WDin WFar WHer WPat
	exigua	Widely available
	fargesii	CAbP CBot CDoC CDul CEnd CFee CMac CWon ELan EPfP GKir LEdu LHop LRHS MAsh MBlu MGos MRav NBid NEgg NPCo SDix SMad SSpi WCru WFar WPGP WPat
	fargesii × ***magnifica***	WPGP
§	× ***finnmarchica***	GAuc GEdr NWCA WAbe
	× ***forbyana***	CWon
	formosa	see *S. arbuscula*
	fragilis	CCVT CDul CLnd EMac IFFs LMaj MRav NWea WDin WJPR WMou
§	- var. ***furcata***	CTri CWon GBin GKev IVic NWCA WPat
	- 'Legomey'	WIvy
	× ***fruticosa*** 'McElroy' (f)	CWiW
	fruticulosa	see *S. fragilis* var. *furcata*
	'Fuiri-koriyanagi'	see *S. integra* 'Hakuro-nishiki'
	furcata	see *S. fragilis* var. *furcata*
	glabra	CWon
	glauca	CNat
	glaucophylloides	CWon
	glaucosericea	EPla
	'Golden Curls'	see *S.* 'Erythroflexuosa'
	gracilistyla	CTho CWon ECrN NWea SCoo SLPl WMou
§	- 'Melanostachys' (m)	Widely available
	× ***grahamii*** 'Moorei' (f)	NWCA
	× ***greyi***	NWCA
	hastata (f)	SWat
	- 'Wehrhahnii' (m) ♀^{H4}	CBcs CWib CWon EBee ECho ELan EPfP GCra GKir IVic LEdu MBlu MMuc MRav MSwo NBir NPCo NWea SPer SWat WCFE WDin WFar
	helvetica ♀^{H4}	CBcs CMac EBee ECho EGxp ELan EPfP GAbr IVic MBlu MMuc MRav NBir NEgg NLar NWea SPer WAbe WDin WFar WPat
	herbacea	ECho GAuc GEdr NMen WAbe
	hibernica	see *S. phylicifolia*
I	***himalayas***	CWon
	× ***hirtei*** 'Delamere'	CWon
	- 'Rosewarne'	CWon

	hookeriana	CDul CLnd CTho CWon EBee ELan MBlu MBrN MBri NLar SLPl SSpi WCFE WIvy WMou WPGP WTin
	humilis var. ***microphylla***	CWon
	× ***hungarica***	CWon
	incana	see *S. elaeagnos*
	integra	CWon
	- 'Albomaculata'	see *S. integra* 'Hakuro-nishiki'
	- 'Flamingo' PBR	SPoG
§	- 'Hakuro-nishiki' (v)	Widely available
	- 'Pendula' (f)	CEnd MAsh MBri
	irrorata	CDul CLnd CWon EBee EPfP GKir IFFs MBlu MRav MSwo SWat WCom
	'Jacquinii'	see *S. alpina*
	kinuyanagi (m)	CWon ELan WIvy
§	***koriyanagi***	CWiW CWon
	'Kumeti'	see *S.* × *doniana* 'Kumeti'
	'Kuro-me'	see *S. gracilistyla* 'Melanostachys'
	× ***laestadiana***	GAuc
	laggeri	CWon
	lanata ♀H4	CBcs CBot CMac CMea CWon EBee ECho ELan EPfP EWTr GAbr GAuc GGar GKir MGos MRav NBir NEgg NHol NLar NMen NWea SPer SWat WAbe WCFE WDin WFar
	- 'Drake's Hybrid'	NMen
	- 'Mrs Mac' (m)	CWon
	lapponum	GAuc GEdr GKir NLar NWCA NWea SRms WAbe
	- (m)	EBee
	lasiandra	CWon
	× ***laurina*** (f)	CWon
	lineariStipularis	CWon
	lucida	CWon
	mackenzieana	CWon
	magnifica ♀H4	CDul CEnd CGHE CLnd CMCN CTho CWon EBee ELan EPfP EPla GKir IDee IFFs LEdu LRHS MSnd NWea SSpi SWat WDin WFar WMou WPGP WSpi
	'Mark Postill' (f)	CDoC CWon EBee EMil GBin GKir LRHS MBNS MMuc
	matsudana 'Tortuosa'	see *S. babylonica* var. *pekinensis* 'Tortuosa'
	- 'Tortuosa Aureopendula'	see *S.* 'Erythroflexuosa'
	'Melanostachys'	see *S. gracilistyla* 'Melanostachys'
	× ***meyeriana***	CWon WIvy
	- 'Lumley' (f)	CWiW
	mielichhoferi	CWon
	× ***mollissima*** var. ***hippophaifolia*** 'Jefferies' (m)	CWiW
	- - 'Notts Spaniard' (m)	CWiW
	- - 'Stinchcombe'	WIvy
	- - 'Trustworthy' (m)	CWiW
	- 'Pheasant Brown' **new**	CWon
	- var. ***undulata*** 'Kottenheider Weide' (f)	CWiW
	moupinensis	CWon EPfP MBri WAbe
	- EDHCH 97.319	WPGP
	aff. ***moupinensis*** from Vietnam	WPGP
§	***myrsinifolia***	EBee MBlu MMuc WJPR
	- subsp. ***alpicola***	CWon
	- 'Cotinifolia' **new**	CWon
	- 'Faucille' **new**	CWon
	myrsinites var. ***jacquiniana***	see *S. alpina*
	myrtilloides 'Pink Tassels' (m)	ECho GEdr MAsh NHar NWCA
	myrtilloides × ***repens***	see *S.* × *finnmarchica*
	nakamurana var. ***yezoalpina***	CEnd CFee CWon EBee ELan EPot EWes GEdr GQui IVic LRHS MBlu MMuc MRav NHar NHol NLar NWCA WAbe WFar WPat
	nigra	CWon
	nigricans	see *S. myrsinifolia*
	nivalis	see *S. reticulata* subsp. *nivalis*
	'Onusta' (m)	EBee
	× ***ovata***	NMen
§	× ***pendulina*** var. ***elegantissima***	CTho CWon SWat
	pentandra	CBot CDul CLnd ECrN GKir IFFs NWea WDin WFar WJPR WMou
	- 'Dark French' **new**	CWon
	- 'Patent Lumley'	CWiW CWon
	petiolaris	CWon
	'Philip's Fancy'	NWCA
§	***phylicifolia***	GKir NWea WJPR WMou
	- 'Malham' (m)	CWiW CWon
§	***purpurea***	CCVT CDul EMac GKir IFFs NWea SRms WDin WGwG WJPR WMou
	- 'Brittany Green' (f)	CWiW CWon
	- 'Continental Reeks'	CWiW WIvy
	- 'Dark Dicks' (f)	CWiW CWon NLar WIvy WSFF
	- 'Dicky Meadows' (m)	CWiW CWon WIvy
	- 'Goldstones'	CWiW NLar WIvy
	- f. ***gracilis***	see *S. purpurea* 'Nana'
	- 'Green Dicks'	CWiW CWon WIvy
	- 'Helix'	see *S. purpurea*
	- 'Howki' (m)	CWon WMou
	- 'Irette' (m)	CWiW CWon
	- 'Jagiellonka' (f)	CWiW WIvy
	- var. ***japonica***	see *S. koriyanagi*
	- subsp. ***lambertiana***	CWiW WIvy
	- 'Lancashire Dicks' (m)	CWiW
	- 'Leicestershire Dicks' (m)	CWiW
	- 'Light Dicks'	CWiW CWon
	- 'Lincolnshire Dutch' (f)	CWiW
§	- 'Nana'	EMac EPfP IFFs MMuc NLar NWea SLPl SLon SPer SPur STre WFar WMoo
	- 'Nancy Saunders' (f)	CDul CTho CWiW CWon EHoe EPla GCal MBNS MBlu MBrN MRav NBir NLar NSti SCoo SMHy WCot WIvy
I	- 'Nicholsonii Purpurascens'	CWon
	- 'Pendula' ♀H4	CCVT CDul CEnd CWib CWon EBee ECrN LRHS MAsh MBri MGos MSwo NWea SBfd SPer WDin
	- 'Procumbens'	CWon
	- 'Read' (f)	CWiW
	- 'Reeks' (f)	CWiW CWon
	- 'Richartii' (f)	CWiW CWon
	- 'Uralensis' (f)	CWiW CWon
	pyrenaica	EWes WAbe
	pyrenaica × ***retusa***	ECho
	pyrifolia	CWon NWea
	rehderiana	CWon
	reinii	CWon
	repens	ECho EMac GAuc NLar NWea SRms STre SWat WDin WGwG
§	- var. ***argentea***	CWon ELan EPfP EWes GAuc IFFs LRHS MMuc MRav NWCA SPer STre WDin WFar
	- 'Armando' PBR	MGos NLar
	- 'Iona' (m)	NLar
	- ***pendula***	see *S.* 'Boyd's Pendulous' (m)
	- 'Voorthuizen' (f)	CWib ECho MGos WDin
	reticulata ♀H4	ECho EPot GKir NBir NMen WAbe
§	- subsp. ***nivalis***	EPot NWCA
	retusa	CTri ECho GAuc NBir

retusa* × *serpyllifolia	NWCA
'Robin Redbreast'	CWon
rosmarinifolia misapplied	see *S. elaeagnos* subsp. *angustifolia*
× ***rubens*** 'Basfordiana' (m)	CDoC CDul CLnd CTho CWiW CWon EWes MBNS SWat WMou
- 'Bouton Aigu'	CWiW
- 'Farndon'	CWiW
- 'Farndon Red'	CWon
- 'Flanders Red' (f)	CWiW CWon
- 'Fransgeel Rood' (m)	CWiW CWon
- 'Glaucescens' (m)	CWiW
- 'Golden Willow'	CWiW CWon
- 'Hutchinson's Brown'	CWon
- 'Jaune de Falaise'	CWiW CWon
- 'Jaune Hâtive'	CWiW
- 'Laurina'	CWiW
- 'Natural Red' (f)	CWiW CWon
- 'Parsons'	CWiW CWon
- 'Rouge Ardennais'	CWiW CWon
- 'Rouge Folle'	CWiW
- 'Russet' (f)	CWiW
× ***rubra***	CWiW
- 'Abbey's Harrison' (f)	CWiW
- 'Continental Osier' (f)	CWiW CWon
- 'Eugenei' (m)	CDul CWon ECrN GQui MBlu SWat WIvy
- 'Fidkin' (f)	CWiW
- 'Harrison's' (f)	CWiW
- 'Harrison's Seedling A' (f)	CWiW
- 'Mawdesley'	CWiW
- 'Mawdesley Seedling A' (f)	CWiW
- 'Pyramidalis'	CWiW
sachalinensis 'Kioryo'	CWon
salviifolia	CWon
× ***savensis***	CWon
Scarlet Curls = 'Scarcuzam'	CWon WPat
schwerinii	CWon
- 'Carin Ehrenberg'	CWon
- 'Hilliers'	CWon
scouleriana	CWon
× ***sepulcralis***	LAst NWea
§ - 'Aokautere'	CWiW
- 'Caradoc'	CWiW
§ - var. ***chrysocoma***	Widely available
× ***sericans***	CWon
× ***seringeana***	CWon
serissaefolia	CWon
serpyllifolia	CTri NHar NMen WAbe WPat
serpyllum	see *S. fragilis* var. *furcata*
'Setsuka'	see *S. udensis* 'Sekka'
silesiaca	CWon
× ***simulatrix***	GAuc NWCA
sitchensis	NWea
× ***smithiana***	CLnd GKir NWea
songarica	GKir
× ***stipularis*** (f)	NWea
'Stuartii'	NMen SRms
subopposita	EBee EBtc ELan EWes MMuc STre WAbe WGwG
thomasii	GAuc
triandra	CWon IFFs WJPR WMou
- 'Black German' (m)	CWiW
- 'Black Hollander' (m)	CWiW CWon NLar WIvy
- 'Black Maul'	CWiW
- 'Brilliant'	CWon
- 'Champion B'	CWon
- 'Grisette de Falaise'	CWiW
- 'Grisette Droda' (f)	CWiW
- var. ***hoffmanniana***	CWon
- 'Houghton's Black'	CWon
- 'Light French'	CWon
- 'Long Bud'	CWiW
- 'Noir de Challans'	CWiW
- 'Noir de Touraine'	CWiW CWon
- 'Noir de Villaines' (m)	CWiW CWon WIvy
- 'Oliveacea'	CWon
- 'Rouge d'Orléans'	CWon EBtc
- 'Sarda d'Anjou'	CWiW
- 'Semperflorens' (m)	CWon NLar
- 'Whissander'	CWiW WIvy
- 'Zwarre Driebast'	CWon
× ***tsugaluensis*** 'Ginme' (f)	CWon SLPl
udensis	NWea
§ - 'Sekka' (m)	CWon EBee ELan EPPr EPfP IFFs LTen MBlu NBir NWea STre SWat WFar WIvy WMou
uva-ursi	WAbe
viminalis	CCVT CLnd CMac CWon ECrN EMac IFFs LBuc NWea SVic WDin WJPR WMou WSFF
- 'Black Satin'	CWon
- 'Brown Merrin'	WIvy
- 'Gigantea' (m)	CWon
- 'Green Gotz'	CWiW WIvy
- 'Reader's Red' (m)	WIvy
- 'Regalis'	CWon
- 'Riefenweide'	WIvy
- 'Romanin'	CWon
- 'Yellow Osier'	WIvy
vitellina 'Pendula'	see *S. alba* 'Tristis' ambig.
waldsteiniana	CWon GAuc NWCA
× ***wimmeriana***	SRms
'Yelverton'	see *S. alba* var. *vitellina* 'Yelverton'

Salsola (*Chenopodiaceae*)

soda	CArn ELau

Salvia ✿ (*Lamiaceae*)

sp.	SPhx
ACE 2172	SPin
CD&R 1141	SPin
CD&R 1162	CAby EPyc
CD&R 1458	SPin
CD&R 1495	SPin
CD&R 3071	SPin
DJH 93T	SPin
PC&H 226	SPin
acetabulosa	see *S. multicaulis*
adenophora	SPin
aerea	CPom
aethiopis	EWes SDnm SPav SPin
§ ***africana***	GGar SPin WDyG
africana-caerulea	see *S. africana*
africana-lutea	see *S. aurea*
agnes	SPin
algeriensis	CSpe SBch SPin
amarissima	SPin
'Amber'	EBee LHop SPin SUsu
ambigens	see *S. guaranitica* 'Blue Enigma'
ampelophylla B&SWJ 10751	SPin WCru
§ ***amplexicaulis***	EPyc LPio MWea NLar SMrm SPin WPer
amplifrons	SPin
angustifolia Cav.	see *S. reptans*
angustifolia Mich.	see *S. azurea*
'Anthony Parker'	MAJR SAga SDys
apiana	CArn EOHP EPyc MHer SAga SGar SPin WHfH
arenaria new	SPin
argentea ♀H3	CArn CBcs CSpe EBee EBla EBrs ECha ELan EPfP GMaP LPio LRHS MSpe SBfd SGar SMrm SPav SPer

		SPin SWat WCAu WCom WFar WJek WMnd WWEG
	arizonica	EPyc GCal MAsh MHom SDys SPin
	aspera	SPin
	atrocyanea	CSpe EPyc EWes EWld LPio MAJR MAsh SDys SGar SPin WHal WWlt
§	***aurea***	CHll CSev CSpe EPyc EShb LPio SAga SGar SPin SPlb SWal
	- 'Kirstenbosch'	CAby CDes CSev CWGN EBee ECtt EWld GBin LPio SDys SPin WGwG WKif WPGP WPer
	aurita	SPin
	- var. ***galpinii***	SPin
	austriaca	SPin
§	***azurea***	CRWN LPio LRHS SPin
	- var. ***grandiflora***	SPin
	bacheriana	see *S. buchananii*
§	***barrelieri***	SPin SUsu
	'Belhaven'	EWld GCal MSpe SPin
	bertolonii	see *S. pratensis* Bertolonii Group
	bicolor	see *S. barrelieri*
	'Black Knight'	CDes CWGN EPyc SDys SPin WPGP
	blancoana	CBot CMea ECha ELau GBar MCot MHer SDys SPin
	'Blausiegel' **new**	EWTr
	blepharophylla	EBee ECtt EPyc EShb LHop LPio MCot MHer MSCN NDov NGHP SAga SBfd SDnm SPav SPin SRkn WCom
	- 'Diablo'	ECtt SAga SDys SPin
	- 'Painted Lady'	CWGN EWld MAsh MSpe SDys SPin WWlt
	'Blue Chiquita'	CWGN SDys SPin
	'Blue Sky'	EWld SDys
	bracteata	SPin
	brandegeei	SPin
	broussonetii	SPin
§	***buchananii*** ♀H1+3	CHll CSWP CSam EBee EPfP EPyc EShb LHop LPio MAsh MHer MRav MSpe NDov NGHP SAga SPav SPin SPoG SRkn WCom WFar
	bulleyana misapplied	see *S. flava* var. *megalantha*
	bulleyana Diels	CPLG CSev EDAr EWes EWld LEdu MDKP MMHG MNrw NGHP NLar SDnm SPav WCru WFar
	cacaliifolia ♀H1+3	CPLG CRHN ECtt EPyc EWld GBar LPio MAsh MHer MSCN NGHP SAga SBch SDnm SGar SPer SPin SRkn SUsu WCom WSHC WWlt
	cadmica	SPin
	caerulea misapplied	see *S. guaranitica* 'Black and Blue'
	caerulea L.	see *S. africana*
	caespitosa	ECho NMen SPin
	campanulata	CPom CPou EWld SPin
	- B&SWJ 9232	WCru
	- DJHC C394	SPin
	- GWJ 9294	SPin WCru
	canariensis	CSpe EShb IDee IGor SPin WHil
	- f. ***candidissima***	SPin
	candelabrum ♀H3-4	CAbP CArn CSpe EWes MHer SAga SBch SPav SPin WKif WWlt
	cardinalis	see *S. fulgens*
	carduacea	SPin
	carnea	EWld MHom SPin
	- from Valle de Bravo, Mexico	SDys
	castanea	SPin
	caudata	SPin
	cedrosensis	SDys
§	***chamaedryoides***	CPBP CSev CWGN EBee EPyc LPio MAsh MHom NDov NGHP SDnm SDys SGar SPet SPhx SPin
	- var. ***isochroma***	IRar MAsh SDys SPin
	- 'Marine Blue'	MAsh MCot SDys SPin
	- silver-leaved	CAby CSpe NDov SPin
	aff. ***chamaedryoides*** B&SWJ 9032 from Guatemala	SPin WCru
	chamelaeagnea	EPyc GFai SDys SHar SPin WPrP
	chapalensis	MAJR SPin
	cheinii	SPin
	chiapensis	CSpe MAJR MAsh SAga SDys SPin WWlt
	chinensis	see *S. japonica*
	chionophylla **new**	SPin
	'Christine Yeo'	CDes EBee ECtt ELon EPfP EPyc EWld GGar LPio MAsh MDKP MHer MSpe NGHP SAga SBch SDys SGar SPin SUsu SWal WHoo WMnd WPGP
	cinnabarina	SPin
	cleistogama misapplied	see *S. glutinosa*
	clevelandii	EWes MHer SPav SPin WJek
	- 'Winnifred Gilman'	CWGN SDys
	clinopodioides	SPin
	coahuilensis misapplied	see *S. greggii* × *serpyllifolia*
	coahuilensis ambig.	CAby LSou MAsh SGar SMrm SPin SRkn WSHC
	coahuilensis Fernald	LHop
	coccinea	CBot SPin
	- 'Brenthurst'	SDys SPin
	- 'Coral Nymph' (Nymph Series)	ECtt EPyc SDnm SDys SPav SPin
	- 'Forest Fire'	SDys SUsu
	- 'Lactea'	CBot
	- 'Lady in Red' (Nymph Series) ♀H3	ECtt SDys SPav
*	- 'Snow Nymph' (Nymph Series)	ECtt
	columbariae	LPio SPin
	compacta	LPio
	concolor misapplied	see *S. guaranitica*
	concolor Lamb. ex Benth.	CDes EWld GCal GGar MHom SPin WPGP WSHC
	confertiflora	Widely available
	corrugata	CBcs CDes CFir CPne CSpe EBee EPyc EShb EWld GCal MAsh MHer NGHP SAga SDys SPin SRkn SWal WPGP WWlt
	'Crème Caramel'	CAby CWGN EPyc MAsh MHom SDys
	cruickshanksii	SPin
	aff. ***curtiflora*** B&SWJ 10356	WCru
	curviflora **new**	SPin
	cyanescens	CMea CPBP EPot EWld SPin
	cyanicalyx	SDys SPin
	cyclostegia	CPLG
	daghestanica	SDys SPin
	'Dale Blue' **new**	EWld
I	***dangitalis***	CPLG
	- SDR 4332	EBee
	darcyi misapplied	see *S. roemeriana*
	darcyi J. Compton	CAby CHll CPLG CSpe EPyc EWes EWld LPio MCot SAga SDys SPin WHil WSHC WWlt
	davidsonii	SPin
	decumbens **new**	SPin
	dentata	SDys SPin
	desoleana	SPin
	'Didi' **new**	NDov
	digitaloides BWJ 7777	SPin WCru
	discolor ♀H1	CBot CFir CPne CSev CSpe ECtt ELan EPyc ERea EShb EWld GCal LPio MAsh MCot MHer NGHP SAga

	SDys SEND SGar SPet SPin SUsu SWal WWlt
* - ***nigra***	CArn CMdw ECtt
disermas	SDys SPin SPlb
- pink-flowered	SPin
disjuncta	LHop SPin
- 'Chimbango'	SDys
divinorum	CBow EOHP EPyc GPoy WHfH
dolichantha	CTsd EBee EDAr EPyc EWld MCot MDKP MMuc NBir NLar SEND SPin SWal WMoo WPtf
- 'Breckland Skies'	EPPr
- pale blue/white	SEND
dolomitica	SPav SPin
dombeyi	CHll CPne EWld SDys SPin WCom
dominica	SAga SPin
dorisiana	CPne ELan EOHP MAsh SDys SPin
eigii	SPin
eizi-matudae new	SPin
elegans	ELau EWes GCra LPio MAJR MHom SAga
- 'Golden Delicious' new	EWes LSou SBfd SPin SPoG
- 'Honey Melon'	CAby EOHP EPyc MAsh NGHP SDys
§ - 'Scarlet Pineapple'	Widely available
- 'Sonoran Red'	CAby SDys
- 'Tangerine'	CArn CPrp CWan ELau EOHP EPyc GBar LPio LSou MHer MNHC MSpe NGHP SBfd SDnm SPin SWal WGwG WJek
evansiana BWJ 8013	SPin
'Eveline'	NCGa NLar
excelsa	SPin
'Fairy Tale' new	CWGN
fallax	SPin
farinacea	EPfP SPin
- 'Cirrus'	CFox
- 'Rhea'	CFox
- 'Strata'	SDys
- 'Victoria' ♀H3	LRHS MCot SDys SGar WHrl
§ ***flava*** var. ***megalantha***	CAby ELan LEdu LSRN NGdn SPin
- - BWJ 7974	WCru
florida	SPin
forreri	CDes EBee EPyc MAsh NDov SBHP SDys SEND SPin WPGP
- 'Karen Dyson'	SDys
§ ***forsskaolii***	Widely available
- white-flowered	SPin
§ ***fruticosa***	CArn ELau EPyc LRHS SIde SLon SPin
§ ***fulgens*** ♀H3	EPyc EWld ILis MAsh MHom NGHP SAga SBHP SBch SGar SPin SRkn WFar WWlt
gesneriiflora	ECtt EPyc EWld SDys SPin WCom WOut
- 'Tequila'	MAJR SPin
gilliesii	SPin
glabrescens	SPin
- B&SWJ 11152	WCru
* - var. ***robusta*** B&SWJ 11147 new	WCru
glechomifolia	SPin
§ ***glutinosa***	CArn CSpe EBee ECtt EPyc EWld GCal GMac IMou MCot MNrw NBro SAga SPav SPin SWal WCAu WCom WGwG WPer
graciliramulosa	LPio SPin
gracilis	SPin
grahamii	see *S. microphylla* var. *microphylla*
gravida	SPin
greggii	ECtt EPyc EWes LRHS MHer NGHP WPer
- CD&R 1148	MCot SDys
- 'Alba'	LPio NGHP SAga SDys SPin WHil
- 'Blush Pink'	see *S. microphylla* 'Pink Blush'
- 'Caramba' (v)	CBow EBee EPyc LHop LRHS MAvo NGHP SAga SDnm WHil
- 'Devon Cream'	see *S. greggii* 'Sungold'
- 'Diane'	MAsh
- 'Icing Sugar'	CCVN CHVG ECtt EPPr EPyc LBuc LRHS MAsh MCot NPri SPoG SRkn SUsu SVil WHil
- 'Lipstick'	CPLG ECtt MAsh
- 'Magenta'	WHil
- 'Magnet'	SPin
- (Navajo Series) 'Navajo Bright Red'	EPyc
* - - 'Navajo Cream'	EPyc SAga
* - - 'Navajo Dark Purple'	EPyc SAga WHlf
* - - 'Navajo Purple'	MCot
- - Navajo Salmon Red = 'Rfds016'	EPyc
* - - 'Navajo White'	EPyc
- 'Peach' misapplied	see *S.* × *jamensis* 'Pat Vlasto'
- 'Peach'	CDes CWGN EBee ELau EPfP EPyc MAsh MHer MLLN NGHP SAga SDnm SEND SGar SPet SPin SPoG WCom WMnd WPGP WWlt
- 'Pink Preference'	MAsh
- 'Raspberry Red' new	MCot
- 'Sierra San Antonio'	see *S.* × *jamensis* 'Sierra San Antonio'
- 'Sparkler' (v)	EPfP EPyc LRHS MAsh SLon SPoG
- 'Stormy Pink'	CAby CDes CHll CSpe CWGN EPyc LRHS MAsh MCot MSpe NDov SAga WCom WPGP WSHC WWlt
§ - 'Sungold'	CWGN ECtt EPfP EPyc LRHS MAsh MHom MWte NDov NGHP SBch SDys SHom SPin SSvw WHil WMnd
- variegated (v)	EHoe SEND
- yellow-flowered	CAby
greggii × ***lycioides***	see *S. greggii* × *serpyllifolia*
§ ***greggii*** × ***serpyllifolia***	CAbP CSpe EPyc MAsh MCot MSpe NDov SAga SDys SGar SPin WPGP
grewiifolia	SPin
§ ***guaranitica***	CBcs CBot CEnt CHEx ECtt EShb EWld GCra GQui LRHS SAga SDnm SDys SPav SPer SPin SWal WKif WPGP WWlt
- 'Argentina Skies'	CHGN ECtt EPPr EPyc LPio MSpe SAga SDys SMrm SPin WWlt
§ - 'Black and Blue'	COlW CPLG CPne CRHN CSWP CSev CSpe CWCL EBee ECre ECtt EPPr EPfP EPyc GCal LHop LPio LRHS MAvo NGHP SAga SBch SDnm SGar SPin SWal WPGP WSHC
§ - 'Blue Enigma' ♀H3-4	Widely available
- 'Indigo Blue'	ECtt EPfP MAsh MLLN SPin WWlt
- 'Purple Emperor'	LPio
- 'Purple Splendor'	EShb EWld
- purple-flowered	CSam
haematodes	see *S. pratensis* Haematodes Group
haenkei	SPin
- 'Prawn Chorus'	CSpe MAJR SAga SPin
heerii	SPin
heldreichiana	SPin
henryi	SPin
hians	CPLG CPom EBee GBar GCra MDKP MNrw NLar SBfd SDnm SGar SPav SPin SRms WPer
- CC 1787	SPin
hierosolymitana	SPin
hirtella	SPin
hispanica misapplied	see *S. lavandulifolia*

	hispanica L.	CSam SPin
	holwayi	SPin
	- B&SWJ 8995	WCru
	horminum	see *S. viridis* var. *comata*
	huberi	SPin
	'Huntsman's Red' **new**	IRar
	inconspicua **new**	SPin
	indica	SPin
	'Indigo Spires'	CAby CHll CMHG CPLG CSpe CWGN ECre ECtt EPyc EShb EWld LPio MAsh MCot MHom MLLN NDov SAga SDys SMrm SPhx SPin SUsu WPen WSHC WWlt
	interrupta	EWld MCot MHer SAga SPin WPen
	involucrata ♀H3	CFir CPom CSev CSpe EPyc GCra LPio MCot MHom NBro SDys SPhx SPin WHrl WSHC
	- 'Bethellii' ♀H3-4	CAby CArn CBot CPne CSev EBee ECtt ELan EPfP EPyc EShb GBar LPio LRHS MAsh MHer SAga SDix SDnm SGar SMrm SPav SPin SRkn WKif WSpi WWlt
	- 'Boutin' ♀H3	MAJR MAsh MHom SAga SDys WWlt
§	- 'Hadspen'	CBot CDes CHll CRHN CSam CSpe EWes GCal MAJR SPin WCom WWlt
	- 'Joan'	CAby CWGN MAsh SDys SPin SUsu
	- 'Mrs Pope'	see *S. involucrata* 'Hadspen'
*	- var. ***puberula***	MAJR MHom SDys SPin
	iodantha	LPio SDys SPin WHil
	- 'Louis Saso'	SPin
	iodochroa	CDes EBee WPGP
	- B&SWJ 10252	SPin WCru
	× ***jamensis***	CWGN EBee ELau EPyc EWes EWld MAvo MWea NPri SAga SDys SMrm SPin
	- 'Californian Sunset' **new**	MAsh
	- 'Cherry Queen'	EBee EPyc MAsh SAga SDys SPin WWlt
	- 'Dark Dancer'	CWGN LPio MAsh SDys SPhx WWlt
	- 'Desert Blaze' (v)	CAbP CAby CBow CDes CWGN ECtt EPPr EPyc LBuc MCot MHer NGHP SDys SMrm SPin WCom WCot WGrn WPGP
	- 'Devantville'	CAby NDov
	- 'Dysons' Orangy Pink'	CAby CSpe NDov SAga SPin
§	- 'Hot Lips'	Widely available
	- 'James Compton'	EPyc SDys SGar SMrm
	- 'La Luna'	CEnt CPom CSam CTri ECtt EPfP EPyc EShb EWld LHop LPio MCot MHer MHom MSpe NDov SDys SEND SGar SPin WCom WMnd WPGP WSHC
	- 'La Siesta'	EBee MAsh NGHP SAga SDys
	- 'La Tarde'	CAby CEnt CTri MAsh MHom NGHP SBch SDys WWlt
	- 'Lemon Sorbet'	SDys
	- 'Los Lirios' ♀H3-4	CPom CSpe CTri EPyc SAga SDys SMrm SPin WCom
	- 'Maraschino'	EBee EPfP EPyc LPio LRHS MAsh SDys SPin WMnd WWlt
*	- 'Mauve'	EPyc NDov SDys
	- 'Moonlight Over Ashwood' (v)	EPyc MAsh SBHP SDys SPin WSHC WWlt
	- 'Moonlight Serenade'	CAby EPyc MAsh MWea SAga SBch SDys
§	- 'Pat Vlasto'	EBee EPyc MHom MWea SDys SPin
	- 'Peter Vidgeon'	CWGN EPyc SDys SPin SUsu
	- 'Pleasant Pink'	CSev EPyc MAsh SAga SDys SPin
	- 'Raspberry Royale' ♀H3-4	CDes CPom CSev CWGN EBee ECtt EPfP EPyc EWoo LHop LRHS MAsh MCot MHer MLLN MMuc NGHP SDnm SEND SGar SMrm SPav SPin WCom WHoo WMnd WSHC
	- 'Red Velvet'	CAby CSpe ECtt ELon EPyc EWld MAsh MHer MHom NGHP SUsu WEas WSHC WWlt
	- 'San Isidro Moon'	WHil
	- 'Señorita Leah'	CWGN EPyc MAsh SDys SUsu
§	- 'Sierra San Antonio'	CDes CWGN ECtt EPfP EPyc LRHS MAsh MHom MWea NDov SAga SBHP SDys SMrm WPGP
§	- 'Trebah'	CDes CPom CSpe ECre EPyc MAsh MCot MHom MWea SDys SGar SMrm SPin SPoG SRot WHil WPGP WSHC WWlt
	- 'Trenance'	CAby ECre EPyc LHop MHom SDys SGar SPin SRot WHil
	- white-flowered	SPin
§	***japonica***	SPin
	- 'Alba'	SPin
	'Jean's Purple Passion'	SDys SPin
	judaica	SPin WGrn
	jurisicii	CArn CWib EBee EPyc MAsh SEND SPav SPin WJek
	- pink-flowered	CSpe SPin
	karwinskyi	SPin
	- B&SWJ 9081	WCru
	keerlii	SPin
	koyamae	SPin
	- B&SWJ 10919	WCru
	'Lady Strybing'	SPin
	lanceolata	SPin WWlt
	lanigera	SPin
	lasiantha	SPin
§	***lavandulifolia***	Widely available
	lavanduloides	SPin
	- B&SWJ 9053	WCru
	lemmonii	see *S. microphylla* var. *wislizeni*
	leptophylla	see *S. reptans*
	leucantha ♀H1	CArn CBow CPne CSev CSpe EBee ELan EPyc EShb GBar GGar LPio MAsh MCot MHer MRav MSCN SAga SDys SEND SOWG SPav SPin SPlb SRkn SWal
	- 'Eder' (v)	MAJR MAsh SDys SPin
	- 'Midnight'	IFoB SDys
	- 'Purple Velvet'	EPyc GGar MAJR MAsh MHer MHom NGHP SDix SDys SPin WWlt
	- 'San Marcos Lavender'	SPin
	- 'Santa Barbara'	CHll CWGN MAsh SDys
	leucocephala	SPin
	leucophylla NNS 01-375	SPin
	littae	SPin
	longispicata	SPin
	longistyla	SPin
*	***luzentzii*** F&W 11499 **new**	IFoB
	lycioides misapplied	see *S. greggii* × *serpyllifolia*
	lycioides A. Gray	CAbP CHll LPio SDys SEND SPhx SPin WCom
	lyrata	EOHP SGar SPin WOut
	- 'Burgundy Bliss'	see *S. lyrata* 'Purple Knockout'
§	- 'Purple Knockout'	CArn CBow CKno EBee EPfP EPyc EShb LAst NGHP SBfd SGar SMrm SPhx SPin
	- 'Purple Vulcano'	see *S. lyrata* 'Purple Knockout'
	macellaria misapplied	see *S. microphylla*
	macellaria Epling	CSam
	macrophylla	GCal SPin WPGP
	macrosiphon	SPin
	madrensis	EPyc SPin
	- 'Dunham'	EBee GCal SDys
	'Magic Potion' **new**	CWGN
	melissodora	SDys SPin

	mellifera	CArn SPin
	merjamie 'Mint-sauce'	CPla LHop LRHS WFar
	mexicana	SPin
	- B&SWJ 10288	WCru
	- T&K 550	CBot
	- 'Lollie Jackson'	MAJR
	- var. ***minor***	EPyc EWld MAJR SPin
	- 'Snowflake'	MAJR
	- 'Tula'	SDys
	meyeri	CPom EWld MAJR MHom SPin WWlt
§	***microphylla***	CArn CChe CMHG CMac CPom CPrp CTri CWan ELau EOHP EUJe EWes GBar LAst LHop MHer MSCN NSti SPet WPer
	- CD&R 1141	SPin
	- 'Belize'	MAsh MSpe NDov NGHP WWlt
	- 'Cerro Potosi'	CMdw CPom CSev CSpe ELon EPyc GKir LPio LRHS MAsh MSpe NGHP SAga SDys SGar SMrm SPin SUsu WClo WPen WWlt
	- 'Dieciocho de Marzo'	SDys
	- 'Hot Lips'	see *S.* × *jamensis* 'Hot Lips'
	- 'Huntington'	EOHP EPyc SPin
	- hybrid, purple-flowered	CPom
	- 'Kew Red' ♀H3-4	CFir CHVG CWGN EWld MNrw MWea NGHP SBch SPin WHoo WPGP WPen
	- 'La Trinidad'	SDys
I	- 'Lutea'	MAsh
	- 'Maroon'	CWGN EPyc SDys SUsu
§	- var. ***microphylla***	CFee CRHN CSev CSpe CTri CWib EBee ECtt ELan EOHP EPfP EPyc LSRN MAvo MCot MHer MNHC MRav NGHP SEND SGar SOWG SPav SPin SRkn WFar WHfH WJek WPer WSHC
	- - 'La Foux'	MCot MWea SBch SDys SMrm SPhx SPoG WCom
	- - 'Newby Hall' ♀H3-4	CAby CDes CPom ECtt EPyc EShb EWes MWea NGHP SDys SPhx WPGP
N	- var. ***neurepia***	see *S. microphylla* var. *microphylla*
	- 'Orange Door'	EPyc SDys
	- 'Oregon Peach'	EPfP LRHS
	- 'Oxford'	NGHP SDys SPin
§	- 'Pink Blush' ♀H3-4	CAby CBot EBee ECtt ELan EPfP EPyc LAst LRHS MAsh MCot MHer MHom MMuc NGHP SEND SMrm SPin SRkn WCom WHil WKif WOut WPGP WSHC WWlt
	- 'Pleasant View' ♀H3-4	CAby EPyc MLLN
	- 'Robin's Pride'	EPyc SDys SUsu
	- 'Rodbaston Current Purple'	MSpe
	- 'Rosy Cheeks'	WOut
§	- 'Ruth Stungo' (v)	ECre IRar
	- 'San Carlos Festival'	CDes CPom EPyc MAsh NGHP SBch SDys SPhx SPin WPGP WWlt
	- 'Trelawny Rose Pink'	see *S.* 'Trelawney'
	- 'Trelissick Creamy Yellow'	see *S.* 'Trelissick'
	- 'Trewithen Cerise'	see *S.* 'Trewithen'
	- 'Variegata' splashed	see *S. microphylla* 'Ruth Stungo'
	- 'Violette'	EPfP EPyc
	- 'Wild Watermelon'	CWGN EPfP EPyc MAsh SAga SDys
§	- var. ***wislizeni***	CPom EPyc SDys SPin WHil WWlt
	- 'Zaragoza'	SPin
	miltiorhiza	CArn CSpe SPin
	miniata	CSev CSpe EPyc MAJR SBHP SDys SPin
	misella	SPin
	mohavensis	SPin

	moorcroftiana	EPyc SDnm
	moschata **new**	SPin
	muelleri misapplied	see *S. greggii* × *serpyllifolia*
	muelleri Epling	EBee EPyc
	muirii	SPin
	'Mulberry Jam'	CDes CHGN CHll CMdw CSev CWGN EBee ECtt EPfP EPyc EWes EWld GCal LPio MAJR MAsh MCot MHer MHom NDov SAga SDys SEND SPin SRkn WKif WPGP WSHC WWlt
§	***multicaulis*** ♀H4	EPyc MAsh SPin WEas
	munzii	CFir SPin
*	***murrayi***	CAbP SPin
	Mystic Spires Blue = 'Balsalmisp'PBR **new**	CSpe SBch
	namaensis	SDys SPin
	nana B&SWJ 10272	SPin WCru
	napifolia	EBee GKev NLar SAga SDnm SEND SPav SPhx SPin WGwG
	'Nazareth'	MAsh SPin
	'Nel'	LHop
	nemorosa	EPyc LRHS SPin SRms
	- 'Amethyst' ♀H4	CHar EBee EBrs ELon EPfP GBBs IKil LAst LRHS MLLN MRav NDov NMoo SAga SDys SMHy SPhx WCAu WCot WWEG WWlt
	- Blue Mound	see *S.* × *sylvestris* 'Blauhügel'
	- 'Caradonna'	Widely available
	- East Friesland	see *S. nemorosa* 'Ostfriesland'
	- 'Kleine Amethyst' **new**	NDov
	- 'Lubecca' ♀H4	EBee EBrs ECGP ECtt EHrv EPfP EShb ETod GQue LHop LRHS MCot MSpe NDov NEgg NLar SMrm SPer WFar WMnd WWEG
	- Marcus = 'Haeumanarc'PBR	EBee ECtt ELan EPfP EPyc LAst LRHS LSRN LSou MBNS MBri NBPC NLar SBfd SDys WFar WSHC
	- 'Midsummer'	EWld
§	- 'Ostfriesland' ♀H4	Widely available
	- 'Ostfriesland Compact' **new**	LRHS
	- 'Phoenix Pink'	SPhx
	- 'Pink Friesland'PBR	EBee ECtt EPPr GQue LHop LRHS LSou MGos NDov NPri SMrm
	- 'Plumosa'	see *S. nemorosa* 'Pusztaflamme'
	- 'Porzellan' ♀H4	ECtt
§	- 'Pusztaflamme' ♀H4	CWGN EBee ECha ECtt EPPr EPfP GQue MSpe SMrm SUsu WCAu WWEG
	- 'Rose Queen'	ECtt GKir LAst LBMP NBir SDys SPer SWat WCot WFar
	- 'Rosenwein'	CAby EBee EBrs LRHS MDKP MNrw NBPC NGdn SPhx
	- 'Royal Distinction'	EBee ECtt
	- 'Schneekönig' **new**	LSou
	- 'Schwellenburg'	EBee LHop LRHS LSou NBPC NLar NMoo SUsu
	- 'Sensation Rose'	CCVN CWGN EBee GBin LLHF LRHS LSou MAsh NDov WCot
§	- subsp. ***tesquicola***	ECha EPyc LSRN MNFA MWhi NBPC NGdn NLar SMrm SPhx WFar WPtf
	- 'Wesuwe'	EBee EPPr ETod NDov
	neurepia	see *S. microphylla* var. *microphylla*
	'Newe Ya'ar' **new**	EPfP
	nilotica	LPio SPin SWal
	nipponica	NLar
	- B&SWJ 5829	SPin WCru
	- 'Fuji Snow' (v)	CBow EPyc
	- var. ***trisecta***	SPin
	nubicola	CPLG EBee GPoy SPin

	- CC 4762	NLar
	nutans	LPio SPin
	oblongifolia	LPio
	- B&SWJ 10315	WCru
	officinalis	Widely available
	- 'Albiflora'	CArn CBod CBot ECtt EOHP GBar SBch SPin WJek
N	- 'Aurea' ambig.	CWib ECho GKir GPoy
	- 'Berggarten'	CArn CPrp EBee ECha ELau EPfP GBar GBee GCal LEdu LHop LPio LRHS MBri MCot MHer MRav SDix SPhx SPin WHer WJek WMnd
	- 'Blackcurrant'	LSou
§	- broad-leaved	CBot CSWP ELau MHer SWat WClo WJek
	- 'Crispa'	EOHP SPin
	- 'Extrakta'	SPhx
	- 'Grete Stolze'	EBee IMou
§	- 'Icterina' (v) ♀H4	Widely available
	- 'Kew Gold'	MRav
	- ***latifolia***	see *S. officinalis* broad-leaved
	- narrow-leaved	see *S. lavandulifolia*
	- 'Nazareth' PBR	ELau WJek
*	- 'Pink Splash' (v)	CBow
	- ***prostrata***	see *S. lavandulifolia*
	- 'Purpurascens' ♀H4	Widely available
	- 'Purpurascens Variegata' (v)	WEas
	- 'Robin Hill'	GBar
	- 'Rosea'	CArn EOHP WJek
	- 'Tricolor' (v)	Widely available
	- 'Variegata'	see *S. officinalis* 'Icterina'
	- variegated (v)	CBow ECho MHer
	ombrophila	SPin
	omeiana	WFar
	- BWJ 8062	SPin WCru
	- 'Crûg Thundercloud'	WCru
	oppositiflora misapplied	see *S. tubiflora*
	oppositiflora ambig.	MAJR SAga SDys SPin
	orbignaei	SPin
	oxyphora	SDys SPin
	pachyphylla	SPin
	'Pam's Purple' **new**	MAsh
§	***patens*** ♀H3	Widely available
	- 'Alba' misapplied	see *S. patens* 'White Trophy'
	- 'Blue Angel'	EWes IFoB MSwo WHrl WWEG
	- 'Cambridge Blue' ♀H3	Widely available
	- 'Chilcombe'	CSam EBee ECtt EPyc EWTr MCot MSpe SDys SPin WCom WWlt
	- 'Dot's Delight'	CPLG CWGN EPyc EWes MAsh NGHP SAga SHar SMrm SPin SPoG SRkn SUsu SVil
	- 'Guanajuato'	Widely available
	- large **new**	SUsu
	- lavender-flowered	MLLN SBch
	- 'Oxford Blue'	see *S. patens*
	- 'Pink Ice'	CPom WOut
	- pink-flowered	MSpe SPin
	- 'Royal Blue'	see *S. patens*
	- 'Southern Lights'	MAJR
§	- 'White Trophy'	CPLG EBee ECtt ELan EPyc EShb EWld LRHS MHer NGHP SDnm SDys SMrm SPer SPin SUsu WCom WFar WHil
	pauciserrata	SPin
	'Penny's Smile' **new**	SPin SUsu
	penstemonoides	SDys
	personata	SPin
	'Peru Blue'	CSpe EPyc EWld SDys
	'Phyllis' Fancy'	CSam CSpe EPyc LPio MAsh SDys SPlb SUsu
	pinguifolia	SPin
	pisidica	SPin
	platystoma	SPin
	plectranthoides	SPin
	pogonochila	SPin
	polystachya	SPin
	- B&SWJ 8985	WCru
	pomifera	SPin
*	'Powis Castle'	MHom
	praeclara	SPin
	pratensis	CArn CWib EBWF EBee ELan EPyc GJos MHer MNHC NChi NGHP SGar SPin
	- 'Albiflora'	CDes
§	- Bertolonii Group	EPyc SPin
§	- Haematodes Group ♀H4	ECha ELan EPyc MNrw NLar SBch SDnm SPav SPin SRms
	- 'Indigo' ♀H4	CDes CPrp EBee ECGP ECtt EPfP EWTr LRHS MCot MRav NDov NEgg NLar SPhx SPin SUsu WMnd WPGP
	- 'Lapis Lazuli'	CDes EBee EWes NBre SPhx SUsu WFar
	- 'Pink Delight' PBR	EAEE EBee LRHS MGos NCGa NDov NLar SPoG
	- 'Rose Rhapsody' (Ballet Series)	CAby EBee EDAr GJos LBMP MHer NCGa SPhx WFar WHil
	- 'Rosea'	ECha SPhx SPin
	- 'Swan Lake' (Ballet Series)	CMHG EPyc NCGa NChi NLar SAga SPhx SPin SPlb WHil
	- 'Sweet Esmeralda' (Ballet Series) **new**	EBee NDov NLar SBfd
	- 'Twilight Serenade' (Ballet Series) **new**	CAby EBee ECtt NDov SBfd
	pratensis × ***transylvanica***	GJos
	procurrens	SPin
	prostrata	EOHP
	prunelloides	SPin
	przewalskii	CPLG CPom EWld GBar LRHS MCCP NMRc SAga SDnm SGar SPhx SPin WPer
	- BWJ 7920	SPin WCru
	pubescens	SPin
	pulchella	MAJR SPin
	'Purple Majesty'	CHll CSev CWGN EPyc EShb LHop LPio MAvo SAga SDys SMrm SPhx SPin SRkn WKif WWlt
	'Purple Queen'	LRHS LSou MSpe SDys SPoG WWlt
	purpurea	LSRN SPin
	radula	SPin
	ranzaniana	SPin
	raymondii	SPin
	subsp. ***mairanae*** **new**	
	recognita	CBot SPin WSHC
	recurva	SPin
	red-flowered B&SWJ 10375 from Guatemala	WCru
	reflexa	SPin
	regeliana misapplied	see *S. virgata* Jacq.
	regeliana Trautv.	NBir SPin
	regla	CAby MAJR NGHP SDys SPin WPGP
	- 'Jame'	SPin
	- 'Mount Emory'	SPin
	- 'Royal'	SPin
	repens	EBee EPyc IGor SDys SPhx SPin
	- var. ***repens***	SGar
§	***reptans***	MAsh SPin
	- from Mexico	SDys
	- from Western Texas	CWGN SDys
	retinervia	SPin
	ringens	SDys SPin
	riparia misapplied	see *S. rypara*

	roborowskii	SPin
§	***roemeriana*** ♀H3	CPBP CSpe EBee EPyc IFoB NWCA SDnm SDys SPin WPGP
	- 'Hot Trumpets'	WHil
	roscida	SPin
	'Rose Queen' ambig.	MRav
	'Royal Bumble'	EPyc IPot LHop NDov
	'Royal Crimson Distinction'PBR	WHlf
	rubescens	SDys SPin
	rubiginosa	SDys SPin
	runcinata	EPyc SPin
	rutilans	see *S. elegans* 'Scarlet Pineapple'
§	***rypara***	CPom SDys SPin
	sagittata	SDys SPin WWlt
*	***sauntia***	SPin
	(Savannah Series) 'Savannah Purple' **new**	SRot
	- 'Savannah Salmon Rose' **new**	IFoB SRot
	scabiosifolia	SPin
	scabra	CSpe SDys SPin
	schlechteri	SPin
	sclarea	CArn CHby ECtt GPoy ITim LRHS MHer MNHC NGHP NGdn SIde SPin WHfH WJek WOut
	- var. ***sclarea***	EBla ECtt
	- short	WHil
	- var. ***turkestanica*** hort.	CSev CSpe EBee ECtt EHrv ELan EPfP LBMP LRHS LSRN MBri MCot MRav NEgg NGdn SBfd SEND SGar SMrm SPav SPer SWat WCAu WCom WEas WKif WMnd
	- var. ***turkestaniana*** Mottet	EBrs MSpe NBPC SPhx SUsu WWEG
§	- 'Vatican White'	EBee EBrs EPfP LRHS MSpe SBch SDnm WJek WMnd
	- white-bracted	CWib NChi NLar SPin SWvt
*	***scordifolia***	SPin
	scutellarioides	SPin
	semiatrata misapplied	see *S. chamaedryoides*
	semiatrata ambig.	EPyc IFoB LPio WHlf
	semiatrata Zucc.	CDes CSpe EWld SAga SDys SPin
	'Serenade'	NDov SPhx
	serpyllifolia	SDys SPin WHil
	sessei	SPin
	setulosa	SPin
	'Shame' **new**	NDov
	'Silas Dyson'	CAby CSpe CWGN EPyc EWld LPio LRHS MHom MWea NDov SAga SBch SDys SPhx SPin SSvw SUsu WPGP
	'Silke's Dream'	CAby CPom CWGN EBee ECtt EPyc EWld MAsh MWea NDov SBHP SDys SPin SUsu WPen WWlt
	sinaloensis	EPyc MAsh SDys SPin WFar
	somalensis	SDys SPin
	spathacea ♀H3-4	SDys SPhx SPin
	splendens	SPin
	- 'Dancing Flame' (v)	EPyc
	- 'Helen Dillon'	EPyc SDys
	- 'Jimmy's Good Red' **new**	CSpe
	- 'Peach'	SDys SPin
	- pink-flowered **new**	WHil
	- 'Salsa Burgundy' (Salsa Series)	CSpe SBch WWlt
	- 'Vanguard' ♀H3 **new**	LAst
§	- 'Van-Houttei' ♀H3	CSpe EBee ECre EPyc EWld GCal MHom SDys SPin WWlt
	sprucei	SPin
	squalens	SPin

	stachydifolia	SPin
§	***staminea***	SDys SPhx SPin
	stenophylla	SPin WHil
	'Stephanie'	EPyc SDys
	stepposa	SPin
	stoteonifera	SDys SPin
	striata	SPin
	styphelus	SDys SPin
	subpalmatinervis	SPin
	subrotunda	EWld SDys SPin
	summa	CPBP
	× ***superba*** ♀H4	CBot CSBt EBee ECtt ELan EPfP EPyc EWld LAst LEdu LRHS MBri MWat SDix SPer SRms WCAu WHoo
	- 'Adrian'	CMHG EBee ECtt LRHS LSRN SMrm SPoG
	- 'Dear Anja'	EBee LHop NDov SAga SPhx
	- 'Merleau'	EPyc LRHS
	- 'Merleau Rose'	EBee WGor
*	- 'Rosea'	EBee
	- 'Rubin' ♀H4	ECtt MBNS NBre SMrm SPhx
I	- 'Superba'	CSev ECha ECtt EHrv MRav SMrm SPhx SRkn
	× ***sylvestris***	LAst SGar SPin
§	- 'Blauhügel' ♀H4	CHar EBee EBrs ECha ECtt ELan EPfP EShb GKir MArl MCot NDov NPri SBch SMrm SPhx WCAu WHoo WPer WWEG
§	- 'Blaukönigin'	EBee ELon EPfP GKev GMaP LAst LBMP LRHS MWat NGBl NLar NMir NVic SBfd SPet SPlb SPoG SWvt WPer WWEG
	- Blue Queen	see *S.* × *sylvestris* 'Blaukönigin'
	- 'Lye End'	ECtt MWat WCot
§	- 'Mainacht' ♀H4	Widely available
	- May Night	see *S.* × *sylvestris* 'Mainacht'
	- 'Negrito'	EBee EWll NGdn NLar SMrm
	- 'Rhapsody in Blue'PBR	EBee LRHS MBNS NDov NLar WFar
	- 'Rose Queen'	CMac EBee ECha ECtt ELan ELon EPfP LHop LRHS NGBl SBfd SCoo SPet SPhx SPoG SWvt WPer WWEG
	- 'Rügen'	CMac EBee EPyc
	- 'Schneehügel'	CMac CSBt EBee ECha ELan ELon EPPr EPfP GKir GMaP LAst LRHS MBNS MRav NBre NCob NEgg NMoo NPri SMrm SPer WCAu WMnd WWEG
	- 'Tänzerin' ♀H4	EBee ELon EPPr EPyc NDov SDys SUsu WHlf
	- 'Viola Klose'	CHar CMHG CPrp CWGN EBee EBrs ECha ECtt LRHS LSRN MBri MCot NCGa NDov NGdn NLar
	tachiei hort.	see *S. forsskaolii*
	'Tammy'	SPin
	taraxacifolia	SDys SPin WHil
	tesquicola	see *S. nemorosa* subsp. *tesquicola*
	tianschanica	SPin
	tiliifolia	SPav SPin SRms
	tingitana	SDys SPin
	tomentosa	SPin
	transcaucasica	see *S. staminea*
	transsylvanica	IMou MSpe SDnm SGar SMrm SPav SPhx SPin STes WPer WPtf
	- 'Blue Spire'	CMea EBee ECtt EWTr GQue MCot MWhi SPad SPav SPur
	'Trebah Lilac White'	see *S.* × *jamensis* 'Trebah'
§	'Trelawney'	EPyc MHom SDys SPin SRkn SRot
§	'Trelissick'	ECre EPyc LHop MAsh MHom MWea SDys SPin SRkn SRot WHil WWlt
§	'Trewithen'	CPLG CPom ECre EPyc SPin SPoG SRkn SRot WHil

	trijuga	SPin
	triloba	see *S. fruticosa*
	tubifera	SAga SPin
§	***tubiflora*** ♀H1+3	CSpe EPyc MAJR MAsh SPin
	uliginosa ♀H3-4	Widely available
	- 'African Skies'	CChe EBee MNrw SPin
	- 'Ballon Azur' **new**	CSpe SDys SMHy
	urica	MAJR SDys SPin
	- short	CMdw CSpe SDys
	'Valerie'	CAby EPyc SDys
	'Van-Houttei'	see *S. splendens* 'Van-Houttei'
	'Vatican City'	see *S. sclarea* 'Vatican White'
	verbenaca	CArn EBWF EBee EPyc ITim MHer NSco SPin
	- pink-flowered	SPhx
	verticillata	EBee EHrv EPyc LEdu MLLN NLar SDys SEND SPin
§	- 'Alba'	CAbP EBee ECtt EPfP EShb GJos GQue LBMP LRHS MCot MLLN MRav NGdn NLar SPer SPin
	- subsp. ***amasiaca***	SGar
	- 'Endless Love' **new**	NDov
	- 'Hannay's Blue'	EPPr SMrm SUsu
	- 'Hannay's Purple'	EPPr
	- 'Purple Rain'	Widely available
	- 'Smouldering Torches'	LHop LPla NDov SPhx
	- 'White Rain'	see *S. verticillata* 'Alba'
	villicaulis	see *S. amplexicaulis*
§	***virgata*** Jacq.	EBee SGar SPin
	viridis	CHby MNHC SPin
§	- var. ***comata***	MCot NGHP SIde WJek
	- var. ***viridis***	WHrl
	viscosa ambig.	EPyc WBox
	viscosa Jacq.	SPin
	- 'Framboise'	MCot
	vitifolia B&SWJ 10236	WCru
	wagneriana	MAJR SPin
	'Waverly'	CDes CHll CSpe EBee EPyc EWld MAJR MAsh MCot SAga SBch SDys SUsu WCom WWlt
	× ***westerae*** **new**	SPin
	xalapensis	SPin
	aff. ***yunnanensis***	SPin
	- BWJ 7874	WCru

Salvinia (*Salviniaceae*)

	sp.	LPBA
	natans	LLWG MSKA

Sambucus (*Caprifoliaceae*)

	adnata	SDix WFar
	caerulea	see *S. nigra* subsp. *caerulea*
	callicarpa	NLar
	ebulus	GKir LEdu NLar SMad
	mexicana B&SWJ 10349	WCru
	miquelii RBS 0265	NLar
	nigra	CArn CBcs CCVT CDul ECrN EMac GKir GPoy IFFs LBuc NWea SBfd SIde WDin WFar WMou WSFF
	- 'Albomarginata'	see *S. nigra* 'Marginata'
	- 'Albovariegata' (v)	CMac EBee SEND WMoo
*	- 'Ardwall'	CAgr GCal
N	- 'Aurea' ♀H4	CBcs CDul CLnd CSBt CWan ELan EMac EPfP GKir IFFs MRav NWea SPer WDin WFar WMoo
	- 'Aureomarginata' (v)	EBee ECrN ELan EPPr EPfP MRav NLar NSti SBfd WCFE WFar
	- 'Bradet'	CAgr NLar
	- 'Cae Rhos Lligwy'	CAgr WHer
§	- subsp. ***caerulea***	EPfP WSpi
	- subsp. ***canadensis*** 'Aurea'	CWib WHar
	- - 'John's'	CAgr
	- - 'Maxima'	EWes SMad SMrm WCot
	- - 'York' (F)	CAgr WCot
	- 'Donau'	CAgr
§	- 'Eva' PBR	Widely available
	- 'Frances' (v)	EPPr WCot WPat
	- 'Franzi'	CAgr
	- 'Fructu Luteo'	NLar
§	- 'Gerda' PBR ♀H4	Widely available
	- 'Godshill' (F)	CAgr SDea
	- 'Haschberg'	CAgr
	- 'Heterophylla'	see *S. nigra* 'Linearis'
	- 'Ina'	CAgr
	- 'Körsör' (F)	NLar
	- f. ***laciniata*** ♀H4	CDul CPLG EBee ELan EPPr EPfP EPla EWTr GCal GKir LRHS MBlu MMuc MRav NBea NLar NSti NWea SDix SLon SPer WCFE WCot WDin WFar WPGP
§	- 'Linearis'	CPMA ELan EPla MRav NLar
	- 'Long Tooth'	CDul
	- 'Madonna' (v)	CMac EBee LRHS LTen MBlu MGos MRav NLBP NLar SBfd WBrE WCot
§	- 'Marginata' (v)	CDul CWan CWib EHoe GKir MHer MRav SDix SPer WCot WDin WFar
	- 'Marion Bull' (v)	CDul
I	- 'Marmorata'	NLar
I	- 'Monstrosa'	NLar
	- 'Nana'	WCot
	- 'Plena' (d)	WCot
	- f. ***porphyrophylla*** 'Black Beauty' PBR	see *S. nigra* 'Gerda'
	- - 'Black Lace' PBR	see *S. nigra* 'Eva'
§	- - 'Guincho Purple'	CBcs CDul CTri CWib EBee ELan EPPr EPfP GKir MCCP MHer MRav NHol NLar SPlb WDin WFar WMoo
	- - 'Purple Pete'	CDul
	- - 'Thundercloud'	CDul CMHG EWes LBMP LRHS MAsh MBri MNrw NChi NLar WCot WFar WMoo
	- 'Pulverulenta' (v)	CBow CWib EPPr EPla GCal GKir LHop MRav NLBP NLar SPer WCot WFar
	- 'Purpurea'	see *S. nigra* f. *porphyrophylla* 'Guincho Purple'
	- 'Pyramidalis'	CPMA EPla NLar
	- 'Robert Piggin' (v)	WCot
	- 'Sambu' (F)	CAgr
	- 'Samdal' (F)	CAgr
	- 'Samidan' (F)	CAgr
	- 'Samnor' (F)	CAgr
	- 'Sampo' (F)	CAgr
	- 'Samyl' (F)	CAgr
*	- 'Tenuifolia'	MRav
	- 'Urban Lace'	CAgr
	- 'Variegata'	see *S. nigra* 'Marginata'
	- f. ***viridis***	CAgr
	racemosa	EPfP NWea
	- 'Aurea'	EHoe
	- 'Crûg Lace'	WCru
	- 'Goldenlocks'	EWes MGos MSwo NLar
	- 'Plumosa Aurea'	CBcs CMac CPLG CSBt CWib EBee ELan EPfP GCra GKir LRHS MBri MRav MSwo NHol NLar NPri NWea SLim SReu SSta WDin WFar
	- 'Sutherland Gold' ♀H4	Widely available
	- 'Tenuifolia'	CPMA ELan EPfP NLar WPat
	tigranii	NLar

Samolus (*Primulaceae*)

	repens	CPBP ECou LLHF
	valerandi	EBWF LLWG

Sandersonia (*Colchicaceae*)

aurantiaca	CAvo CFFs CPne ECho EPot LAma

Sanguinaria (*Papaveraceae*)

canadensis	Widely available
- f. ***multiplex*** (d)	CDes CLAP ECho GEdr GKir IFro LRHS NBir WCom WSHC WWst
- - 'Plena' (d) ♀H4	CBct CSpe CWCL EBee ECho ELon EPot GBin GCra GCrs GKev GPoy LAma NHar NHol NLar NMen NRya SKHP SPer SPoG WAbe WBVN WFar WHil WKif WPGP WPat WTin
- 'Star' new	GCrs

Sanguisorba ✿ (*Rosaceae*)

sp.	NDov NLar SUsu
DJHC 535 from Korea	SMHy
§ ***albiflora***	CCVN CDes CHar CKno EBee EBla EBrs ELan LBMP LPla LRHS MAvo MRav NGdn NLar SEND SMrm SPhx SWat WCom WFar WHil WMoo WPGP
'All Time High' new	NDov
applanata new	WCot
armena	CElw EBee EBla EWes MAvo MLLN MNrw SSvw WTin
benthamiana	CHEx
'Blackthorn'	NDov SMHy
'Burr Blanc'	SMHy SPhx
canadensis	CDes CKno CMac CRow EBee EBla ECha EPPr EPfP GCal GMaP GPoy LPio LPla MAvo NBir NLar NVic SPer SPhx SWat WAul WFar WMoo WOld WTin WWEG
'Cangshan Cranberry' new	SMHy
* ***caucasica***	EBee EPPr EWes LBMP LEdu LPla NBre SPhx
'Chocolate Tip'	EBee EBla ECtt IPot NBro
hakusanensis	CDes CHar CKno EBee EBla GBBs GCal GKev IFro IPot LEdu MAvo MNFA MNrw NBir NBre NBro NChi NDov SUsu WCot WFar WPGP WSHC WTin
- B&SWJ 8709	WCru
'John Coke'	NLar
magnifica	CDes EWes GCal LEdu SUsu WCot WPGP
- *alba*	see *S. albiflora*
menziesii	Widely available
- 'Dali Marble' (v)	CBow CCVN EBee ECtt NBPC NLar SPoG
- 'Wake Up' new	NDov
§ ***minor***	CArn CHby CPrp EBee EBla ELau GBar GKir GPoy MHer MNHC NBro NGHP NMir SIde SPhx SPlb WGwG WHer WJek WMoo
- subsp. ***minor***	EBWF
obtusa	Widely available
- 'Chatto'	EBee ECha
- silver-leaved new	MAvo
- white-flowered	CDes MAvo MMuc WPGP
officinalis	CArn CKno COIW CWan EBWF EBee EBla EHoe EHrv EPPr GBar GQue LPio MHer MNFA NMir SPer SPhx SWat WCAu WFar WMoo WWEG
- CDC 282	SPhx
- CDC 292	GQue WCot
- from Mongolia	LEdu
- 'Arnhem'	CKno CMdw EBla EPPr LEdu LPla NDov SMHy SMrm SPhx SUsu WCot WPGP WTin
- 'False Tanna'	CSpe CWib WFar
- 'Lemon Splash' (v)	CBow EBee EBla MAvo WCom WCot
- 'Martin's Mulberry'	CDes EWes MAvo NDov
- 'Pink Tanna'	CDes CElw CKno CPrp EBee EBla EPPr GBBs LEdu MAvo MCot MDKP MGos MMuc MNFA NBid NBre NBro NDov NSti SEND SMHy SMrm SPhx SUsu WCAu WCot WMoo WTin WWEG
- 'Red Thunder'	CSpe EBee ECtt EPPr IPot LRHS MAvo NCGa NDov NLar WCAu WWEG
- 'Shiro-fukurin' (v)	CDes EBee EWes MAvo NLar WCot
parviflora	see *S. tenuifolia* var. *parviflora*
pimpinella	see *S. minor*
'Pink Brushes'	EBla NDov NLar
'Rock and Roll' new	NLar
sitchensis	see *S. stipulata*
§ ***stipulata***	EBee EBrs GCal GKir LRHS MAvo MNrw
- var. ***riishirensis***	EBee MAvo
'Tanna'	Widely available
'Tanna' seedling	EPPr EShb
tenuifolia	CEnt EBla GBBs GCal GKir IFro LRHS MCot MHer NLar SBHP SMrm SPhx
- var. ***alba***	CKno CPrp EBee EBla EWes GCal GQue IMou LPio MAvo MRav NDov SMad SMrm SPhx WCom WCot WFar WMoo WOld WWEG
- - 'Korean Snow'	MAvo MNFA NDov SMHy SPhx SUsu
- 'Big Pink'	GCal MAvo MNrw
- 'Henk Gerritsen' new	NDov
§ - var. ***parviflora***	CDes EBee LEdu MAvo MNrw NCob NLar WPGP WTin
- - white-flowered	EBla
- 'Pink Elephant'	CDes CHar CKno EBee EBla ECtt EPPr GBin LEdu MAvo NDov NLar SMad WCAu WMoo WPGP WTin
- 'Pink Tickler' new	NDov
- var. ***purpurea***	CDes
- 'Purpurea'	CKno EBee EBla EPPr LEdu MAvo MDun NLar SPhx WCom WCot WFar WPGP
- 'Stand Up Comedian'	EBee MAvo NDov NLar WWEG
- 'Sturdy Guard'	EBee IPot
- 'White Elephant'	EBla

Sanicula (*Apiaceae*)

europaea	EBWF EBee GBar GPoy NSco WHer WTin

Sansevieria (*Dracaenaceae*)

trifasciata	EShb
'Moonshine' ♀H1	

Santolina (*Asteraceae*)

§ ***chamaecyparissus*** ♀H4	Widely available
- var. ***corsica***	see *S. chamaecyparissus* 'Nana'
- 'Double Lemon' (d)	EBee EPfP WSpi
- 'Lambrook Silver'	CArn CDoC EBee ECtt EOHP EPfP LBMP LRHS MAsh NLar SBfd SCoo SLim SPoG WJek
- 'Lemon Queen'	CArn CDoC EBee EPfP GBar LRHS MAsh MGos MNHC MSwo NBir NLar SBfd SIde SWat WFar WGwG WJek WSpi

- subsp. ***magonica***	GKir WAbe
§ - 'Nana' ♀H4	CBar CPrp EBee ECho EPfP LRHS MAsh MHer MRav MSwo SPoG SRms SWat WGrn WPer
- 'Pretty Carroll'	CAbP EBee ECtt ELan EPfP GBar GGar LRHS LSRN LSou LTen MAsh MBri NLar SIde WFar WJek
- 'Small-Ness'	CMea EBee ECho ELan EPfP EWes GBar GEdr LRHS MAsh MHer SPer STre SWvt WAbe WCom WJek WPer
- 'Weston'	ECho
incana	see *S. chamaecyparissus*
pectinata	see *S. rosmarinifolia* subsp. *canescens*
pinnata	CArn CSev MHer MLHP WPer
§ - subsp. ***neapolitana*** ♀H4	CArn CSBt CSev CWib EBee ECha ECho ELan EPfP GBar MBri MMuc MNHC NCob NPri SDix SEND SIde WEas WMnd WTin WWEG
- - cream-flowered	see *S. pinnata* subsp. *neapolitana* 'Edward Bowles'
§ - - 'Edward Bowles'	Widely available
- - 'Sulphurea'	CArn CMea EBee ECGP EPfP LRHS MAsh NCob SBfd SPer SPhx SPoG WKif WPer
rosmarinifolia	CArn CChe CDoC CDul CWan EBee GPoy LRHS MMuc MRav MSCN SEND SLon SPlb SRms STre WCom
§ - subsp. ***canescens***	EBee EPfP WPer
- 'Lemon Fizz'	EBee EPPr LBMP LRHS LSou NPri SBfd SPoG SWvt
§ - subsp. ***rosmarinifolia***	CBar CPrp CSev ECha ECrN ELan EPfP GBar MHer MRav SBfd SDix SIde SPer SWvt WBrE WDin WFar WGwG WHoo WJek
- - 'Primrose Gem' ♀H4	CBcs CDoC CPrp CSBt CSam CTri EBee ECha ECho ECrN EPfP GBar LHop LRHS MAsh MMuc MRav MSwo MWat NCob NLar NPri SBfd SEND SPer SPoG SWvt WJek WSpi
- - white-flowered	SSvw
tomentosa	see *S. pinnata* subsp. *neapolitana*
virens	see *S. rosmarinifolia* subsp. *rosmarinifolia*
viridis	see *S. rosmarinifolia* subsp. *rosmarinifolia*

Sanvitalia (*Asteraceae*)

Aztekengold = 'Starbini'PBR	LAst WGor
'Little Sun'	SPet
procumbens 'Irish Eyes'	CSpe
'Sunbini'PBR	CCCN CSpe LSou NPri SVil

Sapindus (*Sapindaceae*)

saponaria var. ***drummondii***	EGFP

Saponaria (*Caryophyllaceae*)

'Bressingham' ♀H4	ECho ECtt EDAr EPfP EPot LBee NMen WPat
Bressingham hybrid	LRHS
caespitosa	ECho EDAr EWes
× ***lempergii*** 'Max Frei'	CAbP CSam EBee ELon EPPr EWTr LSou MCot MRav NCob SAga SPhx WCot WSHC
ocymoides ♀H4	CMea EBee ECha ECho ECtt EDAr EHon EPfP GAbr GBar GKev LAst LRHS MLHP MMuc MNHC NMen NPri NVic SEND SPer SPlb SPoG SRms SRot SWal WBor WCFE WFar WPer
- 'Alba'	ECha ECho WFar
- 'Rubra Compacta' ♀H4	WAbe
- 'Snow Tip'	ECho ECtt EDAr EPfP NGdn NLar SBch
- 'Splendens'	ECho
officinalis	CArn CBre CPbn CWan EBWF GBar GPoy LEdu MHer MLHP MNHC NPri SIde SPlb WFar WHer WJek WMoo WPer WPtf
- 'Alba Plena' (d)	CBre EBee EWTr GBar GGar MMuc NLar SEND SHar WFar WHer WPer WPtf WTin
- 'Betty Arnold' (d)	EBee ECtt EWes GMac MHer WCot WFar WTin
§ - 'Dazzler' (v)	WHer WWEG
- 'Rosea Plena' (d)	Widely available
- 'Rubra Plena' (d)	CAby CBre ELan EWes MMuc MSCN MWhi NBre SHar WHer WTin
- 'Variegata'	see *S. officinalis* 'Dazzler'
× ***olivana*** ♀H4	CPBP ECho ECtt EPot NLAp NLar NMen
pamphylica	MNrw
persica	ITim
pumila	GKev
'Rosenteppich'	CPBP ECtt WPat
zawadskii	see *Silene zawadskii*

Saposhnikovia (*Apiaceae*)

divaricata	CArn

Sarcocapnos (*Papaveraceae*)

enneaphylla	LSRN

Sarcococca ✿ (*Buxaceae*)

confusa ♀H4	Widely available
hookeriana ♀H4	CPLG EPfP IFoB LAst LRHS LSRN LTen MBlu MDun MSwo NLar NPri SBfd WAbe WFar WPGP
- B&SWJ 2585	WCru
- HWJK 2393	WCru
§ - Sch 2396	CPMA EPla WCru
- var. ***digyna*** ♀H4	Widely available
- - 'Purple Stem'	CPLG CPMA CTri EPfP EPla LRHS MGos MRav NLar NPnk SBfd SCoo SPoG WClo WCru WDin
- var. ***hookeriana***	CPMA LSRN
- - GWJ 9369	WCru
- - Sch 1160	CGHE
- var. ***humilis***	Widely available
- 'Schillingii'	see *S. hookeriana* Sch 2396
orientalis	CAbP CMCN CPLG CPMA EBee ELan EPfP EPla LRHS MAsh MGos SPoG SSpi WFar WPGP WPat WSpi
'Roy Lancaster'	see *S. ruscifolia* var. *chinensis* 'Dragon Gate'
ruscifolia	CBcs CBgR CDoy CDul CMCN CMHG CPLG CPMA CSBt EBee ECrN ELan EPfP EPla EWTr GKir LAst LRHS MAsh MGos MRav NEgg SLim SLon SPer SRms SSpi WCru WFar
- var. ***chinensis*** ♀H4	CPMA CSam EPfP EPla SLon WCru WFar WPGP
- - L 713	EPla
§ - - 'Dragon Gate'	CDoC CGHE CPLG CPMA EBee ELan EPfP EPla LLHF LRHS LSRN MAsh MBlu NLar SChF SLim SLon SPoG SReu SSta WCru WPGP WPat
saligna	CBcs CPMA EBee EBtc EPfP LRHS NLar SLon SPoG WCru

- MF P2056	WCru
vagans B&SWJ 7285	WCru
wallichii	CBcs CGHE CPLG CPMA MBlu SPoG WPGP WPat
- B&SWJ 2291	WCru
- GWJ 9427	WCru
zeylanica var. ***brevifolia*** GWJ 9480 **new**	WCru

Sarmienta (*Gesneriaceae*)

repens ♀H2	CGHE CPLG EBee GKev WAbe WPGP

Sarothamnus see *Cytisus*

Sarracenia ✿ (*Sarraceniaceae*)

× ***ahlesii***	CHew
alata	CHew CSWC EECP MCCP NChu SHmp WSSs
- all green	SHmp
- 'Black Tube'	WSSs
- heavily-veined	SHmp WSSs
- pubescent	EECP NChu WSSs
- 'Red Lid'	CSWC EECP NChu WSSs
- 'Red Lid' × ***flava*** red pitcher	EECP
- wavy lid	SHmp WSSs
- white-flowered	WSSs
alata × ***flava*** var. ***maxima***	CSWC NChu
× ***areolata***	CHew CSWC NChu WSSs
× ***catesbyi*** ♀H1	CHew CSWC NChu SHmp WSSs
× ***courtii***	CSWC NChu
'Dixie Lace'	CSWC
× ***excellens*** ♀H1	CSWC NChu WSSs
× ***exornata***	CSWC NChu SPlb
flava ♀H1	CSWC MCCP MREP NChu WSSs
- all green giant	see *S. flava* var. *maxima*
- var. ***atropurpurea***	EECP WSSs
- 'Burgundy'	WSSs
- var. ***cuprea***	CSWC NChu SHmp WSSs
- var. ***flava***	CHew EECP WSSs
§ - var. ***maxima***	CHew CSWC EECP NChu WSSs
- var. ***ornata***	CHew CSWC EECP NChu SHmp WSSs
- var. ***rubricorpora***	CHew EECP NChu SHmp WSSs
- var. ***rugelii***	CHew EECP SHmp WSSs
- veinless	CSWC
× ***harperi***	CSWC NChu
'Juthatip Soper'	SHmp WSSs
'Ladies in Waiting'	CSWC
leucophylla ♀H1	CHew CSWC NChu SHmp WSSs
- from Okaloosa Co., Florida	SHmp
- 'Deer Park Alabama'	SHmp
- green	WSSs
- green and white **new**	WSSs
- pubescent	WSSs
- 'Schnell's Ghost'	WSSs
- 'Tarnok'	WSSs
leucophylla × ***oreophila***	CSWC EECP NChu
leucophylla × (× ***popei***)	EECP
'Lynda Butt'	CSWC SHmp WSSs
× ***miniata***	EECP SHmp
minor	CSWC EECP NChu SHmp WSSs
- var. ***minor***	CHew
§ - 'Okee Giant'	CSWC NChu WSSs
- var. ***okeefenokeensis***	CHew
- 'Okefenokee Giant'	see *S. minor* 'Okee Giant'
minor × ***oreophila***	CSWC
× ***mitchelliana*** ♀H1	SHmp WSSs
× ***moorei***	CHew WSSs
- 'Brook's Hybrid'	CHew CSWC EECP NChu WSSs
oreophila	CHew CSWC MYeo NChu SHmp WSSs
oreophila × ***purpurea*** subsp. ***venosa***	CSWC NChu
× ***popei***	CSWC NChu
psittacina	CHew CSWC EECP NChu SHmp WSSs
* - f. ***heterophylla***	CSWC
purpurea	MREP SPlb
- subsp. ***purpurea***	CHew CSWC MCCP NChu SHmp WSSs
- - f. ***heterophylla***	CSWC MYeo WSSs
- subsp. ***venosa***	CHew CSWC SHmp WSSs
- - var. ***burkii***	CSWC NChu WSSs
× ***readii***	SHmp WSSs
- 'Farnhamii'	CSWC EECP NChu
× ***rehderi***	SHmp
rubra	CSWC EECP NChu WSSs
- subsp. ***alabamensis***	CHew CSWC NChu SHmp WSSs
- subsp. ***gulfensis***	CHew CSWC NChu SHmp WSSs
* - - f. ***heterophylla***	CSWC WSSs
- subsp. ***jonesii***	CSWC EECP NChu WSSs
* - - f. ***heterophylla***	CSWC WSSs
- subsp. ***rubra***	CHew CSWC WSSs
- subsp. ***wherryi***	CHew CSWC EECP NChu WSSs
- - giant	WSSs
- - yellow-flowered	CSWC WSSs
× ***swaniana***	SHmp
'Umlanftiana'	CSWC
× ***wrigleyana*** ♀H1	MREP

Saruma (*Aristolochiaceae*)

henryi	CDes CLAP CPom EBee LSou MAvo SUsu WCot WCru WPGP WSHC

Sasa (*Poaceae*)

chrysantha misapplied	see *Pleioblastus chino*
disticha 'Mirrezuzume'	see *Pleioblastus pygmaeus* 'Mirrezuzume'
glabra f. ***albostriata***	see *Sasaella masamuneana* 'Albostriata'
kagamiana	NLar
kurilensis	EBee EPla LPal MWhi MWht NMoo WFar WJun
§ - 'Shima-shimofuri' (v)	EPPr EPfP EPla MMoz MWht WJun
- 'Shimofuri'	see *S. kurilensis* 'Shima-shimofuri'
- short	EPla
nana	see *S. veitchii* f. *minor*
nipponica	WJun
oshidensis	EPla
§ ***palmata***	CDul COld CWib EBee EHoe MCCP MMuc MWhi SBfd SEND SLim WDin WFar WHer
- f. ***nebulosa***	CBcs CBct CDoC CFir CHEx EBee EHul ENBC EPfP EPla EWes MBrN MMoz MWht NLar NMoo SAPC SArc WDyG WFar WJun WMoo
quelpaertensis	EPla MWht
tessellata	see *Indocalamus tessellatus*
tsuboiana	CDoC EBee ENBC EPla GQui LPal MMoz MWht NGdn NLar SBig WDyG WFar WMoo WPnP
§ ***veitchii***	CBcs CDoy CKno CTrC EBee ECha EHoe ENBC EPfP EPla GKir LEdu LRHS MMoz MMuc MRav MWht NLar NMoo SEND SPer WDin WFar WJun WMoo
§ - f. ***minor***	EBee MCCP WMoo

Sasaella (*Poaceae*)

glabra	see *S. masamuneana*
§ ***masamuneana***	ENBC EPla WDyG
§ - 'Albostriata' (v)	CDoC CEnt CWib EBee ENBC EPPr EPla LEdu LPal LRHS MCCP MMoz MMuc MWhi MWht NGdn NMoo SBig SEND WDyG WFar WJun WMoo WPGP
- f. ***aureostriata*** (v)	EPla MMoz NPal
§ ***ramosa***	CHEx EPla MCCP MMoz MWht NMoo WDin

Sassafras (*Lauraceae*)

albidum	CArn CBcs CCCN CMCN EBee EPfP LEdu LRHS MBri SBfd SSpi WPGP
tzumu	CGHE WPGP

satsuma see *Citrus unshiu*

Satureja ✿ (*Lamiaceae*)

coerulea ♀H4	CWan ECho EWes NBir
douglasii	EOHP GBar SBfd SHDw WJek
- 'Indian Mint'PBR	CArn MHer NGHP
hortensis	CBod ELau GPoy ILis MHer MNHC SBfd SIde WJek
- 'Selektion'	LLWP
macedonica new	LLWP
montana	CArn CHby CWan ECho ELau EPot GKev GPoy ILis LLWP MBri MHer MNHC NGHP NMen SBfd SDix SEND SIde SRms SVic WHfH WJek WPer
* - ***citriodora***	GPoy LLWP MHer
§ - subsp. ***illyrica***	WJek WPer
- 'Purple Mountain'	GPoy LLWP MHer
- ***subspicata***	see *S. montana* subsp. *illyrica*
parnassica	LLWP WPer
repanda	see *S. spicigera*
seleriana	SDys SPhx
§ ***spicigera***	CArn CBod CPBP CPrp ECho ELau EPot GBar LEdu LLWP MHer NBir NMen SIde WJek WPer
thymbra	CArn SBfd SHDw

Saurauia (*Actinidiaceae*)

subspinosa	CHEx

Sauromatum (*Araceae*)

guttatum	see *S. venosum*
§ ***venosum***	CArn CDes CMea CPLG CStu EAmu EBee ECho EShb GCal LAma LEdu LRHS NLar SBig SHaC WCot WCru WPGP
- CC 3810	WCot

Saururus (*Saururaceae*)

cernuus	CBen CHEx CRow CWat EHon ELan LLWG LPBA MWts SRms SWat WMAq
chinensis	CRow

Saussurea (*Asteraceae*)

albescens	WCot
costus	CArn
deltoidea WWJ 11652	WCru
nepalensis new	CStu
aff. ***superba*** new	GKev
velutina SDR 6176 new	GKev

savory, summer see *Satureja hortensis*

savory, winter see *Satureja montana*

Saxegothaea (*Podocarpaceae*)

conspicua	CBcs CDoC CDul GBin IDee IFFs NLar

Saxifraga ✿ (*Saxifragaceae*)

sp.	NMen WAbe
'Ada' (× *petraschii*) (7)	NMen
'Aemula' (× *borisii*) (7)	NMen
'Affinis' (× *petraschii*) (7) new	CPBP
aizoides (9)	ECho
- SDR 5497	GKev
- var. ***atrorubens*** (9)	ECho
aizoon	see *S. paniculata*
'Aladdin' (× *borisii*) (7)	NMen
'Alan Hayhurst' (8)	WAbe WFar
'Alan Martin' (× *boydilacina*) (7)	ECho MHer NLar NMen
'Alba' (*oppositifolia*) (7)	ECho ELan EWes ITim NHol NWCA WAbe
'Alba' (× *apiculata*) (7)	ECho EDAr EPot MHer NMen NRya SPlb WCom WFar WPat
'Alba' (× *arco-valleyi*)	see *S.* 'Ophelia'
'Albert Einstein' (× *apiculata*) (7)	NMen
'Albertii' (*callosa*)	see *S.* 'Albida'
§ 'Albida' (*callosa*) (8)	ECho MAsh WAbe
'Albrecht Dürer' (Lasciva Group) (7)	WAbe
'Aldebaran' (× *borisii*) (7)	NMen
'Aldo Bacci' (Milford Group) (7)	NMen
'Alfons Mucha' (7)	EPot GCrs NMen WPat
'Allendale Acclaim' (× *lismorensis*) (7)	EPot NMen
'Allendale Accord' (*diapensioides* × *lilacina*) (7)	MAsh NMen NWCA
'Allendale Allure' (*aretiodes* × *stolitzkae*) (7)	NMen
'Allendale Amber' (7)	NMen
'Allendale Andante' (× *arco-valleyi*) (7)	NMen
'Allendale Angel' (× *kepleri*) (7)	NMen WAbe
'Allendale Argonaut' (7)	NMen
'Allendale Ballad' (7)	NMen WAbe
'Allendale Ballet' (7)	NMen
'Allendale Bamby' (× *lismorensis*) (7)	NMen
'Allendale Banshee' (7)	NMen
'Allendale Beau' (× *lismorensis*) (7)	CPBP NMen
'Allendale Beauty' (*aretiodes* × *cinerea*) (7)	CPBP NMen
'Allendale Betty' (× *lismorensis*) (7)	NMen
'Allendale Billows' (7)	NMen
'Allendale Blossom' (× *limorensis*) (7)	NMen
'Allendale Bonny' (7)	NMen WAbe
'Allendale Boon' (× *izari*) (7)	NMen
'Allendale Bounty' (7)	NMen
'Allendale Bravo' (× *lismorensis*) (7)	NMen WAbe
'Allendale Cabal' (7)	NMen
'Allendale Celt' (× *novacastelensis*) (7)	NMen

	'Allendale Charm' (Swing Group) (7)	CPBP NMen WAbe
	'Allendale Chick' (7)	NHar NMen
	'Allendale Comet' (7)	NMen
	'Allendale Dance' (7)	NMen
	'Allendale Desire' (7)	WAbe
	'Allendale Divine' (7)	WAbe
	'Allendale Dream' (7)	EPot NMen
	'Allendale Duo' (*aretiodes* × *georgei*) (7)	NMen WAbe
	'Allendale Elegance' (7)	NMen
	'Allendale Elf' (7)	ITim NMen
	'Allendale Elite' (7)	NMen
	'Allendale Enchantment' (7)	NMen
	'Allendale Envoy' (7)	MAsh NMen WAbe
	'Allendale Epic' (*ferdinandi-cobirgi* × *wendelboi*) (7)	EPot NHar NMen WAbe
	'Allendale Fairy' (7)	MAsh NHar NMen
	'Allendale Fame' (7)	NMen
	'Allendale Fancy' (7)	WAbe
	'Allendale Frost' (7)	NMen
	'Allendale Garnet' (7)	NMen
	'Allendale Ghost' (7)	NMen
	'Allendale Goblin' (7)	NMen NWCA WAbe
	'Allendale Grace' (7)	NMen WAbe
	'Allendale Gremlin' (7)	NMen
	'Allendale Harvest' (7)	NMen
	'Allendale Hobbit' (*matta-florida* × *poluminiana*) (7)	EPot MAsh NHar NMen WAbe
	'Allendale Host' (*andersonii* × *poluminiana*) (7)	NMen WAbe
	'Allendale Icon' (× *polulacina*) (7)	WAbe
	'Allendale Imp' (7)	WAbe
	'Allendale Ina' (7)	NHar NMen WAbe
	'Allendale Joy' (× *wendelacina*) (7)	NMen
	'Allendale Pearl' (× *novacastelensis*) (7)	NMen
	'Allendale Ruby' (7)	NMen
	'Allendale Snow' (× *rayei*) (7)	NMen
	'Alpenglow' (7)	NMen
	alpigena (7)	WAbe
	'Amitie' (× *gloriana*) (7)	CFee NMen
	andersonii (7)	NMen NRya
	'Andrea Cesalpino' (Renaissance Group) (7)	NMen
	angustifolia Haw.	see *S. hypnoides*
	'Anna' (× *fontanae*) (7)	NMen WAbe
	'Anne Beddall' (× *goringiana*) (7)	NMen WAbe
	'Antonio Vivaldi' (7)	NMen WAbe
	× ***apiculata*** sensu stricto hort.	see *S.* 'Gregor Mendel'
	'Apple Blossom' (15)	ECtt GKev NRya WGor
	'Arabella' (× *edithae*) (7)	ECho
§	'Arco' (× *arco-valleyi*) (7)	NMen
	× ***arco-valleyi*** sensu stricto hort.	see *S.* 'Arco'
	× ***arendsii*** purple-flowered (15)	SPlb
§	'Aretiastrum' (× *boydii*) (7)	NMen
	aretioides (7)	NMen
	'Argia Romani' (7)	NMen
	'Ariel' (× *hornibrookii*) (7)	NMen
	'Arthur' (× *anglica*) (7)	NMen
	'Asahi' (*fortunei*) (5) new	IVic

	'Assimilis' (× *petraschii*) (7)	NMen
	'Aufheiter von Eri' (*fortunei*) (5) new	IVic
	'August Hayek' (× *leyboldii*) (7)	NMen
	'Aurea Maculata' (*cuneifolia*)	see *S.* 'Aureopunctata'
	'Aurea' (*umbrosa*)	see *S.* 'Aureopunctata'
§	'Aureopunctata' (× *urbium*) (11/v)	CMac CTri ECha ECho ELan GKev GKir GMaP LBMP LRHS MHer MRav NDov NHol SBfd SPer SPlb SPoG SRms STre WCom WMoo
	'Autumn Tribute' (*fortunei*) (5)	CLAP WAbe WFar
	'Ayer's Rock' (7)	WAbe
	'Balcana' (*paniculata*) (8)	EPot WAbe
	'Baldensis'	see *S.* 'Minutifolia' (*paniculata*)
§	'Beatrix Stanley' (7)	ECho LRHS MHer NHol NMen NRya WGor
	'Becky Foster' (× *borisii*) (7)	NMen
	'Bellisant' (× *hornibrookii*) (7)	NMen
	'Berenika' (× *bertolonii*) (7)	NMen
	'Beryl' (× *anglica*) (7)	NMen
	'Bettina' (× *paulinae*) (7)	NMen
	× ***biasolettoi*** sensu stricto hort.	see *S.* 'Phoenix'
	× ***bilekii*** (7)	ECho NMen
	'Black Beauty' (15)	CMoH MHer
	'Black Ruby' (*fortunei*) (5)	Widely available
	'Blackberry and Apple Pie' (*fortunei*) (5)	CBct CBod CElw CLAP EAEE EBee ECtt GEdr IBal IVic LOck LRHS MBrN MLHP MNrw NMen NMyG SBch SWvt WAul WCot WFar WWEG
	'Blaník' (× *borisii*) (7)	NMen
	'Blanka' (× *borisii*) (7)	NMen
	'Bob Hawkins' (15/v)	EDAr LRHS NHol
§	'Bodensee' (× *hofmannii*) (7)	EPot WPat
	'Bohdalec' (× *megaseiflora*) (7)	NMen
	'Bohemia' (7)	ECho NLar NMen NWCA
	× ***borisii*** sensu stricto hort.	see *S.* 'Sofia'
	'Bornmuelleri' (7)	NMen
	'Boston Spa' (× *elisabethae*) (7)	ECho ECtt LRHS MHer NLAp NLar NMen SPlb WPat
	'Brailes' (× *poluanglica*) (7)	NMen
	'Brian Arundel' (Magnus Group) (7)	NMen
	'Bridget' (× *edithae*) (7)	ECho LRHS NMen
	'Brimstone' (7)	NMen WAbe
	'Brno' (× *elisabethae*) (7)	EPot NMen
	'Brookside' (*burseriana*) (7)	EPot NMen
	brunoniana	see *S. brunonis*
§	***brunonis*** (1)	GKev
	- CC 5315	EWld
	- CC&McK 108	NWCA
	'Bryn Llwyd'	WAbe
	bryoides (10)	ECho
	× ***burnatii*** (8)	LRHS NMen WAbe WGor
	burseriana (7)	ECho NLAp WAbe WGor
	'Buster' (× *hardingii*) (7)	NMen
	'Buttercup' (× *kayei*) (7)	EPot ITim NMen NWCA WHoo
	× ***byam-groundsii*** (7)	WFar
	caesia misapplied (× *fritschiana*)	see *S.* 'Krain'
	caesia L. (8)	SRms WAbe
§	***callosa*** (8) ♀H4	ECho EDAr GEdr MDKP MLHP NHol WAbe WFar WPat WTin
	- subsp. ***callosa*** (8)	ECho

§	- - var. ***australis*** (8)	GCrs GKev NBro NHol NMen
	- var. ***lantoscana***	see *S. callosa* subsp. *callosa* var. *australis*
	- ***lingulata***	see *S. callosa*
	'Cambridge Seedling' (7)	NMen
	'Camyra' (7)	WAbe
	× ***canis-dalmatica***	see *S.* 'Canis-dalmatica'
§	'Canis-dalmatica' (× *gaudinii*) (8) 🏆^{H4}	EChο ECtt GEdr GGar LRHS NHar NHol NMen NWCA WGor WPer
§	'Carmen' (× *elisabethae*) (7)	NMen WAbe
§	'Carniolica' (*paniculata*) (8)	GKir NBro NHol NMen NWCA WCom
	carolinica	see *S.* 'Carniolica' (*paniculata*)
	cartilaginea	see *S. paniculata* subsp. *cartilaginea*
	'Castor' (× *bilekii*) (7)	NMen
	'Caterhamensis' (*cotyledon*) (8)	NHar
	'Cathy Reed' (× *polulacina*) (7)	NMen
	caucasica (7)	ECho WAbe
	cebennensis (15) 🏆^{H2}	NMen NRya
	cespitosa (15)	WAbe
	'Chambers' Pink Pride'	see *S.* 'Miss Chambers'
	'Charles Chaplin' (7)	ECho NHar NMen WAbe
	'Cheap Confections' (*fortunei*) (4)	CBct CLAP EBee ECtt GAbr GBee GEdr LLHF NMen SBch SBfd WBor WCot WFar WMoo WOld WPGP WWEG
§	***cherlerioides*** (10)	NRya WFar
	'Cherry Pie' (*fortunei*) (5)	CBct CLAP EBee GAbr LLHF LOck LRHS NBir NHar NMyG WCot
	'Cherrytrees' (× *boydii*) (7)	NMen WAbe
*	'Chetwynd' (*marginata*) (7)	NMen
	'Chez Nous' (× *gloriana*) (7/v)	NMen
	'Chodov' (7)	EPot NMen
	'Christine' (× *anglica*) (7)	ECho NHol NMen
	cinerea (7)	NMen WAbe
	'Cio-Cio-San' (Vanessa Group) (7)	NMen
	'Citronella' (7)	ECho WAbe
	'Claire Felstead' (*cinerea* × *poluniniana*) (7)	NMen
	'Clare' (× *anglica*) (7)	NMen
§	'Clarence Elliott' (*umbrosa*) (11) 🏆^{H4}	CMea CTri EBee ECho EWes GAbr GCal GJos GKev GMaP MDKP MHer NDov NHol NRya NVic STre WCom WFar WPat WWEG
	'Claude Monet' (Impressio Group) (7)	CPBP WAbe
	'Claudia' (× *borisii*) (7)	NMen
	'Cleo' (× *boydii*) (7)	NMen
	'Cloth of Gold' (*exarata* subsp. *moschata*) (15)	ECha ECho ECtt EDAr ELan GMaP LRHS MAsh MHer NHol NMen NRya SPer SPlb SPoG SRms WAbe WFar
	cochlearis (8)	CTri GEdr LRHS NBro NMen SBch STre WAbe WCom WPer
	'Cockscomb' (*paniculata*) (8)	ECho GEdr NHol NMen NRya WAbe
	columnaris (7)	NMen WAbe
	'Combrook' (× *poluanglica*) (7)	NMen
	'Coningsby Queen' (× *hornibrookii*) (7)	NMen
	continentalis (15)	NWCA
	'Conwy Snow' (*fortunei*) (5)	CLAP NHar WAbe WFar
	'Conwy Star' (*fortunei*) (5)	CLAP NHar WAbe WFar
	'Coolock Gem' (7)	NMen WAbe
	'Coolock Jean' (7)	NMen WAbe
	'Coolock Kate' (7)	NMen WAbe
	'Cordata' (*burseriana*) (7)	NMen
	'Corona' (× *boydii*) (7)	NMen
	'Corrennie Claret' (15)	EWes
	'Correvoniana' Farrer (*paniculata*) (8)	EDAr EPot MHer MSCN WFar
	cortusifolia (5)	CLAP CSpr ECho LRHS
	- B&SWJ 5879	WCru
	- var. ***stolonifera*** (5)	ECho GCal
	- - B&SWJ 6205	WCru
	'Cotton Crochet' (*fortunei*) (5/d)	CBct EBee ECtt GEdr LRHS NMyG SBfd SHeu WBor WCot WFar WOld
	cotyledon (8)	ECho MAsh NHol WAbe WCFE WEas WPer
§	'Cranbourne' (× *anglica*) (7) 🏆^{H4}	ECho EPot LRHS NHol NLAp NMen NWCA WCom WPat
	'Cream' (*paniculata*) (8)	ECho
	'Cream Seedling' (× *elisabethae*) (7)	ECho NMen
	'Crenata' (*burseriana*) (7)	EPot NMen
	'Crimscote-love' (*poluanglica*) (7)	NMen
	'Crimson Diall' (× *irvingii*) (7)	NMen
	'Crimson Rose' (*paniculata*)	see *S.* 'Rosea' (*paniculata*)
§	***crustata*** (8)	ECho MDKP NMen WAbe WThu
	- var. ***vochinensis***	see *S. crustata*
	'Crystal Pink' (*fortunei*) (5/v)	CBct CMil EBee ECtt EHrv GAbr GBBs GEdr IFoB ITim LOck LRHS NBro NHar NMen NMyG NPnk SGSe WCot WFar WGrn WOld
	'Crystalie' (× *biasolettoi*) (7)	LRHS NMen NRya WPat
	'Cultrata' (*paniculata*) (8)	NBro
	'Cumulus' (*iranica* hybrid) (7) 🏆^{H4}	EDAr EPot NMen WAbe
	cuneata (15)	NHol
§	***cuneifolia*** (11)	ECho GGar GKir IMou LBee MHer MWat NHol NWCA WCom WFar WPer
	- var. ***capillipes***	see *S. cuneifolia* subsp. *cuneifolia*
§	- subsp. ***cuneifolia*** (11)	ECtt
*	- var. ***subintegra*** (11)	ECho
	'Cuscutiformis' (*stolonifera*) (5)	CElw CHid EBla EWld GEdr MLLN SBch SMad SMrm SRms WBox WCru WPGP
	cymbalaria (2)	EBur
	dahurica	see *S. cuneifolia*
	'Dainty Dame' (× *arco-valleyi*) (7)	NMen NWCA
	'Dana' (× *megaseiflora*) (7)	NHol NMen
	'Dartington Double' (15/d)	EWes WFar
	'Dartington Double White' (15/d)	NHol
	'David' (7)	NMen
	'Dawn Frost' (7)	NMen
	'Delia' (× *hornibrookii*) (7)	ITim NMen
§	'Denisa' (× *pseudokotschyi*) (7)	NMen
	densa	see *S. cherlerioides*
	'Dentata' (× *geum*)	see *S.* 'Dentata' (× *polita*)
§	'Dentata' (× *polita*) (11)	CSpe ECha ECho GCal GGar MAvo SMHy WMoo WWEG
	'Dentata' (× *urbium*)	see *S.* 'Dentata' (× *polita*)
	desoulavyi (7)	NMen
	'Diana' ambig.	NLar
	diapensioides (7)	WAbe
	dinnikii (7)	NMen WAbe
	× ***dinninaris*** (7)	NMen
	'Dobruška' (× *irvingii*) (7)	NMen
	'Doctor Clay' (*paniculata*) (8)	EPot GEdr GKev LRHS NHar NMen NRya SPlb WAbe

	'Doctor Ramsey' (8)	ECho ECtt EWes GEdr LRHS NBro NHol NMen WAbe WGor WPnn
	'Donald Mann' (15)	EWes
	'Donnington Chalice'	NMen
	'Donnington Gold'	NMen
	'Donnington Veil'	NMen
	'Dorothy Milne' (7)	NMen
	'Drakula' (*ferdinandi-coburgi*) (7)	ECho GCrs LRHS NMen
	'Dubarry' (15)	EWes NRya
	'Dulcimer' (× *petraschii*) (7)	NMen
	'Edgar Irmscher' (7)	NMen
	'Edith' (× *edithae*) (7)	ECho LRHS
	'Edward Elgar' (× *megaseiflora*) (7)	NHol NMen
	'Elf' (7)	see *S.* 'Beatrix Stanley'
	'Eliot Hodgkin' (× *millstreamiana*) (7)	NMen
	× ***elisabethae*** sensu stricto hort.	see *S.* 'Carmen'
	× ***elisabethae*** Sünd. (7)	EDAr
	'Elizabeth Sinclair' (× *elisabethae*) (7)	EPot GKev NMen
	'Ellie Brinckerhoff' (× *hornibrookii*) (7)	NMen
	'Elliott's Variety'	see *S.* 'Clarence Elliott' (*umbrosa*)
§	'Ernst Heinrich' (× *heinrichii*) (7)	NMen
	'Esther' (× *burnatii*) (8)	CMea ECho GEdr GKev LRHS NHol NMen NWCA SRGP WAbe WPnn
§	'Eulenspiegel' (× *geuderi*) (7)	EPot NHol NMen
	'Eva Hanzliková' (× *izari*) (7)	NMen WAbe
	exarata (15)	NMen WAbe
	- subsp. ***moschata*** 'Elf' (15)	ECtt EPfP NHol NMen SRms WGor
	'Excellent' (Exclusive Group) (7)	EPot
	fair maids of France	see *S.* 'Flore Pleno'
	'Fairy' (*exarata* subsp. *moschata*) (15)	CMea ECtt ELan GKir WCom
	'Faldonside' (× *boydii*) (7) ♀H4	NMen NRya WPat
	'Falstaff' (*burseriana*) (7)	NHol NRya
	× ***farreri*** (15)	EPot GEdr
§	'Faust' (× *borisii*) (7)	NMen
	'Favorit' (× *bilekii*) (7)	NMen
§	***federici-augusti*** (7)	GCrs
§	- subsp. ***grisebachii*** (7) ♀H2-3	ECho NSla WAbe WFar
	'Ferdinand' (× *hofmannii*) (7)	NMen
	ferdinandi-coburgi (7) ♀H4	ECtt NRya WAbe
§	- subsp. ***chrysosplenifolia*** var. ***rhodopea*** (7)	ECho GCrs LRHS NMen
	- var. ***pravislavii***	see *S. ferdinandi-coburgi* subsp. *chrysosplenifolia* var. *rhodopea*
	- var. ***radoslavoffii***	see *S. ferdinandi-coburgi* subsp. *chrysosplenifolia* var. *rhodopea*
	'Findling' (15)	EPfP NHol NMen SPoG WAbe
	'Firebrand' (× *kochii*) (7)	NMen WAbe
	'Five Color' (*fortunei*)	see *S.* 'Go-nishiki'
§	***flagellaris*** (1)	NMen WAbe
	'Flavescens' misapplied	see *S.* 'Lutea' (*paniculata*)
	× ***fleischeri*** (7)	NMen
§	'Flore Pleno' (*granulata*) (15/d)	CFir EWes NBir SUsu WAbe WFar
	'Flowers of Sulphur'	see *S.* 'Schwefelblüte'
	'Flush' (× *petraschii*) (7)	WAbe
	fortunei (5) ♀H4	CHEx CLAP CMac ECho EWTr GAbr GKir GMaP NBir NPnk SRms WAbe WMoo
	- B&SWJ 6346	WCru
	- f. ***alpina*** (5)	CLAP
	- - from Hokkaido (5)	CLAP WCru
	- var. ***koraiensis*** (5) B&SWJ 8688	WCru
	- 'Musgrove Pink'	CLAP
	- var. ***obtusocuneata*** (5)	CLAP ECho LLHF NMen WAbe
	- f. ***partita*** (5)	CLAP GEdr WCru
	- var. ***pilosissima*** (5) B&SWJ 8557	WCru
	- pink-flowered (5)	CLAP WAbe WFar
	- var. ***suwoensis*** (5)	CLAP
	'Foster's Gold' (× *elisabethae*) (7)	NMen WAbe
	'Four Winds' (15)	EWes SPoG WCom
	'Francesco Redi' (Renaissance Group)	NMen WAbe
	'Francis Cade' (8)	EPot GAbr WAbe
	'Frank Sinatra' (× *poluanglica*) (7)	NMen
	'Franz Liszt' (7)	WAbe
	'Franzii' (× *paulinae*) (7)	NMen
	'Freckles'	CYeo GKev
	frederici-augusti	see *S. federici-augusti*
	'Frederik Chopin' (7)	WAbe
	'Friar Tuck' (× *boydii*) (7)	NMen
	'Friesei' (× *salmonica*) (7)	EPot NMen
	× ***fritschiana*** (8)	GEdr NMen
	'Fumiko' (*fortunei*) (5)	CLAP WAbe WCru
	'Funkii' (× *petraschii*) (7)	NMen
	'Gaertneri' (× *mariae-theresiae*) (7)	NMen
	'Gaiety' (15)	ECho GKir LRHS SPoG WFar
	'Galahad' (× *elizabethae*) (7)	NMen
	'Galaxie' (× *megaseiflora*) (7)	NMen
	'Ganymede' (*burseriana*) (7)	NMen
	'Gelber Findling' (7)	EPot WAbe
	'Gelbes Monster' (*fortunei*) (5) **new**	IVic
	'Gem' (× *irvingii*) (7)	NMen
	'General Joffre' (15)	see *S.* 'Maréchal Joffre'
	'Geoff Wilson' (× *biasolettoi*)	NMen
	'George Gershwin' (Blues Group) (7)	NMen
	georgei (7)	NMen WAbe
	- hybrid (7)	GCrs
	'Gertie Pritchard' (× *megaseiflora*)	see *S.* 'Mrs Gertie Prichard'
	× ***geuderi*** sensu stricto hort.	see *S.* 'Eulenspiegel'
§	× ***geum*** (11)	CHid MLHP MRav WFar WMoo
	- Dixter form (11)	ECha SMHy WFar WWEG
	'Gleborg' (15)	EWes GAbr SPoG
	'Gloria' (*burseriana*) (7) ♀H4	ECho LRHS NMen WCom WPat
	'Gloriana'	see *S.* 'Godiva'
	× ***gloriana*** sensu stricto hort. (7)	see *S.* 'Godiva'
	'Gloriosa' (× *gloriana*) (7)	see *S.* 'Godiva'
	'Glückliches Mädchen' (*fortunei*) (5) **new**	IVic
§	'Godiva' (× *gloriana*) (7)	NMen WAbe
	'Gold Dust' (× *eudoxiana*) (7)	ECho NLAp NMen NRya WCom
	'Gold Mound' **new**	WNew
	'Golden Falls' (15/v)	EWes LRHS NHol SPlb SPoG
	Golden Prague (× *pragensis*)	see *S.* 'Zlatá Praha'
§	'Go-nishiki' (*fortunei*) (5)	EBee LLHF
	'Gorges du Verdon' (8) **new**	GKev
	'Goring White' (7)	NMen
	'Gothenburg' (7)	EPot LBMP NMen WAbe WPat

'Grace Farwell' (× *anglica*) (7) ECho NHol NLar NMen NRya NWCA WCom WHoo
'Grace' (× *arendsii*) (15/v) see *S.* 'Seaspray'
granulata (15) CRWN EBWF ECho EDAr GJos NMir NSco NSla WAbe WFar
'Gratoides' (× *grata*) (7) NMen
§ 'Gregor Mendel' (× *apiculata*) (7) ♀H4 CMea CSam ECho ECtt LRHS NHol NLAp NLar NMen SRms WAbe WCom WFar WHoo
grisebachii see *S. federici-augusti* subsp. *grisebachii*
- subsp. ***montenegrina*** see *S. federici-augusti*
'Haagii' (× *eudoxiana*) (7) CTri ECho GKev NLAp NLar NMen
'Hare Knoll Beauty' (8) ECho GKev LRHS NHar NLAp NMen NRya NSla WAbe
'Harley' (7) NMen
'Harlow Car' (7) NMen NSla
'Harold Bevington' (*paniculata*) (8) GEdr
'Harold Lloyd' (7) NMen
'Harry Marshall' (× *irvingii*) (7) NHol NMen
'Hartswood White' (15) LRHS MWat
'Harvest Moon' (*stolonifera*) (5) CBow CHEx WHer
'Hedwig' (× *malbyana*) (7) NMen
× ***heinreichii*** sensu stricto hort. see *S.* 'Ernst Heinrich'
'Heisel Kurenai' (*fortunei*) (5) **new** IVic
'Hi-Ace' (15/v) ECtt EDAr MHer SPlb
'Hime' (*stolonifera*) (5) WCru
'Hindhead Seedling' (× *boydii*) (7) LRHS NMen
hirsuta (11) EBla EWTr EWld GGar IFro LRHS MMuc WCru
§ 'Hirsuta' (*paniculata*) EPot
'Hirsuta' (× *geum*) see *S.* × *geum*
'Hirtella' misapplied see *S.* 'Hirsuta'
'Hirtella' Ingwersen (*paniculata*) (8) EPot
'Hirtifolia' (*paniculata*) (8) GJos
'His Majesty' (× *irvingii*) (7) NMen WCom WFar
'Hiten' (*fortunei*) GKev
'Hocker Edge' (× *arco-valleyi*) (7) ITim NMen
'Holden Seedling' (15) ECtt EWes
'Honington' (× *poluanglica*) (7) NMen
× ***hornibrookii*** (7) WPat
hostii (8) ECho EDAr GKev NHol NLAp WTin
- subsp. ***hostii*** (8) GAuc GEdr
- - var. ***altissima*** (8) STre
- subsp. ***rhaetica*** (8) GBin NBro NMen WAbe
'Hradčany' (× *megaseiflora*) (7) NMen
'Hsitou Silver' (*stolonifera*) (5) CFee EBee EPPr MDKP SPhx WCru
'Hunscote' (× *poluanglica*) (7) NMen
hybrid JB 11 NMen
§ ***hypnoides*** (15) SPoG WAbe
hypostoma (7) WAbe
'Iceland' (*oppositifolia*) (7) EWes WAbe
'Icicle' (× *elisabethae*) (7) NMen
'Idlecote' NMen
'Ignaz Dörfler' (× *doerfleri*) (7) NMen WAbe
imparilis (5) CLAP EHrv GEdr WCru
'Ingeborg' (15) ECha
iranica (7) NMen
- pink-flowered (7) CPBP
'Irene Bacci' (× *baccii*) (7) NMen
× ***irvingii*** (7) ECho EPot
× ***irvingii*** sensu stricto hort. see *S.* 'Walter Irving'
'Ivana' (× *caroliquarti*) (7) NMen WAbe
'Jan Neruda' (× *megaseiflora*) (7) NMen
'Jan Palach' (× *krausii*) (7) NMen
'Jason' (× *elisabethae*) (7) NMen
'Jenkinsiae' (× *irvingii*) (7) ♀H4 CFee ECho EDAr EPot LRHS NLAp NMen NRya WAbe WCom WPat
§ 'Johann Kellerer' (× *kellereri*) (7) CFee WAbe
'John Byam-Grounds' (Honor Group) (7) WAbe
'John Tomlinson' (*burseriana*) (7) NMen
'Jorg' (× *biasolettoi*) (7) EPot
'Josef Čapek' (× *megaseiflora*) (7) NMen
'Josef Mánes' (× *borisii*) (7) NMen
'Joy' see *S.* 'Kaspar Maria Sternberg'
'Judith Shackleton' (× *abingdonensis*) (7) NHol NMen WAbe
'Juliet' see *S.* 'Riverslea'
§ ***juniperifolia*** (7) CMea ECho EDAr GAbr LRHS NLAp NWCA SRms
'Jupiter' (× *megaseiflora*) (7) NMen
'Kampa' (7) NMen
'Kanna' (*fortunei*) (5) **new** IVic
karadzicensis (7) NMen
'Karasin' (7) NMen
'Karel Čapek' (× *megaseiflora*) (7) ECho LRHS NMen NRya NSla WAbe
'Karel Stivín' (× *edithae*) (7) NMen
§ 'Kaspar Maria Sternberg' (× *petraschii*) (7) LRHS NMen WPat
'Kath Dryden' (7) ECho ECtt GEdr GKev NHol
'Kathleen Pinsent' (8) ♀H4 ECho NWCA WCom
'Kathleen' (× *polulacina*) (7) WAbe WFar
× ***kellereri*** sensu stricto hort. see *S.* 'Johann Kellerer'
'Ken McGregor' (7) WAbe
'Kestoniensis' (× *salmonica*) (7) NMen
'Kew Gem' (× *petraschii*) (7) ECho NMen
'Kewensis' (× *kellereri*) (7) NMen WAbe
'Kineton' (× *poluanglica*) (7) ITim NMen
'King Lear' (× *bursiculata*) (7) ECho EPot LRHS NMen
'Kinki Purple' (*stolonifera*) (5) EBee EHrv ELon EWld GGar WCru WPGP
'Knapton Pink' (15) ECtt EDAr EPfP NRya SPoG WAbe WCom WFar
'Knapton White' (15) SPoG
'Knebworth' (8) ECho
* 'Koigokora' (*fortunei*) (5) WOld
'Kokaku' (fortunei) LLHF
'Kon Tiki' (7) WAbe
* 'Kosumosu' (*fortunei*) (5) WOld
kotschyi × ***wendelboi*** EPot
'Koukan' (*fortunei*) (5) **new** IVic
§ 'Krain' (× *fritschiana*) (8) ECho
'Krákatit' (× *megaseiflora*) (7) NMen
'Krasava' (× *megaseiflora*) (7) EPot ITim NMen
'Kyrilli' (× *borisii*) (7) NMen
'Labe' (× *arco-valleyi*) (7) EPot NMen WAbe
'Ladislav Čelakovský' (7) NMen
'Lady Beatrix Stanley' see *S.* 'Beatrix Stanley'
'Lagraveana' (*paniculata*) (8) ♀H4 ECho ECtt EDAr LRHS MMuc NRya WGor

× ***landaueri*** sensu stricto hort. — see *S.* 'Leonore'
'Lemon Hybrid' (× *boydii*) (7) — NMen
'Lemon Spires' (7) — NMen WAbe
'Lenka' (× *byam-groundsii*) (7) — NMen NSla
'Leo Gordon Godseff' (× *elisabethae*) (7) — ECho LRHS NMen
§ 'Leonore' (× *landaueri*) (7) — ECho LRHS WFar
'Letchworth Gem' (× *urbium*) (11) — ECho GCal NWCA
'Licht des Cerise' (*fortunei*) (5) new — IVic
'Lidice' (7) — NMen WAbe WHoo
'Lilac Time' (× *youngiana*) (7) — NMen WAbe
lilacina (7) — NMen WCom WPat
lilacina × ***lowndesii*** (7) new — CPBP
'Limelight' (*callosa* subsp. *callosa* var. *australis*) (8) — WAbe
'Lindau' (7) — NMen
lingulata — see *S. callosa*
'Lismore Carmine' (× *lismorensis*) (7) — GCrs NMen
'Lismore Gem' (× *lismorensis*) (7) — ECho NMen
'Lismore Mist' (× *lismorensis*) (7) — NMen
'Lismore Pink' (× *lismorensis*) (7) — NMen
'Lissadell' (*callosa*) (8) — GKev IFoB
* 'Little Piggy' (*epiphylla*) (5) — GEdr WCru
'Lohengrin' (× *hoerhammeri*) (7) — NMen
'Lohmuelleri' (× *biasolettoi*) (7) — GKev
'Long Acre Pink' (*fortunei*) (5) — CLAP
longifolia (8) — ECho GKev NSla WGor
- hybrids — GKev
'Louis Armstrong' (Blues Group) (7) — CPBP EPot NMen WAbe
Love Me — see *S.* 'Miluj Mne'
lowndesii (7) — WAbe
'Loxley' (*poluanglica*) (7) — GEdr NMen
'Ludmila Šubrová' (× *bertolonii*) (7) — NMen
'Lutea' (*aizoon*) — see *S.* 'Lutea' (*paniculata*)
'Lutea' (*diapensioides*) — see *S.* 'Wilhelm Tell', 'Primulina'
'Lutea' (*marginata*) — see *S.* 'Faust'
§ 'Lutea' (*paniculata*) (8) ♀H4 — ECho EDAr EHoe EPot GEdr GGar GMaP NBro NHol WFar
§ 'Luteola' (× *boydii*) (7) ♀H4 — WAbe
'Lužníce' (× *poluluteopurpurea*) (7) — NMen
macedonica — see *S. juniperifolia*
'Magdalena' (× *thomasiana*) (7) — NMen
'Major' (*cochlearis*) (8) ♀H4 — WGor
'Major Lutea' — see *S.* 'Luteola'
'Malý Trpaslík' (*vandellii* × *sempervivum*) (7) — WAbe
'Mangekyo' (*fortunei*) (5) new — IVic
'Marc Chagall' (Decora Group) (7) — CPBP NMen WAbe
§ 'Maréchal Joffre' (15) — GAbr NEgg WCom
'Margarete' (× *borisii*) (7) — NMen
marginata (7) — GCrs WAbe
- var. ***balcanica*** — see *S. marginata* subsp. *marginata* var. *rocheliana*
- subsp. ***marginata*** var. ***boryi*** (7) — EPot NMen WAbe
- - var. ***coriophylla*** (7) — EPot NMen NWCA WAbe
§ - - var. ***rocheliana*** (7) — ITim NMen
'Maria Callas' (× *poluanglica*) (7) — WAbe WGor
'Maria Luisa' (× *salmonica*) (7) — CFee CPBP NMen WPat
'Marianna' (× *borisii*) (7) — CMea NHol NMen
'Maroon Beauty' (*stolonifera*) (5) — EBee ECtt EPPr MDKP NBre SPhx WCot WEas
'Mars' (× *elisabethae*) (7) — NMen
'Marshal Joffre' (15) — see *S.* 'Maréchal Joffre' (15)
'Marsilio Ficino' (Milford Group) (7) — NMen
§ 'Martha' (× *semmleri*) (7) — NMen
'Mary Golds' (Swing Group) (7) — EDAr GKev ITim NLar WGor
matta-florida (7) — NMen
'May Queen' (7) — NMen
× ***megaseiflora*** sensu stricto hort. — see *S.* 'Robin Hood'
'Melrose' (× *salmonica*) (7) — NMen
mertensiana (6) — GEdr NBir WCru
'Meteor' (7) — NRya
micranthidifolia (4) — CLAP WPGP
'Mikuláš Koperník' (× *zenittensis*) (7) — WAbe
'Millstream' (8) — NWCA
'Millstream Cream' (× *elisabethae*) (7) — ECho NMen
§ 'Miluj Mne' (× *poluanglica*) (7) — ECho ITim NHol NMen WHoo
'Minor' (*cochlearis*) (8) ♀H4 — ECho GKev LRHS MAsh NHol NMen NWCA WGor WPat
'Mirko Webr' (Harmonia Group) (*aretioides* × *cinerea*) (7) — NMen WAbe
§ 'Miss Chambers' (× *urbium*) (11) — SMHy WCot WMoo WPen WSHC
'Momo Sekisui' (*fortunei*) (5) new — IVic
'Mona Lisa' (× *borisii*) (7) — NMen WAbe
'Monarch' (8) ♀H4 — GAbr MAsh WAbe
'Moonlight' (× *boydii*) — see *S.* 'Sulphurea'
'Morava' (7) — NMen
Mossy Group (15) — LRHS
* 'Mossy Pink' — SPoG
'Mossy Red' — SPoG WNew
'Mossy Triumph' — see *S.* 'Triumph'
'Mossy White' — GAbr WNew
'Mother of Pearl' (× *irvingii*) (7) — ECho NMen
'Mother Queen' (× *irvingii*) (7) — NMen WPat
'Mount Hood' (*fortunei*) — LRHS
'Mount Nachi' (*fortunei*) (5) — CBct CDes CWCL EBee EBrs EPfP EWes GAbr GEdr GMaP IBal ITim IVic LOck LRHS MLHP NBro NMen NMyG SUsu WAbe WClo WCot WFar WPGP WPer WSpi WWEG
§ 'Mrs Gertie Prichard' (× *megaseiflora*) (7) — NMen
'Mrs Helen Terry' (× *salmonica*) (7) — EPot NMen
'Mrs Leng' (× *elisabethae*) (7) — MDKP NMen
'Myra Cambria' (× *anglica*) (7) — ITim NHol NMen

'Myra' (× *anglica*) (7) ECho NHol NMen NWCA WHoo WPat
'Myriad' (7) NMen
'Nancye' (× *goringiana*) (7) ITim NMen WAbe
§ ***nelsoniana*** (4) NHol
'Nimbus' (*iranica*) (7) NMen
'Niobe' (× *pulvilacina*) (7) NMen
'Nisi' (*fortunei*) (5) new IVic
'Norvegica' (*cotyledon*) (8) ITim WAbe
'Notata' (*paniculata*) (8) NLAp
'Nottingham Gold' (× *boydii*) (7) EPot NHol NMen
'Obristii' (× *salmonica*) (7) NMen NRya
§ ***obtusa*** (7) EPot MHer NMen WAbe
'Ochroleuca' (× *elisabethae*) (7) NMen
'Odysseus' (*sancta*) (7) NMen
'Olymp' (*scardica*) (7) NMen
'Opalescent' (7) NMen
§ 'Ophelia' (× *arco-valleyi*) (7) NMen
oppositifolia (7) ECho GKir MWat NLAp NSla SPlb SRms WAbe WCom WFar
I - 'Holden Variety' (7) NHol NRya
- 'Le Bourg d'Oisans' (7) WAbe
- subsp. ***oppositifolia*** var. ***latina*** (7) ECho
'Oriole' (× *boydii*) (7) NMen
'Orjen' (*paniculata* var. *orientalis*) (8) GEdr
'Ottone Rosai' (Toscana Group) (7) NMen
'Oxhill' (7) NMen
§ ***paniculata*** (8) ECho EDAr EHoe GGar GKev GMaP MAsh MDKP MWat NSla SPlb SRms WAbe WFar WHoo WNew
§ - subsp. ***cartilaginea*** (8) NHol WAbe
- subsp. ***kolenatiana*** see *S. paniculata* subsp. *cartilaginea*
- var minutifolia' (8) CPBP CTri ECho LRHS MSCN MWat NBro NHol NLAp NMen NRya NWCA SPlb WAbe
paradoxa (15) ECho EPot GEdr LRHS NHol WGor
'Parcevalis' (× *finnisiae*) (7 × 9) WAbe
'Parsee' (× *margoxiana*) (7) EPot NMen
'Paula' (× *paulinae*) (7) NMen
'Peach Blossom' (7) GCrs NMen
'Peach Melba' (7) ITim NLar NMen WAbe WFar
* 'Peachy Head' NMen WAbe
'Pearly Gates' (× *irvingii*) (7) NMen
'Pearly Gold' (15) NRya WFar
'Pearly King' (15) GMaP WAbe WFar
× ***pectinata*** Schott, Nyman & Kotschy see *S.* 'Krain'
pedemontana (15) GKev
'Penelope' (× *boydilacina*) (7) ECho EPot GCrs LRHS NLar NMen WCom WHoo WPat
pensylvanica (4) EBee GCal GCra IMou
'Perikles' (7) NMen
'Peter Burrow' (× *poluanglica*) (7) ♀H4 CPBP ECho ITim NMen
'Peter Pan' (15) EDAr EPfP GJos GMaP MHer MSCN NHol NMen NRya SPoG WFar WNew WPat
'Petra' (7) ITim NMen WFar
§ 'Phoenix' (× *biasolettoi*) (7) ECho LRHS WThu
'Pilatus' (× *boydii*) (7) NMen
'Pink Cloud' (*fortunei*) (5) CLAP NHar WAbe WFar
'Pink Haze' (*fortunei*) (5) CLAP NHar WAbe
'Pink Mist' (*fortunei*) (5) CLAP NHar WAbe WFar
'Pink Pagoda' (*nipponica*) (5) CDes CLAP EBee GEdr WCot WCru WPGP
'Pink Pearl' (7) NMen
'Pixie' (15) CTri ECtt LRHS NHol NMen SPoG SRms
'Pixie Alba' see *S.* 'White Pixie'
'Plena' (*granulata*) see *S.* 'Flore Pleno'
'Polar Drift' new WAbe
'Pollux' (× *boydii*) (7) EPot NMen
poluniniana (7) WAbe
poluniniana × 'Winifred' (× *poluanglica*) (7) ECho
'Popelka' (subsp. *marginata* var. *rocheliana*) (7) LRHS NMen
porophylla (7) GCrs NMen
- aff. var. ***thessalica*** see *S. sempervivum* f. *stenophylla*
aff. ***porophylla*** (7) NWCA
'Precious Piggy' (*epiphylla*) (5) WCru
'Primrose Bee' (× *apiculata*) (7) EPot ITim
'Primrose Dame' (× *elisabethae*) (7) ECho MDKP NMen WAbe WCom
'Primulaize' (9 × 11) MHer MWat NMen
'Primulaize Salmon' (9 × 11) NHol WCom WHoo WPer
§ 'Primulina' (× *malbyana*) (7) NMen
primuloides see *S.* 'Primuloides'
§ 'Primuloides' (*umbrosa*) (11) ♀H4 ECho EDAr GKir MMuc NMen SEND SRms SWvt WFar
'Prince Hal' (*burseriana*) (7) ECho EDAr EPot LRHS NMen WCom
'Princess' (*burseriana*) (7) ECho EDAr LRHS NMen WCom
'Probynii' (*cochlearis*) (8) EPot MWat NMen WAbe
'Prospero' (× *petraschii*) (7) NMen
× ***prossenii*** sensu stricto hort. see *S.* 'Regina'
× ***pseudokotschyi*** sensu stricto hort. see *S.* 'Denisa'
'Pseudopungens' (× *apiculata*) (7) EPot
'Pseudoscardica' (× *wehrhahnii*) (7) NMen
'Pseudo-valdensis' (*cochlearis*) (8) WAbe
pubescens (15) WAbe
- subsp. ***iratiana*** (15) CPBP
punctata Sternb. (4) see *S. nelsoniana*
* ***punctissima*** NHol
'Pungens' (× *apiculata*) (7) EPot NMen
'Purple Piggy' (*epiphylla*) (5) CFee CLAP WCru
'Purpurea' (*fortunei*) see *S.* 'Rubrifolia'
§ 'Pygmalion' (× *webrii*) (7) GCrs WGor
'Pyramidalis' (*cotyledon*) (8) EPfP EWTr SRms
'Pyrenaica' (*oppositifolia*) (7) ECho NMen
quadrifaria (7) WAbe
'Quarry Wood' (× *anglica*) (7) NHol NMen
'Radvan Horný' (× *cullinanii*) (7) WAbe
'Rainsley Seedling' (8) EPot GKev NBro NMen
ramulosa (7) NMen WAbe
'Red Poll' (× *poluanglica*) (7) NMen NRya
* 'Regent' WAbe
§ 'Regina' (× *prossenii*) (7) MHer NMen
retusa (7) NMen WAbe
'Rex' (*paniculata*) (8) CYeo NHol
rhodopetala (7) ECho
§ 'Riverslea' (× *hornibrookii*) (7) CPBP NMen WAbe

§	'Robin Hood' (× *megaseiflora*) (7)	CFee CPBP NMen WHoo WPat
	'Rokujō' (*fortunei*) (5)	CLAP EBee IVic NLar NPnk SHeu WFar
	'Romeo' (× *hornibrookii*) (7)	NMen
	rosacea (15)	EDAr
	'Rosea' (*cortusifolia*) (5)	CLAP NHar
§	'Rosea' (*paniculata*) (8) $\mathbb{Y}^{H4}$	GMaP LBMP NBro NHol NSla SRms WFar
	'Rosea' (× *stuartii*) (7)	NMen
	'Rosemarie' (7)	ECho NMen
	'Rosenzwerg' (15)	WFar
	'Rosina Sündermann' (× *rosinae*) (7)	ECho EPot NMen
	'Rote Stadt' (*fortunei*) (5) **new**	IVic
	rotundifolia (12)	EBee GMaP MDKP NHol SBfd
	'Roy Clutterbuck' (7)	NMen
	'Rubra' (*aizoon*)	see *S.* 'Rosea' (*paniculata*)
§	'Rubrifolia' (*fortunei*) (5)	CLAP CSpe EBee ECha ECtt EHoe GAbr GEdr IBal LAst LOck LRHS MBri NMen NMyG NPnk SAga SGSe SMad SPet SWvt WAbe WBor WClo WCot WCru WFar WWEG
*	'Ruby Wedding' (*cortusifolia*) (5)	CLAP WCru WFar
	rufescens (5)	EHrv GEdr
	- BWJ 7510	WCru
	- BWJ 7684	EWld WCru
	'Rusalka' (× *borisii*) (7)	NMen
	'Russell V. Prichard' (× *irvingii*) (7)	NMen
	'Ruth Draper' (*oppositifolia*) (7)	WAbe WFar
	'Ruth McConnell' (15)	CMea WCom
	'Saint John's' (8)	EBur ECho GEdr WAbe
	'Saint Kilda' (*oppositifolia*) (7)	ITim
	× ***salmonica*** sensu stricto hort.	see *S.* 'Salomonii'
§	'Salomonii' (× *salmonica*) (7)	NMen SRms
	'Samo' (× *bertolonii*) (7)	NMen
	sancta (7)	ECho LRHS NMen SRms WAbe
	- subsp. ***pseudosancta***	see *S. juniperifolia*
	- - var. ***macedonica***	see *S. juniperifolia*
	'Sandpiper' (7)	NMen
	'Šárka' (7)	NMen
	sarmentosa	see *S. stolonifera*
	'Sartorii'	see *S.* 'Pygmalion'
	'Satchmo' (Blues Group) (7) **new**	CPBP
	'Saturn' (× *megaseiflora*) (7)	NMen WFar
	'Sázava' (× *poluluteopurpurea*) (7)	NMen
	scardica (7)	EPot NBro NMen WAbe
	- var. ***dalmatica***	see *S. obtusa*
§	'Schelleri' (× *petraschii*) (7)	NMen
	'Schneeteppich' (15)	WCom
	'Schöne Mädchen' (*fortunei*) (5) **new**	IVic
§	'Schwefelblüte' (15)	ECho GMaP LRHS NPri NWCA WCom WPat
	scleropoda (7)	EPot NMen
§	'Seaspray' (× *arendsii*) (15/v)	EWes
	'Seissera' (*burseriana*) (7)	EPot NMen
	'Semafor' (Holenka's Miracle Group) (× *megaseiflora*) (7)	NMen
	× ***semmleri*** sensu stricto hort.	see *S.* 'Martha'
	sempervivum (7)	NGdn NMen WAbe WTin
§	- f. ***stenophylla*** (7)	ECho MHer
	sendaica (5)	CLAP WCru
	- B&SWJ 7448	GEdr
	'Sergio Bacci' (7)	NMen
	'Sherlock Holmes' (7)	WAbe
	'Shinkunomai' (*fortunei*) (5) **new**	IVic
§	'Silver Cushion' (15/v)	CMea CTri ECho EDAr ELan GKir LRHS NEgg NPri SBch SPlb SPoG WAbe WFar WNew
	'Silver Edge' (× *arco-valleyi*) (7)	NMen
	'Silver Maid' (× *engleri*) (8)	GEdr NMen WAbe
	'Silver Mound'	see *S.* 'Silver Cushion'
	'Silver Velvet' (*fortunei*) (5)	CLAP CMil EBee ECtt GEdr IFoB LOck LRHS NMyG SHeu WBor WCon WCot WFut
	'Sissi' (7)	CPBP
	'Slack's Ruby Southside' (Southside Seedling Group) $\mathbb{Y}^{H4}$	MDKP NLAp NSla WAbe WFar
	'Slzy Coventry' (× *proximae*) (7)	WAbe
	'Snowcap' (*pubescens*) (15)	WAbe
	'Snowdon' (*burseriana*) (7)	NMen
	'Snowflake' (Silver Farreri Group) (8) $\mathbb{Y}^{H4}$	WAbe
§	'Sofia' (× *borisii*) (7)	NMen WFar
	'Sorrento' (*marginata*) (7)	NMen
	Southside Seedling Group (8) $\mathbb{Y}^{H4}$	Widely available
	- 'Southside Star' $\mathbb{Y}^{H4}$	WAbe WFar
	spathularis (11)	CEnt WCom WEas
	'Splendens' (*oppositifolia*) (7) $\mathbb{Y}^{H4}$	ECho EPfP NHol NLAp NWCA SRms WAbe WPat
	'Spotted Dog'	see *S.* 'Canis-dalmatica'
	'Sprite' (15)	SPoG
	spruneri (7)	ECho LRHS NMen WAbe WCom
	- var. ***deorum*** (7)	NMen
	'Stansfieldii' (*rosacea*) (15)	LRHS NMen SPlb SPoG WFar
	'Star Dust' (7)	EPot
	stenophylla subsp. ***stenophylla***	see *S. flagellaris*
	stolitzkae (7)	NMen WAbe
§	***stolonifera*** (5) $\mathbb{Y}^{H2}$	CArn CCVN CEnt CHEx CSpe ECho EShb EWTr GBin NBro NPnk SDix SWvt WCot WFar WMoo WPnn
	- large-flowered (5) **new**	WCot
	stribrnyi (7)	NMen WAbe
	- JCA 861-400	NWCA
	'Sturmiana' (*paniculata*) (8)	NMen SRms
	'Sue Drew' (*fortunei*) (5)	LLHF
	'Sue Tubbs' **new**	GKev
	'Suendermannii' (× *kellereri*) (7)	ECho LRHS
	'Suendermannii Major' (× *kellereri*) (7)	ECho LRHS NRya
	'Sugar Plum Fairy' (*fortunei*) (5)	EBee EHrv EShb IVic LOck LRHS SMad WCot
§	'Sulphurea' (× *boydii*) (7)	ECho LRHS NMen WCom WPat
	'Sunset' (*anglica*) (7)	WAbe
	'Superba' (*callosa* subsp. *callosa* var. *australis*) (8) $\mathbb{Y}^{H4}$	MAsh
	'Swan' (× *fallsvillagensis*) (7)	NMen
	'Sylva' (× *elisabethae*) (7)	NMen
	'Symons-Jeunei' (8)	GEdr WAbe
	'Tábor' (× *schottii*) (7)	NMen

	'Tamatsuzuri' (*fortunei*) (5) **new**	IVic
	'Tamayura' (*fortunei*) (5)	CLAP
	'Teide' (Swirly Group) (7)	NMen
	'Tenerife' (Swirly Group) (7)	CPBP NMen
	'Theoden' (*oppositifolia*) (7) 🏆H4	CMea ECho EWes WAbe
	'Theresia' (× *mariae-theresiae*) (7)	NMen
	'Theseus' (7) **new**	CPBP
	'Thorpei' (× *gusmusii*) (7)	NMen
	'Timmy Foster' (× *irvingii*) (7)	NHol NMen
	tolmiei (3) **new**	WAbe
	tombeanensis (7)	NMen
	'Tricolor' (*stolonifera*) (5) 🏆H2	CBow CHEx EBak
§	'Triumph' (× *arendsii*) (15)	ECtt EPfP GMaP NEgg NPri SPoG
	'Tully' (× *elisabethae*) (7)	NLAp WGor WPat
	'Tumbling Waters' (8) 🏆H4	CPBP ECho GAbr LHop LRHS NHol NMen NSla WAbe WFar WGor WPat
§	'Tvoje Píseň' (× *poluanglica*) (7)	ECho GKev NMen WHoo
§	'Tvůj Den' (× *polulacina*) (7)	ECho NMen WAbe
§	'Tvůj Polibek' (× *poluanglica*) (7)	ECho MDKP NMen
§	'Tvůj Přítel' (× *poluanglica*) (7)	ECho
§	'Tvůj Úsměv' (× *poluanglica*) (7)	ECho NLar NMen
§	'Tvůj Úspech' (× *poluanglica*) (7)	ECho GCrs NHol NMen WAbe
	'Tycho Brahe' (× *doerfleri*) (7)	NMen WAbe
	'Tysoe' (7)	ITim NMen
	umbrosa (11)	CMac CTri EBee ECGP ECho ECrN EDAr GKir LAst LEdu LRHS MMuc MRav NDov SBfd SEND SPlb SPoG SRms STes SWvt WCAu WFar WMoo
*	**- *subinteger***	SEND
	'Unique'	see *S.* 'Bodensee'
	× ***urbium*** (11) 🏆H4	CAby CHEx CTri EBee ECho ELan EPfP EWTr GMaP LAst LEdu SBfd SPer SRms STre WBrk WFar WPer WWEG
	'Vaccariana' (*oppositifolia*) (7)	ECho
	'Václav Hollar' (× *gusmusii*) (7)	NMen
	'Vahlii' (× *smithii*) (7)	NMen
	'Valborg'	see *S.* 'Cranbourne'
	'Valentine'	see *S.* 'Cranbourne'
	'Valerie Finnis'	see *S.* 'Aretiastrum'
	'Valerie Keevil' (× *anglica*) (7)	NMen
I	'Variegata' (*cuneifolia*) (11/v)	ECho ECtt EPfP GGar LRHS NHol NVic SPet SPlb SPoG WFar WMoo WPer
	'Variegata' (*umbrosa*)	see *S.* 'Aureopunctata'
I	'Variegata' (× *urbium*) (11/v)	EBee ECho EPfP GGar LAst LRHS MSpe NLar SRms WEas WFar WNew WWEG
	'Večerní Hvězda'	WAbe
	veitchiana (5)	EBee GEdr NBro
	'Verona' (× ***caroli-langii***) (7) **new**	WAbe
	'Vesna' (× *borisii*) (7)	NMen
	'Vincent van Gogh' (× *borisii*) (7)	NMen
	'Vladana' (× *megaseiflora*) (7)	ECho LRHS NMen
	'Vlasta' (7)	NMen
	'Vlasta Burian' (7)	WAbe
	'Vltava' (7)	NMen
	'Volgeri' (× *hofmannii*) (7)	NMen
	'Vreny' (8)	GKev
	'Vysoké Mýto' (7)	WAbe
	'Wada' (*fortunei*) (5)	CAbP CLAP CSam EAEE EBee ECtt ELon GEdr LAst LRHS MCot MNrw NBir NMyG SGSe SPer SPoG WBor WCot WFar WOld WPGP WWEG
	'Waithman's Variety' (8)	GEdr
	'Wallacei' (15)	NMen
	'Walpole's Variety' (8)	WAbe WPer
	'Walter Ingwersen' (*umbrosa*) (11)	SRms
§	'Walter Irving' (× *irvingii*) (7)	EPot NHol NMen WAbe
	'Warmes Herz' (*fortunei*) (5) **new**	IVic
	'Wartosque' (*callosa*) (8)	EPot
	'Wellesbourne' (× *abingdonensis*) (7)	ITim
	'Welsh Dragon' (15)	WAbe
	'Welsh Red' (15)	WAbe WFar
	'Welsh Rose' (15)	WAbe
	wendelboi (7)	GCrs NMen
	'Wendrush' (× *wendelacina*) (7)	NMen
	'Wendy' (× *wendelacina*) (7)	NMen
	'Wheatley Gem' (7)	NMen
	'Wheatley Lion' (× *borisii*) (7)	NMen
	'Wheatley Rose' (7)	ECho LRHS
	'White Cap' (× *boydii*) (7)	NMen
	'White Craggs' (7)	NHol
	'White Imp' (7)	NMen
§	'White Pixie' (15)	ECtt EDAr EPfP GMaP MHer NHol NPri NRya SPlb SPoG SRms WFar WNew
	'White Star' (× *petraschii*)	see *S.* 'Schelleri'
	'Whitehill' (8) 🏆H4	CMea ECho ECtt ELan GEdr GJos GKir GMaP LRHS MDKP NBro NHol NMen NRya SPet WCom WFar WHoo WNew WPat WTin
§	'Wilhelm Tell' (× *malbyana*) (7)	NMen
	'William Shakespeare' (Blues Group) (7)	WAbe
	'Winifred Bevington' (8 × 11) 🏆H4	ECho EDAr LHop LRHS MMuc NBro NHol NLAp NMen NRya WAbe WCom WFar WHoo WPer WPnn
	'Winifred' (× *anglica*) (7)	ECho NMen
	'Winston Churchill' (15)	CElw CTri ECho EPfP LRHS NHol
I	'Winston Churchill Variegata'	LRHS NHol
	'Winton' (× *paulinae*) (7)	NMen
	'Wisley' (*federici-augusti* subsp. *grisebachii*) (7) 🏆H2-3	NLAp NMen WPat
	'Woodside Ross' (15)	ECtt
	'Yellow Rock' (7)	NMen NRya
	'Youkuy' (*fortunei*) (5) **new**	IVic
	Your Day	see *S.* 'Tvůj Den'
	Your Friend	see *S.* 'Tvůj Přítel'
	Your Good Fortune	see *S.* 'Tvůj Úspěch'
	Your Kiss	see *S.* 'Tvůj Polibek'
	Your Smile	see *S.* 'Tvůj Úsměv'
	Your Song	see *S.* 'Tvoje Píseň'
	Your Success	see *S.* 'Tvuj Úspěch'
	'Yuinagi' (*fortunei*) (5)	WOld
	'Yunagi' (*fortunei*) (5) **new**	IVic

	× ***zimmeteri*** (8 × 11)	ECho NMen
§	'Zlatá Praha' (× *pragensis*) (7)	NMen NRya WAbe
	'Zlin' (× *leyboldii*) (7)	NMen

Scabiosa (Dipsacaceae)

	africana	CElw EBee EWes SHar
	alpina L.	see *Cephalaria alpina*
	argentea	EBee EWes LEdu WPGP
	atropurpurea	CEnt SPav
	- 'Ace of Spades'	CWCL EBee EDif SMad SPav WPGP WSpi
	- 'Beaujolais Bonnets'	GKir LAst LRHS SPer
§	- 'Chile Black'	Widely available
§	- 'Chilli Pepper'	CWCL EPfP LHop LRHS MBri MGos NLar WSpi
§	- 'Chilli Sauce'	CWCL EPfP LHop LRHS MGos NLar SPer
	- 'Derry's Black'	CSpe
	- 'Fire King' **new**	MWea
	- 'Nona'	LLHF
	- 'Peter Ray'	CElw ECtt WWlt
	- 'Salmon Queen'	NLar
	banatica	see *S. columbaria*
	'Blue Diamonds'	LRHS WClo WSpi
	Burgundy Bonnets = 'Scabon'[PBR]	EGxp LRHS LSou
§	'Butterfly Blue'	CMHG EBee ECtt EPPr EPfP LBMP LRHS LSRN MAsh MBri NBPC NLar NMoo SCoo SMrm SPer SPoG SWvt WAul WCAu WCot WFar WWEG
	caucasica	CMac EBrs EPfP GKev GKir LAst LEdu WFar WHoo
	- var. ***alba***	CBcs CBot CKno EBee EHrv EPfP GKir NGBl NPnk WFar WHoo
	- 'Blausiegel'	CSam EBee ECtt LAst LBMP MRav NBre NCob NDov NGdn SPet WFar
	- 'Bressingham White'	LRHS
	- 'Clive Greaves' ♀H4	CHar CTri EBee ECha ECtt EHrv ELan EPfP GKir MBri MRav NCob SRms SWvt WCAu WCom WEas WFar WHrl
	- 'Deep Waters'	CSpe EBee LRHS NBre NCGa SPad WPtf
	- 'Fama'	CWib EShb LRHS NBir NGBl NLar SPlb SRms WFar WWEG
	- 'Goldingensis'	GJos MHer NBre NGdn NPri WPer
	- House's hybrids	CSBt GJos NGdn SRms
	- 'Isaac House'	ELon LRHS NLar WBVN
	- 'Kompliment'	GMac NBre NLar SMrm WWEG
	- 'Lavender Blue'	NBPC WFar
	- 'Miss Willmott' ♀H4	CMMP CSam EBee ECha ECtt EHoe ELan EPfP EShb LBMP LHop LRHS MBri MHer MLHP MRav NCob SWvt WCAu WFar WHrl WMnd WWEG
	- 'Moerheim Blue'	EBee
	- Perfecta Series	CWib EBee LRHS MMHG NGdn NLar SPoG SWat WBor
	- - 'Perfecta Alba'	CBar COIW CWib EBee ECtt GJos GKir GMaP GMac LAst LRHS MWat NChi NLar NPri SBfd SMrm SPad SPer SPoG STes SWat WPtf WWEG
	- - 'Perfecta Blue' **new**	CBar
	- - 'Perfecta Lilac Blue'	CWib EPfP GMaP GMac SBfd SPer STes WWEG
	- 'Stäfa'	CMMP EBee ECha EShb EWTr LBMP LRHS MBri MRav NEgg NLar SUsu WFar WHrl WMnd
	'Chile Black'	see *S. atropurpurea* 'Chile Black'
	'Chile Pepper'	see *S. atropurpurea* 'Chilli Pepper'
	'Chile Sauce'	see *S. atropurpurea* 'Chilli Sauce'
	'Chile Spice'	MBri WHlf
	cinerea	SPhx
§	***columbaria***	EBWF EBee LRHS MLLN MMuc MPet NBre NEgg NLan NMir NSco NWCA WHer WJek WSFF WWEG
	- 'Misty Butterflies'	COIW ECtt EDAr EPfP EShb EWll LBMP LHop LSou NBPC NEgg NGdn NLar NMoo SBfd SMrm SPad STes WBor WBrE WFar WWEG
	- 'Nana'	CMdw CMea EBee EShb GEdr NBir NGdn NLar NMen NPri SBch WCFE WFar WHil WHrl
§	- subsp. ***ochroleuca***	CBot CKno CSpe ECha EHrv EShb GBBs GCal GKev LEdu LPio LRHS MCot MLLN MRav MSpe NBir NDov NLar NPri SGSe SMad SPhx SPoG SRms WCAu WFar WHoo WPGP WTin
	- - MESE 344	EBee
	- - 'Moon Dance'	CMea CSam EBee EDAr EPPr EShb GCal LBMP LLHF MSpe NCGa NLar SBfd
	- 'Pincushion Blue' **new**	EWll
	- 'Pincushion Pink'	NGdn NPri SGSe WFar WHil WWEG
	cretica	CSpe
	drakensbergensis	EBee EKen EWes GAbr MAvo SGSe WHrl
	farinosa	CBot CDes ECtt MMuc SAga SEND SGar WFar WSHC
	gigantea	see *Cephalaria gigantea*
	graminifolia	ECho GKev LRHS MDKP NBir NMen NWCA SBch SRms
	- JM 990	EBee
	- ***rosea***	EWes
	'Helen Dillon'	EBee ECtt EWes LSou WWEG
	'Irish Perpetual Flowering'	EBee ECGP ECtt MTis NDov WCot WWEG
	japonica var. ***acutiloba***	SPhx
	- var. ***alpina***	CEnt CPrp EBee GKev IBal MMuc NGdn NHol SBfd SEND SPet SPhx WAbe WHoo WNew WTin
	- - 'Blue Star'	NBre NCGa
	- 'Ritz Blue' **new**	EPfP
	lachnophylla	GCal SPhx
	- 'Blue Horizon' **new**	NDov
	'Little Emily'	ELon SAga SUsu
	lucida	EAEE EBee EBrs ECho ECtt EPfP LRHS MRav NPri WHrl WPGP WPer
	'Midnight'	CMea
	'Miss Havisham'	EBee ECtt EWes LSou NDov WPGP
	'Monita Pink'	CMoH
	montana Mill.	see *Knautia arvensis*
	montana (Bieb.) DC.	see *Knautia tatarica*
	ochroleuca	see *S. columbaria* subsp. *ochroleuca*
	olgae	EBee
	parnassi	see *Pterocephalus perennis*
	'Peggotty'	ECtt
	'Perpetual Flowering'	see *S.* 'Butterfly Blue'
	Pink Buttons = 'Walminipink'	CFir EBee LRHS MWat
	'Pink Mist'[PBR]	CPrp EBee ECtt EPfP EWll LRHS MAsh MBri NBir NLar SCoo SMrm SPer SPoG SRms WCAu

pterocephala	see *Pterocephalus perennis*
rhodopensis	EBee
'Rosie's Pink'	ECtt
rumelica	see *Knautia macedonica*
'Satchmo'	see *S. atropurpurea* 'Chile Black'
speciosa 'Maharajah'	NBre NCGa NLar SPad
succisa	see *Succisa pratensis*
tatarica	see *Cephalaria gigantea*
tenuis	LPio SPhx
triandra	EBee LHop
'Vivid Violet' new	LSou MTis SMrm WCot

Scabiosa × *Cephalaria* (*Dipsacaceae*)

S. cinerea* × *C. alpina	LRHS

Scadoxus ✿ (*Amaryllidaceae*)

multiflorus	CPne CPrp ECho LAma LRHS WCot WGwG
§ - subsp. ***katherinae*** ♀H1	CPne ECho
natalensis	see *S. puniceus*
§ ***puniceus***	CLak

Scaevola (*Goodeniaceae*)

aemula 'Blue Fan' PBR	see *S. aemula* 'Blue Wonder'
§ - 'Blue Wonder' PBR	NPer SWvt
- 'White Fan'	LAst
- 'Zig Zag' PBR	CCCN LAst LSou
Blauer Facher = 'Saphira' PBR	CCCN LHop LRHS
'Brillant' PBR	LSou
crassifolia	SPlb
'Diamond'	LSou
'Mini Blue'	CCCN
'Topaz Pink'	LAst LSou

Schefflera (*Araliaceae*)

actinophylla ♀H1	EUJe
alpina B&SWJ 8247	WCru
- HWJ 585	WCru
- HWJ 936	WCru
arboricola ♀H1	CHEx MMuc SEND XBlo
- 'Gold Capella' ♀H1	MMuc SEND XBlo
- 'Kalahari'	XBlo
brevipedicellata HWJ 870	WCru
§ ***chapana*** B&SWJ 11830	WCru
- HWJ 983	WCru
delavayi	CHEx
digitata	CTrC
elegantissima ♀H1	EShb
enneaphylla B&SWJ 11727	WCru
- HWJ 1018	WCru
fantsipanensis B&SWJ 8228	WCru
- B&SWJ 11666	WCru
fengii new	GLin
gracilis HWJ 622	WCru
hoi B&SWJ 11747 new	WCru
kornasii HWJ 918	WCru
lenticellata B&SWJ 9762	WCru
macrophylla B&SWJ 8210	WCru
- B&SWJ 9788	WCru
microphylla B&SWJ 3872	WCru
rhododendrifolia	CHEx
- GWJ 9375	WCru
taiwaniana	CHEx
- B&SWJ 3575	WCru
- B&SWJ 7096	WCru
- RWJ 10000	WCru
- RWJ 10016	WCru
vietnamensis	see *S. chapana*

Schima (*Theaceae*)

wallichii new	CBcs
- subsp. ***noronhae*** var. ***superba***	CCCN EBee EPfP
- subsp. ***wallichii*** var. ***khasiana***	IDee

Schinus (*Anacardiaceae*)

molle	CArn IDee
polygamus	EBee

Schisandra (*Schisandraceae*)

TH	CHEx
arisanensis B&SWJ 3050	WCru
aff. ***bicolor*** BWJ 8151	WCru
chinensis	CAgr CArn CBcs GPoy LEdu MSwo WBVN
- B&SWJ 4204	WCru
- SDR 3980	GKev
grandiflora	CDoC EBee ELan EPfP LRHS MBlu NLar SCoo SKHP SPer WGwG
- B&SWJ 2245	WCru
- 'Jamu' (m)	WCru
- 'Lahlu' (f/F)	WCru
grandiflora* × *rubriflora	WCru
henryi subsp. ***yunnanensis*** B&SWJ 6546	WCru
aff. ***neglecta*** BWJ 7739	WCru
nigra	see *S. repanda*
propinqua	CBot CMac CSPN LEdu MBlu NLar
subsp. ***sinensis***	WSHC
- - BWJ 8148	WCru
§ ***repanda*** B&SWJ 5897	WCru
- B&SWJ 11455	WCru
rubriflora	CHEx CSPN CTri CWSG EBee EPfP GKir IFFs LRHS MBlu MGos SKHP SLon SSpi WSpi
- (f)	ELan MGos WSHC
- (m)	NHol
- BWJ 7557	WCru
sphenanthera	ELan NLar WSHC
verrucosa	see *Kadsura verrucosa*

Schivereckia (*Brassicaceae*)

doerfleri	MWat

Schizachyrium (*Poaceae*)

§ ***scoparium***	CBod CKno EBee EBrs ECGP EHoe EPPr EPau GCal IFoB LBMP LRHS MWhi NSti SGSe SPhx SUsu WCot
- 'Cairo'	EBee
- 'Prairie Blues'	CKno EBee EPPr GQue SMrm WCot

Schizocarphus (*Hyacinthaceae*)

nervosus new	WCot

Schizocodon see *Shortia*

Schizopetalon (*Brassicaceae*)

walkeri	CSpe

Schizophragma (*Hydrangeaceae*)

corylifolium	NLar
- BWJ 8150	WCru
aff. ***elliptifolium*** WWJ 11905 new	WCru
hydrangeoides	CBcs CDoC CDul EBee ELan EPfP EWTr GKir LRHS MBlu MGos MMuc NPri SLim SLon SPer SPoG SSpi SWvt WDin

- B&SWJ 5489 WCru
- B&SWJ 5732 WCru
- B&SWJ 5954 WCru
- B&SWJ 6119 from Yakushima, Japan WCru
- B&SWJ 8505 from Korea WCru
- B&SWJ 8522 from Ulleungdo, Korea WCru
- 'Brookside Littleleaf' see *Hydrangea anomala* subsp. *petiolaris* var. *cordifolia* 'Brookside Littleleaf'
- 'Cheju's Early' WCru
- 'Iwa Garami' EBee NLar
- 'Moonlight' Widely available
* - f. ***quelpartensis*** B&SWJ 8771 WCru
- 'Roseum' ♀H4 CDoC CDul CMHG CMil CSBt CSPN EBee ELan EPfP EWes GKir IArd LRHS MBlu MBri MGos NCGa NLar SKHP SLim SPer SPoG SSpi SWvt WCru WFar WPGP

integrifolium ♀H4 CBcs CMac EBee ELan EPfP NLar SKHP SPoG SSpi WPGP WSHC
- var. ***fauriei*** NLar WSHC
- - B&SWJ 1701 WCru

Schizostachyum (*Poaceae*)

§ ***funghomii*** EPla MMoz MMuc SEND WPGP

Schizostylis ✿ (*Iridaceae*)

§ ***coccinea*** Widely available
- from Giants Castle **new** CTca
- f. ***alba*** Widely available
- 'Anne' WHoo
- 'Ballyrogan Giant' CFir CTca CYeo ECho IBlr MAvo NCot NHol WPGP WSHC
- 'Big Moma' CPrp CYeo GMac MAvo
- 'Brick Red' MAvo NCot
- 'Cardinal' NHol WFar WMoo
- 'Caroline' NCot
- 'Cindy Towe' MAvo
- 'Countesse de Vere' EBee NCot
- 'Crawshaw Chance' LRHS
- early-flowering **new** NCot
- 'Elburton Glow' CPrp CYeo GMac NCot NLar WFar WHoo
- 'Fenland Daybreak' Widely available
- 'Gigantea' see *S. coccinea* 'Major'
- 'Good White' CYeo EBee MAvo NBir SUsu WCot
- 'Grandiflora' see *S. coccinea* 'Major'
- 'Hilary Gould' CPrp MAvo NCGa WFar WHal
- 'Hint of Pink' MAvo MDKP
- 'Jack Frost' EBee MAvo NCGa WMoo
- 'Jennifer' ♀H4 Widely available
- late-flowering NCot
- 'Maiden's Blush' CPrp EBrs ECGP ECtt EHrv GKir LRHS LSou MAvo MCot MDKP MWea NCot NHol NLar SBfd SPet WFar
§ - 'Major' ♀H4 Widely available
* - 'Marietta' NCot
- 'Mollie Gould' CTca CYeo EAEE EBee EBla ECtt EHrv EKen ELon EShb GCra LBMP LPio MAvo MHer MMHG NBre NCGa NCot NHol NLar SCoo SRms WFar WHil WPrP WTin WWEG
- 'Mrs Hegarty' Widely available
- 'November Cheer' CMac CPrp CSpr CTca CYeo IBlr NBir NCot NLar WFar WWEG
- 'Oregon Sunset' CPrp EBee GMac MDKP
- 'Pallida' CMil CPom CSam CYeo ECha ECtt EHrv ELan MLHP MMuc MRav MWea NBir NCot NLar SEND WFar
- 'Pink Marg' CPrp GMac MAvo NCot NLar
- 'Professor Barnard' CCCN CFee CHar CPrp CSpe CTca CYeo EBee ECho ECtt ELon EPfP EShb GAbr MAvo MBNS MSpe NBir NCot NEgg SApp SRot SWal WFar WMoo WOld WPtf WWEG
- 'Red Dragon' CYeo ECtt GAbr LLHF NCGa NCot NHol WCon WFar WHoo
- 'Salmon Charm' EBrs ECtt GBee GBin LRHS NCGa WFar WMoo
- salmon-flowered LSou NCot
- 'Salome' CPrp GMac NCot
- 'Silver Pink' IBlr
- 'Snow Maiden' CElw ECtt ELon GAbr GGar GKev MAvo NCot SPav
- 'Strawberry' CPrp EBee NCot
§ - 'Sunrise' ♀H4 Widely available
- 'Sunset' see *S. coccinea* 'Sunrise'
- 'Tambara' CMdw CPou CPrp CSam EBee EHrv GAbr LHop MAvo MWea NCot NLar SApp SMrm WFar
- 'Vera' NCot
- 'Viscountess Byng' CBcs CPrp CTca CTri CWCL CYeo EBee ECho ELon EPau IBlr IGor LRHS MSCN NBir NCot NLar SMrm SPav SPer WFar WPer
§ - 'Wilfred H. Bryant' Widely available
- 'Zeal Salmon' CAby CFee CFir CPou CPrp CYeo ECha EPot GAbr GMac MAvo NBir NCot NHol NLar SApp SMHy WFar

'Pink Princess' see *S. coccinea* 'Wilfred H. Bryant'

Schoenoplectus (*Cyperaceae*)

§ ***lacustris*** CWat EBWF GFor MMuc MSKA SEND SVic
§ - subsp. ***tabernaemontani*** EBWF SPer
- - 'Albescens' (v) CBen CKno CWat EBee LPBA MNrw MSKA MWts SWat WHal WPrP
- - 'Zebrinus' (v) CBen CBot CKno CWat ELan EPfP LPBA MMuc MNrw MSKA MWts NPla SPlb SWat WFar WHal WMAq WPrP

Schoenoxiphium (*Cyperaceae*)

'Golden Caterpillars' **new** WBox

Schoenus (*Cyperaceae*)

pauciflorus CWCL EBee EHoe EWes LLWG NOak WMoo WPGP WPrP

Sciadopitys (*Sciadopityaceae*)

verticillata ♀H4 CBcs CDoC CDoy CDul CKen CSBt EHul EPfP ERom GKir IDee LRHS MAsh MBlu MBri MGos MMuc NHol NWea SBfd SCoo SLim SSpi SWvt WDin WEve WFar WHar
I - 'Compacta' LRHS
- 'Firework' CKen
- 'Globe' CKen
- 'Gold Star' CKen
- 'Goldammer' NLar
- 'Golden Rush' CKen ECho MAsh MGos NLar WEve
- 'Goldmahne' CKen
- 'Grüne Kugel' CKen ECho NLar SLim

- 'Jeddeloh Compact'	CKen
- 'Kugelblitz'	WEve
- 'Kupferschirm'	CKen ECho NLar
- 'Mecki'	CKen ECho MBri WEve
- 'Megaschirm'	CKen
- 'Ossorio Gold'	CKen ECho WEve
- 'Perlenglanz'	NLar
- 'Picola'	CKen ECho MAsh NLar
- 'Pygmy'	CKen
- 'Richie's Cushion'	CKen ECho WEve
- 'Shorty'	CKen
- 'Speerspitze'	CKen
- 'Star Wars' **new**	CKen
- 'Starburst'	CKen
- 'Sternschnuppe'	CKen ECho MAsh NLar SLim WEve
- 'Wintergreen'	CKen

Scilla (*Hyacinthaceae*)

adlamii	see *Ledebouria cooperi*
× ***allenii***	see × *Chionoscilla allenii*
amethystina	see *S. litardierei*
amoena	ECho WCot
aristidis from Algeria	ECho
autumnalis	CAvo CDes CPom CStu EBWF EBrs ECho EPot LAma NRya WShi WThu
- JCA 0.872.602	WCot
- from Crete	ECho
- from Morocco	ECho
- subsp. ***fallax***	ECho
bifolia ♀H4	CAvo CFFs CPom CStu CTca EBrs ECho EPot LAma LLWP LRHS SDeJ SPhx WCot WShi
- RS 156/83	ECho WWst
- 'Alba'	ECho EPot SPhx
- 'Norman Stevens'	SCnR
- 'Rosea'	CStu ECho EPot LAma LLWP LRHS MWat SDeJ
bithynica ♀H4	WShi
campanulata	see *Hyacinthoides hispanica*
caucasica	WWst
chinensis	see *S. scilloides*
cilicica	CStu ECho SPhx
greilhuberi	CStu ECho LLHF WAbe WCot WWst
haemorrhoidalis MS 923	WCot
hohenackeri	SPhx WThu
- BSBE 559	WWst
- BSBE 811	WCot
§ ***hughii***	CDes ECho
hyacinthoides	ECho WBVN WCot WWst
ingridiae	ECho WWst
- var. ***taurica***	ECho WWst
italica	see *Hyacinthoides italica*
japonica	see *S. scilloides*
latifolia from Morocco	ECho
libanotica	see *Puschkinia scilloides* var. *libanotica*
liliohyacinthus	CRow ECho GCrs IBlr MMHG WSHC WShi WWst
lingulata	CStu ECho LLHF NMen WCot
- var. ***ciliolata***	CPBP ECho EPot
- var. ***lingulata***	ECho WCot
§ ***litardierei*** ♀H4	CBgR CMea CPom CStu CTca EBrs ECho EPPr EPot LAma MBri NMen SBch SDeJ SPhx WShi
- 'Orjen'	ECho
lutea hort.	see *Ledebouria socialis*
madeirensis	CLak
mauritanica	ECho WWst
melaina	WCot
cf. ***mesopotamica***	WWst
messeniaca	CPom
- HOA 0168	WWst
- MS 38 from Greece	WCot
mischtschenkoana ♀H4	CAvo CHid EBrs ECho EPot IFro LAma MBri WBVN
§ - 'Tubergeniana' ♀H4	CMea ECho GKev SPhx WCot
- 'Zwanenburg'	ECho
monophyllos	CStu ECho
morrisii	ECho
natalensis	see *Merwilla plumbea*
non-scripta	see *Hyacinthoides non-scripta*
numidica	ECho
nutans	see *Hyacinthoides non-scripta*
obtusifolia	ECho WCot
- subsp. ***intermedia***	ECho
persica ♀H4	CPom ECho LPio SPhx WCot
peruviana	Widely available
- S&L 285	WCot
- SB&L 20/1	WCot
- 'Alba'	CBcs CDes CFwr CPrp CSWP CStu CTca ECho LPio LRHS MTho SMrm WCot WWst
* - var. ***ciliata***	WCot
- var. ***elegans***	CDes
- 'Hughii'	see *S. hughii*
- var. ***ifniensis***	WCot
- var. ***venusta***	CDes
- - S&L 311/2	WCot
pratensis	see *S. litardierei*
puschkinioides	ECho
ramburei	ECho
reverchonii	ECho WWst
- from Spain	WCot
rosenii	ECho
§ ***scilloides***	ECho SCnR
- B&SWJ 8812	WCru
siberica ♀H4	CAby CAvo CBro CFFs CFox CTca EBrs ECho EPfP GAbr GKev LAma LRHS MMuc MWat SBch SMrm SPer SPhx WShi
- 'Alba'	CFox CTca ECho EPfP EPot LAma LRHS SBch WShi
- subsp. ***armena***	ECho
- 'Spring Beauty'	CMdw CMea ECho EPot GKev LAma LRHS MBri SDeJ SPhx SRms
'Tubergeniana'	see *S. mischtschenkoana* 'Tubergeniana'
verna	CDes EBWF EBrs ECho WShi WThu
vicentina	see *Hyacinthoides vicentina*
violacea	see *Ledebouria socialis*

Scindapsus (*Araceae*)

aureus	see *Epipremnum aureum*

Scirpoides (*Cyperaceae*)

§ ***holoschoenus***	CRWN EBWF

Scirpus (*Cyperaceae*)

cernuus	see *Isolepis cernua*
holoschoenus	see *Scirpoides holoschoenus*
lacustris	see *Schoenoplectus lacustris*
- 'Spiralis'	see *Juncus effusus* f. *spiralis*
maritimus	see *Bolboschoenus maritimus*
tabernaemontani	see *Schoenoplectus lacustris* subsp. *tabernaemontani*

Scleranthus (*Illecebraceae*)

biflorus	CTrC ECho EDAr EWes GGar NWCA SPlb WPer
perennis	ECho
singuliflorus	WPat

uniflorus CTrC ECho EShb NHol NWCA SMad SPlb WPrP

Sclerochiton (*Acanthaceae*)

harveyanus EShb

Scoliopus (*Trilliaceae*)

bigelowii GCrs SCnR WHal WWst
hallii EBee GCrs GEdr LEdu NMen SCnR WCru WWst

Scolopendrium see *Asplenium*

Scopolia (*Solanaceae*)

carniolica CArn CFir COld EBee ELan EWld GCrs GKir GPoy LEdu MPhe NChi NLar NSti SPhx SPlb WAul WCru WFar WPGP WSHC
- from Poland LEdu
- from Slovenia WCot
§ - var. ***brevifolia*** EHrv EPPr EWld GBin LEdu LRHS SDys SPhx WTin
- - WM 9811 MPhe
- subsp. ***hladnikiana*** see *S. carniolica* var. *brevifolia*
- 'Zwanenburg' EHrv EPPr EPot EWes LEdu NLar SPhx
lurida see *Anisodus luridus*

Scorzonera (*Asteraceae*)

hispanica SVic
suberosa subsp. ***cariensis*** CPBP

Scrophularia (*Scrophulariaceae*)

aquatica see *S. auriculata*
§ ***auriculata*** EBWF LPBA MHer NMir NPer WHer
§ - 'Variegata' (v) CArn CBcs EBee ECha ECtt EHoe ELan EPfP GCal GKir LLWG LPBA LRHS MHer NBid NCob NEgg SBfd SDnm SPer SPoG WFar WSHC
buergeriana 'Lemon and Lime' misapplied see *Teucrium viscidum* 'Lemon and Lime'
buergeriana 'Lemon and Lime' (v) NEgg
calliantha MDKP
grandiflora NBre SAga WCot WFar
nodosa CArn CRWN EBWF EBee GPoy NMir NSco WHer WHfH
- ***variegata*** see *S. auriculata* 'Variegata'
scopolii EBee

Scutellaria ✿ (*Lamiaceae*)

albida EBee
§ ***alpina*** CPBP ECho GJos NWCA SPlb SRms SRot WGor WPer
- 'Arcobaleno' GKev LLHF LRHS NLar SMrm
- 'Greencourt' WPat
- 'Moonbeam' GEdr NLar SMrm
altissima CArn ECha ELan ELon GKev GKir MMuc NBro SBfd SEND SGar SMrm SPlb WPtf
'Amazing Grace' EWes
baicalensis CArn EBee EWld GJos GKev GPoy MAvo SMrm WPtf
barbata CArn
canescens see *S. incana*
columnae EBee
costaricana EShb
diffusa ECtt
formosana 'China Blue' EPfP
galericulata CWan EBWF GPoy MHer
hastata see *S. hastifolia*
§ ***hastifolia*** CTri ECho ECtt
§ ***incana*** CBct CPom CSam EBee ECGP EHrv ELan ELon EPPr GBee GMaP LHop LPla MAvo MWea SMrm SUsu WCot
indica EWld WCFE
- var. ***japonica*** see *S. indica* var. *parvifolia*
§ - var. ***parvifolia*** CPBP EBee EBur ECho EWes GEdr NWCA SRot
- - 'Alba' CPBP ECho LLHF NWCA
lateriflora CArn GBar GPoy MNHC NMun WJek
maekawae EBee WPGP
- B&SWJ 557a WCru
novae-zelandiae ECho ECou
orientalis CArn CMea EBee ECtt GCal WAbe
- subsp. ***bicolor*** ECtt NWCA
- subsp. ***pinnatifida*** ECho NWCA
pontica CPBP EBee EDAr SBch SMrm WFoF
scordiifolia CEnt CMea CSam EBee ECha ECho EDAr GEdr IMou LRHS NRya NWCA SBHP SBch SRms WCom WFar WHal WHoo WTin
- 'Seoul Sapphire' CSpe EWes GAbr LEdu LRHS LSou WBVN WPtf
sevanensis EBee LHop WCot
'Sherbert Lemon' MWea SBfd SRot
suffrutescens 'Texas Rose' CPBP CSpe EBee LLHF LRHS MWea SBch SBfd SRot WNew
supina see *S. alpina*
tournefortii ECtt LLWP
* ***zhongdianensis*** WPtf

seakale see *Crambe maritima*

Sebaea (*Gentianaceae*)

rehmanii SPlb
thomasii GCrs WAbe

Securigera (*Papilionaceae*)

§ ***varia*** CArn EBee LHop MMuc NLar NPri SEND SRms

Sedastrum see *Sedum*

Sedum ✿ (*Crassulaceae*)

'Abbey Dore' EBee EBrs ELan EPfP GCal LPla LRHS NBPC NCGa NWsh SBfd SPoG SRkn WAbb WAul WBor WPGP
acre CTri EBWF ECho GJos GPoy LEdu LRHS MHer MNHC NMir SEND SPlb
- 'Aureum' ECho EDAr EHoe EPfP LAst NLar NPri NRya SPer SPoG WFar WNew WPat
- 'Elegans' ECtt GKir
- 'Golden Queen' ECho LRHS SPlb SPoG
- 'Helvetica' **new** WCot
- 'Minus' ECho EDAr
§ - subsp. ***neglectum*** var. ***majus*** CChe EPfP NLar
- 'Oktoberfest' GJos
adolphi EPfP
aizoon ECho GCal GKir LAst NBre SIde SPlb WFar
- 'Aurantiacum' see *S. aizoon* 'Euphorbioides'
§ - 'Euphorbioides' EBee ECha ECtt ELan MHer MMuc MRav NLar SEND SGar SHar SPer SPlb WFar WTin
albescens see *S. forsterianum* f. *purpureum*
alboroseum see *S. erythrostictum*

§	***album***	EBWF ECho LRHS MMuc NBro NMir SEND
	- 'Coral Carpet'	ECho ECtt EDAr EPfP GJos GKev MRav MWat NRya SFgr SPoG WCot WFar
	- subsp. ***gypsicola***	see *S. gypsicola*
§	- subsp. ***teretifolium*** var. ***murale***	CTri STre
	altissimum	see *S. sediforme*
*	***altum***	NBre WFar
§	***amplexicaule*** subsp. ***tenuifolium***	EBur
	anacampseros	NHol SEND SUsu
	anglicum	EBWF
	athoum	see *S. album*
	atlanticum	see *S. dasyphyllum* subsp. *dasyphyllum* var. *mesatlanticum*
	'Autumn Charm'	see *S.* (Herbstfreude Group) 'Lajos'
	Autumn Joy	see *S.* (*Herbstfreude Group*) 'Herbstfreude'
	balfourii HWJ 824	WCru
	'Bertram Anderson' ♀H4	Widely available
	beyrichianum misapplied	see *S. glaucophyllum*
	bithynicum 'Aureum'	see *S. hispanicum* var. *minus* 'Aureum'
	'Black Beauty' **new**	LRHS
	'Blade Runner'	EBee LRHS
	brevifolium	GGar NWCA
*	- var. ***novum*** **new**	MAsh
§	- var. ***quinquefarium***	WAbe
	burrito **new**	CStu
	'Carl'	Widely available
	caucasicum	WAbb WCot WEas
	cauticola ♀H4	CSpe ECho EDAr GCal GEdr LPio MBrN MHer MRav NBre NHol SRms SRot WAbe
	- from Lida	ECho
	- 'Coca-Cola'	CBct CCVN CWGN ECtt EHoe LAst LRHS NDov NPri SBfd SPhx SPoG SWvt WBor WFar WNew
	- 'Lidakense' ♀H4	CMea ECha ECho ECtt EPfP GKir LRHS MAvo MBri MLHP MSCN NHol NSla SBch SPlb SRot WCot WFar
	- 'Purpurine'	ECho GCal
	- 'Robustum'	see *S.* 'Ruby Glow'
	'Cloud Walker'[PBR] **new**	EBee WCot
	compressum	see *S. palmeri* subsp. *palmeri* tetraploid
	confusum Hemsl.	SChr SEND WFar WHoo
	crassipes	see *Rhodiola wallichiana*
	crassularia	see *Crassula setulosa* 'Milfordiae'
	'Crazy Ruffles'	EBee ECtt MAsh
	cryptomerioides B&SWJ 054	WCru
	cyaneum Rudolph	WAbe
	'Dark Jack'	MGos NDov
	dasyphyllum	ECho EDAr NRya SPlb SRms STre
§	- subsp. ***dasyphyllum*** var. ***mesatlanticum***	GKev NBir
	- ***mucronatis***	see *S. dasyphyllum* subsp. *dasyphyllum* var. *mesatlanticum*
	debile	WAbe
	'Diamond Edge' (v)	EBee ECtt MAsh WWEG
	douglasii	see *S. stenopetalum* 'Douglasii'
	drymarioides	NBre
	'Dudley Field'	MHer
	'Eleanor Fisher'	see *S. telephium* subsp. *ruprechtii*
	ellacombeanum	see *S. kamtschaticum* var. *ellacombeanum*

	'Elworthy Rose' **new**	CElw
§	***erythrostictum***	CBot CWan MTho WAbb
	- 'Frosty Morn' (v)	Widely available
§	- 'Mediovariegatum' (v)	EBee EBrs ELan EShb LRHS MHer MNrw MRav NCob NLar NPnk NWsh SBfd SPad SPoG SWvt WFar WMnd WMoo WWEG
	'Evening Cloud'	EBee ECha
	ewersii	ECho ECtt EDAr LRHS MMuc NBro NHol NLar SPhx SPlb
	- CC 5288	EWld
	- var. ***homophyllum*** 'Rosenteppich'	LRHS MBrN SWvt WCom WMoo
	fabaria	see *S. telephium* subsp. *fabaria*
	farinosum	GGar
	fastigiatum	see *Rhodiola fastigiata*
	forsterianum subsp. ***elegans***	SPlb
§	- f. ***purpureum***	NRya
	frutescens	STre
	furfuraceum	CStu NMen WAbe
	Garnet Brocade = 'Garbro'[PBR]	CCVN ECtt
§	***glaucophyllum***	WFar
	'Gold Mound'	EPfP LAst LRHS MGos NLar SPoG SVil
	'Green Expectations'	ECtt GBin MNFA MRav MWat NBre
§	***gypsicola***	EBee
	'Harvest Moon'	EBur
	(Herbstfreude Group) 'Autumn Fire'	EBee EBrs MAsh
	- 'Elsie's Gold' (v) **new**	EBee MAsh
§	- 'Herbstfreude' ♀H4	Widely available
	- 'Jaws'[PBR]	CKno EBee ECGP ECtt IKil LSou SMrm WClo WCot
§	- 'Lajos' (v)	EBee LRHS LSou MAsh
	- 'Mini Joy' **new**	GKir
	heterodontum	see *Rhodiola heterodonta*
	hidakanum	ECtt EHoe GGar GMaP NBro NHol NMen WHoo WTin
	himalense misapplied	see *Rhodiola* 'Keston'
	hispanicum	ECho EDAr NBre SPlb
	- ***glaucum***	see *S. hispanicum* var. *minus*
§	- var. ***minus***	ECho ECtt MMuc SEND SPlb
§	- - 'Aureum'	ECha ECho EDAr NHol
	humifusum	EBur NWCA
§	***hybridum***	WEas
	'Indian Chief'	see *S.* (Herbstfreude Group) 'Herbstfreude'
	integrifolium	see *Rhodiola integrifolia*
	ishidae	see *Rhodiola ishidae*
	'José Aubergine'[PBR]	CPrp EBee GBin IPot LRHS MBri NCGa WWEG
	'Joyce Henderson'	EBee EBrs ECtt GKir GQue LHop LRHS MCot MRav NCob NLar SPer SRGP SUsu WBrk WCom WCot WEas WMoo WTin WWEG
	kamtschaticum ♀H4	ECho GAuc GJos WFar
	- B&SWJ 10870	WCru
§	- var. ***ellacombeanum*** ♀H4	EDAr LRHS MMuc NMen SEND WCot
	- - B&SWJ 8853	WCru
§	- var. ***floriferum*** 'Weihenstephaner Gold'	CEnt CTri ECho ECtt EDAr EPfP GAbr GEdr GGar GKir GMaP LRHS MHer MMuc MRav MWat NBir NMen NPri SPlb SPoG SRms WAbe WFar
	- var. ***kamtschaticum*** 'Variegatum' (v) ♀H4	CMea ECho ECtt EDAr EHoe EPfP GKir LAst LBMP LRHS MAsh MHer MMuc MWat SPoG SRms SRot SWvt WCom WEas

	kirilovii	see *Rhodiola kirilovii*
	lanceolatum	NBre
	lineare	LAst
	'Little Gem'	see × *Cremnosedum* 'Little Gem'
§	***lydium***	CTri ECho GKir MHer SFgr SPlb
	- 'Aureum'	see *S. hispanicum* var. *minus* 'Aureum'
	- 'Bronze Queen'	see *S. lydium*
	makinoi 'Ōgon'	EBee
I	'Marchants Best Red' ♀H4	SMHy SUsu
	'Matrona' ♀H4	Widely available
	maweanum	see *S. acre* subsp. *neglectum* var. *majus*
	middendorffianum	ECho EDAr GKev MBrN MHer MWat NMen SEND SRms SRot WFar
	'Moonglow'	ECtt NMen
	moranense	MMuc SEND
	morganianum ♀H1	EBak EShb MSCN STre
	'Mr Goodbud'PBR ♀H4 **new**	EBee ECtt GBin MTis NDov SBfd WCot WFut WWEG
	'Munstead Red'	CMea COlW CPrp CWCL EBee EBla EBrs ECha ECtt EHrv EPfP GBin LHop LRHS MRav MWat NGdn NLar SBfd SGar SMrm SPer SPhx SPoG WCom WFar WKif WMnd WMoo
	murale	see *S. album* subsp. *teretifolium* var. *murale*
	nevii misapplied	see *S. glaucophyllum*
	nevii ambig.	SPlb
	nicaeense	see *S. sediforme*
	niveum	NMen
	obcordatum	NMen
	obtusatum misapplied	see *S. oreganum*
§	***obtusatum*** A. Gray	ECtt GGar NBro NSla STre WFar WPnn
	- subsp. ***boreale*** NNS 01-123	NWCA
	ochroleucum	MMuc NBre SEND
	oppositifolium	see *S. spurium* 'Album'
§	***oreganum***	ECha ECho EDAr GAbr GGar GKev GMaP MHer MSCN MWat NMen SPlb SRms SRot STre
	- 'Procumbens'	see *S. oreganum* subsp. *tenue*
§	- subsp. ***tenue***	LEdu NHol NRya WAbe WPat
§	***oregonense***	EBur ECho LRHS NMen
*	***oryzifolium*** 'Minus'	EBur
	oxypetalum	STre
	pachyclados	see *Rhodiola pachyclados*
	pachyphyllum	EPfP WNew
	palmeri	CHEx CSpe LSou MRav NBir SChr SGar SSvw STre
§	- subsp. ***palmeri*** tetraploid	EDAr SEND
	'Pewter'	ECho
	pilosum	NMen
§	***pluricaule***	ECho LRHS NSla SPlb SRms
	populifolium	ECha GCal GJos IMou MHer NLar SPhx STre WCom WPer
	praealtum	GGar SChr SEND STre WCot
	pulchellum	SPlb
	purdyi	see *S. spathulifolium* subsp. *purdyi*
	quinquefarium	see *S. brevifolium* var. *quinquefarium*
	'Red Cauli' ♀H4	CKno EBee ECha EPPr GBin IPot LHop LPio LRHS MAvo MBNS MBri MCot MNFA NCGa NDov NLar SMHy SPhx SSvw SUsu WCot WFar
	reflexum L.	see *S. rupestre* L.

	reptans	ECho NCob
	rhodiola	see *Rhodiola rosea*
	'Ripe Rhubarb' **new**	SMHy
	rosea	see *Rhodiola rosea*
	rubroglaucum misapplied	see *S. oregonense*
	rubroglaucum Praeger	see *S. obtusatum* A. Gray
	× ***rubrotinctum***	CHEx SChr
	- 'Aurora'	SChr
§	'Ruby Glow' ♀H4	Widely available
	'Ruby Glow' variegated (v) **new**	WPer
	'Ruby Port'	CSpe
§	***rupestre*** L.	EBWF ECho GGar MBNS MWat SEND SPlb SPoG WFar
	- 'Angelina'	EBee EPPr EWes IMou LRHS MAvo MGos MHer NBir NDov NHol NPri SPoG SRGP WCot
	- 'Monstrosum Cristatum'	NBir SMad
	ruprechtii	see *S. telephium* subsp. *ruprechtii*
	'Samuel Oliphant' (v)	WCot
	sarcocaule hort.	see *Crassula sarcocaulis*
	sarmentosum	ECho
§	***sediforme***	CArn EDAr EPot LRHS
	- 'Marrakesh' **new**	MSCN
	- ***nicaeense***	see *S. sediforme*
	selskianum	GGar NBre SBch WFar
	sempervivoides	ECho
	'September Ruby'	LRHS
	sexangulare	ECho EDAr EPot GGar MHer MMuc NRya SEND SFgr SPlb SRms STre WFar
	sibiricum	see *S. hybridum*
	sieboldii	ECho
	- 'Mediovariegatum' (v) ♀H2-3	CHEx COlW ECho MHer NCob NPri NSla SPlb WFar
	'Silvermoon'	EBur ECtt NHol
	spathulifolium	CTri ECha ECho MDKP
	- 'Aureum'	EBur ECho ECtt MWat WAbe
	- 'Cape Blanco' ♀H4	Widely available
§	- subsp. ***purdyi***	WAbe
	- 'Purpureum' ♀H4	CEnt COlW ECho ECtt EDAr EHoe EPfP GAbr GGar GKev GKir GMaP LAst LBee LRHS MHer MMuc MWat NHol NMen NPri NRya SEND SPer SPlb SPoG WAbe WFar WNew WPer
	- subsp. ***yosemitense*** 'Red Raver' **new**	CPBP
	spectabile ♀H4	CArn CChe CHEx CPrp CTri EBee ELan EPfP GJos GMaP LRHS MCot MHer MRav NCob NGdn SBfd SGar SPlb SRms WBVN WBor WBrk WCAu WFar WSFF WTin WWEG
	- 'Album'	CHEx NCob
	- Brilliant Group **new**	CBar
	- - 'Brilliant' ♀H4	CAby CBcs CKno CSBt CTri EBee ECha ECtt ELan EPfP GKir LAst LRHS MAsh MBri MGos MMuc MRav NGdn SBfd SEND SMad SPer SPoG SWvt WFar WMoo WWEG
	- - 'Carmen'	EBee LRHS WMoo
	- - 'Hot Stuff'	WCot
	- - 'Lisa'	GBin MAsh NDov NLar
	- - 'Meteor'	CPrp EBee MBNS MWat NLar SMrm WPer WWEG
	- - 'Neon'	EBee EBrs NCGa NDov
	- - 'Rosenteller'	EBee NBre NCGa SMrm WFar
§	- - 'Septemberglut'	EBee NBre NSti WCot
	- - 'Steven Ward'	EBee EWes SRGP

	- 'Iceberg'	Widely available
*	- 'Mini'	ELan MRav
	- 'Pink Chablis' PBR (v)	EBee NLar WCot
	- September Glow	see *S. spectabile* (Brilliant Group) 'Septemberglut'
	- 'Stardust'	CKno CPrp CTri EBee EPfP GKev GMaP LRHS MBNS MHer MRav NVic SMrm SPer SPet SPoG WFar WGor WWEG
	- 'Variegatum'	see *S. erythrostictum* 'Mediovariegatum'
	spinosum	see *Orostachys spinosa*
	spurium	CHEx ECho GJos MMuc NHol SEND SGar SRms STre
§	- 'Album'	NRya
	- 'Atropurpureum'	ECha ECho NCob WMoo
	- 'Coccineum'	ECho GJos LRHS MMuc MNHC SEND
	- Dragon's Blood	see *S. spurium* 'Schorbuser Blut'
	- 'Erdblut'	NMen
	- 'Fuldaglut'	CTri EBee ECho EDAr EHoe EPfP GMaP GQue IPot LRHS MNrw NRya SMrm WFar WMoo WNew WPer WPnn
	- 'Green Mantle'	EBee ECha ECho EPfP
	- Purple Carpet	see *S. spurium* 'Purpurteppich'
	- 'Purpureum'	SRms
§	- 'Purpurteppich'	EBee ECho ECtt GJos MRav NBro NHol NLar SRms
	- 'Roseum'	EWll SRms
	- 'Ruby Mantle'	EWll GKev GKir SBch SPoG SWvt WBVN WMoo
§	- 'Schorbuser Blut' ♀H4	CMea EBee ECho ECtt EPau EPfP GJos GKev GKir MCot MLHP MWat NBir NRya NVic SPlb SRGP SRms WEas WFar WHoo WTin
	- 'Summer Glory'	NLar
§	- 'Tricolor' (v)	CTri EBee ECha ECho EDAr EHoe MHer MLHP MRav NHol NPri NRya SPlb SPoG STre WFar WMoo
	- 'Variegatum'	see *S. spurium* 'Tricolor'
	- 'Voodoo'	CChe CEnt EBee ECtt EWes LBMP MHer MSCN WFar
	stenopetalum	SPlb
§	- 'Douglasii'	MHer SRms
	'Stewed Rhubarb Mountain'	CPrp EAEE EBee EBla ECha ECtt EPfP LHop LRHS LSou MBNS MNFA MRav NBro NCGa NLar SBfd SMrm SPur WFar WMoo WPGP WWEG
	stoloniferum	ECho
	'Sunset Cloud'	CHEx CMHG CSam EBee ECtt EWes GCal IPot LPla LRHS MRav NBre NCob
	takesimense B&SWJ 8518	WCru
	telephium	CArn NBir SRms
§	- Atropurpureum Group ♀H4	COIW EBee ELan EPfP MRav SWvt WCom WCot WEas WWEG
	- - 'African Pearl'	ECtt MCot WCFE WCot WWEG
	- - 'Arthur Branch'	CPrp EBee GBin MTho WWEG
I	- - 'Atropurpureum Nanum'	WWEG
	- - 'Black Emperor'	EBee
	- - 'Bon Bon'	CPrp EBee MBNS
	- - 'Bressingham Purple'	EBrs LRHS
	- - 'Chocolate'	CBcs EBee ECtt EPPr LRHS MAvo MBNS MGos NLar
	- - 'El Cid'	EBee EWes
	- - 'Hester'	EBee WSpi WWEG
	- - 'Karfunkelstein' ♀H4	EBee EPPr GBin MAvo NDov SPhx SUsu WCot
	- - 'Leonore Zuuntz'	EBee NBre
	- - 'Lynda et Rodney'	EWes WCot
	- - 'Lynda Windsor'	CBct CBow EBee ECtt EHrv EPfP GAbr GQue MBNS NLar NMoo NPnk SPoG SRGP SWvt WFar
	- - 'Möhrchen'	EBee EHrv GBin GMaP MRav NGdn NLar NPnk NWsh SBfd SMrm SPoG WCom WFar WMnd WMoo
	- - 'Picolette'	EBee IPot LRHS
	- - 'Postman's Pride' PBR	CKno CWGN EBee ECtt EPfP GQue IPot LRHS MNHC MTis MWat NCGa SPoG SUsu WCot WFut WWEG
§	- - 'Purple Emperor' ♀H4	Widely available
	- - 'Ringmore Ruby'	WCot WWEG
	- - 'Xenox' PBR ♀H4	CWGN EBee EBrs ECtt EKen EPPr EPfP ETod EWll GBin IPot LRHS MAsh MAvo MBNS MCot NLar SBfd SHar SPoG WCot WPGP WWEG
	- 'Bronco' PBR	NDov
	- Emperor's Waves Group	GQue NGdn
§	- subsp. ***fabaria***	MRav NWsh SMrm WAbb WCot WFar WWEG
	- - var. ***borderei***	CAby CElw LPla SBch SPhx SUsu
	- 'Jennifer'	WCot
	- subsp. ***maximum***	CBot
	- - 'Atropurpureum'	see *S. telephium* Atropurpureum Group
	- - 'Gooseberry Fool'	CMea COIW CPrp EBee ECGP ECtt EPfP EWTr GMaP NSti SBch SPhx SPur WFar WWEG
	- 'Roseum'	WWEG
§	- subsp. ***ruprechtii***	CPrp EBee ECha ECtt EPPr EPfP GAuc GMaP LRHS MNFA MRav NSti SPer SPet SPhx WBVN WEas WFar WMoo WPer
	- - 'Citrus Twist'	EBee EBla ECtt LRHS LSou MBNS MRav NPnk WPtf
	- - 'Hab Gray'	CSpe EBee ECtt ETod EWes GBin GQue LAst LRHS MAvo MCot MTis NBPC NLar SAga SMrm SUsu WClo WCot
	- - 'Pink Dome'	ECha
	- 'Strawberries and Cream'	Widely available
	- subsp. ***telephium***	GCra
	- 'Variegatum' (v)	MDKP WHal
	tenuifolium	see *S. amplexicaule* subsp. *tenuifolium*
	- subsp. ***ibericum***	see *S. amplexicaule* subsp. *tenuifolium*
	ternatum	WFar
	trollii	see *Rhodiola trollii*
	urvillei Sartorianum Group	MHer
	ussuriense	EBee ECha EPfP GCal SUsu
	- 'Chuwangsan'	EWld WCru
	- 'Turkish Delight'	EWll GJos
	'Veluwse Wakel'	GBin
	'Vera Jameson' ♀H4	Widely available
	viviparum B&SWJ 8662	WCru
	'Washfield Purple'	see *S. telephium* 'Purple Emperor'
	'Weihenstephaner Gold'	see *S. kamtschaticum* var. *floriferum* 'Weihenstephaner Gold'
	weinbergii	see *Graptopetalum paraguayense*
	yezoense	see *S. pluricaule*
	'Zebra'	LOck LRHS

Seemannia see *Gloxinia*

Selaginella ✿ (*Selaginellaceae*)

	braunii	CLAP WCot
	erythropus	CBty
	var. ***sanguinea*** **new**	

helvetica	CStu IMou
kraussiana ♀H1	CLAP EDAr GGar NHol WRic
- 'Aurea'	CBty CCCN LRHS SMad WRic
- 'Brownii' ♀H1	CBty CCCN ISha LRHS
- 'Gold Tips'	CBty CCCN ISha LRHS
lepidophylla	SVic
moellendorfii	CBty ISha WRic
sanguinolenta	CStu
tamariscina	WAbe
uncinata ♀H1	CBty CLAP ISha WRic

Selago (*Scrophulariaceae*)

flanaganii	WCot
galpinii	CPBP WAbe
serrata new	WCot
thunbergii new	LHop

Selinum (*Apiaceae*)

carvifolium	EBee LRHS
tenuifolium	see *S. wallichianum*
§ ***wallichianum***	Widely available
- EMAK 886	EBee GPoy SDix
- HWJK 2224	WCru
- HWJK 2347	WCru

Selliera (*Goodeniaceae*)

radicans	ECou EDAr GBin GGar

Semele (*Ruscaceae*)

androgyna	CHEx CRHN

Semiaquilegia (*Ranunculaceae*)

§ ***adoxoides***	CPom EBee SHar
'Early Dwarf'	EDif
§ ***ecalcarata***	CBot CDes CPom EBee ECho GBBs GCal GGar GKev GKir LRHS NGdn SBch SRms SSvw WCru WFar WHal WPGP WTou
* - f. ***bicolor***	WCru WFar
- 'Flore Pleno' (d)	WTou
- 'Snowbell'	WCru
simulatrix	see *S. ecalcarata*
'Sugar Plum Fairy' new	EPfP SPoG

Semiarundinaria (*Poaceae*)

from Korea	EPla
§ ***fastuosa*** ♀H4	CBcs CDoC CEnt CHEx CPMA EAmu EBee ENBC EPfP EPla EUJe IMou LMaj LPal MMoz MMuc MWht NMoo SAPC SArc SEND SPlb WJun
- var. ***viridis***	CEnt EPla LPJP MWht SBig WCru WJun
kagamiana	CDoC EBee ENBC EPla IMou MMoz MMuc MWhi MWht NMoo SBig SEND WJun
§ ***lubrica***	MWht
makinoi	CGHE EAmu EPla MWht SLPl WJun WPGP
nitida	see *Fargesia nitida*
§ ***okuboi***	CEnt EBee ENBC EPla LPal MMoz MWht WJun
villosa	see *S. okuboi*
yamadorii	EPla MMoz MWht WJun
- 'Brimscombe'	EPla
yashadake	CEnt EPla WJun
- 'Gimmei'	EPla
- f. ***kimmei***	CDoC CEnt EBee ENBC EPla LRHS MAsh MGos MMoz MMuc MWht NLar NMoo SBig SEND WDyG WFar WJun WMoo WPGP
I - - 'Inversa'	CEnt

Sempervivella see *Rosularia*

Sempervivum ✿ (*Crassulaceae*)

sp. new	SArc
from Andorra	ESem NHol
from Sierra Nova	ESem
'Abba'	EDAr WHal WPer
'Adelaar'	CWil NMen
'Adelmoed'	CWil SFgr
'Adeltruid'	NHol
'Adlerhorst'	NHol
'Aglow'	ESem MHom NMen
'Aladdin'	CWil ESem GEdr NMen SRms
'Albernelli'	NHol SFgr
'Alchimist'	ESem
'Alcithoë'	ESem
'Aldo Moro'	CWil ECha EDAr ESem GAbr LBee LRHS MHom NMen SFgr WIvy
'Alice' new	ESem
'Alidae'	ESem
allionii	see *Jovibarba allionii*
'Alluring'	ESem GAbr
'Alpha'	ESem LBee LRHS MTis NHol NMen SFgr SRms STre WHal WPer WTin
altum	CWil ESem LRHS MHom MTis NMen SPlb
'Amanda'	CWil ECha EDAr ESem MBrN MTis NMen SRms WHoo WPer WTin
'Ambergreen'	ESem NMen
andreanum	see *S. tectorum* var. *alpinum*
'Apache' Payne	see *Jovibarba heuffelii* 'Apache'
'Apache' Haberer	ESem NMen
'Apollo'	NHol SFgr
'Apple Blossom'	CMea ECha ESem NMen
arachnoideum ♀H4	Widely available
- from Cascade Piste 7	ESem
- 'Ararat'	SDys
- 'Boria'	ESem
- var. ***bryoides***	CWil ESem LRHS NMen WAbe WIvy WPer
- 'Cebennense'	ESem
- 'Clärchen'	EPot ESem MSCN NHol NMen NSla SFgr WAbe
- cristate	CWil
* - ***densum***	EDAr LRHS MSCN MTis WAbe WFar
- subsp. ***doellianum***	see *S. arachnoideum* subsp. *tomentosum* var. *glabrescens*
- form No 1	ECho
- from the Abruzzi, Italy	ESem
- 'Laggeri'	see *S. arachnoideum* subsp. *tomentosum* (C.B. Lehm. & Schnittsp.) Schinz & Thell.
- 'Opitz'	WCom WPer
- 'Peña Prieta'	NHol
- red	NMen
- 'Red Wings'	ECha NMen SRms
- 'Rubrum'	CHEx GKir GMaP LRHS SPlb
- 'Sultan'	ESem
- subsp. ***tomentosum*** misapplied	see *S.* × *barbulatum* 'Hookeri'
§ - subsp. ***tomentosum*** (C.B. Lehm. & Schnittsp.) Schinz & Thell. ♀H4	CHEx CWil ESem LRHS MSCN NHol NMen NPer SFgr SPlb SRms WAbe WGor WPer
- - GDJ 92.04	CWil
§ - - var. ***glabrescens***	NMen SDys WPat
- - 'Minus'	NHol NMen
§ - - 'Stansfieldii'	ESem GAbr LRHS NMen SDys STre WHal

	- 'Transsylvanicum' new	ESem
§	- 'White Christmas'	CWil MHer
	arachnoideum* × *calcareum	CWil NHol NMen WIvy WTin
	arachnoideum* × *montanum	see *S.* × *barbulatum*
	arachnoideum* × *nevadense	CWil SDys
	arachnoideum* × *pittonii	CWil MTis NHol NMen WAbe
	arenarium	see *Jovibarba arenaria*
	'Arlet' new	EDAr
	armenum	ESem NMen
	- var. ***insigne***	ESem
	'Arondina'	CWil
	'Aross'	CMea ESem GAbr NMen
	'Artist'	CWil ESem NMen SFgr
	arvernense	see *S. tectorum*
	'Ashes of Roses'	EPot ESem MHom NMen WAbe WGor WPer
	'Asteroid'	CWil ESem NMen
	'Astrid'	CWil
	atlanticum	ESem MHom NMen NSla SRot
	- from Atlas Mountains, Morocco	CWil ESem
	- from Oukaïmeden, Morocco	CWil ESem GAbr NHol NMen WTin
	- 'Edward Balls'	CWil ESem SDys SFgr
	'Atlantis' ambig.	ESem NHol
	'Atropurpureum' ambig.	CHEx CWil EDAr GAbr GEdr MBrN NMen SRms WGor WIvy WPer
	'Aureum'	see *Greenovia aurea*
	'Averil'	CWil
	'Aymon Correvon'	ESem
	balcanicum	CWil EDAr ESem NMen WIvy
	ballsii	LRHS NMen
	- from Kambeecho, Greece	MHom
	- from Smólikas, Greece	CWil ESem MHom NMen
	- from Tschumba Petzi, Greece	CWil ESem MHom SDys
	'Banderi'	ESem
	'Banjo'	ESem
	'Banyan'	ESem LRHS
	'Barbarosa'	CWil ESem
§	× ***barbulatum***	ESem NMen SDys WCom WPer
§	- 'Hookeri'	CTri CWil EPot ESem MSCN NLar NMen SFgr WAbe WPer
	'Bascour Zilver'	CMea CWil ECha ESem LBee SFgr WHal
	'Beaute'	ESem
	'Bedazzled'	ESem
	'Bedivere'	CPBP CWil LBee LRHS NMen SRms
*	'Bedley Hi'	ESem MHom
	'Bella Donna'	ESem MHom NHol NMen WPer
	'Bella Meade'	CWil EDAr ESem NMen SFgr SRms WPer
	'Bellotts Pourpre'	CWil NHol
	'Benny Hill'	CWil ESem
	'Bernstein'	CWil EDAr EPot ESem MHer SFgr WHal
	'Beta'	ESem MHom NHol NMen WAbe WPer WTin
	'Bethany'	CMea CWil ESem NHol NMen WHal
	'Bicolor' ambig.	EPfP
	'Big Mal'	NHol
	'Big Slipper'	ESem NHol
	'Binstead'	ESem NHol
	'Birchmaier'	NMen SFgr
	'Black Beauty'	EPot
	'Black Claret'	NHol
	'Black Knight'	LRHS MHer SPlb SRms WHal
	'Black Mini'	CWil EPot ESem GAbr MDKP NBir NMen SRms WAbe
	'Black Mountain'	CHEx CWil ESem LBee LRHS
	'Black Prince'	ECha ESem
	'Black Velvet'	ESem WCom WIvy WPer
	'Bladon'	WPer
	'Blood Sucker'	ESem WGor
	'Blood Tip'	CHEx CMea CWil ECha ESem GAbr GCra LRHS MHer MSCN NHol NMen NRya SEND SPlb SPoG SRms WFar WGor WHal WHoo WPer
	'Blue Boy'	CWil ECha EPPr ESem GAbr LBee LRHS NHol NMen SFgr SRms WCom WOut WPer
	'Blue Moon'	ESem NMen
	'Blue Time'	ESem GEdr SFgr WHoo WTin
	'Blush'	EDAr ESem
	'Boissieri'	see *S. tectorum* subsp. *tectorum* 'Boissieri'
	'Bold Chick'	ESem
	'Bombardier' new	EDAr
	'Booth's Red'	CHEx NMen WGor
	'Boreale'	see *Jovibarba hirta* subsp. *borealis*
	borisii	see *S. ciliosum* var. *borisii*
	borissovae	CWil ESem MHom NMen SDys
	'Boromir'	CWil EDAr ESem
	'Boule de Neige'	NMen NRya
	'Bowles's Variety'	WCom WPer
	'Braune Maus'	ESem SFgr
	brevipilum from Turkey	ESem
	'Bright Eyes'	ESem
	'Britta'	ESem SDys
	'Brock'	CWil ECha ESem LRHS MHer MHom NHol WPer
	'Bronco'	CDes CHEx CWil ECho ESem GAbr LBee LRHS MHom NMen SRms WCot WFar WHfH WPGP
	'Bronze Beauty'	EDAr
	'Bronze Pastel'	CWil ECha EDAr ESem MHom NMen NSla SEND SFgr SRms SRot WGor WTin
	'Bronze Tower'	NHol
	'Brown Owl'	CWil ECho ESem NHol SRms WFar
	'Brownii'	ESem NMen WPer WTin
	'Brunette'	ECho GAbr
	'Burgundy'	ECha ESem
	'Burgundy Velvet'	ESem
	'Burnatii'	see *S. montanum* subsp. *burnatii*
	'Burning Desire'	WGor
	'Burnished Bronze' new	ESem
	'Butterbur'	ESem
	'Butterfly'	ESem
	'Café'	CWil MSCN NHol NMen SFgr SRms WIvy WPer
	× ***calcaratum***	EDAr SRms
	calcareum	CMea CSam CWil EWll GKir LRHS MAsh MMuc NBro NEgg NMen NWCA SPlb SPoG SRms SRot WFar WHoo WPer
	- GDJ 92.15 from Petite Ceüse, France	CWil
	- GDJ 92.16 from Petite Ceüse, France	CWil
	- from Alps, France	CWil ESem
	- from Calde la Vanoise, France	CWil NMen
	- from Ceüze, France	CWil ESem WIvy
	- from Cleizé, France	see *S. calcareum* 'Limelight'
	- from Col Bayard, France	CWil ESem GAbr NMen

	- from Colle St Michel, France	CWil ESem NMen SFgr
	- from Gorges supérieures du Cians, France	CWil ESem NMen
	- from Mont Ventoux, France	CWil ESem
	- from Petite Ceüse, France	ESem SRot
	- from Queyras, France	CWil ESem NMen
	- from Route d'Annôt, France	CWil ESem NMen
	- from Triora, Italy	CWil ESem NHol NMen
	- 'Benz'	ESem SDys
	- 'Cristatum'	CStu
	- 'Extra'	CHEx CWil ESem GAbr GEdr MSCN SFgr SRot
	- 'Greenii'	CWil ESem GKev LRHS MMuc NHol NMen SEND SPlb
§	- 'Grigg's Surprise'	CWil ESem MHer NMen SPlb WFar
	- 'Guillaume'	CWil ESem NMen SFgr SRot WHoo
§	- 'Limelight'	CMea CWil EDAr LRHS NHol NMen WHal WIvy WPer WTin
	- 'Monstrosum'	see *S. calcareum* 'Grigg's Surprise'
	- 'Mrs Giuseppi'	CWil ECho ESem ETod GAbr LBee LRHS NMen SFgr SRms STre WAbe WFar WPer
	- 'Pink Pearl'	CWil MSCN NMen SDys SFgr WIvy WTin
	- 'Sir William Lawrence'	CMea CPBP CWil ECho EDAr ESem NMen SFgr WAbe WHal WHoo WIvy WPer WThu WTin
	'Caldera'	NHol
*	***calopticum* × *nevadense***	WTin
	'Cameo'	see *Jovibarba heuffelii* var. *glabra* 'Cameo'
	'Canada Kate'	CWil ESem NHol WPer
	'Cancer'	ESem
	'Candy Floss'	CWil NMen WGor
	cantabricum	CWil ESem MMuc NMen SEND WThu
	- from Cue Vas de Sol **new**	ESem
	- from Cuengas Piedras	ESem
	- from Cuevas del Sil, Spain	CWil
	- from Navafria, Spain	CWil NHol WTin
	- from Peña Prieta, Spain	NMen
	- from Piedrafita, Spain	ESem
	- from Riaño, Spain	CWil ESem GAbr
	- from San Glorio, Spain	CWil ESem GAbr NMen
	- from Santander, Spain	NHol
	- from Ticeros	ESem NMen
	- from Tizneros, Spain	CWil
	- from Valvarnera, Spain	ESem NMen
	- subsp. ***cantabricum*** GDJ 93.13 from Peña de Llesba, Spain	CWil
	- - from Leitariegos, Spain	CWil GAbr MHom NMen
	- - from Pico del Lobo, Spain	CWil
	- subsp. ***guadarramense***	see *S. vicentei* subsp. *paui*
	- - from Pico del Lobo, Spain, No 1	SRot
	- - from Pico del Lobo, Spain, No 2	ESem
	- - from Valvanera, Spain, No 1	CWil NMen
	- subsp. ***urbionense***	CWil GEdr
	- - from El Gatón, Spain	CWil
	- - from Picos de Urbión, Spain	CWil ESem NMen
	cantabricum* × *montanum subsp. ***stiriacum***	WEas WTin
	cantabricum* × *montanum subsp. ***stiriacum*** 'Lloyd Praeger'	CWil

	'Canth'	NHol
	'Caramel'	ESem
*	× ***carlsii***	ESem
	'Carmen'	ESem SFgr
	'Carneum'	ESem NHol
	'Carnival'	ESem NMen WPer
	caucasicum	CWil ESem GEdr GKir MHom NMen
	'Cavo Doro'	CWil SFgr
	'Celon'	ESem
	'Centennial'	ESem
	'Cerluke' **new**	ESem
	charadzeae	CWil ESem LBee LRHS NHol
	'Charolensis' **new**	ESem
	'Chartbury' **new**	EDAr
	'Cherry Frost'	ECho NMen SFgr STre WAbe
	'Cherry Glow'	see *Jovibarba heuffelii* 'Cherry Glow'
	'Cherry Tart'	ESem
	'Chivalry'	ESem
	'Chocolate'	ESem NHol WAbe WPer
§	× ***christii***	ESem NHol NMen
	'Christmas Time'	ESem NHol SFgr
	chrysanthum	ESem
	ciliosum ♀H4	CMea CPBP CWil ECho ESem GMaP NMen NRya
	- from Alí Butús, Bulgaria	SDys
	- from Pestani **new**	ESem
§	- var. ***borisii***	EPfP ESem GCal GKev NMen NRya WAbe WHal
	- var. ***galicicum*** 'Mali Hat'	CPBP NMen WPer
	ciliosum* × *ciliosum var. ***borisii***	CTri NMen
	ciliosum* × *grandiflorum	CWil ESem NMen
	ciliosum* × *marmoreum	ESem NMen
	ciliosum* × *tectorum	WTin
	'Cindy'	ESem SRms
	'Circlet'	CWil ESem NMen
	'Cistaceum'	WEas
	'Clara Noyes'	ESem WFar WPer
	'Clare'	ESem MHer
	'Claudine'	ESem
	'Clemanum'	ESem
	'Cleveland Morgan'	ECha ESem MHom NBro NMen
	'Climax' ambig.	ECho EPfP ESem MHom NMen WFar
	'Clisette'	ESem
	'Cobweb Capers'	ESem MHom MTis
	'Cobweb Centres'	ESem NMen
	'Cochise'	ESem
	'Collage'	ESem NHol WPer
	'Collecteur Anchisi'	ESem NHol SDys SFgr
	'Commander Hay' ♀H4	CHEx EDAr EPfP ETod EWes GCra LHop MHom MSCN NDov NMen NPer SRGP SRms STre WEas WHal WIvy WJek WPer
	'Comte de Congae'	ESem MTis NMen
	'Concorde'	LRHS
	'Congo'	ESem NMen SFgr
	'Conran'	NHol
	'Corio'	ESem
	'Cornstone'	ECha ESem NHol
	'Corona'	CWil ESem NHol SFgr SRms WPer
	'Coronet'	ESem
	'Corsair'	CWil ECha ESem GEdr MBrN NMen SFgr WGor WIvy WPer WTin
	'Cranberry'	ESem
	'Cresta'	ESem
	crested	ESem
	'Crimson King'	SFgr
	'Crimson Velvet'	CHEx CMea ESem LBee LRHS NHol SFgr WCom WPer

'Crimson Webb'	ESem
§ 'Crispyn'	CWil ESem LBee LRHS MHer MHom NHol NMen SFgr WEas WPer
'Croky'	ESem
'Croton'	ESem WPer
'Cupream'	CWil ESem SRms WPer
'Czakor'	NHol
'Dakota'	CWil EDAr ESem NHol NMen SFgr
'Dallas'	CWil NHol NMen SRms
'Damask'	CWil LBee LRHS NMen SFgr WPer
'Dame Arsac'	ESem
'Dancer' **new**	ESem
'Dancer's Veil'	ESem
'Darjeeling'	CWil
'Dark Beauty'	CMea CWil ECha ESem LRHS MSCN NMen WAbe WCot WGor WHal WPer
'Dark Cloud'	CWil ESem GAbr LBee LRHS WHoo WIvy WPer
'Dark Point'	CWil ESem MHom NMen SFgr WCom
'Dark Velvet' **new**	CMea
'Darkie'	CWil ESem SFgr WPer
davisii	ECha
'Deep Fire'	CWil ESem NHol NMen SRms WAbe WIvy WTin
× ***degenianum***	ESem GAbr NMen SFgr WPer
'Delta'	MHom NMen WHoo WTin
densum	see *S. tectorum*
'Devon Jewel'	WGor
'Diamant'	ESem
'Diane'	CWil ESem SFgr
'Director Jacobs'	CWil EDAr ESem NHol NMen SEND SFgr WEas WPer WTin
'Disco Dancer'	ESem
'Doctor Roberts'	NHol
dolomiticum	ESem NMen
dolomiticum* × *montanum	ESem GKev NBro NMen SFgr WTin
'Donarrose'	ESem NHol SFgr
'Downland Queen'	CWil ESem NHol
'Dragoness'	ESem
'Duke of Windsor'	NMen SFgr
'Dunscar Hybrid' **new**	ESem
'Dunstan Seedling' **new**	ESem
'Dusky'	ESem
'Dyke'	CTri CWil EDAr ESem GAbr NHol NMen SFgr WHal
dzhavachischvilii	ESem NMen
'Edge of Night'	CWil NHol SRms
'Eefje'	CWil ESem
'El Greco'	ESem
'El Toro'	ECha ESem MHom
'Elgar'	WIvy WPer
'Elizabeth'	ESem WPer
'Elvis'	CWil MHom NMen SFgr
'Emerald Giant'	CWil ESem NHol SFgr SRms WPer WTin
'Emerson's Giant'	CWil ESem NMen
'Eminent' **new**	ESem
'Emma Jane'	ESem
'Emmchen'	CWil
'Engle's'	CMea CTri ECha ESem LRHS MHer MTis NMen SRms WHal WPer
'Engle's 13-2'	ESem NBro NHol NMen
'Engle's Rubrum'	CPBP EPot LBee NHol NMen
erythraeum	CMea ESem LRHS MHom NHol NMen SPlb WAbe WHal
- from Pirin, Bulgaria	NMen
- from Rila, Bulgaria	NMen
'Excalibur'	ESem NMen WIvy
'Exhibita'	CWil ESem SDys SRms
'Exorna'	CWil ECha EDAr ESem MHom NMen SFgr WEas WIvy WPer
'Fair Lady'	CWil ESem MHom MTis NMen
'Fairy'	EPot
'Fame'	ESem NHol
'Fat Jack'	CWil
×***fauconnettii***	CWil EDAr ESem NHol NMen SFgr
- 'Thompsonii'	CWil ESem NHol NMen
'Feldmaier'	ESem GAbr
'Festival'	EDAr ESem NMen
'Fiery Furness'	ESem
'Fiesta' ambig.	WHal
fimbriatum	see *S.* × ***barbulatum***
'Finerpointe'	ESem
'Fire Glint'	CWil ESem GEdr NHol SRms WIvy
'Firebird'	ESem NMen SFgr
'Firefly'	ESem
'First Try'	ESem
flagelliforme **new**	ESem
'Flaming Heart'	CWil EDAr ESem MBrN NMen WGor WPer
'Flamingo'	ECha ESem NMen
'Flanders Passion'	ECha LBee LRHS NMen SRms WPer
'Flasher'	ESem WPer
'Forden'	CHEx MSCN SFgr WGor
'Ford's Amiability'	ESem SDys
'Ford's Shadows'	SDys
'Ford's Spring'	CWil ESem NHol NMen WIvy WPer
'Freeland'	WPer
'Frigidum'	ESem
'Frolic'	ESem
'Fronika'	CWil
'Frost and Flame'	NHol
'Frosty'	CWil ESem SFgr SRms
'Fuego'	CWil ESem MHom SFgr
'Fuji' **new**	ESem
×***funckii***	CHEx CWil EDAr ESem MBrN NHol NMen SDys WPer WTin
'Furryness'	ESem
'Fuzzy Wuzzy'	EDAr ESem MTis
'Gallivarda'	CWil ESem MSCN
'Gambol'	ESem NHol
'Gamma'	CHEx CWil ESem LBee LRHS NHol NMen SDys SRms WEas WTin
'Garnet'	ECho ESem WIvy WPer
'Gay Jester'	CTri CWil ESem SFgr WHoo WTin
'Gazelle'	ESem WIvy WPer
'Genevione'	CWil ESem
'Georgette'	CWil ECha ESem NMen WPer
'Gilosum' **new**	EDAr
'Ginger'	ESem
'Ginnie's Delight'	CWil NMen
giuseppii	LBee MHer NHol NMen WPer
- GDJ 93.17 from Coriscao, Spain	CWil
- GDJ 93.04 from Cumbre de Cebolleda	CWil
- from Coriscao, Spain	LRHS
- from Peña Espigüete, Spain	CWil ESem NMen SDys
- from Peña Prieta, Spain	CWil NMen
'Gizmo'	CWil ESem SFgr
'Gleam'	ESem
'Gloriosum' ambig.	EDAr ESem SFgr WPer
'Glowing Embers'	CWil ESem MHom NMen WHal WPer
'Goldie'	ESem

'Goya' **new**	ESem
'Graceum'	ESem
'Grammens' **new**	ESem
'Granada'	EDAr ESem NMen
'Granat'	CWil ESem LRHS MHer NMen SRms WCom WIvy WPer
'Granby'	CWil ECho LBee LRHS NMen SDys
grandiflorum	CWil ESem NMen WPer
- from Valpine	ESem NMen
- 'Fasciatum'	ESem NMen
- 'Keston'	ESem
grandiflorum* × *montanum	see *S.* × *christii*
'Grape Idol'	CWil ESem
'Grapetone'	ESem MHom NMen SDys WHal
'Graupurpur'	CWil
'Green Apple'	CWil GAbr MHom NMen SDys
'Green Dragon'	ESem LRHS MSCN WOut
'Green Gables'	EDAr ESem WPer
'Green Giant'	ESem
'Green Ice'	CWil
'Greenwich Time'	EDAr ESem NMen
* ***greigii***	EPot
'Grenadier'	ESem
'Grey Dawn'	LRHS MHom MTis
'Grey Ghost'	ESem NMen WIvy WPer
'Grey Green'	CWil NHol
'Grey Lady'	CElw CMea CWil ESem
'Grey Owl'	GMaP LRHS
'Grey Velvet'	CWil
'Greyfriars'	CMea EDAr EPot ESem LBee LRHS MTis NMen SFgr WGor WPer
'Greyolla'	CWil ESem WPer
'Gruaud Larose'	NHol
'Grünrand'	ESem
× ***guiseppe***	ESem
'Gulle Dame'	CWil ESem MHom SFgr
'Hades'	ESem
'Halemaumau'	CWil ESem
I 'Hall's Hybrid'	CWil ESem GAbr NBro SRms STre
'Hall's Seedling'	GKir
'Happy'	CWil ESem NMen SFgr SRms WGor WIvy WPer WThu
'Hart'	CWil NHol SRms WTin
'Havana'	ESem NMen
'Hayling'	ESem LRHS NHol NMen SRms WPer
'Heavenly Joy'	NHol
'Heigham Red'	CWil EPPr ESem LBee LRHS NHol NMen WPer
'Helen' **new**	EDAr
'Heliotroop'	ESem SDys SRot
helveticum	see *S. montanum*
'Hester'	CHEx CWil ECho ESem MBrN NBro NMen SRms WFar
'Hey-hey'	EPot ESem LBee LRHS MBrN NDov NMen SPlb SRms WPer
'Hidde'	CWil ESem SFgr WIvy WPer
'Hidde's Roosje'	ESem NMen
'Hirsutum'	see *Jovibarba allionii*
hirtum	see *Jovibarba hirta*
'Hispidulum'	ESem
'Hookeri'	see *S.* × *barbulatum* 'Hookeri'
'Hopi'	CWil NHol SRms
'Hortulanus Smit'	NMen
'Hot Peppermint'	ESem
'Hullabaloo'	EDAr ESem SFgr
'Hurricane'	CWil ESem MTis WIvy WPer
'Icicle'	CHEx CMea ESem LRHS MSCN NBro NHol NMen SRms WAbe WGor WOut
imbricatum	see *S.* × *barbulatum*
'Imperial'	CWil MHom
'Inge'	see *Jovibarba heuffelii* 'Inge'
ingwersenii	ESem MHom
ingwersenii* × *pumilum	CWil ESem
ingwersenii* × *pumilum from Spain	NMen
'Iophon'	LBee LRHS
iranicum **new**	ESem
'Irazu'	CWil ESem GAbr LRHS NMen SDys SFgr SRms WPer
'Irene'	ESem SFgr
'Isaac Dyson'	SDys SRot
italicum	ESem MHom NMen
'Itchen'	ESem NMen
'Iwo'	CHEx ESem NMen SFgr WIvy
'Jack Frost'	CWil NBro NMen SFgr
'Jacquette'	CWil ESem
'Jade' ambig.	ESem
'Jamie's Pride'	WGor
'Jane'	ESem
'Jasper'	ESem
'Jaspis'	ESem
'Jelly Bean'	CWil ESem NMen SFgr
'Jet Stream'	CWil EPPr ESem LRHS MHom NMen SDys SPlb WGor
'Jewel Case'	CWil ESem LRHS NMen SRms
I 'John Hobbs seedling No. 2' **new**	ESem
'John T.'	ESem WEas
'Jolly Green Giant'	ESem MHom
'Jo's Spark'	NSla
'Jubilee'	CMea CWil ECho EDAr ELan ESem MHer NHol NMen SRms STre WGor WPer
'Jubilee Tricolor'	ESem NHol NMen SFgr WAbe
* 'Julia'	ESem
'Jungle Fires'	CMea CWil EPot ESem ITim NHol SDys SRms WHoo
'Jungle Shadows'	EDAr ESem
'Jurato'	NHol
'Justine's Choice'	CWil SRms
'Kalinda'	ESem MHom NMen
'Kappa'	CTri ESem NBro NHol NMen SDys SRot WPer
'Katmai'	CWil ESem NHol
'Kelly Jo'	CWil ESem NBro NMen WFar WTin
'Kelut'	ESem
'Kermit'	ESem MHom NMen
'Kerneri'	NHol
'Kia' **new**	CWil
'Kibo'	ESem WIvy
'Kimble'	ESem WPer
'Kimono'	ESem
kindingeri	CWil ESem MHom NMen NWCA
'King George'	CTri CWil ECha ESem GKir ITim LBee LRHS NMen SFgr SRms STre WGor WHal WHoo WPer WTin
'King Lear' **new**	ESem
'Kip'	CMea ECha NMen WGor WIvy WPer
'Kismet'	NMen
'Koko Flanel'	CWil ESem SFgr
'Korspel Glory 4'	CWil
'Korspelsegietje'	CWil ESem GAbr
kosaninii	ESem NHol NMen SFgr WPer WTin
- from Koprivnik, Slovenia	MSCN NMen SDys WAbe
* - from Visitor	CWil
- 'Hepworth'	NHol
'Kramer's Purpur'	NMen

'Kramer's Spinrad'	CHEx CMea CPBP CWil ECha ESem GAbr LBee LRHS NMen NWCA SDys SFgr STre WEas WHoo WIvy WTin
'Krater' **new**	ESem
'Kubi' **new**	ESem
'Lady Kelly'	ESem NMen WIvy
'L'Arte' **new**	ESem
'Launcelot'	ECha ESem WPer
'Laura Lee' **new**	ESem
'Lavender and Old Lace'	CHEx CWil ESem GAbr LRHS MSCN NMen SFgr WNew WPer
'Laysan'	CWil NHol
Le Clair's hybrid No 4	NMen
'Lemon and Lime' **new**	ESem
'Lennik's Glory'	see *S.* 'Crispyn'
'Lennik's Glory No.2' **new**	ESem
'Lennik's Time'	ESem
'Lentezon'	ESem
'Leocadia's Nephew'	ESem NMen
'Leon Smits'	CWil ESem
'Les Yielding'	ESem
'Lilac Time'	CMea CWil ESem GAbr LRHS MBrN MHer MSCN NMen SFgr SPlb SRms WHal WIvy WPer
'Lime Frost' **new**	ESem
'Lion King'	CWil ESem MSCN
'Lipari'	CElw ECha EPot ESem NMen SRms
'Lipstick'	ESem NMen
'Little Bo Bo'	ESem
'Little Flirt' **new**	MSCN
'Lively Bug'	CWil EDAr ESem GEdr LBee LRHS MSCN SDys WCom WGor WPer
'Lloyd Praeger'	see *S. montanum* subsp. *stiriacum* 'Lloyd Praeger'
'Long Shanks' **new**	MSCN
'Lonzo'	CWil SRms
'Lynn's Choice'	CWil GAbr SFgr WHal WIvy WPer
macedonicum	ESem NMen WTin
- from Ljuboten, Macedonia/Kosovo	CWil ESem NMen
'Madeleine'	CWil ESem
'Magic Spell'	CWil ESem NMen
'Magical'	CWil
'Magnificum'	CWil ESem NMen WGor
'Mahogany'	CHEx CTri CWil ECho EDAr ESem LBee LRHS MHer NHol NMen NWCA SFgr SRms STre WEas WGor WHal WIvy WNew
'Maigret'	CWil WPer
'Majestic'	CWil ESem LBee LRHS NMen
'Major White'	CHEx
'Malby's Hybrid'	see *S.* 'Reginald Malby'
'Marella'	ESem WPer
'Maria Laach'	CWil ESem
'Marijntje'	CWil ESem NHol NMen WPer
'Marjorie Newton'	CWil ESem WPer
'Marmalade'	ESem
§ ***marmoreum***	ECho EPot LBee LRHS NMen SRms STre WFar WHal WPer
- from Kanzan Gorge, Bulgaria	EPot ESem NHol NMen
- from Monte Tirone, Italy	LRHS SDys
- from Okol, Albania	ESem NMen
- 'Brunneifolium'	CWil ESem GAbr GCal LBee LRHS NHol NMen WIvy WPer
- 'Bruno'	STre
- subsp. ***marmoreum*** var. ***dinaricum***	ESem MHer NMen
- - - from Karawanken **new**	ESem
'Martin' **new**	ESem
'Mate'	ESem NMen
'Maubi'	CHEx
'Mauna Kea'	WPer
'Mauvine'	NHol
'Mayfair' **new**	EDAr
'Maytime'	ESem
'Medallion'	ESem SFgr
'Meisse'	ECho
'Melanie'	CWil ESem MBrN NMen WIvy
'Memorial Merit' **new**	ESem
'Mercury'	CWil ESem GAbr LRHS NBro NHol NMen SRms
'Merlin'	ESem MSCN
'Metallicum'	ESem
'Midas'	CWil ECha ESem GEdr LRHS SFgr
'Milá'	CWil
'Mini Frost'	CWil NMen WPer
'Missouri Rose'	NHol
'Mixed Spice'	CWil
'Moerkerk's Merit'	CWil ESem GAbr MTis NHol NMen
'Mondstein'	CWil ESem GMaP SFgr SRms WIvy WPer
'Monique'	WPer
'Monseigneur Desmet' **new**	ESem
'Montage'	CWil
§ ***montanum***	ESem NMen WPer
- from Arbizion	CWil
- from Gavarnie, France **new**	ESem
- from Ljuboten **new**	ESem
- from Monte Tirone	LBee
- from Monte Tonale, Italy	CWil
- from Windachtal, Germany	CWil NMen
§ - subsp. ***burnatii***	CWil ESem MHom NMen WIvy
- 'Caesar'	MSCN
- subsp. ***carpaticum***	CWil
- - 'Cmiral's Yellow'	MSCN NMen SFgr WAbe WCom WIvy
* - Fragell form	SFgr
- subsp. ***montanum***	CWil
- 'Rubrum'	see *S.* 'Red Mountain'
- subsp. ***stiriacum***	CWil ESem GEdr NMen SFgr
- - from Mauterndorf, Austria	ESem
- - from Puerto de San Francisco, USA **new**	ESem
§ - - 'Lloyd Praeger'	CWil ESem LBee LRHS NMen SDys SFgr WIvy WPer
montanum* × *tectorum var. ***boutignyanum*** GDJ 94.15	CWil
'Moondrops'	CWil
'More Honey'	CWil NMen SFgr SRms
'Morning Glow'	WGor WHal WPer
'Mount Hood'	ESem LRHS SRms WHal
'Mrs Elliott'	ESem
'Mulberry Wine'	CWil ESem LBee LRHS NHol WHoo
'Mystic'	CWil ESem MBrN NMen WPer
'Neon'	CWil
nevadense	CWil EPot NMen SFgr SRms
- from Calar de Santa Barbara, Spain GDJ 96A-07	CWil
- from Puerto de San Francisco	CWil ESem
- var. ***hirtellum***	CWil NMen
'Nico'	CWil SRms
'Night Raven'	CMea MTis WIvy WPer
'Nigrum'	see *S. tectorum* 'Nigrum'
'Niobe'	ESem SFgr WHal
'Noir'	CWil EDAr ESem NBro NMen WAbe
'Norbert'	CWil EDAr SRms WIvy WPer
'Norne'	ESem
'Nouveau Pastel'	CMea CWil ESem NMen WHal WPer

'Novak'	CWil
'Octet'	CWil NMen
octopodes	NBir SIde
- var. ***apetalum***	CWil ESem GAbr MSCN NMen SRms WIvy
'Oddity'	CPBP CWil ECha ESem ETod MBrN MHer NMen WCot WHal WPer
'Ohio Burgundy'	ECha ESem LRHS NMen WAbe WPer WTin
'Old Copper' **new**	ESem
'Olivette'	ECha ESem NMen WPer WTin
'Omega'	WPer
'Ornatum'	EPot ESem MHer MHom NMen SRms WAbe WEas WHal WIvy WPer
ossetiense	CWil EDAr ESem GAbr GKev NMen
'Othello'	CTri EPfP GCra NBir STre WCot WPGP WPer WTin
'Ottelein' **new**	CWil
'Pacific Feather Power'	NMen
'Pacific Purple Shadows'	CWil
'Packardian'	CWil ESem NHol NMen SFgr WIvy
'Painted Lady'	CWil ESem
'Palissander'	EDAr ESem GAbr NMen SFgr WPer
'Pam Wain'	MHom NMen
'Panola Fire'	WFar
'Paricutin'	SDys
'Passionata'	CWil ESem SFgr
'Pastel'	CWil ESem NMen
patens	see *Jovibarba heuffelii*
'Patrician'	CWil ESem LBee LRHS SRms
'Peggy'	CWil ESem WGor
'Pekinese'	CWil EDAr EPot ESem GEdr ITim LRHS MBrN NBro NHol NMen SRms WEas WGor WPer
'Peterson's Ornatum'	SDys
'Petsy'	ESem SRms
'Pilatus'	ECha EWes LBMP SRms WFar WPer
'Pink Astrid'	CWil ESem
'Pink Button'	CWil
'Pink Cloud'	CWil LRHS NMen SRms
'Pink Dawn'	ESem
'Pink Delight'	ESem
'Pink Flamingoes'	ESem
'Pink Lemonade'	CWil ESem MHom
'Pink Mist'	WPer
'Pink Puff'	CWil ESem MHom NMen SRms
'Pippin'	CWil ESem SRms WPer
'Piran'	CWil
pittonii	CMea CWil EPot ESem GAbr NMen WHal
'Pixie'	CPBP CWil ESem NMen SFgr WIvy WPer
'Plum Frosting'	MSCN WGor
'Plum Mist'	NHol
'Plumb Rose'	CWil ESem NMen WIvy WPer
'Pluto'	CWil ESem LBee LRHS NHol
'Poke Eat'	ESem
'Polaris'	CWil ESem MHom
'Poldark'	ESem
'Pompeon'	ESem
'Ponderosa'	CWil
'Pottsii'	CWil ESem
I 'Powellii'	ESem
'Precious'	ESem
'Procton'	ESem
'Proud Zelda'	EDAr ESem GAbr MTis NMen
'Průhonice'	CWil SRms WFar
'Pseudo-ornatum'	LBee LRHS SRms
'Pumaros'	NMen SDys
pumilum	CWil LRHS NMen
- from Adyl-Su, Chechnya, Russia, No 1	CWil
- from Armkhi	ESem SDys
- from El'brus, Russia, No 1	CWil ESem
- from Techensis	CWil NMen
- 'Sopa'	CWil ESem NMen
'Purdy'	MHom MSCN WAbe
'Purdy's 50-6'	CWil ESem GAbr
'Purdy's 70-40'	ESem
'Purple Beauty'	EPot ESem
'Purple King'	CMea MHom MTis SDys
'Purple Passion'	ESem
'Purple Queen'	CWil EDAr ESem LRHS
'Pygmalion'	CWil ESem
'Queen Amalia'	see *S. reginae-amaliae*
'Quintessence'	CWil NHol SFgr SRms
'Racey'	CWil ESem
'Ragtime'	ESem
'Ramses'	ESem SDys
'Raspberry Ice'	CMea LBee LRHS MSCN NBro NHol NMen WPer
'Rauer Kulm'	CWil ESem
* 'Rauheit'	WFar
'Rauhreif'	ESem WFar
'Red Ace'	CWil ECha GEdr NBro NDov NMen SFgr SRms WFar WPer
'Red Beam'	CWil ESem MSCN
'Red Chips'	EDAr MHom
'Red Delta'	CWil NBir NMen SFgr WCot
'Red Devil'	CMea CWil ECha LRHS NHol NMen SFgr SPlb WHoo WPer WTin
'Red Giant'	ESem
'Red Lion'	CWil GEdr SFgr
'Red Lynn'	CWil
§ 'Red Mountain'	CWil ESem LBee LRHS NWCA SRms
'Red Pink'	CWil
'Red Robin'	EDAr ESem GMaP
'Red Rum'	WPer
'Red Shadows'	LBee LRHS WPer WTin
'Red Spider'	CWil EPot MHom NBro NMen
'Red Summer'	ESem
'Regal'	ESem NMen
'Regina'	NMen
reginae	see *S. reginae-amaliae*
§ ***reginae-amaliae***	CWil EPot ESem NHol NMen
- from Kambeecho, Greece, No 1	ESem
- from Kambeecho, Greece, No 2	NMen SDys
- from Mavri Petri, Greece	CWil ESem SDys
- from Sarpun, Turkey	CWil ESem NMen SDys WTin
- from Vardusa, Serbia	CWil ESem SDys
§ 'Reginald Malby'	CTri ECho ESem GMaP LRHS NMen SFgr SRms WIvy
'Reinhard'	CMea CWil ECha EDAr EPot ESem GEdr LRHS MBrN MHer NMen SPlb SRms WFar WHal WHoo WIvy WPer
'Remus'	CWil ECha ELan ESem NMen SDys SFgr SRms WGor
'Rex'	NMen
'Rhône'	CWil ESem LBee LRHS
'Rich 'n' Fruity' **new**	MSCN
'Risque'	CWil ESem LBee LRHS WPer
'Rita Jane'	CWil ECha ESem MHom NMen SFgr WTin
'Robin'	ITim LBee LRHS NBro NHol SRms WTin
'Ronny'	CWil ESem

'Roosemaryn'	EDAr ESem
'Rose Queen'	ESem
'Rose Splendour'	NHol
× ***roseum***	ESem
- 'Fimbriatum'	CWil ESem GAbr LBee LRHS NHol SFgr WEas
'Rosie'	CMea CPBP CWil EPot GAbr GEdr ITim LBee LRHS NHol NMen SRms WHal WHoo WPer WTin
'Rotkopf'	CWil ESem MSCN NHol NMen SFgr SRms
'Rotmantel'	SDys WTin
'Rotsandsteinriese'	ESem
'Rotund'	CWil ESem GEdr
'Rouge'	ESem NMen
'Royal Mail'	ESem
'Royal Opera'	CWil EDAr ESem NMen
'Royal Ruby'	ECha ESem LBee MSCN NMen SRms WIvy WOut
'Royale'	SFgr
'Rubellum'	CWil ESem
'Rubellum Mahogany'	SFgr
'Rubikon Improved'	ESem
'Rubin'	CMea CTri ECha EPfP GGar GKev MAsh MSCN NBir NEgg NMen NPri NWCA SPoG SRms WAbe WClo WEas WNew WOut WPer
I 'Rubra Ash'	CWil ESem NMen WAbe WTin
'Rubrum Ray'	CWil EDAr ESem SRms
* 'Ruby Glow'	EDAr
'Ruby Heart'	EDAr
'Russian River'	CMea WHoo WTin
'Rusty'	CWil ESem SFgr
ruthenicum	ESem LRHS MHom NRya
- 'Regis-Fernandii'	ECho
'Safara'	CWil ESem
'Saffron'	NMen
'Saga'	ESem MHom
'Santis'	ESem
'Sarah'	EDAr ESem NMen
'Sarotte'	CWil
'Sassy Frass'	ESem NMen
'Saturn'	ESem NMen
schlehanii	see *S. marmoreum*
schnittspahnii	ESem
'Seminole'	CWil ESem
'Serendipity' **new**	EDAr
'Shadri'	ESem
'Sha-Na'	CWil
'Sharon's Pencil'	CWil ESem
'Sheila'	GAbr
'Shirley Moore'	CWil EDAr ESem SFgr WTin
'Shirley's Joy'	ESem NMen WTin
'Sideshow'	CWil ESem
'Sigi' **new**	ESem
'Sigma'	ESem
'Silbering'	LBMP
'Silberkarneol' misapplied	see *S.* 'Silver Jubilee'
'Silberspitz'	CWil LRHS MHer MHom NBro NMen SPlb WPer
'Silver Cup'	CWil ESem SFgr WIvy
§ 'Silver Jubilee'	CMea CWil ECha EDAr ESem GAbr LRHS NBro SPlb SRms WGor
'Silver Queen'	CWil ESem SFgr
'Silver Shadow'	WGor
'Silver Spring'	ESem
'Silver Thaw'	CWil ECha EDAr NMen SFgr
'Silverine'	CWil EDAr
'Silvertone'	CWil ESem
'Simonkaianum'	see *Jovibarba hirta*
'Sioux'	CPBP CWil ESem GAbr LBee LRHS MBrN NMen WFar WHal WIvy WPer WTin
'Skrocki's Bronze'	ESem GAbr LRHS WPer
'Slabber's Seedling'	CWil
'Small Wonder'	CWil
'Smaragd'	CWil ECha ESem LBee LRHS WFar
'Smokey Jet'	ESem SFgr
'Snowberger'	CWil EPot ESem LRHS NMen SFgr SRms WGor WHal WPer
'Soarte'	ESem
soboliferum	see *Jovibarba sobolifera*
'Soothsayer'	CWil NMen
sosnowskyi	CWil NMen
'Spanish Dancer'	NMen
'Speciosum'	ESem
'Spherette'	CWil EDAr MBrN MSCN NMen WAbe WPer
'Spider's Lair'	EDAr MHom
'Spinellii'	WThu WTin
'Springmist'	CWil EPot ESem GAbr GMaP LRHS MTis SFgr SRms WGor WPer WTin
'Sprite'	CWil GEdr MTis NMen SDys WIvy WTin
'Squib'	CWil MSCN
stansfieldii	see *S. arachnoideum* subsp. *tomentosum* 'Stansfieldii'
'Starion'	CWil
'Starshine'	MHer NHol NMen SFgr
'State Fair'	CWil EDAr NHol NMen WCom WIvy WPer
* ***stoloniferum***	GAbr
'Strider'	CWil GAbr WTin
'Stuffed Olive'	CWil SDys SRot
'Sun Waves'	CWil ESem NHol SDys SFgr
'Sunray Magic'	WGor
'Super Dome'	CWil
'Superama'	ESem
'Syston Flame'	CWil NMen
'Tamberlane'	EDAr
'Tarita'	CWil
§ ***tectorum*** ♀H4	CArn CHby CSam CTri ECho EDAr ELan EPfP GKir GPoy LBee LRHS MHer MNHC NMen SBfd SIde SPlb STre WFar WJek
- from Eporn	CWil NMen
§ - var. ***alpinum***	CWil ESem LRHS MHom NBro NHol NMen
- - from Sierra del Cadi, Spain	NHol
- var. ***andreanum***	CWil
- 'Atropurpureum'	ECho ELan NHol NMen WCom WTin
- 'Atrorubens'	NHol
- 'Atroviolaceum'	EDAr ESem NHol NLar NMen WFar WIvy WTin
* - 'Aureum'	SFgr
- var. ***boutignyanum*** GDJ 94.04	CWil
- - GDJ 94.02 from Sant Joan de Caselles, Andorra	CWil
- - GDJ 94.03	CWil
- - from Route de Tuixén, Spain	ESem
- var. ***calcareum***	ECho
- subsp. ***cantalicum***	SRms
§ - 'Nigrum'	ESem LBee LRHS MHer NBro NHol NMen SDys SRms WGor WTin
- 'Red Flush'	CWil EDAr GKir MBrN NMen SDys SFgr WFar WPer
- 'Royanum'	ESem GAbr MSCN

*	- subsp. ***sanguineum***	EDAr
	- 'Sunset'	CMea EDAr ESem NMen SDys SFgr WHal
	- subsp. ***tectorum***	ESem
§	- - 'Boissieri'	CWil NMen SRms WIvy
	- - 'Triste'	CHEx CWil LBee LRHS NMen SRms WAbe WFar
	- 'Tokajense' **new**	ESem
	- 'Violaceum'	MHom SRms STre WAbe WGor
	tectorum × ***zeleborii***	WTin
	'Tederheid'	ESem LBMP
	'Telfan'	NMen
	'Terracotta Baby'	CWil ESem SFgr
	'Thayne'	NMen
	'The Platters'	CWil
	× ***thompsonianum***	CWil NHol NMen SFgr
	'Thunder'	CWil ESem
	'Tiffany'	NHol WPer
	'Tiger Bay'	NHol
	'Tina'	WPer
	'Tip Top'	CWil ESem GEdr SFgr
	'Titania'	CWil NBro NMen WHal WTin
	'Topaz'	CWil ECha LBee LRHS NMen SFgr SRms
	'Tordeur's Memory'	CWil LBee LRHS NMen
	'Tracy Sue'	EDAr
	'Trail Walker'	CWil ESem LBee LRHS SRms
	transcaucasicum	CWil
	'Tree Beard'	CWil
	'Tristesse'	CWil EDAr NMen SFgr WGor
	'Truva'	CWil ESem NMen SFgr
	'Tumpty'	WGor
	'Twilight Blues'	CWil ESem LRHS SFgr
	'Undine'	CWil ESem SFgr
	'Unicorn'	ESem
	'Utopian' **new**	ESem
	× ***vaccarii***	CWil NMen
	'Vanbaelen'	CWil NMen SDys
	'Vanessa'	CWil
	× ***versicolor***	NHol
	'Veuchelen'	CWil
	vicentei	MHom NMen WFar WTin
	- from Gaton	LBee LRHS NMen
§	- subsp. ***paui***	NSla
	'Video'	CWil ESem MHom NMen SFgr
	'Violet Queen'	ESem
	'Virgil'	CWil EDAr ESem GAbr MBrN MSCN MTis NMen SDys WAbe WCot WGor WPer WTin
I	'Virginius'	CWil GAbr
	'Warners Pink'	MDKP
	'Warrior' **new**	EDAr
	'Watermelon Rind'	MTis
	webbianum	see *S. arachnoideum* L. subsp. *tomentosum* (C.B. Lehm. & Schnittsp.) Schinz & Thell.
	'Webby Flame'	CWil
	'Webby Ola'	NMen
	'Wega'	NMen
	'Weirdo'	CWil
	'Wendy'	NMen
	'Westerlin'	CWil ECha NMen
	'White Christmas'	see *S. arachnoideum* 'White Christmas'
	'White Eyes'	NMen
	'Whitening'	EDAr GAbr NMen
I	'Woolcott's Variety'	CWil ECho ESem LRHS MDKP MSCN NBir NMen SFgr WFar WPer WTin
	wulfenii	CWil NMen
*	- ***roseum***	EDAr
	'Xaviera'	CWil ESem
	zeleborii	SDys WHal
	'Zenith'	CWil EDAr ESem GAbr SFgr SRms
	'Zenobia'	MHom
	'Zenocrate'	WHal
	'Zepherin'	CWil MSCN
	'Zilver Moon'	CWil NMen
	'Zircon'	EDAr NMen
	'Zone'	CHEx MTis NMen
	'Zorba'	NMen
	'Zulu'	ECha SFgr

Senecio (*Asteraceae*)

	B&SWJ 10703 from Colombia	WCru
§	***articulatus***	EShb SGar STre
	bidwillii	see *Brachyglottis bidwillii*
	buchananii	see *Brachyglottis buchananii*
	chrysanthemoides	see *Euryops chrysanthemoides*
	cineraria 'Ramparts'	EBee
	- 'Silver Dust' 🏆H3	EPfP
	- 'White Diamond'	ECha
*	***coccinilifera***	SBch
	compactus	see *Brachyglottis compacta*
	confusus	see *Pseudogynoxys chenopodioides*
	crassissimus	EShb
	doria	EShb LRHS WFar WHrl
	fistulosus	LEdu
	formosoides B&SWJ 10736	WCru
	formosus B&SWJ 10700	WCru
	- B&SWJ 10746	WCru
	gerberifolius B&SWJ 10357	WCru
	- B&SWJ 10361	WCru
	grandifolius	see *Telanthophora grandifolia*
	'Gregynog Gold'	see *Ligularia* 'Gregynog Gold'
	greyi misapplied	see *Brachyglottis* (Dunedin Group) 'Sunshine'
	greyi Hook.	see *Brachyglottis greyi* (Hook. f.) B. Nord.
	heritieri DC.	see *Pericallis lanata* (L'Hér.) B. Nord.
	hoffmannii	EShb
	integrifolius subsp. ***capitatus***	SPlb
	kleiniiformis	EShb
	laxifolius hort.	see *Brachyglottis* (Dunedin Group) 'Sunshine'
	leucostachys	see *S. viravira*
	macroglossus	CHll EShb WFar
	- 'Variegatus' (v) 🏆H1	ERea EShb
	mikanioides	see *Delairea odorata*
	monroi	see *Brachyglottis monroi*
	niveoaureus B&SWJ 714	WCru
	petasitis	CHEx CTrC
	polyodon	CCCN CSpe CSpr EBla EPPr EShb GAbr GBin GMac LBMP MNrw MWea NCGa NDov NLar SPhx SPoG WMoo WPGP WWEG
	- S&SH 29	CFir EBee
	- subsp. ***subglaber***	EWes
	przewalskii	see *Ligularia przewalskii*
	pulcher	CDTJ CDes CGHE CSam LEdu MNrw SHar SMrm SUsu WCot WPGP
	reinholdii	see *Brachyglottis rotundifolia*
	rowleyanus	EBak EShb STre
	scandens	CBre CCCN CPLG EShb MNrw WPGP
	seminiveus	EBee

§ ***serpens***	CStu EShb SEND
§ ***smithii***	ELan GBee NBid WCot WCru WFar WWEG
spedenii	see *Brachyglottis spedenii*
squalidus	WHer
'Sunshine'	see *Brachyglottis* (Dunedin Group) 'Sunshine'
talinoides	EShb
subsp. ***cylindricus*** 'Himalaya'	
tanguticus	see *Sinacalia tangutica*
§ ***viravira*** ΨH3-4	CWan EPfP EShb MCot SDix SMad SMrm SPer WEas WSHC

Senna (*Caesalpiniaceae*)

alata B&SWJ 9772	WCru
alexandrina	CCCN EBee EShb LRHS WPGP
artemisioides ΨH1	SOWG
§ ***corymbosa***	CBcs CBot CCCN CHEx CRHN CSpe CTri SMrm SOWG
- 'John Bull Amberley' **new**	SGar
didymobotrya	SOWG
×***floribunda***	LRHS
hebecarpa	SPhx
§ ***marilandica***	CArn EBee ELan EWes WHil
retusa	CHEx
septemtrionalis	CCCN EBee LRHS WPGP

Sequoia (*Cupressaceae*)

sempervirens ΨH4	CBcs CDoC CDul CLnd CMCN CMac CMen ECrN EHul EPfP ERom EWTr IFFs LMaj MMuc NMun SAPC SArc SEND SLim STre WDin WEve WMou
- 'Adpressa'	CDoC CTho EHul EPfP EPla IDee IFFs LRHS MAsh MBri MGos NHol NWea SCoo SLim WFar
- 'Cantab'	SLim WMou
- 'Henderson Blue' **new**	SLim
- 'Prostrata'	CDoC GGar LRHS MAsh MMuc SLim WFar
- 'Simpson's Silver' **new**	SLim

Sequoiadendron (*Cupressaceae*)

giganteum ΨH4	Widely available
- 'Bajojeka'	NLar
- 'Barabits Requiem'	GKir IArd LRHS MBlu NLar SLim SMad
- 'Blauer Eichzwerg'	NLar SLim
- 'Blue Iceberg'	CKen
- 'Bultinck Yellow'	MBlu NLar SMad
- 'Cannibal'	NLar
- 'Curley Green' **new**	NLar
- 'French Beauty'	NLar
- 'Glaucum'	CDoC CTho LRHS MAsh MBlu MBri NLar SLim SMad SPoG
* - 'Glaucum Compactum'	MBlu
- 'Greenpeace'	MBlu NLar
- 'Hazel Smith'	SMad
- 'Lightening Green' **new**	NLar
- 'Little Stan'	CKen NLar
- 'Pendulum'	CDoC CDul CKen GKir MBlu MGos NLar SLim SMad SWvt
- 'Philip Curtis'	NLar
- 'Pierie' **new**	NLar
- 'Pirat' **new**	NLar
- 'Powdered Blue'	LRHS NLar SLim
- 'Variegatum' (v)	GKir MGos
- 'Von Martin'	NLar

Serapias (*Orchidaceae*)

lingua	SCnR

Serenoa (*Arecaceae*)

repens	EAmu LPal

Seriphidium (*Asteraceae*)

caerulescens var. ***gallicum***	CEls
§ ***canum***	CEls MHer
§ ***ferganense***	CEls
§ ***fragrans***	CEls
§ ***maritimum***	CArn GGar GPWP ILis MHer
- var. ***maritimum***	CEls
§ ***nutans***	CEls MCot MRav
§ ***tridentatum***	CArn EBee
- subsp. ***tridentatum***	CEls
tripartitum var. ***rupicola***	CEls
§ ***vallesiacum*** ΨH4	CEls EBee ECGP SUsu WEas

Serissa (*Rubiaceae*)

foetida	see *S. japonica*
§ ***japonica***	STre
- ***rosea***	STre
- 'Variegata' (v)	STre
- 'White Snow'	MGos

Serratula (*Asteraceae*)

bulgarica	WCot
coronata	EBee LRHS
- subsp. ***insularis*** f. ***alba***	GAbr
§ ***seoanei***	CKno CMea CPom EBee ECha EDAr LHop LPla LRHS MCot MHer MLHP MRav MWat SBch SDix SPhx SRms SUsu WCot WEas WFar WPGP WPat WPrP WTin
shawii	see *S. seoanei*
tinctoria	CArn GBar NLar NMir SPhx WOut
- subsp. ***macrocephala***	EBee EBrs LRHS
wolffii	EBee

Serruria (*Proteaceae*)

florida	SPlb

Sesamum (*Pedaliaceae*)

indicum	CArn

Sesbania (*Papilionaceae*)

punicea	CCCN CSpe SOWG

Seseli (*Apiaceae*)

elatum	CSpe LPio
gummiferum	CArn CBot CHid CSpe EBee LPio NLar SDix SEND SPhx SPur WPtf
hippomarathrum	EBee LPio SPhx WCot WHrl WPGP
§ ***libanotis***	CSpe EBee IMou LEdu LPio LPla NDov NLar SBch SDix SPhx
montanum	CDes CSpe EBee IMou WPGP

Sesleria (*Poaceae*)

§ ***albicans***	EBee
§ ***argentea***	EHoe
autumnalis	EBee LEdu LPla SPhx
caerulea	CBod CKno CSam EBee EHoe ELan EPfP GFor LEdu LTen MMoz MWhi WPtf
- subsp. ***calcarea***	see *S. albicans*
- 'Malvern Mop'	EBee WHrl WPGP WWEG
* ***candida***	EPPr
cylindrica	see *S. argentea*
glauca	EHoe NLar NOak SBfd
heufleriana	CBod CWCL EBee EHoe EPPr EPla GFor MLLN NLar SMea SPlb WWEG

insularis	EBee EPPr EShb
'Morning Dew'	EBee GCal
nitida	CKno EBee EHoe GFor LBMP LEdu MBrN MMoz SApp SPhx WCot WPGP
rigida	EHoe
sadleriana	EBee EPPr EWes GFor

Setaria (*Poaceae*)

italica	WTou
macrostachya ♀H3	CKno LLWP NDov SBch SPhx SUsu
palmifolia	CHEx CHll CKno SGSe WCot WDyG
- BWJ 8132	WCru
viridis	CSpe NSti WCot WTin

Setcreasea see *Tradescantia*

shaddock see *Citrus maxima*

Sharon fruit see *Diospyros kaki*

Shepherdia (*Elaeagnaceae*)

argentea	NLar

Shibataea (*Poaceae*)

chinensis	CBcs
kumasaca	CAbb CBcs CDoC CEnt CHEx EBee ENBC EPfP EPla GCal IBal LEdu LPal LRHS MBrN MCCP MMoz MWht NMoo SBig SLPl WDyG WJun WPGP
- 'Aureostriata'	EPla
lancifolia	EPla WJun

Shortia (*Diapensiaceae*)

galacifolia	GCrs IBlr
soldanelloides	IBlr
- var. ***ilicifolia***	IBlr
- var. ***magna***	IBlr
uniflora	IBlr NHar
- var. ***kantoensis***	GCrs
- var. ***orbicularis*** 'Grandiflora'	IBlr

Sibbaldia (*Rosaceae*)

procumbens	GAuc GKev GKir

Sibbaldiopsis (*Rosaceae*)

tridentata 'Lemon Mac'	CYeo

Sibthorpia (*Scrophulariaceae*)

europaea	CGHE CHEx CPLG WBor

Sida (*Malvaceae*)

hermaphrodita	EBee

Sidalcea (*Malvaceae*)

'Brilliant'	CBcs EBee EHoe EPfP LAst MDKP MNrw MSCN NBPC NBir NPri SBfd SPer SPoG WMoo WWEG
campestris from Oregon, USA **new**	EPPr
candida	CSam EBee ECtt ELan EPfP GCra GGar GMaP LAst LEdu LHop LRHS MBNS MCot MLLN MMuc MRav MTis NEgg NGdn NLar NSti SEND SMrm SPer STes SUsu WCAu WCot WSpi
- 'Bianca'	CBot CMea EBee EHrv EPfP EShb MSCN NBPC NGBl NLar NPri WFar WHal WMoo WPer WRHF WWEG
'Candy Girl'	EBee
'Croftway Red'	CFir EBee ELan EPfP GCra LRHS MAvo MCot MLLN NBro NCob NGdn NHol SAga SMrm SPer SPet SWvt WAul WFar
cusickii	WOut
'Elsie Heugh' ♀H4	Widely available
hendersonii	EBee
hickmanii subsp. ***anomala***	EBee
hirtipes	EBee
'Little Princess'PBR	CElw CFir EBee EPfP EWes GKir LRHS LSou MAsh NCGa NDov NLar SPoG WFar
'Loveliness'	CMMP EBee ECtt ELan EShb GGar LHop LSou MAvo MRav NBro NCob NGdn NHol NLar SBch
malviflora	SEND SRms WBVN
- 'Alba'	WFar
'Monarch'	MDKP WFar
'Moorland Rose Coronet'	WMoo
'Mr Lindbergh'	EBee EPfP MAvo NHol WFar
'Mrs Borrodaile'	CMac EBee ECtt LAst MLLN MRav NBro NCob NGdn NHol SMrm WFar WMoo WSpi WWEG
'Mrs Galloway'	WFar
'Mrs T. Alderson'	EBee WFar WMoo
'My Love'	NDov
'Oberon'	EBee EBrs LRHS MRav WFar
oregana (Nutt. ex Torr. & A. Gray) A. Gray	NBid NGdn
- subsp. ***spicata***	WFar WMoo
'Party Girl'	Widely available
'Purpetta'	COlW EBee NGBl NLar SBfd STes WPer
reptans	CDes EBee
'Reverend Page Roberts'	MAvo MRav WCot WFar WWEG
'Rosaly'	EBee ELon GAbr IFoB LBMP LRHS NLar SBfd STes WFar WGor WHal
'Rosanna'	EBee EBrs GAbr GMaP LRHS NLar SBfd SPhx WHal WPer WPtf
'Rose Bud'	CElw EBee MAvo
'Rose Queen'	EBee ECha LHop MAvo MCot MRav NBro NCob NHol SPer SRms WCAu WFar
'Rosy Gem'	ECtt NBre WFar
Stark's hybrids	LRHS SRms
'Sussex Beauty'	CPrp CSam EBee EWTr GMac MArl MAvo MCot MLHP MLLN MRav NDov NEgg NGdn SMrm SPer WAul WFar WMoo
'Wensleydale'	LRHS
'William Smith' ♀H4	CPrp CSam EBee ECha ECtt EPfP EWes GKir LAst LRHS MLLN MMuc MRav NBir NChi NCob NGdn NLar SEND SPer SPhx WBVN WFar WMoo WWEG
'Wine Red'	CFir CMHG EBee EShb IPot LAst LLWG LRHS MAvo MCot MDKP MTis NCob NEgg NGdn SWvt WFar WSpi WWEG

Sideritis (*Lamiaceae*)

hyssopifolia	EBee
syriaca	CArn NBre

Sieversia (*Rosaceae*)

§ ***pentapetala***	GEdr WAbe
reptans	see *Geum reptans*

Silaum (*Apiaceae*)

silaus	NMir

Silene (*Caryophyllaceae*)

	CC 5576	GKev
	from Uzbekistan	GCal
	acaulis	ECho EDAr MMuc NLAp NLar NMen SRms WAbe
§	- subsp. ***acaulis***	ECho SPlb SRms
	- 'Alba'	ECho EWes NLan NLar NMen WAbe WPat
	- 'Blush'	ECho NHol NLAp NMen WAbe
§	- subsp. ***bryoides***	NLar
	- 'Correvoniana'	NLar
	- subsp. ***elongata***	see *S. acaulis* subsp. *acaulis*
	- subsp. ***exscapa***	see *S. acaulis* subsp. *bryoides*
	- 'Frances'	CYeo EPot GCrs GMaP NHar NLAp NMen NRya NSla NWCA WAbe
	- 'Francis Copeland'	ECho NMen
	- 'Helen's Double' (d)	ECho EDAr EPot
	- 'Mount Snowdon'	ECho ECtt EDAr ELan EPfP EPot EWes GGar GKir GMaP LBee MMuc NLAp NLar NMen NRya NWCA SPlb SPoG SRms SRot WHoo WPat
	- 'Pedunculata'	see *S. acaulis* subsp. *acaulis*
	alba	see *S. latifolia*
§	***alpestris***	NBre NLar SRms SRot WFar WMoo WThu
	- 'Flore Pleno' (d) ♀^{H4}	CMea EWes LBee LRHS NSla WAbe WPat
	araratica	WAbe
	argaea	GKev WAbe
	× ***arkwrightii***	see *Lychnis* × *arkwrightii*
	armeria	WHer
	- 'Electra'	CSpe
	asterias	GCal GCra IGor MNrw NBid NBre
	- MESE 429	GBin
	atropurpurea	see *Lychnis viscaria* subsp. *atropurpurea*
	bellidioides	WPGP
	caroliniana subsp. ***wherryi***	CMea GAuc WFar
§	***compacta***	NLar
	'Confetti' **new**	CAby
§	***davidii***	CPBP EBee GKev
§	***dioica***	CArn CRWN EBWF LEdu MHer MNHC NLan NLar NMir NVic SPoG SWat WMoo WSFF WShi
	- 'Clifford Moor' (v)	ECtt EHoe NSti SCoo
	- 'Compacta'	see *S. dioica* 'Minikin'
	- 'Firefly'	LRHS LSou
§	- 'Flore Pleno' (d)	GCra MRav NBid NBro NChi NGdn SMrm WEas WFar WHoo WTin
§	- 'Graham's Delight' (v)	MSCN
	- 'Inane'	CDes EBee WAlt WPGP WRHF WWFP
	- 'Innocence'	NChi
	- f. ***lactea***	MHer
§	- 'Minikin'	ECha MAvo WAlt WTin
	- 'Pembrokeshire Pastel' (v)	WAlt
	- 'Purple Prince'	CBow WMoo
	- 'Richmond' (d)	EBee NBre
	- 'Rosea Plena' (d)	CBre NCob
	- 'Rubra Plena'	see *S. dioica* 'Flore Pleno'
	- 'Thelma Kay' (d/v)	CFee CSev ECtt EWes NBre WMoo WPGP WWFP
	- 'Underdine'	EBee EWes
	- 'Valley High' (v)	CBow EBee EWes MMuc WHer
	- 'Variegata'	see *S. dioica* 'Graham's Delight'
	elisabethae	GKir
§	***fimbriata***	CFir CSpe EBee EHrv ELan EPyc EShb LPla MCot MMHG MNFA MRav NChi NSti SBri SMrm WAbb WCot WMoo WPGP WPen WPtf WRHF WSHC WTin
	gigantea **new**	EBee
	hookeri Ingramii Group	WAbe
	inflata	see *S. vulgaris*
	kantzeensis	see *S. davidii*
	keiskei var. ***minor***	CPBP ECho EWes LRHS WAbe
	laciniata 'Jack Flash'	MWea WHrl
§	***latifolia***	CArn EBWF MMuc NMir NSco SEND
	- subsp. ***alba***	MNHC
	maritima	see *S. uniflora*
	maroccana	CRWN
	multifida	see *S. fimbriata*
	nigrescens	GKev
	noctiflora	EBWF
	nutans	CArn EBWF SRms WHer WSFF
	orientalis	see *S. compacta*
	parishii var. ***latifolia*** NNS 03-556	NWCA
	petersonii NNS 06-534	NWCA
	pusilla	CPBP NLar WAbe
	quadridentata misapplied	see *S. alpestris*
	regia	NBre SPhx WPGP
	rubra	see *S. dioica*
	saxifraga	NLar
	schafta ♀^{H4}	CTri ECha ECho ECtt EPfP GGar LRHS MMuc NBid NCob NPri NWCA SRms WAbe WFar WHoo WNew WPer
	- 'Abbotswood'	see *Lychnis* × *walkeri* 'Abbotswood Rose'
	- 'Persian Carpet'	SBch WRHF
	- 'Robusta'	NDov WAbe
	- 'Shell Pink'	ECha EPot EWes GJos LBee LRHS NBid NCob NDov WAbe WCom WHoo
	sieboldii	see *Lychnis coronata* var. *sieboldii*
§	***uniflora***	EBWF ECho ECtt EPfP GGar LRHS MMuc MSCN MWat NBro SBch SEND SPlb SRms SRot WFar WMoo
	- from Madeira	GGar
	- 'Alba Plena'	see *S. uniflora* 'Robin Whitebreast'
I	- 'Compacta'	CEnt ECho EWTr WMoo
§	- 'Druett's Variegated' (v)	CMea CTri ECha ECho ECtt EDAr ELon EPfP EPot EWes LAst LBee LRHS MHer NBid NMen NPri SPad SPet SPlb SPoG SRms WFar WPat
	- 'Flore Pleno'	see *S. uniflora* 'Robin Whitebreast'
§	- 'Robin Whitebreast' (d)	EBee ECha ECho ECtt EPfP GCal MTho NBPC NBid NBro NPri SRms SRot SUsu WMoo WSHC
	- 'Rosea'	EBee ECtt EPfP GGar GKir MMuc SEND SPlb SRot SUsu WFar WPer
	- 'Variegata'	see *S. uniflora* 'Druett's Variegated'
	- Weisskehlchen	see *S. uniflora* 'Robin Whitebreast'
	- 'White Bells'	CTri ECtt WHoo WKif WSHC
§	***vulgaris***	CRWN EBWF ELau LEdu MHer MNHC NLan NMir NSco
	- subsp. ***maritima***	see *S. uniflora*
	wallichiana	see *S. vulgaris*
	'Wisley Pink'	ECtt
	yunnanensis	SPhx WSHC
§	***zawadskii***	GKev MDKP NHol SWal WTin

Siler (*Umbelliferae*)

montanum	see *Laserpitium siler*

Silphium (*Asteraceae*)

integrifolium	EBee NBre SAga SMad SPhx WCot WOld

laciniatum	CArn CWCL EBee NBre NLar SMad SMrm SPhx WCot
perfoliatum ♀H4	CArn COld EBee ELon GPoy IMou NBre NCob NDov NLar SMrm SPhx SUsu WCot WFar WOld WWEG
- var. ***connatum*** new	SPhx
radula	EBee
terebinthinaceum	EPPr SMad SPhx WCot
trifoliatum	WCot

Silybum (*Asteraceae*)

marianum	CArn EBrs ELan EPfP GAbr GPWP GPoy LRHS MNHC NGHP SIde SPav WFar WHer WHfH WOut WTou
- 'Adriana'	SPav

Simmondsia (*Simmondsiaceae*)

chinensis	CArn EOHP

Sinacalia (*Asteraceae*)

§ ***tangutica***	CSam EBee ECha GGar MLLN NBid NBro NChi NLar SDix WAbb WCot WFar

Sinarundinaria (*Poaceae*)

anceps	see *Yushania anceps*
jaunsarensis	see *Yushania anceps*
maling	see *Yushania maling*
murielae	see *Fargesia murielae*
nitida	see *Fargesia nitida*

Sinningia (*Gesneriaceae*)

sp.	EABi
* ***caerulea***	WDib
canescens ♀H1	ERea WDib
§ ***cardinalis***	CSpe EBak WDib
- 'Innocent'	WDib
conspicua	WDib
'Kaiser Wilhelm'	LRHS
nivalis	WDib
speciosa 'Blanche de Méru'	LRHS
- 'Kaiser Friedrich'	LRHS
tuberosa new	MCot
tubiflora	CSpe LPio SUsu

Sinobambusa (*Poaceae*)

§ ***intermedia***	EPla
* ***orthotropa***	EPla WPGP
rubroligula	EPla NMoo WPGP
tootsik	EPla WJun
§ - 'Albostriata' (v)	EPla LPJP WJun
- 'Variegata'	see *S. tootsik* 'Albostriata'

× *Sinocalycalycanthus* (*Calycanthaceae*)

raulstonii 'Hartlage Wine'	CPMA EPfP LRHS MAsh MBri NLar SSpi
'Venus'	EPfP LRHS SSpi

Sinocalycanthus (*Calycanthaceae*)

chinensis	CBcs CMCN CMac CPMA EBee ELan EPfP IArd IDee LRHS MBlu MPkF NLar SSpi WBVN WPGP

Sinofranchetia (*Lardizabalaceae*)

chinensis	CBcs WCru

Sinojackia (*Styracaceae*)

xylocarpa	CBcs NLar WFar

Sinowilsonia (*Hamamelidaceae*)

henryi	NLar

Siphocampylus (*Campanulaceae*)

foliosus RCB RA S-4	WCot

Siphocranion (*Lamiaceae*)

§ ***macranthum***	CDes EBee EWes WPGP

Sison (*Apiaceae*)

amomum	CBre

Sisymbrium (*Brassicaceae*)

§ ***luteum***	WHil

Sisyrinchium ✿ (*Iridaceae*)

× ***anceps***	see *S. angustifolium*
§ ***angustifolium***	CMHG EBur ECha ECho LBMP LPBA MCot NBir NChi NLar SChF SPlb SRms WBrk WPer WPtf
- ***album***	ECho MCot NChi NLar
§ ***arenarium***	CMea CPBP EBur MAvo
atlanticum	EDAr NBro SUsu
bellum hort.	see *S. idahoense* var. *bellum*
bermudiana	see *S. angustifolium*
- 'Album'	see *S. graminoides* 'Album'
'Biscutella'	CBod CKno CTri EBee EBur ECho ECtt EPfP GKir GMaP LEdu LHop NMen NRya SAga SPad SPlb SPoG SWvt WFar WHal WHoo WKif WNew
'Blue France'	EPot
'Blue Ice'	CMea CPBP CWCL EBur EDAr LRHS MAvo WAbe WMoo WPat WPer
boreale	see *S. californicum*
brachypus	see *S. californicum* Brachypus Group
'Californian Skies'	Widely available
§ ***californicum***	CBen EBur ECho EHon EPfP LLWG LPBA LRHS NBro NHol SMrm WFar WMAq WNew WPer
§ - Brachypus Group	CMac EBee ECho ECtt EDAr EPfP GAbr GKir MMuc MWat NBir NLar NPri SGar SPad SPlb SPoG SWal SWvt WMoo
* ***capsicum***	CPLG
coeleste	EBur
coeruleum	see *Gelasine coerulea*
commutatum	ECho SGar
convolutum	GGar NDov
- B&SWJ 9117	WCru
cuspidatum	see *S. arenarium*
'Deep Seas'	MAvo SUsu
demissum	EBur
depauperatum	EBur MNrw
'Devon Blue'	ECho
'Devon Skies'	CHid CTca CWCL CYeo EBur ECho MDKP MNrw MTis MWea NMen SBch SWvt WAbe WFar
douglasii	see *Olsynium douglasii*
'Dragon's Eye'	CKno CMea CPBP CYeo EBur EWes MAvo MBrN MTis NWCA SMHy SMrm SRot SSvw WPer
'E.K. Balls'	Widely available
elmeri	EBur
'Emmeline'	EBur
filifolium	see *Olsynium filifolium*
graminoides	EBur IFoB NBro
§ - 'Album'	EBur NBro
grandiflorum	see *Olsynium douglasii*
'Hemswell Sky'	EBur ECho EHoe GAbr NRya
'Iceberg'	CElw EBur EDAr EShb LPla MWat SBch SMrm

	idahoense	CYeo ECha ECho ECtt EDAr GAbr GEdr LRHS LSou MHer NRya SPlb SRms
§	- var. ***bellum***	CKno EBur ECho EPfP GGar IFro LBMP NPri SGar SPet SRms WCom WMoo WNew WPat
	- - pale-flowered	CKno LPla NDov SMHy
	- - 'Rocky Point'	CElw CSpe EBee EBur EWes GJos LRHS MAvo MMuc NLAp SPoG SRot WCom WFar WHoo WPat
	- var. ***macounii***	EBee EPot GEdr LRHS SPlb WFar
§	- - 'Album' ♀H4	CAby CMea CYeo EBur ECho ECtt EPot GAbr MTho MWat NLAp SPet SPlb WAbe WFar WPat
	iridifolium	see *S. micranthum*
	junceum	see *Olsynium junceum*
	littorale	CPLG EBur NLar
	macrocarpon misapplied	see *S. macrocarpum*
	macrocarpon ♀H2-3	CPBP NMen
§	***macrocarpum***	CFee EBur ECho EDAr MDKP SWal WPer
	'Marie'	EBur
	'Marion'	CElw CKno CMea CPBP EDAr MAvo MBrN NDov NLar SBch SMrm SPet SRot WPer
	'May Snow'	see *S. idahoense* var. *macounii* 'Album'
	'Miami'	EBur
§	***micranthum***	EBur ECho
	montanum	ECho
	montanum × ***nudicaule***	CFee EBur ECho GAbr MNrw MSpe NRya SRot
	'Mrs Spivey'	EBur ECtt MHer NBir
	'North Star'	see *S.* 'Pole Star'
	palmifolium	CAby CBgR CBod CDes CSpe EBee EBur EWTr GAbr LEdu MAvo MDKP MHer MNrw MWea SBch SGar SMad SPoG WCot
	- JCA 2.880.010	WPGP
	patagonicum	CPLG EBur EDAr
§	'Pole Star'	CFee CSpe EBur ECho WFar WPer
	'Quaint and Queer'	COIW CPLG CWCL EBur ECha ECho ECtt EHoe EShb MBrN MLHP MNFA MNrw MTho NBir NBro NChi NLAp SWvt WMnd WMoo WPer WSHC
	'Raspberry'	CMea EBee EBur
	'Sapphire'	CYeo ECtt MTis NPri WFar
	'Sisland Blue'	EBur EWes
§	***striatum***	Widely available
§	- 'Aunt May' (v)	Widely available
	- 'Variegatum'	see *S. striatum* 'Aunt May'
	aff. ***unispathaceum*** B&SWJ 10683	WCru

Sium (*Apiaceae*)

sisarum	ELau GPoy MHer

Skimmia ✿ (*Rutaceae*)

	anquetilia	CMac
	arborescens B&SWJ 11799	WCru
	- subsp. ***nitida*** B&SWJ 8239	WCru
	arisanensis B&SWJ 7114	WCru
	black-fruited B&SWJ 8259 from northern Vietnam (f/m) **new**	WCru
	× ***confusa***	WFar
	- 'Kew Green' (m) ♀H4	Widely available
	japonica	CDul CMHG CMac CWib GQui MGan MGos NPla SReu SSta WDin WFar
	- (f)	CDoy CMac CTri ELan EPfP GGal SRms WCru
	- (m)	GGal WCru
	- B&SWJ 5053	WCru
	- 'Alba'	see *S. japonica* 'Wakehurst White'
	- 'Bowles's Dwarf Female' (f)	CMHG EBee EPfP MBri MGos MRav MWht NHol SLim SLon SPer
	- 'Bowles's Dwarf Male' (m)	CMHG EBee EPla NHol SLim SPer
	- 'Bronze Knight' (m)	CMac EQua MBri MRav NHol SLim WFar
	- 'Cecilia Brown' (f)	WFar
	- 'Chameleon'	NHol
	- compact (f)	GGal
	- 'Dad's Red Dragon'	NHol
	- 'Emerald King' (m)	MBri WFar
N	- 'Foremanii'	see *S. japonica* 'Veitchii'
§	- 'Fragrans' (m) ♀H4	CDoC CMac CSBt CTri CWib EBee ECrN EPfP GKir IVic LRHS MAsh MBri MGos MRav NHol NLar NWea SBfd SLim SPer SPoG SWvt WFar WGob WGwG
	- 'Fragrant Cloud'	see *S. japonica* 'Fragrans'
	- 'Fragrantissima' (m)	WFar
	- 'Fructu Albo'	see *S. japonica* 'Wakehurst White'
	- 'Godrie's Dwarf' (m)	CWSG EBee EPfP LRHS NLar WFar
	- 'Highgrove Redbud' (f)	MGos
	- var. ***intermedia*** f. ***repens***	WFar
	- - B&SWJ 5560	WCru
	- 'Keessen' (f)	WFar
	- 'Kew White' (f)	CAbP CDoC CWib EBee EPfP EQua GKir IArd LRHS MGos NHol NPal SLon SPer SRms SWvt WCFE WDin WFar
	- Luwian = 'Wanto'	EBee LRHS NHol WCFE WFar
	- 'Magic Marlot'PBR (v)	CWSG EGxp EPfP LRHS MAsh MGos NLar SPoG
	- 'Marlot' (m)	EBee EPfP LRHS MAsh NLar SPoG
	- 'Nymans' (f) ♀H4	CDoC CEnd CSam EBee ELan EPfP GKir LBMP LRHS MAsh MBri MRav SBfd SLim SPer SPoG SReu SRms SSpi SSta WBVN WFar WGob
	- 'Obovata' (f)	EPla
	- 'Pigmy' (f)	CPLG
	- 'Red Dragon' (f)	CMac
	- 'Red Princess' (f)	WFar
*	- 'Red Riding Hood'	LBMP MAsh NHol SLon
	- 'Redruth' (f)	CBcs CDoC CMac CSBt CSam EBee EQua GKir MAsh MGos MWat NHol NLar SBfd SEND SSta WFar
§	- subsp. ***reevesiana***	Widely available
	- - B&SWJ 3763	WCru
	- - 'Chilan Choice' (f/m)	EPfP SLim
	- - var. ***reevesiana*** B&SWJ 3544	WCru
§	- Rogersii Group	CMac CTri
	- - 'George Gardner'	EBee LRHS
	- - 'Nana Mascula' (m)	CTri MGos
	- - 'Snow Dwarf' (m)	WFar
	- 'Rubella' (m) ♀H4	Widely available
	- 'Rubinetta' (m)	EBee EPfP GKir IArd LSRN MAsh MGos NHol SLim WFar
	- 'Ruby Dome' (m)	GKir NHol WFar
	- 'Ruby King' (m)	CDoC CSBt EQua IArd LSRN MHav NHol NLar
	- 'Scarlet Dwarf' (f)	EBee NHol
	- 'Scarlet Queen' (f)	CWib
	- 'Snow White'PBR	EGxp MAsh
	- 'Tansley Gem' (f)	EPfP LRHS MAsh MBri MWht SPoG SSta WFar

- 'Thelma King'	GKir WFar
§ - 'Veitchii' (f)	CBar CBcs CDoy CDul CMac CSBt CTri CWit EBee ELan EPfP GKir IArd LRHS LSRN LTen MAsh MGos MMuc MRav MWat NHol NLar SEND SLim SPer SPoG SWvt WDin
§ - 'Wakehurst White' (f)	CBcs CMHG CMac CSBt CTri EPfP GKir LRHS MRav SLim SLon SPer SReu SSpi WFar
- 'Winifred Crook' (f)	EBee GKir MBri SLim WFar
- 'Winnie's Dwarf'	MGos
- 'Wisley Female' (f)	CTri ECtt NHol WFar
laureola	CDoC CPLG CSam EBee MRav NHol SRms WFar WSHC
- GWJ 9364	WCru
- subsp. ***laureola*** HWJK 2095 **new**	WCru
- subsp. ***multinervia*** GWJ 9374	WCru
* ***mica***	SLim
'Olympic Flame'	EWTr GKir LRHS MAsh MBlu MGos SPoG WFar
reevesiana	see *S. japonica* subsp. *reevesiana*
rogersii	see *S. japonica* Rogersii Group

Smilacina see *Maianthemum*

Smilax (*Smilacaceae*)

sp.	WBor
B&SWJ 6628 from Thailand	WCru
F&M 051	WPGP
from Thailand	LEdu
aspera	CArn CMac EShb EWld LEdu WCru WPGP
china B&SWJ 4427	WCru
discotis	CBcs SEND
glaucophylla B&SWJ 2971	WCru
nipponica B&SWJ 4331	WCru
rotundifolia	LEdu
sieboldii	LEdu MRav
- B&SWJ 744	WCru

Smithiantha (*Gesneriaceae*)

'Extra Sassy'	EABi
'Little One'	EOHP WDib
'Multiflora'	EABi WDib
'Santa Clara'	EABi
I 'Temple Bells'	EABi

Smyrnium (*Apiaceae*)

olusatrum	CArn CSev CSpe EBWF EBee GPWP MHer MNHC SIde STre SWat WHer WSFF
perfoliatum	CHid CSpe EBee EHrv ELan ELon EWes LPio NBir SDix SMrm WCot WEas WFar WHal WSHC
rotundifolium	CArn LPio WCot

Solandra (*Solanaceae*)

grandiflora misapplied	see *S. maxima*
hartwegii	see *S. maxima*
§ ***maxima***	CCCN CHII EShb

Solanum (*Solanaceae*)

atropurpureum	CDTJ CSpe
conchifolium hort.	see *S. linearifolium*
crispum	NBir SGar WDin
- 'Autumnale'	see *S. crispum* 'Glasnevin'
- 'Elizabeth Jane Dunn' (v)	WCot WSHC
§ - 'Glasnevin' ♀H3	Widely available
- 'Variegatum' (v)	WGwG
dulcamara	CArn EBWF GPoy WHfH
- var. ***album***	LSRN
- 'Variegatum' (v)	CMac CWan EBee EHoe EPfP MAsh NSti WFar
hispidum	CHEx
jasminoides	see *S. laxum*
laciniatum	CArn CCCN CDTJ CHEx CPLG CSev CSpe EShb EWes GGal GGar MCot SAPC SBfd SBig SBst SEND SGar SPav SPlb WKif WWlt
§ ***laxum***	EBee EShb GGal LRHS MMuc MSwo NSti SPer SPoG SRms SWvt WDin WSHC
- 'Album' ♀H3	Widely available
- 'Album Variegatum' (v)	CWib ELan LRHS NSti WSHC
* - 'Aureovariegatum' (v)	CBar CMac EBee EPfP EShb LBMP MGos NEgg SBfd SLim SPlb
- 'Coldham'	EShb GCal SMad
- 'Creche ar Pape'	ECha
§ ***linearifolium***	CSpe MAsh WCot WPGP
muricatum (F)	CCCN CHII EShb
pseudocapsicum 'Thurino'	EPfP
- variegated (v)	EShb WCot
pyracanthum	CDTJ
quitoense (F)	CDTJ SBig
§ ***rantonnetii***	CCCN CHII ELan EPfP EShb IDee LHop LRHS MREP SEND SOWG SPer SPoG
- 'Royal Robe'	CBcs CRHN
- 'Variegatum' (v)	EShb MSCN WCom WCot
salicifolium	EShb
seaforthianum	EShb SOWG
sisymbriifolium	CDTJ WWlt
aff. ***stenophyllum*** B&SWJ 10744	WCru
virginianum **new**	ELau
wendlandii	CHII EShb

Solaria (*Alliaceae*)

sp.	GCal

Soldanella (*Primulaceae*)

alpina	EBee ECho EWld GCra GCrs GKev GKir MTho NMen SRms WAbe
I - 'Alba'	ECho GEdr WAbe
carpatica	EBee ECho GKev LLHF WAbe
- 'Alba'	ECho MDKP NHar NSla WAbe
- hybrid	NMen
carpatica × ***pusilla***	CPBP ECho NHar NHol NMen NRya WAbe
carpatica × ***villosa***	ECho LEdu MDKP
cyanaster	ECho GEdr GJos GKev NLBP NMen NRya WAbe
dimoniei	CFee EBee ECho GEdr GKev NMen NSla NWCA WAbe
hungarica	ECho MTho WAbe
minima	EBee ECho GCrs GJos GKev NMen
montana	EBee ECho EDAr GEdr GJos LLHF MDun MTho NLar NMen SBch
pindicola	ECho EWes NMen NWCA WAbe WFar
pusilla	GKev
* - ***alba***	ECho
'Spring Symphony'	GEdr
'Sudden Spring'	GEdr WAbe
villosa	CAby CDes EBee ECho GAbr GEdr GGar GKev LEdu MTho NHol NRya SBch WFar WPtf WSHC

Soleirolia (*Urticaceae*)

	soleirolii	CHEx CTri EPot EUJe LPBA MCCP MWhi SMad SPer STre SVic SWvt WHer
	- 'Argentea'	see *S. soleirolii* 'Variegata'
§	- 'Aurea'	CTri EPot STre SWvt
	- 'Golden Queen'	see *S. soleirolii* 'Aurea'
	- 'Silver Queen'	see *S. soleirolii* 'Variegata'
§	- 'Variegata' (v)	EShb LPBA WHer

Solenomelus (*Iridaceae*)

	chilensis	see *S. pedunculatus*
§	***pedunculatus***	CFee WPGP

Solenopsis (*Campanulaceae*)

axillaris	see *Isotoma axillaris*

Solenostemon ✿ (*Lamiaceae*)

'Alice Horn'	NHor
'Angel of the North'	NHor
'Autumn'	NHor
'Autumn Gold'	NHor
'Autumn Rainbow'	WDib
'Beauty' (v)	NHor WDib
'Beauty of Lyons'	NHor
'Beckwith's Gem'	NHor
'Billy Elliot'	NHor
'Bizarre Croton' (v)	NHor
'Black Dragon'	LSou NHor
'Black Heart'	NHor WDib
'Black Prince'	NHor WDib
'Brightness' (v)	NHor
'Brilliant' (v)	NHor WDib
'Bronze Gloriosus' (v)	NHor
'Bronze Pagoda'	NHor WDib
'Brooklyn Horror'	NHor
'Burning Bush'	NHor
'Buttercup'	NHor WDib
'Buttermilk' (v) 𝕐H1	NHor
'Carnival' (v)	NHor
'Carousel' (v)	NHor
'Castle Eden'	NHor
'Chamaeleon' (v)	NHor WDib
'City of Durham' (v)	NHor
'City of Liverpool'	NHor
'City of Middlesbrough' (v)	NHor
'City of Newcastle'	NHor
'City of Sunderland'	NHor WDib
'City of York'	NHor
'Combat' (v)	NHor WDib
'Coppersmith'	NHor
'Crimson Ruffles' (v) 𝕐H1	NHor WDib
'Crimson Velvet'	NHor
'Crinkly Bottom'	NHor
'Crown of Bohemia'	NHor
'Dairy Maid' (v)	NHor
'Dazzler' (v)	NHor WDib
'Display'	NHor WDib
'Doctor Wu'	NHor
'Dracula'	NHor
'Duke of Swirl'	NHor
'Durham Autumn'	NHor
'Durham Gala'	NHor WDib
'Eclipse'	NHor
'Ella's Fire'	NHor
'Etna' (v)	NHor
'Fire Fingers'	NHor
'Firebrand' (v) 𝕐H1	NHor
'Firedance' (v)	NHor
'Firefly'	NHor
'Firelight'	WDib
'Flamenco Dancer'	NHor
'Flirtin' Skirts'	NHor
'Forest Flame'	NHor
'Freckles' (v)	NHor WDib
'Funfair' (v)	NHor
'George Harrison'	NHor
'Gertrude Jekyll'	NHor
'Glennis' **new**	NHor
'Gloriosus'	NHor
'Glory of Luxembourg' (v) 𝕐H1	NHor
'Goody Goody'	NHor
'Grape Expectations'	NHor
'Green Mars' (v)	NHor
'Hannay Harding'	NHor
'Harvest Time' (v)	NHor
'Holly' (v)	NHor
'Illumination'	NHor WDib
'Inky Fingers' (v)	EShb NHor WDib
'Jean' (v)	NHor
'Joseph's Cloak'	NHor
'Joseph's Coat' (v)	NHor
'Juliet Quartermain'	NHor WDib
'Jupiter'	NHor
'Kate Adie'	NHor
'Kentish Fire' (v)	NHor WDib
'Killer Klown'	NHor
'Kiwi Fern' (v)	NHor WDib
'Klondike'	NHor
'Kong Rose' (Kong Series)	NPri
'Laing's Croton' (v)	NHor
'Lemon Chiffon' **new**	WDib
'Lemon Dash'	NHor
'Lemondrop'	NHor
'Leopard' (v)	NHor
'Lindisfarne'	NHor
'Lord Falmouth' 𝕐H1	NHor WDib
'Luminous'	NHor
'Mardigras'	NHor
'Margaret Horn'	NHor
'Masquerade'	NHor
'Melody' (v)	NHor
'Midas'	NHor
'Midnight'	NHor
'Mission Gem' (v)	NHor
'Morris Cullen'	NHor
'Mrs Pilkington' (v)	NHor WDib
'Muriel Pedley' (v)	NHor WDib
'Nettie' (v)	NHor
'Paisley Shawl' (v) 𝕐H1	NHor WDib
'Palisandra'	CSpe
'Panache'	NHor
pentheri	NHor
'Percy Roots'	NHor
'Peter Wonder' (v)	NHor WDib
'Phantom'	NHor
'Picturatus' (v) 𝕐H1	NHor WDib
'Pineapple Beauty' (v) 𝕐H1	CHVG NHor WDib
'Pineapplette' 𝕐H1	NHor WDib
'Pink Chaos'	NHor WDib
'Pink Devil' (v)	NHor
'Pink Shawl'	NHor
'Primrose Cloud' (v)	NHor
'Primrose Spire' (v)	NHor
'Prince Bishop'	NHor
'Red Angel'	WDib
'Red Croton' (v)	NHor
'Red Mars'	NHor
'Red Nettie' (v)	NHor
'Red Rosie'	NHor
'Red Velvet'	NHor WDib
'Redcoat' **new**	NHor

	'Ringleader'	NHor
	'Rose Blush' (v)	NHor WDib
	'Rosie'	NHor
	'Roy Pedley'	NHor WDib
	'Royal Scot' (v) ♀H1	NHor WDib
	'Royal Velvet'	NHor
	'Salmon Plumes' (v)	WDib
	'Saturn'	NHor WDib
	'Scarborough Fair'	NHor
	'Scarlet Ribbons'	NHor
	scutellarioides 'Molten Lava' (v)	NHor
	'Solar Sunrise'	NHor
	'Speckles' (v)	NHor
	'Spire' (v)	NHor
	'Strawberry Jam'	NHor
	'Swinging Linda' **new**	NHor
	'Tabasco' **new**	NHor
	'Tees Valley'	NHor
	'The Cardinal'	NHor
	'The Durham Angel'	NHor
	'The Flume' **new**	WDib
	'Theresa Horn'	NHor
	thyrsoideus	see *Plectranthus thyrsoideus*
	'Tilt and Whirl' **new**	NHor
	'Timotei'	NHor WDib
	'Tom Cooke'	NHor
	'Treales' (v)	NHor
	'Tynesider'	NHor
	'Vesuvius'	NHor
	'Volcano'	NHor
	'Walter Turner' (v) ♀H1	NHor SVil WDib
	'Weardale'	NHor
	'Wearsider'	NHor
	'White Gem' (v)	NHor
	'White Pheasant' (v)	NHor
	'Winsome' (v)	NHor WDib
	'Winter Sun' (v)	NHor WDib
	'Wisley Flame'	NHor WDib
	'Wisley Tapestry' (v) ♀H1	NHor WDib
	'Yellow Croton' (v)	NHor

Solidago (*Asteraceae*)

	Babygold	see *S.* 'Goldkind'
	brachystachys	see *S. cutleri*
	caesia	EBee EWes NBir SMHy WMoo WOld WTin
	canadensis	CTri EBee ELan MMuc NBre SEND SPlb WFar WHer
	- var. ***salebrosa***	LRHS
	- var. ***scabra***	MAvo WOld WTin
	'Citronella'	ECtt EWll NBPC
	'Cloth of Gold'	CMac EBee ECho ECtt GKir LRHS SWvt WMnd
§	'Crown of Rays'	CPrp EBrs ECtt EPfP LRHS MRav WFar WMnd WWEG
§	***cutleri***	EBee ECho ELan GEdr MTho MWat NLar SPlb SRms WFar WPat
I	- ***nana***	ECho EWes
	'Ducky'	EBee NBPC
	'Early Bird'	NLar WFar
	'Featherbush'	EBrs LRHS
§	***flexicaulis***	GMaP
	- 'Variegata' (v)	CWan EBee EBrs ECtt ELan EPfP GKir GMaP NLar NWsh WFar WHer WPer WWEG
	'Gardone' ♀H4	WFar
	gigantea	WFar
	glomerata	EBee NBre NLar SMrm
	Golden Baby	see *S.* 'Goldkind'
§	'Golden Dwarf'	COlW LRHS SPoG WPtf WWEG
	'Golden Falls'	LRHS
	'Golden Fleece'	see *S. sphacelata* 'Golden Fleece'
	Golden Gate = 'Dansolgold'	EBrs LRHS
	'Golden Thumb'	see *S.* 'Queenie'
	'Golden Wings'	CBre
	'Goldenmosa' ♀H4	CAby CMac CSBt EBee ECtt EPfP EWes GKev GMaP MRav SPer SSvw WCot WFar
	'Goldilocks'	NPri SRms
§	'Goldkind'	CAby CMMP CSBt CTri EBee ECho ECtt EPfP EShb GAbr GKir LRHS MCot MMuc MWhi NBPC NEgg SBfd SEND SWvt WBrk WFar WWEG
	Goldzwerg	see *S.* 'Golden Dwarf'
	'Harvest Gold'	CAby CElw
	hybrida	see *S.* × ***luteus***
	latifolia	see *S. flexicaulis*
	'Laurin'	EBee EPfP LRHS MBri NLar
	'Ledsham'	CAby EBee EBrs ECtt EWll LEdu LRHS MCot NBre WMnd
	'Leraft'	EBee
	'Linner Gold'	NBre
	'Little Lemon'	GCal NBPC
§	× ***luteus***	EBee EWTr MBri NBPC SRms WEas WFar WHil
	- 'Lemore' ♀H4	CMea CPrp EBee ELan EPfP GMaP GMac GQue LAst LHop LRHS MBrN MNFA MWat NCGa NPri NWsh SMrm SPer WCot WFar WWEG
	ohioensis	EBee
*	'Peter Pan'	LRHS WFar
§	***ptarmicoides***	CSam EBee EBla LBMP NBre WOld WPer
	- 'Mago'	EBee
§	'Queenie'	ECha ECho MHer MLHP NBre NVic SRms WWEG
	riddellii **new**	EBee
	rigida	EBee LRHS NBre SMrm WCot
	roanensis	EBee NBre
	rugosa	ECha MBNS MMuc NBre SPhx WCot
	- 'Fireworks'	Widely available
	sciaphila	NBre
	sempervirens	WCot WFar
	- 'Goldene Wellen'	EBee
	'Septembergold' **new**	CSam
	shortii	EBee
	simplex subsp. ***simplex*** var. ***nana***	NWCA
	'Sonnenschein'	NBre
	speciosa	LRHS NBre SPhx
	spectabilis var. ***confinis***	EBee
§	***sphacelata*** 'Golden Fleece'	CBcs EBee IMou LRHS NBre WFar WMnd WWEG
	spiraeifolia	NBre
	Strahlenkrone	see *S.* 'Crown of Rays'
	'Summer Sunshine'	WWEG
	'Super'	CAby CPrp WCot
	Sweety = 'Barseven'PBR	LRHS MBri
	'Tom Thumb'	CMac MRav NBir SRms WEas
	uliginosa	EShb NBre
	ulmifolia	EBee NBre
	virgaurea	CArn CSam EBWF EBee GPoy MHer MNHC NBre NLar NSco SMrm WHer
	- subsp. ***alpestris*** var. ***minutissima***	CMea NBre WPat
	- var. ***cambrica***	see *S. virgaurea* subsp. *minuta*
§	- subsp. ***minuta***	GBin
§	- 'Variegata' (v)	CBre EHoe

vulgaris 'Variegata'	see *S. virgaurea* 'Variegata'
'Yellow Springs'	GJos

× *Solidaster* see *Solidago*

hybridus	see *Solidago* × *luteus*

Sollya (*Pittosporaceae*)

fusiformis	see *S. heterophylla*
§ ***heterophylla*** ΨH1	Widely available
- 'Alba'	CBcs CCCN EBee ELan EPfP LRHS MCot MREP SLim SLon SPer SPoG SRms SWvt
- mauve-flowered	ECou
- 'Pink Charmer'	EBee ELan ERea LRHS MAsh SLon SPer SPoG
- pink-flowered	CCCN CHGN CHll CSPN EPfP LBMP LRHS SEND SLim SPad SWvt

Sonchus (*Asteraceae*)

fruticosus	CHEx GGar
giganteus	CHll
pinnatus	SPlb

Sophora (*Papilionaceae*)

§ ***davidii***	CBcs CGHE CPLG CWGN CWib EBee EBtc EPfP EWTr LHop LRHS MBlu MGos MWea SEND SOWG SPoG SSpi WPGP WSHC
flavescens	CArn
fulvida	ECou
godleyi 'Goldie's Mantle' **new**	CBcs
howinsula	ECou IRar
japonica	see *Styphnolobium japonicum*
§ 'Little Baby'	CAbP CWib EBee EPPr EPfP IVic LAst LBuc LRHS LSRN MCCP MGos MWea SBfd SDix SMad SPoG SWvt WGrn WPGP WPat
longicarinata	ECou
macrocarpa	CBcs
microphylla	CArn CHEx CTri EBee ECou EPfP EUJe LHop LRHS MMuc SEND WBVN WPGP
molloyi	ECou
- 'Dragon's Gold'	CBcs EBee ECou ELan EPfP LRHS MAsh SCoo SPoG SSpi SSta WDin
prostrata misapplied	see *S.* 'Little Baby'
prostrata ambig.	CBcs CGHE LRHS MMuc SEND
prostrata Buch.	CBot CMac ECou
Sun King = 'Hilsop'PBR ΨH4	CBcs CCVT CWGN EBee ELan EPfP EWes GKir IVic LRHS LSRN MGos MMuc MWea NCGa NLar NPri SBfd SCoo SEND SLon SPoG SWvt
tetraptera ΨH3	CAbP CBcs CDul CFee CMac CTsd CWit EBee ECou EPfP GGal MMuc MWea SEND SRms WBVN WBor WPGP
viciifolia	see *S. davidii*

Sorbaria (*Rosaceae*)

aitchisonii	see *S. tomentosa* var. *angustifolia*
arborea	see *S. kirilowii*
aff. ***assurgens*** BWJ 8185	WCru
§ ***kirilowii***	CMac CPLG MRav NLar SMad SPer WBVN WDyG WOut
- AC 3433	MSnd
rhoifolia	EPfP
sorbifolia	CAbP CBcs EBee ECrN GAuc GKir IFFs MLHP MMuc NLar SEND SPer SPlb SPoG WDin WFar
- 'Sem'PBR	Widely available
- var. ***stellipila***	SLPl
- - B&SWJ 776	WCru
§ ***tomentosa*** var. ***angustifolia*** ΨH4	CBcs CDul CTri CWan EBee ELan EPfP EWTr GAuc GKir LRHS MMuc MRav NBid NHol SEND SLon SPer WEas WFar WHer WSpi

× *Sorbopyrus* (*Rosaceae*)

auricularis	CTho MCoo
- 'Shipova' (F)	CAgr

Sorbus ✿ (*Rosaceae*)

sp.	CMen
Guiz 119	GKir
MF 96.072	EBee
MF 96072	GKev
alnifolia	CLnd CMCN CPMA EPfP MBlu SLPl
- B&SWJ 10948	WCru
- 'Red Bird'	EPfP MBlu
americana	CLnd NWea
amoena	GKir
- CLD 311	GKir
aff. ***amurensis*** B&SWJ 8665	WCru
anglica	CDul CNat GKir
apiculata	GKir
- CLD 310	GAuc GKir
'Apricot'	CEnd GKir
'Apricot Lady'	GBin GKir MGos
'Apricot Queen'	CLnd EBee ECrN GKir LAst NEgg WBor WFar
aria	CCVT CDul CLnd CSBt CTri EBee ECrN EMac EPfP GAuc GKir IFFs LBuc MGan MGos MMuc MSnd NWea SEND WDin WMou
- 'Aurea'	CLnd EBee MGos WFar
- 'Chrysophylla'	CDul CSBt EBee ECrN MGos NWea SLim SPer SPoG
- 'Decaisneana'	see *S. aria* 'Majestica'
- 'Lutescens' ΨH4	Widely available
- 'Magnifica'	CDoC CTho ECrN ELan LMaj NEgg SCoo WDin WJas
§ - 'Majestica' ΨH4	CCVT CDoC CDul CLnd CMac CTho EBee ECrN LHop MAsh NWea SCoo SPer SPoG WHar WJas
- 'Mitchellii'	see *S. thibetica* 'John Mitchell'
× ***arnoldiana*** 'Cerise Queen'	GKir
- 'Golden Wonder'	see *S.* 'Lombarts Golden Wonder'
aronioides misapplied	see *S. caloneura*
arranensis	GKir
§ ***aucuparia***	Widely available
- 'Aspleniifolia'	CBcs CCVT CDul CMCN CMac CSBt EBee ECrN GBin GKir IFFs LAst LRHS MAsh MGos MRav MWat NPCo NWea SBfd SLim SPer SPoG WDin WFar WJas
- 'Beauty of Banff'	GKir
§ - 'Beissneri'	CAgr CDul CLnd GBin GKir MBri MGos NLar NPCo NWea SCoo SLon SPoG WHCr
- Cardinal Royal = 'Michred'	CCVT CDoC EBee ECrN GKir GQui LRHS MMuc NEgg SBfd SCoo SEND WJas
- 'Crème Lace'	GKir
- 'Dirkenii'	GBin GKir IFFs MAsh WDin WJas
§ - var. ***edulis*** (F)	CDul CLnd CTho EBee ECrN LBuc LMaj MCoo MGos SCoo WDin
- - 'Rossica' misapplied	see *S. aucuparia* var. *edulis* 'Rossica Major'

§	- - 'Rossica Major'	CDul ECrN GQui SCoo WFar
§	- 'Fastigiata'	CEnd CLnd CMac CTri ECrN EPfP GKir LAst LMaj MGos NPCo WDin WFar
	- var. ***heteromorpha***	GAuc
	- 'Hilling's Spire'	CTho GKir
	- 'Pendula'	CDul EBee
	- ***pluripinnata***	see *S. scalaris* Koehne
	- var. ***rossica*** Koehne	see *S. aucuparia* var. *edulis*
	- 'Sheerwater Seedling' ♀H4	CBcs CCVT CDoC CDul CMCN CSBt EBee ECrN ELan EPfP GKir IFFs LAst LHop LMaj MGos MMuc MRav MSwo NPri SBfd SEND SLim SPer SSta WDin WFar
	- var. ***xanthocarpa*** ♀H4	CLnd ECrN EPfP LMaj WDin
	Autumn Spire = 'Flanrock'	CDoC CLnd CWSG EBee GKir LRHS MAsh MBri MGos NLar SBfd SCoo SLim SLon SPoG SWvt WClo WHCr WHar
	'Bellona'	WPat
	bissetii	GKir
	'Boyne Bay'	GKir
	brevipetiolata B&SWJ 11771 new	WCru
	'Brilliant Yellow'	GKir
	bristoliensis	GAuc GKir
	'Burka'	see *Aronia* × *Sorbus*, 'Burka'
	californica	GKir
§	***caloneura***	EPfP GKir MBlu SSpi WPGP WPat
	carmesina 'Emberglow'	GKir
	'Carpet of Gold'	CLnd GKir
	cashmiriana Hedl. ♀H4	Widely available
	chamaemespilus	GAuc WPat
	'Chamois Glow'	GKir MAsh WJas
	'Chinese Lace'	Widely available
§	***commixta***	CBcs CDul CEnd CLnd CMCN CSto CTho EBee ECrN GAuc GKir IFFs LAst MBlu MGos MMuc MSwo NBea NLar SEND SLim SPer SPoG WDin WJas
	- B&SWJ 8496	WCru
	- 'Embley' ♀H4	CBcs CCVT CDul CMCN CMac CSBt CTho CTri EBee ECrN ELan EPfP GKir LHop MBlu MGos MMuc MRav NEgg NPCo NWea SEND SPer SPoG WDin WFar
	- 'Jermyns'	GKir
	- Olympic Flame = 'Dodong' new	EBee GKir LRHS MBri NLar SCoo WHar
	- 'Ravensbill'	EBee GKir MAsh NLar SCoo WHCr WHar WMou
	- var. ***rufoferruginea***	GQui
	- - B&SWJ 6078	WCru
	- - B&SWJ 11486	WCru
	- var. ***sachalinensis*** B&SWJ 8496 new	WCru
	- - B&SWJ 8515	WCru
	conradinae misapplied	see *S. pohuashanensis* (Hance) Hedlund
	conradinae Koehne	see *S. esserteauana*
	'Copper Kettle'	EBee GKir MAsh MBri MWat NLar SCoo SPoG WClo WHCr WHar
	'Coral Beauty'	CDul CLnd
	corymbifera WWJ 11860 new	WCru
	'Covert Gold'	CEnd CLnd
	croceocarpa	CDul GKir
	'Croft Coral'	MAsh NPal
	cuspidata	see *S. vestita*
*	***decora*** 'Grootendorst'	CDul
	- var. ***nana***	see *S. aucuparia* 'Fastigiata'
	devoniensis	CDul CNat CTho GKir
	- 'Devon Beauty'	CAgr
	discolor misapplied	see *S. commixta*
	discolor (Maxim.) Maxim.	CLnd EBee GAuc GKir MBlu NWea SEND WJas
	- MF 96172	GKir
	domestica	CDul EPfP IFFs MMuc SEND SLPl WDin
	- 'Rosie'	CAgr
	'Eastern Promise'	CSam CWSG EBee ECrN EPfP GBin GKir MBlu MBri MWat NLar NWea SCoo SLim WDin WHCr WJas
§	***eburnea*** Harry Smith 12799	GKir GQui
	eminens	CDul CNat
	epidendron	GKir
	- WWJ 11930	WCru
§	***esserteauana***	CTho EPfP WPat
	- 'Flava'	GKir
	'Fastigiata'	see *S. aucuparia* 'Fastigiata', *S. × thuringiaca* 'Fastigiata'
	folgneri	CEnd CPMA
	- 'Emiel'	EPfP MBlu MBri
	- 'Lemon Drop'	CDul CEnd CLnd CPMA EBee EPfP GKir MWya NLar SCoo SMad
§	***foliolosa***	CLnd EPfP GKir NWea
	forrestii	CBcs EPfP GKir MMuc NBea SEND SLPl
*	***fortunei***	CLnd
	frutescens	CEnd CLnd EPfP EWTr GKev GKir NWea
	fruticosa Crantz	CSto GAuc
	- 'Koehneana'	see *S. koehneana* C.K. Schneid.
	'Ghose'	CEnd CLnd EBee GKir SCoo SPer
	glabrescens	CSto GKir
	glabriuscula	GGal GKev
	'Glendoick Gleam'	GGGa
	'Glendoick Glory'	GGGa
	'Glendoick Ivory'	GGGa
	'Glendoick Pearl'	GGGa
	'Glendoick Ruby'	GGGa
	'Glendoick Spire'	GGGa
	'Glendoick White Baby'	GGGa
	glomerulata	LLHF
	'Golden Wonder'	see *S.* 'Lombarts Golden Wonder'
	gonggashanica	EPfP GKir
*	***gorrodini***	CLnd
§	***graeca***	GAuc GKir
	granulosa HWJ 1041	WCru
	harrowiana	GKir WPat
	hedlundii	CPLG EBee EBtc GBin GKir LRHS MGos NWea WPGP
	helenae	GKir
	hemsleyi	CDul CLnd CPLG GKir WPGP
	- 'John Bond'	EBee GKir LRHS MBri NLar NPal SCoo SPoG WClo
	× ***hostii***	CLnd MRav
	hupehensis C.K. Schneid. ♀H4	CBcs CDul CEnd CLnd CMCN CMac CTho CTri EBee EPfP EWTr GKir LHop LRHS MMuc NHol NWea SBfd SEND SLPl WDin WFar WHar WJas WMou WPat
	- MF 96170	EPfP
	- 'November Pink'	see *S. hupehensis* 'Pink Pagoda'
§	- var. ***obtusa*** ♀H4	CCVT CDoC CDul CLnd EPfP GCal GKir NEgg NPCo SSpi WDin
§	- 'Pink Pagoda'	Widely available
	- red-berried	GGal
	- 'Rosea'	see *S. hupehensis* var. *obtusa*
	× ***hybrida*** misapplied	see *S. × thuringiaca*
	hybrida L.	ECrN
	- 'Gibbsii' ♀H4	CDoC CLnd EBee ELan EPfP GAuc GKir MBri SPur WHar

	insignis	EPfP WPat
	intermedia	CCVT CDul CLnd CSBt CTho CTri CWib EBee ECrN GKir IFFs MGos NWea SEND WDin WHar WMou
	- 'Brouwers'	ELan LMaj WMou
	japonica B&SWJ 10813	WCru
	- B&SWJ 11048	WCru
	'Joseph Rock'	Widely available
§	× ***kewensis***	CDul CLnd NWea SPlb
	'Kirsten Pink'	CLnd CWib EBee ECrN SPer WFar
	koehneana hort.	see *S. fruticosa* McAllister
§	***koehneana*** C.K. Schneid. 𝕐H4	CBcs CLnd EBee GKev GKir GQui IDee MMuc NMen NWea WPat WTin
	aff. ***koehneana*** C.K. Schneid.	see *S. eburnea*
	'Kukula'	GKir
	kurzii	GKir
	- KR 1501	GKir
	lanata misapplied	see *S. vestita*
	lancastriensis	CDul CNat GKir
	latifolia	CLnd WDin
	- 'Henk Vink'	LMaj
	'Leonard Messel'	EBee GKir MAsh MBri MWya SCoo WHCr
	'Leonard Springer'	ECrN EPfP GKir
	leptophylla	CDul GKir
	ligustrifolia HWJ 984	WCru
	'Likjornaja'	EPfP
§	'Lombarts Golden Wonder'	CBcs CDul CLnd MMuc NWea SEND WJas
	'Maidenblush'	GKir
	matsumurana misapplied	see *S. commixta*
	megalocarpa	CDoC CPMA EPfP SSpi WPGP WPat
	meliosmifolia B&SWJ 11709	WCru
	microphylla GWJ 9252	WCru
	minima	GKir
	monbeigii (Card.) Yü	GAuc GKev GKir
	moravica 'Laciniata'	see *S. aucuparia* 'Beissneri'
§	***munda***	CMCN GBin GKir
	aff. ***ovalis*** H 1948	EBee
	'Peachi-Ness'	CLnd
	'Pearly King'	CBcs CTho GKir NBea WJas
	pekinensis	see *S. reticulata* subsp. *pekinensis*
§	'Pink Pearl'	CDul GKir
	'Pink Veil'	NLar
	'Pink-Ness'	CWit EBee GKir NLar SCoo SPoG
	pogonopetala Koehne	GAuc GKir
	pohuashanensis misapplied	see *S.* × *kewensis*
§	***pohuashanensis*** (Hance) Hedlund	WPat
	porrigentiformis	CDul
	poteriifolia	GAuc GCrs GKev GKir NHar WPat
	prattii misapplied	see *S. munda*
	prattii Koehne	CDul EBee GKev GKir MMuc WPat
	- var. ***subarachnoidea***	see *S. munda*
	pseudofennica	GKir
	pseudohupehensis	GKev GKir
	pseudovilmorinii	CDul EBee GBin GKir LRHS MBri
	- CLD 1437	GAuc
	- MF 93044	SSpi
	- SDR 82	GKev
	- SDR 4232	GKev
	- MCA 119 from Guizhou **new**	GKir
	randaiensis	CSto EPfP GKev GQui SPlb
	- B&SWJ 3202	NHol SSpi WCru
	'Red Tip'	CDul EWTr MWat
	reducta 𝕐H4	CBcs CEnd CSWP EBee EPfP GAbr GAuc GBee GBin GKev GKir GQui MBlu MMuc NHar NHol NWCA SPer WDin WFar WPat
	reflexipetala misapplied	see *S. commixta*
	rehderiana misapplied	see *S. aucuparia*
	rehderiana Koehne	CDul CLnd GKir
§	***reticulata*** subsp. ***pekinensis***	GKir
	rosea	GAbr GKev GKir
	- 'Rosiness'	CLnd EBee EPfP GKir LRHS MAsh MBri SCoo SLim
	'Rowancroft Coral Pink'	CDul MGos
	rufopilosa	GKir
	'Salmon Queen'	CLnd GKir
	sambucifolia	GAuc SKHP
	sargentiana 𝕐H4	Widely available
	scalaris ambig.	GAuc LAst MGos NWea WMou
§	***scalaris*** Koehne	CBcs CCVT CDul CEnd CTho CTri EBee EPfP GKir MBlu MGos SBfd SCoo SPer SPoG SSpi WDin WJas
	'Schouten'	ECrN GKir MGos
	scopulina misapplied	see *S. aucuparia* 'Fastigiata'
	scopulina Greene wild-collected	GKir
	setschwanensis	GGGa GKir
	'Signalman'	GKir
	simonkaiana	GAuc
	subulata HWJ 579	WCru
	- HWJ 925	WCru
	'Sunshine'	CCVT CDoC CDul EBee GKir LTen MAsh MBri MGos MMuc NLar SEND WJas
§	***thibetica*** 'John Mitchell' 𝕐H4	CAgr CDul CEnd CLnd CMCN CWib EBee EBtc ECrN EPfP GKir LRHS MBlu MBri MGos MRav NBea SLim SPer SPoG WFar WMou WPat
	aff. ***thibetica*** BWJ 7757a	WCru
	thomsonii GWJ 9363	WCru
§	× ***thuringiaca***	GAuc NBea
§	- 'Fastigiata'	CBcs CDul CLnd CMac CSBt EPfP MGos MMuc NEgg SCoo SEND WDin WJas
	tianschanica	GAuc
	torminalis	Widely available
	umbellata	GKir
	- var. ***cretica***	see *S. graeca*
	ursina	see *S. foliolosa*
	× ***vagensis***	CLnd GKir WMou
§	***vestita***	CLnd CTho EPfP MBlu
	vexans	CDul GBin
	vilmorinii 𝕐H4	Widely available
	- 'Robusta'	see *S.* 'Pink Pearl'
	aff. ***vilmorinii***	GKir
	wardii	CBcs CLnd CTho EPfP GKir MBlu
	'White Swan'	ECrN NLar
	'White Wax'	CDul EBee EPfP GKir LAst MGos SPer SPoG WDin WPat
	'Wilfrid Fox'	CLnd EBee GKir SLPl
	wilmottiana	CDul
	wilsoniana	CLnd GQui
	- C 5018	GKir
	- C&H 7122	GKir
	'Wisley Gold'	CWSG EBee MAsh MGos SCoo SLim SPoG WClo WHCr WMou

Sorghastrum (Poaceae)

	avenaceum	see *S. nutans*
§	***nutans***	CBod CKno CRWN CWCL GFor LEdu LRHS SMad SPhx

- 'Indian Steel'	EBee ECha GFor GQue SDix SGSe WWEG
- 'Sioux Blue'	EPPr

sorrel, common see *Rumex acetosa*

sorrel, French see *Rumex scutatus*

Souliea see *Actaea*

soursop see *Annona muricata*

Sparaxis (*Iridaceae*)

sp.	ECho
auriculata	ECho
'Vanrhynsdorp' **new**	
bulbifera	ECho
fragrans 'Napier'	ECho
grandiflora ♀$^{H2-3}$	LRHS
- subsp. ***acutiloba***	EBee ECho
- subsp. ***fimbriata***	ECho
- subsp. ***grandiflora***	CGrW ECho WCot
- subsp. ***violacea***	ECho
'Botriver' **new**	
hybrids	LAma
meterlekampiae	ECho
'Piekenierskloof' **new**	
- 'Rawsonville'	ECho
parviflora	ECho
'Red Reflex'	ECho
tricolor	CFox ECho SDeJ
variegata (v)	ECho
villosa	ECho

Sparganium (*Sparganiaceae*)

§ ***erectum***	CRow CWat EHon LPBA NMir NPer NSco SWat WMAq WSFF
ramosum	see *S. erectum*

Sparrmannia (*Tiliaceae*)

africana ♀^{H1}	CBcs CHEx CHll EAmu EShb LRHS MBri SDnm SPav

Spathipappus see *Tanacetum*

Spartina (*Poaceae*)

'Dafken'	EBee
patens	EPPr
pectinata	CHar GFor LRHS
- 'Aureomarginata' (v)	Widely available

Spartium (*Papilionaceae*)

junceum ♀^{H4}	CArn CBcs CDoC CDul CEnd CTri EBee ECrN ELan ELon EMil EPfP GCal IFFs LAst LRHS MGos MMuc MWat NSti SBfd SDix SGar SPer SPoG SRms WDin
- 'Brockhill Compact'	CDoC EBee IVic LRHS

Spartocytisus see *Cytisus*

Spathantheum (*Araceae*)

orbignyanum	WCot

Spathiphyllum (*Araceae*)

'Viscount'	MBri
wallisii	MBri

Spathodea (*Bignoniaceae*)

campanulata	SPlb

spearmint see *Mentha spicata*

Speirantha (*Convallariaceae*)

§ ***convallarioides***	CAby CDes CGHE CLAP CPom CStu EBee ECho EHrv ELon EPPr LEdu MNrw WCot WCru WPGP WPrP
gardenii	see *S. convallarioides*

Spergularia (*Caryophyllaceae*)

purpurea	ECho
rupicola	EBWF ECho

Sphacele see *Lepechinia*

Sphaeralcea (*Malvaceae*)

ambigua	ELan
'Childerley'	CSpe LHop SAga SMrm
coccinea	SPlb
fendleri	CBot CHll
'Hopleys Lavender'	EBee LAst LHop LSou SAga SWvt WSHC
incana	CSpe SAga WCot
malviflora	CDTJ
miniata	CHll SAga SMrm
munroana	CBot CDTJ CPom CSev ECGP ELan SAga SRkn WSHC
- pale pink-flowered	ECtt
* - 'Shell Pink'	CSpe ECGP
'Newleaze Coral'	CSpe EBee EWld LAst LHop LSou MAsh SAga SPad SPoG SUsu SWvt
'Newleaze Pink'	LHop SAga SRkn
obtusiloba	SAga
remota	CPLG EBee SPlb
rivularis	EBee
umbellata	see *Phymosia umbellata*

Sphaeromeria (*Asteraceae*)

§ ***capitata***	CPBP NWCA

Sphenosciadium (*Apiaceae*)

capitellatum	WCot
NNS 04-449 **new**	
- NNS 05-653	WCot

Spigelia (*Loganiaceae*)

marilandica	EBee EWTr SKHP
- 'Wisley Jester'	CSpr LRHS MBri SChF SCoo SKHP

Spilanthes (*Asteraceae*)

acmella misapplied	see *Acmella oleracea*
oleracea	see *Acmella oleracea*

Spiloxene (*Hypoxidaceae*)

canaliculata	ECho
'Kamiesberg' **new**	
capensis 'Somerset West'	ECho
minuta 'Nay' **new**	ECho
serrata 'Saldanha'	ECho

Spiraea (*Rosaceae*)

SDR 6047	GKev
'Abigail'	CDoC
albiflora	see *S. japonica* var. *albiflora*
arborea	see *Sorbaria kirilowii*
arcuata	EMac
§ 'Arguta' ♀^{H4}	Widely available
× ***arguta*** 'Bridal Wreath'	see *S.* 'Arguta'
bella	SLon WTin
betulifolia	MRav NHol WDin
- var. ***aemiliana***	CBot CWSG EBee ECtt MAsh MGos MMuc SLPl WFar
- 'Tor' **new**	EPPr IVic

	× ***billardii*** misapplied	see *S.* × *pseudosalicifolia*
	× ***bumalda*** 'Wulfenii'	see *S. japonica* 'Walluf'
	callosa 'Alba'	see *S. japonica* var. *albiflora*
	canescens	CPLG
	- AC 1354	MSnd
§	***cantoniensis*** 'Flore Pleno' (d)	SLon
	- 'Lanceata'	see *S. cantoniensis* 'Flore Pleno'
	× ***cinerea*** 'Grefsheim' ♀H4	CDoC CSBt EBee ECtt MBri MGos MMuc SLim SPer SPlb WDin
	crispifolia	see *S. japonica* 'Bullata'
	douglasii	CMac GAuc IFFs
	formosana	WCru
	- B&SWJ 1597	CPLG
§	× ***foxii***	SLPl
	fritschiana	CMac SLPl SLon
	hayatana	SLon
	- RWJ 10014	WCru
	hendersonii	see *Petrophytum hendersonii*
	japonica	GKir WFar
§	- var. ***albiflora***	CBcs CChe CMac CSBt CTri CWib ELan EPfP GKir LBMP LRHS MGos MMuc MRav MSwo MWat NEgg NPri SBfd SEND SLim SPad SPer SRms SWvt WDin WFar WMoo WSpi
	- 'Alpina'	see *S. japonica* 'Nana'
	- 'Alpine Gold'	GBin
	- 'Anthony Waterer' (v)	Widely available
	- 'Barkby Gold'	MGos
	- 'Blenheim'	SRms
§	- 'Bullata'	CFee CMac EPfP EPot GEdr NLar NWCA SRms WAbe
	- 'Candlelight' ♀H4	CSBt EBee EPfP GKir LAst LRHS MAsh MBri MGos NEgg NHol NLar SBfd SCoo SLim SPer SPoG SWvt WMoo
	- 'Crispa'	EPfP WFar WGrn WMoo
	- 'Dart's Red' ♀H4	GKir IVic WFar
	- 'Firelight'	CChe CSBt EBee EHoe ELan EPfP GKir LAst LRHS MAsh MBri MGos MSwo NEgg NHol NLar SCoo SLim SPer SPoG SSta SWvt WDin WFar WHar WMoo
§	- 'Genpei'	CMac MAsh SPer
	- 'Gold Mound'	CBar CMac CPLG CWSG CWib CWit EBee EHoe ELan EPfP GKir LBMP LRHS MAsh MGos MMuc MRav MSwo NHol NLar NPri SBfd SCoo SLim SPer SPlb SRms WDin WFar WHar
	- Golden Princess = 'Lisp'PBR ♀H4	CMac CTri EPfP GKir LBuc LRHS MAsh MGos NEgg SCoo SReu SRms SSta WCFE WDin WFar WMoo
	- 'Goldflame'	Widely available
	- 'Jacobsen's Goldflame' **new**	IVic
	- 'Little Princess'	CBar CBcs CDul CMac CWSG CWib CWit EBee ECrN GKir LRHS MAsh MRav MSwo NHol NWea SCoo SLim SPer SRGP SRms SSta SWvt WBVN WDin WFar WHar WMoo
§	- 'Macrophylla'	WPat
	- Magic Carpet = 'Walbuma'PBR (v) ♀H4	EBee GKir LBuc LRHS MAsh MMuc NLar SCoo SEND SPoG
	- 'Magnifica'	see *S. japonica* 'Macrophylla'
§	- 'Nana' ♀H4	CMac CSBt ECho GEdr MAsh MRav SRms
	- 'Nyewoods'	see *S. japonica* 'Nana'
	- 'Shiburi'	see *S. japonica* var. *albiflora*
N	- 'Shirobana' misapplied	see *S. japonica* 'Genpei'
N	- 'Shirobana'	see *S. japonica* var. *albiflora*
	- 'Snow Cap'	CWib
§	- 'Walluf'	CMac CPLG CTri CWib
	- 'White Cloud'	ELan
	- 'White Gold'PBR	CSBt EBee ELan EPfP GKir LAst LRHS LSqu MAsh MBri NHol SCoo SLim SPer SPoG SWvt WHar WMoo WRHF
	'Margaritae'	SPer SWvt
	micrantha	CPLG
	nipponica	CBcs GKir LAst
	- 'Halward's Silver'	MGos MRav NHol SLPl
§	- 'Snowmound' ♀H4	Widely available
	- var. ***tosaensis*** misapplied	see *S. nipponica* 'Snowmound'
	- var. ***tosaensis*** (Yatabe) Makino	LHop SReu
	palmata 'Elegans'	see *Filipendula purpurea* 'Elegans'
	prunifolia (d)	CMac ECrN ELan GKir LRHS MBlu MRav SPer SPoG WCFE WDin WGrn WPat
§	× ***pseudosalicifolia*** **new**	MMuc
	- 'Triumphans'	MMuc
	salicifolia	MMuc WFar
	'Summersnow'	SLPl
	'Superba'	see *S.* × *foxii*
	tarokoensis	GAuc
	thunbergii ♀H4	CDul CTri CWib EBee ECrN EPfP MMuc MRav NWea SBfd SCoo SEND SLim SRms WDin
	- 'Aurea'	LRHS MAsh
	- 'Fujino Pink'	WDin
	- 'Golden Times' **new**	SPoG
	- 'Mellow Yellow'	see *S. thunbergii* 'Ogon'
	- 'Mount Fuji'	CMac CWib EHoe MGos MMuc MRav WFar
§	- 'Ōgon'	WFar WPen
	trilobata	EBee
	ulmaria	see *Filipendula ulmaria*
	× ***vanhouttei***	CBcs CDul CTri EBee EPfP MMuc MRav MSwo SEND SLim SPer SRms WDin WFar
	- 'Gold Fountain'	CWSG GBin LRHS NHol SCoo SPoG WFar WRHF
	- 'Pink Ice' (v)	CAbP CDoC CWib EBee EHoe EPfP LAst LBMP LRHS MAsh MGos MMuc MRav NHol SBfd SPer SPlb SPoG SWvt WDin WFar
	veitchii	MRav
	venusta 'Magnifica'	see *Filipendula rubra* 'Venusta'

Spiranthes (*Orchidaceae*)

	cernua	NGdn
	- var. ***odorata***	LSou
	- - 'Chadd's Ford'	Widely available
	spiralis	WHer

Spodiopogon (*Poaceae*)

	sibiricus	CKno EBee EHoe EPPr GFor LEdu MWhi NWsh SGSe SMad
	- 'West Lake'	IMou

Sporobolus (*Poaceae*)

	airoides	CKno EBee EHoe EPPr EShb GCal LPio MWea SGSe SMad WCot WHrl
	heterolepis	CKno EBee EHoe EShb GCal LPio MWhi NDov SGSe
	- 'Cloud'	GBin
I	- 'Wisconsin Strain'	EPPr IMou
	wrightii	EBee EPPr MWhi

Sprekelia (*Amaryllidaceae*)

	formosissima	CFir CSpe CStu ECho LAma LEdu LRHS SPav

Stachys ✿ (*Lamiaceae*)

	aethiopica 'Danielle'	see *S. thunbergii* 'Danielle'
§	***affinis***	CArn CFir GPoy LEdu SVic
	albens	EBla IFro
	albotomentosa	CMea EBla MDKP SHar WCot WWlt
	× ***ambigua***	EBWF
	balcanica	CDes EBee GKev
	- MESE	WPGP
	betonica	see *S. officinalis*
§	***byzantina***	Widely available
§	- 'Big Ears'	CBow EBee ECha EPfP EWTr GMaP LHop MBri MGos MLLN MMuc MRav MWat SBch SBfd SEND SGSe SMad SMrm SPhx SPoG SRms WBor WCAu WCFE WCot WFar WHoo WMnd WWEG
§	- 'Cotton Boll'	COIW EBee ECha GCal SBch SPer WCom WFar WWEG
	- 'Countess Helen von Stein'	see *S. byzantina* 'Big Ears'
	- gold-leaved	see *S. byzantina* 'Primrose Heron'
	- large-leaved	see *S. byzantina* 'Big Ears'
	- 'Limelight'	WCot
§	- 'Primrose Heron'	CMoH EBee ECha EPPr GBee GKev LRHS MRav MSpe NBid NLar SMrm SPoG SWvt WFar WOut
	- 'Sheila McQueen'	see *S. byzantina* 'Cotton Boll'
	- 'Silky Fleece'	EBee ECha EDAr EPfP EShb EWTr GKir LBMP NBre SBfd WCAu WWEG
	- 'Silver Carpet'	CBar CBcs COIW EBee ECha EHoe EPfP EWTr GKir GMaP LAst LRHS LSRN MRav NSti SPer SPoG SRms SWat SWvt WCAu WCom WCot WFar WHoo WMnd WWEG
§	- 'Striped Phantom' (v)	CBow EBla WEas
	- 'Variegata'	see *S. byzantina* 'Striped Phantom'
	chamissonis var. ***cooleyae***	EBee
	citrina	CMea EBee GCal
	coccinea	CPla EBee ECtt EHrv EShb MCot SBch SDnm SPav SRkn WMoo
	- 'El Salto'	WCom
	corsica	WPGP
	densiflora	see *S. monieri* (Gouan) P.W. Ball
§	***discolor***	CMea EBee IKil MDKP MLLN NLar SBch WCot WOut
	germanica	CPom EBee GPWP NBre SEND
	- subsp. ***bithynica***	SMrm
	glutinosa	MDKP
	grandiflora	see *S. macrantha*
	'Hidalgo'	CSpe SAga
	lanata	see *S. byzantina*
	lavandulifolia	WAbe
§	***macrantha***	Widely available
*	- 'Alba'	EBee ECha
	- 'Hummelo'	see *S. officinalis* 'Hummelo'
*	- 'Nivea'	CSam EHrv ELan MMHG NBir
	- 'Robusta' ♀H4	CDes ELan GCal LRHS MMuc NBro NGdn SMrm WCot WWEG
	- 'Rosea'	CElw CMHG EBee ELan GBee GMaP LLWP MArl MAvo MLHP SPlb SWat WCFE WEas WPer
	- 'Superba'	CPrp CSpe EBee EBla ECtt EPfP GCra GKev GKir GMaP LAst LBMP LEdu MBri MMHG MRav MWhi NBPC NEgg SPer SWvt WBor WCAu WCom WCot WFar WMnd WMoo
	- 'Violacea'	EBee LRHS MAvo MBrN NChi WCot WPGP
	mexicana misapplied	see *S. thunbergii*
	monieri misapplied	see *S. officinalis*
	monieri ambig.	CAbP CMMP EBee EShb GKev LBMP MSCN NLar NSti
	- white-flowered **new**	GKev
§	***monieri*** (Gouan) P.W. Ball	CEnt GBin LEdu LRHS
*	- 'Rosea'	EBee NBre NDov NLar
	nivea	see *S. discolor*
	obliqua	NBre WOut
§	***officinalis***	CArn CEnt CPrp CRWN CSev CWan EBWF EBee GBar GPoy LEdu MCot MHer MMuc MNHC NLan NMir WClo WCot WHer WHfH WJek
	- 'Alba'	CArn CPrp EBee GKev LEdu MMuc NBro STes WCom WFar WOut WTin
	- dwarf, white-flowered	GCal
§	- 'Hummelo'	CPrp EBee ECtt ELon EPPr EPfP GAbr GQue IKil LHop LPla LSou MDKP MLLN MRav NBPC NDov NLar SAga SMrm SPhx SPoG SUsu WCAu WFar WWEG
	- mauve-flowered	WTin
	- 'Rosea'	CMea GCal GQue NBro STes WCom WFar WSHC WTin WWEG
	- 'Rosea Superba'	EBee ECha MDKP MLLN NBre WCAu WCot WFar
	- 'Saharan Pink'	CMHG EBee EPfP LSou MHer MLLN MMuc WOut WWEG
	- 'Spitzenberg'	SUsu
	- 'Wisley White'	EBee GQue SBfd WClo WCot
	olympica	see *S. byzantina*
	ossetica	CDes EBee
	palustris	CArn EBWF LLWG LPBA MMuc NLan NLar NMir NSco SEND
	- from Islay **new**	SEND
	recta	CEnt NLar
	scardica MESE 362	MDKP
	setifera	EBla NBre
	spicata	see *S. macrantha*
	stricta	LRHS
	sylvatica	CArn EBWF NLan NMir NSco WHer WSFF
	- 'Huskers' (v)	NBre
	- 'Shade of Pale'	WAlt
§	***thunbergii***	CDes CSam EShb LEdu MBrN MDKP MSpe MWhi SBch SPhx SUsu WCot WPGP WPrP
§	- 'Danielle'	CBow CSam EBee ECtt LHop LIMB LRHS LSRN MHer MMuc NBre SRkn WMoo
	tuberifera	see *S. affinis*

Stachyurus (*Stachyuraceae*)

B&SWJ 11508 from Yakushima Island, Japan **new**	WCru
chinensis	CBcs CMCN CPMA CTri CWib IArd IDee IVic MGos NLar SMad SPoG
- 'Celina'	CPMA EMil LRHS MBlu MBri MGos NLar
- 'Goldbeater'	NLar
- 'Joy Forever' (v)	CBcs CDoC CDul CEnd CMCN CMac EBee EMil EPfP IArd IVic LLHF LRHS LSRN MBri MGos NLar SKHP SLim SPoG SSpi SSta SWvt WCot
himalaicus	NLar
- HWJCM 009	WCru
- HWJK 2035	WCru
aff. ***himalaicus*** HWJK 2052	WCru

'Magpie' (v)	CPMA EPfP MBri MGos NLar SAga WCru
praecox ♀^{H4}	Widely available
- B&SWJ 8898	WCru
- B&SWJ 10899	WCru
- var. ***leucotrichus***	CPMA NLar
- var. ***matsuzakii***	CPMA NLar
- - B&SWJ 2817	WCru
- - B&SWJ 11229	WCru
- 'Petra'	CPMA
retusus	CPLG NLar
'Rubriflorus'	CPMA ELan EPfP LRHS MAsh MBri NLar SChF WFar WPGP
salicifolius	CBcs CGHE CPLG CPMA MBri NLar SKHP SSpi WAbe WPGP WPat
sigeyosii	CBcs
- B&SWJ 6915	WCru
- RWJ 10094	WCru
aff. ***szechuanensis***	CPLG
- BWJ 8153	WCru
yunnanensis	CBcs NLar SSpi WPat WSHC

Stapelia (*Asclepiadaceae*)

gettliffei	EShb LToo
grandiflora	CStu
- 'Flavirostris'	EShb
hirsuta	EShb
leendertziae	LToo
marmoratum	see *Orbea variegata*
variegata	see *Orbea variegata*

Staphylea (*Staphyleaceae*)

bolanderi	CBcs
bumalda	CBcs CPMA NLar
- B&SWJ 11053	WCru
colchica	CBcs CDul CPMA EBee EBtc ELan EPfP EWTr EWes LRHS MGos MMHG NPal SMad SPer WCom WDin WKif WSHC
holocarpa	CPMA EBee EPfP MRav WFar
- 'Innocence'	CDul NLar
N - var. ***rosea***	CPMA EPfP MBri SMad
N - 'Rosea'	CBcs CPMA MBlu NLar SSpi WSHC
pinnata	CAgr CEnd CPMA EBtc EPfP IVic NLar SEND SMad WPat
trifolia	CPMA NEgg

Statice see *Limonium*

Stauntonia (*Lardizabalaceae*)

B&SWJ 8223	WCru
aff. ***chinensis*** DJHV 06175	WCru
hexaphylla	CBcs CDoC CHEx CSam CTri CWGN EBee EPfP LRHS MAsh MBri MMuc MWya NLar SKHP SPer SPoG SReu SSpi SSta WBrE WSHC
- B&SWJ 4858	WCru
leucantha KWJ 12218 new	WCru
obovatifoliola B&SWJ 3685	WCru
- CWJ 12353	WCru
purpurea	NLar
- B&SWJ 3690	WCru
yaoshanensis B&SWJ 8223 new	WCru
- HWJ 1024	WCru

Stegnogramma (*Thelypteridaceae*)

pozoi	EFer

Stellaria (*Caryophyllaceae*)

graminea	EBWF
holostea	CArn CRWN EBWF MNHC NMir NSco WShi

Stellera (*Thymelaeaceae*)

chamaejasme SDR 5946	GKev

Stemmacantha (*Asteraceae*)

carthamoides	CArn
§ ***centaureoides***	EBee EBrs ECGP ECha GAbr GCal GQue LPla LRHS MBNS NBid NBre SPhx SUsu WCot WSpi
heleniifolia	CDes
subsp. ***bicknellii*** new	

Stenanthium (*Melanthiaceae*)

gramineum new	EWes
robustum	WPGP

Stenochlaena (*Blechnaceae*)

tenuifolia	WRic

Stenomesson (*Amaryllidaceae*)

§ ***miniatum***	WCot
pearcei	EBee ECho WCot WPrP
variegatum	WCot
- yellow-flowered	WCot

Stenotaphrum (*Poaceae*)

secundatum	EShb
- 'Variegatum' (v) ♀^{H1}	EShb LSou

Stephanandra (*Rosaceae*)

chinensis	SLon
incisa	CBcs CPLG
§ - 'Crispa'	CDoC CDul CMac CTri EBee ELan EPfP EWTr LAst LHop LTen MBlu MRav NEgg NHol NLar SPer WCFE WDin WFar WMoo
- 'Dart's Horizon'	SLPl
- 'Prostrata'	see *S. incisa* 'Crispa'
tanakae	CBcs CDoC CDul CMac CPLG CTri EBee ELan EPfP EWTr LAst MBlu MRav NEgg SLPl SLon SPer WDin WFar

Stephania (*Menispermaceae*)

longa KWJ 12163 new	WCru
rotunda B&SWJ 2396	WCru
sinica BWJ 8094	WCru
aff. ***tetrandra*** WWJ 11896 new	WCru

Stephanotis (*Asclepiadaceae*)

floribunda ♀^{H1}	CBcs CCCN EBak MBri SOWG

Sterculia (*Sterculiaceae*)

rupestris	see *Brachychiton rupestris*

Sternbergia (*Amaryllidaceae*)

'Autumn Gold'	ECho GKev LAma
candida	ECho
§ ***clusiana***	ECho
colchiciflora	ECho
fischeriana	ECho
greuteriana	ECho EPot WWst
lutea	CPBP ECha ECho EPot ERCP EWes LAma LRHS MAsh MCot MHer SChF SDeJ SDix SPhx WEas WTin
- Angustifolia Group	CDes CMea ECho WCot
macrantha	see *S. clusiana*
sicula	EBrs ECho GKev MAsh NRya

- 'Arcadian Sun'	ECho WWst
- var. ***graeca***	ECho
- - from Crete	ECho
- 'John Marr'	WThu

Stevia (*Asteraceae*)

rebaudiana	CArn EOHP GPoy MDKP WCot WJek

Stewartia ✿ (*Theaceae*)

gemmata	see *S. sinensis*
'Korean Splendor'	see *S. pseudocamellia* Koreana Group
koreana	see *S. pseudocamellia* Koreana Group
malacodendron 🏆H4	EPfP SSpi
monadelpha	CMen IDee LLHF MPkF NLar SSpi
ovata	SSpi
pseudocamellia 🏆H4	Widely available
- B&SWJ 11044	WCru
§ - Koreana Group 🏆H4	CBcs CDul CEnd CMCN EPfP GAuc GKir LRHS NLar SSpi WDin WFar
- 'Ogisu'	NLar
pteropetiolata B&SWJ 11726	WCru
rostrata	CBcs CPMA ELan EPfP IArd MBlu MPkF NLar SSpi
serrata	CMen CPMA IArd IVic MPkF
§ ***sinensis*** 🏆H4	CBcs CDul CPMA EPfP LRHS MBlu MBri NLar NMun SSpi

Stigmaphyllon (*Malpighiaceae*)

ciliatum	CCCN
littorale	CCCN

Stipa (*Poaceae*)

sp.	CDes
F&M 248	WPGP
arundinacea	see *Anemanthele lessoniana*
barbata	CKno CMea CSpe ECha EPPr EWes LRHS MAvo SApp SMad SPer SPhx SUsu WClo WKif WPGP
- 'Silver Feather'	NWsh SLim
* ***boysterica***	CFee
brachytricha	see *Calamagrostis brachytricha*
§ ***calamagrostis***	Widely available
- 'Algau'	GBin WCot
- 'Lemperg'	EPPr IMou
canescens	SPhx
capillata	EBee EPPr GCal GFor LRHS SMad
- 'Brautschleier'	CWib SWal WNew WPtf
comata	EBee MSnd
elegantissima	CKno EHoe GFor LRHS
extremiorientalis	CKno ECha EPPr GFor MRav SMad
* ***gerardi***	SApp
gigantea 🏆H4	Widely available
- 'Gold Fontaene'	CDes CElw CFir CKno EBee EPPr EWes MAvo MMoz MNrw NDov SBch SMad SPhx SUsu WCot WMoo WPGP WPrP
- 'Pixie'	NWsh SApp SGSe SPhx
grandis	CKno ECha EPPr GBin GFor WMoo WPer
ichu	CKno SDix SMHy
- F&M 32	WPGP
joannis	GCal
kirghisorum new	WCot
lasiagrostis	see *S. calamagrostis*
lessingiana	CPLG EBee EHoe EHul EPPr MMuc SBfd SEND WMoo WPGP WSpi
offneri	EBee EPPr EWes SSvw
pennata	CKno CSpe EBee EPPr GFor WWEG
§ ***poeppigiana*** new	GCal
pontica	SPhx
pseudoichu	EBee
- RCB/Arg K2-2	WCot
- RCB/Arg Y-1	WCot
pulcherrima	CBow EBee EPPr GAbr GCal LBMP LRHS
- subsp. ***pulcherrima***	SPhx
- 'Windfeder'	CFir
ramosissima	CKno
robusta	EBee EPPr
splendens misapplied	see *S. calamagrostis*
splendens Trin.	WFoF
stenophylla	see *S. tirsa*
stipoides	GGar
tenacissima	EBee EHul GFor SUsu WDin
tenuifolia misapplied	see *S. tenuissima*
tenuifolia Steud.	CHar CMea EBee EHul EPfP LRHS MBri MRav NBir NBro NHol NOak NSti WHal WMoo
§ ***tenuissima***	Widely available
- 'Wind Whispers'	CSpe GBin MLLN SBfd
§ ***tirsa***	CAby LRHS NDov SPhx
turkestanica	EBee NDov SBfd SUsu SWal SWat
ucrainica	GFor
verticillata	CKno

Stokesia ✿ (*Asteraceae*)

cyanea	see *S. laevis*
§ ***laevis***	CMea CPrp EBee ECGP ECha EPfP GKir LRHS NBPC NLar SMrm SPet SPlb WBrE WCAu WClo WFar WMoo WPGP WPer WWEG
- 'Alba'	CMMP COIW CPrp CTca EBee ECha EHrv ELan EPfP EWTr GKir LEdu LRHS MMuc MRav NPnk SPad SPer SPhx STes
- 'Blue Star'	Widely available
- 'Color Wheel' new	EBrs
- 'Klaus Jelitto'	CFwr EBee IPot LBuc LEdu LRHS SHar
- 'Mary Gregory'	Widely available
- mixed	CPou
- 'Omega Skyrocket'	CPou EBee EWTr GBin LRHS NHol NLar SMrm WFar WWEG
- 'Peach Melba'	EBee ECtt NCGa NLar SPoG WMoo
- 'Peachie's Pick' new	NLar
- 'Purple Parasols'	Widely available
- 'Silver Moon'	COIW EAEE EBee ECtt EPfP EShb IPot LAst LPio LRHS MLLN NBir NHol SPoG STes WAul WFar WWEG
§ - 'Träumerei'	CWGN EBee GGar LAst LRHS NHol NLar SBfd SMrm SPet WMnd WMoo WPer WWEG
- 'White Star'	see *S. laevis* 'Träumerei'
- 'Wyoming'	LRHS

Stranvaesia see *Photinia*

× *Stranvinia* see *Photinia*

Stratiotes (*Hydrocharitaceae*)

aloides	CBen CWat EHon LPBA MWts NPer NSco SVic SWat WMAq WPnP

strawberry see *Fragaria*

Strelitzia (*Strelitziaceae*)

alba	CCCN EAmu NPla

juncea	ERea XBlo
nicolai	CAbb CDTJ EAmu EShb EUJe LPal NPer XBlo
reginae 🏆H1	CAbb CBcs ELan ERea EShb EUJe LPal LRHS MMuc MREP NPal NPer NPla SAPC SArc SBig SChr SEND SPlb SRms XBlo
- var. ***citrina***	ERea
- 'Kirstenbosch Gold'	NPal XBlo

Streptocarpella see *Streptocarpus*

Streptocarpus ✿ (*Gesneriaceae*)

'Albatross' 🏆H1	SBrm SDnm WDib
'Alice'	SBrm WDib
'Alissa'	WDib
'Amanda' Dibley 🏆H1	SBrm WDib
'Amanda'[PBR] Fleischle (Marleen Series)	WDib
'Anne'	CSpe MCot SBrm WDib
'Athena'	SBrm WDib
'Awena'	WDib
baudertii	WDib
'Beryl'	WDib
'Bethan' 🏆H1	SBrm WDib
'Bicentenary'	SBrm
'Black Gardenia'	WDib
'Black Panther'	WDib
'Blue Bird'	SBrm
'Blue Gem'	WDib
'Blue Heaven'	SBrm
'Blue Moon'	WDib
'Blue Nymph'	SBrm WDib
'Blue Pencil'	SBrm
§ 'Blue Upstart'	SBrm
'Blushing Bride' (d)	SDnm WDib
* 'Boysenberry Delight'	WDib
'Branwen'	SBrm SDnm WDib
'Brimstone'	SBrm
'Bristol's Black Bird'	SBrm WDib
'Bristol's Daisy Jane'	SBrm
'Bristol's Ice Castle'	SBrm
'Bristol's Petticoats'	SBrm
'Bristol's Red Typhoon'	SBrm
'Bristol's Stormy Skies'	SBrm
'Bristol's Very Best'	WDib
'Buttons'	SBrm
caeruleus	WDib
'Caitlin'	WDib
candidus	WDib
'Carol'	SBrm WDib
'Carolyn Ann'	SBrm
'Carys' 🏆H1	SBrm WDib
'Catrin' 🏆H1	SBrm WDib
caulescens	WDib
- var. ***pallescens***	EOHP WDib
'Charlotte'	SBrm WDib
'Chloe'	WDib
'Chorus Line' 🏆H1	SDnm WDib
'Christine'	SBrm
'Clouds'	CSpe SBrm
'Concord Blue'	WDib
'Constant Nymph'	SBrm WDib
'Copper Knob'	SBrm
'Coral Flair'	WDib
'Cranberry Velvet'	SBrm
'Crystal Beauty'	WDib
'Crystal Blush'	WDib
'Crystal Charm'	WDib
'Crystal Dawn'	WDib
'Crystal Ice'[PBR] 🏆H1	WDib
'Crystal Snow'	WDib
'Crystal Wonder'	WDib
cyaneus	WDib
- subsp. ***polackii***	WDib
'Cynthia' 🏆H1	SBrm WDib
'Dainty Lady'	SBrm
'Daphne' 🏆H1	WDib
'Dark Eyes Mary'	SBrm
'Demeter'	SBrm
denticulatus	WDib
'Diana'	SBrm WDib
'Dinas'	SBrm WDib
'Double Trouble'	SBrm
'Dreamtime'	SBrm
dunnii	SGar WDib
'Eleanor'	SBrm
'Elegance'	SBrm
'Elizabeth'	SBrm
'Ella'	SBrm
'Ella Mae'	SBrm
'Ellie'	WDib
'Elsi'	SBrm SDnm WDib
'Emily'	SBrm WDib
'Emma'	SBrm WDib
'Falling Stars' 🏆H1	CSpe SBrm WDib
'Festival Wales'	SBrm WDib
'Fiona'	SBrm WDib
floribundus hort.	WDib
'Frances'	SBrm
'Franken Alison'	SBrm
'Franken Jenny'	SBrm
'Franken Kelly'	SBrm
'Franken Misty Blue'	SBrm
'Franken Texas Sunset'	SBrm
'Frosty Diamond'	SBrm WDib
gardenii	WDib
'Gillian'	SBrm
glandulosissimus 🏆H1	EOHP WDib
'Gloria' 🏆H1	CSpe SBrm WDib
'Gower Daybreak'	SBrm
'Gower Garnet'	SBrm
'Gower Midnight'	SBrm
'Gwen'	SBrm WDib
'Hannah' **new**	WDib
'Hannah Ellis'	SBrm
'Happy Snappy' 🏆H1	SBrm SDnm WDib
'Heidi' 🏆H1	SDnm WDib
'Helen' 🏆H1	SBrm WDib
'Hope' **new**	WDib
'Huge White'	CSpe
'Ida'	SBrm
'Inky Fingers'	SBrm
'Iona'	WDib
'Izzy'	SBrm
'Jaco's Gem'	SBrm
'Jacquie'	WDib
'Jane Elizabeth'	SBrm
'Jennifer' 🏆H1	SBrm SDnm WDib
'Jessica'	WDib
'Joanna'	SBrm WDib
johannis	WDib
'Josie'	SBrm
'Judith'	SBrm
'Karen'	SBrm SDnm WDib
'Katie'	WDib
kentaniensis	WDib
'Kerry's Gold'	SBrm
'Kim' 🏆H1	CSpe EShb MCot SBrm SDnm WDib
kirkii	WDib
'Kisie'	SBrm
'Lady Lavender'	SBrm
'Largesse'	SBrm
'Laura' 🏆H1	SBrm WDib

'Lemon Ice'	SBrm
'Leyla' PBR **new**	WDib
'Lisa' ♀H1	SBrm
'Little Gem'	CSpe SBrm
'Louise'	SBrm WDib
'Lynette'	SBrm
'Lynne'	SBrm WDib
'Maassen's White' ♀H1	SBrm WDib
'Magpie'	SBrm
'Mandy'	SDnm WDib
'Margaret' Gavin Brown	SBrm WDib
'Marie'	SBrm WDib
'Mary'	SBrm
'Megan'	SBrm WDib
'Melanie' Dibley ♀H1	SBrm WDib
meyeri	WDib
'Midnight Flame'	EShb SBrm WDib
'Mini Nymph'	CSpe WDib
'Misty Pink'	SBrm
'Modbury Lady'	SBrm
modestus	WDib
'Molly'	SBrm
'Mona'	SBrm
'Monica's Magic'	SBrm
'Moonlight'	SBrm WDib
'Muse'	SBrm
'Neptune'	SBrm WDib
'Nerys'	WDib
'Nia'	CSpe SBrm WDib
'Nicola'	SBrm WDib
'Night Beacon'	SBrm
'Olga'	WDib
'Olwen'	WDib
'Orchid Lace'	SBrm
'Padarn'	WDib
'Pale Rider'	SBrm
'Party Doll'	SBrm WDib
'Passion Pink'	SBrm
'Patricia'	SBrm
'Paula' ♀H1	SBrm WDib
pentherianus	WDib
'Pink Fondant'	CSpe
'Pink Leyla' **new**	WDib
'Pink Souffle'	SBrm SDnm WDib
'Pink Upstart'	SBrm
'Plum Crazy'	SBrm
polyanthus	WDib
subsp. ***dracomontanus***	
primulifolius	WDib
- subsp. ***formosus***	WDib
'Princesse' (Marleen Series)	WDib
prolixus	WDib
* 'Purple Passion'	SBrm
'Raspberry Dream'	SBrm
rexii	WDib
'Rhiannon'	SBrm SDnm WDib
'Rosebud'	SBrm WDib
'Rosemary' (d)	WDib
'Roulette Azur' (Roulette Series) **new**	WDib
'Roulette Cherry' (Roulette Series)	WDib
'Ruby' ♀H1	SBrm WDib
'Ruby Anniversary'	SBrm
'Ruffled Lilac'	SBrm
'Ruffles'	SBrm
'Sally'	SBrm WDib
'Samantha'	SBrm
'Sandra'	SBrm SDnm WDib
'Sarah'	SBrm WDib
saxorum ♀H1	CCCN EOHP EShb LSou SRms WDib WFar
- compact	CCCN EOHP WDib
'Seren'	WDib
'Shannon'	SBrm
'Sian'	SBrm SDnm WDib
silvaticus	WDib
'Snow White' ♀H1	SDnm WDib
'Something Special'	SBrm SDnm WDib
'Sophie'	WDib
'Southshore'	SBrm WDib
'Spider'	SBrm
'Spirit' **new**	WDib
'Stacey'	SBrm
'Stella' ♀H1	SBrm WDib
'Stephanie'	CSpe MCot WDib
stomandrus	WDib
'Stormy'	SBrm
'Strawberry Fondant'	SBrm
'Sugar Almond'	SBrm
'Sunsweet'	SBrm
'Susan' ♀H1	WDib
'Swaybelle'	SBrm
'Tanga'	SBrm
'Targa' (Marleen Series)	WDib
'Tatan Blue'	SBrm
'Terracotta'	SBrm
'Texas Hot Chili'	SBrm WDib
'Texas Sunrise'	SBrm
thompsonii	WDib
'Tina' ♀H1	SBrm SDnm WDib
'Tracey'	SBrm WDib
'Turbulent Tide'	SBrm
'Upstart'	see *S.* 'Blue Upstart'
'Vanessa'	SBrm
variabilis	WDib
'Velvet Underground'	SBrm
'Vera'	SBrm
'Violet Lace'	CSpe SBrm
'Watermelon Wine'	WDib
wendlandii	WDib
'Wendy'	SBrm WDib
'White Wings'	SBrm
'Wiesmoor Red'	WDib
'Winifred'	SBrm WDib

Streptopus (*Convallariaceae*)

amplexifolius	EBee ECho NMen WCru
roseus	EBee ECho
streptopoides	EBee

Streptosolen (*Solanaceae*)

jamesonii ♀H1	CHll EBak EBee ELan ERea EShb SAga
- 'Fire Gold'	ERea

Strobilanthes (*Acanthaceae*)

sp.	WBor
CC 4071	CPLG
CC 4573	CPLG
anisophylla	EShb WCot WSpi
atropurpurea misapplied	see *S. attenuata*
atropurpurea Nees	see *S. wallichii*
§ ***attenuata***	Widely available
- 'Aquarella' **new**	NDov
- 'Blue Carpet' **new**	NDov
- dwarf	WCom
- subsp. ***nepalensis***	CHll CLAP MWhi WPrP
dyeriana ♀H1	CAbP EAmu EBak ECtt ELan EShb LSou WCot WHil
flexicaulis	CDes CPou EBee WPGP WPrP
- B&SWJ 354	WCru
gossypinus	EShb
aff. ***inflata*** B&SWJ 7754	WCru

nutans	CDes CLAP CPom CPou EBee LSou NSti WPrP
aff. ***pentstemonoides*** HWJK 2019	WCru
rankanensis	CDes CFir CLAP EBee EPPr NDov SDys SMHy WHil WPrP
- B&SWJ 1771	WCru
violacea	CPrp LHop WPer
§ ***wallichii***	CDes CLAP CMac CSam EBee EWes EWld LLWP LSou NSti SUsu WCot WCru WFar WMoo WOld WPrP WSHC WWEG
'Wollerton'	WWlt

Stromanthe (*Marantaceae*)

sanguinea 'Triostar'PBR (v)	XBlo

Strongylodon (*Papilionaceae*)

macrobotrys	SOWG

Strophanthus (*Apocynaceae*)

speciosus	CCCN CHll EShb

Strumaria (*Amaryllidaceae*)

aestivalis	ECho
chaplinii	ECho
karooica 'Komsberg'	ECho
leipoldtii 'Vanrhynsdorp' **new**	ECho
massoniella 'Reitfontein'	ECho
salteri 'Nardouwsberg' **new**	ECho
truncata	ECho
- 'Garies' **new**	ECho

Struthiopteris (*Blechnaceae*)

niponica	see *Blechnum niponicum*

Stuartia see *Stewartia*

Stylidium (*Stylidiaceae*)

graminifolium	GGar SPlb
- 'Little Sapphire'	NOak SRot
- 'Tiny Trina'	LRHS NCGa NOak

Stylophorum (*Papaveraceae*)

diphyllum	CPBP CPou EBee EWld GEdr IMou MRav NMen WCru WFar WPnP
lasiocarpum	CPLG CPom CSpe CSpr EWes EWld LRHS MWhi NBid SGar WCru WPrP

Styphelia (*Epacridaceae*)

colensoi	see *Leucopogon colensoi*

Styphnolobium (*Leguminosae*)

§ ***japonicum*** ♀H4	CAbP CDul CLnd CWib EBee EPfP LMaj MGos MMuc SEND SPer SPlb WDin
- 'Dot'	LRHS
- 'Pendulum'	CDul EBee ELan LMaj LRHS MBlu MBri MGos

Styrax (*Styracaceae*)

americanus	CBcs GAuc IVic NLar
faberi	CBcs
formosanus	CGHE EBee
- var. ***formosanus***	CPLG EPfP WPGP
- - B&SWJ 3803	WCru
- var. ***hayatiana*** B&SWJ 6823	WCru
hemsleyanus ♀H4	CAbP CBcs CPLG CTho EBee EPfP GBin GKir IArd IDee LRHS MBlu MMuc NLar SEND SPer SSpi WFar
hookeri	CPLG
japonicus ♀H4	CBcs CDoC CDul CEnd CMCN CPLG CTho CTri CWib EBee ELan EPfP GGal GKir LRHS MAsh MBlu MGos MMuc MRav NPal SPer SPoG SReu SSpi SSta WDin WFar WPGP WPat
- B&SWJ 4405	WCru
§ - Benibana Group ♀H4	SSta
- - 'Pink Chimes'	CBcs CMCN CMac CPLG CPMA ELan EPfP IVic MBlu NLar SCoo SSpi SSta
- 'Carillon'	CPMA MBlu
I - 'Compactus'	SSpi
- 'Fargesii'	CBcs CDoC CDul CPLG CPMA CTho EPfP GBin LRHS SCoo SKHP SSpi
- 'Pendulus'	NLar
- 'Purple Dress'	NLar
- 'Roseus'	see *S. japonicus* Benibana Group
- 'Sohuksan'	MBlu MBri NLar SSpi
obassia ♀H4	CBcs CDul CMCN CPne CTho EPfP GBin GKir IDee LRHS MBlu MBri NLar SSpi
- B&SWJ 6023	WCru
odoratissimus	CPLG
officinalis	CBcs
suberifolius WWJ 11868 **new**	WCru
* ***taiwanensis*** **new**	SKHP
wilsonii **new**	CPLG
wuyuanensis	CBcs

Succisa (*Dipsacaceae*)

§ ***pratensis***	CArn EBWF EBee LEdu LLWG MHer MNHC MWea NLan NLar NMen NSco NWCA SBch SGSe SMHy SPhx SUsu WHer WHoo WSFF WTin
- ***alba***	EWes MDKP
- 'Cassop' **new**	GEdr
- 'Derby Purple'	CSpe
- dwarf	NRya WAbe
- 'Peddar's Pink'	EBee EWes SPhx WAlt

Succisella (*Dipsacaceae*)

inflexa	MSpe SPhx
- 'Frosted Pearls'	CSpr EBee EDAr EDif LLWP MBNS MWat WHil

sunberry see *Rubus* 'Sunberry'

Sutera (*Scrophulariaceae*)

(Abunda Series) Abunda Blue Improved = 'Balabimblu'	LAst
- Abunda Colossal Sky Blue = 'Balabolav' **new**	NPri
- Abunda Colossal White = 'Balabowite'	NPri
Cabana Trailing White = 'Sutcatrwhi'PBR (Cabana Series)	WGor
(Cinderella Series) 'Cinderella Lavender' **new**	LAst
- 'Cinderella Pink' **new**	LAst
- 'Cinderella Strawberry'	NPri
(Copia Series) Copia Dark Pink = 'Dancop19'PBR	NPri
- Copia Double White (d)	LSou
- Copia Golden Leaves	LAst NPri

- Copia Great Dark Pink (7) SVil
- Copia Great Purple LSou
- Copia Gulliver Blue Sensation **new** SVil
- Copia Gulliver Lavender = 'Dangul16'PBR LSou NPri
- Copia Gulliver Lilac LSou
- Copia Gulliver White = 'Dangul14'PBR LAst LSou

cordata 'Blizzard' LSou
- Lavender Showers = 'Sunlav' NPri
- 'Olympic Gold' (v) ECtt SCoo SPoG
- 'Pink Domino' ECtt SPet

§ - 'Snowflake' ECtt NPer SCoo SPet SPoG

microphylla CPBP

neglecta SPlb WPGP

Suteranova Big Pink = 'Danova912'PBR (Suteranova Series) NPri

Sutherlandia (*Papilionaceae*)

frutescens CArn CBod CSpe SPlb WJek
- 'Prostrata' MBri

montana WCot

Swainsona (*Papilionaceae*)

galegifolia CHll
- 'Albiflora' SOWG WWlt

sweet cicely see *Myrrhis odorata*

Syagrus (*Arecaceae*)

botryophora XBlo

§ ***romanzoffiana*** CBrP EAmu LPal XBlo

weddeliana see *Lytocaryum weddellianum*

× *Sycoparrotia* (*Hamamelidaceae*)

semidecidua CPMA IArd MBlu NLar WPGP
- 'Purple Haze' MBri NLar

Sycopsis (*Hamamelidaceae*)

sinensis CAbP CMCN CPLG CWib EBee EMil EPfP LHop LRHS MMuc NLar SDnm SKHP SPoG SSpi WDin WFar WPGP WSHC

Symphoricarpos (*Caprifoliaceae*)

albus CDul ECrN EMac GKir MSwo NWea SPoG WDin
- 'Constance Spry' SRms

§ - var. ***laevigatus*** EPfP LBuc

§ - 'Taff's White' (v) WMoo
- 'Variegatus' see *S. albus* 'Taff's White'

× ***chenaultii*** 'Hancock' CBar CMac EBee ECrN ELan EMac EPfP MGos MMuc MRav MSwo SLim SPer WDin

× ***doorenbosii*** 'Magic Berry' IFFs MRav
- 'Mother of Pearl' EBee ELan EMac EPfP GKir IFFs MGos MMuc MRav NWea SPer
- 'White Hedge' CAlb CSBt EBee ELan IFFs LBuc MMuc SPer SPlb

guatemalensis B&SWJ 1016 WCru

orbiculatus SLon
- 'Albovariegatus' see *S. orbiculatus* 'Taff's Silver Edge'
- 'Argenteovariegatus' see *S. orbiculatus* 'Taff's Silver Edge'
- 'Bowles's Golden Variegated' see *S. orbiculatus* 'Foliis Variegatis'

§ - 'Foliis Variegatis' (v) CMac CTri EBee EHoe ELan EPfP MGos MRav SPer WDin WEas WSHC

§ - 'Taff's Silver Edge' (v) EHoe
- 'Variegatus' see *S. orbiculatus* 'Foliis Variegatis'

rivularis see *S. albus* var. *laevigatus*

Symphyandra see *Campanula*

asiatica see *Hanabusaya asiatica*

Symphyotrichum see *Aster*

Symphytum (*Boraginaceae*)

asperum ECha ELan MRav NLar WMoo

* ***azureum*** EBee ELan LTen NLar WCAu WFar WMnd

'Belsay Gold' NBir SDix

caucasicum ♀H4 CElw CMHG EBee ECha GBar GPoy IFro LEdu LRHS SBch SEND SIde SSvw WHer WHil WMoo WOut
- 'Norwich Sky' CKno CPLG EWld

cordatum EBee EPPr LEdu SKHP

'Denford Variegated' (v) NBid

§ 'Goldsmith' (v) Widely available

grandiflorum CArn CMac CTri CWan EBee GPoy LEdu STes WGwG

* - 'Sky-blue-pink' IFro

'Grandiflorum' variegated (v) LRHS

'Hidcote Blue' Widely available

§ 'Hidcote Pink' CBct CPom CPrp EBee ECha ECtt EPla LBMP LRHS MMuc NBir NEgg NWsh SBch SBfd SEND SLPl SPer SPoG WCAu WFar WMnd WMoo WPnP WWEG

'Hidcote Variegated' (v) CMac

ibericum CArn CSam CWit EBee ECha EHrv EPfP EPla GBar GMaP GPoy LRHS MLHP MMuc NSti SEND SGar SRms WJek WMoo WOut
- 'All Gold' CArn EBrs ECha ECtt MHer MNrw WMoo
- 'Blaueglocken' CSev EBee ECha LPla WMoo WPrP
- dwarf CPrp IFro WMoo
- 'Gold in Spring' NLar WFar
- 'Jubilee' see *S.* 'Goldsmith'
- 'Lilacinum' LRHS WHer
- 'Variegatum' see *S.* 'Goldsmith'
- 'Wisley Blue' CBcs CPrp EBee EPfP LLWG NLar WFar WMnd WMoo WWEG

'Lambrook Sunrise' EAEE EBee LEdu LRHS MBri NBro WCot WFar WMoo WWEG

'Langthorns Pink' CPom ELan GCal

'Mereworth' see *S.* × *uplandicum* 'Mereworth'

officinale CArn COld CSev CWan EBee GBar GJos GPoy MHer MNHC MNrw NGHP NPer NPri NSco SBfd SIde SPoG SRms WHer WHfH WJek

* - blue SEND
- 'Bohemicum' ECho
- var. ***ochroleucum*** WHer

orientale CPom GCal MLLN

peregrinum see *S.* × *uplandicum*

'Roseum' see *S.* 'Hidcote Pink'

'Rubrum' CDes CEnt EBee EHrv ELan EPPr EPfP EWes GBin GCra LAst LBMP

	LEdu LRHS MAvo MHer NCGa SPer WCAu WFar WGwG WPGP
tuberosum	CArn CBre CElw CEnt COld CPom CSam EPPr EWTr GPoy LEdu MHer MMuc NHol WBor WCot WFar WHer
§ × ***uplandicum***	CSev CTri EBee ELan GBar GCra GPoy MHer SIde SVic WJek
- 'Axminster Gold' (v)	CDes CEnt CMea EWes LHop SUsu WPGP
- 'Bocking 14'	CAgr CEnt CHby CPbn CPrp EOHP GAbr GBar SIde WSFF
- 'Droitwich' (v)	WCot
§ - 'Mereworth' (v)	CBct LRHS MMuc SEND
- 'Moorland Heather'	MAvo WMoo
- purple-flowered	MMuc SEND
- 'Variegatum' (v) ♀H4	CBot CMac EBee ECtt ELan EPfP EWes MBri NBir NGdn SDix WCot WFar WMoo WSpi

Symplocarpus (*Araceae*)

foetidus	ECho
nipponicus new	WCru
renifolius new	WCru

Symplocos (*Symplocaceae*)

paniculata	see *S. sawafutagi*
§ ***sawafutagi***	CBcs EPfP NLar WCFE WPGP WPat

Syneilesis (*Asteraceae*)

aconitifolia	CFwr CLAP EBee GEdr WCot WPGP
- B&SWJ 879	WCru
palmata	CLAP GEdr LEdu WCot
- B&SWJ 1003	WCru
subglabrata	LEdu
- B&SWJ 298	WCru
aff. ***tagawae*** B&SWJ 11191	WCru

Syngonium (*Araceae*)

podophyllum ♀H1	XBlo

Synnotia see *Sparaxis*

Synthyris (*Scrophulariaceae*)

laciniata NNS 06-540	NWCA
missurica	CDes CLAP GKev LRHS
- var. ***stellata***	CLAP EBee EHrv LEdu NHol NWsh WFar WHal WPGP WWEG
pinnatifida	NBir
reniformis	CLAP WPGP WWEG

Syringa ✿ (*Oleaceae*)

afghanica misapplied	see *S. protolaciniata*
afghanica C.K. Schneid.	IDee IVic
'Alexander's Pink'	WGob
× ***chinensis*** 'Alba'	see *S.* 'Correlata'
- 'Persian Lilac'	WDin WFar WGob WSpi
- 'Saugeana'	EBee NLar SPer
§ 'Correlata' (graft-chimaera)	EBee IArd
emodi	CBot
- 'Aurea'	IArd MGos NLar
- 'Aureovariegata'	see *S. emodi* 'Elegantissima'
§ - 'Elegantissima' (v)	CBcs CDoC CEnd CMac CWGN EBee EPfP GQui LLHF LRHS MAsh NEgg SKHP SPoG SSpi WDin
- 'Variegata' (v)	LRHS
'Hagny'	WGob
× ***hyacinthiflora*** 'Esther Staley' ♀H4	EPfP MRav WGob
- 'Excel'	WGob
- 'Maiden's Blush'	WGob
Josée = 'Morjos 060f'	CDoC EPfP EQua LBMP MAsh NLar SPoG SWvt WFar WGob WPat
× ***josiflexa***	CPLG
- 'Agnes Smith'	LAst NLar WGob
- 'Anna Amhoff'	GBin NLar
- 'Bellicent' ♀H4	CEnd CLnd CMac EBee ELan EPfP GAbr GKir LAst LRHS MMuc MRav NLar NSti SCoo SKHP SPer SPlb SPoG SRms SSpi SWvt WCFE WDin WGob WPat WSpi
- 'James MacFarlane'	NLar WGob
- 'Lynette'	EPla
- 'Redwine'	NLar SKHP
§ - 'Royalty'	LRHS LTen NLar SKHP WGob
josikaea	CMCN CSBt EBee NLar SCoo SPer WBVN WGob WSpi
'Kim'	GKir MRav
komarowii	NLar
- L 490	GGGa
§ - subsp. ***reflexa***	CDul EPfP EWTr LLHF MGos SLon SSpi WDin WFar WGob
§ × ***laciniata*** Mill.	CBot CPMA EBee EGxp ELan EPfP LRHS MGos MMuc MRav MWea NLar SCoo SPer SPoG SSpi WCFE WGor WPGP WSHC
§ ***meyeri*** 'Palibin' ♀H4	Widely available
microphylla	see *S. pubescens* subsp. *microphylla*
'Minuet'	CBcs MGos NLar SKHP WGob
'Miss Canada'	GKir MBri NLar WGob
oblata	CMCN
palibiniana	see *S. meyeri* 'Palibin'
patula misapplied	see *S. meyeri* 'Palibin'
patula (Palibin) Nakai	see *S. pubescens* subsp. *patula*
pekinensis	see *S. reticulata* subsp. *pekinensis*
× ***persica*** ♀H4	CDul CPLG CPMA CSam CTri EPfP EWTr GKir MGos MRav NBea NLar NPal SLon SPer
- 'Alba' ♀H4	CBot CPMA GQui LTen MRav WFar WPat
- var. ***laciniata***	see *S.* × *laciniata* Mill.
pinnatifolia	CBcs CBot GKir IArd MBri NLar
× ***prestoniae*** 'Coral'	WFar
- 'Desdemona'	LRHS SKHP SSta
- 'Donald Wyman'	WGob
- 'Elinor' ♀H4	CMHG EPfP MRav NSti SKHP SPer
- 'Isabella'	MGos SCoo
- 'Nocturne'	MGos WFar WGob
- 'Royalty'	see *S.* × *josiflexa* 'Royalty'
§ ***protolaciniata***	EShb IArd LBMP MGos NLar SKHP WFar
- 'Kabul'	EPfP GKir LRHS NLar
§ ***pubescens*** subsp. ***microphylla***	GKir
- - 'Superba' ♀H4	Widely available
§ - subsp. ***patula***	CMac ECho EPfP LRHS MMuc MRav NWea SEND WFar
- - 'Miss Kim' ♀H4	Widely available
'Red Pixie'	CMac CWGN ELon GAbr LBuc LRHS MAsh MBri MGos MMHG NLar SBfd SCoo SKHP WGob
'Red Prince'	MAsh NPri
reflexa	see *S. komarowii* subsp. *reflexa*
reticulata	MBlu MBri WDin
- 'Ivory Silk'	CWSG EPfP LLHF NLar SKHP WClo WGob
§ - subsp. ***pekinensis***	CBot CMCN GBin GKev WBVN
- - Beijing Gold = 'Zhang Zhiming' new	IArd

- - China Snow = 'Morton'	SKHP
- - 'Pendula'	IDee
- - 'Yellow Fragrance'	NLar
× ***swegiflexa***	CDul CPLG NLar
sweginzowii	IDee SPer WFar WSpi
- 'Superba'	WMoo
tomentella	NWea SRms
velutina	see *S. pubescens* subsp. *patula*
villosa	SPlb WBVN WDin WGob
vulgaris	EMac LBuc NWea
- 'Albert F. Holden'	WGob
§ - 'Andenken an Ludwig Späth' ♀H4	Widely available
- 'Aurea'	EQua LBuc MRav WFar
- Beauty of Moscow	see *S. vulgaris* 'Krasavitsa Moskvy'
- 'Belle de Nancy' (d)	CCCN CDul CMac CWib EBee ELan ELon GAbr IFFs LAst MAsh MMuc MRav NEgg SEND SWvt WDin WGob
- 'Charles Joly' (d) ♀H4	Widely available
- 'Congo'	EBee GKir LSRN MRav NMoo SPer WGob
- 'Decaisne' **new**	SPer
- 'Edward J. Gardner' (d)	ELon MMuc SEND
- 'Firmament' ♀H4	ELan EPfP MMuc MRav NEgg SEND SPer WGob WSpi
- 'Hope'	see *S. vulgaris* 'Nadezhda'
- 'Katherine Havemeyer' (d) ♀H4	Widely available
§ - 'Krasavitsa Moskvy' (d)	EWes GKir IArd LRHS MBri NLar
- 'Lee Jewett Walker'	WGob
- 'Lois Amee Utley' (d)	LRHS
- 'Madame Florent Stepman'	CMac CWSG NLar WGob
- 'Madame Lemoine' (d) ♀H4	Widely available
- 'Masséna'	EBee MRav SPer
- 'Maud Notcutt'	EWes
- 'Michel Buchner' (d)	CBcs CDul CWSG CWib CWit ELan GKir LAst MGos MRav NLar SBfd SCoo SLim SPer WBVN WBor WGob
- 'Miss Ellen Willmott' (d)	IArd MBri MRav NLar
- 'Mrs Edward Harding' (d) ♀H4	EPfP LAst LBuc MGos MRav NLar NWea SCoo SPer
§ - 'Nadezhda' (d)	LRHS
- 'Olivier de Serres' (d)	MBri NLar
- 'Paul Deschanel' (d)	NLar
- 'Président Fallières' (d)	EBee
- 'Président Grévy' (d)	CBar CDoC CLnd CMac EBee EMil MAsh MMuc SLim SPer
- 'Primrose'	Widely available
- 'Prince Wolkonsky' (d)	EBee EMil EPfP LRHS LSRN LTen WFar
- 'Princesse Sturdza'	EMil
- 'Sensation'	Widely available
- 'Souvenir de Louis Spaeth'	see *S. vulgaris* 'Andenken an Ludwig Späth'
- 'Sweetheart' (d)	GKir
- variegated (v)	EWes
- variegated double (d/v)	WCot
- 'Vestale' ♀H4	EWes MRav
- 'Viviand-Morel' (d)	CMac LLHF MMuc NEgg SKHP WGob
- 'Znamya Lenina'	MBri
wolfii	CArn EBtc WBVN
yunnanensis	CPLG GGGa LLHF WSpi
- 'Prophecy'	WGob
- 'Rosea'	WGob

Syringodea (*Iridaceae*)

longituba 'Perdekraal' **new**	ECho

Syzygium (*Myrtaceae*)

sp.	CMen
australe	ERom EShb IDee SArc
jambos	EShb
paniculatum	CMen CPLG EShb IDee

T

Tabernaemontana (*Apocynaceae*)

coronaria	see *T. divaricata*
§ ***divaricata***	CCCN SOWG

Tacca (*Taccaceae*)

chantrieri	CCCN EAmu ECho EGxp
integrifolia	EAmu ECho

Tacitus see *Graptopetalum*

Tagetes (*Asteraceae*)

lemmonii	IMou SBfd SHDw WJek
'Lemon Gem'	WJek
lucida	CArn EOHP IMou WJek
tenuifolia	CArn

Talbotia (*Velloziaceae*)

§ ***elegans***	EPot WFar

Talinum (*Portulacaceae*)

'Kingwood Gold'	CBow CPla
okanoganense	CCCN GKev
paniculatum	CCCN
'Zoe'	CPBP

tamarillo see *Cyphomandra betacea*

tamarind see *Tamarindus indica*

Tamarindus (*Caesalpiniaceae*)

indica (F)	SPlb

Tamarix (*Tamaricaceae*)

africana	EBee EMil
chinensis	CSBt
gallica	CMen CSBt MGos NWea SAPC SArc WSHC
hampeana	SEND
§ ***parviflora***	CMac EMil IVic LRHS MGos SPoG
pentandra	see *T. ramosissima*
§ ***ramosissima***	CCCN CMac CTri ECrN ELan EPfP MAsh MBrN MWhi SLim SLon SRms SSta WDin WSHC
- 'Pink Cascade'	CBcs CCCN CDul CSBt EBee ELon EMil EPfP GCal GKir IVic LRHS MBlu MBri MGos MMuc MREP MRav NEgg SBfd SEND SPer SPoG SWvt WDin
- 'Rosea'	CBcs MGan
§ - 'Rubra' ♀H4	CChe CDoC CWSG EBee EPfP GKir IVic MGos NLar SLon SPer WDin WSpi
- 'Summer Glow'	see *T. ramosissima* 'Rubra'
tetrandra ♀H4	Widely available
- 'Africance'	ERom
- var. ***purpurea***	see *T. parviflora*

Tamus (*Dioscoreaceae*)

communis	CArn

Tanacetum ✿ (*Asteraceae*)

§ ***argenteum***	ECho MRav SIde
- subsp. ***canum***	ECho EWes LRHS SLon
§ ***balsamita***	CArn COld CPrp EBee ELan ELau GPWP GPoy LEdu MHer MNHC WHfH WJek WTin
§ - subsp. ***balsamita***	GPoy SIde
§ - subsp. ***balsamitoides***	CBod CHby CPrp GBar MHer WJek
- var. ***tanacetoides***	see *T. balsamita* subsp. *balsamita*
- ***tomentosum***	see *T. balsamita* subsp. *balsamitoides*
capitatum	see *Sphaeromeria capitata*
§ ***cinerariifolium***	CArn CPrp CWan EBee GBar GPoy MNHC WJek
§ ***coccineum***	NBPC SPoG WFar
- 'Alfred'	EBee
- 'Aphrodite' (d)	ECtt NEgg
- 'Beauty of Stapleford'	NEgg
- 'Bees' Pink Delight'	NEgg
- 'Brenda'	EPfP MRav
- 'Duro'	LRHS
- 'Eileen May Robinson' ♀H4	EBee EPfP LSRN NBre NGdn
- 'Evenglow'	ECtt EPfP
- 'H.M. Pike'	ECtt
- 'James Kelway' ♀H4	EBee ECtt ELan EPfP GKir MRav NBir
- 'King Size'	SGar WFar
- 'Laurin'	LRHS
- 'Mont Blanc'	EBee
- Robinson's, mixed	SBfd WWEG
- - Robinson's crimson-flowered	LRHS
- - Robinson's giant-flowered	GJos SRms
- - Robinson's pink-flowered	CMdw EBee ELan EPfP GKir GMaP NBre SBfd SGSe WRHF WWEG
- - Robinson's red-flowered	CSBt EBee EPfP GKir GMaP MBNS MLHP NBPC NPri NVic SBfd SGSe SMrs SPlb SPur SWvt WClo WWEG
- - Robinson's rose-flowered	MBNS SBfd
- 'Snow Cloud'	ECtt ELan NBre WWEG
- 'Vanessa'	MNrw
§ ***corymbosum***	GCal
- 'Festtafel'	EBee LPla
densum	ECho EDAr EPot WCFE
- subsp. ***amani***	EBee ECha ECho ECre GMaP LRHS MHer MWat NWCA
§ ***haradjanii***	ECho ECtt ELan SBch WHer
huronense	EBee
macrophyllum misapplied	see *Achillea grandifolia* Friv.
§ ***macrophyllum*** Sch.Bip. (Waldst. & Kit.)	ECtt EPPr LPla SPhx
- 'Cream Klenza' **new**	WCot
niveum	ECha WCot
- 'Jackpot'	CMea CWib EBee EPfP EWes SHar SSvw
§ ***parthenium***	CArn CHby CPbn CWan EBWF ELau GPoy MHer MNHC NPer SBfd SIde SRms SVic WHer WJek
- 'Aureum'	CHid CPbn CPrp CRow CWan ECha ELan ELau EWes GBar GPoy MBri MHer MLHP MNHC MSCN NGHP SBfd SPer SPlb SRms WCot WEas WFar WHer WJek WMoo
- 'Cartwheels' **new**	SUsu
- double white-flowered (d)	CSWP GBar MMuc NPer SRms
- 'Golden Ball'	EPfP
- 'Plenum' (d)	EHrv SBch
§ - 'Rowallane' (d)	EBee ELan GMac MMuc SEND WCot
- 'Sissinghurst White'	see *T. parthenium* 'Rowallane'
- 'Snowball' (d)	EPfP
- 'White Bobbles'	LRHS
- 'White Bonnet' (d)	WEas
poteriifolium	EBee EBrs LRHS
§ ***ptarmiciflorum*** ♀H3-4	WCot
- 'Silver Feather'	MNHC WJek
tatsiense	EBee
* ***tommansii***	LRHS
vulgare	CArn CHby CSev ECtt ELau GPoy MHer MNHC NSco SBfd SIde SVic WJek WMoo WSFF
- 'All Gold'	SMad
- var. ***crispum***	CHby CPrp CWan EBee ELau GBar MHer MRav SBfd SIde SMad WFar WJek
- 'Golden Fleece'	CBre CWGN ECtt EWes LRHS LSou MAvo NSti SPer SUsu WCot WFut
- 'Isla Gold' (v)	CBow CHVG EBee ECtt EWes GMaP LHop MHer MMuc MRav NBre SEND SMrm WCAu WCot WFar WJek WMoo
- 'Silver Lace' (v)	CBow CBre EBee GBar MLLN NBid NGHP WFar WHer WJek WMoo

Tanakaea (*Saxifragaceae*)

radicans	WCru

tangelo see *Citrus* × *tangelo*

tangerine see *Citrus reticulata*

tangor see *Citrus* × *nobilis* Tangor Group

Taraxacum (*Asteraceae*)

albidum	GLin
- DJH 452	CHid
coreanum	WPrP
faeroense	EPPr WCot
officinale agg.	CArn
- 'Tapeley' (v)	CNat
rubrifolium	CSpe EPPr

Tarchonanthus (*Asteraceae*)

camphoratus	CTrC

tarragon see *Artemisia dracunculus*

Tasmannia see *Drimys*

Tayberry see *Rubus* Tayberry Group

Taxodium (*Cupressaceae*)

ascendens 'Nutans'	see *T. distichum* var. *imbricarium* 'Nutans'
distichum ♀H4	Widely available
- 'Cascade Falls'PBR	IArd LRHS MBlu MBri MGos NLar NPri SLim
- 'Cave Hill'	SLim
- 'Falling Waters'	LRHS SKHP
- 'Hursley Park'	NLar SLim
- var. ***imbricarium***	CGHE CMCN EPfP LRHS
§ - - 'Nutans' ♀H4	CAlb CBcs CEnd CTho EPfP GKir IArd LRHS MAsh MBlu NLar SCoo SLim SMad

- 'Little Leaf'	NLar SLim
- 'Minaret'	IArd MBlu
* - 'Pendulum' **new**	IArd
- 'Peve Minaret'	CDoC CMen EWTr LRHS MAsh MBri MGos NLar SKHP SLim SMad SPoG
- 'Peve Yellow'	MBlu NLar
- 'Schloss Herten'	LRHS SLim
- 'Secrest'	CBcs MAsh MBlu SLim
- Shawnee Brave = 'Mickelson'	MBlu
mucronatum	CDoC CPLG
- F&M 198	WPGP

Taxus ✿ (*Taxaceae*)

baccata ♀H4	Widely available
- 'Adpressa' (f)	ECho
- 'Adpressa Aurea' (v)	CKen ECho GKir SCoo
- 'Adpressa Variegata' (m/v) ♀H4	CDoC ECho
- 'Aldenham Gold'	CKen
- 'Amersfoort'	CDoC LRHS NHol NLar SCoo SLim
- 'Argentea Minor'	see *T. baccata* 'Dwarf White'
- Aurea Group	CDul NHol SRms STre
I - 'Aurea Pendula'	ECho GKir
I - 'Aureomarginata' (v)	CBcs CBow ECho MAsh NEgg SWvt
- 'Autumn Shades'	CBcs NLar
- 'Bridget's Gold'	CKen
- 'Compacta'	EPla
- 'Corleys Coppertip'	CKen ECho EPot GKir MAsh MRav NHol NLar SCoo SLim WEve WFar
- 'Cristata'	CKen NLar
- 'David'	IArd MBri NLar SCoo WEve
- 'Dovastoniana' (f) ♀H4	CMac NLar SCoo WMou
- 'Dovastonii Aurea' (m/v) ♀H4	CBcs EPfP EPla GKir MBlu MBri MGos NEgg NLar NPCo NWea SCoo SLim WCFE WDin WFar
§ - 'Dwarf White' (v)	SCoo WGor
- 'Elegantissima' (f/v)	CTho ECho ECrN EHul EPfP LRHS NPCo NWea SCoo WFar
- 'Erecta' (f)	EHul
§ - 'Fastigiata' (f) ♀H4	Widely available
- Fastigiata Aurea Group	CLnd CWib ECho EPfP GKev GKir IArd IFFs LBuc LMaj MAsh MGos NHol NPri SRms STre WBrE WFar WHar
- 'Fastigiata Aureomarginata' (m/v) ♀H4	CDoC CDul CMac CSBt CTri ECho EHul EPfP GKir LBee LRHS MBri MGos NWea SAga SBfd SCoo SLim SLon SPer SPoG SWvt WCFE WDin WEve
- 'Fastigiata Robusta' (f)	CDoC CSBt ECho EPfP EPla GKir MBri NHol NLar NPCo SCoo SLim WEve WFar
- 'Goud Elsje'	CKen MBri NLar
- 'Grayswood Hill'	NLar
- 'Green Column'	CKen
- 'Green Diamond'	CKen NLar
- 'Green Rocket'	CDul EMil NLar
- 'Hibernica'	see *T. baccata* 'Fastigiata'
- 'Icicle'	CBcs EPla LRHS MAsh MGos NHol NLar SLim
- 'Itsy Bitsy'	CKen
- 'Ivory Tower'	CBcs CDoC CKen ECho ELan LBee LRHS MAsh MGos NEgg NHol NLar NPCo SLim SPoG WEve WFar WGor
- 'Klitzeklein'	CKen
- 'Litfass' **new**	NLar
- 'Lutea' (f)	SLim
- 'Nutans'	CDoC CKen ECho GKir SCoo
- 'Pendula'	MRav
- 'Prostrata'	CMac WFar
- 'Pygmaea'	CKen
- 'Repandens' (f) ♀H4	EHul IArd NWea WCFE WDin WFar
I - 'Repens Aurea' (v) ♀H4	CDoC CKen CMac ECho EHul EPfP GKir MGos NEgg SCoo WEve WFar
- 'Rushmore'	MBri
- 'Semperaurea' (m) ♀H4	CBcs CDoC CMac ECho EHul EPla GKir LBuc LTen MAsh MBri MGos NHol NWea SCoo SLim SPoG WCFE WDin WFar
- 'Silver Spire' (v)	CKen MDKP
- 'Standishii' (f) ♀H4	Widely available
- 'Stove Pipe'	CKen
- 'Summergold' (v)	ECho EHul ELan EPfP EPla LRHS MBri MGos MRav NBir NEgg NHol NLar SCoo SLim WDin WEve WFar
- 'Washingtonii' (v)	IArd
- 'White Icicle'	MGos WGor
brevifolia	NHol NLar
chinensis	EGFP
cuspidata	CMen ECho GKir
- 'Aurescens' (v)	CKen EPla SRms
- 'Minuet'	CKen
- var. ***nana***	IFFs
- 'Robusta'	EHul
- 'Silver Queen' **new**	SLim
- 'Straight Hedge'	EMil LRHS SLim
× ***media*** 'Brownii'	LBuc
- 'Hicksii' (f) ♀H4	CDul GKir LBuc LMaj LRHS MGos NLar NWea SCoo SLim WFar
- 'Hillii'	LBMP LTen SCoo
- 'Lodi'	LBee LRHS
- 'Nixe'	SLim

Tecoma (*Bignoniaceae*)

× ***alata***	SOWG
capensis ♀H1	EBee MREP SOWG
- 'Aurea'	EShb SOWG
- 'Coccinea'	EShb
- 'Lutea'	EShb
cochabambensis RCB/Arg L-8	WCot
'Orange Glow'	SOWG
ricasoliana	see *Podranea ricasoliana*
stans	SOWG

Tecomanthe (*Bignoniaceae*)

speciosa	CHEx ECou SOWG

Tecomaria see *Tecoma*

Tecophilaea (*Tecophilaeaceae*)

cyanocrocus ♀H2	CAvo CStu ECho EPot GCrs LAma LLHF LRHS NMin SUsu WCot
- 'Leichtlinii' ♀H2	ECho EPot GCrs LAma LLHF LRHS MAsh NMin SCnR
- 'Purpurea'	see *T. cyanocrocus* 'Violacea'
- Storm Cloud Group	ECho LLHF
§ - 'Violacea'	CAvo ECho EPot LLHF LRHS NMin
violiflora	ECho LAma

Tectaria (*Dryopteridaceae*)

gemmifera	WRic

Telanthophora (*Asteraceae*)

§ ***grandifolia***	CHEx

Telekia (*Asteraceae*)

§ ***speciosa***	CFir COIW CSam CSpe EBee EBrs ELan EPPr EPfP GAbr GKir

	LRHS MCCP MLLN MMuc NBro NChi NLar SDix SEND SLPl SPlb WCFE WFar WHer WHoo WMoo WWEG

Telesonix see *Boykinia*

Teline see *Genista*

Tellima (*Saxifragaceae*)

grandiflora	Widely available
- 'Bob's Choice'	WCot
- 'Delphine' (v)	CBow EBee EPPr EWld WCot WOut
- 'Forest Frost'	CBct CBow CMac EBee EPPr GCai LAst LBMP NBre NDov NGdn NHol NLar WClo WMoo WOut
- Odorata Group	CBre ECha MRav NSti WCot WMoo
- - 'Howells'	WOut
- 'Purpurea'	see *T. grandiflora* Rubra Group
- 'Purpurteppich'	EBee EBrs ECha EHrv EPPr LAst LRHS MRav NGdn NVic WMnd WMoo WWEG
§ - Rubra Group	Widely available
- 'Silver Select'	EPPr

Telopea (*Proteaceae*)

'Dawn Fire'	CTrC
oreades	GGal SPlb
speciosissima	CCCN CTrC SOWG SPlb
- 'Red Embers'	CTrC
truncata	CCCN GGal SPlb WCru

Templetonia (*Papilionaceae*)

retusa	ECou

Temu see *Blepharocalyx*

Tetracentron (*Tetracentraceae*)

sinense	CBcs EPfP IArd IFFs MBri NLar WPGP

Tetradenia (*Lamiaceae*)

riparia	EOHP

Tetradium (*Rutaceae*)

§ ***daniellii***	CBcs CCVT CMCN EBee EPfP IArd IDee IFFs LRHS SSpi WPGP
* - ***henryi***	NLar
§ - Hupehense Group	CMCN CTho EBee GBin GKir MBri MSnd NLar WDin
glabrifolium B&SWJ 6882	WCru
- CWJ 12364	WCru
ruticarpum B&SWJ 3541	WCru
* ***velutinum***	NLar

Tetragonia (*Tetragoniaceae*)

tetragonoides	CArn

Tetragonolobus see *Lotus*

Tetraneuris (*Asteraceae*)

scaposa	LRHS

Tetrapanax (*Araliaceae*)

§ ***papyrifer*** ♀H2-3	CBcs CBrP CDTJ CHEx CHGN CTsd CWit ESwi MBri NLar SAPC SArc SBig SBst SPad XBlo
- B&SWJ 7135	WCru
- 'Di-Sue-Shan' **new**	WCru
- 'Empress'	WCru
- 'Rex'	CDTJ CGHE CHEx CHid CPLG EAmu EGFP ESwi ETod EUJe SKHP SMad WCot WCru WPGP
- 'Steroidal Giant'	CDTJ SBig SKHP

Tetrapathaea see *Passiflora*

Tetrastigma (*Vitaceae*)

obtectum	CCCN CTsd CWit EBee ECre ELon EShb EWes
voinierianum ♀H1	EShb SAPC WCot

Tetratheca (*Tremandraceae*)

'Bicentennial Belle' **new**	LRHS
ciliata var. ***alba***	SOWG
thymifolia pink-flowered	SOWG

Teucridium (*Verbenaceae*)

parvifolium	ECou

Teucrium (*Lamiaceae*)

* ***ackermannii***	CMea ECho LBee NMen NWCA WAbe WCom WEas WHoo WPat WTin
arduinoi	MMuc SEND
aroanium	ECho EPot GEdr MWat NMen NWCA
bicolor	EBee
botrys	MHer
canadense	WWEG
chamaedrys misapplied	see *T.* × *lucidrys*
chamaedrys L.	CBar CPom CPrp CWan CWib ECho ELon GBar GMaP GPoy LEdu LRHS LSRN MNHC MSwo NGHP NWCA SBfd SEND SLim SPlb SRms STre WBrk WHfH WJek WTin WWEG
- 'Nanum'	ECho NChi WPat
- 'Rose Carpet'	WCom
- 'Variegatum' (v)	GBar WCom
§ ***creticum***	ECho
divaricatum NS 614	NWCA
flavum	CArn EBee EDAr EPPr NBre SGar WJek
fruticans	Widely available
- 'Azureum' ♀H3	CAlb CBcs CBot CMMP COIW CWSG EBee ELan EPfP LAst LRHS LSRN MMuc MRav SBfd SEND SMad SPer SPoG WCot WEas
- 'Compactum'	CChe CDoC EBee ELan ELon LAst LRHS MCCP MGos SLon SPer SPoG WCFE WPGP
- 'Drysdale'	CDoC CSBt EBee LRHS
hircanicum	Widely available
- 'Paradise Delight'	EBee ECtt EKen MAvo NBPC NLar NPnk WBor
- 'Purple Tails'	CChe COIW CPrp CSpe CWib GQue LSou MCot MNHC NBPC NBir NCob SMad SPoG SWal WWEG
§ × ***lucidrys***	CArn CChe CMea CSev CWan EBee ECha ECho ELan EPfP LAst LRHS MGos MHer MMuc MNHC MRav NGHP SGar SIde SPer SPoG WCFE WEas WHoo WJek
lucidum	GCal
marum	CArn CMea CTri NGHP NMen WJek
massiliense misapplied	see *T.* × *lucidrys*
massiliense L.	EBee WSHC
montanum	GBar WJek
musimonum	EPot
nivale	EBee

polium	CPLG ECho MWat NLAp WCom WJek WPat WThu
pyrenaicum	CMea CPBP CPom EBee ECho EPot EWes GEdr NWCA WPat
rosmarinifolium	see *T. creticum*
scordium	CNat
scorodonia	CArn COld CRWN EBWF GBar GPoy MCot MHer MNHC NLar NMir WHer WJek
- 'Binsted Gold'	EBee EPPr LSou MMoz WAlt
- 'Crispum'	CWan GBar GKir LBMP MHer MMuc MNHC NBro NCob NLar SBch SEND SPer WBrE WClo WGrn WGwG WJek WKif WMnd WMoo WPer
- 'Crispum Marginatum' (v)	CBot COlW EBee ECGP ECha EHoe EHrv EPPr EPfP GBar ILis MNrw MRav NHol NSti SBfd WEas WFar WTin WWEG
- 'Spring Morn'	EBee
- 'Winterdown' (v)	CBow EBee MSCN SBch
subspinosum	ECho GEdr LBee LLHF LRHS MWat NLAp NMen WCom WHoo WPat
§ ***viscidum*** 'Lemon and Lime' (v)	CBow EBee ECtt LSou SDnm
webbianum	ECho
'Winterdown'	LEdu

Thalia (*Marantaceae*)

dealbata	CBen CHEx CMdw CTrC EAmu EUJe LLWG LPBA MSKA MWts NLar SBig SDix SLon WMAq

Thalictrum (*Ranunculaceae*)

CC 4576	CPLG
SDR 1679	GKev
SDR 5944	GKev
from Afghanistan	see *T. isopyroides*
actaeifolium	CLAP CWib GMac MDKP
- B&SWJ 4664	WCru
- B&SWJ 6310	WCru
- var. ***brevistylum***	LSou
- - B&SWJ 8819	WCru
- - 'Twinkling Star'	EBee NCob
- 'Perfume Star'	WCot
adiantifolium	see *T. minus* 'Adiantifolium'
alpinum	EBWF EDAr EPPr SBch
angustifolium	see *T. lucidum*
'Anne' PBR	IPot NDov
aquilegiifolium	Widely available
- var. ***album***	CAby CBot CMea EBee ECha ELan EPfP GCra LAst LBMP LHop MMuc NBid SEND SKHP SPhx SWvt WMnd WPer WSpi WWEG
- 'Gold Lace'	MLLN
* - 'Hybridum'	WFar WMoo WPer
- 'Purpureum'	CPom CSev LBMP LRHS NLar WHoo
* - var. ***sibiricum*** B&SWJ 11007	WCru
- 'Small Thundercloud'	GCal
- 'Thundercloud' ♀H4	Widely available
baicalense	CPom
'Black Stockings'	CKno EBee EShb GBin LBMP LRHS LSou NCGa NPnk SPoG
chelidonii	EBee GMaP LRHS
- HWJK 2216	WCru
clavatum	CLAP WPGP
contortum	SDys
coreanum	see *T. ichangense*
cultratum	CDes WPGP
- HWJCM 367	NLar WCru
dasycarpum	EBee GMac MDKP MLLN NBre NLar WFar WPnP
§ ***delavayi*** ♀H4	Widely available
- BWJ 7903	WCru
- DJHC 473	WCru
- var. ***acuminatum*** BWJ 7535	WCru
- - BWJ 7971	WCru
- 'Album'	Widely available
- 'Ankum'	EBee
- var. ***decorum***	CDes CElw CLAP CPom CWCL ELon EPPr GEdr GMac IMou LPio MCot MLLN NCGa NCob NPnk WCot WCru WPGP WSHC
- - BWJ 7770	WCru
- aff. var. ***decorum*** **new**	GQue
- 'Gold Laced' **new**	NLar
- 'Hewitt's Double' (d) ♀H4	Widely available
- var. ***mucronatum***	WCru
- - DJHC 473	WCru
- purple-stemmed BWJ 7748	WCru
diffusiflorum	CLAP GMac WCru WSHC
dioicum	WPnP
dipterocarpum misapplied	see *T. delavayi*
dipterocarpum Franch.	CMac EBee GKir WMnd
- ACE 4.878.280	CMil
elegans HWJK 2271	WCru
'Elin'	Widely available
fendleri	GBin
- NNS 06-547	WCot
- var. ***polycarpum***	WOut
filamentosum	EBee EPPr GMac IMou
- B&SWJ 777	WCru
- B&SWJ 4145	WCru
- var. ***yakusimense*** B&SWJ 6094	WCru
finetii	CLAP
aff. ***finetii***	CLAP
flavum	CMac CWan EBWF ECtt LRHS NBro SMrm SPhx SWat WBrE WShi WWEG
- 'Chollerton'	see *T. isopyroides*
§ - subsp. ***glaucum*** ♀H4	Widely available
- - dwarf	CDes WPGP
- - 'True Blue'	MNFA NDov
- 'Illuminator'	CDes CTri EBee ELon EPPr EPfP GKir LPio LRHS MArl MHer MRav SBfd SMrm SPoG WCom WCot WFar WPnP WPrP
flexuosum	see *T. minus* subsp. *minus*
foetidum	NBre
- BWJ 7558	WCru
foliolosum HWJK 2181	WCru
grandiflorum	WCot
honanense	EBee SKHP
- BWJ 7962	WCru
§ ***ichangense***	WCot
- B&SWJ 8203	WCru
* - var. ***minus***	WCru
- - 'Chinese Chintz'	WCru
- 'Purple Marble'	WCon WCot
'Illusion' **new**	EBee
§ ***isopyroides***	CFir CPom EBee EBrs EWTr GBin GCal LPio LRHS MCot MLLN MNFA MRav NChi NGdn NLar NMen NPnk WCot WSpi WTin WWEG

	- from Afghanistan new	LRHS
	javanicum	LEdu
	- B&SWJ 9506	WCru
	- var. ***puberulum*** B&SWJ 6770	WCru
	johnstonii B&SWJ 9127	WCru
	kiusianum	Widely available
	- Kew form	WSHC
	koreanum	see *T. ichangense*
§	***lucidum***	CElw CSpe EBee ECtt ELan EShb GBin GCal LOck LPio LRHS MAvo MLLN MMuc MTis NBPC NBre NLar NSti SGar SHar SKHP SPhx WCot WFar
	minus	CArn EBWF EBee ECGP ELan GKir LPio LRHS MLLN MMuc NBre SEND
§	- 'Adiantifolium'	CMac EBee GBin MLLN MRav NBre NCob NGdn NLar SHar SRms WFar WPer WWEG
	- var. ***hypoleucum*** B&SWJ 8634	WCru
	- subsp. ***kemense***	EBee
§	- subsp. ***minus***	NBre
§	- subsp. ***olympicum***	WPer
	- subsp. ***saxatile***	see *T. minus* subsp. *olympicum*
	- var. ***sipellatum*** B&SWJ 5051	WCru
	morisonii	NBid
	omeiense	WPGP
	- BWJ 8049	WCru
	orientale	EWes
	osmundifolium	WCru
	petaloideum	ECha EWll GCal MDKP NLar WCot
	platycarpum B&SWJ 2261	WCru
	polygamum	see *T. pubescens*
	przewalskii	WCru
§	***pubescens***	ECha GAuc GMaP LRHS NBre NCGa NDov SHar SUsu WPrP
	punctatum	CLAP LPio
	- B&SWJ 1272	WCru
	ramosum BWJ 8126	WCru
	reniforme	CFir GMac WCot
	- B&SWJ 2610	WCru
	- GWJ 9311	WCru
	- HWJK 2152	WCru
	reticulatum	IMou WCru
	- BWJ 7407	WCru
	rochebrunianum	Widely available
	rubescens	EBee
	sachalinense	EBee MCCP SWal WOut WPGP
	- RBS 0279	EKen
	shensiense	GEdr
	simplex var. ***brevipes*** B&SWJ 4794	WCru
	speciosissimum	see *T. flavum* subsp. *glaucum*
*	***sphaerostachyum***	CElw GKir GMac MNrw MWhi SMrm WHal
	'Splendide'	CSpe GMac IPot MLLN MNrw MTis NBPC NDov NLar SUsu
	squarrosum	CDes EBee LRHS WPGP
	tenuisubulatum BWJ 7929	WCru
	tuberosum	CElw CMea GCrs LLHF NDov SHar SUsu WAbe WPGP WPat
	- 'Rosie Hardy'	WCot
	tubiferum	EBee
	uchiyamae	CDes CFwr GBin LRHS WCot WPGP
	yunnanense	WCru

Thamnocalamus (*Poaceae*)

	aristatus	CGHE EPfP EPla WDyG WPGP
	crassinodus	EPla SBig
	- dwarf	EPla
	- 'Gosainkund'	CEnt EPla MWht
	- 'Kew Beauty'	CAbb CDTJ CDoC CEnt CGHE EPfP EPla MBrN MMoz MWht NPal SBig WCot WDyG WJun WPGP
	- 'Lang Tang'	CEnt CGHE EPla MMoz MWht WJun WPGP
	- 'Merlyn'	CDoC CEnt EPfP EPla MMoz MWht WJun WPGP
	falcatus	see *Drepanostachyum falcatum*
	falconeri	see *Himalayacalamus falconeri*
	funghomii	see *Schizostachyum funghomii*
	khasianus	see *Drepanostachyum khasianum*
	maling	see *Yushania maling*
	spathaceus misapplied	see *Fargesia murielae*
§	***spathiflorus***	CEnt EPla WJun
	- subsp. ***nepalensis***	EPla MMoz MMuc MWht SBig WPGP
§	***tessellatus***	ENBC EPla MMoz MMuc MWht SEND WDyG WJun

Thamnochortus (*Restionaceae*)

bachmannii	CTrC
cinereus	CTrC WPGP
insignis	CSpe SPlb WPrP
lucens	CTrC SPlb
rigidus	CCCN CTrC
spiciger	CTrC IDee

Thapsia (*Apiaceae*)

decipiens	see *Melanoselinum decipiens*
villosa	CArn

Thea see *Camellia*

Thelypteris (*Thelypteridaceae*)

dentata	SGSe
erubescens new	WRic
kunthii	ISha WRic
limbosperma	see *Oreopteris limbosperma*
palustris	CKel CRWN EBee LPBA NHol NLar NVic SRms WFib WPnP WRic
phegopteris	see *Phegopteris connectilis*

Themeda (*Poaceae*)

japonica	EPPr SGSe SMad

Thermopsis (*Papilionaceae*)

	caroliniana	see *T. villosa*
	chinensis	EBee EBrs LRHS WHil
	- 'Sophie'	LRHS
	fabacea	see *T. lupinoides*
	lanceolata	CMea CTri EBee EPfP GBin LRHS NBPC NCGa NPri NSti SAga SHar SMrm SPhx WAul WFar WHil WHrl WKif
§	***lupinoides***	ECha EHrv EWld MHer NBre
	mollis	CPLG LRHS NBid
	montana	see *T. rhombifolia* var. *montana*
§	***rhombifolia*** var. ***montana***	CMHG CWCL EAEE EBee EBrs ELan ELon EPfP GAbr GCra GGar GMaP LBMP LHop LRHS MSCN MWat NBir NBre NCGa NLar NSti SGSe SPer SPoG WAbb WBVN WHil WPer WWEG
§	***villosa***	CPom CWCL EBee EBrs MRav NBre NDov NGdn NLar SMHy WCot WHil WHoo WPGP

Therorhodion see *Rhododendron*

Thevetia (*Apocynaceae*)

neriifolia	CCCN

Thladiantha (*Cucurbitaceae*)

dubia	EBee GCra SDix

Thlaspi (*Brassicaceae*)

biebersteinii	see *Pachyphragma macrophyllum*

Thryptomene (*Myrtaceae*)

baeckeacea	CCCN
saxicola	ECou

Thuja ✿ (*Cupressaceae*)

	'Extra Gold'	see *T. plicata* 'Irish Gold'
	'Green Giant'	SLim
§	***koraiensis***	GKir IFFs SCoo
	occidentalis	EMac IFFs NWea
	- 'Amber Glow'	CDoC CKen CSBt ECho EPla LRHS MAsh MGos NHol NLar SCoo SLim SPoG WBor WEve
	- 'Aureospicata'	EHul
	- 'Bateman Broom'	CKen
	- 'Beaufort' (v)	CKen EHul
	- 'Brabant'	CDul IFFs LMaj LRHS NLar SCoo SLim WMou
	- 'Brobecks Tower'	CKen LRHS NLar SLim
	- 'Caespitosa'	CKen ECho NHol SCoo WEve WGor
	- 'Cristata Aurea'	CKen
	- 'Danica' ♀H4	CMac ECho EHul GKir MAsh MMuc NWea SBfd SCoo SLim SRms WCFE WEve WFar
	- 'Degroot's Spire'	CKen LRHS NLar SLim
	- 'Dicksonii'	EHul
	- 'Douglasii Aurea' (v)	CKen
	- 'Ellwangeriana Aurea'	MGos
	- Emerald	see *T. occidentalis* 'Smaragd'
	- 'Ericoides'	CDoC CTri EHul MGos SRms
	- 'Europa Gold'	CDoC CDul EHul MGos NHol NLar SLim
	- 'Filiformis'	CKen
I	- 'Globosa Variegata' (v)	CKen
	- 'Gold Drop'	CKen
	- 'Golden Globe'	CDoC EHul LRHS MGos NHol SCoo SLim WDin
	- 'Golden Minaret'	EHul
	- 'Golden Tuffet'	CDoC EHul LRHS MBri MGos SCoo SLim SPer
	- 'Hetz Midget'	CKen ECho EHul LRHS NHol NLar SCoo SLim SPlb WDin WFar
	- 'Holmstrup' ♀H4	CDoC CDul CMac CSBt CTri CWib EHul GKir MAsh SBfd SCoo SLim SPoG SRms WClo WDin WEve WFar
	- 'Holmstrup's Yellow'	EHul LRHS NHol SLim SPoG
	- 'Hoveyi'	CTri EHul
	- 'Linesville'	CKen
	- 'Little Champion'	EHul LBMP NLar
	- 'Little Gem'	EHul MGos NHol NLar SRms WDin
	- 'Lutea Nana' ♀H4	EHul WCFE
	- 'Malonyana'	NLar
	- 'Malonyana Holub' new	SLim
	- 'Marrisen's Sulphur'	EHul
	- 'Meineke's Zwerg' (v)	CKen NLar
	- 'Miky'	CKen
	- 'Mr Bowling Ball'	CDoC LRHS SCoo SLim SPoG
	- 'Ohlendorffii'	CDoC CKen EHul NHol
I	- 'Pumila Sudworth'	NHol NLar
I	- 'Pygmaea'	CKen
	- 'Pyramidalis Aurea'	MGos NHol WEve
	- 'Pyramidalis Compacta'	EHul IFFs NWea WGor
	- 'Recurva Nana'	EHul NHol
	- 'Rheingold' ♀H4	Widely available
§	- 'Smaragd' ♀H4	CDoC CDul CSBt CWib ECho ECrN EHul EPfP GKir IFFs LAst LBuc LRHS MAsh MGos NLar NWea SBfd SCoo SLim SPer SPoG SWvt WCFE WEve WFar WMou
*	- 'Smaragd Variegated' (v)	CKen
	- 'Smokey'	CKen
	- 'Southport'	CKen WEve
	- 'Spaethii'	EHul
	- 'Spiralis'	EHul NLar WCFE
§	- 'Stolwijk' (v)	EHul MGos SCoo
	- 'Sunkist'	CKen CMac CTri CWib ECho EHul EPla GKir LAst MAsh MGos NEgg NHol SCoo SLim SPoG WFar
	- 'Teddy'	CDoC ECho EHul LBee LRHS MAsh NHol SCoo SLim SPoG WFar
	- 'Tiny Tim'	CDoC CMac CSBt CWib ECho EHul GKir IFFs MGos NHol SCoo WEve WFar WGor
	- 'Trompenburg'	CDoC CSBt ECho EHul NLar SCoo
	- 'Wansdyke Silver' (v)	CMac EHul SCoo SLim SPoG
	- 'Wareana'	CMac
	- 'Wareana Aurea'	see *T. occidentalis* 'Wareana Lutescens'
§	- 'Wareana Lutescens'	CWib EHul MGos NHol
	- 'Yellow Ribbon'	CKen CSBt EHul GKir IFFs LRHS NLar SCoo SLim SPoG WEve WFar WHar
	orientalis	see *Platycladus orientalis*
	- 'Miller's Gold'	see *Platycladus orientalis* 'Aurea Nana'
	plicata	CCVT CDoy CDul CMac CSBt EHul EMac EPfP IFFs MGos NWea SLim SPer WDin WMou
	- 'Atrovirens' ♀H4	CDul CTri IFFs LBee LBuc LMaj LRHS LTen MAsh MBri MGos MMuc SBfd SCoo SEND SLim SRms WDin WEve WHar WMou
*	- 'Atrovirens Aurea'	WEve
	- 'Aurea' ♀H4	EHul LBee LRHS MAsh SLim SPoG SRms
	- 'Brooks Gold'	CKen
	- 'Can-can' (v)	ECho NLar SCoo
I	- 'Cole's Variety'	CWib MGos
	- 'Collyer's Gold'	CDul CTri EHul NHol NLar SRms WEve
	- 'Copper Kettle'	CKen ECho EHul LRHS MAsh NLar SCoo SLim WEve WGor
	- 'Cuprea'	CKen EHul
	- 'Doone Valley'	CKen EHul WFar
	- 'Excelsa'	CDul LMaj
	- 'Fastigiata' ♀H4	CDul CMac
	- 'Gelderland'	CTho ECho EHul LRHS LTen NEgg NLar SCoo SLim WFar
	- Goldy = '4ever'PBR	MBri
	- 'Gracilis Aurea'	EHul
	- 'Hillieri'	CDoC CDul
§	- 'Irish Gold' (v) ♀H4	CDul CMac
	- 'Rogersii'	CDoC CKen CMac CTri ECho EHul EPfP GKir MAsh MGos NHol SCoo SPoG SRms WFar
	- 'Semperaurescens' (v)	CMac
	- 'Stolwijk's Gold'	see *T. occidentalis* 'Stolwijk'
	- 'Stoneham Gold' ♀H4	CDoC CMac ECho EHul GKir LRHS MAsh MGos MMuc NHol NPCo SPer SRms WEve

	– 'Sunshine'	CKen
	– Verigold = 'Courtapli'	MMuc SEND
	– 'Whipcord'	CBcs ECho EHul LRHS MBri NLar SCoo SLim SPer SPoG WEve
*	– 'Windsor Gold'	EHul
	– 'Winter Pink' (v)	CKen
	– 'Zebrina' (v)	CBcs CDoC CDul CMac CSBt CTri CWib ECho EHul ELan EPfP GKir LRHS MAsh MGos MMuc NEgg NLar NPri NWea SCoo SEND SLim SPer SWvt WDin WEve WFar WHar
	plicata* × *standishii	CDul

Thujopsis (*Cupressaceae*)

	dolabrata ♀H4	CBcs CDul EHul GKir IFFs MMuc NEgg NLar NWea WDin WEve WFar WPGP
	– 'Aurea' (v)	CDoC CKen EHul LRHS MGos NLar SCoo SLim WEve
	– 'Laetevirens'	see *T. dolabrata* 'Nana'
	– 'Melbourne Gold'	NLar WEve
§	– 'Nana'	CDoC CKen CMac EHul IFFs LRHS MGos NHol NLar SCoo SLim SRms STre WEve WFar
	– 'Variegata' (v)	CFee CMac EHul LRHS MGos NLar NMun SCoo SLim SPoG WDin WEve WFar
	koraiensis (Nakai) hort.	see *Thuja koraiensis*

Thunbergia (*Acanthaceae*)

	alata	CFox EPfP MBri SPoG
	– 'African Sunset'	CSpe EShb SVil WHil
	– 'Lemon'	SVil
	– 'Orange Beauty'	SVil WBor WHil
*	***arborea***	CCCN
	battiscombeii	CCCN ERea EShb SOWG
	coccinea	CCCN ERea
	erecta	CCCN ERea SOWG
	fragrans GWJ 9441	WCru
	grandiflora ♀H1	CCCN CHll ELan ERea EShb SOWG
	– 'Alba'	CCCN CHll EShb
	gregorii ♀H1+3	CCCN CHll ERea EShb SOWG
	– 'Mango' **new**	SVil
	'Moonglow'	CCCN
	mysorensis ♀H1	CCCN ERea SOWG
	natalensis	CCCN ERea EShb
	'Orange Wonder'	CCCN

thyme, caraway see *Thymus herba-barona*

thyme, garden see *Thymus vulgaris*

thyme, wild see *Thymus serpyllum*

Thymus ✿ (*Lamiaceae*)

	from Albania	CArn
	from Turkey	ECho EWes LLWP SBfd SHDw
§	'Alan Bloom'	LLWP
	'Anderson's Gold'	see *T. pulegioides* 'Bertram Anderson'
	azoricus	see *T. caespititius*
	'Bressingham'	Widely available
	'Brigantes'	LLWP
	'Caborn Fragrant Cloud'	LLWP
	'Caborn Greenfinch'	LLWP
	'Caborn Grey Lady'	LLWP
	'Caborn Lilac Gem'	LLWP SBfd SHDw
	'Caborn Pink Carpet'	LLWP
	'Caborn Rosanne'	LLWP
	'Caborn Wine and Roses'	LLWP
§	***caespititius***	CArn ECho EDAr ELau GBar GMaP GPoy MHer NMen NRya SBfd SPlb SRot WAbe WPer WWEG
	caespitosus	CTri GKir
	camphoratus	CArn ELau EWes GBar LAst MHer MNHC NGHP NMen SBfd SPhx WJek WWEG
	– 'A Touch of Frost'	SBfd SHDw
	– 'Derry'	CSpe
	capitatus	CArn MHer
	carnosus misapplied	see *T. vulgaris* 'Erectus'
	carnosus Boiss.	STre
	'Carol Ann' (v)	ECho ELau EWes GBar LLWP MNHC WWEG
	'Caroline'	SBfd SHDw
	'Carshalton'	CWan
	ciliatus	LLWP WClo WPer
	cilicicus misapplied	see *T. caespititius*
	cilicicus ambig.	MNHC NMen WJek WWEG
	cilicicus Boiss. & Bail.	CPBP EWes GBar WAbe
	citriodorus misapplied	see *T.* 'Culinary Lemon'
	citriodorus (Pers.) Schreb. 'Archer's Gold'	see *T. pulegioides* 'Archer's Gold'
	– 'Aureus'	see *T. pulegioides* 'Aureus'
	– 'Bertram Anderson'	see *T. pulegioides* 'Bertram Anderson'
	– ***repandus***	see *T.* 'Rosemary's Lemon Carpet'
	– 'Silver Posie'	see *T.* 'Silver Posie'
	– 'Variegatus'	see *T.* 'Golden King'
	'Coccineus'	see *T.* Coccineus Group
N	Coccineus Group ♀H4	Widely available
§	– 'Atropurpureus' misapplied	LLWP SBfd SHDw
	– 'Bethany'	LLWP SGar
§	– 'Hardstoft Red' (v)	GBar
§	– 'Purple Beauty'	EPot LLWP MHer WWEG
§	– 'Purpurteppich'	LLWP
§	– 'Red Elf'	ECho GAbr GBar MHer SBfd WJek WWEG
	'Coccineus Major'	CMea CWan ECho EDAr LRHS MHer MNHC SIde WJek
	comosus misapplied	SBfd SHDw WEas WJek WPer
	'Cow Green'	LLWP SBfd
	'Creeping Lemon' misapplied	see *T. pulegioides* 'Kurt'
	'Creeping Lemon'	ELau GBar LLWP MHer
§	'Culinary Lemon'	CArn CHby CWan ECho EDAr ELau GBar GKir GPoy LLWP MBrN MHer MNHC MWat NGHP NPri SBfd WBrE WJek WPer
	'Dark Eyes'	SBfd SHDw
	'Dartmoor'	GBar LLWP SBfd SHDw WJek WWEG
	'Desboro'	see *T. serphyllum* 'Desborough'
	doerfleri	ECha LLWP
	'Doone Valley' (v)	Widely available
	drucei	see *T. polytrichus* subsp. *britannicus*
	'E.B.Anderson'	see *T. pulegioides* 'Bertram Anderson'
	'Eastgrove Pink'	LLWP SBfd SHDw
	'Emma's Pink'	LLWP
	erectus	see *T. vulgaris* 'Erectus'
	'Fragrantissimus'	CArn CEnt CMea CWan ELau GBar GGar GPoy LLWP MHer MNHC MWat NGHP SIde SPlb WFar WJek WPer
	'Gibson's Cave'	LLWP
	'Glenridding'	LLWP

§	'Golden King' (v)	CWan ECha ECho EDAr ELan GBar LHop LLWP LSRN MBri MHer NGHP WWEG
	'Golden Lemon' misapplied	see *T. pulegioides* 'Aureus'
	'Golden Lemon' (v)	CArn LLWP WJek
	'Golden Queen' (v)	ECho EDAr GGar MHer MWat NGHP NPri SBfd SPer SPet SRms WFar
	'Gratian'	LLWP SBfd SHDw
	'Hadrian'	LLWP
	'Hans Stam'	see *T. serphyllum* 'Hans Stam'
	'Hardstoft Red'	see *T.* (Coccineus Group) 'Hardstoft Red'
§	'Hartington Silver' (v)	ECha ECho ECtt EPot EWes GBar GKev GKir LBee LHop LRHS MHer MNHC NHol NRya SPlb SPoG WFar WHoo WJek WPer WWEG
	herba-barona	CArn CMea CPrp CTri CWan ECha EDAr ELau GBar GPoy LEdu LLWP MHer MMuc MNHC MWat NGHP NHol SEND SIde SRms STre WJek WPer WWEG
	- 'Bob Flowerdew'	LLWP
	- ***citrata***	see *T. herba-barona* 'Lemon-scented'
§	- 'Lemon-scented'	ECha GBar GPoy LLWP MHer SBfd SHDw SIde WJek
	'Highdown'	ECtt SBfd SHDw
	'Highdown Adur'	SBfd SHDw
	'Highdown Lemon'	SBfd SHDw
	'Highdown Red'	SBfd SHDw
	'Highdown Stretham'	SBfd SHDw
	'Highland Cream'	see *T.* 'Hartington Silver'
	hirsutus	NBir
	'Iden'	WJek WWEG
	'Jekka'	WJek WWEG
	'Kurt'	see *T. pulegioides* 'Kurt'
	'Lake District'	LLWP
I	'Lantanii'	LLWP SBfd
	lanuginosus misapplied	see *T. pseudolanuginosus*
	'Lavender Sea'	ELau EWes LLWP
	'Lemon Caraway'	see *T. herba-barona* 'Lemon-scented'
	'Lemon Curd'	ELau GBar LLWP MHer MNHC NHol SBfd SHDw SIde SPlb SPoG WFar WJek WWEG
	'Lemon Sorbet'	SBfd SHDw
	'Lemon Supreme'	LLWP
*	'Lemon Variegated' (v)	EDAr ELau EPfP GBar MNHC SPer SPoG WWEG
	'Lilac Time'	ECtt EWes GBar LLWP MHer NGHP SBfd SHDw SIde SPlb WJek WPer WWEG
	'Lime'	LLWP
	longicaulis	CArn ECha ELau GBar LLWP MHer WJek
	'Low Force'	LLWP
	'Marjorie'	LLWP
	marschallianus	see *T. pannonicus*
§	'Massa'	LLWP SBfd SHDw WWEG
	mastichina	CArn WPer
	- 'Didi'	MHer
	membranaceus	CPBP
	micans	see *T. caespititius*
	minus	see *Calamintha nepeta*
	montanus Waldst. & Kit.	see *T. pulegioides*
	'Mountain Select'	LLWP SBfd SHDw
	neiceffii	CMea ECha ELau GBar LLWP WWEG
	'New Hall'	SBfd
	nummularius misapplied	see *T.* 'Pat Milne'
	odoratissimus	see *T. pallasianus* subsp. *pallasianus*
	'Orange Balsam'	see *T. vulgaris* 'Orange Balsam'
	'Orange Spice'	LLWP SBfd SHDw SPoG WWEG
	pallasianus	ELau SBfd SHDw
§	- subsp. ***pallasianus***	GBar
§	***pannonicus***	LLWP MHer WPer
§	'Pat Milne'	ELau LLWP
	'Peter Davis'	CArn CMea LHop LRHS LSRN MBNS MHer MNHC NBir NGHP NHol SBfd SIde SPoG
	'Pinewood'	LLWP MHer SIde
	'Pink Ripple'	CBod CMea ECtt ELau EPot EWes GBar LLWP MHer NGHP SBch SBfd SHDw SIde WHal WHoo WJek WPer WWEG
	polytrichus misapplied	see *T. praecox*
§	***polytrichus*** A. Kern. ex Borbás subsp. ***britannicus***	CArn ECho GPoy LSou MNHC SBfd SHDw SPlb WAbe WJek WPer WWEG
	- - 'Minor'	see *T. polytrichus* subsp. *britannicus* 'Nettleton Pink Carpet'
	- - 'Nettleton Pink Carpet'	ECho LLWP WPer
	- - 'Orkney White'	WAlt
§	- - 'Thomas's White' ♀H4	CTri ECho LLWP
	- - 'Timothy's White'	CEnt
	'Porlock'	CMea CPrp CTri CWan ECho ELau EPfP GBar GKir GMaP GPoy LLWP MHer MNHC NGHP SIde SRms WAbe WHoo WJek WPer WWEG
§	***praecox***	EBWF GBar GJos MHer NLan NMir NSco
	- 'Albiflorus'	EPot
	- subsp. ***arcticus***	see *T. polytrichus* subsp. *britannicus*
	- - 'Albus'	see *T. polytrichus* subsp. *britannicus* 'Thomas's White'
§	***pseudolanuginosus***	CArn CTri CWan ECha ECho EDAr EPot GBar GJos GMaP LLWP MBNS MBri MHer MLHP MMuc MNHC NBir NHol SEND SPlb SRms WHoo WJek WPer WSpi WWEG
	- 'Hall's Variety'	GBar
§	***pulegioides***	CArn CBod CHby ELau GBar GGar GPoy LLWP MBri MHer MNHC NPri SBch SBfd SHDw SIde WClo WJek WPer
§	- 'Archer's Gold'	Widely available
§	- 'Aureus' ♀H4	EPot GBar GGar GKir GMaP LAst LLWP LRHS MBri MHer NWCA SBfd SGar SPer SPlb STre WFar WHoo WJek
§	- 'Bertram Anderson' ♀H4	Widely available
	- 'Foxley' (v)	CBod CBow CWan ECho EHoe ELau EPfP GBar LLWP MHer MNHC NGHP NHol NPri SBfd SHDw SIde SPlb SPoG WJek WWEG
	- 'Golden Dwarf'	LLWP
§	- 'Goldentime'	GBar LLWP
§	- 'Kurt'	LLWP SBfd SHDw WJek WNew WWEG
	- 'Sir John Lawes'	LLWP MHer SBfd SHDw
	- 'Tabor'	GBar GMaP MNHC NGHP SBfd SHDw
	'Rainbow Falls' (v)	EPfP GBar LLWP MNHC NGHP NHol SBfd SHDw SIde WRHF WWEG
	'Rasta' (v)	ECtt LLWP
	'Red Glow'	LLWP

	'Redstart'	ECha ELau EPot GBar LBee LLWP MHer SBch SBfd SHDw SIde WJek WWEG
	richardii subsp. ***nitidus*** misapplied	see *T. vulgaris* 'Suditin'
	- - 'Compactus Albus'	see *T. vulgaris* 'Snow White'
	'Rosa Ceeping'	SBfd SHDw
	'Rosalicht'	see *T.* 'Rosedrift'
	'Rosalind'	SBfd SHDw
§	'Rosedrift'	LLWP SBfd SHDw
§	'Rosemary's Early Red' new	LLWP
§	'Rosemary's Lemon Carpet'	LLWP
	rotundifolius misapplied	see *T. vulgaris* 'Elsbeth'
	'Ruby Glow'	CEnt ECtt ELau EPot EWes MHer SBfd SHDw WFar WWEG
	serpyllum misapplied	see *T.* 'Rosemary's Early Red'
	serpyllum ambig.	CArn ELau GJos MBri SIde SPet SPlb SRms WPer
	serpyllum L.	LLWP MMuc WJek
	- var. ***albus***	CPrp ECha ECho ELau GBar GMaP GPoy LAst LLWP LRHS MNHC NGHP NHol NPri SIde SPer SRms WAbe WHoo WJek WWEG
	- 'Albus Variegatus'	see *T.* 'Hartington Silver'
N	- 'Annie Hall'	CWan ECho EDAr ELau EPfP EPot GAbr GBar GGar LAst LLWP LRHS MHer NGHP NPri SBfd SIde SPer STre WCFE WJek WPer
	- 'Atropurpureus'	see *T.* (Coccineus Group) 'Atropurpureus' misapplied
	- 'August Moon'	LLWP
	- 'Barwinnock Snowdrift' (v)	GBar
	- ***coccineus*** 'Minor' misapplied	see *T.* Coccineus Group
	- ***coccineus*** 'Minor' Bloom	see *T.* 'Alan Bloom'
	- 'Conwy Rose'	CPBP LLWP WAbe
§	- 'Desborough'	ECtt GBar LLWP MHer NHol WWEG
N	- 'East Lodge'	LLWP MNHC
	- 'Elfin'	ECho EWes LBee MBri SBfd SPlb WAbe
N	- 'Fulney Red'	EWes
	- 'Goldstream' (v)	CMea ECho ELau EPfP GBar LHop LLWP LRHS MBri MHer NGHP NHol SPlb SRms WHoo WJek WPer
§	- 'Hans Stam'	LLWP
	- 'Minimalist'	see *T. serpyllum* 'Minor'
	- 'Minimus'	see *T. serpyllum* 'Minor'
§	- 'Minor'	Widely available
N	- 'Minor Albus'	ECho GBar
	- 'Minus'	see *T. serpyllum* 'Minor'
	- 'Petite'	EWes LLWP
N	- 'Pink Chintz' ♀^{H4}	CMea CPrp ECha ECho ECtt EDAr ELau EPfP GBar GKir GPoy LLWP LRHS MBri MHer MNHC NGHP NPri SBfd SPer SPlb SPoG WClo WCom WHoo WJek WPer WWEG
	- 'Posh Pinky'	EPot LLWP NMen
	- 'Purple Beauty'	see *T.* (Coccineus Group) 'Purple Beauty'
	- 'Purpurteppich'	see *T.* (Coccineus Group) 'Purpurteppich'
	- 'Pygmaeus'	LLWP
	- 'Red Carpet'	ECtt EDAr NHol
	- 'Red Elf'	see *T.* (Coccineus Group) 'Red Elf'
	- 'Roger's Snowdrift'	LLWP
N	- 'Roseus'	GBar SIde
N	- 'Russetings'	CPrp CYeo ECtt ELau EPfP EPot GBar LLWP MHer MNHC NGHP NHol SBch SBfd SIde SPer SPoG SRms WFar WHoo WJek WNew WWEG
N	- 'September'	LLWP MHer
N	- 'Snowdrift'	CArn CMea CWan ECho ECtt ELau EPfP EPot GBar GKev LLWP MHer MNHC MWat NHol NMen NRya SBch SIde SPlb WCFE WFar WJek WPat WPer WWEG
N	- 'Splendens'	LLWP
	- subsp. ***tanaensis***	CArn
	- 'Variegatus'	see *T.* 'Hartington Silver'
	- 'Vey'	CPBP ECho EPot EWes GBar GMaP LLWP LRHS MHer SBfd SHDw WJek WWEG
	sibthorpii	CArn
	'Silver King' (v)	ECho
N	'Silver Posie'	Widely available
	'Silver Queen' (v) ♀^{H4}	CBcs CSam CWan ECha ECho EDAr ELau EPfP GBar GGar GKev GMaP LAst LLWP MHer MNHC NGHP SBfd SPlb WFar WJek WNew
	'Snowdonia Idris'	LLWP
	'Snowdonia Ifor'	LLWP
	'Snowdonia Imperial Beauty'	LLWP
	'Snowdonia Iorwerth'	LLWP
	'Snowdonia Isolde'	LLWP
	'Snowdonia Istyn'	LLWP
	'Snowdonia Lass'	LLWP SBfd
	'Snowdonia Pedr'	LLWP
	'Snowdonia Pink Gem'	LLWP
	'Snowdonia Pryderi'	LLWP
	'Snowdonia Pwyll'	LLWP
	'Snowdonia Rhiannon'	LLWP
	'Snowdonia Rowena'	LLWP
	'Snowman'	SBfd
	valesiacus	see *T.* 'Massa'
§	***villosus***	ECho
§	***vulgaris***	Widely available
	- ***albus***	see *T. vulgaris* 'Rosemary's White'
	- 'Aureus' hort.	see *T. pulegioides* 'Goldentime'
	- 'Boule'	LLWP
*	- 'Compactus'	CSam GPoy LLWP MNHC MRav WJek
	- 'Deutsche Auslese'	see *T. vulgaris*
	- 'Diamantis'	LLWP
	- 'Dorcas White'	LLWP MHer WPer
§	- 'Elsbeth'	ECho ELau LLWP SBfd SHDw
	- 'English Winter'	GBar SIde
§	- 'Erectus'	CArn GBar MHer WCom WPer
	- French	see *T. vulgaris*
	- French, summer	SIde
	- 'Golden Pins'	GBar MHer
	- 'Lemon Queen'	ECho ELau
	- 'Lucy'	GBar LLWP MHer MNHC
§	- 'Orange Balsam'	LLWP NHol
§	- 'Rosemary's White'	ECho GBar
	- 'Silver Pearl' (v)	ECho
§	- 'Snow White'	ELau EWes LLWP SBfd SHDw WJek
§	- 'Suditin'	STre
	'Widecombe' (v)	LLWP MHer SBfd SHDw
	zygis	CArn

Tiarella (*Saxifragaceae*)

	'Arpeggio' new	EBee
	'Black Snowflake' PBR	EBee NHol
	'Black Velvet' PBR	EBee MLLN SHeu SPer WFar
	'Braveheart'	EBee MGos WWEG
	collina	see *T. wherryi*
	cordifolia ♀^{H4}	Widely available

- 'Glossy'	CBct WPGP
- 'Oakleaf'	CMoH EBee MLLN NBre NBro
- 'Rosalie'	see × *Heucherella alba* 'Rosalie'
- 'Running Tapestry'	EBee
- 'Slick Rock'	EBee EPPr
'Crow Feather'PBR	EBee SHeu
'Cygnet'PBR	CBct CLAP EBee ECtt GCai LHop LRHS MLLN SHeu SPer SPoG SRot WFar
'Dark Star'	ECtt NBre
'Dunvegan'	EBee MLLN
'Elizabeth Oliver'	CLAP EBee
'Freckles'	MRav
'Hidden Carpet'	CHid
'Inkblot'	EBee ELan LRHS MLLN MPnt NBro SHeu WFar WMoo WSpi
'Iron Butterfly'PBR	CBct CLAP CMac CWCL EBee ECtt EPfP GBin GMaP LAst LBMP LRHS LSRN MRav NBro NCGa SGSe SMrm SPer SPoG SRot STes WFar WPGP WSpi WWEG
'Jeepers Creepers'PBR	EBee MAsh MPnt SHeu
* 'Laciniate Runner'	CLAP
'Martha Oliver'	CLAP EBee NBre SBch WPGP
'Mint Chocolate'PBR	CChe CLAP EBee ECha ECtt EHoe EHrv ELan EPfP GMaP LOck LRHS MLLN MRav MSCN NCGa NGdn NLar SPer SPur SWvt WAul WFar WHoo WPGP WWEG
Morning Star = 'Tntia042'PBR	EWll LAst LRHS MBri MPnt SHeu SRot WFar
'Mystic Mist' (v) new	MAsh MPnt SHeu
'Neon Lights'PBR	CBow EBee ECGP EWes MPnt NBPC NPnk SHeu SWvt
§ 'Ninja'PBR	CHid CMac CWCL EBee EBrs ECha ECtt EHrv ELan EUJe GMaP LAst LRHS MRav NLar NSti SPer SWvt WFar
'Petite Pink Bouquet'	ECtt
'Pink Bouquet'	CAbP CBow CLAP CMac CSpe EAEE EBee EBrs ECha ECtt EHrv GJos LBMP LRHS MBri MLLN NDov NHol SBch WFar WMoo WPnP
'Pink Brushes'PBR	CLAP EBee WPnP
'Pink Skyrocket'PBR	CAbP CLAP CMil CWGN EBee ECtt LLHF LOck LRHS LSRN MPnt NCob NGdn NHol NPnk SHar SHeu SMrm SPer WBor WCot WCra WFut WGor
'Pinwheel'	EBrs LRHS MRav NBre
'Pirate's Patch'PBR	EBee LLHF NHol SHeu
polyphylla	CBow EBee ELan NBre NLar SBch SWal WFar WMoo
- 'Baoxing Pink'	CBow CLAP WCru
- 'Filigran'	EBee EPfP LBMP LRHS NHol NLar
- 'Moorgrün'	GCal
- pink-flowered	CLAP CMoH EHrv GBin
- - BWJ 8088	WCru
'Running Tiger'	EBee WWEG
'Sea Foam'	NHol NPnk SHeu WSpi
'Simsalabim'	EBee
'Skeleton Key'	EBee
'Skid's Variegated' (v)	CBow EBee ECtt EShb LRHS MNrw NSti SHeu SWvt WCot
'Spanish Cross'PBR	NHol SHeu
'Spring Symphony'PBR	CLAP CMac CWCL EBee ECtt EShb GBin GCai LAst LBMP LRHS LSou MBri MLLN NCGa NHol NLar NPer NPnk SHar SMrm WFar WSpi
Starburst = 'Tntia041'PBR	LAst SHeu
'Starfish'	NBPC NBre WPrP
'Sugar and Spice'PBR	EBee LSou NHol NPnk
'Tiger Stripe'	EBee EPfP LRHS MPnt MRav NBro NPnk SPer WFar WSpi
'Timbuktu' new	MPnt
trifoliata	MRav NBre WFar
- var. ***unifoliata***	WWEG
'Viking Ship'PBR	see × *Heucherella* 'Viking Ship'
§ ***wherryi*** ♀H4	CBar CBcs COlW CPla EBee ECtt EHrv ELan ELon EPfP GKir GMaP LAst LBMP LRHS NBir NBro NDov NHol NPri SBch SBfd SPer SPlb SRot SWvt WFar WPer WPnP WWEG
- 'Bronze Beauty'	CLAP MRav NDov SBch WFar WPGP WSpi
- 'Green Velvet'	ECha
- 'Heronswood Mist' (v)	CAbP CBct CBow CFir EBee ECtt GEdr MCot SPer SWvt WCot
- 'Montrose'	NBre WPGP

Tibouchina (*Melastomataceae*)

grandifolia	CCCN CRHN EShb
granulosa	SOWG
heteromalla	CCCN
'Jules'	CBcs SOWG
* ***laxa*** 'Skylab'	SOWG
organensis	CCCN CHII CMac SHeu SOWG WCot WPGP
paratropica	CRHN
- RCB/Arg X-4	WCot
semidecandra hort.	see *T. urvilleana*
§ ***urvilleana*** ♀H1	CBcs CCCN CDoC CHEx CKno CRHN CSBt CTri EAmu EBak EBee ECre ELan EPfP IFFs MCot MMuc NCGa SAPC SDnm SEND SOWG SPer SPoG SRkn SRms WCot
- 'Compacta'	CCCN
- 'Edwardsii'	LSou SMrm SUsu WCot
- 'Nana'	CDoC
- 'Rich Blue Sun'	CSpe
- variegated (v)	CCCN LSou SUsu WCot

Tigridia ✿ (*Iridaceae*)

lutea	ECho
orthantha 'Red-Hot Tiger'	WCru
pavonia	CPLG CSpr ECho EDif EWld EWll IGor LAma MBri
- 'Alba'	CSpe EDif
- 'Alba Grandiflora'	EBee
- 'Aurea'	EBee
- 'Canariensis'	CTca EBee SBch
- 'Lilacea'	EBee ECho EWll SBch
- 'Speciosa'	CTca EBee
van-houttei new	WHil

Tilia ✿ (*Tiliaceae*)

americana	CLnd CMCN GKir
- 'Dentata'	CDul
- 'Nova'	CDoC
amurensis	CMCN
- subsp. ***taquetii***	GKir
argentea	see *T. tomentosa*
begoniifolia	see *T. dasystyla*
chenmoui	CMCN EBee EPfP GKir MBlu WPGP
chinensis	CMCN GKir NPCo WPGP
chingiana	CDul CMCN GKir SBir SLon
cordata ♀H4	CBcs CCVT CDul CLnd CMac CSBt CTho CTri EBee ECrN ELan EMac

		EPfP GKir IFFs LBuc LMaj MMuc MSwo NWea SBfd SCoo SEND SPer STre WDin WMou
§	- 'Böhlje'	CDul SLPl
	- 'Dainty Leaf'	CDul
	- 'Erecta'	see *T. cordata* 'Böhlje'
	- 'Greenspire' 🏆^{H4}	CCVT CDoC CDul CLnd CWib EBee ECrN LMaj LTen SBfd
	- 'Len Parvin'	EBee WPGP
	- 'Lico'	CMen LMaj
	- 'Roelvo'	CDul
	- 'Swedish Upright'	CDul CLnd CTho
	- 'Winter Orange'	CDul CEnd CWit EBee ECrN EPfP GKir LRHS MBlu MBri NPCo SBir SCoo
§	***dasystyla***	CMCN WPGP
	- subsp. ***caucasica***	WPGP
	× ***euchlora*** 🏆^{H4}	CBcs CCVT CDul CLnd CMCN EBee ECrN EPfP GKir LAst LMaj NWea SBfd SPer WDin WFar
§	× ***europaea***	CBcs CDul CLnd CRWN ELan NWea
	- 'Koningslinde'	CDul
	- 'Pallida'	CDul CLnd CTho EBee LMaj LTen MBlu NWea
	- 'Wratislaviensis' 🏆^{H4}	CDoC CDul CLnd EBee EPfP GKir MAsh MBlu
§	'Harold Hillier'	MBlu
	henryana	CDoC CDul CEnd CLnd CMCN CTho CWib EBee ECrN EMil EPfP GKir IArd IDee LRHS MBlu MBri MMuc MREP SBir SCoo WDin WPGP
§	***heterophylla***	CMCN WPGP
	- var. ***michauxii***	CLnd GKir
	'Hillieri'	see *T.* 'Harold Hillier'
	insularis misapplied	see *T. japonica* 'Ernest Wilson'
	intonsa	CMCN
	japonica	CDul CMCN GKir WPGP
§	- 'Ernest Wilson'	CMCN GKir MBlu
	kiusiana	CDul CMCN GKir MBlu MBri WPGP
	mandshurica	CMCN WPGP
	maximowicziana	GKir WPGP
	mexicana	EBee WPGP
	miqueliana	CMCN
	'Moltkei'	CLnd CMCN EBee WPGP
	mongolica	CDoC CDul CLnd CMCN EBee EPfP GKir MBlu MMuc SCoo WPGP
	monticola	see *T. heterophylla*
	oliveri	CDul CMCN GKir MBlu NWea SBir WPGP
	'Petiolaris' 🏆^{H4}	CCVT CDoC CDul CEnd CLnd CMCN EBee ECrN ELan EPfP GKir MBlu MSwo NWea SEND SPer WDin WMou
	platyphyllos	CCVT CDul CLnd CMCN CSBt CTho CTri EBee ECrN EMac EMil EPfP EWTr GKir IFFs LAst LBuc MMuc NWea SBfd SCoo SEND SPer WDin WMou
	- 'Aurea'	CDul CLnd CTho ECrN MBlu
	- 'Corallina'	see *T. platyphyllos* 'Rubra'
	- 'Erecta'	see *T. platyphyllos* 'Fastigiata'
§	- 'Fastigiata'	CDul ECrN SLPl
	- 'Laciniata'	CDul CMCN CTho GKir LMaj MBlu
§	- 'Rubra' 🏆^{H4}	CDoC CLnd CTho EPfP GKir LBuc MGos NWea WDin WFar
	- 'Tortuosa'	MBlu WMou
§	***tomentosa***	CDul CLnd CMCN CTho ELan EMil GKir IFFs LMaj MMuc NWea SCoo WDin WMou
	- 'Brabant' 🏆^{H4}	CDoC CDul EPfP LMaj WFar
	tuan	CMCN
	× ***vulgaris***	see *T.* × *europaea*

Tilingia (*Apiaceae*)

ajanensis B&SWJ 11202	WCru

Tillaea see *Crassula*

Tillandsia (*Bromeliaceae*)

	abdita	XAld
	achyrostachys new	XAld
	aeranthos	SChr XAld
	- var. ***alba*** new	XAld
	albertiana	XAld
	albida new	XAld
	arequitae new	XAld
	argentea 🏆^{H1}	XAld
	argentina new	XAld
	baileyi	XAld
	bandensis new	XAld
	bergeri	XAld
	brachycaulos	XAld
	bulbosa	XAld
	butzii	XAld
	cacticola	XAld
	caliginosa new	XAld
	capillaris new	XAld
	capitata new	XAld
	caput-medusae	XAld
	cardenasii new	XAld
	chiapensis new	XAld
	concolor new	XAld
	crocata new	XAld
	cyanea 🏆^{H1}	XAld
	diaguitensis new	XAld
	didisticha new	XAld
	disticha new	XAld
	dodsonii new	XAld
	dorotheae new	XAld
	duratii new	XAld
	dyeriana new	XAld
	fasciculata new	XAld
	filifolia	XAld
	fuchsii new	XAld
	funckiana new	XAld
	gardneri	XAld
	geminiflora new	XAld
	gerdae new	XAld
	harrisii	XAld
	heteromorpha new	XAld
	humilis new	XAld
	ionantha 'Rubra' new	XAld
	- var. ***scaposa***	see *T. kolbii*
	- var. ***stricta*** new	XAld
	ixioides new	XAld
	jucunda new	XAld
§	***kolbii***	XAld
	latifolia new	XAld
	lindenii 🏆^{H1} new	XAld
	lopezii new	XAld
	magnusiana	XAld
	neglecta new	XAld
	remota new	XAld
	streptophylla	XAld
	usneoides	SHmp

Tinantia (*Commelinaceae*)

pringlei	CDes EBee LEdu SDys WPGP WSHC

- AIM 77	WCot WPrP

Titanopsis (*Aizoaceae*)

calcarea ♀H1	CCCN EPfP

Tithonia (*Asteraceae*)

rotundifolia	CSpe
- 'Torch'	CSpe SMrm

Todea (*Osmundaceae*)

barbara	WPGP WRic

Tofieldia (*Melanthiaceae*)

calyculata	NHol
coccinea	GCal

Tolmiea (*Saxifragaceae*)

menziesii	EWld MCot NHol SPer SWal
- 'Goldsplash'	see *T. menziesii* 'Taff's Gold'
- 'Maculata'	see *T. menziesii* 'Taff's Gold'
§ - 'Taff's Gold' (v) ♀H4	CWan EBee EHoe EOHP EShb GMaP MHer NBid NVic SPlb WHoo WTin
- 'Variegata'	see *T. menziesii* 'Taff's Gold'

Tolpis (*Asteraceae*)

barbata	CSpe

Tonestus (*Asteraceae*)

§ ***lyallii***	WPer

Toona (*Meliaceae*)

§ ***sinensis***	CArn CDul CEnd CGHE CTho CWib ELan EMil EPfP MMuc SEND WBVN WFar WPGP
- 'Flamingo' (v)	CBcs EBee EPfP LRHS MAsh MGos NLar SPoG SSta WCot

Torenia (*Scrophulariaceae*)

(Moon Series) Blue Moon = 'Dantmoon'	LAst
- Golden Moon = 'Danmoon16'PBR	LAst
- Purple Moon = 'Dantopur'PBR	LAst LSou SVil
- Rose Moon = 'Dantoromoon'	LAst
- Yellow Moon = 'Danmoon20'PBR	LSou
Summer Wave Series	CCCN SCoo

Torilis (*Apiaceae*)

japonica	CBre EBWF

Torreya (*Taxaceae*)

jackii new	EGFP

Townsendia (*Asteraceae*)

alpigena	GKev
§ - var. ***alpigena***	CPBP EPot GKev
- var. ***caelilinensis*** NNS 06-551	GKev
exscapa	GKev
formosa	ECho GKev
incana	WAbe
leptotes	CPBP
montana	see *T. alpigena* var. *alpigena*
parryi	WAbe
§ ***rothrockii***	EPot GKev NMen
spathulata	CPBP GKev
wilcoxiana misapplied	see *T. rothrockii*

Toxicodendron (*Anacardiaceae*)

vernicifluum	see *Rhus verniciflua*

Trachelium (*Campanulaceae*)

§ ***asperuloides***	WAbe
caeruleum ♀H1	SGar
- 'Black Knight'	CSpe
- 'Purple Umbrella'	CPLG
jacquinii	NWCA WPat
subsp. ***rumelianum***	

Trachelospermum ✿ (*Apocynaceae*)

from Nanking, China	EShb
§ ***asiaticum*** ♀H2-3	Widely available
- B&SWJ 4814	WCru
- 'Golden Memories'	CPLG CWGN EBee EPfP IVic LRHS LSRN LSqu MAsh MGos SKHP SLon SPoG SSpi SSta WCot WPat
- 'Goshiki' (v)	CBow EShb WPat
- var. ***intermedium***	NPal WPGP
- - B&SWJ 8733	WCru
* - 'Kiejiu Chirimen' new	SKHP
- 'Kulu Chirimen'	WCot
- 'Nagaba' (v)	SKHP
- 'Ogon Nishiki' (v)	SKHP
- 'Shirofu Chirimen' (v) new	SKHP
- 'Theta'	SKHP WPat
'Chameleon'	EBee EGxp NPal SKHP
jasminoides ♀H3-4	Widely available
- B&SWJ 5117	WCru
- 'Big White Star'	EPfP
§ - 'Japonicum'	CRHN CSPN LRHS SLon WSHC
- 'Major'	CSPN EBee ELan SEND SSpi
* - 'Oblanceolatum'	GCal
- 'Tricolor' (v)	CBcs SLim SMad SWvt WCot
- 'Variegatum' (v) ♀H3-4	Widely available
- 'Waterwheel'	CWGN EBee ELan IVic LRHS SKHP SPoG SSpi WPGP WSHC
- 'Wilsonii'	CBot CMac CPLG CSPN CSam EBee ELan EPfP EShb GCal LHop LRHS MCCP NLar SEND SKHP SLim SPer SPoG SWvt WCot WCru WHar WPGP WPat
majus misapplied	see *T. jasminoides* 'Japonicum'
majus Nakai	see *T. asiaticum*

Trachycarpus (*Arecaceae*)

sp.	EAmu
from Manipur	EAmu SChr
§ ***fortunei*** ♀H3-4	Widely available
latisectus	CBrP EAmu LPJP LPal SBig
martianus	CDTJ CTrC EAmu LPJP LPal SBig SChr
nanus	LPal
'Nova' new	EAmu
oreophilus	LPal
princeps	LPal
takil	CBrP CDTJ EAmu EPla LPal NPal
wagnerianus	CBrP CDTJ CGHE CHid CPHo CPLG CTrC EAmu EPla ETod EUJe LPJP LPal MREP NPal NPla SAPC SBig SChr SMad WPGP

Trachymene (*Apiaceae*)

coerulea	CSpe

Trachyspermum (*Apiaceae*)

ammi new	CArn

Trachystemon (*Boraginaceae*)

orientalis	CBre CHEx CMac CPLG CSev EBee ECha EGol ELan EPfP EWTr IKil LEdu LHop MAvo MRav NBid NLar SBch SBig SDnm SKHP WCAu WCru WDyG WFar WHer WMoo WPnP

Tradescantia ✿ (*Commelinaceae*)

albiflora	see *T. fluminensis*
× ***andersoniana*** W. Ludwig & Rohw. nom. inval.	see *T.* Andersoniana Group
§ Andersoniana Group	CSpr CWan CWib SPet SWal WHil WPer
- 'Baby Doll'	GKir
- 'Bilberry Ice'	Widely available
- 'Blanca'	WWEG
- 'Blue and Gold'	CBcs COlW CSpe EBee ECtt ELon EPPr EPfP LAst LHop LRHS MNFA MRav NLar NPri NSti SGSe WCot WFar WHil WWEG
- 'Blue Stone'	CMdw CMea CSBt EBee ECha ECtt MAvo MRav NDov NPri SRms WFar WHoo WTin
- 'Bridal Veil'	CHll
- 'Caerulea Plena'	see *T. virginiana* 'Caerulea Plena'
- Carmine Glow	see *T.* (Andersoniana Group) 'Karminglut'
- 'Charlotte'	CTca EBee EBrs ECha ECtt LRHS LSRN NBre NBro NGdn NLar SBfd SRGP WCAu WMnd WWEG
- 'Chedglow'	WWEG
- 'Concord Grape'	Widely available
- 'Danielle'	EBee EPfP GMac
- 'Domaine de Courson'	EBee ECtt
- 'In the Navy'	NBre NLar
- 'Innocence'	CMHG CSBt CTri EBee ECha ECtt ELan EPfP GCra GJos GMaP LAst LHop LRHS MLLN MMuc NBPC NBir NCGa NGdn NPnk NPri NSti SBfd SPer STes WFar WMnd
- 'Iris Prichard'	CPrp CTca EBee ELan EPfP GCra GLog GMaP LAst NBre NCGa NLar SRGP WFar
- 'Isis' ♀H4	CBcs CPrp CTri EBee EBrs ECGP ECtt ELan EPfP GCra GKir LBMP LRHS MMuc MRav NBir NCGa NGdn SBfd SEND SPer WKif WMnd WNew WTin
- 'J.C. Weguelin' ♀H4	EBee EPfP GKir NBir NBre NMRc NPnk SRms WCAu WMnd WWEG
§ - 'Karminglut'	EBee ECtt ELan EPfP GKir GLog GMaP MNrw NBir NGdn NPnk NVic SGSe WHoo WWEG
- 'Leonora'	CWan EBee EPfP LRHS MMuc NLar
- 'Little Doll'	CWCL ECtt GKir GLog GMac LAst MDKP MGos MNFA NBro NLar NPri WFar WWEG
- 'Little White Doll'	CPrp CWCL EBee ECtt GMac LAst MDKP MNFA NBre WFar WWEG
- 'Mariella'	EBee GMac
- 'Mrs Loewer'	MAvo
- 'Navajo Princess'	EBee
- 'Osprey' ♀H4	Widely available
- 'Pauline'	EBee ECtt ELon EPla GKir LAst MNrw MRav NBir NLar WFar WHoo WTin WWEG
- 'Perinne's Pink'	CWCL EBee EBrs EPfP NBPC NDov NLar NPnk NSti SUsu WCAu
- 'Pink Chablis' PBR	CWCL ECtt MAvo NBro NLar NMoo
- 'Purewell Giant'	CMac CMoH CTri EBee GBee GLog LHop LRHS NBro NLar SPer WGor WKif WMnd
- 'Purple Dome'	EBee ECtt EPla GKir GMaP LAst LRHS MMuc MRav NBir NBro NCGa NGdn SBfd SEND STes WMnd WTin WWEG
- 'Red Grape'	CTca EBee EBrs ECtt EWll LRHS MLLN MWhi NSti WBor WWEG
- 'Rosi'	EBee
- 'Rubra'	CPrp CSpr EBee GKir SRms
- 'Satin Doll' PBR	CBcs EBee ECtt EPfP LRHS
- 'Sweet Kate'	CBct CMac CWCL EBee ECtt LRHS LSRN MBNS MCCP NBPC NBro SRGP WBor WWFP
- 'Sylvana'	EBee GMac SApp
- 'Temptation'	ECtt MAsh
- 'Valour'	CSBt EBee WFar
- 'Zwanenburg Blue'	EBee ECha ECtt EHrv ELan GBee GKir GLog GMac LAst LRHS MLHP NCGa NPnk SGSe SPlb WMnd WWEG
'Angel Eyes'	ECtt MDKP MLLN
canaliculata	see *T. ohiensis*
§ ***fluminensis***	SChr
- 'Albovittata'	EShb
§ - 'Aurea' ♀H1	EShb
- 'Maiden's Blush' (v)	CSpe EShb SGar SRms WFoF
- 'Quicksilver' (v) ♀H1	EShb
- 'Variegata'	see *T. fluminensis* 'Aurea'
§ ***ohiensis***	CFee EBee LPBA MAvo
pallida 'Kartuz Giant'	WCot
§ - 'Purpurea' ♀H2-3	EOHP EShb
pendula	see *T. zebrina*
'Purple Sabre'	CBcs LAst SDys SMrm
purpurea	see *T. pallida* 'Purpurea'
sillamontana ♀H1	EOHP
spathacea	EShb
tricolor	see *T. zebrina*
virginiana	CMoH MWhi
- 'Alba'	CMac GCal WPer
* - 'Brevicaulis'	EBee ECha ECtt NBre NBro WWEG
§ - 'Caerulea Plena' (d)	CMHG EBee ELan EPfP EPla MRav NBPC SPer SRms STes WFar WTin WWEG
- 'Rubra'	SPlb
§ ***zebrina*** ♀H1	EShb
- ***pendula***	see *T. zebrina*
- 'Purpusii' ♀H1	SRms

Tragopogon (*Asteraceae*)

RCB/TQ M-1 new	WCot
crocifolius	CCVN CSpe EBee SPhx WCot
porrifolius	EBWF GCal ILis MCot SVic
pratensis	CArn EBWF NMir

Trapa (*Trapaceae*)

natans	CBen

Trautvetteria (*Ranunculaceae*)

carolinensis	CLAP EBee GEdr WCru WPrP
var. ***japonica***	
- - B&SWJ 10861	WCru
- var. ***occidentalis***	EBee GEdr WCru

Triadica (*Euphorbiaceae*)

sebifera	CPLG

Trichopetalum (*Anthericaceae*)

§ ***plumosum***	ECho

Trichostema (*Lamiaceae*)

dichotomum RCB RL 15	WCot

Tricuspidaria see *Crinodendron*

Tricyrtis ✿ (*Convallariaceae*)

	sp.	MWat
	B&SWJ 3229 from Taiwan	WCru
	from Taiwan	WFar
	'Adbane'	CAby CBct CChe CLAP EBee ELan EPPr EWes GKev IKil MMoz NGdn SGSe SMrm WFar WGwG WWEG
	affinis	CLAP GAbr GGar
	- B&SWJ 2804	WCru
	- B&SWJ 5640	WCru
	- B&SWJ 5645	WCru
	- B&SWJ 6182	WCru
	- B&SWJ 11169	WCru
	- 'Early Bird'	LEdu WCru WFar
	- 'Sansyoku'	GEdr
	'Amanagowa'	CLAP
	bakeri	see *T. latifolia*
	'Blue Wonder'	EBee LRHS LSou MSCN NGdn NLar SPer SPet
	dilatata	see *T. macropoda*
	'Empress'	CBct COIW EBee EBla ECha ELon EPfP EWTr EWes IBal LEdu LSou MAvo MSCN NBPC NCob NEgg NHol NSti SGSe SMrm SPet SUsu WFar WWEG
	flava	EBee EBrs LRHS WCru WFar
	formosana $\mathbb{Y}^{H4}$	Widely available
	- B&SWJ 306	CLAP EBla MNrw WFar
	- B&SWJ 355	WCru WFar
	- B&SWJ 3073	WCru
	- B&SWJ 3616	WCru
	- B&SWJ 3712	WCru WFar
	- B&SWJ 6705	CLAP WPrP
	- B&SWJ 6741	WCru
	- B&SWJ 6970	WCru
	- B&SWJ 7071	WFar
	- RWJ 10109	WCru
	- 'Dark Beauty'	CDes CEnt CLAP CPLG CWCL EBee ECtt EHrv EWTr MBri MCot MNrw NBPC NPri SGar SMrm SPad SPur SUsu WFar WPGP WWEG
	- dark-flowered	GAbr NCGa WFar
	- 'Emperor' (v)	EBee
	- 'Gilt Edge' (v)	Widely available
	- f. ***glandosa***	WFar
	- - B&SWJ 7084	WCru
	- aff. f. ***glandosa*** 'Blu-Shing Toad'	WCru WFar
	- var. ***grandiflora*** 'W-Hopping Toad'	WCru WFar
	- pale-flowered	CBct WFar WWEG
	- 'Purple Beauty'	EBee GKev LSou MDKP MNrw NMyG NPnk WClo
	- 'Samurai' (v)	CLAP CMil CWCL EPPr EWes NMoo NPnk WFar
	- 'Shelley's'	CBct CLAP NBro SMrm WFar WPrP WWEG
	- 'Small Wonder'	WCru WFar
	- 'Spotted Toad'	LEdu WCru
§	- Stolonifera Group	CAvo CBcs CMMP CMac EBee EBrs EHrv ELan EPfP GGar LEdu LRHS MCot NGdn NHol SDix WFar WMnd
	- - B&SWJ 7046	WCru WFar
	- 'Taiwan Toad'	WFar
	- 'Taroko Toad'	WCru WPrP
	- 'Tiny Toad'	WCru WFar
	- 'Variegata' (v)	CBct CWan LEdu MMHG NBir WBor WCru WFar
	- 'Velvet Toad'	WCru WFar
	'Golden Leopard'	CBct EBee EPfP LRHS NCGa NMyG NSti SPer SPet
	'Harlequin'	LEdu WAul WFar
§	***hirta***	Widely available
	- B&SWJ 2827	WCru
	- B&SWJ 5971	WCru
	- B&SWJ 11182	WCru
	- B&SWJ 11227	WCru
	- 'Alba'	CMac EHrv LRHS SGSe WFar
	- 'Albomarginata' (v)	CMac CPrp EAEE EBee EPPr EPfP EShb GCra LBMP LRHS MAvo MCot NEgg NHol NLar NMyG NSti SGSe SWvt WFar WPGP
	- 'Golden Gleam'	WCot WFar
	- 'Makinoi Gold'	WFar
	- 'Matsukaze'	CLAP CPom EWes MAvo SUsu WFar
	- 'Miyazaki'	CBct CFir CLAP CMac ECtt IFoB LBMP LRHS MAvo MCot MHer MNrw MTis NCGa NLar SMrs WFar WWEG
	- 'Taiwan Atrianne'	EAEE EBee ECtt IPot LRHS MDKP MNrw MRav NCGa NCob NEgg NHol WFar
	- 'Variegata' (v)	CBct CTri EBrs ELon EWes GCra LRHS MTis WCot WFar WHrl WWEG
N	Hototogisu	CBct CLAP CPom EAEE EBee EBla EBrs ECtt ELan ELon EWTr LHop LRHS MCot MTho NBir NEgg NHol NLar NMyG SDnm SMrs SPav WFar WHil WMnd WSpi WWEG
	ishiiana	CDes CLAP EBla EPPr MMoz SUsu WCot WCru WFar WP3GP WSHC
	- var. ***surugensis***	EBla LEdu WCru WFar
	'Ivory Queen'	WFar
	japonica	see *T. hirta*
	'Kohaku'	CBct CLAP EBla ELan EPPr EWes WFar WPGP WWEG
	lasiocarpa	CAby CBct CLAP LEdu MAvo NMyG WFar
	- B&SWJ 3635	CLAP EBla WCru WFar
	- B&SWJ 6861	WCru
	- B&SWJ 7013	WCru WPrP
	- B&SWJ 7103	WCru
	- 'Royal Toad'	WCru
§	***latifolia***	CAby CDes EBee ELan GAbr GGar GLog GMaP LEdu LRHS MNrw NGdn NLar SGSe WBVN WCru WFar WWEG
	- B&SWJ 10996 from Japan	WCru
	- from Japan	WFar
	- 'Yellow Sunrise'	CBcs EBee ECtt EPPr LRHS MCot NCGa
	'Lemon Lime' (v)	CBct MDKP SGSe WFar WWEG
	'Lightning Strike' (v)	CBct EBee ECtt EWes LEdu LSou MDKP NBPC NCob NHol NMyG NPnk WCot WFar
	'Lilac Towers'	CBct ELan LRHS MAvo WCru WFar WWEG
	macrantha	CMil GGar GKev GLog WCru WSHC
§	- subsp. ***macranthopsis***	CBct CLAP EBla EPot GEdr MDKP WCot WCru WFar
	- - 'Juro' (d)	WCru

	macranthopsis	see *T. macrantha* subsp. *macranthopsis*
N	***macropoda***	CBct EBee EBla ELan EPfP GAbr GLog GMaP LEdu LRHS MAvo NGdn SGSe SMad WFar WMnd WWEG
	- B&SWJ 1271 from Korea	EBla WCru WFar
	- B&SWJ 2804 from Japan	WCru
	- B&SWJ 5013	WCru WFar
	- B&SWJ 5556	WCru
	- B&SWJ 5847 from Japan	WCru WFar
	- B&SWJ 6209	WCru WFar
	- B&SWJ 8700	WCru WFar
	- B&SWJ 8829 from Korea	WCru WFar
	- from Yungi Temple, China	CLAP EBla EPPr MDKP NCGa WFar
	- variegated (v)	CBow
	maculata	WFar
	- HWJCM 470	WCru
	- HWJK 2010	WCru
	- HWJK 2411	WCru
	'Moonlight Treasure'^{PBR}	CLAP NHol WCot
	nana	WCru
	- 'Karasuba'	GEdr
	- 'Raven's Back'	WCru
	ohsumiensis	CBct CDes CLAP CPom EBla ECha GEdr LEdu MDKP MTho NMyG SUsu WCru WFar WPGP
	- 'Lunar Eclipse'	GEdr
	perfoliata	CLAP LEdu WCru WFar
	- 'Spring Shine' (v)	WCru WFar
	'Pink Freckles' **new**	LRHS LSou SPoG
	'Raspberry Mousse'	CDes CLAP CWCL EBee EHrv EKen IFoB IPot LHop LSou MAvo MBNS MWea NMoo NMyG NSti SMrm WPGP
	setouchiensis	WCru WFar
	'Shimone'	CHid CLAP CPom EBee ECha ELan NCGa SGSe WFar
	'Sinonome'	EBee IPot MAvo
	stolonifera	see *T. formosana* Stolonifera Group
	suzukii	WFar
	- RWJ 10111	WCru
	'Taipei Silk'	CMac EBee EKen GAbr IFoB LRHS LSou MAvo NLar SBfd
	'Tojen'	Widely available
	'Tresahor White'	WFar
	'Variegata' (*affinis* hybrid) (v)	WFar WWEG
	'Washfields'	WFar WPGP
	'White Towers'	Widely available
	'White Towers' spotted	WBrE

Trientalis (*Primulaceae*)

	europaea f. ***rosea***	WHil

Trifolium (*Papilionaceae*)

	angustifolium	CArn
	brandegeei **new**	CPBP
	fragiferum	EBWF
	incarnatum	CSpe MHer
	medium	EBWF
	ochroleucon	CAby CElw EBWF EBee EHrv EPPr GMaP LBMP LRHS MAvo MCCP MCot MMuc NSti SBch SGSe SSvw SWal WAul WCAu WCot WFar WMoo WWEG
	pannonicum	CBgR CCVN CMea EHrv GCal MNrw NBre SUsu WFar WTin
	pratense	EBWF MHer NMir NSco WSFF
	- 'Dolly North'	see *T. pratense* 'Susan Smith'
	- 'Ice Cool'	see *T. repens* 'Green Ice'
	- 'Purple Heart'	LRHS
	- 'Speech House' (v)	WAlt
	- 'Splash'	WAlt
§	- 'Susan Smith' (v)	CBre CCCN EBee EHoe EPfP EWes GCal MNrw NGHP NSti WFar
	repens	COld EBWF EHrv NSco SVic WSFF
	- 'Dragon's Blood'	EBee LEdu LLWG SMrm SVil WFar
	- 'Gold Net'	see *T. pratense* 'Susan Smith'
	- 'Good Luck'	MTho
§	- 'Green Ice'	CBre EAEE EBee EHoe LLWG LRHS MBNS NBir NCob NSti WAlt WFar WHal
	- 'Harlequin' (v)	EBee EHoe MHer MTho WAlt WCot WFar WMoo WOut
	- 'Hiccups' (v)	WAlt
	- pale pink-flowered	WAlt
	- 'Purpurascens'	CArn CBre CEnt EAEE ECGP EPfP GGar ILis LLWG LRHS MAsh MAvo MBNS MHer NEgg NSti SPoG WNew
§	- 'Purpurascens Quadrifolium'	CMea CWan EBee ECha ECho EHoe EPau EWes GAbr LBMP MCot NEgg NGHP NMir NPer NPri SPer SPlb WAlt WFar
	- 'Quadrifolium'	EDAr
	- 'Saint Patrick'	CNat
	- 'Tetraphyllum Purpureum'	see *T. repens* 'Purpurascens Quadrifolium'
	- 'Wheatfen'	CBow CRow EBee EHoe NDov NPer
	- 'William'	CBow ECGP LEdu NDov SPur WAlt WCot WFar
	rubens	Widely available
	- 'Drama'	MNrw SUsu
	- 'Peach Pink'	CSpe EBee EPPr EShb LHop MAvo MLLN MMHG NCob SPhx SSvw SUsu WCot
	- 'Red Feathers'	CSpr EPPr LRHS MWat MWea SGSe SMad SMrm WWEG

Triglochin (*Juncaginaceae*)

	maritimum	CRWN EBWF
	palustre	CRWN

Trigonella (*Papilionaceae*)

	foenum-graecum	CArn SIde

Trillidium see *Trillium*

Trillium ✿ (*Trilliaceae*)

	albidum	CWCL EBee ECho ELon GCrs GGar GMaP LLHF LRHS MAvo MNrw NMen SKHP SSpi SUsu WBVN WCot WCru WHal WWst
	angustipetalum	WCru
	apetalon	EBee GEdr WWst
	camschatcense	EBee GEdr LAma WCru
	- from Japan	WWst
§	***catesbyi***	CLAP CWCL EBee ECho EHrv EPot GEdr GKev LAma LLHF NHol NMyG WWst
	cernuum	CLAP ECho GCra LRHS NMyG WCru WSHC
	chloropetalum	EBee GBBs LRHS SSpi WFar WPGP
	- var. ***chloropetalum*** × ***parviflorum***	SKHP
§	- var. ***giganteum*** 🏆^{H4}	CLAP GEdr GKir NMen NSla SSpi WCru WWst
	- var. ***rubrum***	see *T. chloropetalum* var. *giganteum*
	- white-flowered	ECha
	cuneatum	Widely available

decipiens	WWst
decumbens	SKHP WWst
discolor	SKHP WWst
erectum ♀H4	Widely available
- f. ***albiflorum***	CFir CLAP EBee ECho GCrs GEdr GGar LAma MNrw NHol NMyG SKHP SSpi WCru WWst
- 'Beige'	GKev
- f. ***luteum***	CBct EPfP SKHP WWst
- red-flowered	GCrs WBVN
erectum × ***flexipes***	CLAP EBee ECho EHrv GEdr GGar MNrw NBir NMen SKHP SSpi WWst
flexipes	CLAP EBee ECho EHrv EPot GAuc GEdr GKev LAma MNrw NMen SKHP SSpi WCru
- erect	GAbr MNrw NMen WWst
- 'Harvington Selection'	LRHS MBri SKHP WWst
foetidissimum	SKHP WWst
govanianum	EBee WWst
grandiflorum ♀H4	Widely available
- 'Kath's Dwarf'	GEdr
- f. ***polymerum*** 'Flore Pleno' (d)	CLAP ECho MTho SCnR SKHP WCra WWst
- - 'Snowbunting' (d)	EBrs EWes GCrs GKir LRHS MMHG NHar WThu WWst
- 'Quicksilver'	SKHP
- f. ***roseum***	WCra WWst
kurabayashii	CAby CBct CFir CPLG CWCL EBee ECho ELon GCrs LRHS MNrw SKHP SSpi SUsu WBVN WCra WCru WHal WPGP WWst
lancifolium	WWst
ludovicianum	WWst
luteum ♀H4	Widely available
maculatum	EBee WWst
nivale	WWst
ovatum	CLAP CWCL EBee ELon NMen SSpi WBVN WHal
- f. ***hibbersonii***	GCra NMen
- 'Roy Elliott'	EPot
parviflorum	ECho GEdr NMen SKHP
pusillum	CLAP EBee ECho ELan EPot GAuc GBBs GEdr GGar GKev NHol NMen WAbe WWst
* - var. ***alabamicum***	SKHP
- var. ***virginianum***	CLAP LAma WCru
recurvatum	CBcs EBee ECho EHrv EPot GBBs GEdr GKev LAma NHol NMen NMyG NPnk SKHP WCru WFar WPnP WWst
reliquum	WWst
rivale ♀H3	CElw CLAP ECho EHrv GBBs GCrs ITim LLHF NMen WAbe WFar WWst
- NNS 04-460	WCot
- NNS 04-461	WCot
- pink-flowered	GEdr NMen
- 'Purple Heart'	CLAP GEdr
rugelii	CLAP EBee ECho EHrv EWes GAbr GAuc GMaP MNrw NMen SKHP SSpi WCru WWst
- Askival hybrids	EBee ECho MNrw NMen SKHP SSpi WWst
- 'Orchard Pink'	MNrw WWst
rugelii × ***vaseyi***	EHrv EWes MNrw NMen SKHP SSpi WWst
sessile	EBee ECho GBBs GKev GKir LAma NBPC NBir NMen NPnk SKHP SMrm WCot WFar WKif WPnP WShi WWst
- 'Rubrum'	see *T. chloropetalum* var. *giganteum*
simile	CLAP EBee ECho GAbr GCrs LLHF LRHS MNrw SKHP SSpi WWst
smallii	EBee WCru WWst
stamineum	ECho GEdr WCot WWst
stylosum	see *T. catesbyi*
sulcatum	CLAP EBee ECho EHrv EPot GAbr GAuc GCrs GEdr GMaP LRHS MBri MNrw NMen SKHP SSpi WCot WCru WFar WWst
taiwanense B&SWJ 3411 new	WCru
texanum	SKHP
tschonoskii	ECho GEdr LAma NMen
underwoodii	WWst
undulatum	EBee ECho GEdr LAma NHol NMen NMyG WCru WWst
vaseyi	CLAP EBee ECho EHrv EPot EWes GAbr GAuc GBBs GEdr GGar GKev LAma LRHS MNrw NMen SKHP SSpi WCru WWst
- horizontal inflorescence	MNrw WWst
viride	EBla GBBs WFar WPnP
viridescens	EBee ECho EPot GEdr LAma WFar WWst

Triosteum (*Caprifoliaceae*)

erythrocarpum	EBee
himalayanum	CLAP EBee GCal GKev
- BWJ 7907	WCru
- SDR 4406	GKev
pinnatifidum	CLAP CPom EBee GCal IMou

Tripetaleia (*Ericaceae*)

§ ***bracteata***	GAuc

Tripsacum (*Poaceae*)

dactyloides	EPPr

Tripterospermum (*Gentianaceae*)

B&SWJ 11297 from Malaysia	WCru
* aff. ***chevalieri*** B&SWJ 8359	WCru
cordifolium B&SWJ 081	WCru
distylum B&SWJ 11491 new	WCru
fasciculatum B&SWJ 7197	WCru
aff. ***hirticalyx*** B&SWJ 8264	WCru
- B&SWJ 11774	WCru
japonicum	GEdr LLHF WCot
- B&SWJ 8920	WCru
- B&SWJ 10876	WCru
lanceolatum B&SWJ 085	WCru
- RWJ 9918	WCru
taiwanense B&SWJ 1205	WCru
- RWJ 10115	WCru

Tripterygium (*Celastraceae*)

regelii	CBcs NLar
- B&SWJ 5453	WCru
- B&SWJ 10921	WCru
wilfordii	WCru
- WWJ 12009	WCru

Trisetum (*Poaceae*)

flavescens	GFor

Tristagma (*Alliaceae*)

nivale	EBee
- f. ***nivale*** F&W 10284	WCot

Triteleia (*Alliaceae*)

'4U'	CAvo CMea EBee ECho
bridgesii	CAvo EBee ECho GAuc
- NNS 00-731	WCot

californica	see *Brodiaea californica*
§ 'Corrina'	CAvo CFFs CMdw EBee ECho EPot MNrw
grandiflora	ECho NBre WCot
hyacinthina	EBee ECho WCot
ixioides	ECho
- 'Splendens'	EBee ECho NMen
- 'Starlight'	CAvo CFFs CTri EBee ECho EPot ERCP SBch SDeJ SPer
§ ***laxa***	ECho GAuc WBVN
- NNS 98-541	WCot
- 'Allure'	CAvo EBee ECho
§ - 'Koningin Fabiola'	CMea CTri EBee ECho EPfP EPot IPot LAma LRHS MNrw NBir SBch SDeJ SEND SPer WBrE WCot
* - var. ***nimia*** NNS 00-743	WCot
- Queen Fabiola	see *T. laxa* 'Koningin Fabiola'
lilacina	ECho
§ ***peduncularis***	EBee ECho WCot
- NNS 95-746	WCot
'Royal Blue' **new**	CMea ERCP
'Rudy'	CAvo CFFs CHid CMea CPou EBee EBrs ECho ERCP
× ***tubergenii***	ECho
uniflora	see *Ipheion uniflorum*

Trithrinax (*Arecaceae*)

brasiliensis	EAmu LPJP LPal SBig
campestris	CBrP EAmu EUJe LMaj LPal SBig

Tritoma see *Kniphofia*

Tritonia (*Iridaceae*)

crocata 🏆$^{H2-3}$	CPou ECho EPfP SBch
- 'Baby Doll'	CPrp CYeo EBee LEdu WHil
- 'Bridal Veil'	EPot
- 'Pink Sensation'	CDes CSpe EBee ECho EPot WHil
- 'Plymouth Pastel'	CDes WPrP
- 'Prince of Orange'	CPou
- 'Princess Beatrix'	CDes WCot
- 'Riversdale' **new**	ECho
- 'Serendipity'	CDes CPrp EBee WCon
- 'Tangerine'	CDes CPBP EPot
- white-flowered **new**	WHil
deusta **new**	CDes
§ ***disticha***	Widely available
subsp. ***rubrolucens***	
- - pale pink-flowered **new**	CTca
dubia	WCot
flabellifolia	ECho
florentiae	ECho
'Tanqua Karoo' **new**	
hyalina	CPou
karooica 'Middlepos' **new**	ECho
laxifolia	CPrp CTca EBee ECho EPot LEdu
lineata	CDes CPou EBee ECho WPGP WPrP
- 'Parvifolia'	EBee
pallida	ECho SPlb
rosea	see *T. disticha* subsp. *rubrolucens*
securigera	ECho
squalida	ECho

Trochocarpa (*Epacridaceae*)

clarkei	WThu
thymifolia	WAbe
- red-flowered	WAbe WThu

Trochodendron (*Trochodendraceae*)

aralioides	Widely available
- B&SWJ 1651 from Taiwan	WCru
- B&SWJ 6727 from Taiwan	WCru

Trollius (*Ranunculaceae*)

ACE 1187	GEdr
SDR 4816	GKev
acaulis	ECho EPot EWes GKev MTho WFar WPat
asiaticus	EBee ECho GKev LRHS WFar
§ ***chinensis***	ECha GCal GKev GKir NChi SWat
- 'Golden Queen' 🏆^{H4}	Widely available
× ***cultorum*** 'Alabaster'	Widely available
- 'Baudirektor Linne'	ECtt MRav NGdn WFar
- Bressingham hybrids	WFar
- 'Bressingham Sunshine'	LRHS
- 'Byrne's Giant'	EBee ECtt GBin WFar WPnP
- 'Canary Bird'	ELan EPfP GCal NGdn SRms WSpi
- 'Cheddar'	CSpe EBee EBla EBrs ECtt EPPr EPfP GCal GKir GMac LSou MBNS MBri MCCP MMHG MRav NBPC NBro NEgg NLar NPnk NPri SKHP SMrm WBor WFar WSpi WWEG
- 'Commander-in-Chief'	CDes EBee LRHS WFar WPnP
- 'Earliest of All'	CSam EBee EKen GKir MBri NGdn SPer WFar WSHC WWEG
- 'Empire Day' **new**	EBee MBri
- 'Etna'	EBee WFar WPnP WWEG
§ - 'Feuertroll'	CMea EBee ECha ECtt GKir LBMP LLWG LRHS MBri MCot MRav MSCN NBPC NCob NEgg SPoG SUsu WFar
- Fireglobe	see *T.* × *cultorum* 'Feuertroll'
- 'Glory of Leiden'	EBee
- 'Golden Cup'	NBir NGdn
- 'Golden Monarch'	WFar
- 'Goldquelle' 🏆^{H4}	EHon GKir
- 'Goliath'	EWes NCob WFar
- 'Helios'	CSam
- 'Lemon Queen'	CWat EBee ECtt EHrv EPfP GBin GMaP LPBA LRHS MBri MNFA MRav NBPC NLar NPnk SPer SWat WFar WSpi
- 'Maigold'	MAvo
- 'Meteor'	WFar
- new hybrids	WFar
- 'Orange Crest'	EBee GCal GKir WFar WHal WWEG
- 'Orange Globe'	EBee GAbr NBPC NCob SMrm WFar
- 'Orange Glow'	LLWG SMad
- 'Orange Princess' 🏆^{H4}	CElw CWat EBee EPfP GKir GMaP LLWG MCCP NBro NLar NPri SPer SRms
- 'Orange Queen'	SWvt
- 'Prichard's Giant'	CMHG EBee EBla ECtt ELan NBro NEgg NLBP WFar WSpi WWEG
§ - 'Superbus' 🏆^{H4}	CWCL EBee ECho ELan EPfP GKir GMaP LAst LRHS MBNS NGdn SPer WBrE WFar
- 'T. Smith'	NBro WFar WWEG
- 'Yellow Beauty'	WFar
europaeus	CBot COIW CRWN CWCL EBWF EBee ECha GCal GGar LAst LEdu LHop MLHP MMuc MRav NChi NCob NGdn NHol NMir SBfd SPet SRot STes SWat WAul WFar WHoo WTin WWEG
- SDR 5441	GKev
- SDR 5473	GKev
- 'Superbus'	see *T.* × *cultorum* 'Superbus'
farreri	ECho
hondoensis	EBee GCal LLHF LRHS NLar
ircuticus	EBee GKev
laxus	EWes
- 'Albiflorus'	NWCA

ledebourii misapplied	see *T. chinensis*
papavereus	see *T. yunnanensis* var. *yunnanensis*
pumilus	CAby EBee EBrs ECha ECho ELan EPfP GCal GGar GKev GKir GMaP LRHS NLar NWCA SBfd SGSe SPer WAbe WClo WFar WPer
- 'Wargrave'	ECho
ranunculinus	GKev
ranunculoides	GKev
riederianus	LRHS
stenopetalus	CDes EWes GKir MBri MNrw MRav WFar
vaginatus	GKev
yunnanensis	EBee GKev WFar WPnP
- orange-flowered	GKev
§ - var. ***yunnanensis***	EBee

Tropaeolum ✿ (*Tropaeolaceae*)

azureum	CCCN CPla EPot
brachyceras	CCCN EBee ECho EPot GGar WCot
ciliatum $\mathbb{Y}^{H1}$	CAvo CCCN CFir CGHE CPla CSpr CStu EBee ECho ELan EPot GCal MTho NBid NLar SPhx WCot WCru WFar WHer WPGP
incisum	CCCN EBee
lepidum	CPla
majus Alaska Series (v) $\mathbb{Y}^{H3}$	CPrp MNHC SBch SEND SIde WJek
- 'Apricot Twist'	GBee
- 'Crimson Beauty'	CSpe
§ - 'Darjeeling Double' (d) $\mathbb{Y}^{H4}$	GBee GCal
- 'Darjeeling Gold'	see *T. majus* 'Darjeeling Double'
- 'Empress of India'	CPrp MNHC WJek
- 'Hermine Grashoff' (d) $\mathbb{Y}^{H2-3}$	CSWP CSpe GBee GCal NPer
- 'Margaret Long' (d)	CSpe GCal
* - 'Peaches and Cream'	WJek
- 'Red Wonder'	CCCN CSWP CSpe EPfP LSou SMrm
- 'Ruffled Apricot'	CSpe
- 'Sunset Pink'	CPrp
- Tom Thumb mixed	MNHC WJek
pentaphyllum	CAvo CSpe EBee ECho ELan EWes GCal GGar LLHF MTho WCot
peregrinum	CSpe ECho SBfd
polyphyllum	CBcs CCCN EBee ECho EPfP EPot GCrs NBir SCnR SMHy WAbe WBVN WPGP
rhomboideum	EBee
sessilifolium	EBee ECho
smithii **new**	WCot
speciosum $\mathbb{Y}^{H4}$	Widely available
sylvestre	EWld
tricolor $\mathbb{Y}^{H1}$	CAvo CCCN EBee ECho ELan EPot GCal GGar MTho WBor
tuberosum	CEnd ECho GPoy
- var. ***lineamaculatum*** 'Ken Aslet' $\mathbb{Y}^{H3}$	CBcs CCCN CSpe EBee ECha ECho ELan EOHP EPfP EPot GAbr GGar IFro LAma LRHS MTho SPer SPoG WCom WCru WFar

Trymalium (*Rhamnaceae*)

ledifolium	CTrC

Tsuga ✿ (*Pinaceae*)

canadensis	CDul EHul NWea WDin WEve
- 'Abbott's Dwarf'	CDoC CKen MGos NHol
§ - 'Abbott's Pygmy'	CKen
- 'Albospica' (v)	WFar WGor
- 'Arnold Gold Weeper'	CKen
- 'Aurea' (v)	NHol NLar WEve
- 'Bacon Cristate'	CKen
- 'Beehive'	ECho WGor
- 'Betty Rose' (v)	CKen
- 'Birkett's White' **new**	CKen
- 'Brandley'	CKen
§ - 'Branklyn'	CKen
- 'Cappy's Choice'	CKen
- 'Cinnamonea'	CKen
- 'Coffin'	CKen
- 'Cole's Prostrate'	CKen MAsh NHol NLar SLim
- 'Coryhill'	ECho SCoo
- 'Creamey' (v)	CKen
- 'Curley'	CKen
- 'Curtis Ideal'	CKen
- 'Dr Hornbeck'	see *T. canadensis* 'Hornbeck'
- 'Essex'	NHol
* - 'Everitt's Dense Leaf'	CKen
- 'Everitt's Golden'	CKen
- 'Fantana'	ECho LRHS MAsh NHol NLar SCoo SLim WEve
- 'Gentsch White' (v)	MGos NLar SMad
- 'Gracilis'	WThu
- 'Hedgehog' **new**	CDoC NLar
§ - 'Hornbeck' **new**	CKen
- 'Horsford'	CKen NLar
- 'Horstmann' No 1	CKen
- 'Hussii'	CKen NHol NLar
- 'Jacqueline Verkade'	CKen NLar
- 'Jeddeloh' $\mathbb{Y}^{H4}$	CDoC CMac ECho EPla EPot IFFs LRHS MAsh MGos NEgg NHol SCoo SLim SPoG WDin WEve
- 'Jervis'	CKen NHol NLar
- 'Julianne'	CKen
- 'Kingsville Spreader'	CKen
- 'Little Joe'	CKen
- 'Little Snow'	CKen
I - 'Lutea'	CKen
- 'Many Cones'	CKen
- 'Minima'	CKen
- 'Minuta'	CDoC CKen ECho MGos NLar SCoo SPoG WGor
- 'Moon Frost'	NLar
- 'Nana'	WDin
- 'Palomino'	CKen NLar
- 'Pendula' $\mathbb{Y}^{H4}$	CKen ECho EPfP LRHS MAsh SLim WDin WEve WFar
- 'Pincushion'	CKen
- 'Prostrata'	see *T. canadensis* 'Branklyn'
- 'Pygmaea'	see *T. canadensis* 'Abbott's Pygmy'
- 'Rugg's Washington Dwarf'	CKen
- 'Snowflake'	CKen MGos
- 'Stewart's Gem'	CKen
- 'Verkade Petite'	CKen
- 'Verkade Recurved'	CKen NLar
- 'Von Helms' Dwarf'	CKen
- 'Warnham'	CKen ECho LRHS MAsh SCoo
caroliniana 'La Bar Weeping'	CKen
chinensis	CKen
- var. ***chinensis*** **new**	NMun
diversifolia 'Gotelli'	CKen
dumosa **new**	CKen
heterophylla $\mathbb{Y}^{H4}$	CBcs CCVT CDul CLnd EPfP IFFs LBuc NWea SMad SPer STre WDin WEve
- 'Iron Springs'	CKen
- 'Laursen's Column'	CKen
- 'Thorsens Weeping'	CKen
menziesii	see *Pseudotsuga menziesii*
mertensiana 'Blue Star'	CKen NLar

	- 'Elizabeth'	CKen
	- 'Glauca'	CKen
I	- 'Glauca Nana'	CKen
I	- 'Horstmann'	CKen
	- 'Quartz Mountain'	CKen
	sieboldii 'Baldwin'	CKen
	- 'Green Ball'	CKen
	- 'Honeywell Estate'	CKen
	- 'Nana'	CKen

Tsusiophyllum (*Ericaceae*)

	tanakae	see *Rhododendron tsusiophyllum*

Tuberaria (*Cistaceae*)

	lignosa	WAbe

Tulbaghia ✿ (*Alliaceae*)

	acutiloba	CPen CTca EBee MHom NHoy WPrP
	'African Moon'	NHoy
	alliacea	CAvo EBla ECho EShb MHom NHoy WCot
	alliacea × ***violacea***	ECho
	'Bob Brown' new	WPrP
	'Bright Eyes' new	NHoy
	capensis	CPou EBee LPio NBir NHoy WCot WPrP
	capensis × ***violacea*** CGV 1970 new	WPrP
	'Cariad' new	WPrP
	cernua CD&R 199	CDes WPrP
	- hybrid	NHoy WPrP
	cernua × ***violacea***	WPrP
§	***coddii***	EBee MHom NHoy WCot WPrP
	coddii × ***violacea***	NHoy WPrP
	cominsii	CPLG SBch SCnR WCom WPrP
	- 'Harry Hay's Pink'	NHoy
	cominsii × ***violacea***	CAvo CPLG CTca EBee MHom NHoy WPrP
	cominsii × ***violacea*** soft pink-flowered new	WPrP
	'Cosmic'	CPen CPou NHoy WPrP
	'Crystal'	NHoy
	'Dreaming Spires'	NHoy
	dregeana	NHoy WCot
	'Elaine Ann'	NHoy
	'Enigma'	NHoy
	'Fairy Snow'	CDes WPrP
	'Fairy Star'	CDes CTca EBee EShb LEdu NHoy SUsu WCot WPGP WPrP
	fragrans	see *T. simmleri*
	- 'Alba'	ELan EPot EWTr
*	***fragrantissima***	WCot
	galpinii	CPen NHoy NWCA WPrP
	'Grey Dawn'	NHoy
	'Hazel'	CPen CPou NHoy WPrP
	'Janet'	NHoy
	'John May's Special'	CAby CDes CKno EBee EShb MHom NHoy NWCA SUsu WCot WHil WPGP WPrP
	leucantha	CDes CTca EBee MHom NHoy NWCA WPGP WPrP
	- H&B 11996	CDes WPrP
	- from Sentinel Peak, South Africa	WPrP
	'Lilian' new	WPrP
	maritima	see *T. violacea* var. *maritima*
	Marwood seedling	EBee MCot MHom NHoy
	mixed seedlings new	NHoy
	montana	CDes CStu EBee NHoy WCot WPGP WPrP
	natalensis	CPou CPrp EBee ECho NHoy WHoo
	- B&V 421	CDes
	- - clone 1 white	NHoy WPrP
	- - clone 2 pink	NHoy WPrP
	- CD&R 84	NHoy WPrP
	- pink-flowered	CTca ECho MHom NHoy WPrP
	- white-flowered new	CTca
	natalensis × ***verdoorniae***	WPrP
	natalensis × ***verdoorniae*** VOS 1966	WPrP
	natalensis × ***violacea***	NHoy NWCA WPrP
	poetica	see *T. coddii*
	'Premier' new	NHoy
	'Purple Eyes'	WPrP
	'Rainbow'	NHoy
§	***simmleri***	CBgR CPou EBee EBla ECho EHrv EPot EShb EWes GGar LAma LEdu LPio NHoy WPrP
	- 'Cheryl Renshaw'	CDes WPrP
	- pink-flowered	CPen CTca WPGP
	- 'Snow Queen'	CPrp
	- white-flowered	CPen CPou CTca ELon ERCP NHoy WPrP
	'Snowball'	NHoy
	'Suzanne'	NHoy
	verdoorniae	NHoy WHil
	violacea	Widely available
*	- 'Alba'	EBee EBla EPPr GCal LPio MHer NHoy NMRc SWat WFar WHoo WTin
	- 'Dissect White'	NHoy WPrP
I	- 'Fine Form'	CKno NHoy SMHy WKif
*	- ***grandiflora***	CAvo
	- 'John Rider'	NHoy NWCA WPrP
	- 'Lowan'	NWCA WPrP
*	- var. ***maritima***	CPMA CPen CPrp EDif EShb GGar MHom NBid NHoy NWCA SMrm WCot WPrP
	- var. ***obtusa***	NHoy WPrP
	- 'Pallida'	CAvo CDes CMdw CPne CPou CTca ECho LEdu LPio NHoy NWCA WPGP WPrP
	- 'Pearl'	CPou NHoy WPrP
	- 'Peppermint Garlic'	CDes CTca WPrP
	- from RBGE	MHom NHoy
	- var. ***robustior***	CPou CTca EBla EWes NHoy WPrP
	- 'Seren' new	WPrP
§	- 'Silver Lace' (v)	Widely available
	- 'Variegata'	see *T. violacea* 'Silver Lace'
	- var. ***violacea***	NHoy WPrP
	- 'White Goddess'	CPou WPrP
	- 'White Star'	EBee WHil
	violacea × ***violacea*** var. ***maritima*** new	WPrP

Tulipa ✿ (*Liliaceae*)

	'Abba' (2)	LRHS SDeJ
	'Absalon' (9)	LAma
	'Abu Hassan' (3)	CAvo CFFs CMea ERCP LAma MBri SDeJ SPhx
	acuminata (15)	CAvo CFFs CHid CTca EBrs ECho ERCP LAma LRHS MMHG NMin SDeJ
	'Ad Rem' (4)	MBri
	'Addis' (14) ♀H4	LAma
	'African Queen' (3)	LAma
	aitchisonii	see *T. clusiana*
	'Aladdin' (6)	LAma LRHS SDeJ
	'Aladdin's Record' (6)	CAvo CFFs
	albertii (15)	ECho LAma NMin WWst

'Aleppo' (7)	SDeJ
'Alfred Cortot' (12) 🏆H4	LAma SDeJ
'Allegretto' (11)	LRHS MBri
altaica (15) 🏆H4	ECho EPot LAma
amabilis	see *T. boogiana*
'American Eagle' (7)	ERCP SDeJ
'Analita' (13) **new**	LAma
'Ancilla' (12) 🏆H4	CAvo CFFs LAma
'Angélique' (11) 🏆H4	CAvo CFFs CFox CTca EBrs EPfP ERCP LAma LRHS MCot NBir SPer SPhx
'Annie Schilder' (3)	ERCP LRHS
'Antoinette' PBR (5)	LAma LRHS SPer
'Apeldoorn' (4)	EBrs EGxp LAma LRHS MBri SDeJ SPer
'Apeldoorn's Elite' (4) 🏆H4	LAma LRHS MBri SDeJ
'Apricot Beauty' (1) 🏆H4	CFox CHid CTca EBrs EPfP ERCP LAma LRHS MBri MCot NBir SDeJ SPer
'Apricot Impression' PBR (4) **new**	LAma
'Apricot Jewel'	see *T. linifolia* (Batalinii Group) 'Apricot Jewel'
'Apricot Parrot' (10) 🏆H4	CAvo CFFs CFox EBrs EPfP LAma MBri MCot SPer
'Arabian Mystery' (3)	CAvo CFFs CFox ERCP LAma SDeJ
'Artist' (8) 🏆H4	CFox EBrs ERCP LAma
'Attila' (3)	CAvo CFFs CFox EBrs LAma
aucheriana (15) 🏆H4	EBrs ECho EPot LAma LLHF NMin
'Aurea'	see *T. greigii* 'Aurea'
australis (15)	ECho
aximensis (15)	ECho LAma
'Bacchus' (7)	LAma
bakeri	see *T. saxatilis* Bakeri Group
'Ballade' (6) 🏆H4	CAvo CFFs ERCP LAma MCot
'Ballerina' (6) 🏆H4	CAvo CFFs CFox CMea CTca EBrs ECho EPfP ERCP IFro LAma LRHS MBri MCot SPer SPhx
'Banja Luka' (4)	SDeJ
'Barbados' (7) **new**	LAma
'Barcelona' (3) 🏆H4	ERCP
'Bastogne Parrot' PBR (10) **new**	LAma
batalinii	see *T. linifolia* Batalinii Group
'Beau Monde' (3) 🏆H4 **new**	SDeJ
'Beauty of Apeldoorn' (4)	LAma LRHS MBri
'Beauty Queen' (1)	EBrs
'Belicia' (2)	LAma
'Bellflower' (7)	LAma
'Bellona' (3)	SDeJ
'Berlioz' (12)	SDeJ
'Bernadette' (15)	LRHS
biebersteiniana (15)	ECho NMin
§ ***biflora*** (15)	CTca ECho EPot GKev LAma LRHS SDeJ WShi
bifloriformis (15)	ECho WWst
I - 'Maxima' (15)	ECho NMin
- 'Starlight' (15) 🏆H4	ECho WWst
'Big Chief' (4) 🏆H4	LAma
'Big Smile' (5)	LRHS
'Black Hero' (11)	CAvo CFFs EBrs ERCP LAma LRHS MCot SPer
'Black Jewel' (7)	ERCP LAma SDeJ
'Black Parrot' (10) 🏆H4	CAvo CFFs CFox CHid EBrs EPfP ERCP LAma LRHS MBri MCot SDeJ SPer
'Black Stallion' (11)	LAma
'Black Swan' (5)	SDeJ
'Bleu Aimable' (5)	CAvo CFFs ERCP MCot SDeJ
'Blue Diamond' (11)	CAvo CFFs ERCP SPer
'Blue Heron' (7) 🏆H4	CAvo CFFs CFox ERCP LAma MCot SDeJ
'Blue Parrot' (10)	CAvo CFFs EPfP ERCP LAma LRHS SDeJ
'Blue Ribbon' (3)	CAvo CFFs
Blueberry Ripple	see *T.* 'Zurel'
'Blushing Beauty' (5)	SDeJ
'Blushing Bride' (5)	SDeJ
'Boutade' (14)	NPer
'Bridesmaid' (5)	LAma
'Burgundy' (6)	CAvo CFFs CFox CTca EBrs ERCP LAma LRHS SPhx
'Burgundy Lace' (7)	LAma SDeJ
'Burning Heart' (4) **new**	SDeJ
'Café Noir' (5)	ERCP LAma
'Cairo' PBR	ERCP LRHS
'Calgary' (3) 🏆H4	EBrs EPfP LAma LRHS
'Calibra' (7)	LRHS
'Canasta' (7)	LRHS
'Candela' (13) 🏆H4	LAma SDeJ
'Candy Club' (5)	LAma
'Canova' (7) **new**	SDeJ
'Cantata' (13)	LAma
'Cape Cod' (14)	LAma
'Cardinal Mindszenty' (2)	ERCP SDeJ
carinata (15)	ECho LRHS NMin
'Carlton' (2)	MCot
'Carnaval de Nice' (11/v) 🏆H4	CAvo CFFs CTca ERCP LAma LRHS MBri SDeJ SPer
'Cassini' (3)	CFox LAma SDeJ
§ ***celsiana*** (15)	ECho LAma WWst
'China Lady' (14) 🏆H4 **new**	SDeJ
'China Pink' (6) 🏆H4	CAvo CFFs CTca EBrs EPfP ERCP LAma LRHS MBri SPhx
'China Town' (8) 🏆H4	EBrs ERCP LAma LRHS MBri SDeJ
'Christmas Dream' (1)	EBrs SDeJ
'Christmas Marvel' (1)	EBrs LAma
chrysantha Boiss. ex Baker	see *T. montana*
'Claudia' (6)	EPfP
'Cloud Nine' (5)	ECho
§ ***clusiana*** (15)	ECho ERCP LAma MSSP NMin SPhx WHer
- f. ***cashmeriana***	SPhx
- var. ***chrysantha*** (15) 🏆H4	CAvo CFFs CGrW ECho LAma LRHS SBch SPhx WHoo WShi
- - 'Tubergen's Gem' (15)	ECho EPot LAma LRHS MBri SPhx
- 'Cynthia' (15) 🏆H4	CTca ECho EPot ERCP LAma LRHS MSSP NMin SDeJ SPhx
- 'Sheila' (15)	ECho NMin SPhx
§ - var. ***stellata*** (15)	ECho
'Colour Spectacle' PBR (5)	LSou
'Columbine' (5)	ECho LAma
'Concerto' (13)	CFox MBri NPer SDeJ
'Corona' (12)	ECho SDeJ
'Cortina' (9) **new**	SDeJ
'Couleur Cardinal' (3)	EBrs LAma SDeJ
cretica (15)	ECho EPot LAma NMin WWst
'Cum Laude' (5)	LAma LRHS
'Cummins' (7)	CAvo CFFs ERCP
'Curly Sue' (7)	CAvo CFFs ERCP LAma LRHS
'Czaar Peter' (14) 🏆H4	CAvo CFFs CFox EPfP MBri NPer
'Dance' (13) **new**	SDeJ
'Dancing Show' (8)	LAma
dasystemon (15)	ECho LAma
dasystemonoides (15)	ECho WWst
'Davenport' (7)	ERCP
'David Teniers' (2)	ERCP
'Daydream' (4) 🏆H4	EGxp SPer
'Deirdre' (8)	ERCP
'Diana' (1)	CFox
didieri misapplied	see *T. passeriniana*
'Doll's Minuet' (8)	ERCP LAma SPer
'Don Quichotte' (3) 🏆H4	MBri SDeJ
'Donna Bella' (14) 🏆H4	EPfP SDeJ

	'Dordogne' (5) ♀^{H4}	LRHS SDeJ
	'Double Price' (2)	ERCP
	'Douglas Bader' (5)	CAvo CFFs
	'Dreamboat' (14)	MBri
	'Dreaming Maid' (3)	EGxp LAma
	'Dreamland' (5) ♀^{H4}	MBri
	'Duc van Tol Max Cramoisie' (1) **new**	LAma
	'Duc van Tol Primrose' (1) **new**	LAma
	'Duc van Tol Red and Yellow' (I)	WHer
	'Duc van Tol Rose' (1)	LAma
	'Duc van Tol Salmon' (1)	LAma
	'Duc van Tol Violet' (1) **new**	LAma
	'Duc van Tol White' (1) **new**	LAma
	'Early Harvest' (12) ♀^{H4}	CAvo CFFs SDeJ
	'Early Star' (14) ♀^{H4}	CMea
	'Easter Surprise' (14) ♀^{H4}	MBri SDeJ
	eichleri	see *T. undulatifolia*
	'Electra' (5)	LAma MBri
	'Elegans Alba' (6)	LAma
	'Elegant Lady' (6)	CAvo CFFs EBrs EPfP LAma LRHS MCot SPer
	'Esperanto' (8/v) ♀^{H4}	LAma SDeJ
	'Estella Rijnveld' (10)	EBrs EGxp LAma LRHS MBri
	'Esther' (5)	ERCP
	'Eternal Flame' (2)	LAma
	'Exotic Emperor'	LAma
	'Fancy Frills' (7) ♀^{H4}	ERCP LAma LRHS SDeJ
	'Fantasy' (10) ♀^{H4}	LAma
	'Fashion' (12)	EPfP
	ferganica (15)	ECho LAma NMin
	'Fidelio' (3) ♀^{H4} **new**	SDeJ
	'Fire Queen' (3) ♀^{H4}	ERCP LAma
	'Flair' (1)	LAma SDeJ
	'Flaming Parrot' (10)	CAvo CFFs ERCP LAma LRHS MBri
I	'Flaming Purissima' (13)	CAvo CFFs LRHS SDeJ
	'Flaming Springgreen' (8)	CAvo CFFs ERCP LAma LRHS
	'Florosa' (8)	ERCP SDeJ
	'Foxtrot'^{PBR} (2)	ERCP
	'Françoise' (3) **new**	SDeJ
	'Fringed Beauty' (7) ♀^{H4}	ERCP
	'Fringed Family' (7) **new**	SDeJ
	'Fritz Kreisler' (12)	LAma
	'Fulgens' (6)	LAma
	'Für Elise' (14)	SDeJ
	'Garden Party' (3) ♀^{H4}	LAma SDeJ
	'Gavota' (3)	CAvo CFFs CFox EGxp EPfP ERCP LAma LRHS MCot SDeJ SPer
	'Gemma' (10)	LAma
	'Generaal de Wet' (1)	EBrs LAma MBri SDeJ
	'Georgette' (5)	LAma LSou MBri
	'Gerbrand Kieft' (11) ♀^{H4}	ERCP
	'Giuseppe Verdi' (12)	LAma MBri
	'Glück' (12) ♀^{H4}	ECho
	'Golden Apeldoorn' (4)	EBrs LAma LRHS MBri SDeJ
	'Golden Artist' (8)	EPfP LAma LRHS
	'Golden Emperor' (13)	EPfP LAma SPer
	'Golden Melody' (3)	MCot
	'Golden Oxford' (4)	LAma
	'Golden Parade' (4)	LAma
	'Gordon Cooper' (4)	SDeJ
	'Goudstuk' (12)	LAma
	'Green Eyes' (8)	SDeJ
	'Green River' (8) **new**	SDeJ
	'Green Wave' (10)	ERCP LAma LRHS SDeJ
§	***greigii*** 'Aurea' (14)	WWst
	grengiolensis (15)	ECho LAma WWst
	'Groenland' (8)	CAvo CFFs CFox ERCP LAma LRHS MBri MCot SPer
	'Gudoshnik' (4)	LAma
	hageri (15)	ECho LAma MBri
	- 'Red Cup' (13) **new**	NMin
	- 'Splendens' (15)	CFox ECho EPot LAma SPhx WHoo
	'Hamilton' (7) ♀^{H4}	LAma
	'Hans Mayer' (4)	LRHS
	'Happy Family' (3)	LAma
	'Happy Generation' (3)	LAma MBri
	'Happy Hour' (7)	ERCP
	'Havran' (3)	CAvo CFFs ERCP LAma
	'Heart's Delight' (12)	CFox ECho LAma MBri SDeJ
	'Hemisphere' (3)	EPfP ERCP LAma SPer
	'Hermitage' (3)	ERCP LAma
	heweri (15)	ECho LAma NMin
	'Hillstar' (7)	LRHS
	'Holland Bouquet' (3) **new**	LAma
	'Holland Chic'	LAma LRHS
	'Hollandia' (3)	LRHS
	'Hollands Glorie' (4) ♀^{H4}	SDeJ
	'Hollywood' (8)	LAma
	'Honeymoon' (7) **new**	LAma
§	***hoogiana*** (15)	ECho WWst
	'Hotpants' (3) **new**	LAma
§	***humilis*** (15)	CGrW ECho EWTr LAma MBri WShi
	- 'China Carol' (15)	ECho ERCP SPhx
	- 'Eastern Spice' (15)	ECho LAma NMin
	- 'Eastern Star' (15)	ECho GKev LAma MBri NMin SMrm SPhx
§	- 'Lilliput' (15)	CMea ECho EPot GKev LAma LRHS NMin SPhx
	- 'Magenta Queen' (15)	ECho LRHS
	- 'Odalisque' (15)	ECho EPot ERCP GGar GKev LAma LRHS NMin SPhx
	- 'Pegasus' (15)	NMin
	- 'Persian Pearl' (15)	CAvo CFFs CFox EBrs ECho EPfP EPot ERCP LAma LRHS MBri NMin SBch SDeJ SPer
	- var. ***pulchella*** Albocaerulea Oculata Group (15)	CMea CPou CTca ECho EPot ERCP GKev LAma LLHF LRHS NMin SPhx WWst
§	- Violacea Group (15)	CAvo CFFs CFox CMea ECho LAma MBri
	- - black base (15)	ECho EPot ERCP GKev MBri NMin
	- - yellow base (15)	ECho EPot LAma
	- 'Zephyr' (15)	NMin
	'Humming Bird' (8)	LAma
	'Ile de France' (5)	LAma SDeJ SPer
	iliensis (15)	ECho EPot NMin WWst
	'India' (3)	ERCP
	'Indian Summer' (3) **new**	MCot
	ingens (15)	ECho LAma NMin SPhx WWst
	'Insulinde' (9)	LAma
	'Inzell' (3)	EPfP LAma
	'Ivory Floradale' (4) ♀^{H4}	LAma SDeJ
	'Jackpot' (3)	ERCP LRHS MCot
	'Jan Reus' (3)	CAvo CFFs
	'Jazz' (6)	ERCP LRHS
	'Jeantine' (12) ♀^{H4}	EPfP
	'Jewel of Spring' (4) ♀^{H4}	LAma
	'Joffre' (1)	MBri
	'Johann Strauss' (12)	ECho LAma MBri
	'Juan' (13) ♀^{H4}	MBri
	'Judith Leyster' (3)	LRHS
	julia (15)	ECho NMin
	'Karel Doorman' (10)	LAma
	kaufmanniana (12)	ECho EPot
§	'Kees Nelis' (3)	MBri
	'Keizerskroon' (1) ♀^{H4}	LAma SDeJ
	'Kingsblood' (5) ♀^{H4}	EBrs SDeJ
	'Knight Rider' **new**	MCot

kolpakowskiana (15) 🏆^{H4}	ECho EPfP EPot ERCP LAma LRHS MBri SBch WShi
kurdica (15)	ECho LAma SPhx WWst
- purple-flowered (15)	ECho WWst
- red-flowered (15)	WWst
'Lac van Rijn' (1)	EBrs LAma
* 'Lady Diana' (14)	MBri
'Lady Jane' (15) 🏆^{H4}	CAvo CFFs EBrs ECho ERCP MSSP NMin SPer SPhx
'Lady Night' (3)	LRHS
'Lambada' (7) 🏆^{H4}	LRHS
lanata (15)	ECho NMin
'Latvian Gold' (15)	ECho NMin
'Leen van der Mark' (3)	LAma LRHS MBri
'Libretto Parrot' (10)	LAma SDeJ
'Lighting Sun' (4) new	LAma
'Lilac Perfection' (11)	CTca ERCP MBri
'Lilac Wonder'	see *T. saxatilis* (Bakeri Group) 'Lilac Wonder'
'Lilliput'	see *T. humilis* 'Lilliput'
linifolia (15) 🏆^{H4}	CAvo CFFs ECho EPfP EPot ERCP LAma MBri NMin SBch SPhx WShi
§ - Batalinii Group (15) 🏆^{H4}	ECho LAma MBri SPhx
§ - - 'Apricot Jewel' (15)	CGrW ECho EPot GKev
- - 'Bright Gem' (15) 🏆^{H4}	ECho EPot GKev LAma LRHS MBri SBch SPer SPhx
- - 'Bronze Charm' (15)	CAvo CFFs CMea ECho EPot LAma MBri NMin SDeJ SPhx
- - 'Honky Tonk' (15) 🏆^{H4}	CMea ECho NMin SPhx
- - 'Red Gem' (15)	ECho GKev LAma SPhx
- - 'Red Hunter' (15) 🏆^{H4}	ECho ERCP SPer
- - 'Red Jewel' (15)	ECho
- - 'Yellow Jewel' (15)	ECho LAma SPhx
§ - Maximowiczii Group (15)	ECho EPot LAma
'Lipgloss' (3)	LAma
'Little Beauty' (15) 🏆^{H4}	CAvo CFFs CFox CMea CSam ECho GGar GKev LAma LRHS MBri SBch SDeJ WHoo
'Little Princess' (15) 🏆^{H4}	CAvo CFFs CMea CSam ECho EPfP GGar LAma LRHS
'Lovely Surprise' (14)	SDeJ
'Lucky Strike' (3)	MBri
§ 'Lustige Witwe' (3)	SDeJ
'Mabel' (9)	LAma
§ 'Madame Lefeber' (13)	LRHS MBri
'Magier' (5)	MBri
'Maja' (7)	CAvo CFFs CFox MBri MCot
'March of Time' (14)	MBri
'Mariette' (6)	LAma LRHS MBri
'Marilyn' (6)	EBrs ERCP LAma LRHS
marjolletii (15)	CAvo CFFs EBrs ECho LAma NMin SPhx
'Maroon'	ERCP
'Mary Ann' (14)	LAma
'Matchpoint' new	ERCP
'Maureen' (5) 🏆^{H4}	EBrs EGxp LAma LRHS
mauritiana (15)	ECho
- 'Cindy' (15)	ECho NMin
maximowiczii	see *T. linifolia* Maximowiczii Group
'Maytime' (6)	CAvo CFFs EBrs ERCP LAma LRHS MBri MCot
'Maywonder' (11) 🏆^{H4}	MBri MCot
'Menton' (5) 🏆^{H4}	LAma LRHS
Merry Widow	see *T.* 'Lustige Witwe'
'Mickey Mouse' (1)	MBri
'Miskodeed' (14) new	SDeJ
'Miss Holland' (3)	MBri
'Mona Lisa' (6)	LAma LRHS SDeJ
'Monsella' (2)	LRHS
§ ***montana*** (15)	CTca ECho EPfP EPot LAma LRHS NMin
- yellow-flowered	ECho LAma NMin WWst
'Monte Carlo' (2) 🏆^{H4}	CFox LAma LRHS MBri
'Montreux' (2)	ECho LAma
'Mount Tacoma' (11)	CAvo CFFs CFox EBrs EPfP ERCP LAma LRHS MBri MCot SPer
'Mr Van der Hoef' (2)	LAma MBri SDeJ
'Mrs John T. Scheepers' (5) 🏆^{H4}	MCot
'Muriel' (10)	ERCP
'My Support' (14)	LRHS
'Negrita' (3)	CFox EGxp ERCP LAma LRHS MBri MCot SDeJ SPer
neustruevae (15)	ECho EPot NMin SPhx
'New Design' (3/v)	EBrs ERCP LAma MBri
'Ollioules' (4) 🏆^{H4}	SDeJ
'Olympic Flame' (4) 🏆^{H4} new	SDeJ
'Orange Bouquet' (3) 🏆^{H4}	LAma LRHS MBri
'Orange Breeze' (13)	LRHS
'Orange Elite' (14)	MBri
'Orange Emperor' (13) 🏆^{H4}	CAvo CFFs EBrs LAma MBri SDeJ SPer
'Orange Favourite' (10)	LAma
'Orange Princess' (11) 🏆^{H4}	CTca EBrs ERCP LRHS SDeJ
'Orange Triumph' (11)	MBri
'Oranje Nassau' (2) 🏆^{H4}	LAma MBri MCot
'Oratorio' (14) 🏆^{H4}	MBri SDeJ
orithyioides	ECho LRHS NMin
orphanidea (15)	ECho LAma NMin SCnR SPhx
- 'Flava' (15)	CFox ECho EPot ERCP LAma SPhx
§ - Whittallii Group (15) 🏆^{H4}	CAvo CFFs ECho EPot ERCP LAma LRHS MMHG NMin SPhx
ostrowskiana (15)	ECho LAma NMin WWst
'Oxford' (4) 🏆^{H4}	LAma LRHS
'Oxford's Elite' (4)	LAma LRHS
'Page Polka' (3)	MBri SDeJ
'Pandour' (14)	MBri
'Papillon' (9)	LAma
'Parade' (4) 🏆^{H4}	MBri
§ ***passeriniana*** (15)	ECho WWst
'Passionale' (3)	EGxp EPfP SDeJ
patens	ECho
'Paul Scherer' (3)	ERCP
'Peach Blossom' (2)	CFox EBrs ERCP LAma MBri SDeJ SPer
* 'Peaches and Cream'	SPer
'Peppermintstick' (15) 🏆^{H4}	ERCP LRHS NMin SPhx
'Perestroyka' (5)	MBri
persica	see *T. celsiana*
'Philippe de Comines' (5)	LAma
'Piccolo' (15) new	ERCP LAma
'Picture' (5) 🏆^{H4}	ERCP LAma
'Pieter de Leur' (6)	EPfP LAma MBri SPer
'Pimpernel' (8/v)	LAma LRHS SDeJ
'Pink Diamond' (5) new	EPfP SPer
'Pink Dwarf' (12) new	SDeJ
'Pink Impression' (4) 🏆^{H4}	LAma MBri SDeJ SPer
'Pinocchio' (14)	CFox LRHS MBri SDeJ
'Plaisir' (14) 🏆^{H4}	LAma MBri
platystigma (15)	ECho LAma NMin
polychroma	see *T. biflora*
praestans (15)	ECho LAma SPer WShi
- 'Fusilier' (15) 🏆^{H4}	ECho EPfP EPot LAma LRHS MBri NBir SDeJ SPhx
- 'Unicum' (15/v)	CFox ECho EPot ERCP LAma MBri NMin SBch SDeJ
- 'Van Tubergen's Variety' (15)	ECho LAma
- 'Zwanenburg Variety' (15)	ECho
'Princeps' (13)	LAma MBri SDeJ
'Princess Unique' PBR (11) new	LAma

'Princesse Charmante' (14) ♀H4	MBri
'Prinses Irene' (3) ♀H4	CAvo CFFs CMea CTca EBrs EGxp EPfP ERCP LAma LRHS MBri NBir SDeJ SPer
'Professor Röntgen' (10)	LAma LRHS SDeJ
pulchella humilis	see *T. humilis*
§ 'Purissima' (13) ♀H4	CAvo CFFs CFox EBrs EPfP LAma LRHS MBri MCot SDeJ SPer SPhx
'Purple Bouquet' (3) **new**	LAma
'Purple Prince' (5)	CFox EPfP LAma SDeJ
'Quebec' (14)	SDeJ
'Queen Ingrid' (14)	LRHS
'Queen of Marvel' (2)	SDeJ
'Queen of Night' (5)	CAvo CFFs CFox CMea CTca EBrs EGxp EPfP ERCP LAma LRHS MBri MCot SPer SPhx WPtf
'Queen of Sheba' (6) ♀H4	LAma
'Quest' **new**	LAma
'Rajka' (6)	CFox LRHS
'Recreado' (5)	CAvo CFFs ERCP
'Red Emperor'	see *T.* 'Madame Lefeber'
'Red Georgette' (5) ♀H4	LAma LSou MBri NBir
'Red Impression'PBR (4) ♀H4	LRHS
'Red Riding Hood' (14) ♀H4	CAvo CFFs CFox EBrs EGxp EPfP LAma LRHS MBri NBir SDeJ SPer
'Red Shine' (6) ♀H4	CAvo CFFs LAma LRHS MBri
'Red Springgreen' (8)	LAma
'Red Wing' (7) ♀H4	SDeJ
Rembrandt mix (9)	MBri
'Renown Unique' (11)	LAma
rhodopea	see *T. urumoffii*
'Ringo'	see *T.* 'Kees Nelis'
'Rococo' (10)	ERCP LRHS MBri SDeJ
'Ronaldo' (3) **new**	LAma
'Rosy Dream' (13) **new**	SDeJ
'Royal Virgin' (3)	CAvo CFFs
'Salmon Impression'PBR (4)	LRHS
'Salut' (13) **new**	MCot
'Sapporro' (6)	LAma MCot
saracenica	ECho
saxatilis (15)	CArn ECho EPfP LAma MBri SDeJ WShi
§ - Bakeri Group (15)	CPou ECho
§ - - 'Lilac Wonder' (15) ♀H4	CAvo CFFs EBrs ECho EPot ERCP GKev LAma LRHS MBri SBch SPhx
'Scarlet Baby' (12)	EPfP MBri
'Schoonoord' (2)	CFox LAma MBri MCot
schrenkii (15)	CMea ECho ERCP LAma NMin WWst
'Shakespeare' (12)	ECho LAma SDeJ
'Shirley' (3)	CAvo CFFs CFox EBrs EPfP ERCP LAma LRHS MBri MCot SDeJ SPer
'Shirley Dream' (3)	EGxp
'Showwinner' (12) ♀H4	CAvo CFFs LAma MBri
'Silverstream' (4)	LAma
sogdiana (15)	ECho LAma NMin WWst
'Sonnet' (6)	ERCP
'Sorbet' (5) ♀H4	LAma
sosnowskyi (15)	ECho
sprengeri (15) ♀H4	CAvo CFFs CLAP CMea CTca ECGP ECha ECho EPot ERCP LAma SCnR SDix WHal WIvy WShi WTou
- Trotter's form (15)	WCot
'Spring Green' (8) ♀H4	CAvo CFFs CFox EBrs EGxp EPfP ERCP LAma LRHS MBri MCot MMHG SDeJ SPer SPhx
'Spryng' (3) ♀H4 **new**	SDeJ
'Starfighter' (7) **new**	SDeJ
stellata	see *T. clusiana* var. *stellata*
'Stockholm' (2) ♀H4	LAma
'Stresa' (12) ♀H4	LAma
subpraestans (15)	ECho LAma
'Sunwing'	LSou
'Super Parrot' (10)	LAma LRHS
'Swan Wings' (7)	CFox ERCP LAma LRHS SDeJ SPer
'Sweet Harmony' (5) ♀H4	MBri
'Sweetheart' (13)	MBri SDeJ SPer
sylvestris (15)	CAby CArn CFox CTca EBrs ECho EPfP EPot ERCP LAma LRHS MBri MCot NMin SDeJ SPhx WCot WHer WShi
systola (15)	ECho NMin WWst
tarda (15) ♀H4	CAvo CFFs EBrs ECho EPfP ERCP GGar GKev LAma LSou MBri SDeJ SPhx
'Tequila Sun' (3) **new**	LAma
tetraphylla (15)	ECho LAma NMin
'Texas Flame' (10)	MBri SDeJ
'Texas Gold' (10)	CHid LAma
'The First' (12)	CAvo CFFs
'The Lizard' (9)	LAma
'Theeroos' (2)	LAma
'Tinka' (15)	ECho LSou NMin SPhx
'Toronto' (14) ♀H4	CTca LAma LRHS LSou MBri SDeJ
'Toulon' (13) ♀H4	MBri
'Très Chic' (6)	CTca
'Trinket' (14) ♀H4	LAma
'Triumphator' (2)	EGxp
tschimganica (15)	ECho LAma WWst
tubergeniana (15)	ECho
- 'Keukenhof' (15)	ECho
turkestanica (15) ♀H4	CFox CTca EBrs ECho EPfP EPot ERCP LAma MBri SBch SDeJ SPhx WHoo
'Turkish Delight' (14)	NPer
'Typhoon' (3)	LAma
'Uncle Tom' (11)	EGxp EPfP ERCP LAma LRHS MBri
§ ***undulatifolia*** (15)	ECho LAma LRHS
- 'Clare Benedict' (15)	ECho
- 'Excelsa' (15)	ECho
'Union Jack' (5) ♀H4	LAma
'United States' (14)	NPer
urumiensis (15) ♀H4	ECho EPot LAma MBri NMin SBch SPhx
§ ***urumoffii*** (15)	ECho LAma
'Valentine' (3) ♀H4	SDeJ
'Valery Gergiev' (7)	ERCP
'Van der Neer' (1)	SDeJ
'Velvet Lily' (6) **new**	NMin
'Verona' (2)	CFox EBrs LRHS SDeJ
violacea	see *T. humilis* Violacea Group
'Violet Bird' (8)	ERCP SDeJ
'Virichic' (8)	ERCP MCot
vvedenskyi (15)	ECho EPot WWst
- 'Tangerine Beauty' (15) ♀H4	ECho LRHS MBri SBch SPhx
'Warbler' (7) **new**	SDeJ
'Washington' (3)	EBrs ERCP
* 'Water Lily'	ECho
'Weber's Parrot' (10)	MBri
'Weisse Berliner' (3)	EBrs LAma LRHS
'West Point' (6) ♀H4	CAvo CFFs CTca EBrs ERCP LAma MBri MCot
'White Dream' (3)	CAvo CFFs EPfP LAma MBri SDeJ
'White Elegance' (6)	SPer
'White Emperor'	see *T.* 'Purissima'
'White Parrot' (10)	CAvo CFFs ERCP LAma LRHS SDeJ
'White Triumphator' (6) ♀H4	CAvo CFFs CFox CMea EBrs ERCP LAma LRHS MCot NBir SPhx

	whittallii	see *T. orphanidea* Whittallii Group
	'Wildhof' (3) ♀H4	ERCP
	'Willemsoord' (2)	CFox LAma MBri SDeJ
	'William of Orange' **new**	SDeJ
	wilsoniana	see *T. montana*
	'Yellow Crown' (3) **new**	LAma
	'Yellow Emperor' (5)	MBri
	'Yellow Flight' (3)	LAma SDeJ
	'Yellow Present' (3)	CFox
I	'Yellow Purissima' (13) ♀H4	EPfP
	'Yellow Springgreen' **new**	ERCP
	'Yokohama' (3)	EBrs LAma SDeJ
	'Zampa' (14) ♀H4	MBri
	'Zombie' (13)	LAma
	'Zomerschoon' (5)	LAma
§	'Zurel' (3)	CAvo CFFs EPfP ERCP LAma LRHS SPer

tummelberry see *Rubus* 'Tummelberry'

Tunica see *Petrorhagia*

Tupistra (*Convallariaceae*)

	aurantiaca	GEdr WCot
	- B&SWJ 2267	WCru WPrP
	- B&SWJ 2401	WCru
	chinensis 'Eco China Ruffles'	WCot
	fimbriata	WCot
	wattii B&SWJ 8297	WCru

Tussilago (*Asteraceae*)

	farfara	CArn EBWF GBar GPoy MHer NMir NSco WHer WHfH WSFF

Tutcheria (*Theaceae*)

§	***spectabilis***	EPfP

Tweedia (*Asclepiadaceae*)

§	***caerulea*** ♀H2	CBcs CDTJ CSpe CWit SGar SPad SPer WCot WSFF
	- pink-flowered	SPad

Typha (*Typhaceae*)

	angustifolia	CBen CKno CRow CWat EHon GFor LLWG LPBA MMuc MSKA NLar NPer NSco SPlb SWat WFar WPnP
	latifolia	CBen CRow CWat EHon GFor LPBA MSKA NBir NLan NLar NPer NSco SWat WFar WHer WMAq WPnP
	- 'Variegata' (v)	CBen CKno CRow ELan LLWG LPBA MSKA MWts NLar NPla WCot WMAq
§	***laxmannii***	CBen CRow GFor LPBA MSKA NLan NLar WPnP
	minima	CBen CFir CRow CWat EHoe EHon ELan EPfP LPBA MMuc MSKA MWts NLar NPer SCoo SWat WFar WMAq WPnP
	shuttleworthii	CRow
	stenophylla	see *T. laxmannii*

Typhonium (*Araceae*)

	alpinum	EBee
	giganteum	SKHP WCot
	kunmingense	CDes
	var. ***kunmingense*** **new**	
	roxburghii	EBee
	venosum	EUJe SBst WWst

Typhonodorum (*Araceae*)

	lindleyanum	XBlo

U

ugli see *Citrus* × *tangelo* 'Ugli'

Ugni (*Myrtaceae*)

§	***molinae***	Widely available
	- 'Flambeau'	CAgr CBcs CBod EBee ELan EPfP IVic LBMP LEdu LRHS MAsh MGos NLar SBfd SPoG SWvt
	- 'Variegata' (v) **new**	WJek

Ulex (*Papilionaceae*)

	europaeus	CAlb CArn CBcs CCVT CDoC CDul CMac CRWN ECrN ELan EPfP GPoy LBuc MCoo MGos MMuc NEgg NWea SCoo SPer WDin WHar
	- 'Aureus'	NLar
§	- 'Flore Pleno' (d) ♀H4	CAlb CBar CBcs CDoC CDul CMac CSBt EBee ELan EPfP GCal GGar IArd LAst MBlu MGos MMuc NLar NWea SPer SPoG WFar
	- 'Plenus'	see *U. europaeus* 'Flore Pleno'
	gallii	NLar WDin
	- 'Mizen Head'	GCal GGar MWhi SLon

Ulmus ✿ (*Ulmaceae*)

	alata	EGFP
	americana 'Princeton'	CKno
	crassifolia	EGFP
	'Dodoens'	IArd MGos SCoo
§	***glabra***	CDul CRWN ECrN EMac IFFs NWea SCoo WDin
	- 'Camperdownii'	CMac EBee ECrN ELan GKir LAst WMou
	- 'Exoniensis'	CTho
	- 'Gittisham'	CTho
	- 'Horizontalis'	see *U. glabra* 'Pendula'
	- 'Lutescens'	CEnd CTho CTri LRHS NWea SCoo SLim
§	- 'Pendula'	CMac
§	× ***hollandica*** 'Dampieri Aurea'	CBot CDul CEnd EBee ELan ELon EPfP GKir LBuc MAsh MBlu MGos MRav NHol NLar SPer WDin WPat
	- 'Jacqueline Hillier'	CDul CMac CSpe ECho ELan LAst LMaj MGos MMuc MRav NLar SEND STre WCFE WDin WFar WPat
	- 'Lobel'	CCVT CDul MGos
	- 'Wredei'	see *U.* × *hollandica* 'Dampieri Aurea'
	laevis	ECrN
	Lutèce = 'Nanguen'	CDoC
	minor	CDul EMac IFFs
	- 'Dampieri Aurea'	see *U.* × *hollandica* 'Dampieri Aurea'
	- 'Variegata' (v)	EBee
	montana	see *U. glabra*
	'Morton Glossy'	CDul LRHS
	parvifolia	CMCN CMen STre WPGP
	- 'Frosty' (v)	ECho
	- 'Geisha' (v)	ECho ELan MGos MRav WPat
§	- 'Hokkaido'	CMen EWes GEdr LLHF NLar NMen WAbe WPat WThu
	- 'Pygmaea'	see *U. parvifolia* 'Hokkaido'
	- 'Yatsubusa'	ECho EWes LLHF MRav NLar STre WPat

procera	ECrN LBuc MCoo MGos WDin WSFF
- 'Argenteovariegata' (v)	CDul MGos
pumila	EBee
rubra	CArn
'Sapporo Autumn Gold'	CCVT EBee LBuc LMaj MRav WDin
serotina	EGFP

Umbellularia (*Lauraceae*)

californica	CArn CPne EPfP GKir IDee SSpi WSHC

Umbilicus (*Crassulaceae*)

rupestris	CArn CRWN SChr WHer WShi

Uncinia (*Cyperaceae*)

from Chile	GCal
* ***cyparissias*** from Chile	NBir
divaricata	ECou
egmontiana	CBod CHid EBee EBla EHoe EPfP EShb LBMP LRHS MNrw WFoF WGrn WHrl WMnd WMoo WWEG
N ***rubra***	Widely available
uncinata	CBcs CMMP ECha GFor NCob NHol SDix
* - ***rubra***	CFir CKno COIW CTri CWCL EHrv IFro LAst MAsh MMHG MNrw NCob NGdn NPri SBfd SLim SMrm SPad SUsu SWvt WPGP

Ungnadia (*Sapindaceae*)

speciosa NJM 05.054	WPGP

Uniola (*Poaceae*)

latifolia	see *Chasmanthium latifolium*
paniculata	SApp

Urceolina (*Amaryllidaceae*)

miniata	see *Stenomesson miniatum*
peruviana	see *Stenomesson miniatum*

Urginea (*Hyacinthaceae*)

capitata 'Sentinel Peak' **new**	ECho
fugax	EBee
macrocentra	ECho
maritima	CArn CPou EBee ECho LAma LRHS WCot
ollivieri	ECho
undulata	ECho

Urospermum (*Asteraceae*)

dalechampii	CDes CSam ECha LLWP LRHS SGar SUsu

Ursinia (*Asteraceae*)

alpina	CPBP
montana	NWCA

Urtica (*Urticaceae*)

dioica 'Brightstone Bitch' (v)	WAlt
- 'Chedglow 2' (v)	CNat
- 'Danae Johnston' (v)	WAlt
- 'Dayglo Delight'	WAlt
- 'Dog Trap Lane'	CNat
- 'Dusting' (v)	WAlt
- 'Fearnvale Tigertooth' (v)	WAlt
- 'Good as Gold'	WAlt
- OGG mutant	CNat WAlt
- 'Spring Fever'	WAlt
- 'Winter Yellow' **new**	CNat
- 'Worn Gilding' (v)	WAlt
galeopsifolia	WAlt

Utricularia (*Lentibulariaceae*)

sp.	EECP
alpina	CSWC SHmp
australis	EFEx
biloba	CHew
bisquamata	CSWC SHmp
- 'Betty's Bay'	CHew
blancheti	CSWC
calycifida	SHmp
dichotoma	CHew CSWC EFEx
exoleta R. Brown	see *U. gibba*
§ ***gibba***	EFEx
heterosepala	CHew
intermedia	EFEx
lateriflora	CHew EFEx
livida	CHew CSWC EECP EFEx SHmp
longifolia	CSWC SHmp
macrorhiza	CSWC
menziesii	EFEx
microcalyx	CHew SHmp
monanthos	CHew EFEx
nephrophylla	CHew SHmp
novae-zelandiae	CHew
ochroleuca	EFEx
paulineae	CHew
praelonga	CHew CSWC SHmp
prehensilis	CHew
pubescens	CSWC
reniformis	EFEx SHmp
- ***nana***	EFEx
sandersonii	CHew CSWC EECP SHmp
- blue-flowered	CSWC EECP
simplex	CHew
subulata	EFEx
tricolor	CHew CSWC SHmp
uniflora	CHew
vulgaris	EFEx
warburgii	CHew
welwitschii	CHew

Uvularia (*Convallariaceae*)

§ ***caroliniana***	ECho
disporum	EBee ECho
grandiflora Υ^{H4}	Widely available
- dwarf	ECho IBlr
- gold-leaved	CAby WWst
- 'Lynda Windsor'	MAsh SKHP
- orange-flowered **new**	SKHP
- var. ***pallida***	CAby CAvo CBct CLAP CPom EBee EBrs ECha ECho EHrv EPPr EPot GCal GEdr IBlr LEdu LRHS MRav NCGa NHar NPnk SMHy SPhx SUsu WAbe WCru WFar WPGP WPnP
- 'Susie Lewis'	WCru
grandiflora × ***perfoliata***	ECho IBlr NBir
perfoliata	CBct CLAP CPLG EBee ECha ECho EDAr EPPr EPfP EPla EPot EWTr GCrs GGar IBlr IMou LEdu MRav NBir NPnk WAbe WBrE WCru WPGP WPnP
- tall **new**	EPPr
pudica	see *U. caroliniana*
sessilifolia	CBct CLAP CPLG EBee ECho EPot GEdr IBlr IMou LEdu NMen SSvw WCru
- 'Cobblewood Gold' (v)	WCru

V

Vaccinium ✿ (*Ericaceae*)

angustifolium var. ***laevifolium***	GLin
arctostaphylos	NLar SWvt
'Berkeley' (F)	CAgr CCCN CTrh CWib EUJe LBuc LSRN MBlu NPla SDea SPoG WClo
'Bluejay' (F)	CWib GKir LRHS MAsh SCoo SLon
'Blueray' (F)	CWib GPri
'Brigitta' (F)	CTrh ECrN EMil GTwe IFFs MAsh NPla SPoG
'Chandler' (F)	CAgr CMac CTrh ERea GPri LSRN MAsh SBfd SKee WBVN
'Chippewa' (F)	SPoG
corymbosum (F) 🏆^{H4}	CBcs EPfP MGos MNHC SBfd SCoo SReu SSta WDin
- 'Blauweiss-goldtraube' (F)	CSBt CWSG CWib EMil ERea EUJe LRHS LSRN MGos NLar SDea SPoG SVic WBVN WFar
- 'Blue Duke' (F)	LSRN
- 'Bluecrop' (F)	Widely available
- 'Bluegold' (F)	EMil LRHS MAsh MGos
- 'Bluetta' (F)	CAgr CTri CWib GKir GPri GTwe MGos SCoo SPoG WFar
- 'Coville' (F)	CWib NLar
- 'Darrow' (F)	CAgr GKir GTwe LBuc
- 'Dixie' (F)	CSBt MSCN NPla
- 'Duke' (F) 🏆^{H4}	CTrh CWib ELan EPfP GPri LRHS MAsh MGos WClo
- 'Elizabeth' (F)	GPri
- 'Elliott' (F)	LSRN MGos
- 'Grover' (F)	LRHS NLar
- 'Hannah's Choice' (F)	GPri
- 'Hardyblue' (F)	CAgr
- 'Jersey' (F)	CAgr CWib EPfP IFFs LRHS MCoo MGos MMuc NLar SCoo SDea SPer SVic
- 'Nelson' (F)	GPri MAsh SCoo
- 'Patriot' (F)	CAgr CSBt CTrh CWib ECrN GPri GTwe IFFs LBuc LRHS MBri MGos MPkF MRav NPla NPri SBfd SCoo SPoG WClo
- 'Reka' (F) **new**	CAgr
- 'Sierra' (F)	GPri
- 'Spartan' (F) 🏆^{H4}	CTrh CWib EMil GTwe LRHS LSRN MAsh MGos SBfd SCoo SKee SPer
- 'Stanley' (F)	ELan LRHS MAsh
- 'Toro' (F)	CTrh EMil GPri GTwe LBuc LRHS MAsh MGos
- 'Weymouth' (F)	SDea
crassifolium subsp. ***sempervirens*** 'Well's Delight' (F)	LRHS MAsh SPoG
cylindraceum 🏆^{H4}	EPfP NLar WFar WPat
delavayi	ECho LRHS MAsh NMen WAbe WFar WPat WThu
dunalianum	MMuc
- var. ***caudatifolium*** B&SWJ 1716	WCru
- var. ***megaphyllum*** HWJ 515	WCru
'Earliblue' (F)	CAgr CSBt LRHS MBri MGos SDea WFar
floribundum	CBcs CDoC CMHG ECho GKir LRHS MAsh MMuc NLar NMen SSpi WPGP
glaucoalbum 🏆$^{H3-4}$	CAbP CDoC CMac EPfP GGGa GKir LRHS MAsh MRav SMad SPer SPoG SSpi WPat
'Goldtraube 71' **new**	NPla
* ***grandiflorum***	ECho
griffithianum	SReu SSta
'Groover'	LSRN
'Herbert' (F)	CAgr CMac CTrh ECrN GTwe LBuc MGos
macrocarpon (F)	CArn ECho ELan GKir GTwe LRHS MAsh MMuc NHar NWCA SDea SRms
- 'CN' (F)	CAgr MGos NLar
- 'Early Black' (F)	EGxp MGos
- 'Franklin' (F)	CAgr
- 'Hamilton'	GCrs GEdr LLHF NLAp NMen WAbe WThu
- 'Howes' (F)	NHar
- 'Langlois' (F)	NLar
- 'Olson's Honkers' (F)	CAgr NLar
- 'Pilgrim' (F)	CAgr CMac EUJe
- 'Red Star' (F)	CEnd MCCP
'Misty' (F)	CAgr
moupinense	CDoC ECho GKir LRHS MAsh NMen WAbe WPat WThu
- 'Variegatum' (v)	LLHF
myrsinites	ECho
myrtillus	CAgr GPoy NLar NWea WSFF
'Northland' (F)	CSBt CWib GTwe LRHS MBri NLar NPla SCoo SDea SPoG
nummularia	EBee ECho GEdr LRHS MMuc NHar NMen SSpi WAbe WPat WThu
ovalifolium	GAuc
ovatum	CBcs CMHG WThu
- 'Thundercloud'	CAbP LRHS MAsh
§ ***oxycoccos*** (F)	CAgr CArn GPoy MCoo MGos WThu
padifolium	WPGP
pallidum	IBlr
palustre	see *V. oxycoccos*
praestans	NHol
retusum	IRar
'Rubel' (F)	LRHS
'Sunrise' (F)	GTwe
'Sunshine Blue' (F)	CAgr ECrN LBuc LRHS SBfd SKee SLon
'Tophat' (F)	CCCN MPkF
vitis-idaea	ECho EPfP EWes GGar GPoy MGos NWea SPoG SVic WFar
- 'Autumn Beauty'	NLar
- 'Compactum'	EWes LLHF LSou
- Koralle Group 🏆^{H4}	CAgr EBee EPfP MBri MCoo NHol SPoG WPat
- subsp. ***minus***	GCrs GEdr GPri NLar NMen WAbe
- 'Red Pearl'	CSBt EBee EPfP LRHS MAsh MGos
* - 'Variegatum' (v)	EWes
wrightii var. ***formosanum***	ECho

Vagaria (*Amaryllidaceae*)

ollivieri	ECho

Valeriana (*Valerianaceae*)

'Alba'	see *Centranthus ruber* 'Albus'
alliariifolia	EBee GCal NBro WCot
celtica	GPoy
'Coccinea'	see *Centranthus ruber*
coreana	CFee WMoo
dioica	EBWF
jatamansi	GPoy
montana	NBro NRya SRms SWat
officinalis	Widely available

- subsp. ***sambucifolia***	CFee EPPr GCal MNrw MSpe SHar WOut
phu 'Aurea'	CArn CBod CBot CHby CMac EBee ECha EHoe EHrv ELan EPfP LRHS MBri MCot MLHP MRav NBid NBir NBro NEgg NSti SMrm SPer SPhx SRms WCAu WEas WFar WGwG WMoo
pyrenaica	CAby ECha EHrv EPPr GCal LPla LRHS MMHG MMuc MNrw SPhx WCot WMoo
saxatilis	NLar NRya SBch
supina	CPBP NWCA
wallrothii	CDes EBee MAvo WCot

Valerianella (*Valerianaceae*)

§ ***locusta***	CArn GPoy SVic
olitoria	see *V. locusta*

Vallea (*Elaeocarpaceae*)

stipularis	CHll CTsd ILis

Vallota see *Cyrtanthus*

Vancouveria (*Berberidaceae*)

chrysantha	CDes CFir CLAP CPLG CPom EBee ECha EPPr MRav NLar NRya NWCA SKHP SMad WCon WCru WMoo
hexandra	CAby CBct CFir CGHE CLAP CPLG CPom EBee ECha EHrv EPPr EPfP EPla GEdr GKev GKir IMou LEdu LRHS NRya NSti NWCA SKHP WCru WMoo WPGP WWEG
planipetala	CLAP WCru

Vania see *Thlaspi*

veitchberry see *Rubus* 'Veitchberry'

Velleia (*Goodeniaceae*)

paradoxa	ECou

Vellozia (*Velloziaceae*)

elegans	see *Talbotia elegans*

Veltheimia ✿ (*Hyacinthaceae*)

§ ***bracteata*** ♀H1	CHll CLak CMdw CPou EBak EBrs ECho ECre IBlr LToo NPal WCot
§ ***capensis*** ♀H1	CSev
viridifolia misapplied	see *V. capensis*
viridifolia Jacq.	see *V. bracteata*

× *Venidioarctotis* see *Arctotis*

Venidium see *Arctotis*

Veratrum ✿ (*Melanthiaceae*)

album ♀H4	CPne EBee ECha ECho GCal GPoy LEdu MNrw MRav NBid SMad WCru WFar WSHC WWst
- var. ***flavum***	CAby GCal MNrw SPhx WCru
- subsp. ***lobelianum*** **new**	GCal
- 'Lorna's Green' **new**	GCal
- var. ***oxysepalum***	WCru
californicum	CHGN ECha GCal MNrw NBid WCot
- compact	MNrw
dolichopetalum B&SWJ 4195	WCru
formosanum	GEdr MNrw
- B&SWJ 1575	WCru
- RWJ 9806	WCru
grandiflorum B&SWJ 4416	WCru
longebracteatum	WCru
maackii	EBee GEdr NMyG
- var. ***japonicum*** **new**	WCru
- var. ***maackii*** B&SWJ 5831	WCru
- var. ***parviflorum***	GCal
nigrum ♀H4	CAby CBct CBot CFir CPne EBee EHrv GAbr GCal GMaP IKil MAvo MLHP MNrw MRav NBPC NBid NBir NCGa NLar SMad SPhx SPlb WBor WCom WCru WFar WPnP
- B&SWJ 4450 from South Korea **new**	WCru
schindleri	WWst
- B&SWJ 4068	WCru
stamineum	EBee WCru
viride	ECha EWes GCal

Verbascum (*Scrophulariaceae*)

adzharicum	WHoo
Allestree hybrids	EHrv
'Annie May'	EBee EPfP LSRN SUsu
'Apricot Sunset'	EBee SPhx
'Arctic Summer'	see *V. bombyciferum* 'Polarsommer'
arcturus	CFee
'Aurora'	SJoh SPhx
'Aztec Gold'	EBee MAvo SJoh SPhx
* ***bakerianum***	EBla ECtt
'Bill Bishop'	ECho
blattaria	EBWF EHrv NBPC NBir SPav SWat WFar WHer WWEG
- f. ***albiflorum***	CSpe EBee IFro LLWP NDov SGar SPlb SWal WHer WMoo WTin
- yellow-flowered	SPav SWat
'Blushing Bride' PBR	ECtt LLHF
§ ***bombyciferum***	CBre CSev ECha GMaP NBPC NGBl
* - 'Arctic Snow'	SPav SPoG
§ - 'Polarsommer'	CSpe EBee EPfP GKir LRHS MBri NBir NVic SPer SPet SWat WWEG
- 'Silver Lining'	NLar NPer SDnm
'Broussa'	see *V. bombyciferum*
'Buttercup'	EBee ECtt LRHS WFar
'Caribbean Crush'	CBcs CMac EAEE EBee ECtt ELan EPfP EWll GKir LRHS NBPC NLar NMoo SBfd SMrm SPer WHoo WWEG
chaixii	CSam ECha ECtt EHrv GKir MLLN MMHG NBir WFar WMoo
- 'Album' ♀H4	Widely available
- 'Blackberry Crush'	MDKP
- 'Helene Bowles'	CHar
- 'Sixteen Candles'	CSpr ECtt GQue LRHS NChi NLar WHal WHil WPtf
- 'Wedding Candles'	GMac LBMP NLar SMrm WHil
chaixii × 'Wendy's Choice'	MDKP
'Charlotte'	SJoh
'Cherokee'	SJoh SUsu
'Cherry Helen' PBR	EBee EPfP LAst LRHS LSRN MBri NEgg NGdn NLar NMoo NPnk SBfd SPer WSpi WWEG
'Claire'	MAvo SJoh
'Clementine'	SJoh SPhx
'Coneyhill Yellow'	EPPr
(Cotswold Group) 'Cotswold Beauty' ♀H4	CSam CSpe EAEE EBee ECtt EPfP GKir GMac LRHS MRav MWat NDov NGdn SPer WCAu WMnd
- 'Cotswold Gem'	ECtt
- 'Cotswold Queen'	CBcs CMMP EAEE EBee ECtt ELan EPPr EPfP LRHS MDKP MRav MWat NGdn SPer SPet SWvt WCAu WMnd WSpi WWEG

	- 'Gainsborough' ♀^{H4}	Widely available
	- 'Mont Blanc'	EAEE EBee EHrv GMaP LPio LRHS SWat WSpi
	- 'Pink Domino' ♀^{H4}	CBcs CBot CPrp CSam EBee ECtt EHrv ELan EPPr EPfP GKir GMaP LRHS MLHP MRav MWat SDnm SPer SPet SWvt WFar WMnd WSpi WWEG
	- 'Royal Highland'	EBee ECtt EHrv ELan EPfP LPio NGdn NLar SDnm SWvt WFar
	- 'White Domino'	EBee ECtt GKir SPer
	'Cotswold King'	see *V. creticum*
§	***creticum***	CSpe IKil NDov SDnm SGar SPav WCot
	- white-flowered	WCot
	'Daisy Alice'	SPhx
§	***densiflorum***	CArn EBee SPer
	- BSSS 232	WCru
	'Dijon'	ECtt EWes
	dumulosum ♀$^{H2-3}$	EPot GCal WAbe
	'Dusky Maiden'	NWCA
	'Ebenezer Howard'	LPio
	'Eleanor's Blush'	EBrs LRHS
	'Elektra'	SJoh
	'Ellenbank Jewel'	GMac
	epixanthinum	CPla CSpe LRHS MCCP
	- MESE 552	EBee
	'Flower of Scotland'^{PBR}	ECtt
	'Golden Wings' ♀$^{H2-3}$	CPla ECtt ITim NMen WAbe
I	'Harkness Hybrid' **new**	SSvw
	Harptree smokey hybrids	CHar
	'Helen Johnson'	CBcs CMMP EBee EBrs ECtt EPfP GKir LAst LHop LRHS LSRN MGos MRav NBPC NLar NPnk NPri SBfd SCoo SMrm SPer SRkn SWvt WCAu WFar WWEG
	'Hiawatha'	SJoh SPhx
	'High Noon'	EBee MTis SJoh WFut
	× ***hybridum*** 'Banana Custard'	EAEE EBee ECtt GKir MNHC NGBl
	- 'Copper Rose'	EPfP MBri
	- 'Snow Maiden'	CTri EPfP MBNS MHer SDnm WClo
	- 'Wega'	NLar
	'Hyde Hall Sunrise'	EPfP LBuc MGos
	'Innocence'	MDKP
	'Jackie'	CBcs CHar CMac COlW EBee ECtt EHrv ELan GKir LAst LRHS LSRN MBri NCGa NGdn SBfd SCoo SPer SPoG WFar WSpi WWEG
	'Jackie in Pink'	EWes GKir LBuc LRHS NCGa NMoo WFar
	'Jackie in Yellow'^{PBR}	LLHF NMoo
	'Jolly Eyes'	EBee ECtt MBri NPnk
	'June Johnson'	EAEE EBee ECtt LRHS NGdn SHar
	'Kalypso'	SJoh SPhx
	'Klondike'	SJoh
	'Kynaston'	NGdn
	'Lavender Lass'	ECtt NGdn
	'Letitia' ♀^{H3}	CBcs CMea CPla EBee ECho ECtt ELan EWes GCal ITim LRHS MTho NMen NWCA SRot SWvt WAbe WCom WKif WPat
	longifolium	WFar
	- var. ***pannosum***	see *V. olympicum*
*	***luridifolium***	SPhx
	lychnitis	CArn GJos SPhx WHil WMoo
	'Megan's Mauve'	EBee ECtt EWll SWvt
	'Merlin'	EAEE EBee ECtt LSRN MBNS MLLN MTis SHar SJoh WAul WCot WWlt
	'Monster'	CDes EBee WPGP
	'Moonlight'	ECtt
	'Moonshadow'	SJoh SPhx
	'Mystery Blonde'	SJoh SPhx
	nigrum	CArn EBWF EBee ECtt EPfP NGHP NLar WBrE WMnd WMoo
	- var. ***album***	NChi NGHP NLar WMoo
	'Norfolk Dawn'	EBee ECtt EPfP MAvo NGdn SPhx
§	***olympicum***	CSam CWan CWit EBee ECtt ELan EPfP GJos GKir LRHS MAvo MWat NGBl SDix SEND SMrm WBrE WCAu WCot WWEG
	'Pandora'	EBrs LRHS
	'Patricia'	EBee SPhx
	'Petra'	SJoh SPhx
	phlomoides	SPhx
	phoeniceum	CArn ELan EPfP GJos LRHS NBro SGar SPlb SPoG WBrE WEas WMoo
*	- 'Album'	WCom
	- 'Antique Rose'	WHrl
	- 'Flush of Pink'	ECtt
	- 'Flush of White'	CBot EBee ECtt EPPr EPfP GQue LBMP NGBl NLar NPnk SDnm SPav SPoG SSvw WGor WMoo WWEG
	- hybrids	CBot CTri ECtt GMaP NEgg NGdn SRms SWat WFar WGor WPer WWEG
	- 'Rosetta'	EPfP LBMP NGBl SPad WHil
	- 'Violetta'	Widely available
	'Phoenix'	CTsd EBee
	'Pink Glow'	GMac
	'Pink Ice'	MDKP
	'Pink Kisses'	EBee LLHF LRHS LSRN NBPC SBfd
	'Pink Petticoats'	EAEE ECtt LBuc LRHS MGos SPoG
	(Pixie Series) 'Pixie Apricot'	WHlf
	- 'Pixie Blue'	WHlf
	- 'Pixie White'	WHlf
	'Plum Smokey'^{PBR}	EBee ECtt IPot LLHF LRHS SBfd WWEG
	'Primrose Cottage'	MBri SPhx
	'Primrose Path'	ECtt LRHS MPnt NPnk SBfd SHar SRot
	'Purple Prince'	ECtt
	pyramidatum	SPhx
	'Raspberry Ripple'	CMac EBee ECtt ELan LAst LBMP LLHF NDov NMoo SPad
	'Rosie'	LRHS MGos NGdn SPoG
	'Sierra Sunset'	ECtt NPnk WWlt
	'South Country'	SJoh
	'Southern Charm'	ECtt EPfP EWll GJos GKir GMaP MBri MCCP NChi NLBP NPnk SPoG STes WFar WHil WPtf WWEG
	'Spica'	GMac NLar WSpi
	spicatum	CBot
	'Sugar Plum'^{PBR}	CHar EBee ECtt EWll LAst LLHF WWEG
	'Summer Sorbet'	EBee ECtt ELan EPfP GKir LRHS NSti SPoG
	Sunset shades	GJos
	thapsiforme	see *V. densiflorum*
	thapsus	CBgR COld CSev EDAr GPoy MHer MNHC NMir NSco SEND
	'Tropic Blush'	MAvo SJoh
	'Tropic Dawn'	MAvo SJoh
	'Tropic Moon'	SJoh
	'Tropic Rose'	MAvo SJoh
	'Tropic Spice'	MAvo SJoh
	'Tropic Sun'	MAvo SJoh
	'Twilight'	EBrs LRHS WHlf
	'Valerie Grace'	SPhx

'Vernale'	CBot
wiedemannianum	CSpr EBee

Verbena (*Verbenaceae*)

(Aztec Series) Aztec Cherry Red = 'Balazcherd'^{PBR} (G)	LAst NPri
- Aztec Coral = 'Balazcoral'^{PBR} (G)	LAst NPri
- Aztec Dark Pink Magic = 'Balazdapima' **new**	NPri
- Aztec Pearl = 'Balazpearl'^{PBR} (G)	SCoo
- Aztec Pink Magic = 'Balazpima'^{PBR} (G)	LAst
- Aztec Plum Magic = 'Balazplum'^{PBR} (G)	LAst NPri
- Aztec Red = 'Balazred' (G)	SCoo
- Aztec Silver Magic = 'Balazsilma'^{PBR} (G) ♀^{H3}	LAst MWea NPri SCoo SUsu
- Aztec White = 'Balazwhit' (G)	LAst
'Betty Lee' (G)	ECtt
'Blue Prince' (G)	CSpe MAsh SUsu
§ ***bonariensis*** ♀$^{H3-4}$	Widely available
brasiliensis misapplied	see *V. bonariensis*
canadensis 'Perfecta' (G)	CSpe
'Candy Carousel' (G)	SPet
chamaedrifolia	see *V. peruviana*
§ 'Claret' (G) ♀^{H3}	CAby CSev CSpe EBee ECtt ELan ELon EPfP EShb LRHS LSRN LSou MCot MGos MWea SAga SBfd SCoo SMHy SMrm SPhx SPoG SUsu WWEG
corymbosa	CEnt CHid CHll CMMP CWCL EBee ECGP ECha EPPr LRHS MDKP MMuc MSpe NLar SAga SBfd SPer SPoG SWal WCom WPer WPtf WWEG
- 'Gravetye'	EBee NCob WFar
'Derby'	MPet
'Diamond Merci' (G)	WHoo
'Edith Eddleman' (G)	CWGN EBee ECtt EPfP LRHS MWea SHar
'Hammerstein Pink'	EBee EPfP
hastata	CHar CSpe EBee ECtt EPfP GBar LEdu LRHS MCot MNrw NCob NDov NSti SGar SMrm SPhx SPlb SWat SWvt WFar WMnd WMoo WPer WSHC
* - 'Alba'	EBee EPfP GBar GCal MCot MDKP MNrw NBPC NLar SMrm WMoo WOut
- 'Blue Spires'	EPfP LBMP WWEG
- f. ***rosea***	CArn CElw CHar CMea CSpe EBee EHoe ELan EPfP GBar MCot MDKP MLHP MNrw MRav NBPC NChi NCob NDov SBfd SMrm SPhx SUsu SWat WCAu WFar WMoo WSHC WWEG
- - 'Pink Spires'	ECtt EKen EPfP LBMP LHop SPad WWEG
- 'White Spires' **new**	EPfP
'Homestead Purple' (G)	CBar CChe CMac COlW CSev EAEE EBee EBrs ECtt EPfP EShb LRHS LSRN MCot MGos SAga SBfd SMrm SUsu SWvt WEas WWEG
incompta	see *V. bonariensis*
'Jenny's Wine'	see *V.* 'Claret'
'La France' (G)	CHGN EBee ECha ECtt EPfP EShb LRHS LSou MWea SAga SDix SMHy SMrm SPhx SUsu WHal WHoo WMnd WSHC WWEG
lasiostachys	EBee
'Lavender Spires' **new**	SPhx
'Lois' Ruby'	see *V.* 'Claret'
macdougalii	MDKP SPhx
officinalis	CArn CRWN CWan EBWF GBar GPWP GPoy MHer MNHC SIde WHer WJek WPer
patagonica	see *V. bonariensis*
'Peaches 'n' Cream' (G) ♀^{H3}	MPet
§ ***peruviana*** (G)	EBee ELan EPfP LBMP LRHS MAsh SAga SChF SRms
'Pink Bouquet'	see *V.* 'Silver Anne'
'Pink Parfait' (G)	EPfP LAst SAga SBfd
'Quartz Red Polka Dot'	SAga SBfd
'Red Cascade'	SPet
§ ***rigida*** ♀^{H3}	Widely available
- f. ***lilacina***	LSRN NLar
- - 'Lilac Haze'	CBod CMac EBee EPfP LRHS NSti SPoG SRkn WClo
- - 'Polaris'	CHar EBee ELon EPfP EShb IPot LHop LSou MAvo MMuc MNrw MRav SHar SMHy SMrm SPer SPhx SPoG SUsu WClo
Sandy Series (G) ♀^{H3}	MPet
'Seabrook's Lavender'	EPPr EPfP EShb LRHS LSRN MTis MWea NPri SBfd SHar SVil SWvt WSHC
§ 'Silver Anne' (G) ♀^{H3}	ECtt MCot SAga SMrm SUsu
§ 'Sissinghurst' (G) ♀$^{H2-3}$	CFox ECtt LAst MAsh SAga SBfd SMrm SRms
stricta	LRHS MDKP NLar SPhx
(Superbena Series) Superbena Bushy Merlot = 'Usbena5002'^{PBR} (G)	NPri
- Superbena Ruby Red = 'Usbena5122'^{PBR} (G) ♀^{H3}	CHVG SBfd
(Tapien Series) Tapien Salmon = 'Suntapiro'^{PBR} (G) ♀^{H3}	LSou WGor
- Tapien Sky Blue = 'Suntapilabu'^{PBR} (G) ♀^{H3}	LSou
- Tapien Violet = 'Sunvop'^{PBR} (G)	LHop LSou
(Temari Series) Temari Blue = 'Sunmariribu'^{PBR} (G)	LSou
- Temari Burgundy = 'Sunmariwaba'^{PBR} (G)	LSou
- Temari Coral Pink = 'Sunmariripi'^{PBR} (G)	LSou
- Temari Neon Red = 'Sunmarineopi'^{PBR} (G) ♀^{H3}	LSou
- Temari Vanilla = 'Sunmarivani'^{PBR} (G)	LSou
- Temari Violet = 'Sunmariba'^{PBR} (G)	WGor
'Tenerife'	see *V.* 'Sissinghurst'
tenuisecta (G)	NLar
- 'Imagination' (G)	CFox
(Vegas Series) 'Vegas Appleblossom' (G) **new**	LSou
- 'Vegas Purple' (G) **new**	LSou
- 'Vegas Scarlet' (G) **new**	LSou
venosa	see *V. rigida*
Waterfall Blue = 'Dofall'	SMrm

Verbesina (*Asteraceae*)

alternifolia	CArn
- 'Goldstrahl'	EPPr WPer
helianthoides	CSpr

Vernicia (*Euphorbiaceae*)

fordii **new**	SPlb

Vernonia (*Asteraceae*)

§ ***arkansana***	CHGN ECha EWes LRHS MCot MMuc NDov NLar SMad SPhx WBor
- 'Betty Blindeman'	EBee
- 'Mammuth'	CDes EBee EWes LHop NCob SMrm SPhx WPGP
baldwinii	EBee
crinita	see *V. arkansana*
fasciculata	EBee EShb EWes LPla LRHS MRav NLar SMHy SMrm WCot
gigantea	CSpr EBee EWes MMuc MNrw NLar SBHP SMad WHrl
missurica	EBee
noveboracensis	EBee EPPr GQue NLar SGSe SGar SMad SMrm WPer WRHF
- 'Albiflora'	EPPr EWes

Veronica (*Scrophulariaceae*)

amethystina	see *V. spuria* L.
anagallis-aquatica	LLWG NSco
'Anna'PBR	NDov
armena	EBee ECho EWes MDKP MHer MWat NMen SBch SRot WAbe WFar WPat
§ ***austriaca***	MLLN NBre NChi WFar WMoo
- var. ***dubia***	see *V. prostrata*
- 'Ionian Skies'	CPBP CTri EBee ECha ECtt EPPr EWes GKir LBee LRHS MMuc NEgg SEND SGar SMrm SPer WAbe WCom WFar WKif WPat WPer WSHC WWEG
- 'Jacqueline'	NBre
§ - subsp. ***teucrium***	CArn CSam CTri EBee ECho MHav SRms WFar WPer
- - 'Crater Lake Blue' ♀H4	EBee ECtt ELan EPfP EShb GKir LEdu LHop LRHS MCot MNFA MRav NBre NVic SMrm SPhx SPlb SRms WCom WCot WEas WFar WMnd WPer WSHC
- - 'Kapitän'	ECha LRHS MNrw WFar WPer
- - 'Knallblau'	EBee SMrm SSvw WFar
- - 'Royal Blue' ♀H4	EAEE EBee EPfP EShb GMaP LRHS MWhi NCGa NSti SBch SBfd SRms WFar WMnd
'Baby Doll'PBR	LRHS LSou MBNS MBri NLar WCra
bachofenii	WTin
beccabunga	CArn CBen CWat EBWF EHon GPoy LPBA MSKA MWts NMir NPer NSco SWat WHer WMAq WPnP WSFF
- var. ***limosa***	WAlt
'Bergen's Blue'	CMac NLar SHar
Blue Bouquet	see *V. longifolia* 'Blaubündel'
'Blue Indigo'	ELan MNrw NBre NGdn
'Blue Spire'	SWat WPer
bombycina	ECho WAbe
- subsp. ***bolkardaghensis***	CPBP NMen WAbe
caespitosa	CPBP
- subsp. ***caespitosa***	NMen WAbe
candida	see *V. spicata* subsp. *incana*
× ***cantiana*** 'Kentish Pink'	WCFE WDyG WFar WMoo WOut WPer WSpi WWEG
caucasica	MWat
chamaedrys	EBWF ECho NMir
§ - 'Miffy Brute' (v)	NBir
- 'Pam' (v)	CBow ECtt
- 'Variegata'	see *V. chamaedrys* 'Miffy Brute'
- 'Waterrow'	WAlt
- 'Yorkley Wood'	WAlt
'Charming Pink' **new**	LRHS
'Christy' **new**	LBuc LRHS SPoG
cinerea ♀H4	GMaP MLHP SAga SBch WEas WHoo WSHC
dabneyi	CDes EBee WPGP
'Dark Martje'	EBee GBin
'Darwin's Blue'PBR	GAbr LRHS NLar NMoo WHrl
'Ellen Mae'	CElw ECtt EWes WCAu WMnd
'Eveline'PBR	EBee ECtt EPfP LSou MBri NDov NLar
exaltata (D)	CMdw NChi SMHy SMrm WCot WPer WSpi
'Fairytale'PBR	CWGN EPfP IPot LRHS LSou MAsh MBNS MBri MLLN MWea NSti SMrm
'Fantasy'	NDov
filiformis 'Fairyland' (v)	EWes
§ ***fruticans***	ECho GJos NMen
fruticulosa	LLHF
gentianoides ♀H4	Widely available
- 'Alba'	CMea GCal LRHS NBre NChi NSti
- 'Barbara Sherwood'	EBee EBrs EKen GBin GKir GMac LRHS NBre WWEG
- 'Blue Streak'	EWll LRHS SGSe WRHF
- 'Lilacina'	EBee LRHS
- 'Nana'	EBee EPfP
- 'Pallida'	CSpr EBee EPfP GAbr MBrN MMuc MRav NMoo SEND SPlb WBor WFar WWEG
- 'Robusta'	EBee ECtt EHrv GMac LRHS NCGa NCob NEgg SMrm WCom WMnd
- 'Tissington White'	Widely available
- 'Variegata' (v)	CBcs EBee ECha ECho ECtt ELan EPfP GCra GKir GMaP LAst MHer MRav MSCN NBir NEgg NPnk NPri SPer SWat WBrE WCom WEas WFar WMnd WWEG
'Giles van Hees' **new**	WCot
grandis	EBee GAbr IFro LEdu MDKP MMuc MWhi NChi NLar SEND WFar WHrl WMoo WPtf
× ***guthrieana***	CAbP NMen SRms WFar
hendersonii	see *V. subsessilis hendersonii*
incana	see *V. spicata* subsp. *incana*
* - 'Candidissima'	GCal
'Inspiration'	CMdw NBre NDov SMrm
'Inspire Blue'	LSou
'Inspire Pink'	LSou
kellereri	see *V. spicata*
kiusiana	CMHG IFro LPla MAvo MWhi NBPC NLar SAga SPhx WHrl
* - var. ***maxima***	CAby GQue MAvo SGar WPtf
liwanensis	ECho NMen
- Mac&W 5936	EPot MDKP
longifolia	CHar CMea CSBt ECha ELan GCra LRHS MLHP NBPC NSti NVic WClo WFar WMoo
- 'Alba'	EBee ELan LBMP MMuc NLar STes WMoo
§ - 'Blaubündel'	CMdw EBee NGdn
- 'Blauer Sommer'	EAEE EBee EPfP MCot NDov NEgg NGdn
§ - 'Blauriesin'	CCVN CTri EBee ECtt EPfP GMaP MWea NBre NSti SPer SSvw WSpi

	- Blue Giantess	see *V. longifolia* 'Blauriesin'
	- 'Blue John'	EBee GMac NBre NSti WCot
	- blue-flowered	SGSe
	- 'Fascination'	ECtt LAst NGdn
	- 'Foerster's Blue'	see *V. longifolia* 'Blauriesin'
	- 'Joseph's Coat' (v)	CBow EBee MLLN NBre
	- 'Lila Karina'	EBee WPer
	- 'Lilac Fantasy'	EBee ECtt GMac GQue MBri NGdn NSti
	- 'Oxford Blue'	CBar EGxp LRHS WHoo
	- 'Pacific Ocean' PBR **new**	ECtt
	- pink-flowered	EShb STes
	- 'Rose Tone'	GJos MWea NLar SBHP WHal WHrl WMoo
	- 'Rosea'	LAst SBfd WPer
	- 'Schneeriesin'	CPrp EAEE EBee ECGP ECha EHrv EPfP GMaP MRav NBir NLar SPer
	lyallii	see *Parahebe lyallii*
	'Martje'	SMrm
	'Mini Spires Blue'	EPfP LRHS MGos
	'Mini Spires Pink'	MGos
	montana	EBWF
	- 'Corinne Tremaine' (v)	CBar CBow EBee NBir NLar SAga SRms WHer
	officinalis	CArn EBWF
	- 'Cream Crackers' (v)	WAlt
	- 'Pathlight'	WAlt
	oltensis	CPBP ECho EDAr EPot EWes LLHF MHer NMen WAbe WPat
	orchidea	EBee SRms
	orientalis subsp. ***orientalis***	NMen
	ornata	WOld WPer
	pectinata	ECtt
	- 'Rosea'	ECho ECtt EWes
	peduncularis 'Oxford Blue'	see *V. umbrosa* 'Georgia Blue'
	perfoliata	see *Parahebe perfoliata*
	petraea 'Madame Mercier'	SMrm
	'Pink Damask'	CHar CWCL EBee ECtt ELan ELon EPfP GMaP MCot MRav MWat NCob NEgg NLar NSti SMrm SUsu WClo WCom WFar WHoo WMnd WTin WWEG
	pinnata 'Blue Eyes'	LBee
	porphyriana	EBee MWea WClo
	prenja	see *V. austriaca*
	'Prince of Wales Feathers'	NCGa
§	***prostrata*** ♀H4	CMea CSam CTri ECho ECtt EPfP GJos GKev LAst LBee LRHS MLHP NEgg NHar NHol SRms WCom WEas WFar WHoo WMoo WNew
	- 'Alba'	MLHP MWat WFar
	- 'Aztec Gold' PBR	CMac NBro NLar
§	- 'Blauspiegel'	CPBP LRHS SMrm
	- 'Blue Ice'	SMrm
	- Blue Mirror	see *V. prostrata* 'Blauspiegel'
	- 'Blue Sheen'	ECho ECtt GEdr LRHS NBir WFar WMoo WPer
	- 'Goldwell'	LRHS
	- 'Lilac Time'	CBar CSpr ECho EPot GKev GMaP LHop LRHS MTis NBir NLar SRms WRHF
	- 'Loddon Blue'	ECho SRms
	- 'Miss Willmott'	see *V. prostrata* 'Warley Blue'
	- 'Mrs Holt'	CPBP ECho ECtt GEdr LHop LRHS NBir NHol NMen SRms WAbe WBrk WCom WFar WPat
	- 'Nana'	ECho ECtt EPot EWes MWat NMen WAbe
	- 'Nestor'	CTri ECtt WClo WMoo
	- 'Rosea'	ECho MWat WPer
	- 'Shirley Holt'	GKir NBir
	- 'Spode Blue' ♀H4	CBar CMea ECho ECtt GAbr GKev GMaP LHop LRHS MTis NWCA SPoG SRms WFar WMoo
	- 'Trehane'	EBee ECho ECtt EDAr EPfP LBee LHop LRHS MHer MWat NEgg NPri NRya SPlb SPoG SRms WFar WMoo WNew
§	- 'Warley Blue'	ECho
*	***pseudolysimachion***	MHer WMoo
	'Purpleicious'	CWGN EPfP LRHS LSou MAvo MBri MWea SMrm WHlf
	repens	ECho EPfP GJos SPlb
	'Rosalinde'	CBot WPer
	'Royal Pink'	CBct MSCN NLar NSti
	rupestris	see *V. prostrata*
	saturejoides	CPBP SRms
	saxatilis	see *V. fruticans*
	schmidtiana 'Nana'	GKev
	- 'Nana Rosea'	GKev
	selleri	see *V. wormskjoldii*
	'Shirley Blue' ♀H4	CPrp CWib EBee ELan EPfP GAbr GKir LSRN MHer MMuc MWat SPer SPhx SPoG SRms WCFE WClo WPer WWEG
§	***spicata***	CSam EBee ELan EPfP GJos LEdu LRHS MDun NBid NPnk SRms WBrk WCAu WFar WMoo WPer
	- 'Alba'	EBee GJos MRav MWat NLar WPer WTin WWEG
	- 'Barcarolle'	EBee ELan EPfP
§	- 'Blaufuchs'	ECtt
	- 'Blue Bouquet'	NBre NLar NPri WPtf
	- Blue Fox	see *V. spicata* 'Blaufuchs'
§	- 'Erika'	CBct CPrp EBee ECha ECtt EPfP IPot MNrw MSCN MWat NBir NBre
§	- 'Glory' PBR	CPrp CWGN EBee ECtt EPfP GKir LRHS LSou MGos NBre NCGa NEgg NGdn NMoo SMrm SPad SPer SPoG WCot WWEG
	- 'Heidekind'	CCVN CWCL EBee ECho ECtt EDAr ELan EPPr EPfP GKev LAst LHop MLHP MWat NBir NPri NWCA SBfd SMrm SPoG SRms SRot SWat WFar WHoo WTin
	- 'High Five' PBR	EBee
	- subsp. ***hybrida***	WCot WHer
§	- 'Icicle'	CDes EBee NBre SSvw SUsu WHlf
§	- subsp. ***incana***	CMea CWan EBee ECho EHoe ELan EPfP GJos SAga SBfd SPlb SRms SWat WCFE WFar WMoo WPer WSpi WTin WWEG
	- - 'Nana'	ECha MLHP NBir SRms
	- - 'Silbersee'	MLHP WHil
	- - 'Silver Carpet'	CPrp EBee ECtt LAst MRav NBre SPer WCom WMnd
	- - 'Wendy'	EWes GCal LPla
	- 'Nana Blauteppich'	EPfP LRHS NBre NLar NWCA
	- 'Noah Williams' (v)	ECtt
	- 'Pink Goblin'	GQue NBre WPer
	- 'Pink Panther'	EBee MAvo
	- Red Fox	see *V. spicata* 'Rotfuchs'
	- 'Romiley Purple'	EBee LEdu NBre SPer WSpi WWEG
	- 'Rosalind'	NLar
	- ***rosea***	see *V. spicata* 'Erika'
	- 'Rosenrot'	ECho
§	- 'Rotfuchs'	CPrp EBee ECtt EHoe ELan EPfP GKir LAst LRHS LSou MAvo MCot MLLN MMuc MRav NBPC NBir NMoo SBfd SMrm SPer SPoG SRms WFar WPer WSHC WWEG

- 'Royal Candles'PBR	see *V. spicata* 'Glory'
- 'Sightseeing'	CWib GJos NBir NBre SRms WFar
- 'Twilight'	MBri
- 'Ulster Blue Dwarf'	CBct EPfP GAbr LRHS MAsh MAvo MBri MLLN WPtf
- ***variegata*** (v)	NBir
§ ***spuria*** L.	MMuc WPer
stelleri	see *V. wormskjoldii*
subsessilis	WPer
- 'Blaue Pyramide'	EBee NBre WPtf
* - ***hendersonii***	NBre
'Sunny Border Blue'	EBee EPfP NBre NLar WFar
telephiifolia	ECho ECtt EWes MDKP NMen NWCA
teucrium	see *V. austriaca* subsp. *teucrium*
thessalica	ECho
thymoides subsp. ***pseudocinerea***	NWCA
umbrosa	WEas
§ - 'Georgia Blue'	Widely available
virginica	see *Veronicastrum virginicum*
'Waterperry Blue'	LRHS WFar WPer
wherryi	WPer
'White Icicle'	see *V. spicata* 'Icicle'
'White Jolanda'	EBee ECtt EPfP MLLN MSCN NSti
'White Spire'	CBot
whitleyi	MMuc
§ ***wormskjoldii***	EBee ECho ECtt EDAr MBrN NCGa NLar NMen NWCA SBch SRms
- NNS 06-569	WCot
- 'Alba'	EBee MLHP WPer

Veronicastrum (*Scrophulariaceae*)

'Adoration'	SPhx
brunonianum	CDes GCal
japonicum	SGar
- var. ***australe*** B&SWJ 11009	WCru
latifolium	CDes EBee GCal LPio WCot WPGP WSHC
- BWJ 8158	WCru
sibiricum	CSpe ECha EShb GCal GQue LEdu NBid NBre NLar WAul WMoo
- BWJ 6352	WCru
- 'Red Arrows'	NDov NLar SPhx
- var. ***yezoense***	MDKP
villosulum	CDes CPom EWes IMou NBid NBro SMrm WCru WSHC
§ ***virginicum***	CArn CEnt CKno EBee EBrs ECtt EHrv GCra GPoy LRHS MBrN MLHP MMuc NBir NHol SRms WMoo WPer WWEG
- 'Alboroseum'	WTin
- 'Album'	Widely available
- 'Apollo'	CBre EBee EBla ECtt EPPr EPfP GAbr GMaP LAst LPio LTen MBri MCot NBro NDov NLar NSti SMrm SPhx WAul WBor WCAu WHrl WSpi WWEG
- 'Diane'	EBee GMaP LRHS NBre NDov SPhx WSpi
- 'Erica'	CCVN EBee ECtt EKen EPPr EPfP GBin GMac GQue IKil LPio MBri MLLN MNrw NBPC NDov NMoo NPnk NSti SMHy SPur SUsu WBor WCot WWEG WWlt
- 'Fascination'	Widely available
- var. ***incarnatum***	see *V. virginicum* f. *roseum*
- 'Lavendelturm'	CAby CDes CSam EBee EBrs ECha ECtt EPPr GMaP IPot LHop LRHS MCot NDov NLar NMir NSti SMrm SPer SPhx WAul WSpi
- light blue-flowered	MMuc SGSe
- 'Pointed Finger'	GCal GMaP LEdu NBre NLar SMrm SPhx SUsu
§ - f. ***roseum***	CAby EBee EBla ECha ELan GMaP LRHS MRav NBPC NBro NDov SPer SPhx WClo WCot WFar WKif WMoo
- - 'Pink Glow'	Widely available
- 'Spring Dew'	CBre EBee ECtt EPfP GBee LPla NBid NBro WMnd
- 'Temptation'	EBee GBin GMaP LRHS NBre NBro SUsu WTin
'White Jolan'	ECtt

Verschaffeltia (*Arecaceae*)

splendida	XBlo

Verticordia (*Myrtaceae*)

chrysantha	SOWG
longistylis	SOWG
minutiflora	SOWG
plumosa purple-flowered	SOWG

Vestia (*Solanaceae*)

§ ***foetida*** ♀H1	CBcs CCCN CElw CPLG CPom CTsd CWib EBee ELan ELon EMil EPfP LRHS MNrw NChi NLar SBig SDnm SEND SGar SOWG WGob WHil WPGP WSHC
lycioides	see *V. foetida*

Viburnum ✿ (*Caprifoliaceae*)

B&SWJ 10290 from Mexico	WCru
acerifolium	GAuc LLHF NHol WFar WPat
alnifolium	see *V. lantanoides*
annamensis B&SWJ 8302	WCru
atrocyaneum	CDul CGHE CPLG EBee NHol NLar SPoG WFar WPGP WPat
- B&SWJ 7272	WCru
- HIRD 113	WPGP
§ ***awabuki***	CBcs CHEx CPLG CSam EBee EPfP EUJe IArd LRHS MBlu MGos MWea NLar SEND SLim SMad SSpi WClo WPGP WPat WSHC
- B&SWJ 8404	WCru
- B&SWJ 11374 from Wabuka, Japan	WCru
§ - 'Emerald Lustre'	CDoC CHEx WPGP WPat
betulifolium	CAbP CBcs CMCN CPLG CPMA EBee EPfP EQua GAuc NLar SMad WFar WPat
- 'Hohuanshan'	WCru
bitchiuense	CPMA ELan NLar
× ***bodnantense***	CBot CMac CTri CWSG EBee LMaj SAga WBrE WHar
- 'Charles Lamont' ♀H4	Widely available
- 'Dawn' ♀H4	Widely available
- 'Deben' ♀H4	EBee EPfP EQua GKir NLar SPer WDin WFar WPat
bracteatum	NLar
buddlejifolium	CMac EBee EPfP EWes GKir MMuc SKHP WCru WFar WPGP
× ***burkwoodii***	Widely available
- 'Anika'	NLar
- 'Anne Russell' ♀H4	Widely available
- 'Chenaultii'	MRav WDin
- 'Compact Beauty'	CPMA EPfP WPat
- 'Conoy'	CPMA LEdu MWat WPat
- 'Fulbrook' ♀H4	CAbP EPfP GKir LEdu LRHS MAsh MGos NLar WDin WFar WPat
- 'Mohawk'	CAbP CDoC CEnd CPMA CWSG EBee ELan EPfP LEdu LRHS MAsh MBri NHol NLar SCoo

		SKHP SWvt WClo WFar WPat WSpi
	- 'Park Farm Hybrid' ♀H4	CAbP CDoC CMac CPLG CPMA CSam CTri CWib EBee ECrN ELan ELon EPfP GKir LAst LBMP LRHS MAsh MRav MSwo NLar NSti SLPl SPer SPoG SRms WFar WKif WPat WSpi
	× ***carlcephalum*** ♀H4	Widely available
	- 'Cayuga'	LEdu NLar WPat
*	- 'Variegatum' (v)	CPMA
	carlesii	CBcs CMac CTri CWib EBee EPfP GKir IVic LAst LSRN LSou MBlu MGan MGos MRav MSwo SCoo SLim SPer WBVN
	- B&SWJ 8838	WCru
	- 'Aurora' ♀H4	Widely available
	- 'Charis'	CPMA CSBt GKir LRHS NLar
	- 'Compactum'	CPMA NHol
	- 'Diana'	CDoC CEnd CMHG CMac CPMA EPfP GKir LRHS LSRN MAsh MBlu MRav MWya NLar SPer SPoG WPat
	- 'Marlou'	CPMA LEdu NLar WPat
	cassinoides	EPfP GBin GKir WFar WPat
	- 'Bullatum'	EPfP
	- 'Sear Charm'	WPat
	'Chesapeake'	CPMA EWes MMuc SEND WDin
	chingii	CGHE CPMA SLon WPGP
	cinnamomifolium ♀H3	CAbP CBcs CHEx CMac CPLG EBee EPfP GKir LRHS MAsh MBri MMuc SAPC SArc SCoo SEND SLon SPer SPoG SSpi WFar WPGP WSHC
*	'Cornubia'	GGal
	cotinifolium	CPLG NLar WCot
	cylindricum	CBot CGHE EBee EPfP EWTr GAuc GKir LHop LRHS NLar SKHP WCru WPGP
	- B&SWJ 6479 from Thailand	WCru
	- B&SWJ 7239	WCru
	- B&SWJ 9719 from Vietnam	WCru
	- BWJ 7778 from China	WCru
	- HWJCM 434 from Nepal	WCru
	dasyanthum	EPfP GAuc NLar
	davidii ♀H4	Widely available
	- (f)	CBcs CBot CDoC CMac CSBt ELan EPfP LAst MAsh MGos SPer SPoG SReu SRms SSta WPat
	- (m)	CBcs CBot CDoC CMac CSBt ELan EPfP GKir MAsh MGos MRav SPer SPoG SReu SRms SSta WPat
	- 'Angustifolium'	EQua LTen WFar
	dentatum	GAuc
	- Blue Muffin = 'Christom'	MBri
	- Chicago Lustre	see *V. dentatum* 'Synnestvedt'
	- 'Morton' **new**	IArd
§	- 'Synnestvedt'	NLar
	- 'White and Blue'	NLar
	dilatatum B&SWJ 4456	WCru
	- B&SWJ 8734	WCru
	- 'Erie'	EPfP
	- 'Inneke' **new**	NLar
	- 'Iroquois'	EPfP
	- 'Michael Dodge'	EPfP MBri NLar
	- 'Sealing Wax'	NLar
	edule	GAuc
	erosum B&SWJ 3585	WCru
	erubescens	CAbP CPMA GKir IArd MBri NLar WFar
	- B&SWJ 8281	WCru
	- 'Foster' **new**	NLar

	- var. ***gracilipes***	CPMA EPfP IArd
	- - HWJK 2163	WCru
	- 'Ward van Teylingen'	EPfP NLar
	'Eskimo'	CAbP CBcs CMac CSBt CWSG EBee EPfP GKir LAst LRHS LSRN MAsh MBNS MGos MRav NMoo SKHP SLim SPoG SWvt WDin WFar
§	***farreri*** ♀H4	Widely available
	- 'Album'	see *V. farreri* 'Candidissimum'
§	- 'Candidissimum'	CBot CDul CMac EBee ELan EPfP EWTr GKir IArd LHop LRHS MRav NLar SPer SPoG
	- 'December Dwarf'	CPMA NLar
	- 'Farrer's Pink'	CAbP CPMA NHol NLar
	- 'Fioretta'	NLar
	- 'Nanum'	CMac CPMA EBee EPfP LRHS MBrN MRav MWat NHol NLar SKHP WFar WPat
	foetens	see *V. grandiflorum* f. *foetens*
	foetidum	NLar
	var. ***ceanothoides***	
	- var. ***rectangulatum*** B&SWJ 1888	WCru
	- - B&SWJ 3451	WCru
	- - B&SWJ 3637	WCru
	fragrans Bunge	see *V. farreri*
	'Fragrant Cloud'	ECrN
	furcatum ♀H4	EPfP IArd MBri NLar SKHP WPat
	- B&SWJ 5939	WCru
	× ***globosum*** 'Jermyns Globe'	CAbP CCVT CDoC CMHG CMac EBee EPfP GKir LAst MRav NLar SLon SPoG WDin WFar WPGP
	grandiflorum	CPMA EPfP NLar WDin
§	- f. ***foetens***	CPMA EPfP NLar
	harryanum	CAbP CDoy CMHG EBee EPfP MBNS NLar SOWG WCru WFar WSHC
	henryi	CAbP CPMA EPfP IArd IDee MAsh NLar WDin WPat
	× ***hillieri***	CHGN MWhi WFar
	- 'Winton' ♀H4	CAbP CDoC CEnd CMac CPMA CWib CWit EBee EPfP GKir LHop LRHS LSRN LTen MBri NLar NPal SKHP SLon SOWG SPoG SSpi WDin WFar WPGP
	hupehense	GAuc
	'Huron'	EPfP WPat
	ichangense	CPMA NLar
	japonicum	CMac CPLG EBee EPfP LRHS NLar SLon WFar
	- B&SWJ 5968	WCru
	× ***juddii*** ♀H4	Widely available
	koreanum B&SWJ 4231	WCru
	lantana	CCVT CDul CLnd CRWN CTri CWib ECrN EMac GAuc GKir IFFs LAst LBuc MAsh NLar NWea SCoo SEND SPer SPoG SVic WDin WFar WMou
	- 'Aureum'	CMHG ECtt EHoe EPfP MAsh MBlu NLar SCoo
	- var. ***discolor***	NLar
	- 'Mohican'	EBee NLar
	- 'Variefolium' (v)	CPMA
§	***lantanoides***	EPfP GKir NLar SSpi
	lentago	CAbP CMac NLar
	lobophyllum	EPfP NLar
	luzonicum B&SWJ 3930	WCru
*	- var. ***floribundum*** B&SWJ 8281	WCru
	- var. ***oblongum*** B&SWJ 3549	WCru
	macrocephalum	CEnd CPMA IArd SLon WDin

	mariesii	see *V. plicatum* f. *tomentosum* 'Mariesii'
	nervosum B&SWJ 2251a	WCru
	nudum	EBee ECrN EPfP IVic NLar
	- 'Pink Beauty'	CGHE CPMA CWSG EBee EMil GKir LRHS LSRN MAsh MWya NLar WFar WPGP WPat
	- 'Winterthur'	CPMA NLar
	odoratissimum misapplied	see *V. awabuki*
	odoratissimum Ker Gawl. RWJ 10046	WCru
	- 'Emerald Lustre'	see *V. awabuki* 'Emerald Lustre'
	aff. ***odoratissimum*** B&SWJ 3913 from the Philippines **new**	WCru
	'Oneida'	NLar WDin WPat
	opulus	Widely available
§	- var. ***americanum***	MBri
	- - 'Bailey's Compact'	MAsh WPat
	- - 'Phillips'	CAgr
	- - 'Spring Red'	MBri
	- - 'Wentworth'	CAgr
	- 'Apricot'	NLar
	- 'Aureum'	CChe CMac CSam CWib CWit EBee ECtt EHoe ELan EPfP GKir LAst LBMP MAsh MGos MMuc MRav NEgg NHol NLar NMyG SPer SPoG SSta WClo WDin WFar WMoo
	- var. ***calvescens*** B&SWJ 10544	WCru
	- 'Compactum' $\mathbb{Y}^{H4}$	Widely available
*	- 'Harvest Gold'	EBee GKir SCoo SLim SPoG
	- 'Nanum'	CAbP CBcs CMea EBee ELan ELon EPfP EPla EShb GKev GKir LAst MRav NHol NLar NMen WDin WFar WPat
	- 'Notcutt's Variety' $\mathbb{Y}^{H4}$	EPfP GKir MGos SRms WPat
	- 'Park Harvest'	CDul EBee EPfP GKir LRHS NLar SKHP SLPl
§	- 'Roseum' $\mathbb{Y}^{H4}$	Widely available
	- 'Sterile'	see *V. opulus* 'Roseum'
*	- 'Sterile Compactum'	LAst SWvt
	- 'Sunshine'	MBri
N	- 'Xanthocarpum' $\mathbb{Y}^{H4}$	CBcs CDoC CDul CMHG CMac CPLG CSam EBee ELan EPfP LAst LHop LRHS MBlu MGos MMuc MRav MSwo NLar NMyG SBfd SKHP SLPl SLon SPer SPoG SRms SWvt WDin WFar
	parvifolium	NLar
	- B&SWJ 4009	WCru
	pichinchense B&SWJ 10660	WCru
N	***plicatum***	CTri CWib GAuc NLar WDin
	- 'Janny'	WPat
	- 'Mary Milton'	NLar
	- 'Nanum'	see *V. plicatum* f. *tomentosum* 'Nanum Semperflorens'
	- 'Pink Sensation'	CPMA GBin GGal NCGa
§	- f. ***plicatum***	GKir
	- - 'Grandiflorum'	CAbP CDoC EPfP GKir NLar WMoo
	- 'Popcorn'	CAbP CMac CPMA EBee EPfP EWTr LEdu LRHS LSRN MAsh MRav SPoG SReu SSta WPat
	- 'Rosace'	EPfP MBlu MBri NLar SSpi WPat
	- 'Shoshoni'	MBri NLar
N	- 'Sterile'	see *V. plicatum* f. *plicatum*
	- f. ***tomentosum***	EGxp EPfP EWTr WDin
	- - 'Cascade'	EBee EWTr LRHS MMHG MWya NEgg NLar SSpi

	- - 'Dart's Red Robin'	ECtt LLHF NLar WPat
	- - 'Elizabeth Bullivant'	LLHF LRHS MAsh
	- - 'Igloo'	NLar
	- - 'Lanarth'	Widely available
§	- - 'Mariesii' $\mathbb{Y}^{H4}$	Widely available
	- - 'Molly Schroeder'	CPMA MBri NLar
§	- - 'Nanum Semperflorens'	CAlb CDoC CMac ECtt EPla IArd LBMP MGos NHol NLar SBfd SLPl SPoG WFar WPat WSHC
	- - Newport = 'Newzam'	CDoC IVic NLar
	- - 'Pink Beauty' $\mathbb{Y}^{H4}$	Widely available
	- - 'Rotundifolium'	LRHS MRav MWya NLar WPat
	- - 'Rowallane'	EPfP MBri WPat
	- - 'Shasta'	CDoC CMCN EPfP EWTr MBri NLar SKHP WDin WFar WSpi
	- - 'Summer Snowflake'	CDoC CEnd CWGN CWSG EBee ECrN EPfP LRHS MAsh MSwo NHol NLar SKHP SLim SPer SPoG WDin WFar
	- Triumph = 'Trizam'	NLar
	- 'Watanabe'	see *V. plicatum* f. *tomentosum* 'Nanum Semperflorens'
	'Pragense' $\mathbb{Y}^{H4}$	CAbP CBcs CDul CMCN EBee EPfP EQua GKir MGos MMuc NHol SLon SPer WDin WFar WPat
	propinquum	CAbP NLar WFar
	- B&SWJ 4009	WCru
	prunifolium	NLar
	- 'Mrs Henry's Large'	CPMA
	punctatum B&SWJ 9532	WCru
*	'Regenteum'	CWib
	× ***rhytidophylloides***	GKir WFar
	- 'Alleghany'	EBee NLar
	- Dart's Duke = 'Interduke'	SLPl
	- 'Willowwood'	EBee LRHS MAsh NLar SPer WPat
	rhytidophyllum	CBcs CDoy CDul CHEx CMac CTri EBee ECrN EPfP GKir LHop LRHS LTen MGos MMuc MSwo NEgg SBfd SCoo SEND SPer SReu SRms WCFE WDin WFar WMoo
	- 'Aldenham'	GCal LSRN
	- 'Crathes Castle'	NLar
	- 'Roseum'	CBot CPLG SLPl SWvt
	- 'Variegatum' (v)	CPMA NLar WPat
	- 'Wisley Pink'	LRHS MAsh SSpi
	'Royal Guard'	LLHF NLar WPat
	sargentii	GAuc
	- B&SWJ 8695	WCru
	- f. ***flavum***	NLar
	- 'Onondaga' $\mathbb{Y}^{H4}$	Widely available
	- 'Susquehanna'	EPfP NLar
	semperflorens	see *V. plicatum* f. *tomentosum* 'Nanum Semperflorens'
§	***setigerum***	EPfP GAuc IArd NLar SLPl WPat
	- 'Aurantiacum'	EPfP NLar
	sieboldii	GAuc
	- B&SWJ 2837	WCru
	- 'Seneca'	EPfP NLar
	subalpinum	NLar
	taiwanianum B&SWJ 3009	WCru
	ternatum	EPfP
	theiferum	see *V. setigerum*
	tinoides B&SWJ 10757	WCru
	tinus	Widely available
	- 'Bewley's Variegated' (v)	CBcs EBee MRav SPer
I	- 'Compactum'	SWvt
	- 'Eve Price' $\mathbb{Y}^{H4}$	Widely available
	- 'French White' $\mathbb{Y}^{H4}$	CDoC CDul CMac EBee ELan ELon EPfP LRHS MGos MRav SBfd SCoo SLim SPoG SWvt WFar
	- 'Gwenllian' $\mathbb{Y}^{H4}$	Widely available
	- 'Israel'	EBee MBNS NLar SPer WFar

- 'Little Bognor'	EBee NLar
- 'Lucidum'	CBcs CPMA CSam EBee NLar WCFE WDin WFar
- 'Lucidum Variegatum' (v)	CMac CPMA SLim
* - 'Macrophyllum'	EBee EPfP LRHS NLar SPoG SWvt WFar
- 'Pink Prelude'	EPla WSpi
- 'Purpureum'	CBar CSBt EBee ECrN EHoe ELon EPfP EPla GKir IFFs LBMP LRHS MAsh MGos MSwo NEgg NHol SBfd SCoo SLPl SLim SPer SPoG WBrE WDin WFar WGwG WMoo WPat
- Spirit = 'Anvi'[PBR]	CAbP CSBt EBee LRHS LSou MAsh MBri NCGa NLar SBfd SCoo SPoG
- 'Spring Bouquet'	MAsh NHol NLar
- 'Variegatum' (v)	CBot CDul CMac CTri CWib EBee EHoe ELan ELon EPfP LAst LBMP LHop LRHS MAsh MGos NEgg NHol NLar SBfd SCoo SLim SPlb SPoG SWvt WBrE WCFE WDin WFar WPat
tomentosum	see *V. plicatum*
trilobum	see *V. opulus* var. *americanum*
urceolatum B&SWJ 6988	WCru
utile	WFar WPat WThu
aff. ***venustum*** B&SWJ 10477	WCru
wrightii	EPfP MRav NLar WPat
- B&SWJ 8780	WCru
- 'Hessei'	WPat
- var. ***stipellatum*** B&SWJ 5844	WCru

Vicia (*Papilionaceae*)

americana new	EBee
cracca	EBWF NLan NMir NSco WSFF
oroboides	LRHS
sativa	EBWF NSco
sepium	NSco
sylvatica	CBgR CPom EWes
unijuga	CPom

Vigna (*Papilionaceae*)

§ ***caracalla***	CCCN

Viguiera (*Asteraceae*)

multiflora	EBee

Villarsia (*Menyanthaceae*)

bennettii	see *Nymphoides peltata* 'Bennettii'

Vinca (*Apocynaceae*)

balcanica	ILis IMou
difformis 🏆H3-4	CAlb CBgR CHar COIW CPom CTri CWan EBee ECha LLWP LRHS MGos NCGa NPri SBfd SBri SDix WHer
* - 'Alba'	CPom GKir SBch WCom
- subsp. ***difformis***	WBrE
- Greystone form	EPPr EPfP LHop MMuc NHol NLar SEND WGwG WRHF
- 'Jenny Pym'	CAlb CBgR COIW CPom CYeo EBee EPPr EPla EWes GGar LHop LRHS MBNS MMuc NHol SBch SEND SMad SPoG WCom WFar WOut WRHF
- 'Ruby Baker'	EBee LRHS NChi NPri WHrl
- 'Snowmound'	CAlb CBgR COIW CWan EBee LRHS MRav SPoG
'Hidcote Purple'	see *V. major* var. *oxyloba*
major	CBcs CDul CMac CSBt CWib EBee ELan EPfP GKir GPoy LBuc LRHS MGan MGos MSwo NPri NWea SBfd SLim SPer SRms WDin WFar WGwG WMoo
- 'Alba'	CMac CWib WEas
- 'Elegantissima'	see *V. major* 'Variegata'
- 'Expoflora' (v) new	NLar
§ - subsp. ***hirsuta*** (Boiss.) Stearn	CMac
- var. ***hirsuta*** hort.	see *V. major* var. *oxyloba*
- 'Jason Hill'	CAlb
§ - 'Maculata' (v)	CAlb CDoC COIW CSBt EBee EHoe LRHS LSou MGos MLLN MRav MSwo NBPC NHol NPri SBfd SEND SLim SPer SPoG SWvt WFar WMoo
§ - var. ***oxyloba***	CBgR CMac COIW COld CTri ECtt ELan EPla LHop MLLN MRav MWat SPoG SRms WFar WHer
- var. ***pubescens***	see *V. major* subsp. *hirsuta* (Boiss.) Stearn
- 'Reticulata' (v)	ELan
- 'Surrey Marble'	see *V. major* 'Maculata'
§ - 'Variegata' (v) 🏆H4	Widely available
- Westwood form	CFee
- 'Wojo's Jem' (v)	CDoC CMac EBee EWes GKir LBuc LRHS LSRN MBri MGos SCoo SLim SPoG SWvt WCot
minor	CAlb CBar CBcs CBgR CDoC CDul CMac CSBt ECrN ELan EPfP GAbr GKir GPoy LRHS MAsh MGos NWea SBfd SLim SVic WCAu WDin WFar
- f. ***alba*** 🏆H4	CAlb CBcs CBot CDoC CMac COIW EBee ECha EPfP EPPr GBar LRHS LSRN MAsh MGos NEgg NLar SBfd SPer STre WCom WCot WFar
- 'Alba Aureovariegata' Beth Chatto selection	see *V. minor* f. *alba* 'Alba Variegata'
- - 'Gertrude Jekyll' 🏆H4	Widely available
§ - - 'Alba Variegata' (v)	CPLG EHoe GGar GKir LSRN MGos NHol SPer SRms STre WCot WEas WFar WHoo
§ - 'Argenteovariegata' (v) 🏆H4	Widely available
§ - 'Atropurpurea' 🏆H4	Widely available
- 'Aurea'	SPoG WFar
§ - 'Aureovariegata' (v)	CBcs CBot CMac EBee GAbr MGos MRav NHol SLim SPer SPlb WFar
- 'Azurea'	CHid
§ - 'Azurea Flore Pleno' (d) 🏆H4	Widely available
* - 'Blue and Gold'	EAEE ECGP NBre
- 'Blue Drift'	EWes MSwo WSpi
- 'Blue Moon'	ECtt
- 'Bowles's Blue'	see *V. minor* 'La Grave'
- 'Bowles's Variety'	see *V. minor* 'La Grave'
- 'Burgundy'	CFee SRms
- 'Caerulea Plena'	see *V. minor* 'Azurea Flore Pleno'
- 'Dartington Star'	see *V. major* var. *oxyloba*
- 'Double Burgundy'	see *V. minor* 'Multiplex'
- Green Carpet	see *V. minor* 'Grüner Teppich'
§ - 'Grüner Teppich'	WFar
- 'Illumination' (v)	Widely available
§ - 'La Grave' 🏆H4	Widely available
§ - 'Multiplex' (d)	CAlb CYeo EBee ECtt EPPr GBar LBuc NChi NHol SLim SRms WHrl WOut
- 'Purpurea'	see *V. minor* 'Atropurpurea'
- 'Ralph Shugert'	CMac EBee ELon EPPr EPfP EWes LRHS LSRN LSqu MAsh NLar NPri SCoo SPoG WClo
- 'Rubra'	see *V. minor* 'Atropurpurea'

- 'Sabinka'	CHid EPPr
- 'Silver Service' (d/v)	CFee CHid CWan EBee MRav WCot
- 'Variegata'	see *V. minor* 'Argenteovariegata'
- 'Variegata Aurea'	see *V. minor* 'Aureovariegata'
- 'White Gold'	EBee NHol
sardoa	CAlb COIW EBee EPPr EWes

Vincetoxicum (*Asclepiadaceae*)

forrestii	CPLG
fuscum	EBee
§ ***hirundinaria***	EBee EPPr GPoy LEdu WGwG
nigrum	CArn CBcs EBee EWTr GCal NChi NMyG WCot WTin
- I am a Tiny Star = 'Zotista' **new**	MGos
officinale	see *V. hirundinaria*
scandens	CRHN

Viola ✿ (*Violaceae*)

'Admiration' (Va)	WBou
adunca	NWCA
- var. ***minor***	see *V. labradorica* ambig.
§ ***alba***	EWes NMen
'Alethia' (Va)	GMac WBou
'Alice' (Vt)	CGro
'Alice Kate'	MWte WBou
'Alice Witter' (Vt)	CGro EBee ECha NChi
* 'Alison' (Va)	WBou
'Amelia' (Va)	GKir WBou
'Amethyst' (C)	EBee
I 'Amethyst' (Vt)	CGro
I 'Annie' (Vt)	CGro LLHF
'Ardross Gem' (Va)	EBee ECho ECtt GKir GMac WBou
arenaria	see *V. rupestris*
'Arkwright's Ruby' (Va)	SRms
'Ashvale Blue' (PVt)	CGro
'Aspasia' (Va) 🏆H4	GMac WBou
'Avril Lawson' (Va)	GQue SHar WBou
'Baby Franjo'	NVic
'Baby Lucia' (Va)	NVic SRms
'Barbara' (Va)	WBou
'Baroness de Rothschild' misapplied	see *V.* 'Baronne Alice de Rothschild'
'Baroness de Rothschild' ambig. (Vt)	CGro
§ 'Baronne Alice de Rothschild' (Vt)	GMaP SHar WCot
'Beatrice' (Vtta)	WBou
'Becky Groves' (Vt)	CGro
* ***bella***	WEas
§ 'Belmont Blue' (C)	CEnt CSam CSpe CTri EBee ECtt EWes GCal GCra GMac IFro LHop LRHS MHer MMuc MRav MSCN MWte NBir NCGa NDov SPer SRkn SRms WBou WCot WFar WSpi
§ ***bertolonii***	WBou
'Beshlie' (Va) 🏆H4	EBee ECtt WBou WEas
biflora	CMHG CPla MTho
'Blue Butterfly' (C)	CAby GMac
'Blue Horns' (C)	ELon
'Blue Moon' (C)	WBou
'Blue Moonlight' (C)	EBee LRHS MMuc SUsu
'Boughton Blue'	see *V.* 'Belmont Blue'
'Bournemouth Gem' (Vt)	CGro
§ 'Bowles's Black' (T)	CArn CSWP CSpe EPfP GCal LBMP LEdu MMuc NBro NGHP NVic SRms WJek
'Boy Blue' (Vtta)	ECtt
'Bruneau' (dVt)	ECtt EWll WCot
* 'Bryony' (Vtta)	WBou
'Bullion' (Va)	EBee WBou
'Burncoose Yellow'	WBou
'Buttercup' (Vtta)	COIW ECtt GKir GMac LSRN MAsh NEgg SPoG WBou
'Butterpat' (C)	CAby GMac
'Buxton Blue' (Va)	WBou
'Candy' (Vt)	CGro
canina	NBro NMir
'Carol' (Vt)	CGro
'Carol Loxton' (Vt)	CGro
'Catalina'	ELon
'Charles William Groves' (Vt)	CGro ELon
- 'Charles Winston Groves' (Vt) **new**	CGro
'Charlotte'	WBou WJek
'Chloe' (Vtta)	CGro
'Christie's Wedding' (Vt)	CGro
'Christmas' (Vt)	CGro
'Cinders' (Vtta)	GMac
'Clementina' (Va) 🏆H4	MRav WBou
'Cleo' (Va)	WBou
'Clive Farrell' (Vt)	CGro
'Clive Groves' (Vt)	CGro CHid ELon
'Coeur d'Alsace' (Vt)	EBee NCGa NLar WEas WHal
'Colette' (Va)	WBou
'Colombine' (Vt)	CGro
'Columbine' (Va)	EBee ECtt EPfP GKir GMaP GMac LRHS MAsh MHer NBir NDov NEgg NPri SAga SPer SPoG WBou WClo WCot WFar WJek WNew
'Comte de Chambord' (dVt)	SHar WFar
'Connigar'	CSam
§ 'Conte di Brazza' (dPVt)	CGro EHrv SHar WFar WHer
'Cordelia' (Va)	WFar
cornuta 🏆H4	CElw CMea CPla ECho EPot GGar GKir LRHS MLHP MWat NBir NBro NChi NCob NWCA SBch SRms WBou WCom WFar WHoo WTou
- Alba Group 🏆H4	Widely available
- 'Alba Minor'	CAby CEnt EBee ECho EPfP EWes GCal GMac IGor NBro WAbe WFar
- 'Blaue Schönheit'	LRHS
- blue-flowered	ECho MHer MLHP WFar WMoo
- 'Brimstone'	GMac
- 'Cleopatra' (C)	GAbr GMac
- 'Clouded Yellow'	GMac MWte
- 'Compton Lane'	WCom
- 'Gypsy Moth' (C)	GMac
- 'Icy But Spicy'	EBee EHrv EWTr SMrm WBou WCot
- Lilacina Group (C)	ECha MRav SWat WFar WMnd WPtf
- 'Maiden's Blush'	GMac
- 'Minor' 🏆H4	CPla CSam GMac NBro WAbe WBou
- 'Netta Statham'	NDov WBou
- 'Pale Apollo' (C)	GMac
- Purpurea Group	CMea ECha GCal SBch WMnd
- 'Rosea'	ECha
- 'Spider'	CAby GMac
- 'Ulla'	SBfd
- 'Victoria's Blush' (C)	CAby CSpe EBee ECtt ELon EWTr GMaP GMac MMuc NBir NDov WBou
- 'Violacea'	GMac
- 'Yellow King'	EHrv
corsica	CMea CSpe EBee NChi WOut
'Crepuscle' (Vt)	CGro
§ ***cucullata*** 🏆H4	ECho SRms WFar
§ - 'Alba' (Vt)	CGro ECho LLWP NBir SRms
- ***rosea***	EWes
* - 'Striata Alba'	NBre NBro
'Czar'	see *V.* 'The Czar'
'Daisy Smith' (Va)	WBou

	'Dancing Geisha' (Vt)	EHrv EPfP
	'Danielle Molly'	WBou
	'Dawn' (Vtta)	EBee ECtt GKir GMaP NEgg NPri SBch SPoG WBou WClo
	'Delicia' (Vtta)	CAby WBou
	'Delphine' (Va)	NChi
	'Des Charentes' (Vt)	CGro
	'Desdemona' (Va)	GMac WBou
	'Devon Cream' (Va)	GMac WBou
	'Diana Groves' (Vt)	CGro
	'Dick o' the Hills' (Vt)	CGro
	dissecta	WCot
	'Donau' (Vt)	CGro EBee WCot
	'Doreen' (Vt)	CGro
	'Duchesse de Parme' (dPVt)	CGro IFro NWCA SRms
	'D'Udine' (dPVt)	CGro WCot
	'Dusk'	WBou
	'E.A. Bowles'	see *V.* 'Bowles's Black'
	'Eastgrove Blue Scented' (C)	GMaP GMac WBou WEas WOut WPtf WWFP
	'Eastgrove Ice Blue' (C)	WBou WEas
	'Eastgrove Twinkle' (C)	WEas
	eizanensis	MTho
	'Elaine Quin'	EBee ECtt NDov NEgg NPri SPoG WBou WKif
§	***elatior***	CPla CSWP EBee EBla EPPr MNrw WHil WPer WSHC
	'Elizabeth' (Va)	ECtt GKir WBou
	'Elizabeth Lee'	WCot
	'Elliot Adam' (Va)	WBou
	'Elsie Coombs' (Vt)	CGro
	'Emma' (Va)	CAby
	'Emperor Blue Vein'	EBee EPfP LSou
	'Emperor Magenta Red'	GJos LSou
	'Emperor White'	LSou
	erecta	see *V. elatior*
	'Eris' (Va)	WBou
	'Etain' (Va)	COlW EBee ECho ECtt ELan EPfP EWes GMaP LRHS MAsh NDov NEgg NPri SMrm SPer SPoG SUsu WBou WClo
	'Fabiola' (Vtta)	CAby GMac NBir
	'Famecheck Apricot'	CPom
*	'Fantasy'	CAby WBou
	fargesii B&SWJ 6728	WCru
	'Feline' (PVt)	CGro
	'Ferndale' (Vt) **new**	CGro
	'Fiona' (Va)	CAby GMac MCot NChi WBou
	'Fiona Lawrenson' (Va)	WBou
	flettii	WAbe
	'Florence' (Va)	WBou
	(Foiolina Series) 'Foiolina Blue'	LSou
	- 'Foiolina Orange'	LSou
	- 'Foiolina Purple'	LSou
	- 'Foiolina White'	LSou
	'Foxbrook Cream' (C)	CAby WBou
	'Freckles'	see *V. sororia* 'Freckles'
	'Fred Morey' (Vt)	CGro
	'George Lee' (Vt)	CGro
	'Gladys Findlay' (Va)	WBou
*	'Glenda'	WBou
	'Glenholme'	GMac
	'Gloire de Verdun' (PVt)	CGro NWCA
	'Governor Herrick' (Vt)	CGro WCot
§	***gracilis***	NBir WFar
	- 'Lutea'	CSam
	- 'Major'	WBou
	'Green Goddess'^{PBR}	EBee GKev MWea WFar
	'Green Jade' (v)	CPla
	'Grey Owl' (Va)	WBou
	'Grovemount Blue' (C)	CElw CMea
§	***grypoceras*** var. ***exilis***	EBee NGdn NWCA
	- - 'Sylettas'	CBow GGar NBPC
	'Gustav Wermig' (C)	WBou
	'Haslemere'	see *V.* 'Nellie Britton'
*	'Heaselands'	SMHy SMrm
§	***hederacea***	CTsd EBee ECho ECou GQui IFoB SRms WFar WPtf
	'Helen' (Va)	ECtt
§	'Helen Mount' (T)	LBMP
	'Helena' (Va)	WBou
	'Hespera' (Va)	WBou
	heterophylla subsp. ***epirota***	see *V. bertolonii*
*	'Hetty Gatenby'	WBou
	hirsutula	EBla EHrv
I	- 'Alba'	EBla
I	- 'Purpurea'	EBla
	'Hudsons Blue'	CElw WEas
	'Huntercombe Purple' (Va) 🏆^{H4}	ECho LHop LRHS MCot NBir SRms WBou WHal WKif
	'Iden Gem' (Va)	NDov WBou
	'Inverurie Beauty' (Va) 🏆^{H4}	GMaP GMac NDov WBou WKif
	'Irish Elegance'	see *V.* 'Sulfurea'
	'Irish Molly' (Va)	CBot CSpe EBee ECho ECtt ELan EPfP GGar GKev GKir GMac LRHS MHer NEgg NPri SPer SPoG SRms WBou WClo WFar
	'Isabel'	NDov WBou
	'Isabella' (Vt)	CGro
	'Ivory Queen' (Va)	CAby GMac MRav WBou
	'Jack Sampson' (Vt)	CGro
	'Jack Simpson'	WCot
	'Jackanapes' (Va) 🏆^{H4}	EBee ECho ECtt ELan EPfP GKir LRHS NEgg NPri SPer SPoG SRms WBou WFar
	'Jane Mott' (Va)	GMac
	'Janet' (Va)	EBee ECtt NPri SPoG
	japonica	GGar
	jaubertiana **new**	CGro
	'Jeannie Bellew' (Va)	ECtt SRms WBou WFar WSpi
	'Jennifer Andrews' (Va)	WBou
	'Joanna' (Va)	WBou
	'John Raddenbury' (Vt)	GMaP
	'Johnny Jump Up'	see *V.* 'Helen Mount'
	jooi	CGro CPBP ECho EPfP GCrs MWea NBir NMen SPhx SRms WPat WPtf
	'Josie' (Va)	WBou
	'Joyce Gray' (Va)	WBou
	'Judy Goring' (Va)	GMac
	'Julia' (Va)	WBou
	'Julian' (Va)	CAby GMac SRms WBou
	'Juno' (Va)	GMac
	'Katerina' (Va)	WBou
	'Kerry Girl' (Vt)	CGro
	'Kim'	CGro
	'Kitten'	CAby GAbr GMac NChi WBou
	'Kitty White' (Va)	CAby GMac
§	'Königin Charlotte' (Vt)	CGro COlW EPfP GMac LBMP LRHS MCot MHer NChi NEgg NWCA WCot WFar WHil WMoo
	koreana	see *V. grypoceras* var. *exilis*
N	***labradorica*** misapplied	see *V. riviniana* Purpurea Group
N	- ***purpurea***	see *V. riviniana* Purpurea Group
§	***labradorica*** ambig.	CHar ECho GQui LRHS MCot MRav NPri SMrm WCAu WFar
	lactiflora	EBee
	'Lady Hume Campbell' (PVt)	CGro WHer
	'Lady Jane' (Vt)	CGro
	'Lady Saville'	see *V.* 'Sissinghurst'
	'Laura Cawthorne'	EBee
	'Lavender Lady' (Vt)	CGro

	'Lavinia' (Va)	WBou
	'Lees Peachy Pink' (Vt)	CGro EBee
	'Letitia' (Va)	EBee SRms WBou WFar
	'Lianne' (Vt)	CGro EBee LLHF WCot
	'Lindsay'	WBou
	'Lisa Tanner' (Va)	WBou
	'Lise Lazare' (Vt)	CGro
	'Little David' (Vtta) Υ^{H4}	CSam CTri ECtt GMac MCot NDov SRms WBou
	'Lord Nelson' (Va)	EBee
	'Lord Plunket' (Va)	WBou
	'Lorna Cawthorne' (C)	WBou
	'Lorna Moakes' (Va)	SAga
	'Louisa' (Va)	GMac WBou
§	***lutea***	WBou
	- subsp. ***elegans***	see *V. lutea*
	'Luxonne' (Vt)	CGro
	'Lydia Groves' (Vt)	WCot
	'Madame Armandine Pagès' (Vt)	CGro
	'Maggie Mott' (Va) Υ^{H4}	ECho ECtt GMac LHop LRHS WBou WFar WSpi WWFP
	'Magic'	EBee WBou
	mandshurica	NWCA
	- 'Fuji Dawn' (v)	CBow CPla EBee SGSe WCot
	- f. ***hasegawae***	EPPr
	'Margaret' (Va)	WBou
	'Marie-Louise' (dPVt)	CGro GMaP SHar
I	'Mars'	CAbP ECtt GBin LSRN LSou MSCN WFar
	'Mars' (Va)	EBee ECtt SBch SMrm WHer WSpi
	'Martin' (Va) Υ^{H4}	CAby COIW EBee ECha ECtt GMaP GMac LHop LSRN MHer NDov SPer SPoG WBou WClo WCom WFar
	'Mary Mouse'	NDov WBou
	'Mauve Haze' (Va)	WBou
	'Mauve Radiance' (Va)	ECtt GMac WBou
	'May Mott' (Va)	GMac WBou
	'Mayfly' (Va)	CAby WBou
	'Melinda' (Vtta)	WBou
	'Melting Moments' (Va)	NEgg WClo
	'Mercury' (Va)	WBou
	'Milkmaid' (Va)	EBee ELon NBir
	'Miss Brookes' (Va)	WBou
	'Misty Guy' (Vtta)	CAby WBou
	'Molly Sanderson' (Va) Υ^{H4}	COIW CSpe EBee ECha ECho ECtt ELan EPfP GGar GKir LAst LHop LRHS MHer MMuc MRav NEgg NPri SPer SPlb SPoG WBor WBou WClo WFar WNew
	'Moonlight' (Va) Υ^{H4}	ECho ELan GKir LHop LRHS MHer MMuc WBou
	'Moonraker'	GMaP NBir
	'Morwenna' (Va)	ECtt MCot WBou WKif
	'Mrs Lancaster' (Va)	EBee GMaP GMac LHop LSRN NBir NChi NPri SPoG SRms WBou
	'Mrs Pinehurst' (Vt)	CGro
	'Mrs R. Barton' (Vt)	CGro SHar
	'Mulberry' (Vt)	CGro
	'Myfawnny' (Va)	ECho ECtt ELan EWes GKir GMac LRHS NDov SRms WBou WFar WSpi
	'Neapolitan'	see *V.* 'Pallida Plena'
§	'Nellie Britton' (Va) Υ^{H4}	ECho ECtt SRms
	'Netta Statham'	see *V.* 'Belmont Blue'
	'Nora'	NDov WBou
	'Norah Church' (Vt)	CGro
	'Norah Leigh' (Va)	EOHP WBou
	obliqua	see *V. cucullata*
	odorata (Vt)	CArn CBcs CBod CGro CRWN CSWP EBee EPfP GBar GPoy MRav NMir NPri NSco SBfd SIde SPer SRms SVic WJek
	- 'Alba' (Vt)	CPom CSWP CWan EBee ECho ELan EPfP EWTr GBar ILis MHer NPri SEND SRms WMoo
	- 'Alba Plena' (dVt)	CDes EHrv LSou
	- 'Albiflora'	CEnt
	- apricot-flowered	see *V.* 'Sulfurea'
	- 'Dawnie' (Vt)	CGro
	- var. ***dumetorum***	see *V. alba*
	- 'Elsmeer' **new**	WCot
	- 'Katy'	CPom ELon SBch
	- 'King of Violets' (dVt)	EBee ECtt EWll LRHS LSou MTis NCGa NEgg SHar SPer WClo WCot WFar WWFP
	- 'Melanie' **new**	WCot
	- 'Perky' (Vt) **new**	CGro
	- pink-flowered	see *V. odorata* Rosea Group
	- 'Port Breedy' (Vt) **new**	CGro
	- 'Red Devil'	WCot WFar
	- ***rosea***	see *V. odorata* Rosea Group
§	- Rosea Group (Vt)	CDes CEnt CGro CPom EBee EWll GBar GMac IFoB LRHS LSou MMuc MRav MTis NEgg SEND SIde SPer WClo WCot WCra
	- 'Souvenier de Jules Josse' (Vt) **new**	CGro
*	- subsp. ***subcarnea*** (Vt)	SEND
	- 'Sulphurea'	see *V.* 'Sulfurea'
	- 'Vin d'André Thorp'	NBPC WCot
I	- 'Violett Charm' **new**	WCot
	- 'Weimar'	GBin
	- 'Wismar' **new**	WCot
	'Opéra' (Vt)	CGro LLHF
	'Orchid Pink' (Vt)	CGro EBee GMaP
§	'Pallida Plena' (dPVt)	CGro
	palustris	CRWN LLWG WHer WSFF WShi
	'Pamela Zambra' (Vt)	GMaP SHar WPrP
	papilionacea	see *V. sororia*
*	'Paradise Blue' (Vt)	EBee
	'Parchment' (Vt)	CGro
	'Parme de Toulouse' (dPVt)	CGro
	'Pasha' (Va)	GMac
	'Pat Creasy' (Va)	NDov WBou
	'Pat Kavanagh' (C)	CAby NDov WBou
	'Patience'	WBou
	'Pearl Rose'	ELon
	pedata	EBee WAbe WHil
	- 'Bicolor'	WAbe
	pedatifida	MTho
	pensylvanica	see *V. pubescens* var. *eriocarpa*
	'Peppered-palms'	EHrv SGSe
	'Perle Rose' (Vt)	CGro EHrv
	'Petra' (Vtta)	CAby GMac
	'Phyl Dove' (Vt)	EBee
	'Pickering Blue' (Va)	WBou
	'Primrose Dame' (Va)	MHer WBou WCot
	'Primrose Pixie' (Va)	WBou
	'Prince Henry' (T)	MNHC
	'Prince John' (T)	MNHC
	'Princess Mab' (Vtta)	WBou
	'Princess of Prussia' (Vt)	CGro WCot
	'Princess of Wales'	see *V.* 'Princesse de Galles'
§	'Princesse de Galles' (Vt)	CGro CTri WHal
	'Pritchard's Russian' (Vt)	CGro
	'Prolific' (Vt)	CGro
§	***pubescens*** var. ***eriocarpa***	SRms WCot
	'Purple Emperor' **new**	SBfd
	'Purple Wings' (Va)	WBou
	'Putty'	ECou
	Queen Charlotte	see *V.* 'Königin Charlotte'
	'Queen Victoria'	see *V.* 'Victoria Regina'

'Raven' CAby GMac WBou
'Rebecca' (Vtta) CPla CSam EBee ECho ECtt ELan EPfP GKir GMaP GMac LRHS LSRN MAsh MHer NBir NCGa NChi NDov NEgg NPri SPer SPoG SRms WBou WClo WFar
'Red Charm' (Vt) EBee
'Red Giant' (Vt) CGro EBla EHrv MRav NEgg
'Red Lion' (Vt) CGro
'Red Queen' (Vt) CGro
reichei CRWN
'Reine des Blanches' (dVt) EBee ECtt ELon LLWP LRHS MTis NBPC NEgg NGdn SMrm SPer WClo WCot
reniforme see *V. hederacea*
riviniana CArn CRWN EBWF MHer MMuc NSco WHer WSFF WShi
- dark pink-flowered WAlt
- 'Ed's Variegated' (v) CBow EPPr WCot
§ - Purpurea Group Widely available
- white-flowered EBee EWes MMuc WAlt
'Rodney Davey' (Vt/v) CPla
'Roscastle Black' CMea EBee ECtt GMaP GMac LRHS NDov SBfd SMrm WBou WCot WSpi
'Royal Elk' (Vt) CGro
'Royal Robe' (Vt) CGro
'Rubra' (Vt) WPtf
§ ***rupestris*** CTri CWan ECho
* - ***rosea*** CEnt CPla CPom EBee EPfP IFro LLWP MHer NWCA SBch SGSe STre WOut
'Saint Helena' (Vt) WCot
'Sally' (Vtta) CGro
schariensis EWes
selkirkii Pursh ex Goldie CPla GAuc NWCA
septentrionalis see *V. sororia*
'Serena' (Va) CAby WBou
'Sherbet Dip' WBou
'Sidborough Poppet' CStu EWes
§ 'Sissinghurst' (Va) MHer NBir
'Sisters' (Vt) CGro
'Smugglers' Moon' WBou
'Sophie' (Vtta) WBou
§ ***sororia*** EAEE EBee ECho EPPr MLHP MNrw NBir NBro WBrE WPtf
* - 'Albiflora' ♀H4 CHid CSWP EBee ECho EPPr EPfP EWll GGar LEdu MRav NWCA SPhx WCFE WClo WFar WHil WJek
- 'Dark Freckles' EBee ECho LHop SPhx
§ - 'Freckles' Widely available
- 'Priceana' CGro EAEE EBee ECGP ECha EPyc LEdu NBir NChi SMrm WCot WSpi
- 'Speckles' (v) CBow EBla
* 'Spencer's Cottage' WBou
'Staffordshire Blue' **new** NDov
'Steyning' (Va) WBou
stojanowii CSpe EBee ECho
suavis 'Catalonica White' (Vt) CGro
§ 'Sulfurea' (Vt) CEnt CPBP CPMA EBee ECho LBMP LLWP MMHG NRya NWCA WCot WFar WOut WPer
'Sulphurea' lemon-flowered (Vt) CGro
'Sultan' (Vt) CGro
'Susan Chilcott' (Vt) CGro
'Susanne Lucas' (Vt) CGro
'Susie' (Va) WBou
'Swanley White' see *V.* 'Conte di Brazza'
'Sybil' (SP) WBou
'Sylvia Hart' MTho
'Tanith' (Vt) EBee
§ 'The Czar' (Vt) CBre CGro NChi WCot
'Tiger Eyes' (Va) EBee SPoG
'Tom Tit' (Va) ECtt WBou
'Tony Venison' (C/v) CAby EBee MTho NEgg SPoG WBou WFar WHer WSpi WWFP
tricolor CPrp EBWF ECho EPfP GBar GPoy MHer MNHC NGHP NPri NSco SBch SIde WJek
'Vanessa' (Va) GMac
velutina see *V. gracilis*
verecunda CLAP WSHC
- B&SWJ 604a WCru
'Victoria Cawthorne' (C) CElw GMac MCot MHer NDov WBou WEas
§ 'Victoria Regina' (Vt) EPfP
'Virginia' (Va) WBou
'Vita' (Va) CAby GMac SRms WBou
'Wasp' (Va) GMac
'White Ladies' see *V. cucullata* 'Alba'
'White Pearl' (Va) NDov SPhx WBou
'White Superior' LRHS
'White Swan' (Va) NChi
'William' (Va) NDov
'Winifred Jones' (Va) WBou
'Winifred Warden' (Va) WSpi
'Winona Cawthorne' (C) GMac NDov
'Wisley White' EBee EWes WFar
'Woodlands Cream' (Va) GMac MHer WBou
'Woodlands Lilac' (Va) WBou
'Zara' (Va) WBou
'Zoe' (Vtta) EBee ECtt EPfP NEgg NPri SMrm SPer SPoG WBou WFar

Viscaria (*Caryophyllaceae*)

vulgaris see *Lychnis viscaria*

Vitaliana (*Primulaceae*)

§ ***primuliflora*** ECho GCrs GKev NLAp NMen NRya NSla
- subsp. ***assoana*** GKev
- subsp. ***cinerea*** EPot
- subsp. ***praetutiana*** CPBP NMen NWCA WAbe WPat WThu
- subsp. ***tridentata*** NMen

Vitex (*Verbenaceae*)

agnus-castus CArn CBcs COld CWSG EBee EGFP EOHP EShb GPoy LEdu LRHS LSou MCCP MMuc SBfd SEND SLon SPer WDin WFar WHer WSHC
- 'Alba' CDul CWib EPfP LTen
- var. ***latifolia*** CAlb CWib EBee ELan ELon EPfP LRHS LSRN MAsh MGos MHer NLar SBfd SPoG WPGP
I - 'Rosea' NLar
- 'Silver Spire' CDul EBee ELan SPoG WPGP WSHC
incisa see *V. negundo* var. *heterophylla*
lucens CHEx
negundo CArn EOHP
§ - var. ***heterophylla*** EWes

Vitis ✿ (*Vitaceae*)

'Abundante' (F) WSuV
'Alden' (O/B) WSuV
'Alnwick Seedling' (B/G) **new** ERea
'Amandin' (G/W) WSuV
amurensis CAlb EBee EPfP NLar
- B&SWJ 4138 WCru
'Atlantis' (O/W) WSuV
§ 'Aurore' (W) CAgr WSuV
'Baco Noir' (O/B) CAgr ERea GTwe SDea WSuV

	betulifolia new	EPfP
	'Bianca' (O/W)	MCoo WSuV
	'Birstaller Muscat' (W)	WSuV
	Black Hamburgh	see *V. vinifera* 'Schiava Grossa'
*	'Black Strawberry' (B)	CAgr WSuV
§	'Boskoop Glory' (O/B) 𝕐^{H4}	CMac ERea EUJe LBuc MAsh MCoo NLar NPal SCoo SDea WSuV
	'Brant' (O/B) 𝕐^{H4}	Widely available
	'Brilliant' (B)	WSuV
	'Buffalo' (B)	WSuV
	californica (F)	NLar
	'Canadice' (O/R/S)	SDea WSuV
	'Cascade'	see *V.* Seibel 13053
	Castel 19637 (B)	WSuV
	'Chambourcin' (B)	WSuV
	coignetiae 𝕐^{H4}	Widely available
	- B&SWJ 4550 from Korea	WCru
	- B&SWJ 4744	WCru
	- B&SWJ 10882 from Japan	WCru
	- Claret Cloak = 'Frovit'^{PBR}	CBcs EBee ELan EPfP GKir LRHS LSRN MAsh MRav NLar SCoo SMad SPer SSpi WClo WPGP WPat WSpi
	- cut-leaved	CMac
	- var. ***glabrescens*** B&SWJ 8537	WCru
	- Sunningdale form	WSpi
	'Dalkauer' (W)	WSuV
I	'Diamond' (B)	WSuV
	'Duchess of Buccleuch' (G/W) new	ERea
	'Dutch Black' (O/B)	WSuV
	'Edwards No 1' (O/W)	WSuV
	'Eger Csillaga' (O/W)	WSuV
	'Einset' (B/S)	WSuV
	ficifolia	see *V. thunbergii*
	flexuosa B&SWJ 5568	WCru
	- var. ***choii*** B&SWJ 4101	WCru
§	'Fragola' (O/R)	CAgr CMac CTri EBee ECha EPfP GTwe LOck LRHS MAsh MRav NLar SDea SLim SPer SRms WCom WSuV
	'Gagarin Blue' (O/B)	CAgr ERea GTwe SDea WSuV
	'Glenora' (F/B/S)	CAgr WSuV
	'Hecker' (O/W)	WSuV
	henryana	see *Parthenocissus henryana*
	'Himrod' (O/W/S)	CCCN ERea GTwe MGos NPal SDea WSuV
	'Horizon' (O/W)	WSuV
	inconstans	see *Parthenocissus tricuspidata*
	'Interlaken' (O/W/S)	CAgr ERea WSuV
	'Johanniter' (W)	WSuV
	'Kempsey Black' (O/B)	CAgr WSuV
	'Kozmapalme Muscatoly' (O/W)	WSuV
	'Kuibishevski' (O/R)	WSuV
	Landot 244 (O/B)	WSuV
	Landot 3217 (O/B)	WSuV
	'L'Arcadie Blanche' (W)	WSuV
	'Léon Millot' (O/G/B)	CAgr CSBt ERea LSRN SDea WSuV
	'Lucy Kuhlman' (B)	WSuV
	'Maréchal Foch' (O/B)	EGxp WSuV
	'Maréchal Joffre' (O/R)	CAgr GTwe WSuV
	'Mars' (O/B/S)	WSuV
	'Merzling' (O/W)	WSuV
	'Munson R.W.' (O/R)	WSuV
	'Muscat Bleu' (O/B)	CCCN LRHS NLar SLim SPoG WSuV
	'Nero'^{PBR}	CAgr ERea SBfd
	'New York Muscat' (O/B) 𝕐^{H4}	ERea WSuV
	'New York Seedless' (O/W/S)	WSuV
	'Niagara' (O/W)	WSuV
	'Niederother Monschrebe' (O/R)	WSuV
	Oberlin 595 (O/B)	WSuV
	'Orion' (O/W)	LRHS MAsh WSuV
	'Paletina' (O/W)	WSuV
	parsley-leaved	see *V. vinifera* 'Ciotat'
	parvifolia	WPat
	'Perdin' (O/W)	WSuV
	'Phönix' (O/W)	CAgr CCCN GTwe LRHS MAsh MBri MGos NLar SKee SLim SPoG SVic WSuV
	piasezkii	WCru
*	'Pink Strawberry' (O)	WSuV
	'Pirovano 14' (O/B)	GTwe SDea WSuV
§	'Plantet' (O/B)	WSuV
	'Poloske Muscat' (W)	CCCN ERea GTwe WSuV
	pseudoreticulata	WPGP
	purpurea 'Spetchley Park' (O/B)	CAgr WSuV
	quinquefolia	see *Parthenocissus quinquefolia*
	'Ramdas' (O/W)	WSuV
	Ravat 51 (O/W)	WSuV
	'Rayon d'Or' (O/W)	WSuV
	'Regent'^{PBR} (O/B)	CAgr CCCN CWSG GTwe LRHS MBri MCoo MGos NLar SKee SLim SPoG WSuV
	'Reliance' (O/R/S)	CAgr ERea WSuV
	'Rembrant' (R)	CAgr NPal WSuV
	riparia	CArn NLar
	'Romulus' (O/G/W/S)	WSuV
	'Rondo' (O/B)	CAgr WSuV
	'Saturn' (O/R/S)	CAgr WSuV
	'Schuyler' (O/B)	CAgr WSuV
	Seibel (F)	GTwe SDea
	Seibel 5279	see *V.* 'Aurore'
	Seibel 5409 (W)	WSuV
	Seibel 5455	see *V.* 'Plantet'
	Seibel 7053	WSuV
	Seibel 9549	WSuV
§	Seibel 13053 (O/B)	CMac LRHS MAsh SDea SEND WSuV
	Seibel 138315 (R)	WSuV
	'Seneca' (W)	WSuV
	'Serena' (O/W)	WSuV
§	'Seyval Blanc' (O/W)	CAgr GTwe MMuc SDea SEND SVic WSuV
	Seyve Villard ambig.	LRHS NPer
	Seyve Villard 12.375	see *V.* 'Villard Blanc'
	Seyve Villard 20.473 (F)	MAsh NPer
	Seyve Villard 5276	see *V.* 'Seyval Blanc'
	'Sirius' (B)	WSuV
	'Solaris' (O/W)	WSuV
	'Stauffer' (O/W)	WSuV
	'Suffolk Seedless' (B/S)	ERea WSuV
	'Tereshkova' (O/B)	CAgr ERea SDea WSuV
	'Thornton' (O/S)	WSuV
§	***thunbergii*** B&SWJ 4702	WCru
	'Triomphe d'Alsace' (O/B)	CAgr CSBt NPer SDea WSuV
	'Trollinger'	see *V. vinifera* 'Schiava Grossa'
	'Vanessa' (O/R/S)	SDea WSuV
§	'Villard Blanc' (O/W)	WSuV
	vinifera	EAmu EUJe GKir LTen MGos MREP
	- EM 323158B	WSuV
	- 'Abouriou' (O/B)	WSuV
	- 'Acolon' (O/B)	WSuV
	- 'Adelheidtraube' (O/W)	WSuV
	- 'Albalonga' (W)	WSuV
§	- 'Alicante' (G/B)	CMac EGxp ERea GTwe NPal SDea WSuV
	- 'Apiifolia'	see *V. vinifera* 'Ciotat'
	- 'Appley Towers' (G/B)	ERea

- 'Augusta Louise' (O/W)	WSuV
- 'Auxerrois' (O/W)	WSuV
- 'Bacchus' (O/W)	CAgr LRHS MBri NLar SDea SLim SVic WSuV
- 'Baresana' (G/W)	EGxp WSuV
- 'Beauty'	CAgr
- 'Black Alicante'	see *V. vinifera* 'Alicante'
- 'Black Corinth' (G/B/S)	ERea
- 'Black Frontignan' (G/O/B)	ERea WSuV
- Black Hamburgh	see *V. vinifera* 'Schiava Grossa'
- 'Black Monukka' (G/B/S)	ERea WSuV
- 'Black Prince' (G/B)	CAgr WSuV
- 'Blue Portuguese'	see *V. vinifera* 'Portugieser'
§ - 'Bouvier' (W)	WSuV
- 'Bouviertraube'	see *V. vinifera* 'Bouvier'
- 'Buckland Sweetwater' (G/W)	CDul ERea GTwe SDea SLim WSuV
- 'Cabernet Sauvignon' (O/B)	LRHS MAsh MGos NPer SDea WSuV
- 'Canon Hall Muscat' (G/W)	ERea
- 'Cardinal' (O/R)	EMil LRHS WSuV
- 'Carla' (O/R)	WSuV
- 'Centennial' (O/N/S)	WSuV
- 'Chardonnay' (O/W)	CAgr CCCN CChe ERea LRHS MAsh NPer SDea SPer SVic WSuV
§ - 'Chasselas' (G/O/W)	LRHS MAsh SDea WSuV
- 'Chasselas Blanc' (O/W)	SVic
- 'Chasselas de Fontainebleau' (F)	CCCN LRHS
- 'Chasselas de Tramontaner' (F)	ECrN LRHS
- 'Chasselas d'Or'	see *V. vinifera* 'Chasselas'
- 'Chasselas Rosé' (G/R)	CAgr SVic WSuV
- 'Chasselas Rosé Royal' (O/R)	CCCN
- 'Chasselas Vibert' (G/W)	WSuV
- 'Chenin Blanc' (O/W)	WSuV
§ - 'Ciotat' (F)	ERea EShb MRav SDea WSuV
- 'Cot Précoce de Tours' (O/B)	WSuV
- 'Crimson Seedless' (R/S)	ERea LRHS WSuV
- 'Csabyongye' (O/W)	WSuV
- 'Dattier de Beyrouth' (G/W)	WSuV
- 'Dattier Saint Vallier' (O/W)	SVic WSuV
- 'Dolcetto' (O/B)	WSuV
- 'Dornfelder' (O/R)	CCCN CSut NLar SLim SPoG WSuV
- 'Dunkelfelder' (O/R)	WSuV
- 'Early Van der Laan' (F)	CMac
- 'Ehrenfelser' (O/W)	WSuV
- 'Elbling' (O/W)	WSuV
- 'Exalta' (G/W/S)	CCCN WSuV
- 'Excelsior' (W)	WSuV
- 'Faber' (O/W)	WSuV
- 'Fiesta' (W/S)	WSuV
- 'Findling' (W)	WSuV
- 'Flame'	CAgr
- 'Flame Red' (O/D)	CCCN
- 'Flame Seedless' (G/O/R/S)	LRHS WSuV
- 'Forta' (O/W)	WSuV
- 'Foster's Seedling' (G/W)	GTwe SDea SVic WSuV
- 'Freisamer' (O/W)	WSuV
- 'Frühburgunder' (O/B)	WSuV
- 'Gamay Hâtif des Vosges'	WSuV
- 'Gamay Noir' (O/B)	WSuV
- Gamay Teinturier Group (O/B)	WSuV
- 'Gewürztraminer' (O/R)	LRHS MAsh SDea WSuV
- 'Glory of Boskoop'	see *V.* 'Boskoop Glory'
- 'Golden Chasselas'	see *V. vinifera* 'Chasselas'
- 'Golden Queen' (G/W)	ERea
- 'Goldriesling' (O/W)	WSuV
- 'Grizzley Frontignan' (G/R)	ERea
- 'Gros Colmar' (G/B)	WSuV
- 'Grüner Veltliner' (O/W)	WSuV
- 'Gutenborner' (O/W)	WSuV
- 'Helfensteiner' (O/R)	WSuV
- 'Huxelrebe' (O/W)	WSuV
- 'Incana' (O/B)	EBee ELon EPfP GCal MRav WCFE WCom WCot WSHC
- 'Italia' (O/W)	LRHS
- 'Juliaumsrebe' (O/W)	WSuV
- 'Kanzler' (O/W)	WSuV
- 'Kerner' (O/W)	WSuV
- 'Kernling' (F)	WSuV
- 'King's Ruby' (F/S)	ERea WSuV
- 'Lady Downe's Seedling' (G/B)	ERea
- 'Lady Hastings' (G/B)	ERea
- 'Lakemont' (O/W/S)	CAgr CCCN CMac GTwe LRHS MBri MGos NLar SKee SLim SPoG WBVN WSuV
- 'Lival' (O/B)	WSuV
- 'Madeira Frontignan' (G/R) **new**	ERea
- 'Madeleine Angevine' (O/W)	CAgr GTwe LRHS LSRN MAsh NPer SDea SVic WSuV
- 'Madeleine Celine' (B)	WSuV
- 'Madeleine Royale' (G/W)	WSuV
- 'Madeleine Silvaner' (O/W)	CSBt GTwe LRHS MAsh NPer SDea SPer WSuV
- 'Madresfield Court' (G/B)	ERea GTwe SLim WSuV
- 'Merlot' (G/B)	LRHS SDea WSuV
§ - 'Meunier' (B)	WSuV
- 'Mireille' (F)	GTwe SDea WSuV
- 'Morio Muscat' (O/W)	WSuV
- 'Mrs Pearson' (G/W)	ERea
- 'Mrs Pince's Black Muscat' (G/B)	ERea
§ - 'Müller-Thurgau' (O/W)	GTwe LRHS LSRN MAsh MGos NPri SDea SPer SVic WSuV
- 'Muscat Blanc à Petits Grains' (O/W)	SWvt WSuV
- 'Muscat Champion' (G/R)	ERea
- 'Muscat de Lierval' (O/B)	WSuV
- 'Muscat de Saumur' (O/W)	WSuV
- 'Muscat Hamburg' (G/B)	ECrN ERea LHop LRHS LSRN MAsh MGos NPla SDea SWvt WSuV
- 'Muscat of Alexandria' (G/W)	CBcs CCCN CMac ERea LRHS MAsh MRav NPal SDea SLim SVic
- 'Muscat Ottonel' (O/W)	WSuV
- 'Muscat Saint Laurent' (W)	WSuV
- 'Nebbiolo' (O/B)	WSuV
- 'No 69' (W)	WSuV
- 'Noblessa' (W)	WSuV
- 'Noir Hâtif de Marseille' (O/B)	WSuV
- 'Olive Blanche' (O/W)	WSuV
- 'Oliver Irsay' (O/W)	ERea WSuV
- 'Optima' (O/W)	WSuV
- 'Ora' (O/W/S)	WSuV
- 'Ortega' (O/W)	CCCN WSuV
- 'Perle' (O/W)	WSuV
- 'Perle de Czaba' (G/O/W)	WSuV
- 'Perlette' (O/W/S)	CCCN CSut ERea LRHS NPri WSuV
- 'Petit Rouge' (R)	WSuV
- 'Pinot Blanc' (O/W)	CCCN LRHS MAsh SVic WSuV
- 'Pinot Gris' (O/B)	SDea WSuV
- 'Pinot Noir' (O/B)	CCCN SVic WSuV
§ - 'Portugieser' (O/B)	WSuV

	- 'Précoce de Bousquet' (O/W)	WSuV
	- 'Précoce de Malingre' (O/W)	CAgr SDea
	- 'Prima' (O/B)	WSuV
	- 'Primavis Frontignan' (G/W)	WSuV
	- 'Purpurea' (O/B) ♀H4	Widely available
	- 'Queen of Esther' (B)	GTwe MBri NLar SKee SLim WSuV
	- 'Regner' (O/W)	WSuV
	- 'Reichensteiner' (O/G/W)	CAgr SDea WSuV
	- 'Riesling' (O/W)	CCCN MAsh SVic WSuV
	- Riesling-Silvaner	see *V. vinifera* 'Müller-Thurgau'
	- 'Rish Baba'	ERea
	- 'Rotberger' (O/G/B)	WSuV
	- 'Royal Muscadine' (G/O/W)	SPoG WSuV
	- 'Saint Laurent' (G/O/W)	SVic WSuV
	- 'Sauvignon Blanc' (O/W)	CCCN LRHS WSuV
	- 'Scheurebe' (O/W)	WSuV
§	- 'Schiava Grossa' (G/B/D)	Widely available
	- 'Schönburger' (O/W)	SDea SVic WSuV
	- 'Schwarzriesling'	see *V. vinifera* 'Meunier'
	- 'Sémillon'	LRHS MAsh
	- 'Senator' (O/W)	WSuV
	- 'Septimer' (O/W)	WSuV
	- 'Shiraz' (B)	WSuV
	- 'Siegerrebe' (O/W/D)	CAgr GTwe LRHS MAsh NPer SDea SVic WSuV
	- 'Silvaner' (O/W)	WSuV
	- 'Spetchley Red'	WCot WCru WPGP WPat WSpi
	- strawberry grape	see *V.* 'Fragola'
§	- 'Sultana' (W/S)	CAgr CCCN ERea GTwe SDea WSuV
	- 'Theresa'	LRHS MBri NLar SKee SLim SPoG WSuV
	- 'Thompson Seedless'	see *V. vinifera* 'Sultana'
*	- 'Triomphe' (O/B)	SVic
	- 'Triomphrebe' (W)	WSuV
	- 'Vroegeivan der Laan'	NLar
	- 'Wrotham Pinot' (O/B)	ERea SDea WSuV
	- 'Würzer' (O/W)	WSuV
	- 'Zweigeltrebe' (O/B)	WSuV
*	'White Strawberry' (O/W)	WSuV
	'Zalagyöngye' (W)	CAgr ERea WSuV

Vriesea (*Bromeliaceae*)

	splendens ♀H1	XBlo

W

Wachendorfia (*Haemodoraceae*)

	brachyandra	GCal
	thyrsiflora	CDes CFir CHEx CPLG CPen CPne CTsd EBee IGor LEdu WCFE WPGP

Wahlenbergia (*Campanulaceae*)

	sp.	ECou
	albomarginata	ECho ECou EWTr NWCA
	- 'Blue Mist'	ECho ECou
	ceracea	GKev
	congesta	ECho GKev
	cuspidata	GKev
	gloriosa	ECho ECou WAbe WFar
	gracilenta	GKev
	hederacea	GGar
	pumilio	see *Edraianthus pumilio*
	rivularis	GKev LLHF
	- 'Snow-cap'	GKev
§	***saxicola***	ECho
	serpyllifolia	see *Edraianthus serpyllifolius*
	stricta	ECou WAbe
	tasmanica	see *W. saxicola*
	undulata 'Melton Bluebird'	GJos

Walafrida (*Scrophulariaceae*)

	myrtifolia	GFai

Waldsteinia (*Rosaceae*)

	geoides	EBee EPfP LAst LRHS NBre SPer WMoo WWEG
	ternata	Widely available
§	- 'Mozaick' (v)	EBee EWes NBid NBir NBre
	- 'Variegata'	see *W. ternata* 'Mozaick'

Wallichia (*Arecaceae*)

	densiflora	LPal
	disticha	LPal

walnut, black see *Juglans nigra*

walnut, common see *Juglans regia*

Wasabia (*Brassicaceae*)

	wasabi	CArn GPoy LEdu

Washingtonia (*Arecaceae*)

	'Filibusta'	EAmu
	filifera ♀H1	CAbb CCCN CDoC CPHo EAmu EShb ETod EUJe LPal LRHS SAPC SArc SBig SEND SPlb WBrE
	robusta	CBcs CTrC EAmu EUJe LPal LRHS NPal SBst SChr SPlb

Watsonia (*Iridaceae*)

	'African Bride' **new**	CPen
	aletroides	CBgR CDes CPen CTca EBee ECho ERCP GCal GGar NCGa WCot WPGP
	amatolae	IBlr
	angusta	CDes CGHE CPen CPne CPrp CTca EBee IBlr SGSe WPGP
	- JCA 3.950.409	WCot
	ardernei	see *W. borbonica* subsp. *ardernei* 'Arderne's White'
	beatricis	see *W. pillansii*
I	'Best Red'	WCot
§	***borbonica***	CPne CPou CPrp GGal NCot SGar WCot
	- subsp. ***ardernei*** misapplied	see *W. borbonica* subsp. *ardernei* (Sander) Goldblatt 'Arderne's White'
§	- - 'Arderne's White'	CBre CDes CFir CGHE CPen CPrp CTca EBee ECho GGar IBlr WPGP
	- subsp. ***borbonica***	CDes EBee IBlr WPGP
	- 'Paarl' **new**	ECho
	brevifolia	see *W. laccata*
	brick red-flowered **new**	CDes WPGP
	'Bronze Beauty' **new**	CPen
	coccinea Baker	see *W. spectabilis*
	- Herb. ex Baker	CPen WCot WPGP
	- 'Somerset West' **new**	ECho
	'Curly Blooms' **new**	CPen
	densiflora	CPou IBlr WCot
	distans	EBee
	fourcadei	CPen CPne WPGP
	fulgens	CPen CPne LEdu
	galpinii	CFir CPen EBee WPGP
	- lavender-flowered	IBlr

	- pink-flowered	CPrp EBee IBlr
	galpinii × ***knysnana***	IBlr
	gladioloides	WPGP
§	***humilis***	CDes CPen CPou CPrp EBee GCal LEdu SKHP WPGP
	knysnana	CDes CPen CPou CPrp EBee IBlr WCot WPGP
§	***laccata***	CDes CFir CPen CPne CPou CPrp EBee WCot WPGP
	latifolia	IBlr
	lepida	CPou EBee ECho IBlr
	× ***longifolia*** JCA 03.952.850	WCot
	marginata	CDes CPne CPou CPrp EBee ECho GGar WCot WPGP
	- ***alba*** new	SKHP
	meriania	CPen CPou CStu ERCP GGal IBlr NCGa WCot
	- var. ***bulbillifera***	CBgR CGHE CPne CPrp CTca EBee ECho GAbr GCra GGal GMac IBlr SMrm WPGP
*	'Mount Congreve'	CTca
	'Peachy Pink Orphan'	CDes EBee
§	***pillansii***	CAbb CGHE CHEx CPLG CPen CPne CPou CPrp CTca CYeo EBee IBal IBlr NCGa SMrm SPoG WFar WMnd
	- JCA 3.593.609	WCot
	- 'Cathcart' new	ECho
	- hybrid	SAga WHil
	- peach-flowered new	CPen
	- pink-flowered	CPen CPrp IVic
	- red-flowered	GBin IVic
	pink-flowered	CDes EBee SUsu
	pulchra	EBee
	pyramidata	see *W. borbonica*
	roseoalba	see *W. humilis*
	schlechteri	EBee WPGP
§	***spectabilis***	CPne WPGP
	'Stanford Scarlet'	CAby CDes CFir CPne CPou CPrp CSpr ELon GGar GMac IBlr SChF SChr SHom SUsu WPGP WSHC
	stenosiphon	EBee IBlr
	strubeniae	IBlr
	transvaalensis	EBee
	'Tresco Dwarf Pink'	CDes CFir CPrp CSam CTca EBee IBlr LEdu WCot WPGP
	Tresco hybrids	CAbb CBcs CHll CPen CPne GGal LTen SAga SRkn WCFE
	vanderspuyae	CPLG CPen CPne CPou CPrp IBlr NCot WCot WPGP
	'White Dazzler'	SApp
	wilmaniae	CPne CPou CPrp IBlr WPGP
	- JCA 3.955200	SKHP
	- 'Ice Angel'	SKHP
	zeyheri	EBee WHil

Wattakaka see *Dregea*

Weigela ✿ (*Caprifoliaceae*)

	CC 1231	CPLG
	'Abel Carrière'	CMac CTri EBee ECtt EPfP EWes MGos NWea WCFE WFar WSpi
	'Anne Marie'	MGos
	'Avalanche' misapplied	see *W.* 'Candida'
	'Avalanche' Lemoine	see *W. praecox* 'Avalanche'
	'Boskoop Glory'	GQui SPer
§	Briant Rubidor = 'Olympiade' (v)	CDoC CMac CSBt CWSG EBee ECtt EHoe EPfP GKir LAst LRHS MAsh MGos MMuc MNHC MRav NEgg NHol NLar NVic SLim SPer SPlb SPoG WFar
	'Bristol Ruby'	Widely available
§	'Candida'	CTri ELan EWes MRav NHol NLar SPer WSpi
	Cappuccino = 'Verweig2'^{PBR}	CWit LBuc NBro NEgg NLar SPoG
	Carnaval = 'Courtalor'^{PBR}	CBar CBcs CWib EBee EQua GKir LRHS LSou NHol NLar
	'Conquête'	GKir SLon
	coraeensis	CHll MBlu MMHG WPat
	- 'Alba'	SPer
	decora	GQui
	'Eva Rathke'	CAlb CTri GKir NBir NLar NWea
	'Evita'	MGos WFar
	Feline = 'Courtamon'	MBri
	florida	CDul CMac EPfP MGos SPad
	- B&SWJ 8439	WCru
	- f. ***alba***	CBcs WFar
*	- 'Albovariegata' (v)	CPLG LAst WBVN
	- 'Bicolor'	CMac ELan
	- 'Bristol Snowflake'	CDul CMac EBee EPfP GKir MHer MMuc MSwo NBir NHol NLar SLon
	- 'Foliis Purpureis' 🏆H4	Widely available
	- 'Milk and Honey' new	LRHS
	- Minor Black = 'Verweig 3'^{PBR}	LBuc MBri MPkF NBro NLar SPoG WCot WMoo
	- Monet = 'Verweig'^{PBR} (v)	Widely available
	- Moulin Rouge = 'Brigela'^{PBR}	CBcs CDoC CSBt ELon EPfP LBuc LRHS MBri MGos
	- 'Pink Princess'	CBar EBee LRHS MSwo
	- Rubigold	see *W.* Briant Rubidor
	- 'Samabor'	WFar
	- 'Sunny Princess'	EQua NHol NMun
	- 'Suzanne' (v)	MGos
	- 'Tango'	CPMA ECtt LRHS MAsh NHol
	'Florida Variegata' (v) 🏆H4	Widely available
	florida 'Versicolor'	CMHG CMac CPLG CWib GQui SLon SMrm WFar WGor
	- Wine and Roses = 'Alexandra'	CAbP CBcs CDoC CPLG CSBt EBee EHoe ELan EMil EPfP EShb GKir LAst LRHS LSRN MAsh MBri MGos MRav MWat NEgg NLar SBfd SPoG SRGP SWvt WFar WGrn
	'Gold Rush'	EHoe NHol NLar
	'Gustave Malet'	CMCN GQui
	hortensis	CPLG
	japonica 'Dart's Colourdream'	EBee ECtt ELon EWes GKir LAst LSou MMuc NHol SCoo SEND SLim
	'Jean's Gold'	EBee ELan MBlu MGos MRav WCot
	'Kosteriana Variegata' (v)	CSBt EBee LRHS MAsh MMuc NEgg NPri SBfd SEND SLon WFar
	'Looymansii Aurea'	CMHG CPLG CTri EBee ELan EPfP GKir LAst NLar SPer WCom WDin WFar WHar
	Lucifer = 'Courtared'^{PBR}	CDoC NHol
	maximowiczii	CPLG GQui
§	***middendorffiana***	Widely available
	'Minuet'	EBee EPfP LRHS MGos MRav MSwo SLPl
	'Mont Blanc'	CBot MAsh MMHG
	Nain Rouge = 'Courtanin'^{PBR}	CBcs CTri MBri NHol
	'Nana Variegata' (v)	CPLG ECrN ELon EPfP EPla LRHS MBri MHav SBfd SLPl WGwG
	Naomi Campbell = 'Bokrashine'^{PBR}	CBow GBin GKir MMHG MWea NEgg NHol NLar WFar WHar WMoo
	'Newport Red'	EBee GKir MBNS MWat NWea WFar
	Pink Poppet = 'Plangen'^{PBR}	CAbP CSBt CWSG EBee EKen EMil LAst LBMP LRHS LSRN MAsh NHol NLar SBfd SCoo SLim SPoG SWvt

	praecox	ECrN MWte
	- B&SWJ 8705	WCru
§	- 'Avalanche'	ECtt SGar
	'Praecox Variegata' (v) ♀H4	CMac CTri ELan EPfP GKir LAst LRHS MAsh MRav NBir SBfd SDix SPer SPoG SRms WCFE WFar WPat
	'Red Prince' ♀H4	CAlb EBee ECrN ELan LBuc LRHS MGos MSwo NEgg NHol NLar SLim SPoG
	Rubidor	see *W.* Briant Rubidor
	Rubigold	see *W.* Briant Rubidor
	'Ruby Anniversary' new	SLon
	'Ruby Queen'PBR	CMac EPfP
	'Rumba'	CMac MRav
	sessilifolia	see *Diervilla sessilifolia*
	'Snowflake'	CAlb CChe ECrN ECtt EWTr GKir SRms WDin WFar
	'Stelzneri'	MMuc
	subsessilis B&SWJ 1056	WCru
	'Victoria'	CAlb CDul CMac CWib EBee ECrN ECtt EHoe ELan EPfP LBMP LRHS MAsh MGos MSwo NBir NHol SBfd SPer WBrE WFar WGor WHar WMoo

Weinmannia (*Cunoniaceae*)

	racemosa	IDee
	- 'Kamahi'	CTrC
	trichosperma	CBcs EBee EUJe IArd IFFs SAPC SArc SSpi

Weldenia (*Commelinaceae*)

	candida	EBla ECho IBlr LLHF NHar NMen WAbe

Westringia (*Lamiaceae*)

	angustifolia	ECou
	brevifolia	ECou
	- var. ***raleighii***	ECou
§	***fruticosa*** ♀H1	CArn CBcs CCCN CTsd ECou EShb WJek
	- 'Smokie' (v)	CCCN CTsd ECou SOWG WAbe
	- 'Variegata' (v)	MNHC WJek
	longifolia	CCCN ECou
	rosmariniformis	see *W. fruticosa*
	'Wynyabbie Gem'	EBee LRHS SEND

whitecurrant see *Ribes rubrum* (W)

Whiteheadia (*Hyacinthaceae*)

	bifolia 'Nardonwsberg' new	ECho

Widdringtonia (*Cupressaceae*)

	cedarbergensis	CPne

Wigandia (*Hydrophyllaceae*)

	caracasana	CHII

Wikstroemia (*Thymelaeaceae*)

	gemmata	LRHS SCoo SSta

wineberry see *Rubus phoenicolasius*

Wisteria ✿ (*Papilionaceae*)

§	***brachybotrys***	CBcs SLau SLim
§	- Murasaki-kapitan	CEnd CTri CWGN EPfP MAsh SKHP WSpi
	- 'Okayama'	SKHP
	- 'Pink Chiffon'	EPfP LRHS MAsh SKHP
	- 'Shiro-beni'	CTri MGos MMuc SEND
§	- 'Shiro-kapitan'	CBcs CEnd CSPN CTri CWGN EBee EPfP LRHS LSRN MBri MGos MMuc MRav NHol SCoo SLau SLim SPer WPGP WPat WSHC
*	- 'White Silk'	CBcs EPfP LRHS LSRN MAsh MGos NPla WGwG
§	'Burford'	CEnd CSPN CWGN EPfP GBin LRHS LSRN MAsh MBri MGan MWat NHol SCoo SLau SLim WHar WPGP WSpi
	'Caroline'	CBcs CCCN CDoC CSPN CSam CWGN EBee EPfP GKir LRHS LSRN MAsh MGos MRav NEgg NPCo SLau SPer SRms SSpi WPGP WSHC
	floribunda	CBcs CRHN CWib ELan EPfP GGal MMuc NPCo WDin WFar
§	- 'Alba' ♀H4	Widely available
	- 'Black Dragon'	see *W. floribunda* 'Yae-kokuryū'
	- 'Burford'	see *W.* 'Burford'
*	- 'Cascade'	LRHS MBri NEgg WSpi
§	- 'Domino'	CEnd CMac CTri CWGN ELon EPfP IArd LHop LRHS LSRN MAsh MGan MGos MMuc MRav NHol SBfd SCoo SEND SKHP SLau SLim SPer SSta WFar
	- 'Fragrantissima'	see *W. sinensis* 'Jako'
	- 'Geisha'	CBcs CEnd SKHP
	- 'Golden Dragon'	SLim
	- 'Harlequin'	CBcs CSPN EBee ECrN ELon GCal LRHS MAsh MMuc NPCo NPla SBfd SEND WFar
	- 'Hocker Edge'	SLau
	- 'Hon-beni'	see *W. floribunda* 'Rosea'
	- 'Honey Bee Pink'	see *W. floribunda* 'Rosea'
	- 'Honko'	see *W. floribunda* 'Rosea'
	- 'Issai'	LSRN MSwo
	- 'Issai Perfect'	LRHS LSRN MAsh NLar SCoo
	- 'Jakohn-fuji'	see *W. sinensis* 'Jako'
§	- 'Kuchi-beni'	CEnd CSPN EBee ELan GBin LRHS LSRN MAsh MBri MGos NEgg NHol NLar NPCo SCoo SEND SLau SPer SPoG SRms WClo
	- 'Lawrence'	CEnd CSPN CWGN MBri NLar SKHP SLau SLim
	- 'Lipstick'	see *W. floribunda* 'Kuchi-beni'
	- 'Longissima'	see *W. floribunda* 'Multijuga'
	- 'Longissima Alba'	see *W. floribunda* 'Alba'
	- 'Macrobotrys'	see *W. floribunda* 'Multijuga'
	- 'Magenta'	LRHS MAsh
§	- 'Multijuga' ♀H4	Widely available
	- Murasaki-naga	see *W. floribunda* 'Purple Patches'
	- 'Nana Richin's Purple'	CEnd SLau
	- 'Peaches and Cream'	see *W. floribunda* 'Kuchi-beni'
	- 'Pink Ice'	see *W. floribunda* 'Rosea'
§	- 'Purple Patches'	NPri
	- Reindeer	see *W. sinensis* 'Jako'
§	- 'Rosea' ♀H4	Widely available
	- 'Royal Purple'	CEnd LRHS MAsh MBri SPoG WFar WGor
	- 'Russelliana'	CBcs EBee GBin LRHS LTen NLar
	- 'Shiro-naga'	see *W. floribunda* 'Alba'
	- 'Shiro-nagi'	see *W. floribunda* 'Alba'
	- 'Shiro-noda'	see *W. floribunda* 'Alba'
	- 'Snow Showers'	see *W. floribunda* 'Alba'
	- 'Variegata' (v)	CWGN
N	- 'Violacea Plena' (d)	CBcs CDoC CMac ECrN EPfP EQua LTen NLar NPri SKHP SPer SWvt WDin WFar
N	- 'Yae-kokuryū' (d)	Widely available
	× ***formosa***	CEnd MGan SLau SLim
	- 'Black Dragon'	see *W. floribunda* 'Yae-kokuryū'
	- 'Domino'	see *W. floribunda* 'Domino'
	- 'Issai' Wada pro parte	see *W. floribunda* 'Domino'
	- 'Kokuryu'	see *W. floribunda* 'Yae-kokuryū'

- 'Yae-kokuryu'	see *W. floribunda* 'Yae-kokuryū'
frutescens	EBee SLim WFar
- 'Amethyst Falls'^{PBR}	CEnd CWGN IArd LRHS LSRN MGos NPri SCoo
- 'Magnifica'	see *W. macrostachya* 'Magnifica'
Kapitan-fuji	see *W. brachybotrys*
'Lavender Lace'	EBee EPfP LRHS LSRN MAsh NEgg NLar SLau WFar
macrostachya	WHar
'Blue Moon' **new**	
§ - 'Magnifica'	WSpi
multijuga 'Alba'	see *W. floribunda* 'Alba'
'Showa-beni'	CEnd CWGN EPfP LHop MGos SCoo SEND SLau SLim WPGP
sinensis 🏆^{H4}	Widely available
- 'Alba' 🏆^{H4}	CBcs CDoC CDul CMen CWib EBee ECrN ELan EPfP GKir LAst LRHS LSRN MAsh MGan MGos MMuc MNHC MWat NEgg NPla SEND SLau SLim SPer SPoG WDin WFar
- 'Amethyst'	CBcs CEnd CSPN CWCL EBee EPfP LRHS LSRN LTen MAsh MBri MGos MRav MWat NPla NSti SKHP SLau SLim SPer SReu WPat
- 'Blue Sapphire'	CBcs CSPN CWGN EBee LSRN NEgg NPCo NSti SLau SRms
* - 'Caerulea'	GAuc
- 'Consequa'	see *W. sinensis* 'Prolific'
§ - 'Jako'	CEnd EBee NHol SSpi
- 'Oosthoek's Variety'	see *W. sinensis* 'Prolific'
I - 'Pink Ice'	EWTr NEgg NPCo
- 'Prematura'	see *W. floribunda* 'Domino'
- 'Prematura Alba'	see *W. brachybotrys* 'Shiro-kapitan'
§ - 'Prolific'	CDul CMac CSam CTri CWGN CWib EBee ELan EMac EPfP LBuc LRHS LSou MBri MGos MMuc MRav NHol NLar SBfd SCoo SEND SKHP SLim SPer SSpi SWvt WFar WPGP WPat
- 'Rosea'	LSRN MGos SPur SWvt WSpi
- 'Shiro-capital'	see *W. brachybotrys* 'Shiro-kapitan'
'Tiverton'	CBcs EBee NPla WGwG
venusta	see *W. brachybotrys* 'Shiro-kapitan'
- 'Alba'	see *W. brachybotrys* 'Shiro-kapitan'
- var. ***violacea*** misapplied	see *W. brachybotrys* Murasaki-kapitan
- var. ***violacea*** Rehder	see *W. brachybotrys* Murasaki-kapitan

Withania (*Solanaceae*)

somnifera	CArn EOHP ERea GPoy

Wittsteinia (*Alseuosmiaceae*)

vacciniacea	WCru

Wodyetia (*Arecaceae*)

bifurcata	EAmu LPal XBlo

Wollemia (*Araucariaceae*)

nobilis	CDTJ EAmu EPfP ESwi LRHS MAsh MWya WMou

Woodsia (*Woodsiaceae*)

intermedia	WAbe
obtusa	CBty CDTJ CKel CLAP CWCL CWit EBee EFer EMil EWTr LRHS NBro NHol NLar NMyG SRot WPnP WRic WWEG
polystichoides 🏆^{H4}	GQui SRms WAbe

Woodwardia (*Blechnaceae*)

from Emei Shan, China	CLAP
areolata	SKHP WRic
fimbriata	Widely available
martinezii	GLin
obtusa	SBfd
orientalis	CBty ESwi WCot WFib WRic
- var. ***formosana***	CLAP WRic
- - B&SWJ 6865	WCru
radicans 🏆^{H3}	CAbb CHEx CHid CLAP EWes EWld GQui SAPC SArc WFib WRic
unigemmata	CHEx CLAP EWes EWld SAPC SArc SKHP WAbe WFib WHal WRic
virginica	CLAP ISha WRic

Worcesterberry see *Ribes* 'Worcesterberry'

Wulfenia (*Scrophulariaceae*)

carinthiaca	CDes EBee ECho GAbr GEdr GKev NBir NHol NLar SBHP WPer
× ***schwarzii***	CDes EBee WPGP

Wurmbea (*Colchicaceae*)

pusilla 'Sentinel Peak' **new**	ECho
recurva	ECho
spicata 'Rawsonville' **new**	ECho

X

Xanthium (*Asteraceae*)

sibiricum	CArn

Xanthoceras (*Sapindaceae*)

sorbifolium 🏆$^{H3-4}$	CAgr CArn CBcs CBot CMCN CWib EBee ECrN ELan EPfP GKir MBlu NLar SPoG SSpi WDin WPat WSpi

Xanthocyparis (*Cupressaceae*)

§ ***nootkatensis***	ECho
- 'Pendula' 🏆^{H4}	CDoC CDul CKen ECho ELan EPfP EPla GKir LMaj LRHS MAsh MBlu MBri MGos MMuc NEgg NPCo NWea SCoo WCFE WDin WEve WFar

Xanthorhiza (*Ranunculaceae*)

simplicissima	CArn CBcs CGHE CRow EPfP GCal IVic LEdu MBri NLar SDys SPer SSpi WPGP

Xanthorrhoea (*Xanthorrhoeaceae*)

australis	SPlb
fulva **new**	SPlb
glauca	CCCN CDTJ EAmu EUJe
preisii	CDTJ SPlb

Xanthosoma (*Araceae*)

sagittifolium	CDTJ EUJe
violaceum	CDTJ WWst

Xerochrysum (*Asteraceae*)

§ ***bracteatum*** 'Coco'	CMHG CSpe MAJR WWlt
§ - 'Dargan Hill Monarch'	CHII CSpe MAJR SRms WWlt
§ - 'Skynet'	WWlt
- 'Wollerton'	WWlt

Xeronema (*Phormiaceae*)

callistemon	CTrC

Xerophyllum (*Melanthiaceae*)

tenax	GCal GGar IMou NMen

Xylorhiza see *Machaeranthera*

Xyris (*Xyridaceae*)

torta	WPGP

Y

Youngberry see *Rubus* 'Youngberry'

Ypsilandra (*Melanthiaceae*)

cavaleriei	CPLG EBee GEdr WCot
thibetica	CDes CFir CGHE CPLG CSpe EBee EBla GEdr LAma LEdu LLHF NLar SMad WCot WCru WPGP

Yucca ✿ (*Agavaceae*)

SDR 3701	GKev
aloifolia	CCCN CDoC CHEx EAmu ETod MGos MREP SAPC SArc SBfd SBig SChr SEND SMad SPlb
§ - f. ***marginata*** (v)	EAmu LPal MREP SArc SBig
- 'Purpurea'	MAga SPlb
- 'Tricolor' (v)	MREP
- 'Variegata'	see *Y. aloifolia* f. *marginata*
angustifolia	see *Y. glauca*
baccata	CCCN CTrC EAmu ETod
carnerosana	CTrC EAmu EUJe
§ ***elata***	CCCN CTrC EAmu WPGP
§ ***elephantipes*** ♀H1	CDTJ EAmu MMuc SBfd SEND
- 'Jewel' (v)	EAmu EBee MMuc SEND
faxoniana	EAmu MAga WPGP
faxoniana* × *glauca	MAga
filamentosa ♀H4	Widely available
- 'Antwerp'	GCal
- 'Bright Edge' (v) ♀H3	Widely available
- 'Color Guard' (v)	CTrC LAst MBri NLar SChr WCot WFar
- 'Garland's Gold' (v)	CBcs CCCN CDoC MGos SBfd SBig WFar
- 'Variegata' (v) ♀H3	CBcs EPfP MGos SRms WDin WFar
filifera	EAmu ETod EUJe SPlb
flaccida	MGos MMuc SDix
- 'Golden Sword' (v) ♀H3	CBcs CDoC CMac CSBt CTrC CWSG CWit EBee EHoe ELan EPfP GAbr GKir LAst LRHS LSRN MAsh MCCP MGos MSCN MSwo NLar NMoo NPla SBfd SLim SPer SPoG SWvt WCot
- 'Ivory' ♀H3-4	CBcs CDoC CEnd EBee ECtt ELan ELon EPfP GCal GKir LRHS LSRN MBlu MBri MGos MRav NLar SBfd SLPl SPer SRms SSta STre WMoo
× ***floribunda***	SAPC SArc
§ ***glauca***	EBee EPfP GLin IFFs LEdu LRHS MBri SAPC
* - var. ***radiosa***	CTrC
gloriosa ♀H4	CBcs CDoC CHEx CMac CTri EAmu EPfP EPla EUJe LRHS MGos MMuc MREP NPla SAPC SArc SBfd SEND SPer SPlb SPoG SWvt WBrE WBrk
- 'Aureovariegata'	see *Y. gloriosa* 'Variegata'
§ - 'Variegata' (v) ♀H4	Widely available
guatemalensis	see *Y. elephantipes*
linearis	see *Y. thompsoniana*
'Nobilis'	CHEx SDix
pallida	WPGP
radiosa	see *Y. elata*
recurvifolia ♀H4	CHEx EAmu EPfP GCal MGos SAPC SArc SBfd
- 'Gold Stream' (v)	WCot
rigida	CBrP CDTJ EAmu WPGP
rostrata	CBrP CCCN CDTJ CTrC EAmu ETod EUJe LPal MREP SChr SPlb WCot
'Sapphire Star'	CBow
schidigera NNS 03-597	WCot
schottii	CTrC MAga WCot
§ ***thompsoniana***	CDTJ CTrC EAmu LPal
- blue-leaved	EAmu
torreyi	CTrC CWit EAmu SChr
treculeana	EAmu MAga
'Vittorio Emanuele II'	SMad
whipplei	CBcs CBrP CCCN CDoC CTsd EBee ELan IGor LRHS MAga NPal SBig WCot WPGP
- NNS 01-412	WCot
- NNS 05-696	WCot
- subsp. ***caespitosa***	WPGP
- subsp. ***intermedia*** NNS 01-413	WCot
- - NNS 05-697	WCot
- subsp. ***parishii*** NNS 01-415	WCot
- - NNS 05-699	WCot
- subsp. ***percursa*** NNS 05-700	WCot
- subsp. ***whipplei*** NNS 05-701	WCot

Yushania (*Poaceae*)

§ ***anceps***	CBcs CDoC CEnt CHEx CPLG EBee ENBC EPfP EPla GBin MGos MMoz MMuc MWht SAPC SBig SEND WDyG WFar WMoo WPGP
- 'Pitt White'	CEnt CGHE EBee EPla MWht WJun WPGP
- 'Pitt White Rejuvenated'	EPla WPGP
brevipaniculata	EPla WJun
chungii	CEnt EPla MWht WJun WPGP
* ***equatus***	WJun
maculata	CEnt EPla MMoz MWht SBig WDyG WJun
§ ***maling***	EPfP EPla MMoz WJun
Yunnan 5	EPla WPGP

Z

Zaluzianskya (*Scrophulariaceae*)

sp.	NMen
JCA 15665	WAbe
capensis	EBee GKev LPio
'Katherine'	SRot
microsiphon	SPlb
'Orange Eye'	ELon EPot LPio NSla WAbe
ovata	CPBP EDAr EPfP EPot EWld GKev LPio LRHS MSCN MTho NSla NWCA SAga SPlb SPoG WAbe WCom WEas
pulvinata	WAbe
'Semonkong'	GCal LPio LSou SUsu SWvt

Zamia (*Zamiaceae*)

furfuracea	CBrP
muricata	LPal

skinneri	LPal

Zamioculcas (*Araceae*)

zamiifolia	CCCN

Zantedeschia (*Araceae*)

§ ***aethiopica*** ♀H3	Widely available
- 'Apple Court Babe'	CAby CElw CRow CStu ELon GCal MAvo MNrw SMrm WDyG
- 'Caerwent'	CPen
- 'Childsiana'	EBee SApp
- 'Crowborough' ♀H3	Widely available
- 'Gigantea'	CHEx
- 'Glow'	CBct CBgR CMac EBee ECtt LAst LRHS LSou MAvo MNrw MRav NCGa NGdn SMrm SPer WClo WCot WGwG
- 'Green Goddess' ♀H3	Widely available
- 'Little Gem'	SMad WFar
- 'Luzon Lovely'	WCru
- 'Marshmallow'	EAEE EBee ECtt ELan EPfP GGar LRHS NCGa SPet WFar
- 'Mr Martin'	CBct CCCN CHid CMac CStu CTrC EBee ECtt ELon EUJe EWll GAbr LOck LRHS MAvo MNrw NCGa SBfd SBig SMad SWvt WCot WPGP
- 'Pershore Fantasia' (v)	CBct EBee MSKA WCom WCot WFar
- pink-flowered	CHEx
- 'Snow White'	MWat
- 'Whipped Cream'	MDKP MNrw
- 'White Gnome'	WCot WFar
- 'White Mischief'	EBee
- 'White Sail'	CBct CPrp EAEE EBee ECtt GCal ITim LRHS MNrw MRav NGdn SWat WFar
albomaculata	CPLG CTca EPfP LAma LRHS SPlb
'Anneke'	CCCN ECho EPfP WBrE
'Apricot Glow'	CHll
'Black Eyed Beauty'	CTca LAma
'Black Magic'	CCCN CMac ECho EPfP
'Black Pearl'	LAma
'Black Star'	see *Z.* 'Edge of Night'
black-flowered	WCom
'Cameo'	CCCN ECho LAma
(Captain Series) 'Captain Chelsea'	LAma
- 'Captain Palermo' PBR	LAma
- 'Captain Samos'	LAma
- 'Captain Tendens' PBR	LAma
'Carmine Red'	WBrE
'Crystal Blush'	LAma
§ 'Edge of Night'	CCCN ERCP EUJe MGos
elliottiana ♀H1	CBcs CFir CHEx CTri EUJe LAma
'Flame'	EPfP SPad WGwG
'Gabrielle' PBR	LRHS
'Harvest Moon'	LAma
'Kiwi Blush'	CAbP CCCN CFir CHEx CSpe CTca EAEE EBee ECtt ELan ELon EPfP EWll LPBA LRHS MAvo MCCP NGdn NPal SApp SBfd SEND SKHP SPad SPer SPet SRkn SWat WFar WGwG
'Lime Lady'	CBct ECha
'Mango'	LAma WCot
'Mozart'	LRHS
'Picasso' PBR	ERCP LRHS SPad
'Pink Mist'	CAby CBct LAma SWal
'Pink Persuasion'	LAma
'Purple Sensation' **new**	EPfP
rehmannii ♀H1	LAma NLar SRms
'Schwarzwalder' PBR	EGxp ERCP EUJe LRHS
'Selina'	LRHS
'Silver Lining'	LAma
'Solfatare'	ECho EWTr
'White Giant' **new**	WPGP
'White Pixie'	EPfP SAga WViv

Zanthorhiza see *Xanthorhiza*

Zanthoxylum (*Rutaceae*)

acanthopodium GWJ 9287	WCru
ailanthoides	EPfP
- B&SWJ 11115 from Japan	WCru
- B&SWJ 11394 from Japan	WCru
- f. ***inermis*** RWJ 10048	WCru
americanum	ELan LEdu
armatum	CAgr
- HWJK 2178	WCru
bungeanum HWJK 2131	WCru
aff. ***fauriei*** B&SWJ 11080	WCru
- B&SWJ 11371	WCru
* ***giraldii***	GAuc
laetum WWJ 11678	WCru
myriacanthum B&SWJ 11844	WCru
oxyphyllum	WPGP
- HWJK 2199	WCru
piperitum	CAgr CBcs EBee GPoy SEND SPoG WPGP
- B&SWJ 8543	WCru
- purple-leaved	WPGP
schinifolium	CAgr CBcs LEdu
- B&SWJ 8593	WCru
- B&SWJ 11080	WCru
- B&SWJ 11391	WCru
simulans	CAgr CArn CBcs CPLG GBin IVic LEdu MBlu NLar WPGP

Zauschneria (*Onagraceae*)

arizonica	see *Z. californica* subsp. *latifolia*
§ ***californica***	CHll CSam CTri EBee ECho EDAr EPfP MBrN NMen SGar SLon SWat SWvt WHrl WPnn
§ - subsp. ***cana***	EBee ECha SWat
- - 'Sir Cedric Morris'	EPfP LRHS MAsh
§ - 'Dublin' ♀H3	Widely available
- 'Ed Carman'	EBee ECtt ELon LRHS LSou
§ - subsp. ***garrettii***	ECho GAbr NWCA SDys SWat
- 'Glasnevin'	see *Z. californica* 'Dublin'
§ - subsp. ***latifolia***	NWCA
- - 'Sally Walker'	EWes
§ - subsp. ***mexicana***	EPot MHer SRms
- 'Olbrich Silver'	EBee ECha ECtt EShb EWes LRHS MAsh NMen SUsu WAbe WCom WFar WPat
- 'Schieffelin's Choice'	WCom
- 'Sierra Salmon'	WPat
- 'Solidarity Pink'	ECha LHop NMen NWCA WAbe WPat
- 'Western Hills' ♀H4	CFir CSpe CTri EBee ECha ECho ECtt EDAr EPfP LHop LRHS LSou MAsh MMuc MRav NWCA SAga SEND SPhx SWvt WAbe WCom WHoo WPat
cana villosa	see *Z. californica* subsp. *mexicana*
I 'Pumilio'	EPot NMen NSla WAbe
§ ***septentrionalis***	WAbe

Zea (*Poaceae*)

mays 'Quadricolor' (v)	SBfd SGar

Zebrina see *Tradescantia*

Zelkova ✿ (*Ulmaceae*)

carpinifolia	CDul CMCN CMen CTho NHol SPlb WDin
'Kiwi Sunset'	CDul EBee LRHS MGos NWea SCoo
schneideriana	CMCN CMen EGFP
serrata ♀H4	CBcs CDul CLnd CMCN CMen CTho EBee ECrN ELan EPfP GKir IVic LMaj MMuc NBea NHol NMun NWea SBir SCoo SEND SPer STre WDin WFar
- B&SWJ 8491 from Korea	WCru
- 'Goblin'	CPMA NLar WPat
- 'Green Vase'	LMaj MBlu
- 'Urban Ruby'	MGos
- 'Variegata' (v)	CMac CPMA MBlu NLar
- 'Yatsubusa'	STre
sinica	CMCN CMen

Zenobia (*Ericaceae*)

pulverulenta	CAbP CBcs CDoC CDul CMac CSBt EBee ELan EPfP IDee IVic LRHS MAsh MBlu MGos NLar SLon SPer SReu SSpi SSta WAbe WBVN WDin WFar WPat WSHC
- 'Blue Sky'	CAbP CBcs CMCN EPfP LRHS MAsh MBlu MBri MGos NLar SPoG SSpi SSta
- 'Misty Blue'	GGGa
- f. ***nitida***	CMac NLar
- 'Raspberry Ripple'	MBlu MBri NLar SSta
- 'Viridis'	NLar

Zephyranthes ✿ (*Amaryllidaceae*)

atamasca	CStu SKHP
candida	CAvo CFFs CPBP CSpe CStu EBee ECho EPot EShb ITim LAma LRHS SDix SMrm WHil
citrina	CBgR CPLG EBee ECho EPot LAma WCot
drummondii	ECho WCot
flavissima	CPBP EBee ECho WCot WHil WPGP
'Grandjax'	WCot
'La Buffa Rose'	CStu WCot
lindleyana	WCot
mexicana	CDes EBee
minima	CStu EBee ECho LLHF
robusta	see *Habranthus robustus*
rosea	EBee EPot

Zigadenus (*Melanthiaceae*)

elegans	EBee ECGP ECha EDAr GBee GCal LRHS MAvo SMad SUsu WSHC WTin
fremontii	WCot
nuttallii	EBee ECho MDKP WCot
venenosus NNS 03-605	WCot
volcanicus B&SWJ 9110 **new**	WCru

Zingiber ✿ (*Zingiberaceae*)

mioga	CMac EBee GPoy IMou LEdu SChr SPlb WPGP
- 'Crûg's Zing' **new**	WCru
- 'Dancing Crane' (v)	CMac EUJe IFro
officinale	CTsd

Zinnia (*Asteraceae*)

'Red Spider'	CSpe

Zizania (*Poaceae*)

caducifolia	see *Z. latifolia*
§ ***latifolia***	IMou

Zizia (*Apiaceae*)

aptera	WPGP
aurea	SDix SPhx WSHC WTin

Ziziphus (*Rhamnaceae*)

§ ***jujuba*** (F)	CAgr CBcs MWya
- 'Lang' (F)	CAgr
- 'Li' (F)	CAgr
- var. ***spinosa***	CArn
sativa	see *Z. jujuba*

BIBLIOGRAPHY

This is by no means exhaustive but lists some of the more useful works used in the preparation of the *RHS Plant Finder*. The websites of raisers of new plants (not listed here) are also an invaluable source of information.

GENERAL

Allan, H.H., et al. 2000. *Flora of New Zealand.* Wellington. (5 vols).

Ball Colegrave. 2007. *Plant Catalogue 2008.* West Adderbury, Oxon: Ball Colegrave.

Ball Colegrave. 2007. *Seed Catalogue 2008.* West Adderbury, Oxon: Ball Colegrave.

Bean, W.J. 1988. *Trees and Shrubs Hardy in the British Isles.* (8th ed. edited by Sir George Taylor & D.L. Clarke & Supp. ed. D.L. Clarke). London: John Murray.

Beckett, K. (ed.). 1994. *Alpine Garden Society Encyclopaedia of Alpines.* Pershore, Worcs.: Alpine Garden Society.

Boufford, D.E., et al. (eds). 2003. *Flora of Taiwan Checklist.* A checklist of the vascular plants of Taiwan. Taipei, Taiwan: NTU. http://tai2.ntu.edu.tw

Bramwell, D. & Bramwell, Z.I. 2001. *Wild Flowers of the Canary Islands.* (2nd ed.). Madrid: Editorial Rueda, S.L.

Brickell, C. (ed.). 2003. *The Royal Horticultural Society A-Z Encyclopedia of Garden Plants.* (2nd ed.) London: Dorling Kindersley.

Brickell, C.D. et al (eds.). 2004. *International Code of Nomenclature for Cultivated Plants* (7th ed.). ISHS.

Brummitt, R.K. (comp.). 1992. *Vascular Plant Families and Genera.* Kew: Royal Botanic Gardens. http://data.kew.org

Castroviejo, S. et al. (eds). *Flora Iberica.* 1987-2007. (Vols 1-8,, 10, 14, 15, 21). Madrid: Real Jardín Botánico, C.S.I.C.

Cave, Y. & Paddison, V. 1999. *The Gardener's Encyclopaedia of New Zealand Native Plants.* Auckland: Godwit.

Cooke, I. 1998. *The Plantfinder's Guide to Tender Perennials.* Newton Abbot, Devon: David & Charles.

Cronquist, A., Holmgren, A.H., Holmgren, N.H., Reveal, J.L. & Holmgren, P.H. et al. (eds). *Intermountain Flora: Vascular Plants of the Intermountain West, USA.* (1986-97). (Vols 1, 3-6). New York: New York Botanical Garden.

Davis, P.H., Mill, R.R. & Tan, K. (eds). 1965-88. *Flora of Turkey and the East Aegean Island.* (Vols 1-10). Edinburgh University Press.

Goldblatt, P. & Manning, J. 2000. *Cape Plants. A Conspectus of the Cape Flora of South Africa.* South Africa/USA: National Botanical Institute of South Africa/Missouri Botanical Garden.

Greuter, W., Brummitt, R.K., Farr, E., Kilian, N., Kirk, P.M. & Silva, P.C. (comps). 1993. *NCU-3.*

Grierson, A.J.C., Long, D.G. & Noltie, H.J. et al. (eds). 2001. *Flora of Bhutan.* Edinburgh: Royal Botanic Garden.

Güner, A., Özhatay, N., Ekîm, T., Baser, K.H.C. & Hedge, I.C. 2000. *Flora of Turkey and the East Aegean Islands.* Supp. 2. Vol. 11. Edinburgh: Edinburgh University Press.

Hickman, J.C. (ed.). 1993. *The Jepson Manual. Higher Plants of California.* Berkeley & Los Angeles: University of California Press. May 2007. http://ucjeps.berkeley.edu

Hillier, J. & Coombes, A. (eds). 2002. *The Hillier Manual of Trees & Shrubs.* (7th ed.). Newton Abbot, Devon: David & Charles.

Hirose, Y. & Yokoi, M. 1998. *Variegated Plants in Colour.* Iwakuni, Japan: Varie Nine.

Hirose, Y. & Yokoi, M. 2001. *Variegated Plants in Colour.* Vol. 2. Iwakuni, Japan: Varie Nine.

Hoffman, M. (ed.). 2005. *List of Woody Plants. International Standard ENA 2005-2010.* Netherlands: Applied Plant Research.

Huxley, A., Griffiths, M. & Levy, M. (eds). 1992. *The New RHS Dictionary of Gardening.* London: Macmillan.

Iwatsuki, K., et al. 1995. *Flora of Japan.* Vols I-IIIb. Tokyo, Japan: Kodansha Ltd.

Jelitto, L. & Schacht, W. 1990. *Hardy Herbaceous Perennials.* Portland, Oregon: Timber Press. (2 vols).

Krüssmann, G. & Epp, M.E. (trans.). 1986. *Manual of Cultivated Broad-leaved Trees and Shrubs.* London: Batsford (3 vols).

Leslie, A.C. (trans.). *New Cultivars of Herbaceous Perennial Plants 1985-1990.* Hardy Plant Society.

Mabberley, D.J. 2008. *Mabberley's Plant Book. A Portable Dictionary of Plants, their classification and uses.* (3rd ed.). Cambridge: Cambridge University Press.

McNeill, J. et al. (eds). 2006. *International Code of Botanical Nomenclature (Vienna Code).* Ruggell, Liechtenstein: A.R.G. Gantner Verlag. http://ibot.sav.sk. Mar 2007.

Metcalf, L.J. 1987. *The Cultivation of New Zealand Trees and Shrubs.* Auckland: Reed Methuen.

Nelson, E.C. 2000. *A Heritage of Beauty: The Garden Plants of Ireland: An Illustrated Encyclopaedia.* Dublin: Irish Garden Plant Society.

Ohwi, J. 1965. *Flora of Japan.* Washington DC: Smithsonian Institution.

Phillips, R. & Rix, M. 1997. *Conservatory and Indoor Plants.* London: Macmillan. (2 vols).

Platt, K. (comp.). 2002. *The Seed Search.* (5th ed.). Sheffield: Karen Platt.
Press, J.R. & Short, M.J. (eds). 1994. *Flora of Madeira.* London: Natural History Museum/HMSO.
Rehder, A. 1940. *Manual of Cultivated Trees and Shrubs Hardy in North America.* (2nd ed.). New York: Macmillan.
Rice, G. (ed.), 2006. *Encyclopedia of Perennials.* London: Dorling Kindersley.
Stace, C. 1997. *New Flora of the British Isles.* (2nd ed.). Cambridge: Cambridge University Press.
Stearn, W.T. 1992. *Botanical Latin.* (4th ed.). Newton Abbot, Devon: David & Charles.
Stearn, W.T. 1996. *Stearn's Dictionary of Plant Names for Gardeners.* London: Cassell.
Thomas, G.S. 1990. *Perennial Garden Plants. A Modern Florilegium.* (3rd ed.). London: Dent.
Trehane, P. (comp.). 1989. *Index Hortensis. Vol. 1: Perennials.* Wimborne: Quarterjack
Tutin, T.G., et al. (ed.). 1993. *Flora Europaea. Vol. 1. Psilotaceae to Platanaceae.* (2nd ed.). Cambridge University Press.
Tutin, T.G., et al. 1964. *Flora Europaea.* Cambridge University Press. Vols 1-5. http://rbg-web2.rbge.org.uk
Walter, K.S. & Gillett, H.J. (eds). 1998. *1997 IUCN Red List of Threatened Plants.* Gland, Switzerland and Cambridge, UK: IUCN.
Walters, S.M. & Cullen, J. et al. (eds). 2000. *The European Garden Flora.* Cambridge: Cambridge University Press. (6 vols).
World Checklist of Selected Plant Families

General Periodicals

Dendroflora
New, Rare and Unusual Plants.
The Hardy Plant Society. *The Hardy Plant.*
The Hardy Plant Society. *The Sport.*
Internationale Stauden-Union. *ISU Yearbook.*
Royal Horticultural Society. *Hanburyana.*
Royal Horticultural Society. *The Garden.*
Royal Horticultural Society. *The Plantsman.*
Royal Horticultural Society. *The New Plantsman.*
Royal Horticultural Society. *The Plantsman* (new series).

General Websites

Annotated Checklist of the Flowering Plants of Nepal. www.efloras.org
Australian Cultivar Registration Authority. Oct 2007. www.anbg.gov.au/acra.
Australian Plant Breeders Rights – Database Search. May 2006. http://pbr.ipaustralia.optus.com.au
Australian Plant Names Index. Australian National Botanic Gardens (comp.). Mar 2006. www.anbg.gov.au/anbg
Bolivia Checklist. www.efloras.org
Botanical Expedition in Myanmar Checklist. Apr 2003. http://persoon.si.edu/myanmar
Brand, H. UConn Plant Database of Trees Shrubs and Vines. www.hort.uconn.edu
Canadian Ornamental Plant Foundation. Dec 2007. www.copf.org
Canadian Plant Breeders' Rights Office: Canadian Food Inspection Agency. Dec 2007. www.inspection.gc.ca
Catálogo de las Plantas Vasculares de las República Argentina. 2007. www.darwin.edu.ar/Publicaciones
Darwin Checklist of Moroccan Vascular Plants www.herbarium.rdg.ac.uk/
DEFRA Plant Varieties and Seeds Gazette. Nov 2007. www.defra.gov.uk
Fischer France. Apr 2002. www.pelfi.fr
Flora Himalaya Checklist www.leca.univ-savoie.fr
Flora Mesoamericana Internet Version (W3FM). Oct 2006. Missouri Botanical Garden. www.mobot.org
Flora of Australia Online. Jul 2007. Australian Biological Resources Study. www.environment.gov.au/biodiversity
Flora of Chile. www.efloras.org
Flora of China Checklist. Jan 2008. http://flora.huh.harvard.edu/china
Flora of North America Website. Jan 2006. Morin, N. R., et al. www.efloras.org
GRIN (Germplasm Resources Information Network) Taxonomy. Dec 2007. www.ars-grin.gov
Hatch, D. Jan 2008. New Ornamentals Society Database. http://members.tripod.com
Index Synonymique de la Flore de France. Oct 1999. www.dijon.inra.fr
International Plant Names Index. Oct 2007. www.ipni.org
International Plant Names Index: Author Query. Oct 2006. www.ipni.org/ipni
IOPI Provisional Global Plant Checklist. Feb 2005. www.bgbm.fu-berlin.de
Manaaki Whenua: Landcare Research in New Zealand Plants Database http://nzflora.landcareresearch.co.nz
Manual de plantas de Costa Rica. Apr 2001. www.mobot.org
Plants Database. Jan 2008. USDA, NRCS. http://plants.usda.gov
Plants of Southern Africa: an Online Checklist. Jan 2007. http://posa.sanbi.org
New Zealand Plant Variety Rights Office www.pvr.govt.nz
SKUD Database for Cultivated and Utilized Plants. http://skud.ngb.se
Synonymized Checklist of the Vascular Flora of the United States, Puerto Rico and the Virgin Isles. BIOTA of North America Program. Jul 1998. www.csdl.tamu.edu
US Patent Full-Text Database. US Patent and Trademark Office, (comp.). Jan 2008. www.uspto.gov/patft

VAST TROPICOS. Jan 2004. http://mobot.mobot.org
World Checklist of Selected Families. 2007. www.kew.org

GENERA AND OTHER PLANT GROUPINGS

Acer
Harris, J.G.S. 2000. *The Gardener's Guide to Growing Maples.* Newton Abbot, Devon: David & Charles.
Van Gelderen, C.J. & Van Gelderen, D.M. 1999. *Maples for Gardens.* A Color Encyclopedia. Portland, Oregon: Timber Press.
Vertrees, J.D. 2001. *Japanese Maples.* Momiji and Kaede. (3rd ed.). Portland, Oregon: Timber Press.
Actaea
Compton, J.A. & Culham, A. 2000. The Name is the Game. *The Garden* (RHS) 125(1):48-52.
Compton, J.A., Culham, A. & Jury, S.L. 1998. Reclassification of *Actaea* to Include *Cimicifuga* and *Souliea* (*Ranunculaceae*). *Taxon* 47:593-634.
Adiantum
Goudey, C.J. 1985. *Maidenhair Ferns in Cultivation.* Melbourne: Lothian.
Agapanthus
Snoeijer, W. 2004. *Agapanthus. A Revision of the Genus.* Portland, Oregon: Timber Press.
Agavaceae
Irish, M. & Irish, G. 2000. *Agaves, Yuccas and Related Plants.* A Gardener's Guide. Portland, Oregon: Timber Press.
Aizoaceae
Burgoyne, P. et al. 1998. *Mesembs of the World. Illustrated Guide to a Remarkable Succulent Group.* South Africa: Briza Publications.
Allium
Davies, D. 1992. *Alliums. The Ornamental Onions.* London: Batsford
Gregory, M., et al. 1998. *Nomenclator Alliorum.* Kew: Royal Botanic Gardens.
Mathew, B. 1996. *A Review of Allium Section Allium.* Kew: Royal Botanic Gardens.
Androsace
Smith, G. & Lowe, D. 1997. *The Genus Androsace.* Pershore, Worcs.: Alpine Garden Society.
***Anemone*, Japanese**
McKendrick, M. 1990. Autumn Flowering Anemones. *The Plantsman* 12(3):140-151.
McKendrick, M. 1998. Japanese Anemones. *The Garden* (RHS) 123(9):628-633.
Anthemis
Leslie, A. 1997. Focus on Plants: *Anthemis tinctoria. The Garden* (RHS) 122(8):552-555.
Apiaceae
Pimenov, M.G. & Leonov, M.V. 1993. *The Genera of the Umbelliferae.* Kew: Royal Botanic Gardens.
Aquilegia
Munz, P.A. 1946. *Aquilegia:* the Cultivated and Wild Columbines. *Gentes Herb.* 7(1):1-150.
Araceae
Govaerts, R. & Frodin, D.G. 2002. *World Checklist and Bibliography of Araceae (and Acoraceae).* Kew: Royal Botanic Gardens
***Arecaceae* (palms)**
Craft, P. & Riffle, R.L. 2003. *Encyclopedia of Cultivated Palms.* Portland, Oregon: Timber Press.
Uhl, N.W. & Dransfield, J. 1987. *Genera Palmarum.* A Classification of Palms Based on the Work of Harold E. Moore Jr. Lawrence, Kansas: Allen Press.
Argyranthemum
Humphries, C.J. 1976. A Revision of the Macaronesian Genus *Argyranthemum. Bull. Brit. Mus. (Nat. Hist.) Bot.* 5(4):145-240.
Araliaceae
Govaerts, R. & Frodin, D.G. 2002. *World Checklist and Bibliography of Araliaceae.* Kew: Royal Botanic Gardens
Arisaema
Gusman, G. & Gusman, L. 2002. *The Genus Arisaema: A Monograph for Botanists and Nature Lovers.* Ruggell, Leichtenstein: A.R. Gantner Verlag Kommanditgesellschaft.
Pradhan, U.C. 1997. *Himalayan Cobra Lilies* (Arisaema). Their Botany and Culture. (2nd ed.). Kalimpong, West Bengal, India: Primulaceae Books.
Arum
Bown, D. 2000. *Plants of the Arum Family.* (2nd ed.). Portland, Oregon: Timber Press.
Boyce, P. 1993. *The Genus Arum.* London: HMSO.
Asclepiadaceae
Eggli, U. (ed.). 2002. *Illustrated Handbook of Succulent Plants: Asclepiadaceae.* Heidelberg, Germany: Springer-Verlag.
Aster
Picton, P. 1999. *The Gardener's Guide to Growing Asters.* Newton Abbot: David & Charles.
Asteraceae
Bremer, K. et al. 1994. *Asteraceae: Cladistics and Classification.* Portland, Oregon: Timber Press.
Cubey, J. & Grant, M. 2004. *Perennial Yellow Daisies: RHS Bulletin No 6.* Wisley, Surrey: RHS. www.rhs.org.uk/plants/documents/yellowdaisies04.pdf
Astilbe
Noblett, H. 2001. *Astilbe.* A Guide to the Identification of Cultivars and Common Species. Cumbria: Henry Noblett.
Aubrieta
1975. *International Registration Authority Checklist.* Weihenstephan, Germany: (Unpublished).
Bamboos
Ohrnberger, D. 1999. *The Bamboos of the World.* Amsterdam: Elsevier.
Begonia
American Begonia Society Astro Branch Begonia Data Base. Jan 2000. http://absastro.tripod.com
American Begonia Society Registered Begonias. 2007. http://www.begonias.org

Ingles, J. 1990. *American Begonia Society Listing of Begonia Cultivars.* Revised Edition Buxton Checklist. American Begonia Society.

Tebbitt, M.C. 2005. *Begonias: Cultivation, Identification and Natural History*. Portland, Oregon: Timber Press.

Thompson, M.L. & Thompson, E.J. 1981. *Begonias.* The Complete Reference Guide. New York: Times Books.

Berberidaceae

Stearn, W.T. & Shaw, J.M.H. 2002. *The Genus Epimedium and Other Herbaceous Berberidaceae including the Genus Podophyllum.* Kew: Royal Botanic Gardens.

Betula

Ashburner, K. & Schilling. T. 1985. *Betula utilis* and its Varieties. *The Plantsman* 7(2):116-125.

Ashburner, K.B. 1980. *Betula* – a Survey. *The Plantsman* 2(1):31-53.

Hunt, D. (ed.). 1993. *Betula: Proceedings of the IDS Betula Symposium 1992.* Richmond, Surrey: International Dendrology Society.

Boraginaceae

Bennett, M. 2003. *Pulmonarias and the Borage Family.* London: Batsford.

Bougainvillea

Gillis, W.T. 1976. Bougainvilleas of Cultivation (*Nyctaginaceae*). *Baileya* 20(1):34-41.

Iredell, J. 1990. *The Bougainvillea Grower's Handbook.* Brookvale, Australia: Simon & Schuster.

Iredell, J. 1994. *Growing Bougainvilleas.* London: Cassell.

MacDaniels, L.H. 1981. A Study of Cultivars in *Bougainvillea* (*Nyctaginaceae*). *Baileya* 21(2):77-100.

Singh, B., Panwar, R.S., Voleti, S.R., Sharma, V.K. & Thakur, S. 1999. *The New International Bougainvillea Check List.* (2nd ed.). New Delhi: Indian Agricultural Research Institute.

Bromeliaceae

Beadle, D.A. 1991. *A Preliminary Listing of all the Known Cultivar and Grex Names for the Bromeliaceae.* Corpus Christi, Texas: Bromeliad Society.

Bromeliad Cultivar Registry Online Databases. Jan 2007. Bromeliad Society International www.bsi.org

Brugmansia

Wreggitt, L. et al. (comp.). Dec 2007. *Register of Brugmansia Cultivars and Checklist of Names in Use.* American Brugmansia and Datura Society. www.abads.org

Buddleja

Stuart, D.D. 2006. *Buddlejas: Royal Horticultural Society Collector Guide.* Portland, Oregon: Timber Press.

Bulbs

Leeds, R. 2000. *The Plantfinder's Guide to Early Bulbs.* Newton Abbot, Devon: David & Charles.

KAVB Online registration pages http://kavb.back2p.soft-orange.com

Buxus

Batdorf, L.R. 1995. *Boxwood Handbook. A Practical Guide to Knowing and Growing Boxwood.* Boyce, VA, USA: The American Boxwood Society.

Cactaceae

Hunt, D. et al. 2006. *New Cactus Lexicon.* (2 vols.) Sherborne, Dorset: DH Books.

Camellia

Trujillo, D. J. (ed.). 2002. *Camellia Nomenclature.* (24th revd ed.). Southern California Camellia Society.

Savige, T.J. (comp.). 1993. *The International Camellia Register.* The International Camellia Society. (2 vols).

Savige, T.J. (comp.). 1997. *The International Camellia Register.* Supp. to vols 1 and 2. The International Camellia Society.

Campanula

Lewis, P. & Lynch, M. 1998. *Campanulas.* A Gardeners Guide. (2nd ed.). London: Batsford.

Lewis, P 2002. *Campanulas in the Garden.* Pershore, Worcs.: Hardy Plant Society.

Campanulaceae

Lammers, T.G. 2007. *World Checklist and Bibliography of Campanulaceae.* Kew Publishing.

Canna

Cooke, I. 2001. *The Gardener's Guide to Growing Cannas.* Newton Abbot, Devon: David & Charles.

Gray, J. & Grant, M. 2003. Canna: RHS Bulletin No 3. Wisley, Surrey: RHS. www.rhs.org.uk/plants/documents/canna03.pdf

Hayward, K. Jan 2007. http://www.hartcanna.com

Carnivorous Plants

Schlauer, J. (comp.). Aug 2006. Carnivorous Plant Database. www.omnisterra.com

Ceanothus

Fross, D. & D. Wilken. 2006. *Ceanothus.* Portland, Oregon: Timber Press.

Cercidiphyllum

Dosmann, M.S. 1999. Katsura: a Review of *Cercidiphyllum* in Cultivation and in the Wild. *The New Plantsman* 6(1):52-62.

Dosmann, M., Andrews, S., Del Tredici, P. & Li, J. 2003. Classification and Nomenclature of Weeping Katsuras. *The Plantsman* 2(1):21-27.

Chaenomeles

Weber, C. 1963. Cultivars in the Genus *Chaenomeles. Arnoldia (Jamaica Plain)* 23(3):17-75.

Chrysanthemum

Brummitt, D. 1997. *Chrysanthemum* Once Again. *The Garden* (RHS) 122(9):662-663.

Gosling, S.G. (ed.). 1964. *British National Register of Chrysanthemums.* Whetstone, London: National Chrysanthemum Society.

National Chrysanthemum Society. 2000. *British National Register of Names of Chrysanthemums Amalgamated Edition 1964-1999.* Tamworth, Staffordshire: The National Chrysanthemum Society.

National Chrysanthemum Society UK Cultivar Database. Jan 2008. www.nationalchrysanthemum society.org.uk

Cistus

Demoly, J.-P. 2005. The identity of *Cistus* 'Grayswood Pink' and related plants. *The Plantsman* 4(2):76-80.

Page, R.G. Feb 2007. Cistus and Halimium Website. www.cistuspage.org.uk

Citrus

Davies, F.S. & Albrigo, L.G. 1994. *Citrus.* Wallingford, Oxon: Cab International.

Page, M. 2008. *Growing Citrus.* London: Timber Press

Saunt, J. 1990. *Citrus Varieties of the World.* An Illustrated Guide. Norwich: Sinclair

Clematis

Clematis on the Web. Jan 2008. www.clematis.hull.ac.uk

Grey-Wilson, C. 2000. *Clematis: the Genus.* London: Batsford

HelpMeFind Clematis. Nov 2006. www.helpmefind.com/clematis

Johnson, M. 2001. *The Genus Clematis.* Södertälje, Sweden: Magnus Johnsons Plantskola AB & Bengt Sundström.

Matthews, V. (comp.). 2002. *The International Clematis Register and Checklist 2002.* London: RHS.

Supps 1 (2004) & 2 (2006). http://www.rhs.org.uk/learning

Toomey, M. & Leeds, E. 2001. *An Illustrated Encyclopedia of Clematis.* Portland, Oregon: Timber Press.

Conifers

den Ouden, P. & Boom, B.K. 1965. *Manual of Cultivated Conifers.* The Hague: Martinus Nijhof.

Farjon, A. 1998. *World Checklist and Bibliography of Conifers.* Kew: Royal Botanic Gardens.

Knees, S. Feb 2005. Complete List of Conifer Taxa Accepted for Registration. RHS. www.rhs.org.uk/research

Krüssmann, G. & Epp, M.E. (trans.). 1985. *Manual of Cultivated Conifers.* London: Batsford.

Lewis, J. & Leslie, A.C. 1987. *The International Conifer Register. Pt 1. Abies* to *Austrotaxus.* London: RHS.

Lewis, J. & Leslie, A.C. 1989. *The International Conifer Register. Pt 2. Belis* to *Pherosphaera,* excluding the Cypresses. London: RHS.

Lewis, J. & Leslie, A.C. 1992. *The International Conifer Register. Pt 3. The Cypresses.* London: RHS.

Lewis, J. & Leslie, A.C. 1998. *The International Conifer Register. Pt 4. Juniperus.* London: RHS.

Welch, H.J. 1979. *Manual of Dwarf Conifers.* New York: Theophrastus.

Welch, H.J. 1991. *The Conifer Manual.* Vol. 1. Dordrecht, Netherlands: Kluwer Academic Publishers.

Welch, H.J. 1993. *The World Checklist of Conifers.* Bromyard, Herefordshire: Landsman's Bookshops Ltd.

Cornus

Cappiello, P. & Shadow, D. 2005. *Dogwoods.* Portland, Oregon: Timber Press.

Howard, R.A. 1961. Registration Lists of Cultivar Names in *Cornus L. Arnoldia (Jamaica Plain)* 21(2):9-18.

Corydalis

Lidén, M. & Zetterlund, H. 1997. *Corydalis. A Gardener's Guide and a Monograph of the Tuberous Species.* Pershore, Worcs.: Alpine Garden Society Publications Ltd.

Corylus

Crawford, M. 1995. *Hazelnuts: Production and Culture.* Dartington, Devon: Agroforestry Research Trust.

Cotoneaster

Fryer, J. & Hylmö, B. 1998. Seven New Species of *Cotoneaster* in Cultivation. *The New Plantsman* 5(3):132-144.

Fryer, J. & Hylmö, B. 2001. Captivating Cotoneasters. *The New Plantsman* 8(4):227-238.

Fryer, J. 1996. Undervalued Versatility. *Cotoneaster. The Garden* (RHS) 121(11):709-715.

Crassulaceae

Rowley, G. 2003. *Crassula: A Grower's Guide.* Venegono superiore, Italy: Cactus & Co.

Eggli, U. (ed.) 2003. *Illustrated Handbook of Succulent Plants.* Springer.

Crocosmia

Goldblatt, P., Manning, J.C. & Dunlop, G. 2004. *Crocosmia and Chasmanthe.* Portland, Oregon: Timber Press.

Crocus

Jacobsen, N., van Scheepen, J. & Ørgaard, M. 1997. The *Crocus chrysanthus – biflorus* Cultivars. *The New Plantsman* 4(1):6-38.

Mathew, B. 1982. *The Crocus. A Review of the Genus Crocus* (*Iridaceae*). London: Batsford.

Mathew, B. 2002. *Crocus* Up-date. *The Plantsman* 1(1):44-56.

Cyclamen

Clennett, C. Jan. 2003. Register of Cultivar Names. www.cyclamen.org

Grey-Wilson, C. 2003. *Cyclamen. A Guide for Gardeners, Horticulturists & Botanists.* London: Batsford.

Grey-Wilson, C. 2002 Sprenger's Alpine Cyclamen. *The Plantsman* 1(3):173-177.

Cypripedium

Cribb, P. 1997. *The Genus Cypripedium.* Portland, Oregon: Timber Press.

Dahlia

American Dahlia Society website. 2006. www.dahlia.org

Bates, D. Dahlia Plant Finder 2007. Dec 2007. www.dahliaworld.co.uk

National Dahlia Society. 2005. *Classified Directory and Judging Rules.* (28th ed.) Aldershot, Hants: National Dahlia Society.

RHS & Hedge, R. (comps). 1969. *Tentative Classified List and International Register of Dahlia Names 1969.* (& Supps 1-13). London: RHS. Supps 13-17. 2002-06. http://www.rhs.org.uk/learning
Winchester Growers Ltd English National Dahlia Collection website. 2007. www.national-dahlia-collection.co.uk

Daphne

Brickell, C.D. & Mathew, B. 1976. *Daphne. The Genus in the Wild and in Cultivation.* Woking, Surrey: Alpine Garden Society.

Grey-Wilson, C. (ed.). 2001. *The Smaller Daphnes. The Proceedings of 'Daphne 2000', a Conference held at the Royal Horticultural Society.* Pershore, Worcs.: Alpine Garden Society.

White, R. 2006. *Daphnes: A Practical Guide for Gardeners.* Portland, Oregon: Timber Press.

Delphinium

1949. *A Tentative Check-list of Delphinium Names.* London: RHS.

1970. *A Tentative Check-list of Delphinium Names.* Addendum to the 1949 tentative check-list of *Delphinium* names. London: RHS.

Bassett, D. & Wesley, W. 2004. *Delphinium: RHS Bulletin No 5.* Wisley, Surrey: RHS. www.rhs.org.uk/plants/documents/delph04.pdf

Leslie, A.C. 1996. *The International Delphinium Register Cumulative Supp. 1970-1995.* London: RHS.

Leslie, A.C. 1996-2005. The International Delphinium Register Supp. 1994-99. *The Delphinium Society Year Book 1996-2005.* London: RHS.

Dianthus

Galbally, J. & Galbally, E. 1997. *Carnations and Pinks for Garden and Greenhouse.* Portland, Oregon: Timber Press.

Leslie, A.C. *The International Dianthus Register.* 1983-2002. (2nd ed. & Supps 1-19). London: RHS.

Supps 19-23. 2002-06. http://www.rhs.org.uk/learning

Dierama

Hilliard, O.M. & Burtt, B.L. 1991. *Dierama. The Harebells of Africa.* Johannesburg; London: Acorn Books.

Dionysia

Grey-Wilson, C. 1989. *The Genus Dionysia.* Woking, Surrey: Alpine Garden Society.

Douglasia

Mitchell, B. 1999. Celebrating the Bicentenary of David Douglas: a Review of *Douglasia* in Cultivation. *The New Plantsman* 6(2):101-108.

Dracaena

Bos, J.J., Graven, P., Hetterscheid, W.L.A. & van de Wege, J.J. 1992. Wild and cultivated *Dracaena fragrans. Edinburgh J. Bot.* 49(3):311-331.

Echeveria

Schulz, L. & Kapitany, A. *Echeveria Cultivars.* Teesdale, Australia: Schulz Publishing.

Episcia

Dates, J.D. 1993. *The Gesneriad Register 1993.* Check List of Names with Descriptions of Cultivated Plants in the Genera *Episcia* & *Alsobia.* Galesburg, Illinois: American Gloxinia & Gesneriad Society, Inc.

***Erica* (see also Heathers)**

Baker, H.A. & Oliver, E.G.H. 1967. *Heathers in Southern Africa.* Cape Town: Purnell.

Schumann, D., Kirsten, G. & Oliver, E.G.H. 1992. *Ericas of South Africa.* Vlaeberg, South Africa: Fernwood Press.

Erodium

Clifton, R. 1994. *Geranium Family Species Checklist. Pt 1 Erodium.* (4th ed.). The Geraniaceae Group.

Leslie, A.C. 1980. The Hybrid of *Erodium corsicum* with *Erodium reichardii. The Plantsman* 2:117-126.

Toomey, N., Cubey, J. & Culham, A. 2002. *Erodium × variabile. The Plantsman* 1(3): 166-172

Victor, D.X. (comp.). 2000. *Erodium: Register of Cultivar Names.* The Geraniaceae Group.

Erythronium

Mathew, B. 1992. A Taxonomic and Horticultural Review of *Erythronium* L. (*Liliaceae*). *J. Linn. Soc., Bot.* 109:453-471.

Mathew, B. 1998. The Genus *Erythronium. Bull. Alpine Gard. Soc. Gr. Brit.* 66(3):308-321.

***Eupatorium* sensu lato**

Hind, D.J.N. 2006. Splitting *Eupatorium. The Plantsman* (n.s.) 5(2):185-189.

Euonymus

Brown, N. 1996. Notes on Cultivated Species of *Euonymus. The New Plantsman* 3(4):238-243.

Lancaster, C.R. 1981. An Account of *Euonymus* in Cultivation and its Availability in Commerce. *The Plantsman* 3(3):133-166.

Lancaster, C.R. 1982. *Euonymus* in Cultivation – Addendum. *The Plantsman* 4:61-64, 253-254.

Euphorbia

Govaerts, R., Frodin, D.G. & Radcliffe-Smith, A. 2000. *World Checklist and Bibliography of Euphorbiaceae.* Kew: Royal Botanic Gardens.

Turner, R. 1995. *Euphorbias. A Gardeners Guide.* London: Batsford.

Witton, D. 2000. *Euphorbias.* Pershore, Worcs.: Hardy Plant Society.

Fagales

World Checklist and Bibliography Series: About the *Fagales.* Jan 2002. www.rbgkew.org.uk

Fagus

Dönig, G. 1994. *Die Park-und Gartenformen der Rotbuche Fagus sylvatica L.* Erlangen, Germany: Verlag Gartenbild Heinz Hansmann.

Wyman, D. 1964. Registration List of Cultivar Names of *Fagus* L. *J. Arnold Arbor.* 24(1):1-8.

Fascicularia

Nelson, E.C. & Zizka, G. 1997. *Fascicularia* (*Bromeliaceae*): Which Species are Cultivated and

Naturalized in Northwestern Europe. *The New Plantsman* 4(4):232-239.

Nelson, E.C., Zizka, G., Horres, R. & Weising, K. 1999. Revision of the Genus *Fascicularia* Mez (*Bromeliaceae*). *Botanical Journal of the Linnean Society* 129(4):315-332.

Ferns

Checklist of World Ferns. March 2003. http://homepages.caverock.net.nz

Johns, R.J. 1996. *Index Filicum.* Supplementum Sextum pro annis 1976-1990. Kew:Royal Botanic Gardens.

Johns, R.J. 1997. *Index Filicum.* Supplementum Septimum pro annis 1991-1995. Kew:Royal Botanic Gardens.

Jones, D.L. 1987. *Encyclopaedia of Ferns.* Melbourne, Australia: Lothian.

Kaye, R. 1968. *Hardy Ferns.* London: Faber & Faber

Rickard, M.H. 2000. *The Plantfinder's Guide to Garden Ferns.* Newton Abbot, Devon: David & Charles.

Rush, R. 1984. *A Guide to Hardy Ferns.* London: British Pteridological Society.

Forsythia

INRA Forsythia website. Dec 2000. www.angers.inra.fr

Fritillaria

Clark, T. & Grey-Wilson, C. 2003. Crown Imperials. *The Plantsman* 2(1):33-47.

Mathew, B., et al. 2000. *Fritillaria* Issue. *Bot. Mag.* 17(3):145-185.

Pratt, K. & Jefferson-Brown, M. 1997. *The Gardener's Guide to Growing Fritillaries.* Newton Abbot: David & Charles.

Turrill, W.B. & Sealy, J.R. 1980. *Studies in the Genus Fritillaria (Liliaceae).* Hooker's Icones Plantarum Vol. 39 (1 & 2). Kew: Royal Botanic Gardens.

Fruit

Brogdale Horticultural Trust National Fruit Collection. Jul 2007. http://www.brogdale.org.uk/nfc_home.php

Bowling, B.L. 2000. *The Berry Grower's Companion.* Portland, Oregon: Timber Press.

Hogg, R. 1884. *The Fruit Manual.* (5th ed.). London: Journal of Horticulture Office.

Fuchsia

American Fuchsia Society Registration Database. Jan 2008. www.americanfuchsiasociety.org

Bartlett, G. 1996. *Fuchsias – A Colour Guide.* Marlborough, Wilts: Crowood Press.

Boullemier, Leo.B. (comp.). 1991. *The Checklist of Species, Hybrids and Cultivars of the Genus Fuchsia.* London, New York, Sydney: Blandford Press.

Boullemier, Leo.B. (comp.). 1995. *Addendum No 1 to the 1991 Checklist of Species, Hybrids and Cultivars of the Genus Fuchsia.* Dyfed, Wales: The British Fuchsia Society.

Goulding, E. 1995. *Fuchsias: The Complete Guide.* London: Batsford.

Johns, E.A. 1997. *Fuchsias of the 19th and Early 20th Century.* An Historical Checklist of Fuchsia Species & Cultivars, pre-1939. Kidderminster, Worcs.: British Fuchsia Society

Jones, L. & Miller, D.M. 2005. *Hardy Fuchsias: RHS Bulletin No 12.* Wisley, Surrey: RHS. www.rhs.org.uk/plants/documents/fuchsia05.pdf

Stevens, R. Dec 2007. Find That Fuchsia. www.findthatfuchsia.info

Van Veen, G. Nov 2007. Gelderse Fuchsia Info-site. www.geldersefuchsia.info

Galanthus

Bishop, M., Davis, A. & Grimshaw, J. 2001. *Snowdrops. A monograph of cultivated Galanthus.* Maidenhead: Griffin Press.

Davis, A.P., Mathew, B. (ed.) & King, C. (ill.). 1999. *The Genus Galanthus. A Botanical Magazine Monograph.* Oregon: Timber Press.

Gentiana

Bartlett, M. 1975. *Gentians.* Dorset: Blandford Press.

Halda, J.J. 1996. *The Genus Gentiana.* Dobré, Czech Republic: Sen.

Ho T.N. & Liu S. 2001. *Worldwide Monograph of Gentiana.* Beijing: Science Press.

Geranium

Armitage, J. 2005. *Hardy Geraniums – Stage 1: RHS Bulletin No 10.* Wisley, Surrey: RHS. www.rhs.org.uk/plants/documents/geranium05.pdf

Armitage, J. 2006. *Hardy Geraniums – Stage 2: RHS Bulletin No 14.* Wisley, Surrey: RHS. www.rhs.org.uk/plants/documents/geranium06.pdf

Armitage, J. 2007. *Hardy Geraniums – Stage 3: RHS Bulletin No 18.* Wisley, Surrey: RHS.

http://www.rhs.org.uk

Bath, T. & Jones, J. 1994. *The Gardener's Guide to Growing Hardy Geraniums.* Newton Abbot, Devon: David & Charles.

Bendtsen, B.H. 2005. *Gardening with Hardy Geraniums.* Portland, Oregon: Timber Press.

Clifton, R.T.F. 1995. *Geranium Family Species Check List Pt 2.* Geranium. (4th ed. issue 2). Dover: The Geraniaceae Group.

Jones, J., et al. 2001. *Hardy Geraniums for the Garden.* (3rd ed.). Pershore, Worcs.: Hardy Plant Society.

Victor, D.X. 2004. *Register of Geranium Cultivar Names.* (2nd ed.). The Geraniaceae Group.

Yeo, P.F. 2002. *Hardy Geraniums.* (3rd ed.). Kent: Croom Helm.

Gesneriaceae

American Gloxinia and Gesneriad Society. Listing of registered gesneriads. 2005. www.aggs.org

Dates, J.D. 1986-1990. *The Gesneriad Register 1986-1987 & 1990.* Galesburg, Illinois: American Gloxinia & Gesneriad Society, Inc.

Gladiolus

British Gladiolus Society List of Cultivars Classified for Show Purposes 1994. Mayfield, Derbyshire: British Gladiolus Society.

1997-1998. British Gladiolus Society List of European, New Zealand & North American Cultivars Classified for Exhibition Purposes 1997 & 1998. Mayfield, Derbyshire: British Gladiolus Society.

Goldblatt, P. & Manning, J. 1998. *Gladiolus in Southern Africa.* Vlaeberg, South Africa: Fernwood Press.

Goldblatt, P. 1996. *Gladiolus in Tropical Africa.* Systematics Biology and Evolution. Oregon: Timber Press.

Lewis, G.J., Obermeyer, A.A. & Barnard, T.T. 1972. A Revision of the South African Species of *Gladiolus. J. S. African Bot.* (Supp. Vol. 10)

Gleditsia

Santamour, F.S. & McArdle, A.J. 1983. Checklist of Cultivars of Honeylocust (*Gleditsia triacanthos* L.). *J. Arboric.* 9:271-276.

Grevillea

Olde, P. & Marriott, N. 1995. *The Grevillea Book.* (3). Kenthurst, NSW: Kangaroo Press.

Haemanthus

Snijman, D. 1984. A Revision of the Genus *Haemanthus. J. S. African Bot.* (Supp. Vol. 12).

Hamamelis

Lane, C. 2005. *Witch Hazels.* Portland, Oregon: Timber Press.

Heathers

Nelson, E.C. Aug 2007. International Cultivar Registration Authority for Heathers. www.heathersociety.org.uk

Hebe

Chalk, D. 1988. *Hebes and Parahebes.* Bromley, Kent: Christopher Helm (Publishers) Ltd.

Hutchins, G. 1997. *Hebes: Here and There.* A Monograph on the Genus *Hebe.* Caversham, Berks: Hutchins & Davies.

Metcalf, L.J. 2001. *International Register of Hebe Cultivars.* Canterbury, New Zealand: Royal New Zealand Institute of Horticulture (Inc.).

Metcalf, L.J. 2006. *Hebes: A Guide to Species, Hybrids and Allied Genera.* Portland, Oregon: Timber Press.

Hedera

Jury, S. et al. 2006. *Hedera algeriensis*, a Fine Species of Ivy. *Sibbaldia* 4: 93-108.

McAllister, H. 1988. Canary and Algerian Ivies. *The Plantsman* 10(1):27-29.

McAllister, H.A. & Rutherford, A. 1990. *Hedera helix and H. hibernica* in the British Isles. *Watsonia* 18:7-15.

Rose, P.Q. 1996. *The Gardener's Guide to Growing Ivies.* Newton Abbot, Devon: David & Charles.

Rutherford, A., McAllister, H. & Mill, R.R. 1993. New Ivies from the Mediterranean Area and Macaronesia. *The Plantsman* 15(2):115-128.

Heliconia

Berry, F. & Kress, W.J. 1991. *Heliconia.* An Identification Guide. Washington: Smithsonian Institution Press.

Helleborus

Burrell, C.C. & Tyler, J.K. 2006. *Hellebores: A Comprehensive Guide.* Portland, Oregon: Timber Press.

Mathew, B. 1989. *Hellebores.* Woking: Alpine Garden Society.

Rice, G. & Strangman, E. 1993. *The Gardener's Guide to Growing Hellebores.* Newton Abbot, Devon: David & Charles.

Hemerocallis

Baxter, G.J. (comp.). Jun 2007. American Daylily Society Registry of Daylily Cultivars. www.daylilydatabase.org

Kitchingman, R.M. 1985. Some Species and Cultivars of *Hemerocallis. The Plantsman* 7(2):68-89.

Herbs

Page, M. & Stearn, W. *Culinary Herbs: A Wisley Handbook.* London: RHS.

Phillips, R. & Foy, N. 1990. *Herbs.* London: Pan Books Ltd.

Heuchera **and ×** ***Heucherella***

Heims, D. & Ware, G. 2005. *Heucheras and Heucherellas: Coral Bells and Foamy Bells.* Portland, Oregon: Timber Press.

Hibiscus

Noble, C. Apr 2007. Australian Hibiscus Society Database Register. www.australianhibiscus.com/

Hosta

Hammelman, T. 2002. Giboshi.com Hosta Database. www.giboshi.com

Hosta Library. Aug 2006. www.hostalibrary.org

Grenfell, D. & Shadrack, M. 2004. *The Color Encyclopedia of Hostas.* Portland, Oregon: Timber Press.

Schmid, W.G. 1991. *The Genus Hosta.* London: Batsford.

Hyacinthaceae

Dashwood, M. & Mathew, B. 2006. *Hyacinthaceae – little blue bulbs: RHS Bulletin No 11.* Wisley, Surrey: RHS. www.rhs.org.uk/plants/documents/hyacinthaceae05.pdf

Mathew, B. 2005. *Hardy Hyacinthaceae* Pt 1: *Muscari. The Plantsman* 4(1):40-53.

Mathew, B. 2005. *Hardy Hyacinthaceae* Pt 2: *Scilla, Chionodoxa* and × *Chinoscilla. The Plantsman* 4(2):110-121.

Hydrangea

Dirr, M.A. 2004. *Hydrangeas for American Gardens.* Portland, Oregon: Timber Press.

Haworth-Booth, M. 1975. *The Hydrangeas.* London: Garden Book Club.

Van Gelderen, C.J. & Van Gelderen, D.M. 2004. *Encyclopedia of Hydrangeas.* Portland, Oregon: Timber Press.

Hypericum

Lancaster, R. & Robson, N. 1997. Focus on Plants: Bowls of Beauty. *The Garden* (RHS) 122(8):566-571.

Ilex

Bailes, C. 2006. *Hollies for Gardeners*. Portland, Oregon: Timber Press.

Dudley, T.R. & Eisenbeiss, G.K. 1973 & 1992. *International Checklist of Cultivated Ilex*. Pt 1 *Ilex opaca* (1973), Pt 2 *Ilex crenata* (1992). Washington DC: United States Dept of Agriculture.

Galle, F.C. 1997. *Hollies: the Genus Ilex*. Portland, Oregon: Timber Press.

Impatiens

Morgan, R.J. 2007. *Impatiens: The Vibrant World of Busy Lizzies, Balsams and Touch-me-nots*. Portland, Oregon: Timber Press.

Iris

Austin, C. 2005. *Irises: A Gardener's Encyclopedia*. Oregon:Timber Press.

Hoog, M.H. 1980. Bulbous Irises . *The Plantsman* 2(3):141-64.

Keppel, K. (ed.) 2001. *Iris Check List of Registered Cultivar Names 1990-1999*. Hannibal, New York: the American Iris Society.

Mathew, B. 1981. *The Iris*. London: Batsford.

Mathew, B. 1993. The Spuria Irises. *The Plantsman* 15(1):14-25.

Service, N. 1990. *Iris unguicularis. The Plantsman* 12(1):1-9.

Stebbings, G. 1997. *The Gardener's Guide to Growing Iris*. Newton Abbot: David & Charles.

The Species Group of the British Iris Society, (ed.). 1997. *A Guide to Species Irises*. Their Identification and Cultivation. Cambridge: Cambridge University Press.

Jovibarba* see under *Sempervivum

Kalmia

Jaynes, R.A. 1997. *Kalmia. Mountain Laurel and Related Species*. Portland, Oregon: Timber Press.

Kniphofia

Grant-Downton, R. 1997. Notes on *Kniphofia thomsonii* in Cultivation and in the Wild. *The New Plantsman* 4(3):148-156.

Taylor, J. 1985. *Kniphofia* – a Survey. *The Plantsman* 7(3):129-160.

Kohleria

Dates, J.D. (ed.) & Batcheller, F.N. (comp.). 1985. *The Gesneriad Register 1985. Check List of Names with Descriptions of Cultivated Plants in the Genus Kohleria*. Lincoln Acres, California: American Gloxinia and Gesneriad Society, Inc.

Lachenalia

Duncan, G.D. 1988. *The Lachenalia Hand Book*. Kirstenbosch, South Africa: National Botanic Gardens.

Lantana

Howard, R.A. 1969. A Check List of Names Used in the Genus *Lantana. Arnoldia*. 29(11):73-109.

Lathyrus

Norton, S. 1996. *Lathyrus. Cousins of Sweet Pea*. Surrey: NCCPG.

Lavandula

Upson, T. & Andrews, S. 2004. *The Genus Lavandula*. Kew: Royal Botanic Garden.

Legumes

ILDIS. International Legume Database and Information Service. Nov 2005. Version 10.01. www.ildis.org/LegumeWeb

Leptospermum

Check List of *Leptospermum* Cultivars. 1963. *J. Roy. New Zealand Inst. Hort*. 5(5):224-30.

Dawson, M. 1997. A History of *Leptospermum scoparium* in Cultivation – Discoveries from the Wild. *The New Plantsman* 4(1):51-59.

Dawson, M. 1997. A History of *Leptospermum scoparium* in Cultivation – Garden Selections. *The New Plantsman* 4(2):67-78.

Lewisia

Davidson, B.L.R. 2000. *Lewisias*. Portland, Oregon: Timber Press.

Elliott, R. 1978. *Lewisias*. Woking: Alpine Garden Society.

Mathew, B. 1989. *The Genus Lewisia*. Bromley, Kent: Christopher Helm.

***Liliaceae* sensu lato**

Mathew, B. 1989. Splitting the *Liliaceae*. *The Plantsman* 11(2):89-105.

Lilium

Leslie, A.C. *The International Lily Register 1982-2002*. (3rd ed. & supps 1-20). London: RHS.

Supps 20-23. 2002-06. www.rhs.org.uk/learning

Online Lily Register. May 2007. www.lilyregister.com

Lonicera

Blahník, Z. 2006. *Lonicera* Cultivar Names: The First World List. *Acta Pruhoniciana* 81:59-64.

Magnolia

Callaway, D.J. Sep 2001. Magnolia Cultivar Checklist. www.magnoliasociety.org

Frodin, D.G. & Govaerts, R. 1996. *World Checklist and Bibliography of Magnoliaceae*. Kew: Royal Botanic Garden.

Maianthemum

Cubey, J.J. 2005 *The Incorporation of Smilacina within Maianthemum. The Plantsman* N.S.4(4).

Malus

Crawford, M. 1994. *Directory of Apple Cultivars*. Devon: Agroforestry Research Trust.

Fiala, J.L. 1994. *Flowering Crabapples*. The genus *Malus*. Portland, Oregon: Timber Press.

Rouèche, A. Oct 2007. Les Crets Fruits et Pomologie. www.pomologie.com

Smith, M.W.G. 1971. *National Apple Register of the United Kingdom*. London: MAFF

Spiers, V. 1996. *Burcombes, Queenies and Colloggetts*. St Dominic, Cornwall: West Brendon.

Meconopsis

Grey-Wilson, C. 1992. A Survey of the Genus *Meconopsis* in Cultivation. *The Plantsman* 14(1): 1-33.

Grey-Wilson, C. 2002. The True Identity of *Meconopsis napaulensis*. *Bot. Mag.* 23(2):176-209.
Meconopsis Group website www.meconopsis.org
Stevens, E. & Brickell, C. 2001. Problems with the Big Perennial Poppies. *The New Plantsman* 8(1):48-61.
Stevens, E. 2001. Further Observations on the Big Perennial Blue Poppies. *The New Plantsman* 8(2):105-111.

Miscanthus

Jones, L. 2004. Miscanthus: RHS Bulletin No 7. Wisley, Surrey: RHS. www.rhs.org.uk/plant/documents/miscanthus04.pdf

Moraea

Goldblatt, P. 1986. *The Moraeas of Southern Africa.* Kirstenbosch, South Africa: National Botanic Gardens.

Musa

INIBAP *Musa* Germplasm Information System. Dec 2006. http//195.220.148.3:8013/mgis_2/homepage.htm
Musalogue 2: Diversity in the Genus *Musa.* 2001. http://bananas.bioversityinternational.org

Narcissus

Blanchard, J.W. 1990. *Narcissus – A Guide to Wild Daffodils.* Woking, Surrey: Alpine Garden Society.
Kington, S. (comp.). 1998. *The International Daffodil Register and Classified List 1998* (3rd ed. & Supps 1-5, 1998-2002). London: RHS. www.rhs.org.uk/research
Supps 6-9. 2002-06. http://www.rhs.org.uk/learning

Nematanthus

Arnold, P. 1978. *The Gesneriad Register 1978.* Check List of *Nematanthus.* American Gloxinia and Gesneriad Society, Inc.

Nerium

Pagen, F.J.J. 1987. *Oleanders. Nerium L. and the Oleander Cultivars.* Wageningen, The Netherlands: Agricultural University Wageningen.

Nymphaea

Liechti, V. & J. Purcell. George Salford Torrey Herbarium Registration and Checklist of *Nymphaeaceae.* http://collections2.eeb.uconn.edu

Orchidaceae

Shaw, J.M.H. Dec 2007. The International Orchid Register. www.rhs.org.uk/plants

Origanum

Paton, A. 1994. Three Membranous-bracted Species of *Origanum. Kew Mag.* 11(3):109-117.
White, S. 1998. *Origanum. The Herb Marjoram and its Relatives.* Surrey: NCCPG.

Paeonia

HelpMeFind Peonies. Jan 2008. www.helpmefind.com/peony/index.html
Jakubowski, R. 2008. *Peonies 1997-2007. Registered Peony Cultivars, with a Checklist of Peony Names, References and Originators.* Missouri: American Peony Society.
Osti, G.L. 1999. *The Book of Tree Peonies.* Turin: Umberto Allemandi.
Wang, L., et al. 1998. *Chinese Tree Peony.* Beijing: China Forestry Publishing House.

Papaver

Grey-Wilson, C. 1998. Oriental Glories. *The Garden* (RHS) 123(5):320-325.
Grey-Wilson, C. 2000. *Poppies. The Poppy Family in the Wild and in Cultivation.* London: Batsford.

Passiflora

King, L.A. Jan 2008. Passiflora online passion flower cultivar register. www.passionflow.co.uk

Pelargonium

Abbott, P.G. 1994. *A Guide to Scented Geraniaceae.* Angmering, West Sussex: Hill Publicity Services.
Anon. 1978. *A Checklist and Register of Pelargonium Cultivar Names.* Pt 1 A-B. Australian Pelargonium Society.
Anon. 1985. *A Checklist and Register of Pelargonium Cultivar Names.* Pt 2: C-F. Australian Pelargonium Society.
Bagust, H. 1988. *Miniature and Dwarf Geraniums.* London: Christopher Helm.
Clifford, D. 1958. *Pelargoniums.* London: Blandford Press.
Clifton, R. 1999. *Geranium Family Species Checklist, Pt 4: Pelargonium.* The Geraniaceae Group.
Complete Copy of the Spalding Pelargonium Checklist. (Unpublished). USA.
Key, H. 2000. *1001 Pelargoniums.* London: Batsford.
Miller, D. 1996. *Pelargonium.* A Gardener's Guide to the Species and Cultivars and Hybrids. London: Batsford.
Pelargonium Palette: The Geranium and Pelargonium Society of Sydney Incorporated. Varieties – Alphabetical List. July 2000. www.elj.com/geranium
Van der Walt, J.J.A., et al. 1977. *Pelargoniums of South Africa.* (1-3). Kirstenbosch, South Africa: National Botanic Gardens.

Penstemon

Lindgren, D.T. & Davenport, B. 1992. List and description of named cultivars in the genus *Penstemon* (1992). University of Nebraska.
Nold, R. 1999. *Penstemons.* Portland, Oregon: Timber Press.
Way, D. & James, P. 1998. *The Gardener's Guide to Growing Penstemons.* Newton Abbott, Devon: David & Charles.
Way, D. 2006. *Penstemons.* Pershore, Worcs.: Hardy Plant Society.

Phlomis

Mann Taylor, J. 1998. *Phlomis: The Neglected Genus.* Wisley: NCCPG.

Phlox

Harmer, J. & Elliott, J. 2001. *Phlox.* Pershore, Worcs.: Hardy Plant Society.
Stebbings, G. 1999. Simply Charming. *The Garden* (RHS) 124(7):518-521.

Wherry, E.T. 1955. *The Genus Phlox.* Philadelphia, Pennsylvania: Morris Arboretum.

Phormium

Heenan, P.B. 1991. *Checklist of Phormium Cultivars.* Royal New Zealand Institute of Horticulture.

McBride-Whitehead, V. 1998. Phormiums of the Future. *The Garden* (RHS) 123(1):42-45.

Pieris

Bond, J. 1982. *Pieris – a Survey. The Plantsman* 4(2):65-75.

Wagenknecht, B.L. 1961. Registration Lists of Cultivar Names in the Genus *Pieris* D. Don. *Arnoldia (Jamaica Plain)* 21(8):47-50.

Pittosporum

Miller, D.M. 2006. RHS Plant Assessments: *Pittosporum tenuifolium* hybrids & cultivars. www.rhs.org.uk/plants/documents/pittosporum06HI.pdf.

Plectranthus

Addink, Wouter. Dec 2007. Coleus Finder. http://coleusfinder.org

Miller, D. & Morgan, N. 2000. Focus on Plants: A New Leaf. *The Garden* (RHS) 125(11):842-845.

Shaw, J.M.H. 1999. Notes on the Identity of Swedish Ivy and Other Cultivated *Plectranthus. The New Plantsman* 6(2):71-74.

Van Jaarsveld, E.J. 2006. *South African Plectranthus.* Vlaeberg, South Africa: Fernwood Press.

Pleione

Cribb, P. & Butterfield, I. 1999. *The Genus Pleione.* (2nd ed.). Kew: Royal Botanic Gardens.

Shaw, J.M.H. (comp.). Oct 2002. Provisional List of *Pleione* Cultivars. RHS. www.rhs.org.uk/plants/registerpages/Pleione_cv.PDF

***Poaceae* (grasses)**

Clayton, W.D., Harman, K.T. & Williamson, H. Mar 2006. World Grass Species Synonymy. www.kew.org/data

Clayton, W.D. & Renvoize, S.A. 1986. *Genera Graminum.* Grasses of the World. London: HMSO.

Darke, R. 2007. *Encyclopedia of Grasses for Livable Landscapes.* Portland, Oregon: Timber Press.

Govaerts, R. & Simpson, D.A. 2007 *World Checklist of Cyperaceae: Sedges.* Richmond, Surrey: RBG Kew

Grassbase – The Online World Grass Flora. www.rbgkew.org.uk/data/grasses-db.

Grounds, R. 1998. *The Plantfinder's Guide to Ornamental Grasses.* Newton Abott, Devon: David & Charles.

Wood, T. 2002. *Garden Grasses, Rushes and Sedges.* (3rd ed.). Abingdon, Oxon: John Wood.

Polemonium

Nichol-Brown, D. 2000. *Polemonium.* Wisley: NCCPG.

Potentilla

Davidson, C.G., Enns, R.J. & Gobin, S. 1994. *A Checklist of Potentilla fruticosa: the Shrubby Potentillas.* Morden, Manitoba: Agriculture & Agri-Food Canada Research Centre. Data also on Plant Finder Reference Library professional version CD-ROM 1999/2000.

Miller, D.M. 2002. *Shrubby Potentilla: RHS Bulletin No 1.* Wisley, Surrey: RHS. www.rhs.org.uk/plants/documents/potentilla_report.pdf

Primula

Richards, J. 2002 (2nd ed.). *Primula.* London: Batsford.

Primula allionii

Archdale, B. & Richards, D. 1997. *Primula allionii Forms and Hybrids.* National Auricula & Primula Society, Midland & West Section.

Primula auricula misapplied

Baker, G. *Double Auriculas.* National Auricula & Primula Society, Midland & West Section.

Baker, G. & Ward, P. 1995. *Auriculas.* London: Batsford.

Hawkes, A. 1995. Striped Auriculas. National Auricula & Primula Society, Midland & West Section.

Nicholle, G. 1996. *Border Auriculas.* National Auricula & Primula Society, Midland & West Section.

Robinson, M.A. 2000. *Auriculas for Everyone.* How to Grow and Show Perfect Plants. Lewes, Sussex: Guild of Master Craftsmen Publications.

Telford, D. 1993. *Alpine Auriculas.* National Auricula & Primula Society, Midland & West Section.

Ward, P. 1991. *Show Auriculas.* National Auricula & Primula Society, Midland & West Section.

Proteaceae

International *Proteaceae* Register. July 2002. (7th ed.). http://www.nda.agric.za/docs/Protea2002/proteaceae_register.htm

Rebelo, T. 1995. *Proteas.* A Field Guide to the Proteas of Southern Africa. Vlaeberg: Fernwood Press/National Botanical Institute.

Prunus

Crawford, M. 1996. *Plums.* Dartington, Devon: Agroforestry Research Trust.

Crawford, M. 1997. *Cherries: Production and Culture.* Dartington, Devon: Agroforestry Research Trust.

Jacobsen, A.L. 1992. *Purpleleaf Plums.* Portland, Oregon: Timber Press.

Jefferson, R.M. & Wain, K.K. 1984. *The Nomenclature of Cultivated Flowering Cherries (Prunus).* The Sato-Zakura Group. Washington DC: USDA.

Kuitert, W. 1999. *Japanese Flowering Cherries.* Portland, Oregon: Timber Press.

Pulmonaria

Bennett, M. 2003. *Pulmonarias and the borage family.* London: B.T. Batsford.

Hewitt, J. 1994. *Pulmonarias.* Pershore, Worcs.: Hardy Plant Society.

Hewitt, J. 1999. Well Spotted. *The Garden* (RHS) 124(2):98-103.

Pyracantha

Egolf, D.R. & Andrick, A.O. 1995. *A Checklist of Pyracantha Cultivars.* Washington DC: Agricultural Research Service.

Pyrus

Crawford, M. 1996. *Directory of Pear Cultivars.* Totnes, Devon: Agroforestry Research Institute.

Smith, M.W.G. 1976. *Catalogue of the British Pear.* Faversham, Kent: MAFF.

Quercus

Miller, H.A. & Lamb, S.H. 1985. *Oaks of North America.* Happy Camp, California: Naturegraph Publishers.

Mitchell, A. 1994. The Lucombe Oaks. *The Plantsman* 15(4):216-224.

Rhododendron

Argent, G., Fairweather, C. & Walter, K. 1996. *Accepted Names in Rhododendron section Vireya.* Edinburgh: Royal Botanic Garden.

Argent, G., Bond, J., Chamberlain, D., Cox, P. & Hardy, A. 1997. *The Rhododendron Handbook 1998.* Rhododendron Species in Cultivation. London: RHS.

Chamberlain, D.F. & Rae, S.J. 1990. A Revision of *Rhododendron* IV. Subgenus *Tsutsusi. Edinburgh J. Bot.* 47(2).

Chamberlain, D.F. 1982. A Revision of *Rhododendron* II. Subgenus *Hymenanthes. Notes Roy. Bot. Gard. Edinburgh* 39(2).

Chamberlain, D., Hyam, R., Argent, G., Fairweather, G. & Walter, K.S. 1996. *The Genus Rhododendron.* Edinburgh:Royal Botanic Garden.

Cullen, J. 1980. A Revision of *Rhododendron* I. Subgenus *Rhododendron* sections *Rhododendron* and *Pogonanthum. Notes Roy. Bot. Gard. Edinburgh* 39(1).

Davidian, H.H. 1982-1992 *The Rhododendron Species* (Vols 1-4). London: Batsford.

Galle, F.C. 1985. *Azaleas.* Portland, Oregon: Timber Press.

Leslie, A. C. (comp.). 1980. *The Rhododendron Handbook 1980.* London: RHS.

Leslie, A.C. (comp.) 2004. *The International Rhododendron Register and Checklist* (2nd ed.). London: RHS. 1st Supp. 2006. http://www.rhs.org.uk/learning

Tamura, T. (ed.). 1989. *Azaleas in Kurume.* Kurume, Japan: International Azalea Festival '89.

Ribes

Crawford, M. 1997. *Currants and Gooseberries: Production and Culture.* Dartington, Devon: Agroforestry Research Trust.

Rosa

Beales, P., Cairns, T., et al. 1998. *Botanica's Rose: The Encyclopedia of Roses.* Hoo, Kent: Grange Books.

Cairns, T. (ed.). 2000. *Modern Roses XI. The World Encyclopedia of Roses.* London: Academic Press.

Dickerson, B.C. 1999. *The Old Rose Advisor.* Portland, Oregon: Timber Press.

Haw, S.G. 1996. Notes on Some Chinese and Himalayan Rose Species of Section *Pimpinellifoliae. The New Plantsman* 3(3):143-146.

HelpMeFind Roses. Nov 2007. www.helpmefind.com

McCann, S. 1985. *Miniature Roses.* Newton Abbot, Devon: David & Charles.

Quest-Ritson, C. 2003. *Climbing Roses of the World.* Portland, Oregon: Timber Press.

Quest-Ritson, C. & Quest-Ritson, B. 2003. *The Royal Horticultural Society Encyclopedia of Roses: The Definitive A-Z Guide.* London: Dorling Kindersley.

Thomas, G.S. 1995. *The Graham Stuart Thomas Rose Book.* London: John Murray.

Verrier, S. 1996. *Rosa Gallica.* Balmain, Australia: Florilegium.

Roscoea

Cowley, J. 2007. *The Genus Roscoea.* Kew Publishing.

Rosularia

Eggli, U. 1988. A Monographic Study of the Genus *Rosularia. Bradleya* (Supp.) 6:1-118.

Rubiaceae

Govaerts, R. et al. 2005. *World Checklist & Bibliography of Rubiaceae.* http://apps.kew.org

Saintpaulia

Goodship, G. 1987. *Saintpaulia Variety List* (Supp.). Slough, Bucks: Saintpaulia & Houseplant Society.

Moore, H.E. 1957. *African Violets, Gloxinias and Their Relatives.* A Guide to the Cultivated Gesneriads. New York: Macmillan.

Salix

Newsholme, C. 1992. *Willows.* The Genus *Salix.* London: Batsford.

Stott, K.G. 1971 *Willows for Amenity, Windbreaks and Other Uses.* Checklist of the Long Ashton Collection of Willows, with Notes on their Suitability for Various Purposes. Long Ashton Research Station: University of Bristol.

Salvia

Clebsch, B. 2003. *A Book of Salvias.* (2nd ed.). Portland, Oregon: Timber Press.

Compton, J. 1994. Mexican Salvias in Cultivation. *The Plantsman* 15(4):193-215.

Middleton, R. *Robin's Salvias.* www.robinssalvias.com

Saxifraga

Bland, B. 2000. *Silver Saxifrages.* Pershore, Worcs.: Alpine Garden Society.

Dashwood, M. & Bland, B. 2005. Silver Saxifrages: RHS Bulletin No 9. Wisley, Surrey: RHS. www.rhs.org.uk/plants/documents/saxifraga05.pdf

McGregor, M. Jan 2006. Saxbase. Saxifrage Society. www.saxifraga.org

McGregor, M. 1995. *Saxifrages: The Complete Cultivars & Hybrids: International Register of Saxifrages.* (2nd ed.). Driffield, E. Yorks: Saxifrage Society.

Webb, D.A. & Gornall, R.J. 1989. *Saxifrages of Europe.* Bromley, Kent: Christopher Helm.

Sedum
Evans, R.L. 1983. *Handbook of Cultivated Sedums.* Motcombe, Dorset: Ivory Head Press.
Lord, T. 2006. *Sedum* up for assessment. *The Plantsman* 5(4):244-252.
Stephenson, R. 1994. *Sedum.* The Cultivated Stonecrops. Portland, Oregon: Timber Press.
Sempervivum
Diehm, H. Jan 2006. www.semperhorst.de
Miklánek, M. 2002. *The List of Cultivars: Sempervivum and Jovibarba v. 7.01.* Piešťany, Slovakia: M. Miklánek (private distribution).
Miklánek, M. 2000. *List of Cultivars: Sempervivum and Jovibarba* v. 15.1. http://miklanek.tripod.com
Sinningia
Dates, J.D. 1988. *The Gesneriad Register 1988. Check List of Names with Descriptions of Cultivated Plants in the Genus Sinningia.* Galesburg, Illinois: American Gloxinia and Gesneriad Society, Inc.
Solenostemon
Pedley, W.K. & Pedley, R. 1974. *Coleus – A Guide to Cultivation and Identification.* Edinburgh: Bartholemew.
Sorbus
McAllister, H. 2005. *The Genus Sorbus: Mountain Ash and Other Rowans.* Kew: Royal Botanical Gardens.
Snyers d'Attenhoven, C. 1999. *Sorbus* Lombarts hybrids *Belgische Dendrologie*: 76-81. Belgium.
Wright, D. 1981. *Sorbus* – a Gardener's Evaluation. *The Plantsman* 3(2):65-98.
Spiraea
Miller, D.M. 2003. *Spiraea japonica with coloured leaves: RHS Bulletin No 4.* Wisley, Surrey: Royal Horticultural Society. www.rhs.org.uk/plants/documents/spiraea03.pdf
Streptocarpus
Arnold, P. 1979. *The Gesneriad Register 1979: Check List of Streptocarpus.* Binghamton, New York: American Gloxinia & Gesneriad.
Dibleys Nurseries Online Catalogue. Oct 2005. www.dibleys.com.
Succulents
Eggli, U. (ed.) 2002. *Illustrated Handbook of Succulent Plants.* Heidelberg, Germany: Springer-Verlag.
Eggli, U. & Taylor, N. 1994. *List of Names of Succulent Plants other than Cacti Published 1950-92.* Kew: Royal Botanic Gardens.
Grantham, K. & Klaassen, P. 1999. *The Plantfinder's Guide to Cacti and Other Succulents.* Newton Abbot, Devon: David & Charles.
Jacobsen, H. 1973. *Lexicon of Succulent Plants.* London: Blandford.
Syringa
Vrugtman, F. 2000. *International Register of Cultivar Names in the Genus Syringa L. (Oleaceae).* (Contribution No 91). Hamilton, Canada: Royal Botanic Gardens.
Tiliaceae
Wild, H. 1984. *Flora of Southern Africa 21 (1: Tiliaceae).* Pretoria: Botanical Research Institute, Dept of Agriculture.
Tillandsia
Kiff, L.F. 1991. *A Distributional Checklist of the Genus Tillandsia.* Encino, California: Botanical Diversions.
Trillium
Case, F.W.J. & Case, R.B. 1997. *Trilliums.* Portland, Oregon: Timber Press.
Jacobs, D.L. & Jacobs, R.L. 1997. *American Treasures.* Trilliums in Woodland Garden. Decatur, Georgia: Eco-Gardens.
Tulipa
KAVB Online registration pages. http://kavb.back2p.soft-orange.com
Ulmus
Green, P.S. 1964. Registratration of Cultivar Names in *Ulmus. Arnoldia (Jamaica Plain)* 24:41-80.
Vaccinium
Trehane, J. 2004. *Blueberries, Cranberries and Other Vacciniums.* Portland, Oregon: Timber Press.
Vegetables
Official Journal of the European Communities. Dec 2007. Common catalogue of varieties of agricultural plant species: 26th complete ed. http://europa.eu.int
Official Journal of the European Communities. Oct 2007. Common catalogue of varieties of vegetable species: consolidated version. http://ec.europa.eu/food
Viburnum
Dirr, M.A. 2007. *Viburnums: Flowering Shrubs for Every Season.* Portland, Oregon: Timber Press.
Viola
Coombes, R.E. 2003. *Violets.* (2nd ed.). London: Batsford.
Fuller, R. 1990. *Pansies, Violas & Violettas.* The Complete Guide. Marlborough: The Crowood Press.
Perfect, E.J. 1996. *Armand Millet and his Violets.* High Wycombe: Park Farm Press.
Robinson, P.M. & Snocken, J. 2003. Checklist of the Cultivated Forms of the Genus *Viola* including the Register of Cultivars. American Violet Society. http://americanvioletsociety.org
Zambra, G.L. 1950. *Violets for Garden and Market.* (2nd ed.). London: Collingridge.
Vitis
Pearkes, G. 1989. *Vine Growing in Britain.* London: Dent.
Robinson, J. 1989. *Vines, Grapes and Wines.* London: Mitchell Beazley.
Watsonia
Goldblatt, P. 1989. *The Genus Watsonia.* A Systematic Monograph. South Africa: National Botanic Gardens.

Weigela
Howard, R.A. 1965. A Checklist of Cultivar Names in *Weigela. Arnoldia (Jamaica Plain)* 25:49-69.
Wisteria
Valder, P. 1995. *Wisterias.* A Comprehensive Guide. Balmain, Australia: Florilegium.
Yucca
Smith, C. 2004. *Yuccas: Giants among the Lilies.* NCCPG.
Zauschneria
Raven, P.H. 1977. Generic and Sectional Delimitation in *Onagraceae,* Tribe *Epilobieae. Ann. Missouri Bot. Gard.* 63(2):326-340.
Robinson, A. 2000. Focus on Plants: Piping Hot (*Zauschneria* Cultivars). *The Garden* (RHS) 125(9):698-699.
Zingiberaceae
Branney, T.M.E. 2005. *Hardy Gingers. Including Hedychium, Roscoea and Zingiber.* Cambridge: Timber Press.

INTERNATIONAL PLANT FINDERS

NEW ZEALAND

Gaddum, Meg (comp.) *New Zealand Plant Finder* (2009). 46,000 plants and where to buy them. Available online only at www.plantfinder.co.nz

UNITED KINGDOM

Pawsey, Angela (ed.) (27th ed.) 2009-2010, *Find That Rose!* Pub. May 2009. Lists approximately 3,500 varieties available in the UK together with basic type, colour and fragrance, including all forms of standard roses. New varieties are highlighted and cross-referenced, where applicable, to alternative selling names. Gives full details of around 50 growers/ outlets, many offering mail order. Includes useful information on how to find a rose with a particular Christian name, or to celebrate a special event, on charity roses and where to see roses in bloom.
For further information, including price of a CD-ROM version, send sae to 303 Mile End Road, Colchester, Essex CO4 5EA. To order a copy send payment of £3.70 made out to *Find That Rose!* to above address.
Visit the website on www.findthatrose.net

Pawsey, Angela. *What's in a Name* (Sep 2008). Listing the origin of the names of over 500 rose varieties. This is a companion booklet to *Find That Rose!* The simple 40 page booklet includes many roses linked with charities. Packed with interesting stories, this gives the background to how and why many roses get their name. To order send £1.90 made out to *Find That Rose* to Angela Pawsey, 303 Mile End Road, Colchester CO4 5EA.

Nurseries

The following nurseries between them stock an unrivalled choice of plants. Before making a visit, please remember to check with the nursery that the plant you seek is currently available.

Nursery Codes and Symbols

The first letter of each nursery code represents the area of the country in which the nursery is situated.

Geographical Codes

South West **C**
Eastern **E**
Scotland **G**
Northern Ireland & the Republic of Ireland **I**
London Area **L**
Midlands **M**
Northern **N**
Southern **S**
Wales & the West **W**
Abroad **X**

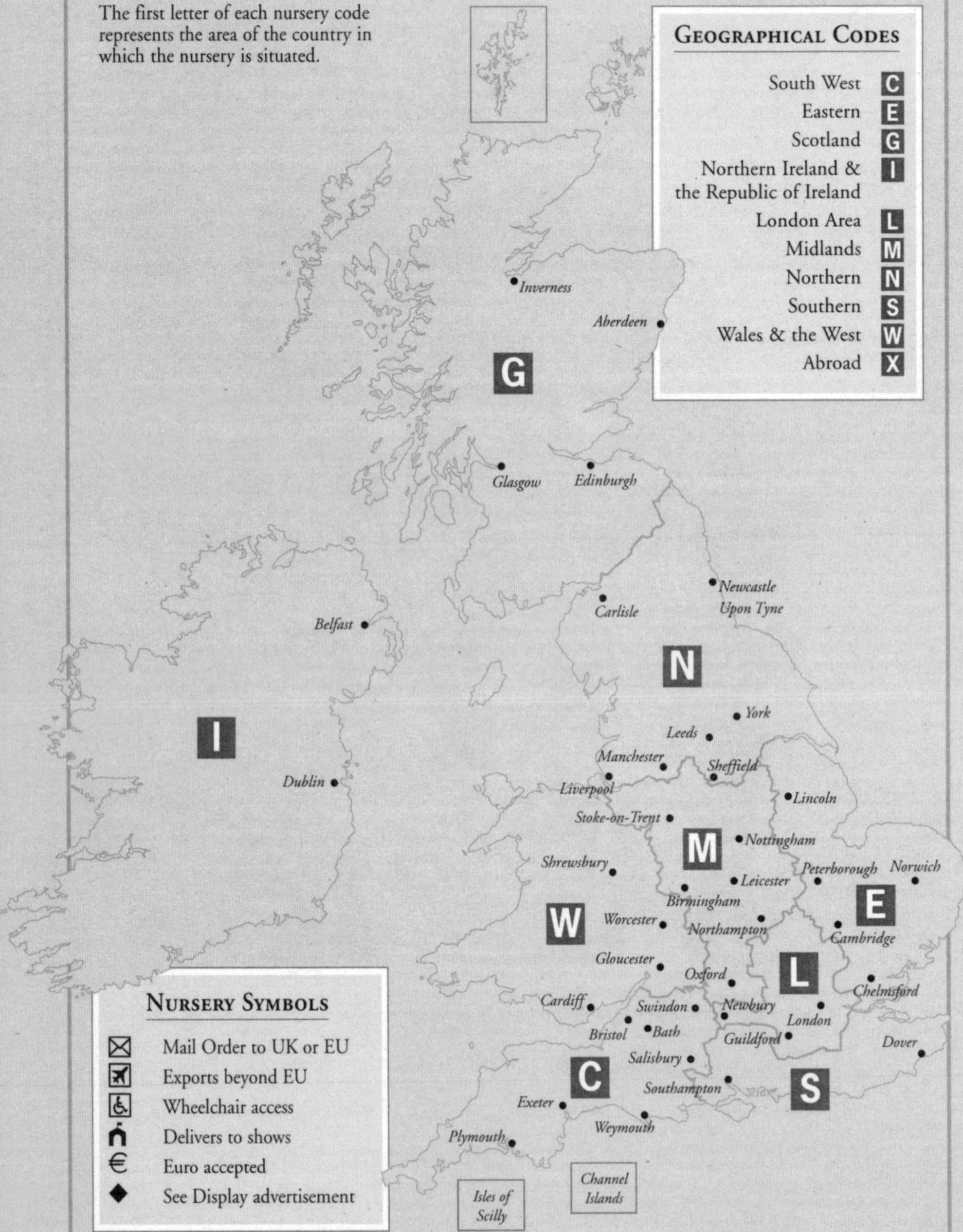

Nursery Symbols

⊠ Mail Order to UK or EU
✈ Exports beyond EU
♿ Wheelchair access
∩ Delivers to shows
€ Euro accepted
◆ See Display advertisement

USING THE THREE NURSERY LISTINGS

Your main reference from the Plant Directory is the Nursery Details by Code listing, which includes all relevant information for each nursery in order of nursery code. The Nursery Index by Name is an alphabetical list for those who know a nursery's name but not its code and wish to check its details in the main list. The Specialist Nurseries index is to aid those searching for a particular plant group.

1 NURSERY DETAILS BY CODE

Once you have found your plant in the Plant Directory, turn to this list to find out the name, address, opening times and other details of the nurseries whose codes accompany the plant.

KEY
⊠ Mail order to UK or EU
Exports beyond EU
Wheelchair access
Delivers to shows
€ Euro accepted
◆ See Display advertisement

Refer to the box at the base of each right-hand page for a key to the symbols

A geographical code is followed by three letters reflecting the nursery's name

WHil HILLVIEW HARDY PLANTS ⊠ € ◆
(off B4176) Worfield, Nr Bridgnorth, Shropshire, WV15 5NT
Ⓣ (01746) 716454
Ⓜ 07974 391608
Ⓕ (01746) 716454
Ⓔ hillview@themutual.net
Ⓦ www.hillviewhardyplants.com
Contact: Ingrid, John & Sarah Millington
Opening Times: 0900-1700 Mon-Sat Mar-mid Oct. At other times, please phone first.
Min Mail Order UK: £15.00 + p&p
Min Mail Order EU: £15.00 + p&p
Cat. Cost: 5 × 2nd class.
Credit Cards: All major credit/debit cards
Specialities: Choice herbaceous perennials incl. *Acanthus* & *Acanthaceae, Albuca, Aquilegia,* auricula, *Primula, Canna, Crocosmia, Eucomis, Ixia,* South African bulbs. Nat. Collection of *Acanthus.*
Notes: Also sells wholesale.
Map Ref: W, B4 **OS Grid Ref:** SO772969

Other information about the nursery

A brief summary of the plants available

The map letter is followed by the map square in which the nursery is located

The Ordnance Survey national grid reference for use with OS maps

2 NURSERY INDEX BY NAME

If you seek a particular nursery, look it up in this alphabetical index. Note its code and turn to the Nursery Details by Code list for full information.

Highdown Nursery	SHDw
Highfield Hollies	SHHo
Hill House Nursery & Gardens	CHll
Hillview Hardy Plants	WHil
Hoecroft Plants	EHoe
Holden Clough Nursery	NHol
Home Plants	SHom
Homestead Plants	MHom

3 SPECIALIST NURSERIES

A list of 32 categories under which nurseries have classified themselves if they exclusively, or predominantly, supply this range of plants.

DROUGHT-TOLERANT

CBot, CKno, CPne, ECha, EHoe, ETod, LLWP, LPal, MBPg, NFir, NHoy, SAll, SDow, SIde, SIoW, SJoh, SMea, SOWG, SPhx, SUsu, WHil, WPnn

How to Use the Nursery Listings

The details given for each nursery have been compiled from information supplied to us in answer to a questionnaire. In some cases, because of constraints of space, the entries have been slightly abbreviated.

Nurseries are not charged for their entries and inclusion in no way implies a value judgement.

Nursery Details by Code (*page 826*)

Each nursery is allocated a code, for example GPoy. The first letter of each code indicates the main area of the country in which the nursery is situated. In this example, G=Scotland. The remaining three letters reflect the nursery's name, in this case Poyntzfield Herb Nursery.

In this main listing the nurseries are given in alphabetical order of codes for quick reference from the Plant Directory. All of the nurseries' details, such as address, opening times, mail order service etc., will be found here.

Opening Times

Although opening times have been published as submitted and where applicable, **it is always advisable, especially if travelling a long distance, to check with the nursery first**. The initials NGS indicate that the nursery is open under the National Gardens Scheme.

Mail Order ⊠

Many nurseries provide a mail order service. **This is, however, often restricted to certain times of the year or to particular genera**. Please check the **Notes** section of each nursery's entry for any restrictions or special conditions.

In some cases, the mail order service extends to all members of the European Union. Where this is offered, the minimum charge to the EU will be noted in the Nursery entry.

Where **'No minimum charge'** (Nmc) is shown, please note that to send even one plant may involve the nursery in substantial postage and packing costs. Some nurseries may not be prepared to send tender or bulky plants.

Where a nursery offers a **mail order only** service, this will be noted under **Opening Times** in the nursery entry.

Export ✈

Export refers to mail order beyond the European Union. Nurseries that are prepared to consider exporting are indicated. However, there is usually a substantial minimum charge and, in addition, all the costs of Phytosanitary Certificates and Customs have to be met by the purchaser.

Catalogue Cost

Some nurseries offer their catalogue free, or for a few stamps, but a large (at least A5) stamped addressed envelope is always appreciated as well. Overseas customers should use an equivalent number of International Reply Coupons (IRCs) in place of stamps.

Increasingly, nurseries are finding it more cost effective to produce catalogues on the Internet rather than printing them. Many nurseries also offer an online mail order facility.

Wheelchair Access ♿

Nurseries are asked to indicate if their premises are suitable for wheelchair users. Where only partial access is indicated, this is noted in the Notes field and the nursery is not marked with the symbol.

The assessment of ease-of-access is entirely the responsibility of the individual nursery.

Specialities

Nurseries list here the plants or genera that they supply and any National Collections of plants they may hold. Please note that some nurseries may charge an entry fee to visit a National Collection. Always enquire before visiting.

Nurseries will also note here if they only have small quantities of individual plants available for sale or if they will propagate to order.

Notes

In this section, you will find notes on any restrictions to mail order or export; on limited wheelchair access; or the nursery site address, if this differs from the office address; together with any other non-horticultural information.

Delivery to Shows

Many nurseries will deliver pre-ordered plants to flower shows for collection by customers. These are indicated by a marquee symbol. Contact the nursery for details of shows they attend.

Payment in Euros €

A number of UK nurseries have indicated that they will accept payment in Euros. You should, however, check with the nursery concerned before making such a payment, as some will only accept cash and some only cheques, whilst others will expect the purchaser to pay bank charges.

Maps

If you wish to visit any of the nurseries you can find its approximate location on the relevant map (following p.939), unless the nursery has requested this is not shown. Nurseries are also encouraged to provide their Ordnance Survey national grid reference for use with OS publications such as the Land Ranger series.

Nursery Index by Name

For convenience, an alphabetical index of nurseries is included on p.931. This gives the names of all nurseries listed in the book in alphabetical order of nursery name together with their code.

Specialist Nurseries (*page 937*)

This list of nurseries is intended to help those with an interest in finding specialist categories of plant. Nurseries have been asked to classify themselves under one or more headings where this represents the type of plant they *predominantly* or *exclusively* have in stock. For example, if you wish to find a nursery specialising in ornamental grasses, look up 'Grasses' in the listing where you will find a list of nursery codes. Then turn to the Nursery Details by Code, for details of the nurseries.

Please note that not all nurseries shown here will have plants listed in the Plant Directory. This may be their choice or because the *RHS Plant Finder* does not list seeds or annuals and only terrestrial orchids and hardy cacti. For space reasons, it is rare to find a nursery's full catalogue listed in the Plant Directory.

In all cases, please ensure you ring to confirm the range available before embarking on a journey to the nursery.

The specialist plant groups listed in this edition are:

Acid-loving
Alpines/rock
Aquatics/marginals
Bamboos
British wild flowers
Bulbous plants
Cacti & succulents
Carnivorous
Chalk-loving
Climbers
Coastal
Conifers
Conservatory
Drought-tolerant
Ferns
Fruit
Grasses
Hedging
Herbs
Marginal/bog plants
Orchids
Organic
Ornamental trees
Peat-free
Period plants
Propagate to order
Roses
Seeds
Specimen-sized plants
Topiary
Tropical plants

Perennials and shrubs have been omitted as these are considered to be too general and serviced by a great proportion of the nurseries.

Deleted Nurseries

Every year some nurseries ask to be removed from the book. This may be a temporary measure because they are moving, or it may be permanent due to closure, sale, retirement, or a change in the way in which they trade. Occasionally, nurseries are unable to meet the closing date and will re-enter the book in the following edition. Some nurseries simply do not reply and, as we have no current information on them, they are deleted.

Please, never use an old edition

Nursery Details by Code

Please note that all these nurseries are listed in alphabetical order by their code. All nurseries are listed in alphabetical order by their name in the **Nursery Index by Name** on page 931.

South West

CAbb **Abbotsbury Sub-Tropical Gardens** ⊠ ♿
Abbotsbury, Nr Weymouth, Dorset, DT3 4LA
Ⓣ (01305) 871344
Ⓕ (01305) 871344
Ⓔ info@abbotsburygardens.co.uk
Ⓦ www.abbotsburyplantsales.co.uk
Contact: David Sutton
Opening Times: 1000-1800 daily mid Mar-1st Nov. 1000-1500 Nov-mid Mar.
Min Mail Order UK: Nmc
Cat. Cost: £2.00 + A4 sae
Credit Cards: Access Visa MasterCard Switch
Specialities: Less common & tender shrubs incl. palms, tree ferns, bamboos & plants from Australia, New Zealand & S. Africa.

CAbP **Abbey Plants** ⊠ ♿
Chaffeymoor, Bourton, Gillingham, Dorset, SP8 5BY
Ⓣ (01747) 840841
Contact: K Potts
Opening Times: 1000-1300 & 1400-1700 Wed-Sat Mar-Nov. Dec-Feb by appt.
Min Mail Order UK: Nmc
Cat. Cost: 2 × 2nd class.
Credit Cards: None
Specialities: Flowering trees & shrubs.
Map Ref: C, B4 **OS Grid Ref:** ST762304

CAby **The Abbey Nursery** ♿ ⌂
Forde Abbey, Chard, Somerset, TA20 4LU
Ⓣ (01460) 220088
Ⓕ (01460) 220088
Ⓔ TheAbbeyNursery@btconnect.com
Contact: Peter Sims
Opening Times: 1000-1700 7 days, 1st Mar-31st Oct. Please phone first to check opening times in Mar.
Cat. Cost: None issued.
Credit Cards: All major credit/debit cards
Specialities: Hardy herbaceous perennials.
Map Ref: C, C4 **OS Grid Ref:** ST359052

CAgr **Agroforestry Research Trust** ⊠
46 Hunters Moon, Dartington, Totnes, Devon, TQ9 6JT
Ⓣ (01803) 840776
Ⓕ (01803) 840776
Ⓔ mail@agroforestry.co.uk
Ⓦ www.agroforestry.co.uk
Contact: Martin Crawford
Opening Times: Not open. Mail order only.
Min Mail Order UK: Nmc
Min Mail Order EU: Nmc
Cat. Cost: 4 × 1st class.
Credit Cards: All major credit/debit cards
Specialities: Top & soft fruit, nut trees including *Castanea, Corylus, Juglans, Pinus.* Also seeds. Some plants in small quantities only.

CAlb **Albion Plants** ⊠ €
Roborough, Winkleigh, Devon, EX19 8TD
Ⓣ (01805) 603502
Ⓕ 08000 112024
Ⓔ huggons@albion-plants.co.uk
Ⓦ www.albion-plants.co.uk
Contact: Neil & Brenda Huggons
Opening Times: Mail order only. Open by appt. for wholesale quantities only.
Min Mail Order UK: Nmc
Cat. Cost: Available by email on request.
Credit Cards: All major credit/debit cards
Specialities: *Vinca, Cornus, Viburnum, Ceanothus.* Specimen-sized shrubs & container-grown trees.
Notes: Also sells wholesale.
Map Ref: C, B3 **OS Grid Ref:** SS584173

CAni **Anita Allen** ⊠
Shapcott Barton Estate, East Knowstone, South Molton, Devon, EX36 4EE

Ⓣ (01398) 341664
Ⓕ (01398) 341664
Contact: Anita Allen
Opening Times: By appt. only. Garden open under NGS.
Min Mail Order UK: Nmc.
Cat. Cost: 5 × 1st class & state which catalogue, Shasta daisies or *Buddleja*.
Credit Cards: None
Specialities: Nat. Collections of *Leucanthemum* × *superbum* & *Buddleja davidii* & hybrids, 70+ cvs. 80+ accurately named Shasta daisies, a few in very short supply. Also many hardy perennials.
Map Ref: C, B3 **OS Grid Ref:** SS846235

CArn ARNE HERBS ⊠ € ♿
Limeburn Nurseries, Limeburn Hill,
Chew Magna, Bristol,
BS40 8QW
Ⓣ (01275) 333399
Ⓔ anthony@arneherbs.co.uk
Ⓦ www.arneherbs.co.uk
Contact: A Lyman-Dixon & Jenny Thomas
Opening Times: 1000-1600 most weekdays, Sat mid-Mar-end Jun. Other times by telephone appt. only.
Min Mail Order UK: Nmc
Min Mail Order EU: Nmc
Cat. Cost: Detailed illustrated catalogue online or A4 sae for free non-descriptive plantlist.
Credit Cards: None
Specialities: Herbs, some very rare. North American, Mediterranean & UK wild flowers. Also plants for reseach, conservation projects & historical recreations.
Notes: Will deliver to Bristol Farmers' Markets. Also sells wholesale.
Map Ref: C, A5 **OS Grid Ref:** ST563638

CAvo AVON BULBS ⊠ ⌂
Burnt House Farm, Mid-Lambrook, South Petherton, Somerset, TA13 5HE
Ⓣ (01460) 242177
Ⓕ (01460) 249025
Ⓔ info@avonbulbs.co.uk
Ⓦ www.avonbulbs.co.uk
Contact: C Ireland-Jones
Opening Times: Mail order only. Open Thu, Fri, Sat, mid-Sep-end Oct & mid Feb-end Mar for collection of pre-booked orders.
Min Mail Order UK: £10.00 + p&p
Min Mail Order EU: £20.00 + p&p
Cat. Cost: 4 × 2nd class.
Credit Cards: Visa Access Switch MasterCard
Specialities: Some special snowdrops are only available in small quantities.

CBar BARTERS PLANT CENTRE & NURSERY ♿
Chapmanslade, Westbury, Wiltshire,
BA13 4AL
Ⓣ (01373) 832694
Ⓕ (01373) 832677
Ⓔ plantcentre@barters.co.uk
Ⓦ www.barters.co.uk
Contact: Giles Hall
Opening Times: 0900-1700 Mon-Thu, 0900-1730 Fri & Sat, summer. 0900-1630 Mon-Thu, 0900-1700 Fri & Sat, winter. 1030-1630 Sun.
Cat. Cost: A4 Sae
Credit Cards: All, except American Express
Specialities: Wide range of shrubs. Ground cover, container trees, ferns, half-hardy perennials, grasses, herbaceous & climbers. Hedging, fruit trees, old fashioned roses & bare-root stock.
Notes: Also sells wholesale.
Map Ref: C, B5 **OS Grid Ref:** ST830480

CBcs BURNCOOSE NURSERIES ⊠ ✈ ♿ ⌂
Gwennap, Redruth, Cornwall, TR16 6BJ
Ⓣ (01209) 860316
Ⓕ (01209) 860011
Ⓔ burncoose@eclipse.co.uk
Ⓦ www.burncoose.co.uk
Contact: C H Williams
Opening Times: 0830-1700 Mon-Sat & 1100-1700 Sun.
Min Mail Order UK: Nmc
Min Mail Order EU: Individual quotations for EU sales.
Cat. Cost: Free
Credit Cards: Visa Access Switch
Specialities: Extensive range of over 3500 ornamental trees & shrubs and herbaceous. Rare & unusual *Magnolia*, *Rhododendron*. Conservatory plants. 30 acre garden.
Notes: Also sells wholesale.
Map Ref: C, D1 **OS Grid Ref:** SW742395

CBct BARRACOTT PLANTS ⊠ € ♿
Old Orchard, Calstock Road, Gunnislake, Cornwall, PL18 9AA
Ⓣ (01822) 832234
Ⓔ GEOFF@geoff63.freeserve.co.uk
Ⓦ www.barracottplants.co.uk
Contact: Geoff & Thelma Turner
Opening Times: 0900-1700 Thu & Fri, Mar-end Sep. Other times by appt.

KEY
⊠ Mail order to UK or EU ⌂ Delivers to shows
✈ Exports beyond EU € Euro accepted
♿ Accessible by wheelchair ◆ See Display advertisement

C

Min Mail Order UK: Nmc
Cat. Cost: 2 × 1st class.
Credit Cards: None
Specialities: Herbaceous plants: shade-loving, foliage & form. *Acanthus, Aspidistra, Astrantia, Bergenia, Convallaria, Disporum, Liriope, Maianthemum, Polygonatum, Roscoea, Trillium, Tricyrtis* & *Uvularia*.
Notes: Also sells wholesale.
Map Ref: C, C3 **OS Grid Ref:** SX436702

CBel **Belmont House Nursery** ⊠ €
Little Horton, Devizes, Wiltshire, SN10 3LJ
Ⓣ (01380) 860510
Ⓔ rcottis@supanet.com
Contact: Gordon Cottis
Opening Times: By appt. only. Please phone.
Min Mail Order UK: £2.50
Min Mail Order EU: Nmc
Cat. Cost: 2 × 2nd class
Credit Cards: None
Specialities: *Helleborus* hybrids & true species, *Galanthus* & *Cyclamen*, some in small quantities only.
Notes: Mail order *Cyclamen* & *Galanthus* only, Nov-Feb.

CBen **Bennetts Water Gardens** ⊠ ♿
B3157 Chickerell Link Road, Weymouth, Dorset, DT3 4AF
Ⓣ (01305) 785150
Ⓔ info@waterlily.co.uk
Ⓦ www.waterlily.co.uk
Contact: James Bennett
Opening Times: 1000-1700 Mar-Oct. Closed Sat.
Min Mail Order UK: Nmc
Cat. Cost: Sae for price list
Credit Cards: Visa Access MasterCard Switch
Specialities: Aquatic plants. Bog Plants. Nat. Collection of *Nymphaea*.
Notes: Mail order Mar-Sep only.
Map Ref: C, C5 **OS Grid Ref:** SY651797

CBgR **Beggar's Roost Plants** ⊠ € ♿
Lilstock, Bridgwater, Somerset, TA5 1SU
Ⓣ (01278) 741519
Ⓕ (01278) 741519
Ⓔ ro@beggarsroostplants.co.uk
Ⓦ www.beggarsroostplants.co.uk
Contact: Rosemary FitzGerald
Opening Times: Any time by appt.
Min Mail Order UK: £10.00
Min Mail Order EU: Nmc
Credit Cards: None
Specialities: Garden-worthy bulbs & herbaceous, incl. heritage *Hemerocallis*, hardy *Nerine*, West Country *Galanthus*, hardy *Fuchsia*, winter interest plants. Small quantities.
Notes: Mail order for specialities: *Crocosmia, Hemerocallis, Iris, Galanthus, Dahlia* (tubers). Ask for lists. No mail order for shrubs.
Map Ref: C, B4 **OS Grid Ref:** ST168450

CBod **Bodmin Plant and Herb Nursery** ♿
Laveddon Mill, Laninval Hill, Bodmin, Cornwall, PL30 5JU
Ⓣ (01208) 72837
Ⓕ (01208) 76491
Ⓔ bodminnursery@aol.com
Ⓦ www.bodminnursery.co.uk
Contact: Mark Lawlor
Opening Times: 0900-1700 Mon-Sat Nov-Mar, 0900-1800 Mon-Sat Apr-Oct. 1000-1600 Sun.
Credit Cards: All major credit/debit cards
Specialities: Herbs, herbaceous & grasses, hardy geraniums & coastal plants. Interesting shrubs, fruit & ornamental trees.
Map Ref: C, C2 **OS Grid Ref:** SX053659

CBot **The Botanic Nursery** ⊠ ṅ € ♿
Atworth, Nr Melksham, Wiltshire, SN12 8NU
M: 07850 328756
Ⓕ (01225) 700953
Ⓦ www.thebotanicnursery.co.uk
Contact: T. Baker
Opening Times: 1000-1700 Tue-Sat, Mar-Nov. Please avoid lunch time if possible.
Min Mail Order UK: £11.00 for 24hr carriage service. At cost for Royal Mail.
Cat. Cost: £1.00 in stamps.
Credit Cards: MasterCard Visa
Specialities: Nursery propagates from large range of lime-tolerant plants in varying quantities all peat free. Nat. Collection of *Digitalis*.
Notes: If travelling, please phone first to confirm specific plant availability. Partially accessible for wheelchairs.

CBow **Bowley Plants** ⊠
Church Farm, North End, Ashton Keynes, Nr Swindon, Wiltshire, SN6 6QR
Ⓣ (01285) 640352
M: 07855 524929
Ⓔ bowleyplants@btinternet.com
Ⓦ www.bowleyplants.co.uk
Contact: Piers Bowley
Opening Times: Some Sat, Mar-Oct, please phone first. Other times by appt.
Min Mail Order UK: Nmc
Cat. Cost: 2 × 1st class.

Credit Cards: None
Specialities: Variegated plants & coloured foliage. Alpines, perennials, shrubs, ferns, grasses & herbs. Some varieties in small numbers.
Notes: Also sells wholesale.
Map Ref: C, A6 **OS Grid Ref:** SU043945

CBre **Bregover Plants** ⊠ ⌂
Hillbrooke, Middlewood, North Hill, Nr Launceston, Cornwall, PL15 7NN
Ⓣ (01566) 782661
Contact: Jennifer Bousfield
Opening Times: 1100-1700 Wed, Mar-mid Oct and by appt.
Min Mail Order UK: Nmc
Min Mail Order EU: Nmc
Cat. Cost: 3 × 1st class.
Credit Cards: None
Specialities: Unusual hardy perennials grown in small garden nursery. Available in small quantities only.
Notes: Mail order Oct-Mar only.
Map Ref: C, C2 **OS Grid Ref:** SX273752

CBro **Broadleigh Gardens** ⊠ € ♿ ⌂
Bishops Hull, Taunton, Somerset, TA4 1AE
Ⓣ (01823) 286231
Ⓕ (01823) 323646
Ⓔ info@broadleighbulbs.co.uk
Ⓦ www.broadleighbulbs.co.uk
Contact: Lady Skelmersdale
Opening Times: 0900-1600 Mon-Fri for viewing only (charity donation). Orders collected if notice given.
Min Mail Order UK: Nmc
Min Mail Order EU: Nmc
Cat. Cost: 2 × 1st class.
Credit Cards: Switch MasterCard Maestro Visa
Specialities: Jan catalogue: bulbs in growth (*Galanthus*, *Cyclamen* etc.) & herbaceous woodland plants (trilliums, hellebores etc). Extensive list of *Agapanthus*. June catalogue: dwarf & unusual bulbs, *Iris* (DB & PC). Nat. Collection of Alec Grey hybrid daffodils.
Notes: Euro payment accepted as cash only.
Map Ref: C, B4 **OS Grid Ref:** ST195251

CBrP **Brooklands Plants** ⊠
25 Treves Road, Dorchester, Dorset, DT1 2HE
Ⓣ (01305) 265846
Ⓔ cycads@btinternet.com
Contact: Ian Watt
Opening Times: By appt. only for collection of plants.
Min Mail Order UK: £25.00 + p&p
Min Mail Order EU: £25.00 + p&p
Cat. Cost: 2 × 2nd class.
Credit Cards: None
Specialities: Cycad nursery specialising in the more cold-tolerant species of *Encephalartos*, *Dioon*, *Macrozamia* & *Cycas*. Also specialist in cold-tolerant palms as well as *Aloe*, *Agave* and *Dasylirion*. Some species available in small quantities only.
Map Ref: C, C5 **OS Grid Ref:** SY682897

CBty **Bentley Plants** ⊠ € ♿ ⌂
1 Bentley Wood Cottages, West Tytherley, Salisbury, Wiltshire, SP5 1QB
Ⓣ (01794) 340775
Ⓕ (01794) 340775
Ⓔ john@bentleyplants.fsnet.co.uk
Ⓦ www.bentleyplants.co.uk
Contact: John Wilson
Opening Times: By appt. only.
Min Mail Order UK: Nmc
Credit Cards: All major credit/debit cards
Specialities: Grows 90 varieties of ferns, a large range of shrubs, incl. more than 20 varieties of *Pittosporum*, bamboos & Japanese maples.
Map Ref: C, B6 **OS Grid Ref:** SU258306

CBur **Burnham Nurseries** ⊠ € ✈ ♿ ⌂
Forches Cross, Newton Abbot, Devon, TQ12 6PZ
Ⓣ (01626) 352233
Ⓕ (01626) 362167
Ⓔ mail@orchids.uk.com
Ⓦ www.orchids.uk.com
Contact: Any member of staff
Opening Times: 1000-1600 Mon-Sun.
Min Mail Order UK: Nmc
Min Mail Order EU: £100.00 + p&p
Cat. Cost: A4 sae + 48p stamp.
Credit Cards: Visa American Express MasterCard Maestro
Specialities: All types of orchid except British native types.
Notes: Please ask for details on export beyond EU.
Map Ref: C, C4 **OS Grid Ref:** SX841732

CCAT **Cider Apple Trees** ⊠ €
Kerian, Corkscrew Lane, Woolston, Nr North Cadbury, Somerset, BA22 7BP
Ⓣ (01963) 441101
Ⓦ www.ciderappletrees.co.uk

KEY
⊠ Mail order to UK or EU ⌂ Delivers to shows
✈ Exports beyond EU € Euro accepted
♿ Accessible by wheelchair ◆ See Display advertisement

C

Contact: Mr J Dennis
Opening Times: By appt. only.
Min Mail Order UK: £9.50
Min Mail Order EU: £9.50
Cat. Cost: Free.
Credit Cards: None
Specialities: *Malus* (speciality standard trees).
Notes: Also sells wholesale.
Map Ref: C, B5

CCCN **CROSS COMMON NURSERY** ⊠ ◆
The Lizard, Helston, Cornwall, TR12 7PD
Ⓣ (01326) 290722/290668
Ⓔ info@crosscommonnursery.co.uk
Ⓦ www.crosscommonnursery.co.uk
Contact: Kevin Bosustow
Opening Times: 1000-1700 7 days, Apr, May & Jun. Reduced hours Jul-Sep, please phone for opening times.
Min Mail Order UK: Nmc
Cat. Cost: Online only.
Credit Cards: All major credit/debit cards
Specialities: Tropical/sub-tropical, coastal plants & conservatory plants. Wide range of grapevines and citrus trees. Some plants available in small quantities only.
Map Ref: C, D1 **OS Grid Ref:** SW704116

CCha **CHAPEL FARM HOUSE NURSERY** € ♿
Halwill Junction, Beaworthy, Devon, EX21 5UF
Ⓣ (01409) 221594
Ⓕ (01409) 221594
Contact: Robin or Toshie Hull
Opening Times: 1000-1600 Tue-Sat, 1000-1600 Sun & B/hol Mons.
Cat. Cost: None issued.
Credit Cards: None
Specialities: Plants from Japan. Also herbaceous. Japanese garden design service offered.
Map Ref: C, C3

CChe **CHERRY TREE NURSERY** ♿
(Sheltered Work Opportunities), off New Road Roundabout, Northbourne, Bournemouth, Dorset, BH10 7DA
Ⓣ (01202) 593537/(01202) 590840
Ⓕ (01202) 590626
Contact: Stephen Jailler
Opening Times: 0830-1530 Mon-Fri, 0900-1500 Sat, Apr-Sep & 0900-1200 Sat, Oct-Mar.
Cat. Cost: A4 sae + 66p stamps.
Credit Cards: All, except American Express
Specialities: Hardy shrubs, perennials, climbers, grasses.
Notes: Debit cards accepted. Also sells wholesale.

CCVN **CULM VIEW NURSERY** ⊠ ⊠ ♠
Waterloo Farm, Clayhidon, Devon, EX15 3TN
Ⓣ (01823) 680698
Ⓕ 0870 7058866
Ⓔ plants@culmviewnursery.co.uk
Ⓦ www.culmviewnursery.co.uk
Contact: Brian & Alison Jacobs
Opening Times: By appt. only for collection.
Min Mail Order UK: Nmc
Min Mail Order EU: Nmc
Credit Cards: None
Specialities: Herbaceous perennials grown in peat-free compost.
Notes: Mail order seed only.

CCVT **CHEW VALLEY TREES** ⊠
Winford Road, Chew Magna, Bristol, BS40 8HJ
Ⓣ (01275) 333752
Ⓕ (01275) 333746
Ⓔ info@chewvalleytrees.co.uk
Ⓦ www.chewvalleytrees.co.uk
Contact: J Scarth
Opening Times: 0800-1700 Mon-Fri all year. 0900-1600 Sat. Closed Sat, Sun & B/hols Jul & Aug.
Min Mail Order UK: Nmc
Cat. Cost: Free.
Credit Cards: All major credit/debit cards
Specialities: Native British & ornamental trees, shrubs, fruit trees & hedging.
Notes: Partial wheelchair access. Also sells wholesale.
Map Ref: C, A5 **OS Grid Ref:** ST558635

CDes **DESIRABLE PLANTS** ⊠ ♠
(Office) Pentamar, Crosspark, Totnes, Devon, TQ9 5BQ
Ⓣ (01803) 864489 evenings
Ⓔ sutton.totnes@lineone.net
Ⓦ www.desirableplants.com
Contact: Dr J J & Mrs S A Sutton
Opening Times: Not open. Mail order only.
Min Mail Order UK: £15.00
Cat. Cost: 6 × 2nd class.
Credit Cards: None
Specialities: Eclectic range of choice & interesting herbaceous plants by mail order.
Notes: Nursery not at this address.

CDob **SAMUEL DOBIE & SON** ⊠
Long Road, Paignton, Devon, TQ4 7SX
Ⓣ 0844 701 7623
Ⓕ 0844 701 7624
Ⓦ www.dobies.co.uk
Contact: Customer Services
Opening Times: Not open. Mail order only.

Phone line open 0830-1700 Mon-Fri (office). Also answerphone.
Min Mail Order UK: Nmc
Cat. Cost: Free.
Credit Cards: Visa MasterCard Switch Delta
Specialities: Wide selection of popular flower & vegetable seeds. Also includes young plants, summer-flowering bulbs & garden sundries.
Notes: Mail order to UK & Rep. of Ireland only.

CDoC **DUCHY OF CORNWALL** ⊠ ◆
Cott Road, Lostwithiel, Cornwall, PL22 0HW
Ⓣ (01208) 872668
Ⓕ (01208) 872835
Ⓔ sales@duchyofcornwallnursery.co.uk
Ⓦ www.duchyofcornwallnursery.co.uk
Contact: Jim Stephens
Opening Times: 0900-1700 Mon-Sat, 1000-1700 Sun & B/hols.
Min Mail Order UK: £14.00
Cat. Cost: None issued.
Credit Cards: All major credit/debit cards
Specialities: *Camellia*, *Fuchsia*, conifers & *Magnolia*. Also a huge range of garden plants incl. trees, shrubs, roses, perennials, fruit & conservatory plants.
Notes: Nursery partially accessible to wheelchair users.
Map Ref: C, C2 **OS Grid Ref:** SX112614

CDoy **CARADOC DOY** ⊠ € ⛺
PO Box 28, Exeter, Devon, EX3 0WY
Ⓣ (01392) 877225
Ⓕ (01392) 877225
Ⓔ info@caradocdoy.co.uk
Ⓦ www.caradocdoy.co.uk
Contact: Caradoc Doy
Opening Times: By appt. only.
Min Mail Order UK: Nmc
Cat. Cost: 6 × 2nd class.
Credit Cards: None
Specialities: Olive trees. Plants introduced by the Veitch Nurseries. Some varieties only available in small quantities.
Notes: Nursery located at Poltimore House, Politmore, Exeter, EX4 0AU. Also sells wholesale.
Map Ref: C, C4 **OS Grid Ref:** SX967964

CDTJ **DESERT TO JUNGLE** ⊠ ♿
Henlade Garden Nursery, Lower Henlade, Taunton, Somerset, TA3 5NB
Ⓣ (01823) 443701
Ⓕ (01458) 250521
Ⓔ plants@deserttojungle.com
Ⓦ www.deserttojungle.com
Contact: Rob Gudge, Dave Root
Opening Times: 1000-1700 Mon-Sun, 1st Mar-31st Oct. Thu, Fri & Sat only Nov-Feb, or phone first.
Min Mail Order UK: Nmc
Cat. Cost: 1 × 1st class sae.
Credit Cards: All major credit/debit cards
Specialities: Exotic-looking plants giving a desert or jungle effect in the garden. Incl. *Canna*, aroids, succulents, tree ferns & bamboos.
Notes: Nursery shares drive with Mount Somerset Hotel. Also sells wholesale.
Map Ref: C, B4 **OS Grid Ref:** ST273232

CDul **DULFORD NURSERIES** ⊠ ♿
Cullompton, Devon, EX15 2DG
Ⓣ (01884) 266361
Ⓕ (01884) 266663
Ⓔ dulford.nurseries@virgin.net
Ⓦ www.dulford-nurseries.co.uk
Contact: Paul & Mary Ann Rawlings
Opening Times: 0730-1630 Mon-Fri.
Min Mail Order UK: Nmc
Min Mail Order EU: Nmc
Cat. Cost: Free.
Credit Cards: All major credit/debit cards
Specialities: Native, ornamental & unusual trees & shrubs incl. oaks, maples, beech, birch, chestnut, ash, lime, *Sorbus* & pines.
Notes: Also sells wholesale.
Map Ref: C, C4 **OS Grid Ref:** SY062062

CEls **ELSWORTH HERBS** ⊠ ♿
Farthingwood, Broadway, Sidmouth, Devon, EX10 8HS
Ⓣ (01395) 578689
Ⓔ john.twibell@btinternet.com
Contact: Drs J D & J M Twibell
Opening Times: By appt. only. NCCPG Open Day 20th Sep 2009.
Min Mail Order UK: £10.00
Cat. Cost: 3 × 1st class or email.
Credit Cards: None
Specialities: Nat. Collections of *Artemisia* (incl. *Seriphidium*) & *Nerium oleander*. Wide range of *Artemisia* & *Seriphidium*, *Nerium oleander*. Stock available in small quantities only. Orders may require propagation from Collection material, for which we are the primary reference source.
Notes: Partially accessible for wheelchairs.
Map Ref: C, C4 **OS Grid Ref:** SY119881

KEY		
	⊠ Mail order to UK or EU	⛺ Delivers to shows
	✈ Exports beyond EU	€ Euro accepted
	♿ Accessible by wheelchair	◆ See Display advertisement

C

CElw **ELWORTHY COTTAGE PLANTS** ♿ ⛫
Elworthy Cottage, Elworthy, Nr Lydeard St Lawrence, Taunton, Somerset, TA4 3PX
Ⓣ (01984) 656427
Ⓔ mike@elworthy-cottage.co.uk
Ⓦ www.elworthy-cottage.co.uk
Contact: Mrs J M Spiller
Opening Times: 1000-1600 Thu & Fri, late Mar-end Aug. Also by appt. Feb-Nov.
Cat. Cost: 3 × 2nd class.
Credit Cards: None
Specialities: *Clematis* & unusual herbaceous plants esp. hardy *Geranium*, *Geum*, grasses, *Campanula*, *Crocosmia*, *Pulmonaria*, *Astrantia*, *Viola* & *Galanthus*. Some varieties only available in small quantities.
Notes: Nursery on B3188, 5 miles north of Wiveliscombe, in centre of Elworthy village.
Map Ref: C, B4 **OS Grid Ref:** ST084349

CEnd **ENDSLEIGH GARDENS** ⊠ ♿ ◆
Milton Abbot, Tavistock, Devon, PL19 0PG
Ⓣ (01822) 870235
Ⓕ (01822) 870513
Ⓔ Treemail@endsleigh-gardens.com
Ⓦ www.endsleigh-gardens.com
Contact: Michael Taylor
Opening Times: 0800-1700 Mon-Sat. 1000-1700 Sun.
Min Mail Order UK: Nmc
Cat. Cost: 2 × 1st class.
Credit Cards: Visa Access Switch MasterCard
Specialities: Choice & unusual trees & shrubs incl. *Acer* & *Cornus* cvs. Old apples & cherries. *Wisteria*. Grafting service.
Map Ref: C, C3

CEnt **ENTWOOD FARM PLANTS**
Harcombe, Lyme Regis, Dorset, DT7 3RN
Ⓣ (01297) 444034
Contact: Jenny & Ivan Harding
Opening Times: Please phone for details.
Credit Cards: None
Specialities: Perennials & bamboos. Selection of shrubs, grasses, herbs & bulbs. Stock propagated & grown at nursery, some in small quantities.
Map Ref: C, C4 **OS Grid Ref:** SY335953

CFee **FEEBERS HARDY PLANTS** ⊠ € ♿ ◆
1 Feeber Cottage, Westwood, Broadclyst, Nr Exeter, Devon, EX5 3DQ
Ⓣ (01404) 822118
Ⓔ Feebers@onetel.com
Contact: Mrs E Squires
Opening Times: Open at any reasonable time by prior telephone arrangement.
Min Mail Order UK: Nmc
Min Mail Order EU: Nmc
Cat. Cost: Sae + 36p stamp.
Credit Cards: None
Specialities: Plants for wet clay soils, alpines & hardy perennials incl. those raised by Amos Perry. Small quantities of plants held unless grown from seed.
Notes: Mail order limited. Nursery accessible for wheelchairs in dry weather only.
Map Ref: C, C4

CFFs **FLORAL FIREWORKS** ⊠
Burnt House Farm, Mid Lambrook, South Petherton, Somerset, TA13 5HE
Ⓣ (01460) 249060
Ⓕ (01460) 249025
Ⓔ info@floralfireworks.co.uk
Ⓦ www.floralfireworks.co.uk
Contact: Carol Atkins
Opening Times: Not open. Mail order only. Orders can be collected by prior arrangement.
Min Mail Order UK: £10.00 + p&p
Min Mail Order EU: £20.00 + p&p
Cat. Cost: 4 × 2nd class.
Credit Cards: All major credit/debit cards
Specialities: Bulbs.

CFir **FIR TREE FARM NURSERY** ⊠ € ♿
Tresahor, Constantine, Falmouth, Cornwall, TR11 5PL
Ⓣ (01326) 340593
Ⓔ plants@cornwallgardens.com
Ⓦ www.cornwallgardens.com
Contact: Glynn Wrapson & Sorcha Hitchcox
Opening Times: 1000-1700 Tue-Sat & 1100-1600 Sun, closed Mon, Feb-Oct. By appt. Nov-Jan.
Min Mail Order UK: £25.00 + p&p
Min Mail Order EU: £40.00 + p&p
Cat. Cost: 6 × 1st class.
Credit Cards: Visa Access Delta Switch
Specialities: Over 4000 varieties of cottage garden & rare perennials with many specialities. Also 80 varieties of *Clematis*. Some rare varieties available in small quantities only.
Map Ref: C, D1

CFol **FOLLY GATE PLANTS** ♿
The Old Post Office, Folly Gate, Nr Okehampton, Devon, EX20 3AF
Ⓣ (01837) 659164
Ⓜ 07831 850086
Ⓔ perrylamb@hotmail.com
Contact: Sara Lamb
Opening Times: 1000-1700, Wed-Sun, Mar-Oct.
Cat. Cost: 2 × 1st class.

Specialities: Hardy herbaceous perennials, shrubs and grasses.
Map Ref: C, C3 **OS Grid Ref:** SX573978

CFox **Foxley Road Nurseries** 🄱 ⌂
Foxley Road, Malmesbury, Wiltshire, SN16 0JQ
Ⓣ (01666) 822171
Ⓔ carol@foxleyroadnurseries.co.uk
Ⓦ www.foxleyroadnurseries.co.uk
Contact: Carol Hinwood
Opening Times: 1000-1600 Mon-Sat Feb, Mar, Jul-Dec. 0900-1700 Mon-Sat & 1000-1600 Sun Apr, May & Jun.
Cat. Cost: Sae.
Credit Cards: All major credit/debit cards
Specialities: Wide range of shrubs & herbaceous perennials, potted bulbs, patio & hanging basket plants, vegetables, herbs & soft fruit.
Map Ref: C, A5 **OS Grid Ref:** ST915865

CFwr **The Flower Bower** ⊠
Woodlands, Shurton, Stogursey, Nr Bridgwater, Somerset, TA5 1QE
Ⓣ (01278) 732134
Ⓔ theflowerbower@yahoo.co.uk
Contact: Sheila Tucker
Opening Times: By appt. only.
Min Mail Order UK: Nmc
Min Mail Order EU: Nmc
Cat. Cost: 2 × 1st class.
Credit Cards: None
Specialities: *Epiphyllum* 500+ varieties, *Hemerocallis*, ferns, *Clivia*. Nat. Collection of *Clivia*, Chinese & Japanese taxa.
Map Ref: C, B4 **OS Grid Ref:** ST203442

CGHE **Garden House Enterprises** ⊠ 🄱
The Garden House, Buckland Monachorum, Yelverton, Devon, PL20 7LQ
Ⓣ (01822) 854769
Ⓕ (01822) 855358
Ⓔ office@thegardenhouse.org.uk
Ⓦ www.thegardenhouse.org.uk
Contact: Jo Selman
Opening Times: 1030-1700 7 days 1st Mar-31st Oct.
Min Mail Order UK: Nmc
Min Mail Order EU: Nmc
Cat. Cost: 4 × 1st class.
Credit Cards: All major credit/debit cards
Specialities: Choice woodland plants & dieramas.
Notes: Mail order seed only, selection from the garden.
Map Ref: C, C3 **OS Grid Ref:** SX496683

CGro **C W Groves & Son Ltd** ⊠ 🄱
West Bay Road, Bridport, Dorset, DT6 4BA
Ⓣ (01308) 422654
Ⓕ (01308) 420888
Ⓔ violets@grovesnurseries.co.uk
Ⓦ www.grovesnurseries.co.uk
Contact: Clive Groves
Opening Times: 0830-1700 Mon-Sat, 1030-1630 Sun.
Min Mail Order UK: Nmc
Min Mail Order EU: £15.00 + p&p
Cat. Cost: 2 × 1st class.
Credit Cards: Visa Switch MasterCard
Specialities: Nursery & garden centre specialising in Parma & hardy *Viola*. Nat. Collection of *Viola odorata* cvs & Parma Violets.
Notes: Mainly violets by mail order. Main display at nursery in Feb, Mar & Apr.
Map Ref: C, C5 **OS Grid Ref:** SY466918

CGrW **The Great Western Gladiolus Nursery** ⊠ €
17 Valley View, Clutton, Bristol, BS39 5SN
Ⓣ (01761) 452036
Ⓕ (01761) 452036
Ⓔ clutton.glads@btinternet.com
Ⓦ www.greatwesterngladiolus.co.uk
Contact: G F & J C Hazell
Opening Times: Mail order only. Open by appt. only.
Min Mail Order UK: Nmc
Min Mail Order EU: Nmc
Cat. Cost: 4 × 1st class (2 catalogues).
Credit Cards: None
Specialities: *Gladiolus* species & hybrids, corms & seeds. Other South African bulbous plants.
Notes: Also sells wholesale.

CHar **West Harptree Nursery** ⊠ € ⌂
Bristol Road, West Harptree, Bath, Somerset, BS40 6HG
Ⓣ (01761) 221989
Ⓜ 07745 442385
Ⓔ bryn@harptreenursery.co.uk
Ⓦ www.harptreenursery.co.uk
Contact: Bryn & Helene Bowles
Opening Times: From 1000 Mon-Sun 7 days.
Min Mail Order UK: Nmc
Min Mail Order EU: Nmc
Cat. Cost: Large sae for free names list.

KEY
⊠ Mail order to UK or EU ⌂ Delivers to shows
✈ Exports beyond EU € Euro accepted
🄱 Accessible by wheelchair ◆ See Display advertisement

C

Credit Cards: MasterCard Visa Maestro Paypal
Specialities: Unusual herbaceous perennials & shrubs. Bulbs & grasses. Many AGM plants.
Notes: Also sells wholesale.
Map Ref: C, B5

CHby **THE HERBARY** ⊠ € ⊠
161 Chapel Street, Horningsham, Warminster, Wiltshire, BA12 7LU
Ⓣ (01985) 844442
Ⓔ info@beansandherbs.co.uk
Ⓦ www.beansandherbs.co.uk
Contact: Pippa Rosen
Opening Times: May-Sep strictly by appt. only.
Min Mail Order UK: Nmc
Min Mail Order EU: Nmc
Cat. Cost: 4 × 1st class or online.
Credit Cards: None
Specialities: Culinary, medicinal & aromatic herbs organically grown in small quantities.
Notes: Mail order all year for organic vegetable seed & large variety of organic bean & herb seed. Also sells wholesale.
Map Ref: C, B5 **OS Grid Ref:** ST812414

CHew **HEWITT-COOPER CARNIVOROUS PLANTS** ⊠ € ♁
The Homestead, Glastonbury Road, West Pennard, Somerset, BA6 8NN
Ⓣ (01458) 832844
Ⓕ (01458) 832712
Ⓔ sales@hccarnivorousplants.co.uk
Ⓦ www.hccarnivorousplants.co.uk
Contact: Nigel Hewitt-Cooper
Opening Times: By appt.
Min Mail Order UK: £10.00 + p&p
Min Mail Order EU: £30.00
Cat. Cost: 1 × 1st class/1× IRC.
Credit Cards: All major credit/debit cards
Specialities: Carnivorous plants.
Notes: Mail order May-Nov.

CHEx **HARDY EXOTICS** ⊠ ♿
Gilly Lane, Whitecross, Penzance, Cornwall, TR20 8BZ
Ⓣ (01736) 740660
Ⓕ (01736) 741101
Ⓔ contact@hardyexotics.co.uk
Ⓦ www.hardyexotics.co.uk
Contact: C Shilton/J Smith
Opening Times: 1000-1700 7 days Apr-Oct, 1000-1700 Mon-Sat Nov-Feb. Please phone first in winter months if travelling a long way.
Min Mail Order UK: £40 + carriage.
Cat. Cost: 4 × 1st class (no cheques).
Credit Cards: All major credit/debit cards
Specialities: Largest selection in the UK of trees, shrubs & herbaceous plants for tropical & desert effects. Hardy & half-hardy plants for gardens, patios & conservatories.
Map Ref: C, D1 **OS Grid Ref:** SW524345

CHGN **HIGH GARDEN NURSERIES** ♿
Chiverstone Lane, Kenton, Exeter, Devon, EX6 8NJ
Ⓣ (01626) 899106
Ⓔ info@highgarden.co.uk
Ⓦ www.highgarden.co.uk
Contact: Chris Britton
Opening Times: 0900-1700 Tue-Fri
Cat. Cost: None issued.
Credit Cards: None
Specialities: Quality shrubs, trees & perennials, some unusual & different.
Map Ref: C, C4 **OS Grid Ref:** SX957836

CHid **HIDDEN VALLEY NURSERY** ⊠ € ♁
Umberleigh, Devon, EX37 9BU
Ⓣ (01769) 560567
Ⓜ 07899 788789
Ⓔ plalindley@itsosbroadband.co.uk
Contact: Linda & Peter Lindley
Opening Times: Daylight hours, but please phone first.
Min Mail Order UK: Nmc
Cat. Cost: None issued.
Credit Cards: None
Specialities: Hardy perennials esp. shade lovers & Chatham Islands forget-me-nots (*Myosotidium hortensia*.)
Map Ref: C, B3 **OS Grid Ref:** SS567205

CHII **HILL HOUSE NURSERY & GARDENS** ⊠ € ♿
Landscove, Nr Ashburton, Devon, TQ13 7LY
Ⓣ (01803) 762273
Ⓕ (01803) 158218
Ⓔ info@hillhousenursery.com
Ⓦ www.hillhousenursery.co.uk
Contact: Raymond, Sacha & Matthew Hubbard
Opening Times: 1100-1700 7 days, all year. Open all B/hols incl. Easter Sun. Closed 24th Dec-7th Jan. Tea room open 1st Mar-30th Sep.
Min Mail Order UK: £25
Cat. Cost: None issued.
Credit Cards: Delta MasterCard Switch Visa
Specialities: 3000+ varieties of plants, most propagated on premises, many rare or unusual. The garden, open to the public, was laid out by Edward Hyams. Pioneers of glasshouse pest control by beneficial insects.
Map Ref: C, C3 **OS Grid Ref:** SX774664

CHVG **Hidden Valley Gardens** ♿

Treesmill, Nr Par, Cornwall,
PL24 2TU
Ⓣ (01208) 873225
Ⓔ hiddenvalleygardens@yahoo.co.uk
Ⓦ www.hiddenvalleygardens.co.uk
Contact: Mrs P Howard
Opening Times: 1000-1800 7 days, 20th Mar-end Oct. Please phone for directions. Garden open as nursery.
Cat. Cost: None issued.
Credit Cards: None
Specialities: Cottage garden plants, *Crocosmia* & many unusual perennials which can be seen growing in the garden. Some stock available in small quantities. Display garden.
Map Ref: C, D2 **OS Grid Ref:** SX094567

CIri **The Iris Garden** ✉ €

Yard House, Pilsdon,
Bridport, Dorset,
DT6 5PA
Ⓣ (01308) 868797
Ⓔ theirisgarden@aol.com
Ⓦ www.theirisgarden.co.uk
Contact: Clive Russell
Opening Times: Open days 1400-1700, 6th & 7th June 2009. Show garden open other times by appt. Please email or phone for details.
Min Mail Order UK: £15.00 + p&p
Min Mail Order EU: £25.00 + p&p
Cat. Cost: 6 × 1st class.
Credit Cards: All major credit/debit cards
Specialities: Modern bearded & beardless *Iris* from breeders in UK, USA, France, Italy & Australia. Nat. Collection of Space Age *Iris*.
Notes: Orders for bearded iris & sibiricas must be received by end Jun & by end Aug for spurias & ensatas.
Map Ref: C, C5 **OS Grid Ref:** SY421988

CJas **Jasmine Cottage Gardens**

26 Channel Road, Walton St Mary,
Clevedon, Somerset,
BS21 7BY
Ⓣ (01275) 871850
Ⓔ margaret@bologrew.demon.co.uk
Ⓦ www.bologrew.pwp.blueyonder.co.uk
Contact: Mr & Mrs M Redgrave
Opening Times: May to Aug, daily by appt. Garden open at the same times.
Cat. Cost: None issued.
Credit Cards: None
Specialities: *Rhodochiton, Lophospermum, Maurandya, Dicentra macrocapnos, Salvia, Isotoma*, half-hardy geraniums.
Map Ref: C, A4 **OS Grid Ref:** ST405725

CKel **Kelways Ltd** ✉ € ♿ ⌂

Langport, Somerset, TA10 9EZ
Ⓣ (01458) 250521
Ⓕ (01458) 253351
Ⓔ sales@kelways.co.uk
Ⓦ www.kelways.co.uk
Contact: Dave Root
Opening Times: 0900-1700 Mon-Fri, 0900-1700 Sat, 1000-1600 Sun.
Min Mail Order UK: £4.00 + p&p
Min Mail Order EU: £8.00 + p&p
Cat. Cost: Free.
Credit Cards: All major credit/debit cards
Specialities: *Paeonia, Iris, Hemerocallis* & herbaceous perennials. Nat. Collection of *Paeonia lactiflora*. Wide range of trees, shrubs & herbaceous.
Notes: Also sells wholesale.
Map Ref: C, B5 **OS Grid Ref:** ST434273

CKen **Kenwith Nursery (Gordon Haddow)** ✉ € ✈ ♿ ◆

Blinsham, Nr Torrington, Beaford, Winkleigh, Devon, EX19 8NT
Ⓣ (01805) 603274
Ⓕ (01805) 603663
Ⓔ conifers@kenwith63.freeserve.co.uk
Ⓦ www.kenwithnursery.co.uk
Contact: Gordon Haddow
Opening Times: 1000-1630 Tue-Sat all year. Closed all B/hols.
Min Mail Order UK: £15.00 + p&p
Min Mail Order EU: £50.00 + p&p
Cat. Cost: 3 × 1st class.
Credit Cards: Visa MasterCard
Specialities: All conifer genera. Grafting a speciality. Many new introductions to UK. Nat. Collection of Dwarf Conifers.
Map Ref: C, B3 **OS Grid Ref:** SS518160

CKno **Knoll Gardens** ✉ ♿ ⌂

Hampreston, Nr Wimborne, Dorset,
BH21 7ND
Ⓣ (01202) 873931
Ⓕ (01202) 870842
Ⓔ enquiries@knollgardens.co.uk
Ⓦ www.knollgardens.co.uk
Contact: N R Lucas
Opening Times: 1000-1700 (or dusk if earlier) Tue-Sun, May-Nov. 1000-1600 Wed-Sat, Feb-Apr & Dec. Open B/hol Mons. Closed 20th Dec 2009 reopens 3rd Feb 2010.
Min Mail Order UK: Nmc

KEY
✉ Mail order to UK or EU ⌂ Delivers to shows
✈ Exports beyond EU € Euro accepted
♿ Accessible by wheelchair ◆ See Display advertisement

C

Min Mail Order EU: Nmc
Cat. Cost: 11 × 2nd class or order online.
Credit Cards: Visa MasterCard
Specialities: Grasses (main specialism). Select perennials. Nat. Collections of *Pennisetum*, *Phygelius* & deciduous *Ceanothus*. Sole UK supplier of *Ulmus americana* 'Princeton'.
Notes: Also sells wholesale.
Map Ref: C, C6

CLak **Lakka Bulbs** ⊠
(Office) 127 Mill Street,
Torrington, North Devon,
EX38 8AW
Ⓣ (01805) 625071
Ⓔ lakkabulbs@tesco.net
Contact: Jonathan Hutchinson
Opening Times: Not open. Mail order only.
Min Mail Order UK: Nmc
Min Mail Order EU: Nmc
Cat. Cost: None issued.
Specialities: Nat. Collections of *Urginea*, *Veltheimia* & *Scadoxus*. Other South African bulbs of families *Amaryllidaceae* & *Hyacinthaceae*. All available in small quantities only.

CLAP **Long Acre Plants** ⊠ ♿
South Marsh, Charlton Musgrove,
Nr Wincanton, Somerset, BA9 8EX
Ⓣ (01963) 32802
Ⓕ (01963) 32802
Ⓔ info@plantsforshade.co.uk
Ⓦ www.plantsforshade.co.uk
Contact: Nigel & Michelle Rowland
Opening Times: 1000-1300 & 1400-1700 Thu only, Feb-Jun, Sep & Oct.
Min Mail Order UK: £20.00 + p&p
Cat. Cost: 3 × 1st class.
Credit Cards: MasterCard Visa Maestro American Express JCB
Specialities: Ferns, woodland bulbs & perennials. Nat. Collection of *Asarum*.
Notes: Some plants available in small numbers only and only seasonally available.
Map Ref: C, B5

CLnd **Landford Trees** €
Landford Lodge, Landford, Salisbury,
Wiltshire, SP5 2EH
Ⓣ (01794) 390808
Ⓕ (01794) 390037
Ⓔ trees@landfordtrees.co.uk
Ⓦ www.landfordtrees.co.uk
Contact: C D Pilkington
Opening Times: 0800-1700 Mon-Fri.
Cat. Cost: Free.
Credit Cards: None
Specialities: Deciduous ornamental trees.
Notes: Mail order maximum size 120cms. Also sells wholesale.
Map Ref: C, B6 **OS Grid Ref:** SU247201

CLng **Longcombe Nursery and Garden Centre** ⊠ ♿
Longcombe, Totnes, Devon, TQ9 6PL
Ⓣ (01803) 863098
Ⓔ info@simplyclematis.co.uk
Ⓦ www.simplyclematis.co.uk
Contact: Linda Clarke
Opening Times: 0900-1700 Mon-Sat, 1000-1600 Sun.
Min Mail Order UK: Nmc
Cat. Cost: Online only.
Credit Cards: All major credit/debit cards
Specialities: *Clematis.*
Notes: Also sells wholesale.
Map Ref: C, C3 **OS Grid Ref:** SX834601

CLoc **C S Lockyer (Fuchsias)** ⊠ € ⊠ ◆
Lansbury, 70 Henfield Road, Coalpit Heath,
Bristol, BS36 2UZ
Ⓣ (01454) 772219
Ⓕ (01454) 772219
Ⓔ sales@lockyerfuchsias.co.uk
Ⓦ www.lockyerfuchsias.co.uk
Contact: C S Lockyer
Opening Times: 1000-1300, 1430-1700 most days, please ring.
Min Mail Order UK: 6 plants + p&p
Min Mail Order EU: £12.00 + p&p
Cat. Cost: 4 × 1st class.
Credit Cards: None
Specialities: *Fuchsia.*
Notes: Many open days & coach parties. Limited wheelchair access. Also sells wholesale.
Map Ref: C, A5

CMac **Mac Pennys Nurseries** ⊠
154 Burley Road, Bransgore, Christchurch,
Dorset, BH23 8DB
Ⓣ (01425) 672348
Ⓕ (01425) 673917
Ⓔ office@macpennys.co.uk
Ⓦ www.macpennys.co.uk
Contact: T & V Lowndes & S Lowndes
Opening Times: 0900-1700 Mon-Sat, 1100-1700 Sun. Closed Xmas & New Year.
Min Mail Order UK: Nmc
Cat. Cost: A4 sae with 4 × 1st class.
Credit Cards: All major credit/debit cards
Specialities: General. Plants available in small quantities only.
Notes: Mail order available Sep-Mar, UK only. Nursery partially accessible for wheelchairs.
Map Ref: C, C6

C

CMCN **MALLET COURT NURSERY** ⊠ € ✈ ♿ ⌂
Curry Mallet, Taunton, Somerset,
TA3 6SY
Ⓣ (01823) 481493
Ⓕ (01823) 481493
Ⓔ malletcourtnursery@btinternet.com
Ⓦ www.malletcourt.co.uk
Contact: J G S & P M E Harris F.L.S.
Opening Times: 0930-1700 Mon-Fri summer, 0930-1600 winter. Sat & Sun by appt.
Min Mail Order UK: Nmc
Min Mail Order EU: Nmc
Cat. Cost: £1.50
Credit Cards: All major credit/debit cards
Specialities: Maples, oaks, *Magnolia*, hollies & other rare and unusual plants including those from China & South Korea.
Notes: Mail order Oct-Mar only. Also sells wholesale.
Map Ref: C, B4

CMdw **MEADOWS NURSERY** ⊠ € ⌂
Hookswood Cottage, Farnham, Blandford Forum, Dorset, DT11 8DQ
Ⓣ (01725) 516394
Ⓔ plants@meadowsnurserymells.co.uk
Contact: Sue Lees & Eddie Wheatley
Opening Times: By appt. only.
Min Mail Order UK: Nmc
Cat. Cost: 3 × 1st class.
Credit Cards: None
Specialities: Hardy perennials, shrubs & some conservatory plants.

CMea **THE MEAD NURSERY** ♿
Brokerswood, Nr Westbury, Wiltshire,
BA13 4EG
Ⓣ (01373) 859990
Ⓦ www.themeadnursery.co.uk
Contact: Steve & Emma Lewis-Dale
Opening Times: 0900-1700 Wed-Sat & B/hols, 1200-1700 Sun, 1st Feb-10th Oct. Closed Easter Sun.
Cat. Cost: 5 × 1st class.
Credit Cards: All major credit/debit cards
Specialities: Perennials, alpines, pot-grown bulbs and grasses.
Map Ref: C, B5 **OS Grid Ref:** ST833517

CMen **MENDIP BONSAI STUDIO** ⊠ ⌂
Byways, Back Lane, Downside, Shepton Mallet, Somerset, BA4 4JR
Ⓣ (01749) 344274
Ⓜ 07711 205806
Ⓔ jr.trott@ukonline.co.uk
Ⓦ www.mendipbonsai.co.uk
Contact: John Trott
Opening Times: Private nursery. Visits by appt. only.
Cat. Cost: Large sae for plant & workshop lists
Credit Cards: All major credit/debit cards
Specialities: Bonsai, Potensai, accent plants & garden stock. Acers, conifers, incl. many *Pinus thunbergii* species. Many plants available in small numbers only. Young trees for garden or bonsai culture.
Notes: Education classes, lectures, demonstrations & club talks on bonsai. Stockist of most bonsai sundries. Mail orders will be normally despatched late Sep/early Oct. Ltd wheelchair access.
Map Ref: C, B5

CMHG **MARWOOD HILL GARDENS** ♿
Marwood, Barnstaple, Devon, EX31 4EB
Ⓣ (01271) 342528
Ⓕ (01271) 342528
Ⓔ info@marwoodhillgarden.co.uk
Ⓦ www.marwoodhillgarden.co.uk
Contact: Malcolm Pharoah
Opening Times: 1100-1630, 7 days. Closed Nov-Feb.
Cat. Cost: 3 × 1st class.
Credit Cards: Visa Delta MasterCard Switch Solo
Specialities: Large range of unusual trees & shrubs. *Eucalyptus*, alpines, *Camellia*, *Astilbe*, bog plants & perennials. Nat. Collections of *Astilbe*, *Tulbaghia* & *Iris ensata*.
Map Ref: C, B3 **OS Grid Ref:** SS545375

CMil **MILL COTTAGE PLANTS** ⊠ ♿
The Mill, Henley Lane, Wookey, Somerset,
BA5 1AP
Ⓣ (01749) 676966
Ⓜ 07851 698759
Ⓔ millcottageplants@tiscali.co.uk
Ⓦ www.millcottageplants.co.uk
Contact: Sally Gregson
Opening Times: By appt. only. Phone for directions.
Min Mail Order UK: Nmc.
Min Mail Order EU: £25.00 + p&p
Cat. Cost: 4 × 1st class.
Credit Cards: All major credit/debit cards
Specialities: Rare *Hydrangea serrata* cvs, *H. aspera* cvs, damp & shade-loving perennials incl. *Epimedium*, *Erythronium*, *Tricyrtis* & ferns.
Map Ref: C, B5

KEY
⊠ Mail order to UK or EU ⌂ Delivers to shows
✈ Exports beyond EU € Euro accepted
♿ Accessible by wheelchair ◆ See Display advertisement

C

CMMP **M & M PLANTS** ♿
Lloret, Chittlehamholt, Umberleigh, Devon, EX37 9PD
Ⓣ (01769) 540448
Ⓕ (01769) 540448
Ⓔ mmplants@mail.com
Contact: Mr M Thorne
Opening Times: 0930-1700 Tue-Sat, Apr-Oct & 1000-1600 Tue-Fri, Nov-Mar. Sat by appt. in Aug.
Cat. Cost: 3 × 1st class.
Credit Cards: None
Specialities: Perennials. We also carry a good range of alpines, shrubs, trees & roses.
Map Ref: C, B3

CMoH **MONITA HOUSE GARDEN** ⊠
Eggesford, Chulmleigh, Devon, EX18 7JZ
Ⓣ (01769) 580081
Ⓜ 07748 563032
Ⓔ monitahouse@tiscali.co.uk
Contact: David Mitchell
Opening Times: 1000-1700, Sun & B/hols, 1st Apr-30th Oct. Please ring first.
Min Mail Order UK: Nmc
Cat. Cost: 4 × 1st class.
Credit Cards: None
Specialities: Small nursery specialising in herbaceous perennials, many available in small quantities only.
Map Ref: C, B3 **OS Grid Ref:** SS681119

CNat **NATURAL SELECTION** ⊠ €
1 Station Cottages, Hullavington, Chippenham, Wiltshire, SN14 6ET
Ⓣ (01666) 837369
Ⓜ 07800 583999
Ⓦ www.worldmutation.demon.co.uk
Contact: Martin Barber
Opening Times: Please phone first.
Min Mail Order UK: £9.00 + p&p
Cat. Cost: 2 × 2nd class.
Credit Cards: None
Specialities: Unusual British natives & others. Also seed. Only available in small quantities.
Map Ref: C, A5

CNMi **NEWPORT MILLS NURSERY** ⊠
Wrantage, Taunton, Somerset, TA3 6DJ
Ⓣ (01823) 490231
Ⓜ 07940 872800
Ⓕ (01823) 490231
Contact: John Barrington
Opening Times: By appt. only.
Min Mail Order UK: Nmc
Min Mail Order EU: Nmc
Cat. Cost: Free.
Credit Cards: None
Specialities: *Delphinium*. English scented varieties of perpetual flowering carnations. Some varieties only available in small quantities & propagated to order. Pinks, Exhibition, Modern & Old World.
Notes: Mail order Apr-Sep for young delphiniums in 7cm pots. Dormant plants can be sent out in autumn/winter if requested.
Map Ref: C, B4

COld **THE OLD MILL HERBARY**
Helland Bridge, Bodmin, Cornwall, PL30 4QR
Ⓣ (01208) 841206
Ⓔ oldmillherbary@aol.com
Ⓦ www.oldmillherbary.co.uk
Contact: Mrs B Whurr
Opening Times: 1000-1700 Thu-Tue 1st Apr-30th Sep. Closed Wed.
Cat. Cost: 6 × 1st class.
Credit Cards: None
Specialities: Culinary, medicinal & aromatic herbs.
Notes: Limited sales of medicinal herbs. Historical site in Area of Outstanding Natural Beauty. SSSI, SAC & AONB.
Map Ref: C, C2 **OS Grid Ref:** SX065717

COIW **THE OLD WITHY GARDEN NURSERY** ⊠
Grange Fruit Farm, Gweek, Helston, Cornwall, TR12 6BE
Ⓣ (01326) 221171
Ⓔ sales@theoldwithygardennursery.co.uk
Ⓦ www.theoldwithygardennursery.co.uk
Contact: Sheila Chandler or Nick Chandler
Opening Times: 0930-1700 7 days, Feb-end Oct. 1000-1600 Mon-Fri, Nov.
Min Mail Order UK: £15.00
Cat. Cost: 4 × 1st class.
Credit Cards: Maestro MasterCard Visa Delta
Specialities: Cottage garden plants, perennials, some biennials & grasses. Some varieties in small quantities only.
Notes: Partially accessible for wheelchairs (gravel paths). Also sells wholesale.
Map Ref: C, D1 **OS Grid Ref:** SW688255

CPar **PARKS PERENNIALS** ⌂
242 Wallisdown Road, Wallisdown, Bournemouth, Dorset, BH10 4HZ
Ⓣ (01202) 524464
Ⓔ parks.perennials@ntlworld.com
Contact: S. Parks
Opening Times: Apr-Oct most days, please phone first.
Cat. Cost: None issued.
Credit Cards: None
Specialities: Hardy herbaceous perennials.
Map Ref: C, C6

CPbn **Penborn Goat Farm** ♿
Penborn, Bounds Cross, Holsworthy, Devon, EX22 6LH
Ⓣ (01288) 381569
Ⓔ penborngoats@toucansurf.com
Ⓦ www.penborngoats.com
Contact: P R Oldfield
Opening Times: Weekends May-Sep.
Cat. Cost: Online.
Credit Cards: None
Specialities: *Mentha, Lavandula, Melissa.* Available in small quantities only.
Map Ref: C, C2 **OS Grid Ref:** SS290021

CPBP **Parham Bungalow Plants** ⊠ € ⌂
Parham Lane, Market Lavington, Devizes, Wiltshire, SN10 4QA
Ⓣ (01380) 812605
Ⓔ jjs@pbplants.freeserve.co.uk
Contact: Mrs D E Sample
Opening Times: Please ring first.
Min Mail Order UK: Nmc
Min Mail Order EU: Nmc
Cat. Cost: Sae.
Credit Cards: None
Specialities: Alpines.
Map Ref: C, B6

CPEN **Pennard Plants** ⊠ € ✈ ⌂
3 The Gardens, East Pennard, Shepton Mallet, Somerset, BA4 6TU
Ⓣ (01749) 860039
Ⓕ 07043 017270
Ⓔ sales@pennardplants.com
Ⓦ www.pennardplants.com
Contact: Chris Smith
Opening Times: 1000-1500 Wed, 1st Mar-31st Oct.
Min Mail Order UK: Nmc
Min Mail Order EU: Nmc
Cat. Cost: 3 × 1st class.
Credit Cards: All major credit/debit cards
Specialities: *Agapanthus, Dierama, Eucomis* & *Gladioli* species. South African bulbous plants.
Notes: Nursery at The Walled Garden at East Pennard.
Map Ref: C, B5

CPhi **Alan Phipps Cacti** ⊠ €
62 Samuel White Road, Hanham, Bristol, BS15 3LX
Ⓣ (0117) 9607591
Ⓦ www.cactus-mall.com/alan-phipps/index.html
Contact: A Phipps
Opening Times: 10.00-1700 but prior phone call essential to ensure a greeting.
Min Mail Order UK: £5.00 + p&p
Min Mail Order EU: £20.00 + p&p
Cat. Cost: Sae or 2 × IRC (EU only).
Credit Cards: None
Specialities: *Mammillaria, Astrophytum* & *Ariocarpus.* Species & varieties will change with times. Ample quantities exist in spring. Limited range of *Agave.*
Notes: Euro accepted as cash only. Specimen-size plants not available by mail order.
Map Ref: C, A5 **OS Grid Ref:** ST644717

CPHo **The Palm House** ⊠
8 North Street, Ottery St Mary, Devon, EX11 1DR
Ⓣ (01404) 815450
Ⓜ 07815 673397
Ⓔ george@thepalmhouse.co.uk
Ⓦ www.thepalmhouse.co.uk
Contact: George Gregory
Opening Times: Mail order only. Open by appt. only.
Min Mail Order UK: £15.00
Min Mail Order EU: £10.00
Cat. Cost: 2 × 1st class.
Credit Cards: All major credit/debit cards
Specialities: Palms.
Notes: Also sells wholesale.
Map Ref: C, C4 **OS Grid Ref:** SY098955

CPHT **Classic Gardener (formerly Pound Hill Plants)** € ♿
Pound Barn, West Kington, Nr Chippenham, Wiltshire, SN14 7JQ
Ⓣ (01249) 783880
Ⓔ info@classicgardener.co.uk
Ⓦ www.classicgardener.co.uk
Contact: Philip Stockitt
Opening Times: 1000-1700 Sat or by prior appt. only.
Cat. Cost: Free
Credit Cards: MasterCard Visa
Specialities: Topiary.
Notes: Also sells wholesale.
Map Ref: C, A5

CPla **Plant World Botanic Gardens** ⊠ € ✈ ♿
St Marychurch Road, Newton Abbot, Devon, TQ12 4SE
Ⓣ (01803) 872939
Ⓕ (01803) 875018
Ⓔ raybrown@plant-world-seeds.com

KEY
⊠ Mail order to UK or EU ⌂ Delivers to shows
✈ Exports beyond EU € Euro accepted
♿ Accessible by wheelchair ◆ See Display advertisement

C

Ⓦ www.plant-world-seeds.com
Contact: Ray Brown
Opening Times: 0930-1700 7 days a week, Apr (Easter if earlier) to Oct.
Min Mail Order UK: £8.00
Min Mail Order EU: £20.00
Cat. Cost: 3 × 1st class or 2 × IRC.
Credit Cards: Visa Access EuroCard MasterCard
Specialities: Alpines & unusual herbaceous plants. Nat. Collection of *Primula.*
Notes: Mail order for seed only. 4-acre garden correctly planted out as the map of the world. Also sells wholesale.
Map Ref: C, C3

CPLG **Exclusive Plants (incorporating Pine Lodge Gardens & Nursery)** ⊠ ♿
Pine Lodge Gardens, Holmbush, St Austell, Cornwall, PL25 3RQ
Ⓣ (01726) 77960
Ⓜ 07775 811385
Ⓕ (01726) 77960
Ⓔ pbonavia3@aol.com
Ⓦ www.exclusiveplants.co.uk
Contact: Paul Bonavia
Opening Times: 1000-1700 7 days all year, except 24th/25th/26th Dec.
Min Mail Order UK: Nmc
Cat. Cost: 3 × 2nd class.
Credit Cards: All major credit/debit cards
Specialities: Rare & unusual shrubs & herbaceous, some from seed collected on plant expeditions each year. Nat. Collection of *Grevillea.*
Map Ref: C, D2 **OS Grid Ref:** SX045527

CPMA **P M A Plant Specialities** ⊠ € ✈
Junker's Nursery Ltd., Lower Mead, West Hatch, Taunton, Somerset, TA3 5RN
Ⓣ (01823) 480774
Ⓔ karan@junker.co.uk
Ⓦ www.junker.co.uk
Contact: Karan or Nick Junker
Opening Times: Strictly by appt. only.
Min Mail Order UK: Nmc
Min Mail Order EU: Nmc
Cat. Cost: 6 × 2nd class.
Credit Cards: None
Specialities: Choice & unusual shrubs incl. grafted *Acer palmatum*, *Cornus*, *Magnolia* & a wide range of *Daphne*. Small quantities of some hard to propagate plants, esp. daphnes. Reserve orders accepted. Planted areas showing how the plants look growing in "real world" conditions. We propagate and grow all our own plants. **Notes:** Partial wheelchair access. Also sells wholesale.
Map Ref: C, B4 **OS Grid Ref:** ST280203

CPne **Pine Cottage Plants** ⊠ € ✈ ⌂
Pine Cottage, Fourways, Eggesford, Chulmleigh, Devon, EX18 7QZ
Ⓣ (01769) 580076
Ⓜ 07718 505053
Ⓔ pcplants@supanet.com
Ⓦ www.pcplants.co.uk
Contact: Dick Fulcher
Opening Times: Special open weeks for *Agapanthus*, 1000-1500 daily 14th Jul-5th Sep excl. Sun. Other times by appt. only.
Min Mail Order UK: £20.00 + p&p
Min Mail Order EU: £50.00 + p&p
Cat. Cost: 4 × 1st class.
Credit Cards: Maestro MasterCard Visa
Specialities: Nat. Collection of *Agapanthus.* 200+ cvs available.
Notes: Mail order *Agapanthus* from Sep-Jun. Also sells wholesale.
Map Ref: C, B3 **OS Grid Ref:** SS683099

CPom **Pomeroy Plants**
Tower House, Pomeroy Lane, Wingfield, Trowbridge, Wiltshire, BA14 9LJ
Ⓣ (01225) 769551
Ⓜ 07895 096564
Ⓔ drsimonyoung@yahoo.co.uk
Contact: Simon Young
Opening Times: Mar-Nov. Please phone first.
Cat. Cost: 2 × 1st class.
Credit Cards: None
Specialities: Hardy, mainly species, herbaceous perennials. Many unusual and often small numbers. Specialities *Allium*, *Salvia* & shade-lovers, esp. *Epimedium.*
Map Ref: C, B5 **OS Grid Ref:** ST817569

CPou **Pounsley Plants** ⊠ € ♿ ⌂
Pounsley Combe, Spriddlestone, Brixton, Plymouth, Devon, PL9 0DW
Ⓣ (01752) 402873
Ⓜ 07770 758501
Ⓕ (01752) 402873
Ⓔ pou599@aol.com
Ⓦ www.pounsleyplants.com
Contact: Mrs Jane Hollow
Opening Times: Normally 1000-1700 Mon-Sat but please phone first.
Min Mail Order UK: £10.00 + p&p
Min Mail Order EU: £20.00 + p&p
Cat. Cost: 2 × 1st class.
Credit Cards: None
Specialities: Unusual herbaceous perennials,

cottage plants & *Clematis*. Comprehensive range of Old Roses. Large selection of South African monocots.
Notes: Mail order Nov-Feb only. Also sells wholesale.
Map Ref: C, D3 **OS Grid Ref:** SX521538

CPrp **PROPERPLANTS.COM** ⊠ ✈ ⛟
Penknight, Edgcumbe Road, Lostwithiel, Cornwall, PL22 0JD
Ⓣ (01208) 872291
Ⓕ (01208) 872291
Ⓔ info@ProperPlants.com
Ⓦ www.ProperPlants.com
Contact: Sarah Wilks
Opening Times: 1000-1800 or dusk if earlier, Tue & B/hols mid-Mar to end-Sep & by appt.
Min Mail Order UK: Nmc
Min Mail Order EU: Nmc
Cat. Cost: 4 × 1st class.
Credit Cards: All major credit/debit cards
Specialities: Wide range of unusual & easy herbaceous perennials, esp. of South African origin. Ferns & grasses. Less common herbs.
Notes: Partially accessible for wheelchair users.
Map Ref: C, C2 **OS Grid Ref:** SX093596

CPSs **PLANTS FOR THE SENSES** ⊠
Corner Cottage, North Street, Dolton, Winkleigh, Devon, EX19 8QQ
Ⓣ (01805) 804467
Ⓔ michaelross@freenetname.co.uk
Contact: Michael Ross
Opening Times: Not open. Mail order only.
Min Mail Order UK: Nmc
Cat. Cost: 1 × 1st class.
Credit Cards: None
Specialities: Some emphasis on scented plants. Some stock in small quantities only.

CQua **QUALITY DAFFODILS** ⊠ € ✈ ◆
14 Roscarrack Close, Falmouth, Cornwall, TR11 4PJ
Ⓣ (01326) 317959
Ⓕ (01326) 317959
Ⓔ rascamp@daffodils.uk.com
Ⓦ www.qualitydaffodils.com
Contact: R A Scamp
Opening Times: Not open. Mail order only. Viewing by appt. only.
Min Mail Order UK: Nmc
Min Mail Order EU: Nmc
Cat. Cost: 3 × 1st class.
Credit Cards: All major credit/debit cards
Specialities: *Narcissus* hybrids & species. Some stocks are less than 100 bulbs.
Notes: Also sells wholesale.
Map Ref: C, D1

CRea **REALLY WILD FLOWERS** ⊠
H V Horticulture Ltd, Spring Mead, Bedchester, Shaftesbury, Dorset, SP7 0JU
Ⓣ (01747) 811778
Ⓕ 0845 009 1778
Ⓔ info@reallywildflowers.co.uk
Ⓦ www.reallywildflowers.co.uk
Contact: Grahame Dixie
Opening Times: Not open. Mail order only.
Min Mail Order UK: £40.00 + p&p
Cat. Cost: 3 × 1st class.
Credit Cards: All major credit/debit cards
Specialities: Native wild flowers for grasslands, woodlands & wetlands. Seeds, orchids & bulbs. Hedge plants & trees. Advisory & soil analysis services.
Notes: Also sells wholesale. Credit card payment accepted for online orders only.

CRHN **ROSELAND HOUSE NURSERY** ⊠ ⛟
Chacewater, Truro, Cornwall, TR4 8QB
Ⓣ (01872) 560451
Ⓔ clematis@roselandhouse.co.uk
Ⓦ www.roselandhouse.co.uk
Contact: C R Pridham
Opening Times: 1300-1700 Tue & Wed, Apr-Sep. Other times by appt.
Min Mail Order UK: Nmc
Min Mail Order EU: Nmc
Cat. Cost: Online only.
Credit Cards: All major credit/debit cards
Specialities: Climbing & conservatory plants. Nat. Collections of *Clematis viticella* & *Lapageria rosea*. Named *Lapageria* in short supply but occasionally available.
Notes: Garden open to the public. Credit cards accepted from mail order customers only.
Map Ref: C, D1 **OS Grid Ref:** SW752445

CRow **ROWDEN GARDENS** ⊠ ✈ ♿
Brentor, Nr Tavistock, Devon, PL19 0NG
Ⓣ (01822) 810275
Ⓕ (01822) 810275
Ⓔ rowdengardens@btopenworld.com
Ⓦ www.rowdengardens.com
Contact: John R L Carter
Opening Times: By appt only.
Min Mail Order UK: Nmc
Min Mail Order EU: Nmc
Cat. Cost: 6 × 1st class.
Credit Cards: None
Specialities: Aquatics, damp-loving &

KEY
⊠ Mail order to UK or EU ⛟ Delivers to shows
✈ Exports beyond EU € Euro accepted
♿ Accessible by wheelchair ◆ See Display advertisement

C

associated plants incl. rare & unusual varieties. Nat. Collections of *Caltha* & Water *Iris*. Some stock available in small quantities only.
Notes: Also sells wholesale.
Map Ref: C, C3

CRWN **The Really Wild Nursery** ⊠ € ⊠
19 Hoopers Way, Torrington, Devon, EX38 7NS
Ⓣ (01805) 624739
Ⓕ (01805) 624739
Ⓔ thereallywildnursery@yahoo.co.uk
Ⓦ www.thereallywildnursery.co.uk
Contact: Kathryn Moore
Opening Times: Not open. Mail order only.
Min Mail Order UK: £10.00 + p&p
Min Mail Order EU: £20.00 + p&p
Cat. Cost: 3 × 1st class.
Credit Cards: Paypal
Specialities: Wildflowers, bulbs & seeds.
Notes: Mail order all year round, grown to order (plants in pots or plugs). Credit card payment accepted via Paypal online only. Also sells wholesale.

CSam **Sampford Shrubs** ⊠ € ♿
Sampford Peverell, Tiverton, Devon, EX16 7EN
Ⓣ (01884) 821164
Ⓔ via website
Ⓦ www.samshrub.co.uk
Contact: M Hughes-Jones & S Proud
Opening Times: 0900-1700 Mon-Sat, 1000-1600 Sun, Feb-Jun. 0900-1700 Tue-Sat, Jul-Oct.
Cat. Cost: A5 sae.
Credit Cards: All major credit/debit cards
Specialities: Large displays of *Pulmonaria* & *Crocosmia*. Nat. Collection of *Helenium*. Plants suitable for naturalistic schemes.
Notes: Mail order only via dedicated ecommerce website. Despatched Oct-Mar.
Map Ref: C, B4 **OS Grid Ref:** ST043153

CSBt **St Bridget Nurseries Ltd** ⊠ ♿ ⌂
Old Rydon Lane, Exeter, Devon, EX2 7JY
Ⓣ (01392) 873672
Ⓕ (01392) 876710
Ⓔ info@stbridgetnurseries.co.uk
Ⓦ www.stbridgetnurseries.co.uk
Contact: Garden Centre Plant Advice
Opening Times: 0900-1700 Mon-Sat, 1030-1630 Sun. Closed Xmas Day, Boxing Day, New Year's Day & Easter Sunday.
Min Mail Order UK: Nmc
Cat. Cost: Free.
Credit Cards: All major credit/debit cards
Specialities: Large general nursery, with two garden centres.
Notes: Mail order available between Nov & Mar.
Map Ref: C, C4 **OS Grid Ref:** SX955905

CSdC **Sherwood Cottage** €
Newton St Cyres, Exeter, Devon, EX5 5BT
Ⓣ (01392) 851589
Ⓔ vaughan.gallavan@connectfree.co.uk
Contact: Vaughan Gallavan
Opening Times: 1400-1700 Sun with Sherwood Gardens or by appt.
Cat. Cost: 1 × 1st class.
Credit Cards: None
Specialities: Magnolias, trees & shrubs. Nat. Coll. of Knap Hill azaleas. Ghent & species deciduous azaleas. Sherwood Garden new Nat. Collection of *Magnolia*. Stock available in small quantities only.
Map Ref: C, C3 **OS Grid Ref:** SX863967

CSev **Lower Severalls Nursery** ⊠ ♿
Crewkerne, Somerset, TA18 7NX
Ⓣ (01460) 73234
Ⓔ mary@lowerseveralls.co.uk
Ⓦ www.lowerseveralls.co.uk
Contact: Mary R Pring
Opening Times: 1000-1700 Tue, Wed, Fri, Sat, Mar-end Sep. Closed Aug.
Min Mail Order UK: £20.00
Cat. Cost: 4 × 1st class.
Credit Cards: None
Specialities: Herbs, herbaceous.
Notes: Mail order perennials only.
Map Ref: C, B5 **OS Grid Ref:** ST457111

CSil **Silver Dale Nurseries** €
Shute Lane, Combe Martin, Devon, EX34 0HT
Ⓣ (01271) 882539
Ⓔ silverdale.nurseries@virgin.net
Contact: Roger Gilbert
Opening Times: 1000-1700 7 days. Closed Nov-Jan.
Cat. Cost: 4 × 1st class.
Credit Cards: Visa MasterCard EuroCard
Specialities: Nat. Collection of *Fuchsia*. Hardy fuchsias (cultivars and species).
Map Ref: C, B3

CSim **Simpson's Seeds Ltd** ⊠ ♿
The Walled Garden Nursery, Horningsham, Warminster, Wiltshire, BA12 7NT
Ⓣ (01985) 845004
Ⓕ (01985) 845052
Ⓔ sales@simpsonsseeds.co.uk
Ⓦ www.simpsonsseeds.co.uk
Contact: Matthew Simpson
Opening Times: 1000-1700 Wed-Sun, Apr-

May. 1000-1700 Tue-Fri & 1000-1230 Sat, rest of the year.
Credit Cards: Visa MasterCard Switch Maestro
Specialities: Large range of hardy perennials, limited quantities of each. Large range of seeds & vegetable plants. Specialities: tomato & pepper.
Notes: Mail order catalogue currently only for seed & veg plants.
Map Ref: C, B5

CSna **Snape Cottage** ⊠
Chaffeymoor, Bourton, Dorset, SP8 5BZ
Ⓣ (01747) 840330 (evenings only).
Ⓔ ianandangela@snapecottagegarden.co.uk
Ⓦ www.snapestakes.com
Contact: Mrs Angela Whinfield
Opening Times: 1030-1700 last 2 Suns in Feb; 1400-1700 last Sat & Sun in month Mar-Aug incl.
Min Mail Order UK: Nmc
Cat. Cost: Sae.
Credit Cards: None
Specialities: 'Old' forms of many popular garden plants. Plantsman's garden open same time as nursery. Stock available in small quantities. Snape Stakes plant supports.
Notes: Mail order *Galanthus* only. List issued in Feb.
Map Ref: C, B5 **OS Grid Ref:** ST762303

CSpe **Special Plants** ⊠ €
Hill Farm Barn, Greenways Lane, Cold Ashton, Chippenham, Wiltshire, SN14 8LA
Ⓣ (01225) 891686
Ⓔ derry@specialplants.net
Ⓦ www.specialplants.net
Contact: Derry Watkins
Opening Times: 1000-1700 7 days Mar-Oct. Other times please ring first to check.
Min Mail Order UK: £10.00 + p&p
Cat. Cost: 5 × 1st class (A5 sae only for seed list).
Credit Cards: All major credit/debit cards
Specialities: Tender perennials, *Pelargonium*, *Salvia*, *Streptocarpus*, hardy geraniums, *Anemone*, *Erysimum*, *Papaver*, *Viola* & grasses. Many varieties prop. in small numbers only.
Notes: Mail order Sep-Mar only.
Map Ref: C, A5 **OS Grid Ref:** ST749726

CSPN **Sherston Parva Nursery** ⊠ € ✈ ♿ ⌂
Malmesbury Road, Sherston, Wiltshire, SN16 0NX
Ⓣ (01666) 840348
Ⓜ 07887 814843
Ⓕ (01666) 840059
Ⓔ sherstonparva@aol.com
Ⓦ www.sherstonparva.com
Contact: Martin Rea
Opening Times: 1000-1700 7 days 1st Feb-31th Dec. Closed Jan.
Min Mail Order UK: Nmc
Min Mail Order EU: Nmc
Cat. Cost: Free.
Credit Cards: MasterCard Delta Visa Switch
Specialities: *Clematis*, wall shrubs & climbers.
Map Ref: C, A5

CSpr **Springfield Plants**
Springfield, Woolsery, Bideford, Devon, EX39 5PZ
Ⓣ (01237) 431162
Ⓔ asta.munro@tiscali.co.uk
Contact: Asta Munro
Opening Times: All year by appt. Please ring for directions.
Cat. Cost: List only, free by email.
Credit Cards: None
Specialities: Hardy perennials for wide variety of situations & plants with interesting foliage. Small quantities only. Hardy geraniums.
Map Ref: C, B2 **OS Grid Ref:** SS347206

CSto **Stone Lane Gardens** ⊠
Stone Farm, Chagford, Devon, TQ13 8JU
Ⓣ (01647) 231311
Ⓔ orders@mythicgarden.eclipse.co.uk
Ⓦ www.stonelanegardens.com
Contact: Paul Bartlett
Opening Times: 0900-1700 Mon-Fri. Collection at w/ends possible. Please phone first if travelling a long distance.
Min Mail Order UK: Nmc
Cat. Cost: £1.75 or 6 × 1st class for colour catalogue with photos.
Credit Cards: None
Specialities: Comprehensive selection of wild origin *Betula* & *Alnus*, both bare-root & in pots. Choice selection of specially grafted cvs. Nat. Collection of Birch & Alder.
Notes: Arboretum open all year with summer sculpture exhibition (charges apply). Planting service available in West Country, details on request. Also sells wholesale.
Map Ref: C, C3 **OS Grid Ref:** SX708908

CStu **Stuckey's Alpines** ⌂
38 Phillipps Avenue, Exmouth, Devon, EX8 3HZ
Ⓣ (01395) 273636
Ⓔ stuckeysalpines@aol.com

KEY
⊠ Mail order to UK or EU ⌂ Delivers to shows
✈ Exports beyond EU € Euro accepted
♿ Accessible by wheelchair ◆ See Display advertisement

C

Contact: Roger & Brenda Stuckey
Opening Times: By appt. only.
Cat. Cost: None issued.
Credit Cards: None
Specialities: Alpines in general. Hardy & half-hardy bulbs. Extensive choice of plants, many available only in small quantities.

CSut **SUTTONS SEEDS** ⊠
Woodview Road, Paignton, Devon, TQ4 7NG
Ⓣ 0844 922 2899
Ⓕ 0844 922 2265
Ⓦ www.suttons.co.uk
Contact: Customer Services
Opening Times: (Office) 0830-1700 Mon-Fri. Also answerphone.
Min Mail Order UK: Nmc
Min Mail Order EU: £5.00
Cat. Cost: Free.
Credit Cards: Visa MasterCard Switch Delta
Specialities: Over 1,000 varieties of flower & vegetable seed, bulbs, plants & sundries.

CSWC **SOUTH WEST CARNIVOROUS PLANTS** ⊠ ✈
Blackwater Nursery, Blackwater Road, Culmstock, Cullompton, Devon, EX15 3HG
Ⓣ (01823) 681669
Ⓕ 0870 705 3083
Ⓔ flytraps@littleshopofhorrors.co.uk
Ⓦ www.littleshopofhorrors.co.uk
Contact: Jenny Pearce & Alistair Pearce
Opening Times: By appt.
Min Mail Order UK: Nmc
Min Mail Order EU: Nmc
Cat. Cost: 2 × 2nd class.
Credit Cards: All major credit/debit cards
Specialities: *Cephalotus*, *Nepenthes*, *Dionea*, *Drosera*, *Darlingtonia*, *Sarracenia*, *Pinguicula* & *Utricularia*. Specialists in hardy carnivorous plants & *Dionea muscipula* cvs.
Map Ref: C, B4

CSWP **SONIA WRIGHT PLANTS** ♿ ⌂
Buckerfields Nursery, Ogbourne St George, Marlborough, Wiltshire, SN8 1SG
Ⓣ (01672) 841065
Ⓕ (01672) 541047
Contact: Sonia Wright & Alison Gee
Opening Times: 1000-1800 Tue-Sat.
Cat. Cost: None issued.
Credit Cards: All major credit/debit cards
Specialities: Grasses, *Iris*, *Euphorbia*, *Penstemon*, old roses.
Notes: Credit cards not accepted over the phone.
Map Ref: C, A6

CTca **TRECANNA NURSERY** ⊠ ⌂
Rose Farm, Latchley, Nr Gunnislake, Cornwall, PL18 9AX
Ⓣ (01822) 834680
Ⓜ 07785 242148
Ⓔ mark@trecanna.com
Ⓦ www.trecanna.com
Contact: Mark Wash
Opening Times: 1000-1700 Wed-Sat all year.
Min Mail Order UK: £20
Min Mail Order EU: £40
Cat. Cost: £1.00
Credit Cards: All major credit/debit cards
Specialities: Hardy South African plants. Good collections of *Crocosmia*, *Eucomis*, *Kniphofia*, *Watsonia*, *Crinum*, *Albuca*, nerines, *Zantedeschia*, *Lachenalia* & *Moraea*. Wide range of dry bulbs from around the globe.
Notes: Talks to garden societies, tours of the nursery. Partial wheelchair access.
Map Ref: C, C3 **OS Grid Ref:** SX247733

CTgr **TREGREHAN GARDEN** ♿
Tregrehan Garden Cottages & Nursery, Par, Cornwall, PL24 2SJ
Ⓣ (01726) 812438
Ⓕ (01726) 814389
Ⓔ info@tregrehan.org
Ⓦ www.tregrehan.org
Contact: Tom Hudson
Opening Times: 1030-1700 Wed-Sun, mid-Mar-end May. 1300-1630 Wed only, Jun-Aug. Other times by appt.
Credit Cards: None
Specialities: *Camellia*, *Rhododendron*, *Nothofagus*, *Myosotidium*, tender trees & shrubs.
Notes: Also sells wholesale (*Camellia*: cuttings & large plants).
Map Ref: C, D2 **OS Grid Ref:** SX0553

CTho **THORNHAYES NURSERY** ⊠ €
St Andrews Wood, Dulford, Cullompton, Devon, EX15 2DF
Ⓣ (01884) 266746
Ⓕ (01884) 266739
Ⓔ trees@thornhayes-nursery.co.uk
Ⓦ www.thornhayes-nursery.co.uk
Contact: K D Croucher
Opening Times: 0800-1600 Mon-Fri. 0930-1400 Sat (Sep-Apr).
Min Mail Order UK: £100
Min Mail Order EU: £100
Credit Cards: All major credit/debit cards
Specialities: A broad range of forms of ornamental, amenity & fruit trees incl. West Country apple varieties.

Notes: Limited wheelchair access. Also sells wholesale.
Map Ref: C, C4

CTrC **TREVENA CROSS NURSERIES** ☒ € ♿
Breage, Helston, Cornwall, TR13 9PY
Ⓣ (01736) 763880
Ⓕ (01736) 762828
Ⓔ sales@trevenacross.co.uk
Ⓦ www.trevenacross.co.uk
Contact: Graham Jeffery, John Eddy
Opening Times: 0900-1700 Mon-Sat, 1030-1630 Sun.
Min Mail Order UK: Nmc
Cat. Cost: Online only.
Credit Cards: Access Visa Switch
Specialities: South African, Australian & New Zealand plants, incl. *Aloe*, *Protea*, tree ferns, palms, *Restio*, hardy succulents & wide range of other exotics.
Map Ref: C, D1 **OS Grid Ref:** SW614284

CTrh **TREHANE CAMELLIA NURSERY** ☒ ♿ ⛺
J Trehane & Sons Ltd, Stapehill Road, Hampreston, Wimborne, Dorset, BH21 7ND
Ⓣ (01202) 873490
Ⓕ (01202) 873490
Ⓔ camellias@trehanenursery.co.uk
Ⓦ www.trehanenursery.co.uk
Contact: Lorraine or Jeanette
Opening Times: 0900-1630 Mon-Fri all year (excl. Xmas & New Year). 1000-1600 Sat-Sun in spring & by special appt.
Min Mail Order UK: Nmc
Cat. Cost: £1.50 cat./book.
Credit Cards: All major credit/debit cards
Specialities: Extensive range of *Camellia* species, cultivars & hybrids. Many new introductions. Evergreen azaleas, *Pieris*, *Magnolia* & blueberries.
Notes: Also sells wholesale.
Map Ref: C, C6 **OS Grid Ref:** SU059000

CTri **TRISCOMBE NURSERIES** ☒ ♿ ◆
West Bagborough, Nr Taunton, Somerset, TA4 3HG
Ⓣ (01984) 618267
Ⓔ triscombe.nurseries2000@virgin.net
Ⓦ www.triscombenurseries.co.uk
Contact: S Parkman
Opening Times: 0900-1730 Mon-Sat. 1400-1730 Sun & B/hols.
Min Mail Order UK: Nmc
Cat. Cost: 1 × 1st class.
Credit Cards: None
Specialities: Trees, shrubs, roses, fruit, *Clematis*, herbaceous & rock plants.
Map Ref: C, B4

CTsd **TRESEDERS** ☒ ♿
Wallcottage Nursery, Lockengate, St. Austell, Cornwall, PL26 8RU
Ⓣ (01208) 832234
Ⓔ Treseders@btconnect.com
Ⓦ www.treseders.co.uk
Contact: James Treseder
Opening Times: 1000-1700 Mon-Sat, 1000-1600 Sun.
Min Mail Order UK: Nmc
Cat. Cost: Plant list available on request.
Credit Cards: All major credit/debit cards
Specialities: A wide range of choice & unusual plants grown in peat-free compost, incl. 200+ *Fuchsia* varieties.
Notes: Also sells wholesale.
Map Ref: C, C2 **OS Grid Ref:** SX034620

CTuc **EDWIN TUCKER & SONS** ☒ ♿
Brewery Meadow, Stonepark, Ashburton, Newton Abbot, Devon, TQ13 7DG
Ⓣ (01364) 652233
Ⓕ (01364) 654211
Ⓔ seeds@edwintucker.com
Ⓦ www.edwintucker.com
Contact: Geoff Penton
Opening Times: 0800-1700 Mon-Fri, 0800-1600 Sat.
Min Mail Order UK: Nmc
Min Mail Order EU: Nmc
Cat. Cost: Free.
Credit Cards: All major credit/debit cards
Specialities: Nearly 120 varieties of seed potatoes, incl. 50 organic varieties. Wide range of vegetables, flowers, green manures & sprouting seeds in packets. None treated. Nearly 200 varieties of organically produced seeds.
Notes: Also sells wholesale.

CWan **WANBOROUGH HERB NURSERY** ♿ ⛺
Callas Hill, Wanborough, Swindon, Wiltshire, SN4 0AG
Ⓣ (01793) 790327 (answering machine)
Ⓔ wanboroughnursery@btinternet.com
Ⓦ www.wanboroughherbnursery.moonfruit.com
Contact: Peter Biggs
Opening Times: By appt. only.
Cat. Cost: £1.00
Credit Cards: None
Specialities: Herbs, herbaceous, esp. culinary. Available in small quantities only.
Map Ref: C, A6 **OS Grid Ref:** SU217828

KEY
☒ Mail order to UK or EU ⛺ Delivers to shows
✈ Exports beyond EU € Euro accepted
♿ Accessible by wheelchair ◆ See Display advertisement

C

CWat The Water Garden ☒ ⬚
Hinton Parva, Swindon, Wiltshire, SN4 0DH
Ⓣ (01793) 790558
Ⓕ (01793) 791298
Ⓔ mike@thewatergarden.co.uk
Ⓦ www.thewatergarden.co.uk
Contact: Mike & Anne Newman
Opening Times: 1000-1700 Wed-Sun.
Min Mail Order UK: £10.00 + p&p
Cat. Cost: 4 × 1st class.
Credit Cards: Visa Access Switch
Specialities: Water lilies, marginal & moisture plants, oxygenators & alpines.
Notes: Also sells wholesale.
Map Ref: C, A6

CWCL Westcountry Nurseries ☒ ⬚ ⋔
Donkey Meadow, Woolsery, Devon, EX39 5QH
Ⓣ (01237) 431111
Ⓕ (01237) 431111
Ⓔ info@westcountry-nurseries.co.uk
Ⓦ www.westcountry-nurseries.co.uk
Contact: Sarah Conibear
Opening Times: 1000-1700 Mar-Sep.
Min Mail Order UK: £10.00
Cat. Cost: 2 × 1st class + A5 sae for full colour cat.
Credit Cards: All major credit/debit cards
Specialities: *Lupinus*, *Lewisia*, *Hellebore*, *Clematis*, cyclamen, acers, lavender, select perennials, grasses, ferns & climbers. Nat. Collection of Lupins.
Map Ref: C, B2 **OS Grid Ref:** SS351219

CWGN Walled Garden Nursery ☒ ⬚
Brinkworth House, Brinkworth,
Nr Malmesbury, Wiltshire, SN15 5DF
Ⓣ (01666) 826637
Ⓔ f.wescott@btinternet.com
Ⓦ www.clematis-nursery.co.uk
Contact: Fraser Wescott
Opening Times: 1000-1700, 7 days Mar-Oct. 1000-dusk, Mon-Fri Nov & Feb. Closed Dec & Jan.
Cat. Cost: 2 × 1st class.
Credit Cards: All major credit/debit cards
Specialities: *Clematis* & climbers, with a selection of unusual perennials & shrubs.
Map Ref: C, A6 **OS Grid Ref:** SU002849

CWib Wibble Farm Nurseries ☒ ⬚
Wibble Farm, West Quantoxhead,
Nr Taunton, Somerset, TA4 4DD
Ⓣ (01984) 632303
Ⓕ (01984) 633168
Ⓔ sales@wibblefarmnurseries.co.uk
Ⓦ www.wibblefarmnurseries.co.uk
Contact: Mrs M L Francis

Opening Times: 0800-1700 Mon-Fri, 1000-1600 Sat. 1400-1600 Sun. All year excl. B/hols.
Min Mail Order UK: Nmc
Min Mail Order EU: Nmc
Cat. Cost: 3 × 1st class.
Credit Cards: All major credit/debit cards
Specialities: Growers of a wide range of hardy plants, many rare & unusual. Display gardens.
Notes: Also sells wholesale.
Map Ref: C, B4

CWil Fernwood Nursery ☒ € ☒ ⬚ ⋔
Peters Marland, Torrington, Devon, EX38 8QG
Ⓣ (01805) 601446
Ⓔ hw@fernwood-nursery.co.uk
Ⓦ www.fernwood-nursery.co.uk
Contact: Howard Wills & Sally Wills
Opening Times: Any time by appt. Please phone or email first.
Min Mail Order UK: Nmc
Min Mail Order EU: Nmc
Cat. Cost: Sae for list.
Credit Cards: None
Specialities: Nat. Collection of *Sempervivum*, *Jovibarba*, *Rosularia* & *Phormium*.
Notes: Mail order for *Sempervivum*, *Jovibarba* & *Rosularia* only. 5 miles from RHS Rosemoor.
Map Ref: C, C3 **OS Grid Ref:** SS479133

CWit Withleigh Nurseries ◆
Withleigh, Tiverton, Devon, EX16 8JG
Ⓣ (01884) 253351
Ⓔ Withleigh@aol.com
Ⓦ www.withleighnurseries.co.uk
Contact: Terry Watling
Opening Times: 0900-1730 Mon-Sat, Mar-Jun, Tue-Sat, Jul-Feb. 1000-1600 Sun, Apr-Jun.
Cat. Cost: None issued.
Credit Cards: All major credit/debit cards
Specialities: Shrubs & herbaceous.
Map Ref: C, B4

CWiW Windrush Willow ☒ € ☒
Higher Barn, Sidmouth Road, Aylesbeare,
Exeter, Devon, EX5 2JJ
Ⓣ (01395) 233669
Ⓕ (01395) 233669
Ⓔ windrushw@aol.com
Ⓦ www.windrushwillow.com
Contact: Richard Kerwood
Opening Times: Mail order only. Open by appt.
Min Mail Order UK: Nmc
Min Mail Order EU: Nmc
Cat. Cost: 2 × 1st class.
Credit Cards: None

Specialities: *Salix*. Unrooted cuttings available Dec-Mar.
Notes: Also sells wholesale.

CWon **The Wonder Tree** ⊠ ⌂
35 Beaconsfield Road, Knowle, Bristol, BS4 2JE
Ⓣ 0117 908 9057
Ⓜ 07989 333507
Ⓔ Kevin@wondertree.co.uk
Ⓦ www.wondertree.co.uk
Contact: Kevin Lindegaard
Opening Times: Not open. Mail order only.
Min Mail Order UK: £8.00
Cat. Cost: Online only.
Credit Cards: Nochex
Specialities: *Salix*.
Notes: Also sells wholesale.

CWri **Nigel Wright Rhododendrons** ♿
The Old Glebe, Eggesford, Chulmleigh, Devon, EX18 7QU
Ⓣ (01769) 580632
Ⓔ wrightrhodos@aol.com
Ⓦ www.wrightrhodos.com
Contact: Nigel Wright
Opening Times: By appt. only. 7 days.
Cat. Cost: 2 × 1st class.
Credit Cards: None
Specialities: *Rhododendron* & deciduous azaleas. 200 varieties field grown, root-balled, some potted. For collection only. Specialist grower. Free advice & planting plans.
Notes: Also sells wholesale.
Map Ref: C, B3 **OS Grid Ref:** SS684106

CWSG **West Somerset Garden Centre** ⊠ ♿
Mart Road, Minehead, Somerset, TA24 5BJ
Ⓣ (01643) 703812
Ⓕ (01643) 706476
Ⓔ wsgc@btconnect.com
Ⓦ www.westsomersetgardencentre.co.uk
Contact: Ms J K Shoulders
Opening Times: 0800-1700 Mon-Sat, 1000-1600 Sun.
Min Mail Order UK: Nmc
Cat. Cost: None issued.
Credit Cards: Visa Solo Maestro MasterCard
Specialities: Wide general range. *Ceanothus*.
Map Ref: C, B4

CWVF **White Veil Fuchsias** ⊠ ♿
Verwood Road, Three Legged Cross, Wimborne, Dorset, BH21 6RP
Ⓣ (01202) 813998
Contact: A. C. Holloway
Opening Times: 0900-1300 & 1400-1700 Mon-Sat, 1000-1300 & 1400-1600 Sun, Jan-Aug. Closed Sat & Sun, Sep-Dec.
Min Mail Order UK: 8 plants of your choice.
Cat. Cost: 4 × 1st class.
Credit Cards: None
Specialities: Fuchsias. Small plants grown from Jan-Apr. Available in small quantities only.
Notes: Also sells wholesale.

CYeo **South Yeo Nursery** ⊠
Poughill, Crediton, Devon, EX17 4LF
Ⓣ (01363) 866740
Ⓜ 07971 412132
Ⓕ (01363) 866740
Ⓔ davidross@eclecticplants.co.uk
Ⓦ www.eclecticplants.co.uk
Contact: David & Penny Ross
Opening Times: Mostly mail order but open most of the year. Please phone for directions.
Min Mail Order UK: Nmc
Min Mail Order EU: Nmc
Cat. Cost: 6 × 1st class
Credit Cards: Paypal
Specialities: Small, family-run nursery specialising in South African & other plants. *Schizostylis*, *Agapanthus*, *Dierama*, *Crocosmia* & *Rhodohypoxis*. Also unusual alpines & other perennials.
Notes: Nursery located in Grade II* listed traditional Devon courtyard.
Map Ref: C, C3

Eastern

EABi **Alison Bilverstone** ⊠ €
22 Kings Street, Swaffham, Norfolk, PE37 7BU
Ⓣ (01760) 725026
Ⓔ a.bilverstone@tiscali.co.uk
Contact: Alison Bilverstone
Opening Times: Not open. Mail order only.
Min Mail Order UK: Nmc
Min Mail Order EU: Nmc
Cat. Cost: A4 sae.
Credit Cards: None
Specialities: *Achemene*, *Kohleria* & *Smithiantha* rhizomes, available Dec to mid-Apr. Stocked in small quantities.

EACa **Alpine Campanulas** ⊠ ⌂
Langham Hall Walled Garden, Langham, Nr Bury St Edmunds, Suffolk, IP31 3EE
Ⓜ 07879 644958
Ⓔ campanulas@btinternet.com

KEY
⊠ Mail order to UK or EU ⌂ Delivers to shows
✈ Exports beyond EU € Euro accepted
♿ Accessible by wheelchair ◆ See Display advertisement

E

E

Ⓦ www.alpinecampanulas.co.uk
Contact: Sue Wooster
Opening Times: 1000-1600 Thu & Fri, 2nd Apr-2nd Oct. Other times by appt. only.
Min Mail Order UK: £10.00
Cat. Cost: Sae or online.
Credit Cards: Paypal
Specialities: *Campanula*. Nat. Collection of Alpine Campanulas. Stock in small numbers only.
Notes: Nursery at the Walled Garden, Langham Hall, nr Bury St Edmunds, Suffolk.
Map Ref: E, C3 **OS Grid Ref:** TL978691

EAEE **AEE** ⊠
38 Church Close, Roydon,
Diss, Norfolk, IP22 5RQ
Ⓣ (01379) 651230
Ⓕ (01379) 651230
Ⓔ aeeloverofplants@fsmail.net
Ⓦ www.aeesupplyingplantlovers.com
Contact: Anne Etheridge
Opening Times: Plant stall 1000-1500 Wed-Thu & Sun, Mar-Sep at Roydon White Hart Garden, Roydon, Norfolk (off A1066).
Min Mail Order UK: Nmc.
Min Mail Order EU: Nmc.
Cat. Cost: 2 × 1st class.
Credit Cards: Paypal
Specialities: Perennials & grasses plus a few enticing alpines & shrubs. Alpines & shrubs available in small quantities only.
Notes: Garden maintenance, spring & autumn pruning. Talks available. Plants may be reserved for collection with a £5.00 deposit. Wheelchair access at plant stall site.

EAmu **Amulree Exotics** ⊠ ♿ ⌂
The Turnpike, Norwich Road (B1113),
Fundenhall, Norwich, Norfolk,
NR16 1EL
Ⓣ (01508) 488101
Ⓔ SDG@exotica.fsbusiness.co.uk
Ⓦ www.turn-it-tropical.co.uk
Contact: S Gridley
Opening Times: 0930-1730 7 days spring-autumn, 1000-1630 7 days autumn-spring.
Min Mail Order UK: Nmc
Cat. Cost: 2 × 1st class.
Credit Cards: Visa MasterCard Electron Solo Switch
Specialities: Hardy & half-hardy plants for home, garden & conservatory. Palms, bamboos, bananas, tree ferns, cannas, gingers & much more.
Notes: Also sells wholesale.
Map Ref: E, B3 **OS Grid Ref:** DX123740

EBak **B & H M Baker** ♿
Bourne Brook Nurseries, Greenstead Green, Halstead, Essex, CO9 1RJ
Ⓣ (01787) 476369
Contact: Clive Baker
Opening Times: 0800-1630 Mon-Fri, 0900-1200 & 1400-1630 Sat & Sun, Mar-30th Jun.
Cat. Cost: 2 × 1st class + 33p.
Credit Cards: All major credit/debit cards
Specialities: *Fuchsia* & conservatory plants.
Notes: Also sells wholesale.
Map Ref: E, C2

EBar **Barcham Trees** ⊠ € ⌂
Eye Hill Drove, Ely, Cambridgeshire,
CB7 5XF
Ⓣ (01353) 720748
Ⓕ (01353) 723060
Ⓔ sales@barchamtrees.co.uk
Ⓦ www.barcham.co.uk
Contact: Keith Sacre
Opening Times: 0900-1700 Mon-Fri. Visits to the nursery by appt. only.
Min Mail Order UK: Nmc
Cat. Cost: Free.
Credit Cards: All major credit/debit cards
Specialities: Containerised trees.
Notes: Also sells wholesale. E-commerce site: www.barchamon-line.co.uk.
Map Ref: E, C2

EBee **Beeches Nursery** ⊠ ♿
Village Centre, Ashdon, Saffron Walden, Essex, CB10 2HB
Ⓣ (01799) 584362
Ⓕ (01799) 584421
Ⓔ sales@beechesnursery.co.uk
Ⓦ www.beechesnursery.co.uk
Contact: Alan Bidwell/Kevin Marsh
Opening Times: 0830-1700 Mon-Sat, 1000-1700 Sun & B/hols.
Min Mail Order UK: £12.00
Min Mail Order EU: £20.00
Cat. Cost: 6 × 2nd class for herbaceous list.
Credit Cards: Visa Access MasterCard Switch
Specialities: Herbaceous specialists & extensive range of other garden plants. Rarieties available in ltd. numbers only.
Notes: Plants dispatched Oct-Feb only. Orders accepted throughout the year. No trees by mail order.
Map Ref: E, C2 **OS Grid Ref:** TL586420

EBla **Blacksmiths Cottage Nursery** ⊠ ♿ ⌂
Langmere Road, Langmere, Dickleburgh,
Nr Diss, Norfolk, IP21 4QA
Ⓣ (01379) 741136/740982
Ⓔ Blackcottnursery@aol.com

Ⓦ www.blackcottnursery.co.uk
Contact: Ben or Jill Potterton
Opening Times: 1000-1700 Thu-Sun & B/hol Mon, Mar-Oct.
Min Mail Order UK: Nmc
Cat. Cost: Online only.
Credit Cards: All major credit/debit cards
Specialities: Over 2000 species grown. Large selection of shade plants esp. *Anemone nemorosa* & *Poygonatum*, also large collection of *Geranium*, *Astrantia* & *Sanguisorba*.
Notes: Coffee Shop & toilets. Barn Garden & bird collection. Group visits by appt.
Map Ref: E, C3 **OS Grid Ref:** TM192821

EBls **Peter Beales Roses** ⊠ ✈ ♿ ⛺
London Road, Attleborough, Norfolk,
NR17 1AY
Ⓣ (01953) 454707 or 0845 4810277
Ⓕ (01953) 456845
Ⓔ info@peterbealesroses.co.uk
Ⓦ www.peterbealesroses.co.uk
Contact: Customer Advisers
Opening Times: 0900-1700 Mon-Sat, 1000-1600 Sun & B/hols.
Min Mail Order UK: Nmc
Min Mail Order EU: Nmc
Cat. Cost: Free to UK. Outside UK £5.00.
Credit Cards: All, except American Express
Specialities: Old fashioned roses & classic roses. Nat. Collection of Species Roses. Some stock available in small quantities only. Other plants on site.
Notes: Shop & bistro.
Map Ref: E, C3 **OS Grid Ref:** TM026929

EBrs **Bressingham Gardens (incorp. Van Tubergen UK)** ⊠ ♿
Bressingham, Diss, Norfolk,
IP22 2AG
Ⓣ (01379) 688282
Ⓕ (01379) 687227
Ⓔ info@bressinghamgardens.com
Ⓦ www.bressinghamgardens.com
Contact: Fiona-Louise Tilden
Opening Times: Mail order 0900-1700 Mon-Fri. Gardens open daily 1030-1730 1st Apr-31st Oct.
Min Mail Order UK: Nmc
Min Mail Order EU: £100
Cat. Cost: None issued.
Credit Cards: Maestro Visa Access MasterCard
Specialities: Bulbs, grafted conifers, grasses & perennials. Nat. Collection of *Miscanthus*.
Notes: Also sells wholesale.
Map Ref: E, C3 **OS Grid Ref:** TM071807

EBtc **Botanica** ⊠
Chantry Farm, Campsea Ashe,
Wickham Market, Suffolk,
IP13 0PZ
Ⓣ (01728) 747113
Ⓕ (01728) 747725
Ⓔ tlc-botanica@btconnect.com
Ⓦ www.botanica.org.uk
Contact: Jon Rose
Opening Times: 1000-1700 6 days summer, 1000-1600 7 days winter.
Min Mail Order UK: Nmc
Min Mail Order EU: £20.00 + p&p
Cat. Cost: 6 × 1st class.
Credit Cards: None
Specialities: Range of rare & unusual hardy plants.
Notes: Also sells wholesale.
Map Ref: E, C3

EBur **Jenny Burgess** ♿
Alpine Nursery, Sisland, Norwich, Norfolk,
NR14 6EF
Ⓣ (01508) 520724
Contact: Jenny Burgess
Opening Times: Any time by appt.
Cat. Cost: None issued.
Credit Cards: None
Specialities: Alpines, *Sisyrinchium* & *Campanula*. Nat. Collection of *Sisyrinchium*.
Map Ref: E, B3

EBWF **British Wild Flower Plants** ⊠ € ♿
Burlingham Gardens, 31 Main Road,
North Burlingham, Norfolk,
NR13 4TA
Ⓣ (01603) 716615
Ⓕ (01603) 716615
Ⓔ office@wildflowers.co.uk
Ⓦ www.wildflowers.co.uk
Contact: Matt Smith
Opening Times: 1000-1600 Mon-Fri. Weekends by appt. Office: 0900-1700 Mon-Fri. Visitors by appt. only.
Min Mail Order UK: Nmc
Min Mail Order EU: Nmc
Cat. Cost: £2.00 + p&p
Credit Cards: All major credit/debit cards
Specialities: Native wild flowers. 400 species. Quantities vary from 1 to 50,000.
Notes: Also sells wholesale.
Map Ref: E, B3 **OS Grid Ref:** TG371101

KEY
⊠ Mail order to UK or EU ⛺ Delivers to shows
✈ Exports beyond EU € Euro accepted
♿ Accessible by wheelchair ◆ See Display advertisement

E

ECGP **Cambridge Garden Plants** ♿
The Lodge, Clayhithe Road,
Horningsea, Cambridgeshire,
CB25 9JD
Ⓣ (01223) 861370
Ⓔ kit@cambridgegardenplants.co.uk
Contact: Kit Buchdahl
Opening Times: 1100-1730 Thu-Sun mid Mar-31st Oct. Other times by appt.
Cat. Cost: 4 × 1st class.
Credit Cards: None
Specialities: Hardy perennials incl. wide range of *Geranium*, *Allium*, *Euphorbia*, *Cyclamen*, *Digitalis*. Also old roses.
Map Ref: E, C2 **OS Grid Ref:** TL497637

ECha **The Beth Chatto Gardens Ltd** ✉ ♿
Elmstead Market,
Colchester, Essex,
CO7 7DB
Ⓣ (01206) 822007
Ⓕ (01206) 825933
Ⓔ info@bethchatto.fsnet.co.uk
Ⓦ www.bethchatto.co.uk
Contact: Beth Chatto
Opening Times: 0900-1700 Mon-Sat, 1000-1700 Sun, 1st Mar-31st Oct. 0900-1600 Mon-Fri, 1000-1600 Sun, 1st Nov-end Feb.
Min Mail Order UK: £20.00
Min Mail Order EU: Ask for details
Cat. Cost: Free plant list.
Credit Cards: Visa MasterCard Maestro
Specialities: Predominantly herbaceous. Many unusual for special situations.
Map Ref: E, D3 **OS Grid Ref:** TM069238

ECho **Choice Landscapes** ✉ ✈ ♿ ⌂
Priory Farm, 101 Salts Road, West Walton,
Wisbech, Cambridgeshire,
PE14 7EF
Ⓣ (01945) 585051
Ⓕ (01945) 580053
Ⓔ info@choicelandscapes.org
Ⓦ www.choicelandscapes.org
Contact: Michael Agg & Jillian Agg
Opening Times: 1000-1300 & 1400-1730 Tue-Sat, 10th Feb-30th Oct 2009. Not open on show dates, please phone. Other times by appt.
Min Mail Order UK: Nmc
Min Mail Order EU: £10.00 + p&p
Cat. Cost: 6 × 1st class or 6 IRC
Credit Cards: Maestro Visa MasterCard Solo
Specialities: Dwarf conifers, alpines, acers, rhododendrons, bulbs, pines, lilies & South African bulbs & seed.
Map Ref: E, B1

ECnt **Cants of Colchester** ✉ ✈ ♿
Nayland Road, Mile End, Colchester, Essex,
CO4 5EB
Ⓣ (01206) 844008
Ⓕ (01206) 855371
Ⓔ finder@cantsroses.co.uk
Ⓦ www.cantsroses.co.uk
Contact: Angela Pawsey
Opening Times: 0900-1300, 1400-1630 Mon-Fri. Sat varied, please phone first. Sun closed.
Min Mail Order UK: Nmc
Min Mail Order EU: Nmc
Cat. Cost: Free
Credit Cards: Visa MasterCard Delta Solo Switch
Specialities: Roses. Unstaffed rose field can be viewed dawn-dusk every day from end Jun-end Sep.
Notes: Bare-root mail order end Oct-end Mar, containers Apr-Aug. Partial wheelchair access.
Map Ref: E, C3

ECou **County Park Nursery**
Essex Gardens, Hornchurch, Essex, RM11 3BU
Ⓣ (01708) 445205
Ⓦ www.countyparknursery.co.uk
Contact: G Hutchins
Opening Times: 1000-1700 Mon-Sat excl. Wed, 1000-1700 Sun Mar-Oct. Nov-Feb by appt. only.
Cat. Cost: 3 × 1st class
Credit Cards: None
Specialities: Alpines & rare and unusual plants from New Zealand, Tasmania & the Falklands. Many plants in small quantities only.
Map Ref: E, D2

ECrc **The Crocosmia Gardens** ✉
9 North Street, Caistor, Lincolnshire,
LN7 6QU
Ⓣ (01472) 859269
Ⓜ 07506 441205
Ⓔ crocosmia@tiscali.co.uk
Ⓦ www.simplesite.com/crocosmia
Contact: Mark Fox
Opening Times: 0800-1900 Mon-Sat.
Min Mail Order UK: Nmc
Min Mail Order EU: Nmc
Credit Cards: None
Specialities: Nat. Collection of *Crocosmia*.
Map Ref: E, A1

ECre **Creake Plant Centre** ♿
Nursery View, Leicester Road, South Creake,
Fakenham, Norfolk, NR21 9PW
Ⓣ (01328) 823018
Contact: Mr T Harrison

Opening Times: 1000-1300 & 1400-1730 7 days excl. Xmas.
Cat. Cost: None issued
Credit Cards: All major credit/debit cards
Specialities: Unusual shrubs, herbaceous, conservatory plants, old roses. Hellebores.
Map Ref: E, B1 **OS Grid Ref:** TF864353

ECrN **Crown Nursery** ⊠ ♿
High Street, Ufford, Suffolk,
IP13 6EL
Ⓣ (01394) 460755
Ⓕ (01394) 460142
Ⓔ enquiries@crown-nursery.co.uk
Ⓦ www.crown-nursery.co.uk
Contact: Jill Proctor
Opening Times: 0900-1700 (1600 in winter) Mon-Sat.
Min Mail Order UK: Nmc
Cat. Cost: 2 × 1st class.
Credit Cards: All major credit/debit cards
Specialities: Mature & semi-mature native, ornamental & fruit trees. Heritage fruit varieties.
Notes: Mail order for small/young stock only. Also sells wholesale.
Map Ref: E, C3 **OS Grid Ref:** TM292528

ECtt **Cottage Nurseries** ⊠ ♿
Thoresthorpe, Alford, Lincolnshire,
LN13 0HX
Ⓣ (01507) 466968
Ⓕ (01507) 463409
Ⓔ bill@cottagenurseries.net
Ⓦ www.cottagenurseries.net
Contact: W H Denbigh
Opening Times: 0900-1700 7 days 1st Mar-31st Oct, 1000-1600 w/ends only Nov-Feb.
Min Mail Order UK: Nmc
Cat. Cost: 3 × 1st class.
Credit Cards: Visa MasterCard Maestro
Specialities: Hardy perennials. Wide general range.
Map Ref: E, A2 **OS Grid Ref:** TF423716

EDAr **D'Arcy & Everest** ⊠ € ♿ ⛺
(Office) PO Box 78, St Ives, Huntingdon, Cambridgeshire, PE27 4ZA
Ⓣ (01480) 497672 answerphone
Ⓜ 07715 374440/1
Ⓕ (01480) 466042
Ⓔ angela@darcyeverest.co.uk
Ⓦ www.darcyeverest.co.uk
Contact: Angela Whiting, Richard Oliver
Opening Times: Wed-Fri, Mar-Sep, except show dates. Coach parties welcome by appt.
Min Mail Order UK: £10.00 + p&p
Min Mail Order EU: £10.00 + p&p
Cat. Cost: 6 × 1st class.
Credit Cards: None
Specialities: Alpines, sempervivums & selected perennials.
Notes: Nursery is at Pidley Sheep Lane (B1040), Somersham, Huntingdon, Cambs.
Map Ref: E, C2 **OS Grid Ref:** TL533276

EDif **Different Plants** ♿ ⛺
The Mellis Stud, Gate Farm,
Cranley Green, Eye, Suffolk,
IP23 7NX
Ⓣ (01379) 870291
Ⓔ nickwtrs@talktalk.net
Contact: Fleur Waters
Opening Times: Sat-Thu by appt. only, closed Fri. Plant stall Eye market Fri 0900-1200.
Cat. Cost: 4 × 1st class.
Credit Cards: None
Specialities: *Mimulus aurantiacus* & hybrids, half-hardy bulbous/cormous perennials incl. *Dietes*, *Aristea*, *Cypella*, *Tigridia* & *Anomatheca laxa*. Bulbs may be available in small quantities only.
Map Ref: E, C3

EECP **Essex Carnivorous Plants** ⊠ ⛺
12 Strangman Avenue, Thundersley, Essex,
SS7 1RB
Ⓣ (01702) 551467
Ⓔ Mark@essexcarnivorousplants.com
Ⓦ www.essexcarnivorousplants.com
Contact: Mark Haslett
Opening Times: By appt. only.
Min Mail Order UK: Nmc
Min Mail Order EU: Nmc
Cat. Cost: 2 × 1st class or online.
Credit Cards: None
Specialities: Good range of carnivorous plants. *Sarracenia*, *Drosera*. Nat. Collection of *Dionaea* forms & cvs. Some stock available in small quantities only. Nat. Collection of *Sarracenia* (hybrids & ssp.).
Notes: Also sells wholesale.
Map Ref: E, D2 **OS Grid Ref:** TQ797875

EExo **The Exotic Garden Company** ⊠ ♿
Saxmundham Road, Aldeburgh, Suffolk,
IP15 5JD
Ⓣ (01728) 454456
Ⓦ http:\\stores.ebay.uk/exoticgardencompany
Contact: Matthew Couchy

KEY
⊠ Mail order to UK or EU ⛺ Delivers to shows
✈ Exports beyond EU € Euro accepted
♿ Accessible by wheelchair ◆ See Display advertisement

E

Opening Times: 1000-1700 Mon-Sat, 1000-1600 Sun, Mar-Oct. 1000-dusk Nov-Dec. Closed Jan-Feb.
Min Mail Order UK: Nmc
Min Mail Order EU: Nmc
Cat. Cost: None issued.
Credit Cards: All major credit/debit cards
Specialities: Palms (hardy & half-hardy), bamboos, tree ferns & other exotics. Extensive range of other garden plants, incl. specimens.
Map Ref: E, C3

EFer **The Fern Nursery** ⊠ ♿
Grimsby Road, Binbrook, Lincolnshire, LN8 6DH
Ⓣ (01472) 398092
Ⓔ richard@timm984.fsnet.co.uk
Ⓦ www.fernnursery.co.uk
Contact: R N Timm
Opening Times: 0900-1700 Fri, Sat & Sun Apr-Oct or by appt.
Min Mail Order UK: Nmc
Min Mail Order EU: Nmc
Cat. Cost: 2 × 1st class.
Credit Cards: None
Specialities: Ferns. Display garden.
Notes: Only plants listed in the mail order part of the catalogue will be sent mail order. Also sells wholesale.
Map Ref: E, A1 **OS Grid Ref:** TF212942

EFEx **Flora Exotica** ⊠ €
Pasadena, South-Green, Fingringhoe, Colchester, Essex, CO5 7DR
Ⓣ (01206) 729414
Contact: J Beddoes
Opening Times: Not open. Mail order only.
Min Mail Order UK: Nmc
Min Mail Order EU: Nmc
Cat. Cost: 4 × 1st class.
Credit Cards: None
Specialities: Exotica flora incl. orchids.

EFtx **Fernatix** ⊠ € ♿
Stoke Ash, Suffolk, IP23 7EN
Ⓣ (01379) 678197
Ⓕ (01379) 678197
Ⓔ mail@fernatix.co.uk
Ⓦ www.fernatix.co.uk
Contact: Steven Fletcher & Kerry Robinson
Opening Times: By appt. only.
Min Mail Order UK: £15.00
Cat. Cost: 8 × 1st or 9 × 2nd class for cat.
Credit Cards: None
Specialities: Ferns, hardy & greenhouse species & cultivars. Some available in small quantities only. Mainly hardy ferns.
Map Ref: E, C3

EGFP **Grange Farm Plants** ⊠ ♿
Grange Farm, 38 Fishergate Road, Sutton St James, Spalding, Lincolnshire, PE12 0EZ
Ⓣ (01945) 440240
Ⓜ 07742 138760
Ⓕ (01945) 440355
Ⓔ ellis.family@tinyonline.co.uk
Contact: M C Ellis
Opening Times: Mail order only. Open by appt. only.
Min Mail Order UK: Nmc
Min Mail Order EU: Nmc
Cat. Cost: 1 × 1st class.
Credit Cards: None
Specialities: Rare trees & shrubs, esp. *Juglans*, *Fraxinus*. Some species available in small quantities only.
Map Ref: E, B2 **OS Grid Ref:** TF382186

EGHG **Goltho House Gardens & Nursery** ♿
Lincoln Road, Goltho, Market Rasen, Lincolnshire, LN8 5NF
Ⓣ (01673) 857768
Ⓔ s.hollingworth@homecall.co.uk
Ⓦ www.golthogardens.com
Contact: Debbie Hollingworth
Opening Times: 1000-1600 Sun & Wed only.
Credit Cards: None
Specialities: Hardy herbaceous perennials.
Map Ref: E, A1 **OS Grid Ref:** TF116783

EGln **Glenhirst Cactus Nursery** ⊠ €
Station Road, Swineshead, Nr Boston, Lincolnshire, PE20 3NX
Ⓣ (01205) 820314
Ⓕ (01205) 820614
Ⓔ info@cacti4u.co.uk
Ⓦ www.cacti4u.co.uk
Contact: N C & S A Bell
Opening Times: Visitors welcome, but by telephone appt. only.
Min Mail Order UK: £5.00
Min Mail Order EU: €15.00
Cat. Cost: 2 × 1st class.
Credit Cards: Maestro Visa MasterCard Switch
Specialities: Extensive range of cacti & succulent plants, incl. orchid cacti.
Notes: Will accept payment in euros online only.
Map Ref: E, B1 **OS Grid Ref:** TF245408

EGol **Goldbrook Plants** ⊠
Hoxne, Eye, Suffolk, IP21 5AN
Ⓣ (01379) 668770
Ⓕ (01379) 668770
Contact: Sandra Bond

Opening Times: 1000-1700, Thu-Sun Apr-Sep, or by appt. Closed during Hampton Court Flower Show. Other times by appt.
Min Mail Order UK: £15.00 + p&p
Min Mail Order EU: £100.00 + p&p
Cat. Cost: 4 × 1st class.
Credit Cards: None
Specialities: Very large range of *Hosta* (1100+), *Hemerocallis*.
Notes: Also sells wholesale.
Map Ref: E, C3

EGxp **GARDENING EXPRESS** ⊠
Mashbury Road, Chignal St James, Chelmsford, Essex, CM1 4UA
Ⓣ 08000 336161
Ⓔ order@gardeningexpress.co.uk
Ⓦ www.GardeningExpress.co.uk
Contact: Chris Bonnett
Opening Times: Not open. Mail order only.
Min Mail Order UK: Nmc
Cat. Cost: Online only.
Credit Cards: All major credit/debit cards
Specialities: 4-acre site growing wide range of perenials and shrubs.
Notes: Also sells wholesale.

EHoe **HOECROFT PLANTS** ⊠ € ♿
Severals Grange, Holt Road, Wood Norton, Dereham, Norfolk, NR20 5BL
Ⓣ (01362) 684206
Ⓔ hoecroft@hotmail.co.uk
Ⓦ www.hoecroft.co.uk
Contact: Jane Lister
Opening Times: 1000-1600 Thu-Sun 2nd Apr-1st Nov or by appt.
Min Mail Order UK: Nmc
Min Mail Order EU: Nmc
Cat. Cost: 5 × 2nd class/£1coin.
Credit Cards: None
Specialities: 290 varieties of variegated and 3850 varieties of coloured-leaved plants in all species. 250 grasses. Free entry to display gardens.
Notes: Nursery 2 miles north of Guist on B1110.
Map Ref: E, B3 **OS Grid Ref:** TG008289

EHon **HONEYSOME AQUATIC NURSERY** ⊠
The Row, Sutton, Nr Ely, Cambridgeshire, CB6 2PB
Ⓣ (01353) 778889
Ⓕ (01353) 777291
Ⓔ info@honeysomeaquaticnursery.co.uk
Ⓦ www.honeysomeaquaticnursery.co.uk
Contact: Mrs L S Bond
Opening Times: At all times by appt. only.
Min Mail Order UK: Nmc
Cat. Cost: 2 × 1st class.
Credit Cards: None
Specialities: Hardy aquatic, bog & marginal.
Notes: Also sells wholesale.

EHrv **HARVEYS GARDEN PLANTS** ⊠ € ♿
Great Green, Thurston, Bury St Edmunds, Suffolk, IP31 3SJ
Ⓣ (01359) 233363
Ⓕ (01359) 233363 & answerphone
Ⓔ admin@harveysgardenplants.co.uk
Ⓦ www.harveysgardenplants.co.uk
Contact: Roger Harvey
Opening Times: 0930-1630 Tue-Sat.
Min Mail Order UK: £25 of plants + p&p
Min Mail Order EU: Please enquire.
Cat. Cost: 8 × 2nd class.
Credit Cards: All major credit/debit cards
Specialities: *Helleborus, Anemone, Epimedium, Euphorbia, Eryngium, Galanthus, Astrantia, Pulmonaria* & other herbaceous perennials. Woodland plants.
Map Ref: E, C2 **OS Grid Ref:** 660939

EHul **HULL FARM** ⊠ ♿
Spring Valley Lane, Ardleigh, Colchester, Essex, CO7 7SA
Ⓣ (01206) 230045
Ⓜ 07900 298366
Ⓕ (01206) 230820
Ⓔ conifers.hullfarm@tiscali.co.uk
Ⓦ www.fryersfarmshop.co.uk
Contact: J Fryer & Sons
Opening Times: 1000-1300 & 1400-1600 Mon-Fri. Closed B/hol.
Min Mail Order UK: £50.00 + p&p
Cat. Cost: 5 × 2nd class.
Credit Cards: MasterCard Visa
Specialities: Conifers, grasses.
Notes: Also sells wholesale.
Map Ref: E, C3 **OS Grid Ref:** GR043274

EIri **IRISESONLINE** ⊠
Slade Cottage, Petts Lane, Little Walden, Essex, CB10 1XH
Ⓣ (01799) 526294
Ⓕ (01799) 526294
Ⓔ sales@irisesonline.co.uk
Ⓦ www.irisesonline.co.uk
Contact: Clare Kneen
Opening Times: By appt. only.
Min Mail Order UK: Nmc.
Cat. Cost: 3 × 1st class or online.

KEY
⊠ Mail order to UK or EU — Delivers to shows
Exports beyond EU — € Euro accepted
♿ Accessible by wheelchair — ◆ See Display advertisement

E

Credit Cards: None
Specialities: *Iris*. Small family-run nursery. Some varieties available in small quantities only.
Map Ref: E, C2 **OS Grid Ref:** TL546416

EJRN **John Ray Nursery** € ♿
36 Station Road, Braintree, Essex, CM7 3QJ
Ⓜ 07826 162406
Ⓕ (01376) 322858
Ⓔ johnraynursery@talktalk.net
Contact: Brian James
Opening Times: 0900-1730 Sat, 1030-1630 Sun & B/Hol.
Cat. Cost: None issued.
Credit Cards: None
Specialities: *Pittosporum.*

EJWh **Jill White** ✉ ♿ ⌂
78 Hurst Green, Brightlingsea, Essex, CO7 OEH
Ⓣ (01206) 303547
Contact: Jill White
Opening Times: By appt. only.
Min Mail Order UK: Nmc
Min Mail Order EU: Nmc
Cat. Cost: Sae.
Credit Cards: None
Specialities: *Cyclamen* species esp. *Cyclamen parviflorum. Cyclamen elegans.* Also seed.
Notes: Also sells wholesale.
Map Ref: E, D3 **OS Grid Ref:** TM088171

EKen **Kenwick Farmhouse Nurseries** ✉ ♿ ⌂ ◆
Kenwick Road, Louth, Lincolnshire, LN11 8NW
Ⓣ (01507) 606469
Ⓕ (01507) 606469
Ⓔ info@kenwicknursery.co.uk
Ⓦ www.kenwicknursery.co.uk
Contact: Janet Elmhirst
Opening Times: 0930-1700 (dusk in winter) Tue-Sat, closed Mon except B/hol. 1000-1600 Sun. Closed Jan.
Min Mail Order UK: £12.00
Credit Cards: None
Specialities: Hardy plants, grown in small quantities.
Notes: Mail order only if stock is available.
Map Ref: E, A2 **OS Grid Ref:** TF342853

ELan **Langthorns Plantery** ✉ ♿
High Cross Lane West, Little Canfield, Dunmow, Essex, CM6 1TD
Ⓣ (01371) 872611
Ⓕ 0871 661 4093
Ⓔ info@langthorns.com
Ⓦ www.langthorns.com
Contact: E Cannon
Opening Times: 1000-1700 or dusk (if earlier) 7 days excl. Xmas fortnight.
Min Mail Order UK: £15.00
Cat. Cost: £1.50
Credit Cards: Visa Access Switch MasterCard Delta
Specialities: Wide general range with many unusual plants.
Notes: Mail order anything under 5ft tall.
Map Ref: E, D2 **OS Grid Ref:** TL592204

ELar **Larkspur Nursery** ✉
Fourways, Dog Drove South, Holbeach Drove, Spalding, Lincolnshire, PE12 0SD
Ⓣ (01406) 330830
Ⓔ info@larkspur-nursery.co.uk
Ⓦ www.larkspur-nursery.co.uk
Contact: Ashley Ramsbottom
Opening Times: Mail order only. Open by prior arrangement.
Min Mail Order UK: Nmc
Min Mail Order EU: Nmc
Cat. Cost: 2 × 1st class.
Credit Cards: None
Specialities: Delphiniums & *Abutilon*. Some varieties in small quantities. Order early to avoid disappointment. Also seed for sale.
Notes: Plants despatched from June in 7 or 8cm pots. See website for details.

ELau **Laurel Farm Herbs** ✉ ♿ ⌂
Main Road (A12), Kelsale, Saxmundham, Suffolk, IP13 2RG
Ⓣ (01728) 668223
Ⓔ laurelfarmherbs@aol.com
Ⓦ www.laurelfarmherbs.co.uk
Contact: Chris Seagon
Opening Times: Please phone or check website for opening hours as times can vary.
Min Mail Order UK: 6 plants + p&p
Min Mail Order EU: 12 plants
Cat. Cost: Online only.
Credit Cards: Visa MasterCard Switch Delta
Specialities: Herbs esp. rosemary, thyme, mint & sage.
Notes: Mail orders accepted by email, phone or post. Nursery will be moving in Oct 2009, check website for details.
Map Ref: E, C3

ELon **Long House Plants** ♿
The Long House, Church Road, Noak Hill, Romford, Essex, RM4 1LD
Ⓣ (01708) 371719
Ⓕ (01708) 346649
Ⓔ tim@longhouse-plants.co.uk

Ⓦ www.longhouse-plants.co.uk
Contact: Tim Carter
Opening Times: 1000-1700 Fri, Sat & B/hols, 1000-1600 Sun, beginning Mar-end Sep, or by appt.
Cat. Cost: None issued.
Credit Cards: All major credit/debit cards
Specialities: Interesting range of choice shrubs, grasses & herbaceous perennials. Many unusual varieties.
Map Ref: E, D2 **OS Grid Ref:** TQ554194

EMac **FIRECREST (TREES & SHRUBS NURSERY)** ⊠ € ♿
Hall Road, Little Bealings, Woodbridge, Suffolk, IP13 6LU
Ⓣ (01473) 625937
Ⓕ (01473) 625937
Ⓔ mac@firecrest.org.uk
Ⓦ www.firecrest.org.uk
Contact: Mac McGregor
Opening Times: 0830-1630 Mon-Fri, 1230 Sat.
Min Mail Order UK: Nmc
Cat. Cost: 2 × 1st class (bare root only).
Credit Cards: None
Specialities: Trees & shrubs. Japanese maples.
Notes: Also sells wholesale.

EMal **MARSHALL'S MALMAISONS** ⊠
Hullwood Barn, Shelley, Ipswich, Suffolk, IP7 5RE
Ⓣ (01473) 822400
Ⓜ 07768 454875
Ⓔ jim@malmaisons.plus.com
Contact: J M Marshall/Sarah Cook
Opening Times: By appt. only.
Min Mail Order UK: £24.00 incl. p&p
Min Mail Order EU: £35.00 incl. p&p
Cat. Cost: 1st class sae.
Credit Cards: None
Specialities: Nat. Collections of Malmaison Carnations & Cedric Morris Irises. *Iris* stock only available in small quantities.
Notes: Also sells wholesale.
Map Ref: E, C3 **OS Grid Ref:** TM006394

EMar **LESLEY MARSHALL** ⊠ ♿
Islington Lodge Cottage, Tilney All Saints, King's Lynn, Norfolk, PE34 4SF
Ⓣ (01553) 765103
Ⓔ daylilies@tiscali.co.uk
Ⓦ www.dazzlingdaylilies.co.uk
Contact: Lesley Marshall
Opening Times: 0930-1800 Mon, Wed, Fri-Sun May-Sep.
Min Mail Order UK: Nmc
Cat. Cost: 3 × 1st class.
Credit Cards: None
Specialities: *Hemerocallis* only, new & old varieties. Some varieties available in small quantities.
Notes: Nursery on A47 east of Tilney All Saints.
Map Ref: E, B1

EMic **MICKFIELD HOSTAS** ⊠ € ♿ 🚚
The Poplars, Mickfield, Stowmarket, Suffolk, IP14 5LH
Ⓣ (01449) 711576
Ⓕ (01449) 711576
Ⓔ mickfieldhostas@btconnect.com
Ⓦ www.mickfieldhostas.co.uk
Contact: Mr & Mrs R L C Milton
Opening Times: For specified dates see catalogue or website.
Min Mail Order UK: Nmc
Min Mail Order EU: Nmc
Cat. Cost: 4 × 1st class.
Credit Cards: All, except American Express
Specialities: Holders of Nat. Collection of *Hosta* containing around 2000 varieties. See website for details of cvs held & latest availability. Will split parent plants for customers if practical. Also operates a waiting list for rarities.
Map Ref: E, C3 **OS Grid Ref:** TM136619

EMil **MILL RACE GARDEN CENTRE** ⊠ ♿
New Road, Aldham, Colchester, Essex, CO6 3QT
Ⓣ (01206) 242521
Ⓕ (01206) 242073
Ⓔ avril.hall@millracegardencentre.co.uk
Ⓦ www.millracegardencentre.co.uk
Contact: Annette Bayliss
Opening Times: 0900-1730 7 days.
Min Mail Order UK: £15.00
Credit Cards: All major credit/debit cards
Specialities: Around 4000 varieties of plants always in stock.
Notes: Trees not sent by mail order.
Map Ref: E, C2 **OS Grid Ref:** TL918268

ENBC **NORFOLK BAMBOO COMPANY** ⊠
Vine Cottage, The Drif, Ingoldisthorpe, King's Lynn, Norfolk, PE31 6NW
Ⓣ (01485) 543935
Ⓕ (01485) 543314
Ⓔ Lewdyer@hotmail.com
Ⓦ www.norfolkbamboo.co.uk

KEY		
	⊠ Mail order to UK or EU	🚚 Delivers to shows
	✈ Exports beyond EU	€ Euro accepted
	♿ Accessible by wheelchair	◆ See Display advertisement

E

Contact: Lewis Dyer
Opening Times: 1000-1700 Fri, Apr-Sep, or by appt.
Min Mail Order UK: £10.00 + p&p
Cat. Cost: 1 × 1st class sae for price list.
Credit Cards: None
Specialities: Bamboos.
Map Ref: E, B2 **OS Grid Ref:** TF683333

EOHP **Old Hall Plants** ⊠
1 The Old Hall, Barsham, Beccles, Suffolk, NR34 8HB
Ⓣ (01502) 717475
Ⓔ info@oldhallplants.co.uk
Ⓦ www.oldhallplants.co.uk
Contact: Janet Elliott
Opening Times: By appt. only. Please phone first.
Min Mail Order UK: Nmc
Min Mail Order EU: Nmc
Cat. Cost: 4 × 1st class.
Credit Cards: Paypal
Specialities: A variety of rare herbs, house plants, *Plectranthus* & *Streptocarpus*. Some plants available in small quantities.
Notes: Partial wheelchair access. Paypal accepted for overseas orders only.
Map Ref: E, C3 **OS Grid Ref:** TM395904

EPau **Paugers Plants**
Bury Road, Depden, Bury St Edmunds, Suffolk, IP29 4BU
Ⓣ (01284) 850527
Ⓜ 07906 618603
Contact: Geraldine Arnold
Opening Times: 0900-1730 Wed-Sat, 1000-1700 Sun & B/hols, 1st Mar-30th Nov.
Cat. Cost: None issued.
Credit Cards: None
Specialities: Hardy shrubs & perennials in large or small quantities.
Notes: Also sells wholesale.
Map Ref: E, C2 **OS Grid Ref:** TL783568

EPfP **The Place for Plants** ⊠ €
East Bergholt Place, East Bergholt, Suffolk, CO7 6UP
Ⓣ (01206) 299224
Ⓕ (01206) 299229
Ⓔ sales@placeforplants.co.uk
Ⓦ www.placeforplants.co.uk
Contact: Rupert & Sara Eley
Opening Times: 1000-1700 (or dusk if earlier) 7 days. Closed Easter Sun. Garden open Mar-Oct.
Min Mail Order UK: Nmc
Cat. Cost: 2 × 1st class.
Credit Cards: All major credit/debit cards
Specialities: Wide range of specialist & popular plants. Nat. Collection of Deciduous *Euonymus*. 20 acre mature garden with free access to RHS members during season.
Map Ref: E, C3

EPGN **Park Green Nurseries** ⊠
Wetheringsett, Stowmarket, Suffolk, IP14 5QH
Ⓣ (01728) 860139
Ⓜ 07909 631143
Ⓕ (01728) 861277
Ⓔ nurseries@parkgreen.co.uk
Ⓦ www.parkgreen.co.uk
Contact: Richard & Mary Ford
Opening Times: 1000-1600 Mon-Sat, 1 Mar-30 Sep.
Min Mail Order UK: £3.00
Min Mail Order EU: £5.00
Cat. Cost: 4 × 1st class.
Credit Cards: Visa MasterCard Delta Switch
Specialities: *Hosta*, ornamental grasses & herbaceous.
Notes: Mail order *Hosta* only.
Map Ref: E, C3 **OS Grid Ref:** TM136644

EPla **P W Plants** ⊠
Sunnyside, Heath Road, Kenninghall, Norfolk, NR16 2DS
Ⓣ (01953) 888212
Ⓔ pw@hardybamboo.com
Ⓦ www.hardybamboo.com
Contact: Paul Whittaker
Opening Times: Every Fri & last Sat in every month, plus all Sats Apr-Sep.
Min Mail Order UK: Nmc
Cat. Cost: Online only.
Credit Cards: All major credit/debit cards
Specialities: Bamboos, grasses, choice shrubs & perennials.
Map Ref: E, C3 **OS Grid Ref:** TM036846

EPot **Pottertons Nursery** ⊠ €
Moortown Road, Nettleton, Caistor, Lincolnshire, LN7 6HX
Ⓣ (01472) 851714
Ⓕ (01472) 852580
Ⓔ sales@pottertons.co.uk
Ⓦ www.pottertons.co.uk
Contact: Robert Potterton
Opening Times: 0900-1600 7 days. By appt. only Nov, Dec & Jan.
Min Mail Order UK: Nmc
Min Mail Order EU: Nmc
Cat. Cost: £2.00 in stamps
Credit Cards: Maestro MasterCard Visa
Specialities: Alpines, dwarf bulbs & woodland plants. Hardy orchids & *Pleione*.

Notes: External talks nationally to garden clubs & societies. Nursery tours by arrangement.
Map Ref: E, A1 **OS Grid Ref:** TA091001

EPPr **The Plantsman's Preference** ⊠ ♿ ∩
(Office) Lynwood, Hopton Road, Garboldisham, Diss, Norfolk, IP22 2QN
Ⓣ Office: (01953) 681439
Ⓜ Nursery: 07799 855559
Ⓔ tim@plantpref.co.uk
Ⓦ www.plantpref.co.uk
Contact: Jenny & Tim Fuller
Opening Times: 0930-1700 Fri, Sat & Sun Mar-Oct. Other times by appt.
Min Mail Order UK: £15.00
Min Mail Order EU: £30.00
Cat. Cost: Online only.
Credit Cards: All major credit/debit cards
Specialities: Hardy geraniums & ornamental grasses. Unusual & interesting perennials incl. shade/woodland. Some choice shrubs esp. *Caprifoliaceae*. Nat. Collection of *Molinia*.
Notes: Nursery is on Church Road, South Lopham, Diss, IP22 2LW.
Map Ref: E, C3 **OS Grid Ref:** TM041819

EPts **Potash Nursery** ⊠ ♿ ∩
Cow Green, Bacton, Stowmarket, Suffolk, IP14 4HJ
Ⓣ (01449) 781671
Ⓔ enquiries@potashnursery.co.uk
Ⓦ www.potashnursery.co.uk
Contact: M W Clare
Opening Times: Pre-ordered plants can be collected by appt. only.
Min Mail Order UK: £12.60
Cat. Cost: 4 × 1st class.
Credit Cards: Visa Delta MasterCard
Specialities: *Fuchsia*.
Map Ref: E, C3 **OS Grid Ref:** TM0565NE

EPyc **Pennycross Plants** ⊠
Earith Road, Colne, Huntingdon, Cambridgeshire, PE28 3NL
Ⓣ (01487) 841520
Ⓔ plants4u@tiscali.co.uk
Contact: Janet M Buist
Opening Times: 1000-1600 Mon-Fri, 1st Mar-31st Oct by appt.
Min Mail Order UK: Nmc
Cat. Cost: 1 × 2nd class for *Salvia* list only.
Credit Cards: None
Specialities: Hardy perennials. Salvias. Some plants available in ltd. quantities only.
Notes: Mail order for young *Salvia* plants only.
Map Ref: E, C2 **OS Grid Ref:** TL378759

EQua **Quaymount Nursery** ⊠ ♿ ∩
The Row, Wereham, Kings Lynn, Norfolk, PE33 9AY
Ⓣ (01366) 500691
Ⓕ (01366) 500611
Ⓔ info@quaymountplants.co.uk
Ⓦ www.quaymountplants.co.uk
Contact: Paul Markwell
Opening Times: 0900-1700 (or dusk if earlier) Mon-Fri, 1000-1600 Sat & Sun. Closed Sun Dec & Jan.
Min Mail Order UK: Nmc
Cat. Cost: 2 ×1st class.
Credit Cards: All major credit/debit cards
Specialities: Wide range of specialist & popular plants. *Hydrangea*.
Notes: Specimen plants collection only. Also sells wholesale.
Map Ref: E, B2 **OS Grid Ref:** TF679006

ERCP **Rose Cottage Plants** ⊠ ∩
Bay Tree Farm, Epping Green, Essex, CM16 6PU
Ⓣ (01992) 573775
Ⓕ (01992) 561198
Ⓔ anne@rosecottageplants.co.uk
Ⓦ www.rosecottageplants.co.uk
Contact: Anne & Jack Barnard
Opening Times: By appt. & for special events (see website for details).
Min Mail Order UK: Nmc
Min Mail Order EU: £20.00
Cat. Cost: Online only.
Credit Cards: All major credit/debit cards
Specialities: Bulbs.
Notes: Mail order, bulbs only (catalogue available online).
Map Ref: E, B1 **OS Grid Ref:** TL435053

ERea **Reads Nursery** ⊠ ✈ ♿
Hales Hall, Loddon, Norfolk, NR14 6QW
Ⓣ (01508) 548395
Ⓕ (01508) 548040
Ⓔ plants@readsnursery.co.uk
Ⓦ www.readsnursery.co.uk
Contact: Stephen Read
Opening Times: 1000-1700, or dusk if earlier, Wed-Sat.
Min Mail Order UK: Nmc
Min Mail Order EU: £25.00
Cat. Cost: Free.

KEY
⊠ Mail order to UK or EU ∩ Delivers to shows
✈ Exports beyond EU € Euro accepted
♿ Accessible by wheelchair ◆ See Display advertisement

E

Credit Cards: All major credit/debit cards
Specialities: Fruit trees, conservatory plants. Nat. Collections. of *Citrus*, figs, *Vitis*.
Notes: Mostly accessible by wheelchair (some gravel paths).
Map Ref: E, C3 **OS Grid Ref:** TM369960

ERhR **RHODES & ROCKLIFFE** ⊠ € ✈
2 Nursery Road, Nazeing, Essex,
EN9 2JE
Ⓣ (01992) 451598 (office hours)
Ⓕ (01992) 440673
Ⓔ RRBegonias@aol.com
Contact: David Rhodes or John Rockliffe
Opening Times: By appt.
Min Mail Order UK: £3.00 + p&p
Min Mail Order EU: £5.00 + p&p
Cat. Cost: 2 × 1st class.
Credit Cards: None
Specialities: *Begonia* species & hybrids. Nat. Collection of *Begonia*. Plants propagated to order.
Notes: Mail order Apr-Sep only.
Map Ref: E, D2

ERom **THE ROMANTIC GARDEN** ⊠ € ✈ ♿ ◆
Swannington, Norwich, Norfolk, NR9 5NW
Ⓣ (01603) 261488
Ⓕ (01603) 864231
Ⓔ enquiries@romantic-garden-nursery.co.uk
Ⓦ www.romantic-garden-nursery.co.uk
Contact: John Powles/John Carrick
Opening Times: 1000-1700 Wed, Fri & Sat all year, plus B/hol Mons.
Min Mail Order UK: £5.00 + p&p
Min Mail Order EU: £30.00 + p&p
Cat. Cost: 6 × 1st class.
Credit Cards: All major credit/debit cards
Specialities: Conservatory. *Buxus* topiary, ornamental standards, large specimens. Hedging. Topiary
Notes: Also sells wholesale.
Map Ref: E, B3

ESem **SEMPS BY POST** ⊠
28 Mill Road, Newbourne, Woodbridge, Suffolk, IP12 4NP
Ⓣ (01473) 736440
Ⓔ Tricia@sempsbypost.co.uk
Ⓦ www.sempsbypost.co.uk
Contact: Tricia Newell
Opening Times: By appt. only.
Min Mail Order UK: Nmc
Min Mail Order EU: Nmc
Cat. Cost: Online only.
Credit Cards: Paypal
Specialities: *Sempervivum*. Some stock available in small quantities.

ESgI **SEAGATE IRISES** ⊠ € ✈ ♿
A17 Long Sutton By-Pass,
Long Sutton, Lincolnshire,
PE12 9RX
Ⓣ (01406) 365138
Ⓜ 07887 856389
Ⓕ (01406) 365447
Ⓔ Sales@irises.co.uk
Ⓦ www.irises.co.uk
Contact: Julian Browse or Wendy Browse
Opening Times: 1000-1700 daily Apr-Sep. Please phone for appt. Oct-Mar.
Min Mail Order UK: Nmc
Min Mail Order EU: Nmc. Carriage at cost.
Cat. Cost: £3.50 or €8.00.
Credit Cards: Maestro Visa MasterCard
Specialities: Different types of *Iris*, bearded, beardless & species hybrids with about 1000 varieties in all, both historic & modern. Nat. Collection of Historic Tall Bearded Irises (pre-1964). Some only available in small quantities. Many container-grown available to callers.
Map Ref: E, B1 **OS Grid Ref:** TF437218

EShb **SHRUBLAND PARK NURSERIES** ⊠ € ⌂
Coddenham, Ipswich, Suffolk,
IP6 9QJ
Ⓣ (01473) 833187
Ⓜ 07890 527744
Ⓔ gill@shrublandparknurseries.co.uk
Ⓦ www.shrublandparknurseries.co.uk
Contact: Gill & Catherine Stitt
Opening Times: 1000-1700 Wed-Sun, Easter-30th Sep. 1000-1400 Wed & Sun from 1st Oct-Easter. Times may vary in 2009. Please ring/check website first.
Min Mail Order UK: £15.00
Min Mail Order EU: £30.00
Cat. Cost: 6 × 1st class or free by email.
Credit Cards: All major credit/debit cards, Nochex, Paypal
Specialities: Conservatory plants, succulents, hardy perennials, climbers, shrubs, ferns & grasses. Large glasshouse & adjacent walled garden with planted display beds. Tender plants available from spring-autumn. Display beds in glasshouse & walled garden.
Notes: For directions phone or see website. nearest postcode for SatNav IP6 0PG. Partial wheelchair access.
Map Ref: E, C3 **OS Grid Ref:** TM128524

ESty **STYLE ROSES** ⊠ ♿ ⌂
10 Meridian Walk, Holbeach, Spalding, Lincolnshire, PE12 7NR
Ⓣ (01406) 424089
Ⓜ 07932 044093 or 07780 860415
Ⓕ (01406) 424089

Ⓔ styleroses@aol.com
Ⓦ www.styleroses.co.uk
Contact: Chris Styles, Margaret Styles
Opening Times: Vary, please phone.
Min Mail Order UK: Nmc
Min Mail Order EU: Nmc
Cat. Cost: Free.
Credit Cards: All major credit/debit cards
Specialities: Standard & bush roses.
Notes: Export to EU during bare-root season Nov-Mar. Other countries subject to plant health requirements. Carriage & export certificates where required charged at cost. Also sells wholesale.
Map Ref: E, B1

ESul **BRIAN & PEARL SULMAN** ⊠ ♿ ⛟
54 Kingsway, Mildenhall, Bury St Edmunds, Suffolk, IP28 7HR
Ⓣ (01638) 712297
Ⓕ (01638) 712297
Ⓔ enquiries@sulmanspelargoniums.co.uk
Ⓦ www.sulmanspelargoniums.co.uk
Contact: Pearl Sulman
Opening Times: Mail order only. Not open except for Open Days 2nd/3rd May & 30th/31st May 2009. Phone for information about 2010 dates.
Min Mail Order UK: £23.00
Cat. Cost: 4 × 1st class.
Credit Cards: Visa MasterCard
Specialities: *Pelargonium.* Some varieties only available in small quantities.
Map Ref: E, C2 **OS Grid Ref:** TL715747

ESwi **SWINES MEADOW FARM NURSERY** € ♿ ⛟ ◆
47 Towngate East, Market Deeping, Peterborough, PE6 8LQ
Ⓜ 01778 343340
Ⓔ info@swinesmeadowgardencentre.co.uk
Ⓦ www.swinesmeadowgardencentre.co.uk
Contact: Colin Ward
Specialities: Hardy exotics, tree ferns, bamboos & phormiums. Wollemi pine stockist. Many specialities available in small quantities only.
Map Ref: E, B1 **OS Grid Ref:** TF150113

ETho **THORNCROFT CLEMATIS NURSERY** ⊠ ✈ ♿ ⛟
The Lings, Reymerston, Norwich, Norfolk, NR9 4QG
Ⓣ (01953) 850407
Ⓕ (01953) 851788
Ⓔ sales@thorncroft.co.uk
Ⓦ www.thorncroft.co.uk
Contact: Ruth P Gooch
Opening Times: 1000-1600 Tue-Sat all year, closed Sun & Mon. Open B/hol Mon.
Min Mail Order UK: Nmc
Min Mail Order EU: Nmc
Cat. Cost: 6 × 2nd class.
Credit Cards: All major credit/debit cards
Specialities: *Clematis.*
Notes: Does not export to USA, Canada or Australia.
Map Ref: E, B3 **OS Grid Ref:** TG039062

ETMg **THOMPSON & MORGAN YOUNG PLANTS LTD** ⊠
Poplar Lane, Ipswich, Suffolk, IP8 3BU
Ⓣ 0844 573 2020
Ⓕ (01787) 882252
Ⓔ ypenq@thompson-morgan.com
Ⓦ www.thompson-morgan.com/plants
Contact: Customer Care
Opening Times: Mail order only. Not open except for Open Weekend 1st/2nd Aug 2009.
Min Mail Order UK: Nmc
Cat. Cost: Free
Credit Cards: Visa MasterCard

ETod **TODD'S BOTANICS** ⊠ ♿ ⛟
West Street, Coggeshall, Colchester, Essex, CO6 1NT
Ⓣ (01376) 561212
Ⓜ 07970 643711
Ⓕ (01376) 561212
Ⓔ info@toddsbotanics.co.uk
Ⓦ www.toddsbotanics.co.uk
Contact: Mark Macdonald
Opening Times: 0900-1700 (or dusk) Thu-Sun. 1100-1600 Sun & B/hols. Open by appt. Mon-Wed. Open by appt. only in Jan.
Min Mail Order UK: Nmc
Cat. Cost: 2 × 1st class.
Credit Cards: All major credit/debit cards
Specialities: Hardy exotics, herbaceous. Bamboos, palms, ferns, grasses, *Canna* & *Hedychium.* Olives, incl. named varieties.
Notes: Also sells wholesale.
Map Ref: E, D2 **OS Grid Ref:** TL843224

EUJe **URBAN JUNGLE** ⊠ ♿ ⛟
The Nurseries, Ringland Lane, Old Costessey, Norwich, Norfolk, NR8 5BG
Ⓣ (01603) 744997
Ⓕ (0709) 2366869
Ⓔ lizzy@urbanjungle.uk.com

KEY
⊠ Mail order to UK or EU — ⛟ Delivers to shows
✈ Exports beyond EU — € Euro accepted
♿ Accessible by wheelchair — ◆ See Display advertisement

E

Ⓦ www.urbanjungle.uk.com
Contact: Liz Browne
Opening Times: 0900-1700 Mar-Oct, 1000-1600 Nov-Feb, 7 days. Closed Xmas Day, Boxing Day & New Year's Day.
Min Mail Order UK: £20.00
Min Mail Order EU: £20.00
Cat. Cost: 2 × 1st class
Credit Cards: All major credit/debit cards
Specialities: Exotic plants, gingers, bananas and aroids. Hardy exotics, conservatory plants, fruit trees.

EWes **WEST ACRE GARDENS** ♿ ⌂
West Acre, King's Lynn, Norfolk, PE32 1UJ
Ⓣ (01760) 755562
Contact: J J Tuite
Opening Times: 1000-1700 7 days 1st Feb-30th Nov. Other times by appt.
Cat. Cost: None issued.
Credit Cards: Visa MasterCard Delta Switch
Specialities: Very wide selection of herbaceous & other garden plants incl. *Rhodohypoxis* & *Primula auricula*.
Map Ref: E, B1 **OS Grid Ref:** TF792182

EWld **WOODLANDS**
Peppin Lane, Fotherby, Louth, Lincolnshire, LN11 0UW
Ⓣ (01507) 603586
Ⓜ 07866 161864
Ⓔ annbobarmstrong@uwclub.net
Ⓦ www.woodlandsplants.co.uk
Contact: Ann Armstrong
Opening Times: Flexible, but please phone or email to avoid disappointment.
Cat. Cost: None issued.
Credit Cards: None
Specialities: Small but interesting range of unusual plants, esp. woodland and *Salvia*, all grown on the nursery in limited quantity.
Notes: Mature garden, art gallery & refreshments.
Map Ref: E, A2 **OS Grid Ref:** TF322918

EWll **THE WALLED GARDEN** ♿ ◆
Park Road, Benhall, Saxmundham, Suffolk, IP17 1JB
Ⓣ (01728) 602510
Ⓕ (01728) 602510
Ⓔ jim@thewalledgarden.co.uk
Ⓦ www.thewalledgarden.co.uk
Contact: Jim Mountain
Opening Times: 0930-1700 Tue-Sun Mar-Nov, 0930-dusk Tue-Sat Dec-mid Feb.
Cat. Cost: 2 × 1st class.
Credit Cards: All major credit/debit cards
Specialities: Tender & hardy perennials, over 1000 varieties, & wall shrubs.
Map Ref: E, C3 **OS Grid Ref:** TM371613

EWoo **WOOTTEN'S PLANTS** ✉ ♿ ⌂
Wenhaston, Blackheath, Halesworth, Suffolk, IP19 9HD
Ⓣ (01502) 478258
Ⓕ (01502) 478888
Ⓔ sales@woottensplants.co.uk
Ⓦ www.woottensplants.co.uk
Contact: M Loftus
Opening Times: 0930-1700 7 days.
Min Mail Order UK: Nmc
Min Mail Order EU: Nmc
Cat. Cost: £2.50 + £2.00 postage.
Credit Cards: Access Visa American Express Switch
Specialities: *Pelargonium*, *Hemerocallis*, *Primula auricula* & *Iris*. Grasses.
Notes: Also sells wholesale.
Map Ref: E, C3 **OS Grid Ref:** TM42714375

EWTr **WALNUT TREE GARDEN NURSERY** ✉ €
Flymoor Lane, Rocklands, Attleborough, Norfolk, NR17 1BP
Ⓣ (01953) 488163
Ⓔ info@wtgn.co.uk
Ⓦ www.wtgn.co.uk
Contact: Jim Paine & Clare Billington
Opening Times: 0900-1800 Tue-Sun Feb-Nov & B/hols.
Min Mail Order UK: Nmc
Min Mail Order EU: £20.00
Cat. Cost: 4 × 1st class.
Credit Cards: All major credit/debit cards
Map Ref: E, B1 **OS Grid Ref:** TL978973

SCOTLAND

GAbr **ABRIACHAN NURSERIES** ✉ ♿ ⌂
Loch Ness Side, Inverness, Inverness-shire, IV3 8LA
Ⓣ (01463) 861232
Ⓕ (01463) 861232
Ⓔ info@lochnessgarden.com
Ⓦ www.lochnessgarden.com
Contact: Mr & Mrs D Davidson
Opening Times: 0900-1900 daily (dusk if earlier) Feb-Nov.
Min Mail Order UK: Nmc
Cat. Cost: 4 × 1st class.
Credit Cards: All major credit/debit cards
Specialities: Herbaceous perennials, old-fashioned *Primula*, *Helianthemum*, hardy geraniums, *Sempervivum* & *Primula auricula*.
Notes: Wheelchair access to nursery only.
Map Ref: G, B2 **OS Grid Ref:** NH571347

GAgs **ANGUSPLANTS** ✉ ♿
3 Balfour Cottages, Menmuir, By Brechin, Angus, DD9 7RN
Ⓣ (01356) 660280
Ⓜ 07972 026109
Ⓔ alison@angusplants.co.uk
Ⓦ www.angusplants.co.uk
Contact: Alison S. Goldie & Mark A. Hutson
Opening Times: By appt. only. Please phone first. Light refreshments provided.
Min Mail Order UK: Nmc
Cat. Cost: 4 × 1st class
Credit Cards: None
Specialities: Predominantly *Primula auricula*, although other *Primula* species are offered. A few available in small quantities only.
Notes: Mail order available all year.
Map Ref: G, B3 **OS Grid Ref:** NO528643

GAuc **AUCHGOURISH BOTANIC GARDEN** ✉ € ♿
Street of Kincardine, by Boat of Garten, Inverness-shire, PH24 3BY
Ⓣ (01479) 831464
Ⓜ 07746 122775
Ⓔ info@auchgourishbotanicgarden.org
Ⓦ www.thebotanicalnursery.com
Contact: Iain Brodie of Falsyde
Opening Times: 1000-1700 Mon-Fri, closed Sat, 1100-1700 Sun, 1st Apr-31st Oct.
Min Mail Order UK: £25.00
Min Mail Order EU: £30.00 + p&p at cost
Cat. Cost: Online only.
Credit Cards: All major credit/debit cards
Specialities: Botanical species. *Betulaceae, Rosaceae, Ericaceae, Iridaceae, Liliaceae* & *Primulaceae*. Nursery is at Auchgourish Botanic Gardens, Boat of Garten. Anchgourish Botanic Gardens are open 1st Apr-31st Oct.
Notes: Mail order despatch Sep-Apr incl. subject to weather. No despatch May-Aug but plants can be uplifted any time by prior arrangement. Credit cards accepted online only. Will deliver to Gardening Scotland show.
Map Ref: G, B2 **OS Grid Ref:** NH955194

GBar **BARWINNOCK HERBS** ✉ €
Barrhill, Girvan, Ayrshire, KA26 0RB
Ⓣ (01465) 821338
Ⓔ herbs@barwinnock.com
Ⓦ www.barwinnock.com
Contact: Dave & Mon Holtom
Opening Times: 1000-1700 most w/ends & Mons, mid Apr-mid Sep. Please phone to confirm.
Min Mail Order UK: Nmc
Min Mail Order EU: Nmc
Cat. Cost: UK free, EU 2 × IRC.
Credit Cards: All major credit/debit cards
Specialities: Culinary, medicinal, fragrant-leaved plants & wildflowers organically grown.
Map Ref: G, D2 **OS Grid Ref:** NX309772

GBBs **BORDER BELLES** ✉ ♿ 🚚
Old Branxton Cottages, Innerwick, Nr Dunbar, East Lothian, EH42 1QT
Ⓣ (01368) 840325
Ⓔ mail@borderbelles.com
Ⓦ www.borderbelles.com
Contact: Gillian Moynihan
Opening Times: 1000-1700, Thu, Fri & Sat, Mar-Sep.
Min Mail Order UK: Nmc
Min Mail Order EU: On request
Cat. Cost: Online only.
Credit Cards: All major credit/debit cards
Specialities: Hardy perennials & woodland plants.
Notes: Mail order Oct-Mar only. Also sells wholesale.

GBee **BEECHES COTTAGE NURSERY** ♿
High Boreland, Lesmahagow, South Lanarkshire, ML11 9PY
Ⓣ (01555) 893369
Ⓜ 07930 343131
Contact: Margaret Harrison, Steve Harrison
Opening Times: 1000-1630 Wed-Sat, Mar-Oct. Other times by appt.
Cat. Cost: None issued.
Credit Cards: None
Specialities: Traditional & unusual hardy & half-hardy cottage garden perennials. Some plants available in small quantities only.
Notes: Wheelchair access to nursery only. Also sells wholesale.
Map Ref: G, C2 **OS Grid Ref:** NS837403

GBin **BINNY PLANTS** ✉ € ♿
West Lodge, Binny Estate, Ecclesmachen Road, Nr Broxbourn, West Lothian, EH52 6NL
Ⓣ (01506) 858931
Ⓕ (01506) 858155
Ⓔ binnyplants@aol.com
Ⓦ www.binnyplants.co.uk
Contact: Billy Carruthers
Opening Times: 1000-1700 7 days. Closed mid-Dec to mid-Jan.

KEY		
	✉ Mail order to UK or EU	🚚 Delivers to shows
	✈ Exports beyond EU	€ Euro accepted
	♿ Accessible by wheelchair	◆ See Display advertisement

G

Min Mail Order UK: £25.00
Min Mail Order EU: £25.00
Cat. Cost: £2.50 refundable on ordering.
Credit Cards: Visa MasterCard EuroCard Maestro
Specialities: Perennials incl. *Astilbe*, *Geranium*, *Hosta*, *Paeonia* & *Iris*. Plus large selection of grasses & ferns.
Notes: Mail order Sep-Apr only. Also sells wholesale.
Map Ref: G, C3

GBut **Butterworths' Organic Nursery** ⊠
Garden Cottage, Auchinleck Estate, Cumnock, Ayrshire, KA18 2LR
Ⓣ (01290) 551088
Ⓜ 07732 254300
Ⓔ butties@webage.co.uk
Ⓦ www.butterworthsorganicnursery.co.uk
Contact: John Butterworth
Opening Times: Mail order only. Open by appt. only.
Min Mail Order UK: £30.00
Cat. Cost: Online only.
Credit Cards: None
Specialities: Fruit trees incl. Scottish apple varieties. Some stock available in small quantities only. All stock is certified organic.

GCai **Cairnsmore Nursery** ⊠ ♿
Chapmanton Road, Castle Douglas, Kirkcudbrightshire, DG7 2NU
Ⓣ (01556) 504819
Ⓜ 07980 176458
Ⓔ cairnsmorenursery@hotmail.com
Ⓦ www.cairnsmorenursery.co.uk
Contact: Valerie Smith
Opening Times: By appt. only.
Min Mail Order UK: Nmc
Cat. Cost: 4 × 1st class.
Credit Cards: None
Specialities: *Primula auricula*, show cultivars. *Heuchera* & *Tiarella*.
Map Ref: G, D2 **OS Grid Ref:** NX756637

GCal **Cally Gardens** ⊠ ♿
Gatehouse of Fleet, Castle Douglas, Kirkcudbrightshire, DG7 2DJ
Ⓣ (01557) 815029 recorded information only.
Ⓔ info@callygardens.co.uk
Ⓦ www.callygardens.co.uk
Contact: Michael Wickenden
Opening Times: 1000-1730 Sat-Sun, 1400-1730 Tue-Fri. Easter Sat-last Sun in Sept.
Min Mail Order UK: £15.00 + p&p
Cat. Cost: 3 × 1st class.
Credit Cards: None
Specialities: Unusual perennials & grasses. Some rare shrubs, climbers & conservatory plants. 3500 varieties growing in an 2.7 acre walled garden built in the 1760s.
Notes: Also sells wholesale.
Map Ref: G, D2 **OS Grid Ref:** NX604549

GCoc **James Cocker & Sons** ⊠ ♿
Whitemyres, Lang Stracht, Aberdeen, Aberdeenshire, AB15 6XH
Ⓣ (01224) 313261
Ⓕ (01224) 312531
Ⓔ sales@roses.uk.com
Ⓦ www.roses.uk.com
Contact: Alec Cocker
Opening Times: 0900-1730 7 days.
Min Mail Order UK: Nmc
Min Mail Order EU: £5.95 + p&p
Cat. Cost: Free
Credit Cards: Visa MasterCard Delta Maestro
Specialities: Roses.
Notes: Also sells wholesale.
Map Ref: G, B3

GCra **Craigieburn Garden** € ♿
Craigieburn House, by Moffat, Dumfriesshire, DG10 9LF
Ⓣ (01683) 221250
Ⓕ (01683) 221250
Ⓔ ajmw1@aol.com
Ⓦ www.craigieburngarden.com
Contact: Janet & Andrew Wheatcroft
Opening Times: 1030-1800 Tue-Sun, Easter-31st Oct. Plus all English & Scottish B/hols. Other times by appt.
Credit Cards: Visa MasterCard
Specialities: *Meconopsis* plants for damp gardens, herbaceous perennials.
Map Ref: G, D3

GCrs **Christie's Nursery** ⊠ € ♿
Downfield, Main Road, Westmuir, Kirriemuir, Angus, DD8 5LP
Ⓣ (01575) 572977
Ⓕ (01575) 572977
Ⓔ ianchristie@btconnect.com
Ⓦ www.christiealpines.co.uk
Contact: Ian Christie
Opening Times: Open by telephone appt. only.
Min Mail Order UK: £18.50
Min Mail Order EU: £28.50
Cat. Cost: 3 × 1st class
Credit Cards: All major credit/debit cards
Specialities: Alpines, esp. gentians, *Cassiope*, *Primula*, *Lewisia*, orchids, *Trillium* & ericaceous.

GEdr **Edrom Nurseries** ⊠ ♿
Coldingham, Eyemouth, Berwickshire,
TD14 5TZ
Ⓣ (01890) 771386
Ⓕ (01890) 71387
Ⓔ info@edromnurseries.co.uk
Ⓦ www.edromnurseries.co.uk
Contact: Mr Terry Hunt
Opening Times: 0900-1700 Thu-Tue (closed Wed), 1st Mar-30th Sep. Other times by appt.
Min Mail Order UK: Nmc
Min Mail Order EU: £20.00
Cat. Cost: 4 × 2nd class. More plants listed online than in printed catalogue.
Credit Cards: All major credit/debit cards
Specialities: *Trillium*, *Arisaema*, *Primula*, *Gentiana*, *Meconopsis*, *Cypripedium*, *Fritillaria*, hardy orchids.
Map Ref: G, C3 **OS Grid Ref:** NT873663

GFai **Fairholm Plants** ⊠ €
Fairholm, Larkhall, Lanarkshire,
ML9 2UQ
Ⓣ (01698) 881671
Ⓕ (01698) 888135
Ⓔ fairholm.plants@stevenson-hamilton.co.uk
Ⓦ
Contact: Mrs J M Hamilton
Opening Times: Apr-Oct by appt.
Min Mail Order UK: Nmc
Cat. Cost: 1 × 2nd class for descriptive list.
Credit Cards: None
Specialities: *Abutilon* & unusual half-hardy perennials esp. South African. Nat. Collection of *Abutilon* cvs. Plants available in small quantities only.
Notes: Mail order for young/small plants.
Map Ref: G, C2 **OS Grid Ref:** NS754515

GFor **Fordmouth Croft Ornamental Grass Nursery** ⊠
Fordmouth Croft, Meikle Wartle,
Inverurie, Aberdeenshire,
AB51 5BE
Ⓣ (01467) 671519
Ⓔ Ann-Marie@fmcornamentalgrasses.co.uk
Ⓦ www.fmcornamentalgrasses.co.uk
Contact: Robert & Ann-Marie Grant
Opening Times: Mail order only. Open strictly by appt. only.
Min Mail Order UK: Nmc
Cat. Cost: 2 × 1st class.
Credit Cards: None
Specialities: Grasses, sedges, rushes. Small orders available.
Notes: Also sells wholesale. Nursery partially accessible for wheelchairs.
Map Ref: G, B3 **OS Grid Ref:** NJ718302

GGal **Galloway Plants** ⊠ ♿
Claymoddie, Whithorn,
Newton Stewart, Dumfries & Galloway,
DG8 8LX
Ⓣ (01988) 500422
Ⓕ (01988) 500422
Ⓔ NICM567@aol.com
Ⓦ www.gallowayplants.co.uk
Contact: Robin & Mary Nicholson
Opening Times: 1400-1700 Fri, Sat & Sun, 6th Mar-27th Sep 2009, other times by prior appt.
Min Mail Order UK: £50.00 + p&p
Min Mail Order EU: £50.00 + p&p
Cat. Cost: 2 × 1st class.
Credit Cards: None
Specialities: Southern hemisphere *Hydrangea*. Available in small quantities only.
Notes: Also sells wholesale.
Map Ref: G, D2 **OS Grid Ref:** NX450377

GGar **Garden Cottage Nursery** ⊠ ♿
Tournaig, Poolewe, Achnasheen, Ross-shire,
IV22 2LH
Ⓣ (01445) 781777
Ⓔ ben@gcnursery.co.uk
Ⓦ www.gcnursery.co.uk
Contact: Ben Rushbrooke
Opening Times: 1000-1800 Mon-Sat mid Mar-mid Oct or by appt.
Min Mail Order UK: Nmc
Cat. Cost: Free.
Credit Cards: Visa Switch MasterCard
Specialities: A wide range of plants esp. those from the southern hemisphere & plants for bog & coastal gardens.
Map Ref: G, A2 **OS Grid Ref:** NG878835

GGGa **Glendoick Gardens Ltd** ⊠ ✈
Glencarse, Perth, Perthshire,
PH2 7NS
Ⓣ (01738) 860205
Ⓕ (01738) 860630
Ⓔ orders@glendoick.com
Ⓦ www.glendoick.com
Contact: P A, E P & K N E Cox
Opening Times: 1000-1600 Mon-Fri only, mid-Apr-mid-Jun, otherwise by appt. 1400-1700 1st & 3rd Sun in May. Garden Centre open 7 days.
Min Mail Order UK: £40.00 + p&p
Min Mail Order EU: £100.00 + p&p
Cat. Cost: £2.00 or £1.50 stamps.

KEY
⊠ Mail order to UK or EU — Delivers to shows
✈ Exports beyond EU — € Euro accepted
♿ Accessible by wheelchair — ◆ See Display advertisement

G

Credit Cards: Visa MasterCard Delta Switch JCB
Specialities: Rhododendrons, azaleas and ericaceous, *Primula* & *Meconopsis*. Plants from wild seed. Many catalogue plants available at garden centre. 3 Nat. Collections.
Notes: Wheelchair access to Garden Centre. Also sells wholesale.
Map Ref: G, C3

GJos **JO'S GARDEN ENTERPRISE** ♿
Easter Balmungle Farm, Eathie Road, by Rosemarkie, Ross-shire, IV10 8SL
Ⓣ (01381) 621006
Ⓔ anne.chance@ukonline.co.uk
Contact: Joanna Chance
Opening Times: 1000 to dusk, 7 days.
Cat. Cost: None
Credit Cards: None
Specialities: Alpines & herbaceous perennials. Selection of native wild flowers.
Map Ref: G, B2 **OS Grid Ref:** NH600742

GKev **KEVOCK GARDEN PLANTS** ✉ € ⌂
16 Kevock Road, Lasswade, Midlothian, EH18 1HT
Ⓣ 0131 454 0660
Ⓜ 07811 321585
Ⓕ 0131 454 0660
Ⓔ info@kevockgarden.co.uk
Ⓦ www.kevockgarden.co.uk
Contact: Stella Rankin
Opening Times: Not open. Mail order & plant stalls only.
Min Mail Order UK: £20.00
Min Mail Order EU: £20.00
Cat. Cost: 4 × 1st class.
Credit Cards: Visa MasterCard Switch
Specialities: Chinese & Himalayan plants. *Androsace, Daphne, Paeonia, Primula, Meconopsis, Iris*, woodland plants, alpines, rock, marginal, bog.
Notes: Also sells wholesale.

GKir **KIRKDALE NURSERY** ✉ € ♿
Daviot, Nr Inverurie, Aberdeenshire, AB51 0JL
Ⓣ (01467) 671264
Ⓕ (01467) 671282
Ⓔ kirkdalenursery@btconnect.com
Ⓦ www.kirkdalenursery.co.uk
Contact: Geoff or Alistair
Opening Times: 1000-1700 7 days (summer), 1000-1600 7 days (winter).
Min Mail Order UK: £30.00 + p&p
Min Mail Order EU: £50.00 + p&p
Cat. Cost: None issued
Credit Cards: Visa Access Switch
Specialities: Trees, herbaceous, conifers. Some plants available in small quantities only.
Notes: Mail order strictly mid-Oct to mid-Mar, carriage at cost.
Map Ref: G, B3

GLin **LINN BOTANIC GARDENS** €
Cove, Helensburgh, Dunbartonshire, G84 0NR
Ⓣ (01436) 842084
Ⓔ jamie@linnbotanicgardens.org.uk
Ⓦ www.linnbotanicgardens.org.uk
Contact: Jamie Taggart
Opening Times: 1100-1700, 7 days.
Cat. Cost: 4 × 1st class or by email.
Credit Cards: None
Specialities: Small plant sales area offering diverse range of plants. Botanic Gardens open (charges apply).
Notes: Wheelchair access to plant sales area but not gardens.
Map Ref: G, C2 **OS Grid Ref:** NS223827

GLog **LOGIE STEADING PLANTS** ♿
Forres, Moray, IV36 2QN
Ⓣ (01309) 611222 or 611278
Ⓕ (01309) 611300
Ⓔ panny@logie.co.uk
Ⓦ www.logie.co.uk
Contact: Mrs Panny Laing
Opening Times: 1030-1700 hours, 7 days, April-end Oct.
Credit Cards: All major credit/debit cards
Specialities: Unusual hardy plants, grown in Scotland for Scottish gardens.
Notes: Logie House Garden open every day. Café, farm shop, gallery, book shop, antiques, river walk.
Map Ref: G, B2

GMac **ELIZABETH MACGREGOR** ✉ ♿
Ellenbank, Tongland Road, Kirkcudbright, Dumfries & Galloway, DG6 4UU
Ⓣ (01557) 330620
Ⓕ (01557) 330620
Ⓔ elizabeth.violas@btinternet.com
Ⓦ www.elizabethmacgregornursery.co.uk
Contact: Elizabeth MacGregor
Opening Times: 1000-1700 Mon, Fri & Sat May-Sep, or please phone.
Min Mail Order UK: 6 plants + p&p
Min Mail Order EU: £50.00 + p&p
Cat. Cost: 4 × 1st class or 5 × 2nd class
Credit Cards: All major credit/debit cards
Specialities: Violets, violas & violettas, old and new varieties. *Campanula, Geranium,*

Eryngium, *Penstemon*, *Aster*, *Primula*, *Iris* & other unusual herbaceous.
Map Ref: G, D2 **OS Grid Ref:** NX692525

GMaP **Macplants**
Berrybank Nursery, 5 Boggs Holdings, Pencaitland, East Lothian, EH34 5BA
Ⓣ (01875) 341179
Ⓕ (01875) 340842
Ⓔ sales@macplants.co.uk
Ⓦ www.macplants.co.uk
Contact: Gavin McNaughton
Opening Times: 1030-1700, 7 days, Mar-end Sep.
Cat. Cost: 4 × 2nd class.
Credit Cards: MasterCard Switch Visa
Specialities: Herbaceous perennials, alpines, hardy ferns, violas & grasses.
Notes: Nursery partially accessible to wheelchairs. Also sells wholesale.
Map Ref: G, C3 **OS Grid Ref:** NT447703

GPoy **Poyntzfield Herb Nursery** ⊠
Nr Balblair, Black Isle, Dingwall, Ross-shire, IV7 8LX
Ⓣ (01381) 610352
Ⓕ (01381) 610352
Ⓔ info@poyntzfieldherbs.co.uk
Ⓦ www.poyntzfieldherbs.co.uk
Contact: Duncan Ross
Opening Times: 1300-1700 Mon-Sat 1st Mar-30th Sep, 1300-1700 Sun May-Aug.
Min Mail Order UK: £10.00 + p&p
Min Mail Order EU: £10.00 + p&p
Cat. Cost: 4 × 1st class.
Credit Cards: All major credit/debit cards
Specialities: Over 400 popular, unusual & rare herbs esp. medicinal. Also seeds.
Notes: Phone between 1200-1300 & 1800-1900 Mon-Sat only.
Map Ref: G, B2 **OS Grid Ref:** NH711642

GPri **Privick Mill Nursery** ⊠
Privick Mill Road, Annbank, Ayr, KA6 5JA
Ⓣ (01292) 521003
Ⓔ jackie@trootnfroot.co.uk
Ⓦ www.trootnfroot.co.uk
Contact: Jackie Jess
Opening Times: By appt. only for collection of plants.
Min Mail Order UK: Nmc
Cat. Cost: Free.
Credit Cards: None
Specialities: Soft fruit bushes. Blueberries. Black raspberries. *Rubus* hybrids. Available in small quantities only. All plants organically grown but not certified by Soil Assoc.
Map Ref: G, D2 **OS Grid Ref:** NS405224

GPWP **Plants With Purpose** ⊠
Middlebank Cottage, Smith's Brae, Bankfoot, Perthshire, PH1 4AH
Ⓣ (01738) 787278
Ⓜ 07871 451579
Ⓔ mail@plantswithpurpose.co.uk
Ⓦ www.plantswithpurpose.co.uk
Contact: Margaret Lear
Opening Times: By appt. only.
Min Mail Order UK: £12.00
Min Mail Order EU: £12.00
Cat. Cost: Online or on application.
Credit Cards: All major credit/debit cards
Specialities: Herbs, esp. *Mentha* & *Artemisia*. Edible plants.
Notes: Credit cards online only. Partial wheelchair access.
Map Ref: G, C3 **OS Grid Ref:** NO067356

GQue **Quercus Garden Plants**
Rankeilour Gardens, Rankeilour Estate, Springfield, Fife, KY15 5RE
Ⓣ (01337) 810444
Ⓕ (01337) 810444
Ⓔ colin@quercus.uk.net
Contact: Colin McBeath
Opening Times: 1000-1700 Thu-Sun, 1st w/end Apr-mid Oct. By appt. only, Nov-Feb. 1000-1400 Sat only, Mar.
Cat. Cost: 4 × 1st class.
Credit Cards: All major credit/debit cards
Specialities: Easy & unusual plants for contemporary Scottish gardens.
Notes: Delivery service available on large orders at nursery's discretion. Also sells wholesale.
Map Ref: G, C3 **OS Grid Ref:** NO330118

GQui **Quinish Garden Nursery** ⊠
Dervaig, Isle of Mull, Argyll, PA75 6QL
Ⓣ (01688) 400344
Ⓕ (01688) 400344
Ⓔ quinishplants@aol.com
Ⓦ www.Q-gardens.org
Contact: Nicholas Reed
Opening Times: By appt. only.
Min Mail Order UK: Nmc
Min Mail Order EU: Nmc
Cat. Cost: 2 × 1st class.
Credit Cards: None
Specialities: Choice garden shrubs & conservatory plants.
Map Ref: G, C1

KEY
⊠ Mail order to UK or EU | Delivers to shows
Exports beyond EU | € Euro accepted
Accessible by wheelchair | ◆ See Display advertisement

G

G

GTwe **J TWEEDIE FRUIT TREES** ⊠
Maryfield Road Nursery, Nr Terregles, Dumfriesshire, DG2 9TH
Ⓣ (01387) 720880
Contact: John Tweedie
Opening Times: Please ring for times. Collections by appt.
Min Mail Order UK: Nmc
Cat. Cost: Sae
Credit Cards: None
Specialities: Fruit trees & bushes. A wide range of old & new varieties.
Map Ref: G, D2

N. IRELAND & REPUBLIC

IArd **ARDCARNE GARDEN CENTRE** € ♿
Ardcarne, Boyle, Co. Roscommon, Ireland
Ⓣ 00 353 (0)7196 67091
Ⓕ 00 353 (0)7196 67341
Ⓔ ardcarne@indigo.ie
Ⓦ www.ardcarnegc.com
Contact: James Wickham, Mary Frances Dwyer, Kirsty Ainge
Opening Times: 0900-1800 Mon-Sat, 1300-1800 Sun & B/hols.
Credit Cards: Access Visa American Express
Specialities: Coastal plants, native & unusual trees, specimen plants & semi-mature trees. Wide general range.
Map Ref: I, B1

IBal **BALI-HAI MAIL ORDER NURSERY** ⊠ € ✈
42 Largy Road, Carnlough, Ballymena, Co. Antrim, N. Ireland, BT44 0EZ
Ⓣ 028 2888 5289
Ⓕ 028 2888 5976
Ⓔ ianwscroggy@btopenworld.com
Ⓦ www.mailorderplants4me.com
Contact: Mrs M E Scroggy
Opening Times: Mon-Sat by appt. only.
Min Mail Order UK: Nmc
Min Mail Order EU: Nmc
Cat. Cost: £3.00 cheque, made payable to Mrs M.E. Scroggy.
Credit Cards: All major credit/debit cards
Specialities: *Hosta*, *Phormium*, *Rhodohypoxis* & other perennials. Tree ferns.
Notes: Exports beyond EU restricted to bare root perennials, no grasses. Also sells wholesale.
Map Ref: I, A3 **OS Grid Ref:** D287184

IBlr **BALLYROGAN NURSERIES** ⊠ € ♿
The Grange, Ballyrogan, Newtownards, Co. Down, N. Ireland, BT23 4SD
Ⓣ (028) 9181 0451 (evenings)
Ⓔ gary.dunlop@btinternet.com
Contact: Gary Dunlop
Opening Times: Only open by appt.
Min Mail Order UK: £10.00 + p&p
Min Mail Order EU: £20.00 + p&p
Cat. Cost: 2 × 1st class.
Credit Cards: None
Specialities: Choice herbaceous. *Agapanthus*, *Celmisia*, *Crocosmia*, *Rodgersia*, *Iris*, *Dierama*, *Erythronium* & *Roscoea*.
Notes: Also sells wholesale.
Map Ref: I, B3

ICro **CROCKNAFEOLA NURSERY** €
Killybegs, Co. Donegal, Ireland
Ⓣ 00 353 (0)74 97 51018
Ⓕ 00 353 (0)74 97 51095
Ⓔ crocknafeola@hotmail.com
Contact: Fionn McKenna
Opening Times: 0900-1800 Mon, Tue, Thu-Sat, closed Wed. 1200-1800 Sun.
Cat. Cost: None issued
Credit Cards: None
Specialities: Bedding plants, herbaceous perennials, rhododendrons, plants for containers, roses, plus shrubs & hedging for coastal areas.
Notes: Also sells wholesale.
Map Ref: I, D2

IDee **DEELISH GARDEN CENTRE** ⊠ €
Skibbereen, Co. Cork, Ireland
Ⓣ 00 353 (0)28 21374
Ⓕ 00 353 (0)28 21374
Ⓔ deel@eircom.net
Ⓦ www.deelish.ie
Contact: Bill & Rain Chase
Opening Times: 1000-1800 Mon-Sat, 1400-1800 Sun.
Min Mail Order EU: €50.00 (Ireland only).
Cat. Cost: Sae
Credit Cards: Visa Access
Specialities: Unusual plants for the mild coastal climate of Ireland. Conservatory plants. Sole Irish agents for Chase Organic Seeds.
Notes: No mail order outside Ireland.
Map Ref: I, D1

IDic **DICKSON NURSERIES LTD** ⊠ ✈
Milecross Road, Newtownards, Co. Down, N. Ireland, BT23 4SS
Ⓣ (028) 9181 2206
Ⓕ (028) 9181 3366
Ⓔ mail@dickson-roses.co.uk
Ⓦ www.dickson-roses.co.uk
Contact: Colin Dickson
Opening Times: 0800-1230 & 1300-1700 Mon-Thu. 0800-1230 Fri. Closes at 1600 Mon-Thu Dec-Jan.

Min Mail Order UK: Nmc
Min Mail Order EU: £25.00 + p&p
Cat. Cost: Free
Credit Cards: None
Specialities: Roses esp. modern Dickson varieties. Most varieties are available in small quantities only.
Notes: Also sells wholesale.
Map Ref: I, B3

IFFs **FUTURE FORESTS** ⊠ € ♿
Kealkil, Bantry, Co. Cork, Ireland
Ⓣ 00 353 (0)27 66176
Ⓕ 00 353 (0)27 66939
Ⓔ futureforests@eircom.net
Ⓦ www.futureforests.net
Contact: Nick Lain
Opening Times: 1000-1800 Mon-Sat (incl. B/hols), 1430-1800 Sun.
Min Mail Order UK: Nmc
Min Mail Order EU: Nmc
Cat. Cost: Free.
Credit Cards: Laser Visa MasterCard
Specialities: Trees, shrubs, hedging, climbers, roses. Fruit trees. Ferns, grasses & perennials.
Map Ref: I, D1 **OS Grid Ref:** W 083587

IFoB **FIELD OF BLOOMS** ⊠ € ♿
Ballymackey, Lisnamoe, Nenagh, Co. Tipperary, Ireland
Ⓣ 00 353 (0)67 29974
Ⓜ 08764 06044
Ⓔ guy2002@eircom.net
Ⓦ www.fieldofblooms.ie
Contact: Guy de Schrijver
Opening Times: Strictly by appt.
Min Mail Order UK: Nmc
Min Mail Order EU: Nmc
Cat. Cost: Free.
Credit Cards: None
Specialities: Hellebores, herbaceous, hardy perennials, ornamental grasses & woodland plants.
Map Ref: I, C2

IFro **FROGSWELL NURSERY** €
Clooncconlon, Straide, Foxford, Co. Mayo, Ireland
Ⓣ 00 353 (0)94 903 1420
Ⓜ 00 353 (0)8621 06166
Ⓔ frogswell@gmail.com
Ⓦ www.frogswell.net
Contact: Celia Graebner
Opening Times: Feb-Oct by appt. Please phone first. Also Garden Open Days & workshops; see website for details.
Cat. Cost: Online list for 2009.
Credit Cards: None
Specialities: A small nursery specialising in shade & woodland plants incl. hybrid hellebores & hardy geraniums, plus unusual perennials for the Irish climate, all raised on site, some in small quantities. Garden visits by arrangement.
Notes: See website for location details.

IGor **GORTKELLY CASTLE NURSERY** ⊠ €
Upperchurch, Thurles, Co. Tipperary, Ireland
Ⓣ 00 353 (0)504 54441
Contact: Clare Beumer
Opening Times: Mail order only. Not open to the public.
Min Mail Order UK: £50.00
Min Mail Order EU: €50.00
Cat. Cost: 5 × 1st class (UK), 5 × 48c (Rep. of Ireland).
Credit Cards: None
Specialities: Choice perennials.
Map Ref: I, C2

IKil **KILMURRY NURSERY** ⊠ € ♿
Gorey, Co. Wexford, Ireland
Ⓣ 00 353 (0)53 948 0223
Ⓜ 00 353 (0)8681 80623
Ⓕ 00 353 (0)53 948 0223
Ⓔ info@kilmurrynursery.com
Ⓦ www.kilmurrynursery.com
Contact: Paul & Orla Woods
Opening Times: 0900-1700 Mon-Fri, Mar-Sep. Wintertime by appt.
Min Mail Order UK: Nmc
Min Mail Order EU: Nmc
Cat. Cost: 3 × 1st class.
Credit Cards: None
Specialities: Herbaceous perennials and grasses.
Notes: Also sells wholesale.
Map Ref: I, C3 **OS Grid Ref:** 3C

ILis **LISDOONAN HERBS** ⊠ € ♿
98 Belfast Road, Saintfield, Co. Down, N. Ireland, BT24 7HF
Ⓣ (028) 9081 3624
Ⓔ b.pilcher@lisdoonanherbs.co.uk
Ⓦ www.lisdoonanherbs.co.uk
Contact: Barbara Pilcher
Opening Times: Please phone for appt.
Min Mail Order UK: Nmc
Min Mail Order EU: Nmc

KEY
⊠ Mail order to UK or EU — Delivers to shows
✈ Exports beyond EU — € Euro accepted
♿ Accessible by wheelchair — ◆ See Display advertisement

Cat. Cost: 2 × 1st class.
Credit Cards: None
Specialities: Aromatics, herbs, kitchen garden plants, period plants, some native species. Freshly cut herbs & salads. Some stock available in limited quantities only. All peat-free.
Map Ref: I, B3 **OS Grid Ref:** J390624

I

IMou **MOUNT VENUS NURSERY** ⊠ € ♿ ⌂
The Walled Garden, Mutton Lane, Dublin 16, Ireland
Ⓣ 00 353 (0)1 493 3813
Ⓜ 00 353 (0)8632 18789
Ⓔ schurmann@ireland.com
Ⓦ www.mountvenusnursery.com
Contact: Oliver & Liat Schurmann
Opening Times: 1000-1800 Mon-Sat, Feb-Nov.
Min Mail Order UK: £20.00
Min Mail Order EU: €35.00
Credit Cards: All major credit/debit cards
Specialities: Specialist perennials. Grasses & bamboos. Unusual woodland plants.
Notes: Also sells wholesale.
Map Ref: I, C3

IPen **PENINSULA PRIMULAS** ⊠ €
72 Ballyeasborough Road, Kircubbin, Co. Down, N. Ireland, BT22 1AD
Ⓣ (028) 4277 2193
Ⓔ Peninsula.Primulas@btinternet.com
Contact: Philip Bankhead
Opening Times: Mail order only. Not open.
Min Mail Order UK: Nmc
Min Mail Order EU: Nmc
Cat. Cost: Free
Credit Cards: None
Specialities: Extensive selection of *Primula* species, plus auriculas.

IPot **THE POTTING SHED** ⊠ € ☒ ⌂
Bolinaspick, Camolin, Enniscorthy, Co. Wexford, Ireland
Ⓣ 00 353 (0)5393 83629
Ⓕ 00 353 (0)5393 83629
Ⓔ sricher@iol.ie
Ⓦ www.camolinpottingshed.com
Contact: Susan Carrick
Opening Times: 1300-1800, Thu-Sun (incl.), Mar-Sep 2009. Other times by appt.
Min Mail Order UK: Nmc
Min Mail Order EU: Nmc
Cat. Cost: 3 × 1st class.
Credit Cards: MasterCard Visa
Specialities: Herbaceous & ornamental grasses.
Map Ref: I, C3

IPPN **PERENNIAL PLANTS NURSERY** ⊠ € ⌂
Nr Ballymaloe, Barnabrow, Midleton, Co. Cork, Ireland
Ⓣ 00 353 (0)21 465 2122
Ⓕ 00 353 (0)21 465 2122
Ⓔ perennialplants@eircom.net
Contact: Sandy McCarthy
Opening Times: Please ring for times.
Min Mail Order UK: Nmc
Min Mail Order EU: Nmc
Cat. Cost: None issued.
Credit Cards: None
Specialities: Many unusual herbaceous, ornamental grasses, tender perennials. Some available in small quantities only.
Notes: Will accept payment in sterling.
Map Ref: I, D2 **OS Grid Ref:** W9568

IPPs **PEONY PASSIONS** ⊠ € ⌂
The Old School House, Bracknagh, Rathangan, Co. Kildare, Ireland
Ⓣ 00 353 (0)5786 29109
Ⓜ 00 353 (0)8724 48636
Ⓕ 00 353 (0)5786 29109
Ⓔ ciaran.flood@gmail.com
Ⓦ www.peonypassions.ie
Contact: Ciaran Flood
Opening Times: Not open. Mail order only.
Min Mail Order UK: £20.00
Min Mail Order EU: £20.00
Cat. Cost: 2 × IRC
Credit Cards: None
Specialities: Chinese tree peonies. *Paeonia suffruticosa* hybrids. *Paeonia rockii* varieties.
Map Ref: I, C2

IRar **RARE PLANTS** ⊠ €
Kinsealy Cottage, Kinsealy Lane, Malahide, Co. Dublin, Ireland
Ⓔ info@rareplants.ie
Ⓦ www.rareplants.ie
Contact: Brian Murphy, Christopher Heavey
Opening Times: Not open to the public.
Min Mail Order UK: Nmc
Min Mail Order EU: Nmc
Cat. Cost: Online only.
Credit Cards: All major credit/debit cards
Specialities: Propagates & raises a range of rare & unusual plants incl. trees, shrubs, herbaceous & alpine. Specialises in difficult to obtain & slightly tender plants. All propagated from superior clones. Only available in small quantities.
Notes: P&P costs on request. Also sells wholesale.
Map Ref: I, C3 **OS Grid Ref:** 0 220 462

IRhd **Ringhaddy Daffodils** ⊠ € ✈
Ringhaddy Road, Killinchy, Newtownards, Co. Down, N. Ireland, BT23 6TU
Ⓣ (028) 9754 1007
Ⓜ 07762 337534
Ⓔ info@ringhaddy-daffodils.com
Ⓦ www.ringhaddy-daffodils.com
Contact: Nial Watson
Opening Times: Mail order only. Not open.
Min Mail Order UK: £20.00 + p&p
Min Mail Order EU: £50.00 + p&p
Cat. Cost: £2.50 redeemable on order.
Credit Cards: Paypal
Specialities: New daffodil varieties for exhibitors and hybridisers. Small stock of some varieties.

ISha **Shady Plants** ⊠ € ♿ ⌂
Coolbooa, Clashmore, Youghal, Co. Cork, Ireland
Ⓣ 00 353 (0)24 96735
Ⓜ 00 353 (0)8605 42171
Ⓔ mike@shadyplants.ie
Ⓦ www.shadyplants.net
Contact: Mike Keep
Opening Times: By appt. only Mar-Oct.
Min Mail Order UK: Nmc
Min Mail Order EU: Nmc
Cat. Cost: €3.00
Credit Cards: Paypal
Specialities: Specialist fern nursery based near the south coast of Ireland.
Map Ref: I, D2 **OS Grid Ref:** 613585

ISsi **Seaside Nursery** ⊠ € ♿
Claddaghduff, Co. Galway, Ireland
Ⓣ 00 353 (0)95 44687
Ⓕ 00 353 (0)95 44761
Ⓔ seaside@anu.ie
Ⓦ www.anu.ie/seaside/
Contact: Tom Dyck
Opening Times: 1000-1300 & 1400-1800 Mon-Sat, 1400-1800 Sun. Closed Sun 1st Nov-31st Mar.
Min Mail Order UK: Nmc
Min Mail Order EU: Nmc
Cat. Cost: €3.50
Credit Cards: Visa MasterCard
Specialities: Plants & hedging suitable for seaside locations. Rare plants originating from Australia & New Zealand esp. *Phormium*, *Astelia*.
Notes: Also sells wholesale.
Map Ref: I, B1

ITim **Timpany Nurseries & Gardens** ⊠ ♿ ⌂
77 Magheratimpany Road, Ballynahinch, Co. Down, N. Ireland, BT24 8PA
Ⓣ (028) 9756 2812
Ⓕ (028) 9756 2812
Ⓔ s.tindall@btconnect.com
Ⓦ www.timpanynurseries.com
Contact: Susan Tindall
Opening Times: 1000-1730 Tue-Sat, Sun by appt.
Min Mail Order UK: Nmc
Min Mail Order EU: £30.00 + p&p
Cat. Cost: £2.00
Credit Cards: Visa MasterCard
Specialities: *Celmisia*, *Androsace*, *Primula*, *Saxifraga*, *Dianthus*, *Meconopsis*, *Cassiope*, *Rhodohypoxis*, *Cyclamen* & *Primula auricula*.
Notes: Also sells wholesale.
Map Ref: I, B3

IVic **Victoria's Nursery & Garden** € ⌂
Upper Kells, Kells, Cahirceveen, Co Kerry, Ireland
Ⓣ 00 353 (0)66 947 7605
Ⓜ 00 353 (0)8791 11465
Ⓔ kellshouse@eircom.net
Contact: Victoria Vogel
Opening Times: 1100-1700 Wed-Sun all year except Xmas. Closed Mon & Tue, except B/hols & by arrangement.
Cat. Cost: None issued.
Credit Cards: None
Specialities: *Rhododendron*, azaleas, *Acer*, treeferns, seaside & woodland plants, South African & Mediterranean bulbs, *Saxifraga fortunei* forms, gentians, campanulas.
Notes: Drive along Ring of Kerry, at Kells follow signs to Kells Bay Garden towards Kells Beach, nursery to left after little bridge.
Map Ref: I, D1

London Area

LAma **Jacques Amand International** ⊠ € ✈ ♿
The Nurseries, 145 Clamp Hill, Stanmore, Middlesex, HA7 3JS
Ⓣ (020) 8420 7110
Ⓕ (020) 8954 6784
Ⓔ bulbs@jacquesamand.co.uk
Ⓦ www.jacquesamand.com
Contact: John Amand & Stuart Chapman
Opening Times: 0900-1700 Mon-Fri, 1000-1400 Sat.
Min Mail Order UK: Nmc
Min Mail Order EU: Nmc
Cat. Cost: 1 × 1st class.
Credit Cards: All major credit/debit cards

KEY
⊠ Mail order to UK or EU ⌂ Delivers to shows
✈ Exports beyond EU € Euro accepted
♿ Accessible by wheelchair ◆ See Display advertisement

L

Specialities: Rare and unusual species bulbs esp. *Arisaema*, *Trillium*, *Fritillaria*, tulips.
Notes: Also sells wholesale.
Map Ref: L, B3

LAst **ASTERBY & CHALKCROFT NURSERY** ⊠ ♿
The Ridgeway, Blunham, Bedfordshire, MK44 3PH
Ⓣ (01767) 640148
Ⓔ sales@asterbyplants.co.uk
Ⓦ www.asterbyplants.co.uk
Contact: Simon & Eva Aldridge
Opening Times: 1000-1700 7 days. Closed Xmas & Jan.
Cat. Cost: 2 × 1st class.
Credit Cards: Visa MasterCard Maestro
Specialities: Hardy shrubs, herbaceous & trees. Please note mail order of plug plants only in the spring.
Map Ref: L, A3 **OS Grid Ref:** TL151497

L

LAyl **AYLETT NURSERIES LTD** ♿ ◆
North Orbital Road, St Albans, Hertfordshire, AL2 1DH
Ⓣ (01727) 822255
Ⓕ (01727) 823024
Ⓔ info@aylettnurseries.co.uk
Ⓦ www.aylettnurseries.co.uk
Contact: Roger S Aylett
Opening Times: 0830-1730 Mon-Fri, 0830-1700 Sat, 1030-1630 Sun.
Cat. Cost: Free.
Credit Cards: All major credit/debit cards
Specialities: *Dahlia*. 2-acre trial ground adjacent to garden centre.
Notes: Also sells wholesale.
Map Ref: L, B3 **OS Grid Ref:** TL169049

LBee **BEECHCROFT NURSERY** ♿
127 Reigate Road, Ewell, Surrey, KT17 3DE
Ⓣ 0208 393 4265
Ⓕ 0208 393 4265
Contact: C Kimber
Opening Times: 1000-1600 Mon-Sat, 1000-1400 Sun and B/hols. Closed Xmas-New Year week.
Cat. Cost: None issued.
Credit Cards: All major credit/debit cards
Specialities: Conifers & alpines.
Notes: Also sells wholesale.
Map Ref: L, C3

LBMP **BLOOMING MARVELLOUS PLANTS** ⌂
Korketts Farm, Aylesbury Road, Shipton, Winslow, Buckinghamshire, MK18 3JL
Ⓣ (01296) 714714
Ⓜ 07963 747305
Ⓔ alex@bmplants.co.uk
Ⓦ www.bmplants.co.uk
Contact: Alexia Ballance
Opening Times: 0900-1700 Wed-Sat & 1000-1600 Sun, 1st Mar-30th Sep. 1000-1600 Sat & by appt. Oct-Dec. By appt. only in Jan & Feb.
Cat. Cost: £1.00 in stamps.
Credit Cards: All major credit/debit cards
Specialities: A mixture of unusual and familiar perennials, shrubs, grasses, ferns & bedding plants, most in more generous sizes than usually found in nurseries.
Notes: Located on the A413 just outside Winslow (heading in the Aylesbury direction). Partial wheelchair access. Also sells wholesale.
Map Ref: L, A2 **OS Grid Ref:** SP777271

LBuc **BUCKINGHAM NURSERIES** ⊠ € ♿ ◆
14 Tingewick Road, Buckingham, MK18 4AE
Ⓣ (01280) 822133
Ⓕ (01280) 815491
Ⓔ enquiries@buckingham-nurseries.co.uk
Ⓦ www.buckingham-nurseries.co.uk
Contact: R J & P L Brown
Opening Times: 0830-1730 (1800 in summer) Mon-Sat, 1030-1630 Sun.
Min Mail Order UK: Nmc
Cat. Cost: Free.
Credit Cards: Visa MasterCard Switch
Specialities: Bare rooted and container grown hedging. Trees, shrubs, herbaceous perennials, alpines, grasses & ferns.
Map Ref: L, A2 **OS Grid Ref:** SP675333

LCla **CLAY LANE NURSERY** ⊠ ⌂
3 Clay Lane, South Nutfield, Nr Redhill, Surrey, RH1 4EG
Ⓣ (01737) 823307
Ⓔ claylane.nursery@btinternet.com
Ⓦ www.claylane-fuchsias.co.uk
Contact: K W Belton
Opening Times: Variable opening times. Please phone before travelling.
Min Mail Order UK: £7.00
Cat. Cost: 3 × 2nd class.
Credit Cards: None
Specialities: *Fuchsia*. Many varieties in small quantities only.
Notes: Mail order by telephone pre-arangement only.
Map Ref: L, C4

LCtg **COTTAGE GARDEN NURSERY** ◆
Barnet Road, Arkley, Barnet, Hertfordshire, EN5 3JX
Ⓣ (020) 8441 8829
Ⓕ (020) 8531 3178

Ⓔ nurseryinfo@cottagegardennursery-barnet.co.uk
Ⓦ www.cottagegardennursery-barnet.co.uk
Contact: David and Wendy Spicer
Opening Times: 0930-1700 Tue-Sat Mar-Oct, 0930-1600 Tue-Sat Nov-Feb, 1000-1600 Sun & B/hol Mon all year.
Cat. Cost: None issued.
Credit Cards: All major credit/debit cards
Specialities: General range of hardy shrubs, trees, fruit trees & bushes, perennials. Architectural & exotics, *Fuchsia*, seasonal bedding, patio plants.
Map Ref: L, B3 **OS Grid Ref:** TQ226958

LDea **Derek Lloyd Dean** ⊠ ✈ ⛺
8 Lynwood Close, South Harrow, Middlesex, HA2 9PR
Ⓣ 0208 864 0899
Ⓔ lloyddeancbtinternet.com
Ⓦ www.dereklloyddean.com
Contact: Derek Lloyd Dean
Opening Times: Not open. Mail order only.
Min Mail Order UK: £2.50 + p&p
Min Mail Order EU: £2.50 + p&p
Cat. Cost: 2 × 1st class.
Credit Cards: None
Specialities: Regal, angel & scented leaf *Pelargonium*. Nat. Collection of Angel *Pelargonium*.

LEdu **Edulis** ⊠ € ♿ ⛺
(office) 1 Flowers Piece, Ashampstead, Reading, Berkshire, RG8 8SG
Ⓣ (01635) 578113
Ⓜ 07802 812781
Ⓕ (01635) 578113
Ⓔ edulis.nursery@virgin.net
Ⓦ www.edulis.co.uk
Contact: Paul Barney
Opening Times: By appt. only.
Min Mail Order UK: £10.00 + p&p
Min Mail Order EU: £50.00 + p&p
Cat. Cost: 4 × 1st class.
Credit Cards: None
Specialities: Unusual edibles, architectural plants, permaculture plants.
Notes: Nursery is at Bere Court Farm, Tidmarsh Lane, Pangbourne, RG8 8HT. Also sells wholesale.
Map Ref: L, B2 **OS Grid Ref:** SU615747

LFCN **Farnham Common Nurseries Ltd** ♿ ⛺
Crown Lane, Farnham Royal, Nr Slough, Bucks, SL2 3SF
Ⓣ (01753) 643108
Ⓕ (01753) 646818
Ⓔ sales@fcn.co.uk
Ⓦ www.fcn.co.uk
Contact: Sadie Cocker
Opening Times: 0800-1700 Mon-Fri, 0900-1700 Sat, 1000-1600 Sun (w/end retail only).
Cat. Cost: No retail cat. issued.
Credit Cards: All major credit/debit cards
Specialities: Good selection of ornamental trees, shrubs & herbaceous perennials, esp. *Pittosporum*, *Phormium*, *Iris* & *Heuchera*.
Notes: Also sells wholesale.
Map Ref: L, B3 **OS Grid Ref:** SU955832

LHel **Herts Hellebores** ⊠ €
(office) Sandersted, Giffords Lane, Haultwick, Hertfordshire, SG11 1JE
Ⓣ (01920) 438458
Ⓔ lorna@herts-hellebore.co.uk
Ⓦ www.herts-hellebore.co.uk
Contact: Lorna Jones
Opening Times: 1000-1600 Wed & Sat only, 14th Jan-28th Mar 2009. Other times during this period by appt. only. Check with nursery for 2010 opening times.
Min Mail Order UK: £18
Min Mail Order EU: £18
Cat. Cost: Free.
Credit Cards: All major credit/debit cards
Specialities: *Hellebore* hybrids. Specialising in developments of double & anemone centred hybrids. Seed-raised plants offered by colour. Some available in small quantities only.
Notes: Nursery at Green Lane Farm, Levens Green, nr Ware, Herts SG11 1HD.
Map Ref: L, A4 **OS Grid Ref:** TL357224

LHop **Hopleys Plants Ltd** ⊠ ♿ ⛺ ◆
High Street, Much Hadham, Hertfordshire, SG10 6BU
Ⓣ (01279) 842509
Ⓕ (01279) 843784
Ⓔ plants@hopleys.co.uk
Ⓦ www.hopleys.co.uk
Contact: Mr Aubrey Barker
Opening Times: 0900-1700 Mon & Wed-Sat, 1400-1700 Sun. Closed Jan-Feb except by appt.
Min Mail Order UK: Nmc
Cat. Cost: 5 × 1st class.
Credit Cards: Visa Access Switch
Specialities: Wide range of hardy & half-hardy shrubs & perennials.
Notes: Also sells wholesale.
Map Ref: L, A4 **OS Grid Ref:** TL428196

KEY
⊠ Mail order to UK or EU — ⛺ Delivers to shows
✈ Exports beyond EU — € Euro accepted
♿ Accessible by wheelchair — ◆ See Display advertisement

LHyd **Hydon Nurseries** ⊠ € ◆
Clock Barn Lane, Hydon Heath, Godalming, Surrey, GU8 4AZ
Ⓣ (01483) 860252
Ⓕ (01483) 419937
Contact: A F George, Rodney Longhurst & Mrs A M George
Opening Times: 0930-1245 & 1400-1700 Mon-Fri Feb-mid Jun & Oct-mid Nov, except Sat Oct-mid Mar 0930-1245 only. Other months 0930-1600 Mon-Fri, 0930-1245 Sat. Sun by appt.
Min Mail Order UK: Nmc
Min Mail Order EU: £25.00 + p&p
Cat. Cost: £2.00 or 7 × 1st class or 10 × 2nd class.
Credit Cards: None
Specialities: Large and dwarf *Rhododendron*, *yakushimanum* hybrids, azaleas (deciduous & evergreen), *Camellia* & other trees & shrubs. Specimen *Rhododendron*. Conservatory: scented tender rhododendrons & camellias.
Notes: Also sells wholesale.

LIMB **I.M.B. Plants** ⊠
2 Ashdown Close, Giffard Park, Milton Keynes, Buckinghamshire, MK14 5PX
Ⓣ (01908) 618911
Ⓔ imbrazier@btinternet.com
Contact: Ian Brazier
Opening Times: Not open. Mail order only.
Min Mail Order UK: Nmc
Credit Cards: None
Specialities: *Helianthemum*. All plants propagated in small quantities. Will propagate to order.

LLHF **Little Heath Farm (UK) (formerly Two Jays Alpines)** ♠
Little Heath Lane, Potten End, Berkhamsted, Hertfordshire, HP4 2RY
Ⓣ (01442) 864951
Ⓔ lhfnursery@gmail.com
Ⓦ www.littleheathfarmnursery.co.uk
Contact: John Spokes
Opening Times: 1000-1700 or dusk if earlier, 7 days.
Cat. Cost: Online only.
Credit Cards: Visa MasterCard
Specialities: Large range of alpines, herbaceous, shrubs, many available in small quantities only.
Map Ref: L, B3

LLWG **Lilies Water Gardens** ⊠ ♿ ♠
Broad Lane, Newdigate, Surrey, RH5 5AT
Ⓣ (01306) 631064
Ⓜ 07801 166244
Ⓕ (01306) 631693
Ⓔ mail@lilieswatergardens.co.uk
Ⓦ www.lilieswatergardens.co.uk
Contact: Simon Harman
Opening Times: 0900-1700 Tues-Sat, Mar-Aug. By appt. only Sep-Feb.
Min Mail Order UK: Nmc but flat rate £10.00 delivery charge.
Cat. Cost: Online only.
Credit Cards: All major credit/debit cards
Specialities: Waterlilies, moist perennials, bog-garden plants, primulas, marginal plants. Ferns, alpines & oxygenating plants. Pond, aquatic, water-garden, floating, stream, deep-water & waterfall plants. Rushes & grasses.
Map Ref: L, C3

LLWP **L W Plants** ⊠ ♠
23 Wroxham Way, Harpenden, Hertfordshire, AL5 4PP
Ⓣ (01582) 768467
Ⓔ lwplants@waitrose.com
Ⓦ www.thymus.co.uk
Contact: Mrs Margaret Easter
Opening Times: 1000-1700 most days, but please phone first.
Min Mail Order UK: Nmc
Cat. Cost: A5 sae + 5 × 2nd class (loose).
Credit Cards: None
Specialities: Plants from a plantsman's garden, esp. *Geranium*, grasses, *Penstemon* & *Thymus*. Some available in small quantities only. Nat. Collections of *Thymus* (Scientific), *Hyssopus* & *Satureja*. *Thymus* ICRA (provisional). *Thymus* propagated to order.
Notes: Mail order *Thymus* only.
Map Ref: L, B3 **OS Grid Ref:** TL141153

LMaj **Majestic Trees** ♠
Chequers Meadow, Chequers Hill, Flamstead, St Albans, Hertfordshire, AL3 8ET
Ⓣ (01582) 843881
Ⓕ (01582) 843882
Ⓔ info@majesticgroup.co.uk
Ⓦ www.majestictrees.co.uk
Contact: Andrew Austin
Opening Times: 0830-1700 Mon-Fri. 1000-1600 (1700 Mar-Oct) Sat. Closed Sun, B/hols & Xmas/New Year.
Cat. Cost: 6 × 1st class.
Credit Cards: MasterCard Visa Switch Maestro
Specialities: Semi-mature & mature containerised trees grown in airpot from 50ltr to 5000ltr.
Notes: Also sells wholesale.
Map Ref: L, B3 **OS Grid Ref:** TL08140815

LMil **MILLAIS NURSERIES** ⊠ ♿
Crosswater Farm, Crosswater Lane, Churt, Surrey, GU10 2JN
Ⓣ (01252) 792698
Ⓕ (01252) 792526
Ⓔ sales@rhododendrons.co.uk
Ⓦ www.rhododendrons.co.uk
Contact: David Millais
Opening Times: 1000-1300 & 1400-1700 Mon-Fri. Sat spring & autumn. Daily in May.
Min Mail Order UK: Nmc
Min Mail Order EU: £100.00 + p&p
Cat. Cost: Free list on request or Online.
Credit Cards: All major credit/debit cards
Specialities: Rhododendrons, azaleas, magnolias & acers.
Notes: Mail order Sep-May only. Also sells wholesale.
Map Ref: L, C3 **OS Grid Ref:** SU856397

LMor **MOREHAVENS** ⊠ ♿
Sandpit Hill, Buckland Common, Tring, Hertfordshire, HP23 6NG
Ⓣ (01494) 758642
Ⓔ morehavens@hotmail.co.uk
Ⓦ www.camomilelawns.co.uk
Contact: B Farmer
Opening Times: Mail order only. Open only for collection.
Min Mail Order UK: £14.00
Min Mail Order EU: £14.00 + p&p
Cat. Cost: Free.
Credit Cards: None
Specialities: *Camomile* 'Treneague' and dwarf variety.
Notes: Also sells wholesale.

LOck **OCKLEY COURT NURSERY** ♿
Coles Lane, Ockley, Surrey, RH5 5LS
Ⓣ (01306) 713576
Ⓜ 07786 998743
Ⓕ (01306) 713755
Ⓔ ma_gibbison@hotmail.com
Contact: Martin Gibbison
Opening Times: 8000-1730 Spring-Autumn, 1000-1600 Winter.
Cat. Cost: £1.00 for stocklist.
Credit Cards: All, except American Express
Specialities: *Clematis* & new herbaceous.
Notes: Also sells wholesale.
Map Ref: L, C3

LPal **THE PALM CENTRE** ⊠ € ✈ ♿ ⛺
Ham Central Nursery, opposite Riverside Drive, Ham Street, Ham, Richmond, Surrey, TW10 7HA
Ⓣ (020) 8255 6191
Ⓕ (020) 8255 6192
Ⓔ mail@palmcentre.co.uk
Ⓦ palmcentre.co.uk
Contact: Martin Gibbons
Opening Times: 0900-1700 (dusk in winter) 7 days. Admin & Order Dept. 0900-1700 Mon-Fri.
Min Mail Order UK: £10.00 + p&p
Min Mail Order EU: £10.00 + p&p
Cat. Cost: Free.
Credit Cards: Visa MasterCard Switch
Specialities: Palms & cycads, exotic & sub-tropical, hardy, half-hardy & tropical. Seedlings to mature trees. Also bamboos, tree ferns & many other exotics. *Trachycarpus*.
Notes: Also sells wholesale.
Map Ref: L, B3

LPBA **PAUL BROMFIELD – AQUATICS** ⊠ € ✈ ♿
Maydencroft Lane, Gosmore, Hitchin, Hertfordshire, SG4 7QD
Ⓣ (01462) 457399
Ⓕ (01462) 422652
Ⓔ info@bromfieldaquatics.co.uk
Ⓦ www.bromfieldaquatics.co.uk
Contact: Debbie Edwards
Opening Times: Mail order only. Order online at website. Office open 1000-1700 Mon-Sat, Feb-Oct. Visitors please ring for appt.
Min Mail Order UK: Nmc
Min Mail Order EU: £100.00 incl.
Cat. Cost: Online only.
Credit Cards: Visa MasterCard Delta JCB Switch
Specialities: Water lilies, marginals & bog.
Notes: Also sells wholesale.

LPen **PENSTEMONS BY COLOUR** ⊠
Peterley Manor, Peterley, Prestwood, Great Missenden, Buckinghamshire, HP16 0HH
Ⓣ (01494) 866420
Ⓕ (01494) 866420
Ⓔ debra.hughes1@virgin.net
Contact: Debra Hughes
Opening Times: Any time by appt.
Min Mail Order UK: £10.00
Cat. Cost: Free
Credit Cards: None
Specialities: *Penstemon*.
Map Ref: L, B3 **OS Grid Ref:** SU880994

KEY
⊠ Mail order to UK or EU ⛺ Delivers to shows
✈ Exports beyond EU € Euro accepted
♿ Accessible by wheelchair ◆ See Display advertisement

L

LPio **Pioneer Nursery** ⊠ € ♿
Baldock Lane, Willian,
Letchworth, Hertfordshire,
SG6 2AE
Ⓣ (01462) 675858
Ⓔ milly@pioneerplants.com
Ⓦ www.pioneerplants.com
Contact: John Hoyland
Opening Times: 0900-1700 Wed-Sat, Mar-Oct. 1000-1600 Thu-Sat, Nov, Dec & Feb.
Min Mail Order UK: £15.00 + p&p
Min Mail Order EU: €30.00
Cat. Cost: Online only.
Credit Cards: MasterCard Visa
Specialities: *Clematis*, *Salvia*, tender perennials, species *Pelargonium*. Wide range of hard-to-find perennials & bulbs.
Notes: Mail order via internet only. Also sells wholesale.
Map Ref: L, A3 **OS Grid Ref:** TL224307

LPJP **PJ's Palms and Exotics** ⊠ €
41 Salcombe Road, Ashford, Middlesex,
TW15 3BS
Ⓣ (01784) 250181
Contact: Peter Jenkins
Opening Times: Mail order only 1st Mar-30th Nov. Visits by arrangement.
Min Mail Order UK: Nmc
Min Mail Order EU: Nmc
Cat. Cost: 2 × 1st clas.
Credit Cards: None
Specialities: Palms, bananas & other exotic foliage plants, hardy & half-hardy. *Trachycarpus wagnerianus* seeds available. Plants available in small quantities.
Notes: Also sells wholesale.
Map Ref: L, B3

LPla **The Plant Specialist**
7 Whitefield Lane, Great Missenden,
Buckinghamshire, HP16 0BH
Ⓣ (01494) 866650
Ⓕ (01494) 866650
Ⓔ enquire@theplantspecialist.co.uk
Ⓦ www.theplantspecialist.co.uk
Contact: Sean Walter
Opening Times: 1000-1700 Wed-Sat, 1000-1600 Sun, Apr-Oct.
Cat. Cost: None issued.
Credit Cards: All major credit/debit cards
Specialities: Herbaceous perennials, grasses, half-hardy perennials, bulbs.

LRHS **Wisley Plant Centre (RHS)** ♿
RHS Garden, Wisley, Woking, Surrey,
GU23 6QB
Ⓣ (01483) 211113
Ⓕ (01483) 212372
Ⓔ wisleyplantcentre@rhs.org.uk
Ⓦ www.rhs.org.uk/wisleyplantcentre
Opening Times: 0930-1700 Mon-Sat, Oct-Feb. 0930-1800 Mon-Sat, Mar-Sep. 1030-1630 Sun all year, browsing from 1000.
Cat. Cost: Online only.
Credit Cards: All major credit/debit cards
Specialities: Over 10,000 plants, many rare or unusual, reflecting the range of the RHS flagship garden at Wisley. Plants subject to seasonal availability. For plants not in stock, we operate a reservation service.
Notes: Programme of free plant events throughout the year. Please ring or check website for details.
Map Ref: L, C3

LSee **Seeds by Size** ⊠ € ✈
45 Crouchfield, Boxmoor,
Hemel Hempstead, Hertfordshire,
HP1 1PA
Ⓣ (01442) 251458
Ⓔ john-robert-size@seeds-by-size.co.uk
Ⓦ www.seeds-by-size.co.uk
Contact: John Robert Size
Opening Times: Not open. Mail order only.
Min Mail Order UK: Nmc
Min Mail Order EU: Nmc
Cat. Cost: Online only.
Credit Cards: Paypal
Specialities: Seeds. 22,000 varieties of flower, vegetable & herb seeds, including sweet peas, pansies, petunias, *Impatiens*, marigolds, ornamental grasses, cabbages, tomatoes, cauliflowers, herbs & onions. Oriental vegetables, hot peppers & sweet peppers in 226 specialities plus other lists.
Notes: Euros accepted as cash payments only. Also sells wholesale.

LShp **Squire's Garden Centre, Shepperton** ♿
Halliford Road, Upper Halliford,
Shepperton, Middlesex,
TW17 8RU
Ⓣ (01932) 784121
Ⓕ (01932) 780569
Ⓔ shepp.plants@squiresgardencentres.co.uk
Ⓦ www.squiresgardencentres.co.uk
Contact: Plant Area Manager
Opening Times: 0900-1800 Mon-Sat, 1030-1630 Sun.
Cat. Cost: None issued.
Credit Cards: All major credit/debit cards
Specialities: Roses.
Notes: Other garden centres in Middlesex & Surrey.

LSou **SOUTHON PLANTS** ☒ ♿
Mutton Hill, Dormansland, Lingfield, Surrey, RH7 6NP
Ⓣ (01342) 870150
Ⓔ info@southonplants.com
Ⓦ www.southonplants.com
Contact: Mr Southon
Opening Times: 0900-1730 Feb-Oct. For Nov, Dec & Jan please phone first.
Min Mail Order UK: Nmc
Cat. Cost: Online only.
Credit Cards: All major credit/debit cards
Specialities: New & unusual hardy & tender perennials, specialising in *Agapanthus*, *Coreopsis*, *Euphorbia*, *Heuchera* and variegated plants.
Notes: Mail order. Please phone/email for details.
Map Ref: L, C4

LSqH **SQUIRE'S GARDEN CENTRE, WEST HORSLEY** ♿
Epsom Road, West Horsley, Leatherhead, Surrey, KT24 6AR
Ⓣ (01483) 282911
Ⓕ (01483) 281380
Ⓔ hors.plants.squiresgardencentres.co.uk
Ⓦ www.squiresgardencentres.co.uk
Contact: Plant Area Manager
Opening Times: 0900-1800 Mon-Sat, 1030-1630 Sun.
Cat. Cost: None issued.
Credit Cards: All major credit/debit cards
Specialities: Herbaceous.
Notes: Other garden centres in Middlesex & Surrey.

LSqu **SQUIRE'S GARDEN CENTRE, TWICKENHAM** ♿
Sixth Cross Road, Twickenham, Middlesex, TW2 5PA
Ⓣ 0208 977 9241
Ⓕ 0208 943 4024
Ⓔ twic.plants@squiresgardencentres.co.uk
Ⓦ www.squiresgardencentres.co.uk
Contact: Plant Area Manager
Opening Times: 0900-1800 Mon-Sat, 1030-1630 Sun.
Credit Cards: All major credit/debit cards
Specialities: *Clematis*.
Notes: Other garden centres in Middlesex & Surrey.

LSRN **SPRING REACH NURSERY** ☒ ♿ ⛺
Long Reach, Ockham, Guildford, Surrey, GU23 6PG
Ⓣ (01483) 284769
Ⓜ 07884 432666
Ⓕ (01483) 284769
Ⓔ info@springreachnursery.co.uk
Ⓦ www.springreachnursery.co.uk
Contact: Nick & Lissa Hourhan
Opening Times: 7 days. 1000-1700 Mon-Sat, 1030-1630 Sun. Open B/hols.
Min Mail Order UK: Nmc
Min Mail Order EU: Nmc
Credit Cards: All major credit/debit cards
Specialities: Shrubs, evergreen climbers, *Clematis*, perennials, roses, grasses, ferns, bamboos, trees, hedging, soft fruit & top fruit. Plants for chalk & clay. Deer & rabbit proof plants. Specimen & acid-loving plants.
Notes: Also sells wholesale. Please ring for mail order details.
Map Ref: L, C3

LStr **HENRY STREET NURSERY** ☒ ♿
Swallowfield Road, Arborfield, Reading, Berkshire, RG2 9JY
Ⓣ (0118) 9761223
Ⓕ (0118) 9761417
Ⓔ info@henrystreet.co.uk
Ⓦ www.henrystreet.co.uk
Contact: Mr M C Goold
Opening Times: 0900-1730 Mon-Sat, 1030-1630 Sun.
Min Mail Order UK: Nmc
Min Mail Order EU: Nmc
Cat. Cost: Free
Credit Cards: Visa Access Switch
Specialities: Roses.
Notes: Also sells wholesale.
Map Ref: L, C3

LTen **TENDERCARE NURSERIES LTD** ♿ ⛺
Southlands Road, Denham, Middlesex, UB9 4HD
Ⓣ (01895) 835544
Ⓕ (01895) 835036
Ⓔ sales@tendercare.co.uk
Ⓦ www.tendercare.co.uk
Contact: Christopher Poole
Opening Times: 0900-1700 Mon-Sat.
Credit Cards: All major credit/debit cards
Specialities: Mature trees, shrubs, hedging, climbers & herbaceous plants.
Notes: Also sells wholesale.
Map Ref: L, B3

LToo **TOOBEES EXOTICS** ☒ € ✈
20 Inglewood, St Johns, Woking, Surrey, GU21 3HX
Ⓣ (01483) 722600

KEY
☒ Mail order to UK or EU | ⛺ Delivers to shows
✈ Exports beyond EU | € Euro accepted
♿ Accessible by wheelchair | ◆ See Display advertisement

Ⓜ 07836 334011
Ⓕ (01483) 751995
Ⓔ bbpotter@woking.plus.com
Ⓦ www.toobees-exotics.com
Contact: Bob Potter
Opening Times: Not open. Mail order & online shop only. Visits by appt. only.
Min Mail Order UK: Nmc
Min Mail Order EU: Nmc
Cat. Cost: Sae
Specialities: South African & Madagascan succulents, many rare & unusual species, *Euphorbia* & *Pachypodium*. Stock varies constantly.
Notes: Credit cards accepted online only.

LYaf **YAFFLES** ⊠ ♿
Harvest Hill, Bourne End, Buckinghamshire, SL8 5JJ
Ⓣ (01628) 525455
Contact: I Butterfield
Opening Times: 0900-1300 & 1400-1700. Please phone beforehand in case we are attending shows.
Min Mail Order UK: Nmc
Min Mail Order EU: £30.00 + p&p
Cat. Cost: 2 × 2nd class.
Credit Cards: None
Specialities: Nat. Collection of *Pleione*. Scientific Award 1999. *Dahlia* for collection only.
Notes: Only *Pleione* by mail order.
Map Ref: L, B3

MIDLANDS

MAga **AGAVE NURSERY** ⊠ € ✈ ⌂
97 Nottingham Road, Somercotes, Derbyshire, DE55 4JH
Ⓜ 01773 605843/07814 787555/07791 627358
Ⓔ jon@agavenursery.wanadoo.co.uk
Ⓦ www.agave-nursery.co.uk
Contact: Jon & Sue Dudek
Opening Times: Mail order only. Open by appt. only.
Min Mail Order UK: Nmc
Min Mail Order EU: Nmc
Cat. Cost: Free
Credit Cards: None
Specialities: *Agave*, *Furcraea*, *Manfreda* & *Yucca*.
Map Ref: M, B2

MAJR **A J ROBINSON** ⊠
Sycamore Farm, Foston, Derbyshire, DE65 5PW
Ⓣ (01283) 815635
Ⓔ argyspot@aol.com
Contact: A J Robinson
Opening Times: By appt. for collection of plants only.
Min Mail Order UK: £14.00
Cat. Cost: 2 × 1st class for list.
Credit Cards: None
Specialities: Extensive collection of tender perennials. Salvias. Nat. Collection of *Argyranthemum*.
Notes: Mail order argyranthemums only.
Map Ref: M, B2

MArl **ARLEY HALL NURSERY** ♿
Arley Hall Nursery, Northwich, Cheshire, CW9 6NA
Ⓣ (01565) 777479 or 777231
Ⓕ (01565) 777465
Ⓦ www.arleyhallandgardens.com
Contact: Jane Foster
Opening Times: 1100-1730 Tue-Sun 22nd Mar-end Sep. Also B/hol Mons.
Cat. Cost: 4 × 1st class.
Credit Cards: All major credit/debit cards
Specialities: Wide range of herbaceous incl. many unusual varieties, some in small quantities. Wide range of unusual pelargoniums.
Notes: Nursery is beside car park at Arley Hall Gardens.
Map Ref: M, A1 **OS Grid Ref:** SJ673808

MAsh **ASHWOOD NURSERIES LTD** ⊠ ♿
Ashwood Lower Lane, Ashwood, Kingswinford, West Midlands, DY6 0AE
Ⓣ (01384) 401996
Ⓕ (01384) 401108
Ⓔ info@ashwoodnurseries.com
Ⓦ www.ashwoodnurseries.com
Contact: Mark Warburton & Philip Baulk
Opening Times: 0900-1700 Mon-Sat & 0930-1700 Sun excl. Xmas & Boxing Day.
Min Mail Order UK: Nmc
Cat. Cost: 6 × 1st class.
Credit Cards: Visa Access MasterCard
Specialities: Large range of hardy plants, shrubs & dwarf conifers. Roses, alpines & herbaceous plants. Also specialises in *Auricula*, *Cyclamen*, *Galanthus*, hellebores, *Hepatica*, *Hydrangea* & *Salvia*. Nat. Collection of *Lewisia*.
Map Ref: M, C2 **OS Grid Ref:** SO865879

MAus **DAVID AUSTIN ROSES LTD** ⊠ € ✈ ♿ ◆
Bowling Green Lane, Albrighton, Wolverhampton, West Midlands, WV7 3HB
Ⓣ (01902) 376300
Ⓕ (01902) 375177

Ⓔ retail@davidaustinroses.co.uk
Ⓦ www.davidaustinroses.com
Contact: Customer Services Dept
Opening Times: 0900-1700, 7 days.
Min Mail Order UK: Nmc
Min Mail Order EU: Nmc
Cat. Cost: Free.
Credit Cards: Switch Visa MasterCard Maestro Access
Specialities: Roses. Nat. Collection of English Roses.
Notes: Also sells wholesale.
Map Ref: M, B2 **OS Grid Ref:** SJ798042

MAvo **AVONDALE NURSERY** ♿ ⛺
(Office) 3 Avondale Road, Earlsdon, Coventry, Warwickshire, CV5 6DZ
Ⓣ (024) 766 73662
Ⓜ 07979 093096
Ⓕ (024) 766 73662
Ⓔ enquiries@avondalenursery.co.uk
Ⓦ www.avondalenursery.co.uk
Contact: Brian Ellis
Opening Times: 1000-1230, 1400-1700 Mon-Fri, 1000-1700 Sat, 1030-1630 Sun, Mar-Sep. Other times by appt.
Cat. Cost: 4 × 1st class.
Credit Cards: All major credit/debit cards
Specialities: Rare & unusual perennials esp. *Aster*, *Eryngium*, *Leucanthemum*, *Geum*, *Crocosmia*, *Sanguisorba* & grasses. Display garden open. Groups welcome.
Notes: Nursery is at Russell's Nursery, Mill Hill, Baginton, Nr Coventry, CV8 3AG.
Map Ref: M, C2 **OS Grid Ref:** SP339751

MBec **BEECHCROFT NURSERIES & GARDEN CENTRE** ♿ ◆
Madeley Road, Madeley Heath, Belbroughton, Stourbridge, West Midlands, DY9 9XA
Ⓣ (01562) 710358
Ⓕ (01562) 710507
Ⓔ mail@beechcroft.com
Ⓦ www.beechcroft.com
Contact: Paul Billingham
Opening Times: 0900-1730 Mon-Sat, 1100-1700 Sun. Close half-hour earlier in winter.
Credit Cards: All, except American Express
Specialities: Shrubs, conifers, rhododendrons, azaleas, heathers, alpine & rockery plants, climbers & *Clematis*, outdoor ferns, wild flowers & trees. Large range of herbaceous perennials & roses.
Notes: Set in beautiful countryside just minutes from the centre of Birmingham & M5 Jct. 4.
Map Ref: M, C2 **OS Grid Ref:** SO951772

MBlu **BLUEBELL ARBORETUM & NURSERY** ⊠ € ♿ ⛺
Annwell Lane, Smisby, Nr Ashby de la Zouch, Derbyshire, LE65 2TA
Ⓣ (01530) 413700
Ⓕ (01530) 417600
Ⓔ sales@bluebellnursery.co.uk
Ⓦ www.bluebellnursery.com
Contact: Robert & Suzette Vernon
Opening Times: 0900-1700 Mon-Sat & 1030-1630 Sun Mar-Oct, 0900-1600 Mon-Sat (not Sun) Nov-Feb. Closed 24th Dec-1st Jan incl. & Easter Sun.
Min Mail Order UK: £9.50
Min Mail Order EU: Nmc
Cat. Cost: £1.50 + 3 × 1st class.
Credit Cards: Visa Access Switch MasterCard
Specialities: Uncommon trees & shrubs. Woody climbers. Display garden & arboretum.
Map Ref: M, B1 **OS Grid Ref:** SK344187

MBNS **BARNSDALE GARDENS** ⊠ ♿ ⛺ ◆
Exton Avenue, Exton, Oakham, Rutland, LE15 8AH
Ⓣ (01572) 813200
Ⓕ (01572) 813346
Ⓔ info@barnsdaleplants.co.uk
Ⓦ www.barnsdaleplants.co.uk
Contact: Nick or Sue Hamilton
Opening Times: 0900-1700 Mar-May & Sep-Oct, 0900-1900 Jun-Aug, 1000-1600 Nov-Feb, 7 days. Closed 23rd & 25th Dec.
Min Mail Order UK: Nmc
Min Mail Order EU: Nmc
Cat. Cost: A5 + 5 × 1st class.
Credit Cards: All major credit/debit cards
Specialities: Wide range of choice & unusual garden plants. Over 160 varieties of *Penstemon*, over 250 varieties of *Hemerocallis*.
Map Ref: M, B3 **OS Grid Ref:** SK912108

MBPg **BARNFIELD PELARGONIUMS** ⊠
Barnfield, Off Wilnecote Lane, Belgrave, Tamworth, Staffordshire, B77 2LF
Ⓣ (01827) 250123
Ⓕ (01827) 250123
Ⓔ brianandjenniewhite@hotmail.com
Contact: Jennie & Brian White
Opening Times: Open by appt. only.
Min Mail Order UK: £6.00
Min Mail Order EU: £10.00
Cat. Cost: 4 × 2nd class.

KEY
⊠ Mail order to UK or EU ⛺ Delivers to shows
✈ Exports beyond EU € Euro accepted
♿ Accessible by wheelchair ◆ See Display advertisement

M

Credit Cards: None
Specialities: Over 200 varieties of scented leaf pelargoniums.

MBri **Bridgemere Nurseries** € ♿
Bridgemere, Nr Nantwich, Cheshire, CW5 7QB
Ⓣ (01270) 521100
Ⓕ (01270) 520215
Ⓔ customer.service@bridgemere.co.uk
Ⓦ www.bridgemere.co.uk
Contact: Keith Atkey, Roger Pierce
Opening Times: 0900-1900 7 days, summer. 0900-1800 winter. Closed 25th & 26th Dec.
Cat. Cost: None issued.
Credit Cards: Visa Access MasterCard Switch
Specialities: Huge range outdoor & indoor plants, many rare & unusual. Specimen shrubs.
Map Ref: M, B1 **OS Grid Ref:** SJ727435

MBrN **Bridge Nursery** € ♿
Tomlow Road, Napton-on-the-Hill, Nr Rugby, Warwickshire, CV47 8HX
Ⓣ (01926) 812737
Ⓔ pemartino@tiscali.co.uk
Ⓦ www.Bridge-Nursery.co.uk
Contact: Christine Dakin & Philip Martino
Opening Times: 1000-1600 Mon-Sun 1st Feb-mid Dec. Other times by appt.
Cat. Cost: Online only.
Credit Cards: All major credit/debit cards
Specialities: Ornamental grasses, sedges & bamboos. Also range of shrubs & perennials. Display garden.
Notes: Also sells wholesale.
Map Ref: M, C2 **OS Grid Ref:** SP463625

MCCP **Collectors Corner Plants** ⊠ ⌂
33 Rugby Road, Clifton-upon-Dunsmore, Rugby, Warwickshire, CV23 0DE
Ⓣ (01788) 571881
Contact: Pat Neesam
Opening Times: By appt. only.
Min Mail Order UK: £20.00
Cat. Cost: 6 × 1st class.
Credit Cards: None
Specialities: General range of choice herbaceous perennials, grasses, shrubs, palms, ferns & bamboos.
Map Ref: M, C3

MCms **Chrysanthemums Direct** ⊠ ✈ ⌂
Holmes Chapel Road, Over Peover, Knutsford, Cheshire, WA16 9RA
Ⓣ (01565) 722116
Ⓜ 07814 519060
Ⓕ (01565) 722740
Ⓔ sales@chrysanthemumsdirect.co.uk
Ⓦ www.chrysanthemumsdirect.co.uk
Contact: Martyn Flint
Opening Times: Not open. Mail order only.
Min Mail Order UK: Nmc
Min Mail Order EU: Nmc
Cat. Cost: 2 × 1st.
Credit Cards: All major credit/debit cards
Specialities: Chrysanthemums. Young plants grown to order. Delivery within 28 days.

MCoo **Cool Temperate** ⊠ ✈
(office) 45 Stamford Street, Awsworth, Nottinghamshire, NG16 2QL
Ⓣ (0115) 916 2673
Ⓕ (0115) 916 2673
Ⓔ phil.corbett@cooltemperate.co.uk
Ⓦ www.cooltemperate.co.uk
Contact: Phil Corbett
Opening Times: 0900-1700, 7 days. Please ring/write first.
Min Mail Order UK: Nmc
Min Mail Order EU: Nmc
Cat. Cost: 3 × 1st class.
Credit Cards: None
Specialities: Tree fruit, soft fruit, nitrogen-fixers, hedging, own-root fruit trees. Many species available in small quantities only.
Notes: Nursery at Trinity Farm, Awsworth Lane, Cossall, Notts. Also sells wholesale.
Map Ref: M, B2 **OS Grid Ref:** SK482435

MCot **Coton Manor Garden**
Guilsborough, Northampton, Northamptonshire, NN6 8RQ
Ⓣ (01604) 740219
Ⓕ (01604) 740838
Ⓔ nursery@cotonmanor.co.uk
Ⓦ www.cotonmanor.co.uk
Contact: Caroline Tait
Opening Times: 1200-1730 Tue-Sat, 1st April (or Easter if earlier) to 30th Sep. Also Sun Apr, May & B/hol w/ends. Other times in working hours by appt.
Cat. Cost: None issued.
Credit Cards: MasterCard Visa
Specialities: Wide-range of herbaceous perennials (3000+ varieties), some available in small quantities only. Also tender perennials & selected shrubs.
Notes: Garden open. Tea rooms. Garden School. Partial wheelchair access.
Map Ref: M, C3 **OS Grid Ref:** SP675715

MCri **Crin Gardens** ⊠ €
79 Partons Road, Kings Heath, Birmingham, B14 6TD
Ⓣ 0121 443 3815
Ⓜ 07504 907553
Ⓕ 0121 443 3815

Ⓔ cringardens@tiscali.co.uk
Ⓦ www.cringardens.co.uk
Contact: M Milinkovic
Opening Times: Not open. Mail order only.
Min Mail Order UK: Nmc
Min Mail Order EU: Nmc
Cat. Cost: 2 × 1st class + 1 × 2nd.
Credit Cards: None
Specialities: Lilies. Limited stock available on first come, first served basis.

MDKP **D K Plants** (Delivers to shows)
(Office) 19 Harbourne Road, Cheadle, Stoke on Trent, Staffordshire, ST10 1JU
Ⓣ Office: (01538) 754460
Ⓜ Nursery: 07779 545015
Ⓔ davidknoxc@aol.com
Contact: Dave Knox
Opening Times: 0900-2000 (or dusk if earlier) Mon-Tue & Thu-Fri. Other times by appt.
Cat. Cost: 4 × 1st class A4 sae plus 44p 1st or 37p 2nd class.
Credit Cards: None
Specialities: Unusual hardy alpines & perennials. All grown on the nursery.
Notes: Nursery is at new roundabout across from Queen's Arms pub, Freehay Crossroads, Freehay, Cheadle, ST10 1TR.
Map Ref: M, B1

MDun **Dunge Valley Hidden Gardens** € ♿
Windgather Rocks, Kettleshulme, High Peak, Cheshire, SK23 7RF
Ⓣ (01663) 733787
Ⓕ (01663) 733787
Ⓔ david@dungevalley.co.uk
Ⓦ www.dungevalley.co.uk
Contact: David Ketley
Opening Times: 1030-1700 Thu-Sun Mar-Jun. 1030-1700 Sat & Sun Jul & Aug. Open B/hols. Otherwise by appt.
Cat. Cost: Online only.
Credit Cards: All major credit/debit cards
Specialities: *Rhododendron* species & hybrids. Azaleas, acers, *Meconopsis*, shrubs & perennials, some rare & wild collected. Some terrestrial orchids.
Notes: Also sells wholesale.
Map Ref: M, A2 **OS Grid Ref:** SJ989777

MFie **Field House Nursery** ⊠ € ♿
Leake Road, Gotham, Nottinghamshire, NG11 0JN
Ⓣ (01159) 830278
Ⓜ 07504 125209
Ⓔ auricula@btinternet.com
Contact: Valerie A Woolley & Bob Taylor
Opening Times: 0900-1600 Fri-Wed or by appt.
Min Mail Order UK: 4 plants.
Min Mail Order EU: £30.00
Cat. Cost: 4 × 1st class or 4 × IRC.
Credit Cards: Visa MasterCard Electron Maestro Solo
Specialities: *Primula auricula* & seed, *Astrantia*, herbaceous perennials. Nat. Collections of *Primula auricula* (Shows & Alpines) & *Astrantia*.
Notes: Mail order for *Astrantia*, *Auricula*, small *Primula*, & seeds.

MGan **Gandy's (Roses) Ltd** ⊠
North Kilworth, Nr Lutterworth, Leicestershire, LE17 6HZ
Ⓣ (01858) 880398
Ⓕ (01858) 880433
Ⓔ sales@gandys-roses.co.uk
Ⓦ www.gandys-roses.co.uk
Contact: Miss R D Gandy
Opening Times: 0930-1630 Mon-Sat.
Min Mail Order UK: Nmc
Min Mail Order EU: £25.00 + p&p
Cat. Cost: Free
Credit Cards: All major credit/debit cards
Specialities: Wide range of rose varieties, hardy nursery stock & fruit.
Notes: Also sells wholesale.

MGos **Goscote Nurseries Ltd** ♿ ◆
Syston Road, Cossington, Leicestershire, LE7 4UZ
Ⓣ (01509) 812121
Ⓕ (01509) 814231
Ⓔ sales@goscote.co.uk
Ⓦ www.goscote.co.uk
Contact: James Toone
Opening Times: 7 days, year round, apart from between Xmas & New Year.
Cat. Cost: Online only.
Credit Cards: Visa Access MasterCard Delta Switch
Specialities: Japanese maples, rhododendrons & azaleas, *Magnolia*, *Camellia*, *Pieris* & other *Ericaceae*. Ornamental trees & shrubs, conifers, fruit, heathers, alpines, roses, *Clematis* & unusual climbers. Show Garden to visit.
Notes: Design & landscaping service available. Also sells wholesale.
Map Ref: M, B3 **OS Grid Ref:** SK602130

KEY
⊠ Mail order to UK or EU — Delivers to shows
Exports beyond EU — € Euro accepted
♿ Accessible by wheelchair — ◆ See Display advertisement

M

MHav **Haven Nurseries Ltd.** ⊠ ♿
Crab Lane, Bobbington, Nr Stourbridge, West Midlands, DY7 5DZ
Ⓣ (01384) 221543
Ⓕ (01384) 221320
Ⓔ info@havennurseries.co.uk
Ⓦ www.havennurseries.co.uk
Contact: Lynda Brettell
Opening Times: 0900-1730 Mon-Sat, 1000-1700 Sun, Mar-Oct. 0900-1630 Mon-Sat, 1030-1600 Sun, Nov-Feb.
Min Mail Order UK: Nmc
Cat. Cost: 4 × 1st class.
Credit Cards: All, except American Express
Specialities: *Fuchsia*, *Geranium*. Wide range of shrubs, conifers, home-grown bedding & many unusual cottage garden plants.
Notes: Also sells wholesale. Mail order bare-root roses only.
Map Ref: M, C2

M

MHer **The Herb Nursery** ♿
Thistleton, Oakham, Rutland, LE15 7RE
Ⓣ (01572) 767658
Ⓔ herbnursery@southwitham.net
Ⓦ www.herbnursery.co.uk
Contact: Peter Bench
Opening Times: 0900-1800 (or dusk) 7 days excl. Xmas-New Year.
Cat. Cost: A5 sae.
Credit Cards: None
Specialities: Herbs, wild flowers, cottage garden plants, scented-leaf pelargoniums. Esp. *Thymus*, *Mentha*, *Lavandula*.
Map Ref: M, B3

MHom **Homestead Plants** ⊠
The Homestead, Normanton, Bottesford, Nottingham, NG13 0EP
Ⓣ (01949) 842745
Contact: Mrs S Palmer
Opening Times: By appt.
Min Mail Order UK: Nmc
Cat. Cost: 2 × 2nd class.
Credit Cards: None
Specialities: Unusual hardy & half-hardy perennials, esp. *Paeonia* species. *Hosta*, *Jovibarba*, *Salvia*, *Sempervivum* & *Heliotrope*. Drought-tolerant asters. Most available only in small quantities. Nat. Collection of *Heliotropium* cultivars.
Map Ref: M, B3 **OS Grid Ref:** SK812407

MJac **Jackson's Nurseries**
Clifton Campville, Nr Tamworth, Staffordshire, B79 0AP
Ⓣ (01827) 373307
Contact: N Jackson
Opening Times: 0900-1800 Mon Wed-Sat, 1000-1700 Sun.
Cat. Cost: 2 × 1st class.
Credit Cards: None
Specialities: *Fuchsia*.
Notes: Also sells wholesale.
Map Ref: M, B1

MJon **C & K Jones** ⊠ € ✈ ♿ ⌂
Golden Fields Nurseries, Barrow Lane, Tarvin, Cheshire, CH3 8JF
Ⓣ (01829) 740663
Ⓜ 07748 316555
Ⓕ (01829) 741877
Ⓔ ck.jones@btconnect.com
Ⓦ www.jonestherose.co.uk
Contact: Keith Jones
Opening Times: Office hours 0930-1600 Mon-Fri. Nursery open 1st w/end in each month only & the Fri & Mon either side. Closed Jan & Feb.
Min Mail Order UK: 1 plant + p&p
Min Mail Order EU: Nmc.
Cat. Cost: £1.00
Credit Cards: MasterCard Visa Maestro Electron Solo
Specialities: Roses.
Notes: Also sells wholesale.
Map Ref: M, B1

MLBr **Leatherbritches Kitchen Garden & Nursery** ♿
(Office) 6 Sycamore Cottages, Parwich, Ashbourne, Derbyshire, DE6 1QL
Ⓣ (01335) 390571 answerphone
Ⓜ 07713 743295
Ⓔ leatherbritchesnursery@yahoo.com
Contact: Bill Whitfield
Opening Times: 1000-1700, 7 days (times vary in winter & poor weather).
Credit Cards: None
Specialities: Herbaceous, shrubs, alpines, bedding.
Notes: Nursery is situated opposite the Bentley Brook Inn, Bakewell Rd (A5056), Fenny Bentley, Ashbourne, DE6 1LF.
Map Ref: M, A2 **OS Grid Ref:** SK185503

MLea **Lea Rhododendron Gardens Ltd** ⊠ ✈ ♿
Lea, Matlock, Derbyshire, DE4 5GH
Ⓣ (01629) 534380/534260
Ⓕ (01629) 534260
Ⓦ www.leagarden.co.uk
Contact: Peter Tye
Opening Times: 1000-1730 7 days 20 Mar-30 Jun. Out of season by appt.
Min Mail Order UK: £15.00 + p&p

Min Mail Order EU: £15.00 + p&p
Cat. Cost: 30p + sae.
Credit Cards: All major credit/debit cards
Specialities: Rhododendrons & azaleas.
Map Ref: M, B1 **OS Grid Ref:** SK324571

MLHP **Longstone Hardy Plant Nursery** ♿
(office) Stancil House, Barn Furlong, Great Longstone, Nr Bakewell, Derbyshire, DE45 1TR
Ⓣ (01629) 640136
Ⓜ 07762 083674
Ⓔ lucyinlongstone@hotmail.com
Ⓦ www.longstonehardyplants.co.uk
Contact: Lucy Wright
Opening Times: 1300-1700 Tue-Sat & B/hols, 1st Apr-30th Sep. 1300-1700 Sat, Mar-Oct. Other times by appt.
Cat. Cost: 4 × 1st class.
Credit Cards: None
Specialities: Specialist peat-free nursery displaying all our own hardy perennials, ornamental grasses, herbs & shrubs, incl. many unusual varieties. Some stock available in small quantities only. Can propagate to order.
Notes: Nursery at Station Road 150 yds on right after turning onto it at the village green. Postcode DE45 1TS.
Map Ref: M, A2 **OS Grid Ref:** SK198717

MLLN **Lodge Lane Nursery** ⊠ ♿
Lodge Lane, Dutton, Nr Warrington, Cheshire, WA4 4HP
Ⓣ (01928) 713718
Ⓕ (01928) 713718
Ⓔ info@lodgelane.co.uk
Ⓦ www.lodgelane.co.uk
Contact: Sue Beesley
Opening Times: 1000-1700 Wed-Sun & B/hols, mid Mar-mid Sep. By appt. outside these dates.
Min Mail Order UK: £10.00
Cat. Cost: By email or online.
Credit Cards: All major credit/debit cards
Specialities: Unusual perennials & shrubs incl. *Achillea*, *Astrantia*, *Campanula*, *Digitalis*, *Penstemon*, *Geranium*, *Heuchera*, *Inula*, *Kniphofia*, *Nepeta*, *Papaver*, *Salvia* & ornamental grasses.
Map Ref: M, A1 **OS Grid Ref:** SJ586779

MLod **Lodge Farm Plants & Wildflowers** ⊠ € ♿ ⛺
Case Lane, Fiveways, Hatton, Warwickshire, CV35 7JD
Ⓣ (01926) 484649
Ⓜ 07977 631368
Ⓕ (01926) 484649
Ⓔ lodgefarmplants@btinternet.com
Ⓦ www.lodgefarmplants.com
Contact: Janet Cook & Nick Cook
Opening Times: Open 7 days all year, except Xmas Day & Boxing Day.
Min Mail Order UK: Nmc
Cat. Cost: Online only.
Credit Cards: None
Specialities: Wildflowers. Vegetable plants, soft fruit. Native trees & hedging. Wildflower seeds. Fruit trees, espalier, fan, stepovers & cordons.
Notes: Also sells wholesale.
Map Ref: M, C2 **OS Grid Ref:** SP223700

M

MMHG **Morton Hall Gardens** ⊠ ♿ ⛺
Morton Hall, Ranby, Retford, Nottinghamshire, DN22 8HW
Ⓣ (01777) 702530
Ⓜ 07940 434398
Ⓔ enquiries@morton-nurseries.com
Ⓦ www.morton-nurseries.co.uk
Contact: Gill McMaster
Opening Times: By appt.only
Min Mail Order UK: £5.00 + p&p
Cat. Cost: 3 × 1st class.
Credit Cards: None
Specialities: Shrubs & perennials.
Map Ref: M, A3

MMoz **Mozart House Nursery Garden** ⛺
84 Central Avenue, Wigston, Leicestershire, LE18 2AA
Ⓣ (0116) 288 9548
Contact: Des Martin
Opening Times: 1000-1300 last Sat of the month, Mar to Sep 2009. Other times by appt.
Cat. Cost: Phone for list.
Credit Cards: None
Specialities: Bamboos, ornamental grasses, rushes & sedges, ferns. Expanding range of shade & woodland plants.
Map Ref: M, C3

MMuc **Mucklestone Nurseries** ⊠ ♿ ◆
Rock Lane, Mucklestone, Nr Market Drayton, Shropshire, TF9 4DN
Ⓜ 07985 425829
Ⓔ info@botanyplants.com
Ⓦ www.botanyplants.com
Contact: Brian Watkins

KEY
⊠ Mail order to UK or EU ⛺ Delivers to shows
✈ Exports beyond EU € Euro accepted
♿ Accessible by wheelchair ◆ See Display advertisement

Opening Times: 0900-1700 Thu-Sun, Mar-Oct. Other times by appt.
Min Mail Order UK: Nmc
Cat. Cost: Online only.
Credit Cards: None
Specialities: Trees, shrubs, grasses & perennials for acid & damp soils of the north & west UK.
Map Ref: M, B2 **OS Grid Ref:** SJ728373

MNew **NEWINGTON NURSERIES** € ♿
Newington, Wallingford, Oxfordshire, OX10 7AW
Ⓣ (01865) 400533
Ⓔ plants@newington-nurseries.co.uk
Ⓦ www.newington-nurseries.co.uk
Contact: Mrs A T Hendry
Opening Times: 1000-1700 Tues-Sun Mar-Oct, 1000-1600 Tues-Sun Nov-Feb.
Credit Cards: Access MasterCard Visa Switch
Specialities: Unusual cottage garden plants, alpines, hardy exotics, conservatory plants & herbs. Nat. Collection of *Alocasia* (*Araceae*).
Notes: Also sells wholesale.
Map Ref: M, D3

MNFA **THE NURSERY FURTHER AFIELD** ⊠ ♿
Evenley Road, Mixbury, Nr Brackley, Northamptonshire, NN13 5YR
Ⓣ (01280) 848808
Ⓔ sinclair@nurseryfurtherafield.co.uk
Ⓦ www.nurseryfurtherafield.co.uk
Contact: Gerald & Mary Sinclair
Opening Times: 1000-1700 Wed-Sat, Apr-mid Sep. Other times by appt.
Min Mail Order UK: £15.00
Cat. Cost: 2 × 1st class.
Credit Cards: None
Specialities: Worthwhile hardy perennials, many unusual. Large selection of *Geranium* & *Hemerocallis*. Nat. Collection of *Hemerocallis*.
Notes: Mail order for *Hemerocallis* only.
Map Ref: M, C3 **OS Grid Ref:** SP608344

MNHC **THE NATIONAL HERB CENTRE** ⊠ ♿
Banbury Road, Warmington, Nr Banbury, Oxfordshire, OX17 1DF
Ⓣ (01295) 690999
Ⓕ (01295) 690034
Ⓦ www.herbcentre.co.uk
Contact: Plant Centre Staff
Opening Times: 0900-1730 Mon-Sat, 1030-1700 Sun.
Min Mail Order UK: Nmc
Credit Cards: All major credit/debit cards
Specialities: Herbs, culinary & medicinal. Extensive selection of rosemary, thyme & lavender, in particular.
Notes: Carriage charge of £9.00 up to 15kg, higher for heavier parcels. Next day delivery. UK mainland only. Signature required.
Map Ref: M, C2 **OS Grid Ref:** SP413471

MNrw **NORWELL NURSERIES** ⊠ ♿ ⌂ ◆
Woodhouse Road, Norwell, Newark, Nottinghamshire, NG23 6JX
Ⓣ (01636) 636337
Ⓔ wardha@aol.com
Ⓦ www.norwellnurseries.co.uk
Contact: Dr Andrew Ward
Opening Times: 1000-1700 Mon, Wed-Fri & Sun (Wed-Mon May & Jun). By appt. Aug & 20th Oct-1st Mar.
Min Mail Order UK: £15.00 + p&p
Min Mail Order EU: £40.00
Cat. Cost: 3 × 1st class or online.
Credit Cards: None
Specialities: A large collection of unusual & choice herbaceous perennials & alpines esp., hardy geraniums, *Geum*, pond & bog plants, cottage garden plants, *Hemerocallis*, grasses, hardy chrysanthemums & woodland plants. One acre garden open.
Notes: Also sells wholesale.
Map Ref: M, B3 **OS Grid Ref:** SK767616

MOld **OLD HALL NURSERY** ♿
Winkhill, Leek, Staffordshire, ST13 7PN
Ⓣ (01538) 308257
Ⓜ 07866 175881
Ⓔ oldhallnursery@hotmail.co.uk
Contact: Sandra Henshall
Opening Times: 1000-1600, 7 days.
Cat. Cost: Not available.
Credit Cards: None
Specialities: Large selection of herbaceous, herbs & alpines. Also shrubs, climbers & fruit trees. All hardy.
Map Ref: M, B2 **OS Grid Ref:** SK051521

MPet **PETER GRAYSON (SWEET PEA SEEDSMAN)** ⊠ ✈
34 Glenthorne Close, Brampton, Chesterfield, Derbyshire, S40 3AR
Ⓣ (01246) 278503
Ⓕ (01246) 278503
Contact: Peter Grayson
Opening Times: Not open. Mail order only.
Min Mail Order UK: Nmc
Min Mail Order EU: Nmc
Cat. Cost: C5 sae, 1 × 2nd class.
Credit Cards: None
Specialities: *Lathyrus* species & cvs. Large collection of old-fashioned sweet peas & over 100 Spencer sweet peas incl. own cultivars and

collection of old-fashioned cottage garden annuals & perennials.
Notes: Also sells wholesale. Mail order for seeds only.

MPhe **PHEDAR NURSERY** ⊠ € ✈
Bunkers Hill, Romiley, Stockport, Cheshire, SK6 3DS
Ⓣ (0161) 430 3772
Ⓕ (0161) 430 3772
Ⓔ mclewin@phedar.com
Ⓦ www.phedar.com
Contact: Will McLewin
Opening Times: Frequent but irregular. Please phone to arrange appt.
Min Mail Order UK: Nmc
Min Mail Order EU: Nmc
Cat. Cost: 2 × A5 envelopes or address labels + 4 × 1st class.
Credit Cards: All major credit/debit cards
Specialities: *Helleborus*, *Paeonia*. Limited stock of some rare items.
Notes: Non-EU exports subject to destination & on an ad hoc basis only. Please contact nursery for details. Credit cards accepted for online orders only. Also sells wholesale.
Map Ref: M, A2 **OS Grid Ref:** SJ936897

MPkF **PACKHORSE FARM NURSERY** ♿ ⌂
Sandyford House, Lant Lane, Tansley, Matlock, Derbyshire, DE4 5FW
Ⓣ (01629) 57206
Ⓜ 07974 095752
Ⓕ (01629) 57206
Contact: Hilton W Haynes
Opening Times: 1000-1700 Tues & Wed, 1st Mar-31st Oct. Any other time by appt. only.
Cat. Cost: 2 × 1st class for plant list.
Credit Cards: None
Specialities: *Acer*, rare stock is limited in supply. Other more unusual hardy shrubs, trees & conifers.
Map Ref: M, B2 **OS Grid Ref:** SK322617

MPnt **PLANTAGOGO.COM** ⊠ ♿ ⌂
Jubilee Cottage Nursery, Snape Lane, Englesea Brook, Crewe, Cheshire, CW2 5QN
Ⓣ (01270) 820335
Ⓜ 07713 518271
Ⓕ (01270) 820335
Ⓔ foxy@plantagogo.freeserve.co.uk
Ⓦ www.plantagogo.com
Contact: Vicky & Richard Fox
Opening Times: By appt. only.
Min Mail Order UK: £7.50 single payment.
Min Mail Order EU: Price on application
Cat. Cost: 4 × 1st class.
Credit Cards: All major credit/debit cards
Specialities: *Heuchera*, *Tiarella*, Nat. Collections applied for. Perennials. Available in small quantities only. Will propagate to order.
Map Ref: M, B1 **OS Grid Ref:** SJ750516

MRav **RAVENSTHORPE NURSERY** ⊠ ♿
6 East Haddon Road, Ravensthorpe, Northamptonshire, NN6 8ES
Ⓣ (01604) 770548
Ⓕ (01604) 770548
Ⓔ ravensthorpenursery@hotmail.com
Contact: Jean & Richard Wiseman
Opening Times: 1000-1800 (dusk if earlier) Tue-Sun. Also B/hol Mons.
Min Mail Order UK: Nmc
Min Mail Order EU: Nmc
Cat. Cost: None issued.
Credit Cards: Visa MasterCard
Specialities: Over 3000 different trees, shrubs & perennials with many unusual varieties.
Notes: Search & delivery service for large orders, winter months only.
Map Ref: M, C3 **OS Grid Ref:** SP665699

MREP **RARE AND EXOTIC PLANTS (FORMERLY PLANTS FOR ALL REASONS)** ⊠ ♿
Woodshoot Nurseries, King's Bromley, Burton-upon-Trent, Staffordshire, DE13 7HN
Ⓣ (01543) 472233
Ⓕ (01543) 472115
Ⓔ sales@rareandexoticplants.com
Ⓦ www.rareandexoticplants.com
Contact: Richard Flint
Opening Times: 0900-1700, 7 days.
Min Mail Order UK: £20.00 + p&p
Cat. Cost: 1 × 1st class.
Credit Cards: All major credit/debit cards
Specialities: *Acacia*, *Agave*, *Bamboo*, *Citrus*, *Cordyline*, *Dicksonia*, *Phormium*, *Pittosporum*, palms, olives, *Yucca*, topiary & specimens.
Notes: Also sells wholesale.
Map Ref: M, B2 **OS Grid Ref:** SK127164

MSCN **STONYFORD COTTAGE NURSERY** ⊠ ♿ ⌂
Stonyford Lane, Cuddington, Northwich, Cheshire, CW8 2TF
Ⓣ (01606) 888970/888128 (answerphone)
Ⓜ 07714 205177
Ⓔ stonyfordcottage@yahoo.co.uk
Ⓦ www.stonyfordcottagenursery.co.uk
Contact: Andrew Overland
Opening Times: 1000-1730 Tue-Sun & B/hol

KEY
⊠ Mail order to UK or EU ⌂ Delivers to shows
✈ Exports beyond EU € Euro accepted
♿ Accessible by wheelchair ◆ See Display advertisement

M

Mons 1st Feb-31st Oct.
Min Mail Order UK: Nmc
Min Mail Order EU: Nmc
Cat. Cost: Not available this year
Credit Cards: All major credit/debit cards
Specialities: Wide range of herbaceous perennials, *Iris*, hardy *Geranium*, moisture-loving & bog plants. *Sempervivum*, *Paeonia*, Candelabra *Primula*.
Notes: Also sells wholesale.
Map Ref: M, A1 **OS Grid Ref:** SJ580710

M

MSKA **Sweet Knowle Aquatics** ⊠ ♿
Wimpstone-Ilmington Road, Stratford-upon-Avon, Warwickshire, CV37 8NR
Ⓣ (01789) 450036
Ⓕ (01789) 450036
Ⓔ sweetknowleaquatics@hotmail.com
Ⓦ www.sweetknowleaquatics.co.uk
Contact: Zoe Harding
Opening Times: 0930-1700 Sun-Fri, closed Sat. Open B/hols.
Min Mail Order UK: Nmc
Cat. Cost: By email only.
Credit Cards: All major credit/debit cards
Specialities: Aquatics. Hardy & tropical water lilies, marginals & oxygenators. 2-acre display garden open to the public (no charge).
Map Ref: M, C2 **OS Grid Ref:** SP207480

MSnd **Sound Garden Rhododendrons (formerly Penton Mill)**
(office) 184 Crow Lane East, Newton-le-Willows, Merseyside, WA12 9UA
Ⓣ 0800 298 0273
Ⓜ 07931 340836
Ⓔ info@soundgardendesign.com
Ⓦ www.s-g-d-uk.com
Contact: Tim Atkinson
Opening Times: By appt. only.
Cat. Cost: 2 × 1st class
Credit Cards: None
Specialities: Species & rare *Rhododendron*. Hardy hybrid rhododendrons, azaleas, primulas.
Notes: Nursery at Middledale Farm, Dale Road, Marple, Cheshire SK6 6NL.
Map Ref: N, B1 **OS Grid Ref:** SJ948901

MSpe **SpecialPerennials.com** ⊠ ♿
(office) Yew Tree House, Hall Lane, Hankelow, Crewe, Cheshire, CW3 0JB
Ⓣ (01270) 811443
Ⓜ 07716 990695
Ⓔ plants@specialperennials.com
Ⓦ www.specialperennials.com
Contact: Janet & Martin Blow
Opening Times: 1300-1700 Fri Mar-Sep & some w/ends. Gardens open for NGS selected w/ends Jun-Sep. See website for details.
Min Mail Order UK: Nmc
Cat. Cost: 1 × 1st class or online.
Credit Cards: None
Specialities: Herbaceous perennials. Large range of *Helenium*, *Hemerocallis*, *Centaurea*, *Geum* & *Salvia*. Some plants available in small quantities only.
Notes: See website for plant fairs attended. Border design service & garden talks available.
Map Ref: M, B1 **OS Grid Ref:** SJ699452

MSSP **S & S Perennials** ⊠
24 Main Street, Normanton Le Heath, Leicestershire, LE67 2TB
Ⓣ (01530) 262250
Contact: Shirley Pierce
Opening Times: Afternoons only, otherwise please phone.
Min Mail Order UK: Nmc
Cat. Cost: 2 × 1st class.
Credit Cards: None
Specialities: *Erythronium*, *Fritillaria*, dwarf *Narcissus* & *Anemone*. Stock available in small quantities only.
Map Ref: M, B1

MSwo **Swallows Nursery** ⊠ ♿
Mixbury, Brackley, Northamptonshire, NN13 5RR
Ⓣ (01280) 847721
Ⓕ (01280) 848611
Ⓔ enq@swallowsnursery.co.uk
Ⓦ www.swallowsnursery.co.uk
Contact: Chris Swallow
Opening Times: 0900-1300 & 1400-1700 (earlier in winter) Mon-Fri, 0900-1300 Sat.
Min Mail Order UK: £15.00
Cat. Cost: 3 × 1st class (plus phone number).
Credit Cards: Visa MasterCard Switch
Specialities: Growing a wide range, particularly shrubs, trees, roses and heathers.
Notes: Trees not for mail order unless part of larger order. Nursery transport used where possible, esp. for trees. Also sells wholesale.
Map Ref: M, C3 **OS Grid Ref:** SP607336

MTho **A & A Thorp**
Bungalow No 5, Main Street, Theddingworth, Leicestershire, LE17 6QZ
Ⓣ (01858) 880496
Contact: Anita & Andrew Thorp
Opening Times: 1000-1700.
Cat. Cost: 4 × 1st class.
Credit Cards: None
Specialities: Unusual plants or those in short supply.
Map Ref: M, C3

MTis **Tissington Nursery** ♿ ⌂
The Old Kitchen Gardens,
Tissington, Asbourne, Derbyshire,
DE6 1RA
Ⓣ (01335) 390650
Ⓜ 07929 720284
Ⓔ info@tissington-nursery.co.uk
Ⓦ www.tissington-nursery.co.uk
Contact: Mairi Longdon
Opening Times: 1000-1700 daily, 3rd Mar-end Oct.
Cat. Cost: 4 × 1st class.
Credit Cards: All major credit/debit cards
Specialities: Choice & unusual perennials esp. *Achillea*, *Geranium*, *Geum*, *Helenium*, *Heuchera*, *Penstemon*, *Sempervivum* & grasses.
Map Ref: M, B1 **OS Grid Ref:** SK176521

MWat **Waterperry Gardens Ltd** ⊠ ♿
Waterperry, Nr Wheatley, Oxfordshire,
OX33 1JZ
Ⓣ (01844) 339226/254
Ⓕ (01844) 339883
Ⓔ management@waterperrygardens.co.uk
Ⓦ www.waterperrygardens.co.uk
Contact: Mr R Jacobs
Opening Times: 1000-1730 summer. 1000-1700 winter.
Min Mail Order UK: £30.00
Cat. Cost: Online only.
Credit Cards: All major credit/debit cards
Specialities: General, large range of herbaceous esp. *Aster*, also Nat. Collection of *Saxifraga* (subsect. *Kabschia* & *Engleria*).
Map Ref: M, D3 **OS Grid Ref:** SP630064

MWea **Wear's Nursery** ♿
(Office) 84 Wantage Road,
Wallingford, Oxfordshire,
OX10 0LY
Ⓣ 07790 425284
Ⓕ (01491) 837803
Ⓦ www.wearsnursery.co.uk
Contact: David Wear
Opening Times: 1000-1700 Mon-Sat, Feb-Oct. 1000-1600 Sun (closed Sun in Aug). 1000-1600 Mon-Sat, Nov-Jan, please telephone first as may be closed on some days in winter.
Cat. Cost: Plant list online only.
Credit Cards: None
Specialities: Unusual herbaceous varieties & shrubs. Large selection of *Geranium*. Some plants only available in small numbers.
Notes: Nursery sited at High Road, Brightwell-cum-Sotwell, Wallingford.
Map Ref: M, D3 **OS Grid Ref:** SU590910

MWhi **Whitehill Farm Nursery** ⊠ € ♿
Whitehill Farm, Burford, Oxfordshire,
OX18 4DT
Ⓣ (01993) 823218
Ⓕ (01993) 822894
Ⓔ a.youngson@virgin.net
Ⓦ www.whitehillfarmnursery.co.uk
Contact: P J M Youngson
Opening Times: 0900-1800 (or dusk if earlier) 7 days, Feb-Nov.
Min Mail Order UK: £5.00 + p&p
Min Mail Order EU: £5.00 + p&p
Cat. Cost: 4 × 1st class.
Credit Cards: All major credit/debit cards
Specialities: Grasses & bamboos, less common shrubs & perennials. Some available in small quantities only.
Notes: £1.00 of catalogue cost refunded on 1st order.
Map Ref: M, D2 **OS Grid Ref:** SP268113

MWht **Whitelea Nursery** ⊠ ♿
Whitelea Lane, Tansley, Matlock, Derbyshire,
DE4 5FL
Ⓣ (01629) 55010
Ⓔ sales@uk-bamboos.co.uk
Ⓦ www.uk-bamboos.co.uk
Contact: David Wilson
Opening Times: By appt.
Min Mail Order UK: Nmc
Cat. Cost: Online only. Price list available 2 × 1st class.
Credit Cards: None
Specialities: Bamboos. Substantial quantities of 45 cvs & species of bamboo, remainder stocked in small numbers only. Ltd stocks of ivies.
Notes: Also sells wholesale. Mail order limited by carrier restrictions, please contact nursery or see website for details.
Map Ref: M, B1 **OS Grid Ref:** SK325603

MWte **White House Plants** ⊠
(Office) The White House, Nicker Hill,
Keyworth, Nottinghamshire, NG12 5EA
Ⓣ 0115 937 2049
Ⓜ 07804 865607
Ⓔ gillyhill@aol.com
Ⓦ www.whitehouseplants.com
Contact: Gillian Hill
Opening Times: Not open. Mail order only.
Min Mail Order UK: £10.00 + p&p
Cat. Cost: Online only.

KEY
⊠ Mail order to UK or EU ⌂ Delivers to shows
✈ Exports beyond EU € Euro accepted
♿ Accessible by wheelchair ◆ See Display advertisement

M

Credit Cards: Paypal
Specialities: *Agapanthus*, *Aster*, *Euphorbia*, *Geranium*, *Iris*, *Kniphofia*, *Miscanthus*, *Papaver orientale*, *Penstemon* & *Phlox*.

MWts **WATERSIDE NURSERY** ⊠ ♠
Sharnford, Leicestershire, LE10 3QD
Ⓣ (01455) 273730
Ⓜ 07931 557082
Ⓕ (01455) 273730
Ⓔ linda@watersidenursery.co.uk
Ⓦ www.watersidenursery.co.uk
Contact: Linda Smith
Opening Times: By appt. only.
Min Mail Order UK: Nmc
Cat. Cost: Online only.
Credit Cards: Paypal
Specialities: Aquatic & moisture-loving plants.

M

MWya **WYATTS** ♿ ♠
Hill Barn Farm, Great Rollright, Chipping Norton, Oxfordshire, OX7 5SH
Ⓣ (01608) 684990
Ⓔ wyatts@callnetuk.com
Ⓦ www.wyattscountry.com
Contact: John Wyatt or Christine Chittenden
Opening Times: 0900-1700, 7 days all year.
Credit Cards: MasterCard Switch Delta Visa
Specialities: Many unusual, rare & exotic plants, shrubs & trees incl. *Daphne*, *Euonymus*, *Viburnum*, *Magnolia*, *Clematis*, *Cornus* & *Acer*. Alpines, fruit trees & cane fruit. Large trees & shrubs. English grown *Buxus*.
Map Ref: M, C2 **OS Grid Ref:** SP317313

MYeo **YEOMANS' EXOTICS** ⊠ € ♿ ♠
2 Carrington Lane, Calverton, Nottingham, NG14 6HQ
Ⓣ 0115 965 4350
Ⓦ www.yeomansexotics.co.uk
Contact: Chris Yeomans
Opening Times: By appt. only Feb-Dec.
Min Mail Order UK: Nmc
Min Mail Order EU: Nmc
Cat. Cost: 1 × 1st class.
Credit Cards: None
Specialities: Carnivorous plants.
Notes: Also sells wholesale.

NORTHERN

NBea **BEAMISH CLEMATIS NURSERY** € ♿
Burntwood Cottage, Stoney Lane, Beamish, Co. Durham, DH9 0SJ
Ⓣ (0191) 370 0202
Ⓕ (0191) 370 0202
Ⓦ www.beamishclematisnursery.co.uk
Contact: Colin Brown or Jan Wilson
Opening Times: 0900-1700 Wed-Mon, closed Tue. Closed Easter Sun & Xmas week.
Cat. Cost: Online only.
Credit Cards: All major credit/debit cards
Specialities: *Clematis*, climbers, shrubs & ornamental trees.
Map Ref: N, B2 **OS Grid Ref:** NZ231535

NBid **BIDE-A-WEE COTTAGE GARDENS** ⊠ ♿
Stanton, Netherwitton, Morpeth, Northumberland, NE65 8PR
Ⓣ (01670) 772238
Ⓕ (01670) 772238
Ⓔ info@bideawee.co.uk
Ⓦ www.bideawee.co.uk
Contact: Mark Robson
Opening Times: 1330-1700 Sat & Wed, 18th Apr-29th Aug 2009.
Min Mail Order UK: £20.00
Cat. Cost: Online only.
Credit Cards: All major credit/debit cards
Specialities: Unusual herbaceous perennials, *Agapanthus*, *Primula*, ferns, grasses. Nat. Collection of *Centaurea*.
Map Ref: N, B2 **OS Grid Ref:** NZ132900

NBir **BIRKHEADS SECRET GARDENS & NURSERY** ⊠ ♿
Nr Hedley Hall Woods, Sunniside, Gateshead, Tyne & Wear, NE16 5EL
Ⓣ (01207) 232262
Ⓜ 07778 447920
Ⓕ (01207) 232262
Ⓔ birkheads.nursery@virgin.net
Ⓦ www.birkheadsnursery.co.uk
Contact: Mrs Christine Liddle
Opening Times: 1000-1700 daily (except Mon) Mar-Oct. Groups by appt.
Min Mail Order UK: £12
Cat. Cost: None issued.
Credit Cards: All major credit/debit cards
Specialities: Hardy herbaceous perennials, grasses, bulbs & herbs. *Allium*, *Digitalis*, *Euphorbia*, *Galanthus* & *Geranium*. Max. 30 of any plant propagated each year.
Notes: Mail order Nov-Feb only. Orders taken all year for winter deliveries.
Map Ref: N, B2 **OS Grid Ref:** NZ220569

NBPC **THE BARN PLANT CENTRE & GIFT SHOP** ♿
The Square, Scorton, Preston, Lancashire, PR3 1AU
Ⓣ (01524) 793533
Ⓕ (01524) 793533
Ⓔ sales@plantsandgifts.co.uk

Ⓦ www.plantsandgifts.co.uk
Contact: Neil Anderton
Opening Times: 0900-1700 Mon-Sat, 1000-1800 Sun.
Credit Cards: All major credit/debit cards
Specialities: 800 varieties of perennials.
Notes: Large gift shop & coffee bar.
Map Ref: N, C1 **OS Grid Ref:** GR501487

NBre **BREEZY KNEES NURSERIES** ♿
Common Lane, Warthill, York, YO19 5XS
Ⓣ (01904) 488800
Ⓦ www.breezyknees.co.uk
Contact: Any member of staff
Opening Times: 1000-1700 7 days (open 1100 Sun), 1st Apr-15th Sep.
Credit Cards: All major credit/debit cards
Specialities: Very wide range of perennials. All can be viewed in 14-acre landscaped garden (open 20th May-15th Sep).
Map Ref: N, C3 **OS Grid Ref:** SE675565

NBro **BROWNTHWAITE HARDY PLANTS** ⊠ ♿ ⌂
Fell Yeat, Casterton, Kirkby Lonsdale, Lancashire, LA6 2JW
Ⓣ (01524) 271340 (after 1800).
Ⓦ www.hardyplantsofcumbria.co.uk
Contact: Chris Benson
Opening Times: 1000-1700, 1st Apr-30th Sep.
Min Mail Order UK: Nmc
Cat. Cost: 3 × 1st class sae for general list. 3 × 1st class for *Hydrangea* catalogue. Sae for auricula list.
Credit Cards: None
Specialities: Herbaceous perennials incl. *Geranium*, *Hosta*, also *Tiarella*, *Heucherella* & *Primula auricula*. Mail order for *Hydrangea*. Nat. Collection of *Ligularia*.
Notes: Follow brown signs from A65 between Kirkby Lonsdale & Cowan Bridge.
Map Ref: N, C1 **OS Grid Ref:** SD632794

NCGa **CATH'S GARDEN PLANTS** ⊠ ♿ ⌂
The Walled Garden, Heaves Hotel, Heaves, Levens, Cumbria, LA8 8EF
Ⓣ (01539) 561126
Ⓕ (01539) 561126
Ⓔ cath@cathsgardenplants.fsbusiness.co.uk
Ⓦ www.cathsgardenplants.co.uk
Contact: Bob Sanderson
Opening Times: 1030-1630 Mon-Fri all year, except Xmas & New Year weeks. 1030-1700 Sat & Sun, Mar-Oct.
Min Mail Order UK: £15.00 + p&p
Min Mail Order EU: £25.00
Cat. Cost: Online only.
Credit Cards: All major credit/debit cards
Specialities: Wide variety of perennials, incl. uncommon varieties & selections of grasses, ferns, shrubs & climbing plants.
Notes: On A590 follow signs for Heaves (not in Levens village).
Map Ref: N, C1 **OS Grid Ref:** SD497867

NChi **CHIPCHASE CASTLE NURSERY** ⊠ ♿ ⌂
Chipchase Castle, Wark, Hexham, Northumberland, NE48 3NT
Ⓣ (01434) 230083
Ⓔ info@chipchaseplants.co.uk
Ⓦ www.chipchaseplants.co.uk
Contact: Joyce Hunt & Alison Jones
Opening Times: 1000-1700 Thu-Sun & B/hol Mons Easter (or 1st Apr)-end Aug.
Min Mail Order UK: Nmc
Min Mail Order EU: Nmc
Cat. Cost: A5 sae for list
Credit Cards: All major credit/debit cards
Specialities: Unusual herbaceous esp. *Eryngium*, *Geum*, *Geranium*, & *Penstemon*. Some plants only available in small quantities.
Notes: Suitable for accompanied wheelchair users.
Map Ref: N, B2 **OS Grid Ref:** NY880758

NChl **CHILTERN SEEDS** ⊠ € ✈
Bortree Stile, Ulverston, Cumbria, LA12 7PB
Ⓣ (01229) 581137 (24 hrs)
Ⓕ (01229) 584549
Ⓔ info@chilternseeds.co.uk
Ⓦ www.chilternseeds.co.uk
Opening Times: Mail order only. Normal office hours, Mon-Fri.
Min Mail Order UK: Nmc
Min Mail Order EU: Nmc
Cat. Cost: 3 × 2nd class.
Credit Cards: All major credit/debit cards
Specialities: Over 4,500 items of all kinds – wild flowers, trees, shrubs, cacti, annuals, houseplants, vegetables & herbs.

NChu **CHURCHTOWN CARNIVORES** ⊠ € ♿ ⌂
8 Sandheys Drive, Churchtown, Southport, Merseyside, PR9 9PQ
Ⓣ (01704) 228175
Ⓔ churchtowncarnivores@yahoo.co.uk
Ⓦ www.churchtowncarnivores.co.uk
Contact: Alan Leyland
Opening Times: By appt. only.
Min Mail Order UK: Nmc

KEY
⊠ Mail order to UK or EU ⌂ Delivers to shows
✈ Exports beyond EU € Euro accepted
♿ Accessible by wheelchair ◆ See Display advertisement

N

Min Mail Order EU: Nmc
Cat. Cost: 2 × 1st class or online.
Credit Cards: None
Specialities: Carnivorous plants. *Sarracenia*, *Dionaea muscipula* & forms, *Darlingtonia*, *Drosera*.
Map Ref: N, D1 **OS Grid Ref:** SD355183

NCob **COBBLE HEY GARDENS** ♿
Off Hobbs Lane, Claughton-on-Brock, Garstang, Nr Preston, Lancashire, PR3 0QN
Ⓣ (01995) 602643
Ⓕ (01995) 602643
Ⓔ cobblehey@aol.com
Ⓦ www.cobblehey.co.uk
Contact: Edwina Miller
Opening Times: 1030-1630 Thu-Mon 1st Feb-24th Dec 2009. Please email or phone before visiting to check stock availability.
Credit Cards: None
Specialities: Wide range of unusual plants grown on hill farm at over 600ft. Specialises in *Phlox paniculata* & geraniums.
Map Ref: N, C1

NCot **COTTAGE GARDEN PLANTS** ⊠ €
1 Sycamore Close, Whitehaven, Cumbria, CA28 6LE
Ⓣ (01946) 695831
Ⓔ expressplants@aol.com
Ⓦ www.cottagegardenplants.com
Contact: Mrs J Purkiss
Opening Times: Open by appt. only for collecting orders & viewing garden. Consult local press & radio for charity openings.
Min Mail Order UK: Nmc
Min Mail Order EU: Nmc
Cat. Cost: 4 × 1st class sae.
Credit Cards: Paypal
Specialities: Hardy perennials incl. *Crocosmia*, *Galanthus*, *Geranium*, *Primula*, *Schizostylis* & bog plants. Small quantities only. Nat. Collection of *Geranium phaeum* Group, open days 1100-1700 13th/14th Jun 2009. Also open by appt.
Map Ref: N, C1

NCro **CROSTON CACTUS** ⊠ € ♿
43 Southport Road, Eccleston, Chorley, Lancashire, PR7 6ET
Ⓣ (01257) 452555
Ⓕ (01257) 452555
Ⓔ sales@croston-cactus.co.uk
Ⓦ www.croston-cactus.co.uk
Contact: John Henshaw
Opening Times: 0930-1700 by appt. only.
Min Mail Order UK: £5.00 + p&p
Min Mail Order EU: £10.00 + p&p
Cat. Cost: 2 × 1st class or 2 × IRCs.
Credit Cards: All major credit/debit cards
Specialities: Mexican cacti, *Echeveria* hybrids & some bromeliads & *Tillandsia*. Some items held in small quantities only. See catalogue.
Notes: Credit card payment accepted for online orders only.
Map Ref: N, D1 **OS Grid Ref:** SD522186

NDav **DAVE PARKINSON PLANTS** ⊠ ⌂
4 West Bank, Carlton, Goole, East Yorkshire, DN14 9PZ
Ⓣ (01405) 860693
Ⓜ 07773 564945
Ⓦ www.daveparkinsonplants.co.uk
Contact: Mary Parkinson
Opening Times: Not open. Mail order only.
Min Mail Order UK: £12 + p&p
Credit Cards: None
Specialities: Hardy orchids. Terrestrial South African *Disa* orchids, species & hybrids.

NDov **DOVE COTTAGE NURSERY & GARDEN** ⊠ ♿
Shibden Hall Road, Halifax, West Yorkshire, HX3 9XA
Ⓣ (01422) 203553
Ⓔ info@dovecottagenursery.co.uk
Ⓦ www.dovecottagenursery.co.uk
Contact: Stephen & Kim Rogers
Opening Times: 1000-1700 Tue-Sun & B/hols Mar-Oct or by appt. at other times.
Min Mail Order UK: £20.00
Min Mail Order EU: £20.00
Cat. Cost: 6 × 2nd class.
Credit Cards: All major credit/debit cards
Specialities: Herbaceous perennials & selected grasses, many displayed in adjoining naturalistic garden.
Map Ref: N, D2 **OS Grid Ref:** SE115256

NDro **DROINTON NURSERIES** ⊠ ⊠ ⌂
Plaster Pitts, Norton Conyers, Ripon, North Yorkshire, HG4 5EF
Ⓣ (01765) 641849
Ⓜ 07909 971529
Ⓕ (01765) 640888
Ⓔ info@auricula-plants.co.uk
Ⓦ www.auricula-plants.co.uk
Contact: Robin & Annabel Graham
Opening Times: Open days in spring, otherwise by appt. only.
Min Mail Order UK: Nmc
Min Mail Order EU: Nmc
Cat. Cost: 4 × 1st class.
Credit Cards: All major credit/debit cards
Specialities: *Primula auricula*. More than 750 cvs of show, alpine, double & border

auriculas. Ltd stocks of any one cultivar.
Map Ref: N, C2 **OS Grid Ref:** SE315753

NEas **East Keswick Plant Centre** ♿
Harewood Road, East Keswick, Leeds, Yorkshire, LS17 9HG
Ⓣ (01937) 573539
Ⓔ nicky@eastkeswickplantcentre.co.uk
Ⓦ www.eastkeswickplantcentre.co.uk
Contact: Mr & Mrs Bowers
Opening Times: 0900-1700 Mon-Sat, 1000-1600 Sun, all year round.
Cat. Cost: Email only.
Credit Cards: All major credit/debit cards
Specialities: Wide selection of *Acer*.
Notes: Also sells wholesale.

NEgg **Eggleston Hall Gardens** € ♿
Eggleston, Barnard Castle, Co. Durham, DL12 0AG
Ⓣ (01833) 650115
Ⓕ (01833) 650971
Ⓔ mbhock@btinternet.com
Ⓦ www.plantsmanscorner.co.uk
Contact: Malcolm Hockham
Opening Times: 1000-1700 7 days. Closed Xmas Day, Boxing Day & New Year's Day only.
Cat. Cost: Online only.
Credit Cards: All major credit/debit cards
Notes: Collection from nursery only. Possible mail order in the next 18 months.

NEqu **Equatorial Plant Co.** ⊠ € ✈ ⌂
7 Gray Lane, Barnard Castle, Co. Durham, DL12 8PD
Ⓣ (01833) 690519
Ⓕ (01833) 690519
Ⓔ equatorialplants@teesdaleonline.co.uk
Ⓦ www.equatorialplants.com
Contact: Dr Richard Warren
Opening Times: By appt. only.
Min Mail Order UK: Nmc
Min Mail Order EU: Nmc
Cat. Cost: Free.
Credit Cards: Visa Access
Specialities: Laboratory-raised orchids only.
Notes: Also sells wholesale.

NExo **Exotic Unusual.co.uk** ⊠ ✈
8 Hoskers Nook, Westhoughton, Bolton, Lancashire, BL5 2RS
Ⓣ (01942) 790027
Ⓔ info@exoticunusual.co.uk
Ⓦ www.exoticunusual.co.uk
Contact: Lou Davies
Opening Times: Not Open. Mail order only.
Min Mail Order UK: £10.00
Min Mail Order EU: £15.00
Cat. Cost: Online only.
Credit Cards: All major credit/debit cards
Specialities: Rare, exotic & unusual plants, particularly *Agave*, chillies & passionflowers. Some plants in small quantities only.

NFir **Fir Trees Pelargonium Nursery** ⊠ ♿ ⌂
Stokesley, Middlesbrough, Cleveland, TS9 5LD
Ⓣ (01642) 713066
Ⓕ (01642) 713066
Ⓔ mark@firtreespelargoniums.co.uk
Ⓦ www.firtreespelargoniums.co.uk
Contact: Helen Bainbridge
Opening Times: 1000-1600 7 days 1st Apr-31st Aug, 1000-1600 Mon-Fri 1st Sep-31st Mar.
Min Mail Order UK: £3.75 + p&p
Cat. Cost: 4 × 1st class or £1.00 coin.
Credit Cards: All major credit/debit cards
Specialities: All types of *Pelargonium* – fancy leaf, regal, decorative regal, oriental regal, angel, miniature, zonal, ivy leaf, stellar, scented, dwarf, unique, golden stellar & species. Also dieramas.
Map Ref: N, C2

NGBl **Garden Blooms** ⊠ ⌂
(office) The Ridings, Netherfield Drive, Guiseley, West Yorkshire, LS20 9DF
Ⓣ 0845 904937
Ⓕ 0870 0528148
Ⓔ info@gardenblooms.co.uk
Ⓦ www.gardenblooms.co.uk
Contact: Liz Webster
Opening Times: Most w/ends Apr-Jun, please check website for up-to-date details.
Min Mail Order UK: £5.00
Cat. Cost: A5 sae or online.
Specialities: Hardy perennials & ornamental grasses. Available in small quantities only.
Notes: Credit cards accepted online only. Nursery at Carlton Lane, East Carlton, Yeadon, LS19 7BE.
Map Ref: N, D2 **OS Grid Ref:** SE213430

NGdn **Garden House Nursery** ♿
The Square, Dalston, Carlisle, Cumbria, CA5 7LL
Ⓣ (01228) 710297
Ⓔ stephickso@hotmail.com

KEY
⊠ Mail order to UK or EU ⌂ Delivers to shows
✈ Exports beyond EU € Euro accepted
♿ Accessible by wheelchair ◆ See Display advertisement

Ⓦ www.gardenhousenursery.co.uk
Contact: Stephen Hickson
Opening Times: 0900-1700 7 days Mar-Oct.
Cat. Cost: Plant list online only.
Credit Cards: None
Specialities: *Geranium*, *Hosta*, *Hemerocallis*, *Iris*, grasses & bamboos.
Notes: Also sells wholesale.
Map Ref: N, B1 **OS Grid Ref:** NY369503

NGHP **Green Garden Herbs** ⊠ ♿ ⌂
13 West Bank, Carlton, North Yorkshire, DN14 9PZ
Ⓣ (01405) 860708
Ⓔ info@greengardenherbs.co.uk
Ⓦ www.greengardenherbs.co.uk
Contact: Sarah Clark
Opening Times: 1000-1600 Sat, Mar-Sep. Other times by appt. Nursery may be relocating during 2009, so please contact before visiting.
Min Mail Order UK: £15
Min Mail Order EU: £15
Cat. Cost: Online only. Plant list free with sae.
Credit Cards: All major credit/debit cards
Specialities: Herbs, aromatic, culinary, medicinal & ornamental, incl. *Salvia*, *Echinacea*, *Monarda*, *Thymus* & wide selection of *Lavandula*. Plants & seed available.
Notes: Also sells wholesale. Credit cards accepted with online orders only. Coaches welcome. Talks given. Plants also available at Bridge Nurseries, Dunwich, Suffolk.
Map Ref: N, D3 **OS Grid Ref:** SE626242

N

NHal **Halls of Heddon** ⊠ ✈
West Heddon Nurseries, Heddon-on-the-Wall, Northumberland, NE15 0JS
Ⓣ (01661) 852445
Ⓕ (01661) 852398
Ⓔ orders@hallsofheddon.co.uk
Ⓦ www.hallsofheddon.co.uk
Contact: David Hall
Opening Times: 0900-1700 Mon-Sat 1000-1700 Sun.
Min Mail Order UK: £10.00
Min Mail Order EU: £25.00
Cat. Cost: 3 × 2nd class
Credit Cards: MasterCard Visa Switch Delta
Specialities: *Chrysanthemum* & *Dahlia*.
Notes: Also sells wholesale.

NHar **Hartside Nursery Garden** ⊠ ⌂
Nr Alston, Cumbria, CA9 3BL
Ⓣ (01434) 381372
Ⓕ (01434) 381372
Ⓔ Hartside@macunlimited.net
Ⓦ www.plantswithaltitude.co.uk
Contact: S L & N Huntley
Opening Times: 1130-1630 Mon-Fri, 1230-1600 Sat, Sun & B/hols, mid Mar-31st Oct. All other times & winter by appt. Times may vary during show season, so please phone before travelling.
Min Mail Order UK: Nmc
Min Mail Order EU: £50.00 + p&p
Cat. Cost: 4 × 1st class or 3 × IRC
Credit Cards: All major credit/debit cards
Specialities: Alpines grown at altitude of 1100 feet in The Pennines. *Primula*, ferns, *Gentian* & *Meconopsis*.
Map Ref: N, B1 **OS Grid Ref:** NY708447

NHaw **The Hawthornes Nursery** ⊠ ♿
Marsh Road, Hesketh Bank, Nr Preston, Lancashire, PR4 6XT
Ⓣ (01772) 812379
Ⓔ richardhaw@talktalk.net
Ⓦ www.hawthornes-nursery.co.uk
Contact: Irene & Richard Hodson
Opening Times: 0900-1800 7 days 1st Mar-30th Jun, Thu-Sun July-Oct. Gardens open for NGS.
Min Mail Order UK: £10.00
Cat. Cost: None issued.
Credit Cards: None
Specialities: *Clematis*, honeysuckle, choice selection of shrub & climbing roses, extensive range of perennials, mostly on display in the garden. Nat. Collection of *Clematis viticella*.

NHer **Herterton House Garden Nursery**
Hartington, Cambo, Morpeth, Northumberland, NE61 4BN
Ⓣ (01670) 774278
Contact: Mrs M Lawley & Mr Frank Lawley
Opening Times: 1330-1730 Mon, Wed, Fri-Sun 1st Apr-end Sep. (Earlier or later in the year weather permitting.)
Cat. Cost: None issued.
Credit Cards: None
Specialities: Country garden flowers.
Map Ref: N, B2 **OS Grid Ref:** NZ022880

NHol **Holden Clough Nursery** ⊠ ✈ ♿ ⌂ ◆
Holden, Bolton-by-Bowland, Clitheroe, Lancashire, BB7 4PF
Ⓣ (01200) 447615
Ⓕ (01200) 447197
Ⓔ info@holdencloughnursery.co.uk
Ⓦ www.holdencloughnursery.co.uk
Contact: P J Foley

Opening Times: 0900-1630 Mon-Fri Mar-Oct & B/hol Mons, 0900-1630 Sat all year. Closed 24th Dec-4th Jan 2010 & Good Fri. Other times by appt. only.
Min Mail Order UK: Nmc
Min Mail Order EU: Nmc
Cat. Cost: 5 × 1st class.
Credit Cards: MasterCard Visa Delta
Specialities: Large general list incl. *Crocosmia*, *Primula*, *Saxifraga*, *Sempervivum*, *Jovibarba*, *Astilbe*, grasses, *Hosta*, heathers & conifers.
Notes: Seasonal mail order on some items. Also sells wholesale.
Map Ref: N, C2 **OS Grid Ref:** SD773496

NHor **HORN'S GARDEN CENTRE** ⊠ ♿
Dixon Estate, Shotton Colliery, Co. Durham, DH6 2PX
Ⓣ (0191) 526 2987
Ⓕ (0191) 526 2889
Contact: G Horn & Theresa Horn
Opening Times: 0900-1730 Mon-Sat 1000-1600 Sun, all year excl. Easter Mon.
Min Mail Order UK: Nmc
Cat. Cost: 3 × 1st class.
Credit Cards: All major credit/debit cards
Specialities: *Fuchsia*, *Solenostemon*. Wide range of trees, shrubs & perennials.
Map Ref: N, B2

NHoy **HOYLAND PLANT CENTRE** ⊠ € ✈ ♿ ⛺
54 Greenside Lane, Hoyland, Barnsley, Yorkshire, S74 9PZ
Ⓣ (01226) 744466
Ⓜ 07717 182169
Ⓕ (01226) 744466
Ⓔ hickman@hoyland13.freeserve.co.uk
Ⓦ www.somethingforthegarden.co.uk
Contact: Steven Hickman
Opening Times: All year round by appt. only.
Min Mail Order UK: Nmc
Min Mail Order EU: Nmc
Cat. Cost: 4 × 1st class.
Credit Cards: None
Specialities: *Agapanthus* (400+ cvs) & *Tulbaghia* (80+ cvs). Some available in small quantities only. Nat. Collections of *Agapanthus* & *Tulbaghia* (Provisional).
Notes: Also sells wholesale. Daily practical workshops available from spring 2009, ring for details.
Map Ref: N, D2 **OS Grid Ref:** SE372010

NLan **LANDLIFE WILDFLOWERS LTD** ⊠ ♿
National Wildflower Centre, Court Hey Park, Liverpool, L16 3NA
Ⓣ (0151) 737 1819
Ⓕ (0151) 737 1820
Ⓔ gill@landlife.org.uk
Ⓦ www.wildflower.org.uk
Contact: Gillian Watson
Opening Times: 1000-1700, 7 days, 1st Mar-31st Aug.
Min Mail Order UK: £30.00 plants, no min. for seeds.
Cat. Cost: Free.
Credit Cards: Visa Delta Access Switch Solo
Specialities: Wild herbaceous plants & seeds.
Notes: Cafe & shop. Visitor centre, admission charge. Also sells wholesale.
Map Ref: N, D1

NLAp **LANESIDE ALPINES** ⊠ € ♿ ⛺
74 Croston Road, Garstang, Preston, Lancashire, PR3 1HR
Ⓣ (01995) 605537
Ⓜ 07946 659661
Ⓔ jcrhutch@aol.com
Ⓦ www.lanesidealpines.com
Contact: Jeff Hutchings
Opening Times: Please contact nursery. Orders can be taken at Shows. Shows list on website.
Min Mail Order UK: £25.00
Min Mail Order EU: £25.00
Cat. Cost: Sae.
Credit Cards: None
Specialities: 100+ species of hardy terrestrial orchids plus composts & cultivation notes. Wide range of alpines.
Notes: Mail order for orchids only during the winter. Also tufa & pumice from the nursery. No mail order for alpines.
Map Ref: N, D1

NLar **LARCH COTTAGE NURSERIES** ⊠ € ♿ ◆
Melkinthorpe, Penrith, Cumbria, CA10 2DR
Ⓣ (01931) 712404
Ⓕ (01931) 712727
Ⓔ plants@larchcottage.co.uk
Ⓦ www.larchcottage.co.uk
Contact: Peter Stott & Joanne McCullock
Opening Times: Daily from 1000-1730 (or dusk in winter), all year round.
Min Mail Order UK: Nmc
Min Mail Order EU: Nmc
Cat. Cost: £7.00
Credit Cards: All major credit/debit cards
Specialities: Comprehensive plant collection in unique garden setting. Rare & unusual plants; particularly shrubs, trees, perennials,

KEY
⊠ Mail order to UK or EU ⛺ Delivers to shows
✈ Exports beyond EU € Euro accepted
♿ Accessible by wheelchair ◆ See Display advertisement

N

dwarf conifers & Japanese maples. *Acer, Hamamelis, Magnolia* & *Cornus kousa* cvs. Old-fashioned roses, bamboo & alpines.
Notes: Terraced restaurant & art gallery.
Map Ref: N, C1 **OS Grid Ref:** NY315602

NLBP **L.B. Plants** ✉ ♿ ⌂
Whitworth Hall Country Park,
Spennymoor, Co. Durham,
DH16 7QX
Ⓜ 07932 159204/07747 895096
Ⓔ enquiries@lbplants.co.uk
Ⓦ www.lbplants.co.uk
Contact: Howard Leslie & Sharon Bartle
Opening Times: 1000-1800 (or sunset in winter), 7 days.
Min Mail Order UK: Nmc
Cat. Cost: 3 × 1st class.
Credit Cards: None
Specialities: Hardy herbaceous & shrubby perennials, incl. lesser known and harder to find plants.
Notes: Also sells wholesale.
Map Ref: N, B2

N

NLLv **Leeds Lavender** ✉
at Greenscapes Nursery, Brandon Crescent, Shadwell, Leeds, LS17 9JH
Ⓣ (0113) 2892922
Ⓦ www.greenscapesnursery.co.uk
Contact: Ruth Dorrington
Opening Times: 1000-1700, Mon-Sun, Feb-Nov. 1200-1600 Mon-Sun, Nov/Dec/Jan.
Min Mail Order UK: Nmc
Cat. Cost: 2 × 1st class.
Credit Cards: None
Specialities: *Lavandula*. Limited numbers of particular varieties available at certain times, esp. at end of summer.
Notes: Wheelchair access difficult in some areas. Only plug plants by mail order.
Map Ref: N, D2

NMen **Mendle Nursery** ✉ ♿ ⌂
Holme, Scunthorpe, North Lincolnshire, DN16 3RF
Ⓣ (01724) 850864
Ⓔ annearnshaw@lineone.net
Ⓦ www.mendlenursery.com
Contact: Mrs A Earnshaw
Opening Times: 1000-1600 Tue-Sun.
Min Mail Order UK: Nmc
Min Mail Order EU: Nmc
Cat. Cost: 3 × 1st class.
Credit Cards: All major credit/debit cards
Specialities: Many unusual alpines esp. *Saxifraga* & *Sempervivum*.
Map Ref: N, D3 **OS Grid Ref:** SE925070

NMil **Millthorpe Nursery**
(Office) 74 Meadowhead, Sheffield, Yorkshire, S8 7UE
Ⓣ 0114 258 4007
Ⓜ 07899 963939
Ⓦ www.millthorpenursery.co.uk
Contact: John & Anne Dawson
Opening Times: 0900-1630 Tue-Sat, 1000-1630 Sun. Closed Mon, except B/hols. Open by appt. only in Jan & Feb.
Credit Cards: None
Specialities: Good range of shrubs, herbaceous, ferns, grasses & edibles.
Notes: Nursery at Millthorpe Lane, Millthorpe, near Holmesfield, Derbyshire S18 7SA.
Map Ref: N, D2 **OS Grid Ref:** SK321767

NMin **Miniature Bulbs & Choice Bulbs** ✉ € ⌂
The Warren Estate, 9 Greengate Drive, Knaresborough, North Yorkshire, HG5 9EN
Ⓣ (01423) 542819
Ⓕ (01423) 542819
Ⓦ www.miniaturebulbs.co.uk
Contact: Ivor Fox
Opening Times: Not open. Mail order only.
Min Mail Order UK: £10.00
Min Mail Order EU: £15.00
Cat. Cost: 2 × 1st class.
Credit Cards: All major credit/debit cards
Specialities: Rare & unusual miniature bulbs, incl. *Narcissus, Tulipa, Iris, Crocus, Fritillaria* & others. Spring bulb list sent out in April. Some stock in small quantities.
Notes: Credit cards accepted online only.
Map Ref: N, C2 **OS Grid Ref:** SE350584

NMir **Mires Beck Nursery** ✉ ♿
Low Mill Lane, North Cave, Brough, East Riding, Yorkshire, HU15 2NR
Ⓣ (01430) 421543
Ⓔ admin@miresbeck.co.uk
Ⓦ www.miresbeck.co.uk
Contact: Judy Burrow & Martin Rowland
Opening Times: 1000-1600 Mon-Sat 1st Mar-30th Sep. 1000-1500 Mon-Fri 1st Oct-30th Nov & by appt.
Min Mail Order UK: Nmc
Min Mail Order EU: Nmc
Cat. Cost: 3 × 1st class.
Credit Cards: None
Specialities: Wildflower plants of Yorkshire provenance.
Notes: Mail order for wildflower plants, plugs & seeds only. Also sells wholesale.
Map Ref: N, D3 **OS Grid Ref:** SE889316

NMoo **Moor Monkton Nurseries** ⊠ ♿
Moor Monkton, York Road, Nr York, Yorkshire, YO26 8JJ
Ⓣ (01904) 738770
Ⓕ (01904) 738770
Ⓔ sales@bamboo-uk.co.uk
Ⓦ www.bamboo-uk.co.uk
Contact: Peter Owen
Opening Times: 0900-1700.
Min Mail Order UK: Nmc
Cat. Cost: 5 × 2nd class or email for details.
Credit Cards: All major credit/debit cards
Specialities: Bamboos, palms, ferns, unusual trees, shrubs & perennials.
Notes: Mail order for bamboos only. Also sells wholesale.
Map Ref: N, C2

NMRc **Millrace Nursery** ♿
84 Selby Road, Garforth, Leeds, LS25 1LP
Ⓣ (0113) 286 9233
Ⓕ (0113) 286 9908
Ⓔ carol@millrace-plants.co.uk
Ⓦ www.millrace-plants.co.uk
Contact: C Carthy
Opening Times: 1000-1700 Tue, Thu-Sat, Mar-Sep.
Cat. Cost: 4 × 1st class.
Credit Cards: None
Specialities: Unusual perennials, especially drought-resistant, incl. hardy geraniums, alliums, campanulas, penstemnons, potentillas & veronicas. Some plants in small quantities only.

NMun **Muncaster Castle** ⊠ ♿
Ravenglass, Cumbria, CA18 1RQ
Ⓣ (01229) 717614
Ⓕ (01229) 717010
Ⓔ info@muncasterplantcentre.co.uk
Ⓦ www.muncasterplantcentre.co.uk
Contact: Jason Haine
Opening Times: 1030-1700, 7 days, 10th Feb-5th Nov. Other times by appt.
Min Mail Order UK: Nmc
Cat. Cost: 2 × 1st class.
Credit Cards: All major credit/debit cards
Specialities: Hardy plants. *Rhododendron*, *Camellia*, *Magnolia*. Some rarer varieties may be in limited supply.
Notes: Mail order mainly Oct-Apr.
Map Ref: N, C1 **OS Grid Ref:** SD103964

NMyG **Mary Green** ⊠ ♿ ⛫
The Walled Garden, Hornby, Lancaster, Lancashire, LA2 8LD
Ⓣ (01524) 221989
Ⓜ 07778 910348
Ⓕ (01524) 221989
Ⓔ Marygreenplants@aol.com
Contact: Mary Green
Opening Times: By appt. only.
Min Mail Order UK: £10.00
Cat. Cost: 4 × 1st class.
Credit Cards: None
Specialities: Hostas, astilbes, ferns & other shade-loving perennials.
Map Ref: N, C1 **OS Grid Ref:** SD588688

NNor **Norcroft Nurseries** ⊠ ♿
Roadends, Intack, Southwaite, Carlisle, Cumbria, CA4 0LH
Ⓣ (01697) 473933
Ⓕ (01697) 473969
Ⓔ stellagbell@btinternet.com
Contact: Keith Bell
Opening Times: Every afternoon excl. Mon (open B/hol), Mar-Oct, or ring for appt.
Min Mail Order UK: Nmc
Cat. Cost: 2 × 2nd class
Credit Cards: None
Specialities: Hardy herbaceous, hostas, *Lilium*, *Aquilegia*, *Papaver*.
Map Ref: N, B1 **OS Grid Ref:** NY474433

NOaD **Oak Dene Nurseries** ⊠ ⛫
10 Back Lane West, Royston, Barnsley, South Yorkshire, S71 4SB
Ⓣ (01226) 722253
Contact: J Foster or G Foster
Opening Times: 0900-1800 1st Apr-30th Sep, 1000-1600 1st Oct-31st Mar. (Closed 1230-1330.)
Min Mail Order UK: Phone for details.
Min Mail Order EU: Phone for details.
Cat. Cost: None issued.
Credit Cards: None
Specialities: Cacti, succulents (*Lithops*) & South African bulbs.
Notes: Also sells wholesale.
Map Ref: N, D2

NOak **Oak Tree Nursery** ⊠ ♿
Mill Lane, Barlow, Selby, North Yorkshire, YO8 8EY
Ⓣ (01757) 618409
Ⓔ gill@oaktreenursery.plus.com
Ⓦ www.oaktreenursery.com
Contact: Gill Plowes
Opening Times: By appt. only.
Min Mail Order UK: £10.00 + p&p

KEY
⊠ Mail order to UK or EU ⛫ Delivers to shows
✈ Exports beyond EU € Euro accepted
♿ Accessible by wheelchair ◆ See Display advertisement

N

Min Mail Order EU: Nmc
Cat. Cost: 4 × 1st class.
Credit Cards: None
Specialities: Ornamental grasses & grass-like plants.
Notes: Will only export seed beyond the EU.

NPal **THE PALM FARM** ⊠ € ♿
Thornton Hall Gardens, Station Road, Thornton Curtis, Nr Ulceby, Humberside, DN39 6XF
Ⓣ (01469) 531232
Ⓕ (01469) 531232 (please phone first)
Ⓔ bill@thepalmfarm.co.uk
Ⓦ www.thepalmfarm.co.uk
Contact: W W Spink
Opening Times: 1400-1700 7 days. Please phone first in winter.
Min Mail Order UK: £11.00 + p&p
Cat. Cost: 1 × 2nd class.
Credit Cards: None
Specialities: Hardy & half-hardy palms, unusual trees, shrubs & conservatory plants. Some plants available only in small quantities.
Notes: Euro payment accepted only if purchaser pays bank commission. Mail order only if small enough to go by post (min. charge £12.50 p&p) or large enough to go by Palletline (min. charge £39.00 p&p). Also sells wholesale.

N

NPCo **PLANTSMAN'S CORNER**
Sunniside, Barningham, Richmond, Yorkshire, DL11 7DW
Ⓜ 07707 694310
Ⓔ plantsmanscorner@btinternet.com
Ⓦ www.plantsmanscorner.co.uk
Contact: Malcolm Hockham
Opening Times: Not yet fully open. Visits by appt. only. Plant orders can be collected by prior arrangement or from Eggleston Hall Gardens (see nursery NEgg for opening hours). Please contact nursery for details.
Credit Cards: All major credit/debit cards
Specialities: *Cornus*, *Ilex*, & Japanese maples. Variable stock levels.

NPer **PERRY'S PLANTS** € ♿
The River Garden, Sleights, Whitby, North Yorkshire, YO21 1RR
Ⓣ (01947) 810329
Ⓔ sharon.perry@virgin.net
Ⓦ www.perrysplants.co.uk
Contact: Pat & Richard Perry
Opening Times: 1000-1700 mid-March to Oct.
Cat. Cost: Large (A4) sae.
Credit Cards: None
Specialities: *Lavatera*, *Malva*, *Erysimum*, *Euphorbia*, *Anthemis*, *Osteospermum* & *Hebe*. Uncommon hardy & container plants & aquatic plants.
Map Ref: N, C3 **OS Grid Ref:** NZ869082

NPla **THE PLANT DIRECTORY (FORMERLY SCAWSBY HALL NURSERIES)** ⊠
Barnsley Road, Scawsby, Doncaster, South Yorkshire, DN5 7UB
Ⓣ (01302) 783434
Ⓔ mail@the-plant-directory.com
Ⓦ www.the-plant-directory.com
Contact: David Lawson
Opening Times: Not open. Mail order only.
Min Mail Order UK: Nmc
Cat. Cost: None issued
Credit Cards: Maestro Visa MasterCard Solo Paypal
Specialities: A wide range of herbaceous perennials, hardy trees, shrubs & indoor plants. Some indoor & aquatic plants in small quantities only.
Map Ref: N, D3

NPnk **PRIMROSE BANK** ⊠ ♿ ⌂
Redroofs, Dauby Lane, Kexby, Yorkshire, YO41 5LH
Ⓣ (01759) 380220
Ⓜ 07774 944447
Ⓔ sue.goodwill@yahoo.co.uk
Ⓦ www.primrosebank.co.uk
Contact: Sue Goodwill
Opening Times: 1000-1700, Thu-Sun, 1st Apr-30th Jun. Every day in Dec. By appt. only at other times.
Min Mail Order UK: Nmc
Cat. Cost: 4 × 1st class
Credit Cards: All major credit/debit cards
Specialities: Unusual hardy perennials, woodland garden & shade-tolerant plants. *Astrantia*, *Echinacea* & *Heuchera*.
Map Ref: N, C3 **OS Grid Ref:** SE695508

NPri **PRIMROSE COTTAGE NURSERY** ♿ ◆
Ringway Road, Moss Nook, Wythenshawe, Manchester, M22 5WF
Ⓣ (0161) 437 1557
Ⓔ info@primrosecottagenursery.co.uk
Ⓦ www.primrosecottagenursery.co.uk
Contact: Caroline Dumville
Opening Times: 0830-1730 Mon-Sat, 0930-1730 Sun (summer). 0830-1700 Mon-Sat, 0930-1700 Sun (winter).
Cat. Cost: 1 × 70p stamp.
Credit Cards: All major credit/debit cards
Specialities: Hardy herbaceous perennials, alpines, herbs, roses, patio & hanging basket plants. Shrubs.

Notes: Coffee shop open daily.
Map Ref: N, D2

NRar **RARER PLANTS** ♿
Ashfield House, Austfield Lane, Monk Fryston, Leeds, LS25 5EH
Ⓣ (01977) 682263
Contact: Anne Watson
Opening Times: Feb, Mar. By appt. only.
Cat. Cost: Sae.
Credit Cards: None
Specialities: *Helleborus.*
Map Ref: N, D2

NRib **RIBBLESDALE NURSERIES** ♿
Newsham Hall Lane, Woodplumpton, Preston, Lancashire, PR4 0AS
Ⓣ (01772) 863081
Ⓕ (01772) 861884
Ⓔ philsd@btinternet.com
Ⓦ www.ribblesdalenurseries.co.uk
Contact: Mr & Mrs Dunnett
Opening Times: 0900-1800 Mon-Sat Apr-Sep, 0900-1700 Mon-Sat Oct-Mar. 1030-1630 Sun.
Credit Cards: Visa MasterCard Delta Switch
Specialities: Trees, shrubs & perennials. Conifers, hedging, alpines, fruit, climbers, herbs, aquatics, ferns & wildflowers.
Map Ref: N, D1 **OS Grid Ref:** SD515351

NRob **W ROBINSON & SONS LTD** ⊠ € ✈ ♿
Sunny Bank, Forton, Nr Preston, Lancashire, PR3 0BN
Ⓣ (01524) 791210
Ⓕ (01524) 791933
Ⓔ info@mammothonion.co.uk
Ⓦ www.mammothonion.co.uk
Contact: Miss Robinson
Opening Times: 0900-1700 7 days Mar-Jun, 0800-1700 Mon-Fri Jul-Feb.
Min Mail Order UK: Nmc
Min Mail Order EU: Nmc
Cat. Cost: Free.
Credit Cards: Visa Access American Express Switch
Specialities: Mammoth vegetable seed. Onions, leeks, tomatoes & beans. Range of vegetable plants in the spring.
Notes: Also sells wholesale.

NRya **RYAL NURSERY** ♿ ⛟
East Farm Cottage, Ryal, Northumberland, NE20 0SA
Ⓣ (01661) 886562
Ⓔ alpines@ryal.freeserve.co.uk
Contact: R F Hadden
Opening Times: 1000-1600 Sun Mar-Jul & other times by appt.
Cat. Cost: Sae.
Credit Cards: None
Specialities: Alpine & woodland plants. Mainly available in small quantities only. Nat. Collection of *Primula marginata.*
Notes: Also sells wholesale.
Map Ref: N, B2 **OS Grid Ref:** NZ015744

NSco **SCOTT'S WILDFLOWERS** ⊠
Swallow Hill Barn, 31 Common Side, Distington, Workington, Cumbria, CA14 4PU
Ⓣ (01946) 830486
Ⓔ scotts.wildflowers@virgin.net
Ⓦ www.scottswildflowers.co.uk
Contact: Ted Scott
Opening Times: 1000-1600 Mar-Oct, 1130-1500 Nov-Feb, 7 days.
Min Mail Order UK: £12.50 + £5.75 p&p
Cat. Cost: 3 × 1st class.
Credit Cards: Maestro MasterCard Solo Visa
Specialities: Native British wildflowers, including aquatics.
Notes: Also sells wholesale.
Map Ref: N, C1

NShi **SHIRLEY TASKER**
6 Sandheys Drive, Churchtown, Southport, Merseyside, PR9 9PQ
Ⓣ (01704) 213048
Ⓜ 07951 834066
Ⓔ shirley@shirleysplants.fsnet.co.uk
Ⓦ www.stbegonias.com
Contact: Shirley & Terry Tasker
Opening Times: By appt. only.
Cat. Cost: 2 × 1st class.
Credit Cards: None
Specialities: Nat. Collection of *Begonia* species & hybrids.
Map Ref: N, D1 **OS Grid Ref:** SD355183

NSla **SLACK TOP NURSERIES** ⊠ € ♿ ⛟
Hebden Bridge, West Yorkshire, HX7 7HA
Ⓣ (01422) 845348
Ⓔ enquiries@slacktopnurseries.co.uk
Ⓦ www.slacktopnurseries.co.uk
Contact: M R or R Mitchell
Opening Times: 1000-1700 Fri-Sun 1st Mar-30th Sep & B/hol Mons 1st Mar-30th Sep.
Min Mail Order UK: £30.00
Cat. Cost: A5 sae.
Credit Cards: None

KEY
⊠ Mail order to UK or EU ⛟ Delivers to shows
✈ Exports beyond EU € Euro accepted
♿ Accessible by wheelchair ◆ See Display advertisement

N

Specialities: Alpine & rockery plants. *Celmisia semi-cordata*, *Saxifraga*, *Hepatica* & native primrose.
Notes: Some areas of garden inaccessible for wheelchairs.
Map Ref: N, D2 **OS Grid Ref:** SD977286

NSti **STILLINGFLEET LODGE NURSERIES** ♿
Stillingfleet, North Yorkshire,
YO19 6HP
Ⓣ (01904) 728506
Ⓕ (01904) 728506
Ⓔ vanessa.cook@stillingfleetlodgenurseries.co.uk
Ⓦ www.stillingfleetlodgenurseries.co.uk
Contact: Vanessa Cook
Opening Times: 1300-1700 Wed & Fri 4th Apr-30th Sep. 1300-1700, 1st & 3rd Sat in each month.
Cat. Cost: Online only.
Credit Cards: None
Specialities: Foliage & unusual perennials. Hardy geraniums, *Pulmonaria*, variegated plants & grasses, interesting climbers.
Map Ref: N, C2

NSum **SUMMERDALE GARDEN NURSERY**
Summerdale House, Cow Brow, Lupton, Carnforth, Lancashire, LA6 1PE
Ⓣ (01539) 567210
Ⓔ summerdalenursery@btinternet.com
Ⓦ www.summerdalegardenplants.co.uk
Contact: Abi Attwood
Opening Times: 0930-1630 Thu, Fri & Sat, 1st Feb-31st Oct. Other times by appt. only.
Cat. Cost: 4 × 1st class.
Credit Cards: All major credit/debit cards
Specialities: Wide variety of pernnials, large collection of *Primula*. Many moist and shade-loving plants incl. *Meconopsis* & hellebores.
Map Ref: N, C1 **OS Grid Ref:** SD545819

NVic **THE VICARAGE GARDEN** ✉ ♿
Carrington, Manchester,
M31 4AG
Ⓣ (0161) 775 2750
Ⓔ info@vicaragebotanicalgardens.co.uk
Ⓦ www.vicaragebotanicalgardens.co.uk
Contact: Paul Haine
Opening Times: 0900-1700 Mon-Sat, closed Thu. 1000-1630 Sun all year.
Min Mail Order UK: Nmc
Credit Cards: All major credit/debit cards
Specialities: Herbaceous, alpines, grasses, ferns.
Notes: Free admission to 7-acre gardens with coffee shop & mini zoo.
Map Ref: N, D2 **OS Grid Ref:** SJ729926

NWCA **WHITE COTTAGE ALPINES** ✉ ♿ ⌂ ◆
Sunnyside Nurseries, Hornsea Road, Sigglesthorne, East Yorkshire, HU11 5QL
Ⓣ (01964) 542692
Ⓔ plants@whitecottagealpines.co.uk
Ⓦ www.whitecottagealpines.co.uk
Contact: Sally E Cummins
Opening Times: 1000-1700 (or dusk) Thu-Sun & B/hol Mon 1st Mar-30th Sep. If travelling far, please phone first. In winter by appt. only.
Min Mail Order UK: Nmc.
Min Mail Order EU: £15.00 + p&p by card only.
Cat. Cost: 4 × 1st class.
Credit Cards: Visa MasterCard Switch
Specialities: Alpines & rock garden plants. Range of American alpines, dwarf willows & an increasing range of South African alpines incl. *Tulbaghia*.
Notes: Euro payments by card only.
Map Ref: N, C3

NWea **WEASDALE NURSERIES LTD.** ✉
Newbiggin-on-Lune, Kirkby Stephen, Cumbria, CA17 4LX
Ⓣ (01539) 623246
Ⓕ (01539) 623277
Ⓔ sales@weasdale.com
Ⓦ www.weasdale.com
Contact: Andrew Forsyth
Opening Times: 0830-1730 Mon-Fri. Closed w/ends, B/hols, Xmas through to the New Year.
Min Mail Order UK: Nmc
Min Mail Order EU: Nmc
Cat. Cost: £2.00 or 7 × 1st class. £2.00 by debit card, £2.50 by credit card.
Credit Cards: All major credit/debit cards
Specialities: Hardy forest trees, hedging, broadleaved & conifers. Specimen trees & shrubs grown at 850 feet (260 metre) elevation.
Notes: Mail order a speciality. Mail order Nov-Apr only. Also sells wholesale to VAT registered customers.
Map Ref: N, C1 **OS Grid Ref:** NY690039

NWit **D S WITTON** ✉
26 Casson Drive, Harthill, Sheffield, Yorkshire, S26 7WA
Ⓣ (01909) 771366
Ⓕ (01909) 771366
Ⓔ donshardyeuphorbias@btopenworld.com
Ⓦ www.euphorbias.co.uk
Contact: Don Witton
Opening Times: By appt. only. Open Day, 1300-1600, Sun 3rd May 2009.

Min Mail Order UK: Nmc
Cat. Cost: 1 × 1st class + sae.
Credit Cards: None
Specialities: Nat. Collection of Hardy *Euphorbia*. Over 130 varieties.
Notes: Mail order plants, Oct-Feb. Mail order seed Oct-June.
Map Ref: N, D2 **OS Grid Ref:** SK494812

NWsh **WESTSHORES NURSERIES** ⊠
82 West Street, Winterton, Lincolnshire, DN15 9QF
Ⓣ (01724) 733940
Ⓔ westshnur@aol.com
Ⓦ www.westshores.co.uk
Contact: Gail & John Summerfield
Opening Times: 0930-1800 (or dusk) w/ends & B/hols, 1st Mar-31st Oct. Other times by appt.
Min Mail Order UK: £15.00
Credit Cards: All major credit/debit cards
Specialities: Ornamental grasses & herbaceous perennials.
Map Ref: N, D3 **OS Grid Ref:** SE927187

NWyk **WYKEHAM MATURE PLANTS** ⊠ €
The Walled Garden, Wykeham Abbey, Scarborough, N. Yorkshire, YO13 9QS
Ⓣ (01723) 862406
Ⓕ (01723) 865643
Ⓔ m.howe@wykeham.co.uk
Ⓦ www.wykehammatureplants.co.uk
Contact: Martin Howe
Opening Times: 0930-1630 Mon-Sat, 10.30-1500 Sun, Mar-May & Nov. Closed throughout Xmas.
Min Mail Order UK: Nmc
Cat. Cost: None issued.
Credit Cards: All, except American Express
Specialities: Trees, shrubs, hedging as mature plants for instant effect.
Notes: Large stock only. Delivery by pallet or large haulage wagon, heavy stock. Also sells wholesale.
Map Ref: N, C3 **OS Grid Ref:** SE959818

SOUTHERN

SAga **BLUEBELL COTTAGE NURSERY (FORMERLY AGAR'S)** € ♿
Agars Lane, Hordle, Lymington, Hampshire, SO41 0FL
Ⓜ 07508 848010
Contact: George Tombs
Opening Times: 1000-1700 (closed Thu), Mar-Sep. Open most days but please phone first.
Specialities: *Penstemon* & *Salvia*. Also wide range of hardy plants incl. hardy & tender shrubs, climbers & herbaceous. Many plants not listed may be available.
Map Ref: S, D2 **OS Grid Ref:** SZ275960

SAll **ALLWOODS** ⊠ ♿
London Road, Hassocks, West Sussex, BN6 9NB
Ⓣ (01273) 844229
Ⓔ info@allwoods.net
Ⓦ www.allwoods.net
Contact: David & Emma James
Opening Times: Office: 0900-1630 Mon-Fri. Answer machine all other times. Nursery: 1st Mar-30th Jun 7 days.
Min Mail Order UK: Nmc
Min Mail Order EU: Nmc
Cat. Cost: 2 × 1st class.
Credit Cards: Access Visa MasterCard Switch Maestro
Specialities: *Dianthus* incl. hardy border carnations, pinks, perpetual, Malmaisons & *D. allwoodii*, some available as seed. Certain lavender varieties. Penstemons.
Notes: Exports seed only.
Map Ref: S, D4 **OS Grid Ref:** TQ303170

SAPC **ARCHITECTURAL PLANTS (CHICHESTER) LTD** ⊠ € ♿ ⛟ ◆
Lidsey Road Nursery, Westergate, Nr Chichester, West Sussex, PO20 6SU
Ⓣ (01243) 545008
Ⓕ (01243) 545009
Ⓔ chichester@architecturalplants.com
Ⓦ www.architecturalplants.com
Contact: Christine Shaw
Opening Times: 1000-1600 Sun-Fri all year. Closed Sat & B/hol Mons. Open Good Fri.
Min Mail Order UK: Nmc
Min Mail Order EU: £150.00
Cat. Cost: Free.
Credit Cards: All major credit/debit cards
Specialities: Architectural plants & hardy exotics esp. rare evergreen broadleaved trees & seaside exotics, spiky plants, yuccas/agaves.
Notes: Second nursery near Horsham, code SArc. Also sells wholesale.
Map Ref: S, D3 **OS Grid Ref:** SU937040

SApp **APPLE COURT** ⊠ € ♿
Hordle Lane:Hordle, Lymington, Hampshire, S041 0HU
Ⓣ (01590) 642130

KEY
⊠ Mail order to UK or EU — ⛟ Delivers to shows
✈ Exports beyond EU — € Euro accepted
♿ Accessible by wheelchair — ◆ See Display advertisement

S

Ⓕ (01590) 644220
Ⓔ applecourt@btinternet.com
Ⓦ www.applecourt.com
Contact: Angela & Charles Meads
Opening Times: 1000-1700 Fri, Sat, Sun & B/hol 1st Mar-31st Oct. Closed Nov-Feb.
Min Mail Order UK: Nmc
Min Mail Order EU: Nmc
Cat. Cost: 4 × 1st class.
Credit Cards: All major credit/debit cards
Specialities: *Hemerocallis*, *Hosta*, grasses & ferns.
Map Ref: S, D2 **OS Grid Ref:** SZ270941

SArc **ARCHITECTURAL PLANTS** ⊠ € ♿ ◆
Cooks Farm, Nuthurst, Horsham, West Sussex, RH13 6LH
Ⓣ (01403) 891772
Ⓕ (01403) 891056
Ⓔ enquiries@architecturalplants.com
Ⓦ www.architecturalplants.com
Contact: Sarah Chandler
Opening Times: 0900-1700 Mon-Sat, closed Sun.
Min Mail Order UK: Nmc
Min Mail Order EU: £150.00
Cat. Cost: Free
Credit Cards: All major credit/debit cards
Specialities: Architectural plants & hardy exotics & rare broadleaved trees, bamboos, spiky plants, ferns & climbers.
Notes: Second nursery near Chichester, code SAPC. Also sells wholesale.

S

SBch **BIRCHWOOD PLANTS** ♿ ⌂
(office) 10 Westering, Romsey, Hampshire, SO51 7LY
Ⓣ (01794) 502192 or (02380) 814345
Ⓔ info@birchwoodplants.co.uk
Ⓦ www.birchwoodplants.co.uk
Contact: Lesley Baker
Opening Times: Open on 27th/28th Mar, 17th/18th Apr, 15th/16th & 29th/30th May. See website for further dates. Plants can be collected by arrangement from nursery or from NCCPG sale at Longstock, Hants on 4th May.
Cat. Cost: Online only.
Credit Cards: None
Specialities: Wide range of plants, mainly herbaceous, many unusual. Large range of Mottisfont herbaceous plants. Good selection of hardy geraniums, salvias & *Dianthus*. Scented plants & those to attract bees & butterflies. Drought-tolerant plants. Some stock available in small quantities only.
Notes: Nursery at Silverwood House, Gardener's Lane, Nr Romsey, SO51 6AD.
Mostly accessible for wheelchairs.
Map Ref: S, D2 **OS Grid Ref:** SU333190

SBfd **BIRCHFIELD NURSERY** ⊠ ♿
Kidders Lane, Henfield, West Sussex, BN5 9AB
Ⓣ (01273) 494058
Ⓕ (01273) 493696
Ⓔ sales@birchfieldnursery.com
Ⓦ www.birchfieldnursery.com
Contact: Clive Parker or Ron Jenkins
Opening Times: 0830-1700 Mon-Fri, 0930-1630 Sat & Sun, all year except Xmas/New Year period. For winter hours please phone first. Please phone before visiting to ensure plant availability & to check opening hours.
Min Mail Order UK: Nmc
Cat. Cost: Online only.
Credit Cards: All, except American Express
Specialities: Very wide general range of plants incl. many unusual & new varieties, plus fruit, young veg. plants & seasonal bedding. Some plants (esp. *Canna*) available in small quantities only.
Notes: Also sells wholesale.
Map Ref: S, D3 **OS Grid Ref:** TQ213178

SBHP **BLEAK HILL PLANTS** ♿
Braemoor, Bleak Hill, Harbridge, Ringwood, Hampshire, BH24 3PX
Ⓣ (01425) 652983
Ⓔ tracey_netherway@btopenworld.com
Contact: Tracy Netherway
Opening Times: 0900-1800, Mon, Tue, Fri, Sat & 1000-1600 Sun, Mar-Oct. Closed Wed & Thu.
Cat. Cost: 2 × 1st class.
Credit Cards: None
Specialities: Hardy & half-hardy herbaceous perennials. Stock available in small quantities.
Map Ref: S, D1 **OS Grid Ref:** SU132111

SBig **BIG PLANT NURSERY** ⊠ ♿ ⌂ ◆
Hole Street, Ashington, West Sussex, RH20 3DE
Ⓣ (01903) 891466
Ⓜ 07957 262845
Ⓕ (01903) 892829
Ⓔ info@bigplantnursery.co.uk
Ⓦ www.bigplantnursery.co.uk
Contact: Bruce Jordan
Opening Times: 0900-1700 Mon-Sat, 1000-1600 Sun & B/hols.
Min Mail Order UK: Please phone for further info.
Cat. Cost: A5 sae with 2 × 1st class.
Credit Cards: All major credit/debit cards
Specialities: Bamboos, hardy exotics & palms,

Ginkgo, *Betula*.
Notes: Also sells wholesale.
Map Ref: S, D3 **OS Grid Ref:** TQ132153

SBir **BIRCHFLEET NURSERIES** ◆
Greenfields Close, Nyewood, Petersfield, Hampshire, GU31 5JQ
Ⓣ (01730) 821636
Ⓕ (01730) 821636
Ⓔ gammoak@aol.com
Ⓦ www.birchfleetnurseries.co.uk
Contact: John & Daphne Gammon
Opening Times: By appt. only. Please phone.
Cat. Cost: 2 × 1st class.
Credit Cards: None
Specialities: Oaks. Beech. *Carpinus*. Nat. Collection of *Liquidambar*.
Notes: Nursery accessible for wheelchairs in dry weather. Also sells wholesale.
Map Ref: S, C3

SBmr **BLACKMOOR NURSERIES** ⊠ ♿
Blackmoor Estate, Blackmoor, Liss, Hampshire, GU33 6BS
Ⓣ (01420) 477978
Ⓕ (01420) 487813
Ⓔ jonmunday@blackmoor.co.uk
Ⓦ www.blackmoor.co.uk
Contact: Jon Munday
Opening Times: 0730-1600.
Min Mail Order UK: Nmc
Min Mail Order EU: Nmc
Cat. Cost: None issued.
Credit Cards: All major credit/debit cards
Specialities: Fruit trees, soft fruit & ornamental trees.
Notes: Also sells wholesale.
Map Ref: S, C3 **OS Grid Ref:** SU779336

SBri **BRICKWALL COTTAGE NURSERY** ⊠ ♿
1 Brickwall Cottages, Frittenden, Cranbrook, Kent, TN17 2DH
Ⓣ (01580) 852425
Ⓔ sue.martin@talktalk.net
Contact: Sue Martin
Opening Times: By appt. only.
Min Mail Order UK: Nmc
Min Mail Order EU: Nmc
Credit Cards: None
Specialities: Hardy perennials. Stock available in small quantities only. *Geum*. Nat. Collection of *Geum*.
Map Ref: S, C5 **OS Grid Ref:** TQ815410

SBrk **BROOKFIELD PLANTS** ⊠ ⌂
Bigelle, Sandyhurst Lane, Ashford, Kent, TN25 4NX
Ⓣ (01233) 624934
Ⓜ 07944 213891
Ⓦ www.brookfieldplants.com
Contact: Paul Harris
Opening Times: Visitors by appt. only.
Min Mail Order UK: Nmc
Cat. Cost: £1.00
Credit Cards: None
Specialities: *Hemerocallis* & *Hosta*. Nat. Collection of *Hemerocallis*.
Notes: Sells at shows.

SBrm **BRAMBLY HEDGE** ⊠
Mill Lane, Sway, Hampshire, SO41 8LN
Ⓣ (01590) 683570
Contact: Kim Williams
Opening Times: By appt. only.
Min Mail Order UK: Nmc
Cat. Cost: Sae for descriptive list.
Credit Cards: None
Specialities: Nat. Collection of *Streptocarpus*. Available in small quantities only.
Notes: Mail order Mar-Aug, small quantities only available.

SBst **BEAST PLANTS**
24 Arundel Road, Boyatt Wood, Eastleigh, Hampshire, SO50 4PQ
Ⓣ 02380 485307
Ⓜ 07887 997263
Ⓔ beastplants@tiscali.co.uk
Contact: Toni & Steve Newell
Opening Times: By appt. only.
Cat. Cost: Free.
Credit Cards: None
Specialities: Exotic, sub-tropical & unusual plants.

SCac **CACTI & SUCCULENTS** ⊠
Hammerfield, Crockham Hill, Edenbridge, Kent, TN8 6RR
Ⓣ (01732) 866295
Contact: Geoff Southon
Opening Times: Flexible. Please phone first.
Min Mail Order UK: Nmc.
Cat. Cost: None issued.
Credit Cards: None
Specialities: *Echeveria* & related genera & hybrids. *Agave*, haworthias, aloes, gasterias, crassulas & aeoniums. (Large range of plants available in small quantities.)

KEY
⊠ Mail order to UK or EU ⌂ Delivers to shows
✈ Exports beyond EU € Euro accepted
♿ Accessible by wheelchair ◆ See Display advertisement

SCam **CAMELLIA GROVE NURSERY** ⊠ € ✈ ♿ ⌂
Market Garden, Lower Beeding, West Sussex, RH13 6PP
Ⓣ (01403) 891412
Ⓔ sales@camellia-grove.com
Ⓦ www.camellia-grove.com
Contact: Chris Loder
Opening Times: 1000-1600 Mon-Sat, please phone first so we can give try to give you our undivided attention.
Min Mail Order UK: Nmc
Min Mail Order EU: Nmc
Cat. Cost: 2 × 1st class.
Credit Cards: All, except American Express
Specialities: Camellias & azaleas. Also rhododendrons & hydrangeas.
Notes: Also sells wholesale.
Map Ref: S, C3

S

SChF **CHARLESHURST FARM NURSERY** ⊠ € ⌂
Loxwood Road, Plaistow, Billingshurst, West Sussex, RH14 0NY
Ⓣ (01403) 752273
Ⓜ 07736 522788
Ⓔ Charleshurstfarm@aol.com
Ⓦ www.charleshurstplants.co.uk
Contact: Clive Mellor
Opening Times: Normally 0900-1730 Fri, Sat, Sun, Feb-Oct, but please ring first before travelling.
Min Mail Order UK: Nmc
Min Mail Order EU: Nmc
Cat. Cost: 2 × 1st class.
Credit Cards: All major credit/debit cards
Specialities: Shrubs including some more unusual species. Good range of daphnes & Japanese maples.
Map Ref: S, C3 **OS Grid Ref:** TQ015308

SChr **JOHN CHURCHER** ⊠ ✈
47 Grove Avenue, Portchester, Fareham, Hampshire, PO16 9EZ
Ⓣ (023) 9232 6740
Ⓕ (023) 9232 6740
Ⓔ churchers.47@tiscali.co.uk
Contact: John Churcher
Opening Times: By appt. only. Please phone or email.
Min Mail Order UK: Nmc
Min Mail Order EU: Nmc
Cat. Cost: None issued.
Credit Cards: None
Specialities: Hardy exotics for the Mediterranean-style garden, incl. palms, tree ferns, *Musa*, hedychiums, cycads, *Agave*, *Aloe*, *Opuntia* & echiums. Stock available in small quantities only.
Map Ref: S, D2 **OS Grid Ref:** SU614047

SCko **COOKOO BOX NURSERY** ⊠ ✈ ⌂
Longfield, 63 Charlesford Avenue, Kingswood, Maidstone, Kent, ME17 3PH
Ⓜ 07749 828168
Ⓔ info@cookooboxchillies.com
Ⓦ www.cookooboxchillies.com
Contact: P Drew-Cook
Opening Times: By appt. only.
Min Mail Order UK: Nmc
Min Mail Order EU: Nmc
Cat. Cost: 2 × 1st class.
Credit Cards: None
Specialities: *Capsicum*

SCmr **CROMAR NURSERY** ⊠ ♿
39 Livesey Street, North Pole, Wateringbury, Maidstone, Kent, ME18 5BQ
Ⓣ (01622) 812380
Ⓔ CromarNursery@aol.com
Ⓦ www.cromarnursery.co.uk
Contact: Debra & Martin Cronk
Opening Times: 0930-1700 daily except Wed. Winter opening 0930-1630 Thu, Fri, Sat, Sun.
Min Mail Order UK: Nmc
Min Mail Order EU: Nmc
Cat. Cost: 2 × 1st class.
Credit Cards: All major credit/debit cards
Specialities: Ornamental & fruit trees.
Map Ref: S, C4 **OS Grid Ref:** TQ697547

SCnR **COLIN ROBERTS** ⊠
Tragumna, Morgay Wood Lane, Three Oaks, Guestling, East Sussex, TN35 4NF
Ⓜ 07933 060905
Contact: Colin Roberts
Opening Times: Not open. Mail order only.
Min Mail Order UK: £20.00
Cat. Cost: 2 × 1st class.
Credit Cards: None
Specialities: Dwarf bulbs & woodland plants incl. many rare & unusual, in small numbers.

SCog **COGHURST CAMELLIAS** ⊠ € ♿ ⌂
Ivy House Lane, Near Three Oaks, Hastings, East Sussex, TN35 4NP
Ⓣ (01424) 756228
Ⓔ rotherview@btinternet.com
Ⓦ www.rotherview.com
Contact: R Bates & W Bates
Opening Times: 0930-1600 7 days.
Min Mail Order UK: Nmc
Min Mail Order EU: Nmc
Cat. Cost: 6 × 1st class.
Credit Cards: All major credit/debit cards

Specialities: *Camellia.*
Notes: Nursery is on the same site as Rotherview Nursery. Also sells wholesale.
Map Ref: S, D5

SCoo **Cooling's Nurseries Ltd** ♿
Rushmore Hill, Knockholt, Sevenoaks, Kent, TN14 7NN
Ⓣ (01959) 532269
Ⓕ (01959) 534092
Ⓔ Plantfinder@coolings.co.uk
Ⓦ www.coolings.co.uk
Contact: Mark Reeve or Dan Short
Opening Times: 0900-1700 Mon-Sat & 1000-1630 Sun.
Cat. Cost: None issued
Credit Cards: All, except American Express
Specialities: Large range of perennials, conifers & bedding plants. Many unusual shrubs & trees. Third generation family business. Display garden.
Notes: Coffee shop.
Map Ref: S, C4 **OS Grid Ref:** TK477610

SCrf **Crofters Nurseries** € ♿
Church Hill, Charing Heath, Near Ashford, Kent, TN27 0BU
Ⓣ (01233) 712798
Ⓕ (01233) 712798
Ⓔ croftersnursery@yahoo.co.uk
Contact: John & Sue Webb
Opening Times: 1000-1700. Closed Sun-Tue. Please check first.
Cat. Cost: 3 × 1st class.
Credit Cards: None
Specialities: Fruit, ornamental trees & conifers. Old apple varieties. Small number of *Prunus serrula* with grafted ornamental heads.
Map Ref: S, C5 **OS Grid Ref:** TQ923493

SDay **A La Carte Daylilies** ⊠ €
Little Hermitage, St Catherine's Down, Nr Ventnor, Isle of Wight, PO38 2PD
Ⓣ (01983) 730512
Ⓔ andy@alacartedaylilies.co.uk
Ⓦ www.alacartedaylilies.co.uk
Contact: Jan & Andy Wyers
Opening Times: Mail order only. Open by appt. only. Difficult to find on an unmade private road.
Min Mail Order UK: Nmc
Min Mail Order EU: Nmc
Cat. Cost: 3 × 1st class.
Credit Cards: None
Specialities: *Hemerocallis.* Nat. Collections of Miniature & Small Flowered *Hemerocallis* & Large Flowered *Hemerocallis* (post-1960 award-winning cultivars).
Notes: Also sells wholesale.
Map Ref: S, D2 **OS Grid Ref:** SZ499787

SDea **Deacon's Nursery** ⊠ ✈ € ◆
Moor View, Godshill, Isle of Wight, PO38 3HW
Ⓣ (01983) 840750 (24 hrs) or (01983) 522243
Ⓕ (01983) 523575
Ⓔ info@deaconsnurseryfruits.co.uk
Ⓦ www.deaconsnurseryfruits.co.uk
Contact: G D & B H W Deacon
Opening Times: 0800-1600 Mon-Fri May-Sep, 0800-1700 Mon-Fri 0800-1200 Sat Oct-Apr.
Min Mail Order UK: Nmc
Min Mail Order EU: Nmc
Cat. Cost: Free.
Credit Cards: All major credit/debit cards
Specialities: Over 300 varieties of apple, old & new, pears, plums, gages, damsons, cherries. Modern soft fruit, grapes, hops, nuts & family trees.
Notes: Also sells wholesale.
Map Ref: S, D2

SDeJ **P. De Jager & Sons Ltd** ⊠ ✈ ♿ ◆
The Old Forge, Chartway Street, East Sutton, Maidstone, Kent, ME17 3DW
Ⓣ (01622) 840229
Ⓕ (01622) 844073
Ⓔ flowerbulbs@dejager.co.uk
Ⓦ www.dejager.co.uk
Contact: George Clowes
Opening Times: 0900-1700 Mon-Fri
Min Mail Order UK: Nmc
Min Mail Order EU: Nmc
Cat. Cost: Free
Credit Cards: All major credit/debit cards
Specialities: Complete range of all flower bulbs.
Notes: Also sells wholesale.
Map Ref: S, C4

SDix **Great Dixter Nurseries** ⊠
Northiam, Rye, East Sussex, TN31 6PH
Ⓣ (01797) 253107
Ⓕ (01797) 252879
Ⓔ nursery@greatdixter.co.uk
Ⓦ www.greatdixter.co.uk
Contact: K Leighton
Opening Times: 0900-1700 Mon-Fri, 0900-1230 Sat all year. Also 1400-1700 Sat, Sun & B/hols Apr-Oct.

KEY
⊠ Mail order to UK or EU — Delivers to shows
✈ Exports beyond EU — € Euro accepted
♿ Accessible by wheelchair — ◆ See Display advertisement

S

Min Mail Order UK: Nmc
Min Mail Order EU: Nmc
Cat. Cost: 5 × 1st class.
Credit Cards: All major credit/debit cards
Specialities: *Clematis*, shrubs and plants. Gardens open.
Notes: Plants dispatched Sep-Mar only. Partially accessible for wheelchairs.

SDnm **DENMANS GARDEN, (JOHN BROOKES LTD)** ♿
Denmans Lane, Fontwell, West Sussex, BN18 0SU
Ⓣ (01243) 542808
Ⓕ (01243) 544064
Ⓔ denmans@denmans-garden.co.uk
Ⓦ www.denmans-garden.co.uk
Contact: Mrs Claudia Murphy
Opening Times: 0900-1700 (dusk in winter) 7 days all year, except 25th & 26th Dec & 1st Jan.
Cat. Cost: None issued
Credit Cards: Visa MasterCard
Specialities: Rare and unusual plants.
Map Ref: S, D3 **OS Grid Ref:** SU944070

S

SDow **DOWNDERRY NURSERY** ✉ € ✈ ♿
Pillar Box Lane, Hadlow, Nr Tonbridge, Kent, TN11 9SW
Ⓣ (01732) 810081
Ⓕ (01732) 811398
Ⓔ info@downderry-nursery.co.uk
Ⓦ www.downderry-nursery.co.uk
Contact: Dr S J Charlesworth
Opening Times: 1000-1700 Tue-Sun 1st May-31st Oct & B/hols. Other times by appt.
Min Mail Order UK: Nmc
Min Mail Order EU: Nmc
Cat. Cost: 3 × 1st class.
Credit Cards: Delta MasterCard Maestro Visa
Specialities: Nat. Collections of *Lavandula* and *Rosmarinus.*
Map Ref: S, C4 **OS Grid Ref:** TQ625521

SDys **DYSONS NURSERIES** ♿
Great Comp Garden, Platt, Sevenoaks, Kent, TN15 8QS
Ⓣ (01732) 886154
Ⓔ info@dysons-salvias.co.uk
Ⓦ www.dysons-salvias.co.uk
Contact: William T Dyson
Opening Times: 1100-1700 7 days 1st Apr-31st Oct. Other times by appt.
Cat. Cost: None issued.
Credit Cards: None
Specialities: Salvias & an eclectic range of choice and uncommon plants.
Map Ref: S, C4

SEND **EAST NORTHDOWN FARM NURSERY** ✉ € ♿ ◆
Margate, Kent, CT9 3TS
Ⓣ (01843) 862060
Ⓜ 07714 241668
Ⓕ (01843) 860206
Ⓔ friend.northdown@btinternet.com
Ⓦ www.botanyplants.com
Contact: Louise & William Friend
Opening Times: 0900-1700 Mon-Sat, 1000-1700 Sun all year. Closed Xmas week & Easter Sun.
Min Mail Order UK: Nmc
Cat. Cost: Online only.
Credit Cards: Visa Switch MasterCard
Specialities: Chalk & coast-loving plants.
Map Ref: S, B6 **OS Grid Ref:** TR383702

SEWo **ENGLISH WOODLANDS** ✉
Burrow Nursery, Cross in Hand, Heathfield, East Sussex, TN21 0UG
Ⓣ (01435) 862992
Ⓕ (01435) 867742
Ⓔ michael@ewburrownursery.co.uk
Ⓦ www.ewburrownursery.co.uk
Contact: Michael Hardcastle
Opening Times: 8000-1700 Mon-Sat. Closed Sun.
Min Mail Order UK: £25.00
Cat. Cost: 4 × 1st class.
Credit Cards: All major credit/debit cards
Specialities: Trees, large & small.
Notes: Also sells wholesale.
Map Ref: S, C4 **OS Grid Ref:** TQ557122

SFam **FAMILY TREES** ✉ ♿
Sandy Lane, Shedfield, Hampshire, SO32 2HQ
Ⓣ (01329) 834812
Ⓦ www.familytreesnursery.co.uk
Contact: Philip House
Opening Times: 0930-1230 Tue, Wed, Fri & Sat mid-Oct-end Apr (closed 15th Dec-15th Jan).
Min Mail Order UK: £10.00
Cat. Cost: Free
Credit Cards: None
Specialities: Fruit & ornamental trees. Trained fruit tree specialists: standards, espaliers, cordons. Other trees, old-fashioned & climbing roses, evergreens. Trees, except evergreens, sold bare-rooted.

SFgr **FIRGROVE PLANTS** ✉
24 Wykeham Field, Wickham, Fareham, Hampshire, PO17 5AB
Ⓣ (01329) 835206 after 1900 hours.
Ⓔ jenny@firgroveplants.demon.co.uk
Ⓦ www.firgroveplants.demon.co.uk

Contact: Jenny MacKinnon
Opening Times: Not open. Mail order only.
Min Mail Order UK: £7.00
Cat. Cost: Sae.
Credit Cards: None
Specialities: Wide range of houseleeks & smaller range of other alpines in small quantities.
Notes: Houseleeks by mail order Apr-mid Oct.

SGar **GARDEN PLANTS** ⊠ ♠
Windy Ridge, Victory Road, St Margarets-at-Cliffe, Dover, Kent, CT15 6HF
Ⓣ (01304) 853225
Ⓔ GardenPlants@GardenPlants-nursery.co.uk
Ⓦ www.GardenPlants-nursery.co.uk
Contact: Teresa Ryder & David Ryder
Opening Times: 1000-1730 summer, 1000-1700 winter. Closed Tues.
Min Mail Order UK: Nmc
Cat. Cost: 2 × 1st class + A5 sae.
Credit Cards: None
Specialities: Unusual perennials, *Penstemon* & *Salvia*.
Notes: Plantsman's garden open to view. Map essential for first visit. Also sells wholesale.
Map Ref: S, C6 **OS Grid Ref:** TR358464

SGSe **GARDEN SECRETS** ⊠ ♿
Boldre Nurseries, Southampton Road, Sway, Lymington, Hampshire, SO41 8ND
Ⓜ 07779 084245
Ⓦ www.gardensecretsnursery.co.uk
Contact: Tim Woodford
Opening Times: 0930-1700 Sat & Sun, Mar-Jan. Other times by appt. only. Please phone first.
Min Mail Order UK: £15.00
Credit Cards: None
Specialities: Perennials, grasses and ferns.
Map Ref: S, D2 **OS Grid Ref:** SZ314981

SHaC **HART CANNA** ⊠ € ♿
27 Guildford Road West, Farnborough, Hampshire, GU14 6PS
Ⓣ (01252) 514421
Ⓕ (01252) 378821
Ⓔ plants@hartcanna.com
Ⓦ www.hartcanna.com
Contact: Keith Hayward
Opening Times: Visitors by arrangement.
Min Mail Order UK: Nmc
Min Mail Order EU: Nmc
Cat. Cost: Free.
Credit Cards: All major credit/debit cards
Specialities: *Canna*. Nat. Collection of *Canna*.
Notes: Also sells wholesale.
Map Ref: S, C3

SHar **HARDY'S COTTAGE GARDEN PLANTS** ⊠ ♿ ♠
Priory Lane Nursery, Freefolk Priors, Whitchurch, Hampshire, RG28 7NJ
Ⓣ (01256) 896533
Ⓕ (01256) 896572
Ⓔ info@hardys-plants.co.uk
Ⓦ www.hardys-plants.co.uk
Contact: Rosemary Hardy
Opening Times: 1000-1700 7 days, 1st Mar-31st Oct. 1000-1500 Mon-Fri, 1st Nov-28th Feb.
Min Mail Order UK: Nmc
Cat. Cost: 10 × 1st class.
Credit Cards: Visa Access Electron Switch Solo
Specialities: Wide range of herbaceous perennials incl. *Achillea*, *Alstroemeria*, *Geranium*, *Hemerocallis*, *Heuchera*, *Paeonia*, *Penstemon* & *Salvia*.
Notes: Accepts HTA Gift Tokens. Offers trade discount.
Map Ref: S, C2

SHDw **HIGHDOWN NURSERY** ⊠ € ✈ ♿ ♠
New Hall Lane, Small Dole, Nr Henfield, West Sussex, BN5 9YH
Ⓣ (01273) 492976
Ⓕ (01273) 492976
Ⓔ highdown.herbs@btopenworld.com
Contact: A G & J H Shearing
Opening Times: 0900-1700 7 days.
Min Mail Order UK: £10.00 + p&p
Min Mail Order EU: £10.00 + p&p
Cat. Cost: 3 × 1st class.
Credit Cards: None
Specialities: Herbs. Grasses.
Notes: Partial wheelchair access. Also sells wholesale.
Map Ref: S, D3

SHea **HEASELANDS GARDEN NURSERY** ⊠ €
The Old Lodge, Isaacs Lane, Haywards Heath, West Sussex, RH16 4SA
Ⓣ (01444) 458084
Ⓜ 07743 939490
Ⓕ (01444) 458084
Ⓔ headgardener@heaselands.wanadoo.co.uk
Ⓦ www.heaselandsnursery.co.uk
Contact: Stephen Harding

KEY
⊠ Mail order to UK or EU ♠ Delivers to shows
✈ Exports beyond EU € Euro accepted
♿ Accessible by wheelchair ◆ See Display advertisement

Opening Times: 0800-1700, Mon-Fri, but please phone first. W/ends by appt. only.
Min Mail Order UK: Nmc
Cat. Cost: Online only. Monthly availability lists.
Credit Cards: None
Specialities: *Rhododendron* hybrids and deciduous azaleas, home-produced from cuttings. Some varieties in small quantities. Nat. Collection of Mollis Azaleas & Knaphill/ Exbury Azaleas.
Notes: Also sells wholesale.
Map Ref: S, C4 **OS Grid Ref:** TQ314230

SHeS **THE HEATHER SOCIETY (PLANT ORDERING SERVICE)** ⊠ €
78 Woodland Way, West Wickham, Kent, BR4 9LR
Ⓣ 020 8777 5161
Ⓜ 07905 825818
Ⓔ allisonfitzearle@yahoo.co.uk
Ⓦ www.heathersociety.org.uk
Contact: Allison Fitz-Earle
Opening Times: Not open. Mail order only.
Min Mail Order UK: Nmc
Min Mail Order EU: Nmc
Cat. Cost: Free.
Credit Cards: None
Specialities: Heathers.
Notes: Mail order plants available year round.

SHeu **HEUCHERAHOLICS (FORMERLY JOOLES PLANTS)** ⊠ ♿ ⌂
(office) The Paddock, Pilley Street, Pilley, Lymington, Hampshire, SO41 5QP
Ⓣ (01590) 670581
Ⓜ 07973 291062
Ⓕ (01590) 670581
Ⓔ cruella@joolesplants.fsnet.co.uk
Ⓦ www.heucheraholics.co.uk
Contact: Julie Burton
Opening Times: By appt. only. Please phone first.
Min Mail Order UK: £7.50
Cat. Cost: None issued.
Credit Cards: All major credit/debit cards
Specialities: Heucheras, heucherellas & tiarellas. Other foliage plants.
Notes: Nursery is located at Spring Hill Nurseries, Shirley Holms Road, Lymington, SO41 8NG.
Map Ref: S, D2 **OS Grid Ref:** SZ310934

SHHo **HIGHFIELD HOLLIES** ⊠
Highfield Farm, Hatch Lane, Liss, Hampshire, GU33 7NH
Ⓣ (01730) 892372
Ⓕ (01730) 894853
Ⓔ louise@highfieldhollies.com
Ⓦ www.highfieldhollies.com
Contact: Mrs Louise Bendall Duck
Opening Times: By appt.
Min Mail Order UK: £60.00
Cat. Cost: £3.50 for illustrated cat.
Credit Cards: None
Specialities: 150+ species & cultivars *Ilex* incl. specimen trees, hedging & topiary. Some in short supply.
Map Ref: S, C3 **OS Grid Ref:** SU787276

SHmp **HAMPSHIRE CARNIVOROUS PLANTS** ⊠ € ⊠ ⌂
Ya-Mayla, Allington Lane, West End, Southampton, Hampshire, SO30 3HQ
Ⓣ (023) 8047 3314
Ⓜ 07703 258296
Ⓕ (023) 80473314
Ⓔ matthew@msoper.freeserve.co.uk
Ⓦ www.hantsflytrap.com
Contact: Matthew Soper
Opening Times: Mail order only. Open by appt. only.
Min Mail Order UK: Nmc
Min Mail Order EU: £50.00 + p&p
Cat. Cost: 2 × 2nd class.
Credit Cards: Visa MasterCard
Specialities: Carnivorous plants esp. *Nepenthes*, *Heliamphora*, *Sarracenia*, *Pinguicula* & *Utricularia*.
Notes: Also sells wholesale.

SHom **HOME PLANTS**
52 Dorman Ave North, Aylesham, Canterbury, Kent, CT3 3BW
Ⓣ (01304) 841746
Ⓔ homeplants@tiscali.co.uk
Contact: Stuart & Sue Roycroft
Opening Times: By appt. only, please phone first.
Cat. Cost: Sae for list.
Credit Cards: None
Specialities: *Phygelius* & unusual South African hardy plants. Limited stock, please phone first.

SHyH **HYDRANGEA HAVEN** ⊠ € YW ⌂
Market Garden, Lower Beeding, West Sussex, RH13 6PP
Ⓣ (01403) 891412
Ⓔ sales@hydrangea-haven.com
Ⓦ www.hydrangea-haven.com
Contact: Chris Loder
Opening Times: 1000-1600 Mon-Sat, please phone first, so we can give you our undivided attention.
Min Mail Order UK: Nmc

Min Mail Order EU: £100.00 + p&p
Cat. Cost: 2 × 1st class.
Credit Cards: Switch MasterCard Visa
Specialities: *Hydrangea.*
Notes: Also sells wholesale.
Map Ref: S, C3

SIde **IDEN CROFT HERBS** ⊠ ♿ ◆
Frittenden Road, Staplehurst, Kent, TN12 0DH
Ⓣ (01580) 891432
Ⓕ (01580) 892416
Ⓔ idencroftherbs@yahoo.co.uk
Ⓦ www.uk-herbs.com
Contact: Tracey Connors-Parry
Opening Times: 0900-1700 Mon-Sat & 1100-1700 Sun & B/hols, Mar-Sep. 0900-1600 Oct-Feb, closed w/ends.
Min Mail Order UK: £10.00
Min Mail Order EU: £25.00
Cat. Cost: 4 × 1st class.
Credit Cards: All major credit/debit cards
Specialities: Herbs, aromatic & wildflower plants & plants for bees & butterflies. Nat. Collections of *Mentha*, *Nepeta* & *Origanum*.
Notes: Wheelchairs available at nursery.
Map Ref: S, C5

SIoW **ISLE OF WIGHT LAVENDER** ⊠ € ♿ ⌂
Staplehurst Grange, Newport, Isle of Wight, PO30 2NQ
Ⓣ (01983) 825272
Ⓕ (01983) 825272
Ⓔ paul@lavender.co.uk
Ⓦ www.lavender.co.uk
Contact: Paul Abbott
Opening Times: 1000-1800 daily, except closed Wed Oct-Mar. Closed Xmas week.
Min Mail Order UK: Nmc
Min Mail Order EU: Nmc
Cat. Cost: 1st class sae.
Credit Cards: All major credit/debit cards
Specialities: Lavender.
Map Ref: S, D2

SIri **IRIS OF SISSINGHURST** ⊠ € ⌂ ◆
Roughlands Farm, Goudhurst Road, Marden, Kent, TN12 9NH
Ⓣ (01622) 831511
Ⓔ orders@irisofsissinghurst.com
Ⓦ www.irisofsissinghurst.com
Contact: Sue Marshall
Opening Times: Contact nursery or see website for opening times.
Min Mail Order UK: Nmc
Min Mail Order EU: Nmc
Cat. Cost: 2 × 1st class.
Credit Cards: None
Specialities: *Iris*, short, intermediate & tall bearded, *ensata*, *sibirica* & many species.
Map Ref: S, C4 **OS Grid Ref:** TQ735437

SJoh **VIC JOHNSTONE AND CLAIRE WILSON** €
43 Winchester Street, Whitchurch, Hampshire, RG28 7AJ
Ⓣ (01256) 893144
Contact: Vic Johnstone, Claire Wilson
Opening Times: By appt. Please telephone first.
Cat. Cost: 2 × 1st class.
Credit Cards: None
Specialities: Nat. Collection of *Verbascum.* Stock available in small quantities.
Map Ref: S, C2 **OS Grid Ref:** SU463478

SKee **KEEPERS NURSERY** ⊠
Gallants Court, Gallants Lane, East Farleigh, Maidstone, Kent, ME15 0LE
Ⓣ (01622) 726465
Ⓕ 0870 705 2145
Ⓔ info@keepers-nursery.co.uk
Ⓦ www.keepers-nursery.co.uk
Contact: Hamid Habibi
Opening Times: Only on a limited number of Open Days & for collection of trees & plants by arrangement.
Min Mail Order UK: Nmc
Cat. Cost: Online only.
Credit Cards: Visa MasterCard Switch Maestro
Specialities: A very large range of fruit trees incl. old & rare varieties as well as modern varieties. Soft fruit plants & nut trees.
Map Ref: S, C4

SKen **KENT STREET NURSERIES** ⊠ € ♿
Kent Street (A21), Sedlescombe, Battle, East Sussex, TN33 0SF
Ⓣ (01424) 751134
Ⓔ peter@1066-countryplants.co.uk
Ⓦ www.1066-countryplants.co.uk
Contact: P Stapley
Opening Times: 0900-1700 Mon-Sat, 1030-1600 Sun.
Min Mail Order UK: £12.00
Cat. Cost: 2 × 1st class.
Credit Cards: All major credit/debit cards
Specialities: *Pelargonium*, bedding & perennials.
Notes: Mail order *Pelargonium* list only.

KEY
⊠ Mail order to UK or EU ⌂ Delivers to shows
✈ Exports beyond EU € Euro accepted
♿ Accessible by wheelchair ◆ See Display advertisement

S

Credit cards not accepted for mail order. Nursery partially accessible for wheelchair users.

SKHP **Kevin Hughes Plants** ⊠ € ✈ ♿
(Office) 89 Ladysmith, East Gomeldon, Salisbury, Wiltshire, SP4 6LE
Ⓣ (01722) 782504
Ⓜ 07720 718671
Ⓕ (01772) 782504
Ⓔ info@kevinsplants.co.uk
Ⓦ www.kevinsplants.co.uk
Contact: Kevin Hughes
Opening Times: 1000-1700 Wed-Sun, 1st Feb-31st Oct. Other times by appt. only.
Min Mail Order UK: £10.00
Min Mail Order EU: £20.00
Cat. Cost: 3 × 1st class
Credit Cards: All, except American Express
Specialities: Less common & new hardy garden plants with a particular emphasis on *Magnolia*, *Trillium*, climbers, *Philadelphus*, *Viburnum* & *Syringa*. We try to select plants that are garden-worthy & attract wildlife. Many plants are slow to propagate & will always be in short supply. None are from wild-dug sources.
Notes: Nursery at Heale Garden, Middle Woodford, Salisbury, SP4 5NT.
Map Ref: S, C1

SLan **Langley Boxwood Nursery Ltd** ⊠ € ✈ ♿ ⌂ ♦
Langley Lane, Rake, Nr Liss, Hampshire, GU33 7JN
Ⓣ (01730) 894467
Ⓕ (01730) 894703
Ⓔ sales@boxwood.co.uk
Ⓦ www.boxwood.co.uk
Contact: Russell Coates
Opening Times: 0800-1630 Mon-Fri, 1000-1600 Sat. Please phone for directions.
Min Mail Order UK: Nmc
Min Mail Order EU: Nmc
Cat. Cost: 4 × 1st class.
Credit Cards: All major credit/debit cards
Specialities: *Buxus* species, cultivars & hedging. Good range of topiary, *Taxus*, and 'character-pruned' specimens. Nat. Collection of *Buxus*. Evergreen topiary & hedging.
Notes: Also sells wholesale. Topiary courses run throughout the summer months. Topiary hire available.
Map Ref: S, C3 **OS Grid Ref:** SU812290

SLau **The Laurels Nursery** ⊠ €
Benenden, Cranbrook, Kent, TN17 4JU
Ⓣ (01580) 240463
Ⓕ (01580) 240463
Ⓦ www.thelaurelsnursery.co.uk
Contact: Peter or Sylvia Kellett
Opening Times: 0800-1600 Mon-Fri, 0900-1200 Sat, Sun by appt. only.
Min Mail Order UK: £20.00
Cat. Cost: Free.
Credit Cards: None
Specialities: Open ground & container ornamental trees, shrubs & climbers incl. birch, beech & *Wisteria*.
Notes: Mail order of small *Wisteria* only. Also sells wholesale.
Map Ref: S, C5 **OS Grid Ref:** TQ815313

SLBF **Little Brook Fuchsias** ♿
Ash Green Lane West, Ash Green, Nr Aldershot, Hampshire, GU12 6HL
Ⓣ (01252) 329731
Ⓔ carol.gubler@ntlbusiness.com
Ⓦ www.littlebrookfuchsias.co.uk
Contact: Carol Gubler
Opening Times: 0900-1700 Wed-Sun 1st Jan-28th Jun.
Cat. Cost: 50p + sae.
Credit Cards: All major credit/debit cards
Specialities: Fuchsias, old & new.
Notes: Nursery located off White Lane in Ash Green.
Map Ref: S, C3

SLdr **Loder Plants** ⊠ € ✈ ♿ ⌂
Market Garden, Lower Beeding, West Sussex, RH13 6PP
Ⓣ (01403) 891412
Ⓔ sales@rhododendrons.com
Ⓦ www.rhododendrons.com
Contact: Chris Loder
Opening Times: 1000-1600 Mon-Sat, please ring first so we can try to give you our undivided attention.
Min Mail Order UK: Nmc
Min Mail Order EU: £100.00 + p&p
Cat. Cost: 2 × 1st class.
Credit Cards: All, except American Express
Specialities: Rhododendrons & azaleas in all sizes. *Camellia* & *Hydrangea*.
Map Ref: S, C3

SLim **Lime Cross Nursery** ⊠ ♿ ♦
Herstmonceux, Hailsham, East Sussex, BN27 4RS
Ⓣ (01323) 833229
Ⓕ (01323) 833944
Ⓔ LimeCross@aol.com
Ⓦ www.Limecross.co.uk
Contact: Jonathan Tate, Anita Green
Opening Times: 0830-1700 Mon-Sat & 1000-1600 Sun.

Min Mail Order UK: Nmc
Min Mail Order EU: £50.00
Cat. Cost: Free of charge.
Credit Cards: All major credit/debit cards
Specialities: Conifers, trees & shrubs, climbers.
Notes: Also sells wholesale.
Map Ref: S, D4 **OS Grid Ref:** TQ642125

SLon **LONGSTOCK PARK NURSERY** ⊠ € ♿
Longstock, Stockbridge, Hampshire, SO20 6EH
Ⓣ (01264) 810894
Ⓕ (01264) 810924
Ⓔ longstocknursery@leckfordestate.co.uk
Ⓦ www.longstocknursery.co.uk
Contact: Peter Moore
Opening Times: 0830-1630 Mon-Sat all year excl. Xmas & New Year, & 1100-1700 Sun Mar-Oct, 1000-1600 Sun, Nov-Feb.
Min Mail Order UK: Nmc
Cat. Cost: 2 × 1st class or email for lists of *Buddleja*, *Penstemon*, roses & fruit
Credit Cards: All major credit/debit cards
Specialities: A wide range, over 2000 varieties, of trees, shrubs, perennials, climbers, aquatics & ferns. Nat. Collections of *Buddleja* & *Clematis viticella*.
Notes: Mail order for *Buddleja* only.
Map Ref: S, C2 **OS Grid Ref:** SO365389

SLPl **LANDSCAPE PLANTS** ⊠ ✈ ♿
Cattamount, Grafty Green, Maidstone, Kent, ME17 2AP
Ⓣ (01622) 850245
Ⓕ (01622) 858063
Ⓔ landscapeplants@aol.com
Contact: Tom La Dell
Opening Times: 0800-1600 Mon-Fri, by appt. only.
Min Mail Order UK: £100.00 + p&p
Min Mail Order EU: £200.00 + p&p
Cat. Cost: 2 × 1st class.
Credit Cards: None
Specialities: Garden & landscape shrubs & perennials.
Notes: Also sells wholesale.
Map Ref: S, C5 **OS Grid Ref:** TQ772468

SMad **MADRONA NURSERY** ⊠ € ♿ ⛟
Pluckley Road, Bethersden, Kent, TN26 3DD
Ⓣ (01233) 820100
Ⓕ (01233) 820091
Ⓔ madrona@fsmail.net
Ⓦ www.madrona.co.uk
Contact: Liam MacKenzie
Opening Times: 1000-1700 Sat-Tue 14th Mar-1st Nov. Closed 1st-14th Aug 2009.
Min Mail Order UK: Nmc
Cat. Cost: Free
Credit Cards: All major credit/debit cards
Specialities: Unusual shrubs, conifers & perennials. *Eryngium*, *Pseudopanax*.
Map Ref: S, C5 **OS Grid Ref:** TQ918419

SMDP **MARCUS DANCER PLANTS** ⊠ ♿
Kilcreggan, Alderholt Road, Sandleheath, Fordingbridge, Hampshire, SP6 1PT
Ⓣ (01425) 652747
Ⓜ 07709 922730
Ⓔ marcus.dancer@btopenworld.com
Ⓦ clematisplants.co.uk
Contact: Marcus Dancer
Opening Times: By appointment only.
Min Mail Order UK: Nmc
Cat. Cost: 3 × 1st class.
Credit Cards: None
Specialities: Wide range of *Clematis*, smaller range of *Daphne*. Some varieties available in small quantities only.
Map Ref: S, D1

SMea **MEADOWGATE NURSERY** ⊠ ⛟
Street End Lane, Sidlesham, Chichester, West Sussex, PO20 7RG
Ⓣ (01243) 641997
Ⓜ 07736 523262
Ⓔ meadowgatenursery@tiscali.co.uk
Ⓦ www.meadowgatenursery.co.uk
Contact: David Allen
Opening Times: 1000-1700 Sat-Wed.
Min Mail Order UK: Nmc
Credit Cards: All major credit/debit cards
Specialities: Ornamental grasses and complimentary perennials.

SMHy **MARCHANTS HARDY PLANTS** € ♿ ⛟
2 Marchants Cottages, Mill Lane, Laughton, East Sussex, BN8 6AJ
Ⓣ (01323) 811737
Ⓕ (01323) 811737
Contact: Graham Gough
Opening Times: 0930-1730 Wed-Sat, 18th Mar-17th Oct 2009.
Cat. Cost: 6 × 2nd class
Specialities: Uncommon herbaceous perennials. *Agapanthus*, *Erodium*, *Sedum*, choice grasses, *Miscanthus*, *Molinia*.
Map Ref: S, D4 **OS Grid Ref:** TQ506119

KEY
⊠ Mail order to UK or EU ⛟ Delivers to shows
✈ Exports beyond EU € Euro accepted
♿ Accessible by wheelchair ◆ See Display advertisement

S

SMrm **MERRIMENTS GARDENS** ♿
Hawkhurst Road, Hurst Green, East Sussex, TN19 7RA
Ⓣ (01580) 860666
Ⓕ (01580) 860324
Ⓔ info@merriments.co.uk
Ⓦ www.merriments.co.uk
Contact: Taryn Cook
Opening Times: 0930-1730 Mon-Sat, 1030-1730 Sun (or dusk in winter).
Cat. Cost: Online only.
Credit Cards: Visa Access American Express
Specialities: Extensive range of unusual perennials, tender perennials, grasses & annuals. Also large selection of roses & seasonal shrubs. 4-acre show garden.
Map Ref: S, C4

SMrs **MRS MITCHELL'S KITCHEN & GARDEN** € ♿
2 Warren Farm Cottages, The Warren, West Tytherley, Salisbury, Wiltshire, SP5 1LU
Ⓣ (01980) 863101
Ⓔ julianm05@aol.com
Ⓦ www.mrsmitchellskitchenandgarden.co.uk
Contact: Louise Mitchell
Opening Times: 1000-1700 Thu, Fri & some Sat, Apr-Oct. Check web or phone to confirm weekly opening times.
Cat. Cost: Online only.
Credit Cards: None
Specialities: Family-run nursery stocking less usual cottage garden plants, esp. hardy geraniums, oriental poppies, *Phlox*, *Echinacea*, heleniums, *Rudbeckia* & Michaelmas daisies. Some items in small quantities. Grown in peat-free compost.
Notes: Despite postal designation, nursery is in Hampshire. Accessible, but difficult, for wheelchairs because of deep gravel. See website for list of shows attended.
Map Ref: S, C2 **OS Grid Ref:** SU261333

SOkt **OAKTREE NURSERIES** ♿
Malt House Farm Bungalow, Queen Street, Sandhurst, Kent, TN18 5HR
Ⓣ (01580) 850859
Ⓕ (01580) 850859
Ⓔ oaktree.nurseries@btinternet.com
Ⓦ www.oaktree-nurseries.co.uk
Contact: Stephen Roff
Opening Times: 0900-1700 Mon-Sat, 1000-1700 Sun.
Credit Cards: All major credit/debit cards
Specialities: Hardy geraniums & Japanese maples, around 50 varieties of each. Expanding plant range.
Map Ref: S, C5

SOWG **THE OLD WALLED GARDEN** ⊠ € ♿
Oxonhoath, Hadlow, Kent, TN11 9SS
Ⓣ (01732) 810012
Ⓕ (01732) 810856
Ⓔ HeatherAngrave@aol.com
Ⓦ www.exoticplantsdirect.co.uk
Contact: John & Heather Angrave
Opening Times: 0900-1600 Mon-Sat, 1st Mar-31st Oct. Other times by appt. only.
Min Mail Order UK: Nmc
Cat. Cost: 6 × 1st class
Credit Cards: All major credit/debit cards
Specialities: Many rare & unusual shrubs. Wide range of conservatory plants esp. Australian. Nat. Collection of *Callistemon*.
Map Ref: S, C4

SPad **PADDOCK PLANTS** ⊠
The Paddock, Upper Toothill Road, Rownhams, Southampton, Hampshire, SO16 8AL
Ⓣ (023) 8073 9912
Ⓜ 07763 386717
Ⓔ rob@paddockplants.co.uk
Ⓦ www.paddockplants.co.uk
Contact: Robert Courtney
Opening Times: By appt. only. Please telephone in advance.
Min Mail Order UK: Nmc
Cat. Cost: Free.
Credit Cards: None
Specialities: Family-run nursery offering interesting range of perennials, grasses, ferns & shrubs, incl. some more unusual varieties. Some varieties grown in small quantities.
Notes: Online descriptive catalogue & ordering. Local delivery by our own transport.

SPav **PAVILION PLANTS** ⊠
18 Pavilion Road, Worthing, West Sussex, BN14 7EF
Ⓣ (01903) 821338
Ⓔ rewrew18@hotmail.com
Contact: Andrew Muggeridge
Opening Times: Mail order only. Please phone for details.
Min Mail Order UK: Nmc
Cat. Cost: 4 × 1st class.
Credit Cards: None
Specialities: Perennials and bulbs. *Digitalis*.
Notes: Also sells wholesale.
Map Ref: S, D3

SPer **PERRYHILL NURSERIES LTD** ⊠ ♿
Edenbridge Road, Hartfield, East Sussex, TN7 4JP
Ⓣ (01892) 770377
Ⓕ (01892) 770929

Ⓔ sales@perryhillnurseries.co.uk
Ⓦ www.perryhillnurseries.co.uk
Contact: P J Chapman
Opening Times: 0900-1700 7 days 1st Mar-31st Oct. 0900-1630 1st Nov-28th Feb.
Min Mail Order UK: Nmc
Cat. Cost: Online only.
Credit Cards: Maestro Visa Access MasterCard
Specialities: Wide range of trees, shrubs, conifers, *Rhododendron* etc. Over 1300 herbaceous varieties, over 500 rose varieties. Unusual & rare plants may be available in small quantities.
Notes: Mail order despatch depends on size & weight of plants.
Map Ref: S, C4 **OS Grid Ref:** TQ480375

SPet **PETTET'S NURSERY** ♿
Poison Cross, Eastry,
Sandwich, Kent,
CT13 0EA
Ⓣ (01304) 613869
Ⓕ (01304) 613869
Ⓔ terry@pettetsnursery.fsnet.co.uk
Ⓦ www.pettetsnursery.co.uk
Contact: T & E H P Pettet
Opening Times: 0900-1700 daily Mar-Jul. 1000-1600 Aug-Oct weekdays only.
Credit Cards: None
Specialities: *Clematis*, herbaceous perennials, alpines, pelargoniums, fuchsias.
Map Ref: S, C6

SPhx **PHOENIX PERENNIAL PLANTS** ♿
Paice Lane, Medstead, Alton, Hampshire, GU34 5PR
Ⓣ (01420) 560695
Ⓕ (01420) 563640
Ⓔ marina@phoenixperennialplants.co.uk
Ⓦ www.phoenixperennialplants.co.uk
Contact: Marina Christopher
Opening Times: 1100-1700 Fri & Sat, 20th Mar-24th Oct 2009. Early openings 2010: 1000-1600 Fri & Sat 5th/6th Feb, 19th/20th Feb, 5th/6th Mar. 1100-1700 Fri & Sat 19th Mar-23rd Oct 2010. Other times by appt. only.
Cat. Cost: 4 × 1st class.
Credit Cards: All major credit/debit cards
Specialities: Perennials, many uncommon. *Achillea*, *Eryngium*, hardy chrysanthemums, *Monarda*, *Phlox*, *Sanguisorba*, *Thalictrum*, *Verbascum*, centaureas, bulbs, prairie plants, grasses & late-flowering perennials.
Notes: Co-located with Select Seeds SSss. Also sells wholesale.
Map Ref: S, C2 **OS Grid Ref:** SU657362

SPin **JOHN AND LYNSEY'S PLANTS** ♿
2 Hillside Cottages, Trampers Lane, North Boarhunt, Fareham, Hampshire, PO17 6DA
Ⓣ (01329) 832786
Contact: Mrs Lynsey Pink
Opening Times: By appt. only. Open under NGS.
Cat. Cost: None issued.
Credit Cards: None
Specialities: Mainly *Salvia* with a wide range of other unusual perennials. Stock available in small quantities only, we will be happy to propagate to order. Nat. Collection of *Salvia* species.
Map Ref: S, D2 **OS Grid Ref:** SU603109

SPlb **PLANTBASE** ⊠ € ♿
Sleepers Stile Road, Cousley Wood, Wadhurst, East Sussex, TN5 6QX
Ⓣ (01892) 891453
Ⓜ 07967 601064
Ⓔ graham@plantbase.freeserve.co.uk
Ⓦ www.plantbase.co.uk
Contact: Graham Blunt
Opening Times: 1000-1700, 7 days all year (appt. advisable).
Min Mail Order UK: Nmc
Min Mail Order EU: Nmc
Cat. Cost: Online only.
Credit Cards: All major credit/debit cards
Specialities: Wide range of alpines, perennials, shrubs, climbers, waterside plants, herbs, Australasian, South African & South American plants in particular.
Map Ref: S, C5

SPoG **THE POTTED GARDEN NURSERY** ♿
Ashford Road, Bearsted, Maidstone, Kent, ME14 4NH
Ⓣ (01622) 737801
Ⓦ www.thepottedgarden.co.uk
Contact: Any staff member
Opening Times: 0900-1730 (dusk in winter) 7 days. Xmas period opening times on website or answerphone. (Closed Xmas Day & Boxing Day.)
Credit Cards: All major credit/debit cards
Notes: Mail order not available.
Map Ref: S, C5 **OS Grid Ref:** TQ810550

SPol **POLLIE'S PERENNIALS AND DAYLILY NURSERY** ⊠ € ♿
Lodore, Mount Pleasant Lane, Sway, Lymington, Hampshire, SO41 8LS

KEY
⊠ Mail order to UK or EU — Delivers to shows
Exports beyond EU — € Euro accepted
♿ Accessible by wheelchair — ◆ See Display advertisement

Ⓣ (01590) 682577
Ⓕ (01590) 682577
Ⓔ terry@maasz.fsnet.co.uk
Ⓦ www.polliesdaylilies.co.uk
Contact: Pollie Maasz
Opening Times: 1000-1730 w/ends & 1400-1730 Mon-Fri during the daylily season, late-May to mid-Aug. Other times by appt. only.
Min Mail Order UK: Nmc
Min Mail Order EU: £20.00
Cat. Cost: 2 × 1st class.
Credit Cards: None
Specialities: *Hemerocallis*, also less commonly available hardy perennials. Stock available in small quantities only. Nat. Collection of Spider & Unusual Form *Hemerocallis*. 1400+ different cvs can be viewed, mid Jun-mid Sep.
Notes: Mail order, daylilies only.
Map Ref: S, D2

S

SPop **POPS PLANTS** ⊠ € ✈ ♿
Pops Cottage, Barford Lane, Downton, Salisbury, Wiltshire, SP5 3PZ
Ⓣ (01725) 511421
Ⓔ mail@popsplants.com
Ⓦ www.popsplants.com
Contact: G Dawson or L Roberts
Opening Times: By appt. only.
Min Mail Order UK: 5 plants.
Min Mail Order EU: 5 plants.
Cat. Cost: £2.00
Credit Cards: None
Specialities: *Primula auricula*. Some varieties in ltd. numbers. Nat. Collection of Show, Alpine, Double & Striped Auriculas.
Notes: Credit cards accepted online only. Min. mail order outside EU, 30 plants.

SPPs **POGS PENSTEMONS** ⊠ €
78 Woodland Way, West Wickham, Kent, BR4 9LR
Ⓣ 020 8777 5161
Ⓜ 07905 825818
Ⓔ Alipog2004@yahoo.co.uk
Ⓦ www.pogspenstemons.co.uk
Contact: Allison Fitz-Earle
Opening Times: Not open. Mail order only.
Min Mail Order UK: Nmc
Min Mail Order EU: Nmc
Cat. Cost: Free.
Credit Cards: None
Specialities: *Penstemon*.

SPur **PURE PLANTS**
Blackboys Nursery, Blackboys, Uckfield, East Sussex, TN22 5LS
Ⓣ (01825) 890858
Ⓕ (01825) 890878
Ⓔ info@pureplants.com
Ⓦ www.pureplants.com
Contact: Brian Fidler
Opening Times: 0900-1700 Tue-Sat. Closed Sun & Mon except B/hol Mon 0900-1700.
Cat. Cost: 2 × 1st class.
Credit Cards: All major credit/debit cards
Specialities: Trees, shrubs, herbaceous, grasses & ferns. Many unusual varieties offered.
Map Ref: S, C4 **OS Grid Ref:** TQ515206

SReu **G REUTHE LTD** ⊠
Crown Point Nursery, Sevenoaks Road, Ightham, Nr Sevenoaks, Kent, TN15 0HB
Ⓣ (01732) 810694
Ⓕ (01732) 862166
Ⓔ reuthe@hotmail.co.uk
Contact: C & P Tomlin
Opening Times: 0900-1600 Thu-Sat. Closed Jan, Jul & Aug.
Min Mail Order UK: £30.00 + p&p
Min Mail Order EU: £500.00
Cat. Cost: £2.50
Credit Cards: Visa Access
Specialities: Rhododendrons & azaleas, trees, shrubs & climbers.
Notes: Mail order certain plants only to EU.

SRGP **ROSIE'S GARDEN PLANTS** ⊠ ✈ ♿
Fieldview Cottage, Pratling Street, Aylesford, Kent, ME20 7DG
Ⓣ (01622) 715777
Ⓜ 07740 696277
Ⓕ (01622) 715777
Ⓔ jcaviolet@aol.com
Ⓦ www.rosiesgardenplants.biz
Contact: J C Aviolet
Opening Times: Not open. Mail order only.
Min Mail Order UK: Nmc
Min Mail Order EU: Nmc
Cat. Cost: Free by post, email or online.
Credit Cards: Visa MasterCard Switch
Specialities: Hardy *Geranium*, *Buddleja* & *Aster*. 'Named' herbaceous & shrubs. Roses.
Notes: Check web or catalogue for dates of shows, talks & Farmers Markets.

SRiF **RIVERSIDE FUCHSIAS** ⊠ € ✈ ♿ ♿
Gravel Road, Sutton-at-Hone, Dartford, Kent, DA4 9HQ
Ⓣ (01322) 863891
Ⓕ (01322) 863891
Ⓔ riverside_fuchsias@btopenworld.com
Ⓦ www.riversidefuchsias.pwp.blueyonder.co.uk
Contact: George & Nellie Puddefoot
Opening Times: 0900-1700, Tue, Wed, Fri, Sat & Sun.
Min Mail Order UK: £1.50 per plant,

10 plants min. order.
Min Mail Order EU: €3.00
Cat. Cost: 3 × 1st class. Addendum available Mar.
Credit Cards: All major credit/debit cards
Specialities: *Fuchsia*. Nat. Collection holder.
Notes: Specimen-sized plants available May-end Jul. Also sells wholesale.
Map Ref: S, B4

SRiv **River Garden Nurseries** ⊠ € ♠
Troutbeck, Otford, Sevenoaks, Kent, TN14 5PH
Ⓣ (01959) 525588
Ⓕ (01959) 525810
Ⓔ box@river-garden.co.uk
Ⓦ www.river-garden.co.uk
Contact: Jenny Alban Davies
Opening Times: By appt. only.
Min Mail Order UK: £10.00 + p&p
Min Mail Order EU: £50.00 + p&p
Cat. Cost: 2 × 1st class.
Credit Cards: All major credit/debit cards
Specialities: *Buxus* species, cultivars & *Buxus* hedging. *Buxus* topiary.
Notes: Also sells wholesale.
Map Ref: S, C4 **OS Grid Ref:** TQ523593

SRkn **Rapkyns Nursery** ⊠ ♿ ♠
Street End Lane, Broad Oak, Heathfield, East Sussex, TN21 8UB
Ⓣ (01825) 830065
Ⓜ 07771 916933
Ⓕ (01825) 830065
Ⓔ rapkyns@homecall.co.uk
Ⓦ www.rapkynsnursery.co.uk
Contact: Steven & Fiona Moore
Opening Times: 1000-1700 Tue, Thu & Fri, Mar-Oct incl.
Min Mail Order UK: Nmc
Min Mail Order EU: Nmc
Cat. Cost: 2 × 1st class.
Credit Cards: None
Specialities: Unusual shrubs, perennials & climbers. Asters, Campanulas, *Ceanothus*, geraniums, lavenders, *Clematis*, penstemons & grasses. New collections of *Phormium*, *Phygelius*, *Crocosmia*, *Anemone*, *Heuchera*, *Heucherella*, *Echinacea*, *Phlox*, *Coreopsis*.
Notes: Postal address: Brinkwells, School Lane, Hadlow Down, East Sussex TN22 4HY. Nursery next door to Scotsford Farm. Mail order Sep-Apr incl. Also sells wholesale.
Map Ref: S, C4 **OS Grid Ref:** TQ604248

SRms **Rumsey Gardens** ⊠ ♿ ◆
117 Drift Road, Clanfield, Waterlooville, Hampshire, PO8 0PD
Ⓣ (023) 9259 3367
Ⓔ info@rumsey-gardens.co.uk
Ⓦ www.rumsey-gardens.co.uk
Contact: Mrs M A Giles
Opening Times: 0900-1700 Mon-Sat & 1000-1600 Sun & B/hols. Closed Sun Nov-Feb.
Min Mail Order UK: £15.00
Cat. Cost: Online only.
Credit Cards: Visa MasterCard Switch
Specialities: Wide general range. Herbaceous, alpines, heathers & ferns. Nat. & International Collection of *Cotoneaster*.
Map Ref: S, D2

SRos **Rosewood Daylilies** ⊠
70 Deansway Avenue, Sturry, Nr Canterbury, Kent, CT2 0NN
Ⓣ (01227) 711071
Ⓕ (01227) 711071
Ⓔ Rosewoodgdns@aol.com
Contact: Chris Searle
Opening Times: By appt. only. Please phone.
Min Mail Order UK: Nmc
Cat. Cost: 2 × 1st class.
Credit Cards: None
Specialities: *Hemerocallis*, mainly newer American varieties.
Map Ref: S, C5

SRot **Rotherview Nursery** ⊠ € ♿ ♠
Ivy House Lane, Three Oaks, Hastings, East Sussex, TN35 4NP
Ⓣ (01424) 756228
Ⓔ rotherview@btinternet.com
Ⓦ www.rotherview.com
Contact: Ray & Wendy Bates
Opening Times: 1000-1700 Mar-Oct, 1000-1530 Nov-Feb, 7 days.
Min Mail Order UK: Nmc
Min Mail Order EU: Nmc
Cat. Cost: 6 × 1st class.
Credit Cards: All major credit/debit cards
Specialities: Alpines.
Notes: Nursery is on same site as Coghurst Camellias. Also sells wholesale.
Map Ref: S, D5

SSea **Seale Nurseries** ♿
Seale Lane, Seale, Farnham, Surrey, GU10 1LD
Ⓣ (01252) 782410
Contact: David & Catherine May

KEY
⊠ Mail order to UK or EU ♠ Delivers to shows
✈ Exports beyond EU € Euro accepted
♿ Accessible by wheelchair ◆ See Display advertisement

S

Opening Times: 1000-1600 Tue-Sat incl. Other times by appt. Closed 25th Dec-mid Jan.
Cat. Cost: None issued.
Credit Cards: Visa Switch Access Delta
Specialities: Roses & *Pelargonium*. Some varieties in short supply, please phone first.
Map Ref: S, C3 **OS Grid Ref:** SU887477

SSpi **SPINNERS GARDEN** € ♿
School Lane, Boldre, Lymington, Hampshire, SO41 5QE
Ⓣ (01590) 673347
Ⓔ info@spinnersgarden.co.uk
Ⓦ www.spinnersgarden.co.uk
Contact: Peter Chappell
Opening Times: 1000-1700 Tue-Sat, Feb-Oct. By appt. only Nov, Dec & Jan.
Cat. Cost: Sae for plant list.
Credit Cards: None
Specialities: Less common trees & shrubs esp. *Acer, Magnolia*, species & lace-cap *Hydrangea*. Bog & woodland plants, esp. trilliums.
Map Ref: S, D2 **OS Grid Ref:** SZ323981

SSPN **SPRING PARK NURSERY** ✉ €
78 Woodland Way, West Wickham, Kent, BR4 9LR
Ⓣ 020 8777 5161
Ⓔ julianfitzearle@aol.com
Ⓦ www.springparknursery.co.uk
Contact: Julian Fitz-Earle
Opening Times: Not open. Mail order only.
Min Mail Order UK: Nmc
Min Mail Order EU: Nmc
Cat. Cost: Free.
Credit Cards: None
Specialities: Heathers.
Notes: Also sells wholesale.

SSss **SELECT SEEDS** ✉ ♿
Paice Lane, Medstead, Nr Alton, Hampshire, GU34 5PR
Ⓣ (01420) 560695
Ⓕ (01420) 563640
Ⓔ marina@phoenixperennialplants.co.uk
Contact: Marina Christopher
Opening Times: Not open. Mail order only.
Min Mail Order UK: £10.00
Cat. Cost: 3 × 1st class.
Credit Cards: All major credit/debit cards
Specialities: Seeds. *Aconitum, Eryngium, Thalictrum, Sanguisorba* & *Angelica*.
Notes: Only sells seed by mail order. Co-located with Phoenix Perennial Plants, code SPhx.
Map Ref: S, C2 **OS Grid Ref:** SU657362

SSta **STARBOROUGH NURSERY** ✉ ♿
Starborough Road, Marsh Green, Edenbridge, Kent, TN8 5RB
Ⓣ (01732) 865614
Ⓕ (01732) 862166
Ⓔ starborough@hotmail.co.uk
Contact: C & P Tomlin
Opening Times: 0900-1600 Thu, Fri & Sat. Closed Jan, Jul & Aug.
Min Mail Order UK: £30.00 + p&p
Cat. Cost: £2.50
Credit Cards: Visa Access
Specialities: Rare and unusual shrubs esp. *Daphne, Acer, Cercis*, rhododendrons & azaleas, *Magnolia* & *Nyssa*.
Notes: Certain plants only to EU.

SSth **SOUTHEASE PLANTS** ♿
Corner Cottage, Southease, Nr Lewes, East Sussex, BN7 3HX
Ⓣ (01273) 513681
Ⓜ 07791 856206
Ⓕ (01273) 513681
Contact: Adrian Orchard
Opening Times: 1100-1700 Wed-Sat, 1400-1700 Sun & by appt.
Cat. Cost: None issued.
Credit Cards: None
Specialities: A small nursery concentrating on *Helleborus* hybrids, grown on the nursery from seed collected from selected plants or obtained from specialist growers. Small quantities only.
Map Ref: S, D4 **OS Grid Ref:** TQ422052

SSvw **SOUTHVIEW NURSERIES** ✉ ♿
Chequers Lane, Eversley Cross, Hook, Hampshire, RG27 0NT
Ⓣ (0118) 9732206
Ⓔ Mark@Trenear.freeserve.co.uk
Ⓦ www.southviewnurseries.co.uk
Contact: Mark & Elaine Trenear
Opening Times: By appt. only, Mon-Fri, Apr-Jun.
Min Mail Order UK: Nmc
Cat. Cost: Free
Credit Cards: None
Specialities: Unusual hardy plants, specialising in old-fashioned pinks & period plants. Nat. Collection of Old Pinks. Pinks collection open in June. Please ring for details.
Notes: Orders by prior arrangement only. Gives talks to garden societies.
Map Ref: S, C3 **OS Grid Ref:** SU795612

SSwd **SPRINGWOOD NURSERY** ✉
5 Southview Drive, Uckfield, East Sussex, TN22 1TA
Ⓜ 07760 152587

Ⓔ springwood.nurserysx@tiscali.co.uk
Ⓦ SpringwoodNurserySussex.co.uk
Contact: Kevin Clift
Opening Times: Mail order only. Open by appt. only.
Min Mail Order UK: Nmc
Credit Cards: Paypal
Specialities: *Hedychium*. Some plants available in small quantities.
Notes: Also sells wholesale.

STas **TASTEFUL PLANTS** € ♿
Macknade, Selling Road,
Faversham, Kent,
ME13 8XF
Ⓣ (01795) 534795
Ⓔ info@tastefulplants.co.uk
Ⓦ www.tastefulplants.co.uk
Contact: William Denne
Opening Times: 1000-1700 Tue-Sun.
Credit Cards: All major credit/debit cards
Specialities: Herbs and hostas.
Notes: Also sells wholesale.
Map Ref: S, C5 **OS Grid Ref:** TR023602

STes **TEST VALLEY NURSERY** ⊠
Stockbridge Road, Timsbury, Romsey, Hampshire, SO51 0NG
Ⓣ (01794) 368881
Ⓔ julia@testvalleynursery.co.uk
Ⓦ www.testvalleynursery.co.uk
Contact: Julia Benn
Opening Times: 1000-1700 Tue-Sun Mar-Oct. Nov-Feb, please phone first.
Min Mail Order UK: Nmc.
Cat. Cost: 3 × 1st class.
Credit Cards: All major credit/debit cards
Specialities: Large range of herbaceous perennials, incl. unusual & new varieties. Some varieties available in small quantities only. Phone first to avoid disappointment.
Notes: Mail order Oct-Feb only.
Map Ref: S, C2

STil **TILE BARN NURSERY** ⊠ €
Standen Street, Iden Green, Benenden, Kent, TN17 4LB
Ⓣ (01580) 240221
Ⓕ (01580) 240221
Ⓔ tilebarn.nursery@virgin.net
Ⓦ www.tilebarn-cyclamen.co.uk
Contact: Peter Moore
Opening Times: 0900-1700 Wed-Sat.
Min Mail Order UK: £10.00 + p&p
Min Mail Order EU: £25.00 + p&p
Cat. Cost: Sae
Credit Cards: None
Specialities: *Cyclamen* species.
Notes: Also sells wholesale.
Map Ref: S, C5 **OS Grid Ref:** TQ805301

STre **PETER TRENEAR** ⊠ ♿
Chantreyland, Chequers Lane, Eversley Cross, Hampshire, RG27 0NX
Ⓣ (0118) 9732300
Ⓔ petertrenear@fsmail.net
Ⓦ www.babytrees.co.uk
Contact: Peter Trenear
Opening Times: 0900-1630 Mon-Sat.
Min Mail Order UK: £7.00 + p&p
Cat. Cost: 1 × 1st class.
Credit Cards: Paypal
Specialities: Trees, shrubs, conifers, bonsai & succulents.
Map Ref: S, C3 **OS Grid Ref:** SU795612

STrG **TERRACE GARDENER** ⊠ €
8 Foxbush, Hildenborough, Kent,
TN11 9HT
Ⓣ (01732) 832762
Ⓔ johan@terracegardener.com
Ⓦ www.terracegardener.co.uk
Contact: Johan Hall
Opening Times: Not open. Mail order only, incl. online & by phone. Telephone orders 0800-1700 Mon-Fri.
Min Mail Order UK: Nmc
Cat. Cost: Free
Credit Cards: All major credit/debit cards
Specialities: Mediterranean trees & plants. Container gardening. Architectural & hardy exotics.

SUsu **USUAL & UNUSUAL PLANTS** €
Onslow House, Magham Down, Hailsham, East Sussex, BN27 1PL
Ⓣ (01323) 840967
Ⓔ jennie@uuplants.co.uk
Ⓦ www.uuplants.co.uk
Contact: Jennie Maillard
Opening Times: 0930-1730 Wed-Sat, 17th Mar-16th Oct. Other times can be arranged but strictly by appt. only.
Cat. Cost: £2.00 + sae or online.
Credit Cards: None
Specialities: Small quantities of a wide variety of unusual garden-worthy perennials esp. *Agapanthus, Echinacea, Erysimum, Euphorbia, Geum*, hardy *Geranium, Salvia, Sanguisorba, Sedum, Thalictrum* & grasses.
Map Ref: S, D4 **OS Grid Ref:** TQ607113

KEY
⊠ Mail order to UK or EU — Delivers to shows
Exports beyond EU — € Euro accepted
♿ Accessible by wheelchair — ◆ See Display advertisement

S

SVic **VICTORIANA NURSERY GARDENS** ⊠ ♿
Challock, Ashford, Kent, TN25 4DG
Ⓣ (01233) 740529
Ⓕ 0203 292 1529
Ⓔ For email, use contact form on website.
Ⓦ www.victoriananursery.co.uk
Contact: Stephen Shirley
Opening Times: 0930-1630 (or dusk) Mon-Fri, 1030-1630 Sat.
Min Mail Order UK: Nmc
Cat. Cost: Free or online.
Credit Cards: All major credit/debit cards
Specialities: *Fuchsia*, 600+ varieties. Also heritage & unusual vegetable plants, seeds, fruit trees & bushes.
Notes: Also sells wholesale.
Map Ref: S, C5 **OS Grid Ref:** TR018501

SVil **THE VILLAGE NURSERIES** € ♿
Sinnocks, West Chiltington, Pulborough, West Sussex, RH20 2JX
Ⓣ (01798) 813040
Ⓕ (01798) 817240
Ⓔ villagenurseries@btconnect.com
Ⓦ www.village-nurseries.co.uk
Contact: Peter Manfield
Opening Times: 0900-1800 or dusk, 7 days.
Cat. Cost: None issued
Credit Cards: All major credit/debit cards
Specialities: Extensive selection of hardy perennials, plus wide range of seasonal patio & bedding plants. Many plants grown in biodegradable pots.
Map Ref: S, D3 **OS Grid Ref:** TQ095182

SWal **WALLACE PLANTS**
Lewes Road Nursery, Lewes Road (B2124), Laughton, East Sussex, BN8 6BN
Ⓣ (01323) 811729
Ⓕ (01323) 811729
Ⓔ plants@wallace-plants.co.uk
Ⓦ www.wallace-plants.co.uk
Contact: Simon Wallace
Opening Times: 1000-1800, Mar-Sep, 1000-1600 Oct-Feb. 7 days, incl. B/hols.
Cat. Cost: 2 × 1st class for availability list.
Credit Cards: None
Specialities: Ornamental grasses, hebes, herbaceous/perennials, shrubs, salvias, penstemons, herbs, cacti & choice, rare & unusual plants.
Map Ref: S, D4 **OS Grid Ref:** TQ513126

SWat **WATER MEADOW NURSERY** ⊠ ♿
Cheriton, Nr Alresford, Hampshire, SO24 0QB
Ⓣ (01962) 771895
Ⓕ (01962) 771895
Ⓔ plantaholic@onetel.com
Ⓦ www.plantaholic.co.uk
Contact: Mrs Sandy Worth
Opening Times: 1000-1700 Wed-Sat, Mar-Jul. 1000-1700 or dusk Fri & Sat, Aug-Oct.
Min Mail Order UK: £10.00 + p&p
Min Mail Order EU: £50.00 + p&p
Cat. Cost: 6 × 1st class or £2.00 cheque.
Credit Cards: All major credit/debit cards
Specialities: Water lilies, extensive water garden plants, unusual herbaceous perennials, aromatic herbs & wildflowers. New Super Poppy Range. Nat. Collection of *Papaver orientale* group & *Papaver* Super Poppy Series.
Notes: Mail order by 24 or 48 hour courier service only. Also sells wholesale.
Map Ref: S, C2

SWCr **WYCH CROSS NURSERIES** ♿
Wych Cross, Forest Row, East Sussex, RH18 5JW
Ⓣ (01342) 822705
Ⓕ (01342) 828246
Ⓔ roses@wychcross.co.uk
Ⓦ www.wychcross.co.uk
Contact: J Paisley
Opening Times: 0900-1730 Mon-Sat.
Cat. Cost: Free
Credit Cards: All major credit/debit cards
Specialities: Roses.
Map Ref: S, C4 **OS Grid Ref:** TQ420320

SWhi **JOHN HALL PLANTS LTD** ⊠ € ♿
Whitehall Nursery, Red Lane (Off Churt Road), Headley Down, Hampshire, GU35 8SR
Ⓣ (01428) 715505
Ⓜ 07714 344327
Ⓔ johnhallplants@hotmail.com
Ⓦ www.johnhallplants.com
Contact: John Hall
Opening Times: 0900-1630 Mon-Fri, 0900-1300 Sat.
Min Mail Order UK: Nmc
Min Mail Order EU: Nmc
Cat. Cost: Email only.
Credit Cards: None
Specialities: *Erica* and *Calluna*.
Notes: Also sells wholesale.
Map Ref: S, C3 **OS Grid Ref:** SU837371

SWvt **WOLVERTON PLANTS LTD** € ♿ ◆
Wolverton Common, Tadley, Hampshire, RG26 5RU
Ⓣ (01635) 298453
Ⓕ (01635) 299075
Ⓔ Julian@wolvertonplants.co.uk

Ⓦ www.wolvertonplants.co.uk
Contact: Julian Jones
Opening Times: 0900-1800 (or dusk Nov-Feb), 7 days. Closed Xmas/New Year.
Cat. Cost: Online only.
Credit Cards: All major credit/debit cards
Specialities: Wide range of herbaceous perennials & shrubs grown on a commercial scale for the public.
Notes: Also sells wholesale. Horticultural club visits welcome by prior arrangement.
Map Ref: S, C2 **OS Grid Ref:** SU555589

Wales and the West

WAbb ABBEY DORE COURT GARDEN € ♿
Abbey Dore Court, Abbey Dore, Herefordshire, HR2 0AD
Ⓣ (01981) 240419
Ⓕ (01981) 240419
Ⓦ www.abbeydorecourt.co.uk
Contact: Mrs C Ward
Opening Times: Garden & nursery may be open any day. A prior phone call is essential if coming any distance.
Cat. Cost: None issued
Credit Cards: None
Specialities: Mainly hardy perennials, many unusual, which may be seen growing in the garden. *Astrantia, Crocosmia, Helleborus, Paeonia, Pulmonaria* & *Sedum.*
Map Ref: W, C4 **OS Grid Ref:** SO388308

WAbe ABERCONWY NURSERY ♿
Graig, Glan Conwy, Colwyn Bay, Conwy, LL28 5TL
Ⓣ (01492) 580875
Contact: Dr & Mrs K G Lever
Opening Times: 1000-1700 Tue-Sun Mar-Sep incl.
Cat. Cost: 2 × 2nd class.
Credit Cards: Visa MasterCard
Specialities: Alpines, including specialist varieties, esp. gentians, dionysias, dwarf *Dianthus, Primula, Saxifraga* & dwarf ericaceous plants. Some choice shrubs & woodland plants incl. smaller ferns.
Map Ref: W, A3 **OS Grid Ref:** SH799744

WAln L A ALLEN ⊠
Windy Ridge, Cerrigwibber, Llandrindod Wells, Powys, LD1 5NY
Ⓔ lesliea@toulansurf.com
Contact: L A Allen
Opening Times: By prior appt.
Min Mail Order UK: Nmc
Min Mail Order EU: Nmc
Cat. Cost: 6 × 1st class.
Credit Cards: None
Specialities: Nat. Collection of *Primula auricula.* Type: alpine auricula, show edged, show self, doubles, stripes. Surplus plants from the Collection so available in small quantities. Occasionally only 1 or 2 available of some cvs.
Notes: Also sells wholesale.

WAlt ALTERNATIVE PLANTS ⊠
The Brackens, Yorkley Wood, Nr Lydney, Gloucestershire, GL15 4TU
Ⓣ (01594) 562457
Ⓔ alternativeplants@tiscali.co.uk
Ⓦ alternativeplants.co.uk
Contact: Mrs Rosemary Castle
Opening Times: Mail order only.
Min Mail Order UK: £10.00
Min Mail Order EU: £20.00
Cat. Cost: 3 × 1st class.
Credit Cards: None
Specialities: Unusual native plants. Small stocks, spring/autumn supply.

W

WAul AULDEN FARM ⊠
Aulden, Leominster, Herefordshire, HR6 0JT
Ⓣ (01568) 720129
Ⓔ pf@auldenfarm.co.uk
Ⓦ www.auldenfarm.co.uk
Contact: Alun & Jill Whitehead
Opening Times: 1000-1700 Tue & Thu Apr-Aug. Thu only in Mar & Sep. Other times by appt. Please phone.
Min Mail Order UK: Nmc
Min Mail Order EU: £20.00
Cat. Cost: 2 × 1st class.
Credit Cards: Paypal
Specialities: Hardy herbaceous perennials, with a special interest in *Hemerocallis* & *Iris.* Garden & nursery open for NGS, see website for details.
Notes: Mail order principally for *Hemerocallis* & *Iris*, other plants available in small quantities.
Map Ref: W, C4 **OS Grid Ref:** SO462548

WBor BORDERVALE PLANTS ⊠ ♿
Nantyderi, Sandy Lane, Ystradowen, Cowbridge, Vale of Glamorgan, CF71 7SX
Ⓣ (01446) 774036
Ⓔ lonytwod@googlemail.com
Ⓦ www.bordervale.co.uk
Contact: Claire E Jenkins
Opening Times: 1000-1700 Fri-Sun & B/hols

KEY
⊠ Mail order to UK or EU — Delivers to shows
Exports beyond EU — € Euro accepted
♿ Accessible by wheelchair — ◆ See Display advertisement

Mar-early Oct. Other times by appt.
Min Mail Order UK: £12.00 + p&p
Cat. Cost: 3 × 1st class.
Credit Cards: None
Specialities: Unusual herbaceous perennials, trees & shrubs, as well as cottage garden plants, many displayed in the 2-acre garden.
Notes: Ltd. mail order, contact nursery with requirements. Garden open May-Sep when nursery open. Also open for NGS. See website for details.
Map Ref: W, D3 **OS Grid Ref:** ST022776

WBou **Bouts Cottage Nurseries** ⊠ € ⌂
Bouts Lane, Inkberrow, Worcestershire, WR7 4HP
Ⓣ (01386) 792923
Ⓦ www.boutsviolas.co.uk
Contact: M & S Roberts
Opening Times: Strictly by appt. only.
Min Mail Order UK: Nmc
Min Mail Order EU: Nmc
Cat. Cost: 1st class sae.
Credit Cards: None
Specialities: *Viola.*

W

WBox **Box Court Plants & Gardens** ⊠
(Office) 1 Anthony's Cross, Newent, Gloucestershire, GL18 1JQ
Ⓣ (01531) 828289
Ⓜ 07771 559429
Ⓔ info@boxcourt.co.uk
Ⓦ www.boxcourt.co.uk
Contact: Paul Hervey-Brookes
Opening Times: 1100-1700, 7 days, 10th Jan-4th Nov.
Min Mail Order UK: Nmc
Min Mail Order EU: Nmc
Cat. Cost: Online only.
Credit Cards: None
Specialities: Herbaceous plants.
Notes: Nursery at Painswick Rococo Gardens, Painswick, Glos, GL6 6TH.
Map Ref: W, C4

WBrE **Bron Eifion Nursery** ⊠ €
Bron Eifion, Criccieth, Caernarfonshire, LL52 0SA
Ⓣ (01766) 522890
Ⓔ gardencottage@talktalk.net
Contact: Suzanne Evans
Opening Times: 1000-dusk 7 days 1st Mar-31st Oct. 1st Nov-29th Feb by appt. only.
Min Mail Order UK: £30.00 + p&p
Min Mail Order EU: £50.00 + p&p
Cat. Cost: None issued.
Credit Cards: None
Specialities: *Kalmia*, *Daphne*, *Embothrium*, plants for coastal regions & wide and interesting range of hardy plants.
Map Ref: W, B2

WBrk **Brockamin Plants** ♿ ⌂
Brockamin, Old Hills, Callow End, Worcestershire, WR2 4TQ
Ⓣ (01905) 830370
Ⓔ dickstonebrockamin@tinyworld.co.uk
Contact: Margaret Stone
Opening Times: By appt. only.
Cat. Cost: Free.
Credit Cards: None
Specialities: Hardy perennials, esp. hardy geraniums and some asters. Stock available in small quantities only.
Map Ref: W, C5 **OS Grid Ref:** SO830488

WBuc **Bucknell Nurseries** ⊠
Bucknell, Shropshire, SY7 0EL
Ⓣ (01547) 530606
Ⓕ (01547) 530699
Contact: A N Coull
Opening Times: 0800-1700 Mon-Fri & 1000-1300 Sat.
Min Mail Order UK: Nmc
Cat. Cost: Free
Credit Cards: None
Specialities: Bare-rooted hedging conifers & forest trees.
Notes: Also sells wholesale.
Map Ref: W, C4 **OS Grid Ref:** SO356736

WBVN **Banwy Valley Nursery** ⊠ ♿
Foel, Llangadfan, Nr Welshpool, Powys, SY21 0PT
Ⓣ (01938) 820281
Ⓔ syd@banwnursery.co.uk
Ⓦ www.banwnursery.co.uk
Contact: Syd Luck
Opening Times: 1000-1700 Tue-Sat.
Min Mail Order UK: Nmc
Cat. Cost: 2 × 1st class or email.
Credit Cards: All major credit/debit cards
Specialities: Perennials, shrubs, incl. climbers, ornamental & fruit trees. Ever expanding range of magnolias & rhododendrons. All grown on the nursery.
Notes: Large specimens not available by mail order.
Map Ref: W, B3 **OS Grid Ref:** SH993107

WCAu **Claire Austin Hardy Plants** ⊠ ✈ ♿
Edgebolton, Shawbury, Shrewsbury, Shropshire, SY4 4EL
Ⓣ (01939) 251173
Ⓕ (01939) 251311

Ⓔ enquiries@claireaustin-hardyplants.co.uk
Ⓦ www.claireaustin-hardyplants.co.uk
Contact: Claire Austin
Opening Times: 0900-1700 Mon-Sat, 1000-1600 Sun, Apr-end Jun. Open by appt. at other times of the year.
Min Mail Order UK: Nmc
Min Mail Order EU: £50.00 + p&p
Cat. Cost: UK £3.50, Europe €7.00
Credit Cards: MasterCard Visa Switch
Specialities: *Paeonia, Iris, Hemerocallis* & hardy plants. Nat. Collections of Bearded *Iris* & Hybrid Herbaceous *Paeonia.*
Map Ref: W, B4

WCFE **CHARLES F ELLIS** ⊠ €
Oak Piece Nurseries, Stanton, Nr Broadway, Worcestershire, WR12 7NQ
Ⓣ (01386) 584077
Ⓕ (01386) 584491
Ⓔ ellisplants@cooptel.net
Ⓦ www.ellisplants.co.uk
Contact: Charles Ellis
Opening Times: 1000-1600 7 days 1st Apr-30th Sep. Other times by appt.
Min Mail Order UK: Nmc
Cat. Cost: None issued.
Credit Cards: None
Specialities: Wide range of more unusual shrubs, conifers & climbers.
Map Ref: W, C5

WChG **CHENNELS GATE GARDENS & NURSERY** ♿
Eardisley, Herefordshire, HR3 6LT
Ⓣ (01544) 327288
Contact: Mark Dawson
Opening Times: 1000-1700 7 days Mar-Oct.
Cat. Cost: None issued.
Credit Cards: None
Specialities: Interesting & unusual cottage garden plants, grasses & shrubs.
Map Ref: W, C4

WClo **CLOSE NURSERY (DUCHY OF CORNWALL)** ♿
Shipton-Moyne Road, Tetbury, Gloucestershire, GL8 8PJ
Ⓣ (01666) 504349
Ⓕ (01666) 504349
Ⓔ OSpencer@duchyofcornwall.gov.uk
Contact: Olly Spencer
Opening Times: 0900-1700 Mon-Sat, 1000-1700 Sun & B/hols.
Cat. Cost: None issued.
Credit Cards: All major credit/debit cards
Specialities: Herbaceous.
Map Ref: W, D5 **OS Grid Ref:** ST884918

WCom **BROWN'S BARN LTD. (FORMERLY COMPTON LANE NURSERIES)** ⊠ ♿
Little Compton, Moreton-in-Marsh, Gloucestershire, GL56 0SJ
Ⓣ (01608) 674578
Ⓕ (01608) 674578
Ⓔ brownsbarn@btconnect.com
Ⓦ www.brownsbarn.co.uk
Contact: Chris Brown
Opening Times: 1000-1700 Wed-Sun, 1st Mar-31st Sep. Other times by appt. only.
Min Mail Order UK: £25.00 + p&p
Min Mail Order EU: £25.00 + p&p
Cat. Cost: 5 × 1st class, sae for separate mail order list.
Credit Cards: None
Specialities: Mainly alpines/herbaceous & a few unusual shrubs. *Saxifraga, Primula* & *Cyclamen.*
Notes: Evening visits for horticultural groups by prior arrangement.
Map Ref: W, C5

WCon **THE CONNOISSEUR'S PLANT CORNER** € ♿
(Office) Bwlchauduon, Ffarmers, Llanwrda, Carmarthenshire, SA19 8JJ
Ⓣ (01558) 650187
Ⓕ (01558) 650187
Ⓔ plantcorner@aol.com
Ⓦ www.norwoodgardens.co.uk
Contact: Brenda Timms
Opening Times: 1000-1800 (closed Tues) 28th Mar-26th Oct.
Specialities: A choice selection of traditional & unusual perennials which can be seen growing in the gardens. Available in small quantities only this year.
Notes: Nursery at Norwood Gardens, Llanllwni, Pencader, SA39 9DU. Tea room open as nursery. Partial wheelchair access to gardens. For special events see website.
Map Ref: W, C3 **OS Grid Ref:** SN492400

WCot **COTSWOLD GARDEN FLOWERS** ⊠ € ♠
Sands Lane, Badsey, Evesham, Worcestershire, WR11 7EZ
Ⓣ Nursery: (01386) 833849 or Mail Order: (01386) 422829
Ⓜ 07812 833849
Ⓕ Nursery: (01386) 49844
Ⓔ info@cgf.net

KEY
⊠ Mail order to UK or EU ♠ Delivers to shows
✈ Exports beyond EU € Euro accepted
♿ Accessible by wheelchair ◆ See Display advertisement

W

Ⓦ www.cgf.net
Contact: Bob Brown/Vicky Parkhouse
Opening Times: 0900-1730 Mon-Fri, 1000-1730 Sat & Sun Mar-Sep. 0900-1630 Mon-Fri, w/ends by appt. only Oct-Feb.
Min Mail Order UK: Nmc
Min Mail Order EU: Nmc
Cat. Cost: £1.50 or 6 × 1st class.
Credit Cards: MasterCard Access Visa Switch
Specialities: A very wide range of easy & unusual perennials.
Notes: Ltd wheelchair access. Also sells wholesale.
Map Ref: W, C5 **OS Grid Ref:** SP077426

WCra CRANESBILL NURSERY ⊠ ♿
White Cottage, Earls Common Road, Stock Green, Redditch, Worcestershire, B96 6SZ
Ⓣ (01386) 792414
Ⓕ (01386) 792280
Ⓔ cranesbilluk@aol.com
Ⓦ www.cranesbillnursery.com
Contact: Mrs J Bates
Opening Times: Not open. Mail order only. Visitors, incl. groups, are welcome but by prior appt. only.
Min Mail Order UK: Nmc
Min Mail Order EU: Nmc
Cat. Cost: 4 × 1st class
Credit Cards: MasterCard Visa Maestro Delta
Specialities: Hardy geraniums & other herbaceous plants.
Map Ref: W, C5 **OS Grid Ref:** 975585

WCre CRESCENT PLANTS ⊠ € ♿
Stoney Cross, Marden, Hereford, HR1 3EW
Ⓣ (01432) 880262
Ⓕ (01432) 880262
Ⓔ june@auriculas.co.uk
Ⓦ www.auriculas.co.uk
Contact: June Poole
Opening Times: Open by appt. Please phone.
Min Mail Order UK: Nmc
Min Mail Order EU: Nmc
Cat. Cost: Free
Credit Cards: All major credit/debit cards
Specialities: Named varieties of *Primula auricula* incl. show, alpine, double, striped & border types.
Notes: Payment by Paypal via website. Orders dispatched post free.
Map Ref: W, C4 **OS Grid Ref:** SO525477

WCru CRûG FARM PLANTS ⊠ ♿
Griffith's Crossing, Caernarfon, Gwynedd, LL55 1TU
Ⓣ (01248) 670232
Ⓔ info@crug-farm.co.uk
Ⓦ www.crug-farm.co.uk
Contact: B and S Wynn-Jones
Opening Times: 1000-1700 Thu-Sun 2nd Sat Mar to last Sun Jun, plus B/hols, then Thu-Sat until last Sat in Oct, or by appt.
Min Mail Order UK: Nmc
Min Mail Order EU: Nmc
Cat. Cost: 5 × 2nd class or free online download.
Credit Cards: All major credit/debit cards
Specialities: Shade plants, climbers, species *Hydrangea, Araliaceae*, rare trees & shrubs, *Convallariaceae*, herbaceous & bulbous. Most self-collected new introductions from the Far East & the Americas. Nat. Collections of *Coriaria, Paris* & *Polygonatum*.
Notes: Delivery by overnight carrier.
Map Ref: W, A2 **OS Grid Ref:** SH509652

WDib DIBLEY'S NURSERIES ⊠ € ♿ ♠ ◆
Llanelidan, Ruthin, Denbighshire, LL15 2LG
Ⓣ (01978) 790677
Ⓕ (01978) 790668
Ⓔ sales@dibleys.com
Ⓦ www.dibleys.com
Contact: R Dibley
Opening Times: 1000-1700 7 days, Apr-Aug. 1000-1700 Mon-Fri, Mar, Sep & Oct.
Min Mail Order UK: Nmc
Min Mail Order EU: Nmc
Cat. Cost: Free
Credit Cards: Visa Access Switch Electron Solo
Specialities: *Streptocarpus, Columnea, Solenostemon* & other gesneriads & *Begonia*. Nat. Collection of *Streptocarpus*.
Notes: Also sells wholesale.
Map Ref: W, A3

WDin DINGLE NURSERIES ♿ ♠ ◆
Welshpool, Powys, SY21 9JD
Ⓣ (01938) 555145
Ⓕ (01938) 555778
Ⓔ info@dinglenurseryandgarden.co.uk
Ⓦ www.dinglenurseryandgarden.co.uk
Contact: Jill Rock
Opening Times: 0900-1700, 7 days.
Cat. Cost: Free plant list.
Credit Cards: MasterCard Switch EuroCard Delta Visa
Specialities: Largest range of trees & shrubs in Wales. Wide seasonal selection of garden plants incl. roses, herbaceous perennials, conifers & bare-rooted forestry, hedging & fruit. All sizes incl. many mature specimens.
Notes: Also sells wholesale.
Map Ref: W, B4 **OS Grid Ref:** SJ196082

WDol **Dolau-hirion Fruit Tree Nursery** ☒
Capel Isaac, Llandeilo, Carmarthernshire, SA19 7TG
Ⓣ (01558) 668744
Ⓔ applewise@tiscali.co.uk
Ⓦ http://users.tinyonline.co.uk/applewise
Contact: Paul Davis
Opening Times: 0900-1800 Mon-Sat by prior arrangement.
Min Mail Order UK: £15.00
Cat. Cost: Free.
Credit Cards: None
Specialities: Small fruit tree nursery in the picturesque Towy Valley selling apple, pear, plum & cherry trees, especially Welsh varieties, incl. Welsh perry & cider trees. Grafting service available.
Map Ref: W, C3 **OS Grid Ref:** SN593267

WDyG **Dyffryn Gwyddno Nursery** ⛫
Dyffryn Farm, Lampeter Velfrey, Narberth, Pembrokeshire, SA67 8UN
Ⓣ (01834) 861684
Ⓔ sally.polson@virgin.net
Ⓦ www.pembrokeshireplants.co.uk
Contact: Mrs S L Polson
Opening Times: By appt. only.
Credit Cards: None
Specialities: Eclectic, yet wide-ranging, from tender salvias & grasses to bog. Peat-free & principled. Plants available in small quantities only. Bamboos. Bamboo collection open by appt. in aid of NGS.
Notes: Also sells wholesale.
Map Ref: W, D2 **OS Grid Ref:** SR138148

WEas **Eastgrove Cottage Garden Nursery** ♿
Sankyns Green, Nr Shrawley, Little Witley, Worcestershire, WR6 6LQ
Ⓣ (01299) 896389
Ⓦ www.eastgrove.co.uk
Contact: Malcolm & Carol Skinner
Opening Times: 1400-1700 Thu, Fri & Sat 23rd Apr-18th Jul, plus May B/hol Sun & Mon. Also Sun 14th Jun. Closed 18th-20th Jun & throughout Aug. 1400-1700 Thu & Fri 10th Sep-9th Oct.
Cat. Cost: Online only.
Credit Cards: None
Specialities: Unique cottage garden & arboretum. Many varieties of *Viola, Iris, Dianthus* & *Aquilegia*, plus a wide range of old favourites & many unusual plants. Small quantities only.
Notes: RHS Partnership garden. See website for directions. 2 acres of arboretum plus grass labyrinth. Home-made ice cream.
Map Ref: W, C5 **OS Grid Ref:** SO795644

WEve **Evergreen Conifer Centre** ☒ ♿ ◆
Tenbury Road, Rock, Nr Kidderminster, Worcestershire, DY14 9RB
Ⓣ (01299) 266581
Ⓕ (01299) 266755
Ⓔ brian@evergreen-conifers.co.uk
Ⓦ www.evergreen-conifers.co.uk
Contact: Brian Warrington
Opening Times: 0900-1630 Tue-Sat (closed Sun & Mon). Please phone before travelling some distance.
Min Mail Order UK: Nmc
Cat. Cost: 4 × 1st class.
Credit Cards: All major credit/debit cards
Specialities: Acers. Dwarf, ornamental, rare & specimen conifers. Hedging conifers. Ornamental trees & heathers.
Notes: Mail order for conifers only.
Map Ref: W, C4 **OS Grid Ref:** SO731737

WFar **Farmyard Nurseries** ☒ ✈ ♿ ◆
Dol Llan Road, Llandysul, Carmarthenshire, SA44 4RL
Ⓣ (01559) 363389
Ⓕ (01559) 362200
Ⓔ richard@farmyardnurseries.co.uk
Ⓦ www.farmyardnurseries.co.uk
Contact: Richard Bramley
Opening Times: 1000-1700 7 days excl. Xmas, Boxing & New Year's Day.
Min Mail Order UK: Nmc
Min Mail Order EU: Nmc
Cat. Cost: 4 × 1st class.
Credit Cards: Visa Switch MasterCard
Specialities: Excellent general range esp. *Helleborus, Hosta, Tricyrtis* & *Schizostylis*, plus shrubs, trees, climbers, alpines & esp. herbaceous. Nat. Collection of *Tricyrtis*.
Notes: Also sells wholesale.
Map Ref: W, C2 **OS Grid Ref:** SN421406

WFib **Fibrex Nurseries Ltd** ☒ ✈ ♿ ⛫
Honeybourne Road, Pebworth, Stratford-on-Avon, Warwickshire, CV37 8XP
Ⓣ (01789) 720788
Ⓕ (01789) 721162
Ⓔ sales@fibrex.co.uk
Ⓦ www.fibrex.co.uk
Contact: U Key-Davis & R L Godard-Key
Opening Times: 0900-1700 Mon-Fri 2nd

KEY		
	☒ Mail order to UK or EU	⛫ Delivers to shows
	✈ Exports beyond EU	€ Euro accepted
	♿ Accessible by wheelchair	◆ See Display advertisement

Mar-31st Aug. 0900-1600 Mon-Fri 1st Sep-1st Mar. 1030-1600 Sat & Sun 7th Mar-26th Jul. Closed last 2 weeks Dec & 1st week Jan. Closed Easter Sun & Aug B/hol Mon.
Min Mail Order UK: £10.00 + p&p
Min Mail Order EU: £20.00 + p&p
Cat. Cost: 2 × 1st class.
Credit Cards: Switch MasterCard Visa Maestro
Specialities: *Hedera*, ferns, *Pelargonium*. Nat. Collections of *Pelargonium* & *Hedera*. Plant collections subject to time of year, please check by phone.
Notes: Also sells wholesale.
Map Ref: W, C5 **OS Grid Ref:** SP133458

WFoF **FLOWERS OF THE FIELD** ⌂
Field Farm, Weobley, Herefordshire, HR4 8QJ
Ⓣ (01544) 318262
Ⓕ (01544) 318262
Ⓔ info@flowersofthefield.co.uk
Ⓦ www.flowersofthefield.co.uk
Contact: Kathy Davies
Opening Times: 0900-1900, 7 days.
Cat. Cost: Online only.
Credit Cards: None
Specialities: Traditional & unusual perennials, grasses, shrubs, trees & herbs. Many varieties of flowers for cutting incl. Oriental lilies, freesias, *Ranunculus* & dahlias.
Notes: Nursery partially accessible for wheelchairs. Also sells wholesale.
Map Ref: W, C4

W

WFut **FUTUREPRIMITIVE PLANTS** ⊠
11 The Leys, Evesham, Worcestershire, WR11 3AP
Ⓜ 07792 376401
Ⓔ sales@futureprimitiveplants.co.uk
Ⓦ www.futureprimitiveplants.co.uk
Contact: Tiggy Fiander
Opening Times: Not open. Mail order only.
Min Mail Order UK: Nmc
Min Mail Order EU: Nmc
Cat. Cost: Free of charge.
Credit Cards: All major credit/debit cards
Specialities: Rare *Aspidistra*. Herbaceous perennials.

WFuv **FUCHSIAVALE NURSERIES** ⊠ ♿ ⌂
Worcester Road, Torton, Kidderminster, Worcestershire, DY11 7SB
Ⓣ (01299) 251162
Ⓕ (01299) 251256
Ⓔ helen@fuchsiavale.co.uk
Ⓦ www.fuchsiavale.co.uk
Contact: Helen Andre
Opening Times: 0900-1700 Mon-Sat, Apr-Jul. 1000-1600 Mon-Sat, Jan-Mar & Aug-Dec. 1000-1600 Sun & B/hols all year.
Min Mail Order UK: £9.00 (6 plants @ £1.50 incl. p&p)
Cat. Cost: Free.
Credit Cards: All major credit/debit cards
Specialities: *Fuchsia*. A good range of shrubs, perennials & trees also available.
Map Ref: W, C5 **OS Grid Ref:** SO843723

WGob **THE GOBBETT NURSERY** ⊠
Farlow, Kidderminster, Worcestershire, DY14 8TD
Ⓣ (01746) 718647
Ⓕ (01746) 718647
Ⓔ christine.link@lineone.net
Ⓦ www.thegobbettnursery.co.uk
Contact: C H Link
Opening Times: 1030-1700, Mon-Sat.
Min Mail Order UK: £10.00
Min Mail Order EU: £50.00
Cat. Cost: 3 × 1st class.
Credit Cards: None
Specialities: *Syringa, Magnolia, Camellia* & *Cornus*. Some varieties available in small quantities only.
Map Ref: W, B4 **OS Grid Ref:** SO648811

WGor **GORDON'S NURSERY** ⊠ ♿ ⌂
1 Cefnpennar Cottages, Cefnpennar, Mountain Ash, Mid-Glamorgan, CF45 4EE
Ⓣ (01443) 474593
Ⓕ (01443) 475835
Ⓔ sales@gordonsnursery.co.uk
Ⓦ www.gordonsnursery.co.uk
Contact: D A Gordon
Opening Times: 1000-1800 7 days Mar-Jun. 1000-1700 7 days Jul-Oct. 1100-1600 weekends only Nov & Feb. Closed Dec-Jan.
Min Mail Order UK: Nmc
Cat. Cost: 3 × 1st class.
Credit Cards: All major credit/debit cards
Specialities: Shrubs, perennials, alpines & dwarf conifers. Some plants available in small quantities only.
Notes: Mail order only available in some cases, please check for conditions in catalogue.
Map Ref: W, D3 **OS Grid Ref:** SO037012

WGrn **GREEN'S LEAVES (FORMERLY LEBA ORCHARD)** ⊠ ♿ ⌂
36 Ford House Road, Newent, Gloucestershire, GL18 1LQ
Ⓣ (01531) 820154
Ⓜ 07890 413036
Ⓔ r.paul.green@hotmail.co.uk
Contact: Paul Green

Opening Times: By appt. only, w/ends preferred.
Min Mail Order UK: £10.00 + p&p
Cat. Cost: 4 × 2nd class.
Credit Cards: None
Specialities: Ornamental grasses, sedges & phormiums. Increasing range of rare & choice shrubs, also some perennials.
Notes: Also sells wholesale.
Map Ref: W, C4 **OS Grid Ref:** SO732273

WGwG **Gwynfor Growers** ⊠ ♿ ⌂
Gwynfor, Pontgarreg, Llangranog, Llandysul, Ceredigion, SA44 6AU
Ⓣ (01239) 654151
Ⓔ info@gwynfor.co.uk
Ⓦ www.gwynfor.co.uk
Contact: Steve & Angie Hipkin
Opening Times: 1000 to 2000 or sunset if earlier, Wed, Thu & Sun, all year round.
Min Mail Order UK: Nmc
Cat. Cost: Free by email or write for current list.
Credit Cards: None
Specialities: Classic & contemporary plants to intrigue & delight plantsmen & garden designers alike. Heritage Welsh fruit trees. Some plants available in small quantities only.
Notes: Plants also available at Aberystwyth & Lampeter Farmers' Markets & Ceredigion Growers' Assoc. plant fairs.
Map Ref: W, C2 **OS Grid Ref:** SN331536

WHal **Hall Farm Nursery** ⊠ € ♿ ⌂
Vicarage Lane, Kinnerley, Nr Oswestry, Shropshire, SY10 8DH
Ⓣ (01691) 682135
Ⓕ (01691) 682135
Ⓔ hallfarmnursery@ukonline.co.uk
Ⓦ www.hallfarmnursery.co.uk
Contact: Christine & Nick Ffoulkes-Jones
Opening Times: 1000-1700 Tue-Sat 1st Mar-31st Oct 2009.
Min Mail Order UK: £20.00
Cat. Cost: Online only.
Credit Cards: Visa MasterCard Electron Maestro
Specialities: Unusual herbaceous plants, grasses, bog plants & pool marginals, late-flowering perennials, foliage plants.
Notes: Nursery partially accessible for wheelchairs.
Map Ref: W, B4 **OS Grid Ref:** SJ333209

WHar **Harley Nursery** ⊠ ♿
Harley, Shropshire, SY5 6LN
Ⓣ (01952) 510241
Ⓕ (01952) 510570
Ⓔ plants@harleynursery.co.uk
Ⓦ www.harleynursery.co.uk
Contact: Nicholas Murphy
Opening Times: 0900-1730 Mon-Sat, 1000-1600 Sun & B/hols. Winter hours 0900-1700 Sun & B/hols.
Min Mail Order UK: Nmc
Cat. Cost: 2 × 1st class.
Credit Cards: All major credit/debit cards
Specialities: Wide range of ornamental & fruit trees. Own grown shrubs, climbers, wide range of hedging plants. Conservation & wildlife plants & native trees a speciality.
Map Ref: W, B4

WHCr **Hergest Croft Gardens**
Kington, Herefordshire, HR5 3EG
Ⓣ (01544) 230160
Ⓜ 07968 435627
Ⓕ (01544) 232031
Ⓔ gardens@hergest.co.uk
Ⓦ www.hergest.co.uk
Contact: Stephen Lloyd
Opening Times: 1200-1730, 7 days, Apr-Oct.
Cat. Cost: None issued
Credit Cards: All major credit/debit cards
Specialities: *Acer*, *Betula* & unusual woody plants.
Notes: Limited wheelchair access.

WHer **The Herb Garden & Historical Plant Nursery** ⊠
Ty Capel Pensarn, Pentre Berw, Anglesey, Gwynedd, LL60 6LG
Ⓣ (01248) 422208 or (01545) 580893
Ⓜ 07751 583958
Ⓕ (01248) 422208
Ⓦ www.HistoricalPlants.co.uk
Contact: Corinne & David Tremaine-Stevenson
Opening Times: By appt. only.
Min Mail Order UK: £15.00 + p&p
Min Mail Order EU: £50.00 + p&p sterling only.
Cat. Cost: Online only.
Credit Cards: None
Specialities: Rarer herbs, rare natives & wild flowers; rare & unusual & historical perennials & old roses.
Map Ref: W, A2

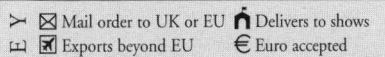

KEY
⊠ Mail order to UK or EU ⌂ Delivers to shows
✈ Exports beyond EU € Euro accepted
♿ Accessible by wheelchair ◆ See Display advertisement

W

WHfH **HERBS FOR HEALING** ⊠ ♿
(Office) Rose Cottage, London Road, Poulton, Cirencester, Gloucestershire, GL7 5JG
Ⓣ (01285) 851457
Ⓜ 07773 687493
Ⓔ herbs@herbsforhealing.net
Ⓦ www.herbsforhealing.net
Contact: Davina Wynne-Jones
Opening Times: 1000-1500 Wed only. Open for NGS in 2009.
Min Mail Order UK: Nmc
Credit Cards: Paypal
Specialities: Medicinal & some culinary herbs. Display garden.
Notes: Courses and workshops on use of herbs. Sells at local farmers markets. Nursery in Clapton's Lane, Barnsley, nr Cirencester, behind Barnsley House Hotel. See web for directions.
Map Ref: W, D5 **OS Grid Ref:** SP048177

W

WHil **HILLVIEW HARDY PLANTS** ⊠ € ⊠ ♿ ⌂ ◆
(off B4176) Worfield, Nr Bridgnorth, Shropshire, WV15 5NT
Ⓣ (01746) 716454
Ⓜ 07974 391608
Ⓕ (01746) 716454
Ⓔ hillview@themutual.net
Ⓦ www.hillviewhardyplants.com
Contact: Ingrid, John & Sarah Millington
Opening Times: 0900-1700 Mon-Sat Mar-mid Oct. At other times, please phone first.
Min Mail Order UK: £15.00 + p&p
Min Mail Order EU: £15.00 + p&p
Cat. Cost: 5 × 2nd class.
Credit Cards: All major credit/debit cards
Specialities: Choice herbaceous perennials incl. *Acanthus* & *Acanthaceae, Albuca, Aquilegia,* auricula, *Primula, Canna, Crocosmia, Eucomis, Ixia,* South African bulbs. Nat. Collection of *Acanthus*.
Notes: Also sells wholesale.
Map Ref: W, B4 **OS Grid Ref:** SO772969

WHlf **HAYLOFT PLANTS** ⊠
Manor Farm, Pensham, Pershore, Worcestershire, WR10 3HB
Ⓣ (01386) 554440 or (01386) 562999
Ⓕ (01386) 553833
Ⓔ info@hayloftplants.co.uk
Ⓦ www.hayloftplants.co.uk
Contact: Yvonne Walker
Opening Times: Not open. Mail order only.
Min Mail Order UK: Nmc
Min Mail Order EU: Nmc
Cat. Cost: Free.
Credit Cards: All major credit/debit cards

WHoo **HOO HOUSE NURSERY** € ♿ ◆
Hoo House, Gloucester Road, Tewkesbury, Gloucestershire, GL20 7DA
Ⓣ (01684) 293389
Ⓕ (01684) 293389
Ⓔ nursery@hoohouse.co.uk
Ⓦ www.hoohouse.co.uk
Contact: Robin & Julie Ritchie
Opening Times: 1000-1700 Mon-Sat, 1100-1700 Sun.
Cat. Cost: 3 × 1st class.
Credit Cards: None
Specialities: Wide range of herbaceous & alpines – many unusual, incl. *Aster, Papaver, Geranium & Penstemon*. Nat. Collections of *Platycodon* & *Gentiana asclepiadea* cvs.
Notes: Also sells wholesale.
Map Ref: W, C5 **OS Grid Ref:** SO893293

WHrl **HARRELLS HARDY PLANTS** ⊠
(Office) 15 Coxlea Close, Evesham, Worcestershire, WR11 4JS
Ⓣ (01386) 443077
Ⓜ 07799 577120 or 07733 446606
Ⓔ mail@harrellshardyplants.co.uk
Ⓦ www.harrellshardyplants.co.uk
Contact: Liz Nicklin & Kate Phillips
Opening Times: 1000-1200 Sun Mar-Nov. Other times by appt. Please phone.
Min Mail Order UK: Nmc
Cat. Cost: 4 × 2nd class.
Credit Cards: None
Specialities: Display gardens showcase wide range of hardy perennials, esp. *Hemerocallis* & grasses.
Notes: Nursery located off Rudge Rd, Evesham. Please phone for directions or see catalogue. Partial wheelchair access. Mail order Nov-Mar only.
Map Ref: W, C5 **OS Grid Ref:** SP033443

WIvy **IVYCROFT PLANTS** ⊠ € ♿
Upper Ivington, Leominster, Herefordshire, HR6 0JN
Ⓣ (01568) 720344
Ⓔ rogerandsue@ivycroft.freeserve.co.uk
Ⓦ www.ivycroft.freeserve.co.uk
Contact: Roger Norman
Opening Times: 0900-1600 Thu, Feb & Apr-Sep. Other times by appt., please phone.
Min Mail Order UK: Nmc
Min Mail Order EU: Nmc
Cat. Cost: 2 × 1st class.
Credit Cards: None
Specialities: *Cyclamen, Galanthus, Salix,* alpines, herbaceous & ferns.
Notes: Mail order for *Galanthus* & *Salix* only.
Map Ref: W, C4 **OS Grid Ref:** SO464562

WJas **PAUL JASPER TREES** ⊠
The Lighthouse, Bridge Street,
Leominster, Herefordshire,
HR6 8DX
Ⓕ (01568) 616499 for orders.
Ⓔ enquiries@jaspertrees.co.uk
Ⓦ www.jaspertrees.co.uk
Contact: Paul Jasper
Opening Times: Not open. Mail order only.
Min Mail Order UK: £40.00 + p&p
Cat. Cost: Online only.
Credit Cards: None
Specialities: Full range of fruit & ornamental trees. Over 100 modern and traditional apple varieties + 220 others all direct from the grower. Many unusual varieties of *Malus domestica* & *Prunus*.
Notes: Regular catalogue updates & notes on website. Also sells wholesale.
Map Ref: W, C4 **OS Grid Ref:** 495595

WJek **JEKKA'S HERB FARM** ⊠ ♿ ⛺
Rose Cottage, Shellards Lane, Alveston,
Bristol, South Gloucestershire,
BS35 3SY
Ⓣ (01454) 418878
Ⓕ (01454) 424907
Ⓔ sales@jekkasherbfarm.com
Ⓦ www.jekkasherbfarm.com
Contact: Jekka McVicar
Opening Times: 4 times a year. Please check website for dates.
Min Mail Order UK: £15 plants
Min Mail Order EU: Seeds only to the EU.
Cat. Cost: 4 × 1st class.
Credit Cards: Visa MasterCard Delta Maestro
Specialities: Culinary, medicinal, aromatic, decorative herbs. Soil Association licensed herb farm.
Map Ref: W, D4

WJPR **JPR ENVIRONMENTAL** ⊠ €
(Office) Unit 2, Breadstone Business Centre,
Breadstone, Berkeley, Gloucestershire,
GL13 9HF
Ⓣ (01453) 811537
Ⓕ (01453) 810646
Ⓔ enquiries@jprenvironmental.co.uk
Ⓦ www.jprwillow.co.uk
Contact: John Robinthwaite
Opening Times: 0900-1700.
Min Mail Order UK: Nmc
Min Mail Order EU: Nmc
Credit Cards: All, except American Express
Specialities: *Salix.*
Notes: Also sells wholesale.
Map Ref: W, D4 **OS Grid Ref:** SO712009

WJun **JUNGLE GIANTS** ⊠ € ✈ ♿
Ferney, Onibury, Craven Arms, Shropshire,
SY7 9BJ
Ⓣ (01584) 856200
Ⓕ (01584) 856663
Ⓔ bamboo@junglegiants.co.uk
Ⓦ www.junglegiants.co.uk
Contact: Michael Brisbane
Opening Times: 7 days. By appt. only please.
Min Mail Order UK: £25.00 + p&p
Min Mail Order EU: £100.00 + p&p
Cat. Cost: Online only.
Credit Cards: Access MasterCard Visa
Specialities: Bamboos.
Notes: Also sells wholesale.
Map Ref: W, C4 **OS Grid Ref:** SO430779

WKif **KIFTSGATE COURT GARDENS** ♿
Kiftsgate Court, Chipping Camden,
Gloucestershire, GL55 6LN
Ⓣ (01386) 438777
Ⓕ (01386) 438777
Ⓔ anne@kiftsgate.co.uk
Ⓦ www.kiftsgate.co.uk
Contact: Mrs J Chambers
Opening Times: 1200-1800 Sat-Wed, May, Jun & Jul. 1400-1800 Sat-Wed, Aug. 1400-1800 Sun, Mon & Wed, Apr & Sep.
Cat. Cost: None issued
Credit Cards: All, except American Express
Specialities: Small range of unusual plants.
Map Ref: W, C5 **OS Grid Ref:** SP170430

WLav **THE LAVENDER GARDEN** ⊠ €
Ashcroft Nurseries, Nr Ozleworth, Kingscote,
Tetbury, Gloucestershire, GL8 8YF
Ⓣ (01453) 860356 or 549286
Ⓜ 07837 582943
Ⓔ Andrew007Bullock@aol.com
Ⓦ www.TheLavenderG.co.uk
Contact: Andrew Bullock
Opening Times: 1100-1700 Sat & Sun. Weekdays variable, please phone. 1st Nov-1st Mar by appt. only.
Min Mail Order UK: £30.00 + p&p
Min Mail Order EU: £30.00 + p&p
Cat. Cost: 2 × 1st class.
Credit Cards: All major credit/debit cards
Specialities: *Lavandula, Buddleja*, plants to attract butterflies. Herbs, wildflowers. Nat. Collection of *Buddleja.*
Notes: Also sells wholesale.
Map Ref: W, D5 **OS Grid Ref:** ST798948

KEY
⊠ Mail order to UK or EU ⛺ Delivers to shows
✈ Exports beyond EU € Euro accepted
♿ Accessible by wheelchair ◆ See Display advertisement

W

WMAq **Merebrook Water Plants** ⊠
Kingfisher Barn, Merebrook Farm,
Hanley Swan, Worcestershire,
WR8 0DX
Ⓣ (01684) 310950
Ⓜ 07876 777066
Ⓔ enquiries@pondplants.co.uk
Ⓦ www.pondplants.co.uk
Contact: Roger Kings & Biddi Kings
Opening Times: Not open. Mail order only.
Min Mail Order UK: Nmc
Min Mail Order EU: £25.00
Cat. Cost: Online only.
Credit Cards: All major credit/debit cards
Specialities: *Nymphaea*, Louisiana irises & other aquatic plants. International Waterlily & Water Gardening Soc. accredited collection.

WMnd **Mynd Hardy Plants** ♿
Delbury Hall Estate, Diddlebury,
Craven Arms, Shropshire,
SY7 9DH
Ⓣ (01584) 841222
Ⓔ myndhardyplants@aol.com
Ⓦ www.myndplants.co.uk
Contact: Mark Zenick
Opening Times: 1300-1700 Wed-Fri, 1000-1700 Sat, 1st Apr-Sep. Other times phone for appt.
Cat. Cost: 4 × 2nd class.
Credit Cards: All major credit/debit cards
Specialities: Herbaceous plants, specialising in American bred, British grown, *Hemerocallis.* Home to New Hope Garden's *Hemerocallis* plants.
Notes: Also sells wholesale.
Map Ref: W, B4 **OS Grid Ref:** SO510852

WMoo **Moorland Cottage Plants** ⊠ ♿
Rhyd-y-Groes, Brynberian, Crymych,
Pembrokeshire, SA41 3TT
Ⓣ (01239) 891363
Ⓔ jenny@moorlandcottageplants.co.uk
Ⓦ www.moorlandcottageplants.co.uk
Contact: Jennifer Matthews
Opening Times: 1030-1730 daily excl. Wed 1st Mar-30th Sep.
Min Mail Order UK: See cat. for details.
Cat. Cost: 4 × 1st class.
Credit Cards: None
Specialities: Traditional & unusual hardy perennials. Many garden-worthy rarities. Cottage garden plants, ferns & many shade plants, moisture lovers, ornamental grasses & bamboos, colourful ground cover.
Notes: Display garden open for NGS from mid-May.
Map Ref: W, C2 **OS Grid Ref:** SN091343

WMou **Mount Pleasant Trees** €
Rockhampton, Berkeley, Gloucestershire,
GL13 9DU
Ⓣ (01454) 260348
Ⓔ info@mountpleasanttrees.com
Ⓦ www.mountpleasanttrees.com
Contact: Tom Locke & Elizabeth Murphy
Opening Times: By appt. only.
Cat. Cost: 3 × 2nd class.
Credit Cards: All major credit/debit cards
Specialities: Wide range of trees for forestry, hedging, woodlands & gardens esp. *Populus, Salix, Tilia* & *Quercus.*
Notes: Also sells wholesale.
Map Ref: W, D4 **OS Grid Ref:** ST654929

WNew **Newbridge Nursery** ⊠ ♿
Crundale, Haverfordwest, Pembrokeshire,
SA62 4EJ
Ⓣ (01437) 731678
Ⓕ (01437) 731678
Ⓔ newbridgenursery@ukonline.co.uk
Ⓦ www.newbridgeplantcentre.co.uk
Contact: Phil & Jane Davies
Opening Times: 1000-1730 daily throughout year.
Min Mail Order UK: Nmc
Cat. Cost: 2 × 1st class.
Credit Cards: All major credit/debit cards
Specialities: Wide range of herbaceous perennials & alpines from the common to the more unusual. Also a selection of coastal & acid-loving shrubs.
Notes: Credit cards not accepted for mail order. Plants also sold at Haverfordwest Farmers Market.
Map Ref: W, D2 **OS Grid Ref:** SM991196

WNHG **New Hope Gardens** ⊠ ♿
Batch Farm, Cockshutford,
Craven Arms, Shropshire,
SY7 9DY
Ⓣ Office: (01746) 712898 or Nursery: (01584) 841222
Ⓔ Newhopegardensmz@aol.com
Ⓦ www.newhopegardens.com
Contact: Mark Zenick
Opening Times: 1300-1700 Wed-Fri, 1000-1700 Sat, Apr-Sep. 1300-1700 B/hol Mons during season. Other times phone nursery for appt.
Min Mail Order UK: Nmc
Cat. Cost: Online only. Plant list on request.
Credit Cards: All major credit/debit cards
Specialities: American bred, British grown, *Hemerocallis.* Ships bare-rooted plants.
Map Ref: W, B4 **OS Grid Ref:** SO510852

WOld **OLD COURT NURSERIES** ⊠ € ♿
Colwall, Nr Malvern, Worcestershire, WR13 6QE
Ⓣ (01684) 540416
Ⓔ paulpicton@btinternet.com
Ⓦ www.autumnasters.co.uk
Contact: Paul & Meriel Picton
Opening Times: 1430-1700 Fri-Sun, May-Aug. 1300-1700 7 days, 1st week Sep-2nd week Oct. Also by appt. May to Oct.
Min Mail Order UK: Nmc
Min Mail Order EU: Nmc
Cat. Cost: 1 × 1st class.
Credit Cards: None
Specialities: Nat. Collection of Michaelmas Daisies. Herbaceous perennials.
Notes: Mail order for *Aster* only.
Map Ref: W, C4 **OS Grid Ref:** SO759430

WOut **OUT OF THE COMMON WAY** ⊠ €
(Office) Penhyddgan, Boduan, Pwllheli, Gwynedd, LL53 8YH
Ⓣ Office: (01758) 721577 or Nursery: (01407) 720431
Ⓔ ziggymen22@tesco.net
Contact: Joanna Davidson (nursery) Margaret Mason (office & mail order)
Opening Times: By arrangement.
Min Mail Order UK: Nmc
Min Mail Order EU: Nmc
Cat. Cost: A5 sae letter rate postage.
Credit Cards: None
Specialities: *Labiates*, esp. *Nepeta* & *Salvia*. *Aster*, *Geranium* & *Crocosmia*. Native plants. Some plants propagated in small quantities only. Will propagate salvias to order.
Notes: Nursery is at Pandy Treban, Bryngwran, Anglesey. Partially accessible for wheelchairs.
Map Ref: W, A2 **OS Grid Ref:** SH370778

WPat **CHRIS PATTISON** ⊠ € ♿
Brookend, Pendock, Gloucestershire, GL19 3PL
Ⓣ (01531) 650480
Ⓕ (01531) 650480
Ⓔ cp@chris-pattison.co.uk
Ⓦ www.chris-pattison.co.uk
Contact: Chris Pattison
Opening Times: 0900-1700 Mon-Fri. W/ends by appt. only.
Min Mail Order UK: £10.00 +p&p
Cat. Cost: 3 × 1st class.
Credit Cards: None
Specialities: Choice rare shrubs & alpines. Grafted stock esp. Japanese maples & liquidambars. Wide range of *Viburnum* & dwarf/miniature trees & shrubs.
Notes: Mail order Nov-Feb only. Also sells wholesale.
Map Ref: W, C5 **OS Grid Ref:** SO781327

WPBF **P & B FUCHSIAS** ⊠ € ♿
Penclawdd Road, Penclawdd, Swansea, West Glamorgan, SA4 3RB
Ⓣ (01792) 851669
Ⓔ sales@gower-fuchsias.co.uk
Ⓦ www.gower-fuchsias.co.uk
Contact: Paul Fisher
Opening Times: 0900-1800 7 days 1 Mar-30 Sep.
Min Mail Order UK: £14.00 (6 plants) incl. p&p
Cat. Cost: 3 × 1st class.
Credit Cards: None
Specialities: Fuchsias. Hybrid & species.
Notes: Cuttings only available Mar-May. Very ltd. quantities of each.
Map Ref: W, D3

WPen **PENPERGWM PLANTS** ♿
Penpergwm Lodge, Abergavenny, Monmonthshire, NP7 9AS
Ⓣ (01873) 840422/840208
Ⓔ boyle@penpergwm.co.uk
Ⓦ www.penplants.com
Contact: Mrs J Kerr/Mrs S Boyle
Opening Times: 1400-1800 Thu-Sun, 2nd Apr-20th Sep.
Cat. Cost: None issued.
Credit Cards: None
Specialities: Hardy perennials.
Map Ref: W, D4 **OS Grid Ref:** SO335104

WPer **PERHILL NURSERIES** ⊠ € ♿
Worcester Road, Great Witley, Worcestershire, WR6 6JT
Ⓣ (01299) 896329
Ⓕ (01299) 896990
Ⓔ perhillp@btconnect.com
Ⓦ www.perhillplants.co.uk
Contact: Duncan Straw
Opening Times: 0900-1700 most weekdays but please phone first if travelling any distance. Closed weekends except by appt.
Min Mail Order UK: Nmc
Min Mail Order EU: £10.00
Cat. Cost: 6 × 2nd class.
Credit Cards: All major credit/debit cards
Specialities: 2000+ varieties of rare, unusual alpines & herbaceous perennials incl.

KEY
⊠ Mail order to UK or EU — Delivers to shows
Exports beyond EU — € Euro accepted
♿ Accessible by wheelchair — ◆ See Display advertisement

W

Penstemon, Campanula, Salvia, Thymus, herbs, *Veronica.*
Notes: Also sells wholesale. Coach parties welcome.
Map Ref: W, C4 **OS Grid Ref:** SO763656

WPGP **PAN-GLOBAL PLANTS** ♿
The Walled Garden, Frampton Court, Frampton-on-Severn, Gloucestershire, GL2 7EX
Ⓣ (01452) 741641
Ⓜ 07801 275138
Ⓕ (01453) 768858
Ⓔ info@panglobalplants.com
Ⓦ www.panglobalplants.com
Contact: Nick Macer
Opening Times: 1100-1700 Wed-Sun 1st Feb-31st Oct. Also B/hols. Closed 2nd Sun in Sep. Winter months by appt., please phone first.
Cat. Cost: 6 × 1st class.
Credit Cards: Maestro MasterCard Visa Solo Delta
Specialities: A plantsman's nursery offering a very wide selection of rare & desirable trees, shrubs, herbaceous, bamboos, exotics, climbers, ferns etc. Specialities incl. *Magnolia, Hydrangea, Bamboo* & *Agavaceae.*
Map Ref: W, D5 **OS Grid Ref:** SO750080

W

WPnn **THE PERENNIAL NURSERY** ⊠
Rhosygilwen, Llanrhian Road, St Davids, Pembrokeshire, SA62 6DB
Ⓣ (01437) 721954
Ⓦ www.droughttolerantplants.co.uk
Contact: Mrs Philipa Symons
Opening Times: 1030-1630 Mar-Oct. Closed Sun & Mon.
Min Mail Order UK: Nmc
Min Mail Order EU: Nmc
Cat. Cost: Online only.
Credit Cards: Paypal
Specialities: *Rosmarinus, Lampranthus,* wind & drought-tolerant plants.
Notes: Also sells wholesale.
Map Ref: W, C1 **OS Grid Ref:** SM775292

WPnP **PENLAN PERENNIALS** ⊠ € ✈ ♿
Penlan Farm, Penrhiw-pâl, Llandysul, Ceredigion, SA44 5QH
Ⓣ (01239) 711102
Ⓜ 07857 675312
Ⓕ (01239) 851244
Ⓔ rcain@penlanperennials.co.uk
Ⓦ www.penlanperennials.co.uk
Contact: Richard Cain
Opening Times: 0930-1730 Fri-Sun & B/hols 1st Mar-30th Jun only. Jul-Feb by appt.
Min Mail Order UK: Nmc
Min Mail Order EU: Nmc
Cat. Cost: Online, or sae for CD-ROM.
Credit Cards: All major credit/debit cards
Specialities: Aquatic, marginal & bog plants. Shade-loving & woodland perennials, ferns, grasses & hardy geraniums, all grown peat-free.
Notes: Mail order all year, next day delivery. Secure online web ordering.
Map Ref: W, C2 **OS Grid Ref:** SN344457

WPrP **PRIME PERENNIALS** ⊠ ⌂
Llety Moel, Rhos-y-Garth, Llanilar, Nr Aberystwyth, Ceredigion, SY23 4SG
Ⓣ (01974) 241505
Ⓜ 07891 333656
Ⓔ liz@prime-perennials.co.uk
Ⓦ www.prime-perennials.co.uk
Contact: Elizabeth Powney
Opening Times: Open by appt. only.
Min Mail Order UK: Nmc
Min Mail Order EU: £12.00
Cat. Cost: 4 × 1st class.
Credit Cards: None
Specialities: Specialist growers of rare, unusual & obscure perennials, ferns, bulbs & grasses. Some plants in small quanitites. Peat free. Grown 650ft above sea level. Nat. Collection of *Tulbaghia.*
Notes: Mail order all year.
Map Ref: W, C3

WPtf **PANTYFOD GARDEN NURSERY** ⊠
Llandewi Brefi, Tregaron, Ceredigion, SY25 6PE
Ⓣ (01570) 493564
Ⓔ sales@pantyfodgarden.co.uk
Ⓦ www.pantyfodgarden.co.uk
Contact: Susan Rowe
Opening Times: Mail order only. Not open, except by prior arrangement.
Min Mail Order UK: Nmc
Min Mail Order EU: Nmc
Cat. Cost: Online only.
Credit Cards: Paypal
Specialities: Hardy geraniums, unusual hardy perennials, black plants, woodland plants, plants for moist soil, all grown largely peat-free. Many plants available in small quantities. Stock changes throughout the year. See website for regular updates or phone/email for availability.
Map Ref: W, C3 **OS Grid Ref:** SN654540

WRHF **RED HOUSE FARM** ♿
Flying Horse Lane, Bradley Green, Nr Redditch, Worcestershire, B96 6QT
Ⓣ (01527) 821269
Ⓕ (01527) 821674

Ⓦ www.redhousefarmgardenandnursery.co.uk
Contact: Mrs Maureen Weaver
Opening Times: 0900-1700 Mon-Sat all year. 1000-1700 Sun & B/hols.
Cat. Cost: 2 × 1st class.
Credit Cards: None
Specialities: Cottage garden perennials.
Map Ref: W, C5 **OS Grid Ref:** SO986623

WRic **WORLD OF FERNS (RICKARDS FERNS LTD)** ⊠ € ✈
Carreg y Fedwen, Lôn Rallt, Pentir, Bangor, Gwynedd, LL57 4RP
Ⓣ (01248) 600385
Ⓜ 07875 093352
Ⓕ (01248) 600385
Ⓔ info@world-of-ferns.co.uk
Ⓦ www.world-of-ferns.co.uk
Contact: Ben Kettle
Opening Times: Open by appt. only.
Min Mail Order UK: £30.00 + p&p
Min Mail Order EU: £50.00 + p&p
Cat. Cost: 5 × 1st class or 6 × 2nd class or online.
Credit Cards: All major credit/debit cards
Specialities: Ferns, incl. tree ferns.
Notes: Also sells wholesale.

WRou **ROUALEYN NURSERIES** ⊠ ♿ ⛫
Trefriw, Conwy, LL27 0SX
Ⓣ (01492) 640548
Ⓔ roualeynnursery@btinternet.com
Ⓦ www.roualeynfuchsias.co.uk
Contact: Doug Jones
Opening Times: 1000-1700 weekdays 1st Mar-31st Aug, 1000-1600 Sat, Sun & B/hols.
Min Mail Order UK: £18.00
Min Mail Order EU: £22.00
Cat. Cost: 2 × 1st class.
Credit Cards: All major credit/debit cards
Specialities: Fuchsias, incl. species.
Notes: Orders may be collected from any of the flower shows listed in current catalogue.
Map Ref: W, A3 **OS Grid Ref:** SH632778

WSFF **SAITH FFYNNON WILDLIFE PLANTS** ⊠ € ♿
Whitford, Holywell, Flintshire, CH8 9EQ
Ⓣ (01352) 711198
Ⓕ (01352) 716777
Ⓔ jan@7wells.org
Ⓦ www.7wells.co.uk
Contact: Jan Miller
Opening Times: By appt. only.
Min Mail Order UK: Nmc
Min Mail Order EU: Nmc
Cat. Cost: 2 × 1st class (list only) or full catalogue online.
Credit Cards: All major credit/debit cards
Specialities: Plants and seeds to attract butterflies and moths. Natural dye plants. Nat. Collection of *Eupatorium*. Stock available in small quantities unless ordered well in advance.
Notes: Percentage of profits go to Butterfly Conservation. Also sells wholesale. Credit cards accepted via website only.
Map Ref: W, A3 **OS Grid Ref:** SJ154775

WSHC **STONE HOUSE COTTAGE NURSERIES** ♿
Stone, Nr Kidderminster, Worcestershire, DY10 4BG
Ⓣ (01562) 69902
Ⓔ louisa@shcn.co.uk
Ⓦ www.shcn.co.uk
Contact: L N Arbuthnott
Opening Times: 1000-1700 Wed-Sat. By appt. only mid Sep-mid Mar.
Cat. Cost: Sae
Credit Cards: None
Specialities: Small general range esp. wall shrubs, climbers & unusual plants.
Map Ref: W, C5 **OS Grid Ref:** SO863750

WShi **SHIPTON BULBS** ⊠ €
Y Felin, Henllan Amgoed, Whitland, Carmarthenshire, SA34 0SL
Ⓣ (01994) 240125
Ⓕ (01994) 241180
Ⓔ bluebell@zoo.co.uk
Ⓦ www.bluebellbulbs.co.uk
Contact: John Shipton & Alison Foot
Opening Times: By appt. only.
Min Mail Order UK: Nmc
Min Mail Order EU: Nmc
Cat. Cost: Sae.
Credit Cards: All major credit/debit cards
Specialities: Native British bulbs, & bulbs & plants for naturalising.
Map Ref: W, D2 **OS Grid Ref:** SN188207

WSpi **SPINNEYWELL NURSERY** ⊠ ⛫ ◆
Waterlane, Oakridge, Bisley, Gloucestershire, GL6 7PH
Ⓣ (01452) 770151 or 770092
Ⓜ 07986 887158
Ⓕ (01452) 770151
Ⓔ wendy.spinneywell@virgin.net
Ⓦ www.spinneywellplants.co.uk
Contact: Wendy Asher

KEY
⊠ Mail order to UK or EU ⛫ Delivers to shows
✈ Exports beyond EU € Euro accepted
♿ Accessible by wheelchair ◆ See Display advertisement

Opening Times: 1000-1600 Mon-Sat, spring, summer, autumn. 1000-1500 Mon-Fri, winter. Alternate Sats 1400-1700, Apr-Nov. Please ring to confirm opening time before visit as these may change during 2009.
Min Mail Order UK: £10.00 + p&p
Min Mail Order EU: £30.00 + p&p
Cat. Cost: Online only.
Credit Cards: All major credit/debit cards
Specialities: *Buxus*, *Taxus* & unusual herbaceous & shrubs. Hellebores, euphorbias, *Ceanothus*, hardy geraniums.
Notes: Plant sourcing service available. Also sells wholesale.
Map Ref: W, D5 **OS Grid Ref:** SO921044

WSSs SHROPSHIRE SARRACENIAS ⊠ € ✈ ♿
5 Field Close, Malinslee, Telford, Shropshire, TF4 2EH
Ⓣ (01952) 501598
Ⓔ mike@carnivorousplants.uk.com
Ⓦ www.carnivorousplants.uk.com
Contact: Mike King
Opening Times: By appt. only.
Min Mail Order UK: Nmc
Min Mail Order EU: Nmc
Cat. Cost: 2 × 1st class.
Credit Cards: Paypal
Specialities: *Sarracenia*. *Dionaea muscipula* & forms. Some stock available in small quantities only. Nat. Collections of *Sarracenia* & *Dionaea*.
Map Ref: W, B4 **OS Grid Ref:** SJ689085

WSuV SUNNYBANK VINE NURSERY (NATIONAL VINE COLLECTION) ⊠ ✈
King Street, Ewyas Harold, Rowlestone, Herefordshire, HR2 OEE
Ⓣ (01981) 240256
Ⓔ Sarah.bell@seabass.co.uk
Ⓦ vinenursery.netfirms.com
Contact: Sarah Bell
Opening Times: Not open. Mail order only.
Min Mail Order UK: £8.00 incl. p&p
Min Mail Order EU: £13.00 incl. p&p
Cat. Cost: Free.
Credit Cards: None
Specialities: Vines. Nat. Collection of *Vitis vinifera* (hardy, incl. dessert & wine).
Notes: EU sales by arrangement.

WTan TAN-Y-LLYN NURSERIES ⊠
Meifod, Powys, SY22 6YB
Ⓣ (01938) 500370
Ⓔ info@tanyllyn-nursery.co.uk
Ⓦ www.tanyllyn-nursery.co.uk
Contact: Callum Johnston
Opening Times: 1000-1700 Tue-Sat Mar-Jun and at other times by appt.
Min Mail Order UK: Nmc
Cat. Cost: 2 × 1st class or online.
Credit Cards: None
Specialities: Herbs, alpines, perennials.
Map Ref: W, B3 **OS Grid Ref:** SJ167125

WThu THUYA ALPINE NURSERY ⊠
Glebelands, Hartpury, Gloucestershire, GL19 3BW
Ⓣ (01452) 700548
Contact: S W Bond
Opening Times: 1000-dusk Sat & Bank hol. 1100-dusk Sun, Weekdays appt. advised.
Min Mail Order UK: £4.00 + p&p
Min Mail Order EU: £10.00 + p&p
Cat. Cost: 4 × 2nd class.
Credit Cards: None
Specialities: Wide and changing range including rarities, available in smallish numbers.
Notes: Partially accessible for wheelchair users. Will deliver plants to AGS shows.
Map Ref: W, C5

WTin TINPENNY PLANTS ♿
Tinpenny Farm, Fiddington, Tewkesbury, Gloucestershire, GL20 7BJ
Ⓣ (01684) 292668
Ⓔ elaine@lime.ws
Ⓦ www.tinpenny.plus.com
Contact: Elaine Horton
Opening Times: By appt. all year round. Moving in 2009, so check website or send email for details.
Cat. Cost: None issued.
Credit Cards: None
Specialities: Wide range of hardy garden-worthy plants esp. *Helleborus*, *Iris* & *Sempervivum*. Small nursery will propagate to order rare plants from own stock. Small quantities only of some plants.
Map Ref: W, C5 **OS Grid Ref:** SO919318

WTou TOUCHWOOD PLANTS ⊠ ✈
4 Clyne Valley Cottages, Killay, Swansea, West Glamorgan, SA2 7DU
Ⓣ (01792) 522443
Ⓔ Carrie.Thomas@ntlworld.com
Contact: Carrie Thomas
Opening Times: Most reasonable days/times. Please phone first.
Min Mail Order UK: Nmc
Cat. Cost: 2 × 1st class.
Credit Cards: Paypal
Specialities: Seeds & plants. Nat. Collection of *Aquilegia vulgaris* cvs & hybrids. Plant stocks held in small quantities. Main stock is

W

seed. Garden & *Aquilegia* Collection open.
Notes: Plants sent bare-rooted at relevant times of the year. Only seed exported beyond the UK.
Map Ref: W, D3 **OS Grid Ref:** SS600924

WViv **VIV MARSH POSTAL PLANTS** ⊠
Walford Heath, Shrewsbury, Shropshire, SY4 2HT
Ⓣ (01939) 291475
Ⓔ mail@postalplants.co.uk
Ⓦ www.postalplants.co.uk
Contact: Mr Viv Marsh
Opening Times: Selected w/ends in spring & autumn. Please phone for details. Other times by appt. only.
Min Mail Order UK: £30.00 plant value
Min Mail Order EU: £30.00 plant value
Cat. Cost: 5 × 1st class or online.
Credit Cards: All major credit/debit cards
Specialities: Specialists in *Alstroemeria, Iris* & *Lathyrus.*
Notes: Wheelchair access with assistance. No disabled toilet.
Map Ref: W, B4 **OS Grid Ref:** SJ446198

WWct **WALCOT ORGANIC NURSERY** ⊠
Lower Walcot Farm, Walcot Lane, Drakes Broughton, Pershore, Worcestershire, WR10 2AL
Ⓣ (01905) 841587
Ⓜ 07780 547983
Ⓕ (01905) 841587
Ⓔ enquiries@walcotnursery.co.uk
Ⓦ www.walcotnursery.co.uk
Contact: Kevin O'Neill
Opening Times: 0800-1700 Mon-Fri. 1000-1300 Sat. Nov-Mar only.
Min Mail Order UK: £12.00
Min Mail Order EU: £30.00 to France, enquire for elsewhere.
Cat. Cost: 1 × 2nd class.
Credit Cards: All major credit/debit cards
Specialities: Organic fruit trees. Also sells wholesale.
Map Ref: W, C5 **OS Grid Ref:** SO944482

WWEG **WORLD'S END GARDEN NURSERY** ⊠ ♿ ◆
Moseley Road, Hallow, Worcester, Worcestershire, WR2 6NJ
Ⓣ (01905) 640977
Ⓕ (01905) 641373
Ⓔ garden@robinpearce.co.uk
Ⓦ www.worldsendgarden.co.uk
Contact: Kristina & Robin Pearce
Opening Times: 1030-1700 Tue-Fri, Mar-Oct. Other times by appt.
Min Mail Order UK: £20.00
Cat. Cost: Online only.
Credit Cards: All major credit/debit cards
Specialities: Wide range of herbaceous perennials, hardy ferns & ornamental grasses. Especially *Hosta, Geum, Leucantheum, Helenium.*
Notes: Also sells wholesale.
Map Ref: W, C5 **OS Grid Ref:** SO815597

WWFP **WHITEHALL FARMHOUSE PLANTS** ⊠ ⛺
Sevenhampton, Cheltenham, Gloucestershire, GL54 5TL
Ⓣ (01242) 820772
Ⓜ 07711 021034
Ⓕ (01242) 821226
Ⓔ info@wfplants.co.uk
Ⓦ www.wfplants.co.uk
Contact: Victoria Logue
Opening Times: By appt. only.
Min Mail Order UK: Nmc
Cat. Cost: 2 × 1st class.
Credit Cards: None
Specialities: A small nursery producing a range of interesting & easy hardy perennials for the garden. Some plants held in small quantities only.
Map Ref: W, C5 **OS Grid Ref:** SP018229

WWHy **WELSH HOLLY** ⊠ € ♿ ⛺
Llyn-y-gors, Tenby Road, St Clears, Carmarthenshire, SA33 4JP
Ⓣ (01994) 231789
Ⓕ (01994) 231789
Ⓔ info@welsh-holly.co.uk
Ⓦ www.welsh-holly.co.uk
Contact: Philip Lanc
Opening Times: By appt. only.
Min Mail Order UK: Nmc
Min Mail Order EU: Nmc
Cat. Cost: 2 × 1st class.
Credit Cards: None
Specialities: Hollies. Limited stock of less common plants.
Notes: Also sells wholesale.

WWlt **WOLLERTON OLD HALL GARDEN** ♿
Wollerton, Market Drayton, Shropshire, TF9 3NA
Ⓣ (01630) 685760
Ⓕ (01630) 685583
Ⓔ info@wollertonoldhallgarden.com
Ⓦ www.wollertonoldhallgarden.com

KEY
⊠ Mail order to UK or EU ⛺ Delivers to shows
✈ Exports beyond EU € Euro accepted
♿ Accessible by wheelchair ◆ See Display advertisement

W

Contact: Mr John Jenkins
Opening Times: 1200-1700 Fri, Sun & B/hols Easter-end Sep.
Cat. Cost: None issued
Credit Cards: All, except American Express
Specialities: Perennials, hardy & half-hardy.
Map Ref: W, B4 **OS Grid Ref:** SJ624296

WWst **Westonbirt Plants** ⊠ € ✉
9 Westonbirt Close, Worcester,
WR5 3RX
Ⓣ (01905) 350429 (answerphone)
Ⓔ office@westonbirtplants.co.uk
Ⓦ www.westonbirtplants.co.uk
Contact: Garry Dickerson
Opening Times: Not open. Mail order only.
Min Mail Order UK: Nmc
Min Mail Order EU: Nmc
Cat. Cost: 3 × 1st class.
Credit Cards: None
Specialities: Bulbs & woodland plants incl. *Anemonella, Arisaema, Colchicum, Corydalis, Erythronium, Fritillaria, Iris* (Juno & Oncocyclus), *Lilium, Paeonia, Roscoea, Trillium* & hardy orchids (*Calanthe, Cypripedium* & *Epipactis*). Many rare plants in ltd. numbers.

W

Abroad

XAld **Aldo Airplants** ⊠ € ♠
Diepestraat 49, 2400 MOL, Belgium
Ⓣ 0032 (0) 4864 06703
Ⓔ aldo.airplant@hotmail.com
Ⓦ www.aldo-airplant.com
Contact: Aldo Ciampitiello
Opening Times: Not open, mail order only. Visits by appt. only.
Min Mail Order UK: Nmc
Min Mail Order EU: Nmc
Credit Cards: All major credit/debit cards
Specialities: Airplants. *Tillandsia.*
Notes: Sells at flowers shows around Europe. Also sells wholesale.

XBlo **Table Bay View Nursery** ⊠ € ✉
(Office) 60 Molteno Road, Oranjezicht, Cape Town 8001, South Africa
Ⓣ 00 27 21 683 5108
Ⓕ 00 27 21 683 5108
Ⓔ info@tablebayviewnursery.co.za
Contact: Terence Bloch
Opening Times: Mail order only. No personal callers.
Min Mail Order UK: £15.00 + p&p
Min Mail Order EU: £15.00
Cat. Cost: £3.40 (postal order)
Credit Cards: None
Specialities: Tropical & sub-tropical ornamental & fruiting plants.
Notes: Due to high local bank charges, can no longer accept foreign bank cheques, only undated postal orders.

XFro **Frosch Exclusive Perennials** ⊠ € ✉
Zielgelstadelweg 5, D-83623 Dietramszell-Lochen, Germany
Ⓣ 00 49 (0)172 8422050
Ⓕ 00 49 (0)8027 9049975
Ⓔ info@cypripedium.de
Ⓦ www.cypripedium.de
Contact: Michael Weinert
Opening Times: Not open. Mail order only. Orders taken between 0700-2200 hours.
Min Mail Order UK: £350.00 + p&p
Min Mail Order EU: £350.00 + p&p
Cat. Cost: Online only.
Credit Cards: None
Specialities: Cypripedium hybrids. Hardy orchids.
Notes: Also sells wholesale.

XPde **Pépinière de l'Île** ⊠ € ♠
Keranroux 22870, Ile de Brehat, France
Ⓣ 00 33 (0)2 96 200384
Ⓜ 00 33 (0)686 128609
Ⓕ 00 33 (0)2 96 200384
Ⓔ contact@pepiniere-brehat.com
Ⓦ www.pepiniere-brehat.com
Contact: Laurence Blasco & Charles Blasco
Opening Times: 1400-1800 spring & summer. Other times by appt. incl. Aug.
Min Mail Order UK: Nmc
Min Mail Order EU: Nmc
Cat. Cost: €6.00.
Credit Cards: None
Specialities: *Agapanthus* & *Echium*. Plants from South Africa, Madeira, Canary Islands.

Nursery Index by Name

Nurseries that are included in the *RHS Plant Finder* for the first time this year (or have been reintroduced) are marked in **bold type**.
Full details of the nurseries will be found in **Nursery Details by Code** on page 826. For a key to the geographical codes, see the start of **Nurseries**.

A La Carte Daylilies	SDay
Abbey Dore Court Garden	WAbb
The Abbey Nursery	CAby
Abbey Plants	CAbP
Abbotsbury Sub-Tropical Gardens	CAbb
Aberconwy Nursery	WAbe
Abriachan Nurseries	GAbr
AEE	EAEE
Agave Nursery	MAga
Agroforestry Research Trust	CAgr
Albion Plants	CAlb
Aldo Airplants	**XAld**
Anita Allen	CAni
L A Allen	WAln
Allwoods	SAll
Alpine Campanulas	**EACa**
Alternative Plants	WAlt
Jacques Amand International	LAma
Amulree Exotics	EAmu
Angusplants	GAgs
Apple Court	SApp
Architectural Plants	SArc
Architectural Plants (Chichester) Ltd	SAPC
Ardcarne Garden Centre	IArd
Arley Hall Nursery	MArl
Arne Herbs	CArn
Ashwood Nurseries Ltd	MAsh
Asterby & Chalkcroft Nursery	LAst
Auchgourish Botanic Garden	GAuc
Aulden Farm	WAul
Claire Austin Hardy Plants	WCAu
David Austin Roses Ltd	**MAus**
Avon Bulbs	CAvo
Avondale Nursery	MAvo
Aylett Nurseries Ltd	LAyl
B & H M Baker	EBak
Bali-Hai Mail Order Nursery	IBal
Ballyrogan Nurseries	IBlr
Banwy Valley Nursery	WBVN
Barcham Trees	EBar
The Barn Plant Centre & Gift Shop	NBPC
Barnfield Pelargoniums	MBPg
Barnsdale Gardens	MBNS
Barracott Plants	CBct
Barters Plant Centre & Nursery	CBar
Barwinnock Herbs	GBar
Peter Beales Roses	EBls
Beamish Clematis Nursery	NBea
Beast Plants	SBst
Beechcroft Nursery	LBee
Beechcroft Nurseries & Garden Centre	MBec
Beeches Cottage Nursery	GBee
Beeches Nursery	EBee
Beggar's Roost Plants	CBgR
Belmont House Nursery	**CBel**
Bennetts Water Gardens	CBen
Bentley Plants	CBty
Bide-A-Wee Cottage Gardens	NBid
Big Plant Nursery	SBig
Alison Bilverstone	EABi
Binny Plants	GBin
Birchfield Nursery	SBfd
Birchfleet Nurseries	SBir
Birchwood Plants	SBch
Birkheads Secret Gardens & Nursery	NBir
Blackmoor Nurseries	SBmr
Blacksmiths Cottage Nursery	EBla
Bleak Hill Plants	SBHP
Blooming Marvellous Plants	LBMP
Bluebell Arboretum & Nursery	MBlu
Bluebell Cottage Nursery (formerly Agar's)	SAga
Bodmin Plant and Herb Nursery	CBod
Border Belles	GBBs
Bordervale Plants	WBor
The Botanic Nursery	CBot
Botanica	EBtc
Bouts Cottage Nurseries	WBou
Bowley Plants	CBow
Box Court Plants & Gardens	**WBox**

SPECIALIST NURSERIES

Nurseries have classified themselves under the following headings where they *exclusively* or *predominantly* supply this range of plants. Plant groups are set out in alphabetical order. Refer to **Nursery Details by Code** on page 826 for details of the nurseries whose codes are listed under the plant group which interests you. See page 823 for a fuller explanation.

ACID-LOVING PLANTS

CBcs, CMen, CTrh, CWCL, CWri, GAuc, GGar, GGGa, IBlr, IPen, ITim, IVic, LHyd, LMil, MBar, MCri, MFie, MGos, MLea, MSnd, MYeo, NHar, NLar, NMun, SCam, SCog, SHea, SLdr, SWhi, WAbe, WRic, WThu

ALPINE/ROCK PLANTS

CEls, CPla, CWat, CWil, CWon, CYeo, EBur, ECho, EDAr, EHoe, EPot, GAgs, GCrs, GEdr, GKev, IBal, IPen, ITim, MCri, NBro, NHar, NHoy, NLAp, NMen, NMin, NRya, NSla, NWCA, SCog, SIng, SPop, SRot, WAbe, WCom, WCre, WGor, WHoo, WPrP, WThu, WWst

AQUATIC PLANTS

CBen, CRow, CWat, EBWF, EHon, LLWG, LPBA, MSKA, MWts, SWat, WMAq, WPnP, WRic, XBlo

BAMBOOS

CAgr, CEnt, CPHo, ENBC, EPla, ESwi, GBin, GLin, IMou, LEdu, LPal, MBrN, MMoz, MMuc, MWhi, MWht, NGdn, NMoo, NPal, SArc, WDyG, WJun, WPGP

BRITISH WILD FLOWERS

CArn, COld, CRea, EBWF, GBar, GPoy, GPWP, MHer, NBir, NExo, NLan, NLAp, NMin, NMir, NSco, SIde, SWat, WAlt, WHer, WHfH, WLav, WSFF, WShi

BULBOUS PLANTS

CAvo, CBro, CFFs, CGHE, CGrW, CLak, CPne, CQua, CTca, CWCL, CYeo, ECho, EPot, ERCP, GCrs, LAma, MCri, MPoH, MSSP, NHoy, NMin, SDeJ, SPhx, WPrP, WShi, WWst, XBlo

CACTUS AND SUCCULENTS

CFwr, CPhi, CTrC, EAmu, EGln, EShb, ETod, LSou, LToo, NCro, NExo, SBst, SCac, SChr, XAld

CARNIVOROUS PLANTS

CHew, CSWC, EECP, MYeo, NChu, SHmp, WSSs

CHALK-LOVING PLANTS

CBot, CSev, CSpe, LOck, LSRN, SAll, SGar, SHar, SJoh, SKHP, SMrs, SSss, SUsu

CLIMBERS

CLng, CRHN, CSPN, CTri, CWGN, ELan, ESCh, ETho, LOck, LSRN, MBlu, MGos, NBea, NExo, NSti, SDea, SKHP, SLau, WCru, WFib, WSHC

COASTAL PLANTS

CBod, CCCN, CHrt, CPne, CTrC, EBWF, EExo, GGar, IBal, ISsi, IVic, NHoy, SChr, SDea, SGar, WPnn

CONIFERS

CKen, CMen, ECho, EHul, EPla, MBar, MBlu, MPkF, NLar, SLim, WEve, WGor, WMou, WThu

CONSERVATORY PLANTS

CBcs, CBrP, CCCN, CEls, CFwr, CLak, CRHN, CSpe, EABi, EBak, EGln, EOHP, ERea, EShb, ESul, EUJe, LHyd, MBPg, NChu, NCro, NFir, SHaC, SOWG, XAld

DROUGHT-TOLERANT

CBot, CKno, CPne, ECha, EHoe, ETod, LLWP, LPal, MBPg, NFir, NHoy, SAll, SDow, SIde, SIoW, SJoh, SMea, SOWG, SPhx, SUsu, WHil, WPnn

FERNS

CBty, CFwr, CGHE, CRow, CRWN, EExo, EFer, EFtx, GBin, GLin, IBal, IMou, ISha, LLWG, LPBA, MMoz, NHar, NMoo, NMyG, SApp, WAbe, WFib, WMoo, WPnP, WRic, WSpi, WWEG

FRUIT

CAgr, CBar, CCAT, CTho, CTri, EBtc, ECrN, ERea, EUJe, GBut, GPri, GTwe, IFFs, LBuc, LEdu, MCoo, SBmr, SCko, SCmr, SCrf, SDea, SFam, SKee, SVic, WDol, WHar, WJas, WWct, XBlo

GRASSES

CBod, CKno, CPla, CWCL, EHoe, EHul, ELan, EPla, EPPr, EPyc, GBin, GCal, GFor, IFoB, IMou, LEdu, LLWP, LOck, MBrN, MLLN, MMoz, MNrw, MWhi, NBea, NBro, NGdn, NOak, NSti, NWsh, SApp, SHDw, SMea, SMHy, SPhx, SSss, SUsu,

SWal, WGrn, WHal, WMoo, WPrP, WSpi, WWEG

Hedging

CBar, CCVT, CRea, CTho, CTrC, CTri, EBls, EBtc, ECrN, ERom, ISsi, LBuc, LTen, MBar, NWyk, SDow, SHHo, SLan, SRiv, SVic, WBuc, WEve, WJek, WJPR, WLav, WMou

Herbs

CArn, CBod, CHby, COld, CPbn, CSev, CWan, ELau, EOHP, GBar, GPoy, GPWP, ILis, LLWP, LMor, MHer, NBir, NGHP, NLan, NLLv, SDow, SHDw, SIde, STas, SWat, WHfH, WJek, WLav, WPnn

Marginal/Bog Plants

CMHG, CRow, CSWC, CWat, CWon, EECP, EHon, GKev, IPen, LLWG, LPBA, MMuc, MSKA, MWts, MYeo, NBir, NCot, SHaC, SMea, WHal, WMoo, WPnP, WSFF, WShi

Orchids

CBur, EFEx, GCrs, GEdr, LYaf, NDav, NEqu, NLAp, WFut, WHer, WWst, XAld, XFro

Organic

CBgR, CHby, COld, CTuc, CWon, EFer, GAuc, GBar, GBut, GPWP, ILis, LEdu, LLWP, MLLN, MLod, MYeo, NHoy, NOak, SFam, SPav, SPol, SRiF, STas, WGwG, WJek, WPnP, WSFF, WShi, WSpi, WWct, XAld

Ornamental Trees

CBcs, CBty, CCVT, CDul, CEnd, CMCN, CMen, CPMA, CSto, CTho, CTri, CWon, EBar, EBtc, ECrN, EGFP, ELan, GAuc, LHyd, LMaj, LMil, LTen, MBlu, MGos, MMuc, MPkF, NBea, NLar, NWyk, SBir, SCrf, SHHo, SKHP, SLan, SLau, SLim, WBuc, WCru, WEve, WHar, WHCr, WJas, WMou, WPGP

Palms

CPHo, EAmu, EExo, ESwi, ETod, LPal, LPJP, MREP, NPal, SArc, SBst, SChr

Peat free

CBgR, CBot, CCVN, CDoy, CElw, CHby, CMdw, CMea, CPHo, CPom, CRHN, CRWN, CSam, CSev, CSNP, CTca, CTho, CTsd, CWon, CYeo, EBtc, EBWF, ECrN, ELau, EMal, EPts, ERea, IBlr, ILis, LEdu, LLWP, MBNS, MCri, MLHP, MLLN, MLod, MMoz, MWhi, NLan, NSco, NWCA, SAll, SBch, SMDP, SMrs, SPav, SRiF, STes, WDyG, WGwG, WHoo, WJek, WPnP, WPrP, WSFF, WShi, WSpi, WWct

Period Plants

CArn, CKel, CSev, EBls, EMal, ESgI, GBut, ILis, IPPs, SAll, SPop, WHer

Propagate to Order

CArn, CCCN, CEls, CElw, CFir, CKel, CMdw, CMen, CPne, CSev, CTsd, CWon, CWVF, EBls, EBtc, ECho, ECrN, EECP, EGFP, EHoe, EMal, EOHP, EPyc, ERea, ERhR, EShb, ESul, GBuc, GKev, GQue, IFro, ILis, IMou, IPPN, IRar, LEdu, LIMB, LLWP, LMil, LOck, MBrN, MJon, MLHP, MLod, MMoz, MNrw, MPnt, MRav, MSpe, NChi, NCot, NCro, NEqu, NHoy, NLan, NLLv, NRya, NShi, NWCA, SAga, SBch, SCam, SDea, SGar, SHDw, SHea, SHyH, SLdr, SPin, SPol, SRiF, SSea, SSwd, STes, SUsu, SWat, WCom, WCru, WDol, WFuv, WGwG, WHer, WHil, WJek, WLav, WPat, WPBF, WPnP, WPrP, WRic, WSFF, WSpi, WSSs, WTin, WTou, WWct

Roses

CBar, CKel, CPou, EBls, ECnt, ESty, GCoc, IDic, LGod, LShp, LSRN, LStr, MAus, MGan, MJon, SFam, SRGP, SSea, SWCr

Seed

CBot, CDob, CGHE, CHby, CKno, CPla, CRea, CSpe, CSut, CTuc, EGln, ETMg, GAuc, GPoy, LSee, MFie, MPet, MPoH, NChl, NChu, NGHP, NLan, SCko, SSss, WHil, WJek, WSFF, WTou

Specimen-Sized plants

CArn, CBar, CBty, CCVT, CKel, CPhi, CPHT, CPMA, CPne, CSWC, CWon, CWVF, EAmu, EBtc, ECrN, EExo, EFtx, EHoe, ELau, EQua, ERea, ERom, EShb, ESwi, EUJe, GAuc, IMou, IPPs, LEdu, LHyd, LMaj, LMil, LOck, LTen, MGos, MLea, MLod, MPhe, MREP, MWht, MYeo, NChu, NCro, NHoy, NLAp, NPal, SArc, SBig, SCam, SFam, SHHo, SHmp, SHyH, SLan, SLdr, SMea, SRiF, SWat, WCru, WEve, WHer, WJek, WPat, WRic, WSpi, XAld

Topiary

CPHT, ERom, LTen, MREP, NWyk, SHHo, SLan, SRiv, WSpi

Tropical

CCCN, EAmu, EShb, ESwi, EUJe, ISsi, LToo, MREP, NPal, SArc, SBst, SHaC, SOWG, SSwd, WCru, WFut, WHil, WRic

INDEX MAP

The maps on the following pages show the approximate location of the nurseries whose details are listed in this directory.

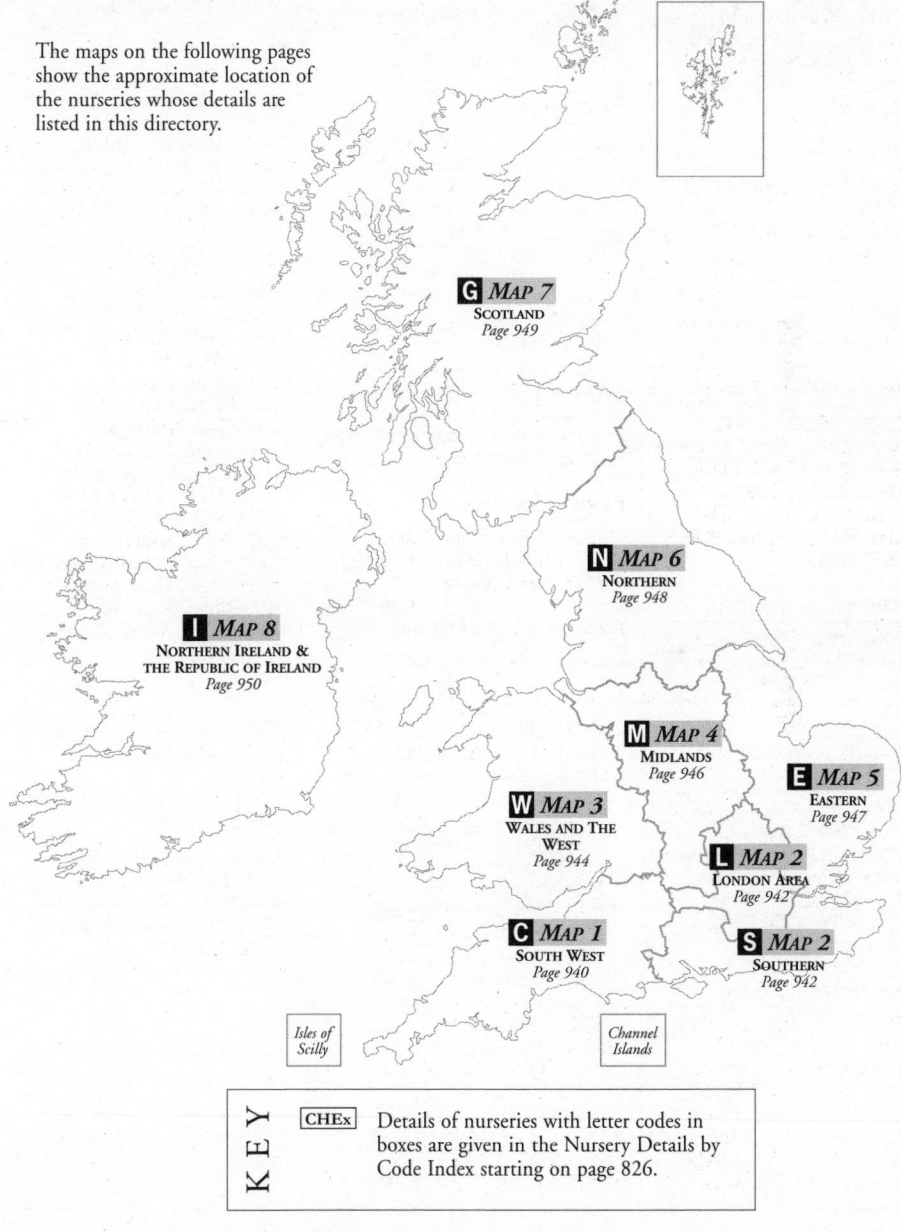

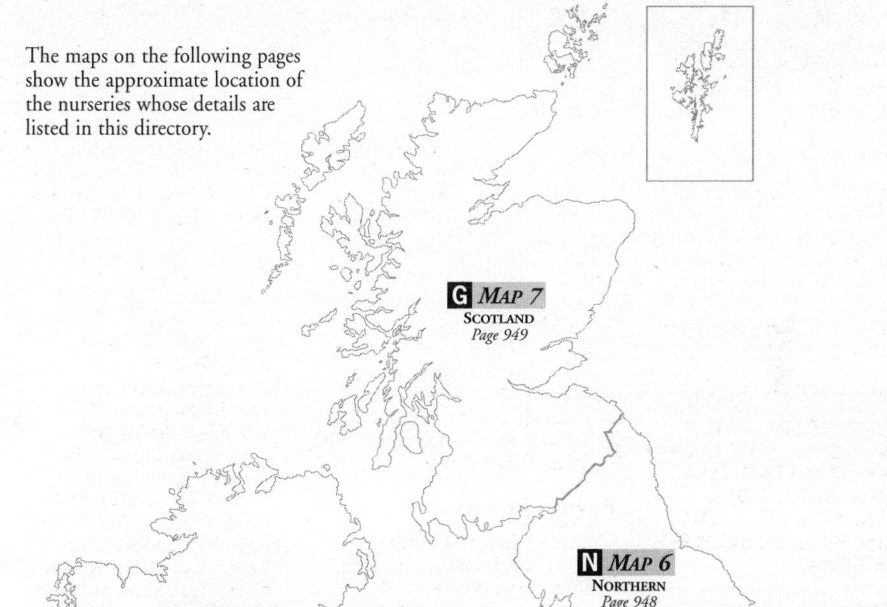

KEY

CHEx — Details of nurseries with letter codes in boxes are given in the Nursery Details by Code Index starting on page 826.

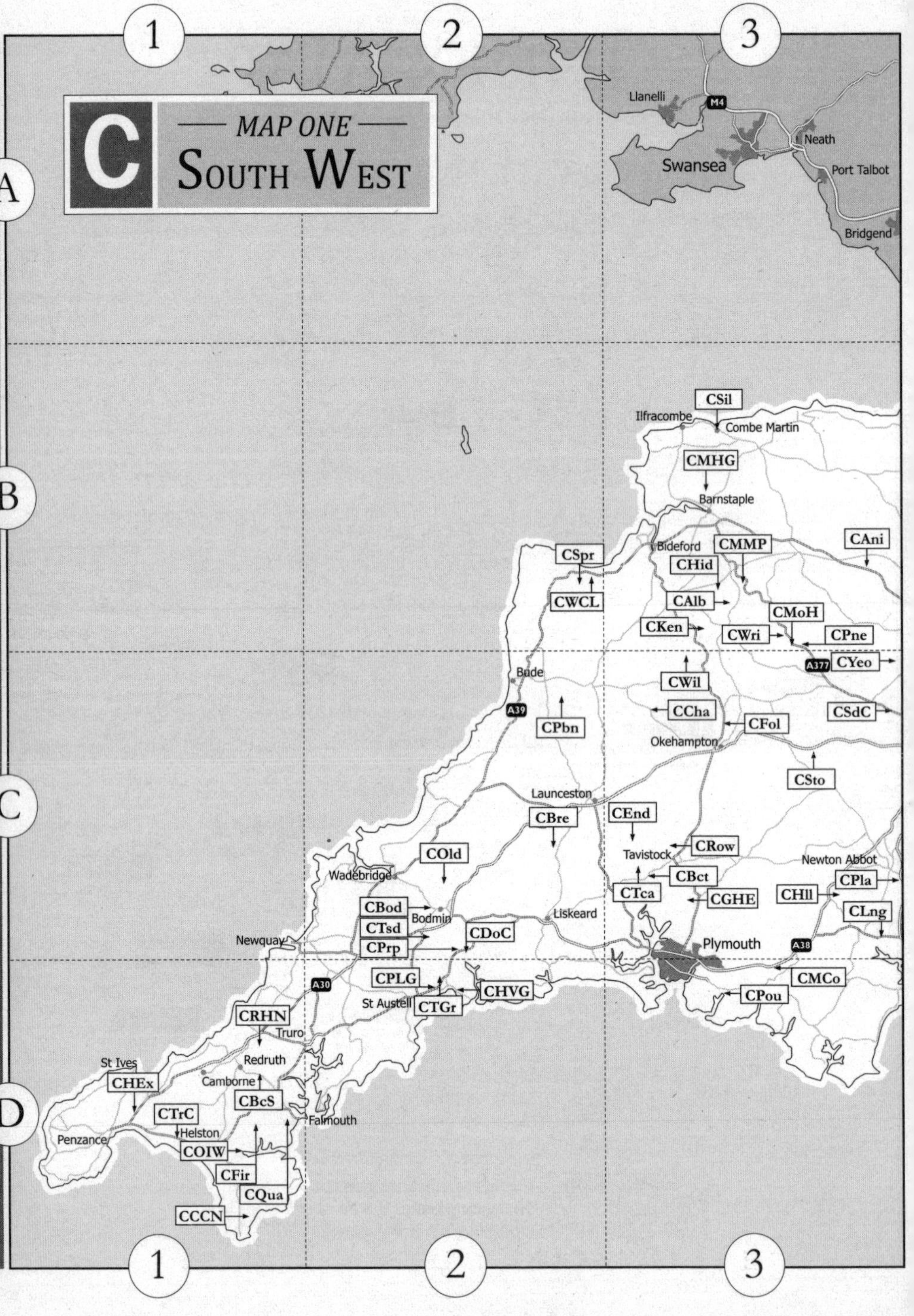
C
MAP ONE
SOUTH WEST
1
2
3
A
B
C
D
Llanelli
M4
Neath
Swansea
Port Talbot
Bridgend
CSil
Ilfracombe
Combe Martin
CMHG
Barnstaple
CSpr
Bideford
CMMP
CAni
CHid
CWCL
CAlb
CMoH
CKen
CWri
CPne
A377
CYeo
Bude
CWil
A39
CCha
CSdC
CPbn
CFol
Okehampton
CSto
Launceston
CEnd
CBre
COld
CRow
Tavistock
Newton Abbot
Wadebridge
CBct
CPla
CHll
CBod
CTca
CGHE
CLng
Bodmin
Liskeard
CTsd
CDoC
Newquay
Plymouth
CPrp
A38
A30
CPLG
CMCo
CHVG
St Austell
CTGr
CPou
CRHN
Truro
Redruth
St Ives
CHEx
Camborne
CBcS
CTrC
Helston
Falmouth
Penzance
COIW
CFir
CQua
CCCN
1
2
3

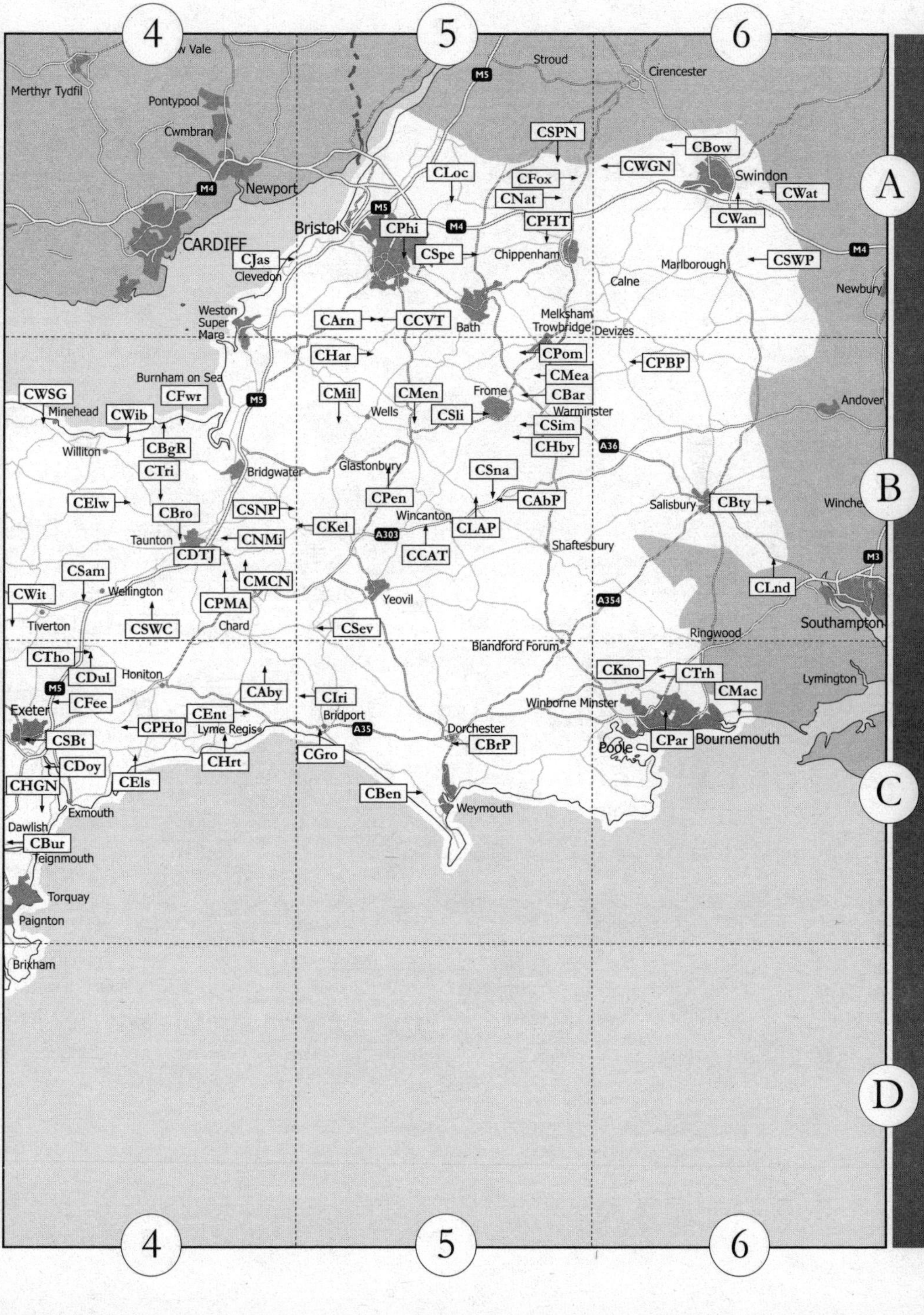
4
5
6
A
B
C
D
Merthyr Tydfil
Pontypool
Cwmbran
Newport
CARDIFF
M4
Stroud
Cirencester
M5
CSPN
CBow
CWGN
Swindon
CWat
CLoc
CFox
CNat
CPHT
CWan
Bristol
CPhi
CSpe
Chippenham
CJas
Clevedon
Marlborough
CSWP
Calne
Newbury
Weston Super Mare
CArn
CCVT
Bath
Melksham
Trowbridge
Devizes
CHar
CPom
CPBP
CMea
Burnham on Sea
CWSG
Minehead
CFwr
CWib
CMil
CMen
Wells
Frome
CBar
Warminster
CSli
CSim
Andover
Williton
CBgR
CHby
A36
CTri
Bridgwater
Glastonbury
CSna
CElw
CBro
CSNP
CPen
CAbP
Salisbury
CBty
Winche
Wincanton
CKel
CLAP
Taunton
CNMi
A303
CDTJ
CCAT
Shaftesbury
M3
CSam
CMCN
CLnd
CWit
Wellington
CPMA
Yeovil
Southampton
A354
Tiverton
CSWC
Chard
CSev
Ringwood
Blandford Forum
CTho
Honiton
CKno
CTrh
Lymington
CDul
CAby
CMac
CIri
Exeter
CFee
Winborne Minster
CEnt
Bridport
CPHo
Lyme Regis
A35
Dorchester
CSBt
CBrP
CPar
Bournemouth
Poole
CDoy
CHrt
CGro
CHGN
CEls
CBen
Exmouth
Weymouth
Dawlish
CBur
Teignmouth
Torquay
Paignton
Brixham

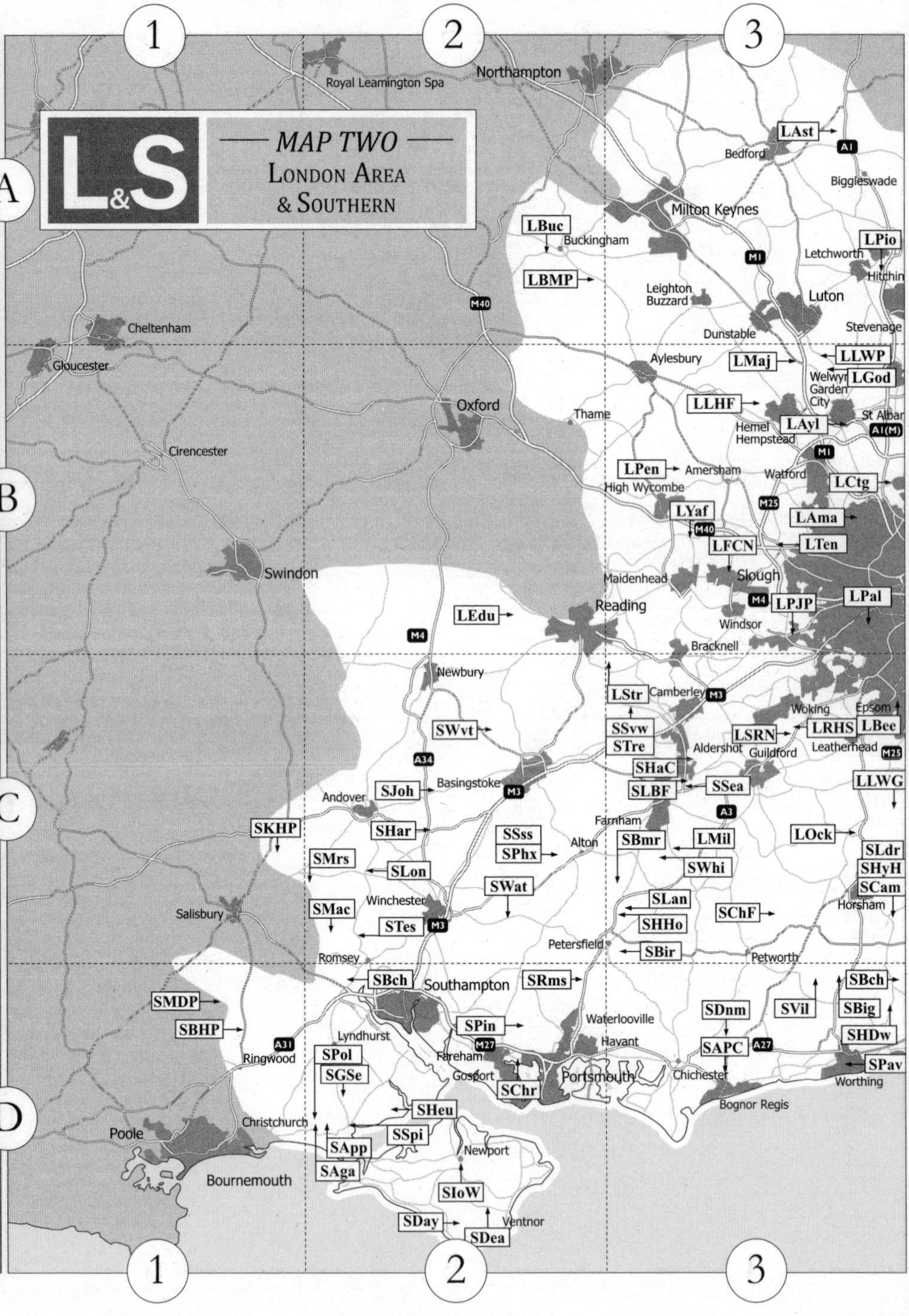
1
2
3
A
B
C
D
L&S
MAP TWO
LONDON AREA
& SOUTHERN
Northampton
Royal Leamington Spa
LAst
Bedford
A1
Biggleswade
Milton Keynes
LBuc
Buckingham
LPio
Letchworth
Hitchin
M1
LBMP
Leighton Buzzard
Luton
M40
Cheltenham
Dunstable
Stevenage
Gloucester
Aylesbury
LMaj
LLWP
Welwyn Garden City
LGod
Oxford
Thame
LLHF
LAyl
Hemel Hempstead
St Albans
A1(M)
Cirencester
LPen
Amersham
Watford
LCtg
High Wycombe
M25
LYaf
M40
LAma
LFCN
LTen
Swindon
Maidenhead
Slough
M4
LPJP
LPal
LEdu
Reading
Windsor
M4
Bracknell
Newbury
LStr
Camberley
M3
Woking
Epsom
SSvw
STre
LSRN
LRHS
LBee
SWvt
Aldershot
Guildford
Leatherhead
M25
A34
SHaC
SJoh
Basingstoke
M3
SSea
LLWG
Andover
SLBF
Farnham
A3
SKHP
SHar
SSss
SPhx
Alton
SBmr
LMil
LOck
SMrs
SLon
SWhi
SLdr
SHyH
SWat
SCam
Winchester
SLan
Horsham
Salisbury
SMac
STes
M3
SHHo
SChF
Petersfield
SBir
Romsey
Petworth
SBch
Southampton
SRms
SBch
SMDP
SDnm
SVil
SBig
SBHP
SPin
Waterlooville
Lyndhurst
M27
Havant
SAPC
A27
SHDw
A31
SPol
Fareham
Ringwood
SGSe
Gosport
Portsmouth
Chichester
SPav
SChr
Worthing
Bognor Regis
SHeu
Christchurch
Poole
SSpi
SApp
Newport
SAga
Bournemouth
SIoW
SDay
Ventnor
SDea
1
2
3

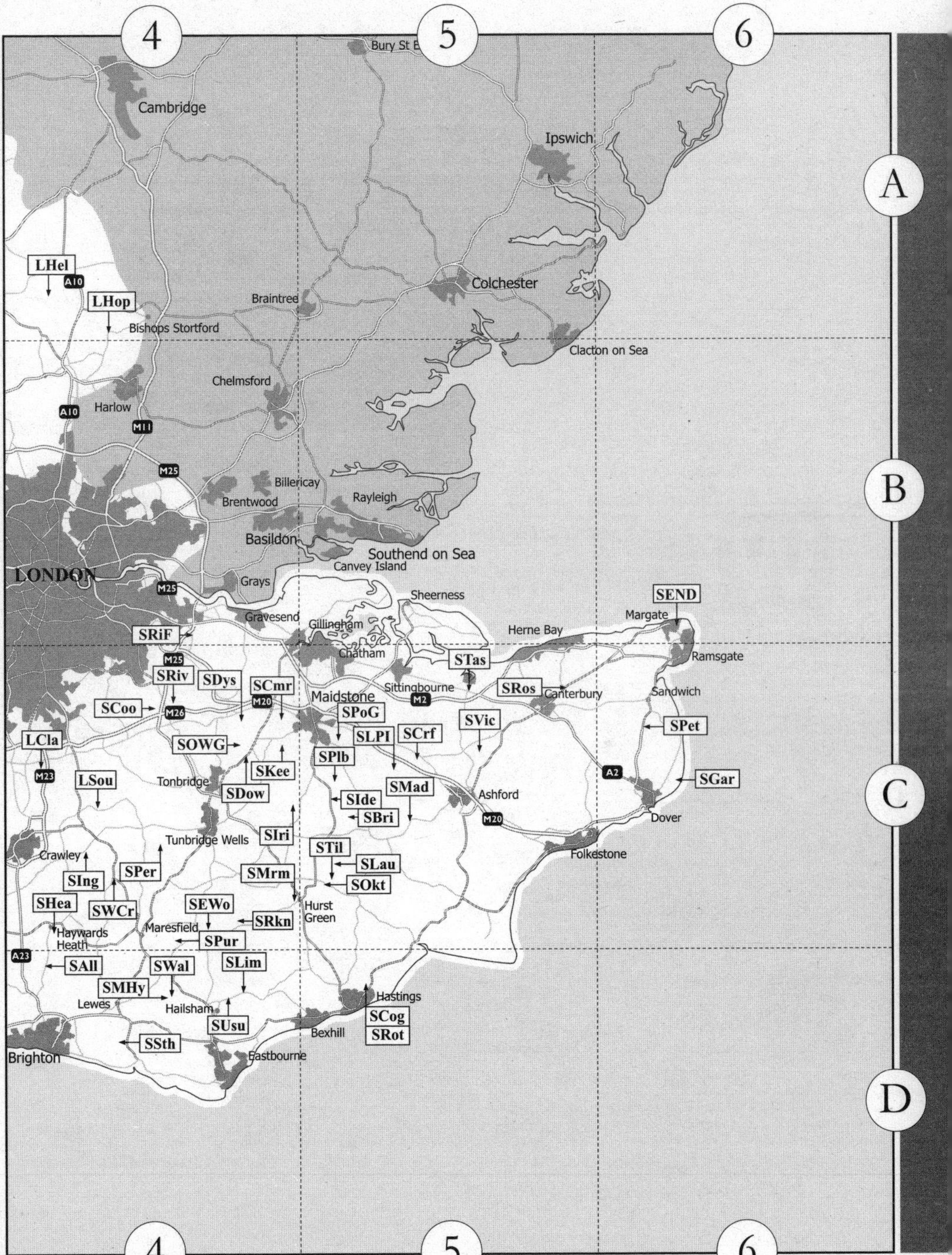
4
5
6
A
B
C
D
Bury St E
Cambridge
Ipswich
LHel
A10
LHop
Braintree
Colchester
Bishops Stortford
Clacton on Sea
Chelmsford
Harlow
A10
M11
M25
Billericay
Brentwood
Rayleigh
Basildon
Southend on Sea
Canvey Island
LONDON
Grays
M25
Sheerness
SEND
Gravesend
Gillingham
Margate
Herne Bay
SRiF
Chatham
Ramsgate
M25
STas
SRiv
SDys
SCmr
Sittingbourne
SRos
Canterbury
Maidstone
M2
Sandwich
SCoo
M26
M20
SPoG
SVic
SPet
LCla
SOWG
SLPI
SCrf
SPlb
SKee
A2
SGar
M23
LSou
Tonbridge
SDow
SMad
Ashford
SIde
SBri
M20
Dover
SIri
Tunbridge Wells
STil
Folkestone
Crawley
SLau
SPer
SIng
SMrm
SOkt
SHea
SWCr
SEWo
Hurst Green
SRkn
Haywards Heath
Maresfield
SPur
A23
SAll
SWal
SLim
SMHy
Hastings
Lewes
Hailsham
SCog
SUsu
Bexhill
SRot
SSth
Brighton
Eastbourne

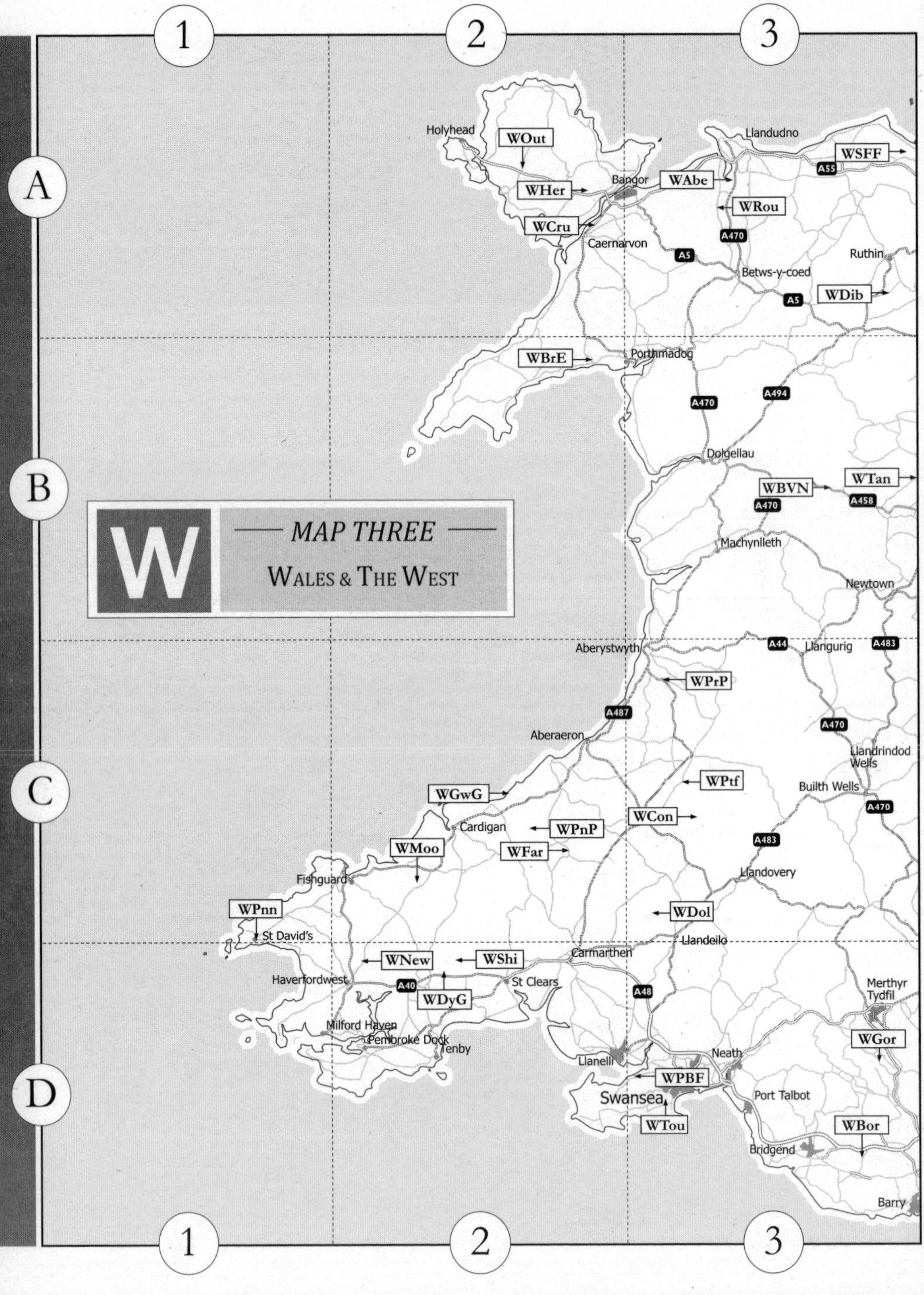
1
2
3
A
B
C
D
W
MAP THREE
WALES & THE WEST
Holyhead
WOut
Llandudno
WSFF
A55
WHer
Bangor
WAbe
WRou
WCru
A470
Caernarvon
A5
Ruthin
Betws-y-coed
A5
WDib
WBrE
Porthmadog
A470
A494
Dolgellau
WBVN
WTan
A470
A458
Machynlleth
Newtown
Aberystwyth
A44
Llangurig
A483
WPrP
A487
A470
Aberaeron
Llandrindod Wells
WPtf
Builth Wells
WGwG
A470
WCon
Cardigan
WPnP
WMoo
WFar
A483
Fishguard
Llandovery
WPnn
WDol
St David's
Llandeilo
Carmarthen
WNew
WShi
Haverfordwest
A40
St Clears
Merthyr Tydfil
WDyG
A48
Milford Haven
Pembroke Dock
Tenby
WGor
Neath
Llanelli
WPBF
Swansea
Port Talbot
WTou
WBor
Bridgend
Barry

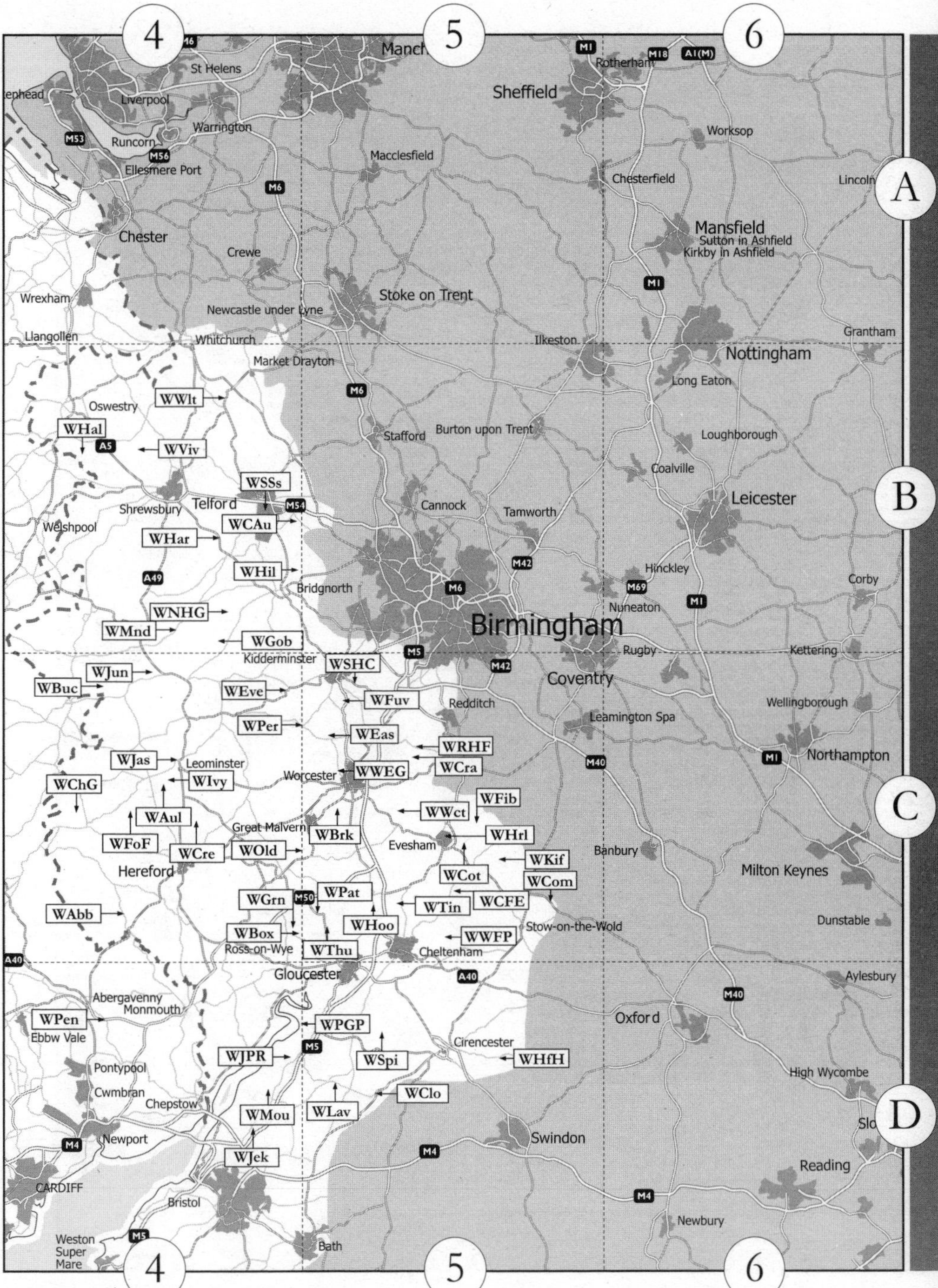
4
5
6
A
B
C
D
Manch
St Helens
Rotherham
Sheffield
Liverpool
Warrington
Runcorn
Ellesmere Port
Macclesfield
Worksop
Chesterfield
Lincoln
Chester
Crewe
Mansfield
Sutton in Ashfield
Kirkby in Ashfield
Wrexham
Stoke on Trent
Newcastle under Lyne
Llangollen
Whitchurch
Ilkeston
Grantham
Nottingham
Market Drayton
Long Eaton
Oswestry
Stafford
Burton upon Trent
Loughborough
Coalville
Shrewsbury
Telford
Cannock
Tamworth
Leicester
Welshpool
Hinckley
Corby
Bridgnorth
Nuneaton
Birmingham
Kidderminster
Rugby
Kettering
Coventry
Redditch
Wellingborough
Leamington Spa
Northampton
Leominster
Worcester
Great Malvern
Evesham
Banbury
Milton Keynes
Hereford
Stow-on-the-Wold
Dunstable
Ross-on-Wye
Cheltenham
Gloucester
Aylesbury
Abergavenny
Monmouth
Oxford
Ebbw Vale
Cirencester
Pontypool
High Wycombe
Cwmbran
Chepstow
Newport
Swindon
Slo
Reading
CARDIFF
Bristol
Newbury
Weston Super Mare
Bath
M6
M1
M18
A1(M)
M53
M56
A5
M54
A49
M42
M69
M5
M50
M40
A40
M4
WWlt
WHal
WViv
WSSs
WCAu
WHar
WHil
WNHG
WMnd
WGob
WSHC
WJun
WBuc
WEve
WFuv
WPer
WEas
WRHF
WJas
WCra
WWEG
WIvy
WChG
WFib
WWct
WAul
WHrl
WBrk
WFoF
WCre
WOld
WKif
WCot
WCom
WPat
WGrn
WCFE
WTin
WAbb
WHoo
WBox
WWFP
WThu
WPen
WPGP
WJPR
WSpi
WHfH
WClo
WMou
WLav
WJek

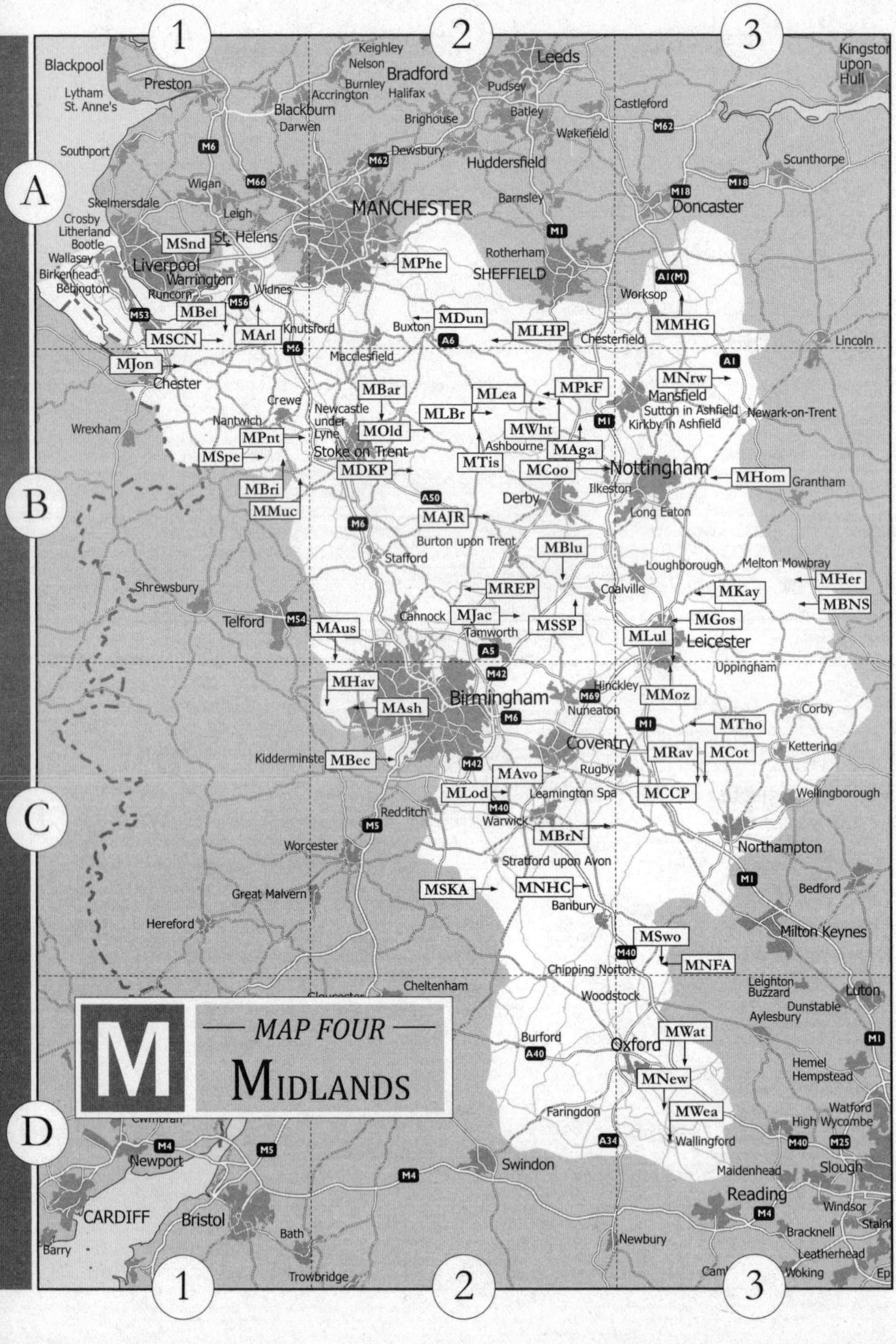
M
MAP FOUR
MIDLANDS
1
2
3
A
B
C
D
Blackpool
Preston
Lytham St. Anne's
Keighley
Nelson
Bradford
Burnley
Accrington
Halifax
Blackburn
Darwen
Leeds
Pudsey
Batley
Brighouse
Castleford
Wakefield
Kingston upon Hull
Southport
Dewsbury
Huddersfield
Scunthorpe
Wigan
Skelmersdale
Leigh
MANCHESTER
Barnsley
Doncaster
Crosby
Litherland
Bootle
Wallasey
Birkenhead
Bebington
Liverpool
St. Helens
Warrington
Runcorn
Widnes
Rotherham
SHEFFIELD
Worksop
Knutsford
Buxton
Chesterfield
Lincoln
Macclesfield
Chester
Crewe
Nantwich
Wrexham
Newcastle under Lyne
Stoke on Trent
Ashbourne
Mansfield
Sutton in Ashfield
Kirkby in Ashfield
Newark-on-Trent
Nottingham
Ilkeston
Grantham
Derby
Long Eaton
Burton upon Trent
Stafford
Loughborough
Melton Mowbray
Shrewsbury
Coalville
Telford
Cannock
Tamworth
Leicester
Uppingham
Birmingham
Hinckley
Nuneaton
Corby
Coventry
Kettering
Kidderminster
Rugby
Leamington Spa
Wellingborough
Redditch
Warwick
Worcester
Northampton
Stratford upon Avon
Great Malvern
Bedford
Banbury
Hereford
Milton Keynes
Chipping Norton
Cheltenham
Woodstock
Leighton Buzzard
Luton
Dunstable
Aylesbury
Burford
Oxford
Hemel Hempstead
Faringdon
Watford
High Wycombe
Wallingford
Newport
Swindon
Maidenhead
Slough
Reading
Windsor
CARDIFF
Bristol
Bath
Barry
Newbury
Bracknell
Leatherhead
Trowbridge
Woking
M6
M62
M66
M18
M1
A1(M)
A1
M56
M53
A6
A50
M54
A5
M42
M69
M40
M5
A40
A34
M4
M25
MSnd
MPhe
MBel
MSCN
MArl
MJon
MDun
MLHP
MMHG
MBar
MLea
MPkF
MNrw
MLBr
MOld
MWht
MPnt
MSpe
MTis
MAga
MDKP
MCoo
MHom
MBri
MMuc
MAJR
MBlu
MHer
MREP
MKay
MBNS
MJac
MSSP
MGos
MAus
MLul
MHav
MAsh
MMoz
MTho
MBec
MRav
MCot
MAvo
MLod
MCCP
MBrN
MSKA
MNHC
MSwo
MNFA
MWat
MNew
MWea

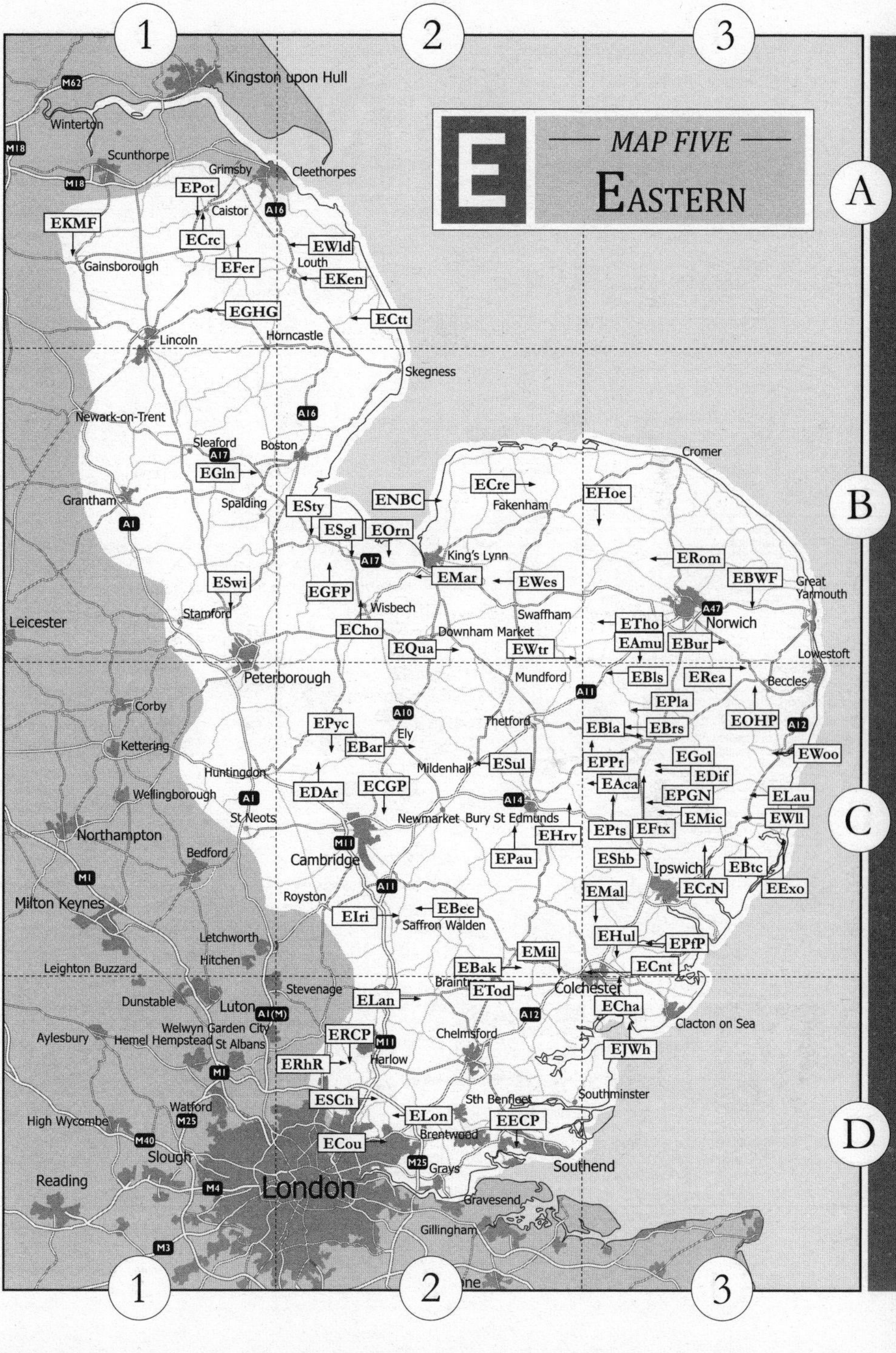

E
MAP FIVE
Eastern
1
2
3
A
B
C
D
Kingston upon Hull
Winterton
Scunthorpe
Grimsby
Cleethorpes
Caistor
Gainsborough
Louth
Lincoln
Horncastle
Skegness
Newark-on-Trent
Sleaford
Boston
Grantham
Spalding
Stamford
Leicester
Peterborough
Corby
Kettering
Huntingdon
Wellingborough
St Neots
Northampton
Bedford
Cambridge
Milton Keynes
Royston
Letchworth
Hitchen
Leighton Buzzard
Stevenage
Dunstable
Luton
Welwyn Garden City
Aylesbury
Hemel Hempstead
St Albans
Harlow
Watford
High Wycombe
Slough
Reading
London
Cromer
Fakenham
King's Lynn
Wisbech
Swaffham
Downham Market
Norwich
Great Yarmouth
Lowestoft
Beccles
Mundford
Thetford
Ely
Mildenhall
Newmarket
Bury St Edmunds
Ipswich
Saffron Walden
Braintree
Colchester
Clacton on Sea
Chelmsford
Southminster
Sth Benfleet
Brentwood
Grays
Southend
Gravesend
Gillingham
M62
M18
A16
A17
A1
A47
A10
A11
A12
A14
M11
A1(M)
M1
M25
M40
M4
M3
EPot
EKMF
ECrc
EWld
EFer
EKen
EGHG
ECtt
EGln
ECre
EHoe
ENBC
ESty
ESgl
EOrn
ERom
EMar
EWes
EBWF
ESwi
EGFP
ETho
ECho
EAmu
EBur
EQua
EWtr
EBls
ERea
EPla
EPyc
EOHP
EBla
EBrs
EBar
EPPr
EGol
ESul
EWoo
EDif
EAca
EDAr
ECGP
EPGN
ELau
EMic
EWll
EPts
EFtx
EHrv
EPau
EShb
EBtc
ECrN
EExo
EMal
EBee
EIri
EHul
EPfP
EMil
ECnt
EBak
ETod
ELan
ECha
ERCP
EJWh
ERhR
ESCh
ELon
EECP
ECou

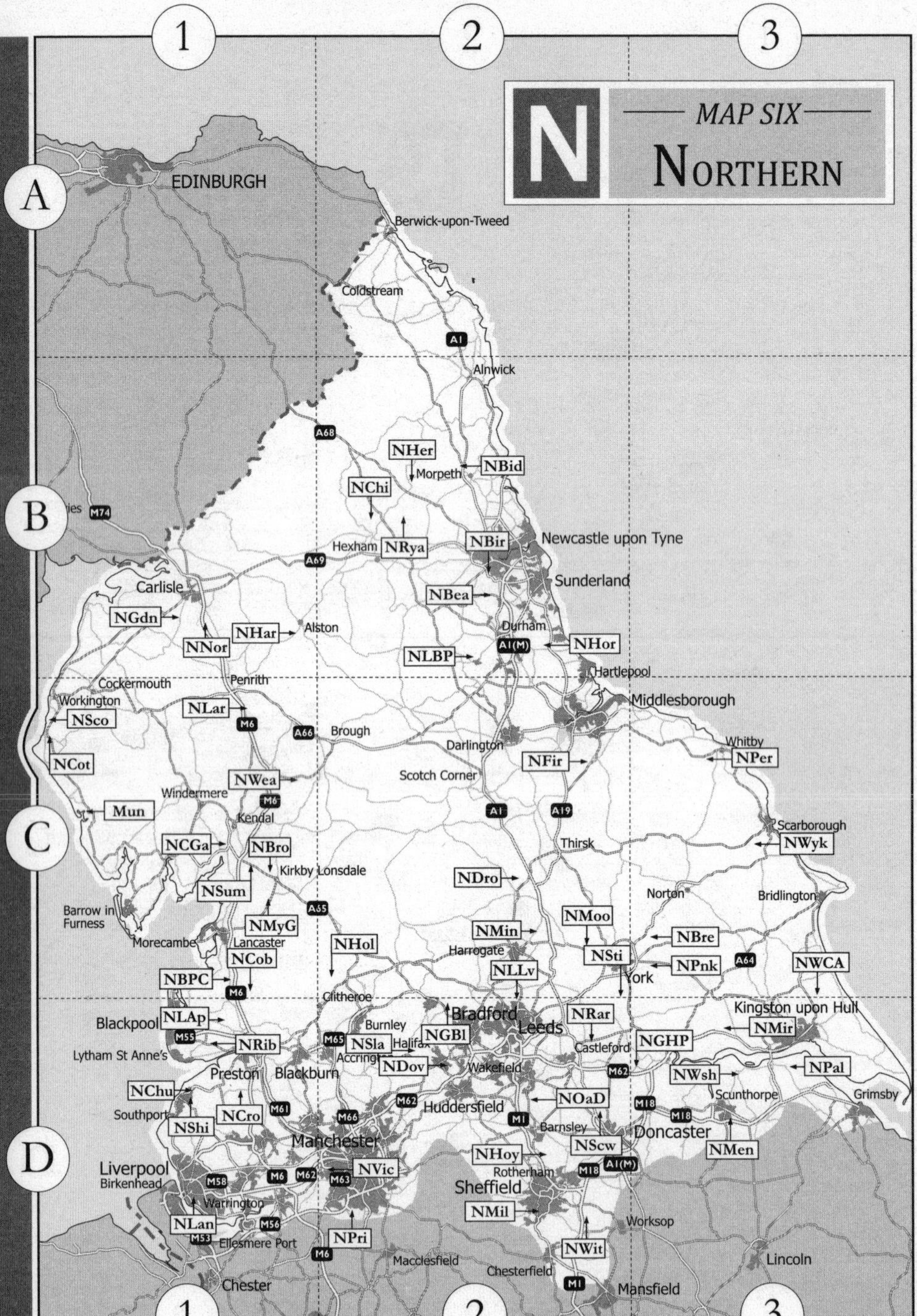
1
2
3
N
MAP SIX
NORTHERN
A
B
C
D
EDINBURGH
Berwick-upon-Tweed
Coldstream
A1
Alnwick
A68
NHer
Morpeth
NBid
NChi
M74
Hexham
NRya
NBir
Newcastle upon Tyne
A69
Sunderland
Carlisle
NBea
NGdn
NHar
Alston
Durham
NNor
NLBP
A1(M)
NHor
Hartlepool
Cockermouth
Penrith
Workington
NLar
Middlesborough
NSco
M6
A66
Brough
Darlington
Whitby
NCot
NFir
NPer
Scotch Corner
NWea
Windermere
M6
Mun
Kendal
A1
A19
Scarborough
NCGa
NBro
Thirsk
NWyk
Kirkby Lonsdale
NDro
NSum
Norton
Bridlington
Barrow in Furness
A65
NMyG
NMoo
Morecambe
Lancaster
NMin
NBre
NHol
NCob
Harrogate
NSti
NPnk
A64
NWCA
NBPC
NLLv
York
M6
Clitheroe
Bradford
Kingston upon Hull
NLAp
NRar
Blackpool
Burnley
NGBl
Leeds
NMir
M55
M65
NSla
Halifax
Castleford
NGHP
Lytham St Anne's
NRib
Accrington
NDov
Wakefield
M62
NWsh
NPal
Preston
Blackburn
Scunthorpe
NChu
M62
Huddersfield
NOaD
M18
Grimsby
Southport
NShi
NCro
M61
M66
M1
M18
Barnsley
Manchester
NScw
Doncaster
NMen
NHoy
Liverpool
Birkenhead
M58
M6
M62
M63
NVic
Rotherham
M18
A1(M)
Warrington
Sheffield
NMil
NLan
M56
Worksop
M53
Ellesmere Port
NPri
NWit
M6
Macclesfield
Chesterfield
Lincoln
Chester
M1
Mansfield

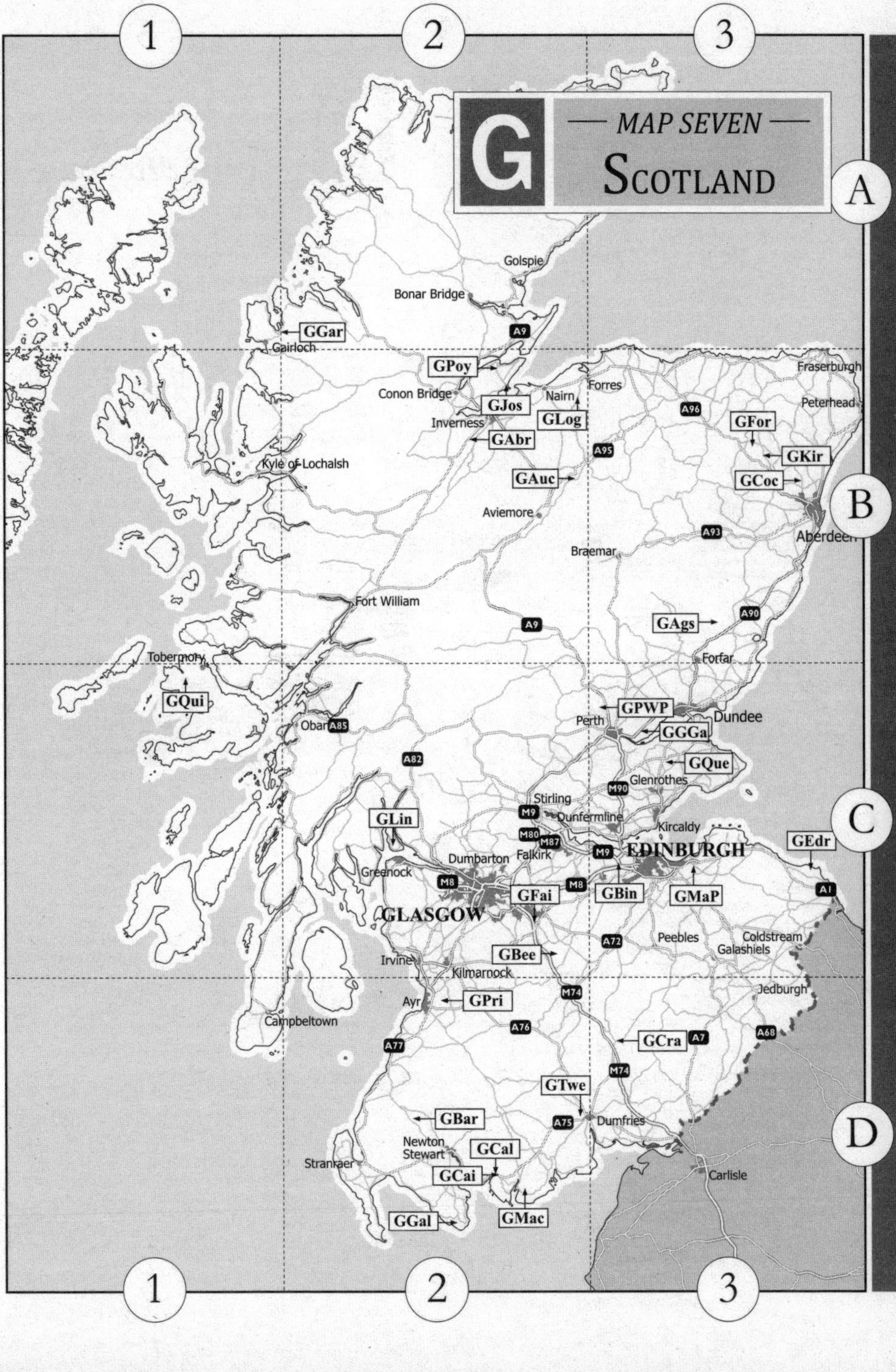
G
— MAP SEVEN —
SCOTLAND
1
2
3
A
B
C
D
Golspie
Bonar Bridge
GGar
Gairloch
A9
GPoy
Conon Bridge
Nairn
Forres
GJos
Inverness
GLog
GAbr
Kyle of Lochalsh
A95
GAuc
Aviemore
Fraserburgh
Peterhead
A96
GFor
GKir
GCoc
Aberdeen
A93
Braemar
Fort William
A9
GAgs
A90
Forfar
Tobermory
GQui
GPWP
Dundee
Perth
GGGa
Oban
A85
A82
GQue
Glenrothes
M90
Stirling
M9
Dunfermline
Kircaldy
GLin
M80
M87
Dumbarton
Falkirk
M9
EDINBURGH
GEdr
Greenock
M8
M8
GFai
GBin
GMaP
A1
GLASGOW
A72
Peebles
Coldstream
Galashiels
Irvine
GBee
Kilmarnock
M74
Jedburgh
Ayr
GPri
Campbeltown
A76
GCra
A7
A68
A77
M74
GTwe
GBar
A75
Dumfries
Newton
Stewart
GCal
Stranraer
GCai
Carlisle
GMac
GGal
1
2
3

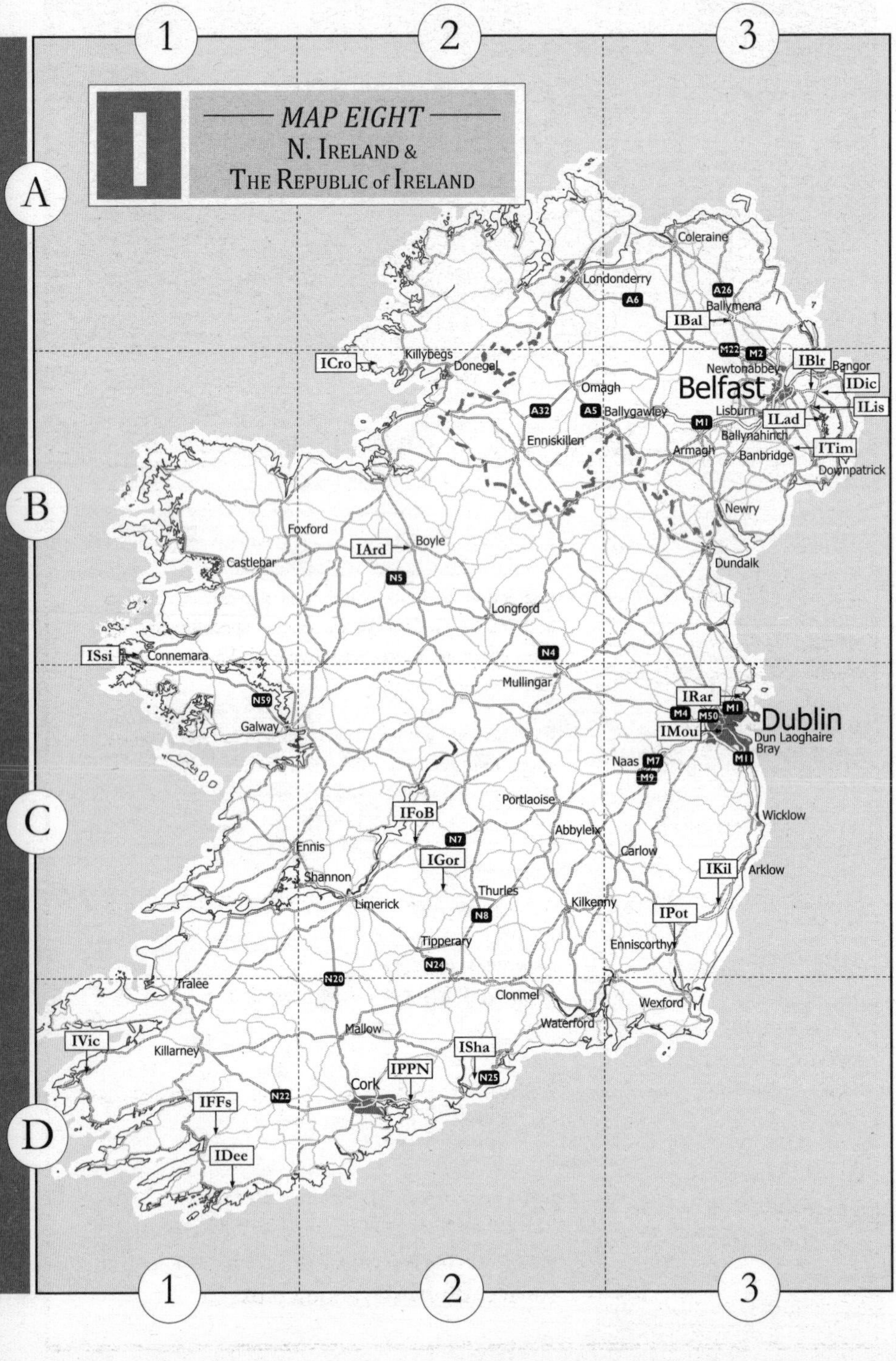
1
2
3
A
B
C
D
I
MAP EIGHT
N. IRELAND &
THE REPUBLIC of IRELAND
Coleraine
Londonderry
A6
A26
Ballymena
IBal
M22
M2
ICro
Killybegs
Donegal
Newtonabbey
IBlr
Bangor
Belfast
IDic
Omagh
A32
A5
Ballygawley
Lisburn
ILis
ILad
M1
Enniskillen
Ballynahinch
Armagh
Banbridge
ITim
Downpatrick
Newry
Foxford
IArd
Boyle
Castlebar
Dundalk
N5
Longford
ISsi
Connemara
N4
Mullingar
IRar
N59
M4
M50
M1
Dublin
IMou
Galway
Dun Laoghaire
Bray
Naas
M7
M9
M11
Portlaoise
IFoB
Wicklow
N7
Abbyleix
Ennis
IGor
Carlow
IKil
Arklow
Shannon
Thurles
Limerick
Kilkenny
N8
IPot
Tipperary
Enniscorthy
N24
N20
Tralee
Clonmel
Wexford
Mallow
Waterford
IVic
ISha
Killarney
IPPN
N25
Cork
IFFs
N22
IDee

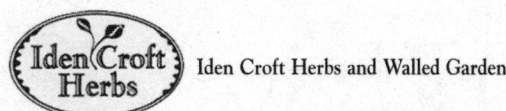

Alpine
garden society
Big ideas for small plants!
Join the world's largest alpine and rock gardening Society and enjoy many benefits:
• Quarterly Colour Journal - informative illustrated articles
• Members' Seed Exchange
• Conferences and Gardening Workshops
• Shows and Plant Sales
• Guided Plant Tours
• Discounted Book Sales
• Local Group Meetings
The Alpine Gardener
Alpinews
Easy Leaflets
See our simple guides to get you started with easy to follow instructions on plants, propagation and techniques.
To join or for more information call or visit our website:
tel: 01386 554790
email: ags@alpinegardensociety.net
www.alpinegardensociety.net

Wide range of Crocosmia, Auricula.
Canna, South African and other
unusual or hard-to-find plants.
Holders of the National
Collection of Acanthus
Hillview Hardy
Plants
For a copy of our full catalogue,
please send 5 x 2nd class stamps
to:
Hillview Hardy Plants (WHil)
Worfield, Nr Bridgnorth,
Shropshire WV15 5NT
Phone/Fax 01746 716454
Email: hillview@themutual.net
www.hillviewhardyplants.com

Triscombe Nurseries
Offer old fashioned quality
value and service
Wide range of plants
our speciality
TREES * SHRUBS * CONIFERS
ROSES * FRUIT * CLEMATIS
HERBACEOUS & ROCK PLANTS
Open 7 days a week, Mon-Sat 9-5.30;
Sundays and Bank Holidays 2-5.30
Tel (01984) 618267
www.triscombenurseries.co.uk
Email: triscombe.nurseries2000@virgin.net
West Bagborough
Taunton, Somerset
TA4 3HG
Turning off A358
at Triscombe
between
West Bagborough
and
Crowcombe

The Dingle
Nurseries
& Garden
We have one of the largest ranges of trees and shrubs in the country, including native trees, hedging, conifers, roses, perennials and fruit. Semi mature and standard trees are also available, as well as specimen shrubs and many rarities all at competitive prices.
Open 7 days a week 9am to 5pm.
DINGLE NURSERIES & GARDEN
Welshpool, Powys, Wales SY21 9JD
T: 01938 555145
E: info@dinglenurseryandgarden.co.uk

Grange Farm Nursery

GUARLFORD
MALVERN
WORCESTERSHIRE. WR13 6NT

SPECIALIST PLANT CENTRE

A small Nursery with an emphasis on Hardy Shrubs and Trees, Climbing Plants, Roses, Conifers and Seasonal Bedding.

WINTER FLOWERING PLANTS

Acer, Cornus, Betula, Sorbus, Magnolia, Hydrangea, Philadelphus, Viburnum, Skimmia, Pieris, Helleborus, Hostas, Phormiums, Grasses, Wisteria.

HERBACEOUS PLANTS

This tiny Nursery, personally run by Carol Nicholls since 1980 is beautifully arranged in seasonal displays, making it a pleasure to visit. The Nursery is set within old farm buildings, located in the beautiful area of the Malvern Hills east on the B4211 in the centre of Guarlford. Open every day except for two weeks after Christmas.

The Horticultural Trades Association HTA Est'd 1899

MALVERN
(01684) 562544

National Garden Gift Vouchers

Email
grangefmnursery@btconnect.com

National Garden Gift Tokens Bought and Exchanged

Primrose Cottage Nursery & Garden Centre

800 Varieties of
PERENNIALS & ALPINES
75 Varieties of HERBS
60 Varieties of CLEMATIS
92 Varieties of CLIMBERS
90 Varieties of ROSES
100 Varieties of
PATIO & BASKET PLANTS
Plus
SHRUBS, CONIFERS, TREES & BEDDING PLANTS

COFFEE SHOP
OPEN DAILY

Ringway Rd, Moss Nook, Wythenshawe, Manchester M22 5WF
Tel: 0161 437 1557
1 mile from Manchester Airport
www.primrosecottagenursery.co.uk

White Cottage Alpines

East Yorkshire's own specialist growers of alpines, rockery plants and low growing perennials.

Excellent mail order service, debit/credit cards welcome.

See nursery details at **NWCA** for opening times.

Find us on the B1244 Beverley-Hornsea Rd. at Sunnyside Nurseries, Sigglesthorne, HU11 5QL

www.whitecottagealpines.co.uk

OVER 2500 DIFFERENT CHOICE AND UNUSUAL HERBACEOUS PERENNIALS & ALPINES

NORWELL NURSERIES AND GARDENS

HARDY GERANIUMS & CHRYSANTHEMUMS, GEUMS, HEMEROCALLIS, GRASSES, WOODLAND & COTTAGE GARDEN PLANTS

www.norwellnurseries.co.uk
Tel: 01636 636337
Norwell Nurseries, Woodhouse Road, Norwell, Newark, Notts NG23 6JX

EAST NORTHDOWN FARM GARDENS & NURSERIES

Comprehensive Plant Range
especially for coast and dry/chalk soils

For details go to
www.botanyplants.com

MARGATE KENT CT9 3TS
Tel: 01843 862060 Fax: 01843 860206

MUCKLESTONE NURSERIES

Comprehensive Plant Range
especially for acid and moist soils

For details go to:
www.botanyplants.com

Nr. Market Drayton, Shropshire. TF9 4DN
Tel. Brian Watkins 07985 425829
Near Loggerheads off the A53, 5 miles from Bridgemere

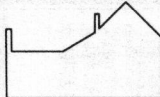

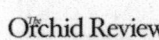

INDEX OF ADVERTISERS

RHS Show Awards 2008

RHS Plant Finder nurseries that were awarded RHS medals at the three major RHS Shows in 2008

Chelsea Gold

Jacques Amand International
Avon Bulbs
Peter Beales Roses
Burnham Nurseries
Dibley's Nurseries
Downderry Nursery
Hampshire Carnivorous Plants
Hardy's Cottage Garden Plants
Harveys Garden Plants
Hewitt-Cooper Carnivorous Plants
Jekka's Herb Farm
Knoll Gardens
Mendip Bonsai Studio
Roualeyn Nurseries
South West Carnivorous Plants
Brian & Pearl Sulman
Thorncroft Clematis Nursery

Chelsea Silver-Gilt

David Austin Roses Ltd
Burncoose Nurseries
Culm View Nursery
The Old Walled Garden
Potash Nursery
Primrose Bank
Rhodes & Rockliffe
The Romantic Garden
Westcountry Nurseries

Chelsea Silver

Aldo Airplants
Barnsdale Gardens
Broadleigh Gardens
Desert to Jungle
Fibrex Nurseries Ltd
Green Garden Herbs
Isle of Wight Lavender
Kelways Ltd
Oak Tree Nursery
Rotherview Nursery
Tendercare Nurseries Ltd

Chelsea Silver Knightian

W Robinson & Sons Ltd

Chelsea Bronze

Big Plant Nursery
The Botanic Nursery
Choice Landscapes
D'Arcy & Everest
C S Lockyer (Fuchsias)

Hampton Court Gold

Jacques Amand International
Avon Bulbs
Dibley's Nurseries
Downderry Nursery
Fernatix
Fernwood Nursery
Fir Trees Pelargonium Nursery
Goldbrook Plants
Hampshire Carnivorous Plants
Hardy's Cottage Garden Plants
Harvey's Garden Plants
Hoyland Plant Centre
Jekka's Herb Farm (& **Best Exhibit in Floral Marquee**)
P W Plants
Park Green Nurseries
Potash Nursery
Roualeyn Nurseries
Brian & Pearl Sulman

Hampton Court Silver-Gilt

Aldo Airplants
The Botanic Nursery
Burncoose Nurseries
Culm View Nursery
Derek Lloyd Dean
Fibrex Nurseries Ltd
Hewitt-Cooper Carnivorous Plants

C S Lockyer (Fuchsias)
Mendip Bonsai Studio
Oak Tree Nursery
The Old Walled Garden
Primrose Bank
Rotherview Nursery
South West Carnivorous Plants
Squire's Garden Centres
Trevena Cross Nurseries

Hampton Court Silver

Big Plant Nursery
Burnham Nurseries
Desert to Jungle
Heucheraholics
Hopleys Plants Ltd
Mallet Court Nursery
Pine Cottage Plants
Plantagogo.com
Todd's Botanics
Trecanna Nursery

Hampton Court Silver Knightian

Cookoo Box Nursery

Hampton Court Bronze

Blacksmiths Cottage Nursery
Highdown Nursery

Hampton Court Festival of Roses Gold

David Austin Roses Ltd
Peter Beales Roses (& **Best Exhibit in Festival of Roses**)

Hampton Court Festival of Roses Silver-Gilt

Style Roses

Hampton Court Festival of Roses Silver

C & K Jones
Seale Nurseries

Tatton Gold

Aldo Airplants
Dibley's Nurseries
Fernatix
Fernwood Nursery
Fir Trees Pelargonium Nursery
Hall Farm Nursery
Hampshire Carnivorous Plants
Elizabeth MacGregor
Mendip Bonsai Studio
Packhorse Farm Nursery
Potash Nursery
Roualeyn Nurseries
Shirley Tasker
Brian & Pearl Sulman
Waterside Nursery

Tatton Silver-Gilt

Broadleigh Gardens
Churchtown Carnivores
Culm View Nursery
Desert to Jungle
Fibrex Nurseries Ltd
Green Garden Herbs
Mary Green
Hardy's Cottage Garden Plants
Hartside Nursery Garden
Heucheraholics
Holden Clough Nursery
Hoyland Plant Centre
Oak Tree Nursery
Pennard Plants
Plantagogo.com
South West Carnivorous Plants

Tatton Silver-Gilt Knightian

Cookoo Box Nursery

Tatton Silver

Barnsdale Gardens
Big Plant Nursery
The Botanic Nursery
Brownthwaite Hardy Plants
Cairnsmore Nursery
Cath's Garden Plants
Mickfield Hostas
White Cottage Alpines

Tatton Silver Knightian

W Robinson & Sons Ltd

Tatton Bronze

Hillview Hardy Plants

The HARDY PLANT SOCIETY

MEMBERSHIP APPLICATION FOR 2009

The Annual Subscriptions are:
Single **£13.00** per year (one member)
Joint **£15.00** per year (two members at the same address)

• Subscriptions are renewable annually on **1 January**.
• Subscriptions of members joining after 1 October are valid until the end of the following year.
• Overseas members are requested to pay in pounds sterling by International Money Order or by credit card. An optional charge of £10.00 is made for airmail postage outside Western Europe of all literature, if preferred.

Please fill in the details in BLOCK CAPITALS, tear off this form and send it with your payment to the Administrator or telephone the Administrator with details of your credit card.

Please tick the type of membership required

☐ Single £13.00 per year (one member)
☐ Joint £15.00 per year (two members at the same address)
☐ Airmail postage £10.00 per year (optional for members outside Western Europe)

NAME/S ....

ADDRESS ....

....

.... POST CODE ....

TELEPHONE NUMBER ....

E-mail ....

I enclose a cheque/postal order* payable to **THE HARDY PLANT SOCIETY** (in pounds sterling ONLY) for £.........

OR

Please debit my Visa/Master Card* by the sum of £ ....
(* delete as required)

CARD NUMBER ☐☐☐☐ ☐☐☐☐ ☐☐☐☐ ☐☐☐☐

EXPIRY DATE ☐☐☐☐

Name as embossed on card ....

Signature ....

Please print your name and address clearly, tear out the page and send it to The Administrator at the address overleaf

The Hardy Plant Society is a Registered Charity, number 208080

Your support ensures the future of endangered plants thr... the guardianship of the National Plant Collections.

We invite you to choose your own level of subscription (minimum £25) from the following range of options.

☐ £25 ☐ £30 ☐ £50 ☐ £125 (Friend)

Please complete in CAPITALS

Title ______ Forename ______________________

Surname ______________________

Daytime Telephone ______________________

Email ______________________

Address ______________________

____

______________________ Postcode ______________________

Where did you get this leaflet? ______________________

- Make cheques payable to NCCPG and send to the address below.
- If you wish to pay by credit card please call us on **01483 447 540**

giftaid it

Gift Aid Declaration:

Are you a UK taxpayer?

If you are, we can claim 28% from the government on your subscription at no extra cost to you.

I would like the National Council for the Conservation of Plants & Gardens to reclaim the tax on any membership subscription or donation that I make/ have made in the previous six tax years and all subscriptions and donations I make in the future, until I notify you otherwise. I have paid an amount of UK income tax or capital gains tax equal to any tax reclaimed. (Remember that if you receive a company pension, income tax may well be paid at source.)

Gift Aid Signature

Date

Pay by Direct Debit and receive 15 months membership for the price of 12

(offer closes 30th September 2009)

Instruction to your Bank or Building Society to pay by Direct Debit

DIRECT Debit

Name and full postal address of your Bank or Building Society

To The Manager Bank/Building Society

Address

Postcode

Name(s) of Account Holder(s)

Bank or Building Society Account Number

Branch Sort Code

Originators Identification Number

9 7 4 2 1 2

Reference Number (Office use only)

Instruction to your Bank or Building Society

Please pay The National Council for the Conservation of Plants & Gardens direct debits from the account detailed in this instruction, subject to the safeguards assured by the Direct Debit Guarantee. I understand that this instruction may remain with the NCCPG and if so, details will be passed electronically to my Bank/Building Society.

Signature(s)

Date

Data Protection Act: Records for each member are kept at NCCPG National Office and by local Group Officers. Under no circumstances are membership records used for purposes other than those connected to the legitimate activities of The National Council for the Conservation of Plants & Gardens.

Please return your form with payment to: Plant Heritage, 12 Home Farm, Loseley Park, Guildford, GU3 1HS.

Tel: 01483 447 540 Email: info@nccpg.org.uk www.plantheritage.com

Plant Heritage is the working name of the National Council for the Conservation of Plants & Gardens. Company Limited by Guarantee. Registered in Cardiff 2222953. Registered Charity Number 1004009.